KT-375-639

Chronicle of Canada

YAR:IN

Withdrawn for sale

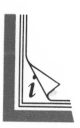

FOR USE IN THE LIBRARY ONLY

Norfolk County Council
LIBRARY
& Information Service

YARMOUTH INFORMATION SERVICES T-15

NORLINK 3 0129
ITEM 015 662 514

Chronicle of Canada

Chronicle
Publications
Montreal, Quebec

ACKNOWLEDGMENTS

Chronicle Publications would like to thank the National Archives of Canada for its special contribution to *Chronicle of Canada.*

The editorial staff would like to acknowledge the following for their help: Margaret Robertson, Vanier Library, Concordia University; Louise Carpentier, Norris Library, Concordia University; the reference staff at McLennan Library, McGill University; Janice Rosen, the Canadian Jewish Congress, Montreal; Catherine Chase, Canadair; Barry Ward, editor of *The Barrie Examiner*; Hugh Halliday, Canadian War Museum; Dr. Richard Harrington, Paleobiology Division, National Museum of Natural Sciences; Derrik Mercer, editor-in-chief, Chronicle Communications; Bronwen Lewis; Keith Crowe; Clifton Daniel; Susan Neale; and J.C. Cooper.

The picture editor and picture research team are grateful to the following for their assistance: Michael Bowie, Lux Photographic Services; Al Stringer, Teal Photographic Specialists; Robert Rohonczy, photographer; Johanna Glover, The Granger Collection; Kate Schellenbac, The Bettmann Archive; Ruth Darby, Chronicle Communications, London; Soeur Marie-Paule Cauchon, Archives du Monastère de l'Hotel-Dieu de Québec; Linda White, Newfoundland photo researcher; Steven McLean, Canadian Press; Andrea Garnier, The Glenbow Museum and Archives; Edward MacDonald, *The Island Magazine,* P.E.I.; Fred Farrell, N.B. Provincial Archives; Janice Rosen, Canadian Jewish Congress, Montreal; Charlie Dougall, Bank of Nova Scotia Archives; Alan Doyle, Nova Scotia Tourism; Terry Mosher, *The Gazette*, Montreal; Roanne Mokhtar, Gloria MacKenzie, Helen De Roia, National Archives of Canada; Chris Kirby, Canadian Museum of Civilization; Le'Anne Frieday, Geological Survey of Canada; Debra Moore, Hudson's Bay Co. Archives; Lynne Champagne-Cormak, Manitoba Archives; John Crosthwait, Metro Toronto Library; Thora Cooke, Western Canada Pictorial Index; Greg Brown, Archives of Ontario; Susan Campbell, National Gallery of Canada; Sandy Cook, The McMichael Canadian Art Collection; Rikki Cameron, Canadian War Museum; Trevor Edwards, Glen Gordon, RCMP Archives; Bonnie Livingstone, Canadian Museum of Natural Sciences; Deborah Morrison, Judy Boundy, Miller Comstock; Carolyn Forcier, Moving Image and Sound Archives; Marlena Wyman, Provincial Archives of Alberta; Jean Goldie, Saskatchewan Archives Board; Nancy Williatte-Battet, CP Rail Corporate Archives; Yoland Toussian, Bank of Montreal Archives.

Most maps and charts which appear in this book were produced by Bull Publishing Associates Ltd. Several others were adapted from Professor Gerald Friesen's book *The Canadian Prairies.* We are very grateful to Prof. Friesen for his kind permission to use these maps.

Our researchers drew on library resources in both Montreal and Ottawa to produce *Chronicle of Canada.* A bibliography would include most standard histories and periodicals, plus scores of other books and pamphlets suggested by our consultants. Specially useful as daily fact-checkers were all the volumes of the *Dictionary of Canadian Biography* , and the four volumes of the revised *Canadian Encyclopedia.* Our researchers also read every issue of the *Toronto Globe and Mail* for the entire 20th century. *The Gazette* of Montreal was an excellent source for both First and Second World Wars.

NORFOLK LIBRARY AND INFORMATION SERVICE

SUPPLIER	H. J.
INVOICE No	026883
ORDER DAT.	10.10.91
COPY No.	

R971

© 1990 Jacques Legrand S.A. International Publishing, Paris for World English rights

© 1990 Chronicle Publications/Editions Chronique, 206 St. Paul St. West, Montreal, Quebec, H2Y 1Z9 - (514)-849-3143

© Harenberg Kommunikation, Dortmund, for the Chronicle system

ISBN 0-920417-16-7

Typesetting: Imprimerie Louis Jean (Gap, France)
Color process work: Sigraph, Christian Bocquez, PHIP, Saga Compoprint
Printing and binding: Brepols (Turnhout, Belgium) - 1rst print

Distributed in Canada by:
Raincoast Books Ltd.
112 East 3rd Ave.
Vancouver
British Columbia V5T 1C8

Printed in Belgium

CHRONICLE OF CANADA

has been conceived and co-ordinated by Jacques Legrand

Editor-in-chief: **Elizabeth Abbott**

Picture editor: **Jutta Duenwald-Dowler**

Chief historical consultant: **Professor J.M.S. Careless,**
Professor Emeritus, University of Toronto

Special Consultant: **Professor Donald B. Smith,**
Department of History, University of Calgary

Historical consultants:

Dr. William Acheson, New Brunswick history, University of New Brunswick;
Dr J. William Brennan, Saskatchewan history, University of Regina;
Harry Bruce, LLD, Nova Scotia history, Nova Scotia;
Dr. Kenneth S. Coates, British Columbia, N.W.T. & Yukon history, University of Victoria;
Keith Crowe, pre-history, Ottawa, Ontario;
Dr. Richard Diubaldo, Inuit history, Concordia University;
Robert Fulford, literature and drama, Ryerson Polytechnical Institute;
Dr. J.L. Granatstein, military history, York University;
Dr. Gerald Killan, Ontario history, University of Western Ontario;
Dr. Henry C. Klassen, Alberta history, University of Calgary;
Dr. Edward MacDonald, Prince Edward Island history, P.E.I. Museum and Heritage Foundation;
Dr. Fernand Ouellet, Quebec history, York University;
Dr. Joy Parr, women's history, Queen's University;
Dr. J. Edgar Rea, Manitoba history, University of Manitoba;
Dr. Shannon Ryan, Newfoundland history, Memorial University;
Dr. George Story, Newfoundland history, Memorial University

Writers:

Louise Abbott, Dr. Robert Beal, Boyde Beck, Peter Black, Ian Bowering, Annabel Bruce, Harry Bruce, Dr. Silver Donald Cameron, James Careless, Rossanna Coriandoli, Marc A. Cooper, Michael D'Arcy, Burt Dowsett, Dorothy Harley Eber, J.W. (Bill) Fitsell, Daniel Francis, Viviane Gray, Dr. Tony Hall, Hugh Halliday, Rita Legault, Cheryl MacDonald, Anne Maxwell, Ian Mayer, Fred McGuinness, Lillian Mein, Stewart A.G. Mein, Geoffrey Molyneux, Dr. David Mulhall, Andrew Neale, Dr. Cameron Nish, Joseph Romain, Dr. Shannon Ryan, Jo Serrentino, Dr. Donald B. Smith, Rachel Vincent

Editorial production: Laurel Sherrer

Assistant editors: Michael D'Arcy, Andrew Neale

Copy editors: Mitchell Axelrad (chief), Marilyn Mill

Assistant picture editor: Sandra Dunkin

Picture research: Anne Maxwell (chief), Geoffrey Molyneux, Cathy Neil, Anya Wasilewski

Chief historical researcher: Jimmy Manson

Research production: Diane Cadieux

Index: Sandra Steiman LaFortune

Production co-ordination: Catherine Balouet, Emmanuelle Berenger, Anne-Marie Viana

Chronicle software: Dominique Klutz

Administration: Mona Tanious, Nevine Messiha

PREFACE

Chronicle of Canada is presented chronologically from the year 4.6 billion B.C., the approximate date of the earth's origin, to December 31, 1989. The opening pages cover billions of years of pre-history, while in the later parts of the book, several pages are often devoted to a particularly eventful year, such as 1867, the year of Canada's birth.

Canada's story is told in concise articles with place and date lines, the latter often approximate in the earliest periods, and indicated by a c. for circa. The stories are written through the eyes of a journalist contemporary to the time of the event, a superhuman "Chronicle reporter" whose beat ranges from the earth's volcanic infancy to the Meech Lake bargaining table. Although nearly omniscient about the present, the Chronicle reporter does not know what lies in the future, and so cannot predict or analyse in relation to events that will happen. He also endeavors to report the facts and to shy away from interpretation, but inevitably, modern perspectives and concerns – environmental, for example – creep into some of his stories. He has limited most of his stories so that he can cover a vast range of events. To follow developments beyond the date of a specific story, the reader is advised to consult the index.

There is also an appendix devoted to stories on issues ranging from restored cities to endangered species, detailed information on each province and territory, and personal historical accounts submitted by Canadians as part of our "My Canada" contest.

One special feature of *Chronicle of Canada* is the single column chronologies included on the left-hand page at intervals throughout the book. These chronologies serve both to list dates such as works of art, inventions, deaths, etc., and to trace events that come between the stories, so if you are reading about the War of 1812, for instance, it is worth reading not only the stories, but also the chronological entries that detail related but lesser events. Particularly important events are covered by both chronology entries and stories. For instance, for the passage of the BNA Act in 1867, there is both a chronology entry and a story.

Wherever possible, we have used pictures or representations contemporary with the story, but of course this is often impossible, and we have used later representations of the story. This is especially true before the advent of photography. Our policy is to indicate when a later photograph has been used to illustrate a story.

For the names of people and places, we have generally used the name current at the time and, if it is different from that used today, we include today's equivalent in square brackets after the name the first few times it is used in the text. In the pre-history chronologies, modern placenames are used in the interest of clarity. Throughout, we have tried to strike a balance between historical accuracy and clarity for the modern reader. We have followed the *Canadian Press Style Guide* in matters of spelling, punctuation, placelines, datelines, etc.

The discrepancy between New Style dates (Gregorian calender, used in Europe after 1582) and Old Style dates (Julian calender, used in England until 1752) presents a problem to books attempting accurate dating. We have tried always to use New Style dates.

We have tried to ensure accuracy by using reliable sources and subjecting the text to the scrutiny of the expert consultants named at the beginning of the book. On the consultants' recommendations, we sometimes changed stories, or included additional stories at the expense of others. History is never an exact science – reliable sources often give a different date for the same event, contemporary witnesses and historians often describe and interpret events differently, and people make mistakes. After running the gauntlet of these and many other difficulties, we believe we have produced an accurate, well-rounded and exciting book.

Elizabeth Abbott

CHRONICLE OF CANADA

CHRONICLE OF CANADA is the story of a nation unique in the world. Canada is politically young but rich with a multitude of traditions, for its people have always chosen cultural diversity over assimilation. Canada is many languages and religions, many races and cultures, many ideologies and legends. To update Lord Durham, Canada is many peoples struggling to coexist in the bosom of a single state.

Canada is also the animals its people coexist with, and often destroy – buffalo and cattle, beaver and prairie dog, dog and wolf, loon and goose, seal and whale, trout and salmon.

Canada is its vast geography of contrasts – Atlantic to Pacific, high Arctic to southern prairie, new Rockies to old Laurentians. It is fruitful orchard and garden, bounteous ocean, barren wasteland. It is luxuriant summer and harsh winter.

Canada shares part of its geography – 4,800 kilometres of transcontinental border – with the United States. Part of being Canadian is relating to the generous, protective, but dominating American economic and cultural presence. A measure of our success is our undefended border, the world's longest.

It is ironic that during this year of CHRONICLE OF CANADA's creation, Canada itself has reached a difficult crossroad. Our nation's political problems have been centuries in the making. Now a constitutional Damocles Sword hangs over us, affecting our collective future.

Understanding this, we have approached our nation's history with love and respect. We have attempted to examine every dimension of its complex development. In presenting our past, we are preserving it forever.

A lavish format gives us almost 1,000 pages for CHRONICLE OF CANADA, and thousands of illustrations. Of course, one book cannot relate the great sweep of events and processes that are Canada. But greedy though we are for more – more of Canada, more of its CHRONICLE – we know that we have created a permanent and vital testimony for our people. We have made sense of things previously ignored, concealed, misunderstood. We feel we have given back to our native peoples something of their original greatness. We have tried to expose wrongs, exalt goodness, and recognize dreams, frustrations, hope, despair, and unquenchable faith.

We hope through CHRONICLE OF CANADA to share with all our readers our love and fascination for this mighty but vulnerable nation. We trust that none who turn the pages of our CHRONICLE will be untouched by the wonders it contains.

Elizabeth Abbott

Elizabeth Abbott

THE EMPRESS
Sightseeing Tours

TABLE OF CONTENTS

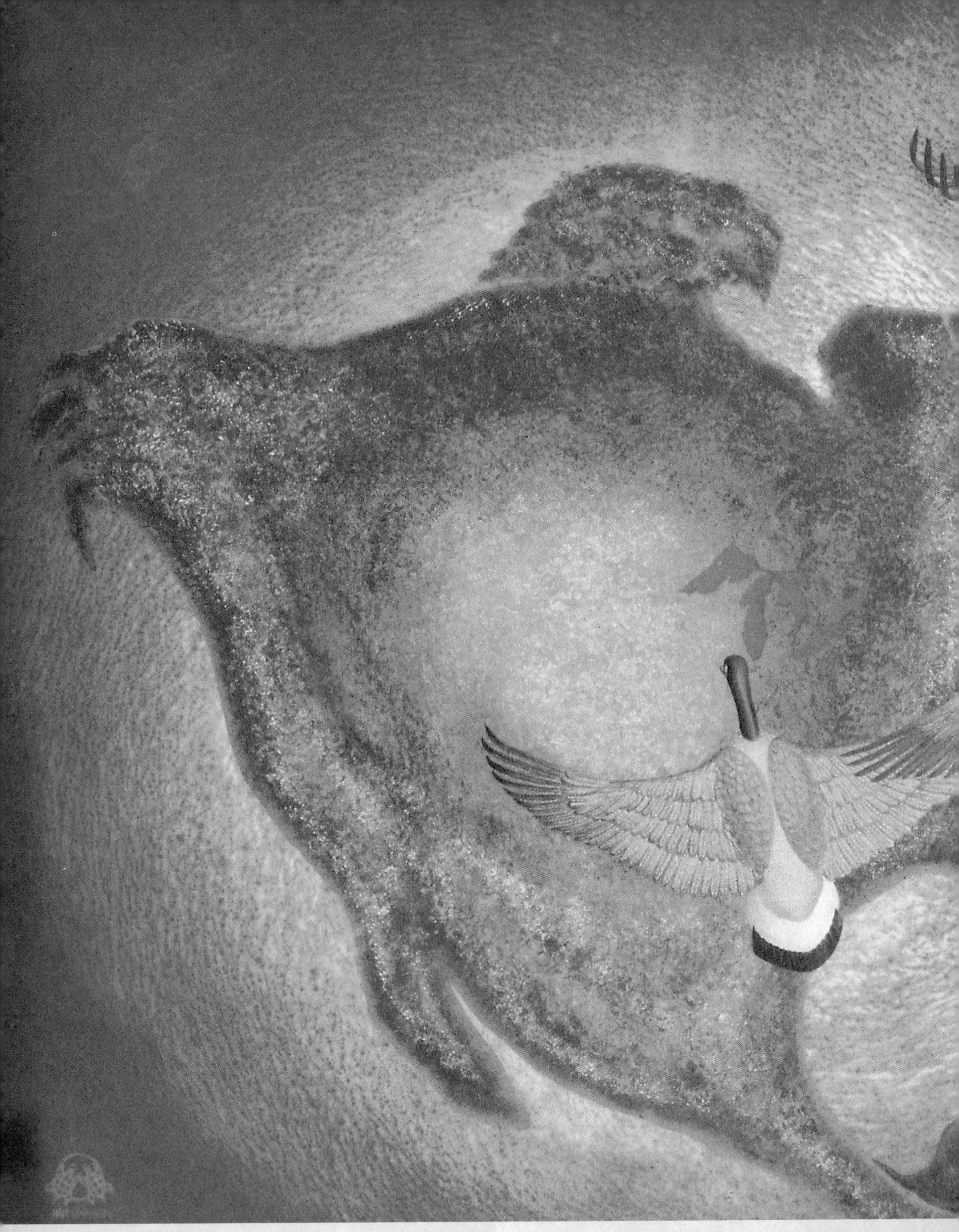

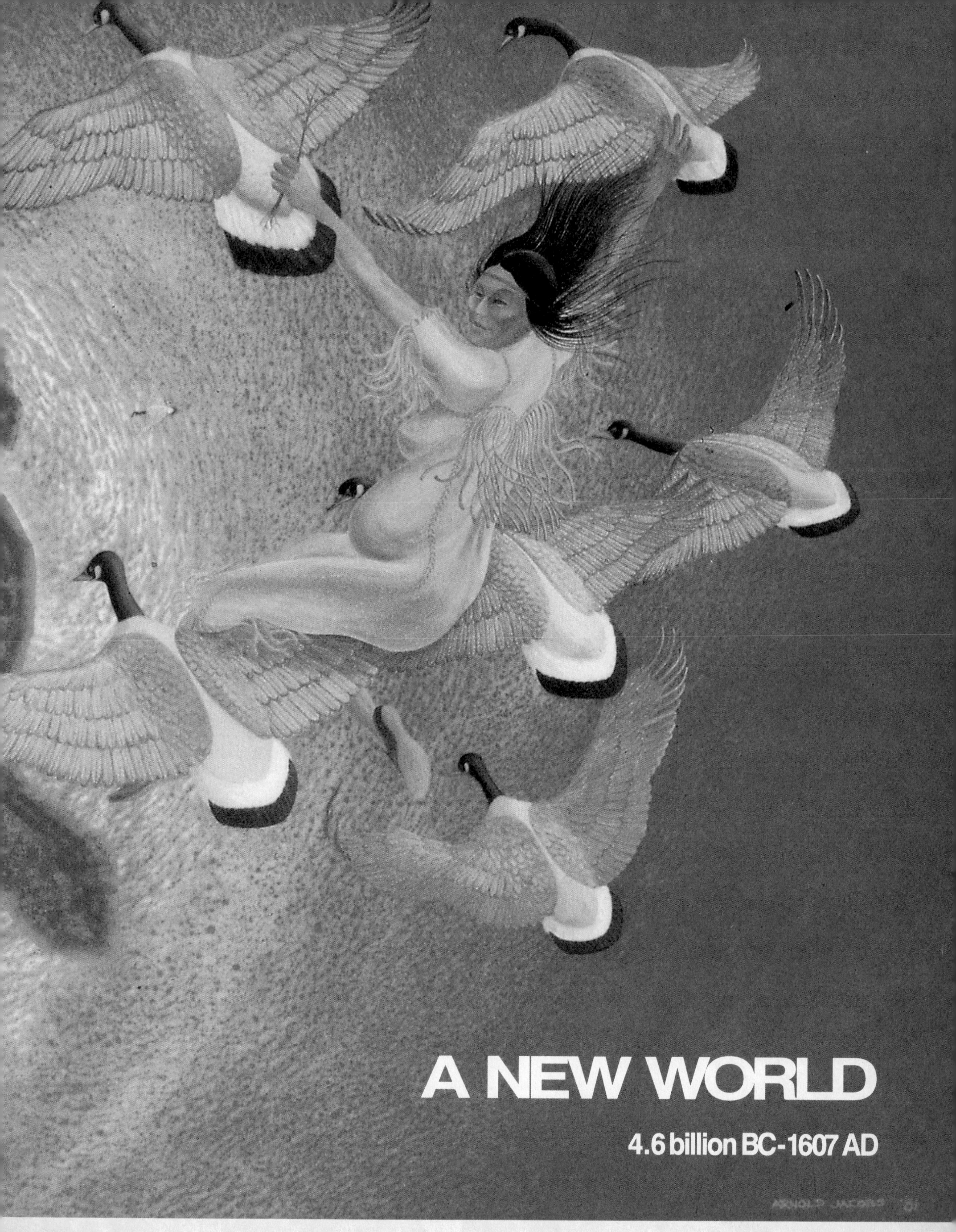

A NEW WORLD

4.6 billion BC-1607 AD

4.6 (4.6B-65M BC)

Milky Way Galaxy, c.4.6 billion BC. Several planets are formed from dust revolving around a small infant star. The dust resolves into blobs that grow larger as they acquire gravitational pull.

Earth, c.4.6 billion BC. Earth is one of the newly formed planets. It is essentially molten. Matter of various weight is found throughout. Gravity slowly pulls the heaviest elements toward the centre, forming a solid iron core, and lighter rocks like basalt and granite rise to the surface.

Earth, c.3 billion BC. Simple bacteria and blue-green algae are alive, the first verifiable life on Earth. The first life probably evolved more than 5 million years ago.

North America, c.2.5 billion BC. Mountain building heats and compresses lavas and sedimentary rocks to the point that they recrystallize, forming the first rocks of the Canadian Shield, the continent's first solid ground.

Earth, c.700 million BC. Species of worms, jellyfish, and soft corals are the first organisms with chromosomes, which makes them the first life capable of sexual reproduction. Sex increases the possibilities of evolution, as it makes natural selection possible.

Earth, c.450 million BC. Small jawless, limbless bottom-dwellers called ostracoderms have appeared in Earth's seas. They have no internal bones, except for a backbone, which makes them the first vertebrates. They are covered with bony plates, which probably developed as a defence mechanism against predators.

Earth, c.275 million BC. A mammal-like reptile called *Lystrosaurus*, a virtually toothless dog-size vegetarian, lives in freshwater swamps on the supercontinent of Pangaea.

Earth, c.130 million BC. The first flowers evolve, perhaps on seed-bearing ferns. Pollen bearing leaves reduce and fuse to become stamens, egg cup bearing leaves become pistils, and outer leaves join to form petals. The first flowering plants in North America are similar to magnolias.

North America, c.88 million BC. Eleven kinds of water birds fish North America's inland sea. Some, like *Ichthyornis*, are good flyers. *Hesperornis* and others are flightless.

New planet is born as sun condenses

c.4.6 billion-650 million BC

EARTH – The planet Earth is in its infancy, a heaving, molten mass probably formed from spinning blobs of dust blown off as the sun condensed from a cosmic dust cloud.

Young Earth is lifeless, but it is in a state of constant activity. Volcanoes spew forth molten lava and hot gases. These gases, containing nitrogen, carbon dioxide, sulphur compounds and water vapor, continuously escape from Earth's centre and are forming a primitive atmosphere surrounding the planet. Rain falls and fills low-lying basins with water, creating Earth's first oceans.

The process of creation continues, and over the years, the Earth's crust or outer skin rises, bends and sinks. As rocks melt, shatter and melt again in Earth's pressurized core, they generate concentrations of such minerals as gold, silver, copper and iron.

It is in this stretch of time known as Pre-Cambrian that the land of [Canada] has been coming into being. In fact, some of the world's oldest known rocks come from the [Northwest Territories], 1,300 kilometres north of [Edmonton, Alberta]. Older rocks from outer space have crashed into the planet, but these [Canadian] rocks, believed to be about 4 billion years old, are the oldest known on Earth.

Portrait of a planet in its infancy: An artist's impression of the surface of the earth as it begins to form an outer crust. This is part of a complex process of creation involving constant activity over billions of years.

Simple life forms appear in Earth's seas

c.3.5-2 billion BC

EARTH – Earth is still barren, but life has appeared in its shallow waters, rich in nutrients. This life consists of procaryotes, single-celled organisms with no nucleus or chromosomes to carry genetic information. Instead, the genetic material is scattered throughout the tiny organisms, which cannot reproduce sexually but simply split apart.

This is a very efficient way to reproduce, but it means that each procaryote is a replica of every other. However, evolution does occur through mutation. Procaryotes reproduce with such speed that recurrent mutation causes considerable genetic variation among individuals. Over a long period of time, procaryotic cells have begun to live together in large groups. Procaryotes include bacteria and blue-green algae.

Earth's atmosphere, virtually devoid of oxygen, can only sustain life forms that do not breathe. Bacteria, which live by fermentation, and algae, which use sunlight for photosynthesis, are therefore well-suited to this environment.

Because procaryotes are soft-bodied, they usually leave few traces. In [Canada], however, some of their remains are permanently embedded in black, fine-grained silica rocks found in outcrops along the shores of [Lake Superior]. Called Gunflint Chert, these rocks contain white rings about a metre across, the fossilized remains of countless blue-green algae and other tiny sea creatures.

Gigantic meteorite collides with Earth

c.1.85 billion BC

EARTH – A meteorite some 10 kilometres wide and travelling faster than the speed of sound has crashed into the ground near [Sudbury, Ontario]. This cataclysmic collision blasted an enormous crater 65 kilometres across, [the Sudbury basin]. Granite flew skyward then settled back into the hole. The crust and lithosphere were shattered. Rocks deep below the Earth's surface melted, and bubbled up into the shattered crust. After cooling, solutions permeated the rim, depositing nickel, copper, gold, silver, iron, palladium, platinum and other metals near the surface. The [Sudbury] crater is the largest nickel deposit in the world.

Earth hosts flourishing life in the seas and on land

Multicellular plants and animals evolve

c.500 million BC

EARTH – The seas are teeming with life. Many-celled plants and animals with tiny phosphate shells have emerged, the first creatures with hard parts that can fossilize in rock. Larger shells composed mainly of calcium are evolving. These shelled animals are swiftly replacing their soft-bodied predecessors, perhaps because of the shells.

A dominant form of life is the three-lobed marine beetle. These trilobites are evolving into thousands of walking, burrowing or swimming species. Some have compound eyes. Some are blind. Most grow no more than five centimetres.

Other new sea creatures are onychophorans, or clawbearers. They are soft-bodied but have the hard claws of the arthropods, a major group that includes marine insects, spiders and crustaceans.

Like their predecessors in [Lake Superior], the new life forms leave permanent traces. The Burgess Shale from [Mt. Stephen] in [British Columbia] preserves the soft parts of around 130 species of strange marine invertebrates.

These marine creatures provide a wonderful insight into the true diversity of life. Nature is experimenting with evolution, and the Burgess Shale is recording the process.

Burgess Shale fossil. It preserves the soft parts of marine invertebrates.

The fossil of a three-lobed marine beetle, known as the trilobite.

The arthropod, a former marine creature, is land's first inhabitant.

First land animals are thriving ashore

c.300 million BC

EARTH – Land has its first occupants: arthropods, the scorpion-like marine creatures with segmented bodies, external skeletons and jointed limbs that evolved more than 200 million years ago in the seas. Arthropods have crawled onto the shores and inhabit plants, the descendants of marine vegetation that emerged from the sea 100 million years ago, when they were rootless, leafless patches of moss.

The forests swarm with 10-centimetre cockroaches and predatory dragonflies, two of the most prolific forms of arthropod. An interesting feature of cockroaches is that they bear wings on their first thoracic segment.

Arthropods are proving to be extremely versatile, evolving to suit every aspect of their environment: crustaceans in coastal nooks and crannies, insects in the air and in the burgeoning forests.

Clearly the present proliferation of life on Earth is a natural outcome of the lack of other competing life forms. This situation is the result of cyclical extinctions, possibly related to environmental changes, in which entire species die out, leaving voids that other life forms fill.

Greening forests are taking root, now rising to heights of nine metres and producing fertile swamps.

Giant continent Pangaea spans the earth

c.275-225 million BC

EARTH – All the continents of the world have now joined in a supercontinent known as Pangaea. Until now, Earth's land has been divided into several continents that straddle the equator. The largest, Gondwana, consisted of [Africa], [South America], [Antarctica], [India] and [Australia]. The others were separate.

The formation of Pangaea was gradual. Slowly – and one by one – the plates carrying Gondwana floated southward, stopping near the South Pole. The plates on which the other continents sat collided with Gondwana, creating a single land mass.

Pangaea extends from the South Pole to high northern latitudes, and along the equator for about 13,000 kilometres. Its formation is proving to have many consequences. Mountains have formed where the continents have pressed together. The shallow seas that existed around the earlier continents have disappeared. Around Pangaea, the sea level has fallen. The seas still teem with life. On land, reptiles have become the dominant animal.

Reptiles emerge as dominant land species

c.225 million BC

EARTH – Reptiles have taken over from amphibians as Earth's dominant life form, principally because of their improved new system of reproduction. While amphibians lay naked eggs in moist or watery places they must patrol to protect their offspring, reptile eggs are coated with a thin shell encasing its own fluid. This means reptilian eggs can be laid on land, are spared attack from marine predators, and can be guarded until they hatch as miniature replicas of their parents.

Alligators, for instance, build nests and defend them. They even try to control the sun's heat by shifting around the nesting materials. Even more important, their reproductive system frees reptiles from limiting their homes to wet places. Now they can roam freely.

Reptiles come in many different forms. The species cotylosaur includes *Hylonomus*, one of the earliest reptiles. Some of its descendants are turtles and the eosuchians. Some cotylosaurs are huge, up to four metres long. Other reptiles include theocodonts, crocodilians and flying pterosaurs.

▷

Supercontinent begins to split apart

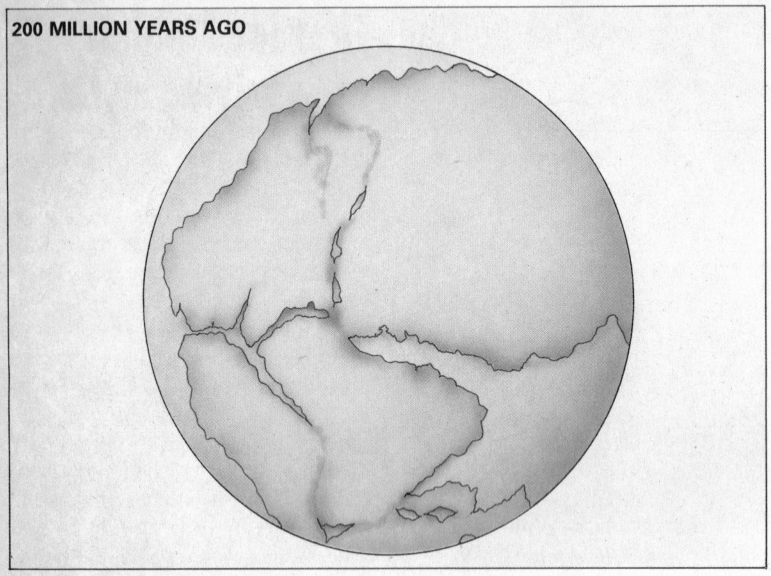

A map of the earth as it appears around 200 million BC. More than 90 per cent of life in the seas, and about half the invertebrates, have become extinct.

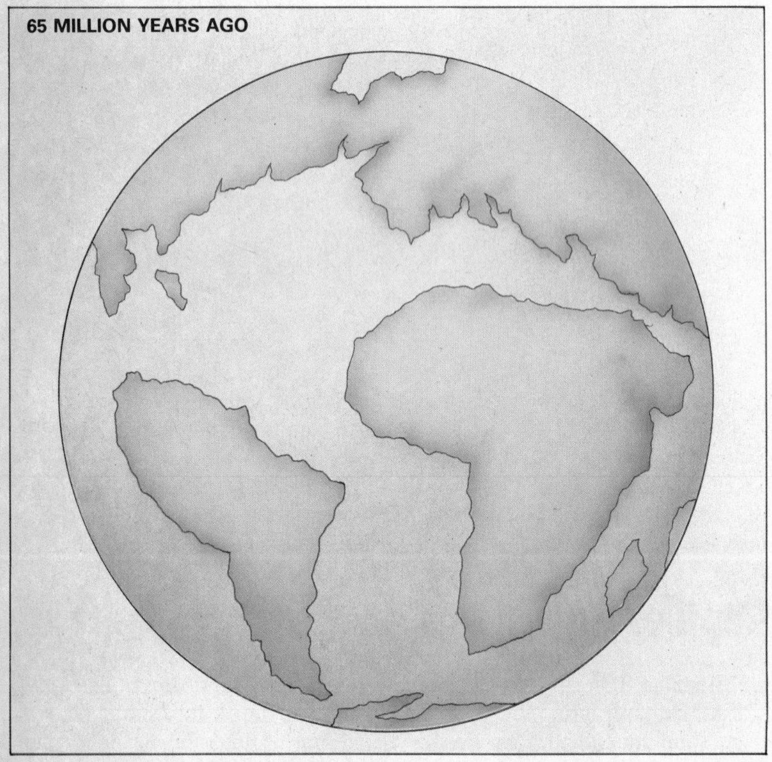

The state of the earth about 65 million BC. The link between [North America] and [Europe] ceases to exist and two new continents slide away from each other.

c.180-160 million BC

EARTH – The vast supercontinent of Pangaea has begun to split apart, the result of a long and complex process that began when it first formed. The land mass is in a constant state of flux. New oceanic crust continually builds up. As time passes, this new crust is pushed aside and fans out in parallel bands. New material slowly rises, propelled by hot convection currents in Earth's mantle. After it moves sideways, it cools and sinks. At the land's edge, new crust is forming. The continents are slowly drifting apart, again becoming separate.

For more than 20 million years the link between [North America] and [Europe] remained, but finally they slid away from each other. [North America] is now developing unique features such as mountains. In the interior, high plains are building up. Savannas are encroaching on the great forests. In the animal world, evolutionary experiments thrive as reptiles and other life forms adapt to changing conditions. Some reptiles, forced off land by stronger, wilier rivals, are even returning to the seas and oceans that now border much of [North America].

The advent of these new marine animals follows almost 200 million years after the Great Marine Disaster of 225 million BC, when more than 90 percent of life in the seas, and more than half the invertebrate species, became extinct. The victims included trilobites, bryozoans and brachiopods.

One probable cause of the disaster was that around the time when Pangaea formed, the shallow seas around the coasts of its merging landmasses disappeared, destroying the habitat of marine life there. Major climatic changes may also have played a part in causing the disaster.

Dinosaurs descend from small reptiles

c.195-135 million BC

EARTH – Many new creatures have appeared, all descendants of the same reptiles. Dinosaurs, which arose from the small springing reptiles called thecodonts, now roam [Alberta] and elsewhere in [Canada]. Dinosaurs are easier to describe than define. Such beasts as *Tyrannosaurus rex* are grotesque and ferocious predators, colossal monsters with thick necks and terrible, jagged-toothed jaws. They crash over the marshy terrain on powerful legs, bent forward and balanced by vast tails lifted up from the ground as they run, hunting down their terrified prey. Their victims, most other dinosaurs, are often large but harmless vegetarians. Some are so tall they can munch leaves from the very top of giant trees.

Brontosaurus, for example, is 80 to 90 feet long and can weigh more than 30 tons. Others are minuscule, measurable in inches and pounds whereas their cousins, up to 80 feet long, weigh up to 30 tons or more. Whether they walk on two legs or four, dinosaur backs are sometimes shielded by a bony ridge. Perhaps this protects them from predators or heat. It is unclear whether they are cold-blooded, hence restricted by their environment, or warm-blooded, able to adapt their internal functions to changing climate. Some smaller, more agile dinosaurs are probably warm-blooded.

Dinosaurs are evolving into two groups – lizard-hipped and bird-hipped. But the hardy beasts are not [Canada]'s only new animals. Others are mammals, innocuous, scurrying and usually furry. Mammals are warm-blooded and can easily adapt to their surroundings. When cold, they can shiver to warm up. In the heat they can pant and sweat. They have four-chambered hearts and a secondary palate that permits them to chew and breathe simultaneously.

Many mammals can suckle their young, giving them the opportunity to develop slowly and safely and to learn from their elders. Mammals at first appeared clumsy, but with time their limbs are strengthening and shifting, giving them increased speed and agility.

First bird fast on its feet, but weak wings keep it grounded

c.140 million BC

EARTH – The first bird has appeared on Earth! *Archaeopteryx* is a small plumed reptile of dinosaur descent, sharp-toothed and balanced by its long, bony tail, which has two rows of feathers. Its clawed wings, short and unsupported by muscle, probably cannot sustain flapping flight, and *Archaeopteryx* uses them as swatters as it runs after its large insect prey.

Sometimes as it races along the coastal mudflats, the wind catches its outstretched wings and lifts it off the ground. Perhaps it climbs trees in its quest for food, moving about by spreading its wings and gliding from one tree to another. *Archaeopteryx* lives in [Europe] and has not been seen in [North America].

Mighty dinosaurs are planet's strongest animals

c.76 million BC

EARTH – Dinosaurs are now the Earth's mightiest animals, dominating all life forms. In [Canada], they are found in [Alberta], [Saskatchewan], [British Columbia], [Nova Scotia], [the Yukon Territory] and [the Northwest Territories]. Many dinosaurs live near insect-rich marshlands in [southern Alberta], on higher ground than swamps inhabited by other reptiles such as alligators, crocodiles, turtles, salamanders and lizards. They roam the fern and moss carpet of [Canada]'s tall forests, past conifers, redwoods, magnolias and palms.

More than 30 varieties of dinosaur inhabit Canada. The most common are duckbills like *Corythosaurus*. The latter have duckbill snouts and call each other by trumpeting through the hollow crests on top of their small-brained heads. The adults, 26 feet long and four-ton vegetarians, shred tough conifer twigs and ferns with hundreds of compressed, rasp-like teeth.

Upright, some duckbills stand 14 feet high. *Lambeosaurines*, from [Alberta], grow up to 49 feet long and weigh more than eight tons. The shape of their four-fingered hands and long muscular tails suggests they also swim.

Other common [Canadian] dinosaurs are carnivorous. *Gorgosaurus*, one of the largest, grows to 30 feet in length, and weighs about eight tons. His cousin, the slender *Albertosaurus*, from [Alberta], is somewhat smaller. These dinosaurs probably hunt by ambushing prey and then catching it in their small forelegs before devouring it with their sharp, curved, jagged teeth. Like most carnivores, *Gorgosaurus* and *Albertosaurus* move much faster than vegetarians, reaching speeds of 43 kilometres per hour as they charge along on their hind feet, balanced by their immense tails.

In [Alberta], the eight-ton *Pachyrhinosaurus* terrorizes its prey, ripping it apart with the huge horns in the middle of its skull. Another [Alberta] dinosaur is the agile, long-necked *Ornithomimus*. Toothless despite carnivore ancestry, it lives on fruits, insects and reptile eggs. *Triceratops*, a three-horned vegetarian, has a huge bony frill over the back of its neck.

Most dinosaurs are egg layers, and some leave their young in nests for weeks while they forage to feed them. Many species live in herds, and most individuals seem to survive only six to 10 years.

The Tyrannosaurus and Edmontosaurus are two of 30 varieties of dinosaurs inhabiting [Canada]'s forests, living among conifers, redwoods and palms.

Disappearance of the dinosaur on Earth a mystery

Dinosaurs and more than half of the earth's life forms are dying off. The reason is unknown. Survivors include insects, small reptiles and mammals.

c.65 million BC

EARTH – Earth has suffered another apocalypse! After 140 million years, the dinosaurs and more than half of Earth's other life forms have died. What killed them is a mystery, but a plausible explanation is the impact of a massive meteorite 10 kilometres in diameter. Everything for 100 kilometres from the point of contact would have been smashed, burned or split. Elsewhere, dust and debris blew into the sky and soon covered Earth. For weeks it blocked the sunlight so that it could not reach the surface. The planet changed into a chill, dark terrain. Acid rain caused by the burning of atmospheric nitrogen where the meteorite had crashed drizzled down. Food chains collapsed. Plants died. Plant-eaters died. Meat-eaters died.

An alternate explanation for the extinction of the great dinosaurs is that a general cooling changed the nature of vegetation so that dinosaurs starved. This cooling may have been caused by a decrease in the amount of sunlight striking the planet, perhaps the result of the clouding of the atmosphere by extensive volcanic activity. Whatever the cause, no species living exclusively on land survived. The survivors include insects, small reptiles and hordes of tiny mammals.

These rodents are beginning to thrive on the ecological disaster. Undeterred as before by giant dinosaurs and reptiles, they scurry everywhere, gorging themselves on eggs, insects, fruit and the dead bodies that lie rotting everywhere. The dinosaurs are gone, and a new era has begun. ▷

Dinosaurs: giant inhabitants of the alluvial plains

Reconstructed skeleton of the Albertosaurus Liberatus of [Alberta], a slender dinosaur, the cousin of another carnivorous dinosaur, the Gorgosaurus.

Albertosaurus Liberatus, the smaller type of carnivorous dinosaur, hunt by ambushing prey and catching it in their small forelegs before eating it.

The reconstructed skeleton of a Chasmosaurus belli dinosaur.

Skull of an Albertosaurus Sarcophagus, from [Alberta], a carnivorous dinosaur which can reach speeds of up to 43 kilometres per hour using its hind feet.

Reconstructed skeleton of a Champsosaurus natator, a plains-dweller.

Stegoceros validus, inhabitant of [Alberta], is one type of dinosaur living in insect-rich marshlands, roaming the fern and moss carpet of the forests.

The Edmontonia, with its heavy shoulder spine, is of ancient derivation. This dinosaur browses on low plants and seems to prefer flatlands, near the sea.

Tyrannosaurus rex is a ferocious predator with a thick neck and jagged-toothed jaw. Some are so tall they can eat leaves from the very top of giant trees.

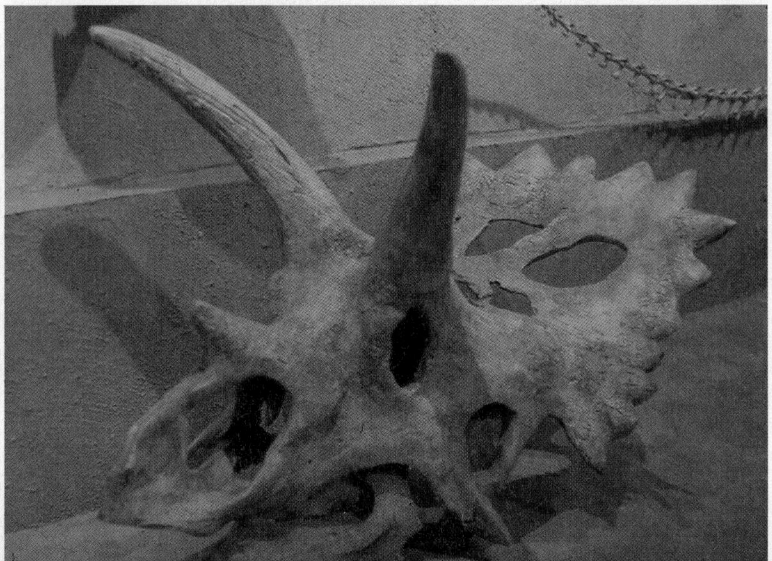

The Anchiceratop ornatus bears a long neck shield and brow horns that are well-developed. The dinosaur inhabits the floodplains inland from the swamps.

The skull of a Triceratops, a great horned dinosaur of [Alberta] which weighs 12 tons and is some 26-feet high - quite large compared to other dinosaurs.

The toothless Struthiominus uses its horny beak to eat its prey while clasping it with particularly strong forearms that have mole-like claws.

65 (65M-20,000 BC)

Earth, c.65 million BC. An unexplained catastrophe extinguishes all animal species weighing more than 20 pounds. Dinosaurs, which have dominated the earth for millions of years, are among the victims. Mammals, which first appeared between 150 and 125 million BC, survive the catastrophe and thrive in the new environment.

Earth, c.50 million BC. The breakup of the supercontinent Pangaea that began around 130 million years ago is virtually complete. Eurasia, North and South America, Africa, and Antarctica have all been formed, along with the Atlantic Ocean.

North America, c.45 million BC. The Rocky Mountains are formed when shifting Pacific and North American plates buckle and override each other. Rivers from the new mountains carry gravel eastward and deposit it on the prairies there, burying the remains of the dinosaurs.

Egypt, c.32 million BC. Several species of primate known as *Propliopithecus* are living in tropical forests. They are primarily fruit eaters.

Ethiopia, c.2.7 million BC. Hominids (two-legged primates) in the Awash river valley in the Afar region of northern Ethiopia are using stone tools, possibly for the first time anywhere, to hunt or cut flesh. The ingenious invention is being passed to other parts of Ethiopia and beyond.

North America, c.1.8 million BC. The first great ice age ever on the continent is under way, known as the Nebraskan. Its cause is mysterious. Ice covers all of Canada and parts of the United States. It locks in water and partially drains the seas. Mammoths enter the continent from Asia on land bridges left by the receding ocean.

Hungary, c.450,000 BC. A *homo sapien* named Vertesszolos Man has a much larger brain capacity than his hominid ancestors. *Homo sapiens*, a species of hominid, are thriving all over the world.

Eurasia, c.30,000 BC. The tough Neanderthals, a *homo sapien* sub-species, have disappeared mysteriously. Since c.130,000 BC they have been the dominant hominid in North Africa, Europe, and Asia. They are succeeded by the agile and clever *homo sapiens sapiens*.

The guard changes: mammals rule

c.65 million BC

EARTH – After the recent global catastrophe, mammals have inherited the earth. When the grotesquely majestic dinosaur was supreme, mammals were diminutive, noctural and inconspicuous. Now they have emerged from their burrows and trees to replace dinosaurs and other extinct reptiles.

Mammals are quickly developing characteristics to help them succeed. Most striking is their brain size, once similar in ratio to that of some dinosaurs. Now, in many mammals it has increased to triple their former brain-body ratio, making them more clever. They need not specialize so much in lifestyle, but can adapt to situations by thought-stimulated actions.

Detail of painting: Lower left, western camel; middle ground, bison and wolves; behind, three [Yukon] horses; in background, a band of caribou.

Another evolutionary advancement is the mammalian method of birth: instead of hatching eggs as their earlier species did, they deliver live babies. The opossum, [North America's] most primitive mammal in evolutionary terms, hatches its eggs in folds of uterine tissue. Thirteen days later, she delivers live babies. All other mammals keep their offspring inside their bodies much longer, nourishing them in a placenta. Far fewer babies are born, but their parents care for them more intensely than any other animal.

From inception, the placental baby is safer than fetuses forming inside eggs, once those eggs have been laid outside the security of the mother's body. The placental infant is usually born helpless. It depends entirely on its mother's milk, so rich in fat and proteins the baby quickly multiplies its body weight. Its total reliance on its mother also gives it another advantage over other animals: a period for training. In its earliest days, the small creature is given information its own parents have learned. This is one of the first cases of non-genetic transference of data, and is a fundamental improvement.

Another significant advantage over rivals is that mammals, usually hairy and with high metabolic rates, can keep their internal temperatures regulated. This means they can hunt food despite the cold of either night or winter. Cold-blooded reptiles, on the other hand, can only react to extreme heat by taking cover from it, or sheltering from cold to avoid freezing. This usually limits them to daytime hunting.

Post-dinosaur mammalian males and females are often different sizes. Usually the male is larger, but many species have developed larger females. In general, however, mammals of both sexes are growing larger. Two examples are [Canada]'s Eastern horse and Pacific horse, both now increasing in size.

Giant mammal species adapts to changes in the environment

c.2.5 million-80,000 BC

EARTH – Mammalian evolution has speeded up – perhaps in response to the cold waves that have begun to chill Earth – and several species have become gigantic. The giant beaver is the largest rodent in the [Americas]. Adults reach 8.2 feet, and weigh about 440 pounds. Their cutting teeth are 15 centimetres long and act as chisels and gougers. Giant beavers flourish near the [Great Lakes] and in the [Yukon]'s [Old Crow] region.

Other large mammals are long-horned bison and horses, found in [British Columbia], [the Yukon], [Alberta] and [Saskatchewan].

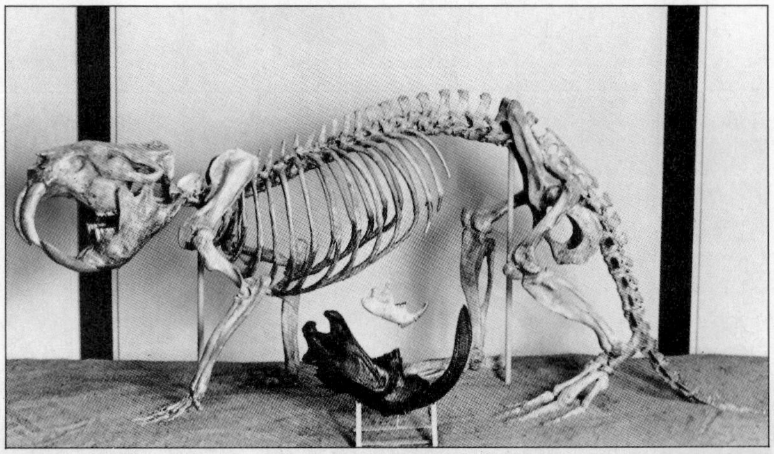

The skeleton of a young giant beaver, Castoroides ohioenis, inhabiting northern [Yukon]. The specimen below it is the right lower jaw of a giant beaver.

Death of primates remains a mystery

c.45 million BC

EARTH – The world's only primates, natives of [North America] and [Europe], have died out. The cause of their demise is unknown. The irony is that 20 million years earlier, at least one order of primate, the small [North American] creature called *Purgatorius*, managed to survive the apocalypse that killed off all the dinosaurs.

Five million years after the apocalypse, four lines of primate had developed. All were small and arboreal, living high in the forests of balmy [North America]. Their tensile paws clutched the branches of trees, and their long tails balanced them while underneath, slow, bulky plant-eaters grazed, and other mammals, carnivorous, hunted less mobile vegetarians.

Mammals crossing over land bridges

c.150,000 BC

EARTH – Ice sheets have spread at the expense of the oceans, drastically lowering the world's sea levels up to 100 metres or more. In some cases, there is a 120-metre drop. [North America] and [Eurasia] are again connected by dry land bridges. The most important are found at the [Bering Strait] which used to divide [North America] from [Asia], and at the [Panamanian isthmus] between [North and South America]. Many mammals are using these links to cross over into [North America].

The musk-ox, a burly, shaggy ruminant, has arrived from [Asia]. Musk-oxen are seldom aggressive, but have excellent defence stratagem. When attacked, they protect themselves by forming a semi-circle, the males facing the enemy with their threatening horns.

The short-faced bear has reached [Canada] from the south. It is long-limbed, agile, fleet and fierce, the largest land carnivore in [North America]. The ground sloth is also a newcomer from [South America]. With the musk-ox, short-faced bear and others, great variety is being added to [Canada]'s mammalian population.

New ice age swallows much of Earth

c.70,000-20,000 BC

EARTH – For the fourth time, sheets of ice are covering much of Earth. The latest glaciation, the Wisconsin, is just beginning. In summer, the average temperature drops just enough to keep snow from melting. Winter after winter, more snow piles up and eventually turns to ice. Most of the northern and southern polar regions of the world are encased in ice up to three kilometres thick. In [North America], it covers about 15.5 million square kilometres. Masses of ice begin to flow and join together.

Locking up so much frozen water on land causes ocean levels to fall. When they do, the [Bering Strait] dries out, creating a bridge of land several hundred kilometres wide that's a northern link between [Eurasia] and [North America].

The ice sheets sweep the land, advancing, standing still and advancing again over thousands of years. As it surges, the ice overrides and grinds down hills, deepening and widening river valleys. It pulverizes boulders and spreads immense sheets of sand, gravel and till over the surface of [Canada]. It scoops out the massive basins of the [Great Lakes]. It pocks the rocky face of the [Canadian Shield] with innumerable lakes, and strips away the mantle from enormous sections.

Silt and clay grow on the beds of the lakes impounded behind the ice dams, forming grasslands and fertile soil. However, in the parts of [Quebec] where the bedrock is hard and breaks into large blocks instead of crumbling, the glaciers deposit large quantities of boulders over the land.

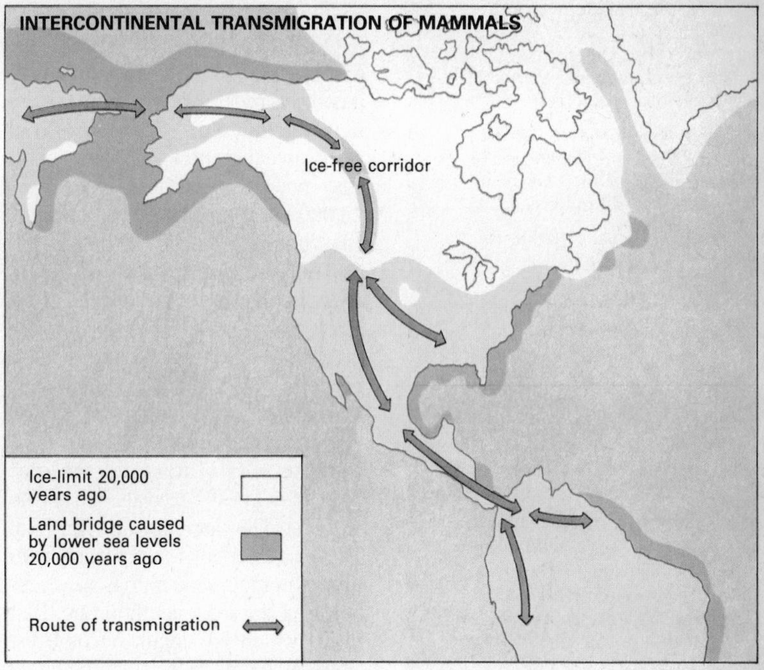

Human beings walk upright, freeing their hands for many uses

c.3.5 million BC

EAST AFRICA – Hominids, who have not appeared in [North America], are walking upright in [East Africa], and three have left their traces in volcanic ash at [Laetoli, Tanzania]. The footprints of two adult hominids are between 17.5 and 24 centimetres long. The depth of their imprints in the ash indicates the hominids who made them are between four- and five-feet tall.

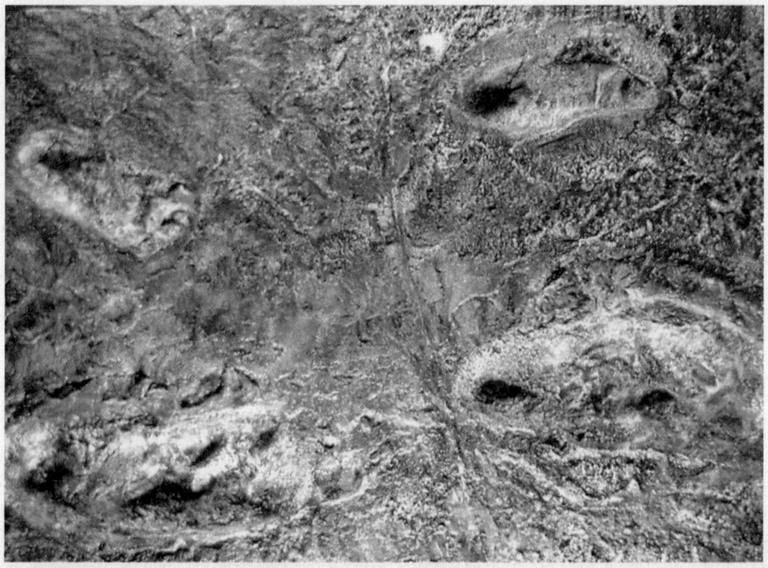

Human footprints in the ash at Laetoli, Tanzania, indicating upright stature.

The footprints reveal that the three hominids interrupted their journey to look to the left. Perhaps they were scouting for predators. Crossing the hominid trail is that of a horse accompanied by a foal.

The ability of hominids to assume an erect position gives them several advantages. The greatest is that it frees their hands for other purposes. Their added height allows them to monitor the approach of carnivorous enemies. Walking upright may also add endurance, enabling them to walk – or even run – for hours, a useful feat in their struggle for survival.

Hominids are the descendants of arboreal primates. They are primarily hunters and scavengers. They can grip with their thumbs and probably use objects such as stones or pieces of wood in their quest for food.

20,000

Europe, c.20,000 BC. Cave painting and engraving are flourishing in southern France and northern Spain. Artists portray their environment with unprecedented realism and mysterious symbolism.

North America, c.18,000 BC. The Wisconsin glaciation covering much of the continent begins to melt and recede.

North America, c.10,000 BC. Groups of PaleoIndian people, originally from Asia, have migrated to the area of the western United States. They travelled along the coast and an inland ice free corridor, avoiding the ice that still covers parts of the continent. They develop a way of life based on hunting large herbivores, such as bison, that graze on grasslands and tundra.

North America, c.9000 BC. PaleoIndians begin to move northward from the western United States into Canada as the southern margin of the glaciation retreats.

Canada, c.8000 BC. PaleoIndians have occupied most southern parts of Canada.

North America, c.6000 BC. A general warming in the climate and the receding glaciation is causing environmental changes. Wind and rainfall patterns alter. Forests replace grasslands in the east, and deserts develop in the central and western regions. Large grazing mammals like mammoths and American camels become extinct. PaleoIndian peoples hunt smaller game and eat vegetables in place of the larger animals.

North America, c.4000 BC. The Wisconsin ice field has disappeared from the continent, except for extreme northern areas, completing the melting that began about 14,000 years ago. As millions of square kilometres of ice melted over the millennia, rivers formed and others like the St. Lawrence swelled beyond recognition. Swirling meltwater carved potholes in the Canadian Shield up to three metres in diameter. The runoff also flooded thousands of kilometres of coastline and covered the Beringian land bridge. Animals and humans can no longer cross overland between Siberia and Alaska.

Egypt, c.3000 BC. Priests and scholars pioneer the use of hieroglyphics, a form of writing using symbols and pictures, to record daily life.

New continent is home to thousands

c.8000 BC

[NORTH AMERICA] – The continent of [North America] now has thousands of permanent inhabitants, immigrants from [Eurasia] who have put down roots in their vast new homeland. For at least 20,000 years, groups of hunters have used the frozen [Bering Strait] or [Beringia] as a land bridge to cross back and forth between [Eurasia] and [North America], on the trail of such arctic game as the herds of caribou, bison and woolly mammoth also roaming the continents in search of food.

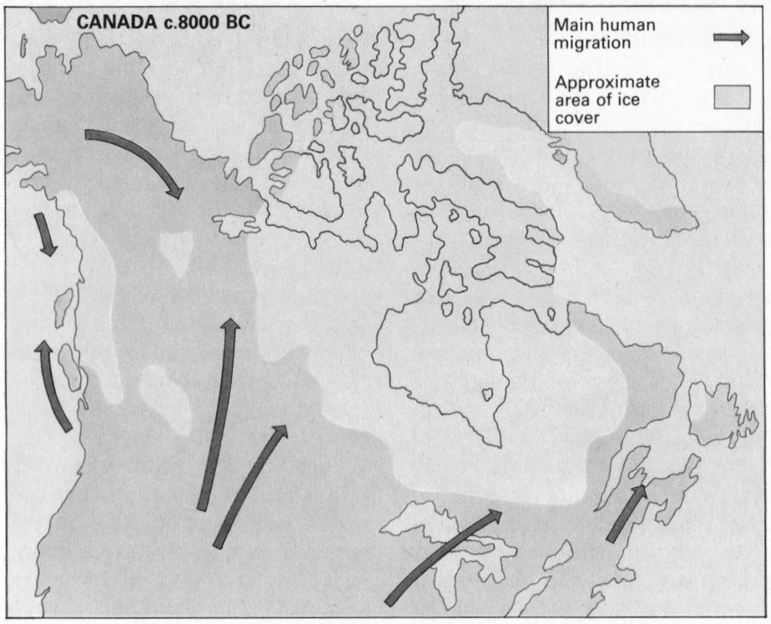

These early visitors did not stay, but the latest arrivals have no choice. The current melting of [North America]'s ice sheets, over three kilometres deep, has drastically raised the sea level, flooding [Beringia] which has again become the [Bering Strait], a sea channel that only those who possess boats can navigate.

The first [North Americans] are PaleoIndians who share a common ancestry. Physically, they vary greatly in height and weight, and in shape of head and nose. They also speak different languages. They do, however, share many common traits: straight, black hair, dark eyes, and reddish-brown skin. They have prominent cheekbones and little hair on their bodies.

[North Americans] are hunter-gatherers. In the warmer weather, they pick fruit and berries and track their prey. Often, their thick-furred dogs help them herd and harass mammoth, caribou and other game into pits and ravines. Their rock cairns, constructed near the shores of glacial lakes where caribou gather to escape swarms of mosquitoes and other biting insects, may be part of their hunting technique, used to channel the animals to where the hunters are waiting. Once trapped, the animals are finished off with spearheads fashioned by chipping rocks.

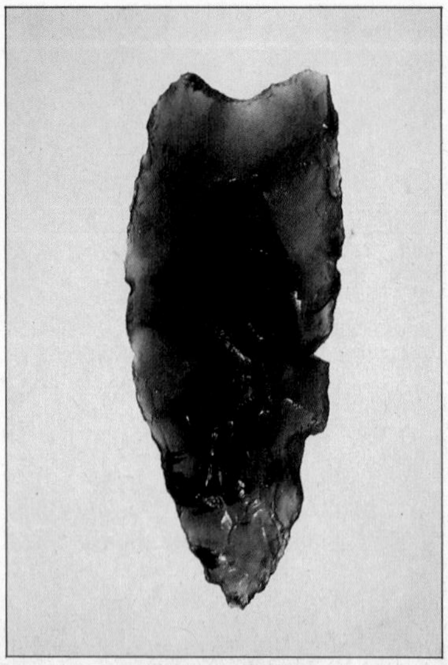

New inhabitants make tools out of rock they carve into fluted points.

The [North Americans] cope well with the harshness and darkness of the prolonged arctic winters. Rarely do they live in caves, preferring to build dwellings, probably domed tents supported by supple saplings and covered with animal skins. They construct their tents over a shallow pit they have already scooped out to keep the interior warmer. They have long possessed the knowledge of fire, and spark it by using flintstones or by rubbing two sticks together. They keep a live fire inside their tents, enduring its smoke so they can warm themselves and cook the food they have preserved and stored during the few months of plenty.

In the [Yukon], hunters sometimes visit the [Bluefish Caves], sheltering overnight in their damp confines before continuing in pursuit of their game. Occasionally, they forget or store things there, tools and the remains of animals they have butchered. Two of their tools, carved out of flint, are the burin and the microblade. They use burins to chisel tools from bones, and microblades to slice and hack meat, and to kill.

The receding glaciation and general warming have provoked many changes in the [North American] way of life. The continent is swiftly becoming divided into different environmental zones with different flora and fauna, and the inhabitants of each region must devise new techniques to suit. On the southern coast of [Labrador], for instance, settlers have discovered the whelping grounds of harpseals, and how easy it is to club them to death.

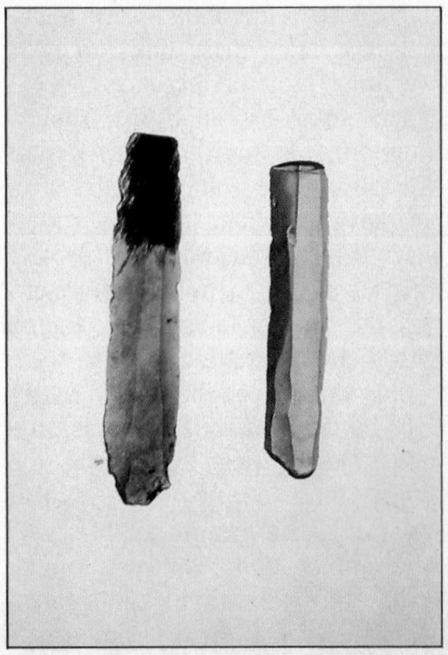

Sharp microblades help inhabitants kill their prey and slice meat.

Musk-ox face new two-legged enemy

c.3000 BC

ARCTIC CANADA – The great musk-ox is falling victim to the growing numbers of its deadly human predators whose weapons and techniques the animal cannot withstand. Musk-ox methods of defence against large northern wolves, in which bulls ring the calves, charge forward and then back into a semi-circle, is totally ineffective against humans, whose spears kill their prey one by one. The musk-ox is surviving only because it lives in remote, isolated areas.

Human clothing is not practical

c.3000 BC

[CANADA] – People in southern [Canada] persist in following impractical fashion trends. Their clothes, mainly leather, are not warm enough for the cold winters. Women wear short leather skirts over bare legs, while men go for leggings. Both sexes sport decorative capes and moccasins. All their clothing is made of skins with the outer fur scraped off.

[Canadians] in northern forests fashion much warmer clothing from animal skins, but the southerners so far have resisted adopting these styles. Instead, they copy the styles of their neighbors to the south [in the United States]. Despite the discomfort of cold, they prefer these revealing garments that show off the tattoos and ornaments they paint onto their bodies as well as their faces.

[Canadian] women learn how to make leather from their mothers, and the process is thus passed on through the generations. First, animal skin must be thoroughly scraped to remove inner layers of skin and outer fur. Next, it is treated with urine or animal fat to ensure the softness of the leather. Then, it is cleaned, smoked and softened, and finally cut into garments. Without this complex process, animal skins become rigid and hard.

Varied cultures take root and flourish

Western peoples adapt to bounty of the land and the seas

3000 BC

PACIFIC COAST – Vast amounts of salmon run up the rivers of [Canada]'s Pacific coast areas in the summertime, and the natives' new techniques for catching and preserving the tasty fish have led to larger and more complex communities.

The sea level has stablized on the west coast and the temperate climate has encouraged the growth of thick stands of cedar. More and more people are settling here. Salmon, readily available, is a main source of food. Also gathered are considerable quantities of shellfish.

Inland, between the coastal mountains and the [Rockies], the Plateau people have evolved as a stable culture. Here, migrating salmon are taken in the late summer and kept in bark-lined pits. Roasted roots are also stored. Together with the salmon, these roots keep people fed during long winters spent in pit-houses. Built with timber frames over excavated pits and covered with an insulating layer of earth, the houses can be as big as 20 metres in diameter and are sometimes clustered in villages of more than 100 people.

East of the [Rockies] the bison, or buffalo, is still the staple food and the principal source of tools. Even its dung is used – to heat the buffalo-skin lodges and the food. As the climate becomes cooler, the grass can support more buffalo, which, in turn, is certain to lead more natives to the area. Hunting buffalo is a highly skilled occupation. The Plains hunters risk their lives and must employ great cunning to drive herds of the skittish and nearsighted beasts over cliffs.

People are interested in personal as well as economic matters. They enjoy decorating themselves, and many adults wear large circular wooden plugs – called labrets – in their lower lips, and skewers in their noses.

People living in coastal [Canada] hunt sea mammals as well as big game.

Life of northern people centres on caribou, musk-ox and bison

2500 BC

NORTHERN [CANADA] – Caribou, musk-ox and buffalo have become integral parts of the diets of [Canada]'s northern peoples on the plateau and in the mountains of the far northwest. Caribou and musk-ox are hunted most often in the summer on barren ground north of the tree line. The encroachment of forests on the grassland the buffalo so desperately need to survive is kept in check with regular and deliberate grass fires.

Since flexibility is crucial for survival in the harsh northern climate, natives often find themselves looking for alternatives to caribou, musk-ox and buffalo when these animals are in shorter supply. At these times it's more commonplace to see the natives hunting small game or fishing to supply themselves with food. On the coast, sea mammals are also hunted.

Tools of these northern peoples include large and coarsely-flaked knives, and, in the [Keewatin] region, large stone spear-points.

Life is similar for people living around [Hudson Bay]. The great herds of caribou and buffalo have followed the retreating glaciers northward, and as might be expected, they are being pursued by the hunters. Bark canoes are used extensively, and seasonal camps are established at the narrow points in rivers and lakes. Migrating caribou crossing at these narrows can easily be spotted and dispatched by the canoe-borne hunters.

Hunting the musk-ox is a highly skilled occupation in parts of [Canada].

Eastern peoples develop technologies for hunting

c.3000 BC

CENTRAL [CANADA] – The glaciers have been gone for some time and the land of central [Canada], now covered with pines and leafy trees, is more bountiful than before.

As a result, a more diversified way of life has emerged to replace that of the PaleoIndians. The people of the new Boreal Archaic culture hunt deer, elk, bear and beaver. In their armory of weapons used for both hunting and warfare are the banner-stone, an ingenious device that adds weight to the throwing board and the spear, which is ejected from a groove in the board. Spear points, small, large, leaf-shaped or triangular, together with knives, chisels and fishing hooks, are made of copper, and they are acquired in trade with the Old Copper people living near the copper deposits on the shores of [Lake Superior].

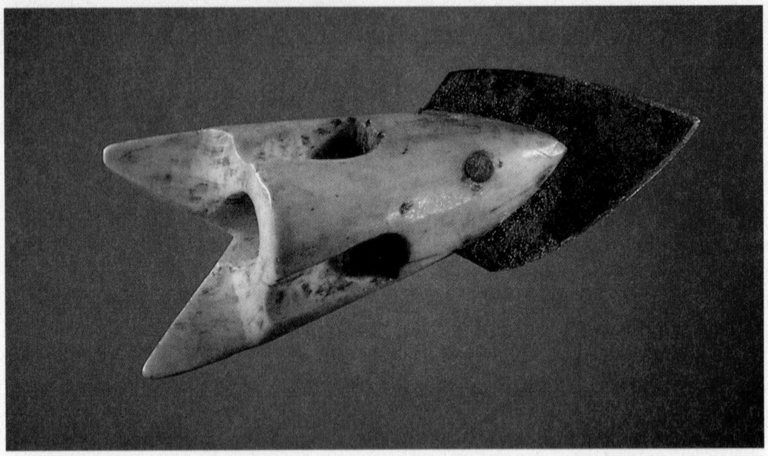

The Maritime Archaic people use harpoons to hunt for seal and to catch swordfish and walrus. They make their tools from ore containing copper.

In what might be the birth of metallurgy in [Canada], ore containing a high percentage of copper – often called "native copper" – is first beaten into the appropriate shape and then heated so as to render it less brittle. Some tools are also being made of slate.

On the east coast, the bills of swordfish and the tusks of walruses sometimes provide the raw material for tools and ornaments. So does a translucent stone, known as Ramah chert, which comes from an outcrop in northern [Labrador]. The highly valued stone is traded for a thousand miles down the Atlantic coast.

To this coast every spring come the Maritime Archaic people to hunt seals basking on the pack ice. Later in the season they harpoon the swordfish and the walrus from their dug-out canoes. In the winter they withdraw into the interior in pursuit of caribou.

The people of this land appear to believe that this annual round continues after death, for with their dead they bury weapons and tools. On the bodies and the gifts that accompany them is sprinkled a layer of powdered ochre, a red clay which has deep religious significance for all the peoples of central and eastern [Canada].

Dorset dwellings popping up in the Arctic

1700-800 BC

ARCTIC – With the arrival of the Dorset people, the type of winter dwelling in [Arctic Canada] is changing again. Dorset people are known for their rectangular homes, sunken into the ground and with walls built of sod – and perhaps blocks of snow for added insulation.

Dorset homes traditionally have two sleeping platforms that flank the cooking area and can accommodate several families. Legend has it the narrow platforms force the Dorset to sleep with their feet propped up against the wall, though it is more likely they sleep next to a source of heat in the home.

Dorset people use shaman masks like the one above in religious ceremonies.

Before 1700 BC, homes of arctic people were designed exclusively for land-based activities. No evidence exists of domed snowhouses, so common to later arrivals. These earlier nomadic people moved from site to site living in tents all year round.

The tents, capable of housing one or two families, were covered with heavy musk-ox skin supported by driftwood poles. Inside these small oval or rectangular dwellings, an open hearth made of stone slabs held the very small fire used to cook food. Basically, the insides of these homes were unheated and the inhabitants huddled under skin blankets for long periods during the winter to keep warm.

Between 1700 BC and 800 BC – just before the Dorset arrived – a number of changes occurred in the type of dwellings seen in the Arctic. They became more circular and were surrounded by a ring of large rocks that held down the edge of the tent. The use of soapstone blubber-burning lamps meant that some form of heating now existed.

Dorset art rich in religious meaning

c.500 BC

ARCTIC – Art is thriving among the Dorset people of northern [Canada]. The art shows a complex view of the universe that is closely attuned to the physical environment, a highly developed aesthetic sensibility, and rich religious feeling. Shamans use detailed and beautiful art objects carved from bone, ivory and wood to perform a variety of rituals that make up the spiritual lives of the people. In one ceremony, they try to ensure good health, weather and hunting with driftwood carvings painted with ochre. The carvings represent animals like the bear, the spiritual allies of the shaman, and sometimes designs of the animals' skeletons are carved in the wood. The shamans, skilled in adapting to different religious performances, act as bears and other animals in various rituals. They put sets of ivory animal teeth in their mouths as part of the ceremony. Other art objects have different meanings in the Dorset culture: shamans use small harpoon heads as spiritual weapons, and kill people magically using carvings of them with holes in the chest. The Dorsets also carve beautiful elaborate wands from antlers with as many as 60 faces represented, maybe dead friends and relatives, or Dorset gods.

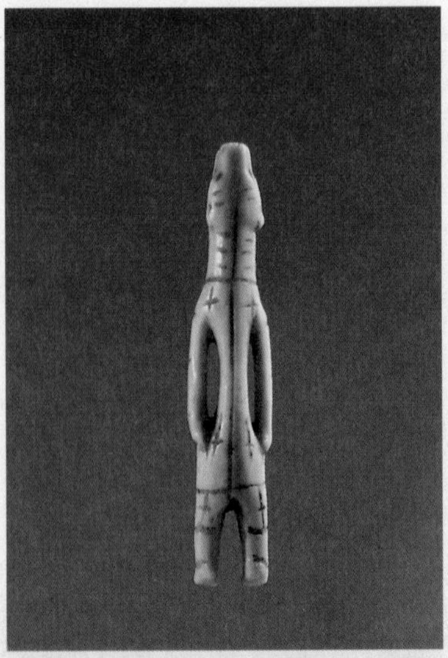

Marks on this Dorset carving of a polar bear represent skeleton, joints.

The Dorsets are descendants of PaleoEskimos who crossed the Bering Strait from Siberia about 1,500 years ago, and then quickly occupied [Arctic Canada]. The Dorsets evolved about 300 years ago, and have a more successful economy than their immediate ancestors.

Arctic architecture: Dorsets adapt to environment

An Inukshuk on Diana Island. Stone structure looks rather like a person.

Two of many cairns - Dorset structures built of stone - on Diana Island.

A Dorset's final resting place is marked by a crude rock structure.

Dorset cairn stands out against the horizon on Diana Island.

Dorset house, a shallow depression surrounded by gravel or stone-block wall.

Dorset stone house on Diana Island will be covered by hides or ice in winter.

1 (1-1400 AD)

Mexico, c.1 AD. Hieroglyphic writing and the highly accurate "Long Count" calendar are developing among the Mayans, who have one of the most advanced civilizations on the continent.

Judaea, April 30, 30 AD. Jesus of Nazareth has been crucified at Golgotha by Roman authorities. His followers call him "the son of God," or Christ (Greek for the Messiah), and credit him with performing many miracles.

Greenland, 985-86. Eric the Red (Eirikr Thorvaldsson), outlawed from his native Norway for murder, leads an expedition of Icelandic colonists to the uninhabited subcontinent of Greenland. They found two settlements.

Atlantic Coast, c.1001. Leif Eriksson's expedition reaches a barren land that he names Helluland [Baffin Island], a wooded land that he names Markland [Labrador], and a temperate land that he names Vinland [located anywhere from Florida to Labrador].

Vinland, c.1002. After wintering at Vinland, Leif sails for Greenland in the spring with a cargo of timber and grapes.

Greenland, c.1004. Thorfinnr Karlsefni, a wealthy Icelandic merchant, leads an expedition consisting of 160 people, four ships, and domestic animals to colonize Vinland.

Hop, c.1005. Thorfinnr's expedition settles for the winter at a bay they call Hop [location unknown]. The weather is mild, wild wheat and grapes grow, and fish and wildlife are abundant.

Hop, c.1006. In the spring, Thorfinnr's colonists meet natives whom they call Skraelings. They trade with them, but fighting breaks out and several settlers are killed.

Atlantic Coast, c.1006. Thorfinnr's expedition sails home, concluding they cannot maintain a colony in the new lands.

Europe, 1348. Hundreds of thousands of people, a third of the population, die from an apparently incurable plague known as the "Black Death."

Huron Country, c.1400. Huron peoples [around the Great Lakes] have been growing corn for the last 400 years and have recently begun growing beans and squash. The crops were developed in Mexico between 5000 and 2000 BC, and were gradually passed north.

Leif Eriksson establishes base camp

1000

VINLAND – An expedition led by Leif Eriksson has set up camp in a new colony it's calling Vinland [anywhere from Florida to Labrador]. The land gets its name from the abundance of grapes and vines. The eldest son of the legendary Eirikr Thorvaldsson (Eric the Red), Eriksson and a 35-man crew left Greenland to search for land trader Bjarni Herjolfsson, sighted in 986 when he was sailing from Iceland to Greenland and a storm blew his ship off course in the Atlantic Ocean. When Eriksson and crew reached Vinland, they decided to build homes and spend the winter. After the houses were built, Eriksson split his forces in two – half to explore the area and half to stay in camp. Eriksson and his men have noticed many things about Vinland. Huge salmon swim in its rivers and lakes, there is no frost in winter, and day and night are of more equal length than in Iceland.

Thorvaldr Eriksson and eight Dorsets killed in Vinland skirmish

1006

VINLAND – A fierce battle with the natives here has taken the life of explorer Thorvaldr Eriksson. Eriksson's last wish as he lay dying from an arrow wound was to be buried on the spot where he had hoped to build his home in Vinland. Eriksson's brother Leif gave Vinland its name in the year 1000 when he became the first Norseman to set up camp here. Leif's return to Greenland in 1001 sparked interest in the new land. Others hoped to visit the place Leif said had dew sweet like nothing else he'd ever tasted. Thorvaldr borrowed Leif's ship in 1002 and sailed to Vinland with 30 men. Their first 18 months here they lived in houses Leif and his men had built. But in the summer of 1004 they set out to search for a suitable place to build a new settlement. They eventually came to an area rich in trees which entranced Thorvaldr. After he picked it for a settlement, Thorvaldr and his men saw nine Dorset tribesmen. They killed eight, but one escaped and roused his tribe. It wasn't long before the Dorset returned in canoes, surrounding the Viking ship and bombarding it with arrows. Thorvaldr lived just long enough to see his men defeat the natives.

Norse explorer Thorvaldr Eriksson battles Dorset Indians after finding a location suitable for building a settlement. Eriksson is killed in the battle.

Norse trader is first Viking on continent

986

GREENLAND – There are reports that a Norse trader headed here has spotted land never seen before by Europeans after a storm drove him off course. Determined to spend the winter with his father in Greenland, Bjarni Herjolfsson and his crew battled a violent storm three days after sailing from Iceland and were driven far south off their course. When the storm abated, Herjolfsson and his men sailed for a day until they sighted a forested and hilly land. That sighting marks the first time Europeans have seen the shoreline of what may be a new continent on the other side of the Atlantic Ocean.

A restored Norse sailing ship. Norse ships are very sturdy to help them survive long voyages of exploration. Explorers such as the Eriksson brothers are interested in colonizing new-found lands.

Inuit story of the orphan's revenge

The Inuit people pass down this story from generation to generation. It is about a young boy named Kaujjarjuk, who goes out hunting seal with his sister and their parents. Unluckily, they are swept out to sea on an ice float. They disappear into the distant waters, and are given up for dead.

After many days, the children land on strange shores. There they are adopted by different families, and are treated badly. Kaujjarjuk is forced to eat and sleep with the dogs. But one older woman is good to him. Using magic, she conjures up a way for the return of Kaujjarjuk's eldest brother, who comes to help him. Kaujjarjuk becomes stronger and takes revenge on the people who abused him. He takes as his wife the older woman who was good to him.

Thule Inuit occupying the Arctic as Dorset people disappear

c.1000

ARCTIC – The Dorset culture has disappeared from [Arctic Canada], its place taken by a new and vibrant people who have introduced to the area a sophisticated sea-hunting culture that comes from [Alaska]. While the disappearance of the Dorset is shrouded in mystery, it appears certain they were either driven out, killed or absorbed by the newcomers, called the Thule Inuit.

The Thule are calling themselves "Inuit," meaning "the people." They speak *Inuktitut,* originate from northern [Alaska] and base their economy and technology on the hunt for the great [Greenland] and [Bowhead] whale. The recent warming trend has reduced the amount of sea ice, allowing these huge mammals, each yielding several tons of meat and blubber, to be hunted further east along the Arctic coast than ever before.

Following the whales, the Thule bring with them a hunting and weapons technology far superior to the people they encounter. Dogs pull their sleds, and they have overcome the problem of snow-blindness and ice glare by inventing slitted snow goggles. Their summer homes are made of logs, and their winter dwellings appear to be perfectly insulated.

It appears the Thule have perfected the art of arctic survival. Coupled with their more aggressive nature, their superiority doomed the Dorset people.

The Thule people build their homes out of whale bones covered with hide.

A mosaic of cultures blossoms in a settled land

c.1000

[CANADA] – There is a colorful mosaic of cultures in this vast land of a third of a million people, of whom nearly half live on the Pacific coast. The linguistic variety is even more marked: there are 50 languages grouped into 11 families, each one distinct from the others. By far the largest language family is the Algonquian, which is spoken from the [Atlantic] coast to the foothills of the [Rockies]. However, often the dialects within the language groups are so different that they are mutually unintelligible.

[North American] languages are extremely complex. Many use prefixes and suffixes added to root words to express such concepts as time, duration, number and category. Some have word forms to convey information about whether an object described is visible to the speaker, or if he has personally experienced what he is speaking about.

But despite linguistic differences, the groups manage to communicate. On the northern shores of [Lake Ontario], the Iroquoian speakers take advantage of their warm summer to grow corn. Perhaps they began to do so after frequent contacts with their southern agricultural neighbors, who learned it from [Mexican] corn-growers.

On the [Pacific] coast the consistency of climate and resource abundance and the ease of communications by sea encourage the development of cultural similarity despite great linguistic diversity. With its densely populated permanent villages and social hierarchy – titled nobles on the top and slaves on the bottom – the Pacific coast culture contrasts sharply with those of the scattered nomads of the Plains and Subarctic.

Peoples like the Plains' Blackfoot or the Cree of the Subarctic forests organize themselves into small bands of relatives whose leaders are "first among equals" and not hereditary aristocrats as on the coast.

Certain common cultural traits have survived the long process of cultural diversification. From the [Atlantic] to the [Pacific] and from the [Great Lakes] to the [Hudson Bay], there is recourse to the shaman to diagnose and cure the sick and to the water vapor "sweat lodge" to purify.

One distinctively common North American trait that's become evident is the passion the people here have for gambling. It usually takes the form of a "hand game," with one player guessing the hand in which his opponent has concealed small carved objects.

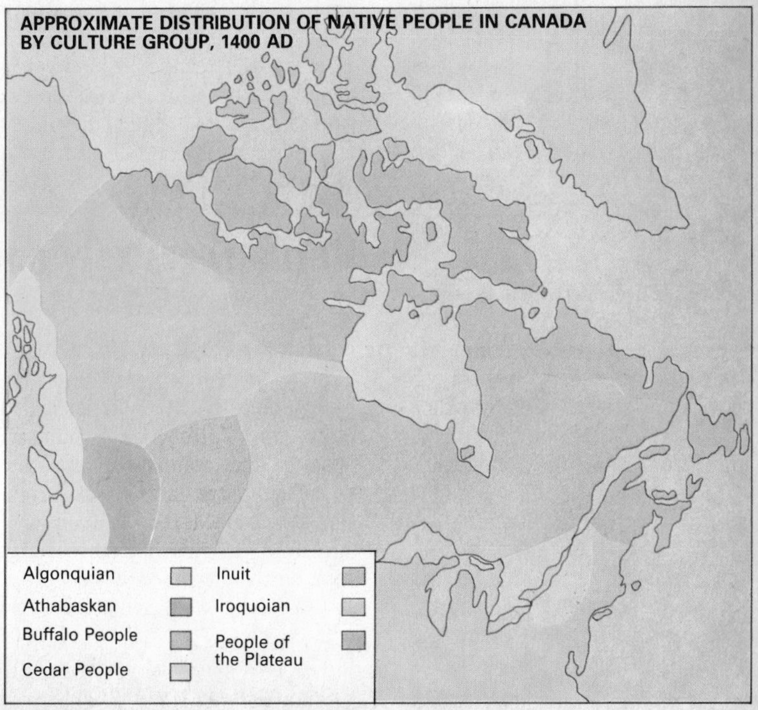

Athabaskan natives are thriving in northern lands

c.1400

NORTHERN [CANADA] – Fifteen groups of native peoples live and hunt in a vast expanse of territory stretching from the northwest valleys of the three great rivers [Yukon, Mackenzie and Peace] eastward to the shores of the inland sea [Hudson Bay]. Collectively known as the Athabaskans and speaking variations of the widespread Athabaskan language, they call themselves Kutchin, Tinneb, Dene and other names, all of them meaning "people."

People of the [Yukon] plateau, who live in dug-out winter houses and wear nose-skewers and battle armor of slate and hide, are gradually adopting the social class systems of their coastal and western neighbors, whom they meet for either friendly trading or fierce fighting. The northern Athabaskans use long stone knives with forked handles, similar to those of their enemies, the Mackenzie Inuit. Also adopted from Inuit clothing are coats with pointed tails and front flaps. The Athabaskans decorate their bodies as well. Some are tatooed, while others adorn themselves with face paint on special occasions.

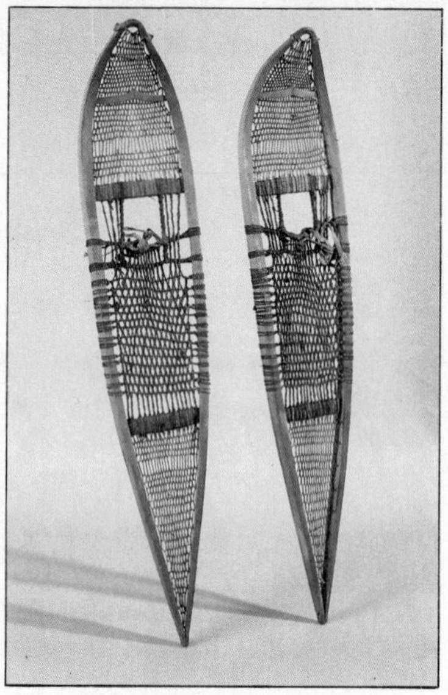

The Athabaskans use snowshoes.

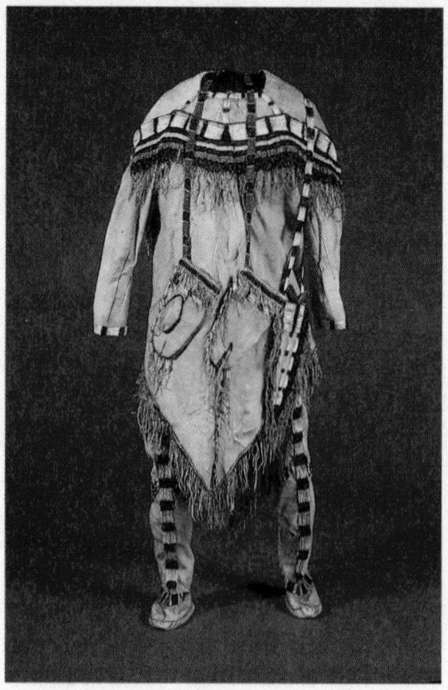

Athabaskans adopt Inuit clothing.

Leadership and organization of everyday living is strongest in the west, but among all Athabaskans the chief's status is more revered than among the Inuit. The children's upbringing is strict: adolescent boys must fast and learn to endure hardship; on reaching puberty, the girls are secluded for several years, living and travelling away from their families.

Athabaskan women work very hard, but their status is generally lower than that of men. Many women achieve considerable power in their households. However, in wrestling matches and gambling, women are sometimes passed from man to man as prizes.

Athabaskan musicians are drummers who play at gambling and dancing events. Skins cover only one end of their small drums.

One of the most popular forms of family entertainment is recounting legends. In one legend, an infant boy is found among musk-ox droppings, then grows up to become a hero. And the Dogrib Athabaskans tell the legend that traces their origin back to a woman who married a dog – a tale strikingly similar to a legend the Inuit tell about their Indian neighbors.

Athabaskan story of the great flood

The Athabaskan Dogrib, or Doné, tell this story about the meaning of the Northern Lights.

The young Cree orphan Caribou-footed has been captured by the cruel and evil Big Man. Hottah, the great moose, helps him escape. Caribou-footed then spends seven suns in the home of Nesnabi the Good Man. When he leaves, Nesnabi gives him a gift of seven arrows. Caribou-footed hunts as he walks, and an arrow sticks into the branch of a tree. He forgets that Nesnabi has warned him not to go after it, and he begins to climb the tree. As he moves upward, so does the arrow. Up, up they move, until Caribou-footed follows the arrow into Sky World.

Now whenever they see the northern lights, the Dogribs say that Caribou-footed is summoning them to the home he has found for them beyond the sky, the home many of them will soon pass to.

Caribou dominate Chipewyan way of life

c.1400

[HUDSON BAY] – At the edge of the forests to the west of [Hudson Bay] live people known to their Cree neighbors as the Chipewyan, meaning "pointed skins" – a reference to the shape of their caribou coats. They call themselves Dene, "the people," and their environment is perhaps the harshest in the world: long, bitterly cold winters and summers hot enough to hatch the hosts of mosquitoes and blackflies which torment both the humans and the caribou on which they depend.

Each summer, carrying light canoes, the Dene follow the herds onto the treeless tundra, where the animals are ambushed crossing rivers. Back in the forest for the winter, caribou are driven into brushwood enclosures equipped with interior mazes and snares at the exits. Caribou hides make clothing, tents, ropes and snowshoes.

Northerners rely on canine companions

c.1400

NORTHWEST [CANADA] – Like all native peoples, the Athabaskans rely on their domesticated dogs for protection, hunting, hauling and companionship. The dogs are large and thick-furred, similar in appearance to their wolf ancestors. To this day, these dogs sometimes interbreed with wolves, just as their southern cousins do with coyotes.

The Athabaskans' relationship with their dogs is traditional: they share food and the warmth of their fires, and in return the animals guard their camps, warn them of intruders and protect them from enemies. The dogs are also valued partners in the hunt, tirelessly sniffing out and tracking game better than any human. In the cold northern forests, they wear harnesses and haul loaded sleds over the snow. Dogs willingly perform all these duties for their masters, whom from puppyhood they have identified as the leaders of their pack.

Story of the big snow in the north

At one time, the Dogrib and Slavey say, animals, fish and birds ate only plants and never thought of eating one another.

One day it grew dark, and a great snowstorm covered all the plants, killing the animals. The chief sent messengers to Sky World to find out why. In Sky World, they met three bear cubs whose mother was out hunting caribou. The messengers were horrified that the animals in Sky World eat one another.

The messengers saw four bags hanging on the wall. One held the powers of the wind, the second the rain, and the third the cold. But the cubs were silent about the fourth bag. The messengers took the bag, and the cubs, back to earth. Inside the bag were the sun, moon and stars, which ended the darkness and dried up the snow. The bear cubs became earth creatures, and the other animals learned to eat animals, birds and fish.

Seasons controlling Algonquin migration patterns

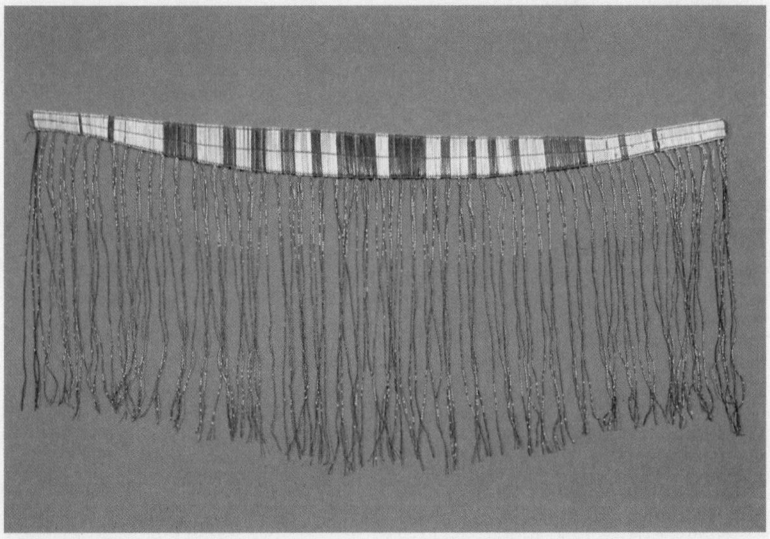

Algonquins make quill embroidery and other crafts, then trade with Iroquois.

Birch bark container made by Algonquins who are living near birch forests.

c.1400
NORTHERN [CANADA] – Like the Athabaskans, the eight principal groups of Algonquian-speaking peoples are hunters, trappers and fishermen following a seasonal circuit around their home territory. This large area, south and east of the inland sea [Hudson Bay], is covered with tundra in the north that gradually gives way in the south to willow, spruce, tamarack and birch forests. Vital winter travelling gear includes snowshoes with a circular design. (The Athabaskan Chipewyans make snowshoes to fit left and right feet.)

While Algonquians hunt with spears and bows and arrows, they trap with snare and dead-fall, by which a heavy weight drops on prey to disable or kill it. They are expert builders of both dug-out and bark-covered canoes, trading some of their craft to the Iroquois in the south. They fish with nets made from root fibre and strips of hide or bark, and spear fish at night, using gum and bark torches to cast light from their canoes.

Beothuk and Micmac peoples have inherited some of the Maritime Archaic culture. They journey many kilometres out to sea in distinctive canoes, built high at the bow, centre and stern, to hunt seals or collect birds' eggs on islands. The people of power (shamans or medicine men), seek guidance for the hunters by scanning cracks on animals' burned shoulder bones.

All of the eight principal groups revere their creator, known as Manitou. Their legends include other spirit-like figures such as the Ojibwa's Nanabozho, otherwise known as the great rabbit, and Wisakedjuk, the Cree's trickster.

Healers summon spiritual helpers

c.1400
[CANADA] – From west of the [Rockies] to the coast of [Labrador], healers – or shamans, as they are called – use the shaking tent ceremony to summon their spirit helpers.

When night falls, the shaman is bound hand and foot with thongs and placed in a small bark or hide tent especially made for the occasion. He then sings to attract the spirits, whose arrival is marked by the shaking of the tent and the casting off of his thongs. Speaking in the spirits' strange and unintelligible language, the shaman asks questions about the location of game or the origin of illness.

To effect a cure, he must know whether the ailment is caused by a malevolent person – a witch – or by an offence against the spirits, such as the breaking of a taboo.

Fish the staff of life for Micmac people

c.1400
ATLANTIC COAST [Maritimes] – Roasted, smoked or boiled but always fish. For most of the year the Micmac diet is supplied largely from the excellent fishing grounds off the Atlantic coast. Besides being rich in fish and shellfish, the ocean is a source of sea birds and water mammals such as seals, whales and porpoises.

In spring people move up river to catch the spawning fish and in fall these rivers yield up eels on their way to the ocean. Only in February and March when migrating fish leave the coast must people rely totally on the few forest animals for food. The movement of the Micmac is so regulated by the animals available for food that the names of the seasons refer to these creatures.

Birch bark canoes are handy for hunting

c.1400
[WOODLANDS] – The native peoples of this land have developed a water craft well-suited to hunting and transportation. The birch bark canoe is, basically, a light wood frame lashed together with roots or rawhide and covered with patches of bark from birch trees. This bark is particularly supple and can be peeled off the tree in great pieces.

A small canoe made in this manner is easy to paddle and light enough for one man to carry. It is repairable on the spot. Different tribes have somewhat different designs. These designs are modified according to the intended use of the craft. Smaller canoes are usually used for hunting while larger ones are made for the transportation of goods.

Micmacs revere mighty Glooscap

One day, four Micmac men visited Glooscap, who created the world, and asked for his help. The first wished to be rich, the second well-liked, the third to lose his wicked temper, and the fourth to live forever.

Glooscap brought them to a river. He sent the fourth man to a rocky point, and transformed him into a gnarled cedar tree. He gave the other three men pouches, which they opened when they reached home. Inside the pouches was a sweet-smelling ointment which they rubbed on their bodies. The man who wanted to be rich discovered he was a good hunter. The bad-tempered man became peaceful and meek. The man who wanted to be liked was now respected and admired by his people.

▷

Fertile land well-suited for the Iroquoian peoples

c.1400

ST. LAWRENCE REGION – The Iroquoian-speaking peoples have settled in the arrowhead of land between the eastern Great Lakes and along the great river [St. Lawrence] to the tidal waters. There, the stony ground of the Canadian Shield gives way to fertile soil covered with pine, cedar, oak and other deciduous trees.

While the Hurons hunt deer and catch fish, as much as three-quarters of their food supply comes from agricultural crops. The men clear the ground with stone tools before the women plant and harvest corn, beans and squash. This regular supply of food enables large groups to live in one place for several years. Tobacco is also cultivated – especially by the people of the southwest – and is traded far afield for use in religious ceremonies or smoked purely for pleasure. When the men are not trading or digging, they are either warring with their enemies or indulging in such pastimes as games of lacrosse.

The Iroquoians regard their world as an ongoing competition between good and evil spirits. In wintertime particularly, their religious societies such as the False Faces hold ceremonies to stave off sickness or ensure good farming in the coming season.

Several families share the long, rectangular residences grouped within palisades surrounded for defence by sharpened poles. Within the compounds, the women grind corn with wooden pestle and hollowed stone mortars. The men make spiked warclubs, bows and arrows and axes of either stone or copper. Because there are fewer birch trees here than in the boreal forest, the Iroquois often have to trade with their northern neighbors for bark canoes and snowshoes.

Women are the heads of families, and elect men to their governing councils. The Mohawks and Oneidas are developing a system of government with the Onandagas, Cayugas and Senecas in the southwest. North of the Great Lakes, several Huron tribes are forming a confederacy. Of all the peoples [of Canada], these organized Iroquoians seem the most likely to change the balance between culture groups – and man and nature.

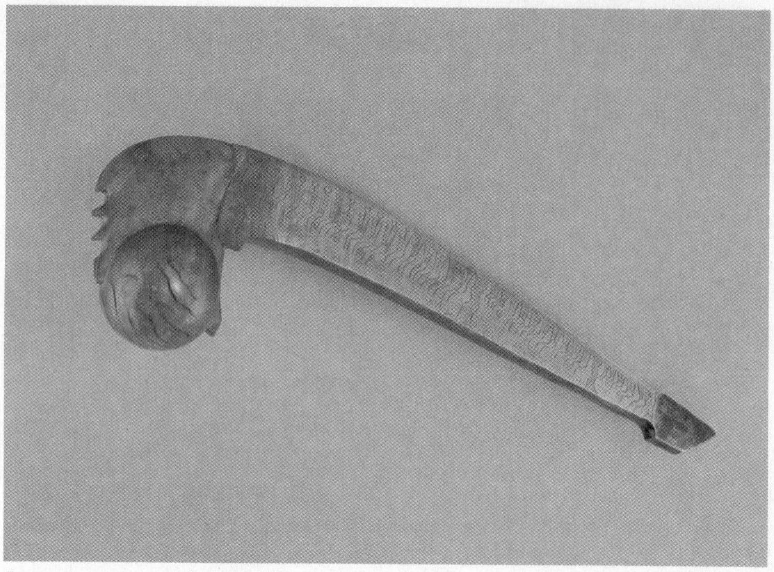

Iroquoian men make spiked warclubs, as well as bows, arrows and axes.

Women rule the roost in Iroquois homes for extended families

c.1400

[EASTERN WOODLANDS] – To the Iroquois woman falls the drudgery and labor, but at home she rules the roost. And what a home it is! A typical longhouse is about nine metres wide and 30 metres long and houses about 10 families.

The Indian longhouses are constructed of a wood frame covered with bark that is held together by saplings. There is a storage area at either end of the house and racks in the centre for the other possessions. The fires are built in a row down the centre. A family lives on either side of each fire. Not only the home but the village and fields are the domain of the women.

A typical Iroquois longhouse constructed of wood frame covered with bark.

The maternal family headed by its matriarch, the senior living woman, has certain control over the children of its sons. It even maintains a stock of first names for its children. These names are usually derived from the first thing seen by the midwife after the birth of a baby.

A matron is elected by the women of each clan. It is she who governs all households of her clan. A clan consists of two or more maternal families who consider the members of each generation to be siblings.

The men concern themselves with matters such as hunting, war, peace and trade. Although the men govern the villages, they attain their offices through female succession. Descent, inheritance and succession pass to family members from their mother. A man belongs to his mother's clan. He must marry outside his clan and when he does he moves to his wife's home. Although the men build the houses and furnishings, these items belong to the women.

Story of earth and Great Turtle

The Iroquoian people tell this story about the creation of the world.

In the beginning, there were only the Sky World and the Water World. The creatures in them understood each other and lived together in peace.

One day, Sky Woman fell from the Sky World. Two loons flying by joined their bodies to cushion her fall, and saved her from drowning. The loons cried out for help, and the Great Turtle, hearing their mournful voices, came to help. He placed Sky Woman on his back.

The sea and sky creatures gathered around, and were amazed at Sky Woman. She was so beautiful and strong! They decided she should have some earth to live on. So, Great Turtle sent the creatures to find it. After many days and nights, Toad found a small bit of earth. Great Turtle took it and placed it on his back. This was the beginning of the Earth World.

People of the plains live in harmony with herds

Buffalo dominates every aspect of life

A buffalo bull. The people of the plains call buffalo meat "the real thing."

c.1400

THE PLAINS – The buffalo dominates the life of the Buffalo people. It provides them with food, and the Blackfoot Indians call its meat "nitapiksisako" – the real thing – as if contemptuous of other kinds. They also depend on the buffalo for clothing and robes, to make shields, and to cover their portable lodges or tepees: an average tepee requires 12 to 14 hides. The Buffalo people even use the animal's bones, fashioning religious objects, drinking vessels and tools from them.

Like other Buffalo people, the Blackfoot are nomads with limited storage facilities, and depend on regular supplies of fresh meat. But the environment sometimes deprives them of it. Terrible blizzards keep them away from the plains where the buffalo are wintering, or the fires that consume the dry prairie brush drive the herds away from the hunters. Then, when their stock of pemmican is exhausted, the people starve.

Grassland people speak four languages

c.1400

THE GRASSLANDS – On vast expanses of grasslands dotted with aspen forests, there are millions of buffalo providing the main – though not the only – livelihood of the people. There are eight groups of Buffalo people, whose way of life has changed little since their ancestors hunted animals within sight of the ice sheets thousands of years ago.

The Buffalo people speak four languages: Athabaskan to the north, Kooteneian to the west, Siouan to the east and Algonquian along the two rivers joining to flow into the inland sea [Hudson Bay].

Buffalo people follow the roaming buffalo herds, with families living year-round in cone-shaped tepees covered with the large hides of the animals that provide their sustenance. In the cooler weather, a mixture of dried buffalo droppings and wood fuels fires in the tents. Families sleep on animal hides, and during the day lean against backrests of woven willow. For emergency food supplies, women pound dried meat with fat and berries into a thick paste called pemmican.

The introduction and refinement of bows and arrows has made hunting buffalo easier. Since the search for food does not allow much time for systematic warfare, animal-hunting weapons are used in skirmishes with other humans.

The land of the Buffalo people is mostly dry, so they only build temporary "bull-boats" of branches and buffalo hides for transporting families across rivers. They dress in deerskin, adding outer garments of rabbit skin blankets and buffalo robes for warmth in winter.

While they live in small groups most of the time, occasionally the Buffalo people come together to drive a herd of buffalo into killing traps or over cliffs. Cliff drives are used more in the summer.

Although the existence of the Buffalo people centres on the animal that provides them with food, clothing and shelter, the eagle is also important in their legends. Its feathers are worn as symbols of rank or to recognize daring deeds.

The Buffalo people's religion is complex and intensely personal. Spirits, some good, others evil, pervade their world. The people begin each day with a prayer, and in all their activities – eating, hunting – honor the spirits. Often they seek direct communication with them, fasting in solitary until the spiritual helper appears. Holy men – the shamans – undertake such contacts to benefit the whole tribe.

Pemmican ideal travelling food

c.1400

WESTERN [CANADA] – If you are travelling, there is nothing better than pemmican as a compact and nourishing food supply. Made from dried buffalo meat, it is a mainstay in the diet of prairie peoples.

Women make pemmican by pounding dried meat with stones until it is almost a powder. Next, they mix it with hot melted buffalo fat. When it cools, they store the finished product in skin bags. For a special touch, crushed berries or peppermint leaves are sometimes added.

Buffalo die en masse in native killing pits

c.1400

THE FOOTHILLS – The native Indians have an effective practice for collecting a store of food, clothing, shelter and other supplies all in one fell swoop, and they have been doing it for thousands of years. A herd of buffalo is driven over a steep cliff into an enclosure. Those not killed instantly in the fall are easily dispatched by the hunters and the gathering begins.

Hides are used for clothing and tent coverings and blankets. Horn and bone can be made into various implements. Hair is braided into ropes or used as stuffing. Sinew is used for sewing and bow strings. Even yellow dye can be made from the gall bladder.

Hunting method calls for herds of buffalo to be driven over a cliff.

The origin of fire revealed in story

Once there was no fire. The people suffered and died. Coyote decided to help them. He climbed to the mountaintop and stole fire from the three Fire Beings. The Fire Beings chased him. Coyote threw the fire to Squirrel. The hot flames turned up his tail. He passed the fire to Chipmunk. The Fire Beings clawed stripes in his back. He gave the fire to Frog. The Beings pulled off his tail. But they could do nothing to Wood, who swallowed the fire. Then Coyote rubbed two dry pieces of wood together, and showed how to make fire.

Plateau people look to fish as main source of diet

c.1400

FAR WEST – Seven main groups of people count on fish as their staple diet in the region that runs between the Rocky and coast mountain ranges and from the northern [Peace] river to the southern [Columbia] river.

Those nearest the west coast rely heavily on the abundant supply of salmon that travel upriver – in a spectacle of breathtaking beauty – to spawning grounds in the interior. Salmon are caught in a number of ways. In the narrow canyons, long-handled gaff hooks and dip nets are more effective than the nets and fish weirs used downstream. Women process the fish, smoking and drying large quantities for the winter. All of the groups catch lake fish with nets, hooks or spears.

The climate and landscape are varied, with forest and desert, rolling grasslands, deep gorges and many long, narrow lakes. Depending on the locality, the people also hunt for meat and hides. Their catches include moose, elk, deer, sheep, cougar and bear.

While people of the plateau live in tents covered with hides, bark or woven rush mats in the summer, in the winter the most northerly groups build cabins of logs and turf.

Within the seven groups, some speak Salishan languages, others Athabaskan. Religious practices and social organization of the plateau people are greatly influenced by the cultural traditions of the people who surround them.

Salish people live in tents covered with hides, bark or woven rush mats.

An Interior Salish tribal chief.

Story of coyote and the old man

Coyote has many magical powers he uses to help human beings, the Thomson River people believe. When Coyote has finished his work in making the earth a safer and better place for humans to live in, he feels it is now time to meet Old Man, who knows many things about the world and could teach Coyote new tricks.

They meet, and Old Man asks Coyote to prove his magical powers by moving rivers and mountains. Coyote does all this in good spirit. To reward Coyote for his sweet nature, Old Man builds a large house of ice and places Coyote in it. No one knows where this house is, but it is said that whenever Coyote turns around in it, the weather turns colder. When it is warm no one mentions his name, for fear the cold will return.

Old Man returned to the upper world. It is said that each time he scratches his back, it rains or snows.

Great salmon runs vital for food supply

c.1400

FAR WEST – In late summer and fall, thousands of salmon work their way up the major rivers to spawn in the tributaries. So numerous are the fish that a few weeks harvest can yield a winter's supply of smoked fish and often a surplus for trading.

The falls offer the best fishing, and people gather from far and near. It is a time for socializing just as much as a time for fishing. Usually a salmon chief supervises the construction of weirs or taps and distributes the catch. In places a willow weir with an enclosure at one end is constructed. The fish which gather in the enclosure are speared. Another method is to hang a large basket above an eddy at the foot of the falls. Fish tend to choose the calmer water from which to make their leap up the rocks. Those that don't jump high enough fall back into the basket.

Food stored high and low for lean seasons

c.1400

FAR WEST – Storing food to use during the lean seasons is a major concern for the people of the plateau. The most common cache is the cellar, where fish and berries are kept. Cellars are circular holes about 1.2 metres deep. Baskets of provisions covered with birch bark are placed inside. Then a roof is laid. It consists of a double row of small poles laid side by side, the first at right angles to the second. The cellar is then buried with pine needles and earth, but an opening is left to retrieve the food as it is needed. Often cellars made just to store fish are built into banks, with an opening left on the side.

Caches are also raised into the air. Some look like small roofed houses being held aloft on 1.5- to 1.8-metre poles, and accessible by ladder. Others are platforms tied by ropes onto the lower branches of trees. The goods stored there are covered with bark and mats. These loft caches protect food from mice and other animals. Tools and other implements are also stored there.

How the animals climbed skywards

The Kootenay people tell this story about how the animals climbed up into the sky.

The animal people decided to journey to Sky World, but didn't know how to get there. Bear advised them to shoot arrows upwards into the sky so as to form a rope. After many tries they succeeded, and then all the animals climbed into the sky except for Glutton, who had gone to check his traps. When Glutton discovered that the others had left him behind, he was angry. He pulled down the rope of arrows, scattering them. These became the Rocky Mountains.

The animals who were visiting Sky World could not return to earth. They stole feathers from Thunderbird but there were not enough, and only some could fly back to earth. These became birds. Others fell to the sea and became fish. Those who could not leave Sky World were killed by the Sky people and changed into stars.

West coast cultures are based on the cedar tree

A wood mask worn by the west coast Cedar people, cut from a cedar tree.

The beginning of the Haida world

After he made the world, the Great Creator placed the Haida people on the beautiful Queen Charlotte Islands. But from the beginning, they quarrel amongst themselves. The Creator comes down from the sky and warns them. If they do not live peacefully, they will be destroyed.

The Haida try to live as the Creator has told them, but greed, jealousy and other evil traits prevent them from peaceful coexistence. The quarrelling starts again.

When the Great Creator comes back a second time, he punishes all the bad people by transforming them into cedar trees. He does this to show the people that when they come to live there in peace, they will use the red cedars for many good things. They will take the wood from the trunk of the cedar to make canoes and houses. They will take the roots to make baskets, mats and medicines. They will take fibres from the bark and weave clothing. They will get food from the inner bark.

This is why cedar trees are so important to the Haida people.

c.1400

FAR WEST – The ocean, rivers and forests of the west coast provide one of the world's richest environments for hunting and fishing. The people of the northwest Pacific coast are divided into six linguistic groups, but share a common culture. Their territory extends as far north and south as the rain forests of giant fir, hemlock and cedar grow.

They can be called the Cedar People, because – of all the assets of the region – the cedar tree is ranked highest. Its wood is easily split into planks for the building of houses or to be hollowed out for the building of canoes up to 12 metres long. The woodworkers use adzes, with blades of polished stone. The bark of cedar is made into clothing and fishing nets. From the tree itself, the people also make storage boxes, utensils and totem poles. Masks, feast dishes and wooden boxes are cut into intricate patterns with instruments that range from heavy knives with stone blades to small tools made from the incisor teeth of beaver and porcupine.

Despite distinct language differences, the six west coast groups appear to outsiders as Asiatic in appearance, and in their clothing, possessions and way of life.

The houses of the people, which can stretch up to about 45 metres long, stand in line between the ocean or river, and the forest. Each house holds several families, with the occupants being divided into three classes: slaves, commoners or nobles. The family crests, and other symbols, of the nobles are carved and painted on the house, totem poles, boxes and other possessions. The images carry historical, social and religious meanings. They also blend symbols of human, animal, reptile, bird and everyday life.

The householders are members of clans, and, among the northern groups, they belong to larger units and cannot marry fellow-members: Raven cannot marry Raven; Eagle cannot marry Eagle. Everyone is involved in netting salmon, jigging for halibut, spinning wool from mountain goat and building canoes. Hunting grizzly bear or cougar wins prestige for the successful, as does the whale hunting, with its strictly followed division of duties.

But because the west coast is so rich and fertile, and food is so readily available, the Cedar people can devote a good deal of time to noneconomic concerns. Art is one of their most important pursuits, and great artists are revered. Every object of daily life may be decorated, even spoons and bowls. Both lifelike and abstract styles are used, but the subject is always recognizable. For example, a broad tail and large gappy teeth represent the beaver, a mouthful of jagged teeth the shark.

In winter, life moves indoors, with games, singing and dancing. This activity often has religious as well as social significance. Secret societies such as the Giants, Grizzlies and Cannibals perform elaborate plays to the sound of whistles, rattles and drums, and create illusions with smoke and trapdoors.

Wealth is obtained by work, war and trade, but the right to titles and ranks is inherited. However, the recipients first have to prove their worthiness. They do so through the potlatch, a large and very special party. A chief invites another chief to attend with all his relatives. They dance and feast, and the host lavishes food and gifts on his guests. Sometimes, to ensure that his potlatch is memorable, the host will even destroy property or sacrifice people. After the potlatch he is respected and impoverished, and must begin again to accumulate wealth.

Potlatches may have other purposes. They may eradicate the shame of the host's capture and enslavement by another nation, or celebrate the creation of a new home or a totem pole.

The Cedar people build their storage boxes and baskets out of cedar trees.

The Haida, one of the Cedar people, make intricately decorated stone bowls. ▷

Inuit lead nomadic lives in search of their prey

c.1400

ARCTIC – A coastal village here is abuzz with activity as the annual Inuit pilgrimage to the south gets under way. With the sheet of winter ice breaking up, it's time once again to say farewell to the seals and set off in pursuit of the caribou. Breaking camp is not a particularly arduous endeavor. Everything has been ready for weeks as the sun gradually returned to the horizon after disappearing for the long winter moons. The village has been far from idle during the season of ice and snow.

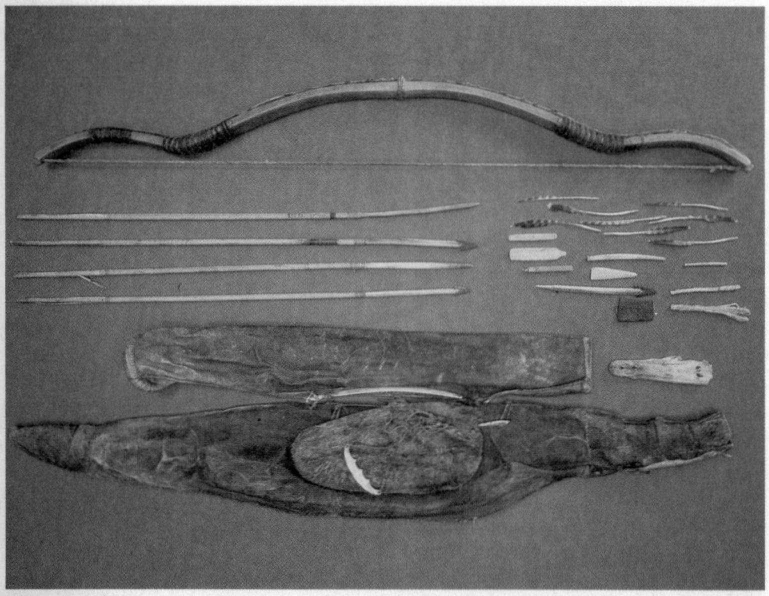

Inuit hunters use various weapons when searching for food for their people. These nomads are very successful in hunting seal and whale in the winter time.

Indeed, hunters have had great success in their forays to the seals' breathing holes, where they've taken an ample supply of the animals to keep up the village's stores of food and materials for clothing and camp utensils. And this winter the village scored a major victory when its whalers killed a huge whale after careful stalking and a lengthy attack with their well-aimed harpoons. The whale provided an abundance of blubber for food, and teeth and bones for tools.

The hunters celebrated their exhausting battle with a feast. Their round, flat and one-sided drums pounded, and their bone rattles rang out. Meanwhile, artisans busily shaped elaborate bone and stone carvings to commemorate the village's triumphs and tragedies over the year.

Now it's time for the Inuit to pack up the village's possessions, place them efficiently on dragging sleds and haul everything inland in search of the huge herds of caribou to the south. The only things left behind by the portable village will be the fleet of skin kayaks used by the whalers.

The Inuit are taking special care to ensure that their precious sculptured stone lamps, pottery and tools are well-stored so they aren't lost or damaged on the their long voyage. The caravan is starting out on snowshoes, for there's still much snow to travel over on the barren terrain. Later, when the weather brings dry terrain on this week's southward trek, the Inuit will be able to travel without snowshoes, and wear just their caribou skin moccasins on their feet.

The Inuit make their hunting hats from the skin of whales and seals, which also provide food for them.

Hunting techniques refined to an art

c.1400

ARCTIC – Considering their limited resources, the Inuit have developed some remarkable hunting techniques that have helped sustain them in their harsh and meagre environment. From their watertight kayaks, the Inuit excel at harpooning seals in open water and caribou at river crossings. They've also perfected an uncanny ability to detect a seal's breathing hole in the winter.

From larger skin-covered boats called *umiaks,* the Inuit brave the terrors of harpooning the dangerous whale. The harpoon itself is attached to inflated sealskin floats which make it difficult for the whale to dive and end up exhausting the huge mammals, allowing for the final kill. The most dangerous prey for the Inuit is the polar bear. Killing it is considered a test of courage, and many die trying.

Fun and games warm cold winter nights

c.1400

ARCTIC – Although Inuit are forced to devote much of their time to survival in this cold northern land, these natives appear to always have time for diversions as well. Such activities not only provide entertainment, but they are also designed to improve Inuit strength and skills so necessary for the hunt.

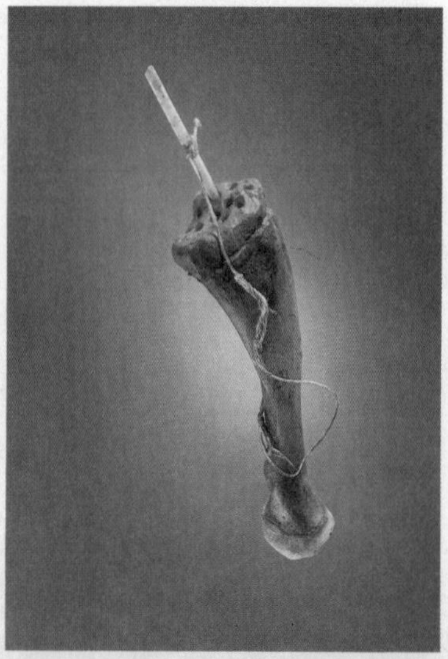

Ring and pin game helps pass time.

Outdoor Inuit games include skin-blanket tossing and the high kick. Wrestling is popular, as is a friendly form of boxing in which each Inuit man takes turns hitting his partner on the side of the head or shoulder. An inflated bladder or sealskin filled with moss serves as a football in other games.

During the long, cold arctic nights, indoor games are a time for fun and cementing ties with family and friends. There are a variety of hole-and-pin games in which contestants try to stick long needles into a suspended and elusive hole-filled bone. On occasion, prizes are given to the most accurate players. Gossip, singing contests, the drum dance and the telling of stories and legends are other essential parts of Inuit evenings.

Inuit story of the woman and dog

There was a young woman who was forced to marry her father's dog because she pridefully rejected all men. The woman lived with her dog husband on an island. Some of their children were humans. Others were dogs. One day when the dog swam to shore to bring food for his family, his wife's father tricked him into carrying stones back to the island. The dog drowned. In revenge, the woman urged her children to kill her father, but he escaped. The woman then sent her children off in a boot to distant lands. Some became Europeans. They learned to make houses, iron and ships. The rest became Itqilit – Indians. They were quick runners and clever hunters who lived much like the Inuit. But their manners were like those of dogs.

From coast to coast: an unspoiled continent

An early snowfall on the west coast [Rocky Mountains] of [British Columbia].

An iceberg on the east coast in [Newfoundland] at [Great Brehat].

[Georgian Bay] in the [Canadian Shield], which has many waterways.

Naturally carved rocks, hoodoos are found in the prairies and west coast.

An arctic landscape at [Button Point] in the [Northwest Territories].

Mainz, Germany, 1455. Johann Gutenburg makes the first publication with the printing press that he recently invented, a revolutionary system that makes use of metal typefaces. Previous printing presses have always involved carved wooden letters. Gutenburg's first publication is a Bible, the first printed version anywhere.

San Salvador, Oct. 12, 1492. "Tierra!, tierra!" Christopher Columbus and his crew reach land after sailing westward for five weeks aboard the *Nina*, *Pinta* and *Santa Maria*. They hope to have reached the coveted western passage to the Indies. He names the island San Salvador [Bahamas] and claims it in the name of King Ferdinand and Queen Isabella of Spain. The crew exchanges gifts with the naked natives.

Bristol, England, May 5, 1497. An Italian explorer Giovanni Caboto (John Cabot) leads an expedition in search of lands to the west. He received letters patent from King Henry VII.

China, 1498. The toothbrush has been invented in China.

London, September 1498. There is still no news of John Cabot's second expedition to North America that left Bristol in May. His fate is a mystery.

Atlantic Ocean, 1501. Portuguese explorer Gaspar Corte-Real is lost at sea after exploring the east coast of Newfoundland and capturing a number of Indians on his second voyage to America.

Atlantic Ocean, 1506. Jean Denys, a captain from Honfleur, Normandy, makes one of the first fishing trips off the east coast of America. He likely stops in Newfoundland.

Saint-Die, Lorraine, April 25, 1507. Cartographers Martin Waldseemuller and Matthias Ringmann publish a new map of the world that, for the first time, shows the New World to be a distinct continent between Asia and Europe. It names the continent America, after the Italian explorer Amerigo Vespucci, who claims to have discovered the mainland in 1497, a year before Columbus.

France, 1508. Thomas Aubert, commander of a fishing voyage to North America, brings back the first Indians to France. They raise many eyebrows with their customs, arms, and canoes. On his trip, Aubert showed the Bonavista fishing banks to Normandy fishermen.

Five Iroquois nations make peace

c.1450

ONONDAGA – A great white pine tree has been planted to mark the dawn of a new era of peace among five nations of Iroquois natives. The Cayugas, Mohawks, Senecas, Oneidas and Onondagas have planted the Tree of Peace near the shore of the Onondaga Lake [Syracuse]. The new peace has inspired a tremendous sense of unity among the fiercely independent natives. While each nation retains its sovereignty, it also gives a measure of authority to the Great Council at Onondaga, where chiefs of the Five Nations will meet to discuss common problems around "the fire that never dies." There are reports crediting Dekanahwideh, the "Heavenly Messenger," with being the founder of the Five Nations confederacy. According to legend, Dekanahwideh was born among the Huron. A messenger sent by the Creator told his virgin mother in a dream that she would bear a son destined to plant the Tree of Peace at Onondaga. Dekanahwideh and his aide Hiawatha faced a difficult task convincing the native nations to accept the peace proposal. Twice Dekanahwideh was called on to perform "miracles." Once he survived a long fall off a cliff overhanging the Mohawk River. Another time he made the sun go out and there was complete darkness. In both instances, Dekanahwideh's feats turned dissident natives skeptical about his peace mission into enthusiastic supporters of the plan.

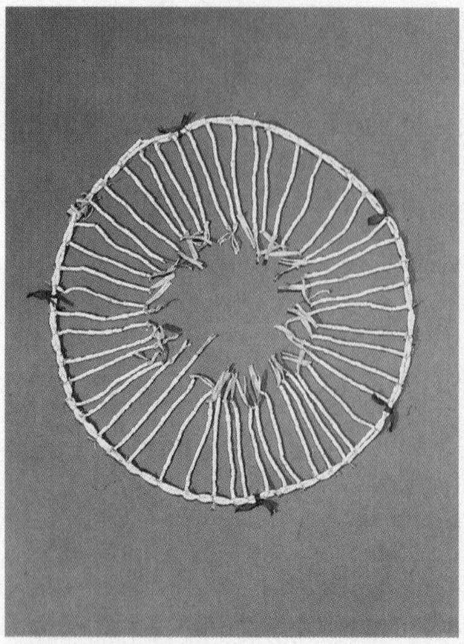

The sacred Iroquois wampum belt is a symbol of peace between the Indian tribes belonging to the Five Nations.

Prosperous European nations eye new riches across oceans

c.1460

EUROPE – The recovery of northwestern Europe from the disasters of the 1300s has been slow and painful. While a series of crop failures and famines has radically reduced the continent's population over the past 150 years, the bubonic plague – or the Black Death – has also ravaged Western Europe. These two factors and the Hundred Years' War between England and France are among the main reasons that about 50 percent of the European population died.

But now, the situation has changed. With the ebbing of fatal diseases and the introduction of more efficient agricultural methods, the population of Europe is again on the upswing and nations everywhere – Spain and Portugal in particular – are entering a new age of economic prosperity and commercial growth. This in turn is leading them to eye new resources and riches across the oceans.

Portugal would appear to be a prime candidate for exploring new horizons. It has entrenched itself as a great sea power under the leadership of Prince Henry, who's sponsored various expeditions that have resulted in the discovery of many new lands.

Henry, known as The Navigator, was an advocate of ocean voyages as early as 1418 when he started promoting trips along the coast of Africa. Under orders from the Crown, Portuguese colonists began to settle the Azores, a small series of islands 1,300 kilometres west of Portugal, in 1440. Despite Henry's many explorations, the one thing his expeditions haven't uncovered is a viable easterly sea route to India. As a result, many Portuguese are now turning their gaze west.

Important advances in shipbuilding and navigation are already under way in Europe: fleets of Portuguese caravels, ideal for coastal navigation but too small to carry provisions for long trips, are now complemented by larger, square-rigged carracks; and Henry has started a school for navigators where in instruments, such as the compass, are being adapted for use at sea.

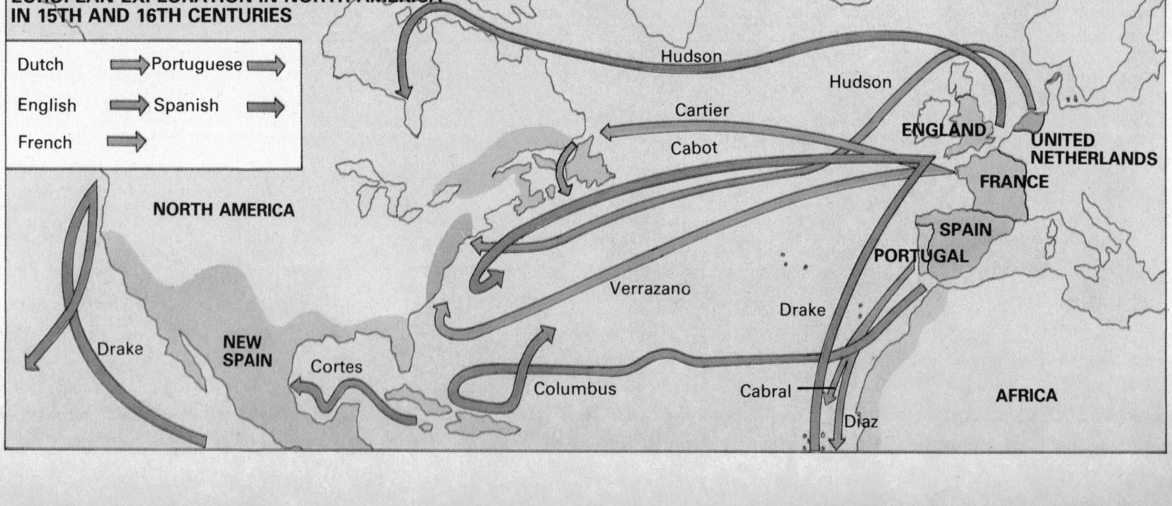

Columbus sails in search of "the land of spices"

Aug. 3, 1492

PALOS, Spain – Forty-year-old Christopher Columbus, a Genoese, set sail today on his long-awaited journey to find a western route to the Indies. Convinced God is with him and that he'll bring Spain glory and riches, Columbus led three small ships – the *Nina,* the *Pinta* and the *Santa Maria* – west into uncharted waters.

Learning from the mistakes of previous explorers, Columbus said he'll avoid the treacherous winds and high seas of the North Atlantic and set his course south toward the Canary Islands before heading west to "the land of spices."

Until recently, it appeared that Columbus's plan was doomed. The charming and enthusiastic seaman got his first opportunity to meet Spain's Queen Isabella to show her his ambitious project back in 1486. Despite Columbus's heartfelt plea, he couldn't persuade the queen to give his plan the go-ahead – at least not for the time being. Isabella turned down the spirited Columbus at that first meeting, though she agreed to set up a commission which would give Columbus's project further study.

While the commission branded Columbus's plan as "uncertain and impossible to any educated person," the queen was more receptive. Distracted until recently by the war with the Moors, she only found time to meet Columbus again in January. The two negotiated until reaching an agreement.

Christopher Columbus asks for ships from Spain's Queen Isabella.

Cabot to explore New World for England

March 5, 1496

ENGLAND – Trailing Portugal and Spain in claiming resource-rich New World lands, England has called on Italian Giovanni Caboto – also known as John Cabot – to explore "all parts, countries and seas of the East, of the West, and of the North."

Letters patent King Henry VII issued today empower Cabot, his sons Lewis, Sebastian and Sancio, their heirs and deputies to sail from Bristol with five ships to "discover and find whatsoever isles, countries, regions or provinces of heathens and infidels, in whatsoever part of the world they be, which before this time were unknown to all Christians."

If Cabot finds new land in the area the letters patent restrict him to, he may follow the coast into the latitudes of discoveries of other nations. While Cabot and his sons are to secure new lands in the name of the king, the letters forbid other English subjects from visiting the areas without first obtaining the proper licence from the Cabots. The Cabots are responsible for their own expenses and can keep 80 percent of any profits they make on the expedition. The remaining 20 percent goes to the Crown.

The main impetus for the expansion of England comes from Bristol merchants familiar with North Atlantic fisheries. It's possible the previous westward probing from Bristol enticed Cabot to move to England in expectation of official support and a base for his voyage to the New World. Bristol, England's westernmost port, is also full of seamen who have mastered the North Atlantic waters.

It appears Cabot was in Portugal last year and may have obtained information about Portuguese explorer Joao Fernandes' voyages.

Giovanni Caboto and his men on the Matthew off the coast of [Canada] while seeking "undiscovered" lands.

Spain, Portugal OK treaty dividing world

June 7, 1494

SPAIN – The Spanish and Portuguese have signed a treaty that divides newly discovered lands – as well as those yet to be discovered – between the two nations.

The Treaty of Tordesillas draws a north-south line at a point 360 leagues west of the Cape Verde Islands. It gives Portugal exclusive rights to all new lands east of the line. Spain acquires rights to those lands west of the line.

The treaty modifies the division of the extra-European world sanctioned by the Pope in 1493. The papal division, established in the two bulls *Inter caetera*, drew the line along the meridian running north and south at a point 100 leagues west of the Azores.

Portugal had been critical of the earlier division and fought hard for the changes brought about by today's treaty, which enlarge its sphere of influence.

A Spanish ship, similar to the kind adventurous sailors receive to travel around the world in search of lands unknown to all Christians. Spain's Queen Isabella gave Christopher Columbus three such ships – the Nina, the Pinta and the Santa Maria – to sail to the Indies in 1492.

Map shows 'Terra Nova'

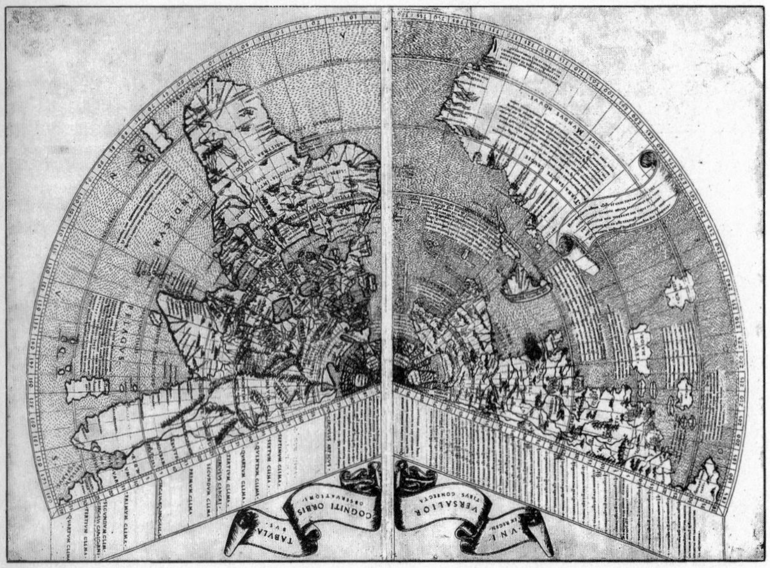

Johannes Ruysch's 1508 map shows "Terra Nova" as being attached to Asia.

June 30, 1508

NEWFOUNDLAND – A map of the New World published in Rome in the most recent edition of Ptolemy's *Geographia* lists a place called Terra Nova – Newfoundland to the English and Terre Neuve to the French. Johannes Ruysch spent much of the past year drawing the map. Born in Antwerp, reports indicate Ruysch is a sailor who once travelled to the New World on an English ship.

The map is well done. It shows the bays and peninsulas on the eastern side of Newfoundland in considerable detail. It is in these bays that the European fishermen gather every summer to use the cod fishery. Ruysch's map clearly defines a gulf to the south and west of Terra Nova.

While the map confirms some of the longheld suspicions that Terra Nova and Greenland are part of northern Asia, there are not enough details to pinpoint exactly where the New World is linked to Asia.

Ruysch employed some unique methods devising his map. He used a conical projection with the apex at the North Pole. The map spreads out like an open fan curved at the bottom. Each half of the curve – or arc – covers 180 degrees. The right side of the map clearly shows that ships can sail around Africa as explorer Vasco da Gama and others have done.

The map describes Asia in considerable detail. It shows India jutting out into the ocean further than in other maps. There is some indication Ruysch used some of the same sources cartographer Gasparo Contarini employed several years ago.

Ptolemy's *Geographia* takes its title from the Greek cartographer Ptolemy (87-150 AD). His geographical guide to making maps was brought to Italy from Constantinople just before invading Turks conquered the eastern Greek empire in 1453.

Over the last 100 years there have been other volumes of the *Geographia* published. Demand for world maps has skyrocketed since the Portuguese began their voyages along the African coast.

Buffalo population numbers 70 million

c.1500

NORTH AMERICA – The various species of North American buffalo are thriving, numbering more than 70 million across the continent. The buffaloes' success seems to lie in their physical prowess and adaptability. Their great size, sweeping horns and thick hide make them more than a match for predators, including humans. Buffalo also acclimatize to different environments and are equally at home in sub-arctic bogs, mountains, prairies and eastern forests.

Cabot sights new continent for England

June 24, 1497

ATLANTIC COAST – Italian explorer Giovanni Caboto – also known as John Cabot – discovered a new continent for England today. Cabot went ashore [probably at Newfoundland or perhaps Cape Breton] and found large trees and pastures gracing the New World.

It has also been reported that the seas surrounding this "new-found-land" are teeming with fish. It is said you can simply lower a basket over the side of a ship and pull it up full of fish. If these reports about the abundance of fish are true, English fishermen will no longer have to depend on Icelandic waters for their catches. England may have found the key to great wealth and power.

Cabot's exact origin is unknown, but he arrived in England from Venice with plans to find a route to Asia by sailing directly westward for a northern route. It seems he had already approached the Spanish and Portuguese governments and was turned down.

King Henry VII accepted Cabot's offer to sail under the English flag. Cabot's charter, granted in March 1496, allows him to take possession of "new-found-lands" for England and turn one-fifth of his profits over to the Crown. While Cabot sailed from Bristol in May 1496, bad weather, a shortage of food and a disagreement with his crew forced him to turn back and wait until this year. He sailed from Bristol once again. His ship – the *Matthew* – arrived in the New World with a crew of 16 or 17 men after a voyage of about 35 days.

For years, Bristol fishermen and sailors have told stories about land in the west where codfish is found in abundance.

Other tales from this seaport tell of the Vikings of ancient times and the colonies they founded in Greenland and Vinland. It's quite possible Cabot has been acquainting himself with these stories since arriving in England in 1495. It's also possible he launched his expedition from Bristol since he knew he would find sailors there who – being familiar with the fishing grounds in the far Atlantic – are not afraid of sailing off the end of the earth.

Giovanni Caboto and his men, who are sailing for England, sight land while looking for a route to Asia.

A bull found in the New World by explorers who landed here while looking for a new route to Asia.

Black bears roam New World forests

c.1520

ATLANTIC COAST – As European explorers increasingly visit the New World, they are sure to encounter black bears, one of the most abundant large mammals in the forests of the northeast. The black bear population is estimated to be at least 100,000 in the general area between the native village of Stadacona and the Atlantic coast. The bears show no fear toward humans, but will rarely attack them, except when mother bears fear their cubs are in danger.

Luther speaks his mind

Oct. 31, 1517

WITTENBERG, Germany – A disgruntled monk has lashed out against what he says are corrupt church practices by nailing a proclamation containing 95 theses to the castle church here.

Martin Luther, a 34-year-old theologian, went public with his long-simmering criticism of church practices, provoked by the open auctioning of pardons by roving Dominican priest Johannes Tetzel.

"I could no longer keep silent about these enormities," Luther explained. The selling of divine forgiveness, what Luther calls "pardon-mongering," had reached a state where indulgence tickets were regularly being slipped across the confession booth by sinners.

By posting the 95 theses, Luther said he hopes to "elucidate the truth" about abuses within the church and bring an end to the selling of divine favors.

Tetzel claims the money raised through the sale of indulgences is for the construction of the new St. Peter's Basilica in Rome. But in one of Luther's theses, the maverick monk said if the pope was aware of Tetzel's pardon-mongering he'd rather see St. Peter's reduced to ashes than built with "the skin, flesh and bones of his sheep."

A disgruntled Martin Luther attacks Roman Catholic church practices.

Luther, a popular professor at the university in this small town on the Elbe River, is one of a growing number of critics of the church. Born in 1483 the son of a wealthy copper miner in Eisleben, Saxony, a religious revelation prompted him to become a monk.

When Luther visited Rome in 1510, the spiritual bankruptcy he found appalled him. Subsequent study of the scriptures strengthened his resolve to pursue reform. His 95 theses are the first public salvo in what Luther predicts will be a hard-fought struggle.

Caribs kill and eat explorer Verrazzano

Explorer Giovanni da Verrazzano.

Spring 1528

WEST INDIES – Italian explorer Giovanni da Verrazzano, sailing in the service of France, has been murdered on an expedition authorized to obtain spices from the Indies, and to find a northwest passage. On a Caribbean island probably near Guadeloupe, Verrazzano and a landing party encountered Caribs, the fierce natives of these islands, who killed then ate him. Verrazzano's crew witnessed this unfortunate event.

Verrazzano was the first European explorer to realize that [Canada] is a part of North America, and that North America is not linked to Asia or Africa. He also contributed important nautical and astonomical data in detailed letters describing his voyage.

Florentine explorer sails coast of America

July 1524

ATLANTIC COAST – There are reports in the New World of a Florentine explorer becoming the first European to sail the coast of America from Florida to Newfoundland. Giovanni da Verrazzano is said to be headed for France "having discovered 600 leagues and more of new land" on his six-month voyage to America.

Though it failed to unveil a passage to China, the trip enabled Verrazzano to be the first to report that the "New World which above I have described is connected together, not adjoining Asia or Africa (which I know to be a certainty)."

A man of distinguished lineage dating back to the Middle Ages, Verrazzano set sail from a deserted islet at the westernmost point of Madeiras in his ship the *Dauphine* on Jan. 17 with a Norman crew of 50. Toward the end of March, Verrazzano spotted "a new land never before seen by anyone" probably close to [Cape Fear, North Carolina].

After sailing south a short way in an unsuccessful search for a harbor, his fear of meeting any Spaniards led Verrazzano to turn back and coast north as far as [Nova Scotia] and "near the land which the Britanni (Britons) found" [Cape Breton]. He went ashore at several places along the Atlantic coast, abducted an Indian boy to take to France, visited New York harbor and spent 15 days in Narragansett Bay. Finding provisions low after reaching Newfoundland, Verrazzano set course for France.

Indians slaughter 200 trapped Micmac

1533

VIEUX BIC [Quebec] – A natural cave cut into the rocks at Vieux Bic was the site of the grisly massacre of 200 Indian men, women and children, perhaps from the Micmac tribe.

A band of these Indians, who live along the great river and who regularly travel the area, was apparently being pursued by an army of Indians from another, enemy tribe. The Indians being pursued knew the area well and sought out the cave, expecting to find refuge there. The men gathered dead wood and built a barrier across the entrance. Thinking the location to be well hidden and themselves to be safe, the entire band retired.

In the middle of the night a bloodcurdling war cry split the dark. As the startled sleepers awakened, the aggressors set fire to the wood in front of the cave. The blaze trapped the surprised people inside and all died except for five men. They managed to slip past the fire and enemy and into the forest. The corpses remain in the cave.

Recent arrivals in the New World try to shoot white [polar] bears.

1534 (1534-1545)

Newfoundland, May 21, 1534. Cartier's crew encounters hordes of spearbills, a species of penguin, at the Isle of Birds [Funk Island] off Newfoundland. They kill many of them.

Canada, July 1534. Cartier meets Iroquoians led by Chief Donnacona [at Gaspé Harbour], who have come from Stadacona [Quebec City] to fish. The Indians accept gifts of trinkets, beads and knives. Their attitude suggests they have already received visits and goods from Europeans. An alliance is concluded with celebrations.

Canada, July 24, 1534. Cartier erects a cross at Penouille Point [on the Gaspé], claiming the land for France. Chief Donnacona protests.

Canada, July 24, 1534. Cartier captures two of chief Donnacona's sons, Domagaya and Taignoagny, whom he hopes will serve as guides and interpreters on future voyages.

Canada, Aug. 13, 1535. Cartier is the first European known to enter [the St. Lawrence River] on his second trip to America, following the instructions of his Indian guides, Domagaya and Taignoagny. He thinks he has found a route to Asia.

St-Malo, France, May 23, 1541. Cartier leaves on his third expedition to North America with five ships and about 1,500 men. Except for a small girl, all the Indian captives he brought to France in 1536 have died, including Chief Donnacona and his sons.

Canada, Aug. 23, 1541. Cartier arrives at Stadacona [Quebec City]. The Indians receive him with demonstrations of joy. Cartier tells them of Chief Donnacona's death but lies about the other Indian captives he took to France, saying they are living there like lords.

Canada, 1542-3. A group of colonists led by Jean-François de La Roque De Roberval winter at Cartier's settlement at Cap Rouge. They suffer from cold, famine and sickness. One day De Roberval hangs six colonists to discourage uprisings. He banishes others to an island, in leg-irons, for petty theft.

East Prussia, May 24, 1543. Nicolaus Copernicus publishes *On the Revolution of the Heavenly Spheres*, in which he argues that the earth is not the centre of the universe, but revolves around the sun, contrary to accepted belief.

Cartier explores 'land God gave Cain'

August 1534

NEWFOUNDLAND – "The land God gave Cain" – this is how French explorer Jacques Cartier describes the region southwest of Newfoundland. His remark sums up a summer's worth of travel on behalf of the king of France, a journey that by all accounts must be judged a failure.

When Cartier left the French port of St-Malo on April 20, with two ships and 61 men, his royal mission was clear: "To voyage to that realm of the *Terres Neufves* to discover certain isles and countries where it is said there must be great quantities of gold and other riches." Such has been not the case, though Cartier was impressed with fertile territory [Prince Edward Island] the expedition spotted in June.

After crossing the Atlantic in 20 days and sailing along uncharted shorelines southwest of Newfoundland, Cartier and his men have found no riches. As for the land that occupied his efforts, Cartier has nothing but contempt.

"It should not be called new land," the explorer says with disgust, but it should have a name describing its "frightful and ill-shapen stones and rocks, for I saw not one cartload of land in all that northern coast."

Despite his disappointment, the Cartier expedition was not a total loss. He has added a lot of territory to the maps.

Explorer Jacques Cartier sailed for the New World from the port of St-Malo.

Jacques Cartier and his crew of explorers land on "the land God gave Cain."

Native youths use the name 'Canada'

Aug. 13, 1535

STADACONA [Quebec City] – Two native youths in explorer Jacques Cartier's sailing expedition referred today to the native village of Stadacona as "Canada." The two boys, sons of Donnacona, the village headman of Stadacona, were directing Cartier near the Island of Anticosti.

Cartier, who had never heard the name before, believes Canada refers not only to Stadacona but to all the land Donnacona controls in the vicinity of the village. The French explorer is making his second voyage here after wintering in France.

Cartier expedition sights a fertile island

June 29, 1534

ATLANTIC COAST [Prince Edward Island] - Sailing from St-Malo with a royal charter to look for a western passage to the Indies and China, explorer Jacques Cartier has sighted what he describes as "one of the best tempered regions" one can see. Sailing westward from the windswept island where he and his men were stranded for 10 days, Cartier sighted land [Prince Edward Island] which he said appeared fertile in comparison to where they had come from.

While Cartier believed he saw two islands at sunset last night, he realized today the land was more extensive than he first thought and is simply one island. After landing at several points ashore, Cartier had nothing but praise for all he saw. It is "best tempered region one can possibly see," he said, "and the heat is considerable."

Cartier navigated around this "mainland" exploring the west and north shores and came on an expanse of water which he decided was a bay. He named it Baie St–Lunaire [Northumberland Strait]. Cartier left St-Malo on April 20 with two ships, 61 men and the charter from the King of France which mandated him to discover various islands and lands widely believed to contain vast quantities of precious metals such as gold.

Cartier captures Donnacona and his sons

The Indians of Stadacona ask Jacques Cartier to release Chief Donnacona.

May 3, 1536

STADACONA [Quebec City] – Stadacona Indians are assembled on the banks of the river tonight, shouting war cries and demanding the French return Chief Donnacona and his sons Taignoagny and Domagaya. Explorer Jacques Cartier and his men captured the Indians earlier in the day and plan to take them to see the king of France.

Stories Donnacona's told about the people and land of "Canada" led Cartier to decide he would not return to France without Donnacona, his sons and the chief's main supporters. Cartier is hoping Donnacona tells his stories to the king, convincing the monarch of the merits of supporting Cartier's future expeditions to Canada.

Cartier has another reason for capturing the Indians. He believes Donnacona's absence from Canada will free the chief's rival, Agona, to rule Stadacona. That, in turn, would strengthen the French position in the St. Lawrence Valley.

Accompanied by a large group of men and women, Donnacona and his sons arrived at the French fort this afternoon. While the uneasy and cautious Indians refused to enter the French camp at first, Donnacona and Domagaya were eventually lured in when Taignoagny went to tell the women to flee. The French seized Taignoagny and the other men Cartier designated when they tried to rescue Donnacona.

Native's cure saves crew

Indians show explorers the virtues of the white cedar tree in curing scurvy.

March 1536

STADACONA [Quebec City] – An Indian is being credited with saving up to 75 of explorer Jacques Cartier's crew from scurvy. About 25 of his 110 men had already died and only 10 were well when Cartier approached Domagaya, son of Stadacona Chief Donnacona, this month to learn about his recent recovery from what appeared to be an attack of scurvy.

When Cartier told Domagaya his servant had scurvy, the native informed him of the remedy *annedda,* made from the bark of common white cedar. Domagaya sent two women to gather the cedar and to show the French how to brew a cure. Within a week of drinking the cure, all of Cartier's men recovered. Some suffering from syphillis say it helped relieve that ailment too.

The winter has been particularly hard on Cartier and his men. His ships have been locked in ice since November and more than four feet of snow have fallen. Despite all attempts to protect themselves, scurvy which first inflicted the Indians has invaded the French camp.

While Cartier prayed before an image of the Virgin Mary and vowed to make a pilgrimage if his men were cured, the scurvy continued to ravage the crew until Domagaya's cure set in. Before he approached Domagaya, fear of an Indian attack led Cartier to mask the desperate condition of his men.

Micmac eager to trade furs with French

July 7, 1534

ST. LAWRENCE REGION – In the first recorded exchange between Europeans and the natives inhabiting the Gulf of St. Lawrence, enthusiastic Micmac Indians traded furs with explorer Jacques Cartier and his men today.

A French longboat encountered two groups of Micmac in some 40 to 50 canoes yesterday. When they saw Cartier's men, the Indians made loud noises and held up furs on the ends of sticks indicating they wished to trade. Since the sight of so many natives frightened the French, they motioned the Indians to move away. When the Indians persisted, the French fired two cannons and scattered fire-lances in their midst to frighten away the natives.

Micmac tribesmen returned today in nine canoes, wary of being fired on but eager to trade. This time the French obliged them and trading ensued. Apparently used to dealing with Europeans, the Micmac quickly bartered furs for iron kettles, knives and other wares.

The natives are not the first Cartier's encountered on his expedition to [Canada]. He reported seeing Indians on June 12 or 13 who came inland to hunt seal and may have been Beothuk people.

More than 1,000 Indians greet Jacques Cartier at Hochelaga, in 1535. The French explorer is impressed as this town is bigger than Stadacona with about 50 longhouses and many well-cultivated cornfields.

Aboriginal traditions new to European explorers

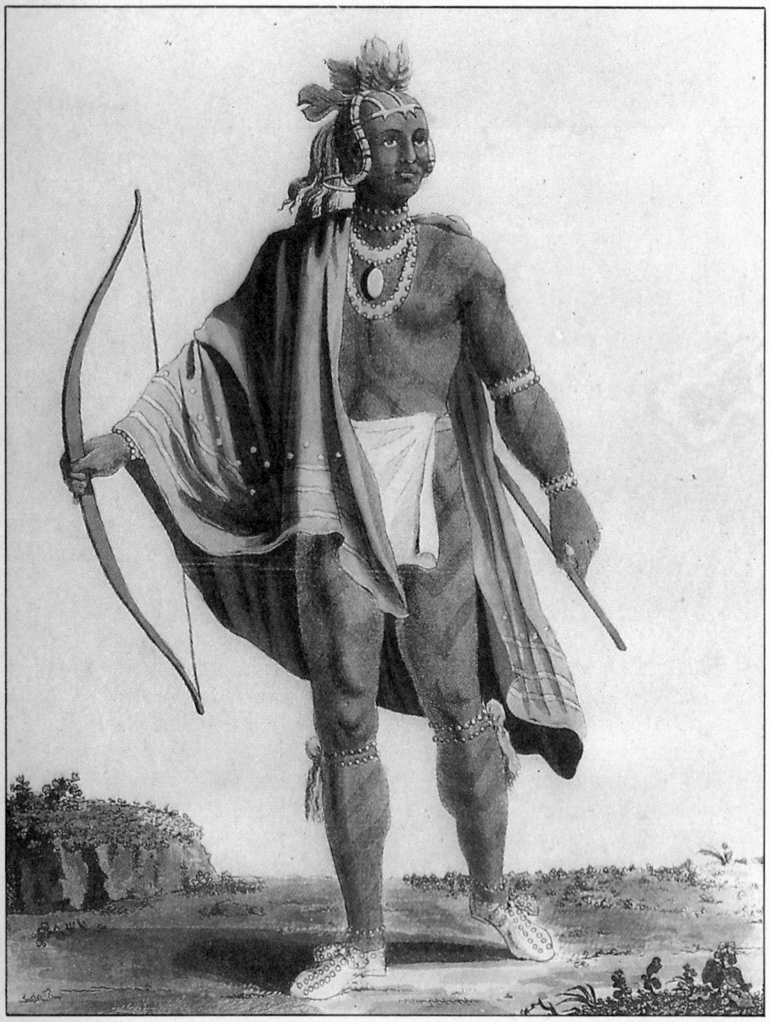

An Indian warrior of the Ottawa nation at the time of Cartier's arrival.

A group of Indians gather to ask their dead relative why he has died.

A marriage ceremony between two Indians from the new French colony.

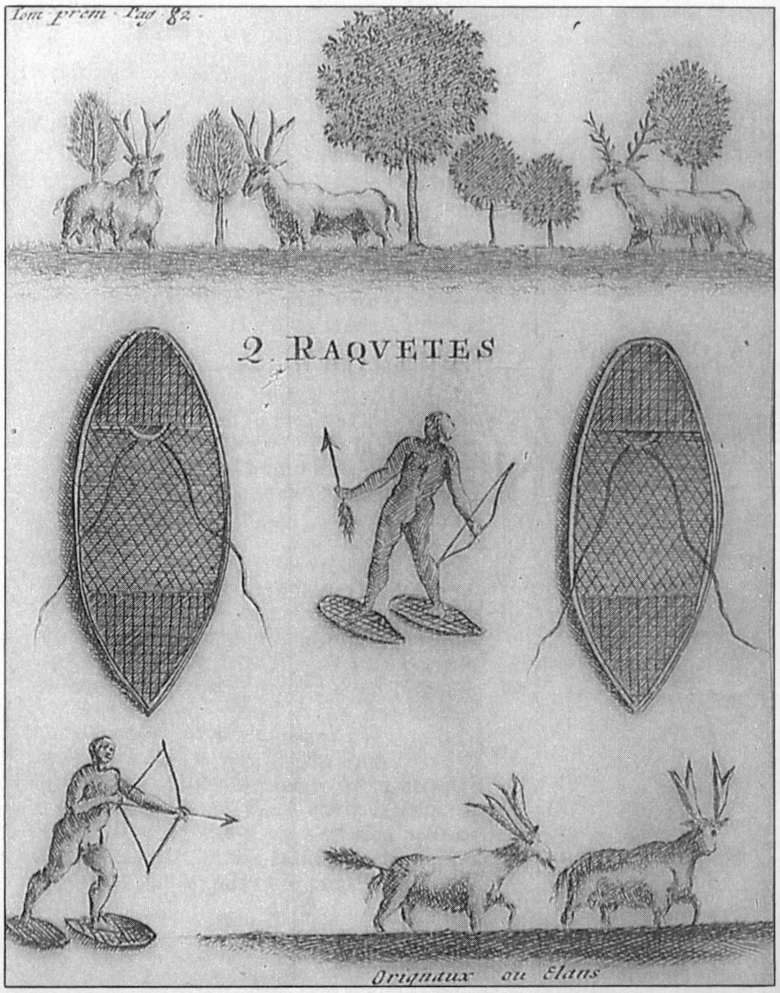

Representation of Indians' use of snowshoes for deer and moose hunting.

Indians torture captured warriors.

Indians attack a French fort.

The ceremony of divorce as practised by a group of natives in [Canada].

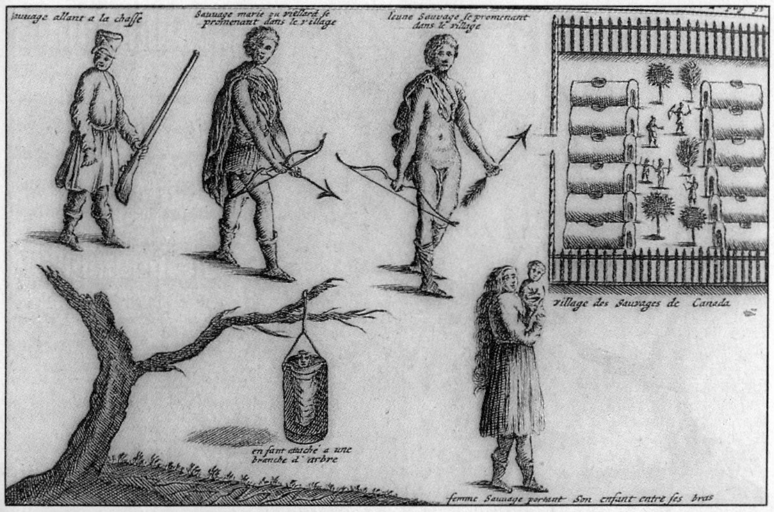

Illustration of some stages of Indian life and one of their villages (inset).

Indian customs differ from those of Europeans. Illustration represents native traditions in hunting, funeral ceremonies and building methods.

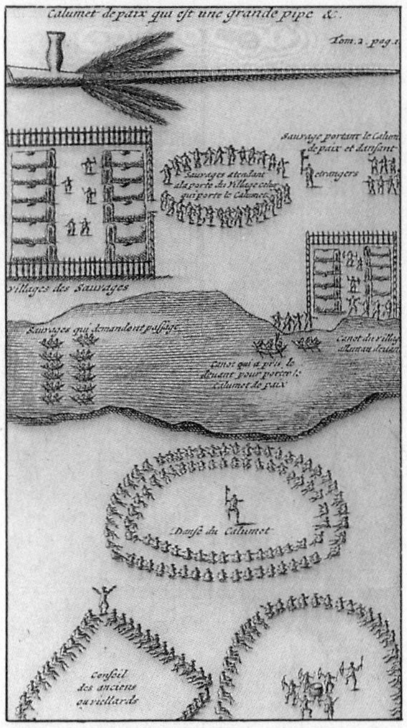

The Indian peace pipe plays an important role in the peace pipe dance as well as other ceremonies.

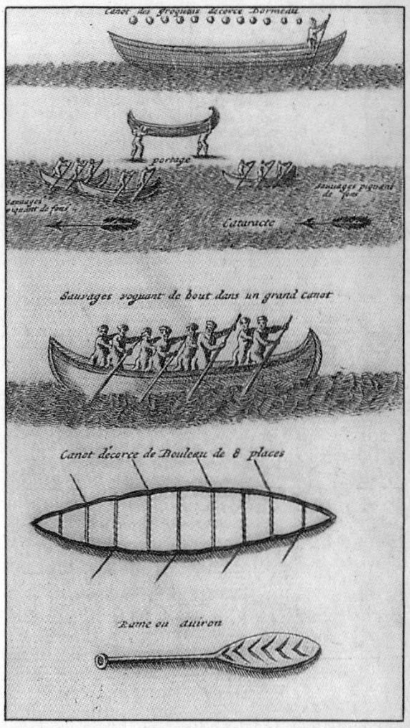

The canoe, which is made of elm tree bark, is important to the Indians for transportation and for fishing.

1546 (1546-1579)

Trinity, Newfoundland, 1558. The first settlers arrive aboard the brig *Hawke*, commanded by Robert Ward.

Florida, October 1565. Spanish troops wipe out the French settlement at Fort Caroline. They kill hundreds of colonists. The massacre culminates years of tension in the area heightened by religious differences.

Ratcliffe, England, June 7, 1576. Martin Frobisher, Christopher Hall, and Gryffyn Owen set sail with a crew of 35 aboard the *Gabriell* and *Michaell* to search for the Northwest Passage to Asia.

London, Oct. 9, 1576. Frobisher returns to England aboard the *Gabriell* after exploring Frobisher Bay. He is greeted with enthusiasm because his ship was presumed lost and people are amazed by his Inuit prisoner. He brings new hope for the existence of the Northwest Passage to Asia.

Blackwall, England, May 25, 1577. Frobisher and crew embark on a second voyage to North America aboard the *Ayde*, *Michaell* and *Gabriell*. They are sponsored by the Cathay Company and Queen Elizabeth I to mine gold at Frobisher Bay and search for the Northwest Passage.

England, Sept. 23, 1577. Frobisher's expedition returns with 200 tons of useless ore and three captured Inuit – a man, a woman, and a child. They entered Frobisher Bay July 19, and stayed for five weeks.

England, October 1577. The three Inuit captured by Frobisher at Frobisher Bay die after a month in England.

Atlantic Ocean, 1578. There are approximately 150 French vessels and 200 ships from other nations fishing off Newfoundland and Labrador, as well as some 30 Biscayan whalers.

England, Oct. 1, 1578. Frobisher's third expedition returns safely. He left with 15 ships to establish a gold mining settlement at Frobisher Bay, and returns with more than 1,000 tons of useless ore.

England, 1579. An English sailor named Thomas Cowles says that a Portuguese mariner told him he discovered the Northwest Passage in 1555. Though the story is a hoax, it contains the first reference to the "Strait of Anian" dividing America from Asia.

Mercator publishes new "Mercator Map" showing Ungava Bay

1569

WESTPHALIA, Prussia – Gerhardus Mercator, former geographer to King Charles V, has just published his world "Mercator Map," a radical departure from previous cartography. Mercator explains in a note, "We have had to employ a new proportion and a new arrangement of the meridians with reference to the parallels." He has spaced the parallels of latitude progressively larger away from the equator toward the poles, in exactly the same proportion as the spreading of the meridians. This new cartographic method, designed to assist navigators by describing the round earth on a plane surface, so severely distorts the north and south extremes that Mercator has not attempted to incorporate the North and South Poles, but sketches them in an inset. He has also drawn in a body of water [Ungava Bay], perhaps from knowledge gleaned from adventurous European fishermen.

Spaniard describes the buffalo skin trade

c.1566

FLORIDA – A letter by Spanish Admiral Pedro Menendez is raising the possibility that buffalo live near the northeast coast. He recently wrote to his king, Phillip II, that in 1665 and for years previously Indians have brought buffalo skins down the Ptomac River and up the coast in canoes to trade with the French at the Gulf of St. Lawrence. In two years, Menendez reports, the French have obtained 6,000 buffalo skins in this trade. Buffalo are known to roam in southern coastal areas [the Carolinas and Georgia], but Menendez's account is one of the only records of them around the northern coast. It is possible he heard the story from a traveller, or he may have made it up himself.

Detail from map showing whaling activities off coast of Canada.

Basque whaleboat sinks in the gulf

Dec. 31, 1565

NEWFOUNDLAND – Reports indicate a Basque whaling ship sailing in the gulf late in the season sank recently. The Basques are noted for their extensive whale fisheries at home. They began cod fishing off Newfoundland in the 1520s and by the early 1540s were whaling in the straits between Labrador and Newfoundland. They capture whales and process their oil in factories they have established on shore, mainly in the well-sheltered harbor of Red Bay.

Whaling ship sails the gulf waters.

Explorer and Inuit trade trinkets for furs

Aug. 19, 1576

ARCTIC [Frobisher Bay] – It didn't take Admiral Martin Frobisher long to start trading with the natives after his expedition landed in a huge bay in the Arctic today. He met Inuit people at the head of the bay and traded bells, looking glasses and toys for clothing made from seal and polar bear skins.

Frobisher took an Inuit man and his peculiar-looking skin boat on board and is bringing them to England. The explorer has been looking for precious metals and has discovered an ore which seems to be almost pure gold. If this turns out to be the case, England may become as wealthy as Spain one day.

Frobisher is an experienced mariner who began his career on a voyage to Guinea. He spent 10 years sailing along the African coast and into the Mediterranean. He received a charter from the Muscovy Company of London last year to search for a northwest passage to Asia.

After fitting out a ship and a crew on June 7, Frobisher left England and was in sight of the southern tip of Greenland by July 11. Soon after that he sailed into the bay, thinking he had discovered a strait leading to Asia.

There is no doubt Frobisher will return to the bay in the near future to continue his explorations and mining operations. Having made contact with the northern natives, it also may be possible to develop valuable fur and ivory trades.

Frobisher names arctic bay after himself

Aug. 11, 1576

ARCTIC [Frobisher Bay] – The Northwest Passage has been found! Sailing directly north from Queen Elizabeth's Foreland, Admiral Martin Frobisher piloted the 20-ton ship *Gabriell* into a "greate gutte, bay or passage" that the explorer believes divides Asia from America.

After sailing some 60 leagues into the passage, Frobisher followed the example of the Spanish explorer Magellan and named the straits after himself. Maintaining for the last 15 years that the passage would be "easie to bee performed," Frobisher's discovery of the straits on his first voyage ranks him second only to Sir John Hawkins as a mariner in this nation of seadogs.

British admiral, Martin Frobisher.

Frobisher captures 3 natives near bay

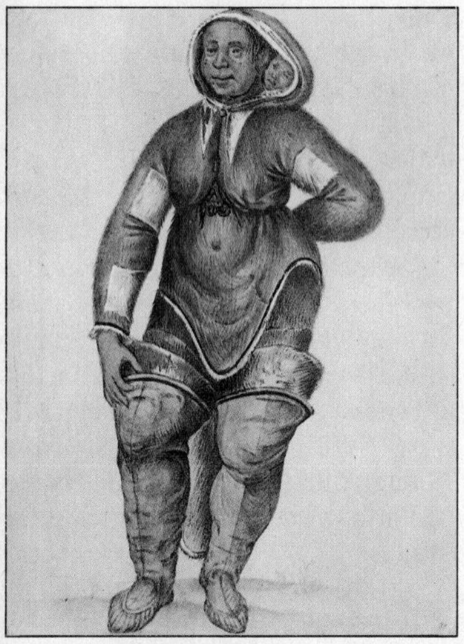

Inuit woman carrying her baby.

Aug. 23, 1577

ARCTIC [Frobisher Bay] – While on an excursion in search of gold in the northern reaches of America, Admiral Martin Frobisher has captured a native man, woman and child. They were seized as Frobisher and crew fought off a group of natives on the west shore of a large bay to which the explorer has given his name.

Frobisher has captured natives before. In 1576, an Inuit in a kayak neared his ship to trade. Frobisher captured him and took him to England. The man eventually died of a cold caught on the voyage.

Merchant returns from Newfoundland

Nov. 13, 1578

NEWFOUNDLAND – Bristol merchant Anthony Parkhurst has just returned home with news of the Newfoundland fisheries. After making four voyages to Newfoundland and exploring the area thoroughly, Parkhurst reports there are about 100 Spanish ships fishing for cod in the island's waters and 20 to 30 vessels engaged in whaling. The whalers are Spanish Basques in the straits between Newfoundland and Labrador.

Parkhurst says there are 50 Portuguese vessels and 150 French and Breton ships in the same waters fishing for cod. He also counted 50 English vessels and says they dominate the harbors despite being outnumbered.

Parkhurst's reports on the Newfoundland fisheries are among the most complete ever received. Based on what he's learned, Parkhurst believes the English should colonize Newfoundland. Advantages include easy access to the fish and the prospect of iron mining and smelting since iron and copper are among the land's natural resources. Converting natives to Christianity is also possible. After experimenting with English fruit, grain and vegetable seeds, Parkhurst says the Newfoundland climate is not unfavorable to settlement.

Island's precious ore believed to be gold

July 1578

ARCTIC [Frobisher Bay] – Admiral Martin Frobisher and his men have started mining a precious ore believed to be gold on Countess of Warwick Island. Frobisher received a hero's welcome on returning to England from his 1577 voyage to America with samples of the ore. He was then equipped with 15 ships and told to bring back 2,000 tons of ore this time and to establish a colony of 120 people.

Frobisher's men are proceeding with the mining on Warwick Island and another island called Best's Blessing in spite of inclement weather, ranging from ice and storms to scorching heat. Plans for colonization have been postponed because one of the expedition's ships carrying most of the building timber sank on the way here after being crushed by ice.

Martin Frobisher and his men try to occupy the islands of Warwick and Best's Blessing, hoping to mine a precious ore believed to be gold.

1580 (1580-1596)

Plymouth, England, Sept. 26, 1580. Francis Drake returns after a three-year voyage of circumnavigation. He is the first captain to sail around the world. His ship is full of captured Spanish treasure.

Canada, c.1581. Merchants from St-Malo begin to trade for furs with natives up the St. Lawrence River.

Plymouth, England, June 11, 1583. Sir Humphrey Gilbert leads an expedition of five ships to search for a site for a colony on the east coast of North America.

Atlantic Ocean, Aug. 29, 1583. The *Delight*, one of Gilbert's ships, runs aground and is lost at Sable Island. Eighty-five people drown in one Canada's first marine disasters.

Atlantic Ocean, Sept. 9, 1583. Sir Humphrey Gilbert drowns when his ship goes down on its return to England.

Dartmouth, England, June 7, 1585. Sir John Davis, explorer and navigator, sets sail with two ships and a royal patent to find the Northwest Passage.

England, Sept. 30, 1585. John Davis returns home. He reached Greenland, crossed the Davis Strait, entered Cumberland Sound, and landed on Baffin Island. He failed to find the Northwest Passage, but is now confident it lies either up Cumberland Sound or Davis Strait.

Dartmouth, England, May 7, 1586. John Davis sails with four ships on his second try to find the Northwest Passage.

England, Oct. 14, 1586. John Davis arrives home after reaching Labrador, where two of his men were killed by Inuit.

England, Sept. 15, 1587. John Davis is back from his third voyage to North America. He charted parts of Greenland, and the coasts of Baffin Island and Labrador. His description of the Inuit is one of the first and most accurate.

France, Jan. 12, 1588. Henry III grants a 12-year trading monopoly for Canada to Jacques Noel and Etienne Cartier.

German States, c.1595. Hundreds of people, mostly women, have been publicly burned in recent years as a result of witch hunts. The fear of witches has been inspired in part by the *Malleus Malificarum*, a misogynistic pamphlet authorized by the pope.

Catholic calendar to follow the sun

Oct. 5, 1582

ROME – Catholics in America and around the rest of the world will follow a new calendar as of today, in accordance with a papal decree. Pope Gregory XIII has reformed the Julian system of calculation, adding 10 days to the calendar. The changes ensure the calendar is more precisely aligned with the sun's rotation of the Earth. The adoption of the new calendar ends 300 years of debate by Catholic experts. Protestant England refuses to use the new system.

Fishery destroyed in surprise attack

Oct. 10, 1585

NEWFOUNDLAND – Reports are circulating that English commander Sir Bernard Drake, a kinsman of the famous Sir Francis Drake, has launched a surprise attack and destroyed the Spanish fishery in Newfoundland waters. Many fear that Drake's offensive could trigger an all-out war pitting England against Spain and Portugal.

Relations between Spain and England have been deteriorating in recent years. Spanish and English ships are preying on each other even when Spain and England consider themselves to be at peace – at least formally.

English fishing merchants in the western counties of Devon and Dorset have lobbied for years for the government to take action to limit foreign fisheries in Newfoundland waters. The merchants have expanded their fishing operations in recent years and desperately need foreign markets for their products. They are supplying France with saltfish and want Spain and Portugal too.

Not only do many navy personnel who have connections in the western counties support the fishing merchants, but so do several government officials – including Her Majesty – who believe a thriving saltfish trade with Spain and Portugal would be an excellent way to strengthen England's economy and make the nation a major maritime force.

Gilbert lays claim to Newfoundland

Sir Humphrey Gilbert claims Newfoundland for the Queen of England.

Aug. 5, 1583

ST. JOHN'S, Nfld. – In a ceremony on the shores of the harbor, Sir Humphrey Gilbert today announced that under the authority of Queen Elizabeth, he is claiming Newfoundland for England. A formal marker – a wooden pillar with the royal arms attached – was erected at St. John's.

Gilbert invited all the captains of the fishing ships in the harbor – English, Spanish and Portuguese – to watch the ceremony. After he had his commission read and interpreted, he proclaimed that the laws of England now apply in the new land. The captains concurred and Gilbert granted them titles to small properties along the shore. Gilbert does not intend to make St. John's his headquarters. He and his small fleet will be leaving shortly to establish the colony's headquarters farther south.

English navigator enters arctic inlet

Aug. 8, 1585

EXETER SOUND, Northern Sea – English navigator John Davis has sailed his ships, the 50-ton *Sunneshine* and the 35-ton *Mooneshine,* into a massive inlet far west of Greenland. It seems to be part of a large island or land mass.

Davis believes the inlet, surrounded by ice-covered mountains, leads to a channel that will take ships to the Indies. He decided not to sail far up the inlet because winter is coming and supplies are short. Officers on the *Sunneshine* estimate the ships will be back in Dartmouth before the autumn gales. Davis left that port on June 7 to seek a path to the Spice Islands free of danger from the Spaniards and Portuguese. On his voyage here he explored Greenland's coast before crossing a 480-kilometre stretch of water to make a landfall in a small inlet. He named it Exeter Sound after the city that is home to some of the west county merchants backing his expedition.

Davis also has some powerful patrons in London, including Sir Francis Walsingham, the queen's secretary. It is said that the idea of the expedition came from Davis two years ago and that Walsingham was persuaded to add his support – and that of the queen, who has a fondness for west country seamen. Wealthy merchants from London and Devon supplied the expedition with ships and money for the voyage.

Many French ships come to Canada and cruise the Atlantic seaboard, often employing natives to help them catch whales found there.

Inuit people at the time of initial European contact

Natives, whom the artist identifies as Inuit, catch water fowl.

Illustration of an Inuit couple with their children, drawn from nature.

Inuit living in the [Labrador] area use canoes to fish and for travel.

Inuit families from the coast of [Labrador] depend on fish to survive.

Original inhabitants of colony use various methods to catch foxes and to fish. Europeans call these people "Eskimos," a term meaning "eaters of raw meat."

1597 (1597-1607)

France, 1599. Henry IV grants a 10-year monopoly of the fur trade in New France to merchant Pierre de Chauvin de Tonnetuit.

Atlantic Coast, 1600. Crude tryworks are commonplace in most fishing harbors on the east coast of North America. Local life forms such as sea mammals and birds are boiled to make oil.

France, 1602. The king gives Chauvin approval to increase ties with the Indians along the St. Lawrence River. Chauvin sees good relations with the Montagnais as crucial to obtaining furs, as they control trading around Tadoussac.

France, 1603. Merchant explorer François Gravé Du Pont brings three young relatives of Montagnais chiefs to France. He treats them generously, and presents them to the king, winning the goodwill of the chiefs.

New France, 1603. To cement their alliance, the Montagnais give François Gravé Du Pont a captured Iroquois woman to take back to France with him.

France, Feb. 8, 1604. Pierre Du Gua de Monts organizes a powerful company with capital of 90,000 *livres* to trade in New France. Henry IV granted him a trading monopoly and appointed him lieutenant-general of New France in 1603.

Le Havre, France, March 1604. De Monts sails with two ships to explore and colonize in New France. Gravé Du Pont is senior officer, and Champlain acts as geographer, though he has no official title.

New France, May 1604. Champlain and De Monts explore a bay that De Monts names the Baie François [Bay of Fundy], and another bay that Champlain names Port-Royal [Annapolis Royal].

New France, June 1604. De Monts and Champlain obtain shelter at Ile Sainte-Croix [Dochet Island]. They settle there, build a palisade and houses, and plant the first wheat in New France.

Atlantic Coast, June 1606. John Knight and three men go ashore [on the Labrador coast] after battling through heavy ice. They are never heard from again, probably killed by Inuit, who attack the ship two days later. Knight's expedition was sponsored by the Muscovy and East India Companies to look for the Northwest Passage.

King names La Roche lieutenant-general

Jan. 12, 1598

CANADA – New letters patent King Henry IV issued today appoint Troilus de la Roche de Mesgouez lieutenant-general of the territories of Canada, Newfoundland, Labrador and Norumbega. Not only do the letters give the Marquis de La Roche-Mesgouez title to the land and a monopoly on the fur trade, but they also forbid others from trading furs without his consent, on pain "of losing all their ships and merchandise." As well, La Roche may recruit hardened criminals for his undertaking.

La Roche first set his sights on developing trade across the Atlantic in 1577, when he received a mandate to acquire any territories "of which he could make himself master." The next year La Roche was named the first viceroy of the "terres neuves" – new lands – and given the right to govern them. After two failed expeditions to the new lands and seven years in captivity during the civil war between the Roman Catholics and Huguenots, last year La Roche finally went back to his plan to develop trade overseas.

Henry IV and wife Marie de Medici.

Tadoussac is picked for fur-trading post

1600

TADOUSSAC, New France – A French military captain has founded the first trading post in Canada at Tadoussac. A gutsy soldier who's proven himself in several wars, Pierre de Chauvin de Tonnetuit and his four-ship expedition arrived in Tadoussac after leaving Honfleur this spring.

Chauvin chose Tadoussac as his destination against the advice of his partner François Gravé Du Pont and passenger Pierre Du Gua de Monts, who'd likely heard of its rugged terrain and extremely cold winters. It's quite probable Chauvin picked Tadoussac because of its strategic location at the junction of the Saguenay and St. Lawrence rivers, the Indian trading routes to the interior, and a harbor. It's also where the Montagnais Indians barter in the summer and a fur-trading and fishing resort for Europeans.

A man of broad interests and a shipowner, Chauvin solicited and received a 10-year monopoly on the New France fur trade from Henry IV in 1599. After La Roche de Mesgouez, who already had been granted the same monopoly, protested, the king issued a new patent this Jan. 15 naming Chauvin a lieutenant of La Roche.

Naval captain builds colony's first house

1600

TADOUSSAC, New France – Pierre de Chauvin de Tonnetuit, a French naval captain with a 10-year monopoly on the fur trade in New France, has built the first house in the new colony. The house in Tadoussac is 7.5 metres long by 4.6 metres wide and 2.4 metres high, covered with boards and has a central fireplace. It is surrounded by a ditch and a fence.

Eastern buffaloes vanishing rapidly

c.1600

NORTH AMERICA – The eastern buffalo, the largest and toughest race of North American buffalo, is rapidly vanishing from coastal areas, hunted down to supply Europe's voracious appetite for buffalo hide. English sailor David Ingram described the animals as "beasts as big as two oxen," with the long ears of a bloodhound and the crooked horns of a ram. They are thriving only in the interior, where they are inaccessible to hunters and traders.

Europeans value buffalo hides for their high quality leather, vastly superior to leather from domestic cattle. Most buffalo hunters are natives who trade with the French near the Gulf of St. Lawrence.

How to kill a whale: A fanciful illustration of techniques used by European whalers in the process of capturing and killing whales.

English explorer Waymouth clears inlet

Aug. 5, 1602

ARCTIC [Hudson Strait] – Capt. George Waymouth has successfully navigated his ships and mutinous crew out of a stormy, ice-strewn inlet [Hudson Strait]. With lookouts watching for icebergs, he plans to sail south and head home for England.

Waymouth sailed from the Thames on May 2 with 35 men in two ships – the 70-ton *Discovery* and the 60-ton *Godspeed.* Since he planned to find a passage to Asia by sailing west, Queen Elizabeth gave him a letter for the Emperor of China. While Waymouth and his crew sighted America at one point, they got lost in the fog and sailed north.

The night of July 19, while Waymouth was asleep in his cabin the crew of the *Discovery* "conspired to beare up the helm for England." The next day, they told Waymouth he was sailing too far north but would carry on if he would limit his exploration to the coast between 57 and 60 degrees N. After punishing the ringleaders, Waymouth sailed south on July 22. Some crewmen narrowly escaped being crushed by an iceberg which cracked apart as they were chipping off blocks of ice for drinking water.

By July 26 Waymouth sailed his ships into the entry of the inlet and headed west for about 480 kilometres. Although Waymouth had "great hope of this inlet," many of his men were ill and he was forced to turn back.

Montagnais leader eager to talk religion

August 1603

TADOUSSAC, New France – It was not your average conversation, even through interpreters. There was French explorer Samuel de Champlain discussing religion with the Sagamore, the tribal leader of a group of Montagnais Indians.

After the native leader explained the Montagnais believe in one God, he took some arrows, placed them in the ground and explained that some represented men and women, others the good and bad elements of the world. Preaching the Christian doctrine, Champlain told the chief God created everything on earth and in the heavens. To the Sagamore's reply that God is both good and evil, Champlain said his God is incapable of evil.

French explorer Samuel de Champlain has spoken with an Indian chief and preached the Christian doctrine.

Only five survive Tadoussac winter

1601

TADOUSSAC, New France – Five of 16 men Tadoussac founder Pierre de Chauvin de Tonnetuit left here over the winter were able to survive the harsh northern climate. All 16 might have died had it not been for Indian hospitality.

Chauvin arrived in Tadoussac early last spring to establish a fur-trading post. After the colonists settled, trading took place until the fall, when all but 16 men sailed for France with a cargo of beaver and other furs. No one is expected to be left behind this winter.

Dance is an integral part of Indian life – an expression of their culture.

Champlain's Des sauvages describes natives, land of Canada

Nov. 15, 1603

NEW FRANCE – Samuel de Champlain's account of his trip as an observer in Canada was released in Paris today. *Des sauvages* provides an admirable description of the natives he met and the areas he explored earlier this year.

Cmdr. Aymar de Chaste, who holds the trade monopoly in New France, invited Champlain to accompany François Gravé Du Pont on an expedition through Canada. When Champlain got on board the *Bonne-Renommée* on March 15, he had no precise function and sailed as a mere observer.

Champlain's accounts reveal that Gravé Du Pont's ships reached Tadoussac from France on May 26. There Champlain witnessed native feasts called the "tabagies." Algonquin women danced naked in these rituals and the male Indians took part in races, with the winners being awarded prizes.

With the fur trading going on from May 26 to June 18, Champlain had ample time to study the native customs. He even gave them a course on religion, and on June 11, travelled up the Saguenay: "It is some gulf of this our sea, which overflows in the north into the midst of our continent."

When the feasts and trading were over on June 18, Gravé Du Pont started up the Rivière de Canada [St. Lawrence River]. Champlain went with him but discovered nothing. While he showed little interest as he passed in front of [Quebec], he did make note of a place [Trois-Rivières] suitable for a "habitation."

Champlain returned to Tadoussac July 11 and left with Gravé Du Pont for Gaspé, where he stayed from July 15 to 19. These days gave Champlain a general idea of the region along the Atlantic coast and time to learn about Acadia, where he hoped to find the route to Asia and the mines Sarcel de Prévert once looked for. The Acadian possibilities – the route to Asia and the mines – fascinate Champlain.

When Champlain returned to France on Sept. 20, he was told de Chaste was dead. He presented a map of the St. Lawrence to the king, gave the monarch a verbal report on all he'd seen in the colony and published *Des sauvages.*

Illustration from Bref Discours, a manuscript attributed to Samuel de Champlain, describing his voyage to the West Indies around 1600.

Asian Sea thought near

July 1603

HOCHELAGA [Montreal] – Not only have the travels of explorer Samuel de Champlain in New France taken him to the town of Hochelaga, but they've also given him the impression the Asian Sea is not far away.

Accompanying an expedition led by François Gravé Du Pont, Champlain has spent the past few days exploring the area west of Stadacona. By questioning the natives in Hochelaga – below the crest of Mount Royal, as Jacques Cartier called it – Champlain's been able to reconstruct the Great Lake network and believes the Asian Sea may be near.

Champlain reached St. Mary's rapids opposite Hochelaga the first Wednesday of July. Since the water was shallow and he had trouble navigating his flatboat, he disembarked several times to push his vessel over the rocks and shallows. Frustrated by such slow progress, he anchored his barge.

Unable to continue by water, Champlain questioned the Indians accompanying him, asking them to draw a map of the rapids, lakes and rivers west of Hochelaga. Their knowledge of the interior was surprisingly accurate. They identified the Ottawa River, Niagara Falls and lakes St. Louis, St. Francis, Ontario, Erie and Huron.

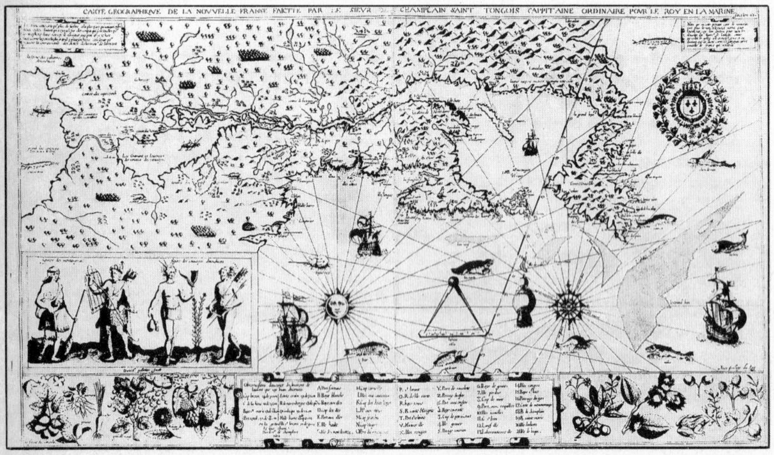

This map by Samuel de Champlain shows the northeast coast of New France.

Montagnais feast after defeating Iroquois

Aug. 3, 1603

TADOUSSAC, New France – Montagnais Indians today invited explorers Samuel de Champlain and François Gravé Du Pont to join them as they celebrated a recent victory over their longtime enemies, the Iroquois. Montagnais warriors killed and scalped about 100 Iroquois. Montagnais Chief Anadabijou began the celebration with a speech and the ceremonial smoking of petum – or tobacco. He passed the pipe to Champlain, Gravé Du Pont and other tribal chieftains. The natives expressed their pleasure and agreement with repeated chants of "ho, ho, ho," meaning "yes, yes, yes."

When the speech ended, the "tabagie" – or feast – began. Eight to 10 kettles, each over a separate fire, were filled with all kinds of meats: moose, which is like beef, bear, seal and wild fowl. While the meat was cooking, an Indian rose and, seizing a dog, danced wildly among the pots and their fires. Then, in front of Anadabijou and to the delight of the crowd, he violently threw the dog on the ground. When one native finished this ritual he was replaced by another until the meal was ready.

When the food was cooked, it was shared among men sitting in two rows, each holding a bowl made of bark. After the feast, one or two natives sang, waving the scalps of their enemies while others clapped their hands. There were many cries of "ho, ho, ho" until the exhausted celebrants fell to the ground from fatigue.

Sailor saves 11 starving island captives

The lake at [Sable Island], where only 11 of 50 men survived their sentence.

Sept. 20, 1603

ATLANTIC COAST [Sable Island] – After failing to bring supplies to this wind-whipped sandbar last year, the French sailor Thomas Chefdostel today arrived to find only 11 survivors of the 50 beggars and petty crooks he and the Marquis De La Roche left here in 1598. The settlers turned on one another and slaughtered their leaders last winter. They lived on seals and dug shelters in the sand. Chefdostel is taking them to France.

Explorer eyes land "ideal" for colony

June 22, 1603

NEW FRANCE [Quebec] – Samuel de Champlain sighted a narrow bend in the Rivière de Canada [St. Lawrence River] today, and he considers the location perfect for a trading post and French colony. The explorer notes that the soil of [Quebec] could be as fertile as the land in France.

Champlain ponders new route to Asia

July 19, 1603

NEW FRANCE [Quebec] – After four days in Gaspé, a brief respite from his travels up the [St. Lawrence River], explorer Samuel de Champlain today expressed interest in finding the two Acadian mines St-Malo merchant Jean Sarcel de Prévert gave him mineral samples from.

[Montmorency Falls] are the highest falls on mainland New France.

First shipbuilders are French captains

March 1604

ACADIA [Nova Scotia] – Two French mariners have launched the first boat of European design built in North America. François Gravé Du Pont and a captain Morel are commanders of ships in Pierre du Gua de Monts' expedition to establish permanent French settlements in America.

Du Pont and Morel built a longboat immediately after landing at English Harbor [Louisbourg]. The work delayed their rendez-vous with de Monts, who was forced to send some of his men and some natives to get reserve supplies from the missing captains.

French sow grain, plant vegetables

1606

PORT-ROYAL, Acadia – Under the direction of colonial boss Jean de Biencourt de Poutrincourt et de Saint-Just and with help from herbalist Louis Hébert and lawyer-poet Marc Lescarbot, freshly arrived French settlers in Port-Royal sowed grain and vegetable seeds in July and saw them sprout in August.

Poutrincourt, who dreamed of an agricultural empire here, has built the first water-driven grist mill in North America. In November, he and his small, happy band rejoiced in the health of their first grain crops.

Union Jack is made the flag of England

1606

LONDON, England – James I of England has proclaimed the Royal Union – also known as the Union Jack – the royal flag. The Union Jack combines the flags of England and Scotland, representing the union of the two kingdoms under James I. The new flag consists of two superimposed crosses, the cross of England's St. George (red on white backing), and the Scottish cross of St. Andrew (white on blue background).

Micmacs dubious of furry "gifts"

1607

PORT-ROYAL, Acadia – Not all the new items the colonists of Port-Royal have introduced to the Micmac natives are as welcome as iron tools, pots, decorations and cloth goods. Brown rats, previously unknown, have disembarked from ships and now infest the new colony and also the lodges where they eat the Micmacs' fish oils. They are also suspected of carrying disease.

The Indians also complain about the disgraceful conduct of traders who loot Micmac graves and steal beaver pelts left there as gifts. Some French observers fear the Indians will grow to despise all Frenchmen.

Select visitor sails to Acadia on Jonas

Jean de Biencourt de Poutrincourt.

May 13, 1606

LA ROCHELLE, France – With backing from local merchants, the elegant Pierre Du Gua de Monts, governor of Acadia, today sent the *Jonas* across the Atlantic to Port-Royal, the Acadian settlement he founded last year. Aboard the 150-ton vessel was Jean de Biencourt de Poutrincourt et de Saint-Just, whom he'd named lieutenant-governor of Acadia. They'd explored its coasts in 1604, and now Poutrincourt is on his way back.

De Monts moves colony

Aug. 1, 1605

PORT-ROYAL, Acadia – Pierre Du Gua de Monts has just moved his infant colony from an island at Ste-Croix [Dochet Island] to Port-Royal, situated on a basin within the peninsula across the great bay. Seventy-nine colonists spent a disastrous winter at Ste-Croix. The weather was extremely harsh, and 35 settlers died of scurvy and other disorders. Another 20 colonists barely survived.

With the arrival of the warm weather this spring, de Monts decided to move the settlement. He spent six weeks exploring the coast to the south for a more promising site before choosing Port-Royal. The ideal site would offer fertile soil, good fishing, mineral wealth, friendly natives and a passage to Asia.

At Port-Royal, colonists have already begun construction of a four-sided habitation and cleared land for vegetables and crops. De Monts holds the rights of settlement, trade and fishery in a territory stretching from the 40th to the 46th parallels of latitude.

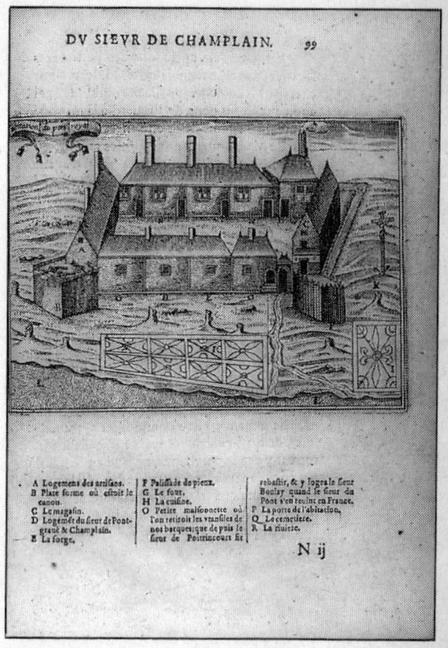

The new colony at Port-Royal.

European drama first in the New World

Nov. 14, 1606

ACADIA [Nova Scotia] – After an exploratory cruise to the south, Jean de Biencourt de Poutrincourt et de Saint-Just and his crew were welcomed home by a trident-bearing Neptune, his six Tritons (male versions of mermaids), and gift-bearing natives. The sea god and his troupe docked their canoes in Acadia under the ship's yardarm and proceeded to perform *Théâtre de Neptune* – the first European drama in the New World.

Visiting French poet Marc Lescarbot wrote the play, complete with trumpets and cannons, and verses in French, Gascon, and Souriquoi (Micmac).

Théâtre de Neptune, the first European drama performed in the New World.

Book details New France

1607

PARIS – No sooner had famed writer, traveller and lawyer Marc Lescarbot published a poem entitled *La défaite des sauvages armouchiquoisis* this year, then he had taken on the task of composing a vast history of French establishments in America. The first edition of *Histoire de la Nouvelle-France* is expected to appear in 1609. It will recount the travels of Laudonnière, Ribaut and Gourges to Florida, Durand de Villegaignon and Jean de Léry to Brazil, and Verrazzano, Cartier and Roberval to Canada.

Born at Vervins in the north of France around 1570, Lescarbot is a man of Renaissance accomplishments. He's a scholar of the classics, member of the Parlement de Paris, diplomat, poet, dramatist and historian. Lescarbot first studied at the Collège in Vervins, then at Laon. He received a thorough classical education in Paris, learned Latin, Greek and Hebrew, and acquired a vast knowledge of ancient and modern literatures. He then studied canonical and civil law.

Lescarbot acquired a temporary distaste for the bar last year after he lost a case. When one of his clients, Jean de Biencourt de Poutrincourt, who was associated with the Canadian enterprises of Sieur du Gua de Monts, proposed to Lescarbot that he accompany them on a trip to Acadia, he was eager to oblige. Before leaving La Rochelle on May 13, 1606, Lescarbot wrote his *Adieu à la France* in verse.

Native funeral rites use European goods

Illustration of native funeral procession which includes a dance ceremony.

c.1600

GREAT LAKES REGION – The Iroquoian peoples around the Great Lakes are increasingly burying their dead along with iron knives, axes and glass beads from Europe. The Iroquoians associate these exotic goods with health and success after death and equip the deceased with them to use in the afterlife, thought to be very similar to this one. They also regard the buried objects as natural substances from the earth, which should rightly be returned to the earth.

The Iroquoians do not appear to discriminate against lower classes in their burial rites. The prized beads and iron articles are placed in the graves of ordinary tribesmen as well as chiefs and their families. But there is sexual discrimination. The Senecans, for example, bury more tools and beads with men and children than with women.

Through intertribal trade, European glass and iron goods began reaching the Iroquoians in the last century. With the growth of the fur trade since 1580, more of the objects have reached them. But most are disposed of in funerals. Rarely are they used in daily life.

There are other distinctive features of Iroquoian burials. The dead are interred with their heads pointed to the west. This practice is probably related to the traditional Iroquoian belief that the land of the dead is in the west.

Colony's first wheat grown at Port-Royal

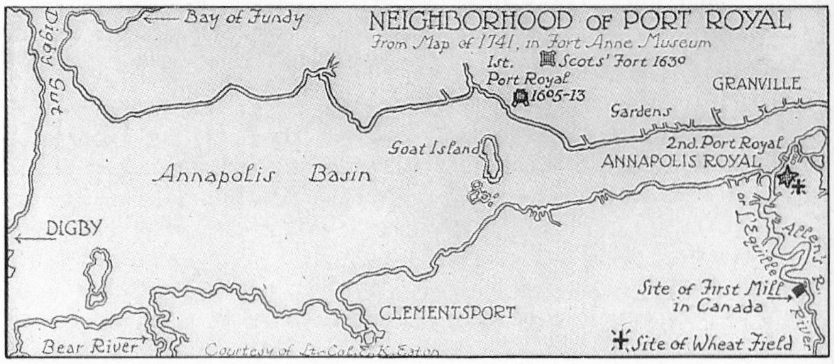

Map shows Port-Royal, site of the first wheat to be grown in Acadia.

1606

PORT-ROYAL, Acadia – Wheat has been successfully harvested at Port-Royal, on land overlooking the junction of L'Esquille [Allen's] River with the Annapolis. This brings Lt.-Gov. Jean de Biencourt de Poutrincourt et de Saint-Just's dreams of an agrarian empire and self-sufficiency another step closer.

It also mitigates earlier disasters at Port-Royal and Ile St. Croix. Poet, author and lawyer Marc Lescarbot is given credit for this triumph. After losing a lawsuit because of interference by a dishonest court official, Lescarbot took the opportunity "to fly from a corrupt world" and try his hand in the New World when Poutrincourt approached him.

Lescarbot arrived at Port-Royal this June 27, only to find two solitary Frenchmen and one native. He immediately set to work at tasks below his station to reap the "fruits of the earth" and set an example. Burning the meadow grass to sow crops of wheat, rye and barley, overseeing the planting of gardens and hoeing the fields by moonlight is not enough. He is also writing the *Histoire de la Nouvelle-France* in his spare time and reading the Scriptures on Sundays, causing many to fear that all this activity will jeopardize his health.

The futile attempt to grow crops on Ile St. Croix in 1604 where "the rays of the sun parched the sand so that the gardens were entirely unproductive" and the decimation of the settlers by scurvy, prompted the colony to move to the mainland. With the wheat capable of "growing under the snow" the colony's future looks bright. Plans are being made to erect Acadia's first grist mill.

Samuel de Champlain has founded the Order of Good Cheer, to keep up settlers' spirits. Members take turns providing fresh game and, as chief steward of the day, leading the ceremonial procession to the table.

Maps show dawning awareness of a vast continent

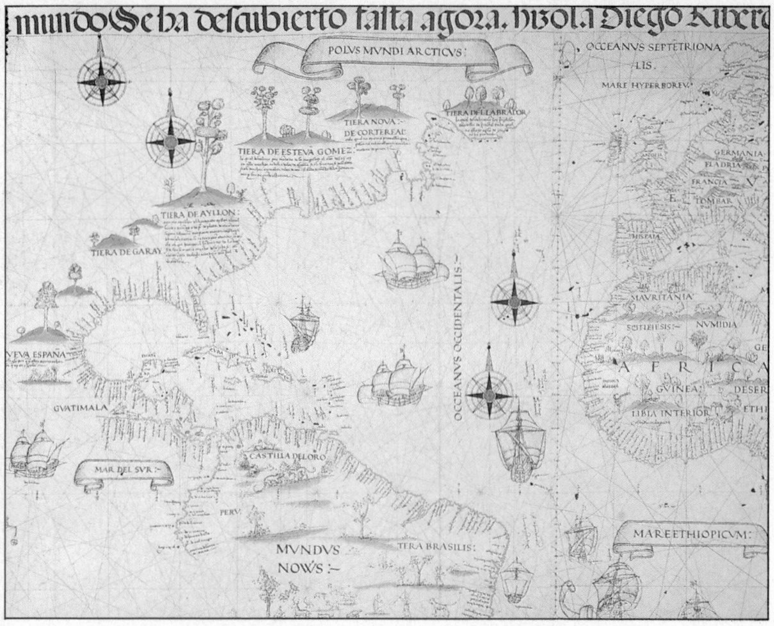

This Diego Ribero map represents the world as it is known now. It is based on explorations in the New World, including those of Giovanni da Verrazzano.

Travels and discoveries: Jacques Cartier and his crew land in Canada.

Guillaume Le Testu's map shows Florida, Canada and Labrador.

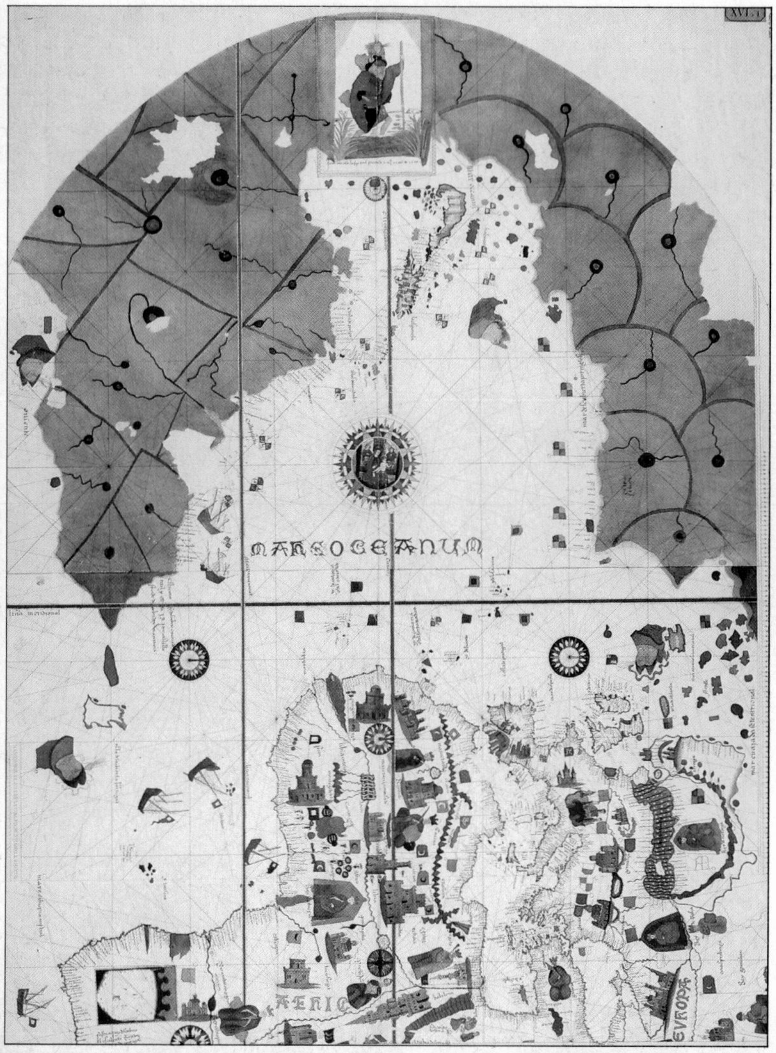

One of earliest maps to show Canada. Flags represent English claims.

Map from Abraham Ortelius' Theatrum Orbis Terrarum includes New World.

FOUNDATIONS

1608-1763

1608 (1608-1609)

France, 1608. Pierre Du Gua de Monts, lieutenant-general of New France, organizes a new colonizing expedition to North America. It involves three ships – one to go to Port-Royal, another to the lower St. Lawrence, and the third to found a settlement at Quebec under Champlain.

Quebec, July 3, 1608. Champlain founds the settlement of Quebec.

Quebec, 1608. The son of Iroquet, an important Algonquin chief, visits the new French settlement at Quebec and tells Champlain about his peoples' war with the Iroquois. Champlain invites the Algonquins to join the French and Montagnais in an expedition against the Iroquois next summer.

Quebec, 1609. The colony at Quebec receives fresh supplies after a disasterous winter marked by a severe scurvy epidemic. Sixteen of the 25 colonists died.

New France, 1609. A group of Huron warriors led by Ochasteguin accompany the Algonquin Chief Iroquet to the St. Lawrence Valley to join the French in a raid on the Iroquois. They are the first Hurons to contact the French in the St. Lawrence Valley.

New France, June 1609. Champlian meets with Algonquins and Hurons assembled to raid the Iroquois. He denies a rumor that he is only interested in trade, and says his sole aim is to help his Indian allies in war.

Paris, 1609. Marc Lescarbot publishes the *Histoire de la Nouvelle-France*, a vast history of French settlements in America. It includes an account of de Monts' settlement in Acadia, and a description of native customs. He sees them as more civilized than Europeans in many ways, but pitifully ignorant of the pleasures of wine and love.

New France, August 1609. Montagnais give Champlain gifts for the king of France.

Manhattan, Sept. 13, 1609. English navigator Henry Hudson sails his ship, the *Half Moon*, up the wide-mouthed river [Hudson River] near Manhattan. He proves it does not lead to the Orient, but establishes its trading potential.

Honfleur, France, Oct. 13, 1609. Champlain returns to report to de Monts and the king.

Champlain makes third trip to New France

Champlain brings back new maps of coast after travelling with Indians.

April 13, 1608

ST-MALO, France – Explorer Samuel de Champlain today set out for a third time to New France, this time carrying the first official function of his Canadian career. The French government recently appointed Champlain lieutenant to another Canadian explorer, Pierre Du Gua de Monts.

A disappointed Champlain returned to France last October, three years and seven months after setting sail for Canada in the hopes of establishing a colony and a fur monopoly for de Monts, his expedition leader at the time. The voyage to Canada was marred by many deaths due to scurvy on Ste-Croix Island and some mortal encounters with Indians.

All was not hardship. Champlain brought back excellent new maps of the coast from Acadia southward to Rivière du Gua [Charles River, Mass.]. And he recalled the good times settlers had in the bountiful settlement at Port-Royal.

Aboriginal dialects confuse newcomers

1608

NORTH AMERICA – A verb with 500 forms. No gender but five states of inanimate. Words and pronunciation used only by females. These are only a few of the complexities facing anyone wishing to learn an Aboriginal language.

It is difficult to pick up a dialect without a knowledgeable teacher to explain the rules in one's own language. Even fluency in one language does not necessarily make learning another easier. What is inanimate to one group of people is considered animate by another.

Many of the languages tend to pack so much information into a word that sometimes several parts have to be altered to attain the meaning one is trying to convey. Something as simple as pitch, tone or accent can change the definition of a word. Other rules of grammar apply that simply do not exist in European languages. Forms in the Athabaskan languages vary depending on the age, sex and the relationship of the speaker to the person spoken to.

Unsuccessful murder plot fails to keep explorer from garden

July 1608

QUEBEC, New France – An unsuccessful plot to murder Samuel de Champlain doesn't seem to have fazed the renowned explorer very much. To test the soil in the new colony, Champlain has been busy planting Quebec's first vegetable garden and sowing wheat and rye. He's also been spotted planting some vines.

Despite Champlain's efforts to get back to the business of colonizing Quebec, tension lingers following locksmith Jean Duval's plot to kill him, hand over the colony to the Basques or the Spaniards, and make a fortune in the process of staging his coup.

Duval's scheme fell through when one of his four fellow conspirators, Antoine Natel, also a locksmith, told the French about the plan. The evening the men hoped to carry out their plot Champlain lured them on board a boat under the pretext of offering them something to drink. Instead, he took them prisoner. While three of the men who plotted against Champlain were condemned to hang in the gallows at first, they were eventually sent back to France for their punishment. Natel was pardoned and Duval has been hanged. As work continues on the settlement, Duval's head is in full view, impaled on the end of a pike at the highest point of the fort.

Champlain's settlement, Quebec.

Champlain built the impressive Quebec fortress this year to defend the new French settlement at the foot of Cape Diamond against the Basques and other European competitors. It is a miniature reproduction of a European fortress.

Unlike its Acadian predecessors in Ste-Croix or Port-Royal, the Quebec fortress Champlain has established here is compact. A gallery and a continuous outside wall unite its three buildings into a single block. A moat surrounding it can only be crossed by a drawbridge. A palisade provides the outermost line of defence.

Fulfilling a longtime desire of his, Champlain founded Quebec on July 3. "I at once employed a part of our workmen," he writes, "in cutting them (the trees) down to make a site for our settlement, another part in sawing planks, another in digging the cellar and making ditches."

Explorer uses firearms to defeat enemy Iroquois

Samuel de Champlain, with two Frenchmen and Algonquins, defeats Iroquois attackers at Ticonderoga.

July 30, 1609

TICONDEROGA – Samuel de Champlain and his Huron Wendat Indian allies today scored an easy victory over an Iroquois war party in the French explorer's first military operation in New France.

The brief battle took place on the shores of a lake Champlain found so stunning in its beauty he decided to give it his own name. The skirmish was a somewhat formal affair, where the Iroquois who paddled out to greet the invaders last night suggested the fight commence in the morning because it was too dark to tell who was the enemy.

Last night both the Iroquois and Champlain's party sang out loud songs of insult to their enemies, and summoned their courage for the next day's battle. This morning the invaders – Champlain, two white companions and 60 Indians – came to shore to greet the 200 Iroquois foes. Champlain was concealed by his Indian allies, while the other two white men hid in the woods. The Indians indicated to Champlain that three robust Iroquois men sporting large plumes were the chiefs and told him "to do what I could to kill them."

Champlain then marched forward to the enemy. When he was within 30 metres of the Iroquois he aimed his arquebus, loaded with four bullets, and felled two chiefs with one blast. Another died later of a gunshot wound. Champlain recounts what happened next: "As I was reloading my arquebus, one of my companions fired a shot from within the woods, which astonished them again so much that, seeing their chiefs dead, they lost courage and took to flight."

Champlain's native allies intercepted fleeing Iroquois, killing several and taking 15 prisoner. The victorious crew celebrated, gorging themselves on cornmeal Iroquois abandoned. Champlain's pleasure with the victory was tempered by the torture his Indian allies inflicted on an Iroquois prisoner, branding him with an iron rod, scalping him and tearing sinews from his arms.

They invited Champlain to take part, but he replied that "we did not commit such cruelties, but that we killed people outright, and that if they wished me to shoot him with the arquebus, I should be glad to do so." Seeing the torture displeased Champlain, the Indians relented and asked him to put the tortured prisoner out of his misery.

Champlain must have forgotten that in France, crimes are often punished by spectacular and public torture. Victims may be flogged, branded, mutilated, broken on the wheel, or their bodies quartered by horses pulling in four directions.

Champlain gives his name to lake on trip into Iroquois country

July 13, 1609

QUEBEC, New France – French explorer Samuel de Champlain came across a huge lake in New France today which he has decided to name after himself. After receiving fresh supplies this spring, Champlain set sail from Quebec on June 28 to explore Iroquois country. Travelling with two Frenchmen and Algonquin, Huron and Montagnais allies, Champlain entered the Rivière des Iroquois [Richelieu River] before taking the Chambly Rapids to [Lake Champlain]. Following his latest discovery, Champlain plans to continue his travels into Iroquois country and is headed for Ticonderoga [Crown Point, N.Y.].

Samuel de Champlain comes upon a large lake and names it after himself.

French start to call native tribe Hurons

June 1609

NEW FRANCE – Traders and colonists have begun calling the Wendat people "Huron." The new name is derived from the French word *Hure* meaning "ruffian" or "boar's head."

The Wendat, or "people of the island," consider European-style facial hair and curls ugly and a sign of second-rate intelligence. The French, in contrast, consider the long, unkempt Wendat hairstyle to be primitive. This difference in taste helps to explain French use of an uncomplimentary name for a people they generally consider intelligent and deserving of respect.

1610 (1610-1619)

Quebec, April 23, 1610. Champlain arrives on his fourth voyage to New France. He finds the wintering colonists in good health.

New France, 1610. Champlain leads a force including Algonquins and Hurons against the Iroquois at the mouth of the Richelieu. Though he is wounded by an arrow, the attack succeeds and the Iroquois flee.

Newfoundland, August 1610. A group of colonists led by John Guy lands and chooses Cuper's Cove [Cupids] as the site for a new colony. James I granted Guy's company a charter to colonize Newfoundland.

The North, November 1610. Henry Hudson's ship, the *Discovery*, is frozen in at [James Bay]. He entered the bay after exploring [Hudson Strait] and sailing along the east coast of [Hudson Bay]. He is the first European to enter the two bays.

Paris, Dec. 30, 1610. Samuel de Champlain, a devout Catholic in his 30s, is betrothed to 12-year-old Protestant Hélène Boullé, daughter of a wealthy secretary to Louis XIII. Of the promised dowry of 6,000 *livres*, he receives 4,500 *livres*, an important contribution to his latest colonizing venture.

New France, May 1611. Champlain travels up the St. Lawrence to the Saint-Louis rapids [Lachine], lands on an island [Montreal], and considers it as "the ground for building." He chooses Pointe Callières for a settlement.

Quebec, June 13, 1611. The Hurons return young Etienne Brûlé after he has spent a year learning their language and customs. Champlain writes "my lad had learned their language very well." In fact, Brûlé's knowledge of the Huron language is limited.

New France, June 1613. Champlain travels up the Grand River [Ottawa River] and visits the Algonquin chief Tessouat. He wants to renew his friendship with the Algonquins and persuade them to trade with French merchants. Tessouat tricks Champlain into ending his explorations.

Acadia, 1613. An English expedition led by Samuel Argall destroys the French settlements in Acadia [Nova Scotia, New Brunswick, and Maine].

Reluctant natives refuse Champlain

June 1610

QUEBEC CITY – Native allies of Samuel de Champlain have balked at fulfilling a promise to help the founder of Quebec explore the Lake Huron area. While Champlain's request that one of his men be allowed to accompany the natives into their territory to explore the Lake Huron area was accepted at first, a tribal council reversed the decision. Champlain hopes to find mines and other rare items at Lake Huron.

Algonquins, Montagnais and Hurons helped Champlain's French companions defeat the Iroquois on June 14. It was after the victory celebrations that the great explorer – wounded in the battle by an arrow which "split the tip of my ear and pierced my neck" – asked the natives to help him in Lake Huron.

Hudson set adrift as crew stages mutiny

June 24, 1611

NORTH [Rupert's Bay] – Mutinous crewmen set English explorer Henry Hudson adrift in a lifeboat today with his son John and seven seamen. After more than a year at sea, the crew of the *Discovery* was afraid that any more of Hudson's "senseless" sailing in the Northern Sea would kill them all.

Hudson after being set adrift.

Discovery sailed from England on April 17 last year to search for the Northwest Passage. The first signs of discord flared up when two crewmen came to blows not long into the journey.

When ice threatened the ship in the fall, the crew built a shelter for the winter. Since food was scarce and most crewmen didn't have enough warm clothing, it was a dismal few months, full of quarrelling.

After the journey home began June 12, Hudson divided rations among his men. The crew was certain he was holding back a reserve supply.

They plotted the mutiny last night, and at daybreak this morning set Hudson and the others adrift, securing much bigger rations of food for themselves.

Feared pirate lands to restock his fleet

June 4, 1614

NEWFOUNDLAND – The feared English pirate Sir Henry Mainwaring arrived in Newfoundland today with eight warlike ships. He's here to recruit men and stock up on fish. Fishing ships and Gov. John Guy's colonists on the Avalon peninsula fear the pirates will inflict heavy losses on them.

Guy's laws protect environment, property

Aug. 30, 1611

CUPER'S COVE [Cupids], Nfld. – Newfoundland's first governor has issued the colony's first laws just before he visits England for a few months. John Guy's legislation protects the forests, harbors and personal property of Newfoundland. It's also aimed at regulating the fishing industry and reforming the disorderly practices of visiting fishermen.

In the one short year since Guy and the other colonists settled in Newfoundland, the governor has seen the problems colonists and migratory fishermen are creating for the environment. The shoreline is an ecological disaster with the destruction of the forests through wasteful building practices and carelessly caused fires. Tons of rock trading ships use for ballast are being thrown into the harbors.

Indian chief, family baptized Catholics

June 24, 1611

ACADIA – Membertou, a Micmac chief, today became the first native baptized a Catholic in New France. Missionary Jessé Fléché performed the ceremony in front of 20 of Membertou's family who followed their patriarch's example and also received the solemn rites. However, it is doubtful that Membertou and his family fully grasp what their conversion implies. Their tutor Fléché, the first Catholic priest in the colony, arrived here less than one month ago and has to rely on interpreters to preach and teach the catechism.

Student exchange opens door for French

1610

NEW FRANCE – Samuel de Champlain has persuaded Algonquin chief Iroquet to accept young Frenchman Etienne Brûlé as a student while the French take in Savignon, a Huron chief's brother. Champlain expects to benefit from what Brûlé will learn about his host tribe's customs and, above all, language: Champlain is painfully aware that he lacks accurate interpreters. However, Iroquet was reluctant to accept Brûlé, one of Champlain's employees, because he feared reprisals should anything happen to his guest. He agreed only on condition that Champlain also accept responsibility for Savignon.

Explorers trade ideas with Hurons.

Huron defeat tarnishes explorer's image

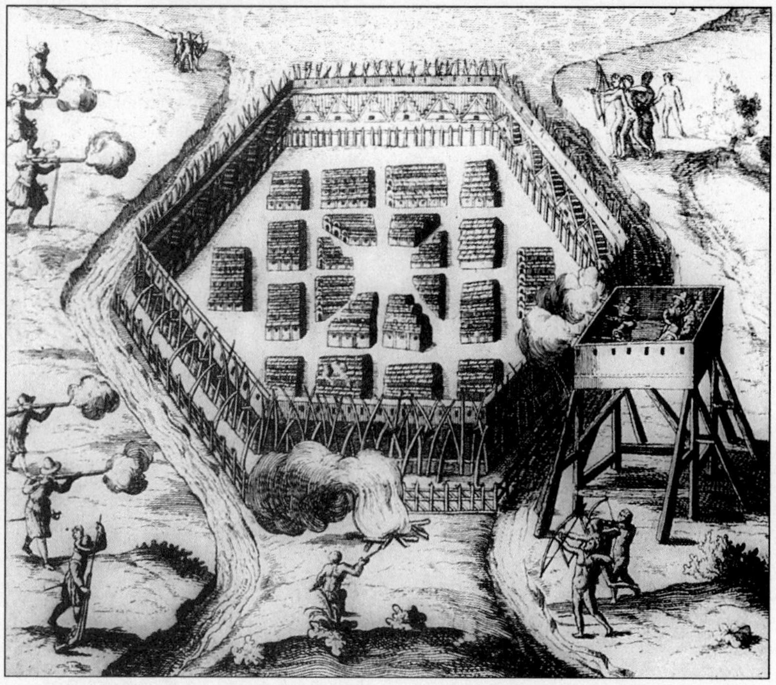

Hurons fail to seize fortified Iroquois village despite help from Champlain.

Oct. 16, 1615

NEW FRANCE [Ontario] – Samuel de Champlain's efforts to coordinate a Huron attack on an Iroquois village have ended in failure. After a one-day offensive, Champlain and the Huron warriors are in retreat. Champlain is demoralized, and fears his prestige is seriously damaged. He does not realize that to his Huron allies, the raid is not the great disaster it is to the French.

The Huron asked Champlain last month for help in their war against the Iroquois. Seizing the opportunity to strengthen the French-Huron alliance, Champlain crossed the eastern end of a giant freshwater sea [Lake Ontario] with a war party. On Oct. 10, the explorer and his allies stumbled across a heavily fortified Iroquois village about 145 kilometres inland.

The village, protected by a stockade nine metres high and a network of gutters to help extinguish enemy fires, has proven impregnable. The Hurons have failed to breach its walls even with the aid of a European-style siege tower.

Hurons awe Champlain

Aug. 1, 1615

HURON COUNTRY – As Samuel de Champlain arrived today at [Huronia], the Hurons' main settlement area and the thriving commercial and agricultural centre of the [Great Lakes], the explorer was astonished to see how prosperous the Indians were. Huronia, 2,070 square kilometres, is the key to a great inland fur trade. It is accessible to the St. Lawrence-Ottawa route, and is at the heart of the Great Lakes system, the reason it is so important to the French.

Champlain has named the magnificent [Lake Huron] *Mer douce*, or Freshwater Sea.

Champlain and his men are astonished at how prosperous Hurons are.

Pirate Easton obtains the king's pardon

November 1612

NEWFOUNDLAND – The notorious pirate Peter Easton has been pardoned by King James for the second time this year.

Easton, who has been terrorizing Newfoundland sailors and settlers since his arrival here last year, was the bane of shippers using the English Channel during the first decade of the century. Easton headed for the New World when the royal navy commissioned Henry Mainwaring to pursue him and bring him to London.

Easton arrived in Newfoundland with 10 ships of war and built himself a fort at Harbour Grace. His main purpose in the area was to repair his ships and capture arms, but he has also plundered fishing fleets and recruited some 500 men for his private army. While many joined Easton voluntarily, others were forced into service.

Easton has not confined his looting to the northern regions of the New World. He also raided the Spanish colony at Puerto Rico, bringing home a Spanish ship stocked with treasure.

It is not unusual for the pirates like Easton to obtain pardons from the king. It is a matter of negotiating a price, a small concern for the now-wealthy Easton.

Tasty sturgeon's a colonial delight

1615

NEW FRANCE [Quebec] – Sturgeon has become one of the most popular foods in the colony. It can grow very large and each part of its body has a different taste.

People prefer the end of the tail and the belly – the darkest and fattest parts are "exquisite," Jesuit Louis Nicolas says. Sturgeon, caught in great quantity, is salted and enjoyed during the winter and Lenten seasons. Colonists appreciate its caviar and jelly made from its stock.

Champlain plans journey to Asia

Feb. 9, 1618

PARIS – Samuel de Champlain, the explorer and geographer from New France, has told the king that the best path to the wealth of Asia lies through New France. The great riches of these lands can be brought to Europe through New France, he pointed out, and the total customs duties to be collected at Quebec would be 10 times those levied in France.

Champlain also wants the king to send 300 families a year to New France to build up the country. He is expected to leave for New France in May to prepare for the families.

Bylot, Baffin map bay, arctic sounds

1616

ARCTIC – English explorers William Baffin and Robert Bylot, searching for the Northwest Passage, have mapped a bay [Baffin's Bay] and entrances to three arctic sounds. Sailing on Capt. Bylot's ship *Discovery*, noted navigator Baffin has guided the expedition to northern points previously unreached by Europeans. While they have penetrated the Smith, Jones and Lancaster sounds, their inability to venture far beyond the entrances has led them to believe the ever-elusive passageway will not be found in these waters.

Explorer and navigator William Baffin employed astrolabe much like Samuel de Champlain's in search for northern passage.

1620 (1620-1629)

France, May 7, 1620. Louis XIII writes to Champlain to tell him to maintain the colony at New France "in obedience to me, making the people who are there live as closely in conformity with the laws of my kingdom as you can."

Quebec, Aug. 18, 1621. A general meeting of settlers authorized by Champlain sends the Recollet Le Baillif as a delegate to present their grievances to the King of France. The colonists' requests include banning the Huguenots from the colony, a seminary for the Amerindians, a more powerful justice system, a stronger military defence, and a raise in Champlain's pension.

England, Sept. 20, 1621. Sir William Alexander is made lord proprietor of a territory to be known as New Scotland, or Nova Scotia [the Atlantic provinces and the Gaspé].

Quebec, Sept. 21, 1621. Ordinances are published, the first legislation in New France.

Quebec, 1622. The Montagnais, persuaded by Champlain to settle and work the land, finish clearing ground near Quebec in the spring. They are hunting and trapping people.

Quebec, June 1625. The first Jesuit missionaries in the colony arrive: Fathers Jean de Brébeuf, Charles Lalemant, and Enemond Massé, and brothers François Charton and Gilbert Burel.

New France, Feb. 28, 1626. Louis Hébert's title to the fiefs of Sault-au-Matelot and St-Joseph is ratified. Both holdings are to be enjoyed *"en fief noble,"* one of the first cases of seigneurialism in New France. Hébert can now support his family independently.

Huron Country, July 1626. Father Brébeuf canoes 1,288 kilometres from Quebec to begin missionary work among the Hurons [in southern Ontario]. He settles at Toanché Island, among the Bear tribe.

France, March 21, 1629. Champlain is made lieutenant in New France of Cardinal Richelieu. Champlain is *de facto* commander of the colony, and at the height of his political career.

Acadia, 1629. William Alexander, Sir William Alexander's son, and Claude de La Tour build Charles Fort at Port-Royal [Annapolis Royal], where Alexander decides to spend the winter.

Medicine at hand, but scurvy fatal for 61

While on west coast of Hudson Bay, Jens Munk and men are struck with scurvy.

June 4, 1620

NORTH [Churchill River] – All the medicine in the world can't save you from scurvy if you don't know how to administer it properly. Danish explorer Capt. Jens Munk learned that lesson the hard way. Scurvy has killed 61 members of Munk's crew since January.

Ironically, Munk's two ships are well-stocked with medicine, herbs and water to treat scurvy. Trouble is no one knows how they should be used. Only Munk and two others have survived the dreaded outbreak of scurvy. While the disease has weakened them, they hope to return to Europe soon.

Munk left Copenhagen last year with two ships – the *Unicorn* and the *Lamprey* – under the orders of King Christian to find a passage to India. He sailed across the North Atlantic seeking the passage across the top of the world. But Munk's navigation was faulty and the ships ended up in an estuary of the west coast of [Hudson Bay]. Munk decided to go ashore to hunt and fish for food for the winter. But it soon became too cold and the men had to go aboard their ships.

In January, scurvy set in and the men's gums started to bleed. Their legs became sore and they could not stay awake. By March half of the men were dead. If successful, the journey back to Europe in the *Lamprey,* with virtually no food and a crew of two, will be a triumph of Munk's skill as a seaman and his determination to survive.

Missionaries turn to breeding pigs

1620

QUEBEC CITY – Recollet missionaries on the shores of the St. Charles river near the settlement of Quebec have turned to pig breeding as a main source of food. Cheap, hardy and almost entirely edible, pigs can be salted, dried, smoked, boiled or pickled. This new resource permits the Recollets, a reformed branch of the Franciscan Friars, to be less reliant on the Amerindians they are striving to Christianize and assimilate.

Angry Indians raid French trade vessel

1623

NEW FRANCE – Montagnais Indians have plundered a French vessel in response to a trader's breach of protocol. The trader met the Montagnais at Tadoussac and began proceedings in customary fashion by first presenting Chief Erouachy with a gift.

Erouachy, however, considered the gift too small and angrily threw it in the river. He then told his people to take what they needed without payment. The trader, realizing his mistake, refrained from defending his goods for fear of disrupting future trade. Indeed, later that evening the Montagnais returned and friendly relations were resumed.

Protestants losing privileges in colony

1627

FRANCE – Helped by Henri de Lévis, Duc de Ventadour and viceroy of New France, the Jesuit Philibert Noyrot has secured permission from Cardinal Richelieu to revoke the Edict of Nantes for the colony. The 1598 edict granted French Protestants, known as Huguenots, considerable religious freedoms and civic rights. Noyrot recently arrived in France representing Catholic interests in the colony that want the Compagnie de Montmorency, largely Huguenot, to lose its monopoly on trade.

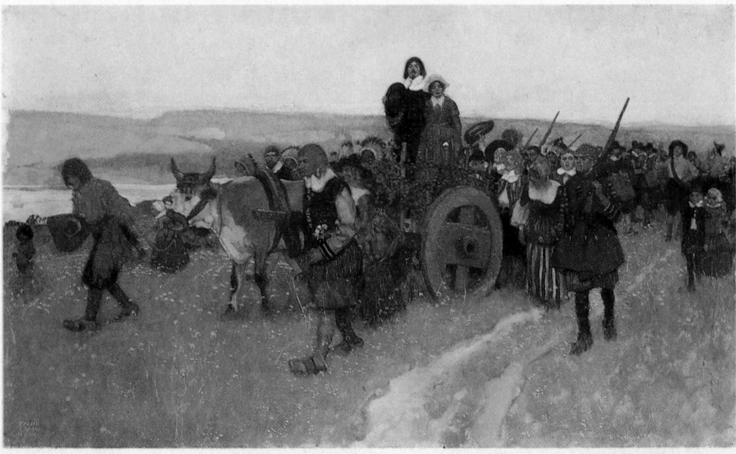

Explorer Samuel de Champlain's wife, formerly Hélène Boullé, joins her husband in Quebec May 8, 1620. Residents escort her to her new home.

English take over French settlements

British troops capture Quebec, weakened by a long and difficult winter.

Champlain surrenders prize Quebec post

July 19, 1629

QUEBEC CITY – The Kirke brothers – a thorn in the side of Samuel de Champlain for years – forced the famous French explorer to hand over his prized Quebec settlement to the English today. Realizing the Quebec *habitants* were on the brink of starvation after a difficult winter, fur trader David Kirke sent his brothers Lewis and Thomas to demand the post surrender.

Champlain founded Quebec in 1608. While the Company of One Hundred Associates was formed in 1627 to strengthen France's hold on Quebec, the Kirkes captured company ships taking men and supplies there on two occasions.

Kirkes spell trouble for colonial settlers

1627

NEW FRANCE – Members of the pirateering Kirke family are wreaking havoc on the *habitants* of New France. Accompanied by his brothers Lewis, Thomas, John and James, David Kirke led a small three-ship fleet that left England this year to sail for New France. In the wake of the war that broke out this same year between France and England, King Charles commissioned Kirke and his expedition to displace the French enemy from "Canida."

The Kirkes sailed up the St. Lawrence and captured the small French settlement at Tadoussac. They seized one supply ship going to Quebec and sent a delegation of Basque fishermen to Quebec founder Samuel de Champlain to demand he surrender his colony. Confident that relief was on its way from France, Champlain refused to surrender. The Kirkes then decided not to attack the fortified colony.

On their trip back to England, the Kirke brothers captured four French vessels carrying supplies and 400 settlers to Quebec. The small settlement was left with little to survive the winter. When news of the Kirkes capturing the French ships reached Paris, the brothers – born in Dieppe and still considered French citizens – were burnt in effigy as traitors to King Louis.

Indians kill priest; Huron eyewitness suffers same fate

June 25, 1625

QUEBEC CITY – Indians have killed a Recollet priest working as a missionary in Huron territory. Father Nicolas Viel, who had been living with the Hurons in the wilderness the past two years, was slain while returning to Quebec with natives planning to trade furs at the port.

Viel was in a canoe in [Sault-au-Récollet] with three Indians when the murder occurred. His body was then thrown into the Rivière-des-Prairies. A young Huron named Ahuntsic who witnessed the event suffered the same fate. The motive for the crime is not known, but hostility to Viel's proselytizing is suspected. His is the first reported Indian murder of a priest.

Indians torture some missionaries.

Seigneurial system introduced to colony

May 6, 1628

NEW FRANCE – King Louis XIII has given royal approval to the new Company of the Hundred Associates, formed on April 29, 1627 by his chief minister, Cardinal Richelieu. The company's mandate is to establish France's empire in North America. It has been granted all the land between Florida and the Arctic, and the Atlantic westward.

The company has been instructed to improve on its predecessors' poor colonization records by bringing out 200 to 300 settlers this year, and 4,000 within the next 15 years.

Old World ways are being used to develop land as more and more settlers arrive in New France.

Frenchman La Tour betrays his country

Nov. 30, 1629

ACADIA [Nova Scotia] – Snared by the English in 1628 while sailing from Acadia to Quebec, French turncoat Claude de Saint-Etienne de La Tour completed the betrayal of his mother country today by becoming one of England's baronets of [Nova Scotia]. He also got a huge land grant in the colony. England now controls all of Acadia except Charles de La Tour's settlement at Cap de Sable. Charles is Claude's son.

Huron fear witches and execute them

1625

NEW FRANCE – Among the Huron, individuals seen as behaving improperly are often accused of witchcraft and threatened with death in a formalized phrase: "We will tear you out of the ground as a poisonous root." Sometimes chiefs hold secret meetings, judge someone guilty, sentence him to death *in absentia*, and appoint an executioner who kills without warning. At times the Huron terror of witches extends to black-robed priests.

1630 (1630-1639)

France, March 1, 1633. Champlain is again made lieutenant of New France, *de facto* commander of the colony. New France was recently returned to French rule.

Quebec, May 22, 1633. Champlain arrives after an absence of almost four years.

Quebec, 1633. Soon after his arrival, Champlain has a chapel built "in honor of our Lady," at the expense of the Company of One Hundred Associates. It is named Notre-Dame-de-la-Recouvrance, and is located on the Cap aux Diamants.

Italy, June 1633. The Inquisition finds astronomer Galileo Galilei guilty of teaching the banned Copernican doctrine, which holds that the Earth is not the centre of the universe, contradicting thought authorized by the Church. He is ordered to recant, which he does.

Quebec, August 1634, Champlain sends Jean Nicollet on a mission of peace and discovery among the tribes bordering the Great Lakes. He wants the Iroquois to be either wiped out or "brought to reason."

Quebec, June 11, 1636. Charles de Montmagny, first titular governor of New France, arrives and immediately goes to the church where the *Te Deum* is sung and he is given the keys to the governor's residence, Fort St-Louis.

England, Nov. 13, 1637. King Charles I grants a charter appointing David Kirke co-proprietor of Newfoundland, along with the Marquis of Hamilton and the Earls of Pembroke and Hamilton.

Connecticut Valley, c.1639. The Iroquois begin to obtain firearms from English traders. They can now raid northern tribes like the Hurons more easily than before.

New France, 1639. Jeanne Enard, wife of Christophe Crevier, arrives at Trois-Rivières. She quickly becomes an established businesswoman and her house becomes the centre of a flourishing traffic in brandy with the natives.

New France, 1639. A smallpox epidemic sweeps through the St. Lawrence Valley in the summer. So many Algonquins die they cannot bury their dead. Huron traders take the epidemic home with them to their country around the Great Lakes.

Treaty allows French to reoccupy colony

July 13, 1632

QUEBEC CITY – The French are reoccupying Samuel de Champlain's beloved Quebec colony – thanks to the recently-signed Treaty of Saint-Germain-en-Laye. While English have let the buildings deteriorate and the post is a shambles, there is little doubt Champlain welcomes the return to French hands of the colony he founded in 1608.

While King Louis XIII demanded the colony's return to France from England as early as April 1630, negotiations dragged on until the treaty was signed earlier this year. Emery de Caën was appointed commandant of Quebec on March 4. Isaac de Razilly was offered the lieutenancy April 20, but refused the post since he considers Champlain more competent.

Champlain has worked to have Quebec returned to the French almost from the moment the Kirke brothers captured it for England in 1629. Champlain reached London that October and pointed out to the French ambassador that the capture of Quebec took place two months after a peace treaty between England and France was signed.

By December Champlain was in France lobbying King Louis and other high-placed officials. He noted the advantages of the colony and emphasized the commercial value of the land, especially if a route to Asia were found.

Playing on religious sentiment, Champlain reminded officials there are a vast number of Amerindians who can be converted to Christianity. He also cited the agricultural potential of the country.

Priest is the first editor of Relations

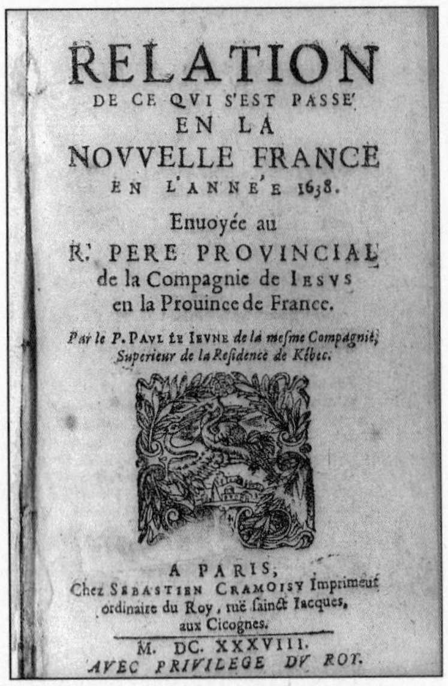
RELATION
DE CE QVI S'EST PASSÉ
EN LA
NOVVELLE FRANCE
EN L'ANNÉE 1638.
Enuoyée au
R. PERE PROVINCIAL
de la Compagnie de IESVS
en la Prouince de France.
Par le P. PAVL LE IEVNE de la mesme Compagnie, Superieur de la Residence de Kébec.
A PARIS,
Chez SEBASTIEN CRAMOISY Imprimeur ordinaire du Roy, ruë sainct Iacques, aux Cicognes.
M. DC. XXXVIII.
AVEC PRIVILEGE DV ROY.

Title page of the Jesuit Relations.

Aug. 28, 1632

NEW FRANCE – Paul Le Jeune, superior of the Jesuits in New France, today became the first editor of the *Relations des Jésuites de la Nouvelle France. Relations* – as it's called for short – is the annual report of missionary activities in the colony.

Le Jeune was born into a Calvinist family in 1591. He converted to Catholicism at the age of 16 and finished his noviciate in 1628. In his first *Relations,* Le Jeune describes the land, inhabitants, settlers and activities of the missionaries, past and present.

Company expands the seigneurial system

Land-ownership expands in Quebec as settlers continue to receive grants.

1634

NEW FRANCE – The Company of One Hundred Associates has granted more than 50 seigneuries of varying sizes along the St. Lawrence River over the past year. The large rectangular estates between Quebec and Ville-Marie front on the river and in most cases extend into the foothills.

Expanding the seigneurial system in the colony is not surprising considering it is the basis of land tenure in France and French immigrants are familiar with it. The seigneurial system was introduced to New France in 1627. The Company of One Hundred Associates was granted ownership and legal and seigneurial rights over New France and obtained the right to allocate the land to its best advantage. Land is granted as fiefs and seigneuries to the most influential colonists, who, in turn, find tenants called *censitaires,* or habitants.

Seigneurs are required to clear some of the seigneury, maintain a manor house and reside there – or have a responsible person live there – throughout the year. Flour mills must be built for the habitants and some seigneuries have a court of law to settle minor disputes.

Treaty ends English hopes in Port Royal

March 29, 1632

FRANCE – By the Treaty of St-Germain-en-Laye, Charles I of England today returned Quebec, Acadia [the Maritime provinces, and some of the Gaspé Peninsula] to France, ending Sir William Alexander's six-year attempt to found a Scottish settlement at Port Royal in western [Nova Scotia].

At outs with his parliament and strapped for cash, the king struck the deal partly to collect the balance of his wife's dowry. She had been Princess Henrietta of France, and the amount owing to her husband was 800,000 crowns.

Interpreter Brûlé is killed by Hurons

June 1633

HURON COUNTRY – The Huron have killed interpreter Etienne Brûlé, Samuel de Champlain's former associate, a great trail-blazer and a longtime inhabitant of Huron territory. His death is believed to be politically motivated.

While Brûlé's skills as an interpreter were essential to French-Huron relations in the early days of the fur trade, in recent years he has fallen into disfavor with both the French and the Indians. On his long stays with the Huron, Brûlé adopted many of their values, alienating colonists with his disregard for European social conventions. Champlain thought he had become "vicious in character, and much addicted to women."

The final wedge between Brûlé and Champlain followed the Kirke brothers' capture of Quebec in 1629. Closer to the merchants and traders than he was to the colonists and missionaries, Brûlé switched sides and began working for the English.

A faction of Huron leaders had suspected Brûlé of trying to establish trade links with their dreaded and hated enemy – the Iroquois – for quite some time. Those Huron suspicious of Brûlé planned his assassination this month knowing that his falling out with Champlain all but eliminated the threat of French retaliation.

Jesuit "Black Robes" take over mission

1634

NEW FRANCE – Three Jesuit priests have been given a mandate to pick up where the Recollets left off in their efforts to set up a mission to the Hurons in New France. Fathers Jean de Brébeuf, Antoine Daniel and Ambroise Davost have been entrusted with the task of choosing a site and setting up a mission to serve as a prototype for future missions needed to bring Christianity to Indians in the colony.

The Jesuits, referred to as "Black Robes" by the natives, began to acquaint themselves with the Hurons in 1626. But this endeavor had to be postponed in 1629, when the Kirke brothers' capture of Quebec for the English forced the missionaries to return to France. Only in 1632, when the French reoccupied the colony, could the religious order continue its efforts to convert the natives.

Brébeuf's superior, Father Paul Le Jeune, has no illusions about the amount of work yet to be done among the Hurons. "Some are astonished that after so many years in New France there has been no word of the conversion of the (Indians)," he said in 1633. "It is necessary to clear, till and sow, before harvesting."

Jesuit priest in New France, 1634.

Control of harbors to fishing admirals

Jan. 24, 1633

NEWFOUNDLAND – The Crown has bowed to the wishes of traders and merchants in England's western counties who want a charter to protect their interests in Newfoundland waters. The Western Charter – based in part on Gov. John Guy's laws of 1611 – says the first captain to arrive in each harbor will be considered the "fishing admiral" for the ensuing season with authority over the harbor. It also lists a number of rules and laws designed to protect property, punish lawlessness and facilitate the fishing industry and trade.

English monarch, King Charles I.

Founder of Quebec dies on Christmas day

Dec. 25, 1635

QUEBEC CITY – Samuel de Champlain died today in Quebec, which he founded in 1608. Records indicate he was in his 50s. Despite a marriage contract with his wife, Champlain willed his furniture to the Virgin Mary, and his share of the Company of One Hundred Associates to Notre-Dame-de-la-Recouvrance church. Champlain's legacy to France, bestowed in his lifetime, was ensuring the St. Lawrence and building the fur-trading empire. Charles Lalemant was with him when he died.

Spurred by fur trade, Hurons exhaust beaver in their territory

1635

NEW FRANCE – The trade of Huron furs for French cloth and metal tools has nearly wiped out the beaver in Huron hunting grounds. To compensate, the Huron are intensifying existing trade with neighboring Algonquins, exchanging European goods and their own corn for furs trapped in Algonquin territory. These furs are then traded to the French. Because the Huron have been traditionally more dependent on fishing and agriculture than on hunting, the loss of their beaver supply has not crippled them economically. Rather, it has transformed them into intermediaries in the fur trade.

Caſtor de 26 pouces de longueur entre
teſte et queue

The beaver is wiped out by trade of Huron furs for French cloth and tools.

Natives fall victim to deadly disease

1636-37

NEW FRANCE – A deadly epidemic of influenza has spread south from the St. Lawrence Valley and killed many Hurons. Influenza is one of several diseases of European origin the Huron have been exposed to, and they lack a natural immunity to it. This epidemic is the severest yet, and their religious leaders and curing societies have been powerless against it. The Hurons, ill and suspicious, refuse such French medical treatments as bloodletting, and have begun to speculate that European witchcraft has caused their misfortune. ▷

Jesuits pick Ihonatiria for Huron mission

Ste. Marie among the Hurons, a Jesuit mission built in 1639.

Sept. 19, 1634

IHONATIRIA, New France – The Jesuits are pinning their highest hopes on a mission Father Jean de Brébeuf chose to locate in Ihonatiria [Saint-Joseph I] today. Brébeuf returned to New France last year following a three-year absence.

After Father Paul Le Jeune entrusted Brébeuf with founding a mission in Huron country earlier this year, Fathers Antoine Daniel and Ambroise Davost accompanied their colleague to Indian territory.

Brébeuf's first act as superior was to choose the place where the mission would have the most impact. After careful consideration, he picked Ihonatiria, a village near Toanché, where he had stayed from 1626 to 1629. It was in those three years that Brébeuf familiarized himself with the Huron people.

Epidemic stirs suspicion

1637

HURON COUNTRY – The Huron are growing more and more hostile toward Jesuit missionaries as an epidemic of influenza cuts its deadly swath through the nation's land. The European disease, only recently introduced to the continent, is attacking the Hurons at an alarming rate – particularly the younger Indians and elder members of the tribe. Lacking a cure, the epidemic has given rise to renewed Huron suspicions of white men in general and Father Jean de Brébeuf and his fellow Jesuits in particular.

Brébeuf and a handful of Jesuits have been working in Huron territory since reopening the mission in 1634. While their efforts to convert Hurons to Christianity have met little success, an air of tolerance and co-operation has developed between the Jesuits and the Indians despite fundamental differences in religious and social values. With the influenza epidemic causing the Hurons to die around them, the Jesuits are working frantically to baptize all they can. Many of those they do baptize are too far gone to protest.

The sight of a healthy Jesuit, apparently immune from contagion, administering rites to a native who dies soon after, has caused many Huron to view the ceremony as an act of sorcery. Consequently, many Huron villages are now barring the "white shamans." The Indians' religious leaders have stirred up the animosity toward the Jesuits with fanatical zeal punctuated by calls for violent action against the missionaries.

Indian medicine man.

Montagnais urged to settle at village

1637

ST. JOSEPH DE SILLERY, New France – Jesuit missionaries are encouraging local Montagnais Indians to settle a 3,500-hectare reserve the priests have established near Quebec. The Jesuits believe that if Algonquian people are to lead Christian lives they must quit their nomadic pursuit of game and grow crops. Using money left to them by Noel Brulat, a former royal minister, they have cleared land and erected a small village seven kilometres from Quebec.

Jesuits are convinced that settling this community, named St. Joseph de Sillery, will help their efforts to convert the Indians in New France to Christianity. It will also provide the Montagnais – destitute since local beaver supplies greatly declined – with food, shelter and clothing.

Nuns found colony's first medical mission

1639

QUEBEC CITY – Responding to an appeal by Jesuit missionary Father Paul Le Jeune, three nuns from the religious Hospitallers in Dieppe have founded the colony's first medical mission for French and native patients. Marie Guenet, Marie Forestier and Anne Le Cointre arrived in early August with a patent letter from King Louis XIII to found the Hôtel-Dieu de Québec. Since their arrival the nuns have been working at a Sillery mission caring mostly for the native population there.

Three French nuns arrive in Quebec to found colony's first medical mission.

Kirke becomes new governor of colony

Oct. 1, 1639

NEWFOUNDLAND – Sir David Kirke is the new governor of Newfoundland. He's taken possession of Lord Baltimore's mansion, making the huge stone house in Ferryland his headquarters. Kirke also seized other property in Ferryland, Baltimore's former colony.

Since Kirke became co-proprietor of Newfoundland in 1637, he has sided with colonists against overseas fishing admirals wanting to bar settlers. The admirals say Kirke dominates them and the Grand Bank fisheries they used to control. They say he rented preferred fisheries to foreigners and disrupted the industry by establishing taverns along the coast though his charter stipulates colonists must live 9.6 kilometres from the sea. Kirke still defends settlers, but has given up authority over the fishing ships.

European religious orders stream to New France

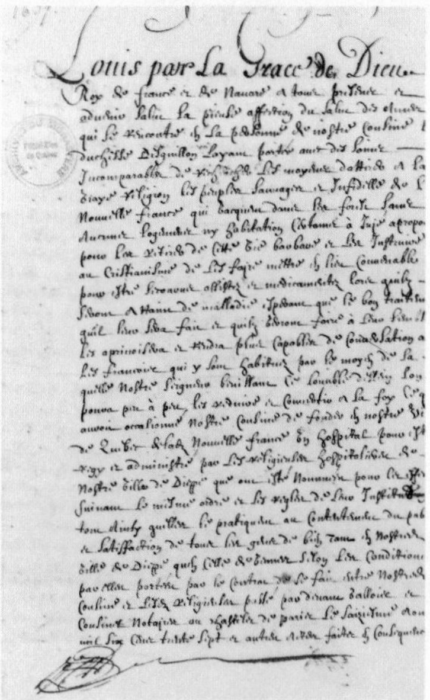
Louis par La Grace de Dieu

A letter patent written by Louis XIII to Augustine missionaries.

Sturdy wood trunks help religious missionaries travelling to French colony transport their belongings to their new home.

The Duchesse d'Aiguillon, founder of Hôtel-Dieu hospital in Quebec.

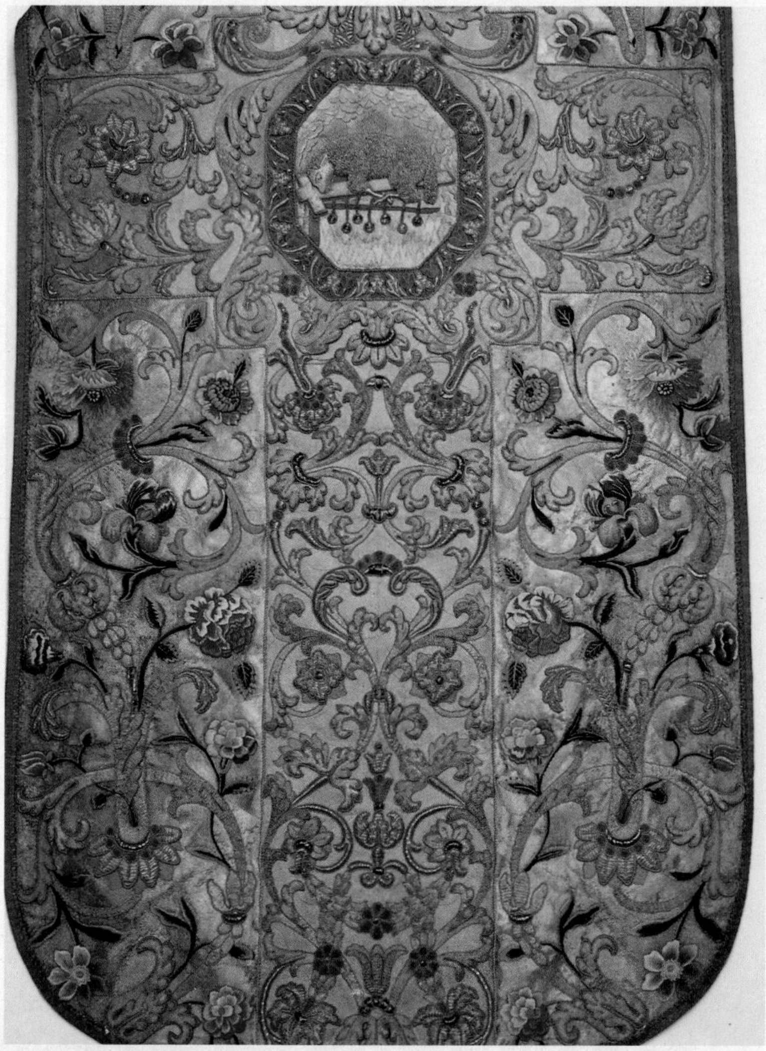

Among the Jesuit possessions brought to the new colony are sacramental robes, many of them decorated and heavily ornate, such as the one depicted above.

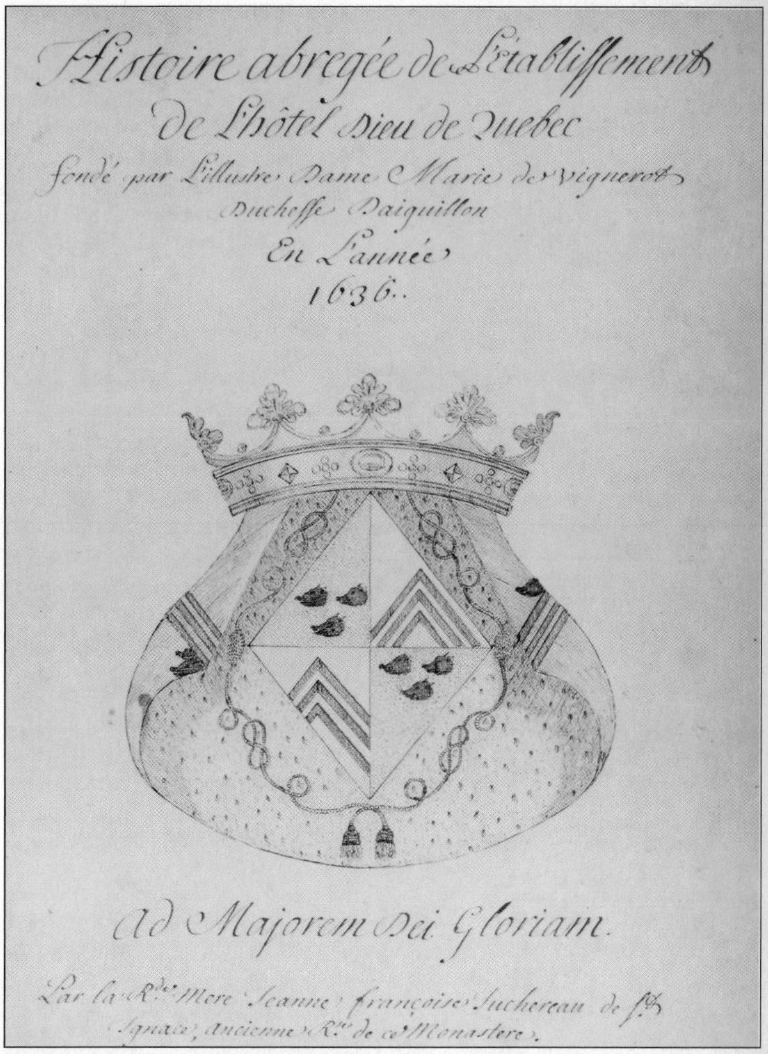
Histoire abregée de l'Etablissement
de l'hôtel Dieu de Quebec
fondé par l'illustre Dame Marie de Vignerot
Duchesse Daiguillon
En L'année
1636.

Ad Majorem Dei Gloriam.

Par la R.de Mere Jeanne françoise Juchereau de S.t
Ignace, ancienne R.re de ce Monastere.

Mother Juchereau de Saint Ignace publishes a history of the establishment of the Hôtel-Dieu hospital in Quebec by the Ursuline nuns.

Huron Country, 1640. A smallpox epidemic kills thousands of Hurons [in southern Ontario] over the winter of 1639-40, more than all the previous Huron epidemics combined. Huron traders carried the disease home from the St. Lawrence Valley.

France, Dec. 17, 1640. The Company of One Hundred Associates grants the entire island of Montreal, with the exception of the mountain and an area to the southwest, to the Society of Notre-Dame of Montreal.

Quebec, August 1641. A band of 40 colonists arrives, en route to colonize the island of Montreal under the auspices of the Society of Notre-Dame. Soldier Paul de Chomedey de Maisonneuve leads the group, which includes 35-year-old Jeanne Mance, who offered her services as housekeeper and nurse.

Montreal, Oct. 15, 1641. Paul Chomedey de Maisonneuve formally takes possession of the island of Montreal for the Society of Notre-Dame.

Ville-Marie, May 18, 1642. Father Vimont celebrates the first high mass at Ville-Marie [Montreal].

Huron Country, Sept. 7, 1644. Father Jean de Brébeuf returns to Huron country [southern Ontario] where he resumes his missionary activities after a two-year stint in Quebec as procurator of the Huron mission.

Quebec, July 3, 1646. Jesuit missionary Isaac Jogues returns from a peace mission among the Mohawks, who were amazed by a mysterious box that Jogues wanted to leave with them.

France, March 5, 1648. A royal edict re-organizes the Council of Quebec, creating a seven-member ruling body.

Huron Country, July 14, 1648. A band of Iroquois attacks the Huron villages of St-Joseph and St-Michel [in southern Ontario], taking advantage of the fact that many Hurons are away trading. They take 700 prisoners, and kill Jesuit missionary Antoine Daniel.

New France, 1648. The Iroquois probably have more than 500 guns, while the Hurons have no more than 120. The guns are clumsy to use, but their loud noise and ability to kill strikes terror in the hearts of adversaries.

Notre-Dame Society given land rights

December 1640

NEW FRANCE – The Notre-Dame Society of Montreal has been granted property rights to Ville-Marie [Montreal] in New France. A humble tax collector in the little town of La Flèche, France, Jérôme Le Royer de La Dauversière is credited with doing much of the groundwork to secure land for the bold project.

De La Dauversière says he was blessed by a supernatural vision in 1635 or 1636. In it he saw an island in New France which could serve as a settlement dedicated to the Virgin Mary and as a base to convert the colony's natives to Christianity.

On the advice of Father François Chauvreau, de La Dauversière went to Paris in 1639 to meet Pierre Chevrier, Baron de Fancamp, a religious zealot interested in missionary work. The purpose of the get-together was to form a society capable of seeing the Ville-Marie project through. At the end of February, de La Dauversière met Abbé Jean-Jacques Olier, a young priest who wanted to work for the conversion of unbelievers.

After a two-hour meeting, de La Dauversière and Olier agreed to found a society to buy the Island of Montreal from Jean de Lauson, an intendant in Dauphiné. Olier knew of a financial backer for the project in philanthropist Baron Gaston de Renty, who was invited to join the society along with the superior of the famous Saint-Sacrament Company and two of Olier's friends.

De Maisonneuve founds Ville-Marie on island of Montreal

May 17, 1642

VILLE-MARIE [Montreal] – An outdoor religious ceremony today marked the founding of Ville-Marie on the island of Montreal by Paul de Chomedey, Sieur de Maisonneuve. Father Barthélemy Vimont, the superior of the Jesuit missions in New France, chanted the *Veni Creator* to commemorate the founding. He also said Holy Mass and exposed the Blessed Sacrament for a happy beginning.

After the ceremony, de Maisonneuve wasted no time having his men secure the new colony by erecting a stronghold of thick stakes. In a symbolic gesture, de Maisonneuve insisted on chopping down the first tree himself.

A group of pious laymen inspired by the idea of founding a mission on the island of Montreal formed the Notre-Dame Society of Montreal in 1639. They secured land for the project and raised funds. The group enlisted de Maisonneuve, a brave young leader and a resolute soldier who overcame hostile opposition from the inhabitants of New France to the foundation of Ville-Marie. "Foolhardy undertaking" was the general outcry. Various religious orders in France have been looking to New France as a field for missionary endeavors. The stated purpose of Ville-Marie is to convert natives to Christianity. It also serves as a western bastion for policing the St. Lawrence River as the primary fur trade artery. Fear that Ville-Marie's location will let it corner the fur trade is clearly what is motivating opposition in New France to the new colony.

FORT OF VILLE MARIE 1642
THIS FORT WAS BUILT ON THE PRESENT SITE OF

De Maisonneuve meets Indians at Fort Ville-Marie on island of Montreal.

Paul de Chomedey, Sieur de Maisonneuve arrives on island of Montreal.

Iroquois intensify raids in New France

1641

NEW FRANCE – Iroquois warriors are intensifying raids on trade posts belonging to New France. Supplied with European goods by Dutch fur traders established along the Hudson River in [New York state], the Iroquois are trying to redirect trade between the French and Huron to their advantage, supplementing their own depleting beaver fur stock with the supply the Hurons now control.

Long before European contact, the Iroquoian tradition of competing rather than trading with their horticultural neighbors established their reputation as warmongers. Now, as the French and Dutch vie to supply Europe with furs, new alliances are being formed between natives and Europeans. The Iroquois are relying on force to secure a place as fur-trade middlemen.

Priest's Xmas carol is the colony's first

Dec. 25, 1641

NEW FRANCE – A song considered to be New France's first Christmas carol has been written in the Huron language.

Father Jean de Brébeuf composed *Jesus, He is Born,* the [*Huron Christmas Carol.*] Brébeuf is the same Jesuit priest who founded the new colony's Huron mission in 1626, mastering the difficult Huron language since then.

Lunar eclipse proof of Jesuit "powers"

Jan. 31, 1646

OSSOSSANE, New France – The principal town of the Huron nation is in a tumult tonight as an eclipse of the moon French Jesuit missionaries predicted began right on time. Natives in Ossossané already converted to the Jesuits' Catholic faith ran from their longhouses to rouse their neighbors. They invited them to look into the night sky for proof of the spiritual power of the bearded priests the Hurons call *ondaki* – demons.

Mme de La Tour surrenders fort to rival

Françoise-Marie de La Tour is forced to watch while her men are hanged.

April 13, 1645

FORT LA TOUR, Acadia – After four days of rallying a handful of men in a gallant defence of her husband's fort, Françoise-Marie Jacquelin today surrendered to her spouse's hated rival for power in Acadia, Charles de Menou d'Aulnay. Said to be the daughter of a barber in France, she married Charles de Saint-Etienne de La Tour at the Acadian capital, Port Royal, in 1640, gave him a son, and proved herself a formidable ally in his violent struggle with d'Aulnay.

Three years before the fall of the fortress, she had evaded d'Aulnay's blockade of the Saint John, sailed to France, and successfully appealed royal orders that her husband be arrested and charged with disloyalty. Now, with her husband in Boston, she was betrayed by a Swiss mercenary who helped d'Aulnay's force penetrate the fort while the defenders were attending an Easter service.

She led her men in a bloody hand-to-hand clash. Losses were heavy on both sides. D'Aulnay finally vowed that if Mme de La Tour would capitulate, he'd "give quarter to all." With food and ammunition running low and Fort La Tour in shambles, the most heroic woman in Acadian history called off her men. They laid down their arms. D'Aulnay's gang arrested them, built gallows, and hanged all but one. The man spared was the hangman. With a rope around her neck, Mme de La Tour was forced to watch the executions.

Three Sioux Indians ready to play the popular sport of lacrosse.

Mance fulfils goal to open a hospital

1642

VILLE-MARIE – Just a few months after Paul de Chomedey, Sieur de Maisonneuve, founded Ville-Marie, Jeanne Mance has opened a hospital in a fort here. The creation of the Hôtel-Dieu fulfils a goal Mance set before arriving in New France last year.

The tireless and pious humanitarian spent her last weeks in France securing funds for the hospital from Angélique Faure, a distinguished and wealthy woman. Opposition to the creation of a post at Ville-Marie left Mance dismayed but undaunted. Iroquois attacks have made the hospital a much-needed facility.

Jeanne Mance, hospital founder.

Ancient wine given to Jesuits as a gift

Jan. 5, 1646

QUEBEC CITY – Jesuits in the new colony will be able to wash down their next meal courtesy of a bottle of wine they received as a New Year's gift today. Robert Giffard de Moncel, the first doctor of the Hôtel-Dieu of Quebec, gave the bottle of hippocras to the Jesuits. Hippocras dates back to the Middle Ages. Though not as common as Spanish wine, it is believed to help digestion and is frequently served at dessert.

Iroquois kill Jesuit priest and aide for "spreading smallpox"

Oct. 18, 1646

IROQUOIS COUNTRY [New York State] – The Iroquois' mystification with the latest smallpox epidemic turned ugly today. The Mohawks killed Father Isaac Jogues, blaming the Jesuit priest for spreading the epidemic. A hatchet blow to the head ended Jogues' life. He was 39. Of all the infectious diseases plaguing the Iroquois, smallpox is the deadliest. It first hit them in 1634, taking hundreds of native lives since then.

Jogues was in Iroquois country on a peace mission – his second of the year. He met the Mohawks in May and departed on good terms a month later, leaving behind a box filled with clothes, sacred vessels and gifts for the natives. When Jogues and his aide Jean de La Lande returned last month, the Mohawks gave them a hostile reception. Both were taken prisoner. The box confirmed Iroquois suspicions about the epidemic's cause. Jogues was accused of spreading smallpox by hiding certain charms in it. The Iroquois also blamed him for the drought and famine which followed the missionary's first visit. He was put to death as a sorcerer and La Lande was also killed.

Jogues is no stranger to Iroquois attacks. The natives ambushed a mission he was on in 1642. After that attack, the Iroquois took Jogues prisoner and tortured him.

Medicine man tries to cure sick.

Iroquois are hard hit by smallpox.

Governor receives colony's first horse

1647

NEW FRANCE – The first governor and lieutenant-general of New France now has the first French horse ever imported to New France. The *Compagnie des habitants* sent Charles Huault de Montmagny the horse as a gift.

While Montmagny's horse is unique in New France, the first French horses brought to the New World were imported into Acadia in 1610. After Jesuits there imported more in 1613, a marauding expedition led by Samuel Argall of the Virginia Company of London carried off most of the Acadian horses in 1616.

There have never been many French horses in Acadia since there are few French settlers there and most are more interested in fisheries than agriculture. The horses families do own are mainly for pleasure and riding.

Council created to ensure order in colony

March 27, 1647

NEW FRANCE – The Sovereign Council adopted legislation today that's being touted as the first political constitution governing the colony of New France. The new law is for "establishing order and surveillance in Canada" and it creates a council composed of the governor of New France, the Jesuit superior and the governor of Ville-Marie.

Everything that concerns the fur trade and the general interest of the colony comes under the council's jurisdiction. It appoints the general and captains of the fleet, the clerks and comptrollers of the fur trade and a secretary able to act as a notary public.

Frenchman "back from dead" as Iroquois

July 1645

TROIS-RIVIERES, – Diplomat Guillaume Couture caused quite a stir at a meeting here between Iroquois and French representatives. Captured by the Iroquois in 1642 after killing a member of the tribe, Couture was given up for dead – or was at least in danger of spending his life in captivity. Instead, he adapted to his new life and is the first Frenchman to win a great deal of influence among the Iroquois.

Like his native companions, Couture dressed Iroquois style for the Trois-Rivières meeting. When his French friends recognized him, they rejoiced as if he had just come back from the dead.

Work is under way rebuilding the Jesuits' College of Quebec

1647

QUEBEC CITY – The Jesuit dream of building a college in Quebec will soon become a reality – again. Work has already started on rebuilding the College of Quebec. Construction will continue through the winter.

Fire destroyed the original College of Quebec in 1640 and the school has operated out of a house since then. The college is devoted to spiritual ends. While the Jesuits initially provided religious instruction only, reading and writing were soon added to the curriculum and at the request of parents so was Latin. Grammar, literature, rhetoric and philosophy are next.

Jesuit college is rebuilt seven years after a fire destroyed the original.

Colony sees first wedding in years

Sept. 3, 1647

QUEBEC CITY – Médard Chouart des Groseilliers married the young widow Hélène Martin in Quebec today, the colony's first wedding in several years. Hélène is the daughter of Abraham Martin, a former mariner and established property owner with 32 acres of land overlooking the St. Charles River from the heights near town.

Groseilliers, who came to the colony from France around 1641, has worked with Jesuit missionaries among the Huron as either a lay helper or soldier. He returned to Quebec last year.

Iroquois destroy Huron nation, overrun missions

Jesuit "sorcerers" tortured to death

March 17, 1649

TAENHATENTARON, New France – Jesuit priests Jean de Brébeuf and Gabriel Lalemant have been tortured to death by Iroquois. The Iroquois believe Brébeuf, founder of the Huron mission in New France, and Lalemant, Jesuit Jérôme Lalemant's nephew, are sorcerers responsible for the Indians' destruction. Iroquois also saw the men as fur trade enemies.

The deaths come in the midst of the Iroquois' struggle to crush the Huron. Iroquois attacks yesterday targeted the villages of Taenhatentaron and St. Louis. More than 1,000 Iroquois attacked Taenhatentaron and killed or captured all but 10 of the 400 people living there. Then they attacked St. Louis, where Brébeuf, 55, and Lalemant, 38, were working. The two missionaries were urged to flee, but refused.

As soon as they captured Brébeuf and Lalemant, Iroquois stripped them of their clothes and tore their nails out. The priests were taken prisoner and carried off to Taenhatentaron, the base from which the Iroquois destroy neighboring hamlets. The Iroquois tortured Brébeuf first. He died at 4 p.m. yesterday. Lalemant died this morning after being tortured overnight. A hatchet blow to Lalemant's head exposed part of his brain. The natives also broiled Lalemant's entire body.

Donné Christophe Regnault describes Brébeuf's torture: "Father de Brébeuf had his legs, thighs and arms stripped of flesh to the very bone; I saw and touched a large number of great blisters, which he had on several places on his body, from the boiling water which these barbarians had poured over him in mockery of Holy Baptism. I saw and touched the wound from a belt of bark, full of pitch and resin, which roasted his whole body. I saw and touched the marks of burns from the collar of hatchets placed on his shoulders and stomach. I saw and touched his two lips, which they had cut off because he constantly spoke of God while they made him suffer."

Iroquois torture Jesuit missionaries to death. The Indians believe the priests are sorcerers bent on destroying the natives.

Huron villages such as the one represented above have been the target of Iroquois attacks, and many of their inhabitants have been killed or captured.

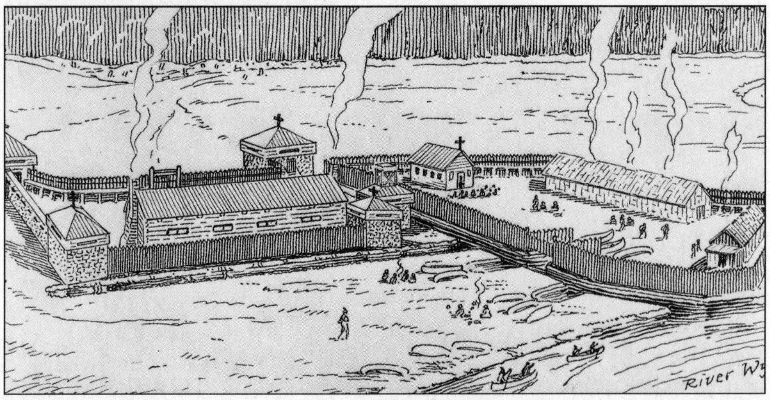

Fort Ste. Marie, a Jesuit mission inhabited by Hurons, was abandoned after attacks by Huron warriors left only 22 lay workers and a few servants.

Jesuits and Hurons abandon Ste. Marie

June 14, 1649

STE-MARIE-DES-HURONS, New France – The Jesuits abandoned Ste-Marie-des-Hurons today. They no longer consider the powerful symbol of the Jesuits' entrenchment in the heart of Huron country a safe place to live.

The threat of an Iroquois attack grows stronger every day. Over the past two years the Iroquois have decimated the Hurons. In 1648 they raided the villages of St. Joseph and St. Michel, and Taenhatentaron and St. Louis were targets this March. Jesuit priests Jean de Brébeuf and Gabriel Lalemant were tortured to death after the attack on St. Louis. Only eight soldiers, 22 *donnés* and seven servants were left at Ste. Marie, so the Jesuits decided to abandon it. They set fire to buildings there and left for Ile St-Joseph with a few hundred Hurons.

The Ste. Marie mission, west of Quebec, was started in 1639 along the east bank of the Wye River on land of the Ataronchronon, a Huron tribe. It grew into a fortified settlement and featured a chapel, residences for priests and lay personnel, carpentry and ironworking shops, a hospital, cemetery, farm, and guest quarters for non-Christians passing through.

At Ste. Marie, Father Jérôme Lalemant, superior of the Huron mission, enforced a strict observance of religious routines among the priests. But while missionaries were sent to preach in Huron towns, Lalemant's hope that Huron converts might be persuaded to settle at Ste. Marie and adopt European customs was never completely fulfilled. Even converts ready to break with their pasts in other significant ways wouldn't totally abandon their culture.

In 1643 permanent Jesuit residences were created in major Huron towns and Ste. Marie started serving as a mission centre for neighboring villages. Missionaries also visited Ste. Marie for spiritual retreats and observances at Christmas, Easter and Pentecost.

1650 (1650-1659)

Quebec, Dec. 30, 1650. The first Ursuline convent at Quebec is destroyed by a fire caused by a careless lay sister. The building was described as "the most handsome and the biggest in Canada."

New France, May 10, 1652. French explorer Jacques Buteux is killed when his expedition is attacked by Iroquois. Buteux set out from Trois-Rivières April 4 in an attempt to reach [Hudson Bay] by land. He was accompanied by some 60 Attikamegue Indians.

France, 1654. Nicolas Denys is appointed governor and lieutenant-general of a vast territory around the Gulf of St. Lawrence, including Cape Breton, the Iles de la Madeleine, and Ile-Saint-Jean [Prince Edward Island].

Acadia, July 1654. An English expedition led by Robert Sedgewick captures the fort of Charles de La Tour, governor of Acadia, at the mouth of the St. John River.

Acadia, September 1654. Robert Sedgewick's expedition captures and plunders the French Fort Pentagouet [Penobscot River, Maine], completing his conquest of Acadia [Atlantic Canada]. He captured Port-Royal [Annapolis Royal] in August.

Ville-Marie, 1657. The Lauson family grants Charles Le Moyne de Longueuil et de Châteauguay a fief of 5,000 acres on the south shore at Ville-Marie [Montreal].

Quebec, March 15, 1657. Mother Giffard de Saint-Ignace dies after terrible suffering. She was the first Canadian woman to take religious vows, at the Hôtel-Dieu in 1646.

Ville-Marie, July 1657. De Maisonneuve returns from France with the first parish clergy for Ville-Marie [Montreal], three Sulpicians led by Abbé Queylus.

Quebec, Nov. 3, 1657. Geneviève-Agnès Skanudharoua is the first native nun. She takes her final vows at the Hôtel-Dieu just hours before her death.

France, March 27, 1659. The king orders François de Laval be recognized as Vicar Apostolic in New France, according to his papal appointment.

Quebec, June 1659. François de Laval arrives as Vicar Apostolic of New France.

Triumphant fur trader returns to Quebec

Groseilliers' brother-in-law, Pierre Radisson, arriving at an Indian camp.

1657

QUEBEC CITY – Trader Médard Chouart des Groseilliers was greeted with much fanfare when he returned to Quebec with a giant cargo of furs. The *coureur de bois* set out in 1654 to make contact with Algonquian people who had no direct trade links with white men, and that's exactly what he accomplished.

Almost 20 years of war and epidemics have seriously depopulated the eastern [Great Lakes] region, an important factor in Groseilliers' decision to push beyond previous trading boundaries. Partly to maximize his profits and partly because he believes local Indians lack the manpower to meet the French demand for fur, Groseilliers hoped trading directly with the Algonquins would allow him to eliminate native middlemen in the fur trade.

Pushing southwest of [Lake Superior] to the [Upper Mississippi] region, Groseilliers accomplished his goal of initiating trade with the local natives. For the return trip down the Ottawa River, he persuaded a group of Algonquins to accompany him.

A 1657 map of [Great Lakes] area.

Renovated hospital like "a mansion"

Aug. 10, 1658

QUEBEC CITY – The Hospitallers nuns today inaugurated the newly renovated Hôtel-Dieu de Québec, a roomy infirmary with eight doors, eight windows and 10 beds. Separated by an aisle, the beds are on both sides of the room as in modern French hospitals. A church and a private chapel for the nuns was also added.

"As we are leaving a slum which resembled a long shack more than a hospital, this is like finding ourselves in a mansion," one nun said.

Renovations, begun in 1654, became essential when the outdated facilities could no longer accommodate the increased population and the number of sick immigrants arriving on French ships. The hospital was first built in 1644, when escalating Iroquois attacks forced the nuns to flee Sillery, just outside Quebec City.

Kidnapped woman weds her rescuer

Aug. 12, 1657

NEW FRANCE – Today's marriage between Lambert Closse and Elisabeth Moyen marks yet another chapter in a true love story. In 1655 when Elisabeth was 16 and living on Iles aux Oies, below Quebec, Iroquois warriors killed her parents and took her and her sister Marie captive. Closse, then 39 and sergeant-major of the Ville-Marie fort, led the troops who rescued the Moyen girls, taken to the Hôtel-Dieu half dead with fear. Closse visited Elisabeth in the hospital, and her feelings of gratitude gradually turned into love.

Quebec City the destination of Jesuit priests and 300 Hurons

June 10, 1650

ILE ST-JOSEPH, New France – Jesuits and 300 Hurons left Ile St-Joseph today and set out in canoes for Quebec. The natives represent the last fragments of the Huron nation in New France. Jesuits brought them to Ile St-Joseph a year ago after the threat of an Iroquois attack forced the missionaries to abandon Ste. Marie.

Problems have plagued the Jesuit mission in Ile St-Joseph. Famine, contagious diseases and Iroquois attacks led to the decision to leave. Huron leaders asked the Jesuits to lead them to Quebec. They told the French that if they support them there until they can harvest their own crops in 1651, they will be able to stay together and remain practising Christians.

After numerous meetings and 40 hours of prayer, the Jesuits decided neither Ile St-Joseph nor the Huron country was defensible. To keep their plans from the Iroquois, the Jesuits thought a quick departure was best. Some 300 Hurons are staying behind till the corn ripens.

Louis XIV slaps ban on brandy trading

1657

NEW FRANCE – Liquor can no longer be used as a trading commodity with Amerindians in New France. The Sovereign Council of King Louis XIV confirmed the ban, part of the colony's first temperance movement.

Brandy traffic has been a contentious issue in New France for a long time. Heavy fines or banishment await those who violate the new law. The trading ban was implemented at the insistence of Bishop François de Laval and Jesuit missionaries. The natives had no fermented beverages before the European arrival, and have no social controls for it. Many regard intoxication as a mystical experience which allows them to communicate with their gods. Some may also drink to boost the self-esteem corroded over decades of contact with Europeans who disparage their ways. But lacking experience with liquor, natives often drink to excess. Some are so eager to obtain alcohol they trade all their furs for a jug or two of brandy. French traders take advantage of this to make a quick profit.

As far back as the 1620s, wine and liquor were supplied to local natives by the independent traders who were operating along the lower St. Lawrence River. Quebec founder Samuel de Champlain strongly opposed such liquor sales.

Radisson, Groseilliers meet the Sioux

Enterprising fur traders moving toward the west meet with Sioux Indians.

A Sioux Indian.

Winter 1659

NEW FRANCE – Fur traders Pierre-Esprit Radisson and Médard Chouart des Groseilliers have pushed beyond the western end of [Lake Superior] and become the first white men to encounter Sioux or Dakota Indians.

Always wary of outside interests that might compromise their own, the two French adventurers quietly left Trois-Rivières in August to avoid bringing one of an insistent Gov. Pierre de Voyer d'Argenson's men along. They reached [Lake Superior] by early fall and ventured inland to spend the winter with Huron and Ottawa refugees, survivors of the epidemics, food shortages and warfare that have plagued the east.

The surrounding area is populated predominantly by the Siouan-speaking Dakota, or "the allies" when defined collectively with the Sioux farther west. Occupying the drainage basins of the [Red, Mississippi and Rainy] rivers, the Dakota live in villages on a semi-permanent basis, depending on wild rice and buffalo for subsistence.

Radisson and Groseilliers have spent six weeks in their country after attending a great Feast of the Dead. Eighteen nations attended the feast, a ceremony the Huron hold to free the souls of relatives who died non-violently. (This winter's heavy snowfall has made hunting difficult and many natives are starving to death.) As an affectionate tribute to the dead, the feast brings people together and is an occasion for the Indians to strengthen existing alliances and perhaps form new ones.

While there's no way of telling for sure, it is probable local Sioux attended the feast and the two Frenchmen arranged to stay with them. It is also likely that Radisson and Groseilliers heard talk of there being vast quantities of beaver roaming the land between their present location and Hudson Bay because they are currently planning a northern trek for next spring.

Sister Marguerite receives first students

April 30, 1657

VILLE-MARIE – Fulfilling a longtime ambition to open a school in New France, Sister Marguerite Bourgeoys today received her first pupils at a stable in Ville-Marie [Montreal]. The founder of Ville-Marie, Paul de Chomedey, Sieur de Maisonneuve, donated the temporary building.

After Sister Marguerite arrived in Ville-Marie five years ago to open a school, she learned there were no children of school age because of the colony's high infant mortality rate. Herself an orphan, the nun is best known for her work establishing the Notre-Dame-de-Bon-Secours church.

Sister Marguerite Bourgeoys.

Visitors report on colonial eating habits: food plentiful, cooking good, meals lavish

1651

QUEBEC CITY – With the abundance of fish and game, the colonists in New France eat much better than French peasants. Even the poorer people here enjoy such plentiful diets that French visitors often express a great deal of surprise about it.

"I wish such good cooking on all of our ruined nobility," France's Baron de la Hontan said. Another French visitor was also astounded at the lavishness of colonial meals. "They offered us cabbage, butter, milk, turnips, plums and chickens," he said.

Eel, another essential part of the daily diet here, has acquired an enviable reputation in New France, where it is praised for its culinary qualities. Caught in great quantities near Quebec City, eel is as much a colonial staple as moose and other game meats.

These meats have familiar tastes. Moose is compared to beef, bear to pork, porcupine to suckling pig and beaver to mutton. Marmot is considered tasty here, and according to one French nobleman the taste of deer surpasses that of all types of venison. Game birds – such as geese – are also popular.

1660 (1660-1669)

Quebec, May 5, 1660. Bishop Laval issues a pastoral letter threatening excommunication for anyone who gives or sells liquor to Amerindians.

France, March 9, 1661. Cardinal Mazarin, *de facto* ruler of France, dies. Louis XIV becomes effective ruler of France. He has been king officially since 1643.

France, Feb. 24, 1663. The Company of New France agrees to turn over control of the colony to the Crown in return for whatever compensation the king gives them. In effect, New France becomes a royal colony.

France, Nov. 11, 1663. Prouville de Tracy receives a royal commission as "lieutenant-general throughout the length and breadth of the continental countries under our authority situated in South and North America, and of the islands and rivers." His mission is to drive the Dutch from the West Indies and to defeat and then reach a truce with the Iroquois in Canada.

Newfoundland, 1663. French settlement begins at Placentia Bay, their main fishing port on the island.

Ville-Marie, 1663. The Sulpicians acquire Ville-Marie [Montreal] from the Society of Notre-Dame.

France, March 8, 1664. King's representative Jean-Baptiste Colbert writes to Bishop Laval in New France that it is necessary "to destroy utterly these barbarians (the Iroquois)."

Quebec, June 30, 1665. Four infantry companies led by Prouville de Tracy arrive from the West Indies to carry out the king's plans to exterminate the Iroquois and are greeted with general rejoicing and festivities. They join four other infantry companies that arrived earlier in the month.

Quebec, Aug. 16, 1665. Twelve mares and two stallions from the Royal Stables of Louis XIV arrive at the colony to form the base of a new breed of horse.

London, October 1669. Groseilliers returns aboard the *Nonsuch* after a fur-trading expedition sponsored by Prince Rupert and London merchants. He reached Hudson Bay, built Fort Charles at the mouth of the Rupert River, and traded with the Indians throughout the winter.

Dollard and troops fall to Iroquois

May 1660

LONG SAULT, New France – The Iroquois have defeated a band of 17 Frenchmen under Adam Dollard des Ormeaux in the battle of Long Sault. All were killed during the battle and its aftermath.

Dollard and his men left Ville-Marie on April 20 to ambush the small bands of Iroquois warriors who every year waylay, massacre and loot furs from convoys travelling down the Ottawa River to the trading factories of the St. Lawrence. Dollard expected the Iroquois, returning from their own hunting expeditions, to be short of ammunition.

Before reaching the Long Sault, northwest of Ville-Marie, Dollard was joined by 40 Hurons and four Algonquins. As his forces were settling into an abandoned Algonquin fort, they were surprised by the arrival of 300 Iroquois with whom they arranged a truce. Dollard was unlucky, for instead of the usual small bands, the Iroquois were on their way to a rendez-vous with 500 warriors whom they now summoned. Negotiations failed after the French panicked and fired on Iroquois emissaries. "Ah, comrades, you have spoiled everything!" cried Annaotaha, the Huron chief. He and most Hurons then fled. The enraged Iroquois assaulted the fort. When they entered it, they found five Frenchmen alive. One was tortured to death immediately, the other four a little later.

Adam Dollard des Ormeaux defending a fort against an Iroquois attack.

Law gives bye boat fishermen the boot

Jan. 26, 1661

NEWFOUNDLAND – The revised Western Charter is a tough pill to swallow for the bye boat fishery. It includes a clause forbidding the transportation of independent boaters on fishing ships. Bye boat keepers are independent boat owners who hire crews of four or five in England and pay for their passage on a fishing ship bound for Newfoundland. Once on the island the crews carry on with the fishery and sell their catch to visiting trading ships.

The bye boat fishery developed in the depression of the 1640s when many old fishing ships went out of business. Others were sunk or captured by enemy ships. Since they could afford the modest investment, captains, mates and others became small operators. They hired experienced fishermen, paid them wages instead of shares, and offered them the comparative luxury of travelling as passengers instead of having to sail the vessel. Fishing admirals and merchants don't like the competition and have convinced the government to ban the bye boat keepers. But since bye boat keepers pay their passage and freight charges, they're popular with the smaller shipowners and the ban will be hard to enforce.

2 killed, 1 whipped for selling brandy

1661

NEW FRANCE – Two men learned the hard way that if you're caught breaking the new colony's temperance law by selling brandy to the natives, you're going to pay the price. Their price was their lives. The two were shot for violating the law. A third man was whipped for committing the same crime. The punishments are the harshest dished out since the law was enacted in 1657. Bishop François de Laval and other Jesuit missionaries led the fight against brandy trading in New France.

French build colony at Placentia harbor

Oct. 1, 1662

NEWFOUNDLAND – There are reports the French have established a small fishing village in Placentia. Isaac Dethick, one of the few English fishermen living there, reports that a "great French ship put into Grand Placentia, where she landed a great number of soldiers and passengers who fortified the harbor with 18 pieces of ordnance." Other reports confirm Dethick's sighting.

The French have been fishing in Newfoundland waters from about 1540. Most of this century they've fished alongside the English in peace. The French maintain both a deep sea and an inshore fishery. With the success of their Quebec colony, in recent years they have pursued the inshore fishery off Newfoundland's south coast. With one colony – New France – based on fur and now a second based on codfish, it's anticipated the French will be able to organize the two activities more efficiently in the future. Unlike English fishermen who are dependent on foreign markets and unable to co-ordinate their activities, the French sell all their fish at their home ports.

Placentia is a beautiful, sheltered ice-free harbor. Unlike most harbors, it has a large beach where fish can be dried. It is hoped relations between the English and French fishermen and the Newfoundland colonists will stay cordial.

Sovereign Council of New France created

Sovereign Council is established to take over government of New France.

April 1663

QUEBEC CITY – The colony is now a royal province of France subject to direct Crown control and with access to the royal treasury. An edict by King Louis XIV has established a Sovereign Council as its new government. This new administrative body succeeds the Council at Quebec formed by the financially troubled Company of One Hundred Associates.

A Crown review of conditions in New France has found the colony desperate for help, poorly populated and inadequately defended. It cannot continue to withstand repeated attacks by the Iroquois. To save the colony, France is reconstructing its institutional authority and injecting financial aid. A governor representing the king will head the new council, working with the settlement's senior ecclesiastic and an intendant. Assigned to oversee the proper application of French law, the council also has a degree of legislative authority.

Law bans the sale of liquor to Indians

Sept. 28, 1663

QUEBEC CITY – Gov. Augustin Saffray de Mézy and the Sovereign Council of New France have outlawed the sale of liquor to the Indians. The new law says anyone caught trading liquor – directly or indirectly – with the Indians is liable to heavy fines or even exile. The edict is one of the first issued by the new Sovereign Council, appointed 10 days ago. Mézy himself just arrived here on Sept. 15.

The law is expected to please Jesuit priests and lift one of the bigger sources of tension in the colony between the church and state. Jesuits have sought liquor legislation for some time. Officials also believe the new law will prove to the Divine Savior that colonists are repenting for their sins and that there is no need for earthquakes such as the one which hit the area in February.

While excommunication, flogging and capital punishment have been used in the past to discourage the brandy trade, nothing's been able to end the practice. The liquor trade upset Msgr. François de Laval so much he went to France to ask King Louis XIV to have Pierre Dubois Davaugour removed as governor in favor of Mézy.

French fur traders, in competition with other Europeans, offer alcohol in addition to other trade items. Their brandy is considered superior to English rum and gin.

The Séminaire du Québec, founded in 1663 by Msgr. François de Laval.

Single women encouraged to immigrate

1663

NEW FRANCE – Royal officials in charge of New France have started a promotional campaign encouraging the immigration of single women to the colony. Calling the women *filles du roi*, or "daughters of the king," the officials are hoping to correct a social imbalance: New France is ripe with eligible bachelors but short on women of marrying age.

While soldiers and traders who wished to settle have relied on the church and the fur-trading monopoly for providing brides until now, over the last 20 years only 230 unmarried women have arrived.

Women take the veil, not husbands.

"Filles du roi" arrive in New France

1663

QUEBEC CITY – God bless the King. He's taking concrete steps to even out the lopsided male-female ratio in New France.

With six bachelors for every woman of marrying age in New France, there's a severe shortage of females in the new colony. But now King Louis XIV is graciously sending his "daughters" to the rescue. Some 30 *filles du roi* are already here. Their mission is to marry quickly and help populate New France. Over the next 10 years about 800 *filles du roi* are expected in New France. They range in age from 12 to 45.

The women are called the *filles du roi* because the king pays their transport and keep. Some are sent by parents who want to get rid of them. Others are orphans or poor. Girls imprisoned for prostitution have also melted into the crowd. Most often their dowry is paid in clothing and household supplies. Some privileged girls receive a cow, utensils and seeds.

Most *filles du roi* find a husband within days of arriving in New France. The women choose their own mates from the abundance of males in the colony. The few *filles du roi* who get pregnant on the two-month crossing from France to the colony are sent back home.

France's King Louis XIV in 1662.

Louis XIV receiving "filles du roi."

"Filles du roi" arrive in Quebec to alleviate the shortage of single women.

French vest rights in West India Company

May 1664

FRANCE – French plans to hasten colonial development have taken a crucial step. Letters patent creating the West India Company have been issued in France. All French property rights are vested in the company. In New France the company has the power to grant lands in fief, build forts, appoint officials, legislate, declare war and make treaties.

Coins issued by the West India Company, established in 1664.

Tithe is instituted: tax on human toil

1663

NEW FRANCE – Tithes, or ecclesiastical taxes, must now be paid by all people of the seigneuries in New France. King Louis XIV has decreed that payments will amount to one-thirteenth of the land's annual produce.

Tithes will be levied on all products of the soil or handiwork made by those living on land owned by the church. Curés will estimate the total crop of each farm to ensure no habitant holds back the church's due portion. While tithes were originally set at one-tenth of annual produce, tenants on land the church owns in New France now find themselves with a higher price to pay for their toil.

Tracy orders army to burn cornfields after Mohawks flee

October 1666

IROQUOIS COUNTRY – The French forces under Alexandre de Prouville de Tracy have set fire to four Mohawk villages and burned all of the Indians' crops in surrounding fields. Consisting of more than 1,000 regular soldiers, some 600 militiamen and 100 Hurons and Algonquins, the force left Quebec Sept. 14 to engage hostile Mohawks in [upper New York state].

After peace talks with the Mohawks failed this summer, New France Intendant Jean Talon ordered an all-out military offensive against them to prevent a combined English-Iroquois attack targeting the colony.

Supported by 300 boats and canoes carrying provisions and arms, Tracy and his men left Fort Ste. Anne, located at the northern end of [Lake Champlain], on Oct. 3. Arriving at the lake's southern tip, the French forces began a rain-soaked march through the forests searching for hostile Mohawks. Instead they found four deserted villages. The Mohawks had been warned in advance of Tracy's approach and chose to flee rather than face his army. Unable to engage the enemy in direct combat, Tracy ordered their cornfields destroyed. The Mohawks now face a winter without adequate supplies of food.

An officer in the French forces.

French and Iroquois sign peace pact

Treaty signed by Iroquois and French helped coureurs de bois and Indians come to terms with each other.

July 1667

QUEBEC CITY – The Iroquois and French have signed their first genuine peace treaty since the days of explorer Samuel de Champlain. Cmdr. Alexandre de Prouville de Tracy deserves much of the credit for getting the Iroquois Indians to come to terms with their longtime enemies.

After the Iroquois approached the French last year hoping to sign a peace pact, the mission went sour when Tracy ordered Mohawk cornfields burned in revenge for the Mohawk murder of his nephew and capture of his cousin. Tracy also recalled the French peace ambassadors and imprisoned 24 Iroquois delegates.

After a perilous trip during which eight men drowned in a storm on Lake Champlain, Tracy reached Quebec on Nov. 5. There he hanged an Iroquois captive, whose name is believed to be Agariata, as a warning to other Iroquois. Then he sent three or four prisoners from each nation back to their people with news of his victory, and to ask them what they intended to do. The answer came only this month, when the Iroquois agreed to make peace not only with the French, but with their Huron and Algonquin allies.

Jesuits eye mission to convert Iroquois over to Christianity

1667

LAPRAIRIE, New France – Jesuit priests in New France plan to set up a mission near Ville-Marie where they can concentrate their efforts on converting the Iroquois to Christianity. The post will be in Laprairie, just a few kilometres away from the growing town of Ville-Marie. Iroquois will be invited to quit their villages and live among the French.

The very idea of moving the Iroquois away from their ancient villages and permanent settlements is a novel one. Recognizing that the task in front of them is a mammoth one, the Jesuits are proceeding with caution. A lot of thought's been put into how to make the transition as easy as possible for the natives.

In Laprairie, the Jesuits believe they have the ideal site for the new mission. Its soil is perfect for growing corn, a crop the Iroquois raise. Bearing in mind that the Iroquois are known to hunt and fish, the mission is situated near an abundance of forests for hunting and Lake St. Louis for fishing. Ville-Marie's proximity gives the natives easy access to the fur company's depot for bartering.

Jesuits believe that as converts to Christianity, the Iroquois will be free to practise their new religion in peace and quiet in Laprairie without having to worry about fellow-tribesmen disrupting them.

Sovereign Council passes hygiene law

April 21, 1664

NEW FRANCE – The Sovereign Council today passed the first hygiene law in New France. It aims to protect public health by banning "straw, manure and everything else" from being thrown on streets.

The lax hygienic standards that have prompted such legislation are also evident in the personal lives of the colonists in New France. They rarely bathe, believing baths will cause colic, fever, headaches and vertigo. Their housekeeping habits are similarly casual.

French women adapt to colonial lifestyle

1665

NEW FRANCE – French women have proved they can adapt to life in New France as well as men. Sometimes better. Some women in the colony run or help run the small businesses that sell imported material, clothes, furs, brandy and utensils. On average, they are also more literate than men. Most women take part in family decisions and accompany their husbands to the notary for matters such as assigning property or signing a lease.

While domestic chores are limited by a lack of furniture, crockery and windows, what sewing, cooking and other household work exists is the responsibility of the woman of the house. When a family moves into a house, both sexes do traditional male chores: burning and clearing land, using a pick, building, harvesting, skinning animals and insulating houses. In the fields and the bush, French women do heavy work and most know how to fire a musket.

French colonists began arriving in New France in 1634. Most women led a life of privation in those early days. Only a privileged few had a change of clothes.

Governor Daniel de Rémy de Courcelle led France to power in [Great Lakes] area in 1666.

1670 (1670-1679)

London, May 31, 1670. The first voyage under the charter of the new Hudson's Bay Company leaves London to establish permanent posts on James Bay and the Nelson River. The expedition includes Groseilliers, Radisson, and Charles Bayly, the first overseas governor of the company.

Great Lakes, June 1670. Daniel de Rémy de Courcelle, governor of New France, arrives at Lake Ontario with a force of 56 volunteers aboard a large flatboat. He warns the Iroquois that if they continue warring against the Algonquins he will return with an army to destroy them. The Iroquois make peace with the Algonquins.

Acadia, July 17, 1670. Hector Andigné de Grandfontaine arrives at Pentagouet as first French governor of Acadia [Nova Scotia, New Brunswick, and Maine] after the English occupation of 1654-70.

Hudson's Bay Territory, October 1670. Governor Bayly of the Hudson's Bay Company arrives at Fort Charles on the Rupert River. He immediately begins building a dwelling, to be known as Rupert House.

Hudson's Bay Territory, July 1, 1671. The first Hudson's Bay Company expedition sails home for England. Governor Bayly could not persuade his men to spend another winter at Rupert House.

New France, July 4, 1671. Explorer Simon François de Saint-Lusson claims an immense territory around the Great Lakes for the king of France in a ceremony at the native village of Sault Ste. Marie attended by representatives of 14 Indian nations and some prominent Frenchmen. They erect a cross "to bring forth there the fruits of Christianity," and a cedar post bearing the arms of France.

France, 1672. Louis de Baude de Frontenac et de Palluau is appointed governor-general of New France in the spring, effectively blocking his creditors' attempts to seize his properties.

Quebec, Oct. 23, 1672. Baude de Frontenac, recently arrived as governor-general of New France, presides at the first Estates General in the colony. The assembly is ostensibly for the people to swear an oath of loyalty to the king, but Frontenac's real purpose is to impress the people with its pomp and ceremony.

Hudson's Bay trading company born

May 2, 1670

LONDON, England – King Charles II signed a 7,000-word charter at the Whitehall palace today incorporating the governor and Company of Adventurers of England Trading into the Hudson's Bay trading company. Made up of the king's cousin, Prince Rupert of the Rhine, a staunch supporter of the king during his exile in France, and 17 other investors, the company is granted sole authority over all the land in the New World with water draining into Hudson Bay. This authority includes a monopoly over the fur trade and rights to the fish and minerals. If it sees fit, the company can also establish a military force for security and defence.

Members of the company have previously underwritten expeditions to the Hudson Bay area to search for a passage into the South Sea and to determine the viability of a fur trade with the inhabitants. Although no one knows the extent of the land holdings, the company has been assured by Pierre-Esprit Radisson and Médard Chouart, Sieur Des Groseilliers, two established fur traders, that the region contains enough animal and mineral wealth to sustain a lucrative enterprise without substantial investment or permanent colonies. A fine cargo of beaver pelts shipped here from Hudson Bay on the ship *Nonsuch* last October would seem to substantiate their claims. The two Frenchmen plan to return to Hudson Bay in the near future for more fur trading.

Prince Rupert is the first governor of Hudson's Bay. He and seven others form a committee running the new company until Nov. 10. From then on, a new governor and committee will be elected annually.

Britain's King Charles II signs charter incorporating Hudson's Bay company.

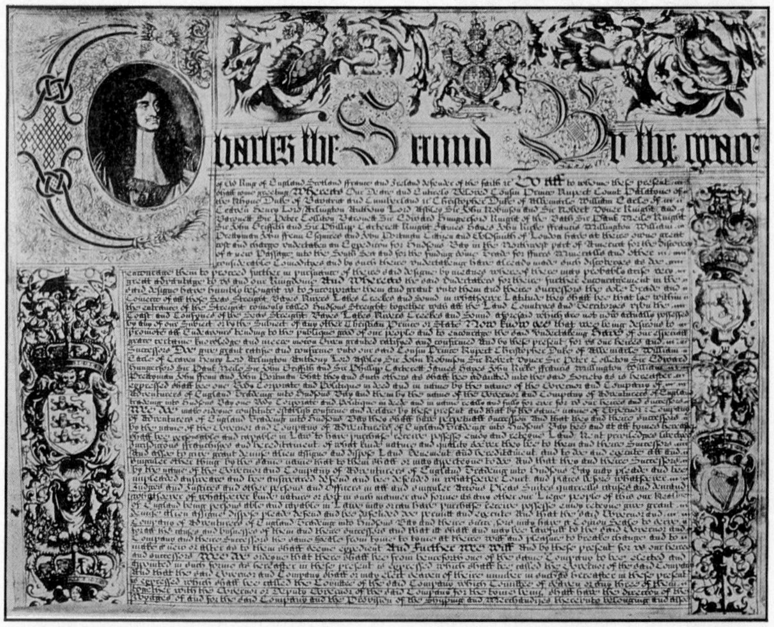

A new charter grants the Hudson's Bay company a monopoly over fur trade.

Priests claim Great Lake region for France

March 23, 1670

NEW FRANCE [Ontario] – On the north shore of Lake Erie, evangelizing Sulpician Fathers François Dollier de Casson and René de Bréhant de Galinée today erected a cross bearing the arms of France and claiming sovereignty over the Lake Erie region in the name of King Louis XIV.

A former cavalry captain, Dollier inspired this voyage of discovery aimed at Christianizing the Potawotomis, Algonquian Indians in the area. Bréhant, a geographer, 22 Europeans and several Algonquian guides assist him. While Dollier once resented being sent to the colony, he now finds the wilderness and forests enchanting. He even says he'd rather die here than with his brothers at the seminary.

No money? Try fur

Sept. 15, 1670

NEW FRANCE – Thanks to a decree just issued by the Sovereign Council, colonists can now pay their debts with beaver and moose hides. This legislation, which comes in response to the colony's scarcity of hard currency, sets the standard for measuring the value of the pelts. Already, colonists use them as barter.

French eye control of Hudson trading

Aug. 6, 1671

HUDSON BAY – Intendant Jean Talon is challenging English control of the fur trade on Hudson Bay. Fathers Charles Albanel and Paul Denys de Saint-Simon left here today for Tadoussac with orders from Talon to find out what is happening in the north. Natives have brought furs from Hudson Bay to New France, telling traders two Frenchmen – Pierre-Esprit Radisson and Médard Chouart, Sieur des Groseilliers – are helping the English establish posts for the fur trade. Albanel and his companion have orders to investigate these reports, establish a fur trade with the natives, take possession of territory, and determine whether it's advisable to set up a warehouse on Hudson Bay to "replenish supplies for the ships which subsequently will be able to use this route to discover the connecting passage between the Northern and Southern Seas."

The expedition is another of Talon's plans to expand the borders of French territory in the New World and to broaden the base of the community's trade and finances. He is particularly interested in directing the growth of industry, agriculture and the fur trade. Albanel, a Jesuit, was chosen for the expedition because of his experience as an explorer and a missionary to the natives at Tadoussac. If he and his party reach Hudson Bay they will be the first Europeans to get there over land from the south.

Some fur traders say Albanel is not the right man for the job since he lacks the skills needed to handle native guides and survive the northern wilderness. Critics note he has no experience in the fur trade and believe he won't know how to set up a trading system and warehouses. "He will spend more time baptizing the Indians than he will exploring the land and dealing with the English," one trader said. Even government officials are worried that Albanel, without soldiers or proof that he is an official envoy, will be captured by the English.

Indian traders transporting furs by canoe from Hudson Bay to New France.

New France Intendant Jean Talon.

Company lays claim to land in the north

September 1670

NORTH [Rupert's Land] – It didn't take the new overseas governor of the Hudson's Bay Company long to lay claim to a tract of northern land [Rupert's Land]. After disembarking from the *Wivenhoe,* Charles Bayly immediately nailed the royal arms to a tree and the deed was done.

Bayly sailed from England in June. Soon after he landed here a strong gale blew up and forced the company party to board the *Wivenhoe* and sail 1,100 kilometres west to Fort Charles. There he found the *Prince Rupert.* It left England with the *Wivenhoe* but storms separated the two ships.

At the urging of Prince Rupert, King Charles granted the Hudson's Bay Company its charter on May 2. An expedition led by Médard Chouart, Sieur des Groseillers, impressed the prince and other merchants: it traded for furs with nearly 300 natives. Without consulting the local native peoples, the charter gives the company the rights to all the land drained by the rivers flowing into Hudson Bay. Much of the territory is unmapped, but the company's backers say this means they have sole claim to all trade conducted west of the bay. Bayly will now direct the establishment of fur trading posts along the shores of Hudson Bay and the vast hinterland.

Smallpox epidemics take toll on natives

1670

NEW FRANCE – The devastating effects of smallpox on the native population in New France cannot be underestimated. Since smallpox was first reported in New France in 1634, it has claimed thousands of lives. One of the most recent smallpox epidemics in 1662 killed more than 1,000 Iroquois.

In one of the earliest and most deadly epidemics, smallpox hit the St. Lawrence Valley in 1639 and killed hundreds of natives trading at Quebec City and Trois-Rivières. That epidemic alone practically halved the Huron population, reducing it to some 9,000 people.

Radisson and Groseilliers establish trade post at Hudson Bay

Radisson and Groseilliers establish English trading post at Hudson Bay.

September 1670

NORTH [Rupert's Land] – The Company of Adventurers is building the Hudson Bay region's first permanent trading post. After they failed to establish one near the Nelson River, Pierre-Esprit Radisson and Gov. Charles Bayly arrived here at Fort Charles to try again. They have been using Fort Charles, located in James Bay, as a seasonal trading post since 1668.

Radisson's brother-in-law Médard Chouart, Sieur des Groseilliers made a concentrated effort to stimulate fur trading with local natives last summer. His success prompted Bayly to order the construction of a new winter dwelling on the same site as the old one. ▷

Frontenac goes behind minister's back to establish a French fur-trading post

Louis de Buade de Frontenac on way to establish trading post at Cataracoui.

May 17, 1674

FORT FRONTENAC, New France – The daring and sometimes brash French soldier Louis de Buade de Frontenac, now governor of New France, has established a fur-trading post [Kingston] on Lake Ontario, at the mouth of the Cataracoui River. Frontenac's move is sure to create an uproar in France. He's built the fort without first informing Minister of Marine Jean-Baptiste Colbert and without the proper authorization.

Frontenac has already incensed the fur traders and *habitants* of Ville-Marie. Fur traders fear the advanced trading post will deprive them of part of the western fur trade. The *habitants* are upset since Frontenac forced them to help him build his fort. When Ville-Marie Gov. François-Marie Perrot protested the use of forced labor, Frontenac had him arrested and sent back to France. Father François de Salignac de La Mothe-Fénelon suffered the same fate when he criticized Frontenac in an Easter sermon.

Frontenac sailed from La Rochelle in June 1672 to take up the post of governor-general of New France. A haughty, imperious and debt-ridden man, Frontenac already had a somewhat turbulent past at that time. His military exploits involved him in numerous conflicts with his superiors.

Not long after Frontenac arrived in the colony, Intendant Jean Talon left for New France. Talon was a proponent of expanding the colony westward. He had sent expeditions to explore the west, claim lands for France and establish trade relations with the Ojibwas, Ottawas and other tribes. He wanted to establish fortified posts in the west and create a vast fur-trading empire extending far into the interior.

Colbert rejected Talon's expansionist ideas. He hoped to firmly establish the French colony in the St. Lawrence Valley before expanding west. Recognizing Colbert's stance and the potential of the western fur trade, Frontenac proceeded to build Fort Frontenac behind the minister's back.

Cataracoui trading post was built without government authorization.

Taps flow at first brewery in colony

Nov. 2, 1671

QUEBEC CITY – The taps at the King's Brewery in Quebec City were turned on today by Intendant Jean Talon. The ale's pegged at six sols a mug. Beer lovers no longer need to drink home-made spruce beer or bouillon, a cheap alcoholic beverage made by fermenting dough in spiced water.

While Father François-Joseph Le Mercier calls beer "wholesome," Minister Jean-Baptiste Colbert said drunkenness "would no longer cause scandal by reason of the cold nature of beer, the vapors whereof rarely deprive men of the use of their judgment." The brewery's 18,000-litre beer-producing capacity will be split between the West Indies and Canada.

Men must marry or lose privileges

Oct. 21, 1671

NEW FRANCE – It seems the young bachelors of New France are not marrying young enough or fast enough for Intendant Jean Talon. So Talon – determined as ever to see the colony populated – today signed an ordinance forcing bachelors to wed the young *filles du roi* arriving here from France, though the close to 1,000 already here have had no trouble finding husbands almost as soon as they landed.

Some stiff penalties await young bachelors who evade matrimony. They can be deprived of their fishing, hunting and fur-trading privileges. But if they marry before turning 21, they can claim a bonus of 20 *livres* Talon provided for in a decree of 1669.

Colony's furs hot item at London auction

London's first auction of furs supplied by Radisson and Groseilliers begins.

Oct. 17, 1671

LONDON, England – London's first auction of furs from the colony of New France was held today. The two enterprising traders who secured the furs for the auction are Pierre-Esprit Radisson and Médard Chouart des Groseilliers. The English call them "Mr. Radishes and Mr. Gooseberry."

Groseilliers arrived in New France around 1641 and settled in Trois-Rivières. While the date Radisson arrived in the colony is not known, his capture by the Iroquois in 1651 indicates he was involved in inter-tribal warfare sometime before then. Like Groseilliers, Radisson also settled in Trois-Rivières.

The two Frenchmen offered their services to the English after an expedition to the Hudson Bay area in 1659-1660. They returned with a huge supply of furs, only to have them seized by French authorities for not having the proper trading licence. Disgusted, they turned to the English. The result was the creation of the Hudson's Bay Company last year.

La Salle expedition launches the Griffon; 45-ton ship is first to sail the Great Lakes

Aug. 7, 1679

NIAGARA FALLS, New France – The first ship to sail in the Great Lakes was launched today above Niagara Falls. Named after the symbol on Frontenac's coat of arms, the *Griffon* weighs 45 tons and carries a crew of 30 and seven guns. The ship was built on orders from French explorer René-Robert Cavelier, Sieur de La Salle, who needs it for his new expedition. La Salle was granted permission in May last year to explore the western half of North America. He's already explored part of the Great Lakes and some areas to the south. It was on one of his previous expeditions that La Salle and his chaplain, Father Louis Hennepin, discovered the falls.

La Salle decided he needed a ship for his new task and brought his men came to Niagara last year to work on it. The *Griffon* was on the stocks in January when La Salle was forced to go to Fort Frontenac [Kingston]. By the time he returned in July, the ship was almost finished. Before heading south to explore the continent's great rivers, La Salle plans to sail the *Griffon* to the Baie des Puants [Green Bay] for furs to bring back to Niagara.

La Salle's ship the Griffon is built to explore western half of North America.

Intendant knocks "idle" life of seigneurs

New France's young settlers are encouraged to become coureurs de bois.

Nov. 10, 1679

NEW FRANCE – The seigneurial class is too interested in a life of leisure to take care of their land properly, says Intendant Jacques Duchesneau de la Dousinnière et d'Ambault. He describes the "idle" life of many seigneurs who "make hunting and fishing their greatest occupation" in a letter addressed to Louis XIV's minister Jean-Baptiste Colbert.

"Since they do not apply themselves entirely to their families and to exploiting their lands, they get mixed up in trade, make debts on all sides and incite their young settlers to become coureurs de bois and send their children into the woods," he said. "And with all that they are in great poverty."

Jean-Baptiste Colbert.

Council lifts ban restricting the sale of liquor to natives

Oct. 28, 1678

NEW FRANCE – Colonists in New France are free to sell liquor to the natives. The Sovereign Council lifted the ban today after meeting 20 leading settlers to discuss the contentious issue. Since most of the 20 are in business, it's not surprising 15 favored an open liquor trade.

Bishop François de Laval is the main opponent in New France to an open liquor trade. He plans to go to France immediately to convince the king to reverse the decision.

New charter addresses fishermen's beefs

Jan. 27, 1675

NEWFOUNDLAND – King Charles II has approved a new charter for Newfoundland to protect the rights of fishing admirals and west country merchants. The charter stipulates settlers are not allowed to "cut down any wood or inhabit within six miles of the shore." While it was never enforced, a similar clause was implemented in Newfoundland in the 1630s when Sir David Kirke was governor. It forces Newfoundland colonists to settle inland, virtually eliminating them as a source of competition in the fishing industry.

Like the original in 1633 and revisions passed in 1661 and 1670, the charter was requested by the fishing admirals and west country merchants. They have experienced severe losses since the 1630s and are convinced unfair competition from their own countrymen is compounding the problem. The charter was amended in 1661 to include a clause forbidding the transportation of independent boat keepers on fishing ships. In 1670 the ban was extended to potential colonists.

The English government is convinced that Newfoundlanders add little to the national wealth. It also believes they do not develop skills as sailors and are of no use to the navy. Whether the six-mile clause will be enforced remains to be seen.

Ville-Marie founder dies after spending his last years alone

1676

VILLE-MARIE – Paul de Chomedey, Sieur de Maisonneuve, Ville-Marie's heroic founder, died in Paris after 11 years in seclusion there. He was 64. De Maisonneuve was a skillful organizer and tireless defender of the colony, but he fell out of favor with the governors-general. This led to his recall to France in 1665, despite his popularity among the colonists. De Maisonneuve's friend Philippe de Turmenys and servant Louis Fin were at his side when he died.

1680 (1680-1689)

Quebec, July 1685. A ship arrives carrying l'Abbé de Saint-Valliers, the new Bishop of Quebec, Brisay de Denonville, the new governor, and many officers and soldiers. The ship is rife with sickness.

Quebec, 1685. Governor Brisay de Denonville writes that "the great liberty of long standing which parents have given youth ... has reached such an excess that from the time children are able to carry a gun, fathers are not able to restrain them and dare not anger them."

Montreal, March 20, 1686. Pierre de Troyes and Pierre Le Moyne d'Iberville lead an expedition to capture Hudson's Bay Company posts in James Bay in retaliation for the loss of Fort Bourbon in 1684. Sponsored by the Compagnie du Nord, the expedition boasts 100 men and 35 canoes.

Hudson Bay Territory, July 17, 1686. The French overland expedition led by de Troyes and Iberville captures Fort Albany on James Bay from the English and changes its name to Ste. Anne. Earlier they captured Moose Factory and Rupert House, and changed their names to St. Louis and St. Jacques.

Europe, November 1686. Louis XIV of France and James II of England agree on the Treaty of Neutrality. It provides for the continuance of peace between the French and English dominions in America, even in the event of war in Europe.

London, 1687. Physicist Isaac Newton publishes his masterpiece, *Philosophiae Naturalis Principia Mathematica*. He defines a universal law of gravitation.

Quebec, April 1688. The Sovereign Council authorizes the establishment of offices for the poor in cities and towns, the first form of public social assistance in the colony.

Hudson Bay Territory, June 17, 1689. Henry Kelsey leads a Hudson's Bay Company expedition sailing north from Churchill in search of natives to trade at Churchill.

Hudson Bay Territory, July 1689. Henry Kelsey and a native boy walk 200 kilometres northward in search of natives after his expedition is blocked by ice. They meet no one, but Kelsey sees a musk-ox, the first European recorded to ever see one.

La Salle claims Louisiana for France

La Salle arrives at mouth of Colbert [Mississippi] River and claims Louisiana.

April 9, 1682

LOUISIANA – To the salvos of muskets, René-Robert Cavalier, Sieur de La Salle, today proclaimed the territory of Louisiana a possession of France. Garbed in a splendid scarlet and gold tunic, La Salle erected a cross at the mouth of the Colbert [Mississippi] River, marking a successful voyage embarked on in early February.

Along the river route, the crew of 23 Frenchmen and 18 Indians had founded an encampment called Fort Prud'homme and had a close scrape with menacing Arkansas Indians whom they later befriended. La Salle caught first sight of the sea on April 6 and the adventurers explored the river delta before declaring it a French possession.

Natives catching on to fur-trading ways

September 1684

NORTH [RUPERT'S LAND] – The Cree and Assiniboine have adapted admirably to the ways of the fur trade in the new domain – as this season's trading shows. More than 300 canoes, carrying 700 natives, recently came to York Factory on the Hayes Estuary and traded furs for 300 muskets, 10,000 knives and hatchets, tobacco, kettles, blankets and other goods.

Most natives were acting as middlemen, buying furs from the tribes to the west and north and then selling them to Hudson's Bay Company traders. Some measure of the profit involved: a Cree might pay the trader 14 prime pelts for axes and knives they would later resell to a Blackfoot for 50; the price of a kettle bought by the middleman for eight beaver pelts might cost the native trapper 20.

The Cree and Assiniboine had been the suppliers of pelts to the French on the St. Lawrence, working through Ojibwa and Ottawa middlemen. As the English opened up Hudson Bay, the Cree and Assiniboine, armed with the muskets they bought with their furs, took control of the Nelson River area trade and forced other tribes and the Hudson's Bay Company to deal with them only.

First Englishwomen arrive in James Bay

September 1683

HUDSON BAY – A ship has arrived at Moose Factory carrying the first three Englishwomen known to have ever come to the James Bay area. The *Diligence* sailed from England with the new governor, Henry Sergeant, his wife, her companion, a Mrs. Maurice, and a maidservant. The Englishwomen are the first to winter in James Bay.

Sergeant succeeds John Nixon as governor of the Hudson's Bay Company's James Bay posts. While he is under orders to make Albany his headquarters, he has made it clear he will winter at Moose. Sergeant seems to be irascible and high-handed in dealing with the Indians and his own men. Within a few hours of arriving, he ranted and raved at his men. He has given few signs of being capable of directing the company's operations. Sergeant has also angered many people by bringing three manservants for his personal service and a massive four-poster bed with him, complete with curtains and canopy. From what they have seen so far, many experienced traders believe Sergeant's term of office will be disastrous for the company.

First Englishwomen to visit James Bay arrive at Moose Factory.

Churchill River post to cut risk of attack on company traders

Hudson's Bay Co.'s John Churchill.

June 17, 1689

HUDSON BAY – Hudson's Bay Company officials, afraid of attacks in the James Bay area, are planning to build a post on the banks of the river named after the company's new governor, Maj.-Gen. John Churchill. Company officials also want to strengthen their hold on the northern tribes and Inuit since furs are more plentiful in the north. This is why Henry Kelsey has been ordered to sail to the mouth of the Churchill and set up a post there.

Three years ago, the Chevalier de Troyes marched with 100 men from the St. Lawrence, seized two company posts and attacked Fort Albany with the guns he had captured. Leading the attack was a dashing young French officer named Pierre Le Moyne, Sieur d'Iberville.

Gov. Henry Sergeant was at dinner with his wife, her companion and his officials and officers when the attack began. One shot from the French guns passed under the arm of a servant, and another whizzed by Mrs. Sergeant, who fainted. Mr. Sergeant, the women and officers ran into the cellar and watched while the chaplain waved a maid's white apron as a sign of surrender. Mr. Sergeant then met the Chevalier de Troyes and agreed to give up the post in return for keeping his possessions and safe conduct for himself and the women.

King permits use of African slaves

May 1, 1689

NEW FRANCE – Louis XIV, King of France, today granted permission allowing his subject colonists to import slaves from Africa. This act officially sanctions a practice in place for more than 60 years. The first African slave brought to the colony, Olivier Le Jeune, arrived in 1628. As the number of slaves grew in succeeding years, a measure was introduced defining their status. The "Code Noir," formulated in 1685, enabled slave-owners to prosecute slaves for acts of violence or escape. It was, however, designed to safeguard an institution, not to establish its legal foundation. Now, with the king's assent, importing Africans may occur unhindered by the possibility, however slight, of legal retribution.

Indian slaves provide free labor supply

1689

NEW FRANCE – The number of Indian slaves in New France is rising as the colony attempts to resolve its chronic shortage of labor. With a European population composed principally of adventurers, entrepreneurs, and Catholic nuns and priests, the colony lacks a sufficient labor force to meet demands in areas such as domestic services. Indian slaves, lower priced and more available than African slaves, are a cheap source of labor bought and sold in the markets of Ville-Marie and Quebec. They are used mainly in convents and hospitals.

The majority of Indian slaves are Pawnee and come from the Upper Mississippi Valley, captured in battle by France's Indian allies. After being acquired by the French, they are often baptized and become well integrated into colonial society. However, the *Panis*, as they are called in New France, still share a common trait with free Indians: they are very susceptible to European diseases. The chances of an enslaved Indian reaching the age of 20 are remote.

Native people of the region sometimes adopt captured enemies and assimilate them into their own social fabric. However, permanent integration is a rare occurrence and most captives either escape or die. French willingness to acquire slaves provides their Indian allies with another commodity they can trade for European goods. The fact that *Panis* can be bought this way also aids the French in their present conflict with the Iroquois: captured Iroquois can be used as hostages and bargaining agents, important if the French are to negotiate from a position of strength.

At least 24 dead in Lachine massacre

Aug. 5, 1689

LACHINE, New France – Terrible warcries awakened the *habitants* of Lachine at dawn today. Doors splintered under the blows of tomahawks. Hideously painted Indian warriors burst into houses. It was the Iroquois. Under the cover of last night's hailstorm, an estimated 1,500 Iroquois crossed Lake St. Louis undetected by sentries and dispersed in small bands among the homesteads of Lachine, a few miles from Ville-Marie.

The attack, in retaliation for a French raid on Iroquois villages two years ago, was sudden and ferocious. Terrified men, women and children were hacked to death and mutilated. Many taken prisoner were later tortured. Houses and barns went up in flames.

Twenty-four Lachine *habitants* died in the attack. Some 70 to 90 are prisoners and 42 are missing. They were either killed or, having been adopted into Iroquois families, chose to remain.

Explorer La Salle shot to death in mutiny

La Salle was killed by members of his expedition at Matagorda Bay, Texas.

March 19, 1687

GULF OF MEXICO [Louisiana] – The great French explorer René-Robert Cavelier, Sieur de La Salle, was killed today by members of his own expedition at Matagorda Bay, Texas. La Salle was in command of an expedition King Louis XIV sent to claim the territory between Fort St. Louis and New Biscay. Navigational errors doomed the party. In the end, La Salle set out from New Biscay to seek help at Fort St. Louis. After shooting his servant and supporters, mutineers ambushed him, shot him in the head and left his naked corpse to be devoured by animals.

French ship seizes Hudson's Bay furs

Oct. 10, 1684

QUEBEC CITY – In the ongoing battle for control of the Hudson Bay fur trade, a French ship has arrived in Quebec City with a cargo of furs captured from a Hudson's Bay Company boat. Commanded by Claude de Bermen de la Martinière, the French ship was returning from an aborted attempt to break the Hudson's Bay Company's control over trade in the interior. La Martinière narrowly avoided capture by a larger English ship.

A La Salle trade expedition.

1690 (1690-1699)

Hudson Bay Territory, June 12, 1690. The Hudson's Bay Company sends Henry Kelsey on an inland expedition from York Factory to persuade natives to trade at York. He is accompanied by a group of Assiniboines.

Montreal, Sept. 4, 1690. A force of Iroquois and English militia from Albany attack a settlement south of Montreal. They destroy farms and cattle, and kill more than 50 settlers and troops working in the fields. The force of 150 is part of an army formed to capture Montreal, while a fleet sails from Boston under Phips to capture Quebec.

Quebec, Nov. 5, 1690. The chapel recently built in the Lower Town is named Notre-Dame-de-Victoire, in honor of the recent French victory against Phips's expedition.

Acadia, 1691. Joseph Robinau de Villebon, appointed governor of Acadia [Nova Scotia and New Brunswick] by Louis XIV, reclaims the colony from the English. He erects the French flag at Port-Royal [Annapolis Royal].

Montreal, June 7, 1691. François le Moyne de Bienville leads 100 volunteers against a group of Oneidas at a deserted house in Repentigny, in retaliation for Iroquois attacks. They massacre about 15 of them, and burn the cabin with the others inside. De Bienville and eight comrades are killed.

Montreal, Aug. 31, 1692. The General Hospital of Ville-Marie is founded.

Hudson Bay Territory, October 1694. A French expedition led by Pierre Le Moyne d'Iberville lays siege to York Factory, which surrenders. It renders 60,000 *livres* worth of beaver pelts. Iberville renames the post Fort Bourbon.

Hudson Bay Territory, Sept. 5, 1696. A Hudson's Bay Company supply expedition recaptures Fort Bourbon (York Factory) from the French.

Quebec, Nov. 28, 1698. Baude de Frontenac, governor of Quebec, dies in office.

London, March 25, 1699. An Anglo-French commission issues letters to the governors of Canada and New York ordering them to cease hostilities with the Iroquois. The letters also order the disarming of the Indians, revealing a total ignorance of their way of life.

French avenge the Lachine massacre

January 1690

SCHENECTADY, N.Y. – A group of French colonists and their Indian allies exacted bloody revenge on English and Iroquois foes in Schenectady, killing at least 60 settlers and razing their homes to the ground.

The shocked mayor of neighboring Albany said "the cruelties committed no pen can write nor tongue express. Pregnant women were ripped up and children were thrown alive into flames." The attack was in retaliation for repeated raids on French settlements in Canada by Indians allied to English settlers, notably a brutal massacre at Lachine several months earlier.

Inhabitants of Schenectady escape flames after French and Indians attack.

New England soldiers capture Port Royal

May 20, 1690

PORT-ROYAL, Acadia – With no guns mounted and his 72 men badly outnumbered by 450 New England soldiers aboard seven vessels, Louis-Alexandre Des Friches de Meneval, French governor of Acadia, today surrendered the tiny colonial capital of Port Royal [Annapolis Royal] to Sir William Phips. Fitted out in Boston, Phips's fleet carries 64 guns. While the fortifications at Port Royal are feeble and unfinished to begin with, Meneval's forces suffered from not having any officers to lead them. After Phips demanded the garrison yield unconditionally, the priest the governor sent to negotiate with the New England commander insisted Meneval, racked with gout, would rather die in battle than behave like a coward.

Phips agreed to let the governor and his men go to Quebec with their weapons and baggage and to allow the local residents to keep their property, religion and church. But once inside the fort, Phips saw how pathetic its defences were and claimed the priest had duped him. He disarmed and imprisoned Meneval and his soldiers, forced Acadian farmers to swear allegiance to the protestant King William and Queen Mary of England, and let his men wreck Port Royal. In the orgy of destruction that followed, neither the priest's house nor the settlement's church was spared.

Molière play draws angry bishop's fire

Molière's Tartuffe is banned.

Feb. 1, 1694

NEW FRANCE – Bishop Jean-Baptiste de La Croix de Chevrières de Saint-Vallier has condemned a planned production of *Tartuffe,* Molière's satire on religious hypocrisy.

In a pastoral letter, the bishop said such plays can't be enacted without "all concerned falling into mortal sin." Saint-Vallier has denounced lead actor Sieur de Mareuil for blasphemy and impiety and denied him the sacraments.

The play is about a hypocrite, Tartuffe, who gains absolute influence over Orgon, the master of the house where the play is set, through his shows of piety. It was attacked by religious opinion in France when it was first presented in 1664, to the indignation of Molière.

Colonists warm up to the "inn" thing

1692

QUEBEC CITY – Despite the small population of the colony, European-style inns and pubs are growing in number and popularity. In a small town like Quebec with a population of 1,800, there are 20 innkeepers. That's one for every 90 inhabitants.

Three-quarters of innkeepers are from France. A good number are trained bakers, pastry chefs or cooks. Many first worked in the homes of governors or intendants.

Jolliet first to map coast of Labrador

October 1694

LABRADOR – Cartographer Louis Jolliet has completed the first maps of Labrador. Best known for discovering the Mississippi River, the famed explorer systematically mapped out the Labrador coastline on the travel log for his recent trip to the Atlantic region.

Jolliet drew 16 sketches and wrote vivid descriptions. He also described its inhabitants, giving the most complete portrayal of the Inuit to date.

French repulse bungling English attackers

Governor Frontenac's defensive strategy saves Quebec from British attack.

Oct. 16, 1690

QUEBEC CITY – Settlers here celebrated today as an English fleet retreated in humiliation after a botched attempt to capture the colony. The English assault, led by Sir William Phips, was bungled from start to finish and never really tested the defensive strategy of New France Gov. Louis de Buade de Frontenac et de Palluau, who had rushed down from Ville-Marie with troops to protect Quebec from the English flotilla advancing up the St. Lawrence.

When Phips arrived at Quebec he sent an emissary to deliver an ultimatum to the French to surrender or face attack by Phips's force of some 2,300 men and 34 ships. Frontenac coldly rejected the ultimatum saying: "I have no reply to make to your general other than from the mouths of my cannon and muskets." The English were thus committed to their attack on Quebec, by then made almost impregnable by 3,000 troops.

Struggling against troublesome tides, French snipers and the cold, a landing force made several clumsy attempts to make a beachhead and mount the imposing cliffs to the main settlement. Meanwhile, English ships were blasting away with cannons on the town, inflicting little damage. Realizing the futility of the mission and plagued by smallpox, the English retreated to the victorious cries of the French.

Girl repels Iroquois attack on father's fort

Oct. 23, 1692

NEW FRANCE – Fourteen-year-old Marie-Madeleine Jarret de Verchères repelled an Iroquois attack on her father's stockade yesterday, and also warned neighboring settlers danger was at hand.

At about 8 a.m., the Iroquois surprised Madeleine and others in the fields. While they took up to 20 prisoners, Madeleine escaped to the fort. Her parents were away, so she fired a cannon, unnerving the Iroquois. Neighbors responded to her gunfire, creating an improvised alarm system. Help arrived from Ville-Marie today, an hour after the Iroquois had withdrawn with their prisoners.

Young Madeleine repels Iroquois.

Kelsey sights huge bears, buffalo herds on prairies southwest of Hudson Bay

August 1690

RUPERT'S LAND [Manitoba] – Explorer Henry Kelsey has sighted a huge species of bear and herds of buffalo in a vast prairie he discovered far southwest of Hudson Bay. Kelsey, a Hudson's Bay Company employee with a gift for native languages, is on a mission to enlist Indians in the west to the fur trade. To that end, he brought guns, hatchets, tobacco and blankets. The 23-year-old adventurer noted an abundance of wildlife on the plain.

Last summer, Kelsey sighted musk-ox near the Churchill River.

Explorer Henry Kelsey is interested in herds of buffalo seen on prairies.

Among the wildlife Kelsey has seen in this region are large species of bear.

French lead attack as St. John's falls

Nov. 30, 1696

ST. JOHN'S, Nfld. – The war in Europe and on the North American mainland has reached Newfoundland in full force – the French captured St. John's today. Quebec Gov. Louis de Buade de Frontenac et de Palluau instructed an army of 400 French soldiers and their native allies to attack the English settlements there. Pierre Le Moyne, Sieur d'Iberville, led the French assault.

French forces left Placentia on Nov. 1 and marched to Ferryland. As they destroyed all the property there, Ferryland inhabitants fled to Bay Bulls and Petty Harbor. The French killed 36 English settlers on Nov. 26 in a battle near Petty Harbor. Two days later 88 Englishmen had little success trying to stop the French advance near St. John's. While 34 were killed, the remaining Englishmen fled to a crude fort near the St. John's shoreline and prepared to defend themselves. A shortage of food and ammunition and the fact that they were outnumbered forced them to surrender after two days.

The spectre of being attacked by the French is haunting all the English settlements in Newfoundland now. It's also clear that relations between the French colony of Placentia and its English neighbors will never be as friendly as they were in the past.

Mysterious calumet is given to Inuit

July 19, 1697

NORTH – As he stepped ashore in the New World to meet nine Inuit his expedition first sighted earlier today, Jean-Baptiste Le Moyne de Martigny et de La Trinité handed a calumet to two of the natives who came forward to meet his men.

Among the Amerindians the calumet is a mysterious symbol of peace. It is a kind of large pipe made of red, black or white stone. The head is polished and in the form of a war club. The stem is ornamented with porcupine quills and little colored threads.

Frontenac besieges enemy Mohawk towns

Governor Louis de Buade de Frontenac performing an Indian war dance.

Feb. 17, 1693

NEW FRANCE – The governor of New France, Buade de Frontenac, has successfully besieged three enemy Mohawk towns, but only time will tell if he reached his original goal. Frontenac wanted to destroy all ties between Indians allied with the French and those allied with the English. After 16 days of travel, his troops reached the first two Mohawk towns yesterday. Among them were mission Indians – Iroquois of the Sault and Mountain, Abenakis from the Chaudière, Hurons from Laurette, and Algonquins from Trois-Rivières.

The two towns were a quarter of a league apart, but Frontenac's forces surrounded them both by night. They waited in silence until no sound could be heard within, then attacked. There was no resistence, as many of the inhabitants were away. One town was burnt down and the prisoners were kept under guard in the other.

The French troops then walked a whole day to reach the third Mohawk town, but remained hidden in nearby woods until night. One of the French Indians then scaled the palisade and opened the town's gate. A short, bloody fight ensued, killing 20 or 30 Mohawks and leaving 300 prisoners, mostly women and children.

Soldiers use snowshoes during war.

St. John's garrison protects the English

June 31, 1697

ST. JOHN'S, Nfld. – England has responded to demands that it beef up security for the English residents of Newfoundland by establishing a garrison in St. John's. The destruction of every English settlement in Newfoundland by the French last winter has caused a great deal of concern among the English community. English colonies on the mainland are demanding England reassert its authority over Newfoundland. The fishing admirals, leaders of the visiting fishermen, are demanding protection for their property. The colonists want protection for their lives and property.

Fishing admirals and merchants for years maintained that Newfoundland did not need governmental protection. They said that with a true migratory fishery there should be nothing on the island to protect in the winter and that the fishing fleet could protect itself in the summer. But in recent years the admirals have discovered that their extensive fishing premises in Newfoundland are valuable and would cost a lot to replace. They seem ready to accept this new military presence. The colonists have always wanted protection.

How effective a garrison in St. John's will be when it comes to defending all the settlements on the the island remains unclear. So does the issue of the force becoming a permanent feature in St. John's. If it does, the garrison will certainly make St. John's a safer harbor.

A view of Quebec around 1699.

Noise does the trick: English fort seized

Sept. 20, 1697

YORK FACTORY – Unarmed and soaked after swimming ashore, French survivors of a naval battle tricked English defenders of York Factory and enabled their French colleagues to capture the post and its stock of furs.

Led by Pierre Le Moyne, Sieur d'Iberville, the sailors made so much noise the English fired on them rather than on the French warships trying to land troops and guns. When the French forces surrounded the post the English surrendered and marched out.

Ships engage in naval battle.

French land extends across the continent

1699

FORT MAUREPAS, Louisiana – French expansionist dreams got a big boost when explorer Pierre Le Moyne d'Iberville entered the Mississippi River from the Gulf of Mexico and built a strategic fort on Biloxi Bay between the Mississippi and a Spanish base in Pensacola. Fort Maurepas extends French claims to the Gulf of Mexico from the Gulf of St. Lawrence, an area now under Indian control.

Iberville's success did not come easily. His expedition left Brest last October after months of delays in which he fell ill and some crew deserted. Iberville arrived in St-Domingue [Haiti] Dec. 4 before heading north to Florida and west along the northern shore of the Gulf of Mexico to the Mississippi.

On March 2 a storm stalled the expedition. Misleading descriptions led Iberville to sail up the river in search of proof that he was indeed on the Mississippi. Only after he met natives who convinced him that Cavalier de La Salle had passed among them in 1682 was Iberville satisfied he was indeed on the right track.

Iberville leads way to stunning victory

Sept. 5, 1697

NORTHERN CANADA [Rupert's Land] – Pierre Le Moyne, Sieur d'Iberville, lived up to his reputation for bravery in a naval battle off the Nelson River today. Iberville's five-ship expedition was trapped in ice until one of his vessels, the *Pelican,* managed to break free.

Iberville sailed to three warships on the horizon, thinking they were part of his fleet. He didn't know they were heavily armed English warships. Outgunned and trapped, Iberville attacked, sinking two English ships. The other fled up the Nelson River.

Reluctant minister gets top-level post

Sept. 6, 1699

NEW FRANCE – The destiny of New France lies partly in the hands of a new minister today. Jérôme Phélypeaux, Comte de Pontchartrain et de Maurepas, has been appointed secretary of state for marine development.

As finance minister, Pontchartrain already has his hands full finding funds to pursue the war in Europe. While he asked not to be given the job looking after colonial interests in New France and elsewhere, King Louis XIV said he doesn't have confidence in anyone else. Despite his protests, Pontchartrain was forced to accept.

Sarrazin colony's first great scientist

March 4, 1699

NEW FRANCE – In Michel Sarrazin, the new colony is boasting its first great scientist. The Royal Academy of Sciences in Paris honored Sarrazin today, naming him a corresponding member in recognition of his work in the fields of botany and zoology.

Sarrazin, 39, was pressed into service in New France almost immediately after coming here from France in 1685 to work as a surgeon. The next year he was named surgeon-major of the troops at Ville-Marie and Quebec City.

Sarrazin's hobby – his scientific endeavors – brought him into contact with the Royal Academy of Sciences. The institution brings together distinguished French and foreign scientists, most of whom are in the prime of life and at the height of their work. Correspondents help the academy learn more about foreign countries.

Sarrazin has compiled a catalogue of more than 200 Canadian plants, with extensive notes on their pharmaceutical properties determined after thorough experimentation. After careful dissections, he also submitted articles on the flora and fauna of the new land. The one animal that defeated Sarrazin is the skunk. He was forced to abandon attempts to dissect and study its anatomy because, as he once noted, "it had a dreadful smell, capable of making a whole canton desert."

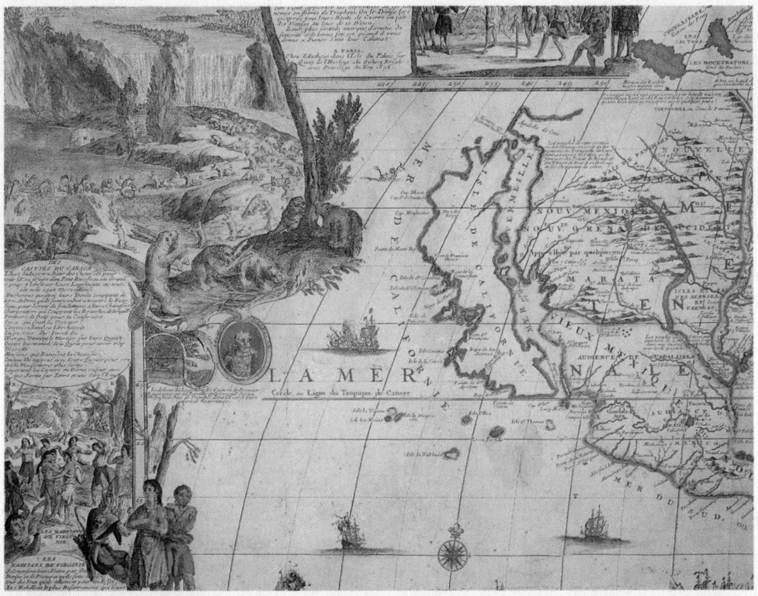

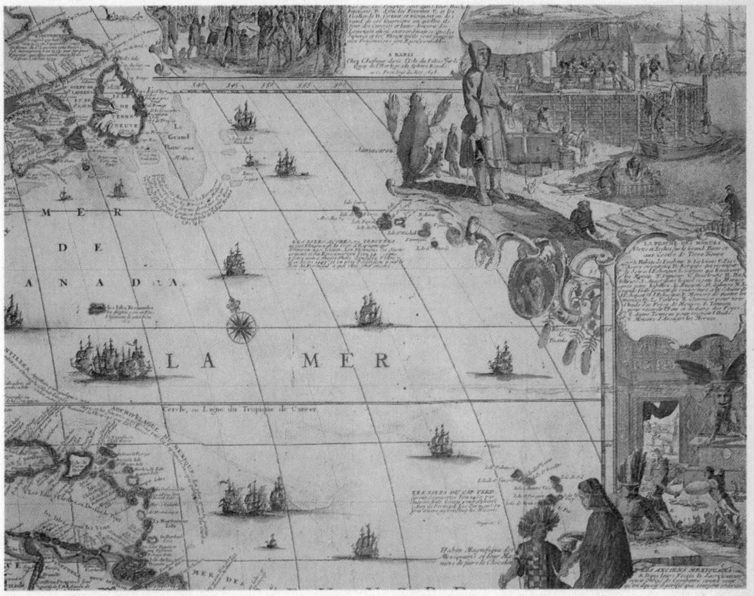

A look at beaver habitat on [Great Lakes] (left) and cod-fishing off the shores of Newfoundland (right) as represented in these two 1698 maps.

1700 (1700-1719)

Quebec, July 1700. Six Iroquois chiefs arrive to announce their desire for peace with the French. Governor de Callières lets Father Bruyas, Chabert de Joncaire and Paul Le Moyne de Maricourt accompany the chiefs to Iroquois country to speak for peace.

Quebec, September 1700. The three French peace ambassadors to the Iroquois return with 19 delegates representing all the Iroquois nations except the Mohawks. They also have 13 French prisoners liberated by the Iroquois as a goodwill gesture. Peace terms are agreed on in a meeting between the French, Iroquois, Abenakis, Hurons and Ottawas.

France, May 31, 1701. Louis XIV issues a dispatch to Callières and Champigny stating his intention to found a settlement at the mouth of the Mississippi in order to slow down the advance of the English on the continent.

France, Oct. 17, 1702. Augustin Le Gardeur de Courtemanche is granted an exclusive 10-year trading and fishing concession for the north shore of the Gulf of St. Lawrence and the coast of Labrador. It paves the way for French settlement of Labrador.

Newfoundland, Aug. 29, 1704. Jean Léger de La Grange leads a French attack against the English port of Bonavista. They burn and capture ships.

Newfoundland, 1704. Le Gardeur de Courtemanche records the massacre of whales by fishermen. He finds "a quantity of bones cast up on the coast like sticks of wood ... the remains of more than two or three thousand whales."

New France, 1705. Le Gardeur de Courtemanche reports that off the north coast of the Gulf of St. Lawrence whales are "in such abundance ... they could be harpooned from the rocks."

Quebec, Sept. 7, 1705. Jacques Raudot arrives with his son Antoine-Denis. They were appointed joint Intendants of New France.

Quebec, May 6, 1708. Bishop Laval, the first Bishop of Quebec, dies.

France, March 20, 1714. An ordinance reiterates the rule that vessels going to Canada and the West Indies must carry *engagés* – indentured workers – on a speculative basis to meet the need for farm laborers in the colonies.

Buffalo hunt demands courage, skill

1700

PRAIRIES – "My grandfather, we are glad to see you, and happy that you are not come in a shameful manner, for you have brought plenty of your young men with you. Be not angry with us; we are obliged to destroy you to make ourselves live." So the Cree welcome the buffalo they corral into pounds for slaughter.

Like all Plains Indians, the Crees' main livelihood is the buffalo hunt. It demands great skill and courage. The usual method is to corral and then kill the huge beasts. Luck is important. So is craftiness. Sometimes the Indians drape wolf skins over their heads and howl, or they bawl like buffalo calves so they can approach the edge of the herd and kill off individuals.

The hunt also requires great endurance. Buffalo roam over great distances which their hunters must cover on foot. This limits their ability to carry large supplies of food, for they have only dogs harnessed to *travois* or wooden litters to transport their belongings.

Recently rumors have circulated about strange animals owned by the Snake Indians to the south. The Snake ride on top of them, and use them to carry much heavier loads than dogs can. However, few Blackfoot or Cree have ever seen such an animal, and still rely on traditional hunting methods to ensure an adequate supply of buffalo meat.

Plains Indians stalking buffalo on foot and in large groups.

Penguins perishing at hands of traders

1700

ACADIA – Spearbills, North American penguins, as big and as tasty as geese, are well on their way to extinction. Fur traders on Hudson Bay have killed thousands. Despite multiplying rapidly, penguins are victims of their own innocence. Heaps of the friendly seabirds, which cannot fly, are clubbed to death or simply driven up planks onto boats.

Governor Philippe de Vaudreuil.

Siege forces French to give up the fort

Oct. 13, 1710

PORT-ROYAL, Acadia – Drums beating and colors flying, French soldiers today surrendered Port Royal after being held under siege for one week by 1,500 New England militiamen supported by seven warships and nearly 30 transport vessels. Port Royal, returned to France in 1697, is the colony of Acadia's administrative headquarters. Now England again controls all Acadia.

Col. Francis Nicholson is particularly pleased at his success because New Englanders failed to retake the Acadian stronghold in 1704 and 1707. Port Royal's pirates and privateers have harassed New England shipping for years.

The commander praised French Gov. Daniel d'Auger de Subercase and his garrison for their courage and spirit. Accepting the keys from the governor, Nicholson noted that when he first called on the French to surrender, the governor replied defiantly he should "come and get the keys of the fort himself." Nicholson has renamed the settlement Annapolis Royal.

Law makes licences a must for doctors

July 7, 1710

NEW FRANCE – To cut down on the growing number of medical abuses in New France, Intendant Jacques Raudot has issued a proclamation penalizing all unlicensed doctors.

The number of medical practitioners in the colony has also been growing and there are many barber-surgeons and midwives. But there are charlatans as well.

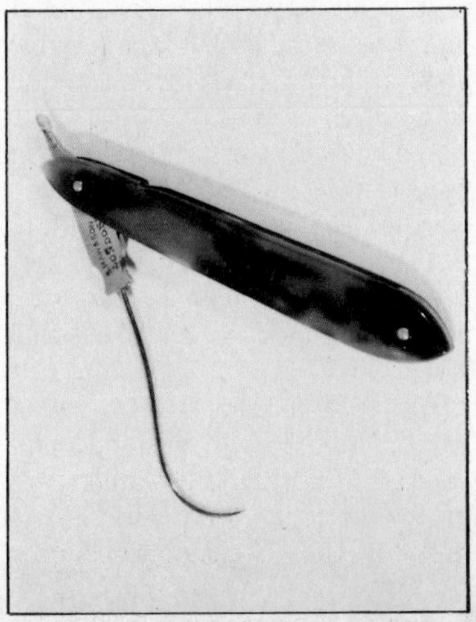

Tools used by New France doctors.

France protecting industries at home

June 14, 1704

VILLE-MARIE [Montreal] – French authorities continue to subordinate the economic progress of the colonies to that of France. Witness the declaration King Louis XIV sent to Ville-Marie Gov. Philippe de Rigaud de Vaudreuil today. The royal document reads: "Anything that could compete with the manufactories in the kingdom must never be made in the colonies, which on the contrary could not be used too much to supply the materials necessary to the manufactories in the kingdom."

The policy underscores the theory that the French government can strengthen the nation's economic interests by protecting industries at home. It also supports the belief that France's main reason for developing the colonies is not to preach the gospel and convert Indians to Christianity, but to gain wealth.

Habitants in valley filling up on bread

1706

NEW FRANCE – Settlers in the St. Lawrence Valley are eating a lot of wheat – mostly in the form of bread. Intendant Jacques Raudot says the average *habitant* of the region eats two pounds of bread per day – and that's a half-pound more than soldier's daily rations of 1.5 pounds.

The diet of rural settlers is restricted. There is a limited variety of grains and vegetables, livestock products – especially milk, butter and eggs – salt pork, some game and fish, passenger pigeons and eels, preserved in salt.

Cabbage, turnip or onion soup seasoned with salt pork or eel eaten with lots of bread is the daily fare in hard times. Many of the poorer *habitants* in the colony survive on a diet of little more than dry bread and water.

Even the well-to-do eat a lot of bread. Bakeries in New France are stocked with an assortment of breads – white, light brown and dark brown, depending on the amount of bran. White bread is reported to be the favorite.

Iroquois leaders meet Queen Anne

Chief Ho Nee Yeath Taw No Row.

Chief Etow Oh Koaw.

Chief Tee Yee Neen Ho Ga Row.

Chief Sa Ga Yeath Qua Pieth Tow.

April 1710

LONDON, England – Four Iroquois leaders were greeted here with regal pomp by the great white monarch, Queen Anne. The leaders, representing the Five Nations confederacy in North America, are in London to appeal to the queen to bolster the British colonies' war effort against the French.

The queen received her guests warmly and presented them with the best in English finery – magnificent scarlet robes edged in gold. The impressed leaders sported the garments over their traditional costumes of skins, beads, feathers and furs. Once the visitors had draped themselves in their new outfits, a portrait artist was summoned to capture the occasion on canvas.

Then it was down to business. The four Iroquois leaders, who live south of Lake Ontario, are allied with Queen Anne's armies in the bitter struggle with the French for control of settlements and the riches of North America. The tribes control trade in the Mohawk and Hudson rivers area and are becoming concerned about French incursions into their territory. They told Queen Anne that if she did not send supplies and reinforcements to her military outposts, she risked losing England's hard-won northern colonies.

The queen seemed impressed by the Indians' pleas and assured them she would meet their requests for a stronger military presence.

Intendant says kids are lacking respect

1708

NEW FRANCE – Intendant Jacques Raudot says children in New France have developed what he calls a "hard and ferocious character" and adds that that they no longer show respect toward their parents, superiors or parish priests.

Raudot says overindulgent parents and the influence of the native culture on *habitants* has meant children never had a proper education. To restrain the licentiousness of youngsters in New France, Raudot has proposed establishing schoolmasters in each parish.

French, Iroquois sign historic peace pact

July 1701

VILLE-MARIE [Montreal] – Feasts throughout the town of Ville-Marie marked the signing of an historic peace pact between Governor-General Louis-Hector de Callières of New France and the Five Nations. The treaty ends almost a century of hostilities between the Iroquois and French settlers and their native allies.

The accord was not won easily. The troublesome issue of prisoners of war took Callières more than two years to resolve. All parties wanted their warriors returned but not all the Iroquois were willing to release theirs. Many French and Indian captives are so integrated into Iroquois tribes that they are considered family members, and refuse to return home. Indian prisoners also constitute a significant part of Iroquois military strength.

To get the Five Nations to agree to serious talks, Callières had to counter English claims that the Iroquois were under their jurisdiction and couldn't sign any treaty without their approval. Callières simply ignored the English and dealt directly with the Iroquois who maintained that they were in no way vassals of the English.

The treaty document is to be presented to Louis XIV shortly.

Tuscaroras flee to Iroquois country

1714

NORTH CAROLINA – Each month more Tuscarora families arrive as refugees in Iroquois country. Only a year ago, this North Carolina Indian tribe lost the final battle in its three-year war against the settlers and their Indian allies from South Carolina. The victors have killed several hundred Tuscaroras and sold more than 400 into slavery. The power of the Tuscarora nation has been broken.

One prominent colonist openly admits the whites had "cheated these Indians in trading, and would not allow them to hunt near their plantations, and under that pretence took away their game, arms and ammunition." The whites also seized the Tuscaroras' lands.

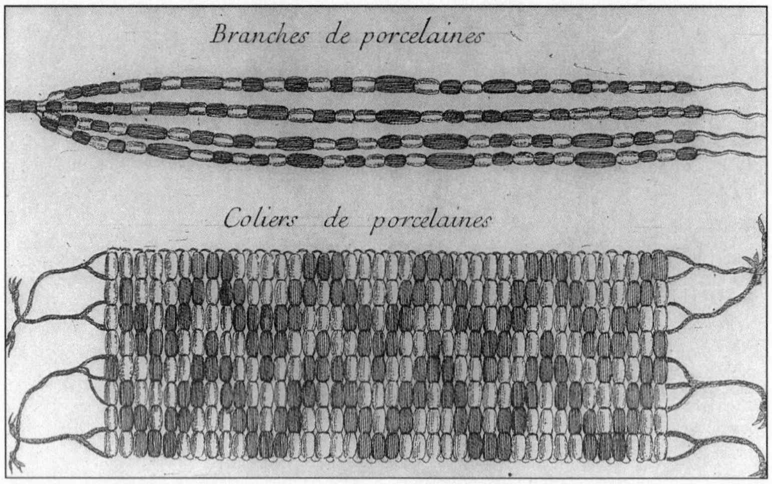

The wampum porcelain necklace and belt symbolize Five Nations unity.

The Tuscarora War began in 1711, when the Tuscaroras rose up, plundering and burning settlers' homes, and killing whites. The whites had no native allies and were unfamiliar with the Indians' guerrilla war techniques. Desperate, they enlisted the Catawba and other Siouan tribes in South Carolina, promising them cheap trade goods if the campaign proved successful. Traditional enemies of the Iroquois to the north, the Siouan tribes willingly struck against the Tuscarora, another Iroquoian-speaking group, and won the war against them.

Now the Tuscaroras want to join the Five Nations. This confederacy – made up of the Seneca, Cayuga, Oneida, Onondaga and Mohawk tribes in the northern part of [New York state] – was created in the late 15th century. The Iroquois use the name "longhouse" to describe their union under the Tree of Peace, a great white pine with roots extending to the four corners of the earth, so that all nations of goodwill can follow the roots to their source and take shelter.

The Seneca are known as the "keepers of the western door," and the Mohawk as the "keepers of the eastern door." Located in the centre, the Onondagas are the Five Keepers, or the hosts of the Confederacy's Grand Councils. The Iroquois believe any tribe which refuses to join the others under the Tree of Peace is evil and hostile. The purpose of the league is to keep peace among nations.

Chipewyan woman turns peacemaker

1713

CANADA – A Chipewyan woman has gone from prisoner to peacemaker and inspired hope that an end to the bitter Cree-Chipewyan rivalry over the fur trade is at hand. After escaping her Cree captors this year, Thanadelthur met Hudson Bay traders who recognized her value as a link between themselves and the fur-wealthy Indians. The result was a Cree-Chipewyan peace mission. The talks stalled, but Thanadelthur's determination carried the day after her constant haranguing forced negotiators to resume talks.

Chipewyan woman, Thanadelthur.

French troops and allies outfox the Fox

1716

MIDWEST [Wisconsin] – A makeshift army composed of spirited *coureurs de bois* and native volunteers has temporarily halted the problems the Fox tribe was causing the fur trade out west. Hoping to retain their status as middlemen in the trade, the Fox were preventing the French from making contact with the Dakota, the Fox's neighbors and enemies. Friction with the French led to open warfare.

After a Ville-Marie expedition sent to deal with the Fox last year failed, a second army made up of some 400 *coureurs de bois* and 400 native volunteers was put under the command of Louis de La Porte de Louvigny this year. It quickly made its way from Ville-Marie to the Fox stronghold in Baie des Puants [Green Bay], where it attacked and forced the natives to agree to terms of a peace pact.

Fox Indian chief.

Louvigny is no stranger to taking on the New World natives. He has distinguished himself against them on several expeditions since arriving here in 1683. His latest exploits against the Fox tribe have earned Louvigny a great deal of praise in New France – not to mention a hefty reward.

Treacherous waters claim 1,000 at sea

Aug. 22, 1711

SEPT-ILES, New France – Dressed in a nightshirt and slippers, British admiral Sir Hovenden Walker looked on helplessly this evening from the deck of his flagship as more than 1,000 sailors and soldiers on seven transport vessels under his command slipped forever beneath treacherous waters at the mouth of the St. Lawrence River.

Walker, leading the largest attack force in British naval history facing the French settlements of the St. Lawrence, inadvertently led his fleet of 72 ships and 12,000 men into shallow water near Sept-Iles. Blaming thick fog, high winds and incomplete maps, Walker said he had no idea his ships were heading for disaster. He will ask for a council of war with his superiors to determine his next move.

Colony feels effects of Treaty of Utrecht

April 4, 1713

CANADA – While the Treaty of Utrecht ends the War of Spanish Succession in Europe, it also has some far-reaching effects here in Canada.

Under the treaty, France recognizes English sovereignty over Hudson Bay, Newfoundland and Acadia. France receives Ile St-Jean [Prince Edward Island] and all islands of the St. Lawrence River and Gulf of St. Lawrence.

The French also retain valuable fishing rights in Newfoundland. The treaty allows France "the right to catch fish and to dry them on land on that part of the Newfoundland coast which stretches from Cape Bonaventure to the northern point of the island, and from thence running down by the western side of Point Riche."

Captured Inuit girls discuss their people

1719

LABRADOR – Through his acquaintance with two Inuit girls, fur trader François Martel de Brouague has become the first European to describe Inuit culture in detail. The girls – one's name is Acoutsina and the other's is not known – were captured in a skirmish two years ago and live with Brouague and his stepmother. Brouague has kept a very detailed account of the conversations he has had with them.

While the girls work as family helpers, they are also considered members of the family. Acoutsina has learned French, which she uses to tell her masters about Inuit customs and traditional legends. She also told the French how certain Europeans had settled among them. One was a shipwrecked sailor called "good old Nicolas" the administration at Quebec tried to get in touch with.

Brouague is the stepson of Augustin Le Gardeur de Courtemanche, the commandant on the coast of Labrador who held an exclusive trading concession in Labrador for 13 years until he died in 1717. Courtemanche was on good terms with the Indians in Labrador but not the Inuit, who interfered with French fishing interests.

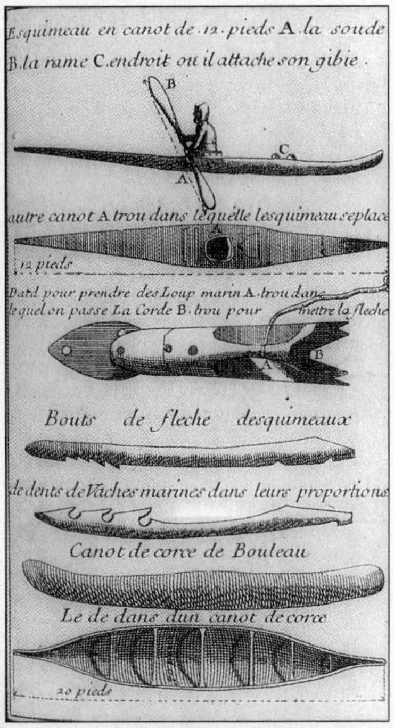

Inuit transportation and tools.

Value of "card money" slashed in half

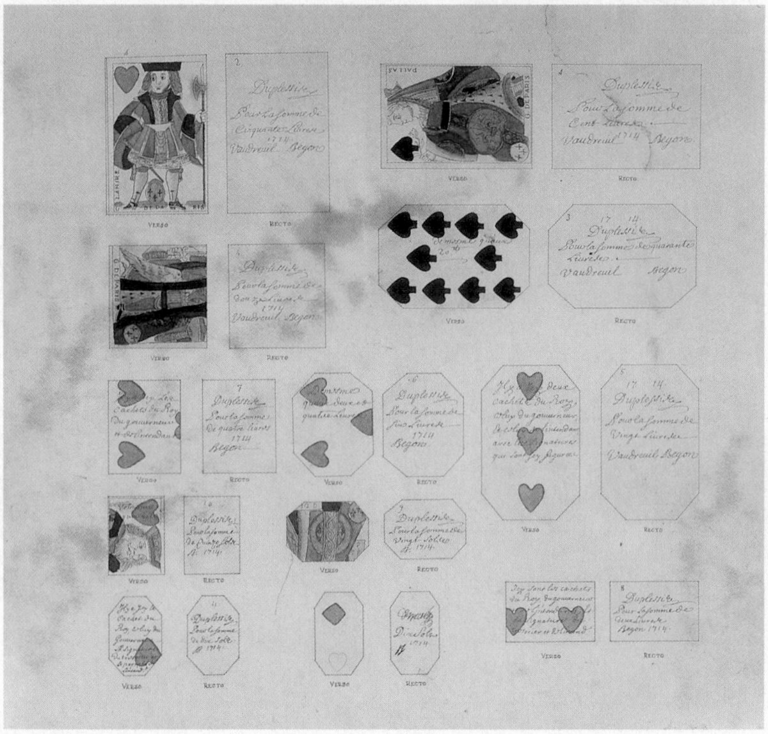

New France authorities are redeeming card money for half its face value.

1719

NEW FRANCE – Card money – the imaginative and ingenious device Jacques de Meulles inaugurated in 1685 when he was intendant of New France – is now being redeemed for just half its face value.

De Meulles invented card money when he needed funds to pay the troops. He took a pack of playing cards and turned them into the first paper money to circulate in the colony by writing an amount on the back with his signature.

He also declared that the cards would be redeemed as soon as ships arrived from France with the annual supply of funds. Until recently, card money had to be accepted at face value.

Acadians saying no to the British oath

Jan. 13, 1716

ACADIA – Despite pressure from English authorities, Acadians in the settlements of Grand Pré and Beaubassin have once again refused to sign an oath of allegiance to the English crown.

Acadians say the French and English governments are negotiating their future. Any declaration of allegiance, they note, could jeopardize negotiations.

In Annapolis Royal, 36 Acadians have signed a conditional oath, valid "as long as I shall be in Acadia or Nova Scotia." While Lt.-Gov. Thomas Caulfield said the conditional oath helps, the government will continue to press Acadians to sign an unconditional oath.

French erect string of northern posts

1717

NEW FRANCE – The French are in the midst of erecting a series of northern trading posts in New France to act as bases for exploration and to strengthen their position in the colony.

One of the colony's best canoeists, Zacharie Robutel de La Noue, is in the governor's service trying to discover the great inland sea linked to the Pacific. De La Noue set out in July with three canoes and orders "to establish the first post on the Kanastigoya River at the western end of Lake Superior, [Thunder Bay], after which he is to go to Takamamisson in the direction of Lac des Christinaux to set up a second, and through the Indians to obtain the necessary information for setting up the third at Lac des Assenipoelle."

De La Noue's past exploits in the colony have earned him a great deal of praise in New France. He's led or escorted several expeditions into native territory and his success played a big part in his being selected for his current assignment in northern Canada.

The governor of New France, Philippe de Rigaud de Vaudreuil, once referred to de La Noue as "a very worthy person and one of the bravest officers in the colony."

Wife and four children of Denis Riverin, Sovereign Council member.

1720 (1720-1729)

Quebec, 1720. Philippe de Rigaud de Vaudreuil, governor of New France, orders the construction of three trading forts [along Lake Ontario] to block trading links between the English settlements in New York and Indians around the Great Lakes.

Newfoundland, June 1720. The feared pirate Black Bart (Bartholomew Roberts) enters the port of Trepassey. His ship, the *Royal Rover*, is identified by a huge black flag with a white skeleton on it.

St. John's Island, Aug. 23, 1720. Some 300 French settlers land at Port La Joie [Charlottetown] to colonize the island [Prince Edward Island].

Hudson's Bay Territory, Aug. 22, 1722. A Hudson's Bay Company expedition to explore the west coast of Hudson's Bay arrives at York Factory after finding traces of James Knight's missing expedition at Marble Island.

Newfoundland, Aug. 29, 1723. Pirate John Phillips and five other men seize a trading schooner in St. Pierre harbor. They sign a set of pirate articles once they are out at sea. The articles provide for the death penalty for those who steal from the company's loot, or molest or rape a woman, and compensation for those who lose limbs in battle.

St. John's Island, 1724. A plague of mice (probably meadow voles) devastates the crops of settlers on [Prince Edward Island].

Arctic, 1725. Danish sailor Vitus Bering is the first European to discover the strait separating Asia and North America [Bering Strait]. Peter the Great of Russia commissioned him to find the point where Siberia meets Alaska.

Quebec, May 18, 1725. Governor Rigaud de Vaudreuil says the *habitants* of the colony have been infected with a "spirit of mutiny and independence."

Quebec, Dec. 26, 1727. Jean-Baptiste de la Croix de Chevrières de Saint-Vallier, bishop of Quebec for the last 42 years, dies at the age of 74.

St. Lawrence River, Sept. 1, 1729. The ship *Eléphant* hits a rock and is wrecked in the lower St. Lawrence. Gilles Hocquart, the new intendant of New France, and Pierre-Herman Dosquet, the new bishop, are both aboard and survive the disaster.

Death is penalty for dumping tots

Feb. 6, 1722

QUEBEC CITY – Intendant Michel Bégon today made legal in New France Henri II's 1708 royal declaration dealing with the timeless problem of abandoned babies. Bégon asked parish priests to read it every three months to remind their congregations about the death penalty for women who conceal their pregnancies, then leave their babies to perish.

While conceiving children out of wedlock is not officially a crime in New France, unmarried pregnant women still face public persecution and go to great lengths to hide illegitimate births.

Often they avoid baptizing their babies, to keep the birth a secret. They thereby risk allowing the infants to die unbaptized, a worse crime than illegitimacy in the eyes of Bégon and the church.

Women also ship illegitimate babies out of the colony to live with poor widows or Indians. The widows often can't afford a wet nurse, and feed orphans cow's milk cut with water.

The midwives whom unmarried mothers use to assist in their deliveries seldom break confidence with their clients, who thus escape detection.

Fighting families disturb the peace

1721

NEW FRANCE – The streets of towns such as Montreal, Quebec and Trois-Rivières are sometimes the setting for some of the most shocking family brawls you'd ever want to witness. Husbands, wives, fathers, mothers, sisters and brothers have been known to make a spectacle of themselves in altercations that are in full view of their fellow-colonists on public streets.

Family members have been witnessed taking their differences outdoors and going at it like a pack of angry wolves, tearing out hair, grabbing throats, kicking, pulling and scratching. At night, their cries and howls can fill the air, sounding just like the wild beasts in the forests and woods.

New France settlements keep growing

Montreal is one of New France's oldest, and one of the colony's busiest ports. The island of Montreal is also the centre of the fur trade.

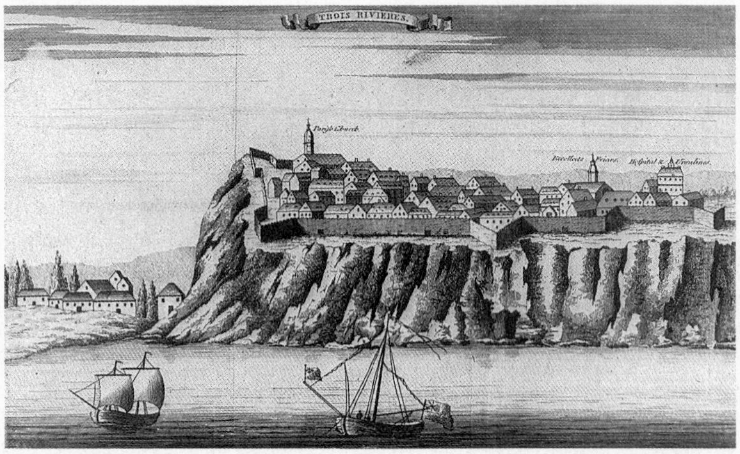

View of Trois-Rivières shows the parish church, the Récollet monastery and the Ursulines' hospital. The city is between Montreal and Quebec.

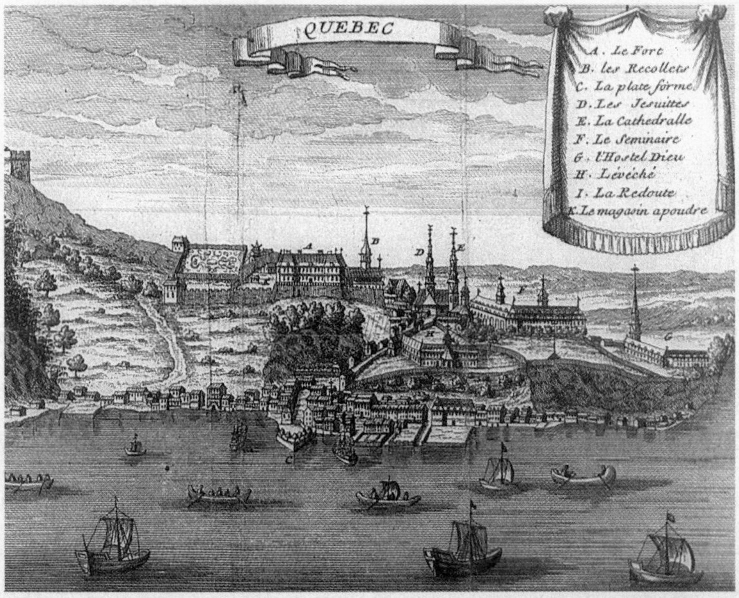

Quebec City from across river. This view shows city's major landmarks.

Acadians take oath of allegiance freely

1727

ANNAPOLIS, N.S. – After years of objecting, Acadians in the district of Annapolis have agreed to take the oath of allegiance to the British Crown freely. The deal they agreed to with Lt.-Gov. Lawrence Armstrong exempts them from taking up arms in case of war. However, Acadians of Minas and Beaubassin on Chignecto Bay have refused to sign the deal, maintaining the governor has no authority in the land and no power to administer oaths.

Acadians must take oath.

Pirate decapitated as prisoners rebel

April 17, 1724

ATLANTIC – Mutinous crew members of John Phillips have tossed the decapitated body of the feared pirate into the sea. Three days ago, Phillips seized a fishing vessel off the coast of New England. Built recently and undergoing minor construction as it sailed for the Grand Banks, the ship was far superior to his own, which he gave to the fishermen.

Phillips forced several captured crewmen to complete unfinished work on the stolen ship. Today, using tools as weapons and aided by rebellious members of the pirate crew, the prisoners recaptured the ship, butchering Phillips and most of his supporters. The murdered man, who had emigrated from England to Newfoundland, turned to piracy less than a year ago after failing to find work as a shipwright.

Newfoundland gets naval governors

April 30, 1729

NEWFOUNDLAND – The British government has decided that in the future convoy commanders will be the new governors of Newfoundland. With few exceptions, ever since the 1650s a naval fleet has been sent to Newfoundland to protect the cod fishery.

In the beginning, commanders had little official authority over the fishing admirals, who jealously looked back on the Western Charter for their authorization. But in 1699, a parliamentary act dealing with Newfoundland allowed parties dissatisfied with rulings of the fishing admirals to appeal decisions to the convoy commanders. This, in turn, gave the convoy commanders more authority.

Since fishing admirals and convoy commanders live in England over the winter, no one with authority is left in Newfoundland to maintain law and order in the colony during those months. The new naval governors will only serve in Newfoundland in the summer. Their responsibilities will include appointing justices of the peace and constables.

Cod fishing, curing and drying.

Inuit show Kelsey relics of missing ships

Aug. 9, 1721

YORK FACTORY, Hudson Bay Territory – Officials here say Inuit have shown Gov. Henry Kelsey some relics of the lost expedition of former governor James Knight. The Knight expedition – whose fate has intrigued Hudson's Bay Company men here, but not, it seems, the directors in London – left Gravesend on June 4, 1719, with orders to explore part of the west coast of Hudson Bay and to claim minerals for the company. Until now, nothing has been heard of the ships – *Albany,* a 100-ton frigate, and the 40-ton sloop *Discovery* – or of Knight and the 39 men sailing with him.

Former colleagues of the 80-year-old Knight – he was in charge of company posts on the bay for many years – wonder why no real search has been ordered. That is why they are so interested in the objects the Inuit have shown Kelsey near Marble Island. There was no love lost between Knight and Kelsey. Indeed, when Knight went to London to seek approval for his expedition he complained about the behavior of Kelsey.

Kelsey left Churchill on July 17 to explore the western shore of Hudson Bay. Ironically, Knight established the post at Churchill as a jumping-off point for trading with the Chipewyans and for his search for the deposits of copper and gold described to him by the Indian slavewoman Thanadelthur. Now everyone here is awaiting news from Kelsey's party, wondering if there is a chance some members of the Knight expedition are still alive.

Bishop's new rules target lay teachers

1727

QUEBEC CITY – Quebec's Bishop Jean-Baptiste de la Croix de Chevrières de St-Vallier has issued a new ordinance prohibiting unmarried lay teachers from instructing members of the opposite sex in rural schools run by the Catholic church. Once run by missionaries and then by parish priests, there are more and more lay teachers in the rural schools of New France.

In addition, the bishop has instructed priests in the colony to make sure teachers are moral individuals. And, the priests have also been told to make sure parents are sending their children to school. Most children, badly needed on the farm, only go to school briefly to prepare for their first communion.

Yankee militia attacks Abenaki village; Jesuit among fatalities

Sept. 3, 1724

ABENAKI COUNTRY, north of New England – Skirmishes between New Englanders and the French-allied Abenaki natives reached a bloody climax today. Almost 30 people were killed as New England militiamen raided the Abenaki settlement of Norridgewock. Among the dead is Father Sébastien Rale, a Jesuit missionary.

Rale was a strong Abenaki ally in the Indians' fight to resist colonial encroachment on their lands. His death is another in a war that has taken many lives on both sides.

Father Sébastien Rale, a Jesuit missionary, is among those killed in raid.

1730 (1730-1739)

Nova Scotia, 1730. Governor Richard Philipps gets the Acadians at Annapolis, Minas, and Chignecto to sign an oath of allegiance to Britain. In return for their oath, he probably promises the more intractable Acadians they will not have to bear arms.

Quebec, Feb. 8, 1734. Intendant Gilles Hocquart issues an ordinance discouraging slaves from escaping.

Quebec, Sept. 6, 1734. Famous physician Michel Sarrazin dies of typhus while living with his family in poverty.

New France, 1734. Dairy products are an essential part of the diet of colonists. Father Navières, parish priest at St-Anne-de-Beaupré, says that milk is to the habitants here what chestnuts are to the peasants of Limousin.

Hudson's Bay Territory, June 18, 1735. Jean-Baptiste Gaultier de La Vérendrye writes to Governor Beauharnois: "I have established a fort at Lac Ouinipigon [Lake Winnipeg], five leagues up the Rivière Rouge." It is called Fort Maurepas.

Quebec, September 1738. Esther Brandeau, 20, is the first Jew to set foot in New France. She is disguised as a ship's boy. When her identity is revealed by chance, she is arrested and taken to the Hôpital Général. According to official policy, non-Catholic immigrants to the colony must be converted or deported.

Ile-Royale, Sept. 22, 1738. Abbé Jean-Louis Le Loutre leaves Ile-Royale [Cape Breton Island] to take up duties as missionary to the Micmacs at the Shubenacadie mission, a vast territory extending from Cape Sable to Chedabucto Bay in the north and [Cumberland Strait] in the west.

Prairies, Dec. 3, 1738. French explorer Pierre Gaultier de Varennes et de La Vérendrye reaches the main Mandan village [near Sanish, North Dakota] after a 2,415-kilometre journey from the east. He is accompanied by his sons, Louis-Joseph and François, and 600 Assiniboines. Louis-Joseph views the Missouri River, which the elder La Vérendrye thinks is the famous River of the West leading to the Pacific.

Quebec, 1739. Pierre Hévé opens the first café in the colony in the Lower Town, imitating Parisian fashions.

Horses change the buffalo hunt

Autumn 1739

PRAIRIES – With the acquisition of horses, many Blackfoot Indians on the [Prairies] are abandoning the surround technique for hunting buffalo. Horsemen have replaced warriors on foot in the drive and they lure buffalo into pounds or over cliffs. Mounted hunters are also beginning to rush straightaway into buffalo herds, singling out an animal, riding beside it on a horse and then killing it at close range with two or three arrows from their bows.

The use of horses has made it easier for Prairie Indians to hunt buffalo.

Horses also allow the Blackfoot to travel further after the herds, and to transport more supplies. They can now carry back far more buffalo meat and hides to their tribes.

The Blackfoot seek five qualities in their buffalo horses: the ability to retain speed over a distance of several kilometres; the ability to respond quickly to commands; the gift of being able to move quickly alongside a buffalo and the agility to stay clear of the buffalo and its horns; the ability to run swiftly without stumbling over uneven ground; and the lack of fear of a stampeding buffalo.

It takes great patience to train a horse to run close alongside a buffalo, and a trained one is worth several simple riding or pack animals. While the Blackfoot are just now beginning to use horses for hunting buffalo, the animals have been a valuable resource in Canada for many years, particularly in the agricultural field, where they haul plows and other heavy loads.

Louisbourg lighthouse lit for first time

April 1, 1733

LOUISBOURG, Ile-Royale – In a quiet ceremony in Louisbourg today, Ile-Royale's [Cape Breton Island] first lighthouse was lit. The light is fuelled by coal from mines at nearby Morien and Spanish River. It's visible six leagues at sea, and is expected to save many lives on this rocky, windswept coast.

The lighthouse is North America's first fireproof concrete building, constructed with cement made from limestone burned in local kilns and slaked for a year. The structure took two years to build.

A round, castle-like tower, the lighthouse is 198 meters high, with four turrets. The walls at its base are 1.8 meters thick, and lightkeepers ascend the tower by means of a circular stairway.

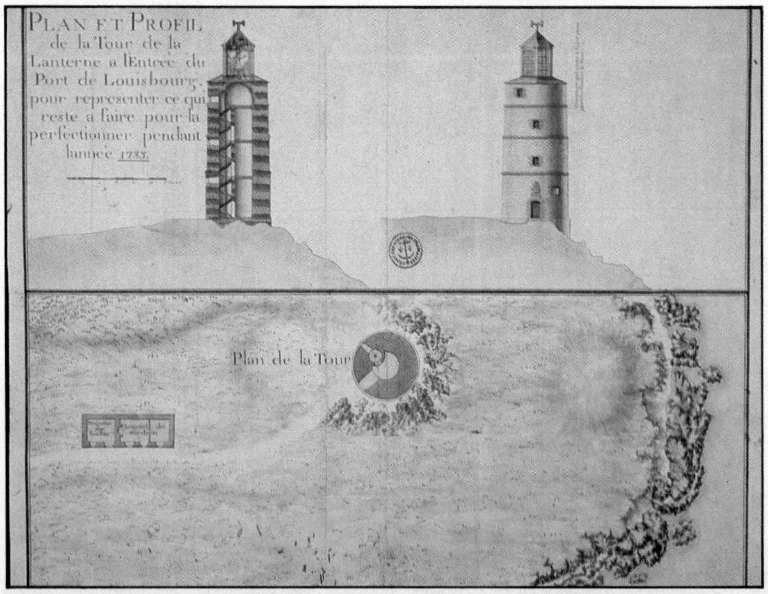

Louisbourg lighthouse is North America's first fireproof concrete building.

Fortress finished, right down to bells

1735

LOUISBOURG, Ile-Royale – Twenty-five years after the first stones were laid, the magnificent fortress of Louisbourg is complete, right down to the bells. The French say it is the strongest fortress in America, and consider it impregnable, despite modern military wisdom that argues against the defence value of forts.

Louisbourg was built as Louis XV's monument to his great-grandfather Louis XIV, the "*roi soleil.*" He invested enormous sums in it, but construction was plagued by problems. Officials embezzled much of the money. For want of civilian laborers, overworked soldiers had to do the actual building.

Louisbourg's fortified walls encircle 57 acres, divided into squares by streets with French royal names. The Château St. Louis of Citadelle, a massive, slate-roofed, four-storey stone building, houses the Governor's residence and the garrison's barracks. It is entered by a drawbridge. Shops, homes, inns and chapels never exceed two storeys, so summer air can ciculate and blow away the stink of drying codfish.

Slavewoman hangs for setting big blaze

June 21, 1734

MONTREAL – A black slavewoman believed to have been planning an escape from Montreal with her lover was hanged today for setting fire to her master's home. Marie-Joseph-Angélique, the slave of François Poulin de Francheville of Saint-Paul, set fire to the Francheville house the night of April 10 to register her protest against slavery in the most dramatic fashion she could imagine. The fire spread, quickly turning into a major blaze that destroyed 46 homes and the Hôtel-Dieu, convent and church.

Marie-Joseph was sentenced on June 4 to make honorable amends, to have her hand cut off and to be burnt alive. When she appealed the case, the sentence was deemed too harsh and reduced: she was to be taken in a garbage cart to the church door, where she was to make a formal confession of her guilt. Then, she was to be hanged and her body burned. Today, this all happened. Before the hanging, Marie-Joseph was tortured. After, her ashes were cast to the winds.

The mother of three small boys, Marie-Joseph supposedly set fire to the Francheville home to cover her escape to New England with her lover Claude Thibault, a white man. She apparently had reason to believe Francheville's widow had plans to sell her.

La Vérendrye constructs Fort la Reine

La Vérendrye and his men go west.

1739

FORT LA REINE, Far West – Pierre Gaultier de Varennes et de La Vérendrye has re-established Fort la Reine [Portage la Prairie, Man.] on the Assiniboine River seven days travel west of the junction with the Red. La Vérendrye had established a fort by the same name last October, only it was east of the present post. It was from this base that he began his trip into Dakota territory to meet the Mandans.

La Vérendrye says there is a substantial advantage in the new site: it is only a brief portage from Fort la Reine to Lake Manitoba, an entranceway to the north.

Intendant's ruling: native slavery OK

May 29, 1733

NEW FRANCE – Intendant Gilles Hocquart has upheld the right of colonists to buy and sell natives as slaves. This practice was recently challenged by a fur trader whose native slave was confiscated as payment for a debt, and then sold to a third party. The trader argued against the transaction on the grounds that his slave was a Christian. Hocquart, however, has ruled the confiscation and sale were legitimate. Though slavery has existed in New France for more than a century, it is not widespread and is limited mainly to domestic service.

Sioux slaughter 21 in attack on French

June 6, 1736

MASSACRE ISLAND, [Ont.] – A wandering band of Sioux last night attacked and killed Jean-Baptiste La Vérendrye, Father Jean-Pierre Aulneau and 19 voyageurs. All were members of the La Vérendrye party, based at Fort St. Charles, in the Lake of the Woods. The heads of La Vérendrye and Aulneau were taken as trophies.

On route to Michilimackinack, the slain men travelled only one day before making camp. It is believed the Sioux are angry that members of the La Vérendrye party had been giving ammunition to other tribes.

Company formed to prop up mining effort

St-Maurice seigneury, owned by François Poulin, is rich in mineral deposits.

Jan. 16, 1733

ST-MAURICE, New France – François Poulin de Francheville formed a company here today he hopes will ensure the development of mineral resources at his St-Maurice seigneury. It's long been Francheville's wish to mine iron deposits in St-Maurice, and in 1730 he was given a 20-year monopoly – as requested the year before – to do just that. Francheville also got the right to exploit cultivated and uncultivated lands adjacent to his own. While he was allowed to simply expropriate uncultivated property, he had to reimburse owners for cultivated land.

The mining project was well under way in 1732 when Francheville realized he needed more funds to bring it to fruition. His request for a loan was granted this month, the same time Francheville decided to form a company to benefit from the favoritism of the colony's upper administrators. His associates include his brother Pierre Poulin and Bricault de Valmur, secretary to Intendant Gilles Hocquart.

D'Youville forms group to help the poor

Dec. 31, 1737

MONTREAL – A group of women led by Marie-Marguerite d'Youville today founded an association dedicated to helping the poor. The group is secular, but Marguerite and her three friends took vows of poverty, chastity and obedience in pursuit of their cause.

The creation of the group ends years of effort on Marguerite's part. Since the death of her husband in 1730, she has devoted herself to prayer and easing the lives of the poor under the direction of her spiritual advisers, Le Pape Du Lescöat and Normant Du Faradon. Just last month, she took Françoise Auzon, an elderly blind woman, into her home to care for her.

Old Grey Nunnery in Montreal, home of secular group that helps the poor.

Hudson's Bay Territory, June 1742. Joseph La France, son of a French fur trader and an Ojibwa woman, reaches the Hudson's Bay Company post at York Factory with a large band of Indians and a cargo of furs. He set out from New France in 1739 to trade with the English at Hudson Bay, after the French denied him a trading licence. En route, he explored Lac Ouinipigon [Lake Winnipeg], Lac des Prairies [Lakes Manitoba and Winnipegosis], and the lower Paskoya [Saskatchewan] River.

Northwest, January 1743. Louis-Joseph Gaultier de La Vérendrye, in search of the western sea, joins a war party organized by the Gens de l'Arc tribe aginst the Gens du Serpent. La Vérendrye hears stories about the Rocky Mountains, but does not reach them. The war party does not find their enemy.

New France, May 1, 1743. The ironworks plant at St-Maurice becomes a state enterprise due to the company's indebtedness to the Crown.

Ile-Royale, Dec. 27, 1744. French soldiers and Swiss mercenaries mutiny at the Fortress of Louisbourg [on Cape Breton] over poor conditions. There is anarchy at the fortress.

Ile-Royale, May 11, 1745. A large force of New Englanders and English arrives off Louisbourg to begin a siege of the fortress.

Atlantic Ocean, May 14, 1747. English ships defeat a French fleet led by La Jonquière sent to recapture Louisbourg. The French lose 800 men and six of their warships are captured.

Aix-la-Chapelle, France, Oct. 18, 1748. The peace of Aix-la-Chapelle ends the War of the Austrian Succession. France and England exchange colonial outposts as part of the treaty, including Louisbourg, which is returned to the French.

New France, June 1, 1749. Father François Picquet founds the post of La Présentation [Ogdensburg, N.Y.], to serve as a village for Indians seeking Christian conversion.

Montreal, Dec. 5, 1749. Pierre Gaultier de Varennes et de La Vérendrye dies. In his career as an explorer and fur trader, he extended the western frontiers of New France [as far as Manitoba].

French yield Louisbourg after siege

June 28, 1745

LOUISBOURG, Ile-Royale – With flags flying and muskets shouldered, defeated French troops marched out of the supposedly impregnable Louisbourg fortress today and victorious New Englanders marched in. After a merciless seven-week bombardment, hand-to-hand skirmishes, sniping by musketeers and military bungling on both sides, the undermanned, undersupplied and underfed bastion of French power on the North American coast fell to a ragtag militia of farmers and fishermen under Boston merchant William Pepperrell's command.

Crucial support came from a crack British naval squadron which, under Commodore Peter Warren, had rushed up from the West Indies. During the siege, land and sea forces of the attackers totalled some 8,000 men, while jammed within the the great walls of the fortress were roughly 2,000 soldiers and 2,000 townsfolk. Many had called the attack "madness," but Pepperrell had inside knowledge. The French had captured some New Englanders in 1744, imprisoned them at Louisbourg, then sent them home. These men spread the word: Louisbourg could be taken. And so it was.

New England fleet attacks Louisbourg, known as an impregnable fortress.

General William Pepperrell and his men at the siege of Louisbourg.

Jewish woman sent out of New France

January 1740

NEW FRANCE – It's been several months now since Esther Brandeau, a Jew, was deported from New France. Jews are barred from Canada, so Esther sneaked here in 1738, disguised as a boy. Before that, she reportedly led an unstable life, in Bordeaux, France.

When Brandeau was revealed as a Jew, New France officials hoped she might convert to Catholicism. But Intendant Gilles Hocquart soon reported that "she is so flighty ... so fickle that at different times she has been as much receptive as hostile to the instructions that zealous ecclesiastics have attempted to give her; I have no alternative but to send her away." Brandeau was deported to France last fall.

Natural resources are colony's big plus

Dec. 31, 1741

NEW FRANCE – As the French colonies and their economic relations with France go, New France is a model its counterparts can learn from. The economic premise guiding France and its colonies is that the mother country should be self-sufficient. France not only uses the colonies as major sources of raw materials, but also as essential markets where goods manufactured at home can be sold.

The aim of this self-sufficiency is to accumulate as many precious metals as possible, such as gold and silver, and to pay other countries as little of the wealth as possible.

What makes New France such a colonial jewel in the economic sense is that many of its natural resources can be profitably exploited at the same time. Furs, the basis of the colony's economy, are the greatest asset. Beaver fur dominates, but the more luxurious otter, mink, weasel, marten and fox are also in demand to trim the robes of clerics and senior officials. Furs are also cheap to obtain. Little capital is required other than trade goods. Lumber, especially for shipbuilding, fish and agricultural products are other assets.

Although in theory the colonies provide France with raw materials only, since 1723 a more supple economic policy has evolved. Entrepreneurs here are encouraged – and even subsidized – to establish industries. The St-Maurice ironworks and the private shipbuilding industries are examples. Less successful were attempts to exploit copper resources and exportation of various other fur and hides.

Disease ravages Louisbourg; 480 dead

April 1746

LOUISBOURG, Ile-Royale – Scores of New England volunteers occupying the conquered fortress at Louisbourg have died from fever, scurvy and the bloody flux. Recent estimates put the death toll at 480.

One soldier reports that "putrid fevers and dysentrys" have been killing people "like rotten sheep." Unsanitary living conditions and a shortage of fresh food are chiefly responsible for the contagion. Gen. William Pepperrell himself is suffering from rheumatic fever, but observers say only his devotion to his men has prevented mutiny in the demoralized garrison.

Battered French armada limps into port

Dec. 7, 1746

PORT LOUIS – Ten battered ships limped into this Breton harbor today, the remnants of a 65-vessel armada which left Brest in May to reconquer Louisbourg and Annapolis Royal in Acadia.

Commanded by the weak-willed, incompetent Duc d'Anville, the fleet carried 6,790 sailors and 3,150 marines. On the Atlantic crossing it was ravaged by storms and bolts of lightning, then by scurvy and typhus. At least 2,400 men were dead before the fleet arrived at Chebucto [Halifax], missing by two days four French warships they expected to reinforce them. Disease raged. Little food was left. Over 1,000 more men died, including Admiral d'Anville, of either a stroke or suicide. His successor, Vice Admiral D'Estournel, ordered an autopsy to quash rumors of poison. Then he too died, piercing his heart with a sword because his officers insisted on trying to retake Louisbourg. The surviving ships sailed for France Oct 13. Gales dispersed them. Their starving crews ate rats and then devoured uncooked sheep taken from an intercepted Portuguese ship.

French pass typhus to Micmac Indians

1746

ANNAPOLIS ROYAL, N.S. – Up to three-quarters of Micmac Indians in western Nova Scotia may have perished from typhus, reports reaching Annapolis Royal this winter indicate.

The Micmac gathered last summer at Chebucto harbor to join Duc d'Anville's expedition against Louisbourg and Boston. Storms delayed d'Anville's fleet, sinking numerous ships and taking many lives. Some survivors who reached Chebucto suffered from scurvy and typhus. At least 1,135 French died. Their clothing and personal items were given to Indians who also contracted typhus and spread it to other Micmac communities.

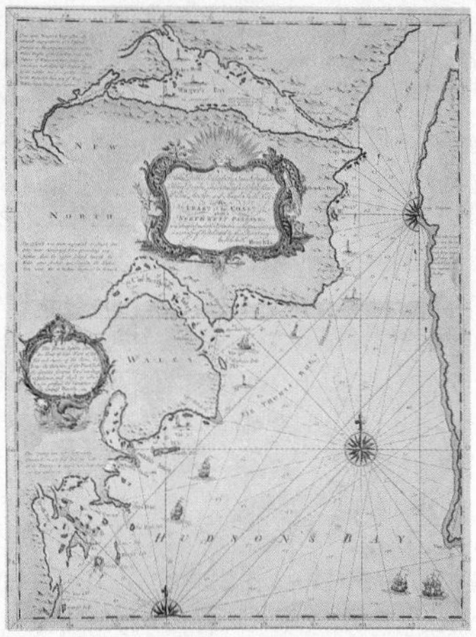

This 1748 chart of Hudson Bay shows Henry Ellis' route taken in search of a Northwest Passage.

Louisbourg fortress returned to France

Oct. 18, 1748

LOUISBOURG, Ile-Royale – Louisbourg, the imposing fortress on the south shore of Ile-Royale [Cape Breton Island], will be returned to France by its British conquerors as part of the peace treaty between England and France. Louisbourg will be exchanged for Madras and other British possessions in India seized in the war.

Meanwhile, New Englanders, who fought to take the fort, are shocked that Louisbourg is being returned to "the enemy."

British dub town Halifax

New settlement is built, named in honor of George Dunk, Earl of Halifax.

July 9, 1749

HALIFAX – Col. Edward Cornwallis, captain-general of the expedition to establish a British town and military base at the harbor of Chebucto, reports the new settlement's streets have been laid out and its perimeter surrounded by a palisade. Some 300 houses have been closed in, ready for the winter. The town has been named Halifax, in honor of George Dunk, Earl of Halifax, the chief Lord of Trade and Plantations. A civil government is expected to be created in the coming days.

Cornwallis, who is also the governor of Nova Scotia, arrived on June 21 with 13 ships carrying 2,576 settlers – many more than were expected when the expedition was announced on March 7. Only one person, a child, died in the crossing.

Cornwallis did not first consult with the Micmacs, who consider this land their own, and he sees no need to purchase the site from them. He also rejected suggestions from the likes of Commodore Charles Knowles, who's an ex-governor of Louisbourg, Capt. Thomas Durell, who had charted parts of Nova Scotia, and officials in England, and chose the site of Chebucto himself.

The townsite is on a narrow passage in the harbor, at the base of a sugarloaf hill which may be fortified in the future. The water is deep at the townsite and a stream from the hill provides fresh water. Construction has already begun on a church – to be named St. Paul's – at the spacious square in the centre of the town.

As a fortified town, Halifax is intended to offset the French fortress of Louisbourg on Ile-Royale, which was returned to France this summer. The former British garrison of Louisbourg has also been moved to Halifax.

The governor says the fisheries along the coasts are "as rich as ever they have been represented" and that "all the officers agree that the harbor is the finest they have ever seen." He is less pleased with the settlers, noting that "the number of industrious active men proper to undertake and carry on a new settlement is very small. Of soldiers there are only 100, of tradesmen, sailors and others able and willing to work, not above 200."

Col. Edward Cornwallis, founder of British town to be named Halifax.

1750 (1750-1754)

Quebec, July 12, 1750. Intendant Bigot imposes a manditory examination on practising doctors, and sets out fines for unqualified doctors. The measures are the colony's first medical code.

Newfoundland, 1750. New England whalers are killing humpback whales with lances in waters off Newfoundland. The whales sink when they die, but rise to the surface after a few days, which allows the whalers to collect their kill.

Halifax, 1750. Indian raids terrify settlers, and halt the growth of the new town of Dartmouth across the harbor.

Britain, 1752. The Gregorian calendar is adopted. The 11 days between Sept. 2 and 14 are omitted. European countries have been using the Gregorian calendar since 1582, but England continued to use the Julian calendar, which is 10 or 11 days behind the Gregorian.

Nova Scotia, 1753. Lunenburg is founded by Protestant settlers from Germany, Switzerland and France.

Hudson Bay, 1753. About 300 Inuit try to attack James Walker's ship south of Marble Island, but he escapes. He was on a routine Hudson's Bay Company trading expedition.

Philadelphia, Nov. 10, 1753. An expedition to find the Northwest Passage to Asia returns. The expedition, sponsored by Benjamin Franklin and others, entered Hudson Strait and explored the Labrador coast.

Ohio River Valley, June 26, 1754. Louis Coulon de Villiers arrives at Fort Duquesne [Pittsburgh, Pa.] with 600 Canadian troops and more than 100 mission Indians. He learns that a party of Canadians under his brother, Jumonville, has been ambushed by George Washington's Virginia militia, even though England and France are not at war. Jumonville and nine other Canadians were killed, and their scalped bodies left as fodder for wolves and crows.

Ohio River Valley, July 3, 1754. Louis Coulon leads a large force of Canadians against Washington's Americans at Fort Necessity. Coulon wants to avenge Washington's attack on Jumonville's party. The Americans surrender after suffering heavy casualties, and agree to abandon the Ohio Valley for a year.

French build Fort Rouillé

Fort Rouillé, a new French outpost on north shore of Lake Ontario.

April 17, 1750

FORT ROUILLE [Toronto] – A new French outpost named Fort Rouillé has been established here on the north shore of Lake Ontario. The fort is part of the continuing efforts of New France's governor-general, the Marquis de La Jonquière, to turn back British incursions into French fur-trading areas.

La Jonquière is concerned about American traders at Chouaguen, on the south shore of the lake. He's been quoted as wanting to drive the "intruders" from Lake Ontario and as saying Fort Rouillé might "disaccustom" the natives "from going to Chouaguen." That, La Jonquière hopes, would convince the English "to abandon that place." In particular, La Jonquière is concerned about American incursions into the Ohio Valley, a lifeline for the French empire.

First Protestant church in Halifax opens

Sept. 2, 1750

HALIFAX – Just 438 days after this outpost of England's imperialism in the northwest Atlantic was founded, the first Protestant house of God north of New England opened its doors today. At the Crown's expense, oak frames and pine timbers for the Church of England's home in the garrison town were shipped from Boston and Portsmouth, New Hampshire. Gov. Edward Cornwallis, 37, a handsome bachelor and good soldier, likes the new church. It reminds him of one in London.

The first Protestant church north of New England has opened its doors.

Prairie river is site of fur-trading post

1750

HUDSON BAY – The La Vérendrye brothers have built an independent trading post on the Saskatchewan River near the Carrot River junction. Fort Paskoyac is on the route to York Factory where the natives, until now, have had to travel to trade with the British Hudson's Bay Company. People are finding it more convenient to trade with the growing ranks of intruders than to travel great distances to reach the Hudson's Bay posts, which have a legal trading monopoly in this area, according to a charter signed by King Charles II.

Meeting of independent fur traders.

Peace hopes dim after Micmac raid

May 1754

NOVA SCOTIA – Peace efforts between Micmac Indians and the British have received a crushing blow. Earlier this month, Micmacs slaughtered the crew of an English sloop sent here to help the Indians move provisions the British had given them. After the massacre, the Micmacs burnt a peace treaty they signed with the British last year.

The Micmacs are taking revenge for the actions of two British sailors who last month robbed them of government provisions. Later when their ship was wrecked, the men received shelter from friendly Indians, but returned the kindness by murdering them.

Company sends Henday inland to meet Blackfoot

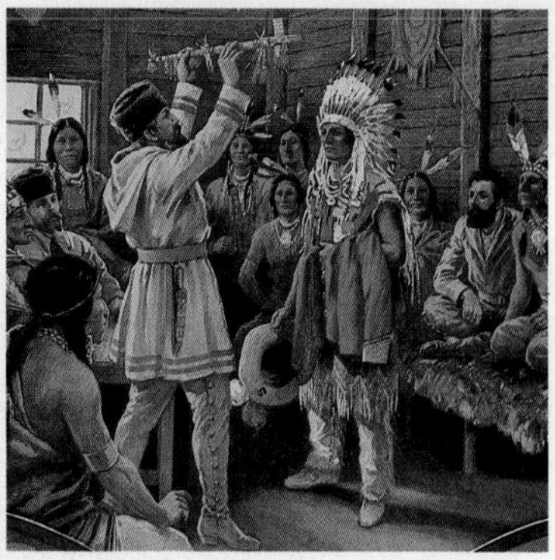

Blackfoot hold ceremony of the pipe when making contact with settlers.

June 26, 1754

YORK FACTORY – Hoping to counter competition from the French fur traders in the western interior, the Hudson's Bay Company today sent one of its employees inland to make direct contact with Indian tribes living there. Anthony Henday, a laborer and netmaker with the company, left the post on foot with a group of Cree Indians who will guide him toward the land of their distant neighbors, the Blackfoot Indians of the Plains.

Ever since the La Vérendrye family established posts on the Saskatchewan River, the HBC has felt the effect of competition from the French who approach the Indians on their trapping grounds and trade for the finest furs. As well, the company wants to silence critics in England saying that it is "asleep by the frozen sea" and not doing enough to explore its chartered territories in Canada. HBC officials hope that Henday will be able to re-establish the company's position with the Indians of the interior.

Anthony Henday meets with interior Indians to establish trade with them.

Blackfoot say no to Henday's offer

Oct. 11, 1754

RED DEER RIVER, Far West – Anthony Henday today become the first European to visit the Blackfoot Indians when he marched into one of their villages south of the Red Deer River in [Alberta]. Advancing down a broad avenue of 200 skin tents, Henday approached the lodge of the leading Indian, who received him surrounded by a council of elders.

No words were spoken as pipes of tobacco were passed hand to hand. After a meal of boiled buffalo meat, Henday's Cree guide explained that the white man wished to invite the Blackfoot to come to Hudson Bay to trade. The Blackfoot were friendly, but uninterested. They had no canoes and did not want to travel so far to obtain goods they did not need. Disappointed, Henday nonetheless admitted the sense of the Blackfoot chief's argument.

Henday's guide is a Cree Indian.

Explorer spending the winter with Indians

Dec. 31, 1754

RED DEER RIVER, Far West – Explorer Anthony Henday is spending the winter on the western Plains in the company of Indian guides, making him the first Englishman to do so since Henry Kelsey. Henday, a trader with the Hudson's Bay Company, has failed in his mission to draw the Blackfoot Indians down to Hudson Bay to trade. But he is gathering useful information about the Indian tribes and the fur trade in the interior.

The Blackfoot word for Frenchmen – "real white men" – indicates that Henday is not the first European they have known. When the ice breaks up in the spring, Henday will return to York Factory.

Nova Scotia, Micmacs bury the hatchet

November 1752

HALIFAX – Nova Scotia Gov. Peregrine Hopson and Micmac Indian chief Major Jean-Baptiste Cope of Shubenacadie have concluded a treaty which says all warlike events between the Micmac and the English should be "buried in Oblivion with the Hatchet."

The Micmac received gifts of blankets, tobacco, powder and shot, which will be renewed each Oct. 1 "so long as they continue in friendship." The Indians are also to have "free liberty of hunting and fishing as usual."

First printing press set up in colonies

Aug. 3, 1751

HALIFAX – Bartholomew Green, Jr. brought Nova Scotia its first printing business when he shipped his types and press from Boston to Halifax today. Green, 51, is in the third generation of a New England family that excelled as printing pioneers in British America. His father published the first authorized newspaper in the New World in 1704, and his grandfather ran an early press at Harvard College, Mass. News that Halifax had no press lured Green to Nova Scotia.

Colony elite gather for a carnival ball

1750

NEW FRANCE [Quebec] – Intendant François Bigot, *officier de plume* and responsible for maintaining food supplies, has wined and dined the colony's elite with yet another carnival ball.

Bigot is renowned for his extravagance, yet other prominent members of society also indulge in expensive and lavish lifestyles. Nowhere is this more evident than at gatherings in Quebec's official residences. There, in stately dining rooms that can accommodate up to 60 guests, local and visiting dignitaries can dine on elaborate and exotic dishes prepared by professional cooks and drink wines from well-stocked cellars.

Annapolis Royal, one of three main points of embarkation for Acadians who are expelled for refusing to become subjects of the British Crown.

1755

Quebec, June 7. A fire, criminally set by two sailors, destroys the Augustine monastery, the hospital, and the church at the Hôtel-Dieu.

Hudson's Bay Territory, June 20. A Hudson's Bay Company overland expedition led by Anthony Henday returns to York Factory with 70 Indian canoes carrying furs. Henday left in 1754 to encourage the Blackfoot to trade at York Factory, and travelled within sight of the Rocky Mountains.

Britain, July 8. Britain breaks off diplomatic relations with France as their land dispute in North America intensifies.

Ohio River Valley, July 9. Some 750 French and Indian troops led by Daniel Beaujeu ambush 1,500 British soldiers sent to recapture Fort Duquesne [Pittsburgh]. The British suffer almost 1,000 casualties, while French and Indian casualties are light.

Nova Scotia, July 18. Governor Lawrence informs British authorities the Acadians will be expelled from the colony unless they abandon their neutrality.

Nova Scotia, July 25. A delegation of Annapolis Royal Acadians are told they must either take the oath of allegiance to Britain or "quit their lands." They refuse.

Halifax, July 28. The Council of Nova Scotia endorses the deportation of all Acadians under British jurisdiction who refuse to take an unqualified oath of allegiance.

Bay of Fundy, October. A convoy of 24 ships leaves with about 5,000 expelled Acadians to be resettled in other British North American colonies. They leave behind possessions accumulated over many generations, including thousands of acres of prime agricultural land recovered from the sea by dike building, and thousands of heads of livestock.

Virginia, Nov. 11. More than 1,000 expelled Acadians arrive at the colony to resettle.

Massachusetts, Nov. 16. A law is passed empowering "Justices of the Peace and Overseers of the poor" to look after the welfare of expelled Acadians in the colony.

Quebec. The population of the city is only about 7,200, but there are 80 innkeepers, a ratio of one for every 90 people. Three quarters of the innkeepers are from France.

French surrender fort to Monckton

June 18, 1755

FORT BEAUSEJOUR, N.S. – Col. Robert Monckton today obtained the surrender of Fort Gaspereau at Baye Verte, completing his conquest of Chignecto, the isthmus forming the *de facto* border between British Nova Scotia and French Acadia.

Monckton's forces arrived in the district June 2. After capturing outlying positions, they laid siege to Fort Beauséjour, the principal stronghold, on June 12. The engagement was relatively bloodless – a "velvet siege," one French officer said – but the garrison was weak and demoralized. The French gave up the fort two days ago.

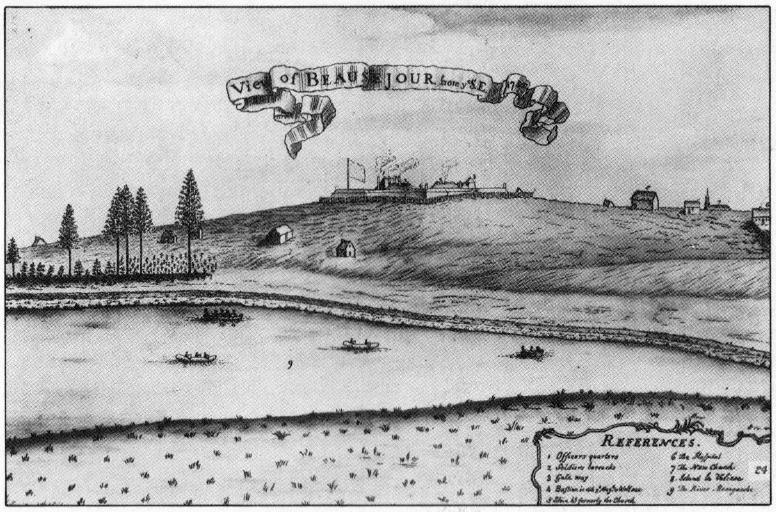

Fort Beauséjour, no longer the principal stronghold of French forces.

Braddock, Beaujeu both fall in battle

July 13, 1755

OHIO COUNTRY – British Maj.-Gen. Edward Braddock died today in Ohio land west of Pennsylvania of wounds inflicted four days ago by French forces led by ex-Acadian officer Daniel-Hyacinthe-Marie Liénard de Beaujeu.

While the victory is expected to make the Ohio region safe for French interests for another few years, it was a bittersweet triumph for the French – they lost Beaujeu in the battle. The British ambushed and killed the French captain as he was preparing his own attack.

Burial of Edward Braddock.

Johnson to secure support of Iroquois

April 1755

NORTH AMERICA – Edward Braddock, commander-in-chief of His Majesty's North American forces, has named William Johnson to manage relations with the Six Nations – or Iroquois Indians – and their confederated tribes. Johnson's immediate task is to secure Iroquois to fight the French.

The 40-year-old Johnson came to North America from Ireland 17 years ago to manage his uncle's estates in the Mohawk Valley of New York. Within a decade of his arrival, the tall, young Irishman became the most important businessman on the Mohawk River. In 1750 he obtained a prize public appointment, being named to the New York Council. Among the Indians of the Six Nations, Johnson has great influence, having learned the Mohawk language and customs, and having lived with several Mohawk women.

Sometime in 1753, Johnson met and courted Mary Brant, a member of a prominent Mohawk family who later became a clan mother, one of the governesses who select their tribe's chiefs. Through her, Johnson has acquired much influence among the Mohawk. No other white man is said to have more influence with the Six Nations than William Johnson – or Warraghiyagey, as the Iroquois call him.

Officer has orders to deport Acadians

Aug. 28, 1755

GRAND PRE, Acadia – John Winslow, recently named lieutenant-colonel of a provincial regiment helping Nova Scotia's Lt.-Gov. Charles Lawrence rid the province of its French influence, arrived in Grand Pré today. Winslow's orders are simple: he is to deport all the Acadians refusing to sign an unconditional oath of allegiance to the British Crown. Winslow played a major role capturing Fort Beauséjour in June and ending French ambitions in the Chignecto region this summer.

Winslow reads deportation orders.

Winslow orchestrates expulsion of the Acadians

Sept. 5, 1755

GRAND PRE, Acadia – Lt.-Col. John Winslow today told the men of this Acadian community who are refusing to take an unconditional oath of allegiance to the British monarch that their land and livestock were being forfeited to the Crown and that they and their families will be removed from the region immediately. Of the 418 Acadian men gathered to hear the decree, Winslow let only 20 depart to explain the decision to the women and children. There have been similar announcements at Piziquid, Minas, Annapolis Royal and Beauséjour – Acadia's chief communities. The decree ousts nearly 10,000 "unreliable" people from Acadia.

A government spokesman in Halifax said Gov. Charles Lawrence has decided not to deport the Acadians to French territories, but to disperse them among other English colonies along the Atlantic coast. The government wants to make sure the deportations don't strengthen its French rivals. The spokesman refused comment when asked if Lawrence might have exceeded his authority by ordering the mass deportation.

Meanwhile, early reports from Annapolis Royal indicate many Acadians in the district have taken to the woods, hoping to harass their tormentors and reclaim their property at a later period. With this in mind, Lawrence has ordered soldiers to burn Acadian homes, barns and churches so stragglers and escapees will not be able to feed or shelter themselves.

While an unconditional oath has been urged on the Acadians for a while, they have always insisted on conditions, notably an exemption from fighting on either the French or English sides in case of a war. As French-speaking residents of a British colony, the Acadians consider themselves neutral.

Lawrence suspects the Acadians of complicity – and even actual participation – in raids the Micmac Indians have staged on British settlers in the region. The Acadians' close and cordial relationship with the Micmac is no secret.

Lawrence is painfully aware of the fact that the Acadian population of Nova Scotia greatly outnumbers the English. "Suppose a French army assaulted Halifax, and the Acadians were whipped forward by the priests and the Micmacs," the government spokesman said. "Could they really stay neutral?"

In Grand Pré, Winslow has said privately that he suspects the Acadians do not believe they will actually be deported. He noted that they have been living under British rule for 40 years without taking the oath, enjoying unmolested tenure of their land and freedom of religion. This time, however, British authorities appear determined to settle the issue once and for all.

Acadians are exiled for refusing to take oath of allegiance to British Crown.

Acadians are being expelled after living under British rule for 40 years.

Acadian refugees safe in Maryland

Nov. 20, 1755

MARYLAND – Some 900 French Acadians the British expelled from Nova Scotia are in Maryland to start a new life. They were lucky to make it safely. Two ships evacuating about 1,200 refugees last month sank in an Atlantic storm. No survivors were reported. The British gave the expulsion order, covering some 6,000 or 7,000 settlers, after the Acadians refused to sign an oath of allegiance to the Crown. Most Acadians were interned in England or relocated in Britain's American colonies.

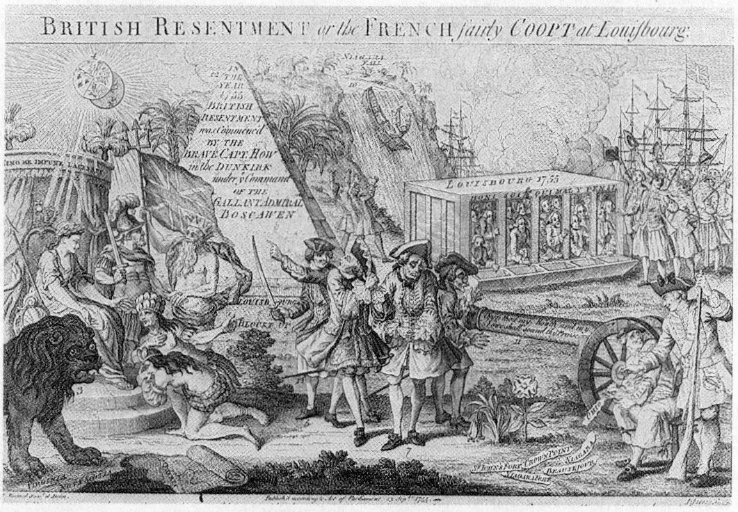

Illustration of British resentment of French shows Britannia attending to injured men (left) and British arms eclipsing French arms (above).

Maple syrup used for making vinegar

1755

NEW FRANCE – A local doctor has come up with an interesting way to produce Canadian vinegar. His unusual recipe was released in a paper presented recently to the Royal Academy of Sciences in Paris. The paper says maple sap enclosed in a barrel turns into vinegar – but not as quickly as the liquor extracted from sugar cane.

"If a barrel is left in the sun over the summer, it turns into very good vinegar," he said. However, the recipe specifies the vinegar must be made from the last sap to be tapped.

1756 (1756-1758)

Massachusetts, April 20, 1756. The government legislates severe penalties for Acadians who attempt to leave the colony without permission.

Lake Ontario, Aug. 14, 1756. French forces led by Louis-Joseph de Montcalm capture Fort Oswego from the British. They capture 1,700 prisoners and a vast quantity of supplies. The French now control Lake Ontario.

New York, Aug. 9, 1757. The British surrender Fort William Henry to a superior French force led by Montcalm.

New York, August 1757. British soldiers from Fort William Henry are attacked by Indians after Montcalm pledged them safe conduct. The Indians kill several of the British, and abduct 500 or 600 of them. The French recover most of those who are seized.

New France, November 1757. Meat is scarce and the government distributes horsemeat. French-Canadians are "repelled by the idea of eating a horse, a friend to man." Montreal women throw the meat at the feet of Governor Vaudreuil.

Halifax, May 25, 1758. Commander James Wolfe holds a lavish pre-attack bash for the town's military brass. His hotel bill lists 25 bottles of brandy, 50 of claret, and 70 of madeira for 46 guests.

Halifax, May 28, 1758. A British fleet of 157 ships and a total of 27,000 men led by Major-General Jeffery Amherst and Admiral Edward Boscawen sails to recapture the Fortress of Louisbourg from the French.

New France, July 8, 1758. The French, led by Montcalm, repulse a British attack on Fort Carillon [Ticonderoga, New York]. The French are outnumbered 15,000 to 3,600. There are 1,944 British casualties.

Lake Ontario, August 1758. A force of 3,000 colonials led by John Bradstreet captures Fort Frontenac [Kingston] from the French. They plunder, burn, and destroy the fort, a crushing blow to French control of the Great Lakes.

Ohio River Valley, Nov. 25, 1758. The French are forced to abandon Fort Duquesne [Pittsburgh], the centre of their control of the Ohio River Valley. The British occupy the fort and rename it Fort Pitt.

Montcalm to command French forces

March 11, 1756

QUEBEC CITY – Hailing from an old and distinguished family of nobility, Louis-Joseph de Montcalm today was appointed major-general of the French forces in New France. The Marquis de Montcalm is the French force's commander in the field only. His commission and instructions explicitly state that the governor general of New France, Pierre de Rigaud de Vaudreuil, has command of the armed forces of New France and that Montcalm is his underling.

After receiving an education from "a despairing private tutor" who considered the young Montcalm "too opinionated," the marquis began his active military career in 1732.

When hostilities broke out in New France last year and French troops under the Baron de Dieskau suffered a humiliating defeat, a replacement was needed. With war looming in Europe, experienced officers dread the thought of serving in such a remote place as North America. France's better known military leaders refused the New France posting before Montcalm, a lesser figure, was chosen.

Louis-Joseph de Montcalm.

Léry's men take Fort Bull with a bang

Gaspard Chaussegros de Léry.

March 27, 1756

FORT BULL – An Anglo-American outpost south of Lake Ontario has been seized by an armed party French-Canadian Gaspard-Joseph Chaussegros de Léry is leading. In fact, "seized" is a weak word for what happened to Fort Bull since it no longer exists.

At 8 this morning, 360 Canadians, natives and soldiers under Léry attacked Fort Bull, killing most of the 60 to 80 Americans inside. Léry's men barely escaped death themselves when the fort's gunpowder magazine blew up, destroying the outpost.

French fort hosts first frontier play

Feb. 1, 1757

THE HOUSE OF PEACE [Fort Niagara] – French troops stationed at the fort called "The House of Peace" have been suffering through a hard winter. Food is short, and so is heat.

But evidently imagination is not, because one soldier has managed to write a play. It's called *The Old Man Duped,* and it's been performed by members of the House of Peace garrison in home-made costumes. The play is believed to be the first staged in a frontier outpost.

British execute former governor of Newfoundland John Byng

March 14, 1757

NEWFOUNDLAND – John Byng, the former governor of Newfoundland, was executed before a firing squad today for "negligence" in his duties as admiral with the British Royal Navy. Byng's failure to attack French ships off the British-held island of Minorca and relieve British Fort St. Phillip led to his arrest and trial by court martial. He was executed on the *Monarch* at Portsmouth.

In his three years as governor of Newfoundland from 1742 to 1745, Byng won local respect trying to stop a trade monopoly in St. John's. He also collected extensive statistical data on the fisheries and information on the living conditions of the local population.

John Byng, former governor of Newfoundland, is executed for negligence.

Legislature meets for the first time

Oct. 2, 1758

HALIFAX – Swarming with New Englanders who demand their rights as Englishmen and believe in running their own affairs, this nine-year-old outpost of Empire in the northwest Atlantic today witnessed the gathering of the first elective assembly in Nova Scotia.

Charles Lawrence, a veteran of fighting in Europe and America, is one of a long line of soldier-governors in British America, and he shares their traditional contempt for civilians who want to govern in garrison towns. He reports to London, "I observe that too many of the members chosen are such as have not been the most remarkable for promoting unity or obedience to H.M. Government here."

The elective assembly of Nova Scotia meets for the first time in Halifax.

Indians trade furs for "luxury" items

c.1756

HUDSON BAY – European goods such as beads, alcohol and tobacco are considered important luxuries by Assiniboine and Cree who trade furs at Hudson Bay.

Each year at York Factory, the Indians exchange their beaver pelts for about 100-200 pounds of beads, 2,000-3,000 pounds of tobacco, and 300-400 gallons of brandy. This might seem like a lot, but the precious goods are shared by hundreds of band members and are probably traded to neighboring tribes. Individuals only get modest portions. Alcohol is saved for a few brief celebrations, like ones the Indians have before hunting migrations.

British forces seize Fortress Louisbourg

General Jeffrey Amherst and his 14,000 British troops capture Louisbourg.

July 26, 1758

LOUISBOURG, Ile-Royale – Vastly outnumbered by 13,000 British soldiers under Gen. Jeffery Amherst and a further 14,000 men aboard a fleet led by his friend Admiral Edward Boscawen, Fortress Louisbourg today surrendered for the second time. It had fallen in 1745, but England, infuriating its New World colonists, handed it back to France in 1748. The French promptly made it stronger than ever, but not strong enough to withstand the onslaught of the past two months.

On June 1, a sudden breeze swept away the fog in Gabarus Bay, and now the French saw Boscawen's mighty fleet. The ships lay at anchor in a menacing crescent. But the fortress, under a tough, new governor, Chevalier de Drucour, was ready. After a week of violent weather, the British tried to land in heavy surf. As their boats neared shore, French emplacements raked them with heavy gunfire. Even the boldest of the British officers, James Wolfe, urged his Highlanders to flee.

But he saw some of them struggle into a tiny cove the French couldn't see, and he furiously drove his boats toward that one chance. As they hit the breakers, he leapt overboard, cane in hand, and led the Scots through the surf, over a ridge, and down on the horrified French. More troops poured ashore, and all along the coast, the French retreated toward the walled city.

Now Louisbourg was doomed. Drucour held out valiantly, and even his wife took her turn firing guns. But once the British were ashore, the outcome was certain. The capitulation looked like the beginning of the end of French power in the New World.

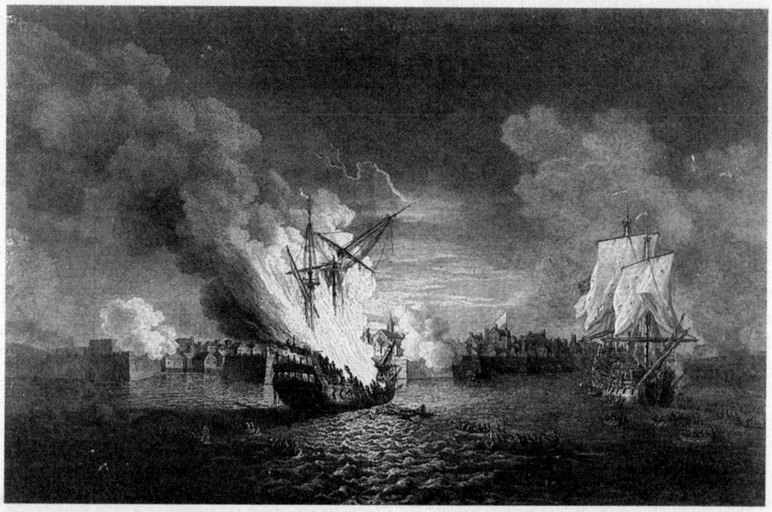

French ships the Bienfaisant and the Prudent are burnt in Louisbourg siege.

British ships sink, Acadian exiles die

Autumn 1758

ATLANTIC OCEAN – Seven hundred Acadians forcibly expelled from St. John's Island [Prince Edward Island] drowned when the British ships *Duke William* and *Violet* sank as they were taking the Acadians to France. Most of the dead Acadians escaped the 1755 expulsions by fleeing to the Island. Late this year, Lord Rollo and 500 British troops arrived and deported 3,000 Acadians. But about 200 hid in the remote Malpeque area, and 1,200 fled to New France. Luckily for them, Rollo left without them.

Food shortages irk women of Quebec

Only the rich can eat well these days.

April 1758

NEW FRANCE – Despite repeated warnings they would be jailed and hanged if they caused any more street riots, women in New France have taken to the streets once again to protest continuing food shortages caused by the war in England.

In the absence of the governor, hordes of women called on the lieutenant-general of the police to protest the dwindling supplies of bread. Daily rations were recently cut to two ounces. The rioters, mostly poor women who are struggling to feed their families, also protested the high cost of the bread.

As a result of the demonstrations, the governor has promised to increase by 30 pounds the 75 he distributes to poor families.

1759

Lake Ontario, July 6. General John Prideaux leads an Anglo-American force of 2,500 to Little Swamp Cove, several kilometres from Fort Niagara, en route to attack the fort.

Lake George, July 21. British General Jeffery Amherst leads an army down the lake to invade New France via Lake Champlain.

Quebec, Sept. 14. British forces celebrate Thanksgiving with an Anglican service in the Ursuline Chapel.

Quebec, Sept. 21. Following the English capture of Quebec, habitants from within a 14-kilometre radius flock to the town to take an oath of allegiance to Britain.

New France, Sept. 24. French forces led by François de Lévy return to Jacques Cartier after bad weather forced them to abandon a march on Quebec.

Montreal, Oct. 1. Rigaud de Vaudreuil, governor-general of New France, arrives with the bishop of Quebec to prepare the city's defences against an expected English attack.

New France, Oct. 4. On the orders of General Jeffery Amherst, Major Robert Rogers leads a British attack on the Abenaki village of Odanak at 3 a.m. when everyone is sleeping. They kill 30 people and burn the village. Rogers believes they have killed at least 200. The Abenaki have been allied with the French in the battle of New France.

France, Oct. 10. A royal decree invalidates paper money of the former French government in New France.

Quebec, Oct. 12. James Murray is appointed governor of the British garrison of Quebec.

Lake Champlain, Oct. 18. General Amherst finally learns of the fall of Quebec. He stops his advance up the lake because he fears the whole French army is encamped at Montreal. Amherst's hesitation in invading New France delays an English conquest of the colony.

New France. Robert Rogers' force retreats down the Connecticut River following their raid on Odanak, pursued by Indians and suffering from hunger. Fifty men die on the expedition, many from starvation.

Quebec, Nov. 12. Governor James Murray establishes English civil law.

Marquis urges tough defence effort

Feb. 8, 1759

QUEBEC CITY – The Marquis de Montcalm, charged with the military defence of New France, is urging Paris to make an all-out effort to defend the colony from British attack. Informed sources in the French capital say the general has sent two aides to plead his case to the government. One, the Comte de Bougainville, has been instructed to ask for reinforcements, to help Quebec City withstand invading forces. Evidently, the Marquis is worried the British, drawing on strong supply lines in the American colonies, may try to strike here in order to decapitate the French empire in North America.

Whether Montcalm's pleas will fall on receptive ears remains to be seen. Even if they do, the fact remains that France itself fears seaborne assaults – something that may persuade the royal government not to part either with ships or men.

Meanwhile, in Quebec City itself, the tensions of war have led to a very busy social calendar in the capital of New France, with the emphasis on parties, romance and gambling. Even government officials are taking part, among them Intendant François Bigot, the colony's top civil servant. Says Montcalm, "there have never been so many balls and so much gambling."

French royal arms, taken by British troops from the gates of Quebec.

Wolfe to command British land forces

Jan. 12, 1759

QUEBEC CITY – A commission issued today appoints a reluctant James Wolfe major-general and commander-in-chief of the British land forces for the expedition against the French in Quebec. Wolfe, 32, has a distinguished military career behind him, fighting his first battle at 16 and serving on the force which captured Louisbourg last year. However, service in America is not popular and the appointment is more than Wolfe "wished or desired."

Nova Scotia clears use of secret ballot

Feb. 13, 1759

HALIFAX – Nova Scotia's fledgling House of Assembly has adopted a resolution, the first of its kind in the British Empire, to apply secret balloting to the election of its members. The assembly's creation last October was a concession to the idea that inhabitants of colonies settled by Englishmen should enjoy English law and be taxed only by the king in Parliament or a legislature in which they were represented. But the authority of the Nova Scotia assembly was limited. Real power still lay with the governor and his hand-picked council.

Montcalm, Vaudreuil back in Quebec City

May 28, 1759

QUEBEC CITY – Both the Marquis de Montcalm, commander of all the military forces in New France, and Gov. Gen. the Marquis de Vaudreuil have returned to Quebec City – a move that can only mean they expect the British to strike here next.

Both men are taking this possibility seriously, judging by the defences springing up around the capital. On the ground, defensive works of trenches and cannons are being extended northwards to the Montmorency River. As well, in the lower town of Quebec, batteries of cannon and trenches are also being put into place.

Since the English are expected to invade using ships, a host of water defences are being assembled. Besides gunboats, the French are building "floating batteries" – literally waterborne cannons! Firerafts are also being readied. These are set on fire, then floated toward attacking wooden ships.

British seize Fort Niagara from French

Fort Niagara surrendered to British Brigadier-General John Prideaux.

July 25, 1759

FORT NIAGARA, Lake Ontario – In a classic display of siege warfare, the British have taken Fort Niagara from its French garrison. Under Brig.-Gen. John Prideaux, their gunners simply smashed away at the fort's earthworks until the French, exhausted and low on supplies, had to surrender.

It's an important event for both sides. For the attackers, especially the Americans, seizing Fort Niagara effectively ends French competition for the western fur trade, and most Great Lakes Indian tribes are leaving the French alliance. For the French, it dashes hopes of regaining military superiority on the Great Lakes. It also shifts the battle eastward, toward Quebec City, now that its western garrisons are lost.

Sisters seek refuge in Hôpital Général

July 13, 1759

QUEBEC CITY – With the British assault on Quebec, the Augustine nuns have been forced to take refuge in the Hôpital Général outside the city's walls. Five sisters have remained in the vaults of the monastery to watch over their possessions.

Most of the sisters and the wounded French soldiers they were treating are now at the general hospital, where they had already sent their beds and provisions. Also taking refuge at Hôpital Général are the Ursuline sisters – except for eight who chose to remain in cloister.

Montreal Grey Nun. Assault on Quebec forces other nuns to join them.

Left bank of Montmorency River occupied

July 9, 1759

QUEBEC CITY – The British fist continues to close around the French capital of Quebec City. In his latest move, Gen. James Wolfe has established a beachhead on the left bank of the Montmorency River, just to the east of the French defensive lines.

This bridgehead is just one of many British encampments surrounding Quebec. Directly across from the city, on the south shore of the St. Lawrence, the invaders have established batteries of cannons at Point Levis. And, on the south tip of the Ile d'Orléans, there's yet another British position. In short, the city is flanked by enemy forces on three sides.

The question everyone is asking is, what will Wolfe do next? The French commander, the Marquis de Montcalm, is said to be certain that his opponent is planning to attack on the city's right flank. This evaluation makes sense, given the British concentration at Point Levis, across the river. Such a strategy, coming in from the west, should be given away by British troop movements in this area. For this reason, Montcalm has detached 700 men to this region to monitor the situation. But this isn't the only option open to Wolfe. He could attack on the left, also a logical conclusion, given the buildup of forces at his Montmorency Falls headquarters. One thing is certain: the next move is up to the British.

George Townshend, commander of a British brigade in occupation.

Ile d'Orléans site of British attack

June 26, 1759

ILE d'ORLEANS, New France – The battle that Quebec City has feared for so long seems to finally be starting, as British ships full of troops have arrived at Ile d'Orléans. The island, just northeast of the French capital, is being taken at this hour by British soldiers under Gen. James Wolfe and his engineer, Maj. Patrick Mackellar. Although there's been some resistance to the invaders, the fact is these forces haven't met any organized opposition on Ile d'Orléans. Given this, there's little doubt the island, so close to the city, will soon be a British military camp.

Charles Saunders of British navy.

Cannons roar as war comes to Quebec

July 12, 1759

QUEBEC CITY – After days of waiting, the war has come to Quebec. British cannons, based across the St. Lawrence River at Point Levis, started firing tonight at the city. The bombardment began after British Gen. James Wolfe fired off a rocket from his headquarters at Montmorency Falls, just east of here. While the first few shells fell short – an incompetence that cheered inhabitants – succeeding cannonballs found their aim. Given enough time, artillery alone may force Quebec's surrender.

British soldiers told they'll get their ale

June 11, 1759

NEW FRANCE – It's official! Two quarts of beer will be issued daily to each man of the Royal Highland Regiment serving in North America. The Daily Order says "Spruce Beer is to be brewed for the health and conveniency of the troops which will be served at prime cost. Five quarts of molasses will be put into every barrel of Spruce Beer. Each gallon will cost nearly three coppers." Rumors persist that these orders will carry into the winter months.

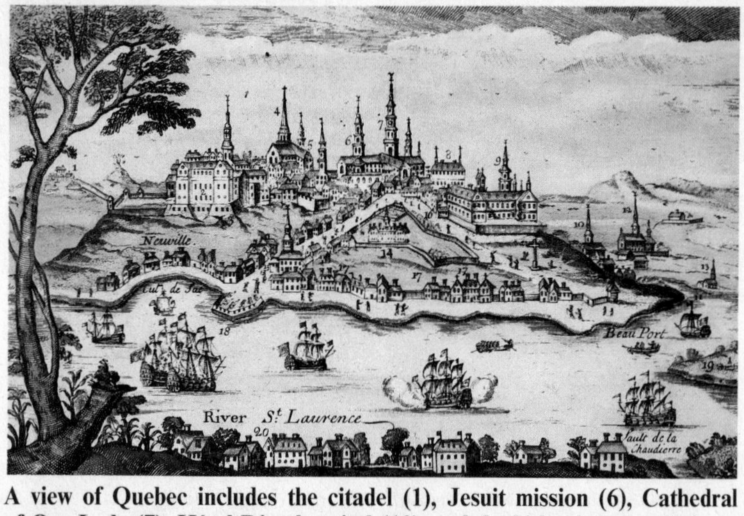

A view of Quebec includes the citadel (1), Jesuit mission (6), Cathedral of Our Lady (7), Hôtel Dieu hospital (10), and the bishop's house (14).

Wolfe tightens grip on Quebec City area

June 30, 1759

BEAUMONT, New France – British Gen. James Wolfe continues to tighten his grip on the Quebec City area. A few days ago, his troop transports anchored off Ile d'Orléans. Now, having survived a botched attack by French fireboats which inflicted no damage on the British fleet, his men have begun to land at Beaumont, on the south shore of the St. Lawrence. It's estimated 3,000 British troops will make their camp here before the day is out. ▷

Amherst leads way to victory over French forts

French troops put up token resistance against British at Fort Carillon.

Aug. 1, 1759

CROWN POINT, Lake Champlain – British troops have seized forts Carillon and St-Frédéric from the French and renamed them Ticonderoga and Crown Point. But to be more exact, the British had the smoking remains of the forts given to them.

The successful conclusion to the inland campaign under British commander-in-chief Jeffery Amherst has to be one of the stranger ones in military history. It began last winter, as his forces made methodical preparations for the capture of Carillon and St-Frédéric. The assembly of men, ships and provisions took a lot of time. So much so, that the expedition to Carillon didn't actually get under way until July 22, when 6,236 men set off at the portage leading to the fort.

Amherst didn't know the French commander at Carillon was waiting to surrender – though not too soon. François-Charles de Bourlamaque, along with 3,100 men, were to stay in Carillon just long enough to persuade the British to waste time building siege entrenchments. When Amherst arrived, they put on a token resistance, keeping him busy until the night of July 26-27. On this night the French slipped away, leaving Carillon in flames. They made for Fort St-Frédéric, which, while Amherst stayed at Carillon, they blew up yesterday before retreating.

Torrential rain a deciding factor in battle

July 31, 1759

QUEBEC CITY – From the heights across the St. Lawrence River, from ships anchored in the channel and from batteries just east of the city at the Montmorency River, the British unleashed a thunderous barrage against French defences here at 5:30 p.m. Under its cover, 13 companies of British grenadiers and a detachment of Royal Americans, all commanded by the sick, skinny, red-haired James Wolfe, slipped inland near the Montmorency on the Quebec side of the St. Lawrence, nabbed a French redoubt, then tried to charge up a cliff. At the top, French regiments mowed them down. The dead kept rolling back on the living, but Wolfe urged his men onward. They closed ranks again and again, and might have made it to the top, but torrential rain delivered the *coup de grace.* It drenched the attackers and their ammunition, and turned the hill as slippery as ice. Wolfe finally ordered a retreat. His dead, missing and wounded totalled 443. From his standpoint, the battle was a disaster. From that of the French commander Lt.-Gen. Louis-Joseph de Montcalm, it was a gift.

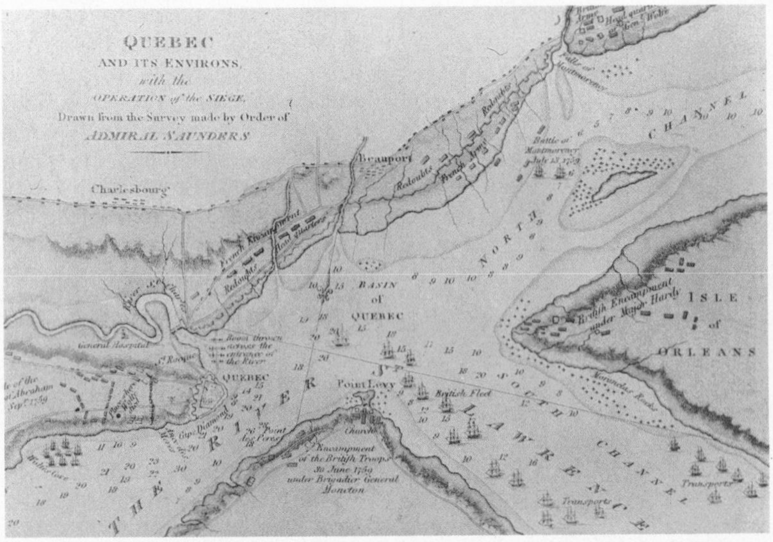

Quebec and surrounding area during the British siege in summer of 1759.

Gen. James Wolfe leads 13 companies of British men and a detachment of Royal Americans in attack on French entrenchments at Montmorency River.

Frustrated Wolfe reviews British strategy

Aug. 27, 1759

QUEBEC CITY – Frustrated in his attempt to force the French to battle, Gen. James Wolfe is in conference today with his senior officers in an effort to find a way to take the capital of New France. So far none of his other strategems have worked, although they have caused much suffering for the French-Canadian colonists.

The continuous shelling of the city by cannons across the river at Point Levis has destroyed its buildings. Brutal raids in the farming communities along the St. Lawrence have caused much death and destruction. But there is still no battle given by the French commander, the Marquis de Montcalm. And, when Wolfe was able to land his troops to take a small cliff from the French on July 31 – a move that was to be the Battle for Quebec – they were driven off not by French resistance, but by the rain, which made their muskets useless, and thus made retreat unavoidable.

So, the question remains: what will Wolfe do? It's rumored that he favors a direct attack on the Beauport lines, east of Quebec. His senior officers are said to be against this, favoring an attack to the west, which would starve out the city by cutting off its supply lines.

British troops prepare for major assault on Quebec

British troops and General James Wolfe prepare to attack landing place at Anse-au-Foulon, near the Plains of Abraham, to the west of Quebec City.

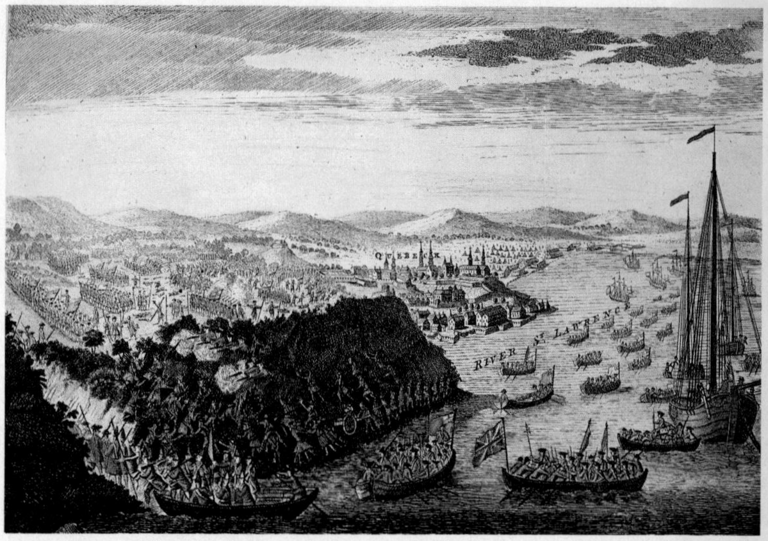

Gen. James Wolfe's forces prepare to land at Anse-au-Foulon, below the cliff. The British officer is reportedly sick and discouraged as battle nears.

Sept. 13, 1759

QUEBEC CITY – "Qui Vive?" shout French sentries. "France!" replies Gen. Alexander Fraser of the 78th Highlanders, and the British convoy of boats is allowed to continue rowing through darkness. It is 4 a.m., and Gen. James Wolfe's troops are heading for Anse-au-Foulon above Quebec and the cliffs under the Plains of Abraham. "The paths of glory lead but to the grave," Wolfe recited last night. Was it an omen when he swore he'd rather have penned Gray's *Elegy* than "beat the French tomorrow?"

It's far from clear that Wolfe will beat them. He's sick and discouraged, and recently reported to Sir William Pitt, "I own myself at a loss" what to do. He's bowed to his brigadiers' demands to forget another direct attack on the Beauport lines, but in planning to land at Anse-au-Foulon, will endanger his army if he fails to cut French commander the Marquis de Montcalm's supply line westward. Wolfe's main advantage stems from his past indecisiveness, for Montcalm still thinks he'll strike again east of the town. In fact, Wolfe's now heading west.

Whatever happens, this will be the last battle in a bitter, protracted campaign. Winter is coming, and Wolfe can't remain at Quebec past September. If he loses, he'll accept defeat and head home to England.

For days Wolfe has been waiting to use his naval power to get above Quebec. Now his men, decimated by desertion and disease, must clutch tree roots and bushes to haul themselves up the treacherous cliffs to the plains, guarded for now by only a token French guard under Capt. Duchambon de Vergor.

The situation is critical. One key question is, what sort of fight will the French put up? Wolfe's 4,500 soldiers, though well-drilled, are hungry and exhausted. Montcalm too commands 4,500, half regular troops, the rest Canadian militiamen. He also has 1,000 Indians, very frightening to their enemies. However, it cheers the English to know many of Montcalm's best soldiers are dispersed to other defensive positions where Wolfe is expected to attack. Will the French general's error on this score be a key to an English victory?

In silence, the English spend the precious night hours scaling the cliffs. They even drag two light cannons with them. But the Plains of Abraham are Montcalm's own ground, a distinct advantage. The English invaders, with few rations, no reserves or doctors, have on their side only surprise. When will Montcalm learn of their arrival? Will he move at once and massacre the invaders with the full force of his troops? Mere hours from now, the fate of Quebec – and so of New France – will be decided. The destiny of North America too may well hang in the balance.

Gen. Alexander Fraser calls on his brigade of Highlanders to attack French.

Gen. James Wolfe and British forces on Plains of Abraham before the attack.

British, French in Battle for the Plains of Abraham

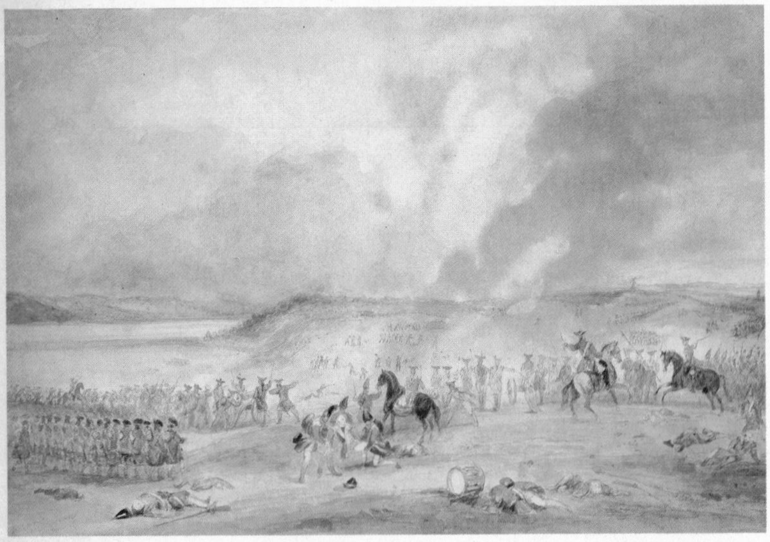

The battle between British and French forces on the Plains of Abraham begins.

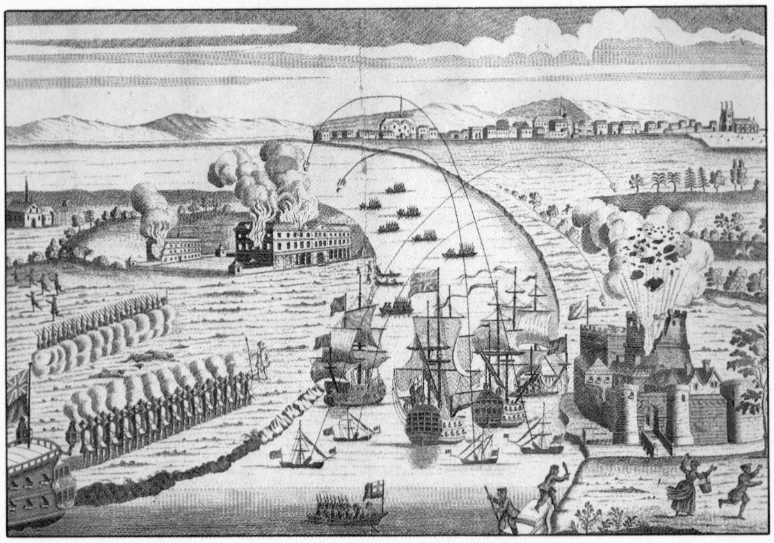

Gen. James Wolfe's forces attack the French at Quebec City.

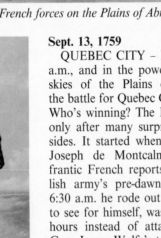

The Marquis de Montcalm orders all his French troops to report to the battleground and defend Quebec.

Sept. 13, 1759

QUEBEC CITY – It's nearly 11 a.m., and in the powder-blackened skies of the Plains of Abraham, the battle for Quebec City is raging. Who's winning? The English – but only after many surprises on both sides. It started when Gen. Louis-Joseph de Montcalm discounted frantic French reports of the English army's pre-dawn landing. At 6:30 a.m. he rode out to the Plains to see for himself, wasting valuable hours instead of attacking before Gen. James Wolfe's troops were in place.

But Wolfe was no better. Though he could and should have occupied commanding heights, he opted for vulnerable lower ground, then waited for Montcalm to attack.

What a match the two generals are proving – Montcalm's timidity and chronic defeatism against Wolfe's indecisive, dysentery-and-alcohol-clouded judgment. But their troops are fighting bravely, despite appalling casualties on both sides. The thick smoke of muskets is blinding. Without the bright colors of their uniforms – British red and French white – they'd be shooting at their own comrades.

At 10 a.m., without waiting for reinforcements from nearby, Montcalm's cheering troops charged. They ran – too fast – in three columns, the five battalions a mix of bush-weary regulars and little-trained Canadian militia. They fired at 120 metres, the Canadians falling to their bellies to reload, breaking ranks. The disciplined British troops waited. At 35 metres they fired by platoons, mowing down the French volley after volley. Wolfe directed them with reckless courage, despite Canadian and Indian snipers on both flanks. Montcalm, high on his charger, was also visible in the thick of battle.

The fighting lasted only minutes. Already the British are pursuing the fleeing French. But Wolfe is bandaging his wrist, torn by a sniper's bullet. He is hit again, in the chest! An officer tells him the enemy is on the run. Satisfied, the wounded general gasps out orders, but in the confusion the French army continues to escape. Now Montcalm is struck! He bends low in his saddle, clutching his belly.

The Marquis de Montcalm's headquarters, with a distant view of Quebec.

The Marquis de Montcalm takes refuge in Quebec, wounded by the British.

French forces at Quebec give up the fight

Sept. 18, 1759

QUEBEC CITY – It's all over. French forces defending Quebec City have surrendered to the British. The capitulation comes after much soul-searching by French authorities. The casualties were heavy on both sides: 58 British killed, 600 wounded, including several senior officers. Gen. Alexander Fraser's 78th Highland Regiment was worst hit, losing 168 to Canadian militiamen whose sniper fire permitted the successful retreat of the defeated French troops across the St. Charles River. French losses total about 600 troops and 44 officers. Both British and French commanders are also dead. The Plains of Abraham was a bloody victory.

Battle injuries prove fatal for Montcalm

Death of Marquis de Montcalm.

Sept. 14, 1759

QUEBEC CITY – The battle that cost it Quebec has also cost France its colonial military commander. The Marquis de Montcalm, wounded in the stomach and thigh during the rout at the Plains of Abraham, today died of his injuries. Montcalm, on horseback, was shot by grapeshot from a six-pound cannon fired by artillerymen in Colonel Williamson's command.

Montcalm died after a summer spent avoiding battle with the eager British Gen. James Wolfe. Montcalm is to be buried in Quebec's Ursuline Chapel, in a shell crater carved out by a British cannon.

General Wolfe shot dead in hour of glory

Sept. 13, 1759

QUEBEC CITY – Young British Gen. James Wolfe has succumbed to his wounds, dying in the hour of his greatest military exploit – the conquest of Quebec.

Wolfe's death is a great loss to the British. Though a flawed strategist, he was a superb battleground commander. He directed operations until his last breath. Then he sighed, "Now, God be praised, I will die in peace," and died surrounded by four horrified officers. Knowing the British had no surgeon, the French sent theirs. But as Wolfe said, "It is needless; it is all over with me."

Wolfe was engaged to be married to Katherine Lowther. His body is to be returned to England on the warship *Lowestoft*.

Death of James Wolfe at Quebec.

Quebec promised "mild and just" rule

Sept. 22, 1759

QUEBEC CITY – The British commander of recently-captured Quebec City is promising its French inhabitants "mild and just government." In a manifesto released today, Cmdr. James Murray also promises Canadians the right to remain Catholic. Murray's declaration may be an attempt to win over French residents and forestall any attempt to recapture the city by French troops who escaped capture and are still at large.

Highlanders warm up to nuns' knitting

1759

NEW FRANCE – Scottish soldiers on guard duty at the Ursuline monastery will be warmer this winter thanks to nuns there. The Highlanders, whose tradition of bare legs under kilts isn't suited to the rigors of the colony's winters, are now wearing wool socks knit by the nuns who felt sorry for them. Gen. Alexander Murray and his wounded soldiers have occupied part of the monastery since the battle on the Plains of Abraham.

Murray orders Jesuit priests to leave city

Oct. 26, 1759

QUEBEC CITY – James Murray, the British military commander at Quebec City, has ordered Catholic priests known as the "Jesuits" to leave the city. The French-speaking Jesuits, known for their missionary work among the natives, are suspected of encouraging discontent among British troops occupying the city. In some cases, it's believed the Jesuits have tried to persuade these soldiers to desert their posts.

New headquarters located in Montreal

Sept. 28, 1759

MONTREAL – The French governor-general, the Marquis de Vaudreuil, has chosen Montreal as his new headquarters. The move comes two weeks after the fall of Quebec City to the British. That defeat essentially deprived the French of their capital in New France and much of its territory. In selecting Montreal, Vaudreuil has picked the heart of whatever land in the colony still belongs to France. Time will tell if Montreal can avoid the defeat that cowed Quebec.

Notre-Dame-de-la-Victoire church after British forces destroyed it during the siege of Quebec in 1759. The church was built in 1695.

British to disarm French-Canadians

Nov. 30, 1759

QUEBEC CITY – French-Canadians living on the south side of the St. Lawrence River are to be disarmed by British troops. That's the word from James Murray, military commander of Quebec City. The move coincides with continuing attacks by French-Canadians and natives loyal to France on British soldiers and civilians. To back up Murray's order, 200 men left today for the river's south shore. They'll also make residents swear allegiance to the British Crown.

1760 (1760-1763)

Quebec, March 24, 1760. Cold weather, food shortages, and war has reduced the number of active British troops to 3,500.

Montreal, April 20, 1760. François de Lévis leads a French army of more than 7,000 up the St. Lawrence to try to recapture Quebec from the British. They have inadequate artillery supplies.

New France, May 16, 1760. French forces led by Lévis are forced to abandon their siege of Quebec when three recently arrived British ships attack and destroy the French frigates supporting the besieging army.

Montreal, June 8, 1760. Dubreuil de Pontbriand, the bishop of Quebec, dies.

Montreal, Sept. 9, 1760. The British army takes possession of the city after the French surrender, ending their conquest of New France. The French army, outnumbered 17,000 to 2,100, lay down their arms on the Place d'Armes.

New France, Sept. 9, 1760. At the time of the French capitulation, there are about 160 clergymen in the colony, including 70 parish priests.

Montreal, Sept. 21, 1760. François Bigot, Intendant of New France, leaves for France following the French capitulation. Pierre de Rigaud de Vaudreuil, governor-general of the colony, left the day before.

Montreal, Sept. 16, 1760. Almost the whole French army at Montreal has embarked on boats bound for Quebec en route to France.

New France, September 1760. Jeffery Amherst, commander-in-chief of British forces in New France, establishes British rule by proclamation. He leaves the colony under military administrators who follow a policy of conciliation with habitants.

New France, 1760. Merchants from the south arrive to supply the needs of the colony.

Halifax, June 25, 1761. In an elaborate ceremony, the Micmacs and British formally conclude the peace treaty signed in 1760. The British think the Micmacs are surrendering unconditionally to their rule, but the Micmacs probably see the treaty as conditional.

Fort Niagara, 1763. General Amherst suggests that smallpox might be introduced among Pontiac's rebellious Indians by way of infected blankets.

French victorious in attack on British

April 28, 1760

STE-FOY, New France – A French force led by François de Lévis defeated Cmdr. James Murray's British troops at Ste-Foy today, but failed to recapture Quebec. The British garrison, beaten and demoralized by a bitter winter battling scurvy and food shortages, is now rampaging through the lower town, smashing into stores looking for liquor.

Murray decided to meet the advancing French army beyond Quebec's ramparts. Outmanoeuvred, he had to retreat. If their navy reaches Quebec first this spring with men and supplies, the French will probably retake Quebec.

A view of Quebec showing the 12 principal buildings of the city.

Murray sends foes English newspapers

May 9, 1760

QUEBEC CITY – It's a sign of the times that the British frigate *Lowestoft* reached the besieged garrison of Quebec today. British Cmdr. James Murray promptly delivered some European newspapers to his French counterpart, Gen. François de Lévis, so he too could read about France's European defeats in its war with England. Lévis' ironic response to Murray was to hope he would soon have the "power to send you more interesting news." But thanks to England's increasing naval superiority, the next headlines may also please Murray more than Lévis.

François de Lévis during battle.

Vauquelin diverts 2 enemy frigates

May 16, 1760

POINTE-AUX-TREMBLES, New France – Without any gunpowder to defend against two pursuing British frigates, French naval officer Jean Vauquelin has deliberately driven his frigate *Atalante* aground at Pointe-aux-Trembles. The wreck ends a chase which saw Vauquelin divert the enemy warships away from French supply depots. The recent arrival of three frigates has given a distinct advantage to British forces defending Quebec. Still, Vauquelin's efforts bought the French much-needed time.

British torch homes of rebellious French

Feb. 26, 1760

NEW FRANCE – Following orders issued today by Cmdr. James Murray, 300 British soldiers are burning the homes of French colonists accused of breaking their oaths of allegiance to King George. The punitive action comes in the wake of recent enemy activity in the area and is meant as a warning against future co-operation with French forces. All the homes lie on the opposite bank from Quebec, stretching six to eight kilometres along the St. Lawrence between the the Etchemin and Chaudière rivers.

Lawrence's death comes as a shock

Oct. 19, 1760

NOVA SCOTIA – The death of Nova Scotia Gov. Charles Lawrence today came as a shock to friends and close associates. That so seemingly robust and healthy a man could be struck down so quickly after catching a chill is a mystery. Born in England in 1709, Lawrence's death prompted Gen. Jeffery Amherst to write Cmdr. James Murray. "I should have taken an annuity on his life as soon as anyone I knew," Amherst wrote. Lawrence was appointed governor of Nova Scotia in 1756.

Strategic Fort Lévis falls to the British

Aug. 25, 1760

FORT LEVIS, New France – After enduring a four-day artillery barrage, the French garrison at Fort Lévis led by Capt. Pierre Pouchot surrendered to the British today. The fall of Fort Lévis, built on an island in the St. Lawrence near [Prescott, Ont.], removes the last remaining military obstacle between a British force 17,000 strong, commanded by Jeffery Amherst, and Montreal. With fewer than 400 men, Pouchot has been trying to impede the advance by firing on passing British troop transports.

British raze hated Louisbourg fortress

Oct. 17, 1760

LOUISBOURG, Ile-Royale – Using powerful explosives, the British began to wreak vengeance on the French fortress they'd captured in 1758 and had long hated. They blasted it into timeless rubble. Powerful British politician William Pitt ordered that "all fortifications of Louisbourg, together with all the works, and defences ... be forthwith totally demolished, and razed, and all the materials so thoroughly destroyed, as that no use may, hereafter, be ever made of the same." The demolition ends English fears of France's reoccupying this dangerous military base.

Female population keeps on growing

Dec. 31, 1760

NEW FRANCE – Of the nearly 70,000 people populating New France, the ratio of men to women is almost equal. Before 1700, the population of New France was disproportionately male. Attracting French women to the colony has been a challenge for the royal government for years. The heaviest pushes were in the 1660s and 1670s when at least 774 *filles du roi* – single women sponsored by the king – came to New France to marry. Childbirth is encouraged, and bachelors are penalized.

Vaudreuil surrenders Montreal to British

French forces surrender Montreal to British without a single shot being fired.

Sept. 8, 1760

MONTREAL – Gov. Gen. Pierre de Rigaud de Vaudreuil de Cavagnial of New France today surrendered Montreal to British Cmdr. Jeffery Amherst. Surrounded by three British armies, the unwalled commercial capital of New France fell without a single shot being fired.

The decision to capitulate ends a debate between military and political leaders over whether terms of the surrender, as proposed by Amherst, should be accepted. The terms maintain civil and religious rights for the people, but treat the military more harshly. Local citizens, clearly in favor of surrender, have won the day.

Treaty's new terms are OK with Micmac

Sept. 13, 1760

HALIFAX – Leaders of the Malecite, Micmac and Passamaquoddy bands were here today to swear allegiance to King George, reconfirming previous ties with England and acquiring a source of much-needed supplies. Today's pledge ends French-inspired hostilities between these Algonquian Indians and English forces. Declining French military investment in the region left Indians without ammunition for last winter's hunt.

Rogers and his men reach Fort Rouillé

Sept. 30, 1760

FORT ROUILLE – Leading 200 of his Rangers, Maj. Robert Rogers today reached Fort Rouillé [Toronto] in Toronto Bay. Less than three weeks ago, British authorities assigned Rogers to take possession of western posts the French abandoned. Fort Rouillé was built as a French trade-post at [the foot of Dufferin Street] in 1750 but destroyed as the French forces prepared to retreat from the region last year. Rogers is impressed with the site. The abundance of game, level fertile land and excellent timber has led him to conclude it is an ideal location for a trade-post.

Major Robert Rogers is assigned to take formal possession of the western posts abandoned by French forces.

Quebec in 1760: At left, a view of the cathedral, the Jesuits' college and the Récollet friars' church, as seen from near the governor's house. At right, a view of the bishop's house and the town ruins as they appear going up the hill from the lower to the upper part of Quebec.

St. John's captured in surprise attack

June 27, 1762

ST. JOHN'S, Nfld. – In a surprise move, the French attacked St. John's today and captured it from the British. An attacking force made up of four warships and 700 troops left France this spring and reached Bay Bulls, which they captured, on June 24. The French force then turned its attention to St. John's, which was protected by 63 soldiers and one English ship. The fort was in bad condition and the soldiers surrendered.

King Louis XV of France is pleased with the French victory in St. John's.

British recapture St. John's from French

Sept. 20, 1762

ST. JOHN'S, Nfld. – Three months of French rule at St. John's ended today. In a decisive battle, the British have recaptured the prized Newfoundland port which they had surrendered to the French on June 27.

Newfoundland's Gov. Thomas Graves was sailing to St. John's in July when he heard of the port's surrender to the French. He immediately altered his destination and headed to Placentia to bolster defences there and at Ferryland.

Lord Alexander Colvill, commander-in-chief of the North American squadron, arrived at Placentia on Aug. 14. Eight days later, Graves sailed with Colvill to blockade St. John's, taking about 50 fishermen from Conception Bay as volunteers.

Colvill's men were joined by troops under Lt.-Col. William Amherst, and on Sept. 11 the British force reached the harbor of St. John's but was unable to enter because the French controlled the entrance from Signal Hill. Instead, the British moved on to Torbay, where they landed despite French opposition. Amherst led his British troops to Quidi Vidi, where there was another battle. He then led an attack against Signal Hill. The French ships escaped during the night and the garrison surrendered.

Respect the French, British officials say

Dec. 12, 1761

MONTREAL – The policy of British North America Gov. Gen. Jeffery Amherst insisting that the French be treated with respect has won strong backing. In a letter to Amherst, Secretary of State Lord Egremont supported the governor general's stand and said nothing is more essential than retaining as many French subjects as possible.

Egremont urged that the French be treated humanely and kindly, enjoy full benefits and that governors give "strictest orders to prevent all soldiers, mariners and others from insulting or reviling any French inhabitants."

Benjamin Franklin opens post offices

1763

MONTREAL – Quebec's beleaguered postal service has received a huge shot in the arm with the establishment of post offices in Quebec City, Trois-Rivières and Montreal by Benjamin Franklin, deputy postmaster-general for the American colonies.

Franklin's visit and subsequent action comes in the first year under British rule. Messengers have carried letters between Montreal and Quebec for 42 years, but mail has been expensive, slow, irregular and infrequent. Franklin has also established a courier service between New York and Montreal.

Gunshot, cannon fire part of trade ritual

1760

YORK FACTORY, Hudson Bay Territory – A gunshot sounds over the water as the rows of Cree canoes near the trading post. In response, the British fire a cannon and raise the Union Jack. This is the start of a typical trading convention in which Indians swap surplus furs for European goods.

The trade has great benefit for both parties. Guns top the Indian shopping list, followed by blankets, cloth, flints, hatchets, knives and beads. These items are highly prized by them. Luxury goods like tobacco and liquor are also traded. For the Hudson's Bay Company, the trade spells money. The furs fetch a pretty price on European markets. The trading reunion is also a time for socializing and celebration. The two peoples exchange lavish gifts, make speeches and smoke the grand calumet (pipe of truth and friendship).

Crees and Assiniboines do most of the Indian trading at York Factory. They serve as middlemen, trading with distant bands and taking the furs to Hudson Bay for a large profit.

This view of Montreal from across the St. Lawrence River shows major buildings: general hospital (5), the Récollet convent (13), the parochial church (14), Hôtel Dieu hospital (15), Jesuit monastery and church (16), Château Vaudreuil (17), the citadel (19), and Montreal's dock (20).

Treaty of Paris gives Britain control of Canada

Feb. 10, 1763

PARIS – The French, British and Spanish today ended three years of negotiations and signed the Treaty of Paris, concluding the Seven Years' War and ceding Canada to the English. According to boundaries set in the treaty, Canada includes the Great Lakes basin and stretches west to the northeastern bank of the Mississippi River.

In accordance with the conditional capitulation of 1760, following the decisive Battle of the Plains in 1759, Britain has guaranteed Canadians limited freedom of worship. Provision has also been made for the exchange of prisoners and Canadians are being given 18 months to emigrate if they wish.

The final disposition of Canada was complicated by the fact that in negotiations neither side appeared to want the colony for its own sake. There was strong pressure in England to take the lucrative sugar island of Guadeloupe instead. In France, there was equally strong pressure to drop the colony because it had proved to be a large financial and military drain. The British desire to knock French imperial power out of North America became the deciding factor.

In addition to Canada, Britain also gets Ile-Royale [Cape Breton Island] from France, and Florida from Spain. France retains fishing rights in Newfoundland and the Gulf of St. Lawrence.

The Treaty of Paris ends the Seven Years' War and sparks fireworks.

Out with New France, in with Quebec

Oct. 7, 1763

QUEBEC CITY – French inhabitants of this city, once the capital of New France, are learning the price of defeat today. By Royal Proclamation, New France no longer exists. In its place is the new province of Quebec, and it's a much smaller territory.

Under the new law, derived from the treaty between England and France, Quebec's borders no longer run south to the Mississippi and east to Newfoundland. Instead, the new province lies in a rectangular region, centred on the St. Lawrence River. All its other lands – the interior, the islands in the Gulf of St. Lawrence and those on the Mississippi – have been carved away. The British have promised Quebec parliamentary rule in the future.

Ojibwa win fort during lacrosse game

June 4, 1763

AMERICA [Michigan] – Two days ago, Ojibwa Indians seized Fort Michilimackinac, the most important British fort north of Detroit, and overpowered its 35 soldiers, killing 20 of them.

In the excitement of a lacrosse game outside the palisade, a warrior hooked a lacrosse ball high over the stockade. The Ojibwa grabbed their weapons and then rushed in after the ball and took the garrison completely by surprise.

Only two years earlier, Minavavana, an Ojibwa chief living near Michilimackinac, warned a British trader: "Englishman, although you have conquered the French, you have not yet conquered us!"

Jewish merchants pay ransom for trader

June 1763

MONTREAL – Jewish fur trader Ezekiel Solomons, captured by Indians along with three of his partners and taken to Montreal, was ransomed this month by other Jewish merchants. Large quantities of goods were reportedly taken from the four partners, who had established two trading posts outside of Montreal. Originally from the province of New York, Solomons settled in Montreal in 1760 after the British made the settlement of Jews in Quebec legal. In 1761, preceding even the British troops who arrived in September to take over the post from French, Solomons established a trading post in Michilimackinac.

Pontiac continues assault on the British

Aug. 5, 1763

CANADA – Britain suffered one of its greatest defeats in the Indian uprising only a few days ago. Chief Pontiac and his warriors ambushed Capt. James Dalyell and his force of 250 soldiers, sent out from Detroit to subdue the Indian revolt. They killed Dalyell and 19 others, and wounded another 40 in the battle of Bloody Run.

Pontiac and his band have seized all but one of the British forts in the upper Great Lakes. It is said that if the French in Louisiana send Pontiac an officer skilled in the art of siege warfare, the Indian chief will try to take Detroit.

Chief Pontiac takes up war hatchet.

Chief Pontiac and his Indians try to take Fort Detroit in 1763.

CONQUEST & CHANGE

1764-1867

Quebec, June 21, 1764. William Brown publishes the first issue of the *Quebec Gazette*, the colony's first periodical. It is bilingual.

Montreal, 1764. There are reportedly 136 male Protestants in the district. 50 of them are merchants.

St. John's Island, Oct. 6, 1765. British surveyor Samuel Holland completes a survey of the island [Prince Edward Island], expected to form the basis for future land distribution and settlement.

Quebec, 1765. Merchants complain of the dearth of French wines, and even see the shortage as an attempt by British authorities to change the drinking habits of Canadians by making available only fortified wines (sherry, port, and Madeira).

Atlantic Coast, 1765. Up to 120 New England vessels are killing whales, mainly humpbacks, in the Strait of Belle Isle, the Grand Banks, and the Gulf of St. Lawrence.

Quebec, April 1766. James Murray, governor of Quebec, is ordered to Britain to account for his actions after the attack on magistrate Thomas Walker, and his administration of Quebec in general. British merchants in Quebec have been petitioning against him.

Newfoundland, 1768. The fishery's production is worth £600,000 a year. About 20,000 are employed, many from outside the colony.

Hudson's Bay Territory, June 3, 1769. British astronomers William Wales and Joseph Dymond observe the transit of Venus at Churchill. The Royal Society of London sent astronomers to points around the world to observe the astronomical event, with the goal of defining the distance between the earth and the sun.

England, June 28, 1769. St. John's [Prince Edward] Island is made a separate colony, after determined lobbying by the island's proprietors.

England, July 14, 1769. Walter Patterson is commissioned as the first governor of St. John's [Prince Edward] Island.

Nova Scotia, 1769. Micmac society is struggling to adapt to the arrival of European settlers. They use European tools for traditional activities, wear traditional and European clothing, and some convert to Christianity.

Murray is new governor of Quebec

James Murray, the flamboyant and popular new governor of Quebec.

Aug. 10, 1764

QUEBEC CITY – After 10 months of waiting, James Murray has been formally confirmed as governor of Quebec. The announcement took place today, in the square near the Château St-Louis. A huge crowd of both Canadians and English conquerers turned out for the occasion, celebrated with troop manoeuvres and cannon fire.

For the French, who have lived under the British since the conquest a few years ago, Murray's appointment is actually good news. He is said to be sympathetic to their plight, and more than willing to to live and let live. Though he denies it, Murray seems to revel in the prestige of his new appointment. He has already bought a handsome coach and formal dinner silver sets by the dozen. His excuse for this "royal" behavior is that "the people here love show – I hate it, but I must not starve the cause."

However, there could be clouds on the horizon for the new governor. In a radical move, Britain separated the civil and military functions, so as civil governor, Murray loses his position as military commander of Quebec, the position he held after the conquest. Now Gen. Jeffery Amherst in New York is his military superior, so Murray doesn't have much power anymore. He lacks as well the influential connections in England that are so important for ambitious officials.

Appointment of Guy Carleton catches many people by surprise

Sir Guy Carleton, new governor.

April 7, 1766

QUEBEC CITY – Guy Carleton was named today to succeed James Murray as lieutenant-governor and administrator of Quebec. Carleton's appointment has caught many people by surprise since he has no previous experience in civil administration. However, he has been well briefed, and has strong political ties in Britain – something Murray lacks – and it is thought these connections will serve the province well. Among those who favor his appointment is King George III, who has described Carleton as a "gallant and sensible man." One other advantage Carleton has over Murray is that he is being given command over all the troops in the colony.

Carleton has experience in Quebec, but it is limited to a military role in the recent war with France. Born in 1724, he began his military career at 17. As he rose through the commissioned ranks, Carleton got to know British army officer James Wolfe, who would later request his services for sieges on Louisbourg and Quebec. Carleton failed to distinguish himself in these campaigns – he was neither an embarrassment nor a hindrance.

First novel published in Canada full of romance and intrigue

1769

CANADA – The first Canadian novel, Frances Brooke's *The history of Emily Montague,* has been well-received by critics in England. Set mostly in Canada, the novel is a collection of 228 fictional letters. The principal correspondents are retired English officer Ed. Rivers, Emily's romantic interest who arrives in Canada in 1766 with plans to settle, and Emily's friend and confidante in England, the coquettish Arabella Fermor. The letters, apart from the romance and intrigue typical of today's European fiction, describe in detail the social customs and manners of French colonists and native people.

Due to social and political commentary in the book, Brooke has expressed concern that it may not be as popular as her only previous novel, *The history of Lady Julia Mandeville*, published in 1763. It was in that year that Brooke first arrived in Canada. There she joined her husband, the Reverend John Brooke, a chaplain assigned to the Quebec garrison in 1760.

Frances Brooke became familiar with many aspects of the colony before returning last year, and has dedicated *The history of Emily Montague* to the new governor, Guy Carleton.

Frances Brooke publishes first book.

British, Pontiac talking peace at Indian congress

July 23, 1766

OSWEGO, N.Y. – The great Indian congress between Sir William Johnson and Pontiac, who is accompanied by about 40 Indian chiefs, began this morning at Fort Ontario here in Oswego. Pontiac's three-year long resistance to British occupancy of the Great Lakes area resulted in the death – and the capture – of at least 2,000 soldiers, traders and settlers.

In the late summer of 1763, Pontiac and his Ojibwa, Ottawa, Potawatomi and Huron allies were able to seize, apart from Detroit, every British fort in the western Great Lakes. The Indian offensive soon broke down due to the reluctance of the French in Louisiana to send an officer, skilled in the art of siege warfare, to help the Indians storm Fort Detroit.

Chief Pontiac meets with other Indian chiefs at war council.

Also hurting the offensive was the resurfacing of old inter-tribal rivalries, destroying the unity of Pontiac's pan-Indian alliance. And finally, the Indians could not repair their own guns, and they needed to make peace to gain access to gunsmiths and ammunition suppliers.

Pontiac maintains the Indians have retained control over their land even though they have lost their war with Britain. He adds that they would willingly give up part of their country for forts and trading posts, provided the British, as the French did, pay for the use of the land, and leave the Indian hunting grounds undisturbed.

In part, the British appear to have recognized this position in a Royal Proclamation issued in late 1763, at the height of the uprising. The document confirmed the legal right of the North American Indian tribes to claim title to the lands which they occupy.

Indian negotiator, Chief Pontiac.

Mysterious "mink" sighted at Belle Isle

Sept. 15, 1766

BELLE ISLE, Nfld. – An "extraordinary animal" likened to a huge mink was spotted by English naturalist Joseph Banks on a visit here to study native wildlife. According to one of Banks' assistants, the creature "came up from the sea" and was "bigger than a fox (and) in make and shape nearest compared to an Italian greyhound, legs long, tail long and tapering."

Trade post and shipbuilding site founded

March 1764

MOUTH OF THE ST. JOHN RIVER, N.S. [New Brunswick] – With the Treaty of Paris having wiped out the last traces of French power in North America, New Englanders James and Richard Simonds brought 30 men to this strategic harbor and started to build a trading post on the spot where Charles de La Tour's fort had stood more than a century before.

Several Massachusetts army officers had been pondering opportunities on the St. John River, but even before the treaty had punctuated the disintegration of French authority, the Simonds brothers had stolen a march on the rest. Like the French before them, they saw lucrative possibilities in fish and fur here, and in 1762, they settled on the harbor shore. They also wangled a 5,000-acre grant of hay-producing marshland.

With William Hazen as their partner back home in Massachusetts and little more than a sloop and a handful of men here in the largely abandoned riverside wilderness, they fished, and traded with the natives for fur. They were so successful they organized a company to "enter upon and pursue with all speed and faithfulness the business of the cod fishery, seine fishery, fur trade, burning of lime and every other trading business that shall be thought advantageous to the company." Those who just arrived, well before spring, prove the company means business.

Attackers flee after cutting off judge's ear

Dec. 6, 1764

MONTREAL – About 20 men with blackened faces attacked Magistrate Thomas Walker in his home on St. Paul Street tonight while he was dining with his wife. The assailants broke into the front room where the Walkers were eating and charged at the baffled judge. Resisting vigorously, he struggled to the room where he keeps his guns, but before he could arm himself, the hoodlums beat him, carved off his ear, and fled.

Walker believes the assault was blacklash from a case in which he and other Montreal justices jailed a Captain Payne for refusing to vacate rooms in a magistrate's house that had previously billeted officers. The incident heightened animosity between the merchant class and the army.

Late tonight, it became clear who attacked Walker when one of the 28th Regiment flung a newly severed ear onto the adjutant's table, and said, "That was for his supper."

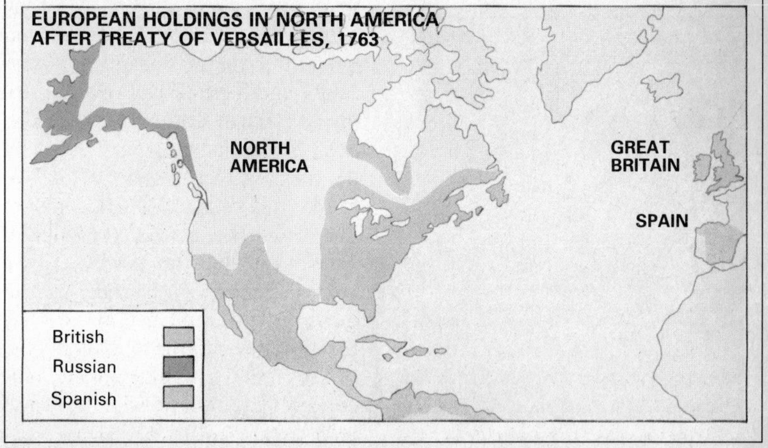

Hearne leads the search for fabled copper mine

Explorer Samuel Hearne's signature, as he engraved it on a rock in 1767.

Hearne's Fort Prince of Wales post, property of the Hudson's Bay Company.

Nov. 6, 1769

YORK FACTORY – Samuel Hearne left the trading post on foot today in search of a fabled copper mine in the vast barren lands to the northwest. Along with two white companions, the 24-year-old employee of the Hudson's Bay Company is guided by Chawchinahaw, a Cree Indian. They go first in search of the famed Chipewyan leader Matonabbee, who is said to know the mine's location.

For decades the Indians have told traders about a rich mine on the banks of a distant river called the Coppermine. Two years ago Indians produced a map of the mine, drawn on a piece of deerskin. No European has ever crossed the treeless barrens. The HBC hopes that Hearne will pinpoint the exact location of the mine and discover whether its ore can be brought out by ship via the Arctic Ocean. As well, the company hopes its emissary will make contact with distant Indians who may have furs to trade.

Trade board favors Catholic right to vote

Sept. 2, 1765

QUEBEC – The British Board of Trade, an official central government body instrumental in shaping colonial policy for the empire, today issued a report on Canada recommending that Roman Catholics be allowed to vote for, but not sit as members in, a proposed assembly. In a second report, the board criticized a judicial ordinance of a year ago for denying Canadians equality with other British subjects in the courts. The report said the ordinance, which abolished local laws and customs, should be replaced.

Montreal's Notre Dame de Bon-Secours Church, built in 1651 to withstand the Canadian winters.

The Board of Trade's stand is another step in what has been an easing of British domination over the colony and its large Roman Catholic population. In June of this year, two Crown officers, Attorney General Sir Fletcher Norton and Solicitor General William de Grey, said English penal laws do not apply to Roman Catholics in the colony. No explanation was given by the men for their position.

Last fall, James Murray, governor of Quebec, started pressing for concessions for the people of the colony. Murray feels there is too much English influence in a colony that still does not have a large English-speaking population, and his concerns are beginning to be heard in Britain.

Lottery gives island to prominent citizens

July 23, 1767

LONDON – All of St. John's Island [Prince Edward Island], a French possession until it passed into British hands four years ago, was today assigned by lottery to a mere 100 lords, military officers, politicians, high-ranking civil servants, wealthy merchants and business adventurers.

In his 1764-65 survey, Samuel Holland, surveyor general of Quebec, divided the island into 67 townships of about 20,000 acres apiece, and today's winners (some in partnerships) each got an entire township for nothing. Some of the lucky ones know King George III, and most are influential. They also share the view that their new holdings are either tomorrow's cash cow or today's speculative opportunity.

Cartwright finds deserted Beothuk camps

August 1768

NEWFOUNDLAND – Capt. John Cartwright has travelled up the Exploits River hoping to contact and befriend the elusive Beothuk Indians, but instead he has found only deserted camps. The Beothuk have traditionally migrated with the seasons, occupying the forested interior from September to May and coastal areas during the summer. That Cartwright expected to find them here, in the heart of Newfoundland's interior, reflects just how little is known about these people.

The Beothuks have long demonstrated a preference to remain isolated from whites. This tendency has prevented the establishment of trade relations and led to friction with white settlers in the region, most of whom are salmon catchers. Gov. Hugh Palliser, having heard talk of conflicts, dispatched Cartwright to soothe relations. The expedition has not accomplished this goal, but has found evidence suggesting the Beothuk population excedes previous estimates. Instead of 200 or 300, Cartwright now suggests they number at least 400.

Acadians returning to Bay of Chaleur

1767

NOVA SCOTIA – Acadians are establishing settlements along the northeastern shore of [New Brunswick] in the Bay of Chaleur, salvaging a cultural identity they have come perilously close to losing. Descendants of early French colonists, these Acadians were expelled from Nova Scotia by the British in 1755. Many tried to establish themselves in the Channel Islands, along the coast of France, even in the Caribbean and Louisiana, but these efforts often met with failure.

Three years ago the British government passed legislation permitting the deported to return, but a migration of New Englanders to areas the Acadians once occupied made resettlement in their former communities impossible. A growing number of Acadians, frustrated in their attempts to settle elsewhere, are now converging on the Bay of Chaleur and the town of Caraquet.

There, far removed from the colonial seats of power in Halifax and Quebec, they feel free to develop the land and harvest the sea without interference from hostile interests. The Acadians, forced as they were to endure the trials and tribulations that so often accompany the dispossessed, seem determined to restore their dignity and place in a land they helped build.

Inuit reveal fate of Knight and crew

Summer 1769

MARBLE ISLAND, Hudson Bay – It was 50 years ago that James Knight and the crews of his two small discovery vessels disappeared without a trace in the treacherous waters of northern Hudson Bay. Today, on this surf-battered island off the mouth of Rankin Inlet, the fate of the Knight expedition was revealed by an elderly Inuk who was a witness to its last tragic days.

A longtime employee of the Hudson's Bay Company, Knight was determined to find the fabled copper mine which Indians told him lay in the interior of the barren lands. Knight decided it should be possible to reach the mine by sailing a ship out of Hudson Bay through an undiscovered northwest passage. In 1719 he sailed into the northwest corner of the bay in search of the passage and never came back. A search was carried out, but no remains were found.

Then, in the summer of 1767, the mystery was partly solved. Whalers found the remains of a hut, a shipwreck and several graves on Marble Island. This year the whalers returned to the island and one of them, Samuel Hearne, spoke to some local Inuit. The Inuit said Knight's ships foundered in the harbor and one by one the men had died of exposure and malnutrition.

An Inuit woman and her child. An Inuk woman revealed Knight's fate.

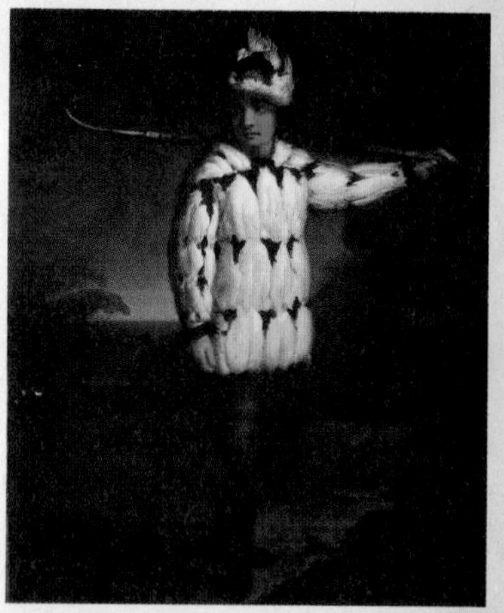

A male Inuit as he would have looked around the time of Knight's death.

Illustration of a group of Inuit living northwest of the Hudson Bay area.

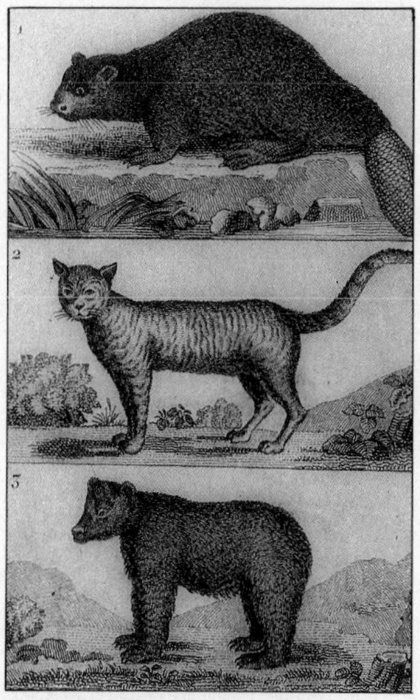

An illustration of the typical Canadian wildlife shows the beaver, the lynx, and the bear.

Quebec upper crust relying on slavery

1766

QUEBEC CITY – William Brown, founder of the *Quebec Gazette*, purchased three black slaves this year. He is just one of many prominent people in Quebec still relying on slavery as a form of inexpensive labor. French capitulation of New France to British forces in 1760 did not weaken institutionalized slavery in the colony. A clause was inserted into the terms of surrender allowing slave owners to retain their privileges. This clause received further ratification in the Treaty of Paris in 1763. Since then, Gov. James Murray, himself a slave owner, has called slavery an economic necessity.

King grants land for Moravian mission

1769

LONDON, England – The king has granted 40,470 hectares of land on the rugged coast of Labrador to a group of missionaries who wish to establish Christian settlements among northern Inuit. When the missions open, it will be the first time that Europeans have settled on the north coast of Labrador, and the first time that any North American Inuit have heard the Christian message from missionaries.

The missionaries are members of the Moravian Brethren from Germany. Active among the natives of Greenland for many years, the Moravians in Labrador are led by Jens Haven, a carpenter by trade. The 45-year-old Haven has won the support of Newfoundland's governor, Sir Hugh Palliser, who hopes that the missionaries will befriend the Inuit and make it easier for the British to establish fishing and trading stations in Labrador.

It was largely through the persuasion of Haven, who has visited Labrador, that the British government agreed to the grant.

The Moravians plan to visit Labrador next summer to consult with local Inuit about establishing their first permanent mission settlement. They will take as a guide the Inuit woman Mikak, who has been living in England since she was kidnapped by British sailors several years ago. The missionaries intend to support their efforts by fishing and trading with the Inuit.

1770 (1770-1774)

Labrador, August 1770. A Moravian missionary expedition led by Francis Mugford meets a large number of Inuit. They trade with them, preach to them, and buy land to found a mission.

St. John's Island, September 1770. The first legislation devised on the island [Prince Edward Island] is an act to regulate the sea cow (walrus) fishery. The animals are being depleted on the island.

The Northwest, Nov. 25, 1770. A Hudson's Bay Company expedition led by Samuel Hearne returns to Churchill after penetrating 500 km inland from Hudson Bay, the furthest sub-arctic penetration yet by a European. It was Hearne's second attempt to look for copper deposits and locate the Northwest Passage.

Arctic, July 17, 1771. On his third Arctic expedition, Samuel Hearne's Indian companions massacre a group of Inuit near the mouth of the Coppermine River.

Arctic Ocean, July 18, 1771. Samuel Hearne is the first European to stand on the north coast of the continent as his expedition reaches the mouth of the Coppermine River.

Labrador, Aug. 9, 1771. A Moravian missionary expedition led by Francis Mugford lands at Nain to establish a permanent mission among the Inuit. The Moravians bought land here the previous year. They immediately begin building a mission house.

Churchill, Aug. 11, 1771. A Hudson's Bay Company whaling expedition led by Thomas Robinson returns. They killed three whales off Marble Island, one of the first instances of arctic whaling.

St. John's Island, July 3, 1773. The island's first assembly meets at the Crossed Keys Tavern in Charlottetown.

Pacific Coast, July 15, 1774. A Spanish expedition led by Juan Pérez Hernandez trades with Haidas [off the Queen Charlottes], the first recorded European contact with the Indians of the northwest coast. The expedition was intended to establish Spanish sovereignty in the area.

Pacific Coast, Aug. 9, 1774. Hernandez's expedition trades with Nootkas after finding an opening in the coast that he names Surgidero de San Lorenzo [Nootka Sound].

Hearne back at Fort Prince of Wales

June 30, 1772

FORT PRINCE OF WALES – Eighteen months and 23 days after leaving this fort on a 5,600-kilometre hike into the far north to promote and extend the trade of the Hudson's Bay Company, to look for a northwest passage and to locate the rumored copper mines, Samuel Hearne has returned. After failing on two previous attempts, Hearne decided to change his strategy. Taking only his quadrant, some tobacco, knives, blanket, gun and a change of underwear, he put himself into the hands of Matonabbee, a Chipewyan chief. Hearne attributes the completion of his trek to the fact that he travelled with and lived as the Indians.

Samuel Hearne, of Hudson's Bay.

Crossing the barrens was always brutal. The ground is soft with moss and filled with sharp gravel. In winter, Hearne and his men were faced with the bitter cold. In summer, mosquitoes and flies made life a misery. At one point they were faced with a snowstorm in July.

It took 19 months of such hardships for Hearne to establish that there is no northwest passage, the Coppermine River will not accommodate company ships and reports of copper seem to be largely myth.

He notes: "Though my discoveries are not likely to prove of any material advantage to the nation at large or indeed to the Hudson's Bay Company, yet I have the pleasure to think that I have fully complied with the orders of my masters and that it has put a final end to all disputes concerning a northwest passage through Hudson's Bay."

Hearne, the first white man to reach the Arctic Ocean by land, discovered a 480-kilometre long lake and a river system, and has received a £200 bonus from the company.

Hearne and crew of Indian guides.

Governor appoints justices of peace

Aug. 8, 1772

ST. JOHN'S, Nfld. – Lord Molyneux Shuldham, governor of Newfoundland, has taken steps to bolster security in the colony by appointing three prominent individuals justices of the peace in the most populated areas: D'Ewes Coke to the Trinity District; Robert Grey to Harbour Grace; and Nicholas Gill to St. John's.

First Highland Scots arrive in Nova Scotia

Sept. 15, 1773

PICTOU, N.S. – A ship-weary group of 178 Scottish immigrants got a first glimpse of their new, Nova Scotia home today. After a dreary 11-week North Atlantic crossing, passengers from the brig *Hector* waded ashore at Pictou harbor to claim the land British authorities had promised them.

Most of the arrivals are economic refugees, poor tenant farmers fleeing high rents and bad harvests in Scotland. Their voyage here was horrible. Food and water were in short supply and storms lashed the tiny vessel. Eighteen children did not live to see Nova Scotia. The survivors are the first large-scale immigration of Highland Scots settlers to the colony. The British authorities in Halifax have made no attempt to purchase land for the newcomers. It belongs to the Micmac Indians, but the officials assume it belongs to the Crown.

Hudson's Bay Company constructs its first inland trading post

Sept. 3, 1774

CUMBERLAND HOUSE – A log building 11.4 metres by 7.8 metres, roofed with planks and caulked with moss, is the first permanent inland trading post of the Hudson's Bay Company. Samuel Hearne, in charge of the project, has named it Cumberland House. He has located it near convenient river connections to [Lake Winnipeg] and to the mountains. This spot is also only about 40 days travel from the company supply base of York Factory. Cumberland House is in direct competition with the many independent pedlars who proliferate in the country. However, these traders are supplied from Montreal, which is a good five months away.

The post offers such trade items such as Brazilian tobacco, gunpowder, shot, brandy and building supplies. Ten men will remain at Cumberland House over the winter, and in the spring furs will be shipped to York Factory.

Work begins on Cumberland House.

HBC trader taught how Blackfoot hunt

Nov. 25, 1772

EAGLE HILLS, Rupert's Land – Matthew Cocking, a Hudson's Bay Company employee, is reported to be living among the Blackfoot Indians of the plains, learning how they hunt the buffalo they depend on for survival.

Cocking left York Factory in June to try to convince the interior Indians to bring their furs to Hudson Bay instead of dealing them to traders from Montreal who recently poured into the fur country. The Indians received the young trader well, but told him they do not intend to make the long trip to the Bay as long as they trap few fur-bearing animals, and rely mainly on the buffalo to support themselves.

American congress slams Quebec Act

Sept. 5, 1774

PHILADELPHIA – The first continental congress of American colonies has called the Quebec Act a flagrant violation of human rights. The act, passed earlier this year, extends Quebec's control over lands – including the fur-trading area of the interior lakes – that the colonies had claimed for themselves.

The colonists see the Quebec Act and its establishment of laws and government over the disputed area as an act of tyranny. Congress's firm stand here underlines fears expressed earlier that rebellion was inevitable. The act has also not gone over well with English merchants in Quebec, who have organized and requested it be repealed.

First meeting of the continental congress of American colonies in Philadelphia.

Quebecers are urged to defy British rule

Carpenter's Hall, location for the continental congress of American colonies.

Oct. 21, 1774

QUEBEC CITY – American colonies are urging Quebecers to defy British rule and join their opposition to the controversial Quebec Act. Congress is asking the province to send delegates to its next meeting, scheduled for May. The Quebec Act, which extends the province's control over most of the interior of British North America, was denounced by the Americans as a violation of human rights.

News of the American stand, taken at the continental congress in Philadelphia last month, is filtering into the province from colonial papers. So far, the *Quebec Gazette* has not run the story, probably fearing the loss of government printing contracts. The Americans' invitation is likely to receive at least some consideration in the province, where English merchants are seeking the Quebec Act's repeal. The merchant lobby is stronger in Montreal, where 162 signatures were obtained, as opposed to just 25 in Quebec.

Angry anglo merchants consider options

June 22, 1774

QUEBEC CITY – English merchants here and in Montreal are enraged at the Quebec Act, and some are even considering extreme action. Their first impulse, sources say, is to join forces with Americans in their fight against imperial rule. But extremists are unlikely to get the upper hand because most merchants, particularly those in the fur trade, are aware of their economic dependence on England.

The Quebec Act, passed this year on the recommendation of Quebec Gov. Guy Carleton, marks the end of any attempt to establish government here based on English models. It marks a return to an authoritarian government and the French seigneurial system. A council of 17 to 23 members is to be appointed, to which the French are to be admitted without restrictions. There is no provision for an elected assembly. A combination of English common law and French civil law is to be used. The act also reaffirms freedom to worship for Roman Catholics, and gives the church the right to collect tithes from all Catholics.

To combat the act, English merchants are starting to form cabals, to produce papers for kings, lords and commons, asking for its repeal. Opposition is particularly strong in Montreal, where the merchants are richer and more radical than their counterparts here.

Cartoon shows the displeasure some people have for the Quebec Act.

1775 (1775-1776)

United States, June 27, 1775. The Continental Congress orders General Philip Schuyler to attack the British in Quebec.

Pacific Coast, Aug. 24, 1775. A Spanish expedition led by Bruno de Heceta to look for the Northwest Passage lands [at Prince of Wales Island] and claims the area for Spain.

Montreal, Nov. 13, 1775. American forces led by Richard Montgomery occupy Montreal after Governor Guy Carleton surrenders the city. British resistance to the American invasion has collapsed in almost all the province, and French-Canadians are remaining neutral.

Quebec, c.1775. The first Norway rats in North America reach the colony aboard ships from Europe. They multiply rapidly.

London, Mar. 9, 1776. Adam Smith publishes *An Inquiry into the Nature and Causes of the Wealth of Nations* in which he argues that economic growth occurs when individuals are left to pursue their self-interest. He provides a theoretical framework for the emerging industrial revolution.

Halifax, March 1776. The British fleet and army from the evacuation of Boston arrive, making the city the temporary centre of British power in North America.

Quebec, March 1776. A worried Governor Guy Carleton informs the British government that fuel and provisions are scarce as a result of an American blockade of the city led by Benedict Arnold.

Trois-Rivières, Quebec, June 1776. British and Canadian forces repulse an American invasion of the city.

Quebec, June 1776. The American army occupying Sorel and Montreal under John Sullivan and Benedict Arnold retreats to Crown Point on Lake Champlain in the face of an advancing British army led by Governor Guy Carleton.

Philadelphia, July 4, 1776. The Continental Congress approves the Declaration of Independence drafted by Thomas Jefferson which declares the American colonies independent from Britain.

Plymouth, England, July 12, 1776. James Cook leads a British naval expedition to search for a northwest passage on the west coast of America.

Act discourages settlement in Nfld.

July 31, 1775

NEWFOUNDLAND – The British government is hoping legislation it recently passed will discourage settlement in Newfoundland and encourage English fishermen in nearby waters to return to Britain at the end of each fishing season. This is because Newfoundland is considered a vital "nursery of seamen" that supplies trained deepwater sailors for British overseas shipping and the navy. The act comes into force Jan. 1, 1776.

People are calling the legislation Palliser's Act, since it includes several rules Sir Hugh Palliser enforced here when he was governor from 1764 to 1768. The number of British fishermen coming here then increased from 7,000 in 1764 to 12,000 in 1768, the total of resident fishermen fell from 10,000 to 7,000, and the number of seamen returning to the British Isles more than doubled from 5,562 to 11,811.

By Palliser's Act, fishing captains will retain one-half of each employee's wages until his ship is home at the end of the season.

Second continental congress addresses British-American crisis

George Washington addresses second continental congress in Philadelphia.

Sept. 12, 1775

PHILADELPHIA – Concerns about defence and the ongoing hostilities with Britain have dominated the second continental congress at its meetings here. The responsibility of protecting the continent has taken more of congress's time than even the yet-to-be achieved independence.

Earlier this year, the continental congress took responsibility for the Massachusetts forces, which were enlarged to be the continental army under Virginia's George Washington. While the prevailing philosophy here is an army should be manned by citizens, not full-time soldiers, Washington believes that his only chance of beating the regular British army is with a similarly trained and organized armed force.

Fort Ticonderoga falls to rebels without a single shot fired

May 10, 1775

FORT TICONDEROGA, Lake Champlain – A strange battle took place here today: British versus British, with the goal being the control of this military outpost. While the garrison slept, Benedict Arnold, Ethan Allen and their force of 100 men walked into the fort, which surrendered without a shot being fired.

The seizure of Fort Ticonderoga and neighboring Crown Point and Fort George came as relations between London and the Thirteen Colonies broke down. Because of this, the "Americans," as they are calling themselves, have decided that the only way to control their own taxes and livelihoods is to gain independence. And the only way to gain independence is by military force. Hence the raid here.

A view of Ticonderoga from the middle of the channel at Lake Champlain.

American rebels suffer a huge defeat at Quebec

Dec. 31, 1775

QUEBEC CITY – With Montreal already in their power, American rebel forces today attacked Quebec City during a pre-dawn blizzard. Leading them were Richard Montgomery, formerly of the British army, and Benedict Arnold, who had left Massachusetts with 1,100 men, and after a gruelling march, had reached Quebec with half of them still alive. The Americans wanted to get on with the bloodshed and complete their conquest of the colony.

The defenders' champion was the unflappable, cautious, yet resourceful Gov. Guy Carleton, 51, who'd been wounded when the British captured this same fortress in 1759. Luckily for him, his meagre forces here were recently bolstered by some Highland soldiers, Newfoundland fishermen, crew off British ships, and both French and British-Canadian militia.

"Come on brave boys, Quebec is ours," Montgomery cried, and led his men into a French-Canadian ambush. He fell at once. His men fled from the murderous gunfire. Meanwhile, Arnold was wounded in another assault. When his men hesitated, the British regrouped and routed them in a bloody street fight. Daylight came. The Union Jack still flew over Quebec, and a patrol found a hand protruding from a snowdrift. The soldiers uncovered Montgomery's corpse.

Quebec's second barrier withstands attack by Benedict Arnold and his men.

Benedict Arnold and his men march through the wilderness toward Quebec.

General Richard Montgomery's death during attack on Quebec by Americans.

Bishop condemns American revolt

May 1775

QUEBEC CITY – American revolutionaries won't get any sympathy from Quebec Bishop Jean-Olivier Briand, and neither will their Catholic supporters here. Briand has condemned all Catholics who sympathize with the revolutionaries, and he's urging his flock to remain obedient to the British king. The bishop warns, in a pastoral letter, that he will excommunicate any Catholic who collaborates with the enemy.

Nova Scotia swears loyalty to the Crown

June 24, 1775

HALIFAX – Shocked by the rebellion against the Crown in Massachusetts, House of Assembly officials today promised king and parliament Nova Scotia was one colony that would stay loyal to the Mother Country. The battles of Lexington and Concord launched the American Revolution in April. Fort Ticonderoga, on Lake Champlain, fell to the Americans in May. One week ago, at the Battle of Bunker Hill, 1,150 redcoats fell.

Horrified by these events, the House of Assembly has just passed an address to king and parliament. In it, the Nova Scotians say they "most humbly acknowledge our gracious sovereign George the third, king of Great Britain, the lords spiritual and temporal, and the commons of Great Britain ... to be the supreme legislature of this province, and of all the British dominions, and that it is our indispensible duty to pay a due proportion of the expense of this great empire." With respect to "this dreadful and alarming crisis," meaning the rebellion, "We tremble at the gloomy prospect before us."

Vandals target bust of King George III

May 1, 1775

MONTREAL – Vandals targeted a bust of King George III at Place d'Armes today, blackening its face and placing a rosary of potatoes around its neck. The unidentified criminals also defaced the monument with the inscription: "Behold, the Pope of Canada, or the English idiot."

Officials suspect the crime was committed by Montrealers who sympathize with anti-British, American sentiments.

American rebels seize Fort Chambly

Fort Chambly capture by American rebels is considered an important victory.

May 17, 1775

CHAMBLY, Que. – American rebels have gained a crucial foothold by capturing Fort Chambly. The invaders battered down the old fort's stone wall and captured the gunpowder and supplies, which the British had failed to destroy. It is feared that if the invaders are able to capture St. Jean next, it would put them in a position to establish themselves at Sorel, at the junction of the St. Lawrence and Richelieu rivers. There, they could effectively cut off Montreal from Quebec and move against either centre.

Chambly's fall is considered a turning point for the Americans, who had experienced some setbacks. Sickness and lack of discipline plagued the invaders, who are now set to move against St. Jean.

Clergy told to urge worshipers to arms

May 30, 1775

MONTREAL – Local priests have been ordered to tell their worshipers they must fight against American invaders advancing up Lake Champlain toward Montreal. At the urging of Quebec Gov. Guy Carleton, Grand Vicar Etienne Montgolfier issued a circular reminding his priests their habitants must obey government orders to take up arms against the invaders. Many habitants are known to be sympathetic to the Americans and their promises of greater liberty.

Ben Franklin fails to annex Canada

American commissioner Benjamin Franklin wants to annex Canada.

Feb. 15, 1776

MONTREAL – Ben Franklin and two fellow American commissioners arrived here to mend fences and pave the way for the annexation of Canada, but their mission has failed. The Americans arrived in response to a Canadian petition to the continental congress at Philadelphia, seeking the re-opening of the woolen cloth trade to the west that had been cut off on Gen. Charles Lee's orders.

Congress had hoped the trade interruption would bring a full Canadian delegation, giving them an opportunity to invite Canada into the union. But the Canadians didn't bite and aren't biting now, even with the expected re-opening of trade by Franklin.

Loyalists quell Fort Cumberland uprising

Nov. 28, 1776

FORT CUMBERLAND, N.S. – A three-week siege by American rebels and their local sympathizers at this fortress on the Isthmus of Chignecto collapsed at dawn after Royal Marines and Boston-recruited loyalists stole out of the fort in darkness, and then pounced on the enemy's sleepy camp. The rebel force was a motley band of ardent revolutionists from Machias, [Maine], swelled by other New Englanders and a bunch of Nova Scotian farmers led by Jonathan Eddy, armed with clubs, pikes, fowling pieces, pistols, swords and other throwbacks to the war with France. Eddy hoped to take Fort Cumberland, gather reinforcements and roll on triumphantly to Halifax, but this morning his "Army of Liberty" was hightailing it through the woods, and the loyal troops were burning farms.

Most other people in this area are staunchly loyal: the south shore's Americans, victims of Revolutionary privateers; Haligonians dependent on imperial trade; Lunenburg's Germans; and Cumberland's loyal Yorkshire Methodists.

Lower Quebec is the residential and commercial centre of city, its expansion limited by development of religious institutions and military installations.

Town hopes to join American rebellion

May 14, 1776

NOVA SCOTIA [New Brunswick] – At a meeting American sympathizers held today, Maugerville, the only large settlement in the St. John River Valley, announced plans to secede from British rule and join the rebellion in New England. Among resolutions passed by 125 townsfolk: a denial of Britain's right to impose laws on the colonies; Maugerville's intention to place itself under the government of Massachusetts; the nomination of a committee to conduct all civil and military matters in the town; and a ruling binding settlers to obey the orders of this new oligarchy, and also to help fund the rebellion. One resolution ostracizes the 13 townsfolk who refused to sign the document: "We will have no dealings ... with any ... persons ... that shall refuse to enter into the foregoing or similar resolutions."

Since many colonists along the St. John River are New Englanders, there's support here for the rebellion. But it took Rev. Seth Noble to inflame settlers with revolutionary zeal. He asked George Washington to capture this colony, but was refused. Undaunted, Noble and his cohorts believe they can conquer the river valley by themselves.

Victory caps off a successful campaign

Oct. 11, 1776

CROWN POINT, Lake Champlain – The American menace which has lurked around Lake Champlain all summer has finally been driven back from the British fort of Crown Royal. Loyal troops under Guy Carleton, the governor of Quebec, have engaged and defeated armed American ships on the lake. As well, they have retaken Crown Royal, or, at least, taken control of its smouldering ruins. The retreating Americans torched the fort before they left.

The victory caps off a successful campaign that started when the rebels invaded Canada last year. It certainly redeems Carleton, who surrendered Montreal to the invaders Nov. 13. That captured town became a base for the rebels, who proceeded to attack Quebec City on New Year's Eve. Only stout resistance by defending British troops and a blinding snowstorm kept them from success.

Events turned with the arrival of spring, and more British reinforcements. The Americans prudently abandoned Montreal on May 9, and have been on the run, more or less, ever since. So much for their easy invasion of Canada.

British navy whips up a Surprise frigate

Benedict Arnold leads rebel force.

May 6, 1776

QUEBEC CITY – "Surprise!" And it wasn't a pleasant one for an American force attacking Quebec, as the frigate *Surprise* sailed into Quebec harbor today, the first ship of a British fleet that is bringing a force of 10,000 men. The invaders, who had failed throughout the winter to take Quebec, retreated immediately. The American force of 800 men led by Benedict Arnold had entered Quebec last year via a little-used route up the Kennebec and by taking the Dead River to the Chaudière, which joins the St. Lawrence above this centre.

His Majesty's armed vessels successfully turn back an American attack.

Mohawk chief Brant a big hit in Britain

June 1776

LONDON, England – Mohawk war chief Thayendanegea (pronounced Tai-yen-da-nay-geh) was a veritable social lion in London this past winter. The young man – known as Joseph Brant in English – came here in December with Guy Johnson, nephew of the late Sir William Johnson, the superintendent of Indian Affairs.

Brant has acted for nearly a decade as an Iroquois interpreter and agent for William Johnson, and now for Guy, his replacement. He came to Britain to present Mohawk land grievances to the British government and learn more about the current civil war in America.

The urbane North American Indian fascinates London. King George III received him at St. James' Palace, and on that occasion Brant wore a splendid Indian costume. George Romney, Sir Joshua Reynolds' rival, painted Brant's portrait, showing him dressed in an Indian blanket and plumes, holding a tomahawk. Society, in general, has adopted and entertained Brant.

Young merchant sets up shop in Montreal

1776

MONTREAL – Simon McTavish, a young merchant in his mid-20s, has moved here from Albany, N.Y., where he has been engaged in business. A native of Scotland, McTavish came to America as a boy and has prospered supplying goods to the fur trade. Now that the War of Independence has erupted in the American colonies, several of their merchants have transferred their business to the northwest. McTavish is known as a lover of "good wine, good oysters and pretty girls."

Polar bears thriving on coast of Labrador

April 1776

LABRADOR – White bears, also known as polar bears, are thriving on the coast of Labrador. One of entrepreneur George Cartwright's men recently "saw the tracks of near a hundred white bears which had lately crossed Sandwich Bay."

Moravian missionary Jens Haven recorded in 1775 that the coast abounded with white bears. Cartwright, the first European to establish a trading post in Labrador, has dismissed the possibility of farming the area because it would be too hard "to fence against the white bears and wolves," apparently the major local predators.

The health of the bears in Labrador is encouraging in view of the fact that humans have largely killed them off in Newfoundland and around the Gulf of St. Lawrence. Europeans and Indians hunt them for their shaggy pelts that fetch a pretty price across the Atlantic. In the interest of obtaining furs, the French have supplied the Indians with guns to hunt the bears. Fishermen kill the bears because they prey on the racks where cod is dried.

Cartwright wearing his snowshoes.

Carleton rewarded with a knighthood

July 6, 1776

QUEBEC CITY – Guy Carleton, governor of this British outpost and commander of troops which drove back an American invasion last year, has been recognized for his efforts with a knighthood. The recognition is a bit half-hearted. Some British officials feel Carleton should have pursued the Americans to their total defeat after routing their invasion last year.

New tax act helps pay for government

April 5, 1775

QUEBEC CITY – A new tax to support the government of this British possession has been introduced. The Quebec Revenue Act revises the range of duties on merchants levied for the old French regime. This became necessary after the merchants didn't pay the old taxes. Britain's Declaratory Act ending colonial taxation means colonies must raise their own monies.

1777 (1777-1779)

Baffin Bay, June 5, 1777. A British naval expedition led by Walter Young turns back after reaching a latitude of 72 degrees north. They were sent to complete a survey of Baffin Bay and investigate if the sea found by Samuel Hearne [Arctic Ocean] can be reached via the bay.

Quebec, June 17, 1777. British General John Burgoyne leads a force of 7,500 down Lake Champlain, planning to split the American colonies in half along Lake Champlain and the Hudson River.

Bennington, Vermont, Aug. 16, 1777. American militia repulse a British raid. The British lose 900 men.

Nova Scotia, November 1777. The British finish building Fort Howe at the mouth of the St. John River [New Brunswick] to defend against Americans and Indians.

Sandwich Islands, Jan. 19, 1778. James Cook's expedition lands on the islands [Hawaii]. They are perhaps the first Europeans on the islands.

Arctic, August 1778. James Cook's expedition sails northeast from the Bering Strait with hopes of finding the Northwest Passage to Baffin Bay, but arctic ice forces them to turn back. They sail south along the west coast of North America, still looking for a northwest passage.

Nova Scotia, Sept. 24, 1778. At Fort Howe, Malecite and Micmac leaders take the oath of allegiance to Britain and agree to shun the American-sponsored rebels at Machias. They give strings of wampum to the British to emphasize the seriousness of their pledge.

The Northwest, July 2, 1779. Independent fur trader Peter Pond arrives at Cumberland House with three canoes laden with furs after wintering on the Athabaska River. He acquired some 8,400 beaver pelts from the Indians, but had to leave most of them behind.

Nova Scotia, 1779. Indian Superintendent Michael Francklin keeps the Micmacs and Malecites on the British side by giving them gifts.

United States, 1779. American troops under General Sullivan invade Six Nations territory to punish the Iroquois for their loyalty to the British. They burn crops and destroy villages. Iroquois warriors retaliate by destroying American farms.

Americans repel British at Saratoga

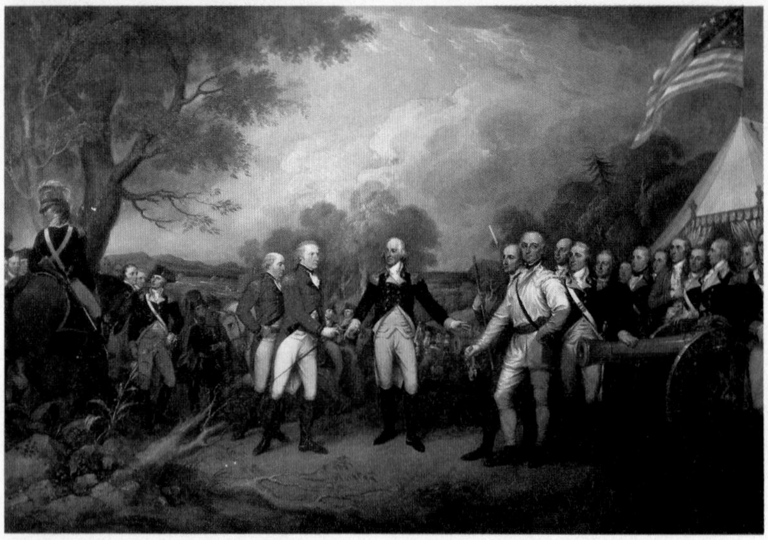

British force General John Burgoyne surrenders to Americans at Saratoga.

Oct. 7, 1777

SARATOGA, N.Y. – A British force Gen. John Burgoyne was leading suffered heavy losses in being repulsed by the Americans here. Reports indicate about 600 of his 1,500 men were killed, wounded or missing. American losses are estimated at just 150. An American observer came across the British in a wheat field, and reported to his superiors that the enemy front was open and that it was also vulnerable in its flanks. Benedict Arnold, who had fallen from favor and was relieved of his command in the American forces, was reluctantly given approval to investigate when fighting broke out, but instead he flung himself into the battle.

Synagogue the first to open in Canada

1777

MONTREAL – Canada finally has its first permanent synagogue. Located in Montreal, the Shearith Israel Congregation, the fourth established in North America, has now moved out of the temporary premises it occupied on St. James Street since Dec. 30, 1768. Shearith Israel, at the corner of Notre Dame and St. James streets, is built on land donated by the family of the late Lazarus David. His son David is the first Quebec-born Jew.

War leading blacks to come to Quebec

1777

QUEBEC CITY – Increasing numbers of blacks, both free and enslaved, are arriving in the colony as a result of the American War of Independence. Loyalists from the Thirteen Colonies are migrating to British-held regions and bringing their slaves with them. At the same time, American slaves are being encouraged to escape to British soil. In 1775, British authorities, hoping to undermine economic productivity in the rebellious colonies, promised freedom to slaves who escaped from their American owners and joined the British forces.

Traders reach fur-rich Lake Athabasca

October 1778

LAKE ATHABASCA – Fur traders in the northwest have succeeded for the first time in reaching Lake Athabasca, the source of some of the richest pelts to come out of the fur country. In June, Peter Pond, one of the Canadian traders on the Saskatchewan River, set off with three canoes in search of a route into the Athabasca region.

Led by Indian guides, Pond and his men struggled up the Churchill River to the Methye Portage. This narrow footpath, 19 kilometres long, traverses the height of land dividing the Mackenzie River basin and the Arctic from rivers flowing to the south. The first white men to cross the portage, Pond and his followers descended the Athabasca River to the great lake which no other trader or explorer has ever been known to see.

A former soldier with a violent temper and a history of dueling, Pond only arrived in the northwest from Detroit three years ago. But he has quickly made a name for himself as an energetic trader with a taste for exploration. He is carrying goods supplied to him by traders who hope he will contact the Indians of the far north.

Competition for furs has become so fierce on the Saskatchewan River that traders are always on the lookout for untapped territories. Pond has built a log post not far from the lake where he will spend the winter trading with the local Chipewyan trappers.

Grand Manan Island in New Brunswick is the largest and the most remote of the three major islands at the entrance to Bay of Fundy.

Haldimand arrives to govern Quebec

June 1777

QUEBEC CITY – The new governor of Quebec, Frederick Haldimand, is here to take up his post. He replaces Sir Guy Carleton, who resigned after ongoing quarrels with provincial administrators. Haldimand, a Swiss-born 58-year-old, is a longtime British army officer. He has been in Canada before – in fact, he was military governor of Trois-Rivières in 1762-63. Friends call him an honest man, but one who demands loyalty and obedience from subordinates.

The tasks facing Haldimand are not simple. First and foremost, he must contend with the American rebellion and attacks on British troops by disloyal forces. In addition, the vastness of the Quebec territory, which runs west to the Great Lakes, and the lack of troops to deal with American traders in this area make control difficult, if not impossible. Finally, France joining the conflict doesn't help.

HBC hires surveyor to map vast empire

April 30, 1778

HUDSON BAY – The Hudson's Bay Company has gone and hired Philip Turnor, the first servant employed solely for the purpose of surveying and mapping the vast company empire. Turnor, a 27-year-old surveyor and mathematician from England, has a signed three-year contract to survey the northwest country. He will keep geographical data, map rivers and locate trading posts.

Turnor brings to the job an interesting concept of surveying. He believes the best strategy is to go inland and follow the rivers all the way to the ocean, rather than the other way around, which is the general practice. His reasoning is that following a river upstream always poses the dilemma of which branch to follow when two streams meet. Which is the main river is not always obvious.

By going downstream there is never any question. As rivers flow to the sea they increase in width and the water runs faster.

Privateers cause food shortages in Nfld.

British naval ship the Milford challenges American marauder in the Atlantic.

1778

NEWFOUNDLAND – When an American vessel is seen plying the waters near The Rock these days, Newfoundlanders find little reason to rejoice. For years the sight of an American ship signalled the arrival of needed foodstuffs; these days it means only harassment, possible loss of ships and equipment, and a grim reminder that food is short.

Food from the American colonies has long been a necessity for the outport communities of Newfoundland, where the barren nature of the land makes agriculture close to impossible. The American Revolution, however, has brought with it a trade embargo, and ships sailing from New England ports now have a new mission in mind. As privateers, they have targeted the Newfoundland fisheries for disruption. Their presence threatens supply ships, and by seizing vessels, the privateers are depriving Newfoundlanders in the outports of both the needs and the means for their livelihood.

Religious revival sweeping rural N.S.

1779

NOVA SCOTIA – The gospel – according to Henry Alline – is spreading like wildfire through rural communities in the Annapolis Valley, delivering New Englanders settled there from two evils affecting their lives: isolation and the threat of political upheaval.

In a land bereft of churches and schools, Alline's New Light movement stresses a sense of pride in both community and the neutral stance most New Englanders here have adopted toward the War of Independence. A self-taught itinerant lay preacher, Alline is organizing prayer meetings and hymn recitals throughout the region with a zeal many find hard to resist.

Washington nixes plan to attack Canada

November 1778

PHILADELPHIA – Plans to attack Canada have been vetoed by Gen. George Washington, thereby ending – at least for now – the threat of another invasion. The attack plan had been formulated in the wake of an alliance between the United States and France. France's Marquis de Lafayette made plans for attacking Canadian posts between Montreal and Detroit, while at the same time naval action in the St. Lawrence was to be launched.

Congress approved the plan, but Washington rejected it because he felt the price for kicking the English out of Canada would be in effect inviting France to resume possession. There is suspicion here that Lafayette's real motive was to keep the U.S. weak and therefore dependent on France for support. Washington is not ready to bite.

The North West Co. to compete for furs

Summer 1779

MONTREAL – A group of Montreal merchants has joined with several experienced inland fur traders to form a new partnership which will give its members added strength in their rivalry with the Hudson's Bay Company. Called the North West Company, the new firm is actually an alliance of nine separate partnerships, each holding two shares in the company. Members of the group include veteran traders like the brothers Benjamin and Joseph Frobisher, Peter Pond and John Ross, and prominent Montreal merchants like Isaac Todd, James McGill, Lawrence Ermatinger and Simon McTavish.

North West Co. armorial bearings.

The North West Company is the end result of a trend that has been evident for several years. The fur trade has extended its reach over 5,000 kilometres into the northwest so that it is very expensive for a single individual to outfit a trading expedition. Instead, "pedlars" have been making informal partnerships, pooling their goods to reduce the costly competition. Pond was backed by one of these partnerships when he made his daring trek to the Athabasca country last year.

Members of the new company agree to spread themselves evenly throughout the fur country, and to divide returns at the end of each season. The agreement is renewable after one year. The new company combines the efforts of some of the most successful fur traders in Canada. It promises to give the Hudson's Bay Company a real fight for control of the interior trade.

Captain Cook and crew land at "Friendly Cove"

British explorer, Capt. James Cook.

March 29, 1778

NOOTKA SOUND – The British naval explorer, Capt. James Cook, has reached the west coast of Vancouver Island. Cook sailed his two ships, *Resolution* and *Discovery,* into Nootka Sound, where he was met with such a welcome from the Nootka inhabitants that he has christened the spot "Friendly Cove."

As the British ships approached the shore, about 30 canoes came out to greet them. The people wore ceremonial dress and offered goods to trade. "They seemed to be a mild inoffensive people, showed great readiness to part with anything they had and took whatever was offered to them in exchange, but were most desirous of iron than anything else," reports the captain.

Cook is on his way to the Arctic to seek a northwest passage around the top of America. He has decided to pause to repair his ships and take on supplies. Already his men have traded several beautiful sea otter pelts from the Indians.

The captain is no stranger to America's British colonies. Twenty years ago, he served at the siege of Louisbourg in Nova Scotia, and later surveyed the coastline of Newfoundland. Since then he has made two great voyages of exploration through the Pacific Ocean.

Capt. James Cook's ships moored at Nootka Sound, Vancouver Island.

Capt. James Cook stops at Nootka Sound and meets the natives.

Wilderness is home for many loyalists

1779

CANADA – The areas most loyalists leave are far more developed than the often-pristine wilderness of [Ontario]. The streams Canadians call "creeks" serve the inhabitants as roads. Fish swim through them, and they are usually clean enough to drink from. Connected to these creeks are swamps that at first discourage would-be pioneers. But when they are drained, the land becomes wonderfully fertile. Ponds also proliferate here, sodeep people can dive into them before swimming.

The waterways also provide fuel in the form of rude peat. Loyalists call it "muck" and hack it off in large chunks. Muck burns with an invisible flame and a fine aroma.

Loyalists share their new homes with abundant wildlife, including swarms of mosquitoes. Wolves, deer and bear are common. So are passenger pigeons and field mice.

Quebec gets first public library in Canada

1779

QUEBEC CITY – Gov. Frederick Haldimand opened Quebec's and Canada's first circulating public library today. The driving force behind the project, Haldimand says having a library is necessary to acquaint Britain's new subjects with English customs and law.

Individual subscription memberships are available at £5 a year. Representing more money than the average laborer here earns in a month, it is feared that this fee is too high. Critics of the high price have suggested that 30 shillings per annum would have been more in line. Canada's oldest college library was founded at the Quebec Seminary in 1668.

Clampdown targets colony's seigneurs

Aug. 28, 1777

QUEBEC CITY – Quebec's sorry state of financial affairs has prompted the government to clamp down on landholders who failed to pay their rent to the Crown. A proclamation was issued today that forces seigneurs to appear at Quebec before December 1778. They will have to pledge loyalty, and exchange deeds and rent rolls for authenticated copies.

THE OLD CHURCH OF ST. ANNE DE BEAUPRÉ.

Quebec's Ste. Anne de Beaupré church has stood since 1676.

Influx of refugees straining resources

Oct. 14, 1778

QUEBEC CITY – The ongoing rebellion in the Thirteen Colonies has resulted in a flood of refugees coming to Quebec. Known as loyalists because of their allegiance to the Crown in the face of their compatriots' treason, they are heading here to avoid persecution.

The influx has strained resources in the colony. So much so, that Gov. Frederick Haldimand wrote the British government for help today. He needs more supplies and government money to resettle these people, whom he calls "loyalists in great distress." To that end, the governor has established a community for them at Machiche, near Trois-Rivières. Local militia are building barracks to house refugees, and merchants are supplying food and clothing. It's estimated 1,000 civilians have fled to Canada this fall, in addition to the 3,000 troops who have also arrived.

British foil rebels' plot to seize river

June 30, 1777

NOVA SCOTIA – A British naval force reached the mouth of the St. John River today and routed an encampment of American rebels and Nova Scotian turncoats who planned to seize the whole river for the American Revolution.

The rebel leader was John Allan, a Nova Scotian who fled the province last August, met George Washington at his headquarters on the Delaware, and got an assignment to enlist Indians in the rebel cause along the St. John.

When Allan arrived here recently, he also counted on the support of sympathizers among the pioneers, but a Colonel Gould had just come up from Halifax, extracted oaths of loyalty to the Crown from the rivermouth settlers, and left.

Aboard three vessels, the British arrived in force today, with Captain Hawker in command. They killed several of Allan's men – he had fewer than 100 – and captured more. Others fled upriver, with the redcoats in hot pursuit. Now, the river remains British in law, if not entirely in the hearts of New Englanders who settled along its shores.

Some unlicensed coureurs de bois are continuing to trade furs.

Nootka people start to move inland

Native of Nootka Sound in far west.

Nootka man at time of Capt. Cook.

A family of Nootka Sound Indians.

August 1778

NOOTKA, Northwest Coast – After a summer spent fishing and hunting whales and sea otters, the Nootka people are starting to move away from the coast to the river inlets inland. Here they will catch salmon going upstream to spawn, and then dry and smoke them for the winter.

After the big ships left, some families urged the chiefs to order a larger sea otter haul. This was needed, they said, to satisfy the men from the ships who will be back soon to trade. The women could prepare the extra pelts and set them aside for the next visit of the ships. But their advice was ignored and the traditional hunting and fishing – by the men – and gathering shellfish and berries – by the women – went on as before.

Soon whole familes will have deserted the houses by the seashore for the fishing camps built by the side of the inland streams. Then, in November, the families will go inland for the winter. Here they can catch deer and bear in traps if they are hungry. Most of the time, however, will be spent feasting and potlatching, for it is usually too rainy to spend much time outdoors.

When the days start to get longer, nearly all the food will be gone and the families will start to move back to the coast for the herring run. This need to move to maintain the food supply is the reason why Nootka chiefs must own property and resources in many places.

War expands in Newfoundland waters

Oct. 5, 1778

NEWFOUNDLAND – Recent fighting in and around Newfoundland has prompted Rear-Admiral John Montagu to strengthen local defences and oversee the capture of St-Pierre and Miquelon islands from France.

The fighting has taken its toll on Newfoundland. An American privateer raided Placentia Bay in May, and more recently a 22-gun privateer schooner caused great destruction on the coast of Labrador. Businesses operated by Noble and Pinsent and by George Cartwright have been destroyed. While missing the privateer, a ship Montagu sent to Labrador captured another vessel, averting more destruction.

Treaty ends Miramichi district hostilities

July 20, 1779

NOVA SCOTIA – Micmac chief John Julian and the British signed a treaty today, ending hostilities in the Miramichi River district of [New Brunswick]. The agreement has forced rebel Micmac chief Caiffe to flee, and it gives Julian's people "licence to occupy" 20,000 acres along the river's northwest branch. However, the Indians have been denied the right to claim ownership over the land, and questions over native land rights were at the root of the recent hostilities.

The trouble began in 1765 when a commercial fishery was granted 100,000 acres along the river. Its fisheries interfered with those of the Miramichi Indians and encroached on the locations of several villages.

Pond finds deposits of black substance

Autumn 1778

LAKE ATHABASCA, Rupert's Land – Peter Pond, fur trader, army officer and explorer, has found an El Dorado of prime pelts in the country near here – and pools of a black pitch-like substance. This substance burns when put on a fire. Pond, who has few companions and fewer friends because of his short-fused temper, plans to spend the winter here, organizing the fur trade for the partners who equipped him with a stock of trade goods.

Pond assembled his goods at Cumberland House and then moved north to the Methye Portage. From there he canoed to the lake and met big groups of Cree and Chipewyans who happily traded with him because they would then not have to make the long trip to Churchill. ▷

British warship blown up in sea battle with French

Battle between French frigate La Surveillante and British frigate Le Quebec.

British frigate Le Quebec burns off coast of Ushant, in Brittany.

Oct. 7, 1779

BRITTANY, France – The British warship *Quebec* was blown up and burned in a fierce battle with a French ship off the coast here. The French frigate, *La Surveillante,* encountered the English frigate near the coast of Ushant, an island off the western tip of Brittany that is also known as Ouessant Island.

While details of the battle and casualties are sketchy as yet, it is known that the French ship enjoyed an edge in firepower. *La Surveillante* had 40 guns, compared to 32 for the *Quebec*. Frigates are three-masted warships, full-rigged with a single gun deck.

The heated battle at sea occurred amid a backdrop of hostility between the two countries, made more volatile by France's support of the American revolutionaries. Ushant Island, a rocky mass which covers about 15 square kilometres in area, is the site of a lighthouse which marks the south entrance to the English Channel.

Cartwright's sport fatal for 6 polar bears

July 22, 1778

LABRADOR – There are six fewer polar bears in Labrador today. Entrepreneur George Cartwright and his comrades shot the animals on an expedition to Eagle River. Cartwright describes the day's slaughter as "the finest sport that man ever had" – though he recovered only a single bearskin.

For the bears, the day was a tragedy. At one point, Cartwright shot a mother in the head as she swam by with her cub. The baby charged, apparently to avenge the death of its mother, but Cartwright shot it twice in the eyes. The bears are abundant here in Labrador, but in the Gulf of St. Lawrence have been hunted almost to extinction.

Harp sealing on the rise in Newfoundland

June 15, 1779

NEWFOUNDLAND – The rise of industry in recent years has led to a growing demand for seal oil – and, indeed, for all kinds of oil – in the British markets. Drying oils, for example, are needed for the paints and varnishes used in the building and furniture industries.

At the same time, non-drying oils are also in great demand. They are used to lubricate machinery, for the manufacture of leather and woollen textiles, and for street and other types of lighting. The increasing demand for non-drying oils has made both British whale oil from the Arctic and seal oil from Newfoundland much sought-after items here and abroad.

Polar bears, or white bears, as they are known, are abundant in Labrador.

Seal oil from Newfoundland is in great demand in the British market.

Navigator James Cook stabbed, beaten to death

Feb. 14, 1779

KEALAKEKUA BAY, Sandwich Islands – Capt. James Cook is dead. The navigator who braved the perils of icebergs in both the southern and northern seas and explored strange lands was stabbed and clubbed to death here by the people he loved and trusted. It is still difficult to find out exactly what happened, for Cook's men are in shock. Apparently there was a dispute with the natives over a stolen pinnace and in the melee Cook stumbled and fell into the water where he was stabbed and beaten.

Cook is best known for voyages that began in 1768 and 1772, during which he explored and mapped the coast of Australia, New Zealand and many of the islands in the south Pacific. On his last voyage, which began in 1776, his orders were to find the Northwest Passage. He reached Nootka Sound in March 1778 and then sailed up the coast into the Bering Strait. But then his ships faced a large wall of ice which forced Cook to turn back and winter in the Sandwich Islands.

Captain Cook is killed by the natives of Kealakekua Bay who had until now loved and trusted the explorer.

Nfld. saltfish trade a bonus for Britain

Oct. 31, 1779

NEWFOUNDLAND – The British fishery in Newfoundland has recovered nicely from the war of rebellion in North America and the disruption it caused in 1776. Ninety-five fishing ships came to Newfoundland this year, and 103 trading ships followed them to take the fish to market. These vessels employed 2,329 men. In addition, these British ships carried a further 226 boatkeepers and their employees, as well as 1,819 men who fished from shore.

Together, these fishermen produced about 7,500 tons of saltfish. An even larger amount, 13,150 tons, was produced by British subjects now making their homes in Newfoundland. Although Spain's participation in war has closed Spanish markets for now, it is hoped the demand for saltfish in Portugal, Italy and the British West Indies will be sufficient to take the year's total production.

Clinton replaces Howe as commander-in-chief in North America

April 1778

PHILADELPHIA – British Gen. Sir Henry Clinton has replaced Sir William Howe as commander-in-chief in North America. Howe's recent defeat at the hands of George Washington's troops in Philadelphia has much to do with Clinton's appointment. Washington disgraced Howe at a time when Clinton had just redeemed Sullivan's Island at Newport. Clinton's star was rising as Howe's was in decline.

When first offered the new position, Clinton hesitated and even tried to resign, saying he would much prefer detached service in Florida to the command-in-chief. But his superiors gave him no choice in the matter, and Clinton received his orders this month to come to Philadelphia and take over from Howe.

The Banks of Newfoundland: ballad portrays crew's plight

18th century

ATLANTIC REGION – *The Banks of Newfoundland* is a popular sea-ballad portraying the plight of a shipwrecked crew as they contemplate cannibalism. This is how it goes:

We fasted for three days and nights, our provisions giving out.

On the morning of the fourth day, we cast our lots about.

The lot it fell on the captain's son; thinking relief at hand,

We spared him for another night on the banks of Newfoundland.

The plight of a shipwrecked crew off the banks of Newfoundland.

18th century civilian and military fashion trends

A Canadian engineer's typical costume around the middle of 18th century.

An officer of the British Army and a Quebec merchant in winter dress.

Illustration shows a French artillery gunner in full uniform of the time.

A member of the French-Canadian militia around mid-18th century.

Illustration shows a private in the Canadian Troupe de la Marine.

Member of a Canadian marine regiment early in the 18th century.

French-Canadian woman in a winter dress, and a Roman Catholic priest.

A young woman's dress could easily be made with a printed material.

This three-piece dress is popular with many fashionable colonial women.

The English lords and counts wore this type of vest and coat in the 1760s.

Women often wear dresses like this one on those special evenings out.

1780 (1780-1784)

Quebec, 1782. Author Friederike Riedesel writes that Canadians do not know how to pickle gherkins (cucumbers). Gherkins are usually salted in the colony, though vinegar marinades have been used in France since the 1600s.

New York, March 1783. News of a preliminary peace ending the American War of Independence sparks a wave of persecutions, confiscations, and proscriptions against loyalists. Thousands of them inform British commissioner Guy Carleton they have decided to go to Nova Scotia.

United States, April 26, 1783. A convoy of 32 ships carrying 2,383 loyalist refugees, known as the Spring Fleet, leaves Sandy Hook for the St. John River.

London, June 10, 1783. The British government orders the governor of Nova Scotia to grant free land to loyalist immigrants.

New York, June 15, 1783. A second fleet departs carrying loyalists to British North America. Eighteen ships carry 2,472 people, mostly going to the St. John River.

Halifax, June 24, 1783. Commissary-General Brook Watson instructs the captain of the *Stafford*, transporting loyalists to Nova Scotia, to issue one pound of bread and 12 ounces of pork per day to everyone aboard the ship. The Nova Scotia government has agreed to supply the loyalists with food during their trip to the colony and for a year after their arrival.

Spain, Oct. 22, 1783. Charles III agrees to pay to transport Acadians in France to join their relatives and compatriots living in Louisiana, now under Spanish rule.

Quebec, May 22, 1784. Ten Mississauga Indians led by Wabakinine sign an agreement surrendering a vast area at the western end of Lake Ontario to the British, reserving only the "Mississauga Tract" between the Credit River and Burlington Bay. They give up about half of their hunting grounds.

Newfoundland, 1784. As a result of an agreement between the British government and the Vatican, Reverend James O'Donnell arrives from Ireland to serve as Prefect Apostolic.

Quebec, 1784. Nuns at the Augustine monastery of the Hôtel-Dieu open a small hospital ward with 18 beds.

Niagara land deal suits British fine

May 9, 1781

NIAGARA – The presence of several hundred white loyalists at Niagara has led the British government to purchase lands on the west bank of Niagara River, just opposite Fort Niagara. The governor is hoping that the loyalist farmers will supply provisions for the fort.

Guy Johnson, the new superintendent of Indian Affairs, obtained the deed today from the Mississauga Indians, one of three Indian signatories being the young Mississauga chief, Wabakinine, a good friend of the British.

Johnson has fulfilled – to the letter – his instructions to make the purchase of the tract of land 6.4 kilometres wide and about 40 kilometres long, "upon the most advantageous terms." To this end, he gave the Indians 300 suits of clothing.

In his letter written today to Gov. Frederick Haldimand at Quebec, Johnson also mentions that an Indian raiding party had just returned to Fort Niagara having killed 16 rebels at Cherry Valley, a New York community in the Mohawk Valley. The war continues to go well for the Crown in the Great Lakes area thanks to the help of the Six Nations Indians, the vast majority of whom back the British in the now seven-year long struggle.

Indian pouch, earrings and knife.

Americans hang high-ranking British officer caught spying

British forces learn that Major John André has been taken prisoner.

Oct. 2, 1780

TAPPAN, N.Y. – "Witness to the world that I die like a man." British officer John André uttered those last words today, just before he was hanged by the Americans for spying. André, who had been adjutant general under British forces leader Sir Henry Clinton, was caught with secret U.S. military papers hidden in his stocking. They described the placement and number of troops around the Hudson River garrison.

André was the middleman in the purchase of the documents by his superiors from Maj.-Gen. Benedict Arnold, who escaped capture by fleeing to the British ship *Vulture*. Arnold was bitter that others had been promoted over him.

Smallpox epidemic hits natives hard

1781

FORT PASKOYAC [The Pas, Manitoba] – A smallpox epidemic which last year spread as far north as the Saskatchewan River system has reached the Athabasca Region and the Barren Grounds.

The native population is highly susceptible to this disease. Explorer-fur trader Samuel Hearne reports it may have killed up to 90 percent of the Chipewyans in the Barren Grounds.

Converting won't get slaves off the hook

1781

ST. JOHN'S ISLAND – Does conversion to Christianity free a slave, who then, theoretically, belongs only to his Creator? Not on St. John's [Prince Edward] Island. Here, when a slave becomes a Christian, he remains a slave. The colony's legislature has just passed an act "declaring that baptism of slaves shall not exempt them from bondage."

On the surface, it seems a strange piece of legislation for the Island, for the colony has few slaves. The law seems to be more a response to external factors. The war with the rebellious Thirteen Colonies is going badly, and loyalist refugees from the conflict are already moving north. Gov. Walter Patterson obviously wants to attract them to his colony, and the law assures the loyalists that property rights, especially those concerning slaves, will be protected. The law further guarantees "that all children born of women slaves shall belong to and be the property of the masters or mistresses of such slaves."

Peace treaty slights native allies: Brant

Summer 1783

GREAT LAKES REGION – "England had sold the Indians to Congress." So said Joseph Brant upon learning Britain had forgotten its Indian allies at peace negotiations with the Americans. A preliminary treaty transfers to the Americans all British-claimed territory south of the Great Lakes from the Appalachian mountains to the Mississippi River, even though Indians occupy almost the entire area. At no point did the British consult their native allies.

A story is circulating that the English and Americans went to war to destroy the Indians, and not each other. The countries operate like a pair of scissors. While it might appear that the blades would destroy each other's edges, in fact they cut only what comes between.

British officers at the Great Lakes garrisons fear the Indians will retaliate for betraying them. But fortunately for the British, the Great Lakes Indians depend on the British for trade goods and gifts, and an attack does not seem likely.

Brant tells Indians it is time to unite

Sept. 7, 1783

LOWER SANDUSKY, Ohio – Joseph Brant continues to play a major role organizing a confederation of Six Nations and Great Lakes Indians to oppose American expansion into Indian territory. Today, the great Mohawk war chief addressed an Indian Council here.

Brant told Hurons, Delawares, Shawnees, Cherokees, Mingos, Ottawas and Ojibwas: "We the Chief Warriors of the Six Nations with this [Wampum] Belt bind your Hearts and Minds with ours, that there may be never hereafter a separation between us, let there be Peace or War, it shall never disunite us, for our Interests are alike, nor should anything ever be done but by the united Voice of us all, as we make but one with you."

The British support Brant's proposal of a union of 35 tribes. A firm native union would help protect Canada and the British fur trade.

Hunters decimate walrus population

Walrus hunting expedition: Young Horatio Nelson commands the second boat.

1780

THE ARCTIC – The view from the boat isn't a pretty one. A wall formed by the carcasses of the first victims of the attack is blocking the escape path to the sea for other walruses. Welcome to the hunt.

Walrus hunting is taking a big toll as European merchant traders take advantage of the herd's vulnerability on accessible beaches. Both commercial hunters and Inuit have sought walruses for their blubber, hide and ivory tusks. Often, the hunt becomes a diversion for sailors on other missions. On a trip a few years ago to explore a northeast polar route to the Pacific, 14-year-old Horatio Nelson went along and took part in a hunt.

York Factory changes hands again as British surrender to French

Hudson's Bay Company ships off the coast of York Factory before invasion.

Aug. 17, 1782

YORK FACTORY, Rupert's Land – A French fleet, commanded by the famous French explorer Comte de Lapérouse, has destroyed this Hudson's Bay Company fort and depot. Thirteen years after it was founded in 1684 on the spit of land between the Hayes and Nelson rivers, it was the scene of a naval battle when Sieur d'Iberville sank some English warships and seized the post.

The Treaty of Utrecht returned York Factory to English hands, and now the post's been taken by the French again. Why the French, in a massive struggle with the English in Europe and the Caribbean, want to detach three warships to attack this post is a mystery.

Governor seeks land for loyal Iroquois

Summer 1783

QUEBEC CITY – Now that Britain has lost the American Revolution, Gov. Frederick Haldimand of Quebec wants to find a suitable home for loyalist Iroquois who want to come to Canada. The governor has sent Samuel Holland, surveyor general of Quebec, to examine the north shore of Lake Ontario.

To obtain land for the Iroquois, Haldimand must deal with the Mississauga, the resident Indians. However, there may be problems. When told the Iroquois intend to settle on Lake Ontario, the Mississauga protested, as they consider their traditional enemies "bad Indians." They say their arrival would "be followed by disputes between them, and must terminate in the one or the other leaving the country."

The Iroquois, in turn, have a low opinion of the Mississauga, who they claim "stink of fish," as they grease their body with fish oil.

Northwest Passage eludes Cook's crew

April 11, 1780

CAPE OF GOOD HOPE – The crew of Capt. James Cook, who died last year, has failed in its latest attempt to fulfil their ex-leader's dream of finding the Northwest Passage. After returning to the Bering Strait, ice prevented the crew from going any further. The men returned to Macao and the Cape of Good Hope, without circumnavigating the globe. ▷

Loyalists fill St. John River district

American loyalists arrive on Canadian shores to found a settlement.

May 1783

NOVA SCOTIA – The mass exodus of loyalists from the American colonies has had a sudden and dramatic effect on the St. John River district of [New Brunswick]. As many as 20 ships lie at anchor, their 2,400 passengers and future settlers either establishing temporary camps ashore or remaining aboard until preparations are complete. Two makeshift settlements have sprung up almost overnight near the river's mouth, transforming an uneven, rocky peninsula into a bustling centre of activity.

The scene is peculiar to the district; apart from Fort Howe, a smattering of cabins and a few cleared lots, the area is rather undeveloped. Its principal asset is the harbor itself, as it reportedly remains ice-free over the winter. The thickly-wooded countryside promises an abundance of valuable lumber, but the rugged hills may hamper farming.

British "rewards" different for blacks

1783

NOVA SCOTIA – At least 3,000 black men, women and children have arrived in Nova Scotia this year, only to have expectations of equality and opportunity dashed to pieces on the rock-strewn land they now call home. They are former slaves who chose loyalty to Britain during the War of Independence in return for promises of freedom, land and provisions.

British authorities are employing a double standard in their loyalist relocation scheme: expecting the same rewards as white loyalists, blacks are instead receiving smaller allotments of land, fewer rations, and inadequate amounts of tools and seed. The land given to them is often thinly soiled and unsuitable for farming. In many instances, it is far away from established settlements, making communication difficult, and isolating black settlers from commercial centres.

Agents luring loyalists to Nova Scotia

Jan. 14, 1783

ANNAPOLIS ROYAL, N.S. – Agents for loyalist losers in the American Revolution wrote to friends in New York to describe juicy opportunities for settlement in Nova Scotia, where the Union Jack still flies against the northern sky. The rebels effectively won the war more than a year ago. Now, in New York, more than 30,000 refugees – people of all classes, with a myriad of reasons for having refused to forsake the Crown – wait to be evacuated with British troops.

Their agents today sent word that, from Annapolis to St. Mary's Bay at the western end of the Nova Scotia peninsula, the soil and fishery are excellent. Moreover, the agents crossed the Bay of Fundy and called the St. John a fine river with a fine harbor at its mouth. The riverside soil "produces crops of all kinds with little labor; and vegetables in the greatest perfection. ... The lands on the river ... are also sufficiently near the cod fishery in Fundy Bay, and perfectly secure against the Indians and Americans. The inhabitants are computed to be near 1,000 men, able to bear arms. Here is a county and court established, and the inhabitants at peace..."

The colony could easily exploit the fisheries, the West Indies trade, and the British market. Fat land grants awaited the intrepid, and it seemed certain that tens of thousands of loyalists, having lost their past in the United States, would bet their future on Nova Scotia.

The coat of arms of the United Empire Loyalists coming to Canada.

Annapolis Royal bulging at fenceposts

Oct. 20, 1782

ANNAPOLIS ROYAL, N.S. – Two men-of-war and nine transport ships from New York unloaded 500 loyalists onto the shores today, and this town, built for the 120 people who live here, bulges at its fenceposts. "Every habitation is crowded and many are unable to procure any lodgings," says Rev. Jacob Bailey, a loyalist who lives here after fleeing from Maine to Halifax in 1779. Sir Guy Carleton is in charge of relocating loyalists assembled in New York, and organized this first exodus to Annapolis Royal. He has indicated it may be the beginning of a much larger wave of pro-British refugees.

Bailey conveys the town's feeling toward these distressed, displaced persons: "Their sufferings on account of their loyalty and their present uncertain and destitute condition render them very affecting objects of compassion."

The town of Annapolis Royal is crowded with the recent arrivals.

Cape Breton Island is declared a colony

May 2, 1784

LONDON, England – By Order in Council, Britain today declared Cape Breton Island a colony. Until the conquest of New France a quarter-century ago, the island was a French possession for generations. It's been an official part of Nova Scotia for 21 years, but until this spring, Britain has shown no interest in seeing it settled.

Cape Breton dozes. Perhaps 300 Acadians live there, and some 400 Newfoundlanders, Irish and others use it as fishing headquarters. Today's decision amounts to London's recognition that, with hordes of loyalist refugees looking for places to settle, Cape Breton's time as a British colony has come at last.

The Cape Breton council must deal with the hordes of loyalist refugees.

55 British loyalists look to Nova Scotia

July 22, 1783

NOVA SCOTIA – A group of 55 British loyalists not only wants to settle in Nova Scotia, but is also asking for field officers' allowances of 5,000 acres each.

In a letter to Gov. Guy Carleton, the men write: "Settling such a number of loyalists, of the most respectable character, who have constantly had great influence in His Majesty's Dominions – will be highly advantageous in diffusing and supporting a spirit of attachment to the British Constitution, as well as to His Majesty's royal person and family."

Colony survives its most challenging year

Loyalist refugees on their way to changing British North America's future.

Dec. 31, 1784

NOVA SCOTIA [Nova Scotia, New Brunswick] – With the arrival since spring of about 20,000 loyalists in peninsular Nova Scotia and Cape Breton Island, and 14,000 more in the territory that includes the St. John River, this colony has endured the most challenging and chaotic year in its history.

The flash flood of humanity doubled the peninsula's population, swamped settlements on the St. John, and dumped stupendous responsibilities on colonial authorities: feeding the hungry, housing the cold; deciding who should settle where; handing out tools, lumber, shingles, bricks, window glass; settling countless land-grant squabbles; and dealing with newcomers whose contempt for Nova Scotians was as fierce as their wrangling among themselves.

The refugees include soldiers and shirkers, the rich and the poor, opportunists and idealists, hard-handed farmers and soft-palmed bankers, 2,000 blacks and 10,000 teenagers and children. The exiles hate the revolution, and the rebel gangsters who persecuted them. They haven't much else in common, but at year's end, it's clear that the future of British North America lies in them.

A group of loyalists drawing lots for the lands in British North America.

British buy land from Mississaugas

Oct., 1783

QUEBEC CITY – The British have bought another section of western Quebec [Ontario] from the Ojibwa or Mississauga Indians living there. Known as the Crawford Purchase, this tract lies between the St. Lawrence and the Grand [Ottawa] rivers to the north. It includes the high rock bluff overlooking Chaudière Falls, a well-known landmark to traders paddling to the interior.

This land surrender is one of several the British have obtained for the influx of loyalists expected to arrive next spring. Gov. Frederick Haldimand wants to populate the "upper country" with loyalists to discourage the Americans from expanding northward across Lake Ontario. Surveyor John Collins will soon arrive to begin laying out townships along the St. Lawrence River and the Bay of Quinte.

The Crawford Purchase follows a series of negotiations with the Mississauga on the northeastern shore of Lake Ontario who have inhabited the area since the 17th century, when they drove out the Iroquois. But it was an error to deal with them rather than the Algonquin Indians in the Ottawa River valley about the south bank of the Ottawa River. The Algonquins will be irate when they learn of this land sale, for which the Mississauga received guns, ammunition and new suits of clothing.

1,500 loyal blacks settle in Shelburne

August 1783

SHELBURNE, N.S. – Veterans of the Black Pioneers, an all-black regiment the British formed in the War of Independence, have arrived at Shelburne with permission to settle around the northwest end of the harbor. The ex-soldiers have arrived with some 1,500 blacks who sailed last month from New York as part of the massive British evacuation of loyalists and troops.

Like other loyalists, the Black Pioneers were promised free land, three years worth of rations, and other forms of aid to settle in British territory.

Mississaugas swap land on Grand River for gifts

Representation of the Six Nations legend of the Tree of Peace, symbolizing the Iroquois concept of good and evil. Tododaho's snakes symbolize evil.

May 22, 1784

FORT NIAGARA – Chief Wabakinine, the war chiefs, and principal women of the Mississauga Indians at the western end of Lake Ontario today ceded the Niagara peninsula and adjacent lands to the British Crown for nearly £900 of European gifts.

The natives understand that, in return for their land, "the farmers would help us." At the king's request, the Mississauga also welcomed the Six Nations, although they had little love for a people they call the *nahdoways,* or snakes.

Nearly 2,000 Iroquois are expected to take up the British offer to settle on the newly-ceded lands of the Mississauga on the Grand River. The land in question runs 9.6 kilometres on either side of the river from its mouth to its sources.

Most of the Mohawk refugees in New York will come, as will a large number of Cayuga and Onondaga. The majority of the Oneida and Tuscarora, who sided with the Americans in the recent war, will stay in New York, as will almost all the Seneca, who, although they fought for Britain, want to hold onto their land in the Genesee Valley of western New York.

Britain wants to put the Six Nations on the Grand River to serve as a western buffer for those British communities already in place, and others expected on the Niagara peninsula and the north shore of Lake Ontario.

Census: 83 people in Niagara region

Aug. 25, 1782

NIAGARA – The first census of this settlement, taken by Col. John Butler, records a population figure of 83. There are 16 families, according to the census, and they are expected to pave the way for further settlement. Butler, a loyalist, fled in 1775 to Canada, where he was named deputy Indian commissioner at Niagara. He also commands Butler's Rangers.

Inspections to determine if regions ripe for loyalist settlements

May 26, 1783

CATARAQUI, Ont. – Acting on orders from Gov. Frederick Haldimand, surveyor general Samuel Holland is inspecting the land around Cataraqui [Kingston] and has sent a surveying party to the Niagara region. Holland's report will determine the suitability of the areas for habitation. Britain's decision to make extensive land grants to loyalists after the American Revolution has made it necessary to find new tracts for settlement.

View of Cataraqui [Kingston], where loyalists may establish a settlement.

British rewards include land, shelter, clothing, tools and seeds

One of the earliest loyalist settlements to be established in [Ontario].

June 16, 1784

CANADA – Some 250 loyalists have been rewarded for their support of the British during the American Revolution with a parcel of land in [Ontario] they plan to turn into a settlement called Adolphustown. Travelling from Sorel in Quebec on ships that were provided by the Crown, the loyalists arrived today at [Lake Ontario] in the Bay of Quinte to establish their new settlement.

The loyalists have big plans for the site. One encouraging fact is that the group is full of capable farmers. Another is that the Crown has given the loyalists shelter, clothing, tools and seeds to help them launch their venture.

Loons are oldest bird in Canada

The loon is Canada's most primitive bird, and has bones very similar to those of its prehistoric ancestors. The loon lives in the lakes of the north woods, where night and day human inhabitants hear its piercing calls and timorous laughs that carry across the water. Some people claim that the loon never sleeps!

The loon is almost impossible to shoot, for despite his clumsy gait on land, he is supremely agile in the water. He can dive at the flash of a bullet and propel himself so fast that in seconds he is a safe 45 to 90 metres distant.

British reward Iroquois with a "safe retreat"

Iroquois Indians read the wampum: The sacred wampums that record Iroquois history are made from shell beads which are woven into symbolic designs.

Iroquois singers: The Iroquois Indians use a small drum filled with water and rattles made from animal horns to accompany the Longhouse singers.

Brant rejects land on Bay of Quinte

May 1784

BAY OF QUINTE – A group of Six Nations Indians has arrived here to take up land the British granted them, but their great war chief is not among them. Joseph Brant has decided against settling on the Bay of Quinte grant, preferring to wait for land further west.

The Indians at Quinte are led by another Mohawk war chief, John Deseronto. The Mohawks are receiving land in compensation for territory lost during the recent revolutionary war.

Oct. 25, 1784

QUEBEC CITY – Gov. Frederick Haldimand today formally awarded a huge tract of land along the Grand River to the Iroquois Indians of the Six Nations as a "safe and comfortable retreat." The award fulfils a promise made to the Indians that they would receive compensation for their territory in Upper New York which was devastated during the recent War of American Independence and then handed over to the Americans in the peace treaty. The new land, located on the peninsula between lakes Ontario, Huron and Erie, amounts to nearly 700,000 acres. The British purchased it from the Mississauga Indians last May.

The 1,800 refugee Indians who will occupy the land are led by the Mohawk war chief Thayendanegea, or Joseph Brant. Brant is in Quebec to sign the proclamation. A friend of the British, the 41-year-old chief was influential in keeping most of his people loyal to their cause during the recent war.

From his base on the Grand River, Brant hopes to unite all the tribes of the Great Lakes into an Indian confederacy which is strong enough to withstand the steady encroachment of the white settlements. He plans to encourage farming among his followers because he is convinced that the Indians must adopt some white ways in order to survive.

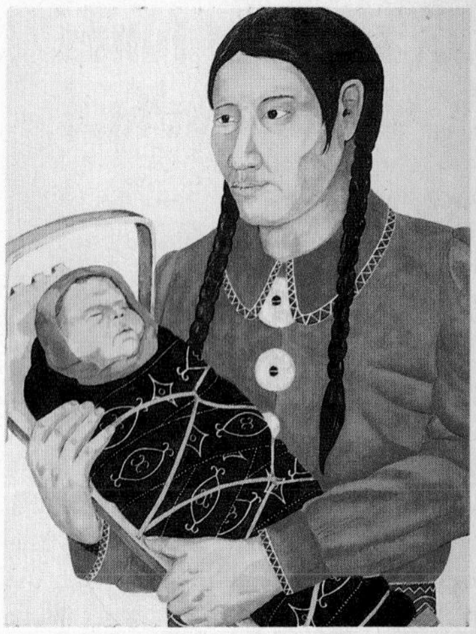

Iroquois women carry their babies on cradle boards to protect the tots and make it easier to tend fields.

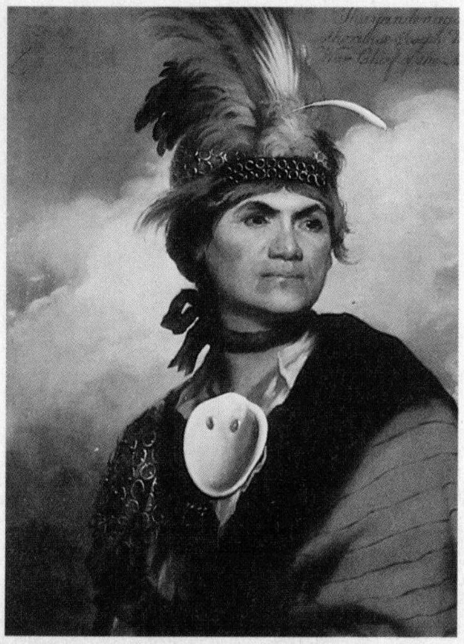

Mohawk war chief Thayendanegea, who is also known as Joseph Brant.

Pond acquitted of murdering fur trader

Winter 1784

MONTREAL – Explorer and fur trader Peter Pond has been cleared of a murder which took place in the far northwest almost three years ago. A court here acquitted Pond of killing Swiss-born trader Jean-Etienne Waddens in March 1782. Pond and the murdered man, rival traders in the Athabasca country, were camped by each other when the events in question took place.

Joseph Faignant, one of Waddens' men, testified that he heard two shots fired on the night of the murder. Faignant said when he went to investigate, he saw Pond and another man leaving the cabin of the dead man. Faignant discovered Waddens lying beside his bed with a gunshot wound in his leg. The Swiss trader lost consciousness and died without naming his assailant, but Faignant also testified that he heard Pond and Waddens arguing earlier that evening.

Since the murder there has been some question about the authority of officials in Canada to investigate matters in such a remote part of the country. The case only came to trial at the insistence of Waddens' grieving widow.

Whites demolish 20 Negro homes

July 1784

BIRCHTOWN, N.S. – Twenty Negro families here have lost their homes after a mob of white, disbanded soldiers rampaged through the settlement and pulled down their houses.

The soldiers became unruly when they found out they either could not find jobs or had to accept work at low wages because Negroes are underbidding them. Infuriated and blaming the free Negroes of Birchtown for their misfortune, the soldiers went on to destroy the homes. ▷

Niagara settled, but falls still mystical for natives

Fort Niagara in 1783, where many loyalists are establishing settlements.

c.1783

NIAGARA FALLS – Many loyalists fleeing the United States are settling in the fertile region around Niagara Falls, the spectacular waterfalls that seem to awe all those who visit here. To the Senecas, however, the falls also have a mystical meaning.

Long ago, the Indians say, a lovely Seneca princess tried to drown herself in the Niagara River rather than marry the ugly old man her father had chosen. But she was rescued by Thunderer, the great chief of clouds and rain. Thunderer then killed the snake monster that poisoned the princess' people. Its huge, uncoiled body became wedged between rocks, and the water cascaded over it to form Niagara Falls.

Legend of the maid of the mists.

Lotto raises funds for Halifax school

September 1781

HALIFAX – After selling the first batch of 5,000 tickets at 20 shillings each, as advertised on Sept. 25, the public school lottery has raised £750 of the £1500 needed to build a school. Prizes totalled £4250, with the biggest set at £2000. The House of Assembly passed an act last October permitting the lottery to defray the cost of erecting "a proper and convenient building."

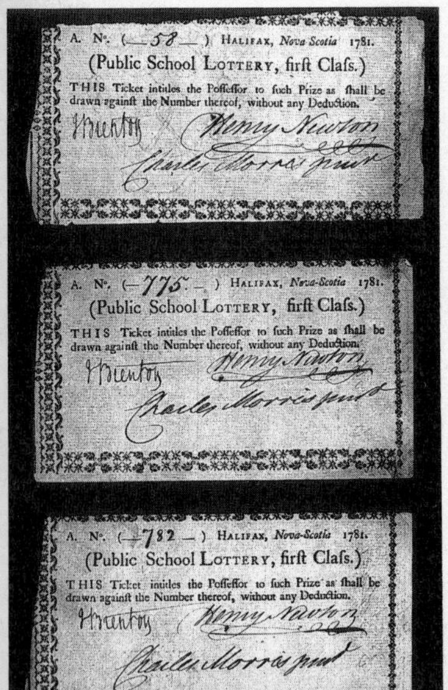

A. N°. (58) HALIFAX, Nova-Scotia 1781.
(Public School LOTTERY, firft Clafs.)
THIS Ticket intitles the Poffeffor to fuch Prize as fhall be drawn againft the Number thereof, without any Deduction.

A. N°. (775) HALIFAX, Nova-Scotia 1781.
(Public School LOTTERY, firft Clafs.)
THIS Ticket intitles the Poffeffor to fuch Prize as fhall be drawn againft the Number thereof, without any Deduction.

A. N°. (782) HALIFAX, Nova-Scotia 1781.
(Public School LOTTERY, firft Clafs.)
THIS Ticket intitles the Poffeffor to fuch Prize as fhall be drawn againft the Number thereof, without any Deduction.

The public school lottery of 1781.

Ceremony marks start of trading season

Trading ceremony at York Factory.

c.1780

HUDSON BAY LANDS – Early each summer, a fleet of Indian fur traders from the west paddles by canoe to the trading posts along the shores of Hudson Bay. Their arrival heralds the beginning of the year's commerce, which begins after an elaborate ceremony. The local post official greets the Indian chief, who changes into European clothes. Then, the chief is escorted to the lodge for the main rituals. Drummers lead the march, followed by servants who carry brandy, bread, prunes, tobacco, pipes and the chief's beaver coats.

Destitute refugees worry the governor

Jan. 15, 1784

HALIFAX – Hordes of squabbling loyalist refugees last year wrecked Gov. John Parr's dream that his job would be easy, and now the last families out of New York are here. He wrote today to Lord North to complain about "the wretched situation" of those on the *Clinton.* They were "destitute of almost everything, chiefly women and children, all still on board, as I have not yet been able to find any sort of place for them, and the cold setting is severe."

Loyalists complain about life in colony

April 29, 1784

MACHICHE, Que. – Unhappy with living in Quebec, many United Empire loyalists in Machiche, near Trois-Rivières, are complaining of bad living conditions and even unfair and cruel treatment.

While Gov. Frederick Haldimand's secretary wrote a letter today to the inspector of the loyalists informing him of the discontent, for the most part the claims are seen as the grumblings of a few malcontents with unreasonable expectations.

A family of Cree Indians at Fort York on their way to the hunt.

Influx of settlers welcome on Island

June 12, 1784

ST. JOHN'S ISLAND [Prince Edward Island] – Attracted by an aggressive recruiting campaign and promises of free land, some 380 refugees from the United States have made their way to the Island. Gov. Walter Patterson has the support of 21 proprietors who have promised to grant a fourth of their lands to these loyalists.

Already experienced settlers and farmers, the refugees are a valuable addition to the colony. A note of caution, however. Many may be unable to get clear title to their land since they have settled on lots the governor seized in 1781 for non-payment of quit rents. A powerful group of proprietors is contesting Patterson's decision to seize their land. If they win their case, will they honor the loyalist titles? Or will the recent arrivals on the Island lose their lands?

Noted American is new council secretary

1784

NEW BRUNSWICK – Noted American satirist, surgeon, educator, Anglican minister and confidential agent Jonathan Odell has been appointed council secretary and registrar for New Brunswick. Born in New Jersey in 1737, Odell is an unwavering and longtime loyalist who remained in the American colonies during the War of Independence before seeking refuge this year in British North America. Prior to the war, Odell was well-known for scathing editorials, laced with satire, denouncing American agitation he felt would lead to an unjust rebellion.

Odell is a talented songwriter and has written ballads – sometimes bawdy – he's hoped would inspire both British troops and fellow loyalists. In December 1776, revolutionary authorities in New Jersey issued a warrant for his arrest on charges of sedition, but he managed to escape with the help of local citizens. While living behind British lines in New York in 1779, Odell became involved in secret talks between the British command and Benedict Arnold, a general willing to defect from the Revolutionary Army.

Confidential agent Jonathan Odell.

King OKs province of New Brunswick

June 18, 1784

NEW BRUNSWICK – King George III today created a new province in North America by partitioning Nova Scotia. New Brunswick will extend from the Isthmus of Chignecto to Quebec province. It will include the Gaspé Peninsula.

The action stems from the arrival last year of 14,000 loyalists in the St. John Valley, chiefly from New York, Connecticut and the other mid-Atlantic colonies. The former hinterland of Nova Scotia has suddenly become well-populated, and sources say the new province was created largely because of the difficulty communicating with the Nova Scotia capital at Halifax.

Officials have suggested the province be called New Ireland, but the king prefers New Brunswick, in honor of His Majesty's German dominions. Col. Thomas Carleton is to be named governor.

Cook's Voyages published posthumously

1784

ENGLAND – Capt. James Cook's own account of his travels in North America has been published, some six years after the man considered to be one of Britain's most renowned explorers died at Kealakekua Bay [Hawaiian Islands]. Appropriately enough, the book is entitled *Voyages*.

Cook's superior, Lord Colville, once described his underling as a man of "genius and capacity." Cook's travels are famed throughout Europe, and in the Pacific thousands of natives know him personally. The book is welcome news to those interested in the commercial impact of the information Cook gathered on his travels.

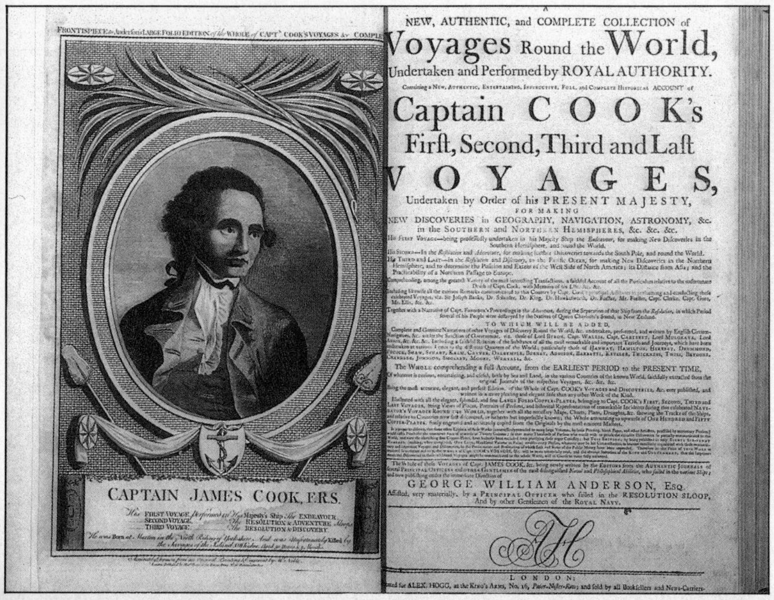

The title page of Voyages with a portrait of its author, Captain James Cook.

New York becomes British control centre

Sept. 1782-Dec. 1783

NEW YORK – Since the preliminary peace of September 1782 between rebel and British forces, Sir Guy Carleton has been directing the affairs of British North America from New York. The former Quebec governor, now commissioner "for restoring peace and granting pardon" in the rebellious colonies, has supervised evacuation of 30,000 troops and 27,000 refugees, including former slaves resettled despite George Washington's objections.

Loyalists dub settlement New Johnstown

June 6, 1784

NEW JOHNSTOWN – The vanguard of 3,700-plus loyalists, destined to settle on the upper St. Lawrence River, arrived today from Lachine. Reunited after seven years of war, Sir John Johnson settled soldiers of the disbanded First Battalion King's Royal Regiment of New York with their families and servants at this army depot on the St. Lawrence. The Royal Yorkers have dubbed the site New Johnstown [Cornwall].

A loyalist encampment in New Johnstown on the banks of the St. Lawrence.

1785 (1785-1789)

New Brunswick, Feb. 22, 1785. Governor Carleton orders the establishment of a town on the St. John's River to be called Fredericks Town [Fredericton], after the popular Frederic, Duke of York. The town is to be the capital of the province.

Montreal, Aug. 25, 1785. Fleury Mesplet, a French printer who was jailed for trying to persuade Quebec to join the American Revolution, publishes the first issue of the bilingual *Montreal Gazette*. The paper shows the growth of the city.

Quebec, 1785. Anglican clergyman John Stuart starts the first school west of the Ottawa River at Cataraqui [Kingston], where he has recently settled with his family. He holds classes in his home, and services in the barracks.

Louisiana, 1785. A total of 1,596 Acadians are resettled in Louisiana from France, with their transportation paid for by Charles III of Spain.

London, April 1786. Guy Carleton, now Baron Dorchester, is commissioned as governor of Quebec, Nova Scotia, and New Brunswick. He is also made commander-in-chief of all these provinces as well as Newfoundland.

The Northwest, June 3, 1789. Alexander Mackenzie leaves Fort Chipewyan with a crew of seven in a birchbark canoe to explore the river that Indians say flows from the west end of Great Slave Lake. He hopes it will lead to the Pacific.

Halifax, June 1789. Clergyman William Cochran publishes the *Nova Scotia Magazine and Comprehensive Review of Literature, Politics, and News*, one of the first periodicals in the remaining British North American colonies.

Pacific Coast, October 1789. A Spanish expedition led by Esteban José Martinez returns to Mexico after waiting in vain for orders to make their base at Nootka permanent. Since arriving in May, they have constructed a battery and buildings, and planted a garden at the Indian village of Friendly Cove [B.C.]

Quebec, 1789. Famine results from a poor wheat crop. Many urban and rural poor die. Montreal is especially hard hit.

Quebec, 1789. Jean-Olivier Briand, the Bishop of Quebec, says the number of literate women exceeds the number of literate men in the province.

Saint John the first city of B.N.A.

Legislature meeting takes place in Mallard House, New Brunswick.

May 18, 1785

SAINT JOHN, N.B. – On the second anniversary of the arrival of the first loyalists, Gov. Thomas Carleton today gave the settlements here a charter of incorporation as a city, renaming this cluster of seaports on the Bay of Fundy, Saint John. Along with the distinction of being first city in British North America, the charter awards Saint John the "powers and privileges usually granted to mercantile towns for the encouragement of commerce," as well as "protection and support of the upright part of the community."

The document is based on New York's colonial charter, with aldermen elected by enfranchised citizens, and a mayor appointed by the government. In this city of tradesmen, Carleton, aligned with elitist loyalists, wants to keep a tight rein on the mayor's office. He distrusts the working class. Many people feel he gave this first-city honor to Saint John to placate citizens disgruntled by his choice of Fredericks Town [Fredericton] over Saint John as the capital of the colony.

Colonists petition for representation

Jan. 7, 1785

QUEBEC CITY – A petition calling for government by assembly was delivered today to Henry Hamilton, administrator of the province in Frederick Haldimand's absence. Messengers have been riding throughout the countryside the few past weeks urging people to support the movement for representation.

Pressure for an assembly is mounting, but opinions differ as to the form the assembly should take. One faction favors the American colonial model. Others prefer a strictly appointed body in the English and French tradition.

Hamilton is known to be sympathetic to the demand for an assembly, and his detractors accuse him of quietly encouraging the movement. The church is taking a position of official neutrality and priests have been ordered not to sign petitions. Hamilton is to submit the petition to London shortly.

Molson starts brewing on "grand stage"

July 28, 1786

MONTREAL – After a lapse of two years, Montrealers will once again have a beer they can call their own. Lincolnshireman John Molson, 22, declared his intent today to start brewing by buying eight bushels of barley malt. Noting that this marked his "commencement on the grand stage of the world," Molson simply said "good ale is all I want."

John Molson hopes to start brewing beer in Montreal by the year's end.

Capitalizing on the large unslaked thirst of the local garrison and emigrant loyalists, Molson believes this philosophy will bring "plenty of customs and good profits." To guarantee success, his fresh beer will cost 25 percent less than the imports. Brewing will take place at Thomas Loid's old brewery opened four years ago at the foot of St. Mary's current. Molson, a former silent partner, acquired the 11- by 18-metre malt and brewhouse constructed from 10-centimetre squared white cedar logs last year.

The enterprising Molson arrived in Montreal from London on May 31, bringing English hops, 46 bushels of barley and seeds, equipment and a copy of John Richardson's *Theoretical Hints on an Improved Practice of Brewing.* Test runs on the ale start at the end of September, with the first brews ready for Christmas. Capacity will be 980 litres a week. Molson has already planned for next year by giving out free barley seeds.

Convention approves United States Constitution

Sept. 17, 1787

PHILADELPHIA – The Constitution of the United States has been signed, sealed and approved after four months of debate on issues ranging from slaves to the presidential election. With the document in place, the former British colonies' transition to an independent federal state seems complete.

Of the 73 delegates appointed to the convention in Philadelphia, 55 attended at one time or another but only 39 signed the document. Of the 12 regular members who were not in attendance at the convention's end and who did not sign, seven are known to have approved of the Constitution and three are known to have disapproved.

Incomplete and inadequate as its creators believe it to be, the Constitution remains a symbol of hope for the United States. Concerning the slave trade, the document prohibits Congress from limiting the importation of slaves by any state until 1808. Delegates also agreed the president of the United States should be chosen by electors.

George Washington presides at convention, where the Constitution remains a symbol of hope for United States.

West Indians eye Canadian rum market

April 5, 1787

LONDON – West Indian merchants and planters want to take over as much of the Canadian rum market as they can. To this end, they resolved at today's meeting at the London Tavern that distilleries in Canada should be prohibited, and the duty on West Indian rum entering Canada should be eliminated. There are four distilleries in Canada, three of them in Quebec.

Fur trade intrigues German immigrant

1787

MONTREAL – Young German immigrant John Jacob Astor has arrived in Montreal, curious about its fur trade possibilities. Astor apparently heard about the city while on the ship *North Carolina* bound for North America. Another older German passenger, who had been to America a few years earlier, taught Astor all about the trade – where to buy furs and how to pack and preserve them.

During the crossing, the German also gave Astor the names of Montreal traders who had amassed great wealth by succeeding in the American fur trade despite the ruthless competition.

Young German immigrant John Jacob Astor comes to Montreal.

William is the first royalty in Halifax

Oct. 5, 1786

HALIFAX – When Prince William, one of King George's rapscallion sons, came ashore from the frigate *Pegasus* at King's Wharf today, Haligonians got their first glimpse of royalty – a red-faced, pointy-headed, 21-year-old rogue known in the navy as "Coconut Head." Gov. John Parr and local dignitaries greeted William with all the pomp befitting a royal visit. Not long into the ceremonies, the young captain asked to be treated as merely a naval officer. He and his crew then embarked on a drunken spree around town, attending cockfights, dueling and wenching – William's favorite folly.

"We drank 28 bumper toasts," one of His Majesty's boon buddies said. "After supper we set to Burton ale. The prince ... sang two or three songs, and for three hours, laughed incessantly." By 8 p.m. all the streets were gaily lit in honor of the royal playboy.

Syphilis targeting Quebec population

1786

QUEBEC CITY – Sexual promiscuity can kill you. People here have discovered this the hard way, as so many fall victim to the syphilis that has raged through the colony for a decade. Syphilis is transmitted through sexual intercourse. The strain of the disease in Quebec is highly contagious and known by various names – *Mal de la Baie St. Paul, Mal Anglois, Lustu Crue.*

The symptoms of syphilis are hideous and unmistakable. It begins with open sores on the face. Facial bones break down, hair falls out, lips swell. The stench increases "till universal putrefaction ends the existence of the unfortunate sufferer." Those who survive its ravages are perhaps unluckier than those who die. They live on "under the united miseries of an injured constitution and a mutilated frame."

Most doctors agree the plague is a venereal disease, but a few disagree, claiming it is a form of pox. ▷

Loyalists petition for a new province

April 15, 1787

QUEBEC CITY – The growing loyalist population, which has brought the level of English speakers in this colony from four to nine percent, is getting tired of living under French law. So much so, that it has petitioned the British government for the creation of a British-style colony in the newly settled Upper St. Lawrence region.

The dilemma is a peculiar one for the Crown. Since the conquest, the lack of immigration to this French outpost has meant that, for all intents and purposes, it's been the Canadians who have been providing all the growth, both in the economy and in population. Because of this, the government has allowed French-Canadians to keep their French laws and way of life.

Enter the loyalists, who find they cannot get British law in a British colony and now want an area where such laws apply. Interestingly, the government may go along with their request to prevent conflict between the two cultures living here.

Trader brings Chinese to Nootka to build trading post, schooner

May 13, 1788

NOOTKA, Northwest Coast – Trader John Meares, once an English naval officer, has arrived here with two ships, the *Felice Adventurer* and the *Iphigenia Nubiana.* Some Chinese carpenters and metal workers are on the ships. Meares has plans to build a trading post here and a small schooner to be used for trading voyages. The Chinese artisans – and some European workers – are to build both.

Meares believes the Chinese, who, he says, eat only fish and rice and accept low wages, will make excellent settlers for the northwest coast. Meares first came to this part of America two years ago on two other ships in an expedition organized by the Bengal Fur Company, which some say belongs to Meares. He traded for furs on the Alaskan coast and spent the winter in Prince William Sound, where 23 of his crew died of scurvy.

Chinese come to Nootka to help build a trading post on the west coast.

Last May, rival British trading captains Nathaniel Portlock and George Dixon found Meares's ships and accused him of trading in territory assigned to the East India and South Seas Companies. They seized him and his ships and released him only after he agreed to sail to Macao and keep away from this coast.

On this trip Meares is sailing under the Portuguese flag – a device that saves him Chinese customs duties. As soon as he landed Meares picked out a site for the trading post and for building the schooner he wants to name the *North West America.* He also told the Nootka he wanted to see their chief to discuss buying land and an exclusive right to trade in timber and sea otter pelts.

Blacks hard-pressed in "Nova Scarcity"

1789

NOVA SCOTIA – Future prospects appear far from bright for black settlers in "Nova Scarcity". Freedom for the thousands of black loyalists escaping the bonds of American slavery has proven it has a price, and a costly one at that. Attempts at drawing sustenance from land unsuited for agriculture have created famine-like conditions, and racial intolerance is limiting job opportunities to the fringe areas of black communities.

A free black wood-cutter working in Shelburne, Nova Scotia, in 1788.

Mackenzie reaches mouth of "big river"

July 12, 1789

ARCTIC – After a 40-day canoe journey, Alexander Mackenzie reached the mouth of the Deh-cho, or "big river" as the local Dene Indians call it, which from now on in English will bear his name. Mackenzie, a trader with the North West Company, set off June 3 from Fort Chipewyan on Lake Athabasca, guided by a Chipewyan Indian known as the "English Chief."

As he travelled down the river, Mackenzie met several Indian tribes which do not take part in the fur trade. Suspicious of the strangers, the Indians warned that huge waterfalls guarded by hideous beasts obstructed the river ahead. Some of Mackenzie's companions were frightened off, but the explorer persevered and reached the mouth of the river, 2,400 kilometres from the trading post, without incident. When Mackenzie reached the ice-covered sea, he first hoped it was a large lake. But when he noticed the tide rising and falling, and saw some whales offshore, he had to admit he had reached the ocean and could go no farther.

Despite the fact that Mackenzie is the first white man to descend the river, he and his employers are disappointed. They hoped the river would lead them westward through the Rocky Mountains to the Pacific Ocean. Instead, it has revealed an unexplored territory and a frozen ocean not navigable by ships.

Alexander Mackenzie names river.

Spaniards use force to claim land on the coast

The Spanish establish a fortified base at Nootka Sound, on the west coast.

The home of a native family in Nootka Sound at time of the Spanish arrival.

May 14, 1789

NOOTKA SOUND, Far West – The Spanish have used force to assert their territorial claim to the northwest coast of America. A few days ago, Capt. Esteban José Martinez arrived in Nootka Sound with two ships and a detachment of 31 marines. The Spaniard has orders to establish a fortified base in the sound and to make it clear that Spain claims the area. The Spanish are worried about the activities of Russian and British traders on the coast.

When he arrived at Nootka Sound, Martinez discovered three trading vessels doing business, two Americans and another, the *Ifigenia Nubiana,* which claimed to be Portuguese but clearly was British. Suspicious, the Spanish captain captured the *Ifigenia,* claiming it lacked the proper licences to be in Spanish waters. Martinez later released the ship on condition that it leave the area immediately. The seizure will doubtless outrage the British, who do not recognize Spanish claims to Nootka Sound, saying Capt. James Cook claimed the area for Britain a decade ago.

Martinez plans to build a fortification in the sound which will be manned by Spanish soldiers who'll keep the coast free of "interlopers."

Bread crisis over; prices rolled back

Aug. 3, 1789

MONTREAL – The bread crisis in Montreal is over. At their monthly meeting today, city magistrates lowered the price of a white loaf of bread from 14 pence to ninepence, where it was in January. Bread – and most foods – have been scarce here the last six months as a result of heavy exports and a poor crop in 1788. Ten thousand barrels of flour, 5,000 barrels of biscuit and more than 265,000 bushels of wheat were exported last year, causing six months of famine for Montrealers. Beef bones have been boiled, re-boiled and shared by several families at a time. Desperate mothers used wild roots and tree bark to feed their families. One visitor to Montreal in the winter wrote that many loyalists have been able "to alleviate Canadian distress with many hundred bushels of wheat at a much lower rate than it could have been bought from their more fortunate countrymen below."

Fort Chipewyan asserts itself in fur trade

Summer 1789

FORT CHIPEWYAN – This new trading post, built by the North West Company last year on the south shore of Lake Athabasca, is quickly establishing itself as the headquarters of the most productive fur-producing area on the continent. Named for the Chipewyan Indians who inhabit the region, the fort lies near the heart of a vast river delta teeming with fur-bearing animals. It was built for the NWC by Roderick Mackenzie, cousin of the explorer Alexander Mackenzie.

It is an open question how long the Hudson's Bay Company will allow its rival to enjoy unopposed the profits from this rich trading area, which draws in all the Indians to the north and west.

Fort Chipewyan, established on Lake Athabaska by the North West Company.

British trader lands a huge load of furs

July 31, 1787

FAR WEST – Capt. George Dixon, a British trader, has made a fabulous haul of furs in a group of islands he has named the Queen Charlottes, after his trading vessel. Dixon arrived at the islands on July 2. The local Haida people came out in canoes and at first they seemed reluctant to trade. But later, Dixon reports, "they fairly quarrelled with each other about which should sell his cloak first." In 30 minutes, the British obtained 300 pelts, and today the hold of the ship has more than 1,800.

The trade for sea otter pelts has been flourishing on this coast since Capt. James Cook's visit in 1778. The Indians are clever traders who demand only quality goods in return for their furs. They especially want iron goods and blankets. Nonetheless, traders are able to sell the furs in China for large profits and more ships flock to the coast every year.

People of west coast enjoy rich artistic life

Haidas use stone tools to carve wood sculptures such as this one of a bear.

An intricately carved wooden spindle whorl made by the west coast Salish.

Mask made by west coast Indian.

Kwagiutl mask of a tribal chief.

Basket woven using swamp grass.

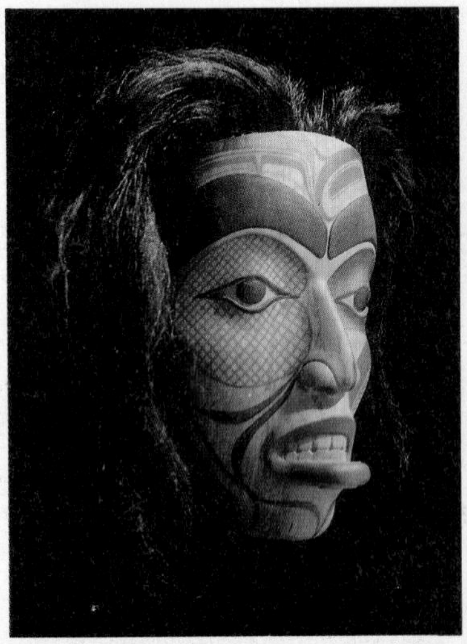

Haida masks sometimes have hair.

A wooden rattle often used by the west coast Indians during ceremonies.

A wooden mask crafted by the Bella Coola Indians of the west coast.

A Chilkat blanket with a repeated killer whale design. This type of design has the distinctive feature of the limbs outstretched in frog fashion.

Wooden mask of the Kwagiutl people which is believed to represent the sun.

Tsimishian Indians use this wooden soul catcher in religious ceremonies. In the mythological world of the coast spiritual forces are always active.

Detail from a comb carved from animal horns by the Tingit people.

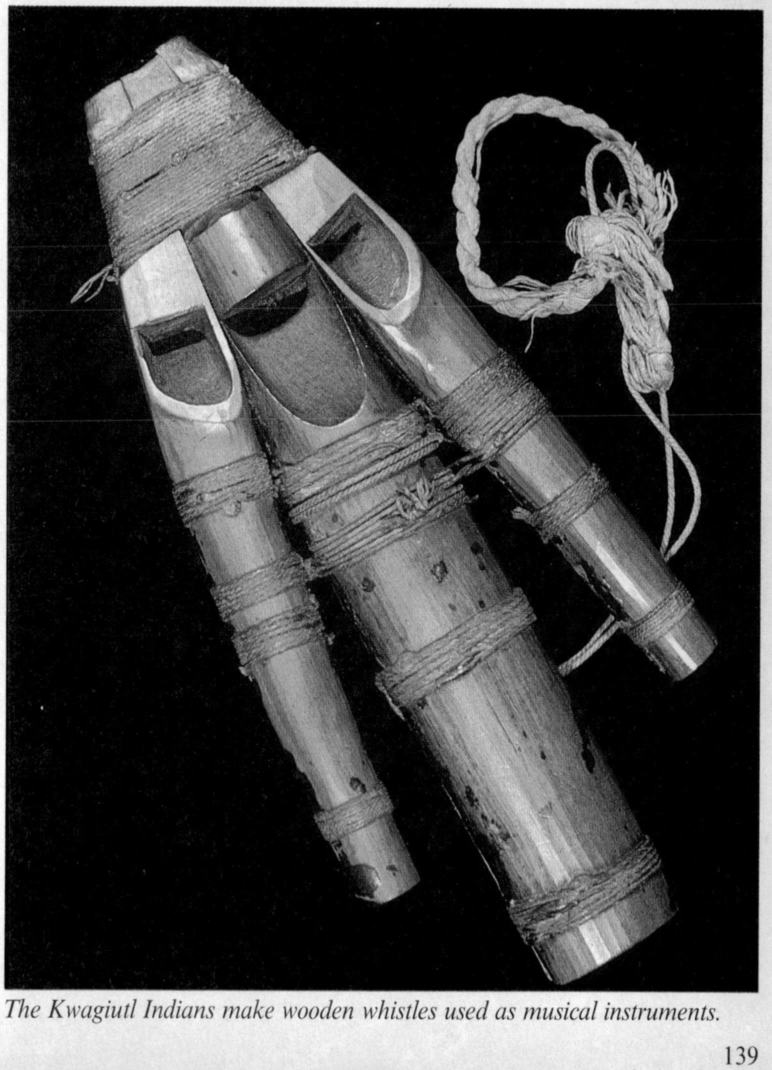

The Kwagiutl Indians make wooden whistles used as musical instruments.

1790 (1790-1794)

Falmouth, England, April 1, 1791. George Vancouver leads a British naval expedition to survey and search for the Northwest Passage on the Pacific coast of North America. They are also to receive property that Spain restored to British subjects by the Nootka Sound Convention, and survey the Sandwich Islands [Hawaii].

Pacific Coast, March 27, 1792. An American fur-trading expedition led by Robert Gray burns the Nootka village of Opitsat on Clayoquot Sound, consisting of some 200 houses, in retaliation for a Nootka plot to seize the American ship and kill her crew. The expedition sailed from Boston in 1790.

Pacific Coast, May 11, 1792. Robert Gray reaches the mouth of a river that he names after his ship, the *Columbia*, giving the U.S. a strong claim to the Oregon country.

Labrador, August 1792. André Michaux is the first naturalist to explore the interior of the Quebec-Labrador peninsula.

Pacific Coast, August 1792. Vancouver visits the Spanish settlement at Nootka Sound. He and the Spanish commander Bodega can't agree on the details of the property transfer provided for in the Nootka Convention.

Quebec, April 1793. A bill to abolish slavery in Lower Canada is tabled and dies.

United States, June 1793. Citoyen Genet, representing the revolutionary French Republic, exhorts French-Canadians to rebel against English rule: "insurrection is the holiest of duties for you."

Quebec, July 7, 1793. Jacob Mountain is consecrated as first Anglican bishop of Quebec.

Newark, Upper Canada, July 9, 1793. The legislature passes a bill for the gradual elimination of slavery in the province. It states that no one is to become a slave from this time, but those who are slaves will remain so for the rest of their lives. The law bans importation of slaves.

Upper Canada, 1793. A wolf bounty is introduced to protect livestock and deer.

Pacific Coast, Aug. 19, 1794. Vancouver finishes a highly accurate three-year survey of the coast at 56 degrees north. He has proven the Northwest Passage from the west coast to inland America does not exist.

Indians surrender land to the British

May 19, 1790

DETROIT – At the request of King George III, representatives of the Ojibwa, Ottawa, Potawatomi and Huron nations gathered here today to surrender their land south of Lake St. Clair and La Tranche [Thames] River, down to the northwestern shore of Lake Erie. The past few years, white squatters have been moving up the Tranche into Indian territory, building log cabins on its banks and planting corn in open spaces. Many more white farmers have awaited today's legal surrender of the valley of the Lower Thames before establishing their farms. The natives received £1,200 for the land.

Government surveyors will soon begin working in the Lower La Tranche area. The dense forest, occasionally intermixed with bogs, marshes and beaver meadows, begins after one passes the luxuriant grasslands at the river's mouth. The overhanging foliage of the giant trees shuts out sunshine and most daylight. In the treaty, the Indians asked for the right to hunt and plant throughout the tract, a request the British have granted.

The French call the river La Tranche – or more properly La Tranchée, meaning "the trench" – as the muddy waterway appears to them to be a trench which slices through the thick forest and the tall grasses near its mouth. The Ojibwa call the river "the Horn," from the appearance of its two branches, which look like the horns of a deer.

Warrior of Ottawa Indian nation.

Trader off to live with Mississaugas

June 4, 1790

CANADA – David Ramsay, the notorious trader who killed eight Ojibwa Indians nearly 20 years ago, allegedly in self-defence, has gone to live among the Mississaugas, Ojibwa-speaking Indians on the northwest shore of Lake Ontario. Ramsay last year appeared in the land registry office at Newark [Niagara Falls] to claim land the Mississaugas granted him at the Twelve Mile [Bronte] Creek.

While he returned today to have the grant confirmed, trouble lies ahead. The Royal Proclamation of 1763 says Indian land can only be surrendered to the Crown.

Fishermen discover seal herds in Arctic

June 15, 1790

NEWFOUNDLAND – The first fishermen believed to ever have travelled to the Arctic ice floes in search of seals have returned, their journey a huge success. The fishermen, who left Conception Bay this spring, discovered herds of these sea mammals and brought back valuable cargoes. Before, the only seals caught were those netted in small numbers near shore.

Spanish expedition re-occupies Nootka

Spanish ships sail into Nootka Sound to re-establish Spain's claim to area.

April 30, 1790

NOOTKA, Northwest Coast – Three Spanish ships have sailed into Nootka Sound to re-establish Spain's claim to this trading centre. Count Revilla Gigedo, the new viceroy of New Spain, arrived in Vera Cruz recently and decided the time for pretence was over.

The English and the Russians had to be shown that the northwest coast of America belonged to Spain, whose God-given task is to bring Christianity to the native people. And so Francisco de Eliza led the frigate *Concepcion,* the sloop *Princess Real* and a supply ship into the sound today. He was relieved to find no other ships or Europeans there and set about building warehouses so that the ships could be unloaded.

The Spanish had left Nootka only a few months earlier. Esteban Martinez, the Spanish commander, had been ordered back home after he had seized some English ships and an Indian chief had been shot. Martinez's troubles began when he arrived on May 5 last year and found a ship at anchor there. He seized it – and two others which arrived later. Then, surprisingly, came the order to leave.

Legislation creates new court in Nfld.

July 31, 1791

NEWFOUNDLAND – The helter-skelter status of Newfoundland's justice system is about to be remedied. Legislation's been passed creating a Court of Civil Jurisdiction to determine "all pleas of debt, account, contracts respecting personal property, and all trespasses committed against the person or goods and chattels" in Newfoundland. Legal adviser John Reeves is the first chief justice.

While fishing admirals, justices of the peace, naval surrogates, the governor and the vice-admiralty court all heard cases in Newfoundland before, recent decisions were overturned in Britain and governors were reluctant to issue rulings.

Law bars women from right to vote

1791

NEW BRUNSWICK – It appears women are being left out of a quiet democratic revolution afoot in the British North American colonies. New Brunswick, for example, has passed a law excluding women from the right to vote. Other colonies haven't followed suit, simply assuming women won't vote anyway. Meanwhile, more men are becoming politically active as the British government introduces elected assemblies and gives men voting privileges.

Judge William Osgoode, chief justice of Upper Canada since 1792, assumed the same position in Lower Canada in 1794.

Constitutional Act divides Canada in two

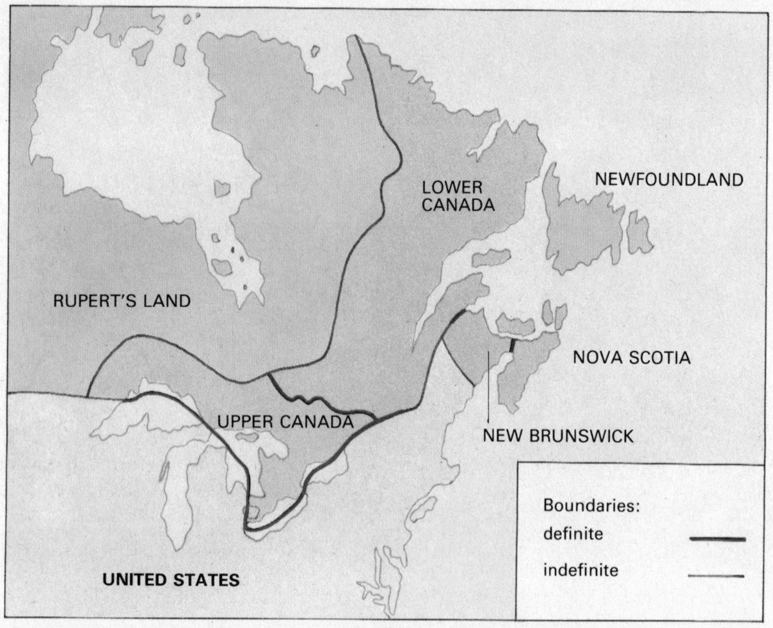

House of Commons members will be elected by the people of Canada.

June 10, 1791

QUEBEC CITY – A fundamental change occurred in this country today. What was once one province, Quebec, is now two: Upper Canada and Lower Canada.

The change is the result of the new Constitutional Act, given royal assent in London today. Politically and socially, it creates a province where the English will dominate. The French hold Lower Canada, the English Upper Canada. In this way, the government hopes to appease loyalist settlers who have been complaining about the French laws that have governed Canada. Now, in Upper Canada, they will live in a British-style society, while Lower Canada stays unchanged.

However, there is a change in the way this colony is governed. Under the new constitution, the governor is still in charge, with two lieutenant-governors under him. One of these will head up Upper Canada, the other Lower Canada.

Advising each lieutenant-governor are appointed executive and legislative councils, the latter a pseudo-House of Lords made up of local worthies. And, rounding it off, is an elected assembly – a House of Commons. Its members will be chosen by the populace, under certain entitlement laws. Those who own land or buildings with an annual income of £2 in the country, or £5 in the city, or pay £10 annual rent, can vote.

Pact settles claims on northwest coast

Oct. 28, 1790

LONDON, England – Spain and Great Britain have stepped back from the brink of war. The two nations have reached an agreement over their competing claims on the northwest coast of America.

The crisis began last year when a Spanish force entered Nootka Sound and seized British ships. Outraged, the British demanded retribution. While Spain called on France to come to its aid and the situation in Europe worsened, no one really wanted a war. Spain backed down and today the Spanish ambassador in London signed the Nootka Sound Convention, which recognizes that both countries have equal rights in the territory.

Post-road extended in both directions

1791

LOWER CANADA – The Montreal-Quebec post-road has been extended eastward to New Brunswick and westward to Kingston, Upper Canada. Until now, the service has consisted of a monthly courier route from Halifax to Quebec, involving a seven-week trip and expenses of about £200.

In Lower Canada, postmasters carry mail in two-wheeled, single-horse carriages. Ships take mail to loyalist settlements on the St. Lawrence River and Lake Ontario.

Mackenzie headed to London to study

June 1790

CUMBERLAND HOUSE, Rupert's Land – Trader Alexander Mackenzie, a North West Company man just back from an expedition down the river that will surely soon bear his name, was insulted here by Philip Turnor, a Hudson's Bay Company surveyor. Mackenzie, said Turnor, didn't really know where he had been. Mackenzie, who plans more exploring to find a path to the Pacific Ocean, told friends he was going to to London to learn more about surveying.

▷

Surveyor reaches Great Slave Lake

July 19, 1791

GREAT SLAVE LAKE, Rupert's Land – Philip Turnor and his party have just arrived here after a long canoe trip down the Slave River from Lake Athabasca. Turnor, a 40-year-old Englishman, is the Hudson's Bay Company's first professional surveyor. He was appointed 13 years ago "to map all the longitudes and latitudes of all ... settlements."

Turnor's task this trip is to survey a route from the Saskatchewan to Lake Athabasca and to determine its position. Some of his party believe Turnor has orders to find a route from Lake Athabasca to the Pacific and that is why he has gone on to the lake here.

Philip Turnor surveys east end of Lake Athabasca for Hudson's Bay Co.

Blacks transported to African colony

Jan. 15, 1792

HALIFAX – A 15-vessel flotilla is slowly edging its way from Halifax harbor today, carrying almost 1,200 black passengers destined for the African colony of Sierra Leone. The departure marks the beginning of a resettlement program carefully planned by a group of Englishmen opposed to slavery.

Forming the Sierra Leone Company last year, the Englishmen chose to recruit their first settlers from destitute black communities in Nova Scotia. There, the majority of "free" blacks are bound by chains of poverty, the legacy of unkept government promises of support which never materialized.

Priest from Canada guillotined in Paris

Sept. 2, 1792

PARIS – Canadian priest André Grasset de Saint-Sauveur was guillotined today as mass violence continued to spread in this troubled city. Since the overthrow of the monarchy less than a month ago, political prisoners have been in jeopardy because of the widespread belief that they were planning an uprising to break out of jail and join a counter-revolutionary plot.

Grasset, who was born in Montreal in 1758 but had been serving as canon of the metropolitan church in Sens, southeast of here, was one of several priests held for refusing to accept the reorganization of the church by the revolutionaries.

Nor'Westers capturing Athabasca trade

July 17, 1792

YORK FACTORY – Philip Turnor, a trader and surveyor with the Hudson's Bay Company, is back from an expedition to Athabasca country. Away for almost two years, Turnor reports that the North West Company post on Lake Athabasca, Fort Chipewyan, has become the "Grand Magazine" of the northern trade. Because the HBC has no post in Athabasca, the Nor'Westers are capturing all the trade, despite reports that they are badly mistreating the Indians.

The situation in Athabasca is typical of much of the fur country, where the HBC is scrambling to keep up with its more energetic opponents from Canada. For many years the British company was content to remain at its posts on Hudson Bay, waiting for the Indians to come down with their furs. This policy changed and the HBC has been building trading posts in Saskatchewan country since 1774.

Still, the company carries on trade, in the words of one observer, "as if it were drawn by a dead horse." Nor'Westers are aggressive and talented, and by all reports they now control three quarters of all the trade. There is even talk that the HBC will soon be forced from the country.

A black Canadian slave woman.

Law bans the sale of liquor in prisons

Oct. 15, 1792

NIAGARA, Upper Canada – The province's first limits on the sale of alcohol became law today, as part of the new penal system. Legislators at Niagara proclaimed "that no licence shall be granted for retailing any Spirituous Liquors within any of the province's Gaols or Prisons, and if any Gaoler ... shall sell, lend, use, or give away or knowingly permit, or suffer any Spirituous Liquors or Strong Waters, to enter ... such Gaol or Prison ... except as prescribed by a regular physician, surgeon, or Apothecary; every such Gaoler ... shall be fined Twenty Pounds."

Simcoe sets terms for free Crown land

Feb. 7, 1792

QUEBEC CITY – A proclamation establishing regulations for receiving free Crown land has been issued by Lt.-Gov. John Graves Simcoe. Conditions include: lands to be granted must be part of a township; one-seventh of the land in townships be reserved for each of the Protestant clergy and Crown; grants should not exceed 200 acres, but with Simcoe's discretion may be as much as 1,000 acres; applicants must till and improve the lands and pledge allegiance to the king and the provincial parliament; the navy have access to coal and timber.

Portrait of John Graves Simcoe.

First bank notes issued in Canada

Aug. 10, 1792

CANADA – Paper money along the lines of that released by the United States has begun circulation here. But while the Canada Banking Company has issued notes, it's an event that hasn't raised much interest, since the money is considered about as valuable as U.S. continental dollars – that is, virtually worthless. Hard coin is still the only currency with real value.

Vancouver explores the west coast for England

Uncharted waters and hazardous conditions have made Vancouver's survey of the coast necessary if trade ships like this are to be saved from the rocks.

Captain George Vancouver and crew, with Indian guides, on way to shore.

Expedition enters the Juan de Fuca Strait

April 29, 1792

ABOARD HMS DISCOVERY, Northwest Coast – Capt. George Vancouver has sailed from the Pacific Ocean into the strait named for that mysterious explorer Juan de Fuca. Now his task is to explore and survey the coast, its capes and inlets, keeping an special eye open for any body of water that might lead into the continent. This, it is hoped, will open up a route to the fur trading posts of the Hudson's Bay Company.

Vancouver sailed in the 300-ton *Discovery* from Falmouth in April last year with the armed brig *Chatham*. They passed the Cape of Good Hope, then skirted South Australia and sighted the American coast north of San Francisco bay. On the way here they saw no sign of the great river said to flow into the ocean south of Juan de Fuca.

First legislature of Upper Canada meets

Sept. 17, 1792

NEWARK, Upper Canada – Upper Canada's first legislature was convened today, with Lt.-Gov. John Graves Simcoe calling on all his speaking skills in his inaugural address. Simcoe said "great and momentous trusts and duties" had been given to members of both Houses. He described the occasion as a reward for loyalty to Britain and predicted the rise of a large agricultural population.

The speech and the legislation in this first session are consistent with Simcoe's vision of Upper Canada as a British province. The first statute introduced called for the establishment of English law to prevail in disputes relating to both property and civil rights. The legislature followed up by repealing parts of the Quebec Act that set up French civil law. Other agenda items before the legislature in its first session include the establishment of a 12-person jury system, jails and courthouses, and the English weights and measurement system.

Open air meeting of Upper Canada Legislative Assembly at Navy Hall.

Inlet named after British naval officer

June 12, 1792

ABOARD HMS DISCOVERY, Northwest Coast – Capt. George Vancouver discovered a large inlet today he thought might lead into the continent. But after exploring both the north and shore coasts he decided that it was just another bay that had no navigable outlet. Despite this, Vancouver named it Burrard's Channel (Inlet) after his friend, Sir Henry Burrard, who is a senior officer in the Royal Navy.

Earlier Lieut. William Robert Broughton in the brig *Chatham* had explored a group of small islands. These lie in a gulf with outlets leading both northwest and northeast that may provide an entrance to the Northwest Passage.

On June 4, during the voyage here, Vancouver formally took possession of the coast, islands and straits from 39 degrees 20 minutes N. to the entrance of the strait of Juan de Fuca and those in the interior sea which he called the Gulf of Georgia. Just before the ships entered Burrard's Channel some of the officers noticed a current coming into the sea and wondered if it came from a large river.

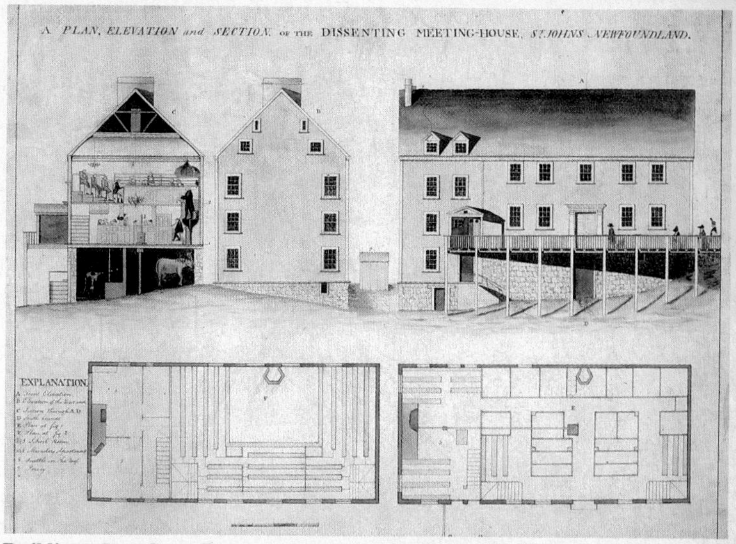

Building plans for a Protestant meeting-house in Newfoundland. A growing number of non-Anglican churches reflects the influence of immigration.

Mackenzie travels overland to Pacific

July 22, 1793

FAR WEST – For the first time, an explorer has crossed North America by land. Twenty-nine-year-old Alexander Mackenzie, the North West Company fur trader, reached the saltwater shore of the Pacific Ocean a few days ago after struggling over Rocky Mountain passes choked with snow, then crossing the rugged interior of New Caledonia [British Columbia].

Today, as Mackenzie and his party prepared to return to Lake Athabasca, he wrote on a slab of rock: "Alex Mackenzie/From Canada by land/22d July 1793." Despite the success of the expedition, it does not appear the route Mackenzie pioneered is useful for the fur trade. The rivers are too swift for safe passage by canoes, and the mountain paths are steep.

Alexander Mackenzie reaches Pacific Ocean after travelling over Rockies.

Traditions of Spain observed in Nootka

1792

NOOTKA SOUND, Northwest Coast – The north Pacific coast is about as far as you can get from the castles of Spain, but the rituals, courtesy, and precedence of the Spanish court are strictly observed in this North American village.

Nootka was established in 1790 by Spain's Viceroy Revila-Gigedo to maintain the Spanish sovereign's claims in the area. It carries on little trade, and depends almost entirely on supplies from Mexico. But the Nootka men don't complain about the village's lack of self-sufficiency nearly as much as they do about the scarcity of women.

Canada gets first Anglican bishop

July 9, 1793

QUEBEC CITY – The Anglican church has appointed Jacob Mountain its first bishop in Canada. While Mountain was named Bishop of Quebec, he will have responsibility of both Canadian provinces. Previously, they had been under a bishop from Nova Scotia. The posting is a partial victory for Upper Canada Lt.-Gov. John Graves Simcoe, who has long pushed for a greater church presence. But Simcoe had hoped that a separate bishop would be appointed for Upper Canada.

Bishop of Quebec Jacob Mountain.

Importing slaves banned in Upper Canada

July 9, 1793

NEWARK, Upper Canada – Slavery in Upper Canada will be gradually phased out, the legislature decided. A bill making this law was passed in parliament, after some opposition. Loyalist settlers who had brought Negro slaves, expected to continue using them.

Advocates of the retention of slavery had argued that the high cost and scarcity of labor should be considered in the decision. But Lt.-Gov. John Graves Simcoe, a strong proponent of the bill, moderated his stand and won passage of the legislation.

The compromise is that slaves already in the province would continue as such for the rest of their lives. But new slaves would not be brought into the province. When children born in Upper Canada to women slaves become 25, they are to receive their freedom. Again on this issue, passed in parliament's second session, Simcoe's will won the day. He had often complained about his lack of influence in parliament, but he usually got his way.

First parliament of Lower Canada meets

Dec. 17, 1792

QUEBEC CITY – The first parliament of Lower Canada is in office and already the balance of power is clearly established. Of the 51 representatives holding office in the assembly the next four years, 30 are merchants, many of them in the fur trade. The military and aristocracy are next in line with nine members. While English-speaking members hold 16 seats, an over-representation going by population figures, the honor of being the first speaker in the legislature's history goes to francophone member Jean Antoine Panet.

The Lower Canadian Legislative Assembly meets for the first time.

Wealthy eat better, Simcoe's wife notes

The first lady, Elizabeth Simcoe.

March 10, 1793

UPPER CANADA – If tidbits of information in the diary of Lt.-Gov. John Graves Simcoe's wife Elizabeth are any indication, the first family of Upper Canada and other upper class citizens in the province are certainly not lacking for food to put on their tables. Eggs, veal, beef, fish and game are all on the Simcoes' diet, as are raccoon and porcupine meat, boiled black squirrel, wild turkey, duck and roasted pigeon. The Simcoes eat much less pork than the lower classes. Loyalists in Upper Canada eat a lot of salt pork, fish and game.

England, the U.S. sign Jay's Treaty

Nov. 1, 1794

LONDON, England – Representatives of the governments of England and the United States have signed Jay's Treaty, settling differences that recently brought the two nations to the brink of war. The treaty is named after Chief Justice John Jay, President George Washington's special negotiator.

One of Jay Treaty's most important clauses is Britain's surrender to the Americans of the interior posts it failed to relinquish after the Treaty of Versailles ended the American Revolutionary War in 1783. The treaty kills all Indian hopes that Britain will support them in any conflict with the Americans.

John Jay effigy burned after treaty.

Land grant aims to hurry settlement

May 17, 1794

YORK – In a move to speed up settlement, Upper Canada's government has granted 64,000 acres to an artist and architect who has set up a community about 30 kilometres north of York [Toronto]. William Berczy has brought about 60 families of German settlers from New York State, where they originally settled two years ago. That experience disappointed them, so Berczy transferred the colony here.

The settlers had to cut their way through forests to get to their new home and plans call for this route to be the basis of a road joining York and Lake Aux Claies [Lake Simcoe], which will serve as a military link to the upper lakes.

This recently cleared farm is similar to those the loyalists are being granted.

Fort Augustus built on the Saskatchewan

1794

FORT AUGUSTUS – A North West Company trading post called Fort Augustus has been built on the Saskatchewan River by John MacDonald, James Hughes and about 20 other men at the forks. Duncan McGillivray, also of the North West Company says, "This is described to be a rich and plentiful country, abounding with all kinds of animals especially beavers and otters which are said to be so numerous that the women and children kill them with sticks and hatchets."

It is hoped that this fort can service the Cree and Assiniboines, while the Plains people will continue to trade 320 kilometres downstream at Fort George and Buckingham House. In this way, perhaps, many awkward moments and outright conflicts can be avoided since it seems the woods Indians and the plains Indians do not care to get along.

The North West Compnay's competition, the Hudson's Bay Company, is building Fort Edmonton right beside Fort Augustus.

Indians supply food at fur-trading posts

c.1790

NORTHWEST – The Assiniboine and Cree, long the middlemen in the fur trade, are assuming a new role as suppliers of food to Europeans at inland trading posts.

The Indians provide buffalo meat and pemmican, a nutritious concoction made from dried, pulverized buffalo jerky and berries, to more than 1,000 hungry laborers at the posts and hundreds more transporting furs in canoes. Fur trade middlemen have been eliminated as the Hudson's Bay and Northwest companies set up inland trading posts.

Simcoe names town of York as the capital of Upper Canada

The town of York, established in Upper Canada on the Bay of Toronto by Lt.-Gov. John Graves Simcoe, will soon be developed as a fur-trading centre.

Aug. 26, 1793

YORK – Strategically located for defence and trade, this centre has been named Upper Canada's capital by Lt.-Gov. John Graves Simcoe. He has named the centre York [Toronto], after the second son of George III, the Duke of York. When informed that Simcoe had changed the name of Toronto, as the Indians have long called the area, Iroquois war chief Joseph Brant commented, "General Simcoe has done a great deal for this province, he has changed the name of every place in it." Recently the English have altered the names of Cataraqui to Kingston, and Niagara to Newark. They also call the La Tranche River the Thames.

Gentleman's coat and waistcoat.

1795 (1795-1799)

Pacific Coast, March 28, 1795. Spain and Britain complete their withdrawal from Nootka Sound in accordance with the Nootka Sound Convention, which says that both countries can erect temporary buildings at Nootka, but not permanent garrisons or factories.

United States, Aug. 3, 1795. Indians and Americans agree to the Peace of Greenville, in which Indians cede a large area north of the Ohio River to the U.S., and recognize the "protection" of the U.S.

London, Oct. 20, 1795. Vancouver's expedition returns after surveying the northwest coast of America, the longest surveying expedition in history. It lasted four-and-a-half years, and covered about 120,000 kilometres. Only six men died on the journey.

Halifax, July 23, 1796. 556 Jamaican Maroons arrive. The descendants of escaped black slaves, they are famous for their courage as warriors. They are well received and immediately put to work reconstructing the city's citadel.

Upper Canada, 1796. John McIntosh, an early settler in Dundas County, transplants a number of wild apple trees, and distributes grafts from one of them throughout the province.

The Northwest, 1796. The British abandon their fur trade posts of Detroit, Niagara, Oswegatachie [Ogdensburg], Oswego, and Michilimackinac to the Americans in keeping with Jay's Treaty.

Fredericton, May 24, 1797. John Coffin and James Glenie, rivals in the legislature, fight a duel over a constitutional dispute. Glenie is wounded.

England, 1798. John Simcoe resigns as lieutenant-governor of Upper Canada. He has had a major impact on the settlement of the province since becoming its first governor in 1792.

Quebec, April 1, 1799. Montreal slave-owners present a petition to the legislature arguing that slavery is legal in the province, and asking for a law to protect them and their property, as their slaves are becoming restless.

Labrador, 1799. George Cartwright, a fisherman and entrepreneur, reports "in Eagle River we are killing 750 salmon a day and we would have killed more had we had more nets."

Work makes way for "Yonge Street"

Dec. 28, 1795

YORK – Work begun by the Queen's Rangers continues on a military highway between Upper Canada's new capital and Lake Simcoe. Directed by William Berczy, axemen are felling the forest along a line that runs north from York [Toronto].

Secretary of war, Sir George Yonge.

This grand new avenue is to be named "Yonge Street," after the secretary of war. It is just one of many routes Lt.-Gov. John Graves Simcoe has planned. He believes that if the Americans invade, these highways will allow easy transport of troops and supplies.

"Dundas Street," named after the secretary of state, is another major military highway being built. It runs from Burlington Bay, at the western tip of Lake Ontario, to the Thames River. Simcoe visited the area in March 1793. He said he wanted to locate the capital at the forks of the Thames, and a government reserve was set aside. Simcoe considers it easier to defend from an attack via Detroit or Lake Ontario.

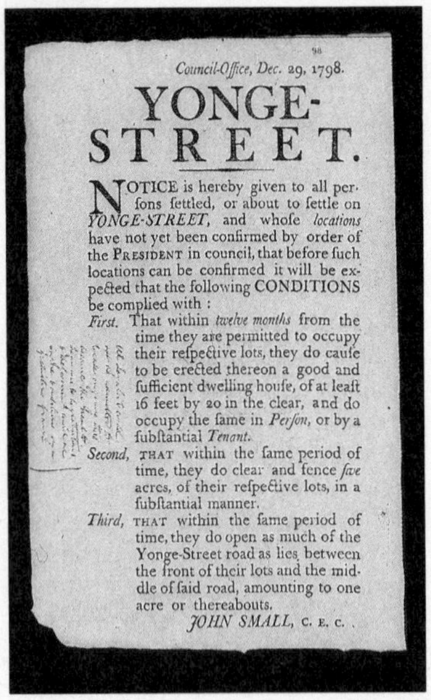

98

Council-Office, Dec. 29, 1798.

YONGE-
STREET.

NOTICE is hereby given to all perſons ſettled, or about to ſettle on *YONGE-STREET*, and whoſe *locations* have not yet been confirmed by order of the PRESIDENT in council, that before ſuch locations can be confirmed it will be expected that the following CONDITIONS be complied with:

First. That within *twelve months* from the time they are permitted to occupy their reſpective lots, they do cauſe to be erected thereon a good and ſufficient dwelling houſe, of at leaſt 16 feet by 20 in the clear, and do occupy the ſame in *Perſon*, or by a ſubſtantial *Tenant*.

Second, THAT within the ſame period of time, they do clear and fence *five* acres, of their reſpective lots, in a ſubſtantial manner.

Third, THAT within the ſame period of time, they do open as much of the Yonge-Street road as lies between the front of their lots and the middle of ſaid road, amounting to one acre or thereabouts.

JOHN SMALL, C. E. C.

Yonge Street settlement regulations are posted for the residents of York.

Capital of Upper Canada is "officially" established in York

Parliament buildings in York, established as the capital of Upper Canada.

Feb. 1, 1796

YORK – The capital of Upper Canada has been "officially" moved to York [Toronto]. Lt.-Gov. John Graves Simcoe named it after the second son of King George III, the Duke of York, who is known to be winning victories against the French in other lands.

York replaced Niagara as the capital because of its military presence, naval harbor, and route north to the fur trade of the Upper Lakes.

Indian clan mother Molly Brant is dead

April 16, 1796

KINGSTON, Upper Canada – The death today of Molly Brant, elder sister of Joseph Brant, widow of the late Sir William Johnson and a leading clan mother among the Mohawk Indians, has caused great sorrow throughout Upper Canada.

Through her relationship with Johnson, and more importantly through her position as the head of the society of Six Nations matrons, Konwatsi'tsiaiénni – which means "someone lends her a flower" – had great influence among the Iroquois. The Indians consulted her on all matters of importance.

Mississaugas angered as chief murdered

Aug. 21, 1796

YORK – The authorities in Upper Canada fear the murder of Head Chief Wabakinine may cause an Indian uprising. Last night on the waterfront, opposite Berry's Tavern, a British soldier violently struck the Indian with a large rock, and then kicked him in the chest. Wabakinine died of his wounds this morning.

The British soldier apparently offered Wabakinine's sister a dollar and some rum to sleep with him. Just before midnight he came for her, accompanied by two male settlers. Once Wabakinine's wife saw the white men dragging her sister-in-law from her resting spot under a canoe, she shook her husband to awaken him. The tall, muscular man staggered up, half asleep and half drunk. He lunged at his sister's attackers, and the soldier then set on Wabakinine and his wife. Wabakinine's wife remains in critical condition at the Mississauga village on the Credit River, 20 kilometres west of York.

The murder of their head chief and the attack on his wife have enraged Mississauga Indians at the western end of Lake Ontario. Runners have left to tell the Ojibwa-speaking bands in the interior of the atrocity. Meanwhile, the provincial government has a garrison of only 135 men to protect York.

Thompson takes up with rival company

May 23, 1797

REINDEER LAKE, Far West – The rivalry between the Hudson's Bay Company and the North West Company took a dramatic turn today when David Thompson, a 13-year veteran with the HBC, defected to the Nor'Westers. A noted surveyor, Thompson was recently given a senior trading position in the HBC, but apparently he believes the rival company is more suited to his skills as an explorer.

Raised in poverty in London, Thompson joined the HBC when he was 14. Four years later, he tumbled down the steep bank of the Saskatchewan River and broke his leg. The accident changed his life. While he was recovering he used the time to study with the well-known surveyor Philip Turnor. This was the beginning of young Thompson's career as an explorer.

The past few years Thompson has been trying to locate a new, "back door" route from Hudson Bay to the Athabasca country which avoids the arduous Methye Portage. He was working on this assignment when he defected to the Nor'Westers. The North West Company will doubtless find useful work for its new recruit. The Montreal-based company has expanded its trade all the way to the base of the Rocky Mountains.

Horse-stealing part of Blackfoot life

c.1797

PRAIRIES – On a dark night, a group of young Blackfoot men steals into the camp of their neighbors, quickly round up the best buffalo-running horses, and drive the captured animals home through the prairie night. The Blackfoot are engaging in a typical horse raid, now an essential part of their society.

These expeditions take lots of courage, skill and patience. The raiders run the great risk of waking the villagers asleep in their tepees. But it is worth the danger for the ambitious young warriors who prove themselves in the raids. Horses, especially trained buffalo-running horses, mean wealth and status among the Blackfoot. Most families have about 10 of them, the number needed to move camp. A wealthy man can have up to 100, while poor families languish with one. A young man from a poor family can make it for himself by taking horses from tribal enemies.

Horses have revolutionized the lives of the Blackfoot. They have changed the buffalo hunt forever, made transportation easier, and expanded horizons. With horses, the Blackfoot follow the buffalo far out onto the prairie, and claim larger territory. They come into closer contact with their neighbors like the Crow, Shoshone, Cree and Assiniboine, and fight over land claims. Horse-raiding has become the great sport of the plains.

Illustration of a Blackfoot chief.

American spy suffers gruesome execution

July 21, 1797

QUEBEC CITY – David McLane was hanged, beheaded and disembowelled before a large crowd outside the city walls today, marking the first time such a gruesome execution has been carried out here. Convicted of high treason, McLane was sentenced to be hanged and disembowelled while still alive. But he'd already died from hanging before he was disembowelled and his head cut off. His body was not dismembered, as had been ordered.

McLane, about 30 years old, a trader from Providence, R.I., had been accused of trying to overthrow the government by enlisting seven or eight influential people and as many others as possible to make a surprise attack on the Quebec garrison. Despite arguments that his two main accusers could not be trusted because they were accomplices, he was convicted. A move to quash the verdict – because as a foreigner, the prisoner could not be charged with treason – also failed.

Rattlers flourishing at Burlington Bay

1797

BURLINGTON BAY, Upper Canada – Most settlers in Upper Canada continue to regard the Burlington Bay area [Hamilton] as one of the most undesirable districts in the province. In the summer, the low-lying wetlands have swarms of mosquitoes, and even more alarming are the rattlesnakes. In 1795, Augustus Jones, a provincial surveyor, reported Burlington Bay settlers killing 700 rattlesnakes that one summer alone. The rattlers live in caves in the escarpment and come down to Burlington Bay to drink in dry weather.

Sketch of Chief Great Sail done by John Graves Simcoe's wife.

Mississaugas refuse to surrender remaining land to British

The King's Head Inn, located in the northwest of Burlington Bay [Hamilton].

Aug. 21, 1797

BURLINGTON BAY, Upper Canada – The Mississauga Indians now realize that to the British, land surrender means the outright surrender of their hunting grounds and fisheries. The Mississauga now refuse to cede their remaining tract of land between the head of the lake [near Hamilton] and York, apart from 3,450 acres on Burlington Bay, where Joseph Brant will build a home. They have great respect for the Mohawk war chief as he "alone knows the value of the land."

Brant now advises them, and despite the traditional enmity between the Mississauga and the Six Nations, may soon be elected one of their chiefs. The British paid £75 for the 3,450 acres.

Danforth cuts road toward Kingston

New roads will make it easier for the pioneers to settle in Upper Canada.

July 26, 1799

YORK – The spate of road building in Upper Canada has gone one step further, with the start of a highway running east from York toward Kingston, under the direction of Asa Danforth. The road is the latest in a series of highways intended to provide easy travel in this pioneer land.

What ready transportation there is right now tends to rely on Lake Ontario – a route that is not easily defended should hostilities resume with the American rebels. With this new road and others, settlers will be able to open up new lands. This, in turn, should improve the economy and encourage immigration.

New law protects native gravesites

Dec. 14, 1797

UPPER CANADA – At long last, the British administration in Upper Canada has acted on the Mississauga Indians' request to protect their gravesites from settlers. A proclamation was issued today protecting the native burial grounds, sternly warning offenders they "shall be proceeded against with the utmost severity." The declaration also protects Mississauga fisheries.

The Mississaugas have repeatedly asked British officials to protect their gravesites. Tomahawks, pipes, silver and brass ornaments, and copper kettles have been taken.

Population of Nfld. is near starvation

Oct. 30, 1798

NEWFOUNDLAND – Gov. William Waldegrave reports that the population of Newfoundland – closing in on the 20,000-mark – is near starvation. The problem stems from the closure of the Spanish saltfish markets because of war. Portugal cannot absorb Spain's share, and the market is swamped with fish selling at a loss.

Meanwhile, the war has caused food prices in Newfoundland to rise considerably. To add to the problem there has been a partial potato failure. To reduce prices, Waldegrave has ordered copper coins from Britain.

St. John's Island renamed after Prince Edward, Duke of Kent

Feb. 2, 1799

PRINCE EDWARD ISLAND – St. John's Island received permission to change its name today. Its new appellation, Prince Edward Island, honors Edward, Duke of Kent, who has recently shown interest in the colony's affairs.

The new name, some argue, is long overdue. As early as the 1780s, officials said that St. John's Island is too easily confused with other "St. John's" in the region. In 1780, Gov. Walter Patterson suggested "New Ireland" as an alternate name, but authorities in London refused this, and instead suggested "New Guernesy" or "New Angelsey." Finally, a compromise was reached in Prince Edward Island.

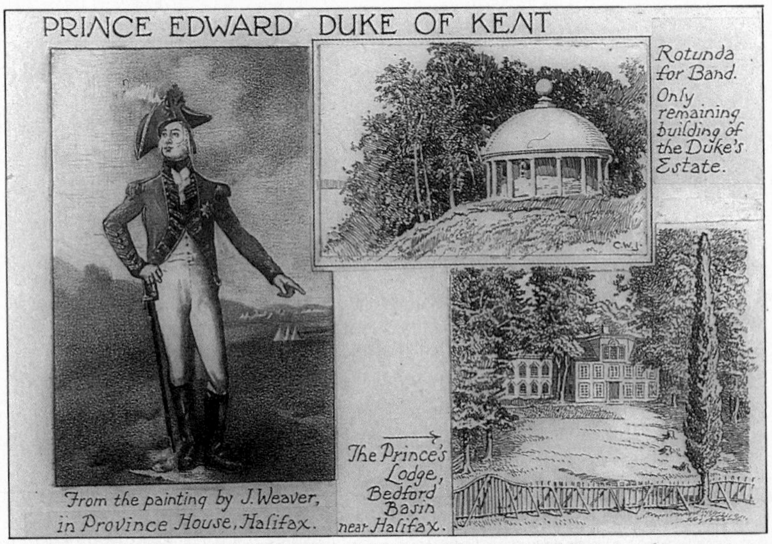
PRINCE EDWARD DUKE OF KENT
Rotunda for Band. Only remaining building of the Duke's Estate.
From the painting by J. Weaver, in Province House, Halifax.
The Prince's Lodge, Bedford Basin near Halifax.

Portrait of Prince Edward, Duke of Kent, and some buildings on his estate.

York's new jail stands on King Street South and Leader Lane. Built in 1799, the jail is part of the great expansion that's under way in York right now.

Tea Gardens offers a host of fine foods

1797

MONTREAL – The British elite of Montreal will be pleased to learn about the opening of a fine new eating establishment in the city, one comparable in comfort and taste to such English pleasure gardens as the Ranelagh in Chelsea and the Vauxhall in London. A Mr. T. Powis is the proprietor of the Montreal Tea Gardens, where the city's genteel population can enjoy a variety of fine foods. Punch, tea, pastries and dinner are served.

Non-Anglicans can perform marriages

Dec. 29, 1798

YORK – Bowing to reality, the government has passed a new law allowing some non-Anglican ministers to perform marriages. In the past, since Anglicanism is the state church of England, only Anglican ministers were authorized to perform the service. However, only a small minority of the Upper Canada population is Anglican. So, as of today, Lutherans, Calvinist and Presbyterian ministers have gained the right to marry couples.

Furniture and various household items of the day

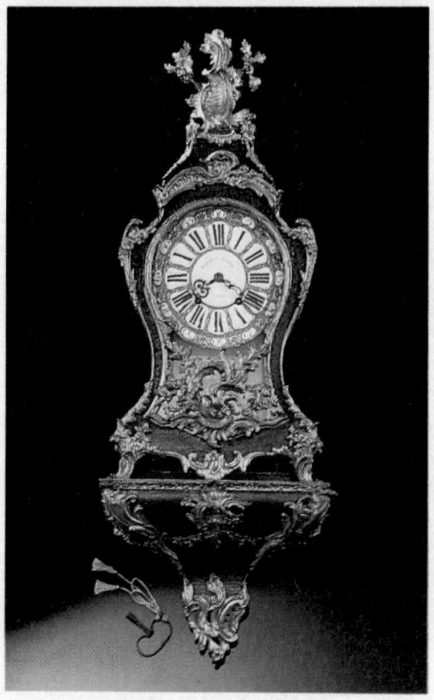

Bracket clock with mechanism made by Charles Le Roy of Paris.

Louis XIII-XIV style settee found in a Quebec City home around 1799.

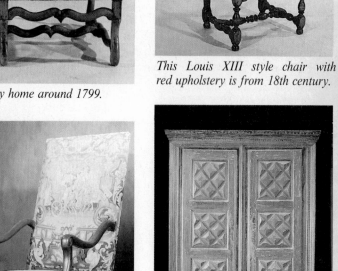

This Louis XIII style chair with red upholstery is from 18th century.

This popular long-case clock is signed Philip Constantin, London.

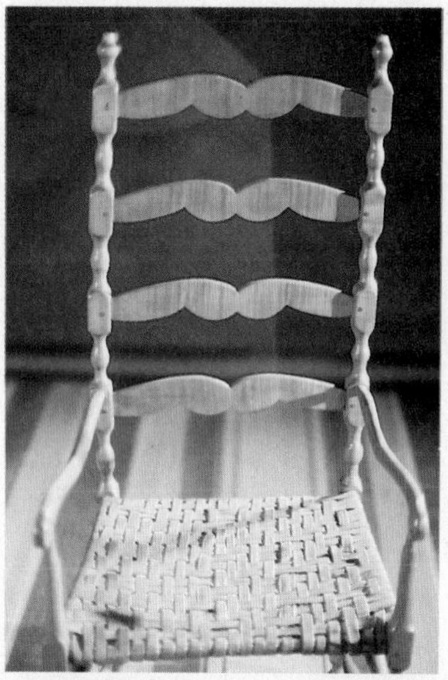

Louis XIII style chair, made of tiger maple with elm-bark woven seat.

Elegant birch armchair with sheep bone pattern is popular in Quebec.

Pine armoire has diamond-point panels and a dark-green finish.

A shelf at a trade depot in York factory is decorated with this painting.

A sundial from [Churchill, Man.].

1800 (1800-1804)

Halifax, Aug. 3, 1800. The 551 Jamaican Maroons exiled to Halifax in 1796 sail for Sierra Leone. Governor Wentworth has employed them improving the city's citadel. After repeated appeals, London has allowed them to go to Africa.

Upper Canada, 1800. As far as their incomes allow, urban and rural residents follow the English custom of serving a variety of meats along with batter puddings for dessert.

Atlantic Provinces, 1800. The courts of both New Brunswick and Nova Scotia deny the rights of slave owners to regain possession of escaped slaves. Slavery is no longer protected by the law.

North America, c.1800. There are an estimated 50 million buffalo left on the continent, most of them west of the Mississippi Valley. There were about 70 million on the continent in 1500, including many in the east which were killed to provide leather for European markets.

Upper Canada, May 1801. Thomas Talbot, an eccentric alcoholic bachelor and veteran of the French Revolutionary War, is granted 5,000 acres on Lake Erie, where he begins settling English immigrants, according to plan that will make him a landed magnate.

Quebec, May 1801. Following a law passed in April relating to insane people and abandoned children, the Augustine sisters take responsibility for abandoned children at the request of the legislature.

Upper Canada, Aug. 1, 1801. It is announced that public coaches will no longer carry mail between Niagara, Queenston, and Chippawa, as post offices have been established with postmasters' stages to carry mail.

Upper Canada, 1801. Mennonites from Pennsylvania settle in Waterloo and York counties. They come with capital, cattle, and furniture, and build mills and substantial farms.

Trinity Bay, Newfoundland, January 1802. Dr. John Clinch has inoculated 700 people for smallpox. He is likely the first person in British North America to administer vaccines.

Lower Canada, 1804. Thomas Moore writes the *Canadian Boat Song* near the rapid of St. Anne. It is based on a song sung by *voyageurs* who are about to leave civilization for the Grand Portage to the west.

"Mad" fur trader puzzles Indians

Summer 1800

ROCKY MOUNTAIN FORT, Rupert's Land – North West Company trader John Thompson has built a post on the Mackenzie River here opposite the mouth of the North Nahanni. But he is finding that the Indians believe he is mad. For them the animals of the forest are there primarily to provide food, not clothing and ornament. They call the pelts he wants for trade "meat with hair."

Although Alexander Mackenzie explored the river that now bears his name more than 11 years ago, the North West Company made virtually no attempt to exploit this new source of furs until four years ago when Duncan Livingston built a post at the outlet of Great Slave Lake. He traded there for three years and then decided to follow Mackenzie's trail himself.

But about 320 kilometres from the Arctic a band of Inuit attacked his party and killed all except one who was thrown into the river with a big stone tied to his neck. Despite the danger, the North West Company decided to continue the development of the Mackenzie region. That is why Thompson has built his fort here and is trading with the Indians – despite their reservations about his sanity. More forts are planned for the Mackenzie.

Voyageurs enjoy the challenge of shooting the rapids from time to time.

Birds of a feather drop together

Passenger pigeons are easy targets.

c. 1800

NORTH AMERICA – Passenger pigeons, abundant on the eastern coast of the continent when Europeans first arrived, continue to be destroyed in what can only be described as a bloodthirsty killing orgy. They have been shot, clubbed, netted, blown up, and burnt with torches. The birds nest in huge colonies that make them easy targets for hunters, who want them only for food.

Passenger pigeons are numerous in the interior. The birds summer in huge flocks in forests of Canada and the northern U.S., and winter in the south. They are long tailed, with a blue back and head, and a red breast. They are graceful, and fly some 100 kilometres per hour.

Insults cost attorney general his life

Jan. 3, 1800

UPPER CANADA – Maj. John Small's wife's honor has been vindicated by John White's death! The province's first attorney general, White died of a gunshot wound received above the right hip in a duel with Small, clerk of the Executive Council.

Nearly involved in an earlier fight with a Capt. Fitzgerald of the Queen's Rangers, White was protected by a court order. This time White refused to withdraw insulting remarks he made about Small's wife. Small felt duty-bound to challenge White to what appears to have been a fair duel.

Judge's ruling frees Lower Canada slave

1800

MONTREAL – Slavery is legal in Lower Canada, but at least one judge has taken it upon himself to fight the longtime practice from the bench. That message comes across loud and clear in Chief Justice James Monk's recent decision to free an escaped slave named Robin.

Monk took the law into his own hands when he released Robin on the grounds that the Imperial Act of 1797 abolished all legislation regarding slavery in the province. Legally, it is a mistaken ruling, as the law provides for the imprisonment of escaped slaves in houses of correction. Robin escaped from his owner last year and went to live with a Montreal tavern-keeper. He was committed to a house of correction at his owner's request.

Ever since becoming chief justice in 1794, Monk has been out to dig the grave of slavery. He freed two Negro slaves in 1798 on legal technicalities, saying slavery did not exist in the province and that he would apply his interpretation of the law to later cases. Just last year, a slave owners' petition argued that slavery is upheld by law.

Plains people herding buffalo over great jumps

1800

WESTERN PLAINS – Plains Indians are stampeding large herds of buffalo over cliffs to their deaths, a hunting technique that is causing considerable waste. While a group of hunters approaches the buffalo from behind to get the herd moving toward the cliff, others on the sides keep it moving by creating noise. Another method to begin the stampede is to set the plains grass on fire, forcing the buffalo to run over the cliff to their deaths. The height of the cliff-drive sites, known as buffalo jumps, is often not great, but is sufficient to cripple the animals.

Indians have no way to control the number of buffalo they are stampeding, and as a result often many more animals than they can use are being chased to their deaths. However, with the buffalo herd estimated at some 50 million to 60 million here this year, the species is in no immediate danger.

Cliff drives are more common in the summer. At this time of year, Indian hunters often build pounds to entrap the animals, taking advantage of their natural urge to seek shelter. A 1.2-metre high fence built from birch stakes forms the perimeter of the pound and the animals are lured into it.

When the hunts are over, women skin and butcher the buffalo. Both jobs are worth the effort because buffalo hides and meat rate highly.

Plains people stampede large herds of buffalo over cliffs to their deaths.

Abandoned tot to be put up for adoption

Nov. 15, 1800

QUEBEC CITY – A seven-month-old baby girl abandoned at the Hôtel-Dieu hospital here will be put up for adoption, the first such case involving the Assembly. The future of the child, who was found by the hospital gatekeeper, will be ironed out in correspondence between Hôtel-Dieu mother superior Sister M.G. de Saint François, advocat general M.J. Sewell and Lt.-Gov. Robert Shore. Sources said the government will take an active role in the child's welfare in this case. The feeling is that the government will provide for her care until parents – either natural or adoptive – can be found or until she is able to look after herself. But the Assembly may take a low profile in the adoption, so other parents will not be encouraged to abandon children.

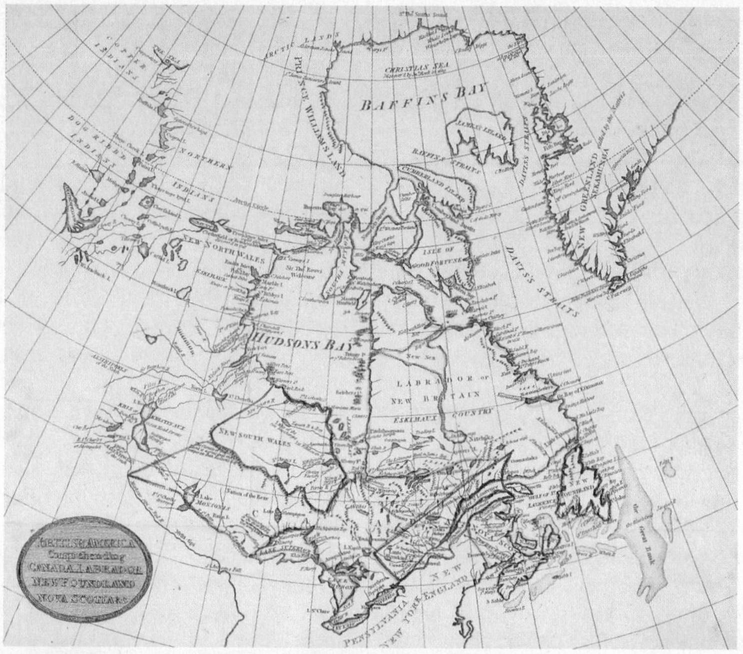

An 1800 map of British North America, including Canada, Labrador, Nova Scotia, Newfoundland, New South Wales, and Hudson's Bay Co. territory.

Rev. Strachan opens academy in Cornwall

Rev. John Strachan heads academy.

July 28, 1803

CORNWALL, Upper Canada – The Reverend John Strachan has opened his all-male academy [high school] in Cornwall. Just ordained a deacon by Bishop Jacob Mountain, former Presbyterian Strachan received his MA at King's College Aberdeen.

Recently put in charge of Cornwall's Anglicans, Strachan is "a young man of competent attainments, of fair understanding and great modesty and worth." He supplements his income by teaching at a school he set up at his home with a few students. Strachan came to Canada in 1799.

Selkirk suggests colonizing the northwest

April 3, 1802

LONDON, England - Thomas Douglas, the Earl of Selkirk, has suggested Britain might relieve itself of some of its "congested and dissatisfied population" through a program of emigration to the British North American northwest.

In a communiqué to the government, Lord Selkirk says although the Atlantic coast of Canada has no large tracts of open land available, save for those he described as "barren and frozen deserts," this is not the case farther inland. In a territory His Lordship described as the "western extremity of Canada," there is "a country which the Indian traders represent as fertile, and of a climate far more temperate than the shores of the Atlantic under the same parallel."

The Selkirk letter says the major impediment to such a colonization is the Hudson's Bay Company monopoly on the territory, but he felt the company might approve of the proposed settlement if it were "amply indemnified."

Selkirk's proposal is now being considered by the colonial secretary. Informed observers say the British people do not look with favor upon emigration.

Two-wheeled carts ease Métis lives

Métis engaged in buffalo hunt now use such carts to carry their loads home.

May 4, 1800

RED RIVER, Rupert's Land – Some of the Métis engaged in the buffalo hunt have found a new way of moving their heavy loads. Instead of tying them on the horses' backs, they move them in two-wheeled carts made of hardwood and fastened together with dowels. Shafts run down both sides of the horse and converge at its collar. Also, the carts are easily taken apart for river crossings.

Early trials with animal grease on axles were found to collect dust. No lubricant is used and the carts are exceedingly noisy, like a thousand fingernails drawn across a thousand panes of glass.

New depot replaces Grand Portage fort

Summer 1803

LAKE SUPERIOR – The North West Company has built a new depot [Fort William] for its inland trade at the mouth of the Kaministiquia River at the western end of Lake Superior. The depot replaces the fort at Grand Portage, 60 kilometres to the south, which now sits in territory adjudged to be American.

The nerve centre of the inland trade, the depot consists of buildings sprawled across 125 acres of lakeshore. It is dominated by the spacious Great Hall where senior partners in the company will gather and hold their annual meetings.

Middle class found to eat lots of meat

1800

QUEBEC CITY – The average middle-class family in the colony spends much of its food money on meat. To feed his wife and a servant, well-known *Gazette* printer John Neilson, for example, buys eight kilograms of meat a week – eating up 40 percent of the food budget. Dairy products account for 28 percent of the Neilson food budget, as they consume a kilogram of butter, 18 eggs and four pints of milk a week. Fruits, herbs and vegetables eat up 10 percent of the budget, cereal four. Drinks include tea, milk and water.

Slaughter targets northern penguins

1802

NEWFOUNDLAND – The last penguin rookery in North America at Funk Island has been destroyed by humans. Jacques Cartier first killed great auks, or North American penguins, in 1534. From the 1700s on, English fishermen have slaughtered them for food and bait, and boiled them to make oil.

Recently, Americans have killed thousands of penguins for their feathers, despite a 1794 colonial office ban against the practice. People also eat penguin eggs. Unfortunately for the friendly, 30-inch high bird, it is flightless and easy to kill.

Fredericton residence of Thomas Carleton, governor of New Brunswick.

Measures to tame notorious death trap

Sable Island should no longer be a death trap to ships sailing nearby.

Oct. 10, 1801

SABLE ISLAND, N.S. – After today, this notorious death trap for seafarers, a skinny sandbar 300 kilometres southeast of Halifax, should be less dangerous than it has been for centuries. James Morris, his family and staff arrived by schooner from Halifax to set up the Sable Island Humane Establishment. As ships pile up on the island and submerged sandbars around it, the establishment will try to rescue people and salvage property.

Morris got his orders from Sir John Wentworth, governor of Nova Scotia, who had lobbied for just such an establishment despite coolness toward the idea in London. Nova Scotians were his strongest supporters. Both the local assembly and council wanted a year-round lifeguard settlement on Sable. Public opinion supported it, and public money paid for it. Nova Scotians set it up, and Nova Scotians will be the rescuers and comforters of the shipwrecked.

The province has grown sick of Sable's horrifying record as a saboteur. Two years ago, the island snared the brig *Frances,* taking to their deaths a Dr. and Mrs. Copeland, their two children, 15 other passengers and a crew of 19. Copeland was surgeon to the personal regiment of Prince Edward, Halifax-based commander of all British forces in North America. Edward's furniture went down with the ship.

Indian attack devastates the Boston

March 22, 1803

NOOTKA SOUND – Nootka Indians at this popular trading spot on the northwest coast of America have attacked and destroyed an American ship, killing almost the entire crew. The trading vessel *Boston* entered the harbor several days ago. At that time Capt. John Salter presented a musket to the local chief, Maquinna, as a gift. The gun turned out to be faulty, an insult which may have motivated the attack. The Indians may also have been reacting to some mistreatment at the hands of another captain at another time.

Since the sea-going trade for furs began along this coast in 1785, relations between traders and local Indians have been amicable for the most part. However, traders are not always friendly in dealing with the Nootka, and this is not the first time the Indians have answered back with violence. Another cause of these attacks is simple misunderstanding between two cultures.

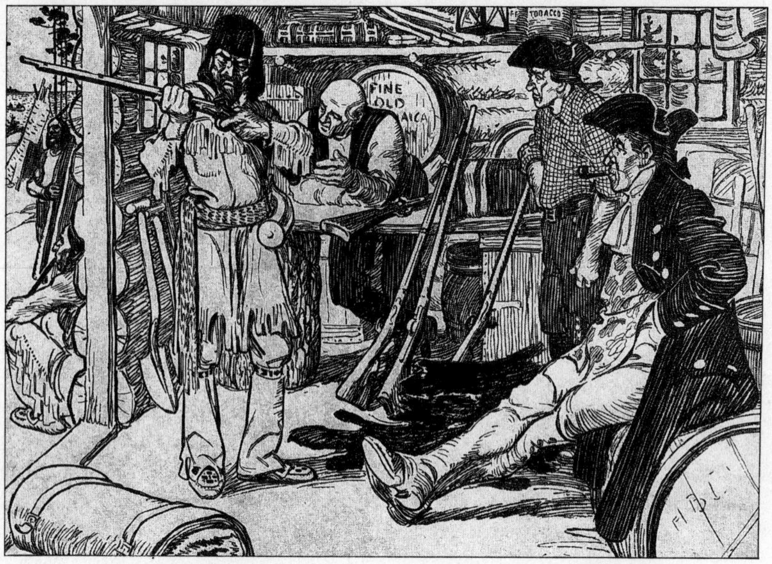

Relations between Canadian traders and Indians are generally amicable.

The two crewmen of the *Boston* who survived the incident are John Jewitt and John Thompson. They are being held captive by Maquinna and his followers. Jewitt is the ship's armorer who was spared because the Indians want him to be their gunsmith and blacksmith. When word of the attack gets out, it will likely discourage trading vessels from visiting Nootka Sound in the near future.

Fur-trading baron McTavish is dead

July 6, 1804

MONTREAL – Simon McTavish, the leading partner of the North West Company, is dead at age 54. He is survived by his young wife and their four children. The body will be buried behind the stone mansion which McTavish was building at the edge of the city.

Though he probably never travelled into the Northwest, McTavish was the most important member of Montreal's fur-trading elite. Known as "The Marquis" because of his autocratic manner, he was one of the founding members of the North West Company in 1779, helping to build it into a successful rival of the Hudson's Bay Company for control of the fur trade.

More recently he has been challenged by the famed explorer and trader Alexander Mackenzie, who has thrown his support behind the upstart Canadian firm, the XY Company. The last six years of competition between these two companies have been marked by falling fur prices, rising wages and violence on the fur frontier.

As long as McTavish remained alive, nursing his dislike of Mackenzie, the two rivals would not make up their differences. One result of the death of "The Marquis" is expected to be a merger of the two companies in the near future.

Cost-cutting Hudson's Bay Company increases whaling efforts

June 24, 1804

RUPERT HOUSE, Rupert's Land – Competition and dwindling fur supplies have forced the Hudson's Bay Company to cut costs. One way is to send company employees on whaling expeditions in the north of the bay. Then the company's supplies of whale oil will be supplied by employees at less cost than that obtained from trading with the Indians.

This is the reason a group led by Thomas Alder is leaving this post on the eastern shore of James Bay to visit other company posts along the shore to try to organize whaling expeditions. Company officials believe their employees, with better boats and weapons than those of the Indians, will do a better job. Then no more whale oil will need to be bought from Indians and trade with them can be limited to furs.

Col. Thomas Talbot, official promoter of settlement in the London District, Upper Canada.

Schooner sinks with court officials, accused Indian on board

Oct. 8, 1804

UPPER CANADA – The man accused of being John Sharpe's murderer will never be tried. Solicitor General Isaac Dey Grey, Judge Thomas Cochrane, lawyers Angus Macdonell and William Weekes, along with court officials, Indian interpreters, witnesses, the crew and the accused Indian Ogtonicut, all perished today without a trace, when a storm arose near their final destination, Presqu'Ile, and sank their schooner *Speedy.*

The native prisoner was to be tried for avenging the murder of his brother by a white man named Cosens. Finding Sharpe alone, at a trading post on Lake Scugog, Ogtonicut is reported to have murdered him.

A storm has destroyed the schooner Speedy near its destination of Presqu'Ile.

1805 (1805-1809)

Quebec, Aug. 14, 1805. Businessmen and civil servants gather to lay the cornerstone for the Union Hotel, a new kind of hotel with an emphasis on lodging, comfort, service, and dining. Currently established hotels are similar to taverns or coffeehouses.

Lower Canada, 1805. Paper is handmade from rags at a St-Andrew mill, the first paper produced in Canada. It is sold to merchants to be used as printing and wrapping paper.

Upper Canada, March 3, 1806. The legislature passes an act for the promotion of science in schools, allocating £400 to buy scientific instruments.

Trois-Rivières, Lower Canada, April 11, 1807. Ezekiel Hart, a Jew, wins a byelection for the House of Assembly. When pressed, he reluctantly signs official documents even though it is the Sabbath for him, omitting the formula "in the year of our Lord."

Upper Canada, Nov. 24, 1807. Thayendanegea, also known as Joseph Brant, illustrious Mohawk interpreter, translator, and chief of the Six Nations Indians, dies [at Burlington].

Northwest, 1807. The North West Company names its principal post Fort William [near Thunder Bay], after its superintendent William McGillivray. Built in 1803, it is the company's major transshipment point.

Trois-Rivières, Lower Canada, June 18, 1808. Ezekiel Hart is re-elected to the legislature.

Atlantic Provinces, 1808. Most slaves in Nova Scotia and New Brunswick have escaped.

London, Sept. 7, 1809. In response to the Ezekiel Hart affair, the colonial secretary confirms that a Jew is not allowed to sit in the legislature.

Montreal, Sept. 17, 1809. A bill from the Beaver Club records that 32 guests consume 62 bottles of wine, 12 quarts of beer, and large amounts of brandy and gin.

Newfoundland, 1809. Labrador is reannexed to Newfoundland.

Saint John, New Brunswick, 1809. The Drury Lane Theatre opens.

Lower Canada, 1809. The Durham boat, a 24- to 27-metre barge with a large carrying capacity, is introduced to the St. Lawrence as a freight carrier by Americans.

Assembly in Lower Canada ousts Jew

March 14, 1808

LOWER CANADA – An odious mixture of political opportunism and anti-Semitism reared its ugly head in the House of Assembly today as members passed a resolution to expel elected representative Ezekial Hart, a Jew. Controversy over Hart's right to sit or vote in the House has raged since his victory in a Trois-Rivières byelection last year. According to his detractors, Hart's initial *faux pas* was his disregard for the customary expression "in the year of our Lord" when writing the date on official documents. Then, at his swearing-in ceremony in January, Hart substituted "Christian" with "Jewish" in the text of his oath; it has been successfully argued that this rendered his oath invalid.

While some House members appear determined to oust Hart simply because of his religion, the controversy has more widespread political implications. One observer, John Lambert, has voiced his suspicions that members of the Canadian party are seizing the opportunity to expel Hart to maintain their majority, and, "if possible, to get a French, instead of an English member in the House." Ironically, Hart was elected in a largely Canadian and Catholic constituency, the same interests that have campaigned for his expulsion.

Jewish representative Ezekiel Hart.

Timber offers hope of valuable new trade

August 1806

QUEBEC CITY – Philomen Wright, an American settler from up the Ottawa River, has arrived here after a harrowing ride down the river on a raft of square timber. It is the first time that wood has been brought out of the upper country this way, and promises to open a valuable new trade in timber for the Ottawa Valley.

The demand for wood is high in Great Britain because the long conflict with the Emperor Napoleon has cut off the Mother Country from its usual supplies from the Baltic.

Wright plans to sell the wood to support his farming colony at the Chaudière Falls. He's been established there since 1800, when he and 27 compatriots arrived from Massachusetts. He hit upon the rafting idea when forced to come up with a way to raise some cash to support the settlement.

Philomen Wright is the first to go up the Ottawa River on a lumber raft.

North West trader establishes outpost

Fall 1805

McLEOD LAKE, Far West – The first substantial outpost west of the Rockies has been built here close to the lake by North West Company trader and explorer Simon Fraser.

Fraser and his companion and lieutenant, John Stuart, have the task of extending the company's operations west of the Rockies. They followed Alexander Mackenzie's route up the Peace and Parsnip rivers and so to the lake here where they hope to start trading soon.

Snafu leaves York ownership in doubt

Aug. 1, 1805

YORK – A sloppily prepared deed has left the ownership of York, the provincial capital, in doubt. When Sir John Johnson executed and recorded the Toronto Purchase of Sept. 23, 1787, he was quite careless: the deed has no signatures and doesn't specify the area of land surrendered. As it does not conform to the Proclamation of 1763, it is invalid.

However, the Mississauga at the Credit River, 20 kilometres west of York, remember the transfer, and for a nominal fee of 10 shillings, they will sign a proper deed today.

Craig fumes as Hart expelled again

May 15, 1809

LOWER CANADA – Gov. James Henry Craig stormed into the Legislative Assembly of Lower Canada today and dissolved the house, hoping an election will undermine the Canadian party's majority. His action comes on the heels of the Assembly's second expulsion of Ezekial Hart last month, and reflects the political struggle being waged in Lower Canada between representatives of the British and Canadian parties. Craig did not interfere last year when Hart, a Jew, was expelled, apparently because of his religion. But since then the governor has become more openly opposed to the Canadians and their attempts at wresting control from the pro-British legislative and executive councils.

The second expulsion of Hart has given Craig the pretext for interfering with the Canadian-controlled Assembly. Hart was re-elected in his Trois-Rivières riding after his initial expulsion.

This time Hart pledged his oath of office "in a Christian manner" and the Legislative Council has recognized his right to sit in the Assembly. In spite of this, the Canadians have expelled Hart, provoking Craig to denounce the "personal animosities" and "unconstitutional" steps taken by the Legislative Assembly.

Fraser makes trip down feisty river

July 1, 1808

MUSQUEAM, Far West – Simon Fraser and his party have survived clinging to the walls of a canyon and canoeing through rapids and whirlpools on their journey down the great river that flows into the sea near here. Today, as they paddle down the estuary near the river's mouth, reflecting on the tumultuous journey, its usefulness as a trade route to the Pacific is in serious doubt.

Fraser and 24 men left Fort George in May despite warnings from Indians of dangers ahead. At one point, steep banks on either side made portaging impossible. Canoes and supplies were cached, but travel overland proved equally difficult. Acquiring canoes from Indians, they took their chances in the treacherous, fast-moving water.

Simon Fraser descends the river.

Adventurers repel hostile Cowichans

Masked dancer in Cowichan garb.

July 1808

FAR WEST – Simon Fraser's expedition has hastily retreated back up the [Fraser] river, escaping harassment from hostile Cowichan Indians. The trouble began soon after his party reached the river's mouth. There, within sight of the Strait of Georgia, Fraser and his company of 24 adventurers encountered the warlike Cowichan.

A quick decision was made to retreat upriver, but the Cowichan followed. Dozens of canoes pursued Fraser, but each attack was successfully repelled. Neither side suffered casualties and the Cowichan gave up the chase near [Hope].

Fleece-bearing dog intriguing to Fraser

June 27, 1808

FAR WEST – Indians in the northwest rely on a type of fleece-bearing dog for some of their clothing needs, explorer Simon Fraser has observed.

While travelling along the treacherous "Great River" in search of a navigable route to the Pacific Ocean, Fraser's party of adventurers passed through the village of Spuzzum. It was there that they noted blankets made of mountain goat hair and the fleece of certain dogs, which appeared to have been recently shorn.

It is common for Indians to keep dogs as companions, watchdogs and pack animals. However, this is the first instance in which Europeans have observed the natives making use of dogs' fur as a raw material for textiles.

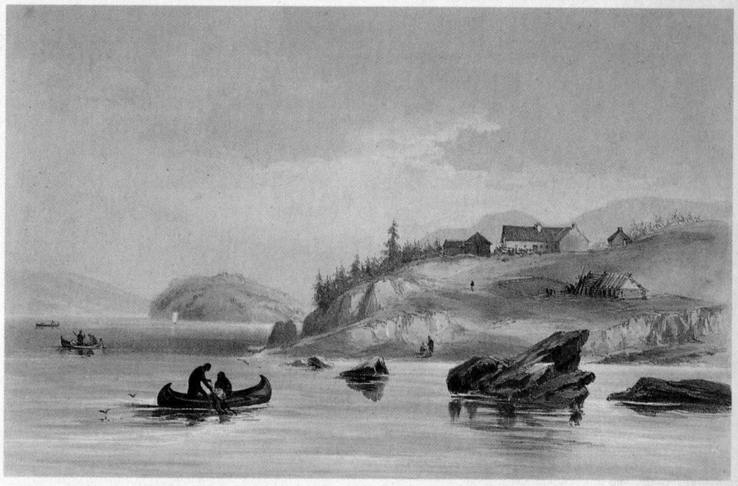

View of Fort George, a new fur-trading post west of the Rocky Mountains. It was set up by Simon Fraser as a base for exploration of the [Fraser River].

Governor questions Americans' loyalty

Jan. 5, 1808

YORK – Loyalty from recently-arrived Americans in the western part of the province cannot be taken for granted in the event of war with the United States, warned Francis Gore, governor of Upper Canada. Gore expresses his concerns today in a letter to his counterpart in Lower Canada, Gov. James Craig.

Gore writes that he is confident he can count on people living between Kingston and the border of Lower Canada. But he could not say the same for those living in this area, as well as Niagara and Long Point on Lake Erie.

"I have to observe that excepting the inhabitants of Glengarry and those persons who have served in the American war and their descendants ... the residue of the inhabitants of this colony consist chiefly of persons who have emigrated from the States of America and in consequence retain those ideas of equality and insubordination much to the prejudice of this government, so prevalent in that country."

Craig will likely receive the letter sympathetically, but it will do nothing to help his growing pessimism. Craig feels that war with the Americans is inevitable and that he he is too old and unhealthy to be in charge of the defence. Adding to his gloom is both a lack of confidence in the ability of French soldiers and his lack of esteem for the French-Canadian population in general.

▷

Molson launches Canadian steamship

Aug. 19, 1809

LOWER CANADA – The age of "steam" has come to Canada. Without ceremony, brewer John Molson launched the all Canadian-made *Accommodation,* North America's third steamship. Measuring 21.6 metres long in the keel, the two paddle wheels are moved by a six horsepower engine. The engines were cast at Forges du St. Maurice, the metal work was done in Montreal and the ship built at Munn's yards.

Fascinated by the industrial uses of steampower, Molson undertook this project after hearing about Robert Fulton's successful Hudson River steamboat service in 1807. Seeing the future in steam-powered navigation along the length of the St. Lawrence, now that plans have been approved to bypass the Lachine Rapids, Molson has formed a partnership with two Englishmen.

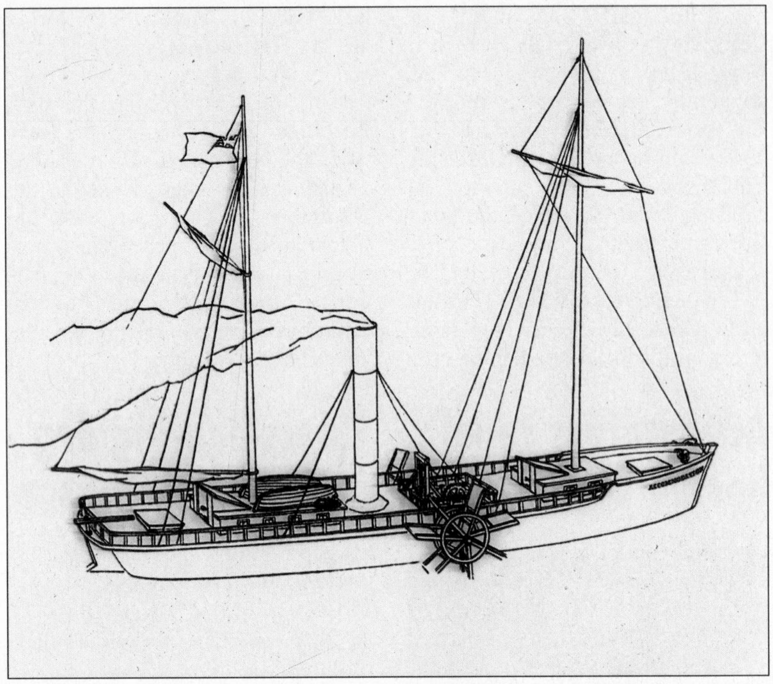

The Canadian-made Accommodation is North America's third steamship.

Woman discovered disguised as a man

Dec. 29, 1806

PEMBINA, Rupert's Land – White women are rare in the far northwest, so it was with a great deal of surprise that the Hudson's Bay Company servants at this remote trading post found a woman living among them. The discovery was made by postmaster Alexander Henry when he was called to the bedside of an ailing servant named John Fubbister.

"He stretched out his hands toward me," Henry recounts, "and in piteous tones begged me to be kind to a poor, helpless, abandoned wretch, who was not of the sex I had supposed, but an unfortunate Orkney girl, pregnant, and actually in childbirth."

It turns out that John Fubbister is actually Isabel Gunn, who has been in the employ of the HBC, masquerading as a man, since the summer. Apparently she resorted to her desperate disguise knowing the company did not hire women, but wishing to follow her lover into the fur country. Unhappily for Isabel, she was assigned to a post a good distance from her lover.

Making the best of her situation, "John" turned out to be a very able servant, but in the final stages of her pregnancy she could no longer keep up the disguise. The company will doubtless send her and her baby out of the country.

"Mr. Edwards" reveals plot to the governor of Nova Scotia

June 16, 1808

HALIFAX – A mysterious visitor has arrived in town from New York. He calls himself "Mr. Edwards," but he is in fact Aaron Burr, 52, hero of the American Revolution, brilliant lawyer, crafty politician, ex-vice-president of the United States, and the man who in 1804 killed U.S. statesman Alexander Hamilton in a duel. Burr today found his way to Government House, got an audience with Nova Scotia's new governor, Sir George Prevost, and outlined a fantastic scheme.

Last year, after conspiring with Gen. James Wilkinson to seize parts of Spanish America and create an independent republic in the American Southwest, Burr was tried for treason, and acquitted. He now wants Britain to help him carve his new nation out of Spanish possessions south of the U.S. Sir George listened to Burr, consulted Vice-Admiral John Warren, then gave the American a letter of introduction to Lord Castlereagh, secretary of war in England.

New governor's arrival surprises the old

Lt.-Gen. Sir George Prevost, the new governor of colony of Nova Scotia.

April 7, 1808

HALIFAX – Sir John Wentworth, governor of Nova Scotia for 16 years, was tending his ailing wife today when William Tonge, a politician he hates, gloatingly informed him Sir George Prevost had arrived in town as the new governor. This was how Sir John learned he'd lost his cushy job.

Britain smells war with the U.S., and Prevost is a general. When he entered the harbor aboard the warship *Penelope,* he was accompanied by transports bearing 3,000 soldiers. He landed at King's Wharf, and was promptly escorted to the noble but exorbitantly expensive Government House, built to please the snobbish Lady Wentworth.

Vaccine fights smallpox in Newfoundland

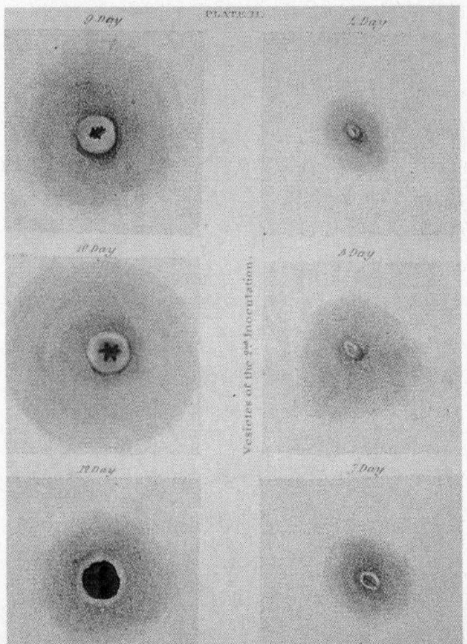

Vesicles of the cowpox inoculation.

1805

NEWFOUNDLAND – Much of the island has been inoculated against smallpox since Dr. John Clinch administered one of the first vaccinations in North America at Trinity Bay in 1798. Four years later, Clinch wrote: "I began by inoculating my own children and went on with this salutary work till I had inoculated 700 persons."

Newfoundlanders can thank an old school buddy of Clinch's, Dr. Edward Jenner, who invented the vaccination in London. Jenner found that fluid from cows infected with cowpox prevented smallpox when injected in humans. He told Clinch about his findings, and sent him threads of vaccine.

Foreign currency making the rounds in Canada

United Kingdom coins of the 1800s are being circulated around Canada.

A hodgepodge of money from different countries around the world is circulating in Canada. Among the coins often seen in use are Mexican ones such as these.

Americans can use their U.S. coins as currency in most Canadian stores.

Portuguese currency, such as these coins, is used to pay for Canadian goods.

Canadians often use Spanish coins being circulated around the British colony.

French coins of the 1800s are common currency here.

Upper Canada, Feb. 15, 1810. The Assembly passes a motion allowing for the conviction of any "stranger" who tries to promote any kind of public entertainment while passing through the province.

Washington, Nov. 2, 1810. President Madison re-establishes freedom of trade with France, after being assured that European ports will be opened to American shipping. The move flies in the face of British attempts to impose a counterblockade on France in retaliation for the French blockade of Britain.

New Brunswick, 1810. The colony exports 87,690 tons of timber to Britain. It becomes an important supplier of timber for industrial development and the Royal Navy after the Napoleonic wars cut off supplies of Baltic timber.

Washington, Feb. 2, 1811. President Madison sends Britain an ultimatum demanding that it revoke its orders in council of 1807 justifying British harassment of U.S. ships during the Napoleonic war.

Fort Astoria, Oregon, May 18, 1811. An American fur-trading expedition sent by John Jacob Astor founds a post called Astoria near the mouth of the Columbia River.

Upper Canada, Oct. 9, 1811. Major-General Isaac Brock becomes administrator and commander of the Upper Canadian forces.

Labrador, October 1811. A Moravian missionary expedition led by Benjamin Kohlmeister returns after exploring Ungava Bay to expand the work of the Moravian Labrador mission. They didn't contact any Inuit.

Washington, Nov. 4, 1811. Congress convenes; the House of Representatives is clamoring for war with Britain.

Fort St. James, Far West, 1811. Daniel Harmon of the North West Company plants a vegetable garden at the eastern end of Stuart Lake, the first attempt at farming on the [B.C.] mainland.

Newfoundland, 1811. The government gives a raise of £100 a year to missionaries who have worked on the island for 10 years, in order to encourage priests to stay.

New Brunswick, 1811. The colony doubles its trade with the West Indies.

Lord Selkirk granted Red River land

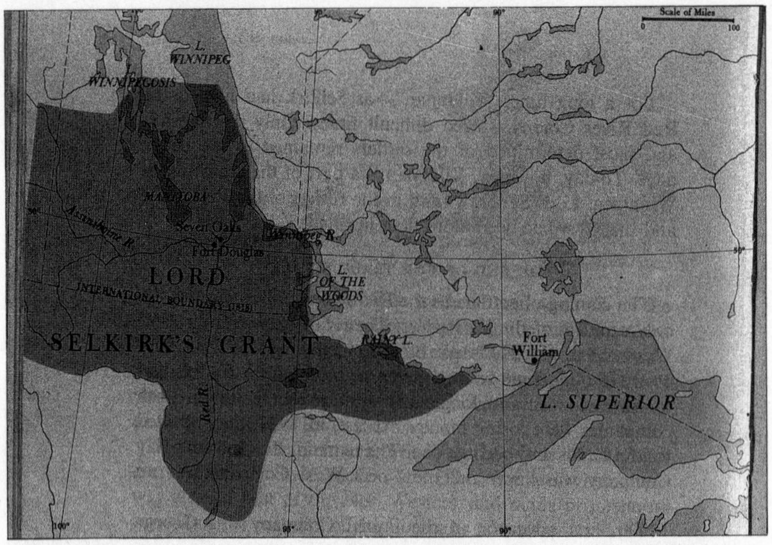

Map of the land grant made by Hudson's Bay Company to Lord Selkirk.

Life in the Red River settlement. A settler's house and oxen-pulled cart.

June 12, 1811

LONDON, England – Amid much controversy, the Hudson's Bay Company has granted Lord Selkirk more than 300,000 square kilometres of land in the Red River country to establish there a colony of Scottish crofters. This will be the third such settlement Lord Selkirk has founded in British North America, the other two being Baldoon in Upper Canada, and one on Prince Edward Island.

There is conflicting opinion as to the quality of the land and the effect a settlement will have on the fur trade. In general, Lord Selkirk and the Hudson's Bay Company feel the land is quite suitable for farming and see the colony as a supplier of goods and services for the company. The North West Company, worthy competitors of the Hudson's Bay Company, fiercely oppose the colony on the grounds it will destroy the fur trade entirely by interfering with major supply routes and that the settlers are being sent into an uninhabitable and dangerous environment.

The terms of the agreement state that Selkirk is to fully finance the bold Red River venture himself. One thousand families are to be settled in the district over the next 10 years. The settlement is to supply 200 men yearly as servants to the Hudson's Bay Company, and officers of the company are to be given 200 acres in the settlement upon retirement.

Explorer Thompson gets travel orders

July 22, 1810

RAINY LAKE, Rupert's Land – David Thompson, the North West Company's surveyor, mapper and trader, was told here to return to Rocky Mountain House to finish his exploration of the Columbia River.

Thompson, 40, is an expert on the Columbia which he first found when he was exploring three years ago with his wife and three children. He has now been told to travel down the Columbia to its mouth to forestall American traders on their way there.

Newspaper printer jailed for sedition

March 17, 1810

QUEBEC CITY – Gov. James Craig took his battle against the Assembly to the streets today, seizing the press of *Le Canadien,* which had opposed his stand, and jailing its editors for sedition. He also put armed patrols in the streets and suspended mail service. It is the aftermath of a long feud between the executive and Assembly. Craig dissolved Parliament this year when it went beyond its powers by passing a resolution to bar a judge from the Assembly, after the Legislative Council ruled he could stay.

Trader big on meat and Scottish haggis

October 1810

QUEBEC CITY – Joseph Frobisher, known for his extravagant lifestyle and posh dinner parties, entertains in the old-fashioned manner of the British upper class – but sets his table for Scottish tastes too. The famous fur trader's food bills prove Frobisher is big on meat and Scottish haggis.

Between June and October, Frobisher purchased 360 kilograms of beef, 17 of veal, 16 mutton, 10 lamb quarters, 80 chickens and various small game. To wash it down, he bought tea and Madeira wine.

Deaths frustrate Buchan's mission

Jan. 30, 1811

NEWFOUNDLAND – Naval officer and expedition leader David Buchan returned to the Bay of Exploits today, exhausted and disheartened after failing to establish friendly relations with Beothuk Indians – a failure that cost the lives of two men in his command.

Last October, Gov. John Duckworth assigned Buchan the task of ascertaining whether or not Indians reportedly seen on the coast were permanent residents or merely temporary visitors from the mainland. Over two weeks ago, Buchan and 27 men set out from the schooner *Adonis* to explore the interior, carrying supplies and gifts over the ice-covered Exploits River on 12 heavy sleds.

Having travelled 200 kilometres upstream, on Jan. 24 they came across 75 Beothuks encamped on [Red Indian Lake]. Neither spoke the other's language, but Buchan felt comfortable taking most of his men back down the river 12 kilometres to retrieve a cache of gifts. He left two marines behind, only to find them both dead and the village deserted when he returned two days later. Seeing his chances of "securing" a Beothuk without bloodshed as next to impossible and fearing for the safety of his men, Buchan led the weary group back to the *Adonis*.

Law eyes a better quality of schools

1811

HALIFAX – To encourage school development and attendance, Nova Scotia and New Brunswick have passed legislation allowing school districts to elect a controlling board of trustees.

The Maritimes have been settled by people of diverse cultural and religious backgrounds, but under British colonial administration the Anglican Church has dominated education. This bias has caused many settlers of different faiths to ignore government-run schools. The new legislation, based on a New England model, is less sectarian and allows for local interests to be represented.

Tecumseh's plans suffer a severe setback

Nov. 7, 1811

PROPHETSTOWN, Indiana Territory – U.S. troops under Gov. William Henry Harrison have just attacked the large Indian settlement on the Tippecanoe River, during Tecumseh's absence. Up to a quarter of the governor's 1,000-man army is dead or wounded. Indian deaths total at least 200.

The battle stems from an ongoing struggle between the Americans and followers of Tecumseh and his brother "The Prophet," for whom this Indian settlement was named. The Americans believe Tecumseh is building an alliance of native bands to stop westward expansion by American settlers. Today, those plans were dealt a serious blow. Prophetstown has been destroyed, and its Indian claims defenders dispersed.

American troops defeat Indians.

Cargo ship surprises French privateers

May 15, 1811

QUEBEC CITY – The British cargo ship *Fortune* sailed triumphantly into port today bearing all the scars of a man-of-war, its crew and passengers bringing news of an amazing victory over a French privateer. War between Britain and France continues to disrupt Atlantic shipping despite the defeat of the French armadas. Smaller warships roam the seas, harassing trade routes to British North America.

A French privateer chanced upon the *Fortune* south of Iceland on April 13. Loaded with cargo and with no chance of outrunning the more heavily armed vessel, the *Fortune* withstood the initial broadside then replied in kind. Although outnumbered 120 to 19, the passengers and crew repelled three boarding attempts. Attack and counterattack continued for over an hour until a chance shot broke the French ship's fore-topmast, ending the battle.

York's first church, St. James, built in 1807 by Anglican pioneers who formed the first known congregation of any denomination in the town.

Pacific is reached via the Columbia

July 15, 1811

FAR WEST – North West Company explorer David Thompson has become the first white man to reach the Pacific Ocean by following the mighty Columbia River to its mouth. Much to his disappointment, however, he finds that the spot is already occupied by a group of American fur traders belonging to John Jacob Astor's Pacific Fur Company. They arrived by ship four months ago and have since put up a log fort, calling it Astoria.

Thompson was ordered by the North West Company to proceed down the Columbia last year. It was hoped he would arrive before the American expedition and establish claim to the region or at least reaffirm his connections with natives of the interior. But his trip suffered a serious delay when he opted to detour around territory occupied by hostile Piegan Indians and cross the Rockies by way of the Athabasca River. To tackle the previously unexplored Athabasca Pass in midwinter was very ambitious, and in fact proved too much for so many of his men, who deserted at various stages of the journey.

David Thompson in Athabasca Pass.

On the banks of the Columbia, Thompson and three men waited until April before continuing down river in a 7.5-metre cedar board canoe they constructed themselves. Arriving today and finding the Americans established at Astoria has no doubt irked Thompson. He now plans to return upriver and convince Indians there to trade with the Nor'Westers.

1812

Washington, June 19. President Madison formally declares war on Britain. The main American grievances are British harassment of American ships, and impressment of American seamen.

New York, June 24. Two Montreal merchants hear about the American declaration of war from trading associates, and immediately relay the news to Governor Prevost in Quebec. It is the first that British North America hears of the American declaration.

Upper Canada, July 12. American Brigadier-General William Hull crosses the Detroit River and takes peaceful possession of Sandwich [Windsor], the first American invasion of the war.

York, Upper Canada, July 28. Brock convenes a special session of the legislature to ask for the repeal of Habeas Corpus, and the imposition of martial law to help in the war. The legislature is unco-operative.

Lacolle, Lower Canada, Nov. 20. Canadian voltigeurs and Caughnawaga Indians repulse a U.S. invasion of 6,000 men.

York, Upper Canada, Nov. 22. Rector John Strachan gives a sermon to raise the city's morale, exaggerating the role of Canadian militia in repelling the American invaders.

Upper Canada, Dec. 15. The Loyal and Patriotic Society of Upper Canada is formed to help families of soldiers fighting the war with the U.S.

Upper Canada, 1812. An American fleet blockades Kingston for the rest of the navigation season after mounting an inconclusive bombardment Nov. 10.

Lower Canada, 1812. The population is 330,000. Montreal, strategically located in transportation routes, is the economic capital of Canada.

Upper Canada, 1812. The population is 90,000. It has grown rapidly as Americans immigrated encouraged by free land grants.

Atlantic Provinces, 1812. The population is almost 100,000. The main industries are timber, fishing and shipbuilding.

North America, c.1812. Beavers have been depleted everywhere east of the Rocky Mountains, but are still abundant to the west.

Angry Americans declare war on Britain

June 19, 1812

WASHINGTON, D.C. – An indignant President James Madison declared war on Britain today on behalf of the 7.5 million white Americans. "Free trade and sailors rights" is the rallying cry of all the "war hawks" in Congress who voted for the war, up in arms against what they see as British bullying on the high seas.

Since Napoleon has blockaded Britain, the English have retaliated by trying to stop the Americans from trading with France, sometimes even resorting to commandeering American vessels. The Americans are also angry at Britain's current policy of stopping American ships and seizing sailors it claims are British seamen who deserted to find better conditions elsewhere. A third American beef has nothing to do with shipping. Since 1811, Tecumseh has been leading an Indian Confederacy in war against thrusts into the American northwest. Americans suspect the British aid Tecumseh.

The war has been conceived mainly on the high seas, but it looks like it will be fought on Canadian soil. The Americans are confident they can easily conquer what they see as the soft underbelly of the British Empire – the fertile peninsula of Upper Canada. They expect the inhabitants who have recently arrived from the U.S. will welcome them as an army of liberation.

Brock, Tecumseh meet for first time

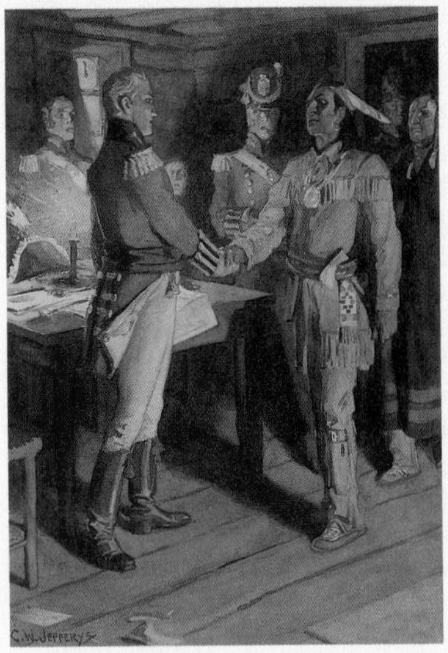

Isaac Brock meets Chief Tecumseh.

Aug. 13, 1812

AMHERSTBURG, Upper Canada – Two titans fighting for a common cause met for the first time here at Amherstburg. Maj.-Gen. Isaac Brock, British military commander for Upper Canada, and the great Shawnee war chief Tecumseh shook hands today. Both were accompanied by their armies: Brock his British troops, and Tecumseh his native warriors.

The Indians greeted the massive, six-foot-three Brock with a musket salute, an honor that alarmed him as it wasted ammunition for the attack on Detroit.

Nova Scotia leader declares "no war"

July 3, 1812

HALIFAX – There may be a war on between Britain and the United States, but it doesn't extend to New England and Nova Scotia. So says Sir John Sherbrooke, lieutenant-governor of the province.

Mindful that New Englanders have expressed no desire to attack Canada – indeed both sides want to keep trading with each other – Sir John has essentially declared "no war" for this section of Canada. He promises Canada will "abstain from molesting" New Englanders and their property, provided the Americans do the same.

Lt.-Gen. Sir John Sherbrooke.

Privateers mistake women for redcoats

1812

CHESTER, N.S. – When three Yankee pirate ships brought the War of 1812 to this tiny port, who'd have thought the freebooters would be scared off by a wisp of women wearing their cloaks inside out? But that's what happened. The townswomen reversed their pelisses to show the red linings, shouldered muskets, and marched round Meeting House Hill. Privateers mistook them for trained British redcoats, and sailed away empty-handed.

British losing control of Lake Ontario?

Nov. 10, 1812

KINGSTON – American Capt. Isaac Chauncey today dealt a blow at British control of Lake Ontario, a crucial issue in the war given the waterway's importance as a British supply route. With a small squadron, he chased the British ship *Royal George* into Kingston harbor. The Americans exchanged fire with the British at Fort Henry, but there was little damage on either side and they left the harbor at dusk. While the exchange was inconclusive, the incident proves the Americans are a force to be reckoned with on the lake. Last June, Americans captured several British schooners – including the *Lord Nelson* – which they converted to warships.

British schooner the Lord Nelson was captured by American forces in June.

British capture fort in Michilimackinac

July 12, 1812

MICHILIMACKINAC – Soldiers from the British fort at St. Joseph's captured Fort Michilimackinac today, a military victory Gen. Isaac Brock considers critical to his overall battle plan against the Americans. Brock, who issued the order for the St. Joseph's commander to launch the attack with his small force, hopes the victory will prompt Indians to join his forces for follow-up, cross-border attacks, possibly against Detroit.

Brock is not satisfied with the size of his fighting force – just 1,600 regulars, two-thirds of them in the 41st regiment, based opposite Detroit. He is counting on Indian support to help his army's chances.

Daring Indians deal Hull a double blow

Aug. 5, 1812

AMHERSTBURG, Upper Canada – A raid by natives loyal to the Crown has snagged the plans of American commander Brig.-Gen. William Hull. Led by the Shawnee chief Tecumseh, two dozen braves slipped across the Detroit River near Amherstburg. Once in hostile territory, they intercepted an American supply convoy protected by a small escort from Ohio. The natives also dealt Hull a second blow, ambushing his convoy then dispersing the troops sent to meet it.

No help for Canada to fight Americans

Aug. 10, 1812

QUEBEC CITY – Canada will get no immediate military help from the Mother Country in hostilities with the Americans, Gov. George Prevost learned today. Prevost's superiors told him he would have to do his best with men and munitions that he had. Fighting Napoleon, mighty conqueror of Europe, Britain has little military aid to spare. Manpower shortages mean offensives into the U.S. will be undertaken only to strengthen a defensive position.

Brock wins Detroit from the Americans

American Gov. William Hull, as he surrenders to Sir Isaac Brock.

Aug. 16, 1812

DETROIT – Gen. Isaac Brock captured this United States centre today without firing a single shot. Michigan Gov. William Hull, who commands the western army, surrendered to Brock and his force of 1,300 regulars, militia and Indians.

Hull was already in retreat when Brock moved his army into place. The U.S. general, who earlier had invaded Upper Canada, withdrew because he was unable to establish communications to the south and also feared an Indian attack from the north. Hull did not challenge Brock because he was concerned about the safety of women and children behind the lines, four of whom had died when a shell hit the officers' mess. Hull also lacked confidence in his inexperienced army.

Wyandot allegiance shifts to the British

Aug. 2, 1812

AMHERSTBURG, Upper Canada – American prestige, hurt by the loss of Fort Michilimackinac at the connection between Lakes Michigan and Huron, got another blow today. The Wyandot – or Huron – Indians, thought to be loyal American allies, have switched their allegiance to the British. It's reported that the Indians, who live near Detroit, are being escorted to Amherstburg by soldiers of the Crown. The loss of the Wyandots has serious implications for the Americans. If one "reliable" tribe can change its allegiance, then so can others.

Triumph over U.S. avenges Brock's death

Artist's representation of the battle of Queenston Heights in Upper Canada.

Oct. 13, 1812

QUEENSTON, Upper Canada – Gen. Isaac Brock was shot dead today as he led a counterattack against American forces that had briefly seized Queenston Heights. His second in command, Gen. Roger Hale Sheaffe, avenged the death, arriving with the main British force and retaking the heights. Brock heard the enemy was crossing the river, perhaps a ploy to attack from Fort Niagara, and raced 11 kilometres from his Fort George base. Before Sheaffe arrived, Brock was killed leading a few men up the escarpment. Sheaffe inflicted heavy losses on U.S. troops.

Lord Selkirk's first colonists arrive to settle near Red River

The Hudson's Bay Co. calendar.

Aug. 30, 1812

RED RIVER COLONY – The first of Lord Selkirk's colonists have arrived at the forks of the Red and Assiniboine rivers after a harrowing trip from Hudson Bay.

The settlers – most of them are poor Scottish folk – are led by Miles Macdonell, a former soldier whom Selkirk has made governor of the new colony. They plan to establish a farming community on the grant of land Selkirk has obtained from the fur-trading Hudson's Bay Company.

Governor Miles Macdonell.

1813

Brockville, Upper Canada, Feb. 7. American riflemen led by Captain Forsyth surprise the Canadian militia post at Brockville, taking 52 prisoners.

York, Upper Canada, May 8. The Americans withdraw to Fort Niagara after occupying the city since April 27.

Fort Meigs, Ohio, May 9. British Major-General Procter is forced to end a 10-day siege of the Americans at Fort Meigs because his militia is deserting.

Upper Canada, May 28. Gen. John Vincent leads a British force of 1,600 in a retreat to Burlington at the head of Lake Ontario. The British have abandoned Fort George, Fort Erie, and Fort Niagara to the Americans, who now control Lake Ontario, and the Niagara peninsula.

Upper Canada, June 24. Some 400 Iroquois Indians defeat 575 American troops sent to attack the British post at Beaver Dams. British troops from Beaver Dams under Lieutenant FitzGibbon arrive to receive the Americans' surrender after housewife Laura Secord warned them of the planned American attack.

Upper Canada. Shortly after their defeat near Beaver Dams at the hands of the Iroquois, the American invaders withdraw from the Niagara peninsula.

Lake Ontario, Oct. 5. American Commodore Chauncey captures six British schooners sailing from York [Toronto] to Kingston carrying reinforcements and sick and wounded.

Detroit, Oct. 17. American Major-General Harrison, fresh from victory over the British at Moraviantown, issues a proclamation permitting civil servants in the Western District of Upper Canada to remain in office provided they take an oath of allegiance to the U.S. during the occupation.

Fort Astoria, Oregon, Dec. 12. British officers take possession of the fort as part of the British-American war, renaming it Fort George, after the king of Britain. The North West Company bought the fort earlier from the American-owned Pacific Fur Company, gaining control of the fur trade from the Columbia to Alaska.

Fort Niagara, Dec. 19. About 550 British troops led by Lieutenant-Colonel John Murray capture Fort Niagara from the Americans in a surprise attack.

British take Ogdensburg in mismatch

Satirical cartoon shows incompetent American soldiers marching to the front during the war encumbered by their women, babies, and household furnishings.

Feb. 22, 1813

OGDENSBURG, N.Y. – Local incompetence and sheer bad luck aided the British today in their conquest of Ogdensburg, across the St. Lawrence River from Prescott, Upper Canada. Before dawn, about 500 troops under Lt.-Col. "Red George" Macdonnell set out across the ice. As the Americans are accustomed to watching the British garrison drill on the mile of ice between the two shores, it wasn't until they were halfway across that the Americans decided to fire.

To make things worse, most of the shots missed and many soldiers ran when the British arrived. It took just a few hours for the British to seize the American fort.

Casualties high as American forces overwhelm British at York

A bird's-eye view showing the arrival of the American fleet prior to the capture of York by U.S. forces.

April 27, 1813

YORK – American troops, backed by 12 armed schooners, have taken York after overwhelming a smaller British force and driving it back toward Kingston. Hundreds were wounded or killed in the raid, in which the retreating British blew up the fort at York.

The explosion came as a surprise to the Americans, since their opponents had left the flag flying at the fort, misleading them into believing that it was still occupied. "The sky rained boulders," is how one eyewitness described the hail of foundation stones from the explosion. As well, the British burned the naval storehouse and a half-built warship, to keep out of American hands the supplies and ammunition they could not take with them.

Artist's representation of the attack on Fort York by American forces.

British regain post in surprise attack; losses are heavy

Jan. 22, 1813

FRENCHTOWN, Michigan – A force led by Maj.-Gen. Henry Procter of Amherstburg has almost wiped out its American foes in a surprise attack, and retaken this British post on the River Raison the U.S. had briefly captured. Frenchtown, 42 kilometres south of Detroit, was defended by 900 American regulars and Kentucky militiamen commanded by Brig.-Gen. James Winchester.

Four days earlier Winchester had easily driven off Frenchtown's few Canadian militiamen and Indian defenders, and he failed to anticipate a counterattack by Procter's men, a makeshift force of 273 regulars, 61 Fencibles, 212 militiamen and 28 Provincial Marine sailors, and 600 Indians.

Procter's gunners focused their attack on the American right side, which retreated across the river ice, only to be cut down by the Indians. Elsewhere, the Americans held, but surrendered to avoid further casualties. The losses were heavy on both sides. Of the American force, estimated to total 900 men, at least 500 were taken prisoner, including Winchester. Most of the others were killed. Thirty men wounded so badly they could not walk were murdered by drunken Indians under Procter. Procter lost 24 soldiers killed, 158 wounded, excluding casualties suffered by his Indian allies.

British attack Sackett's Harbour base

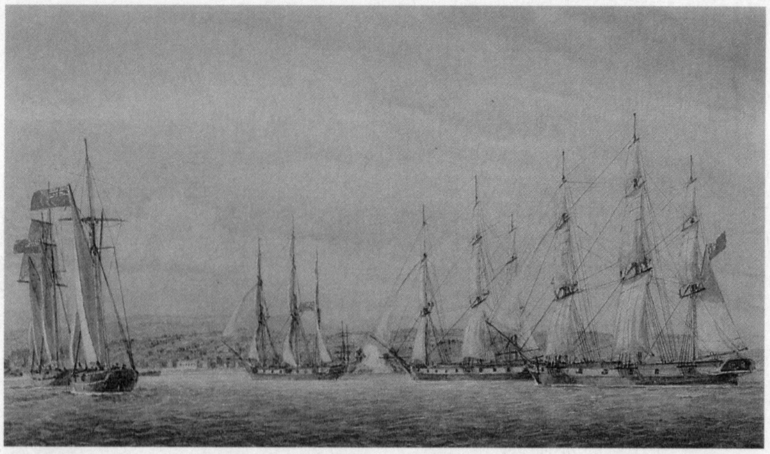

British naval forces attack key American base at Sackett's Harbour, N.Y.

May 29, 1813

SACKETT'S HARBOUR, N.Y. – British troops attacked this key American naval base today. Their raid caused much destruction, but not enough to put the base out of permanent operation.

The British troops, transported here on ships commanded by Sir James Yeo, overcame local opposition without much difficulty, yet they apparently failed to press the attack home. This means the American Great Lakes fleet will still have a place for repair and resupply when it returns from its successful attacks on Upper Canada.

Angry U.S. troops torch Parliament

May 1, 1813

YORK – American troops occupying the capital of Upper Canada have signalled their contempt for British authority by torching the Parliament buildings. The act comes as somewhat of a surprise to the residents of York, who have been enduring a relatively safe occupation. Theft from abandoned houses has been rampant. However, there has not been a single reported rape or murder.

With this first outrage committed after two days of American control, local citizens fear this uneasy calm may be coming to a violent end. The American in charge says the fire was unauthorized.

400 Americans die in Fort Meigs fighting

May 5, 1813

FORT MEIGS, Ohio – Some 400 American soldiers died today trying to rescue Fort Meigs from an ongoing British/Indian siege. The fort, which lies on the Maumee River feeding Lake Erie, has been the home of American Cmdr. William Henry Harrison and his men, who failed to retake Detroit last January. At about 9 a.m. today, 1,200 Kentuckians attempted to relieve Fort Meigs. British losses are estimated at 15 men.

Royal Navy wins battle at Boston Harbour

June 13, 1813

BOSTON – The Royal Navy whipped its American counterpart this afternoon, right on Boston's doorstep. One ship stood for each side: for the British it was the *HMS Shannon.* Commanded by Capt. Philip Vere Broke, it boasts 38 guns and an experienced crew. The *Chesapeake,* commanded by Capt. James Lawrence, has more guns and men, but not the same skill.

The battle was brief and brutal. Meeting outside Boston Harbour, it took *Shannon* 15 minutes to blast *Chesapeake* into submission, and then board her. Forty-eight Americans died, as opposed to 23 British. The *Shannon* is towing *Chesapeake* to Halifax as a prize today.

A Métis and his two wives. Métis are French-speaking people of mixed Indian-European descent. They are active in the fur trade in [Manitoba].

Crew of H.M.S. Shannon board and take the American ship Chesapeake.

Laura Secord hikes through woods to warn British

June 22, 1813

QUEENSTON, Upper Canada – A Queenston woman walked 32 kilometres through enemy lines and treacherous woods and swamps to warn the British of an American attack. Laura Secord, a wife and mother of young children, left her house here on foot to warn Lieut. James FitzGibbon at Beaver Dams that American soldiers were planning a surprise attack on his force of 30 men, volunteers from Gen. Isaac Brock's old regiment.

The U.S. invaders occupied the house of Secord and her husband James, home after being injured in the Battle of Queenston Heights, and she overheard them discussing the planned attack. Secord set out on foot, being careful to avoid the road because it was under surveillance by American soldiers.

Instead, she walked through the swamp and climbed the heights at Twelve-Mile Creek. To get to St. David's, her first stop along the way, Secord had to pass three U.S. sentries, outwitting one with a concocted story of a cow that had strayed and the other two by telling them her brother was sick at St. David's, a true story.

As she worried greatly about the Americans intercepting her, she chose the least frequented route, risking wolves and rattlesnakes, and travelling from daybreak to moonlight. A fallen tree provided her a bridge across Twelve-Mile Creek, swollen by recent rains. Near her destination, she was surprised by Indians, but convinced them she was not a spy and they guided her to FitzGibbon's base, where she delivered her message.

Laura Secord convinces Indians to guide her to a British base so she may warn them of an American attack.

Laura Secord meets Lieut. James FitzGibbon and warns of American attack.

Tip from local scout helps British forces

June 6, 1813

STONEY CREEK, Upper Canada – Acting on a tip from young local scout Billy Green, British forces surprised the American invaders in an overnight raid on their camp near Lake Ontario here. Just before the Americans struck, Green raced to warn the British, returning with a vanguard of troops that turned the tables on the invaders.

The surprise bayonet attack by the British, led by Lt.-Col. John Harvey, was launched at two this morning. Fighting raged until dawn, when the British, though outnumbered 2,000 to 700, triumphed. They captured both American generals, John Chandler and William Winder, and killed about 200. An Indian witness says corpses are strewn about like freshly-caught salmon. The Americans have retreated toward Niagara.

Despite losses of up to 250, the British victory is a turning point. With the central part of the province secured, Kingston-based troops can now thrust eastward.

Fort George falls to invading Americans

May 27, 1813

FORT GEORGE, Upper Canada – After two days of heavy bombardment, the American fleet off this outpost has made its move. Invading troops have seized this British outpost at the mouth of the Niagara River, driving out about 1,000 men under the command of Brig.-Gen. John Vincent.

The victors have not gained much of a prize. Most of Fort George's buildings were destroyed by fire the shelling started two days ago. As well, the departing commander made sure all the cannons were disabled, and any ammunition that could not be taken was destroyed. Vincent, meanwhile, has withdrawn his men to Burlington.

The school in County of Grenville, Upper Canada, erected in 1812. Built in the typical style of frontier settlements, it is a one-room schoolhouse.

Hard workers earn land grants in Nfld.

June 1813

ST. JOHN'S, Nfld. – Newfoundland Gov. Sir Richard Keats has established the first land grants for farming. The land has been given to hard workers outside this community who have been keeping livestock and market gardens. The action by Keats is in recognition of the importance farming has developed in light of the war with the Americans. In the first winter of the war, imported food prices have been exorbitant and starvation conditions have been a problem.

Keats has ordered that 1,000 acres of land be enclosed but that each grant is not to exceed four acres. The little farms are to be used to grow hay, potatoes and vegetables. The land grants make legal what is already a fact of life. The 1699 Act specifying that fishermen have coastal land available to build wharves and dry their fish has been largely ignored. Public opinion, led by the merchants, has maintained that residents have the right to hold or own private property.

British fleet demolished in battle at Put-In Bay

Sept. 10, 1813

LAKE ERIE – An historic first of the most awful gravity occurred today. In a battle at Put-In Bay, American Cmdr. Oliver Hazard Perry captured or destroyed the entire fleet commanded by British officer Robert Barclay. The loss of the *Detroit, Queen Charlotte, Lady Prevost* and three armed schooners makes this lake an American pond.

Barclay, a lieutenant, was ordered by Maj.-Gen. Henry Procter to try to reopen communications with Long Point, where desperately-needed supplies waited to be transported. Dwindling resources, restive Indian allies dependent on the British for food, the approach of winter, and Procter's insistence convinced Barclay. "I shall sail and risk everything to gain so great a point – as that of opening the communication by water," he wrote, and sailed to confront the U.S.'s Perry, whom he knew had double the fleet and armaments.

At first, the long-range cannons on the *Detroit* favored the British. But then the wind changed, allowing the U.S. ships to close and demolish the British fleet, killing 41 and wounding 94. Barclay, badly wounded, was taken prisoner when the Americans captured the British vessels and towed them into Put-In Bay. The American victors lost 27 killed, 96 wounded.

Perry's triumphant fleet has turned Lake Erie into a virtual American pond.

Merchants seeking foreign fishing ban

November 1813

NEWFOUNDLAND – Merchants involved in the saltfish trade recently petitioned the British government to refuse the French and the Americans permission to fish on Newfoundland's coast.

Since 1713, the French have been free to fish and dry their catch on part of the island's coast – the French shore. And until last year, the Americans had an extensive fishery on the Labrador coast and in the Gulf of St. Lawrence. But though Britain is at war with France and the U.S., many fear she will not cut these fishing rights.

Regiment of foot walks for 52 days

April 12, 1813

KINGSTON – Six companies, 549 men of the 104th Regiment of Foot, have arrived here from Fredericton after a 52-day trek over some 1,100 kilometres in extreme cold. They are reinforcements for Lower Canada until Lt.-Gen. Sir John Sherbrooke can replace them with troops from Halifax.

The men travelled on snowshoes, carrying their weapons and personal kits, and pulling toboggans with their supplies. They bivouacked at night. Just one man died en route.

Soldiers turn Halifax into a den of vice

July 3, 1813

HALIFAX – The city is under attack, but not by the Americans. No, the enemy is the 10,000 soldiers stationed here and the "low life" they indulge in. The centre of this drink and debauchery is the upper street, along the base of Citadel Hill, between the north and south barracks. So many brawls take place it's known as "Knock him down" street. It's lined with brothels for soldiers and sailors, where venereal disease eats up the prostitutes. By age 25, most are already dead or too old for the streets.

British recapture the Liverpool Packet

Oct. 5, 1813

HALIFAX – The *Liverpool Packet,* which captured many American ships before being taken herself, was recaptured by the British warship *Fantome* two days ago. The *Packet* is a "privateer," a privately-owned but licensed raider, whose captain, Joseph Baras Jr., makes his living seizing and selling enemy ships for the Crown. The *Portsmouth Packet*, as her American captors had renamed her, was yesterday towed into Halifax.

Attacking a whale and "cutting in." Canadians have entered the field of whale fishing, establishing whaling stations in Newfoundland.

Halifax hears news of British defectors

June 22, 1813

HALIFAX – News has reached the city today of British soldiers defecting to the Americans in a failed assault near Chesapeake Bay, not far from Washington. Many members of the "Canadian Chasseurs" are reportedly defecting after landing at Craney Island.

The behavior of these soldiers comes as no surprise to residents of Halifax, who have had to endure their company. And the Chasseurs, in fact, are not British at all. They are captured French soldiers who chose to join the British army rather than languish in prison.

Vengeful Americans pursue Indian ally

Autumn 1813

FORT MALDEN, Upper Canada – Loyalist Simon Girty, named "White Savage" and "Dirty Girty" by Americans bitter that he champions Indians in land disputes, has escaped Fort Malden – and Americans who want to kill him.

As a child, the now 72-year-old Girty lived with Indians, and during the War of Independence used his knowledge to work for the British Indian Department. Vengeful Americans exaggerated Girty's role in Indian raiding parties.

Americans kill Tecumseh in victory over British

British forces are defeated in the battle of the Thames in Moraviantown.

Americans kill Tecumseh during battle against the British at Moraviantown.

Many Indians have died in the fighting against the American forces.

Oct. 10, 1813

MORAVIANTOWN, Upper Canada – The war may soon end, with the Americans winning. That is what dispirited British soldiers are saying today, following a devastating defeat by the invaders at the Thames River, in Moraviantown.

Whether or not this fiasco marks the defeat of the British army, it certainly marks the death of the great warrior chief and loyal ally of the Crown, Tecumseh. The chief, whose warriors have terrorized the Americans since war began, fell during a pitched battle between the exhausted troops of British Maj.-Gen. Henry Procter and the determined forces of the governor of Indiana territory, William Henry Harrison. The invaders, who outnumbered the British, definitely got the better of the fight. They killed Tecumseh, scattered the defenders, and even caused Procter to run for his life.

This disaster for the British comes just days after the defeat of their fleet at Put-In Bay, on the south side of Lake Erie. These and other setbacks have British troops in Moraviantown openly speculating about a full-scale American conquest of Upper Canada.

De Salaberry and brave voltigeurs turn back wary opponents

Oct. 26, 1813

CHATEAUGUAY, Lower Canada – A small contingent of French-Canadian troops has done the impossible: it has thrown back a much larger American army which invaded here five days ago. Under the command of Lt.-Col. Charles de Salaberry, 1,600 *voltigeurs,* as the French call these light troops, convinced 4,200 Americans to give up after a very short fight.

Why the American general retreated after so little combat isn't officially known. But reports from the battlefield, near the Châteauguay River, say that de Salaberry's tactics, such as blowing horns in the woods to give the impression of a large force, unnerved his opponents. So did the bravery of his men.

Lt.-Col. Charles de Salaberry leads his French-Canadian troops to battle.

Fort Astoria sold to North West Co.

Nov. 30, 1813

ASTORIA, Oregon – With war raging between the United States and Britain elsewhere on the continent, the British naval sloop *Raccoon* arrived here today to wrest the fort and surrounding territory from the American-owned Pacific Fur Company, only to find it is already the property of British subjects. On Oct. 16, the Americans had sold Fort Astoria to the North West Company because they expected the British navy to land anytime to take the fort by force.

When the *Raccoon* appeared, the Nor'Westers feared it was an American vessel, and shipped their furs up the river to avoid losing them.

American invaders lose battle at Crysler's farm

Nov. 11, 1813

UPPER CANADA – Montreal is saved! The thin red line held firm when 800 Canadian and British soldiers defeated 1,800 Americans at John Crysler's farm on the northern shore of the St. Lawrence, 30 kilometres west of Cornwall.

Royal Navy Capt. W. Mulcaster's gunboats opened fire on an American bateau as their army of 4,000 began descending the rapids toward Montreal. U.S. Gen. John Parke Boyd's men faced a "storm of bullets and shrapnel shells."

Repulsing 1,800 poorly-deployed American dragoons and infantry, forces made up of men of the British 89th and 49th Regiments with 200 more voltigeurs, Canadian Fencibles, some Indians and militia, killed 102, wounded 237 and took 100 prisoners. The Canadian-British force suffered 179 casualties. Commanding Col. Joseph W. Morrison, impressed by the conduct of the American 25th Infantry Regiment, sent a note to their commander hoping they might meet as friends after the war.

The death of American General Covington, the illness of commander General Wilkinson, and the lateness of the season coupled with Charles de Salaberry's victory over U.S. Gen. Wade Hampton at Châteauguay will stop the Republic's movement on Montreal.

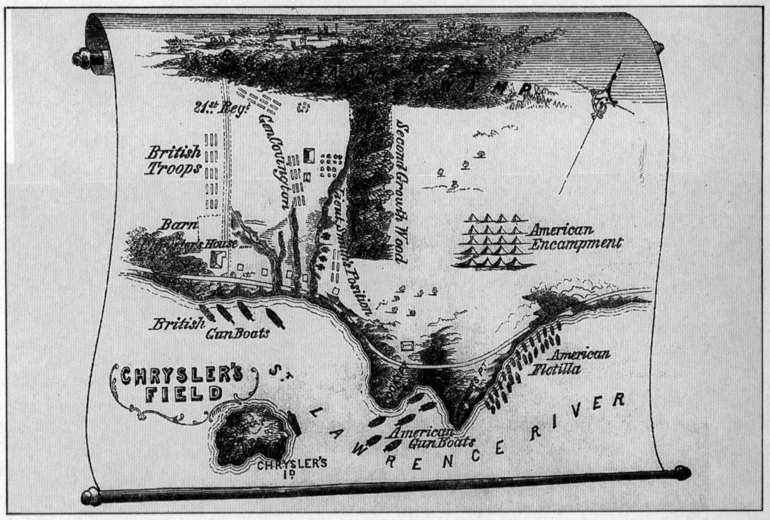

Crysler's field map, from Sir Francis Bond Head's narrative on the battle.

U.S. warship triumphs off South America

Cartoon inspired by American warship Hornet's victory over the Peacock.

Feb. 24, 1813

GUYANA – The British sloop *Peacock* has been destroyed, after its crew put up a fight. The *Hornet,* a heavier-armed American craft, met the *Peacock* while cruising the northern coast of South America at the mouth of the Demarara River. As it flew the British flag, the *Peacock*'s commander, Lieut. William Peake, was tricked into believing it was an allied ship.

The two circled each other, until Capt. James Lawrence felt he had gained the weather gauge, and hoisted the American Stars and Stripes. The two ships played cat and mouse for two hours, then bore down on each other, exchanging broadsides at short range. Peake attempted to cross the enemy's stern, but the *Hornet* turned, caught him and started shooting him to pieces. As some Americans went on board to claim the *Peacock,* the British ship began to sink, taking with it not only its own men but some enemy sailors as well. Against a flaming sunset, the proud *Peacock* sank, leaving behind only its mast.

Americans set fire to two settlements

Dec. 11, 1813

QUEENSTON, Upper Canada – People in Newark [Niagara on the Lake] and Queenston were turned out into the winter night when Brig.-Gen. George McClure and his American army set fire to the settlements. It appears McClure expected a British advance on the Niagara frontier, and being undermanned, used this as his defence. Another actor in the tragedy, whose exact role is unknown, is the ex-member of the Upper Canada legislative assembly Joseph Willcocks. He defected earlier this year and now fights with the Americans.

British forces burn Black Rock, Buffalo

Dec. 29, 1813

BUFFALO – The American villages of Black Rock and Buffalo are all ablaze, as the British have gotten revenge 18 days after Brig.-Gen. George McClure's American troops burned the Canadian settlements of Newark and Queenston. After the British recaptured Fort Niagara, which McClure was trying to prevent when he torched the Canadian towns, Maj.-Gen. Phineas Riall retaliated by destroying Lewiston. Now, with about 1,500 British regulars and Indians, he has burned the two American villages and destroyed four schooners.

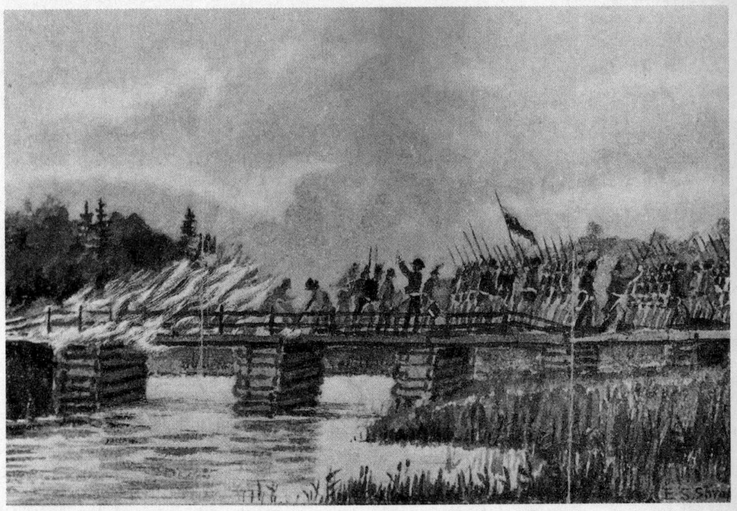

The burning of the Don Bridge at York by American forces.

1814

Upper Canada, May 14. Some 800 Americans land at Port Dover and burn settlements on Lake Erie. Renegade Canadians do most of the damage.

Fort Erie, July 3. Americans under General Winfield Scott capture a poorly defended Fort Erie from the British.

Ohio, July 22. The Shawnee, Delaware, Seneca, Wyandot, and Miami Indians make peace with the U.S., and agree to declare war on Britain.

Upper Canada, July 26. A day after the battle of Lundy's Lane, the bloodiest battle of the war so far, American forces under Gen. Eleazor Ripley and Maj.-Gen. Jacob Brown retreat to Fort Erie, ending their offensive in Upper Canada.

Upper Canada, July. American troops led by Lieutenant-Colonel George Croghan burn a North West Company fur trading post [at Sault Ste. Marie].

Upper Canada, Aug. 4. A force of British, Canadians, and Indians led by Lieut.-Col. Robert McDougall repulse an attack by a superior American force on Fort Michilimackinac.

Ghent, Belgium, Aug. 8. American and British delegations begin negotiations aimed at ending the War of 1812.

Upper Canada, Aug. 15. Lieutenant-General Gordon Drummond leads an unsuccessful British attack on the Americans at Fort Erie. The British lose some 900 men.

Baltimore, Sept. 14. The British end a three-day attack on Baltimore and Fort McHenry. During the bombardment, American lawyer Scott Key writes a poem asking "O say does that star spangled banner yet wave/O'er the land of the free and the home of the brave?"

Upper Canada, Sept. 17. American troops leave Fort Erie to face besieging British forces. The British suffer hundreds of casualties.

Prince Edward Island, Oct. 28. Sancho Byers, a poor Charlottetown black, is sentenced to hang for stealing a loaf of bread and a pound of butter.

Upper Canada, Nov. 5. American forces blow up Fort Erie and evacuate across the Niagara River to New York.

Halifax, 1814. British warships bring 1,700 released slaves from the southern U.S. Most of them settle around Halifax.

British overpower Americans at Oswego

The storming of Fort Oswego. British troops have captured the U.S. depot.

May 6, 1814

OSWEGO, N.Y. – After a short, sharp battle, Lt.-Col. G.A. Mitchell of the Third United States Artillery and his men have withdrawn from here, leaving Oswego with its guns, naval stores and provisions to the British victors.

Commodore James Lucas Yeo and Lt.-Gen. Gordon Drummond of the British forces sailed troops up the Oswego River yesterday. After delaying their attack overnight because of bad weather, Lt.-Col. Fisher and Capt. William Howe Mulcaster led their men up the hill to the American garrison. The British were supported by guns of their own fleet, but still had to face heavy fire from the Americans. As the British reached the top of the hill, the Americans retreated and the battle was over.

British casualties total 18 killed and 73 wounded. Among the captured goods are schooners which are being used to return the booty to Kingston. The victory at Oswego takes out an important American supply depot – the last such depot in the Hudson River-Sackett's Harbor supply line.

Government bans pemmican export

Jan. 8, 1814

RED RIVER COLONY, Rupert's Land – The northwest is in an uproar following today's proclamation by Miles Macdonell that forbids the export of pemmican from this colony for a year without permission granted by his government. The purpose of the Pemmican Proclamation is to ensure that colonists have enough food to survive while they get their farms established. As yet their fields are not producing enough to live on, and the people are hungry.

North West Company fur traders, and their Métis allies, view the measure as an unwarranted interference in the flow of pemmican between the plains and nortwest fur-trade posts. Pemmican is the staple food of western fur traders and Métis are main suppliers. A voyageur eats on the average one-and-a-half pounds a day, equivalent to six pounds of fresh meat.

Nor'Westers believe the colony, owned by Lord Selkirk, is a cover for their rival, the Hudson's Bay Company. The Métis, on the other hand, believe the newcomers intend to steal their land. After today's proclamation, there is fear of violence against the colony.

Dead traitor booted out of Parliament

Feb. 19, 1814

YORK – Joseph Willcocks, a member of Parliament who treacherously sided with Canada's American enemies, has been expelled from the House – even though he is already dead. The action by the other members here expresses their disgust at Willcocks' treason, all the more reviled because he has not the claim of American ancestry as an excuse.

Joseph Willcocks was born in Britain, and when he immigrated, he came to Canada. He worked as an agent for Maj.-Gen. Isaac Brock at the start of the war, and also fought at Queenston Heights, where Brock was killed. Yet, Willcocks turned traitor last year, spending his time leading American raids into Canada until his death.

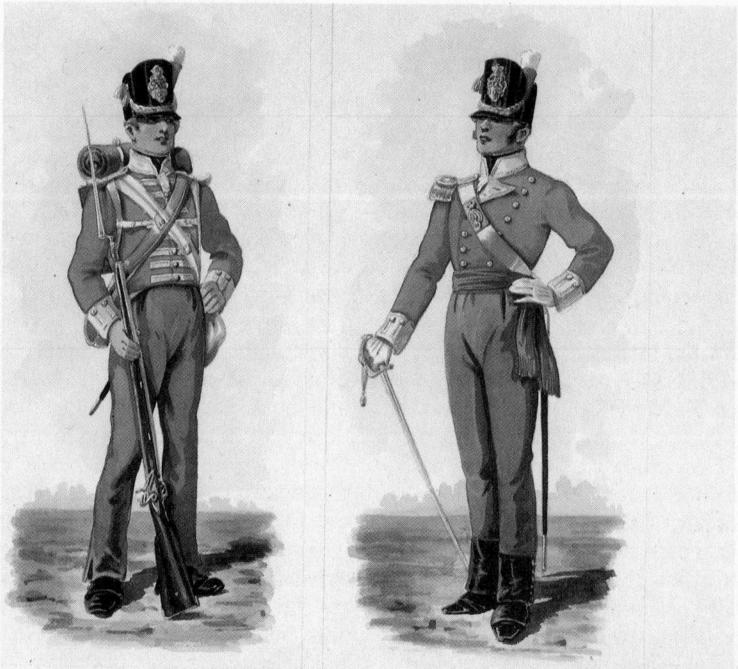

Two soldiers of the British 103 Regiment who served in 1813-14. Illustration shows the uniforms worn at the time by those fighting the American enemy.

Outnumbered Americans win battle at Chippewa

Brig.-Gen. Winfield Scott orders the charge of McNeil's battalion at Chippewa.

Gen. Brown and his American forces during the battle of Chippewa.

July 5, 1814

CHIPPEWA, Upper Canada – Maj.-Gen. Phineas Riall today was forced to withdraw his British troops after engaging Brig.-Gen. Winfield Scott and his Americans at Chippewa. The 8th Regiment of Foot had just arrived from a rest period at York, joining Riall's troops as reinforcements, but even with superior numbers, the British, after doing battle for some time, deemed it wiser to retreat.

Despite fresh British forces and being outnumbered, Scott and his troops capably outmanoeuvred their enemy and advanced with devastatingly accurate fire. However, the British were able to cross the Chippewa River by bridge, tearing up the planks behind them, effectively cutting off pursuit. The river is 135 metres wide at this point and can only be crossed by bridge.

British casualties number 148 dead, 321 wounded and 46 missing, while 48 Americans died and 227 were wounded in the fighting.

Disloyal subjects hang for treason

July 20, 1814

BURLINGTON HEIGHTS, Upper Canada – Any thought that British authorities might be lenient toward disloyal soldiers or citizens was erased here today when eight men convicted of treason to the British Crown died on the gallows. As an example to other would-be traitors, their dangling corpses were cut down, their heads chopped off, and their bodies publicly exhibited.

Today's victims were eight of the 19 tried last June 21 by three judges in Ancaster, in what is now known as the "Bloody Assize." After all was said and done, one pleaded guilty, 14 were found guilty, and four were acquitted.

The innocent ones walked away with their lives. But the others drew sentences of death by hanging, which the judges felt would act as a deterrent to others. In a popular move, they decided to invoke the law's harshest sentence as a means of trying to resolve the ongoing problem of disloyalty by citizens who have been aiding the enemy.

Revenge of the British: public buildings burned in Washington

Aug. 25, 1814

WASHINGTON, D.C. – The capital and the president's official residence, as well as other public buildings in Washington, were set on fire by British troops today in retaliation for the American actions at Niagara and York in Upper Canada. The office of the National Intelligencer and some private residences were also wrecked here.

British troops under Maj.-Gen. Robert Ross have been advancing on Washington since Aug. 19, when they landed and started marching up the Patuxent River. Supporting the land forces was Rear Admiral George Cockburn with a naval division of light vessels. As the British approached, Commodore Joshua Barney of the American fleet destroyed his own gunboats to prevent their capture, and then moved his men, along with hastily gathered militiamen, to defend the road leading from the village of Bladensburg to Washington.

The British charged the defence, and after doing battle for a time the Americans retreated. The British rested for a couple of hours before going on to Washington. Political wrangling had left Washington virtually defenceless. The only defensive action was taken by Commodore Thomas Tingey, commandant of the Washington Navy Yard, who had standing orders to blow up the yard in such an event, which he did.

During the afternoon, a storm moved in which helped put out the fires. The citizens were placed under a curfew, the injured left behind, and the British returned to their ships at night.

The burning of Washington: British troops retaliate against Americans.

Bloodiest battle of the war ends at Lundy's Lane

July 25, 1814

LUNDY'S LANE, Upper Canada – There were a total of 1,735 casualties: 255 dead, the others wounded, captured or missing. And all for naught, it seems, because while this was the site of one of the bloodiest battles of the war to date, it is unclear who the actual victor was of the fighting on this route between Niagara Falls and Lake Ontario.

They're already calling it the battle of Lundy's Lane. Both the Americans and the British claim victory. The Americans say they withdrew to rest. The British point out that they held the field.

American Maj.-Gen. Jacob Brown explains it this way: "I saw and felt that the victory was complete on our part, if proper measures were promptly adopted to secure it. The exhaustion of the men was, however, such as made some refreshment necessary. They particularly required water. I was myself extremely sensible of the want of this necessary article. I therefore believed it proper that General Ripley and the troops should return to camp, after bringing off the dead, the wounded, and the artillery; and in this I saw no difficulty, as the enemy has ceased to act."

As fierce as the fighting was, for the most part it took place in the dark amid considerable confusion. Those manning cannons often retrieved an enemy gun by mistake. There were times when the two sides stood only metres apart, firing at the flashes from enemy muzzles which were the only targets that could be seen in the dark. Among the wounded and captured was British Maj.-Gen. Phineas Riall.

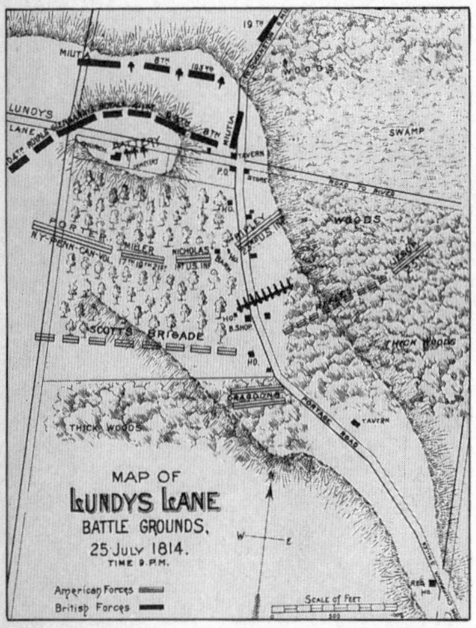

Map of the Lundy's Lane battlefield.

Artist's representation of the bloody battle at Lundy's Lane, Upper Canada.

British retreat ends Niagara campaign

Sept. 21, 1814

FORT ERIE – After several bombardments and weeks spent in siege of American Fort Erie, British commander Lt.-Gen. Gordon Drummond has admitted defeat, ordering his troops to retreat to Chippewa in Upper Canada. He blamed his men's poor health, torrential rains and lack of shelter for his failure to take Fort Erie, but the real reason was his incompetence.

On Sept. 15, Drummond sent five columns to assault the fort after only two days of bombardment. Confusion and bad planning cost the British 57 dead, 309 wounded, and 539 missing, most captured after they became lost in the darkness. The American death toll was 84 officers and men.

Drummond next ignored warnings of an American attack on batteries his men, reinforced by 1,200 troops, had built near the fort. When the attack came, he lost 115 dead, 176 wounded, hundreds captured and two batteries taken.

Drummond's retreat ends the Niagara campaign.

American fleet carries the day in naval battle at Plattsburgh

Sept. 11, 1814

PLATTSBURGH, N.Y. – Misunderstanding and bad judgment on the part of the British have led to their defeat in a naval battle on Lake Champlain. A deciding factor was that the *Confiance,* touted as a superior British fighting frigate, went into battle before it was ready. Her crew was green and the guns were not in top working order.

Leading a naval expedition that included the *Confiance,* Capt. George Downie originally set out to lend support to an attack on Plattsburgh by Lt.-Gen. Sir George Prevost. However, when the land battle did not start at the appointed time, the naval force was left without military support. From there, things went from bad to worse for the British. The wind failed and Downie was not able to align his ships as planned. He was killed early in the battle. The British ships then ran into a series of disasters. The *Chubb* went out of control and had to surrender, the *Preble* and the *Finch* were disabled and drifted away, and the *Confiance* and the *Linnet* were forced to surrender after being severely damaged.

Victorious Americans win the battle on Lake Champlain near Plattsburgh.

Illustration of the battle near Plattsburgh where British forces were defeated.

Treaty of Ghent ends unpopular War of 1812

Dec. 24, 1814

GHENT, Belgium – The War of 1812 is over. Almost five months of negotiations have finally paid off. The Treaty of Ghent signed in Belgium today will bring to an end a war that has become unpopular on both sides. The governments of Britain and the United States – as well as the populations of both countries – have longed for peace for some time.

The treaty sets out the conditions for peace in 11 articles and 3,000 words, though in their haste British and American officials have hammered out an agreement which sometimes lacks clarity. Much of the wording is ambiguous to the point of uselessness. For example, Article 1 merely gives the impression that slaves and private property are to be returned to the rightful owners, yet it doesn't actually come out and say so. It leaves room for dispute.

However, the treaty satisfies both sides since it fulfils its main objective – ending the war. It is an agreement of peace with honor, for very little has changed. All conquered territory is to be returned. American expansionist sentiment has been met by returning to the United States the territory seized by Britain along the Canadian border. Both Britain and the United States agree to cease hostilities against the Indians. According to Article 9, the Indians will be given back their status and territory that they had in 1811.

Several major issues are left for future discussion, others are not touched on at all. There is no mention of neutral rights, fishing rights or impressment (taking former British sailors off American merchant ships and putting them back into British service). Use of the Mississippi River has not been addressed. A joint commission will be set up to deal with boundary problems.

Peace commissioners for the United States were Albert Gallatin, James A. Bayard, Jonathan Russell, Henry Clay and John Quincy Adams. British delegates were Admiral Lord James Gambier, chairman, Henry Goulburn, the parliamentary undersecretary of state for war and the colonies, and William Adams, a doctor of civil law.

The signing of the Treaty of Ghent between Britain and United States of America ends the war in North America.

Trusted paper money to pay army bills

1814

CANADA – The war has cut Canada's access to coins bought on American markets and paid for by bills drawn on London. So the Quebec Executive Council has issued – and fully guaranteed – up to £250,000 in paper army bills to buy supplies and pay soldiers. They are based on Spanish dollars. Denominations are one to 400, and over $25 earn four percent interest.

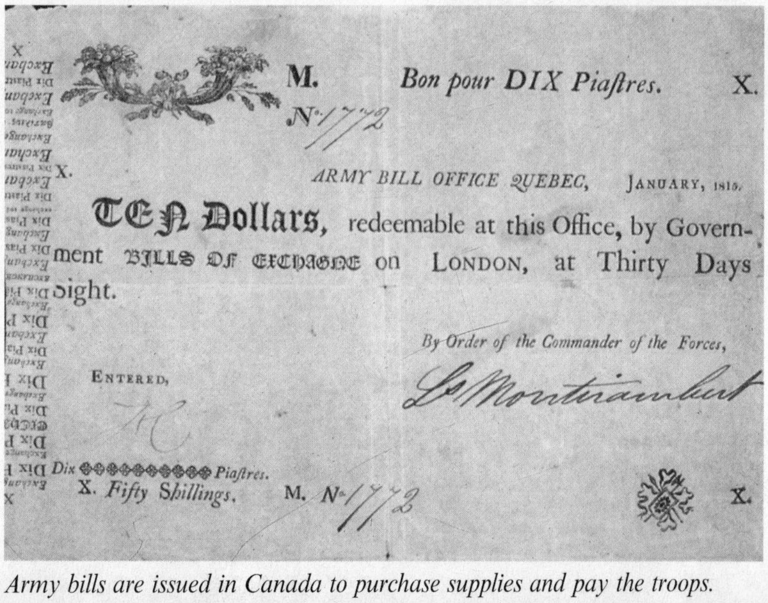

M. Bon pour DIX Piaſtres. X.

No 1772

X. ARMY BILL OFFICE QUEBEC, JANUARY, 1815.

TEN Dollars, redeemable at this Office, by Government BILLS OF EXCHANGE on LONDON, at Thirty Days Sight.

By Order of the Commander of the Forces,

ENTERED,

Dix Piaſtres.

X. Fifty Shillings. M. No 1772 X.

Army bills are issued in Canada to purchase supplies and pay the troops.

Schooner captured in surprise attack

Sept. 5, 1814

MICHILIMACKINAC – The American schooner *Scorpion* was captured today in a surprise attack off Michilimackinac Island [Mackinac Island, Mich.] when it came alongside its sister ship the *Tigress*. Unbeknownst to the *Scorpion* captain and crew, the *Tigress* was already in the hands of British forces led by Lieut. Miller Worsley, whose men quickly boarded and captured the U.S. vessel. The British capture of the two U.S. ships leaves Lake Huron free of American power.

Two nights ago, Worsley, commander of the destroyed British ship *Nancy*, boarded the *Tigress* with four boatloads of men, quickly overpowering the ship's 30-man crew. Of the British detachment, only two men were killed and eight wounded. Worsley then went on to capture the *Scorpion* by sailing the *Tigress* next to it and boarding it in the same manner.

1815 (1815-1817)

Nova Scotia, April 1815. About 800 black refugees from the U.S. arrive in wake of the War of 1812.

Saint John, N.B., May 25, 1815. Some 370 black refugees arrive from the U.S.

Red River, June 1815. Métis led by Cuthbert Grant harass the Hudson's Bay Company settlement. The North West Company has encouraged the actions by voicing the idea of a Métis nation with land rights in opposition to the land claims of the HBC.

Atlantic Colonies, 1815. Thousands of unlicensed squatters are clearing land in the backwoods of New Brunswick and Nova Scotia. Some of them are encroaching on Indian reserve lands. The provincial governments tolerate them.

Halifax, Feb. 14, 1816. Stagecoach service is inaugurated between Halifax and Pictou. The first coach carries six passengers at a charge of $6 each.

Upper Canada, 1816. Sawmills are operating on a large scale. The best in the province, located at Hawkesbury Township, employs 80 men.

Upper Canada, 1816. Common School Acts are passed to regulate the establishment of grammar schools. They provide for the construction of a schoolhouse and the employment of a teacher for six months if there are 20 students available.

Upper Canada, 1817. A road is completed linking Montreal and York [Toronto], making long distance land travel possible for the first time in Canada. Stage-sleighs travel the road in winter, and travellers on horseback use it in summer.

Halifax, 1817. The Halifax Chess, Pencil, and Brush Club folds. Born in 1787, it is the first artists' organization in British North America.

Newfoundland, 1817. A storm claims some 25 vessels and 200 men looking for the main whelping patch of harp seals in the area.

Upper Canada, 1817. A bill gives limited police powers to local authorities in York, Sandwich and Amherstburg.

London, 1817. Parliament recomends the deportation of 5,000 or 10,000 from Newfoundland to help the colony cope with famine.

Selkirk colonists return to Red River

Sept. 15, 1815

RED RIVER COLONY – An attempt to destroy Lord Selkirk's young colony on the Red River apparently has failed. After being driven from the area by angry Métis, refugee colonists returned to their farms this month under the protection of Hudson's Bay Company trader Colin Roberton and his men.

The episode began in the spring when Duncan Cameron, the North West Company commander on the Red River, arrested the settlement's governor, Miles Macdonell, and packed him off to Canada. Meanwhile, Métis horsemen were harassing the remaining settlers, trampling their crops and stealing their livestock. The Nor'Westers and their Métis allies have never made peace with the colony which they believe threatens their livelihood as traders and buffalo hunters. Finally, just last month, all but three colonists left and nothing remained of Selkirk's dream but burned buildings and broken crops.

However, before the fugitive settlers could get very far they met up with Colin Robertson and his brigade of HBC canoes. With this support, the colonists took heart and returned to the tiny settlement, which now has risen like a phoenix from the ashes. It is said that a new governor, Robert Semple, is on his way from England.

Colin Robertson, Hudson's Bay Co.

Métis agree to end Red River attacks

June 25, 1815

RED RIVER COLONY, Rupert's Land – Métis attacks on the colony would appear to be over, but the treaty guaranteeing the peace comes with a price. Led by Cuthbert Grant, the Métis have agreed to stop their wave of destruction in the Red River colony if the remaining settlers here leave the area. Peter Fidler, head of the colony, and his lieutenant, James White, have agreed to the Métis terms. The pact says past acts of violence will be forgotten and peace will reign.

Cuthbert Grant says Métis violence will end if settlers leave Red River.

Governor among Fort Douglas arrivals

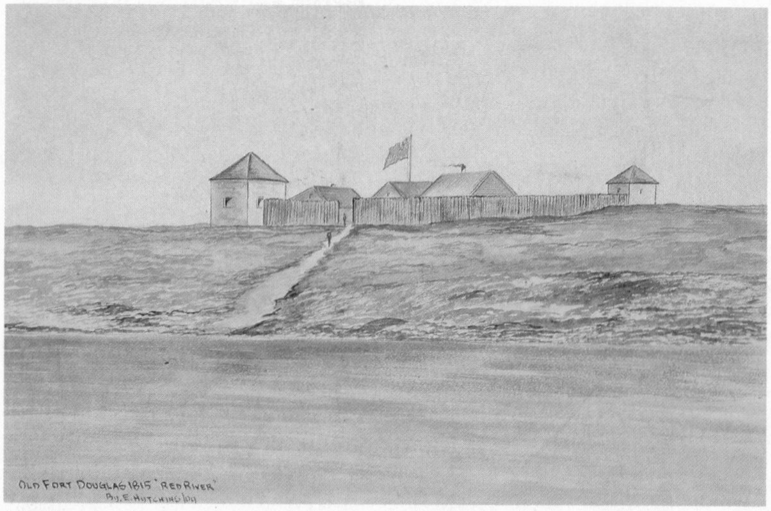

Highlanders have arrived at Fort Douglas in the Red River settlement.

April 11, 1815

FORT DOUGLAS, Assiniboia – The recent party of Highlanders arriving at Red River, via Hudson Bay, has brought the number of settlers to 270.

The first shipload, which arrived at York Factory four years ago, included 70 Highlanders and 20 Irish colonists and company employees. A year later a number of skilled workmen arrived to construct the buildings. This year's party is 84 in number, and among them is the colony's new governor, Robert Semple.

Assiniboia governor surrenders himself

June 17, 1815

FORT GIBRALTAR, Assiniboia – After avoiding arrest for two years, Gov. Miles Macdonell has surrendered himself to Capt. Duncan Cameron at Fort Gibraltar. Macdonell did so after receiving guarantees that the settlers' lives would be protected. Friction between them and Nor'Westers stems from Macdonell's January 1814 one-year ban on exporting foodstuffs from Assiniboia. He said this was to prevent the settlers from starving, but fur traders think it was to starve them out of business.

21 die in massacre at Seven Oaks

Illustration of the battle of Seven Oaks in the Red River colony, a confrontation between settlers and the Métis.

June 19, 1816

RED RIVER COLONY – An armed confrontation between settlers and Métis here today cost the lives of 21 people, including Robert Semple, the governor of the colony. The incident began late in the afternoon when a band of Métis horsemen, led by the noted buffalo hunter Cuthbert Grant, appeared near Fort Douglas, the Hudson's Bay Company post on the Red River.

The Métis have never accepted the presence of the Scottish settlers in their country. The natives fear the newcomers intend to take their land. This particular band was on its way from pillaging an HBC post. They were planning on blockading Fort Douglas to starve the colonists out. Tensions have been high in the colony for some time and when Semple saw the Métis he led a party of armed men out to find out what they were planning.

Marching down the road beside the river, Semple and his followers met the Métis by a clump of trees called Seven Oaks. A Métis emissary advanced to ask Semple what he wanted. An argument erupted, and as the messenger fled back to his ranks, a shot was fired. In a flash, widespread fighting broke out. The settlers, on foot, stood not a chance. Métis riders outnumbered and outflanked them, and within 15 minutes 21 colonists lay dead.

Semple took a bullet in the leg and was finished off at point-blank range, despite Grant's attempt to save him. The Métis suffered one casualty. In the violent history of Red River, this is the bloodiest incident so far.

Young Métis writes Ballad of Frog Plain after great victory

June 19, 1816

RED RIVER COLONY – Today's violent clash at Seven Oaks has already been celebrated in a ballad by the young Métis poet and troubadour Pierre Falcon. For the colony, the incident was a disaster, claiming the lives of 21 men. For the Métis, however, it was a great victory against people they consider to be invaders, and as they sat around their camp fires tonight they listened with pride as Falcon put the triumph to music in a song he has called *The Ballad of Frog Plain*. The ballad will surely become an anthem for the Métis people.

Although Falcon just recently turned 23, he is already known in this country for his song writing. The son of a Cree mother and a French father, he was sent to Montreal for an education and now works in the fur trade for the North West Company.

Nor'Westers are partly responsible for today's fighting. They suspect the Hudson's Bay Company is using the Red River colony as a cover for its fur-trade strategies, and they have been encouraging the Métis in their campaign of violence against the settlement.

Tomorrow the Métis will ask for the surrender of Fort Douglas. Then they intend to transport the colonists out of the country, just as they did last summer.

Poet and troubadour Pierre Falcon.

Negro brothers to hang for petty thefts; one pilfers cash, the other bread, butter

March 8, 1815

PRINCE EDWARD ISLAND – Peter Byers, a Negro, was today sentenced to die, convicted of breaking into a tobacco shop and stealing £5. Byers confessed to the crime after a three-day interrogation, saying he'd "told so many lies on the subject I cannot rest."

Byers is the second in his family to be convicted of a capital crime. Twelve days ago, his brother Sancho received a death sentence for stealing a loaf of bread and a pound of butter. Denied mercy, the brothers will be hanged later this month.

Prince Edward Island's few Negroes came here as slaves of loyalists, the first 16 arriving in 1784. Though slavery is still legal here, most Negroes live as freemen in shacks in Charlottetown, eking out livings as casual laborers, gardeners, chimney sweeps and puntsmen.

Fall frosts damage Red River harvest

October 1817

RED RIVER COLONY, Rupert's Land – Another calamity has beset Red River colonists. Crops promised well all summer, but fall frosts damaged the harvest, as settlers were late with their sowing. What they collected was kept for seed. Despite the reversals, morale has been raised by Lord Selkirk's visit, and the Scots are determined to remain in Red River. ▷

Lord Selkirk visits Red River colony

1817

RED RIVER COLONY, Rupert's Land – After interrupting his inspection of the Red River settlement to take the North West Company post of Fort William and those there he believed responsible for the Seven Oaks Massacre, Lord Selkirk is back with his troops of mercenaries, former soldiers with the disbanded De Meuron regiment that served in the War of 1812.

Selkirk is here to restore order to his four-year-old settlement of Scottish immigrants. His first act was to return the settlers who were banished to Norway House by the Métis. They had been harassed by Métis leader Cuthbert Grant and his men, who believe the Red River colony has no place on the plains. Those settlers suffering huge losses were granted new land.

Meanwhile, land's been set aside here for a church and a school. At present, a temporary building is being erected to serve as both until permanent structures can be built.

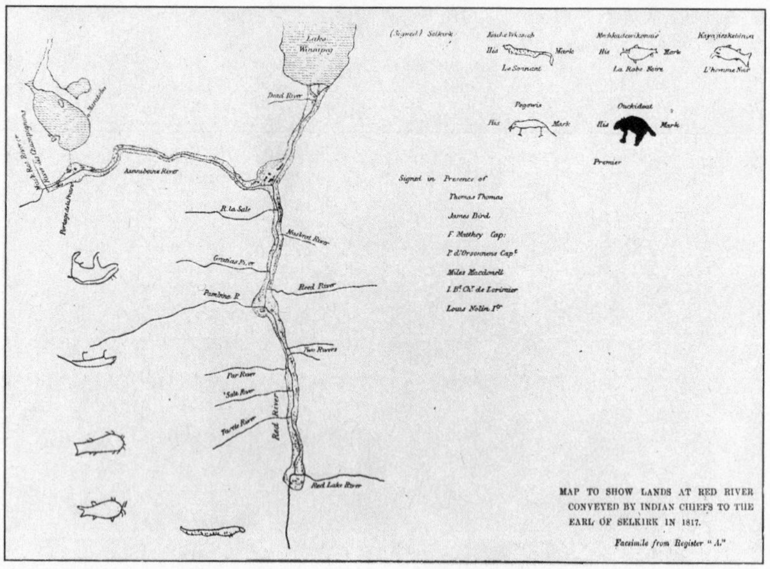

The settlement at Red River in 1817, which Lord Selkirk is visiting.

Selkirk has promised to secure a minister for the church. Roads and bridges – as well as other items important to the running and well being of the settlement – are being discussed, and a general survey of the colony has been ordered. Many of the soldiers who had accompanied Selkirk are now taking advantage of the offer of grants of land in exchange for their services to Selkirk.

Treaty to restrict warships on lakes

April 27, 1817

YORK – Residents here are celebrating news that the days of the "Great Lakes navies" are over. In a treaty between the British and American governments, both sides have agreed to restrict the number of armed ships each is allowed on the Great Lakes.

The pact is nicknamed the Rush-Bagot Treaty in honor of the men who negotiated it – acting U.S. Secretary of State Richard Rush and Sir Charles Bagot, the British minister in Washington. Under its terms, each side is only allowed one armed ship on Lakes Ontario and Champlain, and two more to patrol the Upper Great Lakes. Given these terms, any aggressor would be hard-pressed to put together a fighting force for any sort of surprise attack, since such a buildup would be an obvious violation of the treaty. It's hoped the agreement will slow down the "arms race" between these two former enemies.

Steamship Frontenac makes its debut

Sept. 7, 1816

ERNESTTOWN, Upper Canada – The latest in newfangled technology has come to travel on the Great Lakes. Today, amidst much fanfare, the new steamship *Frontenac* was launched into the Bay of Quinte.

The vessel is a far cry from the small, rough-sailing bateaux that still travel this lake. It is 51 metres long and powered by two giant paddle wheels 12 metres in circumference. As for inside, some refer to it as "a floating palace." The total cost of the vessel was $100,000. The *Frontenac* will run from Prescott to York. Fare is $12 one way, including food; $3 for steerage passengers, who bring their own victuals. And yes, the *Frontenac* does have sails – just in case.

The steamer Frontenac, which has been launched into the Bay of Quinte.

First bank in Canada opens in Montreal "to discount, deposit and issue money"

The Bank of Montreal, the first bank in Canada, formed to discount, deposit and issue money. The bank's rented offices are on St. Paul St.

Nov. 3, 1817

MONTREAL – Canada's first bank has opened. With paid-up capital of £250,000, the new Bank of Montreal is in a rented house at 32 St. Paul St. Spearheaded by fur trader, politician and magistrate John Richardson, Monday's opening represents the culmination of 25 years of lobbying.

Initially opposed by French-Canadians, their attitude toward a regular bank and currency changed due to the prosperity brought by the Army Bills' use in the last war. With the withdrawal of these notes bearing six percent interest rates, it became difficult to finance new ventures because of lack of currency. Without a form of legal tender, Canadians faced wildly fluctuating rates of exchange for the British, French, Spanish, Halifax and American specie in circulation.

Richardson and eight Montreal merchants formed the bank to discount, deposit and issue money. Open weekdays 10 to 3, discount days are Tuesday and Friday.

Cree and Ojibwa sign treaty surrendering Red River holdings

July 18, 1817

RED RIVER, Rupert's Land – The Earl of Selkirk met earlier today with a party of Ojibwa and Cree chiefs and warriors. Through an agreement with them he believes he has extinguished the Indian title to land along the Red and Assiniboine rivers, from the mouth of the Red River as far south as Red Lake River, and along the Assiniboine River beyond Portage la Prairie to Musk Rat Creek.

This is the first treaty made with the Indians in the western interior of British North America. At the signing, Selkirk said the depth of the land Indians are surrendering is the greatest distance at which you could see a horse on the level prairie, or you could see daylight under his belly between his legs. In return for the land, Selkirk promised to pay 100 pounds of good quality tobacco annually to both the Ojibwas and the Cree.

The agreement has not pleased everyone. Some Cree are furious the Ojibwa – latecomers to the region brought here by the North West Company 30 years ago – are included. The angry Cree say their tribe and the Assiniboine, who now live further east, deserve the payment for the settlers' use of Indian land at the Red River.

Chief Peguis has signed the treaty.

Teenager in York killed in gun duel

July 17, 1817

YORK – The illegal and deadly romance of dueling claimed yet another victim today when 18-year-old John Ridout was killed in a contest with Samuel Peters Jarvis. It is not known what the quarrel was between these two scions of the local establishment. What is known is that the duel took place in a meadow near the corner of Yonge and College streets.

It's unclear what, if any, punishment Jarvis will face. While dueling is illegal, juries tend to acquit if they feel it was conducted fairly.

Famine, frost, fire hit St. John's hard

Nov. 21, 1817

ST. JOHN'S, Nfld. – A combination of famine, frost and fire seems determined to destroy St. John's. The present depression began with the end of the last war and continued throughout 1816, when St. John's and the outports were in a state of starvation.

This autumn the situation got worse, with gangs of unemployed, hungry men roaming the streets, breaking into storehouses and threatening the lives and property of those better off. Now, a major fire has destroyed about 300 homes, rendering 2,000 people homeless.

Selkirk arrests 15 after capturing North West Company post

Aug. 13, 1816

FORT WILLIAM, Rupert's Land – Spurred on by news of the Seven Oaks Massacre, in which 21 Red River settlers were killed, Lord Selkirk and his retinue of mercenaries have captured the North West Company's supply post, Fort William, and arrested the 15 Montreal partners in residence for treason, conspiracy and being accessories to murder. Much of the evidence went up in smoke last night as the ailing Selkirk rested in his camp and prisoners burned papers and documents pertinent to the case, though enough evidence remains to warrant sending 14 of the men to Montreal for trial.

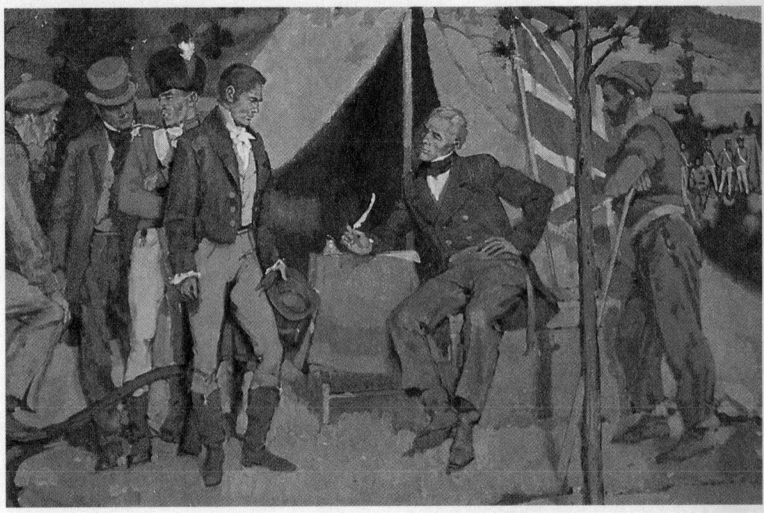

Lord Selkirk captures William McGillivray at Fort William.

American steamer Ontario makes round trip in a record 10 days

American steamship the Ontario has a record that's not in doubt this time.

April 28, 1817

YORK – The plucky little American steamer *Ontario* has set a new speed record for lake travel: a round trip voyage between Ogdensburg, on the St. Lawrence River, and Lewiston, on Lake Ontario, in just 10 days!

The trip marks yet another first for this steamship, and at least one that is not in doubt. Other claims about her – notably that she was the first to be launched on the Great Lakes – have not stood up so well. In fact, while the *Ontario* was being built in Sacket's Harbour, N.Y., that very honor was snatched by the Canadian ship *Frontenac*.

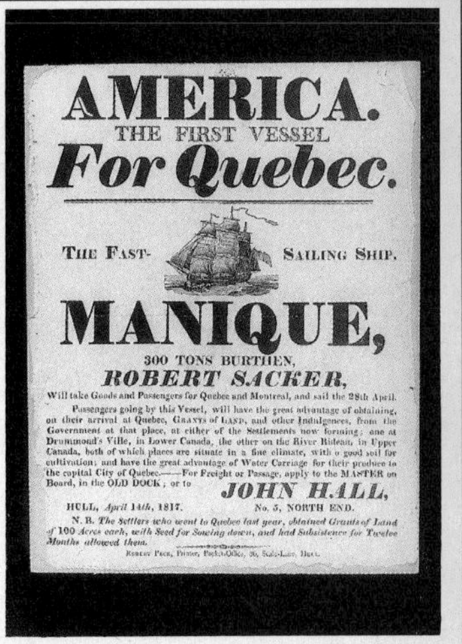

AMERICA.
THE FIRST VESSEL
For Quebec.

THE FAST-SAILING SHIP.

MANIQUE,
300 TONS BURTHEN,
ROBERT SACKER,
Will take Goods and Passengers for Quebec and Montreal, and sail the 28th April.

Passengers going by this Vessel, will have the great advantage of obtaining, on their arrival at Quebec, GRANTS of LAND, and other Indulgences, from the Government at that place, at either of the Settlements now forming; one at Drummond's Ville, in Lower Canada, the other on the River Rideau, in Upper Canada, both of which places are situate in a fine climate, with a good soil for cultivation; and have the great advantage of Water Carriage for their produce to the capital City of Quebec.——For Freight or Passage, apply to the MASTER on Board, in the OLD DOCK; or to

JOHN HALL,
No. 5, NORTH END.

HULL, *April 14th*, 1817.

N. B. *The Settlers who went to Quebec last year, obtained Grants of Land of 100 Acres each, with Seed for Sowing down, and had Subsistence for Twelve Months allowed them.*

Notice for the Manique, a ship which takes immigrants to Quebec where they receive land grants and "other indulgences."

1818 (1818-1819)

Upper Canada, April 2, 1818. Reformer Robert Gourlay publishes an address to resident landowners in which he argues for overturning the system of government, and proposes a plan to organize the the province's reformers.

Niagara, Upper Canada, April 13, 1818. The first official meeting of Upper Canadian reformers is convened by Robert Gourlay and a number of representatives are elected.

Red River, July 16, 1818. Priests Joseph-Norbert Provencher and Sévère Dumoulin arrive at Fort Douglas [Winnipeg] to establish the Catholic church at the colony. They are warmly received.

Red River, July 18, 1818. A grasshopper plague destroys the crops of settlers.

Arctic, Aug. 31, 1818. John Ross leads a British expedition to search for the Northwest Passage into Lancaster Sound, but it turns back when Ross sees a range of mountains to the west and concludes that the sound is enclosed. The mountains are an illusion.

Northwest, 1818. Colin Robertson and John Clarke lead a Hudson's Bay Company expedition to Lake Athabasca to try to break the North West Company's monopoly in the area. North West Company men take Robertson prisoner.

Newfoundland, 1818. The winter of 1817-18 is known as the "Winter of the Rals," or the Rowdies, as the island continues to suffer from a famine that began in 1815 and starving men resort to desperate acts. The situation is aggravated by the continuing arrival of Irish immigrants.

Lower Canada, 1818. Twenty percent of households have at least one servant.

Upper Canada, Aug. 20, 1819. Robert Gourlay is convicted of disobeying a government order to leave the province, and ordered deported.

Prince Edward Island, August 1819. Patrick Pearce bayonets his landlord's agent out of anger at his intransigence. The agent dies from his wounds, and Pearce is hidden by sympathetic neighbors.

Northwest, 1819. John Clarke has two Hudson's Bay Company posts built in the Peace River area. They give the company a foothold in the Athabasca area, dealing a blow to the North West Company.

Doom hovers over Arctic expedition

June 30, 1818

ARCTIC – It is already clear this expedition to find a passage around the northern tip of America will be a failure. A few weeks ago Cmdr. David Buchan sailed from Britain in the barque *Dorothea* with Lieut. John Franklin in command of the brig *Trent.*

Buchan and Franklin set sail to Spitsbergen, on the edge of the Arctic ice cap, to find out if they could take their ships through the ice to reach the Bering Strait and the Pacific. But there seems to be no opening through which any ship can sail.

H.M. brig the Trent is taking John Franklin and his crew on Arctic expedition.

Earlier this year, another expedition, led by Royal Navy officer John Ross, left England for Greenland and Baffin Bay to find a navigable passage from Baffin Bay through to the Pacific. Both these expeditions were planned soon after the war with Napoleon ended.

The war at sea had used all the Royal Navy's resources and ships, and men could not be spared for non-essentials such as expeditions. As soon as there were ships and officers to spare, John Barrow of the Admiralty and Sir Joseph Banks, Capt. James Cook's patron, persuaded the government to resume the search for the Northwest Passage. But it is obvious to the men on Franklin's and Buchan's ships that if a route to the Pacific is found, it will not be through the Arctic ice from Spitsbergen.

British explorer on northern voyage hopes to enlist Inuit aid

April 18, 1818

LONDON, England – Royal Navy officer John Ross, an often-wounded Scottish veteran of the Napoleonic war, is off to the Shetland Islands in the 385-ton *Isabelle.* Ross is in command of one of two expeditions seeking more information about the Arctic and will be searching for a channel to the west through Davis Strait. The other expedition, led by Cmdr. David Buchan, will head for the North Pole ice pack.

Ross is on his way to the Shetlands to discuss details of the expeditions with Buchan. Ross plans to get the help of the Inuit – particularly on the west coast of Greenland – and has an Inuk whaler from Greenland on board to act as an interpreter. No doubt, the Inuit will be seeing Europeans for the first time, and Ross's men will be seeing lands never visited by Europeans. Ross's route, navigators say, will take him through Baffin Bay and Davis Strait – a dangerous trip. They wonder if Ross is the man for such a voyage.

Fledgling Bank of Montreal initiates first foreign exchange deal

Bank of Montreal on St. Paul Street makes its foray into foreign exchange.

January 1818

MONTREAL – The Bank of Montreal, less than a year old, has made its first foray into foreign exchange. The St. Paul Street institution, which has not yet been incorporated by the government, this month sent a convoy to Boston with 130,000 Spanish dollars for the China trade. More than three tons of coins were packed in 65 kegs and hauled by horse and sleigh.

Lacking the government's seal of approval, Bank of Montreal officials had to turn to the United States for subscriptions for almost half of its capital stock.

Convention settles the U.S.-Canadian boundary dispute

Oct. 20, 1818

CANADA – Peace with the United States is definitely a reality here, following the signing of a convention between Britain and America which resolves a number of contentious issues. For one, territorial disputes over fishing rights in the Atlantic Ocean have been worked out.

More importantly, the boundary between Canada and the United States has been agreed to. In the east of the continent, it remains as always – up the St. Lawrence, and through the Great Lakes westward to Lake of the Woods. But, since much of the land beyond this is unsettled, it has been agreed that the 49th Parallel shall serve as the dividing line between both nations, up to the Rocky Mountains. Beyond this, notably in the Oregon Territory, land will be under joint Anglo-American occupation.

Of course, not everyone is pleased with the solution. Fur traders in Montreal say it's "a sell-out." They're angry because the rich fur lands in the Michigan-Wisconsin area, once part of their hinterland, now belong to the Americans. Nor are some Upper Canadians pleased. They say the convention will limit further settlement to the northwest, in the vast, cold Prairies.

Café has treat for high society women

1818

MONTREAL – High society women in the colony, who never miss the chance to take tea, coffee or chocolate in the afternoon, can now get their favorite sweets at the Café Français in Montreal.

At the café, owned by Deshons Montbrun, an apartment is now reserved for women where they can eat creams, iced fruit sorbets and ice creams prepared by a Lefebvre ice cream maker from the old Montansier Café in Paris. Also on the Café Français menu are delicate pastries such as petty-shoes and profiteroles.

Ships spending winter locked in ice

British naval expedition, on the Hecla and Griper, are locked in Arctic ice.

Parry's Arctic expedition has not yet encountered any natives of the north.

The crews of the H.M.S. Hecla and Griper cut a passage through Winter Harbour ice to bring the ships to shelter. The explorers sailed deeper into the Arctic archipelago than any previous expedition before putting in for the winter.

Sept. 26, 1819

WINTER HARBOUR, Melville Island – A British naval expedition is spending a winter locked in Arctic ice 2,000 kilometres from the nearest permanent settlement. It is the first time explorers have ever intentionally passed a winter so far north. The expedition consists of two naval vessels, the *Hecla* and the *Griper*, with 94 men under the command of Lieut. Edward Parry.

Only 28 years old, Parry is already a 16-year veteran of the Royal Navy. Last year he was with Cmdr. John Ross's unsuccessful attempt to locate a northwest passage through the Arctic. The purpose of this year's expedition is once again to search for a passage linking the Atlantic and Pacific oceans across the top of America.

In July, Parry and his ships struggled across ice-choked Baffin Bay and in the first week of August entered Lancaster Sound. Passing the point where Ross turned back last year, they proved that no land barrier blocks this passage. With a favorable wind at their back, the ships managed to sail deeper into the Arctic archipelago than any previous expedition.

In just five weeks, Parry surveyed 1,200 kilometres of new coastline. A week ago, after they had penetrated almost two-thirds of the way through the archipelago, the ships were halted by heavy ice near this harbor on the coast of Melville Island. For several days huge ice floes threatened to crush the vessels against the rocky shore and Parry had to admit that the sailing season was over.

The entrance to this harbor was already blocked by ice, but sailors used saws to cut a long passage to shelter and today the *Hecla* and *Griper* entered their winter quarters. Parry has with him hundreds of cans of meat and vegetables. The navy is experimenting with tinned food in the hope that it will preserve the good health of its crews on long voyages when fresh food is unavailable. Canned goods will provide a welcome relief from the usual diet of beer, bread and salt meat during the long Arctic night.

Parry hopes next summer to continue his search for the elusive Northwest Passage. ▷

Franklin reaches Cumberland House

Inuit people roam the Arctic lands.

The Franklin party on the Hudson's Bay Company ship Prince of Wales.

Oct. 22, 1819

CUMBERLAND HOUSE, Rupert's Land – Royal Navy officer John Franklin and his party – two midshipmen, a surgeon and a seaman – are here after an exhausting trip from York Factory on Hudson Bay. They left London on May 23 in the Hudson's Bay Company ship *Prince of Wales* and reached York Factory at the end of August.

Franklin, under orders to chart the Arctic coast east of the Coppermine River, was promised help from the Hudson's Bay Company. But he learned at York Factory that he could have only one boat to take him, his men and supplies to Cumberland House and had to leave most of his supplies behind. He is not satisfied with the information about his route and plans to snowshoe to a North West Company post to get guides.

Duke of Richmond succumbs to rabies

Aug. 28, 1819

RICHMOND, [Near Ottawa] – The Duke of Richmond, governor-in-chief of Canada, has died. His death is a release from days of fits and physical suffering, believed to be caused by rabies.

Sources close to the duke say he probably contracted the disease two months ago, while touring Fort William Henry in Lower Canada. While on the parade ground, he went to the rescue of his dog, which was fighting a pet fox. The fox bit him deeply in his hand. Although the wound bled profusely, the duke laughed off the injury and continued with his tour.

The symptoms started to show a few days ago. On one day, the duke was full of energy, walking 24 kilometres in a stretch. The next, he was exhausted. And at a tavern on the 26th he said to an aide, "I feel that if I were a dog I should be shot as a mad one." Finally, his condition having worsened, the duke came to a small Richmond farmhouse where he mercifully died.

Hunters find harp seal whelping patch

1819

NEWFOUNDLAND – Harp seals would probably sound a collective whimper if they realized hunters in the Atlantic Ocean recently found their main whelping patch just 160 kilometres off Newfoundland's coast. Uncommonly open ice and huge ice-strengthened boats carrying up to 60 men helped make the discovery.

The boats brought home almost 150,000 whitecoats, and the total year's harvest is 280,000 harp seals. Sealers have looked for this whelping patch since the 1770s. They knew only that the seals whelped on the ice north of Newfoundland.

These finely-carved caribou ornaments are made by Beothuk Indians of Newfoundland, who are believed to number no more than 1,000.

Sedition the charge for jailed reformer

Jan. 1, 1819

NIAGARA-ON-THE-LAKE – Robert Gourlay, the reform advocate who's been a thorn in the side of the appointed provincial government, has been jailed here on a convenient charge of sedition. It's apparently the latest attempt of the conservative establishment to silence this radical who's asking the Prince Regent to inquire into their management – or mismanagement – of government money and administration.

The Scot Gourlay has been charged under the 1804 Sedition Act, actually aimed at that time against Irish rebels penetrating Canada. Since (due to a stay in the United States) he has not been living in the province the last six months and he has not sworn an oath of allegiance to the Crown, he now has to prove to a judge that he is, in fact, a loyal and obedient subject. If the judge doesn't believe Gourlay, he'll be ordered to leave the province. If he refuses, he will be jailed.

It's just the next trial for a man who's been complaining loudly about patronage in government. In pursuit of reform, Robert Gourlay has surveyed the province, compiling statistics to show how the vast tracts of land owned by rich, absentee landlords are preventing effective settlement. He has also organized meetings to elect delegates bearing his complaints to the government in London.

Dalhousie named governor general

September 1819

CANADA – Following the sudden and sad death of the Duke of Richmond, the British government has named the 9th Earl of Dalhousie to succeed him. The earl has some Canadian experience. In fact, until his new appointment, he was Nova Scotia's lieutenant governor.

Born on Oct. 23, 1770, Dalhousie joined the British army at age 18, and he saw action in Spain and France, including the famed Battle of Waterloo. He is expected to give Canada strong, stern – and his critics say – unimaginative rule.

Early 19th century furniture in colonial Canada

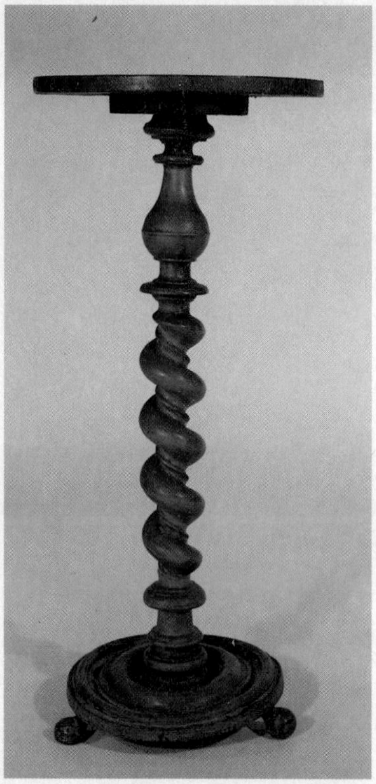

An intricately-wrought candlestand pedestal table seen in many of Quebec's upper class homes in the first half of the 19th century.

A nun's room at the Hôtel Dieu hospital in Quebec contains a variety of wooden furniture in simple, sturdy design.

A wooden sewing table used by Quebec women in the early 19th century is both handsome and practical. The spacious drawer is designed to store the needles, thread, and other sewing notions such as buttons, ribbon and lace.

A "break-front" butternut commode, the elaborate openwork skirt carved with scrolls and stylized foliage in the manner of Louis XV. The rocaille-inspired motifs are typical of what has been called the "Canadian rococo" style.

1820 (1820-1821)

Pau, France, April 8, 1820. Thomas Douglas, Earl of Selkirk, the founder of the Red River colony, dies.

London, May 6, 1820. The British government rules that the Church of Scotland is entitled to support from the government of Upper Canada. The Upper Canadian government already supports the Church of England, and Presbyterians in the province have been petitioning for support.

Northwest, Aug. 15, 1820. Anglican clergyman John West arrives at York Factory on his way to the Red River colony. He is the first Protestant missionary on the shores of Hudson Bay.

Red River, Northwest, November 1820. A month after his arrival, John West opens a school to convert and "civilize" Indians but most of his students are children of colonists.

Atlantic, 1820. There is a lull in American whaling in the Gulf of St. Lawrence and along the coast of Labrador because most of the profitable whales have been exterminated. Greys, rights, bowheads, sperms, and humpbacks have all been depleted.

Carlton House, The Northwest, Dec. 5, 1821. The Hudson's Bay Company receives a royal licence giving it a monopoly on trade with the Indians in selected areas of North America. The licence is intended to prevent competition in the fur trade.

Upper Canada, 1821. Over the years, the Iroquois have sold or lost nearly half the land the British granted them in 1784 for their support in the American Revolutionary War.

Russia, 1821. Tsar Alexander I decrees the Pacific coast from Alaska to 51 degrees N [just north of Vancouver Island] to be Russian territory. Russians have been harvesting seal skins along the Alaskan coast for years, and seals have become depleted in the area.

Montreal, 1821. McGill University is founded by royal charter. It is named after merchant James McGill, who left part of his estate for a college when he died in 1813.

Northwest, 1821. The Hudson's Bay Company adopts Norway House, where the Nelson River enters Lake Winnipeg, as the centre of its transportation system.

Minister to serve in Red River colony

May 27, 1820

RED RIVER COLONY, Rupert's Land – The Reverend John West has been dispatched to the Red River settlement. West is an author, teacher and Church of England chaplain sent here to minister in the colony.

A Catholic mission was established here two years ago when Lord Selkirk obtained the services of Father Joseph Norbert Provencher. It is somewhat ironic that the great majority of the Scottish settlers in the Red River colony are staunch Presbyterians. West and Provencher are among the first clergy to enter Rupert's Land.

Women ignore law and cast their votes

1820

BEDFORD COUNTY, Lower Canada – The participation of 22 married Bedford County women in this year's provincial election has led the Assembly of Lower Canada to nullify results of the vote here. Whether or not their husbands cast ballots, the Assembly ruled voting by wives violates British law.

Many male property owners, whose monopoly on the franchise is entrenched in law, disputed the election, saying the married women duplicated their husbands' votes. Women are also known to have voted in Trois-Rivières this year.

Cape Breton Island part of Nova Scotia

Oct. 16, 1820

SYDNEY, N.S. – A proclamation today ended Cape Breton Island's 36 years as a separate colony and annexed it to Nova Scotia. Sydney unhappily ponders its future not as a colonial capital, but as a provincial backwater.

Annexation rumors had already depressed land values. Some former office-holders have left town, but others have stayed on to form what George Ainslie, the last lieutenant-governor, calls "a family compact" of separatists.

Missionaries push Christian moral code

Illustration of interior of an Indian tent shows life among the Cree people.

Informal lifestyles of western settlers are under attack by the Church.

1820

RED RIVER COLONY, Rupert's Land – What has been accepted as good and natural by the people of the west is now being reviewed by newly arrived Church of England and Roman Catholic missionaries and found to be sinful and impure. Living arrangements which have been happily worked out on an informal basis until now are being uprooted under pressure from the clergy to sanctify these unions by taking part in a Christian marriage service.

Along with the church wedding comes a moral code that is to be adhered to if one is going to be a proper Christian. A wife must be clean and industrious, docile and obedient to her husband, and, above all, sexually pure. Hunting is barbarous, as is the nomadic life. They are both decidedly unChristian.

It seems Christian conduct is closely linked with civilized behavior – which is defined by the behavior of the civilization the missionaries come from. To be a good Christian one must learn the rules of etiquette. Unfortunately there are those who are using this new wave of religiously-sanctified marriages to cast off an old partner and take on a new one. Some of the Hudson's Bay Company chief factors and traders are giving up an Indian or Métis common law wife to legally marry a fair young British girl fresh from the Isles.

People of the Plains: portraits of a way of life

Buffalo meat is dried by the Indians of the White Horse Plains, Red River.

View of Prairie Indian encampment. People of the Plains share the work.

Portrait of an Indian of the Sauteaux tribe living around the Red River.

Sioux Indian Kan-te-was-te-win, meaning a "good broad woman."

Indian burial ground in the [Thunder Bay] area, east of the Great Plains.

Cree Indians watching over a buffalo pound near Fort Carlton, [Alberta].

A Sauteaux Indian travelling with his family in winter near Lake Winnipeg.

▷

Franklin party spending winter at Fort Enterprise

Franklin's men build Fort Enterprise to serve as their winter quarters.

Sept. 1, 1820

FORT ENTERPRISE, Rupert's Land – The Franklin party has built its winter quarters here, close to the Coppermine River, and named their digs Fort Enterprise. They will need all the enterprise they can muster for the task set them by the Admiralty – to sail down the Coppermine River to the Arctic and then explore the coast to the east.

The expedition, which left England nearly 18 months ago, has been plagued by shortages of food, guides and reliable information about the route. And on the way here, Cmdr. John Franklin managed to anger nearly all the party with behavior more suited to the quarter deck than the Arctic.

John Franklin, leader of the expedition planning to sail down the Coppermine River to the Arctic and then explore the coast to the east.

Chief Peguis aids Red River settlers

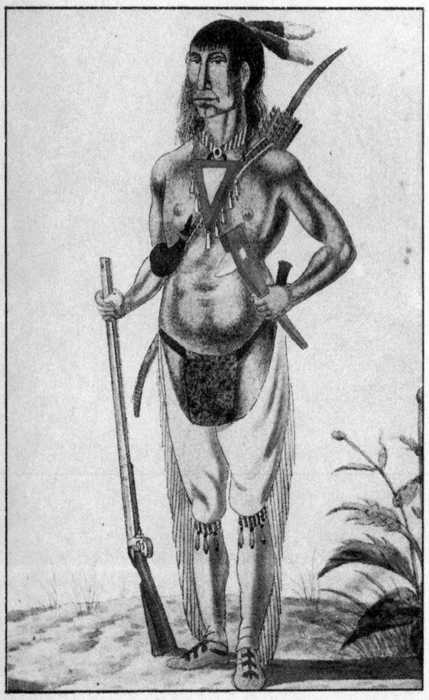

Red River's Chief Peguis.

1820

RED RIVER COLONY, Rupert's Land – Be it with land, pemmican or dried fish, Chief Peguis of the Ojibwa Indians has aided the people of Red River in many ways. At a time when most natives are not particularly friendly, he continues to be of assistance when needed. In times of famine, he has supplied food. When asked for land, he granted it. And in the Seven Oaks Massacre, Peguis even harbored a mother and her children.

Bank of Upper Canada charter approved

1821

YORK – Growing demand for economic expansion has led the Assembly of Upper Canada to approve a charter for the Bank of Upper Canada. Modelled after the First and Second Banks of the United States, the new bank will have four of its 15 directors appointed by provincial solons. The province will own 25 percent of the bank's stock, with the remainder going to private subscribers.

Opposition to the newly-formed institution comes primarily from Kingston merchants who tried to incorporate a bank in their city but were stopped by proponents of the York bank. Shopkeeper-advocate William Lyon Mackenzie is also proving to be a tenacious opponent of the Bank of Upper Canada. The fact that stockholders are liable only to the extent of their investment – and not to the full extent of their private fortunes in the event the bank cannot meet its debts – is what's got Mackenzie's dander up.

Robbery a problem mail carriers facing

1821

UPPER CANADA – Mail carriers in Upper Canada have been plagued by a rash of robberies this year despite improvements deputy postmaster-general Daniel Sutherland has implemented. The Kingston Road to York has seen a number of robberies. Setting up post offices in [Belleville], [Port Hope] and [Cobourg] in recent years has not remedied the situation.

British explorer at Turnagain Point after a terrifying journey

Aug. 18, 1821

TURNAGAIN POINT, Arctic – After a terrifying canoe journey along the storm-swept coastline of the Arctic Ocean, John Franklin reached this landmark on the Kent Peninsula today.

With a party of 20 men in two canoes, the British naval explorer has been travelling eastward along the coast for the past month, surveying what he hopes is part of the Northwest Passage through the Arctic. Franklin wants to continue, but the men have convinced him to turn back to their winter base at Fort Enterprise, 450 kilometres away. The men argued that they are frozen, tired and half-starved, and both canoes are too badly damaged to return along the coast.

The Coppermine River, where the Franklin party built its winter base in 1820.

Hudson's Bay and North West companies merge

Hudson's Bay Co. promisory note.

March 21, 1821

LONDON, England – After some 40 years of fierce competition, the Hudson's Bay Company and the North West Company have merged. The agreement was signed by representatives of the two companies in London today after years of negotiation.

The new company will be known as the Hudson's Bay Company, but Nor'Westers will have equal representation on the board of directors. The merger comes about because the wasteful and violent rivalry between the two companies is proving ruinous to them both. The NWC was never a unified company like its rival. Instead, it was an uneasy partnership of traders in the fur country, the so-called "wintering partners," and their merchant suppliers in Montreal. Winterers were not always happy with their suppliers and it appeared recently that the company was going to disintegrate when its present partnership agreement expired next year. It was this prospect that made some winterers anxious to talk union.

Hudson's Bay Company fur traders.

Conservatives label Bidwell an "alien"

Nov. 24, 1821

YORK – Barnabas Bidwell, a Reform deputy for Lennox and Addington, has been labelled an "alien" by Conservatives trying to keep him out of the House.

The fact is, under the law, his opponents are correct. Bidwell is like about half the populace who were born in the United States and then moved here, most since 1812. (Bidwell came in 1810, fleeing fraud charges.) The current government so fears American influence it withholds citizenship from immigrants who can lose their rights and land, and be deported as aliens any time the establishment pleases.

Simpson banquet reconciles fur traders

October 1821

YORK FACTORY, Northwest – When George Simpson talks, people listen. When he gives a banquet, even guests who have not gotten along in the past behave themselves. It happened tonight. The new governor of the Hudson's Bay Company hosted a gathering of traders, former rivals under the Hudson's Bay and North West companies but now co-workers, since the two companies recently merged.

At first, traders such as Alexander McDougall and Alexander Kennedy split along "company" lines, until Simpson introduced members of each group to the other.

A Methodist camp meeting around 1820 attracts an enthusiastic crowd.

Member of expedition executes murderer

John Franklin's Arctic expedition sailed in the Hudson's Bay Company ship Prince of Wales on the first leg of its voyage. Illustration shows the Prince of Wales and a sister ship meeting another British explorer, Capt. W.E. Parry.

Fall 1821

ARCTIC – John Richardson, a leading member of John Franklin's ill-fated exploration party, has been credited with saving the expedition from perishing of starvation, cold – and perhaps mass murder. The British surgeon and naturalist courageously took matters into his own hands when a French-Canadian voyageur shot and killed British midshipman Robert Hood. To ensure the survival of remaining party members, Richardson personally executed the murderer.

On the terrible trek on foot to Fort Enterprise, with only lichen to eat, nine men starved or froze to death. The motive for Hood's murder may have been desperation for food, even human flesh.

Sir John Richardson, a member of John Franklin's Arctic expedition.

1822 (1822-1824)

Upper Canada, Jan. 4, 1822. Reversing a previous decision, the Assembly votes to expel Barnabas Bidwell, who previously held office in the U.S. and was convicted of felony. The Assembly passes an act disqualifying anyone who has held office, or been convicted of a crime in another country.

Arctic, October 1822. A British Northwest Passage expedition led by William Edward Parry returns to Iglooik to winter with Inuit there after exploring the east coast of Melville peninsula, and finding Fury and Hecla Straits. Ice stopped them from entering the straits, but overland journeys confirmed that they reach the sea [Gulf of Boothia], suggesting they are a shorter Northwest Passage route than Lancaster Sound.

Newfoundland, 1822. William Epps Cormack is the first white man to walk across the island, travelling from Trinity Bay to St. George's Bay.

Montreal, 1822. Laywomen found the Montreal Protestant Orphans Asylum to care for orphans.

Ancaster Township, Upper Canada, June 1823. Peter Jones, son of surveyor Augustus Jones and an Ojibwa woman, is converted to Christianity at a Methodist Episcopal Church meeting. Reverend William Case cries out "now is the door opened for the work of conversion among his nation!"

Montreal, 1824. Laywomen found the Montreal Benevolent Ladies' Society to help poor women and children.

Lower Canada, 1824. The Literary and Historical Society of Quebec is formed. It begins an active program of research and publication.

Upper Canada, 1824. A board of education is created to supervise the province's schools, with Dr. John Strachan as chairman.

Saint John, New Brunswick, 1824. The Philharmonic Society of Saint John is formed.

Upper Canada, 1824. A lot of tea is smuggled into the province. A traveller is told: "of every 15 pounds sold, 13 were smuggled," and that one merchant smuggles 500-1,000 chests of tea annually into the province.

Ottawa River, 1824. Regular Durham boat service is established on the river.

Bank of Upper Canada open for business

The Bank of Upper Canada in town of York is the province's first bank.

July 1822

YORK – Upper Canada's first bank is now open for business, and that's good tidings for all those cash-starved local entrepreneurs who are hoping to capitalize on business opportunities in the rapidly expanding colony. The Bank of Upper Canada is modelled on the British banks, says its president and founder, successful merchant William Allan. The establishment of the bank has the backing of members of the Family Compact as well as key figures in the province's business community.

No fatalities in wreck off Sable Island

May 16, 1822

SABLE ISLAND, N.S. – This skinny, sandy, wind-lashed death trap today wrecked yet another vessel. She was the French man-of-war *L'Africaine,* carrying 44 guns and 250 officers and men.

This time Sable took not a single life. Thanks to the heroism of a few Nova Scotians at the Sable Island Humane Establishment, founded in 1801, every Frenchman got ashore safely. The French were especially grateful to a Captain Darby, master of the schooner *Two Brothers,* for his part in saving them, and also to the rescuers under Edward Hodgson.

Just six years ago, Hodgson begged authorities to "send Captain Darby or some other vessel ... as we are in starving condition." The great storm of 1816 smothered the island's meagre cropland and hay in sand. Many horses died. Recent wrecks vanished, while forgotten ones rose into view.

View of South Saskatchewan River. It is formed in southern [Alberta] by the junction of the Bow and Oldman rivers, flowing past [Medicine Hat].

Royal Navy seamen study Inuit people on Arctic expedition

Feb. 1, 1822

WINTER ISLAND, Arctic Circle – The crew of the Royal Navy ships *Hecla* and *Fury,* which are spending the winter here, have little time to be bored. Performances are held in the Royal Arctic theatre aboard one of the ships, with some of the crew taking on acting roles. In the daytime, classes are held for the seamen.

But perhaps the best learning experience comes from the Inuit band which has just arrived and camped close to the ships locked in the ice. Members of the band have already made it clear that they want to help the British seamen, here on yet another expedition to seek the elusive Northwest Passage. And both officers and men are interested in learning the Inuit language and in learning about Inuit culture and the way they hunt, fish and find shelter.

Inuit have told Cmdr. William Parry, the expedition leader, that there is a stretch of water north of here that leads to the west. The ships left Deptford a year ago and sailed through Hudson Strait and into Repulse Bay. They found their way to the west blocked, and sailed north along the coast of Melville Peninsula until they reached Winter Island. They were locked in the ice in mid-October.

Dalhousie returns, Halifax has a ball

July 25, 1823

HALIFAX – George Ramsay, Earl of Dalhousie, governor of Canada, and former lieutenant-governor of Nova Scotia, was welcomed back to town last night at the most sumptuous ball in the history of Halifax.

Two nights ago he endured a banquet – where men made 40 formal toasts – and left at 12:30 a.m. But at last night's affair in Province House, supper didn't even begin till midnight. A military band played on a platform above the central doors, hundreds of candles twinkled in chandeliers, sofas awaited the weary, and no expense was spared.

Parry expedition studies traditional Inuit lifestyle

Sketch of Inuit and their dog on their way to the seal hunt.

Inuit man and woman carry a child. All are inhabitants of Savage Island.

Three dancing Inuit children of Igloolik in the Arctic region of Canada.

Copper Indian guide and his daughter Green Stockings mend a snowshoe.

Four Inuit women of Igloolik in Canada's Arctic region carry their children.

Inuit men of Igloolik, ready to hunt for food to bring to their families.

Protestant church opens in Red River

View of the new Roman Catholic church at the colony in Red River.

The Protestant church and the mission school at the Red River colony.

June 10, 1823

RED RIVER COLONY, Rupert's Land – The first Protestant church in the Red River area, St. John's Church, was consecrated today by the Rev. John West. Lord Selkirk himself had assigned a lot for the Anglican church within the settlement. There is also room beside the church yard for a cemetery. The structure is a rough log building, but it does have a steeple. It was financed and built by the people of the colony and their government, quite an interesting undertaking in view of the fact that the majority of settlers are staunch Presbyterians.

West is a Church of England pastor who has been in the west only a few years. He was appointed the chaplain to the Hudson's Bay Company in 1820. Since then, he has been ministering to the Protestant colonists and HBC personnel. He has also been doing missionary work among the native people. A large part of his job has been performing marriages, consecrating unions that were already in existence. West was born in Farnham, Sussex, England, about 1775.

Retired Nor'Wester weds trader's niece

May 23, 1823

WILLIAMSTOWN, Upper Canada – Though married "according to the customs of the country" and until recently living with his wife Nancy Small at Gart [Inverarden], John McDonald has wed Amelia Cameron, Williamstown trader Hugh McGillis' niece. A retired Nor'Wester, McDonald married Small, a Métis, in 1799. He left the fur trade in 1814, selling off all of his shares in the company for £10,000, plus £1,000 in credit to the Montreal firm of McTavish, McGillivray and Co.

McDonald, Small and their five children settled in Cornwall in 1816 at their new Regency Cottage and 750-acre estate overlooking the St. Lawrence at Gray's Creek. Several years later, McDonald's daughter Eliza married former Nor'Wester John Duncan Campbell. The house was expanded and McDonald's savings fell to some £1,100. Then McDonald met McGillis' niece, and despite his previous liaison, married her. With McGillis' assistance, the couple plan to build a new home east of Gray's Creek.

Stealing 25 cents costs teen his life

Feb. 21, 1824

SAINT JOHN, N.B. – Patrick Bergen died today in payment of a most serious offence – he stole 25 cents. The 18-year-old male was taken to the gallows this morning, where, as the law states, he fulfilled his sentence of "being hung by the neck until dead."

It was a stern punishment for the offence, but not one at all out of place in British justice. In fact, although applying the death sentence to such a small theft seems extreme, the fact is that death is a common fate for those who fall afoul of the law. Many crimes are covered by this sanction, including forgery and counterfeiting.

Yet it cannot be said the criminal element is entirely unaware of the risks they run. Still, perhaps it would have been better for young Mr. Bergen to have worked to repay his debt 10 times over, than die.

Steam-powered sawmill to boost Saint John lumber industry

1822

SAINT JOHN, N.B. – The first steam-powered sawmill has opened here in what is expected to be a big boost for the local lumber industry. The use of steam power is considered a breakthrough because it will mean faster and more continuous cutting. Early mills used water for power, and sawing was slow. The new sawmill should put the Saint John area in a good position to meet European demand for timber, which has fuelled development and immigration in this area.

The Royal Navy had been one of the markets for local timber, which was being cut for use as large masts. This market started coming into its own in 1808 when France was able to cut off most of Britain's imports of lumber from the Baltic countries during the heyday of Napoleon. At this time Saint John started to lose out in the naval trade to the St. Lawrence and lower Great Lakes area, where forests produced deciduous oak as well as pine. Lumber is available again to Britain from the Baltic area, but the Mother Country has maintained the Canadian trade. While wood is also being used in shingles and barrel staves, most of it takes the form of sawn lumber and square timber. Square timber is shipped to England and often is re-sawn there.

The first steam-powered sawmill in New Brunswick, built in Saint John.

Destitute parents abandoning hundreds of tots

1824

MONTREAL – Hundreds of children, many just days old, are being abandoned here by destitute parents. Responding to this crisis of tragic proportions, groups of Montreal women have formed charitable organizations to provide a modicum of care for the unfortunate infants. Until now, only the nuns of the General Hospital have taken them, and they are overwhelmed by the burden. The government provides no assistance at all.

The abandoned children, who often die within weeks from malnutrition, disease or exposure, are usually left on the doorstep of a women's relief society with just a plaintive note attached to their ragged clothing. A typical note pinned to a baby left at Hôtel-Dieu hospital in Quebec, reads: "This babe is not baptized – her name is Anne Bradie – the father being run away and the mother not being able to support it – born this morning."

Several factors have contributed to this grave situation. In some families, neither parent can find work, and so they resort to ridding themselves of mouths they cannot feed. Many immigrant women arrive here with small children and no means of support.

Poverty has even forced a lot of women into prostitution. A recent survey finds that of Montreal women claiming a profession, six percent said they were prostitutes. The birthrate is another factor. The average family counts eight children – a burden that many cannot handle on a limited income.

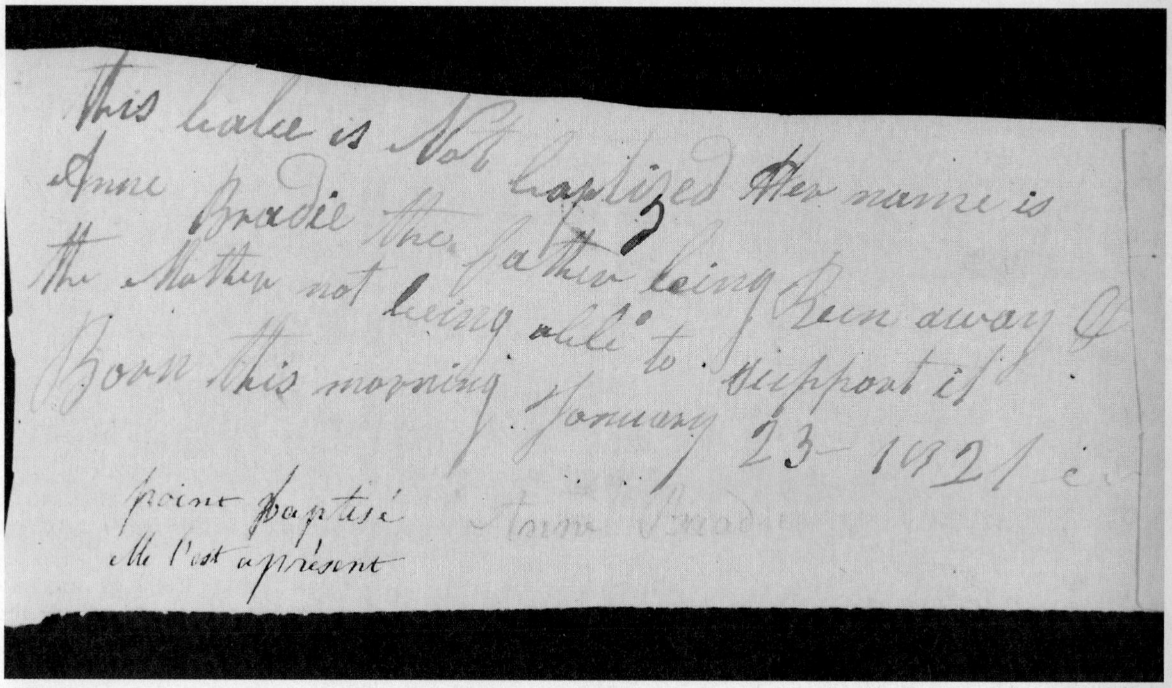
This babe is Not baptized Her name is Anne Bradie the father being run away & the Mother not being able to support it Born this morning January 23 1821
point baptisé
Ne l'est à présent
Anne Bradie

"This baby is not baptized. Her name is Anne Bradie, the father being run away," writes a desperate woman.

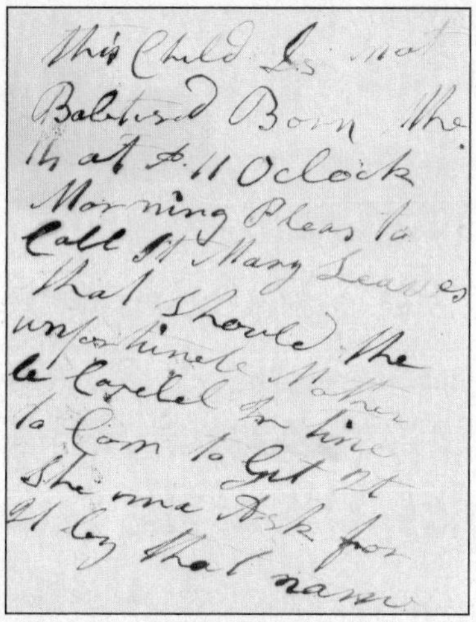
This Child Is not Babtised Born the [illegible] at 11 Oclock Morning Pleas to Call It Mary Leaves that Should the unfortunate Mother be Cared for hire to Com to Get it She may Ask for it by that name

A letter by another single mother.

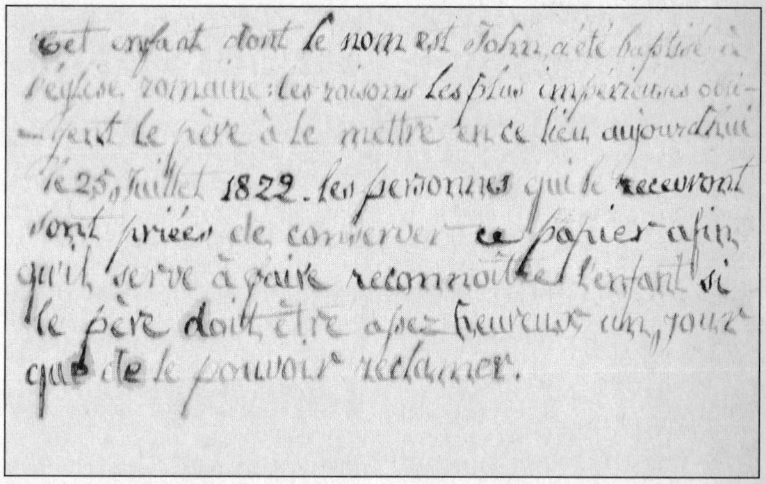
Cet enfant dont le nom est John, a été baptisé à l'église romaine: les raisons les plus impérieuses obligent le père à le mettre en ce lieu aujourd'hui le 25 juillet 1822. les personnes qui le recevront sont priées de conserver ce papier afin qu'il serve à faire reconnoître l'enfant si le père doit être assez heureux un jour que de le pouvoir réclamer.

Written by a French-Canadian father, letter says child must be given away.

Colonial Advocate slams government

May 18, 1824

QUEENSTON, Upper Canada – Eyes of newspaper readers opened wide with astonishment today with the appearance of a new paper called the *Colonial Advocate*. Published by William Lyon Mackenzie, it seems determined to take aim at the government and its friends. In the first edition of his newspaper, Mackenzie has accused the provincial authorities of corruption and patronage.

First canal on the St. Lawrence opens

September 1824

LACHINE, Lower Canada – After years of work, the first canal on the St. Lawrence River is open this summer, at Lachine.

River boatsmen are enjoying the "easy way around the rocks" this boating season, and for good reason. The Lachine lock means that a particularly rough section of portage has been eliminated. Instead of having to haul their freight – and then their boats – overland, the boatsmen can now sail into the lock, and let the water do the work of taking them from one level to another. Work on this lock was started by the French years ago, perhaps as early as 1700. But it was left to Britain's Royal Engineers to finish the difficult job. This year they did just that, bypassing the Lachine Rapids.

Work is also progressing on other locks on the St. Lawrence. Some people dream of the day when the entire length of the river will be passable without a single portage: a chain of locks from the sea to the Great Lakes.

First medical school opens in Montreal

Nov. 10, 1824

MONTREAL – Canada will have its first crop of domestically trained doctors in a few years with the official opening today of the colony's first school of medicine.

The Montreal Medical Institution is beginning its inaugural term, and 25 students have enrolled, hoping to fulfil their dream of becoming doctors, and taking the oath of Hippocrates after successfully passing their final examinations.

1825 (1825-1826)

London, October 1825. A Northwest Passage expedition that left in 1824 under William Parry returns. It reached Lancaster Sound, wintered at Point Bowen, and made important scientific observations.

Upper Canada, Dec. 30, 1825. The Assembly passes a resolution that Americans whose fathers or grandfathers were born British subjects will be considered British subjects as well.

Prince Town, Prince Edward Island, 1825. Presbyterian women found the Prince Town Female Society for Propogating the Gospel. Its missions include distributing Bibles to families of isolated fishermen.

Montreal, 1825. The lavish 1,000 seat Theatre Royal is completed, financed by investors led by John Molson, Sr.

Newfoundland, 1825. A coach road is opened between St. John's and Portugal Cove, the colony's first official highway.

Peterborough, Upper Canada, 1825. Peter Robinson settles some 2,000 Irish immigrants near the new town of Peterborough, which is named after him. The settlers are mostly young farmers and their families, and the community is an immediate success. The British government offered the immigrants free passage and settlement assistance as a way of dealing with mounting poverty and social unrest in Ireland.

Quebec, January 1826. The bilingual *Quebec Medical Journal*, founded by Dr. Xavier Tessier, begins publication. It is one of the first medical journals in Canada.

Northwest, February 1826. George Simpson is made governor of all Hudson's Bay Company Territory in North America.

Upper Canada, April 8, 1826. Joseph Pickering reports great flocks of pigeons flying northward. People kill hundreds of them daily with nets.

Arctic, July 7, 1826. John Franklin's British overland expedition to explore the north coast of the continent meets hostile Inuit near the mouth of the Mackenzie delta.

Upper Canada, 1826. A volunteer fire department is organized in York [Toronto].

Upper Canada, 1826. The first police office in the province opens.

North Pacific trading restrictions set

Feb. 28, 1825

ST. PETERSBURG, Russia – Britain and Russia today concluded an agreement putting restrictions on trading on the North Pacific coast. Russian diplomats claim a triumph. They have told the Russian American Fur Company that Russia has gained recognition to territory in North America, including a strip of land stretching down the coast to 54 degrees 40 minutes N. On the other hand, British diplomats and Hudson's Bay Company officials are pleased that the restrictions placed by the Russians on trading in the Pacific Northwest have been ended, in return for recognition of Russia's territorial claims.

An Inuit grave. The Inuit way of life is being influenced by the Europeans.

The agreement illustrates the problems facing the Hudson's Bay Company and other British fur traders in the land west of the Rockies and on the Pacific coast. The company wishes to trade from its string of posts on the Columbia to close to the Arctic coast. In the south, there are always threats from the ambitious Americans. In the north, there is the Russian American Fur Company. And the government in London is concerned about threats to the land it regards as British property. It has already mounted numerous expeditions to the Arctic to find a northern sea route to these territories.

Davidites start construction on temple in Upper Canada town

1825

SHARON, Upper Canada – "It is right to be delighted with the things of God," according to former Quaker David Willson. Expelled for his love of music and "spirit" by the elders and members of the church as "a wild man" 13 years ago, Willson and 32 Davidites have started constructing their temple in Sharon, 50 kilometres north of York [Toronto].

Believing that "God is peace" and at the centre of the divine-human soul, Willson's Children of Peace search for light or wisdom to find their Eden. The quest for inner light will be symbolized by the temple, which will have 2,952 panes of glass when finished. The three-storey structure will be made of wood. To stress the importance of music, a "Jacob's ladder" staircase will be made for the choir.

Settler buys Fort Douglas, site of the Seven Oaks Massacre

July 9, 1825

FORT DOUGLAS, Assiniboia – Four-hundred pounds is the price settler Robert Logan has paid for a 13-year-old fort that has withstood conflict and strife almost from the time it was built. Fort Douglas was built as Point Douglas in 1812 on the west bank of the Red River just below the spot where the Assiniboine River joins the Red. Three years later it was converted into a fort by adding a palisade and watchtower to provide a haven for the colonists in the event of an attack. Later, in anticipation of trouble from the Métis, logs were taken from Gibraltar, the North West Company post a mile upstream, and rafted down the river to be used to strengthen the fort.

A view of the area around Fort Douglas on the Red River in the summer.

It was here that the unfortunate Seven Oaks Massacre took place in 1816. Métis leader Cuthbert Grant took possession of the fort at that time. It was later recaptured and restored to the Hudson's Bay Company. Fort Douglas was the headquarters of the governor of Assiniboia, but now that the Hudson's Bay Company has bought back interests in the Red River valley, it has decided to sell the fort.

Intermarriage creates new society of Métis people

Governor's Métis son almost killed

Jan. 3, 1825

CARLTON HOUSE, Rupert's Land – The Métis son of Gov. Hogson was attacked at Carlton House and almost killed by Gustavas Aird, who was inebriated at the time of the assault. John Hogson is recovering from the incident.

Carlton House, built in 1790 on the bank of the Assiniboine River, stands on the new route from Fort Garry to the Hudson's Bay Company post at Edmonton. The first to travel this way was HBC governor George Simpson. He initiated the trail on his return journey from the Columbia River area where he had gone to reorganize the fur trade and to establish Fort Vancouver.

Alexander Ross retires to Red River with his Indian family

Alexander Ross's wife, an Okanagan Indian, is in the Red River colony.

1825

RED RIVER COLONY, Rupert's Land – Alexander Ross and his family are here to stay. Ross, always a believer in the settlement being a necessary oasis of permanency and civilized life in the vast wilderness, has brought his Okanagan princess and their children here so the youngsters can be educated.

Ross himself has been a schoolteacher in the past, as well as longtime fur trader. He joined the Pacific Fur Company in 1810 as a clerk and first served in Fort Astoria. When the fort was captured by the North West Company he became a trader in its employ. He later joined the Hudson's Bay Company. Ross was born in Scotland in 1783 and immigrated to this land.

Henrietta, one of Alexander Ross's children, also went to Red River.

White neighbors swindling Indians

1825

UPPER CANADA – Growing government interest in the [Lambton County] district has led to findings that Indians settled in the area have been swindled by unscrupulous white neighbors in recent years. More than 30 years ago, a band of Chippewas, numbering about 300, was brought to St. Mary's [Walpole] Island by the Indian Department; they had fought with the British in the American Revolution and received the island as reward.

Since then, they have been tricked and cajoled into giving away the island's best, most arable land. The region was, and still is, relatively unsettled. But its mild climate and rich, fertile soil make it an attractive region for agricultural development. Whites living in the area recognized the island's potential and fooled the Indians settled there, unaccustomed to the formalities of land transactions, into signing papers that, unbeknownst to them, were actually deeds. If they objected or refused to surrender their land after realizing the true nature of what they'd done, their protests fell on deaf ears and they were forcibly removed.

Earl offers solution to "alien question"

July 22, 1825

LONDON, England – The British colonial secretary, the Earl of Bathurst, has offered a way out of the citizenship issue that is causing social and political havoc in Canada. Under existing laws, American-born settlers are legally considered "aliens." That is, they can neither vote nor sit in the Assembly, nor can they legally own land. The dilemma has enraged the Americans who make up much of the population of Upper Canada.

In an attempt to resolve the "alien question," the earl has proposed that Americans should be confirmed in their right to hold property, but not to play a part in the electoral process. It's a solution that will probably please neither the aliens, nor those who distrust them.

Two chiefs of the Ottawa nation (or Odawa, as they prefer). Their tribes live in Michilimackinac, Lake Huron, and speak Algonquian languages.

Colony encourages Scots to emigrate

June 1826

CANADA – "Come to Canada, and find your fortune!" This is the promise being made to potential immigrants in the Scottish Highlands by both government and private charities, eager to assist in the populating of the new land.

There's also another reason: Scotland is changing. These days the landlords want to bring in sheep to profit from the wool trade. To do this, they often have to get rid of the poor tenant farmers living on their lands. One way to do this is to have these unfortunates leave, to seek their fortunes overseas.

Of course, it's not accurate to assume most Scottish immigrants have simply been dumped here by greedy landlords. In fact, the majority, no matter how poor, still manage to pay their own way to the new country. Of course, they can't afford to pay much, and so they don't get much in the way of onboard accommodations.

Often the quarters are nothing but bare walls in the hold of a ship designed to haul grain or wood. They have to bring their own food, and, as for sanitation – well, it's virtually non-existent.

Historic canoe route's time has gone

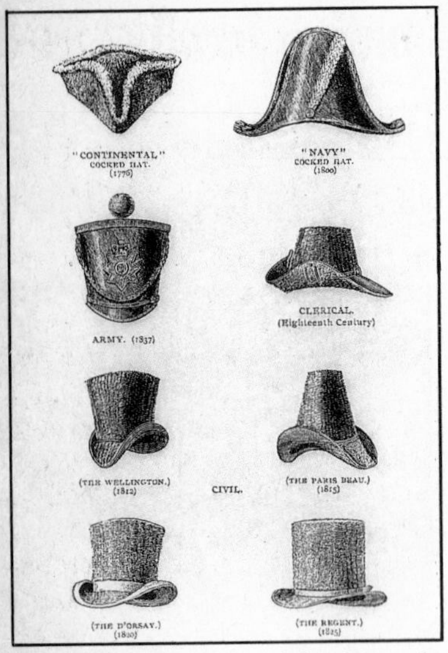

Beaver hats, product of the fur trade.

Traditional canoes are being replaced by York boats, wood-plank vessels.

Summer 1825

LACHINE, Que. – Since the merger of the Hudson's Bay Company and the North West Company four years ago, the historic canoe route between Montreal and the northwest through the Ottawa River has fallen into disuse.

Brigades of bark canoes still leave here for the head of Lake Superior in the spring, carrying mail and passengers into the fur country. But since the merger, most of the furs and bulky supplies travel inland to Lake Winnipeg from York Factory, the combined company's depot on Hudson Bay. Traditional canoes are being replaced by York boats, heavy, wood-plank vessels which can carry a much larger cargo with the same crew.

Rowing a York boat is no work for the feeble or faint-hearted; nor is manhandling the cumbersome craft down rapids and across portages. "The work is so laborious that some kill themselves by it," reports one veteran, "and many are sprung and so disabled that it makes old men of them before they come to the prime of life." For the most part, "tripmen" are Métis from the Red River colony who man the York boats every summer.

An express canoe leaving Lachine, with passengers going west, and three freight canoes are ready to set out.

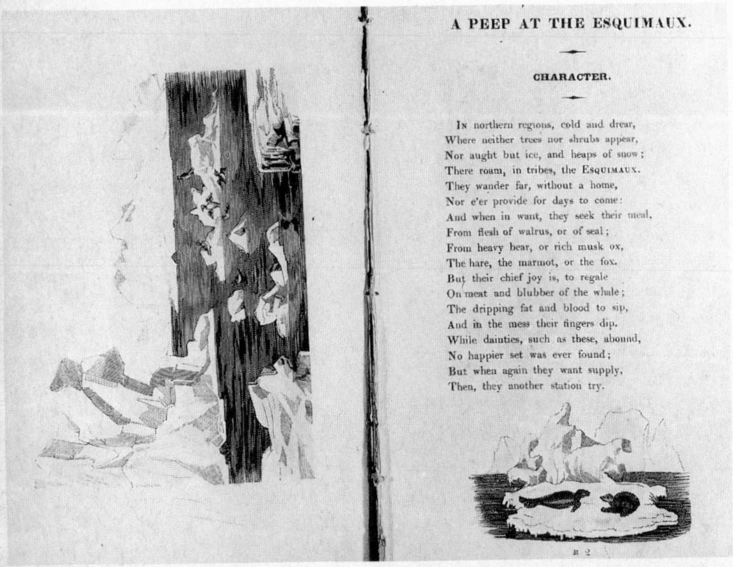

A PEEP AT THE ESQUIMAUX.

CHARACTER.

In northern regions, cold and drear,
Where neither trees nor shrubs appear,
Nor aught but ice, and heaps of snow;
There roam, in tribes, the Esquimaux.
They wander far, without a home,
Nor e'er provide for days to come:
And when in want, they seek their meal,
From flesh of walrus, or of seal;
From heavy bear, or rich musk ox,
The hare, the marmot, or the fox.
But their chief joy is, to regale
On meat and blubber of the whale;
The dripping fat and blood to sip,
And in the mess their fingers dip.
While dainties, such as these, abound,
No happier set was ever found;
But when again they want supply,
Then, they another station try.

B 2

A poem written about the Inuit way of life and their eating habits, "They wander far, without a home, Nor e'er provide for days to come: And when in want, they seek their meal, From flesh of walrus, or of seal. ..."

Council's members banking on success

Sept. 23, 1825

HALIFAX – A meeting of His Majesty's Council will look remarkably like a meeting of the board of Nova Scotia's first bank, incorporated today. Five partners of bank founder Enos Collins are members of the governing council, known as The Twelve.

Other members of The Twelve are either friends or relatives of the owners of the Halifax Banking Company, leaving the bank open to charges of too cosy a relationship with the Nova Scotia government. Located in an ironstone building on Water Street, the bank was established to provide capital for expansion of the province's economy.

Price drop rocks timber merchants

April 3, 1826

SAINT JOHN, N.B. – Timber merchants here are in a state of dismay as they learn that prices for their products have plunged. Reports from London and Liverpool say whole shiploads of timber docked there are worth next to nothing. The crisis is being brought about by a lack of buyers for shipbuilding material, which is in oversupply due to rampant speculation.

The timber and shipbuilding business is the lifeblood of the city, and the prosperity it has brought has created stark contrasts. While fine houses painted in bright colors line the hills, down by the teeming wharves filth and stench prevail.

Rumors are alreading circulating that British exporting houses will soon be looking to liquidate local companies to collect debts accumulated during the boom years.

Government sells ex-native territory to Canada Company

Aug. 19, 1826

LONDON, England – One million acres of Upper Canadian land have been sold by His Majesty's government to the Canada Company. The government recently purchased the block, located in the London and Western districts, from the Ojibwa Indians.

The sale – at a price so low it's really a transfer – comes just a few months after the British parliament created the Canada Company to sell land to settlers, land that has been improved with roads, canals, schools and other amenities. This way, the government rids itself of some of the day-to-day nuisances of opening up new territory. For Canada Company stockholders, the motive is simple: profit.

In addition to the million acres granted to the company, it also has rights to 1.4 million acres of "clergy reserves." These were previously set aside for the Church of England, the province's established religion. The church itself wishes to gain a profit by selling these lands through the Canada Company.

Flames devastate Miramichi region; at least 160 dead

Oct. 7, 1825

NEW BRUNSWICK – Scores of horror-stricken refugees are making their way down the Miramichi River today, survivors of a devasting fire that has turned more than 15,000 square kilometres of magnificent pine forest into a near lifeless, blackened wasteland. The tragic blaze has reduced countless farms and entire towns to ashes, and taken the lives of at least 160 men, women and children who were unable to escape the flames or drowned trying.

Counted among the losses are Douglastown, Newcastle, Moorfields and several other smaller settlements, all north or west of the Miramichi. All told, 595 buildings have been consumed. The fire has failed to leap the river's span, sparing the south side, but the blow it has dealt, economically, is massive: the forest has been the region's lifeblood, a natural resource that has made the district a prosperous world leader in lumber exports.

Sod-turning kicks off canal construction

Col. John By at the Rideau Canal site where construction began today.

Sept. 26, 1826

RIDEAU FALLS, Upper Canada – Construction began today on the Rideau Canal. Lord Dalhousie, governor of British North America, turned the first sod on the project at a small ceremony in Sleigh Bay on the Ottawa River opposite Wright's Town [Hull].

The entrance locks to the system will be built here next summer. A series of eight locks will carry boat traffic up to the height of land above the Rideau Falls. John By is in charge of the project. When completed, the canal will open a second route into Upper Canada from Montreal to Lake Ontario, in case invading Americans blockade the upper St. Lawrence River.

Fredericton native toasts frontier life in her second novel

1825

WATERTOWN, N.Y. – There is nothing like life on the range for Julia Beckwith. The Fredericton-born woman has just published her second novel, *Tonnewonte; or, the adopted son of America*, in which she celebrates the simple virtuous life of the American frontier family.

Beckwith is the author of the first novel written by a native-born Canadian, and the first published in Canada. *St. Ursula's Convent, or the nun of Canada*, was published last year in Kingston, even though Beckwith wrote it in Cornwallis and Fredericton 11 years ago when she was 17. The novel, based on the experiences of her cousin serving as a nun at the Hôtel-Dieu in Montreal, is full of romance, suspense, complicated plots and daring escapades. Critics said it was hard to follow, but still praised Beckwith as a literary pioneer. Beckwith handles suspense more skillfully and shows more depth of feeling in her second novel.

Travellers take chances with tavern food

1826

UPPER CANADA – Where does a weary traveller go for a good meal? Coming from the uninitiated searching for sustenance and rest after a long day, the question invites pity, or possibly derision, for it begs the impossible (barring an invitation for a home-cooked meal).

The tavern is the inevitable, often only option. According to one traveller, one can expect "fried beef or pork, pickles and preserves, teacakes and butter," with no guarantee of quality, all for [19 cents]. Fishcakes and fried bread are common fare. Fortunately, when the food seems almost too bad to swallow, one can always indulge in beer, whiskey or cider to chase it down.

Hudson's Bay Co. traders transport leather through [Yellowhead Pass].

Franklin abandons expedition to Arctic

Aug. 18, 1826

RETURN REEF, Arctic Ocean – A deeply disappointed John Franklin has decided to abandon his attempt to reach Point Barrow along the frozen shore of the Arctic Ocean. The British explorer descended the Mackenzie River to his base camp on Great Bear Lake last summer, planning this season to survey the Arctic coastline westward to a planned rendezvous with the naval vessel *Blossom*, which has entered the Arctic through the Bering Strait. The expedition is part of a larger attempt to find a northwest passage across the top of America.

The 16 members of Franklin's party reached this island after a harrowing six-week journey down the coast. Battered by wind and freezing rains, the men had to work their longboats across ice floes and between the shallow islands that line the shore. A heavy, wet fog reduced visibility almost to zero, and in the end it was this fog which forced Franklin to turn back. After seven days on the island, unable to proceed through the thick mist, the commander decided he could not risk losing the boats and being stranded on the coast with no way of getting back to his base.

View of the base camp established by John Franklin on Great Bear Lake.

1827 (1827-1828)

Kingston, Upper Canada, Sept. 17, 1827. A riot occurs during a procession of Orangemen, pitting Protestants against Catholics.

Upper Canada, Sept. 26, 1827. The Earl of Dalhousie, governor-in-chief of British North America, lays the cornerstone of the Rideau Canal.

Quebec, 1827. Printers found the Quebec Typographical Society to fight for better conditions, one of the first trade unions in Canada.

Montreal, 1827. The Beaver Club closes. Since 1785, it has embraced the heart of Montreal high society. Membership has been restricted to fur traders, mainly from the North West Company, with ships' captains and army officers as honorary members.

Canada, 1827. There are 49 post offices in Lower Canada, and 65 in Upper Canada.

British North America, 1827. The first temperance societies in the colonies are formed in Montreal, and Pictou County, Nova Scotia. They tolerate moderate use of beer and wine.

Lake Erie, 1827. Three ships are wrecked in the same place off Long Point in 1827.

Upper Canada, 1827. Anglican minister John Strachan persuades the British government to let the Upper Canadian Anglican Church sell a quarter of the Clergy Reserves, public lands reserved in 1791 for the "Protestant clergy," a phrase then intended to apply to the Church of England.

Upper Canada, March 20, 1828. The Legislative Assembly adopts an address to the king that declares only a small part of the population belongs to the Church of England, defends Methodist preachers, and recommends the clergy reserves be used for education and internal improvements, rather than to support the Church of England.

Upper Canada, May 22, 1828. The Episcopal Methodist churches of Canada and the U.S. separate.

Newfoundland, July 13, 1828. Ann Harvey, her father, and brother rescue 152 people when a Quebec-bound ship wrecks off Newfoundland.

Lower Canada, 1828. Petitioners question the election of the previous year in Quebec Upper Town because a widow was refused the right to vote.

King's College receives royal charter

March 31, 1827

YORK – Higher education has finally come to this pioneer capital. Thanks to the tireless efforts of Rev. John Strachan, the king has granted a royal charter for King's College [later the University of Toronto] in York.

Strachan, a powerful member of the appointed government, is a champion of the Church of England. A fervent (and some would say reactionary) patriot, he has been working to create a church-based school system in the province for years. The charter for King's College, criticized by many as an outline for an Anglicans-only university, is more liberal than one might expect. Students of all denominations will be admitted.

King's College receives royal charter to operate in Upper Canada's capital.

Farmer charged for hoisting American flag

Sept. 25, 1827

FREDERICTON – A Maine farmer was charged today with conspiracy and sedition for planting an American flag in Madawaska. It's the latest salvo in a simmering border dispute between British and American officials. Charged is John Baker, leader of a Maine political party that refuses British territorial claims defining the New Brunswick-Maine border. Confounding the issue are the vague terms in the Treaty of Ghent.

Fort Vancouver, the capital of the great domain known as the "Western" department of the Hudson's Bay Company, located on the Columbia River.

St. Patrick's parade "wild, roisterous"

March 17, 1828

BYTOWN [Ottawa] – The city's reputation as "a wild and roisterous place" has been confirmed by this year's St. Patrick's Day parade and donnybrook in the Corktown slum. To celebrate their day, 200 laborers – "all drunk, dancing and fighting" – killed one man and seriously injured many others. The Irish live on Crown land near the Rideau Canal in Corktown which is just "two rows of cabins in the swamp."

Frequent patrons of Mother McGinty's tavern, the Irish Shiners, who work on the canal, are the sworn foes of the French-Canadian lumbermen known as Grangers. The exact origin of the term Shiner is unclear. Some say it refers to Irishmen's shiny temples and their greasy, slicked backed hair. Others claim that publicans would serve them only after they had paid for their drinks with a British half crown, called a Shiner. Or Shiner may be an anglicization of the French *les cheneurs,* cutters of oak.

"Jimmy the Wren," a "dead shot with a stone," and his mates terrorize Lower Town, separated from Scottish Upper Town by the canal and a half-mile wide common. The two parts of Bytown were joined by a bridge built in 1827.

HBC founds Fort Langley on the Fraser

July 27, 1827

FORT LANGLEY, Fraser River – The sailing schooner *Cadboro*, under the command of chief factor James McMillan, arrived here today with 25 men and supplies to begin constructing a new trading post for the Hudson's Bay Company. About 50 kilometres upstream from the mouth of the Fraser River, at the highest point of navigation for ships, the post is expected to be the company's major trading depot in this part of the world. It will be named for HBC director Thomas Langley.

The report of an expedition sent in 1824 to investigate the lower Fraser River convinced HBC Gov. George Simpson the waterway will become "the grand communication with all our establishments on this side of the mountain."

Fort Langley is the first post built by the HBC west of the Rockies since it absorbed the North West Company in 1821, and one of several planned for the Pacific coast. The company hopes that a string of trading forts will break the hold of American and Russian traders here. The site is blessed with nearby meadows suited to farming and is close to native fishing villages where the Indians congregate for the salmon run every year.

Central Agricultural Society established

March 1827

PRINCE EDWARD ISLAND – Gov. John Ready has succeeded in establishing a Central Agricultural Society for Prince Edward Island. The popular Ready has been a tireless promoter of the Island's agriculture since his arrival in 1824. He has imported, at his own expense, various thoroughbred animals in an attempt to improve the colony's breeding stock. The governor's support and enthusiasm come at a crucial time. Of late there have been severe criticisms of the colony's farming practices. "The settlers are both indolent and ignorant farmers," one critic writes. The new society has promised to "extend the knowledge and practice of the best and most espoused modes of agriculture."

Anglican minister calls for state church

May 16, 1827

LONDON, England – Rev. John Strachan, a politically powerful Upper Canadian Anglican minister, has issued a rebuttal to members of Parliament here who object to the Anglican church being held as Upper Canada's official church.

In his response, Strachan claims settlers would flock to the church if given a chance, because wherever new ones opened, people deserted other faiths such as Methodism in droves. Strachan also says most non-Anglican ministers in Canada are disloyal to the Crown. As well, he says, his church has more ministers than any of the province's other popular sects. Strachan's claims are sure to raise laughter when they're heard in Upper Canada since most settlers aren't Anglican.

Law settles thorny land rights dilemma

May 28, 1827

YORK – The rights of Americans to live, vote and own land in Canada have been resolved ... at least for those who were already here before 1820. Under a law that received royal assent today, anyone who has a land grant from the government, or held a public office, or sworn an oath of allegiance to the Crown before 1820, is now considered to be a British citizen. Other Americans will be given the same rights after residing in Canada seven years.

This legislation overrides the bill passed last year, which would have forced American-born settlers to register with the government in order to own property. That law, in turn, was the result of an ongoing fight about who in Canada is and isn't a full-fledged citizen, with all the rights that entails.

A view of the Rocky Mountains from the Columbia River, looking northwest. This range is the Canadian part of North America's largest mountain range. Alexander Mackenzie was the first to cross the Rocky Mountains.

Another view of the Rocky Mountains, where Simon Fraser established the first trading post at Hudson's Hope in 1805. This mountain range extends 1,200 kilometres from U.S. borders at [British Columbia] and [Alberta].

Illustration of the Leather Pass in the Rocky Mountains. The Canadian Rockies of song and painting are in the main ranges, near routes that go through two mountain passes. These passes mark the continental divide.

Simpson arrives at Fort St. James

Sept. 17, 1828

FORT ST. JAMES, New Caledonia – Sir George Simpson, governor of the Hudson's Bay Company, arrived here today on his way to Fort Langley on the Fraser route to the sea. Simpson left York Factory on July 12, and, say *voyageurs* in the party, made sure everyone kept up the cracking pace he loves so well. Simpson saw to it that all those in the expedition were woken at two in the morning and travelled for six hours before breakfast. But he does not believe in too much hardship, and brought his "country wife" Margaret Taylor along.

People in the fort here on Stuart Lake knew Simpson was close when they heard gunfire, then a bugle and bagpipes. As the party came near they could see a guide, bearing the British ensign, the band, then Simpson, Dr. Richard Hamlyn and chief factor Archibald McDonald and the rest of the party on foot. James Douglas, in charge of the fort, greeted Simpson.

Fort St. James founder James Douglas welcomes Governor George Simpson.

Stunt has animals going over the falls

Sept. 8, 1827

STAMFORD [Niagara Falls] – A rotting Great Lakes schooner named *Michigan* was pushed over the falls with a cargo of wild animals today, all for the entertainment of 15,000 to 30,000 people and for the profit of three hotel owners who staged the stunt. William (Colonel) Forsyth, who got his financial start from smuggling, got together with John Brown, a rival Canadian innkeeper, and American counterpart Parkhurst Whitney on this venture.

The trio had advertised that they were trying to obtain "animals of the most ferocious kind, such as panthers, wild cats and wolves." As it turned out, they included a buffalo, two small bears, two raccoons, a dog and a goose. The bears, loose on deck, jumped overboard and swam to Goat Island. The others went over the falls, all dying in the loud crash except the goose, which struggled ashore.

College established in New Brunswick

1828

FREDERICTON – Years of effort and saving have paid off with the dedication of New Brunswick's first college. King's College has just been granted a royal charter culminating a drive that began back in 1785 when loyalists here first petitioned then-governor Thomas Carleton for a college.

It wasn't until some eight years ago that the community started to put aside the funds for the institution, and that was only possible because of the prosperity brought by the booming lumber business. The British government, which collects timber trade revenues, allotted $1,000 annually toward the college and agreed to pay half the cost of the college building.

Financing was not the only obstacle in the would-be college's path. Lt.-Gov. Howard Douglas had to get Anglican administrators of the college to agree that students wouldn't be required to subscribe to tenets of Anglican faith in order to be granted admission.

Work completed on York General Hospital

1828

YORK – The York General Hospital is now a *fait accompli*. Construction of the facility, Upper Canada's largest, began in 1820, but when fire destroyed the Parliament buildings four years ago the government temporarily relocated its offices in the unfinished building. Finally, the hospital stands ready to be used as originally intended and can accommodate as many as 100 patients.

The establishment of a civilian hospital, complete with civilian doctors, reflects the political and demographic evolution currently under way in Upper Canada. For years the province's health care has been in the hands of the military. But since the end of the War of 1812, thousands of immigrants have arrived while Britain's military commitment in British North America has remained static at best. This is causing responsibility for public health care to shift from Britain over to the province itself.

York General Hospital is ready to open, accommodating up to 100 patients.

Baptist community academy unveiled

1828

WOLFVILLE, N.S. – The Baptist community has taken a big step forward toward the goal of a full-fledged university, with the opening of a new academy here. Horton Academy is the project of the Baptist Education Society, a group which has split with the Church of England.

Not everyone is pleased with the opening of the break-away academy. Lt.-Gov. Lord Dalhousie has been trying to restrain the establishment of small denominational colleges in the belief they hinder the development of a comprehensive higher education system in Nova Scotia. Under existing laws, the House of Assembly will not provide financial grants to denominational schools. A Protestant group, however, has convinced the Assembly to provide grants for Pictou Academy, but not permanent endowment.

The spread of denominational colleges highlights the clash of religious factions in the province.

Lord Dalhousie's proposal: assimilate the Indians

September 1828

QUEBEC CITY – Gov. Gen. Lord Dalhousie has recommended that the British government work toward the assimilation of the Canadian Indians, as Britain's former military allies no longer are able to support themselves. The example of the Methodist Indian mission at the Credit River, 20 kilometres west of York, proves that wandering hunters can be transformed into successful Christian farmers. The Mississauga converts now live in log cabins. They have short hair, the men wear coats and trousers, they go to church and the children attend school.

The governor general now hopes to duplicate the Methodist success story. He wants to foster in the Canadian Indian, "a love of the country, of the soil on which they are settled and a respect for the government which protects them." Dalhousie's scheme would be financed from the annual payments given for the previous sale of their lands, and from any future sales and leases.

While supportive of Dalhousie's plan, Indian Department officials do not want the Methodists and their Indian workers to run the new program. They regard the Methodists as subversive plotters determined to bring Upper Canada into the American union. Was not the parent body of the Upper Canadian Methodists the American Methodist Episcopal Church?

Dalhousie leaves Quebec for England this month en route to India, where he will take up his new duties as the commander-in-chief of the army. His successor as governor general, Sir James Kempt, will be sworn in shortly after Dalhousie departs for Europe.

Britain wants to assimilate Indians like Nicholas Vincent Iswanhonhi.

Red Lake chief speaks to governor of Red River settlement at Fort Douglas.

A view of Selkirk, [Manitoba], an Indian settlement on the Red River.

Timber exports up thanks to British

1827

BRITISH NORTH AMERICA – Exporting timber is big business in British North America, thanks in large part to the British government. Colonial exports of wood have increased steadily since 1809, when Britain began imposing stiff tariffs on all foreign timber imported into the country except that coming from the colonies. The English wanted to safeguard their timber supplies for the Royal Navy and construction during the Napoleonic Wars by developing colonial timber production. Since the wars ended, they've let preferential duties continue, with changes. Two years ago, an economic downturn in Britain led to a slowdown in the timber industry here in British North America.

Colborne new governor of Upper Canada

Nov. 4, 1828

YORK – Sir John Colborne has succeeded Sir Peregrine Maitland as governor of Upper Canada. Colborne, who joined the British army when he was 16 years old, fought in the French Revolutionary and Napoleonic wars. At the Battle of Waterloo, where Colborne commanded the 52nd Regiment, he greatly distinguished himself. In particular, he is credited with being mainly responsible for the rout of Napoleon's old guard.

Colborne, 50, also served as lieutenant-governor of Guernsey for seven years, until his present appointment. His accomplishments in Guernsey included the restoration of Elizabeth College.

Townsfolk outraged by tar-feather case

Aug. 24, 1827

HAMILTON – A tar and feather case coming to trial today is causing an outrage here. A particularly cruel punishment quite popular in the United States, tarring and feathering is also sometimes inflicted here in Canada by mobs punishing real or imagined crimes.

The victim, often "convicted" by the mob of a perceived moral crime, is placed in front of the fire as the pine tar is melted. When it comes to a boil the unfortunate is stripped to his waist – or further – and the tar is poured over his body. Then, adding insult to injury, feathers are added. Removing the tar can take weeks and is almost as painful, because the skin peels off with it.

Galt gives his OK to roadside taverns

1827

HURON TRACT – Taverns to provide beds and meals for travellers, and shelter for their animals, will be built along the Huron Road. Canada Company superintendent John Galt has described plans for three such taverns, which he calls "houses of entertainment."

The first tavern will be 32 kilometres west of Springer's in Blenheim, and the second and third will be at subsequent 32-kilometre intervals, a convenient distance between stops for travellers the difficult roads oblige to move at a very slow pace. To get the project going, Galt has appointed Col. Anthony Van Egmond the honorary agent for the Canada Company and asked him to obtain the innkeepers, who will be paid a £40 bonus.

1829

New Brunswick, Jan. 1. Governor Howard Douglas opens King's College, the first institution of higher learning in the colony.

Lower Canada, Feb. 7. The legislature passes an act authorizing a Jewish religious corporation, with many powers for its ministers to celebrate marriages, to keep civil registers, and to acquire property for religious purposes.

England, May 23. John Ross leads an expedition to find the Northwest Passage via Lancaster Sound and Prince Regent Inlet.

Montreal, Dec. 23. Merchants meet to protest against the possibility of Britain opening the West Indies to American trade. Opening the West Indies would destroy Canada's privileged trade position.

Upper Canada, December. Tekarihogen, also known as John Brant, Mohawk chief and superintendent of the Six Nations of the Grand River, writes to Governor Colborne: "the dam thrown across the Grand River by the Welland Canal Company has overflowed the Indian Cornfields their Crops laid waste and their winters provision destroyed."

Upper Canada. The Methodist newspaper *Christian Guardian* begins publication with Egerton Ryerson as editor. It is initially confined to religious and moral questions, like the temperance movement, but soon becomes political.

Montreal. Notre-Dame Church is completed, a gothic revival church built to serve the congregation of St-Sulpice. Its innovative design by New York architect James O'Donnell is unique on the continent.

Upper Canada. John McTaggart reports on the houses in the colony: "The orders of architecture baffle all description; everyone builds his cottage or house according to his fancy."

Sable Island. Thomas Haliburton reports that each year lighthouse keepers kill whelping seals on the island with long spiked clubs.

Lower Canada. The government refuses an American request to extradite an escaped Illinois slave on the grounds that his offence does not make him liable to arrest in Canada. Legislative and judicial action has made slavery virtually defunct in British North America.

Welland Canal links two Great Lakes

The Ann and Jane is one of two ships taken up the Niagara Escarpment.

A view of the Welland Canal, which links Lakes Erie and Ontario.

Nov. 29, 1829

PORT COLBORNE, Upper Canada – Niagara Falls has been defeated! After five years of hard work, the Welland Canal, linking Lakes Erie and Ontario, is open. The honors took place today, when two ships, the *Ann and Jane* and the *R.H. Broughton,* were taken south, up the Niagara Escarpment, to Lake Erie.

The Welland Canal consists of 34 locks; water-filled compartments allow ships to "step" their way up or down steep elevations. Each timber-built compartment is 30 metres long and 6.6 metres wide, with a depth of more than 2.1 metres. With this much space, all sorts of passenger and freight ships can move between the lakes, totally bypassing Niagara Falls.

The history of the canal is a long one, first dreamt of by early pioneers who had to portage their goods up the escarpment. The Welland Canal Company had to wait until 1823 to be incorporated by the legislature. This private enterprise, first put forward by William Hamilton Merritt, one of its incorporators, ran into thousands of problems as it progressed. First costed at £40,000, the project eventually came in at £300,000.

Still, the Welland Canal is a big boost for the St. Lawrence-Great Lakes shipping route.

Northwest Passage expedition sails into Prince Regent Inlet

Aug. 11, 1829

SOMERSET ISLAND, Arctic Circle – The steamer *Victory* has just sailed into Prince Regent Inlet here with the Northwest Passage expedition commanded by Capt. John Ross on board. Ross plans to sail south, take on extra provisions from the *Fury,* abandoned in 1825 by the Parry expedition, and then find a place to winter.

Ross has been under a cloud since his return from an 1818 expedition in which, critics claim, he turned back after entering Lancaster Sound. Ross says a range of mountains blocked the channel, but critics believe they were a mirage and an excuse to abandon the expedition. Now, Ross hopes to restore his reputation.

John Ross's depiction of his meeting with the natives of Prince Regent Inlet appeared in A Voyage of Discovery, published soon after his 1818 expedition.

Last known Beothuk Indian in Newfoundland dies

Such a scene may no longer be possible now that Beothuks appear to be gone.

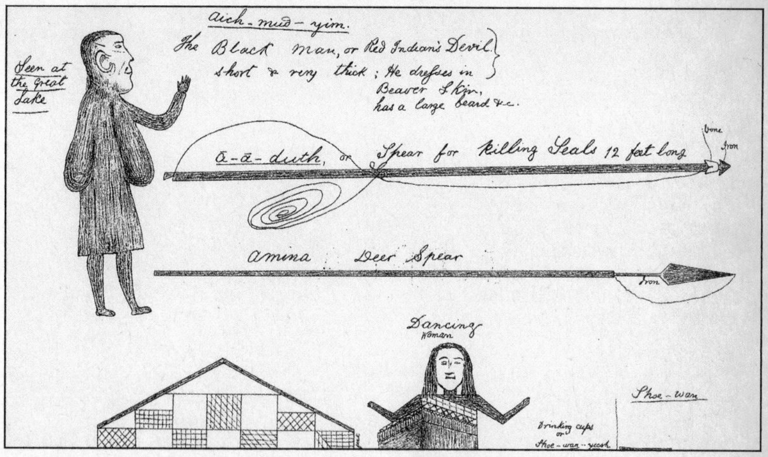

Drawing by Shanawdithit illustrates the old way of life of the Beothuks.

June 6, 1829

ST. JOHN'S, Nfld. – Shanawdithit, the last known survivor of this island's native Beothuk Indians, died here today at the age of 23. She succumbed to tuberculosis, commonly known as consumption, as had the two native women captured with her in 1823.

Shanawdithit worked as a servant in a British settler's household until 1823, when she was brought to St. John's by concerned members of the new Beothuk Institute. Believing she was the last of her people, they encouraged her to compose a vocabulary and to illustrate through pictures a now vanished way of life. Shanawdithit did as her mentors proposed. She also revealed how Beothuks had long mistrusted and feared the Europeans who for centuries encroached on their hunting and fishing grounds, first coming as summer fishermen in the 1500s, but within a century, becoming fur trappers during the winter months as well.

When conflicts developed over such things as the disappearance of fishermen's equipment, there were neither missionaries to act as intermediaries nor government officials to enforce British law. The result was chronic violence. Britain did eventually establish an official presence, but attempts to end mistrust by capturing and befriending Beothuks backfired. The rewards offered for captives prompted fur trappers to murder those who resisted kidnapping. But even Beothuks who eluded capture were no more able than Shanawdithit to resist the ravages of the white man's diseases.

Though it is widely believed that Shanawdithit was the last of her people, it is possible that two or three Beothuk might now be living with the Micmac Indians in southern Newfoundland.

Mary March, a Beothuk woman.

Two commissioners at Canada Co. helm

Jan. 2, 1829

YORK – The Canada Company, which owns 2.4 million acres of unsettled land, has thrown out its sole superintendent in favor of two commissioners. Gone today is John Galt, the man who helped pull this enterprise together a few years ago. In his place is one boss, and one figurehead. Thomas Mercer Jones is the boss, and the Hon. William Allen, president of the Bank of Upper Canada, is the figurehead designed to keep the financial community breathing easy about the company. Insiders in Canada are saying Jones has been instructed not to spend a penny more without the explicit orders of the company's head office in London.

Upper Canada thief banished for 7 years

Aug. 1, 1829

YORK – Harsh justice continues today in this capital of Upper Canada, with news that the courts have sentenced a thief to seven years banishment. It is yet another example of the antiquated savagery of British justice. In this province, a man convicted of grand larceny can expect to be branded; yes, branded, with a red-hot iron on his hand. Petty larceny can bring a public whipping. Those convicted of more heinous crimes can often expect the death penalty.

Without a doubt, the main purpose of such punishments, beyond crude retribution, is to set an example to the populace that criminal activities will not be tolerated.

Boothians and their snow cottages, in the [Northwest Territories]. This year, explorer John Ross took an expedition financed by wealthy distiller Felix Booth to the [Boothia Peninsula], where this group of Inuit lives. It is not known if Ross met them, as he has not been heard from since his departure.

1830 (1830-1831)

Brockville, Jan. 1, 1830. Ogle Gowan founds the Grand Lodge of Orangemen of British North America, a pro-British anti-Catholic organization composed mainly of Irishmen. The Protestant lodges provide mutual aid and organize social events.

Prince Edward Island, April 28, 1830. Catholic Emancipation Act is adopted, freeing Catholics from most civil disabilities. It gives them the right to vote, and the Island's electorate is transformed.

Lower Canada, Oct. 19, 1830. The secretary to the governor notifies Samuel Hart, a Jew, that the Executive Council has refused him an appointment as Justice of the Peace on the grounds that a Jew could not take the oath of qualification.

Quebec, 1830. The first steam railway in British North America is a small line to carry stone from the wharves at Cape Diamond to the Citadel.

Newfoundland, 1830. Some 290 ships carry 5,735 Newfoundland sealers to the ice around the island each spring.

Lower Canada, Jan. 31, 1831. Jews present a petition to the Legislative Assembly arguing they have been deprived of civil rights accorded to other British subjects in the colony, and asking that the situation be rectified.

Upper Canada, Feb. 8, 1831. The British government informs the government of Upper Canada that judges can no longer sit in Canadian executive or legislative councils, except the chief justice, who will continue to sit in the legislative council.

St Andrew's, Prince Edward Island, Nov. 30, 1831. St. Andrew's College, the first Catholic college in the Atlantic provinces, opens in the residence of Angus MacEachern, bishop of Charlottetown.

Upper Canada, Dec. 13, 1831. The Assembly votes to expel reformer William Lyon Mackenzie in retaliation for his criticism of the government.

Lower Canada, 1831. French philosopher Alexis de Tocqueville interviews habitants around Quebec and finds them worried about immigration, and resentful of the seigneurs and clergy.

Upper Canada, 1831. Upper Canada College is founded as a state institution.

Moravian mission to bring Jesus to Inuit

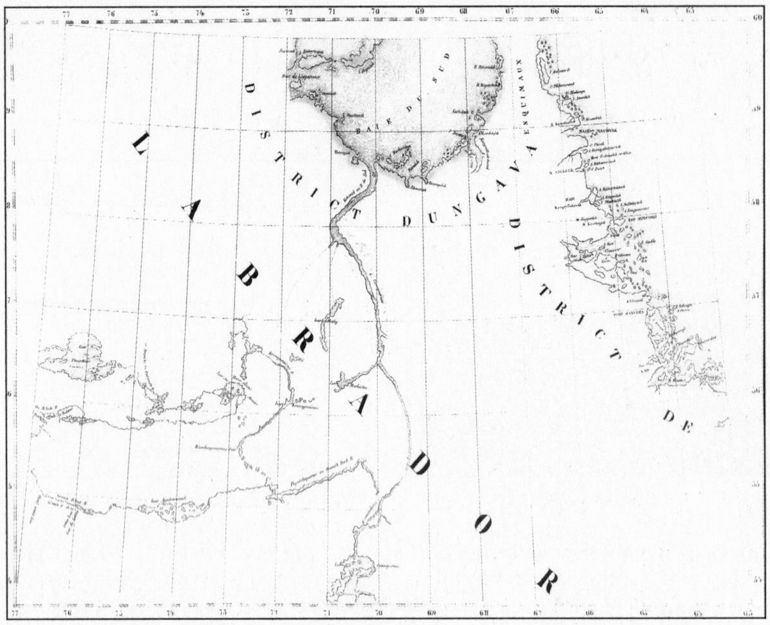

Map of a part of Labrador where the Moravian church is increasing its work.

These Inuit are building a snowhut; Moravians have other projects planned.

July 28, 1830

HEBRON, Labrador – The Moravian church is increasing its services to the Inuit people of Labrador and has just opened its fourth mission in this small community on the coast. Jens Haven opened the first Moravian missionary post in 1771 at Nain, 190 kilometres to the south. Over the next 13 years, Haven established other posts on the coast. At these missions, dedicated to bringing the name of Jesus to the Inuit, the Moravians have built – or plan to build – churches, schools, hospitals, workshops and stores.

The Inuit of Labrador are proud, independent people who live by hunting whales and other large sea mammals, and by fishing. Their reliance on their own devices appeals to the adherents of a religion like that of the Moravian church.

Moravians, who come from central Europe, maintain that theirs is the original Protestant church, in existence before Luther challenged the Catholic church. They believe in service and the need to spread the gospel of Jesus, and have opened branches of the church in Europe and mission posts abroad. The money for the opening of the mission in Labrador came from British branches of the church as part of their avowed support for the foreign mission program.

Citizens and troops play wicket on ice

Feb. 24, 1831

HALIFAX – Large parties of townsfolk and the military have enjoyed the healthy and spirit-stirring game of wicket on the ice at the head of the North West Arm this week. The game, also known as ricket, is played by any number of skaters, who propel a ball or round object with crooked sticks.

They attack or defend goals marked by cobblestones frozen on the ice about 1.2 metres apart and about the same distance apart as wickets in cricket. The side counting a pre-selected number wins.

Officers of the British garrison and Royal Navy are proficient skaters. Whenever the ball is put through a goal, the sound of "game ho" resounds from shore to shore.

York-based bank targeting laborers

June 5, 1830

YORK – In a move to encourage thrift and industry in the lower classes, a group of publicly-minded individuals has banded together to form the Home District Savings Bank.

The bank is aimed at journeymen tradesmen, mechanics, servants and other such laborers of small means. It's meant to encourage them to "make a provision for times of need," says a bank handbill. Deposits can be as small as one shilling and threepence.

Curry spices up life for the upper class

1831

QUEBEC CITY – Curry was only imported to Canada in the beginning of this century, but it has grown in popularity among the British upper class here. This year, the Quebec Driving Club has even included a curry recipe on the menu for one of its banquets. The mixture of spices called "curry" comes from the same tradition as French fine spices such as ginger, pepper and cinnamon, which date back to the Middle Ages.

Colonials, Indians treat their women differently

Men rule the roost, Papineau tells wife

Does Louis-Joseph Papineau believe women are subordinate to men?

Feb. 15, 1830

LOWER CANADA – Was Louis-Joseph Papineau, leader of the Parti Patriote, serious when he wrote his wife a letter quoting St. Paul's epistle to the Ephesians about the role of women, and expressing his own belief that women ought to be subject to the "absolute authority" of their husbands?

In the 1820s, Papineau and other Lower Canadian reformers supported the ideal of votes for women. Could it be that he has changed his mind since then?

Iroquois females hold a position of prestige in their society

An illustration of a Micmac Indian woman living in Nova Scotia.

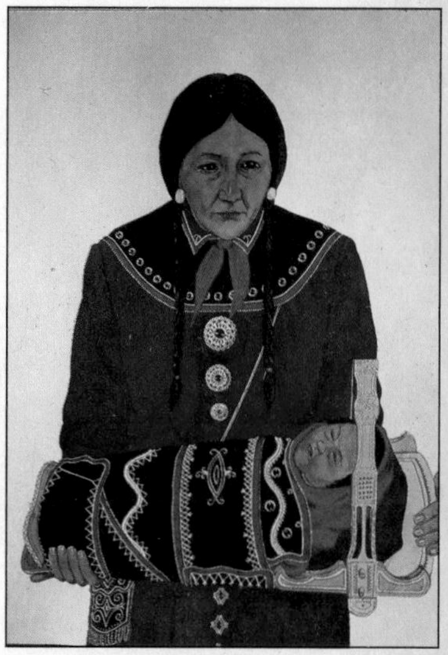

An Iroquois clan mother, who holds much power with her Indian tribe.

1830

GRAND RIVER, Upper Canada – Few settlers in Upper Canada realize the influence and the respect that Six Nations of Iroquois women enjoy in their own society. Pioneer women have no vote, but Iroquois women do, and in fact, they themselves select the Iroquois Confederacy's political leaders.

The Six Nations Indians have organized their society on a clan basis, tracing their descent through the female line. In the Iroquois family the children belong to their mother's clan, and not to their father's. As outsiders, the fathers have no voice in the selection of the political leader of their wife's and their children's clan. The senior women of each clan alone have that privilege. Whenever one of the 49 chiefs of the Iroquois Confederation Council dies, the senior women of his clan nominate his successor. In their society, Iroquois women occupy a position of prestige and are respected by their husbands.

The respect enjoyed by Iroquois women from their husbands is confirmed by Mary Jemison, a white girl captured in 1755 at the age of 12 who has spent the rest of her life living among the Iroquois. A few years ago the then elderly woman described her late Iroquois husband in these words: "During the term of nearly 50 years that I lived with him, I received, according to Indian customs, all the kindness and attention that was my due as his wife. ... He uniformly treated me with tenderness, and never offered an insult." Oh, that all the settlers' wives could claim as much!

Impartial judiciary another step closer

Feb. 2, 1831

YORK – The push for an impartial judiciary, free from political ambition or interference, scored a major victory today.

The British government has announced that it will "nominate no judge to the executive or legislative councils (the appointed bodies which run the province), except the chief justice ... for the purpose of giving legal advice in framing the laws." This is a definite victory for the reformers!

Commercial centre of Montreal isolated in its own province

June 1831

MONTREAL – A paradox is Montreal, at least in commercial terms. It is far more powerful than York, in terms of its commerce and wealth. Yet its bankers and merchants lack in part the power the same group has in the Upper Canadian capital. The explanation lies in the nature of Lower Canada, where the majority of merchants and bankers are English, but where increasingly, those elected to the Assembly are – by-and-large – French. Because of this, the English have remained more isolated from the levers of power. Even with their appointments and deals, they can't get control of the society.

The Assembly in Lower Canada: Its members are by-and-large French.

More and more American slaves fleeing north

Former slave and early black settler in Upper Canada is dead

A view of Brockville, Upper Canada, where many black ex-slaves settled.

Nov. 5, 1830

BROCKVILLE, Upper Canada – Former slave Henry Floyd, one of Upper Canada's earliest black settlers, died in Brockville today. Floyd, known as Black Harry, was born on the west coast of Africa.

Many blacks who settled here were ex-slaves who served in the military in the American Revolution, and in return were given their freedom. Blacks are coming to the forefront more now that the anti-slavery movement is growing and there's more migration from American states where slavery is legal.

Indian Department reorganization includes new reserve system

April 13, 1830

YORK – A system of reserves was established today for Indians in Upper Canada, in which land will be set aside for their use. The action is the first step in the reorganization of the Indian Department, which has been transferred by the colonies' secretary of state to civil authorities in the two Canadian provinces. In Upper Canada, James Givins was appointed superintendent of Indian Affairs. He had previously served as an Indian agent and later superintendent in York since 1797.

The establishment of the reserves and reorganization of Indian affairs come at a time when the province is at a crossroads in its approach to native people. Indians had been valuable allies during the War of 1812, but now in peace their military importance has been diminished. In fact, some hard-liners had urged that the Indian Department be abolished and native people abandoned. However, the new regime has been given a mandate to civilize the Indian tribes.

Editor of Canadian Freeman still in jail

Jan. 21, 1831

YORK – Despite a near-unanimous motion passed by the Assembly demanding his release, *Canadian Freeman* editor Francis Collins is still imprisoned on libel charges at this hour. He stays there at the pleasure of Lt.-Gov. John Colborne, who has seen fit to uphold the questionable sentence of this radical editor.

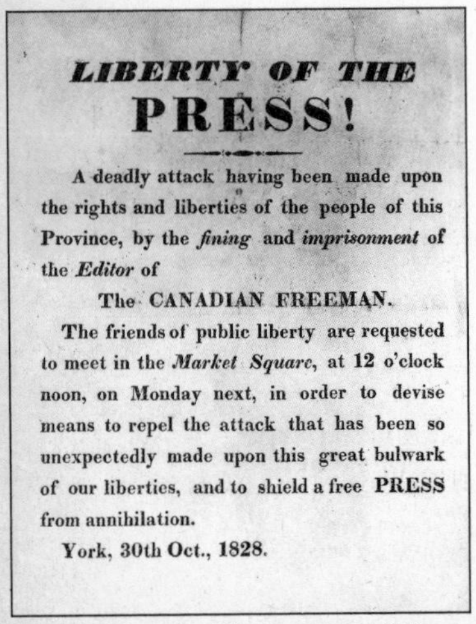

LIBERTY OF THE

PRESS!

A deadly attack having been made upon the rights and liberties of the people of this Province, by the *fining* and *imprisonment* of the *Editor* of

The CANADIAN FREEMAN.

The friends of public liberty are requested to meet in the *Market Square*, at 12 o'clock noon, on Monday next, in order to devise means to repel the attack that has been so unexpectedly made upon this great bulwark of our liberties, and to shield a free PRESS from annihilation.

York, 30th Oct., 1828.

Meeting is called by a group of Upper Canadians against editor's jailing.

Collins' jail stay is the result of a successful libel action brought against him by Attorney General John Beverley Robinson. Ironically, that was based on Collins' report on an earlier libel trial, in which he was acquitted. In that account, he accused Robinson of "open and palpable falsehood" and "native malignity."

Because his sentence demands a large cash payment before he can be released, the relatively poor Collins has essentially been sentenced to indefinite imprisonment. Small wonder that Francis Collins is being touted as a martyr by reformers in Upper Canada. In his brutal sentencing, they see the hand of a reactionary government trying to stifle change at any cost.

Cree chiefs spread the wealth around

c.1830

PRAIRIES – If you are a poor Cree, thanks to a complex system of social assistance you'll probably never go hungry. Cree chiefs, usually the wealthiest members of the band, traditionally give generously to less fortunate tribesmen and their families. After a hunt, the chiefs' wives will leave the best parts of the buffalo at the tepees of the poor. Many chiefs also adopt orphans or sons of poor families.

Gift giving is an important social custom among the Cree. Wealthy men distribute goods among the tribe, which the recipients can give away in turn. In this way, wealth trickles down from Indians who are better off to the less fortunate. While gift giving increases the status of the donor, original owners can ask for their goods to be returned at any time if need be.

Canada new home for escapee Henson

American slave Josiah Henson.

Oct. 28, 1830

DETROIT – Black slave Josiah Henson, his wife and four children flung themselves gratefully on Canadian soil across the river from here today after completing a six-week journey to freedom from Kentucky. Henson had cleverly chosen a time in the plantation's routine when he would not be missed for three days to make good his escape.

Travelling by foot, he crossed the Ohio River to the Indiana shore and proceeded on his journey with his two smallest children in a knapsack on his back. Henson, a preacher, became disenchanted and made plans to escape after his owner reneged on a deal to sell him his freedom for $450.

Cookbook targeting Canadian tastebuds

1831

KINGSTON, Upper Canada – *The Cook Not Mad; or Rational Cookery,* a compendium of 310 recipes "embracing not only the art of curing various kinds of meats and vegetables for future use, but of cooking ... to the taste, habits, and degrees of luxury, prevalent with the Canadian public," has been published by J. Macfarlane of Kingston. The book copies *The Cook Not Mad,* an American work.

Policy says poor settlers can't buy land

Goderich's policy would affect poor settlers, such as these near Chatham.

Nov. 21, 1831

UPPER CANADA – Britain's colonial secretary Lord Goderich has sent a dispatch to the government of Upper Canada outlining a new policy called "systematic colonization." The policy reflects a new school of thought among British colonizers inspired by Edward Gibbon Wakefield, a British consular official in Paris until he was imprisoned five years ago for abducting a 15-year-old girl he wished to marry. While serving his three-year sentence, Wakefield studied colonial settlement problems.

Wakefield argues that granting Crown land to poor settlers who must then pay taxes hampers development by extracting what little capital the settlers may accumulate: it creates a population of destitute farmers and deprives the colony of potential laborers.

To solve this problem, Wakefield proposes that land be auctioned to the highest bidder. The higher price ends the need for settlement taxes, allowing buyers to direct profits solely toward development, and prevents poorer immigrants from acquiring land. For the impoverished immigrant, a chance to own land will come, but only after he accumulates capital by working as a paid laborer. Then – and only then – will the once-poor immigrant be able to responsibly develop land.

Wakefield's plan also responds to the plague of land speculators, who often obtain grants through "dummies" who pose as poor settlers.

Explorer Ross finds North Magnetic Pole

June 8, 1831

BOOTHIA PENINSULA, Arctic Ocean – A British expedition this morning located the North Magnetic Pole, the point to which all compass needles swing. James Clark Ross, the famed Arctic explorer, made the discovery at Cape Adelaide on the remote coast of Boothia Peninsula, precisely at 70 degrees, 5 minutes, 17 seconds N lat. and 96 degrees, 46 minutes, 45 seconds W long.

"It almost seemed as if we had accomplished everything that we had come so far to see and to do," the elated Ross reports, "and that nothing now remained for us but to return home and be happy for the rest of our days."

But there will be no return home for Lieut. Ross, at least not yet. His ship, commanded by his uncle John Ross, is mired in the ice on the far side of Boothia, where it has been trapped already for two winters. The explorers have made friends with the local Netsilik Inuit who have been providing the ship with snowshoes, meat, fish and clothing. As well, the Inuit showed the Englishmen how to manage dogsleds, which James Ross used to reach this magnetic pole.

Despite this discovery, the members of the expedition are frustrated and nervous. If the ice does not release their ship this summer, they are trapped thousands of kilometres from the nearest settlement.

Micmac people inhabiting coastal areas

c.1830

NOVA SCOTIA – The Micmac people, relying on the sea for the bulk of their diet, continue to inhabit coastal areas most of the year. There the men fish for salmon and sturgeon, hunt whales and seals from their sturdy birchbark canoes, and gather shellfish.

When they rove inland they hunt beaver and moose, and gather edible plants. Baskets made by Micmac women from bark and decorated with bright quills are popular trade items. Smoking tobacco made of red willow bark and bearberry leaves is a favored pastime, as is the Waltes dice game.

Micmac Indians such as this one inhabit the coast, fishing salmon and sturgeon, hunting whales and seals, and gathering shellfish.

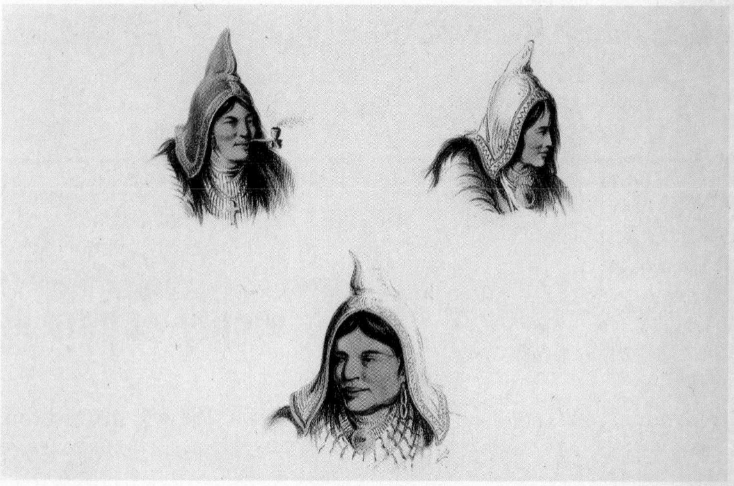

Illustration of three Micmac women, who weave baskets out of bark and decorate them with bright quills to be sold to Europeans. Their settlements are characterized by individual or joint households scattered about.

The interior of a wigwam, the home of Micmac Indians living on the eastern coast. The role of the Micmac leaders is to manage fishing and hunting, and these positions are based on personal prestige. One of the first native peoples to encounter Europeans, the Micmac are experiencing depopulation.

1832

Upper Canada, Jan. 30. After being expelled from the Assembly, William Lyon Mackenzie wins another byelection.

Newfoundland, March 2. The British government issues a new commission to Governor Thomas Cochrane in keeping with the spirit of parliamentary reform in Britain, giving control of almost all Crown revenue to the colony, while requiring a guaranteed civil list to pay for office holders.

London, April 2. The colonial secretary advises Upper Canadian Gov. John Colborne that the Assembly has no power to permanently bar William Lyon Mackenzie.

London, May 25. The Treasury charges Colonel John By with overspending in the construction of the Rideau Canal, and demands he be recalled for questioning.

Quebec, June 3. A brig arrives at the Grosse Isle quarantine station, bringing the first cholera cases to the continent.

London, June 4. A bill for British parliamentary reform is passed, giving the vote to small property owners and middle class tenant farmers, doubling the number of men who are allowed to vote.

Lower Canada, June 15. A law goes into effect stating that Jews are entitled to the same rights and privileges as other British subjects, and can occupy any public office in the province.

Hamilton, Nov. 16. A fire destroys the business centre, causing £13,000 damage.

Upper Canada, November. Mackenzie is elected to the Assembly for a fourth time, despite the fact that he has just been expelled from the Assembly for the third time.

Halifax. The Bank of Nova Scotia is founded.

Upper Canada. There are about 10,000 members of various temperance societies throughout the province.

Montreal. *The Museum of Montreal Magazine* is founded. It's an educational and cultural publication aimed at women.

British North America. Since 1828, Canada's population has increased 50 percent, largely due to Irish immigration.

Quebec. A cholera epidemic claims 3,292 lives in Quebec City. The per capita death rate from the disease is 16 times what it is in London.

Rideau Canal officially open for business

Some British soldiers also worked on construction of the Rideau Canal.

May 29, 1832

BYTOWN, Upper Canada – Lt.-Col. John By and his family arrived here today on the steamer *Pumper*, officially opening the Rideau Canal. The canal links the Ottawa River to Lake Ontario through 200 kilometres of Upper Canadian backwoods. It consists of 47 locks and about 50 dams.

A workforce of 2,000 laborers, many of them Irish immigrants, have been employed for five years cutting trees, digging trenches and hauling stone. In swampy areas, malaria and dysentery swept through the camps, and the backwoods have provided graves for many canal workers. Despite its financial problems, the canal is among the greatest engineering projects in North America.

Assembly expels Mackenzie a third time

Nov. 2, 1832

YORK – The will of the people of York County continues to be flouted by the pro-British, anti-American and Conservative government of Upper Canada. For a third time the Conservatives have expelled Reformer William Lyon Mackenzie from his seat in the Assembly, passing another motion of expulsion through the efforts of their elected colleagues who form the majority in the House. Grounds for the motion are that since Mackenzie has been expelled twice before, he is not fit to sit as a member of Parliament.

Mackenzie is in England now, pressing the British for the removal of the very appointed officials who masterminded the overriding of his legitimate election.

Tale of Canadas is author's latest

1832

UPPER CANADA – The author of *Ecarté,* Queenston-born Maj. John Richardson, just released *A Tale of the Canadas,* popularly known as *Wacousta.*

Printed in three volumes, the Richardson adventure weaves a tale of treachery, romance and revenge on the Canadian frontier during Pontiac's uprising. Wacousta is a white man "turned Indian" after a love affair fails.

New representative government is OK, Newfoundland told

Aug. 22, 1832

ST. JOHN'S, Nfld. – After a campaign involving local merchants, aspiring St. John's politicians and Roman Catholics, Newfoundland has been granted representative government by Britain. While merchants look forward to dominating the new government, Roman Catholics hope to acquire their share of offices and positions under the new Catholic Emancipation Act.

Representative government was opposed by the governor, officials in the Newfoundland colonial service and British merchants. They all argued that, because of the lack of an educated middle class, Newfoundland was not ready for government by election.

Wholesale outlets popping up in York

Oct. 20, 1832

YORK – The commercial umbilical cord between York and Montreal is being cut, according to the *Courier of Upper Canada.* Today the paper ran an editorial citing the appearance of five local wholesale firms as proof that the town has attained some commercial independence from Montreal, the economic capital of Canada. Some York firms prefer to bypass Montreal altogether, getting their goods from the United States.

The Iroquois, a steamer, has a paddle wheel for navigating the rapids of the St. Lawrence. Paddle steamers are useful in Canadian waters.

Devastating cholera epidemic ravages colonies

A view of the quarantine station at Grosse Isle, on the St. Lawrence River.

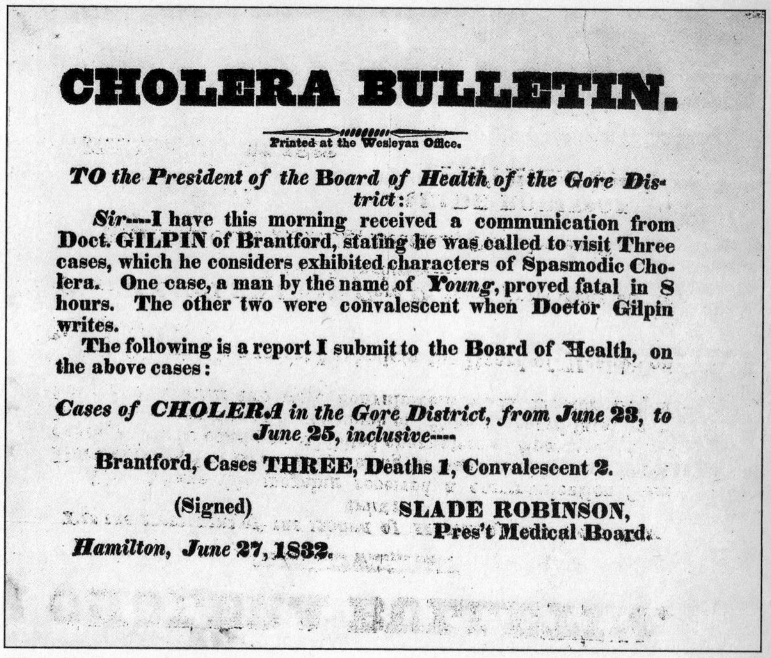

CHOLERA BULLETIN.

Printed at the Wesleyan Office.

TO the President of the Board of Health of the Gore District:

Sir----I have this morning received a communication from Doct. GILPIN of Brantford, stating he was called to visit Three cases, which he considers exhibited characters of Spasmodic Cholera. One case, a man by the name of *Young*, proved fatal in 8 hours. The other two were convalescent when Doctor Gilpin writes.

The following is a report I submit to the Board of Health, on the above cases:

Cases of CHOLERA in the Gore District, from June 23, to June 25, inclusive----

Brantford, Cases THREE, Deaths 1, Convalescent 2.

(Signed) SLADE ROBINSON, Pres't Medical Board.

Hamilton, June 27, 1832.

This Cholera Bulletin shows epidemic's effect on Canadian communities.

Quarantine station to check for cholera

Feb. 25, 1832

QUEBEC CITY – A quarantine station to curb the spread of cholera into Lower Canada will be set up at Grosse Isle, 48 kilometres below Quebec. Legislation making the station law, known as the Quarantine Act, was passed today.

The station will monitor passengers on incoming ships from England. The ships are to stop at a point marked with buoys for inspection and if any passenger or crew member has been in contact with the disease, the vessel is to be brought in to anchor. Cholera victims will be placed under quarantine on the isle. Before a ship is allowed to sail above Grosse Isle to Quebec, a certificate of health must be issued. At Quebec, another inspection is to take place.

Newspaper denounces Irish immigration

August 1832

QUEBEC CITY – A series of stinging editorials in the Quebec *Gazette* attacks Irish emigration to the province, blaming newcomers for unleashing a cholera epidemic.

Declared editorialist M. Rodier: "When I see my country in mourning, and my native land presenting to my eye nothing but a vast cemetery, I ask, what has been the cause of all these disasters? ... It is emigration." Rodier was savaged by Tory writers who claim he in truth feared emigrants would overwhelm the French-Canadian population.

New science says vegetables can cure all

December 1832

YORK – As this year draws to a close, one of its most memorable events has to be the appearance of a new branch of science which claims to cure diseases through the use of vegetables.

Its founder is Samuel Thompson, an uneducated man who styles himself a doctor. His book, *New Guide to Health; or, Botanic Family Physician*, says the body is a great furnace. "All disease is caused by clogging the system" of this furnace, and all cures by clearing the clog, using vegetables.

Disease spreading, Upper Canada hit

June 16, 1832

PRESCOTT, Upper Canada – The cholera epidemic struck Upper Canada today with the first case reported here. The dreaded fatal disease is following the path of immigrant ships coming from the British Isles, where it had spread from Europe late last year. While the first three ships to arrive this spring all lost passengers to the disease, there was no epidemic until the *Carricks* arrived from Dublin, Ireland, earlier this month.

Despite the fact that 42 passengers had died en route, the ship was allowed through Grosse Isle's quarantine station below Quebec. Her passengers sailed on to Montreal on another ship, where the first case of cholera was reported a week ago.

Authorities believe the crowded, unsanitary conditions on immigrant ships, coupled with the fact they're coming from places already under the siege of cholera, are making a bad situation worse. Symptoms include an intermittent and slow pulse, a sick stomach, vomiting and color changes by the entire body, ranging from bluish-purple to deep brown or black, depending on the complexion.

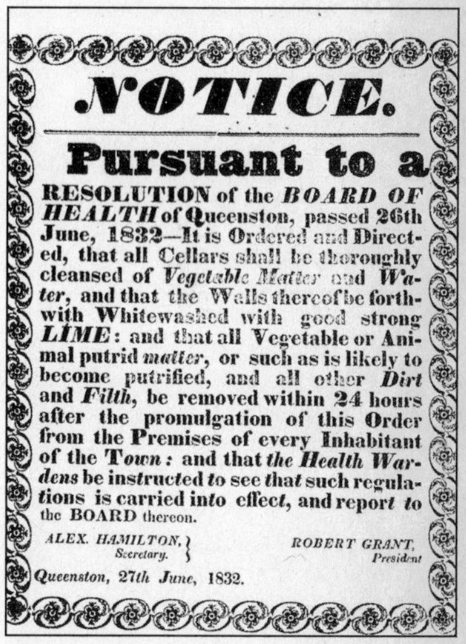

NOTICE.

Pursuant to a RESOLUTION of the *BOARD OF HEALTH* of Queenston, passed 26th June, 1832—It is Ordered and Directed, that all Cellars shall be thoroughly cleansed of *Vegetable Matter* and *Water*, and that the Walls thereof be forthwith Whitewashed with good strong *LIME*: and that all Vegetable or Animal putrid *matter*, or such as is likely to become putrified, and all other *Dirt* and *Filth*, be removed within 24 hours after the promulgation of this Order from the Premises of every Inhabitant of the *Town*: and that *the Health Wardens* be instructed to see that such regulations is carried into effect, and report to the BOARD thereon.

ALEX. HAMILTON, Secretary. *ROBERT GRANT,* President

Queenston, 27th June, 1832.

New rules in effect to fight cholera.

Church bells silent as epidemic sets in

June 14, 1832

QUEBEC CITY – The cholera epidemic has this community in so much fear officials have decided to discontinue the ringing of church bells to mark the death of victims. It is hoped the move will help curb the despair that has become widespread. Cholera was first reported here last week, with eight cases being recorded in the first day. All eight were immigrants and three of them died.

1833 (1833-1835)

Montreal, May 24, 1833. The Montreal Medical Institution grants Canada's first university degree in medicine.

Nova Scotia, June 1833. Naturalist John James Audubon meets collectors who have taken some 40,000 seabird eggs on local islands and are selling them for 25 cents a dozen.

Newfoundland, 1833. Following reforms giving more power to the colony's government, the new government is unable to raise revenue because of a deadlock between the elected Assembly and the appointed Council dominated by British officials. The British treasury is paying the cost of administering the colony until the matter can be resolved.

Upper Canada, 1833. Even in well-built houses, it is very cold on winter nights; water often freezes in bedrooms.

Quebec, 1833. Standard Life, the first life insurance company in Canada, opens.

Quebec, 1833. Due to a drop in wheat production, only a third of the population in parishes of the district has enough food reserves to survive until the next harvest.

Lower Canada, June 24, 1834. Journalist Ludger Duvernay founds the St-Jean-Baptiste Society to inspire nationalist spirit among his countrymen and encourage them to defend their French heritage.

Lower Canada, 1834. The Assembly, dominated by Louis-Joseph Papineau, passes an act regarding controverted elections that prohibits women from voting.

Toronto, 1834. Reformer William Lyon Mackenzie is elected as first mayor of Toronto. He is ineffective in solving the city's problems, mainly because of his incompetence as an administrator.

Upper Canada, 1834. A majority of Reformers is elected to the Assembly. They give notice they intend to tolerate Mackenzie's anti-government positions.

Upper Canada, Feb. 16, 1835. The Assembly votes to erase the record of William Lyon Mackenzie's many expulsions from the journals of the house.

Toronto, 1835. Tory Robert Sullivan defeats William Lyon Mackenzie in mayoralty elections. He begins a program of municipal improvement, including the construction of a much needed sewer system.

Canadian steamer crosses Atlantic

The steam-powered Royal William under construction.

September 1833

GRAVESEND, England – A Canadian-built ship has crossed the Atlantic Ocean by steam. The *Royal William* left Pictou, Nova Scotia, on Aug. 18 with seven passengers and a load of coal, and landed here after a 25-day crossing.

The ship was built for the Halifax Steam and Navigation Company, and launched in 1831 at Quebec by Lord and Lady Aylmer. It plied the route between Quebec and the Atlantic provinces in 1831, but the 1832 cholera epidemic forced it into quarantine, resulting in losses for the ship's owners. The first paddle steamer in Canadian waters was the *Accommodation*, launched in Montreal in 1809.

Mackenzie reelected after four expulsions

Dec. 16, 1833

YORK – Try as they might, the Conservative backers of the appointed Tories who run Upper Canada for the Crown cannot keep the people from reelecting William Lyon Mackenzie. This latest victory for the Scottish firebrand, one of the government's most bitter critics, comes after he was expelled from the Assembly for a fourth straight time.

The ejections comes at the behest of members sympathetic to the government, who wish to deny this voice of reform a position in the House. They have passed motion after motion declaring him unfit and ineligible for office. Interestingly, each successive motion garners a smaller majority in the House, indicating more and more government supporters are doubting the wisdom of their actions. The last expulsion just passed by a slim 18-15 margin on Dec. 2.

Once again, Mackenzie's constituents have responded by reelecting him. In fact, in this latest contest he was unopposed, indicating his justification at claiming to be the "legitimate" representative of his people. Tonight, those electors made their displeasure with the Assembly well known. About 300 of them escorted him to the House.

Ryerson changes tune, attacks Reformers

Oct. 30, 1833

YORK – Egerton Ryerson, editor of the Methodist newspaper *The Christian Guardian*, shocked his readers today by attacking the very Reformers he worked with for years, describing them as little more than American sympathizers. Adding to the shock, Ryerson also champions the very people he's damned for years: the Tories who run this province.

What has changed Ryerson's views? Is it Reformers' support of atheistic British radicals, or fear of pro-Americanism spurring another military crisis – as in 1812-1814?

Newspaper editor Egerton Ryerson.

Surgeon's research focuses on stomach

1833

UNITED STATES – A shotgun wound to the stomach of Alexis St. Martin 11 years ago has led to the publication of a paper by Dr. William Beaumont, a United States army surgeon. The paper is entitled "Experiments and Observations on the Gastric Juice and Physiology of Digestion."

Beaumont was called from Fort Mackinac to Michilimackinac to attend to St. Martin, a French-Canadian trapper who was 19 years old at the time of the accident. The wound, which took a year to heal, left St. Martin with a hole in his stomach that held itself closed and could be opened by simply depressing the surrounding tissue.

Thus, Beaumont was able to observe a person's stomach in action. He used the opportunity to prove his hypothesis that digestion is carried out by chemicals in the stomach. He was able to observe different foods in the stomach and their effect on it. For example, vegetables are the least digestible food and milk coagulates before it is digested.

Beaumont is the first person ever to observe and study human digestion as it occurs in the stomach. Among his discoveries is the fact that alcohol causes inflammation of the stomach's mucous membrane.

Indian's marriage to Englishwoman stirs controversy

September 1833
CREDIT MISSION, Upper Canada – For more than a week now, newspapers in Upper Canada have criticized the marriage of Mississauga Indian chief Sacred Feathers – also known as Peter Jones – to Eliza Field, a wealthy Englishwoman. "Improper and revolting," thundered the Kingston *Chronicle and Gazette*. "We believe that the Creator of the Universe distinguished his creatures by different colors, that they might be kept separate from each other." The St. Catharines *British Colonial Argus* denounces "the amalgamation system." The York *Patriot* terms Eliza an "unhappy, deceived woman."

Sacred Feathers, who'll be ordained a Methodist minister next month, met Eliza on his recent year-long tour of England to raise money for the Methodists' Indian work in Upper Canada. Their paths crossed in Bristol and London before Eliza fell in love with the eloquent lecturer. Sacred Feathers returned to Canada, and earlier this month, married Eliza in New York city's leading Methodist chapel. They will live at the Credit Mission.

The storm of protest against them shows how racial attitudes here have hardened. A generation ago, when Molly Brant's five daughters married respectable Englishmen in Upper Canada, there was no public outcry.

Sacred Feathers' father was also a respectable white man, surveyor Augustus Jones.

Sacred Feathers, or Peter Jones.

Log cabins popular in Upper Canada

One-quarter of the homes in Upper Canada are made out of logs and clay.

1834
UPPER CANADA – Log cabins are becoming more and more common. In fact, about 25 percent of homes here are now of this type. Many Irish settlers build log shanties similar to the wooden and clay huts they had back home. It's easy to pick out the Irish-made cabins from the high earth embankment up against the walls. They are low and look like caves on a hillside.

Wealthy settler Samuel Strickland's log house at Pigeon Lake, Peterborough County is American-style, made "of elm-logs, 36 feet long by 24 feet wide, ... divided into three rooms on the ground floor, besides an entrance hall and staircase and three bedrooms upstairs."

N.B. lumber industry booms at the expense of farms, fisheries

c.1834
NEW BRUNSWICK – Young New Brunswickers are again flocking to the province's lumber camps, lured by the excitement and excellent wages the industry offers. The quality pine indigenous to the region is in high demand after a period of recession that lasted several years, and exports of square and sawn timber to Britain and the West Indies are rising. But while the boom attracts immigrants and capital, it also drains manpower from the farms and fisheries.

New Brunswick has already fallen prey to the dangers of having a one-dimensional economy based on lumber exports. In 1825 the British market temporarily collapsed and quite suddenly New Brunswick was without means to purchase food imports. But the point seems to have missed its mark. The majority of young men are again demonstrating their preference for the short-term gains from lumber over the long-term advantages derived from the relatively dull, yet ever-demanding, life on the farm.

Log booms on the St. John River.

Fire marks the end of St. Louis castle

Jan. 23, 1834
QUEBEC CITY – The Castle of St. Louis, a landmark in Quebec's history, was destroyed by fire today. Built in 1620 by Quebec founder Samuel de Champlain, the fort was turned into a stone fortress by Charles Huault de Montmagny, New France's first governor, and then was erected on its original foundations. It was later redone, then replaced. It was in this building that Montcalm helped plan the colony's defence in the conquest.

Today's terrible blaze points out the ever-present danger of the fires that from time to time devastate the colony's cities, specially in winter.

Great Fish River full of falls and rapids

Aug. 16, 1834
OGLE POINT, Arctic Coast – A British overland expedition led by naval officer George Back has followed the Great Fish River to its mouth on the Arctic coast. Accompanied by Dr. Richard King and eight other men, Back descended the river in a 10-metre open boat through the treeless barren lands. The explorer calculates that this wild river contains no less than 83 falls and rapids. He and his followers are the first Europeans to travel the entire length.

When they set out from England early last year, Back and King were hoping to discover the fate of Cmdr. John Ross, who had been missing with his ship in the Arctic since 1829. But before they began their descent of the river, word reached the explorers that Ross was home safely. The expedition continued, but now its purpose was to reach and explore the Arctic coast.

The boat arrived at the mouth of the Great Fish in Chantrey Inlet on July 29. Proceeding up the inlet, the explorers reached this low, sandy point where they stopped, unable to proceed farther through the compact ice. In the distance they can see land, but whether it is an island or part of the mainland they cannot tell. King wishes to keep on going, but Back is worried about the lack of supplies and plans to return inland to their base camp at Great Slave Lake.

Booming city renamed, incorporated as Toronto

Residents celebrate the incorporation of Toronto, formerly known as "Muddy York," with carriage rides and other activities. York's growing commerce and population demands are largely responsible for the city being incorporated. Its name was changed since many municipalities are already known as York.

A southern view of Upper Canada College, founded in 1829 by Lt.-Gov. Sir John Colborne, and situated in the newly-incorporated city of Toronto.

More efficient style of government sought

March 6, 1834

TORONTO – York has been incorporated as the first city of Upper Canada and its name has been changed back to Toronto, by which it was originally known. In passing the act today, the Legislature noted that York's growing commerce and population demands "a more efficient system of police and municipal government than that now established." The name change to Toronto is because many municipalities are known as York. The lieutenant-governor has been empowered to change the name of any other centre called Toronto, if one is found. At the same time, Toronto's boundaries have been extended west to Bathurst Street, as well as north, 364 metres, to Crookshank Street.

General view of Toronto at the time of its incorporation in 1834. An extensive network of routes has been developed for the lake, with seven operating boats.

Boat routes link Toronto to neighbors

1834

TORONTO – An extensive network of steamboat routes has been developed on the lake, forming this city's main transportation links with outlying communities. There are now seven boats on routes from Toronto, with five of them circling the entire lake, usually covering the distance in a week. Of the other two, one each goes to Niagara and Rochester. The boats connect with stage routes to Montreal and cities in the United States, as well as with other boats plying both the upper Great Lakes and the Rideau Canal.

Cape Spear picked for new lighthouse

Oct. 25, 1834

CAPE SPEAR, Nfld. – This site, the most easterly point in Newfoundland and just a few kilometres from St. John's, has been chosen for the new lighthouse. Up until now, the only lighthouse marking the entrance to St. John's Harbour has been the one at Fort Amherst built in 1810. The Cape Spear light, which will burn whale or seal oil, will be about 60 metres above sea level and visible for a much greater distance.

Decline of wheat crop sparks questions

January 1834

LOWER CANADA – What's wrong with Lower Canadian agriculture? That's the question on many people's minds after last year's disastrous wheat crop. The harvest has gradually worsened the past two decades, to the point where some people in the area below Quebec City starved last year.

Natural causes are partly to blame for the wheat crop's decline. Bad weather, disease, and insects have ravaged crops the last few years. Still, with Upper Canadian farmers boosting their wheat output, some people here are blaming *habitant* farming techniques for the problems. Agricultural specialists blame the *habitants* for not rotating their crops, and for dumping manure in rivers instead of using it for fertilization. In reality, Upper and Lower Canadian farm methods are similar, so it's hard to explain the difference in output.

Habitants now grow more peas, potatoes, oats, and other crops they need for their own daily existence. It may be a good idea, considering the shaky market for wheat at home and abroad.

Mayor orders thief to stand in stocks

1834

TORONTO – In one of his first decisions, Toronto's mayor and chief magistrate, William Lyon Mackenzie, has sentenced a convicted thief to spend two months in prison, breaking stones. The thief must also "stand one hour tomorrow, and one hour tomorrow week, in the common stocks, in the Market Place, and to be banished from the Home District for 12 months."

The case marks the first recorded use of stocks in Toronto.

Reformers to pick election candidates

Nov. 25, 1834

TORONTO – The movement for reform came down to municipal politics today when a local group made plans for the next election. The Constitutional Reform Society decided at its weekly meeting to establish committees in the various city wards to nominate candidates supporting their views and to canvass for them. The purpose of the society is to elect reformers who are both sympathetic to the economy and retrenchment.

The move to the municipal arena follows by seven years a similar action tried at the provincial level. Then, as battle lines began to grow between those in favor of reform and those against, a committee was appointed to nominate a candidate in York who would represent views of the reformers.

Slavery abolished in British Empire

Aug. 1, 1834

BRITISH NORTH AMERICA – Three quarters of a million slaves were set free today, Emancipation Day in British Empire colonies. While there are probably fewer than 50 slaves in North American colonies left to reap the benefits of freedom, it is certain that many blacks are celebrating.

Of the £20,000 set aside to compensate slave owners, nothing has been earmarked for British North America, and the act of abolition makes no mention of these colonies – slavery does not exist here in the eyes of the British government. In fact, slavery has died a slow death here, mainly due to the efforts of judges who have consistently ruled against it even though it was still legal. The late James Monk, who granted freedom to many escaped blacks when he was chief justice in Lower Canada, is considered a hero in the war against slavery.

Many factors have made slavery untenable here. Public opinion has not supported the practice. In the northern climate, slaves have proven expensive to feed and clothe. Most importantly, it has become difficult for owners to keep physical possession of their slaves when they can escape to areas where slavery has been abolished.

Celebrations followed the abolition of slavery in the British Empire colonies.

Logging bees raise hackles of genteel folk

July 1834

UPPER CANADA – Logging bees, seen by many as the epitome of frontier cooperation, are raising the hackles of genteel folk around here. Bees are held whenever there is a lot of hard work to do, such as clearing land. People come from all around to help out, and in return the farmer provides lots of food and whiskey, as well as entertainment. There is usually a dance, or "hoe-down," along with sports and games. Bees are an outlet for all the frustrations of pioneer life.

But, according to more refined settlers, bees often deteriorate into drunken debaucheries full of swearing, and sometimes they end in violence. Susanna Moodie and her husband held a logging bee this month. They supplied a feast for workers consisting of pork, venison, eel, raspberry pie, and plenty of whiskey to wash it all down. Many of the men were drunk by lunchtime. After supper, they broke into song and noisy partying. Their swearing offended the Moodies, sitting in the next room. Some people think that bees are not worth the trouble, considering the amount of work that gets done for the number of people involved.

Neighbors get together to help clear wooded farmland during logging bees in Upper Canada. In return for the help, farmers provide food and drink, as well as entertainment. There are complaints the bees are getting out of hand.

Moccasins combine comfort and beauty

c.1834

UPPER CANADA – European shoes are usually uncomfortable, but Indians have been wearing comfortable and practical shoes called moccasins for years. The Six Nations Indians here make soft-soled moccasins from a single piece of hide.

The shoes are beautiful as well as practical. Since the arrival of Europeans, the Iroquoians have used beads to decorate them, but they traditionally adorn them with porcupine quills and moose hair. The decorations are rich in religious symbolism. Curves may represent the sun and the sky dome, which divide the Earth from the world above, or the celestial tree, associated with the creation of the Earth.

A soft-soled moccasin as made and worn by the Iroquois of Upper Canada using one piece of hide. These shoes are beautiful as well as practical.

Howe triumphs: jury acquits editor in libel case

March 4, 1835

HALIFAX – A jubilant crowd carried Joseph Howe through the streets in triumph today after the journalist won acquittal at his trial for libel. The verdict is considered a strike for freedom of the press in the colony.

Howe, the 30-year-old editor of the Halifax *Novascotian*, was charged after he published a letter accusing local government officials of corruption. Failing to find a lawyer who believed he stood a chance of winning the case, Howe decided to defend himself in court.

The trial began yesterday before the Supreme Court of Nova Scotia. The room was filled with a noisy crowd which adopted Howe as its champion. After the prosecutor introduced the case, it was the turn of the accused. Howe spoke for more than six hours, without notes and without pausing. It was indeed a bravura performance, by turns shrewdly logical, blustery and impassioned. He argued that he had no malicious intent in publishing the letter, only a concern for the public welfare. Local magistrates were, Howe thundered, "the most negligent and imbecile ... that ever mismanaged a people's affairs."

At the end, Howe was exhausted and the chief justice adjourned the court. This morning the trial resumed with Justice Haliburton advising the jury to convict. However, after just 10 minutes, it returned with a not guilty verdict and the court exploded in celebration.

Novascotian editor Joseph Howe.

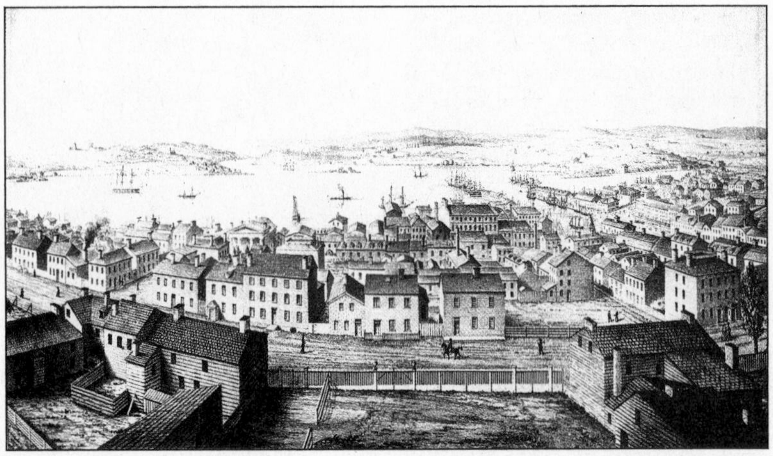

A view of Halifax, where editor Joseph Howe has been acquitted of libel.

Committee's report directs harsh words at Crown patronage

April 10, 1835

TORONTO – Patronage by the Crown is under fire as the Seventh Report of the Committee on Grievances was presented to the House today. The committee, chaired by William Lyon Mackenzie, reported that Crown patronage to the tune of £50,000 a year in salaries and pensions was going on. Also under the gun was the post office, for extravagant charges and for the fact it is not responsible to the House. The report calls for responsible government and criticizes both the constitution and the legislature.

Mackenzie, sitting in the House as one of four York members – all opposed to the government – has been a longtime opponent of the status quo. Nine years ago, as publisher of the *Colonial Advocate,* his attacks on the Family Compact became so aggressive that a group of young men supporting the governing clique raided his printing plant. Some of his equipment was smashed and type was carried out and thrown into the bay. Mackenzie was awarded damages by the courts and his popularity soared.

Rowdy lumberjacks force official to resign

June 15, 1835

BYTOWN – George W. Baker, the magistrate who has been leading the fight against lawless Irish lumberjacks, resigned his post today. The law-abiding citizens were too frightened of the "Shiners" to rally to Baker, who has stepped down to protect his family.

Named Shiners from the French word oakcutters, the lumberjacks do not hesitate to attack law officers, intimidate witnesses, and break their compatriots out of jail. Behind much of this violence are the machinations of an Irish timber baron, Peter Aylen. He supplies the desperately poor immigrants with jobs, liquor and, some claim, even prostitutes from Montreal.

In addition, Aylen encourages the Shiners to drive their competitors, the more experienced and less boisterous French-Canadians, from the Ottawa Valley. They, in return, provide him with the strong arms he needs to take over timber concessions from business rivals and the town of Bytown [Ottawa] from its British leading citizens.

Canadian Alliance appeals for support

Dec. 24, 1834

TORONTO – The Canadian Alliance Society has appealed for the development of branches to support the Upper Canada reform movement. Brockville Reformer A.N. Buell is one of the sympathizers sent a circular from William Lyon Mackenzie in which he outlines a plan of attack. Outlying branches are to send extra funds to the central office and keep it informed of local political feelings.

Americans welcomed at Fort Vancouver

Chief factor John McLoughlin greets Methodist minister Rev. Jason Lee.

Sept. 16, 1835

FORT VANCOUVER, [Oregon] – A party of American settlers led by Methodist minister Rev. Jason Lee was greeted today by Hudson's Bay Company factor Dr. John McLoughlin. With four religious workers, Lee plans to establish a mission here, the first such post on this side of the Rockies.

Also on the expedition are Nathaniel Wyeth, a Boston trader, a Mr. Nuttal, a botanist from Harvard, and a Mr. Townsend, a Quaker ornithologist. Lee is originally from Independence, Missouri.

Filthy ships blamed as cholera spreads

Dec. 15, 1834

MONTREAL – A report by the Special Sanitary Committee of Montreal blames ship owners and captains, who subject passengers in their vessels to filthy conditions, for the cholera epidemic which has claimed nearly one-tenth of the province's population since 1832.

The report concludes: "Common avarice has led many captains, owners and agents in the seaport towns of Ireland into a most horrible traffic in human life."

Incoming governor told he's to reform "real grievances"

Governor Sir Francis Bond Head.

Dec. 5, 1835

TORONTO – The incoming governor of Upper Canada has been told to reform the province's "real grievances" and treat the Assembly with "attention and courtesy."

But the instructions from England to Sir Francis Bond Head are vague. No concessions to the colony are suggested. They reiterated the governor's responsibility to the throne and that of the colony's department heads to him, but forbid him to be decisive in opposition to the radicals. The British stance is in response to a special grievance committee report earlier this year.

Catholics suspected of attacking editor

May 19, 1835

HARBOUR GRACE, Nfld. – The editor of the *Public Ledger* was savagely assaulted and injured today while on his way from Harbour Grace to Carbonear. Henry Winton has been known for his editorials attacking Roman Catholic Liberal politicians and Bishop Michael Anthony Fleming, their major supporter. Last Dec. 25, the St. John's magistrates were forced to call out the militia to protect Winton's house. In today's attack, Winton was travelling over Saddle Hill when he was seized, beaten and had his left ear cut off by disguised assailants. The police are questioning local Catholics.

Crown land put under legislative control

Crown lands such as this are now under New Brunswick's legislative control.

The city of Fredericton in New Brunswick, where a long battle is over.

Sept. 10, 1835

NEW BRUNSWICK – In an attempt to forestall greater unrest, colonial secretary Lord Glenelg has ordered that Crown lands be turned over to legislative control. The ruling marks the end of a long battle for New Brunswick residents.

Making his decision, Glenelg stopped short of giving the delegation he faced all it wanted. Land commissioner Thomas Baillie, who has been particularly unpopular here, escaped with his job but not with his power.

Glenelg refused to lower Baillie's salary, but no longer will he be able to set policy in Crown land matters. Instead, he will receive instructions from the Executive Council, which will be guided by the legislature. However, the colonial secretary promised that the salaries of successors to appointed positions such as Baillie's, would, in certain situations, be reduced.

Canada Company comes under the gun

January 1835

DISTRICT OF HURON, Upper Canada – Protests against the Canada Company and its treatment of settlers have become more organized with the formation of the Huron Union Society. Formed by Col. Anthony Van Egmond, the society has been meeting in settlers' homes. Its complaints against the Canada Company include broken promises involving the building of bridges, canals, roads, churches, schools and wharves.

New penitentiary's first six prisoners arrive to serve time

June 1, 1835

UPPER CANADA – Trading his name for a number, Mathew Tavender has become inmate No. 1 at the Provincial Penitentiary at Portsmouth. He was sentenced to three years for grand larceny. No. 2 is John Hamilton serving three years for felony, No. 3 is Edward Middlehurst, sentenced to five years for grand larceny, No. 4 is John O'Rorke, sentenced five years for grand larcency, No. 5 is John Dayas, and No. 6 is Joseph Bonsette, assigned to the kitchen.

Prisoners' cells are 30 inches wide, and they have a bucket for waste and a bed hinged to the wall. The warden is Henry Smith. Notes one observer: "Mr. Smith's habits of industry and active vigilance make him peculiarly fit for this responsible office."

The opening of the 140-cell block completed in 1834 was delayed because the provincial Assembly forgot to provide funds for prisoner maintenance. Modelled after the American Auburn "congregate" system, inmates spend their days at hard labor and their nights in private cells. The key is deterrence. Convicts will be reformed through reflection, hard labor and fear of punishment. Anyone who is caught communicating will be flogged.

Portsmouth was chosen by Kingstonians J. Macaulay and H. Thomson for the government because of the stone for hard labor, easy access, and proximity of the troops in case of a riot.

An Indian of the Hare nation, who live in the Mackenzie River valley in the [Northwest Territories].

1836

Lower Canada, January. Governor Gosford issues a proclamation dissolving the British Rifle Corps, recently formed by 300 young men opposed to Reformers in the province. The group reluctantly dissolves after a demonstration of 1,000 people.

Upper Canada, Feb. 5. Sir Francis Bond Head, new governor of the province, says in a letter to the colonial office that the Reformers in the province are only interested in getting control of the government for their own financial gain, an oversimplified assessment of the political situation.

Newfoundland, Sept. 1. Cape Spear Lighthouse goes into operation.

Toronto, Oct. 10. The Toronto Political Union is formed to press for constitutional reform.

Toronto, Oct. 12. The Upper Canada Academy [Victoria College] receives a royal charter.

Toronto, November. Printers end an unsuccessful two-week strike. Their demands included higher pay and shorter working hours.

Quebec, Dec. 12. At a general meeting, more than 400 Quebec Tories form a Constitutional Association to protect their interests in constitutional talks with Reformers.

Lower Canada. The Legislative Assembly repeats its demands for political reform, and restricts its grant of funds to the Executive Council to six months. The Council refuses to accept a limited grant, so the province is left without authorized revenue from local sources for a fourth straight year.

Charlottetown, Prince Edward Island. A law is passed specifically excluding women from the franchise.

Prince Edward Island. The provincial government opens Central Academy, a non-denominational institute of higher learning.

Lower Canada. A law authorizes the training of teachers in the province.

Sydney, Nova Scotia. The general Mining Association begins using locomotives instead of horses to pull coal-cars over 9.6 kilometres of rail. Stagecoaches are still the fastest means of travel in the colony.

Upper Canada. The Ottawa Baptist Association is formed.

Sir Francis arrives to assume new post

Jan. 23, 1836

TORONTO – Sir Francis Bond Head arrived here today to assume the post of lieutenant-governor and Reformers are already enthusiastic in anticipation of his professed liberal leanings. Head, who succeeds Sir John Colborne, inherits a province rife with discontent from the Reform movement.

Head, who was at the Battle of Waterloo and who introduced the lasso to the British army, left in 1825 to manage a South American mining venture which proved to be unsuccessful. He was assistant poor law commissioner for Kent in England until his appointment to this position. One report says he is getting this job by mistake, instead of his cousin, Sir Edmund W. Head.

Former Lt.-Gov. Sir John Colborne.

Assembly digs in: motion to withhold supplies is passed

April 18, 1836

TORONTO – The Assembly of Upper Canada voted today to withhold supplies to enforce its demand for responsible government. It is the first time such action has been taken here. The crux of the debate which sparked the drastic measure is a contention by Reformers that the Executive Council's tenure in office should depend on a majority of the Assembly. Those opposed argue this would mean separation from Britain. The resolution on the supplies passed, 31-20.

The issue came to a head in the wake of a report from a select committee of Reformers on responsible government. Like that of a special grievance committee headed by Reformer William Lyon Mackenzie a year ago, this group restated grievances and the case for responsible government. However, unlike Mackenzie's group, the committee says the existing constitution calls for responsible government.

Reformers drafting the report are indignant at the lieutenant-governor, Sir Francis Bond Head, for denying that Upper Canada enjoys that status in the constitution. Head, whose billing as a liberal was warmly received by the Reformers, is beginning to fall from grace.

Facility opens to care for mentally ill

February 1836

SAINT JOHN, N.B. – The first institution in British North America devoted solely to the care of the mentally ill opened here today in the basement of a former cholera hospital on Leinster Street. For years the mentally ill have been confined along with paupers and criminals in gaols and poorhouses throughout the colonies. Recently Reformers have decided that these unfortunate people need an institution of their own where they can receive proper care, not punishment.

The man behind the new facility is Dr. George Peters. As a visiting medical officer at the local almshouse and gaol, Peters was horrified to find deranged inmates mingling with the others. Many were chained up, "some of them perfectly naked and in a state of filth." As a result of his efforts, 14 mentally ill patients were moved to the new building. An equal number of sick paupers are on the floor above.

Supply ship Beaver is first steamship on the northwest coast

Hudson's Bay Company's steamer the Beaver arrives at Fort Vancouver.

April 10, 1836

FORT VANCOUVER, Columbia River – The first steamship on the northwest coast arrived here today after a 204-day passage around Cape Horn from London. The 30-metre *Beaver* arrived under sail, but once its engines are installed, the side-wheeler, under the command of Capt. William McNeill, will serve as a supply boat for Hudson's Bay Company posts along the coast.

Dr. John McLoughlin, in charge of the Columbia District, thinks the vessel is an expensive luxury, but he has been overruled by Gov. George Simpson, who believes steam is more efficient than sail, and besides will impress the Indians with the power of the company.

Fund raising paves way for poorhouse

A new poorhouse will be erected in Toronto, financed by private contributions.

Dec. 1, 1836

TORONTO – Individuals interested in helping the poor have banded together to raise funds through public subscription for a poorhouse. Called a House of Industry, it will be constructed to face a growing need government has yet to meet. The attitude has been that such services are best provided by the private sector. While founded on British law, Upper Canada has had a rider that England's Poor Laws do not apply.

However, the philosophy behind the new House of Industry reflects the thinking behind England's 1834 Poor Laws. Most pertinent is the concept of indoor relief, forcing the poor into institutions so austere only the desperately needy – and not the merely lazy – would enter them. Also involved is the notion that poverty is sinful.

Howe likens government to a "mummy"

1836

HALIFAX – Joseph Howe, poet, orator, journalist and now the Reform candidate for Halifax County, knows his enemies well: the clique of well-fixed Halifax officials who, aided by governors, have run the province their way.

Unlike England, Howe tells voters, where the people have control over their government, "in this country, the government is like an ancient Egyptian mummy wrapped up in narrow and antique prejudices – dead and inanimate, but yet likely to last forever. ... All we ask for is what exists at home – a system of responsibility to the people extending through all the departments supported at the public expense."

Britain pays $1.2M to keep 3,601 slaves

1836

LONDON, England – Britain has agreed to pay the United States $1,204,960, rather than returning 3,601 slaves who came over to her side during the War of 1812. The British action follows a ruling by the emperor of Russia in an international arbitration. The emperor ruled that Vice-Admiral Alexander Cochrane, British fleet commander on the Atlantic coast during the war, acted wrongly carrying away the slaves and that the U.S. should be compensated. Cochrane had proclaimed that all U.S. residents who came to a British ship or military post would have a choice of military service or free transportation to an English colony in North America or the West Indies. Of the 3,601 slaves Cochrane transported, 2,400 were from Maryland and Virginia and the remainder came from North Carolina, Louisiana and Georgia. Nearly 2,000 of the first group of slaves were taken to Nova Scotia.

Selkirk heir sells Assiniboia to the HBC

May 4, 1836

RED RIVER COLONY, Rupert's Land – Lord Selkirk, heir to the original Lord Selkirk who established the Red River colony as a home for displaced Scottish crofters and other immigrants, has sold Assiniboia back to the Hudson's Bay Company for the price of £84,000. That is £83,999 and 10 shillings more than the land was bought for 25 years earlier. While the price has just about doubled, the acreage has gone down. The original land grant was for 300,440 square kilometres, some of which now lies in the Unites States.

Although the inhabitants were not consulted or even informed of the transaction, the Selkirk family has requested that the future of the colony is to be ensured. The Hudson's Bay Company has come to see the value of the settlement. To date, the colony has not paid dividends, but it has become a symbol of ownership, and establishes a presence in the vast wilderness for the trading posts in the west that is much cheaper than importing goods from England.

The sale price of this land was determined after taking into account costs, interest, and profits earned. The Selkirk heir has accepted payment in HBC shares. The deal was initiated by the Hudson's Bay Company.

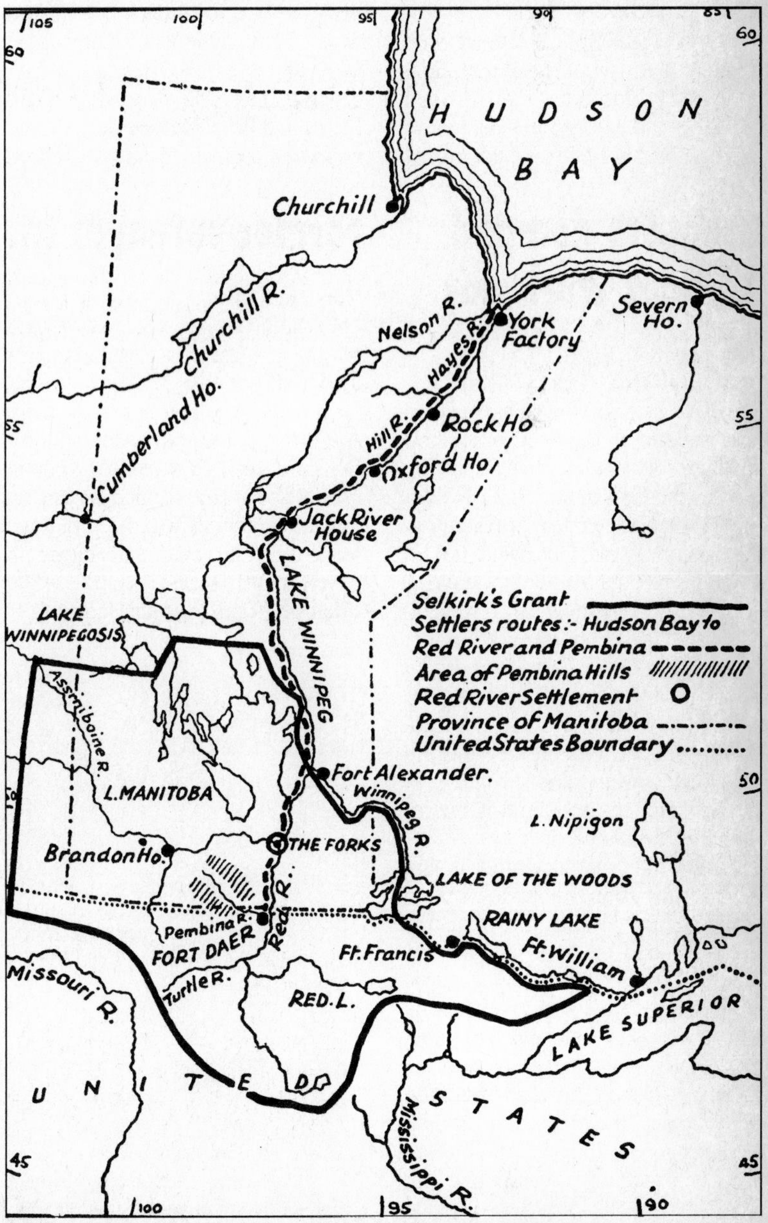

Map of [Manitoba] shows Lord Selkirk's grant to Hudson's Bay Company.

Flogger almost gets a taste of his own medicine

Fort Pembina, south of the Red River colony, is also experiencing discontent.

An official of the Red River colony travelling with guides in a light canoe.

April 28, 1836

FORT GARRY – A man who administered a court-ordered flogging nearly got a taste of his own medicine today when he was forced to run for his life from an unruly mob. Police held back the crowd while the flogging was administered to Louis St. Denis, then had to rescue the man who flogged him. St. Denis had been accused of theft and was tried, convicted and sentenced to receive corporal punishment. The sentence was unpopular and the indignation that followed cost the government a loss of respect, provoking the first feelings in favor of the establishment of representative government. The incident underlines rising discontent with the Council of Assiniboia. Arbitrary decisions by magistrates, who are all members of the government, are worsening the discontentment.

Laborers demand 10-hour work day

July 11, 1836

COBOURG, Upper Canada – Workers in this village have taken a daring step in the fight to improve working conditions. In a meeting held at the Common School House, the assembled signed a resolution that commits each of them not to work more than 10 hours a day.

Says the document: "It was resolved that the number of hours which we now work is nothing better than domestic slavery, is altogether derogatory to the improvement of our moral and intellectual powers and progress in the arts and sciences, and is one of the chief causes of vice."

Under the plan, summer hours would run from 6 a.m. to 6 p.m., with an hour off at 7:30 a.m. for breakfast and an hour at noon for lunch. The winter schedule goes from 7 a.m. to 6 p.m., with breakfast being taken before work.

It remains to be seen whether owners will tolerate this dictation of hours by their laborers. Doubtless, for some, this declaration will seem an act of revolution – an attempt by their employees "to do less work for the same pay."

Former surveyor for Upper Canada dies

Nov. 16, 1836

PARIS, Upper Canada – One of the province's early pioneers died today in his 79th year at his farm a few kilometres east of here. Augustus Jones, an American of Welsh descent, moved to Niagara in 1787. Having studied surveying in New York City, he obtained work as a surveyor and stayed in government service until 1800 when he began full-time farming.

Jones knew both Mohawk and Ojibwa, the language of the Mississauga Indians. He learned Mohawk from Sarah Tekarihogen, his legal wife, and Ojibwa from Tuhbenahneequay, with whom he lived for awhile. Sacred Feathers – also known as Peter Jones – is the younger of Augustus Jones' two Mississauga sons. Peter is a well-known Mississauga chief and an ordained Methodist minister.

Fort Vancouver, Hudson's Bay Company fur-trade post and Columbia district headquarters. Strategically located to protect British interests.

Sir Francis believes Indians "doomed"

Aug. 9, 1836

MANITOULIN ISLAND, Upper Canada – Sir Francis Bond Head, lieutenant-governor of Upper Canada, today presented his new Indian policy to the leaders of the Ottawa and Chippewa tribes gathered here for the annual gift-giving. Head, who has been in the colony less than a year, has concluded the Indians are a "doomed race," destined to disappear as white settlement spreads.

Head believes that for their own protection, the Indians should be removed to some remote location where they can be protected from all communication with whites while they slowly disappear. He has chosen this island at the north end of Lake Huron, where he plans to establish a huge reserve on land belonging to the Indians. He hopes to persuade all the Indians from the southern parts of the colony to settle here.

The lieutenant-governor's plan is a dramatic break with previous government policy aimed at integrating Indians into white society by exposing them to missionaries and teaching them agriculture.

HBC council meets to discuss fur trade

The Hudson's Bay Co. council meets.

June 21, 1836

NORWAY HOUSE, Rupert's Land – Fur trading was the topic at the annual meeting of the Hudson's Bay Company's Council of the Northern Department of Rupert's Land, at Norway House trading post, north of Lake Winnipeg. Discussed were prices, wages for traders, fines and promotions. The council rules British North America's northwest for the HBC.

Government loses non-confidence motion

May 28, 1836

TORONTO – Parliament was dissolved today by Lt.-Gov. Francis Bond Head after the Assembly passed a non-confidence motion. The motion brought to a climax the long-standing hostility between the Reformers in the Assembly and the lieutenant-governor, who has repeatedly gone against their demands for responsible government. The non-confidence vote passed with a 32-18 majority.

Head, in a token gesture earlier this year, tried to appease Reformers by asking Robert Baldwin to join the Executive Council. He agreed only after Dr. John Rolph, a Reformer representing Norfolk in the Assembly, and receiver-general John H. Dunn, were also asked to be members. After three weeks they complained about their lack of input, only to be told by Head if he wanted their advice he would ask. The executive resigned and was replaced quickly by the governor.

But the Reformers' attacks continued in and out of the Assembly. At a public meeting here in which a protest was organized to send to the governor, Head played into their hands by tactlessly telling the people that he would reply to their concern with as much attention as if it had come from the House but would use plainer language. Rolph attacked his "condescension."

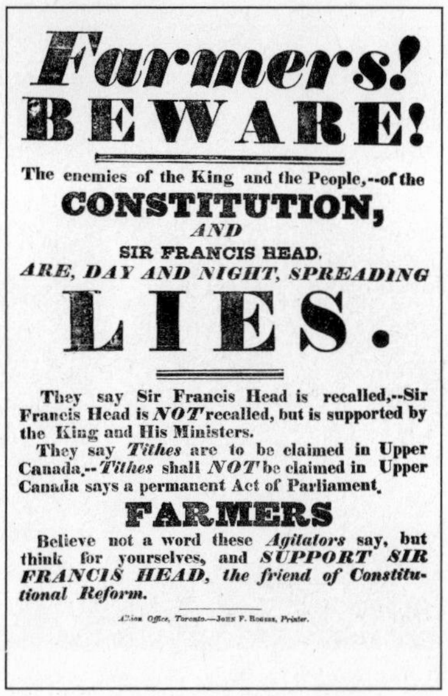

Farmers!
BEWARE!

The enemies of the King and the People,--of the
CONSTITUTION,
AND
SIR FRANCIS HEAD,
ARE, DAY AND NIGHT, SPREADING
LIES.

They say Sir Francis Head is recalled,--Sir Francis Head is *NOT* recalled, but is supported by the King and His Ministers.

They say *Tithes* are to be claimed in Upper Canada,--*Tithes* shall *NOT* be claimed in Upper Canada says a permanent Act of Parliament.

FARMERS

Believe not a word these *Agitators* say, but think for yourselves, and *SUPPORT SIR FRANCIS HEAD, the friend of Constitutional Reform.*

Proclamation puts down agitators.

Delegates discuss the issue of union

June 1836

MONTREAL – A group of constitutionalists meeting here is pushing for a union of Upper and Lower Canada and for the recall of Sir Archibald Gosford, governor-in-chief of British North America. Montreal delegates want a petition taking this stand, and while there is general agreement, so far it has not been drawn up. The decision on the issue of union is expected to bring considerable more debate before a final verdict is reached.

Throughout this past winter, the constitutional movement has been active, with local societies springing up in the Eastern Townships, Trois-Rivières, Beauharnois, Quebec and Montreal. The more moderate Quebec society went on record this spring as being mainly satisfied with Britain's intentions. The Montreal group has been the most vocal, and is pushing hard for Gosford to be recalled to England. It remains to be seen if the societies can make a unified push for union.

Back's ship stranded in the Arctic ice

Sept. 27, 1836

ARCTIC OCEAN, Rupert's Land – The *HMS Terror,* the exploration ship commanded by Capt. George Back, is stranded in the ice southeast of Southampton Island. Strandings such as these are unfortunately common for European-style sailing vessels that stay in Arctic waters after the freeze-up begins.

At present, Back and his crew are not in danger. However, should the ice continue to push against the *Terror*, her hull could be crushed, marooning the explorers.

First Canadian railway off and running

July 21, 1836

LAPRAIRIE, Lower Canada – The first real railway in British North America opened today. The line runs 23 kilometres between this small community opposite Montreal on the south shore of the St. Lawrence River and the town of Saint-Jean on the Richelieu. Called the Champlain and St. Lawrence Railway, the line consists of one locomotive, four passenger cars and 20 freight cars. The track is made of wood. The new railway brings Montreal within 36 hours travel time of New York City.

British ship HMS Terror: The vessel is stranded in the ice in Arctic waters.

The first locomotive to be used on the Champlain and St. Lawrence Railway.

1837

Lower Canada, May. Philippe-Ignace-François Aubert de Gaspé publishes *L'influence d'un livre*, the first French-Canadian novel.

Lower Canada, June 15. Governor Gosford forbids public meetings, as the climate of revolt intensifies.

Lower Canada, July 25. Bishop Lartigue tells priests to warn their flocks that rebellion against legitimate authority is a sin, an attempt to counter the brewing *patriote* rebellion.

Lower Canada, Oct. 24. Bishop Lartigue issues a pastoral letter condemning the reformist goals of the *patriotes.*

Upper Canada, Nov. 15. William Lyon Mackenzie publishes a draft republican constitution based on the American constitution and incorporating elements of radical English reformism and utilitarianism.

Lower Canada, November. Authorities find only five *patriote* leaders after Governor Gosford issues warrants for the arrest of 26.

Toronto, Dec. 4. William Lyon Mackenzie's Patriot rebels assembled at Montgomery's Tavern north of Toronto make a scouting expedition to check on the city's preparedness for attack. They capture Alderman John Powell, who escapes and warns the city of the rebels.

Toronto, Dec. 7. Large numbers of loyalist reinforcements arrive from across the province to help put down Mackenzie's Patriot rebellion.

Toronto, Dec. 7. Loyalist militia march to Montgomery's Tavern and defeat Mackenzie's smaller and badly armed force of rebels, ending Mackenzie's Toronto revolt.

Buffalo, New York, Dec. 11. Mackenzie is enthusiastically received as a political refugee after his recently failed rebellion. He begins recruiting to continue the uprising.

Upper Canada, Dec. 13. Charles Duncombe, leader of a rebel force of 300 gathered near Brantford, orders the rebels to disperse after learning of Mackenzie's Toronto defeat and the approach of a loyalist army under Alan MacNab.

London. Anna Jameson publishes *Winter Studies and Summer Rambles in Canada*, an account of her recent visit. She lambastes the pretentiousness of Toronto, and shows sympathy for Indians.

Indian evidence all right in liquor cases

Indians such as these can now testify in alcohol cases in Assiniboia courts.

Feb. 2, 1837

ASSINIBOIA – The council at Assiniboia has decided to accept evidence given by Indians as valid in cases where traders are charged with selling alcohol to the natives. In fact, half of the fines are to go to people providing information that leads to a conviction.

Assiniboia's governor and council, which was created upon the return of the settlement to the Hudson's Bay Company, have taken an interest in the general well-being of the people, as opposed to simply dealing with matters such as trade, as they did in the past. The council has instituted penalties for such things as starting fires on the plains, allowing livestock to run free, or borrowing a horse without permission. It has established a police force and a court system. The council also deals with such matters as public buildings, roads, agriculture and education.

Resolutions reject demands Assembly made of the British

March 2, 1837

QUEBEC CITY – Anger is the only word that can describe the mood of the elected Assembly, following the rejection of their demands for reform by the British government.

The rejection came in the form of "Ten Resolutions" authored by the British colonial secretary Lord John Russell, and released today. All of the demands of the Lower Canadian House are simply dismissed. As well, the Assembly's one weapon – controlling funds used by the provincial government – is taken away. In his resolutions, Russell authorizes the appointed governor to take what funds he likes from the provincial treasury.

With control of the public purse gone, the people here and in Upper Canada have no more say about how public funds are spent. Appointed officials are no longer accountable to the elected Assembly, spelling the death of what little democracy there was in Canada. Patriots must now either submit, or organize a revolt.

Racial riot erupts over Mosely affair

1837

NIAGARA – As British North America quickly becomes the promised land for slaves in the American south, the influx of blacks to Niagara has stirred a bloody racial riot here.

The violence centres around the threatened extradition of escaped Kentucky slave Solomon Mosely. When Mosely was arrested, mulatto teacher Herbert Holmes led local blacks in a 24-hour vigil to stop the extradition. When the deputy sheriff eventually led Mosely out of jail chained to a wagon, blacks grabbed the reins and guards opened fire. They killed Holmes and another man, while more than 20 blacks were arrested and Mosely escaped. In the aftermath of the riot, cooler heads are prevailing. All blacks have been released from jail, and Mosely has been allowed to return.

Chief Assiginack a man of many talents

UPPER CANADA – Jean-Baptiste Assiginack, Indian chief, interpreter and Catholic preacher, is also a skilled carver. In 1820, he made a metre-long model canoe as a souvenir for Europeans. Seven painted figures sit in the canoe, wearing leggings, breechcloths, garters, sashes and feather headdresses. They represent prominent Indians Assiginack knows.

Wood carving made by Ottawa chief Assiginack as a souvenir for Europeans. The figures, with distinct facial features, represent real people he knows.

Ritual native garb confers blessings

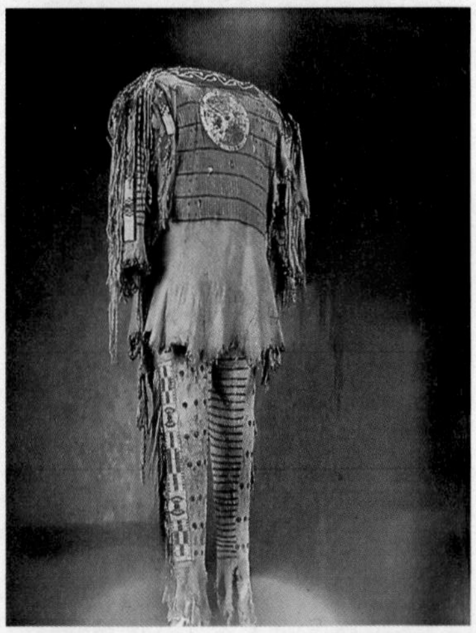

Blackfoot warrior's suit is believed to confer the power of three patrons: the sun, the weasel and the bear.

c.1837

PRAIRIES – For the Blackfoot, a warrior's clothing can pay him great dividends. Ritual costumes connected with spiritual patrons confer blessings and prestige. The Weaseltail Suit, for instance, marked by fringes of weasel fur and painted tadpole symbols, gives its owner the spiritual powers of the underworld.

Ritual Blackfoot costumes cost up to 30 horses. They are passed among warriors, considered sacred, and honored with sweatgrass.

Methodist hymns win Indian's praise

Indian converts have "good clothes."

The governor of Red River takes his family for a drive.

March 10, 1837

ST. CLAIR, Upper Canada – "I am sure one of them is worth more than all the songs and tunes of our fathers." So writes George Henry, or Maungwudaus (Great Hero), of the Methodist hymns he is translating into Ojibwa at the Methodist mission station at Lake St. Clair.

Maungwudaus, a half-brother of Sacred Feathers, is one of the most promising Mississauga Indian converts. Over the last decade he has taught at the Credit Mission Sunday school, been on a mission to Sault Ste. Marie, and acted as a missionary interpreter at Munceytown, near London, and now at St. Clair [Sarnia, Ont.].

In embracing Christianity, Maungwudaus has totally rejected his ancestors' religion and cultural ways. He writes of the Ojibwa Indian converts: "Since the great spirit has blessed them they have good clothes; plates and dishes; window and bed curtains; knives and forks; chairs and tables ... but what is better than all these things they have the religion of Jesus Christ."

Indians before Christian influence.

Upper Canadian banks in trouble

1837

UPPER CANADA – Banks here are more troubled this summer than ever before, as Upper and Lower Canada's private and public financial crisis adds to the commercial depression spreading in Europe, America and in the Canadas.

Lower Canadian banks, on the other hand, have been able to escape the crisis almost scot-free. They've suspended cash payments to clients, averting a serious run on their cash supplies. The main reason banks in Upper Canada are in so much trouble is because they have to contend with the province's lieutenant-governor, who says the banks must fulfil obligations to clients as a point of honor.

Reformers draw up a list of grievances

July 31, 1837

TORONTO – Reformers met today in Toronto, at John Doel's brewery. Their purpose: to adopt a list of grievances against the provincial government and a "plan of organization" drawn up by noted radical William Lyon Mackenzie.

The reform plan aims at bringing all the reformers into a single "political union." What is different about this plan, says Mackenzie, is that the organization "could easily be transferred without change of its structure to military purposes." This clearly hints at open rebellion and won't please the government, already upset at popular unrest.

Patriotes to ask Americans for free trade

May 23, 1837

MONTREAL – The Permanent Central Committee, French-Canadian *patriotes* demanding radical political reform, intends to ask the American Congress for free trade between Canada and the United States. The move is the latest aimed at forcing the Crown to grant the elected Assembly control of the provincial government.

Led by Louis-Joseph Papineau, an Assembly member with reformist tendencies, the PCC wants a boycott of all taxable British goods, in an attempt to starve the government of funds. It is also organizing public rallies across Lower Canada.

Mass patriote rally slams British rule

May 7, 1837

ST. OURS, Lower Canada – Echoing the American Declaration of Independence, 1,200 people gathered here at a *patriote* rally, to approve 12 resolutions advocating self-government in Canada. Staged by the Permanent Central Committee, a *patriote* group spearheaded by Reformer-parliamentarian Louis-Joseph Papineau, the rally targeted the British government's attempt to run the province without the population's consent.

Among the resolutions are inflammatory statements such as, "Regarding ourselves as no longer bound except by force to the English government, we shall submit to it as to a government of force."

Patriote rebels turn back British army at St. Denis

Tired, frost-bitten British troops were no match for rebels at St. Denis.

Nov. 24, 1837

ST. DENIS, Lower Canada – Civil war has broken out here, and so far the *patriote* rebels appear to be winning. Today they routed a British attack led by Col. Charles Stephen Gore.

Inside government sources say Gore's force was supposed to take the *patriote*-held village of St. Denis by surprise last night. However, bad road conditions delayed the regulars, and so this morning hundreds of tired, frost-bitten troops made the charge. They came up against an alert, well-defended rebel garrison at St. Denis, reinforced by other *patriotes* summoned by village church bells.

The fighting raged for five hours, costing the British six dead and 18 wounded. At roll call tonight, it was apparent 100 more had deserted. The *patriote* force of 800 strong, lost 11 men killed, and seven wounded. It also lost its military commander, to cowardice, not death, when rebel leader Louis-Joseph Papineau fled the battlefield during the hostilities. Dr. Wolfred Nelson took his place and led the *patriote* fight.

Attack on government troops ignites war

Nov. 16, 1837

LONGUEUIL, Lower Canada – War has broken out, with an attack near Longueuil on government troops by *patriote* rebels. Soldiers with the Montreal Volunteer Cavalry, en route to St. John's to arrest some *patriote* leaders, were set upon by a rebel force led by Bonaventure Viger and Dr. Timothée Kimber. It appears shots were fired by both sides and there were casualties. The hostility simmering all year has finally led to violence.

Assembly members boycott British goods

August 1837

LOWER CANADA – Patriotic members of the Assembly in Lower Canada are following the advice of rebellion leaders by boycotting British goods – save those smuggled in from the United States.

At the same time, members have been making appearances in unique costumes, too. Edouard Rodier showed up to the opening of the Assembly wearing only a pair of Berlin gloves, a frock coat of granite-colored homespun material, a blue and white striped vest of the same material, a straw hat, and beef shoes with a pair of home-made socks. He wore no shirt, being unable to either make one or smuggle one in. Member Edmund O'Callaghan also made his presence felt with a costume made up of nothing more than a hat, boots, gloves, a shirt and spectacles.

The boycott by Lower Canada *patriotes* is intended to deprive the government of customs revenues, its main source of income.

Policy says no to responsible government

March 6, 1837

LONDON, England – The British government has announced its new Canadian policy based on Lord John Russell's Ten Resolutions and a report prepared by the royal commission sent to Canada to look into the "Canadian situation." The policy rejects Canadian demands for responsible government while maintaining the old doctrines of colonial government.

The British government passed Russell's Ten Resolutions after a three-day debate in the House of Commons. Except for the Radicals, the Commons agreed to support the government proposals.

Russell's resolutions reject outright the idea of responsible government in Canada. However, they also affirm the title of the British American Land Company, offer hope of the revocation of the Tenure Act, and authorize the governor to take provincial funds without the authority of the Canadian legislature.

News of patriote success spreads quickly

Nov. 16, 1837

LONGUEUIL, Lower Canada – More details are in about tonight's attack on government forces by *patriote* rebels. Apparently 15 cavalrymen led by Constable Malo were set upon by 150 *patriotes.* The troops were escorting rebel prisoners, freed in the attack.

News of this *patriote* success is spreading fast. Because of it, rebels are said to be establishing military camps at St. Denis and St. Charles. Rallies are being organized in these areas, in an effort to convince local country people to take up arms and join the rebellion. How many do will determine its outcome.

Patriotes encourage locals to fight.

British troops avenge lieutenant's death

Dec. 1, 1837

ST. DENIS, Lower Canada – British troops have sacked and looted this stronghold of *patriote* support, the site of their defeat a week earlier. Much of the passion that drove them to victory was a desire to avenge the death of Lieut. Jack Weir. He was taken prisoner before the first battle here. Sighting British troops after his capture, Weir was murdered trying to flee.

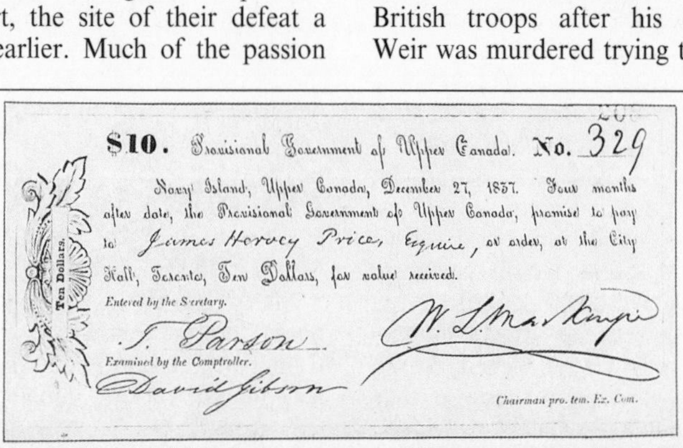

$10. Provisional Government of Upper Canada. No. 329

Navy Island, Upper Canada, December 27, 1837. Four months after date, the Provisional Government of Upper Canada, promise to pay to James Harvey Price, Esquire, or order, at the City Hall, Toronto, Ten Dollars, for value received.

Ten Dollars.

Entered by the Secretary.
T. Parson
Examined by the Comptroller.
David Gibson
W. L. Mackenzie
Chairman pro. tem. Ex. Com.

A $10 note the provisional government of Upper Canada issued is made out to James Harvey Price and signed by William Lyon Mackenzie.

Priest defies bishop by joining patriotes

Nov. 21, 1837

LA PRESENTATION, Lower Canada – The wave of rebellion crashing through Lower Canada is sweeping some of the Roman Catholic clergy along in its wake, despite orders from Bishop Jean-Jacques Lartigue to obey the law. The latest convert was found here today, when an unnamed local priest shed his façade of obedience and declared himself a *patriote* at a secret revolutionary meeting held right in his presbytery. Some other *patriote* priests include Curé Blanchet of St. Charles, who gave absolution to rebels before the battle here, and Curé Demers of St. Denis.

British crush rebel base at St. Charles

Nov. 24, 1837

ST. CHARLES, Lower Canada – British troops have captured the *patriote* base here, a fortified manor house the rebels seized days ago from seigneur Pierre-Dominique Debartzch. In doing so, they razed much of the village of St. Charles, and killed at least 40 rebels.

The rout is a stunning defeat for *patriote* leaders, most of whom fled the battle before it was even over. One fugitive is "General" T.S. Brown, a Montreal carter named to command St. Charles by Louis-Joseph Papineau. He rationalizes the defeat by saying his 200 men had worn-out guns, and that rebels were outnumbered two-to-one.

Inferior weapons and smaller numbers led to patriote defeat at hands of British.

Governor cracks down: warrants issued for leading patriotes

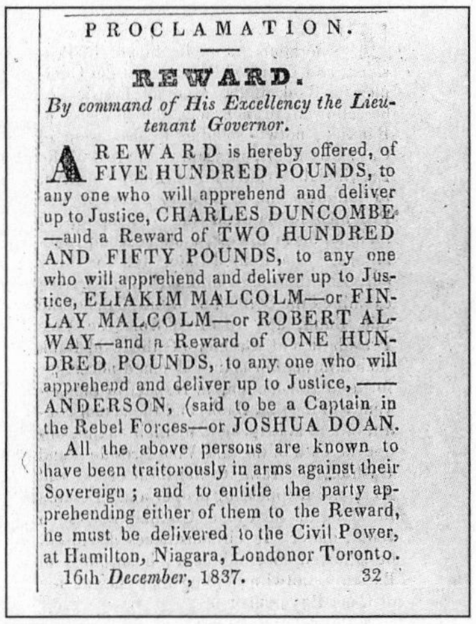

PROCLAMATION.

REWARD.

By command of His Excellency the Lieutenant Governor.

A REWARD is hereby offered, of FIVE HUNDRED POUNDS, to any one who will apprehend and deliver up to Justice, CHARLES DUNCOMBE—and a Reward of TWO HUNDRED AND FIFTY POUNDS, to any one who will apprehend and deliver up to Justice, ELIAKIM MALCOLM—or FINLAY MALCOLM—or ROBERT ALWAY—and a Reward of ONE HUNDRED POUNDS, to any one who will apprehend and deliver up to Justice, —— ANDERSON, (said to be a Captain in the Rebel Forces—or JOSHUA DOAN.

All the above persons are known to have been traitorously in arms against their Sovereign; and to entitle the party apprehending either of them to the Reward, he must be delivered to the Civil Power, at Hamilton, Niagara, Londonor Toronto.

16th *December*, 1837. 32

Proclamation describes the rewards offered for capture of rebels.

A price of £500 has been put on the head of rebel Dr. Charles Duncombe.

Nov. 16, 1837

MONTREAL – Alarmed at the rapid growth of chaos in this city and other areas of Lower Canada, Gov. Archibald Acheson, Lord Gosford, is cracking down on the *patriotes* before the situation breaks into civil war. Following a riot in Montreal a few days ago between *patriotes* and government supporters, he has banned all public meetings and processions.

A government source says Gosford also wants to proclaim martial law, and has written London for its blessing. Most importantly, he has issued warrants for the arrest of 26 *patriote* leaders, including the kingpin, Louis-Joseph Papineau.

Seduced women's interests ignored

1837

UPPER CANADA – The government of Upper Canada believes when a young woman is seduced, it is her family that suffers the most. Consequently, it's not surprising to learn Upper Canada lawmakers recently passed legislation recognizing "the wound given to parental feelings, the disgrace and injury inflicted upon the family of the person seduced." The law ignores the interests of the woman concerned.

The fact that young women often work as servants and are vulnerable to being seduced by their masters is the main reason for the new law.

Nelson encourages an open rebellion

Oct. 23, 1837

ST. CHARLES, Lower Canada – Some 5,000 people gathered here tonight to hear the major *patriote* leaders, including their nominal chief, Louis-Joseph Papineau. One leader, Dr. Wolfred Nelson, encouraged open rebellion, telling the crowd it was time "to melt our spoons into bullets." Young Dr. Jean-Olivier Chenier, from St. Eustache, agreed. Earlier Chenier vowed, "What I say to you I believe and will do. Follow me, and you may kill me if you see me run away."

Opposition growing to appointed Tories

Nov. 11, 1837

ST. THOMAS, Upper Canada – The growing animosity against the appointed Tories who rule this province is crystalizing into organized opposition here and in other parts of the province.

Tonight St. Thomas residents voiced their concerns at a meeting to consider forming a "political union." Such groups are being formed to pressure the provincial government – and London – into granting democratic reforms loyal British subjects are crying for.

A drawing by William H. Wentworth depicts the chaos that reigned during the great fire that hit Saint John, New Brunswick, on Jan. 14, 1837.

Officer dies trying to report on rebels

Col. Moodie is fatally shot while running rebel barricades on Yonge Street.

Dec. 4, 1837

TORONTO – The city of Toronto is under siege by William Lyon Mackenzie's rebels, and, although the attack has yet to begin, there has already been a casualty. Col. Robert Moodie, a loyalist who lived north of Toronto, was fatally wounded tonight as he attempted to reach the city to report on rebel activities at Montgomery's Tavern.

Moodie managed to run the first of three barricades on Yonge Street at the tavern. At the second, Moodie fired his pistol, an action answered by four rebel rifles. Moodie fell from his horse, and died a few hours later while in rebel hands.

Mackenzie poised to attack Toronto

Dec. 4, 1837

TORONTO – At this hour, hundreds of farmers and reform supporters are gathering at Montgomery's Tavern. Here, their leader, William Lyon Mackenzie, is assembling his forces for an attack on Toronto scheduled for Dec. 7.

Initially, this attack was meant to overthrow the government here at the same time as the Lower Canadian administration was being overthrown by force. While that rebellion has been put down, Mackenzie is determined to go ahead.

Rebellion begins as Mackenzie leads march down Yonge Street

Dec. 5, 1837

TORONTO – The long-awaited rebellion has begun. Hundreds of men, under William Lyon Mackenzie, have left their camp at Montgomery's Tavern north of the city, and are marching on Yonge Street hoping to capture Toronto. The attack was set for Dec. 7, but news of reinforcements motivated its leaders to strike now, while the capital is relatively defenceless. However, the rush means the force is poorly-armed; just a few rifles, plus pitchforks and knives.

Mackenzie's chances look good. Since the lieutenant-governor, Sir Francis Bond Head, has refused to take the rebellion seriously, the city is wide open. As usual, only the local militia will oppose this march.

Hundreds of rebels leave Montgomery's Tavern and march down Yonge Street.

Governor declares state of martial law

Dec. 5, 1837

MONTREAL – Martial law has been declared in Lower Canada by the governor, Lord Gosford, for the third time in this province since the 1760 conquest. In this case, it's the *patriote* rebels the governor is trying to suppress. He's already told the populace to give up their arms, and put a price on the leaders of the *patriote* movement.

However, it seems unlikely that this action will have any effect on the temptestuous situation here. Even though the rebels' military campaign has failed, and its leaders are in hiding in the United States, the fact remains that public order in this province is in a state of chaos.

The revolt is over: rebels defeated at Montgomery's Tavern

Rebels led by Mackenzie take a beating from government troops yet again.

Dec. 7, 1837

TORONTO – Rebels-in-arms led by William Lyon Mackenzie have been dispersed by government militia after a half-hour battle at Montgomery's Tavern, on Yonge Street north of Toronto.

Today's rout comes on the heels of yesterday's rebel defeat, when a force several hundred strong ran after exchanging shots with a posse of government supporters at a roadblock above the city's northern limits. Apparently confusion was the major reason the rebels ran. With today's rout, the revolt is over.

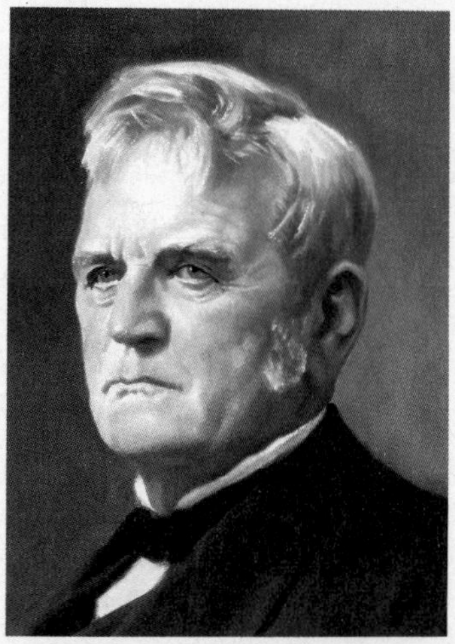

A better plow developed this year by John Deere of Illinois is good news for Canadian farmers.

Government troops set fire to village

Dec. 15, 1837

ST. BENOIT, Lower Canada – Government troops, aided by volunteers, have burnt this village to the ground, despite the fact it surrendered without a fight. And it's not the only village feeling the wrath of the loyalists, many of whom want revenge against the *patriotes*. The village of St. Eustache has also suffered, with more than 100 *patriotes* killed.

The government blames most of the destruction on volunteers, saying its regular troops are well-disciplined. In any case, burnt-out homes and the dead are the legacy the *patriotes* have left behind.

Soldiers overpower remains of the rebellion in Lower Canada

Lower Canadian rebels are dispersed by government troops at St. Eustache.

Dec. 14, 1837

ST. EUSTACHE, Lower Canada – About 2,000 loyalist soldiers under Sir John Colborne today crushed the remains of the Lower Canadian rebellion here at St. Eustache. Their target, for rifles and cannon alike, was the village church, in which 250 rebels had taken refuge. To drive them out, soldiers set fire to the church, then shot those who escaped the flames by jumping out windows. Those remaining inside burned to death.

More than 70 *patriotes* were killed, including young leader Jean-Olivier Chenier, the rest captured. Soldiers celebrated by pillaging and burning the village. In this way end the hopes of the rebellion.

Loyalists strike a blow at the rebellion

Rebel steamboat Caroline is cut loose and set ablaze by loyalists.

Dec. 29, 1837

NIAGARA FALLS – Under a cloak of darkness, seven boatloads of loyalist lads armed with cutlasses and pistols crossed the Niagara River to cut the rebel steamer *Caroline* free. Found on the American side, Royal Navy Capt. A. Drew, risked violating American territory to lead the ship to midstream and set it to the torch.

Isolating William Lyon Mackenzie and his men under the drunk "General" Van Rensselaer on Navy Island, this action has struck a mortal blow at the rebellion. No longer able to secure supplies from American Fort Schlosser, funds from the wealthy citizens of Buffalo, or recruits from the slums, Mackenzie's declaration that he is "chairman pro tem of the provincial government of the state of Upper Canada" has become the boast of a braggart.

Those who resisted were "dealt with according to the usages of war." Those who surrendered were put ashore. One American was killed. Witness Samuel Strickland said "the night was intensely dark, yet every surrounding object was distinctly visible in the wild glare caused by the *Caroline* as she rushed into the thundering abyss (of Niagara Falls) below."

Island proclaimed "Republic of Canada"

Dec. 13, 1837

NAVY ISLAND, in the Niagara River – Today, while many of his supporters are either in hiding or in chains, rebel leader William Lyon Mackenzie has established the "Republic of Canada" on Navy Island. He's also created a new flag for the country, and made himself chief of state.

Navy Island is a good place to start a republic, if one wants to stay away from Canadian authorities. It is a good distance from Canadian shores, yet a stone's throw from Grand Island, N.Y. Since much of Mackenzie's support comes from Americans who wish to see Canada join the Union, it doesn't seem the U.S. will help capture him, or conquer his republic.

As for the flag, it is a tricolor bearing two stars; one symbolizing English Canada, one French. But as to whether this flag will ever fly over all of Canada is another question. The fact is that government forces have thoroughly crushed the rebels in both provinces. A full-blown coup seems impossible now.

Rebel William Lyon Mackenzie.

Swindlers are operating sham Canadian banks, issuing worthless currency such as this $3 note. The notes are circulating mainly in the U.S., where banks have suspended redemption of bank notes in coin, due to a depression.

1838

United States, Jan. 5. President Van Buren issues a proclamation declaring American neutrality in the rebellions of Upper and Lower Canada.

Upper Canada, Jan. 14. Patriot rebels occupying Navy Island since Dec. 14 evacuate in the face of heavy artillery fire from the British.

Buffalo, New York, January. Patriot rebel leader William Lyon Mackenzie is arrested for violating the American neutrality laws.

Lower Canada, Feb. 22. In a letter to Governor Gosford, Archbishop Signay argues that if the province cuts its ties with Britain the Catholic clergy in the province will be doomed.

Upper Canada, May 29. William Johnston and a band of Patriots hijack and burn the steamship *Sir Robert Peel* at Wells Island. Johnston and his men are basically pirates, rather than politically motivated rebels.

London, Sept. 14. Ojibwa leader Peter Jones (Sacred Feathers) has an audience with Queen Victoria at Buckingham Palace.

Quebec, Oct. 16. Five Patriot prisoners led by Dr. Edward Theller escape from the citadel of Quebec, causing general excitement in the city.

Lower Canada, Nov. 3. Some 800 *patriote* rebels take possession of the town of Beauharnois, including the seigneurial manor.

Lower Canada, Nov. 4. Radical *patriote* Dr. Robert Nelson establishes himself at Napierville with about 2,000 men. He issues his proclamation of independence of the previous February, and is proclaimed president of Lower Canada.

Lower Canada, Nov. 4. Lieutenant-General John Colborne proclaims martial law.

Lower Canada, Nov. 10. Government militia disperses *patriote* rebels from their strongholds at Napierville and Beauharnois. They burn Beauharnois, and the houses of known rebels in the area.

Lower Canada, December 19. Ther are 753 *patriotes* in custody, captured by government militia during the recent rebellion.

Upper Canada. The settler population is 400,000, compared to 90,000 in 1812, and 14,000 in 1791.

Nelson leads rebels back into Canada

Wolfred Nelson, a patriote leader.

Robert Nelson, new "president."

Feb. 28, 1838

NOYAN, Lower Canada – After leading hundreds of well-armed Canadian rebels back into Canada from refuge in Vermont, Dr. Robert Nelson, Wolfred's brother, today declared himself president of the provisional government of Lower Canada. The Montreal surgeon read a proclamation demanding an independent republic, an end to seigneurial tenure and the Catholic tithe, and suffrage for all males, including Indians.

Nelson fled after last year's *patriote* rebellion was crushed, and is expected to return to Vermont to prepare a full-scale invasion. Many American filibusterers accompanied him to Canada today.

Blacks join fight against the rebellion

1838

CHATHAM, Upper Canada – The Second Coloured Company of Chatham has been established to help fight against the rebellion William Lyon Mackenzie started in December 1837.

Blacks are playing a larger role in the rebellion than they have in the past. Within a month of the revolt's beginning, about 1,000 blacks volunteered for service. For the most part, their role is to guard bridges and buildings, though many have taken part in capturing rebel ships and guarding forts.

Life goes on: While loyalists and patriotes are engaging in military skirmishes, habitants proceed with their usual early spring routine of tapping maple trees and painstakingly boiling down the sap to make syrup and sugar.

England suspends the constitution of Lower Canada

Feb. 10, 1838

MONTREAL – It seems the rebellions of 1837 may not entirely have been in vain. Today the British parliament suspended Lower Canada's constitution until Nov. 1, 1840. More importantly, the members also appointed Lord Durham the new governor-general, with orders to investigate Canadian grievances and find a solution.

Durham has a reputation as a moderate reformer. It's believed he is committed to returning the Assembly to action as soon as possible, following his inquiries. And it's hoped he will take heed of the violence besetting this land, and offer something different than the answer of previous British administrators, namely more repression.

Meanwhile, Lower Canada is to be ruled by an appointed council, chosen at the moment by the current governor, Sir John Colborne. The elected Assembly is suspended along with the constitution.

Institute to better P.E.I. working men

1838

CHARLOTTETOWN – The latest Mechanics' Institute opened in Charlottetown today. It is one of many which are springing up in England and British North America. The first one was established in England in the 1820s by a Dr. Birkbeck.

Mechanics' Institutes are community-based associations used by working men to better themselves through education. Individual institutes offer their members lectures, reference libraries, study classes and reading rooms. Their purpose is to provide learning that benefits one's work, and to offer general information.

Institutes have already been established in Toronto and Kingston, as well as other centres. The success of the Mechanics' Institutes has led the government to grant a sum of money – proportionate to the amount contributed by members – for the purchase of books.

Durham to tackle political problems

May 29, 1838

QUEBEC CITY – John George Lambton, Earl of Durham, is here to take over as governor of British North America. Durham plans to conduct an inquiry into political problems plaguing Lower and Upper Canada. Known as a reformer and a radical, he is expected to find a solution to the *patriote* rebellion in the province. Durham succeeds Sir John Colborne, who governed with the help of a specially appointed council of 11 English- and 11 French-Canadians.

Lord Durham is in Quebec City.

Reformer Baldwins meet with governor

Spring 1838

UPPER CANADA – The new governor-in-chief, Lord Durham, has personally interviewed lawyer Robert Baldwin and his father Dr. William Warren Baldwin, two of Upper Canada's most respected Reformers. During the brief session, the Baldwins discussed their concept of responsible government, and later Robert submitted a detailed memorandum on the subject.

Robert Baldwin, who recently defended several men accused of participating in the 1837-38 rebellions, believes that by applying Britain's own principles of ministerial responsibility, the colony can achieve self-government while remaining within the imperial system. Foreign affairs would remain the prerogative of Britain.

Lount and Matthews hang for treason

Mrs. Lount pleads with Sir George Arthur to spare her husband Samuel.

April 12, 1838

TORONTO – Rebellion leaders Col. Samuel Lount and Capt. Peter Matthews were hanged today before a huge crowd of onlookers. The pair were executed despite appeals and petitions to Lt.-Gov. George Arthur. Lount and Matthews pleaded guilty to treason and were sentenced by Chief Justice John Robinson.

Lount and Matthews held to their beliefs to the very end and mounted the gallows steps without faltering. According to a fellow prisoner, Charles Durand, Lount had been in good spirits right up until the day of execution, and had declared that he "would do the same thing again" in order that "some day Canada would be free."

The gallows was erected and prisoners were allowed to observe the hangings from their cell windows. They watched as Lount and Matthews knelt in prayer on the gallows before nooses were slipped around their necks. The trap was released and in moments the rebel pair were dead.

Crowd gathers for the public execution of rebels Lount and Matthews.

Trader administers Indian vaccinations

1838

FORT PELLY, Northwest – As Indians start arriving here for the spring fur trade, they are giving warm thanks to Hudson's Bay Company factor William Todd. An experienced physician, Todd has just engineered the first vaccination campaign on the Canadian prairies in an all-out effort to fight a deadly smallpox epidemic ravaging the Indian population.

Todd has been both relentless and professional in his efforts since Cree Indians first informed him of the epidemic last Sept. 20. Even though reports of the disease were not confirmed, he lost no time getting a vaccination campaign under way. He immediately assembled all the Indians of the area, explained the danger of the disease, and proposed his vaccination plans. The Indians readily agreed, and Todd proceeded to inoculate 60 of them. He vaccinated every Indian who came to the post in the fall and winter, except for a few Cree and Assiniboine who refused to be treated. He taught the vaccination procedure to Indians who came to the post, and sent vaccines to other trading posts, along with instructions on how to use them. All these efforts were possible because the Hudson's Bay Company outfitted traders with vaccines and ordered them to be administered in the name of humanity and good business. Unfortunately, few traders have followed the orders until now.

Todd and his collaborators stopped the spread of the disease by late winter. They prevented it from reaching the Woodland Indians, but could not stop it from ravaging the Plains Indians – up to three quarters of the population of some groups died. The Assiniboine, Blackfoot, Blood, Peigan, and Sarcees were especially hard hit. The worst part of the catastrophe, Edmonton House trader John Rowand says, is "to have to witness so much misery without being able to do any good."

Smallpox was first carried into HBC territory by Indians trying to flee an epidemic ravaging the Missouri River Valley, where the disease was introduced by an American Fur Company steamer in June. ▷

British repel American raid on island

March 3, 1838

PELEE ISLAND – British forces have repelled an American raid on Pelee Island, some 30 kilometres from the Canadian shore of Lake Erie between Kingsville and Leamington. About 1,000 mostly-American raiders had been occupying the 11,000 acre island when the British arrived. Cavalry and artillery on horses and infantrymen in sleighs crossed over the 15-inch ice on frozen Lake Erie, but the raiders had fled, their pots of potatoes still boiling in their empty camp. The British pursued, and one eyewitness saw blood staining the snow for a quarter of a mile as the raiders retreated. At least 11 Americans died, and several were captured.

About 1,000 U.S. Patriots are repelled by British troops at Pelee Island.

Short Hills raid spells doom for Patriots

June 1838

SHORT HILLS, Upper Canada – A group of Patriots from the United States faces execution after a failed attack on Short Hills and surrounding area in Upper Canada. Some 34 men crossed the frontier and remained in Upper Canada for 10 days before being detected. They hoped to induce the Grand River Six Nations Indians, British loyalists, to rise up in rebellion.

American rebels attack but are defeated at Dickinson Landing, Upper Canada.

Canadians and British unite to turn back invasion of the "Yankee expansionists"

American invaders took refuge in this windmill, but were forced to surrender.

Nov. 16, 1838

PRESCOTT, Upper Canada – British regulars with two cannons arrived from Kingston and blasted out the walls of a large stone windmill near the U.S. border where American invaders had taken refuge from Canadian militiamen. Before surrendering, about 30 invaders died, and 160 were captured.

The invasion of the 400 "Yankee expansionists," as the local press calls them, began Nov. 11, when they crossed the river at Prescott to help Lower Canadian rebels with an uprising they started last month. But that revolt was short-lived, as the militia had been alerted by magistrates, militia officers and clergymen in Lower Canada.

American prisoners will no doubt be facing some harsh penalties, despite Upper Canada Lt.-Gov. Sir George Arthur's decision to be more lenient with Lower Canadian insurgents. Canada's executive councils have called for severe punishment as the only way to discourage future American invasions into Lower Canada.

The lieutenant-governor opposes capital punishment for Canadian rebels, so some of the worst offenders are getting lengthy terms in penal colonies. Many rebels are being set free, however, to help cool the Lower Canadian *patriote* fire. Arthur is also aware that a fair jury trial is impossible, as French-speaking juries would free all the rebels, and English-speaking juries would see that they are all hanged.

Leaders of rebellion exiled to Bermuda

June 28, 1838

MONTREAL – "By what authority do you chain us like felons?" Wolfred Nelson yelled out today as he was led in shackles from the jail by the waterfront to a ship waiting to take him and eight other leaders of the recent *patriote* rebellions to exile in Bermuda. Nelson was forced to stoop, as he was chained to a shorter man. Meanwhile, cavalry drove back crowds jostling on the street and along the waterfront trying to catch a glimpse of the rebels. And in the end, Nelson's histrionic question went unanswered. Disregarding legal precedent, Lord Durham recently exiled the nine rebel leaders and gave amnesty to other political prisoners, after the leaders signed an ambiguous admission of guilt. The official penalty for Nelson's crime of high treason is death. But Durham feared a storm of protest if he permitted the execution of Nelson and other *patriote* leaders, who since last November's successful battle against the British at St. Denis are heroes to most Lower Canadians.

Battle of Windsor: Prince's militiamen turn back Patriots

Dec. 4, 1838

WINDSOR, Upper Canada – American Patriots scored a short-lived victory over the British in Windsor today. Poorly armed, the 135 men marched into the town ready to take over. The invaders set the British barracks on fire before torching a steamer and two neighboring houses. A black man named Mills, who refused to join the invaders and instead gave three cheers for the queen, was shot.

But then the Patriots entered into battle with Col. John Prince's forces in Windsor. A volley from the British was all that was needed: 44 Patriots were captured, and about 25 were killed. Four militia were killed and four wounded in the attack. Americans watching the battle from across the river say both parties retreated, and neither is claiming victory.

Young rebel hangs on the second try

Dec. 21, 1838

MONTREAL – It's as if Joseph Duquet was hanged twice today. The young *patriote,* whose death sentence Gov. John Colborne had questioned and Bishop Ignace Bourget appealed, had to be supported as he mounted the scaffold. When the trapdoor sprung, the noose slipped and he was thrown against the gallows. He lay moaning, fully conscious, his face pouring blood. The crowd yelled "pardon," but 20 minutes later Duquet was hanged with a new rope.

Duquet is only one of many men executed for their roles in the recent Canadian rebellions. On Dec. 8, Nils Gustaf von Schoultz, a Polish-born rebel "colonel," was hanged in Fort Henry, near Kingston. Schoultz was captured after a battle with Canadian troops at a windmill near Prescott where a force of about 400 made their headquarters until shelling led to their surrender.

In his last letter to his fiancée, Schoultz forgave all of "them who brought me to this untimely death. Let no further blood be shed."

Hudson's Bay Co. monopoly renewed

May 30, 1838

BUCKINGHAM PALACE, England – Queen Victoria has granted an extension of the monopoly enjoyed for the past 168 years by the Hudson's Bay Company. This grant follows the 1821 royal licence obtained from George IV which was due to expire in 1842. He had issued the licence for exclusive trading privileges upon the amalgamation of the Hudson's Bay and the North West fur-trading companies. The new grant, valid for 21 years, allows these privileges to continue and extends the trading area into lands not covered in the original 1670 charter. New areas include land west of the mountains and the Columbia River.

The purpose of the arrangement is to prevent competition which, it has been learned at great expense, causes hardships not only for the company, but for the fur trade and the trappers. It's felt that, in general, the HBC carries on more responsible and fairer trading practices than other companies or independent traders.

HBC governor on an inspection tour.

Bartlett leaves toting Canadian sketches

The Cedars, one of scores of Bartlett paintings depicting Canada in the 1800s.

December 1838

QUEBEC CITY – Renowned English illustrator William Henry Bartlett sailed for England this month, after spending the summer and fall in Canada depicting prominent sites such as Niagara Falls, and Canadians at their daily work. Bartlett's itinerary in the Canadas and any observations he made remain obscure, though he seems to have travelled from here westward to Niagara Falls, and then by way of the Erie Canal to New York state. For one sketch he visited the rapids on the approach to Cedars, a village near the junction of the Ottawa and St. Lawrence rivers.

Durham resigns, sails for England

Nov. 1, 1838

QUEBEC CITY – Lord Durham left for England today after resigning as governor when the British government repudiated his ordinance of June 28 exiling some rebels to Bermuda, and banning others from returning to Canada, though they had not yet been tried. Durham acted illegally, to save the men from execution. Before leaving he declared: "I shall feel anxious only to know how well and wisely I have used ... my great powers." Durham spent five months here.

MURRAY'S

FIRST BOOK FOR CHILDREN.

RE-PRINTED FROM THE

LATEST ENGLISH EDITION.

QUEBEC:

PRINTED AND SOLD BY W. COWAN & SON,

FABRIQUE STREET, UPPER TOWN.

1838.

Educating a young nation: "Murray's First Book for Children" is a sign of growing emphasis on education in Canada.

Nelson flees to U.S. after heavy losses

Nov. 9, 1838

NAPIERVILLE, Que. – Facing mutiny by his ragtag army, rebellion leader Robert Nelson fled to the United States today after failing in an attempt to capture Lower Canada and declare an independent republic.

Nelson retreated as a force of 5,000 troops and Indians marshalled in Laprairie by Gen. John Colborne attacked *patriote* forces here, killing at least 50. Nelson had been named "president" of the provisional government *patriotes* hoped to establish to replace British rule.

1839

Lower Canada, Jan. 2. The government closes *La Fantasque*, one of the only newspapers in the province not shut down during the Rebellions of 1837.

Lower Canada, Feb. 15. The last public execution of leaders of the 1837 rebellion is held.

Lower Canada, April 12. Upper Canadian Reformer Francis Hincks urges Lower Canadian Reformer Louis-Hippolyte LaFontaine to support the proposed union of the two provinces as a way of achieving responsible government.

Lower Canada, May 1. The last trial of leaders of the 1837 rebellions is held. Since last Nov. 28, 108 *patriotes* have been tried, 99 sentenced to death, and 12 executed. Fifty-eight were exiled to Australia, to the indignation of French-Canadians.

Upper Canada, May 11. Construction begins on a provincial lunatic asylum.

London, July 3. Lord John Russell, representing the British government, tells Parliament he opposes Lord Durham's plan for responsible government in Canada.

Northwest, July 4. The Council of Assiniboia establishes a more comprehensive judicial system in the area by increasing the number of judges assigned to each district.

Burlington, Vermont, Aug. 7. *Patriote* in exile Ludger Duvernay, founder of the St-Jean-Baptiste Society in 1834, launches the newspaper *Le Patriote Canadien.*

Arctic, September. British adventurer William Parry, accompanied by Inuit, explores Exeter Sound. He is searching for an inlet known as Tenudiakbeek, reputed to be a good whaling ground, but doesn't find it.

Montreal, Nov. 11. Governor Thomson submits his proposal for the union of Upper and Lower Canada to a Special Council. His terms are unfair to Lower Canada, and French-Canadians are outraged.

Toronto. John Strachan is consecrated as first bishop of the newly formed Anglican diocese of Toronto.

Upper Canada. The province's first comprehensive game law is passed, establishing a closed hunting season for many game birds.

New book to tackle Saulteaux tongue

1839

LOWER CANADA – Father Georges-Antoine Belcourt, who lives among the Ojibwa or Saulteaux Indians, is now in Lower Canada overseeing publication of his book entitled *Principles of the Saulteaux Indian Language.*

Belcourt's gift for Indian languages allows him to converse with Indians who live nearby. Algonquian languages are very challenging to speakers of European languages, which rely less on verbs. For Ojibwa, almost 80 percent of all words are verbs. Belcourt learned the language to try to convert the Indians to Christianity.

Durham: unite Canadas

Feb. 4, 1839

LONDON, England – In a report to the British parliament, Lord Durham, former governor-in-chief of the British North American colonies, has recommended a legislative union of Upper and Lower Canada. This union is necessary, Durham explains, to anglicize the French majority of Lower Canada: "I entertain no doubt of the national character which must be given to Lower Canada; it must be that of the British Empire; that of the great race which must, in the lapse of no long period of time, be predominant over the whole North American Continent."

To Durham, the social assimilation brought about by his proposed political union is as inevitable as it is desirable. French-Canadians, he says, are "destitute of all that can invigorate and elevate. ... They are a people with no history and no literature."

Durham also recommends responsible government for the new united Canadas, arguing for the creation of a responsible executive council to "place the internal government of the colony in the hands of the colonists themselves." But he stops short of recommending full independence, stating that matters such as trade, foreign affairs and disposal of public lands, should come under British control.

LaFontaine blasts Durham plan to assimilate French-Canadians

La Danse Ronde: Is French-Canadian culture threatened by Durham report?

April 21, 1839

LOWER CANADA – Louis-Hippolyte LaFontaine, a popular leader of the reform movement in Lower Canada, is angry about parts of Lord Durham's *Report on the Affairs of British North America.*

In a letter to British Reformer Francis Hincks, LaFontaine vehemently disagrees with the report's proposal to outlaw French in Canada. LaFontaine's letter is in response to one Hincks penned which supports the report's call for responsible government and the union of Upper and Lower Canada. A great Durham supporter, Hincks has been promoting the report with Durham meetings, Durham flags, and Durham songs.

A watercolor painting by Charles Wright shows a view of Château Haldimand and Place d'Armes in Quebec City in the late 1830s.

Russians lease land to Hudson's Bay Co.

February 1839

HAMBURG, Germany – Officials of the Hudson's Bay Company have signed an agreement here governing the fur trade on the Northern Pacific coast. The pact allows the British company to lease a strip of the coast from Russia for 10 years at an annual fee of 2,000 otter pelts and for other benefits. The Russians in Alaska have been hindering the British company's transportation of furs to the coast for export.

Simpson and Dease survey Arctic coast

Aug. 16, 1839

MONTREAL ISLAND, Arctic Coast – Thomas Simpson and Peter Warren Dease today reached this barren island in Chantrey Inlet, discovering a cache left by George Back three years ago.

By reaching the island, Simpson and Dease have almost closed the last gap of knowledge about the Arctic coast. Only a small part of the survey begun by British explorers many years ago is still to be completed. For the two Hudson's Bay Company employees, it is the third season of Arctic exploration.

Thomson arrives with Durham's blessing

Governor Charles Poulett Thomson.

Oct. 19, 1839

QUEBEC CITY – Charles Poulett Thomson has arrived in Quebec as the new governor of British North America. Thomson has come with the blessing of the former governor of the British North American colonies, Lord Durham, who resigned from his post last year when the British cabinet failed to support his orders that rebels be exiled to Bermuda. In Lower Canada, Thomson takes over the administration of Sir John Colborne.

Thomson brings with him the promise of a large guaranteed loan in hopes of gaining Canadian support for a union.

Governor can oust councillors: Russell

Oct. 16, 1839

LONDON, England – The colonial office has told Charles Poulett Thomson, British North America's new governor, not to encourage responsible government in Canada. Lord John Russell grants Thomson power to remove executive councillors from office at will. In his dispatch, Russell states responsible government cannot be reconciled with imperial supremacy, and if councillors' advice runs opposite to England's interests, following it would make the governor an independent sovereign.

Judge opposes moving Indians to island

Schim-a-co-che, a Crow Indian.

April 22, 1839

TORONTO – A judge of the Court of King's Bench has just submitted his report on Indian conditions in Upper Canada. In it, James B. Macaulay categorically rejects suggestions that the Indian civilization policy has failed, and that the Indians must be moved to distant Manitoulin Island.

Joseph Sawyer, head chief of the Mississauga Indians, who farm on their reserve at the Credit River 20 kilometres west of here, is delighted. "If we go to Manitoulin we could not live; soon we should be extinct as a people; we could raise no potatoes, corn, pork or beef; nothing would grow."

Medicine circles: Have efforts to "civilize" Indians in Upper Canada failed?

Border dispute headed for arbitration

March 25, 1839

NEW BRUNSWICK – War will not be waged over the timber rights of New Brunswick's and Maine's lumber barons. Gov. John Harvey and American Gen. Winfield Scott agreed to send the disputed border territory around the Aroostook River to arbitration.

With British regulars at the St. Croix River and Congress poised to send 50,000 men, Scott was dispatched to ease tensions over this British land route with Quebec.

Public officials no longer sitting for life

Aug. 16, 1839

LONDON, England – Sir John Russell, head of Britain's colonial office, has introduced a new concept to the administration of Canada. As of today, new appointees to public office will no longer hold their positions for life: they can stay in office only as long as the representative of the Crown feels they are useful. In other words, a public office is no longer considered a piece of property owned by the person holding it.

Legislation implementing this change will no doubt shock the most conservative of officials in British North America since it indirectly brings a form of responsible government to the colony.

Government House, Fredericton: Public officials are no longer here for life.

1840

Toronto, April 2. The city holds a street ox roast to celebrate Queen Victoria's marriage, inviting people to come cleanly attired, with a "knife, fork, and plate."

Fort Smith, Northwest, June 26. W. Davies returns from a HBC exploring expedition up the Churchill [Hamilton] River to find a supply route to Fort Nascopie. He ascended as far as Churchill [Grand] Falls.

Halifax, July 17. The *Britannia*, the first in a line of steamships to be built by Nova Scotian Samuel Cunard, crosses the Atlantic for the first time, causing much excitement in the city.

Isle of Wight, England, July 28. John Lambton, Earl of Durham, dies. After serving as governor-in-chief of British North America in 1838, he issued a report advocating union of the two Canadas as a way of achieving responsible government.

Queenston Heights, Upper Canada, July 30. Prominent citizens gather to discuss ways to raise money to repair the monument to Isaac Brock, recently blown up by an irate Irish-Canadian.

Nova Scotia, July. The first coal miners strike in the colony erupts.

Lower Canada, Aug. 18. Word arrives that Queen Victoria has signed the Act of Union uniting Upper and Lower Canada. The French-Canadian political community is united against the bill.

England, Aug. 19. Governor Charles Poulett Thomson is given a baronetcy. He is now Lord Sydenham.

St. Lawrence River, Oct. 19. The steamer *Ontario* is the first large vessel to navigate the upper St. Lawrence rapids.

Quebec, Oct. 20. One thousand people, most French-Canadian, oppose the Act of Union, but decide to participate in the coming elections.

Canada. Retired explorer and surveyor David Thompson writes that before Europeans came to North America, the continent "may be said to be in possession of two distinct races of beings, Man and the beaver."

Canada. The death penalty for stealing cows is abolished.

Quebec. Daguerreotypes (photographs) are taken for the first time in Canada.

Ojibwa and Iroquois renew friendship

Jan. 21, 1840

TORONTO – Ojibwa and Iroquois leaders held council today and ceremoniously passed the pipe of peace, renewing a pact of friendship first established between these once-bitter enemies in 1783. At a village on the Credit River, near Toronto, 200 Ojibwa chiefs and warriors and 15 Iroquois headmen ratified four earlier agreements with a treaty so strong "that if a tree fell across their arms it could not separate them or cause them to unloose their hold."

In the 17th century, the Algonquian alliance, to which the Ojibwa belonged, fought the Iroquois for control of the eastern Great Lakes region. By 1700 the Ojibwa had driven their enemy from southern [Ontario]. However, following the War of Independence the Ojibwa generously offered land to refugee Iroquois who wished to remain loyal to Britain. Now the Ojibwa and Iroquois, numbering several thousand, stand united amidst the wave of white settlers rapidly encroaching on their territory.

Missionary takes up post in Edmonton

Oct. 18, 1840

EDMONTON – This frontier town now has its own Christian minister. Rev. Robert Rundle just arrived here today to take up his posting as missionary. Rundle was sent out by the Wesleyan Society of London, and although the clergyman has no experience in the rugged colonial life, he appears to be quite eager to explore the vast area where he will find his converts.

Rundle is not the first clergyman to visit Edmonton. Fathers François Blanchet and Modeste Demers stopped by the settlement two years ago on their way to Fort Vancouver from St. Boniface.

Rev. Robert T. Rundle, missionary.

Egging destroying seabird population

1840

GULF OF ST. LAWRENCE – "This war of extermination cannot last many years more." So writes naturalist John James Audubon about the holocaust of seabirds under way through egging – the collection of seabird eggs for food. Audubon recently accompanied a group of eggers on an expedition to local seabird islands. They shoot birds when arriving on the islands, and proceed to crush and collect every egg they can find. Guillemots, gulls and ducks are among the worst victims of the egging.

Suicide suspected in shooting death of Arctic explorer Simpson

June 14, 1840

RED RIVER COLONY, Rupert's Land – Arctic explorer Thomas Simpson is dead, apparently by his own hand. The body of the Hudson's Bay Company employee was found at his camp south of here. Simpson has spent the past three summers exploring the coastline of the Arctic Ocean with his partner, Peter Warren Dease, in search of the Northwest Passage. Convinced he was close to completing the survey of the passage, Simpson wanted to finish his explorations this year, but the company did not answer his request.

Frustrated, depressed and angry that the company did not appreciate him, Simpson left here last week, on horseback and with four Métis companions, to visit company officials in London. As the party made camp this evening, Simpson shot and killed two of the Métis, saying it was self-defence. The other two men immediately rode off to seek help. Returning, they heard a single shot, and found the explorer dead with a gun in his hand and a massive head wound.

Some people are hinting that Simpson was murdered. Given his gloomy state of mind, however, and his history of bad relations with the Métis, it is more probable that Thomas Simpson is the victim of a combination of his own violent temper and his current deep depression.

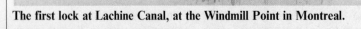

The first lock at Lachine Canal, at the Windmill Point in Montreal.

British act merges provinces to form "Canada"

July 23, 1840

LONDON, England – By an act approved by Parliament here today, Upper and Lower Canada have been merged into one province, called, not surprisingly, "Canada."

The move reflects the government's desire to rectify the political problems that led to the rebellions in 1837 and 1838. The new Province of Canada will be administered through a two-house system, an elected Assembly and an appointed Legislative Council, under an appointed governor general. A cabinet of ministers that is backed by, and responsible to, a majority in the elected Lower House, will put an end to the entrenched oligarchies previously so powerful in the Canadas – and so despised.

What makes this system different is the implicit attempt to swamp the French-Canadians. The House is split along the old lines of Upper and Lower Canada, with each region having 42 seats. However, since there are fewer English in Upper Canada than French in Lower Canada, the deliberate effect is to under-represent the French.

Explosives damage Brock's monument

April 17, 1840

QUEENSTON HEIGHTS, Upper Canada – The tomb of the hero of Upper Canada has been desecrated. Explosives were detonated on Good Friday by Irish-Canadian Benjamin Lett, seriously damaging the 40.5-metre Tuscan column raised in memory of Sir Isaac Brock, who fell "while advancing to repel the enemy" on Oct. 13, 1812.

Lett apparently tried to blow up the monument on Queenston Heights to avenge himself for being banished to the United States by the government for his role in the rebellions of 1837.

Inuit leads whaler to northern inlet

July 27, 1840

BAFFIN ISLAND – With the help of an Inuit guide, Scottish whaling captain William Penny has rediscovered an Arctic inlet last visited by explorers nearly 300 years ago. The guide, Eenoolooapik, grew up in the area, on the shores of Baffin Island, and spent last winter in Scotland perfecting his English as a guest of Penny.

Eenoolooapik reports that large numbers of whales visit the inlet each autumn. Penny hopes that the new whaling ground also will serve as a suitable location for a relief station to aid whaling vessels that get trapped in the Arctic ice. During the past decade many British whalers have died after their ships were wrecked or marooned in the north. Penny is now investigating the inlet, which he is reported to have named Hogarth's Sound [Cumberland Sound].

Carling's ale a hit; brewery opens at urging of local garrison

Thomas Carling, whose beer is reputed to be good, opens brewery on Waterloo Street in Upper Canada.

Carling's brewery, like Bloor's in Toronto (above), has started off modestly.

1840

LONDON, Upper Canada – Former amateur brewer Thomas Carling has opened a brewery on Waterloo Street, across from the barracks in Victoria Park, at the urging of the local garrison. A farmer since he arrived in Canada in 1818, Yorkshireman Carling won many friends for the ale he's provided at numerous building bees. Before long his beer became a favorite in the mugs of the local British garrison. Carling's new professional brewery consists of two potash kettles and a horse to turn the grinding mill. He employs six men, and sons Will and John.

LaFontaine urging Reformers to unite

Aug. 28, 1840

MONTREAL – A ringing appeal for unity in the struggle for responsible government was issued today by Lower Canada Reformer Louis-Hippolyte LaFontaine.

Published in *l'Aurore,* LaFontaine's manifesto denounces terms of union for the two Canadas and calls for his Reform party to fight the next election and then join with the Reformers of Upper Canada to win responsible government "as has been wished for and promised by the Assembly of Upper Canada." LaFontaine believes unification is the only way for French-Canadians to secure lost rights and freedoms.

Not enough women settling in Canada

c.1840

CANADA – Women are wanted in Canada, according to advertisements found in popular immigration literature. "Unmarried women, who have no fortunes, and are active, and industrious, without much pride or vanity, and who relish a quiet and retired life ... have an opportunity of being well married" in Canada. Females are scarce, so "every young farmer or laborer going out (who can pay for the passage of two) should take an active young wife with him."

But immigrants are told to leave behind their corkscrews: "Drinking is the great vice of the country."

Painting of England's Queen Victoria with her new husband, Prince Albert, after the royal wedding in 1840.

1841

Canada, March. Polling begins in Canada East and Canada West [Quebec and Ontario] for the first Parliament since the union of the two provinces.

Kingston, Canada West, August. The *Canadian Farmer and Mechanic* is launched, Canada's first agricultural journal.

Kingston, Canada West, Sept. 3. Reformer Robert Baldwin moves resolutions in the Assembly to make the executive more responsible to the Assembly.

Kingston, Canada West, Sept. 18. A bill for the establishment of non-denominational elementary schools receives royal assent after several amendments are passed.

Kingston, Canada West, Sept. 19. Charles Poulett Thomson, Baron of Sydenham and first governor general of the united Canadas, dies from lockjaw after a wound from a riding accident becomes infected. The accident happened while he was returning from a meeting with his mistress.

Canada West, Sept. 23. Lower Canadian Reformer Louis-Hippolyte LaFontaine wins the former riding of Upper Canadian Reformer Robert Baldwin in a byelection. Baldwin urged his former constituents to elect LaFontaine, and they responded enthusiastically.

London, Sept. 27. Sir Charles Bagot is appointed governor general of Canada.

London, Oct. 16. Queen Victoria grants a royal charter to Queen's College at Kingston.

Toronto. Upper Canada Academy receives a charter as Victoria College, named after Queen Victoria.

Nova Scotia. Baptists found Acadia University.

Canada East. The introduction of land registry offices increases pressure on women to renounce their dowry rights. Dowry rights entitle women to use part of their husband's property after his death, even if it has been sold or mortgaged. The land offices enable prospective buyers to investigate dowry encumbrances of property.

Scotland. The Montreal Curling Club is admitted to the Grand [Royal] Caledonian Curling Club, the international mother curling club.

Nova Scotia. Halifax is incorporated as a city.

Kingston is capital of united Canada

Feb. 10, 1841

KINGSTON – As the Union of the Canadas becomes official today, so too does the selection of this historic city as the capital of the new province. It's a development that, after months of wrangling, leaves Kingstonians delighted, and virtually everybody else discontented.

When word of Gov. Gen. Lord Sydenham's selection of this city came out four days ago, it was condemned by residents of both Toronto and Montreal, the former capitals of the now-defunct Upper and Lower Canadas. Torontonians who had hoped their city would grow even more powerful as the seat of the united Canada are now moaning about real estate depreciation. But Montrealers are less bitter.

Cuvillier elected Assembly's first Speaker

1841

KINGSTON – Augustin Cuvillier has been elected Speaker of the first Legislative Assembly of united Canada. A merchant and banker who is representing Huntingdon in this Parliament, Cuvillier has widespread connections and he speaks English fluently. His election is viewed as a victory for French Canada, although it was secured on the votes of the Reformers in Parliament from Upper Canada. It was Cuvillier's ability to gain support from this group that prompted his nomination, thereby stopping the Tories from electing as Speaker one from their own ranks.

Augustin Cuvillier, first Speaker.

Micmac to queen: "Let us not perish"

Micmacs want England's Queen Victoria to help them get back their land.

Jan. 25, 1841

LONDON, England – "I cannot cross the great Lake to talk to you for my Canoe is too small." So wrote an aged Micmac Indian chief to Queen Victoria in a letter received today at the colonial office in London.

Paul Peminuit from the Shubenacadie reserve in Nova Scotia speaks in desperate terms: "My people are in trouble. ... No hunting grounds, no beaver, no otter. ... All these Woods once ours. ... White Man has taken all that was ours. ... Let us not perish."

Anti-unionist wins Quebec County vote

March 22, 1841

QUEBEC CITY – John Neilson, a respected Scotsman opposed to the Union of the Canadas, has won election to its united Assembly as the member for Quebec County.

It's a bittersweet win for Neilson, a longtime foe of the union who led the French-Canadian majority against it. Neilson was considered a firm ally of the Reformers as well, until their reform boiled over into rebellion a few years ago. Neilson, a newspaper publisher loyal to the Crown, if not its representatives, opposed radicals in the Reform movement, and in 1834 this stand cost him his seat.

Elementary schools guaranteed in bill

July 20, 1841

KINGSTON – Children in Canada will be guaranteed state-aided elementary school education, if a new bill introduced in the Assembly today receives assent. As proposed by Charles Dewey Day, solicitor general and member for Ottawa County, the schools will be non-denominational. In Canada West, funding will come from taxpayers pockets. In Canada East, where the church is the traditional educator, the money will be from the funds of the Jesuit estates, the defunct holdings of a Roman Catholic order the Pope dissolved.

The proposal has come under sharp criticism from French-Canadians and the Roman Catholic church in Canada East. The complaint is that though French will be taught, the bill is still another attempt to assimilate their culture to the English mainstream.

Thomson fights reform as first Parliament opens

June 14, 1841

KINGSTON – The first Parliament of the new Province of Canada opened today in Kingston, in grand quarters built in what used to be a hospital. And, although Gov. Gen. Charles Poulett Thomson has worked hard to ensure a "majority" of supporters in the elected Assembly, it's likely the voice of reform will soon dominate that chamber.

In his effort to control the demand for democracy, Thomson has packed the appointed Upper House, or Legislative Council, as it's called, with his supporters. Although the Assembly is also filled with pro-unionists, even many of these members have sympathy for the need for political reform.

Gov. Gen. Charles Poulett Thomson arrives at Union Parliament in Kingston for the opening of the new Legislative Assembly. Controlling the demand for reform is his main goal.

Kingston Hospital, home of the first Parliament of the province of Canada.

To bee or not to bee: Canadian quilts

1841

CANADA EAST – Quilts have become so essential to settlers in their drafty cabins here that they are in short supply. Women have started cutting fabrics from worn-out clothing to sew over tears and thin spots – in effect developing patchwork quilts.

Settlers are finding that the best way to make quilts is in groups. While piecing and appliqué can be done individually, quilting the finished product is better handled by a group. As a result, women have developed community quilting bees.

Because of the shortage of cloth, new quilts are made of scraps of linen as well as homespun fabrics made from homegrown flax and wool. They are stuffed with anything that's available, including grass, corn husks, straw, hay, milkwood and even letters from home.

On quilting bee days women take their finished quilt tops, along with baskets of food, to the largest home or building in town. While the best quilters work at the frames, others who've gathered are relegated to the kitchen to prepare food. Late in the day, husbands and children – and often the whole community – are invited to join the feast. Seven to eight quilts can usually be completed at each bee.

Quilt made by Maria Steeves in 1840 shows how rags can be put to good use.

Fighting in Toronto fatal for immigrant

May 10, 1841

TORONTO – One man is dead following a clash here between supporters of Reform and government candidates in the recent election.

The clash came in a victory procession for the two successful Reform candidates, J.H. Dunn and Isaac Buchanan. It ended at the North of Ireland Coleraine Inn, an Orange Order hangout on King Street. After the crowd threatened the building, some of its inhabitants fired shots, killing an immigrant named James Dunn (no relation) and wounding several others.

Census: population of P.E.I. at 50,000

Sept. 18, 1841

PRINCE EDWARD ISLAND – The census reports the Island population at 50,000, about 30,000 Island-born. Half are of Scottish descent. The rest are Irish, English, Acadians, and a few hundred loyalists from the 13 Colonies. Lord Durham once wrote that the Island "possesses a soil peculiarly adapted to the production of grain." Agriculture is the main industry, with 100,000 acres under cultivation. Absentee landlords own most of the Island, creating tension.

LaFontaine to sit in English riding

Aug. 15, 1841

NEWMARKET, Canada West – Louis-Hippolyte LaFontaine, the French-Canadian Reform leader prevented from winning a seat in Canada East through the machinations of Gov. Gen. Charles Poulett Thomson now has a seat – and in an English-speaking riding! He won the seat thanks to Reform leader Robert Baldwin convincing his supporters here to elect LaFontaine in his place. This astute move has effectively sealed an alliance between Reformers of both languages in Canada.

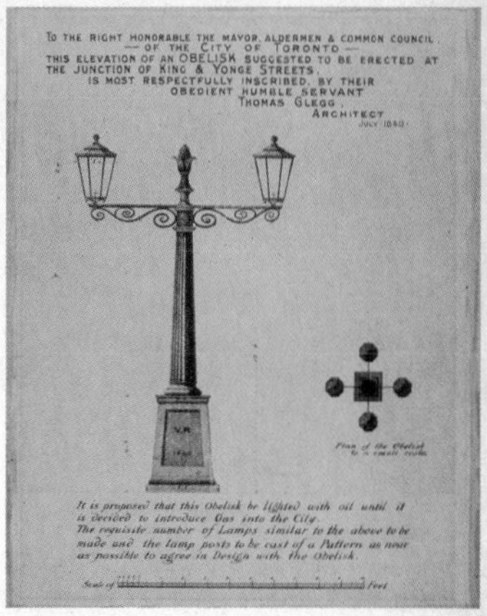

Sketch of the first gas street lamp proposed for Toronto in 1840 by architect Thomas Glegg, for the corner of King and Yonge streets.

1842

Kingston, Canada West, Jan. 10. Sir Charles Bagot arrives to take up duties as governor general of Canada.

Canada, April 27. Currency reform comes into effect. The Halifax currency system is retained with an adjustment in the values assigned coins. The sovereign, American eagle, dollar, and half-dollar are all legal tender. French crowns and half-crowns are dropped from the currency.

Montreal, April. Ignace Bourget, bishop of Montreal, commissions Bishop Gaulin at Kingston to petition Governor Bagot to grant amnesty to French-Canadian rebels exiled after the rebellion of 1837-38.

New Brunswick, April. Geologist and surgeon Abraham Gesner opens the Gesner Museum, one of the first in British North America, in an attempt to get out of debt. The museum features a collection of minerals, wildlife specimens, and ethnological artifacts that Gesner has gathered travelling in the area.

Edmonton, June 19. Reverend Father A. Thibault, an Oblate from St. Boniface, arrives to establish a mission. He hopes to persuade the Métis in the area to settle down to farm, and wants to provide a place for the Crees to practise Christianity in peace, away from hostile plains Indians.

Kingston, Sept. 27. Dr. William Dunlop moves an address in the Assembly for correspondence regarding Nelson Hackett's extradition to Arkansas, which he notes created an uproar in England.

Kinsgston, Oct. 8. Dr. dunlop withdraws his motion regarding Nelson Hackett.

Beauharnois, Canada East, Nov. 9. Edward Wakefield is elected to the assembly on the strength of French-Canadian support. He was an attaché of Lord Durham in 1838, and supported his views on French-Canadian assimilation, but recently became a supporter of French-Canadian rights.

Fort Alexandria, New Caledonia. Catholic missionary Father Modeste Demers builds a small chapel to serve the Indians of the area. It is one of the first churches in [British Columbia].

Montreal. William Edmond Logan founds the museum of the Geological Survey of Canada, one of the first Canadian museums.

Fugitive slave's freedom short-lived

June 1842

SANDWICH, Upper Canada – Fugitive slave Nelson Hackett has been delivered back into slavery in Fayetteville, Arkansas, less than a year after his escape to Canada.

Illustration from the Fugitive's Song, dedicated to Frederick Douglas.

The handsome, articulate valet's freedom was short-lived, because his master, Alfred Wallace, was determined to make him an example for any other would-be runaways. An impetuous and wealthy merchant, Wallace quickly arrived in Canada and charged Hackett with theft of the horse he had escaped on, the clothes and watch he had worn, and even the rape of a "young lady of respectability."

Wallace later withdrew the rape charge, but hired influential politician Col. John Prince to press his case against Hackett, who was arrested in Sandwich, and admitted his guilt. He later recanted, claiming he had confessed only after a severe beating. He pleaded to remain here, for in Arkansas he faced such tortures "that to hang him at once would be mercy".

Hackett remained in jail until January, when the newly-arrived governor, Sir Charles Bagot, authorized his extradition. On Feb. 7, he was sneaked across the Detroit River in the dead of night so other ex-slaves could not rescue him. Aboard ship on his trip back to Arkansas, Hackett so impressed four New Yorkers they helped him escape again. However, a large reward was offered for him, and he was turned in by a man he asked for food. Abolitionists everywhere are very angry about Hackett's case.

An influential politician, John Prince argued the case against Hackett.

Bell leads overland expedition in search of fur-trading tribe

June 23, 1842

FORT McPHERSON, Rupert's Land – Hudson's Bay Company posts here have been ordered to expand their operations west from the Mackenzie River. They have also been told to make sure they control the fur trade, and not leave it to Indian middlemen. That is why trader John Bell recently left here with a double task: first, to find a trade route to the west, and second, to find and trade directly with the tribe or tribes being forced by the Kutchins to trade only with them.

After days of hard going, Bell and his men came to a narrow stream. An Indian guide told them it led to the territories of the Indians who traded with the Kutchins. But when they reached a large river [the Porcupine], the Indians deserted and Bell was forced to return to Fort McPherson.

Governor general mingles with his people

Jan. 12, 1842

KINGSTON – It was a coming out fit for a king – at least a king's representative – as Gov. Gen. Sir Charles Bagot met the people for the first time today at Alwington House. In his first official function since arriving in the capital two days ago, Bagot appeared in court uniform to meet the crowd, estimated in the hundreds. Bagot, who succeeds Lord Sydenham, is known for his personality and good judgment, which will be put to the test here. So will the experience in diplomacy with the Americans that he gained when he was sent as an envoy to the United States in 1815.

Gov. Gen. Bagot met with the people of Canada for the first time today.

Bank loan saves the Cunard empire

April 11, 1842

HALIFAX – The Bank of Nova Scotia has saved businessman Samuel Cunard's empire. The resident director and manager of the General Mining Association has been losing money on his timber tracts, his Prince Edward Island farmlands, and his new steamers.

The bank has approved Cunard's application for a sizable loan, but everything he owns is mortgaged. Two "keepers of his person" have been assigned to make sure Cunard does not leave Nova Scotia without the bank's knowledge.

Indian guide slips away in bid to stop HBC from growing

August 1842

FORT McPHERSON, Rupert's Land – For the second time in two years, Hudson's Bay Company fur trader John Bell has failed to explore west of the Richardson Mountains from the Mac-kenzie to the Yukon River area as directed by Gov. George Simpson. Bell successfully crossed the mountains, but then his Kutchin Indian guide abandoned his party. Bell debated going on anyway, then turned back instead of risking a meeting with hostile Indians or natural hazards such as waterfalls.

Bell's experience is common to other explorers trying to move into the far northwest. Indians promise to guide them, then slip away before doing so. Thus the Indians control HBC expansion, and assure their own role as middlemen in the lucrative fur trade. They fear being replaced by HBC traders and relegated to merely harvesting the furs.

Treaty ends bitter boundary dispute

New Brunswick's Government House presides over newly-redefined territory.

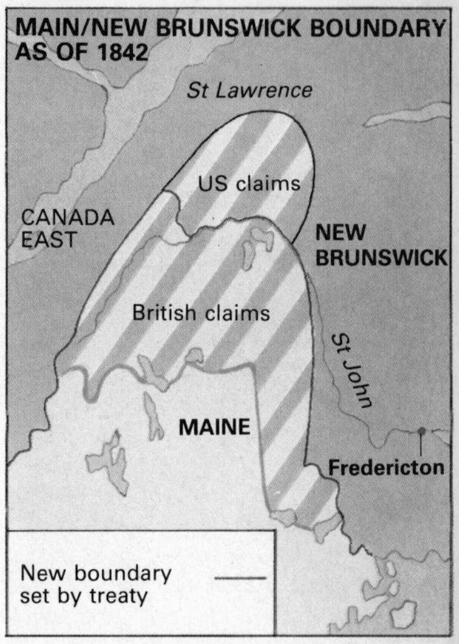

Aug. 9, 1842

NEW BRUNSWICK – After years of wrangling and violence between British and American lumbermen, the boundary dispute between this colony and Maine has been resolved. Under terms of the Webster-Ashburton Treaty, the dividing line in the north is at the St. John River. Through most of the Aroostook territory the boundary runs about 16 kilometres west of the river, and includes some of New Brunswick's best agricultural land.

It's a compromise boundary, for Maine wanted to go much further north, so far that New Brunswick would be almost cut off from other British colonies. The English, on the other hand, were intransigent about the issue of a boundary far further south, so that the link between New Brunswick and the Canadas would be maintained. They were prepared to break off negotiations rather than concede this point. They also wanted to save the Acadian settlements on the south bank of the river, but considered this a less important matter.

Canadien errant remembers exiles

1842

CANADA EAST – M.A. Gerin-Lajoie, a student, has immortalized scores of exiled or fugitive rebels with his song *Un Canadien errant*. Here is an English translation:

A wandering Canadian,
Exiled from his home,
Trudged in tears
Through foreign lands.
One day, sad and pensive,
Beside a stream he sat,
Beside the rushing water
He spoke these words to it:

If you see my country,
My unhappy country,
Go, tell my friends
That I remember them
Oh days so full of charm
You are gone...
And my beloved homeland, alas!
I'll not see you again!
No, but as I'm dying,
Oh my dear Canada,
my final look
will be toward you.

Norfolk County's first settler dead at 89

Feb. 28, 1842

PORT ROWAN, Canada West – John Troyer, Norfolk County's first settler, died today near here. He was 89. Troyer, a businessman, farmer, exorcist and self-taught medical practitioner, arrived from Pennsylvania in 1789. He farmed near Long Point on Lake Erie and established a gristmill. Medically, he practised blood letting and used herbal remedies. He supposedly could banish witches and find water and metals with a divining rod.

Lecture tour brings Dickens to Montreal

1842

MONTREAL – English novelist Charles Dickens is visiting Montreal on a lecture tour. Dickens, a great observer of life, is sampling that offered in this developing society. Staying at Rasco's Hotel near the waterfront, the English writer is often seen on his daily walk near the quay, where immigrants huddle on wharves with their possessions. The author, whose own childhood background was one of poverty as the son of a man committed to debtors' prison, came onto the literary scene in England with the publication of *Sketches by Boz*. Other works include *The Pickwick Papers* and *Nicholas Nickleby*.

Novelist Charles Dickens is staying at Rasco's Hotel in Montreal. He's in the city on his current lecture tour.

Single legislature to govern in Nfld.

Aug. 31, 1842

NEWFOUNDLAND – Britain has signalled its strong disapproval of recent political developments in Newfoundland by imposing a new and rather unusual system of government on the colony. Ever since Newfoundland was granted representative government in 1832, political, religious and economic conflicts have kept the colony in turmoil. In the beginning, the elected house, the Legislative Assembly, was at odds with the appointed house, the Legislative Council – the latter being dominated by officials in the colony.

In recent years, local merchants and their backers have dominated the Legislative Council, while the Assembly has been controlled by Roman Catholics and other reformers. The result has been a deadlock and little legislation. The new amalgamated Assembly will have elected and appointed members, and legislation will be decided by a simple majority.

▷

Tougher guidelines protect emigrants

James Mackenzie Dunkin, a Scottish immigrant, is among the many who survived a difficult overseas voyage.

1842

LONDON, England – Shipping interests that treat emigrants as little more than ballast have been dealt a blow by the colonial land and emigration commissioners.

Ship owners who transport timber from British North America must now adhere to tougher regulations when filling their empty holds with people for the voyage there: provisions and accommodations for the emigrants must be improved and passage brokers must be licensed. It's hoped the measures will end abuses suffered by great numbers of oceangoing emigrants.

The St. Jean Baptiste Society, whose statutes say, "Our institutions, our language and our laws," began in 1842 to boost French-Canadian nationalism.

LaFontaine appointed attorney general

Sept. 10, 1842

QUEBEC CITY – Louis-Hippolyte LaFontaine has been named attorney general of Canada East, in a move aimed at calming fears caused by union of the two Canadas. Debate on the issue arose again this spring. John Neilson, a Lower Canada delegate in the national Assembly, and some Upper Canada Tories, oppose it. LaFontaine hopes to convince French-Canadians that union is in their best interests because they would share power with Upper Canadian Reformers – and so bring about responsible government. A goodwill tour by Gov. Gen. Sir Charles Bagot has helped his cause.

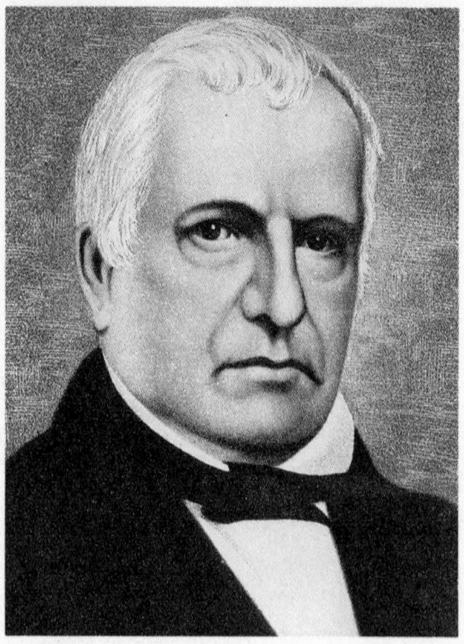

LaFontaine gets Canada East post.

Commissioner sees plight of Micmac

1842

NOVA SCOTIA – Newly-appointed Indian commissioner Joseph Howe began a five-week tour in October of Micmac reserves and encampments in northwestern Nova Scotia, determined to acquire firsthand knowledge of reported deprivations suffered by the province's native people. He has found that little of the 22,000-acre area set aside for the 1,500 or so Micmac is suitable for the encouraged practice of farming and that few schools or churches have been built. Nowhere has he found adequate supplies of tools or seed. In his first report, Howe concludes that without relief the population may be decimated within two generations.

In the 1830s, government assistance did not exceed the donation of a few blankets each year. Then, in 1841, a Micmac chief petitioned Queen Victoria for some desperately needed aid. This initiative led to an investigation that revealed Indian relief in the province to be substandard. This March an Indian Act was passed and the position of commissioner was created.

French speech in Parliament angers Tory

Sept. 12, 1842

KINGSTON – Attorney General Louis-Hippolyte LaFontaine delivered his first speech to the united Assembly in French today, despite Tory member Charles Day's objections. LaFontaine replied in French: "Has the honorable member forgotten that I belong to the nationality so unjustly treated by the Act of Union? He asks me to give my first speech in this chamber in a language other than my maternal language. I am not confident in my ability to speak the English language, but even if I spoke it as well as an Englishman I could do no less than give my first speech in the language of my French-Canadian compatriots."

Queen's College opens in Kingston with a tiny enrolment

March 7, 1842

KINGSTON – Queen's College held its first classes today with 10 students and a faculty of two professors. Using a rented building here as its base of operations, the college was founded by the Presbyterian Church with the association of the Church of Scotland.

Queen Victoria gave the fledgling college its royal charter last Oct. 16 and it was named in her honor. The 40,000 settlers in this area raised a $40,000 endowment fund for the college, which is intended mainly to train candidates for the ministry. It is the second college established by the Methodists, who earlier founded Victoria College at Cobourg. Rev. Liddell of Scotland is in charge of Queen's.

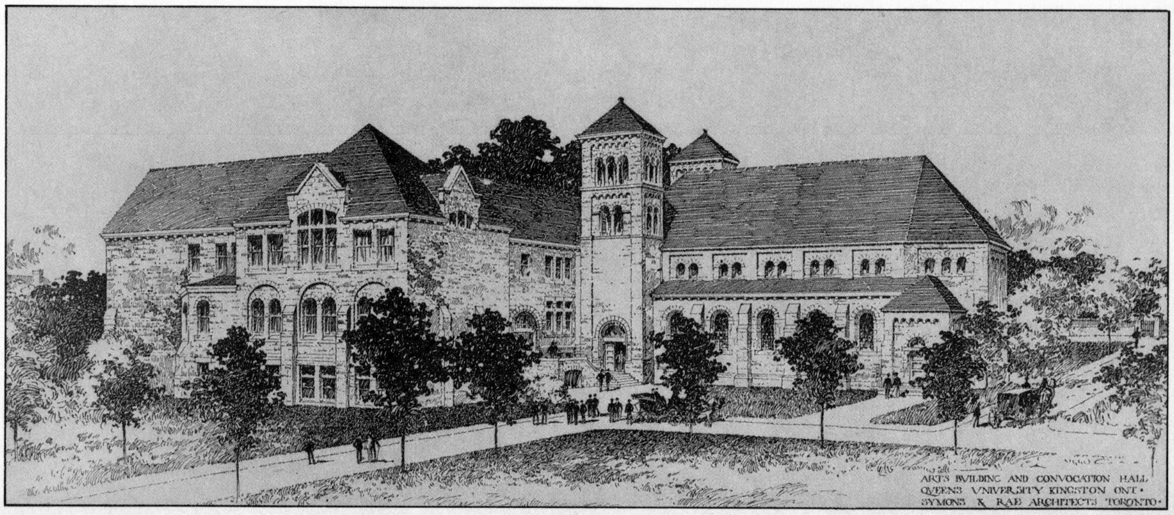

The arts building and convocation hall at Queen's College, which has just recently opened in Kingston.

Bagot government chalks up easy win in confidence vote

Sept. 19, 1842

KINGSTON – The government of Sir Charles Bagot scored a huge victory today, winning a vote of confidence in the Assembly 55-5. The win is a victory for the governor general, and also for Reformers and French-Canadians, whose support the government needed to sustain the elected Assembly's confidence. Above all, it is a vindication of Canada West Attorney General Robert Baldwin's strategy for implementing responsible government, a strategy his French-Canadian Reform ally Louis-Hippolyte LaFontaine, attorney general for Canada East, has accepted.

Cabinet minister Baldwin defeated

Oct. 5, 1842

HASTINGS COUNTY, Canada West – Robert Baldwin, the Reformer who was just made a cabinet minister, has lost a byelection here. Under British tradition, all new cabinet ministers resign when appointed so the public can prove its faith in them through reelection. However, all is not lost. Two years ago Baldwin resigned his seat so French Reform leader Louis-Hippolyte LaFontaine could get elected. Now it's rumored one of LaFontaine's French members will return the favor.

Robert Baldwin, a cabinet minister who has lost a byelection in Hastings County, will try to win another seat.

Popularity of the corset fails to fizzle

1842

CANADA – As slender waists are in vogue this year, most women will resort to every trick in the book to try to make theirs look as slim as possible. Dresses in Canada are now being made with the slender waist look in mind – their bodices have deeper points than before and the gathers of the full skirts are distributed at the sides and back to produce the desired effect.

The use of corsets is the most popular way to make a waist look more slender. Despite changes in fashion, the corset has been worn for centuries, and it continues to be one of the most common pieces of a woman's intimate wardrobe. Corsets are usually made of smooth, elastic materials, although some women have been known to have metal bars added to theirs for a tighter fit.

One authority offers some wise words of advice for modern young women who use corsets. "I agree with the doctors in setting my face against tight lacing, the most dangerous practice a lady can persevere in," the expert writes.

One suggestion to spare the "necessity and agony" as well as injury, of tight corsets, is wearing petticoats made of crinoline, to make the dress look fuller so that it contrasts with the waist.

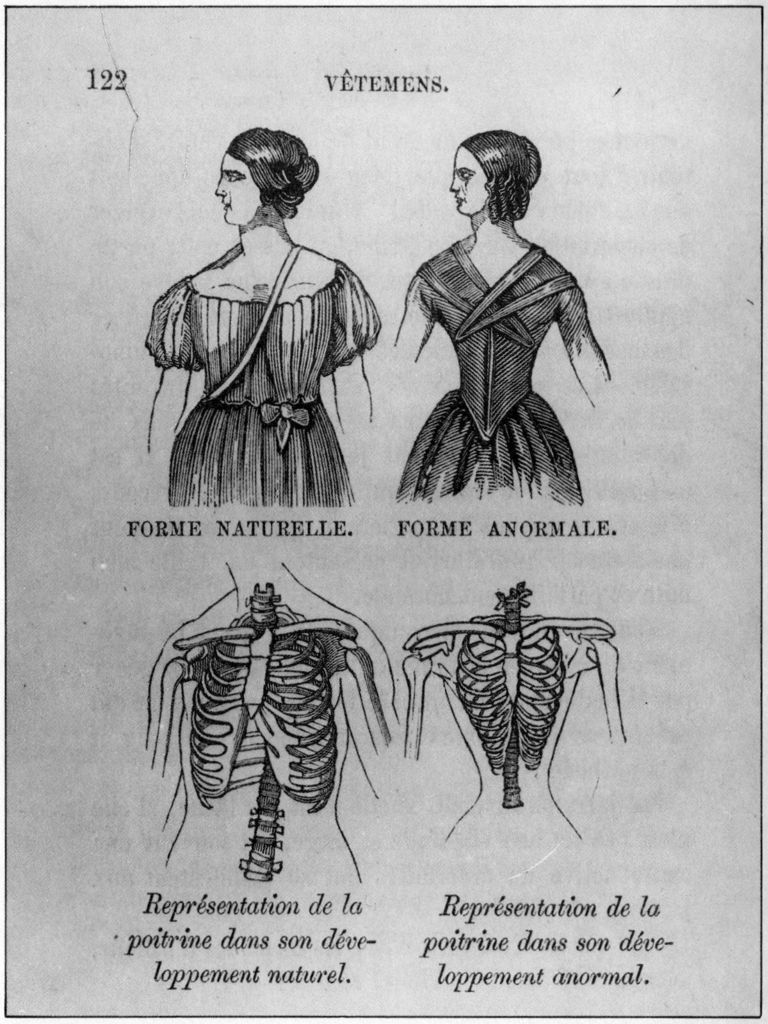

This illustration shows how the corset affects the shape of the female body.

Protesters' plea: repeal the union

March 15, 1842

MONTREAL – "Repeal the Union!" This was the slogan voiced by hundreds of French-Canadians at a public meeting tonight. They jammed Ecole des Glacis to hear speeches by some of the union's most notable opponents, such as John Neilson and Denis Viger. And they approved an open letter asking people to petition the British government to repeal last year's Act of Union.

The chief concern of these protesters is that the new United Province of Canada is politically structured to keep the French in the minority when it comes to the Assembly, whatever their proportion of the population.

Bagot commission to study Indian affairs

Oct. 10, 1842

KINGSTON – Sir Charles Bagot, governor general of British North America, today appointed a commission to report on the administration of the colony's Indian Department. Members of the commission are Rawson W. Rawson, William Hepburn and John Davidson. The unification of the two Canadas last year also united the branches of the Indian Department, and the governor believes an assessment is necessary.

Since about 1830, the government has followed a policy of civilization; Indians have been encouraged to become self-reliant farmers, assimilated into white society. The mandate of the new commission is to find out why this policy is not working.

Illustration of an Indian hunter on snowshoes. The government's policy of encouraging Indians to become self-reliant while being assimilated into white society has failed so far.

1843

London, Feb. 24. Sir Charles Metcalfe is commissioned as governor general of Canada.

Far West, March 15. Fifteen men begin construction on Fort Camosun [Fort Victoria, Vancouver Island], under the direction of James Douglas, chief factor of the HBC's Pacific coast headquarters at Fort Vancouver [Vancouver, Washington].

Toronto, April 13. John Lefroy leaves on an expedition to make a magnetic survey of northern HBC territory [northern Canada] for the British government.

Kingston, Canada West, July 12. Orangemen attack a Catholic church.

Far West, July 30. A Russian surveying expedition led by Zagoskin is forced to abandon an attempt to find the source of the [Yukon River] because of unnavigable waters.

Montreal, Dec. 23. A group of men form a curling club [Thistle Curling Club].

Canada, December. Governor Metcalfe issues a proclamation announcing the move of the Canadian capital from Kingston to Montreal. The British government recently approved the transfer.

Kingston, Canada West. Governor Metcalfe strongly urges the Assembly to work toward establishing an organization to care for the mentally ill.

Canada East. Bishop's University is founded under the sponsorship of George Mountain, Anglican bishop of Quebec. It is intended to provide a liberal education for anglophones in the [Eastern Townships].

Montreal. The Montreal School of Medicine and Surgery is established for the city's francophones.

Canada. The Assembly passes an amendment to the Common School Act of 1841 that set up common schools for Catholics and Protestants. The amendment, only applicable in Upper Canada, states a common school teacher cannot compel a student to participate in religious exercises to which his parents object, and introduces the concept of "separate schools" for Catholic students.

Fort Chimo, Ungava Bay. The HBC closes Fort Chimo, established in 1830 in an attempt to open the Quebec-Labrador peninsula to the fur trade.

Unopposed Baldwin elected in Rimouski

Jan. 30, 1843

RIMOUSKI, Canada East – Robert Baldwin, the English-Canadian Reform leader, has been elected unopposed as the member for Rimouski, a riding which is 99 percent French. His victory repays a debt owed to him by French Reform leader Louis-Hippolyte LaFontaine, for whom Baldwin had found a seat two years ago.

Baldwin's triumph also indicates how the crusade for responsible government has united the two cultures in this province. So strong is this drive, that these French-Canadians voted for a man they have never seen.

Former governor general Bagot is dead

May 19, 1843

KINGSTON – Sir Charles Bagot, the former governor general of Canada, died here today, of heart trouble. He has been ill for some weeks. The death of Bagot is being mourned across the province, particularly by the French, whose great savior he had become in his short term of office. The governor general had appointed many French-Canadians to high positions.

Of Bagot's death, the French newspaper *La Minerve* sadly comments, "Only a memory remains to us now of the great man who was the regenerator of the French-Canadians."

Six strikers killed as labor woes continue

June 11, 1843

BEAUHARNOIS, Canada East – Six strikers were killed today as troops quelled a strike by workers on the Beauharnois Canal. It is the latest in a series of labor problems at the project.

A strike in May for more money and a shorter working day led to the dismissal of several men, reducing the workforce to 19. Troops were also sent in on Feb. 6 during another strike. Laborers went back three days later. A pay increase was promised, but layoffs followed instead, prompting another strike. Striker Martin Donnelly said the laborers think six to seven shillings daily is fair. He took home less than two shillings a week last winter.

Reluctant Metcalfe is governor general

Sir Charles T. Metcalfe succeeds Sir Charles Bagot as governor general.

March 30, 1843

KINGSTON – Sir Charles Metcalfe has arrived to take over as governor general, succeeding the highly-popular Sir Charles Bagot, now near death. While Metcalfe is a career civil servant who has served as governor general of India, he's not looking forward to the job. "All my plans and my hopes of happiness are disappointed," he says, "and such little reputation as I have been able to acquire is, I fear, exposed to shipwreck in the agitated waters of Canada."

Better late than never: King's College finally opens in Toronto

King's College is open for classes, 17 years after it was granted a charter. It took the intervention of the late governor general to get construction started.

June 8, 1843

TORONTO – King's College [University of Toronto] has finally opened for classes, 17 years after the bishop of Toronto, Dr. John Strachan, was granted its charter. The reason for the delay has much to do with the politics of religion in Canada West. Strachan's original college, while non-denominational in membership, was intended to be an Anglican University, with members of England's official religion in charge of operations. This outraged members of other faiths in Canada West, who outnumber the Anglicans. Other people argued for a non-denominational university.

The ensuing struggle meant that 17 years were lost while a compromise was negotiated. It took the intervention of the late governor general Sir Charles Bagot to finally get construction started.

Patronage debate sparks resignation of council members

Nov. 25, 1843

KINGSTON – The "ministry" of Robert Baldwin and Louis-Hippolyte LaFontaine, in reality nine of the 10 members of the Executive Council which acts as a cabinet to the governor general, has resigned *en masse*. At stake is the issue of patronage. Gov. Gen. Sir Charles Metcalfe is insisting that allowing his "ministers" to have any say in this matter would let them use such posts for political purposes. Baldwin and LaFontaine, for their part, insist that controlling patronage is the Assembly's right.

Three-man Executive Council formed

Dec. 12, 1843

KINGSTON – Struggling to put together a ministry in the wake of mass resignations from his Executive Council, Gov. Gen. Charles Metcalfe appears to be resorting to provisional government in the interim. Today it was announced that two more politicians – William Draper and the French-Canadian Denis Viger – would join the sole survivor of the exodus, Dominick Daly, to form a three-man Executive Council. Metcalfe's aim is to act as an intermediary between all political parties, rather than as a figurehead for one with the majority. To do this, he has to split the French-English Reform alliance.

William Draper is one of three men on the new Executive Council the governor general has just unveiled.

Denis-Benjamin Viger is also on the governor general's newly-appointed, three-person Executive Council.

Canada's capital moving from "this hell Kingston" to Montreal

The magnificent Château de Ramezay stands in the new capital, Montreal.

Oct. 6, 1843

KINGSTON – The capital of Canada will be moved from "this hell Kingston" to Montreal, the Assembly voted today. The decision, which was surprisingly opposed by Montreal Tory member George Moffat, still must be approved by England.

Kingston, named capital in 1841, is too small and inconvenient, its detractors feel. Even Sir Charles Bagot, the first governor general who died in May, had thought so. His choice was Montreal or Quebec. Today's vote was not unexpected, because last year the Assembly passed a resolution declaring Kingston to be unsuitable.

Native "Christ" killed and burned

Aug. 30, 1843

RUPERT'S LAND – Abishabis, a self-proclaimed native Jesus Christ, was killed and burned today in his home town, the fur-trading community of Severn on the west coast of Hudson Bay.

For about a year, Abishabis has generated great hopes among natives hard-hit by European diseases and a game shortage caused by the fur trade. He prophesied that the animals would return to the old hunting grounds, and that a wonderful mansion would descend from heaven, for the natives' exclusive occupation. In exchange for predicting these marvels, Abishabis demanded clothes, guns and women. Some gave their daughters, others their wives.

Then the prophecies failed to materialize. Abishabis' disillusioned followers abandoned him. In despair, Abishabis murdered the entire family of an in-law, in order to obtain a canoe, food and a gun to flee to Severn. There the Hudson's Bay Company, aware of his crime, locked him up.

But bars did not keep Abishabis safe from natives who feared he was possessed by the murderous and cannibalistic Windigo spirit. They removed and dispatched him, then burned his body to melt the ice heart through which the Windigo spirit operates.

New snowshoe club set to make tracks

Dec. 14, 1843

MONTREAL – What began as a weekend snowshoe "tramp" by 12 friends a few years ago has been officially turned into the Montreal Snow Shoe Club. The move is only natural, given that more and more people were coming out for the 19-kilometre walks each Saturday. Today, the MSSC has its own president, Col. Charles Oakes Ermatinger, a former fur-trading partner in the North West Company. And it has a new series of races where members compete against natives.

Group established to unite Baptists

June 19, 1843

PARIS, Canada West – The Canadian Baptist Union was borne at a convention here today, providing membership to all Baptist churches and associations. There had been several groups within the church and it was felt a central voice was needed so Baptist concerns could be voiced more effectively in Canada. Rev. J. Winterbotham of Brantford was appointed president of the new organization, while David Buchan of Paris will serve as the group's secretary.

Protesters target Baldwin and Hincks

Nov. 6, 1843

TORONTO – Orangemen livid at the passing of a bill suppressing all secret societies except the Freemasons demonstrated in the streets tonight, hanging effigies of two of their enemies. The effigies, hung from a gallows erected on a cart, were of co-premier Robert Baldwin and Francis Hincks, a member of the Executive Council. Calling the two Reformers "traitors," the mob burned the effigies in front of the home of Baldwin's father, William Warren Baldwin.

1844

Saint John, New Brunswick, March 15. The mayor forbids street processions in light of recent violence between Protestant and Catholic religious organizations.

Saint John, New Brunswick, March 17. A riot breaks out between Catholic and Protestant religious groups.

Atlantic Ocean, June 3. Icelandic fishermen kill two great auks (North American penguins) and smash one of their eggs at Eldey Island off Iceland, perhaps the final extinction of the great auk. The birds were abundant when Europeans arrived in North America.

Yukon, June 21. Zagoskin completes his survey of the Yukon. The Russian is the first European to map the Yukon interior.

New Brunswick, July 19. The colony's first leper hospital opens on Sheldrake Island.

Canada East, July. Antoine Gérin-Lajoie's *Le Jeune Latour*, one of the first French-Canadian plays, receives a special premier showing. It is a historical tragedy set during the Conquest.

Canada West, August. The "College in Connection with the Free Presbyterian Church in Canada" [Knox College] is opened, the result of a split in the Presbyterian Church.

Fredericton, New Brunswick, Sept. 3. A law is passed permitting sale of Indian lands to Europeans and creating a fund to be used for Indians.

Kamouraska, Canada East. Physician Louis-Pascal Taché is shot to death by physician Georges Holmes, who is having an affair with Taché's wife.

Canada West. Seven women manage to vote and the election is upheld, despite the fact that women have not been granted the franchise.

Labrador. In the spring, more than 300 Newfoundland sealing ships work a harp seal whelping patch off the coast of Labrador. They harvest 300,000 to 600,000 pelts, mostly from newborn pups.

Toronto. Printers set up the Toronto Typographical Union to fight for better working conditions, a revival of the York Typographical Society founded in 1832, one of the first unions in Canada. The original union failed after bitter struggles.

Red River Métis petition to join the U.S.

Indian settlement at Red River, from the journal of the Bishop of Montreal.

1844

RED RIVER COLONY, Rupert's Land – The Métis of Red River are so tired of the control which the Hudson's Bay Company tries to maintain over their lives and activities they are petitioning to join the United States.

The petition is the result of a recent company crackdown on free trade that has been flourishing of late. Enterprising young men have found that Americans pay good prices for fur and hide, and in many instances are much closer. The HBC, backed by a local government which finds itself in a position of upholding the law whether it agrees with it or not, has taken such actions as confiscating land of convicted free traders and opening the mail of suspected wrongdoers.

Draper-Viger ticket spurs Tory triumph in national election

1844

MONTREAL – Their strong showing in Upper Canada has carried the Tories to victory in the national election and the Draper-Viger coalition to power. William Henry Draper led the rout in Upper Canada, taking more than twice as many seats as the Reformers.

It was a different story in Lower Canada, where Draper's ally Denis Viger could not penetrate the power base of Reformer Louis-Hippolyte LaFontaine, electing just two French-Canadians to back Gov. Gen. Charles Metcalfe. Eight English Tories did win seats in Quebec's Eastern Townships, riding an appeal for "Metcalfe and loyalty."

In Upper Canada, Robert Baldwin's Reformers paid the price at the polls for a series of actions, among them moving the capital from Kingston to Montreal, the Secret Societies Bill that offended the Orangemen, and the Upper Canada Assessment Bill that provides for higher local taxation.

Brown's new weekly, the Globe, publishes first issue in Toronto

March 5, 1844

TORONTO – The first issue of a new weekly, the *Globe*, hit the streets of Toronto today. It's being published and edited by 26-year-old George Brown, whose father, Peter, publishes the weekly *Banner*. In fact, both are being printed at the same King Street plant.

Unlike the *Banner*, which tends to focus on religious issues, Brown says the *Globe* will be entirely secular. His main concern is politics, being that he is a Reformer himself. Yet Brown intends to champion his own opinions, rather than those of his party. He says that "we write to please no man."

Goings-on at city hall (above) will be sure fodder for Toronto's new newspaper.

George Brown, a Toronto Reformer, has published the first issue of the Globe. Brown intends to champion his own views in the newspaper, rather than those of his Reform party.

Second Parliament meets in Montreal

Nov. 29, 1844

MONTREAL – The second Parliament of the United Province of Canada opened today, this time in the new capital of Montreal. Inside the St. Ann's Market building, Gov. Gen. Sir Charles Metcalfe started the proceedings by delivering the speech from the throne.

Although Metcalfe was resplendent in his blue and gold ceremonial uniform, his speech did not move his audience. Much of this has to do with a facial cancer which has arrested the movement of his mouth, making his speech hard to understand. But the fact is that although Metcalfe has managed to cobble together a Conservative government, the theme of the Assembly is political reform, which he resists.

Sir Charles Metcalfe opens Parliament in the new capital of Montreal.

Seal fishery enjoys a productive year

Sept. 30, 1844

NEWFOUNDLAND – The seal fishery has been remarkably productive this year. Reports indicate 685,530 seal skins, valued at £39,648 sterling [$200,000] and 9,793 tons of seal oil, valued at £244,825 sterling [$1.2 million] were exported since April.

When it began about 150 years ago, the seal fishery – as it is referred to here – was an insignificant industry prosecuted by a few individuals in the northern bays who ventured out on the ice. In recent years, ships from St. John's and Conception Bay have gone in search of the herds and developed an industry supplying Britain with oil.

Lefroy surveys northern magnetic activity

May 25, 1844

FORT SIMPSON, Rupert's Land – British Army officer John Lefroy, a 27-year-old artilleryman, has just completed a series of observations on magnetic activity here. Despite the bitter weather at this trading post on the Mackenzie, Lefroy and his assistant measured magnetic disturbances every hour from March 26 until today. Their work is part of a British government program to measure magnetic activity around the world. It will help determine the exact site of the Magnetic North Pole.

Lefroy left London five years ago and started his work on the island of St. Helena. Then he went to Toronto and made observations there for six months before starting his journey across Canada.

Reformer Drummond wins in rowdy vote

April 17, 1844

MONTREAL – After weeks of violence, the Montreal byelection has been won by Reformer Lewis Thomas Drummond. He outpolled the Tories' choice, brewer William Molson, 1,383-463.

Votes were cast yesterday, after the original April byelection date was cancelled due to violence at the polling stations. Because of the use of open polls, where each voter has to declare his choice publicly, election days have turned into festivals for rowdies of all parties to beat, bully and riot in their efforts to intimidate the voters. In this instance, the cost of democracy is one man dead, and dozens wounded. It was more of a war than an election.

Institut Canadien gets off the ground

Dec. 17, 1844

MONTREAL – About 200 French-Canadian intellectuals met tonight to launch a new institution dedicated to the fostering of their culture. Called the Institut Canadien, it is meant to be a focal point for political and cultural activities. Because of this, the members intend to acquire quarters for their club, with space for debates, a library, and reading rooms.

The founding of the Institut Canadien is yet another example of the rebirth being experienced by French-Canadian culture, partly due to the efforts of the late governor general, Sir Charles Bagot.

Grant negotiates peace treaty with Sioux

These days, the Sioux buffalo hunting grounds are shared with the Métis.

1844

GRANTOWN, Rupert's Land – Métis leader Cuthbert Grant has refused to compensate the Sioux for their dead, but has accepted their peace offering after four years of hostilities between the Sioux and the Métis of the Red River. The buffalo hunts of late have taken the Métis farther into Sioux country. This has resulted in several skirmishes since 1840.

Population of Red River reaches 5,148

1844

RED RIVER COLONY, Rupert's Land – From 90 in 1812, Red River's population has grown to 5,148: immigrants, fur traders, their Métis descendants and Indians. Life here is hard. Twice hostilities have forced residents to leave, but the colony survives. The two largest groups are mixed-bloods: French-speaking Métis, and English-speaking Country-born.

1845

Montreal, Feb. 17. The Speaker of the Assembly rules a motion out of order because it is in French, causing a storm of protest in the House.

Montreal, March 17. The Assembly passes a bill to charter a railway between Montreal and Portland, Maine, the St. Lawrence and Atlantic.

Quebec, April 17. In gratitude for his defence of the use of the French language in Parliament, Thomas Aylwin's constituents carry a message of thanks to his home on a paper 7.5 metres long.

Montreal, Oct. 9. Patriote leader Louis-Joseph Papineau, recently returned from exile, makes a triumphant re-entry to Montreal, where he is welcomed by a large crowd.

St. Boniface, Northwest, Oct. 12. Alexandre Taché is ordained as a priest. He becomes one of the first Oblate priests to work in the Northwest.

New Brunswick, Oct. 16. The leper hospital on Sheldrake Island falls victim to fire.

Quebec, Nov. 26. Governor Charles Metcalfe, near death, returns to England for medical attention.

Quebec, Nov. 26. Earl Cathcart is sworn in as interim administrator of Canada.

Prince Edward Island, Dec. 4. The Point Prim lighthouse goes into operation, the Island's first.

Canada, Dec. 12. An order-in-council sets out conditions for getting a mining licence in Canada West.

London, Dec. 23. William Ewart Gladstone is named Secretary of State for the colonies.

Ireland. A potato blight causes an unprecedented crop failure. Four million Irish people live almost entirely on potatoes. Families emigrate in tens of thousands to America.

Pictou, Nova Scotia. The sheriff builds a 3.3-metre-high wall across the main street to keep Kirkmen and Secessionist religious factions apart. The groups are waging a dispute over Pictou Academy.

Montreal. The Assembly decides to give the money derived from sale of liquor to municipalities, an attempt to appease the prohibition lobby.

Prince Edward Island. The Royal Agricultural Society is formed.

39 patriotes back from 6-year exile

Jan. 19, 1845

QUEBEC CITY – Thirty-nine Lower Canadian *patriote* exiles returned today after more than six years of captivity in Australia. British officials had told them in London that the governor general, Sir Charles Metcalfe, and fellow *patriote* Denis Viger, now a member of the United Canada legislature for Trois-Rivières, negotiated the pardon. On returning, some of the exiles went to Government House to thank Metcalfe, and later went over to Viger's home, where a reception was held to celebrate their return.

Garneau publishes Histoire du Canada

Author François-Xavier Garneau.

August 1845

CANADA EAST – French Canada's first scientific historian, François-Xavier Garneau, has published the first volume of his *Histoire du Canada depuis sa découverte jusqu'à nos jours.*

Garneau learned about the colony and its politics working for the British government. He is the first Canadian to use original sources to write a history which will, he says, rally French-Canadians and "re-establish the truth which has been so often disfigured and to repel attacks and insults ... on the part of men who wish to oppress and exploit them at the same time."

Drinking bout leads to mass street fight

Jan. 6, 1845

STRATFORD, Canada West – Some 80 men brawled in the streets here today after an argument broke out during heavy drinking in a local hotel. Irish Catholics and Irish Protestants belonging to the Orange order were drinking after taking part in elections for town council. Violence between Orangemen and Irish Catholics had first flared in Upper Canada at Perth in 1824.

Businessmen form a Board of Trade

April 29, 1845

TORONTO – The economy seems to be picking up in this city. So much so that local businessmen have formed a Board of Trade. Aimed at encouraging sales and exports of local goods and services, its birth signals the city's recovery from the depression of the 1830s. In fact, Toronto city appears to be moving up generally in terms of its affluence, amenities, and facilities.

French-Canadians get 16 commissions

Dec. 15, 1845

MONTREAL – The weak Conservative government left by Sir Charles Metcalfe, which has been trying to woo French-Canadian voters, has struck out again: it assigned only 16 French-Canadians to the 118 commissions in the reorganized militia. Worse, the military commander, Col. Bartholomew Conrad Augustus Gugy, is hated by the French.

Mixed reviews for colony's corduroy roads

1845

CANADA WEST – Travel in the province is being made easier by corduroy roads – but some settlers are less than happy with the new type of street. Corduroy roads are built with logs which are not squared, flattened or straight, and often far apart.

One traveller notes: "Whole hetacombs of trees are sacrificed to form a corrugated causeway of their round trunks, laid side by side, over which wagons can be slowly dragged or bumped, any attempt at speed being checked by immediate symptoms of approaching dissolution in the vehicle."

Despite the high cost of upkeep and some complaints, corduroy roads are proving to be more than adequate in swampy territory. They are also preferable to existing trails, which are often impassable.

Canada West's corduroy roads are well-suited for swampy territory.

Legislation tabled to charter railway

March 7, 1845

MONTREAL – Railway fever came to the Canadian Parliament today with the introduction of a bill to charter the St. Lawrence and Atlantic Railway. This line, running from Montreal to Portland, Maine, would be the world's first international railway. More importantly, it would link Montreal, Quebec City, and the Townships to an ice-free port, open to Atlantic shipping year-round.

It's because of this that many businessmen are pushing for construction of the St. Lawrence and Atlantic. They want to ensure that Montreal, long a powerful shipping port, doesn't lose out in the brave new world of transport the "iron horse" offers. Whether the Assembly will buy it is another question.

Franklin seeks Passage

May 19, 1845

LONDON, England – The largest seagoing expedition ever sent in search of the Northwest Passage through the Arctic set sail today. Led by Capt. Sir John Franklin, the expedition consists of 134 men on two sailing ships, the *Erebus* and the *Terror*, recently returned from Antarctica and fitted out with small auxiliary steam engines.

A veteran of two previous excursions into the Arctic, Franklin is just back from a seven-year stint as governor of Van Diemen's Land. His orders direct him to travel up Lancaster Sound and then to sail southwest across the uncharted central Arctic to link up with his own, earlier discoveries at the western end of the archipelago.

As the expedition sets off on its journey, everyone is confident that it will complete its mission. "You have no idea how happy we all feel," reports Lieut. James Fitzjames, Franklin's second-in-command, "how determined we all are to be frozen and how anxious to be among the ice. I never left England with less regret."

The one dissenting voice belongs to Dr. Richard King, a veteran of Arctic exploration. King has expressed his disapproval of naval excursions into the ice, warning that Franklin and his men have been sent to the Arctic "to form the nucleus of an iceberg." King, however, does not enjoy the confidence of officials and his dire predictions are being ignored. The Franklin expedition is expected to be away at least two seasons.

Explorer Bell finds river called Youcon

August 1845

FORT McPHERSON, Rupert's Land – John Bell has written to his chief, Hudson's Bay Company Gov. George Simpson, telling him that he has reached the big, fast-flowing river the Indians call the Youcon (White Water). Bell had tried to reach this river before because it is obviously a potential trade route, as well as a route to the Pacific Ocean. He failed, however, because he tried to find a water route across the mountains west of here. This time he left Fort McPherson on foot, and by June 1 had reached the Little Bell River that led him to the Porcupine.

Bell drifted down the Porcupine and reached its mouth on June 16. Ahead was a river nearly 3.2 kilometres across. At first he thought it was a lake, but then the strong grey-colored current showed that he was on a large river. On the bank stood an old Indian woman and a boy. They told Bell that the name of the river was Youcon.

A ship rounds Cape Disappointment, at the mouth of the Columbia River. The river has become a major trade route for the Hudson's Bay Company.

Quebec fires leave thousands homeless

Major fires are occurring with great frequency in Quebec City these days.

June 28, 1845

QUEBEC CITY – Two fires in about a month have devastated the city. The latest blaze occurred when a bush fire hit the Saguenay district today, covering an area about eight kilometres wide by 58 kilometres long. It's left 700 families homeless, and has destroyed plants, crops and farm buildings. Just over a month ago flames left 5,000 residents homeless here, destroying more than 400 tenements, two ships that were under construction, and other property. The illegal and dangerous overcrowding of wood buildings in Quebec was blamed for that fire.

Saulteaux Indian hangs in double killing

Sept. 5, 1845

RED RIVER COLONY, Rupert's Land – The first execution was held here today, as a Saulteaux Indian, tried and convicted of a double murder, was hanged from the wall of the fort. It had been argued at his trial that he shot and killed a Sioux Indian in an act of vengeance, and that he also murdered a fellow Saulteaux.

Authorities decided to hang the man to deter Indians from committing any other violent crimes. Indians and Métis have petitioned the governor, asking him to explain the rule of law as it now exists.

Fort Garry in the Red River colony.

First issue of the Western Globe published

Oct. 16, 1845

LONDON, Canada West – The first issue of the *Western Globe,* also known as the *London, Western and Huron District Advertiser,* has reached Canada West.

The new weekly newspaper published out of Toronto is moving toward "western country" with the help of the recently completed Toronto-Hamilton plank road, which speeds up communication with the London district. It is now possible for local reports to leave London on Monday night and be in Toronto for printing the next morning. The completed newspaper can then be distributed first thing Thursday.

1846

London, Jan. 27. Prime Minister Sir Robert Peel announces that Britain is adopting free trade. Timber imported from British North America will no longer be subject to a preferential duty over other foreign timber.

Montreal, April 24. Earl Cathcart officially takes office as governor of Canada.

Canada, April. F.-X. Garneau publishes the second volume of his *Histoire du Canada depuis sa découverte jusqu'à nos jours*. The first volume, published in 1845, was well-received, but some saw it as anti-Catholic and anti-Canadian.

Canada West, May 18. Kingston is incorporated as a city.

Canada West, June 9. Hamilton is incorporated as a city.

London, June 25. Parliament repeals the Corn Laws, reducing duties on imported grains to a minimum. The Corn Laws gave preferential duties to grains imported from the colonies, so their repeal is expected to hurt British North America.

St. Boniface, Hudson's Bay Territory, July 8. Fathers Laflèche and Taché leave on a mission to convert the Indians of the Northwest.

Montreal, Sept. 12. English, German, and Polish Jews form the first Ashkenazic congregation in Canada [Shaar Hashomayin Congregation].

Canada West, Sept. 29. After finding copper on the site, James Cuthbertson asks the governor general for permission to take possession of and mine land near the mouth of the Thessalon River [Bruce Mines].

Canada East, September. It is announced that James Bruce, Earl of Elgin, is the new governor general of Canada.

Toronto, Oct. 21. The first Provincial Manufacturers and Traders' Exhibition is held to exhibit Canadian-made goods.

Hudson's Bay Territory. Artist Paul Kane travels with an HBC canoe fleet to Fort Garry [Winnipeg], where he sees a great buffalo hunt. He left Toronto to sketch Indians and collect their legends.

Halifax. Theatre Royal opens.

London. The British Possessions Act allows colonial legislatures to reduce or repeal imperial customs duties they are subject to, and allows them to have free trade.

Elgin named governor general of Canada

The Earl of Elgin, governor general.

Oct. 1, 1846

LONDON, England – The Earl of Elgin has been named Canada's new governor general. And, for once, it's an appointment that is likely to be well-received by Reformers who have been agitating for change in Canadian politics.

Lord Elgin is 35, speaks French, and is said to be an intelligent man of principle, capable of great common sense. More importantly, he shares the conviction of many here that the time is ripe for responsible government – that is, government responsible to, and thus controlled by, elected members of the Assembly. Elgin's arrival is expected to mark the onset of true representative government in Canada.

Enforce compulsory education: Ryerson

1846

TORONTO – A report recommending the enforcement of general or common education has been issued by Egerton Ryerson, superintendent of education for Canada West. After a year probing education in England and the continent, Ryerson concludes that: the public should have control of education and resulting legislation; government aid should only be issued in cases where it can be most effective in helping local authorities found schools by local taxes or "rates"; property is the base on which rates should be supported; a thorough inspection scheme is necessary for the school system's efficiency.

Adolphus Egerton Ryerson.

Troops in Red River to keep the peace

Autumn 1846

RED RIVER COLONY, Rupert's Land – Five hundred sappers and artillerymen of the Royal Regiment of Foot have arrived here, and commanding officer Lt.-Col. J.F. Crofton has replaced Gov. Alexander Christie.

The ostensible reason for this increased military presence is the Oregon crisis, but many believe the Hudson's Bay Company has taken advantage of the crisis to protect its trade monopoly.

Raging fire razes most of St. John's

June 10, 1846

ST. JOHN'S, Nfld. – This town was almost totally destroyed yesterday by a fire that burned nearly all the 60 large mercantile operations and left thousands homeless. The fire began when a glue pot boiled over in a cabinet maker's shop and high winds spread flames throughout the town. When the sealing merchants' oil vats caught fire, the conflagration became a terrible force. Even vessels in the harbor caught fire and burned.

Fathers Laflèche and Taché found St. John Baptist mission

St. Boniface Cathedral shows strong Catholic presence in western colonies.

Sept. 10, 1846

ILE-A-LA-CROSSE, Rupert's Land – The Roman Catholic mission of St. John Baptist has opened here. Fathers Louis-François Laflèche and Alexandre-Antonin Taché were sent by the church to minister to the Indians of the north. The church is built of logs and covered with mud, as is the custom of the country. It measures about six metres by six metres and is about two metres high.

A Hudson's Bay Company post built in 1799, Ile-à-la-Crosse is in Rupert's Land on the upper Churchill River. Taché and Laflèche plan to celebrate mass in the new church, and they welcome all who wish to attend.

Gesner invents oil he calls kerosene

Geologist Abraham Gesner.

1846

CORNWALLIS, N.S. – Local geologist Abraham Gesner has begun experiments in which he is distilling coal oil from solid hydrocarbon. Developed in the process is a lamp oil he calls kerosene, which, when burned, emits a light that is both brilliant and white. Kerosene is inexpensive to manufacture and may eventually replace the candle as a source of light for homes.

Harvey instructed on picking cabinet

Nov. 3, 1846

HALIFAX – The final round in the battle for responsible government in Nova Scotia may be over. Bowing to pressure from the Nova Scotian people, the British colonial office has instructed Lt.-Gov. Sir John Harvey to appoint his cabinet from the majority party in the Assembly, and to do their will. Specifically, Earl Grey has told Harvey "it is neither possible nor desirable to carry on the government of any of the British provinces in North America in opposition to the opinion of the inhabitants."

The great Reformer of Nova Scotia, Joseph Howe, is likely to be a major force in any truly responsible government in this province. Like Robert Baldwin of Canada, he believes in self-government at home, and British force abroad, specially to guard against U.S. power.

Treaty sets border at the 49th Parallel

June 15, 1846

LONDON, England – The Oregon Boundary Treaty setting the border between British territory and the United States in western North America as the 49th Parallel was signed today by Britain and the U.S. Negotiated for Britain by Foreign Secretary Lord Aberdeen, it keeps Vancouver Island a British possession by dipping around it. The U.S. Democratic government, whose slogan last year was "fifty four forty or fight," says it has conceded by not pushing the boundary to the 54th Parallel (Alaska). But British North America gave up much, including the Columbia River, best route from inland.

The telegraph era arrives in Canada

Dec. 19, 1846

TORONTO – Canada's first telegram was sent today on a line linking Toronto city hall with Hamilton by the Toronto, Hamilton and Niagara Electro-Magnetic Telegraph Company. Newspaper correspondents expect to be among the first to benefit from this new means of instantaneous, long-range communication, derived from the Greek meaning "writing at a distance." They say their reports will then reach their editors within minutes, and can appear in print right away, instead of days later, as now.

Draper in a bind as Viger resigns

July 1846

MONTREAL – French-Canadian war-horse Denis Viger has resigned from the government. And, with his absence, William Draper, the "sort-of prime minister" of Canada, needs to find new French-Canadian members if he is to maintain the Tories' hold on power.

As most French-Canadian members are allied with the Reformers Baldwin and LaFontaine, the search could be tricky for "Sweet William," so-called because of his legendary powers of persuasion.

Artist sketches scenes from Indian life

Artist Paul Kane uses watercolors to paint Cree or Assiniboine lodges in front of Rocky Mountain Fort in [Alberta]. Both these Indian groups have declining populations due to diseases they caught from Europeans.

Another Kane painting depicts an Indian encampment at Georgian Bay, the northeast arm of Lake Huron. These Indians, who live a largely nomadic life, set up camp near fur-trading posts during the summer, so that they can engage in transporting and trading furs.

In yet another portrayal of Indian life, artist Paul Kane shows Indians of the plains engaging in a buffalo hunt. Buffalo are a main source of food.

1847

Canada West, Jan. 1. Toronto and St. Catharines are connected by telegraph.

Fredericton, N.B., March 28. Governor Colebrooke, recently discredited and about to end his term, prorogues the legislature in the midst of a dispute over the form responsible government will take in the colony.

Hudson's Bay Territory, May 20. The Council of Assiniboia places an additional duty of two shillings a gallon on the import of American alcohol.

Saint John, New Brunswick, June 21. Dr. George Harding reports there are 2,500 sick immigrants in quarantine at Partridge Island off Saint John. Island hospitals cannot accommodate all of them.

Montreal, June. The first Hebrew Philanthropic Society in the city is founded to help Jewish immigrants who arrive in the city.

Montreal, July 28. The government of Canada incorporates the town of Bytown [Ottawa].

Canada West, July 28. A provincial agricultural association is incorporated.

Canada, Aug. 3. The Montreal Telegraph Company inaugurates telegraph service between Montreal and Toronto.

Nova Scotia, Aug. 5. Provincial elections result in unprecedented political excitement. The Liberals win a slim majority over the Conservatives. There is simultaneous polling throughout the colony for the first time.

Montreal, Nov. 19. The Montreal and Lachine Railroad between Montreal and Lachine is officially inaugurated.

Canada. The Montreal Mining Company sends surveyor Forest Shephard to explore mineral sites on Lake Superior, including the property of James Cuthbertson [Bruce Mines], which is rich in copper deposits. Shephard recommends the property for mining.

Montreal. The Montreal Gas Company is established to light the city's streets.

Montreal. Hugh Allan forms the Montreal Telegraph Company to connect Canadian and American cities by telegraph.

Quebec. A total of 90,150 immigrants arrive at the port in 1847, overwhelming the city.

Métis "the cheapest, best servants"

1847

RED RIVER COLONY, Rupert's Land – "The cheapest and best servants we can get." That is how Hudson's Bay Company Gov. George Simpson has described the colony's French-speaking Métis and English-speaking Country-born – the mixed race offspring of European and Indian parents.

The company has an unbending policy against promoting the mixed-bloods to officers. It employs them as laborers, building posts, chopping wood, hunting, and doing other rough tasks. In 1830, 100 to 200 Métis and Country-born represented some 25 percent of the overall HBC laborer workforce. Today, that percentage has roughly doubled to half the workforce.

Labatt and partner buy London brewery

1847

LONDON, Canada West – John K. Labatt and brewmaster Samuel Eccles have purchased the Simcoe Street London Brewery from innkeeper John Balkwill. Founded in 1828, the first brewery burned in 1840. It was replaced with a stone structure boasting a 4,000-barrel capacity. Labatt came from Ireland in 1830. He met Balkwill selling him barley to make malt. Not happy with farming, Labatt went to England to study business. He wrote his wife: "I fancy I should like brewing better than anything."

Brewing the ale: John Labatt wants to get in on the great beer action.

Novelist marries twice in one day

Feb. 15, 1847

MONTREAL – A noted novelist was married twice today to the same woman. Pierre-Georges Prévost Boucher de Boucherville, author of *Une de perdue, deux de retrouvées,* and a founder of *La Revue Canadienne,* first walked down the aisle with Marie-Louise Elizabeth Gregory at First Congregational Church of Montreal, and then later at Notre Dame church. The new Mme de Boucherville is the daughter of a Montreal doctor.

Reform party wins Assembly majority

1847

NOVA SCOTIA – Responsible government has been ushered in peacefully, with the Reformers winning a majority in the Assembly in Nova Scotia. The win would not have been so significant, except for a recent dispatch from the new colonial secretary, Lord Grey, saying the governor of Nova Scotia must accept the control of the party with the majority in the Assembly.

P.E.I. legislature gets new building

January 1847

PRINCE EDWARD ISLAND – Ten years after it was first proposed and five years after the first stone was laid, the Island's new legislature is set to open. Architect Isaac Smith has pronounced himself satisfied with the fine, neo-classical building. "If it were to be erected again, " he writes, "the experience gained would suggest but little variation in the design."

Work starts on HBC post in the Yukon

July 1, 1847

FORT YOUCON, Alaska [Russian America] – Work started today on Fort Youcon, near the junction of the Yukon and Porcupine rivers. All the members of the Hudson's Bay Company party that just reached here are well-armed because the fort they're building is deep within the area claimed by Russia. Some of the Kutchin Indians who watched the Hudson's Bay men at work told them that they had traded with other white men who wanted to buy their dogs.

While trader Alexander Murray is concerned about the possible threat from the Russians, others in the party believe the Indians are lying. Just to be on the safe side, Murray left his pregnant wife Anne behind in Lapierre House, in the care of an Indian woman, when he and his party departed in the *Pioneer,* a large wooden boat specially built for the trip. They drifted down the Porcupine until it met the Yukon, following the route explored by John Bell a year ago. Murray was not impressed by the Yukon, with its low banks, swampy coastline, stunted trees – and mosquitoes which filled the eyes and mouths of everyone in the party.

The Hudson's Bay Company builds Fort Youcon as a new trading post.

The men lit fires, but they were of no use. So to avoid the mosquitoes, the party went back on board the *Pioneer.* They rowed 4.8 kilometres upstream and Murray picked this drier site. Then, while the men started to clear the land, Murray began to draw up plans for the buildings. A 4.5-metre high palisade will surround the bulletproof post. And all the buildings will have loopholes so they can be defended with small firearms.

Elgin woos support of French Canada

Feb. 23, 1847

MONTREAL – Lord Elgin, Canada's new governor general, seems determined to convince all parties here of his sincere interest in developing responsible government in Canada. To this end, he has worked hard to assure French-Canadians they are welcome in any regime formed under his rule.

Elgin is offering the French more seats on the Executive Council. To achieve this, he has sent a secret memo to Augustin-Norbert Morin, a noted Canada East Reformer, asking for names of appropriate French-Canadians who enjoy the "esteem and confidence" of the French population at large.

Bloody riot plagues Belfast byelection

March 1, 1847

PRINCE EDWARD ISLAND – Authorities report three dead and scores injured as a byelection in the Belfast district ended in a bloody riot today. Belfast, split along ethnic, religious and political lines, has a history of voting day disturbances. Violence today started as Irish and Scottish voters set about each other with cudgels, and fought most of the afternoon. "The field was as if a number of butchers had been extensively at work," one shocked observer noted.

Last piece of Arctic coast surveyed

An eyeshade that's worn by Inuits living in the Arctic regions of the north.

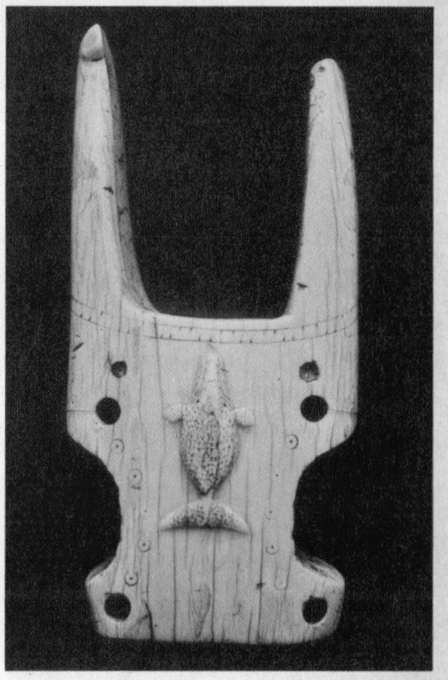

An Inuit harpoon rest. The Inuit are known to be hunters and gatherers.

Inuit wooden mask. Much of the Inuit art has magical and religious meanings.

April 18, 1847

LORD MAYOR BAY, Boothia Peninsula – The last piece of the Arctic coastline of North America has finally been surveyed. Dr. John Rae, an employee of the Hudson's Bay Company, reached this spot today after trekking overland from Hudson Bay. He has seen unbroken coastline all the way, indicating that Boothia is a peninsula, not an island. Ships attempting to navigate a northwest passage will have to seek it on the western side of this frozen land mass. Rae spent last winter in a hut in Repulse Bay, the first time an explorer has wintered so far north without a ship.

Anesthetic easing medical procedures

March 1847

MONTREAL – Anesthetics are now facilitating Canadian medical procedures. Dr. E. D. Worthington of Sherbrooke, Canada East, has just performed a first – he amputated the leg of a patient unconscious from sulphuric ether.

Days earlier, the rehabilitated rebel Dr. Wolfred Nelson, first performed surgery using an anesthetic. Dr. Nelson removed a tumor, while his son Horace administered an ether anesthetic. Horace had demonstrated the painlessness of the technique earlier, using dogs.

Sherwood steps in as Draper calls it quits

May 29, 1847

MONTREAL – William Draper, the nominal prime minister of this province, has had enough. He has resigned, to take up new work as a judge. In his place, Tory members of the Assembly have rallied around Henry Sherwood, a former solicitor general. It is his role to try to stem the tide of full reform which appears to be leading to responsible government in this province.

Sherwood's new ministry has essentially been met with a chorus of yawns by the Reform opposition, and with good reason. Faced with a government that is Conservative, and certain that fresh elections cannot be far off, leaders such as Robert Baldwin and Louis-Hippolyte LaFontaine see little purpose in trying to accomplish a great deal in the next session. Nor is it clear that the session, which begins in June, will last much longer – Sherwood only holds a two-seat majority.

Meanwhile, Lord Elgin waits, intending to extend the powers of responsible government to the politicians who demand it. But, as this policy of the British government cannot be implemented without the consent of the majority party, and as that party, the Tories, remains opposed to it, the governor general's waiting continues.

Ojibwa say miners are on their land

July 5, 1847

CANADA WEST – Ojibwa Indians today protested to the government against mining interests occupying land they consider to be theirs on the north shore of Lake Huron [at Bruce Mines]. The Indians settled the land after the War of 1812, moving there from the south side of the lake because they wanted to stay under British rule. They say they settled the area "with the understanding of the British authorities," and consider the land theirs because they haven't received any remuneration for it.

Typhus takes toll: hundreds of Irish die on way to N.B.

December 1847

SAINT JOHN, N.B. – The latest influx of immigrants is over, and people here are wondering what has hit them. Since May, a record 16,251 immigrants have landed in New Brunswick, almost all of them from Ireland. Some 2,115 immigrants have died in this time, 823 during the crossing, 601 at the Partridge Island quarantine station off Saint John, and the rest elsewhere in the colony. It is a tragedy unprecedented in the colony's short history, threatening to cripple the society the loyalists built after first arriving here in 1783.

Partridge Island has resembled a scene from Dante's *Inferno* over the past months, as sick immigrants, many suffering from typhus, overflowed its meagre facilities. The sick lay exposed to the elements, and corpses accumulated before being buried in mass graves.

British clamp down on liquor imports to stymie trading

Nov. 18, 1847

RED RIVER COLONY, Rupert's Land – Although the use of liquor in trading with the Indians has declined, some traders are still bringing brandy, rum and firewater over the border from the U.S. But now this source has been banned, and liquor brought across the border will be confiscated.

Decades ago, the use of liquor in the fur trade grew by leaps and bounds in the intensifying struggle between the old North West Company and the Hudson's Bay Company – liquor was easier to carry than goods such as blankets or kettles. But some observers say huge quantities of the hard stuff are still brought into fur-trading country each year – several litres for each man, woman and child. Most traders realize liquor destroys Indians just as surely as European diseases. But it has taken many complaints to Britain's House of Commons to cut the supply.

Franklin and crew now believed lost

June 11, 1847

ABOARD HMS EREBUS, Victoria Strait – Sir John Franklin, the commander of the latest British expedition seeking the Northwest Passage, is now believed lost, along with the crew of his two ships.

Franklin sailed the *Erebus* and *Terror* from England two years ago with orders to link together the results of his previous explorations along the Arctic coast – and to sail through the Northwest Passage. The ships spent the winter of 1845-46 on Beechey Island, where a number of men died and were buried. Franklin then led his ships south, but they were trapped in ice west of King William Sound. From 1825-27, Franklin surveyed 645 kilometres of the Arctic coastline, but his record as explorer is not unblemished. In 1818, he was second in command of a foolish attempt to find a passage across the Arctic ice west from Spitsbergen. And in 1819, on his Coppermine expedition, Franklin lost 10 men to hunger and cold because he had insufficient stores and quarrelled with Indian and fur trapper guides. He made no attempt to adapt to conditions by adopting native sleds and clothes. Instead he relied on British linens, silver cutlery, fine china, and unsuitable clothes.

Has Franklin's crew perished?

Le Marchant ready to govern in Nfld.

July 15, 1847

ST. JOHN'S, Nfld. – Sir Gaspard Le Marchant has arrived to take up his duties as governor. He succeeds Sir John Harvey, who is well known for his calming influence and his ability to make the amalgamated Assembly a success.

It is Le Marchant's task to lead the colony back to the system of two legislative chambers that was in force from 1832-41, despite the conflict and violence it stirred between Catholics and Protestants, Conservatives and Liberals.

Toronto school set to teach teachers

Nov. 1, 1847

TORONTO – The first Normal School to train teachers for their profession opened here today in the old Upper Canadian Parliament buildings. The action follows up on a report by Superintendent of Education Egerton Ryerson that good schools are dependent on good teachers, who can only achieve that status through training.

An annual grant of £1,500 will be issued to the new school. Its first headmaster is Thomas Jaffray Robertson.

Canadian railway OKs wider gauge

Sept. 20, 1847

MONTREAL – Shareholders of the St. Lawrence and Atlantic Railway today agreed to use a wider gauge than that of United States lines, in order to discourage competition. It is felt that going to a five-foot, six-and-one-half-inch gauge, compared to the Americans' four feet, eight-and-one-half inches, would make the Montreal-Portland line more difficult for the U.S. to tap by diverting trunk lines from it. Also, the increased load-carrying capacity was an economic edge.

Two Irish Catholics killed in festivities

July 12, 1847

SAINT JOHN, N.B. – Two Irish Catholics were killed today, one in each of Saint John and Fredericton, as violence flared during the traditional July 12 celebrations of William of Orange's 1690 victory over Britain's last Catholic king.

While troops were brought in to restore peace in Saint John, the Fredericton incident occurred when several Irish Catholics came into town from the surrounding countryside. In Woodstock, local Irish Orangemen bolstered by counterparts from across the border in the United States got out of hand and the jail was burned down.

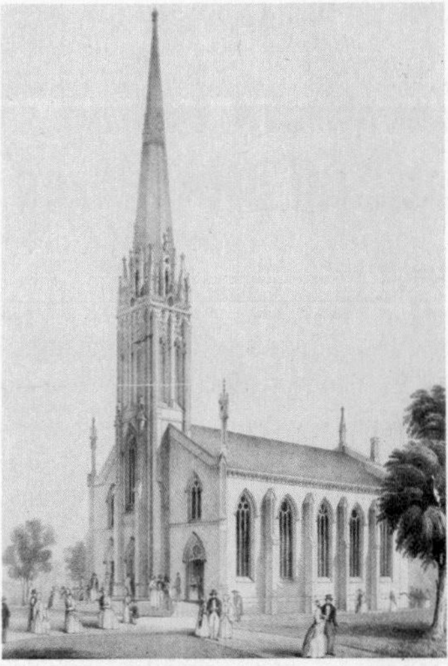

Sunday worship plays an important role in all Canadian towns, regardless of denomination. Notre-Dame-de-la-Victoire Church, left, serves the spiritual needs of Quebec City's Catholics, while Knox Church, right, is one of the Sabbath gathering places for Protestants living in Toronto.

Irish famine taking toll on immigrants to Canada

Aug. 12, 1847

GROSSE ISLE, Canada East – The *Virginius* arrived at the immigrant quarantine base today with grim tidings. Of the 476 Irish immigrants aboard the vessel, 158 died during the gruelling 63-day voyage from Liverpool.

The deaths are becoming typical, as the wave of emigration from Ireland, brought about by famine there, hits the shores of the St. Lawrence in steady waves. The average mortality rate for people aboard ships is 15 percent for those embarking from Liverpool and 19 percent for those coming from Cork. While many die in transit to this island 46 kilometres downstream from Quebec City, scores of others die while they are in quarantine here, from disease, notably bubonic plague [Black Death], cholera or malnutrition.

The recent tide of immigration has swamped the charitable groups organized to help settle newcomers. Although colonial authorities have had ample notice of the impending onrush of immigrants, disputes over settlement policy were never resolved and now they are trying vainly to cope with the problem.

When word of the famine in Ireland reached the colonies more than a year ago, the simple solution seemed to be to welcome the destitute here to help settle and build the colonies. One resolution urged the imperial government to encourage resettlement so that "the surplus population of the Mother Country, instead of remaining a burden at home, may be made to add to the wealth, strength and safety of the colonies of the empire."

Some argued that immigrants should be encouraged to work as agricultural laborers. This would permit them to earn and save money. Then eventually, they would have their own farms. Other people suggested that Irish villages should be "transplanted" here to speed settlement. But *The Examiner,* a Toronto newspaper, disagrees, saying that Irish villages are static, unlike villages in North America.

With the settlement policy still unresolved, ships began arriving after ice break-up last May, with the first of the 100,000 immigrants expected in the Canadas.

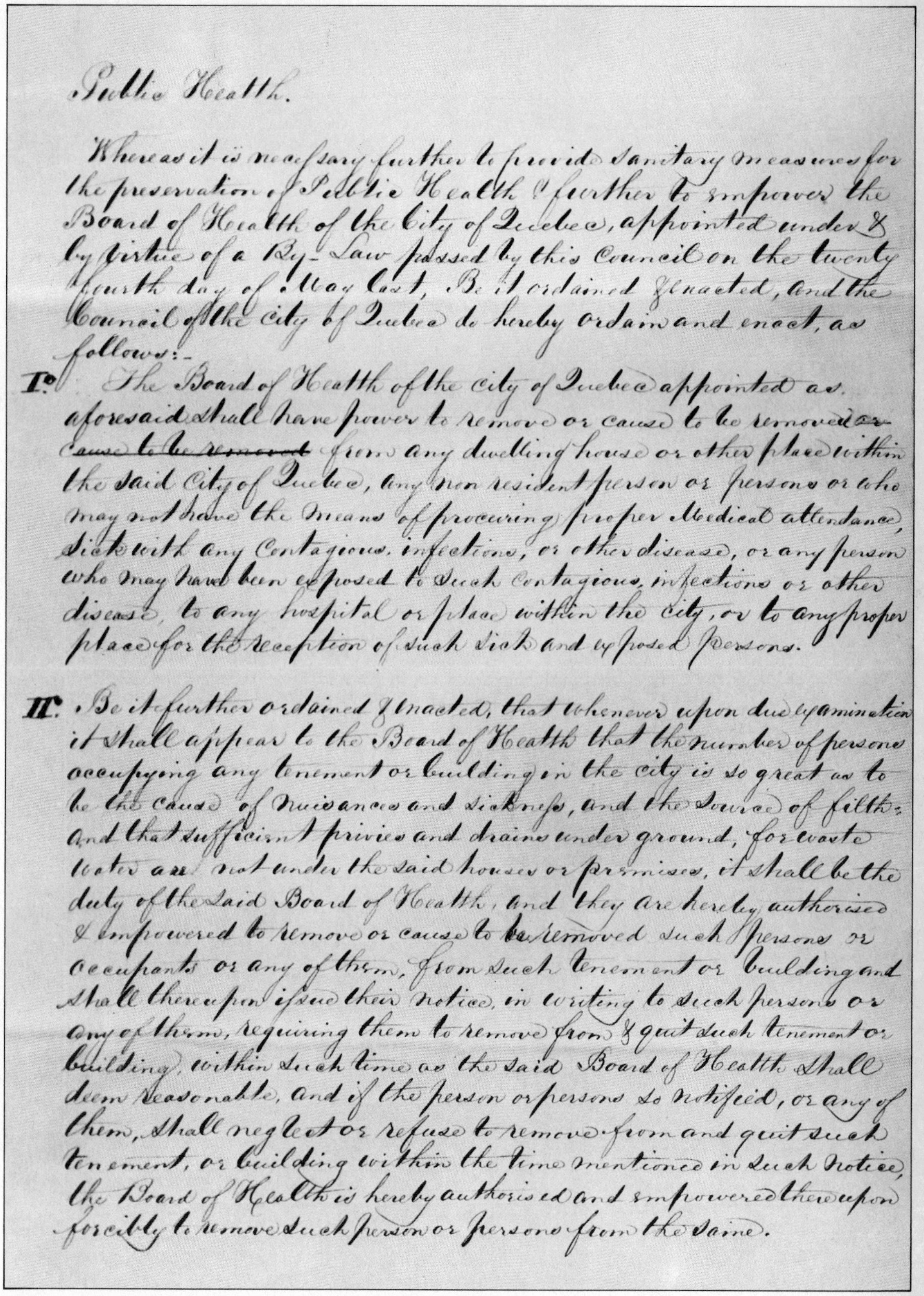
Public Health.

Whereas it is necessary further to provide sanitary measures for the preservation of Public Health & further to empower the Board of Health of the City of Quebec, appointed under & by virtue of a By-Law passed by this Council on the twenty fourth day of May last, Be it ordained & enacted, and the Council of the city of Quebec do hereby ordain and enact, as follows:-

I° The Board of Health of the city of Quebec appointed as aforesaid shall have power to remove or cause to be removed ~~or cause to be removed~~ from any dwelling house or other place within the said City of Quebec, any non resident person or persons or who may not have the means of procuring proper Medical attendance, sick with any Contagious, infectious, or other disease, or any person who may have been exposed to such contagious, infectious or other disease, to any hospital or place within the city, or to any proper place for the reception of such sick and exposed persons.

II° Be it further ordained & enacted, that whenever upon due examination it shall appear to the Board of Health that the number of persons occupying any tenement or building in the city is so great as to be the cause of nuisances and sickness, and the source of filth, and that sufficient privies and drains under ground, for waste water are not under the said houses or premises, it shall be the duty of the said Board of Health, and they are hereby authorised & empowered to remove or cause to be removed such persons or occupants or any of them, from such tenement or building and shall thereupon issue their notice, in writing to such persons or any of them, requiring them to remove from & quit such tenement or building, within such time as the said Board of Health shall deem reasonable, and if the person or persons so notified, or any of them, shall neglect or refuse to remove from and quit such tenement, or building within the time mentioned in such notice, the Board of Health is hereby authorised and empowered thereupon forcibly to remove such person or persons from the same.

"Whereas it is necessary further to provide sanitary measures for the preservation of Public Health and further to empower the Board of Health of the City of Quebec..." So begins sanitary regulation No. 58, passed to deal with the large numbers of immigrants arriving at Canadian shores from Ireland. The regulation was adopted in an attempt to impede the spread of diseases the immigrants are catching while aboard the ships that bring them here from England. It calls for strict housing regulations and the deportation of any sick immigrant without the means of procuring treatment.

1848

Canada East, Jan. 3. Reformer and former *patriote* rebel Louis-Joseph Papineau is elected by acclamation to the Assembly in the riding of St. Maurice.

Cap-Rouge, Canada East, Feb. 1. John Neilson, prominent politician and moderate Reformer, dies.

Seneca Falls, U.S., July 19. "We hold these truths to be self evident: that all men and women are created equal..." So says Elizabeth Stanton at a women's rights convention. She presents a Declaration of Sentiments, listing wrongs done to women.

Niagara, Canada West, Aug. 9. The Suspension Bridge across the Niagara River to the U.S. opens. It is considered a great engineering achievement.

Arctic Ocean, August. A British overland expedition led by John Richardson searches the coast from the Mackenzie to the Coppermine rivers, but finds no trace of Franklin's missing expedition, last seen in 1845.

York Factory, HBC Territory, Sept. 12. The British troops sent to the Red River colony in 1846 during the Oregon Boundary dispute leave for Britain.

Toronto. There are approximately seven inns for every church in the city, due largely to a large influx of Irish men.

Toronto. Brewer turned philanthropist Enoch Turner opens the city's first tuition free school to serve the large number of Irish immigrants in Toronto. Like most of the Irish immigrants, Turner himself is a Protestant.

Toronto. The Royal Lyceum Theatre opens.

Far West. A sawmill is established at Parson's Bridge [near Victoria], the first in the area.

Magdalen Islands. The islands export 136,000 litres of seal oil, almost all of it made from horsehead seals.

Bruce Mines, Canada West. Mining operations begin at the mines, the first commercial copper producer in Canada.

Toronto. Artist-explorer Paul Kane returns from a trip across the continent begun in 1845 that took him as far as Fort Vancouver [Vancouver, Washington]. He drew about 700 sketches of scenery and Indians.

Revolutions sweeping through Europe

Popular protests in Vienna forced the resignation of Prince Metternich.

Spring 1848

BRITISH NORTH AMERICA – Revolutions are convulsing Europe, and newspapers here avidly trace their path. Among the most dramatic developments: French King Louis Philippe escaped to exile in England while an armed mob sacked his palace. In Vienna, unstoppable popular protests forced the resignation of Prince Metternich, Austria's vain chancellor. In Berlin, after a week of violence, erratic King Frederick William IV has himself assumed the role of reformer. Hungary, Italy, England and Ireland are also affected.

Colonies here have avoided Europe's violence, but share the intense desire for change. Here, reform, not revolution, is the order of the day.

Bishop consecrates 8 Sisters of Mercy

Jan. 16, 1848

MONTREAL – Bishop Ignace Bourget has acknowledged the foundation of a new religious order at Montreal. Eight Sisters of Mercy were already occupying a house at the corner of St. Catherine and St-André streets. Founded by Marie-Rosalie Cadron-Jetté, also known as Mother de la Nativité, the order is dedicated to caring for unwed mothers and their infants.

Niagara Falls dry, but just for a day

March 29, 1848

NIAGARA FALLS – The loud thunder of water stopped at 5 a.m. Ice on Lake Erie loosened from the shore by warm east winds, suddenly changed directions when the wind howled down from the west. The ice sealed the mouth of the Niagara River, causing it to dry up, and the falls to stop flowing for the first time in history. The curious explored the riverbed for souvenirs.

Settle Townships, French are urged

April 5, 1848

MONTREAL – About 8,000 people filled Bonsecours Square tonight to witness the birth of a new land settlement association called the Association des Etablissements Canadiens des Townships. The company hopes to persuade French Catholics and Irishmen emigrating to the U.S. to settle in the Eastern Townships of Canada East instead, thus boosting the population.

A wooden revelation mask of the sun used by the Kwakiutl Indians of the northwest coast, who live in the area around Fort Rupert.

Three cheers for the queen, ex-rebel says

Jan. 15, 1848

MONTREAL – As crowds tonight celebrated the victory of the Reformers in the general election, the once-unthinkable happened. Former rebel Dr. Wolfred Nelson incited the revellers to give "three cheers for the Queen!"

Nelson's change of heart, shared by many, stems from respect for Gov. Gen. Lord Elgin's work for responsible government, and his impartiality in the election. Nelson may also be celebrating the money he has learned will be his in a proposed Rebellion Losses deal.

Elgin calls on Reformers to form cabinet

March 4, 1848

MONTREAL – Henry Sherwood's Tory government resigned today after losing a non-confidence motion 54-20. Lord Elgin, meanwhile, cemented the principle of responsible government by calling on the leaders of the majority Reformers, Robert Baldwin and Louis-Hippolyte LaFontaine, to form a new Executive Council. As the council is essentially the cabinet, and as Elgin has made it clear that he will follow its wishes, parliamentary government has finally arrived in Canada.

Potato blight hits Micmac farms hard

1848

NOVA SCOTIA – Three seasons of potato blight have devastated Micmac hopes of establishing successful farming communities. The blight has affected farms throughout the province, but according to Dr. Robert Leslie disease is ravaging the Indians because they have lacked long-term food supplies of nutritional value and still live in "damp lodging on the ground."

While the Indian Act of 1842 brought much-needed government assistance to the Micmac, its lasting effects are now being threatened by the untimely blight, striking as it is while Micmac farm development is in its earliest stages.

Nelson accuses Papineau of cowardice

Louis-Joseph Papineau addresses a crowd. He is accused of cowardice.

May 21, 1848

SAINT-AIME, Canada East – A bitter war of words has erupted between two key players in the 1837 Rebellion. Dr. Wolfred Nelson, who led the rebels in their defeat of government troops at St. Denis, has accused Louis-Joseph Papineau, who inspired the rebellion, of cowardice during the uprising.

Nelson made the charges this morning after mass in this small French-Canadian town. He claims Papineau fled when British troops arrived to crush the rebel stronghold at St. Denis in 1837, a charge often hinted at but only now made publicly. Papineau, for his part, has acknowledged that he did leave, but at Nelson's command. It's an alibi that Nelson disputes.

Liberals in Nfld. demand changes

Dec. 14, 1848

ST. JOHN'S, Nfld. – Gov. Gaspard Le Marchant has opened the legislature under the same rules in force when it was suspended in 1841 – there are two houses, one elected and one appointed.

While there were fears this arrangement would result in a return to confrontation and government paralysis, it is clear now that the Liberals who dominate the elected Assembly have another agenda. Under the direction of leading Roman Catholics, including Bishop Michael Anthony Fleming, the Liberals are beginning to demand that responsible government be accepted, as in mainland provinces.

Asylum not fit for humans, official says

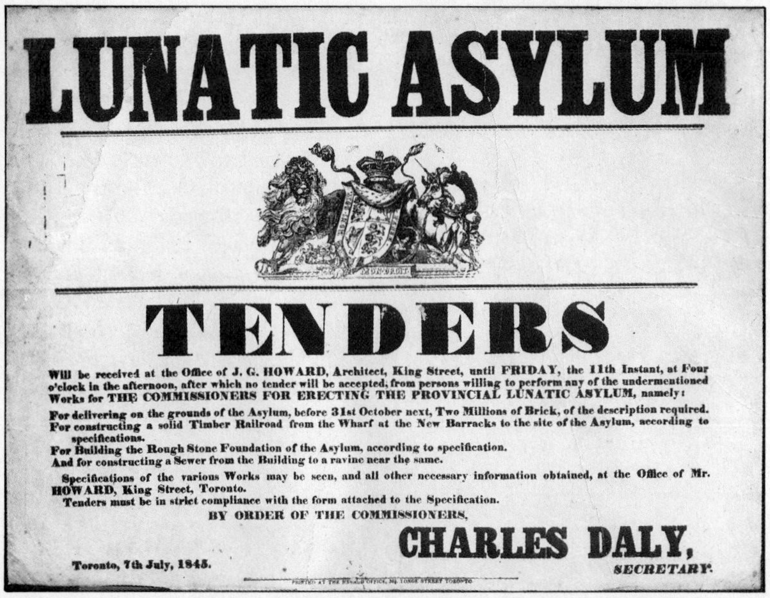

LUNATIC ASYLUM

TENDERS

Will be received at the Office of J. G. HOWARD, Architect, King Street, until FRIDAY, the 11th Instant, at Four o'clock in the afternoon, after which no tender will be accepted, from persons willing to perform any of the undermentioned Works for THE COMMISSIONERS FOR ERECTING THE PROVINCIAL LUNATIC ASYLUM, namely:

For delivering on the grounds of the Asylum, before 31st October next, Two Millions of Brick, of the description required.
For constructing a solid Timber Railroad from the Wharf at the New Barracks to the site of the Asylum, according to specifications.
For Building the Rough Stone Foundation of the Asylum, according to specification.
And for constructing a Sewer from the Building to a ravine near the same.

Specifications of the various Works may be seen, and all other necessary information obtained, at the Office of Mr. HOWARD, King Street, Toronto.
Tenders must be in strict compliance with the form attached to the Specification.

BY ORDER OF THE COMMISSIONERS,

CHARLES DALY,
SECRETARY.

Toronto, 7th July, 1845.

Announcement of tenders for construction of insane asylum in Toronto.

Dec. 26, 1848

TORONTO – Dr. George Park was fired today from his job as medical superintendent of the asylum here, after he had complained about filthy, inhumane conditions in the facility for the insane. The asylum, located in the old jail vacated by prisoners when a new one was built in 1841, was in a bad state when he was hired, Park said. There was not enough clothing to enable patients to change, and some had been naked for months.

These patients were often confined to their cells or could be found on the floor of a filthy attic ward that housed 60 or 70 people. The ward stank, and while others were not as bad, the whole asylum was dirty and poorly maintained, Park said. His dismissal marks the end of a bitter battle between Park and asylum commissioners whom he accused of undermining his authority. In turn, they told the provincial secretary Park had hired a man who had been fired from the hospital for removing a body from a coffin and placing firewood in it. Park's salvo in response prompted his dismissal.

Lack of money closes schools in Toronto

June 30, 1848

TORONTO – City council's refusal to quadruple funding has forced the board of trustees to close down schools for a year. The board asked for an increase from £500 to £2,000 in city taxpayer contributions to schools, but council balked, saying free education was fine in theory but costly in practice. Some members wanted to challenge the council's refusal in court, but the board did not go for the proposal, opting instead to close the schools and dismiss the teachers. Common schools here first obtained public money in 1843, and the board was appointed last year.

New Brunswickers calling for free trade

May 31, 1848

SAINT JOHN, N.B. – The British government has been called upon to gain free trade for New Brunswick with the United States. The action came today at a public meeting conducted by John Robertson, a local mill owner and member of the Legislative Council. It comes in the wake of great indignation here arising from the province of Canada turning a cold shoulder to this area, after it had sought an arrangement providing free trade.

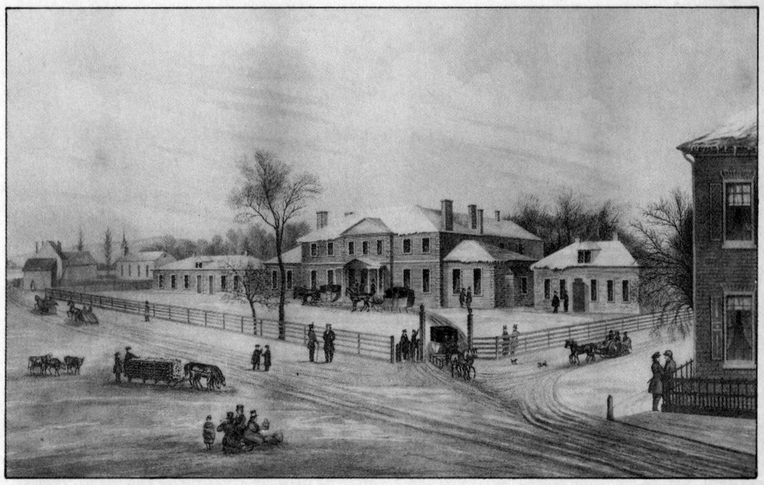

Fredericton, N.B., where merchants want free trade with United States.

1849

New Brunswick, Jan. 1. New Brunswick Electric Telegraph opens to provide telegraph service for the colony.

Montreal, Jan. 18. At the opening of Parliament, Governor Elgin reads the speech from the throne in both French and English, recognizing the legitimacy of French in the Assembly for the first time.

Montreal, Feb. 14. Louis-Hippolyte LaFontaine introduces the Rebellion Losses Bill in the Assembly, which provides for compensation for the Lower Canadians whose property was destroyed during the rebellion of 1837-38 by those acting on behalf of the goverment.

Montreal, Feb. 15. The galleries of Parliament are cleared because crowds are arguing more loudly than members over the Rebellion Losses Bill.

Montreal, April 30. A mob of Tories, outraged by the Rebellion Losses Bill, shower members of the Assembly with vegetables, dead rats, and garbage as they try to walk to the governor's residence. An official is hit in the mouth with an onion when he tries to read the Riot Act.

London, June 14. The British House of Commons proclaims Canada's full achievement of responsible government.

Montreal, July 18. A brawl between Tories and *Canadiens* erupts at a concert when Tories interrupt the singing of *La Marseillaise* with catcalls.

New Brunswick, July 28. The New Brunswick Colonial Association is formed from the Saint John Railway League to lobby for federal union of British North America.

Toronto, August. The Toronto, Simcoe, and Huron Railway Company is incorporated to build the city's first railway, to Georgian Bay.

Canada. The act incorporating the town of Bytown [Ottawa] is vetoed because military authorities fear losing control of the town's affairs.

Canada. A statute authorizes municipal councils to establish separate schools for blacks, legalizing racial segregation.

Canada. The capital of Canada moves from Montreal to Toronto on a temporary basis after Tory mobs burn down the Assembly in Montreal to protest the passage of the Rebellion Losses Bill.

Laws to clamp down on immigration

Jan. 18, 1849

MONTREAL – Canada's lawmakers have decided the time is ripe to clamp down on immigration. The Legislative Council and Assembly of United Canada passed a new set of laws today which say all lunatic, idiotic, deaf and dumb, blind or infirm immigrants arriving at a Canadian port will be deported.

The Acts Concerning the Naturalization of Aliens and Emigration and Quarantine provide for the medical inspection of all newly-arrived immigrants by the medical superintendent. Captains of vessels arriving at Canadian ports must provide authorities with a list of their passengers, including names and ages. Captains must also inform authorities if passengers are accompanied by any relatives.

In addition to the $1 duty payable for each passenger, captains must also pay a $300 bond for each passenger who is infirm, a lunatic, deaf and dumb, or blind. The money will be refunded once the captain has returned the passengers in question to the country they came from. Captains who neglect to pay the bond will be fined $400, and they'll also find that their vessels will not be cleared until the bond and any outstanding fines have been paid. Finally, captains also will be held responsible for court costs.

If a passenger, at any time within three years of arriving in Canada, becomes dependent on the government of Canada, one of its municipalities or charitable institutions, his or her care shall be paid for with the money collected from the bonds deposited by the captain of the vessel which brought them here.

Passengers on ships arriving at Canadian harbors must be kept on board the vessels for 48 hours after docking, along with their luggage. The condition of each ship's passengers will be determined by a medical superintendent, who will also examine the vessel's bill of health, its manifest, log book and any other information considered pertinent.

Each time a captain does not make passenger information available to the collector of customs, a fine of not less than $20 and not more than $1,000 will be levied.

This new legislation, which may prove difficult to enforce, is an attempt to control immigration, and limit it to the self-sufficient. For the past few decades, tens of thousands of men, women and children have arrived in desperate condition, destitute and often critically ill with contagious diseases. Without extended help they risk perishing, and people here have responded selflessly in caring for the newcomers. But many Canadians resent the continuing drain on their economic and human resources, and demand in-depth screening of immigrants, such as this new law prescribes.

NOTICE TO EMIGRANTS,

FOR SALE,

Several good improved Farms in a high state of cultivation, Situated within a short distance of Hamilton and Dundas, in the Gore District and at prices varying from 300 to £1000 and upwards.

For Further particulars Apply to

A. F. BEGUE, *Notary Public.*

Dundas, April 24 1845.

Notices like this have drawn adventurous Europeans to the "new world."

Between the decks of an immigrant ship, where colonists hoping to make a new life instead often contract fatal diseases.

Medal honors work of Père Chiniquy

July 5, 1849

LONGUEUIL, Canada East – Temperance crusader Père Chiniquy was presented with a gold medal wrapped up in four $100 bills today by a crowd of 9,000 people. Inscribed on the medal were the words "To R.P. Chiniquy, apostle of temperance. Homage to his virtues, his zeal and his patriotism."

This year alone, Père Chiniquy has given 500 sermons to 120 parishes and more than 200,000 people. He has established temperance groups throughout the province.

Père Chiniquy, a great believer in temperance, has received a medal for his work for this important cause.

Woman must wear a veil in classroom

1849

FREDERICTON – Martha Hamm Lewis has won her battle to become the first woman here to go to a Normal School and attend class with her male counterparts. However, Martha will not exactly be treated like her male classmates. She is not allowed to mix with male students, and must enter the classroom 10 minutes before the others, sit at the back, and leave before the end of lectures. She must wear a veil at all times, and leave the premises without speaking to male students. Martha appealed to the lieutenant-governor for leave to attend a Normal School, and it took an order-in-council to finally grant her admission.

Rebellion Losses Bill sparks controversy

Feb. 13, 1849

MONTREAL – The test of responsible government has arrived. In the Assembly, majority leader Louis-Hippolyte LaFontaine has tabled the Rebellion Losses Bill. It would indemnify people whose property was damaged in the Lower Canadian rebellion of 1837-38.

Tory supporters are outraged by the bill. They see it as rewarding treason, and long for Gov. Gen. Lord Elgin to disallow it. If he does, responsible government will be proven to be a farce. But if he doesn't, then, despite Tory anger, it will be an unassailable fact.

Cartoon on Rebellion Losses Bill.

New Brunswick adopts tough abortion law

1849

NEW BRUNSWICK – The province has just adopted one of the toughest abortion laws in British North America, making it illegal for women here to have an abortion at any stage of pregnancy. The legislation is unprecedented in Canada. Not only will women who abort their babies be imprisoned, but so will the person who performs the abortion.

Abortion is a contentious issue here. Not long ago, New Brunswick eliminated the distinction between sentences for performing an abortion before the child's movements could be felt, and afterward.

Reform government: women can't vote

1849

CANADA – The Reform government has banned Canadian women from voting, ending years of confusion over the validity of the female franchise.

The decision confirms previous tries to ban women from voting. Back in 1832, an act concerning elections specifically barred women from voting, as did the Reform Act passed later that year. The former measure was overturned for reasons unrelated to a woman's right to vote. But in 1844, seven women were allowed to vote in a Canada West election and the results were not disputed.

The Long Sault Rapids on the St. Lawrence River are one of the three great rapids formed by the movement of the ice in the glacial period.

Tory riots continue to plague Montreal

April 27, 1849

MONTREAL – The madness continues here, as Tories opposed to the Rebellion Losses Bill continue their rampage of violence and vandalism. Today the jail was the focus of their anger. It's where Tory leaders are kept, following their role in riots rocking this capital. A target of the mob's affections was Fire Chief Alfred Perry, who led the attack on the now-destroyed Parliament buildings two days ago.

So intense was the crowd's anger that prison officials deemed it wise to bring out Perry himself to try and calm them. Thus he was paraded before the mob on the prison walls, where the only response to Perry's pleas for peace was a call for him to jump to freedom.

Cartoon shows French-Canadian nationalists tormenting British lion.

King's College now Toronto University

1849

TORONTO – The charter for King's College has been revoked, and in its place the University of Toronto has been established. It will be a non-sectarian provincial university which will affiliate the colleges and abolish the faculty of divinity at King's. Clergymen are excluded from the chancellorship.

King's College, long chartered, was made operational by the late governor Sir Charles Bagot. In 1842, the cornerstone was laid, and the college opened on June 8, 1843. ▷

Outraged Tories burn down House of Assembly

April 25, 1849

MONTREAL – Tory mobs, whipped into a frenzy by the passage of the Rebellion Losses Bill tonight, have sacked and burned the Parliament buildings.

Violence broke out after Gov. Gen. Lord Elgin gave royal assent to an act that the Tories claim compensates those who rebelled against the Crown in 1837. As assent was granted, a groan rose up from the packed gallery of spectators. These people then rushed outside, greeting Elgin with a hail of rocks and garbage. Fortunately, he managed to escape in his enclosed carriage.

Later this evening, a mob of about 1,500 English-speaking Montrealers (since 1831 the majority in the city), gathered outside the House, where the Assembly still sat. They broke into the chamber at about 9 p.m. One declared, "I dissolve this French House," while another took an axe to the throne. They stole the mace, the staff that symbolizes royal authority, and sacked the chamber itself.

At this point it was discovered fire had broken out – the result of smashed lighting-gas mains in the Parliament buildings. In the midst of the chaos, the members gathered around Speaker Morin, not leaving until he formally adjourned the sitting. They left with flames literally at their backs.

Then, as the mob hooted and howled with delight, they stood outside and watched the buildings burn to the ground. No help arrived, for the rioters kept the firemen back, and cut the hoses of those who managed to get through.

The passage of the Rebellion Losses Bill prompts angry Tory mobs to set fire to the House of Assembly in Montreal and to hold firemen back while it burns.

Tories burn the House of Assembly.

LaFontaine speech ridicules Papineau

Jan. 23, 1849

QUEBEC CITY – In a speech mocking his main opponent, Reform leader Louis-Hippolyte LaFontaine today delivered an emotional plea for the Act of Union to a packed Assembly.

Flanked by his allies and under the watchful gaze of his friends in the galleries, LaFontaine proclaimed that had his foe Louis-Joseph Papineau been heeded, efforts to improve the Act of Union would have failed and, he asked "where would our language now be?" In the 90-minute speech, LaFontaine reminded the Assembly he had won the repeal of unjust clauses in the Union Act, had returned the capital to Lower Canada, and had been instrumental in opening up lands for French-Canadians to settle.

LaFontaine's speech was in reply to Papineau, who said the Act of Union had been advanced "with the avowed goal of injuring the Canadian people." Rejecting economic arguments for union, Papineau said the country "has never suffered as much since the union."

Government leader ready for Tory mob

Aug. 15, 1849

MONTREAL – Tory rioters, still infuriated by the Rebellion Losses Bill months after its passage, attempted to storm the home of government leader Louis-Hippolyte LaFontaine. But LaFontaine was ready. Aided by friends, he waited inside his darkened house with rifles at the ready. As the rioters approached, shots rang out on both sides. One protester, William Mason, was killed. Six more were wounded before the mob fled.

Tories vandalize Reformers' homes

April 26, 1849

MONTREAL – The riots that erupted last night over the passing of the Rebellion Losses Bill continued today. Some of the Tory mob's favorite targets were the homes of Reformers who helped steer the bill into law.

Vandalized tonight were the homes of Francis Hincks, Benjamin Holmes, and Louis-Hippolyte LaFontaine. At Hincks' and Holmes' houses, the inhabitants literally fled out the back door while the mob came in the front. At LaFontaine's nobody was home, but plenty of antiques, china, and books were just waiting to be destroyed. LaFontaine's stable was also torched.

Cartoon is "dedicated to Lower Canada as a sample of what the beef and beer of Toronto have done for one of her great men."

Vancouver Island leased to the HBC

Jan. 13, 1849

FORT VICTORIA, Vancouver Island – The British government, worried American settlers from the Oregon Country will move into British territory along the Pacific Coast, has leased Vancouver Island to the Hudson's Bay Company. The rent is seven shillings a year. In this way the colonial office has succeeded in getting the company, the only British institution with any pretence to power out here, to act as a colonizing agent and defender of the territory.

The British government's hand was forced by Mexico's 1848 surrender of California to the conquering United States, and, two years earlier, by the Oregon Boundary Treaty, which set the border at the 49th Parallel, and left the southern tip of Vancouver Island jutting out below the line. Although the colonial office seems to have solved the problems of administration and defence, there is still a puzzle: How will chief factor James Douglas manage to serve both his country and company?

Métis challenge the HBC – and win

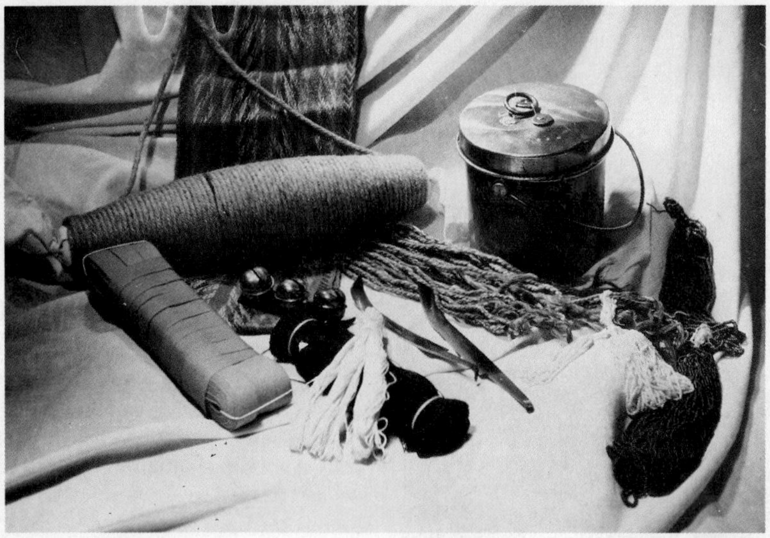

Hudson's Bay Company trade goods include kettle, thread, skeins of beads.

Jug of rye whiskey has HBC label.

May 17, 1849

RED RIVER COLONY, Rupert's Land – Métis traders in this colony won an important court battle with the Hudson's Bay Company today. While an angry mob of about 300 people, many armed with rifles, waited outside the courthouse, charges of illegal trading against three Métis were dropped and a fourth defendant, Guillaume Sayer, was convicted but not punished. When the four accused Métis emerged from the courtroom free men, they were greeted by a wild celebration and cries of "the trade is free."

The HBC took the traders to court in an attempt to assert their monopoly of the fur trade and to prove that free traders who have been taking their business south of the border have been breaking the law. Once the jury found Sayer guilty, the HBC chief factor John Ballenden thought he had made his point and withdrew all the other charges. However, to the dismay of the company, the verdict is being interpreted much differently by the local people who see the result of the trial as a glorious vindication of their right to trade with whomever they want. It looks like the HBC is going to have to outstrip competitors in the field, not the courtroom.

Hudson's Bay Company tea caddy.

Orange Order riots lead to 12 deaths

July 12, 1849

SAINT JOHN, N.B. – Twelve people died today as Orangemen celebrated the "Glorious 12th" by trying to march through Catholic areas. After failing to talk Orange leaders into calling off the march, the mayor tried to defuse potential trouble, but he was attacked and his head split open. At his urging, British troops intercepted the march, getting between the two sides. Despite their efforts, a battle ensued. Both sides were armed with muskets, and the Catholics were on the tops of buildings, shooting and throwing cobblestones down into the narrow street below.

Guarantee Act lends incentive to railways

1849

TORONTO – Canada's fledgling railroad industry got a big boost with the passage of the Guarantee Act. The law provides government aid to all railroads at least 112 kilometres long.

Railway construction in the Canadas has been slowed by the political turmoil of the 1837 Rebellion and the economic recession in its wake. There are now only 106 kilometres of track in Canada, including a 12.8-kilometre portage line around the rapids between Lachine and Montreal built in 1846-47.

British American League nixes annexation

July 26, 1849

KINGSTON – The British American League has said no to annexation to the United States as a solution to trade problems caused by Britain abandoning the preferential colonial system.

At a convention here today, the league passed resolutions calling for a protective Canadian tariff, retrenchment, and that a potential union of British colonies in North America be investigated. Those who are in favor of annexation to the U.S., if this convention is an indication, are still in a minority.

Telegraph helping to move the news

Feb. 21, 1849

SAINT JOHN, N.B. – The telegraph line from Saint John to Boston has become popular with New York newspapers. Newspaper representatives pick up the latest European news from mail steamers stopped in Halifax. They send the news by horse and rider to Digby, where it is ferried across the Bay of Fundy to Saint John. The news is telegraphed to Boston, where it is then published in the newspapers' evening editions.

Merchants, Tories support annexation

Oct. 11, 1849

MONTREAL – Politics makes strange bedfellows! Today the Rouges, free-thinking French-Canadian liberals, and a group of wealthy, English merchants issued a joint manifesto urging annexation to the U.S. The Rouges are attracted by what they see as the greater political liberties in the U.S., and the English feel betrayed by Britain's adoption of free trade.

The manifesto is no surprise. Last May, Montreal women sewed star-spangled banners and on July 4, many city businesses sported the U.S. flag. All four English newspapers here endorse annexation. Recently, 150 annexationists met here and elected sugar manufacturer John Redpath their president.

Cartoon about U.S. takeover of Canadian institutions through free trade. ▷

Gold rush in California too tempting to resist

It's every man for himself in the rush to cash in on California's gold. This cartoon comments on the individualist nature of the gold-seeker, who is "neither a borrower nor a lender," on the road to finding great riches.

Illustration shows gold washers panning in the rivers of California. Many Canadian men have flocked to America's west coast, seeking their fortune.

A cartoon titled "The way they go to California" shows fleets of sailing ships all bound for California and advertising exorbitant prices for passage. Airships and other visionary modes of getting to the gold rush poke fun at gold-seekers' apparent willingness to sacrifice life and limb for the chance to strike it rich on the American west coast.

News of gold rush has come to P.E.I.

1849

CHARLOTTETOWN – Gold fever is starting to grip P.E.I. With letters coming home describing how eight days of work can net $800 in the gold fields, Islanders are flocking to California. Prominent Charlottetown ship owner James Peake, for one, has wished them luck. He does not blame the gold-seekers, observing dryly that the Island was truly a good poor man's country, as it had always kept him poor.

The figure of a gold rush miner.

Two miners inspect nuggets, hoping they've found the real thing.

Miners in the California gold rush.

In search of their fortune: illustration of some men panning for gold in the rivers of California.

Visions of wealth filling their heads

Nov. 12, 1849

CHARLOTTETOWN – The brig *Fanny* sailed from Charlottetown today, her destination being the California gold fields. On board is the California Association, a company of 40 Islanders determined to make their fortunes.

The venture took shape several months ago, when news of the gold rush began to filter onto the Island. A meeting in Charlottetown resulted in the formation of the association, with each of the 40 members paying £100 to join. With the money, they bought the *Fanny,* a 200-ton vessel built of juniper in Charlottetown.

Former owner James Peake calls the *Fanny* his "luckiest and best averaged vessel." The company has outfitted her with a large supply of lumber; two large houses, framed and ready for assembly; and lashed securely amidships, a five-ton cedar built boat. With ordinary commodities selling for extraordinary prices in California, the company is also sailing with a generous supply of foodstuffs, raw materials such as tin, coal and iron, and tools. Many on the *Fanny* are tradesmen. If they cannot find their fortune lying on the ground, perhaps they can make it with their hands.

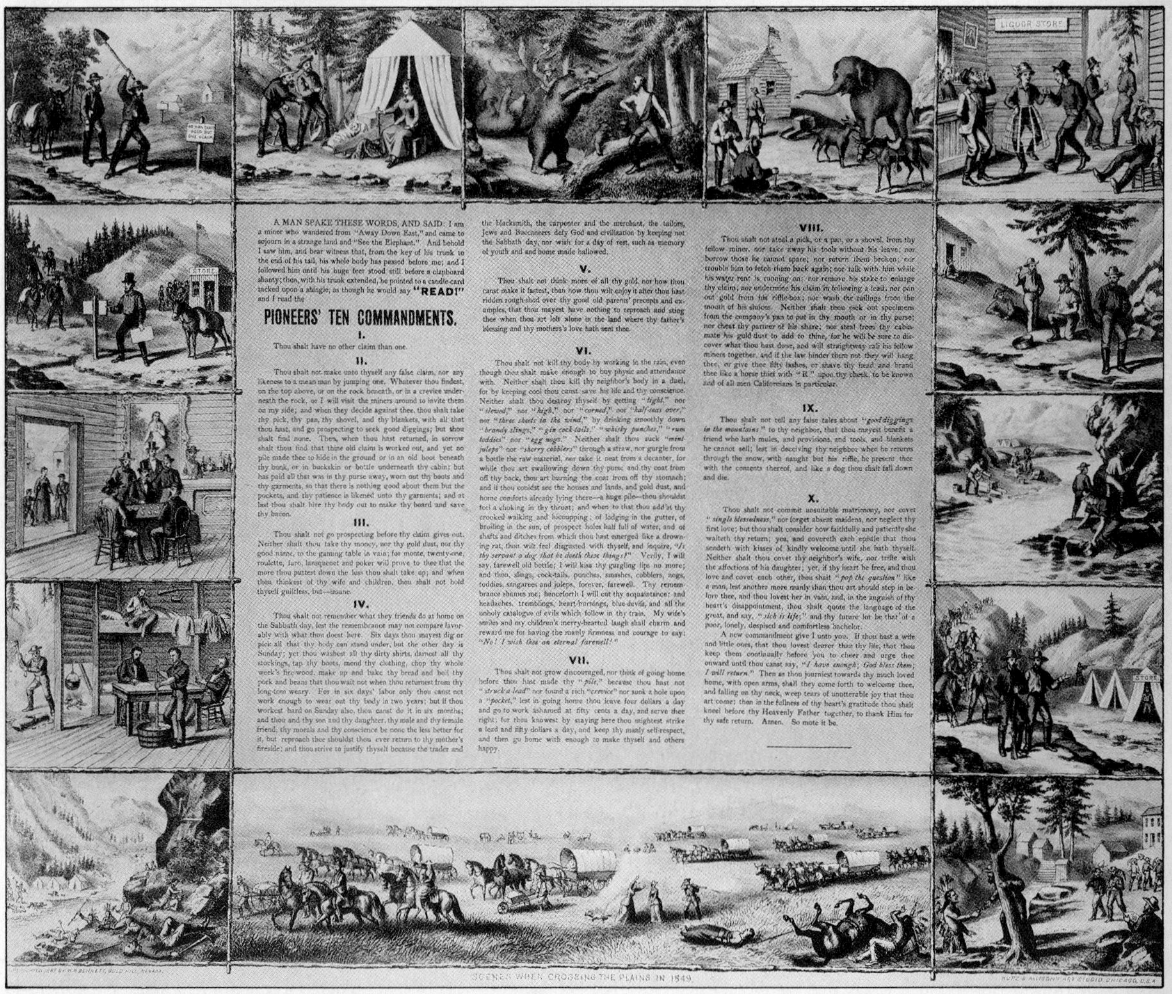

A MAN SPAKE THESE WORDS, AND SAID: I am a miner who wandered from "Away Down East," and came to sojourn in a strange land and "See the Elephant." And behold I saw him, and bear witness that, from the key of his trunk to the end of his tail, his whole body has passed before me; and I followed him until his huge feet stood still before a clapboard shanty; then, with his trunk extended, he pointed to a candle-card tacked upon a shingle, as though he would say **"READ!"** and I read the

PIONEERS' TEN COMMANDMENTS.

I.

Thou shalt have no other claim than one.

II.

Thou shalt not make unto thyself any false claim, nor any likeness to a mean man by jumping one. Whatever thou findest, on the top above, or on the rock beneath, or in a crevice underneath the rock, or I will visit the miners around to invite them on my side; and when they decide against thee, thou shalt take thy pick, thy pan, thy shovel, and thy blankets, with all that thou hast, and go prospecting to seek good diggings; but thou shalt find none. Then, when thou hast returned, in sorrow shalt thou find that thine old claim is worked out, and yet no pile made thee to hide in the ground or in an old boot beneath thy bunk, or in buckskin or bottle underneath thy cabin; but has paid all that was in thy purse away, worn out thy boots and thy garments, so that there is nothing good about them but the pockets, and thy patience is likened unto thy garments; and at last thou shalt hire thy body out to make thy board and save thy bacon.

III.

Thou shalt not go prospecting before thy claim gives out. Neither shalt thou take thy money, nor thy gold dust, nor thy good name, to the gaming table in vain; for monte, twenty-one, roulette, faro, lansquenet and poker will prove to thee that the more thou puttest down the less thou shalt take up; and when thou thinkest of thy wife and children, thou shalt not hold thyself guiltless, but—insane.

IV.

Thou shalt not remember what they friends do at home on the Sabbath day, lest the remembrance may not compare favorably with what thou doest here. Six days thou mayest dig or pick all that thy body can stand under, but the other day is Sunday; yet thou washest all thy dirty shirts, darnest all thy stockings, tap thy boots, mend thy clothing, chop thy whole week's fire-wood, make up and bake thy bread and boil thy pork and beans that thou wait not when thou returnest from thy long-tom weary. For in six days' labor only thou canst not work enough to wear out thy body in two years; but if thou workest hard on Sunday also, thou canst do it in six months; and thou and thy son and thy daughter, thy male and thy female friend, thy morals and thy conscience be none the less better for it, but reproach thee shouldst thou ever return to thy mother's fireside; and thou strive to justify thyself because the trader and the blacksmith, the carpenter and the merchant, the tailors, Jews and Buccaneers defy God and civilization by keeping not the Sabbath day, nor wish for a day of rest, such as memory of youth and and home made hallowed.

V.

Thou shalt not think more of all thy gold, nor how thou canst make it fastest, than how thou wilt enjoy it after thou hast ridden rough-shod over thy good old parents' precepts and examples, that thou mayest have nothing to reproach and sting thee when thou art left alone in the land where thy father's blessing and thy mothers's love hath sent thee.

VI.

Thou shalt not kill thy body by working in the rain, even though thou shalt make enough to buy physic and attendance with. Neither shalt thou kill thy neighbor's body in a duel, for by keeping cool thou canst save his life and thy conscience. Neither shalt thou destroy thyself by getting "*tight,*" nor "*slewed,*" nor "*high,*" nor "*corned,*" nor "*half-seas over,*" nor "*three sheets in the wind,*" by drinking smoothly down "*brandy slings,*" "*gin cock-tails,*" "*whisky punches,*" "*rum toddies*" nor "*egg nogs.*" Neither shalt thou suck "*mint-juleps*" nor "*sherry cobblers*" through a straw, nor gurgle from a bottle the raw material, nor take it neat from a decanter, for while thou art swallowing down thy purse and thy coat from off thy back, thou art burning the coat from off thy stomach; and if thou couldst see the houses and lands, and gold dust, and home comforts already lying there—a huge pile—thou shouldst feel a choking in thy throat; and when to that thou add'st thy crooked walking and hiccupping; of lodging in the gutter, of broiling in the sun, of prospect holes half full of water, and of shafts and ditches from which thou hast emerged like a drowning rat, thou wilt feel disgusted with thyself, and inquire, "*Is thy servant a dog that he doeth these things?*" Verily, I will say, farewell old bottle; I will kiss thy gurgling lips no more; and thou, slings, cock-tails, punches, smashes, cobblers, nogs, toddies, sangarees and juleps, forever, farewell. Thy remembrance shames me; henceforth I will cut thy acquaintance; and headaches, tremblings, heart-burnings, blue-devils, and all the unholy catalogue of evils which follow in thy train. My wife's smiles and my children's merry-hearted laugh shall charm and reward me for having the manly firmness and courage to say: "*No! I wish thee an eternal farewell!*"

VII.

Thou shalt not grow discouraged, nor think of going home before thou hast made thy "*pile,*" because thou hast not "*struck a lead*" nor found a rich "*crevice*" nor sunk a hole upon a "*pocket,*" lest in going home thou leave four dollars a day and go to work ashamed at fifty cents a day, and serve thee right; for thou knowest by staying here thou mightest strike a lead and fifty dollars a day, and keep thy manly self-respect, and then go home with enough to make thyself and others happy.

VIII.

Thou shalt not steal a pick, or a pan, or a shovel, from thy fellow miner, nor take away his tools without his leave; nor borrow those he cannot spare; nor return them broken; nor trouble him to fetch them back again; nor talk with him while his water rent is running on; nor remove his stake to enlarge thy claim; nor undermine his claim in following a lead; nor pan out gold from his riffle-box; nor wash the tailings from the mouth of his sluices. Neither shalt thou pick out specimens from the company's pan to put in thy mouth or in thy purse; nor cheat thy partner of his share; nor steal from thy cabin-mate his gold dust to add to thine, for he will be sure to discover what thou hast done, and will straightway call his fellow miners together, and if the law hinder them not they will hang thee, or give thee fifty lashes, or shave thy head and brand thee like a horse thief with "R" upon thy cheek, to be known and of all men Californians in particular.

IX.

Thou shalt not tell any false tales about "*good diggings in the mountains*" to thy neighbor, that thou mayest benefit a friend who hath mules, and provisions, and tools, and blankets he cannot sell; lest in deceiving thy neighbor when he returns through the snow, with naught but his riffle, he present thee with the contents thereof, and like a dog thou shalt fall down and die.

X.

Thou shalt not commit unsuitable matrimony, nor covet "*single blessedness,*" nor forget absent maidens, nor neglect thy first love; but thou shalt consider how faithfully and patiently she waiteth thy return; yea, and covereth each epistle that thou sendeth with kisses of kindly welcome until she hath thyself. Neither shalt thou covet thy neighbor's wife, nor trifle with the affections of his daughter; yet, if thy heart be free, and thou love and covet each other, thou shalt "*pop the question*" like a man, lest another more manly than thou art should step in before thee, and thou lovest her in vain, and, in the anguish of thy heart's disappointment, thou shalt quote the language of the great, and say, "*sich is life;*" and thy future lot be that of a poor, lonely, despised and comfortless bachelor.

A new commandment give I unto you. If thou hast a wife and little ones, that thou lovest dearer than thy life, that thou keep them continually before you to cheer and urge thee onward until thou canst say, "*I have enough; God bless them; I will return.*" Then as thou journiest towards thy much loved home, with open arms, shall they come forth to welcome thee, and falling on thy neck, weep tears of unutterable joy that thou art come; then in the fullness of thy heart's gratitude thou shalt kneel before thy Heavenly Father together, to thank Him for thy safe return. Amen. So mote it be.

The miner's Pioneer Ten Commandments of 1849, teaching those interested in making their fortune out west to keep their morals intact. Illustration includes scenes when crossing the plains during the Gold Rush.

1850

Toronto, Jan. 1. Bytown [Ottawa] is incorporated.

Vancouver Island, March 10. Richard Blanshard arrives as first governor of the colony of Vancouver Island. He does not have an enviable job: the colony's land is owned by the HBC and all the inhabitants work for the company, which does not welcome the new governor. There is no legislature or judiciary. To top it all off, he gets no salary.

San Francisco, May 23. The brig *Fanny* lands with some 40 gold-seekers from Prince Edward Island eager to take part in the great gold rush.

London, June. The British government says in a dispatch it will not pay for the building of an Intercolonial Railway between the Maritime colonies and Canada.

Vancouver Island, August. Governor Blanshard appoints a Provisional Council of three men. He was instructed to appoint a council of seven, but can't find enough candidates.

Arctic, August. William Penney and Horatio Austin, head of British expeditions looking for Franklin's missing expeditions, find graves and other traces of Franklin's mission at Beechey Island.

England, Oct. 1. An venture led by Charles Forsyth and sponsored by Lady Franklin to look for her husband's missing expedition returns unsuccessfully. They learnt of Austin's discovery of traces of the expedition at Beechey Island.

Vancouver Island, November. Dispirited by his term as governor of the Island, Richard Blanshard tenders his resignation on the grounds of ill health. He spent most of his term travelling along the coast settling disputes between the HBC and its employees.

Europe and America. Railways are spreading throughout Britain, Europe, and America, making travel much faster and promising an economic and social revolution.

Canada. Only a few railway lines totalling 106 kilometres have been built. The most important are the Champlain and St. Lawrence, the Erie and Ontario, and the Montreal and Lachine.

Pacific Coast. Governor Blanshard has an Indian village burnt near Fort Rupert after the Indians kill three deserters from a merchant ship.

U.S. clamps down on escaped slaves

The effects of the Fugitive Slave Bill: tracking down some fugitive slaves.

The discovery of Nat Turner, an escaped American slave, as he tried to make his way to British North America in search of a safe place to live.

The Fugitive Slave Bill in operation: an American slave is taken away.

Sept. 18, 1850

WASHINGTON, D.C. – Runaway American slaves must now reach British North America if they are to be assured of freedom, thanks to a new law passed today by President Millard Fillmore in Washington. By signing the controversial Fugitive Slave Bill, Fillmore has made escaped slaves subject to federal jurisdiction. They will now be denied both trial by jury and the right to testify in their own defence, even in states where slavery has been abolished.

The new law also gives southern slave owners the right to reclaim runaway slaves captured in any part of the country, and any white person found guilty of aiding an escapee is subject to a fine or imprisonment. Federal commissioners who return runaways to their owners get $10 per slave.

Indians urged to maintain way of life

1850

OKANAGAN LANDING, Rupert's Land – A female religious leader is touring the Indian settlements of the Okanagan and Similkameen valleys, calling for a return to the traditional way of life. These valleys, situated about halfway between the Rocky Mountains and the Pacific Coast and blessed with hot summers and crisp winters, have seen many changes in the last 40 years. Soon after the first Europeans came through, the Indians started to work for the fur traders who used the valleys as routes from the Oregon Country. This work interfered little with the traditional way of life. The route has just been closed. But now missionaries are at work, teaching a new religion and frightening the people into abandoning practices that have served them well.

Next, if stories told by Indians from the coast are true, settlers will take over the hunting grounds and spoil the fishing. This is why the Indian visionary warns the Indians that the new ways must be resisted.

Ex-slaves settling at Saltspring Island

1850

SALTSPRING ISLAND, Colony of Vancouver Island – A number of black settlers from the United States have made their home here – the biggest of the islands in the Gulf of Georgia. The ex-slaves plan to start farming. They arrived at Victoria recently from San Francisco and have been assured that after they have lived in the colony for seven years, they can become British subjects.

Elgin Settlement: haven for ex-slaves

Aug. 10, 1850

BUXTON, Canada West – Elgin Settlement, a 9,000-acre haven for ex-slaves near Buxton, was officially given the blessing of the government of Canada and the governor general today.

The settlement, named for the governor general who serves as its patron, was founded by Rev. William King, a Louisiana landowner who inherited slaves from his wife's family. King freed his slaves and accompanied them to Canada to seek refuge from the Fugitive Slave Act in the United States. On their arrival in Canada, King appealed to the Christian community and the government to assist the destitute refugees. They responded with a land grant in Raleigh Township, County Kent, and $18,000 in funds. The land will be divided into 50-acre lots and sold at a nominal fee to the settlers. King was named superintendent of the colony.

Facility for mentally ill opens doors

Jan. 26, 1850

TORONTO – The Provincial Lunatic Asylum in Toronto opened its doors today, British North America's first facility to treat the mentally ill. Before, insane persons have been forced to live among society, often as indigent wanderers, or be confined in jail cells with common criminals, or hidden away in the darker recesses of the building, perhaps the basement. In recent years society has recognized the need for a better solution.

In 1839, an Ottawa Valley petition complained of repeated "appearances among them of maniacs, and insane persons, for the most part strangers to the country, or to the district" and the unavoidable expense "owing to the necessity of confining and maintaining the deranged persons in the Common Gaol of the District." The legislature responded with an act providing for an institution like the asylum which opened here today.

A south side view of the Queen Street Provincial Lunatic Asylum in Toronto.

Over the past decade, the Home County Gaol was converted into a centre where the mentally ill received sustained treatment, and its success rate proves the inadequacy of older forms of care. But the building itself is old and dilapidated, in stark contrast to the new institute.

Unfortunately, there is a problem with the new institute's site – the Mississauga Indians claim it is theirs. Half a century ago, the Credit River band used the site for camping and council purposes, and Head Chief Joseph Sawyer says they have never surrendered "the lot of three acres in the vicinity of Toronto City near or where the Provincial Lunatic Asylum now stands." The province has ignored these claims.

Reciprocity replaces annexationist goal

c.1850

CANADA EAST AND WEST – The thrust for annexation with the United States, which climaxed in 1849 with the Montreal Annexation Manifesto, has now lost most of its force. Britain's condemnation of the manifesto as treasonous has given many annexationists second thoughts. The United States too has shown much less interest in the project it used to encourage. In the Canadas, a surging economy has dampened the appeal annexation once had. However, a new idea is gaining ground – closer economic integration with the U.S., or commercial reciprocity.

Haida potlatch on the Pacific coast. A potlatch ceremony is held to mark any important event in the life of the Haida Indians, such as birth, marriage, death, or new social position. Dancing, feasting, and gift-giving take place.

Blanshard assumes new post at Victoria

March 11, 1850

FORT VICTORIA, Colony of Vancouver Island – Richard Blanshard, a 32-year-old barrister from England, stepped ashore from *HMS Driver* today. There was a 17-gun salute from the warship, and then he walked over the snow to the fort and read a proclamation that made him governor of Vancouver Island.

After the ceremony, Blanshard, who is paid no salary but expects a land grant in its place, met chief factor James Douglas and was told the house he will be provided with has not been built yet. It is difficult to see how Blanshard will do his job – he has no staff, no police and no army. After meeting Douglas, Blanshard went back to his cabin on *HMS Driver* to spend the night.

Fort Victoria, Columbia district headquarters, where British lawyer Richard Blanshard will reside as the first governor of the Vancouver Island colony.

Indians sell land for blankets, cap

Indians of the Pacific coast arriving by canoe for a burial ceremony.

A Kwakiutl woman with a Chilkat blanket and a spruce root hat. The Indians were given blankets and a cap in return for their western land.

May 1, 1850

FORT VICTORIA, Vancouver Island – James Douglas, chief factor of the Hudson's Bay Company, today concluded a series of treaties with the local Indians by which the company purchases all the lands in the vicinity of this fort "entirely and forever" from the Sooke, Songhee and Klallam tribes. These are the first Indian treaties in the colony of Vancouver Island. In return for their land, the natives receive a total of 371 blankets and a cap. The Indians retain title to their village sites and enclosed fields, and have the right to hunt and fish on unoccupied lands.

The HBC has had responsibility for colonizing this island since 1849. It intends to import settlers to begin farming the district near the fort and, wishing to avoid conflict with the local Indians, Douglas decided to purchase title to the land so there would be no question about ownership. Douglas now intends to continue his treaty-making with native inhabitants in other parts of the Island.

Elizabeth Simcoe succumbs in England

Jan. 17, 1850

WOLFORD, England – Elizabeth Simcoe, the popular wife of the first lieutenant-governor of Upper Canada, died today at her family estate. She was predeceased by her husband John Graves Simcoe 44 years ago, in 1806.

Elizabeth Simcoe married her soldier husband in 1782, and 10 years later the couple were transferred to Upper Canada, where they presided until 1796. She kept voluminous diaries, recording all she saw, from the colonial social swirl to its flora and fauna.

Elizabeth Simcoe, who kept a diary.

Toronto drowning in taverns, beer shops

c.1850

TORONTO – Residents here need not go without a drink for long – there are so many drinking establishments in the city it's almost as if you couldn't throw a stone without hitting one.

Every crossroad has at least one place where drinks are served, and the main highways support dozens of drinking establishments. There are 152 taverns and 206 beer shops to keep the city's 30,000 residents and many visitors happy. What's more, these numbers do not include the many inns also serving liquor.

Robinson treaties cede land to British

Sept. 9, 1850

NORTH SHORE OF LAKE HURON – Commissioner William B. Robinson has concluded the second of two treaties with the Ojibwa Indians living north of lakes Superior and Huron. Under the terms of the treaties, the Crown obtains title to 129,500 square kilometres of land between the lakes and the height of land to the north. Negotiations were prompted by the recent discovery of valuable minerals near Sault Ste. Marie.

The Robinson-Superior and the Robinson-Huron treaties – as they are known – grant the Indians 21 reserves, a lump-sum payment of £4,000 sterling, as well as annuities amounting to 96 cents per person. Also, the Crown admits the right of the Indians to continue to fish and hunt throughout the ceded territory. These are the first Indian treaties in the northern part of Canada West.

Shifts in economy affect immigrants

1850

SAINT JOHN, N.B. – Many of the 150,000 Irishmen who have come here since 1815 have suffered from the British government's failure to regulate the flow of immigrants according to economic conditions in the province.

One of the most difficult years was 1842, as thousands of new immigrants were unable to find work due to an economic downturn. They either re-emigrated, became charges of overseers of the poor, or wandered the countryside seeking help. In 1843, as the economy improved and workers were needed, no immigrants arrived.

Variations on a theme: an array of bonnets worn around 1850.

The latest in women's headgear.

Two ships looking for Franklin travel on different routes

June 30, 1850

HONOLULU – The two ships which left England in January in the latest search for explorer Sir John Franklin have gone their separate ways to the Arctic. *HMS Enterprise,* commanded by Richard Collinson, and *HMS Investigator,* with Robert McClure in command, were to have met here and compared plans. (Collinson is in charge of the expedition.) But McClure, whose ship was the faster, waited five days and then went ahead, sailing north for the Bering Strait.

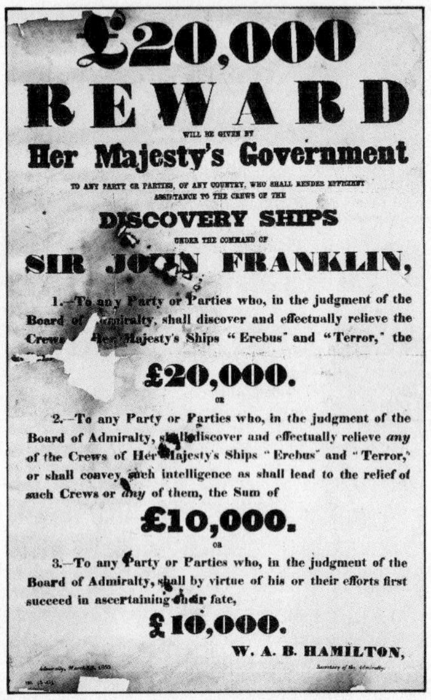

£20,000
REWARD
WILL BE GIVEN BY
Her Majesty's Government
TO ANY PARTY OR PARTIES, OF ANY COUNTRY, WHO SHALL RENDER EFFICIENT ASSISTANCE TO THE CREWS OF THE
DISCOVERY SHIPS
UNDER THE COMMAND OF
SIR JOHN FRANKLIN,

1.—To any Party or Parties who, in the judgment of the Board of Admiralty, shall discover and effectually relieve the Crews of Her Majesty's Ships "Erebus" and "Terror," the

£20,000.

OR

2.—To any Party or Parties who, in the judgment of the Board of Admiralty, shall discover and effectually relieve *any* of the Crews of Her Majesty's Ships "Erebus" and "Terror," or shall convey such intelligence as shall lead to the relief of such Crews or *any* of them, the Sum of

£10,000.

OR

3.—To any Party or Parties who, in the judgment of the Board of Admiralty, shall by virtue of his or their efforts first succeed in ascertaining their fate,

£10,000.

W. A. B. HAMILTON,
Secretary of the Admiralty.

Reward for John Franklin and crew has prompted search expeditions.

Tensions run high in Red River colony as scandal erupts

July 18, 1850

RED RIVER COLONY, Rupert's Land – Allegations of an adulterous affair between the beautiful Mrs. Sarah Ballenden, a Métis, and gallant Irishman Christopher Foss have heightened tensions here between Métis and whites. Today, in an improvised courtroom, Foss was awarded damages in a libel suit filed against Hudson's Bay Company clerk A.E. Pelly.

The remarks that led to the trial are rooted in the attitudes of local English-born women, relative newcomers to the region who are unabashedly keen on excluding Indians or mixed-bloods from the upper echelon of Red River society. They are determined to topple Mrs. Ballenden, wife of a prominent HBC man.

Strachan petitions for Anglican college

April 10, 1850

TORONTO – Bishop John Strachan left for England today toting an 11,700-signature petition asking for an Anglican college to be established here. The bishop is travelling still fuming over the government's decision, effective last Jan. 1, to turn King's College into the non-denominational – and "godless" – University of Toronto.

Cartoon of California gold rush: head of lettuce helps get the horse going.

Discovery of Northwest Passage reported

Sleds arrive at southern depot during Robert McClure's Arctic expedition.

The critical position of HMS Investigator on the north coast of Bering Island.

Oct. 26, 1850

VICTORIA ISLAND, Arctic Circle – Robert McClure, the officer commanding *HMS Investigator,* believes he has discovered the Northwest Passage. McClure, who sailed from England in January, with Richard Collinson as his commander, reached the Arctic well ahead of Collinson.

McClure sailed through Bering Strait and then ran past Banks Island. Seeing there was a wide strait [Prince of Wales Strait] between Banks Island and Victoria Island, McClure started to sail through it but got stuck in the ice. He then explored by sled and found that the strait led to Viscount Melville Sound – and to the east.

Effort made to improve quality of horses

1850

CANADA WEST – Effort is being made to improve the quality of horses and other livestock in Canada. Agricultural societies are encouraging conscientious care and feeding, as well as gentle handling. But despite these efforts, there's still much work to be done. Reports indicate some breeders are continuing to neglect their animals and overwork their horses. On average, horses cost between £15 and £20 in Canada.

1851

Canada, April. With the post office recently transferred from Imperial to Canadian control, Canada issues its first postage stamp, the "Three Penny Red Beaver." True to its name, it features a beaver and costs three pennies.

Moose Factory, Hudson's Bay Territory, Aug. 25. John Horden arrives from London to perform missionary work.

Canada. The Eddy Match Company is founded.

Canada. The Canadian capital is moved from Toronto to Quebec City.

Nova Scotia. A law is passed making it a criminal offence for the woman herself who obtains an abortion at any stage of her pregnancy. The law is unprecedented everywhere except in New Brunswick and New York State.

Nova Scotia. A law is passed specifically excluding women from the franchise.

Liverpool. The *Marco Polo*, launched in Saint John April 17, completes her maiden voyage across the Atlantic in just 15 days. She was stuck in the mud for two weeks after her launch, which caused her keel to sag.

Nova Scotia. Clergyman Norman MacLead sails from St. Ann's on Cape Breton with 135 emigrants bound for Australia.

Canada West. Maple sugar production totals 3,669,874 pounds.

Canada West. The Queenston-Lewiston Suspension Bridge opens.

Canada. A census reports the average age at marriage for women is 23.

British North America. Major cities report disproportionate numbers of young women. Many migrated from Britain by themselves, and most work as domestics.

British North America. More than four fifths of the population lives in rural areas.

Canada West. Fewer than 25 percent of the children of laborers go to school, compared to 46 percent of the children of merchants.

Bruce Mines, Canada West. Reverend George McDougall sets up a Methodist mission to preach among Indians and holds services at a small chapel, pioneering church activity in this northern area.

Métis band rebuffs Sioux attackers

July 14, 1851

RED RIVER COLONY, Rupert's Land – A small band of Métis buffalo hunters succeeded in fighting off a large force of mounted Sioux warriors today southwest of here at a place called the Grand Coteau. The Métis first spotted their Indian rivals two days ago. Realizing that the Sioux meant to attack, the buffalo hunters placed their carts in a circle, then dug trenches to protect the women and children and to serve as rifle pits for the men. About 65 Métis faced an army of several hundred Sioux.

The Sioux attack began yesterday morning. Again and again the mounted Indians tried to overwhelm the circle of carts. But, firing from protected positions, the defenders held them off. Finally, after six hours, the Sioux withdrew. Today, as the Métis retreated, the Sioux attacked again, but still failed to capture the column of carts. After one last volley of gunfire and arrows, the Indians disappeared over a hilltop. In the whole episode, the Métis lost only one hunter.

Jenny Lind packs St. Lawrence Hall

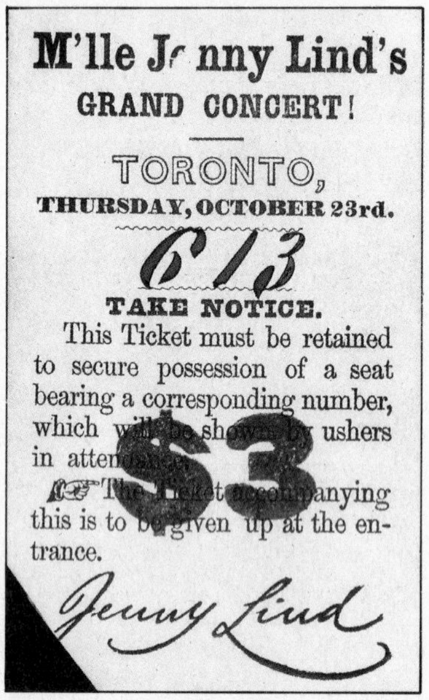

M'lle Jenny Lind's
GRAND CONCERT!
TORONTO,
THURSDAY, OCTOBER 23rd.
613
TAKE NOTICE.
This Ticket must be retained to secure possession of a seat bearing a corresponding number, which will be shown by ushers in attendance.
The Ticket accompanying this is to be given up at the entrance.
$3
Jenny Lind

A ticket to the Jenny Lind concert.

1851

TORONTO – Internationally acclaimed soprano Jenny Lind, known as "the Swedish nightingale," recently packed Toronto's new St. Lawrence Hall, highlighting a revival of opera under way in Canada. Small foreign companies featuring international stars such as Lind have been frequent visitors to Canada in recent years, performing excerpts from operas.

Anglican bishops iron out common woes

Sept. 24, 1851

QUEBEC CITY – Five Anglican bishops meeting here this week have agreed to a declaration intended to iron out organizational problems the church faces in the British North American colonies.

The declaration calls for the formation of diocesan synods to co-operate with bishops, and provincial synods under a Canadian metropolitan council. It also sets out standards for worship, such as an offertory at morning prayer, adherence to the prayer book, the need for a careful selection of psalms and hymns, and Sunday schools under control of the clergy. One contentious issue was that of freewill offerings as opposed to pew rents. Bishop George Mountain of Quebec convened the summit.

Métis buffalo hunt a prairie tradition

1851

RED RIVER COLONY, Rupert's Land – More than 1,000 men, women and children left Red River today in almost 1,000 carts for the annual Métis buffalo hunt, filling the prairies as far as the eye can see. They are expected to kill some 800 buffalo on the prairies to the west in a hunt that has become their main source of livelihood since the Hudson's Bay Company cannot employ as many Métis as it has in the past, and they have not turned en masse to farming.

The success of the hunt depends on strict organization. The Métis elect temporary leaders and submit to strict rules, which helps them ward off Indian attacks.

Rivalry develops over prairie land

1851

PRAIRIES – As the annual Métis buffalo hunt extends further west each year, it is riling up Indians like the Blackfoot and Gros Ventres, who are angry at the Métis for killing buffalo on their territory. Each year they attack the Métis hunting party. But the Métis can more than hold their own – the strict organization of their expeditions makes them the most formidable fighters on the prairies.

This is an artist's interpretation of Victoria Island's first appointed council in 1851. There were three people named to sit on the body.

Economic tiff leads Baldwin to step down

June 30, 1851

MONTREAL – Robert Baldwin, a father of responsible government in Canada, resigned today as co-leader of the Reform government, after a longstanding feud with fellow Reformer Francis Hincks over economic policy.

It was Baldwin who gave his seat to the French-Canadian Reformer Louis-Hippolyte LaFontaine in 1841, cementing the French-English Reform alliance. And it was Baldwin who symbolized the aspirations of English Canada for self-government within the Empire.

Anti-Slavery Society set up in Canada

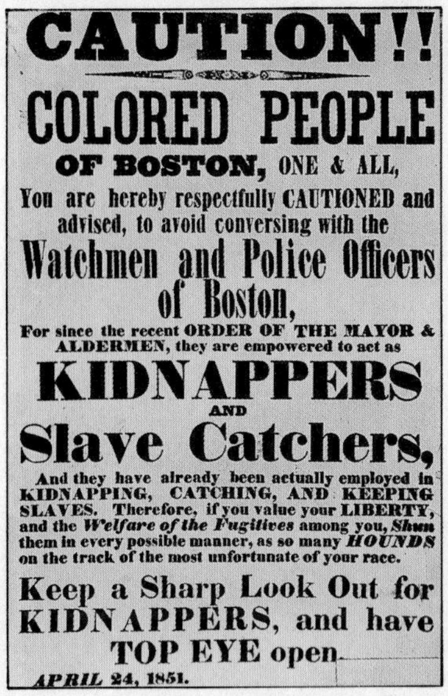

CAUTION!!

COLORED PEOPLE

OF BOSTON, ONE & ALL,

You are hereby respectfully CAUTIONED and advised, to avoid conversing with the

Watchmen and Police Officers of Boston,

For since the recent ORDER OF THE MAYOR & ALDERMEN, they are empowered to act as

KIDNAPPERS

AND

Slave Catchers,

And they have already been actually employed in KIDNAPPING, CATCHING, AND KEEPING SLAVES. Therefore, if you value your LIBERTY, and the *Welfare of the Fugitives* among you, *Shun* them in every possible manner, as so many *HOUNDS* on the track of the most unfortunate of your race.

Keep a Sharp Look Out for KIDNAPPERS, and have TOP EYE open.

APRIL 24, 1851.

This notice was issued by the Vigilance Committee of Boston this year.

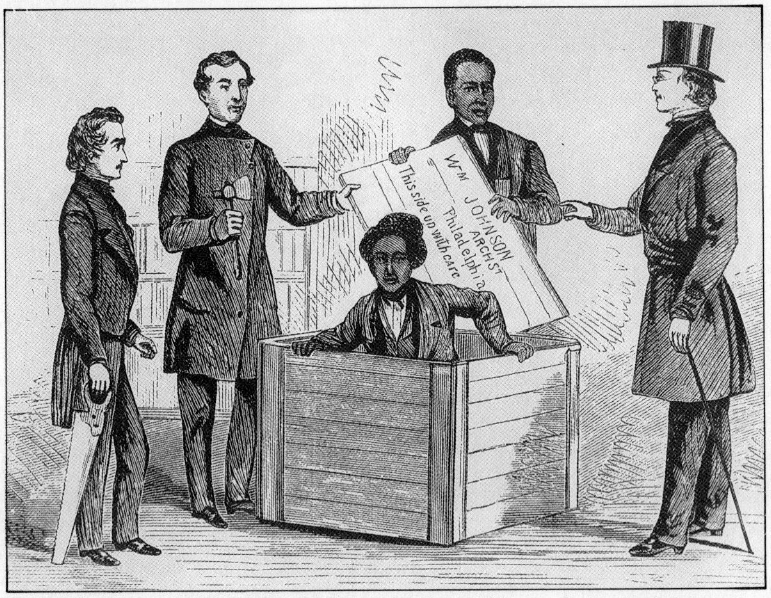

An American slave dispatched to freedom by abolitionists via a wood box.

Feb. 26, 1851

TORONTO – Slaves in the United States have a new friend with the formation of the Anti-Slavery Society in Canada today. Championed by well-known leaders such as George Brown, publisher of the *Globe*, the society's goals are to support the abolitionist movement in the U.S. It also works to provide relief for escaped slaves who have made it to Canada, only to try to start a new life with few possessions and little money.

The creation of the Anti-Slavery Society marks the continuing concern of Canadians over the issue, despite the fact that slavery was effectively abolished in the British Empire in 1834. In Canada West, slavery has been frowned on by the government since 1793.

Fugitive slaves enter union lines in ancient farm wagon called a schooner.

Ex-slave is founder of first newspaper to cater to blacks

Jan. 1, 1851

WINDSOR – The first issue of *The Voice of the Fugitive* was published today to provide news and an exchange of views for the many blacks living in the area who hope to one day return to freedom in the United States.

The paper's founder is Henry Bibb, of Kentucky, son of a white father and slave mother. The name of the paper is no accident – Bibb has escaped from slavery five times. He came to Canada in 1842 and became involved in the anti-slavery movement in the border area and in Ohio and New York.

Besides being publisher of *Voice of the Fugitive,* Bibb is a founder of the Refugee Home Society, which helps slaves on the run settle on Canadian soil. The society has come under attack for its methods of selling land and gathering offerings. Bibb's most outspoken critic is Mary Ann Shadd, a teacher active in the anti-slavery movement. Shadd has denounced Bibb's Home Society as simply the white man's front for exploiting and segregating blacks. She says the society's practice of "begging" for donations is ridden with abuse. The facts tend to support her claims. Society agents take 20 percent commission on proceeds, and its top administrator, a white clergyman, takes 25 percent off the top. Land obtained with proceeds is not passed on directly to blacks, but given on the condition that they purchase an additional large acreage.

Main Trunk railway another step closer

1851

CANADA – The Canadian legislature has passed the Main Trunk Railway Act. It is now up to Britain to guarantee a joint provincial loan to build a railway across Canada and the Maritimes, from Halifax to Quebec. Canada also wants to build its own line extending from Quebec to the very western tip of the province, linking the American midwest to Maritime ports.

Island conceded responsible government

April 23, 1851

PRINCE EDWARD ISLAND – Lt.-Gov. Alexander Bannerman has accepted the resignation of the Island's Executive Council and asked Reformer George Coles to form a government. After four years of bitter squabbling, P.E.I. has finally been conceded responsible government. There is jubilation in the streets, but the colony's proprietor class fears new attempts to strip them of their land rights.

Coles' Reform party has its roots in the land reform movement, and the struggle for responsible government has been closely tied to the land question. Opponents of self-government have argued that most Islanders are too ignorant to govern themselves, and they stayed in power for several years by offering compromises to full responsible government. It is obvious, however, that London has grown tired of their arguments, and that the time has come for Prince Edward Island to govern itself.

Publisher elected to the legislature

Dec. 14, 1851

KENT COUNTY, Canada West – George Brown, publisher and editor of the *Globe*, has been elected as the independent member for the Kent riding. It's a stunning victory for Brown and his "voluntaryist," anti-state church Reformers. There is no doubt that the presence of this powerful speaker in the House should make life uncomfortable for the Hincks-Morin government. ▷

Canada to take over control of the post office

Three-pence stamp, the first postage stamp issue of the Province of Canada.

A view of the post dog trains leaving Fort Garry for St. Paul in 1851.

The first proof from plate of first stamp issued by Province of Canada.

April 12, 1851

CANADA – The British government has passed an act transferring the operation of the domestic post office to the Province of Canada. As well, it has also transferred post offices in New Brunswick and Nova Scotia to legislatures there.

The change should speed up the mail considerably. Under British control, the system was a form of taxation, with charges far outstripping costs. It was slow, relying on a single route from Halifax to Windsor, Canada West. Under provincial control, rates are to be dropped from ninepence to threepence an ounce. As well, the government of Canada intends to open 243 new post offices, to improve service.

The new post office may well generate a deficit, but those in government circles say any additional cost to the taxpayer will be worth it. They see the postal service as an essential public utility, one that has to be available at a low cost to all Canadians to encourage trade and communications.

Trader opens new northern supply route

June 1851

FORT YOUCON, Alaska [Russian America] – Trader Robert Campbell has arrived here after a long journey down the Yukon River from Fort Selkirk. He was trying to develop an easier trading route to this fort and others in the northwest. Campbell had started to explore the Pelly River in 1843 and wanted to continue his exploration, for he believed that the Pelly and the Yukon were the same. But he was ordered to stop. Now he has proved his point and it is hoped his trip will clarify the geography of the northwest region of Hudson's Bay Company territory.

Until now, company officials have tied all their plans to the Colville River, visited in 1837 by Peter Dease and Thomas Simpson. Yet talks with the Indians prove that the Colville flows into the Arctic. And since salmon have been seen in the Yukon, it is equally obvious that it flows into the North Pacific.

Now Campbell has shown that the Pelly-Yukon is the river that provides access to the region west of the Mackenzie and links the posts at Fort Youcon, Fort Selkirk, Pelly Banks and Frances Lake. Campbell had an easy trip down the Yukon to here – and a short one, too, for at this time of the year there is little darkness and he travelled day and night.

Douglas named governor of island colony

May 16, 1851

VANCOUVER ISLAND – James Douglas, chief factor for the Hudson's Bay Company at Fort Victoria, is the new governor of the colony of Vancouver Island. He succeeds Richard Blanshard, the first governor, who resigned after a year in the country. Douglas will keep his position with the HBC, a company he has served for 30 years.

Certainly no one knows the Island better than the new governor. He organized the establishment of Fort Victoria in 1843, and has been in charge of the fur trade there since 1845. His biggest job as governor will be to supervise the settlement of colonists coming to the Island.

The new governor, James Douglas.

Island politicians try to settle score with a formal duel

June 21, 1851

PRINCE EDWARD ISLAND – Premier George Coles and the leader of the opposition, Edward Palmer, are used to fighting in the legislature. But tonight they took their battle beyond the House of Assembly, to a field near Government Farm to settle their differences with pistols, in a formal duel.

The cause of the duel is not known, but feelings have been running high with the turmoil over responsible government. The affair was settled with honor, but no bloodshed. Palmer fired first, and missed. Coles responded by raising his arm, and firing into the air.

Marco Polo launched in Saint John

April 17, 1851

SAINT JOHN, N.B. – The *Marco Polo* was launched today with a squish. The handsome clipper, built here at the yard of James Smith, was like a dog that refuses to heel, as it flew down the ways into the water so fast it could not be checked, finally landing in the mud as the cheering crowd assembled for the event looked on in surprise. It looks like the ship was a little overanxious to be off and running before the Atlantic wind.

The *Marco Polo*'s innovative design continues the proud tradition of ships built in Saint John. It combines the underwater body of a clipper with the midship sections of a cargo vessel. The ship is built out of tamarack and pitch pine.

Marco Polo, a ship with an innovative design, is launched from New Brunswick.

Hincks and Morin agree on coalition

Oct. 28, 1851

CANADA – Francis Hincks and Augustin-Norbert Morin today became co-premiers of the Province of Canada, continuing the coalition of Upper and Lower Canadian Reformers first established by their predecessors, the recently resigned tandem of Robert Baldwin and Louis-Hippolyte LaFontaine.

Hincks and Morin both endorse responsible government, but their moderate position has angered more radical Reformers who desire a U.S.-style presidential system. Hincks, in fact, has been accused by some within his own party of being a political opportunist.

Cartoon on choosing the capital.

White colonists ignoring the Indians' knowledge of medicine

British medicine often calls for such methods as the head wrap.

An Indian healer treats a sick man, attributing illness to the spiritual world.

c.1851

BRITISH NORTH AMERICA – In the first half of this century, a great deal of emphasis has been placed on the establishment of medical schools in the colonies. But by modelling schools only after English, Scottish, and American institutes, colonists are guilty of one major oversight: the fount of medical knowledge that exists within their own back yard, Indian medical practices that for centuries have successfully battled accident and illness.

Indian medical communities have gone largely ignored – even condemned – since the earliest days of European settlement. Colonists praise certain Indian medical practices, and adopt a few: early French settlers often used Indian-style sweat lodges and herbal medicines, for example. But usually colonists reject Indian medicine. One reason is that they cannot relate to the crucial spiritual dimension of the Indian healing, with its emphasis on shamanistic rituals based on non-Christian belief systems.

However, there are aspects of Indian medicine that could serve white settlers well. For example, Indians have long understood the need to cleanse wounds and keep them clean, whereas the European medical practitioners have only recently begun to recognize the importance of doing so. Indians have always been expert bone setters and also display considerable surgical skill. They possess an impressive pharmacopoeia, and can treat scurvy, rheumatism, venereal disease, colic, bowel disorders, and even the common cold, all common among colonists, who rely instead on less effective, often bogus, remedies. ▷

Sod-turning kicks off work on railway

Oct. 15, 1851

TORONTO – Construction of the Ontario, Simcoe and Huron Railway is under way, as Lady Mary Louisa Lambton, wife of the governor general, Lord Elgin, performed the official sod-turning.

The railway got off to a rocky start last year with a scandal arising out of the project's financing which implicated Francis Hincks. The city of Toronto offered a loan to railway developers on the condition they establish terminals in the city. Hincks became entangled when he bought city of Toronto debentures, which the municipality urged the railway to use to pay off contractors. The deal died, but Hincks profited from sale of the debentures.

Lady Mary Louisa Lambton, wife of the governor general, at sod-turning.

First Presbyterian minister in colony

Sept. 19, 1851

RED RIVER COLONY, Rupert's Land – Scottish settlers brought here by Lord Selkirk are rejoicing at the prospect of worshiping in the church of their forefathers. After being obliged for 40 years to join Anglicans for worship, colonists are looking forward to services Rev. John Black, the first Presbyterian minister west of the Great Lakes, will be conducting.

Ordained at Knox Church in Toronto on July 31, Black set out immediately for the Red River settlement by means of rail, stagecoach and birch-bark canoe. He arrived today and was welcomed into the home of Alexander Ross.

John Black, first resident minister.

"Great American Gale" claims 130 men and 80 ships at sea

Oct. 10, 1851

PRINCE EDWARD ISLAND – It is already called "The Great American Gale." As the wreckage is assessed, the tally is 80 vessels and at least 130 men lost in last weekend's terrible windstorm. The prelude to the storm was innocuous. Last Friday, several hundred boats from the American fishing fleet, annual visitors to Island waters, were trying their luck in the shallows off the north coast, hoping for one last big catch before the winter. Instead, they were pinned to the coast by a northwest wind, then smashed on it by one of the worst storms in memory.

All weekend the storm raged, subsiding only late Sunday evening. Some crews managed to beat out to sea, and ride out the gale. Others resorted to desperate measures to get ashore. Many, as grim evidence shows, were not so lucky. Monday morning, many communities woke to the sight of beaches littered with shattered vessels, and the bodies of drowned fishermen. It is P.E.I.'s greatest natural disaster ever.

Maungwudaus and his troupe thrill their audience in Toronto

April 21, 1851

TORONTO – Ojibwa Indian Maungwudaus today appeared at Toronto's St. Lawrence Hall with his celebrated performing troupe. Maungwudaus, born in 1810, was baptized George Henry as a youngster and educated by Methodist missionaries. A great proponent of European ways, he held a promising future with the ministry. But it was not to be. In 1840 he quite suddenly abandoned missionary work and further shocked those he knew by organizing a performing troupe comprised mostly of immediate family members.

The troupe began to tour Europe in 1845, and led by Maungwudaus's enterprising skills, they performed in theatres and for royalty, feeding popular imaginations and enthralling audiences everywhere with native dances, feats of archery, and even simulated scalpings.

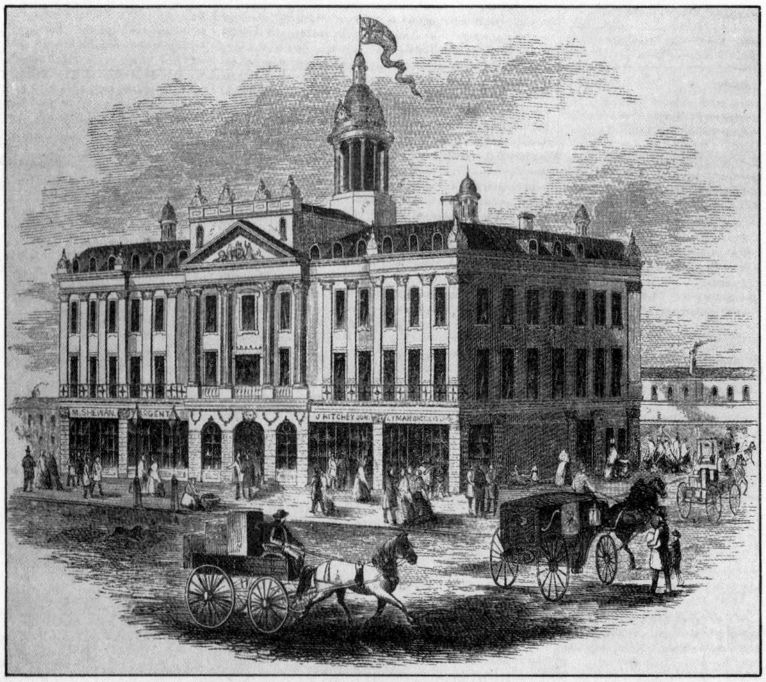

St. Lawrence Hall, where Maungwudaus dance troupe has thrilled audience.

First YMCA opens in Baptist church

Nov. 25, 1851

MONTREAL – There should be less idleness among youth in the city streets thanks to a new organization founded today. The Young Men's Christian Association (YMCA) has opened its first North American chapter at St. Helen Baptist Church. The YMCA, founded in 1844, is dedicated to the spiritual and physical well-being of young men. A branch is to open in Boston next month, and plans are under way to open branches in Toronto, Halifax and Saint John.

Habitants know how to have a good time in winter

People enjoy sleigh rides and skating at Montmorency Falls, near Quebec City.

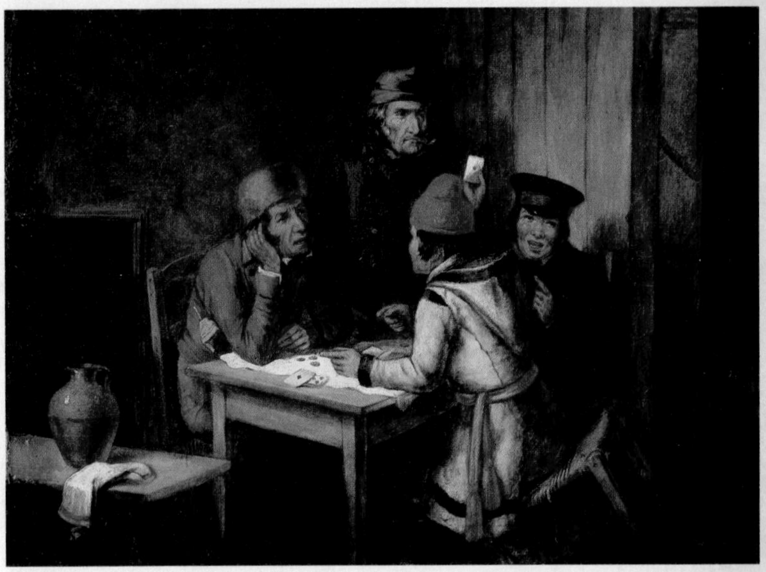

Habitants know a game of cards can help pass time during cold winter days.

Dashing through the snow isn't so chilling when you invite some friends.

A habitant family gathers around the stove to while away the winter months.

Having a drink is one way to keep warm on those cold winter evenings.

A Canadian habitant wearing a blue tuque and enjoying his pipe tobacco.

A sleigh ride through the countryside can mean close encounters with wildlife.

1852

Toronto, Jan. 15. Trinity College opens.

Quebec, February. During the winter carnival, Abbé Girroir of the Seminary of Quebec wins a skating match against the U.S. champion "Albumazar."

Toronto, February. Tailors go on strike protesting against the advent of the sewing machine.

Newfoundland, March 6. A telegraph line is inaugurated connecting St. John's and Carbonear.

Kingston, Canada West, May. Stonecutters go on strike, opposed to the hiring of convict labor.

Melbourne, Australia, Sept. 18. Saint John built ship *Marco Polo* arrives with 930 passengers after a trip of only 76 days from Liverpool. Previous trips have taken 100-120 days. James Baines recently converted the ship to a luxury passenger vessel to carry emigrants to Australia.

Montreal, Sept. 20. Regular rail service is inaugurated between Montreal and Plattsburgh, New York.

Vancouver Island, Oct. 6. The Legislative Council of the colony decides to regulate the sale of alcohol by issuing wholesale and retail licences.

Gulf of St. Lawrence, Nov. 22. Frederick Gisborne lays the first submarine telegraph cable in North America from Cape Tormentine, New Brunswick, to Carleton Head, Prince Edward Island. He plans to lay a transatlantic cable.

Red River, HBC Territory. The colony suffers from a disasterous spring flood of the Red River.

Toronto. The Toronto Locomotive Works is established, one of the first large scale factories in the city.

Toronto. Businessmen form the Toronto Stock Exchange to create a market in industrial securities. They meet informally in their offices.

Montreal. Dr. Wolfred Nelson reports that 47 percent of those incarcerated in the city's prisons are women, many of them unwed mothers.

Toronto. The Canadian Institute of Toronto is founded.

Scotland. Canada and Nova Scotia are granted their own branches of the Royal Caledonian Curling Club.

Canada East. The Montreal-Sherbrooke Railway is opened.

Massive floes crush whaling vessel

July 7, 1852

DAVIS STRAIT – The Connecticut whaling vessel *McLellan* has foundered in the ice off Greenland. The crew has abandoned the vessel, which was crushed between two massive floes and is slowly sinking, and is returning home with other ships in the whale fleet. The accident leaves in doubt the fate of a small group of sailors that the *McLellan* left on Baffin Island last summer. The men, commanded by first mate Sydney Buddington, were planning to winter in Cumberland Sound so as to get an early start on whaling from the ice edge in the spring. When it sank, the *McLellan* was on its way to rescue these winterers.

Capt. William Quayle has taken passage aboard the *Truelove* and is going to Cumberland Sound to find out the result of his experiment. If the men have survived in good health and have managed to kill some whales, other ships will probably begin leaving wintering parties to live among the Inuit and hunt whales from shore.

Book details family's struggle in the bush

1852

BELLEVILLE, Canada West – *Roughing it in the Bush,* a first person account of an English immigrant family's struggle against the element in the Canadian backwoods, has been published by town resident Susanna Moodie.

Susanna describes how she, her husband and small children tried and failed to scrape a living from "the green prison of the woods." The Moodies arrived in Canada in 1832 and made a first dismal attempt at farming near Cobourg. They then tried to hack farmland out of forest near Peterborough but gave up in 1840 and moved here, where they have since prospered.

Susanna Moodie, book's author.

Schoolteacher woos blacks to Windsor

June 1852

WINDSOR – A pamphlet entitled *Notes of Canada West* is recommending blacks settle here. Author Mary Ann Shadd is the daughter of abolitionist Abraham Shadd. The black schoolteacher says: "No settled country in America offers stronger inducements to colored people. The general tone of society is healthy, and there is an increasing anti-slavery sentiment."

Downtrodden fill Montreal prisons

1852

MONTREAL – The city's prisons are actually holding pens for a raft of down and outers ranging from the insane to unwed mothers, whose only crime is their marginal position in society. The homeless, old, and sick are often incarcerated on vague charges to get them off the streets. These are some of the revelations in a study by Dr. Wolfred Nelson, provincial jail inspector.

Lacombe makes it to Fort Edmonton

July 8, 1852

ST. BONIFACE, [Manitoba] – Reports are circulating that Father Albert Lacombe reached Fort Edmonton today. The popular priest made the journey via Cumberland House in the company of Chief Factor Rowand and a party of 80 in 10 York boats. In his years of duty at Pembina and St. Boniface, Lacombe twice served as chaplain to the annual buffalo hunt. Local records show he was on the hunt in 1850 when 800 animals were killed. That same year he was instrumental in mounting a wooden cross on top of the Turtle Mountains.

Lacombe, a secular priest, was assigned to Fort Edmonton on orders from Bishop Joseph-Norbert Provencher. He was nominated the replacement for Father Jean-Baptiste Thibault, who has returned to St. Boniface after 10 years on the western frontier.

Father Albert Lacombe has arrived in Fort Edmonton from St. Boniface.

Canadians to get "a real Irish porter"

1852

TORONTO – "Canadians need a real Irish porter." To satisfy this demand and to capture the Toronto market, Patrick Cosgrave and John Moss have opened a brewery on the Credit River, just west of Toronto at Pucky Huddle [Erindale].

Cosgrave and Moss chose this spot to be near a ready source of barley. The Irishmen's drink of choice, porter is brewed with roasted unmalted barley. Recent Irish migrations have made this sweet, dark, roasty tasting beer almost as popular as English brown ales.

Royal charter granted to Laval University

Laval University, in Quebec City, has just received its royal charter.

1852

QUEBEC CITY – Queen Victoria has granted a royal charter making Laval University the first French-language Roman Catholic university in North America. Laval emerges from the Séminaire de Québec, founded in 1663, and is modelled on French universities. With faculties of medicine, theology, civil law, and arts, it is the second university in Canada East after McGill, which was founded at Montreal in 1821.

British assert grip on Queen Charlottes

July 9, 1852

VICTORIA, Vancouver Island – With American miners from the California gold fields flocking to the Queen Charlotte Islands, the government in London has given Gov. James Douglas an additional commission as lieutenant-governor to assert British dominion over the islands, some 800 kilometres north of here.

An Indian woman discovered gold on Moresby Island two years ago. The Haida resent the Vancouver Island miners who blasted rocks to get at the ore-bearing lode. To them, neither British nor American newcomers have any right of dominion over their lands. No agreement has been made with the Haida concerning the invasion, but they have found a practical solution – they wait until after the blast to run in and grab gold for themselves.

Record-setting ship arrives in Liverpool

Dec. 26, 1852

LIVERPOOL, England – The ship *Marco Polo* arrived here today after a record-shattering voyage around the world to the Australian gold fields and back in just five months and 21 days. The ship was built in Saint John, N.B., by James Smith. Under Capt. James Nicol "Bully" Forbes, the *Marco Polo* left Liverpool July 4. She reached Melbourne in 76 days, beating the steamer *Australia* by a week. The return voyage took just 76 days.

First Indian joins Anglican ministry

July 1852

RED RIVER COLONY, Rupert's Land – Henry Budd was ordained an Anglican priest today, the first Indian to be so appointed in North America. The 40-year-old Budd, son of an Indian father and Métis mother, is well known in this area, having been a farmer, a teacher and a clerk with the Hudson's Bay Company. In his two years as a deacon, Budd has been called "one of the most dedicated missionaries in the northwest."

Real life an improvement for Uncle Tom

Harriet Beecher Stowe, author.

1852

CANADA WEST – Real life sometimes turns out better than fiction. Just look at Josiah Henson, "the real-life Uncle Tom." An escaped American slave who came to Canada in 1830, Henson is supposedly the model for the hero of Harriet Beecher Stowe's anti-slavery novel *Uncle Tom's Cabin, or, Life Among the Lowly*, currently setting sales records in the U.S. In the novel, the slave protagonist is beaten to death by his master. Henson, on the other hand, has lived to found a successful black settlement at Dawn Township, and he's become a spokesman for Canada's blacks.

Seal fishery suffers through tough year

April 30, 1852

NEWFOUNDLAND – This has been a disastrous year for the seal fishery. It began on an ominous note in February, when four men of a crew of five were lost while sealing on the Funk Islands. Then, early this month, many of the vessels engaged in the offshore seal fishery were caught in a gale and "running ice."

While several ships were crushed in the ice, others were swept onto shoals and rocks. All told, 40 vessels were lost. Some of those abandoned by their crews were salvaged by others. About 1,500 men were forced to leave their ships and escape over ice to shore. Shipwrecked crews are still arriving daily.

Chilkats ransack HBC's Fort Selkirk

August 1852

FORT SELKIRK, Hudson Bay Territory – Chilkat Indians have ransacked this Hudson's Bay Company post at the fork of the Pelly and Lewes rivers. Trader Robert Campbell is inspecting the empty, damaged buildings to see if anything can be done to keep the post operating. If Fort Selkirk is abandoned, it is expected most of the men will winter at Fort Yukon.

Campbell will go to Fort Simpson to get more supplies – and permission to get revenge on the Chilkats. The Chilkat attack took place when Campbell had only two *voyageurs* and two Indians to help him defend the post. His other men were away trading.

The arts building at King's College, Fredericton. Formerly called the University of New Brunswick, its name was changed to King's College in 1828.

U.S. slaves come to Canada telling tales of horror

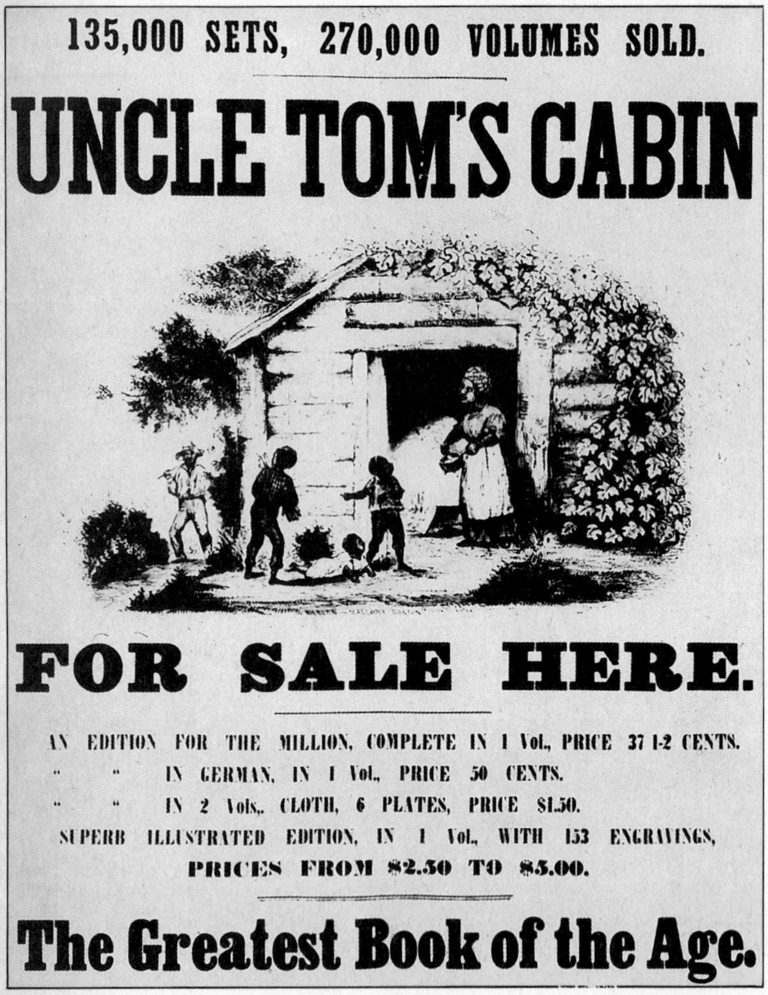
135,000 SETS, 270,000 VOLUMES SOLD.
UNCLE TOM'S CABIN
FOR SALE HERE.
AN EDITION FOR THE MILLION, COMPLETE IN 1 Vol., PRICE 37 1-2 CENTS.
" " IN GERMAN, IN 1 Vol., PRICE 50 CENTS.
" " IN 2 Vols., CLOTH, 6 PLATES, PRICE $1.50.
SUPERB ILLUSTRATED EDITION, IN 1 Vol., WITH 153 ENGRAVINGS,
PRICES FROM $2.50 TO $5.00.
The Greatest Book of the Age.

An advertisement for Harriet Beecher Stowe's novel Uncle Tom's Cabin. Her story of an American slave may be based on the life of a Canadian.

Owners display different forms of cruelty

1852

TORONTO – Slave owner cruelty comes in different forms, explains Patrick Snead, who escaped to Canada after being cleared on a bogus murder rap in Buffalo.

Snead, who fled from slavery in Georgia, reports: "There is a great difference in the modes of treating slaves, according to the character of the owners. ... I saw a man in Savannah, who had been whipped severely, and thrust into a dark hole or dungeon in a cellar. The maggots got in his flesh, and he was offensive to the sense. ... I saw a Methodist minister who had a colored woman for a cook. Something which her mistress told her to cook did not suit. The mistress complained to the minister; he shut up the cook in a stable and beat her, having first tied something over her mouth."

Snead says slaves in Georgia "don't know their condition. It is ignorance that keeps them there. If they knew what I know, they could not be kept there for a moment."

Family braves cold in flight to freedom

1852

LONDON – With a $500 price on his head, Henry Morehead and his family fled slavery in Kentucky nearly succumbing to cold on the way to their new home in London.

Morehead, one of thousands of fugitive slaves, recounts his journey via the underground railroad: "I was longer on the road than I should have been with my burden: one child was nine months old, one two years old, and one four. The weather was cold, and my feet were frost-bitten, as I gave my wife my socks to pull on over her shoes. With all the sufferings of the frost and the fatigues of travel, it was not so bad as slavery."

Morehead, now comfortably supporting his family after more than a year as a free man, is bitter about being denied an education by slavemasters: "My owners used to object to my going to school, saying that I could learn rascality enough without it. I went to a night school, at my own expense of course, to learn how to spell and read. My owners found out and set policemen to break the school up. This ended my schooling."

Children not spared the lash: ex-slave

1852

CHATHAM – Children in slavery were shown no special mercy, recalls Mary Younger, now living in freedom in Canada.

"Many a time I have looked out in the moonlight, and seen my little children, just able to walk in the fields, carrying buckets of water. They used to carry the buckets on their heads: they would wear off the hair, and I used to make pads to protect the sore places. Where I was raised, my children were often whipped till the blood ran."

Women were just as barbarous as the men, Mary recalls. "A woman who lived near us whipped at different times three of her slave women to death."

Man says beating took off his skin

1852

QUEEN'S BUSH – "I was a slave long enough, and tasted it all," declares John Little in a horrifying account of his days in bondage in North Carolina under a particularly beastly master.

"The master marked on me with his cane where the overseer was to begin and said 'Whip him from there down.' He struck me a hundred lashes right off before he stopped. The master said 'Now you cursed son of a b–, your running about will spoil all the rest of the niggers.' He told overseer 'put it on him like the very devil.' I know that from the small of the back to the calves of my legs they took the skin clear off, as you would skin beef."

The escape of Eliza and her child on the ice in an illustration from Uncle Tom's Cabin, a book about American slavery by Harriet Beecher Stowe.

"Ignorance keeps the slaves down," fugitive concludes

1852

ST. CATHARINES – Ignorance is as strong a weapon as the whip in keeping slaves in bondage, says Dan Josiah Lockhart, a fugitive slave from Virginia, one of thousands to tell their shocking stories now that they are free in Canada. Slaves more often than not were denied any education, and those who were able to read and write were frequently taught by children of slavemasters – as it was in Lockhart's case.

Lockhart notes how Virginia's slaves are ignorant about Canada. "I was told before I left Virginia – have heard it as common talk – that the wild geese were so numerous in Canada, and so bad, that they would scratch a man's eyes out; that corn wouldn't grow there, nor anything else but rice; that every thing they had was imported.

"It is ignorance that keeps the slaves down." Lockhart concludes. He had been fortunate in his early years to have worked his way up to overseer of a tool shop, and enjoyed some degree of liberty. "The management was pretty much left to me. I would carry my gun down into a hollow, and have a book – the children had taught me to read." But his situation soon slipped into a nightmarish series of whippings of himself, his wife and 10 children. Lockhart then decided to flee north via the underground railroad.

Uncle Tom and Eva, an illustration from Harriet Beecher Stowe's popular book, Uncle Tom's Cabin.

Mother sold away from her children

THE SEPARATION OF THE MOTHER AND CHILD.
"The old men of the company, partly by persuasion and partly by force, loosed the poor creature's last despairing hold, and, as they led her off to her new master's waggon, strove to comfort her."—Page 103.

The separation of mother and child: scene from Uncle Tom's Cabin shows white men taking a slave child, while other slaves try to comfort the mother.

1852

ST. CATHARINES – "Where I came from, it would make your flesh creep, and your hair stand on end, to know what they do to the slaves," recounts fugitive slave James Seward. He says of the brutal sins of slave owners, none was worse than separating mother from child. "I had a niece, who was married and had two children; one at her breast. The estate being in debt ... her owner concluded to sell her. She was taken away from her children, handcuffed and put into jail where I was. She was in great grief, crying all the time, 'Oh my children!' till it appeared to me she would kill herself for grief. She was sold and carried away, leaving her children behind."

Fugitive recalls beatings as "the wickedest thing a man can do"

1852

ST. CATHARINES – "It is the wickedest thing a man can do to hold a slave," says Isaac Williams, a fugitive slave who has the horrible experiences to prove it. Williams, who just arrived in Canada after a harrowing dash to freedom, recalls the brutality of his master on a Virginia plantation.

"He was a sharp man – whipped me with cowhide. I've seen him whip women and children like oxen. My master owned a yellow girl, who, he feared, would run away. I was his head man and had to help do it. He tied her across the fence, naked, and whipped her severely with a paddle bored with holes, and with a switch. Then he shaved the hair off of one side of her head and daubed cow-filth on the shaved part, to disgrace her. ...

"The last time he whipped me was for stealing corn for bread for Christmas. George was with me. He tied our wrists together about a tree, and then whipped us with a carriage whip. He whipped till he tore the lash off; then he tied a knot on the end, and gave me a blow that laid me up limping three weeks – the blood ran down into my shoes. I have seen him strip my wife and whip her with a cobbing board or cowhide."

Williams fled to Canada after his owner sold him to a slave pen.

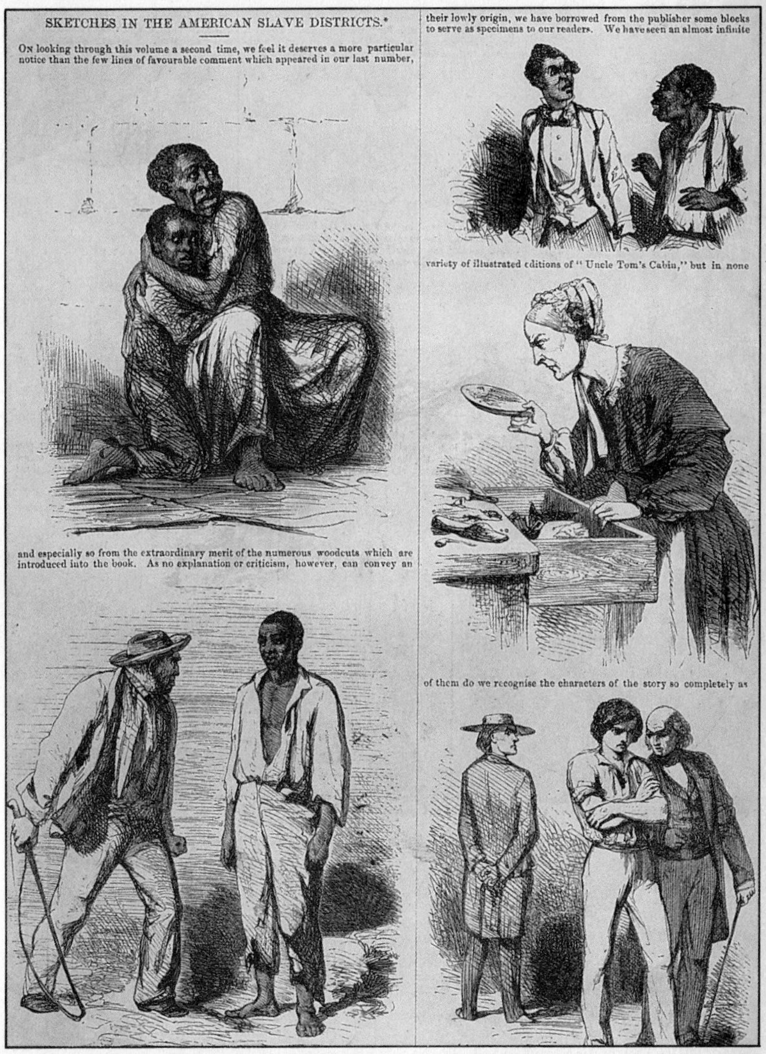
SKETCHES IN THE AMERICAN SLAVE DISTRICTS.*
On looking through this volume a second time, we feel it deserves a more particular notice than the few lines of favourable comment which appeared in our last number,
and especially so from the extraordinary merit of the numerous woodcuts which are introduced into the book. As no explanation or criticism, however, can convey an
their lowly origin, we have borrowed from the publisher some blocks to serve as specimens to our readers. We have seen an almost infinite
variety of illustrated editions of "Uncle Tom's Cabin," but in none
of them do we recognise the characters of the story so completely as

Sketches of the American slave scenes inspired by Uncle Tom's Cabin.

1853

Prince Edward Island, Jan. 20. The first telegraph message is sent on an underwater cable between P.E.I. and New Brunswick.

Vancouver Island, March 29. The Legislative Council of the colony sets a fee of £100 for wholesale liquor licences and £120 for retail licences.

Vancouver Island, March. James Douglas, recently named lieutenant-governor of the Queen Charlottes, proclaims the Crown's ownership of gold on the islands, and issues rules requiring miners to pay a monthly licence fee. Gold has just been found on the islands.

Fredericton, April 2. The legislature passes a law allocating funds for the teaching of civil engineering.

Toronto, April 16. The *Toronto*, the first locomotive built in Canada, moves out of the James Good plant to be used on the Ontario, Simcoe, and Huron Union Railroad, the first steam-operated railway in the province.

Montreal, May 12. A banquet is held to celebrate the arrival of the *Genova*, the first transatlantic steamship to visit the city.

New Brunswick, Sept. 4. The first sod is turned in the construction of the European and North American Railway, the colony's first railway.

Vancouver Island, Sept. 23. A supreme court is instituted in the colony.

Toronto. The *Globe* newspaper goes daily. Since its founding in 1844, it has become popular with the educated and business community.

British North America. YMCAs open in both Toronto and Halifax.

HBC Territory. Three Métis are appointed to the Council of Assiniboia, giving the Métis a role in government decisions.

Toronto. The medical faculty of King's College and the Toronto School of Medicine are incorporated under the leadership of Dr. John Rolph.

Canada. In winter, it takes eight to 11 days to send a letter from Quebec to any post office in Canada West beyond Toronto.

London. Joseph Howe borrows £1 million for the Nova Scotia government to build a railway from Halifax to Truro and Windsor, the colony's first railroad.

Crew rescued after 3 years in Arctic

April 6, 1853

MERCY BAY, Banks Island – Capt. Robert McClure and his crew aboard the ship *Investigator*, lost in the Arctic for the past three years, have been found alive. Help arrived barely in time. Trapped in this remote Arctic harbor, members of the naval expedition were slowly starving to death and fewer than a dozen are still healthy enough to perform routine chores. In fact, a party of survivors was planning to set off overland by sled to seek help. But the arrival of today's relief party makes that desperate gamble unnecessary.

The rescuers are a sledding party from another British naval vessel, the *Resolute*, which is wintering across Melville Sound at Dealey Island. Both ships are taking part in the search for the missing Franklin expedition. Having given up hope of rescue, McClure was perplexed to see the sled approaching across the bay today. At first he thought it was a bear, then he decided it must belong to a native. "Had the skies fallen upon us, we could hardly have been more astonished than when the dark-faced stranger called out, 'I'm Lieutenant Pim, late of the *Herald*, and now in the *Resolute*.' "

Arctic waters are dangerous for ships exploring British North America's lands.

Law signals defeat for Protestant pols

1853

TORONTO – Churches have been granted the right to establish charitable institutions under a new law passed by the legislature of the United Canadas.

The Ecclesiastical Corporations Act, piloted through the House by the Roman Catholic majority from Canada East, reflects the prevailing view there that church and state are indivisible. The act is a defeat for Protestant politicians led by George Brown who favor stricter control of public welfare by granting official charters and small subsidies to institutions which would raise funds from the private sector.

Canada West has, to date, assumed little responsibility for social welfare programs. Under municipal acts dating back to 1849, the burden of caring for the poor falls on municipalities which usually raise the funds for relief through special levies. Canada West's contribution to social welfare is limited to small grants to hospitals and orphanages, and to Toronto's House of Industry, established in 1837 to provide permanent institutionalized poor relief on the English model.

Maple sugar an annual springtime treat

1853

CANADA WEST – Sugar is expensive here, so any settler with even just a few maple trees turns to making maple sugar each spring. Using methods they learned from the Indians, settlers insert wooden taps into trees to collect sap which is then boiled in iron or copper kettles, day and night, until it forms a thick syrup or sugar. Once ready, the maple sugar is poured into pans or wooden moulds. Indeed, it is a tasty treat.

Legendary soldier and developer dies

Feb. 5, 1853

CANADA WEST – Legendary drinker, soldier and land developer Col. Thomas Talbot has died at 82. Refusing to do business after noon, to prevent interference with his libations, and labelling temperance groups "damned cold water drinking societies," Talbot was responsible for settling 50,000 people on half a million acres in 27 townships extending 210 kilometres along the north shore of Lake Erie from Long Point to Detroit, and north to the Huron Tract from 1803 to 1837.

Responsible for building the 480-kilometre long Talbot Road to link the interior, Talbot was often seen as a despotic recluse because he insisted that settlers fulfil their obligations or be dispossessed.

Two views of New Brunswick.

Vancouver Island gets first schools

March 31, 1853

VICTORIA, Vancouver Island – There may be complaints here about the lack of good housing for settlers – but there can be no complaints about schools. Chief factor James Douglas first asked the Hudson's Bay Company's governors in London to provide a "middle-aged married couple" who could give the children a sound education. Then he persuaded the company to pay the schoolmaster's salary. And so a boys' school opened in Victoria and a girls' school at Colwood Farm. Now the Legislative Council has borrowed some money from land sales and opened a new school on the school reserve lands.

Male teachers earn more than women

1853

CANADA EAST – One step forward, two steps back. Women have entered the teaching profession here with a thud – there are now more women than men teachers in Canada East, but a woman teacher only makes about 40 percent of her male colleague's salary. There is also a clear hierarchy in schools: women teachers are relegated to the lower grades, taking care of younger students, while male teachers look after higher grades, or become inspectors.

Women who want to work professionally have little option. Teaching is really the only profession which does not bar them.

An Indian's caribou-skin coat.

New Brunswick law bans importing booze

Jan. 1, 1853

NEW BRUNSWICK – Importing alcoholic beverages into New Brunswick is illegal as of today. A dry province is a triumph for the Sons of Temperance, led by politician and lifelong temperance advocate Samuel Leonard Tilley. The group has lobbied for an anti-booze law for five years, to combat what it claims is excessive drunkenness on the part of lumber camp workers. The legislature adopted the law after getting a 9,000-name petition.

Flag conveys international flavor of lake

Oct. 27, 1853

SHERBROOKE, Canada East – Sherbrooke has agreed to donate a flag to be flown on the summit of Mount Owl's Head, overlooking Lake Memphremagog. The boundary between the United States and Canada runs through the lake, some 9.6 kilometres north of Newport, Vermont. Insignias of both Canada and the U.S. will adorn the flag. The British Cross of St. George will appear on one side, the American Stars and Stripes on the other.

Royal charter given to Bishop's College

Jan. 1, 1853

LENNOXVILLE, Canada East – After a long fight, Bishop's College in Lennoxville has won the right to confer degrees. The university was granted a royal charter today, giving it the same status as its counterparts in Great Britain and Ireland.

A first effort to secure a charter failed in 1847. So did a second in 1850 with petitions from the university, the Church of England and English-speaking Lower Canadians. The charter was finally granted after concerted lobbying.

Hunting deer for pleasure a fashionable sport in Canada West

This illustration shows a group of deer, a wild animal which is found in abundance throughout Canada West.

1853

CANADA WEST – Hunting deer strictly for pleasure rather than sustenance has become increasingly popular in Canada West. The joys of the sport were recently lauded by Samuel Strickland in his book *Twenty-Seven Years in Canada West*. Though the hunt may jeopardize the future of the deer population, Strickland and others have been seduced by its charms. "I do not know anything more pleasant than these excursions (to Stoney Lake, Deer Bay, or the River Trent), especially if you have agreeable companions, a warm camp, and plenty to eat and drink," he wrote. Large numbers of deer are often killed on the expeditions. Strickland says he and his companions once killed 17 deer in three days, and that people he knows have killed 32 deer in two weeks. ▷

Anti-Catholic speech sparks a riot

June 9, 1853

MONTREAL – Ten people are dead and at least as many wounded following an assault on the Zion Church by Irish Catholics. The throng of Catholics had descended on the church to disrupt a speech by Alessandro Gavazzi, a charismatic anti-papist on a tour of Canada East. The killings resulted when troops called in to quell the riot fired a volley into the Protestant congregation leaving the church.

The altercation follows one in Quebec three nights ago in which a mob broke into the Free Presbyterian Church where Gavazzi was delivering his impassioned anti-Catholic oratory. A brawl broke out, but soldiers were able to restore order before any serious injuries were inflicted. Gavazzi, an imposing figure in his black monk's robe, had to be escorted from Quebec under the protection of 60 armed guards.

The Gavazzi riot in Montreal sees Irish Catholics assault the Zion Church.

Gavazzi's crusade, in which he hopes to raise funds for the Italian patriot cause in the wake of the 1848 revolution, has stoked up already explosive religious tensions in the United Canadas. Before his visit to Quebec and Montreal, he had swept through Canada East, whipping up anti-Catholic sentiment as the legislature remains embroiled in a dispute over separate school funding.

Dorothea Dix visits hazardous sandbar

July 1853

SABLE ISLAND, N.S. – The doughty Dorothea Lynde Dix, a 51-year-old Boston philanthropist and mental health reformer, spent three days here at "the graveyard of the Atlantic," 300 kilometres east-southeast of Halifax, and witnessed the latest of some 200 shipwrecks on this treacherous sandbar. When the 132-ton *Guide* ran aground on the island's south shore, Miss Dix rode to the beach on horseback. Sailors on the last boat to land said the captain had gone mad, and refused to abandon ship.

Miss Dix intervened, begging the crew to row over to the wreck, tie up the captain, and bring him back. When they did, she loosened his ropes, and persuaded him to thank his men. She also vowed to raise funds in the U.S. to get better boats and life-saving gear for the Sable Island Humane Establishment.

Train service kicks off in Canada West

May 16, 1853

TORONTO – The locomotive *Toronto* worked up a full head of steam today on a two-hour trip from Toronto 48 kilometres northward to Machell's Corners [Aurora], kicking off the first regular train service in Canada West. It pulled four cars, carrying a chest of tea, 12 brooms, a barrel of salt, and a gaggle of passengers who paid a dollar each for the thrill of it all.

It seems like only yesterday that Lady Elgin turned the first sod for the railway back on Oct. 15, 1851. You could feel the electricity in the air on that day – 20,000 people watched the parade before the ceremony, drawn by the allure of a new technology that has changed travel forever in Europe, and now promises a social revolution. So far, only a few kilometres of railway line have been built in Canada.

The steam engine Toronto is the first locomotive constructed in Canada West.

Rae leads search for Sir John Franklin

Illustration of York Factory. John Rae left York Factory on June 25, 1853.

June 25, 1853

LONDON, England – John Rae, explorer, surgeon and Hudson's Bay Company trader, is on his way to the Arctic in yet another search for Sir John Franklin. Rae, 40 years old, has spent a good part of the last seven years in various Arctic expeditions and is well-known for his ability to successfully overcome the worst conditions.

Rae has just returned from leading a search party for Franklin in which he explored the south and east coasts of Victoria Island and went up the Coppermine River. He crossed over to Great Bear Lake and canoed up the Mackenzie River. For the trip back home, Rae and his men trudged south on snowshoes for 2,800 kilometres, past Fort Garry and into the U.S.

When Rae got back to England after this epoch-making expedition which covered 8,600 kilometres, he told the Hudson's Bay Company another expedition should be organized. This one would complete the survey of the Arctic coast and look for the Franklin expedition. The company agreed, and so he is off on another expedition.

Railway links Montreal to Portland

July 1853

MONTREAL – This great port now has a seaport that, unlike the St. Lawrence River, never freezes up in winter. Today, Montreal is linked to the ice-free port of Portland, Maine, thanks to the completion of a 450-kilometre rail line. It's the first international railway ever built in North America, and proof that the often-stormy relations between Canada and the U.S. have finally started to settle down.

Because it's an international railroad, this company has two names. On the Canadian side, it's known as the St. Lawrence & Atlantic, while, south of the border, it's the Atlantic & St. Lawrence. But what it really is, is a boon for merchants in Montreal, and the rural communities that the line passes through.

The St. Lawrence & Atlantic started as a vague dream in the early 1840s. It took the pioneering campaigning of a Portland promoter, John Poor, to get people along the proposed route interested, as well as drawing capital to the project. The two railroads were incorporated in 1845, but, being short of cash, work was delayed. In fact, it wasn't until the Canadian government passed the Guarantee Act, which guaranteed a return for investors, that money came in. Today, the fruit of this labor is a steel ribbon to the sea.

Grand Trunk Railroad (above) amalgamated with St. Lawrence and Atlantic.

Workmen at the Grand Trunk Railroad shop in St. Charles assemble an engine.

Rideau Canal ruling a boon for Bytown

July 1853

BYTOWN, Canada West – Gov. Gen. Lord Elgin's visit to Bytown has been a success, with residents giving him a warm reception. It's been a banner year for Bytown, because the British government decided to allow vessels from the United States to use the Rideau Canal. This has boosted trade here, especially the export of lumber.

The Rideau Canal was originally built to provide an alternate route to bypass the St. Lawrence River in case of a war like that of 1812-14 – and thus to avoid the risk of American attack.

Great Western rail begins new service

Dec. 15, 1853

HAMILTON – After years of delays, money problems, and broken promises, service on the Great Western Railway between Hamilton and London opened today.

The hoopla heralding the new trains helped erase the memory of the last 19 years, when the Great Western sat idle, hungry for money, and going nowhere. Chartered in 1834 as the London and Gore Railway company, it was not until 1851, when the American capital came in, that work actually began.

New rail service starts today: a timetable for the Great Western Railway.

Mail steamer sinks, 7 passengers dead

Oct. 7, 1853

PICTOU ISLAND, N.S. – Seven of 13 passengers died tonight when the *Fairy Queen* foundered off Pictou Island in the Maritimes. The mail steamer began taking on water after battling heavy seas. A fight to keep it afloat ensued, but by late afternoon water in the hold had extinguished her boilers.

As it became apparent the vessel was doomed, the captain ordered her lifeboats lowered. At 11 o'clock he and all but three of his crew took to these boats, and, as horrified passengers watched, began pulling for shore. Survivors had to cling to wreckage after the ship capsized.

Jury settles island colony's cattle dispute

Sept. 20, 1853

VICTORIA, Vancouver Island – There is more evidence that this colony is getting all the accoutrements of civilization. The first jury trial was held here today to settle a dispute about the detention of some cattle. In Webster vs. Muir the jury ruled in favor of the plaintiff and awarded $2,213 and costs.

The administration of justice in the colony, it must be admitted, is not proceeding too smoothly. Mention was made at the trial about the lack of proper records. And a group of lay magistrates, appointed to the Court of Petty Sessions by Gov. James Douglas earlier this year, has not proved to be a very satisfactory bunch.

But the small, vocal group of would-be reformers, always critical of Douglas, seems to forget that this colony was only a Hudson's Bay Company outpost a few years ago. Change from the arbitrary kind of justice appropriate to the fur trade and the frontier to a sophisticated judicial system, with the proper checks and balances, must be gradual if law and order is to be maintained.

There is also a shortage of the kind of people who can participate in, and administer, such marks of civilization as representative government and a British-style justice system. Nevertheless, Douglas has plans to create a Supreme Court of Civil Justice soon.

1854

Canada West, January. The Great Western Railway opens its main line connecting Niagara Falls, Hamilton, London, and Windsor. It has been promoted by Hamilton merchants and financed by British and American capital.

Europe, March 28. Britain and France declare war on Russia, joining their ally the Ottoman Empire already opposed to Russia in the Crimean War.

New Brunswick, April 20. The lieutenant-governor is informed of the existence of cholera in Saint John.

New York, June 27. Canadian chemist Abraham Gesner patents his process for distilling kerosene from petroleum.

Vancouver Island, Aug. 8. The sale of alcohol to Indians is made illegal.

Prince Edward Island, Aug. 13. The Bank of Prince Edward Island, the Island's first locally owned bank, opens. Its founders want to provide Islanders with their own currency and help them control their financial system.

Quebec, Sept. 8. Francis Hincks and Augustin-Norbert Morin resign from the Legislative Assembly after their Reform government, recently re-elected with a minority, is defeated in the House.

Quebec, Nov. 6. The Canadian legislature prohibits interments in burial grounds within the limits of the city of Quebec as a measure against cholera.

Canada East. William Rhodes introduces the sparrow to the province, importing 25 couples from Britain.

Canada East. French-Canadian poet Octave Crémazie publishes his first volume of poetry, celebrating the Anglo-French alliance during the Crimean War as an example for Canadians. The poems oppose American annexationism, and declare French-Canadians would fight against it on the side of the British.

New Brunswick. The first steam foghorn in the world, invented by a Scot emigré named Robert Foulis, is erected on Partridge Island off Saint John.

Prince Edward Island. The Island Telegraph System is inaugurated.

Montreal. The port receives 174 sailing ships during the navigation season, but only six ocean steamers.

Rae learns of Franklin's fate from Inuit

April 21, 1854

PELLY BAY, Far West – The first eyewitness account of the fate of the Franklin expedition, missing for almost a decade, has emerged from the Arctic. On an overland trek toward Boothia Peninsula, the indefatigable northern traveller Dr. John Rae has met some Inuit with an astonishing tale to tell.

They say that several years ago another party of Inuit were hunting seal near King William Island when they saw a large number of *kabloonas*, white men, crossing the ice. The strangers, about 40 of them, were dragging a boat and some sledges. Communicating by sign language, they told the Inuit that their ships were wrecked and that, having run out of supplies, they were heading for the mainland in search of caribou to kill. The men looked weak and hungry.

John Rae at Pelly Bay with an Inuit who tells him of John Franklin's fate.

Later that spring the Inuit came across many corpses and some graves in a cove on the mainland side of the strait. The Inuit also told Rae that the mutilated state of some of the corpses leaves little doubt that the sailors were driven to cannibalism in their last days.

St. Francis Xavier gets a new home

October 1854

ANTIGONISH, N.S. – St. Francis Xavier academy and seminary, founded last year by Bishop Colin MacKinnon, is coming up in the world, from rented rooms in Arichat, Cape Breton, to a made-to-order home in the heart of this Scottish-Catholic county. As carpenters complete the building, Arichat students and teachers prepare for the move. The bishop says the school will be for "the training of missionaries for service in this Diocese," and the instruction of "young people in this district in letters and good moral conduct." This is good news for the Roman Catholic Highlanders in eastern Nova Scotia. However, many non-Catholics here say they would also like to study at the new university.

Racial prejudice in the Canadas frowns on Indian ancestry

April 25, 1854

PROVINCE OF CANADA – If you have Indian blood in your veins, your best chance of success in the Canadas lies in downplaying your ancestry. Toleration – one side of the racist coin – depends on family status, achievements, and degree of assimilation. The mixed-blood who is accepted should be prepared to live a white man's life.

Some prominent mixed-bloods in the Canadas are John Baptist Askin, an influential official in London, Canada West, and president of the Middlesex Agricultural Society. Norman Bethune, a Toronto doctor, is the son of a fur trader and his Indian wife. So is Montreal's William Ermatinger, the city's police superintendent for nearly 15 years, recently named field inspector of the militia in Canada East.

In face of prevailing racial prejudice, none of these men advertises his Indian heritage. But what really galls white society is intermarriage, specially when the woman is well-bred and white. The Upper Canadian press almost uniformly condemned the 1833 marriage of Eliza Field and Sacred Feathers, the Mississauga chief. Two years ago, Emily Howells' marriage to George Johnson, a young Six Nations chief, also raised public ire.

Kildonan Presbyterian Church opens its doors to worshippers

The Kildonan Presbyterian Church, founded in 1854 in the Red River colony.

Jan. 5, 1854

RED RIVER COLONY, Rupert's Land – Scottish settlers here now have their own new church, not to mention a recently-wedded minister to tend to the congregation. The Kildonan Presbyterian Church officially opened today, with construction costs of £1,050 already paid off. Rev. John Black, who married Country-born Henrietta Ross a few weeks after his return to the Selkirk settlement in November, will take to the pulpit.

The church is modelled after Kildonan Church in Helmsdale, Scotland. Prior to the completion of the Kildonan church here, Presbyterians worshipped at St. John's Anglican Church.

Canadian's courage noted in tragic Crimean battle

Oct. 25, 1854

LONDON, England – A Canadian who took part in the heroic and disastrous charge of the Light Brigade at Balaclava is being cited by observers as the most courageous officer there. Lieut. Alexander Roberts Dunn of the 11th Hussars, "one of the handsomest men of his day, and also ... one of the finest swordsmen and horsemen in the army" – according to the *London Gazette* – "having emptied his revolver at the Russians, he flung it at them and resorted to his sabre, which he used to such good effect" that he saved a sergeant major's life by cutting down several Russians. (Dunn stands 6-3 and used a sword longer than regulations permit.)

Dunn also saved another life by "cutting down a Russian Hussar, who was attacking Private Levett, of the 11th Hussars." Dunn was one of the 607 men who rode out in the morning sun toward the assault which had such a bloody ending that by nightfall, only 198 had survived. One French general

Lieut. Alexander Roberts Dunn.

A Canadian officer takes part in the 1854 charge of the Light Brigade. Lieut. Alexander Dunn's exploits in the battle have won him a reputation for bravery.

commented, though the battle was "magnificent, it was not war."

Tragically, the foolhardy charge of the Light Brigade resulted from a confusion over orders. Instead of being sent to recapture British guns on Causeway Heights, the cavalry was ordered to advance on the Russian guns at the end of the North Valley to prevent them from being carried away. In brave obedience, the brigade charged 2.4 kilometres down a narrow valley directly into the mouths of Russian guns, as artillery batteries blasted them from either side as well, mowing down riders and horses. The poorly-provisioned British won, but paid a terrible price for their victory in the battle which had absolutely no military value. It was the second victory since Britain, France, Turkey and Sardinia landed in the Crimea six weeks ago to attack the Russian Black Sea naval base at Sebastopol.

Alexander Dunn is the son of John Henry, former receiver-general and member of the executive and legislative councils of Upper Canada, and Charlotte Roberts.

Trains collide in fog; 52 dead, 48 injured

Oct. 27, 1854

BAPTISTE CREEK, Canada West – The worst train wreck since the Great Western Railway was built last year killed 52 people and injured 48 about 24 kilometres west of Chatham early this morning. Poor visibility due to fog is being blamed for the accident, as an express train toppled off the track after hitting a fully-loaded gravel train. Eyewitnesses say the express rolled over, trapping a mass of passengers in the wreckage.

Octave Crémazie, founder of the Institut Canadien, owns a French bookstore in Quebec City.

Doctor kills himself after patient dies

Winter 1854

BRUCE MINES – Wracked with guilt over the death of a patient, Dr. David Rintoul, the town's only doctor, committed suicide with his dueling pistol.

Rintoul, 24, the son of Rev. William Rintoul, a noted Montreal theologian, had visited a pregnant woman in the countryside, finding her near labor but in good condition. The next day he returned to discover the woman and the baby had both died due to complications in childbirth. After consoling the distraught father, Rintoul went home and shot himself.

Canada-U.S. trade deal torpedoes tariffs

June 6, 1854

WASHINGTON, D.C. – The United Province of Canada and the United States today reached a trade agreement which eliminates tariffs on a wide range of goods.

The deal was some 10 years in the making, with negotiations breaking off as protectionist sentiment in the United States grew. The Democratic administration of Franklin Pierce finally was able to strike a deal with Gov. Gen. Lord Elgin, who took charge of negotiations for Canada last month. This 10-year Reciprocity Treaty allows products such as grain, lumber, coal, livestock, meat and fish to be traded across the border duty-free. The United States also gains access to Atlantic fisheries north of the 36th Parallel, as well as free use of the St. Lawrence and Canadian waters in Lake Michigan. The pact can be cancelled on one year's notice. The agreement, which must be ratified by provincial legislatures, comes into effect next Jan. 1.

Coalition assumes power in the Assembly

Sept. 11, 1854

QUEBEC CITY – Sound economic and political sense appears to have prevailed today with the appointment of a Liberal-Conservative, Anglo-French coalition government. Led by Sir Allan MacNab and Augustin-Norbert Morin, the administration hopes to transcend the sectionalism that divided and sabotaged the Reform party's policies. The new coalition is a synthesis of diverse interests that have long lacked a common denominator. They now stand combined, the sum of their equation promising economic prosperity. Moderate Conservatives, liberal Reformers, commercial interests, and some leading French politicians are all uniting under MacNab's dictum "my politics now are railroads," construction of which, it is thought, will hold the fragile union together.

Coalition passes bill to secularize Clergy Reserves

Nov. 23, 1854

MONTREAL – The Conservative-Liberal coalition today passed a bill to secularize Clergy Reserves and to transfer the funds from them over to the municipalities. The bill, introduced by John A. Macdonald, brought an end to privileges Protestant clergy gained from the Constitutional Act of 1791, which had reserved for them the income from one-seventh of the sale of public lands of Upper Canada. Macdonald's bill passed despite being attacked from both sides.

A group of Tories tried to save at least part of the endowment from the state for the clergy. But George Brown and his followers, Liberals who are not part of the coalition, objected to a clause in the bill that permits stipends currently paid to the clergymen to be commuted into permanent capital funds to be used by their churches. This clause, to Brown's group, opens the door to continue at least some of the endowment. But the bill's opponents did not have the numbers to pose a serious threat and the legislation was easily passed.

The Clergy Reserves have been a bone of contention almost from the outset. John Strachan, a Presbyterian who had turned Anglican and became the first bishop of Toronto, contended that all the land should go to the Anglican church because it was the only "established" one. He talked former governor John Colborne in 1836 into his way of thinking and 44 of a planned 57 Anglican rectories were endowed before other denominations stepped in to stop the practice.

Both Presbyterians and Methodists staked claims. The dispute was resolved by governor Lord Sydenham in 1840, when he ruled Anglicans and Presbyterians would share half the money from the future sale of the land and the other half would go to other denominations, with shares based on their numbers. But this compromise did not satisfy either Anglicans in Tory ranks or Reformers who wanted nothing short of secularization. Today's bill should put an end to what has been a long battle.

Instructions issued to combat cholera

Feb. 27, 1854

SAINT JOHN, N.B. – The Board of Health has issued a list of instructions to be followed in hopes of avoiding an epidemic of cholera that is sweeping Europe. Cleanliness being the first defence against the disease, the city is to be inspected and filthy sites cleaned immediately. Pigs and other animals are banned from the city. House to house visits will be instituted to detect the disease in its early stages and sufferers will be given immediate treatment.

The city has its work cut out for it, especially in the overcrowded slums where there are no sanitary arrangements and the streets are awash in household refuse, often mingled with slaughterhouse waste.

Cholera claims German laborers.

Lavish celebration marks railway opening

The Hercules, a Hinckley locomotive, was built in 1854.

Dec. 29, 1854

PETERBOROUGH – A feast fit for a king celebrated the official opening of the newly-completed railway link from Cobourg. The crowd of 200 – among them Cobourg dignitaries on the inaugural run – dined on fresh cod and venison, washed down with the "best and costliest" wines, and heard speeches paying tribute to the new 46.5-kilometre railway, built at an estimated cost of $1.1 million.

The line is expected to greatly increase Cobourg's importance as a shipping port handling lumber, grain and flour destined for burgeoning markets in the United States. It runs through a scenic valley and features a 4.8-kilometre trestle bridge over Rice Lake.

Citizens of Cobourg financed the project, which had been first discussed in 1834. The economic depression and political unrest in the intervening years delayed start-up of the railway, and the charter for the line wasn't issued until 1852. The sod-turning took place early last year, on Feb. 7.

A tradition ends: French seigneurial system abolished

Nov. 23, 1854

MONTREAL – Parliament abolished the seigneurial system of Lower Canada today, ending more than two centuries of dependency by habitants on the privileged land owners known as seigneurs. A total of $1.5 million will be paid as compensation to seigneurs, Parliament decided, but it will be paid by the community and not the habitants, or *censitaires*, as they are sometimes called. Habitants must still pay an annual fee for their land, but ownership can be achieved by making lump-sum payments.

The seigneurial system dates to 1627, when, inspired by the feudal system, it was established in Lower Canada as a means to distribute and occupy land, and to create a hierarchical society. Seigneuries, often five by 15 kilometres in area, were given to nobility, military officers, administrators and to religious orders such as the Sulpicians. Seigneurs, by dividing their holdings into long, narrow strips, usually fronting the river, distributed lands to *censitaires*, who were forever subject to seigneurial dues.

Censitaires had several obligations to the seigneur. They had to pay rent as well as tax on the grain ground at the mill operated by the seigneur. In some cases, habitants had to work for seigneurs a given number of days each year. In the early days, seigneurs proved to be lax in clearing and settling the lands that had been granted to them.

Over the passage of time, the system had become more exploitative, and few tears are likely to be shed over today's legislation. The significance of the vote is best understood by looking at the population of Lower Canada, where until recently, 80 percent of the people were concentrated in the seigneurial area. It takes in most of both banks of the St. Lawrence River between Quebec and Montreal, as well as the Richelieu and Chaudière valleys.

This stranglehold on choice land has led to increasing urbanization and an exodus to the U.S., although some people have opted to settle in the Eastern Townships or around Lake St. John.

Kutchin Indians adapting to fur trade

1854

RUPERT'S LAND – The Athabascan-speaking Kutchin people of the western sub-Arctic, North America's northernmost Indians, have been adapting to development of the fur trade here for more than a decade. The Hudson's Bay Company is spreading westward and in 1840 established its first post in the region, Fort McPherson.

Like the Algonquians of the eastern woodlands, the Kutchin have depended on fur-bearing animals as their resource base. Caribou, moose, muskrat, snowshoe hare, fish and waterfowl have long been staple to their diet; hides of the larger game are used for clothing and for tents. Traditionally dependent on the availability of game, the Kutchin have seldom stayed in one location more than a month. They have acquired extensive knowledge of the region's landscape and fauna. But by shifting priority of the hunt from subsistence to trade in recent years, the Kutchin are also changing their way of life. By concentrating more on one species, the beaver, they travel less. As the beaver is best trapped by smaller groups, individual family units, rather than larger groups, hunt them. Boundaries have changed, as families develop their own territories based on traplines.

Fully-attired Indian hunters of the western sub-Arctic Kutchins.

Saviah, senior member, or chief, of one of many Kutchin bands.

The dance of the Kutchin Indians: regional bands assemble for annual festivities and ceremonies to celebrate their traditional spiritual beliefs.

Graveyard of the Atlantic claims U.S. ship

Illustration of the wreck of the Arcadia off the shores of Sable Island.

1854

HALIFAX – R.W. Fraser, consul for the United States in Halifax, has filed an official complaint over government involvement in the sale of property salvaged from the American vessel *Arcadia*. The ship foundered earlier this year off Sable Island, the infamous Graveyard of the Atlantic.

The desolate, crescent-shaped island lies in the midst of the Gulf Stream trade route. Submerged sandbars stretching from its eastern and western tips shift periodically, threatening sea traffic. Because of the frequency of wrecks, Nova Scotia has established life-saving stations on Sable, the only form of settlement there. Crews of the government-funded stations use the island's horses, living legacies of earlier wrecks, to assist in their rescue and salvage operations.

Canadian fur trader Peter Ogden dies

Sept. 27, 1854

OREGON CITY – Peter Skene Ogden, who was born in Quebec and lived by the credo, "Necessity has no laws," died today at age 64. This scrappy fellow did whatever it took to advance his interests. Happily for him, many of those interests coincided with those of the fur-trading companies for which he worked, first the North West then the Hudson's Bay after the merger.

Ogden rose in the company because he identified what needed to be done and then did it. He explored many areas of the far western United States, overcoming natural hazards, American competitors, and hostile Indians, as he studied the area's complex geography.

Treaty opens peninsula to white settlers

Oct. 13, 1854

SAUGEEN PENINSULA, Canada West – "We the chiefs, sachems and principal men" of the Saugeen and Newash band of the Ojibwa Indians "make a complete surrender unto the Crown of that peninsula known as the Saugeen [Bruce Peninsula, Ont.]."

Signed at the Indian Mission Church, on the Saugeen Reserve, Treaty No. 72 marks the last major land transfer by the Indians in the southern part of Canada West, and opens up the rocky peninsula to white settlement. Under the terms of the treaty, the Indians reserve a triangular block of land around the Saugeen River to Lake Huron on the west and north to Sauble Beach. They also reserve Chief's Point and Cape Croker. Indian Agent L. Oliphant and a missionary signed as witnesses.

1855

Ottawa, Jan. 1. Bytown is officially incorporated as a city, adopting the name of Ottawa to commemorate the 200th anniversary of the re-opening of the Ottawa River for peaceful navigation by the Ottawa Indians after it was closed by the Iroquois.

Prince Edward Island, Jan, 17. St. Dunstan's College opens, dedicated to educating young men for the Catholic clergy, and as lay leaders for the Island's Catholic society.

Quebec, January. A Liberal-Conservative coalition government led by Etienne-Pascal Taché and Allan MacNab comes to power.

New Brunswick, March 27. A law is adopted to prohibit alcoholic beverages in the colony.

Prince Edward Island, March. A storm overtakes an ice boat, resulting in two deaths. The boats are the Island's only way of communicating with the mainland in winter, and the disaster shows the Island's winter isolation.

Prince Edward Island, April 17. Charlottetown, the capital of the colony, is incorporated as a city. Its population is 6,500 people.

Canada East, August. The corvette *La Capricieuse* brings the French flag to the St. Lawrence for the first time since the Conquest.

Canada East, August. Poet Octave Crémazie writes *Vieux Soldat Canadien*, during the visit of the *La Capricieuse*. In the final address of the poem, he urges the crew of the ship to report in France that French-Canadians have preserved their heritage and their hearts still belong in France, even though their allegiance is to England.

Toronto, October. The capital of Canada returns to Toronto from Quebec City.

Toronto. The Toronto General Hospital is described in the this way: "The floors, walls, and ward appurtenances are extremely filthy, the patients swarming with vermin."

Toronto, December. The city is connected with the Great Western Railway system serving London, Windsor, Niagara Falls, and Hamilton.

Red River. The Grey Nuns build a hospital at the colony. The Grey Nuns, founded in Montreal, are a non-cloistered order dedicated to nursing.

Train crosses Niagara River bridge

Great Western Railroad train exiting from the Niagara suspension bridge.

March 9, 1855

NIAGARA FALLS – The new suspension bridge across the Niagara River was crossed by a train for the first time today, marking the culmination of a four-year building project. Construction began in 1851 on the bridge, which covers a span of 255 metres. It was designed by John Roebling. The initial crossing comes one day after the bridge was declared officially open.

Apart from the engineering feat, the new bridge is expected to have a major economic impact on Canada, gaining it U.S. trade, especially in the winter when waterways are closed. Most of a rail route linking Buffalo, N.Y., a crucial shipping point at the west end of the Erie Canal, and the Michigan centres of Detroit and Port Huron, will be on Canadian soil.

The main line of the Great Western Railway from the bridge here to Windsor, across the border from Detroit, was completed in January. A spur line between Toronto and Hamilton is also planned to link up with this new international route, connecting Toronto with New York.

Anderson to verify Franklin discoveries

June 2, 1855

GREAT SLAVE LAKE, Rupert's Land – John Anderson, the Hudson's Bay Company's chief factor here, is leading an expedition to check John Rae's discoveries about the fate of Sir John Franklin. Last year Rae reported he had talked to Inuit at Repulse Bay about Franklin and bought some relics from them. Rae concluded the Franklin party died near King William Island. Anderson will look for evidence along the Arctic coast.

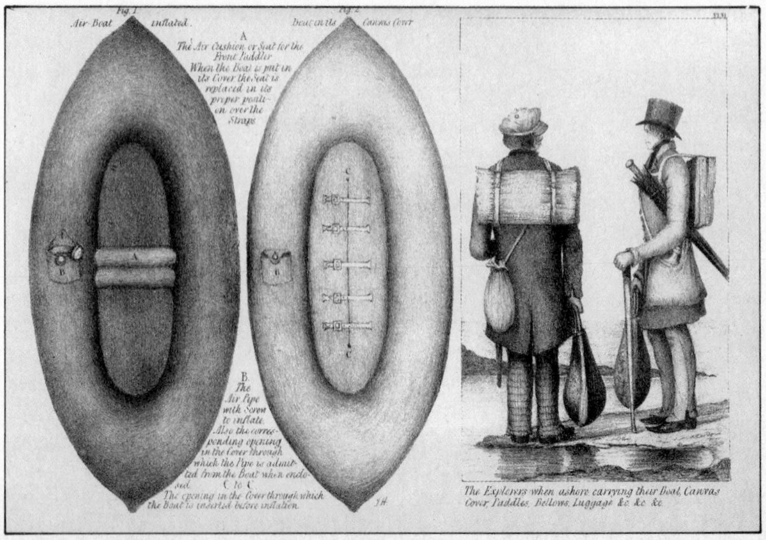

An inflatable boat used on the journey in search of Franklin expedition.

Railway's steamers work Lake Ontario

June 25, 1855

HAMILTON – The steamers *Canada* and *America* have been put in service on Lake Ontario between this centre and Oswego, N.Y., by the Great Western Railway. Shipping has been developing rapidly on the lakes this century, particularly since the development of the screw propeller in 1839. All steamships were driven by paddle wheel until 1841, with the *Vandalia*'s launch at Oswego. It was the first propeller ship on Lake Ontario.

A mail service using steamships developed and by 1853, the Royal Mail Line had four vessels carrying mail from Toronto and Hamilton to Kingston, linking up there with other mail ships. Besides passenger and mail service on the lakes, three lines of freight steamers are operating this year between Toronto and Montreal. But with the completion of the railway to Toronto next year, the steamers' role may decline.

Government OKs Catholic schools; act angers Brown

May 30, 1855

TORONTO – Against the opposition of George Brown and other Reformers in Canada West, the government has passed a law which now allows the full establishment of Roman Catholic separate schools in Canada West. The Supplementary School Act, which came in response to petitions from the Catholic church and Lower Canadians, allows for the establishment of separate school boards to run these facilities. As well, it allows Roman Catholics to divert their school taxes to support this system, rather than the non-denominational public schools.

The act has sparked a regional row that is remarkably bitter. Led by Brown, opponents of the bill want the complete disallowance of any such separate schools. Lurking behind their objections is a fear of French-Canadian domination, an ever-present terror mirrored by a similar French-Canadian paranoia toward the English.

Howe files report on mission in U.S.

May 8, 1855

HALIFAX – Joseph Howe, the most dominant politician in Nova Scotia, today reported to Lt.-Gov. Gaspard le Marchant on his bizarre stint as an army recruiter. To strengthen Britain in its struggle against Russia in the Crimean War, Howe tried to persuade Americans to join the British army in Halifax. With the full backing of Britain, he spent weeks ducking in and out of Boston, New York, Philadelphia, and Washington. His activities were illegal. Moreover, he complained, the U.S. was "as much a Russian stronghold as Sebastopol."

U.S. lawmen arrested his assistant, paralysed his agents with fear, and charged Howe with a misdemeanor. Using phoney names, hiding in New Jersey hotels, and walking the streets day and night, the greatest orator in Nova Scotia kept himself out of Yankee hoosegows. But his mission was a flop.

Priest says he's found a cure for cancer

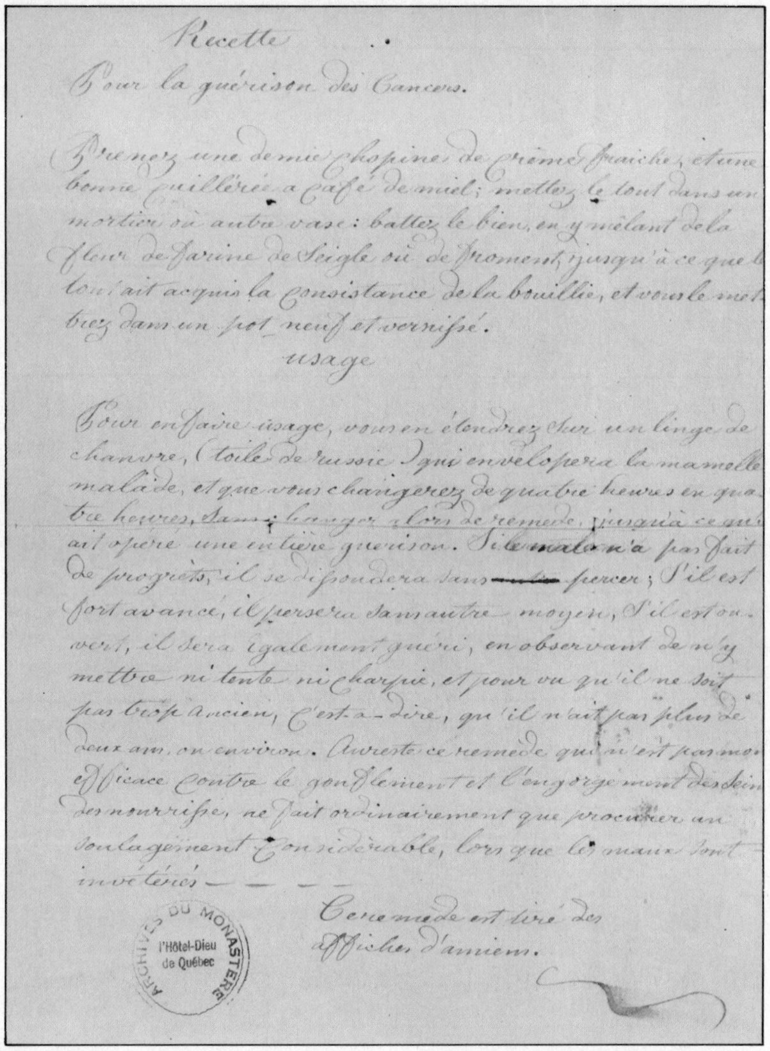

Recette

Pour la guérison des Cancers.

Prenez une demie chopine de crême fraiche, et une bonne cuillérée a caffé de miel; mettez le tout dans un mortier ou autre vase: battez le bien, en y mêlant de la fleur de farine de Seigle ou de froment, jusqu'à ce que le tout ait acquis la consistance de la bouillie, et vous le mettrez dans un pot neuf et vernissé.

usage

Pour en faire usage, vous en étendrez sur un linge de chanvre, (toile de russie) qui enveloppera la mamelle malade, et que vous changerez de quatre heures en quatre heures, sans changer alors de remede, jusqu'à ce qu'il ait opéré une entière guerison. Si le mal n'a pas fait de progrès, il se dissoudera sans percer; S'il est fort avancé, il percera sans autre moyen, s'il est ouvert, il sera également guéri, en observant de n'y mettre ni tente ni charpie, et pour vu qu'il ne soit pas trop ancien, c'est-à-dire, qu'il n'ait pas plus de deux ans ou environ. Au reste ce remede qui n'est pas moins efficace contre le gonflement et l'engorgement des seins des nourrisses, ne fait ordinairement que procurer un soulagement considerable, lorsque les maux sont invétérés — — — —

Ce remede est tiré des affiches d'amiens.

ARCHIVES DU MONASTÈRE
l'Hôtel-Dieu de Québec

In his own handwriting, priest's cancer cure calls for cream and honey.

1855

QUEBEC CITY – Cream and honey a cure for cancer? That's what a local priest and amateur doctor is claiming. Pierre-Joseph Compain is said to have cured dozens of cancer sufferers in his parishes using a mixture of cream and honey saturated in a cloth, which is then applied directly to the affected area. Compain studied medicine in the army, but he never completed his medical training.

Since becoming a priest, Compain has continued to apply his medical knowledge for the care of his flocks. He practises another cancer treatment using powdered arsenic, which is applied to the area of the tumor.

Grand Trunk links Montreal to Brockville

Sept. 17, 1855

MONTREAL – Railroad service between this city and Brockville began today as the first phase in the Grand Trunk Railway's Montreal-Toronto linkup took to the tracks. The completion of the route joining the two major cities is not expected until next year, but the Brockville trip gave a hint of what is to come: the train is expected to average an incredible 25 kilometres an hour. Commuters are already talking hours instead of days in discussing time en route.

Tracks between Montreal and Brockville follow a relatively level route along the St. Lawrence River. But the biggest challenge for builders on the route is a major bridge now under construction across the St. Lawrence River here.

Sheep stirs dispute over San Juan isle

June 21, 1855

VICTORIA, Vancouver Island – Americans on San Juan Island have seized a sheep belonging to a British settler, Gov. James Douglas has reported to the Legislative Council. Douglas is especially concerned about this seizure because the ownership of the island has been in doubt since the signing of the Oregon Boundary Treaty nine years ago.

The border follows the 49th Parallel on land, but then dips south of Vancouver Island, leaving the ownership of some islands in limbo. The Reciprocity Treaty, signed last year, has accentuated the commercial rivalry between Americans and other inhabitants of the west coast.

First Charlottetown city council elected

Aug. 7, 1855

CHARLOTTETOWN – It is "a memorable day," in the words of one local newspaper, as Charlottetonians today elected their first city council.

Sitting in a converted flour market, the new municipal government takes over a community lacking "some of the commonest comforts of life." The city badly needs improved streets, proper police protection, and an adequate sewer system. Addressing these problems will be difficult, for the council has a £1000 ceiling on yearly spending.

Capital of Canada is back in Toronto

Oct. 20, 1855

TORONTO – Toronto is the capital of Canada – again! The Legislative Assembly has voted to alternate the status of capital city between Toronto and Quebec, the result of an alliance between members of these two locales. The move was sanctioned by Gov. Gen. Sir Edmund Walker Head over cries of the appointed Legislative Council, in line with the principles of regional government. The council wants the "road show" stopped.

1856

Canada East, January. Bishop Charbonnel issues a pastoral letter declaring that Upper Canadian Catholics who do not vote in favor of separate schools for Catholics are guilty of mortal sin.

Canada East, February. A French-Canadian judge and a Catholic jury acquit seven Irish Catholics of murder, despite strong evidence that they beat to death an Irish Protestant named Corrigan. The verdict causes anger in Canada West.

Paris, March 30. Britain, France, Russia, the Ottoman Empire, Piedmont, Austria, and Prussia sign the Treaty of Paris, ending the Crimean War and securing the neutrality of the Black Sea.

Vancouver Island, June 4. A meeting of the Legislative Council is called to consider a British proposal for the establishment of an elected assembly for the Island.

Toronto, Sept. 7. The orthodox Sons of Israel Congregation is founded, the first Jewish congregation in the city.

Canada West, Dec. 31. Since March 1, 15,364 passengers have travelled on the recently completed Cobourg-Peterborough railway.

Toronto. A newspaper claims that "Protestantism may be said to be the genius of Upper Canada."

Canada. Governor Edmund Head makes remarks in Hamilton about the "superiority" of the British race that built Canada West. The French-Canadian newspaper *L'Avenir* responds that French-Canadians have been insulted.

Montreal. A museum is founded at McGill University.

Canada West. Game laws are re-written and extended to fur-bearing animals.

London. Queen Victoria institutes a bravery award, called the Victoria Cross, for officers and men of her British and colonial forces. The award is cast from bronze derived from Russian cannon captured in the Crimean War, and the first recipients are veterans of the Crimean War.

London. Lieut. Alexander Dunn is the first Canadian to receive the Victoria Cross for his bravery during the charge of the Light Brigade.

Red River. The population of the colony, mostly Métis, is 6,691.

Photographer opens studio in Montreal

A picture of Quebec City taken by Montreal lensman William Notman.

William Notman, who has opened a photographic studio in Montreal.

1856

MONTREAL – William Notman has opened Montreal's newest photographic studio at 11 Bleury St. Trained in drawing and painting in Glasgow, Notman pursued photography as a hobby. He left Scotland, where he was wanted for fraud for trying to save the family cloth business from bankruptcy, to start his life over in Canada.

Arriving here in August, Notman was hired by dry goods merchants Ogilvy and Lewis, who helped him get started by loaning him money to set up his gallery. Producing paper calotypes, Greek for beautiful impression, and glass ambrotypes, Notman works alone in his studio. His wife Alice acts as receptionist.

Cobourg a booming transportation centre

1856

COBOURG, Canada West – Cobourg has been transformed into a booming transportation centre, due largely to the Cobourg to Peterborough railway and the Reciprocity Treaty signed between Canada and the U.S. in 1854. This year, some 4.2 million metres of lumber and 200,000 bushels of wheat have been exported from the port after being shipped here via the railway.

Map shows British, Russian and Danish territory in North America.

U.S. denies entry to Métis hunters

1856

PEMBINA, Rupert's Land – Gone are the days of free and easy movement over the prairies as dictated by trade and commerce, the quest for food, or simply the pull of one's heart strings. Evidence of this fact is that the United States army under Col. C.F. Smith has been prohibiting Métis from crossing the border to hunt buffalo in the U.S.

An American military post has been established just across the border at the new Métis settlement of St. Joseph's on the Pembina River, just inside the border. The Americans are working to maintain border control and prevent free movement of people and trade back and forth between the two countries.

Recently there have been hostilities between the Métis and the American Sioux. The peace negotiated by Métis leader Cuthbert Grant with the Sioux is still in force, but no doubt its chances of continuing will increase if the two groups do not compete for the ever diminishing buffalo herds which the Métis have been following farther and farther south on their biannual hunts.

Renowned crusader is excommunicated

1856

KANKAKEE, Ill. – Charles Chiniquy, a Roman Catholic priest who became famous in Quebec for his temperance crusades, has been excommunicated by the church. Charges of sexual escapades, arson and embezzlement led to the action by the church against the priest, who came to this community about 80 kilometres south of Chicago after earlier scandals.

In the 1840s, in one 18-month period in Quebec, Chiniquy is credited with converting 200,000 people to temperance in 120 parishes. But here, he has been accused of propositioning a young teacher several times, trying to corrupt women who came to his confessional, eating meat on Friday saying the Pope wouldn't know, and setting fire to the chapel after removing valuable vases. He was put under interdict, defied it and was excommunicated.

Cavalry recruiting young Canadians

Feb. 2, 1856

TORONTO – "The cavalry is coming! The cavalry is coming!" Such a cry can be heard in the streets of Toronto today. But, this time, it doesn't foretell of an American assault like that of the War of 1812. Instead, Capt. Robert Denison is hosting a meeting this afternoon, in a hotel in nearby Weston, aimed at enlisting young volunteers in a new squadron of cavalry, and, as well, a battery of artillery.

The recruitment is a sign of the times. First, the growing British desire for colonies to defend themselves means Canadian troops are needed. Second, while the law says it's compulsory for all males of reasonable age to serve in time of war, the lack of training for such conscripted soldiers has resulted in poor quality troops. Hence the call for volunteers; men willing to fight. Third, unrest last year between the U.S. and Britain – after the Mother Country tried to recruit soldiers there for the Crimean War – means there is a need for more troops to protect this country from invasion when tensions run high.

It is expected the government will have little trouble raising this new company of volunteer militia across the country. They won't replace the British regulars, but they will make this country more secure.

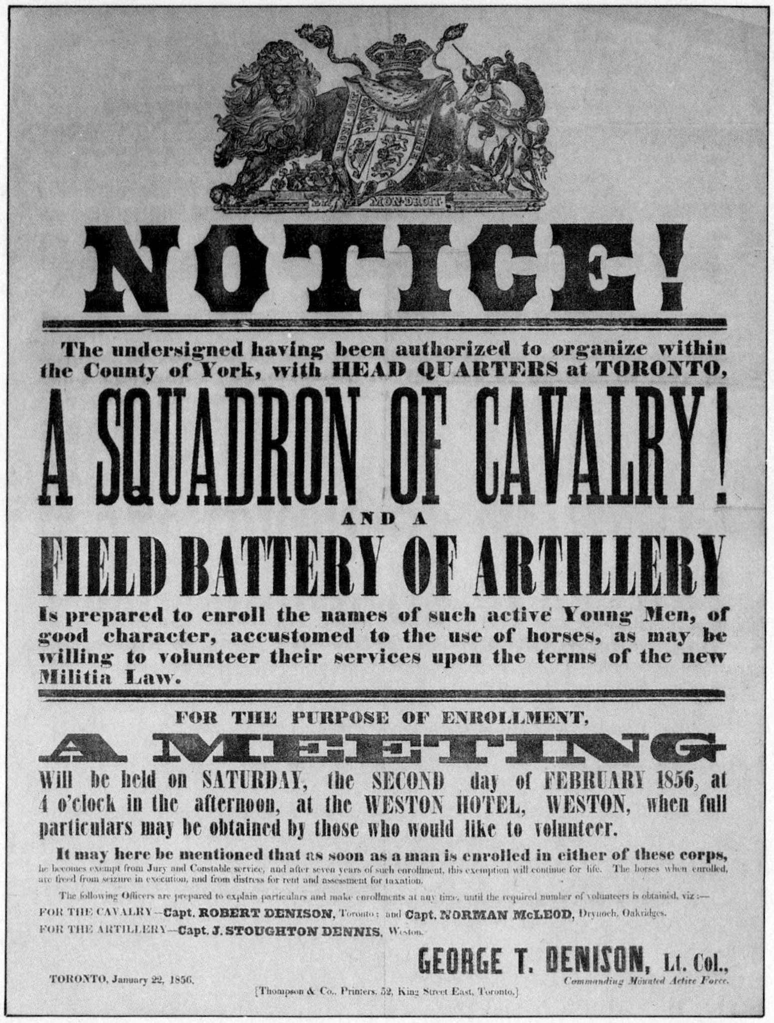

NOTICE!

The undersigned having been authorized to organize within the County of York, with HEAD QUARTERS at TORONTO,

A SQUADRON OF CAVALRY!

AND A

FIELD BATTERY OF ARTILLERY

Is prepared to enroll the names of such active Young Men, of good character, accustomed to the use of horses, as may be willing to volunteer their services upon the terms of the new Militia Law.

FOR THE PURPOSE OF ENROLLMENT,

A MEETING

Will be held on SATURDAY, the SECOND day of FEBRUARY 1856, at 4 o'clock in the afternoon, at the WESTON HOTEL, WESTON, when full particulars may be obtained by those who would like to volunteer.

It may here be mentioned that as soon as a man is enrolled in either of these corps, he becomes exempt from Jury and Constable service, and after seven years of such enrollment, this exemption will continue for life. The horses when enrolled, are freed from seizure in execution, and from distress for rent and assessment for taxation.

The following Officers are prepared to explain particulars and make enrollments at any time, until the required number of volunteers is obtainid, viz:—

FOR THE CAVALRY—Capt. ROBERT DENISON, Toronto; and Capt. NORMAN McLEOD, Drynoch, Oakridges.

FOR THE ARTILLERY—Capt. J. STOUGHTON DENNIS, Weston.

GEORGE T. DENISON, Lt. Col.,
Commanding Mounted Active Force.

TORONTO, January 22, 1856.

[Thompson & Co., Printers, 52, King Street East, Toronto.]

Notice urges men to join the Canadian cavalry and field battery of artillery.

Elected members added to council

March 1856

TORONTO – The government has made a strange change to the Upper House of Parliament, known as the Legislative Council. To make this appointed body more responsive to the voters, and presumably more in tune with the ruling party, it has passed a bill which enlarges the council by adding elected members to its chamber.

The move is odd because, in a spirit of compromise uniquely Canadian, it has mollified its Conservative critics by allowing current councillors to retain their seats until they die, when elections will replace them. The result will be an Upper House with a peculiar mix of appointed and elected members, which won't for years mirror the political balance of the Assembly.

Government leader post to Macdonald

May 23, 1856

TORONTO – John A. Macdonald has replaced Allan MacNab as the government leader for Canada West. Macdonald's move up comes after the government both won and lost a vote of confidence in the house. That is, it won overall, 70-47. However, when the vote is broken down into Canada West and Canada East, the Tories lost in the west by six votes. In order to rebuild the government's support, MacNab quit, to give a more popular leader to the coalition ministry.

Former government leader MacNab. ▷

Sacred Feathers dies after long illness

June 29, 1856

BRANTFORD, Canada West – After a long illness, Sacred Feathers – also known as Peter Jones – died early this morning at the age of 54. Born in a wigwam, he died in a stately English-style house. For some time, Mississauga Indians from his own reserve at New Credit have come to sing, in a neighboring room in his house, three kilometres from here, the grand old Methodist hymns he had translated for them into Ojibwa.

In his lifetime, Sacred Feathers accomplished a great deal for his people as a chief and an ordained Methodist minister. Before his conversion to Christianity in 1823, the 200 or so Mississauga Indians at the western end of Lake Ontario had appeared on the verge of extinction, their strength diminished by disease and by alcohol abuse, forced off their land by tens of thousands of settlers. This son of an American surveyor and a Mississauga Indian woman had helped them, and other Ojibwa-speaking bands throughout Upper Canada, to adjust to the European presence, by teaching them how to lead a settled life, and how to farm.

Not all his people supported him. From age 14 to 21, Sacred Feathers had lived away from them, with his father, and had become very "Europeanized." Even in his own community, about one-third of the Christian converts opposed him, as one too willing to adopt the newcomers' customs. Sacred Feathers is survived by his wife Eliza and their four sons.

N.B. law prohibits liquor consumption

Jan. 1, 1856

SAINT JOHN, N.B. – As of today, it is illegal to consume alcoholic beverages in New Brunswick. The law is the result of concerted lobbying by the Sons of Temperance, an anti-drink pressure group backed by the evangelical churches in the province.

Prohibition has torn New Brunswick in two, with the population divided nearly evenly on each side of the question. That's why tremendous problems may arise, if the dries decide to spy on those who oppose the law, and who say privately they still intend to take a drop. Under the law, fines and imprisonment can be meted out to offenders for what was once entirely legal.

Cable link to speed up the news

Ships struggle to lay telegraph cable from Newfoundland to Cape Breton.

1856

NEWFOUNDLAND – Several days will be cut off the transmission time for news travelling from Europe to mainland North America now that a telegraph line connects Cape Breton and Newfoundland islands. The line means telegraphs can now replace the much slower method of transporting messages by boat.

The cable link was laid by engineer Frederick Newton Gisborne. It runs under Cabot Strait from Cape Ray, Nfld.

A.P. Salter surveys his first meridian

July 28, 1856

WHITEFISH LAKE – Provincial land surveyor Andrew Pellew Salter has started to survey his first meridian in this area. Meridians are charted in a north-south line and serve as reference points. In beginning his survey, Salter's compass experienced severe anomalies, possibly caused by the presence of nickel. Nickel was first discovered here 10 years ago, but further exploration did not take place until this year.

Pasteur: disease spread by germs

1856

PARIS – A Paris chemist of humble origins and little formal training named Louis Pasteur is proposing an incredible new idea. Basing his claims on experiments on putrefying and souring food, he says that disease spreads via tiny living organisms called germs.

It is very hard to believe. For years people have thought that disease is transmitted by poisonous gases called miasmas, so doctors take little care to keep their operating coats and instruments clean to protect against the spread of the "germs" Pasteur is talking about. Indeed, it is even considered bad etiquette for doctors to wash their operating coats.

Interest in lacrosse skyrockets; club boosts sport in Montreal

1856

MONTREAL – A group of sports enthusiasts interested in the centuries-old Indian game of *baggataway*, or lacrosse, has founded the Montreal Lacrosse Club, the first such organization devoted to the game. Formation of the club comes in the wake of sporadic and informal matches held in recent years with Indians from nearby Caughnawaga.

Long before European contact, *baggataway* was played as a ritual honoring fallen warriors or the sick. Hundreds of ceremoniously-dressed participants would play a single match on a field with few boundaries. Only since the turn of the century have its rules been adjusted to make the game playable on a strictly recreational basis.

Indians and whites take part in the vigorous and popular game of lacrosse.

View of Fort Victoria, originally founded as a headquarters for the Hudson's Bay Company and now the residence of the governor of Vancouver Island.

Englishmen open commercial malt house

1856

GALT, Canada West – Englishmen Thomas Peck and John G. Dykes have opened Canada's first commercial malt house. Built of local granite, it has two sloped malting floors, one kiln, a barley chamber and a stone pump-house fed by spring well water. Capable of turning 20,000 bushels of barley into malt for brewing, observers believe the local brewing industry will thrive now that brewers will no longer have to malt their own barley. At present, Galt has one brewery and seven distilleries.

Governor reports to London on gold finds

April 1856

VICTORIA, Vancouver Island – Gold miners have moved over the border of the United States and are working in the north Columbia River area, Gov. James Douglas has told the colonial office in London. They are earning from £2 to £8 a day, he says. It is still too early to tell if the gold finds are substantial, but someone should be named to keep peace in the area.

New play reflects political reformism

1856

BROCKVILLE – Caralee Candidus has just published one of the first Canadian plays dramatizing a contemporary local event. The *Female Consistory of Brockville*, about a group of women who plot to oust a local minister because of his bad attitude toward women, may be a satire on the real-life suspension of a minister named White. But some suspect it is a Reform-inspired satire on local politics.

Montreal festivities celebrate rail link

Nov. 11, 1856

MONTREAL – Thousands of passengers arrived in special trains today to celebrate the completion of the Montreal-Toronto rail link, setting off the first of three days of festivities. Montreal sent out invitations for the celebrations, which include banquets. The Grand Trunk Railway included tickets for free transportation to guests from Canada and the New England states.

Great Route to the West!
1857. 1857.
GRAND TRUNK
VICTORIA RAIL ROAD BRIDGE
ENTIRE LENGTH 7000ft. BEING THE LONGEST BRIDGE IN THE WORLD.
RAIL ROAD
55 Miles Saved between Maine & the West.
AN EXPRESS TRAIN LEAVES PORTLAND & DANVILLE JUNCTION, FOR
Montreal, Quebec & Toronto
EVERY MORNING, making a Direct Connection (at Toronto,) with the GREAT WESTERN RAILROAD, and forming the MOST EXPEDITIOUS, PLEASANT AND ECONOMICAL ROUTE TO
HAMILTON, LONDON, BUFFALO
DETROIT, TOLEDO, CLEVELAND
PITTSBURG, CINCINNATI, CAIRO,
ST. LOUIS, CHICAGO
MILWAUKEE, DUNLEITH, ST. PAUL,
Madison, Iowa City, Burlington, Peoria, Quincy,
AND ALL PARTS IN THE WEST AND SOUTH.
Rates of Fare and Freight Lower
THAN BY ANY OTHER ROUTE.
Travelers generally, and Families in particular, moving out West, will find this Route by far the Most Comfortable and Economical. They will have neither expense nor trouble in Transferring their Baggage between the Station or Port of Embarkation and that of Destination.
The GRAND TRUNK RAILROAD is a BROAD GAUGE TRACK, and for SPEED, SAFETY and COMFORT, is not excelled by any Road in America. Large and Commodious First and Second Class Dining Saloons have been established at convenient Stations along the Road, where all kinds of Refreshments can be procured at very Moderate Charges.
Only One Change of Cars between Portland & Toronto
THROUGH TICKETS, and every information can be obtained of the undersigned, or at any of the Railroad and Steamboat Offices east of Portland, and also on board the BANGOR and ST. JOHNS' Steamers.
GEO. DARTNELL, General Agent, Buffalo, N. Y.
WM. FLOWERS, Ticket Agent, Bangor, Me.

Grand Trunk Railway schedule advertises "Great Route to the West."

Vancouver Island's first Assembly meets

Aug. 12, 1856

VICTORIA, Vancouver Island – Victoria's expanded Legislative Assembly today met for the first time. Gov. James Douglas had received orders from the colonial office in London in February telling him such an Assembly would have to be organized. He and his Legislative Council did not have the power to legislate, colonial office lawyers had decided.

Despite some of his own personal misgivings about the suitability of a representative system in Vancouver Island, Douglas got the council to decide on a property qualification for membership in the new Assembly (£300 freehold) and to organize four electoral districts.

Since only 40 property holders got the right to vote, most of the elections outside Victoria were actually nominations. But seven representatives have been chosen, and at their first meeting today Douglas told them what their duties are in the Assembly.

The first Assembly meets in Victoria.

Pressure to annex Rupert's Land grows

Dec. 18, 1856

TORONTO – In the Canadas, the movement to annex Rupert's Land is growing fast. A group of members of the Reform party, now popularly known as Clear Grits, ("grit" is an American term implying firmness of character) has called for annexation, and the British government would be wise to pay attention. The Reformers speak for a broad-based movement widely supported by businessmen, farmers, newspaper editors, radicals, and politicians such as George Brown of the *Globe,* and his new assistant, the clever, idealistic young lawyer, William McDougall.

The businessmen are interested in the virgin lands of the west for settlement, development and profit-making. Some are even interested in the declining fur trade. Others see a railway to the west, through the annexed territory, as carrying in farm settlers and opening up new markets. The radicals champion the Indians, claiming they have been exploited by the Hudson's Bay Company. And the politicians see the HBC as a bastion of privilege that should be destroyed.

Champlain Street below the Citadel in Quebec City. Built hastily and out of wood, the houses in this area often fall victim to major fires.

Editor publishes his first book of poetry

1856

KINGSTON – Newspaper editor Charles Sangster has published his first book of poetry, *The St. Lawrence and the Saguenay and Other Poems*. Sangster, 34, holds the position of sub-editor at Kingston's *British Whig*.

Published in the *Literary Garland* and in this, his first book, Sangster shows a great love of the natural world and an intensely religious nature.

Editor and poet Charles Sangster.

P.E.I. school set to train teachers

Oct. 1, 1856

PRINCE EDWARD ISLAND – Since the Free Education Act of 1852, the number of schools in Prince Edward Island has risen to 268, and student enrolment has grown to 11,000. Last year, however, only about one in five Island children received formal schooling. Perhaps the main problem has been the lack of trained teachers, so today, the colony officially opened a Normal School.

Though it's non-denominational, the school will feature daily prayers and Bible lessons. This appeals to Protestants reluctant to see a "godless, secular education." But it may upset Catholics, who feel religious instruction has no place in a denominationally mixed school system. They also fear their children will be taught from Protestant Bibles.

1857

Longueuil, Canada East, Feb. 10. David Thompson, retired Canadian explorer, fur trader, surveyor and author, dies.

London, Feb. 18. With the HBC trade monopoly in North America due to expire in 1859, a Select Committee of the House of Commons meets to study the HBC and the lands it controls.

Canada West, March 12. The steam engine *Oxford* derails while crossing a swing bridge, plunging 59 people to their deaths in the icy waters of the Desjardins Canal.

Delhi, May 11. Thousands of Indian troops, resentful of British dominance in their country, mutiny against the British army and capture the city of Delhi.

Australia, Aug. 14. New Brunswicker Sam Napier and his brother find one of the world's biggest gold nuggets.

Kekerten, Baffin Island, August. Moravian missionary Mathias Warmow lands and establishes winter quarters to work among the Inuit. He is the first Christian missionary to be stationed on the island.

Lucknow, India, Nov. 16. Black Canadian William Hall acts with exceptional courage while fighting with British troops against Indian mutineers during the Siege of Lucknow, a key battle in keeping India in the Empire.

Canada, Dec. 31. Governor Head is informed that the queen has chosen Ottawa as the future capital of Canada.

Toronto. Lola Montez, a notorious European actress who has fascinated such men as Franz Liszt and King Ludwig I of Bavaria, draws packed houses at the Royal Lyceum theatre.

Canada. Parliament adopts the Matrimonial Causes Act, establishing a double standard for getting a divorce. It says that a husband can get a divorce if his wife is a proven adulterous, but a wife can only get a divorce if her husband is guilty of adultery along with either desertion without reason, extreme cruelty, incest, bigamy, sodomy, or rape.

Nova Scotia. Passenger pigeons are extinguished in the province by humans.

Canada East. The first Normal Schools open in the province.

Canada West. Oil is discovered at Lambton County.

Largest fleet ever gets set for yearly Nfld. seal fishery

Feb. 2, 1857

NEWFOUNDLAND – The largest ever fleet of ships is fitting out for the annual seal fishery. Ever since its beginning more than a half-century ago, the seal fishery has been expanding in spite of several disastrous seasons.

This year it is reported that 370 ships carrying 13,600 sealers will go "to the ice" in search of the seal herds. It is feared, however, that the days of the big profitable voyages are over because the seal herds have been overly exploited and are now in decline.

Palliser to explore vast unknown land

John Palliser and James Hector.

March 3, 1857

LONDON, England – Capt. John Palliser and his party, including geologist James Hector, have left for North America to explore the unknown land from Lake Superior to beyond the Rockies. A 40-year-old Irish bachelor, Palliser spent 1847 and 1848 hunting buffalo in Missouri and thought someone should find out what lay in British territory above the border.

Palliser has no money of his own, but persuaded the Royal Geographic Society to support his plan. When the British government decided to finance the expedition, its terms of reference were expanded to include transcontinental transportation and agriculture.

HBC monopoly on land rights in doubt

May 11, 1857

RED RIVER COLONY, Rupert's Land – Rumors abound in the colony today that a committee of the British House of Commons will inquire into the "general position and prospects" of the Hudson's Bay Company. If true, it could end what western nationalists see as the company's monopoly.

The territory known as Rupert's Land, draining into Hudson Bay, came into HBC possession by charter, but land outside Rupert's Land was secured by a licence which must be renewed every 21 years.

Hudson's Bay Co.'s Cumberland Mission, in the colony of Rupert's Land.

Grand Trunk governs Canada, Globe says

April 22, 1857

TORONTO – "The Grand Trunk Railway governs Canada at the present moment," says today's Toronto *Globe*. As the paper is edited by Reform leader George Brown, who believes the railway to be nothing more than a profit-making scheme for a corrupt government, the charge is hardly surprising. Still, it stands as the fiercest attack by a politician who has tried, fruitlessly and for years, to stop the ever-more expensive railroad.

Fire destroys ship; death toll near 250

June 26, 1857

CAPE ROUGE, Canada East – Some 250 people are feared dead in the wake of a fire that destroyed the river steamer *Montreal.* The ship, which left Quebec City at 5 p.m. yesterday, caught fire off the coast of Cape Rouge. The steamer *Napoleon* gave the crew and its 500 passengers every assistance, saving from 175 to 200 people on board. Capt. J.C. Rudolph and his crew are among those rescued. Most of the passengers were Scottish immigrants who had just landed at Quebec on their way to the west.

Form new cabinet, Macdonald is told

Nov. 26, 1857

TORONTO – John A. Macdonald, nominal head of the defunct Macdonald-Taché government, has been called on to form a new cabinet, now that Etienne-Paschal Taché and three others have resigned. Without a doubt his most important move has been to appoint George-Etienne Cartier as the formal head of the cabinet's Canada East section. He has also selected L.V. Sicotte, N.F. Belleau, and T.J.J. Loranger, ensuring the four vacancies from Canada East have been filled by French-Canadians.

Racial prejudice thrives in the remote northwest

Dec. 28, 1857

VANCOUVER ISLAND – James Douglas is a mulatto, born of Scottish and West Indian parents. He is married to the half-breed daughter of a fur trader. He is also the governor of Vancouver Island. Today he announced stringent regulations to control prospecting in the Crown colony. These measures are being unilaterally imposed to control an expected influx of American gold-seekers. And they are being implemented solely on the authority of Douglas.

That a man of his racial background should achieve near absolute power in the colony is nothing short of remarkable, for it has been achieved in an age and land rife with racial prejudice. That he espouses the manner and form of a stoic, gentrified Englishman has no doubt aided his rise in rank, helping make him an exception to the rule.

A popular belief among colonial officials is that Victorian England has risen above "savagery" and "barbarism" and become the pinnacle of civilization. Popular too is the notion that any product of miscegenation, any child of mixed-blood, is intellectually inferior, the least fit of the fittest.

Sir James Douglas, the governor of Vancouver Island, is the son of a free colored woman. He married the part-Indian daughter of the chief factor.

The half-breed wife of Gov. James Douglas, Lady Amelia, and her family.

In the remote northwest, fur traders often marry Indian or mixed-blood women, producing Country-born or Métis offspring. But still, many of these marriages are informal and are considered temporary aberrations. At Red River, Hudson's Bay Company Gov. George Simpson has concealed his past liaisons with "bits of brown" from his Englishborn wife. He has also discouraged Métis from attempting anything but unskilled labor. Alexander Ross, fur trader and politician, and happily married to an Indian, still considered their 13 children genetically inferior.

While James Douglas has achieved much in the face of similar attitudes, his aloofness is thought to stem from sensitivity over both his and his wife's racial backgrounds.

Bill proposes end to Indian reserves

May 1857

TORONTO – The Canadian Assembly this week debated the new civilization bill, introduced by Attorney General John A. Macdonald, to eliminate the Indian reserves. The bill says any adult male Indian judged to be educated, free from debt, and of good moral character, may apply to be a citizen with the right to vote. If he proves all this during a three-year probation period, he can become a citizen. But he must transfer his land from the reserve into freehold tenure, cease to belong to his band, and sign away his rights as an Indian.

George Brown and Antoine Dorion, Liberal opposition leaders, praise the bill. But other opposition members do not. William Lyon Mackenzie says it aims "to get the lands of the Indians and not to civilize them." Indians contacted, even Christian converts, agree.

Governor issues ordinance declaring goldfields Crown property

Dec 28, 1857

VICTORIA, Vancouver Island – Fears that the mounting gold rush on the Fraser and Thompson rivers might provide the Americans with a pretext for annexing the area have prompted Gov. James Douglas to declare the goldfields Crown property. Douglas today issued an ordinance to that effect.

Already many Americans are moving into the interior mainland, and Douglas fears that if the number of Americans gets much bigger they will take over. The colonial office in London shares his view. But the closest arm of the British government is in Victoria, on Vancouver Island, and Douglas has no power to act in mainland matters – and no troops to keep order.

Religious teaching stirs Island battle

Sept. 7, 1857

PRINCE EDWARD ISLAND – The battle lines are hardening over religious instruction in Island schools. While Protestants want compulsory morning Bible readings, Catholics say their children "shall not kneel in prayer under a master not of their own creed." The Liberal government is caught in the middle. If it refuses the call, it will be accused of "outlawing the Bible." If it concedes, it stands to lose its large Catholic base.

Dec. 31, 1857: A view of Ottawa, which colonial officials announced today as Queen Victoria's choice to be the capital of the Province of Canada.

1858

Prince Edward Island, Feb. 19. At a "Great Protestant Meeting" attended by evangelicals, speakers say they will work to defeat politicians who do not support compulsory Bible study in schools.

Victoria, April 25. The *Commodore* arrives from San Francisco with 450 gold-seekers en route to the Fraser Valley, more than doubling the town's population. The town has no hotels, so the newcomers turn it into a sea of tents.

Toronto, July. Alexander Galt introduces resolutions in the Assembly calling for a federal union of British North America. Members agree in principle, but don't think union is possible at this time.

Toronto, July 29. The government led by John A. Macdonald and George-Etienne Cartier resigns after being defeated in the House over its plans to move the Assembly to Ottawa.

Toronto, Aug. 4. A non-confidence motion forces the resignation of the government of George Brown and Antoine-Aimé Dorion only two days after they are sworn in.

Toronto, Aug. 6. A government led by George-Etienne Cartier and John A. Macdonald is sworn in, only a week after they resigned.

Atlantic, Sept. 2. The first transatlantic telegraph cable running from Britain to the U.S. via Newfoundland breaks down after only 28 days of operation.

Montreal, Nov. 10. The remains of John Rowand, an Edmonton fur trader, are finally buried four years after his death. He died while travelling to Montreal, where he wished to be buried. When HBC Governor George Simpson heard of his wish, he had Rowand's body shipped to Montreal.

Victoria, Dec. 31. Some 10,000-20,000 Americans have come to Victoria in the last seven months, most of them on their way to the mainland to look for gold. Some of them stay in the town to speculate on land or open businesses.

Montreal. Photographer William Notman documents the construction of the Victoria Bridge across the St. Lawrence, the longest tubular bridge in the world.

Sackville, N.B. Mount Allison University allows women to attend classes.

Gold rush lures thousands to B.C.

Hudson's Bay Company ship the SS Beaver brings gold-seekers to B.C.

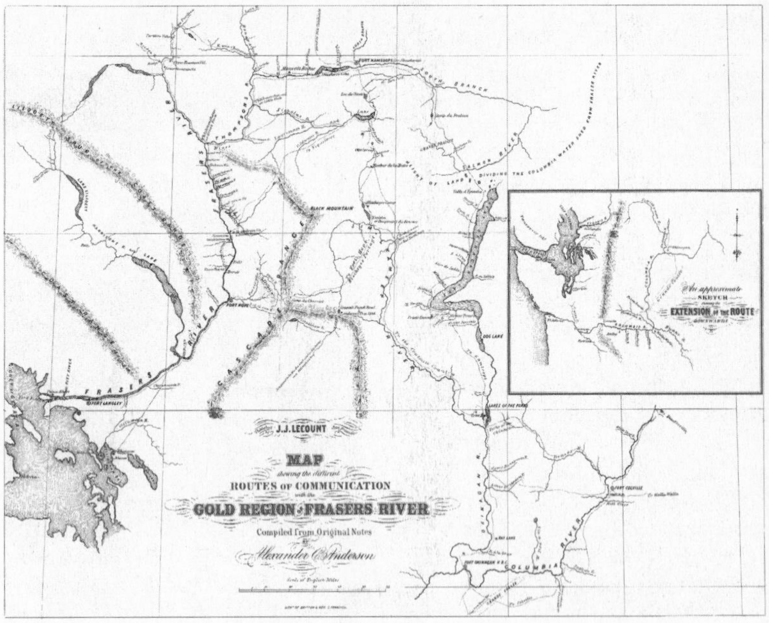

Map published this year details gold region of the Fraser and Thompson rivers.

Gold country just too much to resist

March 5, 1858

OLYMPIA, Wash. – Some sensational headlines in the local *Pioneer and Democrat* newspaper here about gold discoveries on the Fraser River have touched off a serious case of gold fever. Men are leaving jobs and families to board ships heading north up the coast to "gold country." There are reports of soldiers and sailors deserting their posts to join the rush. Not since the famous California rush of 1849 has excitement been so intense.

Rumors of gold discoveries are nothing new. Miners have been working on the Thompson River for at least two seasons, and Indians along the Fraser River commonly trade gold dust with the Hudson's Bay Company. However, just last month the HBC shipped 22 kilograms of gold to the mint in San Francisco, where the fever is also building, and gold-seekers are convinced that this time the rumors will turn out to be true.

Panning popular among the prospectors

August 1858

FORT YALE, B.C. – Along the banks of the Fraser and Thompson rivers and their tributaries, thousands of prospectors are panning nuggets of gold from the sand and gravel that have hidden them for centuries. This type of mining requires little capital, and, for equipment, only a pan to wash the river gravel – and a strong back. The product of panning is usually small flecks and tiny nuggets of gold, but the ease of extraction means a day's work can be worthwhile. As the river banks and bars are cleaned out, miners must move slowly upriver to seek new deposits. There are fewer finds but the size of the gold fragments is bigger.

Americans come north in search of wealth

Nov. 30, 1858

VICTORIA, Vancouver Island – Officials here, overwhelmed by the rush of gold miners through the city, estimate that about 27,000 men have left goldfields in the United States to join the search for gold on the Fraser. The news of the gold find first reached the California fields in the spring. Since most of the miners there were finding it harder to get a good haul, they quickly began to head north on ships from San Francisco. Between May 15 and June 1, at least 10,000 men started up the Fraser.

B.C. system for licensing mine operations comes into effect

February 1858

VICTORIA, Vancouver Island – James Douglas, the governor of Vancouver Island, has vested ownership of the goldfields on the mainland in the Crown. Starting today, miners will have to buy a licence from Victoria costing 21 shillings ($5) a month.

Douglas suggested this course of action when gold was first found in the Queen Charlotte Islands, but he was refused power to act. Then, last year, Douglas showed some gold from the Thompson River to his officials in Victoria. And while he warned London that there might be trouble, with thousands of Americans travelling north to the goldfields on the mainland, he got little support. So, last December, Douglas decided to protect British interests and forestall a possible annexation by the Americans.

Douglas issued an ordinance last Dec. 28 declaring the goldfields Crown property – even though he was exceeding his powers. Next day came the licensing ordinance that comes into effect today.

Maritimes will be asked to consider union with Canada

Aug. 16, 1858

TORONTO – Strange parliamentary events have preceded today's announcement by Gov. Gen. Sir Edmund Walker Head that the Maritime provinces will be asked to join in federation with the United Province of Canada. Only 10 days ago, the government responsible for this overture, led by John A. Macdonald and George-Etienne Cartier, was sworn into office. One week before, the same administration had resigned.

This political flip-flopping has provoked great anger, most notably from Liberal George Brown. Although the resignation occurred after a plan to move Parliament to Ottawa was rejected, some consider July's introduction of a plan for confederation as the root cause of the government's collapse. While most approve the proposal in principle, many believe it is premature and wish to see it dropped for now.

Overthrow of U.S. government planned

May 8, 1858

CHATHAM, Canada West – Old John Brown has a lot of gumption! Now in his late 50s, the fanatical Kansas abolitionist thinks he can overthrow the American government and the whole slavery system along with it. Tonight he held a secret meeting at the British Methodist Episcopal Church to outline his outrageously daring plans to attack the arsenal at Harper's Ferry, Virginia, arm his men, and proceed south to outmuscle the American government and set himself up as provisional ruler. As the meeting drew to a close, Reverend Walter Toyer, who let Brown use the church, rose to withdraw his support and warned his flock to have nothing to do with Brown's plans "in case they ended this life before a firing squad."

It doesn't look like people here are taking Toyer's advice. Since Brown hit town nine days ago with 13 supporters, local blacks, many escaped American slaves, have welcomed him with open hearts. He is staying at the home of James Bell, a well known black writer. Others have signed up to fight alongside Brown at Harper's Ferry. Appropriately enough, Brown has been drilling his men at Tecumseh Park, named after the great Indian leader who fought against the Americans during the War of 1812. Friends say Brown has turned into an "old man" since he started his crusade.

Brown conducts meeting in church.

Bishop condemns Institut Canadien

March 3, 1858

MONTREAL – Bishop Ignace Bourget has attacked the Institut Canadien, a young man's literary and public affairs club, accusing it of disseminating "bad books, lying publications and irreligious discourses." The charges are contained in a pastoral letter from the conservative top bishop in Montreal.

The institute has been heading for a collision with Bourget since it opened its doors in 1844 to offer French-Canadian youths a place to read, hear lectures and host debates. Among its 700 members are Dr. Louis-Antoine Dessaulles, a nephew of Reformer Louis-Joseph Papineau, and Eric Dorion, brother of Antoine-Aimé Dorion, leader of the Rouge party. The institute has a reputation for encouraging free thinking and speech. Bourget is reportedly incensed by the group's tolerance of non-Catholic opinion, including reading matter, prompting him to issue his letter denouncing the Institut Canadien.

"Conductor" Harriet Tubman back in U.S.

1858

CANADA WEST – Harriet Tubman has moved back to the United States after an illustrious career as a "conductor" on the "underground railway" bringing escaped slaves from the American south to Canada. The underground railway is a route fugitive slaves use to flee from former masters. The "tracks" are lined with abolitionists who shelter slaves from the clutches of authorities trying to return them to bondage.

An escaped slave herself, in 1851 Mrs. Tubman moved to St. Catharines, Canada West, which she has used as a base as she guides slaves to the province. On her 15 or so trips to the south, Mrs. Tubman has rescued more than 300 slaves. There are almost none left in her home town of Bucktown, Maryland, since most escaped with Mrs. Tubman's help or inspiration. Her elderly parents are among those she helped to freedom.

American governments are not at all happy about her accomplishments, not to mention the rash of escapes. Southern states placed an incredible bounty of $40,000 on her head, and the federal government passed the harsh Fugitive Slave Bill in 1850, an attempt to ensure swift return of all escaped slaves to their owners. Mrs. Tubman has this to say: "I wouldn't trust Uncle Sam with my people no longer. ... I brought 'em all clar of to Canada."

Harriet Tubman, a former slave.

Canada to have its own currency soon

Dec. 10, 1858

CANADA – The province will soon have its own money. To trade with the United States and to finally remove the confusion over the value of money, Canadian decimal currency will replace pounds and shillings. To make this change, silver 5, 10 and 20 cent pieces will be minted. This move stems from the Currency Act of 1854 which demonetized all foreign coins except British gold and silver, and American gold coins, which were valued at 1841 rates. An 1857 law says all government accounts should be recorded in dollars and cents, ending the use of sterling.

A 20-cent piece: Canadian decimal currency will replace pounds and shillings. ▷

British Columbia gets colonial status

Nov. 19, 1858

FORT LANGLEY, B.C. – It has rained all day here and the ceremony inaugurating the Hudson's Bay Company's James Douglas as first governor of the mainland colony of British Columbia has been forced indoors. Parliament in London created the government of British Columbia in August, and Queen Victoria then appointed Douglas – governor of the enlarged colony of Vancouver Island – its first governor.

Many British politicians – and quite a few people on Vancouver Island, where Douglas has governed for five years – fear he will be in conflict of interest. His resignation from the HBC was a condition of his appointment, but Douglas's critics fear this will not be enough.

At any rate, Douglas came to his inauguration in style. He left Victoria on the Royal Navy's *HMS Satellite*. With him were Rear Admiral Barnes, David Cameron, the chief justice of Vancouver Island, and Matthew Begbie, who recently arrived from England to be the first judge of the new colony. Douglas transferred to the Hudson's Bay Company ship the *SS Otter* and travelled the last few kilometres in the historic *Beaver,* the first steamship on the Pacific coast.

A crowd of about 100 heard Douglas give Begbie his judge's commission. Begbie then read the royal commission making Douglas governor. Douglas announced that the special privileges of his old company had been revoked, and then proclaimed the new colony.

James Douglas leaves Fort Langley after being inaugurated as B.C. governor.

Amor De Cosmos starts new paper

October 1858

VICTORIA, Vancouver Island – The benevolent despot of Vancouver Island, Gov. James Douglas, has another critic. He calls himself Amor De Cosmos – Lover of the World – though he was born William Smith in Nova Scotia. De Cosmos has started *The British Colonist*, a weekly newspaper dedicated to winning responsible government.

De Cosmos has a long, black beard and piercing eyes. He is tall, so obsessed by politics he has few other interests, and plans to use his paper to gain political power. De Cosmos, who recently left the California goldfields, promises to fight for responsible government.

Amor De Cosmos launches paper.

Pass named after bucking bronco attack

Aug. 29, 1858

ROCKY MOUNTAIN HOUSE, Rupert's Land – Dr. James Hector, the 24-year-old geologist with Capt. John Palliser's expedition, was almost killed while exploring a pass through the Rockies. Reports reaching here state that Hector's horse stumbled in a stream in the mountains and then kicked him in the chest. When his Indian guides, believing he was dead, laid him in a shallow grave, Hector managed to wink at them, and they quickly pulled him out. In great pain, Hector forced himself to get on his horse, for everyone in the party was exhausted and short of food. At the next camp the men decided Kicking Horse Pass would be an appropriate name for the pass, considering the accident.

The Palliser expedition includes Hector, a British Army Crimean War veteran, the French botanical collector Eugène Bourgeau, and Thomas Blakiston, a magnetical observer. The group left England last year to explore this western territory. One of its tasks is to see if it is possible to build a railway linking the Atlantic and Pacific coasts. Hector, for one, believes it is not.

New this year: Stamps with perforations to ease separation.

Cattle herd arrives at B.C. destination

August 1858

FORT KAMLOOPS, B.C. – The miners in the goldfields are going to get their beef. Gen. Joel Palmer has just arrived near here with a herd of cattle and wagons pulled by oxen. Palmer is originally from Upper Canada. He emigrated to Oregon and wrote the standard book of advice for would-be settlers there. He heard about the goldfields from miners travelling through Oregon, and realized that whoever could feed thousands of miners would make lots of money.

Palmer and his men gathered their cattle and wagons in Washington territory in June. They followed the Okanagan River and worked their way up the west coast of Okanagan Lake, and then struck east to open land near here. The cattle are grazing now, and after selling them Palmer will go back for another herd next year.

Keeping the peace on governor's mind

August 1858

VICTORIA, Vancouver Island – Officials here estimate there are about 10,000 miners at work in the goldfields on the nearby mainland – many of them Americans – and want to ensure that no Indian wars take place. The violence that has accompanied the movement of settlers and miners into the American west has not been seen here, and Gov. James Douglas is determined to see that it is avoided. He has considered using marines to keep the peace, but it seems that London favors a mainland government.

Hind and Dawson explore northwest for Canada

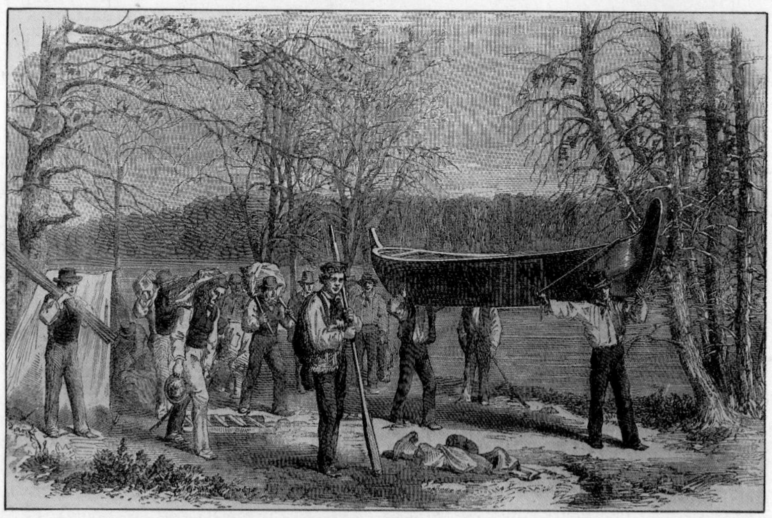

While exploring the northwest, Henry Hind's party draws upon the skills and knowledge of Iroquois guide Charlot Skanasah, pictured in the foreground.

On the banks of Red River: Assiniboine and Saskatchewan exploration.

1858

RUPERT'S LAND – Geologist Henry Hind and civil engineer S.J. Dawson have been sent out by the Canadian government to explore the northwest with an eye to the feasibility of a transport link from Canada which does not entail entering the United States. The only route at present is by water and trail. Hind will also report on conditions pertaining to agriculture and settlement.

So far Hind has suggested that a connection could be made between the Qu'Appelle and South Saskatchewan rivers by diverting the water, thus making a navigable shortcut. He has also found two distinct land types. One is an arc of good soil that runs from the Red River northwest to the Sasktchewan River valley and on to the mountains. The other is a triangular area that extends from the United States into the prairies. This he reports to be quite arid and desert-like.

Doing similar explorations and having similar findings to date is John Palliser, who is working for the British government.

Canadian pols ponder Maritime question

Sept. 9, 1858

TORONTO – Should the Maritime provinces join Canada, and form a federation of British North American states? That question is being pondered by British North American politicians and Gov. Gen. Sir Edmund Walker Head.

In fact, Head has gone beyond musing. On behalf of all concerned, he's asked the British colonial office to authorize a meeting of colonial delegates to consider "the subject of Federative Union, and reporting on the principles on which the same could be properly based."

Strong winds put a damper on canoe race

Sept. 17, 1858

GORE'S LANDING, Rice Lake – If it had been a sailing race, the winds would have been welcome. Instead, the gale force winds and rough waters seen today at Gore's Landing pretty well washed out the event. Only two competitors, using heavy dugout canoes made from single logs, were able to compete.

There was one highlight: a new design of canoe built by John Stephenson of Peterborough. The Peterborough canoe, made out of cedar wood stripes and canvas, is strong, flexible, yet easy to portage.

Reformer Baldwin meets a quiet end

Dec. 9, 1858

TORONTO – Robert Baldwin, one of the architects of responsible government in Canada, died today at his family home in Spadina. It was a quiet end for the Canada West politician who, by giving French Reformer Louis-Hippolyte LaFontaine his parliamentary seat in 1841, forged the French-English Reform coalition in Canada. That coalition managed to move a reluctant British government to granting responsible government. Baldwin was co-premier of Canada with LaFontaine in 1842-43 and 1848-51.

Hamilton to build a replica of the glass-walled Crystal Palace

Oct. 30, 1858

HAMILTON – The city will construct a scaled-down version of London's glass-walled Crystal Palace, which in 1851 housed an exhibition so successful it spawned replicas throughout North America.

Hamilton, in the midst of a recession, won the right to hold an exhibit after two local members of the legislature fought legislation limiting fairs to London, Kingston and Toronto. One MP says the fair will "prevent property from going further wrong in value." Unlike the Toronto glass building inspired but not copied from the Crystal Palace, Hamilton wants an exact replica.

Toronto's Crystal Palace, inspired by, but not a replica of, the London version.

1859

Perth, Canada West, Jan. 25. The first train on the Brockville & Ottawa railway line arrives from Brockville after a nine-and-a-half hour trip that was supposed to take three-and-a-half hours.

Victoria, British Columbia, Jan. 26. The Philharmonic Society, a group specializing in choral music, holds its first meeting.

Prince Edward Island, March 19. Conservatives defeat the incumbent Liberals in a provincial election thanks to support from evangelical Protestants in favor of compulsory Bible study in schools.

Victoria, British Columbia, April 25. The first black settlers in the colony arrive.

Fort Simpson, HBC Territory, June. The arrival of York boats with supplies is greeted with wild parties. Priests call the fort the "Babylon of the North," and "Devil's Island."

Prince Edward Island, July. The Island's streets are lighted by gas for the first time. Gas lighting was installed in houses and shops in 1854.

Harpers Ferry, Virginia, October. John Brown is captured after leading a raid on a government arsenal, the first step in a plan to seize the American government and overturn the slavery system. He planned the raid from Chatham, Canada West.

British Columbia, Nov. 3. As instructed by the colonial office, Governor Douglas revokes the HBC's exclusive trade licence for B.C., making the area a Crown colony.

London, November. Charles Darwin publishes the *Origin of Species by Means of Natural Selection*, in which he argues that species evolve into other species by mutation from a common ancestor. The controversial book sells well.

Canada. The legislature gives legal recognition to homeopathic medical practitioners and creates the first Homeopathic Medical Board.

Canada. The province establishes a Board of Prisons, Asylums, and Public Charities to look after social welfare.

Canada. Until 1859, some 230 offences are punishable by death in Canada under British law. They include treason, rape, murder, stealing turnips, being found disguised in a forest, and unlawful abuse of a girl under 10.

Grand Trunk hails railway's opening of the Sarnia link

January 1859

SARNIA – Now that the Grand Trunk Railway's main line has been finished to this city at the mouth of the St. Clair River, the 1,282-kilometre route from here to Portland, Maine is almost complete. The only interruption is at Montreal, where a 3.2-kilometre bridge across the St. Lawrence River is expected to be completed late this year. The significance of the Sarnia link is that this centre is Canada's closest shipping port to Chicago, a major United States city and port.

Incorporated in 1852 by Parliament, the Grand Trunk grew to this proportion after original intentions were only to link Hamilton and Toronto with Montreal. But former prime minister Sir Francis Hincks and his government pushed for the extension to Sarnia. Construction of the line has not been without problems. Subcontractors east of Toronto often treated their workers poorly. They endured bad working conditions and sometimes did not get paid, or when they did, it was in supplies from the company store. Deaths from cholera occurred and strikes were frequent.

Law allows wives to own property

1859

CANADA WEST – Married women in Canada West may now own property, thanks to a new law giving them more financial freedom from their husbands. Although women still cannot sell common property, a wife's consent is now required before her husband does so.

The law, similar to a British proposal and a New York law, follows concern in cases where drunken or neglectful husbands could dispose of a woman's earnings, savings and other assets. A petition supporting the legislation notes that lower-class women are hardest hit by common law which deprives them "of all pecuniary resources." Early drafts of the law included permission for married women to keep their own earnings.

New Brunswicker invents steam foghorn

1859

SAINT JOHN, N.B. – Saint John engineer T.T. Vernon-Smith has been granted permission to erect a coded steam foghorn on Partridge Island. The apparatus will be the first one installed anywhere in the world, and will undoubtedly save countless lives by permitting navigators to distinguish the location of each alarm bell, previously impossible.

But Smith's technical coup is a bitter one for Robert Foulis, the foghorn's real inventor. In 1854, Foulis applied to the Commissioners of Light for permission to install it on the island. Last year, commissioner Isaac Woodworth gave Foulis's plans to Smith, who altered and claimed the design engineering genius Foulis had invented.

Robert Foulis, Maritime inventor.

Fire destroys downtown core of Halifax

Sept. 9, 1859

HALIFAX – Fire destroyed the heart of this wooden city's commercial district today. The blaze roared along Granville Street, and consumed dozens of buildings, including shops of jewellers, furriers, tailors, haberdashers, and china merchants. Yesterday, Granville was Halifax's finest avenue; today, it's a smouldering ruin. Between Duke and Buckingham streets, there remains hardly a building.

The city had barely recovered from the New Year's Day inferno of 1857, which wiped out much of nearby Hollis Street. That fire razed Mather's Church, first used by dissenters among the Yankee immigrants of a century ago.

A view of Halifax after the great fire that destroyed its commercial district.

Construction ends on the Victoria Bridge

Dec. 17, 1859

MONTREAL – Today Montreal notables celebrated the opening of the Victoria Bridge by riding a train across the "world's eighth wonder," a link in the Toronto-to-Montreal stretch of the Grand Trunk Railway. The bridge took 3,000 workers, including Mohawks from nearby Caughnawaga, five years to finish. Floating dams anchor it to the St. Lawrence floor.

San Juan dispute heats up; 60 U.S. soldiers on island

July 27, 1859

VICTORIA, Vancouver Island – Sixty American soldiers have landed on San Juan Island, between Vancouver Island and the American mainland. There is talk of war with the United States here because the ownership of the island is in dispute and the Americans have seized the advantage. The trouble began when a pig belonging to a Hudson's Bay Company farm on the island got into an American settler's garden. He shot it and the company demanded compensation.

Queensborough is site of new capital

First government offices in mainland British Columbia at Queensborough.

Feb. 14, 1859

VICTORIA, Vancouver Island – Gov. James Douglas has accepted the proposal of Col. Richard Moody, of the Royal Engineers, and has picked a site for a new capital on the Fraser River, about 32 kilometres from the sea. He calls the site Queensborough, but everyone expects a new name will be chosen soon.

The selection of Queensborough over Derby – the old Fort Langley – has angered many people who bought lots around the old fort at a sale Douglas ordered. Moody said he selected the Queensborough site because it is easily defended.

Clergymen to sing the temperance blues

April 1859

RICHMOND HILL, Canada West – Choirs will be singing the works of the masters, and when they take a break the clergy will be singing the blues about the evils of drinking alcoholic beverages. The movement for temperance in Canada West has taken to music. Next Wednesday, choirs from St. Paul's Church and St. Michael's Cathedral of Toronto will sing at the Roman Catholic church here, but the real purpose is to provide a forum for a temperance lecture at intermission by Rev. Ouelette of St. Michael's.

The temperance movement has its roots in the United States, but it spread into Canada in the second quarter of the 1800s. Prompted by brawling and family abuse blamed on drunkenness, temperance societies have been appearing in growing numbers in Canada West this decade. They have provided many with entertainment and a social outlet. But they have also had a more practical impact, brought on by problems in frontier life. For instance, fear that barns were not the only things getting high at barn raisings, has prompted some groups to abolish liquor at bees.

GRAND MUSICAL

ENTERTAINMENT

Will take place at RICHMOND HILL, on the Evening of Easter Wednesday, the 27th APRIL, 1859, at 7 30, p.m.

A number of Pieces from the best Masters will be performed by several Ladies and Gentlemen of the Choirs of St. Michael's Cathedral and St. Paul's Church, of Toronto, particulars of which will be given in a Programme.

During the intervals a Lecture on

TEMPERANCE!

Will be delivered by the Rev. Mr. OUELETTE, Rector of St. Michael's Cathedral, and

PIECES RECITED by Several Children

Selected for the occasion. Arrangements will be made in the

RICHMOND HILL ROMAN CATHOLIC

CHURCH, for the purpose, and no pains spared to make it a Highly Instructive and Moral Entertainment.

To meet expenses the following admission fees will be charged: Adults, 37½ cts.; Children, 12½ cts.

RICHMOND HILL, April 21, 1859.

PRINTED AT THE YORK HERALD OFFICE, RICHMOND HILL.

Announcement of entertainment event to help sell Canadians on temperance.

Early treatment for insane said to be vital

January 1859

TORONTO – "Denying to the insane the benefits of early treatment is very erroneous public economy," says the medical superintendent of the Provincial Lunatic Asylum at Toronto. In his annual report to the legislature, the superintendent decries the underfunding of the mental health care system, saying that, if early treatment were available, three of four insanity patients could be cured. Canada West has 250 new cases a year.

Abolitionist hangs for treason and murder

Dec. 2, 1859

CHARLESTOWN, West Virginia – John Brown, a Kansas abolitionist who planned to overthrow the American government and the slavery system from Canada, was hanged here today after being convicted of treason and murder. Brown was captured after leading an unsuccessful raid on Harper's Ferry. Some Canadians see him as a martyr to freedom.

Last records of Franklin expedition found

Aug. 10, 1859

BELLOT STRAIT, Arctic – Francis McClintock and his crew sailed for home today after finding written records concerning the fate of the Franklin expedition, missing since 1845 when they entered Lancaster Sound to look for the Northwest Passage.

McClintock's men found two notes the expedition wrote. One, dated May 1847, reports all is well. The other, found by William Hobson on King William Island, tells of John Franklin's death on June 11, 1847, the expedition's discovery of the Northwest Passage, and their abandoning their ships in 1848. Many expeditions have tried to discover the fate of Franklin's voyage.

Relics of the Franklin expedition.

Steamer chugs into Red River land

Steamer the Anson Northup, the first stern-wheel, steam-powered vessel to navigate the waters of the Red River from Minnesota to the Red River colony.

Anson Northup, the ship's owner.

June 10, 1859

RED RIVER COLONY, Rupert's Land – Modern technology has arrived! The unfamiliar sound of a steamer's whistle sent residents of Fort Garry scurrying to the banks of the Red River today. In the distance there was the odd shape of a stern-wheeler chugging its way toward the settlement's docks, a sight never before seen in this remote part of the northwest.

The captain and crew of the *Anson Northup* are being given a hero's welcome, and deservedly so – their feat unprecedented and extraordinary. They dismantled the steamer last year, transported it 240 kilometres overland, then reassembled it on the Red. Success of the enterprise pleases the Hudson's Bay Company – the transportation of goods from the hinterland will now cost less and be faster than ever.

Future of Canada is front-and-centre as Reformers meet

Nov. 9, 1859

TORONTO – Today, some 600 delegates from across Canada West descended on Toronto for the convention of the opposition Reform party. Many issues are on the agenda, such as the party's desire for "Rep by Pop"; that is, "representation by population" in Parliament, which would give Canada West a majority voice, rather than the current equal division of seats between Canadas East and West.

But the issue expected to dominate the convention, and perhaps split the party, is the fate of the United Province of Canada. The moderates – like party leader George Brown – want the union replaced with a federation, recreating the two separate Canadas East and West, bound to each other by a central government. But other, more radical, voices want outright dissolution, with each province left to go its own way.

First black elected to a public office

1859

RALEIGH TOWNSHIP, Canada West – Abraham Doras Shadd has been elected to the Raleigh town council, becoming the first black to hold public office in British North America. Shadd fled the United States with his family shortly after the American Fugitive Slave Bill was passed in 1850. He began farming in Raleigh Township, Kent County, and actively campaigned against racism and slavery while in his adopted country. He has also worked with fellow black settlers to establish Masonic lodges throughout the region.

Kent County is the centre of the abolition movement in Canada West. The principal town, Chatham, was the terminus point of the "underground railway." Close to 2,000 blacks now live there. But, even in Chatham, blacks are still often made to feel like second-class citizens, banned from many hotels and other public places simply because of their color.

Bylaw to protect "public moral" in Perth

Dec. 23, 1859

PERTH COUNTY, Canada West – Perth's county council passed a bylaw this week containing 24 provisions designed for the "preservation of public moral." Woe be to all those who enjoy a bet at the horse races or gambling tables, or who frequent dens of "ill-fame." Such activities shall be tolerated no more, on any day of the week. As for Sundays? Well, forget about fishing, hunting, marbles, cricket, skittles, ball, racket, footraces, dancing "or any noisy game." Nice to know that with work also prohibited, one should at least have plenty of free time.

This is the scene of an accident on the G.W. Railway, near Dundas, Canada West, the morning of March 19, 1859. Seven people died in the accident, caused by an embankment having been washed away by recent rains.

Island legislature shoots down union

April 12, 1859

PRINCE EDWARD ISLAND – Today's throne speech suggests the possibility of a meeting to consider a union of British North American colonies. The suggestion was noted, and declined. Though Canadians seem keenly interested in such a union, Islanders are less than enthusiastic. Declaring the issue involves "interests of too extensive a character" to permit proper discussion, the Assembly has refused to consider it during the current session.

The legislature's lukewarm response reflects the present political climate. This session promises to turn on the bitter schools question, and the need to negotiate an end to the colony's leasehold land tenure system. Even if these issues were not so pressing, the Assembly has little desire to court union with Canada. The colony is enjoying unprecedented autonomy and a booming economy. Union, many feel, may threaten both.

Nova Scotia native gets Victoria Cross

Oct. 28, 1859

QUEENSTOWN HARBOR – Able Seaman William Hall, born in Horton, N.S., today became the first black decorated with the prestigious Victoria Cross. Hall joined the Royal Navy in 1852, and on Nov. 16, 1857, played a vital role in the defeat of 30,000 Sepoy rebels at Lucknow, India. Hall entered the fray after volunteering to serve with a heavy-artillery gun crew laying siege to a rebel-held mosque. Moving to within 18 metres of the fortification, the gun-crew was decimated by constant enemy fire. Single-handedly Hall maintained a barrage that collapsed a section of wall and enabled troops to successfully storm the position.

Able Seaman William Hall has been decorated with the Victoria Cross.

Tightrope walker takes on Niagara

Aug. 19, 1859

NIAGARA FALLS – French tightrope walker Blondin, who is renowned for performances above the Niagara Gorge, raised the stakes of terror today when he crossed between the Canadian and American sides with his manager on his back.

About 100,000 people turned out to see the daredevil carry Harry Colcord along 300 metres of five-centimetre wide rope, at a height of 45 metres above the churning waters with no net below. It was a tense crossing, but they made it.

First Red River paper moves by mail

Dec. 28, 1859

FORT GARRY, Red River Territory – The first edition of *The Nor'Wester*, the Red River's first newspaper, has appeared just in time to catch today's mail packet. *The Nor'Wester*, to appear every two weeks, already has several subscribers paying $3 annually. Delivering it to them won't cost its editors William Coldwell and William Buckingham a cent – to encourage the new paper, the Council of Assiniboia has granted all Red River newspapers free postage.

Getting *The Nor'Wester* out was no easy task. Last night editors Buckingham and Coldwell wetted down their newsprint, then awoke this morning to find it had frozen solid overnight. Somehow, they still managed to produce a four-page paper, 22 by 15 inches. This first issue has more advertisements than news, with businesses in St. Paul supplying more than half, and Toronto and local merchants the rest.

News-wise, *The Nor'Wester* offers local and foreign news, and miscellaneous tidbits. The King of Siam has named his son George Washington, for instance.

Editorially, the paper announces that "the time has arrived when this fertile and magnificent country, thrown open to the people of all lands, needs an exponent of its opinion, its feeling, its varied yet common interests, through the medium of the Press."

The Nor'-Wester.

Red River's The Nor'Wester.

William Coldwell, paper's co-editor.

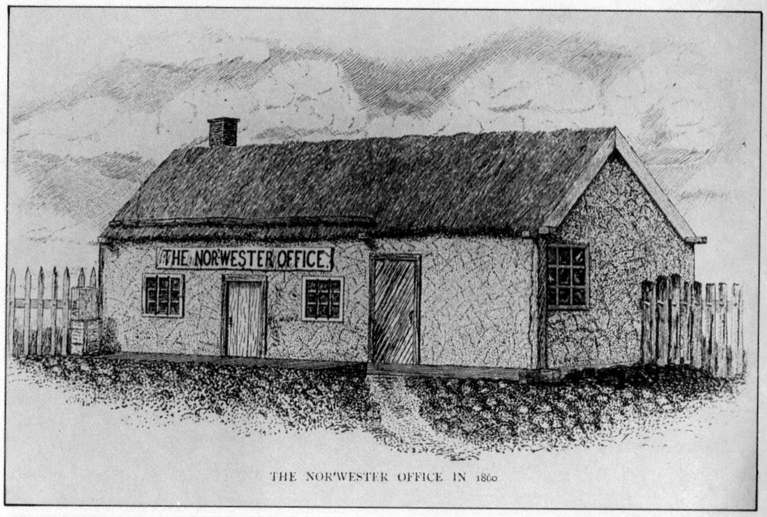

The Nor'Wester office building, situated in Red River territory.

Curator set to lead expedition to north

April 28, 1859

CHICAGO – Robert Kennicott, the museum curator at Northwestern University, has agreed to lead an expedition to look at the wildlife of the sub-Arctic. Kennicott was approached by Spencer Fullerton Baird of the Smithsonian Institution.

High hopes are held for this expedition, for Gov. George Simpson of the Hudson's Bay Company is expected to make certain that Kennicott's party can travel with fur brigades and use company posts in the Mackenzie and Yukon areas as their bases.

Sod turned for new legislature buildings

Dec. 20, 1859

OTTAWA – After years of political wrangling, the sod has been officially turned on the site of the new legislature buildings in Ottawa. It's a ceremony that would have been inconceivable just a year ago. Then, the ruling Macdonald-Taché ministry, under Sir John A. Macdonald, was defeated on this issue by George Brown, leader of the opposition "Clear Grits." But now John A. is prime minister once more, and Ottawa, the personal choice of Queen Victoria herself, has become the capital of Canada.

Newspaper editors form Canadian Press

Sept. 27, 1859

KINGSTON – A group of leading newspaper editors has come together to form the Canadian Press Association. The men have elected Hamilton *Spectator* editor and owner William Gillespie as their president, while a nine-person executive has also been chosen. Although the association includes only 17 men right now, the group believes a time will come when the Canadian Press membership will number in the hundreds.

1860

San Juan Island, Far West, March. British marines land to take up joint occupation of the island with American troops according to an agreement between the two countries involved in a boundary dispute in the area.

St. John's, Newfoundland, July. The Prince of Wales visits the colony on the first leg of a royal visit to British North America. He is very friendly with Catholics in St. John's, leading the Protestant Orange Order in Canada to expect special treatment as well.

Portsmouth, England, Nov. 20. An expedition led by Francis Mclintock returns after surveying the depth of the Atlantic and nature of the bottom between the Faroe Islands and Labrador in preparation for the laying of a transatlantic telegraph cable.

Brockville, Canada West, Dec. 31. The Brockville Tunnel under the town – Canada's first railway tunnel – opens.

Canada. During his visit to Canada, the Prince of Wales becomes interested in a young Six Nations Indian named Oronhyatekha and invites him to study in England.

Montreal. Photographer William Notman records the royal visit of the Prince of Wales as he open the Victoria Bridge. Notman also habitually roams the streets looking for interesting subjects.

Canada. Seventeen-year-old George Beers establishes the first set of rules for lacrosse. He is the goalkeeper in a lacrosse game played before the Prince of Wales.

Hamilton. The Prince of Wales opens a steam-powered pumping station. It provides clean water, so it helps prevent cholera, and makes fire insurance less expensive because plentiful water is now available from hydrants.

Newfoundland. The last 30 years have been prosperous for the sealing industry. Some 13 million seals have been landed, and maybe twice that many have been killed.

Canada. There are 10 railways in Canada. In Canada West, there are 2,226 kilometres of track, most on the Grand Trunk and Great Western lines.

Toronto. The city has more people who are Irish by birth than English. Most of the Irish are Protestants.

Gold rush heats up in the Cariboo

Minnesota man poses with tools of a gold miner, down to the bag of gold.

Fall 1860

LYTTON, B.C. – Gold miners have moved east from the Quesnel River to the hills around Cariboo and Quesnel lakes. The rush to the Cariboo began last year when a Chilcotin Indian told miner Peter Dunleavy there was gold east of Lac La Hache. Dunleavy took the Indian's advice and was soon panning gold on the Horsefly River. Benjamin McDonald, also a miner, found plenty of gold around the same time in the gravel of the Quesnel. Then, as miners followed the gold trail, some big strikes were made. The news brought a stampede of dance hall girls, tavern-keepers, barbers and gamblers to a settlement called Keithley Creek.

News of these finds in the Cariboo region has reached the United States, and is expected to reach England and Europe soon, and then more miners and hangers-on can be expected. The gold nuggets are larger than those found down river, leading the miners to believe they are close to the mother lode.

American union founds local in Canada

1860

CANADA – The Iron Moulders is the first American union to found a local in Canada. Canadians may find membership opens job opportunities for them in the United States. At the same time, they can improve the Iron Moulders status by increasing its numbers. Last year, the first international union, the British Amalgamated Society of Engineers, also enlisted Canadians.

Entrepreneur staking his future on oil

1860

HAMILTON – Canada's first oil well is open in Petrolia. Sensing the potential for oil as a lubricant and for lamps, Hamilton entrepreneur James Miller Williams has decided to stake his future on oil, even though no one is sure of its potential or how to effectively recover, refine and transport it.

Williams entered the oil business when he acquired the "gum beds" used to produce asphalt near Oil Springs from the Tripp Brothers in 1857. The Tripps' asphalt earned honorable mention at an exhibition in Paris, but they were unable to finance their firm. Williams has the money, and has opened a refinery in Hamilton.

Photograph of oil wells at Petrolia.

Legislature opens in a "bird cage"

March 3, 1860

VICTORIA, Vancouver Island – The transformation of this community from frontier fort to colonial capital became reality today. The Legislative Assembly opened its second session in the magnificent new courthouse built on the south side of the harbor. The courthouse is one of a number of public buildings distinguished by pagodas and balconies painted red. Locals call them the "bird cages."

While the builders have been at work, building wreckers have started to tear down the old fort which was erected to protect the settlement and act as the headquarters of the Hudson's Bay Company. The northeast bastion of the fort is disappearing, and the rest of the fort will go soon to make way for the stores, hotels and other buildings more suitable for a city that is expanding to serve the development of the goldfields on the mainland, the farming and lumbering on the island – and government.

Prince of Wales makes a royal splash in Canada

Illustration of the Prince of Wales descending a timber slide in Ottawa while on a visit to Canada in 1860.

Edward Albert, Prince of Wales, who thrilled Canadians with the first official royal visit to the colonies.

Governor George Simpson entertains H.R.H. Prince of Wales at Lachine.

Sept. 20, 1860

BRITISH NORTH AMERICA – The Prince of Wales left Canada for the United States today, ending a two-month visit to British North America and leaving the colonies in the midst of an exciting but painful adolescence. The 18-year-old Edward Albert, not far from adolescence himself, has had all the style and charm expected of a future king since landing at St. John's July 23. Royal princes have been in the colonies before, but this is the first official royal visit.

The prince immediately became king of the dance floor at Halifax and Newfoundland balls. "Fairyland" is how a Halifax newspaper described the city ballroom. Montreal was not to be outdone. It built a ballroom 90 metres in diameter, to host 6,000 dancers: "It has risen literally by magic, with its artificial streets of water and plantations of trees. ... Around the orchestra were some half-dozen jets of various perfumes, in which the fairer half of the brilliant assemblage could dip their tiny handkerchiefs." Fairyland indeed!

When he wasn't burning up the dance floor, the prince moved from one royal event to the next, meeting with dignitaries and many ordinary people, breathing in something of the essence of Canadian life. In Montreal he drove the last rivet into the Victoria Bridge, an engineering wonder by any standard. He laid the cornerstone for the new Parliament buildings at Ottawa, where he was met by 1,000 lumbermen paddling 150 birch canoes. He also watched lacrosse games, met 200 Indians at Sarnia, and saw a man walk over Niagara Falls on a tightrope.

The queen authorized the royal visit to recognize the growth of British North America, and it definitely marks a coming of age for the colonies. The visit would have been impossible 10 years ago. Since then, roads, railways, and steamships have made it possible for most people to see the prince, and because of the telegraph people can read about his adventures in newspapers. The fairyland celebrations at Montreal and Halifax were possible because of the recent advent of gas lighting. But fairyland has to give way to real life after awhile, and it eventually rained on the prince's parade. As his steamer neared Kingston, the Loyal Order of Orangemen, a pro-British anti-Catholic group, strung their banner across the wharf as a way of showing their loyalty to the British Crown and receiving recognition from the Prince of Wales as he entered the city.

The prince's attendant, the Duke of Newcastle, opposes the order and is determined that the prince stay impartial. He ordered the banner down, the Orangemen refused, and the prince continued down the lake without coming ashore. The incident sparked a storm of protest, and has revived talk of the dissolution of the Canadas.

Escaped U.S. slaves live in Canada West

1860

CANADA WEST – It has been estimated that anywhere from 15,000 to 75,000 fugitive American slaves are living in Canada West, and while most whites consider the higher total to be more accurate, evidence suggests the lower figure is more correct. Either way, no figure can be conclusively discerned.

There are two camps responsible for popularizing the higher estimate: abolitionists who wish to emphasize Canada's effort on behalf of the enslaved; and anti-black groups hoping to turn public opinion against black settlement.

Is it possible black fugitives consider British North America the new Canaan, the Promised Land? Many do. Several black songs or folk tales tell of the Canadas in this context, referring to them as the "Northern Star" fugitives should follow. Owners, fearing their slaves will take this route, try to convince them that Canada is a rugged land far away, cold and unaccommodating for blacks.

Southern newspapers do not recognize the provinces as the goal of most fugitive slaves. And even with a lot to gain by exaggerating losses, last year the New Orleans *Commercial Bulletin* estimated that at the outside 75,000 slaves escaped the previous 50 years. Certainly only a small percentage of these made it to British North America, let alone Canada West.

Black volunteer militia OK, governor says

The black volunteer military company in Victoria, B.C. is formed.

Spring 1860

VICTORIA, Vancouver Island – Civic-minded blacks are happy Gov. James Douglas has accepted their plan for a volunteer militia corps. Earlier they were rebuffed when they tried to join the volunteer fire brigade. Douglas is concerned about the colony's lack of defences during the San Juan Island dispute with the Americans. The corps is now seeking a drill hall.

Captain Palliser readies a second report

1860

LONDON, England – Capt. John Palliser and his party have finished their examination of the western hinterland of Canada, and he is now preparing a second report – the first was made last year. The two major components of the reports concern transportation and settlement. Palliser believes that building a transcontinental railway on British territory would be difficult and expensive. Better by far, Palliser says, would be a route through the United States with branches north to Canada.

Palliser's hinterland survey also reveals that there is a semi-arid tract of land in the southwest of the Prairies, surrounded by a large tract of land suitable for agriculture and settlement.

Victoria race riot: seven under arrest

Nov. 3, 1860

VICTORIA, Vancouver Island – Seven men, five of them black, have been arrested here after a riot at the Colonial Theatre. Just before the curtain rose two blacks tried to buy tickets to the stalls. They were refused because blacks are restricted to the gallery.

Reports of what went on next vary, but it seems that the two blacks forced their way into the theatre, where they were attacked by both spectators and actors, who jumped down from the stage. Then, it appears, other blacks armed with sticks started attacking spectators before police came to restore order.

Demotion enrages college ex-principal

Jan. 23, 1860

NEW BRUNSWICK – Edwin Jacob, one-time principal of King's College, is not celebrating the founding of the University of New Brunswick. This winter the college was transformed into a nondenominational provincial university. However, the theology chair Jacob held for 30 years was abolished, and he was demoted to professor of classical and moral philosophy.

The elderly Jacob has bitterly resisted the change, taking up residence in King's College with his daughter and refusing to budge.

Troops in San Juan, border talks go on

March 21, 1860

SAN JUAN ISLAND – British marines landed today on the island of San Juan, off the coast of British Columbia. Britain and the United States previously agreed to a joint military-naval occupation of the island with limited forces while boundary negotiations continue.

San Juan's strategic location between Vancouver Island and British Columbia put it in the middle of a dispute which arose while determining the international border west of the Rocky Mountains as defined in the treaty of 1846.

P.E.I. act creates a secular college

May 1, 1860

CHARLOTTETOWN – The Prince of Wales College Act passed third reading before the House of Assembly today, raising Central Academy, a publicly-supported grammar school in Charlottetown, to the status of college, named in honor of Edward, Prince of Wales, a visitor to the colony this year.

The act ensures the college is a purely secular institution without any religious instruction, sparking much dissent in the House on the part of Liberal Catholic assemblyman Francis Kelly.

View of Nanaimo, B.C. Once called Colvile Town, Nanaimo was first settled by 24 families who emigrated from England in 1854.

Chinese immigrants flock to west coast

April 1860

VICTORIA, Vancouver Island – The Norwegian ship *Hebe* has arrived here from Hong Kong with 265 Chinese immigrants – one a young female. More shiploads of Chinese are on the way here, it is learned, despite the danger of pirate attacks in the South China sea. The immigrants must also endure hardships on the trip because the ship owners often take their money – about $30 – but fail to provide food or proper accommodation.

Some Chinese who worked in the goldfields have just gone home with $500 or so (about five years pay) in their pockets. Others will want to follow their example.

Typical Chinese wedding costume.

Brown makes pitch for a "federation"

April 30, 1860

TORONTO – George Brown, leader of the opposition Reform party, has introduced a parliamentary motion that the current United Province of Canada be dissolved. In its place he wants a federation, made up of the old regions of Upper and Lower Canada.

This is the Reformers' or Clear Grits' latest attempt to change the nature of Canada, giving a bigger voice to Canada West. The proposal would give this region more members in a "general" parliament than Canada East, because its population is bigger, but the two Canadas would also have their own parliaments for provincial affairs.

Canada controls expenses on Indians

1860

CANADA – As of this year, the United Province of Canada is financially responsible for the native people of British North America. The transition from British to colonial control comes in the wake of an imperial financial crisis. It also reflects, at least in part, confidence that the Indian Civilization Act, adopted in 1857, will successfully eliminate government expenditure on Indians in the near future. The act encourages the assimilation of the reserve Indians into the dominant white society. Indians have called for the repeal of this destructive act. They are concerned that the Canadian government is only interested in seizing their lands.

Illustration of Montagnais and Naskapi Indian lodges at Seven Islands. The Canadian government now plans to take over control of Indian affairs which until now has been left up to the colonial department in Britain.

More women training to satisfy the huge demand for teachers

Dec. 31, 1860

CANADA – Because of the dire need for teachers in Canada, more women than ever before are being allowed into Normal Schools, the teacher training colleges. In the past, women have not been formally trained as teachers. A would-be schoolmistress simply advertised in a newspaper that she wished to give instruction in certain skills – reading, writing, sewing or French were standards – and she then taught whoever happened to respond to her advertisement.

Today, the number of women entering teacher training colleges is increasing. But these women are few compared to the number of men enrolled. In addition, they are among the few women in Canada getting a higher education, as few can afford the tuition fees.

As more women are being allowed to teach, debate rages about the admission of female students into Normal Schools. There is also the question of whether girls should be allowed to attend state-subsidized schools, and whether they're worth a full government subsidy or only one-half that paid for boys.

Merits card used in public schools.

Farm women, such as these two, cannot afford to get higher education.

Lynch named new "Ontario" bishop

April 26, 1860

TORONTO – The Roman Catholic church has made Father John Joseph Lynch bishop of the "Ontario" – Canada West – see. He is the third clergyman to hold the office since it was created.

Lynch has extensive experience. Born in Ireland in 1816, he was ordained as a priest in 1843, and worked as a missionary in that country until 1846. After that, Lynch crossed the ocean to serve Texas and Missouri. In 1856 he came to Niagara Falls, New York, where he established the Seminary of Our Lady of the Angels.

Bishop says Kent ignoring outports

June 30, 1860

ST. JOHN'S, Nfld. – John Thomas Mullock, the Catholic bishop of Newfoundland, has levelled charges against the Liberal government led by prominent Catholic politician John Kent.

While in New York, the bishop and Chief Justice Philip Francis Little arranged to charter a steamer to travel between St. John's and the outports. Although the government initially agreed to foot the bill, when push came to shove it refused to hire the steamer. Mullock condemned the government for lacking interest in the outports.

First Queen's Plate is run near Toronto

June 27, 1860

TORONTO – Some 4,000 Torontonians came out to a race track in nearby Carleton today to watch a horse race sponsored by Queen Victoria herself. The Queen's Plate, as it is being called, saw a strong field of horses run the oval track for the honor of claiming a special commemorative silver plate. Also awarded was the princely sum of 50 guineas. The triumphant steed which took first place was a fast, flashy horse named Don Juan. Due to its popularity, the race will be held again next year.

Thousands of Irish flock to Canada

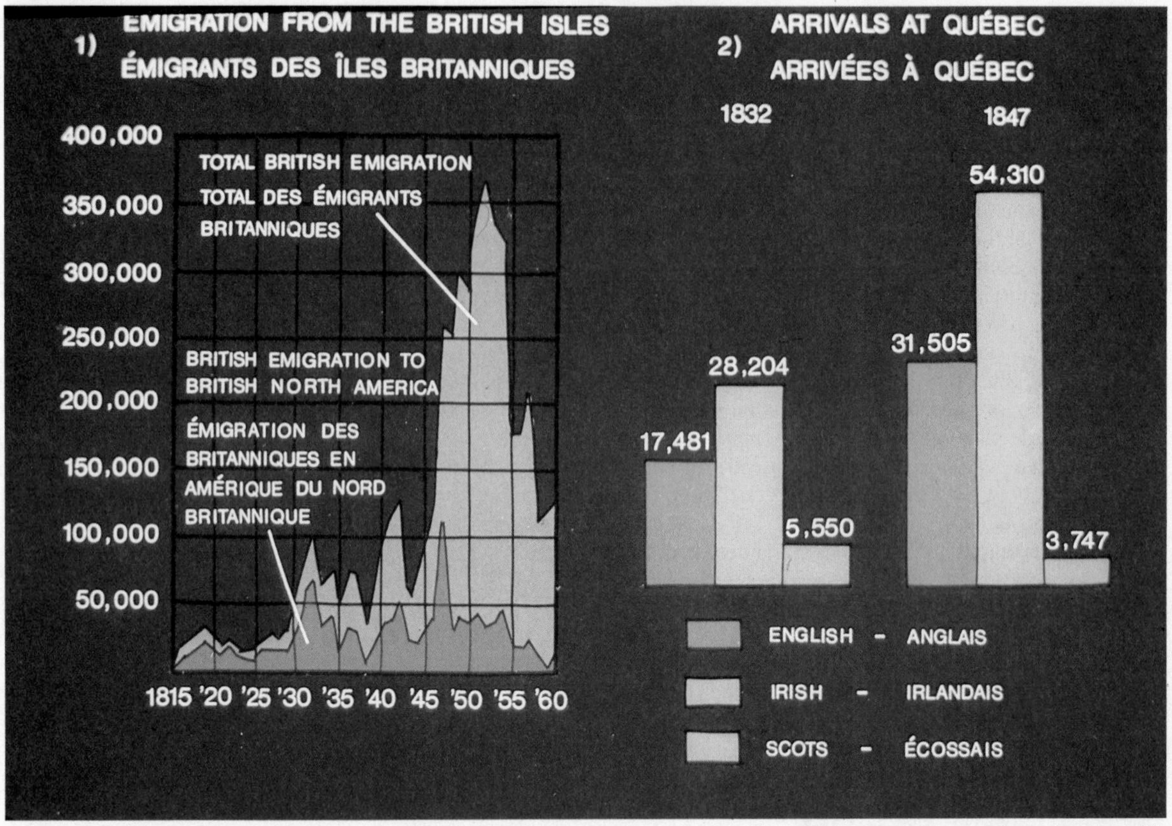

Figures for emigration from the British Isles to British North America (1) and immigration to Canada East (2).

1860

CANADA – Over the past two decades, Canada has been the recipient of thousands of immigrants – its biggest influx since Europeans first began settling here. A lot of these new "Canadians" are from Ireland, where potato famines the 1840s forced millions to flee.

In Lower Canada, as in such American centres of heavy Irish immigration as Boston, most of these Irish newcomers are Roman Catholic. In Upper Canada, on the other hand, most are Protestant. Both Roman Catholics and Protestants tend to settle in rural areas where they usually become successful farmers. The rest end up in cities where they join an easily exploited industrial labor force.

Total eclipse of the sun keeps Red River colony in the dark

July 17, 1860

RED RIVER COLONY, Rupert's Land – There was an unreal, almost eerie silence in the community for part of today. Even the birds fled to their nests during a total eclipse of the sun.

The weather accompanying this phenomenon proved a major disappointment to astronomer Simon Newcombe. This Canadian-born scientist led an expedition into the northern part of the territory to make observations at the location of maximum darkness, but clouds obscured the view.

Newcombe is a mathematical genius, who reportedly was extracting cube roots at the age of seven. He now is engaged by the *American Nautical Almanac.*

An illustration of a total eclipse of the sun. In Red River colony, the 1860 eclipse brought the whole community to a standstill for part of the day.

Prince leads cornerstone ceremony

Sept. 1, 1860

OTTAWA – A crowd of thousands turned out in Ottawa today to watch the Prince of Wales [Edward VII] lay the cornerstone for the new Parliament buildings. The ceremony was held under a Gothic-arched canopy, in front of which was the white marble cornerstone. The stone was suspended from a giant wooden crown, and lowered into place using a gilted pulley.

After the ceremony, His Highness enjoyed an outdoor luncheon with various dignitaries. Then, no doubt wishing for some entertainment, he went to a nearby lumber chute, and spent the afternoon operating it with his own hands.

A view of Ottawa. The new seat of government will have Parliament buidings.

American whalers turn to cannibalism

October 1860

LABRADOR – Reports are circulating that seven American whalers are conducting themselves shamefully as they pass through mission communities in northern Labrador. It has also been reported that these same men resorted to cannibalism last month, eating two of their own party of nine.

The men were in the icy Cumberland Sound when, in early August, they fled in a small whaleboat, fed up with miserable conditions on their ships. By September, their supplies exhausted, a member died and was eaten. A second was soon killed, and he was eaten as well.

Doctors get to the root of the problem

1860

CANADA WEST – Stay away from regular physicians when you are sick. That's the advice of many people who live here and a growing body of medical men called "root doctors," or botanics, who treat illness with vegetable cures that include roots and herbs.

The most popular system of root doctoring was developed by a doctor named Thomson. He believes in steaming his patients, and administers six classes of vegetable-based medicines. Would-be Thomsonian doctors attend classes and buy patent rights from him to practise the system. Besides the Thomsonians, in many towns there are also "friendly botanical societies" that offer members unlimited care for a set fee. Root doctors, Thomsonian or otherwise, publish their own medical journals to help themselves stay abreast of the latest innovations in their profession.

"Root doctors" prescribe cures based on vegetables, including roots and herbs.

Naturalist studies birds of the north

1860

NORTHWEST TERRITORY – American naturalist Robert Kennicott is travelling extensively in the [Mackenzie District], the first English-speaking scientist to collect zoological specimens of wild fowl in the Yukon basin. His fact-finding tour has aroused great excitement among the American scientific community, and is being financed by the Audubon Society and the Smithsonian Institute.

U.S. whaling ships enter Hudson Bay

July 1860

CHURCHILL, Rupert's Land – Until now, British ships have dominated whaling in the Arctic – particularly in Davis Strait and Lancaster Sound. But now American whalers are entering an area once the domain of the Hudson's Bay Company – the bay itself. This summer American whalers are active in the bay's northwest corner, for the easy whaling days are over. New grounds must be found.

View of Fort Chambly, now abandoned by British as it is in poor condition.

1861

Red River, February. *The Nor'Wester*, the settlement's first newspaper, dispenses with pretensions of unbiased reporting as a lead editorial says the paper's role is to foment public opinion against the colony's governing council. The paper opposes continued HBC rule in the colony.

Washington, April 15. President Lincoln declares a state of "insurrection" in the U.S., and appeals for volunteers for military service, following the surrender of Fort Sumter to Confederate forces yesterday. It is the opening of civil war.

Prince Edward Island, July 18. The Land Commission makes its final report on the land tenure problem on the Island. It recommendations favor tenants in their struggle against the absentee landlords.

Toronto, July 23. An editorial in the *Globe* newspaper endorses the North in the American Civil War.

Toronto, Aug. 26. William Lyon Mackenzie, former radical Reform politician and a leader of the Rebellions of 1837-38, dies.

Frobisher Bay, August. American Charles Hall sails around Frobisher Bay. He finds relics of Frobisher's expeditions of the 1570s, and discovers that the bay has no western outlet, as had been believed.

Toronto, October. Famous midget entertainer Tom Thumb holds four receptions at St. Lawrence Hall from Oct. 21-24.

Boston, October. An American expedition led by Isaac Hayes returns after failing to reach the North Pole. It reached Greenland, Ellesmere Island, and made important meteorological, magnetic, and other scientific observations.

Atlantic, Nov. 8. The Northern navy seizes two Confederate emissaries en route to London aboard the *Trent*, a British merchant ship. The seizure violates British neutrality in the American Civil War.

Toronto, Dec. 31. Alexander Easton's street railway company reports it has built 9.6 kilometres of track which transport an average of 2,000 passengers daily.

Canada West. Anderson Abbott becomes the first Canadian-born black to receive a licence to practise medicine.

Red River. There is a serious flood of the Red River.

Douglas orders survey of Indian reserves

1861

VICTORIA, Vancouver Island – Gov. James Douglas has ordered a survey of all the Indian reserves on Vancouver Island and on the mainland. On Vancouver Island, only a dozen existing treaties deal with small tracts of land.

Some property owners fear Douglas will allow the Indians more land and prevent the development of agriculture and ranching in the colony. They recall when the reserves were allocated, and Douglas ordered the surveyors to respect Indian wishes about the location and size of the reserves.

Sir James Douglas, B.C. governor.

Swearing-in held for Negro soldiers

July 1861

VICTORIA, Vancouver Island – The black militia company, now known as the Victoria Pioneer Rifle Company or, to local wags, as the African Rifles, has been sworn in at a ceremony here. The corps has been operating for some months and has become popular here; so popular that some white men have volunteered – and were rejected. The Negro community has provided some funds, and the colonial government has allocated $250 to the militia unit.

Maid of the Mist conquers the treacherous Whirlpool Rapids

Maid of the Mist proves its worth to prospective buyer by surviving plunge.

June 6, 1861

NIAGARA RIVER – The *Maid of the Mist* etched her way into maritime history today – led by the renowned Niagara riverman Joel Robinson, the sturdy sidewheel steamer became the first vessel to conquer Niagara's thundering Whirlpool Rapids. Manned by Robinson and two others, the boat plummeted down the narrow, 200-metre long gorge, then circled the whirlpool three times before escaping its deadly pull.

The tumultuous trip was planned after a Montreal firm agreed to buy the former tour boat on condition it be transported to Lake Ontario. With little to lose, its indebted owner offered $500 to anyone crazy enough to chance the rapids.

Book to highlight history of Ojibwas

1861

LONDON, England – A.W. Bennett Publishers have published the *History of the Ojebway Indians: With Especial Reference to their Conversion to Christianity,* by the late Sacred Feathers, a Mississauga, or Ojibwa, chief. It has this description of how Mississauga elders view nature: "They suppose that all animals, fowls, fish, trees, stones, etc., are endowed with immortal spirits, and that they possess supernatural power to punish any who may dare to despise or make any unnecessary waste of them."

A painting by William Armstrong shows the Athabasca River in the Rockies.

Five Haida arrested in west coast clash

May 17, 1861

CAPE MUDGE, Vancouver Island – About 400 Haida Indians barricaded themselves behind a stockade here and held off attacks from the Royal Navy gunboat *Forward* for several hours. The Haida, who take their canoes south to Victoria to trade in the spring, often rob settlers on the way north. This time, after some robberies on Saltspring Island, the *Forward* was sent after them.

As the gunboat approached, the Haida fired muskets at it, while the sailors fired one shell in the air to intimidate the Indians and others which reduced the village to rubble. Five Haida were arrested.

Court frees escaped slave from Missouri

1861

CANADA WEST – John Anderson, an escaped Missouri slave charged with murder, is a free man; the Court of Common Pleas recently rejected the warrant of a Detroit man committing Anderson.

Anderson stabbed a white man to death while attempting to escape in 1853. He came to Windsor, and lived peacefully in Canada until 1860, when he was arrested, released, arrested again, and tried twice for murder. The case has highlighted Canadian sympathy for escaped slaves. Meetings in Toronto opposed the trial, and armed police were assigned to the court to prevent violent demonstrations.

Canada has been a haven for escaped American slaves since the early part of the century when slavery began to crumble here due to judicial and legislative action. The passage of the Fugitive Slave Act in the U.S. in 1850, which made it easy for owners to capture escaped slaves, increased the flow of escapees to Canada. Canadians have occasionally shown prejudice and fear toward the fugitives, but mostly they have sympathized with the plight of the homeless Negroes.

Canadians formed the Anti-Slavery Society in 1851, and have participated in the "underground railway" bringing American slaves to the province. Harriet Beecher Stowe's anti-slavery novel *Uncle Tom's Cabin*, published in the U.S. in 1852, has contributed to Canadian opposition to slavery.

Streetcars serving Montreal, Toronto

November 1861

MONTREAL – Horse-drawn streetcars have brought modern urban transit to Montreal. The City Passenger Railway promises fast, efficient service on either its single- or double-decked cars.

So does the Toronto railway opened two months ago by entrepreneur Alexander Easton. His Yonge Street line, running from the northern community of Yorkville south to the city core, has regular horsecars every half-hour. Easton plans to run streetcars along Queen Street, from Yonge west to the Mental Asylum, and along King Street, from Bathurst east to the Don River.

American conciliation ends Trent Affair

Dec. 30, 1861

TORONTO – The threat of war between Britain and the United States, with Canada as the battlefield, seems to have faded following the resolution of the Trent Affair. The confrontation between the two major North American powers was named for the British steamer the *Trent.* On Nov. 8, the ship was carrying two Confederate envoys, James Mason and John Slidell, to Europe to take up diplomatic posts in England and France, respectively. However, the *Trent* was waylaid by the U.S. Union warship *USS San Jacinto.* Under the orders of its captain, Charles Wilkes, the two southerners were seized and taken to the North.

It was feared that this violation of a neutral British ship would lead to war. Certainly, the British prime minister, Lord Palmerston, was itching for a fight, unless the men were released and an apology issued by the American government. However, given that the war-torn Union was elated by the capture, such a resolution seemed unlikely. In fact, what first happened was the mobilization of troops on both sides of the Canada-U.S. border.

But, thankfully, cooler heads have prevailed in this matter. Today the U.S. government, already busy with its battle with the rebellious South, released Mason and Slidell, avoiding apologies but at the same time mollifying the British.

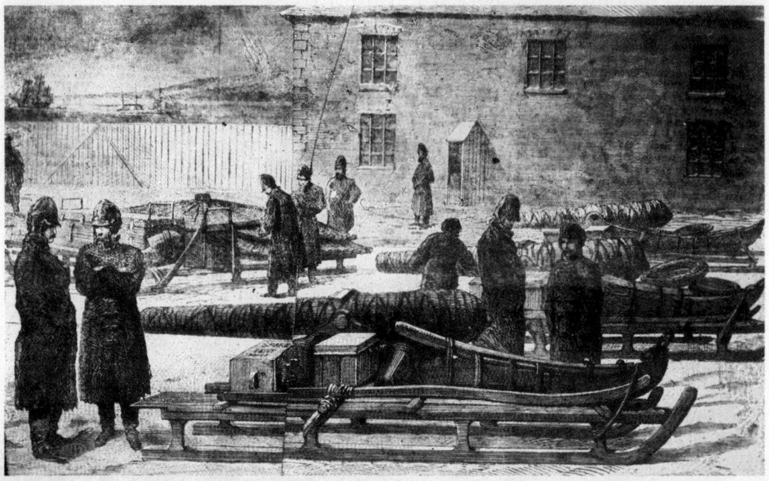

British troops in St. John prepare for trek to the Canadas during Trent Affair.

Monck replaces Head as governor general

Gov.-Gen. Charles Stanley, Lord Monck, and his family at Rideau Hall.

Oct. 25, 1861

TORONTO – The new governor general is Charles Stanley, fourth Viscount of Monck in Ireland. He replaces Sir Edmund Head, who didn't live up to Canadian expectations. Monck is reputed to be a pragmatic manager of men and property, according to those who live on his Irish estates. He is also said to be impartial, fair-minded, and easygoing.

Representation by population rejected

April 5, 1861

TORONTO – Representation by population threatens French-Canadians by upsetting the balance of the United Canadas, Conservative George-Etienne Cartier has charged in a heated debate on a motion by T.R. Ferguson, an Upper Canadian Conservative.

Pressure is mounting for change in the way seats are distributed in the legislature. Under the terms of union, Upper and Lower Canada have an equal number of Assembly seats. Cartier affirmed "the principle of the union to be that the two provinces should coexist with equal powers."

▷

Indians of the Pacific coast maintain rich culture

Halibut fishing gear of the Kwakiutl, or "kwakwaka'wakw" as they call themselves. These Indians live in the coastal areas of British Columbia.

West coast Indian totem poles. Coastal people often fish and hunt according to the seasons, holding their ceremonial and artistic activities in winter.

A woven basket made by the Salish people of the northwest Pacific coast.

The interior of a Kwakiutl Indian home on the northwest Pacific coast.

Arts and crafts of the Haida Indians, of coastal British Columbia. Their culture and art is distinctive within northwest Pacific coast traditions.

Haida Indians' works of art. Haida publicly proclaim clan membership displaying inherited family crests carved on furniture and other objects.

Southern Kwakiutl Indian cannibal bird masks are ceremonial objects which hold religious significance.

A Tsimshian chief. Totem poles and potlatch feasts are part of the way of life for the Tsimshian Indians.

Southern Kwakiutl Indian cave exhibits traditional animal masks. Because of their substitution of an inhuman for a human face, masks are the most spectacular of all articles used in ceremonies and religious observances.

An ivory totem pole, serving as the Haida Indians' signboard, genealogical record and memorial.

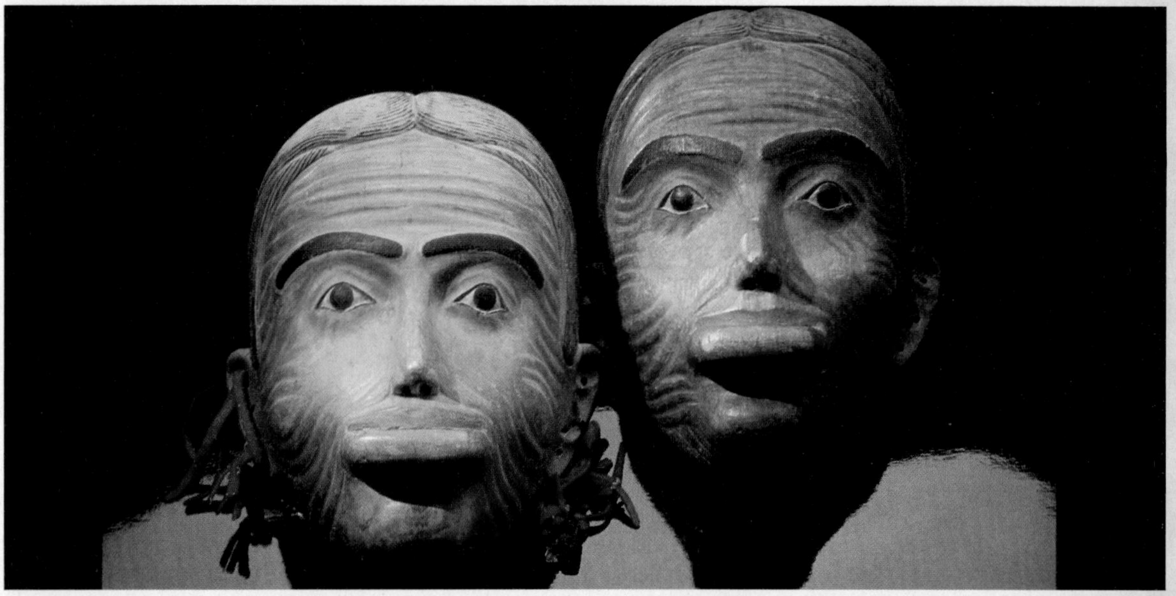

Portrait masks of two women, fashioned by the Haida Indians of the west coast using abalone shell and wood.

Coastal religious leader's equipment includes masks and other items.

West coast Indians sometimes use clothing, such as the dress, moccasins and gloves shown above, as trade goods when dealing with Europeans.

A west coast Salish Indian weaving a typically-intricate blanket.

1862

Fort Garry, HBC Territory, June. The Overlanders, a group of some 150 settlers from Canada West led by Thomas and Robert McMicking, leave with carts and horses on a trek across the continent to the Cariboo goldfields.

London, July 19. Following the discovery of gold on the Stikine River, [B.C.], an order-in-council organizes the Stikine Territories north of the colony of B.C., removing the area from HBC control. The governor of B.C. is named administrator of the area.

Hamilton, Canada West, Aug. 8. Allan MacNab, former premier of the Canadian government, dies.

Williams Creek, B.C., August. With the creek swamped by gold-seekers, William Barker pioneers deep digging in the area, drawing gold from a 15.6-metre shaft.

Victoria, Sept. 23. The first City Ordinances are to regulate "privies" and prohibit littering.

Quebec, September. Leaders of Canada, Nova Scotia, and New Brunswick agree on financing for the construction of an Intercolonial Railway connecting the colonies.

U.S., Nov. 4. Gatling patents a gun that fires hundreds of rounds a minute by using a cluster of rotating barrels.

Gulf of St. Lawrence. In the spring, sealers from the Magdalen islands kill 15,000-20,000 seals in five days.

Williams Creek, B.C. Gold miners strike it rich with deep digging at the creek, begun by William Barker. The creek is established as a stable gold producer, and contributes much of the $2,656,903 officially credited to B.C. gold mining in 1862.

British Columbia. During a smallpox epidemic, lay missionary William Duncan leads several hundred Indians to Metlakatala Pass, an ancestral Tsimshian village, to found a Christian settlement.

Fort George, B.C. The Overlanders arrive [at Prince George] after a perilous descent of the Fraser River by raft, ending a trek across the continent from Fort Garry [Winnipeg]. Six of them died on the trip.

Canada East. Jean Rivard publishes his novel *Jean Rivard, le défricheur canadien*, extolling a rural destiny for French-Canadians.

Smallpox killing hundreds of Indians

May 14, 1862

VICTORIA, Vancouver Island – A terrible epidemic of smallpox has struck the Indian population of Vancouver Island and British Columbia, leaving hundreds – perhaps thousands – of natives dead. The disease arrived in this city in March, transmitted by a sailor from San Francisco. It soon took hold in the Indian settlements on the outskirts of the town.

Not too many Indians are fishing these days due to the smallpox epidemic.

Since the gold rush boom of 1858, more and more natives visit Victoria each summer, some from their territories far to the north. They trade furs, handicrafts, fish and game animals with the local people, and sometimes take jobs as laborers before returning to their villages for the winter. Smallpox has spread like wildfire through their crowded camps, and early this month white settlers began to urge that the Indians be driven away from the city. As a result, authorities have evicted the Indians and burned their houses.

Northern Indians have decided to return home, and they will surely carry the highly infectious disease with them, spreading it up the coast and into the interior. The Indians have no immunity to smallpox and whole villages stand the risk of being wiped out once the infection reaches them. It is the worst calamity to hit the natives of this coast since the arrival of whites.

Store owner snubs lure of Fort Garry

1862

RED RIVER COLONY, Rupert's Land – Recent events here suggest commercial development will not take place at either Upper Fort Garry or Lower Fort Garry, but rather part way in between.

Giving proof to this prospect is the location of the first major general store at neither of the established locations. Henry McKenny is building the new structure at the junction of the Main Road and the Portage Trail.

Fort Garry, in Red River settlement.

Report slams British on P.E.I. land rights

1862

PRINCE EDWARD ISLAND – The long-awaited Land Commission Report has been released. The three-man body was created to suggest remedies to the chronic and bitter land question. The commissioners have criticized the imperial government for its handling of the issue, and recommend it loan the Island £100,000. The money will let the colony purchase the remaining proprietal lands, and in turn resell them to resident tenants. Commissioners have also included a plan detailing how tenants will become freeholders on easy terms.

Islanders have received the report with enthusiasm, though their feelings may not be shared by the imperial government, especially when it sees the price tag attached.

A ball at Upper Fort Garry at the home of the governor of Rupert's Land.

Monck's decision: Macdonald, Sicotte to lead government

May 24, 1862

QUEBEC CITY – John Sandfield Macdonald, the moderate Reformer, and Louis-Victor Sicotte have been named leaders of a new Canadian government by Gov. Gen. Monck. The appointment comes after the Macdonald-Cartier regime's defeat over the issue of a paid and trained militia.

The British government, alarmed by growing American hostility and the costs of maintaining troops in Canada, wants Canada East to assume most of its own defence as part of the cost of self-government. However, the majority in Parliament, objecting to the price, threw the government out. Despite Sandfield Macdonald's opposition to the bill, Monck chose him because he has wide support in the Assembly.

John Sandfield Macdonald.

Nest of rare bird seen in the Arctic

1862

ARCTIC – Roderick MacFarlane has discovered the first known Hudsonian Godwit nest in the Canadian High Arctic. The long-legged wading bird was once common along the Atlantic seaboard. However, its members there have been decimated by settlers who collected Hudsonian Godwit eggs for food and shot adult birds during the mating season.

Ice makes going tough for sealing ships

St. John's sealing fleet waits to depart for the northern ice fields, but the ice is making it difficult for the ships to make it to their destination.

April 30, 1862

ST. JOHN'S, Nfld. – This year has been one of the most unusual in sealing history. Many sealing ships became jammed in the ice earlier this month, and after futile attempts to free them crews were forced to abandon the vessels.

What makes the situation so remarkable is that all the crews – with one exception – burned their boats, claiming they were a hazard to shipping. There is strong evidence to suggest that the owners wanted to collect the insurance and feared that if their ships were simply abandoned other crews would salvage them – as happened in 1852. Losses will probably exceed £100,000 sterling, and many ships will never be replaced.

Meanwhile, northeast winds have driven Arctic ice floes with old and young seals into Green Bay and White Bay. Ice is tight against the land, and the few people from the small scattered outports in the area can harvest as many seals as they can kill and haul ashore. Their stamina decides the size of the catch.

Landsmen are enjoying a bonanza season, with women and children participating in order to take as many seals as possible before the ice moves off. Already, firms in St. John's and Conception Bay are planning to send ships to the area to buy the seal pelts as soon as the ice clears. Many local commentators are referring to this season as a "Green Bay spring," a freakish but not entirely unknown development.

This illustration of the SS Retriever, a sealing ship, shows some crew members killing and pelting the seals before carrying the pelts back onto the ship.

Renowned explorer Simon Fraser dead

Aug. 19, 1862

ST. ANDREW'S, Canada West – The man who explored the Fraser River to the Pacific and established Britain's claim over British Columbia, is dead. Simon Fraser, 86, died yesterday. His wife Catherine Macdonell, 72, died today at St. Andrew's, Canada West. They'll be buried in a single grave in the town's Roman Catholic cemetery.

Fraser is one of the last surviving partners of the North West Company. He is best remembered for his trip down the Fraser River. Starting in May 1808 on what he believed to be the Columbia River, Fraser wrote "the rapids were very bad. ... I scarcely ever saw anything so dreary, and seldom so dangerous in any country." He reached the Gulf of Georgia on July 2 to find he was not on the Columbia at all.

Pamphlet targets "The Black Town"

April 9, 1862

HALIFAX – An anonymous pamphleteer today published *Halifax: Its Sins and Sorrows,* claiming the little port known as "The Black Town" boasts 340 booze shops, and 1,000 whores. It says, "Old and young, black and white, mothers, sisters, daughters, are engaged in the horrid commerce." His challenge: "Christian ladies of Halifax, will you arise, and save The Black Town? ... Home is not in the vocabulary of the drunkard. Home! The fallen of your sex have none. Shall it always be so in Halifax?"

New Brunswick 20-cent piece. Foreign currency is still in use throughout Canada, however.

The Cariboo won't be the same after the gold rush

A painting of a gold miner in the Cariboo goldfields in the fall of 1862.

Man carried by camel, sometimes used by gold miners as pack animals.

A gold miner in British Columbia.

Camels brought in to work in Cariboo

May 1862

LILLOOET, B.C. – Getting supplies to the goldfields is a tough task – and it's proving to be an expensive one, too. It costs $825 a ton to move freight from Victoria to the goldfields.

And so, an entrepreneur named Frank Laumeister has imported camels from the United States for use as pack animals on the road from the Fraser River to the mines. Most people believe that the camels won't last long, for the road is rocky and the camels, used to sand, will soon go lame.

Individual miners on their way out

Fall 1862

YALE, B.C. – Gold mining in the Cariboo country is fast becoming an industry, demanding capital and forcing out one-man firms with few resources.

In the first stages of British Columbia's gold rush the ore was found in river banks and gravel bars. Only a pan and strong arms were needed to shake the surface gold from the gravel. Now, as the miners move up the rivers, they find that they have to sink shafts or bring water to gold deposits sunk in bluffs above high water.

A horse and wagon round China Bar Bluff, on the way to Cariboo Road.

Sluicing for gold: Two miners in British Columbia search for gold nuggets in a system of sluices they have built to divert the river water.

Dutch Bill leads gold rush to the interior

July 1862

WILLIAMS CREEK, B.C. – From dawn to sunset, the creek is crawling with gold diggers. Williams Creek, never seen by white men before last year, is the richest find yet in the massive gold rush to the interior. William "Dutch Bill" Dietz and his companions discovered it in the spring of last year, ending a long and relentless search, as thousands of miners pushed up the Fraser River and its tributaries in their quest for that ever elusive mother lode.

Since Dutch Bill's discovery, the creek has been flooded with gold diggers, from the North American colonies, the U.S., and across the Atlantic. Everyone wants a piece of the magical gold finds, a discovery that will make a man rich according to his wildest dreams. But most of them are disappointed. The best claims around here yield an average of $2,000 worth of gold a day, but many don't even pay expenses.

Williams Creek shares mining action with nearby Lightning, Antler, and Lowhee creeks. "Creek diggings" are the main method of mining in the area, shallow diggings of only a few feet. So far, miners haven't tried to go any deeper.

Overlander delivers a first in British Columbia

October 1862

KAMLOOPS, B.C. – The first white child born in the interior of British Columbia arrived today. Her parents, Catherine and Augustus Schubert, are Overlanders, pioneers who have trekked from Red River across the plains and the Rockies to join the Cariboo gold rush. Catherine Schubert was the only woman in the party, and she brought her other three children with her.

The Overlanders took all summer to make the trek, enduring the stifling heat and dust of the prairies, and the freezing cold of high mountain passes. When they arrived at the North Thompson River, the Schuberts made a raft and got here the day before the baby was born.

Painter William Hind, who went to B.C. to paint the gold miners there.

Some miners leaving Fort Garry for the gold mines of British Columbia.

Milton and Cheadle to explore the west

Aug. 23, 1862

FORT GARRY, Rupert's Land – Two English adventurers, Viscount Milton and Dr. Walter Butler Cheadle, set out from Fort Garry today in search of a northwest passage by land. But unlike the Overlanders, gold-seekers from Canada West who left Fort Garry on a similar trek in early June, Milton and Cheadle are in no rush; they are undertaking the journey for pleasure, and do not plan to cross the Rockies.

Explosives business gets off the ground

June 14, 1862

HAMILTON – The Hamilton Powder Company has held its first directors' meeting. The creation of the explosives company was inspired by the success of Canadian mining, stumping, and harbor-building.

James Watson, textile manufacturer, and associates Peter Carroll and Matthew Leggatt started the company, whose charter lists the right to produce acids other than those used to make black powder.

Canada should defend itself, Monck says

July 3, 1862

MONTREAL – Canada is an independent country which has been "protected at others' expense." So declared Gov. Gen. Monck at a banquet held in his honor tonight in Montreal. His comments came as a surprise to the crowd, which is accustomed to governors general who do little more than mouth the sentiments of their Canadian ministers.

As always, Monck spoke the mind of the British government, which is furious with Canada for not taking responsibility for its own defence. London is not impressed by the passage of the recent Canadian Militia Bill, which only increases the force of volunteers from 5,000 to 10,000. It wants this country to cover most of its defence costs, which would likely bankrupt the Canadian government.

Bustling Victoria declares itself a city

Aug. 2, 1862

VICTORIA, Vancouver Island – This growing settlement on the southern tip of Vancouver Island declared itself a city today. Founded as a fur-trade centre by the Hudson's Bay Company in 1843, Victoria has been booming since the gold rush on the Fraser River four years ago. It is now an outpost of the British Empire on this coast, an important port and business capital for the gold rush which continues in the Cariboo.

Colonial secretary OKs railway plan

Oct. 14, 1862

LONDON, England – Colonial secretary the Duke of Newcastle has given his blessing to the proposed Intercolonial Railway. The line, designed to link the Maritime provinces of New Brunswick and Nova Scotia with the province of Canada, was given the go-ahead by delegates from all the provinces at a conference in Quebec last month. Under the deal, Canada will pay five-twelfths of the cost, and the Maritimes will split the rest.

Inside Montreal's Victoria skating rink: ice skating is considered quite appropriate for women, and it has become an important social pastime.

1863

Washington, Jan. 1. President Abraham Lincoln signs the Emancipation Proclamation, proclaiming all slaves in the Confederate south free. Lincoln does not have the constitutional power to abolish slavery, but the proclamation shows his moral resolve.

London, Jan. 10. The world's first underground railway opens, to relieve traffic.

Rustico, Prince Edward Island, April 21. Led by Father Georges Belcourt, a former Red River missionary, Acadians establish the Farmer's Bank of Rustico, the smallest bank ever chartered in British North America.

Canada East, April. Philippe-Joseph Aubert de Gaspé publishes his historical romance *Les Anciens Canadiens*. It is an instant success.

Quebec, May. Sandfield Macdonald's government loses a non-confidence motion and the Assembly is dissolved. The government is defeated over its bill to provide for a Canadian militia, its failure to deal with the issue of representation by population, and its chilly handling of the Intercolonial Railway project.

London, July 31. The colonial secretary tells Arthur Gordon, lieutenant-governor of New Brunswick, to work toward the union of the Maritime colonies.

British Columbia, July. The boundaries of the colony are redefined, and most of the Stikine Territories [northern B.C.], created last year at the height of the gold rush, are absorbed into the colony.

Gettysburg, U.S., Nov. 20. President Lincoln gives an address pledging that "government of the people, by the people and for the people shall not perish from this earth", while dedicating a cemetery for the nation's war dead.

Canada. Canada withdraws from the agreement with New Brunswick and Nova Scotia to build an Intercolonial Railway between the colonies because of a snag in financial arrangements. The Maritime colonies are angry.

Hudson Bay. Steam-powered American whaling ships begin hunting bowhead whales, abundant in the bay.

Montreal. Jewish poet Isadore Gordon Ascher publishes *Voices from the Hearth and Other Poems*.

Controversial bill expands privileges of Catholic schools

Dec. 31, 1863

QUEBEC CITY – As the progress of Parliament for 1863 is surveyed, one of the more contentious pieces of legislation has to be a private member's bill expanding the privileges of Catholic education. Introduced by Richard Scott of Ottawa, the bill expanded funding for separate schools to include monies from both provincial and municipal grants.

As with an earlier act passed eight years ago, opposition to the bill came from English-speaking members in Canada West. And, as before, the passage of the bill was made possible by majority support from the members of Canada East; the western majority was against it. The bill was passed by 76-31, with a whopping 26 members absent from the House when the legislation came to a vote.

Forest fire engulfs town in Canada West

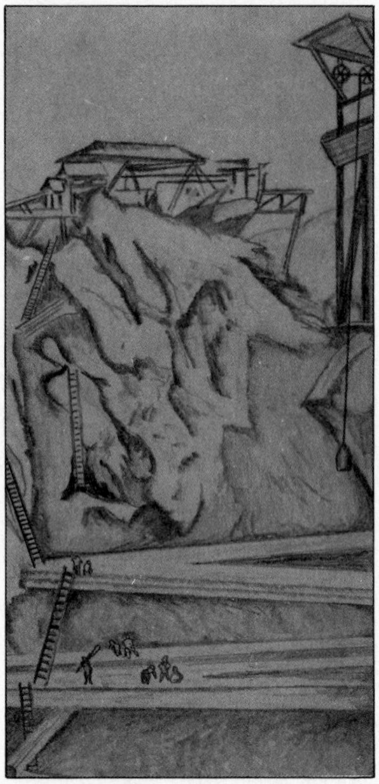

Mining methods of Bruce Mines.

July 1863

BRUCE MINES, Canada West – Residents of Bruce Mines can be seen digging for buried treasure in and around town these days, but their quest is not for the riches of legend or lore. Rather, they are retrieving valuables they themselves hastily buried only a few short days ago in the face of a forest fire that was racing toward them.

Fanned by a strong wind, the fire has swept through the town destroying everything in its path. Most of the copper-mining community's buildings were engulfed by flames, but there has been no reported loss of life. Bruce Mines is located on St. Joseph Island, at the northwestern tip of Lake Huron, and the townspeople found refuge from the fire in boats. The community has few horses, and this made transporting personal possessions to the waterfront difficult. Instead, valuables were buried and are now being retrieved, unscathed by a fire that has destroyed so much.

Long-serving chief justice Robinson dies

Jan. 31, 1863

TORONTO – Sir John Beverley Robinson, Canada's longest-serving chief justice, died today at his home.

A Family Compact leader, Robinson mistrusted responsible government as "servile and corrupt." As chief justice, he was impartial but severe in criminal cases. In 1860, he ordered fugitive slave John Anderson extradited to the U.S., a controversial judgment later reversed on a technicality.

Fredericton's Christ Church Cathedral, built in 1846.

Steamers bought to help seal hunt

March 15, 1863

ST. JOHN'S, Nfld. – Two St. John's fishing/sealing firms have each invested in a steamer for this year's seal fishery. Last year two steam whaling ships from Dundee participated in the seal fishery off Newfoundland, and while they had little success, the experiment was observed by local firms.

It is obvious that steamers will be easier to manoeuvre among the ice floes, and therefore more successful than the sailing ships. It is expected that many more will be purchased. The use of steamers, however, will benefit big firms at the expense of the smaller, and may hasten the decline of the herds.

Pals storm prison, clergyman set free

April 1863

RED RIVER COLONY, Rupert's Land – Rev. G.O. Corbett, of Headingley, convicted and jailed for attempted abortion, was freed when schoolmaster James Stewart and a party of friends stormed the jail. Stewart was arrested, but he too went free when two Country-born leaders, John Bourke and William Hallett, led a second armed party to the jail.

P.E.I. set to hear proposals to unite

April 14, 1863

CHARLOTTETOWN – Prince Edward Island will listen to proposals to unite the British North American colonies. The Assembly adopted a resolution today "that the government will be prepared attentively to consider any proposition emanating from the neighboring colonies ... which may have as its object union of the British North American colonies."

Confederates and Americans rattle their sabres

Captured steamer in Nova Scotia waters

Mid-December 1863

HALIFAX – With the Civil War raging, and the U.S. growing prickly over the use of British ports by Confederate naval raiders, the seizure by Southerners of a U.S. steamer may draw Halifax into an international dispute.

Bound for Portland, Maine, the *Chesapeake* left New York on Dec. 5, but several "passengers" were Confederate sailors in disguise. At nightfall, they drew pistols, killed at least one officer, put the crew in irons, and left for Halifax. Running short of coal, the *Chesapeake* is in a bay near the harbor mouth. She's in Nova Scotia waters, but one of the U.S. cruisers watching the port has an eye on her.

U.S. cruiser recaptures the Chesapeake

December 1863

HALIFAX – The *Chesapeake,* the U.S. steamer seized by Confederates off New York and anchored near here, was retaken by the Union government on Dec. 12. Though she was in Nova Scotia waters, a U.S. cruiser captured and sent her to the British Vice-Admiralty Court in Halifax for disposal.

A furore arose in the U.S., and a legal duel in Halifax. The South claimed the *Chesapeake* was a prize of war; the North said her seizure was piracy. The case has aroused great bitterness between partisans of both sides of the Civil War here. Judge Alexander Stewart ordered the immediate return of ship and cargo to their owners.

Indian Rebellion on Manitoulin Island is resolved peacefully

An Indian Department effort to convince Indians to give up their nomadic way of life in favor of farming has led to discord on Manitoulin Island.

July 1863

CANADA WEST – A dispute over native fishing rights on Manitoulin Island erupted this month. It is one more confrontation few anticipated in 1835 when the Indian Department initiated a program to "civilize" natives by establishing model communities on Manitoulin. There, the Ottawa, Ojibwa, and Potawatomi people would become "yeoman farmers," on the island which would forever remain theirs.

But the soil proved unsuited to extensive farming, and tribal conflicts created political and religious tensions. Infighting was compounded by rival Anglican and Catholic missionaries, each dominating one of the two main villages of Manitowaning and Wikwemikong. To survive, Indians reverted to hunting and fishing, and by the 1850s many had abandoned the communities.

By 1860, land-hungry farmers in Canada West wanted to open the island to settlement. When eastern business interests demanded it be opened to development, fishing rights were granted to several commercial firms. The Indians responded angrily. Last October Treaty Commissioner William McDougall, the veteran Canada West politician, convinced the Indians at the western end of the island to sign a treaty relinquishing their lands, but the Indians around Wikwemikong at the eastern end refused to sign.

Only this summer, the Indian Department granted a fishing licence in the unceded eastern section. Department officials, protected by armed constables, managed to quell the uproar at Kikemikong by agreeing to further negotiations.

"Brain fever" fells Scottish-born giant

Aug. 8, 1863

ENGLISHTOWN, N.S. – At seven feet nine inches tall, with hands as big as dinner plates, Angus MacAskill seemed unbeatable. But after a week-long bout of "brain fever," the 38-year-old Scottish-born strongman died today in this Cape Breton village, not far from his boyhood home in St. Ann's. Famous for his superhuman strength, "the gentle giant" is said to have once shouldered a 2,700-pound anchor on a bet.

MacAskill joined a travelling show in 1849, and in one act, joined the equally famous midget Tom Thumb. In an unforgettable duet, Thumb, 35 inches tall, danced on MacAskill's palm.

In 1853 MacAskill came home, started a business, and shared his wealth, proving he was not only gentle, but generous, too.

Macdonald, Dorion form latest coalition

June 22, 1863

QUEBEC CITY – Is Canada ungovernable? Or will John Sandfield Macdonald, who has managed to assemble yet another in a series of fragile coalitions, retain his hold on power?

Macdonald, whose former coalition was defeated on May 8 over a non-confidence motion moved by Conservative leader John A. Macdonald, will now attempt to govern with Antoine-Aimé Dorion as leader of the Canada East majority – former leader Louis Sicotte, the Irish and discontented Bleus in the cabinet all had to go. Dorion is the old Parti Rouge leader with a love of American institutions and experience as co-government leader in the 1858 Brown-Dorion ministry. Macdonald has patched together a working majority – a patchwork majority of many views, that is.

Institute a boost for unwed mothers

Society denies illegitimate children the simple pleasures of childhood.

Jan. 16, 1863

MONTREAL – It was 15 years ago today that the widow Marie-Rosalie Cadron-Jetté and a group of dedicated women took religious vows at a small house on St. Simon Street, founding the Institute of the Sisters of Mercy to care for unwed mothers and their infants. Since then, the community has sheltered more than 3,000 of the women society usually treats like moral lepers. The nuns' humanity toward them has been largely inspired by Marie-Rosalie.

Marie-Rosalie founded the community with the support of Bishop Ignace Bourget, concerned about the plight of unwed mothers in rapidly growing Montreal. The public has recently started to recognize the value of her work.

Ways to get around town, river and countryside

The Red River cart can be used to transport crops in the far west.

Horse-drawn sleighs are not only an efficient and comfortable mode of transportation on ice-covered streets, but they are also part of the trappings of upper-classdom, conveying a sense of the owner's rank in society.

Steamers such as the Great Britain are useful for inland navigation – on the Great Lakes, for instance – as opposed to deep-keeled, oceangoing steamships.

Canoeing around the Great Lakes area often requires tiresome portaging. Europeans learned various techniques involved in canoeing from Indian guides.

Ships such as these sailboats have often been used by Europeans in Canada, but by 1863 more convenient methods have been found – such as steam power.

Sailboats such as the one above have been known to be used for dangerous stunts on the Lachine Rapids, but they are better suited for gentler waters.

An ice boat at Penetanguishene, Lake Huron. In a region where the cold can put a damper on transportation, ice boats such as these can save the day.

Cariole sleds are often used by fur trappers to transport their pelts. The lack of roads through the country in the wintertime makes the cariole quite popular.

Two habitants going through a toll gate. These people know the usefulness of the horse-drawn sleighs, which can speed them over snow-covered roads.

Massive ocean-going vessels transporting people and freight to and from Europe are a common sight at Canada's ports. The English colonist transport ship, the Wellington, brought a large number of immigrants to Canada from Britain.

A North West canoe on Lake Ontario. Indians developed this longer version of the canoe to transport larger numbers of people.

Canadian natives use birch-bark canoes on lakes and rivers, as they can easily be carried over portages.

The sleigh (top) and sled (botton) shown here are two ways to travel during the cold, snowy winter.

1864

Montreal, April 5. Marie-Rosalie Cadron-Jetté, founder of the Institute of the Sisters of Mercy to care for unwed mothers, dies.

Quebec, June 14. The minority Conservative government led by Sir Etienne-Paschal Taché and John A. Macdonald is defeated, epitomizing the deadlock in the Canadian political system as neither Conservatives nor Reformers can form a stable government.

Quebec, June 14. Reform leader George Brown, chairman of the parliamentary committee to study constitutional questions, advocates the federative union of the British North American colonies.

Quebec, June. Gov. Gen. Monck urges John A. Macdonald to negotiate with George Brown to form a coalition government to work for British North American union.

Maritimes, July 9. The governors of New Brunswick and Nova Scotia tell Governor General Monck that Canadian delegates will be welcome at the Charlottetown Conference on Maritime Union.

Niagara Falls, Canada West, Aug. 8. Daredevil Signor Guilermo Farini, originally Willie Hunt of Port Hope, gets stuck trying to walk the rapids above the falls on stilts. He is dragged to shore with a rope.

Charlottetown, Sept. 7. The Charlottetown Conference adjourns. Canadian delegates stole the show with their arguments for British North American union.

Quebec, Oct. 28. Canadian and Maritime delegates end the Quebec Conference by adopting 72 Resolutions aimed at uniting the British North American colonies.

Charlottetown, Dec. 30. The *Islander* newspaper states "the majority of people appear to be wholly averse to Confederation." People are opposed because they are resentful toward Britain for the absentee landlord system, and because they see little in Confederation for the Island.

Newfoundland, December. Many Newfoundlanders support the Quebec Resolutions for British North American union as way out of mounting poverty in the colony, but St. John's merchants are opposed.

Canada. Legislation is passed protecting birds considered beneficial to crops.

Tenant League formed on the Island

Prince Edward Island farm tenants pledge to withhold their rents until the Island's land question is solved.

May 19, 1864

CHARLOTTETOWN – The colony's tenants are tired of waiting for the government to solve the land question, and are taking their own steps toward land reform. Today they formed a Tenant League, and have pledged to withhold rent until their lands are freehold. All townships are to have local committees to negotiate "a fair and reasonable price" to offer proprietors.

Unlike previous tenant movements, the league does not advocate expropriation without compensation. It has even resolved that "any tenant who refuses to make a fair offer ... shall forfeit the sympathy and all the advantages of this union." It is not known how long this moderation will last.

Tupper eager to discuss Maritime union

March 29, 1864

HALIFAX – Will indifference kill off the latest attempt at Maritime union? Yesterday Charles Tupper, Conservative premier of Nova Scotia, persuaded a sluggish House of Assembly to name five delegates to discuss Maritime union with Prince Edward Island and New Brunswick. Supporters include New Brunswick's Lt.-Gov. Arthur Hamilton Gordon, and bluenoses who yearn for the restoration of Nova Scotia's 18th-century boundaries, which included P.E.I. and New Brunswick. Union is also advocated by those interested in an intercolonial railway.

HON. CHARLES TUPPER, C. B., M. D., L. R. C. S., ETC.
M. P. pour Cumberland.

N.S. Premier Charles Tupper.

Monck eyes invitation to Charlottetown

June 30, 1864

QUEBEC CITY – Canada's governor general, Lord Monck, has written the lieutenant-governors of the three Maritime provinces, in an effort to wring an invitation to the Maritime union conference in Charlottetown this fall. Monck and his ministers hope to persuade their Maritime counterparts to expand their vision beyond a united "Acadia" of New Brunswick, Nova Scotia and Prince Edward Island.

The governor general is reported to have asked "whether the proposed Union might not be made to embrace the whole of the British North American Provinces."

Longtime foes form "Great Coalition"

June 22, 1864

QUEBEC CITY – Today was a scene of highest emotion in the Canadian Assembly, as government Tories and opposition Reformers announced they have joined hands to form a coalition government with a single goal: to unite British North America into one nation. John A. Macdonald and his chief rival, George Brown, have agreed to suspend their political conflicts in the hopes of ending the recurring governmental collapses that now plague Canada.

Brown's speech today was his greatest ever, and provoked wild cheers, and embraces from French-Canadian members. "We have two races, languages, two systems of religious belief, two sets of laws, two systems of everything," Brown began, referring to the realities that make governing a united Canada an apparent impossibility.

Brown then urged national unity to end the crisis, and compliment ed as great statesmen the French-Canadians in the new coalition.

Reaction is mixed to Great Coalition

June-July, 1864

CANADA EAST AND WEST – Public reaction to the Great Coalition is intense and divided – wildly enthusiastic in Upper Canada, disapproving to cautiously optimistic in Lower Canada.

Upper Canadians have responded with almost uniform joy to both the coalition and its goal of Confederation. Nine out of 10 newspapers, both Reform and Conservative, have come out in favor of both. The holdouts, such as the Conservative *Northern Advance*, question the coalition as being "rather embarrassing in a country where politics run high and where a few days since every man, woman and child knew their political creed by heart, but are now, as it were, brought to a standstill."

Lower Canadian Conservatives support the coalition, but feel defensive because their Rouge opponents charge that French-Canadian ministers in the new government are traitors.

Canadians crusade for Confederation

Aug. 13, 1864

HALIFAX – One hundred Canadians, under the leadership of cabinet minister Thomas D'Arcy McGee, enjoyed a sumptuous dinner in the Drill Shed tonight – the latest event in their "crusade for Confederation." This isn't the official name of their tour first to Saint John, N.B., and then here. But listen to what the Canadians are saying – the politicians, journalists, and other tourists – and it's more than clear that they're selling the gospel of Confederation as well as they can to the "political pagans" of the Maritimes.

On this tour the Canadians have feasted in Saint John, been the guests of New Brunswick Lt.-Gov. Arthur Hamilton Gordon, and danced on the deck of the *HMS Duncan* off the port of Halifax. But, through it all, they've stuck to their message of unity. No matter who talks, no matter what's going on, Confederation is foremost in their minds.

Charlottetown readies for conference

Sept. 1, 1864

CHARLOTTETOWN – Having steamed from Quebec City in three days of superb weather, the *Queen Victoria* at noon brought eight Canadian cabinet ministers to town for the Charlottetown Conference. The Nova Scotian delegates arrived yesterday afternoon, the New Brunswickers at 11 last night.

The ostensible purpose of the conference is to debate Maritime union, but the Maritimers want to hear Canadian proposals for a bigger Confederation. They met at 2 p.m. without the Canadians, deferred the Maritime matter, then invited the Canadians to join them before adjourning till morning. Canadians John A. Macdonald and George-Etienne Cartier will speak.

N.B. delegation leaves Fredericton on first leg of journey to Charlottetown.

All that's left is setting "wedding" date

Sept. 3, 1864

CHARLOTTETOWN – On the steamer *Queen Victoria,* which arrived two days ago from Quebec, eight Canadian cabinet ministers today held a lavish, late-afternoon lunch for the Charlottetown Conference. At formal sessions, the Canadians had already made a warm, forceful case for a union of the British North American provinces. Now, the Maritimers' suspicions were melting. It was Saturday. Work was over till Monday. Though lunch didn't begin till 4 p.m., the fare was delicious, the champagne bubbly, and the speeches no less eloquent for being spontaneous – "in vino veritas?"

Once again, French-Canadian leader George-Etienne Cartier and Toronto publisher George Brown talked of a glorious new country. Nation-building fever hit everyone, and peaked in the jolly reading of banns of union. So now the engagement is official, though the wedding date is still unknown.

26 sealing vessels lost in Arctic storm

April 27, 1864

NEWFOUNDLAND – A disastrous storm has caught many Newfoundland sealing vessels in Green Bay, and at least 26 are lost. When the storm struck, the ships did not have room to manoeuvre, and consequently were driven on the rocks and shoals. Many others are reported jammed in the ice, and about 1,500 shipwrecked sealers have reached Greenspond.

Delegates no longer consider Confederation a distant notion

Some Fathers of Confederation photographed at Charlottetown Conference.

Sept. 6, 1864

CHARLOTTETOWN – Today the 23 delegates wrapped up the Charlottetown Conference, discussing details of the Confederation the Canadians had spoken of so glowingly in previous days. What a change from a few days ago, when Prince Edward Islanders preferred to attend the touring Slaymakers and Nicols' Olympic Circus rather than greet their Maritime and Canadian conference guests!

Then Confederation was a dull and distant notion. Today, it inspires in its new converts the most luminous hopes and dreams! Ironically, the Charlottetown Conference was originally mandated to discuss only Maritime union. ▷

Conference ends in Charlottetown

Sept. 7, 1864

CHARLOTTETOWN – The conference convened to discuss Maritime union has now ended, with strange results. The delegates from Prince Edward Island, Nova Scotia and New Brunswick today decided such a union is hopeless, but they unanimously agreed that if satisfactory terms could be agreed on, a broader Confederation of British North America is highly desirable. Their Canadian guests spent the afternoon touring, sea-bathing, and congratulating themselves at the success of their mission.

More champagne on the long road

Sept. 13, 1864

HALIFAX – Fresh from Prince Edward Island, the Charlottetown Conference last night enjoyed a feast in the Halifax Hotel, proving again that Maritimers and Canadians both have a prodigious appetite for champagne. In a fine speech, Canadian John A. Macdonald said he'd long endured "the dreary waste of colonial politics. I thought there was no end, nothing worthy of ambition, but now I see something which is well worthy of all I have suffered." He saw the union of British North America.

P.E.I. names delegates

View of Charlottetown, where Quebec Conference delegates have been selected.

Sept. 27, 1864

CHARLOTTETOWN – The Executive Council has named seven delegates, four Conservatives and three Liberals, to represent Prince Edward Island at next month's Quebec Conference.

Col. John Hamilton Gray is currently premier of the province. Edward Palmer, a former premier, is now attorney general. William Henry Pope edits the influential newspaper *The Islander,* and is a member of the ruling party. George Coles led the Island's first responsible government, and attends this conference as leader of the opposition in the Lower House. Andrew A. MacDonald leads the opposition in the Executive Council. These five represented the Island at the recent Charlottetown Conference.

The two new delegates are T. Heath Haviland and Edward Whelan. Haviland has served as provincial secretary, solicitor general and Speaker. Whelan publishes the reform newspaper *The Examiner.*

Cheese factory first to open in Canada

The first cheese factory in Canada West has opened in Oxford County.

June 1, 1864

OXFORD COUNTY, Canada West – What was once a pioneer pastime is now an industry, with the opening of this province's first cheese factory in Oxford County. The project is the brainchild of Harvey Farrington, a local entrepreneur who believes there's an untapped urban market for quality cheddar. Farrington is using milk from farms throughout the area.

99 feared dead as train plunges into river

Swing bridge open; Grand Trunk train falls into Richelieu River.

June 29, 1864

ST. HILAIRE, Canada East – A Grand Trunk train carrying 458 passengers failed to stop for a swing bridge open over the Richelieu River near here, and plunged into the water, killing up to 99 riders. As many as 100 people were injured in the train, which was carrying German and Polish immigrants to their new homeland. A barge passing below the bridge was struck.

Vancouver Island lumber exports rising

1864

VICTORIA, Vancouver Island – Ships have been taking timber out of Vancouver Island for almost 100 years. Capt. James Cook repaired his ship's masts at Nootka Sound in 1778. Then other ships took spars home with them to be used in shipbuilding. Fifteen years ago the first general cargo of timber was shipped to San Francisco. Now timber is being exported to southern Australia as the local sawmills expand and produce more lumber.

Sawmills at work on the Island for 20 years have been joined by new mills at New Westminster and Burrard Inlet. Large loads are going to San Francisco and Peru as well as Australia. Smaller loads are being shipped to Mexico, China, Hawaii and England.

Military struts stuff as civilians look on

Sept. 25, 1864

SAINT JOHN, N.B. – More than 3,000 civilians came out to see a military review at Camp Torryburn today featuring 1,400 soldiers, both British regulars and New Brunswick militia. To bolster declining numbers of soldiers in the province, former New Brunswick governor John Manners-Sutton urged the creation of militia units at danger points along the border in 1859. The units have grown in popularity, particularly in Saint John and other towns in the province.

Macdonald woos uneasy Maritimers

Oct. 13, 1864

QUEBEC CITY – Maritime provinces will be well-represented in an appointed Upper House of Parliament. So promises John A. Macdonald, chief Canadian negotiator at a conference here to discuss uniting the Maritime provinces and Canada into one country.

Maritimers are uneasy that in such a union, seats in the Lower House, or "Commons," are likely to be based on population. To allay their fears, Macdonald said today that a third of Upper House seats would go to the Maritimes.

72 Resolutions adopted in Quebec

The Fathers of Confederation. Painting combines the delegates to the Charlottetown and Quebec conferences.

Oct. 28, 1864

QUEBEC CITY – After weeks of strenuous discussion, debate and deal-making around the crimson, book-strewn table in the spacious, second-floor reading room of the Legislative Council, delegates from Canada, New Brunswick, Nova Scotia, Newfoundland, and Prince Edward Island have adopted 72 resolutions aimed at uniting British North America.

The Quebec Resolutions will soon be published and presented to each legislature for approval. But most details of the agreement are already known, and are being excitedly discussed. As George Brown exulted to his wife Anne in a private note, "All right!!! – constitution adopted – a most creditable document – a complete reform of all the abuses and injustices we have complained of!"

The resolutions were hammered out through exhausting days in dreary, rainy weather, fought over, altered and finally agreed upon after every pressure, political and personal, was brought to bear. At nighttime balls, indefatigable Canadian politicians waltzed the wives and daughters of Maritime delegates over the dance floor, and the next day at the conference, reaped the rewards of their evening charm.

Prince Edward Island leading Maritime resistance to union

Oct. 21, 1864

QUEBEC CITY – If words were money, then Quebec City would be rich, thanks to the ongoing discussions of politicians in town to discuss uniting British North America into one country. Since Oct. 10, delegates from the Maritime provinces and Canada have been debating, criticizing and even ridiculing some proposals the Canadians put forward.

Resistance is being led by Prince Edward Island, whose delegates see little advantage in trading colonial status for only a small part in a "confederation." They're suspicious of the Canadian plan, and rightly so. Parliamentary seats, for example, would be based on "representation by population." As Canadians far outnumber Maritimers, their delegates foresee powerlessness in government, despite promises from Canadian John A. Macdonald that they'll get enough seats in an appointed Upper House. For the Prince Edward Islanders in particular, resolving this question satisfactorily was crucial to the entire Confederation issue. Ominously, Edward Palmer has written a note to a Charlottetown editor complaining, "I am thoroughly disgusted at the course things have taken here."

As well, all the Maritimers worry about increased taxes, losing customs duties to the proposed federal government, and at the failure to buy out their absentee landlords. Still, there's a general feeling that Confederation may win the day.

One Quebec Conference delegate is Sir Etienne-Paschal Taché.

Canadians capture Confederate raiders

Oct. 23, 1864

MONTREAL – Fourteen Confederate raiders who robbed three banks in Vermont of $200,000 and killed one citizen before fleeing across the border to Montreal, were arrested today by Canadian militia. So far, just $19,000 of the loot has been recovered.

The band of Southerners, escaped prisoners of war who had hidden out in Canada, re-entered the U.S. and made the raid in St. Albans, Vermont, four days ago. Canada's neutrality in the American Civil War was not compromised making the arrests – though the robber/murderers operated in Vermont, their raid was initiated here. ▷

Mactavish takes on difficult double role

Governor William Mactavish.

1864

FORT GARRY, Assiniboia – Poor William Mactavish! The 50-year-old Hudson's Bay Company trader and administrator has a double role – and is unpopular in both. These are difficult times for those in authority in the Red River area and Mactavish, who has served the company since he was 18, is both a company administrator (governor of Upper Fort Garry) and political boss (governor of Assiniboia and Rupert's Land).

The gradual decline of the company in the west has complicated life for Mactavish, for since 1857 he has been governor of Upper Fort Garry, governor of Assiniboia, and now governor of Rupert's Land.

Polish immigrants to become farmers

1864

CANADA WEST – Canada's first group of Polish immigrants has settled in Renfrew County, on land between and west of Round and Golden lakes. They call their settlement Wilno, after the Polish city of the same name. Seeing land as the route to security, the new arrivals will be farmers.

Individual Poles have been coming to Canada for centuries. Some even say Polish explorer Johannes Scolvus reached Labrador before Columbus discovered America.

Confederation debate is heating up

Rouge leader says resolutions a sham

Nov. 7, 1864

MONTREAL – The Quebec Conference resolutions for a Canadian Confederation are a sham, charges Rouge leader Antoine-Aimé Dorion in today's *L'Avenir.*

"This is not the confederation we were proposed," Dorion writes, "but simply a legislative union disguised under the name of confederation." Dorion fears a strong central government will leave provincial legislatures only minor powers.

"A question of life or death for P.E.I."

Nov. 16, 1864

CHARLOTTETOWN – "It is a question of life or death for Prince Edward Island." Premier John Hamilton Gray uttered these words today in a powerful appeal for Confederation.

Gray feels union would solve the Island's bitter land question, and "make our tenantry happy and free." He also appealed to a sense of common nationality: "Shall we form part of a great nation extending from Halifax to Vancouver?"

Saint John gives union a cool response

Saint John, N.B., where Leonard Tilley called pro-Confederation meeting.

Nov. 17, 1864

SAINT JOHN, N.B. – A meeting to promote Confederation drew a lukewarm response at the hall of the Mechanics' Institute today. The meeting was called by the Liberal New Brunswick leader Leonard Tilley, who along with Conservative J. H. Gray, is pushing the cause in this province.

New Brunswick is badly divided on the issue of union. The hall was full but the audience was quiet and gave no indication of support. Tilley hopes to prove to New Brunswickers that it is in their financial interest to be part of a united Canada. However, he does not appear effective on the financial aspects of the Quebec Resolutions, and spoke in vague terms about how the proposed federal government is expected to discharge the large responsibilities it will be committed to. Unfortunately for Tilley, Saint John, the province's economic and press centre, is critical for the success of his pro-Confederation campaign.

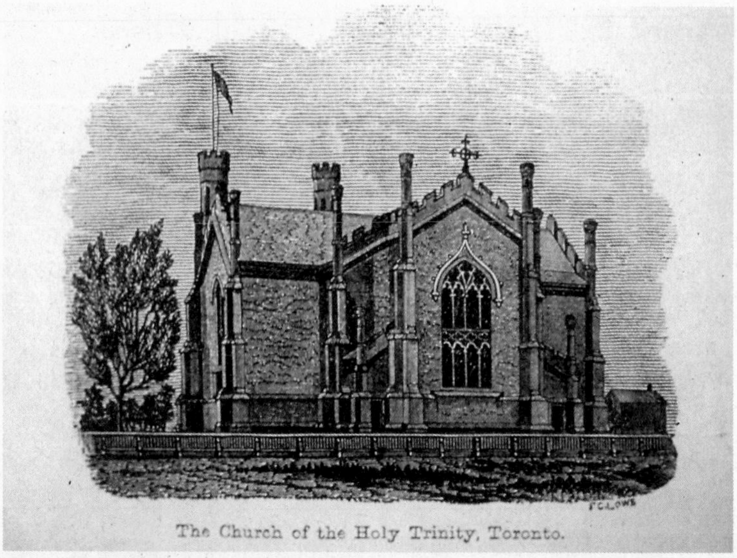

Holy Trinity Anglican Church in Trinity Square, Toronto. This engraving was given as a reward to Sunday School children of the congregation, on December 31, 1948.

Galt speech tackles Quebec Resolutions

Nov. 23, 1864

SHERBROOKE, Canada East – Today Alexander Tilloch Galt, the romantic and idealistic nationalist with a genius for finance, spoke for three hours to a crowd of 300, and explained better than anyone else just what the Quebec Resolutions mean. He unravelled the financial complexities of the proposed federation. He also elucidated its fundamental legal and constitutional implications, which were "to go back to the fountainhead, from which all our legislative powers were derived – the imperial Parliament." That is, the colonial legislatures have only to ask the Queen for an act uniting them.

Brown in London to gather support

Dec. 2, 1864
LONDON, England – Canadian Reform leader and Confederation advocate George Brown has arrived here today, on a very important mission. He is going to try to win imperial government support for Confederation, specifically the fast-track Canadian proposal.

Such support goes beyond securing approval for the scheme. Brown also hopes the British colonial office will persuade its lieutenant-governors in the Maritimes to support Confederation and convince politicians there to do the same. At present, opposition to a possible union with Canada is so strong in Nova Scotia that tensions are nearing the point of violence.

Reform leader George Brown.

Gray resigns as leader

Dec. 16, 1864
CHARLOTTETOWN – A big supporter of union, Premier John Hamilton Gray has staked his political future on Confederation. Today he admitted defeat, and resigned as premier. Most Islanders are overwhelmingly opposed to the scheme of union with Canada. The issue threatens to split the ruling Tory party, as members of Gray's own government have opted for the anti-confederate platform.

Edward Palmer, Gray's attorney general, has dismissed union "as a mere glittering delusion. I would be disposed to sit by the waters of Babylon and weep," he states, "if I thought our Island people would be taken in by the scheme."

Gray has appealed equally passionately for the union, but the anti-confederates are winning the day. At the Quebec Conference Gray became convinced P.E.I. ought to join Confederation. But his cabinet is split on the issue, and he feels he cannot retain both his honor and the premiership. Former premier Palmer may form a new cabinet.

Passports needed to visit the States

Dec. 17, 1864
WASHINGTON, D.C. – British North Americans now need passports to enter the United States, President Abraham Lincoln ordered today. Pressure in the U.S. has been mounting for retaliation against the British colonies for such grievances as releasing the St. Albans raiders – Confederate agents.

As relations deterioriate, some U.S. newspapers boast of the Union war machine's power, and urge war with Canada.

Thousands expected to use Cariboo road stagecoach service

1864
YALE, B.C. – Francis Jones Barnard, who has been delivering mail and supplies to the Cariboo goldfields with packhorses, is starting a stagecoach service. He is using two sizes of coach – one, drawn by six horses, carries 14 passengers; the other, with four horses, carries six. Barnard has also ordered freight wagons with up to 12 mules to pull them up the Cariboo road. At first he intends to go no further than Soda Creek, where both passengers and freight will transfer to a river steamer. But he also has future plans to extend the service to Quesnel and then east to Barkerville.

Barnard's service is already very popular, and thousands of passengers are expected to travel in his coaches over the next few years. He has had plenty of experience in the industry. He was working as a purser on steamships going up the Fraser when he realized how much the men in the mines looked forward to receiving mail and newspapers. Barnard decided to service this need himself. Because he could not afford a horse, he walked 1,200 kilometres from Yale to Barkerville, charging $2 for a letter. After a year he bought a packhorse and walked beside it on the road. Now he has his own stagecoach service.

Popular stagecoach service is now available on the Cariboo road.

Confederation debate heats up in Nfld.

December 1864
ST. JOHN'S, Nfld. – Should Newfoundland enter Confederation with British North America? And if so, will the island become "the contemptible fag-end of such a compact," as the St. John's *Patriot* claims, or will Confederation bring an end to the "nurtured, fostered, cherished pauperism" imposed on most Newfoundlanders by the monopoly of "merchant princes" in St. John's, as is speculated by the popular *Day-Book*?

These questions are heard more and more frequently these days throughout the Avalon Peninsula, from St. John's to Harbour Grace. Here live the majority of Newfoundlanders, most of whom are destitute, some of whom are even starving. Newfoundland's economy is based almost entirely on fishing – The Rock has only 168 square kilometres of cultivated land – and the past few seasons have been poor for both inshore and Grand Banks fisheries. Those against Confederation say Newfoundland will lose the power of "independent legislation"; those in favor point out that any legislature, independent or not, can do little when one-third of its revenue is spent on direct relief.

The 76-metre high Montmorency Falls are the highest in Canada East.

1865

Charlottetown, Feb. 16. The main opponents in the Island's Confederation debate reach a truce when anti-Confederation Attorney General Edward Palmer apologizes to Premier James Pope and former premier John Gray for remarks he made against them.

Appomattox, Virginia, April 9. Confederate Gen. Robert E. Lee surrenders unconditionally to federal Gen. Ulysses S. Grant, ending the Civil War.

Charlottetown, April. The legislature passes an address to the queen outlining why the colony should not have to pay the salary of the lieutenant governor.

London, May. Prominent Canadian ministers John A. Macdonald, Alexander Galt, George Brown, and George-Etienne Cartier leave for home after getting the British government to try to persuade the Maritime colonies to support Confederation.

St. Thomas, Canada East, July 30. Sir Etienne-Paschal Taché, trusted statesman and premier of the pro-Confederation Canadian government, dies.

Charlottetown, Aug. 6. Some 130 British troops arrive from Halifax to defend against a feared tenants' revolt over the absentee landlord system.

New Westminster, B.C., Aug. 15. A public library is opened, one of the first in the colony.

Washington, D.C., Dec. 7. The 13th Amendment to the U.S. Constitution abolishes slavery.

Montreal. One of the first games of rugby football played in Canada pits English officers against civilians, mainly from McGill University.

Montreal. A city bylaw is passed prohibiting the playing of baseball in city parks or public places.

Canada. Only murder, treason, and rape are now capital offences.

British Columbia. The colony exports about 30 million board feet of lumber.

Montreal. Charles Heavysege publishes his poem *Jeptha's Daughter*, based on a biblical theme.

Canada East. Folklorist Ernest Gagnon publishes the first part of his *Chansons populaires du Canada*, a collection of French-Canadian folk music, preserving a rich oral tradition, and alerting the world to French-Canadian folk music.

Confederation plan doomed to failure, Howe's letters say

Nova Scotian Joseph Howe.

January 1865

HALIFAX – In his Botheration Letters, Joseph Howe – no longer an elected politician but still a mighty voice – has been attacking the Quebec Resolutions for most of this month. The resolutions are the foundation of what many dream will be the new nation of British North America. But Howe says there's no skill in the design, and no cohesive qualities in the material, and therefore, "unite what you will ... there is no strength."

Within five years, Howe predicts, French Canada will "escape from the confederacy as Belgium did from Holland." Nova Scotia would be foolish to run away, above tidewater, to "the will-of-the-wisp at Ottawa, which will land us in a Slough of Despond."

Thoughts of union targeted in P.E.I.

Jan. 18, 1865

CHARLOTTETOWN – Pro-confederate Edward Whelan has conceded P.E.I. is "dead set against union in all shapes and forms." Last night's public meeting seems to confirm this. Participants agreed union poses little more than higher taxes, decreased representation and a threat to the colony's trade. The meeting concluded the scheme "is of no possible advantage to us."

Island minister Palmer "forced to go"

Jan. 7, 1865

CHARLOTTETOWN – Three weeks ago, it looked as if Edward Palmer would succeed John Hamilton Gray as premier of Prince Edward Island, his chief task to reunite his party, badly split by the Confederation issue, and his own behavior. Today, amid great controversy, Palmer quit the cabinet.

The controversy stems from his activity at the Quebec Conference. Previously one of the Island's most eloquent anti-confederates, critics say at Quebec he waxed just as eloquently in favor of the scheme. Such inconsistency implies dishonor. Unable to form a cabinet in such circumstances, he was, in the words of the press, "forced to go."

N.B. vote to decide Confederation stance

Jan. 19, 1865

SAINT JOHN, N.B. – Tempers, including that of Lt.-Gov. Arthur Hamilton Gordon, are high in New Brunswick over Confederation. So, in a move to settle the issue and get on with the political business of the province, he's persuaded Premier Samuel Tilley to go along with a general election.

It's a concession Tilley may live to regret. A pro-confederate who attended the Charlottetown and Quebec conferences as a delegate, he's up against an opposition that is gaining strength every day.

Canada not taking sides in U.S. Civil War

Jan. 19, 1865

QUEBEC CITY – The speech from the throne opening a new session of the legislature calls for measures to enforce Canadian neutrality in the U.S. Civil War. The speech proposes to amend the Alien Act to grant the government powers to expel any aliens without trial. What this means is Canada won't allow itself to be a refuge for sympathizers of either side of the conflict between the Union and the Confederacy. The government gave assurances it would not abuse the sweeping power.

Decline of goldfields sparks call for union

Jan. 26, 1865

VICTORIA, Vancouver Island – All the signs are there. The good times brought about by the goldfields are almost over. Both the colonies, Vancouver Island and the mainland, are losing people, as there is less work and less money. No other industry has yet emerged to take the place of gold. But the signs of decline are harsher on the Island, and, led by the fiery Amor De Cosmos, the House of Assembly has made it clear that it wants union of the two colonies. It now seems certain this will occur soon.

Victoria, on Vancouver Island, feels the decline of gold rush prosperity.

Tupper moves to save Confederation

April 10, 1865

HALIFAX – In a ploy to avoid outright rejection of Confederation, Premier Charles Tupper of Nova Scotia today moved an alternative scheme, Maritime union. Premier Leonard Tilley's pro-Confederation party in New Brunswick recently suffered a shocking defeat, and Joseph Howe's Botheration Letters in the Halifax press have poisoned Nova Scotians against Confederation. It is, Howe gloats, "as dead as Julius Caesar."

In today's debate, Tupper offered much background on Confederation, little of it new or gripping. But due to "circumstances over which we have no control," it was pointless to propose resolutions on Confederation. Still, Maritime union seemed like a good idea.

Will these gold-washers in Lunenberg, N.S. soon be part of a Maritime union?

Anti-union Smith rallies for support in Tilley country

Jan. 31, 1865

SAINT JOHN, N.B. – Albert Smith, leader of the forces opposing Confederation, rallied supporters tonight in the heart of Tilley country: the Mechanics' Institute in Saint John. The crowd cheered wildly whenever Smith attacked Premier Leonard Tilley and his Confederation scheme. Still, Smith was caught off guard when the premier himself appeared on stage, and challenged him to a debate two nights hence. Smith refused! Could it be that he fears Tilley's legendary powers of mustering facts, arguments and – ultimately – support for his pet schemes just when the going is the toughest?

Confederation debate could last weeks

Feb. 3, 1865

QUEBEC CITY – The 72 Resolutions, adopted last year at a conference in this city, have been introduced by the government as an act of Parliament. If approved, the act will allow Canada to join the Maritime provinces to form a federated state. Debate on the issue has been exhaustive. Every single point and every qualification is being explored by speaker after speaker. The debate could take weeks before Parliament puts the bill to the test.

London refuses to pay governor's salary

Feb. 18, 1865

CHARLOTTETOWN – Britain, determined to pressure Prince Edward Island into Confederation, today announced that, Confederation or not, it will stop providing funds for the lieutenant-governor's salary. Prince Edward Island has no revenue from Crown lands; in 1767 London granted them all away, covering the salary with an annual sum. Islanders term today's decision "a confederate screw unfairly put upon us."

New Brunswickers say no to union

March 4, 1865

SAINT JOHN, N.B. – Final returns are in from the New Brunswick election. And the result is a clear-cut defeat for Premier Samuel Tilley and his Confederation policy. The premier lost his seat, as did two other delegates to the Confederation conferences.

Anti-confederate leader Albert Smith won his seat, as did many others sharing his views. The result is summed up by Lt.-Gov. Arthur Hamilton Gordon, who said "the government is practically overthrown, and the scheme of union virtually defeated."

What's caused Confederation's defeat? It seems New Brunswickers are obsessed with fears that such a union would increase taxation. As their local politics tend to revolve around taxation issues, their present concern is not surprising.

Toronto shutdown to mourn assassination of President Lincoln

April 18, 1865

TORONTO – City council has ordered all Toronto businesses to close for two hours on the afternoon of Abraham Lincoln's funeral, in mourning for the popular United States president who was assassinated four days ago. The resolution passed by council also acknowledged regret for his death. Just one councillor opposed the motion. His hostility to the North, which Lincoln led, was well known.

When news of the killing first broke, members of the American community living here met and selected a delegation of three to go to Washington for the funeral. There were some sour notes as well. A few Southerners toasted John Wilkes Booth, Lincoln's assassin.

U.S. President Abraham Lincoln.

A solemn funeral procession for the slain president in New York City.

Pro-Confederation forces win the day; motion supported

March 11, 1865

QUEBEC CITY – After five tense weeks of debate, members of Parliament lobbying for Confederation have won the day. However, final analysis of voting reveals a split between Canada West and Canada East that could widen and fuel the flames of discontent in French Canada. Members from Canada West have overwhelmingly supported Confederation, 54-8, but in Canada East the margin of victory was 37-25, with 21 of 48 French-Canadian members opposed.

Antoine-Aimé Dorion, leader of the liberal-reform Rouge party, has led the attack on Confederation, saying French-Canadian interests will be ignored in a House of Commons dominated, at least numerically, by members from English Canada. He says the "disallowance of local legislation" will make the preservation of French-Canadian culture impossible, despite George-Etienne Cartier's assurances that Confederation will mean "political nationality," not "cultural." Cartier, reluctant to mix politics with religion but wary of defeat, has elicited support from the influential Catholic clergy, at odds with the Rouges, in his campaign.

Booth hinted of murder in Montreal

John Wilkes Booth fires fatal shot at President Lincoln in Ford Theatre.

May 7, 1865

NEW YORK – Startling new evidence reveals that President Abraham Lincoln's assassin, John Wilkes Booth, dropped hints the act was impending long before the actual killing three weeks ago. *The New York Times* today published an account of a conversation Booth had at Montreal's St. Lawrence Hall hotel last October.

While playing a game of pool, an intoxicated Booth is quoted as saying he would "bag the biggest game this side of ..., just remember my address – you'll hear of a double carom one of these days." He went on to say that Lincoln "would get his goose cooked."

Huge $1M budget for defence OK'd

March 17, 1865

QUEBEC CITY – Parliament today approved an unprecedented defence budget of $1 million. Confederation is unlikely this year and tensions are running high with the United States. It is hoped the move will support the imperial cabinet's argument with Britain's House of Commons for a continued military commitment to a staunchly loyal British North America.

18 men rescue "tallest girl in the world"

1865

NEW YORK – When P.T. Barnum's museum burned down, it took 18 men with a block and tackle to rescue one living exhibit. She was Nova Scotia-born Anna Swan, "the tallest girl in the world."

At 18 or 19, Anna stands 7-6 and weighs 352 pounds, but Barnum advertises that she's even bigger. Three years ago, she went to work for him for $1,000 a week, and a chance to hire a private tutor to further her education.

Scarlet fever killing hundreds of Indians

July 1865

PEEL'S RIVER POST, Rupert's Land – The Indians of the Mackenzie and Yukon valleys, already weakened by European diseases, are dying by the hundreds of scarlet fever, brought in by the Hudson's Bay Company's supply boat crews. As the boats went down the Mackenzie, they took the disease to the various Indian camps. Then the supply expedition to Fort Yukon spread the disease east as it trekked over the mountains.

Annual spring ice jam at Montreal causes damage to several buildings.

Montrealers act to save river's salmon

1865

MONTREAL – Habitant Napoleon Comeau has been hired by a handful of Montreal businessmen and politicos to guard salmon in the Godbout River, on the north shore of the St. Lawrence River, about 320 kilometres below Quebec. Comeau wages war up and down the river, dealing harshly with all poachers, including the native Indians whose ancestors fished for salmon in these waters for many centuries.

First of 15 oil refineries built in Petrolia

1865

PETROLIA – The first of 15 oil refineries has been constructed in this village southeast of Sarnia. It was here in 1862 that Hugh Shaw, a Strathroy photographer, hit it big with the first free-flowing oil gusher. It was almost too big, with 2,000 barrels of oil a day gushing out, filling creeks and spreading into the fields. Fortunately, a traveller from Titusville, Pennsylvania, which had its own oil wells, came by and demonstrated how to cap a well.

Colonies should pay for defence: British

June 1, 1865
LONDON, England – British officials today stressed that the North American colonies "must recognize a right, and admit an obligation" to assume part of their own defence. The colonial office considers Confederation a vital step toward this goal.

"Preparations for material defence," it states, "would be easily undertaken by a province uniting in itself all the population and all of the resources of the whole."

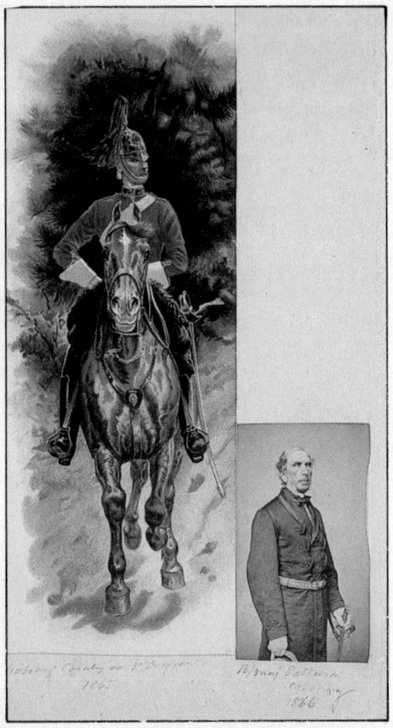

Uniform of Cobourg Cavalry.

Ministers lobby for defence dollars

Prominent Canadians seek British support for major defence projects.

May 1, 1865
LONDON, England – Four prominent Canadian ministers are here today to try to convince the British to fund a series of military defence projects in the colony. John A. Macdonald, Alexander Galt, George Brown and George-Etienne Cartier are trying to gain imperial backing for a network of canals, railways, forts, and munitions factories aimed at making Canada impervious to American attack.

Galt estimates the cost at £8 million to £10 million. It's a price tag the British government, which has a slim majority, is unlikely to swallow. Last year the best it could offer was a mere £50,000.

Americans to end Reciprocity Treaty

March 17, 1865
WASHINGTON, D.C. – The United States gave notice today that it intends to terminate the Reciprocity Treaty with British North America, an agreement for free trade in a number of natural products. It also allowed mutual access to certain fishing waters.

The treaty, signed in 1854, was to run at least 10 years, after which it could be terminated by either party by giving a one-year notice. Northern resentment at alleged British favoritism of the South in the Civil War, contributed to this decision.

Britain urges Gordon to push for union

N.B. trains soldiers to prove it does not need Confederation for defence.

June 24, 1865
LONDON, England – Britain's government has urged New Brunswick Lt.-Gov. Arthur Hamilton Gordon to do everything in his power to push the Maritimes into Confederation. Today's official letter comes after reports that the colonial office believes "selfish interests of small men in small provinces" are delaying Confederation. A recent New Brunswick election voted in a government against Confederation. But the letter should quiet those who insist union would end the link with Britain.

Dundas to farmers: avoid Tenant League

March 22, 1865
CHARLOTTETOWN – In response to the growing power of the Tenant League, Gov. George Dundas has issued a proclamation urging all farmers "to abstain from all such unlawful associations."

Prince Edward Island's tenant farmers have been growing restless since 1861, when it became obvious London was not going to act on the popular Land Commission Report. Members of the league have pledged to withhold rents until proprietors agree to sell their lands at "just prices."

Passports no longer needed to enter U.S.

March 6, 1865
WASHINGTON, D.C. – The United States today revoked last December's order requiring British North Americans to carry a passport when entering the U.S. The move soothes Canadian and Maritime anxieties over the threat of an American invasion, but the British imperial office and London press remain nervous and continue to speculate over the possibility.

P.E.I. committee frowns on Confederation

April 3, 1865
CHARLOTTETOWN – Union based on the Quebec conference resolutions will "prove disastrous to the best interests and future prosperity of Prince Edward Island." So says a committee of the legislature charged with assessing the matter.

Existing terms do not give the Island adequate representation in a union parliament. It is also feared that union would ruin the Island's economy and give "no satisfactory return" for the extra taxes Islanders would have to pay. Finally, the committee says the Island's defences are sound, and it need not look to Canada for protection.

D'Arcy McGee slams Fenian brotherhood

May 15, 1865

WEXFORD, Ireland – Canadian politician D'Arcy McGee took a few shots at a favorite target, the Fenians, in a speech to the Young Men's Society in his home town. In Ireland to represent Canada at the Dublin International Exposition, McGee dismissed his background as an Irish rebel as "the follies of one and twenty," and added that he had never seen "a specimen of the genus Fenian in Canada."

Taking a shot at the U.S., where in New York the Fenian brotherhood was organized six years ago to push for Ireland's independence, McGee, who once lived in the U.S., said the Irish were not accepted as social equals in that country.

Parliament of Canada now in Ottawa

The new Parliament Buildings now nearing completion overlook the Ottawa River. The logs in the river illustrate the industrial basis of the city.

Oct. 20, 1865

OTTAWA – Eight years after Queen Victoria selected this city as the permanent capital of the Province of Canada, Parliament has been moved to Ottawa. Thus ends the long dispute over which city should be the seat of government. Ottawa won the queen's approval in a five-way race with Quebec, Montreal, Kingston, and Toronto.

The bid was helped by former governor general Edmund Head. His memorandum to London said Ottawa was the only place acceptable in both Upper and Lower Canada as a fair compromise. Construction work on the Parliament Buildings is in progress. The project, begun in 1860, was put on hold from 1861-63 when funds ran out.

Brown wants new reciprocity treaty

July 15, 1865

TORONTO – Canada will send a delegation to Washington to try to renew the reciprocity treaty, it was decided at a stormy cabinet meeting today. At the insistence of George Brown, two ministers – Alexander Galt and W.P. Howland – will open talks on extending the treaty, due to expire in March. Americans, incensed by the St. Alban's raid by Confederate troops from B.N.A. soil, want to cancel the treaty in retaliation.

P.E.I. farm revolt threatens to erupt

Aug. 7, 1865

CHARLOTTETOWN – Disturbances centred on the Tenant League's activities are reaching a critical point. As authorities have tried to collect the rents farmers have refused to pay, the league's policy of peaceful negotiation has collapsed. There have been many instances of violence.

The colony's militia is suspect, and administrator Robert Hodgson has lost faith in their ability to quell the unrest. Fearing a general revolt, he has appealed to Halifax for a company of regular troops.

London instructs Gordon to toe the line

Oct. 28, 1865

SAINT JOHN, N.B. – Lt.-Gov. Arthur Hamilton Gordon, once a notorious anti-confederate, returned home today with a new wife and, insiders say, strict instructions from the imperial government to lobby for Confederation, like it or not. In fact, rumor says Gordon was recalled to London to be chewed-out by the colonial secretary for his anti-Confederation beliefs.

Wine-maker woos Niagara churches

W. W. KITCHEN'S
PURE GRAPE WINE,
WHOLESALE
AND RETAIL.
PURE
GRAPE WINE
FOR SALE BY
W.W. KITCHEN. GRAPE GROWER
& WINEMAKER GRIMSBY C.W.
Took a SPECIAL PRIZE at the PROVINCIAL EXHIBITION in HAMILTON, 1864.
TOOK THE HIGHEST PRIZES
AND AWARDED THREE DIPLOMAS,
At the last PROVINCIAL EXHIBITION in LONDON,
And tested by the Committee of Management of the MONTREAL GENERAL HOSPITAL, who report it to be a pure article, good for Medicinal purposes.
Now in use by some Hundreds of Churches,
FOR SACRAMENTAL SERVICES.
It is sold by most of the principal Chemists in Canada East and West.
PRICE, $2 50 per Gallon. 10 gallons and over, 25 per cent. Discount.
Kegs and Barrels furnished at $1 25 each. Money may be sent with the order at my risk, if duly registered, or paid to Express Company on receipt of the Wine.
Direct all orders to
W. W. KITCHEN,
GRIMSBY, C. W.
N.B.—GRAPE VINES AT LOW RATES BY THE 1,000.
[103]

W.W. Kitchen of Grimsby proudly advertises award-winning product.

Nov. 8, 1865

GRIMSBY, Canada West – Wine-making is on an upswing in the Niagara area and one local producer is actively promoting his product. W.W. Kitchen, who started growing grapes on his farm near here in 1858 and opened his winery last year, claims to be selling wine to hundreds of churches. His wine, which has won prizes at provincial exhibitions, sells for $2.50 a gallon.

Subsidies are lower for female students

1865

CANADA WEST – Many Ontario school trustees are critical of the current criteria for disbursing public monies to grammar schools, because subsidies are much lower for female students. They believe both boys and girls should attend grammar school at taxpayers' expense. Dr. Egerton Ryerson disagrees. Ryerson states that grammar schools are not primarily designed for girls. The result: numerous young women across the province are deprived of the benefits of higher education.

Unusual design graces new stamp in B.C.

Nov. 1, 1865

VICTORIA, B.C. – The British Columbia Postal Service issued a new threepence stamp today. The unusual design, approved last year, is based on the uniform buttons worn by the Royal Engineers. The stamp also bears Her Majesty's initial and the Crown.

The designer's identity is something of a mystery. One source credits Capt. William Driscoll Gosset of the Royal Engineers. However, another rumor suggests it originated with the agents general for the colonies in London.

New 3d British Columbia stamp.

Pro-confederate wins byelection

Nov. 6, 1865

YORK COUNTY, N.B. – Charles Fisher achieved a near-miracle tonight. An avowed supporter of Confederation in an anti-confederate province, he nevertheless defeated rival John Pickard tonight in a byelection. It's fair to say that Fisher, an old political veteran, used every trick in the book save truth to win this seat over the inexperienced Pickard.

Minister wraps up pro-union pep tour

Nov. 28, 1865

HALIFAX – Canadian cabinet minister George Brown left Halifax today, completing a pro-Confederation pep tour of this city and Saint John. Brown wants to bolster support for Confederation in an area generally opposed to it. However, opposition is crumbling, as the anti-confederates propose no constructive alternative, and Britain is determined its colonies unite.

Brown quits over treaty

Dec. 22, 1865

QUEBEC CITY – George Brown has resigned from the government following a dispute over the Reciprocity Treaty. The treaty, which has provided 10 years of low duties on U.S.-Canadian trade, expires soon. And, given U.S. anger at Canada for its supposed favoring of the defeated Confederate States, in border incidents, it is unlikely to be renewed unless Canada makes some major concessions. This is apparently what happened, or what Brown believes happened, when Alexander Galt, Canada's finance minister, proposed legislative reciprocity (interlocking laws) between the two countries. Brown, the Liberal, felt that Galt, the Conservative, was actually giving Canada away to the United States by the economic terms he was prepared to accept.

Railway extension sparks controversy

Nov. 8, 1865

SAINT JOHN, N.B. – The railway's "western extension" – to link up with U.S. lines in Maine – had its official sod-turning today, but one of its champions was pessimistic. Timothy Warren Anglin, member for Saint John in the Assembly, had pushed for the line but opposed having it built by private enterprise – American at that – when the government could not raise funds for the project itself.

Stamp opens mill on Burrard Inlet

Nov. 30, 1865

BURRARD INLET, B.C. – The Vancouver Island Spar, Lumber and Sawmill Company opened today on the swampy shores of Burrard Inlet. The steam-powered mill, owned by itinerant sea captain Edward Stamp, has a store and a loading wharf. Stamp owns timber rights to a large area. But he moved here because the Whoi Whoi village Indians feared for the sanctity of their burial ground.

Missionary heals as replacement arrives

Dec. 25, 1865

FORT SIMPSON, Rupert's Land – William Carpenter Bompas, a 34-year-old curate from England, arrived here today to replace missionary Robert McDonald, who has been seriously ill. But Bompas had hardly unpacked when he learned that McDonald, who worked out of Fort Yukon, was getting better.

The Anglican Church Missionary Society has been working with the Hudson's Bay Company to keep the Catholic Oblates of Mary Immaculate from getting a foothold among the fur traders and Indians in the Yukon. McDonald's illness left a void, and to fill it, Bompas was brought over from England. Now some work must be found for Bompas, for he is a determined, restless, young man.

Work must now be found for curate William C. Bompas (later photo).

Montagnais Indians struggle to survive

The Montagais Indians are struggling to survive in a land depleted of resources.

c.1865

CANADA EAST – Montagnais Indians have not signed a treaty. They have not been offered one. Shunted aside as the fur trade spread west during the last century, these people, once proud allies of the French and so important to the post-contact fur trade economy of the St. Lawrence region, now struggle to survive in a land depleted of game. With no land on which to farm, small bands inhabit coastal regions where they must compete with salmon fisheries that offer little, if any, employment.

West Coast Indian models potlatch regalia and carries talking stick.

1866

Saint John, N.B., Jan. 28. Robert Foulis, inventor of a steam-operated foghorn with a coded system of signals, dies in poverty even though he was a man of great genius.

North America, March 17. The Reciprocity Treaty between Canada and the U.S. ceases operation after being abrogated by the U.S. It was signed in 1854 to lower tariffs between the two countries.

St. John's, Nfld., March. The Assembly passes a resolution postponing the issue of Confederation indefinitely, a reflection of anti-Confederation feeling. The government has no authority to take part in Confederation negotiations.

New Brunswick, April. British soldiers and local militia easily repulse a Fenian invasion from Maine. The Fenians only succeed in seizing a Union Jack from a customs house.

Niagara Falls, Canada West, June 3. Fenian invaders retreat over the Niagara River to the U.S. after occupying Fort Erie on June 1. They are captured by American authorities.

Pigeon Hill, Canada East, June 9. British soldiers and Canadian militia chase a group of Fenians across the border to the U.S. after they invaded two days ago.

New Brunswick, June. Pro-Confederation forces led by Leonard Tilley win a heated election on the issue of Confederation. The Fenian invasion of the colony increased support for Confederation.

Montreal, Dec. 29. *The Saturday Reader* declares "skating has obtained of late years, especially among the fairer portion of our population, an unwonted popularity." Skaters strut their stuff at the four-year-old Victoria Rink, one of the first and biggest indoor rinks on the continent.

Canada East. The Roman Catholic church declares that marriage for Catholics is dissoluble only by death.

Canada East. The new Civil Code states that no dower rights are valid unless registered, increasing pressure on women to renounce their dower rights which entitle them to use their husband's land after his death even if he has sold or mortgaged it.

Montreal. A rugby football club is established. British soldiers and settlers introduced the game to Canada.

Volunteers poised to fight Fenians

British Volunteer Cavalry and Fenians meet in conflict near Frelighsburg, Canada East, on June 8, 1866.

March 7, 1866

TORONTO – Arms have been put into the hands of 10,000 volunteers for a period of three weeks to ensure the Fenians a warm reception if they invade British North America on St. Patrick's Day. Heeding the words of Maj. G.T. Denison of Toronto about the possibility of attack, authorities are putting the Militia Act of 1863 to the test, by placing the militia at the exposed points along the frontier.

Believing they can free Ireland by invading Canada to distract the imperial government, the Fenian Brotherhood came to North America in 1857 when it was founded by Col. John O'Mahony. Idle in the Civil War, the group sent money and arms to the Irish Republican Army. In 1865 the organization split to form the Secret Wing of the Fenian Brotherhood under Col. William Roberts, and Secretary-of-War Sweeney. At a convention held in Cincinnati the Fenians decided to invade Canada. Headquartered in New York, the "Irish Republic" has successfully recruited former Irish Union soldiers to their cause. The American authorities wink at their hostile activities.

St. Paddy's Day invasion never comes

March 17, 1866

CANADA EAST AND WEST – The hotly-awaited St. Patrick's Day has passed uneventfully in cities and villages everywhere, as volunteers standing at the ready in barracks fought boredom as deadly as any Fenian. In Toronto, only 618 showed up to march. Brantford, Ingersoll, Chatham, Perth, Peterborough, Stratford, Kingston and Sarnia were also peaceful and calm.

British believe Confederation is desirable

March 8, 1866

FREDERICTON – Britain's government believes that Confederation is desirable, the speech from the throne said today. While the union of Britain's North American colonies seems inevitable, there has been little excitement here. But more and more New Brunswick residents are becoming resigned to the fact, particularly in light of the Fenian threat.

N.B. council asks for Confederation

April 7, 1866

FREDERICTON – The New Brunswick Legislative Council has issued a statement asking the queen for Confederation. The Upper House said today it would agree to any measure, but it favors the Quebec Resolutions. The letter was drawn up with a push by Lt.-Gov. Arthur Hamilton Gordon, who felt his chances were better in the Upper House, controlled by opponents of the Smith government, than with the vacillating Albert Smith.

Pro-confederates to govern in N.B.

April 17, 1866
FREDERICTON – Pro-confederates formed a government in New Brunswick today, one week after Albert Smith's administration resigned. Lt.-Gov. Arthur Hamilton Gordon asked confederate protagonist Peter Mitchell to form the government, but the group's real leader is Leonard Tilley.

Smith had wavered on union so long Gordon finally lost patience and asked for his resignation. At first he refused but later complied. Tilley will assume his former position of provincial secretary in the new administration. Robert Duncan Wilmot, who had been in the Smith government, will also figure in this regime.

Nova Scotia votes to support union

April 18, 1866
HALIFAX – Unnerved by news of an army of Irish Americans (Fenians) in Eastport, Maine, the Nova Scotia Assembly, after 15 hours of debate, voted 31-19 for Premier Charles Tupper's resolution to arrange "a scheme of union" with other provinces of British North America. One Confederation convert hoped he'd "never live to see the Stars and Stripes floating over Citadel Hill."

Fenians invade British North America

Fenian invaders carry the Irish flag in a clash with British regulars and militia at the Battle of Ridgeway.

June 2, 1866
NIAGARA FALLS – Canada has been invaded and Fort Erie is occupied. Fenian "general" John O'Neill, formerly of the Union Army, and a band of some 800 Fenians crossed the Niagara River the night of May 31. Landing a mile below Fort Erie "colonel" Starr raised the Fenian flag at 4 a.m.

Catching Canadian forces off guard, O'Neill occupied Fort Erie without resistance. To secure the landing, he ordered the reeve to provide rations for his men, the cutting of telegraph lines, and the tearing up of railway tracks. The main body moved to Frenchmen's Creek yesterday, terrorizing the countryside on their way. Hearing of the invasion, Gen. George Napier ordered the regulars and militia under colonels George J. Peacocke and Alfred Booker forward.

President's proclamation slams Fenians

June 6, 1866
WASHINGTON, D.C. – Fenian hopes for a successful invasion of British North America received a serious setback today as U.S. President Andrew Johnson issued a proclamation condemning their "high misdemeanors, forbidden by the laws of the United States." The decision officially ends American neutrality and denies the Fenians safe refuge on their own side of the border. U.S. troops under generals Ulysses S. Grant and George C. Meade are under orders to seize Fenian arms and ammunition.

P.E.I. to resume debate on Confederation

May 7, 1866
CHARLOTTETOWN – Under extreme pressure from the colonial office, the Prince Edward Island legislature has agreed to resume debate on Confederation. It appears that the scheme is in for rough time, for the resolutions are worded in extremely anti-confederate terms. As Premier J.C. Pope warns, "99 out of every 100 of the people are against Confederation. I think we, as their representatives, are bound to express their wishes."

A William Henry Bartlett engraving shows farmers tending to their land and livestock, with Fredericton, New Brunswick, in the background.

Telegraph links tiny town to Europe

July 27, 1866

HEART'S CONTENT, Nfld. – The transatlantic telegraph cable was hauled ashore here today, and messages began to move between England and this tiny fishing village. It was a victory for Cyrus Field, the brains behind the operation, who had failed on three earlier attempts.

The most recent failure was last year when the cable snapped less than one day out of Newfoundland after fraying beneath the hull of the *Great Eastern.* Field reorganized, raised £600,000 and set sail in June. His first attempt, in 1857, ended when the cable broke some 480 kilometres out of Ireland. His second attempt worked briefly before the flawed cable went dead.

Sailors drag ashore the transatlantic telegraph cable at Heart's Content.

American bill's aim is to annex Canada

July 2, 1866

WASHINGTON, D.C. – A bill clearing the way for the annexation of Canada was introduced in Congress today. The bill calls for the "admission of the states of Nova Scotia, New Brunswick, Canada East and Canada West and for the organization of the territories of Selkirk, Saskatchewan and Columbia." It also urges the U.S. to build or enlarge canals to improve navigation on the St. Lawrence River.

While the bill is not likely to pass, there is mounting pressure to expand, particularly in the press. Tension between England and the north mounted in the Civil War, and now papers such as the New York *Herald* and Chicago *Tribune* are pushing for annexation.

"The Canadians," the *Tribune* writes in its Jan. 6 edition this year, "will stay out in the cold for a few years and try all sorts of expedients, but in the end will be constrained to knock for admission into the great Republic." Two weeks later the Chicago paper said Canada would be "snatched up by this Republic as quickly as a hawk would gobble up a quail." On the east coast, the legislature of Massachusetts passed a resolution promoting annexation, and a state assemblyman was greedily looking forward to new potential markets in Canada for New England products he felt would be the spoils of annexation. The fisheries of Canada's Maritime provinces were being coveted at the same time by U.S. revenue commissioners.

Vancouver Island and B.C. to unite

June 8, 1866

VICTORIA, Vancouver Island – The British government is going ahead with legislation to unite the colonies of Vancouver Island and British Columbia, it is understood here. As far as London is concerned this is the only solution to the economic, financial and constitutional crisis facing the island colony.

The colonial office has consulted with Frederick Seymour, governor of British Columbia, who is in Europe on leave from New Westminster. He has recommended that the government of British Columbia take over the Island.

Horseless carriage debuts at parish picnic

June 24, 1866

RUSTICO, P.E.I. – Father Georges Belcourt, the popular pastor of Rustico, shocked his flock today by arriving at a parish picnic in a horseless carriage. The steam-powered carriage, imported from New Jersey, is believed to be the first of its kind in British North America. It has allowed Belcourt to score two "firsts" in one day. He is the first to own a horseless carriage, and he is also the first to have an accident in one. After a half-mile run his vehicle lost control, and veered into a nearby field.

Grand vicar stresses importance of French

June 24, 1866

OTTAWA – Canadians must retain their language or forfeit their Catholic faith, a senior Quebec priest told a St-Jean Baptiste Day crowd here. The grand vicar, Louis-François Laflèche, noted for his advocacy of close links between the church and state, said at the French-Canadian gathering that learning English is "the heaviest tax imposed upon us by the Conquest. Let us pay it loyally but let us pay only when necessary."

Charlottetown fire worst in city history

July 15, 1866

CHARLOTTETOWN – The city has been devastated by the worst fire in its history. The blaze broke out early this morning in a house near the corner of King and Pownall streets. Fanned by a strong westerly wind, the fire quickly marched toward the centre of town.

Though virtually every citizen turned out to help the fire department, the flames died down only after consuming 200 buildings. Four blocks are reduced to ruins.

Hudson's Bay Company establishment at Fort Rupert, British Columbia.

"Copper" now gold in Madoc Township

Aug. 15, 1866

MADOC TOWNSHIP – When copper turns to gold: Marcus Herbert Powell, a court clerk, and an oldtimer known only as "Snider" have been told the ore they thought was copper is gold. So stunned were they by their find, all they could do was swear. With the discovery of the gold, on James Richardson's farm in Madoc Township, prospectors have just started to tap the mineral wealth of the Canadian Shield, known for its iron, lead and marble.

Confederation talks in the homestretch at London meeting

Dec. 4, 1866

LONDON, England – It's a raw and cold day here in the heart of London, and the 16 men sitting around a long table inside the Westminster Palace Hotel are warmed only by the urgency of their mission – to convince the imperial government to legislate into reality the long-delayed, hotly-contested union of British North America.

Six Canadians led by John A. Macdonald and George-Etienne Cartier will hammer out the final details with five New Brunswickers and six Nova Scotians. Basically, they will adapt the 72 Resolutions adopted at Quebec into a workable piece of British legislation. The Maritimers are edgy – they have been waiting since August for the Canadians to arrive. The Nova Scotians are particularly impatient, for an election must be held there before June 1867. In politically-battered Canada, further delay may cause the fragile, governing coalition to dissolve.

But circumstances beyond their control prevented the Canadians from setting sail until early November. They had waited until it was clear the Fenians would not launch any major attacks. Also, U.S. congressional elections resulted in an overwhelming Republican majority, removing immediate worry that British North America would be a pawn in American politics.

London Resolutions ready for perusal

Dec. 24, 1866

LONDON, England – Three exhausting weeks after the London Conference opened, Canadian delegate John A. Macdonald has notified Lord Carnavon, the new colonial secretary, that the London Resolutions are ready to be sent to the colonial office. Basically, they echo the 1864 Quebec Resolutions. Minor alterations clarify dubious points, or satisfy delegates' qualms.

Now it is just a matter of waiting. The delegates believe they – and Confederation – will prevail, despite the attempts of anti-confederates such as Joseph Howe, in London to sabotage the scheme. Howe has even stooped to sending Lord Carnavon George Brown's *Globe* article, "Drunkenness in High Places," describing a drunken Macdonald clinging to his desk in Parliament to keep from falling.

Macdonald and his colleagues George-Etienne Cartier and Alexander Galt have countered with personal visits to Lord Carnavon. He is an idealist, without the cynicism of many British officials who favor the union as an easy way to shrug off colonial problems. Carnavon sees instead a new and great British North American nation.

After one trip to Carnavon's Highclere Castle, Macdonald fell asleep in his hotel bed, reading the newspapers, and his candle set afire his bedding. Despite serious burns, he cheerfully chaired the next day's meeting. Not even painful injury would delay Confederation!

John A. Macdonald.

George-Etienne Cartier.

Delegates tackle the thorny issue of a future Upper House

Dec. 13, 1866

LONDON, England – Today the thorny issue of a future Upper House, or Senate, dominated the agenda of the London Conference. It has always provoked bitter controversy, all the more difficult to resolve because the Upper House is at the heart of the proposed federal system. Says Jonathan McCully of New Brunswick, "I feel that we are now touching the very life of the whole scheme." Three aspects of the issue are crucial: will representation be by region or province; will the 24 seats allotted to the Maritimes at the Quebec Conference be reduced because P.E.I. has withdrawn; and will members be appointed, or elected?

After intense debate, it was decided the Senate will have regional representation, a guarantee against the brute force of numbers in the Lower House. The Maritimes retain their 24 seats, divided equally between Nova Scotia and New Brunswick pending P.E.I.'s final decision. And despite vociferous Reform objections, the Senate will be an appointed body of 72, chosen by the central government, to sit for life. Also, the number of members may not be changed – this alone allays fears of less populous regions that they may be swamped.

Monck telegraphs for reinforcements

Sept. 11, 1866

OTTAWA – A request for British military reinforcements to stave off cross-border raids by the Fenians was sent to England today via the transatlantic telegraph line. Gov. Gen. Charles Monck is asking for three infantry battalions, one cavalry and artillery and engineering units. Despite John A. Macdonald's skepticism, both Monck and Sir John Michel, commander-in-chief of British forces here, worry about the Fenians, who since 1865 have stepped up their rhetoric.

A Kwakiutl chief in his colorful traditional costume.

Kwakiutl Indians of the west coast dance and sing in a traditional ceremony.

1867

London, Feb. 16. British North Americans in the city gather at St. George's Church for the marriage of John A. Macdonald and Susan Agnes Bernard.

Halifax, February. The Assembly passes anti-Confederation resolutions and authorizes a delegation to join Joseph Howe in London to seek the colony's release from Confederation.

British Columbia, March 18. The Legislative Council asks Governor Frederick Seymour to work toward the admission of B.C. to Canada.

London, March 29. Parliament passes the British North America Act, providing for the union of Nova Scotia, New Brunswick, and Canada [Ontario and Quebec] into a self-governing nation, to be known as the Dominion of Canada.

Washington, D.C., April 9. The U.S. agrees to buy Alaska from Russia for $7.2 million.

Canada West, May 10. The Canadian Bank of Commerce opens its first branches.

Montreal, June 10. Some 10,000 workers demonstrate in support of bakers involved in a labor dispute. The Great Association for the Protection of Canadian Workers, founded by Médéric Lanctot, organized the event.

Toronto, June. Liberals hold a large convention, organized by George Brown, to work for party unity against John A. Macdonald's government.

Canada, July 1: The BNA Act goes into effect. A public holiday, Canada's first Dominion Day, is held to celebrate the birth of the new nation. John A. Macdonald, Canada's first prime minister, has formed a new federal coalition government of Liberals and Conservatives.

London, Sept. 14. Karl Marx publishes *Das Capital*, in which he argues that capitalism will collapse from its own contradictions, and be followed by a dictatorship of the proletariat.

Kingston, Ont. There are 907 prisoners at Kingston Penitentiary. Overcrowding is undermining disciplne. New prisons are needed.

Canada. There are 3,667 kilometres of railway in Canada, an increase of only 322 kilometres in 10 years.

Paris. A New Brunswick crew wins a race at the Paris International Exhibition, Canada's first major rowing victory.

Queen gives BNA Act royal assent

March 29, 1867

LONDON, England – The delegations from British North America, in London seeking fulfilment of their Confederation proposal, today saw their long fought-for goal of unity to preserve the northern part of the continent from the U.S. achieved. Three weeks to the day after third reading of the bill passed through Britain's Parliament without a word of debate, Queen Victoria gave royal assent to the British North America Act. The new Dominion of Canada, composed of four provinces – Ontario, Quebec, New Brunswick and Nova Scotia – is now a reality.

For the Canadians, several in London since last July, the queen's signature today vindicated years of hopes, dreams, and often-bitter struggle. The act embodies the 72 Resolutions drafted at the 1864 Quebec Conference, and modified by the London delegates last winter. It outlines the executive powers of the federal and provincial governments, and the division of representation. It also allocates revenues, and provides for eventual construction of an intercontinental railway. But, just as it was not unanimously endorsed in 1864, so rumblings of discontent are heard now. For many new Canadians, the Confederation debate is by no means over. The system of self-government, for instance, remains ill-defined – while the central government resembles the former colonial legislatures, all wrapped up into one, the powers now vested in the individual provinces are unclear. As a constitutional document, the BNA Act is strong on principle, vague on application. How the pieces will fit together is far from clear.

What is certain is that this new nation is the realization of the collective dream of a powerful political elite. With the exception of Canada West, now Ontario, it is doubtful the agreement could have passed the electoral test. But though it may not reflect the wishes of most British North Americans, it does satisfy its Mother Country eager to be rid of responsibility for its North American colonies. Canada is a nation born prematurely and not whole. But now, at least, it can build its own transcontinental future.

First female doctor practising illegally

1867

TORONTO – Canada's first female doctor is practising illegally in this city. A former teacher who has supported her family since her husband got tuberculosis, Emily Howard Stowe recently graduated from New York Medical College for Women. Foreign-trained physicians are required by law to attend lectures and pass Canadian exams. However, Dr. Stowe was previously turned away by Canadian medical schools. The mother of three intends to risk the $100 fine for practising medicine without a licence.

Dr. Emily Howard Stowe of Toronto.

De Cosmos wants B.C. in federation

The distinctive Government Buildings of B.C. are nicknamed the "Bird Cages."

March 18, 1867

VICTORIA, B.C. – Amor De Cosmos, the mercurial editor of the *British Colonist* newspaper, today introduced a motion in the Legislative Council promoting the union of British Columbia with the Canadian federation now being discussed. The motion asks that before it is passed, the British North America Act be worded to allow the eventual inclusion of this colony.

Just as he fought hard for the establishment of responsible government, the eccentric De Cosmos, originally from Nova Scotia, is now leading the charge toward Confederation. He belongs to a vocal party of "Confederationists" who believe that union with the east will bring significant economic benefits to this heavily indebted colony. Gov. Frederick Seymour seems to agree, and public opinion favoring Confederation is also rising; D.W. Higgins, editor of the *British Colonist*, wrote recently that "were the colony polled tomorrow there is little doubt that the vote in favor of a close communion with our brethren on the other side of the Rocky Mountains would be 10 to one."

Date of Confederation is July 1, Monck reveals

June 21, 1867

QUEBEC CITY – Gov. Gen. Lord Monck is back from England, and upon landing here today he issued a proclamation, in the queen's name, which declares that the BNA Act, creating the new Confederation of Canada, comes into effect July 1. While overseas, Monck helped shape the BNA Act.

In this new country, Monck will retain his post as governor general. John A. Macdonald will become prime minister, and with him he'll bring a cabinet specially chosen from all regions of the country: four from Canada West, four from Canada East, and two apiece from Nova Scotia and New Brunswick. As well, a new federal, or "dominion," Parliament will be elected.

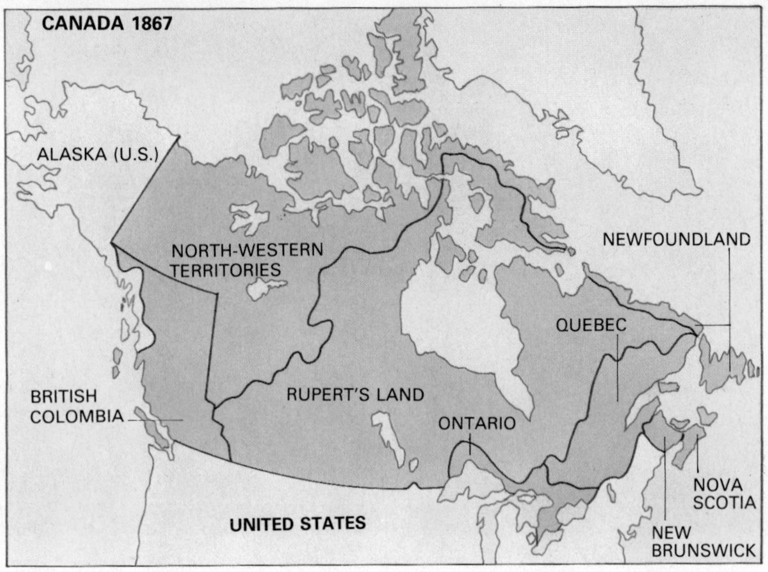

The Dominion of Canada with its four provinces as of July 1, 1867.

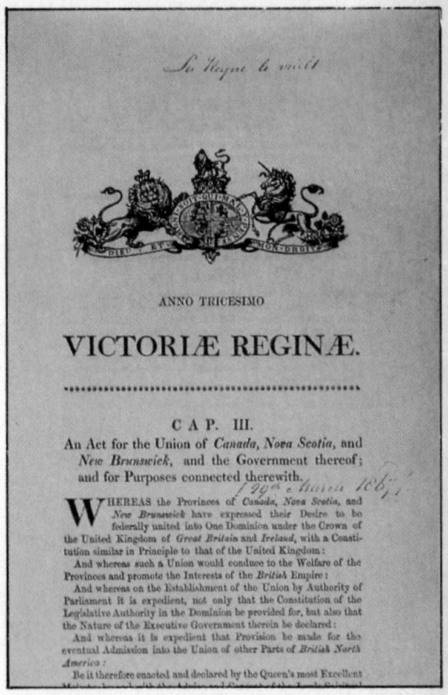

ANNO TRICESIMO

VICTORIÆ REGINÆ.

CAP. III.

An Act for the Union of *Canada, Nova Scotia*, and *New Brunswick*, and the Government thereof; and for Purposes connected therewith.

WHEREAS the Provinces of *Canada, Nova Scotia*, and *New Brunswick* have expressed their Desire to be federally united into One Dominion under the Crown of the United Kingdom of *Great Britain* and *Ireland*, with a Constitution similar in Principle to that of the United Kingdom:

And whereas such a Union would conduce to the Welfare of the Provinces and promote the Interests of the *British* Empire:

And whereas on the Establishment of the Union by Authority of Parliament it is expedient, not only that the Constitution of the Legislative Authority in the Dominion be provided for, but also that the Nature of the Executive Government therein be declared:

And whereas it is expedient that Provision be made for the eventual Admission into the Union of other Parts of *British North America*:

Be it therefore enacted and declared by the Queen's most Excellent

The British North America Act.

Surveying goes on for telegraph line

March 11, 1867

FORT YUKON, Rupert's Land – A survey expedition preparing for the construction of a telegraph line overland to Russia has completed most of its work. Now it is up to the construction crews, who have already built large stretches of the line in the south.

The expedition, financed by the Western Union Telegraph Company, is led by Michael Lebarge and Frank Ketchum. Earlier it lost American William Kennicott, who led a Smithsonian zoological expedition to the sub-Arctic seven years ago. He collapsed and died on the banks of the Yukon.

Alaskan Finns come to British Columbia

March 1867

VICTORIA, B.C. – Word has just been received here that a number of Finns living in Alaska, unhappy at Russia's sale of the territory to the United States, are moving to British Columbia. The Finns like a peaceful, co-operative life and were left alone by the Russians. They fear the aggressive Americans will force their ways on them, and so are coming to British Columbia.

Whaleship free after nightmarish winter

March 17, 1867

IN THE NORTH ATLANTIC – The British whaleship *Diana* steamed into open water off Labrador today after 175 days trapped in the Arctic ice. The ordeal began last September when the vessel became separated from the rest of the whaling fleet. Unable to bull its way through the ice, the ship was gripped by the pack which began to carry it slowly southward.

As autumn deepened into winter, the temperature below deck dropped to -30C. Wine froze in the bottle, and ice formed on the walls of the cabins. The men survived on scanty rations of salt meat and hard bread, and scurvy afflicts almost every member of the crew.

Every once in a while the ice would tighten around the ship, threatening to crush it. But just as the crew prepared to jump overboard, the ice relaxed and the ship stayed afloat. Now that it is free the *Diana* must still sail to England. The captain and one crewman are already dead, and it is feared that more of the crew will not survive.

Island crisis over; British troops leave

June 27, 1867

CHARLOTTETOWN – Some 18 months after they were brought in to quell a possible rebellion, British troops are returning to Halifax. Authorities seem satisfied the crisis has passed, and report "although the animosity of the tenantry on the rent question has not subsided, the dread of incurring heavy costs has induced many to come forward." Though the idea of collecting rent "at the point of a bayonet" is repugnant to most Islanders, it appears the repression has been successful in breaking the power of the Tenant League.

Scientist finds skull of extinct elephant

June 23, 1867

PASTOLIK, Yukon Delta, Alaska – A serious and dedicated young American scientist named Dall has found the skull of an extinct elephant on the beach near this temporarily deserted Inuit village. Natives here are not familiar with any animals larger than moose or reindeer, so they regard huge bones like those from an elephant as the remains of "devils," and treat them as valuable trade goods.

Queen Victoria receives the new prime minister of Canada, John A. Macdonald, in a private audience at Buckingham Palace, London.

Fathers of Confederation see fruits of their labor

3 conferences laid all the groundwork

1867

OTTAWA – Achieving federal union was an arduous and lengthy process involving dozens of the men now referred to as Fathers of Confederation. Much of their work was done in their home provinces, in both local assemblies and among the general public. But in addition, three historic conferences marked definitive stages in their progress, and those who attended established their place in history as Fathers of Confederation.

The first of these conferences was held at Charlottetown, in 1864. All of the men represented on the next two pages participated at Charlottetown, and some would go on to the other conferences as well.

G. Coles.

A.T. Galt.

G.A. Adams.

A. Campbell.

G. Brown.

G.-E. Cartier.

R.B. Dickey.

E.B. Chandler.

J. Gray.

W.A. Henry.

J.H. Gray.

H.R. Langevin.

J. McCully.

A.A. MacDonald.

J.A. Macdonald.

W. McDougall.

J.M. Johnston.

C. Tupper.

E. Palmer.

T. D'Arcy McGee.

W.H. Pope.

W.H. Steeves.

S.L. Tilley.

And then there was Quebec – for conference No. 2

The second stop on the long road

1867

OTTAWA – The Quebec Conference, which followed the Charlottetown Conference, marked the second stage of the long, paper-strewn path to Confederation.

The Quebec Conference differed from Charlottetown in two important respects. Firstly, delegates came to hammer out the principles and, where possible, the mechanics of British North American union, while in Charlottetown the official issue was Maritime union. Only later, at the behest of politicians with a different vision, was it expanded to explore the feasibility of a far broader project – federation of all British North American colonies.

Secondly, the Quebec Conference sponsors organized a far more lavish affair than its predecessor, with ladies invited to accompany their menfolk, and glittering social activities programmed for their enjoyment. So the 19 Maritime Fathers of Confederation came with five happy wives and nine bonny daughters, 14 Mothers of Confederation whose enthusiasm for the project contributed mightily to its success.

All the Fathers of Confederation represented on this page attended the Quebec Conference. Several also participated at Charlottetown and London.

P. Mitchell.

O. Mowat.

E.P. Taché.

J.C. Chapais.

J. Cockburn.

E. Whelan.

C. Fisher.

J.A. Shea.

R.D. Wilmot.

F.B.T. Carter.

Parliament Buildings nothing short of magnificent

July 1, 1867

OTTAWA – Just over one year ago, the magnificent Parliament Buildings, designed in the Victorian Gothic style and perched high above the Ottawa River, officially opened their doors. Today, bathed in the warm radiance of a fine summer day, they are ready to accommodate the federal offices of the newly formed Dominion of Canada.

The architectural splendor of the buildings, the lancet windows, pointed arches, pinnacles and exposed buttresses, all stand in stark contrast to Ottawa, a lumber-town described last year by Joseph Howe as "a shabby imitation of Washington" with a "turbid river full of slabs and sawdust." Most visitors are able to overlook the town's shortcomings, its principal attraction being so grand.

Queen Victoria chose Ottawa as the seat of government for the United Province of Canada in 1857. This site on a promontory overlooking the Ottawa River was selected as the location for the new Parliament Buildings. Construction was completed in 1866 in time for the last legislative session of the Province of Canada.

New song lauds British heritage

Alexander Muir, author of new song.

1867

ONTARIO – Alexander Muir, a schoolteacher, has written a new song, *The Maple Leaf Forever.*

In days of yore from Britain's shore
Wolfe the dauntless hero came,
And planted firm Brittania's flag
on Canada's fair domain.
Here may it wave, our boast, our pride, and join in love together,
The thistle, shamrock, rose entwine
the Maple Leaf forever.

The Centre Block of the Parliament Buildings of Canada was designed by Thomas Fuller in the Gothic Revival style. This elaborate structure with its many turrets and pointed arches is reminiscent of the British Houses of Parliament. The central tower is called the Victoria Tower in honor of Queen Victoria, who chose the lumber town of Ottawa as the capital of Canada over several of the country's larger and more developed cities.

Ontario at Confederation: cities and towns thrive

London, on the banks of the Thames River, is quickly becoming a major commercial centre for the southwestern area of the province of Ontario.

The White Trillium which grows in profusion in the rich soil of Ontario's forests in the early spring is the floral emblem of this province.

Province knee-deep in natural resources

1867

ONTARIO – The diversity of the natural resources of this province continues to evolve, and as the final third of the 19th century approaches, the next frontier could well be the development of minerals many believe will be found in quantity in the north.

The fur trade gave way to the lumber industry early in this century and lumber accounts for 28 percent of Ontario's revenue today. The square-timber trade of mid-century is no longer dominant, having been replaced by sawn lumber. A major resource has been the rich farmlands of Southern Ontario. And in Lambton County in the southwest, oil was found.

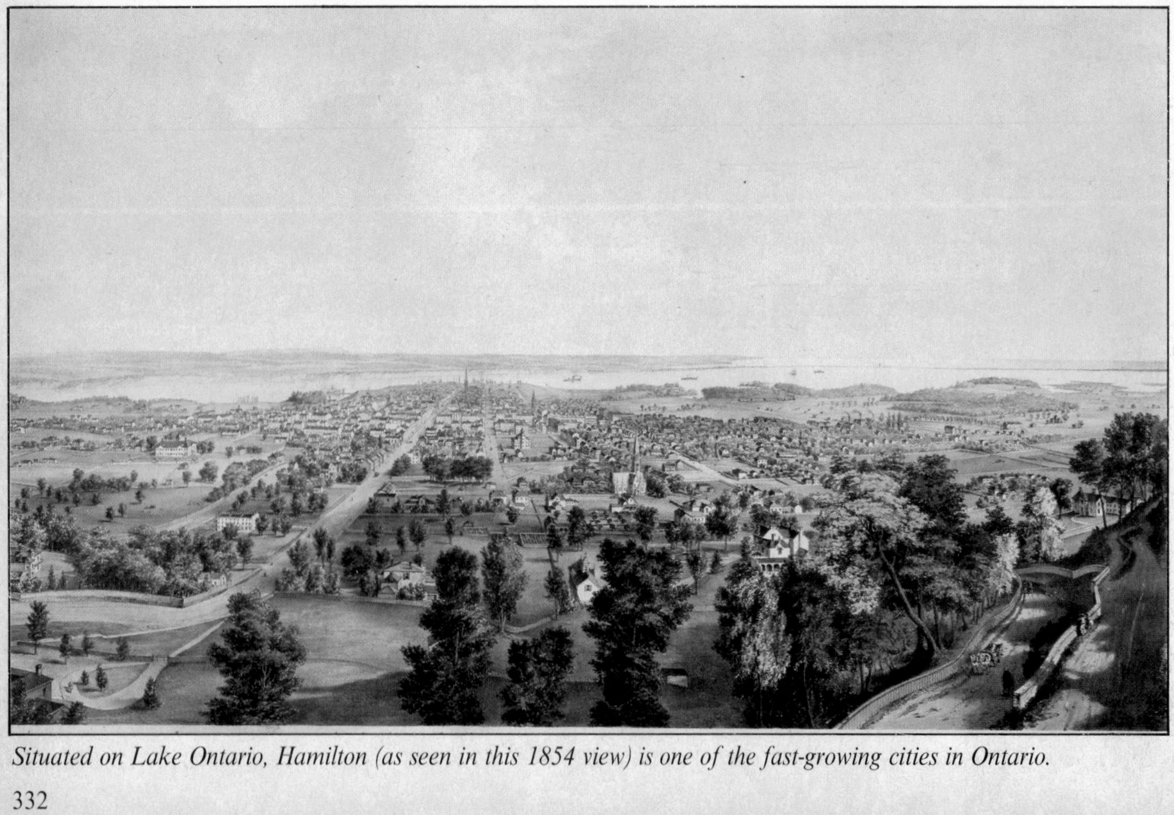

Situated on Lake Ontario, Hamilton (as seen in this 1854 view) is one of the fast-growing cities in Ontario.

Transport industry aids development

1867

ONTARIO – Lumber, wheat, agriculture and transportation have been the major industries in Ontario this century, with advances in the latter playing a big role in developing the province. Canal construction dominated the transportation industry for 30 years until 1850. Welland Canal bypassed Niagara Falls, opening up commerce by linking lakes Erie and Ontario.

Now railroads are doing for inland areas what canals did for ports. The rail industry boomed in the '60s with four major railway companies on the scene. However, agriculture and lumbering remain dominant. A kingpin in lumbering is John R. Booth, who owns sawmills, a railway, a pulp and paper mill, and river barges.

Quebec: St. Lawrence River lifeblood of province

Montreal has been a significant port since the earliest days of colonization.

Industrialization still in its early stages

1867

QUEBEC – Industrialization is still in its infancy in this province, which goes into Confederation with an economy based primarily on agriculture. Of Quebec's population of just over one million, only 20 percent live in cities. The urban population is clustered mainly in Montreal, with 90,000 people, and Quebec City, with almost 60,000. But the industrial sector that has developed is reasonably diverse. It involves railways, shipping, shoes, clothing, textiles as well as lumber and agricultural-related industries.

Montreal is clearly developing as the province's economic capital and the centre of the developing transportation industry. A canal system developed along the St. Lawrence River in mid-century has enabled direct access to Lake Ontario to shipping. A vast network of railways that has spread out from here in more recent years also is starting to have an impact on the economy.

However, with Confederation and the prospect of more Canada-wide trade, Ontario may develop faster industrially as it is closer to western and American Great Lakes markets. From the outset, Quebec has been a trading province, with fur its first staple. That has given way to agriculture.

The Market Place is an important centre in any Canadian city. This one in Quebec City is dominated by the Catholic church (1832 view).

The White Garden Lily (Fleur-de-Lis) is the floral emblem of Quebec.

Lumber tops list of natural resources

1867

QUEBEC – Lumber remains as Quebec's primary natural resource, with 500,000 square kilometres of this province covered in forests. While the lumber and agricultural resources have been tapped, many others have great potential. They include iron ore, gold, asbestos, limestone, peat, silica, granite and mica. How well these resources will be developed is yet to be seen.

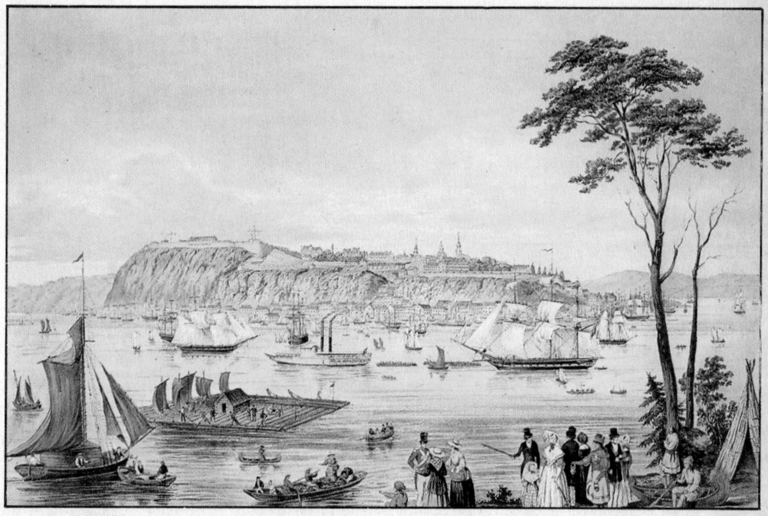

Quebec City is situated on Cape Diamond and overlooks the St. Lawrence.

New Brunswick: loyalist colony in Confederation

The city of Saint John, here seen as it was in 1851, is an important port.

The floral emblem of the province of New Brunswick is the Purple Violet.

Province has a wealth of forests and fish

1867

NEW BRUNSWICK – Almost 90 percent of the province is forested, making lumber the most valuable resource. Large rivers and their tributaries are important related resources critical to the lumbering industry. Coastal water fish are also important. It is said more than half of the province's land is suitable for farming, though a good deal is not cultivated.

The Barracks and Market House overlook the St. John River in Fredericton, the capital of New Brunswick.

Lumbering industry on the downswing

1867

NEW BRUNSWICK – Lumbering, traditionally this province's biggest industry, is in decline in this Confederation year. The shipbuilding industry, supplying the British navy's lucrative timber markets, flourished from the 1850s until recently. But now the use of iron and steam on the world's oceans presages a decline in wooden ships. As the age of railways comes into its own, the hope is for more industrialization to offset current losses.

Agriculture is developing in the province and potatoes are a major product, particularly along the fertile St. John River valley. But more farming development is needed. Both deepsea and inshore fisheries are important to the economy. Haddock, cod and halibut are among the catch in the deepsea fishery. Inshore catches include salmon, herring, mackerel and lobsters.

Nova Scotia: the colony by the sea enters union

The Mayflower is the floral emblem of the province of Nova Scotia.

Halifax was established early as a important port and military centre.

Fish is top natural resource in province

1867

NOVA SCOTIA – It was this province's fisheries that attracted many Europeans, and fish remains its most valuable natural resource. Timber is a close second, a resource exploited heavily early this century during the Napoleonic wars.

Good agricultural land is not found in abundance, with just 10 percent of the land considered good for farming, primarily in the Annapolis Valley and in northern Nova Scotia. The coal resource is starting to play a more important role, particularly because a lot of it is near the surface. Other minerals include salt, gypsum and even gold.

Fishing, lumbering critical industries

1867

NOVA SCOTIA – Fishing and lumbering, which have been traditional economic bases of this province, are still critical in this Confederation year, but the railway era may usher in new industrial opportunities. In the last decade, railways have developed, linking the city of Halifax with such centres as Truro and Windsor.

Offshore and inshore, fishing is king here, especially haddock, cod and lobster. The fishing industry gave rise to a related one, shipbuilding. A lot of lumber was shipped overseas earlier this century, with the British navy being a big customer. And the Nova Scotia schooner and clipper became famous on the Atlantic. In terms of farming, Fundy tides have created areas of marsh, which Acadians developed agriculturally. Coal may develop as a major industry here this century.

The capital of Nova Scotia is Halifax. This port city is viewed here from across the bay (1840 image).

▷

Dominion of Canada Parliament open

Nov. 7, 1867

OTTAWA – Amid much pomp and splendor, the first Parliament of the Dominion of Canada opened in its sparkling new Ottawa home today. Outside the Parliament Buildings, a huge crowd stood, held back by long rows of soldiers.

Inside, Gov. Gen. Lord Monck read the first speech from the throne in the new Parliament. On his right, dressed in his formal "court costume," was the prime minister, Sir John A. Macdonald, the key man in the campaign to bring into being the very country he now leads. Around him, equally formal, were his cabinet and coalition partners. Across the House were a number of familiar faces: opposition leader John Sandfield Macdonald, Antoine-Aimé Dorion of the Parti Rouge, and Alexander Mackenzie. A grand turnout, for a grand day in Canadian history.

Governor General Lord Monck reads the first speech from the throne.

Macdonald breezes to election victory

Sept. 20, 1867

OTTAWA – The final results from the joint federal-provincial election are in, and the verdict is a resounding victory for Sir John A. Macdonald and his Tories. With the exception of Nova Scotia, pro-confederate candidates swept the new nation. At final count, the government has 130 seats in the new Parliament, while the handful of opposition parties have 51.

Still, this does not guarantee smooth sailing for the new government, especially when it comes to Nova Scotia. With the exception of cabinet minister Charles Tupper, all of the Nova Scotia contingent are anti-confederate.

B.C. saloon flies flag of dominion

July 20, 1867

GASTOWN, B.C. – "Gassy Jack" Deighton hoisted the flag of the Dominion of Canada over his saloon today, perhaps conveying to the other residents of this tiny hamlet on Burrard Inlet where he stands on the simmering issue of Confederation. An ex-gold prospector and river pilot, Jack opened the Deighton House only a few days ago. He floated a barrel of whisky ashore, then used it to persuade some mill hands to put up the building for him in a single day. Jack earned his nickname by talking so much behind the bar.

National Lacrosse Association established

Members of the Toronto Lacrosse Club pose for this early photo.

Sept. 26, 1867

KINGSTON – The first major lacrosse league and a set of rules to play by were established at a convention of the sport here today. Dr. W. George Beers, of Montreal, is the author of the rules, which set dimensions for the playing field, the goal, specify the number of players per side and define illegal play and the game's duration. The National Lacrosse Association will realize Beers' dream of expanding the sport to Ontario.

Country of Canada is officially born

July 1, 1867

OTTAWA – There's a new country on the planet: Canada. As of today, the British North America Act has come into force. It abolishes the old United Province of Canada, as well as the separate colonial entities of New Brunswick and Nova Scotia. In its place is a new nation, comprised of the above territory – a federal state with its capital in Ottawa.

Toronto named the capital of Ontario

July 1, 1867

TORONTO – This city, once the capital of Upper Canada, and then the temporary capital of the disbanded Union of Canada, is a capital once more. It is home to the legislature of Ontario, the old Canada West. This government, under the premiership of John Sandfield Macdonald, returns to Toronto some of the glamor lost when the national capital moved to Ottawa.

French newspaper first in the Maritimes

July 8, 1867

SHEDIAC, N.B. – The inaugural edition of *Le Moniteur Acadien,* the first French-language newspaper in the Maritimes, rolled off the presses today. The paper – which has a motto of "Our language, our religion and our customs" – is a big step for French Roman Catholic Maritimers, voters since the 1790s, but eligible to run for office only since 1829-30.

Influential Whelan dies on the Island

Edward Whelan of P.E.I.

Dec. 10, 1867

CHARLOTTETOWN – The colony lost one of its most influential journalists and politicians today. Edward Whelan, who came to Prince Edward Island in 1843, is dead. In founding his first newspaper, Whelan gave notice he was a Reformer who intended "to investigate and assail, if not remedy, the evils which have grown out of the Land-ocracy system." For the next 25 years, as both publisher and politician, Whelan campaigned not only for land reform, but for free education and religious tolerance.

Recently, Whelan's calls for moderation isolated him politically. The resulting disappointments may well have contributed to his death at the unseemly age of 43.

Cockburn elected Speaker of House

Nov. 6, 1867

OTTAWA – James Cockburn, a man known for his courtesy and tact, has been elected Speaker of the House of Commons for Canada's first Parliament. Cockburn, who represents Northumberland West, is a former solicitor general for Upper Canada and was a delegate at the Quebec Conference, where a lot of the groundwork for Confederation was laid. Born in England in 1819, he came to this country in 1832.

Minister wants Rupert's Land in Canada

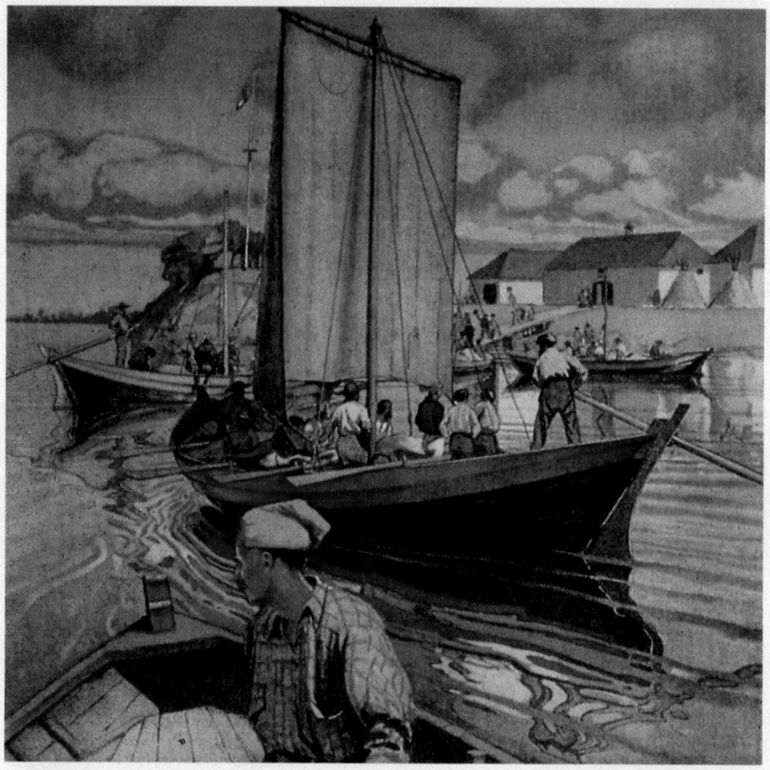

A brigade of Hudson's Bay Company York boats arrives at Norway House.

Dec. 4, 1867

OTTAWA – Public Works Minister William McDougall has been in the forefront of the fight to take Rupert's Land from the Hudson's Bay Company. Today he had a banner day, moving a seven-part resolution in the new House of Commons calling for the cession of the territory to Canada.

McDougall, 45, founded the Clear Grit newspaper the *North American.* When the paper was taken over by George Brown of the *Globe,* he became an ally of Brown, particularly in the drive for expansion to the west. It is now expected that McDougall will go to England to implement the transfer of Rupert's Land to Canada.

Howe demands N.S. be let out of union

Nov. 10, 1867

OTTAWA – Joseph Howe, leader of the 17 anti-confederate Nova Scotia MPs in the Commons, made it very clear today that he wants his province out of Confederation. In a speech in Parliament, the fiery politician reiterated his determination to agitate against "a mere act of Parliament" – that is, the British North America Act which brought Canada into being.

What Howe can do about secession, beyond talk about it, is an interesting question. He is aided in his crusade by the fact that the new provincial government in Nova Scotia is also against the union. Perhaps they might join forces.

Bishop of Toronto John Strachan dies

Nov. 1, 1867

TORONTO – John Strachan, the great bishop of Toronto, has died. Strachan, described by some as an "arch Tory" who believed firmly in the Crown and his beloved Anglican church, can rightly be called a giant in Canadian history.

Born in Scotland in 1778, he came to Canada in 1799, working first as a teacher, then as a priest. Strachan boosted Tory loyalism, using his position in government to strike at "Yankee influences." He was a great teacher who helped establish both schools and colleges.

Rough Riders meet Senators in football

Sept. 16, 1867

OTTAWA – An oval shaped ball you carry under your arm past a gauntlet of opponents! Some call it football, but its real name is rugby and it's sacrilege to soccer purists. The Rough Riders, named for lumberjacks who ride logs down the Ottawa River, and Senators got together today to show capital residents what a game of this new version of football is like. The sport was first played in Canada in 1865 in Montreal between some English officers and McGill students.

This Old Church of the Récollets has just been demolished in Montreal. It was built in 1695 by this religious order of the Franciscan family.

CP
CANADIAN PACIFIC

NATION BUILDING

1868-1913

1868

Portage la Prairie, Rupert's Land, Feb. 9. A local government set up by settlers informs the colonial office of its existence in order to secure imperial recognition. Young Montrealer Thomas Spence has recently been elected president of the government.

Canada, March 8. Governor General Monck writes to the colonial secretary requesting steps be taken to bring B.C. into Confederation.

Ottawa, March. The government withdraws its proposal to extend the currency of Canada to Nova Scotia and New Brunswick, as a way of pacifying opposition to Confederation in the two provinces.

London, May 3. The colonial secretary tells Joseph Howe and W.H. Smith, in town to lobby for Nova Scotia's release from Confederation, that the British government has no intention of supporting release.

Prince Edward Island, May 19. Lieutenant-Governor Dundas informs the colonial secretary that anti-Confederation feeling is stronger than ever on the Island.

London, May 30. The British government informs Thomas Spence's government at Portage la Prairie that it has no legal authority.

Yale, B.C., Sept. 14. A Confederation League Convention, organized by Amos De Cosmos and attended by delegates from diverse social backgrounds, calls for democratic reform and union of the province with Canada, and declares the current B.C. government "a despotism."

Halifax, Oct. 26. Joseph Howe begins a series of public letters in the *Morning Chronicle* advocating negotiation with Canada to readjust the terms of Confederation.

Canada. Confederation has led to a slew of legal hassles as the government tries to reconcile differences in the laws of the provinces. For instance, Canadian law requires the death penalty for more crimes than Nova Scotia law. Canadian law is usually extended to the Maritimes, causing resentment in those provinces.

Ottawa. Most civil servants in the new Canadian government are from Ontario and Quebec. Of 500 civil servants, only two are from Nova Scotia.

Quebec. The Quebec Academy of Music is founded.

Gunman assassinates D'Arcy McGee

April 7, 1868

OTTAWA – D'Arcy McGee, the silver-tongued orator of Parliament, was gunned down in the street early this morning by an unknown assailant. McGee, a close friend of Prime Minister John A. Macdonald, was returning to his lodging house after a late-night Parliament session. He was bending to put his key into the lock of his front door when someone shot him in the head at point-blank range.

The murder is widely considered to be the work of those revolutionary Irishmen, the Fenians, who are believed to have hated McGee because of his public campaign targeting them. An invasion of Fenians across the border is hourly expected, and other prominent politicians are protecting themselves with bodyguards.

Crowds watch the funeral cortege of Thomas D'Arcy McGee in Montreal.

Domestic mail rate is 3 cents a letter

One of the first Canadian stamps.

April 1, 1868

OTTAWA – New stamps from the Post Office Department at Ottawa are now on sale throughout Canada. The stamps were created by the Post Office Act of 1867, which establishes uniform postal prices. Rates for prepaid postage are three cents for domestic letters, six cents to the United States, and 12.5 cents to Britain.

The new stamps are designed by the British American Bank Note Company. A portrait of Her Majesty Queen Victoria's profile is featured on the domestic stamp.

First fish hatchery in Ontario now open

1868

NEWCASTLE, Ont. – The province's first fish hatchery – and one of North America's earliest – is open in Clarke Township. It is said that locally, Wilmot's Creek was "famous for salmon, great numbers of which frequented it every autumn for the purpose of spawning. They were so plentiful, often a thousand were caught in the course of one night."

Henson's settlement for blacks disperses

1868

DRESDEN, Ont. – The settlement at Dawn is no more. Since 1834, the fugitive slave community provided practical education to children and adults, assisted by funds from abolitionist groups and profits from the settlement's gristmills and sawmills. But dissension has plagued the community of late, and the management of founder Josiah Henson has been criticized.

Grasshoppers threaten Red River crops

Summer 1868

RED RIVER COLONY, Rupert's Land – There is no doubt the entire crop is in danger of being wiped out by grasshoppers. The infestation is many times worse than that of 1867. Authorities are planning for the eventuality there will be no grain for flour or seed. Appeals are being made to Britain, the eastern provinces, and the United States for supplies to offset famine.

Papal Zouaves to defend Pope's Rome

February 1868

MONTREAL – A contingent of 135 Catholic crusaders has set sail for Rome to help defend the Pope's Rome from an Italian nationalist army led by Garibaldi.

The French-Canadian troops, known as Papal Zouaves, were given a rousing send-off during three days of religious ceremonies. They plan to join forces with their counterparts in Paris.

Cold-shoulder treatment greets PM

Prime Minister John A. Macdonald.

George-Etienne Cartier, Macdonald's political partner.

Aug. 2, 1868

HALIFAX – Hostile silence greeted Prime Minister John A. Macdonald as he stepped off a train here yesterday. Only 13 months have passed since his Canada was born, and less than a year since Joseph Howe led Nova Scotia's anti-confederates to a stunning victory in the first federal election.

Lt.-Gov. Charles Doyle held a banquet last night to honor Macdonald and his party, but the Nova Scotia cabinet boycotted it. Macdonald has a secret: Howe agreed that, after church today, he'd meet him. Is the arch-enemy of Confederation finally weakening?

Far Westerners split on Confederation

July 1, 1868

BARKERVILLE, B.C. – As Canada celebrated its second Dominion Day today, the debate about whether British Columbia should join Confederation heated up at a noisy open meeting in this Cariboo gold town. Union with Canada enjoys a lot of support in the Cariboo, where many inhabitants come originally from the east. However, there were the usual criticisms heard at the meeting that Confederation is just a plot to allow government officials to hold onto their jobs a bit longer. There is strong anti-Confederation feeling in Victoria, where many people depend on long-standing trade relations with the United States.

Fire destroys capital of Cariboo gold rush

Sept. 16, 1868

BARKERVILLE, B.C. – The capital of the Cariboo gold rush was destroyed by fire today. In less than two hours, the fire, which began this afternoon in Barry and Adler's saloon, wiped out almost the entire settlement, leaving thousands homeless and reducing the business district to ashes.

The town is only six years old. It burst to life in the summer of 1862 after gold was discovered below the canyon on Williams Creek. Prospectors flooded into the area, and for a while Barkerville was the largest town north of San Francisco. It is named for Billy Barker, the English seaman who made the original strike.

Snow ordered to construct western road

Sept. 18, 1868

RED RIVER COLONY, Rupert's Land – John A. Snow, a federal government road contractor currently residing in Red River, received orders today from William McDougall, Canada's minister of public works, to begin construction of a road from Fort Garry to Lake of the Woods. The move comes as a surprise, for Canada as yet does not possess title to the land; negotiations for its purchase from the Hudson's Bay Company are still in progress. The proposed route has been planned by engineer Simon Dawson, with the HBC's knowledge and permission, but actual road building prior to the transfer of authority is a different matter, particularly when no request to begin work has been made. Snow is planning to use Canadian and American workers for the project, and there is speculation this will not go over well with local Métis.

New patriotic group puts Canada First

Spring 1868

OTTAWA – A patriotic group, Canada First, has been formed in the wake of national enthusiasm for a new Canada. Influential members George Denison, Dr. Henry J. Morgan, William A. Foster, Robert J. Haliburton and Charles Mair want Canada to play a larger role in the British Empire, but their main concern is – Canada first! They seek more power for Canadian army officers, and freer Canadian trade.

Beaver on the table at Christmas dinner

Dec. 25, 1868

STIKINE RIVER, N.W.T. – Roast beef and turkey are not always available on the frontier, so traveller Charles Frederick Morrison found himself enjoying an unusual Christmas dinner today – stuffed beaver with all the trimmings. Up on the Stikine River, the beaver was stuffed like a suckling pig and roasted till tender.

People in the Northwest Territories compete for the tail, a delicacy which, Morrison says, is still enjoyed by discerning natives. The beaver tail is removed from the body, blanched in boiling water and peeled, before it is placed on a roasting pan and baked for about 30 minutes.

Champion brothers skate in Montreal

March 25, 1868

MONTREAL – The celebrated Meagher brothers of Kingston, Ont., gave their final figure skating exhibition at the Victoria Skating Rink here tonight. Decorated with medals won throughout Canada and the United States, John and Daniel Meagher entertained for close to three hours without doing the same figure twice.

Over the past two seasons, after exhibitions in Chicago, Philadelphia and New York, the brothers were praised for their skill, grace and beauty, and saluted as "The Champion Skaters of America."

George A. Meagher, expert skater.

Church blacklists institute yearbook

May 14, 1868

MONTREAL – The yearbook published by the Institut Canadien, a haven for liberal thinkers, has been blacklisted by the Catholic church. Bishop Ignace Bourget got the Vatican to put the institute's book, which contains a eulogy on free thought, on its index of banned literature. The bishop took the action after institute members complained to the Pope of Bourget's harassment. Bourget believes true Catholics must refrain from reading works the institute carries.

1869

Ottawa, Jan. 30. PM John A. Macdonald announces new financial terms for Nova Scotia in Confederation, negotiated for Nova Scotia by Joseph Howe, who accepts a federal cabinet post.

Ottawa, April 26. The noon day gun is fired for the first time.

London, April. The Hudson's Bay Company accepts terms for the surrender of Rupert's Land [northwestern Canada] to the Crown, to be transferred to Canada. Some 25,000 Indians and 15,000 mixed bloods live on the prairies, but nobody consulted them in negotiations.

Promontory, Utah, May 10. The last spike is driven as the Union Pacific line meets the Central Pacific line, the first railway across the continent.

Ottawa, September. William McDougall is named the first lieutenant-governor of Rupert's Land. Canada is due to take possession of the territory Dec. 1, but McDougall has already ordered a survey of the Red River settlement, alarming Métis in the area, who are concerned about land rights.

Italy, Oct. 20. Some 150 young Canadian volunteers arrive at Civitta Vecchia to serve in the Papal Zouaves.

Red River, Rupert's Land, Nov. 6. On the invitation of Métis leader Louis Riel, representatives of the Country-Born meet with Métis leaders, who are planning to resist Canadian authority which has been imposed without their consent. The meeting ends in disagreement.

Red River, Rupert's Land, Dec. 1. At a convention of Country-Born and Métis, Riel presents a list of Métis demands to be met in a union with Canada. It includes representation in the Canadian Parliament, a bilingual legislature, a bilingual chief justice, and plans for free land grants and Indian treaties.

Pembina, Rupert's Land, Dec. 18. William McDougall, designated lieutenant-governor of Rupert's Land, returns to Ontario after the Canadian government informs him it has postponed its takeover of the territory until the HBC can guarantee a peaceful transfer.

Canadian Prairies. Smallpox kills thousands of Indians.

Canada. Prison inmates are at last allowed to have lights in their cells to read by.

Federal government alters Indian policy

Thunder Cape, Lake Superior, represents the Creator in Ojibwa legends.

Natives near Kingsclear, New Brunswick, in traditional costume.

June 22, 1869

OTTAWA – The governor general today gave royal assent to a bill which greatly alters current federal Indian policy. Section 6 of the Act for the Gradual Enfranchisement of Indians concerns Indian women marrying non-Indians.

A clause in the new act states that from now on, "any Indian woman marrying any other than an Indian, shall cease to be an Indian within the meaning of this act," as will be the children "of such marriage." What this means is that any Indian woman who marries a non-Indian will lose her Indian rights, as will her children. In contrast, all Indian men marrying non-Indians are allowed to retain their Indian rights. Children of these unions also keep theirs.

The Indian population was not consulted about this bill at any time. Indian spokesmen have complained about this fact, and request that, "Indian women may have the privilege of marrying when and whom they please; without subjecting themselves to exclusion or expulsion from their tribes." Regardless of any protests, the federal government intends to implement its new legislation.

Nova Scotia lured with sweetened pot

Jan. 15, 1869

PORTLAND, Maine – Here on neutral ground in Yankee New England, John Rose, minister of finance for Canada, and Joseph Howe, leader of the anti-confederate movement in Nova Scotia, met today to cut a deal.

Rose has Prime Minister John A. Macdonald's authorization to offer Nova Scotia "better terms," meaning more money, for its entry into Confederation. But Canada wants Howe to abandon his rabid followers, who urge the repeal of Confederation, and join the federal cabinet. In his heart, Howe knows his cause is lost. He needs a deal he can take home with honor.

Velocipedes: they make for wheel fun

1869

MONTREAL – Canadians are taking to wheels with shipments of velocipedes arriving here this year. These velocipedes, or bicycles, have wooden wheels and are driven by pedals that are powered by the legs of their riders. Developed in Paris earlier this decade by Pierre Michaux, the bicycles are already showing their potential as a means of exercise and recreation. But comfort is not high on their list of attributes. The rough ride has earned them the nickname "boneshakers." The bicycle, with the pedals attached directly to the front wheel, has gained great popularity through the rise of clubs, lessons and rinks.

Copway dies before his first communion

January 1869

MONTREAL – Kah-ge-ga-gah-bowh, "Firm Standing," or George Copway, an ex-Methodist preacher and once popular author and lecturer on the North American Indians, has died at the Lake of Two Mountains [Oka, Que.]. The 50-year-old Mississauga Indian died just before his first communion as a member of the Roman Catholic church was to take place.

Thousands watch as Fenian hangs for killing McGee

Patrick James Whelan, convicted assassin of D'Arcy McGee.

Feb. 11, 1869

OTTAWA – After uttering his last words – "God save Ireland and God save my soul" – Patrick James Whelan plunged 2.7 metres through the gallows trapdoor to his death in a hanging 5,000 people watched this morning. Whelan, a Fenian, was convicted of murdering politician D'Arcy McGee, shot from behind on April 7 last year as he unlocked the door of his home.

The crowd started to gather at dawn outside the jail here for the 11 a.m. hanging. Speaking in a high, trembling voice from the gallows, Whelan asked for forgiveness from the crowd, then concluded with his salute to Ireland.

Farmers pledging to rebuild brewery

1869

NEUSTADT, Ont. – Woe is Neustadt! While no German community is complete without a brewery, a fire which targeted Henry Huether's 10-year-old brewery has left Neustadt high and dry. To remedy the situation, and provide an outlet for their spare grain, local farmers have pledged to rebuild Huether's Crystal Spring Brewery with their fieldstones.

Queen graces the Great Seal of Canada

The new Great Seal of Canada will appear on all official documents.

1869

OTTAWA – The Great Seal of Canada has been designed to be attached to all important documents executed by the government, conveying royal authority. Some 12.6 centimetres in diameter, the seal shows her Majesty Queen Victoria seated, crowned, and holding a scepter in her right hand and the orb in her left. Around her are the coats of arms of the four provinces.

Penitentiary report stirred bitter feud

April 1869

KINGSTON – Twenty years ago this month, George Brown completed his report on the Kingston penitentiary. After Dr. James Sampson, a prominent surgeon, complained to authorities, a commission was formed to look into prison conditions. As commission secretary, Brown uncovered serious abuses – all listed in his report. Events following the publication of the report are largely responsible for the bitter feud between Brown and Sir John A. Macdonald.

Brown's report found that under warden Henry Smith, prisoners were required to be silent at all times. Food was poor and punishments severe. An inmate could be flogged with a cat-o-nine-tails for laughing. Smith's son Frank, keeper of the prison kitchen, threw potatoes and stones at prisoners and shot at some with blunt arrows. One prisoner lost his eye. However, the Tories felt compelled to protect Henry Smith, a political appointee. Macdonald acted as chief spokesman as Brown, a Reformer, was accused of falsifying information.

Trade talk earns P.E.I. a reprimand

March 13, 1869

CHARLOTTETOWN – The Island has received a sharp rap on the knuckles for entertaining an American trade delegation. Since Confederation, the Island's strategic position in the gulf fishery has become quite apparent. The Americans are eager to negotiate a separate trade treaty with P.E.I. This would give them complete access to the gulf fishery, without the bother of making a deal with Canada.

The Island, smarting under British pressure to join Confederation, is equally eager to resurrect free trade with the U.S., and breathe life into a flagging economy. Last fall an informal delegation met to discuss these possibilities. Today the colonial office voiced "its most serious objection," reminding both sides that Prince Edward Island's foreign policy is formulated in London, not Charlottetown.

Surveyor is critical of Red River Métis

January 1869

RED RIVER COLONY, Rupert's Land – Charles Mair is not the most popular man around here. A member of the federal survey party that arrived last year to build a road from Upper Fort Garry to Lake of the Woods, and a friend of government minister William McDougall, Mair has just published articles in Ontario newspapers criticizing the French-speaking Métis, who are very numerous here. He denounces the mixture of French and English cultures at the settlement, and wants to see people flooding here from Ontario – and drowning the Métis.

Railway locomotive has to push huge snowplow to clear the tracks after a fierce winter storm in the vicinity of Quebec.

HBC transfers Rupert's Land to Crown

Nov. 19, 1869

LONDON, England – Hudson's Bay Company officials today signed a deed transferring the huge territory of Rupert's Land back to the British Crown. The Crown has already agreed to give the territory to Canada on Dec. 1. The surrender, arranged for in the Rupert's Land Act of 1868, ends 200 years of company privileges in the area.

Canada has agreed to compensate the HBC by paying it $1.5 million and also one-twentieth of the region's fertile land. As well, the HBC retains title to its 120 trading posts. Canada's plans are to annex the new territory and open it up to agricultural settlement. The new lieutenant-governor, William McDougall, is already on his way to Red River.

Fort Edmonton was established by the Hudson's Bay Company in 1795.

Hall finds graves of Franklin's men

May 12, 1869

REPULSE BAY, Arctic Circle – An American expedition, led by explorer Charles Hall, claims to have found the graves of some men on the Franklin expedition. This is Hall's second trip to look for traces of Sir John Franklin and his men. In the early 1860s, Hall spent two winters with Inuit stuck in the ice of Baffin Island, finding no traces of Franklin on that trip.

Hall then persuaded the American Geographical Society to back another expedition and arrived in the Arctic nearly five years ago. He set up a base in the Repulse Bay area, and from there made a number of trips, interviewing Inuit about the Franklin expedition and collecting relics from them.

Smallpox epidemic ravages plains Indians

Fall 1869

PRAIRIES – A murderous smallpox epidemic is devastating plains Indians. The disease has killed thousands of Bloods, Piegans, Blackfoot, Assiniboines and Crees, and has also spread to the Métis. The epidemic began on the Upper Missouri River [Montana], apparently when some Crow Indians caught it from infected whites who came upriver in a steamboat. The disease then spread quickly northward.

Many Wounds, a Sarcee Indian, describes how smallpox attacked his band. "Some became red all over, but their skin did not break out into open sores; others were covered with red sores oozing pus. Some were attacked in the throat; their tongues swelled and they suffocated. Others felt pain in the spine and died in one night."

Killer Dowie hangs on third attempt

April 6, 1869

CHARLOTTETOWN – It took three tries, but convicted murderer George Dowie was hanged today. On the first try the rope broke. A dazed Dowie was returned to the gallows, and dropped again. On this try the rope was too long, and he was able to reach the ground with his feet. Several men hauled him back into the air, and, as the assembled booed the executioner, George Dowie breathed his last.

Institut Canadien under interdiction

August 1869

ROME – Bishop Ignace Bourget, here attending the Vatican Council, has proclaimed that anyone who remains a member of the liberal Institut Canadien will be excommunicated. Bourget's edict is the latest salvo in a battle in which he accuses the institute of "promoting dangerous errors" through books and papers in its library. The Vatican has banned the institute's recent yearbooks.

Soprano makes triumphant debut in Sicily

Emma (Lajeunesse) Albani.

1869

MESSINA, Italy – A Canadian soprano has made a triumphant debut in Sicily. Emma Lajeunesse, who uses the stage name Emma Albani, recently appeared as Oscar in *Un Ballo in maschera.*

The native of Chambly, Que., has trained as a musician since childhood. She was among the artists who entertained the Prince of Wales on his visit to Montreal in 1860. A student of Gilbert-Louis Duprez of Paris and Francesco Lamperti of Milan, Mademoiselle Albani, 22, is now preparing for the role of Amina in *La Sonnambula.* According to Duprez, "she has a beautiful voice and the sacred fire. She is the kind of wood from which great flutes are made."

Aerial view of the complex of Hôtel-Dieu buildings in Quebec City.

Fort Youcon in U.S. territory: engineer

Aug. 12, 1869

FORT YOUCON [Yukon] – Hudson's Bay Company officials here feigned surprise today when American engineer Capt. Charles W. Raymond, currently undertaking a survey of the region, informed them that, according to his astronomical observations, Fort Youcon is actually situated in United States territory. The HBC men already knew this, but wished to save themselves from the rather embarrassing situation.

Raymond has taken possession of the buildings, raised the U.S. flag and ordered all trade conducted between the HBC and local Indians to cease. The HBC men have offered no resistance, and are preparing to move their people and possessions back up the Porcupine River to Rampart House.

"Wandering Willie" is N.W.T. governor

Sept. 28, 1869

OTTAWA – Known as "Wandering Willie" because of his frequent changes of political loyalty, William McDougall is leaving today to be lieutenant-governor of the North-West Territory.

The government passed legislation in June creating a temporary government for the former Rupert's Land. Now McDougall, who was once the public works minister, is to try to administer the territory – including the Red River settlement where his survey was so unpopular.

Howe fails in bid to restore peace

Oct. 16, 1869

RED RIVER COLONY, Rupert's Land – Joseph Howe, secretary of state for the provinces in the federal cabinet, left for Ottawa today following an unsuccessful bid to reassure the anxious colony. One of Howe's final acts was to send a message to Louis Riel explaining that Canada has only peaceful intentions. Riel currently leads the resistance to annexation.

Riel says no to Red River surveying

Métis of the Red River area, whose land is being surveyed for settlement.

Oct. 11, 1869

RED RIVER COLONY, Rupert's Land – Louis Riel, accompanied by 16 unarmed Métis, today stopped a group of Canadian surveyors dead in their tracks with a defiant "You go no further" and by placing his moccasined foot firmly on the survey chain. The incident took place on land behind the farm of André Nault. Earlier in the day Nault attempted to tell members of the survey party they were trespassing on his land, but because he spoke no English, his complaints were ignored.

Last July, William McDougall, prior to his appointment as lieutenant-governor of the North-West Territory, ordered Col. J.S. Dennis to "select the most suitable localities for the survey of townships for immediate settlement." The survey recommended was the acre-and-section type used in the United States. It gives no consideration to the system in use here.

Priest refuses to give Institut Canadien member his last rites

Nov. 18, 1869

MONTREAL – Joseph Guibord died today. In the annals of the Roman Catholic church, Guibord's name will undoubtedly live on in infamy. In the history of Canadian liberalism, he will become a hero. The 69-year-old printer was a member of the Institut Canadien, and a free-thinker. Just three months ago, Bishop Ignace Bourget, opposed to the institute's liberalism, issued an ordinance refusing its members last rites. But a priest actually administered Guibord's last rites, before learning he belonged to the institute. The cleric then demanded that Guibord resign from the organization. When Guibord refused, his last rites were revoked, and he will be denied a religious burial. The incident is sure to draw criticism from the institute.

People say Guibord was a good man. He raised at least 10 children with his wife, Henriette Brown, and was an able typographer.

Voyageurs led the way in opening up the west. Métis are descendants of these men and native women.

▷

Council formed to represent Métis

Oct. 16, 1869

RED RIVER COLONY, Rupert's Land – Local Métis have established a committee to represent them in the negotiations concerning the transfer of Red River land to the government of Canada.

The new body is called the National Council of the Métis of Red River. The first president is John Bruce, and Louis Riel is secretary. The decision to form the council comes as a result of an incident at André Nault's farm in which a group of Métis forced a government survey party to stop its work. One of the council's first undertakings was to mobilize manpower. In the first three days, 500 men responded to the call.

Louis Riel is seated in the centre of the National Council of the Métis.

Illustrated News uses photographs

Prince Arthur on front of first issue.

Oct. 30, 1869

MONTREAL – Georges-Edouard Desbarats published the first edition of *The Canadian Illustrated News* today, introducing the world to its first periodical printing half-tone photographs in place of artists' engravings. The revolutionary new process was only recently developed by Desbarats and engraver William Leggo. Desbarats worked as queen's printer in Ottawa, a position his family has held since 1799, before resigning earlier this year to start the new weekly.

Rye brings children in need to Canada

Oct. 28, 1869

LIVERPOOL, England – Maria Susan Rye, an Englishwoman, set out for Canada today aboard the ship *Hibernian* along with 68 children she gathered from the workhouses and streets of London and from the Kirkdale Industrial School here in Liverpool. Miss Rye's charges are orphans or the sons and daughters of parents unable to care for them.

In Canada, Miss Rye will place these children with farmers who, in return for what help the children can provide, must promise to treat them like members of the family. Children nine years old or younger will be considered for adoption. Children 10 years of age or older will be indentured to the farmers until they reach 16, 18, or 21, depending on the laws of the province where they live.

Youths sort the ore at the Huntington Copper Mining Co., Bolton, Quebec.

McDougall banned from the Northwest

Hon. William McDougall.

Oct. 31, 1869

RED RIVER COLONY, Rupert's Land – When William McDougall arrived today at Pembina, a Métis courier handed him a note which caused the governor-designate to fly into a rage. The note read: "The National Committee of the Métis of Red River orders Mr. William McDougall not to enter the Territory of the Northwest without special permission of this committee. By order of the president, (signed) President John Bruce and Louis Riel, secretary."

The letter was drafted at a meeting of the committee a few days after the incident in which Riel stood on a government surveyor's chain and forbade the members of Col. J.S. Dennis's survey crew to go any farther. At that point, Dennis told his surveyors not to work near Métis farms.

Still, the fact that the survey was in progress made the Métis more determined than ever to oppose the transfer of colony land to Canada. They are even preparing for armed resistance – if this is necessary. There are reports emanating from the committee meetings that the Métis have drawn up lists of up to 500 men armed with rifles and equipped with horses.

Observers believe Bruce will not remain president of the national committee much longer. He is likely to be succeeded by Riel, who is acknowledged to be both better educated and much more eloquent.

Macdonald tries to upset Riel's plans

Nov. 22, 1869

OTTAWA – The prime minister has asked London to postpone the transfer of Rupert's Land and the Northwest Territories from the Hudson's Bay Company to Canada. Sir John A. Macdonald made the request when he heard that William McDougall, the first lieutenant-governor of the N.W.T., has been prevented by Métis leader Louis Riel from entering the area. Macdonald says Canada has a right to a peaceful transfer of the land.

Believing the land was already transferred – illegally – Riel set up a provisional government. Since Canada refuses to take over, Riel's government fills a vaccuum, and under international law, is the local community's legitimate response.

Sir John A. Macdonald and Lady Macdonald make a public appearance.

New government to replace council

Nov. 22, 1869

RED RIVER COLONY, Rupert's Land – It was learned today that Louis Riel has decided to form a new government to replace the Council of Assiniboia. Apparently, Riel is being encouraged to do so as a way of forestalling the argument that the appointment of William McDougall as governor-designate of the government of Canada is the only alternative to rule by the Hudson's Bay Company.

It is believed that Riel is taking advice from priests Joseph-Noel Ritchot and Georges Dugas. It will strengthen Riel's hand if he is able to resolve the obvious differences between the two language groups, the English and the French.

Louis Riel's troops occupy Fort Garry

Nov. 2, 1869

RED RIVER COLONY, Rupert's Land – Louis Riel and his troops today took possession of Fort Garry. This bold move took place while armed members of the Métis brigade were escorting the governor-designate, William McDougall, back to Pembina. Some observers feel Riel was virtually forced to take Fort Garry because of the strong response to his recent call to arms.

Assiniboia council is not dead yet

Nov. 27, 1869

RED RIVER COLONY, Rupert's Land – Louis Riel appears to be giving consideration to the idea that the Council of Assiniboia be permitted to continue as the legislative body controlling public affairs in the colony. That would put Riel in close co-operation with English-speaking residents. It is said that Riel has given his tentative approval, provided that English-speaking settlers support it.

A west coast Indian mother demonstrates a method of rocking her baby.

Newest "whisky fort" in N.W.T. opens

Indians gather in front of the most famous whisky fort, Fort Whoop-up.

December 1869

FORT HAMILTON, N.W.T. – The newest "whisky fort" in the west opened today. Fort Hamilton, just completed, is situated at the junction of the St. Mary and Oldman rivers. John Healy and A.B. Hamilton, both of Fort Benton, are the investors in this venture. They hope to serve the area between Fort Benton and Fort Edmonton. The trading post is a collection of log huts built in a semicircle and connected by a picket fence.

Free trading has been going on for some time in this area. Individuals have found the business to be more lucrative when operating as independents, rather than being associated with a company. As businessmen, some have cut overhead costs by going directly to the people rather than waiting for the people to come to them. Instead of maintaining a post, they carry their goods with them and conduct business right at Indian encampments. However, on occasion, as a result of whisky or unfair treatment, traders have been known to lose all their goods – and sometimes their lives. This has led to a number of hastily constructed trading posts called "whisky forts" being built.

Riel's men capture Canadian Schultz and his followers

Dec. 7, 1869

RED RIVER COLONY, Rupert's Land – Dr. John C. Schultz, leader of the small but vocal Canadian Party, and up to 48 of his supporters are prisoners of Louis Riel and his Métis band. Riel's partisans last evening surrounded the Schultz home and unloaded two cannons, as if they wanted to destroy the house and its occupants. Influential businessman and Riel supporter A.G.B. Bannatyne interceded, urging the Métis to avoid bloodshed. In reply, Riel gave Schultz and his followers 15 minutes to decide: surrender or fight. The Schultz crew surrendered immediately and was marched to Fort Garry under the escort of armed Métis. The men are now in the cells.

Through this bold move Riel has quieted for a while the tension which might have led to armed battle. Schultz has met with some success in recent times creating division between English- and French-speaking residents. He has been working recently to have William McDougall established as governor, and surveyor J.S. Dennis appointed conservator of the peace with authority to raise an army. The imprisonment of the Canadians effectively silences Riel's most troublesome opponents.

Nfld. voters reject plan to join Canada

Dec. 7, 1869

NEWFOUNDLAND – In a bitterly fought campaign, the anti-confederate party won the recent election by a 21-9 seat margin over the confederates. It was an extraordinary election because most of the leading members of the Assembly – both in government and opposition – favor the plan which would see Canada take over most of the services the colony is now financing. However, the elderly Charles Fox Bennett, politician and mining promoter, won by convincing voters that taxes would rise. Newfoundland will not yet become part of the dominion.

Canada offers P.E.I. its best terms yet

Ships of all sizes and types use the good harbor of Summerside, P.E.I.

Dec. 16, 1869

CHARLOTTETOWN – The Canadian government has offered its best terms yet for Prince Edward Island to join Confederation. The deal includes: a yearly operating grant for the local legislature, a guarantee of "continuous steam communication" with the mainland, compensation for the Island's lack of Crown lands, and legislation enabling the local government to buy out the remaining proprietors. The terms are in addition to those in the Quebec Resolutions. Lord Granville, of the colonial office, anticipates the Island "will receive favorably such propositions."

Smith appointed special commissioner

Hudson's Bay Company's Donald A. Smith meets with natives in the west.

Nov. 28, 1869

OTTAWA – Prime Minister John A. Macdonald has appointed Donald A. Smith, an officer of the Hudson's Bay Company, a special commissioner of the Canadian government. With the help of would-be Lt.-Gov. William McDougall and Hudson's Bay Company Gov. William Mactavish, Smith's job is to ensure the peaceful transfer of the HBC's land and government to Canada. He will journey to the west to calm suspicion and resolve the dispute at Red River. He will also assure the inhabitants of Canada's good intentions, and deal with Louis Riel's provisional government.

Eaton's new store open on Yonge St.

Toronto merchant Timothy Eaton.

1869

TORONTO – A new store is open at 178 Yonge St. Proprietor Timothy Eaton has experience with stores in Stratford and the Huron Tract. However, observers predict the new enterprise is doomed. The location is unfashionable. Eaton offers goods at a fixed price, and no credit is available. Amazingly, he also pledges: "Money Refunded if Goods are not Satisfactory."

Globe points finger at the government

Dec. 31, 1869

TORONTO – The Toronto *Globe* today blamed most of the recent trouble at Red River on the dominion government, citing its failure to recognize "the opinions and feelings of the inhabitants" as the principal cause of political unrest there. The French-speaking Métis are afraid an onslaught of English-speaking settlers from the east will deny them rights to land and their way of life. This fear was exacerbated when the government irresponsibly sent surveyors to the region this fall. The general impression they created was that Métis claims will go ignored. This has prompted the *Globe* to ask Ontarians if, were they in a similar situation, they too "would not have felt indignant!"

Riel leads provisional government

Dec. 27, 1869

RED RIVER COLONY, Rupert's Land – Louis Riel today became the new leader of the provisional government here. His appointment was automatic following the resignation of John Bruce. Louis Schmidt, a lifelong friend of Riel's, succeeds him as secretary.

These dramatic events follow a month of tense negotiations. On Dec. 10, Riel, with the help of close associates Ambroise-Dydime Lépine and W.B. O'Donoghue, hoisted the flag of the provisional government on the pole in the centre square of Fort Garry. In design, the standard of the new assembly is a fleur-de-lis on a white background.

Riel now heads the colony's only effective government. While some observers doubt that he has a solid foundation for an adminstration, there can be no question Riel has met his first objective – to keep Canada from establishing William McDougall as the governor of a territory annexed to Canada.

Also today, Donald Alexander Smith, appointed by the Canadian government as a special commissioner, arrived in the colony, ostensibly on Hudson's Bay Company business.

LIST OF RIGHTS.

1. That the people have the right to elect their own Legislature.
2. That the Legislature have the power to pass all laws local to the Territory over the veto of the Executive by a two-thirds vote.
3. That no act of the Dominion Parliament (local to the Territory) be binding on the people until sanctioned by the Legislature of the Territory.
4. That all Sheriffs, Magistrates, Constables, School Commissioners, etc., be elected by the people.
5. A free Homestead and pre-emption Land Law.
6. That a portion of the public lands be appropriated to the benefit of Schools, the building of Bridges, Roads and Public Buildings.
7. That it be guaranteed to connect Winnipeg by Rail with the nearest line of Railroad, within a term of five years; the land grant to be subject to the Local Legislature.
8. That for the term of four years all Military, Civil, and Municipal expenses be paid out of the Dominion funds.
9. That the Military be composed of the inhabitants now existing in the Territory.
10. That the English and French languages be common in the Legislature and Courts, and that all Public Documents and Acts of the Legislature be published in both languages.
11. That the Judge of the Supreme Court speak the English and French languages.
12. That Treaties be concluded and ratified between the Dominion Government and the several tribes of Indians in the Territory to ensure peace on the frontier.
13. That we have a fair and full representation in the Canadian Parliament.
14. That all privileges, customs and usages existing at the time of the transfer be respected.

All the above articles have been severally discussed and adopted by the French and English Representatives without a dissenting voice, as the conditions upon which the people of Rupert's Land enter into Confederation.

The French Representatives then proposed in order to secure the above rights, that a Delegation be appointed and sent to Pembina to see Mr. Macdougall and ask him if he could guarantee these rights by virtue of his commission; and if he could do so, that then the French people would join to a man to escort Mr. Macdougall into his Government seat. But on the contrary, if Mr. Macdougall could not guarantee such rights, that the Delegates request him to remain where he is, or return 'till the rights be guaranteed by Act of the Canadian Parliament.

The English Representatives refused to appoint Delegates to go to Pembina to consult with Mr. Macdougall, stating, they had no authority to do so from their constituents, upon which the Council was disolved.

The meeting at which the above resolutions were adopted was held at Fort Garry, on Wednesday, Dec. 1, 1869.

Winnipeg, December 4th, 1869.

A List of Rights has been published by Louis Riel's provisional government.

Painter to create Christmas scenes

Self-portrait by Robert Harris.

December 1869

CHARLOTTETOWN – A promising young artist has been charged with creating scenes for the first Christmas celebration in St. Peter's Cathedral. Robert Harris, 20, has lived on the Island since emigrating from Britain with his parents in 1856. He is currently employed as a bookkeeper for lawyer E.J. Hodgson, and also does some surveying work. In his spare time, Harris draws portraits from photographs for a small fee.

The red-haired Harris, who recently lectured on art at the Charlottetown YMCA, is a talented musician and a member of the cathedral choir. He plans to pursue his artistic studies in Boston.

Popular Nfld. song lauds independence

c.1869

NEWFOUNDLAND – Charles Fox Bennett, with the manipulating grace of a skilled propagandist, has enlisted the support of Newfoundland's outport communities in his fight against Confederation with Canada. Appealing to their sense of independence, wrought from isolation and Irish nationalist sentiment, Bennett has brought his message of higher taxes, competition, and Canadian self-interest to outporters. The result is clearly reflected in a popular ballad of today:

Newfoundland's face turns to
Britain, her back to the Gulf,
Come near at your peril,
Canadian Wolf.
For a few thousand dollars
Canadian gold
Don't let it be said that our
birthright was sold

Red River's only newspaper shut down

December 1869

RED RIVER COLONY, Rupert's Land – Louis Riel and his supporters have closed the office of the *Nor'Wester,* the colony's only newspaper. The move is one in a series of events in which the provisional government is seeking to impose its authority on the troubled colony. In this same week, all Winnipeg shops have been cleared of guns and ammunition.

In silencing the *Nor'Wester,* Riel has effectively shut down the principal means of public communication. In recent editions the newspaper had met with some success in creating a breach between the English and French here. Its final edition appeared Nov. 24.

Bonsecours Market busy on Christmas Eve

Dec. 24, 1869

MONTREAL – The Bonsecours Market bustles with activity year-round, but as last-minute shoppers stock up on edibles, gifts and necessities for the holiday, Christmas Eve is its most vibrant, mad time of year. Housed in and around city hall, crowds gather indoors or roam the perimeters where pedlars and farmers have placed their stalls and their horse-drawn sleighs. Everywhere can be heard the din of bargaining and banter. At street level, beneath corporate offices and the council chambers, are the "flesh" market and its variety of meats; in the basement butter, vegetables, and crockery can be found, and at the stalls everything from small wares to fruits and Indian trinkets.

Abortion a serious offence in Quebec

1869

QUEBEC – Pregnant women who undergo abortions face lengthy imprisonments, possibly life sentences, if convicted by authorities in Quebec. Anyone who aids in the operation risks a similar fate. But what is being done to prevent abortions? Offenders are being punished, but the root cause is not being addressed. Sexuality has long been a topic of utmost discretion for both church and state, and diffusion of sexual knowledge long suppressed; the public remains largely unaware of methods for birth control.

1870

Red River, Rupert's Land, Feb. 3. A convention of Métis and Country-Born residents called by Riel approves a List of Rights to take to negotiations for union with Canada.

Red River, Rupert's Land, Feb. 10. Métis and Country-Born settlers set up an assembly to govern the settlement temporarily. Riel becomes president of the provisional government.

Fort Garry, Rupert's Land, Feb. 15. Residents arrest a force of 48 Canadians from Portage la Prairie led by John Schultz, Charles Mair, and Thomas Scott trying to topple the provisional government.

Ontario, April. Schultz and Mair, recently arrived from Red River, foment widespread hatred against Riel and his government for the execution of Thomas Scott on March 4. Their campaign is anti-French and anti-Catholic.

Ottawa, April. The Red River delegates led by Father Noel Ritchot secure most of the demands of Riel's government in negotiations for the entry of the territory into Confederation. But Ottawa won't grant an official amnesty to Riel and his followers because of political pressure fomented by Schultz and Mair.

Ottawa, June 15. Prime Minister Macdonald is out of danger after a serious gallstone attack last month.

Red River, Rupert's Land, June 24. Riel's government approves the terms of the Manitoba Act.

Manitoba, July 15. The province enters Confederation under the Manitoba Act. The population is divided almost equally between Indians and mixed-bloods, with only about 1,000 non-native settlers.

Red River, July. Archbishop Alexandre-Antonin Taché writes to Gov. Gen. George Young that Riel and members of the provisional government have been offered more than $4 million plus arms and men to back annexation to the U.S. They stay loyal to Canada.

Winnipeg, Sept. 2. Adams Archibald arrives as first lieutenant-governor of Manitoba. The city is in chaos as militia, under Col. Garnet Wolseley, threaten or assault supporters of Riel's movement.

Saint John, N.B. The first Canadian Young Women's Christian Association opens.

Hundreds brave cold to hear debate

Jan. 20, 1870

RED RIVER COLONY, Rupert's Land – One of the most unusual political meetings ever conducted in this area concluded today in the centre square of Fort Garry. It was the culmination of a two-day debate on the future of the colony and was held outdoors in -28C weather. More than 1,000 people attended the meetings each day and shivered in the square because there was no building large enough to accommodate such a crowd.

The principal speaker was Donald A. Smith, who has been in Labrador for decades and is now a special commissioner appointed by the Canadian government to look into what Prime Minister Sir John A. Macdonald describes as the "armed obstruction" at Red River.

Crowds listen to Donald Smith present the Canadian government's position.

Hincks introduces banking guidelines

Royal Bank first meeting minutes.

March 1, 1870

OTTAWA – Finance Minister Sir Francis Hincks introduced his resolutions on banking and currency in the Commons today, measures aimed at making banking laws uniform across the country. Among the issues expected to bring heated debate is a proposal by the minister requiring banks to post $1 million, with $200,000 required up front before starting business. The rest is to be posted in $200,000 chunks every year until the total is reached.

Jews taxed for schools of other faiths

Rabbi Alexander Abraham de Sola, prominent Montreal religious leader.

1870

QUEBEC – According to a new law passed this year, Jews living in Quebec have the choice of paying school taxes to either Protestant or Catholic school boards. By virtue of the Education Act of 1841, Jewish children must attend a school run by one Christian faith or the other.

Jewish leaders are growing vexed by this situation and, with Jewish immigration rapidly rising, calls for the establishment of secular schools are being heard.

P.E.I. says no to Canadian Confederation

Jan. 7, 1870

CHARLOTTETOWN – Despite the "better terms" recently offered by the Canadian government, Prince Edward Island still refuses to join Confederation.

In the words of the colony's Executive Council, union should depend "upon the free and unbiased consent and approval of the contracting parties," and not on an arrangement between "candidates and a bribed constituency." The council feels the financial aspects of the latest offer will have no effect in swaying a people.

Man jailed 10 days for stealing turkey

1870

TORONTO – The theft of a turkey has netted a felon 10 days, with each alternate day in solitary confinement. While many believe solitude is "no barrier whatever to sin," it is frequently enforced. Last year a man received 20 days "each alternate day in confinement, except Sunday." And in 1868 a man was sent to gaol for 20 days for contempt, in solitary.

PM: show of force will crush uprising

Jan. 25, 1870

OTTAWA – Prime Minister John A. Macdonald is convinced the situation in the west calls for an immediate show of force. It is time to end Métis resistance, and to let the United States know Canada means to annex the territory. The Métis, outnumbered by English-speaking Country-Born, are trying to hold on to a government based on a shaky alliance of factions, and this may cause them to overreact.

Macdonald has recommended to London that a military expedition proceed west to seize control of the area and to establish a presence. He requested a force composed of British regulars and Canadian militia, conveying a message to the U.S. that Britain supports Canada's extension of authority over the British American northwest.

Of late, the west has shown anti-colonial and separatist tendencies. It's also rumored American Fenians are in contact with the Métis. The U.S. government shows great interest in local affairs. Several Hudson's Bay Company servants support American ownership. Even some of Louis Riel's officials favor annexation to the U.S.

Musgrave supports B.C. joining Canada

Feb. 16, 1870

VICTORIA, B.C. – An expectant crowd filled the legislature here today to listen while Gov. Anthony Musgrave urged the colony to join the new Canadian Confederation. The address was actually delivered for him, since Musgrave is bedridden with a broken leg he suffered in a riding accident last November.

The governor's support of union with Canada comes as no surprise. It is widely known that the imperial government would like to transfer responsibility for this debt-ridden colony to Canada, and Musgrave was sent here as governor last year with the express job of convincing the colonists to agree to Confederation. Much of the opposition to union has melted away under the firm persuasion of the governor.

Prince makes his residence in Montreal

Prince Arthur attends elegant skating party at the Victoria Rink in Montreal.

March 1, 1870

MONTREAL – Prince Arthur is the toast of the town. Queen Victoria's third son is making Montreal his temporary residence, and he has been warmly welcomed. The prince arrived three months ago, drawing an adoring crowd.

The city was festooned with flags to welcome the prince, returning from a tour of western territories. After Mayor William Workman's welcome address, Prince Arthur replied saying "the selection of Montreal as my residence is a sufficient proof of the confidence Her Majesty places in the devotion of citizens to her throne."

First edition of The New Nation published

The Red River cart, seen here at Calgary, is used across the west now.

Jan. 7, 1870

RED RIVER COLONY, Rupert's Land – The settlement has a new newspaper. Copies of the first edition of *The New Nation* were snapped up today by residents eager for reports on these troubled times. *The New Nation* is printed on equipment formerly owned by the *Nor'-Wester,* shut down last month by the provisional government. *The New Nation*'s editor is Henry M. Robinson, an American living in Winnipeg, and a leader of the small group looking to an American takeover. There is no official connection between Robinson and the provisional government. It is hoped the paper's name appeals to the Métis sense of nationality.

New List of Rights gets top priority at first convention

Jan. 25, 1870

RED RIVER COLONY, Rupert's Land – Forty newly elected members convened today for the first meeting of the provisional government. With the exception of the representatives of five English-speaking parishes, and a scattering of others, the members represent an almost solid front of Riel supporters. The few French-speaking dissidents, including Charles Nolin, George Klyne and Thomas Harrison, represent a small body of anti-Riel Métis.

Following the nomination of Judge John Black as assembly chairman, the first order of business was the appointment of a committee to prepare a new List of Rights. There is general agreement that the original list was written in undue haste. The new committee of six preparing the list includes three members from each of the language groups. Riel is one of the six.

The new List of Rights will become the virtual constitution of the Red River settlement. Among the items members will wish to see included are those specifying the need for improved communication with Ottawa. It is becoming increasingly bothersome to many residents that they now have to depend on U.S. facilities for their connection with eastern Canada.

Another sensitive topic for the committee to consider is the best type of administration for the colony. Some members now favor a form of provincehood with specific areas of local control which will eliminate eastern domination.

Much of the first session was taken up by Donald A. Smith, the Canadian special commissioner who read from official documents.

Meanwhile, Métis leader Louis Riel repeated earlier statements about his desire to have negotiations for the sale of Rupert's Land taken out of the hands of the Hudson's Bay Company and turned over to the people of the colony. Riel also urged that Rupert's Land not accept territorial status, but that it demand full status as a province as a condition for accepting annexation. ▷

Execution makes an "example" of Thomas Scott

The fatal shot is fired at close range in the execution of Thomas Scott.

Crowds stand out in the cold to watch the execution of Thomas Scott.

March 4, 1870

RED RIVER COLONY, Rupert's Land – Thomas Scott was executed today after a tribunal appointed by the provisional government convicted him of insubordination in the Fort Garry prison cells.

The tribunal was a traditional prairie-style, buffalo-hunt court martial, with a presiding officer, a secretary, and a jury of six. Witnesses reported that Scott refused to submit to the provisional government, struck a captain of the guard, and overtly scorned people of mixed-blood – in buffalo-hunt justice, all capital crimes.

Scott, an Irish Orange Lodge devotee, came here from Ontario seven years ago. He had served briefly in the Hastings Battalion of Rifles. At Red River, Scott became a supporter of John Schultz, and was with Schultz when the so-called "Canadians" were imprisoned early in December. Scott was one of the prisoners who escaped Jan. 9.

Among those who urged the provisional government to revoke Scott's death sentence was Methodist minister Rev. George Young, who got Donald A. Smith to speak to Louis Riel. But the Métis leader was adamant: "I must make an example to impress others," he said.

Canadians have twice tried to overthrow the provisional government. Charles Boulton was recently sentenced to death for his role, but Riel pardoned him. Scott publicly sneered at the pardon, labelling it cowardly, and insulted his Métis guards. It was the guards who insisted that Scott be tried.

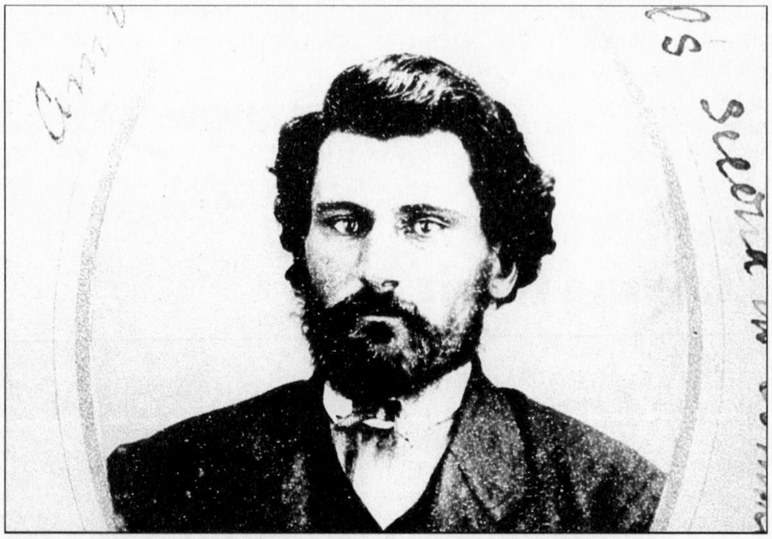
Ambroise-Dydime Lépine, second-in-command in provisional government.

B.C. Legislative Council endorses union

March 12, 1870

VICTORIA, B.C. – After a three-day debate, this colony's Legislative Council has voted to endorse the idea of union with Canada. The legislature, partly elected and partly appointed, accepted the draft terms of union drawn up by the Executive Council. These terms seek eradication of the colony's heavy debt load and the construction of a transportation link with the rest of Canada.

At the very least, colonists hope a carriage road across the mountains could be built immediately. But there is a widespread feeling that if the Canadians offer to build a railway, Confederation will be a sure thing. A delegation is going to Ottawa this summer to discuss the terms with Canadian officials.

Assiniboia reps to discuss List of Rights

March 23, 1870

ASSINIBOIA – Joseph-Noel Ritchot and Alfred H. Scott, delegates of the provisional government of Assiniboia, set out for Ottawa today to be followed by John Black tomorrow. Ritchot, a priest, Black, a judge, and Scott, a bartender, were chosen to represent French, British and American elements of the population. They go to settle the details of the List of Rights submitted earlier by Louis Riel.

Each received a commission yesterday from Thomas Bunn, secretary of the Riel government, authorizing him to present to the federal government the list of propositions and conditions upon which Assiniboia will consent to enter into Confederation with the other provinces of the dominion.

U.S. mulls motion to annex Red River

April 22, 1870

WASHINGTON, D.C. – The American Congress, which has been watching Louis Riel's resistance in the Red River area with much interest, has been presented with a motion to offer to annex the rebellious territory to the United States. Under its terms, Congress would send commissioners to the area west of Ontario to negotiate with the settlers directly.

No action is expected on the motion at present, and Capitol Hill watchers downplay its ever being passed in the House. But even its introduction indicates American desire to grab the Canadian northwest. Powerful elements, including railway capitalists, are for it.

UNCLE SAM AND HIS BOYS.

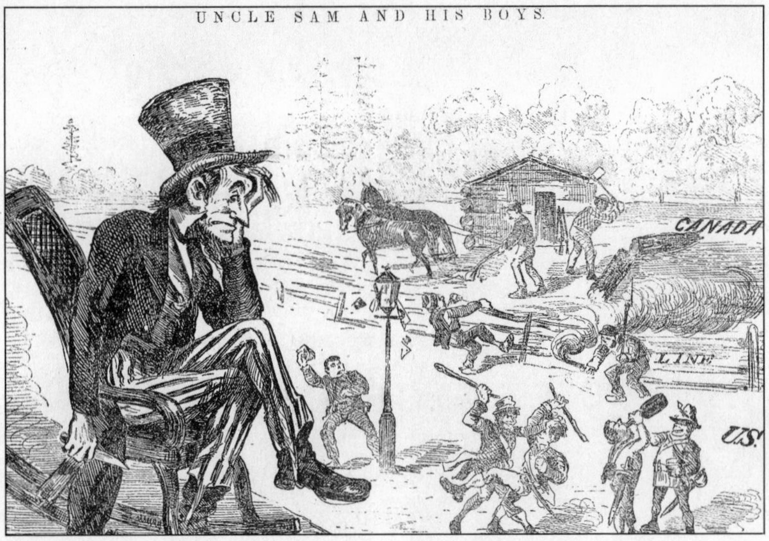

The cartoonist's view of American interest in annexing the Canadian west.

Ritchot and Scott out of detention

April 23, 1870

OTTAWA – Father Joseph-Noel Ritchot and Alfred Scott, two diplomatic emissaries from Louis Riel's provisional government at the Red River settlement, have been released from detention. Ritchot and Scott were arrested and charged with the murder of Thomas Scott, the fiercely rowdy Orangeman Riel had executed for "treason."

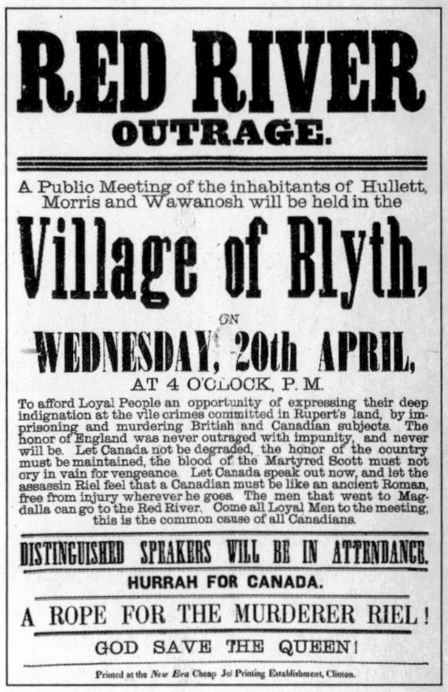

RED RIVER

OUTRAGE.

A Public Meeting of the inhabitants of Hullett, Morris and Wawanosh will be held in the

Village of Blyth,

ON

WEDNESDAY, 20th APRIL,

AT 4 O'CLOCK, P. M.

To afford Loyal People an opportunity of expressing their deep indignation at the vile crimes committed in Rupert's land, by imprisoning and murdering British and Canadian subjects. The honor of England was never outraged with impunity, and never will be. Let Canada not be degraded, the honor of the country must be maintained, the blood of the Martyred Scott must not cry in vain for vengeance. Let Canada speak out now, and let the assassin Riel feel that a Canadian must be like an ancient Roman, free from injury wherever he goes. The men that went to Magdalla can go to the Red River. Come all Loyal Men to the meeting, this is the common cause of all Canadians.

DISTINGUISHED SPEAKERS WILL BE IN ATTENDANCE.

HURRAH FOR CANADA.

A ROPE FOR THE MURDERER RIEL!

GOD SAVE THE QUEEN!

Printed at the New Era Cheap Job Printing Establishment, Clinton.

Ontario reacts to Scott's execution.

Gallstone attack near-fatal for PM

May 6, 1870

OTTAWA – Prime Minister Sir John A. Macdonald narrowly escaped death today, after falling prey to a serious attack of gallstones. The PM collapsed in his office at lunchtime. According to his physician, Macdonald's condition is extremely serious; so serious that, for the time being, he cannot even be removed from his parliamentary office. His wife, Agnes Macdonald, has thus started to convert it into a sickroom.

B.C. names terms for joining Canada

April 6, 1870

VICTORIA, B.C. – British Columbia has named its terms for joining Canada. Gov. Anthony Musgrave now has to pick three delegates to go Ottawa to see if the terms are acceptable. Since British Columbia is cut off from the rest of Canada by thousands of kilometres of wilderness with no roads or railways, the delegates will travel to Ottawa through the United States on the new transcontinental railway opened last year. They plan to leave Victoria May 10 for San Francisco, where they will board a Union Pacific train, and are expected to reach Ottawa at the beginning of June. There they are expected to meet the prime minister, Sir John A. Macdonald, if he is well enough, or Sir George-Etienne Cartier, if he is not.

Basically, British Columbia's terms are these: B.C.'s population (about 55,000) is to be regarded as 120,000 for grants; all of B.C.'s debts are to be assumed by Canada; surveys must be started at once for a railway; a wagon road must be constructed through the Rocky Mountains within three years.

Manitoba to enter Canadian dominion

May 12, 1870

OTTAWA – The Manitoba Act has received royal assent and will take effect July 15, when Manitoba, carved out of the northwest once ruled by the Hudson's Bay Company, enters Confederation as the fifth province, joining Nova Scotia, New Brunswick, Quebec and Ontario. To influence the transfer and governing of their land, future Manitobans wrote a List of Rights, most of which the act meets.

English and French language rights are maintained. The right to education in French or English was denied, but Protestant and Catholic educational rights are protected. Land is granted to Métis and their children. Canada will control natural resources and sell vacant land to help finance the Pacific railway.

British and Canadian troops to keep the peace in Red River

May 7, 1870

TORONTO – A force of 400 British regular troops and 800 Canadian militiamen left here today for the Red River. Although their instructions are to keep peace in the Red River settlement – which is now quiet – many militiamen are seeking revenge on the Métis for the killing of Thomas Scott.

Sir Garnet Wolseley, the British war hero, will be leading his men over an all-Canadian route to the Red River, soon to be part of Canada if negotiations are successful. The route runs from Toronto into Lake Superior, then along roads, trails and portages and through the Lake of the Woods to St. Boniface.

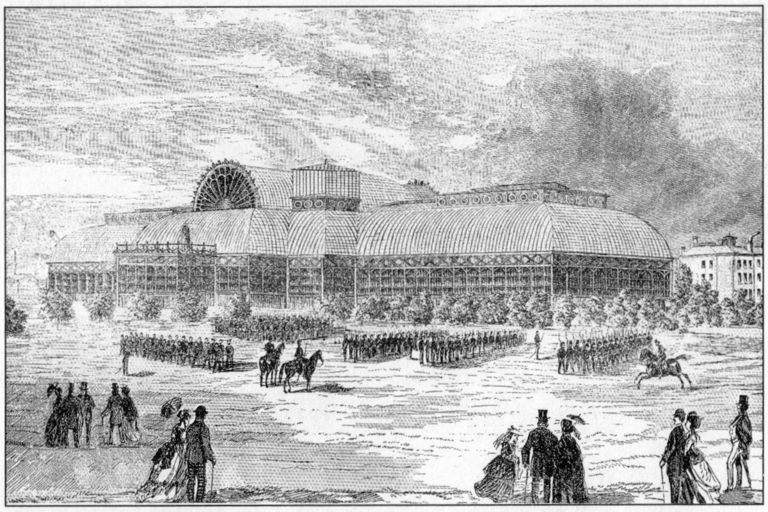

Volunteers drill in Toronto's Crystal Palace before leaving for Red River.

Manitoba: fifth province to enter Confederation

The buffalo was a staple of prairie life before the development of farming.

The Prairie Crocus is the floral emblem of the new province of Manitoba.

Farm land develops as important resource

1870

MANITOBA – Rich farming lands are starting to develop as this province's most important natural resource. Fertile black soil underlies both the mixed grass prairie in the southwest and the Red River lowlands' tall-grass prairie. Fur is no longer prominent. Mining is uncommon, but iron ore and salt are known to exist and it is believed there is coal and gypsum as well.

The corner of Portage and Main is becoming a popular gathering place in the growing centre of Winnipeg.

Agriculture grows, fur trade fizzles

1870

MANITOBA – The purchase by Canada of Hudson's Bay Company territories here this year and the resulting creation of this province, is the first step in the emergence of farming as Manitoba's major economic resource. The industrial revolution and its resulting urbanization is spreading to Canada, and as a result large agricultural bases are needed to provide food for workers in cities. A migration of farmers, mainly from Ontario, is beginning to settle the fertile rural areas. A whole new wheat frontier, of wide farms and flourishing small towns, may hope to attract millions more to the new west.

The farming explosion comes as Manitoba's former economic standby, the fur industry, continues to decline after peaking about 1850. Beaver is no longer in great demand in Europe. Also, buffalo, once hunted in great numbers here, is scarce.

Bishop questions amnesty guarantee

July 1870

TORONTO – Bishop Alexandre-Antonin Taché of St. Boniface has met with Gov. Gen. Sir John Young, hoping to acquire a document guaranteeing amnesty for Louis Riel and members of Red River's provisional government. Instead, he has received only a verbal promise that amnesty will be forthcoming. The unwillingness of the governor general to commit this promise to writing concerns Taché – the bishop knows an armed force of British regulars and Canadian militiamen is nearing Red River, and he is uncertain their mission is one of peace.

Last March, Prime Minister John A. Macdonald asked Taché to act as intermediary between Riel and the federal government. Macdonald authorized Taché to inform Riel that the seizure of Fort Garry and the establishment of the provisional government would be forgiven, that "not only will there be a general amnesty, (but) the Canadian government will stand between the insurgents and all harm."

But since then Taché has received no document proclaiming amnesty, no proof of the verbal promises he was asked to – and did – reiterate to Riel. Now, a disheartened Taché is preparing for his return west, conscious that public outcry against the "rebel" Riel has intensified in Ontario, particularly since Thomas Scott's execution.

Canadians turn back Fenian invasion

Volunteer militia defends against a Fenian invasion near Cook's Corners.

Another Fenian attempt to invade Canada takes place at Trout River.

May 25, 1870

ECCLES HILL, Que. – Canadian preparations against a possible Fenian invasion paid off today, as the country's militia easily drove back an attack led by John O'Neill. Since the Fenian invasions of 1866, Canadians have been vigilant in training their own troops and monitoring Fenian activity. However, the arrival here of dynamic Fenian leader O'Neill spurred the Fenians to launch their latest invasion from Vermont. The Fenians also hoped to take advantage of the fact that many Canadian troops have been sent to put down the Red River uprisings.

In their quest to capture Canada and hold it ransom in return for liberating Ireland, the Fenians have pushed relentlessly. The Americans have only looked on and allowed it.

"The Great Fenian Scare."

Bill clears land for rail link to Canada

May 15, 1870

WASHINGTON, D.C. – The American Congress, which is viewing the unresolved conflict at Red River with an eye toward annexing the northwest for the United States, has approved a bill granting land to aid in the construction of a railway from Minnesota to Canada. In particular, the bill seems to be aimed at assuring rebellious settlers there is a place for them in America.

Despite the actions of Congress, the administration in Washington is keeping a low profile, in an effort not to antagonize Britain.

Blaze leaves 5,000 homeless in St. Roch

May 24, 1870

QUEBEC CITY – Five thousand people are homeless after an inferno ripped through the crowded St. Roch suburb. The fire started about 1 a.m. and then, fuelled by a powerful eastern wind, quickly spread over an expanse of 12 streets. The fire brigade saved Jacques Cartier hall, which houses the marketplace. Winds dropped and rain began at about 4 a.m., and firemen, aided by soldiers from the Artillery and 69th Regiment, contained the blaze. By 6 a.m., they had the fire under control.

Canada owner of Rupert's Land, N.W.T.

June 23, 1870

LONDON, England – Queen Victoria has signed the order-in-council transferring Rupert's Land and the North-West Territory to Canada. Earlier, the Canadian government had paid the Hudson's Bay Company £300,000 for its rights to the area. Now Ottawa can send troops to maintain law and order in the Red River settlement there. The Manitoba Act admitting the N.W.T. into Canada will take effect July 15 – before the troops reach the Red River.

These decisions and manoeuvres, all interdependent, result from a complex set of negotiations among London, Ottawa and the company. They were sparked by disturbances in the Red River, fear of U.S. expansionism, Upper Canada's need for more markets, and the new government's desire to rule all Canada.

The most pressing problem was in the Red River area of Rupert's Land where long-simmering rivalries among settlers, the Métis, and the company had turned violent. Despite apparent calm in the settlement this spring, both London and Ottawa have been preparing a military expedition to send to the Red River. But London had reservations about using British troops before the territory was transferred.

B.C. delegates agree to terms for joining Canada

British Columbia natives use weirs across the rivers to catch salmon.

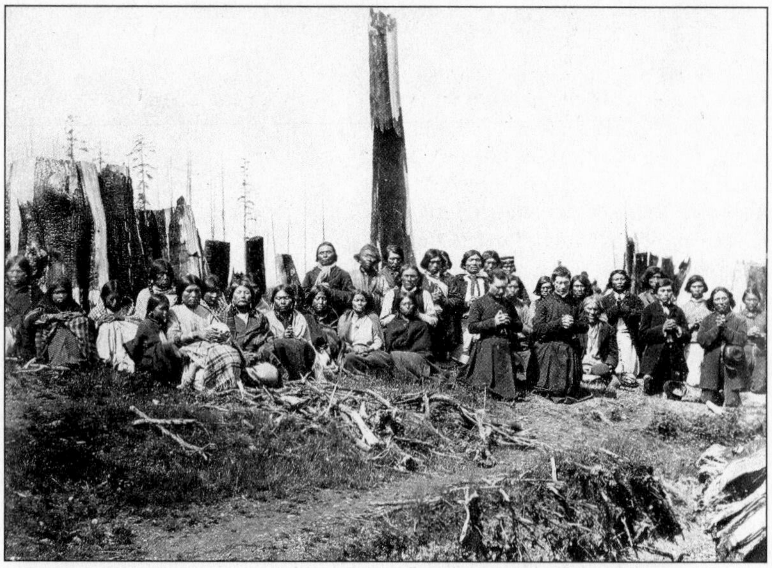

British Columbia natives assemble for a Roman Catholic prayer meeting.

July 7, 1870

OTTAWA – The union of British Columbia with Canada came another step closer today when a delegation from the Pacific colony agreed to terms offered by the Canadian government. The delegates – Robert Carrall, Joseph Trutch and J.S. Helmcken – have been in the capital for a month meeting with George-Etienne Cartier and other members of the government. (The prime minister is in Prince Edward Island.)

Agreement was reached much more quickly than the colonists expected. They came east with a list of demands, including the construction of a road link between their colony and Canada. Much to their surprise, the Canadians offered instead to build a railway, which pretty much sealed the deal. Cartier promises to begin construction of the line within two years, and to complete it within 10.

As well, the Canadians agree to take over the colony's debt and to make several other subsidies. British Columbia will be free to adopt responsible government and will receive full provincial status. The delegates leave this city exultant at the treatment they have received. There will now be elections in the colony to endorse or reject the terms, but there is not much doubt that Confederation will take place.

B.C. civil servants assured of pensions

July 1870

VICTORIA, B.C. – It has been made clear to the colonial civil servants here that they will get pensions if their jobs are affected when British Columbia joins Canada. Large numbers of civil servants have been recruited here from the ranks of the middle class settlers who came to the colony of Vancouver Island. They claim to have devoted most of their lives to the colony, and if they lose their jobs there will be little else for them to do. This group has been a powerful watchdog over the negotiations to join Canada, and a settlement of the pension problem will ensure that they do not disrupt the changeover.

It now seems certain a statement protecting the civil servants will be included in the terms to be ratified by a specially-elected legislature of B.C. and the government of Canada. British Columbia's delegates in Ottawa are happy that virtually all of B.C.'s conditions have been accepted – including special financial assistance and the construction of a railway.

Joseph Royal, a spokesman for French-speaking Manitobans, and the founder of Le Métis.

No say for Indians in future of colony

Aug. 30, 1870

VICTORIA, B.C. – The majority of whites in British Columbia are thought to welcome today's announcement that representatives have agreed to terms of Confederation, but what of the Indians? They far outnumber whites, comprising at least 25,000 of B.C.'s 37,000 residents. Yet they have been offered no role in the negotiations, nor even been consulted. They do not possess the franchise, and while many have adjusted to white intrusions, economically and culturally, they have no political say in the colony's present state, let alone its future.

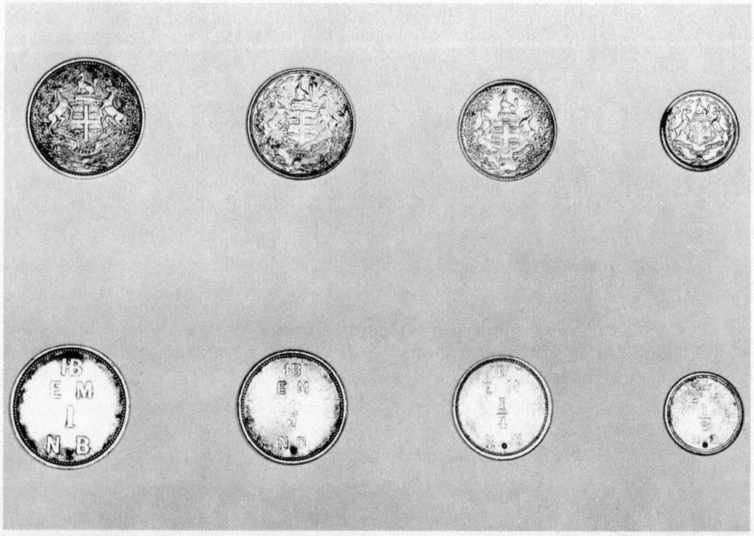

The Hudson's Bay Company issued tokens representing beaver skins for use in the fur trade. They bore the company's coat of arms and monogram.

Riel, Métis gone as Red River expedition arrives

Aug. 24, 1870

RED RIVER, Man. – The rain fell in sheets all day. Col. Garnet Wolseley and his 250 green-coated British regulars landed at Point Douglas and advanced in battle formation on Upper Fort Garry, only to find it empty. No flag flying, no Métis resistance. Wolseley and his men were bitterly disappointed. After an arduous trip from Toronto that took more than three months, they were ready for a fight.

The expedition is a politically motivated act of revenge. There is no good military reason for it, since Red River peacefully entered Confederation in July under the Manitoba Act and Lt.-Gov. Adams Archibald is due to arrive here any day to establish civilian authority. But many people in Ontario are still angry about last March's execution of Thomas Scott at Red River, by Métis led by Louis Riel, and it looks like Prime Minister John A. Macdonald wanted to give Scott's supporters satisfaction. Some 800 militiamen, most from Ontario, accompanied Wolseley, and many of them went to spill Métis blood.

Wolseley seems to share the men's feelings. Publicly, he has called the expedition a mission of peace, but privately, he wrote to his wife, "I have such a horror of rebels and vermin of his (Riel's) kidney, that my treatment of him might not be approved by the civil powers."

People are saying that Riel fled the settlement this morning in the middle of his breakfast after learning that the approaching troops wanted to lynch him. As he left St. Boniface, he told Bishop Alexandre-Antonin Taché he'd been deceived, an understandable reaction considering government ministers assured Métis ambassador Father Noel Ritchot that an amnesty would be granted to Riel and his followers. Riel also told Taché that "no matter what happens now, the rights of the Métis are assured by the Manitoba Bill; it is what I wanted – my mission is finished."

Col. Garnet Wolseley's camp at Prince Arthur's Landing.

Seal fishery fears American competition

The SS Walrus lands seal pelts on the south side of St. John's, Nfld.

March 24, 1870

NEWFOUNDLAND – Reports are circulating that American sealing and whaling companies are planning to enter the local seal fishery. Americans are already involved in the Pacific seal industry and could easily adapt their fleets to work in the ice off Newfoundland.

Ever since the Scottish whaling and sealing steamers began to take seals in this colony's traditional waters, there have been concerns about Newfoundland not being able to protect its second principal resource from foreign exploitation. Furthermore, local firms fear American sealing steamers could enter Newfoundland's ports and offer sealers higher wages and improved working conditions.

However, informed sources say the Americans think the seal fishery is too risky to lives and ships, especially with seal oil prices declining. The sources believe Americans will be reluctant to invest in a seal fishery off Newfoundland.

Indians in bloody battle on the plains

Late Fall 1870

PRAIRIES – News has just reached the Red River of one of the biggest Indian battles ever fought on the northern plains. According to Métis traders arriving from the Qu'Appelle Valley, a large party of Crees and Assiniboines set out a few weeks ago with their chiefs Big Bear, Little Pine, and Piapot to attack their enemy, the Blackfoot Confederacy, recently weakened by the smallpox epidemic. About five kilometres from the whisky traders' Fort Whoop-up [Lethbridge, Alberta], they located a small Blood camp on the Oldman River. The Cree and Assiniboine swept down on their enemies before sunrise, not knowing a larger group of Peigans were just upstream. The Peigans had repeating rifles, far superior to their opponents' inferior muzzle-loaders. When reinforcements arrived, just after dawn, the Bloods pushed back their attackers. The Crees and Assiniboines suffered huge losses, an estimated 200 to 300 warriors killed, while the Bloods and Peigans lost about 40. That day, the water of the Oldman River ran red with blood.

Joseph Bloor operates a brewery at this location in Toronto.

1871

Winnipeg, January. It is announced that the first legislature of Manitoba will be held in the house of merchant Andrew Bannatyne, "the best and most commodious building in Winnipeg."

Toronto, Feb. 3. The *Daily Telegraph*, Toronto's first evening paper, reports a circulation of 25,700.

Dakota Territory, U.S., February. In exile following the arrival of British and Canadian soldiers at Manitoba, Louis Riel becomes seriously ill, over-worried about his safety and his family.

Boston, April 1. Alexander Graham Bell begins using his father's system of "visible speech," a written code that shows how human vocal sounds are produced, to teach deaf people.

Victoria, B.C., July 10. Canadian government engineers arrive to make surveys for the building of railways in the province.

British Columbia, July 20. The province enters Confederation under the terms of an imperial order-in-council.

Prince Edward Island, Sept. 7. The Island government awards the contract to build a railway from Alberton to Georgetown to Collingwood Schreiber.

Ontario. The Act to Improve Common and Grammar Schools, the crowning achievement of Egerton Ryerson's career as superintendent of schools, entrenches the principle of free compulsory education for every child and advances a pragmatic and egalitarian approach to Ontario education.

Toronto. Various unions form the Toronto Trades Assembly, one of the first city-based labor councils in Canada.

Canada. Keronaire, a famous Indian snowshoe racer, sets a record of two miles in 11 minutes and 30 seconds. Indians dominate long distance snowshoe races.

Ontario. With the establishment of free provincial public schools, there are about the same number of girls and boys in elementary schools. But post-secondary education for women is only available at private colleges that train women in "the arts and graces of life."

Toronto. The city has a population of just over 56,000, and 497 industries.

Railway tempts Prince Edward Island

"Feeling here is strong," Robinson says

March 24, 1871

CHARLOTTETOWN – Lt.-Gov. William Robinson suggests Canada offer P.E.I. a railroad to join Confederation. "So strong," he writes, "is the feeling here for a railroad, the want of which is now much felt in consequence of the increasing productions of the colony, and the extreme badness of the roads, that I believe such a proposal would go far to reconcile the people to the change."

If the tenor of some recent remarks are any indication, people need a lot of reconciling. Referring to the Canadians' most recent offer, anti-confederate Edward Palmer asked: "Are there three men in the Island who can read and write who are such absolute asses as to make such a sacrifice?" Robinson warns the Canadians to wait and time their offer carefully. He suggests delaying it until P.E.I.'s government has started the work "and the people begin to feel heavy taxation which will be thereby occasioned."

An express ticket to boost economy

March 17, 1871

CHARLOTTETOWN – Railway mania has gripped the Island. Reflecting the public mood, Premier J.C. Pope predicts a railway will boost tourism, foster factory construction and even bring new land under cultivation. "Every way I look at it," he enthuses, "I see advantages ... Men would be more profitably employed (and) labor would be more in demand."

Armstrong making tracks: snowshoe king sweeps major meets

Snowshoeing is a very popular sport in the city of Montreal. These members of the Montreal Snowshoe Club take part in the annual carnival.

Club members, out for a pleasure trek, snowshoe in Indian file.

Feb. 11, 1871

MONTREAL – Snowshoe champion J.D. Armstrong made an impressive comeback this season, sweeping races at all the major area competitions. Armstrong has beaten all comers with his outstanding performances. He broke a record in the dash race at the Montreal Snowshoe Club races, beating top competitors Wood and Young in 11 seconds. He set another record at the Maple Leaf races, overtaking Massey in the quarter mile with a time of one minute, four seconds. His most stunning victory also came at the Maple Leaf meet, when he outraced the Indian Keraronwe by 40 yards in the quarter mile.

Although illness kept him out of competition last year, Armstrong made a roaring return to the snowshoeing scene this season in the Athletic races in October, winning the quarter-mile dash in 58 seconds, 30 yards ahead of the Prescott champion Fraser.

Armstrong, Canadian-born of English, Irish, Scottish and French-Canadian lineage, comes from Lanaudière in Maskinongé County. At five-foot-eleven and 144 pounds, the 22-year-old athlete is lean and muscular, and says he doesn't require training to prepare himself for the winter's snowshoe competitions. He's a former employee of the mercantile house Leeming & Cowie, but is now involved in other business interests which will take him out of Montreal for the next several years.

Census pegs population of Canada at 3.6 million

April 1871

OTTAWA – It's not everything you've ever wanted to know about Canada, but it's still fascinating reading. It's the first census of the new Dominion of Canada and it's hot off the press this month. It's full of population statistics and analyses – did you know there are 41 brothels in Montreal? Unfortunately, your friendly government census-taker left out many people, including most of Canada's Indians, so bear that in mind when evaluating the following statistics. Canada's population is 3,689,257, 60 percent of British origin and 31 percent French. Provincial populations: Ontario 1,620,851; Quebec 1,191,516; Nova Scotia 387,000; New Brunswick 285,594; Manitoba 10,000. The census includes Prince Edward Island's 94,021 people, and British Columbia's 36,247, whom Canada hopes will soon join Confederation. Please note, B.C. also has about 36,000 Indians, Manitoba an unknown number.

The census was taken under the authority of the Census Act, passed May 12, 1870. There is no permanent staff but people were hired as they were needed. Facts they gathered are as they existed on April 2 of this year. Information was collected under nine schedules.

They include: statistics on the living, with names, sex, birthday, place of birth, religion, origin, profession, marital status and education; data on the dead, including cause of death; returns on public buildings or institutions, acreage of farmland and town lots owned, ownership of buildings, carriages and farm implements; agricultural statistics on land and farm products; livestock, animal products, fabrics and furs; industries, employees and wages, and products; forest products; fisheries and shipping; and mineral products.

In terms of religion, the census-takers found that Roman Catholics were the largest single denomination, with 42.8 percent. The Methodists followed with 16.3 percent, Presbyterians 15.6 and Anglicans 14.2 percent. Canada also has 1,333 Jews. Occupationally, Canada's largest group, 13.8 percent of the wage-earning population, was employed in farming. The others were: industrial 6.1 percent, unclassified 4.1, commercial 2.2, domestic 1.7, and professional 1.1.

A breakdown of the industrial sector shows women and children are 42 percent of the workforce in Montreal, and 34 percent in Toronto. The degree of industrialization in the provinces is reflected by the percentages of people in urban areas. Ontario is the most urbanized – 20.6 percent of its people live in cities or towns, followed by Quebec at 19.9. The average for Canada is 18.3 percent. The correlation between industry and urbanization is shown in Toronto, where 497 industries support a population of more than 56,000 people.

Old Regulus: "It is necessary, Bridget, that you should inform me of your age and origin that I may comply with the law in filling up the census." Bridget: "It is me age y're wantin' to know sir? Ah, faith, I've often heard me mother say I was born the same day as Mrs. Maloney's Pat that killed hisself with drink; but me origin, faith, your honour, I'ven't the least idea of me origin."

Nothing, it seems, is sacred to census-takers, even marital fertility rates. From top to bottom on the list, defined by national background: Scottish and French-Canadian, Irish and German, and lastly, English. The government enumerators collected their data house to house in 206 census districts, subdivided in turn into 1,701 census sub-districts. But settlers are limited to about 5 percent of the geographical extent of the new country, and little is known about the other 95 percent. So now the data has been collated for your consumption. It's not very accurate, but like Canada itself, it's a beginning.

Canada's last slave John Baker is dead

Jan. 17, 1871

CORNWALL, Ont. – John Baker, Canada's last ex-slave, died today in Cornwall at age 93. His Quebec-born mother Dorinda was brought to Canada by the Gray family in 1776. John grew up near Cornwall. When Solicitor General Robert Isaac dey Gray died in 1804, Baker's family was freed and inherited land and money. Baker enlisted and served in Canada and at Waterloo. After Denmark, Canada was the first western country to legislate against slavery in 1793. It was fully abolished in 1833.

B.C. accepts terms for joining Canada

Jan. 20, 1871

VICTORIA, B.C. – The 15 members of British Columbia's newly-elected Legislative Council have unanimously accepted the terms of union with Canada. These were reached in discussions last summer between B.C. delegates and the cabinet. The agreement in principle by the new council paves the way for a formal agreement this summer when a delegation from B.C. will travel to Ottawa. Under the terms of union, the province would make its own decisions on responsible government.

Indians use birch-bark to construct both wigwams and canoes.

World's richest coal is in Cape Breton

May 20, 1871

CAPE BRETON – The International Coal and Railway Company of Nova Scotia is producing 3,000 tons a day of what top geologists call the world's richest coal.

The mines at Bridgeport are tapping into reserves estimated at 80 million tons of coal, which produces "more gas than the coals from Newcastle and of a high illuminating power." A 21-kilometre railway to a loading pier allows the company to fill seven large vessels at once. Cape Breton now mines about two-thirds of Canada's coal.

Prairies surveying: a simple solution

April 1871

OTTAWA – The federal government has established a system for surveying the Canadian prairies, an important prelude to settlement. The system is simple, uniform, and, since it's based on astronomical observations, accurate.

The prairies will be divided into square mile sections. A quarter section, a half-mile square, will make up a homestead. Thirty-six sections, six miles square, will comprise a township. Townships will be numbered according to a common system from base lines at the 49th Parallel and the Fort Garry meridian. Settled land along the Red, Assiniboine and other rivers will be exempted from the survey.

Bishops urge flock to vote for Tories

April 20, 1871

MONTREAL – In a move seen as an effort to set up a Catholic political party, powerful ultramontane bishops Ignace Bourget and Louis-François Richer Laflèche issued a statement today urging Catholics in Quebec to support certain candidates in the upcoming federal election. The Catholic Program orders the faithful to vote for Conservatives over Liberal Party "opportunists." In the event there is a Conservative candidate who rejects the ultramontane line, Catholics should "refrain from voting."

Manitoba attracts settlers from east

April 26, 1871

WINNIPEG – Cheap land and rumors of thriving crops have attracted settlers from Canada along the newly opened Dawson route and by Lake Superior and the railway to Red River. A group from Southampton, Ont., has just arrived in Winnipeg. The women and children will wait in town with the household effects while the men look for land. When they find what they are looking for, the men will return to pick up their families.

Treaty of Washington costs Canada

May 8, 1871

WASHINGTON, D.C. – Neither brilliant sunshine nor the bloom of spring flowers could cheer Prime Minister John A. Macdonald this morning as he added his signature to the Treaty of Washington. No amount of fine weather can compensate for the blow just delivered Canada's rich inshore fisheries, where Americans have been granted free access. Canada has received no significant concessions, and demands for compensation for the Fenian raids have been ignored.

Macdonald, a reluctant member of the British commission that negotiated the treaty, had little choice but to sign; it's what Britain wants. From the outset, the four other commissioners appeared willing to sacrifice Canadian interests to end hostilities between Britain and the United States. Macdonald's only consolation, significant but overshadowed, is that the U.S. now officially recognizes Canada's boundaries. He's also secured British financial aid for the construction of Canada's transcontinental railway.

Steamboat Selkirk arrives at Fort Garry

The steamer Selkirk makes its way down the Red River in Manitoba.

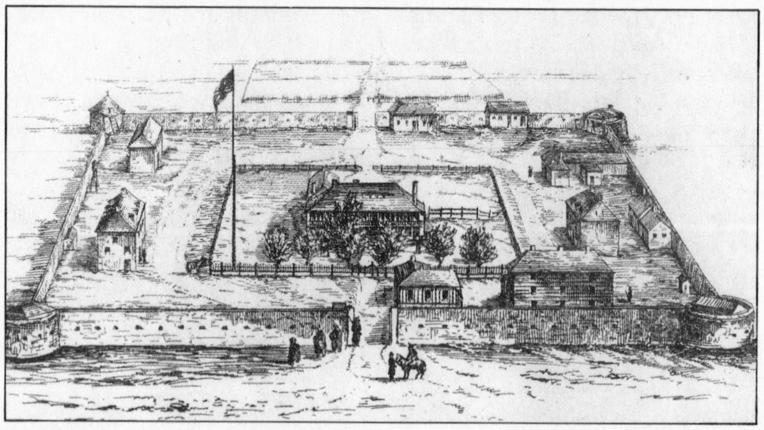

Lower Fort Garry is one of two forts by the same name on the Red River.

May 1871

FORT GARRY, Man. – The steamboat *Selkirk,* owned by James J. Hill of St. Paul and his partners, reached Fort Garry today. It is only the second steamboat to enter the Red River, and will be competing for freight and passengers with the *International,* which has been operating since 1859.

The *Selkirk* is a sternwheeler built at McCauleyville. It burns wood and runs only in daylight. The trip from Moorhead, railhead of the Northern Pacific, to Winnipeg takes 60 hours down river. It is a 660-kilometre trip by water, 340 by land.

Hill is a Canadian immigrant who moved to the United States at an early age. Now, he's making his mark in transportation.

Promise of rail link sways delegates; B.C. joining Canada

July 20, 1871

OTTAWA – British Columbia formally agreed to join Canada today, swayed primarily by a promise to build a railway to the west coast province. After three days of negotiations, Canada approved a rail link. "They do not consider that they can hold the country without it," said John Sebastian Helmcken, a member of the Legislative Council of B.C. and one of the delegates here. The railway is to be started within two years, beginning simultaneously at both ends of the route. It is to be completed in 10 years.

The swiftness of the negotiations has greatly impressed the B.C. delegation, and will assuredly silence talk in the province of annexation by the United States. As well as the rail link, Canada has agreed to assume the provincial debt.

Dusty Dawson Road a vital link out west

June 15, 1871

ON THE DAWSON ROAD – One look at the Dawson Road tells you that this is no Yonge Street. Little more than a dusty trail, it stretches from the northwest corner of the Lake of the Woods westward 120 kilometres to Fort Garry [Winnipeg] in the Red River district.

Despite its humble appearance, Dawson Road is vital. It links this fledgling nation not only to Fort Garry, but to the prairie region of Rupert's Land. The reason why is simple: the prairies are flat, and travel is easy beyond the Red River.

Resource-rich B.C. enters Canadian Confederation

The city of Victoria is named after the popular queen. Its sheltered harbor has been used by the natives of Vancouver Island for many years.

Province gains market for lumber, fish

1871

BRITISH COLUMBIA – Confederation offers this province new markets in the rest of the country for its lumber and developing fishing industry. A diversifying economy in British Columbia is helping fishing as a provision industry. Before union, gold was a critical export. In a seven-year period ending in 1865, gold exports were estimated in excess of $18 million. Coal, another export, was in decline as Confederation approached.

The floral emblem of the new province of British Columbia is the Pacific Dogwood. This beautiful plant thrives in the Pacific coastal areas where the precipitation is plentiful and the winter temperatures are mild.

Where the money grows on trees

1871

BRITISH COLUMBIA – Money grows on trees in British Columbia, Canada's newest province. Not literally, of course, but with its territory, except mountains, covered with trees, forests are its most important natural resource. In terms of animal resources, sea otter pelts from coastal regions and furs from the interior were important earlier in the century but now fishing is coming into its own.

Gold, first discovered in the Queen Charlotte Islands in 1852, was quickly exhausted. But another gold find four years later on the Fraser River developed into an important resource. So is coal, which was put into production near Nanaimo 20 years ago. Other minerals include silver, copper, iron, lead and zinc. Only an estimated three percent of the soil is fit for farming.

Established as a Hudson's Bay Company trading post in 1843, Victoria was incorporated as a city in 1862. With its good natural harbor, this city has become a significant business centre for the west coast.

Treaty hands over Indian territory

Indian and government representatives assemble at Lower Fort Garry.

Chippewas and Swampy Crees listen to explanation of first Indian treaty.

Aug. 3, 1871

FORT GARRY, N.W.T. – The first Indian treaty negotiated by the Dominion of Canada was signed here today. The lieutenant-governor of Manitoba, Adams Archibald, and Indian commissioner Wemyss Simpson signed the treaty on behalf of the government. Signing for the Ojibwa and Cree Indians of southern Manitoba were chiefs Red Eagle, or Henry Prince, Bird Forever, Flying Down Bird, Centre of Bird's Tail, Flyinground, Whippoorwill and Yellow Quill.

Under terms of the treaty, the Indians surrender 43,250 square kilometres of their traditional territory to the government. In return they receive reserves amounting to 160 acres of land for each family of five, along with an annuity of $3 per person. Initially, the Indians had no idea of the reserve concept, and asked the government for two-thirds of the province of Manitoba. The government also promises to maintain a school on each reserve if the Indians want one, and to prohibit liquor sales on reserves. At the insistence of the Indians, Simpson also agreed to provide farm implements, seed and livestock.

This treaty is the first that the government plans to make with the 35,000 Indians living in the western plains. The purpose of the pacts is to secure clear title to the land in anticipation of an influx of farm settlers to the area. For their part, the Indians are eager to obtain help adjusting to a new way of life they realize is inevitable. The buffalo herds are disappearing and the first trickle of settlers is already here. The Indians do not accept simply being dispossessed of their land and had already begun blocking the progress of settlers until some kind of agreement was reached.

English rower dies in loss to Canada

Aug. 23, 1871

SAINT JOHN, N.B. – A four-man crew from this Maritime city proved it was the fastest in the world today in a race marred by an unexpected tragedy. As the Canadian rowers pulled away from their English opponents, a member of the English crew suddenly collapsed in his seat. The stricken athlete, was brought hurriedly to shore, but he was declared dead an hour later.

The calamity has put a damper on the victory celebrations. The Saint John foursome first came to prominence in 1867 by winning the Paris Regatta. Since that time they have won several races, and the contest with the English was for the world championship.

First sod is turned for P.E.I. Railroad

Oct. 5, 1871

CHARLOTTETOWN – Today the first sod was turned in the construction of the P.E.I. Railroad. In view of the benefits it anticipates, the government feels the Island can easily support the extra debt and taxes the work will entail.

But the railroad's few opponents are not so confident. They have criticized the "railway speed" with which the project has proceeded, and fear an expensive railroad will not secure the Island's independence, but deliver it straight into Confederation.

Montreal club wins world lacrosse title

Sept. 23, 1871

MONTREAL – The Montreal Shamrocks defeated the Toronto 12 today to win the world lacrosse championship in front of 8,000 spectators. Organized in 1866, the Shamrocks are still a young team. Since last year, they have won 15 matches, a feat unequalled by any other team. This summer, they went on a United States tour with another top Montreal team, the Caughnawaga Indians. The Shamrocks won every game.

Cabinet members postpone talks with railway entrepreneurs

Oct. 5, 1871

OTTAWA – Two businessmen wishing to build the Pacific railway learned today the Canadian government is not set to start negotiations on the project. Hugh Allan, millionaire owner of a Montreal steamship company, and Chicago entrepreneur George McMullen were told of the delay in a meeting with some cabinet members.

Allan, who is president of the Merchants' Bank and about 15 other corporations, became interested in building the Pacific route when Finance Minister Francis Hincks told him some Americans wanted to carry out the project. One was McMullen, a Canadian-born U.S. newspaper owner whose interests include railways and canals. Allan approached him and they set up a company last month. But they face a fight from George-Etienne Cartier, Prime Minister John A. Macdonald's Quebec lieutenant, who opposes U.S. involvement.

British troops withdraw from Canada

Nov. 11, 1871

QUEBEC CITY – To the tune of *Auld Lang Syne,* Royal Artillery regiments and Royal Engineers today marched from their garrison at the Citadel above Cape Diamond to St. Andrew's Wharf, and thence to England. They were among the last British military forces in Canada, now to be defended by its own militia. The withdrawal, which began last year, has caused anxiety among Canadians who fear continued harassment from Fenians in the east. Despite the Treaty of Washington recognizing Canada's southern border, they also fear American designs on territories in the west. Halifax and Esquimault naval bases still have imperial troops.

The last British regiments in Canada march out of the Citadel.

Three newspapers open in Manitoba

Dec. 14, 1871

WINNIPEG – One of the three newspapers that started up this year in Manitoba is *Le Métis,* a French-language journal. The two others – both English papers – are the *Newsletter* and the *Manitoban.* The newspapers are just three of the many businesses and industries that have opened up in Winnipeg this year alone. The village also boasts a school, butchers, bakers, cabinet-makers, insurance companies, lawyers and a brewery. A telegraph line between Manitoba and Ontario became operational this year. It is a welcome addition.

LE METIS

DIEU ET MON DROIT.

French language paper Le Métis.

Investors found Merchants' Bank of P.E.I.

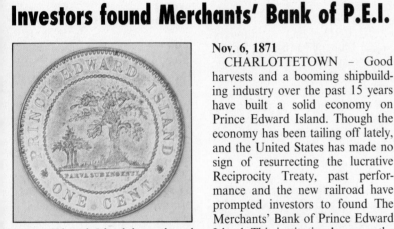

Prince Edward Island has adopted the decimal currency. The Island's one cent piece is shown here.

Nov. 6, 1871

CHARLOTTETOWN – Good harvests and a booming shipbuilding industry over the past 15 years have built a solid economy on Prince Edward Island. Though the economy has been tailing off lately, and the United States has made no sign of resurrecting the lucrative Reciprocity Treaty, past performance and the new railroad have prompted investors to found The Merchants' Bank of Prince Edward Island. This institution becomes the fifth bank on the Island, joining the Bank of P.E.I. and three others.

American explorer dies on Arctic trip

Nov. 8, 1871

THANK GOD HARBOUR, Greenland – After a brief illness, American explorer Charles Francis Hall died today at this remote Arctic harbor aboard his ship the *Polaris.* Hall was wintering in Thank God Harbour in preparation for his attempt to reach the North Pole next year. Before his death, the explorer claimed that someone was poisoning him, but no evidence was found. This was Hall's third expedition into the Arctic.

Tory government ousted in Ontario

Dec. 19, 1871

TORONTO – After days of backroom manoeuvring and delaying, the Ontario government of John Sandfield Macdonald was defeated today on a non-confidence motion carried by one vote. That vote came from Edmund Burke Wood, known as "Big Thunder" in the House and a government member who recently quit the cabinet. The move ends four years of Conservative rule, which began as a coalition. The new premier is the Liberal leader, Edward Blake. He's a wealthy Toronto lawyer, renowned for his courtroom oratory.

Fenians forced to withdraw after capturing unoccupied HBC fort

The commandant addresses the recruits as they prepare for Fenian raids.

Oct. 5, 1871

MANITOBA – William B. O'Donoghue led a band of Fenians into Manitoba today to capture the small Hudson's Bay Company post of Pembina. However, the victory turned out to be a hollow one – and short-lived at that. The fort O'Donoghue conquered was unoccupied, and even then it wasn't long before American troops were on the scene to escort him and his men back over the U.S. border. The Métis did not help O'Donoghue as he had hoped they would. Indeed, the two people who took him prisoner and turned him over to the Americans were both Métis. The invasion lasted one day.

1872

Northwest Territories, April 5. American Thomas Hardwick, a fanatic Indian hater, fires on a group of Assiniboines in the Sweetgrass Hills [Alberta], killing four and injuring 10.

Toronto, April 8. Representatives of industry issue a manifesto defying printers and other workers who are threatening to mount a general strike for a nine-hour working day.

Toronto, April 16. Fourteen leaders of the printers' strike are arrested for conspiring to keep other workers from their jobs after George Brown of the powerful *Globe* newspaper and master printers lay charges. Labor unions are illegal.

Manitoba, June. Riel returns to the province after a voluntary exile in the U.S. Prime Minister Macdonald gave him $1,000 to persuade him to stay out of Canada.

Niagara Falls, Ont., August. Famous buffalo hunter Wild Bill Hickok is a big hit in a Wild West show.

Winnipeg, Sept. 14. George-Etienne Cartier, prominent Quebec minister and a champion of Manitoban French language rights and amnesty for Louis Riel, is elected locally as MP.

Canada, September. In a general election, Conservatives led by John A. Macdonald win 103 seats to the Liberals' 97 to form a majority government.

Prince Edward Island, Nov. 16. Lt.-Gov. William Robinson writes to Canadian Gov. Gen. Lord Dufferin to find out what terms Canada will offer P.E.I. to enter Confederation.

Ontario. Premier Edward Blake offers a reward of $5,000 to anyone who brings about the arrest of the "murderers" of Thomas Scott.

Montreal. Bishop Ignace Bourget issues a condemnation of theatre.

St. George, N.B. Citizens form a company to try to capture a monster in Lake Utopia.

New Brunswick. Every summer the province ships 675,000 kilograms of fresh salmon to U.S. markets.

Ontario. According to a list of rules for teachers published in the *Glengarry News*, male teachers are allowed to go courting one or two nights a week, and female teachers who marry or engage in "unseemly conduct" will be dismissed.

Stop the presses: Printers on strike

March 25, 1872

TORONTO – Spearheading the fight for a nine-hour workday, the Toronto Typographical Union has pulled its workers from newspapers across town. The deadline for acceptance of its demands passed today, with all newspapers, except the *Leader*, refusing to give in. The printers want $54 a week for a 54-hour week; the newspapers offered them that wage for 60 hours.

It's generally agreed the Typos, as they are known, want changes desired by most unionized workers in all trades. Newspapers will be pressured by business not to give in.

Lands act now in force

1872

OTTAWA – Parliament has passed the Dominion Lands Act, expected to lay the foundation for settlement of the prairies. To attract settlers to the west, the act offers them each a homestead of 160 acres, or a half mile square, for only $10, thus establishing the principle of the free Canadian homestead. The landmark legislation is modelled on the American Homestead Act of 1862, which offered settlers the same deal. Settlers must live on the land for three years before they are granted clear title. They must also build a home and cultivate a certain amount of land over a period of three years. The Lands Act was made possible when the federal government gained control of prairie land in 1870. It acquired Rupert's Land, and when Manitoba became a province the federal government kept control of its public land.

Ottawa is pursuing national objectives – it wants to use prairie land to promote settlement and the creation of a national railway. It has reserved a large strip to be sold to finance the railway. There are other claims on prairie land. Some of it is reserved for the Hudson's Bay Company and some will finance prairie education.

Yellowhead Pass chosen for rail route

Botanist John Macoun is part of a government survey crew in 1872.

April 1872

VICTORIA, B.C. – Surveyor Walter Moberly has learned by telegram that the Canadian Pacific Railway will use the Yellowhead Pass route through the Rockies. It looks as if this is the end to any chance of using the Eagle Pass, which is Moberly's choice and which he has surveyed, and he is bitterly disappointed.

The Yellowhead Pass, named after a blonde Iroquois trapper, Tête Jaune, cuts across the Great Divide at an altitude of 1,050 metres. It has been used for years as a pathway from the prairies into British Columbia. Moberly and his work crews are now expected to go up the Thompson and Columbia rivers to join Sandford Fleming near the pass. It will be a lively meeting!

The Canadian Pacific survey party includes Sandford Fleming (centre).

Tough times befall Nfld. sealing fleet

April 30, 1872

ST. JOHN'S, Nfld. – The present season has been a disastrous one for the sealing fleet – more than 100 lives have been lost, along with two new steamers and several sailing ships. The *Huntsman* from Bay Roberts sank in a storm off the Labrador coast, taking Capt. Robert Dawe, his son and 40 crew members with it. The *Village Belle* of Brigus disappeared without a trace with Capt. John Antle and 18 crew members, and the *Dundanah* of St. John's under William Jenkins also disappeared, with its captain and 31 sealers.

The loss of the *Huntsman* and the *Village Belle* will undoubtedly hurt the already faltering seal fisheries in Bay Roberts and Brigus. To make matters worse, Bay Roberts and Brigus also lost other sailing vessels and lives. The *SS Retriever* and the *SS Bloodhound* sank, although their crews were picked up by neighboring ships.

For the first time in Newfoundland's history, sensation mongers in New York have published wildly exaggerated accounts of disasters here. The *New York Times* writes: "Over forty vessels ... total wrecks, having been dashed to pieces amid huge icebergs and plains of ice during a terrific hurricane ... out of 4,000 human souls only 175 have been accounted for." Officials are correcting these reports.

A woman's mission is to teach children – or is it?

Women resorting to contraception

1872

OTTAWA – It is commonly held by respectable society that it is woman's moral and social duty to bear children. However, there is increasing evidence many women in Canada are engaged in the practice of unnatural methods of contraception. Since 1851, the country's birthrate has been declining at an alarming rate.

Numerous methods of contraception are used by the women of Canada. When it is necessary, due to health reasons, to limit reproduction, doctors recommend natural methods, including abstinence and prolonged nursing of young children. Another alternative is confining intercourse to the safer period of a woman's cycle, which doctors say occurs in the middle of the menstrual cycle.

While they're not recommended by physicians, various unnatural methods of contraception are also in use. When pregnancy occurs, women may turn to quinine, tansy, pennyroyal or ergot to set themselves right. Others resort to more violent means, such as bleeding, hot baths, heavy exercise, or the insertion of catheters or other instruments. If these methods fail, certain midwives and doctors can be found to perform abortions.

As for contraception, in 1823 Francis Place recommended the use of a small sponge, attached to a ribbon, inserted prior to sexual relations and withdrawn afterwards. Dr. George Drysdale, who wrote *Elements of Social Science* in 1854, suggests the sponge, plus douching in tepid water after intercourse. Some rely upon pessaries or vaginal suppositories made from various ingredients.

Canadian physicians agree that these means are the practices of libertines and prostitutes, as is masturbation and *coitus interruptus.* As the *Lancet* stated in 1869, "a woman on whom her husband practises what is euphemistically called preventive copulation is necessarily brought into the condition of mind of a prostitute."

These women enjoy a rare moment of leisure in the Red River settlement.

Property act lets wives control earnings

1872

TORONTO – Married women in Ontario now have the right to control their earnings. Single women who have achieved the age of majority have always had this privilege, as have widows. And now, under the Married Woman's Property Act, a wife's earnings from any trade or occupation, or artistic or scientific endeavors, will be her separate property. Still, a husband must give explicit or implied consent to his wife's employment. A husband also has the right to order the termination of that employment. Employers who refuse to comply are subject to legal action.

Married women also have some legal rights to make contracts, such as for the purchase and sale of property. A husband's compliance is needed because of his inherent interest in his wife's property.

Wife to husband: "You are complaining, my poor husband, about your 10 hour work day. I've already been working for 14 hours and I haven't yet finished my day's work!"

Official says role of female is limited

1872

VICTORIA, B.C. – John Jessop may be a good superintendent of education – and future generations of children may well bless his name – but he knows little about women. Woman's mission, Jessop says, is to educate babies and children. This is the female's role in life. The men here all agree, though to judge by their interest in some of the females who flaunt themselves around town, they would add another function.

But most Victoria women wonder if Jessop has the slightest idea of the work performed by women. None of the women interviewed would allow their names to be made public. They feared they would be tagged as troublemakers, at best, or given a drubbing by their husbands or fathers. But the women of Victoria agree: the female population of the island and mainland can do a lot more than just teaching babies and children. Good, nearby examples are their Indian sisters, many of whom enjoy high rank among the Haida and other tribes. In matrilineal Indian society, property also passes through the female line.

It is true Lady Douglas restricts herself to caring for her family and the sick, but this may be due to her ancestry and early background. Many female settlers play powerful roles in the life of British Columbia. Take, for example, Mrs. John Muir and her daughter who landed here in 1849 after a six-month voyage from London. They worked as hard and as well as the Muir men in the family, building up a farm and then a sawmill business.

Thousands of other women had to learn how to tend animals, clear the forest, make clothes and defend themselves and their families against natives and wild animals. Four nuns came here 14 years ago to tend the sick. They sailed from Montreal down the Atlantic coast, then crossed the Panama isthmus on foot and sailed up the Pacific coast to Victoria – a journey that would daunt most men. Only good for teaching babies, Mr. Jessop? ▷

Macdonald leads Tories to narrow victory in election

Sept. 1, 1872

OTTAWA – John A. Macdonald's Conservatives have been returned to office, but by the narrow majority of 103 seats to 97. The victory is nevertheless sweet for Macdonald. With great political savvy, he has led the Tories to an electoral victory few would have predicted a year ago. And he has done so without the trump card he tried hard to obtain the last six months. Macdonald wanted to run this summer's campaign with financial backing for the transcontinental railway in his back pocket, but he only partially succeeded.

The British government has promised a guaranteed loan of £2.5-million sterling for construction of railways and canals. The loan is in lieu of American compensation for the Fenian raids, and has allowed Macdonald to salvage some credibility for signing the much-criticized Treaty of Washington.

Macdonald is determined to have private enterprise build the railway. Montreal shipping magnate Sir Hugh Allan has pursued the contract, but he is thought to represent American interests, and Macdonald has stated "that no American ring will be allowed to get control." Allan refuses to align with a rival Toronto syndicate, fuelling speculation over his ambitions.

John S. Macdonald dies of tuberculosis

June 1, 1872

CORNWALL, Ont. – John Sandfield Macdonald died "a good Catholic" today, surrounded by family at his home in Ivy Hall. After a long illness, tuberculosis finally claimed the veteran politician and lawyer at age 59. Known as the "poor boy from Glengarry," his estate is valued at $200,000.

Macdonald, long a moderate Liberal, was elected to the first Assembly of the United Province of Canada in 1841. He was elected Speaker in 1852, served as premier of Canada West from 1862-64, and premier of Ontario from 1867-71.

First immigrant from Iceland in country

Sept. 12, 1872

WINNIPEG – It was learned today that the first known Icelander to come to present-day Canada since Lief the Lucky has landed at Quebec City, and soon will be en route to Winnipeg. Newcomer Sigtryggur Jonasson told reporters many of his countrymen are interested in emigrating, and that he is headed west on their behalf.

Iceland has recently been hit by calamities, including disease, volcanic eruptions, crop failures and starvation. The Danish government, which controls the island, invited Icelanders to Denmark, but many prefer North America, where the sagas say a few migrated via Greenland about 1000 AD.

Icelander Sigtryggur Jonasson.

Mob attacks polling booth, newspapers

Sept. 14, 1872

WINNIPEG – The election by acclamation of Sir George-Etienne Cartier to the federal Provencher riding had an angry aftermath today when a mob attacked a polling booth and the offices of the *Manitoban* and *Le Métis* newspapers.

A speech by lawyer F.E. Cornish angered the mob. Cornish launched a scathing attack on alleged wrongdoings of Gov. Adams George Archibald, and French-speaking residents and former Hudson's Bay Company employees who support him. During this verbal attack, Donald A. Smith attempted to remonstrate, but members of the audience quietened Ottawa's special commissioner by throwing clumps of mud at him. The mob then crossed the river to St. Boniface where its members attacked a polling booth and the offices of the two newspapers. Both offices suffered severe damage.

Cartier, defeated in Quebec, was offered this Manitoba alternative. His election, *in absentia*, seems a major victory for Prime Minister John A. Macdonald. But it indebts him heavily to Louis Riel, nominated to run against Cartier but who withdrew in Cartier's favor.

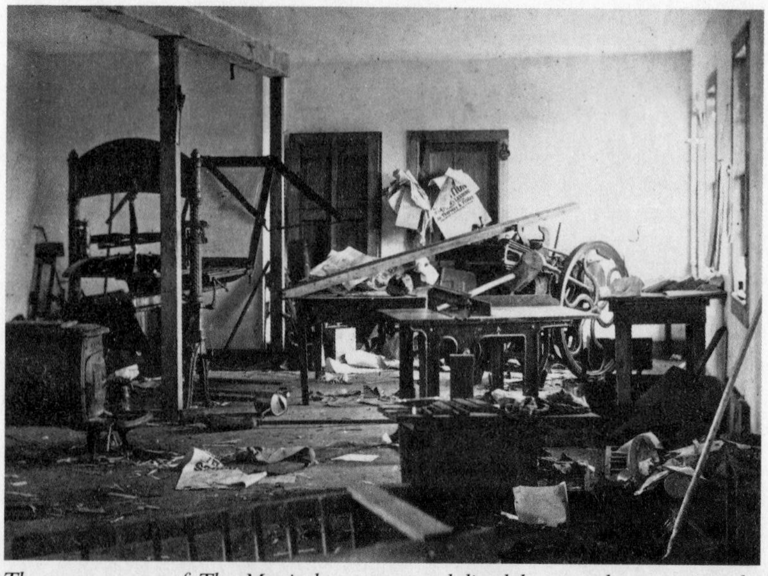

The press room of The Manitoban was vandalized by a mob protesting the recent election of George-Etienne Cartier in the federal riding of Provencher.

Mowat to succeed Blake as premier

Oct. 31, 1872

TORONTO – Oliver Mowat, the vice-chancellor of Ontario, has resigned his judicial position to succeed Edward Blake as the province's Liberal premier. Blake himself has resigned, either to go into federal politics or other endeavors.

Mowat, although most recently a judge, is actually a political veteran. He was a member of the old Union of Canada Parliament from 1857 to 1864, and held a number of cabinet posts there. Mowat also aided in framing the Quebec Conference federal resolutions in 1864. He still has to win an easy riding to gain a seat in the House.

New Ontario Premier Oliver Mowat.

Act of Parliament makes unions legal

June 14, 1872

OTTAWA – Labor has won a major victory in Canada. Thanks to an act passed in Parliament today, it is now legal to unionize. The Trade Unions Bill presented by Sir John A. Macdonald's Conservative government mirrors similar legislation passed in Britain. Under the law, union members can no longer be prosecuted for the simple act of being members.

The end of this loophole means 14 typographical workers charged April 15 for belonging to a union will have the charges against them dropped. It's a welcome triumph for workers, particularly the "Typos" who have been striking for a nine-hour day.

Wilhelm I hands San Juan to U.S.

Oct. 21, 1872

VICTORIA, B.C. – Wilhelm I of Germany has sided with the Americans and has given them San Juan Island. For nearly 13 years the ownership of the island has been in dispute. Once Gov. James Douglas had wanted to invade the island after the Americans had stationed some troops there. But he was persuaded to wait by the local naval commander, Rear Admiral R. L. Baynes.

The dispute was caused when the Oregon Boundary Treaty failed to set a clear line through the islands between Vancouver Island and the American mainland. Dr. John Helmcken, one of B.C.'s delegates to Ottawa to set the terms of union, believes Wilhelm decided correctly based on the evidence before him. The American case was presented excellently; the Canadian was not.

Railroad a strain on Island coffers

The P.E.I. economy, which relies heavily on the fishing industry, is being severely strained by railway costs.

Dec. 20, 1872

CHARLOTTETOWN – Two years ago, the railroad was being trumpeted as the savior of Prince Edward Island's economy and independence. Today it has turned into its nemesis. There have been charges of patronage and corruption as the line has turned into a friendly little road that meanders, at great cost, from one politician's home town to another. A little over a year since the work commenced, the strain is proving too much for the colony's fragile financial apparatus. Government revenues are falling off, and the debentures it floated to finance the scheme are coming due. As bankruptcy stares it square in the face, the Island's legislature has re-opened talks with Canada on Confederation.

Lt.-Gov. William Robinson, a staunch pro-confederate, predicted the railroad would lead to this. He warns the Island legislature not to let anti-confederates "prune them down into anything short of an unequivocal application for admission into the union."

Manitoba Free Press starts to publish

ADVERTISEMENTS.
Manitoba
Free Press,
DAILY & WEEKLY.
KENNY & LUXTON, PUBLISHERS.
WM. F. LUXTON, EDITOR & MANAGER.
Daily issued every lawful day at 5 P.M.; and Weekly every Saturday.
SUBSCRIPTION RATES.
DAILY, 25 cents per week; WEEKLY, $2.50 per annum.
The FREE PRESS is the only daily published in Manitoba; and the Weekly Edition has a larger circulation than all other papers in the Province combined.
KENNY & LUXTON, WINNIPEG.

The Manitoba Free Press promotes circulation with this advertisement.

Nov. 9, 1872

WINNIPEG – The first issue of the *Manitoba Free Press* is on sale today. The paper is owned by W.F. Luxton and published in Winnipeg.

Winnipeg is a town with an economy based on the fur trade but looking toward agriculture. The town's population has increased more than tenfold the last two years. Real estate is a booming business. All sorts of enterprises connected with settlement have been established. There are agencies to lure people to the area, others to accommodate land sales, yet others to outfit them, and, of course, land speculation abounds. Lumber and flour are two other industries which have sprouted up.

B.C.'s second premier: Amor De Cosmos

Dec. 23, 1872

VICTORIA, B.C. – Amor De Cosmos, the fiery reformer and newspaper editor, has agreed to become British Columbia's second premier. He will succeed John McCreight, who resigned four days ago after losing a vote of confidence. His opponents maintain McCreight was under the thumb of Lt.-Gov. Joseph Trutch.

De Cosmos has spent a good part of the past year in Ottawa, for he is a federal MP for Victoria as well as a member of the Legislative Assembly. He has also had an impressive set of electoral successes. In November 1870 De Cosmos was named to the Legislative Council. Then, in October 1871, Victoria voters elected him to the new Legislative Assembly. Two months later he was chosen as an MP. Now he is provincial premier as well.

The YMCA building in Saint John, N.B. was destroyed by a hurricane.

1873

Ottawa, Feb. 5. The government awards the Canadian Pacific Railway Co. headed by Sir Hugh Allan a $30 million subsidy, 50 million acres of land, and a charter to build a railway to the Pacific.

Ottawa, April 2. M.P. Lucius Seth Huntington charges the government with corruption in the awarding of the CPR charter [sparking the Pacific Scandal].

London, England, May 20. Sir George-Etienne Cartier, Father of Confederation, and former prime minister of the Province of Canada, dies. He was largely responsible for reconciling French Canadians to Confederation.

Ottawa, May 21. Parliament approves the entry of P.E.I. into Confederation.

Pictou County, N.S., May. An explosion rips through a coal mine and 60 people die in Canada's first mine disaster.

Prince Edward Island, July 1. The Island enters Confederation. The *Patriot* newspaper states "among the people who thronged the streets there was no enthusiasm."

Canada, Sept. 25. Recruitment and appointment begins for the North West Mounted Police.

Edmonton, Oct. 22. John and David McDougall set out with 25 half-breeds and John's family to establish a combined Methodist mission and ranch among the Stoney Indians in the southern foothills.

Winnipeg, October. Louis Riel is elected to Parliament by acclamation, even though a warrant was issued for his arrest a month ago.

Ottawa, November. Alexander Mackenzie forms Canada's first Liberal government after John A. Macdonald's government is brought down by the Pacific Scandal.

Hull, Que. After coming this far, Louis Riel decides not to enter Ottawa to take his seat in Parliament, probably because he fears assassination or arrest for the "murder" of Thomas Scott. He goes to the U.S.

Nova Scotia. A minimum age of 10 is established for male laborers in the mines.

Canada. The economy enters a severe depression, part of an international economic crisis.

British Columbia. Women property holders, married and unmarried, become the first Canadian women to win the right to vote in municipal elections.

North West Mounted Police formed

May 23, 1873

OTTAWA – Parliament today passed an act establishing a new police force for the Northwest Territories. The force, known as the North West Mounted Police, is looking for able-bodied recruits between the ages of 16 and 40 who know how to ride a horse. Pay has been set at 75 cents a day for sub-constables, $1 for constables.

The force is modelled on the Royal Irish Constabulary. It will be the advance guard of settlement, created to bring law and order to the vast western territory, some of it formerly British, some of it taken over by Canada from the Hudson's Bay Company in 1870. Lately, traders from south of the border have been disrupting the lives of the western Indians by trading them cheap whisky, and the force's first job will be stamp out this illegal whisky trade.

The force's original name was the North West Mounted Rifles, but at the last minute Prime Minister John A. Macdonald changed the word "rifles" to "police." Macdonald has been directly responsible for establishing the force. He hopes it will avoid the bloody warfare which has characterized westward expansion south of the border. He also wants it to be a symbol of Canadian sovereignty in the sparsely-settled region. Members of the new force will live at log posts being built across the west.

NWMP commissioner G.A. French.

Chief Constable Samuel Steele of the North West Mounted Police force.

Cartier dies, prime minister mourns ally

May 20, 1873

OTTAWA – Sir John A. Macdonald, already under siege since April's public revelations about his relations with CPR railway charter holder Sir Hugh Allan's company, has received another blow. His old colleague, Sir George-Etienne Cartier, the Quebec parliamentarian, close friend and steadfast ally in the House, has died in London of Bright's Disease.

The news comes at a bad time for the prime minister. His government is faltering, yet his own party won't let him retire, because there's no one to take his place. It is said Macdonald is again drinking heavily.

The Cartier funeral procession passes up St. James Street in Montreal.

Island reps headed to Ottawa for talks

May 6, 1873

CHARLOTTETOWN – Faced with a crushing railroad debt and a slumping economy, P.E.I. has sent a delegation to Ottawa to negotiate terms for confederation. The mood on the Island is fundamentally changed from nine years ago. Then, pro-confederates were in a decided minority. Now, even violent anti-confederates like Edward Palmer concede the need for union. "I would be an opponent to the present terms," he writes, "if it were not that we are ready to be submerged by our great railway, but inasmuch as the government of Canada has liberally agreed to take that vast undertaking off our hands. ... I have no hesitation in accepting them."

J.C. Pope and T.H. Haviland, longtime confederates, are accompanying former anti-confederate G.W. Howlan to Ottawa. They will base their negotiations on the 1869 "Better Terms" proposal and drive as hard a bargain possible, but there is no doubt as to the outcome.

Ship sinks off Nova Scotia; 547 dead

The Atlantic lies aground on Meagher's Island as survivors struggle ashore.

Two men make a valiant effort to rescue a woman from the wreck of the Atlantic off the coast of Nova Scotia. The raging seas make the rescue bid very dangerous.

April 1, 1873

PROSPECT, N.S. – Sailing from Liverpool to New York, the *SS Atlantic* this morning struck Meagher's Island near here. In the hours that followed, 547 men, women and children drowned, or were pounded to death as furious waves smashed them against rocks. Local fishermen managed to save some 300 lives.

The *Atlantic* turned for Halifax to get coal, and that was the end of her. She boasted a marble dance floor and 21 pianos, and was called "one of those floating palaces" that make a trip to or from Europe a pleasant episode. Among the survivors was Capt. James Williams, who cried, "Would to God even one woman had been saved."

P.E.I. in Canada: Maritime province drives hard bargain

July 1, 1873

CHARLOTTETOWN – "Make the best of it," warns one Islander, "for you go in as paupers." Today, after nine years of resistance, P.E.I. joined Confederation. Ceremonies were accompanied by a *feu de joie*. "So far as powder and metal could do it," observes one local paper, "there was a terrible din. But among the people who thronged the streets there was no enthusiasm."

Islanders are displaying a blend of satisfaction and disappointment. Economic necessity – more than anything else – has brought confederation. They had taken great pride in their autonomy, and hoped to retain it. However, they're proud they were able to drive a hard bargain and enter under better terms than those of 1867. Perhaps their attitude is best summed up by the Union Proclamation. An official read the document from the balcony of Province House, reports the *Patriot*. "The audience consisted of three persons, and even they did not appear to be very attentive."

Government faces charge of scandal

April 2, 1873

OTTAWA – Sprawled comfortably at his seat in the House of Commons and toying with a pencil, Prime Minister John A. Macdonald waits for an oppressive silence hovering over the chamber to break. Just moments ago, in a brief prepared statement, Liberal member Lucius Seth Huntington charged Macdonald and members of his Conservative government with accepting illegal payments from American business interests in connection with construction of Canada's national railway. In response, Macdonald exudes a manner of detached, guilt-free indifference.

Huntington, a handsome man of commanding presence, has surprisingly brought forward no documented evidence supporting his accusation that the payoffs were used to finance last year's Conservative election campaign.

Survivors of Hall expedition rescued after six months adrift

April 30, 1873

LABRADOR – The Newfoundland steamer *Tigress* today picked up 19 crew members of the *Polaris* just off Grady Harbour, Labrador, survivors of an ill-fated Arctic expedition led by Charles Francis Hall, an American. Miraculously, the group managed to survive almost six months adrift on an ice floe after becoming separated from their ship.

Had they not been helped by two longtime Inuit friends of Hall's, the 19 men almost certainly would have perished. As for Hall, he died five months after the expedition set out in July 1871, reportedly of apoplexy, although there are rumors he was deliberately poisoned with arsenic.

Howe representing the Crown in N.S.

May 10, 1873

HALIFAX – Joseph Howe, 68, the dominant politician in Nova Scotia for 30-odd years, today was sworn in as lieutenant-governor, but the honor came too late for him to enjoy. Some old friends snub him. They see him as a traitor because he abandoned the anti-Confederation cause four years ago, joined the federal cabinet, and now, as the queen's representative, wallows in his final payoff. He also suffers lung trouble.

Golf is becoming very popular in Canada. Here golfers line up to tee off at the Royal Montreal Golf Club while others watch the sport.

Prince Edward Island: weak sister in Canada?

The port of Charlottetown, Prince Edward Island's largest community, can boast several impressive buildings in its downtown area.

The delicate Lady's Slipper is the floral emblem of Prince Edward Island.

Established trade links an Island plus

1873

PRINCE EDWARD ISLAND – This province goes into Confederation with established trade links both along the Atlantic seaboard and to Great Britain. They include the exporting of farm products to the United States. Another major industry on the Island since mid-century has been shipbuilding, with lumber being supplied from the forests here. Ready access to the sea has been a major factor in getting products to market.

But there are some ominous signs for the P.E.I. economy. It does not have the coal to sustain industry, which puts the Island in a bad spot as the industrial revolution gathers momentum. Also, wooden ships are about to be replaced by steam-powered steel vessels and the shipbuilding industry here may be in jeopardy because the raw materials are not available to change with the times. There are fears that in joining Canada this year P.E.I. may become the weak sister, thanks to westward expansion and the industrialization of Ontario. But debt incurred in building a railway across the Island and Canada's promise to pay it off, prompted P.E.I. to join Confederation.

Province's rich soil is top natural resource

1873

PRINCE EDWARD ISLAND – Forests are giving way to fertile soils as the top natural resource of this new province. Despite two centuries of clearing, there is still a lot of woodland, particularly in upland areas. But the Island's rich soil is king, with up to 90 percent of its land having potential for farming. The sea, which offers fishing and commerce, is another key resource.

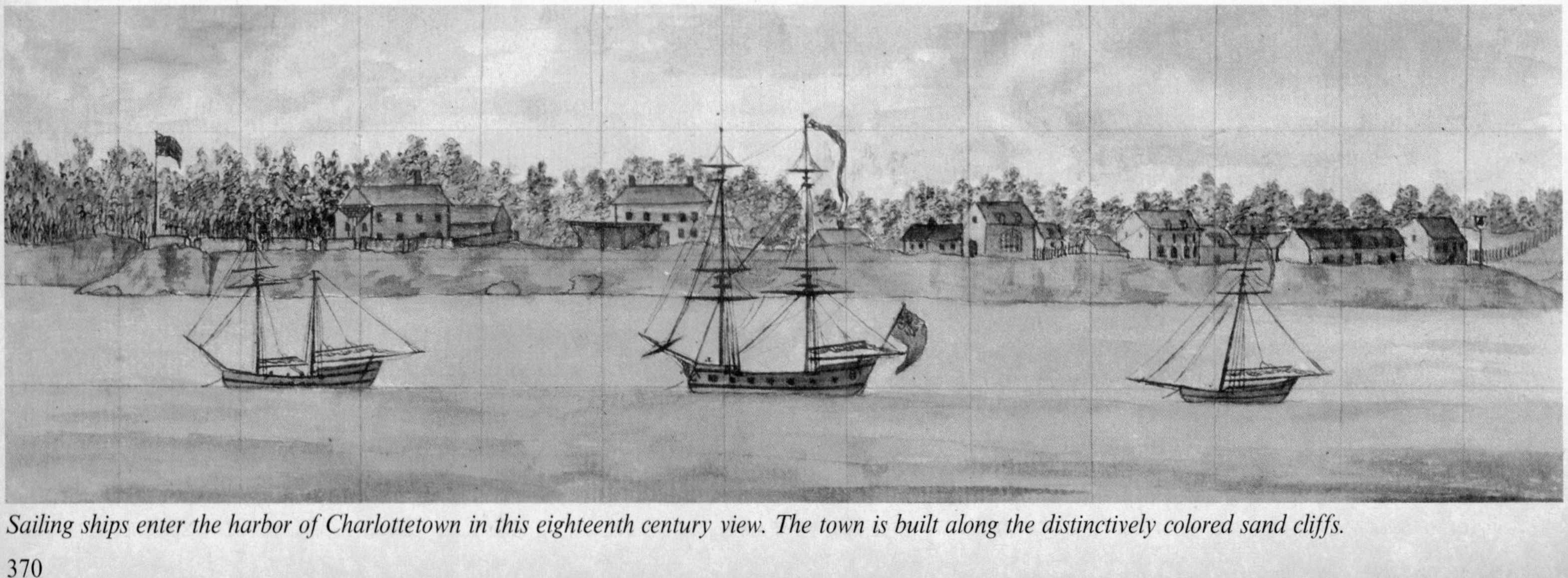

Sailing ships enter the harbor of Charlottetown in this eighteenth century view. The town is built along the distinctively colored sand cliffs.

Pacific Scandal explodes in the press

Macdonald asks innocently if his actions in CPR scandal are wrong.

July 4, 1873

OTTAWA – The long-simmering controversy over the relationship between the Conservative government and Sir Hugh Allan's Canadian Pacific Railway exploded in the press today. This morning both the Toronto *Globe* and Montreal *Herald* gleefully revealed correspondence from Allan that reveals him openly bribing the government to award him the railway charter.

In the correspondence, sent to a hitherto-unknown group of American financiers – fuelling fears that giving the railway contract to the CPR was, in fact, giving it to the Americans – Allan boasts he openly compromised the late Sir George-Etienne Cartier, Macdonald's Quebec leader. He did it first by buying supporters in Cartier's riding before the August election. Then, having done so, he coerced Cartier into changing his opposition to the CPR by threatening to use these voters to defeat him. Cartier gave in, and accepted funds from Allan to rebuy his supporters. Cartier isn't the only one damned in Allan's correspondence. Other public figures are mentioned as individuals who would have to be bought off with CPR stock. Names range from George Brown, whose *Globe* broke the story, to Donald A. Smith, chief commissioner of the Hudson's Bay Company. There's no proof, however, these men were corrupted; only that Allan believed an attempt should be made.

The reason for all these intrigues is simple: the government's railway contract is worth millions of dollars and Allan wants it at all costs. And according to his letters, the government has signed a secret agreement with the CPR to make him president of the railway project and his cronies majority stockholders.

Macdonald proclaims his innocence as he stands on the back of Canada.

American says Macdonald and others were "lent" thousands

July 21, 1873

OTTAWA – The Pacific Scandal has gotten bigger. Today, the Toronto *Globe*, Montreal *Herald* and Quebec *l'Evénement* published an amazing "historical narrative" by the American financial connection of the CPR's Sir Hugh Allan. George McMullen says government officials, including Sir John A. Macdonald, were "lent" thousands of dollars for their political campaigns, "with very good knowledge that it was never to be repaid."

Secret telegrams reveal everyone involved knew the government was trading political influence for election donations. Macdonald himself telegraphed the CPR lawyer on Aug. 26, 1872, writing "I must have another 10,000 ... do not fail me."

Governor general hears of scandal brewing in Ottawa

July 7, 1873

CHARLOTTETOWN – Gov. Gen. Lord Dufferin, in P.E.I. to welcome the newest province into the dominion, heard news today of a major scandal brewing in Ottawa. Three days ago, the newspapers in Montreal and Toronto began publishing the revelations of George McMullen. The Canadian-born McMullen is a powerful businessman in Chicago, and until recently part of a conspiracy to sell out the new national railway to U.S. interests. McMullen says he gave Sir Hugh Allan some $350,000 to use as bribes to sway Canadian shareholders and politicians into letting the Northern Pacific Railway buy control of the planned railroad.

Rages Senator David MacPherson, who headed a rival syndicate hoping for the contract, "One of the most unpatriotic conspiracies ever entered in this Dominion. An audacious, insolent, unpatriotic and gigantic swindle." Apparently Sir Hugh, head of a major Canadian railway syndicate, acted with American backers for whom he hoped he could secure control of the Canadian railway. McMullen says much of the money went to buy the Conservatives' victory in last year's election. He exposed the scheme when he realized Allan would double-cross his American cohorts.

Esquimalt named western terminus

July 19, 1873

VICTORIA, B.C. – Sir John A. Macdonald, ever the wily politician, has declared that Esquimalt will be the western terminus of the Canadian Pacific Railway. In the terms of union it was agreed that construction of the railway would start within two years. Yet the surveyors are still entangled in the mountain forests, unable to determine a route. And so Sir John A., a few days before the two-year deadline is up, has chosen Esquimalt and ordered a sod-turning ceremony to convince the people of Victoria that the railway is coming. ▷

Hunters kill 20 Indians in massacre

June 1, 1873

CYPRESS HILLS, N.W.T. – The tranquility of these rolling hills was shattered today when a band of Assiniboine Indians was attacked by American wolfers. Over 20 Indians died in the fight, apparently sparked by the disappearance of a horse from a nearby trading post. Thinking that the Indians had stolen the animal, the wolfers came north in search of Indians who had stolen their mounts just outside of Fort Benton in Montana.

It turned out the missing horse had simply wandered away, but the wolfers, who had been drinking heavily, did not wait for an explanation. They opened fire on the Indians, including women and children, sending them scurrying for cover in a hail of bullets. After the survivors fled, the Americans stormed the camp and celebrated the victory by placing the severed head of an Indian corpse on a lodge pole. Four native women were captured and taken away to the hunters' post. Fearing reprisals, most of the Americans will return back across the border tomorrow. Even before this massacre, Indians have loathed wolfers, who use strychnine to poison their prey, a technique which often kills the Indians' dogs.

Cypress Hills lie on the eastern edge of "Whoop-up Country," the plains area where Indians and traders from the south have co-existed in an uneasy peace for several years. The Americans come north to trade furs and buffalo pelts, to kill wolves and to sell cheap liquor to the Indians. This vile brew is known locally as "Whoop-up bug juice," a horrible blend of whisky, chewing tobacco and spices.

The unofficial capital of the area is Fort Whoop-up [Lethbridge, Alberta] itself, located at the junction of the St. Mary and Oldman rivers, but there are other tumbledown trading posts dotted about the territory. One of these is operated by Abe Farwell, a Montana native who gets on well with the Indians.

Assiniboine Indians, killers' target.

Before today's massacre, Farwell tried to warn the Indians to flee, but he was too late.

Because of incidents like this, the Canadian government will create a new police force to bring law and order to the Northwest Territories.

Lake of the Woods Ojibwa finally sign treaty with Ottawa

Oct. 3, 1873

LAKE OF THE WOODS, Ont. – The federal government's treaty commissioners have found the Lake of the Woods Ojibwa to be difficult negotiators. The past two years the Indians turned down federal offers and asked the Dominion to improve its terms, but after protracted and difficult talks this year the government has secured a treaty for land west of Lake Superior and east of the Red River.

A Lac Seul chief reveals how anxious the Ojibwa were to sign a treaty. "We would ask you to assist us with every kind of implement to use for our benefit, to enable us to perform our work; a little of everything and money. We would borrow your cattle; we ask you for this support; I will find whereon to feed them. The waters out of which you sometimes take food for yourselves, we will lend you in return."

Many men are employed at the Gatling Gold Mines at Marmora, Ontario. This prosperous operation has several buildings surrounding the pit.

Artist Susanna Moodie painted this picture of the first operating mine in the province of Ontario at Marmora, Hastings County.

Sir John urges MPs not to desert ship

Nov. 3, 1873

OTTAWA – Sir John A. Macdonald made the speech of his life tonight. A five-hour impassioned plea, couched both in terms of defiance and apology, it was aimed at convincing his dwindling band of MP supporters not to abandon his ship and vote down the government.

The speech before the packed Commons started at 9 p.m., and ended at two with the words, "I leave it (victory or defeat) to this House with every confidence. I am equal to either fortune."

Legislators neglect Micmacs of P.E.I.

July 1873

CHARLOTTETOWN – Of all the provinces in Canada, it is perhaps in the newest, Prince Edward Island, where Indians have been neglected the most. As elsewhere in the Maritimes, British settlers did not acknowledge the Indians' title to their lands, but at least in Nova Scotia and New Brunswick colonial legislators set aside numerous reserves for resident natives. On the Island, however, as late as 1867 the 300 resident Micmacs only had some 200 acres of reserve land.

Canadian Labor Union founded in Ontario

Sept. 23, 1873

TORONTO – Representatives from 31 unions came together today to form the Canadian Labor Union, an umbrella organization to help labor improve working conditions. The Toronto Trades Assembly played a big role in putting together the central body, which will represent unions from eight Ontario towns. But the CLU hopes this province is just the beginning. It intends to expand into a national organization, as its name suggests.

The formation of the CLU is the second step in the development of labor federations. The first was the Toronto Trades Assembly, which was established in 1871, linking 15 local unions.

Macdonald, cabinet resign in the wake of railway scandal

Nov. 5, 1873

OTTAWA – Sir John A. Macdonald and his Tory government accepted the inevitable today. Despite a brilliant five-hour speech the other night in Parliament and despite hopes the public would forget his part accepting under-the-table campaign donations from Sir Hugh Allan's American-backed Canadian Pacific Railway, the prime minister has finally faced reality. Enough government members have deserted his party in the House to make defeat unavoidable. And so, this morning, Macdonald and his cabinet decided to resign.

In his place, as a new government, comes the Liberal party led by Alexander Mackenzie – a move made by the governor general without calling an election. It's an uneasy victory for Mackenzie. The party is not really ready to govern. As well, its move from minority to majority in the House only comes as a result of the migration of disaffected Tories to its side, members who can just as easily abandon it when they disagree with policies.

New political party gets off the ground

Dec. 6, 1873

TORONTO – The Canada First movement, an Ontario group dedicated to the advancement of Canada as a nation, has formed its own political party aimed at forwarding its views in Parliament. The Canadian National Association, as it's called, wants Canada to have more say in treaties affecting the country. That's a response to the 1871 Treaty of Washington between Britain and America, in which the imperial government gave the U.S. access to Canadian fisheries without Canada's consent.

The new political party also wants closer trade relations, and eventually political ties, with the British West Indies, secret voting (to end intimidation and corruption at the polls), the encouragement of immigration and a Canadian-controlled militia.

Winnipeg becomes Manitoba's first city

Nov. 8, 1873

WINNIPEG – The provincial legislature today approved the bill incorporating Winnipeg as Manitoba's first city. Passage of the bill ends the dispute which has divided the community over the past several years. Many residents had been urging incorporation so they could elect their own leaders and collect the taxes necessary for sorely needed improvements. However, such action had been opposed by the major property owners. One of their leaders was Donald A. Smith, of the Hudson's Bay Company.

When the bill was first proposed in the House, Speaker J.C. Bird rejected it on a technicality. So strong was the public reaction to this that one night, unknown assailants waylaid and tarred him. They are still at large despite a reward of $1,000 for their apprehension.

At the time of incorporation, Winnipeg has 900 buldings, and a population in excess of 3,000. Its area is eight square kilometres. It is anticipated that within weeks the campaign will begin for the election of the first city council. The incorporation also settles the controversy concerning the city's name. In the debate in the House, suggested alternatives included Assiniboia, Barry, and Selkirk.

The famed Red River cart has been called into action in a new role now. The city of Winnipeg uses a Red River cart as its first water cart.

Water supply for the new capital of Manitoba is drawn from the river, transported into the city by ox-cart and sold by the gallon to residents.

Mounties get their first men; whisky traders in custody

The new North West Mounted Police have a very striking uniform.

December 1873

WINNIPEG – Six men are in custody at the Stone Fort at Lower Fort Garry. They have the dubious distinction of being the first people arrested by the new North West Mounted Police force.

Patrols were prompted when word reached the post that whisky traders were doing business around the western shore of Lake Winnipeg. NWMP commissioner George Arthur French assigned Inspector J.F. Macleod to investigate. Macleod took with him a constable and three subconstables whom he first instructed in snowshoeing and survival. They travelled in horsedrawn bobsleighs. Two dog sleds carried their camping equipment and supplies. The police found the culprits in a log shack that served as headquarters for the traders. The round trip took several days, and the party arrived back at Fort Garry on Christmas Eve.

The Stone Fort was leased by the government from the Hudson's Bay Company to be used as a police post. It houses 150 men – three divisions – who were sworn in on Nov. 3 of this year.

1874

Canada, May 3. Reverend William Bompas is consecrated as the first Anglican Bishop of Athabasca.

Winnipeg, July. The *Manitoba Free Press* goes daily, becoming the only daily west of Toronto. *The Manitoba Weekly Free Press*, a farm paper, appears.

London, Ont., Aug. 27. The Earl of Dufferin officially opens Victoria Park.

Manitoba, September. Louis Riel is re-elected to Parliament following his expulsion from the House in April. He sees the election as a victory for French and Catholic rights in western Canada.

Ottawa. Riel does not take his seat in the House of Commons, and is expelled for the second time.

Northwest Territories, Oct. 14. Col. James Macleod and his North West Mounted Police begin building a fort on an island in the Oldman River to serve as their headquarters [Fort Macleod, Alberta].

Maitland, N.S., Oct. 27. The 73-metre *William D. Lawrence*, the largest ship built in Canada, is launched. The ship is named after her owner.

Quebec, November. French-speaking Quebecers are furious at the conviction of Ambroise-Dydime Lépine in Winnipeg for the murder of Thomas Scott, and newspapers demand amnesty for Lépine and Riel.

Ontario. Printer Daniel O'Donoghue, vice-president of the Canadian Labour Union, is elected to the legislature as an independent workingman. The Canadian Labour Union is largely responsible.

Northwest Territories. Methodist missionary John McDougall reports there were 42 fatalities among the Blackfoot [in Alberta] following drinking bouts during the past winter.

Toronto. The Toronto Argonauts football team is formed.

Ontario. Dr. Mack founds the Mack Training School, the first nursing school in the province. He was advised by Florence Nightingale.

Toronto. The Prisoners' Aid Association of Toronto is formed to help former inmates adapt to life on the outside.

Montreal. Led by McGill principal Dr. William Dawson, 50 worshippers walk out of Erskine Presbyterian Church to protest organ playing during church services.

Liberals triumph in federal election

Jan. 22, 1874

OTTAWA – The ruin of the Conservatives, begun last year with the revelation of the Pacific Scandal, is now complete. Across the country, Liberal candidates have routed their rivals, garnering 133 seats to the Tories' 73.

It is a stunning defeat for Sir John A. Macdonald, but not an unexpected one. The indignation of the Canadian public at his corruption, and the alternative offered by the undeniably honest, upright, and high-principled Alexander Mackenzie, doomed his party from the outset. Sir John had a tough fight to retain his seat in Kingston, and even that victory isn't certain yet. His opponent has petitioned for another election, charging Macdonald with vote buying, and other electoral malpractices.

"Guiding force" Blake quits cabinet post

For many Liberals, Prime Minister Alexander Mackenzie was the second choice to lead the party.

Feb. 13, 1874

OTTAWA – Edward Blake, the guiding force of the Liberals, has resigned from the federal cabinet. The move pleases no one, least of all Prime Minister Alexander Mackenzie. In fact, when the Liberals assumed power, Mackenzie wanted Blake to become prime minister. But the former premier of Ontario refused, and so Mackenzie, judged by many as inferior to Blake in his talents, took the lead role instead.

Since then, the prime minister has tried to get Blake to play a larger role in the government. Blake, professing the need to remain at his law firm, has only been willing to be a minister without portfolio. Now, having pulled the Liberals through their victorious election campaign, he has given up that post. And even though he was elected as a Liberal MP, Edward Blake will sit as a private member.

Commission conducts survey of boundary

1874

WESTERN CANADA – Two years ago, a joint British-American commission established the western boundary separating Canada and the United States along the 49th Parallel. Last year, the Boundary Commission sent surveyors to the region, their goal being to establish the first international borderline based not on natural geographic features, but according to a pre-designed, geodetic concept.

The project is ambitious. Plans are that nearly 1,450 kilometres of terrain, from Lake of the Woods, Ont., to the Rocky Mountains, will be surveyed by the end of this year. More than half the distance was covered last year. Stone cairns, earth mounds, and innumerable timber markings, some already in place, will stand as peaceful symbols of a continent divided in two.

An earth mound is built to mark the border between Canada and the U.S.

Edgar and Walkem address B.C. crisis

March 9, 1874

VICTORIA, B.C. – A near-riot last month when former premier Amor De Cosmos tried to water down the terms of union in an indication of how important are talks going on now between James Edgar, a federal Liberal leader, and Premier George Walkem.

B.C. needs the railway to restore prosperity, but there is great rivalry between the island and mainland over the route it should take. Prime Minister Alexander Mackenzie has Edgar working on a compromise.

Grange establishes outpost in London

Feb. 27, 1874

LONDON, Ont. – The Grange, an American farmers' association dedicated to improving agricultural techniques, has established an outpost in this town. Known as the Advance Grange, it was put together through the efforts of local editor William Weld, and Eben Thompson, a young Vermonter travelling the country preaching the gospel of farm improvement.

North West Mounted Police at work

June 11, 1874

FORT GARRY, Man. – The new North West Mounted Police force has left here on its way to bring Canadian law to the southwest corner of the Northwest Territories. The force, which has been set the task of policing 777,000 square kilometres of land, consists of 275 officers and men, 339 horses, 142 oxen, 189 wagons, some cannon and field kitchens.

The NWMP was created last year. Prime Minister John A. Macdonald introduced a bill on April 28 to form a police force for the Territories. He was responding to pressures to protect the Indians against the whisky traders and other American ruffians operating in Canada – and to preempt American control of the southern half of the Territories. As one fur trader in Fort Edmonton said of the American whisky traders: "They said that as there was no force to prevent them, they would do as they damn well please."

The North West Mounted Police force faces a journey of around 1,600 kilometres across virtually unknown country before it reaches the Oldman River. On the way it will root out the American whisky forts. A small force will stop at Fort Edmonton on the trip.

North West Mounted Police badge.

NWMP begin trek west to stop Fort Whoop-up whisky trade

July 8, 1874

FORT DUFFERIN, Man. – A long caravan of members of the North West Mounted Police wound its way out of Fort Dufferin this morning, beginning a 1,200-kilometre march across the plains to the foothills of the Rocky Mountains. The 275 troopers, wearing red tunics and armed with pistols, carbines and light field artillery, are heading for Fort Whoop-up, the notorious whisky post on the Oldman River just west of the Cypress Hills where American traders illegally sell cheap liquor to the Indians. Last year the Cypress Hills were the scene of a terrible massacre when American wolfers slaughtered more than 20 natives.

Sub-Inspector John French reads orders for the North West Mounted Police.

The police are hoping to eradicate the whisky trade and bring Canadian law and order to the region. The troopers are riding at the head of a parade of ox carts, wagons, cattle and artillery that's more than six kilometres long. Most members of the force are from eastern Canada, veterans of the British army and Canadian militia. The force was created by Parliament last May. Recruits began gathering last summer at Fort Garry where they spent the winter marching and drilling. A second contingent arrived from Toronto this spring.

Once they bring the whisky traffic under control, the troopers will be stationed at log posts at strategic locations across the west. Their job will be to pacify the Indians and assist pioneer farm settlers.

Government makes secret ballot law; bars to close polling day

May 26, 1874

OTTAWA – The new Liberal government has ended the days of election-day bribery and voter intimidation with a single action: it has made the secret ballot law. Under the new election law, party supporters won't be able to tell how people vote until the count is taken. By depriving them of this power, election-day violence and vote-buying are sure to become extinct!

As an added precaution, the government has moved to close all bars on polling day, and made it illegal to offer ribbons, posters and flags when the vote is being taken. Finally, all election expenses must be reported two months after the vote. Any victories won through corrupt practices will be declared invalid.

Riel risks capture for his swearing-in

March 30, 1874

OTTAWA – Fugitive Métis leader Louis Riel sneaked into the House of Commons today and managed to get himself sworn in without being discovered. Riel won a parliamentary seat in a Manitoba riding in the recent federal election, but he's a wanted man in Ontario and has been reluctant to claim his place in the House of Commons.

The Ontario government has charged Riel with the murder of Thomas Scott in 1870 and is offering a $5,000 reward for his capture. After today's daring escapade, Riel did not linger in the House – he darted to the Quebec side of the border where French-Canadians fête him as a national hero.

MPs vote to expel Riel from Commons

April 9, 1874

OTTAWA – Louis Riel, the only member of Parliament with a price on his head, was expelled from the House of Commons today. The vote pitted Riel's French-speaking supporters against his more numerous English-speaking detractors. The fugitive Métis leader, elected to represent a Manitoba riding in the recent federal vote, was ordered to appear in Parliament to face certain questions. But since he is wanted for murder in Ontario, Riel was a no-show and his fellow MPs expelled him.

McGill team plays new form of rugby

May 15, 1874

CAMBRIDGE, Mass. – Rugby and its oval leather football was introduced to the United States today when McGill University and Harvard played to a scoreless tie in three half-hour periods. The McGill men had been experimenting with this new form of rugby, but today's match was the first to be played in the U.S. Yesterday, the two sides played a traditional soccer game with a round ball, with Harvard winning 3-0. ▷

Russian Mennonites reach Winnipeg

The first group of Mennonite immigrants arrives at Winnipeg on board the steamer International.

July 31, 1874

WINNIPEG – The steamer *International* arrived in Winnipeg today, loaded with Mennonites. They are the first influx of what will become a major addition to the province's farming population.

The newcomers will settle on a reserve north and east of the Rat River. Their arrival here was preceded by special orders-in-council passed by the federal government which guarantee the Mennonites freedom of religion, exemption from military service, and the right to conduct their own schools, "so far as the law allowed." These Russian colonists emigrated from Europe when the Russian imperial government revoked their exemption from military service. After this decision, the Mennonites sent out emissaries to search for suitable land to settle.

Bell tells his dad he's working on "telephone" idea

July 24, 1874

BRANTFORD, Ont. – He's already taught the family dog to "talk," and now Alexander Graham Bell, 23, is planning an invention to allow people to talk to each other over great distances. While spending the summer in Tutelo Heights, Bell explained his "telephone" idea to his father, Melville Bell, the inventor of a symbolic code for vocal sounds. Alexander, who teaches deaf children, has shown his father diagrams for his telephone.

The Bell family has been in Canada for four years, coming here from Scotland to seek fresher air after Alexander's brother Melville died from tuberculosis.

Alexander Graham Bell, a brilliant inventor (later portrait).

Central Prison open for Ontario inmates

June 1, 1874

TORONTO – The Central Prison opened here today with 147 inmates being transferred from smaller jails in the counties. The new facility is for short-term prisoners and it was built in the wake of concerns about conditions in county jails. Initially, Ontario had planned to build three central prisons, but opted for one after meeting with opposition. The prisoners' labor – at 50 cents a day per inmate – has been sold to Canada Car Company.

McDougall brothers bring 100 head of cattle to N.W.T. mission

June 1874

MORLEYVILLE, N.W.T. – Methodist missionary John McDougall and his brother David have driven a herd of 100 head of cattle up the trail from Fort Benton, Montana, to this Stoney Indian mission in the valley of Bow River.

The McDougall herd is one of the first in the Canadian foothills, but others will surely follow as the region has fine grass and many well-watered valleys. As well, the North West Mounted Police, expected here later this summer, will mean a steady demand for butchered meat. The McDougalls set up the mission here last year.

The cartoonist's view of the Canadian political situation. Liberals and Conservatives dance together at the New Year's Dance of Reconciliation.

Hodgson takes up plum post in P.E.I.

July 4, 1874

CHARLOTTETOWN – P.E.I. got its first native-born lieutenant-governor today in Robert Hodgson. Entering public life in 1824, he quickly became a powerful member of the Island's family compact.

Hodgson is no stranger to the vice-regal office, having served three times as colonial administrator in the absence of a governor. The governorship is his third "first" as an Islander. In 1852 he became its first native-born chief justice, and in 1869 he was the first Islander to receive a knighthood.

Cree, Saulteaux surrender rich land

Sept. 15, 1874

QU'APPELLE VALLEY, N.W.T. – The Cree and Saulteaux (Ojibwa) tribes of the Qu'Appelle Lakes agreed today to a surrender of their rich, fertile land in the Saskatchewan region north of the American border. Terms of Treaty No. 4 duplicate those in Treaty No. 3, signed last year with the Lake of the Woods Ojibwas, namely a gratuity of $12, and an annuity of $5, for each band member. Commissioner Alexander Morris also promised the Qu'Appelle Indians a reserve of 2.59 square kilometres for every five Indians, a school on each reserve, and livestock.

A tense moment in the talks came when Chief Pasquash, a Plains Cree, asked why the Hudson's Bay Company received £300,000 for Rupert's Land. The money, he said, should have been paid to the Indians, because the land belonged to them. Morris rejected this demand.

It is difficult to believe the Cree and Saulteaux Indians fully understand the carefully chosen legal phrases in the agreement. Yet, their marks now appear on a document which states: "The Cree and Saulteaux Tribes of Indians, and all other Indians inhabiting the district hereinafter described and defined, do hereby cede, release, surrender and yield up to the Government of the Dominion of Canada, for Her Majesty the Queen and Her successors forever, all their rights, titles and privileges whatsoever, to the lands included within the following limits. ..."

Address from the Grand General Council of the Indians of Canada, Sarnia.

Americans flee fort before police arrive

Oct. 9, 1874

FORT WHOOP-UP, N.W.T. [Lethbridge, Alberta] – A column of North West Mounted Police located this whisky trading post in the southwestern prairies today, only to find that the American traders who occupied it had left before their arrival. The police arrived ready for a fight. Field guns were moved into position and the men prepared to storm the log fort. But apparently word had reached the traders that the NWMP was on its way, and when the police burst in, all they found was one old man and three or four Indian women.

The NWMP arrived ragged and weary after being on the trail since early July. The men, many of them greenhorns from eastern Canada, will not forget their first taste of life in the west. On the march from Manitoba, food supplies ran out and the horses became as skinny as walking skeletons. At times the sun beat mercilessly down on the men; at other times they dragged their wagons through knee-deep mud. Then in September, it snowed. Métis guide Jerry Potts, hired at the American settlement of Fort Benton to the south, helped the NWMP to find the fort. From here, the column will proceed west to an island in the Oldman River and build a permanent post.

Red tunic, pillbox hat give NWMP officers an impressive appearance.

Davis seeks economic relief from Ottawa

Aug. 3, 1874

WINNIPEG – When Premier Robert Davis stood for election, he promised to strive to improve the provincial economy. But he could not have foreseen the difficulty he now faces. On top of a debt in excess of $100,000, another poor grain crop has placed Manitoba's economy in a near-perilous position. Davis, a popular hotel proprietor, says that some form of relief from Ottawa is the only way to solve the growing problem.

Rumor says that Davis and Joseph Royal, a member of his cabinet, plan to travel to Ottawa to petition Prime Minister Alexander Mackenzie for direct assistance. The province needs a large sum of money to continue improving roads and extending public services.

Those who know of these plans say Davis wants "better terms" for the province, and he believes Mackenzie will be interested in a cost-cutting plan to abolish the legislative council, or "Petty House of Lords," which many residents now view as a needless expense.

When Manitoba joined Canada, one condition of union was a subsidy in lieu of natural resources retained by Ottawa for "purposes of the Dominion," but even a few years of experience show it to be inadequate for the needs of the small new province.

In Canada, public hangings such as this one often draw large crowds of interested spectators.

Lépine sentenced to die for murder

Nov. 2, 1874

WINNIPEG, Man. – Ambroise-Dydime Lépine today was found guilty and sentenced to death for his part in March 4, 1870 murder of adventurer Thomas Scott at the Red River settlement. Due to the uncertain state of government in the colony there were lengthy delays both in bringing Lépine to justice, and in conducting the trial.

Lépine was president of the Métis court martial which condemned Scott to death on a charge of insubordination. A warrant for Lépine's arrest was issued on the basis of information laid by William Farmer, once held prisoner by the provisional government of Louis Riel. It is common knowledge the Lépine arrest was instigated by lawyer Francis Evans Cornish, in hopes of securing a reward being offered by Ottawa.

Following his arrest in February, Lépine spent a month in custody after which he was released on $8,000 bail.

Booming year for Nfld. cod fishery

Oct. 31, 1874
NEWFOUNDLAND – The colony has just experienced the best cod fishery since 1857. It was in '57 that production reached almost 71 million kilograms, a figure which compares to this year's more than 81 million kilograms. The huge take is encouraging because the catch was down throughout the 1860s, dropping to a low of 47 million kilograms in 1866. In fact, it was at this point that many people began to look to Confederation with Canada as the only answer to Newfoundland's economic woes. But a slight recovery in the cod fishery in 1869 helped convince voters the colony could manage on its own, and the pro-confederate party was defeated in an election. However, failures in the cod fishery have led to an exodus of fishermen to Boston. Many go while still quite young to work seasonally, returning to Newfoundland only periodically. Others settle south of the border. It is hoped an improving cod fishery will stop this drain of population from the colony.

Church must bury "liberal" Guibord, Privy Council says

Nov. 28, 1874
MONTREAL – More than four years after his death, the Privy Council has ordered the Catholic church to allow Joseph Guibord to be buried in holy ground. Guibord had been a member of the Institut Canadien, a club which fosters liberal thinking and provides reading materials Bishop Ignace Bourget considers contrary to the ultramontane doctrine of church supremacy over the state. When Bourget had the Vatican ban the institute, all of its members were denied the rites of the church, including burial in a consecrated cemetery.

Pleas from Guibord's widow fell on deaf ears, and a subsequent appeal was thrown out on grounds that the decision to deny Guibord a Roman Catholic burial was a church matter. That ruling was brought to the Privy Council which decided in favor of the Guibord family today. Guibord's remains have been interred in a Protestant cemetery in Montreal while the case was before the courts.

The Guibord affair symbolizes yet another battle between Bishop Bourget and Rouges faction in Quebec. The bishop fears the liberal attitudes of the Rouges will undermine the traditional French-Canadian lifestyle, a lifestyle he feels the Conservative party protects.

Bennett defeated in Newfoundland

Dec. 1, 1874
NEWFOUNDLAND – The tenure of Charles Fox Bennett as premier of Newfoundland is over. The man who first guided his party to victory in 1869 by leading the campaign against Confederation has lost the election to Frederick B.T. Carter. Bennett was returned to power last year, but his government quickly disintegrated. In the absence of Confederation as an issue, this time around Bennett was not able to produce a platform that would unite his diverse anti-confederate supporters.

Southern plains buffalo near extinction

1874
GREAT PLAINS – Hide hunters and sportsmen have killed well over three million buffalo on the American plains the last two years. It is one of the most gutwrenching episodes in the long line of atrocities perpetrated by humans against North American animals.

Since the late 1860s, when the "iron horse" first cut across the plains, people have been gunning the animals down from railway cars for the sheer fun of it. Railway companies even supply passengers with guns, and slow their trains when they come to a buffalo herd so riders can amuse themselves. The scores of voluminous black carcasses sprawling in blood are hardly ever used, except when the railways serve tongues from the dead animals to passengers as they relax in the dining car, a memento of a satisfying hunt.

There are other reasons for the slaughter of the plains buffalo the past few decades. Buffalo have been killed to supply the growing market for leather, for industrial belting for lathes in eastern American factories, and as a source of food for railway workers in the 1860s. Authorities in the American army also feel they can exterminate the Indians by killing the buffalo, their main source of livelihood. Gen. Philip Sheridan summed up this attitude when he told Congress it should strike a medal honoring hide hunters with a dead buffalo on one side and a dead Indian on the other.

The demise of the plains buffalo, once the most common large mammal on Earth, has happened overnight in terms of nature's evolutionary calendar. Indians still tell stories of riding for days in a row and never coming to the end of a herd, and as late as 1830 there were an estimated 40 million buffalo on the plains.

James Sutherland advocates the American Brotherhood and civil rights in this skating costume. Many Canadians have shown a lot of interest in this issue.

Bandits disguised as KKK rob train

Nov. 13, 1874
TORONTO – A Great Western Railway train was robbed of about $45,000 today by five bandits who were wearing the robes of the Ku Klux Klan. The robbers boarded the train between Toronto and Port Credit and made the hoist. So far, authorities have no clue as to their identity. It marks the first time that a train has been held up in Canada.

Today's robbery, especially if the culprits are not apprehended, could signal the start of more such holdups. Stagecoaches in the U.S. have long been the target of highwaymen who are now taking aim at trains.

A new settlement takes shape in the backwoods of Canada. Settlers clear the land, and use the logs to make simple dwellings for themselves and their livestock. This hard work will bring a brighter future for most.

Canada having a tough time attracting immigrants

1874

OTTAWA – Many people in Europe would like to emigrate, but Canada is failing to enamor them of the charms of life here. Since 1867, the government has been making a concerted effort to attract certain kinds of immigrants – namely, hard-working farmers with some money. It passed the Free Grants and Homestead Act in 1868, providing free land for settlers. And two years ago, it launched an extensive $700,000 advertising campaign in preferred countries like Britain. Ottawa has also sponsored the Passenger Warrant System to reduce passenger fare to Canada by a third.

These efforts have lured some people here, but not in large numbers. It is hard to attract settlers to a sparsely populated and relatively undeveloped country like Canada. The depression that struck North America and Europe last year is also to blame. With bankruptcies and unemployment a daily fact of life here, Canada is not exactly a greener pasture from the point of view of hardworking Europeans eagerly looking to start a new life in the new world.

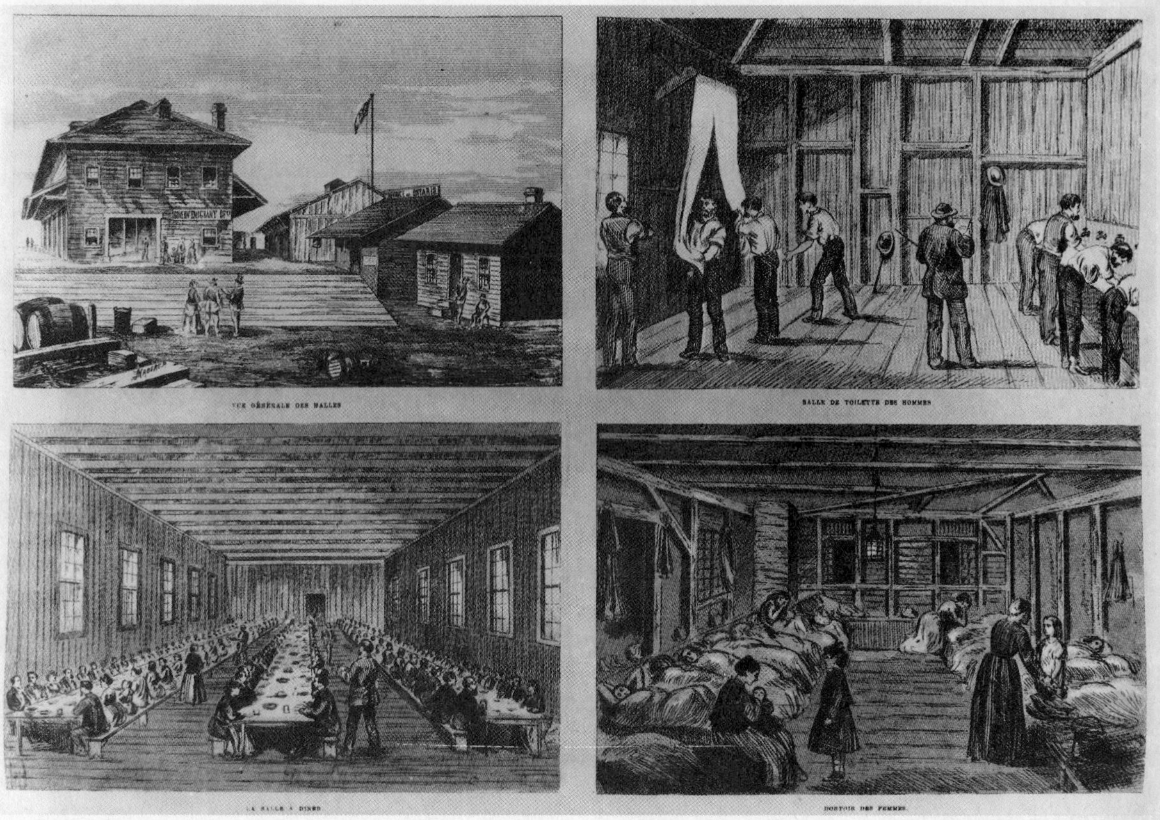

The Quebec Immigration Hall showing the men's washroom, the dining room, and the women's dormitory.

Canadian immigration has also suffered from a lack of accurate information about Canada abroad, and many foreign newspapers paint an overly bleak picture of life here. But it is no wonder people have a bad opinion of Canada. The country's advertising efforts have always been badly organized, and Canadian immigration agents have a well-earned reputation of misrepresenting the facts about Canada to attract immigrants. Case in point: a certain "man from Kent," living in Toronto, recently wrote to Britain's *Reynolds Newspaper* accusing immigration agents of luring hordes of unfortunates to Canada "under false pretences." The government is trying to restore credibility to its immigration advertising by warning the unfit not to come here.

Canada is not alone in the race to attract immigrants. It faces stiff competition, especially from the United States. The Americans have a highly skilled public relations machine. There is hardly a village in Britain that is not plastered with posters extolling the greatness of American life. American immigration officials have been just as dishonest at wooing Europeans as their Canadian counterparts, but they've also been far more successful at bagging immigrants. One Canadian observer says American efforts make it "very difficult for Canada to get any immigrants."

An immigrant's life is often quite difficult. This family buries a loved one in a log-framed grave with a home-made cross at the edge of the woods.

Immigrants wait with their baggage to board a steamer of the Allen Line.

1875

Canada, Jan. 1. Total assets of Canadian banks reach $180 million.

British Columbia, January. Three women, recently granted the franchise in municipal elections, cast their votes despite "jibes and catcalls."

Ottawa, January. Gov. Gen. Lord Dufferin commutes the death sentence of Ambroise-Dydime Lépine for the "murder" of Thomas Scott to two years' imprisonment.

Sackville, N.B., May 25. Grace Lockhart receives a Bachelor of Science from Mount Allison University, the first woman in Canada to get a university degree.

Ontario, June 1. The first sod is turned for the Canadian Pacific Railway at Fort William [Thunder Bay].

Toronto, June 13. The first B'nai B'rith Lodge in Canada is established.

Montreal, July 14. Bishop Ignace Bourget writes to Louis Riel: "I have the deep-seated conviction that you will receive in this life, and sooner than you think, the reward for all your mental sacrifices. ... For He has given you a mission which you must fulfil in all respects," confirming Riel's belief in his spiritual mission.

Prince Edward Island, Aug. 21. George Coles, Father of Confederation and first premier of the Island under responsible government, dies.

Ellesmere Island, Sept. 1. British naval ship *Alert*, commanded by George Nares, lands at Floeberg Beach. At 82 degrees N, it is the highest latitude ever reached by ship.

Montreal, Sept. 2. An unruly crowd prevents the reburial of Joseph Guibord in a Catholic cemetery after the Privy Council ordered the reburial.

Montreal, November. Bishop Ignace Bourget declares the grave of Joseph Guibord "under an interdict and separate from the rest of the cemetery" after Guibord's remains are reburied in a Catholic cemetery.

Northwest Territories. North West Mounted Police officers are reportedly frequenting brothels. The force is made up of single men under 30.

Montreal. The chief of police says there are about 400 prostitutes working in the city: 245 in brothels, 100 kept women, and some 50 vagabonds.

Land Purchase Act passes in P.E.I.

1875

CHARLOTTETOWN – The long fight for land reform on P.E.I. is over. The legislature has passed a Land Purchase Act, compelling the province's remaining proprietors of over 500 acres to sell their estates. The government began buying land years ago under the 1853 Land Purchase Act. But by the 1860s those proprietors who wished to sell had done so, and no law compelled the rest. A compulsory Land Purchase Act and a Canadian federal grant to fund it were key to the Island's joining Confederation.

The roots of the land problem lay in the Island's formation as a British colony. In 1767 Britain tried to make the Island self-supporting by granting land to interested proprietors. In theory, this promoted settlement and provided quit rents to support the civil establishment. In practice, it deprived the Island of its Crown lands and sparked a long, bitter fight for land reform.

From 1790 to 1840, land reformers noted original proprietors had not met terms of their grants, and were subject to escheat, or seizure and redistribution. Though Britain condemned escheat as too radical, it was willing to let the Island buy back its own land. The end of leasehold is in sight; the way is clear to solve a century-old problem.

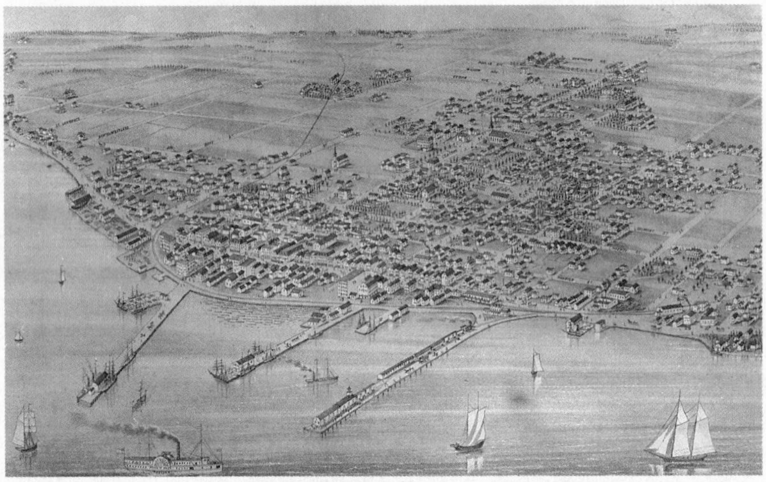

A panoramic view of Summerside, Prince County, Prince Edward Island.

Temperance group forms Canadian local

1875

PICTON, Ont. – Letitia Youmans has founded the first Canadian local of the Women's Christian Temperance Union in this town 160 kilometres east of Toronto. Youmans learned her first "temperance lesson" as a child, seeing the rotting dead body of a local drunk "swarming with worms." Such firsthand knowledge of the effects of alcohol has brought many Canadian women to the forefront of the temperance movement.

Also, as wives and mothers, they often take on the cause of prohibition because their economic survival depends on a husband, father or son. Canadian women have seen many of their counterparts lose home and family after their husbands drank everything away.

The WCTU operates a refreshment booth at the Provincial Exhibition.

Mowat government returned in Ontario

Jan. 19, 1875

TORONTO – Sir Oliver Mowat's Liberals returned to power today in Ontario's first provincial election fought on distinctly party lines. The premier holds a clear majority, with 51 seats, compared to 33 for the opposition Conservatives and four independents. An astute politician and devout Presbyterian, Mowat has enjoyed political support from both his fellow churchmen and Roman Catholics.

In this election, the Liberals ran on their record in power. Helping railways extend rail links throughout the province, has been one of this government's pluses. Also, they reaped advantage from the federal Conservatives' fall from grace in the Pacific Scandal. Federal Liberals accused the Macdonald administration of awarding a charter to Montrealer Hugh Allan to build the Pacific railway in return for donations to the party.

Mowat, who had earlier served as a member of the federal Parliament, retired from politics in 1864, but assumed the provincial Liberal leadership when Edward Blake resigned as the premier.

Editorial in praise of stouter women

Journalist decries large crinolines.

August 1875

HALIFAX – The *Acadian Recorder,* 62 and still feisty, has come out thundering against the thin, pale model of beautiful womanhood. Like Americans, many Nova Scotians of both sexes now prefer women to look both voluptuous and athletic. The *Recorder* roundly denounces the pallor and languor of "pale and weak young ladies who exhibit loads of expensive dry goods upon their persons." It advises parents not to raise "any more girls of that kind," praises "rosy cheeks and stout figures," and warns all "feeble women" that "young men ridicule the idea of tying themselves for life to sickly girls." New programs of diet and exercise could help the "fish-like girls" of Nova Scotia become graceful, robust, and truly womanly.

Among Maritime journalists, virtually all males, the clothing, shape, and health of young women are favorite themes. A New Brunswick scribe recently visited a Pictou County, N.S., church at West River, and raved in print about "the plainest, neatest congregation ever I saw." It pleased him to see "no crinoline rising over the the top of the pew doors when ladies were entering," and he suggested, "If any New Brunswick boy wants a wife, not afraid to work, let him go to West River, and there he will find the red-cheeked Scotch lassie. The piano they play at this time of year is the hay rake, which goes far to make them so healthy and hearty."

"Fly" bridge helps surveyor cross river

July 14, 1875

BUTE INLET, B.C. – Marcus Smith, the 60-year-old CPR surveyor in British Columbia, was forced to build and use an Indian "fly" bridge to cross the Homathko River north of here. Smith, an ardent proponent of the Bute Inlet route, was trying to blaze a trail from the Chilcotin country to the Homathko Pass and so down to tidewater at Bute Inlet.

Smith's partners were working their way inland from the inlet, bridging streams and opening up the trail. But Smith found torrents destroyed bridges they made, and he and his crew spent seven hours building a "fly" bridge (a pole and line) across Homathko Canyon.

Ross a graduate of medical college

March 11, 1875

MONTREAL – Montrealer Charlotte Whitehead Ross was graduated today as a doctor of medicine by the Women's Medical College of Pennsylvania. She is the mother of four children and the wife of David Ross, a railway construction contractor. Born in England in 1843, Ross is the daughter of engineer Joseph Whitehead, associated with George Stephenson in building the first steam locomotive.

Parliament grants amnesty in Scott case

Feb. 12, 1875

OTTAWA – After months of delay, Parliament has voted to grant amnesty to Louis Riel, W.B. O'Donoghue, and Ambroise-Dydime Lépine for their roles in the March 1870 death of adventurer Thomas Scott at the Red River settlement. O'Donoghue is granted amnesty outright. Riel and Lépine are granted that same privilege after "five years banishment from Her Majesty's Dominions." Lépine in November had been convicted and sentenced to die for his part in the murder, though the sentence was commuted to a short prison term last month.

This case has gone from Manitoba to the Dominion of Canada to the imperial government. At the time of the final vote, two MPs tried to have the three men granted unqualified pardons, but their amendment failed to carry. Gov. Gen. Lord Dufferin writes: "This is the most thorny business I have ever had to deal with, thanks to the imbecility of almost everyone who has hitherto meddled with it."

CPR surveyor Marcus Smith.

First indoor game of hockey played

March 3, 1875

MONTREAL – J.G.A. Creighton's team defeated Fred Torrance's squad 2-1 tonight in the first game of indoor hockey at the Victoria Skating Rink. Nine-member teams, including some of the city's best skaters, attempted to shoot a flat block of wood, between two poles frozen in the ice, about 2.4 metres apart. The block was introduced in place of the usual rubber ball of the outdoor game.

The game ended when a fight broke out among the spectators over some boys who were skating about during play.

The Toronto Temperance Reformation Society has many supporters. A speaker denounces the evils of liquor at a recent meeting.

Hospital in Toronto is just for children

March 1, 1875

TORONTO – The British Empire's second hospital for sick children is open at 31 Avenue St. General hospitals are not skilled at treating infantile diseases: half the deaths in this city are of children under 10. The hospital will treat children 12 and under, but none suffering from smallpox or other incurable ailments. Its foundress, Elizabeth McMaster, 28, believes she has been led by God to establish a hospital for sick children.

Mountie fort built at junction of two N.W.T. rivers

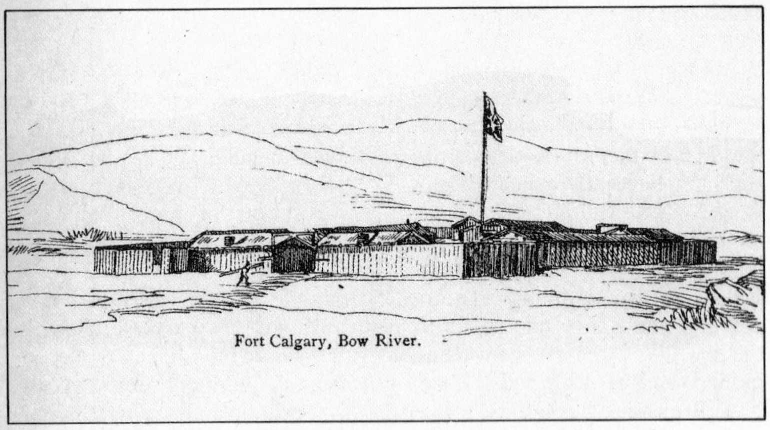

The new NWMP fort on the Bow River, a deterrent to whisky traders.

A group of Blackfoot chiefs meets with the North West Mounted Police.

September 1875

ELBOW [Calgary], N.W.T. – The construction of a North West Mounted Police fort has begun on the southwestern side of the junction of the Bow and a smaller river joining it on its south bank. Métis workers are building the small palisaded structure on high ground, on a site covered by long prairie grass and shrubs. The fort will deter whisky traders from visiting here.

Indians have come to this meeting point of the two rivers for some time. They find they can make excellent bows from the elastic wood of the young Douglas fir trees here. In winter, the Indians also appreciate the shelter afforded by the Bow's high banks, and those of the smaller river, which joins the Bow at the angle of an elbow. The Blackfoot, Sarcee, and Stoney call the smaller river and the settlement springing up at its junction with the Bow, "Elbow" [Calgary].

Indian land policy questioned in B.C.

May 1875

VICTORIA, B.C. – With British Columbia's entry into Canada in 1871, the question of the province's lack of Indian treaties arose. The federal government in 1873 requested Victoria to acknowledge Indian land titles, and allot at least 80, instead of 10, acres for each Indian family of five.

But the province denies existing land allotments are inadequate. Two years ago, Premier George Walkem even said Indians already had more than enough property. Others disagree. When one of his own provincial committees on Indian lands and reserves published the Papers Connected with the Indian Land Question 1850-1875, Walkem tried to suppress the document, as it pointed to many injustices against the B.C. Indians. The provincial government continues to ignore the report, and carry on as if, by right of the settlers' arrival, it owns all of B.C.

Supreme Court of Canada now a reality

Sept. 19, 1875

OTTAWA – In 1868, when noted Canadian nationalist Edward Blake asked John A. Macdonald if the Conservative government planned to establish a Supreme Court of Canada, the prime minister replied, "Yes, certainly." Today, roughly seven years later, this important judicial body is a reality. And although its creation reflects a great deal of Macdonald's work, it is the present Liberal government, led by Alexander Mackenzie, that has guided it through.

Establishing a Supreme Court is a big step toward greater Canadian independence from Britian; it replaces the Crown-appointed Privy Council as Canada's final judicial authority. It would have been formed sooner, but French-Canadian Tories opposed it, saying that having only two of seven judges from Quebec, as was proposed, wouldn't adequately represent French civil law. French-Canadian Liberals, on the other hand, think this representation is better than none at all, as was the case on the Privy Council.

Prince Edward Island Railway in business

May 12, 1875

CHARLOTTETOWN – With surprisingly little fanfare and only 20 passengers, the P.E.I. Railway made its inaugural run today. The railway has been an expensive undertaking. Cost overruns from a vastly expanded number of trunk lines placed an unbearable strain on the Island's economy; a major factor in the colony's entry into Confederation. The idea of a railway first gripped the Island in 1870, and construction began Oct. 5, 1871. A few, cautious opponents warned the colony could not afford the project, hinting it was little more than a confederate plot. Supporters of the scheme argued a railroad was vital to the Island's economic future.

British expedition sets out for Arctic

May 29, 1875

PORTSMOUTH, England – About 200,000 people crowded the naval harbor here to see the ships of the latest Arctic expedition move out into the Channel. The Queen has sent congratulations to the expedition's commander, George Nares. His task: to plant the Union Jack at the North Pole. Nares is expected to take his ships up the Kennedy Channel between Ellesmere Island and Greenland and then head for the Pole.

Under Prime Minister Benjamin Disraeli, British policy has become very expansionist. A new Arctic expedition was, then, a matter of national policy. Officially, of course, it was to be a scientific expedition but everyone, especially the readers of the new brand of popular newspapers, knew that the Pole was the target. Critics, however, have pointed out that the expedition's ships, equipment and training are years behind the times.

Long dispute ends: Guibord finally gets his Catholic burial

Nov. 16, 1875

MONTREAL – A six-year dispute over the burial of Joseph Guibord, whom the Roman Catholic Church excommunicated, ended peacefully today. The remains of Guibord, a member of the Institut Canadien, a liberal club condemned by Bishop Ignace Bourget, were reburied in Côte-des-Neiges Catholic cemetery under the protection of 1,235 soldiers.

The burial took place without incident, unlike an attempt in September in which hostile Catholics along the route of the funeral procession heaped insults on the passing cortege. Angry cries of "God damn Guibord" from the menacing crowd forced the funeral party to return to the Protestant cemetery where Guibord's remains had been buried pending a court battle for his right to a Catholic burial.

235 Icelanders to settle in Manitoba

Oct. 21, 1875

WINNIPEG – A party of 235 Icelanders arrived today on the steamer *International* to take up land on the west shore of Lake Winnipeg. It's been three years since the arrival in Winnipeg of Sigtryggur Jonasson, who conducted a search for land suitable for the relocation of his fellow countrymen. Jonasson's decision to establish a colony on Lake Winnipeg led to extensive negotiations with the Dominion of Canada since the land he chose is outside the existing Manitoba boundaries and therefore without what Ottawa views as adequate administration.

The party which arrived today will be moved to their new homesite on flat-bottomed barges. Meanwhile, it is anticipated that a further 1,000 or more Icelanders will arrive here next summer. The relocation has been triggered by a series of disasters which have plagued their homeland. Volcanoes have erupted, and crop failures have resulted in starvation. Settlers now coming to Canada have chosen not to accept an offer from the Danish government to settle in Denmark.

Local officials view the arrival of the Icelanders as a major coup for settlement in the area. The newcomers have a reputation for being industrious and being a strong family people, with a tradition of cooperation in their communities.

The first group of Icelandic immigrants comes ashore at Willow Point.

Riel has mystical experience; sees himself as a divine prophet

Dec. 8, 1875

WASHINGTON, D.C. – Exiled Métis leader, Louis Riel, experienced a mystical vision in church this morning, convincing him that "God anointed him with his divine gifts and fruits of his Spirit, as prophet of the New World." Standing at his pew, Riel was seized by great joy, then plunged into depression so deep he cried out in grief. Riel is in Washington trying to convince the Americans to support his planned armed invasion of Manitoba. Earlier this year Riel was banished from Canada for five years. His friends fear he has suffered a nervous breakdown.

Cree and Ojibwa sign land treaty

September 1875

LAKE WINNIPEG – The latest treaty with the Indians has secured for the Canadian government Ojibwa and Cree land on both sides of Lake Winnipeg and in the Lower Saskatchewan Valley. Ojibwa and Cree hunters and trappers in the area, many of them living in small, isolated communities, gave the government treaty party little opposition. There have been, in fact, few substantive negotiations, partly because the treaty party has arbitrarily joined together several bands for the talks. It's been difficult, in many cases, for the newly created larger bands to select a common chief.

Did the Indians understand the treaty, which involves the concept of a land surrender, something alien to their culture and expressed in a foreign tongue to boot? One government official thought not, "because they have very dark ideas of our language and only slowly comprehend our bargains with them no matter how clearly we explain matters to them."

Company growing: E.B. Eddy's business skills hard to match

1875

HULL, Que. – In the 24 years since he arrived here from Vermont with $40 in his pocket, Ezra Butler Eddy has set the town on fire – business-wise. Besides matches, doors and frames, the E.B. Eddy company, now North America's biggest forest products industry, annually produces 600,00 wooden pails, 45,000 basins and 75,000 zinc washboards. Eddy employs over 1,700 workers and 400 tree-cutters.

The company can cut 12 million metres of red and white pine a year with its 243 saws in its four sawmills. It leads Ottawa area lumbermen in destroying the forests, leaving more land open for agriculture. Sadly, no one replants the decimated forests. Eddy, 48, sits in the Assembly for Ottawa County.

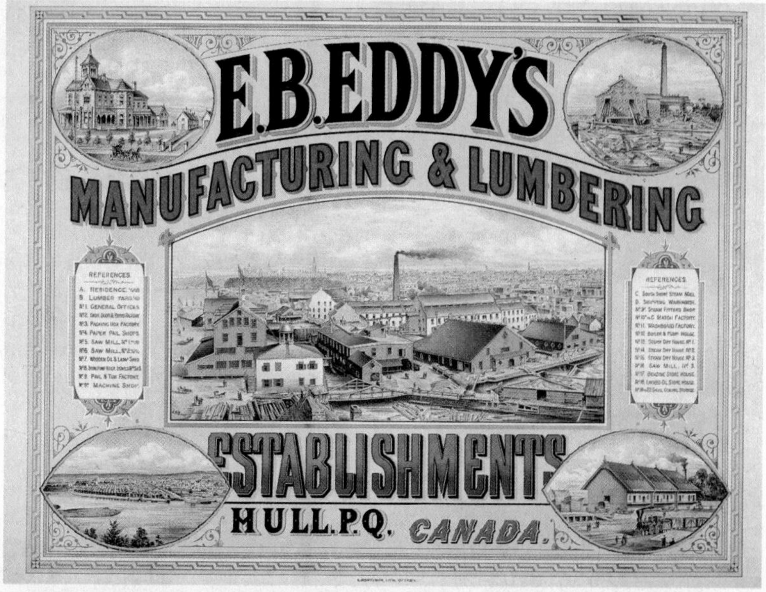

The various buildings and facets of E.B. Eddy's business at Hull, Quebec.

1876

British Columbia, Jan. 10. The province rejects Ottawa's latest financial offer to compensate for delays in building the CPR, and threatens secession from Confederation.

Ontario, February. Egerton Ryerson resigns after 22 years as superintendent of education in the province. He has fought for free universal schooling.

Montreal, March 6. Louis Riel is admitted to the Longue-Pointe mental asylum under the name of Louis David. Riel's worsening religious hysteria drove his friends to get him admitted.

Boston, March 10. Inventor Alexander Graham Bell achieves the first electric transmission of the human voice when he spills battery acid on his leg and uses a transmitting instrument to call to his assistant, "Watson, come here, I need you!"

Battleford, Northwest Territories, April 6. The first message is sent on the new telegraph line between Battleford and Winnipeg.

Montreal, May 24. Mount Royal Park is officially opened with a royal salute fired by the Montreal Field Battery.

Floeberg Beach, Ellesmere Island, June 14. A sledge expedition led by Albert Markham returns to the *Alert* after reaching a record latitude in an attempt to get to the North Pole.

Moose Factory, Northwest Territories, Sept. 7. Rev. Edmund Peck arrives from London to do missionary work among the Inuit.

Northwest Territories, December. Some 1,500 Sioux arrive from the U.S., fleeing American retaliation for the Sioux victory at the Battle of the Little Big Horn.

British Columbia. A Christian missionary visits Haida territory and threatens them with jail if they don't stop building totem poles, which he says God wouldn't approve. He also tells them to live in European-style houses instead of large decorated dwellings.

Toronto. Dr. Emily Stowe, Canada's first woman doctor, sets up the Toronto Women's Literary Club. A screen for suffrage activity, it is Canada's first suffrage group.

Nova Scotia. The Society for the Prevention of Cruelty to Animals, founded in England in 1824, comes to the province.

Calgary new name of Mounties' post in the northwest

Summer 1876

FORT CALGARY, N.W.T. – Since the NWMP founded a post last fall at the junction of the Bow and Elbow rivers, the fort and settlement have had three names: Elbow, Brisebois, and now Calgary. Inspector Ephraim Brisebois, the local commander of the post, did not like Elbow, and renamed the fort after himself.

The new title, in turn, upset A.G. Irvine, Col. James Macleod's successor as assistant commissioner of the NWMP, and he's recommended a Scottish title, one Macleod suggested years ago when he visited Calgary House on the Isle of Mull on Scotland's west coast. Calgary means "bay farm" in Gaelic.

George McDougall dies in snowstorm

Jan. 25, 1876

CALGARY – George Millward McDougall, missionary and pioneer, died at age 55 in a blizzard north of Calgary while out hunting. He died of either a stroke or a heart attack. McDougall endured many hardships to bring Christianity and education to the Indians. He was born in 1821 in Kingston, Upper Canada, of Scottish parents. He was ordained a Wesleyan Methodist deacon in 1852 and minister in 1854.

Rev. George Millward McDougall.

Bell sends first-ever telephone message

Spectators watch anxiously as the world's first long distance telephone call is made from Dominion Telegraph Office in Brantford, Ontario.

Alexander Graham Bell receives the world's first long distance telephone call. The phone call is made from Brantford to Paris in the province of Ontario.

Aug. 10, 1876

BRANTFORD, Ont. – Alexander Graham Bell, 29, a tall, slender, Scottish-born speech therapist, has pulled off a scientific miracle. Exploiting the principle of telephony – the electrical transmission of sound over wires – Bell and assistant Thomas Watson today sent the world's first telephone message. Using Dominion Telegraph Company wires, they managed to make the human voice travel 12.8 kilometres between Brantford and Paris, Ont. The transmission went only one way, but the young scientist expects to perfect two-way telephone communication before the year is out.

Bell fell in love with a deaf patient, a proper Bostonian named Mabel Hubbard whose father urged Bell to try inventing a device for the multiple transmission of telegraphic messages. During this experimentation, the inventor stumbled on telephony, and Mr. Hubbard will soon have a rich son-in-law.

Indians are wards of the government, federal law states

April 12, 1876

OTTAWA – Parliament today passed the Indian Act, perhaps the most important piece of Indian legislation in this century. The act makes few radical departures from previous laws or policies, but it consolidates the many Indian laws now on the statute books, a measure the government claims is in the Indians' best interests.

The act puts Indians in a separate legal category as minors or special wards of the government, and does not give bands full control over their reserve lands. Bands must meet several conditions before they can sell or lease any of their reserves. The act also says that money raised from the sale or lease of reserves or the natural resources on them will go into an Indian Trust Fund to be managed by the government on behalf of Indian bands. At the request of Indian chiefs, the act also prohibits Indians from consuming alcohol.

Ultimately, the act is designed to promote Indian assimilation. It says that any "sober and industrious" male Indian can, after a probationary period, apply to give up his rights as an Indian, including his right to live on a reserve, in return for British citizenship with full legal privileges and the right to vote. Western Indians are excluded from this provision; apparently the government considers them too "uncivilized" to be assimilated.

Bishop Feild dies after short illness

June 8, 1876

NEWFOUNDLAND – Bishop Edward Feild, the greatest Church of England prelate the colony has ever had, died today in Bermuda after a short illness. He was 75. After his arrival here in 1844, Feild concentrated his efforts on developing an organized church based on High Church principles with control over its own schools. His policies resulted in a Roman Catholic-Methodist alliance that was to dominate the colony in the 1850s.

Hanlan rows to victory in single sculls

Torontonian Edward "Ned" Hanlan wears his distinctive blue costume as he practises for the single sculls competition, an event he excels in.

Sept. 4, 1876

PHILADELPHIA – Toronto's Edward "Ned" Hanlan beat some of North America's best oarsmen today to win the centennial single sculls event on the Schuylkill River. Hanlan, 21, has been the best oarsman in Ontario for the last three years but until today was unknown elsewhere. At five-foot-eight and weighing no more than 155 pounds, Hanlan is often pitted against much bigger rivals.

The son of a hotel owner on Toronto Island, as a boy he spent his off-hours helping his father by fishing or rowing around Toronto harbor. His first rowing shell was a home-made one, consisting of a five-centimetre plank that was sharpened at each end, with a seat and outriggers mounted on it. Today's victory should propel Hanlan into the rowing spotlight. A handsome man with a distinctive blue rowing costume, he is modest off the water but has a flair for the dramatic when in a rowing shell.

Mountie to reserve site for police post

March 25, 1876

BATTLEFORD, N.W.T. – Sub-Inspector Edmond Fréchette of the North West Mounted Police arrived today by dog sleigh in the middle of a bad storm. He was sent to Battle River by commissioner George A. French to choose a site for a police post. Inspector L.N.F. Crozier was out earlier this year to ascertain the suitability of this area for a detachment. He was satisfied with what he found and plans to establish a post are going ahead.

Fréchette has been ordered to stake out 1,000 to 2,000 acres of land in anticipation of the town becoming the headquarters of the mounted police. He is looking for "a position sheltered for quarters and stables from prevailing winds in winter and at the same time, not sunk in a hollow, or place liable to be infested with mosquitoes in summer." The men of the force require good land with enough wood for fuel and fencing, and, of course, good water. They also must have access to hay.

Though no treaty has yet been made with the resident Indians, this community, near the mouth of the Battle River, has already been chosen as the territorial capital, and official buildings will be erected.

City's heritage pays off: Kingston to get Royal Military College

June 1, 1876

KINGSTON – This city's rich military heritage is paying off with the establishment of Royal Military College here. Fort Henry, at Kingston's east end, was investigated as early as two years ago by Prime Minister Alexander Mackenzie as a potential site. The other city in the running was Quebec.

It is the country's first military college and will be far more intensive than earlier facilities here, as well as in Toronto, Montreal and Quebec. Training at these schools did not exceed three months and was strictly military. However, this new college will be styled along the model of West Point in the United States. The education it offers will include military tactics, fortifications, engineering and science related to the military profession.

The new Royal Military College in Kingston will be housed in this large limestone building. The grassy area in front will serve as a parade square.

Indians win bloody battle in Custer's last stand

General George Custer's last stand at the Battle of the Little Big Horn.

Chief Crazy Horse in war paint is seen at the top centre of this pictograph.

June 25, 1876

LITTLE BIG HORN, Dakota – The American government's efforts to force the Indians off the plains and back to their reserves were dealt a bloody blow today. Thousands of Sioux, Cheyenne, and Arapaho Indians, forced from their reserves by starvation and angry at American treaty violations, have just killed Gen. George Custer and every one of his 265 troops in a battle on the Little Big Horn River. Custer's force was the key to American plans to get the Indians to return to their reserves.

An estimated 10,000 Indians are encamped at the Little Big Horn. When they saw the cloud of dust put up by Custer's advancing troops they had no time to hold a proper council of war; braves mounted their horses and rode off to meet Custer. An Indian observer said the movement of braves was like a hurricane, or a swarm of bees.

Custer expected only a handful of Indians as he led his troops along the river. They rounded a bend and came face to face with the massive army led by Crazy Horse and Sitting Bull. With more Indians behind him, Custer had little choice but to raise his sword and yell "charge." After a short battle, Custer's body was found on the top of the hill where he made his last stand, the corpses of his men strewn all around. The Americans will surely retaliate against the Indians.

The price of sugar is sky high, as the shelf location in this store suggests. This merchant sells sugar only to customers who purchase other goods.

Rail crisis concerns British Columbians

Sept. 9, 1876

VICTORIA, B.C. – The governor general, Lord Dufferin, and his wife are enjoying the balls, regattas, entertainment and trips on their visit to British Columbia. They have toured Victoria and the island, visited the Queen Charlottes, Bute Inlet, Fort Simpson and Burrard Inlet. But everywhere they go they are made aware of the railway crisis. Many British Columbian settlers believe their politicians have been tricked by Ottawa. They doubt if the promised railway will ever come. On Vancouver Island they have a special concern. They want the CPR to come down Bute Inlet and then cross over bridges and islands to reach a terminus at Esquimalt.

Lord Dufferin proposed this trip to see if he could find a solution to the struggle between Ottawa and B.C. But the politicians in Ottawa did not want Dufferin involved in domestic politics. He has told his aides, however, that while he is disturbed by the parochial, money-grubbing attitudes he has found in B.C., he will press the dominion government for some concessions when he returns to Ottawa.

B.C. sulks because railway not built.

Cree Indians cede land to Canada in Treaty No. 6

Moderates prevail over Poundmaker

August 1876

FORT CARLTON, N.W.T. – One of the most heated exchanges in all of the plains Indian treaty negotiations occurred this week. About 2,000 Cree gathered here in the North Saskatchewan River valley on Aug. 18. The verbal attack came the next day, just after treaty commissioner Alexander Morris explained that Treaty No. 6 Indians would get the same size reserves as Treaty No. 4 Indians to the south. At this point, a Cree warrior named Poundmaker yelled: "This is our land, it isn't a piece of pemmican to be cut off and given in little pieces back to us. It is ours and we will take what we want."

Morris feared the radical warrior spoke for all the plains Cree, but he soon learned the majority were moderates who favored acceptance if slightly better terms could be secured. They were, and the treaty was signed.

Cree Indians assemble around Fort Carlton while they wait for the formal signing of Indian Treaty No. 6.

Fort Pitt chiefs sign pact; Big Bear furious on his return

Sept. 10, 1876

FORT PITT, N.W.T. – Plains Cree chiefs at Fort Pitt signed Treaty No. 6 yesterday, impressed by the fact that Cree chiefs at Fort Carlton accepted the deal just last month. The Fort Pitt chiefs who signed the treaty are mainly moderates close to Christian missionaries in the area.

Luckily for treaty commissioner Alexander Morris, Chief Big Bear and a group of buffalo-hunting Indians, still free from the missionaries' influence, were on the prairie during the negotiations. It was to no one's surprise that Big Bear was furious when he returned today. He believes the Indians have given up valuable hunting grounds in return for very little from the Canadians.

Manitoba exports wheat to Ontario

Oct. 21, 1876

WINNIPEG – A shipment of 857 bushels of hard spring wheat left Winnipeg today en route to Toronto. It will travel by water to St. Paul, by rail to Duluth, and again by water to Sarnia. From Sarnia it travels to Toronto via rail.

This shipment is being made by R.C. Steele, of the firm Steele-Briggs, who arrived in Winnipeg a year ago and became its principal grain trader. He believes that when eastern millers learn about the bread-making qualities of high-protein wheat, it will lead to a steady demand for more of the product from Manitoba farms.

Steele had hoped he could ship as many as 5,000 bushels of Red Fife, but the Winnipeg firm of Higgins and Young could not fill an order of that size. A crop failure in Ontario, due to drought, is threatening that province's supply of seed wheat for the coming year.

Irish Christian Brothers to establish schools in Newfoundland

1876

NEWFOUNDLAND – The Roman Catholic Order of Irish Christian Brothers established by Edmund Rice has accepted an invitation from the colony's Roman Catholic church to set up branches here. They plan to establish schools – and even a college for boys – in St. John's. They also intend to run a residence for boys from isolated outport communities.

Newfoundland has a large Irish-Catholic population, and ever since the Education Act of 1843, the colony has moved toward denominational education. Catholics here have their own state-funded schools, and the presence of the Irish Christian Brothers will undoubtedly promote this system.

Laird takes oath for N.W.T. post

Nov. 26, 1876

WINNIPEG – David Laird, born in New Glasgow, P.E.I., was sworn in today as the lieutenant-governor of the North West Territories. He is 43 years old.

Laird was editor of a newspaper in Charlottetown before entering politics. He became a Liberal leader in the Island legislature and was elected to the House of Commons in 1873 as one of P.E.I. first members of Parliament. He was minister of the interior from 1873 to earlier this year.

Signorina Maria Spelterini crosses the Niagara Rapids on a tightrope.

1877

Halifax, Jan. 2. Senator and judge Jonathan McCully, a Father of Confederation, dies.

Nebraska, U.S., May 6. Sioux Chief Crazy Horse, along with 800 warriors, surrenders to American troops after leading the Sioux victory in the Battle of the Little Big Horn last year.

Northwest Territories, May 7. Sioux Chief Sitting Bull joins the other Sioux refugees near the Cypress Hills who came to Canada last year to escape American retaliation for the Battle of the Little Big Horn.

Prince Edward Island, June 5. Construction begins on the Prince Edward Island Hospital for the Insane.

Lundi, Man., Sept. 10. Sigtryggur Jonasson publishes *Framfari* (Progress) in a log cabin, the first Icelandic newspaper in North America.

Hamilton, Ont., Oct. 18. The first leases for private telephones in Canada are signed.

New Jersey, U.S., Dec. 15. Inventor Thomas Edison files a patent for a machine that reproduces the human voice, called the "phonograph."

Northwest Territories. In order to conserve the rapidly vanishing buffalo, the Council of the Northwest Territories forbids the traditional Indian killing technique of driving them over cliffs into pits. It also forbids killing them for sport or solely for getting tongues, choice cuts, or robes.

British Columbia. Miners form the Miners' Mutual Protective Society, a federation of mining unions to establish common terms of employment.

Victoria. Manzo Nagano is the first Japanese immigrant to reach British Columbia.

Britain. Queen Victoria gets her wish as Canadian celebrity Josiah Henson visits her at Windsor Castle. He is supposedly the basis for the main character of *Uncle Tom's Cabin*, and is founder of the defunct black settlement at Dawn Township.

United States. Canada Bill Jones, the famous card shark who coined the phrase "it's the only game in town," dies.

North America. The trumpeter swan has been virtually extinguished in recent years as swan skins became valuable trade articles and the HBC took control of the trade. The population has decreased from 1,312 in 1854 to 122.

Sulpician priests say fire at church started by Iroquois

June 15, 1877

LAKE OF TWO MOUNTAINS, Que. – Mysteriously, the Roman Catholic church in this Indian community 50 kilometres west of Montreal has burnt down. The Sulpician priests who claim the land on which the more than century-old Indian mission stands say Chief Joseph Onasakenrat and his Iroquois followers started it. The priests, in fact, will press arson charges against the 31-year-old chief, his father, and a dozen other Iroquois. Chief Joseph says he and the other Iroquois only arrived on the scene of the fire after it started.

Trouble between the priests and Iroquois has been brewing since the late 18th century when the Iroquois first publicly protested the Sulpician claim to ownership of their reserve at Lake of Two Mountains. The Sulpicians say the land was given to them by the king of France to care for the Indians, not to the Indians themselves.

University of Manitoba receives charter

Winnipeg member college of the newly chartered University of Manitoba.

Feb. 28, 1877

WINNIPEG – With the granting of its charter today, the University of Manitoba becomes the first institution of higher education to be established in western Canada. The new institution is a self-governing federation of independent member colleges – St. Boniface, St. John's, and Manitoba. All teaching takes place in the member institutions, while the university is assigned such tasks as conducting examinations and awarding degrees.

The granting of the charter concludes a lengthy period of development for senior learning here. St. Boniface College was established in 1821, and St. John's College was set up in 1849.

Mountie meets Sioux leader Sitting Bull

The red tunic of the North West Mounted Police is very impressive to Indians and settlers alike.

June 2, 1877

WHITEMUD CREEK, N.W.T. – A tense confrontation between 5,000 fugitive Sioux Indians and a handful of North West Mounted Police ended without any violence today on the southern plains just north of the American border. The Indians, led by Chief Sitting Bull, have been drifting across the border since defeating Gen. George Custer and his cavalry at the Little Big Horn last year. Pursued by the Americans, the Sioux have been seeking safe haven here in Canada. Superintendent James Walsh of the NWMP visited the Sioux camp to explain the conditions on which they will be allowed to remain here.

The situation is volatile. Across the border, American troops are just waiting to get at Sitting Bull. The Sioux are mistrustful of white authority. Furthermore, Canadian Indians are upset at the newcomers invading their hunting grounds. But Walsh has proven to be a good diplomat, and Sitting Bull has agreed to respect Canadian law.

Statistics released on mortality rates

1877

QUEBEC – The province's working class French-Canadian population had an extremely high mortality rate this year, especially compared to that of Irish and British residents in Quebec. Studies in working class neighborhoods found the mortality rate among French-Canadians to be 44.3 percent, as opposed to 27.5 percent in Irish and 26 percent in British areas.

The infant mortality rate in Quebec – high among all three groups – is the highest north of the Rio Grande. Experts say the reason is simple: the province's cities lack proper sewage systems. In Quebec City, sewage is discharged into St. Charles River, and in Montreal the St. Lawrence River is the recipient. Inspectors, meanwhile, aren't very enthusiastic about the future. They say the situation will persist despite hygiene regulations, mostly because laws are being ignored by the people they are trying to protect.

Fire devastates Saint John; thousands homeless

Tall chimneys and smouldering ruins are all that remain of a large part of the city of Saint John, N.B., after the great fire which began yesterday. Houses and businesses were destroyed and dozens were injured or killed.

Orange flames light up the night sky over Saint John, New Brunswick.

June 21, 1877

SAINT JOHN, N.B. – Sparks from a lumber mill ignited some hay in an Irish slum yesterday afternoon, and the fire, whipped by an unseasonal no'wester, ripped through town in 10 hours. It killed 18 people, injured dozens more, left 13,000 homeless, caused damage of $28 million, and wiped out the Customs house, city hall, churches, post office, banks, businesses, factories, warehouses, docks and hundreds of houses. Some 1,600 buildings went up in smoke. Saint John had basked in weeks of strangely sunny weather, and the millions of shingles on its buildings were like tinder awaiting a match. Warehouses stored canvas, tar, oil, gunpowder, lumber. The fired leapt across streets, and generated such heat that houses, even before the blaze touched them, burst into flames. Sucking air, the firestorm created a hideous wail. Prosperous yesterday morning, Saint John is a smouldering wreck today.

Mountie meets his death in quicksand

June 19, 1877

RED DEER FORKS, N.W.T. – Members of the North West Mounted Police detachment and neighbors were saddened today by the death of one of the force. Sub-Constable George Mahoney met his end in the quicksand at Red Deer Forks. Quicksand is a bed of wet, loose sand in which heavy objects will sink but are difficult to retrieve because of the force of suction.

"Father of B.C." James Douglas dies

Aug. 2, 1877

VICTORIA, B.C. – Sir James Douglas, the man who built the colonies of Vancouver Island and British Columbia, died today. He was 73. Douglas complained of chest pains and his son-in-law, Dr. John Helmcken, came to see him. While they were chatting, Sir James' head dropped on to his chest and he died. For most of his life Douglas worked for the Hudson's Bay Company.

Autumn sale at Eaton's falls into place

Autumn 1877

TORONTO – T. Eaton & Co. is holding a fall sale. Among the items on sale are men's white shirts at $1, and wool socks for 15 cents. For the women there are beautiful, one-button kid gloves costing between 20 to 25 cents a pair. In the corset department, the stock comprises "The True Fit," "The Cheap Fit," and "The Model Fitting and Durable Corset," second to none in the dominion, as the advertisement states, from 25 cents to $1.75.

Can you trust Eaton's advertisements? It is certainly hoped so. The ads themselves say you must "use no deception in the smallest degree – no – nothing you cannot defend before God or man."

The T. Eaton Co. of Toronto claims wholesale prices, first-quality goods.

A skillfully carved totem pole and a colorful painting adorn the Indian village at Skidegate, Queen Charlotte Islands, British Columbia.

Stoneys, Blackfoot Confederacy sign Treaty No. 7

Sept. 22, 1877

BLACKFOOT CROSSING, N.W.T. – Commissioners James Macleod and David Laird, lieutenant-governor of the Northwest Territories, have concluded the last great treaty on the Canadian prairies, sealing the deal today at Blackfoot Crossing, 9.6 kilometres east of Fort Calgary. Blackfoot, Blood, Peigan, Sarcee, and Stoney tribes gave up 129,500 square kilometres, bounded by the Red Deer River to the south, the Rockies to the west, the Cypress Hills to the east, and the American border to the south. As reserve lands, they retain 2.59 square kilometres for each family of five, in all about three percent of their former hunting territories.

Crowfoot, Chief of the Blackfoot.

Crowfoot addresses a gathering of Blackfoot Indians about the new treaty.

Constantine Scollen, a Roman Catholic missionary at the meetings, believes the Indians do not have a full understanding of Treaty No. 7, yet they signed because they trusted the North West Mounted Police. Chief Crowfoot acted as the Blackfoot Confederacy's spokesman at the talks. He told the commissioners: "If the police had not come to this country, where would we all be now? Bad men and whisky were killing us so fast that very few, indeed, of us would have been alive today. The police have protected us as the feathers of the bird protect it from the frosts of winter." In the end, only one chief, Medicine Calf, a Blood war chief, publicly opposed the government.

Terms of the treaty signed today are the same as those of Treaty No. 6, agreed to last year by the Plains and Woods Crees: it too assures medical aid and food in case of "any pestilence" or "general famine." Also included in the terms is a $1,000 grant – enough for three years' provisions – for Indians who take up farming. Acceptance of these terms indicates that Chiefs Old Sun, Red Crow, Bear's Paw, Morning Plume and, of course, Crowfoot, are hoping to make the best of a bad situation. They are, in effect, anticipating a bleak future for the plains Indians' traditional way of life. The rapid disappearance of the buffalo, on which their people have depended for centuries, means they must adapt.

Laurier defends his beliefs eloquently

June 26, 1877

QUEBEC – "The principle of Liberalism is inherent in the very essence of our nature, in that desire for happiness with which we are all born into the world, which pursues us through life, and which is never completely gratified this side of the grave" – so declared Wilfrid Laurier, federal Liberal government minister, in an address today to the Canadian Club on liberalism.

In a stirring speech, Laurier distinguished European liberalism, whose history "has been written in blood," and moderate British liberalism, which he extolled and cited as the model for Canadian liberalism. Laurier's concern for human freedom and aspirations rang all through his words. But the Liberals have a tough row to hoe in Quebec: the conservative Catholic establishment sees liberalism as nothing short of evil, and has waged a war of persecution against it.

Laird in Battleford taking up residence

August 1877

BATTLEFORD, N.W.T. – Lt.-Gov. David Laird has arrived to take up residence at this police post which last year was named the new capital of the Northwest Territories. The town, located at the junction of the Battle and Saskatchewan rivers in the territory of the Cree Indians, was founded only last summer when work began on buildings to house the governor and his officials. As well, several crude log barracks house a detachment of the North West Mounted Police.

Battleford is the fifth post established by the force in the Territories, and the headquarters of the Saskatchewan District. A sizable townsite is expected to grow up around the government buildings. Laird is the first governor of the Territories since their administration was separated from Manitoba in 1875. He is also responsible for Indian affairs in the region.

Manitoba now the Keystone Province?

Sept. 29, 1877

WINNIPEG – Manitoba may have a new nickname: the Keystone Province. In a speech at Winnipeg city hall today, Gov. Gen. Lord Dufferin said, "From its geographical position, and its peculiar characteristics, Manitoba may be regarded as the keystone of the mighty arch of Canadian provinces which spans the continent from the Atlantic to the Pacific."

City hall in Winnipeg, Manitoba, where Lord Dufferin spoke today.

Local scholars explain that the description is apt. The keystone is a term used by stonemasons, and describes the final stone they must shape when constructing an arch. For its location in the centre, in shape it must be wider at the top than at the bottom. There is agreement at city hall that "Keystone Province" is several cuts above the "Postage Stamp Province," another sobriquet that's often been applied to Manitoba.

During Dufferin's stay in Winnipeg, he and his wife each drove a silver spike into the first tie of the rail network that was to be laid across the west. They then boarded the vessel *Minnesota* and sailed to Fisher's Landing where they saw the first locomotive to arrive in this territory. The new rail line fulfils Ottawa's pledge to underwrite improved transportation for the west.

Young lad's death a tragic first for Nova Scotia mine

Nov. 3, 1877

SPRINGHILL, N.S. – David Ferguson, a 12-year-old pit boy, today left his post as a "trapper" – one who pulls open a ventilation door to allow pit ponies to pass – and foolishly climbed up a balance way. A counterbalance box ran over him, killing him instantly.

Most trappers are boys. They work alone in the dark, waiting for the noise of coal cars, and listening to the echoes of distant explosions. David's death was the first in the mines since coal was found here. That was in 1834, but large-scale mining began only five years ago.

Roddick: antiseptic a must in surgery

1877

MONTREAL – Dr. T.G. Roddick of the Montreal General Hospital has aroused great excitement – and controversy – among this city's medical community, by insisting carbolic spray be used in surgery. The spray is carbolic acid, an antiseptic developed more than 10 years ago by Scottish surgeon Joseph Lister. If Roddick has his way, and his persistent and energetic character suggests he will, the uniforms of doctors and nurses, their hands, the tools they use, the operating room itself, and even the patients, will be scrubbed and sprayed with the solution before surgery.

But this revolutionary new practice has its detractors; not all physicians are convinced the transfer of bacteria to patients causes fatal blood poisoning, despite statistics that show 85 percent of Lister's patients survive while 80 percent of those operated on without antiseptic die. Awed by such figures, a growing number of doctors have been converted to "Listerism," but some perhaps too fervently. It has been reported some that European surgeons use so much disinfectant, operating personnel must wade through saturated floors in rubber boots. This has aroused complaints by doctors who claim such conditions make surgery more difficult.

Manitoba's first steam locomotive arrives

The first steam locomotive in Manitoba is unloaded at St. Boniface today.

The new Countess of Dufferin enters St. Boniface under its own steam.

Oct. 9, 1877

ST. BONIFACE, Man. – The first steam locomotive in Manitoba arrived this morning at Winnipeg by barge down the Red River from the south. Winnipeg welcomed the locomotive, named the *Countess of Dufferin* because the Countess is now here touring the area, with excited fanfare. The day was declared a public holiday. The screeching blast of a steam whistle drew crowds of curious onlookers to the riverbank to witness the arrival of the barge carrying the *Countess*, six flat cars and a caboose.

For two hours people were allowed to climb all over the shiny black engine with its cone-shaped smokestack. Mill whistles hooted and cathedral bells chimed. Then the barge proceeded a short distance down river where a length of track was laid down to the water. Under its own steam, the *Countess* puffed up the slope and into St. Boniface where it will be used by the Canadian Pacific Railway to help build the new rail line between Selkirk and the American border.

Newspaper editor George Ham noticed an Indian rather stoically watching the mad celebration and wondered if the native realized the arrival of this "iron horse" meant the "wild, free, unrestrained life" of his people was nearing an end.

The railway is to border one of several stretches of the proposed transcontinental line to the Pacific.

Sitting Bull, Sioux not leaving Canada

Oct. 17, 1877

FORT WALSH, N.W.T. – An American commission failed today in its attempt to persuade Chief Sitting Bull and his Sioux followers to return to the United States. The Indians have been living in Canada for several months, seeking safe haven after their defeat of Gen. George Custer and the American cavalry at the Little Big Horn last year. The presence of so many Sioux in the west presents a diplomatic problem for the Canadian government, and it was at the request of Canadian authorities that the American commission travelled here to talk to Sitting Bull.

The meeting, which took place in the officers' mess at the fort, was dramatic, but unproductive. The Sioux chief hates the Americans and would hardly even look at the visitors as he sat smoking disdainfully while they presented their message. Gen. Alfred Terry, the leader of the delegation, promised the Sioux that if they put down their guns, returned to the U.S., and agreed to live on reservations, they would not be harmed. But Sitting Bull was not impressed and rejected the American offer. "You come here to tell us lies," he said, "but we don't want to hear them. Go back where you came from. This country is mine and I intend to stay here." Some of the other Indians spoke, then they filed out of the council, still refusing to shake hands with the Americans.

Chief Sitting Bull of the Sioux.

1878

British Columbia, May. George Walkem is elected as premier on a platform of "fight Ottawa," and secession from Confederation.

Quebec. June 12. Two strikers are killed when the armed forces intervene against a strike by workers constructing the province's new parliament buildings.

Ottawa, July 12. The Mackenzie government selects the Fraser River-Burrard Inlet route for the B.C. section of the CPR.

Battleford, Northwest Territories, Aug. 11. Patrick Laurie establishes the Saskatchewan *Herald*, the first newspaper in the Territories.

British Columbia, August. Premier Walkem introduces a resolution in the legislature stating that B.C. will have the right to withdraw from Canada if construction of the transcontinental Canadian Pacific Railway does not begin by May 1879. The railway was one of the terms of B.C.'s entry to Confederation, and so far Ottawa has reneged.

Canada, Sept. 17. In a federal election, John A. Macdonald's Conservatives defeat Alexander Mackenzie's Liberals 137 seats to 69, but Macdonald loses his Kingston seat.

St. John's, Nfld., Sept. 26. George Tyson arrives after leading an American expedition to Cumberland Sound and collecting important scientific and geographical information. The expedition was part of a failed plan to establish a permanent scientific colony at Ellesmere Island.

Manitoba, Nov. 11. Train service is inaugurated between Minnesota and Manitoba, as the first train of the St. Paul and Pacific Railroad arrives at Emerson from Minnesota.

Northwest Territories. The ordinance passed in 1877 to preserve the prairie buffalo is repealed; the regulation is impossible to enforce because of the vastness of the territory and the large number of Indians who rely on the buffalo for food.

Quebec. Canadian asbestos production begins at Thetford Mines.

British Columbia. The first penitentiary in the province is built near New Westminster.

London, Ont. Western University of London [University of Western Ontario] is founded.

Montreal cyclists boasting new club

Various types of high wheelers can be seen when the Montreal Bicycle Club members go on an outing.

1878

MONTREAL – Montrealers were amazed four years ago when A.T. Lane rode a socket-steering high wheeler through the streets. Now Lane, one of the first to use rubber tires on a bicycle, has helped set up the Montreal Bicycle Club.

Only two other North American cities, Bangor, Maine, and Boston, Mass., boast organizations for wheelmen. The Montreal group, which has its own bugler, is planning various outings. Bad weather is unlikely to stop them – boneshakers with spiked front wheels and skates have already been seen on the St. Lawrence River.

Teetotallers triumph: Temperance Act keeps tight rein on liquor

May 10, 1878

OTTAWA – Teetotallers have their first victory since Confederation. The Canadian Temperance Act introduced by R.W. Scott has become law. Under the terms of the act, "on a petition from one-fourth of the electors in any county or city, an election is to be held, and if a majority of the votes poll in favor of the act, it will be brought into force for three years after the date of expiration of any existing licences."

The Scott Act prohibits the sale of liquor except as specifically provided for, and supersedes bylaws passed in the Dunkin Act of 1864. To combat the temperance tide, the Canadian Brewers and Maltsters Association has been formed.

Natives swap furs for guns and other merchandise at Hudson's Bay store.

Big John conquers the Lachine Rapids

Jan. 1, 1878

LACHINE RAPIDS, Que. – Big John Canadien, a Mohawk from Caughnawaga, today took advantage of the unseasonably warm weather to reaffirm his title as master pilot of the Lachine Rapids, shooting the turbulent whitewater in his own nine-metre craft.

The bulwarks of his boat coated with ice both inside and out, Big John and his two companions received a warm reception at the harbor of Montreal, greeted by thrilled spectators. Big John is the latest – perhaps greatest – of the Indian pilots who have traditionally led excursions through the rapids.

Mental institution releases renowned Métis leader Riel

Jan. 23, 1878

BEAUPORT, Que. – Louis Larochelle has been released from the mental hospital at Beauport, outside of Quebec City, after being institutionalized for close to two years. A patient's departure from a hospital normally merits little attention, but this case is an exception. Larochelle is really Louis Riel, the Métis leader of the first provisional government in the Red River in 1870.

Apparently, Riel had a mental breakdown while visiting his uncle, John Lee, in Montreal early in 1876; the 31-year-old Métis kept insisting he was a prophet. He demanded to go to church to proclaim his mission, and when denied, tore his clothes and his bed coverings. Convinced his nephew needed medical attention, Lee committed him at Longue Pointe, and to detract attention, Riel was registered as Louis R. David. Two months later he was transferred to Beauport under a new alias, Louis Larochelle.

U.S. fishermen raid Nfld. herring stock

Feb. 12, 1878

FORTUNE BAY, Nfld. – At least 12 American fishing ships entered Long Harbour here in Fortune Bay last month and began to take herring to use as bait in their cod fishery. The herring had arrived in large numbers, and the Americans joined seines together to make a barrier across the harbor. Their actions broke several Newfoundland laws, including one prohibiting herring from being taken between Oct. 20 and April 25, and another barring herring from being taken on a Sunday.

Some 200 Newfoundlanders who were present and required by law to refrain from taking herring objected. An American captain threatened them with a revolver, and the crowd reacted by destroying the seines and allowing about 2,000 barrels of herring to escape. Newfoundland is determined to protect its herring stocks.

John Deere shipment reaches Winnipeg

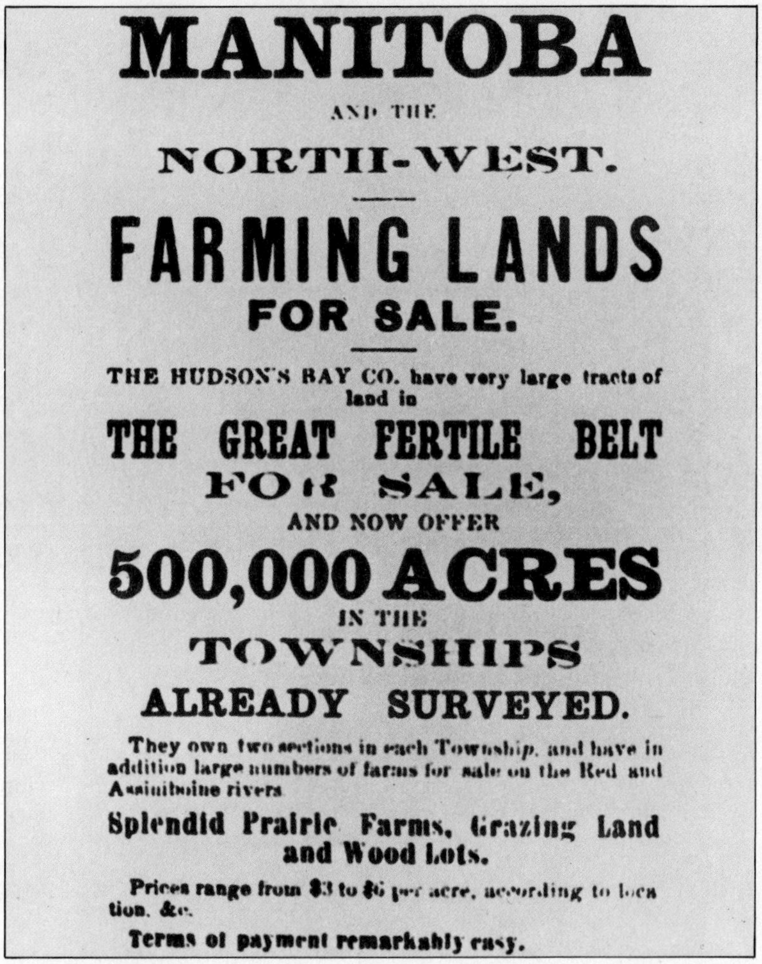
MANITOBA
AND THE
NORTH-WEST.
FARMING LANDS
FOR SALE.
THE HUDSON'S BAY CO. have very large tracts of land in
THE GREAT FERTILE BELT
FOR SALE,
AND NOW OFFER
500,000 ACRES
IN THE
TOWNSHIPS
ALREADY SURVEYED.
They own two sections in each Township, and have in addition large numbers of farms for sale on the Red and Assiniboine rivers.
Splendid Prairie Farms, Grazing Land and Wood Lots.
Prices range from $3 to $6 per acre, according to location, &c.
Terms of payment remarkably easy.

The Hudson's Bay Company offers fertile farm lands for sale in Manitoba.

April 26, 1878

WINNIPEG – The first shipment of implements from the John Deere Company has arrived in this district of Manitoba. The local implement house, Westbrook and Fairchild, ordered them from the Deere headquarters at Moline, Illinois. The shipment travelled by rail to St. Paul, and then down the Red River by steamer to Winnipeg.

A Westbrook and Fairchild spokesman says this equipment was selected because Manitoba soil is similar to that of the midwestern United States. Another reason is Deere's size. Westbrooke and Fairchild believe that in the future, when railroads make possible the opening of more farmland in the Canadian west, there will be a need for larger orders.

The new implements are now in storage in the warehouses of Westbrook and Fairchild. The partners, H.S. Westbrook, and brothers Isaac and Frank Fairchild, are convinced the John Deere plows are ideal for local farms. This Deere line of chilled steel plows has a reputation for being tougher, sharper, more resistant and able to shed sticky prairie soil, which makes them suitable for the heavy moist gumbo soils of the Red River valley. Iron tools tend to clog or break in heavy, root-massed prairie fields.

Post office is first set up in Edmonton

March 1, 1878

EDMONTON – Richard Hardisty has been named postmaster of the town's first post office, to be known as the Fort Edmonton station. He takes over responsibility for mail into the settlement from the detachment of North West Mounted Police which has handled the duty for about two years.

The post office here is a sign of confidence in Edmonton's future, springing from the rapid rate of settlement in surrounding farmlands, opened up through land grants. Edmonton is already the northern terminus for steamships on the North Saskatchewan River. The *Northcote* was the first steamer to visit Edmonton three years ago.

Ontario civil service set to hire women

1878

TORONTO – The government of Ontario is now hiring women in the civil service, mostly in clerical positions. The federal civil service has employed female public servants for years, the first two being the matron and deputy matron who began working at Kingston Penitentiary in 1870. The next year, a woman was hired to work on the lock at the Williamsburg Canal.

Better educated women and fears that the class of men seeking civil service positions is declining are two reasons the Ontario government is hiring females.

This settler near Carberry, in Assiniboia, has prepared fields for crops, built fences and a log home for his family and started to raise livestock.

▷

Macdonald, Tupper battle with Smith on Commons floor

May 10, 1878

OTTAWA – Even seasoned observers of a normally feisty Parliament were shocked today by the pure venom flowing between government minister Donald Smith and opposition leaders Sir John A. Macdonald and Charles Tupper. The issue was Smith's three-months-delayed answer to charges that his support for a bill giving an American railway rights to run into Winnipeg is motivated by his owning shares in the St. Paul's and Pacific Railway, most likely to build the line. Specifically, he has been attacked by Sir John, whose own cabinet Smith resigned from in 1873 over the Pacific Scandal.

In the House today, Smith denied the charges. He then accused Macdonald of once boasting that all of Ontario's votes could be bought if the money were right. At this, Sir John leapt to his feet, and accused Smith of lying. But Smith persisted, referring to Macdonald's drunkenness before his marathon speech in 1873. This brought in Charles Tupper, who also accused Smith of lying. In seconds, the affair was a shouting match. Later, in the lobby, Sir John reportedly roared, "I can lick you, Smith, faster'n Hell can frizzle a feather!"

Orangemen furious as leaders detained

July 12, 1878

MONTREAL – Under provisions of the new Crimes of Violence Prevention Act, Montreal Mayor Jean-Louis Beaudry today authorized police to detain leaders of the Orange Order, in town to participate in a parade. The law prohibits carrying dangerous weapons, and Beaudry hopes to avert the violent confrontations between Catholics and Protestants that marred a similar demonstration last year.

Orangemen have responded angrily, and there is talk they will vent their frustrations on Prime Minister Alexander Mackenzie's Liberal party, responsible for the law, in the next federal election.

Treaties change Indians way of life

Indians gather at St. Peter's Manitoba at "treaty time" and await the payment of the arranged annuities.

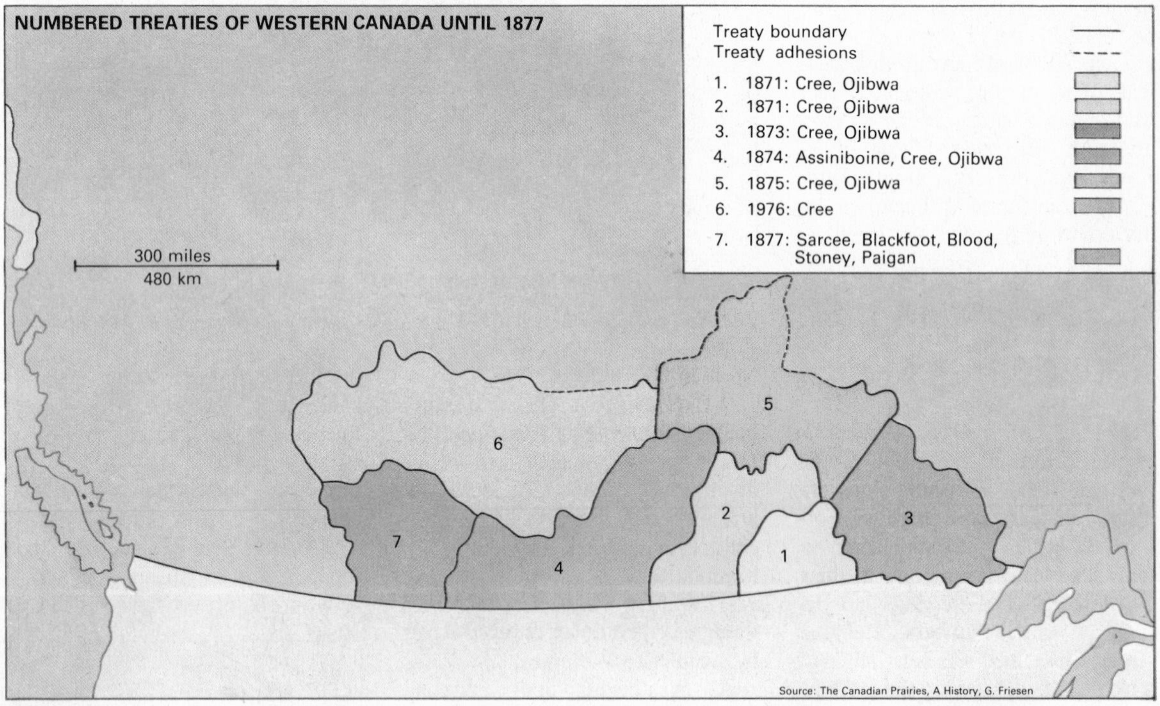

Map shows how the Dominion of Canada's treaty system restricts Indians to specific areas of the prairies.

1878

NORTHWEST TERRITORIES – A way of life is coming to an end for the aboriginal people of the northern prairies. The diminishing buffalo herds are making it harder and harder for them to carry on the lifestyle of the past. They also face the inevitable encroachment into their territory by immigrant farmers looking for land.

The Indians had to choose between resisting the influx of farmers and accepting assistance to adjust. For the 35,000 Indian inhabitants of the west, the choice was to make treaties with the Canadian government in which they were to restrict themselves to certain areas in exchange for such things as schools, farm equipment, hunting and fishing rights, and the prohibition of trading in alcohol on reservations.

When the Dominion of Canada purchased Rupert's Land and the N.W.T. from the Hudson's Bay Company in 1870, part of the deal was that the new country would be responsible for the protection and well-being of the indigenous people. It was also the duty of the federal government to compensate the Indians for their interest in the annexed territories. Out of this grew the treaty system as a way of acquiring legal use of the land until then occupied by the native Indians. A number of the plains Cree and Blackfoot tribes believed treaties 6 and 7 to be peace treaties, rather than land surrenders, a concept foreign to their culture.

Manitobans elect Norquay premier

Oct. 16, 1878

WINNIPEG – John Norquay was elected today to succeed Robert Atkinson Davis as Manitoba's premier. Supporters say Norquay is capable of doing the big jobs, and he certainly has a wide range of talents. Prior to entering public life, he was a teacher, farmer, trapper, merchant and fur trader.

Norquay is a descendant of Hudson's Bay Company servants. His maternal grandmother was the child of a marriage between an HBC officer and an Indian or Métis woman. It is an indication of Norquay's high standing that when he stood for election to the High Bluff constituency, he was elected by acclamation. He now represents the constituency of St. Andrew's.

Manitoba Premier John Norquay.

Lorne named new governor general

Oct. 5, 1878

OTTAWA – The new governor general of Canada will be the Marquis of Lorne, due to take up his new post next month. Lorne has sat in the British House of Commons and, once he succeeded to the dukedom of Argyle, the House of Lords. His appointment brings royalty to Canada, since his wife is Princess Louise, Queen Victoria's fourth daughter. Lorne replaces the retiring Lord Dufferin.

Exciting election returns Sir John A.

Election poster shows voter options.

Estranged wife (Canada) offers husband (Sir John A.) a second chance.

Oct. 17, 1878

OTTAWA – Five years after the Liberals drove him from power, Sir John A. Macdonald is once again Canada's prime minster. In the general election of Sept. 17, his Conservatives smashed their Liberal adversaries 142-64, sweet revenge for the humiliating aftermath of the Pacific Scandal which swept Alexander Mackenzie into office. Sir John's own Kingston riding rejected him, by a mere 144 votes, but he quickly won a "safe" by election in Victoria, B.C.

Macdonald recovered thanks to the Great Depression that struck the western world in 1873. Newly healthy and sober, he hammered at the desperate Mackenzie's inability to cope with economic distress, and offered his appealing national policy instead. He also wooed electors in two summers of political picnics, where thousands washed down hearty buffets with raspberry cordial, lemonade and iced wine. The picnics paid off, and in their first secret ballot, Canadians swarmed to vote for the old chieftain.

Marguerite Bourgeoys declared venerable

Dec. 19, 1878

MONTREAL – Marguerite Bourgeoys, founder of the Congrégation de Notre-Dame, has been declared venerable by Pope Leo XIII, 178 years after her death. A native of Troyes, France, Marguerite came to Montreal in 1657 where she soon opened a girls school in a stable. She also founded a boarding school for girls as well as a school for Indian girls at the Sulpician reserve at La Montagne.

Marguerite served as chaperon for the *filles du roi,* marriageable young women sent to New France as brides. She helped establish domestic arts and primary schools in Quebec City. She died in 1700 after two years in meditation.

Marguerite Bourgeoys.

Labatt ale captures gold medal in Paris

Oct. 21, 1878

PARIS – The French have discovered something Canadian beer drinkers have known all along – that Canadians brew the world's best suds. John Labatt's India Pale Ale has won a gold medal at the International Exposition in Paris.

Developed from a recipe Labatt obtained while learning the "art and mystery of brewing" from a brewmaster in West Virginia in 1865, IPA is Labatt's answer to lager. A light colored ale, capable of travelling well, IPA has won three previous awards. Labatt's of London also brews stout, X, XX, and XXX ales in wood and bottle.

1879

Winnipeg, Jan. 4. The Winnipeg Board of Trade is registered.

Toronto, June. The first telephone directory in Canada appears.

Foxe Basin, Arctic, Aug. 7. A U.S. whaling voyage led by John Spicer sights a group of islands [Spicer Islands] while beset by bad weather.

Hamilton, Ont., Aug. 15. A telephone exchange opens, the first in Canada and the British Empire and ninth in the world.

Northwest Territories, Aug. 16. Cree Indian Swift Runner is arrested and charged with murder and cannibalism in connection with the deaths of his wife, children, brother-in-law, and mother-in-law.

St. Eleanor's, P.E.I., Oct. 7. William Pope, a Father of Confederation and judge, dies.

New Jersey, U.S., Oct. 21. Thomas Edison demonstrates an electric light bulb that burns for more than 13 hours.

Charlottetown, P.E.I., Oct. 23. Roman Catholic Bishop Peter McIntyre establishes the Charlottetown Hospital, the first on the Island. It is open to all denominations, but islanders label it "Catholic."

Northwest Territories. Edgar Dewdney is appointed first Indian Commissioner of the Northwest to ensure observance of all treaty obligations. He urges Indians to select reserve lands, and offers government help in farming.

Northwest Territories. Indian Commissioner Dewdney reports that several prairie fires have been "started at different points almost simultaneously." Probably set by the U.S. army, the fires keep the buffalo from returning to Canada in their annual migration.

Nova Scotia. Miners form the Provincial Workingmen's Association, a federation of unions to work for better working conditions.

Ontario. The first inter-urban telephone service in Canada is established between Hamilton and Dundas.

Falconwood, P.E.I. A Hospital for the Insane is established.

Prince Edward Island. Women are admitted as students to Prince of Wales College.

Hamilton, Ont. James Jermy of England's Christian Mission [Salvation Army] arrives to preach on city streets.

Fleming pushes time zone proposal

Sir Sandford Fleming, who has presented a paper promoting the idea of dividing the world into 24 time zones.

The Royal Canadian Institute considers Fleming's standard time proposal.

Feb. 8, 1879

TORONTO – A paper proposing that the world be divided into 24 time zones was presented to the Royal Canadian Institute today by Sir Sandford Fleming. He told the RCI, a scientific society based in Toronto, that each time zone would consist of 15 degrees. They would start from a prime meridian drawn through the Pacific Ocean so land masses would be avoided. A surveyor, engineer and scientific researcher, Fleming felt the issue should be addressed at an international level. He is expected to get some backing in this country, as the governor general is sending copies of his paper to various scientific organizations throughout the world.

The push for developing a workable system of time zones has become greater this century as communication times shrank with technology such as the underwater telegraph cables linking this continent with Europe. Fleming himself proposed this year that a Pacific cable be laid linking Canada and Australia. Railway construction, in which Fleming has played a major role in this country, has also shrunk the world and created the need for a more workable way of keeping time in more than one centre. The futility of the existing situation is best underlined in England where special watches with multiple dials have been developed, each showing the time in a different city.

Developing the concept of time zones is just another facet of Fleming's diverse talent. Coming to Canada from Scotland in 1845, he was granted his land surveyor's licence four years later and set up shop in Toronto. But no job was too small or too big for him. In terms of the former, he designed Canada's first postage stamp – the three-penny beaver. Railroad construction soon took over. Among his projects is the trouble-plagued Pacific rail route that he charted out for the government. While Fleming was an innocent bystander in the cross fire of the infamous Pacific Scandal, he treads a more perilous path with his time zone concept because it would affect every country in the world.

"The Last Polar Wave" – images of a typical Canadian winter storm.

Lornes wintering just like Canadians

Winter 1879

OTTAWA – The Marquis of Lorne and his wife, the Princess Louise, are delighting people here as they throw themselves enthusiastically into enjoying the unfamiliar Canadian winter. Every day the petite and elegant princess dons her stout walking boots, size three, and strides briskly through town, dropping unannounced into local shops. At home at Rideau Hall, the Lornes skate and curl on the skating pond, Lorne with icicles sparkling in his beard. They specially love gliding down the giant toboggan slide.

Tories introduce a National Policy

March 14, 1879

OTTAWA – Today Minister of Finance Leonard Tilley introduced a protective tariff, part of what he called a National Policy to build our new nation. The tariff, an issue in last fall's elections, will increase on most foreign imports. Besides this protection, the legislation also benefits Canadian manufacturers by reducing customs duties on raw materials and semi-processed goods imported into Canada.

The tariff flies in the face of British policy and is more in line with American thinking. In a reply via telegraph received just 48 hours before the budget speech, the British government expressed regret but noted the decision was up to Canada, subject to treaty obligations.

Prime Minister John A. Macdonald explained earlier on the campaign trail he wanted a tariff readjustment, not increase. Later, when forming his government, he argued that the tariff's primary purpose was to raise revenue. Certainly he'll need lots of that to meet some of the projects he promised as part of the National Policy – completion of a transcontinental railway, and settlement of the west. While Macdonald is confident, the issue is likely to be debated at length in Parliament before it comes to a vote. In fact, every argument has been presented many times since the tariff question first was discussed by politicians three winters ago.

The finance minister's egg dance.

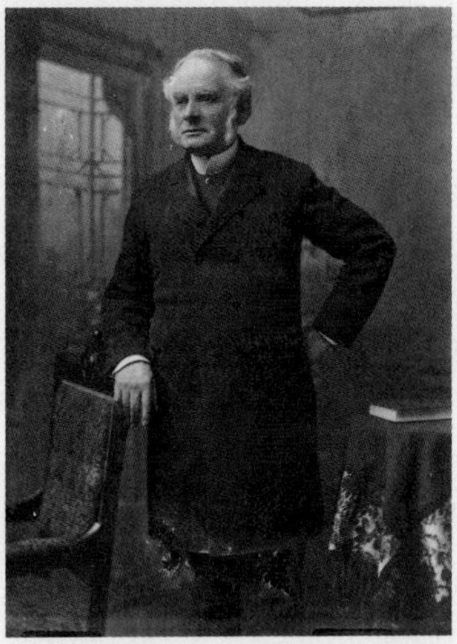

Leonard Tilley, Canada's minister of finance, introduced a National Policy in his budget speech today.

What did happen at Rideau Hall?

Feb. 19, 1879

OTTAWA – What happened last night at the first Government House state ball hosted by the Marquis of Lorne and Princess Louise? Is it true Sir John A. Macdonald – among others – imbibed too freely of the potent champagne punch and insulted the princess? Was Lady Agnes Macdonald also disrespectful to Queen Victoria's most beautiful and accomplished daughter? Here in Ottawa, tongues are wagging about these disagreeable incidents – if they actually happened – and others that did, such as the drunken Senator Carroll's kicking aside the trailing folds of the princess' gown. Sir John is trying to scotch the rumors, and so is Lorne, but rumor-mongering in the capital is too popular a pastime to control, and is just one of the crosses the royal couple has had to bear.

The Lornes are also childless after eight years of marriage, and though Lorne family intimates believe Louise is infertile, others blame Lorne's preference for gentlemen over ladies. The Lornes are artists *manqués*, he a novelist-poet, Louise a sculptress whose passionate relationship with her instructor, commoner Joseph Edgar Boehm, pushed Queen Victoria to find her a suitable husband. Ottawa is a hard post for this couple.

Free government land grants lure hundreds to northern Ontario

June 15, 1879

BRUCE MINES, Ont. – Pioneers by the hundreds are flowing into this rough terrain in northern Ontario, eager to grab their share of free land. The offer is a government scheme to encourage settlement. Any married man with children under 18 years old is allowed to occupy 200 acres of Crown land. If some of it is unworkable, extra land will be awarded to him. Then, to gain title to it, he must clear and farm 15 acres of it within five years of possession. He must also build a good house. Unmarried men and those without children can also get land – 100 acres in this case.

Money from land sales to pay for railway

May 10, 1879

OTTAWA – The new railway across Canada will be paid for by selling the farmlands of the western plains, Railways Minister Charles Tupper announced today. "We believe that we have there the garden of the world," said Tupper. He generously estimated there are 180 million acres on the prairies, adding that their fertility and grain-growing abilities are unsurpassed.

The sale of this land would mean the line could be constructed without raising taxes. Tupper said selecting Burrard Inlet as the west coast terminal is premature and announced that the most difficult 200-kilometre section of track in B.C. will be built first, to break the backbone of the job.

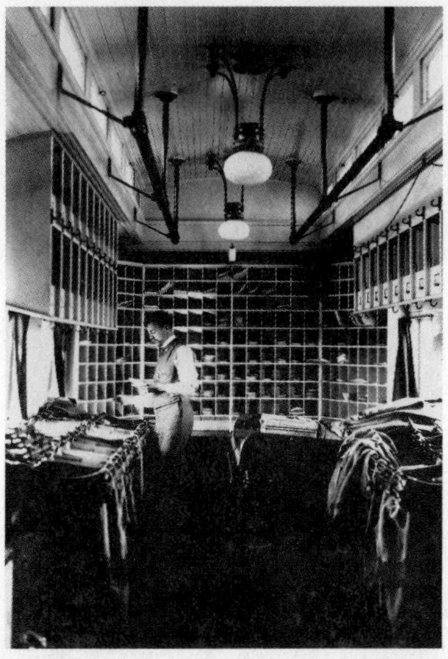

Postal services can be improved with more railway postal cars like this.

Birks' new shop in Montreal a real jewel

March 1, 1879

MONTREAL – Customers are finding it hard to believe their ears. Henry Birks has just opened a jewelry store that only takes cash, and offers fixed prices for merchandise. No more bartering, no more credit. The tiny Birks store is on St. Jacques Street in Montreal and boasts three employees. Birks, tall, white-haired, and dressed in black, is an unmistakable presence as he chats with customers.

For 26 years Birks worked for Savage and Lyman, considered the top jewellers in Canada until they folded last year in the midst of the depression sweeping North America. It looks like Birks is trying to avoid the fate of Savage and Lyman with innovative sales techniques.

Henry Birks has just opened a jewelry store in Montreal. He has plans to become one of the country's major dealers in jewelry, using innovative sales techniques and promotions.

Macdonald ousts Lt.-Gov. Letellier from Quebec post

July 25, 1879

QUEBEC CITY – In an act of political revenge, pure and simple, the Macdonald government has succeeded in firing Quebec Lt.-Gov. Luc Letellier de St. Just. The Tories have sought Letellier's head ever since the former federal Liberal minister tossed out the provincial Conservative government of Charles de Boucherville in March last year.

Letellier used a controversial bill demanding municipalities to pay railway costs as a pretext to dismiss de Boucherville's administration and replace it with a minority Liberal government led by Henri Joly de Lotbinière. Macdonald's Conservatives were outraged by the questionable move, coming as it did on the eve of federal elections. Indeed, federal Conservatives campaigned in the September election on a pledge to remove Letellier.

Cree cannibal Swift Runner hanged

Police have recovered the remains of the victims of Swift Runner, commonly known as the Cree Cannibal.

Dec. 20, 1879

FORT SASKATCHEWAN, N.W.T. – Cree cannibal Swift Runner was hanged this morning in bitter -42 degree weather. His surviving relatives and specially invited chiefs sat in a circle, drumming furiously and singing a death song to speed their departing brother to the happy hunting grounds. Standing on the scaffold, Swift Runner thanked the North West Mounted Police who arrested him and the priests who had welcomed him into the Roman Catholic church after his trial, and warned others to learn from his fate.

Weeks ago, Swift Runner confessed he had "made beef" of his wife, children, brother-in-law, and mother-in-law. He killed and ate them even though he had sufficient dried animal meat to eat. At his murder trial, people said he had been gentle and trustworthy, a good father and husband. But Swift Runner himself said he was tortured for years by dreams of an Indian spirit urging him to take up cannibalism. Tragically, he obeyed it.

Canada takes steps to annex Arctic land

Nov. 4, 1879

OTTAWA – Canada is prepared to assume ownership of the vast Arctic territory lying north of its mainland coast. Parliament today passed an order-in-council providing for the transfer of the region from the British, who lay claim to it by virtue of the fact that British seamen explored most of it. If the British Parliament approves the order, the transfer will take place Sept. 1, 1880. The government is acting to record its claim to the Arctic not because it has plans for the region but mainly to forestall any ambitions the Americans might have in that direction.

Western Canada's first country elevator for handling grain can be found in Niverville, Manitoba.

Northern route it is for railway to west

Oct. 14, 1879

OTTAWA – The railway to the Pacific will take a northerly route through Edmonton, a Conservative order-in-council today says. The plan calls for the line to go through the fertile belt to Edmonton, then head west via the Yellowhead Pass and follow along the Fraser River to the Pacific at Burrard Inlet. The alternative is a southern route that would follow across prairie grasslands and cross the Rockies west of Calgary. The Yellowhead-Burrard route has been endorsed by cabinet. Both have been discussed at length.

Indians cope with decline of the buffalo

1879

CANADIAN PRAIRIES – Hunters have killed off the buffalo herds of the Canadian prairies, and the lives of the plains Indians, who have depended on the animals for thousands of years, will never be the same. The slaughter of the buffalo by American hunters and Canadian Indians to supply U.S. leather markets is largely responsible for the animals' sudden disappearance. Most of the surviving buffalo have been driven to the U.S.

The American army, it would seem, has also contributed to the buffalo's extinction here. It is alleged the army blocked the annual buffalo migration to Canada by setting a string of prairie fires as a way of starving Sitting Bull and his Sioux who took refuge here after the Battle of the Little Big Horn in 1876.

Indians of the western prairies have been the worst hit. Many of the Blackfoot led by Chief Crowfoot were close to starvation by the spring. Old people and children died. Desperate, the Blackfoot ate gophers, rabbits and badgers, and killed their horses, the animals they were once so proud of for their role in the buffalo hunt. They slaughtered the cattle of ranchers around Calgary and Fort Macleod. Crowfoot sent a delegation to the Indian Department at Battleford, and Indian commissioner Edgar Dewdney responded by bringing food to the Blackfoot. Dewdney saw "1,300 Indians in a very destitute condition, and many on the verge of starvation." He saw people eating grass, and tearing a steer to pieces to eat it raw. Meanwhile, food was being rushed to North West Mounted Police forts. The police at Fort Macleod fed 7,000 Indians a day.

The buffalo hunt lives on, a ghost of its former self. Cree, Assiniboine, and Blackfoot are hunting the few remaining buffalo in the Cypress Hills and have crossed the border to the U.S. in pursuit of the harassed animals. Crowfoot and his followers have found enough buffalo to last the winter in Montana's Judith Basin. Unfortunately, they have also found whisky traders. Fights, drunken orgies, and killings have resulted. The future is bleak for all the plains Indians.

Settlers carve out first homes as a nation emerges

Settlers fell trees in a girdled clearing in western Canada. The stumps are burned and the logs are trimmed and used for building houses and barns.

The settler's first home is usually a one-room log cabin in the clearing. Other logs are used to make the snaking rail fence that marks his or her land.

Timber is collected and stored for shipping to the European markets at this Timber Depot in Wolfe's Cove, near Cape Diamond, Quebec City.

Many of Canada's native peoples retain their traditional lifestyles. This Ojibwa camp is located in the Spider Islands on Lake Huron, Ontario.

The Kootenay River is one of the many beautiful waterways of the Canadian west. The magnificent Rockies can be seen in the background of this sketch.

1880

Ontario, March 6. Governor General the Marquis of Lorne presides over an exhibition of works of Canadian artists [future members of the Royal Canadian Academy].

Northwest Territories, June 7. The Saskatchewan *Herald* reports the appearance of two new kinds of early ripening wheat: White Russia and Red Fern.

London, Nov. 15. Canadian sculler Edward Hanlan beats the Australian sculling champion to win the world's professional rowing championship. He is Canada's first great sports hero.

Edmonton, Dec. 6. Frank Oliver publishes the Edmonton *Bulletin*, the first real newspaper in the area [Alberta]. Its slogan is "Read the Bible and the Bulletin."

Quebec. French-Canadian students are ecstatic at the arrival of French actress Sarah Bernhardt, but Montreal Bishop Fabre forbids his parishioners to attend her performances.

Toronto. Dr. Emily Stowe, the first Canadian woman doctor, is finally licensed to practise medicine after setting up practice 13 years ago.

Canada. The Royal Canadian Academy of Arts (RCA) is founded under the patronage of the Marquis of Lorne and his wife HRH the Princess Louise to foster the visual arts in Canada. Some of the country's most accomplished visual artists are among its charter members.

Canada. The National Gallery of Canada is founded with the participation of the RCA and the Marquis of Lorne. Its collection is made up of diploma works of RCA members.

Montreal. The annual mortality rate in working class areas of the city is 35 deaths per 1,000 people, higher than in working class areas of London Paris, Brussels, or Rome.

Canada. A revision to the Indian Act allows Indians with university degrees to choose to become citizens with full voting rights and give up their special tax free rights as Indians.

Ontario. The Canadian Association of Amateur Oarsmen is founded and holds its first annual regatta in Toronto.

Northwest Territories. The first Total Abstinence League in the area [Alberta] is formed.

Emigration crisis hits Canada hard

1880

OTTAWA – The lifeblood of Canada continues to flow steadily across the border. For years now, droves of Canadians, many of them young people in search of their future, have been emigrating to the United States. The exodus includes both native-born Canadians and newly arrived immigrants. Nobody keeps records of Canadian emigration, so it is impossible to determine the exact numbers, but it is clear the country is in the midst of an emigration crisis. Economic conditions in Canada are partly to blame. The depression of the '70s put many out of work. Mechanization in manufacturing and changes in eastern agriculture have also meant fewer jobs. Quebec has suffered the most, where it is said the "flower of the back counties" have gone south. For decades, New England textile and shoe factories have been sponges for the province's surplus labor. Quebecers have flooded New England cities to escape poverty at home, and they have found better wages and steady work. New Englanders call them the "Chinese of the East" because they are willing to work long hours for wages low by local standards.

Droves of Canadians are crossing border to find work in New England factories.

Quebecers aren't the only adventurous ones. Many of Ontario's native sons and daughters have left their homeland for the lure of cheap homesteads in the American midwest or Manitoba. At the same time, many Manitobans have settled across the border in Dakota.

Maritime principal writes book of poems

Fall 1880

CHATHAM, N.B. – The bearded, 20-year-old principal of the local school, Charles G.D. Roberts of Fredericton, has made Canadian literary history with his first book, *Orion, and Other Poems.* Published in Philadelphia, the book won applause in Parliament, and praise from American and Canadian critics. The Montreal *Gazette* predicts Roberts will confer "lasting honor" on Canada. The poet sent copies to Tennyson, Swinburne, Longfellow, Walt Whitman, and Oliver Wendell Holmes.

The St-Jean Baptiste Society in Quebec organizes special events every year on June 24 in order to stimulate the French heritage.

Fire destroys N.B.'s legislature building

Feb. 2, 1880

FREDERICTON – Seventy-five years of parliamentary history was destroyed today, as fire swept through the provincial legislature building. In a few hours, the entire structure, consisting of a central building and two wings, was gutted.

Gone is the site of the House of Assembly, the Legislative Council, and the province's Supreme Court. As well, the Legislative Library was penetrated by the flames. Fortunately many of the books and the parliamentary records were rescued. The fire comes on what was to be the first day of Parliament.

Donnelly murders end longtime feud

Feb. 3, 1880

BIDDULPH, Ont. – A simmering feud erupted into bloody murder today as five members of the Donnelly family were shot and brutally beaten to death by an aroused band of vigilantes wielding pitchforks, clubs and guns. The Donnellys have been notorious in this part of southwestern Ontario for decades. Their brawling and thievery have won them many enemies, and several members of the family have served time in prison.

But the blame is not all on one side. Many of their neighbors defend the Donnellys as hardworking people who are being victimized by vigilante justice. The mob that attacked the family's farm tonight was led by James Carroll, a bitter foe of the Donnellys. The masked men massacred four of the family at the farm – James, his wife Johannah, his son Tom and his niece Bridget. Then, they burned the house to the ground before moving on to the home of another son to continue the killing.

Bell Telephone gets federal charter

April 29, 1880
TORONTO – The Hamilton District Telegraph Company has received a charter to own and operate the National Bell Telephone Company. The company's head office will likely be in Montreal, as Andrew Robertson, who has already agreed to be its president, is also chairman of the Montreal Harbour Commission. Bell Telephone has secured authorized capital of $500,000.

Alexander Graham Bell, who conceived the fundamental idea of the telephone in Brantford, Ont., in 1874, passed the patent rights on to his father, Alexander Melville Bell, who later leased telephones in pairs to be used on private lines. It was Bell senior who licensed the Dominion Telegraph Company to establish telephone exchanges in large centres. When Bell the father wanted to join Bell the son in the United States last year, he convinced National Bell Telephone of Boston to buy the rights. By this time, Hugh C. Baker, head of Hamilton District Telegraph Company, had applied for a charter for the Bell Telephone Company of Canada. The incorporation of Bell Telephone by federal charter gives the company the right to construct telephone lines alongside all public rights-of-way in Canada, a most valuable privilege.

First female operator, M. Warren.

Operator wears 6 1/2 lb. headset.

Ex-Globe employee shoots Brown in leg

March 25, 1880
TORONTO – George Brown, the fiery Reformer and editor of the Toronto *Globe*, was shot today by a disgruntled ex-*Globe* employee. The attack took place this afternoon, at Brown's editorial offices. Police say a man named George Bennett came to see Brown after being dismissed from the paper. Brown did not know Bennett was drunk, with a history of drunkenness and wife-beating. Nor did he know he was armed. Apparently Bennett pulled a revolver on Brown after an argument. When Brown grabbed the pistol, a relatively harmless shot hit him in the leg.

Mackenzie resigns as Liberal leader

April 27, 1880
OTTAWA – Alexander Mackenzie, the "serious Scot" who was the prime minister from 1873 to 1878, has stepped down as leader of the defeated Liberal party. To be more precise, say Liberal insiders, he has been deposed by the caucus. Apparently, the MPs are disgruntled with Mackenzie's leadership.

Tension came to a head today, when the caucus voted to ask Mackenzie to "consider the question of the leadership." Angered and embittered, Mackenzie announced his resignation tonight. He is to be replaced by his former finance minister, Edward Blake.

Edward Blake, former finance minister under Alexander Mackenzie, is the new Liberal party leader.

Bullet wound fatal for Reformer Brown

May 9, 1880
TORONTO – George Brown, the Reform lion of the Toronto *Globe*, died today of complications from a bullet wound in his leg. He was shot in March in his newspaper office, in an altercation with drunken ex-employee George Bennett.

Brown's death brings to a close a great chapter in Canadian history. For, without George Brown, there well might not be any Dominion. It was Brown who, as leader of the opposition Reformers in the pre-Confederation Parliament of 1864, agreed to join Sir John A. Macdonald and the Tories in a Great Coalition, provided the government find a way out of the constitutional deadlock that was stalemating the then United Province of Canada.

As well, Brown has to be remembered as the leading proponent of Rep by Pop, or representation by population, which means that the share of power any region has in Parliament should be based on its share of the overall population. This was a principle opposed by Canada East before Confederation was proposed, because it feared being swamped by the English majority of Canada West.

Contractor arrives to direct B.C. rail work

April 22, 1880
YALE, B.C. – Contractor Andrew Onderdonk has arrived here to direct the start of work on the Emory Bar-Savona section of the Canadian Pacific Railway. Ottawa hopes now British Columbia will stop talking secession, realizing the railway will go through.

Onderdonk is the young American contractor from the state of New York who gained a reputation for speed and determination when he built a sea-wall and ferry slips at San Francisco. He has substantial backing from U.S. financiers and, since the low bidders for the B.C. sections of the railway were in trouble, was permitted to buy them out for $215,000.

Fleming "released" from CPR position

May 22, 1880
OTTAWA – Sandford Fleming, engineer-in-chief of the Pacific Railway project, has been given the "Golden Handshake" by the government of Sir John A. Macdonald. It has "released" him from his duties with thanks, and a going-away present of $30,000.

This polite send-off was only motivated by the government's desire to stay on good terms with Fleming, should he be needed in the future. However, that hardly seems likely. The "brilliant Scots engineer," as some have called him, has been strongly identified with the former Liberal government.

Women and children get added protection

1880
HALIFAX – The Nova Scotia Society for the Prevention of Cruelty, founded four years ago to protect animals, has expanded its mandate to include women and children. Its secretary-agent is John Naylor, an Anglican, freemason, teetotaller, charter member of the Nova Scotia Kennel Club, and owner and defender of horses. Halifax boasts so many signs for his real estate business, that a wag joked the city seemed to belong to God and John Naylor. In the violent slums, women and children need both.

Railway funds available: Macdonald

Railways provide much needed access to new areas for goods and settlers.

These immigrants en route to Canada will board trains to reach new homes.

June 29, 1880

BATH, Ont. – There's money available for the long-delayed railway to the Pacific, Sir John A. Macdonald told a cheering crowd of supporters at a political picnic here tonight. In fact, said the prime minister, there's so much interest from investors the government intends to send a team of ministers to London to open negotiations.

If this is true, it marks a tremendous turnaround for the Pacific Railway project, especially as outside capital has been lacking for years. What has probably made the real difference is the fact that the Great Depression of the '70s, as it's being called, is now over. Capitalists from both the United States and Britain are stepping forward.

Chief among those offering support in return for government subsidies and land is Duncan McIntyre. He heads up the Canada Central Railway, which would connect with the Pacific line at Lake Nipissing, and take it to Ottawa. McIntyre is backed by the money and directors of the St. Paul, Minneapolis and Manitoba Railway, headed by Montreal investor George Stephen. Other possible funding sources come from the British railway promoter Brassey, a group put together by shareholders of the old land-owning concern the Canada Company, and even a somewhat shady syndicate figureheaded by British aristocrat Lord Dunsmore.

British hand control of Arctic to Canada

July 31, 1880

LONDON, England – The bustling streets of London are a universe away from the harsh tundra and glaciers of the North American Arctic. While Londoners rush to and from factories and offices, the Arctic lies cold and fog covered. But today these two worlds crossed paths, as the British government passed an order-in-council giving Canada possession of the Arctic islands after years of negotiations between the two nations. Nobody consulted the Inuit who live in the Arctic.

Canada has no immediate use for the Arctic, and the transfer is only being made because British and Canadian authorities fear the U.S. taking possession of the vast area. The Americans have been making whaling voyages and explorations in the Arctic since the 1850s, and it is widely believed they are itching to get their hands on the territory.

The British are pussyfooting in the transfer because they are scared of negative American reaction. The transfer lacks political teeth because it is has been made by an order-in-council rather than an act of Parliament. The wording of the order is also vague; it gives Canada all of Britain's Arctic possessions, but doesn't define the area involved. Because of this pussyfooting, other nations may not even recognize Canada's claim.

Whisky trader dies in Ontario shootout

July 1880

HAWK LAKE, Ont. – Whisky trader Dan Harrington has been gunned down by a Canadian Pacific Railway constable outside a bawdy tent in this small, frontier community. Confronted by a CPR official and the police, Harrington retreated to the tent and re-emerged with two revolvers. A constable, quick on the draw, fired and struck Harrington in the heart. It is said the trader's last words were, "I'd rather be shot than fined." The CPR has been trying hard, often in vain, to control the disruptive flow of whisky to work camps.

"Voyageur priest" Father Lacombe arrives at Rat Portage

Nov. 2, 1880

RAT PORTAGE – Father Albert Lacombe arrived here today as an emissary of the Archbishop of St. Boniface. Alexandre-Antonin Taché dispatched Lacombe with instructions to become the first chaplain to the 2,000 men constructing the main Canadian Pacific Railway line. The archbishop's motivation is to serve that one-third of the laborers who are French-speaking Roman Catholics.

This is a challenging new assignment for Lacombe, widely known in the western territories as one of the "voyageur priests." He has spent 30 years on the prairies, enduring the worst of the weather.

The fast-growing community of Rat Portage has built this log jail.

New bill proposes a privately-owned CPR

The railway flanger is invented by John Hamilton and used in Fredericton.

Dec. 10, 1880

OTTAWA – The government of Sir John A. Macdonald has introduced a bill that would turn over the construction of the Canadian Pacific Railway to a group of Montreal and American investors. The group is led by Duncan McIntyre and Sir George Stephen, both with ties to the St. Paul, Minneapolis and Manitoba Railway.

Under the bill, the privately-owned Canadian Pacific Railway would receive a sizable number of benefits from the government for building the 3,220-kilometre line. In particular, Macdonald proposes giving the CPR a $25 million subsidy, plus 25 million acres of fertile land along the railroad's right of way. In essence, the CPR will own every second block of 640 acres along its line, up to a distance of 38.6 kilometres on either side of the track. As well, the railway is to be given duty-free status on all its materials, and perpetual tax-free status on its buildings, machines, and capital. Donated lands will be tax-free for 20 years, or until sold.

Syndicate, government sign railway deal

Oct. 21, 1880

OTTAWA – After months of negotiations, the Canadian government has signed a deal with a private company to take over the construction of the Canadian Pacific Railway. The syndicate is led by Sir George Stephen, a Montreal financier with a reputation for getting things done.

Stephen, president of the Bank of Montreal, is one of a group of Canadians who revived the American-based St. Paul, Minneapolis and Manitoba Railway a few years ago. So it's not surprising the prime minister views him and his syndicate as a force that can get this long-delayed project completed. It's not known what the government agreed to give the Stephen syndicate, but rumors of millions of dollars worth of cash subsidies and land are floating around the capital.

Catholic church interference annuls vote

Nov. 30, 1880

OTTAWA – By a unanimous decision, the Supreme Court has annulled an 1878 election in Quebec's Berthier riding because of undue influence by Roman Catholic clergy. The decision adds fuel to the flames of the Holy War that Quebec's ultraconservative Catholics, or ultramontanists, have waged against all forms of liberalism.

Led by Bishop Louis-François Laflèche, the ultramontanists believe in the supremacy of the church in political and social affairs, and so they see nothing wrong with the clergy influencing elections. In the provincial and federal elections of 1878, Catholic clergy swayed their flocks by telling them from the pulpit that heaven is *bleu* and hell is *rouge*, referring to the Conservative and Liberal parties, respectively.

1,162 kilometres of CPR track in place

Dec. 31, 1880

OTTAWA – At the end of a busy year for railroad construction in Canada, it seems appropriate to review just how much has been done in the quest to build twin steel ribbons to the Pacific Ocean. Since work on the Canadian Pacific began in 1874, 1,162 kilometres of line have been completed.

But this number doesn't represent one continuous stretch. Instead, it is the total of four. The longest section runs 660 kilometres from Fort William [Thunder Bay] to Selkirk, Man. From there, south to the U.S. border and rail lines there, is an unfinished 137-kilometre stretch to Emerson, another one further west 161 kilometres long running toward the west coast, and 204 kilometres of track in British Columbia. There are some advantages to this piecemeal approach, the main one being it's faster to have four teams building sections, rather than just one pushing through. However, it doesn't compensate for years of delays caused by the political wrangling in Ottawa. Alexander Mackenzie's Liberal government, 1873-78, thrifty and anti-corruption, viewed the project with caution and doubt.

Overall, however, the Canadian Pacific Railway seems to finally be going "full steam ahead." In particular, money from investors is now becoming available. So much so, that it's rumored a private company may take over the job from a reluctant government.

Canadian Pacific Railway construction crews are at work in the Rockies.

Many new railways such as this one on the ice at Montreal are being built.

1881

Ottawa, Feb. 1. The House of Commons passes the bill approving the contract with the CPR to build a transcontinental railway.

Fort Buford, Montana Territory, July 20. Sioux Chief Sitting Bull, who has been in Canadian exile for five years since leading the Indian victory against General Custer and his troops at Little Big Horn, surrenders to American authorities. He proclaims his "love" for Canada and says he hopes his children will grow up in Canada and not the U.S.

Winnipeg, July 20. The first CPR train arrives in the city.

Memramcook, N.B., July 21. The National Society of Acadians is founded.

London, Ont., Oct. 6. Western University opens for classes.

Prince Edward Island, Nov. 28. The Bank of P.E.I., opened in 1854 as the Island's first native bank, suspends payments in the midst of financial crisis.

Ottawa, Dec. 14. Charles Tupper, minister of railways and canals, moves resolutions authorizing a cash subsidy and land grant to the CPR.

Ontario. Six Nations Indian Oronhyatekha, also known as Peter Martin, becomes supreme chief ranger of the Independent Order of Foresters. He is Canada's first Iroquois physician, and one of the first Indians to get a degree from a Canadian university.

United States. While in exile, Louis Riel marries a Métis named Marguerite Monet. Riel has been wandering the Montana territory as a trader and interpreter. He finds hardship and demoralization among the Métis of the area.

Montreal. There are two Italian noodle manufacturers in the city, one of them Mario Catelli. Macaroni is commonly used in soups, or with cream or tomato sauce.

Quebec. The first Quebec branches of the Knights of Labor are formed. The Knights were founded in the U.S. in 1869 to work for working class consciousness by organizing workers by industry rather than trade.

Toronto. The city has a population of 86,000, and 932 manufacturing establishments.

Canada. There are 11,803 kilometres of railway in Canada.

Mistreated Métis decide Manitoba is not for them

1881

WINNIPEG – When Manitoba entered Confederation 11 years ago, its population was largely Métis. Today it is dominated by Ontario settlers of British descent. The Métis have become alienated in their homeland and have left the province in droves after Louis Riel and others fought so hard to protect their rights here in negotiations for Manitoba's entry to Canada.

The decline of the buffalo hunt forced many Métis to leave Manitoba in the 1870s. Each year Métis hunters had to travel further west in search of the rapidly vanishing herds. Métis set up communities on western rivers like the Saskatchewan to be closer to the herds.

But Métis have also left Manitoba because they have been badly mistreated here. Following the arrival of the Red River expedition in August 1870, Ontario militiamen and members of the settlement's Canadian faction threatened and assaulted Métis in revenge for the execution of Thomas Scott. They even killed François Guillemette and Elzéar Goulet. Witnesses reported men "rolling and fighting in the miry mudholes of Winnipeg."

In recent years, many Métis and some Country-Born have left the province to look for farmland to the west because they have been denied land here. They have received a mere fraction of the 1.4 million acres granted them by the Manitoba Act. Through government corruption or neglect, the grant has suffered delays and confusion, and most of the land has gone to speculators. The Manitoba Act also assured the Métis and Country-Born security of tenure for the land they occupied in 1870. They were required to apply to dominion officials for title to the land, but officials have rejected many Métis claims, in some cases because the Métis occupy the land for only a few weeks a year and spend the rest of the year away on the buffalo hunt.

The Canadian government added insult to injury in its treatment of the Métis by stalling its granting of amnesty to Riel and others in the Red River uprising.

CPR officials opt for more southerly route

Accommodation for railway construction crews is provided in modified cars.

Feb. 17, 1881

OTTAWA – Canadian Pacific Railway has just announced a major decision – the CPR will not cross the northwestern prairies. Instead, the line will run some 320 kilometres south of the route proposed by former engineer-in-chief Sandford Fleming, near the American border.

Probably three considerations for fixing this new route dominated CPR directors' thinking. First, the CPR expects to save money, by beating the speculators and by the sale of town lots. Second, this route will be 150 kilometres shorter. Third, the route solves CPR directors' fears of competition from the new Northern Pacific Railroad, south of the border.

The CPR wants its line to be able to pick up all east-west trade in Canada, effectively keeping the Americans out. Another, less important reason for deciding on this new route is that coal deposits near Lethbridge are available for fuelling the trains. For all these reasons, Fleming's route, charted over 10 years at a cost of more than $4 million to taxpayers, has been rejected. And this has been done though the CPR does not know if it will find a suitable pass through the southern Rockies.

Changing the route means the Canadian Pacific Railway will now run through a prairie region described by many as a desert, though others say it is well-watered. It also means the fertile lands around Edmonton, in the northwest, will be without a line.

The imposing Dorchester Penitentiary under construction in 1881 in New Brunswick. When completed, this federal institution will house criminals from Nova Scotia, New Brunswick and Prince Edward Island.

Population tops 4-million mark in latest census

Settlers work together in a logging bee to clear land for farming in Muskoka.

Education is an important consideration in a new and growing country. Students pose proudly in front of their new school – Edmonton's first.

April 4, 1881

OTTAWA – More than 4.3 million people live in Canada, the census of 1881 says – 2,188,799 males and 2,136,031 females. The census, compiled over the last year by 3,183 enumerators, is intended to give the government information on which to base policies. For the settled areas, it is probably fairly accurate. Among the data collected are: the sizes of the various provinces; the sexes, ages, religions and occupations of the population; and details about farm animals and crops.

So what has Ottawa learned? First, the country covers 8,987,937 square kilometres. The province with the highest population is Ontario, with 1,923,228 people, followed by Quebec with 1,359,027. The smallest population is in British Columbia – 49,459 people. The largest group is French; 1,299,161 people, with more than a million living in Quebec. Surprisingly, the next largest is not English, but Irish: 957,403, to be exact. Canadians of English origin are third, with 882,894 souls. Meanwhile, on the other end of the population scale, Canada has 1,172 people of Spanish or Portuguese origin, 1,009 Icelanders, and 667 Jews. No figures are given for native peoples.

More fascinating facts from the number counters: there are 37 towns and cities with more than 5,000 people in Canada. However, with the exception of Victoria, B.C. (5,935), none lie west of Winnipeg (7,985). The largest city is Montreal with 140,747 souls, followed by Toronto at 86,415.

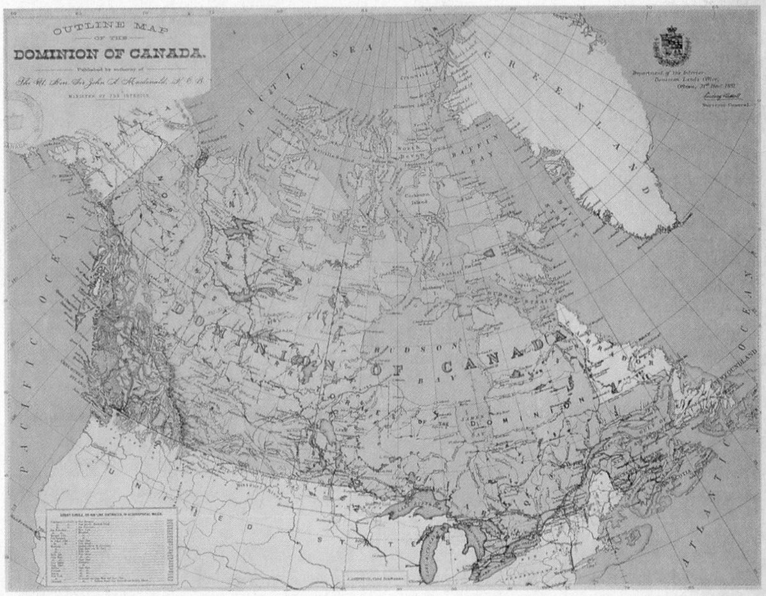

Map of the Dominion of Canada prepared by the Department of the Interior.

Doctor says prime minister recovering

May, 1881

LONDON, England – Canada's ailing Prime Minister Sir John A. Macdonald is in London to consult medical doctor Andrew Clark. In late March, Macdonald "broke down, pulse at forty-nine, and great pain and disturbance in liver and bowels." Canadian Dr. James Grant feared cancer, but Dr. Clark diagnoses "catarrh of the stomach, with a gouty state of body, not amounting to gout." He prescribes a simple diet and lots of rest.

Three McLean brothers hang for murder

Jan. 31, 1881

NEW WESTMINSTER, B.C. – The three McLean brothers, Archie, Allan and Charley, were hanged here today for murder. Archie, the youngest, was 17. The boys were the sons of chief trader Donald McLean and Sophia Grant, an Indian, who raised them herself after McLean was killed in the 1864 Chilcotin uprising to defend Indian land rights.

The sons soon proved to be uncontrollable and were arrested in 1879 on a charge of horse theft by the government agent of the Kamloops district, John Ussher. But a friend, Alex Hare, helped them escape from jail and joined them as they terrorized local ranchers.

Ussher, with William Palmer, a rancher whose horse the gang had stolen, John McLeod and "Ammo" Shumway, set out after the four outlaws, finding them holed-up near Brigade Lake and calling on them to surrender. McLeod was shot in the face, but survived. Ussher was killed. A large posse was formed and captured the young men at Nicola Lake. They were brought to New Westminster, found guilty of murder, and hanged.

12 public hospitals serve all of Ontario

March 1, 1881

TORONTO – There are 1.9 million people in Ontario, and only 12 public hospitals to serve them all. Worse yet, all but two of these are in Toronto, Hamilton, London, Kingston and Ottawa. Recent government figures indicate only one in every 350 Ontarians used a public hospital last year. As well, since the births and deaths handled by these institutions come to 343 and 300, respectively, it's obvious most Ontarians are relying on home care.

Manitoba boundary extended to include disputed territory

Aug. 15, 1881

WINNIPEG – The lieutenant-governor of Manitoba today signed a proclamation extending provincial jurisdiction eastward to the community of Rat Portage [Kenora]. The Manitoba government hopes the move will end the ongoing controversy between this province and Ontario based on the uncertainty as to which province can claim Rat Portage as its own. That community is located in Ojibwa Indian country through which the boundary between the neighboring provinces has never been surveyed.

Part of the motivation for the Manitoba proclamation has to do with liquor control. Drunkenness is a serious problem among the 2,000 men engaged in work crews building the main line of the Canadian Pacific Railway across Canada. The abuse of liquor now is so serious that it has become almost impossible to keep the construction work on schedule. This problem is likely to continue until one province or the other can send in police and liquor inspectors to control the flow of illicit spirits.

9,000 cows grazing near foothill towns

June 1, 1881

CALGARY – The fledgling cattle business continues to grow in western Canada. Cattlemen here estimate that there are at least 9,000 head in the herds around Calgary, High River, Pincher Creek and Fort Macleod. Since some experts have recently forecast profits of 60 percent for cattle ranchers, it is not surprising that there are large numbers of applications for leases of ranchland now being considered by the government in Ottawa.

The government, of course, is eager to see the land taken up, for it needs immigrants, settlements and successful businesses to help the Canadian Pacific Railway pay its own way. The Indians and Métis still greatly outnumber whites here. And Canadian settlement will cool American expansionist ambitions.

Governor general meets Blackfoot

Crowfoot addresses the Marquis of Lorne at a Blackfoot Crossing powwow.

Sept. 10, 1881

BLACKFOOT CROSSING, Alta. – Gov. Gen. the Marquis of Lorne attended a morning powwow with starving Blackfoot Indians who greeted the man they call Great Brother-in-Law with ceremonial dances and peace pipes. Young braves, nearly naked but for body paint, boasted of bravery in war and described their tragic plight: disappearance of the buffalo and loss of their lands to white men. Then Chief Crowfoot, in ragged robes, pleaded for more rations and help for his destitute people. Lorne advised him to turn to farming, saying the old ways of life were over.

Cochrane Ranch Company incorporated

May 1881

CALGARY – The Cochrane Ranch Company has been incorporated with capital of $500,000. Senator Matthew Cochrane, who owns a big leather and shoe business in Montreal, bought 1,000 shares at $100; his son James 500; and Dr. Duncan McEachran, also of Montreal, bought 1,000. Former North West Mounted Police superintendent James Walker will be the resident manager. He bought 100 shares. Now Cochrane's task will be to select the land for the ranch. From his conversations here, he is expected to look around the area 40 kilometres to the west and north of the Elbow River.

Cochrane was born in Compton, Que., an area known for breeding fine cattle. He did well in the leather business and was appointed to the Senate by Sir John A. Macdonald in 1872. Cochrane always wanted to be a successful stock breeder, and bought a 1,100-acre farm near his birthplace and started to stock it with prize cattle. He was one of the first cattlemen to see the opportunities created by the CPR and wrote to Sir John A. two years ago asking about stock farms in the Northwest Territories.

Lucius O'Brien painted his famous Sunrise on the Saguenay as his diploma piece for the new Royal Canadian Academy of Arts in 1880. O'Brien then deposited this work with the new National Gallery of Canada.

Witty Mark Twain on Montreal visit

1881

MONTREAL – "This is the first time I ever was in a city where you can't throw a brick without breaking a church window." Famous American writer Mark Twain delivered this witticism tonight to a group of the most eminent Montrealers, gathered at the Windsor Hotel in his honor. Twain has been in town for the last six months, in which time he has tried to speak French. He admits he has never been mistaken for a Frenchman – except maybe by a horse.

Steamer tips; 181 feared to be dead

May 24, 1881

LONDON, Ont. – There are 181 people missing and feared drowned following tonight's capsizing of the steamship *Victoria* on the Thames River. The ship was bringing Victoria Day celebrants here following events at the waterworks park. About a mile from harbor, the overloaded *Victoria* suddenly careened to one side. The boiler broke loose, throwing the ship offbalance, and it flipped, tossing hundreds of people into the river. Many of these were trapped underwater by the upper deck, which broke loose. Charges are said to be pending against the owner.

Natives a minority in Manitoba, census reveals

Historic Old Fort Garry, seen here in former days, has just been demolished.

Spectators gather along the street in Portage La Prairie, Manitoba, to watch the last ox train pass through their community en route to new settlements.

Sept. 15, 1881

WINNIPEG – Officials of both the city of Winnipeg and the province of Manitoba admit to having great difficulty in validating aspects of the recent provincial census. What is clear, however, is that natives are now in the minority, a startling development when one considers they constituted 90 percent of the population only a decade ago. The recently released report, which reflects numbers inside the new provincial boundaries, states the provincial population has topped the 65,000 mark. The difficulty in pinpointing exact numbers arises from the rate at which Manitoba is being settled. In the late 1870s, more than 6,000 Mennonites and 1,446 Icelanders arrived. While 1876 was an oddity, in that comparatively few immigrants arrived, the influx continued in subsequent years with totals of 11,500 in 1879, 18,000 in 1880, and 28,600 in 1881. A serious agricultural depression in the British Isles greatly increased immigration from that source. In that same period, some 2,000 French-Canadian families arrived from the United States.

Observers say immigrants have settled much of the best land in southwestern Manitoba. More recent arrivals are crossing the province's western boundary in search of homesteads in the Northwest Territories.

A feature of the settlement has been the arrival of major parties of colonists from one area of Europe who prefer to settle together in the new land. One such group, called simply the "Whellams party," has settled in the valley of the Little Saskatchewan. Other large parties of farmers and their families have settled near the new community of Shoal Lake, and along the banks of the Birdtail River. Students of civic and provincial growth report that the rapid population growth is forcing an accelerated rate of change on Winnipeg's available services. New parties of settlers often must sleep on the floors of unfinished buildings. The Métis, Country-born and Indian populations are now greatly outnumbered.

Posters attract many new settlers.

Newfoundland OKs railway to interior

Aug. 9, 1881

NEWFOUNDLAND – After years of debate, the colony has decided to proceed with a railway to Hall's Bay on the northeast coast, with a branch line to Harbour Grace. The government of William Whiteway is convinced Newfoundland cannot survive if it continues to depend exclusively on the fisheries. The government wants to develop the interior and provide access to the vast mineral, timber and agricultural resources found there. The fish merchants have opposed the plan, claiming it will lead to higher wages and higher taxes.

Signs of disaster plague Arctic expedition

Sept. 29, 1881

LADY FRANKLIN BAY, Ellesmere Island – The American Arctic expedition has been in its base on the north shore of the bay here for only six weeks – and there are already signs of disaster. The expedition, consisting of 24 Americans and two Inuit, is led by a Civil War veteran called Adolphus Washington Greely. His task is to establish a U.S. base as part of the International Polar Year campaign. From the base scientists will take observations to add to man's knowledge of the Arctic. But Greely has a second task: to reach the North Pole, or to go farther north than the British have done.

Soon after the base was set up Greely noticed that his two lieutenants, James Lockwood and Frederick Kislingbury, stayed in bed long after the enlisted men were at work. Greely admonished both officers and Kislingbury asked to be sent home. But the *Proteus,* the ship that brought the expedition, had unloaded the stores and left for the south as Kislingbury was trudging across the ice to get on board. So Greely has as one of his two officers a man who hates him and will not accept orders. In addition, one of the scientists, Dr. Octave Pavy, has an obsession – to reach the North Pole at any cost, and he, too, refuses to accept orders from Greely.

5,000 attend first Acadian congress

July 21, 1881

MEMRAMCOOK, N.B. – Some 5,000 people attended the first "national" congress of Acadians. Hundreds participated in talks on various subjects, including the "Acadianization" of the church. Quebec supported the nationalist movement last year when it invited Acadians to its gathering of North American francophones, calling the Maritimers "an invincible race that neither war nor exile has been able to curb or destroy, a branch full of sap, violently torn from a large tree, but now reborn under the sun of freedom."

1882

Brandon, Man., Jan. 19. Will White publishes the first edition of the Brandon *Sun*.

Ottawa, April 21. The House of Commons passes the Costigan resolutions respectfully requesting that the British grant Ireland home rule.

Dublin, May 6. Two British cabinet ministers are murdered by Irish extremists, exacerbating British outrage against the Costigan resolutions.

Prince Edward Island, May 30. The Bank of Prince Edward Island, the Island's first native bank, files for bankruptcy. It was ruined by dishonesty, recession, and poor administration.

Canada, May. Several thousand Jewish refugees fleeing anti-Jewish pogroms in Russia arrive in Montreal and Toronto, more than doubling the cities' Jewish populations.

Arctic, Aug. 1. The first International Polar Year kicks off. The international scientific venture will involve 12 stations scattered throughout the Arctic to make magnetic and meteorological observations.

Regina, Aug. 23. The settlement at Pile of Bones Creek is named Regina, and the CPR reaches the area for the first time.

Toronto, November. The first Canadian Rugby Football Union championship is played with Osgoode Hall defeating the Montreal football club.

Nova Scotia. The Nova Scotia Steel Company produces the first steel ingots in Canada.

Northwest Territories. The Russo-Jewish Committee of London tries to settle 27 Jewish farmers on homesteads near Moosomin [Saskatchewan]. The attempt fails because of bad planning and the settlers' lack of experience. They find work in Winnipeg.

Fort Calgary, Northwest Territories. The first white woman homesteader arrives from eastern Canada.

Ellesmere Island. A U.S. sledge expedition from Fort Conger led by James Lockwood reaches a record northern latitude off the north coast of Greenland, part of International Polar Year.

Winnipeg. There are 86 hotels, along with 64 grocery stores, selling whisky. Police jail more than 2,000 drunks in 1882.

Halifax. Women are admitted to Dalhousie University.

Prairie portion of N.W.T. divided in four

Settlers break land for crops on this prairie area in the southern N.W.T.

May 8, 1882

OTTAWA – The government today divided the prairie section of the Northwest Territories into four provisional districts. A federal order-in-council authorizes the designation of Assiniboia, Saskatchewan, Athabasca and Alberta. The first three names are of longstanding significance on the plains, while the fourth is one of the given names of Her Excellency Princess Louise, the wife of the Marquis of Lorne, the governor general.

In making this announcement, the federal government released no information concerning possible representation from the new districts. However, observers of the territorial government believe designating the four new areas is the first step in the extension of public services for the growing number of settlers living there.

New CPR manager on the job today

Jan. 1, 1882

WINNIPEG – William Cornelius Van Horne has begun work as the new general manager of the Canadian Pacific Railway. The former superintendent of the Chicago, Milwaukee and St. Paul lines is famous in railway circles, "a man of wonderful power and shrewdness," according to the *Railway Journal*.

When CPR president George Stephen asked for a man with the skill and experience to drive the line through to the Pacific, executive committee member J.J. Hill recommended Van Horne. "You need a man of great mental and physical power to carry this line through," he said. "Van Horne can do it." Last fall, Van Horne inspected the rails from Winnipeg to the end of the line. An avid gardener, he is said to be impressed with the quality of soil and crops along the railway's path. Informed sources say Van Horne's first move will be to warn land speculators against buying lots until he confirms the locations of future CPR stations.

Horse-drawn streetcar debuts in Winnipeg

Oct. 20, 1882

WINNIPEG – James Wilson was at the controls this morning when a horse-drawn streetcar made its initial run. The track now in use is on the west side of Main Street from the site of Lower Fort Garry to the new city hall. The track of 16-kilogram steel meets the terms of the contract in which The Winnipeg, Portage Avenue and City Park Street Railway Company agrees to have at least 1.6 kilometres of track in operation within six months.

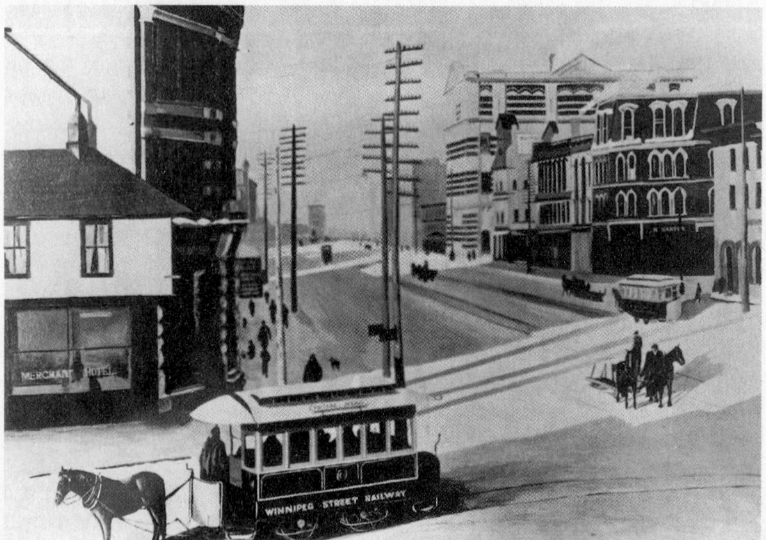

The Winnipeg Street Railway is now offering a horse-drawn streetcar service.

MPs nix Ontario's Rivers-Streams Act

April 14, 1882

OTTAWA – The Commons sat into the night to debate Ontario's Rivers and Streams Act, before disavowing the legislation for the second time. Last year, the Ontario legislature initially passed the act which would protect the public's access to rivers, streams and creeks. It was to give everyone the right to transport logs down streams, if they paid a toll set by cabinet to persons who made stream improvements such as dams or timber slides.

The federal government, which under the British North America Act may disallow provincial legislation within a year of receiving it, rejected the act and now is turning thumbs down on its re-enactment by Ontario this year. The Ontario Liberal government had introduced the act at a time when a Liberal and a Conservative lumberman were battling in the courts over the Liberal's right to use stream improvements made by the Conservative.

Postal service expands west along with railway

The Canadian Pacific Railway moves a house near Birds Hill, Manitoba.

The Canadian Pacific mail train is making its way further and further west. Postal service will be greatly improved when the railway is complete.

1882

CALLENDER, Ont. – Canadian Pacific Railway's push to link the country in a steel transportation network is breaking new ground as construction starts on the line west from this official terminus. Indeed, the CPR's expansion has already opened new horizons for the postal department. As the railway pushes west this decade, a moving post office known as "End of the Line" goes with it, providing mail and financial services for new settlers.

This summer, 5,000 workmen have been employed to work on the transcontinental railway. Funding has been given a boost with Ottawa's decision to provide a grant of $3,200 a mile to selected railways, replacing an earlier subsidy offered by Quebec and Ontario.

Further west, a decision to abandon the Yellowhead Pass route has been approved by an act of Parliament, and the Canadian Pacific Railway will follow a more southerly route through the Rockies.

Mail is delivered by "mud wagon" in areas where the railway does not go.

Qu'Appelle Valley Farming Co. born

May 12, 1882

QU'APPELLE, N.W.T. – W.R. Bell has a plan, and if it works, in the next six years there will be close to 300 families living east of Qu'Appelle. Bell, of Brockville, Ont., is the general manager of the Qu'Appelle Valley Farming Company, just incorporated today.

With government assistance, Bell and his colleagues have bought 23.3 square kilometres of land along the Canadian Pacific Railway. They had to buy the even numbered sections from the government and the odd numbered from the CPR, at a cost of $1.25 per acre. The land will be parcelled into 213-acre farms which will be somewhat improved before being sold to settlers. President of this enterprise is John Northwood, and secretary-treasurer is H.J. Eberts.

Bank of N.S. opens branch in Winnipeg

April 15, 1882

WINNIPEG – The Bank of Nova Scotia today became the fifth eastern bank with a branch in this community. E.H. Taylor is general manager, and David Forgan is accountant of the new office which is operating under straitened circumstances. Taylor brought $40,000 in cash with him as he made his way here from Toronto via Chicago and Minneapolis. At the time of opening, this cash was all he had to work with, for his package of account books failed to arrive. Taylor and Forgan today were recording their transactions on wrapping paper.

Until the security is improved at their new office, Taylor will have to sleep in front of the safe, and he has let it be known that he is armed with a revolver.

Statutes incorporate electric companies

May 17, 1882

OTTAWA – Parliament passed statutes incorporating two Canadian electric companies today, ushering in a new age in power to this country. One company, the Edison Electric Light Company of Canada, is a subsidiary of the Edison Electric Light Company of New York.

The Canadian arm was formed because patent laws in this country require that equipment for electrical installations must be made here if owners of foreign inventions wish to maintain Canadian patent rights. Three Canadians were listed among Edison's shareholders. Thomson-Houston Electric Light Company of Canada, based in Montreal, was also incorporated.

Ryerson dies after career as educator

Feb. 19, 1882

TORONTO – Egerton Ryerson, a major player in the development of public education in Ontario, died today at 78. Ryerson was appointed Upper Canada's chief superintendent of education back in 1844. During his 32 years of service, he established and edited the *Journal of Education.* Prior to becoming superintendent, he was the first head of the University of Victoria College, then in Cobourg.

Ryerson's early career was as a minister, the first Methodist missionary to reside on the Mississauga Indian Reserve west of Toronto, and as editor of the *Christian Guardian,* the church's publication. Politically, his early support for the Reform party waned in response to the extremes of William Lyon Mackenzie, whom he later opposed. ▷

247 Russian-Jews escaping pogroms arrive at Winnipeg

June 1, 1882

WINNIPEG – They're a long way from the shetls of Russia, but it's home just the same for 247 Jews who arrived in this bustling railroad centre today. The Jews, refugees from brutal pogroms perpetrated against their native towns in Russia, have been offered free land to settle, although no government officials were able to confirm when the newcomers would be able to get their land and begin homesteading. While they wait, the penniless, weary group has been taken under the wing of the small local Jewish community, which celebrated their arrival with a kosher meal. The refugees will stay at an immigration shed at the mouth of the Assiniboine River.

The Winnipeg Jews are among the 1,000 Canada has agreed to accept as refugees as a humanitarian effort in response to the growing concern about Russian pogroms against Jews. Jewish immigration to Canada is being co-ordinated by the Montreal-based Jewish Immigrant Aid Society, which greets the refugees before they're sent off to their new homes.

Salvation Army starts Canadian corps

Jack Addie and Joe Ludgate organize Salvation Army activities in London.

Lieut. Bathgate, Capt. Churchill and Cadet Jones of the Salvation Army.

July 15, 1882

TORONTO – The Salvation Army has launched a campaign against Canada. At the request of founder William Booth, formerly a Methodist preacher, Maj. Thomas Moore has established the first official Salvation Army corps in the country.

It's likely that residents of this city and London, Ont., are already familiar with the street meetings conducted by the "soldiers" of this army. Mr. and Mrs. William Freer, "Irish Annie" Maxwell, and Mrs. Shaw have frequently appeared on Toronto street corners. In May, English immigrants Jack Addie and Joe Ludgate organized an outdoor meeting in London.

A Salvation Army assault on a town is a sight to behold. Dressed in motley uniforms, playing cornets and thumping on bass drums, the soldiers march through the streets, singing evangelical messages to popular beer hall tunes. Often they are rewarded by a shower of tomatoes, rotten eggs and other missiles. To be fair, however, it must be stated that the Salvation Army has carried out some fine work in Britain, sheltering the homeless, feeding the hungry, and rescuing fallen women and drunkards.

Artist Fred Finley depicts a fleet of York Boats of the Hudson's Bay Company. First developed about 1826 at the York Factory Post, these uniquely Canadian vessels were designed to carry large loads of furs and supplies. Made of selected spruce, they were powered by sails or long oars depending on the conditions of the weather and water.

Tories crush Liberals in federal election

June 20, 1882

OTTAWA – John A. Macdonald got the mandate he wanted to complete an ambitious project, as the prime minister's Conservatives crushed the Liberals in the federal election today. The Tories won 139 seats, to 72 for the Liberals, down slightly from the 142-64 edge they enjoyed previously. The result will assure Macdonald up to five more years in power, by which time the Canadian Pacific Railway across the country, which the PM has pushed, will be almost completed.

Expecting a tough fight in Ontario from Liberal leader Edward Blake and the province's Liberal premier, Oliver Mowat, Macdonald gave up his British Columbia seat to return to a riding in Ontario (Lennox) for this election.

Rail line to link Fort William and Selkirk

June 7, 1882

FORT WILLIAM, Ont. – The federal government has issued a contract to complete the Canadian Pacific Railway between this centre in northwestern Ontario and Selkirk, Man. The government's contract calls for this section of the line to be finished by July 1 of next year.

A related proposal is the construction of a line linking Sault Ste. Marie and the Canada Central, and the establishment of ship service on the upper Great Lakes to Fort William. This would in effect give Canadian Pacific a combined railway-ship route linking the communities of Selkirk and Montreal.

Big Bear signs pact for starving Cree

Big Bear, chief of the Plains Cree.

Dec. 8, 1882

FORT WALSH, N.W.T. – The last major Canadian plains Indian chief outside of the treaty system finally adhered to Treaty No. 6 today. Starvation has brought Big Bear and his band to the treaty council fire.

Just recently, Dr. Augustus Jakes, the NWMP physician, visited Cree camps, Big Bear's included, around Fort Walsh. He reports: "They are literally in a starving condition and destitute of the commonest necessaries of life. The disappearance of the buffalo has left them not only without food, but also without robes, moccasins and adequate tents or tepees. ... Their clothing for the most part was miserable and scanty in the extreme. I saw little children at this inclement season, snow having fallen, who had scarcely rags to cover them. Of food they possessed little or none."

Big Bear, in effect, had to sign in order to become eligible for government rations. If he did not, the 57-year-old chief and his band would starve to death over the coming winter.

N.W.T. government focused in Regina

The NWMP badge. The force's headquarters are now in Regina.

Dec. 6, 1882

REGINA – The political structure of the Northwest Territories is gradually falling into place. The new lieutenant-governor, Edgar Dewdney, is concentrating the government at Regina on the revised CPR line, instead of at Battleford. The North West Mounted Police headquarters has moved here, and the police barracks and Government House will be built adjacent to land owned by Dewdney.

Battleford was chosen as territorial capital in 1876 because it was located on the projected route of the transcontinental railway. When the CPR changed plans last year, the search for a new capital began.

Renowned aesthete Oscar Wilde lectures in Charlottetown

Oct. 11, 1882

CHARLOTTETOWN – Irish poet and Aesthetic Movement spokesman Oscar Wilde tonight spoke at Market Hall, where he was politely received, though some hecklers' asides inspired one irate citizen to shout, "Two-thirds of the young men in Charlottetown are rogues." Wilde declined to pursue the theme. A newspaper described the leader of the beauty cult: "We saw him make his appearance from the back staircase, we saw his intense look of Pre-Raphaelite wonder as he viewed the walls, gazed on the beauty of the platform, and sniffed the redolent smells of stale eggs, butter and cabbage."

Not all Charlottetown gentlemen are as well-behaved as these in Queen Square.

Minister John Lake names Saskatoon

Aug. 18, 1882

SASKATOON – John Lake, a Methodist minister with the Temperance Colonization Company of Toronto, has named the site for a settlement here "Saskatoon," the Cree name for a berry. Lake headed a survey team that selected the site on the South Saskatchewan.

Temperance advocates are attracted to the land in Saskatchewan district of the Northwest Territories because it is well north of the railway and temptations are fewer there – away from the hothouse activity brought by railway construction and development. Settlers will arrive in Saskatoon next year.

Canadian Rugby Football Union founded

Oct. 21, 1882

TORONTO – The Canadian Rugby Football Union was formed today, giving the fledgling sport its first national organization. William Hamilton Merritt, Junior, of Toronto was appointed president.

The new league follows on the heels of the formation of the Quebec Rugby Football Union in February of this year, with teams from Montreal, Britannia, McGill University, Quebec and Bishop's College. The Quebec league was Canada's first, which is appropriate, because the modern-day adaption of English rugby was first played in the province by students at McGill.

Moose Jaw Creek to be future rail centre?

July 2, 1882

MOOSE JAW CREEK, N.W.T. – James Hamilton Ross and Hector Sutherland are gambling on hearsay and their mathematical skills. They arrived here today from Winnipeg, and calculate that, if the rumor is true that the railroad will build divisional points about every 400 kilometres, this will be the location of a future rail centre.

If Ross and Sutherland decide the land is suitable, they will bring out a group of permanent settlers.

Woman's lost love is subject of novel

1882

QUEBEC CITY – A novel by a Quebec woman is being hailed as a literary breakthrough. Laura Conan's *Angéline de Montbrun* describes the anguish of a woman's lost love – a sharp departure from the typical historical and religious themes of Quebec literature to date.

A native of La Malbaie whose real name is Félicité Angers, the author has already produced several historical novels focusing on lesser known figures. *Angéline de Montbrun,* however, deals with the struggle of a heroine trying to find expression for her love – a subject local clergy will no doubt condemn.

1883

Montana Territory, U.S., March. In exile since 1878, Louis Riel becomes an American citizen.

Northwest Territories, July 28. Langdon and Shepard crews lay a record 10.27 kilometres of track in one day near Strathmore, using a new device, the "Railway Track-layer," a conveyor system that moves tracks and ties forward from a railway flatcar.

Winnipeg, Dec. 19. A meeting of the Farmers' Protective Union of Manitoba drafts a Bill of Rights demanding "provincial rights" for Manitoba from Ottawa, including the control of public lands.

Canada, Dec. 31. The CPR has spent $59 million on its railway, and received $21 million from the government in cash and bonds.

Ontario. Robert Harris is commissioned to paint *The Fathers of Confederation*.

Cobourg, Ont. Augusta Stowe-Gullen graduates from Victoria College, becoming the first woman to get a medical degree in Canada. Her mother, Emily Stowe, Canada's first woman doctor, had to go to school in the U.S.

Toronto. The Toronto Women's Literary Club, formed in 1876 by Emily Stowe to work for women's suffrage, is renamed the Toronto Women's Suffrage Association.

Sudbury, Ont. Sudbury is founded and a huge deposit of copper and nickel ore is found during digging for the CPR.

Ottawa. The Privy Council finds Ontario liquor legislation valid as it deals with a local matter. Ontario and Ottawa have been disputing whether liquor control is a provincial or federal matter.

Canada. There are 12 crimes punishable by death in Canada, including murder, rape, arson, theft, and burglary.

Ottawa. PM John A. Macdonald gives widows the vote.

Kingston, Ont. Dr. Jennie Trout, the first licensed woman doctor in Canada, helps found the Women's Medical College at Queen's University.

Canada. Military schools are laying the groundwork for a permanent Canadian military force. There are artillery schools at Kingston, Quebec, and Victoria, and infantry schools at Fredericton, St. Jean, Toronto, and Winnipeg.

Winnipeg's city hall is going to pieces

City hall in Winnipeg, built on unstable ground, has to be propped up.

April 15, 1883

WINNIPEG – Officials at Winnipeg city hall are prepared to confirm what the ratepayers have for some months suspected – the municipal building they conduct their business in is crumbling. Ever since its official opening in March 1876, Winnipeg's city hall has been in a state of accelerated decay. The trouble began with faulty foundation work which caused cracks to appear as the building settled. In 1881 and 1882 walls had to be shored up. Late in 1882 an addition was built, but part of the brickwork was completed following freeze-up, and the mortar did not set.

If the structure is condemned, it will be a tremendous blow to civic pride. Part of the motivation for its construction was the building boom at the end of the last decade. The structure exemplified the city's optimism. That boom has collapsed, just as city hall appears to be doing.

Booze pours into west along with settlers

June 10, 1883

WINNIPEG – If this city fails to provide some recreational activities, more men will continue to spend more money and more nights in the saloons. This is the message Rev. A.A. Cameron is preparing for parishioners. Cameron, a Baptist minister, recently made a tour of 30 of this community's growing number of watering holes. By actual count, he found 20-30 tipplers in the smaller saloons, and up to 150 or more in larger ones. In his quest for reasons why their time was spent this way, he was told it was for lack of any alternative.

Cameron's study and his sermons may force the city council into action. Only a few weeks ago the Manitoba branch of the Dominion Temperance Alliance convened a meeting which was attended by the heads of local churches. These religious leaders plan to make a presentation to the provincial government concerning the need for controls on liquor sales. It is anticipated that the public will support their efforts.

Ontario's Mowat in with reduced majority

Feb. 27, 1883

TORONTO – Premier Oliver Mowat and his Liberal government have been returned to power, although with a reduced majority. The Grits have an edge of 12 seats, as opposed to 23 before dissolution.

Much of the change is attributed to a pamphlet entitled *Facts for Irish Electors*. In it, an appeal was made to Catholics not to vote for the Liberals. It said the governing party had given the higher civil service posts to Protestants. As well, it cited quotes by George Brown, late Liberal editor of the *Globe*, to "prove" the Grits are "anti-Catholic." Obviously some voters agreed.

Grand Opera House full for Lillie's show

1883

TORONTO – An affair with the Prince of Wales did nothing to hurt Lillie Langtry's box office appeal, as the English entertainer performed before a full house at the Grand Opera House last night. Tickets for the performance and two others here, had been sold out long before she arrived.

Lillie met the prince, heir to the British throne, six years ago, and a relationship soon developed. She became the first society woman to go on stage in 1881, when she played in *She Stoops to Conquer* at the Haymarket Theatre, in London, England. Initially, some critics greeted Lillie with skepticism, but now she is developing as an actress.

Lillie Langtry, English entertainer and friend of the Prince of Wales.

Argos are league's first rugby champs

1883

TORONTO – Ten years after the team was formed from members of Toronto's Argonaut Rowing Club, the Argonauts have won the first championship of the Ontario Rugby Football Union, which was formed in January of this year. The Argonauts, who wear uniforms of double (light and dark) blue, the colors of Oxford and Cambridge universities in England, will meet the Quebec Rugby Football Union champion next to decide the overall Canadian champion.

Buffalo sightings become a rarity

Fall 1883

MANITOBA – In southwestern Manitoba, everywhere the prairie is dotted with old buffalo skulls. It is now roughly 20 years since the last big herds were killed off in this area, although some stragglers have since been seen. Just last year C.C. Helliwell of Brandon saw eight buffalo near Souris, the largest number seen in a decade.

This fall there was one sighting, perhaps the last that will ever be witnessed in this province. A.S. Barton of Boissevain saw an old buffalo bull crossing the Souris plain. Only a handful of the millions of wild plains buffalo that once ranged the Canadian prairies are left.

The buffalo hunt as it was once known on the prairies is a thing of the past.

Eleven Islanders sign up for phones

1883

CHARLOTTETOWN – "The city is a little one, the lawyers' offices are clustered around the courthouse, and the merchants do not seem disposed to bear the expense." Despite an initially gloomy assessment, Bell has installed the Island's first telephone exchange. Bell representative Robert Angus has signed 11 subscribers at $30 a year. Though it estimates it needs 25 for a viable exchange, Bell hopes the service will catch on.

This version of the telephone was invented by Cyrille Duguet in 1878.

First locomotive chugs into Medicine Hat

June 10, 1883

MEDICINE HAT – The first locomotive chugged into Medicine Hat today, completing another link in the construction of the Canadian Pacific Railway's transcontinental line. That leaves about 290 kilometres of prairie yet to have tracks laid over it. The line should be completed to the Rockies later this year. The rail project was unified under one control this spring when contractors hired by the government offered to step aside and turn the remainder of the job over to the CPR. The CPR took control a month ago under the same contract terms, except for a 15-percent deduction to account for preliminary work already completed by the contractors. On the section through the prairies, the railway was raised above the surface to protect the tracks from drifting snow during the winter.

But construction in the Rockies will be a much greater challenge. From the summit, it will follow river valleys westward, including those of the Kicking Horse River, Columbia and Beaver rivers to the Selkirks. From there the line will follow the Illecillewaet River to pick up the Columbia River again at Revelstoke, B.C. The railway's highest point will be some 1,600 metres above sea level, at the summit of the Rockies.

Capital of N.W.T. moved to Regina

March 27, 1883

REGINA – An order-in-council has been passed transferring the capital of the Northwest Territories from Battleford to Pile of Bones Creek – or Regina, as it was recently renamed. The move puts the N.W.T. capital on the Canadian Pacific Railway, which was to follow the Saskatchewan River past Battleford but was instead built across the southern plains.

The decision to move the capital has sparked many rumors. There are hints of land speculation, vested interests in the railway and political influence.

Canada Cotton Mill enlightens guests

April 6, 1883

CORNWALL, Ont. – Noted guests were "electrified" when the lights were turned on today in Canada Cotton Mill's new weave shed, making it the first plant in Canada to use electrical lighting. Designed by the "Wizard," Thomas Edison, the inventor of the light bulb, this installation takes place just one year after the first commercial incandescent lighting plant in the world was put into operation.

Electrical work at the Cornwall plant was done by local contractor John MacMillan. Measuring 150 metres by 36 metres, the shed can operate 24 hours a day, and, consequently, the mill's output of cottenades, ducks and flannelettes is expected to increase dramatically. Power for the plant is supplied by two Corlis engines.

CPR grain elevator in Port Arthur has 300,000-bushel capacity

Sept. 1, 1883

PORT ARTHUR [Thunder Bay], Ont. – The Canadian Pacific Railway has decided there's more to business than trains. So this year it built the first grain elevator at this shipping point, one capable of holding 300,000 bushels of wheat. The CPR has pushed hard to get this job down. The reason for the dedication is simple: the company wants to store wheat hauled on its railway from Manitoba, for shipment by its own freighters. These will sail between Port Arthur, and Owen Sound starting next season.

The S.S. Athabasca docks in front of Port Arthur's CPR grain elevator.

Scores look on as first CPR train arrives in Calgary

Ranchers living near Calgary seem to prefer horses to the new railway.

A home near Calgary. Trains may be the key to greater prosperity in the area.

Aug. 12, 1883

CALGARY – The first Canadian Pacific Railway train steamed into Calgary yesterday, as townspeople, some of whom had never seen a train before, watched from the hillsides around the tiny settlement. With the arrival of the CPR, the community of several hundred doubled in size in one day. A tent city has grown up overnight on the east bank of the Elbow River amid the assortment of tents and shacks already there.

Until yesterday, Calgary was an economic outpost of Montana. All vital supplies came from Fort Benton, the steamboat depot on the Missouri River to the south. All Calgary mail carried U.S. stamps, as it was posted south of the border. Now Calgary has economically become part of Canada. With its own rail link, the hamlet hopes to become the distribution centre for Canadian land north and south.

Just one major question remains – where will the CPR place its station? Most Calgarians believe it will be built where the settlement is now, on the east bank of the Elbow River, opposite the NWMP post. But nothing is certain. Everyone awaits the CPR's decision, one which will determine where the heart of the townsite will be.

Calgary records birth of first white child

Nov. 19, 1883

CALGARY – Yesterday Sarah Toyi Costello, wife of William H. Costello, gave birth to the first white child born in Calgary, a settlement of between 400 and 500 people, which was only reached a few months ago by the Canadian Pacific Railway. The 35-year-old Mrs. Costello and William, her Irish-born husband, only moved to Calgary earlier this year from Renfrew county, in the Ottawa Valley in Ontario. Father M.E. Claude baptized the day-old baby boy today at St. Mary's Roman Catholic church. At the parents' request, he named the child John Calgary Costello.

Meanwhile, another member of the Costello family, Sarah's sister-in-law Elizabeth Copps Costello, is in her eighth month of pregnancy. Elizabeth and her schoolteacher husband only arrived in August. With their baby on the way, John Calgary Costello will soon have a new cousin, and Calgary itself will celebrate the birth of the second white child born in the settlement.

Men dismount to get a closer look at the first white child born in Calgary.

Crew rescued as Marco Polo runs aground

July 25, 1883

CAVENDISH, P.E.I. – The *Marco Polo,* known as "the fastest ship in the world," was wrecked and abandoned in stormy weather today off this village on the north coast of Prince Edward Island. All her crew were saved by local residents. The old ship was rotten, explained Capt. P.A. Bull, and she began to come apart in the storm. To save themselves, the crew drove her on to the beach under full sail. The ship ran aground and was stranded 910 metres from shore.

The *Marco Polo* was built in Saint John, New Brunswick, in 1851. Under Capt. "Bully" Forbes of the Black Ball Line, she once made the arduous round trip between Liverpool and Australia in 152 days, becoming the first ship to circumnavigate the world in less than six months.

American canoeists compete in Ontario

Aug. 24, 1883

STONEY LAKE, Ont. – The American Canoe Association met today at this lake near Peterborough for its annual regatta, marking the first time the event has been held in Canada. American canoeists from Maine to Colorado were in the big meet. The Knickerbocker Canoe Club of New York City travelled by rail in a parlor car, and then transferred to a steamboat. More ardent canoeists paddled and portaged, as is their custom.

Publication begins for Calgary Herald

Aug. 31, 1883

CALGARY – This community now has its own weekly newspaper. The first edition of the *Calgary Herald, Mining and Ranche Advocate and General Advertiser,* hit the streets today, the product of a handpress located in a tent near the junction of the Bow and Elbow rivers. The first edition is four pages in size. It is owned and produced by Andrew Armour and Thomas Braden. Copies will be delivered by the NWMP Postal Service.

Tupper summoned back from London

Dec. 5, 1883

OTTAWA – Faced with the continuing financial woes of the Canadian Pacific Railway, Prime Minister Sir John A. Macdonald has decided he needs help in his bid to push through government aid. So he has recalled Charles Tupper from London, where Tupper was representing Canada. Tupper is also the minister of railways and canals, and so, as Sir John said to him in a recent telegram, "You should be here."

The fact is that CPR stock is suffering the fate of most stocks these days; it is falling, as world prices decline. This means the company, now short of cash, is unable to raise money on the exchange. Only the government can save it.

Women at work in "sweating system"

1883

MONTREAL – The reality out on the streets of today's Quebec is that a husband's wages are often not enough to support his family. Mothers and daughters are picking up the slack, working in factories or in the home for wages. Hordes of Quebec women take in sewing to do in the home.

The clothing industry has become one of the largest industries in Quebec. The backbone of the industry is the thousands of French-Canadian and Jewish women working at home or in small workshops. It is called the "sweating system." Families work together, mothers and daughters, and they are paid by each piece of clothing they sew, rather than by the hour. Many women own their own sewing machines; others rent.

Most of the clothes made in Montreal are produced this way. A few large clothing factories concentrate in cutting clothes, which are then sent out to be sewn. Because of the railway, clothing companies can send work to rural women, as far as 48 kilometres from Montreal.

Women who work in the home are badly underpaid. Many slave away for 60 hours a week, earning only a few dollars each week, a fraction of what men make in such trades as carpentry. But the sweating system does have advantages for them. It lets women combine paid employment with housework and child raising. The women can also organize their time as they wish, because they are paid by the piece instead of the hour, so an otherwise exploitive system gives them a measure of freedom.

This medical school is for women only

Oct. 1, 1883

TORONTO – The first medical school for Canadian women has opened. Dr. Michael Barrett, professor of physiology at the Toronto School of Medicine, is president. Three of the seven members of the board of directors are women, and women will also serve on the faculty. Among the faculty members is Dr. Augusta Stowe-Gullen, who has been appointed demonstrator in anatomy. Dr. Stowe-Gullen is the daughter of Dr. Emily Howard Stowe, one of the founders of the new medical school.

The Toronto school is affiliated with the University of Toronto and Trinity College. Plans are already afoot to organize a second medical college for women in Kingston.

Christopher Winter's home in Birtle, Manitoba is made of sod. Settlers often find that this material is the most convenient for their first homes.

After one year in the bush of Manitoba, a settler has built a sod hut and a log cabin, and has begun to clear and fence his land for farming.

After 15 years in the bush, a settler has a comfortable log home, and wheat growing in his large fields. Roads and bridges provide good access.

The progress achieved in 30 years of settlement is illustrated by the large modern home, many farm buildings, good roads and fine carriages.

1884

Calgary, Feb. 18. The town's first school opens, attended by 12 children. The arrival of wives and families from the east led to the school opening.

London, July. The British Privy Council establishes the Ontario-Manitoba boundary along Lake of the Woods and the Albany River.

Duck Lake, Northwest Territories, August. Cree chiefs led by Big Bear meet in opposition to the Canadian government's Indian reserves policy, and agree to hold a larger council next summer.

Northwest Territories, summer. Indian Commissioner Edgar Dewdney tells PM John A. Macdonald that "sheer compulsion" is the only way to handle unco-operative plains Indians. He gets Macdonald to support an increase in the size of the Mountie force, and an amendment permitting the arrest of any Indian caught on a reserve other than his own without government approval.

Saint John, N.B., Sept. 7. German Franz Boas arrives after a year-long expedition exploring Cumberland Sound and Baffin Island with Inuit.

Calgary, Nov. 17. The town is incorporated; the population is over 500 and growing.

Winnipeg, Dec. 20. Westerners form the Manitoba and Northwest Farmers' Union, and draft a list of grievances against Ottawa.

Ontario. The province passes legislation to protect women and youth factory workers. It sets the minimum age for female workers at 14, and for male workers at 12. Women and youths may work for a maximum of 10 hours a day.

Hamilton. Woollen mill operatives, including women, form a Knights of Labor union local. The Knights have encouraged women members with "socials" for male and female workers.

Northwest Territories. The *Prince Albert Times and Saskatchewan Review* reverses its editorial policy in support of Riel after being bribed by Indian Commissioner Dewdney.

London. Hiram Maxim invents the machine-gun.

Montreal. Women are admitted to McGill University.

Canada. The various Canadian Methodist churches join together in a unified church.

Tyrrell unearths huge dinosaur skull

Joseph Tyrrell and his Geological Survey crew take a rest from their work.

Spring 1884

CALGARY – A battered buckboard sent by geologist Joseph Tyrrell has rolled into town bearing an unusual cargo – the fossilized skeletal remains of a very large, very old reptile. Tyrrell, 24, has been working for the Geological Survey of Canada in western and northern Canada for three years. He arrived in the badlands of the Alberta district this spring, and it was while searching for coal deposits that he came across a huge dinosaur skull. The remarkable discovery led Tyrrell to continue digging in search of further evidence of prehistoric life. Indeed, the sum total of his find is so great several wagon trips will be required to transport it all to Calgary.

Ontario-Quebec Railway leases create "right arm of the CPR"

This horse is frightened by the train crossing the frozen St. Lawrence.

Jan. 4, 1884

MONTREAL – The Canadian Pacific Railway vastly expanded its eastern Canadian operations today, leasing the Ontario and Quebec Railway. The deal not only gives the CPR access to O & Q terminals and facilities, but includes a major network owned by O & Q, including the Credit Valley from Toronto to London, and the Toronto, Grey and Bruce from Toronto to Owen Sound. As well, the O & Q is planning a line from Toronto to Montreal, via Peterborough and Smith Falls. According to CPR financier George Stephen, the deal establishes the "right arm of the CPR."

Seven survivors of Arctic expedition found

June 21, 1884

CAPE SABINE, Ellesmere Island – Rescuers have located the seven surviving members of an American scientific expedition into the Arctic camped at this bleak point of land in Smith Sound at the top of Baffin Bay. Starved, and so weak they could hardly move, the seven explorers have been in the north for three years.

Led by Lieut. Adolphus Greely of the American army, the expedition, which originally numbered 26 men, was stationed at Lady Franklin Bay at the northeast corner of Ellesmere Island. It had been sent to carry out experiments as part of the First International Polar Year, 1882-1883. When their relief ships did not arrive as expected, however, Greely and his men abandoned the station last August and made their way southwards in small boats.

As food supplies ran out, several of the men died of starvation. One committed suicide and another was executed for stealing rations. When rescued, survivors were gnawing on sealskin clothing and sipping on the last bottle of brandy. One man had lost both his hands and feet.

The cornerstone for Winnipeg's second city hall was laid in 1884. Nicknamed Winnipeg's Gingerbread House, this Victorian-style structure is topped with turrets and a picturesque clock.

$25 million federal loan saves the CPR – for now

Many northern Ontario natives still maintain traditional lifestyles. A CPR survey crew meets with these natives near the Hudson's Bay Company post.

The CPR Mountain Creek Bridge is now under construction in the Selkirks.

Feb. 28, 1884

OTTAWA – The Canadian Pacific Railway will not fold, at least not for a while. Relief comes in the form of a $25 million loan by the Macdonald government to the ailing railroad, which has been unable to raise its own money due to the poor state of the stock market.

The 11 resolutions that comprise the "CPR Bailout," as some are calling it, were introduced by the minister of railways and canals, Charles Tupper, on Feb. 1. Since then, the House has been the scene of loud and acrimonious protests over the measure by the opposition, chief among them its leader, Edward Blake. Blake seems to have enjoyed pillorying the government over the railway, a source of trouble to Sir John since the Pacific Scandal in the '70s. The opposition leader denounced the CPR in total, from its monopoly to its route changes and alleged invasions of other railways' territory.

The opposition has not been the only source of discontent for the government. Forty-two Conservative MPs from Quebec, backing their provincial government's campaign for more federal funding, hinted they might desert the government over the CPR issue if Macdonald didn't give in. This dissension has been well-reported in the media, something that has not helped CPR attempts at gaining more loans from private sources.

Indian revolt brewing on western plains

June 1884

BATTLEFORD, N.W.T. – The Northwest was one shot away from an Indian war today as 60 Mounties and about 20 volunteers squared off against 200 Cree, most armed and furious warriors on the adjoining reserves of chiefs Little Pine and Poundmaker near here. A massacre was narrowly averted when chiefs Big Bear, Little Pine, and Poundmaker shouted "Peace! Peace!" The incident occurred during perhaps the largest meeting of plains chiefs ever. To stir up opposition to the Canadian government's reserves policy, Big Bear sent runners to all the plains Indians, inviting them here to the meeting he called a Kawechetwemot or Thirst Dance, the major Cree religious ceremony, and a social and political event. The police were called when violence erupted between a young Cree and a government official.

People consider Big Bear the most important Indian leader on the prairies. He is a stunning man, courageous and eloquent, with a penetrating intellect. With chiefs Little Pine and Piapot, he has united the Cree against the government. He is accusing Ottawa of reneging on its treaty agreements, and asks for a new treaty negotiated with a new concept of reserves. The Cree chiefs want a large Indian territory set up on the prairies, where different tribes could live on adjoining reserves in autonomy from white society. They feel this would help protect their people from the domination of white culture.

But the government is against this idea because it sees a large Indian territory as a military threat and wants to keep Indian reserves separated. The government's goal is to make the Indians self-sufficient by transforming them into farmers, and eventually to "civilize" them. As the Indians have been threatened by starvation with the disappearance of the buffalo, the government has used food rations to coerce chiefs to sign treaties and retreat with their people to reserves. Big Bear and Little Pine have both signed treaties to get government rations for their people.

Eaton's catalogue already a "best-seller"

1884

TORONTO – Timothy Eaton has released a catalogue of the products sold in his Toronto store, giving Canadians, particularly those in rural farming regions and other remote areas, access to a variety of merchandise without having to leave their communities. On the catalogue's cover is a picture of Eaton's store on Yonge Street.

The T. Eaton Co. has just released this catalogue for mail order sales.

There are no illustrations in the 32-page publication, nor are there long descriptions of the goods for sale, but the simple list of items and their cost should be enough to give an idea of what is available. The catalogue is already a "best-seller," as it means people living in the remote areas of Canada can now buy items of the same quality as people living in downtown Toronto.

The reason for the appearance of the catalogue at this time is explained on the first page: "Owing to the immense increase in our Mail Order Department, we find it necessary to issue a catalogue in this style." Eaton's mail order department consists of two people working from behind wooden planks set up on empty cartons. It is tucked away in as inconspicuous a corner as possible. Clerks walk through the store, the shopper's list in hand, and pick up the items requested. ▷

Court frees woman from insane asylum

December 1884

MONTREAL – Rose Lynam won her freedom from the mental asylum at Longue Pointe today following a sordid court case that exposed the brutality of the present system of caring for the mentally ill. Mrs. Lynam entered the hospital in April 1882, after threatening her husband with an axe. In spite of the fact that some doctors found her to be perfectly sane, she has been held in Longue Pointe ever since then.

Evidence at the trial suggests her husband may have paid to keep her locked up. In any case, testimony revealed she was beaten by the nuns who run the asylum, handcuffed, stripped and kept in solitary confinement for long periods of time. Mrs. Lynam secured her freedom through the efforts of Alfred Perry, her former employer.

Amendment bans potlatch ceremony

April 19, 1884

OTTAWA – The governor general of Canada today gave royal assent to an amendment to the Indian Act which will outlaw the British Columbia native ceremony known as the "potlatch." According to the prime minister, Sir John A. Macdonald, the potlatch is a "debauchery of the worst kind," and the government is banning it under pressure from missionaries.

This traditional west coast Indian potlatch ceremony has just been banned.

The clergymen claim that as long as the natives are allowed to engage in these "give-all-away" feasts, which allegedly last for weeks and involve the consumption of alcohol, "orderly habits" and European notions of property accumulation will never take root among the Indians.

Liberal opposition leader Edward Blake conceded that the custom was harmful. He said that he had read accounts of how some natives' "considerable wealth ... is all dissipated in the insane exuberance of generosity." Yet Blake reminded the prime minister the Indian custom is an ancient and "inveterate" one, and he urged the government to use the law in an educative rather than a punitive manner. Experts, meanwhile, also urge caution. They believe that the potlatch is fundamental to the natives' culture, since it alone serves to validate newly inherited titles.

Loneliness and isolation a problem for women living out west

1884

HIGH RIVER, N.W.T. – Life may be rough for the men of the ranching country around here – but the women have a far rougher row to hoe. Not that there are very many women out here. One rancher claimed at a party that he could name only four unmarried white women living between here and the border. Many of the hardships affect both men and women. The hard winters; the monotonous diet and landscape; the dangers of accidents, disease and poor medical attention; and hard work for long hours. But society here is very masculine, offering men more purpose, greater freedom and many more opportunities for entertainment in the bars and brothels of the settlements and towns.

Mrs. F.C. Inderwick, rancher's wife.

For women, however, the thread that runs through their lives is loneliness. Mary Inderwick, originally from Ontario and who married rancher Charles Inderwick last year, wrote to her sister: "I ... long for a woman to come and live near me. ... I am at present the only white woman on this river, or the next, for that matter, as the next ranch is owned by a bachelor. I am 22 miles from a woman and though I like all the men and enjoy having them, I simply long to talk to a woman." But even when there was a woman to talk to she might not be too pleasant. "There are so many Englishmen here and a couple of Englishwomen," Mrs. Inderwick told her sister. "The latter are very different types, but the men are almost all nice."

The long days and nights of loneliness make the women who live on the ranches look forward all the more eagerly to a trip to town, or to a neighboring ranch, for the balls and dances held every two or three weeks. Dances are informal, with everyone, including local Indians, welcome. Food consists of coffee and sandwiches, served by wives in the kitchen or hall. The balls, for the elite, follow a far stricter code of conduct and provide an excuse to show off new dresses.

F.C. Inderwick, North Fork Ranch.

Métis leader Riel is back from exile; speech stirs crowd

July 19, 1884

PRINCE ALBERT, N.W.T. – The largest crowd in this town's history – about 500 people – turned out tonight to hear Louis Riel, recently returned from political exile in the United States. Riel told the crowd that all people in these territories, regardless of race, are oppressed by the federal government and should work together for redress.

It was a moderate, soft-spoken speech by the former leader of the Manitoba uprising of 1869-70, one his audience received enthusiastically. Riel said the people of the territories should first demand responsible government and the creation of provinces in the Northwest. He also said there should be compensation for the Indians, land grants for the Métis and relaxed land regulations for white settlers.

Métis of the Batoche area and their English half-breed neighbors brought Riel back to Canada earlier this month to agitate with the government on their behalf. Riel said he won't condone violence.

Toronto college admits first women

Oct. 1, 1884

TORONTO – University College at the University of Toronto has admitted its first female students, stirring the ongoing debate about the need for Canadian women to get a higher education. Many Canadians argue there is no need; however, a growing number of girls have been educated since the establishment of free public schools in 1871, the inevitable result being that some now have an insatiable thirst for learning.

University College is not the first college in Canada to admit women, an honor that belongs to Victoria College in Cobourg. Women have attended Queen's in Kingston since 1878. And, in 1882, Miss Hattie B. Stewart graduated from Mount Allison, New Brunswick, becoming the first woman to earn a bachelor's degree at a Canadian university.

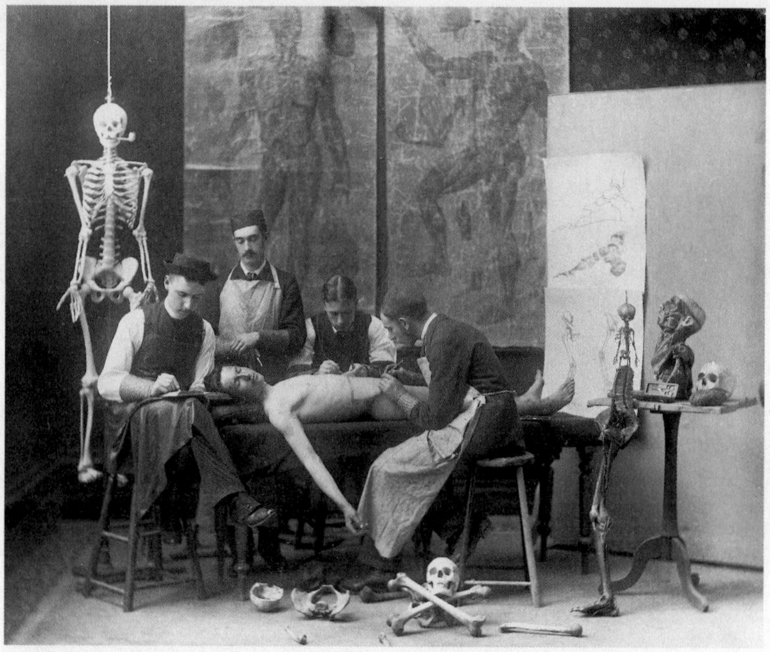

University medical classes are usually considered unsuitable for women.

Barnardo children reach Peterborough

August 1884

PETERBOROUGH, Ont. – The first group of Barnardo children has reached this Ontario town. Last November, railway executive George A. Cox donated Hazelbrae, a large home on the outskirts of Peterborough, to Dr. Thomas John Barnardo, the famous child rescuer. Barnardo opened his first shelter for homeless waifs in London in 1870, and in recent years has sent many children to Canadian farms. His slogan is: "No destitute child ever refused admission." In 1882, a small group of Barnardo boys was sent to a temporary shelter in Hamilton.

The diminutive and dynamic Barnardo is currently visiting this country, speaking on the benefits of his work and assuring critics the children are well-trained.

Acadians focus on protecting their culture

Aug. 15, 1884

MISCOUCHE, P.E.I. – In recent years, Acadian leaders have feared that the pressures of modern society were succeeding, where last century's deportations failed, in destroying their culture. Today the second National Acadian Convention met here in an attempt to check this decay.

Talk ranged from the problems of out-migration and agriculture to the selection of a flag and anthem. "The flag will be our rallying symbol," declared one observer, "and the song the expression of our attachment to all that is related to religion and to our native land." The delegates settled on a French tricolor with a gold star in the blue section, and an anthem based on the latin hymn *Ave stella Maris.*

Sheep farming restrictions anger ranchers

October 1884

CALGARY – Influential cattlemen, close friends of the government in Ottawa, have persuaded the territorial government to restrict the area available to sheep farmers. The order states that sheep farming may not be conducted north of the Bow River – so that the land is left free for cattle. But ranchers with sheep believe that Senator Matthew Cochrane is behind the order and that he is protecting his own interests. They claim that the order will soon be lifted, once the politics are sorted out.

Sheep, in any quantity, have been brought into the land south of Calgary only recently. Sheep ranching has not proved successful because of the harsh winters and heavy lambing losses.

Wolseley leads voyageurs, Indians to Egypt to aid British force

Sept. 7, 1884

WINNIPEG – Gen. Garnet Wolseley and a force of 386 men left today en route to Egypt. Their assignment is to provide relief for British Gen. Charles Gordon, now under siege at Khartoum.

Wolseley describes the members of his expeditionary force as *voyageurs.* Many of them are French-Canadian and some are Indians. Once Wolseley decided that the Nile River was the most likely approach to Khartoum, he selected individuals he knew to have considerable practical experience on the lakes and rivers of Canada West. Wolseley is well known in the area, having been in charge of the Red River expedition in 1870.

Wolseley's "voyageurs" pose for photo at Ottawa before setting out for Egypt.

Petition to Ottawa has Métis demands

Dec. 16, 1884

ST. LAURENT, N.W.T. – The Northwest can "be neither prosperous nor happy" unless major changes are made, the government has been told. The Métis and English half-breeds of this area today sent a petition to Ottawa with their demands, asking that provinces be created in the Northwest, that the Indians be treated better, and that the Métis receive land grants. The petition, drafted by Louis Riel and settlers union secretary Will Jackson, also demands government action on other matters, mainly land and economic issues, that have concerned white settlers here for years.

1885

St. Laurent, Northwest Territories, March 15. During a mass, Louis Riel argues with the priest, Vital Fourmond, making a break from the church. Fourmond threatens to withhold the sacrament from Métis involved in an uprising.

Batoche, Northwest Territories, May 12. Canadian militia defeat the outnumbered Métis rebels led by Riel and Gabriel Dumont, ending their rebellion that began March 19.

Northwest Territories, May 15. Riel surrenders to the NWMP, who describe him as "careworn and haggard."

Ottawa, July 6. The Commons passes the Dominion Franchise Act, establishing criteria for voting. Widows, spinsters, and some Indians in eastern Canada who have gained the franchise can't vote anymore. The property qualification for voting is lowered.

Montreal, July 20. Large crowds welcome soldiers home from putting down Riel's rebellion in the west.

Montana Territory, U.S., July. Indian and Métis rebels take refuge here after being defeated by Canadian troops. Dumont joins the Buffalo Bill Wild West Show as a marksman.

Ottawa, Nov. 11. After many appeals, cabinet rules that Riel must hang as sentenced. They have received thousands of petitions to commute the sentence, and many counter with petitions from Ontario.

Regina, Nov. 16. Riel is hanged for high treason for his role in the recent rebellion.

Ottawa, November. The government reserves Banff Hot Springs to develop as a tourist attraction. CPR workers found the springs this year.

St. Boniface, Man., Dec. 11. People converge from all over the area for Riel's funeral, many of them in tears.

Canada. Robert Harris finishes *The Fathers of Confederation*, a group portrait commissioned by the federal government.

Hudson Bay. Since 1863 there have been 146 U.S. whaling voyages in the bay. Crews kill whales with fragmentation bombs. Many of the slaughtered whales are not recovered.

Kingston, Ont. The first hockey league is formed.

Canada. The government sends some 5,000 troops and spends more than $5 million to put down the Riel rebellion.

Trouble in N.W.T.: provisional Métis government set up

March 19, 1885

BATOCHE, N.W.T. – Métis here established a provisional government today and declared their independence from Canada, most likely bringing them a step closer to a violent clash with Ottawa. Last night, Métis seized stores, cut some telegraph lines, and took a number of prisoners. Their military forces had the area well-secured before the provisional government was proclaimed this afternoon.

Louis Riel was not named to the 15-member provisional government council, but he is clearly the leading force behind the movement. Gabriel Dumont, the famous leader of the Métis buffalo hunts and president of a community government here in 1873-75, was named the government's military commander. Dumont immediately formed the Métis and Indians here into military companies. In a speech, Riel said England will soon go to war with Russia. Therefore, now is the best time for the Métis and Indians to defend their territory, he said.

Quebec labor law is province's first

March 8, 1885

QUEBEC CITY – Quebec's first labor law, passed today by the Assembly, puts limits on hours of work and provides measures for safety in the workplace. The Manufacturers Act sets the maximum hours worked by young women and children at 10 hours a day. However, if an employer chooses to grant Saturdays off, those hours may be prolonged.

Although hailed as a reform, the act contains exemptions which give employers special powers. For example, in the event of a slowdown in work due to a breakdown in machinery or an accident in the factory, the act authorizes employers to increase work hours to recoup time lost. In effect, children, girls and pregnant women can be made to work up to 12 and a half hours a day, and up to 72 and a half hours per week.

Annual winter carnival opens in Montreal

A magnificent ice palace is the focal point of the Montreal Winter Carnival.

Jan. 26, 1885

MONTREAL – Once again, Montreal has outdone itself with its third annual winter carnival. Scores of city residents bundled up to attend the opening ceremony today, apparently following the advice of Dr. George Beers, who was instrumental in organizing the city's first carnival. At that first carnival, Beers urged Montrealers "not only to look Jack Frost in the face, but force him to become our companion in sport rather than our master in misery." This year's organizers would surely echo his sentiments.

Rift grows between Riel, Catholic church

March 2, 1885

ST. LAURENT, N.W.T. – Louis Riel's support among the Roman Catholic clergy has all but evaporated. Late tonight, Riel had a loud argument with Father Alexis André, the senior priest here. André refused Riel's request to bless the Métis provisional government, and angrily told him to leave. The priest had been one of Riel's warmest supporters, but over the past two months the two had heated theological and political disputes.

Gordon's death at Khartoum worries PM

Gen. Charles Gordon being killed.

Feb. 6, 1885

OTTAWA – The death of Gen. Charles "Chinese" Gordon at Khartoum was announced today, and Canadians are reeling under the shock of this tragic blow to the British Empire in the far-off Sudan. Particularly shaken is the prime minister, Sir John A. Macdonald, who's worried Gordon's death will trigger a large-scale war and demands upon Canada to contribute arms and men to defend the empire. Canada's military force is small and relatively undeveloped; with the threat of a rebellion in the Northwest Territories, looming larger since last Christmas, few trained soldiers can be spared.

Indians canvassed for military support

March 23, 1885

BATOCHE, N.W.T. – The Council of the Métis provisional government has sent runners to Indian bands throughout the territories requesting military support in case of a clash with government forces. Many chiefs blame government insensitivity for deplorable conditions on reserves. Last year, there were several large meetings at which the chiefs expressed anger. Young warriors are particularly impatient and dangerous.

Militia on march anticipating fight

March 25, 1885

OTTAWA – A militia contingent is moving west from Winnipeg tonight in anticipation of a clash with Louis Riel's forces at Batoche. For this national expedition, the government mobilized Winnipeg's 90th Battalion and field battery. Militia units throughout Canada are in a state of readiness, and forces can be moved quickly from Ontario and Quebec. Gen. Frederick Middleton, militia commander, will be in Winnipeg in two days.

Métis loot suspected spy's store in attack

March 25, 1885

DUCK LAKE, N.W.T. – Métis militia forces have moved across the South Saskatchewan River and seized this village about 9.6 kilometres west of their headquarters at Batoche. They looted the store of Hillyard Mitchell, suspected of spying for North West Mounted Police superintendent L.N.F. Crozier. The Métis have secured the Carlton Trail, the main road in this district which runs just north of Duck Lake, and they may move on Fort Carlton, where Crozier is established with about 50 men.

North West Rebellion begins at Duck Lake

North West Mounted Police and volunteers battle with rebels at Duck Lake.

March 26, 1885

DUCK LAKE, N.W.T. – The North West Rebellion began today, and the rebels got much the best of the first engagement. About 100 Métis and Cree under Louis Riel and Gabriel Dumont defeated a similar number of North West Mounted Police and volunteers under superintendent L.N.F. Crozier. The battle, on the Carlton Trail just north of here, lasted only half an hour, but it was bloody. The police and volunteers lost 12 killed; the rebels lost six.

The battle began just before noon as Crozier's force moved from Fort Carlton toward Duck Lake, which rebels occupied yesterday. Rebels held strong positions on either side of the Carlton Trail while Crozier's force established a barricade across the road itself. Crozier quickly realized advance was impossible and ordered a retreat. Shortly after Crozier arrived back at Fort Carlton, so did NWMP commissioner Acheson Irvine. Tonight, Irvine is considering abandoning Fort Carlton and moving to Prince Albert.

Rebellious Indians kill 9

The peaceful village of Frog Lake is attacked by Chief Big Bear's band.

April 2, 1885

FROG LAKE, N.W.T. – Nine people are dead after a rampage by warriors of Chief Big Bear's band in this village about 48 kilometres northeast of Fort Pitt. The dead include two priests, the band farm instructor, and the local Indian agent. The warriors took control of the band yesterday, and just after dawn this morning they rounded up all the whites. The killings began about 10 a.m. when War Chief Wandering Spirit shot and killed Indian agent Tom Quinn. The war chief then ordered his followers to kill the other whites. Chief Big Bear tried to intervene but could do nothing. A few escaped death.

Hudson's Bay Company employee Bill Cameron and the wives of two of the dead men, Theresa Delaney and Theresa Gowanlock, are prisoners of the Indians. Henry Quinn, nephew of the slain agent, fled moments before his uncle was killed. Some warriors talk of moving against Fort Pitt.

Commission formed to make land grants

March 30, 1885

OTTAWA – The government today appointed a commission empowered to make land grants to the Métis of the Northwest Territories. Its three commissioners will hurry west to begin their work. The land grant issue is one of the chief reasons for the North West Rebellion. However, most observers say the government action today will have little effect now that fighting has begun. A plan to appoint the commission was first unveiled in January, but it made little impression on Louis Riel and his followers.

Ontario to protect Niagara Falls area

March 30, 1885

TORONTO – Premier Oliver Mowat has introduced a bill aimed at both preserving and restoring the land around Niagara Falls, one of Ontario's great landmarks. Under the bill, three commissioners are to be appointed to select and purchase lands for a provincially-controlled park. It's believed the commission will offer bonds for sale to pay for scenic railways and elevators at the site. Landowners should not bother resisting the commission. It will be able to expropriate lands.

Hundreds of Cree besiege Battleford

March 30, 1885

BATTLEFORD, N.W.T. – Residents here have fled to the safety of the North West Mounted Police fort, as the Indians are in possession of the town. All day, settlers watched from the fort as hundreds of Cree ransacked their stores and homes across the Battle River. Chiefs Poundmaker and Little Pine invited the Indian agent to a meeting but he refused to cross the river. Word arrived this evening that Stoney Indians murdered two white men and will join the Cree.

General's troopers head to Edmonton

April 20, 1885

CALGARY – The first contingent of Gen. T.B. Strange's column left here today for Edmonton, before moving down the North Saskatchewan River to Fort Pitt, near where Big Bear's Cree are camped. This column consists of one battalion from Montreal and one from Winnipeg. Two local groups composed of cowboys and North West Mounted Police accompany the column. The Quebec City battalion will remain here in case the Blackfoot Indians join the rebellion.

Meanwhile, the column under Col. W.D. Otter is nearing the Eagle Hills, just south of Battleford. Gen. Frederick Middleton's troops are moving toward Batoche.

Rebels stall militia in Fish Creek battle

April 24, 1885

FISH CREEK, N.W.T. – Rebels today stopped Gen. Frederick Middleton's advance on Batoche, inflicting heavy casualties on the militia. Fighting began here, about 29 kilometres south of Batoche, at about 8 a.m. and ended late this afternoon. Of a force of 400, six militiamen are dead and almost 50 wounded. Rebels lost five dead and a small number of wounded. After the battle, Middleton camped a short distance south of Fish Creek.

Rangers to fight Louis Riel, rebels

April 25, 1885

PINCHER CREEK, N.W.T. – Capt. John Stewart is preparing to lead his Rocky Mountain Rangers to fight against Louis Riel and the rebels. Stewart, who comes from a prominent Ottawa family, went to the capital to get permission to form a defence force to help the police against the Métis and, perhaps, the Indians. He got approval to raise four troops of mounted men and now has 114 men drilled, trained and ready to march off. Most of the men, who get free carbines and saddles, are cowboys from nearby.

Canadians rout rebels at Batoche

Canadian troops outnumber the Métis and capture the town of Batoche.

The Métis flee from the Battle of Batoche. Their inferior weapons are no match for those of the military.

May 12, 1885

BATOCHE, N.W.T. – Batoche has fallen. After three days of inconclusive fighting, Gen. Frederick Middleton's militia overran the rebel stronghold shortly after noon today. Colonels Arthur Williams and H.J. Grasett led the charge that routed the rebels from their fortified positions and drove them back to the village. Most of the Métis and Indian fighters fled north or across the river, leaving the troops in possession of the village. Some rebel leaders have been captured, but Louis Riel and Gabriel Dumont have not been seen. It is said that Williams and Grasett undertook the charge without orders from Middleton, who was at lunch when it occurred.

The battle of Batoche began the morning of May 9 when the advance of Middleton's troops was stopped on the ridge overlooking the southeast approach to the village. The Métis and Indians had built a series of rifle pits to defend their headquarters, and these proved difficult to overrun. It was only the steady fire of the Gatling gun that prevented the militia from being routed in their first advance. The next two days saw little heavy fighting. The general established his own line facing the main rebel position and tried unsuccessfully to find an easier approach from the north. Last night, it is said that the colonels, impatient with the general's cautious tactics, met to plan today's charge, which took the rebels by surprise.

Eight militiamen died in the battle. Fourteen Métis and Indians were killed, as was a little girl shot by mistake in the fight for the village of Batoche.

Cree, Stoney warriors repel militia at Poundmaker's reserve

May 2, 1885

BATTLEFORD, N.W.T. – Cree and Stoney warriors soundly defeated militia under Col. W.D. Otter on Chief Poundmaker's reserve today. Shortly after dawn, the 325 men under Otter found themselves hemmed in by the enemy on a long, steep hill near Cut Knife Creek, about 48 kilometres west of here. Much credit is given to young war chief Fine Day, who used his forces sparingly but effectively.

The militia's position was hopeless. Retreat would have been close to impossible if Poundmaker had not persuaded the warriors to let the militia retire unmolested. Eight militiamen and five or six Indians were killed. Otter attacked to retaliate for Battleford's sacking.

Canadian troops attack Chief Poundmaker's camp at Cut Knife Creek.

Poundmaker surrenders

Louis Riel is discovered and taken prisoner by scouts Armstrong and Howe.

May 26, 1885

BATTLEFORD, N.W.T. – Poundmaker and his followers surrendered today to Gen. Frederick Middleton. The chief led his band across the Battle River to the flats below the fort where he and his leading men presented themselves before the general's tent. When Middleton appeared, Poundmaker moved forward, hand outstretched. The general refused the gesture, saying he did not shake hands with rebels. He then upbraided the chief for murdering settlers.

Poundmaker, a man of great dignity, was clearly offended. He replied that he had not murdered anyone, and he had only defended himself when the militia attacked his camp. He and his councillors were giving themselves up, and all they asked was that the women and children of the band not be harmed. Poundmaker and some of his men are now in custody.

Meanwhile, the Canadians appear to have the North West Rebellion under control. Métis leader Louis Riel is in jail in Regina, and most members of the rebel council at Batoche are also in prison. Some Métis and Indian leaders, including Gabriel Dumont and Poundmaker's War Chief Fine Day, have fled to the United States.

Poundmaker and his tribe surrender to General Middleton at Battleford.

Battle near Frenchman Butte a stalemate

May 28, 1885

FRENCHMAN BUTTE, N.W.T. – Gen. T.B. Strange's column met Big Bear's Cree today with indecisive results. The militia found the Cree a short way north of Frenchman Butte, where they were strongly dug in. From across a deep gully, Strange brought his artillery to bear on the Indian position on the opposite hill, to little effect. The two forces traded shots for hours, then retired. Strange moved back to Fort Pitt and the Cree moved north. No militia were killed, but one Indian was mortally wounded.

TB epidemic claims Crowfoot's daughter

May 29, 1885

NORTHWEST TERRITORIES – Tuberculosis has taken another child of Blackfoot Chief Crowfoot. One of his daughters died today, a victim of the epidemic sweeping through this area. Crowfoot, born a Blood but brought up as a Blackfoot, played an important part in the Treaty No. 7 negotiations in 1877. He is known both for his bravery and his diplomatic skills. Crowfoot has made peace with the Cree, and has a good relationship with fur traders and the North West Mounted Police. The chief is refraining from joining the present North West Rebellion.

Crowfoot is a shortened version of "Crow Indian's Big Foot," a name he acquired when at an early age he showed great bravery in battle by entering the enemy Crow camp and striking a painted tepee.

Chief Crowfoot with his family last year before the loss of his daughter.

Cree suffer heavy losses in brief skirmish

June 3, 1885

LOON LAKE, N.W.T. – Sam Steele's scouts caught up with the Cree bands under chiefs Big Bear and Cut Arm here this morning and fought a brief battle. Superintendent Steele and his 65 men surprised the Indian camp near the south shore of this lake, about 64 kilometres northeast of Fort Pitt. The battle lasted only 30 minutes, but Cree losses were heavy. Five died, including Woods Cree Chief Cut Arm, one of the leading pacifists among the Indians. Cut Arm was killed as he stepped from his tepee at the start of the battle.

There were many wounded. A daughter of Hudson's Bay Company factor W.J. McLean, whose family is among the Indian prisoners, narrowly escaped death helping an Indian child to safety. None of Steele's men were killed, but four were seriously wounded. The Indians suffered their greatest loss moving their camp across a ford separating two parts of the lake.

Americans refusing to pay fishery bill

July 1, 1885

WASHINGTON, D.C. – The United States gave Canada an unwelcome birthday present today, abrogating the fisheries clauses on the 1871 Treaty of Washington. The Americans are refusing to honor payments they agreed to make to Canada for the use of its fisheries on the Atlantic coast. Part of the reason for that refusal may be the price tag; under an arbitration held at Halifax in 1877, the Americans were billed $5.5 million. With the treaty now abrogated, the once-settled issue of Canada-U.S. trade is an issue once more.

Cree Chief Big Bear agrees to surrender

July 2, 1885

FORT CARLTON, N.W.T. – Chief Big Bear gave himself up here today to three surprised policemen who just happened to be at the ruined fort. While hundreds of militia searched for him far to the north, the Cree chief appeared here accompanied by his 12-year-old son. It is said he surrendered to the only three people in the Northwest not looking for him. Big Bear could have easily escaped to the United States, but he believes he must stay to support his band and take responsibility for his actions in the North West Rebellion.

Workers closing rail gap

Workers lay ties in Fraser Valley.

July 1885

FARWELL, B.C. – Workers are rapidly closing the gap near here between the track from the east and that from the west. When they meet in a couple of months, the Canadian Pacific Railway will run from Montreal to the Pacific.

Contractor Andrew Onderdonk has just completed his government contract section from Port Moody through the Fraser Canyon to Savona's Ferry. He hopes to finish the section covered by his CPR contract, from Savona's Ferry to the end of track from the east, in two months. Then all of Onderdonk's work on the railway will be done.

Women escape from their Indian captors

Mrs. Gowanlock of Frog Lake observes her captors as she awaits rescue.

Juen 3, 1885

FRENCHMAN BUTTE, N.W.T. – Two white women, captured after the Frog Lake massacre, are free again. Scouts in Gen. T.B. Strange's column found Theresa Delaney and Theresa Gowanlock camped north of here tonight with some half-breeds. Both women are safe. They and their companions managed to slip away from the Indians a few days after the battle of Frenchman Butte.

Two days ago, Hudson's Bay Company employee Bill Cameron and Rev. Charles Quinney were also found safe, in the company of a small group of Woods Cree. Mrs. Delaney and Mrs. Gowanlock, meanwhile, are the widows of two of the men killed in the Frog Lake tragedy of April 2. The women deny rumors about ill-treatment at the hands of the Indians. They say half-breeds in the camp protected them, and while being forced to stay with the Indians was a considerable hardship, chiefs Big Bear and Cut Arm took an interest in the safety and comfort of the captives. HBC factor W.J. McLean, his family and most of the others taken captive at Fort Pitt on April 15 are apparently still with the Indians.

Riel sentenced to die for high treason

Aug. 1, 1885

REGINA – Louis Riel is under sentence of death. A jury today found the Métis leader guilty of high treason, and the judge imposed the only penalty available under law, though the jury made a strong recommendation for mercy and there remains a possibility the federal government will commute the sentence.

There is little doubt about Riel's leadership in the North West Rebellion. But while his lawyers raised an insanity plea, Riel himself destroyed that argument when he addressed the court at length and in a very eloquent manner. He wanted his actions defended on political grounds, not an insanity plea. But since there is no defence of justification to a treason charge, Riel's lawyers believed the insanity plea held the only hope for their client. Consequently, the defence called medical witnesses to testify about Riel's mental state.

If the jury had doubts about Riel's sanity, they disappeared as he spoke. He thanked his lawyers for doing their best, then deliberately demolished the defence they tried to establish. He also justified the rebellion on the grounds that the government had forced his people to take violent action. Riel's speech made a strong impression. There were tears in the jury foreman's eyes as he returned the verdict. The defence may appeal.

Riel takes the stand in his own defence at his trial for treason in Regina.

Collision with train fatal for Jumbo

Jumbo, the circus elephant, lies dead by the side of the tracks in St. Thomas.

Jumbo the elephant was a featured star in the P.T. Barnum travelling circus for the last several years.

Sept. 15, 1885

ST. THOMAS, Ont. – The world's most famous elephant, seven ton, 12-foot-high Jumbo, died today after a freight train struck him. He and Tom Thumb, the miniature clown elephant, were strolling with Jumbo's trainer Matthew "Scotty" Scott along the Grand Trunk railway track near their circus cars. Tom Thumb's hind leg broke, but the locomotive rammed into the enormous Jumbo. A tusk pierced his brain and killed him.

Jumbo was born in 1861 in Africa, acquired by Paris' Jardin des Plantes, then traded to the London Zoological Gardens. On June 26, 1865, the filthy and emaciated little elephant arrived. Under Scotty he flourished, but in maturity grew so moody and violent, except with Scotty, that in 1882 he was sold to American showman Phineas T. Barnum to star in The Greatest Show on Earth. Jumbo died embracing Scotty in his trunk.

Death-by-dynamite spells the end for hefty Maritime bullfrog

Fred Coleman trains his pet bullfrog to do tricks at his Fredericton hotel.

1885

FREDERICTON – Gloom not cheer is the fare today at Barker House Hotel, where owner Fred Coleman is inconsolable at the death-by-dynamite of his 42-pound pet bullfrog. Coleman found the oversized frog, then weighing seven pounds four ounces, in Killarney Lake. Over the years he cemented their friendship – and plumped up his friend – with daily gifts of buttermilk, fresh cornbread, and some say, whisky. The frog also dined on June bugs and fireflies carried to the lake by hotel guests.

Sometimes the frog sulked, and refused to emerge from his murky resting place. But usually he followed Coleman, doing such tricks as leaping over orange crates. Men fishing with dynamite killed the frog by mistake. Coleman is so lonely he says he'll have his friend stuffed and at his side forever.

Psychiatric pioneer killed by lunatic in model asylum

Aug. 16, 1885

KINGSTON, Ont. – A psychiatrist who fought for humane treatment for mental patients died today at Rockwood Asylum after an inmate named Maloney stabbed him in the abdomen. "Oh, I'm killed!" gasped Dr. William G. Metcalfe to his horrified colleague and brother-in-law Dr. C.K. Clarke, and fell bleeding to the floor. The noontime murder occurred as Clarke and Metcalfe were entering the dining room after visiting patients. In an attempt to save the wounded man from another blow, Clarke grappled with Maloney, who tried to knife him too. Clarke frightened the lunatic away, then carried his friend to safety in his office, but at 3:10 p.m., Metcalfe, 38, expired.

The nature of Metcalfe's death is specially ironic in light of his advanced views on mental illness. With his superior Dr. R.M. Buck, Metcalfe rejected the idea of a lunatic asylum as "an immense prison full of all sorts of horrors. Speaking generally, we rely more on regular exercise, good food, regular hours, kindness and firmness rather than drugs." Maloney, Metcalfe's patient and beneficiary of his reformist spirit, apparently turned on his psychiatrist without cause. Crazed, he stood waiting to assault anyone who came close to him. Tragically, young Dr. Metcalfe did.

Martha Moore.

Vaccinations spark Montreal protests

Sept. 28, 1885

MONTREAL – The militia was called in today after mobs protesting an anti-smallpox vaccination program attacked city hall and businesses on St. Catherine Street. The program, with fines for refusal to submit to vaccination, will immunize citizens against the rampaging disease. Although smallpox claimed some 3,000 Montrealers this year, including former prime minister Sir Francis Hincks, French-Canadians are ignorant about and greatly fear vaccination. ▷

CPR tracks extend to Rocky Mountains

Workers' camp at Beaverfoot in the Kicking Horse Pass of the Rockies.

October 1885

CALGARY – The Canadian Pacific Railway is now running trains from the east as far as the eastern slopes of the Rockies. In the summer, gaps in the line, chiefly around Lake Superior, were closed. Troops which came west to put down the rebellion travelled home in comfort – a contrast to their journey west when they had to travel in horse-drawn sleighs or walk between sections of the railway.

Now everyone here is waiting for the final finishing touches on the track in the mountains between Roger's Pass and Eagle Pass. This is expected to be ready next month. Then people from Calgary can go by train to the Pacific – as well as to the east.

Riel records thoughts on death row

Oct. 17, 1885

REGINA – Louis Riel has not been idle while awaiting either a successful appeal, a commutation of his sentence, or his date with the hangman. From his jail cell here in Regina, the Métis leader has been busy writing. He has written numerous letters, a long diary and is working on a series of essays outlining the history of the Métis. The diary is a curious document. It contains mainly religious matters and a large number of "revelations."

Some of his entries indicate that Riel, who has always been deeply religious, if unorthodox, believes that God is on his side in his present struggle. Today he wrote, "human justice still leaves me eight days to live. But I have learned from the visit of my guardian angel that, by the grace of God, I have more time than that left." Riel also wrote that God wants the names of the oceans, continents, planets and stars changed. His diary contains many other ideas of this sort that most people would consider bizarre. But on other matters, Riel seems quite sensible. His history of the Métis is an eloquent statement of the struggles of his people.

Meanwhile, Riel's appeal to the Judicial Committee of the Privy Council will be heard on Oct. 22. It is not expected that the appeal to the highest court in the British Empire will be successful. But the federal government is under considerable pressure to commute the rebel leader's sentence.

Louis Riel is permitted daily exercise under guard outside the Regina jail.

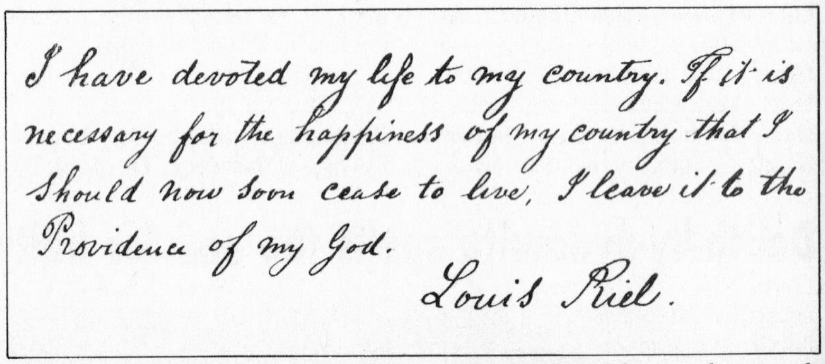

I have devoted my life to my country. If it is necessary for the happiness of my country that I should now soon cease to live, I leave it to the Providence of my God.

Louis Riel.

Apparently resigned to his impending execution, Louis Riel wrote these words in a firm hand in the diary he is keeping in his Regina jail cell.

Police arrest police in Farwell flare-up

Sept. 26, 1885

FARWELL, B.C. – This rip-roaring settlement on the Canadian Pacific Railway has just enjoyed a legal farce in which policemen arrested policemen. As befits Farwell's reputation, the fuss was about beer. Now that it is all over it is obvious that the federal magistrate and a foolish constable were at fault. They seized some bottles of beer under federal law. But the provincial police, saying liquor was in their jurisdiction, arrested the constable for theft.

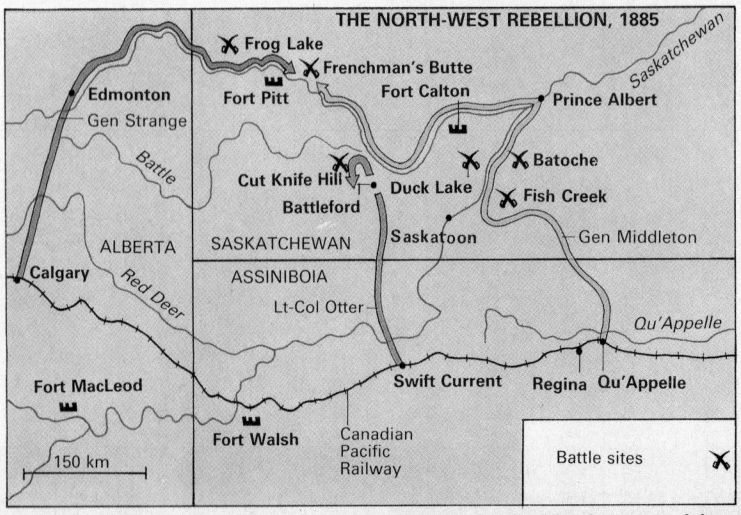

Map shows battle sites and movement of troops in the Northwest uprising.

Fierce gale sweeps 300 to their death

Oct. 12, 1885

LABRADOR – A fierce gale swept the coast today, and there are reports that dozens of vessels, vast quantities of saltfish and, worst of all, more than 300 lives were lost. Families come to this coast every summer from Conception Bay in Newfoundland. At the end of the fishing season, they leave their bleak and exposed fishing stations and return home for the winter. The storm struck when the last of the crews were preparing to leave. A similar storm occurred in 1866.

Smith drives home the last spike

Nov. 7, 1885

EAGLE PASS, B.C. – At nine this morning the last piece of rail was measured and ready. Workers and officials then waited for the official party to arrive. Up puffed a tiny locomotive – No. 148 – pulling one car, and Donald Smith, Sandford Fleming and William Cornelius Van Horne got out. Smith, the senior director, was given the honor of driving the last spike, an ordinary piece of iron. He bent the spike on his first stroke and another one, kept ready for such a situation, was put in place. The photographer's shutter clicked, and Smith drove the spike home.

Donald Smith drives the ceremonial last spike of the CPR at Eagle Pass, B.C.

Winnipeg aldermen mull over problems

Sept. 15, 1885

WINNIPEG – City councillors are wrestling with some decisions for which there are no precedents. One of the topics concerns the wages of civic employees who are fighting in the North West Rebellion. There is a belief that council should pay the difference between militia wages and the income these men would receive as civic workers.

The absence of city engineer H.N. Ruttan, a member of Gen. Garnet Wolseley's army, is also causing problems. Without him at home to supervise the construction of the new city hall, a number of serious errors have been made.

Canada is weighed down by the huge public debt of the CPR.

Riel hanged reciting the Lord's Prayer

Sir John A. Macdonald seems to be in a quandary over the Riel sentence.

Nov. 16, 1885

REGINA – Louis Riel today paid the supreme penalty for high treason. The Métis leader was calm as he mounted the scaffold, even comforting Father Alexis André, who could not keep from weeping. Riel wanted to make a speech from the gallows, but André persuaded him not to. The trap was sprung at a predetermined time, as Riel was reciting the Lord's Prayer.

Few were allowed to witness the execution. But outside the jail was a large crowd, among whom tasteless comments were passed. The reaction in Quebec will be vastly different than that here. Already this morning, Montreal city council plans an emergency meeting. Riel's body will be transported to St. Boniface, Man., for burial.

PM tries to please opposing factions.

Eight Indians hang for part in rebellion

Nov. 27, 1885

BATTLEFORD, N.W.T. – Eight Indians were hanged this morning for murders committed in the North West Rebellion. Six were Cree, convicted of the Frog Lake killings of April 2. The other two were Stoney Indians who killed a farm instructor and a settler south of Battleford on March 30.

Wandering Spirit, the war chief of Big Bear's band, was the most prominent of those hanged. He was the only one who pleaded guilty at his trial. Yesterday, the war chief gave a speech in which he thanked the police for their kind treatment. The Indians went to their deaths singing war songs, and were buried in a common grave.

Electric lights on in Charlottetown

Dec. 21, 1885

CHARLOTTETOWN – Last fall the council hired Royal Electric of Montreal to update street lighting here. Tonight the town switches on the first electric lights on P.E.I. Most applaud the move. *The Examiner* writes, "There is no doubt that ere long electricity will become as familiar to us as gas or kerosene, and it behooves us to keep pace with the times and not remain forever in our sleepy hollow."

Execution sparks Montreal protest

Nov. 22, 1885

MONTREAL – The largest demonstration in this city's history took place tonight as thousands thronged the Champ de Mars to protest Louis Riel's execution. Prominent Liberal Wilfrid Laurier told the angry crowd that if he lived in the Northwest Territories, he'd have taken up arms with the rebels. Quebec Liberal leader Honoré Mercier called for a coalition dedicated to overthrowing Conservative governments in Ottawa and Quebec. Riel's death "raised a cry of pity from the hearts of all civilized people," Mercier said.

1886

Victoria, April 6. The legislature incorporates Vancouver as a city, named after explorer George Vancouver.

United States, May 1. More than 100,000 workers walk out across the country in a general strike for shorter working hours.

Halifax, May. The legislature passes resolutions moved by Premier William Fielding for the release of Nova Scotia from Confederation.

Rome, June 7. At the urging of the Canadian government, Pope Leo XIII makes Elzéar-Alexandre Taschereau the first Canadian Cardinal, giving him great prestige in Canada.

Ottawa, July. The government grants amnesty to all those involved in the rebellion of 1885, except for murderers.

Ontario, Nov. 20. The Toronto [Royal] Conservatory of Music is incorporated.

Ottawa, December. The government appoints a royal commission to study the relations of labor and capital in Canada.

Montreal. One in three infants dies before the age of six months. Children under the age of five years old account for 60 percent of all deaths.

Canada. The whipping of female inmates is abolished.

Quebec. The first stud book for the Canadian horse breed is created.

Ottawa. The Department of Agriculture publishes a report discussing the threat posed to wildlife in the western interior by advancing settlement.

Canada. The Canadian Rugby Football Union (CRFU) folds after the Ontario Rugby Football Union secedes from it. A rule dispute prevented the CRFU championship last year.

Ottawa. The government falsifies the report of three doctors appointed secretly last October to find out if Riel was sane enough to be hanged. Two of the doctors said he was sane, but the other disagreed. The government reports all three of them found him sane.

Montreal. The Trades and Labour Council of Montreal is formed.

Yukon River Valley, Northwest Territories. The first important gold discovery in the area [Yukon] occurs at the junction of the Forty Mile and Yukon rivers.

MP levels charges at Indian Dept.

This elderly Haida woman's generation was less influenced by the white man than are younger Indians. Wearing an Indian mouth ornament, but non-Indian clothing, she laboriously weaves a straw hat.

These Queen Charlotte Islands women still cling to traditional way of life.

April 16, 1886

OTTAWA – Today in Parliament, MP Malcolm Cameron charged that Indian Department employees in the Northwest buy young Indian women. He quoted Rev. John McDougall, a Methodist missionary in the Alberta district, saying that whites buy Indian girls for $10 or $20, though the minister did not claim that Indian Department employees were involved.

But last month, Rev. Samuel Trivett, a missionary on the Blood reserve, said that white men come to the reserve and buy young women from their parents. When they tire of them, these men turn the girls out into prostitution at Fort Macleod.

Today, Minister of Public Works Sir Hector Langevin said an investigation uncovered no instance of "the actual purchase of an Indian girl" by department employees. He added that charges may have arisen from a misunderstanding of native marriage customs. Another experienced missionary has called the allegations "claptrap."

Doc Kelley launches medicine road show

April 14, 1886

ONTARIO – Part circus, part theatre and part dispensary, the Shamrock Concert Company is all set for its first performance. In a country hamlet 160 kilometres west of Toronto, a temporary stage has been hastily erected in the middle of a field. Families from miles around have gathered. Children wait impatiently by the foot of the stage, faces lit by the glow of gas torches on either side, and behind them stand the adults, dressed in country homespuns and calico dresses.

Attention focuses on Doc Kelley as he lectures about his New Oriental Discovery, a special blend of herbs that promises, for a small price, "long life, strong bodies, good health." Then comes song, banjo-picking, pratfalls and jokes, performed free of charge by the four-man company. The show goes well, and sales are brisk.

Ontario OKs workmen's compensation act

March 25, 1886

TORONTO – The Ontario government struck a blow for the workers today, passing the Workmen's Compensation for Injuries Act. However, since the act requires workmen to prove employers or managers were negligent before awarding compensation, it doesn't seem likely to improve the situation that much for labor.

Still, the WCIA is evidence of growing government concern for the welfare of the working class. Back in 1874, the government required the owners of threshers and other machines to provide safety covers over moving parts. In 1881 similar safety provisions were enforced upon railway companies. And three years later, the Factories Act prevented women and children from working in dangerous conditions, and limited hours to 10 a day.

Des Voeux in, Shea out as Nfld. governor

Feb. 5, 1886

NEWFOUNDLAND – Reports the colony was getting its first native-born governor would seem to be a bit premature. The colonial office has rejected the appointment of Newfoundlander Sir Ambrose Shea as the new governor, selecting Sir William Des Voeux instead.

It appears religion was a factor. Reports in December and January indicated the job belonged to Shea, a participant in local government since his first election in 1848. Despite being a Roman Catholic in a society where there has been a great deal of religious antagonism, Shea has always had the respect of Protestants. Therefore it was surprising to learn Prime Minister Thorburn objected to the appointment on the grounds that Shea is a Catholic.

Cardinal condemns Knights of Labor

Cardinal E.-A. Taschereau.

May 14, 1886

MONTREAL – Any Catholic associating with the Knights of Labor organization will be excommunicated, Cardinal Elzéar-Alexandre Taschereau decreed in a letter issued to his priests throughout Quebec today. The Knights, an American organization fighting for abolition of child labor, an eight-hour work day and other labor reforms, already boast more than 700,000 members in the U.S.

"Having learned that agents of the Knights of Labor have tried to recruit members in some areas of the province," Taschereau's statement reads, "we believe we have the duty to warn you against them." The cardinal claims the leaders of the Knights are exploiting workers to enrich themselves under the guise of promoting charity and mutual protection. He said the organization and its undermining of religious faith have spread calamity in the United States, England and France. To subscribe to the Knights will only make the workers' lot worse and lead to the "total ruin of industries which sustain their lives," Taschereau says.

The cardinal ordered priests to announce his policy outlawing the Knights at next Sunday's masses. He urges anyone who has already signed up with the Knights to seek forgiveness by way of confession to the parish priest.

Fire ravages Vancouver; 50 feared dead

June 13, 1886

VANCOUVER – A freak squall blew the flames from a forest clearing fire onto a shed this Sunday afternoon, and in a few hours Vancouver had disappeared. Buildings just vanished in a sheet of flame. Whole families, with their pets, ran into the water of False Creek. Others managed to escape along the CPR embankment or down the Westminster road.

Virtually every building in the mostly wooden village of huts and cabins was destroyed, and at least 20 bodies were found. But officials say the toll will be closer to 50 as many people were reported killed trying to get into blazing buildings to save other people or belongings.

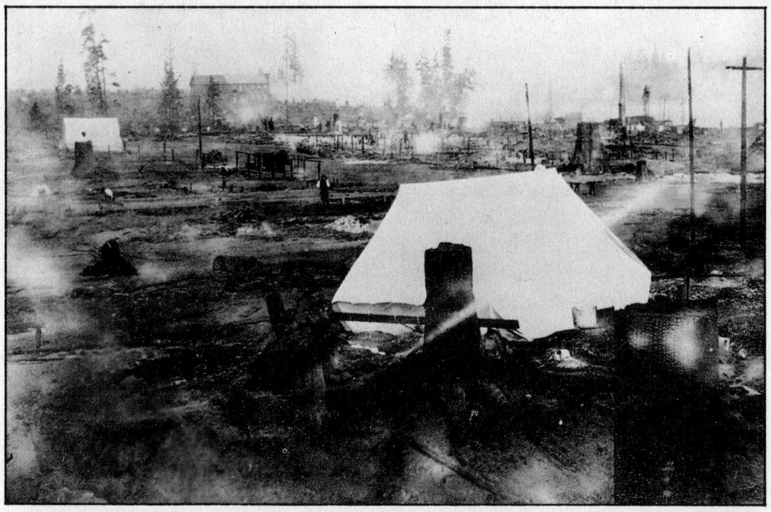

A few tents are set up among the smouldering ruins of the city of Vancouver.

Governing body to rule in amateur hockey

Dec. 8, 1886

MONTREAL – The Amateur Hockey Association of Canada, the first governing body formed since hockey was introduced here a decade ago, was organized today at a meeting in the Victoria Skating Rink. The object of the association is to improve, foster and perpetuate the game in Canada, and protect it from professionalism. The season will run from Jan. 1 to March 15.

T.D. Greene, a Mohawk Indian and noted Ottawa hockey player, was elected president by delegates from Ottawa and four Montreal clubs. Quebec City was not represented. Rules call for seven-man teams and 1.2-metre goal posts fixed in the ice 1.8 metres apart.

National congress to represent labor

Sept. 14, 1886

TORONTO – Trade unionists meeting in Toronto have agreed to form a new national umbrella group for all the unions in Canada. It will be called the Trades and Labour Congress of Canada, and will be a representative body, made up of delegates from various unions. The formation of an umbrella group signals the desire of organized labor to form itself into a single body, capable of wielding power and influence in Canadian politics.

Fielding's Grits win vowing to pull N.S. out of the country

June 15, 1886

HALIFAX – Promising to take Nova Scotia out of Confederation, ex-journalist William S. Fielding led the Liberals to a decisive victory in a provincial election. The score: Grits, 29; Tories, 8; Independent, 1. Once managing editor of the Halifax *Morning Chronicle,* Fielding was first elected to the legislature in 1882, and became premier in 1884. He seems obsessed by the precarious finances of Nova Scotia, and the federal government's refusal to help the province.

Prime Minister John A. Macdonald, Tory champion of Confederation, told Lt.-Gov. M.H. Richey if he allowed Fielding to call a snap election on the repeal of Confederation, he'd be remiss in his duty as a Dominion officer. Richey ignored this gratuitous warning, and Macdonald himself is partly at fault for the sorry showing of local Tories. They endure blame for the federal government's fiscal and tariff policies, yet receive scant sympathy from Nova Scotia members of the federal cabinet.

As recently as 1878, Conservatives outnumbered Liberals in Nova Scotia's legislature 30-8. But Macdonald didn't help Tory premiers when they called, and his cavalier attitude toward Fielding gave the premier campaign ammunition. However, Fielding may find winning an election easier than taking a province out of Canada.

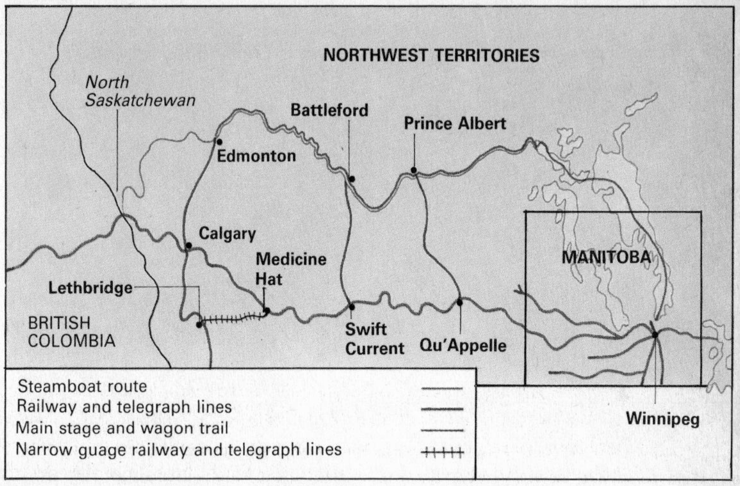

Map shows travel routes and means of communication in the west in 1886.

First transcontinental train chugs into Port Moody

En route to the west coast, the CPR train arrives in Port Arthur, Ontario. This train is making the first complete transcontinental rail trip in Canada.

The first CPR through train completes its cross-country trip at Port Moody.

July 4, 1886

PORT MOODY, B.C. – The Canadian Pacific Railway's first transcontinental passenger train arrived here at 12:01 p.m. today – just 139 hours after leaving Montreal, 4,670 kilometres away. This small community on Burrard Inlet celebrated in gala fashion, as more than 1,000 people came by boat up the inlet from Nanaimo, New Westminster and Victoria.

Ladies showed off their dresses, bought from London stores, as they listened to the Victoria Brass Band. A visiting Italian opera company sang appropriate arias, and everyone forgot about their sometimes bitter rivalries over the site of the CPR's Pacific terminus.

The first eastbound train is due to leave here tomorrow for Montreal. Now ships from the Orient with tea, silk and rice in their holds are expected to steam up the inlet, past Vancouver, to unload their cargoes here for shipping by rail to New York. But some people here – and the land speculators who have invested heavily locally – fear that the CPR is bent on moving its terminus to Vancouver.

Métis leader Dumont nixes return to Canada despite amnesty

July 22, 1886

OTTAWA – Gabriel Dumont, the Métis military commander in last year's North West Rebellion, won't accept the Canadian government's offer of amnesty. Dumont, touring the U.S. with Buffalo Bill's Wild West Show, says he has no reason to return to Canada, and is wary of government promises.

On learning news of the amnesty today, Buffalo Bill Cody planned a feast in celebration. Meanwhile, Chief Poundmaker, pardoned and released from jail earlier this year with several others involved in the rebellion, is said to be seriously ill. Chief Big Bear remains in prison.

A Cree family is on the move – the woman uses a tumpline to carry a heavy bundle on her back. The dog drags a travois with the other supplies.

American in barrel goes over the falls

July 11, 1886

NIAGARA FALLS, Ont. – An American cooper went over Niagara Falls today – deliberately. Carlisle D. Graham of Philadelphia took the drop in a reinforced barrel he crafted specifically for the purpose of braving the falls and the dangerous whirlpool at its foot.

Made of oak, the barrel is 2.1 metres long. Inside, it has a canvas-and-string bag, a sort of pilot's chair for the occupant. This is where Graham sat for his harrowing journey, one he survived unharmed. Past adventurers haven't been so lucky. In fact, many have died just trying to swim the rapids past the whirlpool. Waves are so strong, they literally press the life out of anyone caught in them.

Inspectors protect women, children

1886

TORONTO – Two years after provincial legislation restricted women and children to working no more than 60 hours a week, inspectors have been appointed to enforce the law. A similar Quebec law passed last year sets the limit at 72 hours. There have been excesses involving women and children in the workforce in both provinces. Workers at the Stormont Cotton Mill at Cornwall, including children, have been known to work up to 11 hours a day. Elsewhere in Ontario, reports tell of girls sewing in garment shops and being paid as little as 80 cents weekly for 60 hours labor.

Conditions have been as bad or worse in Quebec, where children are reportedly whipped for real or perceived infractions in the workplace. Cotton and tobacco factories are among the industries accused of exploiting workers. In one tobacco factory, workers who rebelled were punished by being thrown into a basement cell resembling a coal box. Still another disciplinary measure in some factories is fines, at times exceeding wages.

Walker named GM of Commerce bank

Oct. 12, 1886

TORONTO – Byron E. Walker, a former clerk, has been named general manager of the Canadian Bank of Commerce. Considered by many to be an up-and-comer, Walker is expected to bring many new ideas to the Commerce. He is an advocate of changes some consider radical, among them, the division of banks into departments, which can be properly supervised. His professionalism is seen as a breath of fresh air in the Canadian banking world, a place that has been tainted many times with bankruptcy, incompetence, and outright fraud.

Through prudent management, the Commerce has avoided this stigma. Founded in 1867, with William McMaster its leading figure, it has offices in London, St. Catharines, and Barrie. Head office is in Toronto, where the new general manager will be based, and the full force of his changes soon felt. Some old-timers, fearful of this "new broom," are said to be eyeing other professions ... just in case.

Poundmaker dies, Crowfoot grieves

July 4, 1886

BLACKFOOT CROSSING, N.W.T. – Cree Chief Poundmaker died today. The chief, known for his oratory and political skill, was released from prison a short time ago. He had been serving a sentence for his part in last year's North West Rebellion and was released because he was ill. When he died, Poundmaker was visiting his adoptive father, Blackfoot Chief Crowfoot.

Chief Crowfoot (centre) poses with Indian leaders and Father Lacombe and Jean L'Heureux in Ottawa.

Crowfoot, who adopted Poundmaker years ago to replace a son lost in battle and as a gesture aimed at keeping peace between the Cree and Blackfoot, is grief-stricken. Earlier this year, two of his natural sons became ill and died. Because of his ties to Poundmaker, Crowfoot had mixed feelings during the rebellion. He sent a much-publicized telegram of loyalty to Prime Minister John A. Macdonald, but it is known that Crowfoot wanted to help Poundmaker.

It is believed the major reason for Crowfoot's eventual neutrality was that Blood Chief Red Crow, who heads the most powerful of the Blackfoot-speaking tribes, refused to assist his traditional Cree enemies. In any case, the government gave Crowfoot a present of $100 and also made monetary rewards to other Indians who did not join the rebellion. Reliable sources indicate that, for the same reason, Canadian Pacific Railway officials are considering giving Crowfoot a lifetime railway pass, though he often complains about the CPR.

Crowfoot, photographed in October 1886 with CPR lifetime pass, a gift for abstaining from recent Rebellion.

Poundmaker died while he and Crowfoot were attending a Sun Dance religious ceremony.

Wrigley is first steamer on the Mackenzie

Sept. 24, 1886

FORT SMITH, N.W.T. – The first steamer to operate on the Mackenzie River is the *Wrigley*. She has been working on the Athabasca River the past two years, and now serves communities down river from Fort Smith. Until now York boats – taking very small loads – have been used to handle the supplies for exploration and development on the river.

The steamer Wrigley is now serving communities on the Mackenzie River.

Site picked for future Mormon settlement

Oct. 24, 1886

DISTRICT OF ALBERTA, N.W.T. – Charles Ora Card today chose a site between the Belly and St. Mary rivers for future Mormon settlement. Card, a member of the Church of Jesus Christ of Latter Day Saints, and two colleagues were chosen by a group of 40 Mormons, currently in Utah, to find land in Canada suitable for farming. The group, eager to escape religious persecution, hopes to journey north next year.

Flames destroy 14 places of business

Nov. 7, 1886

CALGARY – A major fire destroyed 14 places of business here, including four stores, three warehouses, three hotels, one tinsmith shop, and a saloon. The blaze began in a log structure on the north side of Atlantic Avenue, and it quickly spread from one tinder-dry building to the next.

The volunteer "bucket brigade" proved completely ineffective. What stopped the blaze was the fireguard created when still more volunteers literally dismantled George Murdoch's harness shop.

Sitting Bull and Buffalo Bill.

1887

Medicine Hat, Northwest Territories, Jan. 6. Cascade Lodge No. 342 of the Brotherhood of Locomotive Firemen is formed, the first union in [Alberta].

Peterborough, Ont., Feb. 12. Isabella Valancy Crawford, Canada's first major female poet, author of *Malcolm's Katie*, dies. Critics have called her work too masculine.

Northwest Territories, April 4. Cree Chief Big Bear, imprisoned during the uprising of 1885, is released from jail.

Halifax, April 27. The legislature passes a motion postponing the idea of repealing Confederation in light of federal election results in the province that go against repeal.

Nanaimo, B.C., May. A coal mine explosion kills 150, highlighting brutal working conditions in mines.

Winnipeg, July. 16. On PM Macdonald's orders, the lieutenant-governor disallows the Red River Valley Railway Act, passed by Premier Norquay to build a railway to the U.S.

Ontario, Sept. 23. John Bayne Maclean starts publishing the *Canadian Grocer* [beginning his publishing empire].

Stony Mountain, Man. There are 68 semi-domesticated plains buffalo here, maybe the only left in Canada. There are thousands of wood buffalo left.

Quebec. Louis-Honoré Fréchette, the unofficial poet laureate of French Canada and son of an illiterate contractor, publishes *La Légende d'ùn peuple*, a series of historical poems tracing the history of French Canada from Jacques Cartier to Louis Riel.

Annette Island, Alaska. Lay missionary William Duncan leads Tsimshian Indians to form a Christian utopian community called New Metlakatla. Duncan founded a successful utopian community in 1862 at Metlakatla, B.C., but an Anglican bishop challenged his authority there.

United States. Scientists measure the speed of light, and claim that this speed is the same throughout the universe.

Montreal. The eight-storey New York Life Insurance Co. Building may be the first Montreal skyscraper.

Northwest Territories. [Alberta] merchant D.W. Davis sends his Indian wife back to her reserve after white neighbors oppose the marriage.

Vancouver loses charter because of riots

Chinese railway workers live in camps such as this one at Kamloops, B.C.

Feb. 24, 1887

VICTORIA, B.C. – The provincial government has suspended Vancouver's charter after a mob attacked Chinese workers' camps on False Creek and the outskirts of the city. The Chinese were driven out of town.

Trouble began when a contractor hired some Chinese men, for 75 cents a day, who had been working on the CPR. White laborers wanted $2. A local trade union, newspapers and some businessmen incited the workers, and after some protests the camps were attacked. Some Vancouver citizens blame the trouble on a gang of American burglars who, they say, started the riots to cover their tracks.

Macdonald and Tories returned to power

Feb. 22, 1887

OTTAWA – Sir John A. Macdonald has done it again. Despite public grumbling over the cost of the CPR, provincial election losses in Nova Scotia, Ontario and Manitoba, and other obstacles, he and his Conservatives were returned to power in today's federal election. The Tories won 123 seats, to the Liberals' 92.

Of course, Macdonald's success is another man's failure. In this case, that man is Liberal leader Edward Blake, who relied on a rational and uninspired approach in the campaign. It's the second time Blake has lost to Macdonald.

John A. Fraser's watercolor Summit Lake near Lenchoile, Bow River.

Parti National wins election in Quebec

Jan. 29, 1887

QUEBEC CITY – Simmering French-Canadian outrage over the execution of Métis leader Louis Riel has reached the boiling point, spilling beyond ethnic adversity and into the political arena: the Parti National, led by Honoré Mercier, assumed office today as the new provincial government. Mercier used the 1885 execution to fan the flames of French discontent with English Canada: last November, Montreal's popular *La Presse* declared, "Henceforth there are no more Conservatives, nor Liberals, nor Castors. There are only *Patriots* and *Traitors* – the National Party and the Party of the Rope."

Honoré Mercier, head of the Parti National, which took office today.

Port of Vancouver business booming

Aug. 11, 1887

VANCOUVER – About a year after a major fire levelled Vancouver, the port here is booming. Locally, the port, close to the Pacific terminus of the CPR, supplies camps and communities on Vancouver Island and up the coast to Alaska with goods from the east. Internationally, CPR's Pacific shipping line, built to use the fast route to the Far East, carries tea, silk, mail and passengers between Vancouver and the Orient. On special CPR trains, silk can be in New York 21 days out of Yokohama.

Canada seeks help of British in sealing tiff with Americans

April 17, 1887

OTTAWA – Britain has been asked by Ottawa to protest the seizure of Canadian sealing ships by the Americans in the north Pacific. A big sealing industry was developed by the Russians on the Pribilof Islands in the Bering Sea, but then the U.S. bought Alaska from Russia in 1867 and took over the sealing industry.

In recent years, however, the number of seals on the islands has fallen sharply, and so sealers are deserting the shores and are, instead, hunting seals out in the ocean. But here too, stocks are shrinking, and so the competition for seals is fiercer. That is why the Americans are zealously guarding the seal fishing grounds and trying to scare off Canadian sealers. The cat and mouse game in the ocean will go on until limits are set. Now everyone loses, including the seals.

Americans retaliate against Canadians

March 3, 1887

WASHINGTON, D.C. – The United States moved to exclude Canadian ships from its waters and to ban imports from its northern neighbor today. The action was implemented with the passing of a Fisheries Retaliation Act.

The act comes in the wake of Canadian legislation last year to exclude U.S. ships from commercial use of ports in Canada. Canadians took the action after the U.S. did not respond to overtures to negotiate an agreement on the issue.

Alberta cattle die of cold, starvation

March 1, 1887

PINCHER CREEK, N.W.T. – The cattle on the ranches around here are dying of starvation and cold in the worst winter in memory. Part of the appeal of ranching in the Alberta district of the Northwest Territories lies in the fact that cattle can survive the relatively mild winters. But last Christmas the temperature fell rapidly, and it has stayed down since then.

Chinooks have made matters worse, for they melt snow only for it to freeze again as ice coating the grass. Some cattle are eating twigs and shrubs which puncture their stomachs. Others have been killed by trains as they seek refuge from the snowdrifts on the tracks.

An Alberta rancher demonstrates how to lead an unwilling cow. With this winter's bad weather, ranchers are worried about the survival of their cattle.

Laurier at the helm of federal Liberals

June 7, 1887

OTTAWA – Wilfrid Laurier, a French-Canadian MP from Quebec, has been chosen to succeed Edward Blake as leader of the federal Liberal party. Laurier, a gifted bilingual speaker with a reputation for charm, has long been recognized as the party's most important and powerful Quebec member. He has government experience, having briefly served as minister of inland revenue in the Liberal regime of Alexander Mackenzie in the 1870s.

Laurier faces a tough task in trying to build a winning federal party. In fact, the Liberals have only defeated the Tories once since Confederation. That victory came in 1874, and only because of the Pacific Railway Scandal. So victory, if ever, is a long way off for Laurier and his Liberals.

Nanaimo has become a major shipping centre for the important coal mining industry on Vancouver Island. Here sailing ships wait their turn to load up at the busy Nanaimo coal wharves.

Coal mining is a very dangerous occupation, as this photo illustrates. Women and children wait anxiously for news of the men below after a recent explosion at the Vancouver Coal Mining Co. in Nanaimo, B.C.

Railway a kind of "Northwest Passage"

June 23, 1887

VANCOUVER – One of the dreams of the founders of the Canadian Pacific Railway is coming true. They saw the railway as providing a link between Europe and the Orient – a kind of Northwest Passage. Now mail, freight and passengers from the Orient are on their way to London, via Vancouver and the railway to Montreal, and then ships across the Atlantic Ocean.

The first of a series of voyages by fast ships between Vancouver and Japan was completed nine days ago when the 3,800-ton steamer *Abyssinia* arrived here. Two other ships have been chartered by the Canadian Pacific Railway to maintain a regular service.

New laws both protect and exploit

June 23, 1887

CANADA – This year has seen unprecedented government action in the field of conservation, culminating in today's decision by both Houses of Parliament to pass the Rocky Mountains Park Act. In April, Ontario created Queen Victoria Falls Park at Niagara Falls, and earlier this month North America's first bird sanctuary was established at Last Mountain Lake in the District of Saskatchewan. But have the governments responsible for these parks taken giant steps toward conserving the scenic wonders and wildlife of Canada, or are they merely taking advantage of one more bankable resource? The answer, to both questions, is a qualified yes.

The Banff Springs Hotel in the beautiful Canadian Rockies in Alberta.

With the exception of Last Mountain Lake, commercially motivated interests in both private and public sectors have played a decisive role in creating the parks, a greater role than the ideals of conservation and preservation. In government and business circles, to "preserve" is to protect a natural resource not from, but for exploitation. The federal government hopes Rocky Mountains Park, located near Banff in the District of Alberta, will attract tourists; park regulations control but do not prohibit mining or lumber interests in the area, nor do they prevent hunting. Similarly, plans are for the area surrounding Queen Victoria Falls Park to be more of a tourist resort than nature reserve.

Ex-premier of P.E.I. Col. John Gray dies

Aug. 13, 1887

CHARLOTTETOWN – P.E.I. has lost its most dignified statesman, former premier Col. John Hamilton Gray, who died today at age 76. Gray had a distinguished career in the British army before retiring to the Island in 1856.

Building an equally notable political career, Gray was premier in 1864 when the issue of the decade broke out. Confederation, for Gray, was as bitter as any army battle. He was convinced union would solve the Island's political and sectarian quarrels, but was forced to resign since few shared his view. Gray had the satisfaction of seeing P.E.I. join Confederation in 1873.

Col. John Hamilton Gray.

Lady Macdonald lays bridge cornerstone

Aug. 18, 1887

FREDERICTON – Lady Agnes Macdonald, Prime Minister Sir John A. Macdonald's wife, today laid the cornerstone for this city's first railway bridge. It crosses the St. John River, linking the city with Saint John and railways west and north. But Macdonald is furious that in Manitoba, Premier John Norquay defied the federal government, and recently turned the first sod of a line to the U.S. border. Because it rivals the CPR's Pembina line, a furious Macdonald got Ottawa to disallow the Red River Valley Railway Act, but Norquay's mad scheme has already threatened the economic future of the entire Canadian northwest.

Lady Macdonald lays cornerstone for the new Fredericton railway bridge.

Liberal premiers air common grievances

Oct. 20, 1887

QUEBEC CITY – The premiers of the five Liberal-led provinces – Ontario, Quebec, Nova Scotia, New Brunswick and Manitoba – are in town today. They're here for an inter-provincial conference; a place where they can air their grievances against the federal government, and try to work together to change things.

Among the resolutions said to be on the table are motions supporting the notion of freer trade with the United States. As well, it's expected that Manitoba will push for an agreement to abolish disallowance, a principle that lets the federal government disallow provincial laws when the two conflict. Ottawa recently exercised this right to prevent Manitoba from chartering its own railroad.

Beyond this, the premiers can be expected to do as Canadian premiers often do – that is, call for more restrictions of Ottawa's powers, and an increase in federal grants for the provinces.

Commercial union with U.S. backed

Oct. 12, 1887

INGERSOLL, Ont. – Sir Richard Cartwright, the most powerful Ontario MP in the federal Liberal party, has declared himself a supporter of "commercial union" with the United States. He made his views clear today, at a meeting in his constituency.

Commercial union means a massive reduction in protective tariffs and duties, something the Liberals believe will help bring prosperity to Canada. But it's a policy that is violently opposed by Sir John A. Macdonald, the country's Conservative prime minister.

Icelandic settlers heading west again

Fall 1887

MANITOBA – Icelandic immigration to the province, slowed by the North West Rebellion of 1885, is rising again. And unlike the last wave in 1883, the majority of recent arrivals are not poor but have brought "sizable" amounts of capital. This is good news, for while Icelanders have always displayed the "honesty, industry, and frugality" that has made them attractive as settlers, a series of calamities tarnished their reputations and, indeed, their own vision of Canada.

The first western Icelandic settlement was established in 1875. The following year a smallpox epidemic devastated the community. Then successive crop failures and floods left Icelanders in desperate need of government assistance, leading some to argue that as settlers, they were a financial liability. Others said the Icelanders were merely unfortunate, and pointed to their contributions, such as the establishment of schools, newspapers, churches and agricultural societies.

Inspector: Blackfoot progress slow

Sept. 13, 1887

GLEICHEN, N.W.T. – The inspector of Indian agencies and reserves left here today after a five-day visit to the Blackfoot Indian reserve. Alexander McGibbon said he was pleased with the progress Chief Crowfoot's people have made during the past year, but added that there is much room for improvement. McGibbon said the Blackfoot crops are somewhat better this year, but bad weather has caused low yields. This, combined with a scarcity of small game, means the Indians continue to rely heavily on government rations for sustenance.

While Inspector McGibbon was here, he observed the annual treaty payments and the butchering of cattle for use as rations. This beef is most welcome to the Indians as a change from the often-rancid bacon that in previous years formed the bulk of their rations. The Blackfoot continue to have many fewer acres under cultivation than do other Indians in the Northwest. The 2,000 people on this reserve have cultivated only 235 acres. This compares with the more than 1,000 acres cultivated by about half that number of people on the Battleford Cree reserves. But, as white settlers know full well, this part of the country is more suited to ranching than to agriculture. Also, the government has not provided the Blackfoot with cattle. Instead, neighboring white ranchers supply cattle for the Indians to butcher.

Inspector McGibbon was most critical about the lack of progress in the Indian schools, which he complained do not offer their students a comfortable atmosphere.

Officials carefully weigh and record food rations being given to Blackfoot.

Salvation Army operating coast-to-coast

Dec. 18, 1887

VANCOUVER, B.C. – The Salvation Army realized its dream of establishing a line of salvation outposts across Canada when a facility was opened in an opera house here today. In August, the army had established itself in Calgary. The advance of the army westward involved holding open-air meetings to rally support until the group obtained a building. Arthur Young, who had established the army in the Maritime provinces last year, led the push west. The cross-Canada effort took five years.

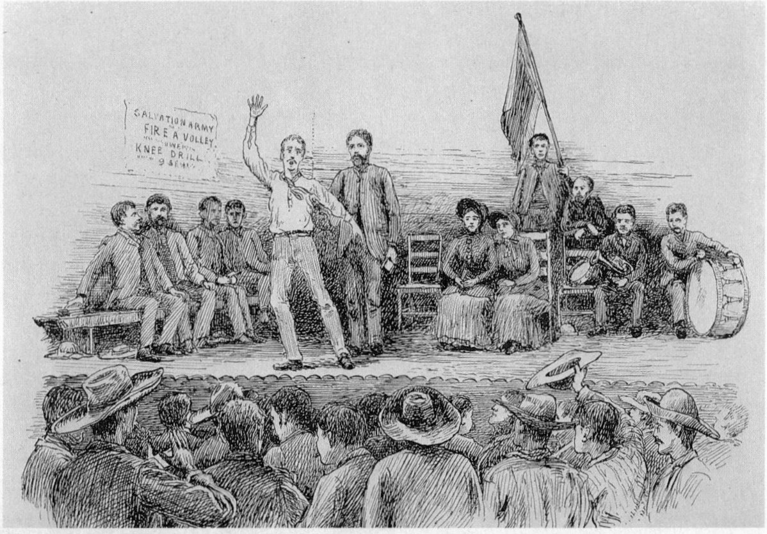

The Salvation Army wins new converts at a recent meeting in Calgary.

First long distance call made on prairies

Nov. 1, 1887

NORTHWEST TERRITORIES – Alex Taylor of Edmonton and Hugh Richardson of Battleford today made telephone history, completing the first long distance call on the prairies. Battleford is 492 kilometres east of Edmonton. Telegraph services link the two communities, but the North West Rebellion of 1885 revealed there was a need for better communications.

Saturday Night magazine hits the streets

Dec. 13, 1887

TORONTO – *Saturday Night,* a weekly magazine targeted at Toronto's upper middle class, has been founded by Edmund Sheppard. The magazine is initially being published in newspaper format, and it hits the street at 6 p.m. on Saturdays. The first issue sold out all 9,500 copies printed.

Sheppard, who is signing his editorials "Don," has been editor-in-chief of the Toronto *News* for the last four years. Born near St. Thomas in 1855 and educated as a minister, Sheppard worked in his youth as a stagecoach driver and cattle herder in Mexico and Texas. He returned to Canada at age 23.

Edmund Sheppard is the founder of the new Saturday Night magazine.

1888

Halifax, Feb. 1. Sir Hugh Hoyles, first native-born prime minister of Newfoundland, chief justice, and knight, dies.

Winnipeg, March 31. The Winnipeg Press Club holds a reunion bringing together the most important figures in Winnipeg journalism.

Nova Scotia, May 3. William Alexander Henry, a Father of Confederation, dies.

Quebec, Sept. 26. Alphonse-Télesphore Lépine, a printer and member of the Knights of Labor, becomes the first labor MP elected in Quebec.

Victoria, Oct. 1. Richard McConnell arrives after making a surveying expedition to the Yukon. One of three men sent by the Canadian government to survey the Yukon in 1887, he recorded valuable data about geology, flora, and fauna.

Regina, Oct. 31. The first legislature of the Northwest Territories opens.

Sudbury, Ont. The Canada Copper Company starts smelting operations. Copper mining has just begun in the area.

Northwest Territories. Johnny Franklin, ranked the best bronco buster in Alberta, gets $75 a month for his efforts.

Vancouver. The Vancouver Rowing Club is founded.

Northwest Territories. There are only six plains buffalo still alive in Alberta.

New York. *A Strange Manuscript Found in a Copper Cylinder*, by Canadian James De Mille, is published posthumously and anonymously. It is an adventure story that satirizes the search for rank and wealth.

Northwest Territories. Montreal's Allan interests own a ranch in Alberta with about 10,000 cattle that pays annual dividends of 20-35 percent. The western cattle industry, controlled by eastern Canadian capital, is prospering because of British market demand, the coming of the railway, and the refrigerated ship.

Calgary. Calgary is the centre of the cattle industry. Ranchers control the town's affairs.

Ontario. Canon Henry Scadding founds the Pioneer Association of Ontario [Ontario Historical Society].

Canada. The CPR inaugurates its mail service between eastern Canada and the Orient.

Lord Stanley is new governor general

Lord Stanley of Preston.

May 1, 1888

OTTAWA – Lord Stanley of Preston is the new governor general of Canada, succeeding the Marquis of Lorne. Lord Stanley is reputed to be a quiet, almost shy man. He comes from a family that has held the Derby peerage in England since 1139, making it the second-oldest peerage still in existence. Lord Stanley has been a Conservative member in the British parliament, serving in numerous cabinet positions. In Canada, Stanley is expected to play a low-key role.

Big Bear recalled as a man of peace

Jan. 17, 1888

LITTLE PINE RESERVE, N.W.T. – Big Bear, a plains Cree chief who in his lifetime fought hard for the preservation of his people, died today. He'll long be remembered as a peaceful man, at times too peaceful for his followers. After a band of his men overrode his wishes in 1885 and killed eight whites and a mixed-blood at Frog Lake, Big Bear was convicted of inciting a rebellion and sentenced to three years in the Stony Mountain Penitentiary. A broken, sick man by then in his early 60s, Big Bear served two years of the term and was released on March 4, 1887.

Credited on many occasions with trying to do the impossible for his people, two of Big Bear's concerns were the disappearance of the buffalo and trying to ensure fair treaty terms for the Indians.

Lampman publishes Among the Millet

1888

OTTAWA – Critically acclaimed poet Archibald Lampman, 27, has further captured the imaginations of a small but discerning audience with his self-published collection *Among the Millet and other poems*. The young postal clerk lives in Ottawa and often finds inspiration in the surrounding countryside. The following lines are taken from the poem *Heat*:

I lift mine eyes sometimes to gaze:
The burning skyline blinds
my sight:
The woods far off are blue
with haze:
The hills are drenched in light...

And yet to me not this or that
Is always sharp or always sweet;
In the sloped shadow of my hat
I lean at rest, and drain the heat;

Nay more, I think some blessed
power
Hath brought me wandering
idly here:
In the full furnace of this hour
My thoughts grow keen and clear

Poet Archibald Lampman.

Liberals push for free trade with the U.S.

March 14, 1888

OTTAWA – The Liberal party, apparently seeking a policy to unite it after the divisions caused by the Riel issue, has decided to advocate unrestricted free trade, or unlimited reciprocity, with the United States.

In Parliament today, Liberal Sir Richard Cartwright moved for "the largest possible freedom of commercial intercourse" between the two countries. It's a motion that welcomes defeat by the majority Tories, and has a lot of political pundits wondering where the Liberals are coming from. After all, many of those advocating free trade are known to be annexationists – supporters of Canada joining the U.S. These are people hardly likely to ever command the majority of public opinion in Canada.

The debate over Cartwright's motion should actually benefit Prime Minister John A. Macdonald. It will allow him to play upon his loyalty to Britain, something that English-speaking voters love.

In this Hudson's Bay trading store, some natives barter with the company clerk while a NWMP officer exchanges news with a local fur trader.

Women, children targeted in most cases of cruelty

Dec. 31, 1888

HALIFAX – More than two-thirds of the cases handled this year by the Nova Scotia Society for the Prevention of Cruelty involved not animals, but women and children. The caseload included dozens of children who were neglected or abused by drunken parents and cruel foster parents, as well as women whose husbands had beaten or deserted them.

The society rescues starving youngsters from impoverished or uncaring parents, frightened women from violent men, and abused old people from their own callous offspring.

Secretary-agent John Naylor says 80 percent of those he cautions or prosecutes are drunkards, and that almost all his cases involve family problems. Andrew Doyle of Halifax has repeatedly been jailed for assaulting or threatening his mother, sister, his sister-in-law, brother-in-law, brother, and his father. Naylor also prosecuted him for assaulting a small girl. However, even such ruffians appeal for help. Doyle has complained to Naylor about the cruelty of the Halifax prison.

This "prie-dieu," or prayer stool, from Quebec illustrates the late nineteenth century popularity of the Victorian style of furniture.

Plan targets Montreal flooding problem

Residents use rowboats at St. Paul and McGill streets during Montreal flood.

March 1888

MONTREAL – The federal government will study a plan to deal with the flooding problem the St. Lawrence River causes in this city each spring. Flooding in April 1885 was the greatest in 12 years. No trains could leave for New York, a hackman drowned on Centre Street, so many boats and rafts were used they were colliding at street corners, and people in flooded areas had to have bread tossed to them through upper windows.

Catholic church to be paid for Jesuit land

Sept. 12, 1888

QUEBEC CITY – The Parti National government of Honoré Mercier has passed a bill settling claims of Catholic Jesuit priests for the loss of their lands. The complicated issue arose when the Pope suppressed the Jesuit order in 1773. In 1800, the Jesuit estates were turned over to the Lower Canadian government, which used them to fund education. However, in the 1860s, the Jesuits returned and reclaimed their land. The government has compensated the Catholic church $400,000.

Prostitute shoots drunken Mountie

Oct. 28, 1888

EDMONTON – The calm of Nellie Webb's house of prostitution was violently shattered tonight, when two drunken Mounties tried to force their way in.

Mounties, most of them single men under 30, are among the prostitutes' best customers, but tonight Nellie refused to let two in – maybe because they were so drunk. She says they threatened to wreck her house and kill her, and when they started to kick down the door, she shot one of them in the thigh. Nellie has been arrested on charges of malicious shooting.

Giant circus star Anna Swan dies

Aug. 5, 1888

SEVILLE, Ohio – Only death could render an uncommon woman such as the seven-foot-six Anna Haining Swan common. The Nova Scotia-born giant, once billed by P.T. Barnum as the world's biggest girl, died today of tuberculosis.

Born in 1846, she joined Barnum's circus at 16. In 1868 she was presented to Queen Victoria alongside Kentucky giant Martin Van Buren Bates. The queen gave Swan a gold watch, and Swan gave Bates her hand in marriage. They settled at Seville where they built a house with tall ceilings.

Giants Anna Swan and husband.

Charlottetown artist Robert Harris depicts a school choir in Local Stars.

Sea creatures in trouble

Shouldering their clubs, sealers drag their laced-up catch across the ice.

1888

NORTH AMERICA – There is a crisis in Canadian waters, as sea creatures buckle under the weight of centuries of slaughter by Europeans and their descendants. An 1840 testimonial by a professor who boarded the sealer *Topaz* at the main harp seal whelping patch on the ice off Newfoundland, is still valid today: "One of the men hooked up a young seal with his gaff. Its cries were precisely like those of a young child in the extremity of agony and distress. ... I saw one poor wretch skinned while yet alive, and the body writhing in blood after being stripped of its pelt."

This incident occurred in the "great days" of the Newfoundland seal hunt, days that provided a livelihood for many Newfoundlanders, and made some rich. From 1830 to 1860, about 13 million seals were landed, and twice as many killed.

A humpback whale sinks like lead when it dies, but decomposition makes its body temperature rise. After a few days, the corpse shoots to the surface because of the gases produced. In the 1700s, American whalers in the Gulf of St. Lawrence put these facts to good use with a wasteful but profitable whaling technique. They lanced whales indiscriminately, expecting to recover their corpses when they rose to the surface. By the 1820s, American and European whaling had made naturally abundant whale species scarce in the gulf.

Since the 1700s, fishermen have blocked off the spawning rivers of the Atlantic salmon with nets and weirs, scooping handfuls of the fish ashore. Now the salmon are showing the first signs of depletion. People would do well to heed the words of English observer John Rowan, who recently warned: "Canadians will spend large sums of money in, perhaps, fruitless efforts to bring back that which they could now so easily retain."

Supplies of the popular and once plentiful salmon are beginning to diminish.

Hunt takes heavy toll

Misuse of the "iron horse" has helped hasten the disappearance of the buffalo.

1888

NORTH AMERICA – This year, in the District of Alberta, only six buffalo have been sighted. Yet short decades ago, millions of buffalo roamed the great western plains. In the first half of this century, pioneer Susanna Moodie was struck by the notion that many men in this land consider "hunting and fishing as the sole aim and object of life." For such men, life must now be far less satisfying. More efficient at killing than ever, thanks largely to the advent of the repeating rifle, they have little left to shoot at – the myth of an inexhaustible supply of game has been shattered. The largest, most devastating animal killing spree in history is over.

The buffalo have fallen in the wake of the railway and the stream of settlement trailing behind, and in the face of hunters greedy for the rich bounty of their hides. At the beginning of this century pronghorn antelope were as abundant as buffalo; now they also are perilously close to extinction. Further west, the foraging grizzly bear, perceived as a threat by settlers, is often shot on sight. So too the wolf and mountain lion. In many areas of eastern Canada beaver have been trapped to the point of extinction. Cougars are considered vermin and killed whenever possible. Deer and elk, long valued for their meat and once so plentiful in parts of Canada, are scarcely ever found near settlements anymore.

Hunted, trapped and poisoned for food, clothing, for their valuable fur, or because they are a nuisance, the slaughter of Canadian wildlife has occurred unregulated: there are no government controls – no quotas to limit hunting or restrict it to certain areas. Since mid-century, the attack has been relentless, sudden in its swiftness, and foolish in view of its consequence.

The killing continues: many bird species in danger

Spring 1888

CANADA – The regenerating rays of the spring sun summon many species of birds to Canada, where great flocks settle to perpetuate their species in the tranquil and plentiful landscape of the Canadian wilderness. But the destiny of many is recast each year when greedy humans decimate entire flocks for profit.

One species particularly affected is the passenger pigeon. It is the nature of these birds to congregate at favorite and mysteriously chosen roosting places throughout the Canadian forest where they return night after night. Although the pigeons fly in large numbers in close formation with breathtaking skill at an average speed of 100 kilometres an hour and are able to dart in and out of trees with grace and ease, they become easy targets once they land to roost in trees.

Market hunters set up encampments and wait for the huge flocks to descend to their doom. No special skills or weapons are needed. Roosting trees are felled or set on fire, bringing thousands of pigeons crashing to their death, and piling singed and multilated carcasses of adult and young birds to be harvested for pure profit.

The meat from adult birds is a staple of the North American market, while squabs excite the sophisticated palate and fill the pockets of market hunters. Gizzards, blood and dung are concocted into medical cures for ailments ranging from stomach pains to epilepsy. The roosting places of the passenger pigeon are veritable gold mines that can be looted by anyone wishing to make a quick gain from an effortless slaughter.

Passenger pigeons account for about 40 percent of the North American bird population. A typical flock can extend 9.6 kilometres in width and 515 kilometres in length, containing more than 1,000 million birds. Relentless hunting is diminishing populations to such an extent that only a few hundred birds are returning to known nesting and roosting sites.

On the Atlantic coast, curlews suffer a similar fate in late spring when they gather to roost on the beaches of Newfoundland. Without even using ammunition, market hunters kill large numbers of Arctic curlews. The men walk among the Arctic birds under the cover of darkness, stun them with the light from lanterns, and strike them down using sticks and clubs.

The carcasses of the "dough-birds," so named because of the fat they accumulate from their Labrador feeding, are salted down in barrels and brought to market to be sold as gourmet delicacies. The continual plundering of roosting and nesting places is taking its toll on the Arctic curlew; populations are being decimated at an alarming rate. Every year the species gets closer to the vanishing point.

Collectors eager for skins of the whooping crane support bird slaughtering forces by offering a price of $2.50 per skin and up to $18 for a skin in perfect condition. The long-legged, graceful marsh birds can walk as fast as man, yet can only protest by blowing loud buglelike noises from their vermilion-smudged beaks as human predators lift the one or two eggs from their nests for a sound profit of $2 an egg, and then grab the adults for their skins.

Colonies of the great snowy-white birds all over North America are dwindling, and known nesting places in the Saskatchewan marshes are becoming scarce, placing the whooping crane on the threshold of extinction.

The passenger pigeon, once abundant on this continent, now faces the very distinct possibility of extinction.

The flightless Great Auk could once be found nesting along the North Atlantic shores, but it has now been hunted to extinction by man.

The whooping crane, tallest bird in North America, is also in danger.

1889

Montreal, Jan. 18. A large crowd gathers for the funeral of eccentric philanthropist "Joe Beef" (Charles McKiernan). It is the most impressive Montreal funeral since that of Thomas D'Arcy McGee.

Kingston, Jamaica, June 3. The Bank of Nova Scotia opens a branch here.

Toronto, June. D'Alton McCarthy forms the Equal Rights Association to work for the repeal of the Quebec Jesuits' Estates Act and for equal rights before the law for Protestant and Catholic denominations. McCarthy's real goal is the supremacy of the English language.

Quebec, Sept. 19. A massive rockslide smashes much of Champlain Street, killing 45.

Nova Scotia. Murdock McLeod, a Springhill miner with 20 years experience underground, tells a royal commission that he began mine work at the age of nine.

Winnipeg. The Shaare Zedek Synagogue, the first synagogue in the northwest, is built.

Montreal. Royal Victoria College is completed, intended to serve as a social, academic, and administrative centre for female students. It was established with a gift of almost $1 million from Donald Smith (Lord Strathcona).

Toronto. St. Paul's Catholic Church is consecrated, one of the finest examples of Romanesque architecture in the country.

Canada. The CPR opens a line across northern Maine from Montreal to Saint John, providing the railway with direct access to an all-weather Atlantic port.

British Columbia. The salmon industry is booming: 9,054,957 kilograms of salmon are packed in 1889.

Ontario. On average, women workers without dependants work 54 hours a week for 259 days a year and earn $216.71 a year. A woman's average annual cost of living is $214.28.

Canada. In the 1880s, a full 20 percent of Canada's industrial leaders were born in Scotland, and another 28 percent had Scottish fathers. Scots are dominant in Canadian economic affairs.

Northwest Territories. George Ross of Little Bow Ranch forms Alberta's first polo team.

Only 635 bison left, most in captivity

A buffalo hunter skins one of the many huge animals he has just killed.

c.1889

NORTH AMERICAN PLAINS – Hunted to near-extinction by hide and meat hunters, only about 635 plains bison survive, almost all in captivity. The last of the great buffalo herds ended on the Canadian plains in 1879 and on the American plains in 1883. Bleached bones still litter the plains, and as late as 1882, a heap 12 metres across and 1.8 metres high stood on the present site of Regina. Gathering buffalo bones is now big business. Bones are shipped east and made into phosphate fertilizer. Also, carbon is extracted for sugar refineries.

Woodland Cree bands sign Treaty No. 6

Feb. 11, 1889

MONTREAL LAKE, N.W.T. – Treaty 6 has just been extended to include a 28,490-square-kilometre portion of land between the North Saskatchewan and Churchill rivers, north of Prince Albert. The Montreal Lake and Lac La Ronge Woodland Cree Indian bands today signed an adhesion to Treaty No. 6. The Woodland Crees signed the treaty as they sought to make a formal agreement with the Crown before large numbers of non-natives enter their territory.

Archdeacon John Alexander Mackay, an Anglican missionary of part-Cree background, translated the legal document from English into Cree for the Indians. Mackay might be able to help with clarifying a linguistic problem emerging from the original Treaty 6 negotiations in 1876. Which word was used in the original negotiations to translate the English word "land" into Cree? The Cree language requires great precision in the use of prefixes to specify exact meanings. Did the government interpreters use the prefix indicating "surface" land to explain what the settlers needed for farming? Many Treaty 6 elders recall that the Canadians used the Cree word for surface land. Consequently, they believe that they have only sold the surface rights to their land.

Due to the constant danger of avalanches in the Rockies, snow sheds have been built over the CPR tracks at the most dangerous locations.

First dogs register with Kennel Club

1889

TORONTO – The first two dogs have been registered with the Canadian Kennel Club, established to control the purity of Canadian purebreds. Nichi, a male Eskimo dog, is owned by R.J. Inglis. Jumbo, a male Newfoundland dog, is owned by S.T. Ami.

Both Eskimo and Newfoundland breeds are uniquely Canadian. Eskimo dogs descend from animals kept by Thule people. They are sled and transport dogs, and also hunt. Newfoundlands, large, heavy, and black-coated, are excellent companions and guardians.

Campbell publishes new book of poems

1889

SAINT JOHN, N.B. – William Wilfred Campbell, 31, has published his second book, *Lake lyrics and other poems*. He continues to examine nature, but less as God's gift to man than as a force in itself, powerful and even threatening. This stanza is from *The Winter Lakes*:

Lonely hidden bays...
Fringed by forests and crags,
haunted by shadowy shores;
Hushed from the outward strife,
where the mighty surf is grinding
Death and hate on the rocks, as
sandward and landward it roars.

Windstorm topples Niagara bridge

Jan. 10, 1889

NIAGARA FALLS – The suspension bridge over the Niagara River collapsed during a windstorm into the gorge below tonight. The structure, built 21 years ago, lies beneath about 45 metres of water, although some of the ruins are visible on the banks on either side. The bridge had been prone to swinging during heavy winds. The structure had undergone many renovations in its short life. Both the 30-centimetre square pine timbers of the towers and the wood bottom cord were replaced by steel. Last year, the 680-metre bridge was widened to accommodate two-way traffic.

A train passes over the Niagara River on the famous suspension bridge.

Alberta's first Jewish settler arrives with plans to set up shop

1889

CALGARY – The first Jewish settler has arrived in Alberta. However, Jacob Lion Diamond, 30, from Vilna, Poland, is not a new arrival to Canada. A decade ago he established himself in the Canadian east, and only now has he again pulled up stakes to try his luck in the west. Like most other East European Jewish settlers, Diamond is not interested in farming; he plans to open a liquor store.

Diamond will probably fare better as a merchant than farmer, if recent experiences in western Canada are a guide – several idealistic but badly-organized attempts to create Jewish farming communities have failed dismally, partly because few Eastern Europe Jews, even rural ones, have agricultural backgrounds. Most were petty traders.

Mr. and Mrs. Jacob Diamond are the first Jewish settlers in Alberta. Like most Jews from Eastern Europe, they are more interested in commerce than farming.

Special home opens for drunken women

March 1889

TORONTO – The Salvation Army has turned its attention to female inebriates. Prostitutes and other fallen women are already cared for in the Salvation Army Rescue at Wilton and Victoria. Seeking to separate women with a chronic thirst for strong drink from other unfortunates, Salvationists have put aside two cottages as the home for inebriates and outcasts.

This painting by J.D. Kelly depicting the uniforms of the Canadian Militia was given with the Christmas Globe this year. In the centre are a Grenadier Officer and a member of the Governor General's Body Guard.

Vote in Parliament refuses to disallow Jesuits' Estates Act

March 28, 1889

OTTAWA – The federal Parliament has voted overwhelmingly not to disallow Quebec's Jesuits' Estates Act, despite ongoing protest against the measure by hard-line Ontario Protestants.

The decision was expressed in the House today as the 188-13 defeat of a motion tabled by renegade Conservative W.E. O'Brien. That motion asked the government to use its power to disallow the law, on the grounds that it appropriated public funds to a religious organization. In the end, O'Brien managed to attract only seven other Conservatives and five Liberals, all English-speaking Protestants. For his part, Sir John voted against it.

To explain why this law has caused so much grief is far from easy. The story begins in 1773, when the Jesuits, a Roman Catholic order of priests prominent in Quebec, were disbanded by the Pope. Their estates were turned over to the Crown, which means that, as time passed, these lands eventually became the property of the province. The money from them was used to endow both Catholic and Protestant education in Quebec.

However, the Jesuits were re-established, returning to Canada in 1842. Understandably, they wanted their land back, something the Quebec government refused to do. After years of negotiation, Quebec passed the Jesuits' Estates Act last August giving the Jesuits $400,000 for their claims. As well, $60,000 was given to the Protestant Council of Public Instruction, as their share of the settlement.

What has raised the ire of many an Ontario Protestant is that the distribution of the $400,000 has been left to the Pope, who many of them openly revile. They fear the act constitutes foreign interference in Canadian affairs, and, worse yet, interference by the head of the dreaded French Catholics! It's just the sort of thing to feed the fears of those who improbably worry about the French minority overrunning the country; a passion that has led to major protest meetings in Toronto and other centres.

Manitoba planning to abolish its dual educational system

Aug. 1, 1889

SOURIS, Man. – The provincial government intends to move quickly to abolish Manitoba's dual system of education. An announcement to this effect was made today by James Smart, minister of public works. Smart announced the decision as if it were a new government policy. He is currently on a speaking tour in the southern part of the province, and he has been in touch with a number of school boards, many of which are in difficult financial straits. He said Catholic schools now were receiving more than their share of the provincial schools budget and an obvious answer to a vexing problem was to create one uniform, non-denominational system of public schools.

The announcement came as a surprise to the educational establishment. Recent information emanating from the legislative buildings has suggested that Premier Thomas Greenway, Smart, and the attorney general are the leaders of a movement to end education in French, but no action in this regard was expected as it is understood the subject has never been discussed with other members of cabinet.

Prairie game rapidly disappearing

Furs are not as plentiful as they once were at HBC posts like Fort Pitt.

1889

PRAIRIES – Game is rapidly disappearing from the prairies, contrary to the popular belief that it is abundant here. That is the substance of a letter written by NWMP Commissioner Lawrence Herchmer to the minister of the interior. Herchmer says elk, bears, and antelope are all suffering, and there are only six plains buffalo known to be alive in the territory. He blames Indians and whites who hunt and trap out of season. Herchmer's assistant says wild fowl are being depleted by market hunters and others who rob their nests of eggs.

Old foes Macdonald and Mowat honored

June 7, 1889

TORONTO – Two of Canada's foremost political enemies shared a platform today in a rare display of common purpose. Conservative Prime Minister John A. Macdonald and Oliver Mowat, Liberal premier of Ontario, were among the first group of recipients of honorary LLD degrees from Toronto University. Both men referred to their personal efforts in nurturing the university, and both were obviously proud of the institution's progress.

Some of the loudest cheers of this afternoon's convocation exercises were reserved for the five female graduates of the arts faculty. It was also noted with approval, and some surprise, that women won two of the three academic medals awarded in the arts faculty. Edward Blake, the university's chancellor and a longtime leader of the federal Liberal party, was also to receive an honorary degree today, but he was unavoidably absent. Macdonald made fun of his being an old man but a new graduate. His son is a previous graduate of the university.

Catholic privileges anger Manitoba MP

Aug. 5, 1889

PORTAGE LA PRAIRIE, Man. – The discussion over the formation of a single, non-denominational school system took an angry turn today as MP D'Alton McCarthy made a fiery attack on the Roman Catholics. In doing so, the outspoken MP added a new and unpleasant tone to an issue causing a furore across the province.

McCarthy's speech was based on what he describes as the growing political influence of the Roman Catholic clergy. He called for federal disallowance of the Jesuits' Estates Act, a Quebec law concerning the disposal of lands owned by the Jesuit order. Manitoba's attorney general was on the platform when McCarthy spoke.

MP D'Alton McCarthy opposes the growing Roman Catholic influence.

Switch to standard time has some Island residents fuming

The latest news is spread by the town crier in Queen Square, Charlottetown.

May 9, 1889

PRINCE EDWARD ISLAND – Islanders are calling the "imposition" of standard time a greater violation of Island life than Confederation ever was. Many believe standard time, in use in Prince Edward Island as of today, will affect life here more than joining the rest of Canada ever did.

Standard time was introduced in Canada to ease the difficulties encountered when making up railway schedules due to different time zones. The confrontation intensified when the local schedule of the Prince Edward Island Railway was changed to suit the standard time schedule of the Intercolonial Railway. Island residents are especially angry because their province has changed to eastern standard time, the same as Quebec and Ontario.

New Yorker guilty of suicide attempt in Niagara hoax

Sept. 8, 1889

NIAGARA FALLS, Ont. – New York saloonkeeper Steve Brodie today allowed himself to be convicted of attempting suicide for what was probably a hoax. Brodie claimed he was deliberately swept over Horseshoe Falls at 5:30 a.m. yesterday to demonstrate the effectiveness of a rubber suit he intends to sell. This afternoon, he was tried on a charge of attempted suicide. The police magistrate said he believed the affair was a hoax and that if Brodie signed a statement admitting he did not go over the falls he would be discharged. Brodie refused. Only one of his friends testified. The magistrate ruled Brodie had to post a bond of $500 and keep the laws of Canada for one year.

CP to take British mail to the Orient

July 15, 1889

HALIFAX – Canadian Pacific has signed a contract to provide a mail service using railways and ships to link Britain and the Orient via Canada. Ships will run from Britain to Halifax in winter and up to Quebec in summer. From these points, the mail will be transported by train to the west coast, then to Hong Kong. Previously, the England-Canada route's slowness stopped a North Pacific route.

Ontario-Manitoba border tiff settled

Dec. 9, 1889

WINNIPEG – The boundary dispute between Ontario and Manitoba has been settled in Ontario's favor. The decision was announced in Ottawa today and is the conclusion of a long-smouldering dispute over the point at which the boundary between the two provinces intersects the 49th Parallel. At one time both provinces tried to extend public services into Rat Portage [Kenora], the community in the centre of the disputed territory.

Father of Confederation dies in P.E.I.

Nov. 3, 1889

CHARLOTTETOWN – Edward Palmer, one of P.E.I.'s Fathers of Confederation, is dead. In a way, it is ironic to call Palmer a "Father" of Confederation, for in the 1860s he was one of its most bitter opponents. A political realist, Palmer was often criticized for his pragmatism. In 1865, for instance, he let his opposition to union transcend party loyalty, and managed to topple his own leader, pro-confederate J.H. Gray. Several years later, though, circumstances persuaded him union was, after all, a good thing.

Edward Palmer of P.E.I.

Grisly murder lands 14-year jail sentence

Mid-July 1889

CALGARY – The protracted Rosalie murder trial has ended with William Fisk's manslaughter conviction. On Feb. 28, the massive blacksmith, nicknamed Jumbo after the gigantic elephant, took Cree prostitute Rosalie to a room above a local saloon for "immoral purposes." Afterward he mutilated her, ripped open her abdomen, and left her to bleed to death. Fisk, sentenced to 14 years hard labor at Stony Mountain Penitentiary in Manitoba, denies his guilt, and some settlers here believe him. Others are unsure. A third group contends that as victim Rosalie was "only a squaw," her death did not much matter.

Plains Indians ignore ban on Sun Dance

Summer c.1889

PRAIRIES – Canada's plains Indians continue to perform the Sun Dance despite a government ban placed on the ritual in 1885. For the Blackfoot, Cree and Sarcee, the Sun Dance has long been a significant spiritual ceremony through which individuals seek guidance from the supernatural world. It also represents a coming of age for young warriors, and has a communal function – in summer, bands gather at a predetermined location to renew bonds of kinship and exchange gifts.

The ceremony usually lasts eight days: four for preparation, three for erecting the sacred lodge and sacred dance pole, and one for the actual dancing. The dancing symbolically represents four phases of warfare – capture, torture, captivity and escape – and is an essential step for a young male plains Indian hoping to attain warrior status.

The sacred dance pole and the sacred lodge of the Sun Dance.

Americans in north enter Beaufort Sea in search of whales

Aug. 12, 1889

HERSCHEL ISLAND, N.W.T. – For the first time, American ships have entered the Beaufort Sea in search of whales. A small fleet of seven whalers today arrived at this island, not far from the mouth of the Mackenzie River, after making the treacherous voyage eastward along the top of Alaska from Point Barrow.

The whalers are following the lead of a trader named Joe Tuckfield, who spent last winter camping with Inuit near the Mackenzie. Tuckfield returned with news that bowhead whales were "thick as bees" in the Beaufort. This was all the whalers needed to overcome their reluctance to risk their ships in the Arctic ice. Herschel Island appears to have a safe harbor and plenty of driftwood for fuel, and the whaling captains are considering the possibility of wintering over at the island instead of returning to the west in the fall.

American whalers have been cruising through Bering Strait since 1848 and reached Point Barrow some years ago. But until this summer, they have always considered the voyage into the Beaufort too risky an undertaking.

Tax collector holds CPR train hostage

December 1889

PORT ARTHUR, Ont. – One of the most unusual hostage-taking incidents in Canada's history has ended, the ransom paid. For several days an eastbound CPR train has been held captive by Port Arthur, its locomotive chained to the tracks by order of the town's tax collector.

At the time of the construction of the railway, the town granted the CPR an exemption from paying half its municipal taxes. However, that privilege was revoked earlier this year, and a newly elected town council demanded the CPR pay $15,000 in back taxes. The bitter dispute has finally drawn to a close, the CPR agreeing to pay $12,800 in exchange for the train's release.

1890

Ottawa, Jan. 22. D'Alton McCarthy introduces Bill 10 to annul the Northwest Territories Act that granted the French language equal rights before the courts and the legislature in the west.

Victoria, Feb. 22. A streetcar system is inaugurated, the third in Canada and the first west of Ontario.

Toronto, September. The Salvation Army opens the Prison Gate Home for ex-convicts, Toronto's first halfway house.

Washington, D.C., Oct. 6. The McKinley tariff goes into effect, increasing tariffs on imported goods an average of 48 percent. It is expected to hurt Canadian exporters.

North Dakota, U.S., Dec. 15. Indian police murder Sioux Chief Sitting Bull as they are trying to arrest him on U.S. army orders. Sitting Bull recently became a believer in the Ghost Dance, a mystic rite, alarming government officials who fear the Ghost Dance will unite the Indians.

South Dakota, U.S., Dec. 29. U.S. cavalry massacre 153 Sioux, half of them women and children, at Wounded Knee Creek. Violence erupted when the soldiers tried to disarm the Sioux, who came here after the murder of Sitting Bull.

St. Petersburg, Russia. Montrealer Louis Rubenstein wins the unofficial world figure skating championship.

Northwest Territories. Acting on pressure from Protestant clergy, the Mounties begin to take action against prostitution. When a complaint is made, they raid the brothel and arrest the prostitutes. Mounties are among the brothels' best customers.

Lennoxville, Que. Women are admitted to the faculty of medicine at Bishop's University.

Ottawa. The government prohibits killing of wildlife in Rocky Mountain Park at Banff Hot Springs. Exceptions could be made on the authorization of the park superintendent.

Nova Scotia. Of a total mine workforce of 5,000, more than 1,100 are under 18 years old.

Ontario. Journalist Sara Jeannette Duncan publishes her first novel, *A Social Departure*.

North America. Since 1880, millions of wild ducks, geese, and swans have been sold on North American markets. Market hunting is big business.

Schools Act passes in Manitoba after long, bitter debate

March 19, 1890

WINNIPEG – The controversial Schools Act passed today in the legislature with a recorded vote of 25-11, marking the end of public funding for Catholic schools in Manitoba. The act also ends a debate in the province noteworthy for both its length and its bitterness.

Opposition was led by former minister of education J.E.P. Prendergast. While he and his colleagues were hopelessly outnumbered, they were resolute in battle and managed to extend the debate by six days. In the dying minutes of the debate they attempted to have the legislation referred to the Supreme Court of Canada to have its constitutionality determined, but lacking numbers, they were unable to force this on the government. They argue that the legislation contravenes the British North America and Manitoba acts, and withdraws Roman Catholic educational privileges guaranteed in the Public School Act of 1871.

Early thaw spoils beef headed east

March 1890

CALGARY – Sir John Lister-Kaye's attempt to ship 800 dressed carcasses of beef to England via the Canadian Pacific Railway has come a cropper – because of an early thaw. Virtually all the shipment, destined for Liverpool via Halifax and refrigerated ships across the Atlantic, has been spoiled by the unseasonably warm weather.

Lister-Kaye, a tall, blond, blue-eyed baronet from Yorkshire, came to the Calgary area from Regina, where he owned a large ranch. Before that he had worked on a land resettlement scheme in California. He bought more than 100,000 acres along the railway between Calgary and Moose Jaw and stocked them with cattle, horses, sheep and pigs. Blizzards in January this year made grazing impossible, so Lister-Kaye had 800 cattle slaughtered and then left to freeze outside before being put on rail cars.

Furs "taken illegally" by Gen. Middleton

Trader Colin Fraser sorts fox, beaver and mink furs at Fort Chipewyan.

May 12, 1890

OTTAWA – Alexander McNeil, chairman of the Select Committee, reported to Parliament that Gen. Frederick Middleton, general officer commanding the Canadian militia, was found to have acted illegally in the confiscation of furs during the North West Rebellion. The furs were taken from Charles Bremner, a fur trader and farmer.

During the inquiry, Middleton himself admitted that in hindsight his actions were not justifiable. The Select Committee reports that Middleton was operating under a misperception of his powers. Bremner will receive $4,500 compensation.

The Massey Manufacturing Company of Toronto is winning recognition at exhibitions around the world for the efficiency of its farm machinery.

Cowboys rank Lethbridge the best in the west

Bull teams line up at Lethbridge. A mine tipple can be seen in the distance.

The streets of Lethbridge are busy as the Fort MacLeod stagecoach arrives.

1890

LETHBRIDGE, N.W.T. – The cowboys and settlers around here rank this town's sporting houses the best. And the girls and madams return the compliment. They say the cowboys and settlers are more generous than their other clients, such as miners or railway workers. And the good folk of Lethbridge? They are not upset by what goes on inside the brothel bedrooms; they object only to being wakened by the loud, happy singing and the noisy piano playing. Some local women feel sympathy for the girls but they are in a minority and there are few, if any, complaints of cruelty in the sporting houses.

The brothels at Lethbridge, on a section of land called The Point, on the west side of town, are homes away from home for the men. The brothels not only supply the men with women, at prices ranging from $2 to $5, but they also provide a warm, home-like atmosphere with pleasantly-decorated bedrooms, a parlor for meeting the girls, and a kitchen complete with Chinese cook. Compared to the Spartan bunkhouse, tent or home built of sod, the sporting houses are the height of comfort and luxury. And the girls offer sympathy and an attentive ear for the man who wants to talk away his troubles.

Of course, brothels are not the only places where cowboys and settlers can let off steam. Bars and pool halls also offer light, warmth, company and fun.

A young cowboy and his horse pose in front of an Alberta log dwelling.

Teams tie in first P.E.I. hockey game

Feb. 7, 1890

CHARLOTTETOWN – Ice hockey, which has been played as an organized sport in Montreal since 1875, is spreading to the Maritimes. Two years ago games were organized in Halifax, and today the first game in P.E.I. was played at Hillsborough Rink. Two teams from the Hillsborough Hockey Club faced off against each other. Each team has seven players: goaltender, point, centre point, centre, right wing, left wing and rover. Evenly matched, they played to an 8-8 tie. It was an "interesting and exciting game," reports the Charlottetown *Patriot*.

Island pair breeding silver foxes for pelts

1890

CHARLOTTETOWN – Charles Dalton is a farmer from Alberton. Robert Oulton, also a farmer, is originally from New Brunswick. Both are avid woodsmen with a consuming interest in the exotic silver fox. Likened to "a brunette born into a family of redheads," the silver fox is actually black. A strain of the red fox, it is the most highly prized of all wild furs. Fetching more than $100 per pelt, these rarities have been fairly well hustled out. In recent years several concerns, including the mighty Hudson's Bay Company, have tried to breed silver foxes in captivity, but with little success. They should have asked Dalton and Oulton.

Earlier this year the two men formed a partnership. "We had hunted and fished together," Dalton observes, "and he was altogether a man after my own heart." They started with a pair of wild foxes captured alive. "Our style of den was a hollow log," Oulton explains, "for in such places Dalton and I had, in our hunting expeditions, usually found wild fox dens."

In these "practically natural conditions," and after careful observation of their habits, the two have succeeded in breeding a strain of "absolutely perfect, blue-black pelts." As Dalton maintains, "such furs have never before been seen, and never could have been produced except by selective breeding."

Great plains Indian Chief Crowfoot dies

April 25, 1890

BLACKFOOT RESERVE, N.W.T. – Plains Indian leader Chief Crowfoot, 60, died today after years of illness. Few other Canadian Indians have so captured the popular imagination as this Blackfoot chief with his proud bearing and lean, hawklike face. As a youth, Crowfoot was known for courage – he went to war 19 times and was wounded six times. Yet as chief he was a peacemaker. He welcomed the NWMP when they came west to end the whisky trade. He approved Treaty 7 in 1877, but grew disillusioned when the government reneged on promises. ▷

"Little Chocolate" boxes way to title

June 27, 1890

LONDON – Canadian boxer George "Little Chocolate" Dixon knocked out Nunc Wallace today to capture the world bantamweight title. The victory made Dixon, from Halifax, $2,000 richer and gave him the distinction of becoming the first black man to win a world boxing title. Boxing is starting to evolve as being more respectable in Canada after being considered an outlaw sport for many years. Many of the early bouts were scheduled by the army in military towns.

George "Little Chocolate" Dixon.

Baron de Hirsch Institute planned

1890

MONTREAL – A Jewish community group here will turn a building into a free school for Jewish children and a shelter for Jewish immigrants. The new Baron de Hirsch Institute was bought with money donated by French philanthropist Baron Maurice de Hirsch.

Pogroms and persecution forced many Russian Jews to flee. Russia's loss is Canada's gain – 6,501 Jews moved here last decade. Canadian immigration officials like Alexander Galt welcomed these skilled newcomers, Jewish philanthropists paid their passage, and Canadian Jews helped them settle.

High-speed electric streetcars make debut

The first electric street railway in Canada is introduced in Toronto.

Aug. 15, 1890

TORONTO – Today's Civic Holiday was made all the more enjoyable this year by the introduction of the latest in public transportation to this fair city. After years of enduring old-fashioned horse-drawn streetcars, high-speed electric cars have been introduced here.

The inaugural run of the Toronto Railway Company's new conveyance began at 3:30 this afternoon, in front of city hall [St. Lawrence Market]. A car full of politicians and prominent citizens enjoyed the cheers of crowds on Sherbourne Street as they headed north. Just 12 minutes later, it reached the bridge at North Sherbourne Street [Bloor Street], the end of the line.

The old-fashioned horse-drawn streetcar will be gradually replaced.

NWMP send first patrol to far north

Aug. 23, 1890

YORK FACTORY, District of Keewatin – NWMP Inspector J. W. Begin has arrived here on a visit of inspection. He plans to appoint a justice of the peace and to investigate various allegations. Begin and his detachment left Winnipeg July 2 on this trip – the first NWMP patrol into the far north and the first to reach Hudson Bay.

They started their trip in a small sailing boat, the *Keewatin,* and after a month's patrol along the shore of Lake Winnipeg, Begin went ashore to establish a detachment at Norway House. He told his men to continue their patrol in the *Keewatin* until the end of August before returning to Winnipeg. Then he canoed down the Nelson River to this fur-trading post. Begin plans to return in a few days to Lake Winnipeg to rejoin his men on the *Keewatin* and then sail back with them to Winnipeg.

General Middleton refuses to resign

June 28, 1890

OTTAWA – Canada's militia commander today denied recent rumors he will resign. Gen. Frederick Middleton has been under intense pressure since last May when a House of Commons select committee severely criticized him. In the rebellion of 1885, Middleton seized furs belonging to an accused rebel and then appropriated the furs for himself. This, the committee said, was improper and illegal. Most observers believe that if Middleton doesn't resign, the government will be in the awkward position of having to dismiss him to satisfy strong public opinion.

American whaleships set to spend winter locked in Arctic ice

Sept. 18, 1890

PAULINE COVE, N.W.T. – A trio of American whaleships is preparing to winter at this remote island harbor in the western Arctic, frozen in the ice. The ships are acting on last year's reports of plentiful bowhead whales in the Beaufort Sea. But the hunting ground is distant from their San Francisco home base, so the whalers will overwinter here on Herschel Island to get an early start at the whaling when the ice breaks up in the spring.

The tiny flotilla, two steam vessels owned by the Pacific Steam Whaling Company – the *Grampus* and the *Mary D. Hume* – and a small sailboat – the *Nicoline* – are the first whalers to overwinter in the Beaufort. Their base, Pauline Cove, offers shelter from the ice, driftwood for fuel, and seems close to the local caribou population.

Last spike links Prince Albert to CPR

Oct. 22, 1890

PRINCE ALBERT, N.W.T. – The last spike in the long-awaited Qu'Appelle, Long Lake and Saskatchewan Railway was driven in by Lt.-Gov. Joseph Royal in Prince Albert today. Nicholas Flood Davin, the MP for Assiniboia West who worked so hard to bring the railway here, gave a rousing speech. The branch line, to be operated by the Canadian Pacific Railway, runs from Prince Albert to Regina, where it links with the CPR.

This CPR train was snowed in for two days near Regina during the winter.

The railway has been a long time coming to Prince Albert, and for many years a branch line seemed an impossible dream. Until now the nearest station was Troy [Qu'Appelle], 322 kilometres away. Eight years ago the first CPR surveyors arrived. From then until August of last year, when the first sod was turned on the line, many companies made plans that did not come to fruition. In 1882 alone the Rapid City Central Railway, the Saskatchewan and Peace River Railway, the Winnipeg and Hudson's Bay Railway and Steamship Company, and the Portage, Westbourne and North-Western Railway all showed interest in the Prince Albert line. In 1883, the Souris and Rocky Mountain Railway and the Wood Mountain and Qu'Appelle Railway also had plans for a branch line to Regina.

Coal mines reopen as "pit boys" end strike at Springhill

Dec. 2, 1890

SPRINGHILL, N.S. – At 2 this afternoon, the Committee of Boys marched into the office of Henry Swift, general manager of the Springhill coal mines, and calmly informed him they are returning to work. The decision ends a strike precipitated by the mine's discharge of a young worker; redress for the alleged wrongful dismissal will be sought by the boy's father in court.

Springhill's coal miners are well-known for their staunch independence, yet the hazardous nature of their work has also nurtured a collective approach to issues such as safety, job security, and wages. Sons follow fathers into the mines, and from an early age learn the value of collective bargaining to settle disputes with management.

The "pit-boys" are anywhere from 12 to 16 years of age. Although their roles are limited they nevertheless perform essential duties: they work as "trappers," opening and closing ventilation doors, or "turn the fan," providing the shafts with fresh air. They also work the horses. Only at 17 or 18 do they advance to the physically demanding work of "the picks."

Wood buffalo near extinction after a series of severe winters

1890

NORTHWEST TERRITORIES – The wood buffalo are verging on extinction. Wood buffalo are larger and have shorter hair than their cousins the plains buffalo. They also range further north, from the Athabasca district to Great Slave Lake. Abundant in the early 1800s, the animals have been declining since then. While hide hunters are responsible for the disappearance of the plains buffalo in the 1870s, wood buffalo have not suffered large scale extermination at human hands. It appears a series of harsh winters around the middle of the century has sped their demise more than anything. Wood buffalo depend on being able to feed through snow in the winter, so deep snowfalls or ice on the ground has disastrous repercussions for them. Many wood buffalo probably starved to death these years. In this situation, even limited hunting has been hard on the wood buffalo.

A desk truly fit for a prime minister

Sir John A. Macdonald's desk is truly fit for a prime minister! It is over two metres high, walnut with decorative maple veneer, and boasts two stacks of drawers, hinged at the back, which Sir John can either open to create a double-pedestal desk, or close to give the effect of two panelled doors. The words "Dominion Secretory," carved on the drawers between desk and bookcase, play on the words "secretary" and "Tory," which Sir John is. In fact, the desk was a gift from admirers, and has an honored place at Earnscliffe in the study he calls his workshop. The desk gets good use – Sir John sits at it every morning before leaving for the Commons.

Sir John A. Macdonald's desk.

Inquiry condemns jailing the poor

Dec. 31, 1890

TORONTO – Perhaps one of the greatest changes in Ontario's notion of social responsibility came this year, with a report by a provincial royal commission investigating prison conditions. The commission strongly condemns the current tendency to lock up the poor in jails just to keep them off the streets. It also demands the establishment of "poor houses" – places where the homeless can live – in every county. Further, the commissioners recommend that "it shall be unlawful ... for a magistrate or justice to commit to a common gaol as a vagrant any homeless and destitute person ... unless such person has committed an offence."

This native child is wrapped in a beautifully embroidered cover and carried about on the convenient cradleboard.

1891

Northwest Territories, Jan. 12. The Lady Aberdeen Association for the Distribution of Literature to Settlers in the West begins sending out literature.

Winnipeg, Feb. 2. The court of Queen's Bench upholds the Manitoba Schools Act, passed last year to provide for non-denominational public schools in the province.

Peterborough, Ont., April 20. The Edison Electric Plant [Canadian General Electric] has its grand opening.

Montreal, May 21. The Henry Morgan and Co. Department Store moves from St. James Street to St. Catherine Street, highlighting the move uptown of many Montreal merchants.

Canada, May. The first accredited Salvation Army Hospital is opened.

Ottawa, June 6. John A. Macdonald, Canada's first federal prime minister, dies.

Ottawa, June 16. Conservative John J.C. Abbott succeeds John A. Macdonald as PM.

Ontario, Oct. 21. The Grand Trunk Railway opens the St. Clair Tunnel between Sarnia and Port Huron, U.S., the first large underwater train tunnel in Canada.

Montreal, Dec. 19. Delegates from the Quebec and Ontario Rugby Unions form the Canadian Rugby Union. The Manitoba Rugby Union is also formed.

Yale, B.C. The All Hallows School for Girls advertises that it keeps Indian and white students strictly separated. The school used to mix Indian and white students.

Calgary. The town has a more balanced proportion of women to men in the 20-40 age bracket than most other towns in the territories, which have far more men than women.

Nova Scotia. The minimum age of boy laborers in mines is raised to 12.

Nova Scotia. The Intercolonial Railway adds the Cape Breton Railway to its lines, with ferry service across the Strait of Canso.

Ontario. Commercial studies are introduced in schools.

Vancouver. A 1,200-seat opera house opens.

Toronto. For the first time, a woman applies to the Benchers of Ontario for admission as a law student. She is refused.

Teen captures plight of the Marco Polo

February 1891

CAVENDISH, P.E.I. – Lucy Maud Montgomery, a 16-year-old native of Prince Edward Island, has sold a stirring account entitled *The Wreck of the Marco Polo* to the Montreal *Witness*. The fact-based story captures with dramatic intensity the running aground in 1883 of Canada's most prized sailing ship, and, not surprisingly, bears all the markings of an eyewitness account: Montgomery spent most of her youth in Cavendish, the shoreline community nearest the disaster.

The raging sea, the plight of the sailors, the helplessness – and hopes – of the community watching from shore are vividly described, interspersed with anecdote and commentary, following the crew's rescue, that is often humorous. The story is Montgomery's first to be bought by a major newspaper.

Phantom voters fill Ontario electoral list

March 1, 1891

TORONTO – The typically competitive federal election has not been helped by the revelation that there appear to be 34,000 men on Ontario voting lists above and beyond the number actually allowed to vote in the province. This absurdity is just the latest fallout from federal control of the voting lists. Due to a variety of loopholes in the 1885 Franchise Act, which allows men of a certain property and above to vote, both the Conservatives and Liberals have been able to place more names on the list than they should – names that come from dead men, people living in two ridings, and emigrants. Such is the low level of Canadian politics.

Bachelors hold bash for hospitable wives

March 1891

FORT MACLEOD, N.W.T. – Planning has already begun for the Easter dance, an annual affair arranged by the bachelors of the community. There will be a meeting in town soon to set the final details of the dance, a thank you designed by single men around here who have been entertained, fed and helped by the wives of the ranchers. For single men, ranch life is often lonely and rarely softened by the feminine touch. Wives of local settlers have gone out of their way to invite single men to dinner and a chat. They have helped mend clothes, listened to problems, and, sometimes, arranged romantic meetings which have led to marriage.

123 die in blast at N.S. coal mine

Feb. 21, 1891

SPRINGHILL, N.S. – A suspected coal gas explosion deep underground at the Springhill Mine has killed 123 miners. The disaster occurred shortly after 12:30 p.m., when the crews had returned to slopes [shafts] one and two after lunch. Witnesses say "a loud roar" was heard, and "the earth shook." In an instant, slopes one and two were transformed into tombs. The miners who died were either lost in the original blast, or poisoned by toxic gases it released. What may have raised the death toll is a ventilation shaft 390 metres down that links the two slopes. Its existence ensured that the gases would fill both slopes.

Rescue work began immediately. By 6 p.m., all the wounded were recovered from the mines, sections of which were now very dangerous due to the destruction of support timbers. Since then, the recovery of the dead has been postponed until 11 p.m., to allow fresh air to circulate down below and to avert the chance of another explosion.

Coal gas explosions are a recurrent danger in mining, but few have caused so much loss of life in Canada. For residents of Springhill, the ghastly accident is another reminder of how the coal they depend on for their livelihood is also one of the worst threats to their own lives.

Fort St. John's is a Hudson's Bay Company trading post on the Peace River in the Athabasca district.

"Old Policy" Tories defeat Liberals

March 5, 1891

OTTAWA – "The Old Flag, The Old Policy, The Old Leader." That's what Sir John A. Macdonald and his Conservative government have been offering the voters, and that's what the voters have chosen. In what has been one of the most difficult elections in a country noted for rough politics, the Tories have gained 123 seats in the House, compared to the Liberals' 92.

Conservative campaign poster.

The victory is a vindication of Macdonald's policy of protective tariffs, and a blow against the Liberals' professed support of freer trade with the United States. Macdonald has portrayed this policy as an American plot, aimed at luring Canada into the Union. Liberals under Wilfrid Laurier say this was not the case, but their credibility was damaged by the discovery of a pamphlet written by Edward Farrer of the Liberal newspaper the Toronto *Globe*. In that document, Farrer proposed ways in which the Americans could hurt Canada's economy to force it to join the United States. Farrer says he only wrote the pamphlet to examine the current Canadian-American trade situation from a U.S. standpoint.

Nevertheless, Sir John A. has been able to ride the fears that the Farrer pamphlet raised to another majority, by stressing his commitment to the imperial connection. As he has said throughout the campaign, "a British subject I was born – a British subject I will die."

Sir John A. Macdonald, Father of Confederation, is once again prime minister of the country which he helped to create in 1867.

Author's new book is critical of Canada

Dec. 31, 1891

TORONTO – A review of the year in Canada would not be complete without mention of Goldwin Smith's proposal to turn this country into the "Scotland of North America." Such is the gist of his new book *Canada and the Canadian Question* criticizing the nation.

Smith, long acknowledged as an intellectual powerhouse, is a former professor at both Oxford and Cornell universities who settled in Toronto back in 1871. Since then he has played a strong part in the Canada First movement, an Ontario nationalist organization. More recently, he has become a believer in the "undoing of the American Revolution," advocating a union of the Anglo-Saxon peoples, a move that would mean the annexation of Canada by the United States.

Reaction to Smith's book has been mixed. Although his argumentative genius is acknowledged by most who have read it, not that many agree with his conclusions.

Census: population is over 4.8 million

April 5, 1891

OTTAWA – The population of Canada is 4,833,239 according to the latest census data. Ontario is by far the most populous province with 2,114,321 citizens, followed by Quebec with 1,488,535. The data, compiled over the last year by some 4,000 enumerators, gives populations as follows: British Columbia, 98,173; Manitoba, 152,506; New Brunswick, 321,263; Nova Scotia, 450,396; Prince Edward Island, 109,078; and the Northwest Territories, 98,967.

There are 1,404,974 French-Canadian citizens, although officials say that number may be misleadingly low because it does not accurately reflect the number of persons of French origin outside Quebec, notably Acadians. There may also be more Indians in the Territories than estimated. The most populous city is Montreal with 216,650 inhabitants; next is Toronto with 181,220. Quebec is third with 63,090 citizens.

CPR ship crosses Pacific in record time

April 28, 1891

VANCOUVER – The gleaming white *Empress of India* sailed into harbor here after a record trip across the Pacific from Yokohama. The 6,000-ton liner, 146 metres long, left England this month soon after she was built in the Naval Construction and Armament Company's yards at Barrow. She sailed through the Suez Canal to Yokohama and then left for Vancouver, cutting the time taken to cross the Pacific from 19 to 17 days.

The *Empress of India* is the first of three CPR ships – the others are the *Empress of Japan* and *Empress of China* – which will run regularly between Vancouver and ports in the Orient.

The CPR's Empress of India will provide a regular service to the Orient.

Byelection victories put Peters in power

April 21, 1891

CHARLOTTETOWN – After a series of byelection defeats, the Conservatives have turned the reins over to Frederick Peters' Liberals. A longtime Liberal supporter, the 40-year-old Peters won his first election to the House last year. Now, relations with Ottawa, especially the transportation issue, are expected to dominate his administration. Islanders are demanding the Dominion government honor its 1873 promise to "maintain efficient and continuous steam communication with the mainland."

In recent years Ottawa has subsidized a series of steamships, but the Island considers these neither "efficient" nor "continuous" – especially when they are locked in port by winter storms and ice. Instead, Islanders want a tunnel under the Northumberland Strait. A rail tunnel, they argue, would cost a mere $5 million – a fraction of the price tag for the recently completed transcontinental railway. ▷

Canada united in mourning Sir John A. Macdonald

June 6, 1891

OTTAWA – Sir John A. Macdonald, the great architect of Canadian Confederation, is dead. He died peacefully at his Ottawa home, Earnscliffe, after suffering a second stroke last Friday. For days the country held its breath, waiting for news of this century's greatest Canadian politician. When the end finally came at 10:15 this evening, the outpouring of grief and respect started. Canadians of all political stripes are honoring the memory of this all-too-human man. They recognize that, for all his wily dealings, his role in the Pacific Scandal, his personal problems with alcohol, Sir John A. was a man who devoted his life to Canada, even to his death.

Plans are being put together for a state funeral to honor Macdonald. Meanwhile, the government he's left behind is wrestling with the question of a successor. The smart money has it that Senator John Abbott, a brilliant lawyer who fell in the 1873 Pacific Scandal, is most likely to be selected by the caucus to take the reins. Other contenders include John Thompson, minister of justice; Mackenzie Bowell; and Nova Scotia's own Father of Confederation, Charles Tupper.

Hon. John Joseph Caldwell Abbott.

Sir John Alexander Macdonald.

Dutch immigrating to western Canada

Manitoba seeks Dutch immigrants.

1891

WESTERN CANADA – A growing number of Dutch immigrants are settling in western Canada, but unlike most newcomers the Dutch are familiar with their new surroundings. Most have already adapted and honed their skills in the American midwest, where since mid-century they have been establishing successful farm communities. But rising costs and decreased availabilty of land there are limiting expansion. For the Dutch, ownership of land is a priority, a means to maintain economic stability: to achieve that goal, more and more are moving to Canada.

Calgary, Edmonton linked by railway

Aug. 11, 1891

EDMONTON – The railway has finally come north to Edmonton – or, rather, to Strathcona, just across the river. The completion of the Calgary and Edmonton Railway means 310 kilometres of track have been laid between both towns. More importantly, Edmonton has been finally linked to the Canadian Pacific Railway, leaseholder of the C & ER. Farmers up here, in this rich country, are now able to ship their products across Canada, and beyond.

The line is just one of a series being built by the CPR off the main track. Last year, 410 kilometres of steel were extended from Regina to Prince Albert. The new lines should open up these regions for farming.

Salvation Army's Rescue Home open

Spring 1891

WINNIPEG – The Salvation Army brought its unique form of social assistance to the prostitutes, unwed mothers and deserted wives of Winnipeg late last year when it opened the Rescue Home and Children's Shelter. Now, demands for its services are so high staff members are roving the city's market square seeking not just the needy, but the well-to-do, soliciting much-needed donations of food.

Ukrainian immigrants reach Edmonton

Sept. 16, 1891

EDMONTON – The first party of Ukrainian settlers arrived here today by train. Immigration authorities believe this party is only the first of many groups of peasants from the provinces of Galicia and Bukovyna in the Austro-Hungarian Empire. It is anticipated that the newcomers will remain in Edmonton over the winter, and in the spring relocate to holdings reserved in their name in the Edna-Star district east of the capital.

Today's arrivals come as a result of pioneering activities by two venturesome Galicians, Ivan Pylypiw and Vasyl Eleniak. They travelled extensively through Manitoba and the district of Assiniboia looking for land suitable for settlement by large numbers of their countrymen. Pylypiw and Eleniak said that emigration appeared to be the only answer for the thousands of Galicians and Bukovyians who are literally starving due to repeated crop failures and overpopulation. For persons such as these, the enticing offer of 64 hectares of farmland for a registration fee of $10 is something they cannot overlook.

Many Ukrainian families are beginning to arrive in the Canadian west.

Schools Act killed in Supreme Court

Oct. 28, 1891

OTTAWA – The Manitoba Schools Act today was struck down by the Supreme Court of Canada. This case began in Winnipeg in November 1890 when a private citizen, J.K. Barrett, issued a legal challenge to a Winnipeg municipal bylaw which required him to pay taxes to the non-denominational public school system.

Barrett launched and lost his case in magistrate's court, and the decision was confirmed by the Manitoba Court of Queen's Bench and the Manitoba Court of Appeal before being overturned by the Supreme Court.

Mercier ousted in Quebec rail scandal

Dec. 16, 1891

QUEBEC CITY – The Baie des Chaleurs Railway scandal today claimed Honoré Mercier. The Liberal premier was dismissed by Lt.-Gov. A.R. Angers following a royal commission inquiry into allegations of kickbacks from railway contractors to government officials.

While the commission exonerated Mercier of personal involvement in the scandal, Angers believes the Liberal government has been irreparably disgraced, and he has called on aging Tory leader Charles de Boucherville to form a government. Mercier, outraged, claims the lieutenant-governor dumped him for partisan reasons. "You will soon receive from your master (Prime Minister J.J.C.) Abbott the prize for your national treason," Mercier declared.

The scandal concerned payments of $100,000 by contractor C.N. Armstrong to Liberal members, who mostly paid off election expenses with the funds. The money, ironically, was part of $175,000 in subsidies the Mercier government had given the Baie des Chaleurs Railway project. At the hearings, Philippe-Olivier-Ernest Pacaud, one of Mercier's ministers, accepted blame for the scandal. The mess is welcome news for federal Tories, embroiled in the Langevin Block construction scandal in Ottawa.

Ousted Premier Honoré Mercier.

Canada puts duties on fish from Nfld.

Dec. 8, 1891

NEWFOUNDLAND – Relations between Canada and Newfoundland have dropped to a new low. Newfoundland recently negotiated a free-trade agreement with the United States, but Britain, under pressure from Canada, vetoed it since it might complicate Canada's efforts to obtain a similar agreement. In retaliation, Newfoundland imposed restrictions on the sale of bait to Canadian bank fishermen. Now Canada has responded by imposing heavy duties on imports of Newfoundland saltfish.

Western brides younger than those in the east, census says

1891

CANADA – The further toward the industrialized east a Canadian woman lives, the longer she'll postpone marrying, according to this year's census. Whereas the average age for brides in British Columbia is 22.3 years, it increases to 23.8 years in Manitoba, 25.3 in Quebec, 26.6 in Ontario, 26.3 in New Brunswick, 26.4 in Nova Scotia, and 27.9 in P.E.I. Overall, women now marry at about 26 years, three years later than in 1851.

Several factors explain this trend to delayed marriage. Higher education for women is one. Generally, those admitted to advanced professional programs either wait or even avoid marriage altogether.

Women also marry later to limit the number of children they will bear. Though various methods of contraception are known, abstinence is still seen as the safest and most respectable – and so much easier to practise outside wedlock!

Canadian invents game of basketball

Dec. 28, 1891

SPRINGFIELD, Mass. – Two half-bushel baskets were nailed to the gymnasium balcony to serve as goals as Canadian James Naismith introduced a new game he has invented called basketball to students at the YMCA training school here. Today is the first time the sport has been played. Naismith, of Almonte, Ont., is a theology graduate of McGill, where he played four sports. An assistant physical education director here, he was assigned to invent an indoor game to fill the gap between football and baseball.

Small grass fires are often fanned into major conflagrations on the wide open and windswept prairies.

Canada adapts to the rise of industrialization

The exterior of the Marysville Cotton Mill in New Brunswick.

Rows of weaving looms line the interior of the Marysville Cotton Mill.

Manufacturing on the upswing in east

1891

CANADA – Industry is thriving in eastern Canada. Factories pump out goods that are shipped by rail across Canada along a trade axis sheltered by a wall of protective tariffs. Prime Minister John A. Macdonald introduced the National Policy in 1879 to boost Canadian industry, and it has worked. Since 1870, there has been steady growth in Canadian manufacturing. Output has grown an average of 4.6 percent a year, slowing down in the depression of 1873-79.

The development of the domestic consumer market has been crucial to Canadian industrialization. With the completion of the CPR in 1885, goods from eastern factories can be shipped as far east as the Atlantic, and as far west as the Pacific. National Policy tariffs have protected Canadian industry from foreign competition. Most Canadian manufacturing is in Ontario and Quebec. Output has increased at about the same rate in the two provinces. Consumer industries such as clothing, shoes, and food processing have led the way in both provinces.

But there are important differences between Ontario and Quebec industry. Ontario industry is scattered throughout the province in various cities and towns, while Quebec's is concentrated around Montreal and Quebec City, close to large pools of cheap labor and railways. Capital goods industries producing iron and steel, tools, and farm implements are more important in Ontario than Quebec, probably because Ontario is closer to sources of iron and coal in the U.S. For reasons hard to fathom, manufacturing wages are lower in Quebec than in Ontario. Finally, many French Quebecers are disturbed that their industry is ruled by anglophones.

The Maritimes have developed textile and steel industries, but industrialization of the area has been hampered by poor access to markets. Winnipeg has several small-scale factories, the only significant manufacturing in the west.

Several types of businesses have been established on Craig Street in Montreal.

Poverty often part of life in the big city

1891

CANADA – Poverty, overcrowded living conditions, and the plight of the new industrial proletariat – all manifestations of this century's Industrial Revolution – are conditions no longer confined to the manufacturing centres of Europe and the eastern United States; they are now an established, growing part of the Canadian milieu. Parallel with the development of manufacturing industries here, thousands of Canadians have abandoned rural life for work in the cities. Many newly arrived immigrants are finding their niche not on the vast, open prairies of the west, but in the sweatshops of Montreal and Toronto, Canada's two principal commercial and industrial centres. This year 40 percent of Ontario's more than two million residents live in urban centres, up 10 percent from 20 years ago.

And as their populations grow, Canada's cities are being subdivided into areas of affluence and poverty, opulence and filth, between those who own and those who rent. Many of Toronto's working-class live in the squalid, delapidated cottages and tenements of St. John's ward; in Halifax they occupy the north end; in Winnipeg, the north side of the tracks. Open sewers and outdoor "pit privies" are common. Similar conditions are found in Montreal's English-speaking district of Griffintown and the French district of St. Henri. Most families, generally five in number, live in cramped one- or two-room apartments that have little ventilation, light, or heat during winter.

At the workplace, increased mechanization has replaced physical brawn, creating jobs for women and children. But unsafe conditions are largely to blame for the high rate of industrial accidents, and government controls to prevent the abuse of workers, particularly of children, are not easily enforced. The typical factory job lasts 10 to 12 hours a day, six days a week, 52 weeks a year, with no security.

Immigration: it's the key to Canadian growth

Expatriates lured back from the U.S.

1891

CANADA – In recent years, so many Canadians, newly arrived immigrants and native sons and daughters alike, have flocked to the United States that emigration has become as grave a concern for the Canadian government as immigration. Indeed, there are now one million ex-Canadians, or 17 percent of Canada's population, living south of the 49th Parallel.

But there is also a concerted effort under way to sway the tide and to bring the expatriates back. Quebec was hit hardest by the exodus. Now a growing number of French-Canadian emigrés are returning to Canada, escaping a depressed American economy that has deprived them of jobs in New England's manufacturing centres and the melting pot mentality that threatens to stamp out their cultural identity.

Aided by the Colonization of Manitoba Society, an organization able to provide reduced transportation costs, by last year 3,000 repatriates had settled in 18 parishes along the Red and Assiniboine rivers. Also, many Canadians who left Manitoba and the Northwest Territories to settle in western states in the 1870s are filtering back having learned that frost, drought, and taxes can take as high a toll in the U.S. as in Canada.

Immigrants huddle apprehensively on the decks of the SS Parisian en route to their new homes in Canada.

Cartoonist's view of the surprises awaiting the new immigrants in Canada.

Mennonites and Icelanders build thriving western communities

1891

MANITOBA – With the Canadian government's failure to attract British immigrants to the west, the successful Mennonite and Icelandic settlements here sparkle like diamonds cast on the otherwise bleak, sparsely populated countryside. Hundreds of new Mennonite immigrants have arrived this year, attracted by the success of Mennonites who first came here in 1874.

The first Mennonite settlers faced awesome, daunting conditions, as one 1878 report attests: "These people were put down on the naked prairie in the middle of the summer, barely three years ago. ... They had to dig wells for water for their daily use on their arrival, and sleep, with their women and children, under the shelter of their wagons." By 1878, the Manitoba Mennonites numbered more than 7,000, with a large community at Rat River, southeast of Winnipeg. They had built substantial houses and buildings, and carried on prosperous wheat growing and mixed farming operations. Just two years ago, it was reported that "the large Mennonite communities in Manitoba continue to flourish." Mennonites have succeeded because they're industrious and community spirited. A Rat River visitor reported seeing "men, women, and children going out into the fields to work before the morning was grey." The Icelanders, who first came to Manitoba in 1875, have had similar success, but only after many initial years of hardship. Most are farmers, others laborers, tradesmen or professionals. They have established schools, churches, a library, literary society, and a newspaper, the *Leifur*. Due to a massive influx since 1887, they now number more than 7,000, mostly at their settlement at Gimli on the southwest shore of Lake Winnipeg.

The fate of Jewish immigrants to the west has not been so bright. Sponsored by London's Mansion House Fund, hundreds of destitute Polish and Russian Jews arrived at Montreal in 1882, en route to settle in the west. They eventually settled near Moosomin, [Saskatchewan], but, by 1887, miserably equipped for farming and woefully inexperienced, they had all left for urban areas like Winnipeg. The same fate probably awaits the many destitute Jewish immigrants who have arrived in Winnipeg this year.

1892

Northwest Territories, May. Forty-seven Jewish families settle on a farm at Hirsch, [Saskatchewan], sponsored by the Young Men's Hebrew Benevolent Society of Montreal and Baron Maurice de Hirsch.

London, July 30. The Judicial Committee of the Privy Council reverses the Supreme Court of Canada's decision to overturn the Manitoba Schools Act, upholding the validity of the act.

Toronto, October. In the first Canadian Rugby Union Championship, Osgoode Hall defeats the Montreal Football Club.

Nova Scotia, Dec. 14. Sir Adams George Archibald, a Father of Confederation, dies.

Ontario. A provincial statute permits women to study and practise law.

Toronto. Three women are elected to the Toronto School Board as trustees.

Ottawa. Parliament adopts the Canadian Criminal Code, based on a codification of English criminal law. It defines criminal activities, and establishes punishments for them.

Ottawa. The Criminal Code makes it an indictable offence to promote articles to prevent conception or cause abortion. Concern about the falling birthrate among English-Canadians gave rise to the law.

Ontario. Of the 42 daily newspapers published in the province, 36 openly identify themselves with one of the two political parties.

Alberta. Mormons buy a big chunk of Cochrane Ranch.

North America. Medical missionary Wilfred Grenfell lectures in Canada and the U.S. to raise money for a hospital for Labrador fishermen.

London. The British government authorizes all Canadians to fly the Red Ensign with the Canadian crest on it, and authorizes Canadian naval vessels to fly the Blue Ensign with the Canadian crest on it.

Ontario. The Ontario government broadens and strengthens its game and fish acts, and hires full-time game wardens, as a result of the MacCallum Royal Commission on Fish and Game, which drew attention to the plight of vanishing wildlife in Ontario.

Canada. A summary says there was an average of 45 rapes or attempted rapes reported each year in Canada since 1877.

Arbitration seen as way to settle Bering seal spat

Feb. 29, 1892

WASHINGTON, D.C. – Britain and the United States, embroiled in a dispute over sealing rights in the Bering Sea, have decided to submit the dispute to international arbitration. The decision is the result of a treaty signed between the two powers today, with Britain acting on behalf of Canada.

The gist of the dispute is simple: the Americans want exclusive trapping rights to Alaskan seals. They not only want these rights on land and within the 4.8-kilometre international limit, but they say all seals found outside that limit should be considered their "domestic animals," temporarily gone astray. Canadian trappers say the Bering Sea is part of the Pacific Ocean, and, as such, seals swimming in international waters can legally be killed by anybody. They dispute the Americans' history of seizing sealing boats in international waters, actions that have led to fines, imprisonments, and more than a few Canadian schooners being left to rot on American beaches.

Of the seven arbitrators, two are to be chosen by the United States, and two by Great Britain. France, Italy, and Sweden will each contribute one arbitrator apiece.

Mohawk poetess thrills sell-out crowd

Mohawk poetess Pauline Johnson.

Feb. 19, 1892

TORONTO – A promising stage career was launched tonight at Association Hall when Mohawk poetess Pauline Johnson read her Indian poems to an enthusiastic sold-out audience. It was Pauline's first solo performance, but she has already been hailed by the poet Charles G.D. Roberts as "the aboriginal voice of Canada."

The 31-year-old Pauline is a native of Brantford, Ont., where her father was a Mohawk chief. She has been writing since she was a teenager, and several of her poems have been published.

Top prof publishes medical text in U.S.

1892

BALTIMORE – Canadian physician William Osler, first professor of medicine at Johns Hopkins University, has published his book *The Principles and Practice of Medicine.* He is an expert in the diagnosis of diseases of the heart, lungs and blood. Osler grew up in Dundas, Ont. He trained at the University of Toronto, at McGill University, in England and Europe. Osler has taught at McGill and the University of Pennsylvania, and he is known for his work in medicine and education.

From gunpowder to high tops ...

April 21, 1892

FORT QU'APPELLE, N.W.T. – Do you need some gunpowder or a pair of high tops? Donald Gunn did, so he went to the Hudson's Bay post at Fort Qu'Appelle. The current price for a keg of gunpowder is $6. A pair of high top boots goes for $3.55. While he was there he also bought 61 yards of seven-ounce duck which cost $8.78.

The Fort Qu'Appelle post carries everything anyone could want for survival and many items that make life more comfortable. Goods can be bought or traded.

Collector cleans up and carts away tons of old buffalo bones

A huge pile of buffalo skulls awaits shipping at a Saskatoon railway siding.

April 22, 1892

MOOSE JAW, N.W.T. – Mr. B.M. Hicks of the North West Bone Syndicate, operating out of Minneapolis, has returned to the Northwest Territories for one of his last hauls of buffalo bones. This load is a good one – 1,000 railway cars – but time is running out for this very lucrative trade. Prices are declining because freight rates are high, bones have become harder to find after years of collection, and, of course, buffalo herds disappeared more than a decade ago.

The bones are shipped to the U.S. for use in sugar refining, and for making fertilizer and cutlery handles. Buffalo bones are sought by sugar refineries because the oil has been bleached out of them.

Thompson new PM after ailing Abbott

John Sparrow David Thompson.

Nov. 24, 1892

OTTAWA – John S.D. Thompson is the new prime minister of Canada. He takes over from John J.C. Abbott, who resigned due to ill health. Abbott succeeded John A. Macdonald after his death in 1891.

Thompson was born in Halifax in 1844. He trained as a lawyer and entered politics as a Liberal-Conservative for Antigonish in the Nova Scotia Assembly. He became attorney general, then premier in Nova Scotia. When defeated he was appointed judge of the Supreme Court of N.S., and later justice minister in the federal government.

Poisoner to gallows for killing 3 women

Nov. 15, 1892

LONDON, England – The notorious Canadian poisoner Tom Cream went to the gallows this morning without confessing his guilt in the deaths of three young women. Cream was born in Scotland but moved to Canada in 1868 and studied for a medical degree at McGill University. He got into trouble in a Toronto abortion case and moved to Chicago in 1880. Soon he was convicted of poisoning his lover's husband and sentenced to life in prison. Pardoned in 1891, he moved to England and set up his vile practice. Cream prescribed fatal doses of strychnine to seven women, three of whom died. He tried to blackmail the druggists who filled the prescriptions.

Fire leaves town of St. John's in ruins

July 10, 1892

ST. JOHN'S, Nfld. – Late in the afternoon of July 8, careless smoking resulted in a fire in a barn on the corner of Freshwater and Pennywell roads. By a terrible coincidence the main water supply had been shut off to effect repairs and had not been turned back on long enough to build up pressure. In addition, the reservoir, usually kept filled, had been emptied during a fire brigade practice.

By 5 p.m. yesterday, 75 percent of the town lay in ruins. Property worth $20 million has been destroyed, and 11,000 people rendered homeless. St. John's hasn't seen the likes of a fire like this since the big blaze of 1846, which also left thousands of people homeless.

Brick walls and chimneys are all that remain of many St. John's homes.

Compliments to the chef and electricity

Aug. 29, 1892

MONTREAL – Dinner guests at the Windsor Hotel last evening were participants in an historic event: they were the first Canadians to enjoy a meal cooked entirely with electricity. The food was prepared on a stove designed and built by Thomas Ahearn, president of the Ottawa Electric Company. Electrical facilities in the kitchen of the Windsor Hotel are viewed by observers as harbingers of a massive move toward the use of electricity in a myriad of forms. Certainly there have been many improvements being made in uses of electricity in a brief span of years.

It is only eight years since J.J. Wright of Toronto designed an arc light system, a model of which was used in the store of Timothy Eaton. In the case of this particular type of lighting, arc lamps were soon determined to have a greater usage in the outdoors, and within a few years the central streets of major cities were being illuminated in this manner. Early arc lighting was installed in Ottawa and powered by three dynamos driven by a waterwheel.

The harshness of arc lamps on the human eye motivated many inventors to work on an incandescent style of lamp in which the lighted filament is enclosed in a glass globe.

Dogs a part of North American way of life

c.1892

BRITISH NORTH AMERICA – From coast to coast and north to south, the humans who inhabit Canada and Newfoundland share their igloos, longhouses, pioneer shanties, farmhouses and colonial mansions with dogs. These animals earn their keep in different ways. Harnessed in teams, they pull sleds in the frozen north. Singly, they trot over the prairies hauling travois. Everywhere they hunt and retrieve, and many Canadians who earn their livelihood hunting rely on their canine colleagues' superior sense of smell. Dogs also guard the people they live with, waking from characteristic light sleep to growl or bark to warn of intruders. Most of all, dogs are loving and loved companions, integral members of their human families. Fittingly, they are often included in family portraits.

Electricity is being used more and more as an efficient source of power. The Winnipeg Street Railway has just inaugurated its new electric cars.

Canadians and their dogs: ruffing it in the bush

A team of sled dogs rests after bringing in a loaded toboggan to Fort Garry. Oxen and horses may carry heavier loads, but the sled dogs are still popular for winter transport in the inhospitable northern districts.

While the team of sled dogs must sleep outside in the snow, the family's pet is allowed to sit by the fire in the igloo while the mother cooks the meal and the rest of the family busies itself with other activities.

Even formal portraits by the famed Notman Studio often include the owner's favorite dog.

Proud owners such as a certain Mr. Thurston have their dogs' portraits done at the Notman studio.

Lt.-Col. W.H. Cotton shoots snipe near Quebec with his trusty pointer.

The traditional dog sled is still a popular mode of winter travel between St. Paul's and the Red River area.

Both dog and owner are dressed in ruffles for this formal photograph.

Children love to play with dogs, and this boy is no exception to the rule.

Two Newfoundland dogs serve as sled dogs for this child's outing.

These dogs get a break from pulling a loaded sled. A child walks behind.

The dog team rests while the masters prepare a snow shelter and a dinner.

1893

France, February. Canada and France sign a commercial treaty allowing French wines to enter Canada at a low duty.

Montreal, February. Montreal Amateur Athletic Association (AAA), champions of the Amateur Hockey Association, is the first team awarded the Stanley Cup.

Prince Edward Island, March 4. The first women's hockey game on the Island is played.

Charlottetown. The Legislative Council is incorporated into the Legislative Assembly, creating a unique political system. Each constituency elects a councillor and an assemblyman. Property owners elect the councillor, and all males elect the assemblyman. People who own property in more than one constituency can vote in each one.

Brampton, Ont. The *Conservator* notes that Lillie Roberts is the town's first lady bicyclist: "The graceful appearance she presents while passing through the town on her wheel will no doubt lead others to take up the healthy pastime."

Winnipeg. The Manitoba branch of the Women's Christian Temperance Union stages a "Mock Parliament" to encourage support for women's suffrage.

Halifax. Leaders of the Halifax Women's Christian Temperance Union form a Local Council of Women to work for female suffrage.

Montreal. Lord Stanley of Preston, at the end of his term as governor general, gives the Montreal Amateur Athletic Association a trophy [the Stanley Cup] to serve as a hockey challenge cup.

Chicago. Thomas Allen ("Allie") Brick of Peace River wins championship honors for his wheat at the World's Fair.

Toronto. A pay box is installed for the public telephone at Joseph Lee's Pharmacy. Users pay five cents a call, according to the honor system.

Victoria. A bill for the enfranchisement of women is defeated in the legislature.

Toronto. Frederick Fetherstonaugh exhibits an electric car.

Nanaimo, B.C. The first Finnish Lutheran Church in Canada is founded.

United States. As a result of a stock market crash, 15,000 businesses, 600 banks, and 74 railways collapse.

Ontario legislature OKs law to prevent cruelty to children

May 27, 1893

TORONTO – Ontario's legislature has passed An Act for the Prevention of Cruelty to, and Better Protection of, Children. Persons neglecting or abusing children are now liable to serious penalties. Under the new law, judges may remove abused children from parents and guardians, and place them in the care of the Children's Aid Society. The society will inspect industrial schools and temporary homes for children, and supervise children in foster homes.

Ontario has also created a superintendent of neglected and dependent children; John Joseph Kelso has been named to the post. For years, Kelso has campaigned for better treatment of children. He is a founder of the Children's Aid Society, and was instrumental in preparing the Children's Protection Act of 1888, which allowed juvenile offenders to be tried separately from adults.

Stanley Cup winners turn down their prize

The MAAA (later photo) finally accepts the 1893 Stanley Cup – in 1894.

Nov. 27, 1893

MONTREAL – The Stanley Cup, awarded in February to the champions of the Amateur Hockey Association, the Montreal Amateur Athletic Association, has not yet been presented. The MAAA, or Montreal Hockey Club, first-place finishers over Ottawa during the regular schedule, declined to accept the $50 silver bowl donated by Lord Stanley of Preston, the sixth governor general of Canada. The dispute arose over an alleged slight to the Montreal team committee.

Stanley announced in March of 1892 that the cup would be given to the leading amateur club in Canada. Subsequent winners would be decided by the challenge method.

National Council of Women off the ground

This Kingston women's surgery class is indicative of women's changing role.

Oct. 27, 1893

TORONTO – About 1,500 women met here today to form the National Council of Women. Inspired by a similar group which met at Chicago's World's Fair last year, the organization is a federation of Canadian women's groups. Its president is Ishbel, Lady Aberdeen, wife of the new governor general, who said, "By means of such a federation a more intimate knowledge of one another's work will be gained." Lady Gzowski, Dr. Emily Howard Stowe and Adelaide Hoodless are among the prominent organizers.

Stringer in Yukon to open a mission

1893

HERSCHEL ISLAND, Yukon – Isaac Stringer, an Anglican missionary, has arrived here to open a mission to the Eskimos. He is 27, straight out of Toronto's Wycliffe College, and will divide his time between Herschel Island and Eskimo communities at Peel River and other settlements.

Stringer has been made welcome by officers of the American whaling ships using the island as a base. But the whalers often trade with the Eskimo and sell them such controversial items as repeating rifles and liquor. They also, Stringer charges, seduce, or buy from their parents, young Eskimo girls. Stringer is already horrified by the drunkenness and degradation of the Eskimo and has threatened to send a report to Ottawa about the activities of the crews of the whaling ships. He plans to preach a sermon on the evils of drink and to persuade the whalers to mend their ways.

Indians obtaining liquor too easily, bishop complains

1893

FORTY MILE, Yukon – William Carpenter Bompas, Bishop of Selkirk, has written to Thomas Daly, the superintendent general of Indian Affairs, complaining about the ease with which Indians can get alcohol. As prospecting and trading activity increase along the Yukon River, many Indians come to this settlement to trade or to visit. Many whites sell Indians liquor, Bompas charges. And some of them use liquor as bait to get Indian women – either by making them drunk, or by offering liquor to husbands and fathers in exchange for wives and daughters.

Bompas, who's been in the north more than 25 years, has made the protection of the Indians his life's work. He opened the Buxton Mission here two years ago as part of his plan to protect Indians against the effects of an alien society. But many whites say Bompas is simply a whiner who devotes all his time to the Indians and neglects the whites.

Scandinavians are settling in Alberta

1893

ALBERTA – The Scandinavians have come! Around Olds, and east of Wetaskiwin, Scandinavians have made their mark on the landscape the last two years; the Wetaskiwin group has occupied almost 780 square kilometres of free land.

The Scandinavians have been like beavers, carving their livelihoods from the countryside. They make their homes and furniture from poplar trees. For food, they catch rabbits in pits, and shoot partridges or prairie chickens. For mattresses, they stuff sacks with grass or straw. Many sell wheat in Edmonton to buy basic necessities. Families often buy whole bolts of cotton that mothers and daughters sew clothes from. Families often show up at church on Sundays wearing almost identical clothing because it has all been sewn from the same bolt of cotton.

Beerage to peerage for John Carling

The Carling Brewing and Malting Company is a major employer in London.

Sir John Carling, London brewer, has long served his city in various federal and provincial governments.

1893

LONDON, Ont. – In the British tradition, brewer-turned-politician Sir John Carling has risen from beerage to peerage in just two generations. President of Carling Brewing and Malting Co., founded here in 1840 by his father Thomas, John Carling started work at the brewery at age 12. He won acclaim for rebuilding it 10 weeks after a fire destroyed a new $250,000 plant in 1879. Known as Honest John after Sir John A. Macdonald remarked "John, no one could be as honest as you look," Tory Carling has won provincial and federal seats, and held cabinet positions.

Bishop John Horden devoted years to serving people of north

Jan. 12, 1893

MOOSE FACTORY, Ont. – John Horden, who has served this settlement as a missionary for 40 years, is dead. Horden was sent here by the Church Missionary Society, arriving on the *Prince Albert* in 1851. He was ordained priest in 1852 by David Anderson, bishop of Rupert's Land.

Horden used Moose Factory as a base from which to visit settlements around James Bay, and he did not go on leave until 1865 when he went home to England. Seven years later the diocese of Rupert's Land was split up, and on Dec. 5, 1872, Horden was appointed the first bishop of Moosonee. Bishop Horden devoted the rest of his life to serving the people of the north.

Catholic "privileges" anger Orange Order

March 23, 1893

SAINT JOHN, N.B. – Angered by what they see as "special privileges" for Acadian Catholics, supporters of the English Protestant Orange Order have gathered 10,000 names on a petition demanding that these "privileges" be revoked. The petitions were presented to the provincial legislature today by opposition member Herman H. Pitts, editor of the influential *New Brunswick Reporter and Fredericton Advertiser*. More importantly, he's Grand Master of the New Brunswick Loyal Orange Order, a Protestant group that historically has had little love for Roman Catholics.

Pitts won election to the House last October. He ran against the government, saying it had allowed Catholics in Bathurst, N.B., to fund a religious convent school using public school funds, and that it ignored complaints of the Protestant minority in that town about this arrangement. Aiding his fight was a pamphlet put out by C.H. LaBillois, a government minister, in his last campaign. It suggested LaBillois' refusal to override the actions of the local Catholic school trustees proved he was a friend of the Acadian Catholics in New Brunswick, and thus they should support him against the pro-Protestant Conservative party. What Pitts really wants is an English-only Canada; one where publicly-funded French Catholic schools are illegal.

The Massey-Harris Company of Toronto makes bicycles as well as its popular farm machinery.

Medical missionary Grenfell at work in small hospital

1893

BATTLE HARBOUR, Labrador – Wilfred Grenfell, the Oxford-trained surgeon who tended sick and injured fishermen on the Labrador and Newfoundland coast last year, is back to work at a small hospital in Battle Harbour. Grenfell had spent three years in a small hospital ship cruising the North Sea, caring for the fishermen there, when he was asked by the National Mission for Deep-Sea Fishermen to take a medical mission ship to Labrador and Newfoundland.

Grenfell arrived off the coast in the *Albert* on Aug. 4 last year and worked until late October, when ice forced his ship back to St. John's. He was honored for his work by the people there and asked to return this year. Two fishing companies offered to build two hospitals for Grenfell, one here and one at Indian Harbour.

Back in London, Grenfell managed to persuade the mission to continue the work. Then he set out to raise the extra money for doctors, nurses, medical equipment and a steam launch to visit fishing villages on the coast. Grenfell's stories about the hardships faced by Labrador and Newfoundland fishermen and their families touched many hearts in England, and it was not long before he had collected the money he needed to return.

Political convention unites Liberal party

June 1893

OTTAWA – The Liberal party has wound down its national convention, the first any Canadian political organization has ever held. Under the guiding hand of leader Wilfrid Laurier, the convention became a unifying event for the party. Chief among the changes implemented was the party's abandonment of unrestricted reciprocity – free trade – with the U.S., replaced by a more cautious desire for "a fair and liberal reciprocity treaty (that) would develop the great natural resources of Canada."

Noted scribe Mary Ann Shadd dies

An Emancipation Day Parade is held annually in Amherstberg, Ontario.

Mary Ann Shadd Carey was editor of the Provincial Freeman paper.

June 5, 1893

WASHINGTON, D.C. – Mary Ann Shadd Carey, the first female newspaper publisher in North America, has died. Mrs. Carey, 69, was a freeborn woman of color who trained as a teacher. In 1851, she moved to Canada West, where she combined teaching with writing. Her pamphlet *Notes on Canada West*, published in 1852, advised Negroes to emigrate from the U.S. to Canada. She served as publisher, editor, reporter, and subscription agent of the *Provincial Freeman*, an abolitionist newspaper published in Windsor and Toronto. Following the Civil War, she returned to the United States, resumed her teaching career, and later worked for women's suffrage.

Algonquin Provincial Park: where wildlife and nature are safe

May 27, 1893

TORONTO – An enormous park where wildlife and nature will be protected from the ravages of timbering has been established by the provincial government of Premier Oliver Mowat. To be known as Algonquin Provincial Park, it encompasses about 115 square kilometres of virgin forest in the Nipissing District. It is named Algonquin after the native tribe which hunted in the area, said to teem with wildlife.

The move addresses increasing concern about declining wildlife populations in Ontario and the environmental impact of logging. A recent royal commission, recommending the establishment of Algonquin park, warned "the wholesale and indiscriminate slaughter of forests brings a host of evils ... it turns plains into arid tracts.

"If nothing is done to change the situation," it says, "the waste of one generation must be atoned for by the enforced economy of the next."

Earthenware dishes featuring Canadian scenes such as Montmorency Falls and Bytown were made in British potteries and sold around the world.

Carman publishes new book of poetry

1893

NEW YORK – New Brunswick poet Bliss Carman, now a journalist in New York, has published *Low Tide on Grand Pré*. Like many popular Canadian poets, Carman links passion and spirituality with the natural landscape. The following stanza is from the title poem:

The night has fallen, and the tide
Now and again comes drifting home,
Across these aching barrens wide,
A sigh like driven wind or foam:
In grief the flood is bursting home.

Beef-heavy Calgary is first Alberta city to be incorporated

Sept. 16, 1893

CALGARY – This centre of about 4,000 people has been incorporated as Alberta's first city. Calgary got its start when the North West Mounted Police established it 18 years ago on the Bow River. The Canadian Pacific Railway's arrival is a big factor in its development, but the surrounding beef ranching industry has had an even greater impact. Calgary beat out Fort Macleod for control of the beef economy, and cattlemen have played a big role in developing the city. It already has electric lights, sewers and waterworks. But the current depression has slowed down building and prompted some Calgarians to sell their homes.

The "Big Cheese" is off to the fair

The Canadian dairy industry is well represented by this mammoth cheese.

April 17, 1893

PERTH, Ont. – A gigantic wheel of cheddar cheese – weighing 9,900 kilograms – left the Dominion Experimental Dairy Station today on a special CPR Cheese Train bound for the World's Columbian Exposition at Chicago. There it will form part of a pyramid of Canadian products on display. The "Big Cheese" is six metres around and 1.8 metres high.

Tyrrell brothers explore N.W.T. lake

Aug. 7, 1893

DUBAWNT LAKE, N.W.T. – Joseph and James Tyrrell, brothers who are surveying the remote parts of Keewatin district, have arrived at this lake, which was visited by Samuel Hearne 120 years ago. They travelled from the east by train to Edmonton and then set off in canoes to the northeast, going down the Athabasca River to Lake Athabasca and Black Lake. They left Black Lake on July 8 to explore the unknown country to the north and went down the Chipman River to Selwyn Lake and then down the Dubawnt River to here.

The Tyrrells plan to spend the next week or so exploring the lake and trying to find the other outlet of the Dubawnt River. After they have done this they will be exploring the area west of Chesterfield Inlet that leads into the west side of Hudson Bay. Once on the shores of the bay they will begin to canoe down the coast, if weather permits, to Churchill before the worst of the winter sets in. They will then travel from Churchill back to Winnipeg, if all goes well, having completed a journey of some 4,000 kilometres in which they will have collected botanical specimens, observed Eskimo settlements, and made geological observations.

Winnipeg all-stars 8-3 on eastern tour

Feb. 27, 1893

WINNIPEG – The city's all-star hockey team was given a rousing reception here today on its return from a three-week excursion to Ontario and Quebec. In the first major tour in the history of hockey, the Winnipeggers won eight of 11 games and outscored the opposition 70-37. Only the leading teams in Ottawa, Montreal and Toronto managed to record victories.

The touring squad, picked from the city's three senior clubs, introduced "The Winnipeg Scoop" – a long clearing shot – leg guards and a new face-off system to the eastern teams. The visitors were applauded for their forward combination play and hard shooting.

Seal slaughter suspended on Sundays

May 24, 1893

ST. JOHN'S, Nfld. – Seals may no longer be killed on Sundays, according to the latest act of the local legislature. For years killing seals on Sundays has been a contentious issue, with some captains and crews engaging in the practice and others refraining. The captains who don't allow the killing of seals on Sundays and men who refuse to do so have always been known as "Sunday men." Conflicts have arisen between the groups over shares and wages.

It is hoped this new measure will help conserve Newfoundland's declining seal stocks and create uniform practices in the industry.

Women's suffrage put on the shelf

April 19, 1893

HALIFAX – The Nova Scotia House of Assembly today refused to debate the women's suffrage bill, probably killing the measure – at least for now. The House accepted a committee report recommending deferral for three months. A motion not to accept the report but to debate the bill was defeated by a single vote. The legislature has been inundated this year with petitions demanding that women property holders be granted the vote. Many of these are the result of efforts by the Women's Christian Temperance Union. Earlier, it caused a lively debate in the legislature.

Zorra quintet leave mark in tug of war

July 4, 1893

CHICAGO – Five burly farmers, "neither young nor handsome," from the Ontario townships of East Zorra and West Zorra today stunned a huge crowd gathered at the World's Fair in Chicago, outpulling an American team to capture the world's tug of war championship. The teams came head-to-head after a series of contests eliminated other entries from Great Britain, France, Belgium and Germany.

The five men, not one standing under six-foot and all of Scottish Highland descent, have been pulling as a team for 12 years and have not once tasted defeat. True to their record and with endurance beyond measure, they won despite being outweighed 25 pounds per man.

A painting by Edward Roper shows Indian women fishing from the Fraser River in British Columbia. In the background is an Indian cemetery.

1894

Winnipeg, Jan. 2. Joseph and James Tyrrell arrive after surveying the remote interior of the Keewatin district for the Geological Survey of Canada. They also made geological observations, and notes on the Inuit.

Quebec, Jan. 8. The Quebec Industrial Establishments Act is passed to protect workers, replacing the 1885 Factories Act and incorporating the principle of the civil responsibility of employers. Work done in the home, a big part of the clothing industry, is exempted.

Montreal, March 22. Montreal AAA defeat Ottawa Generals 3-1 for the Stanley Cup.

Montreal, December. The city has 10,000 unemployed.

Ontario. The Ontario Good Roads Association begins a campaign to awaken the public to the need for road improvement in the province.

Ontario. Six Nations Indian Oronhyatekha, also known as Peter Martin, publishes *History of the Independent Order of Foresters*. He has been successful as supreme chief ranger of the order since 1881.

Prince Edward Island. The charter of the Farmers' Bank of Rustico expires. Federal banking legislation of 1891 doomed the tiny but successful bank, founded by Acadians in 1863.

Campobello Island, N.B. A sea mink is killed, one of the last of the mysterious mammals.

Europe. The technique of vaccinating against infections is being widely practised.

Canada. The National Council of Women resolves to lobby for domestic science courses in schools, to further women's education, and to provide better trained domestics.

New Brunswick. The Women's Enfranchisement Association of New Brunswick is formed to work for equal rights for women.

Montreal. Belgian violinist J.-J. Goulet and 40 other musicians found a Montreal Symphony Orchestra.

Ontario. Rondeau Provincial Park is established on Lake Erie. The park protects the area's abundant plant, animal, and bird life.

Ottawa. The House votes down a petition for women's suffrage presented by the Women's Christian Temperance Union.

Supreme Court says Schools Act beyond federal jurisdiction

Feb. 20, 1894

OTTAWA – The federal government has failed in its appeal to the Supreme Court of Canada to overturn the controversial Manitoba Schools Act. Today the justices ruled 3-2 that the law abolishing public funding of denominational schools is outside federal jurisdiction. In 1891, the court struck down the act itself, but in 1892 the Judicial Committee of the Privy Council reversed that ruling, thus validating the act.

Because the Manitoba government declined to argue the case or to appoint counsel, the federal government engaged lawyers to plead the provincial position – ultimately successful – that Ottawa was powerless to act in this instance.

Snow much fun: Winter Carnival delights

Quebecers in their colorful costumes enjoy skating on the St. Lawrence.

Feb. 2, 1894

QUEBEC CITY – This year's Winter Carnival has once again proved that Quebec City knows how to do things in style. This major annual event has seen thousands of visitors to the city turn up for the shows and activities. Between the annual parade, fireworks, and snowshoe races, participants and spectators alike enjoyed one of the best carnivals ever. Meanwhile, visitors were the lucky recipients of Quebecers' warm hospitality.

Police told publishing names of hookers' clients will do the trick

WANTED, 2,000,000 BOYS!

HAVE you a boy to spare? The saloon must have boys or it must shut up its shop. Can't you find one? It is a great factory, and unless it can have 2,000,000 from each generation, for raw material, some of these factories must close up, and the operatives be thrown out upon a cold world, and the public revenue dwindle! One family out of every five must contribute a boy in order to keep up the supply. Will you help? Which of your boys shall it be? Are you a father? Have you given your share to keep up the supply for this great public institution that is helping pay your taxes and kindly electing public officers for you? Have you contributed a boy? If not, some other family has had to give more than its share. Are you selfish? Voting to keep the saloon open to grind up boys and then doing nothing to keep up the supply? Ponder these questions, ye voters, and answer them to God, to whom you will one day give an account for votes as well as prayers. And ye mothers, wives, and daughters, are you by precept, example, and influence in every possible direction doing all you can to save the boys from the enticements of the horrible liquor saloon, and to hasten the day when it shall be outlawed, and curse our fair land no more? If not, why not?

—*Selected.*

The Women's Christian Temperance Union campaigns against liquor sales.

1894

ONTARIO – The Women's Christian Temperance Union of Ontario wants police to publish the names of prostitutes' clients. Members say it's the only way women can protect themselves and their children. Some doctors estimate that 15 percent of all female disorders, including sterility, are the result of diseases transmitted by husbands who frequent prostitutes. Publishing the names of such men could prevent much tragedy.

The original goal of the WCTU was to abolish the sale and manufacture of liquor, but in recent years members have promoted women's suffrage as the only means of winning votes for prohibition. Today, almost any concern of the fair sex is of interest to the WCTU. Members stress they're not "new women." They believe a woman's proper sphere is the home, and that sexual purity is important.

However, many innocent girls now seek work in cities, where they are prey for immoral men. Moreover, not all girls have loving and protective mothers. Knowledge is the only protection against immorality, say WCTU members, who believe educators and mothers must explain sexual matters.

Paper's editorials may be to blame for midnight bomb

June 29, 1894

MONTREAL – An explosion shook downtown Montreal early this morning, after an attempt to put the *Witness* out of business. Shortly after midnight, a bomb was thrown through a window into the newspaper's pressroom. It blew out the building's windows, but miraculously, the brand new press was only slightly damaged.

The *Witness,* one of this country's best-read newspapers, is an energetic crusader for temperance and Protestantism, among other causes. The attack may have been the work of one of the many targets of *Witness* editorials. *La Patrie,* a French-language paper, blames it on anarchists. Police have no suspects. Damage is estimated at $300.

Grand new theatre unveiled in Toronto

June 14, 1894

TORONTO – This city has entered the world rank of concert stages, with tonight's opening of a grand new theatre on Shuter Street. Massey Hall – named for the family that donated funds to build it – is a remarkable setting for classical music. The acoustics are already called "among the best in the world." The Festival Chorus and orchestra performed tonight.

Colonel Massey of Toronto.

Quebec hotel designed "château" style

The magnificent new Château Frontenac overlooks the St. Lawrence River.

1894

QUEBEC CITY – The Château Frontenac, Quebec's imposing new hotel, is now in operation. Construction began in 1892, and was completed in 1893. The Château, inspired by the châteaux of the French Renaissance, was financed the Château Frontenac Co., a consortium of mostly CPR board members, including William Van Horne, R.B. Angus and Donald Smith, who commissioned American architect Bruce Price to design it on the site once occupied by the Château St. Louis, residence of New France governors.

Price already had a respected reputation for CPR hotels he designed in Vancouver and Banff.

Winnipeg workers still back strikers

July 7, 1894

WINNIPEG – The terrible violence that erupted today in Chicago does not appear to have dampened support for the American railway strikers among this city's unionized workers. But there appears to be little chance that the death and destruction south of the border will spill across the line. This afternoon, federal troops clashed with the Pullman strikers and their supporters in Chicago. The exact death toll is uncertain but it is large. Workers here blame the deaths directly on the intervention of the federal troops.

At a large meeting here just a few days ago, this city's unionized workers were enthusiastic in their support of their American compatriots. CPR workers have joined the boycott of railways using Pullman cars, refusing to handle cars belonging to the American Northern Pacific Railway. But Canadian workers say they will not take other action to further this clash that many see as leading to civil war in the United States.

NWMP pair arrive to police the Yukon

May 1894

FORTY MILE, Yukon – Inspector Charles Constantine and Staff Sgt. Brown of the NWMP are here to begin policing the Yukon. The government in Ottawa ordered them north in response to the complaints Bishop William Carpenter Bompas voiced concerning the corrupting influence of the alcohol sold by traders to the Indians. Local businessmen have also written to Ottawa about the need to preserve Canadian sovereignty and maintain law and order.

Constantine, who served with the Wolseley expedition in 1870 and as Manitoba's police chief, has been given these tasks: regulating the liquor trade; administering the gold claim process; and collecting customs duties. The NWMP men climbed the Chilkoot Pass to get to Forty Mile, and on the way Constantine lost no time in collecting customs duties from the miners, who grumbled but paid.

Moravians in Edmonton to inspect land

July 6, 1894

EDMONTON – Weary, sick and hungry, a group of Moravians has arrived here from Russia. Disappointed by the land offered them in western Russia, they left their homes in Volhynia and trudged to Libau on the Baltic coast. Then they waited 13 days for a ship to take them to England. They sailed from Liverpool to Halifax and a month later arrived here. Now the men are to inspect the land offered them by Ottawa.

Flames close, but McIntosh tree OK

1894

DUNDELA, Ont. – For apple lovers everywhere, near-tragedy struck when one side of the original McIntosh apple tree was scorched by fire. The 64-year-old tree was the victim of a conflagration that gutted Allan McIntosh's home just five metres away. The Mac is the apple Ontario gave the world. John McIntosh, Allan's father, discovered about 20 apple trees when he was clearing his land in 1811. He transplanted several, one of which produced a superior fruit he first called "Granny" after his wife.

The Crazy Quilt was originally created to make use of irregular bits of leftover fabric. However, the style has now developed into a creative art form, as seen above.

Island introduces a 1% income tax

May 15, 1894

CHARLOTTETOWN – Because of the current depression, the P.E.I. government has been forced to develop new ways to raise revenue. So, in addition to traditional debentures and taxes, Islanders are now invited to pay an income tax of 1 cent per dollar on "all income, gains and profits derived from any investment or from any trade, employment, profession or vocation, or from any source whatever." Many Islanders, however, will be exempt from the tax, for it applies only to yearly incomes over $350.

Labor Day declared an official holiday

Sept. 3, 1894

OTTAWA – Parliament has sanctified the primacy of all workers by declaring Labor Day an official holiday. Five years behind Europe, where labor is honored in May, Canadians moved their activities, unofficially organized since 1872, to September to create a summer wrap-up weekend. Spearheaded by Tory politician, journalist and former Knights of Labor leader Alexander Whyte Wright, labor usually marks the day with rallies and parades in Toronto and Ottawa. It has been celebrated at the Toronto Exhibition since 1886.

Domestic science school opens doors

September 1894

HAMILTON – Canada's first school of domestic science is now operating. Cooking, sewing, dressmaking and millinery classes are conducted at the YWCA building on Main Street West. The driving force behind the school is Adelaide Hoodless, who favors domestic science education in public schools. "A nation cannot rise above the level of its homes," she insists. To scoffers who say girls learn household skills from their mothers, Mrs. Hoodless shoots back, "How can a woman teach what she does not know herself?"

Bank crisis cripples Nfld. economy

Dec. 10, 1894

ST. JOHN'S, Nfld. – The colony's two principal banks have suspended business, and the economy is in a state of crisis. The Union Bank, established in 1854, and the Commercial Bank, created three years later, have closed, and their bank notes have been rendered, at least temporarily, worthless.

For the last 10 years the Newfoundland economy has suffered from the decline in the seal fishery and severe competition on the cod market. A number of fish exporters borrowed heavily to finance their trade, and the borrowing was allowed – even encouraged – by senior partners who were also directors of the banks. When a London bank declined to cover further withdrawals, demands were made and the banks could no longer meet them. The banks, in turn, called in loans owed by their mercantile customers, and when these could not be met the banks and firms closed. The banks should be able to pay a percentage of the face value of their notes, but many firms will close.

American ethnologist Russell arrives in Yukon to study Inuit

An Inuit man displays a harpoon; a woman carries her child in her hood.

Music for this Inuit dance is provided by traditional musical instruments.

July 9, 1894

HERSCHEL ISLAND, Yukon – American ethnologist Frank Russell, on an expedition to the Mackenzie district sponsored by the University of Iowa, has arrived here. Russell spent most of last year travelling with Indians, noting their way of life and collecting ornithological specimens. He started at Fort Chipewyan and went down the Slave River to Fort Resolution by steamer and then crossed Great Slave Lake. Here he joined an Indian to canoe up the Yellowknife River and then went back to Fort Resolution with a band of Indians.

Next, Russell accompanied some Dogrib Indians on a musk-oxen hunt for two months. At the end of the hunt he went to Fort Rae. From there he canoed alone down the Mackenzie to Fort Resolution, where he met another explorer with whom he went down to the Mackenzie Delta and out into the Arctic Ocean. They headed west to Herschel Island in time to meet the whaling ships which have come for the season. Russell plans to make trips from Herschel Island to settlements on the mainland so that he can meet the Inuit there as well as the ones who come to the island for trading with the whalers.

Missionaries Peck and Parker bring the word of God to Inuit

Aug. 21, 1894

BLACKLEAD ISLAND, Cumberland Sound – The European mission societies are determined to bring the word of God to Baffin Island, it seems. Nearly 30 years ago, a Moravian missionary called Warnow was brought from Aberdeen, Scotland, to Kekerten, near here, by a British whaling ship. Warnow spent the winter with the Inuit, but after he reported to his mission society, the members decided not to establish a mission here.

Now another whaling ship, the *Alert,* from Peterhead, near Aberdeen, has brought two more missionaries, Edmund Peck and J.C. Parker. They will see if they can establish a mission here, close to the whaling station. They plan to care for the Inuit and to try to bring them the word of God.

Peck and Parker, of the Church Missionary Society, will also use Blacklead Island as a base from which to visit other whaling stations, particularly in Frobisher Bay, to see if they can start missions nearby.

Beautiful Joe sales at near-record level

1894

HALIFAX – Canadian author Margaret Marshall Saunders' latest novel, *Beautiful Joe: The Autobiography of a Dog,* is selling phenomenally well in the U.S. and Canada, and seems likely to equal records set by Anna Sewell's 1877 best-seller *Black Beauty,* about a black stallion.

Though critics point out that *Beautiful Joe* is mawkishly sentimental and didactic, the general public has fallen in love with the mangled mongrel whose "beauty" lies entirely in his serene nature. Joe, the book's narrator, tells a horrendous tale of animal abuse. In puppyhood, his brutish master, the milkman Jenkins, slaughtered the whole litter except Joe, whose ears and tail he hacked off. Fortunately for the bleeding, suffering pup, a minister's children rescue him, and Joe becomes an adored and adoring member of their family. "I don't believe that a dog could have fallen into a happier home than I did," Joe muses.

Joe's subsequent experiences are testimony to how animals can teach humans compassion and selflessness. He also exposes the horrors of animal abuse, though his own abuser Jenkins escapes with a mere $10 fine for "cruelly torturing and mutilating a dog."

Tapeworm remover nothing but a sham

1894

ONTARIO – Tapeworm eating away at you? You might try Dr. Kelley's famous Shamrock Tapeworm Remover. It probably won't do the trick, since it's only a pea soup mixture that leaves a bitter taste in your mouth, but at $7 a crack it is guaranteed to remove money from your pocketbook.

Doc Kelley is part of a travelling medicine show, one of many such shows now popular in Ontario. He tours around with other "doctors" dispensing his wonder remedies. Most travelling medicine men make their cures from alcohol, believed to be the only immediate cure for colds and coughs.

Poll suggests Ontarians oppose drinking

PROHIBITION PLEBISCITE!
CONVENTION
FOR THE
COUNTY OF YORK.

All prohibitionists and friends of temperance in general in the County of York, are requested to meet in the

Mechanics' Hall, Aurora,
ON
TUESDAY 31ST OCT.

For the purpose of organizing in connection with the plebiscite for prohibition and endeavoring to get out the largest vote possible on the 1st of JANUARY, 1894

The Convention will commence at 10 o'clock, and let each municipality in the County be fully represented.

A MASS MEETING!
WILL BE HELD
IN THE EVENING.
Chair taken at 8 o'clock. Collection taken up to defray expenses.

Let all friends of temperance rally and work for "God, Home and Country."

REV. H. S. MATTHEWS,
COUNTY CONVENER.

Aurora, October 24th 1893 — Aurora Banner Print

Prohibitionists held public meetings such as the one advertised here in advance of this month's plebiscite.

Jan. 30, 1894

TORONTO – Ontarians are against drinking – that's what the results of a plebiscite held this month suggest. "Suggest," because although 60 percent of the males who voted did so for a dry Ontario, only half of the male population overall turned out for the plebiscite. So did a number of property-owning women who also have the franchise. Some 13,000 of them also want liquor made illegal.

The fact is that booze has resulted in serious social problems, and now an increasing number of Ontarians are wondering if the best solution to the misery caused by the "demon rum" would be to ban it altogether – if such a law would actually work.

Townsfolk seek stricter controls on fires

Sept. 13, 1894

MOOSE JAW, N.W.T. – The leading citizens of this town are trying to drum up support for stricter regulations to control prairie fires. In a document they are circulating, they claim that in the past two years the frequency of prairie fires has much increased. If nothing is done, the document warns, the good ranching and farming land in this area "will soon be transformed into a sandy desert."

The people here blame the fires directly on the railways. People here want the railways forced to build firebreaks on both sides of their lines, wide plowed areas with the grass burnt between the rail line and the fireguard. They also want a fire police force established to patrol the rail lines across the prairies. Once they have taken hold, grass fires on the prairies are extremely hard to stop. Most people believe there has been a great increase as the result of sparks from locomotives.

Ozias Leduc of St. Hilaire, Quebec, painted this famous work entitled Le Petit Liseur. His younger brother served as model for the masterpiece.

PM Thompson dies at Windsor Castle; Bowell new leader

Prime Minister Mackenzie Bowell.

Dec. 22, 1894

OTTAWA – Sir Mackenzie Bowell yesterday became Canada's sixth prime minister, filling the void left by Sir John Thompson's sudden death. Having been sworn in as a member of Her Majesty's Privy Council by Queen Victoria Dec. 12, Thompson, 49, fainted over lunch in the Octagon Room. He was helped to a nearby room, given water and brandy, and seemed to recover. But on returning he felt a chest pain, slumped against the royal doctor, and, to the horror of the queen and her guests, died.

Ottawa puts a ban on killing buffaloes

1894

OTTAWA – Parliament has passed the Unorganized Territories Game Preservation Act to protect the game of the northern prairies, a big step against wildlife abuses. The act prohibits buffalo killing for the next six years, without exception, sets closed seasons for various birds and mammals, and restricts taking wildfowl eggs and the use of poison by trappers. But the act does allow Indians, travellers, explorers, and surveyors to kill mammals – except buffalo – and take wildfowl eggs. The act is not intended to protect game for its own sake, but rather to help Indians and Inuit who depend on game for survival.

1895

London, January. The Judicial Committee of the Privy Council rules in the case of Brophy vs. Attorney General of Manitoba that the Canadian government has the power to take remedial action against the Manitoba Schools Act.

Ottawa, March 21. An order-in-council promises a separate state-funded Roman Catholic school system in Manitoba, flying in the face of the Manitoba Schools Act.

Prince Edward Island, Sept. 11. Thomas Heath Haviland, Jr., a Father of Confederation, dies.

Quebec, Dec. 16. French millionaire Henri Menier buys Anticosti Island.

Canada. The first breeders' association for the Canadian horse breed is formed.

Canada. Edmonton, Fort Saskatchewan and Strathcona play the first scheduled rugby football games on the prairies.

Northwest Territories. Ukrainian Dr. Joseph Okeskow visits the prairies, and writes a pamphlet called *On Emigration and About Free Lands*, which is widely read in the western Ukraine.

Ontario. The Sault Ste. Marie Canal, bypassing the rapids of the St. Mary's River between Lakes Superior and Huron, is re-opened, becoming the largest canal in Canada. The original canal for fur trade canoes was destroyed during the War of 1812.

Northwest Territories. The town of Bienfait, [Saskatchewan], is named from the oath of a French-Canadian railway worker who, legend has it, put down his hammer on this section of the CPR and yelled "C'est vraiment bien fait!"

Northwest Territories. Waterton Lakes Park, southwest of Calgary on the Canada-U.S. border, is created as a forest preserve. The park includes both prairie and mountain.

Canada. The periodical *Le Passe Temps* allows Canadians to read about the music scene in Canadian cities.

Canada. The Associated Board, a British musical examination board, is set up in Canada.

Germany. Scientist Wilhelm Roentgen discovers a new form of radiation he calls "X-rays."

Montreal. Montreal Victorias, champions of the Amateur Athletic Association, win the Stanley Cup for 1895.

Priests urge Ottawa to kill Schools Act

Jan. 26, 1895

WINNIPEG – Archbishop-elect Adelard Langevin of St. Boniface and a priest from Winnipeg, Father Cherrier, are two of the Roman Catholic clerics engaged in continuing opposition to the Manitoba Schools Act. It is their belief that it is not too late for the federal government to disallow the provincial legislation, and it is to this end that they attempt to lobby the new prime minister, Mackenzie Bowell, and the members of his cabinet.

One of the archbishop's close confidants is Col. Alphonse Audet, the archivist of the secretary of state. In an exchange of correspondence between Audet and the archbishop, the archivist stated that the recent decision of the Privy Council in the Brophy case had determined that a man named Brophy, as a spokesman for the minority of Manitoba Roman Catholics, indeed had a right to appeal to the governor-general-in-council.

The Roman Catholic clergy now believe that if disallowance is not acceptable for political reasons, it should be possible for the cabinet to introduce some remedial legislation which would serve to mitigate the more arbitrary aspects of the Manitoba Schools Act. Clouding this contentious matter further is the uncertain life of the Bowell administration in Ottawa.

Seal hunt cuts into Sable Island herds

Seal skinners show how they prepare the skins by scraping the fat away.

1895

SABLE ISLAND – A seal hunt that went on all summer here has seriously reduced herds off this Atlantic island, 290 kilometres east of Halifax. It is unknown at this point how long it will be before herds recover to the levels they were at before the slaughter. Seals have become popular as a source of food, skins and oil, although the last may decline in importance as the petroleum industry establishes itself. The species hit hard by this hunt has been the smaller dotar.

The sealing history of this island of sand goes back 150 years to when large numbers of seals were found in Sable's central lagoon. Before long, despite hazardous waters around the island, the sealers started to arrive. One hunter from Nova Scotia established a factory here, although he was later run off by American hunters.

Seal hunting evolved along Canada's east coast in the early days of the 18th century when the animals were netted along the shores. By mid-century small boats were being used in the hunt for the first time. These were replaced by sailing ships, which in turn gave way to steamships in the 1860s.

The magnificence and tranquillity of the Rocky Mountains are portrayed in this Edward Roper painting.

Niagara power shuffles off to Buffalo

Detail of an Edward Roper painting of the world-famous Niagara Falls.

October 1895

NIAGARA FALLS, N.Y. – A transmission line that will carry the hydroelectric power produced by generators here to Buffalo, N.Y., is being contracted out by the Niagara Falls Power Company. Power will be transmitted by an alternating current (AC) system, and if this 32-kilometre transmission is a success, it could be a breakthrough for the hydro industry here.

Buffalo's population of 250,000 and position as a large industrial city presents an important market for hydro. Electricity was produced here as early as 1881, but transmitting it has been another story. The Niagara Falls Power Company offered prizes to anyone coming up with a good idea on transmission, but opted for the AC system being tried in Europe. The firm hopes to produce power by building a large, deep tunnel through which water would flow and drive turbines.

Confederation talk fizzles out in Nfld.

May 16, 1895

NEWFOUNDLAND – A second round of Confederation talks between Canada and Newfoundland has gone sour, and now it appears the issue is a dead one. The latest chapter in the Confederation saga began in February – just weeks after the December bank crash. The Newfoundland government decided the time was right to ask to join Canada.

Four delegates from the colony, Edward Morris, George Emerson, Robert Bond and William Horwood, met with a Canadian delegation in Ottawa on April 4 to discuss terms under which Confederation could take place. Newfoundland's most important demand was money to pay debts and local services, so when the Canadian government refused to provide the necessary funding, Newfoundland delegates broke off negotiations.

This is the second serious attempt by Newfoundland politicians to take the colony into Confederation, and it was made at considerable personal political risk because this has never been a popular option with the local voters. Observers believe that Canada's refusal to show some generosity toward its small neighbor will not be forgotten soon. It is quite likely that future politicians will use these aborted negotiations to attack the idea of Confederation whenever it should arise.

Low priority given to controversial act

April 18, 1895

OTTAWA – Today's speech from the throne clearly suggests the Manitoba Schools Act will not be a matter of prime importance at this session. The remedial bill is not being withdrawn, as was suggested by several candidates in the recent election, but certainly it has been relegated to a minor spot on the parliamentary schedule. The throne speech said little more than the Privy Council made its decision in this matter and that an order-in-council was sent to Manitoba.

Even if Prime Minister Mackenzie Bowell does not place the Manitoba Schools Act at the top of the order paper, this does not mean he has forgotten it or is in any way discounting its importance. It is possible he is stalling for time, hoping tempers cool. A further consideration is that the prime minister cannot be assured that all the members of his party are of one mind on this troublesome issue. What began as an internal matter in one province has reached out not only across the nation, but as far as Westminster and the Vatican.

U of T students boycotting their classes

Feb. 15, 1895

TORONTO – Students at the University of Toronto have decided to boycott classes, as a power struggle between them and the university administration continues. The students have numerous grievances, including bad teaching, an attempt to suppress the student-run *Varsity* newspaper by suspending its editor from lectures, and, today, the dismissal of a professor who had gone to the media to complain about the administration's incompetence.

Students leading the revolt are: T. Hamar Greenwood, James A. Tucker, the suspended editor, and William Lyon Mackenzie King. They organized the mass meetings that led to the boycott.

Canadian bankers set sights on Nfld.

Jan. 31, 1895

ST. JOHN'S, Nfld. – Following the failure of its two banks, Newfoundland is welcoming the Canadian banks that have decided to set up operations here. The Bank of Nova Scotia has opened a branch in St. John's and another in Harbour Grace. The Royal Bank of Canada has opened a branch in St. John's as well – its first outside mainland Canada. The Bank of Montreal, which seems set to become the government's banker, has also established a branch in St. John's. It is expected that these banks will be more cautious with their loans.

Mills were important businesses in early Upper Canada. Kingston Mills, shown here, is the site of Upper Canada's first mill, erected in 1784.

Manitoba refusing orders to change status of schools

June 15, 1895

WINNIPEG – Manitoba will refuse to comply with the federal order-in-council concerning the Manitoba Schools Question – so says a communication the province sent to Ottawa today. It is now evident that when the provincial government adjourned the legislative session on May 9, it was so members could determine how to word a response to the order concerning Catholic education in Manitoba. The province's communication is based upon alleged inferior educational services; it states that in Roman Catholic schools "conduct, management, were defective. ... Many people grew up in a state of illiteracy."

This position has considerable public support, largely because of Manitoba's changing demographics. By 1890, when Manitoba abolished its dual education system, tolerating denominational schools but denying them public funding, the English-speaking, Protestant population had increased tenfold, while the Roman Catholic had not.

New railway serves rich mining district

1895

KASLO, B.C. – The Kaslo and Slocan Railway has opened between this town on Kootenay Lake and Sandon in the Slocan district. Sandon is the richest mining settlement in an area being developed for its silver and other ores. The new railway, 47 kilometres long and built to a three-foot gauge, is a spectacular engineering feat, with tracks clinging precariously to the walls of canyons and leaping over rivers on seemingly rickety bridges.

Much of the money to build the Kaslo and Slocan is said to come from the Great Northern Railway below the border which has been trying to get traffic from the mines in Canada to smelters in the U.S. The Canadian Pacific Railway also has a line running into Sandon, and competition between the railways is expected to be fierce.

National body of the YWCA created

Many homeless women end up in jails such as the Carleton County Jail.

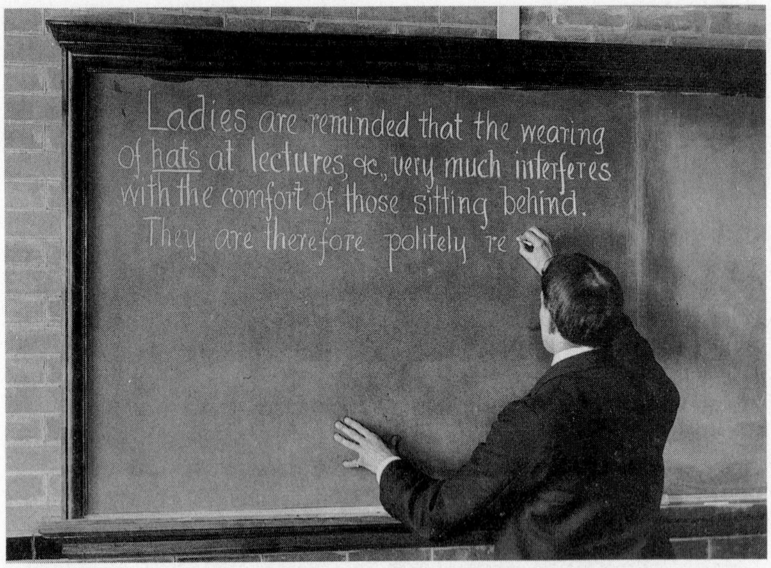

Some new, unexpected problems arise with women's presence in classrooms!

1895

SAINT JOHN, N.B. – Twenty-five years after the first Young Women's Christian Association branch in Canada opened here in 1870, a national YWCA body has been created. The YWCA has its origins in a shelter for nurses established by Lady Kinnaird in London, England, at the time of the Crimean War and the formation of the prayer unions by Emma Robarts. Since the Saint John branch opened, similar organizations have been founded in major Canadian cities such as Montreal, Ottawa, Toronto and Hamilton.

Along with providing shelter for women travelling away from home seeking employment, the YWCA branches function as employment centres. Many of the best domestic workers in Canada have been recommended by the YWCA. Several branches also offer classes in cooking, sewing, physical education and typewriting.

YWCAs act as social centres for young women far from home, ensuring the continued adherence to Christian principles through Bible studies and prayer circles. Members of YWCAs are also involved in other works. The Hamilton branch, for example, has protested the sale of liquor to children and petitioned for the appointment of a police matron to handle juvenile and female prisoners.

Work was begun to form a Dominion YWCA in 1892, after delegates of several local YWCAs attended the Chicago World's Fair. The national association includes some of the most prominent women in Canada. Currently, the president is Adelaide Hoodless of Hamilton, well known for her efforts to introduce domestic science education into public schools.

Women at work in the ironing room of Ottawa's Home for Friendless Women.

New Zealand treasurer proposes free trade with Canada

Aug. 12, 1895

OTTAWA – New Zealand has proposed free trade with Canada. It was learned here today that in his budget speech, New Zealand treasurer J.G. Ward made the trade proposal. Ward recently visited this country briefly to investigate the possibilities for more commerce between his colony and Canada. If Ward succeeds in his plan, New Zealand will become the first British colony to take advantage of the British parliament's allowing colonies to make preferential trade deals. New Zealand's chief export to Canada in a trade deal would be long wool used to make tweeds.

Work is under way on Mountie post as inspector arrives

July 24, 1895

FORTY MILE, Yukon – Inspector Charles Constantine, the tough incorruptible NWMP officer who came here last year to investigate complaints about lawlessness and corruption of Indians, has arrived back in Forty Mile. This time he has brought his wife, another NWMP inspector and his wife, a police surgeon, and 17 men. They have started to build a police headquarters and barracks called Fort Constantine.

The inspector plans to become the voice of authority in the Yukon, and to confirm Canadian sovereignty over the region. He says, wryly, that he is "chief magistrate, commander-in-chief, and home and foreign secretary."

Are you the perfect woman of today?

Dec. 28, 1895

HALIFAX – Are you a perfect woman? The *Acadian Reporter* today describes the ideal female proportions, based partly on the Venetian Venus. According to an article by Lady Jane, reprinted from the *New York Weekly*, the earthly goddess is five-foot-five and weighs 138 pounds, although another 10 pounds are acceptable if a woman is well-formed. "A woman of this height should measure 24 inches around the waist and 34 inches around the bust, if measured from under the arms, and 43 if over them."

Black hair, eyebrows, lashes and pupils are considered ideal features, along with white skin and teeth, red lips and cheeks. You must have a round head, neck, arms, ankles and waist, long back, fingers, and limbs, a large forehead, large eyes and lips, small ears, bust and hands, and narrow eyebrows, nose and feet.

Could this be the perfect woman?

Montreal triumphs in Stanley Cup bid

March 9, 1895

MONTREAL – In the first challenge match for the Stanley Cup here tonight, Queen's University of Kingston lost 5-1 to Montreal AAA. The collegians, champions of the Ontario Hockey Association and the Intercollegiate league, looked fierce in their tiger stripe uniforms of yellow, red and blue, but Montreal easily beat them to defend their 1894 championship. Queen's players were hampered by the large ice surface and the difference between the Quebec and OHA rules. Three goals were called back on the offside rule.

Haviland Routh, leading scorer of the Amateur Hockey Association of Canada, scored two goals for Montreal. Queen's seven-man club was led by its 30-year-old point player and captain, Guy Curtis.

Rail feud explodes in B.C. mining town

Dec. 16, 1895

SANDON, B.C. – The rivalry between the railway barons of the west, Cornelius Van Horne of the CPR and J.J. Hill of the Great Northern, has turned into violence in this little mining town. The CPR, which operates a standard-gauge spur line into town, had begun to build a new depot. As a crowd watched and the CPR crew ate a meal, workers of the Kaslo and Slocan Railway, a Hill-financed narrow-gauge line, wrapped a cable around the depot and hitched it to one of their locomotives. A few puffs and down went the building. Then, the Kaslo men started to wreck the CPR trackage.

CPR officials say they will try to get a warrant for the arrest of the officials who allowed the depot to be wrecked, but public opinion is all in favor of the little railway and against the massive CPR – David over Goliath. A boom in the mining communities near here has provoked fierce competition in the mine ore traffic, for the railways are also involved in the smelting business.

Deadline nears for St. John's 58 saloons

Oct. 31, 1895

ST. JOHN'S, Nfld. – Local saloons, all 58 of them, that plan to stay in business must renew their licences today. Most St. John's watering holes – 35 of them, in fact – are on Water Street, and there are 10 more on Duckworth. The rest are on various side streets and in neighborhoods far-removed from the waterfront, with only one on the south side of the harbor where the sealskin and oil factories have been located since 1846.

St. John's has always had a large number of saloons, frequented by fishermen from the outports, sailors from all over the world, and the locals – especially workers on the waterfront. Several brands of local beer, imported Irish stout, and rum from the British West Indies are the favorite beverages served in these establishments.

The fishing industry is the mainstay of the Maritime provinces' economy. Women are employed in fish processing plants such as this lobster cannery.

Northwest Territories split up – again

Oct. 2, 1895

OTTAWA – The federal government cannot make up its mind about the proper division of territory and authority in northern and western Canada. Since the cession of Rupert's Land to Canada 30 years ago there have been frequent changes in the names and divisions of the land. Now there are some more. The Northwest Territories below the 60th Parallel, a chunk of land lying north of Prince Albert, have been absorbed by the district of Athabasca. The Northwest Territories above the parallel are being divided into four provisional districts. In the west is the Yukon district, with the Mackenzie district to its east. Two other districts get names evocative of natives and an explorer – Ungava and Franklin.

These changes are mostly administrative and hardly affect the lives of the settlers, miners and ranchers and traders who live in northwest Canada, for Ottawa will still rule the area with a tight hand. But as the population of these northwest areas grows, the people will probably demand some kind of locally-run government.

1896

Montreal, Feb. 14. Winnipeg Victorias beat Montreal Victorias 2-0 for the Stanley Cup.

Winnipeg, April 4. Canadian government commissioners return to Ottawa after failing to negotiate a settlement to the Manitoba Schools Question.

Athens, April. The Olympic Games are revived after a gap of 1,500 years. The original games were held in ancient Greece in honor of Zeus.

Ottawa, May 1. Conservative Charles Tupper becomes PM following the resignation of Mackenzie Bowell.

Toronto, May. The Eddy Match Co. announces in the *Globe* newspaper that it is making 28,000 matches a day.

Yukon, June 18. Summer mail service is inaugurated between Juneau and Forty Mile. Mail is to be delivered three times a season by lively 73-year-old William Moore.

Manitoba, Aug. 11. Twenty-seven Ukrainian families settle in southern Manitoba [near Stuartburn], the first Ukrainian settlement in the province.

Forty Mile, Yukon, Sept. 6. Surveyor William Ogilvie tells the Canadian government of George Carmack's rich gold find on Bonanza Creek.

Montreal, Sept. 16. Of 1,000 Canadian emigrants about to leave for Brazil, some 600-700 decide at the last minute not to go after *La Presse* alerted them to the miserable conditions they would face in Brazil.

Forty Mile, Yukon, Nov. 20. NWMP inspector Charles Constantine reports that the worst crime problem in the area is the trading of liquor to Indians. He also says whalers at Herschel Island are trading whisky to natives "for furs, walrus ivory bone, and their young girls."

Winnipeg, Dec. 30. Montreal Victorias beat Winnipeg Victorias 6-5 in a challenge for the Stanley Cup after Winnipeg beat them in February.

Dawson City, Yukon. Following Carmack's gold find, Joseph Ladue founds a town at the mouth of the Klondike River in anticipation of a gold rush. He names it Dawson City, after government geologist George Dawson.

Canada. Timothy Eaton Co. publishes its first Christmas catalogue.

Canada. Immigration to Canada is 16,855.

7 federal ministers quit Bowell cabinet over schools issue

Jan. 3, 1896

OTTAWA – Seven of Prime Minister Mackenzie Bowell's cabinet members resigned today over the Manitoba Schools Question. All are Protestant, and all gave as their excuse the prime minister's prolonged failure to fill the cabinet vacancy created by the earlier resignation of Charles Anger, the MP from La Malbaie. Only two days after the speech from the throne, the following members have left the cabinet: Messrs. Foster, Haggart, Montague, Tupper, Dickey, Ives, and Wood.

In an effort to strengthen his cabinet and cool down the heat generated by the Manitoba problem, Bowell shuffled some cabinet portfolios last month. He raised the positions of controller of customs and controller of inland revenue to cabinet rank. News of the cabinet revolt reached the prime minister while he was conferring with the governor general.

Foxy breeders try peddling their pelts

Valuable black silver fox skins fill this warehouse in Summerside, P.E.I.

1896

CHARLOTTETOWN – Several years ago, Robert Oulton and Charles Dalton were the first to successfully breed the rare silver fox in captivity. Now they have decided to see how their foxes fare in the marketplace, though they have been obsessed with secrecy since the project's beginning. Visitors to their Cherry Island ranch are discouraged, and a hired guard patrols at night. Not even Oulton's wife and daughters know the results of the breeding experiments.

Their obsession is understandable. With the pelts fetching more than $100 each, they want to be able to control the supply and prices of furs as long as they can.

Ski racing, ski jumping catch on in B.C.

1896

ROSSLAND, B.C. – Ski racing and ski jumping, Canada's newest winter sports, are becoming popular in this area. Local jumpers and some from nearby Revelstoke have been meeting for informal competitions. Skiing got its start in Scandinavia, and spread to Canada with Norwegian immigrants. It developed as a means to enlarge the foot surface so travel through soft snow would be easier. It is particularly popular in logging areas.

The huge trees of British Columbia forests are not only a valuable natural resource, but also serve to make sturdy corduroy roads in lumber camps.

U of T graduate designs new tools

Jan. 6, 1896

TORONTO – Mining engineer Herbert E.T. Haultain announced today that he has designed and built two devices known as the superpanner and infrasizer, which are instruments to be used in dressing ore. Haultain, a native of Brighton, England, graduated from the University of Toronto and went on to serve as a mining engineer in South Africa, Ireland and Bohemia, as well as in the western United States and Canada.

Mining is beginning to come into its own in Canada with the development of rail service and industrialization. So far, a lot of Canada's iron ore is going directly to the U.S. In particular, ore from mines in the Kootenay Lake area between the Purcell and Selkirk ranges of British Columbia has been going to smelters in the U.S. Similarly, in the last two decades several mines north of Lake Ontario shipped iron ore to Cleveland.

Louis Cyr triumphs in strongman bout

March 31, 1896

CHICAGO – Canadian Louis Cyr today defeated August W. Johnson of Sweden to win the world championship of strongmen. The competition, which lasted for three hours, carried a prize of $1,000. Johnson, obviously in awe of Cyr's phenomenal strength, remarked afterwards that he had beaten opponents from around the world, "but this is the first time I have met an elephant."

Cyr, 32, of Montreal, in 1894 lifted a platform of men that weighed a total of 4,562 pounds.

Louis Cyr, Canadian strongman.

Schools issue up in air

April 23, 1896

WINNIPEG – Provincial rights supporters here welcome the dissolution of the federal Parliament. But the large Catholic minority in Manitoba is extremely disappointed. Just before dissolution, after a raucous debate and filibuster, the government withdrew remedial legislation designed to restore Catholic school rights in Manitoba.

In 1890, the provincial government ended the province's dual school system, withdrawing support from Catholic schools. This was seen as contrary to the Manitoba Act of 1870, which brought the province into Confederation. But an appeal to the Judicial Committee of the Privy Council in London failed to have the legislation declared unconstitutional.

Earlier this year, Mackenzie Bowell's government prepared the remedial legislation, but it was seen, even among some Catholic supporters, as unwelcome interference in provincial affairs. It seems likely that the prime minister will resign as Conservative leader in the face of a cabinet revolt. Many prominent Conservatives openly oppose their party's position. Liberal leader Wilfrid Laurier promises to negotiate a compromise on the schools issue if he wins the upcoming federal election.

Lost in the schools uproar is the fact that also in 1890 the Manitoba government abolished French as an official language. Many see this as another denial of a constitutional right and an issue that will continue to fester.

Judge dismisses Orange Lodge lawsuit

March 17, 1896

BATHURST, N.B. – A lawsuit launched by the Bathurst Orange Lodge over school trustees' failure to comply with non-sectarian education regulations has been dismissed by an Equity Court judge. The lodge was challenging the right of the trustees to tax its property, contending the board did not comply with provincial law on non-sectarian education.

The legal action was the latest in a series of disputes involving the trustees' actions. It started when the trustees took the convent school under their wing, meaning it would be tax supported. Local Protestants brought a petition to the province to intervene, but it ruled that trustees did not break an 1875 common schools act which legalized sectarian schools within the non-sectarian system.

Colorful Jerry Potts loses battle to TB

Jerry Potts, who served the NWMP for years, has succumbed to TB.

July 14, 1896

FORT MACLEOD, N.W.T. – One of the west's most colorful characters is dead. Jerry Potts, 56, a North West Mounted Police interpreter and guide since the force began, lost a battle with tuberculosis at home here this morning.

Potts, the hard-drinking son of a white fur trader and a Blood Indian mother, led Peigan warriors in the last great Indian battle on the Canadian plains in 1870. He never wasted words: he translated one Indian chief's long, eloquent speech welcoming the NWMP to the west as "He damn glad you're here."

Lacombe helps establish Métis reserve

July 15, 1896

SAINT - PAUL - DES - METIS, N.W.T. – The Métis of western Canada are truly Canada's forgotten people. Many have lost land to white newcomers and have great difficulty supporting themselves. Unlike status Indians, or Indians under the federal Indian Act, they get no federal aid and they have no land base.

Veteran Roman Catholic missionary Albert Lacombe, "the Man of the Good Heart," as the natives call him, proposed a short while ago that a reserve be established for the most destitute Alberta Métis. Ottawa has acted on his suggestion and set aside land north of the Saskatchewan River. Eight Métis families are expected to settle on the selected townships this year, and eventually perhaps as many as 100 will relocate there. Today the missionaries began the construction of the chapel at the site now known as Saint-Paul-des-Métis.

Lacombe has printed trilingual circulars in English, French and Cree directed to those Métis "who have no longer any home and who do not know how to earn a living." They say land will be loaned to those Métis who come, and promise that the missionaries will build a school to train the Métis children in agriculture and ranching. The greatest challenge facing the new Métis community is the financial one. Ottawa has approved the scheme, but it has only provided a modest one-time grant of $2,000.

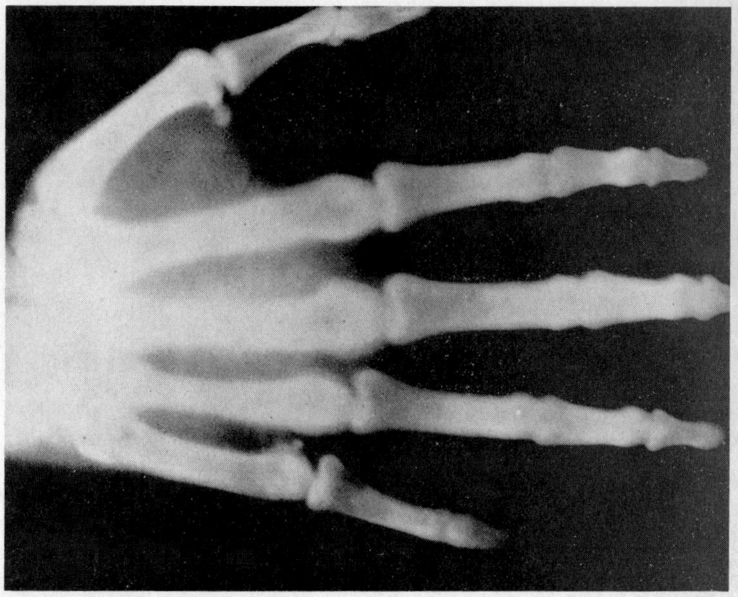

This photograph of the bones of a human hand is one of the first X-rays taken in Canada. It was taken at McGill University in Montreal, Quebec.

French-Canadian Laurier new PM

Cartoonist's view of Laurier policies.

During the recent election campaign, Laurier supporters organized rallies like this one at Amherstburg, Ontario, where people could hear and meet the man who would eventually become the next prime minister of the country.

July 11, 1896

OTTAWA – Wilfrid Laurier is Canada's new prime minister, the first French-Canadian since Confederation. He was sworn in this morning, after a short delay as Sir Charles Tupper tried to retain power despite the results of the recent election. It appears the Liberals won 117 seats to the Conservatives' 89 in the June 23 election.

There have been four short-term Conservative prime ministers since John A. Macdonald's death in 1891. But of more immediate effect was the Liberals' deft political handling of the Manitoba schools issue. Overriding provincial legislation, the Conservative government tried to pass remedial legislation to restore Manitoba's publicly-funded Catholic schools. In the acrimonious debate, many Conservatives refused to support their own party. Laurier has said he will seek a compromise on the issue. This pleased voters in Ontario and Manitoba who oppose Catholic schools. But the Liberals also pleased Quebec voters by promising to seek a political solution that would protect Catholics to a greater extent than would remedial legislation.

Carmack, Indians stake their claims to major gold find

Aug. 17, 1896

RABBIT CREEK, Yukon – George Carmack and his Indian friends – Skookum Jim and Tagish Charlie – have today staked claims along the creek here. They believe they have made a major gold discovery. The gold, they say, was lying in cracks of rock "thick between the flaky slabs, like cheese sandwiches."

Two of the four claims are for Carmack, who says he saw the gold first. After he staked the claims, Carmack ripped some bark off a tree and wrote on it: "I name this creek Bonanza. George Carmack." The three men had gone up Rabbit Creek earlier and found only small flakes of gold. But after a visit to the camp of Robert Henderson, who had been prospecting in Rabbit Creek earlier, the three went back and found the gold.

And there are stories that Henderson saw the gold in Rabbit Creek before any of them. He offered to share his find with Carmack, the stories say, but not with his Indian friends.

Sifton unveils plans for biggest immigration push of the century

Nov. 27, 1896

OTTAWA – Clifford Sifton, the federal minister of the interior, has decided Canada needs to actively promote immigration to the prairies. So he's announced plans for the biggest promotional campaign ever seen in this country to do just that. Sifton is a westerner; a relatively young minister who believes in the future of the west. But he has also seen how things are going – how, even with the railway in place, more people are leaving than coming to Canada.

Sifton has several ideas to speed up immigration. First, he's promised to cut through Ottawa's red tape to make it easier for people to acquire free land grants. As well, Sifton has decided immigrants need to be sought actively, so he's offering government officials a bonus for each new person they recruit to Canada. He's also sending out millions of brochures extolling the virtues of the prairies all over America and Europe. Journalists are being taken on promotional trips through the prairies and being encouraged to write about them back home.

This Mennonite family has already built a house and a barn on their farm.

There is, of course, a slight catch to this "open door policy" – namely, that it's not so open door. The minister is determined to bring in good farmers, like Americans, British, and some European nationalities. But Orientals, Italians, Jews and blacks are not favored because "they don't farm well."

Three ex-premiers in Laurier's cabinet

July 14, 1896

OTTAWA – Prime Minister Wilfrid Laurier has appointed political heavyweight Oliver Mowat to his cabinet as the new minister of justice. Mowat, premier of Ontario since 1872, joins former premiers W.S. Fielding of Nova Scotia and A.G. Blair of New Brunswick in the new cabinet.

The move ends fears that Laurier, whose Liberal party has been in opposition for the last 18 years, suffers from a lack of experienced administrators. Mowat's presence reassures the business community. So does new finance minister Fielding, though Laurier chose him over free-trade advocate and party loyal Sir Richard Cartwright, a minister under former PM Alexander Mackenzie. Laurier's new cabinet also quells doubts about his loyalty to the British connection.

Manitoba schools: agreement reached

Nov. 19, 1896

OTTAWA – Prime Minister Wilfrid Laurier today released the terms of the agreement he reached with Manitoba Premier Thomas Greenway in the contentious matter of Catholic schools. The new compromise pleases the two politicians, but it may not appease the many Canadians hotly divided on the issue. Catholic separate schools are not to be restored. But the agreement allows employing Catholic teachers in certain circumstances, and some religious instruction will be allowed. It is likely Catholic supporters will view the compromise as too little and too vague.

55 on streetcar die as bridge collapses

May 26, 1896

VICTORIA, B.C. – A bridge over the harbor here collapsed as a crowded streetcar was crossing, and 55 people have drowned. The victims were on the way to watch a military display which was a part of the celebration of the queen's birthday. Three years ago this same bridge had buckled when a streetcar went over it, and so the supports were strengthened.

Obviously the job was not done properly, for today the bridge fell into the water and took the streetcar with it. Many of the passengers were riding on the streetcar's platforms and were saved by boats.

Film show attracts hundreds in Ottawa

July 21, 1896

OTTAWA – The first public screening of a moving picture in Canada took place this evening at West End Park. Hundreds of patrons, who paid 10 cents for their seats, thrilled to a series of brief films, each less than a minute. The highlight of the show was a film called *The Kiss*. The showing was sponsored by the Holland brothers, local businessmen who have the Canadian rights to the Vitascope, a projection machine.

Land lease system on the way out

1896

CALGARY – The old lease system favoring the growth and operation of large cattle ranches near here is being phased out. The changes reflect the appointment of Clifford Sifton as minister of the interior. Sifton sees the Canadian west as an empty land awaiting the civilizing influence of settlers and farmers – mostly immigrants. The generous practices of the past, in which vast tracts of land were made available to cattlemen for grazing, are now history.

The battle between settlers and ranchers has been going on in earnest since the early 1880s, and the chief cause of conflict has been access to open water – something the ranchers have been quite unwilling to give up.

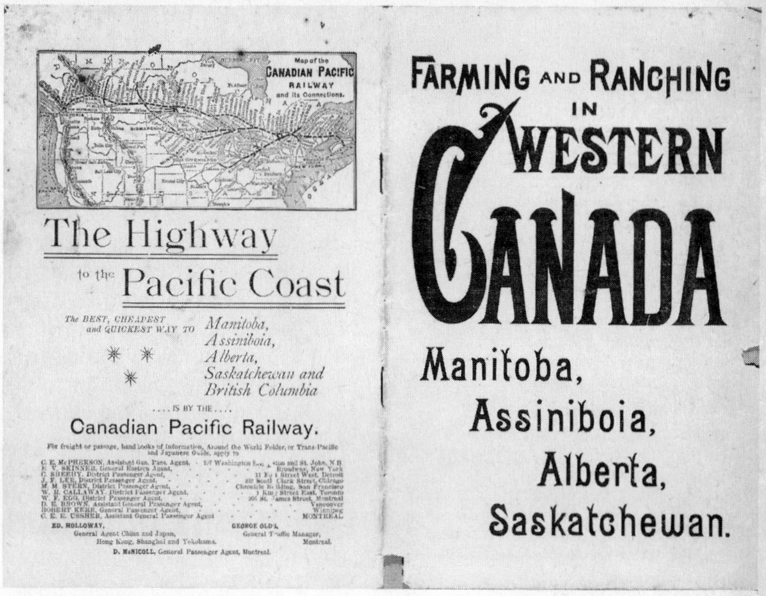

This booklet provides information on farming and ranching in the west.

Former U.S. slave John Ware adapts to life as a cattleman

John Ware's ranch at Millarville has a comfortable house and large corrals.

Cattleman John Ware with his wife and family in front of their home.

1896

PINCHER CREEK, N.W.T. – The story of John Ware, the black cattleman who runs a ranch on the Sheep Creek near here, is typical of the attitudes that are shaping the west. Ware was born a slave in South Carolina and was freed at the end of the American Civil War. He made his way west, working first as a cowboy in Texas and gradually gaining the experience that was to make him a first-rate rider, roper and cattleman.

Ware came to Canada in 1882 when he joined a North West Cattle Company herd coming from Idaho. Despite his experience and skill, he was hired as a cook's helper until he asked for a better horse to ride. He was given a wild bronco, rode it until it quieted down, and from then on was respected and promoted to lead cowboy. Ware was said to have never been thrown by a horse, yet his riding style was awkward and he always seemed to be bouncing off the saddle.

He was an expert hunter, and shot and once trapped a giant wolf that had been killing foals. He then killed it with one shot through the head and draped it over his saddle to bring it back to the ranch on which he was working. The wolf measured seven-and-a-half feet from nose to tail, and Ware won a $50 reward being offered to the wolf's killer.

Ware moved to his own ranch on Sheep Creek with the 9999 brand in 1891, but still competed in steer-roping and other cowboy contests. In Calgary in 1893, riding a horse with no bridle, Ware roped a steer in 51 seconds. His two competitors on that particular day took three and four minutes.

1897

Lethbridge, Northwest Territories, July 14. The CPR begins construction on its Crowsnest Pass Railway to southeastern B.C.

Seattle, August. Some 2,800 people sail for the Klondike in one week. About 3,000 have already reached Skagway and Dyea [on the Alaskan Panhandle], going to the Yukon.

Dawson, Yukon, August. The population has grown to 4,000 as gold-seekers flood in.

Edmonton, Nov. 11. P.D. Campbell and J.R. Brenton, sent by the Edmonton Board of Trade to study the possibility of a road to the Yukon, return. They ran out of supplies before finishing their survey.

Montreal, Dec. 27. Montreal Victorias beat Ottawa Capitals 14-2 for the Stanley Cup.

Ottawa. Responsible government is established in the Northwest Territories [Saskatchewan and Alberta]. Lawyer Frederick Haultain is premier.

Manitoba. James Freer, a Manitoba farmer, makes the first Canadian films, depicting life on the prairies.

St. John's, Nfld. Local merchants and Norwegian whalers form the Cabot Whaling Co. to harvest rorqual whales in the Gulf of St. Lawrence. Norwegians have developed new techniques for killing rorquals.

Stoney Creek, Ont. A Women's Institute is formed to organize farm women.

Montreal. Businessman Herbert Ames publishes *The City Below the Hill*, a study of urban conditions, drawing attention to problems such as poverty.

Montreal. Georgiane and Léontine Génereux and Agalée Laberge found the Sacré-Coeur hospital for the disabled and people with cancer.

British Columbia. James McConnance converts a Victoria store to a cinema, and John Schuberg opens the Edison Electric Theatre in Vancouver, some of the first cinemas in Canada.

Ontario. Former premier Oliver Mowat is named lieutenant-governor.

Quebec. George Foote Foss, a bicycle repairman, builds Canada's first gasoline-driven car.

British Columbia. Sandon reaches a population of 2,000 due to the Slocan silver rush.

Victorian Order of Nurses now a reality

1897

OTTAWA – The Victorian Order of Nurses has been formed, the brainchild of Ishbel, Lady Aberdeen. On her cross-country travels she noted a need for nurses who can care for patients in remote districts where doctors are scarce. Drawing on the example of English cottage hospitals and a similar system in the U.S., the nurses will tend patients and practise midwifery. The National Council of Women looks on this scheme as a fitting way to commemorate Queen Victoria's Diamond Jubilee, an opinion Prime Minister Wilfrid Laurier shares.

VON founder Lady Aberdeen.

Canadians abandon bid to settle in Brazil

Feb. 22, 1897

MONTREAL – A ragged group of 43 Canadians returned home today after a disastrous effort to establish a settlement in Brazil. The group, the second to beat a retreat from what they call an inhospitable country, is furious at agents of the Brazil League who organized the expedition promising riches and an easy life. That's hardly been the case, according to survivors' descriptions of the experience. The Canadians say they found it impossible to cope with the customs of the native population and that they were stricken by the ravages of tropical diseases. Several families left loved ones behind who fell victim to sickness. Father Trudel, who accompanied the group to Brazil, has fled to France, survivors report.

Women get degrees at St. Francis Xavier

1897

ANTIGONISH, N.S. – Higher education for women took a huge step forward this year. St. Francis Xavier University has become the first Catholic university in North America to grant degrees to women, recognizing the work of four students from its affiliated girls' school, Mount St. Bernard College. The precedent-setting decision will do much to further the cause of women who wish to achieve recognition that has long been denied.

The main building at St. Francois Xavier University, Antigonish, Nova Scotia.

Fugitive Indian Almighty Voice caught and killed

May 30, 1897

BATOCHE, N.W.T. – Almighty Voice, the Cree Indian who for almost two days withstood a siege by the North West Mounted Police, was killed this morning. The entire affair took the lives of three Indians, two policemen, and one civilian. Several were wounded.

Almighty Voice, wanted for the murder of a policeman, and two companions were chased into a thicket of woods a short distance northeast of here two days ago. As many as 100 police and volunteers, with two field guns, surrounded the thicket and traded shots with the Indians. After a cannonade early this morning, the police found the bodies of the three Indians. Almighty Voice was wanted for murdering Sgt. Colin Colebrook last October. Colebrook tried to stop Almighty Voice from walking away from an unlocked jail cell at Duck Lake. The Indian was arrested for stealing a cow, which, it turns out, was of uncertain ownership.

Officers extending NWMP jurisdiction

Jan. 4, 1897

FORT SASKATCHEWAN – Two NWMP officers left here on a patrol that will extend NWMP authority into the Mackenzie district for the first time. From this fort, northeast of Edmonton, the men, A.M. Jarvis and W. Hetherington, plan to go by dog team down the valley of the Athabasca River until they reach Fort Chipewyan and Lake Athabasca. After a rest they will head north again, following the Slave River to Great Slave Lake and Fort Resolution. This will take Jarvis and Hetherington up to the middle of February, when they plan to return by way of Peace River, Lesser Slave Lake and Athabasca Landing.

The Mountie patrol is one of a series of exploratory trips made by NWMP men to extend the area of their jurisdiction as the federal government gradually organizes the administration of the north.

Steamer Excelsior carries Yukon gold to San Francisco

July 14, 1897

SAN FRANCISCO – This city is already known for its gaiety and love of the good life – for those who can afford it. Now it has a new reason for celebration: the steamer *Excelsior* has just arrived from St. Michael, Alaska, with a crowd of weather-beaten miners from the Yukon. They have brought their gold with them – suitcases and boxes full of it. Some of them have so much they could buy and sell many of the city's rich families. They are already in the bars telling tales of the riches of the Klondike, the river where the gold was found. There are fortunes to be made, the miners are telling everyone, for there is gold in the rocks and creeks just waiting for men to stake a claim and get it out.

The miners left Dawson more than a month ago and sailed down the Yukon on two rickety river steamers called the *Weare* and the *Alice* to St. Michael on the Bering Sea. Between them they carried close to three tons of gold packed in containers ranging from old cocoa tins to trunks. At St. Michael the miners cleared the little town's supply of fruit and vegetables, for they had eaten nothing but beans and hardtack for months. Now the city talks only of gold. Thousands are booking passages to the north.

The Massey-Harris Company is sure that these children are fascinated by their new bicycle line.

Edmontonians want road to Yukon

Sept. 9, 1897

EDMONTON – Road engineer T.W. Chalmers set out today to investigate the possibility of building a road from Edmonton to the Yukon. Chalmers, acting on behalf of the Northwest Territories, heads the third such party to explore the route in the last 10 days. On Aug. 31, P.D. Campbell and J.R. Brenton were sent north by the Edmonton Board of Trade, while a North West Mounted Police group set out on Sept. 4 on behalf of the federal government.

Edmontonians have been pressuring authorities for such a route. The attraction is the Klondike region of the Yukon, where gold was discovered on Aug. 17 last year. Edmonton hopes to cash in on the gold rush by directing gold-seekers through here. It would be an alternative to the coastal route by sea.

Edmontonians such as Mrs. Gardner are anxiously awaiting a land route to the Klondike. Inhabitants of this city feel a land route through Edmonton would also be of great economic benefit to those who choose to stay at home.

U.S. posts officers at Alaskan border

May 15, 1897

ALASKA – The U.S. placed customs officers at mountain summits along what Canada recognizes as the Alaskan border, backtracking from its earlier insistence that the border was at Lake Bennett, inside Canadian territory. The dispute arose as miners crossed borders en route to Klondike goldfields. Canadians complained of steep tariffs they had to pay for crossing a narrow strip of U.S. land before re-entering Canada.

Crow's Nest Pass Agreement signed

Sept. 6, 1897

OTTAWA – The CPR and the government have signed the Crow's Nest Pass Agreement, a basis for further development of the west. The agreement gives the CPR a \$3.3-million cash subsidy and the right to build a line over the Crowsnest Pass into southeastern B.C. In return, the CPR will reduce, in perpetuity, eastbound freight rates on grain and flour, and westbound rates on specified "settlers' effects."

MFTC to represent workers in Montreal

1897

MONTREAL – The Montreal Federated Trades Council is now the strongest voice of labor in Montreal. The MFTC, affiliated with the powerful American Federation of Labor, will represent workers in the construction and printing trades. The founding president of the new union is Joseph Ainey, the former leader of a carpenters' union who led a one-month strike in 1894 which won a nine-hour day and a minimum wage of 20 cents. The formation of the MFTC is a blow to the dominance of the Montreal Central Trades and Labour Council, an affiliate of the Knights of Labor organization, which is rapidly losing ground to the AFL in the U.S. The MFTC was formed largely by the construction unions which broke from the MCTLC in 1892 after years of turmoil.

The Carpenters' Union of Montreal held this meeting in front of the Drill Hall last year before it joined the Montreal Federated Trades Council.

News of Klondike strike triggers Yukon gold rush

The rivers of the Klondike are swarming with prospectors panning for gold.

Access to the Klondike is hazardous. Those seeking to make their fortune have to carry all their equipment and travel over treacherous mountain passes.

Sept. 10, 1897

SEATTLE, Wash. – North America has become gold crazy, and the name of a small river in the Yukon – the Klondike – is part of every conversation. The centre of this madness is Seattle, the port supplying Alaska. The steamer *Excelsior,* carrying Yukon miners laden with gold, reached San Francisco two days before another ship with a similar cargo, the *Portland,* arrived here. But then Seattle took over. Soon after the *Portland* docked here, nine ships were full of men waiting to go to the goldfields.

Business has been slow in North America for the past 20 years, and since 1893 something close to panic has gripped the nation's financial institutions. The depression has hit the Pacific northwest, with few resources or manufacturing industries, very hard. For the unemployed, the underpaid and the struggling businessman, the news from the Klondike is a godsend. Men are leaving their jobs, their stores and their families in droves. Students at universities are asking for examinations to be advanced so that they, too, can go to the Yukon. Many women are going north. Some of them are respectable women seeking work.

Unfortunately many are going just to suck money from miners' pockets. Very few fortune seekers will reach the goldfields before next summer, for the freeze-up will start soon, but that has not stopped newspapers and hucksters from extolling the ease with which a fortune can be made on the Klondike.

Part of the trip to the Klondike can be made on the Athabasca River.

New trade policy in Britain's favor

April 23, 1897

OTTAWA – The Liberal government has announced a new policy that, in effect, will favor trade with Great Britain. The policy announced today by Finance Minister W.S. Fielding promises to reduce duties on imports to Canada up to 25 percent, provided the exporting country offers Canada an equivalent preference. And, since Britain already believes in free trade, it will automatically receive lower tariffs.

Law aims to protect poor working women

1897

TORONTO – Legislators in Ontario have taken steps to protect working women who are poor. It was once generally believed that the poor were responsible for their own suffering. Today, with one in three residents of industrial cities living in poverty, the enlightened view is that the poor and underprivileged are victims of circumstance.

To that end, the Shops Regulation Act of 1888 has been amended. Women can now work between 7 a.m. and 6 p.m. only. Also, because of the physical strain under which shop clerks work, employers must provide seats when salesgirls are not busy with customers. While more fortunate than factory workers, shop girls are among the most poorly paid of workers.

Meanwhile, the Act to Regulate the Immigration in Ontario of Certain Classes of Children will also protect the unfortunate. Agencies bringing poor children to Ontario must qualify for a provincial charter. Also, the homes to which these children go will be inspected.

Northern Quebec, Labrador surveyed

1897

OTTAWA – Massive outcrops of iron and a thundering falls on the Hamilton [Churchill] River are just some of the discoveries made by Albert Peter Low on his geological survey of northern Quebec and Labrador. Low has been exploring the regions since 1892, in one year alone travelling 8,790 kilometres, 1,610 of them by foot. He reports huge iron formations in the region north of the Manicougan River.

Council established to help keep law and order in Yukon

Sept. 16, 1897

DAWSON, Yukon – Miners are coming back to Dawson for the winter, and a flood of new inhabitants is expected now that the world knows about the gold on the Klondike. So, a judicial council has been appointed to help Inspector Charles Constantine and the NWMP keep order. James Morrow Walsh, an inspector with the NWMP for 10 years, has returned to the police force and has been appointed commissioner of the Yukon. However, it is doubtful he can reach Dawson before the freeze-up and will probably start work next summer.

Curlew population is on the decline

1897

NORTH AMERICA – The Eskimo curlew is fast disappearing. The amazing birds, with long legs and beautiful downward curving beaks, make an annual migration that takes them from the Arctic tundra in the summer, to the Maritime provinces, to their wintering grounds in South America, then north over the great plains in the spring. Curlews used to be known for their vast dense flocks that darkened the skies, but these clouds are a thing of the past thanks to hunters on both continents.

Geographic Board of Canada formed

Dec. 18, 1897

OTTAWA – In an attempt to end duplication in town names across Canada – which causes much confusion to the average map reader – the federal government has established the Geographic Board of Canada.

Its function is to standardize the names of locations and features in Canada, and to provide information on the origin of these names to the public. It's expected that the board will issue an annual report to make its decisions widely known.

Ship-rail service developed in Nfld.

Oct. 19, 1897

ST. JOHN'S, Nfld. – Newfoundland has finally been able to establish a reliable system of transportation from St. John's to the Intercolonial Railway at North Sydney. The railway across the island is completed after 16 years, and the *SS Bruce,* a modern passenger steamer, was built in Glasgow to serve as a ferry between the Newfoundland railway terminal in Port aux Basques and North Sydney. The new system will greatly enhance travel between this colony and the mainland which up to now has been irregular and ad hoc. In particular, it will allow Newfoundlanders working in Boston to visit their families more often. The new terminal being constructed in Port aux Basques will not be ready until next year, and meanwhile the *Bruce* will operate, beginning today, between Placentia and North Sydney twice a week. Placentia is some 80 kilometres from St. John's, but it is on the south coast, which is usually ice-free all year round.

It is ironic that the man who made Newfoundland's railway his lifelong ambition, Premier William Whiteway, will probably lose next week's election. Whiteway's dream, beginning in the 1870s, has been to open up the forest, agricultural and mineral resources of the island and lead an industrialized Newfoundland into the 20th century.

The SS Rosedale, a steel steamship, is a fine example of modern shipbuilding.

Food situation in Dawson: supply plummets as prices skyrocket

December 1897

DAWSON, Yukon – Dawson City has all the trappings of a boom town, but with the arrival of winter it sadly lacks an essential commodity – food. With the gold-seekers who arrived this past summer came hotelkeepers, bartenders, dance hall girls and gamblers, all aiming to strike it rich one way or another. They will have to wait. For now, because food is so short, Dawson's 5,000 inhabitants pay $18 per dozen eggs, $1.50 per pound of beans, and a sack of flour has jumped in price from $15 to $75. Mounties are rationing supplies, and this fall gave 900 destitute prospectors three months provisions to make the long 1,200-kilometre journey back to Skagway, Alaska, where food is cheaper and a dollar goes further than here. Now the prospectors have a better chance of surviving.

New rugby football league is founded

Nov. 24, 1897

KINGSTON – The new Canadian Intercollegiate Rugby Football Union was formed today, with seven colleges fielding teams. The league will include Queen's College from this city, McGill, University of Toronto, McMaster, Bishop's, Ontario Agricultural College at Guelph, and St. Andrews School.

McGill pioneered the sport at its Montreal base and introduced it to Harvard in the U.S. Now, there is enough interest in Canada to create the university league. Football is taking over from soccer on campus because it can be played later into the fall, as field conditions are not as critical. Also, its season does not conflict with other sports.

U.S. to compensate Canadian sealers

Dec. 22, 1897

OTTAWA – After years of debate, the Bering Sea Claims Commission in Ottawa has decided the U.S. should pay $463,454 compensation to Canadian sealers whose boats were unlawfully seized off Alaska. The decision comes at the end of the arbitration process over conflicting claims to sealing rights off Alaska. The Americans claimed all seals on and offshore as theirs, while Canada said those outside the 4.8-kilometre international limit were "wild animals" open to all. In pressing their claims, the Americans seized Canadian ships and jailed crews. The compensation will not make up for their time, nor the loss of revenue.

The Diamond Jubilee of Queen Victoria is cause for celebration.

1898

Washington, D.C., April 25. The U.S. declares war on Spain, discouraging many prospective gold-seekers from going to the Klondike and causing others to return home.

Toronto, summer. Massey-Harris Co. shows one of the first publicity films in the world at the National Exhibition. It was shot on an Ontario farm by Edison Studios.

Yukon, fall. Some 1,500 gold-seekers have left Edmonton for the Klondike since last year, but only a few have arrived.

London, Dec. 25. The Empire stamp rate comes into effect; a half-ounce letter can now be sent through much of the British Empire for two cents.

Kootenay Lake, B.C. The *SS Moyie*, a 400-passenger sternwheeler, begins service, joining other sternwheelers in service on the lake.

Lake Ontario. An Atlantic salmon is netted near Toronto, one of the last of the millions that once spawned in rivers draining into Lake Ontario. Fishing has caused their demise.

Britain. The CPR shows James Freer's films on Manitoba to promote immigration.

Winnipeg. The Manitoba government grants a charter to William Mackenzie and Donald Mann to build a railway to Lake Superior [the Canadian Northern] as an outlet for western grain.

Canada. The Trades and Labour Congress, the largest labor group in Canada, supports the abolition of female labor "in all branches of industrial life." Male workers say women are competing for their jobs.

Quebec. An inquiry by William Lyon Mackenzie King finds that three-quarters of the clothes made in Montreal are sewn in workshops and homes by underpaid Jewish and French-Canadian women.

Canada. Single-cylinder automobiles, considered a novelty, are imported from the U.S.

Toronto. The province passes a bill declaring all pine timber cut in Ontario must be sawn in Canadian mills, an attempt to spur the Ontario sawmill industry.

Canada. Montreal Victorias win the Stanley Cup as champions of the Amateur Hockey Association.

Family thinks girl is long-lost child last seen in 1894

March 20, 1898

WINNIPEG – John and Adelaide Turton, of Cannington Manor, district of Assiniboia, arrived in Winnipeg today from the United States accompanied by the girl they believe is their long-lost daughter.

The Turtons last saw daughter Mathilde in 1894 when her mother sent her out to find her father, working in the fields. The girl was never seen again, despite an intensive search of the area surrounding the family's farm. The only possible lead they had was that some searchers were passed by a wagon containing an Indian family, and a child could be heard crying in the back. It was the crying child which led the Turtons to suspect their daughter had been kidnapped.

The hopes of the Turton family were raised when they learned a girl believed to be white had been taken away from an Indian family in South Dakota. The Turtons travelled to Sioux City and were given the young girl by state authorities.

Still, one huge question remains concerning the girl the Turtons have now: is she in fact their daughter? The child they lost was blonde and fair-skinned. The girl in their possession has dark hair and a swarthy skin.

Steele takes command of NWMP in Yukon

Superintendent Sam Steele of the North West Mounted Police force.

February 1898

DAWSON, Yukon – Superintendent Sam Steele, a strong-willed veteran with a quarter-century service with the North West Mounted Police, is now in command of the 200 or so NWMP men in the Yukon. He is a veteran of the 1866 Fenian troubles in Ontario and the 1870 Red River expedition.

Steele, who has a reputation for hardiness and loves working long hours, will have enough work in the Yukon to keep him busy. Most of the people flocking to the goldfields are American, and Steele, like most Mounties, is determined that the kind of frontier justice that has plagued American mining camps will not be allowed to take root on British soil. Steele likes to take command, and he is not afraid to make laws if there are none that suit the occasion.

"Kit" Coleman in Cuba to cover the war

1898

CUBA – Kathleen Blake "Kit" Coleman has reached Cuba. The well-known author of the Woman's Kingdom page in the Toronto *Mail* is the world's first accredited female war correspondent.

Shortly after the Spanish-American War between Cuba and the United States broke out in April, Mrs. Coleman travelled to Washington and convinced American Secretary for War Russell Alger to issue her credentials. Opposition remained strong – Mrs. Coleman spent six months waiting in Florida and was purposely left behind when male reporters sailed for Cuba. Her reports vividly describe the carnage of war, the heat, and the American army of boys who are "not nearly ready" to do battle.

Miss Hamilton has a fine collection of dolls, dollhouses and doll furniture.

Province of Quebec given HBC territory

1898

QUEBEC CITY – The province of Quebec now stretches from Labrador to the shores of Hudson Bay, because of a federal government decree. Some 306,765 square kilometres have been added to Quebec territory, land transferred from the Hudson's Bay Company to the federal government in 1870. It includes the Abitibi region as far as the Eastmain River, which flows into James Bay.

On the other hand, the federal decree reduces Quebec's long reach into the remote northeast. The new Quebec region (Ungava) and the eastern coast of Hudson Bay are still in Ottawa's hands.

Park to protect animals on the brink of extinction

Four donated buffalo are first inhabitants

1898

ALBERTA – Rocky Mountain Park, known for its mineral springs and its breathtaking scenery, now offers visitors the opportunity to see indigenous wildlife at a close range. Four buffalo donated by a Toronto lawyer will be the first animals to be displayed in a recently erected animal paddock. Since his appointment as superintendent of the Rocky Mountain Park in 1897, Howard Douglas recognized the role wildlife plays in making a Dominion park more appealing to the public. The country's restored economic health, new Liberal government, and the present concern within the Department of the Interior for the conservation of natural resources favored Douglas' plans to create a wildlife display centre. The enclosed animal paddock provides the almost extinct buffalo, or plains bison as they are sometimes called, with a suitable environment in which to breed and naturally multiply under the park's protective policies, while it functions as a popular and profitable tourist attraction.

Douglas estimates that the animals are the most attractive and interesting feature of Rocky Mountain Park and that the presentation of species indigenous to Canada, especially those on the verge of extinction, is an economically sound investment that will more than pay for development and maintenance costs. Douglas hopes to attract more donated wildlife for his enclosure in order to turn Rocky Mountain Park into a wildlife preserve where people can witness the revival of endangered species.

The plains buffalo, now almost extinct, has long been a very useful animal. Natives hunted them for their meat and their skins. Now the bones left from these massacres are being shipped by rail to various manufacturing industries.

Yukon Field Force to help maintain order

Newcomers to the west, some living in tent cities, have boosted crime concerns.

May 6, 1898

GLENORA, B.C. – The Yukon Field Force, on its way to help keep order and show the flag in the Yukon, has disembarked here. The 200 men will now march up the old telegraph trail to the Yukon River. The force has brought two Maxim guns, ammunition, and 100 tons of food. Four women, members of the Victorian Order of Nurses, are with the force to set up a hospital and help the surgeons.

Ottawa has sent the men, almost a quarter of the Canadian army, to strengthen the hand of Canadian officials and the NWMP in the collection of customs duties, to help control crime, and to bolster Canadian claims to the present borders.

Dawson sees debut of Klondike Nugget

May 27, 1898

DAWSON, Yukon – Dawson's first newspaper, the *Klondike Nugget,* was published today. True, it is only a typed bulletin, for the *Nugget*'s editor, Gene Allen, had come by dog sled over the ice to Dawson, leaving his printing press to follow on a steamer. The press of a rival newspaper, the *Midnight Sun,* is also coming by steamer, sharing space in the hold with a lot of cash belonging to two Canadian banks, the Bank of Commerce and the Bank of British North America. As soon as Allen's press is set up he will publish regularly. The charge will be 50 cents a copy, he says.

Territorial status granted to Yukon

June 13, 1898

DAWSON, Yukon – The Yukon district is now the Yukon Territory. This move by Ottawa will make some degree of self-government possible. It will also prevent the Northwest Territories government in Regina, which had some nominal power in the Yukon when it was a district, from making a fortune selling liquor licences in Dawson. The Yukon's first commissioner, NWMP James Walsh, a pioneer of over 25 years in law enforcement on the prairies, has just arrived here. He will appoint members of the Territorial Commission from local administrators.

Train runs on White Pass and Yukon line

July 22, 1898

SKAGWAY, Alaska – The first work train has started to run on the tracks of the new White Pass and Yukon Railway. The line will go from here to the head of navigation on the Yukon. The narrow-gauge White Pass and Yukon Railway was organized by British investors in April and construction started at once. Many of the 200 men working on the line are miners and prospectors who have given up searching for gold. The railway hopes to be in full operation next year, and will then be able to carry the people and cargoes now going to the Klondike over the Chilkoot Pass.

Willow Bunch Giant joins circus shows

1898

WILLOW BUNCH, N.W.T. – Edouard Beaupré, the Willow Bunch Giant, has left his home town to exhibit his great size and strength in circus-type shows held across Canada. Beaupré, just 17 years old, stands 8-foot-3, weighs more than 300 pounds, has a 58-inch chest, and wears size 24 shoes.

Shy but intelligent, Beaupré speaks fluent French, English, Cree and Sioux. He was the first child baptized in Willow Bunch, located 125 kilometres south of Moose Jaw, and was of normal size until the age of seven.

The Willow Bunch Giant, aged 17.

Books, magazines free for the asking

1898

OTTAWA – Free reading material will be sent to anyone who wishes to apply to the Aberdeen Association. You will be asked to fill out a questionnaire to establish your requirements and taste. After that you will receive, free of charge, items such as magazines, papers and books that have been donated to the association. Volunteers collect, pack and mail the material. The organization was first conceived by Lady Aberdeen, wife of the governor general, when she visited the homes of Scottish Crofters and saw the lack of amenities.

Minto appointed next governor general

The Earl of Minto.

July 30, 1898

OTTAWA – News has reached here concerning the replacement for retiring Gov. Gen. Lord Aberdeen. The eighth governor general to serve in Ottawa is to be the 4th Earl of Minto.

Minto knows Canada well. He lived here once before, when he was military secretary to then-governor general Lord Lansdowne. No less a person than Sir John A. Macdonald told Minto then that "I shall not live to see it, but some day Canada will welcome you back as governor general." Minto comes from a long line of soldiers and statesmen. He is a veteran soldier who's served in Afghanistan, Egypt, and Canada.

Mormons bring irrigation to Lethbridge

August 1898

CARDSTON, N.W.T. – It has taken little more than a decade for the Mormons in the Cardston area to make successful and prosperous lives for themselves in this country. Now they are using their technical skills in irrigation to build a canal to bring water from the St. Mary River to Lethbridge.

In this area of extremely limited rainfall, it has been found that oats and wheat are suitable for dry land farming, but trees, vegetables and forage crops need extra moisture. The land, when irrigated, seems to be particularly suitable for sugar beets.

In 1886, Charles Card, John W. Hendricks and Bishop Zundell came to Lethbridge looking for land. They explored the area and settled in the district between the Belly and St. Mary rivers.

The following year Card brought out 40 members of the Church of Jesus Christ of Latter Day Saints from Utah. They travelled in covered wagons, carrying their belongings and equipment, and herding their horses and cattle. Later in the year others of their faith followed and a headquarters was established in Cardston, 22 kilometres north of the United States boundary. Co-operative businesses were started and a couple of years later the first irrigation canals and ditches began to appear. The Mormons developed a system that serviced the whole community from the St. Mary River to Lethbridge.

Canada's first automobile, purchased by John Moodie Jr. of Hamilton.

More than 30,000 catch gold fever, head to Dawson

August 1898

DAWSON, Yukon – There's gold in these here hills, and this summer more than 30,000 people have visited Dawson either looking for gold, or just for the ride. Trader Joseph Ladue founded this city at the junction of the Klondike and Yukon rivers two years ago after George Carmack, Skookum Jim, and Tagish Charlie discovered gold on Bonanza Creek near here. Now Dawson is in the middle of the swiftest boom in Canadian history, and has become the largest city west of Winnipeg overnight.

The gold rush really began in July 1897 when ships landed in Seattle and San Francisco bearing the first successful Klondike prospectors. In the next few months, thousands left the west coast for the Klondike, and last winter 100,000 people set out from various destinations. Many sailed up the British Columbia coast to the Alaska Panhandle, then made the treacherous journey over the White or Chilkoot passes to the promised land of the Klondike. More than 30,000 made the trek up and down the icy slopes of these passes carrying their own supplies, a toil for the Gods. Most of the men reached Dawson at the beginning of June in 7,000 boats travelling down the Yukon River. About 5,000 are now busily working the surrounding creeks for gold. Eldorado and Bonanza creeks alone have produced about $8.5 million worth of gold since the spring.

Dawson has all the exciting facilities of a modern city, and then some. Saloons are highly popular, oases where exhausted and dusty prospectors can relax and swap stories over a stiff whisky. Brothels, dance halls, gambling houses, theatres, and shops all pulse with activity. Inflation is rampant. Dawson is a many colored creature, a rugged frontier city where you can easily get the best French wines and the latest fashions from Paris and New York. Fortunes change hands at all hours of the day, in gambling, drinking bouts, and business deals. The North West Mounted Police have done a heroic job maintaining law and order.

Rugged Yukon transformed by booming gold rush

Klondike dance halls feature such stars as Snake-Hips Lulu, above.

These ladies known as the Goddesses of Liberty claim to be "enlightening" Dawson in the Yukon Territory. The American flag is prominently displayed.

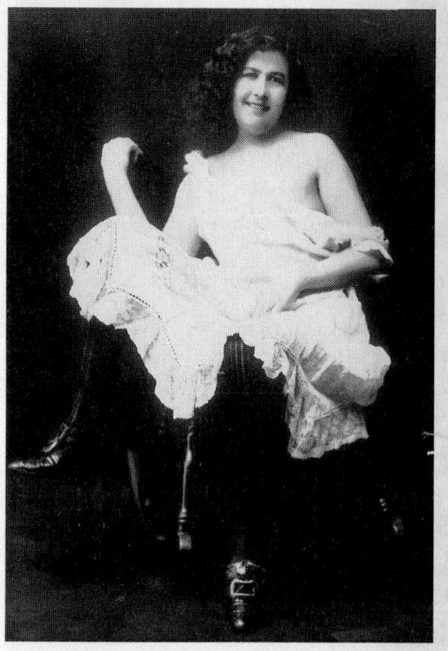

One Klondike dance hall girl bills herself as the Belgian Queen.

Dawson City is growing rapidly. Street signs are now needed to direct Klondikers to the many services available, such as the outfitters and the dentist.

Dawson City is a meeting place for the gold miners. Great crowds gather here on their way to and from the goldfields. Businesses are prospering.

This man has set up an apparatus called a "grizzly" for washing gold from the rich Klondike riverbeds.

These Klondike miners have set up their camp at Glenora, by the Stikine River. They hope to find enough gold to make their hardship worthwhile. Because all equipment has to be brought in, campers improvise if possible.

A steady line of gold-seekers files over the Chilkoot Pass. Spring avalanches make the trip dangerous.

1899

Montreal, Feb. 23. Violence erupts at Windsor Station between police and Chinese immigrants headed to Mexico.

Montreal, March 14. Montreal Shamrocks defeat Queen's University 6-2 to win the Stanley Cup.

Alberta, April 29. South Edmonton is incorporated and named Strathcona, after Donald Smith, Lord Strathcona.

Ellesmere Island, April 29. Otto Sverdrup leads a Norwegian exploring expedition to the head of Bay Fiord. They are the first Europeans to see [Axel Heiberg Island].

Montreal, August. The world cycling championships are held in the city, highlighting a cycling craze on the continent.

Dawson, Yukon, August. The discovery of gold at Nome, Alaska, causes a huge exodus from the town. Some 8,000 people leave in a single week.

South Africa, Oct. 12. War breaks out between the British and the Boers from the Transvaal and Orange Free State.

Ottawa, Oct. 18. Quebecer Henri Bourassa resigns his seat in the House to protest against possible Canadian participation in the Boer War.

Lunenberg, N.S., Dec. 12. W.C. Smith and Co. is incorporated as a fishing company. Lunenberg is a world-famous fishing port, mainly producing dry saltfish for southern markets.

Canada. Dr. Williams' Pink Pills for Pale People, made by the Fulford Co. of Brockville, are the most talked about remedy on the market.

Dawson, Yukon. With the departure of many gold-seekers, the population is reduced to 9,000. Gold mining continues, but the town is declining.

Canada. Parole is introduced to the penal system.

Prince Edward Island. An act makes women eligible for appointment to school boards.

Alberta. Donald Smith, Lord Strathcona, donates 16 more buffalo to the paddock built last year in Rocky Mountain Park, making a total of 20.

Toronto. Toronto's impressive new city hall opens.

Montreal. A French Catholic Normal School for women opens.

Canada. The first Hutterites arrive in Canada.

Lesser Slave Lake Indians accept treaty

The treaty commission leaves Edmonton en route to sign Treaty No. 8.

June 21, 1899

LESSER SLAVE LAKE, N.W.-T. – The Treaty No. 8 commission reached Lesser Slave Lake two days ago on its way to negotiate the surrender of a huge land area north of Treaty 6. Negotiators will travel along the Athabasca and Peace River waterways this summer and next with a view to contact as many Indian groups as possible. Lesser Slave Lake Indians accepted the treaty today after being assured of hunting and fishing privileges. Said Father Albert Lacombe: "Your forest and river life will not be changed by the treaty, and you will have your annuities, as well, year by year, as long as the sun shines and the earth remains."

Journey takes its toll on herd of reindeer

January 1899

DAWSON, Yukon – By any standard, the reindeer is an enduring animal that thrives in the most adverse conditions, but for 539 reindeer the rigors of a long journey proved to be a calamity. Last year, funds were appropriated to buy reindeer from the herds of Norway. They were transported by steamship and railroad to Haines Mission, where Norwegian and Lapp herdsmen took up the task of walking them to Dawson. When they reached their destination this month, the great sea of antlers was reduced to 114 debilitated creatures. The other 425 died en route.

Yukon missionary Father Judge dies

Jan. 16, 1899

DAWSON, Yukon – Father William Judge, the Jesuit missionary who worked long and hard caring for the sick and dying in his little hospital here, has died of pneumonia. Judge had been in the Yukon for some years when, by chance, he had to come to Dawson and saw the need for a hospital. He bought a site and sent away for nuns and lay helpers. The hospital, however, was ready before the nuns and helpers arrived, and Judge had to care for the sick himself until, exhausted, he too became ill.

Imperial controlling Sarnia oil refinery

Feb. 23, 1899

SARNIA, Ont. – Imperial Oil today took over the Sarnia refinery, as well as all of Standard Oil's other Canadian resources. Imperial, founded in September 1880 in London, Ont., sold controlling interest to Standard Oil last year in a desperate attempt to acquire more capital. At the time of the sale, Standard, an American company, had already penetrated the Canadian market through various regional affiliates such as the Bushnell company which ran the refinery here in Sarnia.

Longest covered bridge in the world spans the St. John River

Hartland, N.B., now proudly claims the longest covered bridge in the world.

Dec. 1, 1899

HARTLAND, N.B. – Local residents love to boast about their new covered bridge. Almost a quarter-mile long, the bridge over the St. John River is believed to be the longest of its kind in the world. It costs three cents to cross it, if you're walking, and eight cents for a team of horses on a carriage. The reason the bridge is covered is simple: to save the beams and planks from the weather. Professional builders say an unprotected wooden bridge will only last 10 to 15 years, as compared to 70 to 80 for a covered one. The cheap-to-build roofing and siding save on maintenance and snow shovelling. As well, it's said that horses prefer covered bridges.

Free land lures 7,427 Doukhobors to N.W.T.

The Lake Huron is bringing the first Doukhobors to new homes in Canada.

Traditionally, Doukhobor women do the farm work. Here they separate the valuable grain from the chaff in a laborious process called winnowing.

1899

SASKATCHEWAN – Minister of Interior Clifford Sifton's policy of *vilni zemli* free land has netted this district of the Northwest Territories 7,427 Russian immigrants known as the Doukhobors. Sponsored by Count Tolstoy and Professor James Mavor of the University of Toronto, the Department of the Interior, using the Dominion Lands Act of 1872, has given these agrarian settlers 300,000 hectares of land. An order-in-council exempts them from military service.

The Doukhobors will homestead around Yorkton, Prince Albert, Blaine Lake and Langham. Properly called the Christian Community of Universal Brotherhood, this sect broke away from the Russian Orthodox church in the 18th century.

This migration underlines Canada's new immigration policy aimed at attracting Eastern Europeans living as peasants in Slavic speaking parts of the Austro-Hungarian and Russian empires. Sifton's agents value Doukhobors for their farm experience, strong backs and fecund wives. Free land makes Canada their Promised Land.

Dominion Iron and Steel Company formed

March 1899

HALIFAX – Local investors are bullish on Nova Scotia's future as a steel producer following the incorporation of the Dominion Iron and Steel Company in Halifax this month. The move indicates the increasing prosperity of Nova Scotia's mining industry, which has traditionally been based on coal. And although iron mining has been taking place here on a small scale since before Confederation, the creation of the company means that the industry is about to take a huge leap into the Canadian market.

Jewish immigrants arrive in Saint John

April 1899

SAINT JOHN, N.B. – More than 300 Jewish immigrants arrived here from Eastern Europe on the *SS Gallia,* as Saint John continues to develop as a port of entry. The main reason is the location on Partridge Island in the harbor here of an inspection-quarantine station. The island's isolation helps authorities prevent the spread of any contagious diseases that they may detect carried by immigrants or the crews of visiting ships. One year this decade, almost 75,000 sailors and immigrants went through here.

Firemen on strike as blaze hits Yukon

April 26, 1899

DAWSON, Yukon – A fire that started in the room of a dance hall girl is sweeping through the business district here. The firemen are on strike for higher wages and have let the fires in the boilers of the fire engines go out, so there is virtually no firefighting equipment working. Some men are trying to break the ice on the river so water can be pumped on the flames, but the temperature is 45 below. Many prostitutes have been seen running, naked and terrified, into the streets as their cribs burned down.

Hunters convicted for killing buffalo

1899

FORT SMITH, N.W.T. – Patrolling the region between Edmonton and Fort Resolution, Insp. A.M. Jarvis of the North West Mounted Police found the natives ignorant of the Unorganized Territories Game Preservation Act of 1894 protecting buffalo. Although this is understandable as the Indians have not as yet surrendered their lands by treaty, the NWMP enforced the law and two hunters were convicted of killing buffalo in Fort Smith. It is hoped that Treaty 8 will be signed here this year.

Van Horne named first CPR chairman

June 12, 1899

OTTAWA – William Van Horne was appointed the Canadian Pacific Railway's first chairman today, after resigning as president. He will be succeeded as president by Thomas Shaughnessy. It was under the leadership of Van Horne, 56, that the trans-Canada railway construction was completed. Born in the U.S., Van Horne had worked for American railways before joining the CPR seven years ago. Ironically, one of Van Horne's biggest challenges here has been the threat of a U.S. line to move into Canada.

Oxen Drinking, by the acclaimed Canadian artist Horatio Walker.

Railway inches closer to Whitehorse

July 6, 1899

CARCROSS, Yukon – The White Pass and Yukon Railway has now reached this settlement on Lake Bennett. Engineers say they will get to Whitehorse – 177 kilometres from the docks at Skagway – in about a year. Construction of the railway has been difficult so far because it's had to climb 840 metres from sea level in 34 kilometres through hostile terrain. Track has been laid through deep canyons and on the sides of steep cliffs. One bridge had to be built 75 metres above Dead Horse Gulch. One other problem: workers often left the railway and headed north when there were reports of gold strikes on the creeks upriver.

These miners test paydirt samples for gold during the Klondike gold rush.

Boer forces attack; Canada mulls over British call for help

Oct. 12, 1899

CAPE TOWN, South Africa – Forces from two Boer (Afrikaner) republics – the Transvaal and Orange Free State – have invaded Cape Colony and Natal, British territories. The attack follows the expiration of the republics' ultimatum demanding that Britain declare a "hands off" policy regarding the external control she still held over their affairs – an issue dating back 65 years. During this time there have been Boer migrations and the Anglo-Boer War in 1880-81, as the Afrikaners tried to rid themselves of British influence.

Expecting a crisis, the British government canvassed its colonial cabinets for military units on Oct. 3, as a means of demonstrating imperial unity. New Zealand and four colonies on the Australian subcontinent are eager to take part. The Canadian response has been lukewarm as the government balances imperialist and French-Canadian nationalist sympathies. The outbreak of fighting is expected to force the cabinet of Sir Wilfrid Laurier to make a decision – presumably a Canadian compromise.

Parliament says OK to Pacific cable link

March 16, 1899

OTTAWA – The crusade by Sir Sandford Fleming to run a telegraphic cable underwater from Canada to Australia is a step closer to reality, with Parliament approving the endeavor. The cable would be laid in sections from Vancouver Island to Fiji, Australia, and New Zealand. It will allow telegraph operators to access this part of the globe far quicker than by the current Canada/London-and-beyond Atlantic route. Still, it remains to be seen if money for the 3,455 nautical miles of cable can be found.

Mountie finds bodies of 2 prospectors

October 1899

DAWSON, Yukon – The men of the North West Mounted Police here have to be police, administrators, gold commissioners and protectors of the old and weak. And they still find time to search for those who get lost from the settlements along the rivers.

Word has just been received that NWMP officer G.M. Skirving has found the bodies of two missing prospectors at Bell River. He believes a third man has drowned. The men were on their way to the Klondike and their friends reported them missing. Skirving got to Bell River by going down the Yukon and up the Porcupine to Old Crow River by steamer and canoe. Then he hired a dog team. Now he plans to report to Fort McPherson.

Relieved Klondike King goes bankrupt

July 29, 1899

DAWSON, Yukon – Alex McDonald's reign as the Klondike King is over. The pioneer entrepreneur today declared insolvency. He has debts of $6 million, which his assets will not cover. McDonald has made a fortune consolidating gold claims and making technical innovations in mining them. He also tried to monopolize northern transportation and provisioning services. But bankruptcy does not dishearten McDonald. It was too worrisome being a millionaire, he said.

This patent medicine bottled in Crosby, Ontario, by Thomas H. Singleton makes claim to cure every health problem, including sciatica, headaches, rheumatism, kidney and liver ailments, and both diarrhea and constipation.

The Church at Ste. Anne de Beaupré, Quebec, is becoming a haven for people seeking cures for serious diseases. The stacks of crutches in the shrine attest to the miraculous cures which have taken place at the site.

Canadians off to South Africa to fight Boer forces

The city of Winnipeg bids farewell to the Manitoba Transvaal Contingent.

The members of the P.E.I. Transvaal Contingent are ready for South Africa.

Oct. 30, 1899

QUEBEC CITY – With thousands cheering from dockside this afternoon, Canadian soldiers sailed for South Africa aboard the *SS Sardinian,* an aging Allan Line vessel. The Canadians will help take on Boer forces which invaded two British territories in South Africa earlier this month. More than 1,000 fully-equipped men – as well as four female nurses and seven horses – boarded the *Sardinian* after inspection by Gov. Gen. Lord Minto, Prime Minister Sir Wilfrid Laurier, Minister of Militia Sir Frederick Borden, and Maj.-Gen. E.T.H. Hutton, the British general officer commanding this country's militia.

Officially known as the 2nd (Special Service) Battalion, Royal Canadian Regiment, the force is commanded by Lt.-Col. W.D. Otter, a veteran of North West Rebellion service. Volunteers all, the men are drawn from across Canada. They are the first troops to be sent from Canada since Confederation.

Emily Blake hangs for killing employer

Dec. 27, 1899

BRANDON, Man. – Emily Hilda Blake was hanged today at the Brandon jail. In a brief trial, she had pleaded guilty to the murder of Mary Lane, the woman for whom she worked. Blake was a 20-year-old domestic servant. On the day Mrs. Lane was shot to death, Emily told police that the crime was committed by a "tramp," of whom she gave a detailed description. This information led to an extensive police roundup of all transients in the district, but the search was called off when Chief Const. James Kirkcaldy found the murder weapon in the alley at the rear of the Lane residence.

Emily was an English orphan, one of the "state" children sent into domestic service in Canada. When she was sentenced, her story elicited a wave of sympathy from across the continent, but to no avail. Authorities paid no heed to the petitions sent by women's groups, or to the many editorials in which capital punishment was decried.

North American cougar vanishes from the Canadian wilderness

1899

EASTERN CANADA – One of the largest of the new world cats, the cougar, has vanished from the Canadian wilderness. The last recorded sighting was of a cougar shot in Ontario in 1884; since then, none have been seen in the forests of eastern Canada. Although cougars prey mostly on deer, they will track down and kill domestic livestock. To protect their livelihood, farmers often held silent vigil in the dark of night and shot to kill any cougar that stalked their animals. Relentless pursuit by stockmen and bounty hunters has steadily reduced the Canadian population. Virtually powerless against man's weaponry, the species has fallen victim to insidious extinction.

Canadian universities not doing their proper job, educator says

1899

TORONTO – Educator Alfred Fitzpatrick thinks this country's universities have not been doing their proper job. So, he said today, he intends to do it himself. The university's responsibility, Fitzpatrick said, is to provide education to those who really need it. But the universities have been unwilling "to stoop down and fraternize with the worker." Therefore, he is establishing a new institution [Frontier College] to send teachers to live and to work among the "bunkhouse men" of Canada's lumber camps. "To the university unquestionably falls the task of redeeming the labor of the hands from the disrepute into which it has long fallen," he said.

The Frontier College reaches some of its remote students by railway car.

Dressed to thrill in turn-of-the-century fashions

The proper maiden of the late 19th century wears high necklines, and velvet ribbons around her neck.

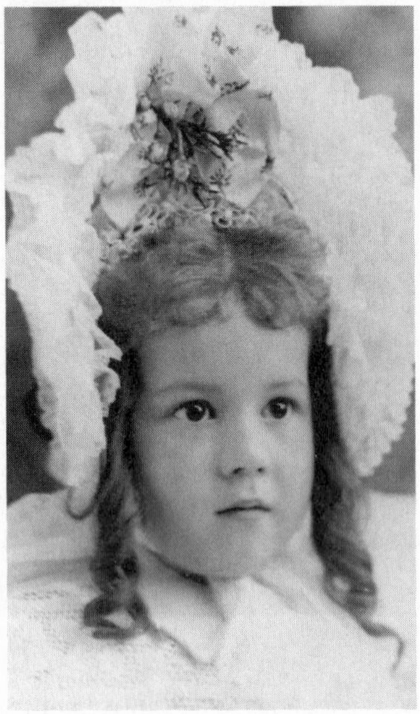

Ringlets and a very ornate bonnet frame the face of this sedate young lady, whose name is Miss Heaton.

The beautiful blond daughter centres this portrait of the H. Joseph family. The child wears a ruffled white dress that contrasts with the adults' sober colors.

Boys' fashions are scarcely less ornate than those of little girls these days. Master Molson is dolled up in velvet with elaborate lace collar and cuffs.

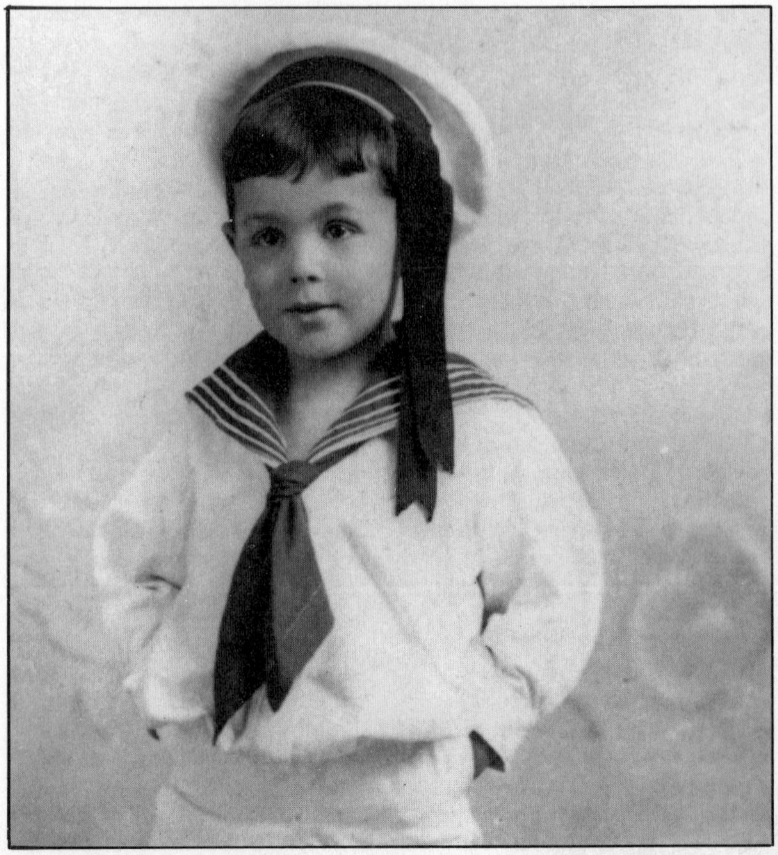

Master McMichael proudly shows off his sailor suit. This traditional suit is very popular with little boys who like to feel that they are quite grown up.

Canadian gents strut their stuff in latest styles

Mr. Anderson wears a collared vest under his long jacket. His starched white shirt and bow tie complete his outfit. Beards are still very popular.

Mr. G.C. Wintle is clean shaven and carries a gentleman's walking stick.

Joseph Drury shows the appropriate dress for the sport of cycling.

George Belford wears a Homburg hat and a tweed overcoat with a cape.

Gentlemen like Col. Strathy proudly wear their dress military uniforms.

This gentleman with his waxed moustache is fashionably dressed in a cut-away morning coat, with contrasting collared vest and a very high starched collar.

Apparel for specific sports such as riding is becoming quite important.

A traditional Quebec costume is suitable for the sport of snowshoeing.

19th century fashions: clothes make the woman

The typical Victorian wedding dress is white or ivory in color and demure in style. This 1884 dress is made of pure silk and features a full-length veil. The color, the veil and the spring flowers symbolize the purity of the bride.

Long skirts and calf-length fur coat keep this fashionable lady's legs warm, while a woolly shawl and fur muff keep ears and fingers toasty.

Fur is part of this elegant velvet costume. The skirt is draped smoothly in front, but the back is gathered for a bustle effect. Sitting is not easy!

The hat has replaced the bonnet, and small waistlines are much in vogue.

Voluminous skirts over huge crinolines are popular in the 1860s.

The bustle back and the heavy lace trim are typical of the 1880s style.

Women often enjoy the sport of cycling, but skirts can be a problem.

Hats sit on top of the head and are trimmed with ribbons and feathers.

This elegant evening outfit shows all the elements of the Victorian look.

Women are asking for less fullness in their riding costumes these days.

"Miss Photography" outfit for a costume ball features camera hat.

In 1895, tiny waists are accentuated by large sleeves and ornate skirts.

An 1867 lady would never show her crinoline and "unmentionables"!

Silk ruffles and a bustle are the highlights of this 1870 evening dress.

This young lady wears an ostrich-feather hat and short curls.

In the 1890s, more women are eligible for graduation caps and gowns.

Fringed panels and ruching trim this beautiful silk 1870s afternoon dress.

This ornate 1885 bonnet is tied on with an enormous satin ribbon.

A shorter fur jacket is worn over this 1865-style, crinolined, layered skirt.

An 1850s-style summer dress is made of lighter fabric with fringed cape and sheer undersleeves.

The bloomer costume, introduced in the 1850s, met with fierce opposition. ▷

Interior designs distinguish Canada's well-to-do

A Victorian drawing room is an ornate room. Heavy laces and rich brocades are the fabrics of choice. Family treasures and photographs cover the tables, and the piano and fireplace are focal points in the room.

The Victorian love of decoration is very evident in this living room fireplace and mantle. The interior of the fireplace is lined with decorative tiles and the exterior is trimmed in marble and finished with various types of wood moldings. The lamps on each side are supported by elaborate brass mounts. The owner's prized collectibles are displayed everywhere.

This bedroom has a large sitting area. The variety of patterns and textures as well as the rich dark wood give this room a warm but heavy appearance.

This dining room is almost completely panelled in wood. The white table linen and the rich table settings and candelabra add the only touches of brightness.

Affluent Canadians spare no expense on homes

The Trutch Family plays croquet in front of their Victoria, B.C., home.

The Irving Family home in Victoria features an immense front veranda.

William Campbell's Georgian-style mansion in Toronto was built in 1822.

This stately Toronto brick home, known as The Grange, was built in 1817.

The Dunsmuir family's Craigdarroch Castle, Victoria, B.C., is romantic gothic.

Casimir Gzowski's Italianate Toronto home, The Hall, is light-colored brick.

1900

Fredericton, Feb. 13. The Imperial Order of the Daughters of the Empire, a women's patriotic and philanthropic organization, is established.

Montreal, March 7. Montreal Shamrocks defeat Halifax Crescents two games to none to win the Stanley Cup.

Boston, April 19. Jim Caffery, Bill Sherring and Frank Hughson of Hamilton are the first Canadians to run in the Boston Marathon, finishing first, second and third.

Ottawa, June 14. The poll tax on Chinese immigrants is raised from $50 to $100. No such tax applies to Japanese immigrants, as Britain wants to keep Japan as an ally.

London, Ont., Sept. 10. Mastodon remains are found.

Vienna, Oct. 14. Sigmund Freud publishes *The Interpretation of Dreams*, which argues that dreams are "the royal road to the unconscious."

Klondike, Yukon. Gold production reaches a peak of about $22,275,000 worth. The richest creeks around Dawson have been exhausted.

Yukon. The White Pass and Yukon Railway connecting Skagway and Whitehorse is completed.

Ottawa. William Lyon Mackenzie King is made editor of the *Labour Gazette*, recently established by Ottawa to give the public information about labor disputes.

Ontario. The National Council of Women of Canada publishes *Women of Canada: Their life and Work*, the first national portrait of Canadian women.

Saint John, N.B. The Boys and Girls Clubs of Canada begins operations.

Paris. Canadian Joe Orton wins a gold medal at the Olympics as a member of the U.S. team. Canada is not participating.

Canada. The best players in Canada's "amateur" hockey leagues get about $200 for an eight-game season.

Canada. The Socialist Labor Party and the Canadian Socialist League, a more moderate Christian socialist group, have both been established in Canada.

Canada. Most women property owners have been granted the vote in municipal elections.

Canada. Hunting has almost killed off the trumpeter swan.

Union reps want limits on alien labor

Railway cars such as this bring immigrant laborers to the prairies.

March 19, 1900

OTTAWA – Union leaders this morning pressed Prime Minister Wilfrid Laurier to act on their concerns about alien labor. Led by Dominion Trades Congress vice-president John Flett, the five-man delegation asked Laurier to exclude illiterate immigrants and increase the head tax on Chinese. The labor leaders accuse the immigrants of strike-breaking activities. They also asked Laurier to permit union labels to be registered as trademarks. The only promise Laurier made was to amend the Chinese head tax.

Horses and beans off to South Africa

Jan. 7, 1900

OTTAWA – More than Canadian troops are bound for the war in South Africa. Through Canada's high commissioner in London, Lord Strathcona, Britain has communicated its willingness to buy some 1,000 horses and 1,000 cases of beans – 10,800 kilograms – for the forces now deployed. The need for horses is evident, given the mobile nature of the fighting. Most of the animals will likely come from western Canada. It is hoped that further orders of foodstuffs will establish Canada more firmly as a supplier to the Mother Country.

Major fires teach Dawson a lesson

Feb. 11, 1900

DAWSON, Yukon – Dawson is a well-built town now – after the lessons learned in the big fires of 1897 and 1898. But the frigid temperatures and special kind of people who live, for short periods, in the town make fires frequent happenings here. This latest blaze has destroyed many important buildings downtown despite the work of the fire brigade. The fire, unfortunately, will hasten the decline of Dawson, for although the mining industry is still strong, the miners and prospectors who kept Dawson alive have gone to the new goldfields at Nome, and now more will follow.

Canadian tells of ordeal as Boer prisoner

Minnie Affleck, Canadian Nursing Sister, with her patients in South Africa.

Jan. 26, 1900

TORONTO – A young Canadian doctor has returned from South Africa recounting his horrifying experiences as a Boer prisoner. Dr. F.J. Livingstone, of Collingwood, Ont., a medical missionary in Zululand since 1895, escaped Dutch captors he describes as "brutal and ignorant, knowing nothing except how to handle a gun and ride a horse." The Boers "showered (him) with abuse," and threatened him with death. While he was detained, the Boer invaders robbed and destroyed Livingstone's home. "What I regretted most was the loss of a fine camera and collection of photographs ... to illustrate lectures on my return to Canada."

Canadian "flour king" W.W. Ogilvie dies

Jan. 12, 1900

MONTREAL – The flour king of Canada is dead. W.W. Ogilvie died suddenly at his home here this afternoon, apparently of a heart attack. He was 64 and leaves his wife Helen and three sons. Ogilvie inherited the company founded by his grandfather at Quebec in 1801. Under his guidance, the company expanded rapidly and introduced many innovations to the milling industry. Ogilvie mills produce 7,500 barrels of flour daily, mainly from company elevators in Manitoba and the Northwest Territories. A few years ago, Ogilvie refused an offer of $8 million for the company.

Ontario approves Niagara power deal

Jan. 27, 1900

NIAGARA FALLS, Ont. – The Niagara Parks Commission, set up by the province to develop a tree park at Niagara Falls, has approved plans to build a massive hydroelectric generating station on the Canadian side of the Niagara River. The project, which is funded by both Canadian and American capitalists, aims at generating 200,000 horsepower worth of electricity through the use of falling water. The water will be diverted from the Welland River, to a point at the edge of the Niagara Gorge.

This first fall will drive turbines that will, in turn, generate electricity, and by this means the first half of the horsepower will be delivered. Then, by ingeniously routing this same water to another place where it can fall some more, the second half of the electricity will be generated.

This plan for generating hydroelectricity mirrors an existing development on the American side of the Niagara River, one that has made that region prosperous.

Students at McGill riot over Boer War

March 1, 1900

MONTREAL – McGill University students and French-Canadian youths today ended the three-day riot which has thrown the city into a turmoil. It began as McGill students celebrated the relief of Ladysmith, then turned ugly when French-Canadian students protested against the suggestion that Canadian soldiers fight for Britain in the Boer War. Once they learned that England had asked for Canadian help, they said they would refuse to fight someone else's war. The issue, they said, was imperialism versus nationalism.

Early in the disturbance civic officials, mistrustful of the municipal police, called in the militia. The situation was exacerbated when the governor general, the Earl of Minto, reportedly said that strong leadership would help the French-Canadian "throw in his lot with the go-ahead Anglo-Saxon race."

More volunteers sail for South Africa

The Edmonton Volunteer Contingent before its departure for South Africa.

Jan. 21, 1900

HALIFAX – More Canadian volunteers sailed today for South Africa. The second contingent will be more varied than the first, consisting of two mounted regiments (1st Canadian Mounted Rifles, Lt.-Col. F.L. Lessard commanding, and 2nd Canadian Mounted Rifles, Lt.-Col. L.W. Herchmer, ex-NWMP, commanding), plus three batteries of field artillery (Lt.-Col. C.W. Drury commanding).

More than 1,300 officers and men are involved. Three ships are needed to transport this group, as well as 1,172 horses and equipment such as rifles, ammunition, wagons, tools. As was the case with the first contingent, the troops will be paid by Britain while out of Canada.

Royal Canadian Regiment helps secure victory over Boer troops

This farmhouse at Paardeberg Drift serves as field hospital to the wounded.

Regiments ford the Paardeberg Drift downstream from the Boer position.

Feb. 27, 1900

PAARDEBERG, South Africa – Some 4,000 Boer troops under Gen. Piet Arnoldus Cronje surrendered here today to Field Marshal Lord Roberts following a nine-day siege. The victory is specially sweet because it comes 19 years to the day after the battle of Majuba, where Afrikaners routed British forces.

The Royal Canadian Regiment played a prominent role in the battle. It suffered heavy losses, with 19 killed and 63 wounded during a river crossing and assault on Feb. 18, plus two killed and four wounded in subsequent fighting. On the final day, the RCR suffered 13 killed and 36 wounded. Among the wounded was Maj. O.C.C. Pelletier, the No. 3 officer in the regiment, hit in the shoulder. The Boers were excellent marksmen; they stopped the RCR attack cold on the 18th, and surrendered only after they had been shelled and starved for many days.

Many of the Canadians have been singled out for their brave conduct in the battle, including Surgeon Maj. Eugene Fiset and Pte. R.R. Thompson, both of whom saved lives while under fire. Pte. J.L. Hornibrook, unarmed, took a Boer soldier prisoner while pretending to have a pistol and hidden assistants. The prisoner turned out to be one of Cronje's adjutants and an important officer.

Boatload of Jewish immigrants lands in Saint John

Many Scots immigrate to Canada.

Immigration brings a variety of new manners and lifestyles to Canada. Here, a Ukrainian woman keeps her culinary traditions using an outdoor bake oven.

This baggage represents some of the many immigrants to Canada (top to bottom): French pine chest, German trunk, a Doukhobor carpetbag, and Norwegian and English trunks.

March 15, 1900

SAINT JOHN, N.B. – The *Lake Megantic* arrived in port today, carrying 480 Russian Jews to their new home in Canada. But before passengers are allowed to set foot on the mainland, they will be inspected by doctors for signs of disease, particularly smallpox, typhus, and cholera. If disease is found, passengers will be kept at Partridge Island in St. John Harbor for up to 40 days while the sick are treated and the ship cleaned and fumigated.

Thanks to advances in medicine and transportation, there is less concern now about the spread of infectious diseases than there was during the waves of immigration in the 1830s and 1840s. Nevertheless, with increasingly larger numbers of newcomers passing into Canada through Saint John, immigration authorities are taking no chances.

According to a report by Dr. John E. March, some 74,906 immigrants and crew were inspected at Partridge Island in 1893-94. Island facilities were allowed to deteriorate over the past several decades, but with the recent rise in immigration and many people coming from Eastern Europe, buildings have been expanded.

Jewish immigrants aboard the *Lake Megantic* will find a small but vigorous community of their faith in Saint John which has organized the Hebrew Benevolent Society. New arrivals are met at their ship and taken into homes where they are fed and clothed while they figure out their next move. The city also boasts a newly constructed synagogue, Ahavath Achim, built two years ago at a cost of $10,000. Rabbi Tobkin is the first resident rabbi to conduct regular services in the city. Although there were only 34 Jews in Saint John according to the 1894 census, the exodus from Eastern Europe has increased that number greatly. Indeed, last year the *SS Gallia* brought 300 Jews from Eastern Europe to the port here.

Lacking skills and speaking little if any English, Jews are rarely given jobs by gentiles. Many have taken to peddling, for which a section of Saint John's business district has been set aside. Earlier arrivals have established businesses, mostly on Main Street.

Worst fire in country's history leaves 3 dead, 15,000 homeless

April 26, 1900

HULL, Que. – Three people are dead, 15,000 homeless, and $100 million worth of property has been lost in both Ottawa and Hull, following the worst fire in Canada's history. Like so many others, the blaze, on the Hull side of the river, started as a chimney fire. But before it could be contained, it was driven throughout the wooden town by high winds. Within a few hours, two-thirds of Hull was destroyed. The winds also managed to blow sparks across the 1.2-kilometre wide Ottawa River.

This tragedy has been repeated all too many times in crowded neighborhoods where wooden structures are the norm and fire-fighting services non-existent.

The Eddy Mill in Hull is one of the many buildings devastated by the worst fire in Canada's history. The blaze destroyed two-thirds of Hull in a few hours.

B.C. House empties as members resign

March 1, 1900

VICTORIA, B.C. – The members of the British Columbia legislature walked out when Lt.-Gov. Thomas McInnes came in to prorogue the House. This political crisis began a week ago when Premier Charles Semlin's government was defeated by one vote.

As the premier was trying to form the province's new government, McInnes demanded his resignation, charging that he was inefficient and extravagant. McInnes called on Joseph Martin, a colleague of Semlin, to form a government, but the legislature quickly declared that it had no confidence in McInnes nor in Martin.

Bourassa's speech condemns Boer War

March 13, 1900

OTTAWA – Henri Bourassa, the rebellious Liberal MP who quit Parliament last year to protest the government sending troops to the Boer War in South Africa, marked his return to the House today with a three-hour speech condemning that same campaign. In his tirade Bourassa reiterated the fundamental objection of French-Canadians to the conflict; namely, that it is a British war, unnecessary for the defence of the empire. It is unjust, unpopular in Quebec, and, by sending troops, the Laurier government has set the dangerous precedent of committing Canada to future British military endeavors.

Henri Bourassa, Liberal MP.

Militia off to protect Japanese fishermen

One of the main catches of the Fraser is the famed British Columbia salmon.

July 24, 1900

VANCOUVER – Two companies of militia sailed early this morning on the steamer *Comox* to Steveston, a fishing village 22.6 kilometres south of here. Their orders are to protect the 1,500 Japanese fishermen at work on the Fraser despite threats from striking white fishermen. The militia commander has warned the strikers that his men are ready to shoot, and so far the strikers have not interfered with the Japanese.

Steel, coal breathe life into Cape Breton

Aug. 25, 1900

SYDNEY, N.S. – Cape Breton, the island that slipped into obscurity following the French surrender to Britain, has come alive. The reasons are coal and steel, resources providing jobs and wealth for the residents of Sydney. Ever since the Dominion Iron and Steel Company was formed a few years back, this quiet village has turned into an industrial powerhouse. So much so that extra labor has been brought in from Newfoundland.

Tupper steps down as Tories defeated in federal election

Nov. 10, 1900

MONTREAL – With cheers of triumphant Liberals still ringing in his ears, today opposition leader Sir Charles Tupper accepted defeat and announced his retirement from politics. It was a sad farewell for the old Conservative war-horse, one of Sir John A. Macdonald's right-hand men and a Father of Confederation. But, having seen his party lose for a second time under his leadership – the first being in 1896 – Tupper decided that now is the time to throw in the towel.

Wilfrid Laurier's Liberals defeated the Tories 132-88 three days ago, taking Tupper's seat in their landslide. While a number of Tory MPs have offered the leader their seats, he has refused. Speaking to supporters in Montreal today, Sir Charles said, "I am deeply moved by these expressions of goodwill, but my decision is final."

As he left the crowd, Tupper promised that "in the quiet of my home life I will not be an indifferent spectator of public events." Still, he will not hold the power he once did. In the 1860s, for example, he played a leading role keeping his disaffected province of Nova Scotia in Confederation. With Tupper's resignation truly ends the Macdonald age of Canadian politics.

Japanese to control flow of emigrants

July 25, 1900

VICTORIA, B.C. – British Columbians are pleased with the latest news from Ottawa concerning Japanese immigration. The federal government has been told by Japan that orders have gone out to governors of the 47 prefectures and to immigration agents to limit the number of Japanese going to Canada to 10 a month for each prefecture. Japan's action comes after federal officials discovered 4,000 Japanese had landed in Victoria in one month. Japanese immigrants are mostly young men who quickly find jobs in farming and fishing, at the expense of white Canadians.

CPR labor dispute slows western lines

Aug. 3, 1900

WINNIPEG – The western Canadian employees of the CPR have gone on strike. A labor dispute which began in Calgary has spread all across western lines. It is not easy to learn the state of efforts to end the strike. Company officials refuse to comment; union members are behind locked doors apparently discussing strategy.

The basis of the grievance is a contractual arrangement giving the unionists a periodic opportunity to talk to company officials. When the union officials appealed for a meeting to discuss rescheduling of work, company representatives refused.

Homer Watson's The Floodgate exemplifies why he was often called "the Canadian Constable." Although his style is reminiscent of the great British landscape painter, John Constable, he was inspired by Canada's landscape.

1901

Ontario, Jan. 2. The Merchants Bank changes its name to the Royal Bank.

Britain, Jan. 22. Queen Victoria dies and is succeeded by her son Edward VII. In her honor, 101-gun salutes will be fired in nine Canadian cities.

Montreal, Jan. 31. Winnipeg Victorias defeat Montreal Shamrocks two games to none to win the Stanley Cup.

Toronto, Feb. 28. The newly organized Toronto Orchestra [Toronto Symphony Orchestra] gives its first performance.

British Columbia, March 9. A court decision upholds the right to vote of naturalized Japanese British subjects.

Ontario, March 14. There has been a decrease in school attendance in the last year, seen as a result of more employment opportunities in cities.

Boston, April 19. Hamilton's Jim Caffery wins the Boston Marathon in record time.

Ottawa, April 29. PM Wilfrid Laurier designates May 24 as Victoria Day, a public holiday honoring the late queen.

Yukon, May 3. Miner Aaron Ewing dies after being bitten by a rabid dog, the first fatality from a mad dog epidemic.

Toronto, June 16. Some 1,500 boys and girls assemble to hear lectures sponsored by the Anti-Cigarette League.

Toronto, Sept. 2. The federal government launches the *J. Israel Tarte*, the world's largest hydraulic suction dredge.

Toronto, Sept. 24. The *Globe* receives the first press dispatch from Dawson over the Canadian Pacific telegraph line.

Japan, Oct. 3. The Diet passes a law forbidding Japanese emigration to the U.S. or Canada.

Niagara Falls, Ont., Oct. 24. Fifty-year-old Annie Taylor goes over Niagara Falls in a barrel and survives.

Sault St. Marie, Ont., Oct. 26. The Michigan Lake Superior Power Company's canal is complete, the world's greatest water-power development.

Ontario. The Good brothers start the first Canadian car factory and build 32 LeRoy cars.

Niagara Falls, Ont. A bust in honor of Laura Secord, a Canadian heroine in the War of 1812, is unveiled at Lundy's Lane Battlefield Cemetery.

Canada. The population is 5,371,315.

Queen Victoria mourned

Britain's new king, Edward VII, and his wife, Queen Alexandra.

Jan. 22, 1901

TORONTO – The big bell at city hall led the other bells of this city all afternoon, mourning the death of Queen Victoria. Business is suspended and flags are at half-mast. A memorial service was held this evening in the chapel of McMaster University.

News of the queen's death arrived here via the Atlantic cable a scant two minutes after she died. City council held an emergency meeting to plan public displays of mourning. It is likely that businesses will close and services be held the day of the funeral.

The popular Queen Victoria.

Ontario sets aside huge forest reserve in northern Ontario

Jan. 7, 1901

TORONTO – The Ontario government today set aside a huge forest reserve in Temagami that is roughly 5,800 square kilometres in extent. The new Temagami Forest Reserve is geographically centred on Lake Temagami, one of northern Ontario's largest lakes. Lumbermen have never reached the lake, which is surrounded by primeval stands of red and white pine forest.

Only one complication exists, namely that the new forest reserve includes about two-thirds of the aboriginal hunting grounds of the Teme-augama Anishnabai – the deep water people – a band of nearly 100 Ojibwa Indians who have never adhered to a treaty and have no reserve of their own. Ontario has unilaterally created the Temagami Forest Reserve without consulting the Indians or setting aside a reserve for them.

Striking Pictou coal miners win dispute

Jan. 3, 1901

HALIFAX – The strike by Pictou coal miners was settled today, with management caving in to the miners' demands – chief among these being a pay increase of 12 percent. The prompt settlement indicates just how important the industry is to Nova Scotia, in the midst of an iron and steel boom. Last year, 2.5 million tons were mined; this year, that figure is expected to approach 4 million. The demand also explains why management didn't fight the workers. In fact, it's the second pay raise in four months, bringing the total hike over that time period to 22 percent.

Blast furnace boosts pig iron production

Feb. 2, 1901

SYDNEY, N.S. – The first of four new blast furnaces was started today at the Dominion Iron and Steel Company here. Pig iron production will begin, with the furnace operating fully late in the week. The remaining three furnaces will be operating in two months. The project, costing almost $10 million, started 18 months ago. When the operation is up to speed, it will have a production capability of 500,000 tons a year.

Election day debut for automatic voting machine is a success

Jan. 7, 1901

OSHAWA, Ont. – It only took seven minutes to add up the votes in today's municipal election, thanks to four new voting machines invented by an Oshawa resident. Dr. A.A. Farwell's Imperial Automatic Voting Machine was used in place of paper ballots to determine the six new members of the town council. And voters agreed the test was a resounding success.

Dr. Farwell's machine is perfectly simple. It consists of a series of levers, one beside the name of each candidate. Because of the machine's ingenious design, no more than six votes (one for each position) can be cast. At day's end, the results are read from steel wheels inside the voting machine.

Tory caucus picks Borden as leader

Robert Borden, Conservative leader.

Feb. 6, 1901

OTTAWA – The Conservative caucus has chosen Robert Borden to replace Sir Charles Tupper as opposition leader. The news came tonight, after a meeting of over three hours. Conservatives are making much of the fact that the vote for Borden was unanimous – despite the very lengthy discussion.

The steely-eyed Nova Scotian lawyer has quite a task ahead of him rebuilding the Conservative party, which has not been the same since the death of Sir John A. Macdonald. As well, he still has to be voted in as party leader at a Tory convention.

Ontario report condemns child labor

Feb. 11, 1901

TORONTO – The head of the Ontario Bureau of Labour condemns the practice of child labor in the bureau's first annual report, released this week. In the report, bureau secretary Robert Glockling notes the prevalence of child labor, as well as long working hours and monthly payments. He also recognizes the difficulty in enforcing legislation protecting children from abusive working conditions, notably cases where exceptions may be warranted.

"Individuals must be sacrificed for the sake of the general object of keeping children out of the mills and factories. If we make the exception we break down the whole law," Glockling writes. "We do not have the chance to enforce a law in the cases where it meets with our approval, and let it go in the cases where it works hardship. A single acknowledged exception weakens its force; it takes but a short series of such exceptions to make it a dead letter."

Glockling calls on labor organizations to help enforce child labor laws by bringing abuses to the attention of authorities, particularly in cases where an individual would be put at personal risk.

The secretary's report, in its general examination of labor conditions, notes a low incidence of strikes in the year ending Sept. 1, 1900. Glockling notes there were 35 strikes and two lockouts, with 14 conflicts still unresolved.

This young miner is only a child.

Desjardins opens caisse populaire doors

Jan. 23, 1901

LEVIS, Que. – Entrepreneur Alphonse Desjardins today opened the doors of the caisse populaire he founded just last month. Having extensively studied similar institutions in Germany, Italy, France and right here in Canada, Desjardins' new co-operative is an innovative mix of different banking systems, and it is aimed primarily at helping the lower classes deal with their financial difficulties. The former journalist started the operation because he was unhappy with what he considers inadequate services at the nation's more prominent banking institutions. Desjardins cites easy credit access for self-helping farmers and laborers as the primary objective of his new venture. On this, its first day of operations, the Caisse populaire de Lévis took in $26.40.

"Metric system is right for Canada"

Feb. 13, 1901

TORONTO – "The metric system is the one for Canada!" was tonight's sentiment at a dinner held by the Canadian Manufacturers' Association. Speaker after speaker advocated the advantages of metric, and more than one wondered aloud as to why Britain, Canada and the United States had yet to adopt it. At meeting's end, the CMA endorsed a resolution proposing an international conference between these countries aimed at making metric the worldwide standard.

Mastodon remains found near Dawson

Feb. 11, 1901

DAWSON, Yukon – Dawson residents had a flashback to a much earlier era, as the remains of a mastodon were brought into town. The bones, weighing about two tons, were discovered 16.5 metres below the surface of a placer mining claim near here.

The find includes a massive skull missing the lower jaw but with the upper part of the head in good condition and holding two 4.5-kilogram teeth. Giant ivory tusks were long and curved, ending in smooth tips. Huge leg, shoulder and thigh bones outlined the impressive skeleton that needed only the vertebrae to complete the frame of the beast that roamed the Yukon so long ago.

These two boys are considered to have been cured of the dreaded tuberculosis of the spine.

Man's brain tumor removed surgically

1901

MONTREAL – A 37-year-old Ontario resident is recovering at the Royal Victoria Hospital after surgery to remove a brain tumor. Levi Poulain of Brockville was experiencing attacks of speechlessness and headaches when admitted to hospital, and after careful study of Poulain's case, Dr. James Stewart diagnosed a brain tumor and recommended surgical removal.

Dr. James Bell, clinical professor of surgery at McGill University, performed the delicate operation, excising a hard irregular tumor several centimetres in diameter. The patient has completely regained his speech, and his writing has gradually returned to normal.

Trading, transport companies merge

April 16, 1901

DAWSON, Yukon – The large corporations are taking over in the Yukon. Businessmen and officials here have just learned that four of the largest companies have merged into two – one for trading, the other for transport.

The Alaska Exploration Co., the Alaska Commercial Co., the Seattle-Yukon Transportation Co. and the Empire Transportation Co. are now doing business as the Northern Navigation Co. and the North American Commercial Co. ▷

Niagara power tapped

Niagara Falls is a source of power.

May 6, 1901

NIAGARA FALLS, Ont. – Development of Niagara's hydro-electric potential started today with the signing of an agreement between the Niagara Parks Commission and the Cataract Construction Company. Under the deal, water will be diverted to a generating station where it will drive turbines to create 25,000 horsepowers worth of electricity. Some 10,000 of this will be transmitted over special pole-mounted wires to Toronto, where it will probably be used to power streetcars. An equal amount will be reserved for sale to American customers.

Rail strike ends; union gains recognition

Aug. 30, 1901

MONTREAL – Railway workers will be back on the job tomorrow, ending an 11-week strike on the Canadian Pacific Railway. An agreement was reached today between the Trainmen's Brotherhood, led by J. Lennan, and CPR vice-president D. McNicholl.

The pact doesn't raise wages, but it does recognize the union as the official representative of workers. The deal only applies to foremen, and first and second men of one year's service. In addition, 13 railway workers fired during the strike were granted the right to appeal their dismissal.

Collision with iceberg sinks the Islander

Aug. 18, 1901

VICTORIA, B.C. – The steamer *Queen* docked here last night with the news that the *Islander,* on her way to Victoria from Skagway, had hit an iceberg and sunk. About 45 of her 107 passengers and 47 crew have drowned, it is feared.

The *Islander,* pride of the Canadian Pacific Navigation Company fleet, was full of passengers from the Yukon and was going at full speed, survivors say, when she hit the iceberg. She sank in 15 minutes. Some passengers managed to get ashore near Juneau but died of exposure. Others were picked up by other ships.

Canadian Pacific steamer the Islander was used on the Pacific coast route.

Pioneers flock to settle in New Ontario

Manpower is provided by neighbors in barn raisings like this one in Ontario.

May 21, 1901

TORONTO – Pioneers are pouring into the wild lands of New Ontario, says the Hon. E.J. Davis, provincial commissioner of Crown lands. "The records of our department show that the number of settlers going into New Ontario (the northern part of the province) in the past 12 months has been largely in excess of the same period of any time in the history of the province." Davis says that most interest is focused on the Timiskaming region, as well as the townships around Port Arthur [Thunder Bay]. Such is the curiosity of potential farmers that they all can't be taken on a government-sponsored railway trip to the region next week.

The boom means good times for agriculture in New Ontario, assuming that the weather and the soil co-operate. Such an influx of settlers will result in rapid clearing of the wilderness, and thus a smooth transition from forest to farming. And, as Davis says, the people are there who want to do the job. In fact, there are so many that "we have abundant evidence that the flow of young men from Ontario (looking for work) to the United States is practically stopped."

Indians burn items condemned by church

July 28, 1901

HAZELTON, B.C. – As the climax of an intense three-day Roman Catholic revival meeting known as a "mission," hundreds of Carrier Indians tonight made a huge bonfire of their masks, rattles, and other paraphernalia condemned by the church as "pagan."

In a ceremony presided over by Bishop Dontenwill from Vancouver but orchestrated by Father Adrien-Gabriel Morice, the local missionary, all objects associated with healing rites or the potlatch were removed by the Carrier people from their houses and cast into flames. Then, as the sparks leapt upwards into the dark, still night, the bishop formally condemned the potlatch, an important native ritual at which property is given away to validate the inheritance of titles.

The church regards the potlatch as an exhibition of sinful "pagan" pride, and Morice has been trying for many years to suppress the ritual. His cause was greatly aided by an influenza epidemic that swept this area last summer, killing about 15 percent of the population. The people, apparently encouraged by the missionary, saw the scourge as divine punishment for their refusal to abandon their old ways. And as for Morice, he's known to have said at the time, "Oh! What a good preacher is sickness."

Housing shortage plaguing Toronto

Oct. 11, 1901

TORONTO – Toronto needs 1,500 more houses – now. Without them, low-rent housing ranging from $8-$25 a month is virtually impossible to find. As well, due to the boom in real estate sales, practically no new houses are being built for the tenant market. It's so bad that up to 2,000 families are believed to be looking for a place to live. Many are out-of-towners who put furniture in storage last spring while they looked for a house ... and they're still looking. The problem is Toronto's booming economy, one that provides jobs without any guarantee that newcomers will be able to find an affordable place to live.

Wireless message heard across ocean

Marconi waits for the message from England in Cabot Tower, Signal Hill.

Dec. 12, 1901

ST. JOHN'S, Nfld. – A message which originated in England was received today at Cabot Tower on Signal Hill in St. John's without the use of wires. Credit the work of Guglielmo Marconi, the Italian physicist and inventor of the telegraph, for today's events. Marconi has been able to concentrate radiated electrical energy into a beam which travels through air.

During the America's Cup in 1899, Marconi equipped two ships with his invention to report the progress of the yacht race. He has now increased the range by using two ballons which hold aloft a vertical wire. Marconi is looking for a location for a permanent station.

Voice of the N.W.T. shoots self in hotel

Oct. 18, 1901

WINNIPEG – Nicholas Flood Davin, 58, committed suicide today. He shot himself in his hotel room. Davin was the first member of Parliament for Assiniboia West. He was first elected in 1887, and served in that post for 13 years. He became known as the champion of the Territories, and was instrumental in having federal services extended to that area. The former MP was a graduate in law. However, his career was based upon his founding of the Regina *Leader,* one of the first papers in the Territories.

First steel is tapped at plant in Sydney

Dec. 1, 1901

SYDNEY, N.S. – Two-and-a-half years after construction of the plant began, the first steel was tapped today at the Sydney Steel Corporation here. The plant, founded by Dominion Iron and Steel Company, owes its existence to Cape Breton coal and iron ore brought in from Wabana, Nfld. Limestone, also used in the process, comes from a local quarry. Steel company management plans to produce pig iron and semi-finished steel, with the majority of the products bound for export markets.

The Duke and Duchess of Cornwall and York are on a Canadian tour. They are seen here in the Royal Carriage at the dock in Victoria, B.C.

Launch of the Huronic hails new industry

The Huronic is a 248-metre-long steel-hulled passenger and freight steamer.

Sept. 12, 1901

COLLINGWOOD, Ont. – Steel shipbuilding has come to Collingwood, on Georgian Bay, with the launch this afternoon of the *Huronic.* A great throng of spectators cheered as the 248-metre-long steamer, the largest freshwater ship ever built in Canada, slid sideways into the bay from its dry dock.

Constructed by the Collingwood Shipbuilding Company, the *Huronic* is a combination freighter and passenger ship capable of carrying more than 250 souls. She features electric power.

Grain growers in Indian Head area unite

Dec. 18, 1901

INDIAN HEAD, N.W.T. – Prompted by the loss of three-quarters of their crop this fall, farmers in the Indian Head area have formed the Territorial Grain Growers' Association.

A record crop of about 60 million bushels was produced on the prairies this year – almost twice the normal harvest. The railway was not prepared to handle the overload, and nearly half the prairie wheat spoiled while waiting to go to market. Farmers are not only upset that elevator companies got priority for whatever boxcars were available, but also with the hold elevator companies have over pricing and marketing in general.

More Canadian women than ever in the workforce

Nursing in hospitals is one of the newer occupations now open to women.

This woman has a rather unusual job. She delivers mail by horseback.

Former journalist Sara Jeannette Duncan is now a successful novelist.

Many work in factories or as domestics

1901

OTTAWA – One in six Canadian workers is a woman. Although there are people today who remember when women were rarely found at work outside the home, this has changed dramatically. Today, 25 percent of all manufacturing and mechanical workers are females. One in 20 clerical workers is a woman. Half of professionals, mostly teachers and nurses, are women.

Although a handful of women have made inroads into previously male professions, including medicine and law, the majority are domestics, teachers, factory workers and sales clerks. For native-born Canadians, domestic service has less appeal than it once did, although a general servant can earn from $8 to $14 a month in eastern Canada and from $10 to $20 in the west. With the exception of farm girls newly arrived in the city, most domestic positions are filled by immigrants. The lack of privacy and the greater availability of other jobs for the Canadian-born are two reasons cited for this change.

Factory work is one way many modern women earn a living. Sometimes wages are good, especially if a worker is skilled and fast. However, many factory girls are paid for piece work, and employers base their rates on what the fastest workers can do. Consequently, many earn less than they need to survive. In one notorious instance, a Toronto woman earned less than two cents an hour. Because of such abuses, factories have been subjected to close government scrutiny, with inspectors appointed to ensure that good light, ventilation and drinking water are available. Many groups, including the National Council of Women, fear that poor conditions, including the physical demands of certain tasks and the long hours, will adversely affect women's childbearing capacities.

Outside of factories, increased opportunities exist for educated women. Nursing is one occupation open to females. A growing number are also employed as clerical workers. Typists, stenographers, and bookkeepers can earn as much as teachers. As for teaching, three-quarters of all employees in this field are women, although females hold few positions in high schools and almost none in universities.

Farm women are the least recognized female workers. They may do farm work and domestic tasks, but for statistical purposes they are considered to have no occupation.

The executive of the Manitoba Equal Suffrage Club works for women's rights.

Women's activist Adelaide Hoodless.

Women challenge traditional dress.

Risking life and limb to provide images of the war

"Special artists" on the battlefield

1901

OTTAWA – Newspapers carry photos of the South African war, but artists who accompany Canadian troops also provide images of the fighting. Since the Crimean War – when mechanical presses allowed mass newspaper runs and increasing literacy created a mass reading public – publishers have dispatched "special artists" as well as "special correspondents" around the world to cover major events.

Military campaigns attract many special artists. They share the soldier's hardships and dangers, plus a few of their own. At least one such artist was detained by a mob in the Franco-Prussian War when his sketching aroused suspicions he was a spy. The *Canadian Illustrated News* employed several artists during the North West Rebellion of 1885 – one of the best covered Canadian events of the century. Decades earlier, the American Civil War was fully covered by artists. American artist Frederic Remington recorded much of the recent Spanish-American war.

Special artists usually send many rough sketches to their papers with notes or news stories. Other artists, such as Canada's A.H. Hider, complete the work for final publication. Some of the drawings are reprinted for sale to interested individuals.

Hider's Surrender of Commander Botha to the Second Canadian Dragoon is based on another artist's sketch.

Woodville's Dawn of Majuba Day.

Sergeant braves heavy cross fire to rescue wounded comrade

July 5, 1901

WOLVE SPUIT, South Africa – Sgt. Arthur Richardson, a former Mountie now serving in Lord Strathcona's Horse, performed an exceptionally brave act today, observers report. Richardson's group of 38 troopers came into contact with 80 Boers who engaged them at close quarters. The order to withdraw was given. As the outnumbered men retreated, one of Richardson's comrades was wounded and his horse killed. Despite heavy cross fire and though his own horse was injured, Richardson rode to within 270 metres of the enemy, picked up the stranded trooper, and got safely away.

Lord Strathcona's Horse, commanded by the famous ex-Mountie Lt.-Col. Sam Steele, left Halifax on March 16.

This painting, Victoria Cross, by an anonymous artist depicts the rescue of a horseless soldier by a fellow trooper. The rescued trooper seems to be taking a last look at his fallen mount and watching for signs of the enemy.

1902

Winnipeg, March 17. The Montreal AAA defeat the Winnipeg Victorias two games to one to win the Stanley Cup.

Ellesmere Island, Aug. 6. Otto Sverdrup's Norwegian expedition sails for home after four years exploring the high Arctic [including Sverdrup Islands].

Toronto, Sept. 9. Leading educationists choose Toronto publishers George N. Morang and Co. to publish educational texts for Canada and the U.S.

Ontario, Sept. 9. Six Nations Indian Dr. Oronhyatekha, supreme chief ranger of the Independent Order of Foresters, gives a collection of Indian and other historical curios to the order.

Nova Scotia, Sept. 17. A U.S. expedition led by Robert Peary arrives after four years exploring the high Arctic and trying to reach the North Pole.

Ontario, Dec. 4. In the Liquor Act Referendum, most voters favor prohibition, but prohibitionists don't get the necessary majority they are seeking.

Montreal, Dec. 20. The first Québécois comic strip, Raoul Barré's *Pour un dîner de Noël*, appears in *La Presse*.

Cape Breton, Dec. 21. Guglielmo Marconi establishes permanent radio communication across the Atlantic to Britain.

Montreal. British physicists Ernest Rutherford and Frederick Soddy develop the disintegration theory of the atom while at McGill University.

Toronto. The Children's Fresh Air Fund, aimed at giving children of the poor an outing away from the city, is one of the most popular charities in the city.

Canada. The Trades and Labour Congress affiliates with the American Federation of Labour, giving the AFL control over Canada's unionized workers.

Ottawa. The ban on wood buffalo hunting is extended until 1907.

Sudbury, Ont. The Consolidated Copper Co. joins with several American companies to form the International Nickel Co. of Canada (INCO).

Canada. Canada's first film production company, the Bioscope Co., is formed to produce *Living Canada*, a series of films depicting Canadian life. The CPR sponsored the films to show in Britain to promote immigration.

Doukhobors not model settlers to all

1902

YORKTON, N.W.T. – The 7,400 Russian Doukhobors who arrived in the Assiniboia district three years ago have established four settlements near Yorkton. Impoverished when they arrived, through industry and thrift they have made remarkable progress. But are they the model settlers Canada has been striving to attract? Some say yes, but there are also those who think them anything but.

No one can argue the Doukhobors are not diligent, skilled farmers. The homesteads provided them have flourished. They have stockpiled enough grain that if this or even next year's harvest are poor, their communities will remain self-sufficient. They are hospitable and gracious, but they are also aloof and abide according to their traditions.

The Doukhobors live communally. They view free enterprise as a hindrance to social well-being. And they live according to strict interpretations of the New Testament, with a fervor that some say broaches fanaticism; they have in some cases refused to recognize secular authority, particularly the homestead and marriage laws. One eastern paper summed up a growing volume of opinion last year: "Better let the prairie lie fallow ... than plant them with residents who will be in, but not of, Canada."

Immigrants pose in front of a Doukhobor hotel on the prairies.

Canadian Mounted Rifles off to S. Africa

Personnel of the Canadian Mounted Rifles are en route to South Africa.

Jan. 14, 1902

HALIFAX – More Canadian troops sailed from this port today to the battlegrounds of South Africa. The *Manhattan* is carrying members of the Canadian Mounted Rifles, as well as 22 bulls and 125 sheep that will be slaughtered on the long journey to provide food for the troops. The Canadians are part of continuing support being lent to the empire's fight with the Afrikaner Boers. It's a duty that has fallen to English-Canadians, as most French-Canadians refuse to fight in a "British war."

Official advocates shots for smallpox

Jan. 31, 1902

TORONTO – Vaccination is the chief defence against smallpox, especially in the wilds of New [Northern] Ontario. So warned Dr. C.A. Hodgetts tonight at a meeting of the University of Toronto Medical Society. Hodgetts is a provincial health inspector who has spent a great deal of his time trying to fight this dreaded disease. In his talk, he discussed the problems and progress of smallpox treatment in the pioneer districts and logging camps in the north. The main problem, says Hodgetts, is with unvaccinated people, 153 of whom were taken to the hospital in Sudbury for treatment last year. Many of these people, either through ignorance or stubbornness, refused to take advantage of vaccines which could have prevented their sufferings.

In his lecture, Hodgetts repeatedly returned to the importance of vaccination as the key to eradicating smallpox from Ontario. He also criticized the failure of many doctors to properly diagnose the disease, thus delaying or preventing proper care for some sufferers.

Drink up! Manitobans defeat prohibition

About half of rural Manitobans voted against prohibition. Temperance groups had expected more support from sober-minded, hard-working country folk.

April 2, 1902

WINNIPEG – Manitobans today decisively defeated prohibition. Returns from the provincewide referendum show about 16,600 votes against prohibition and some 10,600 in favor. As expected, Winnipeg and other populous centres voted strongly against. But what surprised anti-liquor campaigners was the strength of the pro-liquor vote in the countryside, where the two positions ran almost even.

French-Canadian areas and those where foreign-born voters dominate, including Mennonite communities, were heavily against banning the sale of liquor. The turnout was large, indicating that a campaign by a faction of the temperance movement to boycott the referendum had little effect.

Mob gives happy hangman a hard time

March 20, 1902

HULL, Que. – Nobody likes a happy hangman. At least not in Hull, where a mob beat up a hangman named Radcliffe this morning. Apparently the attack occurred after people overheard Radcliffe and his cronies whooping it up at a local hotel, with ribald songs and jokes that implied the hangman truly enjoyed his profession. After a skirmish outside the hotel, police escorted the hangman to jail, where he was locked up for his own safety.

A Dennis Gale painting shows a moose attracted by a bush fire at night.

Nfld. sealers end strike

March 12, 1902

ST. JOHN'S, Nfld. – After two furious days with 3,000 sealers roaming the streets in a threatening mood, the first sealers' strike in more than 40 years has been settled. Sealers have seen their incomes decrease in recent years as the price of seal oil continues to decline and as the seal herds diminish. This year they walked off the ships at the last moment before sailing and refused to board until the berth money was eliminated.

Sealers have been paying $3 per man for their berths. This practice originated in the days when sealers were co-investors on small ships, but in recent years the charge has become unpopular. Today the merchants agreed to eliminate the berth money and the ships sailed. Local residents breathed a sigh of relief, because there were reports that the strike would soon turn violent.

Young sealers with ropes and gaffs.

Cattle town performance ends in a riot

The theatre may be a bit too sophisticated for men who live the cowboy's life.

May 1902

HIGH RIVER, N.W.T. – Albertans have never done anything by halves, and the reaction to the first blossoming of theatre in the province proves that very point. The first performance of a play in Alberta was 20 years ago, and since then audiences have been showing their enthusiastic approval – or disapproval – in various ways.

Here is an example from High River, a cattle town: as the curtain was coming down on a fine performance of the *Cowboy's Romance,* the audience, obviously made up of the worst elements of male and female society, started to throw eggs at the stage. The director of the Great Bostock Theatrical Company, to protect his cast, grabbed a club and rushed toward the audience. The performance ended in a riot. Hopefully this unseemly affair will not deter other touring companies from coming to Alberta. ▷

"Promised Land" lures immigrants

April 30, 1902

HALIFAX – The largest boatload of immigrants ever seen in Canada landed today in Halifax. The 2,692 men, women and children arrived from Europe today on the steamer *Bulgaria.* Many are Jewish, Ukrainian, Italian or German, all coming to start a new life in the "Promised Land." The voyage is said to have been relatively uneventful. Only two children died en route, and eight families came down with measles.

Most of the immigrants will settle new lands in the northwest. The first of these headed out this afternoon by train. Most of the others are still being processed by government officials and will leave soon.

Blast at B.C. mine kills at least 125

May 22, 1902

FERNIE, B.C. – At least 125 coal miners were killed last night by an explosion at the Coal Creek mine eight kilometres from here. A plume of coal dust and flames rose 300 metres above the mine when scorching fumes raced through the pit. Virtually all the men underground were killed at once, officials say, for no one could have survived such a blast, caused by fire damp.

Rescue attempts are dangerous because the fumes will kill within a few minutes. Most of the bodies will have to stay in the mine until the ventilating system, destroyed in the blast, is repaired. Then the fumes will be drawn out of the mine and it will be safe to enter.

War in South Africa over

The Second Canadian Military Regiment is preparing to leave Durban soon.

May 31, 1902

LONDON, England – The war in South Africa is over. A treaty signed today admits British sovereignty over the former Afrikaner republics. The Boers will be granted self-government at the earliest possible moment, with their language and religious rights protected. The Boers will also receive some £3 million in compensation for ruined farms. Described by British papers as "generous" and "magnanimous," these terms reflect the empire's desperate need to end the war. The tough Afrikaners, grimly defending black subservience, faced huge armies outnumbering them 12 to 1, waged guerrilla warfare, and exacted a heavy toll in British blood, money, and self-respect.

In the course of this war, Canada has sent 8,300 men – infantry, mounted troops and artillery – of whom 252 were wounded and 135 died, some from disease. Four Canadians have been awarded the Victoria Cross, and one man, Pte. R.R. Thompson, Royal Canadian Regiment, has received the Queen's Scarf, an honor so rare only four men have ever gotten it.

The Ottawa Hockey Club plays one of Canada's favorite winter sports.

Charles Gorman, world champion, is poised to start a speedskating race.

Northern Ontario railway in works

May 12, 1902

NORTH BAY, Ont. – The first sod was turned today on a new pioneer railway aimed at opening up Ontario's north. The Temiskaming and Northern Ontario Railway will run from here, starting at Trout Lake, up 409 kilometres to Cochrane. The railway is being built by the provincial government, which wants to bring in settlers. As well, it's believed that this region has a wealth of minerals just waiting to be pulled from the ground. Only a railway can provide the access needed to make commercial mining a possibility.

Atom not smallest particle, prof says

May 28, 1902

TORONTO – McGill University physics professor Ernest Rutherford told members of the Royal Society here today that he has found particles smaller than atoms. Rutherford's statement met with some skepticism at the society, but the Montreal professor is involved with ongoing research in atomic physics. His hypothesis involves the spontaneous disintegration of atoms. He has been working with Frederick Soddy, a McGill chemistry professor, on radiation experiments. Born in New Zealand, Rutherford, 30, came to teach at McGill in 1898.

Pacific Cable links the British Empire

Oct. 31, 1902

VICTORIA, B.C. – "Delighted to congratulate you on completion of great work, Pacific cable ... forging further link to advantage our empire." These words, sent by Premier Richard Seddon of New Zealand to the federal government's Sir Sandford Fleming in Ottawa, constitute the first official message sent over the just completed Pacific Cable. Public figures are celebrating this triumph, the final component of a communications network, all within the realm of the British Empire, that now spans the globe.

The Anglin laid the Pacific Cable at Doubtless Bay, New Zealand.

Deal brings an end to streetcar strike

June 24, 1902

TORONTO – The short but violent Toronto Street Railway strike is over, thanks to the Board of Trade. Board members mediated between the two sides and worked out a deal which sees some, but not all, of the workers' demands met.

In its three-day run, the strike led to riots at the TSR's three depots, as strikers literally destroyed any streetcars management brought out of the yards. So bad was the violence that 1,400 troops were called up in case it continued.

Halifax police clash with drunk soldiers

Sept. 26, 1902

HALIFAX – A gang of drunken soldiers from the Royal Canadian Regiment, celebrating a brief respite from the rigors of military life, caused quite a stir this evening as they battled police before hundreds of spectators near city hall. Two of the rowdy offenders were arrested, but this did little to quell the disturbance – their comrades threatened to storm the police station and, jostled by onlookers, the possibility of a street battle between soldiers and civilians loomed large. Police officials quickly sent an appeal to imperial authorities and 50 troops arrived to restore peace.

NWMP cut Doukhobor pilgrimage short

Nov. 8, 1902

MINNEDOSA, Man. – As many as 600 Doukhobors marched into this town yesterday, passing through on a great pilgrimage to convert the world and find a new Promised Land. They will go no further, at least for the time being. This morning they emerged from the local rink, where they had been lodged by civic authorities, to find themselves prevented from continuing their eastward trek; instead, a train of six empty coaches and three cars of North West Mounted Police were waiting to transport them – by force if necessary – back to their settlements in Saskatchewan.

Since their arrival in Canada four years ago, many Doukhobors have expressed dissatisfaction with what they view as government, or secular, interference with their temporal way of life; a great wave of religious fanaticism swept over their communities this fall, exacerbating this discontent. Not all individuals have been affected: only 20 percent of the estimated 7,500 Doukhobor settlers have resorted to such extremes as freeing livestock and burning garments made of leather, determined to stop what they deem as the unnecessary, and sacrilegious, exploitation of animals. In September, government officials authorized the sale of released Doukhobor livestock, a decision some see as the final provocation leading to the pilgrimage.

Newfoundland, U.S. OK free-trade deal

Oct. 18, 1902

NEWFOUNDLAND – Today is an historic day for Newfoundland and for Prime Minister Robert Bond, as the colony and the United States have agreed on a free-trade deal. For decades, Newfoundland has been seeking an agreement that would allow its saltfish exports to enter the United States duty free. In 1900-01 Bond negotiated such a treaty, but Canada and Britain vetoed it. Now, Britain is going to permit the new pact. The main benefit for the United States lies in the fact that its fishermen will be able to purchase bait here for their banks fishery.

The interior of the Anglican Mission School on a Blackfoot Reserve.

Indian boys on the steps of their school in Metlakatla, British Columbia.

1903

Montreal, March 1. French-Canadian nationalists form *La Ligue Nationaliste* to work for Canadian autonomy from Britain and provincial autonomy from Ottawa.

Ottawa, March 10. Ottawa Silver Seven beat the Montreal Victorias for the Stanley Cup.

Saskatoon, April 17. Some 2,000 English colonists arrive en route to settle [western Saskatchewan] under the leadership of Rev. Isaac Barr.

Toronto, April 19. Sir Oliver Mowat, lieutenant-governor and former premier, dies.

Quebec, April 25. The legislature passes an act stating that Jews will be treated in the same way as Protestants for school purposes, and that no Jewish students can be compelled to take part in religious exercises to which their parents or guardians object.

Toronto, April 30. Emily Stowe, Canada's first female doctor, dies.

Northwest Territories, July. The Barr colonists name their first town Lloydminster, after Rev. George Exton Lloyd, who assumed leadership of the colony when Rev. Barr resigned amidst controversy.

Hudson Bay, Sept. 24. The North West Mounted Police establish a detachment at Cape Fullerton, their first outpost in the eastern Arctic, to extend Canadian jurisdiction to American and Canadian whalers wintering in the bay.

Sault St. Marie, Ont., Sept. 28. Ex-employees of the recently closed Consolidated Lake Superior Company riot because the company hasn't paid them, prompting the imposition of martial law. The company laid off 3,500 workers when it closed.

Kitty Hawk, U.S., Dec. 17. Wilbur and Orville Wright make the first motor-driven flight.

Canada. There are 178 cars registered.

New Brunswick. Black lawyer A.B. Walker begins editing *Neith*, an Acadian magazine.

Toronto. The Municipal Houses of Refuge Act makes it mandatory for counties to provide houses for the poor.

Canada. C.A.E. Harriss organizes the Cycle of Musical Festivals of the Dominion of Canada, involving more than 4,000 singers and musicians in 15 communities.

Icy Maritime waters hard on ships

Government steamer Stanley cuts ice-bound vessels out of Bridgewater, N.S.

The bad winter has created this ice jam at the public wharf, Fredericton.

Feb. 25, 1903

GEORGETOWN, P.E.I. – For two long, terrifying days this week, the steamer *Minto*, a government ferry that travels between Prince Edward Island and Nova Scotia, was held fast by ice in the frozen waters of Northumberland Strait. Earlier today the ship smashed its way free and this evening pulled into Georgetown harbor, unable to make the crossing. Despite Canadian assurances that transportation to the mainland would be maintained year-round, first made when P.E.I. entered Confederation in 1873, lack of an efficient icebreaker has long been a source of frustration for Islanders.

The plight of the *Minto*, typical of ships bound for the mainland during the winter months, pales in comparison with that of the steamer *Stanley*, imprisoned in the ice and carried helplessly by tides and storms for 45 days now. The crew of the *Minto*, after freeing their ship earlier today, steered to within a mile of the *Stanley* where they cached provisions of food and coal for the stranded men.

With the *Minto*'s arrival at Georgetown has also come word of a perilous, hair-raising adventure experienced by three young women and four men. Yesterday, after initial efforts to free the ship failed, they crossed the ice-field by foot to Pictou Island, N.S. Climbing over huge ice-crags, skirting stretches of open water and half-blinded by the sun's glare, they managed to reach their destination that night.

Police poked a hole in the perfect alibi

Feb. 11, 1903

BATHURST, N.B. – It was the perfect alibi. You can't steal from a store when you're already in jail. Or can you? Ask Fred Thibodeau, who is in jail awaiting trial for breaking into a jewelry store last month. Police probing two recent burglaries found the prime suspect right under their feet. Loot from the two stores was found in Thibodeau's jail cell, where a hole was cut in the floor beneath his bed, enabling him to come and go as he pleased.

Grain growers band together in Manitoba

March 4, 1903

BRANDON, Man. – The Manitoba Grain Growers' Association was formed here today. The 22 separate local associations now in existence will operate under the jurisdiction of the new provincial body. The constitution of the new association will be modelled closely upon that of the first such farmers' rights group, the Territorial Grain Growers' Association formed two years ago in the district of Assiniboia. At one time it was believed the Manitoba association should be part of the territorial body, but the first board of directors voted to remain independent.

The first move toward formation of the Manitoba association was taken in Virden on Jan. 7, when a local association was formed. At the meeting, W.R. Motherwell and Matthew Snow represented the territorial group and told the assembled farmers there was no reason farmers should not organize for the maintenance of producers' rights.

While Motherwell also attended the Brandon meeting, the main speaker was J.W. Scallion, elected the first president later that day.

Mississauga, Six Nations settle conflict

June 1903

SIX NATIONS RESERVE, Ont. – The Mississauga Indians of the New Credit Reserve and the Six Nations Indians near Brantford, Ont., have resolved a long-standing disagreement. The issue arose with the removal in 1847 of the Mississauga Indians from their home at the Credit River, 20 kilometres west of Toronto, to the Six Nations Reserve. There the Mississauga selected a fertile tract they called New Credit. The land, the Mississauga believed, was given freely – until in the mid-1880s the Six Nations, on account of their own growing population, wanted it back. Finally there's been a compromise. The Six Nations have accepted a Mississauga offer of $10,000 for the undisturbed occupancy of New Credit.

An Indian family greets visitors arriving at their log cabin.

The naked truth: Doukhobors jailed

May 21, 1903

YORKTON, N.W.T. – Twenty-eight Doukhobor men were arrested and charged with nudism after they and a group of 17 women and children arrived in Yorkton yesterday naked as the day they were born. They say they are free men and wish to show their freedom. After refusing to dress, the Doukhobors were "jailed" by police in an immigration hall. The police nailed open the doors and hung up lamps to attract mosquitoes. By morning, all the Doukhobors were clothed.

Chinese immigrants turned away in B.C.

May 21, 1903

VICTORIA, B.C. – Provincial authorities seem to have found a way to stop the flood of Chinese immigrants. New laws state newcomers to the province must fill out forms which presume some knowledge of English. There are also other special requirements which have the effect of barring Chinese immigrants. These laws are part of a continuing attempt by B.C. to keep out Asians by trying to legislate in the area of immigration – an area Ottawa zealously defends.

Starving horse dies moments after rescue

May 1903

FRANK, N.W.T. – One month after it killed 70 miners and 16 horses, the terrible Frank rockslide has also claimed Charlie, the miners' horse. Trapped alone in the stinking, gas-filled blackness, Charlie slurped filthy water, and gnawed mine timber and his leather harness. Then the men dug him out. Charlie swallowed the brandy and oats his cheering rescuers offered, but so great was the shock, he sank to his knees and died.

N.W.T. rockslide a killer

Rescued miners are escorted uptown; wounded miner is driven to hospital.

April 29, 1903

FRANK, N.W.T. – At 4:10 this morning, millions of tons of rock came hurtling down the eastern slope of southern Alberta's Turtle Mountain, devastating the small mining community of Frank. At least 70 of the community's 600 people are thought to have lost their lives. The rockslide, believed to have been caused by an earthquake, has swept almost two kilometres across the valley, destroying the rail line and cutting the town off from immediate aid.

Survivors spent the day frantically trying to free those trapped beneath the rubble, and indeed 23 men, women and children have been rescued. And late this afternoon, 17 miners trapped in a shaft by the slide emerged unexpectedly after a desperate 13-hour struggle. The disaster ends, at least temporarily, two years of profitable coal mining in the area.

This bar in the Alberta Hotel in Calgary is known as the longest bar in Alberta. Spittoons and towels line the front of the bar. Sparkling glassware and gleaming mirrors add a touch of elegance to this popular meeting place.

Fox turns out to be a rich mineral find

Sept. 1, 1903

LONG LAKE, Ont. – A wealth of minerals, including what may be the world's richest vein of silver, has been discovered here by a worker on the Temiskaming and Northern Ontario Railway. Local gossip says blacksmith Fred Larose discovered the minerals at night when he threw his hammer at what he believed to be the eyes of a fox. But instead of a yelp he heard a clang, because the light was actually reflecting off copper in the rocks. Larose realized what he had found and kept it secret until he filed his claim on the site.

A variety of minerals have since been found here – cobalt, copper, nickel, and, of course, silver. Lots of silver. In fact, it's suspected this area is so rich in silver that eager prospectors have begun to flow in.

NWMP establish Herschel Island post

Aug. 7, 1903

HERSCHEL ISLAND, N.W.T. – Two members of the North West Mounted Police arrived at this remote whaling outpost on the Yukon coast today to establish the first permanent police post north of the Arctic coast. The officers, Sgt. Francis Fitzgerald and Const. F.D. Sutherland, have already arranged to occupy a pair of sod huts and a storehouse.

For more than a decade, American whaleships have used Pauline Cove on Herschel Island as a convenient base for their activities, and the Canadian government recently has become concerned that the Americans may have territorial ambitions in the Arctic. Canada has claimed the area since 1880, but has done almost nothing to establish an official presence. As well, there is evidence the liquor trade with the Inuit is rampaging unchecked along the northern coast. The liquor is imported into the western Arctic by the whaling ships and by trading vessels that visit the area.

The NWMP are also establishing a post in northern Hudson Bay. According to the commissioner of the force, the presence of the police will show that "no matter what the cost or how remote the region, the laws of Canada will be enforced."

Sgt. Fitzgerald (second from left) will head the new Herschel Island post.

Government expedition sails for the north

A.P. Low (fifth from right, front) and his Neptune crew in winter dress.

Aug. 23, 1903

HALIFAX – A Canadian government expedition left Halifax today aboard the 465-ton steam vessel *Neptune*, bound for Hudson Bay and the whaling grounds of the eastern Arctic. Commanded by A.P. Low, a geologist with the Geological Survey, the expedition has been sent north to assert Canadian sovereignty over the Arctic archipelago. The *Neptune* will land a six-man North West Mounted Police detachment in the northwest corner of Hudson Bay, where the vessel will pass the winter.

Next spring Low and his crew will cruise north to the whaling grounds off Baffin Island where they will collect customs fees from the Scottish and American whalers and formally declare the area part of Canadian territory. At the same time the government is setting up a police detachment at the other end of the Arctic on Herschel Island.

Artist in court over painting's accuracy

Aug. 7, 1903

TORONTO – An American artist is in a legal dispute with a local hotel over accuracy in Canadian history. William de Leftwitch Dodge wants the New York Supreme Court to prevent his employer, the Tiffany Company, from completing work for the King Edward Hotel.

Dodge was commissioned to paint a mural of British army officer Gen. James Wolfe leading his troops to the heights of Quebec back in 1759. Hotel architect E.J. Lennox rejected the mural because it was too dark.

Dodge refused to re-do the scene as if it had been daylight, which, historically, it was not. In an interview today, Lennox said he did not object to Dodge making the Wolfe scene a night one, "but he should have painted it for a place which would be suitable for a picture of that tone."

Birds of a feather: this Klondike girl in ostrich feathers and Cree warrior in a headdress made of Canadian birds' plumage suggest that the exploitation of wildlife for the sake of ornamentation knows no cultural bounds.

Canadian reps object to Alaska boundary decision

Oct. 19, 1903

LONDON, England – The two Canadians on the Alaska Boundary Commission today refused to sign the commission's decision. After some sharp words with British commissioner Lord Alverstone, Louis Jetté and A.B. Aylesworth walked out of the signing ceremony. Alverstone and the three American commissioners signed, making the decision binding.

The commission was established to set the vague and controversial boundary between Canada and Alaska. Canadian commissioners say virtually all American positions were accepted. Press and political reaction in Canada has been quick and bitter, especially in Quebec. Montreal's *Le Canada* said today that because of the British desire to please the Americans, Canada did not stand a chance of being heard. Canadian commissioners are working on a statement of their objections for release tomorrow, when the decision becomes official.

Grand Trunk Pacific goes coast-to-coast

Oct. 20, 1903

OTTAWA – What is being called "Canada's first truly transcontinental railway" was approved by the Senate today. The Grand Trunk Pacific, which will run from coast to coast – unlike the CPR, which officially ends at Montreal – is a joint project between the Laurier government and the Grand Trunk Railway.

The government is not only helping with funding, but building the less profitable part of the line from Moncton to Winnipeg. This "National Transcontinental Railway" will be leased to the GTR for 50 years. The GTR, meanwhile, is building the line west, following a more northerly route. It will service the rich farmlands around Edmonton, ending at Port Simpson, on the British Columbia coast. The project has the full backing of the government, which sees increased immigration and profit from a line to the northwest.

Immigration total for year at 121,115

Slavic immigrants such as these make up part of the flood of newcomers.

Nov. 5, 1903

OTTAWA – Some 121,115 immigrants came to Canada in the first 10 months of this year hoping to find a better life in a bountiful land. The largest group – 47,541 – is from Great Britain. The next largest – 39,046 – is from the U.S. The rest – 34,528 – is from Europe; a veritable patchwork of different languages and nationalities.

With such an impressive influx, officials hope that within a few years the northwest will be a productive agricultural area and a market for eastern Canadian manufactured goods, making Canada truly a nation from sea to sea.

Priest's treatment of Indians criticized

Nov. 10, 1903

QUESNEL, B.C. – Father Adrien-Gabriel Morice, the missionary who sees himself as the uncrowned king of the Carrier Indians, was told today he'll be replaced. The move follows complaints about Morice's authoritarian ways and his neglect for Carrier spiritual and educational needs.

A priest sent to assist Morice reported that "from the height of his grandeur he treated the Indians like slaves." They want to learn English to compete with whites, but Morice would prefer them to remain his untutored "children of the woods." His concern to enhance his international reputation as a linguist, explorer and anthropologist has also prompted him to take time away from his priestly duties. Yet he refuses to delegate authority to younger priests, who are deemed to be too inexperienced and linguistically incompetent for anything but kitchen duties.

Ladies chastised for cussing on the links

July 22, 1903

HALIFAX – Some female members of the church who take communion with sanctity on Sundays swear like troopers on the golf course the next day, an Anglican minister charged in his Sunday sermon. Rev. W.J. Ancient, speaking at St. Luke's Cathedral, asks: when women accept profanity, what can be expected of men, who usually apologize if they swear in front of them? The women golfers demanded that Ancient retract his charges. He not only refused, but said in an interview he had heard some women also smoke on the golf course.

These three gentlemen represent the Mormon community in Cardston, N.W.T.

Crew catches whale then heads for hunt

1903

NEWFOUNDLAND – The steamer *Puma* has embarked on a gruelling 28-hour hunt after harpooning a large blue whale 9.6 kilometres from Placentia. The wounded whale towed the steamer, which ran with its engines at half-speed astern, for 1.6 kilometres. Even after a second line was attached and the vessel regained its full speed, the crew and whale fought all night, each with intractable tempers. Despite its injuries, the great whale fought on with surprising vigor for another half day, until it was killed by the captain's lance.

1904

Winnipeg, January. A former officer of Louis Riel claims that Riel's men dumped the body of Thomas Scott in the Red River after his execution in 1870.

Ottawa, March 11. Ottawa Silver Seven beat the Brandon Wheat Kings two games to none to win the Stanley Cup.

Canada, March. Canada's peacetime regular army and militia number 46,063, with the capacity to expand to 100,000 in wartime.

St. Louis, May 14. Montreal policeman Etienne Desmarteau wins Canada's first Olympic gold medal, in the hammer throw. George Seymour Lyon wins Canada's only other medal, a gold in golfing. It is Canada's first time participating in the Games.

Sydney, N.S., June 11. The steamer *Turbinia* arrives, becoming the first turbine merchant ship to cross the Atlantic.

Medicine Hat, Northwest Territories, June 15. Drillers strike a tremendous flow of natural gas, expected to lead to a boom.

Ontario, June 18. The last square timber raft departs down the Ottawa River.

Ottawa, June 24. The designation "Royal" is extended to the North West Mounted Police.

Canada, June. Women journalists set up the Canadian Women's Press Club.

Halifax, Oct. 12. A Canadian Arctic patrol aboard the *Neptune* commanded by Albert Low arrives after asserting Canadian sovereignty over the Arctic and Hudson Bay. They established a North West Mounted Police detachment at Cape Fullerton.

Windsor, Ont. The Ford Motor Co. of Canada begins building cars.

Cape Fullerton, Hudson Bay. The new police detachment here stops illicit trading between whalers and Indians in the area.

Ottawa. The head tax for Chinese immigrants is set at $500. The tax keeps Chinese women from coming to Canada because Chinese men cannot afford to pay for their wives, and single women cannot afford to pay for themselves.

Newfoundland. Forest fires destroy $20 million worth of marketable timber.

Rail commissioners have wide powers

Feb. 1, 1904

OTTAWA – A new Board of Railway Commissioners is in place today, following the passing of an enabling act in Parliament. It is, without a doubt, the supreme authority for railways in the country, with wide powers at its disposal. The BRC is in charge of regulating all freight and passenger rates throughout Canada. It can tell the railroads what types and qualities of services they have to offer the public, and it will be the watchdog on how they build their lines. As well, the board is the court where blame for railway accidents will be decided. It is, in short, the prince of the railways, comprised of three members: the Hon. A.G. Blair, former minister of railways, the Hon. M.E. Bernier, former minister of inland revenue, and James Mills, for many years president of the Ontario Agricultural College.

The Board of Railway Commissioners is expected to travel the Canadian Pacific and all of its branches. Commissioners will travel the Canadian Northern to Port Arthur [Thunder Bay], and inspect grain handling there. And doubtless they'll also want to get a look at the construction of the new Grand Trunk Pacific, which is due to be finished in 1911.

Murderer back in prison

The Daily Herald

Special Edition.

Cashel the American Desperado Captured this Afternoon.

SURROUNDED BY POSSE AND DRIVEN OUT BY FIRE.

GRAPHIC STORY OF THE MOST SENSATIONAL CASE IN THE HISTORY OF CANADA.

Calgary paper reports the capture.

Ernest Cashel in Calgary.

Jan. 24, 1904

CALGARY – A murderer who escaped from jail a few days before his Dec. 26 date with the hangman was recaptured today at a house just outside Calgary after exchanging gunfire with a police officer.

Ernest Cashel, who was sentenced to death for the murder of an Alberta rancher, was found hiding in the cellar of the house. He fired two shots at an unarmed officer, who retreated upstairs, grabbed a gun, and met the fugitive on the stairs. Cashel was shot in the heel, but returned to the cellar. Cashel, of Montana, threatened to kill himself, but he surrendered when police set the house on fire. He said he could have escaped to the U.S., but stayed in the Calgary area to rescue his brother John, who had been convicted of aiding his escape.

Cashel escaped after he was ordered out of his cell so it could be searched. When he was told go to back in, he waved two guns in the faces of three policemen, locked them in the cell, unlocked his shackles and walked off.

Canadian Pacific Railway buys 11 Ontario, 10 Quebec engines

The Canadian Pacific Railway needs more engines. One of their current ones is seen crossing the trestle over Surprise Creek in the Mountain subdivision.

March 29, 1904

MONTREAL – The Canadian Pacific Railway appears to be turning into a bit of a nationalist institution. At least that's how some people are interpreting the move by the CPR to purchase its new locomotives in Canada. The decision is a real change for the company, which, in the past, has purchased most of its engines from the United States and Scotland. But today the CPR announced that it is buying its next 21 locomotives at home.

Eleven will be built in Ontario, at the Kingston Locomotive Works. Ten more will be made at the plant in Longue Point, Que. All of the engines will be of the heavy freight class. They'll be used primarily to handle the shipment of western crops east to the docks at Montreal.

Mount Royal Club goes up in flames

Jan. 5, 1904

MONTREAL – The "Millionaires Club" was destroyed early this morning in a blaze that left one fireman and an unidentified occupant dead. Fireman James Hutt, 22, died when he attempted to penetrate the blazing Mount Royal Club at Stanley and Sherbrooke streets. Hutt was crushed when a granite cornice collapsed on him and a fellow firefighter who was taken to hospital with severe head injuries. A badly burnt body was found in the charred ruins of the opulent club and is presumed to be that of the night guard.

Ottawa disallows legislation in B.C.

March 25, 1904

OTTAWA – The federal government has disallowed British Columbia legislation aimed at reducing jobs available to Japanese and keeping them for white Canadians. Increases in immigration from Japan and the fact that most Japanese coming here are young literate men able to handle a variety of jobs have produced a surge of protests from unions, newspapers and devotees of racial purity. Few politicians resist this kind of pressure, and so voluntary limitation by the Japanese might be the answer.

Protests expected as Sikhs reach B.C.

July 1, 1904

VICTORIA, B.C. – Another contingent of Sikhs has arrived on a CPR liner from the Orient. The first group of Sikhs to reach B.C. arrived in April, and officials are bracing themselves for a flood of protests as a new kind of immigrant joins the Chinese and Japanese here. Sikhs have been leaving villages in northern India to look for work since the 1880s. Thousands of them are already working on farms in Australia. Now, the expanding economy here is attracting the Sikhs to B.C., and the CPR's ships make it easy to get here.

French Shore dispute settled in Nfld.

July 9, 1904

NEWFOUNDLAND – After nearly 200 years of fishing on the French Shore, the French government has finally relinquished its rights over part of the Newfoundland coast. In 1713, a treaty between Britain and France granted French fishermen the right to fish and dry their fish on the north and east coasts of the island of Newfoundland. The French agreed not to build permanent structures and not to stay on the island during the winter. The British agreed that British-Newfoundland fishermen would not interfere with the French. In 1783, the boundaries of the French Shore were adjusted somewhat, with the result that it consisted of all of the west coast and the Northern Peninsula.

Atlantic cod fishermen bring their catch to shore for the drying process.

The French Shore became a contentious issue after Newfoundland acquired responsible government in 1855. The French objected to any Newfoundlanders residing or fishing there, and the Newfoundland government resented the fact that the entire area was outside its jurisdiction. By the late 1800s, however, the French fishery on the Grand Banks had become much more important than its inshore fishery on the French Shore. Therefore, when the Anglo-French agreement was signed recently, France gave up its rights on the French Shore. In return, French rights over territories in West Africa were recognized.

Fire destroys Toronto wholesale district; $10M damage caused

The aftermath of the Toronto fire as seen on Bay Street north of Wellington.

April 19, 1904

TORONTO – Twelve hectares of downtown Toronto have been reduced to smouldering ruins, following a $10-million blaze in the wholesale district tonight. Miraculously, no lives were lost in the blaze, which began at 8:04 p.m. on the second floor of the E & S Currie Neckwear factory. In minutes flames spread from this Wellington Street building to the Gale Building next door. Whipped by high winds, it quickly moved to the area bounded by Bay and Yonge streets. Although the 200-man Toronto fire force was aided by men and equipment brought from London and Buffalo, the lack of adequate water pressure made the hoses seem like little more than squirt guns.

Laurier raises eyebrows by calling British general a "foreigner"

June 11, 1904

OTTAWA – An incident in the House of Commons yesterday shows how fragile are French- and English-speaking relations in this country. To make an impact on the unilingual English-speaking members, French-Canadian MPs must speak in English, as there are no simultaneous translation facilities in Parliament. Prime Minister Wilfrid Laurier, for instance, always speaks in English.

Yesterday, however, one small linguistic blunder cost the PM dearly, at least in imperialistic circles. Laurier referred to the British general in charge of the Canadian militia as a "foreigner" when he meant to say "stranger." Tories and Ontario newspapers have denounced the French-Canadian prime minister for describing an Englishman as a foreigner in Canada. ▷

Grey named next governor general

Earl Grey, the governor general.

Sept. 29, 1904

OTTAWA – The fourth Earl of Grey will succeed his brother-in-law Lord Minto as governor general of Canada. Grey was born to the service of royalty – literally. He was born in the Royal Palace at St. James, where his father was private secretary to Queen Victoria.

Grey's sister Lady Minto recently disclosed a curious family tie. On a visit to the Blood Indian reserve in Alberta, she claimed to be a descendant of Pocahontas and Englishman John Rolfe, who wed the Virginian Indian princess in 1614.

Grey, friendly and intelligent, sat in the Commons as a Liberal, and later, in the Lords as a peer. A staunch imperialist, he was commissioner of Rhodesia [Zimbabwe].

Giant hydraulic liftlock in operation

July 9, 1904

PETERBOROUGH, Ont. – One of the engineering feats of the modern world, the giant hydraulic liftlock on the Otonabee River, opened today. A huge crowd on the river bank waited out a heavy rainstorm to watch the steamboat *Stoney Lake* as it rode the lock chamber like an elevator from the upper river to the lower channel. The liftlock took eight years to build. It is the latest lock on the Trent-Severn Waterway, and allows boat traffic to travel from Rice Lake up the Otonabee through Peterborough to the Kawartha Lakes.

Work on the waterway began 70 years ago. When finished, it will run 386 kilometres across the height of land between Lakes Ontario and Huron, using rivers, lakes and manmade channels. Steamboats now use the waterway, and each spring thousands of logs are driven downstream to lumber mills.

Basically, the liftlock consists of two large water-filled chambers sitting on steel rams which slide up and down in deep wells. The two rams are connected in a closed hydraulic system. After a vessel enters the upper chamber, water is added and the additional weight causes it to descend. As it does so it pushes the other chamber upward. With a lift of almost 20 metres, the lock is the largest in the world. Builders used 20,000 cubic metres of concrete and 15,000 tons of metal in its construction. Another hydraulic lock is planned for Kirkfield.

A ship waits to be raised in the hydraulic liftlock in Peterborough.

Notorious bandit Bill Miner holds up train bound for Vancouver

Sept. 10, 1904

MISSION, B.C. – The notorious holdup artist Bill Miner has struck again. The Canadian Pacific transcontinental train, bound for Vancouver, was stopped near here this evening by a trio of masked men. The leader was described as elderly and grey-haired and can only be the wily Miner, wanted for a train robbery south of the line a year ago.

The men stopped the train by crawling over the roofs of several cars to the locomotive, where they held engineer Nat Scott at gunpoint. They ordered the fireman to unhook the passenger coaches and rode down the line with the mail and express cars. Threatening to blow up the train, the bandits compelled the clerk to open the safe and made off with an estimated $7,000 in cash and gold. The men escaped across the Fraser River in a rowboat and have vanished across the border without a trace.

Sealing steamer's back from Antarctic

Aug. 16, 1904

PLYMOUTH, England – A former Newfoundland sealing vessel arrived here today after relieving Robert Scott's Antarctic expedition. The *Terra Nova,* 450 tons, was built in Dundee in 1884 as a whaler/sealer, and was sent to the Newfoundland seal fishery the following year and subsequent years up to 1903 by St. John's sealing firms. The steamer had a successful career, and in its best season – 1891 – it brought in more than 35,000 seals. Britain last year purchased the ship as an icebreaker.

Spring floodwaters cover parts of Fredericton, N.B. Residents here assess the damage to property.

Alien Labour Bill to control immigration

Aug. 6, 1904

OTTAWA – The House of Commons has passed a new Alien Labour Bill, aimed at controlling various forms of immigration to Canada. The bill, in particular, makes it illegal to "falsely represent" the opportunities available in Canada to potential immigrants in other lands. Such frauds are perpetrated from time to time by unscrupulous agents who merely wish to sell more one-way tickets to this land to those who can least afford it. Just a few weeks back a number of Italians arrived in Montreal on the basis of such a lie.

The bill also stipulates that contractors, laborers, and even capital on Canadian railways be British in origin. Lawmakers fear foreigners – namely Americans – would be inclined to import any necessary items from their own countries, to the detriment of Canada.

As well, the bill allows government officials to exclude "undesirable immigrants" from entering the country, a term that is worrying some because of its vagueness and potential for discrimination. And, finally, the legislation answers American restrictions on Canadian contract laborers working in that country, by making the reverse case illegal here.

Officials tell farmers birds of prey are their greatest allies

Nov. 13, 1904

OTTAWA – The fruit division of Ottawa has stressed the role birds of prey play protecting orchards from destruction by mice, and officials have warned farmers not to kill owls and hawks, explaining they are the farmers' greatest allies. These birds feed almost exclusively on the small rodents that ravage orchards every year. In one night, a barn owl can catch as many mice as a dozen cats. Hawks favor rodents but also consume insects that devastate crops.

While owls work at night and hawks wage war on rodents day and night, both birds are of value; they can save an orchardist up to $50 a year in rodent damage.

Great horned owls are among the birds of prey that are useful to man.

Laurier-led Liberals win federal election over Borden, Tories

Nov. 3, 1904

OTTAWA – Sir Wilfrid Laurier has done it for a third time. He and his Liberals have swept the country in the general election, retaining their term in office that began eight years ago. The Liberals have won 139 seats, compared to the Tories' 75. It's a larger majority than the government held at dissolution, and is, without a doubt, a major embarrassment for Conservative leader Robert Borden.

However, Borden has other embarrassments to keep him occupied. Perhaps the most pressing is the fact that he himself was defeated in his own riding in Halifax. Close behind is the fact that his party, which held 18 Nova Scotian seats when the election was called, now has not even one in his home province.

Liberals across the country are beside themselves with joy. So are newspapers supporting them, most notably the Toronto *Globe*. Its front-page coverage, featuring silhouettes of men carrying brooms under the headline "Liberals Sweep the Country," is excessive in its pro-Liberal reporting. Included are phrases such as, "The Government has swept the country in a wonderful way," "Quebec is still wedded to Liberalism," and "Ontario is the least satisfactory spot in the record," because the province still has many Tory ridings.

Edmonton grows: gateway to Klondike incorporated as a city

The Great West Implement Co. is one of Edmonton's thriving businesses.

Nov. 7, 1904

EDMONTON – This centre of 8,350 people was incorporated as a city today and its boundaries have been extended. The Northwest Territories legislature granted the request for city status by Edmonton, which will add 960 hectares to its jurisdiction. Edmonton, first settled in 1795 when a fur-trading centre was established by the Hudson's Bay Company, came into its own in 1897 as a supply base in the gold rush, proclaiming itself the gateway to the Klondike. Despite the expansion, Edmonton is smaller than its southern rival, Calgary, which has a population of 12,000.

Ontario's Liberals discussing strategy

Nov. 24, 1904

TORONTO – This city's been taken over by the Liberals! That's an assessment any visitor might make today, following the arrival of 5,000 party delegates for a provincial convention. Delegates are here to help Premier George Ross and his government figure out the strategy for the next election campaign. The premier has made it plain that he wants to increase the narrow margin of seats by which he holds power. The Liberals will also be discussing temperance, railways, and roadbuilding in Ontario.

Imperial dockyards close; 300 jobs lost

Dec. 15, 1904

HALIFAX – Almost 300 skilled workmen will lose their jobs with the closure of the imperial dockyards. The British admiralty today announced closure by cable to the chief storekeeper. The facility, opened in 1770, is strictly for navy use and can provide speedy repairs to its warships. Some of the workers served for up to three decades at the imperial dockyards and its demise will be a big blow to the economy of Halifax. Still, Canadian forces will take over control of the great base.

Motorized vehicles such as this Model A Ford are becoming more common.

1905

Niagara Falls, Ont., Jan. 2. The Canadian Niagara Power Co. opens its new power house at Queen Victoria Park.

Dawson, Yukon, Jan. 20. Mining offices are closing as the town declines.

British Columbia, March 9. Indians on the Nass River are getting around a ban on Indian liquor consumption by using non-Indian names to order booze from mail order firms.

Ottawa, March 11. Ottawa Silver Seven beat Rat Portage [Kenora] Thistles two games to one for the Stanley Cup.

Canada, April 6. It is announced that all ships of the Canadian Pacific Atlantic fleet will be equipped with cold storage facilities to deliver perishable products to Britain.

Toronto, April 24. Kivas Tully, noted architect of prominent Ontario institutional buildings and churches, dies.

Montreal, June 4. Daily CPR service to Vancouver begins.

Ontario, July 12. Cree and Ojibwa Indians sign Treaty No. 9 with the federal and Ontario governments, surrendering a vast area of land in northern Ontario.

Quebec, July 24. Canadian and U.S. surveyors find that a strip of land home to about 4,500 people is not part of Vermont, as previously thought, but belongs to Canada.

Brockville, Ont., July 25. James Walsh, Royal North West Mounted Police superintendent and commissioner of the Yukon district during the Klondike gold rush, dies.

Canada, Sept. 1. Alberta and Saskatchewan become provinces under the Alberta and Saskatchewan Acts.

Germany. German physicist Albert Einstein proposes the theory of relativity. Embracing time, space, and motion, it says there are no absolute motions in the universe.

Ontario. The Ontario Rugby Football Union makes rule changes: it reduces teams to 12 men per side, adopts the snapback system of putting the ball into play, and requires the offensive team to make 10 yards on three downs.

Quebec. Wilfrid Picard travels around the province showing films, mostly religious ones.

Ontario. John Bayne Maclean buys the *Busy Man's Magazine* [*Maclean's*].

Tories topple Liberals in Ontario vote

Jan. 25, 1905

TORONTO – The Conservatives are back in power in Ontario after a 32-year absence. The long Liberal rule was broken today as the Tories, led by James P. Whitney, ousted Premier George Ross in a stunning landslide. Some 69 seats went Conservative, while only 29 went Liberal. The Tories evidently appealed to urban Ontario, and the party swept most urban ridings.

Five Liberal ministers were defeated, although Ross held on to Middlesex-West. The Liberal political machine that ran Ontario for decades is in shambles. Only weeks ago the party drew 5,000 delegates to a Toronto convention at Massey Hall. In that heady atmosphere, it seemed another term was assured. Now the bubble has burst, and Liberals are trying to figure out what went wrong. Some blame awful weather for keeping voters at home. But it seems that with a Liberal regime in Ottawa, Ontarians simply felt a strong Conservative government in Toronto would best protect their interests.

Battered brig back after 134-day journey

March 22, 1905

ST. JOHN'S, Nfld. – The brig *Grace* arrived yesterday after a journey from Italy that lasted 134 days. The *Grace* was sent by its owners, saltfish exporters Goodridge & Sons, with a cargo to Italy last September. It left Sicily with a load of salt on Nov. 6 bound for Barbados, and then home.

The *Grace* was battered by a number of storms from all points of the compass for 68 days, arriving in Barbados – as it was sinking – on Jan. 16. After repairs were made, the *Grace* loaded a cargo of molasses and arrived here safely. The captain reports that the voyage was one of the longest and hardest he has ever experienced. He and the crew will spend time at home before returning to sea.

Longfellow's Evangeline is off curriculum

Jan. 5, 1905

VANCOUVER – *Evangeline,* the sad story of lost love set against the backdrop of the British expulsion of the Acadians in 1755, will not be taught in British Columbia schools anymore. The superintendent of the board of education made the announcement tonight at a meeting of the Coast Teachers' Institute. Teachers said *Evangeline,* by American Henry Wadsworth Longfellow, is tainted with an anti-British spirit, and has become stale to them after many years of teaching it. Charles Lamb's *Tales from Shakespeare* is also being cut from the curriculum. Teachers said it does not encourage students to read Shakespeare.

While his cycling friends pause for a drink of water at the well, one young man is going to receive a whole jug full of water from some spying children.

Sifton quits cabinet over education law

Hon. Clifford Sifton, MP.

Feb. 28, 1905

BRANDON, Man. – Clifford Sifton yesterday submitted his resignation to Prime Minister Wilfrid Laurier, who accepted it this morning. This action has been rumored widely the past few days. Sifton's disagreement with his cabinet colleagues is based on Section 16 of the education legislation being proposed for Alberta.

The part of the legislation which Sifton finds offensive reaffirms the principle of separate schools, as is the case in the Northwest Territories Act of 1875. It permits a Protestant or Catholic minority to establish separate schools and to have an entitlement of a proportional share of public money.

Sifton says that new provinces should be permitted to establish their own school system in the style of their choice. By having Parliament establish the rules for education, the power of central Canada is being imposed upon those who live in each new province.

MP predicts Six Nations Indians to be absorbed

Jan. 27, 1905
OTTAWA – Today Frank Cockshutt, a Conservative opposition MP from Brantford, Ont., spoke most encouragingly in Parliament of the Six Nations Indians' educational progress. He foresaw that within three to five generations the Six Nations Indians will be absorbed into the Canadian nation.

For many years the Six Nations have been considered the showcase of Canada's Indian Department. Many Iroquois, particularly among the Mohawk, Tuscaroras and Oneidas, have adopted Christianity and have begun farming. In the summer, several large Indian farms employ a number of men, such is the scale of their operations.

Cockshutt is certain that further education will lead many Iroquois to enfranchise, the term used to describe the individual abandonment of Indian status and rights that exist under the Indian Act. The Six Nations have their own school board and run more than 10 schools on the reserve. Already a number of Iroquois children have gone on to high school in Brantford. A few farmers' sons have attended the agricultural college at Guelph. Other Iroquois students have entered the provincial Normal School in Toronto for teacher training. A Six Nations man obtained an engineering degree at McGill some years ago, and another from the reserve has earned his MD.

U.S. lumbermen block river, tempers flare

Mills such as Sinclair's Mill process great quantities of N.B. lumber.

May 27, 1905
GRAND FALLS, N.B. – Tempers flared on the St. John River today as Canadian lumbermen blew up a U.S. log boom blocking the Canadian side of the river and were stopped at gunpoint as they approached another. Levi Pond, in charge of N.B. lumber drives on this stretch of river bordering the U.S., told his foreman, a constable, to arrest the U.S. foreman for carrying a gun on Canadian soil. The Americans threatened to shoot.

A dancing bear entertains spectators in this New Brunswick town.

Farmer strikes oil thanks to a horse

April 3, 1905
WINDSOR, Ont. – Farmer William Angus has long believed that oil exists under his property near here. Repeated exploratory drilling failed to find it, but today a horse proved Angus right. It sunk almost out of sight while plowing a field. When it was dug out, oil followed it in a gushing stream. It seems the oil was so close to the surface, only a bit of topsoil kept it from bursting through. Now the oil is found and Angus is rich.

Acts creating prairie provinces approved

July 20, 1905
NORTHWEST TERRITORIES – The Alberta and Saskatchewan Acts today received vice-regal assent, clearing the way for the formation of two more distinct provinces within the Dominion of Canada. The legislation, introduced and passed by both the House of Commons and the Senate earlier this month, is set to go into effect on Sept. 1 of this year.

Most westerners are rejoicing over the news – but not all. While both new provinces will have exclusive rights to control the justice system and to administer and create laws governing municipal institutions, private property, civil rights, and public health, critics point out that neither will have control over public land and natural resources. Similarly, some are opposed to federal control over – and guarantees of – minority rights, particularly if it involves separate schools.

Nfld. fumes as free-trade deal cancelled

March 24, 1905
NEWFOUNDLAND – Yesterday morning instructions were given to customs officials in charge of dispensing bait licences to withhold them from American fishermen till further notice. Newfoundland is upset that the U.S. Congress recently cancelled the free-trade agreement negotiated by Prime Minister Robert Bond and the American secretary of state. Bond is convinced that Newfoundland needs free trade with the United States because of its potential as a market for the colony's fish. He offered supplies of bait as an inducement to free trade, and is now determined to withhold bait supplies until the Americans yield and agree to free trade. Observers are pessimistic this will happen.

Blunden Harbour is a Kwakiutl village on the British Columbia coast.

Indian traditions still alive at turn of the century

Otokuyicokoan, Sarcee Indian.

Nootka method of spearing fish.

This Cree hunter makes use of an auditory decoy to attract moose.

An elderly west coast Indian woman makes baskets in a traditional style.

The cradleboard is still a popular way for Indian mothers to carry children.

Cree Indian wears ornate headdress.

This Sarcee Indian camp in Alberta combines the modern and the traditional.

A totem pole stands in front of each family's dwelling in this B.C. village.

A Slavey Indian woman fishes through a hole in the ice at Hay River, N.W.T.

A group of Dogrib Indian boys at Great Slave Lake, Northwest Territories.

This Sarcee family clings to much of the traditional plains way of life.

Siupakic and Sikunnacio, Sarcee Indian girls, in front of their tepee.

A west coast woman prepares the family's catch of salmon.

Some Slavey Indian women tan hides at Hay River, Northwest Territories.

Saskatchewan brings 50,000 farms into the fold

Wheat, oats, barley and rye are grown

Sept. 1, 1905

SASKATCHEWAN – By a federal act given royal assent on July 20, the province of Saskatchewan today came into being as part of Confederation. Saskatchewan's economy is dominated by agriculture. More than 40 percent of its soil is arable, and wheat is the major crop. This year 460,000 hectares were planted in wheat and the yield has been 26 million bushels. Oats, barley and rye are also grown. Railway building across Canada is ushering in further development of the wheat farming base here as outside markets are opening up. This is critical if the province is to reach its potential as a wheat producer.

Soil and a favorable climate are the big factors in the developing wheat economy, but low production costs and good prices have helped. To provide a population base for the expanding agricultural economy, immigration has been increasing since the turn of the century, spurred by the free homestead policy. Great Britain and Europe, as well as eastern Canada and the United States, have provided many of the new settlers. In 1901, there were just over 13,000 farms in the newly created province. The total now is believed to be approaching 50,000. Saskatchewan is also developing livestock farming, particularly in cattle and hogs.

Rapidly expanding settlement is giving rise to a small but important forestry industry. Local lumber is being used for farm buildings as well as for ties in railway construction. Mining is another aspect of the economy of the new province, dating back to the 1880s when coal was mined on the Souris River banks near Estevan. By the turn of the century, production was 80,000 tons. The coal produced is lignite, and it is believed the Estevan field could become one of the biggest in Canada. So far, there has been little other mineral development.

Saskatchewan's isolation, together with its dependence on wheat and outside markets for it, leave the economy in a potentially vulnerable position. Developing the economy costs money, and therein lies the biggest plus of this new status as a province. For although Saskatchewan has not been given control of its natural resources, it is in a better position to borrow money and receive subsidies from Ottawa.

The vibrantly colored Western Red Lily is Saskatchewan's floral emblem.

Many Saskatchewan pioneers arrived in the territory by Red River cart trains such as the one shown here.

Saskatchewan soil has huge potential

1905

SASKATCHEWAN – Fertile soils on the plain south of the pre-Cambrian shield form the most important natural resource of this new province. It is here that the grain belt is located and growing of wheat is on the increase. It has the potential to be the largest producer in the world. In the southwest corner of the province lie higher and more rolling plains, where livestock farming is developing. Between the pre-Cambrian shield in the north and the grain belt is a belt of softwood forest. Coal in the Estevan area is being mined in increasing quantities. Saskatchewan is drained by four major basins, and the river bearing its name is Canada's fourth largest.

Agriculture reigns supreme in province of Alberta

Economy has close ties with railway age

Sept. 1, 1905

ALBERTA – With the railway network established and a new rust-free strain of wheat expected to be a success, Alberta gets the icing on the cake today with its creation as a new province of Canada. Agriculture is king of the economy here, thanks to suitable soil and rapidly expanding immigration. Hopes are specially high because of a new variety of hard spring wheat that is quick to mature and free of rust. The wheat, called Marquis, was developed last year by crossing Hard Red Calcutta with Red Fife. The completion of the CPR 20 years ago gave the area a means to take its wheat to market. Livestock raising is next in importance to the Alberta economy, with cattle, sheep, swine and poultry operations growing.

Coal, first mined in the Lethbridge area in 1872, is becoming an important mineral resource. In fact, Alberta's deposits of lignite, bituminous, and semi-anthracite coal may be the largest in Canada. By 1901, Blairmore, a community on the Crowsnest Pass on the CPR line, developed coal mines that attracted miners from Europe. Other minerals are not yet major factors in the economy. They include salt, limestone, sodium phosphate, peat moss and sulphur.

Surprisingly, the forestry industry has been slow to expand, despite the fact that half the province is covered with trees. Timber quality is not high and so far there has been little demand for it.

The economy of Alberta is linked closely with the railway age, and later this year a second major transcontinental line, the Canadian Northern Railway, will reach Edmonton and push west to the coast. It is expected to open up the northern part of the province, much the same as the CPR has in the south, and set the stage for Edmonton to grow as an economic rival to Calgary.

With the promise of future economic prosperity in the air, Edmonton residents ushered in provincial status today with a parade that included floats, hundreds of flags, and at least 1,500 schoolchildren. At the exhibition grounds, Gov. Gen. Earl Grey told the crowd that the federal government and "the energy of your own stout arms" made the creation of the province of Alberta possible.

The province of Alberta has as its floral emblem the beautiful Wild Rose.

Cattle ranching and wheat farming are taking over the Alberta plains, where herds of buffalo once roamed.

Oil and gas on tap in newest province

1905

ALBERTA – Oil and natural gas are believed to be the finds of the future in this new province. A prairie in the south, parkland in the central regions, boreal forest in the north and the Rocky Mountains in the west form the four main physical regions of Alberta. While the province supports both wheat farming and ranching, these industries may be surpassed some day by mineral resources. Coal is already well established, but oil and natural gas are believed to be plentiful. Natural gas was first found in 1883 by a CPR crew drilling for water near Medicine Hat. By 1903, the people in the town were cooking with gas. Further drilling elsewhere produced more gas but so far no oil. ▷

Wild robin banded to trace bird's path

Sept. 24, 1905

TORONTO – The gardens of Ontario residents seem to be the favorite nesting sites of the American robin. James Henri Fleming of Toronto took advantage of this circumstance when he placed a band on the leg of a robin nesting on his property. It is the first wild bird in Canada to be marked with a numbered, catalogued band. Fleming suspects that robins winter near Toronto. He hopes that someone will recover the marked bird in its winter habitat and communicate its whereabouts so that he may begin to trace the robin's path.

Blaze destroys 100 Summerside homes

Oct. 10, 1905

SUMMERSIDE, P.E.I. – It was a night of terror for the people of Summerside. A fire, beginning at the rail yards, rampaged through the town's residential district. The Summerside and Charlottetown fire departments brought the blaze under control, but not before it destroyed more than 100 homes. Fearing for their charges' safety, authorities let prisoners out of the courthouse jail, and those citizens who could not run from the flames had to seek safety "behind the lee side of board fences," says one witness.

Nanaimo miners end 5-month strike

March 9, 1905

NANAIMO, B.C. – A crippling strike which has closed the coal mines here for about five months is over. Miners are sadly preparing to go back down the pits. Sharp divisions between capital and labor are plaguing this province and causing anxiety for investors in Europe and North America. The politicians worry that the conflict is holding back the full development of B.C. resources. Who is to blame for the conflict? Supporters of each side blame the other. Workers argue that employers such as James Dunsmuir, whose family developed the mines near here, are growing rich by employing Oriental laborers to depress wage levels and by ignoring safety regulations. Employers in their turn accuse agitators of stirring up the men.

Now that the strike is over, the McBride government – and the employers – hope that the United Mineworkers of America, which led the strike for better pay and conditions, will be forced out of British Columbia.

Bourassa targets immigration policy

1905

OTTAWA – Immigration is threatening the Canadian dream of a bilingual nation, says Henri Bourassa, leading spokesman for Quebec's Nationalist party. He has taken a hard line against the settlement of newly opened territories by people whose mother tongue is neither English nor French.

Bourassa fears that these immigrants will join the English-speaking community in Canada, thus weakening the percentage, and position, of French-speaking Canadians. He says an English-speaking majority could easily impose its will on a French-speaking majority. The integration of large numbers of newcomers into the English-speaking community would, in Bourassa's opinion, make it impossible to create a bilingual nation from coast to coast.

Well-known Canadian authors Bliss Carman and his cousin Charles G.D. Roberts. Both were poets, but Carman worked as a journalist in the United States and Roberts wrote fiction, in particular animal stories.

Bernhardt interview sparks angry protest

Reclining Sarah Bernhardt in the final scene of La Dame aux Camélias.

Dec. 6, 1905

QUEBEC CITY – A mob of more than 100 threw stones and eggs at celebrated French actress Sarah Bernhardt here early this morning. The missiles missed the actress but hit members of her entourage as they emerged from the theatre after the evening performance. One of the many police on hand to protect her was also hit.

The violence came after the publication of an interview in which Bernhardt allegedly said French-Canadians were not really French, but descended from Iroquois. This, Bernhardt denies saying. But she stands by her statements that Canada is backwards when it comes to the arts. She was quoted as saying that Canada has "no painters, you have no literature, you have no sculptors, you have no poets. You have no men. You have no men!"

Edmonton celebrates as last track is laid

Nov. 24, 1905

EDMONTON – The Canadian Northern Railway line to Edmonton was completed this morning, putting the city on a transcontinental line at last. After the last piece of track was laid at 10:30 a.m., a public holiday for the afternoon was declared. Thousands of onlookers watched as Alberta Lt.-Gov. George H.V. Bulyea drove home the silver spike securing the first rail to reach the station.

The line's roots go back to 1896, when Donald Mann and William Mackenzie bought the charter of the Lake Manitoba Railway and Canal Company. Direct access from here to Winnipeg on this new line is now possible in just 25 hours. Eventually, it will be extended west to the British Columbia coast.

Bell's kite carries man up and away

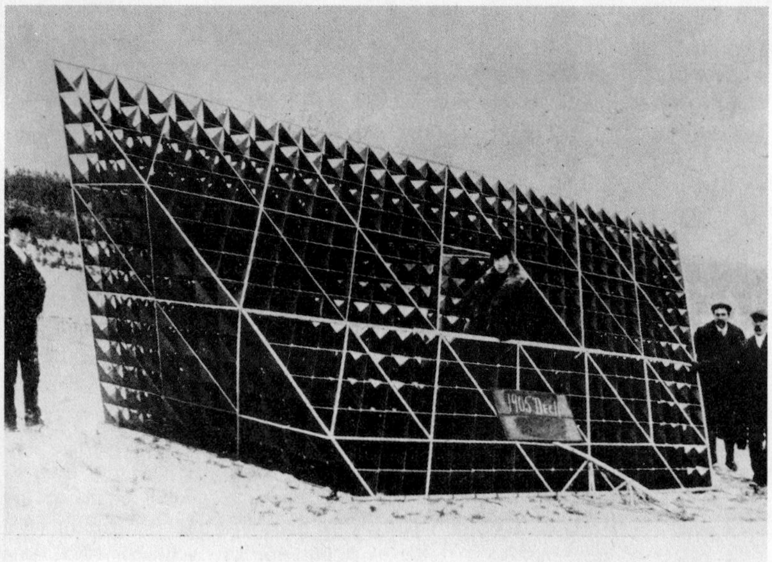

One of Dr. Alexander Graham Bell's experimental kites, Siamese Twins.

Dr. Bell lectures to a group of scientists on the principle of his tetrahedral kites and his theories of flight.

Dec. 28, 1905

BADDECK, N.S. – Alexander Graham Bell's tetrahedral cell kite lifted a man nine metres into the air above this Cape Breton village today. Riding the kite was Neil McDermid, who weighs 165 pounds. Bell has done a lot of experimental work with the tetrahedral design, which has four plane surfaces.

He also did experiments with heavier-than-air flight before the Wright brothers first flew in 1903. Flight is just one of the interests of Bell, who moved from his native Scotland to Brantford, Ont., in 1870. Most famous for inventing the telephone, Bell has spent much of his life teaching the deaf to speak. He now lives in the U.S. but has a summer home here.

Scott leads Liberals to victory in first Saskatchewan vote

Dec. 13, 1905

REGINA – Walter Scott and his Liberals have won the first provincial election in Saskatchewan, garnering 16 seats and 52.2 percent of the popular vote. Led by Frederick W. Haultain, the Provincial Rights party took the remaining nine seats in the Assembly. Scott was appointed provisional premier by Lt.-Gov. Amédée Forget on Sept. 5, the day after the inauguration of the province and the swearing-in of Forget himself as lieutenant-governor. Haultain, who advocates no party government, had been the premier of the Northwest Territories.

Great preparation went into this first election in the new province of Saskatchewan. Immigrants were wooed and those eligible were even made citizens. Campaign literature was printed in several languages. Status Indians, of course, do not have the right to vote.

Liberals in Alberta win by a landslide

Sept. 11, 1905

EDMONTON – The Liberals swept to victory today in the first election in the newly created province of Alberta. Even Conservative leader Richard B. Bennett fell victim to the landslide. Not all the results are yet in, but the Liberals, the governing party by appointment since the new provincial government was formed 10 days ago, will likely hold 20 of the 25 seats in the first parliament. The Liberals lead in 18 seats and are assured of at least one more as both candidates in Peace River riding support Premier A.C. Rutherford's Liberals.

Bennett lost in Calgary to Liberal W.H. Cushing, formerly minister of public works in the territorial government. Bennett ran in a Conservative city, but was unpopular with leading members of his party in Calgary. Also, with the Grand Trunk Pacific under construction, Liberals had questioned his neutrality on railway issues because of his position as solicitor for the CPR.

Last of the Cariboo camels imported from California is dead

1905

KAMLOOPS, B.C. – The last of the Cariboo camels has died on a ranch near here. It was one of the 23 imported from California more than 40 years ago to carry supplies up the Cariboo Road to the goldfields. The camels could carry some 180 kilograms, more than any of the horses or mules in use at that time could carry. In 1863, after about a year's work, the camels were let go because the rough rocky tracks damaged their feet and their smell terrified the oxen, horses and mules so much that they stampeded and upset their loads. The camels also upset the humans. They were hard to handle, spat when angry, and, like goats, would eat soap or clothes. Some camels were sold, others killed for meat, and some roamed wild, living off the land. One was bought by its handler and lived on his ranch for 40 years. The other day it leaned against a tree, and, still on its feet, died.

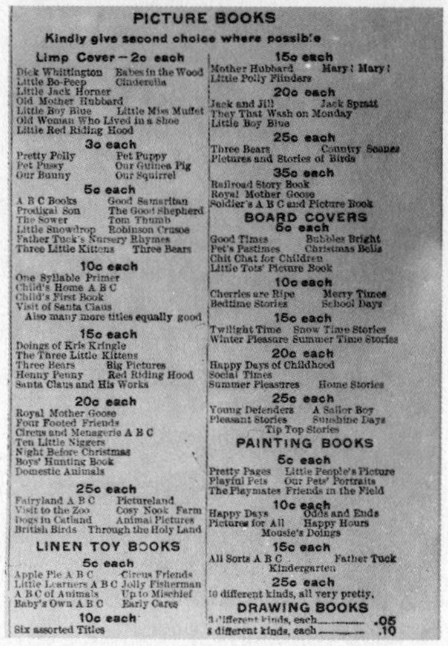

PICTURE BOOKS

Kindly give second choice where possible

Limp Cover – 2c each

Dick Whittington, Babes in the Wood, Little Bo-Peep, Cinderella, Little Jack Horner, Old Mother Hubbard, Little Boy Blue, Little Miss Muffet, Old Woman Who Lived in a Shoe, Little Red Riding Hood

3c each

Pretty Polly, Pet Puppy, Pet Pussy, Our Guinea Pig, Our Bunny, Our Squirrel

5c each

A B C Books, Good Samaritan, Prodigal Son, The Good Shepherd, The Sower, Tom Thumb, Little Snowdrop, Robinson Crusoe, Father Tuck's Nursery Rhymes, Three Little Kittens, Three Bears

10c each

One Syllable Primer, Child's Home A B C, Child's First Book, Visit of Santa Claus

Also many more titles equally good

15c each

Doings of Kris Kringle, The Three Little Kittens, Three Bears, Big Pictures, Henny Penny, Red Riding Hood, Santa Claus and His Works

20c each

Royal Mother Goose, Four Footed Friends, Circus and Menagerie A B C, Ten Little Niggers, Night Before Christmas, Boys' Hunting Book, Domestic Animals

25c each

Fairyland A B C, Pictureland, Visit to the Zoo, Cosy Nook Farm, Dogs in Catland, Animal Pictures, British Birds, Through the Holy Land

LINEN TOY BOOKS

5c each

Apple Pie A B C, Circus Friends, Little Learners A B C, Jolly Fisherman, A B C of Animals, Up to Mischief, Baby's Own A B C, Early Cares

10c each

Six assorted Titles

15c each

Mother Hubbard, Mary! Mary!, Little Polly Flinders

20c each

Jack and Jill, Jack Spratt, They That Wash on Monday, Little Boy Blue

25c each

Three Bears, Country Scenes, Pictures and Stories of Birds

35c each

Railroad Story Book, Royal Mother Goose, Soldier's A B C and Picture Book

BOARD COVERS

5c each

Good Times, Bubbles Bright, Pet's Pastimes, Christmas Bells, Chit Chat for Children, Little Tots' Picture Book

10c each

Cherries are Ripe, Merry Times, Bedtime Stories, School Days

15c each

Twilight Time, Snow Time Stories, Winter Pleasure, Summer Time Stories

20c each

Happy Days of Childhood, Social Times, Summer Pleasures, Home Stories

25c each

Young Defenders, A Sailor Boy, Pleasant Stories, Sunshine Days, Tip Top Stories

PAINTING BOOKS

5c each

Pretty Pages, Little People's Picture, Playful Pets, Our Pets' Portraits, The Playmates, Friends in the Field

10c each

Happy Days, Odds and Ends, Pictures for All, Happy Hours, Mousie's Doings

15c each

All Sorts A B C, Father Tuck, Kindergarten

25c each

10 different kinds, all very pretty.

DRAWING BOOKS

different kinds, each .05

different kinds, each .10

Page from an Eaton's catalogue.

J. Eaton and his builder, Jack McGee, lay the last stone in Winnipeg's new Eaton store in 1905. Timothy Eaton opened his first shop in Toronto in 1869 with the slogan "one price for all." As his business prospered, he added a mail order catalogue so that he could reach customers across the country. Now, with the opening of the Winnipeg store, he is looking to expand.

1906

British Columbia, Jan. 24. 120 people drown when the steamer *Valencia* sinks after hitting a reef off the west coast of Vancouver Island.

Los Angeles, February. Canadian Tommy Burns defeats Marvin Hart in 20 rounds to win the world heavyweight boxing chamionship, the first Canadian to win the title.

Britain, March 8. A government publication states the British Empire occupies a fifth of the globe's land and has a population of 400 million.

Quebec, March 9. The legislature legally recognizes caisses populaires (credit unions).

Ottawa, March 17. Montreal Wanderers beat Ottawa Silver Seven for the Stanley Cup.

Winnipeg, April 9. A strike against the Winnipeg Electric Railway ends when conductors and motormen accept the company's offer for wage increases and a regulated 10-hour day.

Athens, May 1. William Sherring of Hamilton wins the Olympic marathon.

Saskatchewan, May 19. Gabriel Dumont, Louis Riel's first lieutenant and military director of the Northwest Rebellion, dies on his farm near Batoche.

Esquimalt, B.C., May 22. British troops leave the naval base at Esquimalt, the only remaining permanent British military presence in Canada except for Halifax naval base.

Canada, May 30. Statements of Canadian chartered banks show that Toronto is the chief banking centre of Canada.

Hamilton, Dec. 7. The bitter and violent Hamilton street railway strike ends as strikers return to work, pending arbitration.

United States, Dec. 24. Canadian inventor Reginald Fessenden makes the first public radio broadcast of music and voice. Earlier in the year, he made the first two-way voice transmission by radio.

Regina. Canada's motto, From Sea to Sea, is officially used for the first time when it is engraved on the mace of the legislature.

Ottawa. The government grants Tagish Charlie, an Indian, the privilege of drinking intoxicants, exempting him from the law prohibiting Indians from drinking in consideration for his role in starting the Klondike gold rush.

Burns boxes way to heavyweight crown

Champion boxer Tommy Burns.

Feb. 23, 1906

LOS ANGELES – Boxer Tommy Burns became the first Canadian to win the world heavyweight championship today when he won a 20-round decision over former champ Marvin Hart. Burns, who stands just 5-foot-7 and weighs less than 175 pounds, taunted Hart from the outset, prompting him to lose his temper and ultimately his crown. As an enraged Hart chased Burns wildly around the ring, the Canadian scored with sharp punches. Both fighters were standing at the end, but the decision was not in doubt. Burns, born near Hanover, Ont., took up boxing after punching out a big second mate on a Lake Erie boat on which he worked.

British transfer garrison over to Canada

June 18, 1906

HALIFAX – Gen. Sir Charles Parsons today handed over imperial military property to Col. C.W. Drury of the Canadian militia, a transfer that marks another step in Canada assuming full responsibility for her own defences.

British garrisons have been located in Canada for 200 years. Most were removed by 1871, however, the naval bases at Esquimalt, B.C., and Halifax remained under British army control until this year. Canada offered to take over for the bases, which have declined in importance as the Royal Navy concentrated its ships in home waters to face Germany's growing fleet.

The formal transfer actually changes very little. In the South African War, Canada supplied the troops for the Halifax garrison, freeing imperial units for combat. Since then the garrison has been composed largely of Canadians paid for by the British government. The new arrangements give Canada full title to the bases, but also mean formal expansion of the Canadian militia with costs being borne by Canadian taxpayers.

The first legislature of the new province of Alberta took place on March 15 of this year. The first premier is Alexander Cameron Rutherford.

New co-operative set to market grain for prairie farmers

Jan. 27, 1906

SINTALULTA, Sask. – Prairie farmers now have their own grain-marketing co-operative. A large and enthusiastic gathering of farmers today voted to form the Grain Growers' Grain Company. The function of the new co-operative will be to sell the grain purchased from producers by their local grain co-operatives.

Many men were responsible for making this dream a reality. The leaders who did the preliminary work on the new association are E.A. Partridge, David Railton, Sr., A.J. Quigley, William Hall, and Thomas S. McLeod. All of them have been working on the proposal for several months.

The members of the Grain Growers' Grain Company expect that their ambitious new executive will purchase a seat on the Winnipeg Grain Exchange in order that the company may engage in active grain trading. The stock shares are currently being sold at $25 each, with a limit of four shares per person. No matter what number of shares are held, the shareholders are limited to a single vote. No action will be taken to appoint a provisional board of directors until sufficient stock has been sold to assure incorporation.

Captain conquers Northwest Passage

Aug. 30, 1906

POINT BARROW, Alaska – After three winters in the Arctic, a Norwegian ship commanded by Capt. Roald Amundsen rounded Point Barrow today to become the first vessel to travel the Northwest Passage across the top of America.

The 42-ton *Gjoa*, with a crew of six and only a 13-horsepower engine, began its journey in Davis Strait in the summer of 1903. After spending two winters iced in at King William Island, the vessel reached King Point near the mouth of the Mackenzie River. But before it could continue, it was again forced to stop for the winter.

Bruchési's crusade targets Sunday fun

Feb. 18, 1906

MONTREAL – Archbishop Paul Bruchési has struck a blow against booze by calling for a ban on many Sunday activities. The powerful archbishop launched his temperance crusade in a pastoral letter issued today.

The statement calls for citizens to refrain from such popular activities as horse racing, baseball, political meetings, public excursions, theatrical performances, concerts, dances and functions organized for charitable purposes. Bruchési believes such public gatherings lead to the intemperate consumption of alcohol. The ban will not be well-received in the east end of Montreal, where the prohibited activities are particularly popular.

Free trip abroad not so free after all

Feb. 6, 1906

PORTLAND, Maine – Several independent shipping lines today reported that unscrupulous and deceitful shipowners are luring indigent Canadians onto cattle ships headed for England and Europe. Ads for the voyage promise that good wages will be paid for a little work aboard ship; instead, the men – many from Toronto – are paid a pittance and the work is arduous.

French author wins in copyright battle

March 23, 1906

MONTREAL – In a decision favoring Parisian novelist Jules Mary, a Montreal judge ruled today that the international copyright act overrides Canadian copyright law. Mary had filed a suit against the Literary Production Co. of Montreal, charging that it had pirated the use of his book, *La Tante Berceuse*. The international copyright act cited was drawn up in 1886, when it was approved at a Berne, Switzerland, convention. It was later ratified by Britain's parliament. The books will be confiscated and damages awarded.

Railway strike in Winnipeg turns ugly

March 30, 1906

WINNIPEG – Soldiers have set up a machine-gun at the corner of Main and Henry to maintain what Mayor Thomas Sharpe calls "order upon the streets and public places of the city" following two days of bitter violence in the strike at the Winnipeg Electric Railway Company. The company's motormen and coachmen are the ones who are on strike, but it is the citizens of Winnipeg who are taking their fight to the streets with all the zeal of a crusade.

When the company tried to maintain service with strikebreakers yesterday, most citizens refused to go along for the ride and walked to work sporting "We Walk" tags on their lapels and hats to show their solidarity with the strikers. Violence flared yesterday morning outside city hall, where two carts had conveniently broken down on the railway tracks. When a railway car manned by axe-wielding strikebreakers rolled up, a crowd of strike sympathizers surrounded it, smashed its windows and fenders, and put it out of service. Crowds chased the cars still in operation through the streets, until by one in the afternoon the system was shut down.

Similar violence erupted today when the company tried to mount service again. The mayor read the Riot Act standing on the back seat of his car, and ordered the soldiers of the Canadian Mounted Rifles to clear the streets. The soldiers ran into problems, but dispersed the crowd. The strike is unresolved.

Cars are being damaged in the current Winnipeg streetcar workers' strike.

Ontario approves formation of Hydro-Electric Power Commission

May 14, 1906

TORONTO – The move to provide Ontarians with electricity at the lowest possible cost took a major step today, with the Hydro-Electric Power Commission of Ontario [Ontario Hydro] being created. The commission was formed by the Tory government of Premier James Whitney, who has long been an advocate of taking electricity from profit-oriented private companies and getting it to the people as cheaply as possible.

The major focus of this action is Niagara Falls, a site where some hydroelectric generating stations are already in operation. The commission's first likely project is to send some of this power to Toronto via "transmission wires."

Winter Evening, Quebec by Maurice Cullen shows impressionist influence.

MPs vote to keep their high salaries

May 9, 1906

OTTAWA – In a move that was not unexpected, the House voted overwhelmingly against an attempt to override the pay increases given to them in the last session of Parliament. The vote was 167-9 against repeal, with both Prime Minister Wilfrid Laurier and opposition leader Robert Borden voting to keep their wages at a healthy $483 a month. In 1867 an MP earned the equivalent of $173 a month, in 1895 it was $250, and today it is $483. Those defending the raise argue that public office must pay well to attract suitable candidates.

B.C. Indian chiefs take beefs to king

July 12, 1906

WINNIPEG – Three British Columbia Indian chiefs passed here last evening on their way to see King Edward VII. At a brief stop at the railway depot here, the delegation's leader, Squamish Chief Joe Capilano, said they will lay grievances concerning land claims before the king. He says B.C. Indians have not got what they were promised from Canada and Britain. He also complains of the activities of government Indian agents.

Island's 3 counties all for prohibition

July 6, 1906

CHARLOTTETOWN – All of Prince Edward Island's counties have voted to abide by the 1900 Act Prohibiting the Sale of Intoxicating Liquor. The act could not go into effect until all of the counties had voted to accept its provisions. Queen's County accepted the legislation immediately, and now, with the agreement of Prince and King's counties, P.E.I. is the first to embrace provincewide prohibition.

Mounties nab train robbery suspects

The posse returns to Kamloops after capturing suspected train robber Bill Miner. Miner is seated in the democrat, wrapped in a blanket.

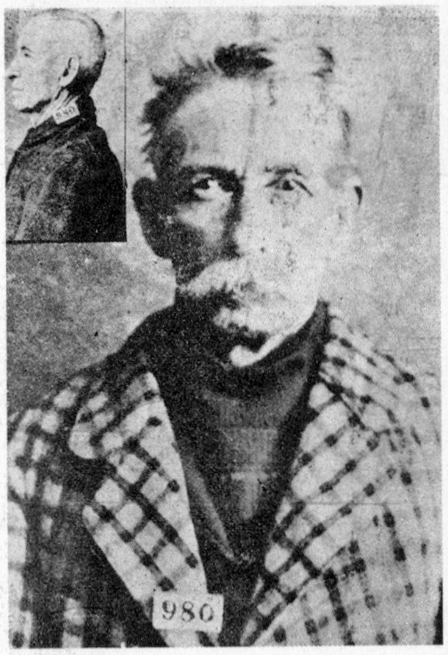

A 40-year career of robbery has made William Miner, the "Gentleman Bandit," a legendary figure.

May 14, 1906

QUILCHENA, B.C. – Const. W.L. Fernie and a contingent of Mounties today captured three alleged train robbers, suspects in last week's daring holdup of the Canadian Pacific Railway's westbound Imperial Limited. Although the bandits took less than $100 – overlooking more than $30,000 in the process – their arrest follows the largest manhunt in B.C. to date, launched by the CPR as an attempt at saving face.

Fernie first confronted the three, one of whom's age and description matches that of legendary American outlaw Bill Miner, at their campsite. Not convinced they were prospectors, as the three had claimed, Fernie returned later with the Mounties. One of the three suspects panicked and fled into the bush. The police pursued and shot the desperado in the leg.

The latest robbery bore all the trademarks of a Bill Miner holdup. Known as "The Gentleman Bandit" for his polite nature, Miner has made a career of robbery that has spanned 40 years. He is thought to be responsible for a similar robbery in B.C. two years ago.

Lord's Day Act makes sure Sunday is an official day of rest

St. Paul's Roman Catholic Church is in Toronto at the corner of Power and Queen Streets. The church has supported the Lord's Day Alliance of Canada.

July 11, 1906

OTTAWA – Sunday has officially been made a day of rest in Canada. Today the Senate passed the Lord's Day Act, already approved in the Commons by Sir Wilfrid Laurier's government. The act restricts activities on Sundays to prevent business interests from turning it into another work day.

Support for the bill has come from a diverse group. The idea originally came from the Lord's Day Alliance of Canada, organized by the Presbyterian church in 1888. Backed by many Protestant faiths, it aimed to reverse the increasing secularization of Sunday.

Over the years the Lord's Day Alliance managed to win the support of the Roman Catholic church, and labor to boot. Labor's motivation wasn't religious. Its leaders saw the campaign as a way to ensure a legislated day of rest.

Close finish ends ships' race to port

June 29, 1906

QUEBEC CITY – Spectators gathered at Dufferin Terrace and lined the docks today as two transatlantic steamers, the recently-built Allan turbine *Virginian* and the older, government-owned *Ottawa*, raced into port neck-and-neck, the latter forging a slight lead at the end, proving herself the faster ship.

The two began the impromptu race nine days ago, leaving Liverpool, England, within two hours of each other. Once across the Atlantic, the race continued up the St. Lawrence despite each vessel being required to make separate stops: the *Ottawa* took the lead as the *Virginian* delivered mail to Rimouski, fell behind after stopping at the Grosse Ile quarantine station for 35 minutes, then managed to catch up at Ile d'Orléans.

Chipewyan, Cree to sign Treaty 10

Fall 1906

SASKATCHEWAN – The Chipewyan and Cree of northern Saskatchewan and Alberta have been brought into the treaty process. Treaty No. 10 covers an area of roughly 220,150 square kilometres in the northern portions of these two western provinces.

The natives themselves had first called for treaty negotiations more than 20 years ago, as they wished that the annuity payments, medical care, and other treaty benefits given to the Treaty 6 Indians to the south be extended to them. As the land, like much of that in the Treaty 5 and 8 areas, is unsuitable for agriculture, the Canadian government was reluctant, at first, to extend treaty provisions to the area. It was the creation of the provinces of Alberta and Saskatchewan last year that helped to convince the federal government to proceed with Treaty 10. Once it is signed all of Alberta and Saskatchewan will be covered under treaty.

Mining boom ends "harvest excursions"

"Harvest excursion" trains like this no longer pass through Cape Breton.

Aug. 24, 1906

SYDNEY, N.S. – The ongoing mining boom on Cape Breton has resulted in a war for workers ... one the mine companies have won for now. Each summer the Canadian Pacific Railway organizes "harvest excursions" – westbound trains taking unemployed eastern laborers to the prairies to help in the harvest. Well, such is the demand for miners here, that the CPR has been forced to stop staging these trips from Cape Breton. The pressure resulted after the first train went through, taking with it hundreds of men from Glace Bay. The second train was cancelled.

The whole situation is a telling sign of the boom taking place here on Cape Breton Island. Gone are the sleepy days. Instead of unemployment, men are in demand for both the coal and steel industries.

Power of Niagara expected to boost industry in Toronto

Nov. 19, 1906

TORONTO – The power of Niagara – electric power – is now driving lights and streetcars in Toronto. Today electricity started to flow on transmission lines running from the generating station at Niagara, along the lakeshore to the city. A current capable of supplying 10,000 to 15,000 horsepower is now a reality, one that is jointly utilized by both the Toronto Electric Light Company and the Toronto Street Railway. The cost is running at $35-$40 per horsepower.

The arrival of such cheap electricity heralds a new era in Toronto's industrial history. As more transmission lines are constructed from the falls, more and more companies will be able to switch from steam power or expensive privately-generated electricity to this plentiful form of power. It will likely result in an industrial boom, as the costs of production are reduced.

Immigration to Quebec pegged at 96,000

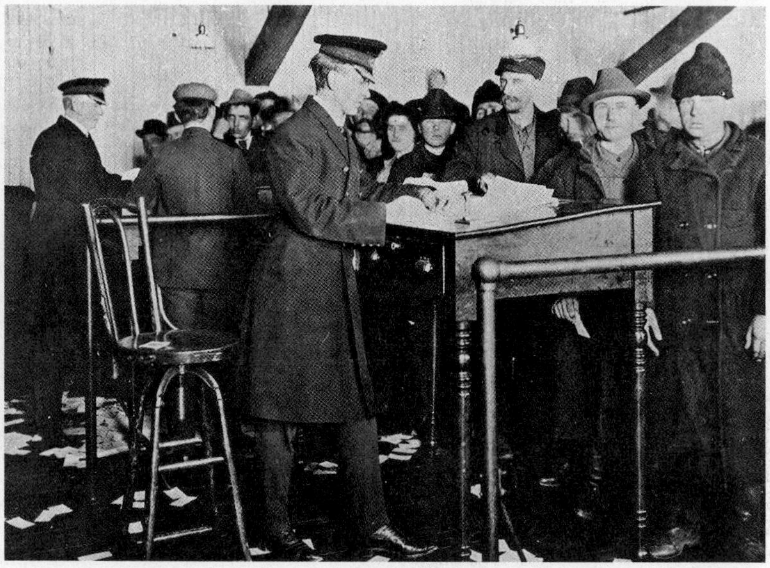

Record numbers of new arrivals are keeping immigration officials hopping.

Sept. 20, 1906

QUEBEC CITY – The first nine months of the year have seen the largest influx of immigrants to Quebec in the history of the St. Lawrence. Immigration officials report that to date 96,000 newcomers have passed through the St. Lawrence, 85 percent of them of British origin. Officials note that of the total number of new arrivals, only six percent plan to move on to the United States. With the immigration season not yet over, another 8,000 settlers are expected on ships bearing their full quota.

Rioting plagues Hamilton streetcar strike

Nov. 23, 1906

HAMILTON, Ont. – About 10,000 people took to the streets tonight as the Hamilton Street Railway Company strike worsened. So vast were the crowds, and so angry was their mood, that the police could do little to stop their rioting and looting. So bad is the situation, that 110 regular soldiers are being brought to Hamilton, and the city is to be put under military rule. The heart of the problem is the HSRC's decision to use strikebreakers to run its streetcars. As it turns out, there are only enough available to run on the King Street East line, and so that's where all the trouble has been focused. The cars have been pelted with volleys of rocks and bricks as they try to pass through the mob.

Health board fears smallpox epidemic

Oct. 30, 1906

MONCTON – It is feared that the smallpox outbreak in Kent County north of here will spread. The Moncton Board of Health said today an investigation has turned up at least 100 cases. Quarantine was not imposed quickly enough and some people exposed to the disease have left. These include four lumber camp workers believed to be in this city and for whom the health board is searching.

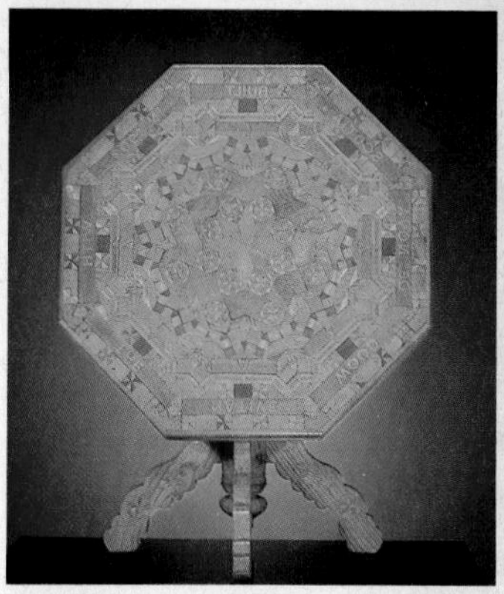

This tilt-top table has a complex inlaid design made with oak, maple, birch, ash, beech and cherry.

1907

Montreal, Jan. 21. The Kenora Thistles defeat the Montreal Wanderers to win the Stanley Cup.

Toronto, Jan. 31. Timothy Eaton, founder of T. Eaton Co., dies.

Savannah, Georgia, March 3. Oronhyatekha, one of Canada's first Indian doctors and successful supreme chief ranger of the Independent Order of Foresters, dies.

Winnipeg, March 25. The Montreal Wanderers defeat the Kenora Thistles to win the Stanley Cup. The cup is awarded twice in 1907.

Los Angeles, May 8. Canadian Tommy Burns defeats American Jack O'Brian in 20 rounds to win the world's light heavyweight boxing championship.

Cobalt, Ont., July. Some 2,500 members of the Cobalt Miners Union go on strike in Ontario's first mining strike.

New Westminster, B.C., Aug. 8. American train robber Bill Miner, captured last year, escapes from prison and returns to the U.S.

Baddeck, N.S. Alexander Graham Bell, J.A.D. McCurdy, F.W. Baldwin and a group of engineers found the Aerial Experiment Association to experiment in flying machines.

Toronto. Pharmacist and bottler John J. McLaughlin develops Canada Dry Ginger Ale.

Victoria. The legislature passes the Natal Act, designed to restrict Asian immigrants, but Lt.-Gov. James Dunsmuir refuses to approve the act.

Quebec. The National Saint-Jean Baptiste Federation is founded to link the province's few French-speaking laywomen's groups.

Quebec. Catholic trade unions are formed in various dioceses under the leadership of the clergy who fear the left-wing and anti-clerical bent of international unions.

Ottawa. The government passes the Industrial Disputes Investigation Act. The act delays strikes and lockouts in public utilities and mines until conciliators investigate the dispute.

Ontario. Many residents of the Thunder Bay and Rainy River districts support secession from Ontario.

Toronto. The Royal Alexandra Theatre, designed by John Lyle, is completed.

Coal strike leads to one cold winter

Jan. 19, 1907

GRENFELL, Sask. – The Saskatchewan prairies seem colder than usual this winter. The Alberta coal strike last year has left people without means to heat their homes. So bad is the situation that some people are dismantling furniture and buildings to burn in heaters.

Near Grenfell, some men, desperate but honest, tapped the only source of coal available to them. They stopped a train and asked to buy some of its coal. When they were refused, they chained a log to the track to prevent the train from moving. The men then took the picks and shovels they had hidden in the snow and helped themselves to the coal car. They left enough fuel to keep the train going until it could restock. Each man kept track of the amount of coal he had taken. They then went into town and reported themselves to the authorities, giving their names and the amount of coal they had taken, and offering payment.

Wife snubs spouse to live in Canada

June 22, 1907

DETROIT – Patriotism won out over love in a marital dispute between a Canadian woman and her American husband. A Michigan court judge granted William Roepke a divorce on the grounds of three years estrangement when his wife Anna refused to accompany him to live in the United States.

"She said she didn't like the country, wouldn't live here and under no circumstances would have children on American soil," the husband testified. "She declared she was a good Canadian for that. I replied that I was too good an American to have my children born under the British flag."

Roepke says he and his wife then quarrelled, and she finally left for Winnipeg. He followed her there and offered to bring her to the U.S. and set her up in a good home. "This she wouldn't agree to so I left her there," Roepke told the court. The ultra-patriotic couple were married in Cleveland in 1903.

Cattle starving to death

Cattle that live unprotected on the ranges are suffering this winter.

Jan. 29, 1907

LETHBRIDGE, Alta. – The heyday of the large cattle ranches is over, a development brought about by a natural tragedy. Thousands of steers and cows have starved to death as a blizzard sweeps southern Alberta. Very few ranchers will escape large losses this winter – the worst in 20 years. Last week some 10,000 cattle stampeded through Lethbridge, seeking food and shelter from the wind and snow. Houses, stores and barns were damaged before the animals could be driven out onto the range. Now it is learned that 6,000 starving cattle have invaded Macleod, causing widespread damage before cowboys managed to drive them out.

The cattle industry here has flourished for two reasons, the first being the generous treatment afforded investors in the ranching business. They were given control of large tracts of government land and were protected, until recently, by policies which slowed the flow of settlers. This policy's now changed. The second reason is the climate. Southern Alberta has relatively mild winters, and snow is usually melted by chinooks (warm winds). This means that there is some winter grass, and so ranchers can leave their cattle out in winter to forage for themselves. In fact, some ranchers do not even put up any hay for the cattle.

It is this trust in the weather that will cost the ranchers dearly. For the poor, starving cattle it means painful deaths in gullies and along railway tracks as they huddle to escape the blizzards. The occasional chinook melts the snow, but then the bitter cold returns and freezes the melted snow into ice. The cattle, wildly searching for food when the winds die down, crash through the ice and cut their hooves and legs.

Operators find long shifts too stressful

Jan. 31, 1907

TORONTO – Almost 400 female telephone operators have walked out on the Bell Company, claiming that a new work schedule is too demanding. The company wants the operators to work eight hours straight, instead of the present five. The operators refuse, saying the work is too stressful to stand for such a period of time. Their union is working toward a settlement through William Lyon Mackenzie King, deputy labor minister.

Cities compete for Alberta university

March 13, 1907

EDMONTON – The government has pledged to establish the University of Alberta by 1908. The news heightens speculation about the site of such an institution – already a big concern in Edmonton and Calgary. Edmontonians say the logical place would be beside the Saskatchewan River, opposite the site of the new legislature. But Calgarians argue that since Edmonton became the provincial capital, they deserve the university.

Top court in Sask. will sit in Regina

Aug. 3, 1907

REGINA – Saskatchewan now has its own Supreme Court, thanks to an act passed in the legislature. The new court in Regina will have five judges to hear both original and appeal cases. As well, the province has been divided into eight District Court regions, each with its own judge. And the act increases juries from six to 12 members.

Meanwhile, the Law Society has been reorganized into a provincial body with the power to decide who will be admitted to the bar in the province.

Longboat triumphs in Boston Marathon

Distance runner Tom Longboat.

April 19, 1907

BOSTON – Tom Longboat, an Onondaga Indian from the Six Nations Reserve near Brantford, Ont., has won the Boston Marathon. Longboat, 19, completed the course in two hours, 25 minutes and one-fifth of a second. Early in the race, he trailed several runners, but before the competitors reached the 10-kilometre mark, it was all down to three men – Sam Mellors, Charlie Petch and Longboat.

After Mellors was knocked down by a cycling spectator, Petch kept the lead until it began to snow. When he faltered near a long hill, Longboat sprinted to the fore. He was ahead by close to 400 metres when he crossed the finish line.

Rave reviews for new hybrid wheat

Dominion cerealist C. Saunders.

Dr. Charles Saunders examines a plot of his experimental Marquis wheat.

Aug. 29, 1907

CANADIAN PRAIRIES – A new hybrid wheat has proven its worth on the Canadian prairie. Many wheat crops failed this year because of frost early in the season, but one notable exception is Marquis wheat. Charles Saunders, son of Dominion Experimental Farms director William Saunders, is responsible for the new, durable variety of wheat. A graduate of the University of Toronto and Johns Hopkins University, he is a cerealist with Dominion Experimental Farms Service.

Marquis wheat, which results from crossing Red Fife with Hard Red Calcutta, is a hardy hybrid. It ripens early, its head is resistant to strong winds, and the flour it yields is excellent. This was the first year it was tested extensively on the prairies, and as a result of its proven superiority it is expected to be introduced commercially in the near future.

This virtually uninhabited section of the British Columbia coast is being planned as the western terminus of the new Canadian Pacific Railway. As a result of the expected boom, a new town is rapidly springing up in the wilderness. It is to be known as Prince Rupert, and although its makeshift dwellings and tangle of freshly cut lumber and brush may not leave a very positive impression now, the hope is that this town will soon rival Vancouver.

Alta. cattle dealer denies price fixing

June 25, 1907

CALGARY – The principal cattle dealer and exporter in the west told the beef commission today that there has never been a cattle combine in the history of Canada. "The prices which I give are open to the world and are higher than the prices which prevail in Winnipeg and in other places," Pat Burns testified. The commission set up by Alberta and Manitoba is to probe allegations of a cattle dealers' combine and to determine why consumer prices are rising while producers' revenue is declining. Ranchers have also complained about poor rail service for cattle transport.

Quebec bridge collapses; 84 feared dead

Quebec bridge falls into river.

Aug. 29, 1907

QUEBEC CITY – Eighty-four men are feared dead after the inexplicable collapse today of the unfinished Quebec bridge across the St. Lawrence. At 5:45 p.m. the south support column and the 240-metre steel span it was holding suddenly twisted and fell into the river. It happened so fast workers had no chance to escape. More than 30 of the ironworkers are Iroquois from Caughnawaga, near Montreal.

No one knows why the bridge collapsed. It's believed that a locomotive and three cars containing steel had just driven on to the bridge when it fell. The city is devastated by the loss. The community of Caughnawaga is in mourning.

Ex-Mountie finds Black Deer's body

Aug. 22. 1907

BOW RIVER, Alta. – Plans are being made this evening by the Stoney tribe to lay the remains of the great hunter Black Deer to rest, 17 years after his disappearance. The funeral, to be held on the Stoney reserve 70 kilometres west of Calgary, will be an elaborate one – Black Deer is the most famous hunter in the history of the tribe.

The remains were found early this morning on the banks of the Bow River during excavations for a new bridge. A former Mountie who knew the hunter recognized several trinkets and other paraphernalia still in evidence on the skeleton.

Oldfield sets auto racing record for mile

July 20, 1907

WINNIPEG – Famed auto racer Barney Oldfield broke the Canadian record here this afternoon. From a rolling start, his car did the mile in 1:19.5, clipping a full 1.5 seconds off the old mark for a mile on a half-mile track. Oldfield averaged more than 45 mph.

Oldfield's machine is little more than a seat on low frame and a tremendously powerful engine. In a two-mile exhibition race, Oldfield also beat racing partner Bruno Seible, winning handily in 2:47. In an exciting afternoon of races, the heaviest betting was reserved for an unscheduled grudge match staged by agents of the Ford and Maxwell companies, each of whom claimed his car was faster over long distances. In the 25-mile race, the lead changed hands several times. The Ford developed carburator trouble in the early going, but at 18.5 miles had opened up a good lead. Then, the Ford's battery wiring failed and the Maxwell took over. But that lead did not last long. The Maxwell ran out of water and before more could be got, the Ford romped to victory by a mile.

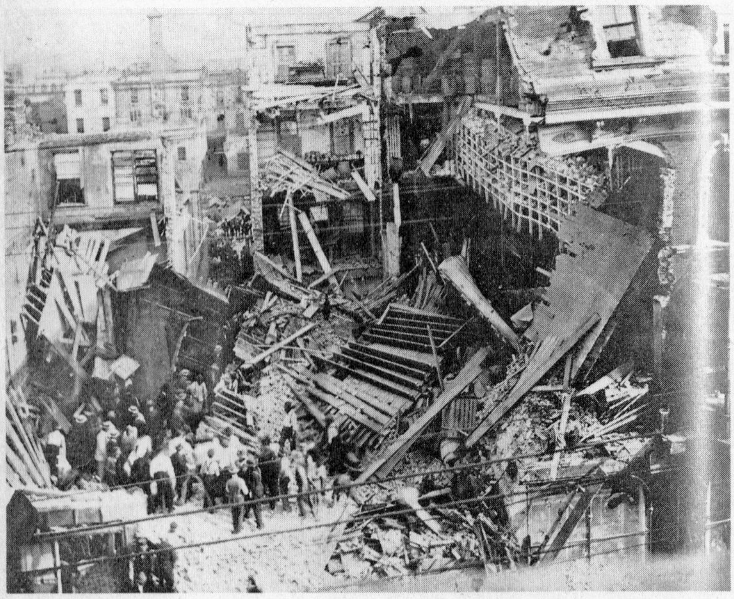

Three buildings collapsed on July 16 in London, Ont., causing seven deaths.

Pablo buffalo herd to come to Canada

Buffalo are being rounded up for shipment to Canada to start a new herd.

Sept. 10, 1907

MISSOULA, Montana – Loading gangs have begun to round up the famous Pablo buffalo herd – the largest remaining herd on the continent – preparatory to moving it to Canada. With only about 1,000 plains buffalo left on the continent, the Canadian government has decided to buy this herd of around 400 from Métis Michael Pablo and move the animals in boxcars to a park near Edmonton. When their journey is complete, it is hoped the buffalo will graze and multiply, free from the slings and arrows of human barbarity and greed that have brought them to the verge of extinction.

Unfortunately, the Pablo herd is not co-operating in the enterprise. Many buffalo are scattered in the mountains after crossing the Powder River in search of food. Pablo is hot on their trail at this very moment with 15 Mexican cowboys, intending to drive them down to Ravalli, where they could be loaded. Coralling and loading the herd will be a herculean effort. Pablo estimates it will take two weeks, with crews working 15 hours a day.

Asians the target of rampaging Vancouver mob

Orientals beaten in riot, stores pillaged

Sept. 7, 1907

VANCOUVER – An angry mob of several hundred people went on a rampage through Vancouver's Oriental districts tonight, smashing store windows and beating up residents. The riot occurred following a public meeting of the Asiatic Exclusion League at city hall. The league, formed last August, wants a halt to Asian immigration to Canada and is supported by many prominent whites in the city, including the mayor.

After burning an effigy of the premier, the mob marched on to Chinatown, where several stores and homes were attacked. Then it moved a few blocks west to the Japanese section of town, where it met strong resistance from a group of Japanese residents armed with sticks, bottles and knives to protect their homes. Several people were injured in the melee, and damage has been estimated at several thousand dollars.

The riot is a culmination of anti-Oriental feeling building in British Columbia all summer. Whites are concerned that they will lose jobs and status to the Oriental newcomers; they fear that the province will become predominantly Asian if immigration is not stopped. "I can see without any difficulty the province of British Columbia slipping into the hands of Asiatics," local member of Parliament R.G. Macpherson warns, "and this part of western Canada no longer a part and parcel of the dominion."

Damage at Japanese grocery store.

Damage toll to be probed, Laurier vows

Oct. 12, 1907

OTTAWA – Prime Minister Wilfrid Laurier announced today an investigation into damages suffered by Asian-Canadians during last month's riot in Vancouver. The prime minister appointed William Lyon Mackenzie King, the deputy minister of labor, to hold hearings on property losses and to set the amount of money individuals will be reimbursed. Laurier also said he is sending the minister of labor to Japan to negotiate restrictions on the number of Japanese allowed into this country, a measure long called for by many people in British Columbia.

Last month's disturbances occurred following a public meeting protesting the growing number of Orientals in the province.

Many Asian-Canadians are in railway work gangs like this one in B.C.

Catholics told to shun the cinema Sundays

Scene from the 1906 motion picture film Madeleine de Verchères.

Dec. 1, 1907

MONTREAL – Catholics have been ordered to shun the cinema on Sundays. Archbishop Paul Bruchési issued an edict today banning attendance at movie theatres by his flock, saying films violate the holiness of the Lord's Day. Theatre owner Ernest Ouimet, who recently opened his second Ouimetoscope, plans to get around the ban by selling candy to customers outside his theatre and then inviting them in to see the movies.

Mounties complete new trail to Yukon

Sept. 23, 1907

DAWSON, Yukon – Two years of labor by the North West Mounted Police have yielded a route from Edmonton to Dawson. A 2.4-metre wide trail cut from Peace River runs through the Rockies to Hazelton, where it joins the trail along the Yukon telegraph lines into Dawson. The trail provides access, admittedly still difficult, to the Yukon entirely on Canadian territory.

Travelling on Canadian land strengthens the justice system, especially when transporting prisoners who would be able to take advantage of territorial law if brought across old routes which cross American territory. The trail also provides a Canadian connection to the Yukon, which, if upgraded, would be strategically important in the event of a war.

Ruler of Abyssinia slams color barrier

Oct. 30, 1907

MONTREAL – Commandant Benito Sylvain, a doctor of law and aide-de-camp of Emperor Menelik of Abyssinia, today fired a broadside at Montreal hotels after being refused a room because of he is a "gentleman of color."

Sylvain is in Canada to encourage the dismantling of racially-motivated color barriers, and he has launched his campaign with a strong statement aimed not only at Montreal hotelkeepers but at society in general: "It is absolutely odious and scandalous that a country imbued with the generous traditions of France, and which claims to be under the English law, reputed to be so liberal, can adopt principles ... still prevalent among the upholders of the slavery system in the southern States."

1908

Montreal, Feb. 4. The Marconi Wireless Telegraph Company announces it will accept messages from the public for transmission to Britain at a rate of 15 cents a word.

Montreal, March 14. Montreal Wanderers beat the Toronto Maple Leafs 6-4 for the Stanley Cup.

Montreal, May 30. Louis-Honoré Fréchette, the unofficial poet laureate of French Canada, dies.

Trois-Rivières, Que., June 23. Fire destroys half the city, leaving 1,000 homeless and causing $2 million damage.

Edmonton, September. Classes begin at the University of Alberta, with 45 students.

New York, Dec. 15. Canadian Six Nations Indian Tom Longboat wins the professional marathon championship.

Sydney, Aust., Dec. 26. American Jack Johnson knocks out Canadian Tommy Burns, the world heavyweight boxing champion, becoming the first black to win the championship.

British Columbia. Peter Verigin leads a group of Doukhobors from Saskatchewan to southeastern B.C. He buys land and founds a community of 6,000 people.

Kingsville, Ont. Conservationist Jack Miner, once an avid hunter, establishes one of the first bird sanctuaries in North America at his farm.

Ontario. The Hydro-Electric Power Commission enters agreements with 14 municipalities to provide power at cost.

Stockholm. British physicist Ernest Rutherford is awarded the Nobel Prize in chemistry for his work at Montreal's McGill University on the disintegration theory of the atom.

Montreal. Lawyer Robert Weir writes an English translation of *O Canada!* The French version appeared in 1880.

Prairies. The last railway land grants are selected in the federal system of granting western land to finance railway construction. Since 1872, 12.8 million hectares have been set aside to finance railways.

Victoria. The legislature passes an act founding the University of British Columbia.

Nova Scotia. The federal government sends 1,620 live lobsters to B.C., hoping to transplant the lucrative lobster industry to the west coast.

First gold sovereign struck at Royal Mint

The rolling operation at the new Royal Canadian Mint in Ottawa, Ontario.

Jan. 2, 1908

OTTAWA – The first coin was struck at the new Royal Mint building today, ending years of importing Canadian currency from England. The coin, a gold sovereign, valued at about $7, was struck by Lord Grey, the governor general. The new stone building that houses the mint sits on a bluff overlooking the Ottawa River. Security is critical at the fortress-like mint, which was completed last year. Until now, most coin issues for Canada came from the Royal Mint in London, England, and some from the Heaton mint at Birmingham. Ottawa's mint is a branch of the Royal Mint.

The one-cent piece is one of the first coins to be minted in Ottawa.

Japan to limit emigration flow to Canada

Jan. 21, 1908

OTTAWA – The threat of a "yellow" British Columbia has diminished due to an agreement announced today with the Japanese government to restrict emigration, federal officials say. Following a visit to Japan by federal minister Rodolphe Lemieux, the Japanese have agreed to suppress the emigration of railway workers. Less than 1,000 Japanese coolies a year will be allowed to travel to Canada, the agreement states.

Ottawa to release immigrants in B.C. held by Natal Act

Feb. 13, 1908

OTTAWA – The Liberal government has told Justice Department officials in Vancouver to use *habeas corpus* writs to free any immigrants held under B.C.'s new Natal Act. When an official copy of the act reaches Ottawa it will be immediately disallowed, cabinet officials say. This new Natal Act is, in effect, a replica of a 1907 act, designed to exclude Asian immigrants. The 1907 act was reserved by Lt.-Gov. James Dunsmuir, but B.C.'s attorney general, W.J. Bowser, reintroduced the legislation after strong pressure from Premier Richard McBride, who has made the exclusion of Asian immigrants an important plank in his platform.

Dunsmuir's blocking of the 1907 legislation was widely criticized in British Columbia, for he has employed many Chinese at low wages in his coal mines. In the summer, Asian immigrants flocked to B.C., prompting the formation of the Asiatic Exclusion League.

Abortion likened to "race suicide"

1908

TORONTO – "God abhors the spirit so prevalent nowadays which condemns motherhood. How it must grieve Him when He sees what we call race suicide." So says Rev. C. Ensor Sharp. According to a Toronto newspaper, many doctors become wealthy by performing abortions. Just how widespread the practice is cannot be known, since abortions are rarely brought to the attention of authorities unless the mother's death results.

What is known, however, is despite the fact that the practice of abortion and other methods of contraception are illegal under Section 179 of the 1892 Criminal Code, many Canadians are deliberately limiting the size of their families. Both medical men and spiritual leaders have condemned this reduction of healthy British stock as immoral and certain to result in race suicide.

Oshawa firm to mass produce motor cars

The McLaughlin-Buick combines a McLaughlin body and a Buick engine.

One of Sam McLaughlin's designs – the McLaughlin Motor Car Model D-45.

1908

OSHAWA, Ont. – Local carriage builder R. Samuel McLaughlin has signed a contract with the Buick Motor Company that gives him rights for 15 years to engines built by the Flint, Mich., firm. The deal is expected to have a dramatic impact on the automobile business in Canada because it gives McLaughlin the push he needs to go into mass production of the new motor cars. The Oshawa firm expects to produce 200 cars this year. The deal with Buick Motor owner William Durant signals the end of McLaughlin's drive to build an all-Canadian car, but with other auto firms failing, it was more important for McLaughlin to align himself with a good engine builder. The car will be called a McLaughlin-Buick.

Juvenile Delinquents Act offers protection for all children living across the country

1908

OTTAWA – Canada's first federal legislation dealing with juvenile delinquents has become law. Although various legal provisions regarding child criminals and neglected children have been made over the past 50 years, the act now offers protection for all children across the country.

In recent years, there has been a dramatic change in methods used to deal with delinquent children, such as legislation requiring child offenders be tried separately from adults. At one time, the main concern was the protection of society, and out of this concern reformatories and other institutions emerged. More recently, due to the influence of child savers, a different attitude has prevailed. Under the Juvenile Delinquents Act, special courts have been established to ensure the welfare of a child. In effect, courts take the place of parents when dealing with juvenile criminals. It is now understood that undesirable behavior in children is the result of upbringing and family circumstances, and children must be saved from unfortunate situations, not punished for their misdeeds or those of their parents.

Baldwin takes off in an "aeroplane"

March 12, 1908

HAMMONDSPORT, N.Y. – Frederick W. Baldwin today became the first Canadian to fly an "aeroplane" when he took off from a frozen lake here. The machine, called the *Red Wing,* was designed by telephone pioneer Alexander Graham Bell. It flew 9.5 metres. Born in Toronto, Baldwin is a 26-year-old University of Toronto engineering graduate.

Members of the Aerial Experiment Association with the Red Wing aircraft.

Legislature bans all cars on the Island

March 26, 1908

CHARLOTTETOWN – The first car in the colonies was owned by an Islander: Father Georges Belcourt. His experience, however, was not a good one, and P.E.I. in general has not taken well to the automobile. Rural Islanders say the contraptions tear up the roads, and terrorize horses, cattle and small children. Their MLAs tend to agree. Today, in a rare instance of non-partisan unanimity, the legislature voted to ban all automobiles from P.E.I. The few but enthusiastic motorists on the Island are expected to challenge the constitutional validity of the act.

Alberta buys out Bell Telephone Company

March 31, 1908

EDMONTON – The provincial government has announced it will buy the Bell Telephone Company in Alberta for $675,000. The move makes Alberta the second province to own its telephone service as a public utility. Manitoba was the first, and Saskatchewan is believed to be next. Alberta's buyout comes after years of criticism of Bell's service in Canada. Bell has been accused of refusing to extend lines into less profitable rural areas. And, in regions where competition arose, Bell fought back by offering free phone service, leading to government regulation.

"Anarchist Queen" facing deportation

Emma Goldman gives a speech.

April 7, 1908

EMERSON, Man. – The "Anarchist Queen" Emma Goldman is here today, refused entry to the United States and facing deportation from Canada. American officials say her naturalization papers are void because of her residence in Russia, and they refuse to allow her to return home. Goldman was apparently warned American authorities would give her trouble. She posted notices in Winnipeg saying her scheduled lectures were postponed because of illness and would resume when she recovered. Then she tried to cross the border two days earlier than scheduled. Canadian officials say she can't stay here and will be deported.

Imperial Tobacco sets up in Montreal

June 11, 1908

MONTREAL – A new company has entered Canada's growing cigarette trade, buying one of the country's largest tobacco manufacturers – the American Tobacco Co. of Canada Limited. The new company, Imperial Tobacco of Canada, has acquired American Tobacco's modern Montreal plant on St. Antoine Street, as well as its many holdings.

According to government figures, Canada produces more than 66 million cigarettes a year.

Ghost train seen prior to collision

July 8, 1908

MEDICINE HAT, Alta. – This morning two CPR trains smashed head-on about 3.2 kilometres out of Medicine Hat, killing 11: the two engineers, a fireman, a conductor, and seven passengers. One train was a single engine en route to to pick up the Spokane Flyer to haul from Dunmore to Swift Current. The other was passenger train No. 514 from Lethbridge.

Terrifyingly, the tragedy had been foreseen. Twice before, CPR trainmen saw a phantom train at exactly the spot of the real collision. It would screech toward the oncoming train, then veer onto nonexistent tracks and speed past pulling ghostly coaches. Stunned trainmen now believe the visions were other-worldly warnings.

Laurier's Liberals are returned to office

Laurier campaigns at Tilbury, Ont.

Oct. 26, 1908

OTTAWA – "They might as well give up on elections in Canada, since the same party always wins!" That's what some wits are saying tonight about the latest election triumph of Sir Wilfrid Laurier's Liberals, in power since 1896. The government has picked up 132 seats to the Conservatives' 82. Seven seats are still to be decided.

This time Tory leader Robert Borden managed to win his seat and his party did well in Ontario, where they got 47 seats to the Liberals' 39. It's likely the Conservatives will also dominate Manitoba and British Columbia. Still, the election is not even a moral victory for the Tories, who haven't tasted power since the last century. The fact is that nobody has been found who can fill the void left by the death of Sir John A. Macdonald.

Booze merchants and makers can't sway voters: N.B. stays dry

April 30, 1908

FREDERICTON – Attempts by local distillers, brewers and tavern owners to overturn local prohibition laws failed tonight. In what has been called the most sharply contested vote in the city's history, Fredericton voters turned out to approve retaining the "dry" law by a margin of 178 votes.

The decision is a victory for local temperance workers, who feared the powerful "booze lobby" would be able to buy votes. Indeed, at least two people were charged for impersonation at the polling booths. Many liquor merchants now say they're going to leave the province.

Defender of the Cree Chief Piapot dies

May 1908

QU'APPELLE VALLEY – Chief Piapot, one of the last of the great plains Indian chiefs of the 1870s and 1880s, has died at the age of 92. The Cree chief has had a remarkable life story. As a young child Sioux warriors kidnapped him, and he lived with them for 14 years. After his release, he himself led war parties against his captors, the Sioux, and also against the Blackfoot.

Piapot was very wary of the Canadian government and refused to sign Treaty No. 4 in 1874. It was only in the following year that he finally agreed to adhere to it. Despite his many disappointments with the Canadian government's way of honoring the agreement, Piapot kept his treaty pledge inviolate, and did not join in the North West Rebellion of 1885, although many of his tribesmen wanted to participate.

However, in the religious domain Piapot never compromised a single belief. To his death he resisted the entreaties of Christian missionaries who invited him to join their denominations. Piapot remained faithful to his ancestral religion.

Cree chief Piapot.

Iroquois delegation eyes elected council

April 24, 1908

OTTAWA – Today a delegation of Six Nations men approached Frank Oliver, the minister of the interior, and requested that an elected council be instituted on the Six Nations Reserve. Since Confederation the Canadian government has accepted the Six Nations Confederacy Council as the legitimate governing body on the reserve. This ancient body, hundreds of years old, is composed of hereditary or life chiefs, as well as a few outstanding men, or "pinetree" chiefs, appointed on their own merit.

Young Iroquois say all the council members should be accountable through elections, and selected on the basis of achievement and not because their families inherited certain titles. It appears the Iroquois reformers are supported by about 25 percent of Six Nations members.

Fishermen in Nfld. form common front

Nov. 3, 1908

HERRING NECK, Nfld. – An historic meeting was held yesterday in Herring Neck, near Twillingate, which may be the beginning of revolutionary change in Newfoundland. Local farmer William Coaker called a meeting of neighboring fishermen and convinced them to join him in creating a Fishermen's Protective Union. Coaker suggested a program that caught everyone's attention, and already plans are in progress for local and regional councils to be formed. The FPU intends to create co-operatives for selling fish and buying supplies in bulk, it intends to elect its own representatives to the House of Assembly, and it plans to work for social and educational reforms. There are also plans for a newspaper.

The fishermen of the northeast coast have seen their incomes decrease in recent years, as the seal fishery which used to provide one-third to one-half their income has been in decline. Meanwhile, shipbuilding and ship ownership in the outports have declined, and firms have gone bankrupt. Coaker told fishermen they are being preyed upon by a horde of parasites who live in St. John's, and it appears that the fishermen are convinced a union will improve their lives.

Anne of Green Gables is published

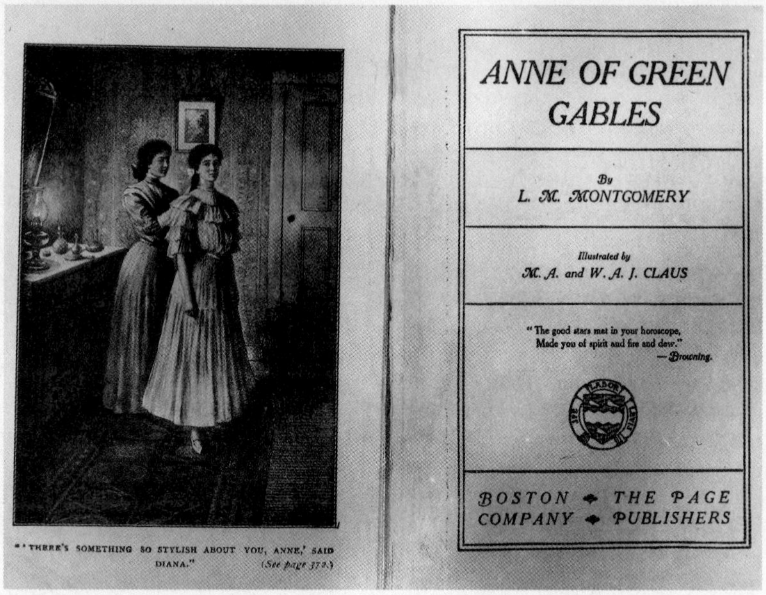

The novel Anne of Green Gables has just been published in Boston. Its author, Lucy Maud Montgomery, is a native of Prince Edward Island.

Writer Lucy Maud Montgomery.

1908

CAVENDISH, P.E.I. – A book by an Island farm woman promises to be one of the best-selling novels of the year. *Anne of Green Gables* was recently published by L.C. Page Co. of Boston. The manuscript by Lucy Maud Montgomery, a 33-year-old former schoolteacher, was rejected by five other publishers before Page offered a contract. Miss Montgomery, who has already published various magazine stories, has also agreed to write several more books for Page Co. in the coming years.

The novel tells of Anne Shirley, a red-haired orphan with a vivid imagination. When elderly Prince Edward Island siblings Matthew and Marilla Cuthbert request a boy to help on the farm, Anne is sent by mistake. The adventures that ensue are alternately hilarious and heart-rending. Due to Miss Montgomery's skill, Anne is no paper heroine, but a flesh-and-blood girl with a sharp tongue, a quick temper, and a soft heart.

There are several similarities between the author and her creation. Like Anne, Miss Montgomery was orphaned at an early age and sent to live with her grandparents. Like Anne, she also had a burning desire to write. This novel is the result, and a delightful one no one who has fond memories of youth can afford to miss.

Scientists head to the Arctic to study Inuit, animal kingdom

American scientist R. M. Anderson.

This Inuit girl from the Mackenzie River area is about nine years old.

May 1, 1908

TORONTO – Two American scientists departed for the western Arctic today on expeditions that are expected to keep them in the north for two years. Vilhjalmur Stefansson is an ethnologist, recently back from an earlier excursion to the Arctic on which he lived with an Inuit family. On this trip he intends to continue his studies of the Inuit, and in particular to make contact with the natives on Victoria Island who are totally unknown to the outside world.

Stefansson is accompanied by zoologist Rudolph Anderson, who will be studying animal life on the excursion. The expedition is supported by the American Museum of Natural History and the Geological Survey of Canada.

Quebec celebrates its 300th birthday

July 31, 1908

QUEBEC CITY – Celebrations of Quebec City's 300th birthday ended today, bringing 10 days of fireworks, naval reviews, military ceremonies and historical pageants to a close. The arrival of Quebec City founder Samuel de Champlain in 1608 has been recreated daily, and historic figures such as Bishop François de Laval and Louis de Buade de Frontenac have returned to life. Soldiers in the uniforms of James Wolfe's and Louis-Joseph de Montcalm's armies have paraded together. Warships from Britain, France, and the United States have fired salutes, while the Prince of Wales and the American vice-president were honored guests.

1909

Ottawa, Jan. 11. The Moral Reform Committee of the Anglican Church takes steps for the criminal prosecution of anyone caught selling "immoral" literature.

North Pole, April 6. An expedition led by U.S. Navy Commander Robert E. Peary is the first to reach the North Pole.

Montreal, April 29. Police arrest popular Oriental dancer Millie De Leon for indecent exposure while dancing, the first such arrest in Montreal in 12 years.

Toronto, May 1. Licence Commissioners reduce the number of establishments allowed to sell liquor by 41 in a radical step against drinking.

Montreal, July 12. Annie Waminolet, a 16-year-old Abenaki Indian, wins first place in the Dominion College of Music examination.

Calgary, Oct. 19. The Calgary Power Company Ltd. is organized by R.B. Bennett and others to provide hydro-electric power for the city.

Toronto, Dec. 4. University of Toronto defeats the Toronto Parkdale Canoe Club 26-6 in the first Grey Cup game for the Canadian football championship. Earl Grey, governor general of Canada, donated the trophy for the championship, but forgot to place an order with silversmiths to make the cup, so it can't be presented.

Ottawa. William Lyon Mackenzie King becomes Canada's first minister of labor in PM Laurier's government.

Ottawa. Parliament establishes the Conservation Commission to investigate Canada's natural resources and make recommendations for their development and conservation.

Edmonton. Police arrest 64 men and 28 women in a raid on a brothel where sex and gambling are offered.

Montreal. Le club de hockey Canadien is founded, symbolic of the arrival of French-Canadians in hockey.

Ottawa. The Ottawa Senators win the Stanley Cup as champions of the Eastern Canada Hockey Association.

Quebec. More than 10,000 leave for the U.S. in 1909 to look for jobs. Most go to work in New England factories.

Canada. Toronto's Thomas Ryan invents five-pin bowling.

McCurdy flight first in British Empire

Feb. 23, 1909

BADDECK, N.S. – The first airplane flight in the British Empire was made today by John Alexander Douglas McCurdy before an astounded crowd on an ice-covered lake in this small Cape Breton town. The most renowned resident of Baddeck, inventor of the telephone Alexander Graham Bell, has been responsible for work carried on by the Aerial Experiment Association and is given much of the credit for this historic achievement.

J.A.D. McCurdy at the controls of the Silver-Dart near Baddeck, Nova Scotia.

Reporter Charles Fox describes the scene: "About three o'clock the *Silver-Dart* was wheeled from her shed to the outer bay. Crowds then began to congregate in front of and along the line of advance of the machine (and) it became necessary to appoint police to keep the ice clear, thereby avoiding accidents. The wind shifted and it was decided to take the machine further up the bay. As most of the laboratory staff were on skates, this was done very quickly. Before some of the people realized what was taking place, the buzz of the engine could be heard and the machine was seen advancing rapidly. She had gone about 90 feet along the ice when she rose gracefully into the air to an elevation of about 20 to 30 feet at about 40 miles an hour (for half a mile) before she glided down. ... Everyone seemed dumbfounded."

Canada and the U.S. agree to preserve beauty of Niagara Falls

Jan. 11, 1909

OTTAWA – With matchless splendor, Niagara Falls is poised between two countries gushing its power with such magnificence that governments wish to protect it from the exploits of industry. Now, Canada and the United States have come together in an effort to preserve the scenic beauty of the falls, placing restrictions on the use of Niagara water for power purposes.

The joint effort of both governments has resulted in an agreement of the provisions limiting the use of Niagara water by electrical companies. William Pugsley, minister of public works for Canada, and the British ambassador met with the United States secretary of state in Washington to embody the agreement in a treaty, which has been signed on behalf of the Canadian and the American authorities.

Settlement on a Hillside, by Marc-Aurèle de Foy Suzor-Coté.

Smooth sailing for int'l waters treaty

Jan. 11, 1909

WASHINGTON, D.C. – A treaty aimed at settling disputes over shared international waters has been signed by Canada and the United States. The Boundary Waters' Treaty says navigation should not be restricted in boundary waters and allows each country to retain control of waters on their land that flow up to the border region. The treaty has created an International Joint Commission of six commissioners, three from each country. The IJC will rule on any disputes over the use, obstruction or diversion of boundary waters. Difficulties the IJC can't resolve will be referred back to the governments.

Minister's book addresses the immigrant problem

The Immigration Office in Edmonton is decorated for its inauguration.

The first party of Doukhobor immigrants to Canada on its march to Yorkton.

1909

WINNIPEG – James Shaver Woodsworth, a Methodist minister at the All People's Mission in the north end of Winnipeg, recently published a book dealing with the immigration problem. *Strangers Within Our Gates* examines immigration to English-speaking Canada, its causes and effects. The book also looks at how restriction and assimilation can solve the most serious problems caused by the arrival of thousands of foreigners.

Woodsworth looks at many different groups of immigrants, including those who are Jewish, Italian, or Oriental, and others from southeastern Europe or the Balkan states. His discussion of the Poles points out that there are now between 10,000 and 12,000 Polish immigrants in Canada, as many as 3,000 in Winnipeg alone. Most are peasants or working men, "poor, illiterate, and with a code of morals none too high." Although some become farmers, most take on menial jobs, finding employment in work camps and factories. Women are frequently employed as domestics.

Under Canadian law, paupers, the mentally or physically unsound, and criminals may not immigrate to this country. However, there is no legal way to screen out those who are simply not suited for life in Canada. Reformers have pointed to a certain class of immigrant as a causative factor for a rising crime rate and unsanitary conditions in Canadian cities.

There are other problems, too. After three years of residence, an immigrant is able to vote. Too often, however, he can neither read nor speak English. How can such a man, one who is just emerging from serfdom, says Woodsworth, understand representative government? And is it right that the vote of such a man should cancel out that of one reared in British traditions?

The book notes that immigrants tend to band together at work and in social and benevolent organizations, and that they maintain their language, their customs and religion. It also suggests that in the long run, this is undesirable. Only immigrants who can be assimilated into the fabric of Canadian society should be made welcome.

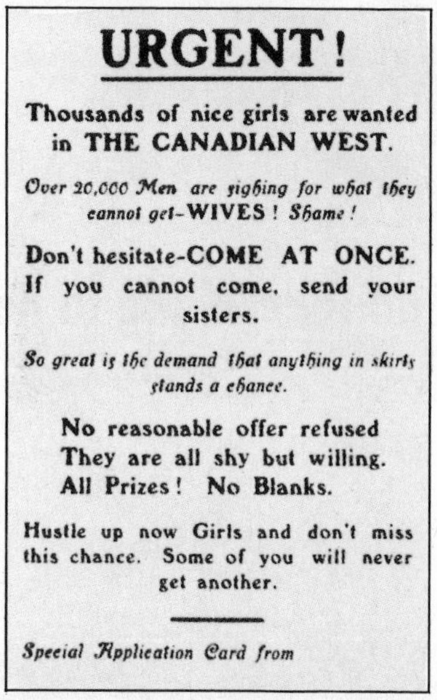

URGENT!

Thousands of nice girls are wanted in THE CANADIAN WEST.

Over 20,000 Men are sighing for what they cannot get–WIVES! Shame!

Don't hesitate–COME AT ONCE. If you cannot come, send your sisters.

So great is the demand that anything in skirts stands a chance.

No reasonable offer refused
They are all shy but willing.
All Prizes! No Blanks.

Hustle up now Girls and don't miss this chance. Some of you will never get another.

Special Application Card from

Women are scarce among settlers.

This homesteading couple seems to be happy with their situation, but the first years in a new settlement are difficult for immigrants. The work is heavy and the climate is harsh.

A young Icelandic family poses for a photo, perhaps to send back to relatives in the old country.

The first home for an immigrant family is often a sod hut like this one.

▷

Arctic archipelago claimed for Canada

July 1, 1909

WINTER HARBOR, Melville Island – In a solemn ceremony on the shores of this frozen harbor, Arctic navigator Joseph-Elzéar Bernier unveiled a tablet claiming the entire Arctic archipelago for Canada. It is Dominion Day, and the expedition's ship, which is still locked in ice in the harbor despite the lateness of the season, is decked out with flags. Bernier and his men celebrated the holiday with a banquet, and after the unveiling a loud three cheers were given in honor of the prime minister.

This is the captain's third official excursion into the eastern Arctic since the government decided in 1903 to establish a presence there. Canada has claimed the archipelago since 1880, but has done almost nothing to administer the region, which is visited by traders and whalers from Britain and the U.S. As well as making claims to territory, Bernier is expected to patrol the whaling fleets and collect customs on goods imported for trade. The captain and his crew have spent the winter at Melville Island, living on ducks, caribou and musk-ox. As soon as the ice releases their ship they will return to the south.

Bobby Kerr of Hamilton won the 220-yard and the 100-yard gold medals at the 1908 Olympic Games in London, England.

Housing shortage plagues Winnipeg

Sept. 1, 1909

WINNIPEG – A report released today by the city's health inspector may shock the councillors, but it proves what many citizens have known for some time: there is a serious housing shortage. The report includes mention of an after-hour call on one rental property where the civic official found a dozen occupants in a single room. And there are hints this is not all that unusual in Winnipeg. What exacerbates the normal problems of growth in a relatively new community is the nature of the current construction. Earlier commercial facilities are being replaced by new ones of a size never before known in western Canada.

One example is the Ashdown Hardware store. When the original headquarters burned down in 1904, its replacement was many times the size of the original and is now considered one of the finest hardware stores in all of Canada. With explosive growth of this type, the city became a magnet for newcomers who flocked to a centre which could provide employment.

Figures from the city and the province clearly show that in little more than a single decade, the population of Winnipeg trebled. Even with an increase in construction, the rate of residential construction has never fully matched the pace at which the population has grown.

On arrival in Winnipeg, immigrants often have difficulty finding lodgings.

Six CPR police, four strikers shot in riot

Aug. 13, 1909

FORT WILLIAM [Thunder Bay], Ont. – The Riot Act was read in Fort William today after 10 people were shot during a confrontation between Canadian Pacific Railway police and striking CPR dockworkers.

The latest trouble started at 9 a.m., when about 30 CPR special constables arrived to guard company property. By the time they reached the railway sheds a huge crowd of strikers had gathered, itching for a fight. When the constables went into the boarding house for breakfast, the gauntlet was thrown down. The strikers told the constables they wouldn't be allowed to leave the boarding house. When they tried to leave at 11:30 a.m., shots were fired from the crowd. The constables tried to return to the house for cover, but were ordered to go out and return fire. In the shooting spree that followed, six officers and four strikers were wounded. Since then, the mayor has read the Riot Act and decreed martial law.

No federal aid to help Peck teach Inuit

Efforts are being made to bring Christianity to isolated Inuit communities.

February 1909

EASTERN ARCTIC – Rev. E.J. Peck has received an answer to his request for federal aid for his mission school on Blacklead Island – "it is not the intention of the government to assist in educational work amongst these people." The government policy of leaving Inuit education in the hands of Anglican, Catholic, and Moravian missionaries remains unchanged. Peck has spent years in the far north, introducing Christianity to the Inuit. He has translated the New Testament into Inuktitut, using the syllabic form first developed for the plains Cree in the 1830s.

East and west combat spread of TB

Freud discussed, doctors in shock

Sigmund Freud.

Nov. 24, 1909

ST. CATHARINES, Ont. – A visiting British doctor has brought the theories of Sigmund Freud to Canada, and the medical fraternity here is in shock. Ernest Jones, a young Welsh psychiatrist, delivered a lecture today in which he summarized the views of Freud. The audience was particularly offended at Jones' remarks about the sexual lives of children.

Jones has been working in Toronto for the past year, and his arrogant attitude toward his Canadian colleagues has already earned their dislike. This is Canada's first exposure to Freud's controversial views, and the reaction so far is summed up in Dr. Charles Clarke's comment that Freud "advocates ... a relapse into savagery."

Earl Grey, governor general of Canada since 1904, works at his desk in Rideau Hall. Grey promotes strong links with England.

Montreal institute open for business

1909

MONTREAL – With the push of a button more than 6,400 kilometres away, the Royal Edward Institute – for treating tuberculosis patients – was opened by its namesake today. Using the latest in cable technology, King Edward triggered a device from Colchester, England, to open the new institute's doors and flood the entrance with light – much to the amazement of a crowd of dignitaries.

The institute, located in Belmont Park, was built with a generous donation from Lt.-Col. Burland and his sisters. Sir Charles Fitzpatrick delivered a message on behalf of Gov. Gen. Earl Grey, who could not attend the ceremony. He said the institute would play an important role treating and eventually eradicating tuberculosis, which, he noted, claimed 30 million lives in the 19th century, whereas all wars had taken less than half that number. Sir George Drummond is the institute's first president.

Tranquille sanatorium gets its first cases

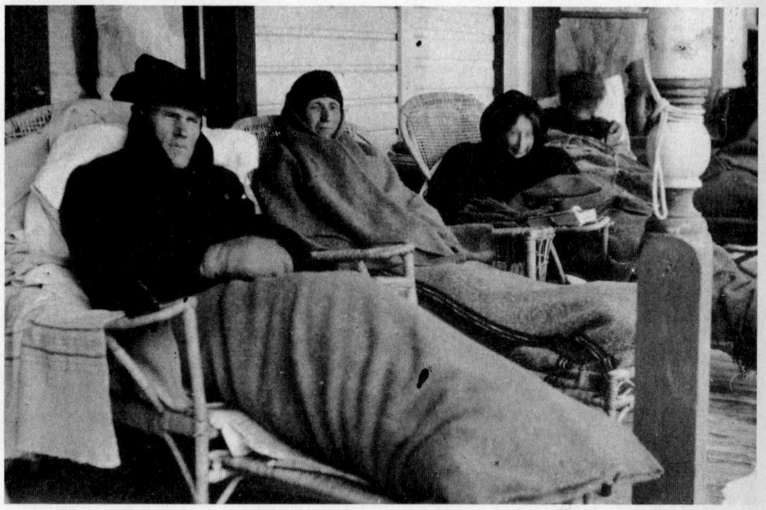

Tuberculosis patients need dry air such that found in the Kamloops area.

Sept. 15, 1909

KAMLOOPS, B.C. – The Tranquille sanatorium for people with tuberculosis now has patients. The new buildings, just completed, will be expanded in the next two years or so.

Tranquille is on the northeast corner of Kamloops Lake and has a perfect climate for curing TB patients – it's dry and sunny with only about 25 centimetres of rain a year and many hot days. Indians used the land for a winter campsite until an Overlander called William Fortune built a ranch there in the 1860s. The B.C. Anti-Tuberculosis Society bought the ranch two years ago for $60,000 and used the ranch-house as a primitive hospital.

Riel's onetime secretary in Prince Albert

Summer 1909

PRINCE ALBERT, Sask. – A colorful veteran of the North West Rebellion of 1885 has returned to western Canada from Chicago, 22 years after the Battle of Batoche. His name is Will Jackson, or as he is now known, Honoré Jaxon. Old-timers may remember the idealistic Ontarian who volunteered to be Louis Riel's English-language secretary when the Métis leader returned to Canada in 1884. Although Jaxon was committed to the insane asylum at Lower Fort Garry after the rebellion, he soon escaped and settled in Chicago.

Jaxon is here to see his wife and family, and to interview participants in and collect documents about the rebellion. He wants to write a history of the 1885 uprising.

Minister of militia cleared in sex scandal

Oct. 15, 1909

KENTVILLE, N.S. – Walter Carruthers of the newspaper *The Eye Opener* has been found guilty of libelling Sir Frederick Borden, the federal minister of militia. The verdict relates to allegations in *The Eye Opener* that Sir Frederick was "keeping" for sexual purposes a woman named Hestor Chalefour at a house at 362 Palace Street, Montreal. He was also alleged to have paid her $2,000 for her services.

During the case, Crown Attorney Roscoe proved that Sir Frederick was not even in Montreal during at least one of the times he is alleged to have stayed with Miss Chalefour. And the defence's reliance on Miss Chalefour as a witness was fatal: she contradicted herself numerous times.

Up to 30 Japanese die in train crash

Nov. 28, 1909

SAPPERTON, B.C. – A train carrying Japanese workers on their way to repair a stretch of railway track has crashed through a bridge into the Brunette Creek. At least 20 – and probably 30 – men have been killed.

Last night's rain and wind, the worst in years, damaged stretches of the Great Northern track near here. A special train, carrying a track repair machine and a car to carry the workers, was made up and headed by Locomotive 456. As it got near the Brunette Creek, the train started to plow through floods covering the tracks. It was on the bridge before the engineer realized, and the wagon with the machinery crashed through the bridge, dragging the workers' car into the flooding water. The locomotive reached the other side safely.

1910

Ottawa, January. Some 1,000 delegates of the *Association Canadienne-Française d'Education d'Ontario* support more and better French-language schooling in Ontario.

Rogers Pass, Alta., March 5. An avalanche swallows up a work crew, killing 62.

Baddeck, N.S., March 7. Aviation pioneer John McCurdy breaks all Canadian aviation records.

Montreal, March 12. The Montreal Wanderers beat the Berlin [Kitchener] Union Jacks 7-3 to win the Stanley Cup.

Toronto, March. The Grey Cup is officially turned over to the University of Toronto for their victory in the first Grey Cup game last year.

Ottawa, April 20. PM Wilfrid Laurier's government passes the Naval Service Bill to establish a small Canadian Navy to be put under imperial control "in case of war." French-Canadian nationalists oppose the bill, and anglophone imperialists criticize it for doing too little.

New Jersey, Aug. 27. Thomas Edison demonstrates talking motion pictures.

Hamilton, Nov. 26. University of Toronto beats the Hamilton Tigers 16-7 for the Grey Cup.

Ottawa, Dec. 12. A deputation of 1,000 farmers from across Canada demands reciprocity with the U.S. and government ownership of railways and grain elevators.

Weston, Ont. John McCurdy crashes his plane in a field, perhaps the first Canadian to crash a powered flight plane.

Dundas, Ont. The first McIntosh apple tree, transplanted by John McIntosh around 1810, dies.

Ontario. Francophone and anglophone wings of the Roman Catholic church clash, with Bishop Michael Fallon leading Irish Catholic opposition to bilingual schools.

Toronto. Weston's Biscuits is incorporated by baker George Weston.

Canada. The CPR hires the Edison Co. to make 13 story films to promote Canadian immigration.

United States. American filmmakers are using Canada as a setting for story films featuring villainous French-Canadian lumberjacks, Métis, gold miners, and noble Mounties.

Manitoba Sanatorium to treat TB patients

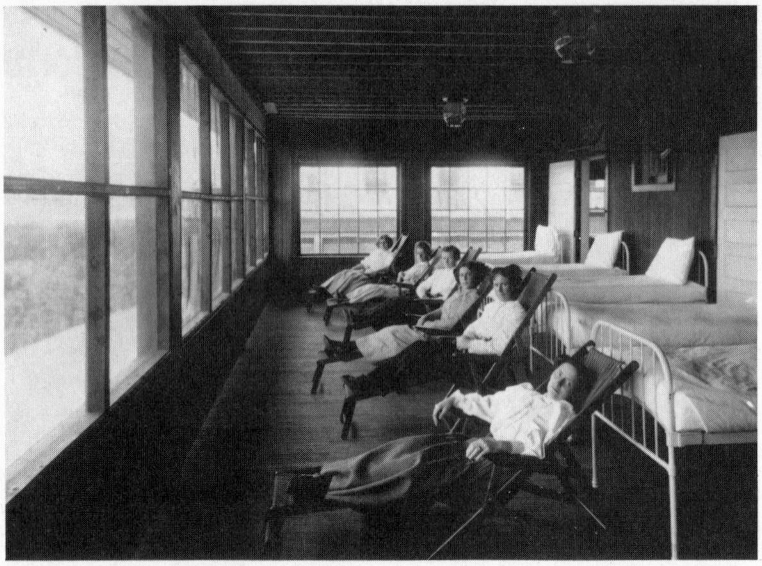

The interior of a sleeping pavilion at the new sanatorium at Ninette, Man.

May 24, 1910

NINETTE, Man. – The official opening ceremonies were held here today for the Manitoba Sanatorium, a 65-bed hospital for tuberculosis patients and the second facility of its type west of Gravenhurst, Ont. It cost $75,000 to build.

At the ceremonies, a number of speakers paid tribute to the man largely responsible for changing the public attitude toward tuberculosis. Dr. David A. Stewart, a graduate in both theology and medicine, is a former tuberculosis patient who since his cure has been a vigorous advocate for TB treatment centres.

Founder Dr. David A. Stewart.

Le Devoir founded; paper comes out swinging at Laurier

Jan. 10, 1910

MONTREAL – The first edition of *Le Devoir* hit the streets today, and the newspaper has already become identified as the personal platform of its founding director, Quebec nationalist leader Henri Bourassa. Financed by 172 shareholders, *Le Devoir* bears the motto "Fais ce que dois (Do what you must)." Bourassa's name is displayed below the masthead.

Bourassa, member of Parliament for St. Hyacinthe, used the occasion to deliver a blistering attack on the naval policy being proposed by the Liberal government of Prime Minister Wilfrid Laurier. The PM's policy would create a Canadian navy available to Great Britain in the event of war. Bourassa, backed by Quebec Conservative Frederick Dabartzch Monk, wants to limit any navy fleet solely to coast guard activities.

Although its debut was a broadside at the Laurier government, *Le Devoir* plans to advocate other pan-Canadian ideals. These, as defined by Bourassa, are: Canadian autonomy, loyalty to British ideals, minority rights throughout Canada, provincial autonomy, and the promotion of bilingual public service and laws.

13 unlucky number for 13 N.S. sailors

Feb. 8, 1910

HALIFAX – Thirteen seamen landed here today after being rescued from a burning sailboat, the *Calcium*, a 13-year-old bark which sailed on the 13th of the month. The crew never want to hear that number again. Fire broke out on the voyage from French Guinea to New York, and for five days they manned the pumps of the leaking vessel ablaze from bow to stern.

The British steamer *Syrian* arrived in response to frantic distress signals, and, despite violently high-running seas, managed to lower a lifeboat and save the entire crew. Only one of the 13 was hurt, suffering three broken ribs.

Outbreak of rabies afflicts Ontario dogs

Even house pets are under restriction in the new regulation against rabies.

Feb. 6, 1910

OTTAWA – The veterinary director general reports that close to 3,000 dogs carrying rabies are living in scattered parts of the western peninsula of Ontario. Yesterday, an order was issued by the Department of Agriculture requiring all dogs lying west of the eastern boundaries of York and Simcoe counties to be chained in a locked outbuilding or muzzled. Violation of the regulation can result in fines of up to $200.

Canada prepared: the Boy Scouts arrive

Col. Sir Henry M. Pellatt presents new flag to the Canadian Boy Scouts.

1910

CANADA – The three-year-old scouting movement, started by British Lt.-Gen. Robert Baden-Powell after his success with a boys' camp in England, has spread to Canada. As their motto "be prepared" illustrates, the Boy Scouts value responsibility, resourcefulness and strength of character; attributes which are instilled through a series of group and community activities. Canada's governor general, Earl Grey, serves as a model for the boys. He is referred to as "Chief Scout."

Slim majority of Blackfoot OKs land sale

June 15, 1910

GLEICHEN, Alta. – The Blackfoot tribe, in a tight 69-64 vote, decided today to sell nearly half of its reserve. The vote fulfils Indian Act requirements which say that a land surrender must secure the consent of a majority of the adult males living on the reserve.

Those Blackfoot in favor of the surrender apparently have accepted Indian Department arguments that the Indians must sell land to finance new farming operations. With cash in hand they could obtain houses and barns like the settlers, and buy good horses and wagons. The sale would also ensure that each band member got improved rations. As one pro-sale Blackfoot said, "Selling land means we shall have farmland and money and will live good."

Indian Department officials are anxious to free up more land for settlement, as hundreds of thousands of immigrants have come to the northwest over the last decade and good land is at a premium. At the same time, the Blackfoot population continues to decline, and, in fact, it has fallen from more than 2,000 in 1877 to about 800. Once the surrendered lands are sold to settlers, it is believed that the Blackfoot will become the richest Indian band in Canada.

A Blackfoot chief.

Incorporation OK'd for Dome Mines Co.

March 23, 1910

TIMMINS, Ont. – The Dome Mines Company, whose rich deposits of gold ore were discovered in the Porcupine ridge 12.9 kilometres east of here last year, was incorporated today. The discovery was staked by Jack Wilson and Barney McEanney after Wilson noticed something yellow glistening. The vein was 45 metres wide and several hundred metres long. The company name is derived from the quartz dome where gold was found.

Steel Co. of Canada founded by Aitken

June 8, 1910

MONTREAL – Financier Max Aitken formed the Steel Company of Canada [Stelco] today by merging the Hamilton Steel and Iron Company, Montreal Rolling Mills, and finishing works in Quebec and Ontario. By controlling overall operations, the company is less vulnerable to United States Steel, which was in a position to either flood Canada with finished products or charge finishing plants here top rates for primary steel.

Government to keep watch over business

April 26, 1910

OTTAWA – The federal government has passed the Anti-Combines Bill, so nicknamed because it will allow the government to investigate unethical business practices, monopolies and mergers. In the House, Labor Minister William Lyon Mackenzie King gave examples of how the bill might be used, such as to prevent the use of patents to create monopolies or to ensure steamship companies receiving federal subsidies don't fix passenger rates. In answer to criticism from the Tories, King said the bill's intent was not so much prosecution as publicity: businesses caught in immoral practices will be shamed into proper behavior.

Campbellton fire leaves 4,000 homeless

These men have built a shack as a refuge after the Campbellton fire.

July 11, 1910

CAMPBELLTON, N.B. – A raging inferno that broke out in a shingle mill and spread rapidly through this prosperous seaport has virtually wiped it off the map. Four thousand people are homeless, and most of them are utterly ruined. One woman, two men and an infant, all unrelated, died in the horror. The damages are estimated at about $2.5 million.

French count first to fly over Toronto

July 13, 1910
TORONTO – Aviation history was made here today as Count De Lesseps of France became the first man to fly over the city. The event was part of a Toronto air show, in which the count and his famous airplane *La Scarabee* are a featured attraction. The historic flight started at 8 p.m. when the Count took off in his Blériot monoplane. In the next half-hour he flew 38 kilometres, passing over the heart of Toronto. Phone lines at newspapers and city hall alike were jammed with reports of his flying overhead.

French university grants woman a BA

Oct. 1, 1910
MONTREAL – The University of Montreal has become Quebec's first French-language university to grant a bachelor of arts degree to a woman. The unidentified graduate was a student at the Marguerite Bourgeoys College.

French-language universities in Quebec lag far behind their counterparts in other Canadian provinces when it comes to the education of women. Mount Allison University, New Brunswick, granted a bachelor of science to a woman in 1875.

Weddings such as this late 19th century one in Saskatchewan are occasions for family portraits. The bride is centre front.

Fisheries ruling favors Newfoundland

Sept. 7, 1910
NEWFOUNDLAND – The Hague Tribunal has ruled that Newfoundland may regulate the fisheries used not only by its fishermen, but by Canadians and Americans in its territorial waters as well. Furthermore, the tribunal has ruled that Newfoundland's territorial waters include the bays and three nautical miles outside a straight line drawn across the mouth of each bay. Consequently, complaints by American fishermen that they were unfairly and illegally treated by Newfoundland when the colony attempted to regulate its herring fishery will be put to rest.

Conflict with the U.S. fishermen on the Newfoundland coast began after 1783, when the Americans insisted they retain the right to fish along the coast of Newfoundland and Labrador. In 1818, a treaty between the United States and Britain allowed Americans to fish on parts of these coasts.

As the century progressed, Newfoundland acquired representative and then responsible government by 1855. During the same time, the Americans developed an extensive bank – or offshore – fishery for which they needed large quantities of bait, especially herring. The Newfoundland government began to insist it had jurisdiction over the herring fishery in its bays, and in the 1870s passed legislation to preserve the stocks. Matters came to a head in 1878 when clashes occurred in Fortune Bay.

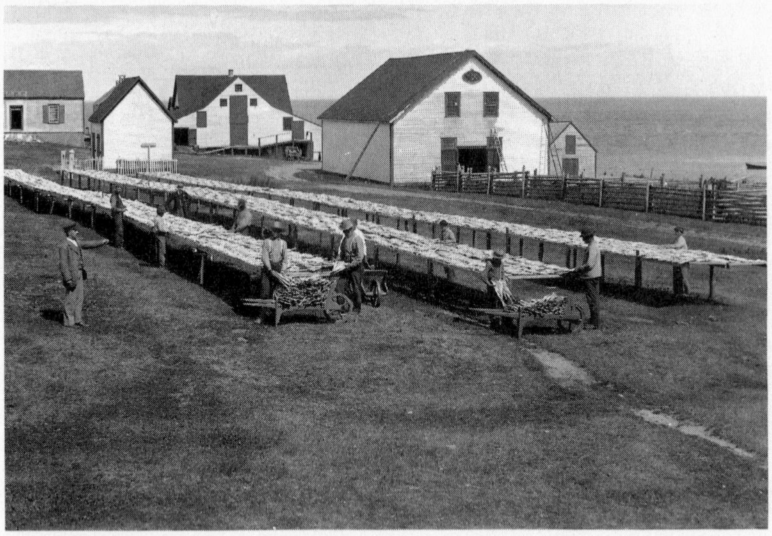

Atlantic fishermen bring their catch ashore and dry the fish on long racks.

Newspapers found the Canadian Press

Nov. 8, 1910
TORONTO – A co-operative news gathering service to be called Canadian Press was founded today by daily newspapers in this country. The wire service, which will be launched Jan. 1, is to take over the responsibilities of the Associated Press in Canada. Canadian Press will have subsidiary organizations throughout the country for reporting local or regional news. There will be one such organization for the Maritime provinces, another for Ontario and Quebec, a third for the prairie provinces, and a fourth for British Columbia.

Stories gathered by members of the news service will be added to the Associated Press report for distribution. The Toronto *Globe*'s J.F. MacKay will be the first president of Canadian Press. Its formation follows on the heels of two earlier regional organizations, the Eastern Press Association (Maritime dailies and those in central Canada) in September of this year and the Western Associated Press in 1907.

Flagship crowns Canada's new naval fleet

The Canadian navy's first battleship – the HMCS Niobe.

Oct. 21, 1910
HALIFAX – Canada's new navy welcomed its flagship today as the first-class cruiser *Niobe* steamed into Halifax harbor. Purchased from the British, the 138-metre *Niobe* weighs 11,000 tons. She has 16 six-inch guns, 14 12-pounders, and three torpedo tubes.

The arrival of the *Niobe* was greeted with great fanfare in the port today. Leading the cheers was L.P. Brodeur, marine minister. In a speech welcoming the ship, he said the *Niobe* proves that Canada is willing to provide her own naval defence and to share in the defence of the British Empire.

Western Canada feels sharp rise in immigration

Immigrants skip to pass the time on board the SS Empress of Britain.

1910

OTTAWA – There has been a sharp increase in the number of immigrants arriving in Canada – and especially the west – since 1902. The figures reveal that while 89,102 immigrants reached Canada in 1902, the number rose to 173,694 last year. And, another 170,000 – at least – are expected this year.

Since 1901, the populations of Alberta and Saskatchewan have quintupled. While 60 percent of the new arrivals are of British stock, and so fit easily into the fabric of Canadian society, they are less likely to settle on the prairies. Here, immigrants from northern, central and eastern Europe are numerous, threatening to displace those of British origin. At one time, most immigrants were farmers who arrived with their families. Now, however, more and more of the new arrivals are unskilled laborers. Often, they are single men, or family men who have come to this country alone. Many head for the Canadian west in the expectation of finding employment suited to their limited skills.

Some observers say the presence of too many foreigners will have a detrimental effect on Canadian society. The federal government's stand on the matter is ambiguous. For instance, official encouragement of Ukrainian immigration stopped in 1899, yet the government quietly continues to pay European shipping agents a bonus for up to 5,000 immigrants per year.

This image is from the cover of a promotional booklet published by the federal Department of the Interior.

A group of homesteaders has put down roots at Lipton, Saskatchewan.

Immigrants to Canada like to settle in communities with others of the same origin so they can keep their own culture and traditions alive. This makes them more comfortable in a new and strange land. These men of Scottish origin have formed a pipe band and wear traditional highland costume.

PM's policy subject of student debate

Nov. 25, 1910

MONTREAL – The Imperialists beat the Nationalists in a heated debate last night between teams from McGill and Laval universities. McGill students, speaking in English, defended the naval policy of Prime Minister Sir Wilfrid Laurier, while Laval debaters, speaking in French, attacked the policy and backed nationalist leader Henri Bourassa. The discussion became lively at times, with both teams often switching languages. In the end, the audience of both French and English voted 65-15 in favor of the McGill team.

Emily Murphy writes the popular Janey Canuck books. Her newest one, Janey Canuck in the West, has just been published. She is also keenly interested in legal reform and women's suffrage.

Explosion at Alberta coal mine kills 35

Dec. 11, 1910

FRANK, Alta. – Thirty-five men are dead as the result of an underground explosion at the Bellevue coal mine, 4.8 kilometres east of here. Thirty-three of the dead were miners, killed in the initial explosion at 7 p.m. last night. The two others were in a rescue party which was trapped after a rock collapse in the damaged shaft.

The rescue effort was heroic. For example, there was Jack Hutton, a local miner who went down in the first rescue party. Once inside, he learned that his brother Ike was among the men trapped below. Jack Hutton worked until 3 a.m., clearing and searching, pushing through bodies in the search for Ike. Fortunately he found him alive, sheltering in a side gallery (a small tunnel off the main shaft). They had just set out together when a second fall of rocks forced them to retreat to the same gallery. Hours later they were found by the second rescue party. Jack Hutton was conscious; his brother was not. So Jack carried his brother back to the surface. Both will recover.

The disaster, which affected so many miners, may have been caused by an underground fire which was thought to have been extinguished last October. Such fires can smoulder in the coal for months, resulting in explosions.

1911

Washington, D.C., January. Canada and the U.S. reach a reciprocity agreement, agreeing to pass concurrent legislation to lower tariff barriers between the two countries.

Toronto, Feb. 14. David Boyle, a leading archeologist, dies.

Ottawa, March 16. The Ottawa Senators defeat the Port Arthur Bearcats 13-4 to win the Stanley Cup.

Ontario, March 21. Shell Canada is incorporated.

Toronto, March 24. The legislature passes the Theatres and Cinematographs Act to regulate the film industry, giving the lieutenant-governor wide powers to censor films.

Toronto, May 2. Hydro-electric power from Niagara Falls is officially inaugurated in the city.

Ottawa, May 9. The government awards Adam Graham $562 as compensation for losses incurred while he was a prisoner of Louis Riel during the Red River resistance.

Nova Scotia, May 27. The long and bitter 22-month Springhill coal miners' strike ends. The strikers failed to secure their demands for pay raises and union recognition.

Ottawa, May 31. In response to complaints from the Edmonton Board of Trade, the minister of the interior suggests blacks be prevented from entering Canada for a year.

Edmonton, Sept. 19. The first synagogue in the city is erected.

London, Ont., Nov. 6. Sir John Carling, millionaire brewer and politician, dies.

Toronto, Nov. 25. University of Toronto beats the Toronto Argonauts 14-7 in the Grey Cup.

Canada. Popular mixed-blood poetess Pauline Johnson publishes *Legends of Vancouver*, inspired by Squamish legends.

Quebec. Jesuits found *L'Ecole sociale populaire* to encourage Catholic trade unionism.

Toronto. John Bayne Maclean's *Busy Man's Magazine* is renamed *Maclean's*.

Toronto. Casa Loma, the largest castle in North America, is completed. It was designed by E.J. Lennox.

Victoria. The legislature establishes a minimum age of 15 for mine work.

Canada. The population is 7,206,643.

Laurier defends proposed trade deal

March 7, 1911

OTTAWA – Speaking with the eloquence for which he is renowned, Prime Minister Sir Wilfrid Laurier gave a stirring defence of the proposed International Reciprocal Trade Agreement being hammered out between Canada and the United States. Addressing fears that reciprocity will end Canadian economic independence, Laurier said the Tories were active advocates of the policy in the early days of Sir John A. Macdonald. Where were their fears about "American economic imperialism" then?

More importantly, the PM said freer trade between both nations will benefit both, without weakening Canada's ties to the British Empire. "Our policy has been, is, and will be ... to seek markets wherever markets are to be found." Whether Laurier has the support of the Canadian people on this, as he says he has, remains to be seen.

RECIPROCITY TREATY
SIR WILFRID—"UNCLE, WOULD YOU ALSO ACCEPT THE CHAIRMANSHIP OF THE CANADIAN CONSERVATION COMMISSION?"

The cartoonist suggests that reciprocity will mean greater U.S. influence.

Treaty protects fur seals in north Pacific

July 7, 1911

WASHINGTON, D.C. – Canada, the United States, Russia, and Japan signed a treaty of historic proportions today, protecting fur seals in international waters in the north Pacific from commercial hunters. The annual seal slaughter will take place on rocky rookeries under controlled conditions.

The importance of the fur seal industry rose with the formation of the Alaska Commercial Co. after the United States bought Alaska. Non-company ships – especially Canadian – hunted the seals in international waters, much to the dismay of the Americans. The ACC and its successor called in U.S. revenue cutters, which arrested the non-company ships on the high seas despite Canadian and British protests. Now, profits from the rookeries must be shared, and only native Indians and Aleuts may hunt seals in international waters.

The seal seems very small beside the sea lion caught by these sealers.

Forest reserve law protects fish, game

1911

ALBERTA – The enactment of the Dominion Forest Reserves and Parks Act establishes the whole eastern slope of the Rocky Mountains in Canada as a forest reserve. The act re-defines the boundaries of existing parks, reducing the areas of the Rocky Mountain, Waterton Lakes and Jasper parks. The new boundaries, as delineated by order-in-council under the act, locate the reserve between two parallel lines drawn to and 16 kilometres from the Grand Trunk Pacific Railway, giving the new reserve an approximate area of 2,590 square kilometres.

Superintendent of forestry R.H. Campbell says the new limits are not intended to reduce the area in which game is protected, but rather to restrict the area to which free access is given to visitors and potential poachers, affording greater preservation of fish and game provided under forest reserve regulations. The well-defined boundaries will facilitate administration of the parks, and make thorough patrolling of the entire reserve achievable.

Life is a nightmare for poor living in city slums

People live in very crowded conditions in the older parts of Canada's cities. Petit Champlain Street in Quebec City offers little room for children to play.

This Winnipeg slum district illustrates typical living conditions of the poor in big cities. Scrap lumber is used to build shelters for extra people.

1911

WINNIPEG – The poor, especially new immigrants, face a life of horror in the city slums of Canada. In his latest book, *My Neighbour*, reformer James Shaver Woodsworth describes the dismal conditions that have become common in Canadian urban centres.

J.J. Kelso, founder of the Children's Aid Society, defines a slum as "a lane or alley, a series of lots about 150 feet deep, with three or four houses, hovels or shacks erected, one behind the other." In these hovels may be found all the miseries known to mankind. Woodsworth presents case after case of overcrowding, of parents and four or more children jammed into a single room, sometimes sharing one bed. In one instance, a Winnipeg health inspector found a boarding house in which 32 men were crowded into four rooms, amid filthy furnishings and bedclothes.

Immorality, murder and violence are rife in Canadian slums. In Winnipeg, one woman, a morphine addict, allowed messenger boys free access to her rooms. Another man, Louis Liew, convinced an innocent girl of 17 to marry him, then, through brutal beatings, forced her into prostitution. More than once, adulterous liaisons have resulted in murder and suicide. There has also been a significant increase in illegitimate births. In Toronto, the Haven sheltered 302 maternity cases in one year alone. One-third of these were married women who had been deserted or were too poor to care for themselves. The remainder were unmarried: three-quarters of them were feeble-minded, and nearly half gave birth to babies who were diseased or defective, according to Haven records.

Children are the most pathetic victims of poverty and ignorance. Neglected by their parents, they starve or are forced into a life of crime. Some succumb to illness, such as consumption, while others are abandoned. Given these conditions, Woodsworth writes, "women who have true sympathy and men who are not devoid of all chivalry cannot but feel impelled to do something to relieve the misery and banish the evils which are so prevalent in our midst."

This young girl has collected a bag of coal from beside railway boxcars.

The children of affluent city families are well-dressed and have the latest toys, such as this replica of the new transportation success – the automobile.

Homemakers' Club takes reform tack

Jan. 31, 1911

SASKATOON – The new Homemakers' Club, formed at a meeting today, aims to bring information and education to rural areas. The club also hopes to serve as a vehicle for cultural and moral reform through discussion on matters of importance such as temperance and votes for women. Today's meeting here was called by a member of the University of Saskatchewan. The 42 invited women included influential journalists Lillian Beynon and Cora Hind, and author and activist Nellie McClung.

Town waging battle against weed seeds

Feb. 25, 1911

McGEE, Sask. – McGee has declared a war on weeds. The town is offering a $500 reward for information leading to the conviction of any person bringing in noxious weed seeds with grain or feed. Farmers spend a great deal of time and energy to combat weeds, mostly by cultivation. One way to help control weeds is to cut down on the amount of seeds that make their way into the fields in the first place. Authorities say seeds cause more losses than pests or plant diseases combined.

Reform committee blasts Sunday fun

April 25, 1911

WOODSTOCK, Ont. – Movies and bridge are forms of vice that should be outlawed, at least on Sundays. So says the report of the Social and Moral Reform Committee, presented to the Hamilton and London Synod meeting here today. As the committee is comprised of clergymen, it's hardly surprising that it feels Sunday should be reserved for worship and nothing else. Picnics, teas, and visiting are frowned upon. As for movies, they are seen as encouraging vice since films sometimes contain violence and illegal acts. Bridge, meanwhile, is portrayed as a form of gambling.

Although there are laws against business on Sunday, and public sympathy for it as a day of rest, it's not likely the committee recommendations will become law.

"Negroes undesirable," farmers say

ALBERTA
THE LINE
Sunny Al Welcomes the Horde of Investors and Settlers From the South

Despite the message of this poster, not all U.S. immigrants are welcome.

April 29, 1911

EDMONTON – Deeming "Negroes undesirable as fellow citizens," the Edmonton chapter of the United Farmers of Alberta has joined the drive led by the Edmonton Board of Trade to ban settlement of blacks from Oklahoma in the province. The secretary of the Board of Trade, F.T. Fisher, has argued against the growth of the black community in Alberta, saying "those Negroes who have been here some time have had a square deal and been treated as whites. But if you would get a thousand more in, conditions would be much changed. They would then be treated as they were in the south."

Fisher says 3,400 people signed a petition asking for a ban on black settlement. Other boards of trade in Alberta and Manitoba also want black settlement banned.

Public interest first, Indian rights second

A Cree woman prepares food at an inside fireplace at Lesser Slave Lake.

May 1911

OTTAWA – Parliament has once again drastically reduced the rights of Canadian Indians, in a new amendment to the Indian Act. Under Section 49A of the act, the government of Canada can approve the expropriation of any Indian reserve near a town or city of 8,000 or more inhabitants regardless of any previous treaty or written agreement. The expropriation is subject only to judicial review by the Exchequer Court of Canada. Reserves the legislation may affect include the Chippewa [Ojibwa] reserve at Sarnia, Ont., and the Caughnawaga [Kahnawake] reserve near Montreal. As Calgary expands, the eastern section of the Sarcee reserve may be in question. Frank Oliver, the Liberal minister of the interior, says that reserves blocking urban growth must be eliminated, as Indian rights "must give away to the public interest."

Report tells of lost Mounties' tragic fate

May 16, 1911

OTTAWA – A full report of the tragic deaths of four Royal North West Mounted Police officers reached here today. The deaths took place in February on a routine patrol from Fort McPherson, near the mouth of the Mackenzie River, to Dawson in the Yukon.

The patrol, led by Inspector Francis Fitzgerald, a 22-year veteran of the force, left the post on Dec. 21. Travelling light in hope of making a speed record, the four men encountered heavy snow and low temperatures. As their supplies ran out, they wandered off the trail and had to eat their sled dogs to survive. Eventually, Fitzgerald and two others starved to death. The fourth man committed suicide.

When the patrol was overdue at the end of February, a search party was sent out and located the bodies. Rescuers found a diary on Fitzgerald's frozen corpse, along with a will he had written with a burned twig on a torn scrap of paper.

The search party returns to Fort McPherson with the bodies of the lost patrol.

U.S. Senate approves Reciprocity Bill

July 22, 1911

WASHINGTON, D.C. – The U.S. Senate approved reciprocity with Canada today 53-27. Voting came after balloting on 16 amendments to the act, many devised by enemies of reciprocity to hamstring it. After all were defeated, Vice-President James Sherman asked, "Are there any more amendments?" Answered by silence, he continued, "The motion is for the passage of the bill. As many as favor it will say aye." Fifty-three said aye, and reciprocity, already passed by Congress, became law, at least in the United States. Said Senator Penrose of Pennsylvania, who guided the bill through the House for U.S. President William Howard Taft, "It is hoped that the Canadian Parliament will able to perform their part at an early date."

Certainly Prime Minister Wilfrid Laurier and his Liberal government believe people want reciprocity – a deal that will eliminate duties on raw materials, and cut duties on secondary imports and exports. But so strong is Conservative opposition to the bill – charging that it is nothing but a plot to bring Canada into the American union – that it's uncertain if Laurier will try to ram the reciprocity bill through Parliament before the next election. In fact, some sources speculate that the prime minister himself may take the issue to the people, to ensure that he has the support necessary to affect such a radical shift from the protective tariffs policy of the past.

In the meantime, the president and his supporters are said to be delighted by the passage of the Reciprocity Bill. With it in place, they hope to see lower-priced foodstuffs come into America, thus easing the shopping bill of the average city dweller. It's a move that's sure to win votes for the Republican Party, although perhaps not from American farmers.

Canadians say no to reciprocity: Grits ousted from office

Sept. 22, 1911

OTTAWA – Across the land this morning, Conservatives are laughing and Liberals are weeping as they survey a political landscape that has been radically altered by yesterday's federal election that swept across Canada with all the force of an advancing and retreating tidal wave. In an election dominated by the Liberals' proposed reciprocity deal with the U.S., Robert Borden's Conservatives have upset Wilfrid Laurier's Liberal government 134 seats to 87.

Borden led the opposition to reciprocity, the general of a political force that included such unlikely allies as prominent Liberal businessmen from Toronto and French-Canadian nationalist Henri Bourassa. The businessmen issued a manifesto arguing reciprocity would "weaken the ties that bind Canada and the Empire ... and make it more difficult to avert political union with the U.S." The political war was fought largely on this emotional terrain. Laurier was crushed in Ontario, where manufacturing communities feared the impact of reciprocity, and he lost seats in Quebec because of his naval policy. The prairies were one of his few bright spots – its farmers have long opposed high Canadian tariff rates and support reciprocity.

At least 300 dead as flames sweep through Northern Ontario

July 11, 1911

TIMISKAMING, Ont. – Hundreds have died in Northern Ontario, as a wall of flames has swept through the bush country, egged on by high winds, dry trees, and no rain anywhere. Nothing can stop the blaze, which has seared Cochrane, Pottsville and South Porcupine off the map. Worse yet is the human tragedy: at least 300 dead, 200 in South Porcupine alone.

Surrounded by flames, townspeople here took refuge in the lake. Due to the crush from the shore, many were pushed into deep waters and drowned. Still others died when their boats capsized.

Volunteers carry the bodies of the many casualties in the Porcupine fire.

PM puts together Conservative cabinet

Oct. 10, 1911

OTTAWA – Some two weeks after sweeping away the Laurier regime in a fiercely-fought election over reciprocity, Prime Minister Robert Borden has put together his Conservative cabinet. In fact, the cabinet was sworn in today by the departing Gov. Gen. Earl Grey. It was his last official act in Canada.

Borden's cabinet reflects the debt he has incurred because of the political alliance he crafted, notably with the Quebec Nationalists, to defeat Sir Wilfrid Laurier. It's a case of politics making strange bedfellows, since the Nationalists are opposed to the existence of the Royal Canadian Navy, especially since that force can be transferred to Britain in times of emergency. Borden is a staunch Tory committed to imperial defence.

Still, both sides wanted Laurier out and so the Quebec Nationalists threw their support behind the Conservatives to defeat him. Three French-Canadians have been named to the new cabinet: W.R. Nantel, minister of inland revenue; L.P. Pelletier, postmaster general; and F.D. Monk, public works minister. Insiders predict a cabinet split over the navy issue before long. Meanwhile, this new government signals two realities: reciprocity is dead, and so is the Laurier regime which ruled Canada since 1896.

The installation of HRH the Duke of Connaught as the new governor general of Canada takes place in the council chamber at Quebec City.

1912

Ottawa, March 21. Prince Edward Island Senator Andrew Archibald Macdonald, one of the last surviving Fathers of Confederation, dies.

Winnipeg, June 2. A convention of Canadian YMCAs forms the National Council of YMCAs of Canada.

Nome, Alaska, Aug. 18. Vilhjalmur Stefansson and Rudolph Anderson complete their four-year expedition studying the Inuit and exploring the Arctic.

Kingston, Ont., Sept. 24. Sir Richard Cartwright, veteran parliamentarian and esteemed statesman, dies.

Hamilton, Nov. 30. The Hamilton Alerts defeat the Toronto Argonauts 11-4 to win the Grey Cup.

Quebec, Dec. 4. Abitibi Pulp and Paper Co. is incorporated.

New Brunswick, Dec. 9. The Bank of New Brunswick merges with the Bank of Nova Scotia.

Canada. Tom Longboat, a Six Nations Indian long distance runner, sets a professional record of 1:18:10 for 15 miles.

Alberta. The first Canadian discovery of a complete duck-bill dinosaur skeleton is made.

Montreal. Carrie Matilda Derick of McGill University is named professor of morphological botany, the first woman in Canada made a full professor.

Saskatchewan. The annual meeting of the Saskatchewan Grain Growers' Association rejects a motion to extend homesteading privileges to women.

British Columbia. More than 700 Doukhobor school-age children are getting no formal education because Doukhobors reject systems of formal education.

Edmonton. A royal commission is set up to look into the problem of brothels, considered to be out of hand.

Canada. There are more than 50,000 motor vehicles registered.

Germany. Geologist Aldred Wegener, expounding his new theory of "continental drift," says that the world's continents are constantly moving. He also says there used to be just one continent.

Quebec. Quebec Bulldogs defeat the Moncton Victorias two games to none to win the Stanley Cup.

Auto shows set to go into high gear

Feb. 21, 1912

TORONTO – The automobile age is here in full force, with two rival auto shows gearing up to display their wares to Toronto consumers. Venues are the Armouries and the St. Lawrence arena.

Cars valued at a total of about $1 million will be displayed at the Armouries. There will be more than 150 different models, about half of them built in the United States. One exhibit features a fire truck built in England. The Armouries will be literally waving the flag for Great Britain at its show. On the ceiling hangs a large Union Jack, which will be illuminated by 6,000 electric lights at night. A crown 4.5 metres high and 4.2 metres across hangs from the building's roof.

The Rauch and Lang electric car is one of the new ideas in automobiles.

Leacock pokes fun at fictional town

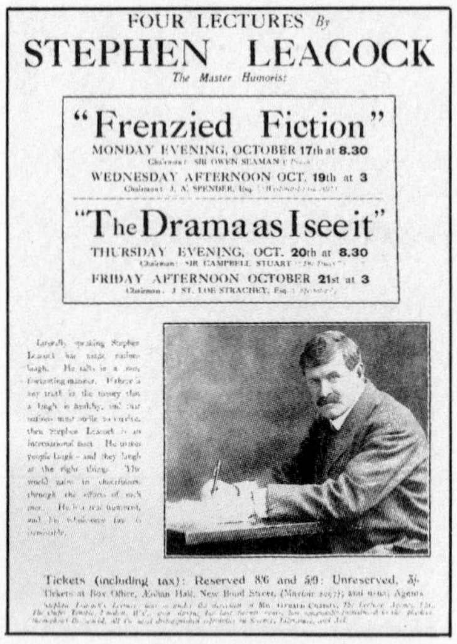

Poster advertises Leacock lectures.

1912

MONTREAL – Professor Stephen Leacock has published his third book of humor. *Sunshine Sketches of a Little Town* is a satirical look at a small Ontario community. Leacock, head of the political science department at McGill University, describes some hilarious events in his latest literary effort, including a bank robbery, a courtship, and an election. Rumor has it that events and characters in Orillia inspired the book. However, Leacock states unequivocally that "Mariposa is not a real town."

New board inspects grain, regulates trade

July 10, 1912

WINNIPEG – The Canadian grain trade is now under the jurisdiction of a Board of Grain Commissioners. The new agency is authorized by the Canada Grain Act, and is under the direct control of the minister of trade and commerce. The new board, to be located at Fort William, has sweeping powers over farmers, grain handlers and grain dealers alike.

Beginning immediately, it will be compulsory that all car lots of grain en route to terminal elevators at the Lakehead be inspected in order to facilitate storing the lots in bins upon their arrival. New and rigid regulations have been established for all aspects of the grain trade. These include regulating equipment to be used, procedures employed in cleaning and handling, and strict standards for every grade of each specific grain.

Several governments over a number of years have attempted to develop legislation which would meet the requirements of this important export industry.

Political Equality League is founded

March 17, 1912

WINNIPEG – Political observers anticipate that the Political Equality League will have a direct influence upon activities in the provincial legislature.

Lillian Beynon is credited with being the driving force behind the new organization. She carries on the organizational work begun 12 years ago by Margret Benedictsson of Selkirk, Man., and kept alive through her periodical, the magazine *Freyja.* The twin pillars upon which the Political Equality League are based are prohibition and universal suffrage.

Biggar, Sask., is named for Grand Trunk lawyer W.H. Biggar.

Abdul-Baha brings the Baha'i message

1912

EASTERN CANADA – Following the recent Canadian visit of Abdul-Baha, son of the Baha'i religion's founder Baha'u'llah, Canada's Baha'is are responding enthusiastically to Abdul-Baha's giving them and American Baha'is responsibility for expanding their faith on the international level. One facet of their plan is to build at least two houses of worship here.

The central teaching of the Baha'i faith, begun in 1844 in Persia [Iran], is that mankind is one single race that must be unified. Other elements are equality of men and women and the right to universal education. A major Baha'i goal is to establish a world government.

Newsprint industry gets started in B.C.

April 12, 1912

POWELL RIVER, B.C. – The first rolls of newsprint made in B.C. have been processed here and are on their way to customers. A Vancouver newspaper, the *Province,* is printing some issues this month on Powell River newsprint to show its support for this new industry on the coast north of Vancouver.

The Powell River Company is an American firm, typical of the U.S. investors who are leading the development – some say exploitation – of B.C. timber resources. Construction of the mill and a town for the workers began three years ago.

Police chief fired for "charity" work

Sept. 9, 1912

LETHBRIDGE, Alta. – City council has fired its police chief, after a judicial inquiry found he solicited money from brothel owners for charity. The case is an odd one, as the parade of madams who testified made it clear the chief never took money for himself. Instead, if a poor man needed cash, the madams coughed it up. The chief once escorted a Salvation Army woman to them for cash.

Iceberg downs "unsinkable" Titanic

April 15, 1912

NORTH ATLANTIC – A calm sea and cloudless sky belie the tragedy that occurred on the frigid waters of the Newfoundland banks last night – 20 minutes before midnight, the massive White Star liner *Titanic* struck an iceberg. The glancing, 10-second blow, barely felt by those aboard, is thought to have torn a 90-metre gash along the ship's starboard side. Three hours and 55 minutes later, the world's largest vessel afloat, dubbed "unsinkable" because of 16 watertight compartments built into its hull, was plunging bow first to the bottom of the sea. At least 1,500 passengers and crew are believed to have lost their lives. An estimated 700, mostly women and children, have been rescued.

Titanic survivors are rowed to safety after the ship struck an iceberg.

The tragedy is unequalled in the annals of marine history. The *Titanic* was four days out of Southampton, England, bound for New York on its maiden voyage. A ship in a class all its own, many prominent figures were to be found in its elegant ballrooms and staterooms, among them American millionaire Col. John Jacob Astor and Canadian Charles M. Hays, president of the Grand Trunk Railway. Neither is thought to have survived.

The Cunard liner *Carpathia* reached the scene of the disaster at daybreak and has led rescue efforts. Accounts by survivors tell how the *Titanic* was abandoned in an orderly fashion, the few disturbances caused by women who refused to leave their husbands. One witness has stated that indomitable faith by those aboard in the technological wonder of this advanced steamship precluded fears that may have induced panic – even the band stoically played on following the order to abandon ship. All the *Titanic*'s lifeboats are thought to have been recovered, fuelling speculation the ship was inadequately equipped for an emergency, carrying too few lifeboats for those aboard. Given that most who made it to the boats survived, many deaths may well have been avoidable.

Regulation 17 throws fuel on Ontario's ongoing language debate

Dec. 31, 1912

TORONTO – As the year 1912 draws to a close, one issue Ontarians still talk about is the use of French in provincial schools. Due to an influx of French-speaking Canadians into the Ottawa Valley, many schools there have become bilingual, or have even begun giving instruction in French, leaving English as just another subject on the curriculum. This has outraged many English-speaking Ontarians, as well as the government.

The response from the Whitney Conservative government has been to issue Regulation 17, limiting the use of French in the classroom to the first two years of schooling, and thereafter relegating it to the status of a subject, like geography or math. The decision has outraged Franco-Ontarians, throwing fuel on the language debate.

Toy trains are popular with Canadian boys. These trackless models are meant to be pulled on the floor.

Boundaries extended on three fronts

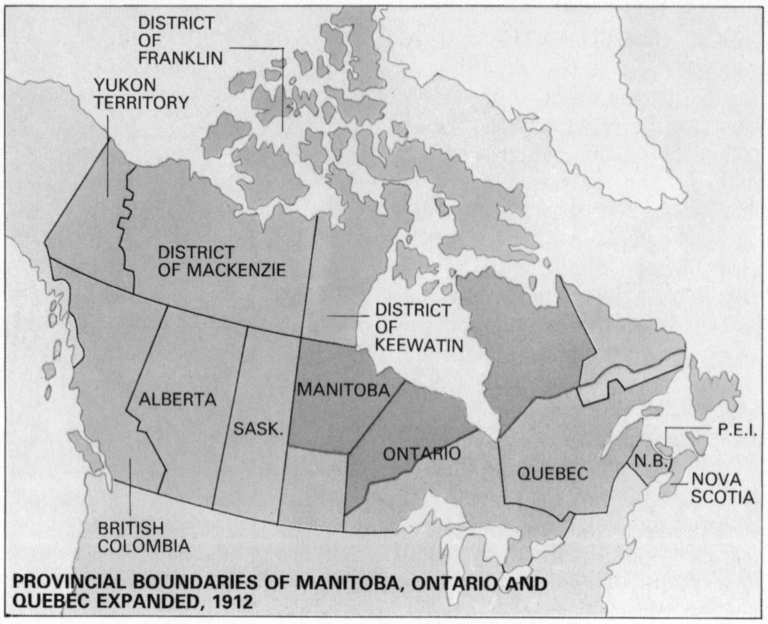

May 15, 1912

OTTAWA – Prime Minister Robert Borden's Conservative government divested itself of responsibility for policing and surveying vast tracts of northern land today by granting boundary extensions to Manitoba, Ontario, and Quebec. And the three provinces are all pleased. Manitoba's demand for more territory, fermenting since the creation of the other prairie provinces in 1905, has been appeased, and Ontario and Quebec stand to gain from promising, but as yet largely untapped, resources.

The broadening of provincial jurisdiction is also a sign of the times: having cleared the path toward development, the federal government is ready to hand the provinces greater autonomy.

Ont. mourns death of former premier

March 1, 1912

TORONTO – Edward Blake, former premier of Ontario and once federal Liberal leader, has died. Blake was an accomplished lawyer who entered politics as a provincial Liberal in 1867. He became leader in 1868, and three years later defeated the Tory government of John Sandfield Macdonald. Within a year he turned the post over to Oliver Mowat and left for Ottawa. In 1873 he refused the federal Liberal party leadership, only to take over as party leader in 1880, losing the elections of 1882 and 1887.

Quebec maps losing Indian place names

1912

QUEBEC CITY – Led by the Geographical Commission of Quebec, a campaign has begun to wipe out North American Indian names from Quebec maps. The urgency arises from the fear that visitors to the province obtain from these names the impression that Quebec is populated primarily by Indians. Four years ago Eugene Rouillard, the secretary of the Geographical Society of Quebec, initiated debate on the subject when he suggested Quebec, an "essentially French province," was "saturated" with Indian geographical names.

A display including several items used by the Kwakiutl Indians in the now illegal potlatch ceremony.

Killer cyclone rips through Regina: 28 dead, 2,500 homeless

June 30, 1912

REGINA – It took only three minutes for a rampaging cyclone to kill 28 people, injure 200, leave 2,500 homeless, and destroy 500 buildings. At 4:50 in the afternoon a cyclone set down and moved north then northeast, cutting a five-block-wide path through the city. Among the buildings destroyed were the CPR freight shed, three churches, the telephone exchange, the YMCA, the YWCA, and the public library. Total damage is estimated at $4 million to $5 million, and it is believed half of the business district will have to be rebuilt.

Huge buildings in Regina were overturned and smashed by the cyclone.

"Tribe of white people" found in Arctic

Sept. 29, 1912

VICTORIA ISLAND, N.W.T. – The Seattle *Daily Times* has just reported that explorer and anthropologist Vilhjalmur Stefansson has found a "tribe of white people" on Victoria Island which is "purely of Norwegian origin," remnants of the Norse Greenland colony which disappeared in the 15th century. Stefansson says their European looks – red and blond beards, dark brown hair, and blue eyes – might be due to climatic factors such as sun bleaching and repeated attacks of snowblindness, but he suggests their true origin came from the hitherto unexplained disappearance of Europeans from Greenland.

Stefansson has put forth a bold new theory which may set the world's scientific community on its head. It says the remaining whites of Greenland were absorbed by conquering Inuit, and after centuries of nomadic wanderings, reappeared in assimilated form in the Coronation Gulf area. Reactions to Stefansson's sensational finding are mixed, ranging from enthusiasm to caution. Some call him a headline hunter and charlatan.

Le Devoir founder speaks his mind

July 16, 1912

MONTREAL – French-Canadians would be better protected under the American Constitution, says Henri Bourassa, founder of *Le Devoir* newspaper. In an article published today, Bourassa says that in Canada, French-Canadians are restricted to Quebec just as the Indian is confined to a reservation, a situation causing many Quebecers to favor annexation to the U.S. There is also greater religious tolerance in the U.S., Bourassa says.

Ride 'em, cowboy! First Calgary Stampede begins

These Blackfoot and Blood Indians are in ceremonial dress for the parade. Bob Riding Black Horses, of the Blood tribe, carries the lance.

Sept. 2, 1912

CALGARY – A giant parade with pioneers, cowboys, cowgirls, colorful Indians from six tribes, Mounted Police and local bigwigs opened the first Calgary Stampede today. The hour-long parade through downtown Calgary was watched by 75,000 people.

More than 100 cowboys are in Calgary to compete in the traditional contests which start after the parade. The governor general, the Duke of Connaught, is expected here Thursday to watch some of the roping, bulldogging and stagecoach racing. Tickets for that day are already sold out. The bucking bronc contest is set for later this week, and one of the horses is the famous black bucker Cyclone. Tom Three Persons, a Blood Indian cowboy, has drawn this horse.

The front cover of the program prepared for the first Calgary Stampede. The organizers are featured.

Guy Weadick rides his horse through the streets of Calgary. Weadick is an organizer and the manager of the new attraction in town – the Stampede.

Tom Three Persons is a Blood Indian cowboy from Macleod, Alberta. He has come to Calgary to compete in the bronc busting competitions.

The Midway at the Stampede is a mixture of old and new. The Oasis Café is in the foreground and Indian tepees at the back represent tradition.

In the wild cow milking contest, cowboys first have to rope the cows. In the background can be seen the main buildings for the Stampede activities.

More women join the workforce despite obstacles

In a traditional role, women prepare huge meals for the men at a barn raising.

Some women work in canneries such as E.D. Smith's at Winona, Ontario.

Women occasionally find employment working as clerks in general stores.

White women must not work for Chinese

Dec. 12, 1912

REGINA – Working women in Saskatchewan now face a new obstacle. The provincial government has made it illegal for white women to work in restaurants and other businesses owned or managed by Chinese. This act was passed allegedly to preserve the morality of white women. Those in desperate need of money may have been tempted to gain employment in such establishments but will now be protected from their own actions.

The Chinese themselves, however, are still welcome in this province. As the chief justice of British Columbia, Matthew Begbie, said in a royal commission report of 1885, "They do and do well what women cannot do, and do what white men will not do." But an attempt is now being made to regulate Chinese immigration and employment so that other Saskatchewan workers will not be replaced by an oversupply of cheap labor.

The new law will affect every town in the province, for most have Chinese restaurants and laundries. But the number employing white women is estimated to be quite low.

These two women homesteaders have built a neat dwelling for themselves.

Women are employed to dip chocolates at the Whitworth Confectionery.

Prospectors strike gold in wilderness

Sept. 30, 1912

KIRKLAND LAKE, Ont. – Gold has been discovered here by a trio of prospectors. Harry Oakes and the Tough brothers, George and Tom, have been rewarded for spending many days clearing the wilderness here in sub-zero temperatures in their quest for the prized mineral. The richness of the ore is inspiring some people to say that this could be one of the biggest gold finds ever in North America.

So how did they find it? Oakes says that by carefully analysing geological reports, he figured out where all the veins discovered elsewhere met – then he claimed it.

New grain elevator is largest in world

Oct. 2, 1912

MONTREAL – The largest concrete grain elevator in the world opened today at a luncheon in its honor. Elevator No. 2 is capable of holding 2.5 million bushels, an amount equal to the current capacity of all the other elevators in the Port of Montreal.

City officials say the extra capacity comes in the nick of time, as the amount of grain going through the port has increased 26-fold in the last five years alone. As well, since this trend is expected to continue, they're already planning an addition to No. 2 that will expand its volume to 5 million bushels.

Thousands attend temperance talks

Nov. 24, 1912

TORONTO – About 50,000 people in Toronto listened to anti-alcohol sermons today. Delivered in 96 Protestant churches, the sermons were part of a "field day" staged by the temperance group Dominion Alliance, which wants to do away with the barrooms of Ontario. To further this end, now that plebiscites have shown public support for prohibition, the alliance is looking to find ways to turn this sentiment into legislation.

Children mistreated in the workplace

This 14-year-old miner faces a dismal future. With little or no education, he will probably spend his life in the mines, where the danger of explosion and cave-in is ever present.

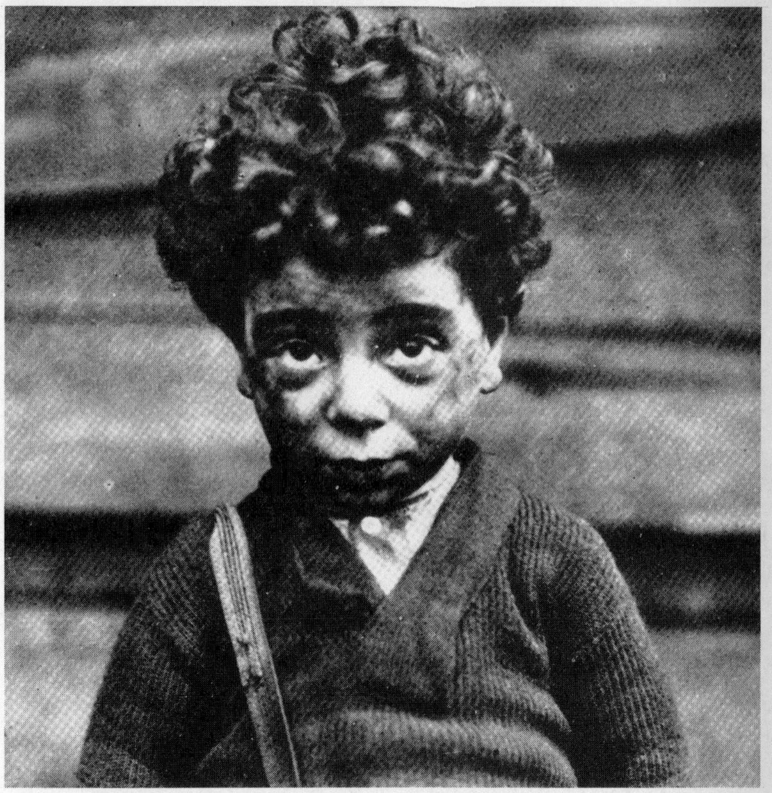

This boy appears in the Manitoba government's report on neglected children.

1912

OTTAWA – Reforms have been introduced in many areas in Canada, but children are still badly mistreated in the workplace. In factories, little skill is required. Young boys and girls are trained on the job, at high cost to their health and schooling. Furthermore, the youth and inexperience of these workers make them easy victims for cruel and uncaring bosses and factory owners, and, sometimes, even their own families. Factory legislation introduced in 1885 forbade boys under 12 from working. However, with falsified documents, many youngsters still go to work.

Because it is felt the boisterous high spirits of youth interfere with production, children are often punished for shouting, running, tardiness, or absenteeism. They are spanked, put into dark cellars, and otherwise tormented.

In Canadian mines, boys are in constant danger, but at least it can be said they are training for a better position. Such is not the case in some cities, where messenger boys, newspaper vendors and others often work at jobs that provide little income and no future. Compulsory education has reduced the number of children in the workforce, but there are still thousands who, through necessity or their parents' greed, are condemned at an early age to a life of drudgery.

Boys are part of the pit crew, seen at the mouth of a mine at Coal Creek, B.C.

A poor child wears ragged cast-offs.

1913

Calgary, Jan. 12. Fire destroys the large P. Burns and Co. meat packing plant, with losses of more than $2 million.

Quebec, March 10. The Quebec Bull Dogs defeat the Sydney Miners two games to none to win the Stanley Cup.

Quebec, April 12. Henri Bourassa lectures on the French-Canadian "capitulation to materialism" and its consequences for French-Canadian culture.

Fort Erie, Ont., July 30. On the 100th anniversary of the destruction of Fort Erie by American invaders, Americans and Canadians hold joint celebrations of the Canadian-American peace since then.

Victoria, Aug. 6. John Bryant is killed in Canada's first fatal plane crash.

Detroit, Oct. 7. Henry Ford launches a new production process called the "assembly line," expected to revolutionize car production.

Ottawa, Oct. 8. W. Robinson makes the first commercial inter-city flight in Canada from Montreal to Ottawa.

Hamilton, Nov. 29. Hamilton Tigers defeat Toronto Parkdale 44-2 to win the Grey Cup.

Quebec. The Victoria Cougars beat the Quebec Bull Dogs in an exhibition series in the first meeting between eastern and western hockey champions.

Nanaimo, B.C. Troops are called in when more than 1,000 miners riot to protest the hiring of Chinese and Japanese laborers as strikebreakers.

Halifax. The Canadian Bioscope Co. makes the first Canadian feature film, *Evangeline*, based on a Longfellow poem about the expulsion of the Acadians.

Victoria. Painter Emily Carr has produced a large number of works on Indian themes, but can't live from her art work.

Edmonton. The province sets a five-year closed hunting season on the pronghorn, now threatened by overhunting.

Montreal. The Young Women's Hebrew Association is organized.

Prairies. There are 17,746 convictions for drunkenness in the three prairie provinces.

Ottawa. Parliament incorporates the National Gallery, formally severing ties between the gallery and the Royal Canadian Academy.

Famed Indian writer Pauline Johnson dies

Poetess Pauline Johnson.

March 8, 1913

VANCOUVER – Pauline Johnson, one of the most popular Canadian writers, the author of *The Song My Paddle Sings, Legends of Vancouver* (1911) and *Flint and Feather* (1912), has died of cancer. She was 51.

The daughter of a Six Nations Indian chief and his English-born wife, Pauline, or to use her Iroquois name, Tekahionwake, was born on the Six Nations Reserve in Ontario in 1861. She first came to prominence in the early 1890s, when the Indian writer began a series of speaking tours across Canada, the U.S. and England. In 1908 she retired from performing and made her permanent home in Vancouver.

Canadian Arctic Expedition in the works

Feb. 23, 1913

OTTAWA – The Canadian government is launching an ambitious scientific expedition into the western Arctic. Led by the controversial ethnologist Vilhjalmur Stefansson, the Canadian Arctic Expedition will explore the Beaufort Sea and gather information on the region's native inhabitants, its minerals, and its animal and plant life. The expedition originally was sponsored by the National Geographic Society and the American Museum of Natural History, but Canadian officials took it over as part of their desire to assert sovereignty over the Arctic territory.

A veteran of two previous northern excursions, Stefansson is most famous for his claim to have discovered a new race of "Blond Eskimos" on Victoria Island. His second in command is the American zoologist Rudolph Martin Anderson. The plan is for Stefansson to concentrate on the Beaufort Sea area, while Anderson focuses on the region along the Arctic coast east of the Mackenzie Delta. The expedition is expected to be away several years.

Nass River valley still belongs to us, Nishga Indians say

Jan. 22, 1913

KINCOLITH, B.C. – The Nishga Indians today adopted a statement which reaffirms their tribal ownership of the Nass River valley. They contend their homeland was never conquered by the British, nor have they ever made a treaty with the British Crown, the provincial government of British Columbia, or the federal government of Canada, surrendering it.

The province disputes the Indians' claims. In 1884, then premier William Smithe declared that the government of British Columbia owned the province, and that the Indians had received their reserves "from the queen's land as a matter of charity." Premier Richard McBride himself reiterated this stand only two years ago at an Indian conference in Victoria, and ever since then Nishga elders have continued to meet to discuss the land question. The Nishga statement today reaffirms their position that they never surrendered the title to their homeland.

Only last September, McBride agreed with the federal government to establish a royal commission to make a final adjustment of all matters relating to Indian Affairs in British Columbia. The commission has just begun its investigations.

Naval cadets take first-class honors

Jan. 24, 1913

OTTAWA – Canada's first group of naval cadets is full of first-class sailors. So says Minister of Naval Affairs John D. Hazen, speaking today in the House of Commons. Hazen says graduates of the Halifax Naval College, trained on Canada's new flagship *Niobe,* took first-class honors in examinations that were set out by the British admiralty.

The success of the cadets means the purchase of the *Niobe* from the British was a good investment for Canada, at least when it comes to putting together a trained group of navy officers.

A prospector's camp in the Cariboo Region. Dogs are used to pack in the supplies. The prospector has to use his rifle to hunt for fresh meat.

Freighter launched amid much hoopla

The gigantic new steamship, the James Carruthers, built at Collingwood.

May 22, 1913

COLLINGWOOD, Ont. – The largest freighter ever built in the British Empire was launched here today, amid much hoopla. The *James Carruthers* is a 165-metre-long steamship capable of carrying 15,000 tons of cargo in her holds. She's the pride of the Collingwood Shipbuilding Co.

The launching was occasion for a public holiday in Collingwood. Hundreds turned out to see the event. At precisely 4:15, eight men chopped through the lines holding the *Carruthers,* mounted on a huge cradle, in place. She slid down the ways without a hitch. As soon as her massive hull hit the water, all the docks and buildings nearby were flooded, a testimony to the ship's colossal size.

Conservatives abandon attempt to limit debate on controversial Naval Aid Bill

March 15, 1913

OTTAWA – The Conservative government has retreated from its attempt to limit debate on the Naval Aid Bill. The Liberals have bitterly opposed the bill, which proposes giving Britain $35 million to purchase three dreadnought "all big-gun" battleships. The Liberals oppose aiding Britain when Canada's own fledgling fleet is starved for funds. But the Conservatives, fearing Germany will win the naval race and knowing even a reinforced Canadian fleet will count for little, want their money to matter. Also, Prime Minister Robert Borden has tied this naval aid to Canada's having a say in foreign policy-making.

Debate in the Commons the last few days has been downright nasty. The central theme of the conflict – limiting discussion on the bill, and getting on with a vote the government is certain to win – has led to insults more suitable to barroom brawls: "rattlesnakes," "rebels," and "western broncos," along with "shut him up" and "arrest him."

Tensions rose to fever pitch tonight when the Speaker "named" (made to expel) Dr. Michael Clark, Liberal member for Red Deer, for questioning his attempt to limit the debate. After an uproar, Borden soothed the House, saying Clark had been named by mistake, and the action was withdrawn. Still, it was clear the attempt to end the debate would fail, so instead Borden asked for an adjournment before the vote on the Naval Aid Bill.

Sask. road workers get $0.25 an hour

April 12, 1913

ROZILEE, Sask. – Need work? No experience necessary, just ambition and a strong back. The Rural Municipality of Rozilee is now paying 25 cents an hour to laborers. If you have a team of horses, bring it along: the RM pays 50 cents an hour for a man and his team to do roadwork.

Many farmers will be taking advantage of the work offered to supplement their farm income or even support their farm. A man, serious about agriculture, may find the going tough at times in this new land. Perhaps he picks a bad homestead or he is ignorant of the ways of a prairie farmer and so sabotages his own efforts. Or maybe he has grand dreams and wants to hurry them along by pouring capital into his venture. But most likely the farmer who joins the road laborers will be saving up against a rainy day, or trying to recover from a drought.

P.E.I. allows autos three days a week

April 24, 1913

CHARLOTTETOWN – Prince Edward Island is softening its stand on automobiles. Banned entirely the past five years, motorists will now be allowed on Island roads on Mondays, Wednesdays and Thursdays. The rest of the week – market days and the Sabbath – Islanders will still be protected from the loud, vile-smelling contraptions. Drafted to address fears the automobile ban was hurting tourism, the law also imposes heavy licence fees on motorists, with the revenue going toward maintaining roads.

Before coming into effect, the law must be passed by plebiscite. This may be a long process, judging by the mood in some communities. "Those Judas Iscariots and Simon Peters!" writes a farmer feeling betrayed by the looser restrictions. Cries another: "We're going to keep them cars out if we have to take a pitchfork to them!"

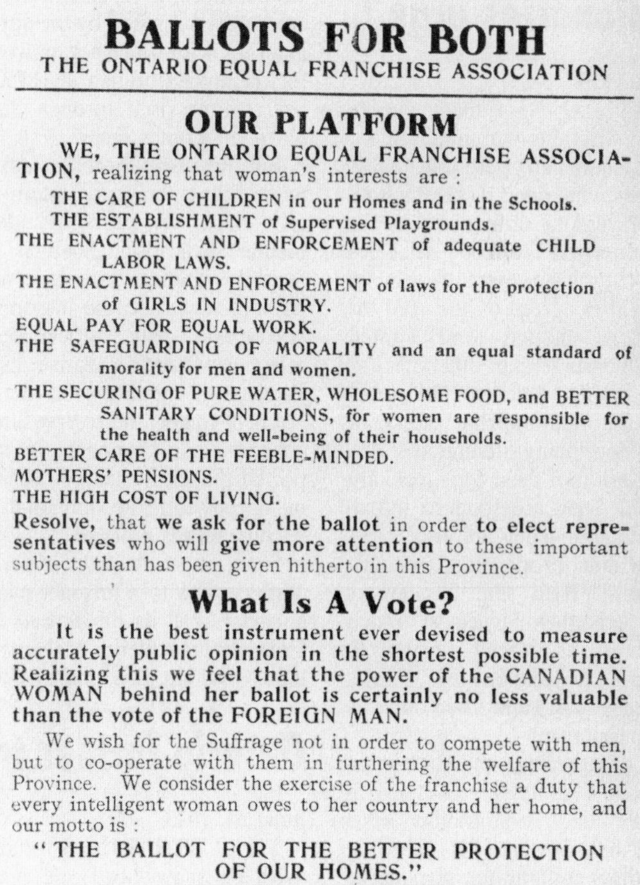

BALLOTS FOR BOTH

THE ONTARIO EQUAL FRANCHISE ASSOCIATION

OUR PLATFORM

WE, THE ONTARIO EQUAL FRANCHISE ASSOCIATION, realizing that woman's interests are :

THE CARE OF CHILDREN in our Homes and in the Schools.
THE ESTABLISHMENT of Supervised Playgrounds.
THE ENACTMENT AND ENFORCEMENT of adequate CHILD LABOR LAWS.
THE ENACTMENT AND ENFORCEMENT of laws for the protection of GIRLS IN INDUSTRY.
EQUAL PAY FOR EQUAL WORK.
THE SAFEGUARDING OF MORALITY and an equal standard of morality for men and women.
THE SECURING OF PURE WATER, WHOLESOME FOOD, and BETTER SANITARY CONDITIONS, for women are responsible for the health and well-being of their households.
BETTER CARE OF THE FEEBLE-MINDED.
MOTHERS' PENSIONS.
THE HIGH COST OF LIVING.

Resolve, that we ask for the ballot in order to elect representatives who will give more attention to these important subjects than has been given hitherto in this Province.

What Is A Vote?

It is the best instrument ever devised to measure accurately public opinion in the shortest possible time. Realizing this we feel that the power of the CANADIAN WOMAN behind her ballot is certainly no less valuable than the vote of the FOREIGN MAN.

We wish for the Suffrage not in order to compete with men, but to co-operate with them in furthering the welfare of this Province. We consider the exercise of the franchise a duty that every intelligent woman owes to her country and her home, and our motto is :

" THE BALLOT FOR THE BETTER PROTECTION OF OUR HOMES."

ONTARIO FRANCHISE CAMPAIGN COMMITTEE
205 YONGE STREET, Room 30, TORONTO

The women's suffrage campaign is heating up. This poster was printed by the Ontario Franchise Campaign Committee, one of several active groups.

Kennel registers a new breed of dog

1913

TORONTO – The Canadian Kennel Club has now recognized the flat-coated retriever as a new breed of Canadian dog, and has registered Kite, a two-year-old prize-winning bitch, as Canada's first. The flat-coated retriever was first developed by crossing continental water dogs, probably of poodle origin, with land spaniels and Newfoundland dogs. The new line was stabilized in the 1880s, when it began to breed true.

Flat-coats are medium-sized dogs of 60 to 70 pounds, with black or liver coats. They have an intelligent expression, and a unique coat – dense, with a fine quality of texture, and as flat as possible.

Curb immigration, missionaries urge

June 3, 1913

TORONTO – Canada needs more restrictions on immigration, Presbyterians here were told today. Ministers experienced in missionary work among immigrants in Canada addressed the 4,000 delegates at the church's General Assembly. Missionaries agreed on the need for restrictions, though some wanted tighter measures than others.

Rev. W.D. Reid of Montreal noted the demoralizing effect of having too many immigrants. "A large portion of these foreigners are illiterate. They are fond of intoxicating liquors. They are also bringing in and propagating socialist doctrines." Reid said immigrants bring with them twice as much criminality as already exists in Canada, two-and-one-half times as much disease, and three times as much pauperism.

While agreeing in the main with Reid's comments, Rev. W.S. Kinsdale said responsibility rests with Anglo-Saxons for allowing immigrants to continue in patterns set in foreign, mainly Roman Catholic, countries. Kinsdale, a missionary among western immigrants, said Protestant churches must keep immigrants from falling into "the clutches of the rum-seller, the Jewish usurer and the slave-driver."

Indian Affairs veteran named to top post

One of the jobs of the Indian Affairs Department is payment of treaty money.

October 1913

OTTAWA – Duncan Campbell Scott, a prominent figure in Canadian literary circles as both a poet and editor, has been named superintendent-general of Indian Affairs by Prime Minister Robert Borden's Conservative government. Insiders are hardly surprised by the appointment – Scott first began working for the Indian branch in 1879, and has steadily risen through the department's ranks since.

But there is more to this appointment than mere recognition of a civil servant's years of departmental dedication. Scott is ideal for the position, from a government point-of-view, because his opinions correspond with official policy affecting Canada's native people. Pressure is mounting on the government to open up reserve land for economic development. It is expected that Scott will do everything in his power to accommodate and encourage this process.

Scott is a staunch imperialist. With regard to Canada's past, he considers "all its life flowed either from the old world or New England." Within this context he believes strongly in assimilation, that Indians should be absorbed into white society and "civilized." In official reports he has denounced their traditional way of life, and in several of his poems the only good Indian is a Christian Indian.

Tom Three Persons and wife Lily.

Ontario grappling with coke problem

Aug. 26, 1913

TORONTO – Is the province of Ontario teetering on the brink of a serious health problem due to cocaine abuse? The registrar-treasurer of the Ontario College of Pharmacy, provincial inspector W.B. Graham, said in an address delivered at the annual druggists' convention today that more than "2,000 ounces of cocaine were sold during the past year ... far more than is necessary for surgical use and prescriptions."

Cocaine is recognized as an addictive drug that debilitates habitual users. In 1908, the Canadian government took measures to either prohibit altogether or restrict under criminal law the importation and sale of cocaine, opium and morphine. The results, says Graham, have been less than satisfactory. Unsavory and unscrupulous agents continue to distribute the narcotics, selling them "on the highway and in secret places." According to Graham, part of the blame also rests with pharmacists who legitimately order excessive quantities of cocaine and then distribute them unwisely.

To rectify this, Graham proposes stricter law enforcement, suggesting the appointment of a dominion inspector with a specific mandate to end illegitimate sales will do the job. Graham points out that while a great deal of provincial and federal money is spent on restricting liquor sales, "nothing is being done to prevent our fellow men from becoming addicted to drug habits which are equally if not more ruinous." That Graham enjoys a great deal of support is unquestionable – his audience greeted his demand with loud applause.

Ontario farmer traps bald eagle suspected of killing chickens

June 24, 1913

ST. CATHARINES, Ont. – With its snowy-head and piercing eyes, the American bald eagle rules the skies. But that doesn't stop the majestic creature, immortalized on the Great Seal of the United States, from swooping down to kill domestic fowl – or being punished for it.

After several chickens had disappeared, a farmer west of here used a dead chicken as bait in his attempt to trap a bald eagle he had seen in the vicinity of his farm. This morning, William Peacock succeeded in capturing a live 16-pound bald eagle. The feathered suspect was brought to St. Catharines and handed over to a former alderman from Niagara Falls, N.Y., who will take the bird across the border to the United States.

Attempts were made to catch the eagle's mate, also seen circling Peacock's farm, but bald eagles mate for life and without its lifetime companion the bereaved bird flew away from its usual territory to roam the skies, perhaps in search of its lost partner.

Thousands attend exhibition in Man.

July 15, 1913
BRANDON, Man. – Thousands of visitors from all over the continent attended today's official opening of the Dominion Exhibition. The ceremonies were performed by Premier Sir Rodmond Roblin. What in most years would be the annual edition of the Provincial Exhibition of Manitoba has been elevated to "dominion" status thanks to a grant of $50,000 from the federal government. The money has been spent on new facilities, from barns and show-rings to a 5,000-seat grandstand.

The feature which brought some visitors thousands of kilometres was the livestock classes. Now housed in 12 new barns is the greatest collection of purebred cattle, sheep, and swine ever displayed in any city in western Canada.

On the weekend before the opening, 200 boxcars filled with animals arrived in a 24-hour period. A number of carload lots of entries are on hand from farms as far east as Quebec. The prize-winning animals will be offered for sale following the judging classes. Another attraction is the presence of the youthful Alfred Blakely, who is offering rides in his airplane.

Crossing Canada on the Transcontinental Highway is tricky, as this automobile driver finds.

Storm spells trouble on Arctic mission

Inuit family which sailed on the Karluk on the Canadian Arctic Expedition.

Workers carry a umiak, or skin-boat, to the Karluk, which is stuck in the ice.

Sept. 21, 1913
COLLINSON POINT, Alaska – The Canadian Arctic Expedition received a terrible blow today when its ship, the *Karluk*, was swept away in a storm, leaving most of the expedition stranded with no command vessel. The *Karluk*, a 250-ton wooden whaling ship commanded by the famous Newfoundland sealer Bob Bartlett, has been mired in the ice off the coast of Alaska for a month, and yesterday the leader of the expedition, Vilhjalmur Stefansson, left the vessel, crossing the ice to the mainland to go hunting. While he was away the storm blew up and the ice began to drift away to the northwest, carrying the *Karluk* with it.

The incident fulfils the worst fears of many members of the expedition who did not believe that the old whaling ship was suitable for the rigors of Arctic exploration. The disappearance of the ship will seriously hamper Stefansson's plans to explore the northern reaches of the Beaufort Sea.

Meanwhile, the southern section of the expedition, under the command of Rudolph Martin Anderson, has established a base camp at Collinson Point. It intends to carry out scientific and ethnological investigations along the coast in the Coronation Gulf area. Stefansson and his marooned colleagues will have to reconsider how to carry out the aims of the expedition now that the *Karluk* is gone. The expedition plans to continue its investigations in the Arctic for four years.

Judge rules Hindus free to enter Canada

Nov. 30, 1913
VANCOUVER – Ottawa's orders-in-council which have stemmed the flow of Hindus into British Columbia are illegal, Chief Justice Hunter has ruled here. Officials claim this means that shiploads of Hindus will be reaching the province very soon.

Hindus are British citizens, and Hunter says they may only be prevented from entering Canada if it can be shown they are mentally defective, have no money, are sick or have a criminal record. These disqualifications would keep any such person from entering this country, not just Hindus. Hunter was dealing with the case of Bhagwin Singh, detained by officials when he landed. Three days ago the chief justice ordered his release in a verbal judgment, and now he has given a written explanation outlining his reasons for freeing the Hindu.

If the British Columbia judge's decision stands, those concerned about the flood of Hindus into this country maintain that regulations to keep them out of Canada can't be made without challenging their British citizenship.

Disastrous storm hits Great Lakes

Nov. 10, 1913
ONTARIO – The entire province is recovering from 36 hours worth of blizzard and gale-force winds. On the Great Lakes, the conditions turned ships into icebergs, says Capt. W.J. Stroy of the *Maricopa*. "It was necessary at times to thaw it away from the front of our wheelhouse in order to see."

One freighter capsized in Lake Huron, with no sign of her crew, while a Tomlinson Line steamer sank off Sault Ste. Marie.

1914

London, Jan. 14. Donald Smith, 1st Baron Strathcona and Mount Royal, dies. He was a major backer of the CPR, a prominent politician, and Canadian High Commissioner in Britain at his death.

Alberta, Feb. 15. More than 1,500 buffalo are thriving in Dominion parks.

Toronto, April 1. The provincial government passes the Workmen's Compensation Act, arguably Canada's most far-reaching labor legislation ever.

Canada, June 12. The Canadian General Council of the Boy Scout Association is incorporated, a branch of the international Boy Scout Association.

Sarajevo, Bosnia, June 28. Austrian Archduke Franz Ferdinand is assasinated by a Serbian nationalist [precipitating World War I].

Quebec, July 11. A commission investigating the *Empress of Ireland* tragedy finds the Norwegian collier *Storstad* responsible for the collision.

London, Aug. 4. Britain declares war on Germany, and Canada enters the war alongside Britain.

Ottawa, Aug. 5. The government orders the enlistment and mobilization of a Canadian army division of 21,000 men.

Winnipeg, Sept. 9. The Grand Trunk Pacific railway is opened from Winnipeg to Prince Rupert.

Quebec, Sept. 14. French-Canadian nationalist Henri Bourassa questions Canada's participation in the war. Many Canadians say he is disloyal.

Toronto, Sept. 25. Sir James Whitney dies in office after serving as premier since 1905.

Ottawa, Oct. 5. Lt.-Col. F.M. Gaudet is made commander of a special French-Canadian army unit, the 22nd Battalion.

Toronto, Dec. 5. Toronto Argonauts beat University of Toronto 14-2 for the Grey Cup.

Toronto. The Duke of Connaught, governor general of Canada, officially opens the Royal Ontario Museum.

Edmonton. A madam says there are 400-500 prostitutes working in the city.

Toronto. Toronto Blueshirts beat Victoria Cougars three games to none to win the Stanley Cup, the first east-west confrontation for the cup.

Trade depression ups unemployment

Jan. 15, 1914

TORONTO – At least 15,000 men are out of work in Toronto, victims of the current international trade depression. It is believed to be the worst unemployment situation in this city since six winters ago, when hundreds of workers were at plants looking for a day's work. Of the current situation, one union leader estimates that for every union man out of work, three non-union workers face the same plight.

Despite the bleak job market, demands on charitable organizations have been remarkably limited. Relatively good economic times in the last few years have enabled people to save, it is believed, and this could be why they have not yet been forced to rely on charity. Also, some plants are dividing jobs among two or three workers.

Adjutant H.R. Hankirk of the Salvation Army's labor bureau, reports that the bureau has found 82 men temporary jobs since the first of the year. In the same time frame last year, only seven men applied and he had to advertise to find temporary workers.

Back home on the range

The antelope population is declining rapidly throughout its range.

1914

CANYON, Alta. – Since the end of the 19th century, reports from detachments of the North West Mounted Police have echoed with warnings about the condition of animal life in Saskatchewan and Alberta. Daily patrols of the forested interior confirm the steady decline of game in these areas. Antelope are particularly scarce, falling prey to difficult winters and native and white poachers.

With the hope of shoring up the antelope herd, a decision was recently taken to create a protected range of country land large enough for these animals to propagate freely, in a protected environment. The federal government will dedicate two reserves to the preservation of the antelope – the first right here in Canyon and the second in Maple Creek, Sask.

Suffragette writes War and Women

1914

TORONTO – Give women political power and they would do away with war. So claims suffragette journalist Flora Macdonald Denison. Mrs. Denison, who is the president of the Canadian Suffrage Association, just recently published *War and Women*. And in it, she writes that "war is a crime committed by men and, therefore, when enough people say it shall not be, it cannot be. This will not happen until women are allowed to say what they think of war."

Mrs. Denison, who has worked as a high fashion dressmaker and recently as a writer for newspapers and magazines, is active in the women's suffrage movement. Her views are more in tune with the militant stance taken by British suffragists, notably Emmeline Pankhurst, than with the moderate tactics of most Canadian feminists.

Southern Cross feared lost in fierce storm

The SS Southern Cross is now feared lost in the Gulf of St. Lawrence.

April 2, 1914

ST. JOHN'S, Nfld. – The *SS Southern Cross*, two days overdue in port, is feared lost in the fierce storm which battered the coast for nearly two days. If so, this is the worst sealing disaster in Newfoundland's history. The sealer was in the Gulf of St. Lawrence, bound for home. It had a full cargo of 17,000 seals and 173 men. People think the wooden partitions dividing the hold broke loose in the storm and the seals shifted, capsizing the sealer.

No voting for men in Mock Parliament

Jan. 28, 1913

WINNIPEG – Patrons of the Walker Theatre were treated to a hilarious Mock Parliament today. Sponsored by the Manitoba Political Equality League, the play featured women in the role of legislators listening to a group of men petition for the vote.

As "premier," writer and suffragist Nellie McClung rejected the idea. "Man is made for something higher and better than voting," she said. "Men were made to support families. What is a home without a bank account?" Mrs. McClung, who has crossed swords with Premier Rodmond Roblin many times, mimicked him so well the audience often roared with laughter.

Deaf want off list of "undesirables"

June 30, 1914

LONDON, Ont. – "Deaf people should not be labelled as undesirable immigrants!" That's the message from the Ontario Association of the Deaf, ending its biennial convention here. The deaf want the federal government to remove this classification from the immigration laws, arguing that it is discriminatory. The association also wants Ontario to provide a special home for aged and infirm deaf people.

A poster touts Victory Bonds.

Dingman well strike sparks oil fever

Dingman Wells, near Calgary, Alta.

An oil well blows in a spectacular fashion near Turner Valley, Alberta.

May 16, 1914

CALGARY – The city is in a state of frenzy today as speculators rush to cash in on a major oil strike at the Dingman well. Reports say oil is gushing high in the sky from the oil pocket discovered at the 810-metre level on the site 48 kilometres southwest of Calgary. A.W. Dingman, a Toronto engineer, says "the character of the oil is high grade, and it appears to be coming into the well at a fairly steady rate at the present time. As to the capacity of the well, it is premature for anyone to pass an opinion as to the amount of the flow."

Dingman's caution hasn't deterred oil-crazed Calgarians from storming the offices of oil brokers, looking for oil shares and a chance to pick up an interest on a lease. Oil stocks have also soared with the news of the strike. A steady procession of cars is streaming out to the Dingman property bearing people curious to view the gusher and scout out properties in the area.

At the moment, seven drilling companies are at work in the oil-rich fields. A smaller find at less than 600 metres at Dingman's property last fall sparked a considerable burst of excitement, but last night's discovery makes that oil fever pale by comparison.

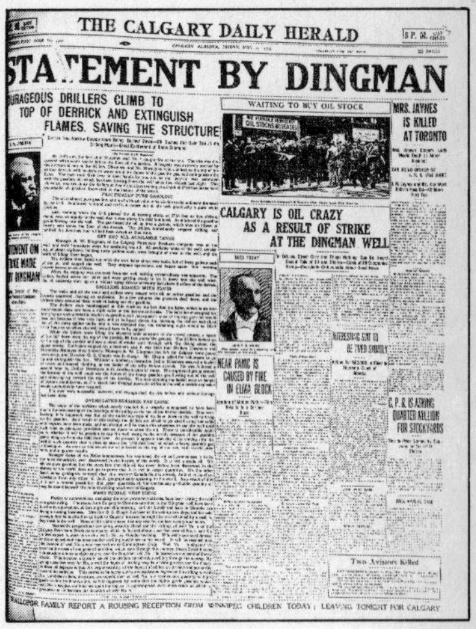

THE CALGARY DAILY HERALD

STA.TEMENT BY DINGMAN

URAGEOUS DRILLERS CLIMB TO TOP OF DERRICK AND EXTINGUISH FLAMES, SAVING THE STRUCTURE

WAITING TO BUY OIL STOCK

MRS. JAYNES IS KILLED AT TORONTO

CALGARY IS OIL CRAZY AS A RESULT OF STRIKE AT THE DINGMAN WELL

NEAR PANIC IS CAUSED BY FIRE IN ELMA BLOCK

C.P.R. IS ASKING QUARTER MILLION FOR STOCKYARDS

Two Aviators Killed

FAMILY REPORT A ROUSING RECEPTION FROM WINNIPEG CHILDREN TODAY; LEAVING TONIGHT FOR CALGARY

Calgary paper announces oil strike.

Collision at sea: 950 are presumed dead

May 29, 1914

QUEBEC CITY – At least 950 people are presumed dead after the Canadian Pacific ocean liner *Empress of Ireland* was rammed by a Norwegian coal ship. The tragedy is the greatest marine disaster in Canadian history. The *Empress* was struck at about 1:30 a.m. near Father Point on the St. Lawrence River, where it had anchored to wait out dense fog. The coal steamer *Storstad* was heading toward Quebec at high speed when it hit the *Empress* in the side, opening an immense, gaping hole well below the water line.

The huge liner immediately began to sink, trapping passengers in their berths below deck. The ship began to list on her side rapidly, severely hampering desperate efforts to launch lifeboards. Fourteen minutes after she was struck, the *Empress* had sunk down to the bottom of the river, with hundreds of passengers trapped inside. Most who escaped the sinking vessel fared little better, dying later of exposure from the icy waters.

Among the passengers were 200 members of the Toronto Salvation Army band who had played the song *God Be With You Till We Meet Again* as the doomed ship left Quebec. So far 250 bodies have been recovered, and survivors are being transported to Montreal.

Storm takes its toll on steamer's crew

April 2, 1914

ST. JOHN'S, Nfld. – The same storm believed to have claimed the *Southern Cross* has also resulted in the loss of 78 crew members on another sealing steamer, the *Newfoundland*. The *Newfoundland*'s crew was sent a considerable distance to kill seals and was caught in a storm that lasted two nights. The ship's captain, Westbury Kean, assumed his men were on board his father's vessel, but Capt. Abram Kean had ordered them to kill the seals and head back to their own steamer. Besides the dead, many are horribly maimed and crippled. ▷

Ship leaves Vancouver carrying 354 Sikhs

The HMCS Rainbow watches the Komagata Maru in Vancouver harbor.

Sikhs aboard the Komagata Maru hope to be allowed to enter Canada.

July 23, 1914

VANCOUVER – Under the watchful eyes of the naval cruiser *HMCS Rainbow,* the tramp steamer *Komagata Maru* sailed away from Vancouver harbor today carrying its cargo of 354 Sikh immigrants back across the Pacific to the Far East. The departure of the steamer ends a two-month standoff which has fuelled a summer of racial tension in the city.

The *Komagata Maru* arrived here on May 23, chartered by a Sikh businessman intent on challenging Canadian regulations limiting immigration from South Asia. Government officials, determined to refuse entry to the ship's passengers, put the vessel in quarantine, allowing no one to come ashore while the matter was settled in the courts. Passengers were even refused food and water.

In the city, the Sikh community staged several rallies in support of the would-be immigrants, while the mayor countered with an anti-Asian meeting of his own. In June a board of inquiry heard the test case of one of the Sikh passengers, and ruled that he and all the others were inadmissible. But without supplies for the return voyage, the ship would not leave. Last week, an armed boarding party of government officials stormed the ship, but failed to capture it. The navy was called in and the captain of the *Komagata Maru* agreed to leave.

Europe on brink of war

July 31, 1914

OTTAWA – Prime Minister Robert Borden is hurrying back to the capital tonight as war looms close in Europe. The prime minister cut short his summer vacation in the Muskoka region of Ontario and has called an emergency cabinet meeting for tomorrow afternoon. The cabinet is expected to tell the British government that this country can put 20,000 men on British soil quickly and get 100,000 there within a month. While there appears to be no problem finding soldiers, there is a lack of both trained officers and proper equipment.

Rumors of war have grown much more persistent and anxious in the past few days. In Canada, press reaction has been generally cautious. But the Ottawa *Free Press* produced a startling front-page headline. In five-inch, red-flared type, the bold headline proclaimed, "Hell's Let Loose." Meanwhile, Canadians have been crowding the windows of newspaper offices to read the latest cables.

It is expected that the German Kaiser will make a decision on war next Tuesday, Aug. 4. Austrians and Germans living in Canada have begun preparing to return to Europe, expecting that their services will be needed.

Patrols in Atlantic to monitor icebergs

July 28, 1914

OTTAWA – Canada will take part in Atlantic patrols to monitor the movement of icebergs in shipping lanes. The patrols are in response to the loss of the *Titanic,* which sank in 1912 after hitting an iceberg at night.

In addition to the patrols, new radio towers being built at Cape Race will keep both patrol ships and ocean liners heading to New York informed of the location, size, and speed of ice as it moves through the region. Thanks to the size of the towers, these radio signals will travel up to 800 kilometres out to sea, enough distance to prevent another disaster like the *Titanic.*

Militia Council set to mobilize troops

July 30, 1914

OTTAWA – Should Britain become involved in the current European conflict, Canada is also ready to send troops. That's the word from the Militia Council, which met today under the chairmanship of Sam Hughes, colonel and minister of militia.

In preparation for such a contingency, the council is pulling together plans to mobilize 25,000 troops from across the country. Units based in Halifax and Esquimalt have been ordered to stand by. So have smaller outfits at other points. In giving these orders, however, the government has stressed that these plans are merely precautionary.

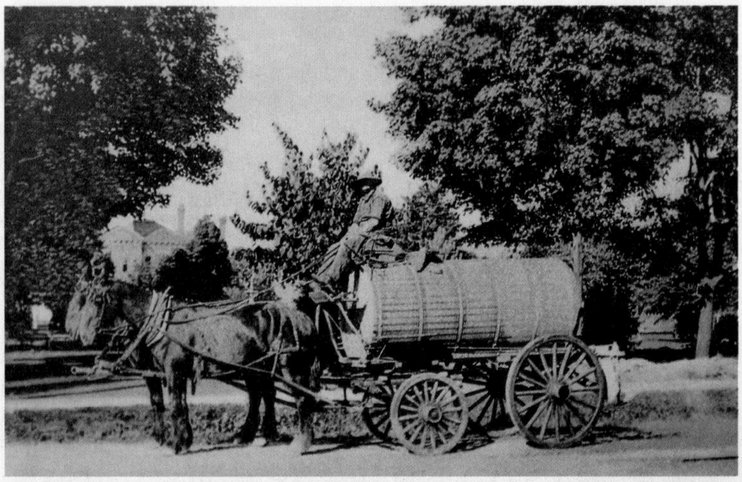

This Preston, Ontario, drayman is idle after the passing of the Local Option.

Government acts to conserve gold

Aug. 3, 1914
OTTAWA – In view of the outbreak of war in Europe, it was announced today that bank notes are to be considered legal tender in their own right, instead of being redeemable for gold. The move is an attempt to conserve the gold supply in Canadian banks. It has the effect of increasing public confidence in the system, since it shows that the government is backing the banks.

Canada enters war alongside Britain

Aug. 4, 1914
OTTAWA – Britain has declared war on Germany following the German invasion of Belgium. In doing so, Britain honored an 1839 treaty to protect Belgian neutrality.

The war was expected. European nations have long been suspicious of one another: France wants to regain provinces lost in the Franco-Prussian War in 1870-71; Austria considers Serbia a haven for terrorists operating against the Austro-Hungarian Empire; Britain fears the growth of German power, the navy in particular; and Germany is aggressively expansionist.

Complex alliances and treaties have ensured a chain reaction once one country declares war on another. Constitutionally, Canada as part of the British Empire was automatically at war with Germany the moment that Britain declared war. However, Canadians will decide how much – or little – they will participate. Public reaction has been enthusiastic; most Canadians view the war as just. With France and Britain allied, the two largest Canadian groups also find common cause, while Germany's offensive through Belgium is seen as unprovoked aggression.

The Canadian militia has an authorized strength of 77,323 officers and men. Only 3,110 are permanent force regulars; the rest are partially trained reservists.

Death toll nears 200 in tragic Hillcrest coal mine explosion

June 19, 1914
HILLCREST, Alta. – There are 193 men dead or presumed dead after an horrific explosion inside Mine Shaft No. 1 of the Hillcrest coal mine. The blast occurred at 9:30 this morning. It was so powerful that it blew the roof off a concrete building nine metres from the mouth of the pit.

There were 232 men in the mine when the blast took place. Most were in No. 1, the main shaft. Of these, only the men near the mouth of the pit and somewhat sheltered from the explosion survived. As for those buried deeper, there's little hope of reaching them in time. The interior of the shaft is a maze of timber, rock, and railroad tracks. Added to the debris are the grisly remains of dead animals and men.

For the grief-stricken families now gathered at the mouth of the pit, there's very little to go on. Little information on how the blast happened. Little chance of seeing their loved ones alive. And little financial aid for the widows of this mining region who must now, somehow, raise their families alone.

But for the moment, these considerations are side issues. What matters is the attempt to get a rescue team down into the mine. It's an extremely dangerous job, since the explosion has made the possibility of further collapses very likely, along with the additional hazards of fire and suffocation. What adds to this tragedy is the fact that, in the mining world, explosions are not uncommon, especially in this region, where just a few years ago a blast at the nearby Bellevue mine killed 35 men.

Bodies were brought up from the mine, washed and searched for identification. Then they were wrapped in shrouds and taken by wagon to the Miners' Hall.

Mass funerals are taking place as there are so many dead in this mine disaster. Many men are still missing in the mines, and the grim search for remains goes on while the families alternately mourn and hope for possible good news.

More than 100,000 volunteer for war

Aug. 12, 1914
OTTAWA – At least 100,000 Canadians have already volunteered to serve in the war, exceeding the most optimistic predictions. In announcing the figures today, Minister of Militia Sam Hughes also said Canada will likely form a second division quickly. The first contingent of 25,000 men will be organized at Quebec next week.

The west leads the way in recruitment. Winnipeg regiments will probably make up a disproportionate number in the first contingent. The Winnipeg troops have already begun training in advance of their departure for Quebec. Pay of $1 per day begins tomorrow for those slated to be among the first 25,000.

HMCS Niobe ready to take on enemy

Sept. 1, 1914
HALIFAX – The 11,000-ton cruiser *HMCS Niobe*, pride of the navy on the east coast, is ready for action. Acquired in 1911 as a Canadian navy training vessel, she has been through sea trials, and her magazines are fully stocked with ammunition. A full crew is aboard – 707 men, including 107 Newfoundland naval reservists. Sailing orders will send her north soon, looking for enemy ships. Unfortunately, most potential targets are long gone. On Aug. 5, in a sporting gesture, the Canadian government granted German merchant ships 10 days grace to leave port.

WAR AND PEACE

1914-1945

$50 million set aside for "defence and security"

A recruiting poster for the war.

Aug. 18, 1914

OTTAWA – The Conservative government intends to appropriate $50 million for conduct of the war that has broken out in Europe. Today, at the opening of the first "war session" in Canada since the War of 1812, Prime Minister Robert Borden gave notice of the government's intention to allocate these funds for "the defence and security of Canada." Specifically, the $50 million will be used to fund Canada's contribution in troops and material to the British war effort, and to keep international trade moving.

As well, the government moved that it be empowered to raise the money needed under the appropriations through loans. Perhaps because many believe the war will be over by Christmas, the government has decided not to disrupt the economy by introducing a new series of taxes to pay for it. Instead, through short-term loans, the cost of the conflict can easily be deferred until it's over, allowing the nation to pay it off without any serious economic disruptions.

There's little doubt that these measures will pass the House, and not just because the government has a majority. As is common in such crises, the opposition has rallied around to the same cause; namely, driving the Germans back behind their borders. Because of this, a degree of co-operation missing in peacetime is now to be found in Parliament. Just this afternoon, Borden walked across the floor to confer with his old adversary, Sir Wilfrid Laurier, the Liberal leader.

The Canada Food Board is urging Canadians to become a conserving society in view of Canada's commitments to the war in Europe.

"Alien" dilemma is causing concern

Aug. 29, 1914

OTTAWA – There's considerable concern here as to the treatment of German-Canadians sympathetic to the cause of the enemy; specifically, what should be done with them. Already, there's talk of the government forbidding these "aliens" from leaving the country, in order to keep them from joining the German army. Other measures contemplated include registering all aliens and making them report to the government once a month.

B.C. buys two subs to defend coastline

Aug. 4, 1914

VICTORIA, B.C. – British Columbia has purchased two submarines from a Seattle shipyard to defend the province's coastline. The sale was sealed today when a naval officer inspected the submarines which had been quickly moved into Canadian waters to beat any U.S. neutrality ban. The submarines were built for Chile, but Ottawa and London, which had been told of the plan, are expected to take them over and pay B.C. the $1.15 million it cost to buy them.

Princess Patricia's Canadian Light Infantry all set for action

Aug. 29, 1914

MONTREAL – While most militia units are still scrambling to get organized, a new Canadian regiment, Princess Patricia's Canadian Light Infantry, sailed today from this port. Formation of the unit was proposed by Capt. A. Hamilton Gault, a Canadian Mounted Rifles veteran of the South African War who contributed $100,000 to the project. Recruiting began on Aug. 11 and included posters distributed in Montreal, Toronto, Ottawa, Winnipeg, Calgary and Edmonton. It was concluded nine days later. Nearly 3,000 applicants were interviewed for the 1,098 finally selected. Of these, 1,049 are Canadian and British servicemen with experience from colonial wars.

The PPCLI takes its name from the daughter of the governor general, the Duke of Connaught, and its first commanding officer is Lt.-Col. F.D. Farquhar, Coldstream Guards, military secretary to the duke. Gault is second in command with the rank of major. Mobilized at Ottawa, the regiment received its first banners from Princess Patricia before entraining for Montreal. Although the PPCLI are the first Canadians ready for action, British convoy schedules are likely to delay their actual transatlantic crossing for two months.

Princess Patricia's Canadian Light Infantry in a 1915 photo.

Princess Patricia reviews the PPCLI after the regiment's arrival in England.

Provinces must recognize federal charters

Oct. 26, 1914

LONDON, Ont. – Canadian provinces can't prevent companies without a provincial charter from doing business if the companies have been chartered by the federal government. Such is the decision made today by the British Privy Council, the final authority on Canadian constitutional matters.

The ruling follows British Columbia trying to block the operation of the federally-chartered John Deere Co., on the grounds that a firm of the same name was already registered provincially. Beyond the loss of registration revenues to the province, the decision reinforces the fact that the federal government has power over the provinces.

Contingent leaves to help fight war

Oct. 3, 1914

GASPE, Que. – Canada's first contingent for overseas service – more than 31,000 men – is en route to Britain. Thirty merchant ships packed with troops, weapons, vehicles, horses, and an airplane sailed at 3 p.m. The 33-kilometre convoy needed three hours for all ships to leave harbor.

Col. Sam Hughes, minister of militia, has been enthusiastic in rallying troops, but he has also been something of a "bull in a china shop," discarding pre-war mobilization plans for his own schemes, and pushing more men into camps than can comfortably be handled.

Nfld. Regiment off for war in Europe

Oct. 4, 1914

ST. JOHN'S, Nfld. – The first contingent of the Newfoundland Regiment sailed from this port today on the *SS Florizel* bound for the war in Europe. The Newfoundland Regiment was raised and drilled by the Newfoundland Patriotic Committee under the chairmanship of the colony's governor. The local government has not seen fit to establish a department under a minister for this purpose, placing the war effort in the committee's hands.

William Coaker, leader of the Fishermen's Protective Union, says Newfoundland should contribute to the Royal Navy, not the army.

Surviving members of the Karluk rescued

Crushed in ice and unable to break out, the Karluk finally sank.

Sept. 7, 1914

WRANGEL ISLAND – The surviving members of the sunken vessel *Karluk* were rescued today when a relief ship arrived at this island off the north coast of Siberia. Caught in the ice off Alaska about a year ago while carrying members of the Canadian Arctic Expedition, the *Karluk* and 25 crew members drifted northwest for five months before the vessel sank. After camping on the ice for a month, the castaways decided to cross the icefields 120 kilometres to this island. Eight men died in the attempt.

Leaving the survivors on Wrangel, Capt. Bob Bartlett and an Inuit companion set out to find help. Crossing to the Siberian mainland, they trekked eastward 1,120 kilometres along the coast to Bering Strait, where they alerted the world by telegraph to the *Karluk*'s fate, the worst Arctic disaster since the disappearance of Sir John Franklin.

Troops arrive in Britain

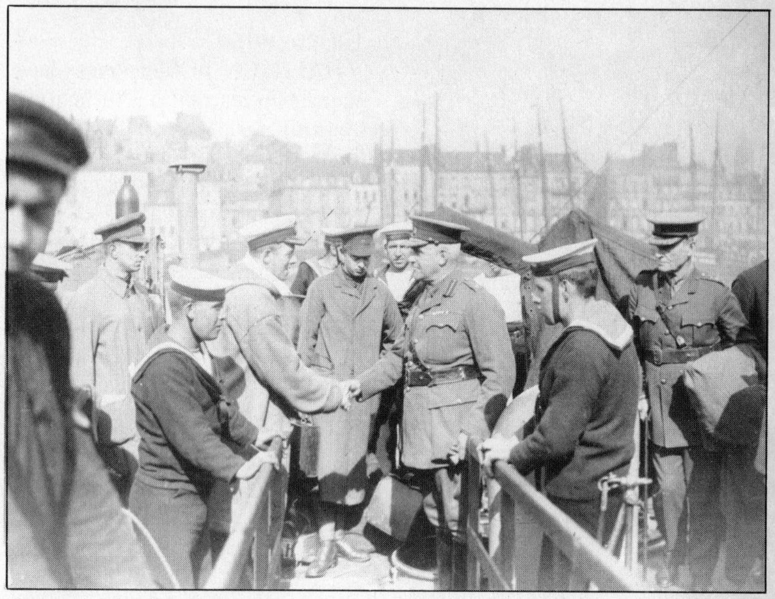

Minister of Militia Sam Hughes meets the men on a Canadian troopship.

Oct. 14, 1914

PLYMOUTH, England – The first Canadian troops to reach Britain to fight in the war sailed into harbor this morning. It is expected that all ships carrying the contingent will be docked within the next two days. On the crossing, the convoy was enlarged by adding ships carrying volunteers from Newfoundland. The force so conveyed was the largest single military contingent ever to cross the Atlantic in either direction, exceeding even Gen. James Wolfe's army of 1759 and British contingents sent to fight the American Revolution. While keen to fight, the Canadians are not yet ready for battle. Many officers have had only weeks to learn about their men, including the vital company sergeants. The vast majority of troops need more training, while much of their equipment must be replaced by British pattern material, to allow easier maintenance in the field. The newcomers will be sent to Salisbury Plain to be trained as a normal division. Lt.-Gen. E.A.H. Alderson, an experienced British officer, has been put in charge of the force.

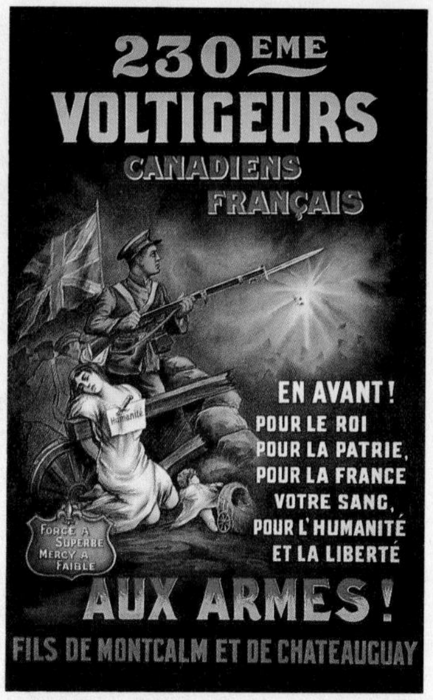

The 230th Voltigeur regiment is seeking recruits for the campaign.

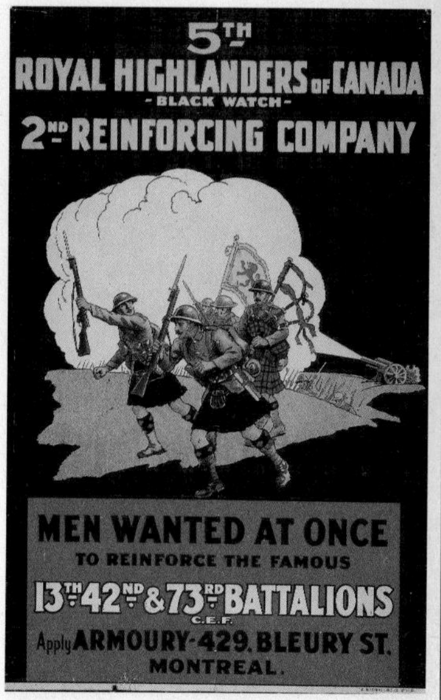

Men are also needed for the Royal Highlander Regiment of Canada.

1915

France, Jan. 4. The first Canadians enter the line on the western front. They are from Princess Patricia's Canadian Light Infantry.

Ottawa, Jan. 20. The government orders the purchase of 150,000 pairs of new and improved boots for the Canadian expeditionary forces.

Montreal, March 28. A conference of the Canadian Jewish Alliance attended by 71 Jewish groups votes to form a Canadian Jewish organization to represent Jewish interests.

Edmonton, April 17. The legislature gives Alberta women the vote in municipal elections.

Saskatchewan, July 1. Liquor legislation goes into effect. Government liquor stores replace privately-owned bars, wholesalers, and clubs.

Toronto, July 14. The first aircraft to go into Canadian production, the Curtis JN-3, is test flown.

Manitoba, Aug. 24. The Mathers Commission submits a report implicating the former Conservative government of Rodmond Roblin in defrauding the treasury of over $800,000.

Deseronto, Ont., Sept. 29. At the 30th annual convention of the Council of the Tribes, Indians condemn liquor as a threat to Indians.

Britain, Oct. 30. Sir Charles Tupper, the last surviving Father of Confederation, dies.

Toronto, Nov. 20. Hamilton Tigers defeat Toronto Rowing 13-7 to win the Grey Cup.

Canada, November. Canada launches its first domestic war loan campaign.

Victoria, Dec. 15. Sir Richard McBride resigns after serving as Conservative premier for 12 and a half years.

Britain. *Punch* publishes the poem In Flanders Fields, written by Canadian medical officer John McCrae at Ypres.

Oshawa, Ont. Chevrolet of Canada is established.

Alberta. The Farm Women of Alberta is established to improve rural health services and education.

Alberta. Namiskam National Antelope Park is created to preserve the threatened antelope.

Vancouver. Vancouver Millionaires beat Ottawa Senators three games to none for the Stanley Cup.

Relief ship is fourth to sail for Belgium

Jan. 26, 1915

HALIFAX – Canadians have once again reached out to help the war-torn population of Belgium. A fourth relief ship, with more than $450,000 worth of food contributed by the people of Canada, left Halifax harbor today en route for Rotterdam, where it will discharge its cargo.

Ravaged by the war, Belgium fell to the Germans last fall when the battle moved from France to Flanders as German troops worked their way up to key positions on the channel coast. While the Belgian armed forces escaped after blowing up the forts – the population left behind is destitute.

McClung leads push for equal suffrage

Suffragist Nellie McClung.

Feb. 26, 1915

EDMONTON – Heading one of the largest delegations ever assembled in the Alberta legislature, well-known suffragist and author Nellie McClung today presented the Liberal-dominated House with a petition demanding that Alberta women be given the right to vote in provincial elections.

McClung, who has received substantial support from local men, including Liberals, says women's suffrage is "in the tide," and that it is only a matter of time before it reaches women here. "Always in Alberta there is a fresh wind blowing," the longtime equal suffrage activist raised on a homestead in Manitoba says optimistically.

Canadians fight in Ypres

Many Canadians lost their lives in the Battle of Ypres, in Belgium.

April 26, 1915

YPRES, Belgium – Troops of the 1st Canadian Division have fought hard here against fierce German attacks. The enemy offensive began four days ago with clouds of poisonous chlorine gas. The Canadians attempted to counter the clouds of noxious gas by breathing through handkerchiefs soaked in urine. Even this was only a partial solution.

The Canadian tasks were difficult because other posts were abandoned by French colonial troops who faced denser gas clouds. Canadians not only had to hold their own ground, but had to try to recapture territory lost by others.

Canadian officers learned a lot about the "fog of war." Battles are confusing affairs to manage: orders are misunderstood or changed, and both sides make mistakes. In some cases, confused troops dug in facing the wrong way. Artillery and machine-gun fire have been deadly, and losses have been terrible. Some 5,000 Canadians have been killed, wounded, or taken prisoner.

Dominion Alliance seeks prohibition laws

March 5, 1915

TORONTO – About 1,000 members of the pro-temperance Dominion Alliance group met with Premier William Hearst today to ask him to pass laws prohibiting the liquor traffic in the province. They also asked if alcohol sales could at least be suspended immediately for the duration of the war.

The premier's response: "You suggest that, without a moment's notice, without any mandate from the people, without the question having been submitted in any way, directly or indirectly, we should immediately prohibit, as far as this province is concerned, the selling and dealing in intoxicating liquors. Now, whether the effect of such a measure as that would ultimately make for permanent advancement of the temperance question, is to my mind open to doubt."

Girl acquitted in death of her employer

Feb. 27, 1915

TORONTO – In one of the most dramatic court scenes ever, English servant Carrie Davies was acquitted today in the shooting death of her employer, Charles Massey. Amid loud cheers from the emotionally-charged courtroom, a frail-looking Davies thanked the teary-eyed 12-man jury for freeing her. In his address to the jury, Chief Justice Sir William Mulock said he had no doubt Davies killed Massey, but believed she acted in self-defence following an attack by her boss. The jury took 30 minutes to deliberate before returning with a not guilty verdict.

"Paper bag" boots come under the gun

March 16, 1915

OTTAWA – Canadian soldiers are issued boots that are little better than paper bags, says a witness to the inquiry into military footware. In testimony today, one captain told of just how poorly these boots resisted water. Asked about the condition of 172 pairs worn by troops in a routine march, he said, "After a march the uppers looked like soaked brown paper. One man showed me a hole in his boot, and I asked him how it happened. He said, I wagged my big toe."

The remark was greeted with hoots of laughter, but underlying it is the serious issue of contractors taking government money and then turning out shoddy merchandise. What makes it worse is the fact that the men who are suffering through these scams are the ones taking the greatest of all risks for Canada, while those who profit from it are living safely at home.

German sub torpedoes British liner

May 7, 1915

QUEENSTOWN, Ireland – A German submarine torpedoed the British liner *Lusitania* just off the coast here today. About 1,200 of her passengers and crew drowned, officials say, and 764 have been picked up by boats and brought to land. The *Lusitania,* pride of the Cunard fleet, left New York last Saturday. Many Canadians were on board, and families and friends are now frantically trying to get news about them.

The *Lusitania,* Cunard officials believe, could outrun any German submarine in the Atlantic and was not protected by a convoy. After leaving New York she maintained an average of about 800 kilometres a day, but there was fog off the Irish coast and the liner slowed down. While passengers ate lunch, two torpedoes – some say only one – hit the ship and the *Lusitania* immediately began to list to starboard. Many lifeboats on the starboard side were shattered, for the ship started to list while still going forward. And some of those on the port side could not be launched because they were quickly raised too high above the water.

Estimates about the time the *Lusitania* remained afloat vary from eight to 20 minutes, but even in this short time the crew managed to get many women and children to safety. There are reports that some officers told first class passengers the ship would not go down.

The British liner Lusitania, seen here on trials in 1907, has just been sunk.

Recruits on the run in meningitis scare

April 3, 1915

BELLEVILLE, Ont. – Fear of an outbreak of spinal meningitis is apparently responsible for the stampede of 200 recruits from the army camp last night.

The soldiers, among some 1,200 recently mobilized members of the 39th Battalion stationed in a canning factory in Belleville, were alarmed after one of their comrades died of meningitis. The runaways were persuaded to return to their camp by superiors who reassured them they would be billeted in other quarters.

The commanding officer of the 39th downplayed the breakout, saying only 50 men were involved. He speculated the soldiers, having recently been paid, got drunk and decided to bolt the barracks.

Battle of Ypres claims 6,000 Canadians

May 3, 1915

YPRES, Belgium – Some 6,000 Canadian troops were lost at the Battle of Ypres, according to figures released today. Horrific in themselves, the numbers do not even come close to conveying the fearfulness of the week-long battle that started here April 22. That day, about 100,000 Germans attacked, aided by clouds of poisonous chlorine gas driving back French and colonial troops.

In a bid to stop the advance, Canadians moved to fill the gap. Although thinly spread, and, at times, attacked from three sides, they held on against the numerically superior German forces. Through this, and a series of counter-attacks, they fought the Germans to a standstill, until the invaders were driven out.

Mohawk C.D. Brant dies on battlefield

April 24, 1915

ST. JULIEN, France – Lieut. Cameron D. Brant, a direct descendant of famed Six Nations leader Joseph Brant, died on the field of battle last night while leading his men on a mission to fortify the 4th Battalion's position. Earlier in the day, Brant's commanding officer had slated him for a captaincy.

Brant was born in 1887 on the New Credit reserve in Ontario. A successful tinsmith in Hamilton, he enlisted four days after Canada went to war alongside Britain.

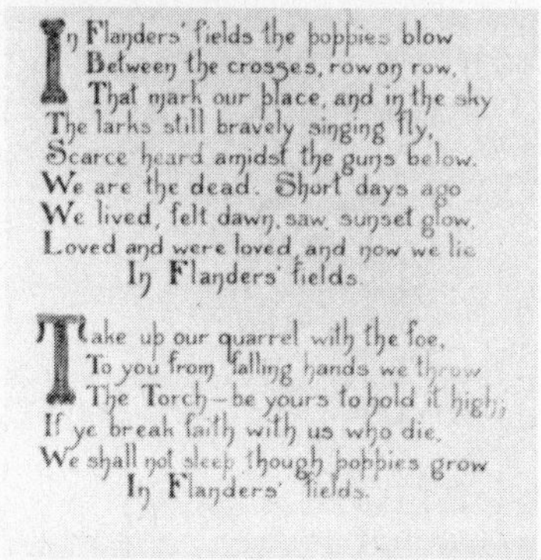

In Flanders' fields the poppies blow
Between the crosses, row on row,
That mark our place, and in the sky
The larks still bravely singing fly,
Scarce heard amidst the guns below.
We are the dead. Short days ago
We lived, felt dawn, saw sunset glow,
Loved and were loved, and now we lie
In Flanders' fields.

Take up our quarrel with the foe,
To you from failing hands we throw
The Torch – be yours to hold it high;
If ye break faith with us who die,
We shall not sleep though poppies grow
In Flanders' fields.

While witnessing the carnage of the second Battle of Ypres in 1915, John McCrae, a Canadian doctor, wrote In Flanders Fields, a poem about soldiers who died in the terrible fighting.

Off-duty Lieutenant-Colonel John McCrae relaxes with his dog Bonneau.

Albertans decide it's time to go "dry"

July 21, 1915
EDMONTON – Alberta will go "dry" as of July 1, 1916, thanks to the victory of anti-liquor forces in a plebiscite held throughout the province. Prohibitionists took city after city in the polling. In Edmonton, dry forces got 39,020 supporters, while wets garnered 20,104. In Calgary, drys were well ahead at the latest report by 12,000 votes. And in Antler Hill, drys shut out the wets 37-0.

What this all means is that by next July, it will be illegal to sell alcohol in Alberta. The only exception will be liquor for medicinal or religious purposes. A warning to drinkers hoping to get around the law through this loophole: this alcohol will be sold through government channels. In addition, the province will abolish 320 hotel, club, and wholesale licences. The only way someone will be able to get a drop in Alberta by that point will be to bring it in from outside.

The vote ends a month of vigorous campaigning by both sides of the issue. Given the result, one would think that Albertans don't like to drink.

Roblin out, Norris in as Manitoba premier

May 12, 1915
WINNIPEG – Tobias C. Norris is the new premier of Manitoba. In a move unprecedented in provincial history, the Liberal party will form a government without having to win an election. Premier Norris is in power today because his predecessor, Sir Rodmond P. Roblin, resigned in the company of his entire cabinet. To permit Norris to conduct business in the legislature, a sufficient number of Conservatives will vacate their seats so Norris will have a majority. It is also understood that members of the Roblin cabinet will not stand for re-election.

These dramatic moves come in the wake of an inquiry into the construction of the provincial legislative buildings. That public inquiry and subsequent stormy meetings of the Public Accounts Committee have disclosed irregularities in the relationship between contractor and government. The full extent of these is not yet publicly understood. Roblin's final act in office was to write a statement commenting widely on his 35 years of service to Manitoba.

Women contributing to the war effort

The staff of the Canadian Field Comforts Mission at Shorncliffe, England.

1915
OTTAWA – The contribution of Canadian women to the war effort can't be overestimated. Across the country, women are stepping into jobs left vacant by departing men. Generally, they are paid less than men, and it's expected they will return to their homes when the war ends. Meanwhile, female volunteers knit socks and make bandages for soldiers. Women's Institute branches are active preparing food and showing members how to deal with shortages. Through the IODE, the Red Cross and other organizations, women also offer financial assistance and friendship to soldiers' families.

A Volunteer Reserve member.

Anti-German mob goes on rampage

May 8, 1915
VICTORIA, B.C. – A rampaging mob of 400 or 500 this evening destroyed a large amount of property associated with Germans in this community. Incensed by the sinking of the Cunard liner *Lusitania* yesterday, the mob first raided the German club here. Led by soldiers in uniform, they paraded downtown, then proceeded to the Blanshard Hotel, formerly the Kaiserhoff, where they destroyed the bar. They also damaged two other businesses thought to be owned by Germans.

Police were unsuccessful trying to quell the riot. The fire department was ordered to turn its hoses on the mob, but refused. No one was seriously hurt. It is expected anti-German demonstrations will take place across Canada the next few days as a result of the sinking.

Baby swept away in Edmonton flood

June 28, 1915
EDMONTON – The flooding of the Saskatchewan River has taken one life, left 2,000 people homeless, and caused about $750,000 worth of damage. The only fatality was a baby carried away by the current after it was dropped by its mother, who was trying to make her way along a floating sidewalk.

The areas worst hit were Fraser's, Ross's, and Galligher's flats. Fifty homes were swept away by the water, as well as the Edmonton Lumber Company's mill and Walter's mill, along with their log booms. The high water reached the city boilers and put out the fires, leaving the city without electricity or water.

The bridge has been closed to traffic. There is speculation it may collapse if the flood waters do not abate soon.

Proud owner with one of the first eight-cylinder Chevrolet automobiles.

Language problem flares up in schools

Aug. 4, 1915

OTTAWA – The war over French-language instruction – or the provincially-mandated lack of it – has escalated further here. First, the Ottawa Separate School Board, dominated by French Catholic sympathizers, refused to recognize Regulation 17, which says French may not be the language of instruction, with certain minimal exceptions. In addition, it insists that English be treated not simply as just another subject, as was the case in these schools.

As mentioned, the school board refuses to abide by these rules. It also refuses to discipline those of its teachers who are defying it by continuing to teach French-speaking children in their own language. In retaliation, the Department of Education tried to overrule the board by superseding its authority with a three-man commission appointed by the government to force the regulation through. And this is where the conflict now stands.

This action may prove to be meaningless, however. Short of withholding funds to pay the teachers, there's little the provincial government can do to force these trustees to teach their children in English, a language their parents don't want. Still, given the usual level of tension between the two language communities, and the determination of English-speaking Catholics in Ontario to keep the French "in their place," this issue won't just go away.

Petition supports universal suffrage

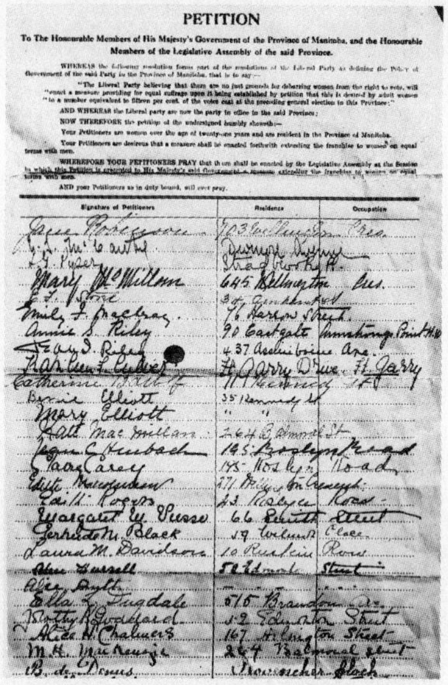

PETITION

To The Honourable Members of His Majesty's Government of the Province of Manitoba, and the Honourable Members of the Legislative Assembly of the said Province.

WHEREAS the following resolution forms part of the resolutions of the Liberal Party as defining the Policy of Government of the said Party in the Province of Manitoba, that is to say:—

"The Liberal Party believing that there are no just grounds for debarring women from the right to vote, will "enact a measure providing for equal suffrage upon it being established by petition that this is desired by adult women "to a number equivalent to fifteen per cent. of the votes cast at the preceding general election in this Province;"

AND WHEREAS the Liberal party are now the party in office in the said Province;

NOW THEREFORE the petition of the undersigned humbly showeth:—

Your Petitioners are women over the age of twenty-one years and are resident in the Province of Manitoba.

Your Petitioners are desirous that a measure shall be enacted forthwith extending the franchise to women on equal terms with men.

WHEREFORE YOUR PETITIONERS PRAY that there shall be enacted by the Legislative Assembly at the Session in which this Petition is presented to His Majesty's said Government a measure extending the franchise to women on equal terms with men.

AND your Petitioners as in duty bound, will ever pray.

Signature of Petitioners	Residence	Occupation

Political Equality League petition for enfranchisement of women.

Manitoba suffragists and their huge petition to the provincial government.

Dec. 23, 1915

WINNIPEG – When Premier Tobias C. Norris entered the public meeting room in the legislative buildings last night, he found a large and enthusiastic crowd of petitioners awaiting him. The petition they presented him with contains the names of roughly 45,000 Manitobans who support the idea of universal suffrage.

It is widely known that the premier's opinion on universal suffrage differs from that of his predecessor, Sir Rodmond Roblin. Former premier Roblin curtly refused earlier petitions on the subject on the grounds that the imperial government had not seen fit to extend the vote to women of the British Isles.

Department of Militia sends Larrigans to troops in the trenches

Dec. 7, 1915

OTTAWA – The Department of Militia is sending Larrigan boots – developed for lumberjacks and almost 100 percent waterproof – to Canadian troops. Boots have long been a problem for Canadian troops, whose first footwear fell apart in wet weather training on Salisbury Plain. Shipment of the Larrigans is yet another example of how Sir Sam Hughes, minister of militia, is determined to have Canadian troops issued with distinctive Canadian equipment.

However, there are many who complain that Sir Sam's policies, however well-meaning, result in the issuance of inferior Canadian items. Last year, for example, he arranged for troops to take 25,000 MacAdam shovels with folding handles overseas; in practice, the shovels proved inferior to British entrenching tools. Some fear the Canadian-made Ross Rifle might also prove inadequate.

Opera star's show supports war effort

Oct. 4, 1915

TORONTO – World-famous opera singer Nellie Melba gave a concert here tonight as part of her campaign to support the war effort. About 4,000 people attended and $9,000 was raised for the Canadian Red Cross. Nellie has been touring the British Empire at her own expense. She was made a life member of the Canadian Red Cross, and a wounded soldier presented her with a bouquet designed to represent the society's emblem.

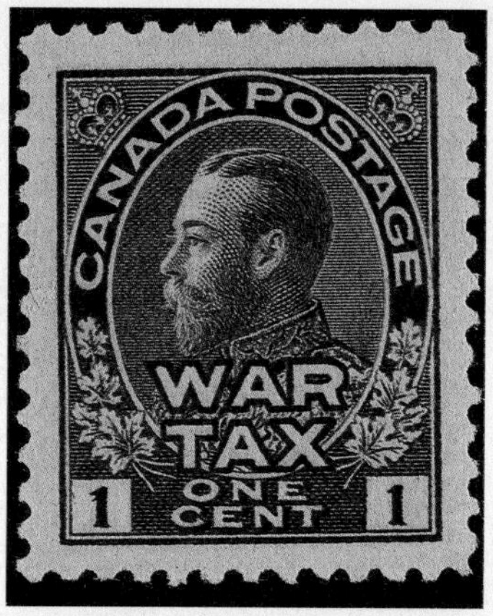

The Special War Tax Revenue Act imposed a surtax of one cent on certain letters and postcards.

Alberta leads the drive to recruit troops

Aug. 11, 1915

OTTAWA – Alberta leads the way in the drive to recruit troops for the war in Europe. According to figures released by Ottawa today, Alberta has recruited some 14,200 men to date, or 3.73 percent of its total population. Overall, as of June, some 106,000 Canadians have signed up to join the fight, or 1.32 percent of the total population of 8 million. The majority of those enlisting are British-born immigrants, many of them recent arrivals. Runners-up to Alberta are Saskatchewan and Manitoba, which combined have recruited 24,000 troops, 2.78 percent of their populations. Third is British Columbia, where 2.55 percent have signed up, followed by Ontario with 1.44 percent. The Maritimes and Quebec lag well behind with 0.79 percent and 0.61 percent, or 7,400 and 13,300 men, respectively.

Ontario has contributed more than 40,000 men to the fight. Officials say if the current pace holds, the services should hit the 300,000 target before the end of the war. Some 10,000 men are believed to have enlisted since June.

1916

Ottawa, Jan. 7. French-Canadian parents occupy the Guiges school to back demands for bilingual education for their children.

Montreal, March 30. The Montreal Canadiens defeat the Portland Rosebuds three games to two to win the Stanley Cup.

Kapuskasing, Ont., May 15. About 1,200 "alien" prisoners clash with 300 Canadian soldiers at an internment camp. One prisoner dies, nine are wounded.

Berlin, Ont., June 28. Citizens vote to change the city's name to Kitchener, a reflection of anti-German feelings.

Edmonton, July 1. The provincial government closes Alberta beer houses and liquor parlors.

Ontario, July 29. Fire destroys many northeastern communities around Porcupine, killing up to 200 people.

Edmonton, Aug. 2. The Edmonton *Bulletin* reports that during the first month of prohibition, savings accounts rose by 100 percent.

Camp Hughes, Man., Aug. 16. Military authorities grant 11,000 soldiers 30 days leave to harvest the wheat crop.

Manitoba, Aug. 21. Manitoba schools open with teaching in French, German, and Ukrainian no longer permissible.

Winnipeg, Aug. 28. The trial of three former cabinet ministers charged with defrauding the Crown during the Roblin government ends with a hung jury. A new trial is ordered.

Midnapore, Alta., Dec. 12. Father Albert Lacombe, Oblate priest, missionary to the plains Indians, and church spokesman for the prairies, dies.

Winnipeg. The Manitoba Temperance Act prohibits the sale of booze in bars, but allows people to consume it in homes.

Ottawa. The government establishes the Honorary Advisory Council for Scientific and Industrial Research [National Research Council].

Ottawa. The government creates the War Office Cinematographic Committee to film the war.

Ninette, Man. Returning soldiers are especially vulnerable to tuberculosis and they strain facilities at the Ninette sanatorium. Some veterans need respiratory care after undergoing German gas attacks.

Prairie women get the right to vote

Leading the way: Manitoba the first

Jan. 27, 1916

WINNIPEG – Manitoba women are the first in Canada to win the right to vote in provincial elections. They are also eligible to hold office. For more than 20 years, since a suffrage campaign was launched by Icelandic women in the 1890s, the women of Manitoba have been working toward this goal.

Since the founding of the Winnipeg Political Equality League in 1912, steady progress has been made. The support of the Manitoba Grain Growers' Association, to which women have been admitted since 1915, has also helped considerably. Although the Conservative party, under former premier Rodmond Roblin, opposed votes for women in its 1914 campaign, the fall of the Tories and the Liberal victory under Tobias C. Norris virtually assured women's suffrage.

Lillian Beynon is one of the women who worked tirelessly for the women's suffrage movement in Manitoba.

Suffrage movement triumphs in Alberta

Women farm, tend animals, and even play cards. Now they can also vote.

April 17, 1916

EDMONTON – Following the lead of Manitoba and Saskatchewan, Alberta women have been granted the right to vote. Many factors have contributed to the success of the suffrage movement in the province, including the example of workers elsewhere on the prairies and the support of the United Farmers of Alberta. The active participation of women in the war effort has proven that they are capable of shouldering heavy responsibilities, and this, too, helped pave the way for the new legislation.

It is expected that other Canadian provinces will eventually follow the example set by the prairies and grant the vote to women. Undoubtedly, the dominion franchise will quickly follow.

Women of Saskatchewan can cast ballots

March 14, 1916

REGINA – Less than two months ago, the women of Manitoba became the first in Canada to win the right to vote in provincial elections. Today, their Saskatchewan sisters were also granted that privilege.

Unlike Manitoba's former longtime premier, Rodmond Roblin, Saskatchewan Premier Walter Scott supports the principle of women's suffrage. However, he felt it necessary for suffragists to overcome the apathy of the majority of women before the vote could be granted. This was a difficult task in a largely rural province, but the support of the Grain Growers' Association, and the publicity given to the cause in the *Grain Growers' Guide*, helped achieve the goal.

Regulation 17 sparks a strike at bilingual schools in Ottawa

Feb. 3, 1916

OTTAWA – Seventeen bilingual schools, manned by 122 French teachers, went on strike today in this city. The issue is simple: no wages. The Separate School Board has been unable to pay the teachers, because the city withheld $83,000 in Separate School taxes. The city is acting at the request of a three-man commission Ontario named to supersede the Ottawa board because of its continued defiance of Regulation 17. By withholding the tax money, the province hopes to force the rebellious board to heel.

In the meantime, 4,000 French-speaking schoolchildren are on the street, while their English-speaking counterparts continue their education. As always, it is the innocent bystanders who pay the price; in this case, children suffer while adults bicker. And the kids may suffer for a long time, as there's no sign of compromise. The province is determined to stamp out French instruction through Regulation 17, while the Ottawa Separate School Board will not back down.

Conditions made safer for sealers

May 4, 1916

ST. JOHN'S, Nfld. – Legislation passed by the local Assembly today attempts to make conditions for sealers safer and a little more comfortable. Companies are now required to make sure sealers are not on the ice after dark or in dangerous weather; that all captains, mates and master watches possess appropriate certificates before they take up their positions; that a doctor is available on each ship; that injured sealers are compensated; and that good cooks are hired.

The legislation is long overdue – it has already been proved that the living conditions of sealers are disgraceful and the work conditions dangerous. Meanwhile, sealing employers make huge profits. While the government of Edward Morris and his People's Party are trying to take credit, the public knows the Fishermen's Protective Union and its leader, William Coaker, are responsible for the legislation.

St. Eloi craters site of latest battle

April 18, 1916

ST. ELOI – Several giant craters, created when British tunnellers exploded mines under German positions, have been the object of fighting as the new Canadian Corps tries to dislodge German troops. Some 1,373 Canadians have been killed, wounded, or taken prisoner at the St. Eloi craters.

The Battle of the Craters marks the first time large numbers of Canadian troops wore steel helmets. It has also been marked by friction between the corps commander, Lt.-Gen. E.A.H. Alderson, and Canadian officers; reports speak of "some feeling against the English" on the part of Canadians, and "a serious feud between the Canadians and the British."

Ontario introduces legislation to make liquor virtually illegal

March 22, 1916

TORONTO – The provincial government has introduced a bill that would, for all intents, make liquor illegal in Ontario. Bill 100 calls for the closing of all bars, clubs, and liquor stores for the duration of the war. It will even be an offence for hotels, offices, or boarding houses to have liquor on the premises. Only private homes will be exempt from supervision. Alcohol will be available through government dispensaries, for religious, scientific or medical reasons. Permanent prohibition will not be voted on until war's end.

A half-mile long line of barmen protest prohibition in Toronto, Ontario.

Fire breaks out at Parliament Buildings

Feb. 4, 1916

OTTAWA – Apart from a pall of smoke still hovering overhead this evening, from a distance the Parliament Buildings look unscathed. But behind darkened walls and beneath the rubble of fallen roofs, one of the most picturesque public buildings in North America lies partially in ruins – the fire that broke out at 1:30 this morning destroyed the Centre Block, and it came close to taking the superb library as well.

The cause of the fire is still unknown, but rumors that German agents were responsible are running rampant. More than 1,200 soldiers are now standing guard over the Parliament House grounds.

Soldiers hurl snowballs at prohibitionists

March 8, 1916

TORONTO – Several hundred convalescing soldiers found enough energy to express their opinion of prohibition today, hurling snowballs and abuse at a procession of temperance supporters. The marchers, on their way to Queen's Park with a petition 1,038 metres long calling for prohibition, fought back with equal resolve, and both sides suffered slight injuries.

The trouble began early when soldiers tried to attach a banner declaring "We fought for you; why deprive us of our liberty" on the procession's wagon. Failing, they nevertheless continued with their harassment, spurred on by some civilians in the crowd.

MOO-CHE-WE-IN-ES.
PALE FACE, MY SKIN IS DARK BUT MY HEART IS WHITE FOR I ALSO GIVE TO
CANADIAN PATRIOTIC FUND

Native support for Patriotic Fund.

Native members of the Canadian Expeditionary Force with tribal elders.

Blacks in Canada get own battalion

July 5, 1916

PICTOU, N.S. – Canadian Negroes, so often told they were not wanted for this "white man's war," can now enlist in their own battalion. The Department of Militia and Defence has authorized the formation of No. 2 (Negro) Construction Battalion, with 1,049 men. Negro soldiers – under white officers – will do manual labor such as logging, milling and shipping. Recruitment will be Canada-wide. However, Cape Breton Negro coal miners are ineligible.

Byng to command the Canadian Corps

Lieutenant-General Julian Byng.

May 9, 1916

OTTAWA – Lt.-Gen. Julian Byng will take over command of the Canadian Corps. "Bungo," as he is known to his friends, is said to be a common sense officer who wastes little time on ceremony or the privileges of rank. He is expected to firm up the leadership in a command many say has made a lot of mistakes the past few months – mistakes which have cost the Allies dearly in men and arms.

Loggers play a part helping war effort

May 13, 1916

LONDON, England – Canadian loggers are playing a part in military operations overseas. Earlier this year the British government requested of Canada that it organize a forestry battalion overseas. By logging British and French forests, space normally used for timber cargoes, can be filled with munitions from North America.

The Canadian government was quick to answer the call. It recruited 1,600 men in six weeks, organized them into the 224th (Canadian Forestry) Battalion, and sent them overseas. The first sawn lumber was produced today at a mill which did not exist a month ago. Additional forestry units are expected to be formed.

Canadians triumph at Mount Sorrel

June 13, 1916

MOUNT SORREL – A flat knoll, ironically named Mount Sorrel, has been the scene of an unqualified Canadian victory. In 12 days of fighting, the Canadian Corps sustained some 8,000 casualties. One unit – the 4th Canadian Mounted Rifles – suffered 89 percent losses. Another, Princess Patricia's Canadian Light Infantry, sustained 400 casualties, including 150 dead. When the enemy overran the 5th Battery, Canadian Field Artillery, gunners did not surrender, but defended themselves with revolvers to the last man.

Much of the fighting was with Wurtemburger troops, determined to show they were tougher than the average German soldier, just as the Canadians tried to demonstrate their superiority over the average British infantryman.

The battle began when German troops, preceded by devastating artillery barrages, tried to capture Canadian trenches. In hand-to-hand combat, Canadians halted the enemy, then counter-attacked and drove them back. The battle was marked by intense use of artillery and aircraft. Yesterday, the Canadian troops mounted four heavy barrages without attacking. When a fifth barrage was fired, the enemy assumed it was another bluff, but this time it was followed by a Canadian assault.

New names have entered Canada's military history – Sanctuary Wood, Observatory Ridge, Maple Copse, and Top Tor.

Crowds read the war news in front of the Edmonton Journal bulletin board.

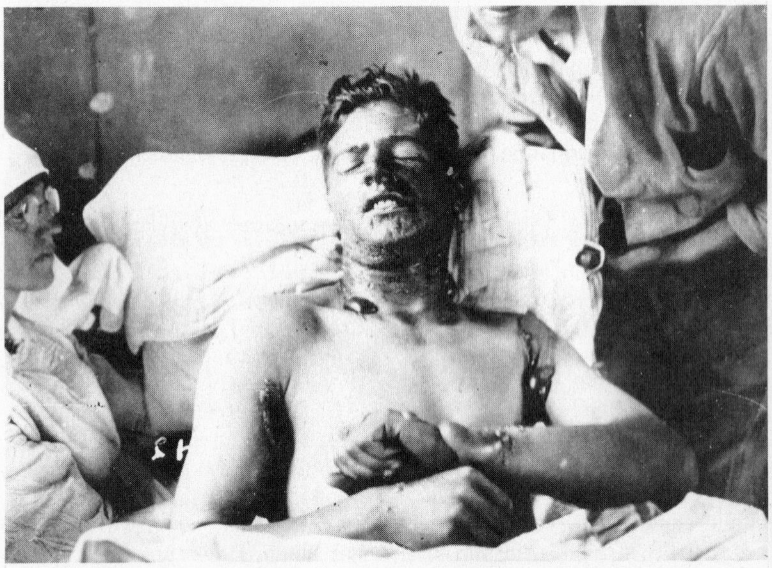

Mustard gas burns are extremely painful, as this injured soldier can attest.

Language used in schools up to Ontario

Nov. 2, 1916

LONDON, England – The Judicial Committee of the British Privy Council has ruled the Ontario government does have the right to decide what languages are and are not to be used in provincial schools. The decision means the Ottawa Separate School Board can no longer resist Regulation 17, which forbids using French as the language of instruction, except in certain restricted cases. The Privy Council also ruled the three-man commission set up by the province to supersede the school board was also unconstitutional, a small victory for the French trustees who defied this government action.

The council rejects the notion that French-language instruction is a right granted under the Canadian Constitution, known as the British North America Act. In part, the judgment says "the only Section in the BNA Act which relates to the use of English and French language does not relate to education, and is directed to entirely different subject matter." With this decision, the language battle in Ottawa-area schools can be said to be ended.

Munitions workers want a 9-hour day

June 12, 1916

HAMILTON, Ont. – Despite government censorship, word is spreading about a strike here by 1,500 munitions workers. They're demanding their employers abide by the recommendations of a royal commission to cut their working day to nine hours. However, the bosses show no sign of doing so. In fact, they've responded to the strike by taking out huge newspaper ads, accusing the workers of being influenced by enemy agents.

Minister criticizes Quebec war effort

July 15, 1916
LINDSAY, Ont. – Sir Sam Hughes, minister of militia, has done it again. Known for "shooting from the lip," the colonel took time out from laying the cornerstone of a building here to insult French Canada. While praising Lindsay, he said, "With all due regard to the province of Quebec, in this great war, it has not done its duty as it should and would if the young manhood of the province had been taken in hand by the proper people, who have benefitted so much from British institutions."

Canadian soldiers ditch Ross rifles

July 18, 1916
OTTAWA – Militia headquarters has announced that Canadian troops overseas will replace Ross rifles with Lee-Enfields, the standard British infantry weapon. Sir Sam Hughes, minister of militia, has long defended the Canadian-designed and manufactured Ross. Yet in battle, Canadian soldiers have discarded them whenever possible, even seizing Lee-Enfields from dead British troops. The very accurate Ross is a good sniper rifle. However, it jams in battle and is easily clogged by mud or dust.

Wartime memories are recalled in this promotional poster for the Victory Bond sales campaign.

Newfoundlanders suffer major losses

Fierce fighting took place around this gun emplacement in Sanctuary Wood.

German dead lie in these trenches demolished by Canadian artillery.

July 1, 1916
BEAUMONT HAMEL – The Newfoundland Regiment, fighting its first major action in France, suffered huge losses today. At 9:05 this morning, 801 men in the unit attacked enemy lines. Although the regiment was to advance on a front 910 metres wide, there were few gaps in the German barbed wire. The Newfoundlanders bunched up and were mowed down by machine-guns. Only a few of them got close enough to throw grenades into the German trenches; fewer still got into those trenches. All told, the regiment suffered 684 casualties, including 310 dead.

The losses are part of a much bigger tragedy. The Newfoundlanders were participating in a general British offensive that began today with more than 57,000 men killed, wounded or missing – and with no gain of enemy-held ground. One may well ask why the Newfoundlanders were sent "over the top" at all; other attacking regiments had been cut to pieces an hour before. The 1st Battalion, Essex Regiment, which was to have advanced with the Newfoundlanders, had been unable to move because its own trenches were clogged with dead and dying.

For a small, relatively poor colony, Newfoundland is playing a significant role in the war. The infantry regiment raised in 1914 saw limited action at Gallipoli before being sent to France. Hundreds of Newfoundlanders are in the Royal Navy or with Forestry Corps units.

Canadian troops pull out of Ypres Salient

Aug. 15, 1916
FRANCE – Canadian divisions are leaving the Ypres Salient, a position they have held for the past 17 months. Over time they have seen farms and villages gradually reduced to rubble by incessant fighting. They have also marvelled at the stubborn resilience of the land and its people. Even the swans have refused to abandon Ypres Moat, despite frequent shelling.

Since arriving here, the Canadian Corps has grown to three battle-ready divisions totalling 90,000 fighting men. A fourth division will soon join the corps. Since May the corps has had a new commander – Lt.-Gen. Julian Byng.

The move out of Ypres can only be associated with the Somme offensive some 80 kilometres away. Australian and British forces – including Canadian cavalry units attached to imperial formations – have suffered major losses, while the Canadian infantry divisions have been working in a relatively quiet sector throughout the summer. The Canadian Corps can expect renewed action when it enters the Somme battle.

Heatstroke claims soldier on parade

July 11, 1916
CAMP BORDEN, Ont. – The official opening of Camp Borden today was marred by the tragic death of Pte. John Campbell of the 204th (Beaver) Battalion from heatstroke. Another 35 soldiers were struck down by the 32C temperatures. The troops suffered because they weren't allowed to carry water bottles on parade, for fear of spoiling their appearance. All told, 34,000 men paraded before Minister of Militia Sir Sam Hughes.

Pact hikes wages to offset inflation

August 1916

ALBERTA – A supplementary agreement to increase employees' wages has been signed by the Western Coal Operators' Association and the United Mine Workers of America. The miners had demanded readjustments to the rates agreed to last year because western Canada has been hit hard by inflation triggered by the Great War. The mine operators also agreed to abide by the demand that the operators not hire any more Japanese labor for the time being, on the condition that other sources of labor are available.

The mud-spattered heroes of the Somme trenches return to camp.

Piper J.C. Richardson has won a posthumous Victoria Cross.

Canadians in Battle of the Somme

First aid treatment in the trenches.

Canadians escort German prisoners on the Somme to the prisoners' cage.

Sept. 15, 1916

FLERS-COURCELLETTE – The Canadian Corps re-entered the fighting in the war today as Field Marshal Sir Douglas Haig launched an offensive with two full armies on a 16-kilometre front. Much of the fighting has been brutal hand-to-hand combat using bayonets. Lt.-Col. T.L. Tremblay, who is commanding the French-Canadian 22nd Battalion, writes, "If hell is as bad as what I have seen at Courcellette, I would not wish my worst enemy to go there." The Canadian Corps has made continual use of its armored cars to provide covering machine-gun fire.

The battle is marked by new tactics. These include a "creeping barrage," by which troops advance only a short distance behind a rain of artillery shells directed at the enemy trenches. Another new feature is the motorized, tracked, armored vehicles carrying machine-guns directly into the battle; they are called "tanks" – a word previously used to conceal their nature from the enemy.

These Canadians are returning happy after their victory at Courcellette.

Not all senior officers are certain of the effectiveness of the tanks. Lt.-Gen. Julian Byng, commanding the Canadian Corps, describes them as "a useful accessory to the infantry, but nothing more." On the other hand, Maj.-Gen. Richard Turner, commanding the 2nd Canadian Division, is much more enthusiastic about them.

Migratory Bird Treaty a monumental step for conservation

Aug. 16, 1916

WASHINGTON, D.C. – In the last century, migratory birds have been ruthlessly hunted for sport and profit, their nesting and roosting grounds mercilessly pillaged. The result of such unbridled hunting has been the extinction of many species of birds common to the United States and Canada. Today, governments from the U.S. and Great Britain – acting for Canada – came to the aid of migratory birds. Officials met in Washington to sign the Migratory Bird Treaty, granting migratory birds international protection.

The treaty is a monumental step for conservation. It prohibits the killing of endangered birds, and protects the nesting and roosting sites of migratory birds, outlawing savage hunting practices. The passage of the Migratory Bird Treaty bans the trade of plumage plucked from protected species and forbids egg collecting.

Christmas mail delivered to the front

Dec. 22, 1916

FRANCE – It seems no Canadian soldier will be forgotten this Christmas, as festively decorated trucks bearing gift parcels join the convoys of war materials making their way to the troops in northern France. The mail delivery has been organized by none other than former British postal workers who are now "Tommies" in the army.

The services boast that mail posted in London will reach its anxious recipient at the front within 48 hours. By the same token, the army mail service is sending back home as heavy a volume of packages as comes overseas. The average normal daily volume of 1.1 million letters and 11,000 parcels is about three times that volume during the Yule season.

Soldiers prepare grave marker.

Hughes out of cabinet

Gen. Sir Sam Hughes inspected the ruins at Arras during a visit to the front.

Nov. 11, 1916

OTTAWA – Sir Sam Hughes, Canada's colorful, egotistical, and eccentric minister of militia, has resigned. After many arguments with Prime Minister Robert Borden, fellow ministers, British leaders and Canadian generals, the final break came over formation of an overseas ministry to handle Canadian military affairs. That would have cut Hughes' powers. Sir Sam was agreeable to the move only if one of his close friends was selected to lead the ministry, but he would not accept Sir George Perley.

Hughes has been his own best publicist and worst enemy for years. Typical of his feuds is one with Lt.-Gen. E.A.H. Alderson, former Canadian Corps commander, over promotions and battle tactics.

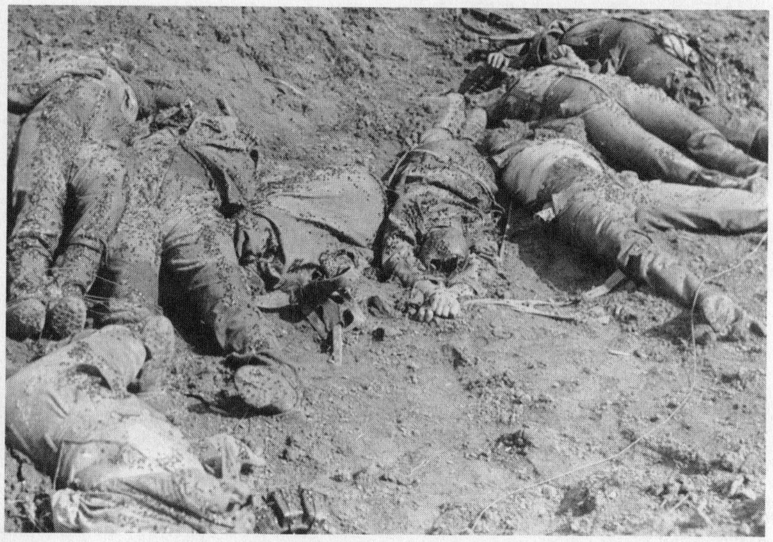

Gruesome battlefield scenes such as this are common at the front.

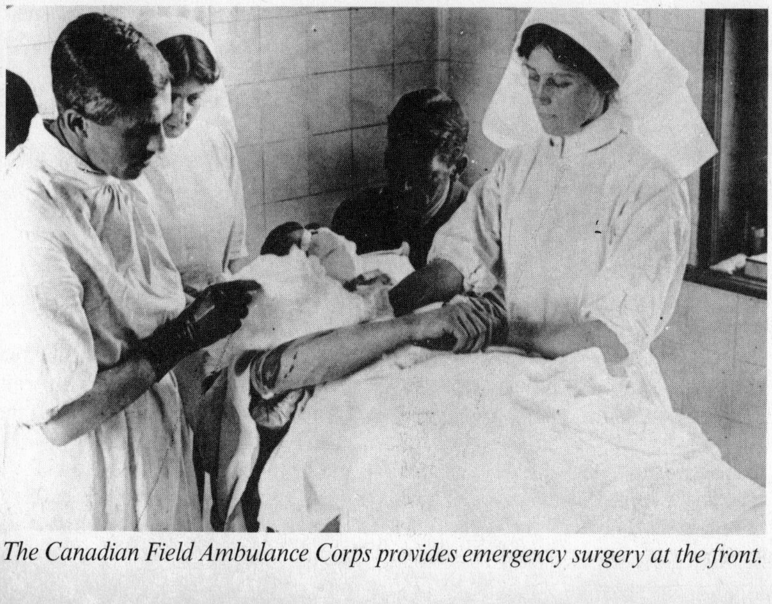

The Canadian Field Ambulance Corps provides emergency surgery at the front.

Grain growers unite in western Canada

Nov. 30, 1916

WINNIPEG – In a single day, the Grain Growers' Grain Co. went through a massive increase in size. At a meeting attended by more than 500 farmers, shareholders of this company voted to join forces with three other grain producers' associations: United Farmers of Alberta, Alberta Farmers' Co-operative Elevator Co., and the Manitoba Grain Growers' Association. The decision was virtually unanimous, with only six of those present voting against the proposal.

The united body now assumes a new name: United Grain Growers Ltd. Its capitalization has been more than doubled to meet its new dimensions, to $5 million from $2 million. With a single exception, the officers of the Grain Growers' Grain Co. will preside over the amalgamated body.

Connaught Tunnel longest in Canada

Dec. 9, 1916

REVELSTOKE, B.C. – The CPR has just opened the Connaught Tunnel near here. It is the longest tunnel in Canada and will eliminate the dangers and bottlenecks of Rogers Pass in the Selkirks. The tunnel, eight kilometres long, was bored through Mount Macdonald and provides a straight run instead of the loops and steep grades that have plagued locomotive crews and passengers travelling between Field and here.

Pressure to build the tunnel has always been strong because of difficulties taking big trains up the grades in an area famous for massive snow slides. But it was the slide of 1910 that forced the CPR into action – 62 men died when snow roared down as they cleared the track. Work on the Connaught Tunnel started in summer 1913.

1917

Western Front, Europe, Jan. 1. Winter brings the bloody fighting of 1916 to an end with little accomplished. The Allies have failed to make a breakthrough on the Somme and have lost more than 50,000 men.

Alberta, March 1. The Alberta Provincial Police take over law enforcement in Alberta from the RNWMP.

Victoria, April 5. The legislature gives women the vote in provincial elections.

Washington, D.C., April 6. The U.S. declares war on Germany.

Saskatchewan, May 1. May 1 is declared Gopher Day, as students from 980 schools kill more than 50,000 gophers. The gopher holocaust is engineered to increase food production for the war effort.

Amherst, N.S., May. Russian revolutionary Leon Trotsky is released after being interned for a month in a prisoner-of-war camp and preaching revolution to the other interns. British marines detained him en route to Europe.

Europe, June 2. Canadian Capt. Billy Bishop attacks a German aerodrome and shoots down three enemy planes.

Europe, June 9. Gen. Arthur Currie becomes the first Canadian commander of the Canadian Corps.

Ottawa, July 23. Parliament passes the revised Northwest Game Act to protect the game of the Northwest Territories. Musk-ox, white pelicans, and wood buffalo are protected.

Petrograd, Russia, Nov. 7. The Bolsheviks (radical communists) led by Vladimir Lenin oust the provisional government in a bloodless coup.

Montreal, Nov. 26. Professional hockey teams form the National Hockey League.

Alberta. Louise McKinney, women's rights and temperance advocate, is one of the first women elected to a Canadian legislature.

Trenton, Ont. The Adanac Production Co. opens the first Canadian film studios.

Ottawa. Parliament passes the Migratory Birds Convention Act to ratify the treaty signed with the U.S. in 1916 to protect migratory birds.

Seattle. The Seattle Metropolitans defeat the Montreal Canadiens three games to one to win the Stanley Cup.

Canadians launch Vimy Ridge attack

April 9, 1917

ARRAS, France – The Canadian Corps, now grown to four divisions, this morning attacked German positions on Vimy Ridge as part of a general British offensive before Arras. Gen. Julian Byng, commanding the corps, is using all branches of Canadian arms.

The ridge, some 135 metres high, is important for the surrounding ground it commands. The Germans captured it in October 1914, and since then it has been attacked by French and British troops. The enemy has had two years to fortify its positions. It is a key sector of the Hindenburg Line, and will be defended vigorously.

Home defence unit plans abandoned

PM Borden may have to conscript.

July 31, 1917

OTTAWA – Formation of a Home Defence Force, previously announced on March 16, has been cancelled because of lack of public interest and the absence of any threat justifying such a force.

The Home Defence Force, recruited from militia units in Canada, was to have freed training personnel in Canada for overseas service, and perhaps have gained a few recruits for the Canadian Expeditionary Force. It is now clear, however, that just about everybody who wants to fight has already enlisted. Maintaining CEF strength in this unexpectedly bloody war may require the government to enforce compulsory military conscription.

Canadians capture strategic Vimy Ridge

The wounded are gathered at the light railway on the battlefield at Vimy.

The Battle of Vimy Ridge as depicted by artist Richard Jack.

April 14, 1917

ARRAS, France – Six days of fighting concluded on Vimy Ridge today with the Canadian Corps holding all their objectives. The Canadians moved up to this sector last March and spent a month in intense preparation. After suffering heavy losses in battles in 1915 and 1916, all ranks, from privates to commanding general Sir Julian Byng, were determined to succeed. As a result, the Vimy Ridge attack was a model of planning, preparation, and training, and the Canadians have gained more guns, more ground and more prisoners than any previous British offensive.

Today's attack began at 5:30 a.m. with a thunderous artillery barrage mounted by 983 guns and mortars, followed by carefully timed and co-ordinated infantry assaults. The weather was on the Canadians' side; wind, snow and sleet were at their backs and in the enemy's face. Artillery shells forced most of the Germans to take cover while the infantry was advancing toward them. Still, the many shell craters later slowed the Canadian troops, and made it difficult to move heavy guns forward for additional advances. Most of the ridge was captured on the first day of fighting, April 9, but fighting and mopping up action continued until today.

Canadians have advanced 4,095 metres and taken 4,000 prisoners. Losses have been 10,602, including 3,598 killed. King George V has sent a telegram: "Canada will be proud that the taking of the coveted Vimy Ridge has fallen to the lot of her troops."

Borden proposes conscription to House

May 18, 1917

OTTAWA – Prime Minister Robert Borden, just returned from England, has announced in the House that compulsory military duty, or conscription, will be implemented in Canada as soon as possible. The policy, long dreaded in Quebec and rural Canada, as well as by various ethnic communities, comes as the figures for voluntary recruitment continue to spiral downwards. "If any effort to stimulate voluntary recruiting still remains to be made," Borden said this afternoon, "I would like to know what it is." The goal is to conscript 50,000 troops to start, with an eventual target of 100,000.

Opposition leader Wilfrid Laurier pledged careful consideration. Laurier himself opposes the draft, but he's aware that English-speaking Liberals support it.

Montreal residents march in an anti-conscription parade at Victoria Square.

The bear facts: Winnie at London Zoo

1917

LONDON, England – Winnipeg, the gregarious Canadian black bear, is now the London Zoo's great darling and star attraction. Nicknamed Winnie by thousands of her admiring fans, Winnipeg [Winnie-the-Pooh] is so friendly she gives children piggyback rides around the zoo grounds and nibbles treats from their hands.

Winnipeg is from White River, Ont., where Capt. Harry Colebourn, an army veterinarian surgeon from Winnipeg, bought her for $20 from a hunter who had killed the cub's mother. Man and bear then travelled together to England, where Winnipeg slept under Colebourn's cot. But in 1915 Colebourn was ordered to the front lines in France. He donated his beloved bear to the zoo, and visits her whenever he is on leave in England.

Canadian black bear Winnie.

Conscription splits Grits

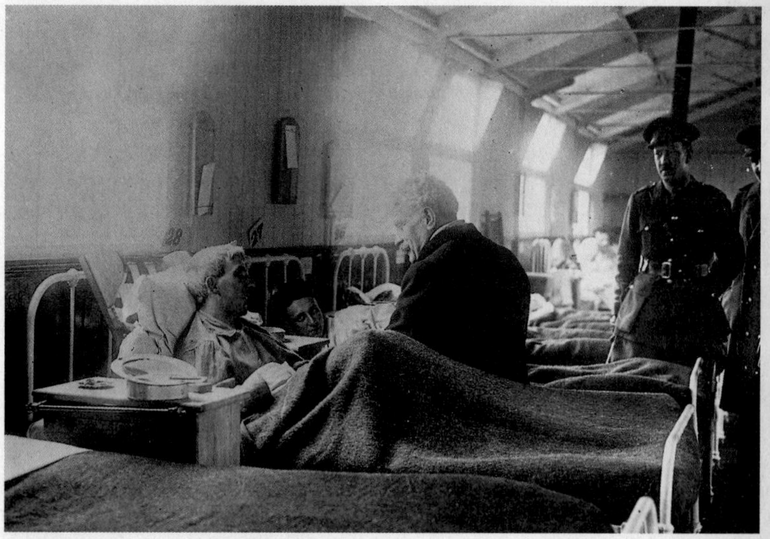

Borden, seen here during a visit to the front, is now considering conscription.

June 1, 1917

OTTAWA – The Liberal party of Sir Wilfrid Laurier is splitting along French-English linguistic lines over conscription, which Prime Minister Sir Robert Borden is expected to introduce this month.

When the war began, nobody thought it would be so long or terrible. After the enlistment rushes of 1914-15, recruiting has not kept up with losses. In a period when the Canadian Expeditionary Force suffered 23,939 casualties, only 11,790 men joined the army. Plans to expand the CEF have been scrapped. Borden wants to keep the Canadian Corps at its present strength, even if it means conscription. He also knows that keeping the CEF strong by conscripting troops will not be a popular move and could thus cripple the long-term electoral prospects of his party.

Opposition to compulsory military service is widespread. But while Ontario and prairie farmers resent it, the most hostile opposition is in Quebec, which is also upset about the anti-French-language school policies in Ontario. Thousands of French-Canadians have enlisted, but conscription is repugnant to all, especially as casualty lists indicate senseless slaughter in the trenches. Laurier himself supports the war effort in all respects except conscription, and refuses to participate in any coalition government dedicated to such a move.

Women in Ontario win right to vote

Feb. 27, 1917

TORONTO – The women of Ontario today were granted the right to vote. Suffrage has been a burning issue in Ontario for many years. In view of the contribution women have made to the war effort, many believed it was only a matter of time before they were enfranchised. Although Premier William Hearst once publicly opposed votes for women as "a responsibility and a burden," the example of the four western provinces could not be ignored. Ontario women still cannot sit in the legislature, though.

Liberals won't join coalition: Laurier

June 6, 1917

OTTAWA – Liberals will not join the ruling Conservatives in a grand coalition government, says Liberal leader Sir Wilfrid Laurier. His negative answer comes after Prime Minister Robert Borden privately courted his approval of a new cabinet drawn equally from both parties. Borden's term of office is running out and he is anxious to avoid an election, say his close confidants, because the touchy issue of conscription would essentially be put to a vote. The result might divide the country.

Roblin, ministers are off the hook

June 25, 1917

WINNIPEG – The criminal charges against former Manitoba premier Sir Rodmond Roblin and two members of his cabinet, J.H. Howden and George Coldwell, have been dropped. Roblin and Howden are excused from trial on grounds of ill health. Crown officials believe no purpose will be served by continuing with charges against Coldwell. Various inquiries have determined these men are personally honorable, but because of their high positions, became engulfed in the fraud surrounding the construction of the Legislative Buildings.

Government to buy Canadian Northern

Aug. 1, 1917

OTTAWA – The government is going to bail out the ailing Canadian Northern Railway by buying it, Finance Minister Sir Thomas White told the House of Commons today. The government, which already owns $40 million in CNR stock, will spend $60 million more to buy out the rest of the stockholders. Once in public hands, the financing of this transcontinental system can be reworked to make it profitable ... or so the government believes. A loan of $7.5 million to the equally ill Grand Trunk Pacific is also being contemplated.

"Fiddlers" to stay on prohibited list

Aug. 2, 1917

OTTAWA – The now notorious pamphlet *The Fiddlers* alleging the spread of alcoholism and disease among Canadian troops overseas will remain on the prohibited list following a report to Parliament by surgeon general J.T. Fotheringham. The booklet by Arthur Mee was first published in England. Any Canadian citizen found possessing it faces a maximum penalty of a $5,000 fine and five years imprisonment. Fotheringham says it is a gross libel of Canadian soldiers and unkind to their families.

Tom Thomson dies; drowning suspected

July 16, 1917

ALGONQUIN PARK, Ont. – The body of Tom Thomson has been found in Canoe Lake. A promising landscape artist, Thomson, 42, was last seen nine days ago as he left on a canoe trip. A 10-centimetre cut on his right temple suggests Thomson lost his balance, struck his head, and drowned. The artist, who was an enthusiastic outdoorsman, will be buried in Algonquin Park.

Artist Tom Thomson.

Victoria Cross goes to pilot Billy Bishop

Captain William "Billy" Bishop at the controls of his aircraft.

Aug. 12, 1917

LONDON, England – Capt. William "Billy" Bishop, a 23-year-old pilot from Owen Sound, Ont., has been awarded the prestigious Victoria Cross for his military exploits. Bishop, who has 36 kills to his record to date, won the highest honor of the British Empire for his attack on a German airfield this June 2.

Early that morning, Bishop set out alone to the enemy airfield, 19.3 kilometres behind the lines. He bombed it first, and then took after four German planes that just happened to be taking off. He shot down the first at a height of 18 metres. Then Bishop forced the second plane to crash into a tree. The third one he downed at 300 metres up, and he put so many bullets into the fourth German aircraft that it retreated. He then returned to base, followed by four more enemy planes 300 metres above him. Perhaps not surprisingly, they chose not to attack.

Mission possible: travelling Chautauqua show arrives in B.C.

June 28, 1917

MISSION, B.C. – Chautauqua has come to Canada! The brown tents, so familiar south of the border as symbols of high class entertainment and education, are now visible in the Canadian west. Promoter John M. Erickson proposed a Canadian Chautauqua last fall. When Erickson convinced the citizens of five prairie towns to sign a contract agreeing to pay for any deficit arising from insufficient ticket sales, the stage was set.

The Chautauqua program includes Ruthven MacDonald, a Canadian baritone, the Waikiki Hawaiian Quintet, and W.J. Hindley's lecture on the "Reign of the Common People." Chautauqua Week in Mission will last six days, after which the charming and attractive performers will move on across the prairies and into the northern United States.

This Chatauqua group includes Agnes McGillis (centre), a Métis performer.

Canadians overwhelm German defences at Hill 70

Gen. Currie watches his men marching to rest camp after taking Hill 70.

Canadian messenger carries his bicycle through mud caused by a recent storm.

Traffic is blocked as Canadian troops under Gen. Currie attack Hill 70.

Aug. 15, 1917

LENS, France – Today at dawn, Gen. Arthur Currie, the Canadian Corps' first Canadian commander, launched his fresh, seasoned troops in a well-rehearsed assault against the bleak, treeless chalk ridge called Hill 70. For Currie it was a double victory; he had been ordered to take the town of Lens, but had correctly judged that the high ground on its left was more important. He argued for a change of plans, and was successful.

The battle demonstrated Currie's mode of fighting – massive use of 160 machine-guns to force the enemy to take cover, and trench mortars and howitzers to kill them in their trenches, thus sparing Canadian lives. He also used feint attacks and thick, oily smoke screens to hide the movements of some troops. And for the first time, our artillery was directed by observers using radios. Still, we suffered 1,056 killed, 2,432 wounded, and 39 taken prisoner. Our losses would have been worse but for heroic stretcher bearers retrieving casualties under fire. Pte. M.J. O'Rourke was exceptionally courageous.

Hill 70 gives the Allies a clear, distant view of German positions in Lens itself. The enemy have fiercely counter-attacked, but our artillery is savaging them. In many battles of this war, land has been captured at great cost, then lost to enemy counter-attacks. Just as at Vimy Ridge, the Canadians are showing they can both take and hold key points.

Inuit pair found guilty of murdering two Oblate missionaries

Aug. 25, 1917

CALGARY – In a courtroom filled to capacity, the celebrated murder trial of two Inuit from the remote Coppermine region of the Northwest Territories has ended. Sinnisiak and Uluksuk, the first Inuit tried in a Canadian court, have been convicted of murdering two Oblate missionaries in 1913.

The Inuit pair were acquitted of the same charge last week in Edmonton. There's no doubt they killed the missionaries – they admit it openly – but they see it as self-defence, and the jury in Edmonton agreed. But the Crown, determined to introduce Canada's justice system to an area considered lawless by Canadian, though not Inuit, standards, arranged for a retrial.

Wartime poster urges Canadians to resist the urge to hoard.

Military Service Act passed to bolster Canadian armed forces

Aug. 28, 1917

OTTAWA – The Military Service Act is now law. It was signed into life today by Canada's governor general, the Duke of Devonshire. The bill defines six classes of men eligible for conscription. The first class, unmarried men or childless widowers between the ages of 20 and 34, will be used for the first selection of 100,000 conscripts. To lessen criticism, the government has allowed for many exemptions. Among these are men working in essential war occupations, whose conscripting might cause their families "serious hardship," and conscientious objectors.

New Elections Act says who can vote

Sept. 14, 1917

OTTAWA – The Conservative government has pushed through a new War-Time Elections Act, one that promises to have sweeping implications for Canadian politics. Using closure to limit what amounted to just three days worth of debate, Prime Minister Robert Borden has taken away the vote from about 25,000 naturalized citizens from enemy countries. He has also awarded the franchise to a half million women whose brothers, husbands, or sons have served or are serving overseas.

What's also keeping Ottawa hopping is the move to tax income. This "temporary measure," long rejected by Finance Minister Sir Thomas White, mainly hits those with income above $6,000. Corporate profits will also be taxed at a rate of four percent. However, the Tories are leaving numerous loopholes in this tax. They say it will only be in effect for the duration of the war.

Canadians end Passchendaele attack

Nov. 10, 1917

PASSCHENDAELE, Belgium – Canadian attacks in this sector ended today. Fighting in Flanders, which has preoccupied British armies since July, is slowing down.

Canadian troops entered this particular battle in mid-October when they relieved Australian and New Zealand forces. They took over an area where months of shelling had destroyed the natural drainage system, creating a sea of mud blighted by unburied corpses.

Approach trenches could not be dug, so men and mules moved to the front over exposed wooden sidewalks and risked drowning in mud if they fell off. The Canadians built wooden roads through the mud in order to use the heavy artillery which Gen. Arthur Currie insisted be deployed in maximum strength. Currie knew that losses would be heavy and was determined that they would at least be justified by success in battle.

German troops held the higher and drier ground, and fought from strong positions, including concrete bunkers. While preparing to attack, the Canadians were harassed by enemy gas shells. Eventually they made four assaults – on Oct. 26-28, Oct. 30, Nov. 6 (which took Passchendaele itself), and today. The attacks alone cost 8,000 Canadian casualties, including 2,623 dead. The Germans launched several counter-attacks. Their shelling killed many of their own men who had been captured.

Canadians carrying trench mats at Passchendaele go by German prisoners.

Borden the leader of Union Government

Oct. 12, 1917

OTTAWA – Tory Prime Minister Robert Borden has emerged as the leader of the new Union Government. The name derives from the fact that it is comprised of both Tories and pro-conscription Liberals, standing in opposition to their own party. In the cabinet itself, besides the PM, there are 12 Conservatives, eight Liberals, and one Labour representative.

Canadians are reminded to save food for the fighting men overseas.

Pro-conscription Union returned to power

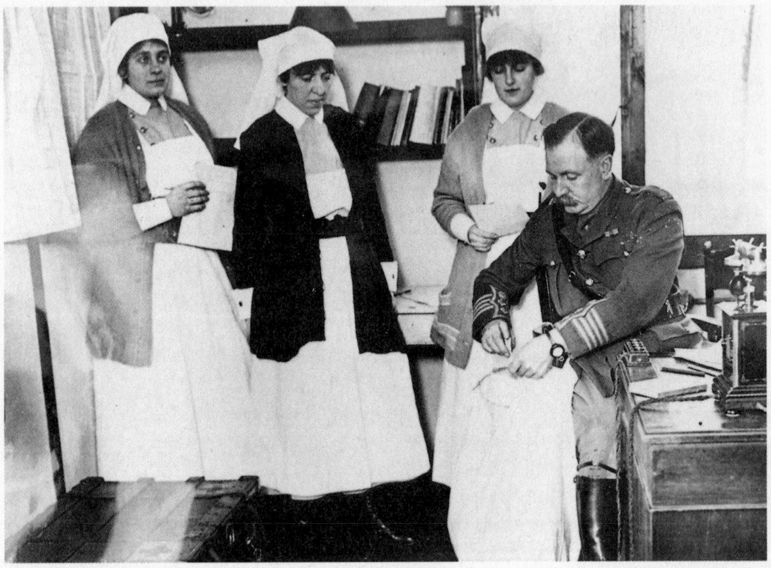

Military voters no doubt supported Robert Borden's pro-conscription stand.

Dec. 15, 1917

OTTAWA – Robert Borden has swept back to power on the strength of his Union campaign against the remains of Sir Wilfrid Laurier's Liberal party. There were 113 Conservatives and 39 Liberal Unionists, as they're called, elected to the government benches, as opposed to 82 Laurier Liberals. Most of these were elected in Quebec: 62 as opposed to three Unionists. The split indicates the animosity over conscription, which became the central issue of the campaign. The overall cost of Borden's victory is the political isolation of anti-conscription French Canada.

Death toll tops 1,000 as explosion rocks Halifax

Soldiers search for survivors.

The city of Halifax as viewed from the waterfront after the great explosion.

Dec. 6, 1917

HALIFAX – A French munitions vessel, the *Mont Blanc,* exploded in Halifax harbor this morning, levelling the city's north end and killing more than 1,000 people. Hundreds of others are still trapped in ruined buildings. They are at the mercy of fires raging through the wreckage of the district's wooden homes.

Naval authorities warn that the flames now threaten the main garrison magazine, and a second explosion is feared. While rescuers claw frantically at ruins, battered and bleeding citizens are evacuating the city. Many have been mutilated or blinded by flying glass, and the city's hospitals are choked with the injured and dying. Among the victims are many children who were killed or mutilated as schools collapsed and shattered classroom windows flew inward.

Six thousand of the city's 50,000 people are homeless, and very few homes are undamaged. Many people are expected to perish from exposure in a blizzard forecast to begin this evening. The blast demolished many of the city's industries, including the naval dockyard, the railway station, and the sugar refinery, as well as wharves, breweries, printing houses, foundries, and warehouses.

Working in makeshift morgues, undertakers have begun sifting through tubs of charred human remains, searching for rings, dentures and other means of identification. Rescuers say it will take months to remove the rubble and determine the final death toll, but officials fear the number could reach 2,000.

What appears to be the worst manmade explosion ever recorded to date occurred shortly after the *Mont Blanc* collided in the harbor's narrowest stretch with the Belgian relief steamer *Imo.* Sparks from the collision ignited oil stored on the *Mont Blanc*'s deck, setting it afire, and the flames quickly spread to the holds below. Then in a chain reaction, almost 3,000 tons of explosive materials were set off, including TNT. Rumors of sabotage have swept the city, but the true cause of the collision is unknown.

Ottawa bans use of grain in liquor

Nov. 5, 1917

OTTAWA – The use of grain to manufacture liquor has been prohibited by an order-in-council, and the "dry spell" may continue until the end of the war. The order states that after the end of this month, no grain such as rye, barley and corn – or any other that can be used for food purposes – may be used for making potable liquor. The only exception is that the food controller may license the making of alcohol from wheat if it is to be used for manufacturing or munitions.

The order will not be rescinded until the current "abnormal conditions" have been declared to be over by the governor general in council. The order carries a penalty of a fine not exceeding $5,000, or up to six months in prison, or both. Compliance is not expected to be a problem because distilleries have been mainly manufacturing industrial alcohol with grains for months.

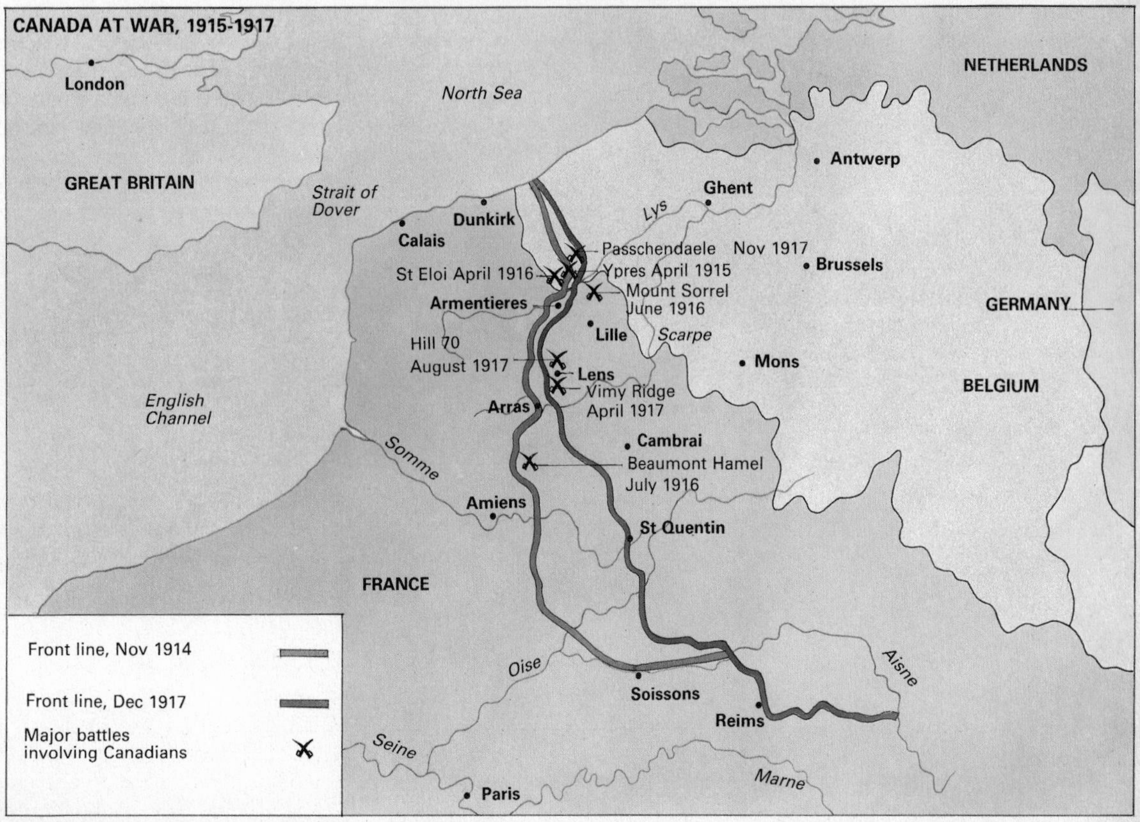

Minimal advances were made between 1914 and 1917 despite seven major battles involving Canadians.

Paintings offer a firsthand look at the Great War

A Tragic Accident While Training, Borden, by Frank Johnston. Johnston covered air training scenes.

Plan allows artists to cover the battle

1917

EUROPE – Canada's war effort is being recorded by artists. Canadian-born press baron Lord Beaverbrook has already publicized the troops' efforts using books, articles, newsreels, a newspaper for the soldiers, and front line photographers. His latest plan allows British and Canadian artists to paint all aspects of the war, from portraits of Victoria Cross heroes to grim pictures of wounded soldiers. He hopes it will all be housed in some type of museum one day.

Shipbuilding, Polsen Yard, Toronto, by Gagin.

The Sunken Road, Hangard, a painting by Maurice Cullen, illustrates the devastation of the war zone and creates a mood of eerie stillness.

Canadian women contribute to war effort

1917

OTTAWA – Since the start of the war, women have taken on new responsibilities at home and contributed to the war effort overseas. Perhaps the most selfless contribution has been made by nurses of the Canadian Army Medical Corps. Soon after the war began, Margaret Macdonald was called from Kingston to succeed Georgina Pope, the Army Medical Corps' first matron. With her staff, Miss Macdonald selected nurses from thousands of volunteers.

No one can deny the nurses are true sisters-in-arms to the soldiers. Nicknamed the "Bluebirds" for their distinctive blue uniforms, they not only care for the wounded and ill, but they also experience the cold, hunger and disease that is the soldier's lot, and are even at risk from air raids and poisonous gas.

Canada's Answer, by N. Wilkinson, shows the transport of Canadian troops.

Women Making Shells, by Henrietta Mabel May, depicts women's war work.

Detail of The Stretcher Bearer Party, by Cyril Henry Barraud. Soldiers carry their wounded back from the front over the muddy battlefield.

Detail of Canadian Gunners in the Mud, by A.T.J. Bastien.

Canadian Monument, Passchendaele Ridge, by Mary Riter Hamilton.

Felling a Tree in the Vosges, by Sir Alfred Munnings.

Detail of the painting called A Night Shoot, by Thurston Topham.

1918

Regina, Jan. 4. The provincial government orders the reporting of all venereal diseases.

Pictou County, N.S., January. An mine explosion at the Allan Shaft kills 88.

Ontario, March 4. The federal government places troops along the Niagara border to prevent those eligible for military duty from crossing into the U.S.

Ottawa, March 11. An order-in-council prohibits the manufacture or import of liquor containing more than 2.5 percent alcohol until one year after the end of the war.

Ottawa, April. In response to Quebec anti-conscription riots, cabinet passes orders-in-council that suspend *habeas corpus* and authorize the governor general to declare martial law.

Quebec, April 13. A jury finds military authorities mainly responsible for anti-conscription riots.

Ottawa, April. With the Allies suffering heavy casualties, PM Robert Borden calls a secret session of Parliament to announce the end of exemptions from military service.

Winnipeg, May 13. With strikes threatening to shut down Winnipeg, city council passes the Fowler Amendment, which challenges the workers' right to strike.

Ottawa, May 15. Some 5,000 farmers demonstrate against federal plans to cancel exemptions from military service.

Europe, June 19. Canadian airman Billy Bishop shoots down five German planes.

Victoriaville, Que., Sept. 1. About 400 teachers and students come down with Spanish flu as returning troops bring the disease to Canada.

Vladivostok, Russia, Oct. 27. Some 4,000 Canadian troops arrive to help fight against the Bolshevik Revolution.

Canada, October. Several provinces ban public meetings as a measure against the Spanish flu epidemic.

Compiègne, France, Nov. 11. An armistice ends the war. The Canadian army overseas numbers 418,000.

Ontario. Point Pelee National Park is created on Lake Erie, a major bird-watching spot.

Toronto. Toronto Arenas beat the Vancouver Millionaires three games to two to win the Stanley Cup.

Draftees expected to register today

Jan. 3, 1918

MONTREAL – The first draftees selected under the Military Service Act are slated to report today at both the Guy and Peel street barracks. About 250 men aged 20-34 are expected to register with military authorities. Any who refuse to show will be classified as deserters, and face a prison term of five years at hard labor. Government officials are keeping the names of the 250 secret, notifying each of them by registered mail.

Separation for Quebec?

Jan. 17, 1918

QUEBEC CITY – Provincial legislators today discussed a motion by J.N. Francoeur recommending that Quebec, if perceived as "an obstacle to the union, progress and development of Canada" by the other provinces, should break the 1867 Confederation pact and form a sovereign country.

The proposal, which has received much media attention since it was made public late last year, is the manifestation of increased tensions between English- and French-Canadians. Much of this friction stems from trouble related to the implementation of the Military Service Act in Quebec and from the conviction that the province's priorities are internal, not external. In presenting his proposal, Francoeur cited defamatory statements appearing in numerous English-Canadian newspapers as evidence that a problem exists. The proposal reveals a fundamental weakness in Canada's Confederation; conflicts about differences in language, faith and tradition have yet to be addressed.

War restrictions have Canadians eating more fish, less meat

Jan. 4, 1918

OTTAWA – In keeping with wartime restrictions on food, Canadians are consuming more fish and less meat. The consumption of white flour has also dropped. According to reports sent to the food controller by leading hotels and restaurants, the per capita consumption of beef in November 1917 was 58.4 percent of that in November 1916.

Fish consumption has increased, especially in private homes. The use of white flour is down dramatically, and there has also been a slight increase in the consumption of corn meal and oatmeal.

Censor board bans frivolous funny films

Jan. 22, 1918

WINNIPEG – Members of the Manitoba Moving Picture Censor Board apparently don't fancy frivolity. They have banned comedy films from motion picture houses on the grounds they make the audience too frivolous. A local clergyman, commenting on a film on the life of Evelyn Thaw, said that while Canadian men were overseas fighting, those at home should have more to do than watch pictures of a "New York strumpet."

Alexander corner, 8th Avenue and 1st Street West, Calgary. Note Regent Theatre, left, and Calgary Municipal Railway checkpoint box on pole, right.

Toronto shuts down to conserve on fuel

Feb. 11, 1918

TORONTO – Some 100,000 workers are idle here. Thousands of businesses, stores, and factories are closed. A general strike? No! Simply the observance of fuel conservation in Toronto, as ordered by C.A. Magrath, Canadian fuel controller. The three-day shutdown, which ends at midnight tonight, is aimed at saving precious coal, so that more of it can be used for wartime purposes.

Conscription riots erupting in Quebec

April 1, 1918

QUEBEC CITY – The Archbishop of Quebec has appealed for cool heads as Ottawa is poised to declare martial law to crush anticonscription rioting here. Troops called in from outside the city have tried to neutralize frenzied crowds surging through the streets. Several innocent bystanders, including a young girl, have been injured in the violence. Rioters failed in an attempt to capture the city armory.

Railway employees strike in Winnipeg

May 21, 1918

WINNIPEG – When 4,000 railway workers went on strike today, the current labor unrest came close to reaching the level of a general strike. The railway employees, machinists, moulders, blacksmiths, and other members of the non-running trades, are supporting earlier walkouts by a wide variety of workers in Winnipeg.

Ninety civic employees from the city's light and power department laid down their tools May 2 when their demand for wage increases was denied. The following day the city's electricians and waterworks employees left their jobs. On May 7, the Teamsters struck, and one week later they were followed by the firemen.

Provincial employees entered the shutdown May 16 when the telephone operators abandoned their switchboards. To date, 7,000 workers representing 14 trades in government and industry have walked off their jobs.

Despite the number of workers on strike, not all proponents of labor are in support of the current action. Editor A.W. Puttee of *The Voice,* a labor paper, only a week ago described the threatened strike as "too precipitate," and he says that all avenues of conciliation and arbitration have not yet been explored. Opposing Puttee's moderate view is the opinion of R.J. Johns, who says that "we have the might, let us use it."

Women to vote in federal elections

"For Home and Country" is the motto of the Federated Women's Institutes.

Women in the Eaton's catalogue.

Katherine Stinson is a woman in a man's field. She is Canada's first female airmail pilot.

May 24, 1918

OTTAWA – Canadian women have won the right to vote in federal elections. Every female British subject over the age of 21 may now vote, providing she meets property requirements in provinces where they exist.

Shortly after the opening of Parliament in March, Prime Minister Robert Borden introduced Bill 3. At the second reading on March 22, he said, "I concede that women are entitled to the franchise on their merits, and it is upon that basis that this bill is presented to Parliament for its consideration."

Much discussion took place when the bill reached the committee of the whole. In Quebec, where women still may not vote in provincial elections, there is widespread opposition. Critics say women's suffrage is contrary to the laws of God and nature. Some members of Parliament also oppose the idea of women holding office. When Lt.-Col. William F. Cockshutte said, "I would rather run against two men than against one woman," Borden emphasized that the legislation granted the right to vote, not to serve as members of Parliament.

A great deal of discussion on the suffrage bill also took place in the Senate. One senator attempted to limit the franchise to unmarried women. Another suggested only women over 30 be eligible. But all these obstacles were eventually overcome, and royal assent was given today.

CAA stats reveal Canada has the third most cars in the world

This automobile was a novelty in 1912, but now cars are plentiful in Canada.

May 8, 1918

HAMILTON, Ont. – Canadians own and operate more than 200,000 motor cars, the third highest number in the world, the Canadian Automobile Association reported today at its annual meeting. CAA president L.B. Howland said the total represents an increase of 100 percent over last year.

Western farmers, using cars to speed up food production, accounted for some of the increase, Howland says. He added that the fuel controller had no immediate plans to ask for jurisdiction over gasoline consumption in Canada.

Food official warns of farm labor crisis

June 17, 1918

OTTAWA – Warning that conservation and lowered consumption are only part of the battle, Canada Food Board chairman H.B. Thomson today drew attention to the farm labor crisis. Calling the harvest of this year's crop an "emergency service," Thomson appealed to Canadians to volunteer for farm service. Earlier this year, farmers responded to calls for increased food production by sowing new land, but without new laborers, the food will rot in the fields.

Pilot delivers first air mail to Toronto

June 24, 1918

TORONTO – The first airmail in Canada has been delivered here from Montreal in a biplane piloted by Capt. Brian Peck of the Royal Air Force. Peck was returning to Leaside base after a weekend in Montreal. The idea of bringing 120 pieces of mail back with him was the result of quick thinking by members of the Aerial League of the British Empire in Montreal. The league arranged for the post office to release the letters and to stamp them "Inaugural service – Via Aerial Mail, Montreal." The flight, with stopovers for fuel, took six hours to complete.

Papers in enemy languages banned

Oct. 1, 1918

OTTAWA – The ongoing campaign against "enemy aliens" – Canadians of German or Austro-Hungarian descent – has been taken a step further by the government. Today it was announced that books, newspapers, or other material in the languages of the "enemy powers" are forbidden in Canada, unless published under a licence from the secretary of state. The move effectively censors such publications before they ever make it into the public domain. Presumably, it will prevent "undesirable elements" working against the Allied cause by whipping up dissent inside Canada.

Winnipeg drops Fowler Amendment

May 24, 1918

WINNIPEG – The so-called Fowler Amendment has been abandoned. Winnipeg city council can now proceed to negotiate a contract with its employees. Councillors today rejected a motion by Alderman F.D. Fowler which would have denied civic workers here the right to strike. Any likelihood of an early settlement of threatened labor action was impossible as long as Fowler's troublesome amendment remained on the books.

Council's actions today came about as a direct result of federal intervention. Senator Gideon Robertson, special assistant to the federal minister of labor, came to Winnipeg to appeal to councillors to strive for peaceful settlements in a period of labor distress which is achieving national prominence.

City council appointed a committee on May 9 to engage the workers in negotiations. Progress was made, and with the defeat of the Fowler Amendment, it is expected that negotiations will continue today.

Did Canadian gun down the Red Baron?

April 21, 1918

LONDON, England – Baron Manfred von Richthofen, the most successful fighter pilot in Germany, has been shot down and killed in a low-level combat over France. Australian troops claim the famed Red Baron fell to them; others say a Canadian pilot, Capt. Arthur Roy Brown of No. 209 Squadron, gunned the enemy pilot down with the aid of fellow Canadian Wilfrid "Wop" May.

Brown has previously been credited with eight victories and was awarded the Distinguished Service Cross last year. He is one of more than 800 Canadian pilots serving in Britain's air forces. Since 1915, Canadians have been appearing in growing numbers and doing ever more tasks – bombing, strafing troops, directing artillery, looking for submarines, and shooting down the enemy airships and aircraft that raid Britain. In Brown's service unit, for example, two of the three flight commanders are Canadian, and the third one is an American with Canadian roots.

Canadian Arthur Roy Brown, who some say shot down the Red Baron.

The British think so highly of Canadian airmen that last year they started a recruiting and training program in Canada. Flying and tactical schools at Camp Borden, Beamsville, and in the area around Toronto are now turning out hundreds of RAF personnel.

Labor "holiday" turns into a riot

Aug. 2, 1918

VANCOUVER – It started as a "holiday" but ended as a riot. The "holiday" was a work stoppage called by the Vancouver Labour Council to mark the funeral of Albert "Ginger" Goodwin. He was a union organizer who was shot while hiding in the woods on Vancouver Island to avoid being called up for military service. Goodwin had led a strike at the Trail smelter, but when it was over he was given a call-up notice.

Labor leaders say Goodwin was a martyr and ordered union members to stop work at noon today. This comes after a summer of labor unrest in which thousands of workers went on strike for higher wages. It was too much for the veterans who had come back from France. About 700 of them stopped streetcar drivers taking their cars back to the depot. Fights started, and the police and army were called out to restore order.

The Dominion Conference of Women at Ottawa was well attended.

Stefansson makes a triumphant return

Sept. 16, 1918

VANCOUVER – Famed explorer Vilhjalmur Stefansson has returned from a five-year excursion into the Arctic. The government-sponsored expedition, which began in tragedy in 1913 with the destruction of the *Karluk*, ends in triumph. Stefansson and his party have located four new islands in the far north, the world's last major land masses to be put on the map. As well, they have charted the floor of the Beaufort Sea and a large section of the continental shelf north of Alaska.

Stefansson's co-leader of the expedition, Rudolph Anderson, was ordered back from the north two years ago. Similar orders went out to Stefansson, but he was intent on completing further discoveries and managed to avoid receiving the orders. More than once he disappeared on the ice, and it was widely believed that he would never be seen again. But he always turned up, safe and sound. This spring officials finally caught up with the controversial explorer when he was hospitalized on Herschel Island with typhoid and pneumonia.

Canadian Corps storm through Hindenburg Line

Tanks advance. Prisoners wearing gas masks carry in wounded at Amiens.

Canadians rest in captured trenches in front of Arras in August.

Oct. 1, 1918

BELCOURT, France – After five days of fighting, the Canadian Corps, 100,000-strong, have pushed through German defences called the Hindenburg Line, opening the way for an Allied advance on Cambrai. Canadians have been on the move ever since the British offensive began with the Battle of Amiens Aug. 8, one successful battle following another. These have included the Battle of the Scarpe Aug. 26-30, and the attack on the D-Q (for Drocourt-Quéant) Line Sept. 2-3. Even on "quiet days," combat casualties have seldom been less than 100.

The latest battle began in the early morning darkness of Sept. 27, when Canadian troops, supported by tanks and a rolling artillery barrage, fought their way across swampy land occupied by the uncompleted Canal du Nord and seized Bourlon Wood. Canadian field guns followed the troops, and as soon as the infantry had advanced to the limit of artillery range, the guns were moved forward to provide continuing covering fire.

The advance slowed after Sept. 27; enemy defences were strong and counter-attacks frequent. At one time or another, the four Canadian divisions met nine full German divisions and parts of three others. One enemy officer described the 27th as the "blackest day" in the history of his regiment, and the day when he "buried all our hopes of victory." In fact, the Canadians captured more than 7,000 prisoners and 205 heavy guns.

Observers note that the five days of fighting included many actions so heroic they predict several Victoria Crosses will be awarded.

Cavalry Brigade leads the charge on German line at Le Cateau

Canadian 18-pounders move forward toward Boulon Wood to cover the infantry advance at a recent battle.

Oct. 9, 1918

LE CATEAU – The Canadian Cavalry Brigade, consisting of Lord Strathcona's Horse, the Fort Garry Horse, and Royal Canadian Dragoons, have fought a series of actions today lasting from 9:30 a.m. until nightfall, advancing 12.9 kilometres and taking more than 400 prisoners. Guns of the Royal Canadian Horse Artillery supported the brigade. The day's action cost the Canadians 168 men and 171 horses killed, wounded, or missing.

The action is most striking because cavalries have little chance of employment on the Western Front. Machine-guns, tanks, and barbed wire render them obsolete. Canadian cavalry charges, though successful, are anachronistic.

Vancouver battles deadly Spanish flu

Oct. 22, 1918

VANCOUVER – Spanish flu is raging in Vancouver – 522 cases were reported today. Hospitals are so overcrowded that the University of British Columbia is serving as an infirmary. Doctors and trained nurses are scarce, although 200 untrained women have volunteered to care for the sick. Meanwhile, the price of medicine is rising. Camphor, which sold for 40 cents a pound in September, now costs $6.50. The epidemic has nearly stopped mail delivery, and people have been asked to use telephones only for emergencies.

This is not the first time flu has devastated Canada – in the 19th century, at least seven epidemics killed thousands, most very young or old. But the present worldwide scourge fells even strong adults. ▷

Hospitals hit hard by war, Spanish flu

Oct. 25, 1918

OTTAWA – Overcrowding caused by war casualties and an influx of Spanish flu victims is a critical problem in military and civilian Canadian hospitals, according to testimony presented today before a government commission. The inquiry was set up after complaints were lodged by the relatives of patients who died in hospital.

One case was that of Cadet F.N. Davidson, whose death put into question the Toronto Base Hospital's ability to care for its patients. The death in the same hospital of Capt. Roy Kain, a minister from Niagara Camp, prompted his widow to make a written complaint to Ottawa. In her letter, Mrs. Kain quoted her husband's last words: "Canada can be well ashamed of the way she has treated her men." Mrs. Kain had moved her husband, who had Spanish flu, from Niagara to the Toronto hospital so that he could receive better care.

Although Davidson and Kain both died in the same hospital, their experiences represent a national problem. Maj.-Gen. W.A. Logie also told the inquiry that overcrowding in hospitals leads to serious fire hazards.

Steamer goes down with passengers, crew

The Princess Sophia sank after running aground on Vanderbilt Reef.

Oct. 25, 1918

VICTORIA, B.C. – The CPR steamer *Princess Sophia* sank in Lynn Canal this evening and took all her 346 passengers and crew with her into the icy water. The *Sophia* left Skagway Wednesday night filled with passengers from the Yukon and Alaska who were leaving for the "outside" before winter came. The community of the Yukon will be hit hard by the loss of so many officials, professionals, and business leaders.

The 2,300-ton ship built in Scotland six years ago ran into a blinding snowstorm four hours out of Skagway on her trip south to Vancouver. She obviously lost her course, and hit Vanderbilt Reef in the Lynn Canal. Her speed and the high tide drove her up onto the reef, so that although her bottom was damaged, she was high and dry. Boats and ships soon came, but the seas were so rough passengers and crew had to stay on the *Sophia* the rest of Wednesday and Thursday.

On Friday morning, the U.S. lighthouse tender *Cedar* got close to the *Sophia,* but her anchors would not hold and she had to move to safer waters. Then, at 8 p.m. the *Cedar* picked up a wireless message from the *Sophia.* She'd been driven off the reef and was sinking fast.

Government selling Victory Loan bonds

Oct. 27, 1918

TORONTO – More than 25,000 people gathered in Queen's Park today to mark the inauguration of the government's second Victory Loan campaign. The gathering was characterized by strong patriotism and optimism for Canada's post-war future. Leaders spoke of supporting the new economy and of doing one's patriotic duty by buying bonds. Public prayers for the success of the nation and frequent singing marked the event.

The government has launched this campaign as a way of overcoming the economic problems which Canada is bound to face the next few years. Many of the men who went overseas did so at the cost of apprenticeships, jobs, and educations, and will have to be retaught upon their return. Furthermore, the job market that these men now face is different from the one they left behind. On top of this, Canada faces huge debts and the need to address looming social problems, such as unemployment. As today's rally shows, however, Canadians have the patriotism and determination to conquer these problems and to render Canada healthy once again.

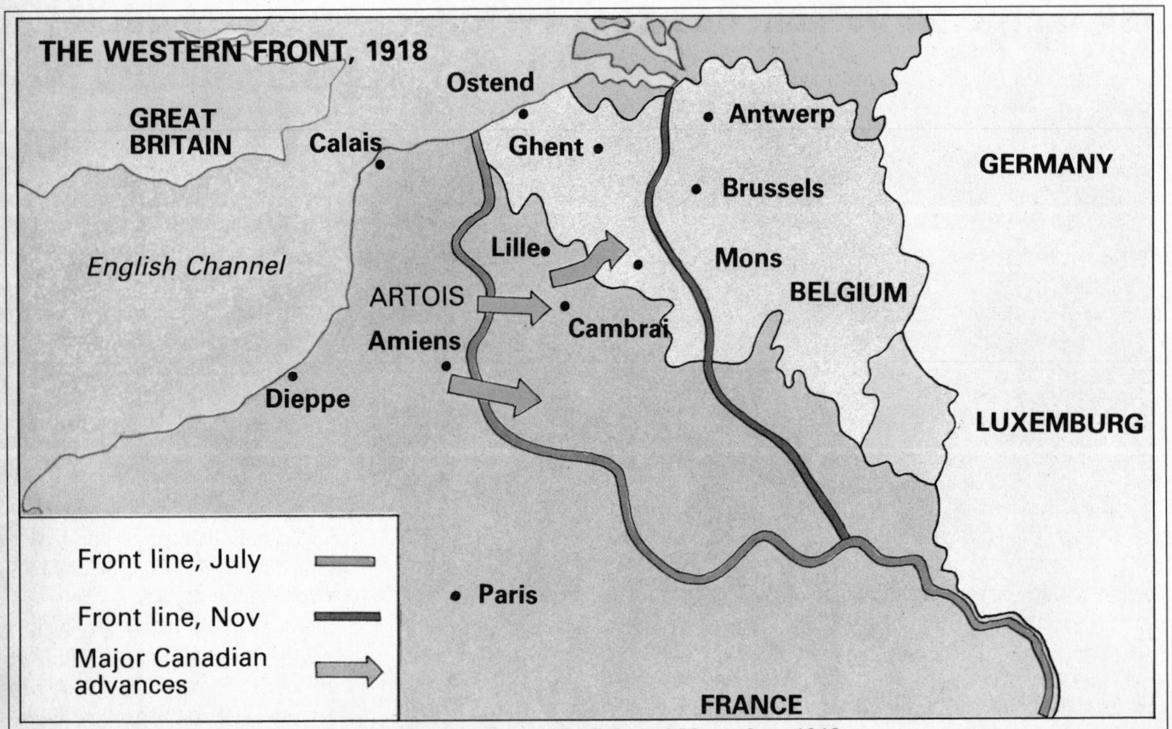

Map indicates location of western frontlines in Europe in July and November, 1918.

Religious leaders boost public morale

Sept. 12, 1918

TORONTO – Canadian and U.S. religious leaders boosted morale with rousing speeches made earlier tonight in front of a capacity crowd in Massey Hall. The clergymen have just returned from extensive travels including into Europe's worst battlefield trenches.

The Right Reverend J.M. McCormick of Western Michigan moved the crowd into a standing ovation when he reminded them that American troops in Europe will soon number 3.5 million. The mood, while remaining optimistic, turned somewhat sombre as the Right Reverend J.A. Richardson of New Brunswick announced that after visiting soldiers in the trenches, he was certain the Canadian sacrifice would be remembered.

Armistice ends the fighting in Europe

Spectators watch Canadian troops led by General A. Currie enter German territory en route to the Rhine.

Fire set by the retreating enemy.

Canadians march through the streets of Mons, the morning of the armistice.

Nov. 11, 1918

MONS, Belgium – The fighting has stopped. At 11 a.m. today an armistice came into effect, although a peace treaty must still be negotiated. German troops will withdraw to their own country, now torn by revolution. When the end came, Canadian troops had just liberated Mons. British and German troops first clashed here in August 1914, and the last of Canada's 229,000 casualties – including nearly 60,000 killed – were sustained here.

Men of the 29th Battalion, CEF, report a touching story. While celebrating with songs, they were approached by a little girl who told them, "I know an English song." Although shy, she sang her song: *It's a Long Way to Tipperary.* Asked how she knew this after living four years under German occupation, the child said that in 1914, before retreating, some English troops had taught her the words and told her to remember them. They said they would return and ask her to sing the song for them. The Canadians, who, steel helmets aside, wear much the same uniform as the "Tommies" of 1914, kept a promise on behalf of their anonymous English comrades. The girl kept her promise by remembering.

In spite of recent influenza epidemics, celebrations are in full swing in all Allied countries. Joy and relief mingle as the most terrible war in human history is over. At least 13 million people have died in the struggle, the vast majority of them young men. Four empires – Russian, German, Turkish and Austro-Hungarian – have fallen. Even the victors had great difficulties. New taxes – including general income taxes – have been needed to pay for the war. The United States abandoned its long-standing policy of isolation to take part in what many considered a European quarrel. Early in 1917, the French army was racked by mutinies. Canada experienced conscription riots. Everyone hopes that this has truly been the "war to end wars."

Newfoundland teen gets Victoria Cross

Private Thomas Ricketts, VC.

Dec. 23, 1918

LONDON, England – It was announced today that Pte. Thomas Ricketts of the Royal Newfoundland Regiment will be awarded the Victoria Cross for bravery in battle. At 17 years old, Ricketts is the youngest ever to receive the medal. He enlisted at 15, and has been a soldier for more than two years.

Ricketts' regiment is part of the Allied advance through Belgium. On Oct. 14, he ran about 100 metres through enemy fire to obtain vital ammunition. Later, he and a corporal drove German gunners from their posts, saving the lives of many Newfoundlanders.

THE TORCH; BE YOURS TO HOLD IT HIGH!
IF YE BREAK FAITH WITH US WHO DIE
WE SHALL NOT SLEEP, THOUGH POPPIES GROW
IN FLANDERS FIELDS.
McCRAE.

A memorial to the Canadians at Vimy and an inspirational line from John McCrae's poem.

Spanish flu fatal for 262

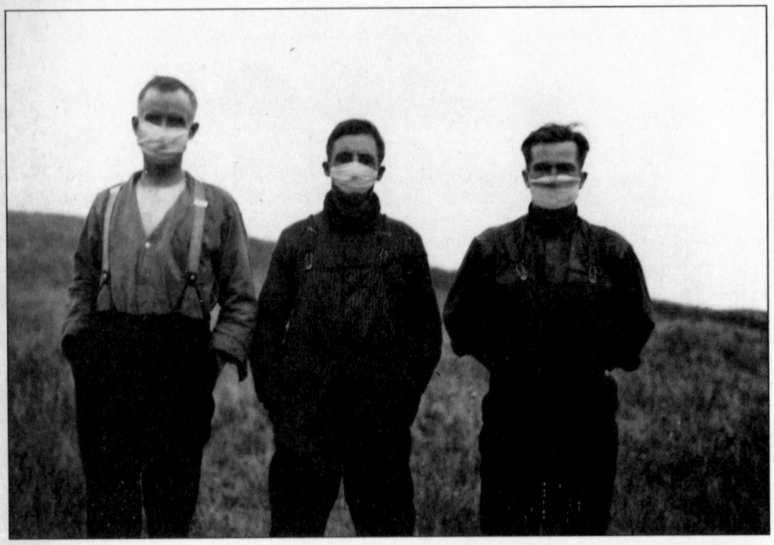

These Alberta men are wearing masks, hoping to avoid contracting the flu.

Nov. 11, 1918

EDMONTON – Last month, Edmonton suddenly fell victim to the Spanish flu epidemic. On Oct. 19, 41 cases were reported. Now, little more than three weeks later, the death toll is at 262. The epidemic sweeping across the country is highly contagious. While schools, churches, theatres and public buildings in Alberta have been closed since Oct. 18, it still spreads.

Symptoms of the infection include a feeling of lassitude, accompanied by a headache. Muscular pains are also typical. Delirium may follow, along with spitting up blood. In some cases the victim is dead within 48 hours. The disease has no respect for age. In fact, many of the dead are young men and women in the prime of life. There have also been instances where whole familes – father, mother and children – succumbed to the disease.

Farm reps suggest sweeping changes

Nov. 28, 1918

WINNIPEG – Farmers from four provinces have joined forces in urging a new national policy of reconstruction. Representatives of farm associations in Alberta, Saskatchewan, Manitoba, and Ontario, meeting as the Canadian Council of Agriculture, have adopted sweeping recommendations they will present to the federal government.

The farmers debated for four days before reaching their conclusions. They finally agreed on a set of proposals which are close in alignment with those which have long been urged by Thomas A. Crerar, the president of the United Grain Growers and minister of agriculture in the Union government.

The council's recommendations include: substantial reduction of customs tariffs; a half-rate for all goods imported from Britain; a free rate for all fuels and agricultural implements; and a requirement that all petitions for relief from tariff be heard in public. The farmers believe the tariff protects the privileged urban class at the expense of rural Canadians. Other requests include the reform of Senate and an end to patronage.

PM seeks a greater role at peace talks

Canadian delegates at June meeting.

Dec. 31, 1918

LONDON, England – At a meeting of the Imperial War Cabinet, currently considering the empire's stand in peace negotiations with Germany, Canadian Prime Minister Robert Borden has insisted that each of the prime ministers in Britain's dominions should take turns representing the empire at the upcoming talks. His demand, which essentially asserts that Canada should be treated as an independent Allied power, is backed by ministers of dominions such as Australia, New Zealand, and South Africa.

Borden's stance exemplifies his ardent nationalism throughout the war. He insists Canada be rewarded for its support of the Allies in the Great War – Canada has already spent more than a billion dollars in the war effort, and the costs of demobilization and resettlement are yet to come – and warns of dire consequences to the empire if such recognition is not forthcoming. What he wants, as do other prime ministers here, is the evolution of the empire into an association of nations under the British Crown, rather than a group of colonies dominated by the Mother Country.

In his quest for Canadian independence, Borden has refused to merge the Canadian navy into a single imperial force under British control. He has also pushed for the dominions to have permanent presentation at the War Cabinet, and for direct communications between the British and dominion PMs.

Dominion Parks and Forest Reserves hires its first ornithologist

Dec. 11, 1918

OTTAWA – The federal government has named Hoyes Lloyd supervisor of wildlife protection, making him the first ornithologist employed by the Dominion Parks and Forest Reserves. Lloyd's responsibilities include the investigation and determination of the extent of wildlife resources, especially the status of waterfowl and other migratory birds. In recent years, Canadian parks have given naturalists and ornithologists unusual opportunities to study birds. Written studies often result.

One such report by a conservation group recommending the preservation of waterfowl habitats is what spurred Lloyd's appointment, which is designed to bring a high level of scientific knowledge, scholarship, and practical administration to the department. Lloyd will report his assessments and his recommendations directly to the commissioner of national parks. He will have administrative powers, especially concerning the Migratory Birds Convention Act and the authority to impose bag limits and enforce all aspects of that act, as well as other wildlife policies.

Manitoba labor leaders slam provincial, federal governments

Dec. 22, 1918

WINNIPEG – Manitoba's labor leaders aired their grievances this afternoon before a mass rally in the Walker Theatre. The meeting was organized by the Winnipeg branch of the Socialist Party of Canada. Speakers railed against policies of both the provincial and federal governments.

The tone of the meeting was set by William Ivens, an English immigrant and former Methodist minister who broke with his church because of his pacifist views. Ivens now is the editor of *Western Labor News*. His particular cause at the moment is the number of Labor party members who, because of their beliefs, are being held as political prisoners. "I am here," Ivens told the crowd, "to champion the rights of humanity. The imperial system must go."

Robert Boyd Russell, a machinist and one of the most important members of the Winnipeg Trades and Labor Council, and Sam Blumberg of the Socialist party also addressed the meeting.

War images: the good, the bad, the unforgettable

Canadian troops en route to the line pass Gen. Mewburn, minister of militia.

A Canadian artilleryman tries to comfort this orphaned Belgian child.

A padre conducts a church service from the cockpit of an RAF aircraft.

The burial of Canadian nurses who were killed in a German air raid.

Mail bags are transported from a dugout east of Arras.

Military cemetery is where the funeral of Sister G.M.M. Wake takes place.

These three Canadians seem to be happy about the news they are reading.

1919

Montreal, Feb. 27. Painter Robert Harris, known for *The Fathers of Confederation*, dies.

Winnipeg, May 15. A general strike is launched in support of striking workers in the building and metal trades.

Winnipeg, May 17. Influential manufacturers, bankers, and politicians form the Citizens' Committee of 1,000 to oppose the general strike.

Winnipeg, May 27. The Citizens' Committee newspaper argues the general strike "is in reality revolution," trying to stir up fears the strike is a Bolshevik conspiracy.

Archangel, Russia, June 11. Most Canadian troops in Russia depart. Western intervention has failed to stop the Bolshevik Revolution.

Ottawa, June 14. On the basis of reports from federal ministers Arthur Meighen and Gideon Robertson, investigating the Winnipeg General Strike, PM Borden writes that the strike is a plot "to overthrow the government of the country." Meighen and Borden refused to meet with the Strike Committee.

Winnipeg, June 17. Federal authorities arrest eight strike leaders and four European Canadians. The Europeans are not strike leaders, but their arrest gives credence to charges the general strike is an alien conspiracy.

Winnipeg, June 30. J.S. Woodsworth, charged with sedition for his role in the general strike, describes Labor church services near Winnipeg: "The atmosphere was a great religious revival. The movement is a religious revival."

Ottawa, July 7. In reaction to the Winnipeg General Strike, Parliament passes Section 98 of the Criminal Code outlawing groups intending to bring about change by force. Anyone attending meetings of such groups will be presumed guilty "in the absence of proof to the contrary."

Nova Scotia, Sept. 9. The HD-4 hydrofoil boat, built by Alexander Bell and Casey Baldwin, sets a world speed record of 114.04 km/h.

Copenhagen. The Danish government says Ellesmere Island is a no man's land, challenging Canada's Arctic sovereignty.

Seattle. The Spanish flu halts the Stanley Cup final between the Seattle Metropolitans and the Montreal Canadiens.

Canada holds first wildlife conference

Jack Miner feeds a Canada goose at his bird sanctuary near Kingsville, Ontario.

Native Canadian animals like the caribou are suffering from loss of habitat.

1919

OTTAWA – The capital is geared up for the first national wildlife conference. Over the last decade, concern for wildlife has been taking shape in the federal government. The efforts of dedicated senior civil servants working in the Dominion Parks and Forest Reserves branches of government have turned wildlife issues into government policy. The realization that Canada's wildlife is limited and that many species are on the brink of extinction has prompted the federal government to assume responsibility for protecting Canada's wildlife.

The Commission of Conservation has played an important role in the process. It is a non-partisan advisory body, comprised of both provincial and federal officials, that gathers information about natural resources and makes recommendations to Parliament. Two conflicting philosophical viewpoints have emerged so far: one calls for more efficient development, the other for more energetic conservation. It was in large part due to the influence of the commission that the government convened the wildlife conference in Ottawa.

Issues to be discussed include: the preservation of particular wildlife species; better methods of conservation in all Dominion parks and forest reserves; the relationship between forest reserves and game reserves; and the formal development of government policy for the advancement of conservation.

Former Liberal PM Wilfrid Laurier dies

Feb. 17, 1919

OTTAWA – Former prime minister Sir Wilfrid Laurier, a champion of Canadian nationalism, died this afternoon at his home in Ottawa. It marked the end of a great statesman, who was Liberal prime minister of Canada from 1896 to 1911. Notable among his many achievements was the completion of the second transcontinental railway, and promotion of immigration to the west. Laurier will lie in the Senate chamber, and then be buried in a state funeral.

Western labor supports One Big Union

March 15, 1919

CALGARY – A large conference of western Canadian labor leaders wrapped up in Calgary today with heavy support for the creation of One Big Union. Such a union would unite workers from all industries into a single, militant organization.

The Calgary conference was called after the Trades and Labour Congress last year defeated various reform proposals presented at its national meeting. Impatient with the conservatism of eastern unionists, leaders from western Canada are spearheading the fight for the OBU. Delegates at the Calgary meeting agreed to hold a referendum asking union members if they wished to secede from the old organizations and form the OBU.

Government officials are reacting with dismay to the workers' militancy. They believe the leaders of the movement are radical socialists who wish to inspire a violent, Bolshevik revolution in Canada. In response, the government has banned foreign-language publications, outlawed certain political organizations, and created a network of secret agents which has infiltrated different radical groups.

Unionism triumphs as strike is settled

May 8, 1919

OTTAWA – Unionism has won a mighty victory in Ottawa, with the end of the building trades strike. Building trade workers won a 20-percent wage hike. As well, their work day has been reduced to eight hours, and all overtime has been eliminated. Adding to the triumph is an agreement between the Building Trades Council – the workers' body – and the Canadian Builders' and Contractors' Association to set up a joint council in Ottawa aimed at resolving further disputes through arbitration. The creation of such a body with employer participation means the unions are being taken seriously, and that employers are deserting earlier attempts to combat unionism by trying to destroy it.

Generally, unionism in Canada is growing rapidly, with 378,000 members as of this year. The increase is due to a few factors: the shift of labor to urban industries; the growing political power of the working class; and the movement among employees to band together to make common cause.

As has been demonstrated in Ottawa, unionism is working for the workers. Only a few years ago, the notion of obtaining a nine-hour day seemed to be just a pipe dream. As well, few would have dreamed "the bosses" could be brought to heel so effectively through strikes.

Winnipeg metalworkers go on strike

May 2, 1919

WINNIPEG – Metalworkers employed by three of the largest employers in this city have gone on strike. Vulcan Iron Works, Manitoba Bridge and Iron, and Dominion Bridge and Iron are closed as a result of the labor stoppage. At issue is the matter of a citywide collective agreement. It is understood that management at the three firms was prepared to negotiate with their own employees, but they refused to have anything to do with collective bargaining with the employees of the three shops working in concert, especially when any contracts negotiated were subject to ratification by the Metal Trades Council.

Immediately after the metalworkers referred their case to the Winnipeg Trades and Labor Council, workers in the building trades also struck for higher wages. In the latter case, there is a seasonal factor, for the carpenters and bricklayers state that the exigencies of Manitoba weather are such that they must make sufficient money during the building season to maintain their families during winter. Following a lengthy debate, the Trades and Labor Council voted in favor of a sympathetic strike in order that all workers might show their support for the metalworkers and the members of the building trades union.

Franchise granted to women of N.B.

April 17, 1919

FREDERICTON – Two years ago, an attempt to legislate votes for women was defeated. A second attempt last spring also failed, but today, the women of New Brunswick were finally granted the right to vote.

On March 21, J.P. Byrne introduced a bill by which women would be allowed to vote on the same terms as men. Matters proceeded smoothly until discussion by the committee of the whole on March 25. Although none of the lawmakers opposed votes for women, some questioned whether the bill would allow women to hold office. It does not, a situation which other members of the Assembly consider too conservative.

The Wayside Cross, Autumn, by Quebec artist Clarence Gagnon.

Historians label Indians a backward race

Lionel Groulx draws a crowd as he delivers a speech at Carillon, Quebec.

May 24, 1919

QUEBEC – Racial tensions between French-Canadians and native Indians continue to grow as prominent Quebec academics lash out against Indian and Métis culture and traditions 259 years after folk hero Adam Dollard des Ormeaux died fighting the Iroquois.

In a newly published book, the popular Quebec historian Lionel Groulx severely criticizes those who accept the story that the French-Canadians have Indian blood. He is joined by geographer Eugène Rouillard, who's adamantly opposed to the use of Indian place names in the province. Both men continually refer to what they consider to be a backward race which threatens the purity of the province's inhabitants.

Impatient soldiers stage a riot overseas

March 5, 1919

KINMEL PARK, England – Some 800 Canadian soldiers, impatient at the slow pace of repatriation home, rioted here for two days. Troops fired on their comrades to restore order, killing five and wounding 23. Seventy-eight soldiers have been arrested on charges of mutiny.

Kinmel Park is one of several centres where soldiers finish demobilization documentation and wait for ships returning them to Canada. The government promised a policy of "first over, first back," but exceptions have been made. Men at Kinmel Park, some overseas for four years, have protested departures from the rule.

Winnipeg paralysed as general strike hits the city

May 15, 1918

WINNIPEG – The long-threatened Winnipeg General Strike began this morning. At 11 sharp, streetcars returned to the barns, and rail workers left the Weston and Transcona shops. Within an hour telegraphers, telephone operators, and postal workers had left their posts.

Those rail workers who do not work on the trains, being more numerous and better organized, seemed to be in total support of the shutdown. The trains continued to operate, but there were no express, freight, or baggage services.

Strike leaders have pledged that essential services, such as light and water, will not be affected by the stoppage. Newspapers are not publishing today, and there are no milk or bread deliveries, but citizens have been assured their property will be protected, for city police responded favorably to a request of the Strike Committee that they remain on duty to protect property.

Borden vows to maintain law and order

The ONE BIG UNION is Bolshevism Pure and Simple

NOTE THE STRIKING PARALLEL

Bolshevism

[illegible] the constitution of "The Federation of Unions of Russian [illegible] the U.S. and Canada," the simon pure Bolshevik organization plant[illegible] by paid agents of Lenine and Trotzky.

Fundamental Principle of the Federation

"The struggle between the classes still continues at the present time and will terminate only when the laboring masses are organized into ONE UNION and USE FORCE to take possession of all wealth through the violence of Social Revolution."

[illegible]

One Big Union

Extract from the official stenographic record of the proceedings at the Western Canada Labor Conference at Calgary last March, where the One Big Union movement was launched by labor delegates from all western cities, including 29 from Winnipeg.

Resolution Creating the One Big Union

"Resolved that this conference place itself on record as favoring the immediate re-organization of the workers along industrial lines, so THAT BY VIRTUE OF THEIR STRENGTH, the workers may be better prepared to ENFORCE ANY DEMAND they consider essential to their maintenance and well-being."

Note the striking parallel between the fundamental principle of Bolshevism, given in the constitution of the Russian Federation, and the fundamental principle of the One Big Union given in the Calgary resolution creating the One Big Union. Even the name, "One Union," was taken by the Calgary convention from the Bolsheviki constitution. [illegible]

This flyer was published by the opponents of One Big Union.

May 27, 1919

WINNIPEG – Leaders of the Winnipeg General Strike have given no indication they will be swayed by the prime minister's pledge to maintain law and order. News dispatches arriving here relate how there was thunderous applause from his followers when Sir Robert Borden declared the government is "absolutely determined that law and order shall be maintained." Officials at strike headquarters have heard rumors the Winnipeg postmaster has been instructed to tell his employees that those who fail to return to work will be discharged.

Sympathy strikes called across the west

May 27, 1919

WINNIPEG – Reports being received at strike headquarters tell of sympathy strikes all across western Canada. While a few of these out-of-province stoppages were based at least in part on local grievances, there is a strong belief that actions in Winnipeg have strengthened the resolve of labor leaders in other cities as well. In Toronto, there is a strong possibility the metal trades will soon strike. They are after an eight-hour day and a 44-hour week. The Toronto Trades and Labor Council has voted to support a general strike. In Calgary, the streetcars are no longer running and many hotels and restaurants are closed.

Labor unrest in growing in the west. Calgary miners were on strike last year.

Police attack peaceful protesters; 2 dead

June 21, 1919

WINNIPEG – Portage and Main streets are stained with blood this sad Saturday afternoon after Royal North West Mounted Police attacked a peaceful parade of general strike sympathizers. At this moment, militia are patrolling the streets in trucks with mounted machine-guns, two men are dead of gunshot wounds, many are wounded, and it looks like the general strike has been dealt a death blow.

Workers and returned soldiers organized the silent parade down Main Street to protest the arrest of 10 alleged strike leaders four days ago and Ottawa's refusal to hear the strikers' case. The mayor read the riot act, but the crowd refused to disperse. The Mounties, armed and on horseback, charged the crowd. The demonstrators threw rocks and sticks, the Mounties fired back and cleared the streets.

Today's violent police intervention in what has until now been a mainly peaceful strike reflects the stated fears of government and business leaders that the strike is the first step to a Bolshevik style revolution. Winnipeg businessmen have sponsored newspaper ads across the country, claiming the strike is about whether "the Union Jack or the Red Flag" will prevail.

Miners at Drumheller are in one of the many labor groups on strike now.

General strike in Winnipeg rumored to be over

The RNWMP brought in to control strikers charge down a Winnipeg street.

After the arrest of the strike leaders, there are mass protests in Winnipeg. A long line of marchers in support of the leaders passes Winnipeg city hall.

June 25, 1919

WINNIPEG – While it has not been confirmed, it is generally understood that the sympathetic Winnipeg General Strike will be called off at any moment now. Informed sources believe workers will return to their jobs at 11 a.m. tomorrow. If the strike does end as forecast, it will have lasted six weeks, to the hour. It began Thursday, May 15, at 11 a.m. sharp.

While rumors about the end of the strike persist, negotiations continue between the Police Commission and its former employees. The employees are policemen who were dismissed when they refused to sign a pledge that they would not participate in sympathetic strikes. The dismissed policemen have now offered to separate themselves from the Winnipeg Trades and Labor Council if they are reinstated, and to recognize no other authority than that of the commission.

Elsewhere in Winnipeg, there are positive signs that strikers are ambivalent about their once-solid support for their walkout. There were 30 streetcars operating today, and transportation officials state more than 100 workers have returned to work. This number includes both drivers and support workers.

This afternoon a meeting of close to 800 returned men was held on the Norwood baseball grounds under the leadership of the Soldiers and Sailors Labor League. Many of those present were interested in forming an official body with a constitution resembling that of a similar body set up three weeks ago in Vancouver. It is the common aim of these bodies to have official representatives in municipal, provincial, and federal governments.

Organized workers in this city feel keenly that public authorities overstepped their rights when they decided to suppress the *Western Labor News,* the official organ of the Central Strike Committee. A new publication, *The Western Star,* which appeared today for the first time, said in defence of the *Labor News* that "it had endeavored to tell the truth, the whole truth, and nothing but the truth. ... Apparently British fair play is a thing of the past in Winnipeg."

Mounted police clear Portage Ave.

British duo in Ireland after first non-stop flight across Atlantic

June 15, 1919

CLIFDEN, Ireland – Britain's Capt. John Alcock and Lieut. Arthur Brown completed the first non-stop flight across the Atlantic Ocean today when they landed in a bog near here, 16 hours and 12 minutes after taking off from Newfoundland. Neither British officer was injured in the 8:40 a.m. crash landing after the 3,059-kilometre flight, but their Vickers-Vimy biplane was damaged. Pilot Alcock opted to land here instead of pressing on to London below low clouds. They had narrowly averted disaster in bad weather over the ocean.

Brown (left) and Alcock (centre) with their Vickers-Vimy aircraft before flight.

Canadian National Railways founded

June 6, 1919

OTTAWA – Canadian National Railways is the new name in the railroad business. Thanks to an act of Parliament, the government line running from Winnipeg to Halifax, and the Canadian Northern, taken over a year ago due to its shaky financial health, will be consolidated together into one publically-owned system. The new CNR, built out of the deficit-ridden ruins of the old lines, is expected to have money problems of its own – a $49 million deficit is projected for 1919. ▷

Liberals pick King to succeed Laurier

William Lyon Mackenzie King.

Aug. 7, 1919

OTTAWA – After three sweltering ballots, Liberal delegates have chosen William Lyon Mackenzie King as their new leader, succeeding the late Sir Wilfrid Laurier. It was by no means an easy victory for King. Although he led the first and second ballots, he needed other candidates' delegates to make it over the top. These he got through Nova Scotian D.D McKenzie, who threw his 60 supporters King's way primarily because he hated King's nearest rival, William Stevens Fielding. On the third ballot, of a field of 949, King got 476 votes to Fielding's 438.

Treaty of Versailles ends Great War

June 28, 1919

PARIS – In a brief 25-minute ceremony, delegates to the Peace Conference today concluded the treaty that formally ends the Great War. First to affix his signature was American President Woodrow Wilson. The treaty was signed in the Hall of Mirrors, Versailles Palace, once the home of French monarchs. Here, in 1871, Imperial Germany forced upon France a harsh treaty concluding the Franco-Prussian War. Crowds outside applauded, with the loudest cheers for the grizzled French army veterans of that conflict. Celebrations are planned for various cities, including a 101-gun salute in Montreal.

By its terms, Germany acknowledges guilt for having started the war. She loses 10 percent of her territory and population, mostly to France and Poland, and will pay heavy reparations to France and Belgium. The Rhineland will be demilitarized, with no forts within 50 kilometres of the river. The German army is reduced to 100,000 men, and Germany is forbidden to build military aircraft, armored vehicles, or submarines.

The treaty also establishes a new body, the League of Nations, as a forum for international debate and discussion. The precise role of the league is unclear, but it is the greatest advance in international law since the 1907 establishment of an International Court in The Hague. Scores of countries sent delegates, but the conference was dominated by those from the United States, France, and Great Britain. Even the Germans were excluded from meaningful discussions; they were presented with a final draft and ordered to sign, with the further warning that normal relations – including the lifting of a blockade – would begin only with formal ratification by their government. German delegates signed under protest. A South African delegate, Gen. J.C. Smuts, declared as he signed that the terms were too harsh. Canadians are particularly interested because Prime Minister Sir Robert Borden and three colleagues served on the British delegation and signed separately for Canada following British signing. Canada thus had a modest part to play in international diplomacy.

Other countries, notably the United States, regard the Canadian voice as being a British echo rather than an independent one. But when Parliament ratifies the treaty, that will be a clear statement of Canada's advance in world status.

The Allies are seated around the conference table in Paris, France.

Returned soldiers fill divorce courts

Aug. 21, 1919

WINNIPEG – In a month from now, Manitoba's court system is likely to be plugged solid by divorce cases. Six judges from the Court of King's Bench have been assigned to hear 1,100 such cases when the autumn assizes open Sept. 15.

It appears domestic bliss was not the universal state for a lot of Canada's soldier heroes returning from France. The majority of these suits involve men who came back to Canada from the war only to learn their wives had been unfaithful. Divorces are an expensive business, according to local lawyers. The costs begin at $200.

Bush pilot "Wop" May aids in manhunt

Having served as a fighter pilot in the war, Wilfrid "Wop" Reid May is now operating his own airline company serving the north out of Edmonton.

Aug. 30, 1919

EDMONTON – The latest job taken on by May Airplanes Ltd., the new airline company formed by the famous "Wop" May and his brother Court, is to fly Detective J. Campbell from Edmonton to Coal Branch, Alta. Campbell is hot on the trail of a murderer.

Wilfrid Reid May is the decorated Royal Air Force pilot who, with Roy Brown, is said to have put the Red Baron out of business in the Great War, when flying was dangerous business as British and British Empire pilots were not issued parachutes. May himself has 13 enemy planes to his credit. May Airplanes now does charters, stunt flying, and barnstorming.

Commons approves terms of Versailles

Sept. 12, 1919

OTTAWA – The House of Commons today voted unanimously to accept the Treaty of Versailles. Discussion of the treaty lasted for days, with much soul searching on its impact on Canadian independence. Many MPs expressed concern the League of Nations might infringe on Canadian sovereignty just as the country is gaining more freedom within the British Empire.

The day before ratification, a Liberal party motion saying Canadian forces should not be committed to any war without prior approval of the House of Commons was defeated 102-70.

Strike leader gets two years in jail

Dec. 24, 1919

WINNIPEG – Robert Boyd Russell, a prominent leader of the Winnipeg General Strike earlier this year, was convicted today of seditious conspiracy and sentenced to two years in prison. The eight strike leaders appeared in court in November, but the Crown elected to try Russell separately.

Russell is Manitoba's most popular labor leader. On the strike committee he represented the International Association of Machinists. He was also a spokesman for One Big Union. Russell, who is Scottish born, was one of those whom the Citizens' Committee of 1,000 came to view as "alien scum."

The Crown claimed that Russell and the other accused had participated in a seditious conspiracy, of which the Winnipeg strike was a part. The defence maintained that the accused were not even in the same union, and indeed were members of different political parties.

Golden Boy adorns dome of legislature

The Golden Boy now has a home.

Nov. 21, 1919

WINNIPEG – The strange odyssey of the Golden Boy is over. After years of travel, the five-ton, four-metre bronze statue has found a home atop the Legislative Buildings. The statue was cast in France and shipped on a freighter. The ship was commandeered for wartime purposes, and the Golden Boy spent two years as ballast travelling back and forth across the Atlantic.

Lives lost to Spanish flu

Dec. 31, 1919

OTTAWA – As the decade draws to a close, many are remembering the 60,000 Canadians who died in the war. Others recall those who lost their lives to a quieter demon. Newspapers and government have consistently downplayed the significance of the Spanish flu epidemic of 1918-19, but the hellish fact remains that this flu has killed more people, more quickly than any war or disease in history: 15 million to 25 million deaths worldwide, including 30,000 to 50,000 Canadians.

Returning soldiers brought the highly contagious disease to Canada in the spring and summer of 1918. The first major civilian outbreak began in September at Quebec's Victoriaville College when 400 students contracted the disease. The flu spread its tentacles to every part of the country as fast as trains could carry infected people. The disease travels fast and it can kill fast. A woman in Paris, Ont., caught the flu at a lecture one night; her roommate found her dead in bed the very next morning. But the flu itself does not usually kill people. Most victims die when pneumonia develops as a complication. Flu traditionally kills the young and elderly, but this epidemic has claimed many in the 20-40 age bracket.

As the disease spread, people faced painful choices – to help friends or relatives with the flu or stay home and protect their families from infection? Doctors and nurses worked until they could not stay awake anymore. Medical facilities just couldn't deal with all the illnesses, and volunteers set up makeshift hospitals in schools and hotels.

Provincial and municipal authorities shouldered much of the burden of dealing with the disease. Western municipalities tried to quarantine themselves. Some provinces banned public meetings, and cities required people to wear gauze masks outside of homes.

Farmer-Labour coalition wins in Ontario

Oct. 20, 1919

TORONTO – Ontario voters have ousted the provincial Tories of William Howard Hearst. In fact, Hearst himself lost his Sault Ste. Marie seat as a coalition of labor and farmers grabbed the lion's share of the votes in today's election. The United Farmers of Ontario, which is more a movement than a political party, won 45 seats, and its Labour partner garnered 11. In view of their combined electoral successes, the coalition now has enough support to override even an unlikely Liberal-Conservative merger, as the two traditional parties managed to get only 54 seats between them.

One of the major issues in this election has been temperance. Although Hearst himself was a strong supporter of the Ontario Temperance Act, his party was divided by the liquor issue. And Ontario voters want the act to remain in force; they supported it in a referendum held at the same time as the general balloting. Hearst also alienated female voters with his lukewarm position on women's suffrage, and many farmers were hostile to his pro-Union government, pro-conscription stance.

The new government is led by a social movement espousing rural values. The UFO has no leader, so Ontario is without a premier. One man being touted for the job is Ernest Drury, a Barrie farmer emerging as a UFO leader. However, he is not an elected MPP – yet.

Barrie farmer Ernest Drury, a UFO leader, is being touted by many as the next premier of Ontario.

Government repeals wartime restrictions

Dec. 20, 1919

OTTAWA – The federal government has decided the war is over, and so it's moved to repeal most restrictions passed during the war. Changes include a general amnesty for those people who illegally avoided conscription into the armed services: those imprisoned will be released, and those not apprehended will be pardoned.

Liquor will once more be allowed shipment across provincial boundaries, at least for the time being. This means people in dry areas will be able to restock – at least until prohibition is extended, if it ever is, on a national scale. Betting will also be allowed once more at race tracks. Censorship, internment of enemy aliens, and "no trade with the enemy" are still in force.

The Prince of Wales goes hunting with native guides on his visit to Canada.

1920

Ottawa, Jan. 1. An order-in-council divides the Northwest Territories into three provisional districts – Mackenzie, Keewatin, and Franklin.

Canada, Feb. 1. The Royal North West Mounted Police and Dominion Police merge to form the Royal Canadian Mounted Police, responsible for federal law enforcement.

Winnipeg, Feb. 16. Charges against J.S. Woodsworth for his role in the Winnipeg General Strike are dropped.

Ottawa, Feb. 26. The new Centre Block of the Parliament Buildings opens.

Canada, March. *The Great Shadow*, shot by Canada's Adanac Production Co., opens and is a big hit.

Ottawa, April 3. The government orders the organization of the Canadian Air Force.

Winnipeg, April 6. Five of six men convicted of leading the Winnipeg General Strike are sentenced to a year in jail.

Ottawa, April 18. The Department of Labor reports the cost of living for the average Canadian family is $15.98 a week, more than double what it was before the war.

Ottawa, July 13. The government asks Danish authorities to stop Greenland Inuit from hunting musk-ox on Ellesmere Island, asserting its claim to sovereignty on the island.

Lévis, Que., Oct. 31. Alphonse Desjardins, founder of the Caisse populaire, dies.

Moscow, Nov. 16. The civil war that began in 1917 is over, with the triumph of Lenin's Bolsheviks.

Toronto, Dec. 4. University of Toronto beats the Toronto Argonauts 16-3 for the Grey Cup. There was no Grey Cup game the last four years because of the war.

Toronto. Frank Underhill, Charles Sissons, Barker Fairley, and other writers found *Canadian Forum*, a nationalist and progressive magazine.

British Columbia. The province votes for government control and sale of liquor rather than prohibition.

Toronto. Ontario adopts the Mother's Alllowance Act. Widows or wives of disabled men get up to $45 a month.

Toronto. The Ottawa Senators defeat the Seattle Metropolitans three games to two to win the Stanley Cup.

Canada helps found League of Nations

Jan. 16, 1920

GENEVA – Canada was among the many nations gathered here today to witness the birth of a new world organization dedicated to peace throughout the globe. The League of Nations, as it's called, aims to foster peace through international discussions of issues, rather than conflict. In fact, Article 10 of the Covenant, the document each subscribing member pledges to uphold, specifies that members must preserve each other's independence. As well, the Covenant indicates that an act of war against any member is an act against all members, and response from all can be expected.

Bulldogs bite thanks to Malone's 7 goals

Jan. 31, 1920

QUEBEC CITY – "Phantom" Joe Malone, ace centre for the Quebec Bulldogs of the National Hockey League, scored seven goals tonight to lead his team to a 10-6 romp over the Toronto St. Pats. Malone victimized St. Pats' goalkeeper Vern Forbes for all seven goals, including three in the space of two minutes. The victory enabled the Quebec team to close out the first half of the 1920-21 season on a winning note.

Phantom Joe used a lightning quick wrist shot to fool Forbes on three of the shots. Malone's seventh marker was the prettiest goal of the night, as he cleverly deked Forbes out of the net before firing the puck into the empty cage.

Canadiens hockey star Joe Malone.

Federal government to buy Grand Trunk

Feb. 19, 1920

OTTAWA – Shareholders in the Grand Trunk Railway today ended speculation by voting to accept the federal government's offer to purchase the troubled corporation. The agreement doesn't place a fixed purchase price on each share, but instead calls for a meeting between government and GTR officials to set an amount. All of the services of the GTR will immediately be combined with those of the Canadian National Railways, and all competing routes will be eliminated.

The Grand Trunk Railway was incorporated in 1852, with a line from Montreal to Toronto inaugurated in 1856. The corporation has expanded steadily since then, either through more building or, as was more often the case, through the purchase of smaller regional railways. GTR was operating 13,158 kilometres of track until today.

The decision to accept the government's purchase offer was far from unanimous. After the vote was taken, a resolution protesting the terms of the deal was passed by some irate GTR shareholders.

Cuts on the horizon for Canada's navy

March 20, 1920

OTTAWA – Canada's navy will be cut. While Canada will accept three ships from Britain to replace older vessels, the number of persons engaged will drop from 1,303 to 521. The new navy will have a cruiser, two destroyers, and two submarines to serve on both coasts. Dockyard services will be cut, and the Royal Canadian Naval College will be shut. Vice-Admiral Sir Charles Kingsmill will be replaced as chief by an officer of lower rank.

Canadiens goalie Georges Vézina.

The Winnipeg Falcons won the Olympic gold medal at this year's Olympic Games, which were held in Antwerp, Belgium.

Group of Seven paintings go on exhibit

May 7, 1920

TORONTO – The first exhibition of the Group of Seven at the Art Gallery of Ontario has opened. Some 114 paintings by group members Frank Carmichael, A.Y. Jackson, Arthur Lismer, F.H. Varley, J.E.H. MacDonald and Lawren Harris are on display, along with works of other artists. According to the exhibition catalogue, the pictures were all painted in Canada in the past year. The works of the Group of Seven have been criticized in the past, and the artists have been referred to as "The Hot Mush School." Although the paintings strike many as unusual or unattractive, the Group of Seven artists state in the foreword of the catalogue, "We have as little desire to be revolutionary as to be old-fashioned. The painter must rely on paint and not on adjectives."

The Jack Pine, by Tom Thomson, inspired members of the Group of Seven.

Overalls Brigade gains momentum

April 19, 1920

OTTAWA – A movement that started in the United States protesting against the high cost of clothing is rapidly spreading across Canada. Latest to join the ranks of the Overalls Brigade are the male members of the dominion command of the Great War Veterans' Association, who say they'll start wearing only denim as of tomorrow.

In Hamilton, Ont., a clerk in the city's waterworks department has led the trend by showing up for work in overalls and a smock which he said cost him only $6.50. He says he intends to wear the outfit every day, even to attend church.

Witnesses abuzz as Human Fly falls

June 24, 1920

ST. CATHARINES, Ont. – The "Human Fly" hung between life and death today after suffering serious injuries in a 22-metre fall during an attempt to climb the wall of Welland House. Charles Hutcheson was entertaining some 2,000 spectators with his aerial stunts when his hands suddenly lost hold of the rope and he plunged to the veranda floor. The crowd, assuming the tumble was part of the act, applauded – then shrieked in horror as they realized what had happened. Investigators say the cause of the fall was a loose knot, tied by Hutcheson himself before the show.

Borden out, Meighen in

July 10, 1920

OTTAWA – Sir Robert Borden, prime minister since 1911, has formally resigned, giving his notice this morning at the governor general's residence. Surprisingly, Sir Robert didn't seem at all depressed at relinquishing power. In fact, he met reporters outside Rideau Hall sporting a big grin!

Sources say that Borden, having guided the country through the Great War, is tired of office and wants to do something else for a change. Meanwhile, the new prime minister is Arthur Meighen, sworn in 15 minutes after Borden resigned. Meighen, acting justice minister during the Winnipeg strike and number two man in the cabinet, will form a new cabinet Tuesday.

New Canadian PM Arthur Meighen.

Commission to probe Tory timber sales

April 12, 1920

TORONTO – The Timber Commission appointed by United Farmers of Ontario Premier Ernest Drury is about to get under way. But even though testimony has yet to be given, the general drift of the inquiry is already clear. It's targeting the sale of timber by the former Conservative government of Sir James Whitney, specifically to lumber companies.

What is expected to be proven is what has been alleged for years – that much of northern Ontario's timber rights were given away by the Tories to friends and cronies, without following proper tendering procedures. Worst yet, much of the land was undervalued as to the amount of timber on it, reducing provincial income on the licences. To top off the mess, it's believed some lumber companies managed to literally steal trees by taking them away from mining claims and "homestead" grants, thus avoiding provincial duties. Finally, adding to the complications is the fact that the government's own records on timber rights are in chaos, and its own offices are understaffed.

Radio CNRW broadcasts from the Fort Garry Hotel in Winnipeg, Man.

Alberta, Saskatchewan and Nova Scotia all vote to go "dry"

Oct. 25, 1920

REGINA – The provinces of Alberta, Saskatchewan, and Nova Scotia have all voted to go "dry." Under an amendment to the Canada Temperance Act of November 1919, the provinces are free to hold referendums to determine if they are to allow liquor. The two Prairie provinces and Nova Scotia have taken advantage of this legislation and voted to go dry. Ontario will vote on the matter next spring.

The date when prohibition will become effective is to be fixed by an order-in-council passed by the federal government. From that date onward, it will be illegal to bring into the "dry" provinces any intoxicating liquor. It may only be transported through the province by common carrier on water or rail, and must remain sealed during transportation.

During the Great War, the Canadian government ceased making and selling liquor. Most people accepted prohibition at the time as a sacrifice for the war effort and part of their patriotic duty. After the armistice, when the federal government re-established the liquor trade, there was a push by temperance organizations to once again adopt prohibition as a means of curing a number of social ills.

Liquor is seen by prohibitionists as the cause of much crime and family hardship. The opposing view is that illegal trade in liquor will flourish with the same results.

In Elk Lake, Ontario, a dry zone, police raid a "blind pig."

Alleged killer saves self from lynch mob

Aug. 17, 1920

ST. CATHARINES, Ont. – A man accused of murdering a five-year-old girl pleaded for his life yesterday after a huge lynch mob from Thorold torched the town hall to force him out. The ruckus broke out after David McNeil was committed to trial in the slaying of Margaret Beaurock. The judge had left the courtroom in the town hall, when some of the 500 spectators, led by the victim's father, began throwing chairs at McNeil. Several court officials were injured.

The crowd outside grew in size and impatience in the afternoon, setting fire to the town hall and smoking out McNeil. As the crowd ran a rope up a pole, McNeil pleaded that he didn't kill the girl – "only a degenerate would do such a thing." Finally, cooler heads prevailed and McNeil was released to the custody of police.

Compulsory enfranchisement introduced

July 1, 1920

OTTAWA – Under an Indian Act amendment which comes into effect today, the federal cabinet can, on two years notice, remove the Indian status of any Indian over 21 who the superintendent general of Indian Affairs thinks is fit for enfranchisement or for citizenship. Those selected get title to reserve lands they occupy and their share of the band's money, and they also get the right vote. Says Duncan Campbell Scott, deputy superintendent of Indian Affairs: "Our object is to continue until there is not a single Indian in Canada that has not been absorbed into the body politic, and there is no Indian question, and no Indian Department."

Sources believe Scott wants to enfranchise Fred Loft, the Iroquois organizer of the League of Indians of Canada. Loft would lose his credibility, and the league, Scott believes, would be leaderless.

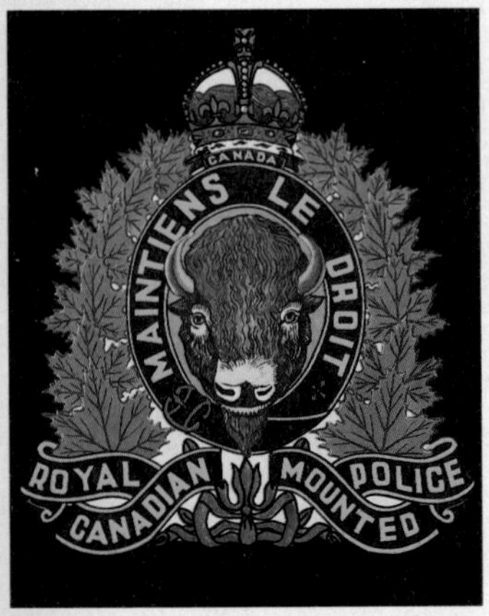

The Royal North West Mounted Police have been re-named the Royal Canadian Mounted Police.

Gala dance benefits jailed bootleggers

July 24, 1920

BLAIRMORE, Alta. – The Blairmore Opera House hosted 70 couples at a gala dance which raised $160 in aid of jailed bootleggers. Revellers were all members of the Crowsnest Pass Bootleggers Association, which owes its existence to Alberta's ban on booze. Although a large majority of Albertans voted for prohibition, many towns in the south bucked the trend and have become havens for the cross-border "rum-running" trade.

Barnardo children headed for new homes

Dr. Barnardo organized the immigration of large numbers of boy immigrants.

July 1920

CANADA – A group of 200 Barnardo children, some orphans from rural England, others street urchins from London's slums – all of them at one time impoverished, abandoned, or abused – is making its way to new homes here. Early this month a small steamer left Liverpool bearing this precious cargo of 150 boys and 50 girls. Once at their new homes, they will each be adopted into a new family and a new way of life.

Dr. Thomas Barnardo started a mission for London's homeless children in 1870, providing them with shelter, sustenance and education. Within 10 years, his efforts on their behalf included a program for resettlement. In the years since – apart from a respite during the war – thousands of Barnardo-sponsored children have arrived here.

Go west young men: new wave flocks to prairies

These people are off to the west to create new homes in a developing area.

British favored as Canadian immigrants

1920

CANADA – After a lull in immigration caused by the Great War in Europe, the federal government is once again on the campaign trail, hoping to populate Canada's vast western prairies with promises of land and opportunity. But there is a striking difference between the current drive and that carried on during the pre-war years. The war rendered many Canadians, politicians and electorate alike, xenophobic – intolerant of ethnic minorities, weary of "enemy aliens."

The ideal of a mosaic has given way to that of a melting pot. In consequence, the British immigrant is once again favored. Last year, more restrictions were added to the Immigration Act. Passing an English literacy test is now a prerequisite. And British ex-servicemen are being offered the same benefits that Canadians get through the Land Settlement Act.

This poster suggests that hard work will bring prosperity in the Canadian west.

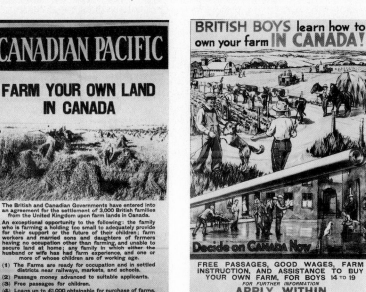

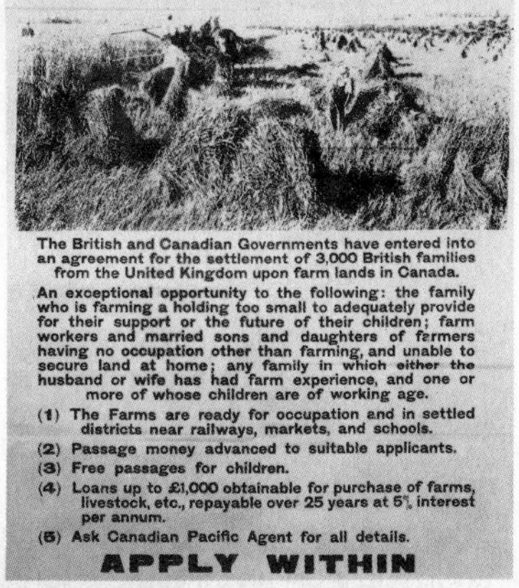

The CPR promotes immigration.

British youth is one group which is being actively recruited for the development of agriculture in Canada.

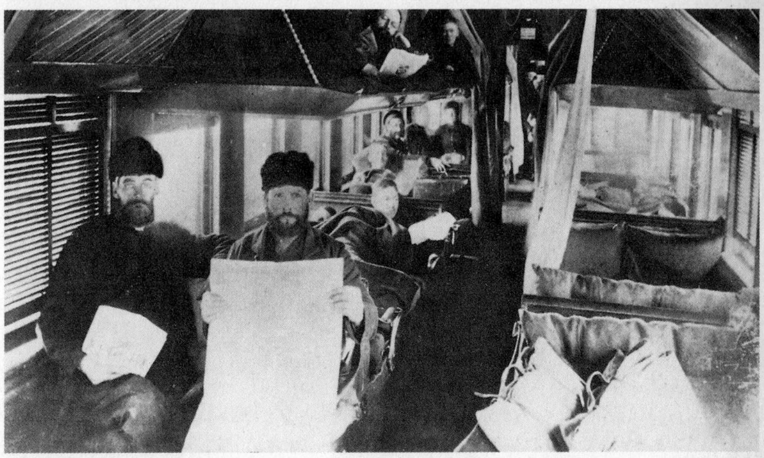

Settlers head west in immigrant railway cars such as the one seen here.

1921

Winnipeg, Feb. 13. Judge Edward Brown prohibits the public exhibition of moving pictures or slides on Sundays. The projection of printed hymns is allowed.

British Columbia, March 1. Federal authorities use a plane to monitor ship movements in an attempt to stop illegal importation of drugs.

Ottawa, March 14. Pte. James Thompson is recognized as the youngest soldier in the Great War. He was 13 years and four months old when he enlisted in 1917.

Lunenburg, N.S., March 26. The *Bluenose* is launched.

Prince Edward Island, April 27. The Potato Growers' Association of Prince Edward Island is incorporated.

Guelph, Ont., June. The Communist Party of Canada is founded, a secret organization.

Yukon, July 12. The territory votes in favor of importing liquor, nullifying the prohibition law of 1920.

London, Ont., Sept. 15. Frederick Classens invents a portable X-ray machine.

Quebec, Sept. 24. The Canadian Catholic Federation of Labour [Confederation of National Trade Unions] is founded.

Edmonton, Oct. 29. The city hears a concert program transmitted from San Francisco, the longest wireless transmission ever over land.

Toronto, Dec. 3. The Toronto Argonauts beat the Edmonton Eskimos 23-0 in the Grey Cup.

United States. Canadian Mary Pickford, "America's Sweetheart," is one of the most popular movie actresses.

Sydney, N.S. West Indian immigrants found Canada's first African Orthodox Church.

Ninette, Man. Expanded facilities are under construction at the Manitoba Sanatorium in response to the admission of almost 1,000 war veterans.

Canada. The population is almost nine million, and 47.4 percent live in cities.

Canada. The maternal mortality rate is 4.7 per 1,000 live births, higher than in most other western countries.

Vancouver. Ottawa Senators defeat the Vancouver Millionaires three games to two for the Stanley Cup.

The write stuff: Canadian authors unite

Some Canadian authors of today.

March 12, 1921

MONTREAL – The fight against proposed copyright legislation has given birth to an organization representing Canadian writers. The Canadian Authors Association was officially founded at a dinner to publicize the battle against a clause in proposed copyright revisions that would deprive authors of the sole right to reproduce their works.

Stephen Leacock, the renowned humorist, has been instrumental in organizing the association, whose founding president is John Murray Gibbon, head of public relations at the Canadian Pacific Railway.

Entry Ordinance governs access to N.W.T.

Jan. 28, 1921

EDMONTON – Authorities in Alberta confirmed today that travellers cannot get into the Northwest Territories this spring without a special certificate proving they can take care of themselves. The new regulation, called the Entry Ordinance, was announced last October. It states that no person may enter the Territories who is "likely to become a public charge" while he is there.

Persons visiting the region are issued a clearance certificate stating they are "mentally and physically able, and properly equipped and outfitted." The certificate must be presented at police posts along the way. The ordinance comes in the wake of last summer's oil strike on the Mackenzie River.

Ontario makes it illegal to import liquor

July 19, 1921

TORONTO – A bill passed by the legislature today makes it illegal to import liquor into Ontario, cutting off the chief way around the Ontario Temperance Act. The bill comes following a referendum held last April, when a majority called for a ban on imports.

Meanwhile, the Quebec government has bowed to political realities, at least when it comes to booze. So instead of trying to prohibit it and thus leave the market open for bootleggers, the government has taken over selling alcohol itself. As well, it has restricted the sale of alcohol in restaurants to wine and beer, and only when a meal is being served.

The YWCA Boarding House in Toronto is home to many single women.

Freight rates to dip 10% on Alberta coal headed for the east

May 21, 1921

ALBERTA – Freight rates on coal mined in Alberta and headed for eastern markets will be reduced 10 percent, thanks to a decision today by the Board of Railway Commissioners. The action is expected to boost the coal industry here, because freight rates kept Alberta coal from being competitive on the central Canadian market with that produced in Pennsylvania.

Bad timing has also plagued rail transportation of coal. The demand for the fuel is at its highest in the fall and early winter, exactly when trains are being used to transport prairie grain crops east to link with Great Lakes shipping, before the ice closes the waterways to traffic for the winter season.

Meighen opposes treaty with Japan

June 29, 1921

LONDON, England – Canada continues to play a strong hand at imperial conferences, this time taking issue with Britain's intent to renew its treaty with Japan. Speaking for Canada, Prime Minister Arthur Meighen opposed the renewal on the grounds that it was opposed by the United States and would therefore damage Anglo-American relations. He requested British PM Lloyd George to instead convene a conference between the U.S., Britain, and Japan to work out a new Pacific treaty, thus allowing America to protect its own Pacific interests while maintaining good relations with Britain. Meighen is deeply disturbed by the growing rift in Anglo-American relations, which he believes are "the touchstone of British policy, and the hope of the world."

Meighen's stance is remarkable for a few reasons. First, it makes a new role for Canada as an intermediary between Britain and the U.S. Second, it is the first time a dominion has formulated imperial policy. And third, it casts the Canadian PM in the role of an international statesman, not a colonial servant.

United Farmers of Alberta in power

THE MORNING ALBERTAN CITY EDITION

U.F.A. Sweeps Province of Alberta

FARMERS CAPTURE 38 OF THE 61 SEATS IN THE LEGISLATURE

THE FIVE NEW CALGARY MEMBERS

CALGARY ELECTS TWO LABOR, TWO INDEPENDENT, AND ONE GOVT. CANDIDATE FOR HOUSE

DE VALERA HAS WASHED HIS HANDS OF CONFERENCE

SUMMARY OF PROVINCE AT MIDNIGHT

Farmers	38
Government	15
Labor	4
Independents	4
	61

PRISONERS BREAK BONDS WHEN FIRE IS STARTED

Farmer Members Will Meet to Discuss Question of Leadership

Standing of the City Candidates in Order of Vote

Premier Stewart Will Resign as Soon as U.F.A. Leader Is Chosen

The Morning Albertan announces the victory of the United Farmers in the provincial election.

Elected members of the United Farmers of Alberta in front of the legislature.

July 18, 1921

EDMONTON – The United Farmers of Alberta have swept aside the Liberal government of Premier Charles Stewart, taking 39 of the 61 seats available. The Liberals got 14, Labour (which supports the UFA) four, and the Conservatives one. Three independent members were also elected. The UFA has no formal leader, but Herbert Greenfield will likely become premier, since the UFA's most potent voice, Henry Wise Wood, doesn't want the job. The UFA will continue to promote agricultural concerns, such as establishing a co-operative provincial elevator storage program as was done in 1913, ironically in co-operation with Stewart's Liberal government.

The UFA also wants a Highway Commission, improvements in education and health care, and control of liquor prohibition through direct public votes. The next premier must also quickly choose a cabinet.

Former militia minister Sam Hughes known for his many feuds

Aug. 24, 1921

OTTAWA – Sir Sam Hughes is dead. Considered mad by some and dull by none, the eccentric former militia minister was famous for his feuds and quarrelled with anyone who disagreed with him. He hated Sir Arthur Currie, Canada's most distinguished general, saying Currie's reputation was based on propaganda rather than merit.

Hughes championed Canadian military equipment, most notably the Ross Rifle long after it had proven inadequate or inferior. His last Commons speech defended the right of MPs to make patronage appointments to the civil service.

Lord Byng named new governor general

Aug. 10, 1921

QUEBEC CITY – Lord Byng, Canada's new governor general, arrived here on the *Empress of France* and received a tumultuous welcome from the crowd. Byng is a popular choice for the position. As Sir Julian Byng, he commanded the Canadian Corps in France during the Great War, a command in which he won much respect from soldiers and politicians alike.

Despite his position, Byng is a plainspoken man, not given to ceremony. Speaking today in Montreal, he said, "I've never done anything like this, you know, and I expect I'll make mistakes."

Lord Byng of Vimy.

Roosevelt's ailment diagnosed as polio

Aug. 25, 1921

NEW BRUNSWICK – The illness which has kept U.S. politician Franklin Delano Roosevelt bedridden for about two weeks has now been diagnosed by a specialist as polio, and doctors say he may never walk again. Roosevelt came to his beloved Campobello Island with his family for a long rest earlier this month, a year after losing his campaign for the vice-presidency on the Democratic ticket. A local doctor first diagnosed a common cold. Analysts fear Roosevelt's disease will end his political ambitions.

Fishing schooner Bluenose triumphs in race at Halifax

Oct. 24, 1921

HALIFAX – As thousands of onlookers cheered, the Lunenburg fishing schooner *Bluenose* defeated the New England schooner *Elsie* today to win the best-of-three International Schooner Championships in two straight races. She was more than 4.8 kilometres ahead at the finish line. *Elsie* stayed close on the downwind legs of the course, but *Bluenose* took a decisive lead when the vessels turned to windward. Capt. Angus Walters, her skipper, said he had never seen a schooner to equal *Bluenose* in windward work.

The races were inaugurated last year at the instigation of Senator William Dennis, publisher of the Halifax *Herald* and donor of the International Trophy. Last year's race was won by the Gloucester schooner *Esperanto,* lost off Sable Island in June. *Esperanto* and *Elsie* were skippered by Marty Welch.

Bluenose was constructed last winter by the Smith and Rhuland yard. Her designer, William Roue, freely admits she was built to win races – but she was also required to be a successful Grand Banks fishing vessel. Walters is pleased on that score, too. In her first season, *Bluenose* proved herself a "highliner," and on one recent trip she brought home the largest catch ever landed in Lunenburg.

The schooner Bluenose in full sail.

Meighen's cabinet members sworn in

Sept. 21, 1921

OTTAWA – After a long night of intense negotiating, Prime Minister Arthur Meighen's new cabinet was sworn in by Gov. Gen. Lord Byng at 8:30 this morning.

Hastily put together three weeks after the campaign was officially launched, the new cabinet is the result of desperate last-minute concessions. The prime minister, who has been unpopular in Quebec ever since he drafted the conscription bill, managed to attract prominent Quebecer Dr. L. P. Normand by offering him the presidency of the Privy Council.

Critics cite lack of experience – of four French-Canadians sworn into the new cabinet, not one currently holds a seat in Parliament – and lack of cohesiveness as the main weaknesses of Meighen's new cabinet. With support unlikely in Quebec and the prairies, Meighen is expected to concentrate his efforts on getting Ontario votes.

King leads Liberals to minority win

Tories fall to third in federal election

Dec. 6, 1921

OTTAWA – The Tory government of Arthur Meighen, who only took over as prime minister from Sir Robert Borden last year, has gone down to a stunning defeat. In the new House of Commons the Tory party will be the third largest, with only 50 seats. The winners are the Liberals under new leader W.L. Mackenzie King. With 117 seats, they form Canada's first minority government. The second largest party, the Progressives under former Tory cabinet minister Thomas Crerar, took a lot of votes from the Tories to win its 64 seats.

Meighen has been much criticized for taking the position of prime minister without going to the electorate for approval. He is also held responsible, fairly or not, for the current business depression.

Will MP Agnes have to doff her cap?

Dec. 8, 1921

OTTAWA – A puzzling question has arisen among parliamentarians. For the first time in its history, the House of Commons has a female member, Agnes Macphail. A 31-year-old schoolteacher from Ontario, Miss Macphail became the representative for South-East Grey in the recent election. She was one of four women to seek office Dec. 6, in the first Canadian election in which women have been eligible to vote or hold office. Miss Macphail is a member of the Progressive party.

MP Agnes Macphail.

Rule 16 of Rules of Debate states, "Every member desiring to speak is to rise in his place, uncovered, and address himself to Mr. Speaker." However, scriptures and accepted standards of behavior dictate that women should not appear in public with their heads uncovered. It is expected that Miss Macphail will follow the example set by Lady Astor, who wears her hat when speaking to the British House of Commons. Further discussion may take place when Parliament opens in March.

Rail helps logging operations to expand

Special logging railways are solving transportation problems in the industry.

Spring 1921

EASTERN CANADA – Logging railways are beginning to penetrate the woods because most of the hardwood trees have been cut from areas adjacent to the rivers in the resurgence of operations after the end of the Great War. Trees that were felled in the winter have been dragged by horses to the railway spurs to be lifted onto flatcars by steam-operated cranes.

Police arrest 45 Kwakiutl in potlatch raid

December 1921

BRITISH COLUMBIA – Police recently raided a Kwakiutl potlatch being held in a remote coastal village, arresting 45 band members and confiscating rattles, whistles, masks, and other items related to the traditional native ceremony banned by the federal government in 1884. All the seized goods are currently being prepared for shipment to the Victoria Memorial Museum in Ottawa.

Since imposition of the ban, experts have warned that strict enforcement would strain relations between native groups and the government. Indeed, some Kwakiutl are angry and resentful that property seized without payment is destined for an institution celebrating their cultural heritage.

This farm kitchen has indoor water pump and electric washing machine.

Census to reveal the ethnic makeup of Canada

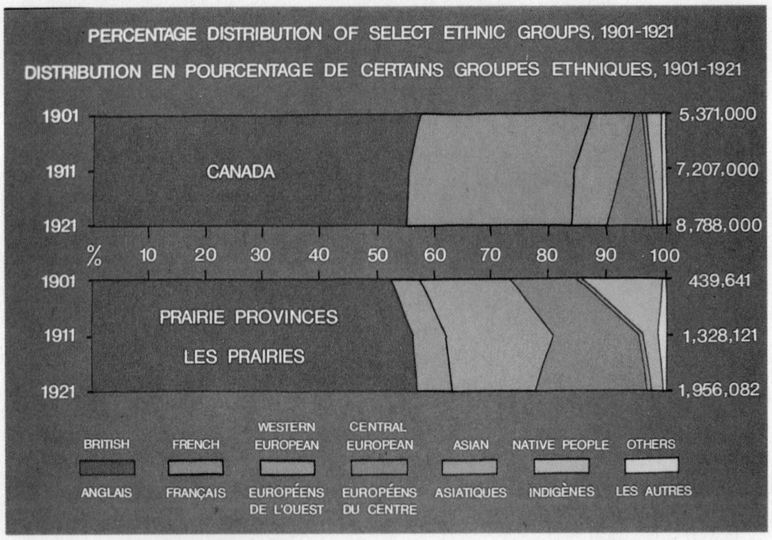

Figures may affect immigration policies

December 1921

CANADA – An army of 12,000 enumerators began work on Canada's Sixth Decennial Census last June, an undertaking Dominion statistician R.H. Coats has called "the largest peacetime operation ever organized by the Canadian government." And although the final analysis has not yet been published, news detailing the ethnic origin of Canada's population in both numerical and regional terms is eagerly awaited – its effect may be staggering, particularly on immigration policies.

Question No. 21 of the census asks the respondent's "racial or tribal origin," stipulating that to answer "Canadian" will not suffice. The question is designed to measure the extent of the "foreign" (non-British and non-American) invasion that occurred during the pre-war years, and it reflects a general and growing opinion that, as stated in the Manitoba *Free Press*, Canada's "open door policy must give place to the melting pot."

The census will help pinpoint groups of immigrants unwilling or unable, possibly for religious reasons or perhaps because of settlement patterns already in place, to assimilate into the Canadian context – that is, the vision of Canada as defined by the country's political elite and captains of industry, the majority of whom are of British descent. Its bird's-eye view will identify, more specifically, the needs of the nation as judged by its leaders.

A Scottish immigrant family arrives at the port of Quebec. They seem a bit apprehensive about their prospects in a new country.

An Icelandic immigrant.

German immigrants at Quebec.

These immigrants are bound for Canada. Since the beginning of the century, Canada has attracted many settlers.

Ethnic groups like to settle in communities such as this Doukhobor village.

1922

Canada, February. The Workers' Party is founded, the public alter ego of the secret Canadian Communist party.

Ottawa, April 21. The government announces Canada's national parks brought $18 million into the country last year, mostly through tourists.

Hobbema, Alta., June 29. Some 1,500 plains Indians meeting at the Samson Reserve form the League of Indians of Canada to oppose Ottawa's Indian policies and promote religious freedom for Indians.

Hamilton, Sept. 11. The Association of Canadian Clubs calls for the "purification" of motion pictures.

Toronto, Sept. 15. John and Alfred Billes open the Hamilton Tire and Rubber Ltd. store [Canadian Tire].

London, September. The British government asks Canada to help against "Turkish aggression" in Constantinople. French-Canadians oppose Canadian involvement.

London, October. Andrew Bonar Law, born in New Brunswick, becomes prime minister, the first colonial to become PM of Great Britain.

Kingston, Ont., Dec. 2. Queen's University beats Edmonton Elks 13-1 to win the Grey Cup.

Gloucester, Massachusetts. The *Bluenose* wins the International Fisherman's Trophy, emblematic of the sailing championship of the North Atlantic fishing fleets, for the second year running.

Newfoundland. The Newfoundland Railway is inefficient compared to the Canadian Pacific Railway. The CPR can move a ton of freight one mile for less than a cent; the cost to the Newfoundland line is more than seven cents.

Ellesmere Island, Northwest Territories. An RCMP detachment is established at Craig Harbour to assert Canadian sovereignty in the Arctic.

Northwest Territories. Wood Buffalo National Park is founded. Indians are allowed to kill game other than buffalo in the park.

Prairies. Nemiskam, Canyon Reserve and Maple Creek antelope preserves are given national park status.

Toronto. Toronto St. Pats defeat the Vancouver Millionaires three games to two to win the Stanley Cup.

Insulin gives diabetes victims hope

Feb. 11, 1922

TORONTO – Four doctors at the University of Toronto have discovered an internal secretion of the pancreas that is being heralded as a life-saver for victims of diabetes. They call the substance insulin. The research team consists of Dr. Frederick Banting, physiologist Charles H. Best, biochemist James Bertram Collip, and Dr. J.J.R. Macleod, a physiologist who had been supervising the research. It was Banting, then practising as a physician in London, Ont., who came up with the idea on Oct. 31, 1920. He had been reading a medical journal that night when he jotted down an idea to isolate the secretion from the pancreas.

Dr. Frederick Banting and Dr. Charles Best, discoverers of insulin.

Banting, who began research on the project last May at the U of T, was joined by Best after he won a coin toss with a classmate. Collip, currently on sabbatical from the University of Alberta, last month discovered a way to produce an anti-diabetic pancreatic extract that is non-toxic.

Insulin is a hormone the pancreas produces, and its function is to help burn sugar or glucose found in the blood, and, in turn, convert that sugar into energy. The disease known as diabetes results when too little of this hormone is produced by the pancreas. The next step in this medical miracle is to develop mass production of insulin.

Just in the nickel of time: Royal Mint making five-cent pieces

Jan. 3, 1922

OTTAWA – With pomp and ceremony befitting a grand occasion, the Canadian branch of the Royal Mint today produced Canada's first five-cent pieces. The new coin is the same size as the American equivalent, but unlike its U.S. counterpart – made mostly of copper – Canada's five-cent pieces are pure nickel. Each weighs 70 grains and is 2.12 centimetres in diameter.

Ladies Mary and Elizabeth Byng, grandnieces of Gov. Gen. Julian Byng, Viscount of Vimy, this afternoon operated the presses that made the first two coins; the "nickels" were then placed in a plush case and presented to His Excellency the governor general and his wife Lady Byng as souvenirs. Byng commanded the Canadian Corps for part of the Great War and led the attack on Vimy Ridge in April 1917. While at the Royal Mint today he reviewed war veterans now working at the plant.

Newfoundland seal herds first to be located using an airplane

Sealers waiting for the order to go overboard and begin the day's work.

March 17, 1922

ST. JOHN'S, Nfld. – The airplane meets new challenges every year, and it has now had its attention turned to the local seal hunt, which has defeated men and ships on many occasions. An attempt was made last year to use an airplane to find the seal herds, but there were so many problems with frozen radiators and landing gear that nothing was accomplished.

Over the past year, Maj. Sydney Cotton, originally from Australia, has been flying an airplane under extreme weather conditions, and this year he located the seal herds. However, it is doubtful there is time to work out an agreement with the companies in time for them to take advantage of his information.

Island women can vote, run for office

May 3, 1922

CHARLOTTETOWN – While votes for women have been advocated as early as 1892, the Island legislature has resisted for 30 years – until today, that is. It has finally given in to pressure from the numerous women's groups and joined the trend toward female suffrage.

Island women now hold the same voting rights as men. Provided they meet the age, residency and property requirements, they can both vote and run for office. Quebec is left as the lone province to resist the extension of the franchise to women.

Premiers' attempt to resurrect the Canadian Wheat Board fails

1922

REGINA – Prairie farmers must continue to battle low grain prices without federal help. Charles Dunning, Liberal premier of Saskatchewan, and his Alberta counterpart, UFA Premier Herbert Greenfield, made a valiant try at reinstating the Canadian Wheat Board, but they have failed. Their governments passed the necessary legislation, but the Canadian Wheat Board Act requires participation of all Prairie provinces. Manitoba chose not to support the proposal, and thus marketing remains in the realm of free enterprise.

From 1917 to 1920, the Canadian government controlled grain marketing. It made one payment upon delivery of the crop by the farmer and a final payment at the end of the year after the last load was in. This system was meant only as a temporary measure and was abandoned in 1920.

After 1920, a drop in demand led to a drop in prices. Discontented farmers began to push for another government wheat board. The National Progressive Party gained prominence as a result of this agrarian discontent. The lack of strong central leadership led the agricultural community to look provincially for a solution. They are still looking.

An agricultural-based economy.

Documentary film Nanook of the North examines life of Inuit

Coronation Gulf Inuit in front of their summer tent homes.

June 11, 1922

NEW YORK – An unusual documentary film about the Inuit of Canada's Arctic received its premiere here today. *Nanook of the North* was made by Robert Flaherty, an American geologist and filmmaker. The film recreates everyday life among the Inuit of northern Quebec, using the native residents of the area as "actors."

Sponsored by the French fur-trading company Revillon Frères, the 38-year-old Flaherty lived with the Inuit for a year making the film under very primitive conditions. An earlier version, filmed on Baffin Island from 1913 to 1916, was destroyed by fire.

Caledonia "ghost" finally laid to rest

March 16, 1922

HALIFAX – Tonight the investigator sent to pierce the mystery of the two-month-long rash of fires in the home of Alex MacDonald of Caledonia Mills revealed in his long-awaited report that the arsonist had human and not ghostly hands. Besieged by reporters from every major North American newspaper, Dr. Walter Franklin Prince emerged into public after two days closeted with eyewitnesses he grilled about the incidents that have thrilled the popular imagination.

Though Prince, from the American Research Service of New York, has debunked the theory that a ghostly agency used psychic means to start the fires, his report suggests that young Mary Ellen MacDonald, identified as the human perpetrator, acted on orders from a supernatural power.

Prince bases this on the fact that Mary Ellen experienced dreams or "altered states which were shared by two persons, and were not assignable to any known existing cause." He believes a series of raps and noises not humanly explicable indicates an incarnate presence in the MacDonald house. He confirmed this by subjecting eyewitness Mr. Whidden to a psychic test – automatic writing. Dictating through the medium of Whidden, a spirit readily confessed to Dr. Prince that it caused the fires and other mischief as well.

Showdown with government avoided at Six Nations Reserve

May 15, 1922

SIX NATIONS RESERVE, Ont. – The threat of violence between a faction of Six Nations Indians and government forces has been defused after federal Minister of the Interior Charles Stewart met with reserve leaders today and acknowledged the legitimacy of several grievances. The trouble has been brewing for some time, but came to a head 10 days ago when the Six Nations Council learned of a government plan to use military force, if necessary, to evict an Indian war veteran from his farm.

Because the farmer failed to make his first payment to the Soldiers Settlement Board, he was accused of illegally possessing public land. But the Six Nations Council, some of whom dispute Canada's claim to sovereignty over the reserve, ruled he could remain.

This prompted the ultimatum that Stewart now claims emanated from unofficial and misguided sources. To further soothe relations, Stewart assured chiefs David Hill and Levi General that compulsory enfranchisement, a controversial policy adopted in 1920, would soon be eliminated and that title to reserve land would always be a council responsibility. Stewart also said alleged misappropriation of Indian funds by government officials would be investigated.

Iroquois council chief.

Bracken becomes Manitoba premier

Premier John Bracken.

Aug. 1, 1922

WINNIPEG – John Bracken today became the premier of Manitoba. His United Farmers party will form an administration to replace that of Tobias C. Norris.

Manitoba's first experiment with a farmers' government will undoubtedly bring some major changes to this province. The United Farmers' candidates during the campaign placed little stress on provincewide policies, choosing instead to repeat their promise to reflect the wishes of their constituents. It was also unusual that the United Farmers fought the election without a leader.

Bracken has a distinguished record as an authority on dryland farming. Prior to this election, his interest in public life was limited.

King to Britain: Canadians won't fight in war against Turkey

Sept. 18, 1922

OTTAWA – Prime Minister William Lyon Mackenzie King has responded to Britain's call for Canadian troops should a war break out with Turkey. That response is, in a word, "no." To be precise, King says his government could not send troops without the approval of Parliament, and that frankly he didn't believe the standoff between Turkey and British forces at Chanak warranted asking for it.

The response is a clear-cut departure from the old days of Canadian policy. But now, bolstered by a sense of nationalism that has resulted in a seat at the League of Nations and Canada's own control of her own external affairs, King has made it clear that a British war is not automatically a Canadian war as well. It's a position that is not likely to be appreciated in Britain, especially among those empire supporters who believe Canada should be "more loyal."

Telephone inventor Bell buried in N.S.

Aug. 4, 1922

BADDECK, N.S. – Alexander Graham Bell, who died two days ago, was buried today in a grave carved into the rock of his summer estate here called Beinn Bhreagh (Gaelic for beautiful mountain). He was 75. The Bell telephone system stopped phone service for one minute during the funeral as a way of honoring the man who had invented the phone at Brantford, Ont., almost 50 years ago.

The telephone was only one aspect of Bell's career. An authority on speech, Bell researched the subject and taught deaf children to speak. A native of Scotland who immigrated to Canada, Bell would later become a U.S. citizen. But it was on the frozen Bras d'Or Lake here that he would establish another first on Feb. 23, 1909, when Douglas McCurdy, in the Bell-built *Silver-Dart,* became the first person to fly an airplane in Canada.

Coal mine strike in Cape Breton gets ugly

Aug. 18, 1922

SYDNEY, N.S. – Cape Breton County has been declared a police district, and 1,000 special police officers are to be recruited in the wake of violence surrounding a strike by coal miners in the area. The order was issued today by the lieutenant-governor-in-council after a train carrying Halifax troops to protect the mines was stoned by a mob in Sydney yesterday.

There are encouraging signs of a break in the stalemate, as J.L. Lewis, the United Mine Workers of America's U.S. president, urged members to protect mine property. An agreement to do so was reached. Yesterday, water was flowing into the workings, but crowds armed with clubs tried to prevent safeguarding the mines. A strike mandate of 96 percent in favor passed last month, as workers rejected proposals for pay cuts because of low coal prices and reduced markets.

Attracted by free or cheap land, settlers arrive by train on the prairies. This group has just arrived.

Campaign against Chinese gets worse

Chinese railway laborer in B.C.

Sept. 7, 1922

VICTORIA, B.C. – The campaign against the Chinese has come to the school system here. The anti-Chinese movement, led by provincial politicians, including the dour Scotsman Attorney General A.M. Manson, and federal MPs, is based on charges that the Chinese are depriving white Canadians of business profits, jobs, and places in the school system. Some white families complain their children are forced to study in overcrowded classrooms because of Chinese children being admitted.

The Chinese, of course, recognize that equality in education leads to economic equality. This fear that education is helping the Chinese to compete with white children is behind the recent decision here to open a separate school for Chinese children. But the Chinese students are boycotting the special school and want to return to the regular system.

Forest fire rages; death toll tops 50

Oct. 5, 1922

COBALT, Ont. – A devastating forest fire has claimed upwards of 50 lives, firefighting officials fear. It is uncertain how and when the fire started, but over the last few days it has become one of the most destructive blazes in Canadian history. The Cobalt region of Northern Ontario has been completely overrun, and 16 townships have already been razed by the inferno. Rescue teams are now out combing the remains of 100 square kilometres of land in the hope of finding some survivors. The region continues to burn despite heavy rains.

Armenians demand help for refugees

Oct. 2, 1922

OTTAWA – Canadian Armenians, led by G. H. Alexander, today appealed to the government to help save 750,000 Armenian refugees cornered in Constantinople. The Turkish army, which has brutalized and deported well over a million Armenians since 1915, now threatens to take the British-held city. Naturalized Canadian Armenians want the government to table the issue in Geneva and to pressure the British government into evacuating the refugees alongside the British nationals now leaving the city.

Wildlife conference now a yearly event

Dec. 6, 1922

OTTAWA – Canada's second national conference on wildlife protection is taking place in the capital. It is a giant step for wildlife conservation in Canada, marking the establishment of wildlife conservation as a regular part of government policy and the beginning of annual conferences.

This year the conference is limited to federal and provincial delegates implicated in natural resource administration. Discussions will stress the development of a policy of wildlife preservation throughout the Dominion.

Deskaheh leads Six Nations' struggle

Dec. 22, 1922

NEW YORK – Deskaheh, or Levi General, a Cayuga chief and the speaker of the Six Nations Hereditary Council of Brantford, Ont., is leading the struggle to gain international recognition of the Six Nations' sovereignty. He has argued in the past that the Six Nations are an independent people. They have always been allies – not subjects – of the British Crown, hence, the federal government has no jurisdiction over them. And today Deskaheh located an historic wampum belt in the Museum of the American Indian in New York. The belt, he argues, proves that Britain in the late 18th century recognized Iroquois sovereignty.

Deskaheh visited London last year to seek British support for his claim that the Six Nations were allies of the Crown, and not subjects. In August 1921 he presented a petition to the colonial office. Winston Churchill, the secretary of state for the colonies, has forwarded this document to the governor general, adding that these Indian grievances were an internal matter and must be addressed by Ottawa.

Churchill must have experienced a strange feeling writing about North American Indian matters. The well-known British politician believes that he has a dash of North American Indian blood in his veins, for his American grandmother, Clara Jerome, had an Iroquois great-grandmother on her mother's side. At least this is the Jerome family tradition which Churchill has told his own children.

This medallion shows the council circle of the Iroquois Confederacy with 50 feathers representing the chiefs. In the centre is the Tree of Peace, which is part of the wampum belt design that records the formation of the confederacy.

London-born Paul Peel's famous After the Bath coming home

Nov. 26, 1922

LONDON, Ont. – After two years of negotiations, renowned art critic James Colerick has purchased Paul Peel's painting *After the Bath* from the Hungarian National Art Gallery in Budapest. It will be returned to London, Peel's home town. The price was not disclosed, but the greatly devalued Hungarian currency probably means a good deal for both sides. *After the Bath* won a medal at the 1890 Paris Salon. It is a wonderful representation of Peel's skill with light and color. Known for his sentimental studies of children, Peel is one of the first Canadians to paint nudes.

New Brunswick-born Dennis O'Leary runs a popcorn-making machine.

Drug addiction: It's a growing problem

Dec. 21, 1922

OTTAWA – Drug addiction is a growing problem in Canada, according to the deputy minister of health. Speaking to St. John Ambulance Association officers, Dr. J.A. Amyot reported that there are between 12,000 and 15,000 drug addicts in Canada. Amyot said drug addiction is one of the most critical problems the Department of Health faces today, and that the department is working hard to battle the problem. He explained that people are entirely untrustworthy when under the influence of drugs, and that they are a dangerous menace.

1923

Nova Scotia, May 8. Twenty-seven people walk across 12.9 kilometres of floating ice to reach shore after their steamer, the *Kyle*, is icebound for more than 10 days.

Montreal, May 8. Agnes Macphail, Canada's only female MP, denounces certain passages in the marriage service as relics of the old servitude imposed on women.

Nova Scotia, July 1. RCMP seize the rum-runner *Veda M. McKeown* and impound its cargo of 7,718 litres of rum, 190 cases of Scotch, and 35 cases of gin.

Cape Breton, N.S., July 28. Troops leave the island after striking mine and steel workers return to work.

British Columbia, Aug. 15. Dominion archeologist Harlan Smith announces the discovery of ancient picture writing on cliffs in the Bella Coola region.

Toronto, Aug. 17. The Home Bank of Canada closes after 20 years. "Bad and doubtful debts" caused the bank's financial crisis.

Toronto, Sept. 1. The provincial government makes free insulin available to diabetics who are unable to pay for it.

Alberta, Nov. 5. The province votes for government control of liquor, ending prohibition.

Alberta, Nov. 15. Leasehold seekers file claims on 1,600 hectares in the Wainwright area following reports of an oil strike by British Petroleum.

Toronto, Dec. 1. Queen's University defeats Regina Roughriders 54-0 to win the Grey Cup.

Ottawa. The Exhibits and Publicity Bureau, formed in 1917, is renamed the Canadian Government Motion Picture Bureau and begins making tourist films like *Where Nature Smiles*.

Halifax. The *Bluenose* wins the International Fisherman's Trophy for the third year running.

Nova Scotia. Boys under 16 years old are prohibited from working in the mines.

Ontario. Noranda Mines Ltd. is incorporated.

Canada. All provinces except Quebec allow women to practise law.

Vancouver. Ottawa Senators defeat the Vancouver Millionaires and Edmonton Eskimos in separate series to win the Stanley Cup.

MPs shoot down motion to scrap RCMP

March 1, 1923

OTTAWA – James S. Woodsworth, the Labor MP representing Winnipeg North Centre, put forth a motion in the House today to disband the RCMP, but it was easily shot down 108-47. Liberals have been unhappy with the force for a while, and some even blame the Mounties for the violence in the 1919 Winnipeg General Strike. Since the force has taken on more duties and increased in strength in recent years, the cost of maintaining it has reached $4 million a year. One alternative to scrapping the force altogether is reducing its size.

James S. Woodsworth.

Grand Trunk now under the CNR banner

Jan. 30, 1923

OTTAWA – The government-run Canadian National Railways has a new component – the now-defunct Grand Trunk company. Floundering under the costs of operating its western line, this venerable old railway has come under government control, leaving the Canadian Pacific as the last privately-held line in Canada. The new CNR is a bit of a monster. It's made up of old lines like the GTR and the Intercolonial in the Maritimes – routes that are not only in need of repair, but, since the lines were once competitors, also are often duplicated.

Murray resigns after 27 years as premier

Jan. 4, 1923

HALIFAX – George Henry Murray, the Liberal war-horse of Nova Scotia, has resigned as premier. He ends a term of office that has run uninterrupted since 1896. Murray is said by many to have been the "ultimate consensus politician," always trying to please the electorate in whatever he did, and always trying to make sure he antagonized as few people as possible. He will be remembered for his introduction of workmen's compensation, women's suffrage, and his support of prohibition.

Susan Maxwell dies as oldest Canadian

Feb. 11, 1923

RICHMOND HILL, Ont. – An extraordinary life's journey ended today with the death of Canada's oldest citizen, former slave Susan Augusta Maxwell. She was 117. Mrs. Maxwell fled to Canada more than 70 years ago via the underground railroad. She had several brushes with danger, including an escape from kidnappers and surviving a killer blizzard. The Pennsylvania native was predeceased by her husband and four children several years ago. She was active until recently, working as a laundress.

A herd of reindeer is being imported to Anticosti Island, Quebec.

Hockey broadcast ends a long day for Foster Hewitt

March 22, 1923

TORONTO – He shoots! He scores! With those words and the immediacy of radio, Foster Hewitt brought the excitement of hockey to people's homes tonight with his broadcast of the intermediate playoff game between Toronto Parkdale and Kitchener.

Norm Albert was the first to broadcast part of a game on Feb. 8 this year, and on March 14 Pete Parker broadcast a complete game. But Hewitt's broadcast has sports fans buzzing. Working in a 1.2-metre square glass box that the Toronto *Star*'s new radio station, CFCA, set up in three rail seats next to the penalty box at the Mutual Street Arena, Hewitt called the play for three regulation periods, three 10-minute overtimes, and talked through the intermissions.

When the final buzzer sounded, it marked the end of a long day for Hewitt. At 5:45 p.m., he was talking with fellow *Star* reporter Gordon Sinclair after a long shift that had begun at 7 a.m. when he was told by radio editor Basil Lake that he had another assignment. Hewitt went to the rink, bought a hot dog and a program, and entered the glass booth designed to shield radio listeners from crowd noise. The booth steamed up, impairing his view, so Hewitt perched on a stool to broadcast the contest.

Law to cut number of Chinese settlers

Chinese laborer crushing stone.

July 1, 1923

OTTAWA – An immigration act which became law today will, in effect, stop the Chinese from settling in Canada. After discussions with China's government, Ottawa introduced legislation which excludes all Chinese except students, merchants, and consuls.

This means that those Chinese immigrants who left their wives and children in China cannot bring them into Canada. A single man cannot bring a woman over to be his wife. But British Columbians are already protesting. They want total exclusion.

Canada, U.S. sign Halibut Treaty

March 2, 1923

OTTAWA – Prime Minister W.L. Mackenzie King is delighted by the latest success in his campaign to forge an independent foreign policy. Canada today signed a treaty with the United States governing fishing rights in the North Pacific. Halibut stocks were the treaty's chief concern.

Canada has signed commercial treaties before, but British diplomats have always participated in the negotiations and ceremony. In the case of the Halibut Treaty, Canada both negotiated and signed the agreement without any participation from the Mother Country.

Britain wanted to play a part in the process but King refused to permit this and threatened to open Canadian diplomatic offices in the United States if Britain did not back down. Canada has been trying to work its own foreign policy since the 1870s, when Sir John A. Macdonald was on a British team negotiating with the U.S. But it was not until the 1921 Imperial Conference that Canada started to reassert its rights. And two years ago King's Liberals won all 65 Quebec seats in the federal election. Since Quebec is basically isolationist, this pushed King to further assert Canadian independence.

Bootlegger and mistress hang for murder of police sergeant

May 2, 1923

LETHBRIDGE, Alta. – Alberta's powerful bootleggers suffered a blow today as one of their colleagues, Emilio Picariello, and his mistress Florence Lassandro were hanged for the Sept. 21 murder of Provincial Police Sgt. Stephen Lawson. Appeals to the Supreme Courts of Alberta and Canada were unsuccessful. Victim Lawson was gunned down from a McLaughlin Buick in front of the Coleman police barracks in the Crowsnest Pass.

Picariello, owner of the Alberta Hotel in Blairmore, and Lassandro, the wife of one of his associates, had been prime suspects in the case from the outset. But his lawyer, McKinley Cameron, defended him so well the outcome of the case appeared to be in question.

Picariello, one of Alberta's most important bootleggers, was widely known as Emperor Pic. Newspaper reports about the case describe him as a gangster, and Lassandro as his gun moll. But like many of his ilk, he cultivated a reputation as a local benefactor, and after the trial residents of southern Alberta described Picariello as a generous man who always helped people in financial trouble. Picariello was also rumored to hold many promissary notes from Alberta provincial policemen who had turned a blind eye to his rum-running business.

Emperor Pic or Emilio Picariello (right) and his partner Charles Lassandro.

A Toronto streetcar and a car cannot seem to share the street corner.

A Toronto streetcar was used for a home after last year's fire in Haileybury.

Experts say bones are a mastodon's

June 26, 1923

LONDON, Ont. – Experts are claiming today that the skeletal remains of a large animal recently unearthed on a farm in nearby Delaware township are actually those of a 30,000-year-old mastodon. This would date the remains to the Pleistocene Age, or that just prior to the coming of man.

A local farmer discovered parts of the skeleton on his property and immediately notified London's Western University. An expert from the school, Professor Robertson, carried on further excavations and found the animal's cranium, lower jaw, vertebrae, and rib cage. The teeth and tusks are 30 centimetres and three metres long, respectively, and the jawbone weighs 18 kilograms. Total weight of the animal is estimated to have been 30 to 50 tons.

President Harding visits Vancouver

July 26, 1923

VANCOUVER – President Warren G. Harding has arrived here on an American cruiser on his way home from Alaska. After a drive down Burrard and Georgia streets, he will take a stroll in Stanley Park and then attend a civic luncheon at the Hotel Vancouver, with Premier John Oliver and the mayor as his hosts.

Harding, who is the first American president to visit Canada, was given full military honors when he arrived in the harbor, with a full complement of army and navy officers, soldiers, and naval ratings on parade. When his visit ends this evening, the president will sail south to San Francisco. Officials have already noticed that although Harding is always smiling, he looks pale and tired. Reports of scandals in Washington have dogged him on the trip.

The U.S. president greets spectators as he arrives in Vancouver harbor.

Renowned architect Frank Darling dies

May 18, 1923

TORONTO – Frank Darling, architect extraordinaire, is dead at the age of 73. Darling was born in Toronto and attended Upper Canada College before going to England, where he studied architecture with G.F. Street.

Darling's accomplishments are many. In 1885, he co-designed the Bank of Montreal at Front and Yonge streets, an early example of French Beaux Arts classicism in Toronto. The next year he was elected a fellow of the Royal Canadian Academy. In 1893, Darling became the senior member in the Toronto firm Darling and Pearson, Architects. The firm, which excelled in bank designs and office buildings, became one of the most successful in its field in Canada, and is responsible for many Toronto and Montreal public buildings – for example, the Toronto General Hospital, the Hospital for Sick Children, the Union Building, and many of the University of Toronto buildings. The firm also designed Winnipeg's Bank of Commerce building. In 1915, Darling was awarded the King's gold medal for architecture.

Ferguson leads Ontario Tories to victory

Tory leader George Ferguson.

June 25, 1923

TORONTO – The Conservatives under George Ferguson have smashed their way back to power in Ontario, routing Premier Ernest Drury and his United Farmers of Ontario party. Returns are a bit sketchy, due to an electrical storm in southwestern Ontario that has delayed results coming in on the telephone lines. However, it is known that Ferguson has at least 77 seats, compared to the Liberals' 16, the UFO's 13, and Labour's one. The victory comes after growing dissatisfaction with the UFO's running of the province.

Squires quits amid rumors of corruption

July 23, 1923

ST. JOHN'S, Nfld. – Premier Richard Squires responded to the threatened resignations of four cabinet ministers today with his own unexpected resignation. Ever since the election on May 3, rumors have been circulating about corrupt and illegal activities on the part of certain government ministers and supporters. One minister, Alex Campbell, is reported to have spent his department's funds without proper authorization during the election campaign. Squires is alleged to have received money from the Liquor Board, and funds are missing from other departments.

Public opinion has grown so unfavorable recently that four prominent ministers, led by Justice Minister William Warren, called on Squires to fire Campbell or they would resign. Squires quit instead, and advised the governor to call on Warren to form a government.

Manitoba adopts Liquor Control Act

July 22, 1923

WINNIPEG – Manitoba today passed the Government Liquor Control Act, legislation which effectively places all aspects of the liquor trade under provincial control. The action was taken as a result of a plebiscite conducted earlier this year. By a vote of 108,000-69,000, Manitobans showed that they wanted state-operated liquor outlets throughout the province. In those province-run outlets, sales will be made only to those who hold valid permits, and quantities will be limited. Permits can be purchased by those persons 21 years of age and over for the price of $1. A record will be kept of all purchases made by each permit holder.

When the Bracken government decided to pass the liquor legislation, it had to make some difficult political choices. Many of those 69,000 plebiscite ballots were cast by prohibitionists who do not want any liquor available in the province under any circumstances. Offsetting this feeling, however, were the requirements of the exchequer, for the new law will bring a flow of cash into provincial coffers.

Cows stagger home after one too many

Oct. 8, 1923

CARGILL, Ont. – You won't hear another one like this till the cows come home, the saying goes. Well, one Greenock township farmer's cows did come home tonight – drunk. The theory is that they came across a still in a swamp near this Bruce County centre, taste-tested the wares, liked it better than their own product and, well – had one too many. They staggered home, behaving in much the same fashion as drunken humans. News travels fast. Rural telephone lines were buzzing over the cows' buzz, and everyone came out to see the show. No peace for a cow with a hangover.

King advocates Canadian independence

Oct. 22, 1923

LONDON, England – At the Imperial Conference here in London, where the prime minister of Britain and the dominions are meeting, Canadian Prime Minister W.L. Mackenzie King has stood out as a quiet yet immovable advocate of Canadian autonomy. In private discussions he has made it clear Canada will decide its own foreign policy. As well, given that Canada has already signed a treaty with the United States concerning halibut – an independent initiative unheard of in the past – he's also made it clear that Canada is quite determined to conduct its own external relations, provided they do not impinge on Britain.

PM King arrives in England.

Banting, Macleod to get Nobel Prize

Oct. 25, 1923

STOCKHOLM, Sweden – Two University of Toronto doctors who discovered insulin last year will become the first Canadians to receive a Nobel Prize. The Council of Teachers of the Karolinska Institute decided tonight to honor both Dr. Frederick Banting and Dr. J.J.R. Macleod for the discovery that has given diabetics a new lease on life. The Nobel Prize for medicine is valued at $40,000. Macleod supervised the work, but the idea of isolating the secretion from the pancreas was Banting's. Two others, J.B. Collip and Charles Best, also worked on the project.

Edmonton girls take basketball tourney

Edmonton Commercial Grads championship basketball team.

1923

EDMONTON – The Edmonton Commercial Grads girls' basketball team has won the Underwood Challenge Trophy, defeating Cleveland in this competition's first international series.

Formed in 1915 of graduates and students of McDougall Commercial High School here, the Grads have carved an impressive record under coach Percy Page. "They have won because the spirit of the prairie is born and bred in them," Page said of his team. The Grads may compete in the 1924 Olympics.

Ontario buys Ojibwa land for $500,000

November 1923

TORONTO – The Williams Commission has been busy visiting Ontario Indian reserves from Oct. 31 to Nov. 21. It's been at Georgina Island, and Rama, on Lake Simcoe; Christian Island on the Georgian Bay; Rice Lake, Alderville, and Mud Lake in the Peterborough area; and Lake Scugog northwest of Toronto. It has arranged with these Ojibwa bands for the formal surrender of 25,900 square kilometres of land lying between the 45th Parallel, the Nipissing and Ottawa rivers, and Georgian Bay, as well as a large tract of hitherto unceded Ojibwa land on the north shore of Lake Ontario, from the Don to the Trent rivers. This southern tract includes a portion of the city of Toronto. The Ontario government has acquired the Indian lands for $500,000.

Alberta Wheat Pool opens Calgary office

Oct. 29, 1923

CALGARY – The United Farmers of Alberta, with a membership of 35,000, have formed the Alberta Wheat Pool, an agency intended to sell wheat for the farmers and pay them fair prices. The United Grain Growers will handle the wheat, and with financial backing from the province and a $15-million line of credit, the pool is in business. Its office is here in Calgary.

Fifteen teams of horses pull six wagon-loads of grain to an elevator.

Staged buffalo kill turns into real thing

Nov. 15, 1923

WAINWRIGHT, Alta. – Thirty tame buffalo were killed when a staged scene went wrong during the filming of an American movie in the National Park. The plan was for the buffalo to be driven toward a coulee by 14 Cree actors from the Hobbema reserve. Sharpshooters were to pick off 10 of the buffalo, but someone fired too soon, causing confusion. Cowpunchers fired more shots into the swirling mass. Crew and cast were not harmed.

1924

Montreal, Jan. 10. The CNR announces that its transcontinental dining cars will serve buffalo tongues and tails.

Alberta, Jan. 17. The United Farmers of Alberta oppose a resolution calling for the secession of the western provinces from Canada.

Newfoundland, March 1. Aircraft are used successfully for the first time to spot Atlantic seal herds.

Vancouver, May 24. The first Canadian parachute jump from an airplane takes place.

Ottawa, June 29. The first national postal strike ends as workers return to their jobs pending settlement of the dispute by cabinet.

Ottawa, July 7. The Crow's Nest Pass Agreement to provide lower western freight rates is restored after being suspended a year ago. It will now cover grain and flour moving eastward and basic commodities moving westward.

Ontario, July 25. Some 800 Mennonites from Russia are settling in Waterloo County. The Non-resistant Relief Committee and the CPR brought them to Canada as part of a plan to bring 5,000 of them.

The Hague, Oct. 2. In an expression of Canadian isolationism, Raoul Dandurand, Canadian delegate to the League of Nations Assembly, says "we live in a fireproof house, far from inflammable materials."

Toronto, Nov. 29. Queen's University defeats Toronto Balmy Beach 11-3 for the Grey Cup.

Boston, Dec. 1. The first NHL game played outside Canada takes place.

Montreal, Dec. 24. The huge cross recently erected on top of Mount Royal is lit for the first time.

Ontario. A court upholds the right of a London restaurant owner to refuse service to blacks.

British Columbia. Socialists found the Canadian Birth Control League to provide birth control education.

Canada. Frank Neighbor is the first recipient of the Hart Trophy for the most valuable player in the National Hockey League.

Ottawa. Montreal Canadiens defeat Calgary to win the Stanley Cup.

Red Ensign unfurled as official flag

Jan. 26, 1924

OTTAWA – The Red Ensign, showing the Canadian crest on a red flag with the Union Jack in the upper corner, has been chosen by the government as Canada's official flag. It's a choice that surprises no one, as the flag has been in use since 1892. Officially, it was to be used by Canadian ships; unofficially, it was seen throughout the country. Now it will officially be flown on Canadian government buildings, both here and abroad.

The original ensign, minus the Canadian crest, was assigned to British merchant ships in 1707 by Queen Anne. It is just one of a host of flags that can be seen throughout the British Empire these days, all possessing the Union Jack.

Detail from Canada's new official flag, the Red Ensign.

Salvation Army assigns British teens to Winnipeg farm homes

The Salvation Army also sponsors groups of women to settle in Manitoba.

March 18, 1924

WINNIPEG – A party of 28 British teenage boys arrived today as part of a contingent under the direction of the Salvation Army. They will be sent to farm homes in Manitoba as a learning experience. Most of the boys are destined for the province's Brandon and Killarney districts.

The English party which arrived in Halifax a week ago on the *SS Regina* consisted of 60 boys and girls. As it moved westward, various members disembarked from the Canadian National Railways train and were assigned to farm homes in the eastern provinces. Salvation Army officials believe these disadvantaged boys will eventually become permanent settlers.

Inuit hanged as long arm of Canadian law reaches the Arctic

Feb. 1, 1924

HERSCHEL ISLAND, N.W.T. – Ottawa has decided to teach all Inuit a lesson. Up to now, Inuit charged with murder have been dealt with leniently, with death sentences commuted to life imprisonment and prisoners released after a short time in jail. The goal was not to alienate or intimidate the Inuit, but to "secure their confidence." Now, the government believes leniency has not had the desired effect of reducing murders. The tough new policy is evident in the case of Alikomiak and Tatimagana, who were originally incarcerated for the 1921 murders of four Canadian Gulf Inuit.

The Inuit compounded their guilt while in custody, killing two white men, including Cpl. W.A. Doak of the RCMP. The police and government were outraged by Doak's death, and this time the full measure of the law was played out in a showcase and very public trial held here. The two Inuit were found guilty, and both were hanged.

There is some embarrassment about how the trial proceeded. Before it began, the Inuits' defence lawyer said "that the law should take its course and those Eskimos found guilty of murder should be hanged in a place where the natives will see and recognize the outcome of taking another's life." Graves were dug before the verdict was in.

Canada steers clear of Lausanne treaty

March 24, 1924
OTTAWA – Prime Minister William Lyon Mackenzie King today took a legal step that will reinforce the issue of Canadian sovereignty. This time the issue was the Treaty of Lausanne, negotiated by the European powers to clear up the chaos generated by the Treaty of Versailles after the Great War. British Prime Minister Ramsey Macdonald's claim that all dominions concurred with the treaty brought a quick denial from King, who says "that having not been invited, or having been represented directly or indirectly, and not having signed, Canada has no obligations. Therefore, we do not feel it necessary to submit the matter to Parliament for approval."

It's worth noting that Canada did play a direct role in the conference that resulted in the Treaty of Versailles, including having signed the treaty itself.

Report leads to the arrest of Newfoundland's former premier

April 22, 1924
ST. JOHN'S, Nfld. – After taking over as premier from Richard Squires last July, William Warren was forced to set up an inquiry into the many allegations and rumors surrounding his predecessor's resignation. With no credible person available locally to lead the inquiry, Warren looked to the British government, which, in turn, recommended Thomas Hollis Walker, KC, for the job.

The report, published last month, found misconduct in public spending. When word reached Warren that several of his supporters were going to vote against him and defeat his government, Warren had Squires and several others charged with larceny and arrested. However, Warren's government does not appear to have enough support to last much longer.

New board controls Alberta liquor sales

May 10, 1924
EDMONTON – The Liquor Control Board starts work today, and the sale of liquor is now a provincial government monopoly. Last year, the people of Alberta voted 93,000-61,000 to end prohibition and start a system of selling liquor in government stores. Beer would be sold in pubs. Prohibition began in Alberta in 1915. Liquor stores close to the border expect a brisk business as "dry" Americans buy booze to take home.

Frustrated western farmers form co-op

May 31, 1924
REGINA – Farmers, frustrated with the unsatisfactory marketing of their crops, have finally contracted enough members to form their own marketing pool. An act of the Saskatchewan legislature last year formed the Saskatchewan Co-operative Wheat Producers Ltd. However, it took until now to sign up 51 percent of wheat acreage needed to make the pool work. This fall farmers will receive the same price for the same grade of wheat, the average price received for the grade when it was sold.

The Ferry, Quebec, by James Wilson Morrice. Morrice was born in Montreal but spent much of his life in Paris. He died this year in Tunis.

Toronto postal workers walk off the job

Stamp presses at the Canadian Bank Note Co. may be idle due to the strike.

Mail is still delivered by the stage on the old Dawson Trail in the Yukon.

June 19, 1924
TORONTO – As a symbol of sympathy for their Montreal brethren, Toronto postal workers have walked off the job. Their main grievance is the salaries that have been offered them by the Civil Service Commission. Postal workers consider the offer "totally inadequate."

Adding an important dimension to the walkout is the fact that it's been joined by clerks who sort letters in railway mailcars. This means that, for all intents and purposes, the nerve centres of Canada's postal service are paralysed. In response, the government is trying to bring in strikebreakers.

Prohibition law to bite the dust in Sask.

Temperance advocates built this fountain on the street in Montreal.

July 16, 1924

REGINA – Prohibition legislation in Saskatchewan passed in 1916 will be scrapped in favor of government control of the sale of liquor. A majority vote of 38,956 favors the end of eight years of prohibition and the control of the sale of liquor by the province. However, the sale of beer by the glass was rejected by voters. Liquor stores will be established under the control of a provincial liquor board. The presence of these stores in a community will be subject to local referendums.

Pilot conducts aerial survey of prairies

RCAF crew of a Vickers Viking aircraft at Victoria Beach, Manitoba.

July 20, 1924

WINNIPEG – Squadron leader Basil Hobbes has begun an aerial survey of water routes in northern Manitoba and northern Saskatchewan. He and three crewmen will photograph from a new Vickers Viking flying boat.

During the war, aircraft mapped enemy trench systems and directed artillery fire. In 1919, a Quebec company used an airplane to survey timber and spot forest fires. Since 1920, the RCAF has tested ways to apply airborne cameras to peacetime work. With more than half of Canada unmapped, Hobbes and his colleagues have a lot of work to do.

Majority OKs formation of United Church

June 27, 1924

OTTAWA – Union of Methodist, Presbyterian, and Congregational churches to form what will be known as the United Church of Canada was approved today by Parliament. In a vote of 110-58, Parliament passed an amendment legislating the new church's corporate existence on June 10, 1925. The amendment, moved by J.L. Brown, a Progressive member from Lisgar, deletes clauses that would delay the union by two years.

While union is now a reality, there will be some rifts to heal after the debate. Most opposition's been within Presbyterian congregations, where some non-union members say the courts of the church do not have the authority to vote for the extinction of the church.

Airplane delivers treaty money to north

Banks are getting into air services also – this one to Black Diamond, Alberta.

Aug. 1, 1924

ATTAWAPISKAT – A Vickers Viking airplane carrying an Indian Affairs official with treaty money for area reservations landed here today, as aircraft continue to make inroads into the north. The plane, piloted by R.S. Grandy, flew up the west shore of James Bay to this Indian settlement, its last stop on the trip. The dispensing of the money has taken two weeks in the aircraft, a job which took months by canoe. Since the end of the Great War, there has been a push to find civilian uses for planes. Travel in the north by planes equipped to land on water is growing.

Experts wonder if Martians sent signal

Aug. 22, 1924

VANCOUVER – A strange signal has been received at the Point Grey wireless station here. Some experts wonder if Martians are trying to make contact as the Earth passes between Mars and the sun on its path to the equinox. The signal received at the government station blots out all other messages and occurs at regular intervals. "The signal has been noticed at the same hour practically every day for a month," says C.W. Mellish, an operator at Point Grey. Mellish said the signal comes in four groups of four dashes, and is so powerful that it cannot be tuned out.

In London, a 24-valve receiver was set up and tuned to 30,000 metres. At 1 a.m. it picked up a signal sounding like Morse code dots. Experts say it could not have come from any station on Earth. But Prof. A.S. Eddington, the famous astronomer from Cambridge University, dismisses the reports as nonsense. A signal could not cross the vast space between Mars and the Earth, he says.

Doukhobor leader Verigin is mourned

Nov. 2, 1924

NELSON, B.C. – Nearly 8,000 people sang and wept at the funeral of Doukhobor leader Peter Verigin near here. It was a moving, colorful ceremony. Verigin, now called Peter Lordly, was buried in a sepulchre blasted out of the rock. From early morning till night, Doukhobor mourners sang dirges that rang out like chants played on a massive organ. Most mourners came from different villages, and some held bouquets of flowers above their heads for hours on end; others carried massive evergreen boughs. Most of the women were wearing colorful dresses, but a few small groups wore black.

From time to time, the chanting mourners sank to their knees in the mud and prayed for the spirit of Verigin, who, they believe, descends from the Holy Spirit. The ceremony, mostly in Russian, was led by Anastasia, Verigin's niece.

Six Nations back Hereditary Council

Oct. 14, 1924

SIX NATIONS RESERVE, Ont. – If the elections today on the Six Nations Reserve prove anything, it is that the majority of male Iroquois still endorse the right of their centuries-old Hereditary Council to govern the reserve. Only about one-fifth or so of the eligible Iroquois males voted.

For years a struggle has been waged by a group of Iroquois in favor of the establishment of an elected council. Most recently a number of Six Nations Great War veterans have led the campaign to unseat the traditional chiefs. Viewing the introduction of an elected council as a progressive move, the Indian Department and the federal cabinet recently approved the removal of the Hereditary Council from power. Only three weeks ago, Indian agent C.E. Morgan, without first holding a reserve-wide referendum, read the order-in-council expelling the Hereditary Council. The RCMP then seized the Hereditary Council's sacred wampum belts, used to sanction their meetings, as well as council records.

The poor voter turnout proves the strong support the Hereditary Council enjoys on the reserve. The building of RCMP barracks on the reservation, the hasty expulsion of the Hereditary Council, and the seizure of the wampum belts have antagonized many Iroquois.

The first elective council of the Six Nations, at Oshweken, Ontario.

Pair fined $600,000 in Ontario fraud case

Oct. 24, 1924

TORONTO – The Supreme Court of Ontario today imposed the biggest fines ever levied by a Commonwealth court in a decision against former province of Ontario treasurer Peter Smith and businessman Aemilius Jarvis Sr. The two men, convicted on charges of conspiracy to defraud the province and of theft, were ordered to pay fines totalling $600,000. Smith, who must serve three years in jail, and Jarvis, sentenced for six months, will have their prison terms extended until such time as they are able to pay their fines. Jarvis' son Aemilius Jarvis Jr. and businessman Harry G. Pepall, also charged, were both acquitted.

Canadiens triumph in their Forum debut

Nov. 29, 1924

MONTREAL – Hockey fans in Montreal were doubly thrilled last night, as their beloved Canadiens opened the season and the new Forum with a win over the Toronto St. Patricks. The Canadiens have traditionally played their home games at the Mount Royal Arena, but as no ice was available for the opening of the season, president Leo Dandurand transferred the game to the recently constructed building on St. Catherine Street. Some 8,000 fans poured into the Forum to see the world champion and Stanley Cup holding Habs thrash the Toronto boys 7-1. Billy Boucher led Montreal scorers with three goals.

St. Joseph's Oratory is under construction in Montreal, Quebec.

Edmonton Commercial Grads, basketball champs, are en route to Paris.

1925

Moncton, N.B., Feb. 2. The Canadian National Railways' centre transmits the first regular Canadian radio program to be heard in Britain.

Ottawa, April 23. The government sets up an interdepartmental Northern Advisory Board out of alarm at the threat to Canadian sovereignty posed by a planned exploration of the Arctic by American D.B. MacMillan.

St. John's, Nfld., May 24. A boom in construction work, including the building of the Newfoundland Hotel, reduces unemployment in the city.

Niagara Falls, Ont., May 25. Twenty-four high-powered electric lamps illuminate the falls at night for the first time.

Tuscarora Reservation, New York, June 25. Deskaheh, Cayuga chief and speaker of the Six Nations Hereditary Council, dies. He fought for international recognition for the Six Nations as a sovereign Indian nation.

Toronto, June 10. Some 7,000 Methodists, Presbyterians, and Congregationalists attend the first service of the United Church of Canada, formed from a union of the three denominations.

London, July 28. Three B.C. Indian chiefs, representing 25 other B.C. Indian leaders, arrive to appeal to King George V for just treatment of Canadian Indians.

Geneva, Sept. 7. The sixth Assembly of the League of Nations opens with the unanimous election of Canadian Senator Raoul Dandurand as president.

Ottawa, Dec. 5. Ottawa Senators beat Winnipeg Tammany Tigers 24-1 for the Grey Cup.

Ottawa. The 1897 Crow's Nest Pass Agreement reduced freight rates on grain and flour are reinstated on lines west of Fort William, but the reduced rate on basic manufactured goods moving westward is cancelled.

Windsor, Ont. The Chrysler Corp. of Canada is incorporated and builds 4,474 cars.

St. John's, Nfld. The Newfoundland government gives women the right to vote.

St. John's, Nfld. The government establishes government sale and control of liquor.

Victoria. Victoria Cougars defeat the Montreal Canadiens three games to one to win the Stanley Cup.

Fruit growers say import tax a must

Jan. 8, 1925

ST. CATHARINES, Ont. – The federal government is being asked to impose an import tax of at least 20 percent on fruits and vegetables coming into Canada before Canadian products are ripe, and to tighten up anti-dumping laws.

Resolutions urging this course of action were passed today at the annual meeting of the Niagara Peninsula Fruit Growers' Association. It suggests the tax be dropped after Canadian products are ripe. U.S. producers dumping fruit led to the second resolution.

Royal Bank moves into Latin America

Feb. 2, 1925

NEW YORK CITY – The Royal Bank of Canada, which has long competed with American banks for business in South America, has upped the stakes of the game by purchasing the Bank of Central and South America. The BC&SA does business in Peru, Venezuela, Costa Rica, and Colombia, with 17 branches overall.

The Royal Bank, founded in the 1860s as the Merchants Bank of Halifax, opened its first international branch in Bermuda in 1882.

Inuit dependent on white man's wares

May 4, 1925

OTTAWA – Danish explorer Knud Rasmussen, just back from Canada's Arctic, sadly observes that nearly all the Inuit of Canada are dependent on the white man's goods, including food and high-powered hunting rifles. Rasmussen reports that not only have the Inuit lost their ability to hunt with bows and arrows, kayaks, and spears, but the rifle has led to wanton overkill of food and game to satisfy the demands of the trading companies and Inuit cravings for goods that only these agencies can supply.

Rasmussen believes overkilling and high-powered rifles should be discouraged. If Inuit are kept self-sufficient by the retention of traditional hunting techniques, not only is game conservation achieved, but there will be less dependency on white man's goods.

Fish is a traditional Inuit staple food.

Demand for caviar wiping out sturgeon

Jan. 14, 1925

OTTAWA – An insatiable desire for caviar by the gourmets of Europe is depleting Canada's valuable sturgeon fisheries practically to the point of extinction. A report just prepared by federal authorities says, "This depletion occurring during the past 45 years was precipitated by such factors as the wanton destruction in early days of sturgeon that did not contain ova fit for the manufacture of caviar, and the premium that was paid for the eggs of ripening sturgeon."

The report says propagation has proved difficult, and there is little hope of restoring the mighty sturgeon to its place as a commercial fish. The report cites figures showing the catch of sturgeon in some areas is down 98 percent.

Ontario motorists put their two cents in protesting gas tax

Automobile owners may have to do less driving with the proposed new tax.

Feb. 23, 1925

TORONTO – Several hundred members of the Ontario Motor League received a stern lesson in political reality today. They came to the legislature to meet with Premier George Howard Ferguson and protest the proposed new two-cents-a-gallon tax on gasoline – only to be informed by the premier that the tax was to be three cents a gallon, not two.

Despite their shock, the OML members were firm in their conviction that motorists already pay enough for road upkeep through licence fees and other taxes that together raise nearly $5 million a year for the provincial treasury. The new gas tax would bring in another $3 million a year.

Inquiry appointed, miners back on the job

Aug. 10, 1925

HALIFAX – The new government of Premier E.N. Rhodes will appoint a royal commission to look at the province's coal industry, still reeling from a five-month strike. Nova Scotia had been paralysed since March 6, when 14,000 unionized miners struck the British Empire Steel Corporation, the province's largest coal concern. The dispute was over wages: BESC wanted the workers to take a cut in pay, which the miners refused.

For the first 13 weeks the strike was calm. Then violence broke out on June 11 between strikers and company police at the New Waterford Power House. One miner was killed; scores of miners and police were injured. The government sent 500 troops and a squadron of police to Sydney to handle the situation – a move that is said to have cost the taxpayers $6,600 a day.

The strike ended last week when both sides ratified a government deal calling for some wage cuts, pending an inquiry into the coal industry and BESC's claim that wage cuts are necessary to keep prices low.

Beck brought hydroelectric power to Ont.

Aug. 16, 1925

LONDON, Ont. – The Hydro Knight is dead. After struggling for many months against pernicious anemia, Sir Adam Beck died at Headley, his London home.

Born in Baden, Canada West, in 1857, Beck entered his father's iron foundry as a youth and later started his own box-making factory. After moving to London, he served as mayor for two years, then as a member of the provincial legislature. But Beck is best known for bringing hydroelectric power to the people of Ontario. He was knighted in 1914. Beck will be buried in Hamilton beside his wife, the late Lady Lillian Beck.

Sir Adam Beck of London, Ontario.

The first Chrysler car is introduced in New York. It features a revolutionary 6-cylinder engine, a replaceable oil filter, and 4-wheel hydraulic brakes.

Buffalo reach new home

Buffalo are rounded up for the trip to Wood Buffalo National Park.

June 1925

ALBERTA – After determining that the deteriorated condition of the range at Buffalo National Park at Wainwright could no longer support the increased animal population, the Department of Dominion Parks and Forest Reserves has transferred surplus plains buffalo to Wood Buffalo National Park, established in 1922 to protect the last herd of wood bison.

The plains buffalo were shipped north from Wainwright to Waterways by railway. From Waterways, the buffalo were transported by scows down the Athabasca and Slave rivers to La Butte and neighboring areas on the west bank of the Slave River. The animals were released in the vast area north and south of Hay Camp that embraces grassy plains and meadows peppered with great reaches of abundant forest. Some of the buffalo crossed the Peace River and headed south.

Mine workers form a Canadian union

June 1, 1925

BLAIRMORE, Alta. – A convention of provincial mining delegates today announced the formal inauguration of the Mine Workers' Union of Canada. The new union, created largely out of growing dissatisfaction with the representation provided by the British-based United Mine Workers, presents Canadian miners with the option of being represented by a Canada-only organization.

Members of the Communist party, the convention's organizers, were quick to note that the new union is not a uniquely communist organization, but rather a conglomeration of groups united in opposition to the UMW's stance on issues such as wages. The new union, likely to be a success due to its Canada-only makeup, plans its first convention in September.

British commander now an Indian chief

July 10, 1925

CALGARY – Earl Haig, the British Empire's military commander-in-chief during the final years of the Great War, has become an Indian chief. Big Plume of the local Sarcee tribe did the honors today assisted by Buffalo Child Long Lance, a Great War veteran himself. Long Lance translated Chief Big Plume's words from Sarcee into English for thousands of onlookers.

Several long-standing acquaintances of the highly successful western Canadian writer expressed genuine surprise at their friend's ability to understand Sarcee, a difficult tongue. Yet this Indian writer, who now identifies himself as a Blackfoot, is full of surprises. Sources remember that only six years ago, when he first came to Calgary, he claimed to be a Cherokee Indian from Oklahoma!

Tories win most seats in federal vote

But will they form the next government?

Oct. 29, 1925

NORTH YORK, Ont. – Surprise is the key emotion here at the headquarters of Prime Minister W.L. Mackenzie King, now that the election results are in. Instead of winning a majority, the Liberals have been cut down from 117 to 101 seats. The Conservatives have risen from 50 to 116, giving them the largest number of MPs. The Progressives, who hold the balance of power, have tumbled from 64 to just 24 seats.

Adding to the shock is King's loss of his North York seat by a mere 494 votes to Conservative T. Herbert Lennox, an old-style municipal politician of the "kissing babies" school. King commented about his defeat: "To be beaten by Lennox is more a reflection on the people than myself – it reveals what money and whisky can do."

King is not expected to step down as prime minister. Instead, some Liberal in a "safe seat" will give up his riding to King. Still, this personal defeat and the loss in the nation overall have seriously compromised his leadership. Although a number of Liberals are confident that, in the short term at least, enough Progressives will support them, their situation as a minority government would be precarious.

King is staying on as prime minister

Oct. 29, 1925

OTTAWA – Although the Liberals lack a clear majority in the House of Commons, or even the status of largest minority party, which is held by the opposition Conservatives, W.L. Mackenzie King has decided to stay on as prime minister. It's a sticky situation with no constitutional precedent. In theory, since the Tories under Arthur Meighen hold the most seats, they should be allowed to rule. But the third-party Progressives are likely to support the Liberals, giving them a functional majority.

Flue-cured tobacco grown with success

1925

LEAMINGTON, Ont. – After years of experimenting, the first successful crop of flue-cured tobacco has been grown in the Lake Erie area. The success could be a springboard to further production in sandy soils beside the lake.

The push to develop flue-cured tobacco here was led by two North Carolina brothers, William and Francis Gregory, who immigrated to the Leamington area early this century. Working for Empire Tobacco Co., William started to experiment with planting Virginia tobacco. Only burley tobacco was being grown here then. His work was augmented by U.S. farmers who came to teach better methods.

Wild camel sighting recalls past glory

1925

KAMLOOPS, B.C. – Memories of the exciting days of the Barkerville gold rush and the Cariboo Road have been revived by the report that a camel has been seen in the bush. Camels were imported as pack animals in 1862 but worked for only a year or so. Their feet were cut by the sharp rocks and they frightened other pack animals, so they were turned loose or sold. The last of the original camels died on a ranch in 1905.

The Cunard Shipping Line tries to make all passengers happy.

Special trains bring education to children isolated in the bush

1925

ONTARIO – The government of Ontario will not only continue but expand its imaginative scheme to bring education to children isolated in the bush. Because they cannot travel to rural schools, students are seeing the classrooms come to them on special trains. Three railroads have donated cars turned into one-room rolling schoolhouses including living quarters for teachers. Eventually there will be seven of these school cars, each serving a different part of the north. Among the first of the teachers, and the only man-and-wife team, were the Bells, with their two children.

Florence Bell recalls the early days of the project: "On our line, we'd make a stop for a week and then move on, leaving five weeks of homework for the children of trappers, prospectors, lumber workers and railwaymen. In the beginning, we had some stops for only a couple of students, but eventually we were teaching 60 students along the line – with 28 different languages between them. All our early fears on the difficulties of the young ones to learn, and to handle the homework with little if any help from the parents, were groundless." At the end of the first year, a school inspector said of the roving rooms: "They're better than my best rural school and as good as any urban one."

These children attend classes in a railway car in a remote area of Ontario.

CNR's oil-electric car in Vancouver after a record-setting trip

Nov. 4, 1925

VANCOUVER – Canadian National Railways' oil-electric car arrived at the station here this morning after a record-setting 67-hour trip from Montreal. The time established a world record for the transcontinental trip, the longest non-stop train voyage made by an engine, which was never shut down during the journey. The train averaged 70 kilometres an hour.

The oil-burning engine operates an electric generator that provides power to the wheels. The car, which is 18 metres long and will hold 57 passengers, will be put in service in British Columbia. A similar car has been in service between Hamilton and Guelph for the last month. CNR officials who made the trip in the car speculated that it might mark the beginning of a new power source to replace the steam engine.

Many Jewish immigrants settle in western Canada

Jewish farm girls in Saskatchewan.

This group of 350 Jewish immigrants has just arrived at the port of Halifax on board the SS Asia.

Farm community dispels long-held theory

1925

EDENBRIDGE, Sask. – This tiny Jewish farm community goes a long way toward disproving the widespread and prejudicial view that Jews make poor farmers or, indeed, do not farm at all. Two-thirds of Canada's Jews live in metropolitan areas, giving popular credence to recent discriminatory immigration policies against Jews by a federal government eager for farmers. But at Edenbridge, in less than 25 years, Jews have established one of the more stable farm communities in Saskatchewan, one of many successes largely ignored.

Most of the settlers at Edenbridge emigrated from Lithuania, England, Poland, Russia, and Galicia, many because of religious persecution, some – particularly those from London – to escape the urban squalor they found repulsive. They were not the ideal pioneers. Most were blacksmiths, tailors, pedlars, storekeepers, butchers, or unskilled laborers who knew little about farming. But with perseverance and courage, by 1923 they enjoyed great prosperity. Numbering more than 200 men, women, and children, the net value of their labors equalled the substantial amount of $256,004.

W.B. Cohen builds a log and sod stable on his farm in Lipton, Saskatchewan.

These Jewish orphan boys are also looking for new homes.

The Cohens of Edenbridge, Saskatchewan, have developed their farm and erected several buildings on it – some of sod and others of logs.

1926

London, Jan. 27. Engineer John Logie Baird demonstrates transmission of moving pictures by wireless, a process he calls "television."

New York, Feb. 18. Prohibition enforcement officers find 138 cases of champagne hidden under a shipment of P.E.I. potatoes. Canadian potatoes will now be suspect, as is already the case with other goods.

Banff, Alta., April 7. Townspeople and railway workers save the Banff Springs Hotel, one of the largest resorts of its kind in the world, from a potentially disastrous fire.

Ottawa, June 14. The Supreme Court rules that peaceful picketing in the course of a strike is a criminal offence.

Northwest Territories, July 19. The Arctic Island Preserve, encompassing the Arctic Archipelago, is created to preserve game.

Nova Scotia, Aug. 10. The schooner *Sylvia Mosher*, high liner of the Lunenburg fleet, runs aground on the north side of Sable Island.

Cranbrook, B.C., Sept. 19. Searchers capture Charlie Ed, the last of five escaped circus elephants still free. He has been free for about six weeks.

Ontario, Dec. 1. Voters re-elect Tory Premier George Howard Ferguson, giving him a mandate to introduce government control of liquor sales in place of prohibition.

Toronto, Dec. 4. Ottawa Senators beat the University of Toronto 10-7 for the Grey Cup.

Northwestern Ontario, Dec. 27. H.A. "Doc" Oaks, a bush flying pioneer, flies supplies from Hudson to Narrow Lake for Bathurst Mines.

Ottawa. The Senate defeats a bill passed in the House by the Liberal government and two Labour MPs that would have provided for means tested old age pensions at age 70.

Charlottetown. The legislature passes its first general marriage act, containing marriage regulations. Parental consent is required until age 21, and divorce is almost impossible.

Winnipeg. Grain merchant James A. Richardson forms Western Canada Airways [Canadian Airways].

Montreal. Montreal Maroons beat the Victoria Cougars three games to one for the Stanley Cup.

Fire rages through Château Frontenac

Jan. 14, 1926

QUEBEC CITY – Fire that raged for more than five hours tonight through the illustrious Château Frontenac hotel has caused an estimated $2 million damage. Five firemen and one guest were treated in hospital for minor injuries and smoke inhalation. Most damage was in the older portion of the castle-like hotel, in the wing overlooking the St. Lawrence. The new portion in the central tower suffered only smoke and water damage.

Cause of the blaze has not yet been established, and the efforts of the city's fire-fighting force were hampered by a strong wind. All guests were evacuated and spent the night in a special CPR train.

Windows of the Château Frontenac are illuminated by the raging fire inside.

B.C. Indian chiefs hope to see the king

June 22, 1926

LONDON, England – Three Indian chiefs from the Kamloops area in southern British Columbia have come to lay their grievances before King George V, if he will see them. One of the three men, Chief William Pierish, is a veteran of the Great War. He lost an arm in the bloody battle of Cambrai. Accompanying the three men is Mrs. Charles Williams, the daughter of one of the chiefs. Mrs. Williams, who has attended mission school, speaks English and is acting as the interpreter for the group.

Without any success, the chiefs came last year as well to try to meet the king and to explain their claim to large tracts of land in B.C. Indians on the British Columbia mainland, apart from those in the northeastern corner of the province who entered Treaty 8 in 1899, have never signed a treaty. The provincial government has adamantly, for over a half-century, denied the Indians have any land rights in B.C.

Art Gallery receives a Thomson painting

Feb. 10, 1926

TORONTO – *West Wind,* a painting by Tom Thomson, was today presented to the Art Gallery by the Canadian Club of Toronto. The painting, it is hoped, will be the foundation of a magnificent collection of Canadian work at the Art Gallery. Dr. George H. Locke, a past president of the Canadian Club, described it as "shot through with Canadian atmosphere."

Coal deal to help unemployed miners

Jan. 25, 1926

OTTAWA – The government-owned Canadian National Railways will buy 120,000 tons of coal from Cape Breton this year to provide unemployed miners there with work. The news came in the House of Commons today, after numerous speeches on the plight of the Nova Scotia miners. Thousands are unemployed and facing starvation.

The government will also "pay the freight" to ship an additional 15,000 tons of coal to Montreal on the CNR, at $1 a ton. Still, this is only a temporary solution, in a country where alternatives such as electricity have cut the demand for Canadian coal by 25 million tons.

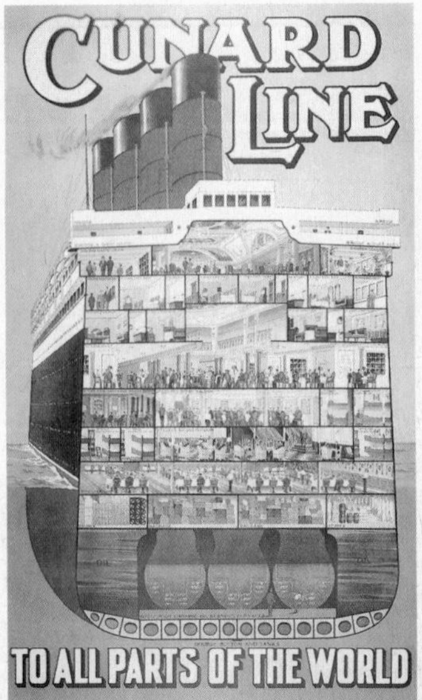

Cunard Line ships offer luxurious accommodation for world travel.

Red Lake the scene of latest gold rush

Feb. 7, 1926

RED LAKE, Ont. – Gold fever has seized this region of northwestern Ontario, creating an atmosphere reminiscent of the Klondike days. As soon as the outside world learned gold was discovered here, men headed north as soon as possible. In their wake, they brought money, a need for food, equipment, and some of the seamier pleasures of life. The result has been to turn formerly isolated trading posts into bustling communities, despite the difficulties involved in getting here. The nearest railway line is 225 kilometres away, which means the only way in is by dog sled or, more recently, by gas-powered tractor.

New technique used to smash icebergs

July 23, 1926

MONTREAL – The iceberg-buster is back after a successful mission. Dr. Howard T. Barnes of McGill University is back from Newfoundland, where he applied his technique to explode icebergs and remove the gigantic hazards from shipping lanes.

Barnes and his crew use the powerful combustive chemical thermite to do the job. In one case they scaled an iceberg 150 metres long and planted a charge. "Intense heat is rapidly developed, the thermite becoming a seething mass of 5,000 degrees Fahrenheit, cracking the ice as a flame will crack annealed glass, and causing it to explode," Dr. Barnes explained.

King's Liberal government collapses

June 29, 1926

OTTAWA – History is being made here today, following the collapse of Progressive support for Prime Minister W.L. Mackenzie King's government, itself a direct result of widespread corruption in the Customs Department. Adding to the drama is the fact that Gov. Gen. Baron Byng refuses to allow the prime minister to dissolve Parliament and call another election so soon after the last one.

Byng will probably exercise his right to ask opposition leader Arthur Meighen to form a Conservative government, sparing the country the expense of another contest. In fact, Meighen has met with Byng, and sources say he has agreed to assume power. But nationally conscious Canadians are unhappy that the British-appointed Byng is invoking a procedure seen here as outdated and inappropriate.

Whatever happens has to happen soon. At present, Canada is essentially without a government – this afternoon in the House, King tendered his government's resignation. If Meighen agrees to replace him, observers foresee major problems. One major concern is that Meighen, having been appointed without the approval of the electorate, would be prevented by parliamentary tradition from sitting in the House without being re-elected in his own riding. More importantly, it is far from certain that the third party Progressives under Robert Forke will support Meighen.

Prime Minister Mackenzie King.

Willingdon named governor general

Viscount and Lady Willingdon.

Aug. 5, 1926

OTTAWA – The appointment of Viscount Willingdon to succeed retiring Gov. Gen. Baron Byng is causing sighs of relief in Ottawa. Indeed, many politicians wish Byng had left earlier this year, instead of playing a pivotal role in the constitutional crisis that gripped Canada in June. Byng refused to allow then-prime minister W.L. Mackenzie King to dissolve Parliament, resulting in the three-day government of Conservative Arthur Meighen and an election this fall.

Meighen defeated on non-confidence vote

July 2, 1926

OTTAWA – Arthur Meighen, sworn in as prime minister Tuesday, was defeated today in the House of Commons on a non-confidence vote by a margin of 96-95. His three days in office ties the 1858 Brown-Dorion government's record for the shortest term of any Canadian government to date.

Meighen's defeat came over a Liberal motion aimed at forcing five cabinet members to respect parliamentary tradition; namely, that new ministers about to receive privileges and payment from the Crown must seek immediate re-election to assure public support for their appointments. With the support of 13 Progressives, the motion squeaked through. With it came the defeat of Meighen's short-lived Conservative government. As he had time to announce the dissolution of Parliament before his defeat, an election is assured.

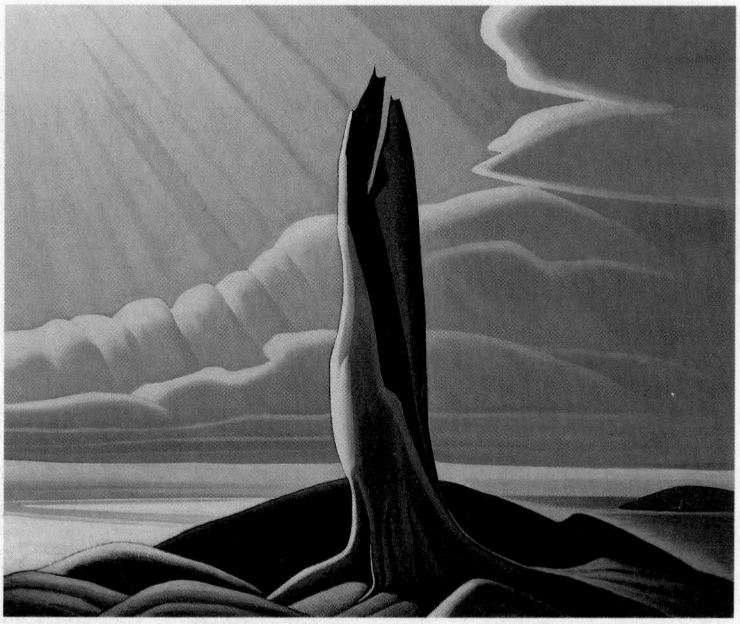

North Shore, Lake Superior, by Group of Seven artist Lawren S. Harris.

Three-day Wonder names his cabinet

July 13, 1926

OTTAWA – Although he is technically the leader of a defeated government, Prime Minister Arthur Meighen is still in charge – at least until an election is held this fall. So, in a move designed to win votes, the "Three-day Wonder" – referring to his short-term in office before being defeated on a non-confidence vote – has put together a new cabinet aimed at impressing both the Maritimes and Ontario, where he needs votes.

Bad booze blamed as unlucky 13 die

July 26, 1926

TORONTO – Thirteen people are dead and another is in critical condition in a tragedy that police think is the result of drinking wood alcohol. Bert D'Angelo of Hamilton has been arrested on a charge of manslaughter. A second man, William Maybee of Oakville, was arrested Saturday morning in a probe of the incident, but he became ill and died, it is believed of wood alcohol poisoning. Two victims are from Toronto, three from Allanburg near St. Catharines, and four each from Hamilton and Oakville.

King leads Liberals to victory at the polls

King campaigns in Victoria, B.C.

Sept. 14, 1926

OTTAWA – William Lyon Mackenzie King has won what many said was unwinnable: 128 seats in the House of Commons versus the Tories' 91. He's still in a minority, but as he only needs the support of six of the 11 Progressives for a majority, a Liberal government in Ottawa seems assured.

The victory is a master stroke for King, who turned the campaign from an exposé of Liberal toleration of Customs Department corruption into a fight over Canada's independence. He said former governor general Baron Byng's refusal to let him dissolve Parliament denied Canada's independent status.

KKK members guilty in church explosion

Oct. 14, 1926

BARRIE, Ont. – William Skelly, a member of the racist Ku Klux Klan, has been convicted of causing an explosion at St. Mary's Roman Catholic church here on June 10. In addition, KKK official Clare Lee was found guilty of helping to put explosives in the church and being a principal in the crime. According to testimony, Skelly was chosen by lot to dynamite a Catholic site on June 9. Damage to St. Mary's was extensive.

Lawyer's will signals start of Stork Derby

December 1926

TORONTO – Lawyer Charles Vance Millar, well known for his love of sports and practical jokes, has left behind his biggest prank of all by creating the Stork Derby. The bachelor's will bequeaths the bulk of his large estate to the Toronto woman who produces the most children in the decade following his death. The will also stipulates that if two or more women tie for first place, the money is to be divided equally among them.

Massey appointed first foreign diplomat

Vincent Massey gets prestigious post.

Nov. 26, 1926

OTTAWA – Canada has achieved a new level of political independence with the appointment to Washington of its first foreign diplomat, Vincent Massey, a former Liberal cabinet minister. England too is pleased at the initiative.

Massey will essentially be Canada's ambassador to the United States. The Liberals argue that he is eminently suited for the position, both from his experience as president of the Massey-Harris Co. and his work with the federal government at the end of the Great War. Others suspect his appointment is a political reward after his defeat in the last federal election.

Balfour Report adopted

Ernest Lapointe, Prime Minister King, Vincent Massey, and Peter Larkin.

Nov. 19, 1926

LONDON, England – Canada will soon be legally equal to Britain. This momentous news, in the form of a statement of policy, is the result of the adoption of the report by British cabinet minister and former prime minister Lord Balfour, which has been the subject of debate by the Premiers' Committee of the Imperial Conference here in London. The committee is just what the name implies: a body made up of prime ministers from around the empire – or commonwealth, to use its new name – including Canada's William Lyon Mackenzie King.

In backing Balfour's recommendations as to the future relations between Britain and her former colonies, the premiers have allowed dominions such as Canada, Australia, New Zealand, South Africa, and the Irish Free State to legally mature into full nationhood. The text of the Balfour Report puts it best: "They are autonomous Communities within the British Empire, equal in status, in no way subordinate one to another in any aspect of their domestic or external affairs, though united by a common allegiance to the Crown, and freely associated as members of the British Commonwealth of Nations."

One result of this is that the governor general will no longer be the representative of the British government in Canada. Instead, he will represent the king directly, leaving all matters of state to the elected Parliament.

Blow proves to be fatal for Harry Houdini

Harry Houdini, master escape artist.

Oct. 31, 1926

DETROIT – Harry Houdini, the magician who made a career of defying death, succumbed today to a ruptured spleen, the result of a punch a McGill student threw a week ago at the Princess Theatre in Montreal. Two students asked Houdini if it was true he could shrug off body blows. Houdini said yes, but before he could brace himself, the fatal blow was dealt.

Houdini had perfected such feats as escaping from locked underwater boxes while handcuffed.

The Roaring Twenties: footloose and fancy free

Travel and taste take on new meaning

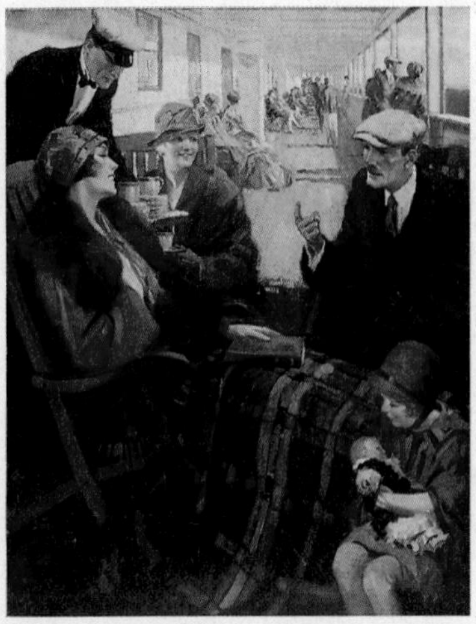

Tourism flourishes: Cunard advertises rates for sailing to Europe.

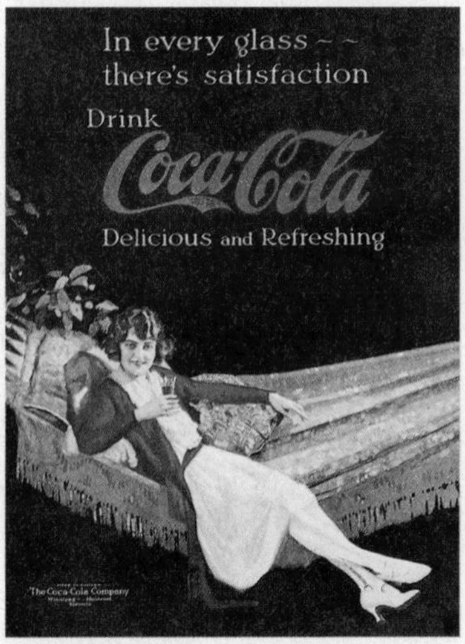

Maclean's magazine touts Coke.

1926

CANADA – Cunard crossings, Coca-Cola and the car craze – what perfect symbols of the effervescence of our liberated, new age!

The end of the Great War has hastened the racier lifestyle of so many middle-class urbanites – but not country dwellers – with spread refrigerators and vacuum cleaners, electricity and running water, and the greater disposable income of post-war prosperity. Younger Canadians, especially females, have rejected the constraints of their parents' generation. Women, too, can now earn money, drink, smoke, and even drive wonderful cars.

The car culture has revolutionized Canada. More than 75,200 kilometres of road are now paved, so people flock to the once-far countryside, visiting further and further afield. Car-related businesses are springing up. Tourism, a byproduct, is also booming, as the freedom of cars replaces rigid railway travel.

Tourism even spills out over national boundaries – if vast Canada can be ours, why not Europe? For a price more and more can afford, Cunard echoes: why not?

One danger in Canada's Roaring Twenties is that Americanization will swamp its national character. It's a troublesome notion, all right, perhaps one to reflect on as we sip our next Coke.

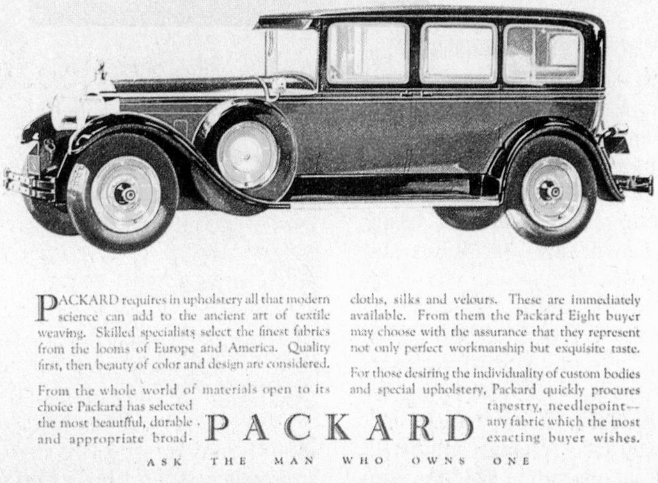
PACKARD requires in upholstery all that modern science can add to the ancient art of textile weaving. Skilled specialists select the finest fabrics from the looms of Europe and America. Quality first, then beauty of color and design are considered.
From the whole world of materials open to its choice Packard has selected the most beautiful, durable and appropriate broad-cloths, silks and velours. These are immediately available. From them the Packard Eight buyer may choose with the assurance that they represent not only perfect workmanship but exquisite taste.
For those desiring the individuality of custom bodies and special upholstery, Packard quickly procures tapestry, needlepoint— any fabric which the most exacting buyer wishes.
PACKARD
ASK THE MAN WHO OWNS ONE

Cars usher in a new era of travel, free from confines of the railways.

Flapper style is the latest fashion craze

Sleek new dresses assert women's equality by forsaking frills and furbelows.

1926

CANADA – What's slender, long-waisted, flat-chested, leggy, crop-haired, and red of cheek and lip? The young Canadian flapper, that's what – and sometimes her older, forward-looking sisters.

Since folding away the last flared skirt of the Great War, women have asserted their equality in dress and deed. Going, going, gone are the breathless rigors of the corset – today's woman binds her breasts and belts her hips, so her silhouette is now like her brother's, when he was a boy. Gone are the frilly white collar, the 17 metres of full and long skirt plus its army of underclothes, the fancy pompadours and millinery confections pinned atop them, scrubbed faces and God-given eyebrows.

Today's Canadian woman wears a short, straight, untrimmed dress over minimal undies. She shingles and bobs her hair into a sleek helmet she hides under the cloche hat pulled down over her plucked and pencilled eyebrows. She paints her lips and rouges her cheeks, bares her arms and rolls her flesh-colored silk stockings nearly down to her knees. She strides about on high heels, her cigarettes, holder, car keys, face powder, and money safe in the handbag she clutches in kid gloves. Her sisters made the ammunition that won the Great War, and also the vote. She's equal to her men, and has the look to prove it.

1927

Prince Edward Island, Feb. 7. Bernard and George Leslie kill a black bear near Souria Line Road, one of the Island's last.

Ottawa, April 14. Ottawa Senators defeat Boston to win the Stanley Cup.

Canada, July 1. A coast-to-coast radio network is improvised, involving 23 stations, to carry the celebrations for the Diamond Jubilee of Confederation at Ottawa.

Nova Scotia, Aug. 24. The "August Gale" claims five schooners and 100 fishermen at Sable Island.

Geneva, Sept. 15. Canada is elected to a non-permanent seat on the Council of the League of Nations.

Toronto, Sept. 21. A special committee appointed to study the province's bilingual schools recommends restoring separate schools because of the failures of the current system.

Winnipeg, Oct. 9. Three Mennonite families, the vanguard of a colony of 900, return to western Canada after leaving nine years ago for South America.

Winnipeg, Oct. 12. Conservatives choose R.B. Bennett to succeed Arthur Meighen as federal leader at a convention.

Toronto, Nov. 26. Toronto Balmy Beach beat the Hamilton Tigers 9-6 to capture the Grey Cup.

Ottawa, Dec. 7. Southam Publishing Co. is incorporated to consolidate the various publishing interests controlled by the Southam family.

Montreal, Dec. 12. University of Montreal receives a papal bull decreeing its autonomy from Laval University.

Toronto. Edward, Prince of Wales, opens Union Station, noted for the influence of beaux-arts style in its design.

Ottawa. Section 141 of the Indian Act prohibits Indian bands from using band funds to pursue land claims.

Canada. A national men's curling championship is inaugurated, sponsored by W.D. Macdonald Co., for a trophy called the Macdonald Brier Tankard.

Ottawa. Homogenized milk is sold successfully for the first time in North America.

Toronto. Hamilton Tire and Rubber Ltd. is incorporated and renamed Canadian Tire Corp. Ltd.

Privy Council awards Labrador to Nfld.

March 2, 1927

LONDON, England – A 25-year dispute over the international boundary between Canada and the British dominion of Newfoundland has been settled in the latter's favor. The disputed land is Labrador, claimed both by Quebec and Newfoundland. Now, after five years of deliberation, the Judicial Committee of the Privy Council has decided the issue.

At the heart of it all was the definition of the word "coast," which, in a document dated 1763, was transferred to Newfoundland. Canada argued coast meant one mile from the shore, while Newfoundland claimed all lands with rivers flowing to the sea.

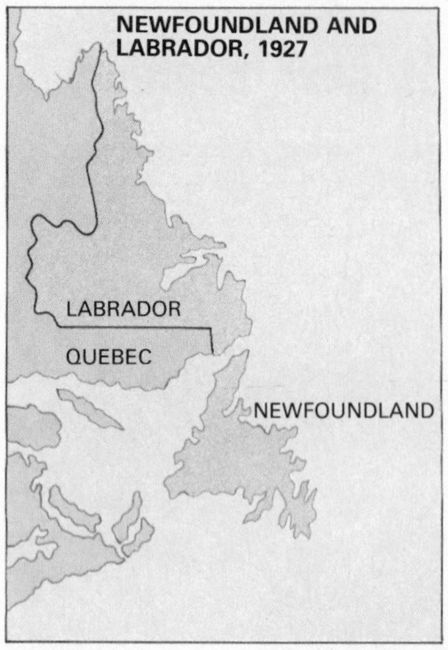

Newfoundland wins Labrador.

Ontario to control the sale of liquor

March 30, 1927

TORONTO – Conservative Premier George Howard Ferguson has got his way: liquor is going to be offered for sale once more in Ontario, through stores controlled by the government. The reintroduction of liquor sales follows Ferguson's recent re-election on a platform to change the Ontario Temperance Act to put bootleggers out of business and protect the public from booze. Under the system, people who want to buy alcohol must purchase a government permit and be over 21. Municipalities which have voted themselves "dry" will not have to allow liquor sales.

Neither rain, nor sleet, nor snow...

April 8, 1927

EDMONTON – Eight weeks is record time for the mail to move from Aklavik to Edmonton. That's a week ahead of schedule. This is no mean feat considering the first 2,576 kilometres of the trip are by dog sled and that initially time was lost due to difficult travelling conditions. From Fort McMurray to Edmonton the mail rides the Alberta and Great Waterways Railway. This will be the last mail of the season. Delivery will resume after freeze-up next fall.

Canadian inventor patents AC radio

1927

TORONTO – Edward Samuel Rogers has received a patent on his new alternating-current (AC) radio tube, an invention which does away with the need for batteries. Until Rogers' invention, re-chargeable acid-filled batteries were necessary to operate home radio receivers. Rogers' invention enables the construction of radios that can be plugged into an electrical outlet in a home, turned on, tuned in, and listened to. Rogers, 27, of Toronto, has always loved radio. At age 13, one of his radios was judged best amateur-built in Ontario.

Fire causes stampede; 76 children killed

Jan. 9, 1927

MONTREAL – The bodies of 76 boys and girls, many as yet not identified, lie in the morgue tonight after a minor fire set off a panic-stricken stampede this afternoon in the Laurier Palace Theatre. There are scores of other children and a few adults being treated for scars, burns, and shock in four hospitals, and the death toll is expected to climb during the night. Witnesses say the alarm was sounded by an usher who spotted smoke curling from under the balcony. Scores of children were stampeding down one of the two staircases when several in the front ranks tripped, fell, and caused a massive, screaming pileup only steps from safety.

Young pockets $25,000 for channel swim

Jan. 16, 1927

WILMINGTON, Calif. – Seventeen-year-old Toronto swimmer George Young stepped ashore on California mainland $25,000 richer early this morning, becoming the first person to swim the 35-kilometre San Pedro Channel. Young beat 95 of the top swimmers in the world to claim the prize put up by William Wrigley Jr. He was the only swimmer to finish the race.

Young, the Canadian amateur champion, covered the distance separating Santa Catalina Island and the mainland in 15 hours and 45 minutes, arriving at 3:06 a.m. He changed course five times to counteract the tide. One-third of the way across, he had to swim through an oil slick, and 90 metres from the finish he stroked through large seaweeds. Young's mother, a widow, had given him $135 to get to California for the race and told her son not to fail.

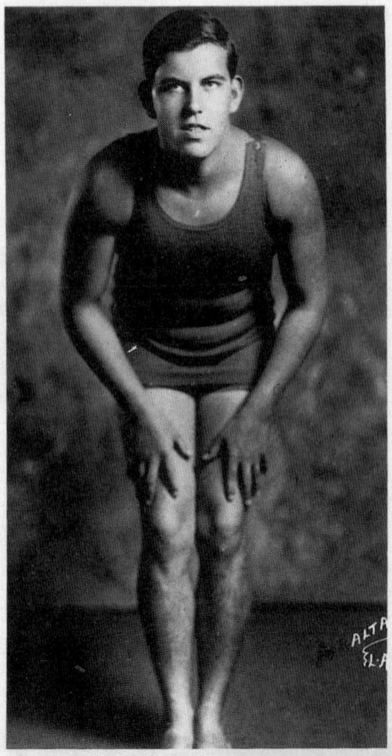

Toronto swimmer George Young.

Report rejects B.C. Indian land claims

April 9, 1927

OTTAWA – A special joint committee of the Senate and the House of Commons has rejected the claim by a group of British Columbia Indians that they retain title to most of the land in the province. The claim was presented by the Allied Indian Tribes of B.C. and its leaders, Andrew Paull and Peter Kelly. It dates back at least to 1913 when the Nishga Indians of the Nass River area sent a petition to Ottawa asserting that they had never given up title to their land.

The Allied Tribes, a political alliance formed in 1916, took up the issue, arguing that the government had no authority to make decisions about land in B.C. without first negotiating with the natives. The Allied Tribes hoped to obtain a hearing before the Judicial Committee of the Privy Council in London, but instead the parliamentary committee was set up last year to examine the claim.

In its report issued today, the committee states categorically that the Indians "have not established any claim to the lands of British Columbia based on aboriginal or other title," and concludes that "the matter should now be regarded as finally closed."

Though impressed with the testimony of Paull and Kelly, the committee says the Indians were manipulated by their white advisers. The report does recommend that $10,000 a year be spent in B.C. for the benefit of the Indians, in lieu of money they would have received if treaties had been signed in B.C. as they were elsewhere in western Canada. The committee's decision is a serious blow to the land claims movement in the province.

West coast Indian woman.

Mazo de la Roche's Jalna is published

1927

ONTARIO – *Jalna*, the latest book by Mazo de la Roche, is a riveting account of Ontario's country gentry. The Whiteoaks live at Jalna, a rural estate that has lost some of its former glory. With his parents dead, Renny Whiteoak leads a family which includes his brothers and sister, his domineering 99-year-old grandmother, Adeline, and other assorted characters. Renny's sister Meg is a reclusive spinster, their half-brother Eden a poetic dreamer, and his brother, Piers, a plodder.

The romantic entanglements and personal crises of Whiteoak family members shape the plot. Renny, for example, has never married, though he has had numerous liaisons. Meg broke her engagement to a neighbor, Maurice Vaughan, after learning he had fathered a child, Pheasant. As a young woman, Pheasant gets involved with Piers Whiteoak, Meg's half-brother. The family saga is set against a backdrop of British imperialist sensibilities. The Whiteoaks have no doubt the English way of life is far superior to the American. This is most clearly illustrated in their reaction to Eden's new American wife.

Miss de la Roche, who published *Possession* in 1923 and *Delight* last year, draws heavily on her own observations. Although born in Toronto, she spent many years near the city on a farm near Bronte and in a cottage on a rural estate near Clarkson.

Novelist Mazo de la Roche.

Typhoid epidemic linked to milkman

April 22, 1927

MONTREAL – A man who remained a carrier of typhoid fever for more than 20 years is the only source authorities have been able to uncover in the epidemic that began March 4 and lasted for more than a month. There were 2,415 cases of typhoid fever reported; 189 lives have been lost.

The man had applied for and got a job in a local dairy. He was fired as soon as it was learned he was a carrier. The facts have been given to the United States consul to be forwarded to Washington in the hope there will be a speedy lifting of the U.S. embargo on milk produced in Montreal and the surrounding district. A new metropolitan health commission is under consideration.

Prohibition platform lifts P.E.I. Liberals

May 26, 1927

CHARLOTTETOWN – The Island's on-again, off-again temperance law is on again. The oft-amended and contested temperance legislation was at centre stage in the recent provincial election. Conservative Premier James D. Stewart wanted to scrap the law. Liberal Albert C. Saunders countered with a promise of stricter enforcement, and bolstered his campaign with a number of powerful church and temperance groups. The result? A landslide for the Liberals. Going into the election with four members, they captured 24 of 30 seats. Despite the win, Saunders hopes to hold a plebiscite on continued prohibition for Prince Edward Island.

Sea serpents blamed for scarcity of fish

April 26, 1927

VANCOUVER – Two sea serpents, nine metres long, are driving the fish away from Howe Sound, about 80 kilometres west of here. Both residents and visiting fishermen say the sea serpents are making fishing off Gibson's Landing impossible. Frederick Parnell of Vancouver says he was fishing from a rowboat off Gibson's Landing when the sea serpents broke surface nearby. Their heads were two feet wide with a huge mouth and bulging eyes. Parnell said he was too frightened to move at first, but then called out to his brother on shore. The sea serpents vanished immediately.

New national park established to preserve forests and wildlife

May 9, 1927

OTTAWA – Charles Stewart, minister of the interior, announced today the establishment of Prince Albert National Park, created for the purpose of preserving in perpetuity a portion of primitive forest and lake country of northern Saskatchewan. The southern border of the park lies 50 kilometres north of the city of Prince Albert. The park lies in Prime Minister W.L. Mackenzie King's riding of Prince Albert, where he was elected in 1926.

Prince Albert National Park takes in 3,874 square kilometres of boreal forest and prairie grassland. The park contains many interesting glacial features, and is inhabited by elk, moose, deer, wolves, caribou, badgers, and beavers. More than 195 species of birds have been identified, including white pelicans and double-crested cormorants.

Noted poet, patriot Charles Mair dies

July 7, 1927

VICTORIA, B.C. – Charles Mair, writer, civil servant, and ardent nationalist, has died in Jubilee Hospital here. He was 90. His death will be the signal for a battle between those who believe he was Canada's first poet and those who say he was a dangerous rabble-rouser. Mair was a member of a group called Canada First and represented Upper Canadian contempt for Métis claims in the Red River colony. He went there in 1869 and was jailed, but escaped.

New variable-pitch propeller is tested

June 6, 1927

CAMP BORDEN, Ont. – A variable-pitch aircraft propeller developed by a Canadian engineer underwent successful flight testing today. Wallace Rupert Turnbull's invention is more efficient than the fixed-pitch propeller because it enables pilots to select a pitch most appropriate for each phase of flight.

Flight Lieut. G.G. Brookes piloted the Avro biplane on which Turnbull's propeller was mounted. A small electric motor enables the pilot to vary the pitch of the propeller blades.

Pensions planned for senior citizens

September 1927

OTTAWA – Many of Canada's senior citizens have something to smile about these days. For the first time, the federal government has entered the field of social welfare on a non-emergency basis, and old-timers are the ones who stand to gain. The federal Old Age Pensions Act was approved by British Columbia this month, and although negotiations are still continuing with Ontario, Quebec, and the Maritimes, the three remaining western provinces are ready to follow suit. The legislation depends on provincial approval because it calls for a 50-50 split on expenditure.

But while the act represents a milestone in government responsibility for health and welfare on a continuing basis, it is less comprehensive than many wish. Pension recipients must be British subjects over the age of 70, residents of Canada for at least 20 years, and must have an annual income of less than $125 from all sources to be eligible for the $20 per month pension payment. Worst is last – on decease, a recipient's personal assets will be sold to repay the pension plus a five percent compound interest.

Moose Jaw site of Ku Klux Klan rally

Ku Klux Klansmen in their white robes meet for a rally.

June 7, 1927

MOOSE JAW, Sask. – Moose Jaw was the site of the first and largest Konclave of the Ku Klux Klan ever held in Canada. Many citizens see the ultra-conservative, secret fraternal organization as a way of cleaning up the city, River Street in particular. The city has come to have an unsavory reputation due to a number of illegal activities instigated by Chicago gangsters who come up on the Soo Line when they need a place to hide out.

The KKK is promoting Protestantism, racial purity, gentile economic freedom, just laws, separation of church and state, freedom of speech, law and order, higher moral standards, and one public school. The gathering drew people from as far away as Weyburn and Shaunavon. Memberships sell for $13.

Union Jacks hang in Union Station, Ottawa, as preparations are made for the visit of His Royal Highness, the Prince of Wales.

Europeans in west prefer the city life

Sept. 8, 1927

OTTAWA – Canada is going to stop allowing Europeans to immigrate here, the federal government says. The shift in policy comes as a result of complaints from cities in the prairies. Officials there say European immigrants are not staying on their farms – the reason they were allowed into Canada – preferring to move to the city in the hopes of making a good wage. This unexpected "internal immigration" is said to be adding to unemployment problems in the cities. So, to forestall this, Europeans will be kept out of Canada, although settlers applying from the British Isles will still be accepted.

Strangler reaches the end of his rope

Earl Nelson is led away by officials.

1927

WINNIPEG – The Strangler's spree of rape and murder has come to an end. Earl Nelson was captured just north of the U.S. border when he hopped aboard a southbound train and into the arms of the special police posse on his trail.

Nelson was wanted in connection with a series of brutal slayings stretching across the continent from Winnipeg to Santa Barbara. Citizens here were sent into a frenzy of fear when William Patterson of Elmwood discovered his wife's body under the bed. She had been raped and strangled. The killing was soon connected to others and a manhunt was launched. Winnipeg chief detective George Smith, acting on a hunch, chartered a train to track down a vagrant who escaped custody. That fugitive is thought to be the Strangler.

Airmail service is getting off the ground

First load of overseas airmail is ready for flight from Father Point to Ottawa.

Dec. 31, 1927

OTTAWA – This will be remembered as the year airmail service started to take off in Canada. By year's end, a variety of routes opened: Moncton to the Magdalen Islands, Moncton-Charlottetown, Leamington-Pelee Island, Murray Bay-Anticosti Island, and Rolling Port-Red Lake. Many routes have winter service in previously impassable terrain. Others, such as the experimental Rimouski-Montreal-Ottawa route, are designed to speed the delivery of mail brought overseas by ship.

Autos change Canadian life and landscape

Washing automobiles in the Humber River, near Lampton, Ontario.

1927

CANADA – These days at Sunday picnics, chances are that Dad will choose a riverside spot not just idyllic but convenient – for washing the newest family member, the Model T. There are some 400,000 passenger cars in Ontario, and Canada has more than 80,000 kilometres of surfaced roads. The car is changing the Canadian way of life, just as the train did over half a century ago, by creating jobs and an unprecedented boom in tourism.

Alberta limits public travelling privileges to curb the spread of infantile paralysis

Sept. 15, 1927

EDMONTON – In a desperate attempt to curb the epidemic spread of infantile paralysis, a mysterious new disease, provincial legislators in Alberta today restricted public travelling privileges. Children under 18, the main victims of the scourge, must stay within their municipalities until further notice. Guidelines for travel are to be posted across the province.

Infantile paralysis has been raging through Alberta and parts of British Columbia for the past three weeks. Medical authorities in Edmonton, unable to determine the cause of the disease or to prevent its spread, have appealed for help to the health division of New York's Rockefeller Foundation.

With 11 children already dead and 77 quarantined in Edmonton alone, it is unlikely that children will be permitted to return to school on Sept. 18, the date the government had originally set for schools to reopen.

N.W.T. responsible for welfare of Inuit

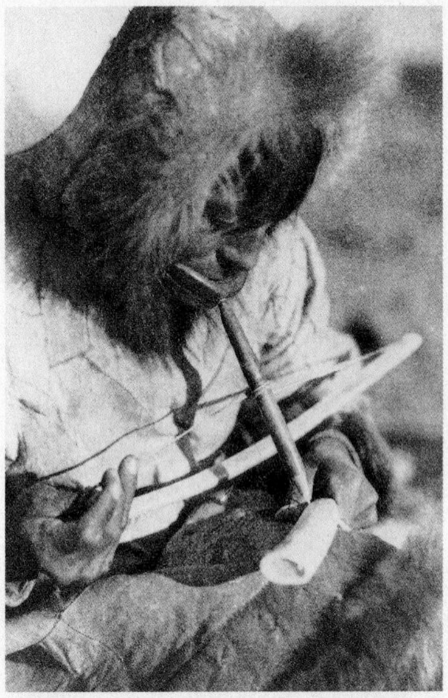

Inuit uses traditional drill for ivory.

Aug. 31, 1927

NORTHWEST TERRITORIES – Confusion over who should look after Inuit welfare has finally been cleared up, as the commissioner of the Northwest Territories was given the responsibility today. The problem is one officials have wrestled with for decades. As recently as 1924, the Indian Department was given charge of Inuit affairs, but the government avoided giving Inuit special status akin to the Indians.

Indeed, the status of the Inuit has still not been cleared up. Legally they are ordinary Canadian citizens. Yet the government, worried by their precarious situation, treats them like children and exercises a control other Canadian citizens would never tolerate.

This 3-cent stamp commemorates the 60th anniversary of Confederation.

1928

Ottawa, March 1. Eileen Vollick is the first Canadian women to get a pilot's licence.

Montreal, March 2. Samuel Bronfman acquires control of Joseph Seagram and Sons Ltd.

Toronto, April 5. De Havilland Aircraft of Canada, Ltd., is incorporated as a sales and service operation of the British parent company.

Montreal, April 14. New York Rangers beat Montreal Maroons three games to two for the Stanley Cup.

Fort Simpson, N.W.T., July 26. The RCMP confirm that an influenza epidemic is decimating Indians from the Mackenzie Delta to northern Alberta.

Quebec, Aug. 20. The attorney general prohibits dog racing in the province.

Vancouver, Sept. 8. Squadron leader A. Earle Godfrey of the RCAF lands after making the first direct mail flight across Canada, flying from Ottawa.

Vancouver, Oct. 20. The talking picture *Mother Knows Best* premieres, one of the first shown in Canada.

Canada, October. The CNR network carries the Thanksgiving Day Service from Westminster Abbey, the first transatlantic radio signal broadcast across Canada.

Hamilton, Dec. 1. Hamilton Tigers beat Regina Roughriders 30-0 for the Grey Cup.

Prairies, Dec. 10. Western Canada Airways begins regular mail, express, and passenger service between Regina, Calgary, and Edmonton.

Toronto. *Carry on Sergeant!* premieres, one of the most expensive silent films ever made in Canada ($500,000).

Ottawa. The government restricts Japanese immigration to 150 persons annually. Japanese in B.C. are denied the vote and entry to professions.

Canada. Maclean Hunter Ltd. launches *Chatelaine*, a women's magazine.

Ottawa. The government sets up a royal commission under Sir John Aird to advise on the future of Canadian broadcasting. Canadian radio broadcasting is in its infancy.

Canada. West coast artist Emily Carr travels to eastern Canada, where she is included in a national exhibition and meets members of the Group of Seven. Their support helps renew her artistic ambition.

Canada strikes gold in Olympic hockey

Feb. 19, 1928

ST. MORITZ – Canada completed a three-game cakewalk to the Olympic hockey gold medal today with an easy 13-0 victory over Switzerland. Coupled with earlier 11-0 and 14-0 wins over Sweden and England, respectively, Canada, represented by University of Toronto Varsity Grads, scored 38 goals and gave up none. Dave Trottier with five goals and Hugh Plaxton with four led today's rout of the Swiss team before 7,000 spectators. In the three games, Plaxton had 10 goals. The outcome was never in doubt and play was good-natured. In fact, in the game against England, even Canadians in the crowd were cheering for Britain.

Savings are pooled in Killam co-operative

1928

KILLAM, Alta. – The Killam Co-operative Association no longer gives credit. It doesn't need to – members of the association can now apply for a loan at the savings and loan department of the Killam Co-operative Store.

The co-operative spirit which has emerged on the prairies is now extending to financial institutions. By pooling their savings, a group of people can then make loans to those in need. The interest received on loans is, in turn, used to pay interest on savings at a lesser rate.

William Halsall, manager of the Killam Co-operative Association, initiated the establishment of the institution. A savings service is also offered. It is operated according to the caisse populaire founded in Quebec by Alphonse Desjardins.

Desjardins studied financial co-operatives in Europe and blended in his own concepts of economic co-operation and mutualism to create a local version that would serve the unique needs of Canadian people. One of Desjardins' goals was to obtain greater economic independence for French-Canadians.

Enraged man's bite worse than his bark

March 25, 1928

MONTREAL – One woman is dead, another woman and a man are injured, and a second man is delirious and in serious condition after an enraged man with infected teeth bit them. Sarah Marcoux died today from infection of the bites she received during a quarrel at a St. Patrick's Day party. Albert Shutes, 56, is in police custody pending an inquest into the woman's death.

Board to determine films kids can see

March 28, 1928

TORONTO – If an amendment to the Theatres and Cinematographs Act becomes law, a special board of censors will classify films suitable for children under 16. Aurelian Belanger, MPP, introduced a bill to amend the act and make it illegal for children under 16 to attend films designated unsuitable. Belanger believes the rise in crimes committed by youths under 20 is directly related to films, especially movies featuring guns. "Parents have a right to look to this legislature for protection against films which work harm to their children," he said.

Heroic pair rescue German plane crew

April 16, 1928

QUEBEC CITY – Two heroic flyers have succeeded in rescuing crewmen of the German airplane *Bremen* who were grounded on a desolate island in the Belle Isle Straits after completing the first ever east-west transatlantic flight.

"Duke" Schiller and Dr. Louis Cuisiner flew the Canadian Transcontinental Airways plane from Sept-Iles to the lonely island in the Canadian north, where the stranded *Bremen* waits for spare parts.

Charles Gorman, world champion speed skater, retires this year. The New Brunswick-born Gorman holds seven world records.

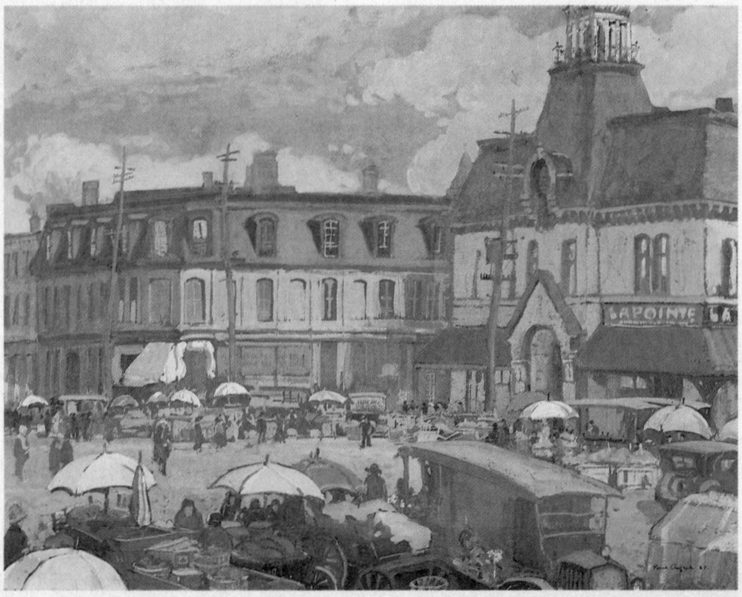

The Byward Market Place in Ottawa as painted by Paul Alfred.

Women not persons: Supreme Court

A non-person keeps house.

April 24, 1928

OTTAWA – Women are not considered persons. That is the unanimous decision of the Supreme Court of Canada. A judgment rendered this morning states that at the time the British North America Act was created in 1867, only "fit and qualified persons" were deemed eligible for appointment to the Senate. The Supreme Court judgment further states "by the common law of England, women were under a legal incapacity to hold public office."

Minister of Justice Ernest Lapointe announced this afternoon the Canadian government would seek to amend the BNA Act to allow women to enter the Senate.

The Supreme Court ruling arises from a petition drafted by five "persons from Alberta" last fall. After eight years of requests from women's organizations to have female senators appointed, no progress had been made.

Five prominent Albertans, Henrietta Muir Edwards, Emily Murphy, Irene Parlby, Nellie McClung, and Louise McKinney, decided to petition the government for a decision from the Supreme Court as to whether women were indeed qualified for the Senate.

Mrs. Edwards is well known for her work with the National Council of Women law committee. Parlby, McClung and McKinney have all served in the Alberta legislature, and Judge Emily Murphy is active in many areas affecting women.

Hofer Brewery sells beer to Americans

1928

LA SALLE, Ont. – The Volstead Act, which turned America "dry," has given this border town in Ontario a new industry. The town's former mayor and innkeeper, Vital Benoit, has opened the Hofer Brewing Co. next to his famed Château La Salle, on the Seven Mile Road from Windsor, to sell beer to the mob in Detroit. Regarded as a giant of the rum-running fraternity, Benoit plans to start producing pure and natural 4.4 percent ale and lager for "exportation."

Ice cream stats: here's the scoop

May 25, 1928

OTTAWA – If every scoop of the 31,316,057 litres of ice cream consumed by Canadians was served as five-cent ice cream cones, each person, on average, would have eaten 43.4 cones last year. Such is the news from the Dairy Branch of the Department of Agriculture. Overall, 45,985 cows were required to satiate Canada's ice cream lust. Still, Canadians are abstemious compared to Americans. Figures show the latter consume, per capita, three times as much ice cream.

Orillia officials itching to rid town of annual mosquito problems

May 4, 1928

ORILLIA, Ont. – Operations have been launched to kill mosquitoes that swarm through Orillia every summer, making outdoor living unbearable for residents. Lowlying swamp lands at the south end of town will be treated with an oily compound guaranteed to destroy mosquito larva and pupa. About 18,000 litres of the oily pesticide will coat every square centimetre of the 240 hectares of swamp land in and around Orillia. The campaign mirrors methods used in Ottawa's anti-mosquito campaign. Officials here hope to enjoy similar success.

Planes are being tested for use in dusting for insect control programs.

Legislative Council is abolished in N.S.

May 31, 1928

HALIFAX – The Legislative Council, a last vestige of colonial control, has been abolished in Nova Scotia. In pioneer days, its members, named by a British-appointed governor, often overruled decisions of a democratically elected Assembly. Now, since the queen's representative is little more than a figurehead, the Legislative Council is essentially a political body without relevance. It is not surprising even its members saw the wisdom in supporting its extinction.

Pilot "Punch" Dickins back from north

Aug. 28, 1928

WINNIPEG – Pioneer bush pilot C.H. "Punch" Dickins flew back into Winnipeg today after a 12-day tour of uncharted, unmapped sections of the Northwest Territories. The purpose of the flight was to determine the working conditions under which geologists and their prospecting parties are forced to work. The trip out followed a route through Churchill, Chesterfield Inlet, Baker Lake, and Lake Athabasca as far as Fort Smith. On the return flight Dickins' course was by way of Reindeer Lake, Lake Kississing, and The Pas.

Flight enthusiasts view the trip as a triumph of organization. It was necessary to have precise measurements of distance in order that Dickins could put down where drums of fuel had been cached. Where radio or telegraph connections made it possible, advance arrangements were made for weather reports.

The lack of ground facilities presented real problems for both pilot and passengers. Every litre of fuel had to be hand-pumped. Dickins' passengers were Col. MacAlpine, president of Dominion Explorers, and journalist R. Pearce.

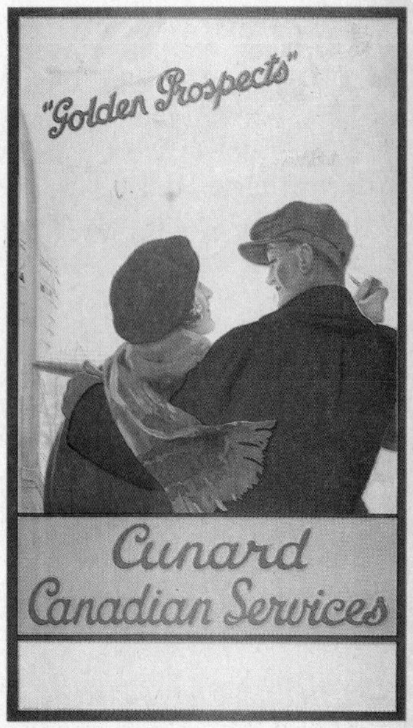

Cunard Canadian Services promotes the glorious future awaiting immigrants to this golden land.

Canadians capture 4 gold medals in Amsterdam

Percy Williams wins gold in the 100-metre sprint. He also captured first place in the 200-metre race.

Ethel Catherwood of Toronto shows her winning style in the high jump.

Aug. 11, 1928

AMSTERDAM – Canadian athletes at the Ninth Olympiad in Amsterdam have outshone past Olympic performances by capturing four gold, four silver, and seven bronze medals. Perhaps the biggest stars of this year's Olympics are the Canadian women, who came out first in overall points with two first-place, two second-place, and one each of third-, fourth-, and fifth-place finishes.

This is the first year women have been admitted to the track and field competition. And it was in track and field that Canadian women won all of their medals. Four Toronto women captured the gold medal in the women's 400-metre relay, beating a world record that they themselves had set only yesterday in the trials. They finished just ahead of the American team with a time of 48.1 seconds. The crack athletes are Fanny Rosenfeld, Ethel Smith, Jane Bell, and their team captain Myrtle Cook. Rosenfeld will also be bringing home a silver for the 100-metre dash, and she came in fifth in the 800 metres. Cook was disqualified in the 100 metres after two false starts.

Fanny "Bobbie" Rosenfeld, lead runner on the women's relay team, holds Canadian records in the running and standing broad jump and in the discus. The 23-year-old was born in Russia.

A gold medal and a world's record were captured by Ethel Catherwood of Toronto in the running high jump. Catherwood's jump of 1.59 metres far exceeded her 17th place showing in the qualifying round. However, she had set a record of 1.6 metres at the Canadian championships in Halifax earlier this year. The 18-year-old "Saskatoon Lily" wrapped herself in a red blanket during the three hours of competition, only taking off her sweatsuit after the bar had reached 1.5 metres.

The Canadian men's team came sixth in the overall standings. Percy Williams of Vancouver put on a brilliant performance winning a gold medal in both the 100-metre and 200-metre sprints. He won the 100 metres with a time of 10.2 seconds, one-tenth of a second short of the world's record. Williams' accomplishments are made all the more impressive by the fact that the 126-pound runner competes with a damaged heart. He suffered from rheumatic fever as a child.

James Ball of Winnipeg brings home a silver for the 400-metre run. Nearing the finish line he glanced behind to check out his competition, an act which some believe cost him first place. Ball also gets a bronze for his part on the 400-metre relay team along with Alexander Wilson of Montreal, Philip Edwards of Hamilton, and Stanley Glover of Edmonton.

The Toronto Argonaut rowing club takes home two medals. Jack Guest and Joseph Wright came in second, five lengths behind the winners in double sculls. The club takes a bronze in the eight-oared shell with coxswain.

The four-member 200-metre freestyle relay swimming team of E. Munro Bourne, James Thompson, Garnet Ault, and Walter Spence, won the bronze.

A silver and three bronze medals were garnered by Canadians in wrestling. Don Stockton of Montreal gets the silver, and bronze goes to Jim Trifunov of Regina, Maurice Letchford of Montreal, and Raymond Smillie.

Ethel Smith (left) and Fanny Rosenfeld (second from left) win the bronze and silver medals, respectively, in the 100-metre race at the Amsterdam Olympics.

Edmonton Commercial Grads win the World Championship in basketball.

"Penny postage" returning for Christmas

Dec. 23, 1928
OTTAWA – Canadians are going to get a Christmas present from the post office this year: the restoration of "penny postage" for letters sent within the British Empire. So, as it was before the Great War, the rate will be two cents per letter. Still, at present 20 million letters are sent from this country, so it's hard to see why a rate cut should be needed. The two-cent service will cost the post office about $200,000 in lost revenue.

Airmail plane crashes just after takeoff

Oct. 23, 1928
CALGARY – The pilot and four passengers on an airmail plane escaped serious injury today when their aircraft crashed shortly after takeoff near Calgary. In an attempt to land the giant de Havilland after difficulties taking off, pilot W.J. Buchanan swerved sharply to avoid automobiles and people, and flew under telephone lines and over a barbed wire fence. The plane broke into flames on impact. The plane was the first to establish a regular airmail and passenger service between Winnipeg and western cities.

With the increase in the airmail services, accidents are starting to occur.

St. Roch toils for RCMP

The St. Roch arrives at Herschel Island as an RCMP floating detachment.

July 30, 1928
HERSCHEL ISLAND – The RCMP schooner *St. Roch* has become a floating detachment in the western Arctic. She joins Herschel Island, Cambridge Island, Aklavik and others as bases for the RCMP's operations in the north.

The *St. Roch* was designed for service in the Arctic, and she was launched earlier this year in a North Vancouver shipyard. She sailed here directly after the launch and will soon be visiting small settlements along the coast.

The *St. Roch*'s role as a floating detachment was explained by Inspector V. Kemp, who commands the force in the north. He said the ship, commanded by Sgt. F. Anderton, with Henry Larsen as first mate, will provide policing (which means anything from dispensing justice to helping the sick) to the Inuit living east of Herschel Island. The ability to move quickly is essential at the present time since many of the communities along the coast are enjoying a boom in the fur trade, Kemp said.

Four found alive a week after crash

Sept. 23, 1928
EDMONTON – Squadron Leader Earl Godfrey and three others were found today, seven days after their plane went missing on a flight between Peace River in northern Alberta and Fort Smith in the Northwest Territories. Only one minor injury was reported – a bruised leg.

The plane was forced down near Carcajou on the Peace River. It had flown from Ottawa to Vancouver and was returning when the accident occurred. The Hudson's Bay Company put its resources to good use. It lent both manpower and boats for use in the search.

Making beautiful music: medieval instruments fit as a fidla

1928
Medieval instruments, now gone from their homelands, have been preserved in Canada. The oldest, a box zither, comes from the Atlantic fidla which the Inuit copied after seeing it played by Hudson's Bay Company workers in the late 1600s.

Other instruments include the Icelandic langspil and the Norwegian Hardanger fiddle. The langspil, played on a table or in the lap, was used in Scandinavia until the end of the last century. As for the Hardanger fiddle, it resembles a violin with sympathetic strings for greater resonance.

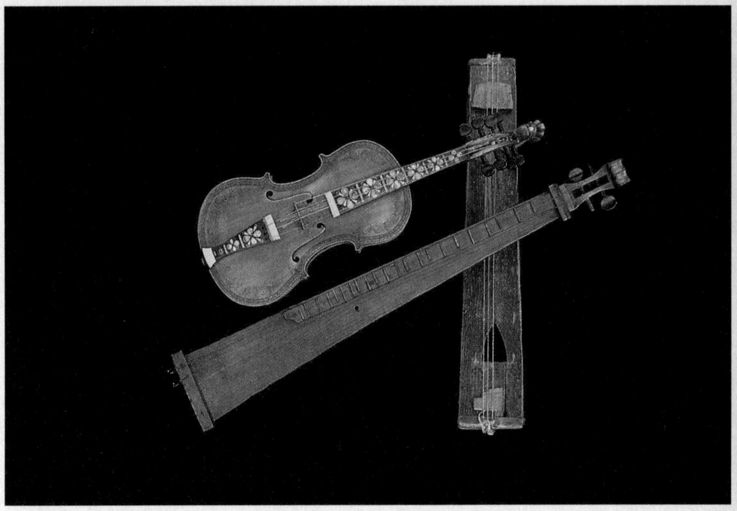
Inuit box zither (behind), Manitoba langspil, and Hardanger fiddle.

1929

Ottawa, Jan. 2. Canada and the U.S. sign a treaty allowing increased diversion of water from the Niagara River for hydroelectric purposes, and providing for extensive work to preserve Horseshoe Falls and the surrounding area.

Edmonton, January. "Wop" May and Vic Horner return after flying in anti-toxin to treat diptheria in the northern community of Fort Vermilion. The flight was dangerous, and 10,000 people give them a hero's welcome on their return.

Northwest Territories, January. Western Canada Airways has established regular air service down the Mackenzie River from Fort McMurray.

Gulf of Mexico, March 22. The U.S. Coast Guard sinks the Canadian schooner *I'm Alone*, suspected of carrying contraband liquor, off the coast of Louisiana.

Quebec, March 28. Lt.-Gov. Sir Jean-Lomer Gouin, former premier of the province and federal cabinet minister, dies.

Winnipeg, March 29. Sir Hugh John Macdonald, former premier of Manitoba and federal cabinet minister, and son of John A. Macdonald, dies.

United States, March 29. Boston Bruins beat the New York Rangers two games to none to win the Stanley Cup.

Ottawa, Sept. 1. The Aird Commission submits its report on Canadian broadcasting to Parliament. It proposes a publicly owned corporation similar to the British Broadcasting Corporation.

Regina, Sept. 9. J.T.M. Anderson becomes premier, heading the Co-operative government, a coalition of Conservatives, Progressives, and Independents.

Canada, Oct. 29. The Montreal and Toronto stock markets suffer the worst crash in Canadian history.

Canada, October. A national survey reports that the *raison d'être* of nursing schools is to provide cheap labor for hospitals. Nursing students work 12 hours a day.

Hamilton, Nov. 30. Hamilton Tigers defeat Regina Roughriders 14-3 for the Grey Cup.

Windsor, Ont. The Ambassador Bridge opens, spanning the Detroit River between Windsor and Detroit. It is the world's longest international suspension bridge.

Police tear-gas Doukhobors; 10 arrested

Jan. 28, 1929

GRAND FORKS, B.C. – Police had to use tear gas before they could arrest 10 Doukhobors here. About 50 of them, men and women, had gathered in a house to protect one of their leaders, a man called Strepnikoff. Twenty-six policemen and a school inspector tried to seize Strepnikoff, but there was a struggle and police had to use tear gas before they could drag Strepnikoff and his wife, both naked, outside. Eventually more Doukhobors were arrested. At stake here is the education of Doukhobor children. Their parents refuse to send them to public schools, and when police went to arrest the Doukhobors last week they were driven off.

Northern Indians facing starvation

Feb. 15, 1929

WINNIPEG – Indians living on two northern reserves face starvation, according to reports arriving here today. The news of the imminent tragedy came from Rev. H.E.W. Hutty, a missionary of the United Church located at Nelson House, and Matthew Wood, a councillor from the Nelson reserve.

The two men report that 1,317 residents of the Nelson House and Norway House reserves are without food because their natural sources have failed. They say there are no Arctic deer or rabbits to be found, nor are there fish to be caught in the lakes and rivers. One possible source of food is the beaver, but currently these animals are protected by legislation.

Last spike driven on the Bay Line

April 3, 1929

WINNIPEG – The steel now is complete on the Hudson Bay Line. The last spike was driven today. The story on the Bay Line reaches back to the turn of the century and has been marked by changes of government and interprovincial disputes. In recent years the unflagging support of the vocal On-to-the-Bay Association has been a decisive factor of the line which reaches north 819 kilometres from The Pas.

The construction is a considerable feat of engineering, for the terrain involved is marked by miles of muskeg over permafrost. It is hoped that before this winter there will be a shipment of grain through Churchill to the European markets.

Unemployed stage a peaceful protest as police look on

Feb. 14, 1929

EDMONTON – A group of 500 unemployed men today marched peacefully on the province's Parliament Buildings. Police on hand, strong in number and armed with tear gas grenades, watched from the sidelines as threatened violence and rioting failed to materialize. A small group dispersed quietly after being warned that their threatened actions would be illegal.

But Alberta Provincial Police officials relied less on intimidation than on positive measures. They calmed the jobless crowd by distributing meal and bed tickets outside the province's Parliament Buildings. The provincial government offers each unemployed man a bed and two meals daily, helping many to survive during the present economic crisis.

Today's demonstration shows that the unemployment problem in Alberta, as in the rest of Canada, appears to be getting worse. Economists warn that short-term solutions such as providing bed and meal tickets are rapidly becoming inadequate, and they urge long-term solutions, if Canada is to avoid future violence.

Vancouver is home to large numbers of immigrants from the Orient, as is evidenced in this street scene.

Two-way phone call from train is a first

May 5, 1929

ONTARIO – Canada has again assumed centre stage in an age of scientific wonders, this time on a Canadian National Railways train just outside Toronto. At 3:45 this afternoon, for the first time in history a two-way simultaneous telephone conversation was held from a moving train.

The demonstration was conducted before a score of reporters from here and the United States, as well as representatives from Europe's news services. The new system is a combination of telephone and radio technology, with variations in radio-wave frequency allowing for contact with different trains.

North under strict watch

A Canadian land expedition prepares to explore the Foxe Basin, Baffin Island.

June 10, 1929

OTTAWA – Canada is zealously guarding its sovereignty of the north. It is certainly not going to permit American explorers to fly over unexplored parts of Canada just to give them American names. This was the message given to the Senate here today by the Hon. George Graham.

Unexplored lakes, bays, or other landmarks can only be given names that are authorized by the Geographic Board of Canada, and to ensure that this is so foreign explorers can only enter the Northwest Territories if Ottawa agrees. Their plans and trips must be supervised by members of the Royal Canadian Mounted Police.

According to a report from Buffalo, a Commander McDonald wrote to the Royal Geographical Society in England recently with details of his plans to fly over Baffin Island this summer. The society referred him to the Department of the Interior in Ottawa, which explained its policy to McDonald. He has found that there are no planes available for his trip and has given up the idea for now. If he does eventually fly over Baffin Island, McDonald will be under Canadian supervision, and any names given to lakes or bays will be Canadian.

The Canadian Burwash Expedition camps at the Magnetic North Pole.

Police arrest 200 Doukhobors in B.C.

Sept. 21, 1929

NELSON, B.C. – Two hundred Doukhobors, members of the Sons of Freedom sect living in tents outside the city, were arrested here today and charged with resisting arrest and vagrancy. Police had ordered the Doukhobors to leave the camp after officials reported it was unsanitary. The Doukhobors refused to move and the Riot Act was read to them. They still refused to budge, and 30 policemen moved in and arrested them. The Doukhobors, singing hymns, then marched peacefully to jail. Police said they concentrated on seizing the leaders. Once the Doukhobors saw them in custody, they gave in.

Thousands protest killings in Palestine

Sept. 4, 1929

TORONTO – Three thousand Jews attended a protest meeting in Massey Hall, where memorial services were held for several hundred Jews killed in Palestine. Speeches in Yiddish and English criticized British policy and delays in creating a Palestinian homeland. However, M. Gelber, president of the Ontario Zionists, stressed loyalty to Britain. Funds were raised to aid survivors of the massacre.

Committee ruling: women are people

Oct. 18, 1929

LONDON, England – The Justice Committee of the Privy Council of England has ruled Canadian women are persons. The decision was unanimous and removed all restrictions on the appointment of women to the Senate. After the Supreme Court of Canada ruled that women were not persons in April 1928, the decision was appealed. The appeal was debated for three days in July and the decision announced this morning. In announcing the ruling, Lord Chancellor Sankey called the bar against women "a relic of days more barbarous than ours."

Flight marks start of service in north

Bush pilot "Punch" Dickins.

July 1, 1929

AKLAVIK, N.W.T. – "Punch" Dickins, known for his work opening up the north by air transport, landed his Fokker Super Universal plane here today by the light of the midnight sun. He was greeted by 50 Inuit and a handful of trappers and RCMP men. Dickins' plane was the first to land at Aklavik, and one old Inuit woman told him she didn't believe his plane could really fly because it could not flap its wings.

Dickins is leading a group of pilots flying all over the north, carrying prospectors, trappers, officials, the sick and injured, and supplies. This particular flight marks the start of a regular service down the Mackenzie from Edmonton. ▷

The 1920s: a decade of development nears an end

A cluster of grain elevators at Leduc, Alberta attests to a thriving agricultural economy in the Canadian west. Trains play a vital role in the transport of goods.

Hydroelectric plants in remote locations, such as this one at Shawinigan Falls, are producing electricity in great quantities for industry and home use.

Favorite Canadian meals, such as pork and beans, now come in cans.

Canadians in step with modern age

1929

CANADA – Canada is right in step with the rest of the western world when it comes to industrial and technological development. The modern age might not have reached the four corners of the earth yet, but it certainly has arrived here. The harvesting of natural resources, whether the grain of western Canada, the rivers of Quebec, or the gold from northern streams, is continuing at a furious pace, ushering in a new age of luxury goods and services.

Billboards advertise the latest conveniences available to the Canadian consumer. This one suggests dry-cleaned clothes for the beautiful life.

Airmail services are being established in all areas of this vast country.

Men hoping to strike it rich in the goldfields still use reliable time-tested equipment. This man uses what is known as a grizzly to pan for gold.

Deadly tidal wave hits outports of Nfld.

The tidal wave tore this house from its foundation and left it in the harbor.

Nov. 22, 1929

ST. JOHN'S, Nfld. – Hope that the massive tidal wave that struck the Burin Peninsula spared human lives was dashed today. As many as 36 lives are now believed lost in the tiny outports along the rocky coast. In Point Augaul alone at least eight died as the crushing wave, caused by a rupture in the Fundian fault, struck with awesome force. People were swept from their homes and drowned. Fishing boats and buildings were demolished in the wave's wake. Seven deaths have been reported in Port-au-Bras, four in Taylor's Bay, four in Lord's Cove, and three in Kelly's Cove. The full extent of the tragedy will not be known until relief ships arrive.

Massive destruction was caused by the tidal wave on the Burin Peninsula.

Stock markets go thud

Oct. 29, 1929

MONTREAL – Prices on the Montreal and Toronto Stock Exchanges have plunged in the worst collapse ever witnessed in Canadian financial history. Matching the panic that's gripped Wall Street in unnerving declines on stock markets since last Thursday, there was a veritable tidal wave of liquidation in Toronto and Montreal, where a slump of 525,000 shares has been the most drastic ever. Hundreds of undermargined trading accounts have cracked under the strain after successfully withstanding the tremendous pressure of earlier breaks. In Toronto, anxious clients scanned the boards at brokerage houses for any sign of recovery, but apart from a few brief intervals in which some stocks made temporary gains, there was nothing to relieve the general depression.

In Ottawa, Prime Minister W.L. Mackenzie King, asked for a statement on the situation, said: "While a number of people have suffered owing to the (stocks') sharp decline, the soundness of Canadian securities generally is not affected. Business was never better."

Emergency relief to help starving Inuit

These Inuit are dining on a meal of raw seal meat at Port Burwell, Quebec.

Dec. 31, 1929

OTTAWA – The governments of Quebec and Canada are working together to help the Inuit of Quebec, many of whom are dying from starvation. Arrangements have been made for the federal government to provide the Inuit with emergency relief supplies. Quebec, in turn, will reimburse Ottawa. The relief effort will be carried out through the Northwest Territories administration. The plight of the Inuit is attributed to two factors: the decline of the northern fur trade over the past decade, and the disappearance of the large herds of caribou on which they depend.

Banks move to prop up stock markets

Nov. 13, 1929

MONTREAL – Canada's leading banks announced this evening they plan measures to try to help the nation's stricken stock markets recover from the disastrous slump. The banks will reduce the call loan rates to brokers to 15 percent on stocks selling at about 30, and to $10 a share on stocks under that. The head of the Standard Stock and Mining Exchange, Norman Urquhart, says "this is one of the biggest things the banks ever did. It means the banks are satisfied the country's prospects are sound."

U.S. magazine tells of near-perfect P.E.I.

Dec. 15, 1929

CHARLOTTETOWN – No divorce. Little crime. A pastoral community with zero unemployment and no poverty. Sound like paradise? According to a recent issue of *The American Magazine*, this is Prince Edward Island. A correspondent reports: "The stores are prosperous, houses are painted, lawns are cropped and streets are clean." Filled with God-fearing, hard-working farm folk, the writer adds, the Island is inviting and easy to live on – "made so by work and by courage." ▷

The Group of Seven captures Canada on canvas

Use of bold colors part of their style

1929

ONTARIO – The most inspired works of art in Canada today are produced by the Group of Seven. Although the members do not paint landscapes exclusively, it is the subject for which they are best known. Their work, a departure from the naturalism of traditional schools, is influenced by the post-impressionists. The artists work to capture not only the physical image, but their own reactions on canvas.

They achieve this through a variety of methods. Their early work is characterized by bold, bright colors and thickly applied paint. In recent years, changes have occurred, with thinner applications of paint and more simplified renderings of shapes. Much of their work focuses on the north, including the critically acclaimed *Fire Swept – Algoma* by Frank Johnston, which is now in the National Gallery.

Self-promotion, friends at the Arts and Letters Club and the *Canadian Forum,* and the National Gallery's support have helped the group's influence spread steadily.

The Solemn Land, by J.E.H. MacDonald, represents a favorite locale of the Group, the Algoma District.

Frederick Varley's Stormy Weather, Georgian Bay is representative of the themes and techniques used by the Group of Seven in the early part of this decade. Strong colors are used to portray the elemental forces of nature. This painting is Varley's best-known landscape. He's also a skilled portrait painter.

Fog Lifting, by A.J. Casson. Casson joined the Group of Seven in 1926. The Group had actually had a membership of only six since 1920 when Frank Johnston had left. Casson is using the now familiar techniques of the others.

Autumn in Orillia, by Frank Carmichael. Vivid colors and strong brush strokes characterize this dramatic work. Carmichael is from Orillia.

Detail of Snow, by Lawren Harris. Although this is a winter scene, the Group of Seven artist has still used strong colors to bring life to his work.

Detail of Rain in the North Country, by Arthur Lismer.

Lake Superior Country, by Alexander Young Jackson. Jackson has used strong colors and simplified form to portray the beautiful Canadian north.

Work shows a profound love for Canada

1929

TORONTO – Critics may rage at their techniques, but few would dispute the work of the Group of Seven reveals a profound love for Canada. Their northern landscapes show the spectacular beauty of this country, along with the artists' own emotional reactions.

The group, founded in Toronto in 1920, originally consisted of Frank Carmichael, Lawren Harris, A.Y. Jackson, Frank Johnston, Arthur Lismer, J.E.H. MacDonald, and F.H. Varley. Tom Thomson, who drowned in Algonquin Park in 1917, was a friend whose work influenced the group. After Johnston resigned in 1920, he was replaced by A.J. Casson in 1926.

Except for Harris, who is independently wealthy, all members of the group earn their livelihood from their art. Their work received international acclaim at the Wembley Exhibition in 1924.

Detail of Fire Swept – Algoma, by artist Frank Johnston. Johnston was a member of the Group of Seven for their first exhibition only in 1920.

1930

Quebec, Feb. 19. The legislature votes down a bill that would amend the statutes to allow women to practise law in Quebec.

Montreal, April 3. Montreal Canadiens beat the Boston Bruins two games to none for the Stanley Cup.

Sudbury, Ont., May 1. Police arrest 13 alleged communists when several hundred people try to stage a May Day parade. An angry crowd demands their release and is dispersed with fire hoses.

Canada, July 1. An amendment to the Canada Export Act comes into effect, placing a total embargo on liquor shipments from Canadian ports to countries under prohibition.

Vancouver, Aug. 9. Canadian sprinter Percy Williams sets a world record of 10.33 seconds for the 100-metre dash.

Hamilton, Aug. 16. About 17,000 people attend opening day of the British Empire Games, the first held in an overseas dominion.

Ottawa, Sept. 8. The Dept. of Marine announces the establishment of radio stations at Coppermine and Chesterfield Inlet. There is now a radio chain stretching from the Arctic to the Atlantic and Great Lakes regions.

Edmonton, Oct. 1. Alberta gains control of its natural resources. The other Prairie provinces also gained control of their resources this year.

Toronto, Dec. 6. Toronto Balmy Beach beat the Regina Roughriders 11-6 to win the Grey Cup.

Ottawa. An amendment to the Indian Act makes it an offence for an Indian to frequent a pool room excessively, on or off the reserve, where he might "misspend or waste his time."

Norway. Norway formally abandons its claim to the Sverdrup Islands in the Arctic. Ottawa pays Norwegian Otto Sverdrup $67,000 for the records of his expeditions in the islands, securing Canada's claim to them.

British Columbia. There are two Haida villages, containing 650 people, compared to an estimated population of 10,000 before Europeans arrived.

Great Bear Lake, N.W.T. Gilbert Labine finds a valuable deposit of silver mixed with pitchblende (an ore containing radium and uranium).

Poverty spreads as depression hits

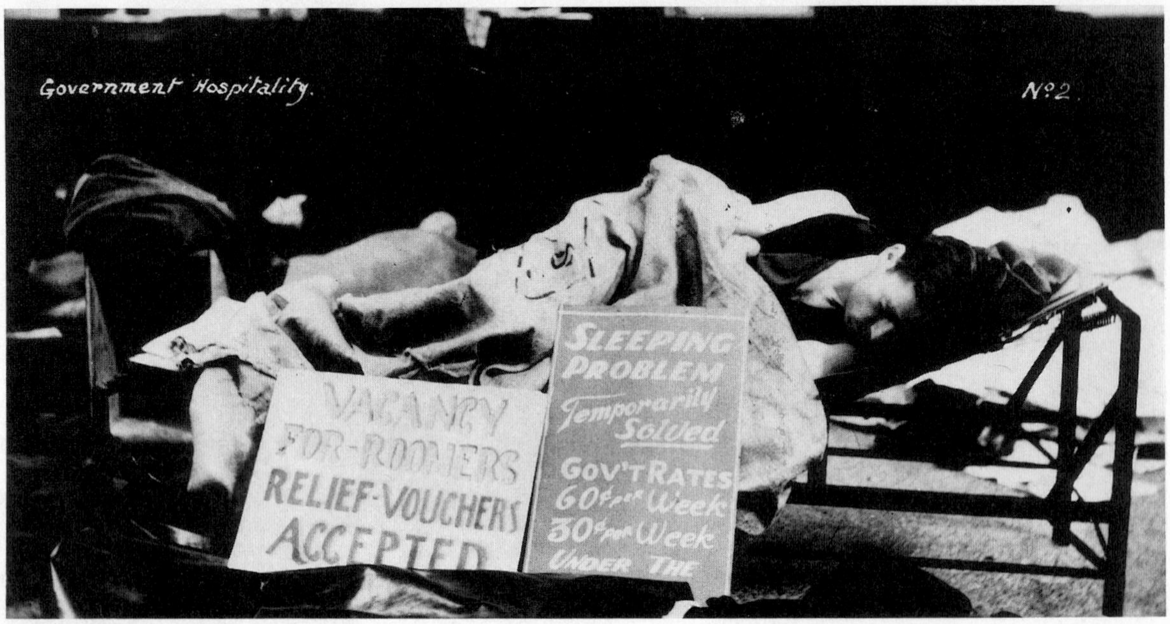

Government Hospitality - cots are set up in offices to provide overnight accommodation for the homeless.

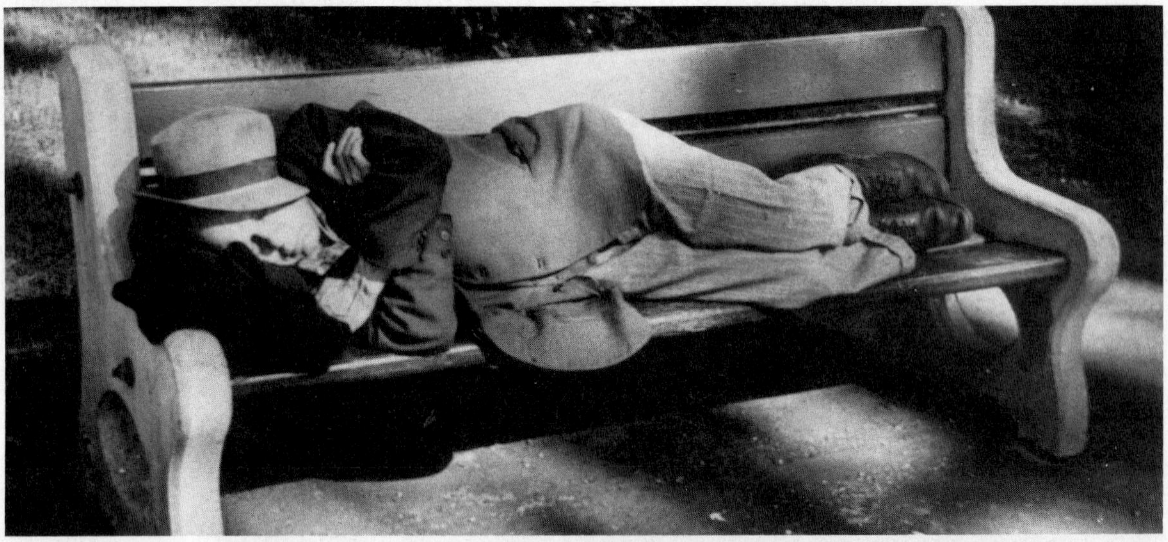

Park benches are the only beds available to some people in this time of unemployment and extreme poverty.

Shipments of relief food from Ontario arrive in the west, where the effects of the depression are most severe.

Ranks of unemployed swell as economy worsens

The east, though suffering from unemployment, still sends relief food west.

Job situation bleak in hard-hit Hamilton

Jan. 10, 1930

HAMILTON – Unemployment is becoming a big issue in Hamilton. At present, 800 job-seekers are listed with the city, while 1,200 men and 500 women are registered with the Ontario Employment Bureau. And hundreds, if not thousands, more unemployed have not bothered to register.

The problem, civic officials say, is a mixture of the traditional winter job slump and bad economic times. Making things worse is the fact that newspapers outside the city reported earlier this year that Hamilton was having an economic boom, with lots of jobs available. The reality is that there's as little work here as there is in other hard-hit regions in Canada, and that there are men, and families, currently suffering destitution and deprivation in this industrial city.

Economic conditions are placing more and more people's fates in the hands of charity. Food kitchens are being established across the country.

Police disperse crowd demanding relief

Jan. 29, 1930

VANCOUVER – A crowd of jobless men was surrounded and dispersed by Vancouver police officers earlier today. Many of the demonstrators, who gathered in Stanley Park to try to intimidate city relief workers, were taken into the police station, and 29 were charged with vagrancy.

Police were sent in on motorcycles and horseback after it was learned that a section of the unemployed crowd had decided to attack those city workers who have accepted the relief wages of $2 a day for a married man and $1 a day for a single man. The crowd moved to Stanley Park, where one of the city's relief workers was struck before police could surround and disperse the mob. Some of the jobless fled into the alleyways when authorities arrived, but they were soon apprehended. Most, however, gave up peacefully.

Local observers report that those who decided to harass the city workers were primarily pro-communist members of the jobless crowd who believe the low wages are unfair to desperate workers.

Hundreds of horses starving to death

Jan. 29, 1930

REGINA – Horses are being fed a mixture of molasses, straw, and wheat on Saskatchewan farms, in a desperate bid to keep them from starving to death. Farmers are virtually out of feed, due to last year's poor harvest. Making the situation critical is the fact that heavy snow has prevented farmers from driving their animals to winter pastures. Thousands of horses are reported to be suffering from malnutrition, and hundreds are said to have already starved to death. It's reported some farm animals are being shot, because there's no longer anything left to feed them.

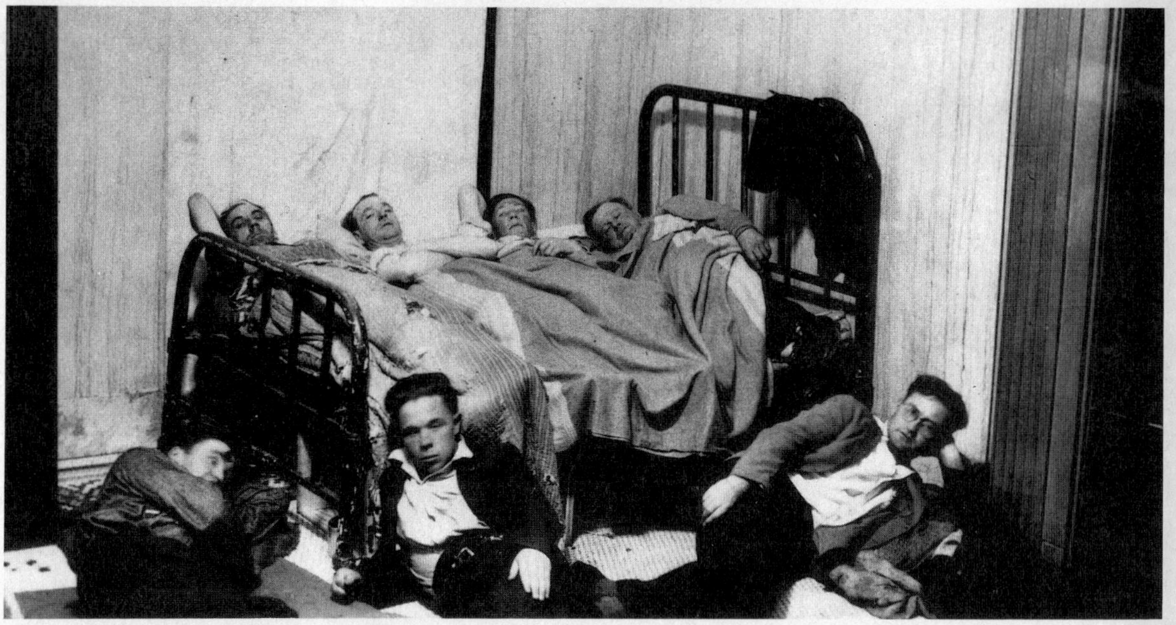

Many people cannot afford their own living quarters. Seven men share this one cramped room to sleep.

Woman to sit in Senate

The swearing-in ceremony of Canada's first female senator, Cairine Wilson.

Feb. 5, 1930

OTTAWA – Six months ago, Canadian women were not legally eligible to serve in the Senate. Today, in light of last October's decision of the Justice Committee of the British Privy Council, Prime Minister William Lyon Mackenzie King announced the appointment of Canada's first female senator, Cairine Wilson of Ottawa.

Mrs. Wilson, 45, an English-speaking Montrealer, is the daughter of the late senator Robert Mackay. Her husband Norman is a former Liberal member of Parliament. Mrs. Wilson has also been a devoted worker for the Liberal party. Two years ago she was instrumental in forming the National Federation of Liberal Women of Canada. Currently, she is involved in the organization of the Twentieth Century Liberal Association, a group for young Liberals.

Regardless of her impressive record of service for her party, Mrs. Wilson has always put family duties first, and, unlike many other prominent women, did not seek a position in the Senate. "All this publicity overwhelms me," she told a reporter following the prime minister's announcement. Mrs. Wilson reinforces her policy of shunning the limelight by avoiding interviews.

Senator Cairine Wilson.

Ku Klux Klansmen stage bizarre raid

Feb. 28, 1930

OAKVILLE, Ont. – Seventy-five members of the racist Ku Klux Klan staged a bizarre raid here. The white-robed and black-hooded Klansmen marched tonight into this small town of roughly 4,000 people, erecting and lighting a huge cross at the foot of a main street. Once it burned to the ground, the Klansmen went to a house occupied by a white woman and a black man. They took the girl and escorted her to her parents' home. The black man was similarly escorted, without violence, to his parents' house. (In the U.S., such "escorts" have often led to lynchings.) After their frightening visitation, the Ku Klux Klansmen left Oakville.

Indians challenging Ontario legislation

March 2, 1930

PORT ARTHUR Ont. – Two Indians are challenging a provincial law that may conflict with treaties signed between natives and the British Crown. Joe Padgema and Albert Quesawa were fined $600 last year for possessing beaver skins without a permit. Their lawyer argued on appeal here today that the Robinson-Superior Treaty, signed in 1850, gives Indians the right to hunt in any of the unoccupied territory they ceded to the Crown. The provincial government cannot put restrictions on that right, he said, and the provincial law under which the two were convicted is unconstitutional. The treaty gave the Crown land north of Lake Superior.

Spiritualist helped PM with timing of vote

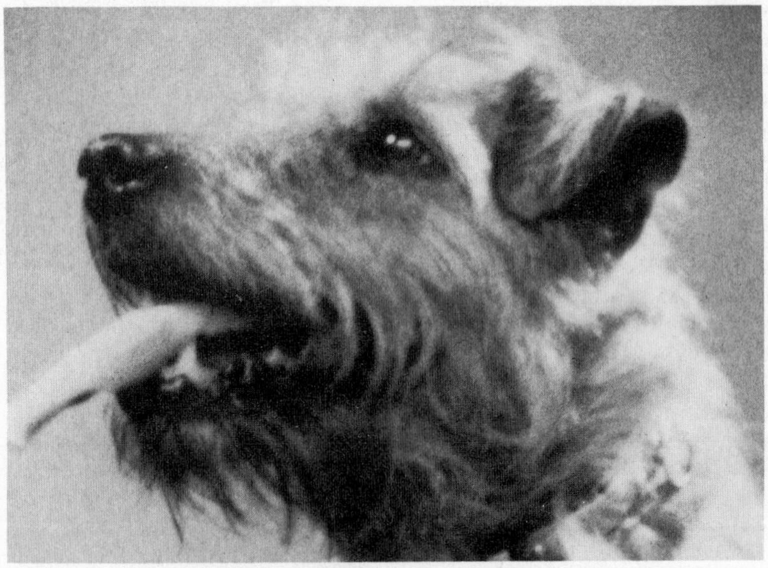

Irish terrier Pat was King's constant companion. The prime minister believed that Pat helped him communicate spiritually with his dead mother.

February 1930

OTTAWA – Only a tiny circle of intimates who share Prime Minister William Lyon Mackenzie King's fascination with the occult are aware that he called an election for this summer rather than next year on the advice of a spiritualist he often consults. King was uncertain about when to schedule the next federal election, but Kingston fortune-teller Mrs. Bleaney told him his chances of winning are stronger this year than next.

King, one of the only surviving members of what was once a very close-knit family, often seeks the advice of spiritualists. In addition to "fortune telling," the PM has sought clairvoyant advice on the nature of his dreams and emotions. He and Bleaney, for example, often discuss such matters.

However, King does not allow the general public to know to what extent spiritual advisers influence his political judgment. In any case, it will be Canadian voters, and not a crystal ball, that will decide the PM's fate on July 28.

Klansman guilty of being disguised

March 10, 1930

OAKVILLE, Ont. – A Ku Klux Klansman has been convicted for his role in a raid here Feb. 28 in which a white woman was abducted from the house of a black man she was living with. Under an obscure Criminal Code section intended to deter burglary, William Phillips was found guilty of being disguised at night to commit an unlawful act. Co-defendants Ernest Taylor and Harold Orme were acquitted. The raid was caused by the woman's mother, who asked the Klan to retrieve her daughter.

Silent Enemy debut a hit in New York

May 19, 1930

NEW YORK – Critics are raving about a silent film from Canada that received its world premiere at the Criterion Theatre today. Called *The Silent Enemy,* the film depicts the lifestyle of the Ojibwa Indians of northern Ontario, using actual native actors, including the famous writer and socialite, Chief Buffalo Child Long Lance.

The Silent Enemy tells the story of the rivalry between a mighty hunter and an Indian shaman, set against the affliction of a terrible famine – the "silent enemy." The film was shot on location in Ontario by Douglas Burden, a young American explorer-ethnologist.

Deals with natives cover all of Ontario

July 28, 1930

WINISK, Ont. – Treaties with natives now cover all of Ontario. Today, the small Cree band here, south of Fort Severn, became the latest, and perhaps the last, Indian band to sign over its land rights. The Winisk band joined three other groups which have during the past year signed adhesions to Treaty No. 9, first signed in 1905. The adhesions cover the vast territory of northern Ontario north of the Albany River, 332,348 square kilometres. The eight bands now adherent to the treaty will receive reserves totalling about 815 square kilometres. There are about 1,500 or 2,000 Indians involved.

Treaty 9, also called the James Bay Treaty, gives Indians an annual payment of $4 each. They have some hunting rights in territory they ceded, and the government is to provide educational services.

Provinces gain control over immigration

March 4, 1930

OTTAWA – Tired of being blamed for causing unemployment by assisting immigration to Canada, the federal government has decided to throw the entire problem over to the provinces. In the near future, Ottawa will only act as a clearing house for immigrants, leaving it to the provinces to decide who will be allowed into their territory. The policy is bound to be a mixed blessing for provincial authorities. They will be able to ensure that only the sort of workers they need will immigrate there.

Prairie farmers cope with severe drought

This Alberta farmer is harvesting his drought-stricken wheat crop.

Autumn 1930

REGINA – After a record crop in 1928 the prairies have done a complete turnabout and farmers have been cursed with a drought that started last season and continues to spread. Hot dry winds are blowing away the topsoil. There are accounts of black blizzards that are so bad it is unsafe for children to venture to school. The tumbling Russian thistle banks against the fences, and when the dirt packs around it the cattle walk over it and out of the fence.

To add to the hardship, prices for farm products have fallen. Foreign markets have been declining at the same time production has been escalating. Many farmers have run up debts in better times, thinking the good crops would continue. Experts have cautioned against specializing in wheat, expanding acreage and neglecting summer fallow and other moisture conservation practices.

Unemployment abounds. The federal government is providing emergency funds to relieve people. Prime Minister Richard Bennett, whose Conservatives won the recent national election, has assured the country that the present economic crisis is manmade and thus controllable.

Provinces to control natural resources

July 15, 1930

WINNIPEG – Sixty years to the day after attaining provincehood, Manitoba has come into full possession of its natural resources. While the same privilege is also being given to the younger provinces of Saskatchewan and Alberta, Ottawa's action has a special meaning in the Keystone Province.

After 15 years of on-again, off-again negotiations, Ottawa finally accepted the recommendation of a royal commission to proceed with the transfer and pay Manitoba compensation of $4,584,212.29.

Bennett-led Tories win federal election

Prime Minister Richard B. Bennett.

July 28, 1930

OTTAWA – Richard Bedford Bennett, the first Conservative leader elected by the party's rank and file, is the prime minister of Canada. Although the returns are still coming in, it's clear Bennett has won a smashing victory over William Lyon Mackenzie King's Liberals. The Conservatives have made gains everywhere, including the Liberal stronghold of Quebec. The Liberals, in turn, have lost at least five cabinet ministers.

The key to King's downfall is the Great Depression which has swept both this country and the world in general. The continuing lack of jobs has motivated many voters to heed Bennett's promises of a better future. It remains to be seen if he can reverse a worldwide trend alone. ▷

Seventeenth-century Jesuits first North Americans canonized

June 30, 1930

VATICAN CITY – Eight Jesuit martyrs became saints today, the first North Americans to be canonized. Ceremonies were held here, in Ottawa, and in Midland, Ont., where the Martyrs' Shrine stands on the site of Ste-Marie-Among-the-Hurons where Jesuits served as missionaries in the first half of the 17th century.

The eight, led by Father Jean de Brébeuf, were tortured and killed near the mission headquarters. Besides Brébeuf, the saints include Father Gabriel Lalemant, Father Noel Chabanel, Brother René Goupil, Brother Jean de La Lande, and Father Charles Garnier.

At the Vatican, Pope Pius XI presided over canonization ceremonies. All over Canada, masses commemorated the first Europeans in Canada to achieve sainthood.

Conservative move limits immigration

British immigrants are still welcome.

Aug. 15, 1930

OTTAWA – Bowing to public pressure – and perhaps prejudice – the Conservative government will limit immigration to Canada. Exceptions will be made for families joining established heads of households here, and rich farmers.

Immigration Minister Wesley Gordon said "the purpose is to prevent persons coming to this country who will not be able to find work on arrival and to protect the people of Canada from the burden of such unemployment." Maybe so. But then why does the new law not apply to British or American citizens?

Judges clamp down on armed robbers

Oct. 2, 1930

MONTREAL – Two judges in the criminal courts are sending a message to armed robbers: crimes of violence will be punished by the lash as well as jail terms. The warning came after Judges Perrault and Lacroix imposed sentences on three robbers totalling 13 years and 52 lashes. Thomas Eric Jones and Eric Thurston, who pleaded guilty to the armed robbery of a taxi driver, were each sentenced to five years in jail and 18 strokes of the lash. Armand Vaillancourt was sentenced to 16 lashes and a three-year term after a holdup.

Unemployment Relief Bill is adopted

Sept. 20, 1930

OTTAWA – The Bennett government has passed an Unemployment Relief Bill, although nowhere in the bill are there any actual relief benefits for the unemployed. Instead, the government plans to spend $20 million on "make-work" projects, focusing mainly on highways, wharves, railways, and other public projects. The government is considering helping provincial and local governments with similar projects, by covering interest costs on loans. Prime Minister Richard Bennett estimates his measures will create from 25,000 to 30,000 jobs.

In addition to the make-work aspects of the bill, Bennett is going to raise tariffs. He hopes to "prevent the importation of goods at ridiculous prices into the markets of this country, thereby throwing people into idleness and destroying their employment, and the co-relative of that, namely, the importation to this country of large quantities of goods which can be made in this country if our people were subjected to fair competition."

One million Canadians catch a glimpse of British airship R-100

Aug. 13, 1930

MONTREAL – The giant R-100 airship that's been visiting the city rumbled away from her tall mooring mast at St. Hubert this evening for the flight back to England. More than one million people saw the R-100 on her two-week stay in Canada, and about 3,000 people toured the airship. On the flight back to Britain, her crew of 30 are joined by several Canadian reporters and officials.

The R-100 reached Montreal on Aug. 1, 77 hours after leaving Britain. Most of her visit was spent at the mooring mast, but on Aug. 10 and 11 she flew to Ottawa, Niagara Falls, and Toronto.

Airmail letter signed by the crew commemorates R-100's transatlantic flight.

Police mobilized to quell Communist riots

The Communist Party of Canada is growing in numbers and influence.

Oct. 21, 1930

PORT ARTHUR [Thunder Bay], Ont. – Port Arthur has become an armed camp, following riots by Communists and unemployed workers demanding relief payments from city council. They want a dollar a day for single men, and $2 for the married unemployed. Things have turned ugly after a mob assaulted Chief George Taylor and a sergeant, and released a prisoner they were holding in custody. Every available policeman is on duty, plus 30 special officers, and RCMP reinforcements.

Boyd pilots plane over the Atlantic

Oct. 10, 1930

LONDON, England – J. Erroll Boyd has become the first Canadian to fly the Atlantic in an airplane. Piloting a Bellanca WB-2 monoplane, he took off from Harbour Grace, Nfld., yesterday bound for London. Unhappily, the engine faltered after 23 hours and 40 minutes due to a loss of oil. Up to that point the flight was uneventful. Boyd made an emergency landing on a beach in the Scilly Islands, just short of Land's End. He'll complete the flight to London tomorrow.

Boyd was accompanied by Harry P. Connor, an American naval officer who acted as navigator. The airplane, named *The Maple Leaf,* was making its second Atlantic crossing. In June 1927, under the name *Columbia,* it flew from New York to Germany with an American crew at the controls.

Motion picture shot at the seal fishery

May 4, 1930

ST. JOHN'S, Nfld. – The *SS Viking* arrived yesterday with the American film crew which has been filming a motion picture on location at the seal fishery. Varick Frissell, the director, arrived here Jan. 16 and shot much of the movie in nearby Quidi Vidi, on Signal Hill and along the waterfront. In March he and his crew, including Newfoundland's Capt. Bob Bartlett, starring as Capt. Bob Barker, went to the seal fishery on board the *SS Ungava,* commanded by the well-known Capt. Billy Winsor.

Scenes were filmed on the ship and on the ice, and when the *Ungava* returned to St. John's on April 17, the *Viking* picked up the film crew and continued its work. *Ungava*'s crew enjoyed the presence of the American film-makers and took part in the activities. Crew members received $5 from Frissell besides the $77.86 each made sealing.

Sask. farmers fume over tax sales

Nov. 12, 1930

REGINA – Boycotting tax, foreclosure, and sheriff sales are just some of the proposals included in the resolutions and recommendations passed at a meeting of farmers from the Buchan, Keys, Sliding Mills, and Goodlake municipalities. The group went on record as protesting against "tax sales imposed on us by the Saskatchewan government through the Department of Municipal Affairs in time of the present capitalist economic crisis and (we) demand cancellation of arrears of taxes."

Other recommendations to come out of the meeting suggest: that the Saskatchewan government discuss with the province of Alberta the possibility of developing oil wells as public enterprises and putting the product on the market at cost; that the federal government launch an investigation into flour-milling operations and setting a standard price for flour; that the government set a standard price on all farm products based on the cost of a reasonable standard of living; that the provincial government hire farmers in place of contractors for the construction of highways. MLA Anton Morkin and MP Milton N. Campbell were both at the meeting.

In Strasbourg, secession of the west from Canada was the solution proposed by the Last Mountain Provincial Progressive Association.

Western farmers are upset by the government's new tax sales proposal.

Underwater tunnel joins Windsor, Detroit

Nov. 2, 1930

WINDSOR, Ont. – An underwater international tunnel opened today, allowing cars to drive between this city and Detroit via a tube under the Detroit River. U.S. President Herbert Hoover pressed a button in Washington that activated gongs on both sides of the river, saluting the occasion. Ceremonies began at 10:30 a.m. on the Canadian side with an invocation that was heard in Detroit via a telephone-loudspeaker hookup.

Corner of Kitwancool Village, by B.C. artist Emily Carr.

Eaton's expanding, new store is open

Oct. 28, 1930

TORONTO – Thousands of people gathered at the corner of College and Yonge streets today to watch the opening of the new Eaton's store. Using an ornate gold key, John David Eaton, grandson of founder Timothy Eaton, opened the main door of the establishment.

Accompanied by his mother, Lady Eaton, the young man then entered the building, where he was greeted by company president R.Y. Eaton, a nephew of the founder. R.Y. later expressed his pleasure at the firm's ability to keep up with progress. The store is one of the finest and most imposing in Canada – and perhaps in the world.

Wawakesy Park to protect the antelope

1930

ALBERTA – The recovery of the pronghorn antelope has initiated the transfer of resources to the province of Alberta. Canyon Reserve, which accommodated pronghorn antelope in the past, has been returned to provincial jurisdiction.

The enactment of the Alberta Natural Resources Act this year transfers certain lands previously vested under the government of Canada back to the province for purposes of wildlife preservation. Canyon Reserve, originally under the authority of the government for forestry purposes, has become a Dominion park, notably Wawakesy National Park, and returned to Alberta. The province has taken the position that Wawakesy National Park will be kept as a wildlife reserve, particularly for the purpose of protecting the antelope.

Ludovine, by Edwin Holgate, who joined the Group of Seven as its eighth member in 1930.

Footprints to end newborn mix-ups

Dec. 8, 1930

LONDON, Ont. – New moms at the city's Victoria Hospital need never worry that they've been sent home with the wrong baby. At least they'll have that assurance soon, when the hospital starts making ink footprints of babies' feet at birth. The system, which costs $34.65 a year, makes it possible to identify babies easily and accurately, because footprints, like fingerprints, are never the same. Mothers will be fingerprinted to prevent confusion.

1931

Ottawa, Feb. 27. The Department of National Revenue prohibits importation of goods from the Soviet Union as a protest against its Communist government.

Montreal, April 14. Montreal Canadiens beat the Chicago Blackhawks three games to two to win the Stanley Cup.

Victoria, April 22. Police seize 40,000 tickets for a Canadian National Lottery, foiling the launching of a sweepstakes involving more than $1 million.

Toronto, Aug. 11. Authorities arrest leaders of the Canadian Communist party, including national secretary Tim Buck, on charges of belonging to an illegal organization.

Bienfait, Sask., Sept. 8. Coal miners go on strike for restoration of wages cut by the mine operators, for better working conditions, and for recognition of the newly formed Mine Workers' Union of Canada.

Bienfait, Sask., Oct. 22. Miners vote to accept an agreement ending their strike, even though the settlement satisfies few of their demands. The RCMP and Attorney General M.A. MacPherson intimidated them in their voting.

Halifax, October. "The wood ain't growin' yet that'll beat *Bluenose!*" Capt. Angus Walters makes good his boast once again as his *Bluenose* beats the *Thebaud* for the International Fisherman's Trophy.

Toronto, Nov. 12. At the opening of Maple Leaf Gardens, a crowd of 13,542, the largest ever to attend a hockey game in Toronto, watch the Chicago Blackhawks beat the Toronto Maple Leafs 2-1.

Montreal, Dec. 5. Montreal AAA Winged Wheelers beat the Regina Roughriders 22-0 for the Grey Cup.

London, Dec. 11. At the dominions' request, Parliament passes the Statute of Westminster, clarifying the powers of the dominion parliaments and giving the dominions full legal freedom, except in areas in which they choose to stay subordinate to Britain. At Canada's request, the British Parliament retains the power to amend the BNA Act (the Canadian Constitution).

British Columbia. Haida Indian Alfred Adams founds the Native Brotherhood of British Columbia to represent Indian interests.

Romance of Canada debuts on radio

These men created sound effects for the Henry Hudson program on CNR radio.

Tyrone Guthrie recently arrived in Canada to produce this radio series.

Jan. 31, 1931

MONTREAL – The historical serial *The Romance of Canada* premiered on the CNR radio network today, marking the debut of Canadian drama on the airwaves. The play, produced and directed by the renowned Tyrone Guthrie, was presented out of the rail company's studios in Montreal. The inaugural production, about explorer Henry Hudson, was written by Merrill Denison, an ex-NBC writer commissioned by the network to pen 25 scripts on Canadian history.

There were few professional actors in the play, with many of the characters portrayed by eager amateurs recruited by Guthrie and his assistant Rupert Caplan. Among their recruits was a bellhop from the Windsor Hotel. *The Romance of Canada* is the brainchild of CNR radio boss Austin Weir.

Director among 24 killed in explosion

March 16, 1931

ST. JOHN'S, Nfld. – Word has been received that the *SS Viking* has blown up and sunk, taking 24 lives with it. The steamer was sailing to the seal fishery with 142 sealers, movie director Varick Frissell, and Frissell's small film crew. Frissell made a movie at the ice fields last year, but wanted more action footage. He was carrying a considerable amount of explosives and planned to film exploding icebergs. Frissell's explosives and those of the ship were stored in the back of the steamer. A massive explosion blew off the ship's stern, but the intervening pounds of coal protected the sealers up front.

Frissell and a 12-year-old stowaway are among the dead or missing. Many men were injured, including Capt. Abram Kean Jr. Some survivors reached the nearby Horse Islands, where a wireless operator reported the tragedy.

Six in hospital as jobless, police clash

April 15, 1931

WINNIPEG – Six demonstrators are in hospital today after yesterday's riot between police and the unemployed. The trouble began when a crowd of 6,000 gathered at the Legislative Buildings. Inside their leaders were meeting with Premier John Bracken, to whom they presented their appeals for assistance. Their principal request is for a non-contributory form of unemployment insurance.

When the meeting ended, members of the crowd left the legislative grounds, and in some instances disrupted traffic. When the police attempted to intervene, a demonstrator hurled a rock at one of them and the riot ensued. The struggle took place on downtown streets, with the result that many of the rocks thrown broke the windows of cars and shops. The end came when a number of demonstrators were taken into custody.

Government bans Tolstoy niece from B.C.

April 9, 1931

VICTORIA, B.C. – Alexandra Tolstoy, niece of the Russian novelist, will not be allowed to come to British Columbia. She wanted to edit a Doukhobor newspaper.

B.C. officials discussed Miss Tolstoy's plans with federal agents who agreed to bar her, the legislature was told here today. In fact, the B.C. government wants all Doukhobors banned from coming to the province because the Sons of Freedom, a small, radical element, refuse to send their children to the schools that are being provided for them and persist in committing acts of civil disobedience such as stripping in public to protest government policy. Even worse, this sect bombs and sets fire to schools, bridges, and railway tracks.

Storms bring tons of silt to Winnipeg

June 18, 1931

WINNIPEG – Two dust storms this week deposited at least 6,000 tons of silt on this city. The topsoil flew in from the drought-stricken farms in southern and central Saskatchewan, as well as the two Dakotas. The calculation of tonnage was made by Professor J.J. Jackson, of the Manitoba Agricultural College in Winnipeg. Jackson collected the dust from one square yard of a downtown street and made his calculations accordingly. There was little comfort for Winnipeggers when a severe windstorm, with winds from the east, blew much of the silt and topsoil out of town again.

Nova Scotia, Ont. at odds over trade

April 29, 1931

SYDNEY, N.S. – Local breadmaker L.L. Snell has started a small war between between this province and Ontario. He suggests Maritimers punish Ontario for not buying enough of their goods by boycotting Ontario goods. The Mechanics' Local of the United Mine Workers intends to follow the plan by buying goods made in Quebec, where their coal is sold. But others aren't committing themselves.

IT SAYS
MAMMA AND PAPA
WHEN YOU PULL THE STRING
EYES OPEN AND CLOSE
Wrigley's
ADVERTISING
OFFER "C"
A BEAUTIFUL DRESSED
TALKING DOLL
FREE
WITH ONE BOX
WRIGLEY'S
SPEARMINT
PEPSIN GUM
FOR 85¢
EACH DOLL PACKED IN A NEAT BOX
SIZE 16 INCH WITH HAT
SOLD FROM JOBBERS
STOCK ONLY
WM. WRIGLEY JR. COMPANY.
LIMITED
TORONTO, CANADA.

The William Wrigley Jr. Co. of Toronto offers a beautiful talking doll free to all customers who buy a box of its chewing gum.

Relief camps a result of the depression

Mines are hard hit by the depression. Their markets are disappearing.

September 1931

VANCOUVER – The depression has hit British Columbia hard. The province's economy, resource-based with a high proportion of wage earners employed in large lumber mills and plants, was particularly vulnerable in a worldwide slowdown. Unemployment in B.C. is around the 28-percent mark – bad enough, but the numbers seeking food, shelter, and work have been swollen by thousands attracted by the temperate climate.

To help the province, Ottawa is now providing money and other resources, and relief camps are being set up in remote areas of the interior. This action is the result of pressure from politicians, businessmen and the public in Vancouver, and the towns on the mainline railways where transient jobless men gather and threaten trouble. Officials hope that the men can be set to work building roads and airports, but no level of government has the money to even start such projects.

About 12,000 men are already in the camps, but it is expected that the number will double soon for there are few signs of any real improvement in the economy. Meanwhile, all levels of government wonder how long they can afford to feed the men.

Bennett dismisses Communist group's plea for the dole

April 15, 1931

OTTAWA – Prime Minister Richard Bennett minced no words when he met a group of unemployed men today who are demanding that the government institute "the dole," that is, payments to the unemployed. A few of the delegates were self-styled "Reds," or Communists, and it was on this point that Bennett grilled them. While he refused to pay their train fare home, he offered each a one-way ticket to the "workers' paradise" in the Soviet Union. None accepted.

Bennett made his position on the dole clear. "This government will not put a premium on idleness, and will not put Canadians on the dole. ... You have observed it has been done in Britain. If you knew what I know about conditions in Britain you would agree with me that no new country should think of the dole, for that would be tantamount to committing suicide." Commenting on the delegation's "Red" beliefs, Bennett added, "I may say here we have a system of government that is not likely to displaced by another very soon."

The PM's dismissal of the men's arguments doesn't change the fact that many Canadians, no matter how loyal, believe much more has to be done to help the unemployed.

Grey Owl busy as a beaver working in second conservation film

June 1931

RIDING MOUNTAIN NATIONAL PARK, Man. – The amazing Indian nature writer Grey Owl will star in his second film, *The Beaver Family,* currently being shot here by National Parks film-maker Bill Oliver. Last year the National Parks branch shot the highly successful film *The Beaver People* with Grey Owl and his tame beaver at Cabano, Que., where he lived at the time. The parks administration liked the picture so much they hired Grey Owl as the "caretaker of park animals" at Riding Mountain, where he moved this spring. The part-Apache Indian has given up trapping to work for the conservation of the beaver.

Grey Owl, conservationist turned actor, feeds a pet beaver.

▷

Western wheat to relieve plight of hungry

July 14, 1931
OTTAWA – Prime Minister Richard Bennett today announced the purchase of two million bushels of wheat, part of the relief promised to starving prairie residents. Bennett said numerous representations had been made to him concerning cases of near-starvation. Describing the situation as "practically a national calamity," Bennett told of some municipalities in Saskatchewan in which 98 percent of the residents are on relief.

Red Cross to aid drought-stricken west

July 6, 1931
OTTAWA – Federal and Canadian Red Cross officials yesterday described drought conditions in southern Saskatchewan as the "most serious emergency Canada has ever known." The Red Cross has placed all of its resources at federal disposal to aid drought victims. Chairman Norman Sommerville said the drought affects 3,885 square kilometres in Saskatchewan, where 150,000 people are desperate for food, clothes, and fuel.

A farmer surveys the devastating effects of drought on his Saskatchewan farm.

Dust forms a drift along a fence between Cadillac and Kincaid, Saskatchewan.

Spirit of co-operation deals with crisis

Prime Minister Bennett (right), chats with Ontario Premier G.H. Ferguson.

July 1, 1931
OTTAWA – On Canada's 64th birthday, Prime Minister Richard Bennett announced that before prorogation, he'll submit bills granting an estimated $25 million in relief to drought-stricken prairie farmers.

Immediately, Liberal opposition leader W.L. Mackenzie King was on his feet pledging "co-operation in the fullest measure." Progressive and Labour members also promised speedy passage of the bills.

King reiterated that federal drought relief should be vested in a "national relief board," not Parliament, but Bennett sees major legal obstacles to that plan.

Sask. Indians revive illegal rain dance

Drought conditions have prompted prairie Indians to revive the rain dance.

July 15, 1931
REGINA – Desperate drought conditions on Indian reserves have forced some natives to turn for help to the sacred rain dance, long prohibited by officials of the Indian Affairs Department. Seeing their cattle herds without food or water, the natives decided to call upon the Great Spirit.

Directed by Chief Buffalo Bow of the File Hills Reserve, Indians danced the forbidden ceremony for two days and nights, non-stop. Soon after, all of southern Saskatchewan was drenched in rain for two days.

Liberals take heat in power project scandal on the Hill

July 28, 1931
OTTAWA – In a city that thrives on political scandal, the current brouhaha over the Beauharnois Power Project, and how $864,000 was raised by company president Robert O. Sweezey for donation to the Liberal party's campaign, has everybody talking. Particularly delighted by the scandal is the Conservative government.

Details of the campaign contributions came out today in a report submitted to the House by a special committee charged with investigating the scandal. It details how the money was funnelled through two Liberal senators, both of whose actions have been disavowed by party leader W.L. Mackenzie King. He's basically taking the position that two of his lieutenants acted improperly without telling him.

The benefit to Sweezey and other promoters of the project was a return of more than $2 million in cash profit and one million Class A common shares worth up to $17 million on the stock market. In short, this project was a cash cow for the promoters, which may explain their concern in helping the then-Liberal government gain re-election.

But the Liberals didn't win, and the Conservatives are in a position to exact some revenge. Vengeance or not, the government will take over the project in the near future.

Searchers discover relics of Franklin expedition to the Arctic

Remains of Franklin's men found.

Fragmented skeletons found by William Gibson of the Hudson's Bay Company.

July 1931
KING WILLIAM ISLAND, N.W.T. – A search for remains of the Franklin expedition has discovered a number of fragmented skeletons scattered about the limestone shingle and soft sand of King William Island's southern shore. That they belong to the ill-fated crew of Franklin's party is beyond doubt. Sir John Franklin, naval officer and Arctic explorer, set out from England in 1845 to sail the Northwest Passage. Neither he nor his crew ever returned. Documents discovered since tell of Franklin's death off King William in 1847. This summer's search was led by the Hudson's Bay Company's William Gibson. It has been undertaken without great hopes of finding further records of the tragedy, but rather to bury the remains reportedly seen there by Inuit.

Illegal mine strike leads to 3 deaths, 23 injuries, 14 arrests

Sept. 29, 1931
ESTEVAN, Sask. – Three killed, 23 wounded, and 14 arrested is the price paid by mine workers who staged an illegal strike in Estevan. What started out as a march to bring attention to the need for better wages, better working conditions, and the recognition of the Mine Workers' Union of Canada turned into a brawl when strikers attacked police, who were barring their advance on the town hall.

The strikers swung iron bars, wrenches, and clubs, and they hurled rocks. When the march turned violent police fired warning shots, which went unheeded. A dousing with the fire hose did not deter the mob either. As the 45-minute riot continued, three strikers were killed by police bullets. The wounded include police, workers, and bystanders.

Destitute men live in island "jungle"

Sept. 18, 1931
SAULT STE. MARIE, Ont. – Some 200 destitute men have taken shelter in a "jungle" on a nearby island. The men, some as old as 68, have given up hope of finding jobs and occupied Whitefish Island, living in dugouts and improvised shelters. They're surviving off the generosity of city households, which are also feeling the pinch of economic conditions. Many of the "jungle" dwellers are weakened by deprivation and ill health and have been taken to hospital. Some men are longtime residents of the Soo.

Squatters camp out in legislature halls

Sept. 23, 1931
WINNIPEG – Nineteen families, including 40 children, have taken up residence in the Legislative Buildings, victims of the maze of regulations which cover the destitute. They have been forced off farms and out of small towns because of the drought, but have not been in Winnipeg long enough to qualify for relief payments.

It will not be easy to evict these squatters. A crowd of 150 men has gathered at the exits, determined to keep authorities from forcing the families back out into the streets.

Mr. and Mrs. David Cardinal, a Cree Indian couple from Calling River, Alberta.

Seven Communists jailed for 5 years

Nov. 14, 1931
TORONTO – Seven Canadian Communists have been sentenced to five years in jail for being members of an unlawful organization and involved in a seditious conspiracy. Judge Wright said, "I have in view the deterrent effect on others of like mind with you." Wright admitted the guilty were not common criminals, a view echoed by one of the defendants, Tim Buck, who said, "I will take whatever sentence your Lordship gives me, I hope, with the same spirit I have tried to advance the cause I believe in."

1932

Alberta, March 19. Three men ski down the peak of the Snow Dome, topographical centre of the Columbia Ice-Fields. The ski-ascent, to an altitude of over 3,300 metres, is the highest achieved in Canada.

Arcadia, Calif., March 20. Buffalo Child Long Lance, celebrated Blackfoot writer who worked in Winnipeg and Calgary as a journalist, is found dead. Apparently he took his own life. Rumors circulate that he was an imposter, a man classified as colored, and not a plains Indian at all.

Toronto, April 9. Toronto Maple Leafs beat the New York Rangers three games to none to win the Stanley Cup.

British Columbia, June. Some 600 Doukhobors are arrested for nude marching and sent to a penal colony at Piers Island in the Strait of Georgia.

Ottawa, Oct. 29. Sixty theatre representatives vote to create the Dominion Drama Festival, a co-lingual annual theatre competition.

Quebec, Nov. 7. About 150 prisoners at the St. Vincent de Paul Penitentiary near Montreal cause $500,000 damage trying to escape. It is the worst prison riot ever in Canada.

Hamilton, Dec. 3. Hamilton Tigers beat Regina Roughriders 25-6 for the Grey Cup.

Canada. Poet Dorothy Livesay and 34 others found the Progressive Arts Club, linking writers of the left to work for social change.

Canada. Left-wing intellectuals, including Frank Underhill and F.R. Scott, found the League for Social Reconstruction to work for social and economic change through education and political means.

Regina. The provincial government amends the Mines Act and the Workmen's Compensation Act in favor of workers as a result of the Estevan miners' strike, but refuses to recognize the miners' union.

Canada. The price of wheat falls to a record low of 34 cents a bushel because of a world surplus and restrictions placed on the import of wheat by European countries. Farmers and wheat pools suffer financial disaster.

London. The Judicial Committee of the Privy Council upholds a Supreme Court of Canada ruling that radio communication is a federal jurisdiction.

"Mad Trapper" killed after long chase

Feb. 17, 1932

RAT RIVER, Yukon – One of the longest manhunts in northern history ended in a hail of gunfire today as police shot and killed Albert Johnson, the so-called "Mad Trapper of Rat River." A posse of RCMP officers and local trappers has been on Johnson's trail for eight weeks, ever since he shot and wounded a policeman who came to his remote cabin to investigate complaints that he was disturbing Indian traplines. When police returned to the cabin in force, the eccentric hermit escaped across the snow. A few days later he was located hiding in a rough fortress about 30 kilometres from his cabin.

Another gun battle took place, and when Johnson stopped firing the police thought they had killed him. However, the fugitive suddenly appeared from cover and fatally shot one of the policemen, driving the others away. Then he vanished once again. The ensuing chase covered 240 kilometres, in temperatures as low as 40 below. While a posse tracked him on the ground, the famous bush pilot "Wop" May kept an eye on him from the air. When the posse caught up with him this morning, Johnson still resisted, wounding another policeman before he was killed.

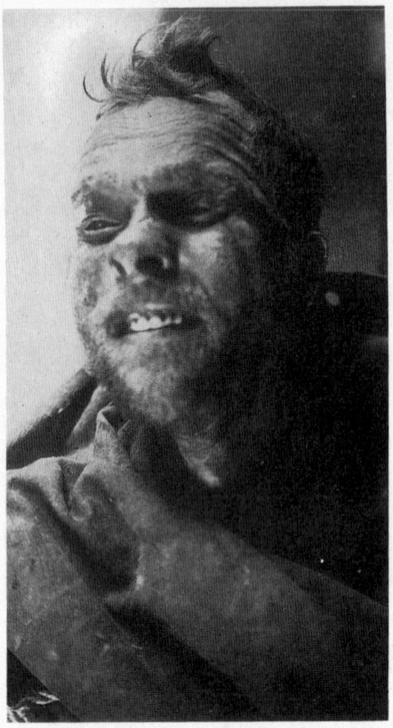

The Mad Trapper after death.

Not much is known about the strange hermit. About 40 years old, he lived alone in his cabin near the delta of the Mackenzie River and seldom had anything to do with anyone else.

Indian health woes cited by prospector

Feb. 28, 1932

OTTAWA – The acute Indian health problems in northwestern Ontario, an area only brought into Treaty 9 in 1930, have been brought to light by John Butterfield, a veteran prospector. Last week he was quoted in a leading Toronto newspaper to the effect that Indian children in the area were dying from tuberculosis, hundreds were going blind with trachoma, and others were on the verge of starvation.

The Department of Indian Affairs has just replied to the prospector's report, terming the charges "grossly exaggerated." The reply also says: "We are doing the best we can with the money available." The department is coping with a budget cut of nearly $1 million in Indian health for the current year.

A prominent civil servant who's visited many reserves blames "Parliament, which for its part, contents itself with voting whatever amount of money seems necessary to fulfil Canada's treaty obligations toward its aborigines and then promptly forgets them, because their number is small and they exercise no influence at the ballot box."

Ships in El Salvador as civil war erupts

Jan. 23, 1932

ACAJUTLA, El Salvador – Royal Canadian Navy ships today are part of an international presence in El Salvador, where civil war has erupted. The RCN's west coast division, destroyers *Skeena* and *Champlain,* was conducting a winter cruise to the West Indies via the Panama Canal when fighting broke out in El Salvador. The ships were ordered to this port to protect foreigners who might be endangered by the fighting. Few Canadians are in El Salvador, and those who are here are chiefly missionaries and telephone workers.

Lt.-Cmdr. Victor B. Brodeur, in charge of the two Canadian ships, expects to remain a week. Ten British subjects have taken shelter aboard the vessels. American and British warships are also proceeding to Salvadoran ports.

Alberta force latest absorbed by RCMP

The RCMP provide provincial police services as well as ceremonial displays.

April 1, 1932

OTTAWA – The Alberta Provincial Police Force is the latest of five provincial forces absorbed by the RCMP. Earlier this year forces in Manitoba, Nova Scotia, New Brunswick, and Prince Edward Island were taken in. This move fits well with Commissioner James Howden MacBrien's effort to develop the force into a professional organization with modern equipment and methods for fighting modern crime. Districts have been regrouped. Each province and territory will become a division. In the last year the force's strength has increased by 1,100 members.

Civil servants taking a 10% pay cut

May 16, 1932

OTTAWA – If times weren't so bad, one could think it was a joke – politicians cutting all civil servant salaries by 10 percent, even their own! But the federal policy is anything but funny, especially for those affected. It cuts the public paycheque by 10 percent for civil servants with salaries above $1,200, with those below that rate getting a five percent cut. Exempted are the military, judges, and the RCMP. They will be subject to a special tax.

One would think the opposition wouldn't dare oppose a pay cut. But such is not the case. All of the opposition members in the House are against the measure, primarily because they fear it will set a dangerous example for the private sector. Prime Minister Richard Bennett says the cut applies only for the current year. After that, Bennett intends to cut the size of the public payroll, as it is "greatly overmanned." Whether it is or not, the result will be even more unemployment, and fewer people with money to spend in the economy.

Devoted sled dogs help save trappers

Sled dogs such as these often show outstanding devotion to their masters.

May 10, 1932

SMOOTH ROCK, Ont. – Two devoted sled dogs lightened the outcome of an accident that occurred on the north country winter trails. A toboggan with three trappers fell through the ice on Ground Hog River, carrying the rear dog and one passenger under the icy current. Chance struck the other two men when their mittens stuck to an ice floe, which acted as a buoy. Two remaining dogs managed to chew through their harness and set out to Fauquier, where they raised a ruckus, alerting villagers to follow them to the scene of the accident. The two men recovered.

CRBC to build a new national network

May 24, 1932

OTTAWA – "The airwaves belong to the people." That's the sentiment Prime Minister Richard Bennett had in mind when he proposed to set up a publicly funded national radio service earlier this year, a proposal that became law today. The creation of the Canadian Radio Broadcasting Commission [forerunner of the CBC] is the government's answer to the arguments over who should be allowed to make radio broadcasts in this country. Bennett is calling for a national chain of public stations, modelled on the British Broadcasting Corporation (BBC).

The new CRBC will be ruled by three commissioners appointed by the government. It is their duty to build the new network, which will be interconnected by telephone line. They will also regulate whatever private stations are allowed to stay on the air, and restrict advertising to no more than five percent of on-air time.

Thousands protest at Nfld. Assembly

March 5, 1932

ST. JOHN'S, Nfld. – The House of Assembly building was attacked today by a crowd, estimated at about 10,000, demanding an investigation into government corruption. When its delegation was refused entry, the crowd began to stone the building, breaking the windows. Mounted police attempted to push people back, but the officers were in turn stoned and knocked from their horses. Then the crowd stormed the building, beating down the doors.

Police kept the people from the Assembly chamber but could not protect the offices, which were broken into and ransacked. Contents of the offices were then thrown through windows. Meanwhile, the premier, Sir Richard Squires, once arrested and charged with larceny, escaped through a rear door and fled the city by taxi.

Nude parades land Doukhobors in jail

Small, radical sects unfortunately give other Doukhobors a bad name.

May 5, 1932

NELSON, B.C. – Nude parades earned a three-year sentence for each of 118 Doukhobor sect Sons of Freedom here today. Thirty-four were women who admitted in court they had taken off their clothes. But, they said, they were praying. The Doukhobors were arrested Sunday morning after they paraded nude at Thrums near here. The RCMP and provincial and railway police have stepped up security on bridges, schools, and public buildings in the area around here after some dynamite was stolen at Ashcroft and a school was burned down at Asquith.

Moravian families such as this one have established Labrador settlements.

McNaughton jumps for gold at Olympics

Canada's Olympic team poses for an official photo at the Ninth Summer Olympics, taking place in Los Angeles, California.

Aug. 1, 1932

LOS ANGELES – Duncan McNaughton won the Olympic gold medal in high jumping for Canada today, edging Bob Van Osdel of the United States. Both were the only competitors to clear the bar at 6 feet, 6 inches, but both failed at 6 feet, 7 inches and 6 feet, 6.5. Officials lowered the bar to 6 feet, 6 inches again and McNaughton succeeded on his first try. Van Osdel failed in three tries.

McNaughton, a Cornwall native raised in Vancouver, made it to the Olympics thanks partly to Van Osdel, his teammate at the University of Southern California. He was disqualified two years ago from the British Empire Games for an illegal technique, but Van Osdel helped him master an accepted style.

High jumper Duncan McNaughton.

Locals relax on a wharf on the south side of St. John's harbor.

Economic treaties signed

Aug. 20, 1932

OTTAWA – The nations of the British Empire reached new trade agreements today. But no one, perhaps not even delegates to the Imperial Economic Conference here, appears to understand the implications. There were 12 treaties signed here today, the majority between Britain and various of her colonies. Most of the details remain secret. It appears that Britain has agreed to give Canadian goods a greater preference in its markets.

Britain has agreed to raise tariffs on some food and primary products while keeping the Canadian tariffs on those goods at a very low level. On some other products, Britain has agreed not to lower the tariffs to other countries without Canada's consent. In return, Canada has given British exporters the right to appeal to this country's tariff board. Canada has also undertaken not to try to protect industries that do not have a reasonable assurance of success, but the details released on this point are vague.

The agreement between Britain and Canada has already raised hackles in Washington. Wheat, lumber, and copper are included in the U.K.-Canada deal. Those are products the U.S. exports to Britain. American producers are expected to protest the new arrangement, which will likely see their exports sales drop.

Prime Minister Richard Bennett said "these agreements constitute a definite advance towards closer empire economic association." But not everyone agrees. The British textile industry is reported to be disappointed, and it is thought the British delegation had hopes of a wider entry into Canadian markets.

Labor and farmers form the CCF party

Aug. 1, 1932

CALGARY – The Co-operative Commonwealth Federation was formed today in Calgary at a conference of laborites and farmers from five different provinces. This new political organization was created with the intention of changing the present economic system. J.S. Woodsworth, Labour MP from Winnipeg North Centre, won the presidency uncontested. Norman F. Priestley, vice-president of the United Farmers of Alberta, was unanimously declared secretary.

The CCF advocates socialization of health services, financial systems, utilities, and natural resources, and equal economic opportunity despite sex, nationality, or faith.

J.S. Woodsworth, the Labour MP from Winnipeg North Centre.

Treaty OKs seaway on the St. Lawrence

July 18, 1932

WASHINGTON, D.C. – After months of negotiation, Canada and the United States have agreed to develop the St. Lawrence River into a seaway capable of taking ships into Lake Ontario. The St. Lawrence Deep Waterway Treaty was officially signed here by William D. Herridge, Canadian plenipotentiary to the United States, and H.L. Stimson, U.S. secretary of state. The Canadian share of the work is estimated at $38 million, and that is after Ontario kicks in $67 million for the right to hydroelectricity generated by the project's dams. In addition to the dams, powerhouses, and canals that must be built, many people living in low-lying areas will have to be moved, and their towns rebuilt on higher ground.

Bullets miss Buck in riots at prison

Oct. 20, 1932

KINGSTON – Tim Buck, former leader of the Communist Party of Canada, is believed to have been prominent in the second outbreak of prison riots at Portsmouth Penitentiary this week. While officials refuse to discuss Buck's part, unconfirmed reports say guards fired three bullets and 10 buckshot pellets into Buck's cell on Range 4D. An unnamed source says sometime after dark, rioting and shooting broke out again in Blocks F and E. Suddenly, the guards were coming over to D. One man yelled, "Duck boys, they're going to shoot in here," followed by a bullet whizzing by just below Buck's left ear.

Funding cut leaves Inuit out in the cold

1932

QUEBEC CITY – The Quebec government has cut off funds to its impoverished Inuit population in the north of the province. The decision comes in the middle of a heated dispute between the provincial and federal governments over which has the responsibility to provide services to the Inuit, who, unlike Indians, are not directly under Ottawa's jurisdiction. Until 1929, the federal government provided for the Inuit, but then passed the buck to Quebec. Now the Inuit are left out in the cold as Ottawa continues to pay, but as little as possible.

An Inuit woman and child.

Work camps to provide 2,000 jobs

The depression in the west is made worse by the drought and dust storms.

A Bennett buggy on the dusty prairie.

Oct. 8, 1932

OTTAWA – The Department of National Defence has the green light to help Canada's unemployed by setting up camps that will put 2,000 civilians to work at a cost of $1 per man per day, starting immediately. The authorization was given today in an order-in-council after the cabinet of Prime Minister Richard B. Bennett had studied a memorandum on the proposal by Gen. Andrew McNaughton.

In his capacity as chief of the general staff, McNaughton's spent the summer and early fall visiting various centres across Canada. He reported seeing hundreds of men without work wherever he went. Nearly a quarter of the labor force is unemployed. Of these, an estimated 70,000 men are destitute and homeless. The army's senior officer proposed that volunteers be accommodated, clothed, and fed in the work camps until they can find jobs on their own.

Manifesto calls for economic equality

Nov. 1, 1932

MONTREAL – Les Jeunes-Canada has published a manifesto calling for French-Canadians to reject their proletarian status and seize their fair share of economic power in Quebec and Canada. Written by André Laurendeau, son of prominent nationalist Arthur Laurendeau, the manifesto of the young generation declares: "In all domains of national life let the ardent concern awake to reconquer lost positions, to make the future better. ... Let us remember that we shall be masters in our own house only if we become worthy of being so."

The manifesto, published in *Le Quartier Latin,* the University of Montreal student newspaper, denounces the "foreign capitalists" who impose on French-Canadians "the worst of dictatorships" and relegate French-Canadian workers to roles as servants and laborers. "We ask today what we shall exact tomorrow," the manifesto warns.

Sewer blasts leave thousands terrified

Nov. 30, 1932

MONTREAL – Fire officials are amazed no lives were lost tonight as dozens of explosions in the city sewer system destroyed buildings, ripped roadways, and kept thousands terrified in their homes. Several people in a building on St. Denis Street were propelled by a blast into the street, yet escaped serious injury. The explosions ripped along St. Denis, blowing manhole covers as far away as three kilometres. One gas station was destroyed by a blast. A fire that ignited a gas line is being blamed.

Quebec puts bounty on all white whales

1932

QUEBEC – There is now a $45 bounty on every white whale in Quebec waters. The provincial government has instituted the bounty as a way of addressing the complaints of commercial fishermen, who are blaming the white whales for depleted salmon supplies. Before the bounty was announced, the white whale was relentlessly stalked by fishermen and sportsmen. But now it will be pursued even more – the bounty makes the white whale fair game for anyone.

Freight travel ban ups shelter demand

Oct. 8, 1932

PORT ARTHUR [Thunder Bay], Ont. – Thanks to the government's enforcement of the Canadian Railway Act, which bans free rides on freight trains, this town is rapidly filling up with unemployed men. The reason: there are no highways out of Port Arthur, and so there's no way for the penniless transients here to leave. The result is that applications for shelter at the charitable Sailors' Institute have gone up 300 percent since enforcement of the act began Oct. 1.

1933

Germany, Jan. 30. Adolf Hitler becomes chancellor.

Toronto, April 13. New York Rangers beat the Toronto Maple Leafs three games to one to win the Stanley Cup.

Winnipeg, May 16. Police raid the western headquarters of the pro-Hitler, anti-Jewish Canadian Fascist Party.

Ottawa, May 23. Parliament passes the Canadian National-Canadian Pacific Act, directing the CPR and CNR to agree to co-operate to make rail service more economical.

Kingston, Ont., Aug. 26. The first non-stop flight across Canada is completed, from Vancouver.

Montreal, Sept. 20. J. Anaclet Chalifoux, president of the Federation of Labor Clubs of Quebec, announces the organization is being renamed the Fascist Party of Canada. Its reported 25,000 members wear Hitler-style brown shirts and salute with the outraised arm.

British Columbia, Nov. 2. Liberal Thomas Dufferin ("Duff") Pattullo, an advocate of "socialized capitalism" to deal with the depression, is elected premier.

Stratford, Ont., Nov. 4. The strike of furniture workers and meat packers ends. All the workers have returned to their jobs after securing small wage increases. The government called in troops to oppose the strike, but the move only succeeded in gaining public sympathy for the strikers.

St. John's, Nfld., Nov. 28. Faced with financial crisis, the legislature votes to relinquish Newfoundland's dominion status, or self-government, and revert back to colonial status, or government by commission appointed by Britain.

Sarnia, Ont., Dec. 9. Toronto Argonauts beat Sarnia Imperials 4-3 for the Grey Cup.

Ottawa. A revision to the Indian Act reinstates the compulsory enfranchisement clause revoked after Indian protests in 1922. Those chosen for forced enfranchisement become citizens with voting rights and relinquish their special tax-free rights as Indians.

Blairmore, Alta. Supporters of the revolutionary Workers Unity League win municipal elections and rename the main street Tim Buck Boulevard.

United States. Canadian Fay Wray stars in *King Kong*.

Prestigious prize for Skinner's flower

Lilium Maxwill Lily.

Dr. F.L. Skinner has just won the Cory Cup for developing this new lily.

1933

ENGLAND – For the first time in history, the prestigious Cory Cup, bestowed by the Royal Horticultural Society, has been awarded to an entry from outside the United Kingdom. The honored recipient was Dr. Frank Leith Skinner, a Scotsman now residing in Dropmore, Man.

Skinner is a respected horticulturist best known for his work with lilies. He captured the Cory Cup with his exquisite Lilium Maxwill, a hybrid of the Chinese and Korean lilies. Skinner dusted the stigma of the Chinese Lily with the pollen from a Korean Lily precisely at the peak of each flower's development. His painstaking efforts generated an Oriental-looking flower that bears the hardiness of the Korean Lily and the graceful appeal of the Chinese Lily.

Controversial law tackles "Red menace"

Feb. 23, 1933

OTTAWA – Fear about the so-called "Red menace" appears to be gaining strength, as police continue to use the contested Section 98 of the Criminal Code to round up Communists. Section 98, passed in 1919 at a time of considerable labor strife, is still in force despite attempts to repeal it. The latest effort was led by J.S. Woodsworth, Labour MP for Winnipeg North Centre. Woodsworth introduced a repeal motion in the House on Feb. 14, arguing that Section 98 allowed imprisonment of Canadians on the basis of their beliefs, rather than their actions. "We have been taught that a man can be convicted only when he has actually committed some crime," Woodsworth said, "but these men have not been convicted of any crime." Despite arguing that Communists should be subject to the same law as all other Canadians, Woodsworth's repeal motion was defeated 89-45, giving a victory to the "Red-haters."

Dorchester inmates go on the rampage

Jan. 8, 1933

DORCHESTER, N.B. – The chill of winter is felt by all Dorchester Penitentiary inmates this morning as the wind howls through hundreds of shattered window panes, a result of the worst rioting in the history of the Maritime provinces. The five-hour uprising last evening involved 300 of the penitentiary's 476 convicts. All except for five now in the infirmary have been led back to their cells – past the toilets, basins, chairs, and lockers that litter the prison yard.

A tip-off from an undisclosed source ensured the riot would be contained by the prison's 40-odd guards, but officials are puzzled over what started it all. Overcrowded conditions in the prison may have contributed, and cries of "we want more food" were heard when the trouble began.

Russian letters tell of Communist evil

March 16, 1933

REGINA – Members of the Saskatchewan legislature listened as colleagues read excerpts of letters sent to their constituents by friends and relatives in Russia. The letters told of hardships caused by the Russian government. One letter reported that starving people were sent to Siberia because they had taken food from their own farms. Another said a family had shot their parents rather than let them suffer. People are said to be searching the garbage for fish scales and making soup from grass.

Members used the opportunity to point out the evils of a Communist government, noting that as troubled as Saskatchewan is, people here are still much better off than the millions of people suffering in Russia.

The discontented "are shot or put into jail and tortured. We have not even a cow or goat, pig, hen, dog or cat," went one letter. "Think of our children, how they plead and we have nothing to give them."

Thousands condemn Hitler, Nazi brutality

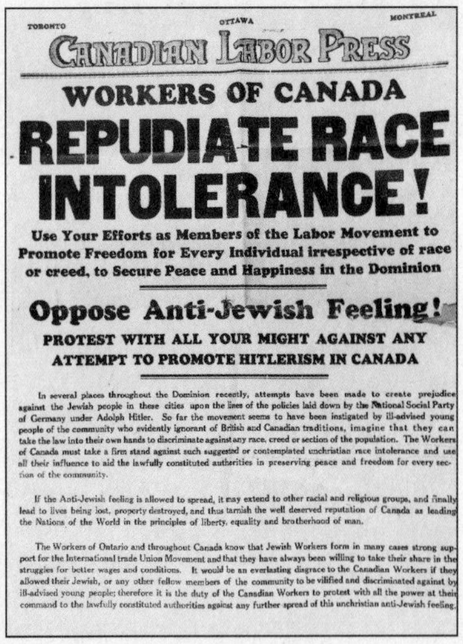
TORONTO OTTAWA MONTREAL

CANADIAN LABOR PRESS

WORKERS OF CANADA

REPUDIATE RACE INTOLERANCE!

Use Your Efforts as Members of the Labor Movement to Promote Freedom for Every Individual irrespective of race or creed, to Secure Peace and Happiness in the Dominion

Oppose Anti-Jewish Feeling!

PROTEST WITH ALL YOUR MIGHT AGAINST ANY ATTEMPT TO PROMOTE HITLERISM IN CANADA

In several places throughout the Dominion recently, attempts have been made to create prejudice against the Jewish people in these cities upon the lines of the policies laid down by the National Social Party of Germany under Adolph Hitler. So far the movement seems to have been instigated by ill-advised young people of the community who evidently ignorant of British and Canadian traditions, imagine that they can take the law into their own hands to discriminate against any race, creed or section of the population. The Workers of Canada must take a firm stand against such suggested or contemplated unchristian race intolerance and use all their influence to aid the lawfully constituted authorities in preserving peace and freedom for every section of the community.

If the Anti-Jewish feeling is allowed to spread, it may extend to other racial and religious groups, and finally lead to lives being lost, property destroyed, and thus tarnish the well deserved reputation of Canada as leading the Nations of the World in the principles of liberty, equality and brotherhood of man.

The Workers of Ontario and throughout Canada know that Jewish Workers form in many cases strong support for the International trade Union Movement and that they have always been willing to take their share in the struggles for better wages and conditions. It would be an everlasting disgrace to the Canadian Workers if they allowed their Jewish, or any other fellow members of the community to be vilified and discriminated against by ill-advised young people; therefore it is the duty of the Canadian Workers to protest with all the power at their command to the lawfully constituted authorities against any further spread of this unchristian anti-Jewish feeling.

Poster urges racial tolerance.

1933

CANADA – Canadian Jews, in an effort to curb the growing tide of international anti-Semitism and to consolidate Canadian efforts against Adolf Hitler's brutal Nazi regime, have resurrected the Canadian Jewish Congress.

In Toronto, thousands of people of all faiths gathered to sing in sorrowful prayer for victims of the Nazis and to call for the Canadian government to impose economic sanctions on fascist Germany. In Montreal, 10,000 people – Jews and gentiles alike – heard appeals for Hitler to abide by terms of the Geneva accord and end the abuse of the Jewish minority in Germany.

Many Jewish immigrants settle in communities such as Edenbridge, Sask.

CCF debates manifesto

July 19, 1933

REGINA – Pacificists won here today in a battle with hardliners in the Co-operative Commonwealth Federation. The CCF party's provisional executive presented what is being called the Regina Manifesto, which advocates fundamental social change. But, in achieving that change, the manifesto declares: "We do not believe in violent change." A good number of delegates to the conference here wanted that clause struck out. Toronto labor activist William Moriarity says "if the ruling class opposes the will of the people, we must use a method suitable to the occasion."

But most delegates agreed with CCF leader J.S. Woodsworth that the new socialist party must pursue peaceful avenues. The Regina Manifesto advocates, above all, a socialization of the economic order. It proposes nationalizing all financial institutions and all services essential to social planning. It supports security of tenure for farmers and removal of farmers' debts. Taxes should be designed to lessen income inequality, it says.

The manifesto proposes a gradual nationalization of key industries, beginning with those involved in transportation, commerce, and electric power. Once these industries are nationalized, a CCF government would move to state-ownership in the industries of mining and pulp and paper, and the distribution of milk, bread, coal, and gasoline. The manifesto declares that "no CCF government will rest content until it has eradicated capitalism." The CCF manifesto also supports increased social services.

RCMP inspector killed as jobless protest

Cramped dormitories in relief camps lead to unrest among the workers.

May 8, 1933

SASKATOON – Inspector L.J. Sampson of the RCMP was killed and three other officers injured when Mounties and city police clashed with about 300 unemployed protesters in Saskatoon.

Trouble has been brewing for some time in the relief camp, an establishment set up to house and feed physically fit single unemployed men until they can find work. The environment was ripe for activists seeking followers in their bid for social reform. When officials decided to transfer 50 men from the overcrowded camp to Regina, including some of the more militant leaders, the men refused to go and staged a demonstration when they were not served supper. The police were called in, and 15 minutes of violence left one dead and several injured. Men of the camp threw stones and wielded planks. Police used nightsticks, causing numerous head cuts. Sampson was thrown from his horse and struck his head on a pole. Twenty-five men will be charged with unlawful assembly.

Hunger leads men to steal food in Nfld.

June 7, 1933

LITTLE CATALINA, Nfld. – Hunger drives people to do unexpected things. Yesterday hungry people entered shops in this village and helped themselves to food. The government precipitated the crisis when it ordered all unemployed men to work on government projects in return for government assistance of six cents per day per person. The men had no objection, but the jobs to which they were assigned are 10 kilometres away and they are expected to walk there and back each day.

The government of Frederick Alderdice has shown little sympathy for the plight of the fishermen, who are bearing the brunt of the collapse in world trade and are on the verge of starvation. Meanwhile, 40 policemen have been sent from St. John's to make arrests.

Ottawa, Quebec fight over who should care for starving Inuit

Aug. 3, 1933

QUEBEC – While many Inuit are starving in Quebec, the provincial and federal governments are squabbling over who should pay for relief and medical supplies. Quebec's minister of justice has notified Ottawa that the care of Inuit is a federal responsibility, as Inuit are Indians and, hence, under the terms of the British North America Act, wards of the Canadian government. Ottawa rejects this view.

An agreement was worked out in 1929 whereby Ottawa would help Quebec's Inuit and the province would reimburse the federal government, but Quebec now says it will not continue to make payments beyond this year.

Inuit in Quebec suffer while federal and provincial governments squabble.

Six under arrest as rioting erupts at Winnipeg march

July 20, 1933

WINNIPEG – Two policemen were injured and six demonstrators arrested yesterday following riots near Winnipeg's city hall. The demonstrators took to the streets on the basis of two specific complaints. They object to the closure of the outpatients' department at Winnipeg General Hospital, and to a recent announcement of changes in the payment of emergency relief. Earlier this week the Relief Commission issued an order stating that henceforth any relief payments paid to transients will be for two days duration only.

When a crowd of marchers chanting "We want medical aid" headed for city hall, a small group of policemen headed them onto Main Street, where a larger force of police officers tried to get the marchers to disperse. The reserves were called, arriving with batons and tear gas.

Police make sure Jews don't encounter anti-Semitic Swastikas

Aug. 1, 1933

TORONTO – The anti-Jewish fervor sweeping Germany turned up in Toronto's Beaches district tonight. There, a group of anti-Semites united under the banner of the Swastika party marched up and down the Boardwalk, looking to rid the area of "undesirables." They might have found their version of the term had they run into a group of 60 to 70 Jews who came down to the Beaches earlier in the evening to meet the challenge. Fast work by police, however, meant the Jews left the area before the 200 or so Swastika supporters marched onto the scene.

Mayor of Toronto bans Swastika emblem

Aug. 17, 1933

TORONTO – Those wearing the Swastika emblem in Toronto will be viewed as troublemakers and charged as such. That's the gist of a statement by the mayor in which he bans the wearing of the Swastika badge in Toronto. Ostensibly, wearers of the badge are members of a citizens' group in the Beaches, aimed at keeping "undesirables" off their waterfront. But, as a recent clash between Jews and gentiles illustrates, this symbol of nazism has become identified with the same ideology of hatred and intolerance by its wearers over here that it has in Germany.

A radio broadcast by the Four Porters on station CNRV, Toronto.

Reindeer herd arrives after four-year trip

The government has just moved a large reindeer herd to a new home.

Aug. 20, 1933

NORTHWEST TERRITORIES – The government-instituted project to relocate 2,100 reindeer ended today, after a four-year trek across wolf-ridden, icy trails. The reindeer purchased by the Canadian government as a source of food and clothing for natives of the Northwest Territories were led by Andy Bahr. Bahr and his assistants brought the herd from the Kotzebue Sound region of western Alaska to the government's experimental station on Richard Island at the northwestern tip of the N.W.T.

Strikebreakers are given a hard time

Oct. 12, 1933

STRATFORD, Ont. – The strike among furniture workers and chicken pluckers that has run for a month here continued its ugliness today, as office workers and strikebreakers crossing a picket line were pelted with rotten tomatoes, apples, and plums. All that was unique was that, for the first time, police were able to arrest one of the pickets. Until the militia was brought into Stratford, attempts at strikebreaking and making arrests were effectively foiled by members of the Workers' Unity League union.

Strikers are after higher wages and are willing to risk their jobs to get them, despite the fact that work is hard to find these days.

Workers ridicule the mayor and his militia during the Stratford strike.

Crafty canine leads officer to stolen car

November 1933

BASSANO, Alta. – A case involving the apprehension of a suspected car thief was tossed out of court early this month, the judge refusing to accept as evidence the tracking skills of a German shepherd named Dale. But credit Sgt. J.N. Cawsey of the RCMP and his well-trained canine companion for innovation in the line of duty.

With the family pet Dale fitted in a specially designed tracking harness, complete with 13-metre leash, Cawsey followed the dog's lead on an eight-kilometre trail through snow and mud until the stolen car was found. Minutes later the suspect was found in a nearby cabin.

Camel-like sea serpent spotted in B.C.

Oct. 5, 1933

VICTORIA, B.C. – Vancouver Island has a sea serpent – and it dwarfs the legendary Ogopogo of Okanagan Lake in the interior. Five people, among them a clerk of the B.C. legislature, say they have seen "Caddy," a 24-metre greenish-brown monster in the sea near Cadboro Island, just off Victoria.

A few days ago, Maj. W.H. Langley, a legislature clerk and well-known Victoria lawyer, and his wife say they saw the monster, which looked, in profile, like a camel. Now Mr. F. Kemp, who works for the provincial archives, says he, his wife and son saw the monster a year ago in the same place. Kemp said he did not report the sighting before because he was afraid he would be laughed at.

Nfld. surrenders responsible government

Nov. 28, 1933

ST. JOHN'S, Nfld. – Betrayed by spineless politicians and ungrateful Britain, Newfoundland lost its democracy and its independence today when the Assembly accepted the Amulree Report and surrendered responsible government.

Premier Frederick Alderdice has tried to reduce interest payments on the public debt of $100 million – much of it borrowed to assist Britain in the Great War – but Britain refused. Instead she lent the money and appointed a royal commission under Baron Amulree to assess the situation. Amulree ignored the collapse in world trade, at the heart of Newfoundland's troubles and the reason she cannot raise her own revenues, and recommended government by a British commission.

Prohibition policy is repealed in U.S.

Dec. 5, 1933

WASHINGTON, D.C. – Liquor is once again legal in the United States. Prohibition – the attempt to regulate the public good by banning booze – is now one of history's failures. Today President Franklin D. Roosevelt signed the proclamation that officially struck Prohibition from the United States Constitution.

Ending Prohibition means many things. It should spell the end of bootlegging, now that legal, high-quality booze is available. This should strike hard at the gangster empires that have built their power on "bathtub gin." It will also open a new area for government control, although the emphasis now isn't so much on temperance, as it is on protecting domestic producers.

Unable to afford gas for their cars, westerners are using "horsepower" to pull their Bennett buggies.

1934

Toronto, Feb. 14. A team of NHL all-stars plays the Maple Leafs in a benefit game for former Leaf Ace Bailey, whose career was ended last year when he suffered a concussion during a game.

Quebec, Feb. 25. Archbishop Georges Gauthier denounces the CCF and socialism in general in a pastoral letter.

Fredericton, March 9. Women are granted the right to stand for provincial office.

Chicago, April 10. Chicago Blackhawks beat the Detroit Red Wings three games to one to win the Stanley Cup.

Northwest Territories, June 1. The Hudson's Bay Co. relocates 52 destitute Baffin Island Inuit on Devon Island in an attempt to improve their lives [the attempt ends in failure].

London, England, June 3. Canadian Dr. Frederick Banting, one of the discoverers of insulin, is knighted.

Ottawa, July 3. Parliament passes the Bank of Canada Act, creating the Bank of Canada, a central bank.

London, England, July 12. Winnie-the-Pooh, a tame black bear from Ontario and the basis of A.A. Milne's *Winnie the Pooh*, dies at London Zoo.

Quebec, July 13. Indians on the Caughnawaga Reserve near Montreal complain to police about whites holding nude bathing parties on the reserve.

Toronto, July 26. The attorney general blocks plans to exploit the Dionne quintuplets, breaking a contract signed by their father to exhibit them at the Chicago Century of Progress Exposition.

California, July 29. Canadian film star Marie Dressler dies.

Toronto, Sept. 24. The province extends the residency requirement for municipal relief from three months to one year. Authorities hope the change will stop towns from secretly transferring destitute citizens to other centres.

Montreal, Nov. 16. Legislature member Athanase David announces the creation of the Société des Concerts symphoniques de Montréal [Montreal Symphony Orchestra].

Toronto, Nov. 24. Sarnia Imperials beat Regina Roughriders 20-12 for the Grey Cup.

Hamilton, Dec. 25. A train collision kills 18 people and injures 30 more.

Bennett plans changes to BNA Act

April 11, 1934

OTTAWA – Prime Minister Richard Bennett today announced to the House of Commons his intention to seek changes to the British North America Act. The main thrust of Bennett's proposals is to get the provinces to relinquish their jurisdiction in matters of social problems, notably old age, illness, minimum wage, and working hours and conditions. Bennett also hopes to seek agreement on how the BNA Act can be amended.

The prime minister has called for a dominion-provincial conference before the end of the year and has asked the provinces to submit their ideas and suggestions for other discussions. Bennett has already hinted he expects resistance to his proposals from some provinces, particularly from Quebec.

Bennett's case for constitutional reform got the official blessing of former Conservative prime minister Arthur Meighen, the government's leader in the Senate, who said the BNA Act was more suitable for the "horse and buggy days of Confederation" and doesn't take into account modern social and business conditions.

Bennett wants to reduce the duplication of efforts of the federal and provincial governments in the areas where jurisdiction is not defined very clearly. Foremost among these areas are social policy, health, and agriculture. Bennett also hopes to "reduce the evils of double taxation and provide a more logical allocation of sources of revenue."

In Saskatchewan, during hard times, people will move anywhere to find work.

Six-person commission to govern Nfld.

Feb. 16, 1934

ST. JOHN'S, Nfld. – Today in the Newfoundland Hotel, Premier Frederick Alderdice signed the document which ended this dominion's 79 years of self-government. Replacing the elected Legislative Assembly and the council will be a commission of six individuals appointed by the British government. These commissioners – three from Newfoundland and three from Britain – and the governor will form the new government. It is agreed that when Newfoundland is self-supporting again, responsible government will be restored on request. Meanwhile, people here say bitterly that ending Newfoundland's democracy won't improve the fish trade.

All Star, "Stars" in the Ace Bailey Benefit Game 1934
BACK ROW LEFT TO RIGHT — THE LATE CHUCK GARDINER, RED DUTTON, EDDIE SHORE, ALLEN SHIELDS, BILL BRIAN, LIONEL CONACHER, CHING JOHNSON, NELS STEWART, FRANKIE FINNIGAN.
FRONT ROW LEFT TO RIGHT — NORMIE HIMES, LARRY AURIE, HOOLEY SMITH, JIMMIE WARD, LESTER PATRICK, LEO DANDURAND, BILL COOK, HOWIE MORENZ, AURIEL JOLIAT, HERB LEWIS, MASCOT, HOWIE MORENZ, JR.

This all-star team played against the Maple Leafs in a benefit game for Ace Bailey, who was seriously injured in a game with the Boston Bruins.

Students search for Sasquatch in B.C.

April 8, 1934

VANCOUVER – Two young American medical students left today on a hunt for the legendary Sasquatch, the hairy monster said to live in the coastal mountains. The students, J.F. and C.K. Blakeney, brothers who attend the University of California, read reports of the Sasquatch and decided to try to photograph or capture one in the Harrison Lake area.

Chief chases officer from Oka Reserve

April 26, 1934

OKA, Que. – A police officer trying to serve a warrant at the Oka Reserve was forced to withdraw after a confrontation with the chief of the Tribal Council, which claims jurisdiction on the reserve. Const. Henri Daoust was seeking Tom Martin on charges of illegally chopping trees on monastery property when the chief threatened to have warriors forcibly remove him.

Gargantuan tumor removed in surgery

June 21, 1934

KINGSTON, Ont. – A tumor weighing 55 pounds was removed today from a 41-year-old woman by staff of the Kingston General Hospital. It is believed to be the largest tumor ever surgically removed from a human body. The woman weighed 115 pounds when she entered hospital. Doctors says there is a good chance she will make a full recovery.

The Flying Bishop sets a new record

July 12, 1934

WINNIPEG – Rev. Archibald Lang Fleming, known as The Flying Bishop, set a new record by covering 2,095 kilometres in one day in a preaching blitz in the Arctic. Embarking from Aklavik in a Canadian Airways craft, Fleming, the Anglican bishop of the Arctic diocese, touched down at such farflung locales as Coppermine, Fort McMurray, and Cameron Bay.

Ontario woman delivers quintuplets

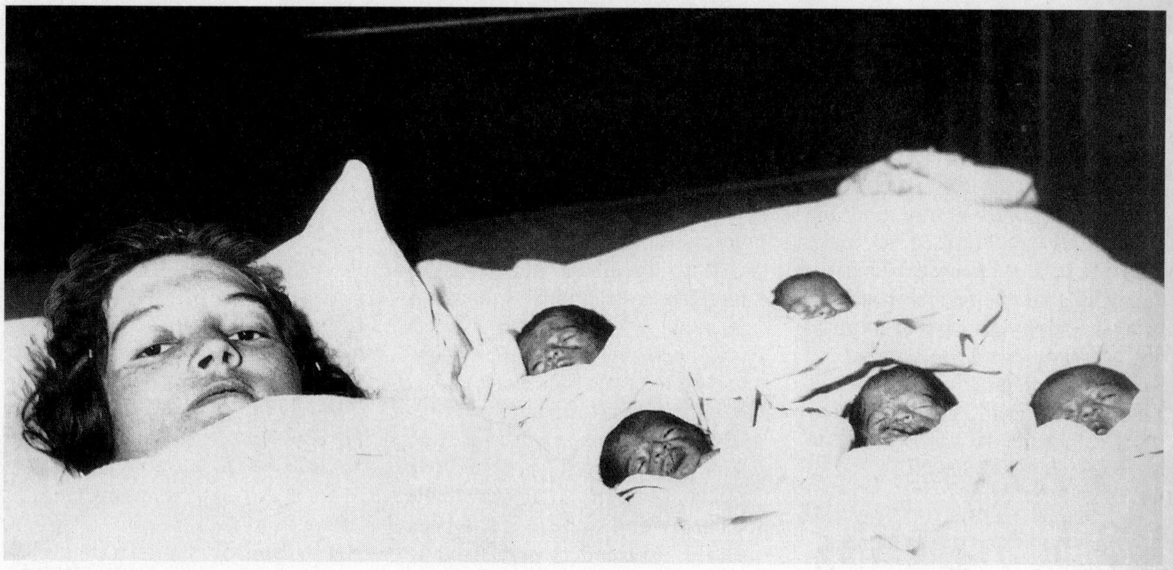

The Dionne quintuplets have their first picture taken with their mother, in their Northern Ontario home.

May 28, 1934

CORBEIL, Ont. – Five tiny baby girls in makeshift cradles in a farmhouse in this northern community near North Bay are the focus of worldwide attention tonight as Oliva and Elzire Dionne continue to receive congratulations on the birth of Canada's first quintuplets. All five were born within half an hour early this morning, three before Dr. Allan Roy Dafoe arrived to attend the 24-year-old mother.

When Mr. Dionne was asked by a throng of reporters if he felt proud, he replied: "I'm the kind of fellow they should put in jail." He then put the babies on a potato scale, calling out the weights to the journalists. All five totalled only 13 pounds, six ounces.

Since her marriage in 1924 at the age of 15, Mrs. Dionne has given birth six times before; five survive. Dionne, who went into debt to buy the farm, is now worrying how he'll feed five more mouths.

Cost to farmers may be in millions as "black blizzard" strikes

May 11, 1934

WINNIPEG – A "black blizzard" swept across the Prairie provinces yesterday, leaving farmers in trouble and city dwellers covered with dust. The storm, the third of the present season, gathered on the east slope of the Rockies and swept to the east, as far as the Great Lakes. Its 65-kilometre-per-hour winds picked up the parched topsoil to such an extent that it blocked out the sunlight. Motorists were forced to drive with their headlights on. Some rail tracks were covered so completely that train crews were required to shovel sand off the lines.

A severe dust storm has partially buried this tractor and farm building.

The economic results will not be known for some time, but the cost may run into the millions. Along with the topsoil went grain seeds planted only a few days before. The severity of the current dry spell is such that some farmers will be reluctant to seed their land again unless there are intervening rains. Adding to the farmers' woes are the reports of the weather forecasters, who anticipate no precipitation in the near future.

For the city residents the storm was little more than a major inconvenience. It was not possible to walk outside without being covered with the powdery dust. The flying particles were so fine that in many instances they penetrated closed windows, bringing despair to housewives and distress to workers in plants and offices.

There are reports from Saskatchewan of motorists stranded on side roads which were covered with up to 60 centimetres of unpacked sand and grit.

Miners vote to end strike in Flin Flon

July 14, 1934

FLIN FLON, Man. – The miners' strike at Flin Flon is over, after the Mine Workers' Union of Canada voted 201-18 to return to work. The stoppage began on June 9 and was only partially complete. By vote time, almost 1,000 workers had returned to duty.

When the first shift reported for duty at 4 p.m. today, members of the RCMP lined the route to the plant. Ninety members of the federal force have been here since June 9, when 1,300 miners struck the plant of Hudson Bay Mining and Smelting Co. to protest labor conditions. During the strike, miners separated into two warring camps, nicknamed the "reds" and the "whites." The militant "reds" have refused to return to work without better wages and working conditions. They are believed responsible for acts of intimidation and for obstructing police investigations. ▷

Kidnappers release brewer John Labatt

Aug. 17, 1934

LONDON, Ont. – The wealthy brewer John Labatt is home with his family today, but there are few details of the kidnap plot in which he was held hostage for more than 60 hours. Lawyers representing the millionaire have refused to make public details of his ordeal, and it is indicated that the silence has been brought on by threats of reprisal against members of the Labatt family. A ransom note, signed Three-Fingered Abe, had been received by the family, and it was believed to have demanded $150,000.

Indians trespassing on former reserve

Aug. 12, 1934

SELKIRK, Man. – Old grievances were aired in court yesterday when 17 Indians were found guilty of trespassing. Their leader was fined $2,015 or three months in jail. The Indians are members of the former St. Peter's Reserve. In 1907 federal authorities negotiated a deed of surrender of this land and moved occupants to Hodgson, but slowly the Indians have moved back. In their defence, the Indians claim St. Peter's was given them by the "Great White Mother."

Storm devastates Alberta wheat crop

Aug. 15, 1934

LETHBRIDGE, Alta. – Thousands of hectares of a promising crop of wheat were wiped out Wednesday night by a devastating storm. The early estimates place damage at well over $500,000, and few of the farms involved were covered by insurance.

The swath of the storm was 16 kilometres wide and 80 kilometres in length. It struck the districts of Connemara, Okotoks, Cayley, and Nanton, and narrowly missed Champion and Carmangay. It began with a brief deluge of rain which was followed by destructive hail. Much of the grain was ready for harvest and some of it had been swathed. The binders were standing in the fields when the storm hit. The crops that were ruined gave promise of yielding in excess of 50 bushels to the hectare.

It is estimated that a few farmers suffered damage to the extent of 100 percent. It is known that 4,800 hectares in the Nanton district suffered 40 percent loss, while 2,400 hectares near Cayley are damaged to the extent of 15 percent.

An idea of the severity of the storm may be gathered by reports in some localities of hail standing in the fields 10 centimetres deep. Fields were turned into ice-covered lakes. The farmers were not the only ones affected by the devastating storm. Thousands of birds were killed by the hailstones.

Relief camp projects are instituted in the west as farm conditions worsen.

Ayling, Reid complete non-stop transatlantic flight to England

Aug. 9, 1934

LONDON, England – Aviation history was made with the completion today of the first non-stop transatlantic flight from central Canada to England. Hoping to set the long distance flying record, James Ayling and Leonard Reid left Wasaga Beach yesterday with 2,724 litres of gasoline in *The Trail of the Caribou* for Baghdad. Faulty carburetors consumed nearly twice as much fuel as expected, and fog forced the pair to land today at Heston, near London.

Flying 5,955 kilometres in 30 hours and 55 minutes, Reid said their black-winged biplane "followed the St. Lawrence to Belle Isle," which was covered with fog. Flying blind, they sighted Ireland "almost at the exact spot we expected." For now, Ayling and Reid plan to have "a good sound sleep."

Leader like Mussolini needed: Groulx

Benito Mussolini, a model of strong leadership, according to Groulx.

Sept. 1, 1934

MONTREAL – French-Canadians need a strong leader to restore national pride, Abbé Lionel Groulx argues in an article published in *l'Action Nationale,* a magazine published by ultra-nationalist French-Canadians.

Abbé Groulx, who teaches at the Jesuits' Collège Ste. Marie, writes in the article titled "Language and Survival" that Quebec needs a national leader with the qualities of present European strongmen. He lauded "the de Valera, the Mussolini, whose politics are open to discussion, but who in 10 years have psychologically remade a new Ireland and a new Italy, as a Dollfuss and a Salazar are remaking a new Austria and a new Portugal."

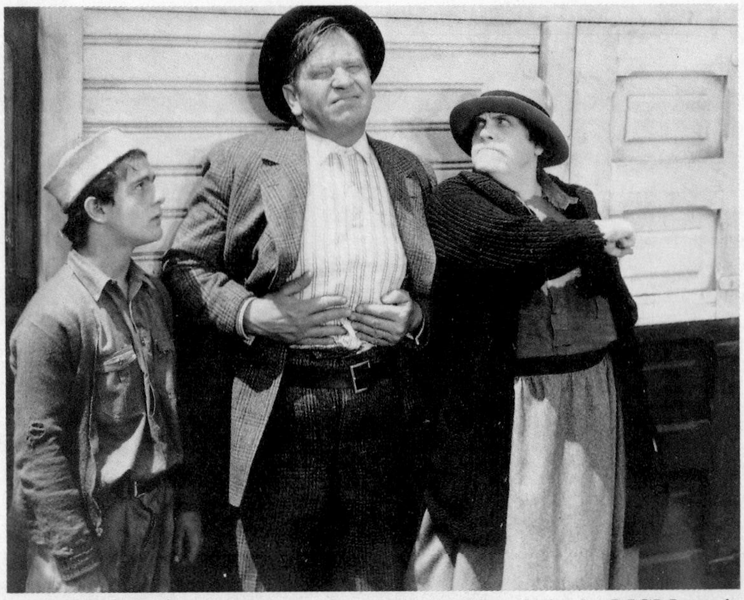

Marie Dressler, from Cobourg, Ont., has the title role in the MGM movie Tugboat Annie. She is also well-known as a stage actress in New York.

Stevens steps down as minister of trade

Oct. 26, 1934
OTTAWA – Henry Herbert Stevens has resigned as minister of trade and commerce and as head of the committee investigating the practices of big business in Canada. His resignation comes after a flurry of public controversy concerning a pamphlet he wrote summarizing some of the committee's findings before its report had been released.

In his pamphlet, Stevens attacks both the buying and labor management strategies of Canadian big business. He accuses them of maintaining "sweatshop" working conditions for employees and of selling goods at a loss, thus hurting independents who can't afford to match such prices, and other abuses.

Although the government of Richard B. Bennett managed to suppress the pamphlet for a time, eventually it turned up in the Winnipeg *Free Press*. The resulting uproar from businessmen forced the PM to distance himself from Stevens by recommending he "correct his misstatements" today at the first meeting of the Prices Spreads and Mass Buying Commission – the body that has superseded the original investigating committee. For his part, Stevens has refused, choosing instead to act only as a commission member, rather than as its chairman.

Quints get a new home

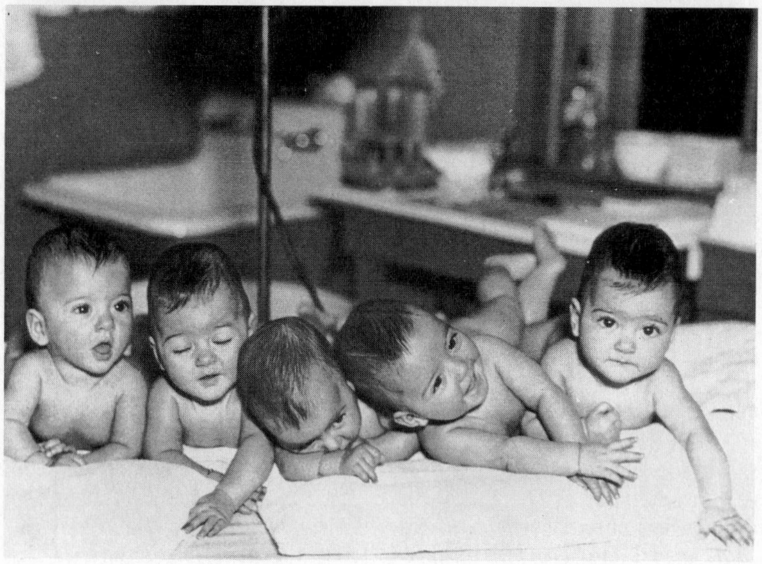

The famous Dionne Quintuplets are shown during a recent photo session.

Sept. 22, 1934
CALLANDER, Ont. – The famous Dionne Quintuplets, not yet four months old, were moved from their parents' home to a special, newly built nursery today where they will be housed under the watchful eye of their government-appointed guardian, Dr. Allan Roy Dafoe.

The decision to relocate the infants has been made out of concern for their health and safekeeping. It's a precautionary move to protect the quints from potentially fatal viruses, as well as to shield them from unscrupulous private interests bent on exploiting them. Dafoe is immensely relieved over now having what he calls "a fair chance to protect the lives of the little babies." He announced he intends to have a high fence built around the nursery. A special constable was on hand during the move to prevent spectators from handling the children.

Parents Oliva and Elzire Dionne were not present for the move, having left early this morning for an undisclosed location. Similarly, neither parent attended last week's nursery opening, pleading shyness.

Colored All-Stars win baseball title

Oct. 23, 1934
CHATHAM, Ont. – The Chatham Colored All-Stars are the toast of town today, after winning this city's first Ontario Baseball Association Intermediate B championship. The All-Stars beat Penetang in the finals. Formed two years ago to give the players something to do in the depression, they barnstormed in this area, attracting big crowds at exhibition games. This year they joined the City Baseball League, losing only once, before advancing to the OBA playoffs.

Scientists examine dead sea creature

Nov. 22, 1934
PRINCE RUPERT, B.C. – The remains of a strange sea creature have been found near here. As scientists start to examine what is left of the nine-metre creature, some experts wonder if the remains are those of Caddy, the sea serpent often seen off Cadboro Bay near Victoria. Caddy was last seen about three months ago. The remains will be taken to the local fisheries experimental station for a full examination. The flesh still sticking to the backbone was red, indicating that the creature was a mammal.

Germany's 1,000-year Reich: can anything stand in its way?

Sept. 5, 1934
NUREMBURG, Germany – At a Nazi rally here today, Adolf Wagner, a prominent Bavarian, claimed that with "the National Socialist revolution, the German form of life has been definitely settled for the next thousand years." Seated next to Wagner was Adolf Hitler, chancellor and president of Germany, chief architect and leader of the Third Reich – unmatched in popular support, and, more importantly, seemingly unstoppable.

In less than two years, the flamboyant, power hungry, anti-Semitic Hitler has attained total political dominance over Germany. By early spring last year, Hitler had become the most powerful chancellor in German history: he and his National Socialist cabinet had enough power to pass laws by decree and without Reichstag approval.

In the late spring of 1933, Hitler's government seized control over trade unions, outlawed the Social Democratic and Communist parties, and in July introduced a plan for the "purification of the Aryan race." Last month, after all opposition was silenced, a plebiscite gave Hitler 90 percent support in his bid to become president. He has authority over the army and all legislative and executive affairs.

The official Nazi position on democracy is government *for* the people, not *by* the people. Is the "1,000-year Reich" a possibility? Much more frightening is who – or what – is left to stop it?

Adolf Hitler with young admirers.

Warrant charges 61 in bootlegging case

Dec. 12, 1934
MONTREAL – The Royal Canadian Mounted Police have issued a blanket warrant charging 61 Canadians, including the four Bronfman brothers, with conspiracy to evade payment of more than $5 million in customs duties on smuggled liquor. The police say the hunt extends over five provinces and into the United States. Supt. F.J. Mead, head of the Mounties' Quebec division, went even further in the first press conference he has ever given. He said: "The affair has indications of being the biggest case in the history of the RCMP ... extending from Prince Edward Island to British Columbia."

1935

Quebec, Jan. 6. Indians meet at Caughnawaga in opposition to Ottawa's edict forcing the reserve to be governed by an elected council.

Montreal, April 9. Montreal Maroons defeat the Toronto Maple Leafs three games to none for the Stanley Cup.

Toronto, May 1. A May Day parade attracts 10,000 people.

Ontario, May 7. The Post Office Department announces its disapproval of chain letters, a fad sweeping North America.

Nova Scotia, Aug. 4. Micmac Indians on a reserve near Truro defend their right to cut basket wood on any unenclosed lots in the province, contrary to a ruling by the Department of Indian Affairs.

Toronto, Sept. 4. Charlotte Acres of Vancouver wins the women's five-mile swim at the CNE, the first Canadian victory in the event.

Edmonton, Sept. 24. Premier William Aberhart announces his government will sell "prosperity bonds" in an effort to clear the provincial debt of $150 million in 10 years.

Ethiopia, Oct. 3. Fascist Italy, led by Benito Mussolini, invades Ethiopia.

London, Ont., Oct. 25. Justice G.F McFarland sentences Jack Bannon to 15 years in prison for the kidnapping and robbery of brewer John Labbatt.

Quebec, October. Dr. A.L. Richards reports on the appalling health conditions of the eastern Arctic Inuit: at Fort Chimo, half have serious dental problems, many have pyorrhea and eye problems.

Hamilton, Dec. 7. Winnipeg beats the Hamilton Tigers 18-12 for the Grey Cup.

Washington, D.C. The U.S. government apologizes to Canada for the sinking of the rum-runner *I'm Alone* in 1929, and pays damages to its captain and crew.

British Columbia. Since 1932, some 365 Doukhobor children have become wards of the B.C. government because their parents were imprisoned for refusing to send them to school.

Canada. Between 500,000 and 600,000 unemployed Canadians are on public relief, one-tenth of the population.

Newfoundland. Forty-five percent of the working male population is employed in various branches of the fishery.

David Dunlap Observatory founded

May 7, 1935

RICHMOND HILL, Ont. – The newly completed David Dunlap Observatory is home to the second largest reflector telescope in the world. The 74-inch pyrex disc was cast by the Corning company of New York to test methods used in the manufacture of a 200-inch telescope.

Named in honor of Toronto financier David Dunlap, the observatory is the brainchild of Dr. Clarence A. Chant. Chant, who received his PhD from Harvard, was teaching at the University of Toronto when he became convinced that a teaching observatory was necessary. The war and a lack of funds delayed progress for many years. In 1922, Dunlap, whose own interest in astronomy was inspired by a lecture given by Chant, expressed interest in donating funds. After Dunlap's death in 1924, his widow agreed to support the project. The official opening of the observatory caps an illustrious career for Chant, 70, who has announced his retirement.

Reindeer herd's five-year journey ends

Feb. 21, 1935

NORTHWEST TERRITORIES – An incredible, more than five-year journey across the far north ended when a herd of reindeer guided by a few Lapp herdsmen reached its final destination. The purpose of the trek across the barren Arctic was to bring 3,000 reindeer, bought by the Canadian government from the Lomen Brothers Corp. of New York, from the Kotzebue Peninsula in Alaska to a government station near Kittigazult, east of the Mackenzie delta.

The migration confronting Arctic blizzards and hungry predators claimed the lives of more than one-quarter of the reindeer and discouraged many herdsmen. But veteran Laplander Andrew Bahr kept his crew together. His endurance was rewarded four days ago, when the herd crossed the last obstacle of the journey, the frozen Mackenzie River. Bahr and his men enjoyed a personal triumph when they arrived at their destination on the eastern side of the Mackenzie delta with an estimated 2,200 reindeer. It is hoped to develop a domestic reindeer industry in the delta.

Rubber horseshoes to muffle clip clops

June 14, 1935

ST. CATHARINES, Ont. – It'll soon be easier to sleep here, thanks to a new noise pollution law. Businesses using horses and wagons for deliveries must now equip their steeds with rubber shoes and their wagons with rubber wheels. Hopefully, this will reduce the loud night-time "clip clop" of horses' hooves. Next on the agenda – monster trucks roaming the streets.

Wilfrid Pelletier, pianist and conductor, is a leader in encouraging Quebec youth to appreciate music.

Jobless protesters read the Riot Act

April 23, 1935

VANCOUVER – Mayor Gerry McGeer read the Riot Act to 2,000 angry unemployed men today after they had fought police in the Hudson's Bay store and caused thousands of dollars damage. The men left their relief camps in the interior a few weeks ago and called on local officials to give them food and shelter. In today's protest march they pushed their way into the Hudson's Bay store and were only forced out after a long battle with police. Then they marched back to Victory Square, where the Riot Act was read and the men dispersed.

Buchan's next step is governor general

Governor General John Buchan.

March 27, 1935

LONDON, England – John Buchan, the noted author of the mystery novels *The 39 Steps* and *Greenmantle*, and an experienced parliamentarian, has been named governor general of Canada, succeeding the Earl of Bessborough. In an interview here today, Buchan, an Oxford graduate who served as an intelligence officer in the Great War, told the press he had been to Canada before, on a fishing trip in the Maritimes.

Buchan, whose novels reveal a keen sense of adventure, is enthusiastic about the appointment, which will allow him to travel all over Canada. The Scottish-born writer has been an MP in Britain's Parliament since 1927. Says the new governor general, "I am extremely proud to have been chosen as His Majesty's representative in Canada, and not less proud to be given a chance of serving Canada."

Bennett's New Deal not such a great deal after all

June 28, 1935

OTTAWA – The Employment and Social Insurance Act received royal assent today. It is the centrepiece of a series of reforms to deal with the depression. The reforms are known as the Bennett New Deal, after the man who initiated them, Prime Minister Richard B. Bennett. They are reminiscent of President Franklin D. Roosevelt's New Deal in the U.S. The reform legislation the government's passed thus far is only a shadow of the sweeping measures that Bennett announced in January, as most of his planned reforms either have not been introduced or have been watered down. The government has passed labor reforms to improve the lot of workers, but the unemployment insurance plan provides very limited protection for workers.

Bennett took to the airwaves in January, spewing left-leaning rhetoric as he revealed reform plans. The millionaire capitalist, who looks like everyone's most hated robber baron, shocked the nation when he said "I am for reform. I nail the flag of progress to the mast. I summon the power of the state to its support." He slammed "avaricious industrialists, unscrupulous big business wizards and financial promoters who exploited the people." People gathered around radios for "Bennett parties" to listen to his grandiose plans that have been diluted almost beyond recognition.

Hepburn promises help for the poor

July 27, 1935

TORONTO – After touring the homes of poverty-stricken relief recipients in Toronto, Ontario Premier Mitchell Hepburn has pledged increased aid for the city's poor. Hepburn wants to curb the problem by buying 20,000 new mattresses and increasing the amount of the food dole, which is a voucher used by relief recipients to buy groceries. Asked if the present voucher was enough, one Ontario woman replied, "I'm getting $4 a month less for food now than I did under the old relief system."

The new measures, which are likely to be implemented in the near future, will doubtless increase Hepburn's already remarkable popularity in the province.

Government hopes to stop On-to-Ottawa protesters in Regina

A trainload of unhappy relief camp workers is heading for Ottawa.

June 12, 1935

REGINA – The On-to-Ottawa trek will stop here if the government has its way. It was learned today that Ottawa has ordered the RCMP to take the trekkers from the freight cars when they arrive and put them in a camp here. The 1,500 protesters, most of them unemployed men from B.C., are travelling by train across the country to present their grievances to Prime Minister Richard B. Bennett.

The Saskatchewan government has already protested Ottawa's decision. Premier J.G. Gardiner telegraphed the prime minister that Saskatchewan did not want to be saddled with the protesters. The CPR, Gardiner said, "delivered these men in Saskatchewan en route to Ottawa, and we expect them to carry through."

PM: trekkers led by communists plotting government's demise

During a stop in Regina, more protesters join the march to Ottawa. The prime minister is suspicious that communists are organizing this effort.

June 24, 1935

OTTAWA – The government is taking steps to prevent a resumption of the On-to-Ottawa trek. In the Commons today, Prime Minister Richard B. Bennett said the protesters now in camps at Regina are led by communists who want to overthrow the government. The 2,000 unemployed men arrived in Regina more than a week ago from the west. There, they were put in camps, preventing them from continuing their journey to the capital.

The trekkers now say they intend to resume the journey because the government has refused their demands for better relief camp conditions and a work-and-wages program. About 500 railway police and RCMP are charged with keeping the trekkers off the trains.

Canadian Wheat Board established

July 5, 1935

OTTAWA – The Canadian Wheat Act has received royal assent, bringing into existence the Canadian Wheat Board, which will stand as a marketing option for producers who do not wish to depend on the open market system. It is emphasized that the government agency will in no way interfere with private enterprise. Farmers are now guaranteed a minimum price for their wheat.

Since the Great War, farmers have sought a government wheat marketing agency. When in the past they went unheeded, they organized their own wheat pools, which collapsed under the harsh economic climate of the early '30s. ▷

New party born; Stevens at helm

July 19, 1935

HAMILTON, Ont. – A new political party was launched here tonight under the leadership of Henry Herbert Stevens, the former Conservative minister who quit the government during its inquiry into Canadian big business. The Reconstruction party was cheered by 1,200 people who heard Stevens decry Prime Minister Richard B. Bennett for not keeping his promises on eliminating sweatshops and helping the poor.

For his part, the new Reconstruction leader pledged to implement these promises. He also wants a Trans-Canada Highway to link national parks; to eliminate level crossings, which have caused fatalities due to car-train collisions; and to replenish Canada's forests.

First four-legged officer joins RCMP

Dale, proud sire of first RCMP dog.

May 25, 1935

CANADA – The Royal Canadian Mounted Police today welcomed its first four-legged officer, as Black Lux, an adult German shepherd, joined two-legged partner Const. W. H. Billington to fight against crime. RCMP officials, citing the success of European police dogs, expect Black Lux to be an excellent officer with speed, discipline, and a discerning nose. Lux's sire Dale, an experienced crime fighter, will also join the force.

On-to-Ottawa trekkers, police clash

Relief camp men, mostly from B.C. and Alberta, commandeered trains to take their grievances to Ottawa.

July 1, 1935

REGINA – A riot here tonight has left one policeman dead and several dozen police and civilians injured. The jails are full. At about 9 p.m. a battle began between a strong contingent of police and a large group of On-to-Ottawa trekkers, unemployed relief camp men who have been attempting to journey to Ottawa to present their grievances. The police moved on a meeting of about 300 people in this city's market square on orders from Ottawa to arrest the trek leaders. Tear gas dispersed the meeting, and for the next two hours trekkers and their supporters stormed through Regina streets assaulting police with rocks and clubs. The police replied with gunfire.

Arthur Evans, one of the main leaders of the 2,000 relief men now staying at the Exhibition Grounds, was arrested along with more than 100 others.

The trekkers, mainly from British Columbia and Alberta, arrived here more than two weeks ago. They were taken from the trains they had commandeered and prevented from moving farther east. In the past few days, the trekkers decided to try to get out of town to resume their journey. But police blocked all exits.

Prime Minister Richard B. Bennett has refused to negotiate with the relief men, believing that they are part of a communist plot to overthrow the government. There is considerable sympathy among citizens here for the trekkers.

Trekkers march along a road near the Manitoba-Ontario border.

Liberals bat 1,000 in P.E.I. election

July 23, 1935

CHARLOTTETOWN – Islanders have granted Walter Lea a rare parliamentary privilege – no opposition. Campaigning on a platform of fiscal restraint, his Liberals won all 30 seats, making Commonwealth history. Voters perceived the Tories under William J.P. MacMillan as too extravagant, mostly due to the rebuilding of a college and insane asylum razed by fire.

Social Credit party wins Alberta election

Aug. 23, 1935

EDMONTON – Under the leadership of William Aberhart, the Social Credit party has scored an overwhelming victory in Alberta, capturing 56 of the 63 seats in the provincial legislature. The United Farmers of Alberta, who have been in power the last 15 years, failed to win a single seat. The Liberals snared five and the Conservatives two. A record 302,000 people cast ballots in the election, compared to 188,000 in the last vote. The record turnout and landslide victory are no doubt directly related to the Social Credit promise of a $25 dividend per person per month.

Social Credit members enter the legislature with no political experience. Aberhart himself, a respected high school principal and a gifted preacher, is new to the fields of economics and politics. Still, the party has raised among the people high expectations of low interest rates, full employment, and a respectable standard of living.

Food shipments to help starving farmers

Nov. 12, 1935

WINNIPEG – By late this evening food shipments will be en route to starving farm families on the northwestern shore of Lake Winnipeg. It is estimated that as many as 40,000 individuals may be without food in six rural municipalities: Gimli, Bifrost, Armstrong, Eriksdale, Coldwell, and Rockwood. These are farm families for whom this year's crop was a total failure.

The severity of the problem was outlined today by W.C. McKinney, member of the legislature for Rockwood. He explained that there is no grain to be ground into flour, the schools are closed, and the families in many cases have no winter clothing. While crop failures in earlier years were not unknown, these mixed farmers previously have been able to subsist on their own homegrown food. This year there was literally nothing to harvest.

Police break up noisy anti-Hitler protest

Dale/Winnipeg/Free Press/6 July 1935

Summer Styles, 1935

The cartoonist's view of the rising popularity of dictators.

Dec. 5, 1935

TORONTO – Police were called in tonight to quell a noisy demonstration against Canada's participation in next summer's Berlin Olympics. About 200 protesters waving placards and banners convened at the Royal York Hotel, where a reception was held by officials of Hitler's Nazi government. The officials, representatives of the state railways and an acting consul general, held the reception to boost Canadian interest in the Olympic Games. Two men were arrested for obstructing police efforts to disperse the crowd. Following the reception, the German officials were given a police motor escort on their way to Montreal.

Trade treaty to benefit Canada and U.S.

Nov. 15, 1935

WASHINGTON, D.C. – After decades of mistrust and political bickering, Canada and the United States have today signed a mutual trade treaty which will make cross-border sales much easier for both sides. Initialled into law here by U.S. President Franklin Roosevelt and Canadian Prime Minister W.L. Mackenzie King, the deal will let Canadian farmers, fishermen, and lumber merchants make more profits off American sales by lowering the tariffs they have to pay to enter that market.

King's Grits crush Tories

W.L.M. King is happy to be once again the prime minister of Canada.

Oct. 14, 1935

OTTAWA – It wasn't an election, it was a massacre. And the victims were members of the governing Conservative party. That's the best way to sum up tonight's national election, in which the government of Prime Minister Richard B. Bennett was annihilated. When the vote was called, the Tories had 113 seats in the House. Now, based on the latest results, they have only 41. Meanwhile, the Liberals under William Lyon Mackenzie King, who only had 88 seats, now have a commanding majority of 165.

The loss is nothing less than a repudiation of Bennett's policies. Perhaps, in good economic times, his business-like approach would have suited the nation. But, given that Canada is in its sixth year of economic chaos, all the people want now is answers, and help from the government, now thrown over to that old veteran, W.L.M. King.

Coal miners die in underground explosion

Dec. 9, 1935

COALHURST, Alta. – A fiery underground explosion claimed the lives of 16 coal miners here today. It is believed the men died when sparks from a telephone circuit in the mine ignited the gas which caused the explosion. The mine, about 15 kilometres northwest of Lethbridge in Alberta's coal country, belongs to the Lethbridge Collieries Ltd. It is the first major disaster in the 52-year history of the coalfields.

The Catelli Company makes the public aware of its newest product.

1936

British Columbia, Feb. 13. About 2,000 women petition for a free birth control clinic.

Toronto, Feb. 19. Before 15,000 screaming fans, the largest indoor boxing crowd ever in Canada, Phil "Red" Munroe is crowned the "White Hope" champion of Canada.

New Brunswick, March 19. An ice jam sweeps away a CNR bridge spanning the St. John River, cutting off rail communication between Fredericton and Saint John.

Toronto, April 11. Detroit Red Wings beat the Toronto Maple Leafs three games to one to win the Stanley Cup.

Alberta, June 16. R.A. (Bob) Brown discovers a gusher at Turner Valley, turning it into a major oil field overnight.

Ontario, July. A heat wave in early July causes hundreds of deaths in southern Ontario.

Spanish Morocco, July 17. General Franco leads an uprising against the Republican Spanish government [beginning the Spanish Civil War].

Ottawa, Aug. 23. The Department of National Defence says Canada is not prepared for an air attack.

Winnipeg, Oct. 9. About 1,000 single unemployed men declare they are ready to aid the Spanish government against Franco's rebellion, and petition Ottawa to provide them with transportation to Spain.

Ottawa, Dec. 6. The government established the Canadian Broadcasting Corporation (CBC) to offer programming and regulate private stations.

Spain, Dec. 25. Some 600 Canadians, including Dr. Norman Bethune, have joined the Republican forces to fight against Franco's rebellion.

Ottawa. Dorothea Palmer, a field worker for the birth control organization Parents' Information Bureau, is arrested for distributing birth control information in a low-income suburb [subsequently acquitted].

Canada. All nine provinces have entered the old age pension system established by Ottawa in 1927 when it passed the Old Age Pension Act.

Canada. Lydia Gruchy is the first female minister in the United Church of Canada. >

Ottawa to spend $125M

April 22, 1936

OTTAWA – Finance Minister Charles Dunning today announced that in the next fiscal year the government will spent $60 million on development and public works projects, $26 million on relief for those crippled by the depression, and another $39.9 million on loans to the Canadian National Railways.

Relief project puts men to work.

The main thrust of the spending will be in western Canada, where the administration will foster countless resource exploitation projects. With $200,000 set aside for intense geological surveying, Dunning expects that new mineral resources will be discovered and exploited, thus creating jobs and restoring prosperity to the region. Meanwhile, $2.5 million of public funds are expected to attract new settlers to the vast prairie fields.

Weary from years of hard times and unsuccessful quick-fix programs, many Canadians are greeting the announcement with a wait-and-see attitude.

MPs often invited to quilting parties

March 9, 1936

OTTAWA – Members of Parliament are being flooded with donation requests from across the country. A typical letter reads, "Please belong to our quilting party, we would so much like the honor of having your name on our quilt." The MP is asked to donate a small sum, perhaps 25 cents. His name is then written on a silk square, embroidered, and sewn into the quilt. Other organizations use other tactics in soliciting money for their favorite causes.

War is inevitable in Europe, PM told

March 5, 1936

WASHINGTON, D.C. – "War is inevitable in Europe." These dramatic words are being credited to U.S. Secretary of State Cordell Hull. Insiders say he spoke them in a long, frank discussion with Canadian Prime Minister W.L. Mackenzie King, who's in town to visit his old friend, President Franklin Roosevelt. Hull, along with the president, is said to believe that the demands of dictators like Hitler and Mussolini are bound to go too far one day.

Canada settles for 2nd in Olympic hockey

Feb. 16, 1936

GARMISCH-PARTENKIRCHEN, Germany – Dave Neville's goal gave Canada a 1-0 win over the United States today, but it was only good for second place behind England in Olympic hockey. It was the first hockey title for England, bolstered by six Canadian players. Today's Canadian win helped the English, because the U.S. had held England to a tie. England beat Canada 2-1 in the semifinal and because of scheduling, Canada did not get another shot at the English. The Canadian team, which had threatened to withdraw in a dispute over the scheduling, had won all three previous Olympic tournaments, in 1924, 1928, and 1932.

Alberta defaulting on bond payments

April 1, 1936

EDMONTON – The Social Credit government of "Bible Bill" Aberhart has defaulted on the principal of a $3.2-million bond. Aberhart announced Alberta's intention to only pay interest with the words, "We haven't the money. I'm sorry; we must default."

The failure to repay the bond makes Alberta the first province to default in Canada. It could have avoided the failure by receiving aid from the federal government. But such a deal would allow the feds a say in how the province spends its money, and that's something Social Crediters don't want. It's unclear whether this failure will prevent others from lending to Alberta.

Prairie farmers are losing their farms – literally. Drought conditions have caused the dry topsoil to blow away, leaving barren sandy fields.

Survivors of mine disaster unearthed

April 22, 1936

MOOSE RIVER, N.S. – After 10 days of frantic digging, volunteers have freed two Toronto men who had been trapped 42 metres below ground in the Moose River Gold Mine. Dr. D.E. Robertson and Alfred Scadding were pulled out today, escaping flood waters that were threatening to drown them underground. A third man, H.R. McGill, died while trapped below with them.

The rescue caps a series of astonishing events at Moose River. For the past few days the trapped men have been fed through a rubber hose, ingeniously sunk down to their level by rescuers. They've also been able to talk to the surface above through the tube, something that has allowed them to comfort their wives, both of whom have been keeping a vigil at the mine.

Also keeping a vigil for the two trapped men were radio listeners across North America. In a feat unheard of in radio, Canadian Radio Broadcasting Commission reporter J. Frank Willis has been sending non-stop reports from the site via telephone for 69 hours. He's been heard over an ad hoc network of 58 Canadian stations, and 650 in the United States. Willis' own super-human effort equals those of the rescuers, who have been working for more than a week now to free these men.

A telephone company employee listens for word from men trapped in the mine.

Dionne quints to do Hollywood movies

May 28, 1936

NORTH BAY, Ont. – The Dionne quints, rapidly becoming North America's favorite children, today marked their second birthday with the announcement that they will star in three 20th Century-Fox movies to be made before the end of 1938. The contract, signed by the quints' guardians, brings the two-year-olds a total of $300,000, which works out to about $10,000 an hour, and 10 percent of the movies' profits, ensuring the financial security of the family for years to come. Meanwhile, fashion designers around the globe are scurrying to create baby designs that duplicate the styles worn by the proud little celebrities.

Two of the Dionne quintuplets (later photo), Canada's favorite children.

Duplessis leads UN to landslide victory

Aug. 17, 1936

QUEBEC CITY – Maurice Duplessis' Union Nationale scored a crushing victory over the scandal-tainted Liberal party led by Joseph-Adélard Godbout. Duplessis, who campaigned on a reform program promising honest elections, took 76 of the legislature's 90 seats. Godbout himself went down to defeat in the UN landslide, which ends 39 continuous years of Liberal rule.

Bungled burglary Red Ryan's last job

May 23, 1936

SARNIA, Ont. – Norman "Red" Ryan, the bandit who talked his way out of jail by convincing authorities he had gone straight, died after being shot in a bungled liquor store robbery here today. Before being shot, Ryan managed to kill Const. John Lewis, who'd been alerted to the holdup by a passerby. Also killed was one of Ryan's cohorts, still unidentified.

Canadian war memorial unveiled at Vimy

Widows and wives of Canadian soldiers attend the Vimy Memorial opening.

July 26, 1936

VIMY, France – King Edward VIII today unveiled the Vimy Ridge Memorial, the largest of several Canadian monuments in Europe to honor Canada's Great War dead. It is on the site of one of the Canadian Corps' greatest victories. Some 100,000 people, including 6,000 former Canadian soldiers and families, watched the ceremony.

Designed by Toronto sculptor Walter S. Allward, the monument was chosen from 160 proposals and took 11 years to build. While it honors all of Canada's 60,000 war dead, the base lists the names of 11,285 men with no known grave.

Plane crash kills 6 in northern Quebec

May 25, 1936

NORTHERN QUEBEC – A General Airways Bellanca today crashed in a remote bush and rock wilderness area near Chibougamau Lake, killing all six passengers, most leading mining officials. W.H. Clarke, general manager of the airline, is also dead. The men, whose bodies have not yet been recovered, were going to prospective mining sites when their plane was forced down by a giant windstorm.

Thousands visit the Dionne Quintuplets

Aug. 8, 1936

CALLANDER, Ont. – Last month more than 140,000 people called at the Dafoe Hospital to see the Dionne Quintuplets, born on May 28, 1934. The 141,342 visitors came to Callander in 30,216 cars, 235 automobiles with trailers, and 67 buses. The staggering total was double-checked by the quints' chief guardian, Welfare Minister David Croll. From auto licence plates, townspeople estimate that about 70 percent of the cars are from the United States, but they say that the Canadian automobiles carry more passengers. The minister of welfare pointed out that as many as 6,000 visitors had called in at the Dafoe Hospital on a single day.

Dr. Allan Roy Dafoe, who attended Elzire Dionne, said on the day of the births he saw no reason why all the babies should not live if given the proper care. The quints weighed a total of only 13 pounds, six ounces; the first-born weighed three pounds, four ounces. There are five other children in the family, all single births. The Dionnes were married in 1924, when the quints' mother was 15 years of age.

Gandhi told to pay taxes or lose land

Mahatma Gandhi.

Sept. 9, 1936

BRIDGEWATER, N.S. – Even spiritual leaders have to pay their taxes. That's why this town is threatening to confiscate four hectares of land owned by Mahatma Gandhi, the renowned Indian leader, unless he pays $375 of back taxes. Gandhi may not know he has property here. It was left to him by Mary Chesly, a local woman who became one of his followers.

Anti-Semitism lives across the country

1936

CANADA – On golf courses in Nova Scotia, outside exclusive resorts in Quebec, or at clubs and beaches in Manitoba and British Columbia, signs warning "No Jews or Dogs Allowed" or "Christians Only" are found. Across Canada, anti-Jewish sentiment is expressed unabashedly and with regularity by leading newspapers, the business community, politicians, and the Catholic and Protestant clergy.

Discrimination against Jews is rampant in most aspects of life. Land ownership is restricted, as are education and employment opportunities at universities, factories, professional firms, and institutions.

Canadian anti-Semitism is not a new phenomenon. Quebec nationalists have long been suspicious of the province's Jewish community. In Ontario and the west, Jews are perceived as unwilling to assimilate, reluctant farmers who commonly abandon their homesteads and migrate to the cities to swell the ranks of the unemployed. Canadian immigration policies reflect these prejudices. Like Orientals and blacks, Jews are now deemed "undesirable."

PM hurt League of Nations, editorial says

Oct. 1, 1936

WINNIPEG – In an editorial in today's Winnipeg *Free Press,* John W. Dafoe accuses Prime Minister William Lyon Mackenzie King of having undermined the validity of the League of Nations. Dafoe's comments were based on King's speech in Geneva on Sept. 29, in which the prime minister stated that Canada would not support automatically all league actions.

Edward VIII to abdicate

Dec. 11, 1936

LONDON, England – Edward VIII, who stunned, shocked, and saddened his subjects around the globe yesterday by announcing that he has decided to give up the throne so that he will be free to marry a twice-divorced American citizen, is to give royal assent today to the Act of Abdication. He will then have his wish and cease to be king. The Canadian Broadcasting Corporation will carry his farewell address from the BBC to the world today at 5 p.m. EST.

Tomorrow morning, the Accession Council will meet to discuss the situation, and in the afternoon, the Duke of York – under the title of George VI – will be proclaimed king, "by the Grace of God, of Great Britain, Ireland, and of the British Dominions." It is assumed that the new king George VI's consort will be known as Queen Elizabeth, and the coronation date is likely to be May 12.

Rumors have raged for weeks that Edward was planning to marry American socialite Wallis Simpson as soon as her divorce from her second husband, Ernest, was final. Mrs. Simpson is now staying with friends in a villa in the south of France. She said in an interview yesterday that "there is not a chance in the world of the king coming here" when he leaves England immediately after his radio address. Mrs. Simpson's food is being tested for poison because she has received hundreds of letters threatening her life. Edward had lunch yesterday with his three brothers. It was, quite possibly, the last time they will be together.

Mrs. Wallis Simpson, twice-divorced American socialite.

His Majesty King Edward VIII, soon to give his farewell address.

Japan, Germany and Italy form alliance

Nov. 25, 1936

BERLIN – World tensions increased today as Japan announced that it had signed the Anti-Comintern Pact. This, in effect, extends a year-old alliance between Italy and Germany to include Asia's aggressive power.

The bonding of these three nations into one alliance is particularly disturbing given their actions of the last six years. Japan has repeatedly invaded China; Italy has conquered Ethiopia in ruthless fashion; Germany has occupied the previously demilitarized Rhineland and is openly re-arming. Germany and Italy have sent troops and aircraft to aid nationalist rebels in Spain. Other European countries are re-arming. Even Canada has increased its defence budgets – slashed to the bone in 1931-32 – and begun to procure modern aircraft, machine-guns, and military vehicles.

Bethune leads innovative blood transfusion unit

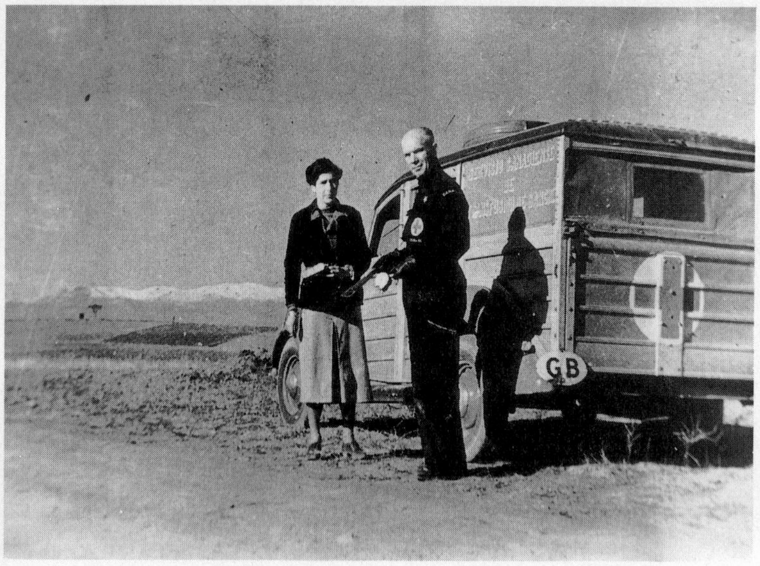

A Canadian blood transfusion unit in Spain is run by Dr. Norman Bethune.

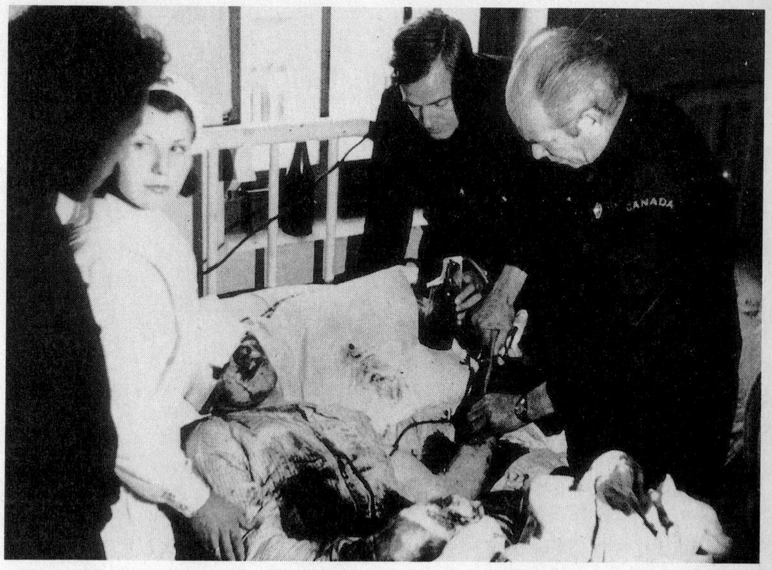

A casualty of the Spanish Civil War is given blood by Dr. Bethune.

Dec. 23, 1936

MADRID, Spain – Night has fallen on battle-weary Madrid, and amidst the deafening roar of an artillery barrage and the shuddering impact of shells, a station wagon weaves its way toward the front line trenches. Emblazoned on both sides of the vehicle are the words "Instituto Hispano-Canadense de Transfusion de Sangre" – Spanish-Canadian Blood Transfusion Institute. Inside sit Canadians Dr. Norman Bethune and Hazen Sise, an assortment of medical instruments, and an electric refrigerator stocked with glass bottles which constitute a transportable supply of blood.

This is Bethune's first night out with the mobile transfusion unit, a first of its kind in medical history. He began organizing it more than a month ago and his painstaking efforts have immediately paid off: tonight, the dozen transfusions he administered mean, in all probability, a dozen lives have been saved.

For centuries, casualties of war have died on the battlefields from loss of blood, or been so weakened by the same that later operations had little hope of success. Now, with fresh quantities of blood being brought directly to the front lines, the injured who might have once died have a better chance of living to fight another day.

For the besieged defenders of Madrid, another day might make all the difference. And it is their cause that the 46-year-old Bethune is firmly allied with. A highly respected thoracic surgeon, outspoken humanitarian, and socialist, he resigned from numerous – and lucrative – positions at various Montreal medical institutes early this fall. He then left Canada for Spain, determined to aid the Spanish Republican forces in their battle to preserve democracy against the onslaught of fascist rebels led by Gen. Francisco Franco.

In October, he resolved to form the blood transfusion unit. He fought with dogged determination for approval of his plan. He had to – what he proposed was unprecedented and, therefore, considered "impractical." But his forceful arguments won over the skeptics, and tonight he has saved a dozen lives. In the days to come, he fully expects to save hundreds.

Remains of ancient man found in Sask.

Nov. 14, 1936

BRADWELL, Sask. – Skeletal remains of what is being called the Bradwell Man have been found by Pius Fischer while digging road gravel in a pit near here. By the time experts arrived, the gravel had been removed from around the bones, thus eliminating evidence that could have helped determine the age of the remains. However, the bones are considered to be the oldest ever found in Saskatchewan.

The skeleton was in a flexed position facing downward. The bones are stained a reddish brown with iron oxide. They are heavy, and a "taste test" indicates considerable mineralization has taken place.

Transaction creates the Globe and Mail

Nov. 8, 1936

TORONTO – Officials at the *Globe* today announced that they had purchased *The Mail and Empire* newspaper. Starting next week, Torontonians will be reading one daily morning paper, the *Globe and Mail*. The new publication will be Canada's largest daily newspaper, and will be printed in a new facility to be erected on the corner of King and York streets this summer. The merger follows three days of negotiations, and gives the *Globe* full control over all of the *Mail and Empire*'s assets. What sort of newspaper will the new *Globe* be? Its directors are calling it "Canada's National Newspaper."

Little mothers can have their own Dionne Quintuplets with this set of dolls.

1937

Montreal, Jan. 13. An estimated 18,000 attend the funeral of Brother André, credited with supernatural healing powers.

London, England, January. The Judicial Committee of the Privy Council declares most of Richard B. Bennett's New Deal *ultra vires.*

Ottawa, February. The Commons defeats a resolution introduced by CCF leader J.S. Woodsworth to have Canada remain strictly neutral in the event of a war.

Ottawa, March 1. The Commons passes a motion to make old age pensions available to blind persons over 40.

Montreal, March 8. Montreal Canadiens star Howie Morenz dies as a result of injuries suffered in a hockey game.

Detroit, April 15. Detroit Red Wings beat the New York Rangers three games to two to win the Stanley Cup.

Ottawa, April. In order to prevent Canadian involvement in the Spanish Civil War, the government passes the Foreign Enlistment Act, outlawing Canadian participation in foreign wars, and the Customs Act, providing for government control of arms exports.

Berlin, June 30. PM King concludes a visit with Hitler and other German leaders. King says he has successfully promoted "understanding, friendship, and goodwill."

Albacete, Spain, July 1. The Mackenzie-Papineau Battalion, composed of Canadian volunteers, is mustered into the XVth "English-Speaking" International Brigade to fight for the Republicans in the war.

Ottawa, Aug. 14. In response to the financial strains imposed on the federal system by the depression, the government establishes the Royal Commission on Dominion-Provincial Relations [Rowell-Sirois report] to study the system.

Toronto, Aug. 22. The federal government announces the CBC will provide 16 hours a day of national broadcasting instead of the present six.

Toronto, Dec. 11. Toronto Argonauts defeat the Winnipeg Blue Bombers 4-3 to win the Grey Cup.

Ottawa. A wave of strikes hits Canada. The *Labour Gazette* reports 72,000 Canadians on strike or locked out in 1937, a conservative estimate.

1.2 million Canadians are on relief

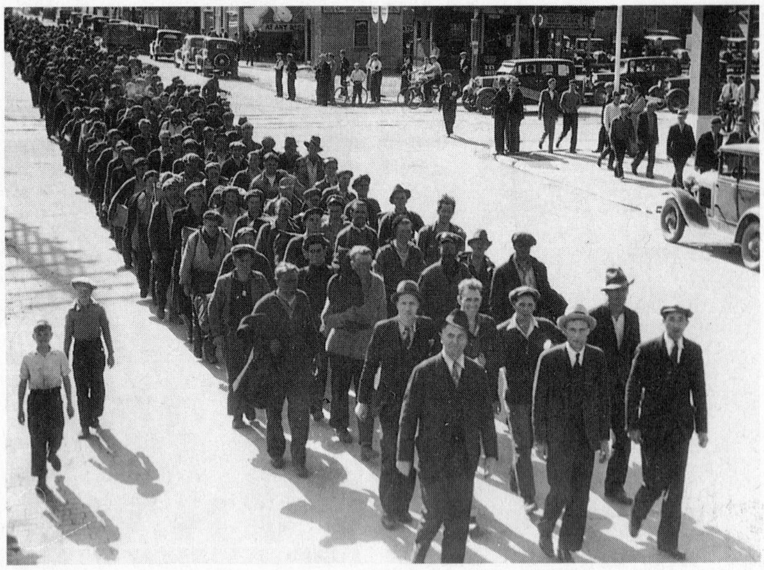

Unemployed march in Calgary. More than 1 million Canadians are on relief.

March 31, 1937

OTTAWA – More than one million Canadians receive relief payments – and that's less than last year! Figures released by Norman Rogers, minister of labor, reveal that 1,265,925 Canadians get financial assistance. Many have jobs on relief projects such as the Trans-Canada Highway.

The figures are an improvement over last year, when nearly 1.5 million people were receiving relief. However, the improvement isn't a national trend. In fact, 8,000 more people on the prairies are on the relief rolls, indicating that things are getting worse, not better, in the west. But overall the figures are good news in a world where the depression seems to be unending.

Sit-down strike marred by violence

March 2, 1937

SARNIA, Ont. – A sit-down strike by 70 workers at the Holmes Foundry here quickly turned bloody today. The men, mostly new immigrants from Eastern Europe, were beaten up by 300 policemen and armed citizens. Police stood by during the assault, only intervening to arrest strikers who escaped the violence for trespassing. This strike is symbolic of employee anger in the auto industry over low wages.

MPs approve trade deal with Germany

April 8, 1937

OTTAWA – The House of Commons today approved a temporary trade deal with Germany, despite a warning about dealing with Adolf Hitler's Reich. Samuel Factor, a Toronto Liberal member, made an impassioned plea against the Nazi persecution of Jews. But economic concerns prevailed.

Trade between the two countries flourished fewer than 10 years ago, with the balance much in Canada's favor. But total trade has diminished substantially and the balance has shifted dramatically. Now, Canada imports about twice as much from Germany as it exports to that country. It is in an effort to reverse this trend that the government came to the agreement.

Opposition leader Richard B. Bennett questioned Germany's ability to make payments. Told that Canada would rely on Germany's good faith, Bennett replied: "You can leave out the question of good faith." The agreement contains an escape clause by which either party can cancel it if dissatisfied.

Dark horse takes Arctic Dog Derby

Feb. 26, 1937

CAMERON BAY, N.W.T. – The dark horse entry of Maurice Evans drove his team of huskies to victory here today in the inaugural running of the 15-mile Arctic Dog Derby. In a thrilling ending, with the cheers of a colorful crowd of prospectors, miners, trappers and Indians ringing in his ears, Evans mushed across the finish line one minute and 10 seconds ahead of the favored Arden entry. Following the race, everybody attended a caribou meat barbecue, where the trophy was presented to Evans by the mine manager's wife, Mrs. Emil Walli.

The funeral of hockey great Howie Morenz is held at the Montreal Forum.

Rival unions clash on Montreal docks

April 29, 1937

MONTREAL – What began as a stand-off between rival unions today deteriorated into a full-fledged riot in which scores were injured. Members of Local 373 of the International Longshoreman's Association blockaded themselves in a shed that members of the rival union, Local 375 of the ILA, were under contract to use to unload the contents of British freighter *Kenbane Head.* Violence quickly ensued, proving that a tentative pact signed by union leaders has done nothing to curb the animosity between the two groups, which has been growing ever since both were granted the right to work Montreal's docks. A police horse had to be shot after it was injured by a gang plank overturned by rioters trying to keep the city's riot police out of the fight.

CIO rumors spark gold price collapse

April 19, 1937

TORONTO – Gold prices collapsed today on the Toronto Stock Exchange, hounded by rumors of union organization in Ontario's mining industry. At the heart of the rumors is the American-based Committee for Industrial Organization. The CIO, which has played a big role in organizing the GM strike in Oshawa, is feared by stock buyers and managers because its workers want higher wages, which would mean smaller profits.

UN's Padlock Law fights communism

April 24, 1937

QUEBEC CITY – A law to stamp out communist propaganda was passed today by the Duplessis Union Nationale government. The bill, known as the Padlock Law, allows police to shut down the offices of any group found to be preparing or distributing communist or Bolshevik literature. Workers fear the law, which does not say what "communism" means, could be used against the unions.

Labor woes plague Oshawa car plant

United Auto Workers walk off the job

Consumers may not get their new Cadillacs this year. GM is on strike.

April 8, 1937

OSHAWA, Ont. – After weeks of fruitless negotiations, members of United Auto Workers, Local 222, walked off their jobs this morning at General Motors here in Oshawa. The employees are going after many things, but, at this point, the key factor is just to get GM to recognize the rights of the union to negotiate with the company on the workers' behalf. That right the company seemed to have agreed to just yesterday. But today GM vice-president George Chappell said the company would only offer "verbal commitments" to the workers, not a contract.

The situation is not being helped by the interference of Liberal Premier Mitchell Hepburn, who wants to "send in the troops" – or police, to be exact – to suppress the strike.

GM strike settled after two weeks

April 28, 1937

OSHAWA, Ont. – After 15 days, the General Motors strike in Oshawa is over. Today, members of United Auto Workers, Local 222, ratified their first deal with GM by a vote of 2,205-36.

Who won this industrial standoff is hard to say. On paper, the UAW achieved every one of its demands, including a minimum wage, a 44-hour work week, a seniority system, the establishment of grievance procedures, and a promise from GM not to discriminate against union members.

But, to gain this, the union's negotiators had to sign the contract as representatives of the "employees of the company at Oshawa." No mention of the UAW, or its parent union, the American-based Committee for Industrial Organization, can be found anywhere in the document. In this sense, then, the company succeeded in denying recognition to the union, even if, by signing the deal, it has already done so in practice. This is also a victory for Premier Mitchell Hepburn, who's been decrying the CIO as "communist agitators."

Happy Gang radio show a hit with CBC's lunchtime listeners

Summer 1937

TORONTO – The CBC has got a hit show on its hands with *The Happy Gang,* broadcast on the network at lunchtime every weekday. It's a successful mixture of popular music and comic sketches, with a cast of highly talented performers.

The show, first aired in mid-June, is run by founder Bert Pearl, a pianist and vocalist who moved to Toronto from Winnipeg last year. The other regulars include theatre organist Kathleen Stokes; violinist Blain Mathe; Bob Farnon on the trumpet and vibraphone; and Eddie Allen, the singing accordionist. The show's infectious light-heartedness, its ad-lib spontaneity, and its "hot music" have won it thousands of fans from coast to coast in a few short weeks.

Performers of the popular new radio show, The Happy Gang.

Bombardier issued snowmobile patent

June 29, 1937

OTTAWA – A Quebec inventor who has designed a car-like "snowmobile" has had his design recognized by the Canadian Patent Office. With the patent, Armand Bombardier can now manufacture his unique snow machines without competition for 17 years.

What makes the Bombardier snowmobile unique is its use of tank-like tracks, which drive it through any depth of snow. Already machines like the seven-passenger "B7" are becoming a common sight in Quebec. Functional outside, inside they're like any car, with comfortable seats and a heater that provides a great deal of warmth on cold winter days.

Bethune attacks fascism

A Canadian soldier in Spain.

June 14, 1937

TORONTO – "Friends and comrades, salutations from the anti-fascists of Spain to the anti-fascists of Canada. Salute!" With these words and a clenched fist raised above his head in the anti-fascist salute, surgeon, humanitarian, and political activist Dr. Norman Bethune of Montreal greeted a gathering of about 2,500 people at Queen's Park tonight.

The soft-spoken, 47-year-old Bethune is touring Canada hoping to raise money for the Republican forces currently at war with the fascists in Spain. He only just returned from that beleaguered country, where he successfully organized the first mobile blood transfusion service.

Blueberry season has welfare on hold

Aug. 14, 1937

CLARKE'S BEACH, Nfld. – Local people threatened to take supplies from the shops by force when they learned the government had discontinued welfare payments during the blueberry season. The Department of Health and Welfare decided the six cents per day per person which is currently paid to those who are destitute would not be paid while blueberries could be picked and sold for 18 cents per gallon. Police reinforcements, consisting of 25 men under the command of a head constable, arrived from St. John's by truck and arrested four ringleaders. The government insists it wants to encourage the blueberry industry.

First regular London-Canada flight lands

July 8, 1937

BOUCHERVILLE, Que. – History was made here today, as the first regular London-Canada flight completed its voyage by landing in the St. Lawrence River. The water landing was no accident, because the aircraft in question is a "flying boat." That is, the four-engine *RMS Caledonia* is a large seaplane, designed to land and take off from water.

It took less than a day for the first Imperial Airways flight to make its voyage, having stopped over in Botwood, Nfld., for fuel. When it arrived, the gigantic aircraft drew gasps of wonder from spectators, as it performed aerial manoeuvres that were worthy of a small fighter. Finally, the "ship" commanded by Capt. A.S. Wilcockson made a long, low run over the river, landing like some giant bird. Soon, such sights will be a common occurrence.

Buchenwald the latest concentration camp

1937

GERMANY – The fate suffered by "enemies of the state" held at Nazi Germany's Buchenwald concentration camp differs little from that suffered by those held at Dachau, Sachsenhausen, or Lichtenburg. In all the camps, prisoners are provided with sparse quantities of food – many lose as much as 50 percent of their body weight. Minimal shelter is provided. Weakened by hunger and susceptible to illness through constant exposure to the elements, they are nevertheless forced to continue working.

Buchenwald is the latest addition to the list of concentration camps put into use by the Nazis since 1933. Prisoners are mostly communists and Jews, but also homosexuals. How many are held in these camps is uncertain, but it is known each camp requires 1,500 guards, suggesting the number of prisoners may total in the thousands.

Cross-country test flight publicizes TCA's new national service

Trans-Canada Airlines has purchased five of these Lockheed 10A Electras.

July 30, 1937

VANCOUVER – After almost 18 hours, a two-engined Lockheed from Montreal touched down here today, ending a publicity-grabbing test of Trans-Canada Airlines' new national service. On board was Transport Minister C.D. Howe, a big player in the government's establishment of TCA as a part of Canadian National Railways.

Howe and his TCA crew had a long, if uneventful, flight across Canada. They left Montreal at 4:01 a.m. EDT, but had to return to the field due to stormy weather. Leaving again at 5:18, they made stops in Kapuskasing, Sioux Lookout, Winnipeg, Regina, Lethbridge, and finally Vancouver. The trip covered 4,025 kilometres.

Despite the depression, hopeful immigrants such as these are still arriving in Canada.

Ottawa to shoot down Alberta laws

Aug. 7, 1937

OTTAWA – The federal government will disallow Alberta's contentious legislation intended to control banks and restrict civil rights. This decision brings to an end a bitter exchange of letters and telegrams between Ottawa and Edmonton over the validity of the laws passed by the Social Credit government of William Aberhart.

The Alberta legislation gives the province the right to license all banks and bank employees. As well, the legislation bars any court challenge of provincial legislation. However, Ottawa can disallow any provincial act within a year of its being passed.

Alberta, home of oil fields, coal and wheat, wants control of its banks.

Alberta announces new minimum wage

Sept. 13, 1937

EDMONTON – Beginning in two weeks time, Alberta will have the second highest minimum wages in Canada. It was announced today by Ernest C. Manning, Alberta's minister of trade and industry, that effective Oct. 1 the new basic rate for men will be 33.3 cents per hour and $15 per week. Only British Columbia, with a minimum of 35 cents, will have a higher rate.

The rates apply to men with more than one year of experience in the work in which they are currently engaged. Four separate rates apply, and they vary with the length of the work week.

Growth proves Inuit can get cancer, too

Dec. 13, 1937

OTTAWA – An Inuit man has cancer and so has dashed the hopes of doctors that the Inuit were immune from the killer disease. Cancer is virtually unknown among Inuit people and medical experts hoped this immunity could lead to a cure for, or an understanding of the causes of, cancer. Several doctors have spent years in the Arctic studying the Inuit to see if their way of life and, in particular, their diet could offer clues to help in the fight against cancer. Now that a growth taken from a man living on Baffin Island has been diagnosed in Montreal as malignant, these hopes have been dashed.

Canadians among the millions shocked by Japanese atrocities

Oct. 14, 1937

CANADA – Canadians are among the many reacting with shock and anger to reports and newsreel footage of Japanese atrocities committed against Chinese civilians at Shanghai.

Today's *Life* magazine estimates that more than 136 million people have seen H.S. "Newsreel" Wong's haunting photo of a bloodied Chinese baby, an innocent casualty of a ruthless and brutal attack by Japanese bombers, in newspapers around the world. The picture was taken immediately following an air raid on a Shanghai train station crowded with more than 1,800 refugees, the majority of them women and children, late last August. It is thought less than 300 survived.

The famous picture, The Baby in the Shanghai Railroad Station.

Governor General's Awards make debut

Nov. 18, 1937

TORONTO – Gov. Gen. Lord Tweedsmuir, himself a successful novelist and poet, presented the first of the Governor General's Awards for literature at Convocation Hall's Canadian Poetry Night this evening. Winning publications for the year 1936 were chosen by the Canadian Authors Association.

Bertram Brooker, whose *Think of the Earth* was chosen as the best novel of 1936, was on hand to receive his award. In the prize-winning work, Brooker, who was born in England, uses vivid descriptions of a small Manitoba town to weave an increasingly intense psychological thriller. His novel will no doubt enjoy renewed popularity.

The medal for best general literature was awarded posthumously and presented to George Robertson on behalf of his late father, T.B. Robertson. The elder Robertson's newspaper pieces were judged to be the best in the country. The Governor General's Awards for literature are to be presented to Canada's best writers annually.

Plan proposes 5 provinces instead of 9

Dec. 2, 1937

WINNIPEG – A new design for the Canadian provinces will be discussed by the Royal Commission on Dominion-Provincial Relations. It calls for five provinces instead of nine, and is believed to represent major savings in the costs of government at senior levels. Commission chairman N.W. Rowell says he will introduce the proposal as a result of similar suggestions made by individuals and associations. In general, the recommendations urge that the Maritime provinces be merged into a single unit; that the Prairie provinces become a single unit; that British Columbia join with the Yukon; and that Ontario and Quebec remain as present.

Even before the debate begins, there are doubts being expressed about the plan. While Manitoba Premier John Bracken supports the proposal, he's found no public support, and even some stated opposition. Winnipeg's business leaders feared a new capital for combined Prairie provinces would be located somewhere other than Winnipeg.

Chicago, April 12. Chicago Blackhawks beat the Toronto Maple Leafs three games to one to win the Stanley Cup.

New York, June. Superman, created by Toronto *Star* artist Joe Shuster and American Jerry Siegel, makes his first appearance in Action Comics.

Ottawa, July 1. PM King, addressing the possibility of RAF training schools in Canada, says his government opposes the operation of any military establishments in Canada not owned and controlled by Canada, except in case of war.

Montreal, July. More than 5,000 people attend the first summer concert of *Les Concerts symphoniques de Montréal* on Mount Royal, conducted by Wilfrid Pelletier.

Ontario, Aug. 22. RCMP pull up and destroy about one ton of marijuana growing in the Tecumseh district.

Niagara Falls, Ont., Sept. 12. The Canadian Trades and Labour Congress demands a Canada-wide boycott of German, Italian, and Japanese goods, and a government embargo on arms shipments to these countries.

Spain, September. The Mackenzie-Papineau Battalion withdraws from conflict in the civil war after serving in five major campaigns.

Munich, Sept. 30. Leaders of France, Germany, Italy, and Britain agree to German occupation of the Sudetenland in Czechoslovakia, allaying fears of war.

Toronto, Dec. 10. Toronto Argonauts beat the Winnipeg Blue Bombers 30-7 for the Grey Cup.

China. Canadian Dr. Norman Bethune joins the communist 8th Route Army fighting against Japanese invaders in the Shanxi-Hobei border area. He serves as a surgeon and propagandist.

Quebec. Gratien Gélinas' theatre revue *Fridolinons*, or *Fridolinades*, starring the character Fridolin, is presented for the first time.

Canada. After 10 years in government film-making in England, John Grierson accepts an offer to study the Canadian government's use of film.

Guelph, Ont. Tests of artificial insemination on cows are conducted at Ontario Agricultural College.

B.C. deals with anti-Asian sentiment

MP slams Japanese Canadian fishermen

The large Oriental population of the west coast is unpopular with whites.

Feb. 23, 1938

OTTAWA – A Liberal MP from British Columbia accuses Japanese Canadian fishermen of exercising forceful control of the fishery at the mouth of the Fraser River. Thomas Reid, a longtime opponent of Asian immigration, told the House of Commons that the Japanese were assaulting white fishermen, cutting their nets, and wrecking their boats to drive them out of business. Reid wants Ottawa to reduce the number of fishing licences granted to Japanese Canadians. In a long, angry speech, Reid said that "those of Japanese origin have themselves to blame if there is any ill feeling against them in British Columbia."

Duff wants Oriental immigrants banned

March 16, 1938

VICTORIA, B.C. – In a submission to the Royal Commission on Dominion-Provincial Relations today, B.C. Premier Duff Pattullo urged a ban on Oriental immigration into Canada and asked that as many Chinese and Japanese as possible be repatriated to their native countries. The premier admitted that the royal commission had no responsibility for immigration, but his recommendation reflects the anti-Asian sentiment so prevalent in the province recently.

Restrictions on Asian immigration would be nothing new. Chinese newcomers used to have to pay a head tax of $500 before being allowed to enter Canada. Since 1923, immigration from China has been virtually halted, and in 1928 Canada restricted Japanese immigration to just 150 persons per year. Nonetheless, many British Columbians still believe Asian newcomers pose a threat to white control of the society and economy.

Ottawa takes aim at fascist groups

Feb. 22, 1938

OTTAWA – The federal government is taking stern action against members of fascist-style groups such as the 11,000 strong Canadian Nationalist Party (CNP). In the House of Commons today, Justice Minister Ernest Lapointe pointed out that it was a criminal offence for any persons to carry out any sort of military exercises without federal permission.

The law in question is an old one left over from the Great War two decades ago which was never repealed. It is now being applied to groups like Quebec's National Christian Socialist Party, which has carried out illegal drills, Ontario's CNP, and a similar group in Manitoba. All these groups are openly anti-Semitic. The announcement has received the endorsement of all four parties in the House.

Honeymoon is over for Niagara bridge

The collapsed Honeymoon Bridge at Niagara Falls.

Jan. 27, 1938

NIAGARA FALLS, Ont. – Niagara's Honeymoon Bridge has been torn down by a sea of ice that has been pressing against its support pillars for days. Thousands who watched feeble attempts to free the ice jam saw Mother Nature deliver the *coup de grâce* as the 372-metre bridge was ripped away from its moorings. The disaster was expected, as chunk after huge chunk of ice was swept over the falls, adding pressure to the ice jam.

Roosevelt pledges help in case of war

Aug. 18, 1938

KINGSTON, Ont. – America won't stand by if Canada is invaded by European enemies. That's the assurance President Franklin D. Roosevelt gave to a cheering crowd of 5,000 at Richardson Stadium. The president was there to receive an honorary degree from Queen's University. Roosevelt pledged "the United States will not stand idly by if domination of Canada is threatened by any other empire." The assurance is good for Canada, but also wise for the U.S., which hardly wants Nazis as neighbors.

President Franklin Roosevelt.

Stork Derby ends in a four-way tie

May 29, 1938

TORONTO – Today, more than 11 years after lawyer, sportsman, and financier Charles V. Millar died of a heart attack in 1926, four mothers became wealthy beneficiaries of his bizarre last will and testament. Each received $75,000 as winners of the Stork Derby.

Among the curious aspects of Millar's will, none captured the public's interest more than the Stork Derby. Millar bequeathed brewery shares to noted temperance supporters, race track stock to anti-gamblers, but he also left a small fortune to the Toronto mother(s) who had the most children over the 10-year period after his death. Each winner had nine.

Grey Owl dies; secret is finally told

Grey Owl (Archibald Belaney).

April 22, 1938

WINNIPEG – Grey Owl is a legendary white man, not an Indian! All week the story of whether Grey Owl is really the English-born Archie Belaney, who married an Ojibwa Indian woman in Temagami, Ont., in 1910 and abandoned her a year later, has been discussed in newspapers on both sides of the Atlantic.

The North Bay *Nugget* raised the issue the day of his death on April 13. Then on April 19, a reporter with the Hastings office of the Brighton *Evening Argus* interviewed Ada and Carrie Belaney of Hastings. Three more days of cross-checking in Britain confirmed the Belaney women raised their nephew Archie. Grey Owl was really one Archibald Stansfeld Belaney, a full-blooded Englishman. As a boy he fantasized about Indians, and at 17 he left for Canada to become one.

From 1931 to 1938 Grey Owl looked after the beaver conservation program in Manitoba's Riding Mountain National Park and later Saskatchewan's Prince Albert National Park. This famous Canadian wrote four books. But is his work jeopardized by his masquerade? No, the vast majority of Canadian newspaper editorialists have responded. As a great Canadian conservationist, he deserves a place in the annals of his adopted country.

Tear gas helps police disperse squatters

June 19, 1938

VANCOUVER – Police today used tear gas bombs and riot sticks to get hundreds of squatters out of the Main Post Office and the Art Gallery. Two policemen were injured and about 40 unemployed were treated for minor injuries.

The men had been occupying the lobby of the post office and the gallery, about a kilometre away, for a month. The police, consisting of almost the entire city force and a detachment of RCMP, surrounded the post office at 4 a.m. and gave the squatters 20 minutes to get out. They refused to move and the tear gas bombs were tossed in. There was silence. Then the men started to break windows to let in clean air and the police stormed through the doors. After battling the police the men retreated along Hastings Street, breaking hundreds of store windows on their way. At the art gallery the men were prepared for the tear gas and had wrapped blankets around their heads to protect themselves from the fumes. They, too, refused a demand to leave, but lasted 20 minutes before they started to depart, without causing any damage. The men plan to send a delegation to Victoria to squat on the legislature steps until a public works program starts.

Policemen break up anti-fascist protest

July 4, 1938

TORONTO – Police this evening broke up an anti-fascist street demonstration and arrested four people. The loud demonstration of about 850 people at a downtown intersection was held to protest a nearby meeting of 2,500 fascists. Police feared the crowd intended to attack the fascist meeting.

At the same time, 10,000 people gathered at Maple Leaf Gardens to applaud speakers who denounced fascism as a danger to democracy. One of the features of the fascist meeting was a tirade against Jews.

TCA to employ nurses as stewardesses

1938

OTTAWA – Trans-Canada Airlines will employ stewardesses on their airplanes. Lucile Garner, a registered nurse, has been hired to establish a stewardess training department. All TCA stewardesses will be registered nurses. Their duties will include seeing to the comfort of passengers, serving box lunches and beverages, and administering first aid. They'll also answer passengers' questions about the weather and emergency procedures. Stewardesses will wear navy blue uniforms, which will cost them $30. A stewardess's monthly salary will be $140.

First two TCA stewardesses.

Death rate from TB high among Indians

May 30, 1938

OTTAWA – Indians are dying partly because the government does not provide enough funds for hospitals, the director of the Indian Affairs branch said today. H.W. McGill told the Rowell Commission probing federal-provincial relations that the death rate from tuberculosis is 11 times higher among Indians than it is among whites. McGill agreed that "sufficient funds are not available for hospitalizing all known cases." Several submissions have dealt with the Indian tuberculosis situation. ▷

Canada, U.S., U.K. sign new trade deal

PM King signs the trade treaty.

Nov. 17, 1938

WASHINGTON, D.C. – Some American manufactured goods will cost less as Canada shifts its pattern of exports and imports. In an agreement signed today by the Canadian, British, and American governments, Canada will forgo some preferences in British markets and reduce tariffs on some American imported goods. In return, the U.S. will lower tariffs on some Canadian goods. This means, for example, that American wheat will be more competitive with Canadian wheat in Britain, but Canadian fish will enter the U.S. at less cost.

Americans eye new international road

Sept. 8, 1938

TORONTO – Alaskan civil engineer Donald MacDonald today urged Canadians to allow the construction of an international highway linking Seattle, Washington, and Fairbanks, Alaska, via British Columbia. MacDonald argued that if it were built, the highway would help tap vast resources in remote parts of B.C. It would also provide an ideal defence against a possible invasion from Asia. Americans are so excited about the project they are willing to share the cost of building the 1,450 kilometres of Canadian road, and are ready to proceed as soon as the Canadian government approves the project.

Magazine muffed, fashion experts say

Oct. 31, 1938

TORONTO – Fashion experts here are scoffing at the suggestion made recently by a popular United States magazine that this season's boom in muff sales means war is imminent. Yes – strange but true – every major war during the last 150 years has been preceded by a muff epoch. But Toronto stylists attribute the latest craze to a mere resurgence of Victorian fashions.

King praises Hitler pact

PM W.L. Mackenzie King.

Germany's leader, Adolf Hitler.

Sept. 30, 1938

OTTAWA – British Prime Minister Neville Chamberlain's success – or sellout, depending on one's point of view – in reaching a deal with Hitler over the dismembering of Czechoslovakia has been greeted with relief by many Canadians, including Prime Minister W.L. Mackenzie King. In a cable to Chamberlain, obtained via anonymous insiders, King lauds the British PM: "Your achievements in the past month alone will assure you an abiding and illustrious place among the great conciliators."

King and other politicians who support Chamberlain believe that all Hitler wants is the return of German populations who live in other lands. So, reason the appeasers, it only makes sense that the Nazis acquire areas, like the Sudetenland in Czechoslovakia, where these ethnic Germans live. Once these people are back within German territory, Hitler will be satisfied, having redressed the arguably harsh peace terms of 1918. Doubters of Nazi sincerity point to their demands for the free city of Danzig, for parts of Poland with German minority populations, and for the Lithuanian port of Memel.

Berlin Jews victims of "Crystal Night"

Nov. 9, 1938

BERLIN, Germany – Anti-Semitism raged in full fury through the streets of Berlin tonight, and more than 90 people, mostly Jews, are dead as a result. Nazis, angered by the assassination of a German official in Paris by a young Polish Jew, began the killing spree, looting, wrecking and burning Jewish stores, homes, and places of worship. Thousands of shattered windows earned this night its name, Kristallnacht (Crystal Night). Before the attacks, efforts by Berlin's Jewish leaders to calm the rising storm by voicing opposition to the Paris assassination were stymied by a Nazi ban on Jewish publications.

Bluenose defends title for International Fisherman's Trophy

Nova Scotia is proud of her famous schooner, The Bluenose.

Oct. 26, 1938

BOSTON – The captain and crew of the *Bluenose*, the pride of Nova Scotia's fishing fleet, are whooping it up after sailing to a triumphant win earlier today in defence of the schooner's International Fisherman's Trophy title. The margin of victory was narrow – the *Bluenose* completed the 57-kilometre course just under three minutes ahead of the challenger, the *Gertrude L. Thebaud*, queen of the Gloucester fleet. Today's race was the fifth and deciding contest.

The *Bluenose* has continued to stave off challenges from newer ships for 21 years now, but the years have taken their toll and there is talk she will soon be retired from international competition.

Group says restrict the influx of Jews

Nov. 19, 1938

TORONTO – A major organization of Canadian soldiers has pleaded with the government to restrict Jewish immigration. The Canadian Corps Association today sent a letter to Prime Minister W.L. Mackenzie King outlining its views. The letter, signed by association president Col. Charles R. Hill, says his organization opposes any plans to make it easier for Jews made homeless by recent events in Europe to come here.

The association fears a "forced mass immigration" of Jews. Any action the British Empire takes to relieve the burden on European Jews should be concentrated in eastern and northeastern Africa, the letter says. Canada's immigration laws should "ensure that our future citizens will be predominantly British, the remainder to be those whose racial origin permits of rapid and complete assimilation."

Cabinet debates Jewish immigration

Dec. 13, 1938

OTTAWA – Thomas Crerar, Liberal mines and resources minister responsible for immigration, shocked his cabinet colleagues just two weeks ago by recommending 10,000 European Jews be allowed into Canada. Today, Crerar once again delivered a statement on the subject, but this one bore little resemblance to his first on Dec. 1. This time he urged no major change to the government's closed-door immigration policy. Crerar merely suggested that regulations be eased slightly and interpreted "as liberally as possible."

Today's statement returns Crerar to the ranks of the status quo. Finding himself alone without any cabinet support, he has rescinded his earlier position, unable to sway opinion from the oft-repeated argument that Canada cannot accommodate an influx of immigrants given the economy's poor state. He also met with resistance from the government's Quebec wing, opposed to Jewish immigration because of its unpopularity among influential Quebec nationalists.

Frederick Blair.

Vincent Massey.

Guarding the government position is immigration director Frederick Blair. An inflexible bureaucrat determined never to bend the rules, even for the most extenuating of circumstances, Blair is openly contemptuous and critical of Jews as potential immigrants. Similarly, Canada's high commissioner to London, Vincent Massey, displays little sympathy for European Jews anxious to escape Nazi persecution.

Berlin paper slams abuse of Indians

Nov. 19, 1938

BERLIN – Canada has no business criticizing German policy toward Jews as long as it treats its native Indians badly, an influential newspaper editorialized today. The *Voelkischer Beobachter,* the newspaper of Chancellor Adolf Hitler, said that Canada has launched a "campaign of hatred" against Germany and is overreacting to the Jewish situation. But, the newspaper said, Canadians should take a look at their own Indian reserves, where "they will find out what inhuman treatment really means, see how the old native Indian population was destroyed by starvation and liquor."

Hitler's literary mentor on North American Indians was author Karl May. May, who died in 1912, wrote about the American west before ever visiting North America. May's Indians are total and ludicrous misrepresentations. Attacks here on the western democracies have become more vocal as complaints grow about Germany's treatment of its Jewish population.

Tory leader opposes immigration if Canadians are out of work

Oct. 14, 1938

QUEBEC CITY – The new Conservative leader said today he will not support immigration as long as Canadians are out of work. R.J. Manion used his first political meeting in Quebec as leader to discount what he said were rumors he favored immigration. He said in 1934, as head of the Canadian delegation to the League of Nations, he opposed admitting German refugees. He said he has not changed his mind, despite pleas to admit those being persecuted in Germany, particularly Jews.

Manion said that Canada should allow no immigration "so long as we have hundreds of thousands of people in this country out of work on relief." But Canada is a large country with a small population, and once the depression ends it might need immigrants, he said.

Trapper Archie White trades in his pelts for provisions and equipment at the local Hudson's Bay Company store at Cameron Bay in the Northwest Territories. HBC manager Andy Reid is behind the counter.

Swift fox all but gone from Alberta

1938

ALBERTA – The swift fox does not live up to its fox-like reputation as being the symbol of cunning. As its name implies, the swift fox is capable of great speed, escaping danger with remarkable bursts of energy, but its trusting nature leaves it quite unsuspecting of man, and often caught in traps or shot. The absence of sightings of this five-pound grey fox proves that the creature's innocence has darkened its destiny. This year, only one swift fox has been seen in Alberta, and it is thought to be the last of its kind. The species is believed extirpated from the Canadian wilderness.

1939

Port Arthur, Ont., Jan. 4. Hundreds turn out for the opening of the world's first skating rink made of milk.

Madrid, March 28. Franco's Nationalist forces take Madrid, winning the civil war. Some 1,300 Canadians fought with the International Brigades on the Republican side, mostly in the Mackenzie-Papineau Battalion. About half of them died.

Boston, April 16. Boston Bruins beat the Toronto Maple Leafs four games to one for the Stanley Cup.

Canada, June. The government gives away 10 tons of year-old surplus butter to unemployed Canadians. One million Canadians are on relief.

Winnipeg, June. A ballet club formed by Gweneth Lloyd and Betty Farrally [Royal Winnipeg Ballet] makes its first public performance.

Ottawa, Sept. 7. An order-in-council gives the newly created Wartime Prices and Trade Board power to seize any supply of food, fuel, or other necessities it deems "unreasonably held from the market."

Ottawa, Sept. 10. Canada declares war on Germany, entering the fighting alongside Britain and France.

Halifax, Sept. 16. The first Canadian convoy leaves for the war in Europe.

Ottawa, Sept. 21. The Department of National Defence bars from enlistment men with university training in medicine, engineering, agriculture, and other sciences, and certain skilled industrial workers.

Ottawa, September. The government forms Defence Industries Ltd. to provide explosives and munitions for the war.

Ottawa, Oct. 5. Gen. Andrew G.L. McNaughton is named commander of the first Canadian Infantry Division overseas.

Ottawa, Dec. 9. Winnipeg Blue Bombers beat Ottawa Rough Riders 8-7 in the Grey Cup.

Ottawa. The government spends $29,480 on Inuit health care (about $4 per Inuit), an inadequate sum considering Inuit health problems.

Ottawa. The Supreme Court upholds a Quebec tavern owner's right to refuse to sell beer to a black.

Edmonton. Alberta's government creates the 3,600-hectare Greene Valley Game Preserve in the Peace River area.

Soldiers back from Spanish Civil War

Girl welcomes home her brother.

Members of the Mackenzie-Papineau Battalion return to Canada.

Feb. 4, 1939

TORONTO – Most grim-faced and teary-eyed, despite the cheers or perhaps because of them, 120 Canadian veterans of the Spanish Civil War, all members of the Mackenzie-Papineau Battalion, were welcomed home tonight at Union Station by a crowd at least 10,000 strong. As a brass band played and the crowd cheered, the scene resembled the welcome given returning troops 20 years ago.

But the resemblance ends there. There are no uniforms made dazzling with decorations. The soldiers are dressed in the nondescript manner of civilians, just as they left. And their cause, ignored for so long in Canada by the government and people alike, appears almost lost. These soldiers committed themselves to the fight against fascism on their own accord. Forced to slip out of Canada as if, according to one observer, "running away from the police," their welcome tonight indicates that many Canadians who "didn't understand at first ... understand now" why they left.

Germany violates pact; war looms

March 15, 1939

PRAGUE – Gemany's seizure of Czechoslovakia, in violation of last September's Munich Pact, makes war ever more likely. Adolf Hitler may make more demands, but others now insist that the German leader be resisted. The Czech state was previously forced to give up a fortified frontier area, the Sudetenland, because Hitler demanded that ethnic Germans should be under German rather than Czechoslovak rule, while Poland seized Teschen, a small corner of Czechoslovakia. On March 10, German tanks and troops occupied what was left of the republic.

The fate of Czechoslovakia unites Europe in the belief that Hitler cannot be trusted. Further German threats will almost certainly be met with force, including a British declaration of war, backed by Commonwealth nations.

United Farmers of Alberta quit politics

Jan. 19, 1939

CALGARY – After 20 years of hectic activity, the United Farmers of Alberta have abandoned the political field. When the decision was taken by standing vote at yesterday's convention, approximately 25 of 272 voting delegates stood in opposition. The move was recommended to the body of delegates by the board of directors. It was obviously a difficult decision to make, for the UFA once formed the government of Alberta, and at one time it had sent a dozen of its members to Parliament.

In making its non-political move and severing all of its party affiliations, the United Farmers of Alberta now join with the United Farmers of Manitoba and the Saskatchewan section of the United Farmers of Canada, who earlier took a similar step.

King condemns German invasion, Hitler

March 20, 1939

OTTAWA – Prime Minister W.L. Mackenzie King today joined other western democratic leaders in denouncing the German seizure of Czechoslovakia. In a statement to the Commons, King called Adolf Hitler's action "wanton and forcible." Tory leader R.J. Manion said Hitler is "mad with a lust for conquest." King pledged Canada's support of Britain if war ensues. "If there were prospects of an aggressor launching an attack on Britain, with bombers raining death on London, I have no doubt what the decision of the Canadian people and Parliament would be."

CCF leader J.S. Woodsworth called for an embargo on exports of war materials to Germany and a heavy tax on German imports.

Students demand answer about draft

March 28, 1939
QUEBEC CITY – Hundreds of angry French-speaking university students this afternoon raided the National Assembly to confront an equally angry premier. The students wanted assurance that, in the event of war, overseas service would be voluntary. The students smashed locks on the doors of the public galleries and shouted questions at Premier Maurice Duplessis on the floor of the Assembly. Duplessis refused to answer questions, and when he reprimanded the students they became quiet. Still, they got no answer.

Quebec court rules Padlock Law is OK

May 31, 1939
MONTREAL – Quebec's Padlock Law, designed to fight communism, is constitutional, the province's Superior Court has ruled. Chief Justice R.A.E. Greenshields said that by passing the law the Quebec legislature did not infringe on the federal government's jurisdiction over criminal law. He said the law was designed to prevent crime, not punish offenders. The law lets Quebec close for one year any building used to "propagate communism or bolshevism" and to confiscate communist propaganda. The judgment will be appealed.

War vet is leading race against horse

April 12, 1939
EDMONTON – Contending it is "a well-known fact a man can beat a horse in a race of this kind," R. Bower is brimming with confidence entering the second quarter leg of a six-day horse-versus-man endurance race. As of today, the 45-year-old war veteran boasts a 15-lap lead after finishing 100 laps on the 0.8-kilometre track. Bower is no stranger to long-distance running. Among his previous feats, he claims to have run 161 kilometres in 16 hours, 28 minutes in 1924, an unofficial world's record.

Prairie Farm Assistance Act passed

Drifted sand covers this prairie farm.

Farmers come to town in Saskatchewan to receive grasshopper poison.

Sandbanks surround this abandoned Saskatchewan farm.

June 3, 1939
OTTAWA – The federal government has offered farmers another weapon in their ongoing struggle to make the western prairie desert productive. It has just passed the Prairie Farm Assistance Act, which offers a type of crop insurance in the event of low prices or low yields in a given area.

A one-percent levy will be collected on sales of wheat and coarse grains. These funds will be used to make payments to farmers in areas that could be declared to be in a state of emergency, because the average price of wheat is less than 80 cents per bushel, or where a crop failure has been declared when the average yield in a number of townships dips below two bushels per hectare. Payments will not be large by any means – the intention is simply to put some cash into a given hard-hit district.

The last few years have seen a concerted effort by farmers, government, and scientists to make agriculture on the prairies a possibility. Now the emphasis is on conservation of soil and water, developing a suitable strain of wheat, pest control, and an insurance safety net for the years when all else fails. The 1930s have been a hard test of the abilities and the spirit of all involved.

Supreme Court rules Inuit are Indians

April 5, 1939
OTTAWA – Inuit are Indians, the Supreme Court of Canada has declared. In a decision handed down today, the high court unanimously settled a dispute between Ottawa and Quebec. The federal government said Quebec Inuit were a responsibility of the province, even though Indians are exclusively a federal concern.

At a hearing before the Supreme Court last year, the federal lawyer pointed to some dictionaries that exclude "Inuit" from the definition of "Indian." But in a series of decisively-worded judgments replete with much historical background, the court ruled that the use of the term "Indian" in the British North America Act referred to all the original peoples of Canada. Justice Patrick Kerwin wrote that when the act confined authority to the federal government for those described as Indians, "the intention was to allocate to it authority over all the aborigines."

Ottawa announces creation of the NFB

May 2, 1939
OTTAWA – The federal government, acting on a recommendation tabled by British film producer John Grierson, today announced the creation of the National Film Board of Canada. Known for his talent and for the creation of a new film genre – the documentary – Grierson is expected to take on the responsibility of running the new organization himself.

Immigration policy angers nation's Jewish leaders

March 1939

OTTAWA – Despite their most concerted efforts on behalf of German refugees, including a recent media campaign that succeeded in arousing a measure of public outcry against the Liberal government's stringent anti-Jewish policies, Canada's Jewish leaders have walked away from the latest round of talks with officials thoroughly dismayed.

When Jewish leaders began meetings with Minister of Mines and Resources Thomas Crerar and immigration director Frederick Blair last month, "a definite and favorable decision" was expected. But all they procured was a curt reiteration, tempered by polite sympathy, that nothing will be done to ease the plight of Europe's Jews.

Frustration over these talks has led the director of the Jewish Immigrant Aid Society, M.A. Solkin, to conclude "the government is as far from admitting (Jews) as they ever were and that any attempt to obtain a general relaxation in immigration is doomed to certain failure." The only hope, Solkin says, is the election of a new federal government, one that "would no longer have to placate the whims of anti-Semitic Quebec or ... other reactionary elements."

Solkin's pessimism is warranted. The government's stand against Jewish immigration, nominally due to unemployment and, according to Blair, because Jews "do not ... take to farming," carries little weight. Earlier this year, in an editorial critical of the King administration's policy toward Jews, the Windsor *Star* pointed out that "what has taken place in Palestine shows that Jewish farmers ... have made that country a garden and the products of Jewish farms are being exported throughout the world."

But the stubborn, generalized view of Jews as non-agriculturalists persists, and no amount of qualifications, capital, or evidence to the contrary seems able to change this opinion. In February, 200 Jewish farm families from Czechoslovakia with combined assets of more than $1 million were denied entry. The same month, the immigration department granted admission to roughly 3,000 political, non-Jewish German refugees from the Sudeten. They applied and have been accepted as a group. The Czechoslovakian Jews also applied as a group. They, presumably, should have known better – Canada accepts Jews "on individual applications only."

Larger cities have Hebrew schools. Here the Calgary Hebrew School holds a picnic in Bowness Park.

These Jewish orphans immigrated to Canada from Poland in 1926. They attended a Jewish-sponsored agricultural school in Ontario.

The Canadian Jewish Farm School at Georgetown, Ontario, was established to help new immigrants learn the techniques necessary to develop farms in their new land. Here a group poses at the school in 1929.

The Canadian Jewish Congress gives help to new immigrants, such as these refugees Yankel and Mendel Szapiro. Here the men proudly stook the first wheat grown on their new farm near Lydiatt, Manitoba.

Jewish refugees are turned away at every port

Don't let the St. Louis dock, minister says

June 7, 1939

OTTAWA – Finance Minister Ernest Lapointe today "emphatically opposed" allowing the liner *St. Louis* and its cargo of Jewish refugees to dock at a Canadian port. His stand is typical of the hard-line government approach to the issue – it is also politically necessary. He is Prime Minister W.L. Mackenzie King's Quebec lieutenant, and as such must consolidate Liberal support in French Canada.

To accomplish this he must bow to the pressures of public opinion, and right now that opinion is firmly entrenched in the right-wing ideology of the Union Nationale. While anti-Semitism is not confined to Quebec, nowhere else is it so blatant or scathing in its attack.

Papers such as *L'Action Nationale, La Nation,* and *L'Action Catholique* have led the way. *L'Action Catholique* has given Hitler credit for snatching Germany "from the hands of the communists ... very many of whom ... were Jews." This link between anti-communism and anti-Semitism is at least partly to blame for the fact that since 1933 Canada has allowed fewer than 4,000 Jews to immigrate – the lowest total among western nations.

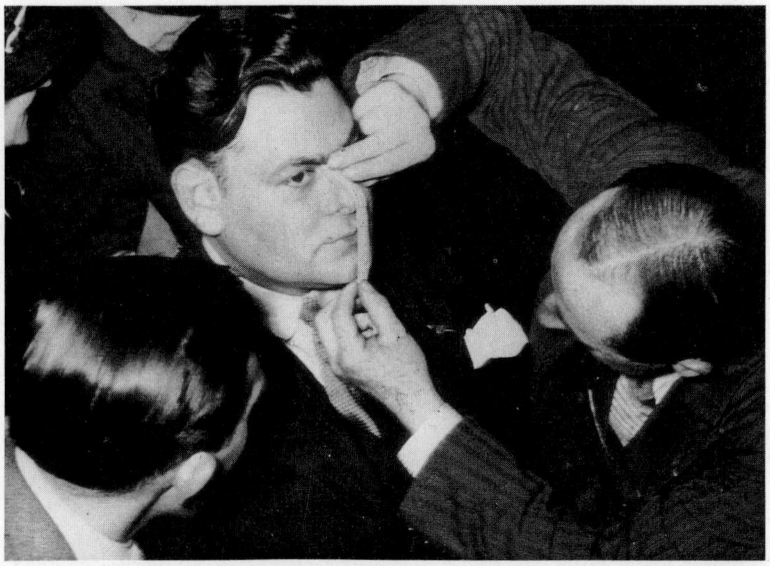

German government official measures a man's nose to see if he is Aryan.

Jewish shops in Berlin have been vandalized by organized gangs.

Canada the latest country to refuse liner

Refugees on the St. Louis are hysterical on being refused sanctuary in Cuba.

June 8, 1939

OTTAWA – With a characteristic note of indifference for European Jews displaced and dispossessed by the dictates of Nazi Germany, the Canadian government has chosen to ignore the plight of 907 refugees in limbo off the east coast of Canada. For the passengers on the Hamburg-American liner *St. Louis*, including more than 400 women and children, Canada represented their last hope of finding a safe haven. Now they have little choice but to return to Europe.

That they even applied for admission into Canada, a country known for its tough policy restricting immigration, particularly to Jews, is a measure of their desperation. In May the ship left Germany bound for Cuba, but once there it was turned away after all entreaties, including a threatened mass suicide, were dismissed.

Within two days, appeals by Jewish organizations to have the refugees admitted to Argentina, Paraguay, Panama, or Uruguay were similarly refused. The United States was then approached, but the Americans' only response was to send gunboats to keep the ship at such a distance that it could not run aground nor its passengers swim ashore.

Nazi soldiers surround elderly Jew.

King George VI and Queen Elizabeth sail away

King George VI and Queen Elizabeth are warmly greeted in Winnipeg.

The royal visitors descend from the Empress of Australia at Quebec City.

Queen Elizabeth lays the cornerstone of the Supreme Court building in Ottawa.

Couple's month-long tour of Canada ends

June 15, 1939

HALIFAX – King George VI and Queen Elizabeth sailed from Halifax tonight, ending a month-long tour of Canada that can only be described as a masterstroke of public relations. Toronto's *Globe and Mail* called the tour "a Royal crusade as colorful and commanding as when a Richard stirred to conquest for humanity's sake and marched in England's name, with justice at his sword-point and with freedom on his shield." Montreal's *Le Devoir* was not quite so enthusiastic: "By the smile of a Queen and the French words of a King the English have conquered once again the cradle of New France."

The king and queen arrived at Quebec May 17, becoming the first of the 17 sovereigns who have ruled Canada to cross the ocean. They immediately endeared themselves to French-Canadians with their fluent French. Speaking near the Plains of Abraham, where the English and French shed each other's blood 180 years ago, the king reflected "it is here today that the two great races live happily side by side." After visiting nine provinces and greeting 2.5 million doting subjects, the king and queen have cemented the bonds of empire, bonds that are now crucial with the spectre of war looming in Europe.

Dedicating War Memorial, Ottawa.

The royal couple talk with a wounded war veteran in Edmonton, Alberta.

Unemployed flock to the tobacco belt

July 31, 1939

DELHI, Ont. – This town of 2,300 is currently jammed with 3,000 transients, all hoping for work in the tobacco fields. And the people here aren't alone in their dilemma – overall, 9,000 people have come to the tobacco belt for the same reason. Police Chief Platt and his one constable are all that's available to handle the situation. Around them, crowded into whatever shelter can be found, are the unemployed. The majority of these jobless transients are basically honest, says the chief. Only a small percentage are troublemakers.

Trouble ranges from vegetables pilfered from gardens to stolen cars. Overall the scene is like a giant refugee camp, with no jobs in sight. That's because this year's crop is a small one, meaning that most of the work can be done by local labor, with no hope for the transients.

PM urges restraint in European conflict

Aug. 25, 1939

OTTAWA – Prime Minister W.L. Mackenzie King has cabled European belligerents, pleading with them to act with restraint. To German Chancellor Adolf Hitler and Polish leader Ignacy Moscicki, King said Canadians "are prepared to join what authority and power they may possess to that of the other nations of the British Commonwealth in seeking a just and equitable settlement of the great problems with which nations are faced." While it clearly refers to the grave situation between Germany and Poland, officials here admit they are perplexed as to the specific meaning of that passage.

King appealed to the two leaders "in the firm hope that your great power and authority will be used to prevent impending catastrophe by having recourse to every possible peaceful means to effect a solution." In a separate message, the prime minister asked Italian leader Benito Mussolini to use his "great power and influence" to intervene and preserve peace between Germany and Poland.

War Measures Act goes into effect

Sept. 1, 1939

OTTAWA – The federal government has assumed wartime powers, even though war has not been declared. Early today, a cabinet order was presented to the governor general proclaiming the War Measures Act. That legislation, first used in the last world war, gives the government sweeping powers of arrest and detention, censorship, and control of shipping and transportation. Also today, the government announced that the country's militia has been called to active service on a voluntary basis.

In a prepared statement, Prime Minister William Lyon Mackenzie King declared "it is now apparent that the efforts which have been made to preserve the peace of Europe are likely to be of no avail."

If Britain becomes engaged in another war, King said "the government of Canada has unanimously decided as soon as Parliament meets, to seek its authority for effective co-operation by Canada at the side of Britain." Officials have been engaged in a flurry of meetings during the past few days as the threat of war increases. The prime minister met today with the governor general, the British high commissioner, and the leader of the opposition.

War production has already begun in parts of the country. High-explosive artillery shells are to be produced at the arsenal at Lindsay, Ont. The Ottawa Car Company has begun building heavy bombers.

Canadian writer pens Hardy Boys novels

1939

WHITBY, Ont. – "After the help we gave Dad on that forgery case, I guess he'll begin to think we could be detectives when we grow up." In 1926, when Whitby writer Leslie McFarlane wrote these words, the opening of *The Tower Treasure*, the first Hardy Boys novel, he had no idea he was giving birth to one of the most popular juvenile fiction series ever. Since then, McFarlane has written over 15 Hardy Boys books under the pen name of Franklin W. Dixon, and the books have sold and sold. Young people can't get enough of Joe and Frank Hardy and their bloodless, sexless, clean spoken, yet always harrowing adventures.

Bayport, U.S., the fictional home of Joe and Frank, may as well be on a different planet. While North Americans have just suffered through a terrible depression, Joe and Frank whiz about in their boat, the *Sleuth*, always eat well from Aunt Gertrude's kitchen, and keep raking in rewards, usually about $1,000, after they solve the mystery at the end of each book. Back in real life, author McFarlane has never driven a car and has been so broke he had to borrow money from his son to send manuscripts to publishers. The Stratemeyer Syndicate, the American publisher of the Hardy Boys books, has paid him about $100 for each book he has written, and has gotten him to sign a contract relinquishing all rights to the books and promising never to reveal he is their author.

Illustration from Hardy Boys novel.

105 couples marry as 20,000 look on

July 23, 1939

MONTREAL – With Archbishop Georges Gauthier officiating, 104 supporting priests, and some 20,000 spectators, 105 young French-Canadian couples were married today at the Montreal Stadium. Father Henri Roy, leader of the youth organization which planned and sponsored the event, completed the ceremony by reading the high mass.

Standard-bearers carrying the multi-colored flags of Jeunesse Ouvrière Catholique ringed the baseball diamond, where the brides in white and the grooms in blue suits stood and knelt at centre field.

Montreal-born Norma Shearer, whose latest film performance as Marie Antoinette is receiving rave reviews, has come a long way from being Miss Lotta Miles in advertisements for tires.

Airmail service with Britain takes flight

July 5, 1939

BOTWOOD, Nfld. – Regular airmail between Canada and Britain began officially today – in both directions. The Pan American aircraft *Clipper III* left here today en route to Foynes, Ireland, loaded with passengers and mail. At the same time, Imperial Airways' *Caledonia* left Foynes, heading west to its landing point here. Apparently, both ships passed each other over the Atlantic tonight at 11 p.m. With favorable winds, the 3,204-kilometre one-way trip averages 15 hours and 9 minutes.

Clothing, blankets needed for children

Sept. 5, 1939
LONDON, England – British authorities today pleaded for Canadian women to help children evacuated from British cities. They need clothing and blankets. The children were evacuated from London and other large urban centres as the possibility of heavy bombing looms. An official in charge of the evacuation said many of the children are from poor families. Not only were they evacuated quickly, but they did not own the means of keeping warm in the countryside. "The first cold night will present real hardships," he said.

Stay out of conflict, Woodsworth argues

Sept. 6, 1939
OTTAWA – J.S. Woodsworth, leader of the Co-operative Commonwealth Federation, committed unavoidable political suicide in the House tonight by arguing for Canadian abstention from the European conflict. Citing his Christianity, and clearly conscience-stricken, Woodsworth urged nonviolence on a House ready to join Britain at the soonest opportunity. It was a noble speech that will surely cost the veteran labor politician his control of the CCF. The left-leaning party will likely support war.

Chamberlain reveals Britain at war

Sept. 3, 1939
LONDON, England – Britons today began grimly and resolutely preparing for the task of war. In a brief radio announcement this afternoon, Prime Minister Neville Chamberlain told the nation that a state of war now exists with Germany. "You can imagine what a bitter blow this is to me that all my long struggle to win peace has failed," the prime minister sadly reported. But it is certain that German Chancellor Adolf Hitler "can only be stopped by force, and we and France are today, in fulfilment of our obligations, going to the aid of Poland." The British government had previously handed to the German leadership a note saying that if the Germans, by 11 a.m. London time today, did not begin at once to withdraw from Poland, war would be declared.

There was no sign of public excitement after the prime minister's announcement. London was much quieter than usual. On the streets, about half the pedestrians carried gas masks, following the example set by Chamberlain. Children were not playing in the parks this Sunday. There was only a small crowd at Victoria Station and at Buckingham Palace, where people normally gather on historic occasions.

One noticeable change is that the guards at the royal palaces in the city have changed their red uniforms to khaki. There were no anti-war sentiments expressed on the soap boxes of Hyde Park, the traditional place for expressing unpopular views. But there were demands for the conscription of wealth to aid the war effort.

British Prime Minister Chamberlain en route to a meeting of Parliament.

German sub sinks British passenger liner; 90 feared dead

Sept. 3, 1939
THE HEBRIDES, England – Canada registered its first war casualties near here tonight when a German submarine sank a British passenger liner. The *SS Athenia* was carrying about 1,400 people, many of them trying to find safety from the European war. Many were North American, including an estimated 200 Canadians. About 90 people are believed to have died. But many rescue ships are still at sea and reports are confusing. Berlin denies a submarine sank the ship. But survivors report seeing the sub, which surfaced after torpedoing the *Athenia* at about 7:30.

Red Cross feeds white and half-breed children evicted from Caughnawaga.

Godbout's Liberals crush Duplessis, UN

Oct. 25, 1939
QUEBEC CITY – Beaten but unrepentant, Premier Maurice Duplessis vowed to "continue to fight for the autonomy of the province." Duplessis tested his stand against the federal War Measures Act, by which he claims Ottawa will usurp provincial powers, at the polls, and his Union Nationale was tossed from office, winning only 15 seats to 68 for the Liberals led by former premier Joseph-Adélard Godbout.

Seven of Duplessis' ministers lost their seats, though he held on to his. "You know I am not a quitter," Duplessis told his supporters.

Bethune succumbs to blood disease

Nov. 12, 1939
HUANG SHIKO, China – Canadian Dr. Norman Bethune, outspoken humanitarian, political activist and founder of the world's first mobile blood transfusion clinic, died today in northern China of septicemia. Bethune arrived in China last year to aid communist guerrilla fighters, led by Mao Zedong, against Japanese invaders. In makeshift hospitals and clinics, often behind enemy lines, Bethune performed surgery under the most gruelling conditions. He contracted the fatal blood poisoning as he operated without disinfectant.

Canada joins in the war

Sept. 10, 1939

OTTAWA – Canada has joined Britain in war against the German Reich. Early this morning, the pronouncement of war was cabled to Buckingham Palace. It followed almost unanimous approval in the Commons last night. A few isolationist members opposed the motion. The Senate was unanimous.

Quebec MP Maxime Raymond warned the war might divide Canada: "The French-Canadian of Quebec is attached to the soil he tills and recognizes only the obligation to defend his own soil." But Raymond did not oppose declaring war. Minister of Justice Ernest Lapointe said war will protect Canada from "the tyrannical doctrines of nazism and communism."

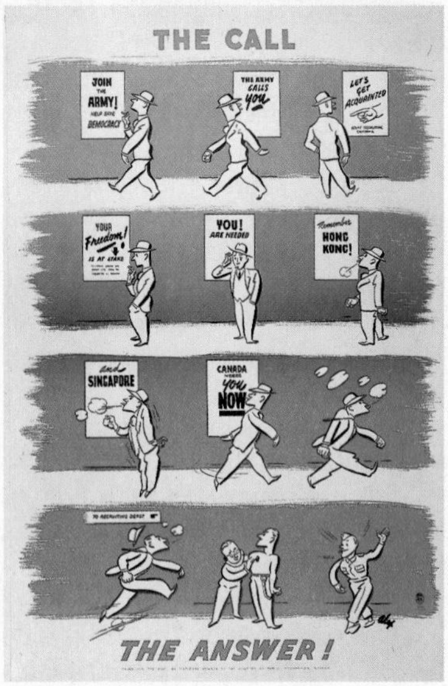

Canadian recruiting poster.

Canadians sign up to serve overseas

September 1939

CANADA – Overwhelming numbers of Canadians have volunteered for overseas service in this first month of war. Already some 58,300 have joined the army, and thousands more have signed up for the navy and air force.

This response, perhaps due to unemployment, has led the Defence Department to stop recruiting in such centres as Ottawa, Montreal, and Toronto. And almost three weeks ago, regiments stopped advertising because of inadequate facilities and equipment. In Nova Scotia, some farm sheds now must serve as mess halls, and in Edmonton, proper military training is difficult because rifles are unavailable.

Thousands of jobs created by the war

Sept. 30, 1939

VANCOUVER – The war means more than just new employment opportunities in the military service. Civilian jobs are also appearing, with thousands of newly created jobs for British Columbia's unemployed, and already shipyards, iron foundries, aircraft plants, and engineering shops are hiring workers and planning expansion. Two new shipyards, one in North Vancouver and the other on False Creek, are currently being built to provide and repair ships for the navy. The manager of one shipyard which now employs 400 says that soon he will need about 10,000 men – and women – to fill the orders expected from Ottawa.

House of Commons approves war taxes

Sept. 12, 1939

OTTAWA – The House of Commons today approved a series of tax increases designed to further the war effort. Cigarettes, liquor, soft drinks, tea and coffee will cost more, personal income taxes will rise 20 percent, and business will pay higher general taxes and a new excess profits tax. The war budget allows tax deductions for donations to patriotic organizations, up to half a taxpayer's income.

Canadians needed for the air force.

Four eager to "get a bead on Hitler" after trek from Arctic

Nov. 15, 1939

MONTREAL – Determined to "get a bead on Hitler," four eager soldiers-to-be arrived here this week after a 5,635-kilometre trek from the eastern Arctic. William Ford, Patrick Baird, Jack R. Ford, and Jack T.D. Ford travelled by dog sled, whaleboat, steamship, and finally train to join the war effort. (The Fords are related, but not brothers.)

William Ford, 26, has not seen civilization for 10 years. Baird is a Cambridge-trained geologist and a member of the team mapping Baffin Island. The four have enlisted with the Royal Canadian Artillery.

Canada plays role in air training plan

Dec. 17, 1939

OTTAWA – Air power is sure to play a major role in this war, and Canada will be prominent developing that power. An agreement signed today binds Australia, Britain, Canada, and New Zealand to operate a massive air training scheme. Soon this country will be humming as dozens of schools are opened across the Dominion, turning out pilots, navigators, bomb aimers and air gunners for the Commonwealth Air Forces. The RCAF, which entered the war with 4,060 personnel and 270 airplanes, will be the principal organizer, teacher, and administrator of the plan.

Unlike the last war, Canadian airmen overseas will have the chance to serve in uniquely Canadian units. Article XV of the agreement, inserted at Canadian insistence, calls for the formation of distinct national squadrons in the war theatres of Europe.

German conquest complete: Warsaw falls

Nazi soldiers search Poles after the German invasion of Poland.

Oct. 2, 1939

WARSAW – Nazi troops occupy this ruined city today, making the conquest of Poland complete. Throughout Germany, demonstrations celebrate the success of the invasion that brought France and the British Commonwealth to war. The Poles have formed a government-in-exile based in Paris and are organizing an army to liberate their country. Meanwhile, the Polish consul general urges Poles living in Canada to join the effort.

1940

Ottawa, Jan. 25. In an unprecedented and unexpected move, PM King dissolves Parliament and calls an election hours after the session opens.

Britain, February. Convoys bring the number of Canadian troops in Britain to 23,000. They are mostly untrained.

Toronto, April 13. New York Rangers beat the Toronto Maple Leafs four games to two for the Stanley Cup.

Quebec, April 25. Quebec is the last province to give women the vote in provincial elections.

Toronto, May 10. Militant anarchist and feminist Emma Goldman dies after a career in the U.S.S.R. and the U.S.

Europe, May 10. The Germans begin an offensive in Belgium and Holland.

France, June 4. 338,226 British, French, and Belgian troops complete the evacuation of Dunkirk, fleeing certain annihilation by the Germans.

Ottawa, June 5. An order-in-council outlaws 16 organizations, including the Communist party and the National Unity Party, under the Defence of Canada Regulations.

Italy, June 10. Italy declares war on Britain and France, which, with their allies (including Canada) reciprocate.

Canada, June 11. Princess Juliana of the Netherlands arrives to spend her exile in Canada after the German occupation of her country.

Ottawa, June 18. Parliament passes the National Resources Mobilization Act, providing for the conscription of able-bodied men for home defence.

Ottawa, Dec. 7. Ottawa Rough Riders beat Toronto Balmy Beach 12-5 for the Grey Cup.

Halifax, December. The first Canadian-built corvettes leave for Britain. Ottawa has ordered the building of 64 corvettes, and 24 minesweepers.

British Columbia. The Big Bend Highway, built by relief workers, is opened between Golden and Revelstoke, providing the shortest road route through the Rockies.

Canada. The All-Canadian Congress of Labour and the Canadian section of the Congress of Industrial Organizations merge to form the Canadian Congress of Labour.

Ottawa. The Canadian army rejects blacks for service.

Liberals back in power

March 26, 1940

OTTAWA – The Liberals under W.L. Mackenzie King have been swept back to power, easily gaining a majority in the federal election tonight. They trounced the National Government party (the renamed version of the Conservatives), even unseating its leader, Robert J. Manion.

King signs election-day autographs.

The victory allows Prime Minister King to point to the possibility of maintaining democracy even during war. Speaking on the radio tonight, King declared he was proud to "have shown to the British Empire and others that it has been possible to carry on an election without impairing the war effort of a united country."

That unity may well be a fiction, at least when it comes to relations between English and French-speaking Canadians. So far King has managed to keep Quebec onside by refusing to conscript Canadians to fight in Europe. But should events turn out as they did in the last war, with more men being required than are joining voluntarily, he may have to conscript after all, thus risking a national crisis.

Madly keen Bea entertains troops

Jan. 28, 1940

ALDERSHOT, England – As a Canadian-style blizzard described as the worst in living memory raged through the countryside, Canada's fighting men were entertained by Toronto-born comedienne Beatrice Lillie here tonight. In the warm theatre, the weather, war, and even Adolf Hitler were forgotten as Bea gave the troops a medley of old hits and a new number written especially for her by Noel Coward, entitled *I'm Madly Keen to Entertain the Troops.* Wild enthusiasm from the boys brought many encores.

Comedienne Beatrice Lillie.

6 Nations won't lease land for air school

March 14, 1940

OTTAWA – The federal government will begin expropriation against Six Nations Indians at Brantford, Ont., after they refused to lease land for a Commonwealth flying school. The government surveyed the 480 hectares proposed for the school without consulting the Indian owners. This angered the elected Six Nations Council, which last week voted to oppose government plans. The Indians "are fighting for the same rights for which Canada's soldiers went overseas," a spokesman said. The natives fear the school might be the first step to losing the lands permanently. A dozen farmers on the reserve would be displaced for the school.

Hepburn bans Canada at War screenings

Ontario Premier Mitchell Hepburn.

March 4, 1940

TORONTO – Saying it is "nothing but political propaganda of the most blatant kind," Ontario Premier Mitchell Hepburn has banned the March of Time film *Canada at War* from screening in Ontario cinemas.

Ontario's Liberal leader says the film will not be shown here "until after the election," in order not to influence voters. This verdict has amazed both the March of Time producers, who have an international reputation, and about 800 Ottawa residents who saw the film tonight at a preview. Most applauded its upbeat, yet dignified portrayal of the war effort.

Experts examining one-ton "monster"

Feb. 8, 1940

HALIFAX – The "monster" of Peggy's Cove is dead – but experts are still stumped as to its origins or identity. The one-ton creature was killed by fishermen using axes after it became jammed under a wharf in nearby Seabright. Now the carcass is stuck in the back of the truck that brought it to the Dominion Fisheries Experimental Station here. Insp. R.A. McKenzie says he thinks it is a whale, but he can't tell what species "without looking in its mouth." The mouth, of course, is wedged tightly in a corner of the truck, to the annoyance of the truck's owner.

PM visits Roosevelt for "a social call"

April 24, 1940

WARM SPRINGS, Ga. – Prime Minister W.L. Mackenzie King met President Frankin D. Roosevelt here today and yesterday. But there will be no official word on details of their talks. King said he is here on vacation and paid "just a social call" on the president. Roosevelt said the prime minister will not give a press conference because that act might be seen as a violation of American neutrality. It is thought King probably pressed the president to have the provisions of the Neutrality Act relaxed.

Canadian soldiers return to England

June 18, 1940

LONDON, England – Canadian troops are back in England today after a brief foray into France. Units of the 1st Division went to Brittany five days ago to help stem the German invasion. They withdrew when it became clear France's army had collapsed and her government was seeking an armistice from the enemy. The Canadians managed to bring almost all their equipment, artillery included, safely back to Britain. During their stay in France, one man was killed and one was taken prisoner.

Communist party illegal, judge rules

May 15, 1940

OTTAWA – A judge of the Ontario Supreme Court today declared the Communist party an illegal organization. After sentencing a party member to jail for distributing anti-war pamphlets, Justice E.R. Chevrier granted an Ontario government request that the party be declared illegal. The declaration was made under the wartime powers of the Defense of Canada Regulations and may set a precedent for other provinces.

Under the wartime regulations, Communists might be placed in enemy alien internment camps. Chevrier sentenced the party member to three years in jail and imposed a $2,000 fine. The Communist party has been legal since 1936 after being outlawed in 1931.

Police sort documents seized in a raid on a suspected Fifth Column office.

Rowell Commission submits its findings

May 3, 1940

OTTAWA – The Rowell Commission probing federal-provincial relations, chaired by N.W. Rowell and Joseph Sirois, today made its report to Prime Minister W.L. Mackenzie King. It's a landmark in Canadian federalism and perhaps the most exhaustive study of a working government ever done.

With the federal system under severe financial strain because of the depression, the government commissioned the report in 1937 to re-examine "the economic and financial basis of Confederation and the distribution of legislative powers in the light of the economic and social developments of the last 70 years." The report's recommendations include a stronger federal government with full control over taxation and responsibility for unemployment insurance and contributory pensions, and a system of grants to poorer provinces.

Britain depending on Commonwealth

June 24, 1940

LONDON, England – France signed an armistice today with Germany and Italy. With no European allies left, Britain faces the Axis supported only by a few governments in exile, representing subjugated nations such as Norway, plus her empire and the Commonwealth. But dominions such as Canada, Australia, and New Zealand stand firmer than any formal allies.

German prisoners of war transferred from Britain to Canada

German prisoners of war are seen here at the train station in Quebec.

Sept. 1, 1940

QUEBEC CITY – A large group of German prisoners of war arrived here today. They are the first PoWs to be transferred to Canada from Britain. It was feared that if left in Britain they might assist an invasion. There are thousands of them, but the exact number transferred remains secret.

After leaving the ship, the PoWs were put on trains for internment camps in various parts of Canada. British officers in charge said the voyage was tense. There are a number of merchant seamen among the PoWs capable of handling the ship if it had been taken over. One prisoner jumped through a porthole to his death on the voyage.

The Canadian beaver is ready to fight alongside the British lion.

Cabinet orders ban on religious group

July 4, 1940

OTTAWA – The Jehovah's Witnesses have been declared an illegal organization. A federal order was published today banning the religious group under wartime regulations. The government has been under pressure, mainly from the Catholic church in Quebec and other mainstream religious organizations, to curb Witness activity.

While taking a firm anti-Nazi stand, the Witnesses are devout pacifists whose religion prevents them from swearing allegiance to any nation. Their critics say their expressing their belief that a nation's law should not be recognized if it conflicts with God's law might undermine Canada's war effort.

U.S. swaps ships for military leases

Sept. 3, 1940

WASHINGTON, D.C. – The United States will trade 50 old destroyers to Britain in return for 99-year leases on eight military bases on British land. President Franklin D. Roosevelt told Congress today the deal is the biggest the U.S. has made since it bought Louisiana. The bases will protect the eastern and southern boundaries of the U.S., creating a defensive line from Newfoundland to British Guyana. The destroyers will help the British fleet cover the Atlantic.

Canadian comics feature the heroine Nelvana.

A Canadian comic male hero is Dixon of the Mounted.

Unemployment insurance legal now

July 11, 1940

OTTAWA – The British parliament has changed the BNA Act to allow the federal government to bring in a much-awaited system of unemployment insurance. The new benefits are not a "dole," or free handout, to the unemployed. Instead, they are aimed at being a stopgap for workers between jobs. As well, to be eligible, workers have to donate to the unemployment insurance fund while they're working, as do their employers.

The federal government, under former prime minister Richard B. Bennett, first tried to bring in a similar scheme in the '30s. But it was derailed by the British North America Act, which states that such relief is the responsibility of the provinces. Now, with these changes, Ottawa can finally create some security for workers.

Canada, the U.S. sign defence pact

Aug. 18, 1940

OGDENSBURG, N.Y. – Canada and the United States will be partners in the defence of North America. This was announced after a two-day meeting between President Franklin D. Roosevelt and Prime Minister W.L. Mackenzie King. Roosevelt brought only his secretary of war to the negotiations. The prime minister was assisted neither by cabinet colleagues nor professional civil servants.

The most tangible sign of today's announcement will be the formation of a Canada-U.S. Joint Defence Board, composed of senior officials from both countries. The board will deal with many issues, including the delivery of arms from American factories to Canadian forces, free exchanges of defence information, and drawing up joint plans should either Japan or Germany threaten this continent. This may include joint coastal defences, highway schemes, and airfields used by forces of both countries.

Montreal mayor arrested under war law

Aug. 5, 1940

MONTREAL – Mayor Camillien Houde has been interned as "a person prejudicial to the public safety." When Houde stepped out of Montreal city hall at 11 tonight, police arrested him on a warrant from the federal justice minister. The arrest was made under the wartime regulations. It follows Houde's statement three days ago that he opposed the law imposing registration for military service and suggested that others defy the law.

Earlier today, the executive committee of city council defeated Houde's efforts to refuse space in municipal buildings for the national registration. The popular mayor was whisked through darkened streets to an undisclosed internment camp north of Montreal. Then, police raided his offices.

Houde publicly opposes conscription.

Men marry in a hurry to avoid the draft

July 15, 1940

OTTAWA – Canadian men rushed to the pulpit over the weekend and jewellers ran out of wedding rings. Last week, the government announced that for the purposes of military service registration it would define "single men" as those single on July 15, 1940. In one three-hour period in Vancouver Saturday, 100 marriage licences were issued. In the province of Quebec, there were about 800 marriages on the weekend. Single men in Ontario and Saskatchewan were out of luck. Regulations in those two provinces specify a waiting period between issuing a marriage licence and the ceremony, making it impossible to meet the deadline.

Germans and Italians lose citizen status

Aug. 23, 1940

OTTAWA – Thousands of people of German and Italian origin who were Canadian citizens yesterday are not citizens today. The government has cancelled naturalization of people from those two enemy countries who took out their papers after Sept. 1, 1922. The deadline had been 1929. After the last world war, the heaviest immigration from Germany and Italy took place between 1922 and 1929. All those who became naturalized Canadian citizens in that period must now report to the police as enemy aliens. They may be issued a certificate of exemption if they can convince the registrar-general they have been loyal subjects.

ANZAC airmen train in Canadian schools

Oct. 25, 1940

VANCOUVER – The first Australian and New Zealand airmen arrived today. They received basic air training at home and will be trained to "wings" standards at Canadian schools prior to overseas postings. Canadians welcome the ANZAC airmen, and are specially charmed by New Zealand's Maoris. They will find a few surprises. Winter will be one, and muddy, unfinished schools will be another.

Ferry service moves bombers to Britain

Nov. 10, 1940

GANDER, Nfld. – This evening seven Hudson bombers manufactured by Lockheed Company of Burbank, Calif., will depart for Britain under the command of Capt. D.C.T. Bennett. This is the beginning of an operation which will involve the ferrying of military aircraft from North America to the United Kingdom. The new airbase here will play a major role in this effort to defend Britain.

Compulsory training experiment begins

Oct. 9, 1940

OTTAWA – The federal government's compulsory military service experiment goes into high gear today as nearly 30,000 single men, aged 21 to 24, report to 31 army centres across Canada for 30 days military training. The short course is dictated by a lack of modern weapons. The men, raised under the authority of the National Resources Mobilization Act, passed June 21, will be available for home defence duties should the need arise. Although conscripted for service in Canada only, authorities hope many of the men will volunteer to fight' overseas.

This young child does not want to be separated from his soldier father.

Evacuee kids doing well

These British evacuee children arrived safely in Montreal.

Sept. 13, 1940

WINNIPEG – Children evacuated from Britain to safety in Canada are doing well here. A report presented by the Manitoba provincial committee for evacuee children today showed the program running smoothly. There have been 167 children placed in Manitoba, 139 of them in Winnipeg. The only problem was the necessity to separate siblings in a few cases.

Medical authorities described the children's health as excellent when they arrived here. All of them had had their first inoculation for diphtheria. A dentist reported that the children's dental health was "much better" than the average for Manitoba children. The committee has had no trouble finding families willing to take the children.

On their arrival in Canada, evacuee children meet a Canadian Mountie.

"Battle of Britain" fought in the skies

Oct. 31, 1940

LONDON, England – Hitler isn't coming. That's the word now that it is clear the Germans will not invade Britain this year. The enemy was forced to change its mind because RAF Spitfire and Hurricane fighters inflicted heavy losses on the German air force, particularly in August and September. The "Battle of Britain," then, has been one fought through air power alone.

Some 100 Canadian fighter pilots saw action in this climactic period. Most enrolled in the RAF before the war, but 35 were RCAF pilots flying Hawker Hurricanes in No. 1 (Canadian) Squadron. The unit reached Britain in June, went into action Aug. 26, and destroyed some 30 enemy aircraft for the loss of three pilots killed and 10 wounded.

Three members were awarded the Distinguished Flying Cross – the RCAF's first gallantry decorations of the war. Top scoring Canadian of the battle was Pilot Officer W.L. McKnight (RAF), of Calgary, credited with seven kills while serving with No. 242 Squadron.

1941

Canada, Jan. 1. The CBC inaugurates its news service, ending its reliance on the Canadian Press news service.

Ottawa, Jan. 15. At a dominion-provincial conference, the provinces won't accept the recommendations of the Rowell-Sirois report.

Ottawa, Feb. 25. PM King orders the thumbprinting of all Japanese in Canada, and the distribution of registration cards without which Japanese won't be able to work.

Detroit, April 12. Boston Bruins beat the Detroit Red Wings four games to none for the Stanley Cup.

Hyde Park, New York, April 20. PM King and President Roosevelt agree to close collaboration in the production of war materials.

Ottawa, April. Finance Minister J.L. Isley announces the government is raising personal and corporation income taxes, taking over provincial claims in these fields in line with the recommendations of the Rowell-Sirois report, to raise money for the war effort.

Montreal, May 22. The first Canadian-built tank rolls off the assembly line.

U.S.S.R., June 22. Germany invades the Soviet Union.

Ottawa, July 2. The RCAF announces it will form a women's branch, the Canadian Women's Auxiliary Air Force.

London, July 13. Britain and the U.S.S.R. conclude a mutual assistance pact after Germany invades the U.S.S.R. Canada is now allied with the U.S.S.R.

Arvida, Que., July. Workers at the Aluminum Co. of Canada plant strike for almost a week, a serious wartime production disruption.

Toronto, Nov. 29. Winnipeg Blue Bombers beat the Ottawa Rough Riders 18-16 for the Grey Cup.

Washington, D.C., Dec. 11. Following its declaration of war on Japan on Dec. 8, the U.S. declares war on Japan's allies Germany and Italy.

Europe, December. Pilot Officer John Gillespie Magee Jr., an American serving with the RCAF, writes the poem *High Flight,* inspired by his flying.

Canada. West coast painter-writer Emily Carr wins a Governor General's Award for her first book, a collection of short stories called *Klee Wyck.*

Banting dies in plane crash off Nfld.

Feb. 23, 1941

MUSGRAVE HARBOR, Nfld. – It is now certain Sir Frederick Banting died in a plane crash near here two days ago. A search party brought the plane's injured pilot and the bodies of his three passengers to this community tonight.

The discoverer of insulin, Banting was flying to England with the results of his research into aviation medicine. It is known that a device has been perfected at the Banting Institute in Toronto to prevent pilots from blacking out, but details are a war secret. One of the plane's engines failed over the Atlantic 80 kilometres from Newfoundland Airport. The pilot flew back inland, the other engine failed, and the plane crashed on a frozen lake.

Site of the Newfoundland air crash which killed Sir Frederick Banting.

Policy switch lets 1,000 go to labor camps

May 29, 1941

OTTAWA – Some of those who object to military service on religious grounds will be sent to labor camps, the government announced today. In a reversal of policy, about 1,000 21-year-old men will no longer be required to attend military camps for non-combatant training. Instead, they will go to the labor camps for three or four months and earn 50 cents a day, less than half what they would earn at the military camps.

Those affected are Mennonites, Doukhobors, and conscientious objectors. The two religious communities are classed separately because when they immigrated to Canada they were guaranteed they would not have to perform military service. Conscientious objectors, who must prove their personal beliefs, are the smallest of the three groups.

Sorry Batman, but here's Johnny Canuck

Summer 1941

TORONTO – Thanks to action by the federal government, Johnny Canuck has replaced Batman as the comic book hero of Canadian kids. Last Dec. 6, Ottawa passed the War Exchange Conservation Act, banning the importation of certain non-essential items from non-sterling countries. The ban included comic books from the U.S. – and Toronto publisher Cy Bell was quick to spot the chance to fill the void with all-Canadian comic book heroes.

Bell and his brother Gene bought their own printing press, and hired their first artist, Edmund Legault. Some months later, illustrator Leo Bachle came up with Johnny Canuck. The sorely deprived Canadian youngsters made the infant comic book industry here an instant hit.

A real Canadian-made hero – Leo Bachle's Johnny Canuck.

Lombardo's pops are tops in U.S.

Feb. 5, 1941

NEW YORK – Guy Lombardo and his orchestra have done it again! For the 10th consecutive year, the band leader from London, Ont., and his Royal Canadians have been judged top of the pops by the New York *World Telegram*'s radio poll. It seems music lovers throughout the United States, despite ever-changing trends, still find Lombardo's "sweet" music just too good to resist. The Royal Canadians have been the Roosevelt Hotel's house band since 1929.

Training program upped to 4 months

Feb. 3, 1941

OTTAWA – Compulsory military training for fit men is being extended from one to four months to allow for more thorough instruction, including training with advanced equipment. Men so trained may be posted to home defence units or placed in reserve units while returning to civilian duties. The new scheme strengthens the home army, but experience shows about eight percent of those called out will be immediately released for health reasons.

Soldiers stage riot at amusement park

Sept. 31, 1941

TRURO, N.S. – About 500 soldiers rioted here tonight and virtually demolished an amusement park. Only the Ferris wheel was left standing. The riot occurred in retaliation for the shooting yesterday of a soldier in a dispute with the park's owner. A rumor circulated that the soldier had died. Military police finally succeeded in dispersing the mob, as thousands of townspeople watched. No one was seriously hurt. Meanwhile, police arrested the park owner for shooting the soldier, who remains in hospital but is not seriously wounded. A large contingent of military police is guarding the park.

Women free to join Canadian army

All services are recruiting women.

June 27, 1941

OTTAWA – Women are to be enrolled as members of the Canadian army. The decision has thus been to create a female branch for each of the fighting services, rather than a single, unified women's corps reinforcing the army, navy, and air force. Recruiting will begin in September and may be expected to exceed 21,000.

The women will not serve in combat, but will be trained for a host of roles, including drivers, mechanics, administrators, cipher clerks, and food service officers. By so doing, they will make hundreds of men available for battle.

Women have previously served in the Canadian forces, but only as Army Medical Corps nurses. Others assisted the First World War effort as civilian workers, including ambulance drivers. Britain set the pattern in 1938-39 by organizing women's auxiliary branches to her forces.

Since the outbreak of war, several voluntary but unofficial women's military groups have been formed in Canada. The new Canadian Women's Army Corps, distinct from all these, will draw many unofficial groups. Its members will be true service personnel in all respects but one – women will be paid two-thirds the rate of men in equivalent ranks. The RCAF and RCN are expected to form their own women's corps shortly.

British Columbians prepare for invasion

Coastal defence gun installation in British Columbia.

1941

BRITISH COLUMBIA – People across the province are preparing for a possible Japanese invasion, which some analysts fear is imminent. The growing threat across the Pacific has prompted numerous defence moves by Canadian and B.C. officials. Bunkers and gun stations are being set up in strategic hilltop positions along the coast, and it is rumored the government may commandeer civilian boats to help patrol the coastline. All defence efforts are carried out in co-operation with American authorities.

Government plan to protect jobless

July 1, 1941

OTTAWA – Canada's unemployed are now protected by a government insurance scheme. The new Unemployment Insurance Act comes into effect today, providing a portion of normal earnings to workers unemployed through no fault of their own. Money will be collected from employers and employees to go into a fund from which the benefits will be paid. To be eligible, workers must contribute to the fund for 180 days. The government expects the scheme to have a stabilizing effect on the economy.

Highlands National Park opens in N.S.

July 1, 1941

INGONISH, N.S. – Premier A.S. MacMillan cut a MacDonald plaid ribbon today to open Canada's newest national park. Highlands National Park straddles the northern tip of Cape Breton Island just west of this community. Mines and Resources Minister T.A. Crerar, who represented the federal government at the ceremony, declared this to be the finest park in Canada because of the beauty and variety of the landscape. After the ribbon-cutting, Crerar opened the luxurious golf course in the park.

A children's knitting club in Moose Jaw knits socks for soldiers overseas.

Dried apple sale to Britain largest ever

July 8, 1941

KENTVILLE, N.S. – Canada has made a tentative sale to Britain of more than 6 million kilograms of dried Annapolis Valley apples. It is the largest volume of dried apples ever sold. Previously, the largest sale to Britain was 31,500 kilograms. Producers, hit hard by the war economy, say they'll now be able to pay their way this year. The value of the sale was not disclosed.

Documentary lands NFB its first Oscar

June 1941

HOLLYWOOD – A short documentary film, part of the *Canada Carries On* series which catalogues the Allies' war effort, has become the first Canadian film to win an Academy Award. The winning film, a documentary of the Battle of Britain called *Churchill's Island*, is the work of the National Film Board of Canada's Stuart Legg.

Under the leadership of John Grierson, the two-year-old NFB has grown tremendously, feverishly churning out documentaries which often play before enthralled audiences all over the allied world.

Many fathers serve the war effort by working in military industries.

This poster appeals for support for the Victory Bond sales campaign.

Britain, U.S. target "Nazi tyranny"

Aug. 14, 1941

THE ATLANTIC – After an historic conference at sea, the leaders of Britain and the United States have agreed to work together for the "final destruction of Nazi tyranny." Prime Minister Winston Churchill and President Franklin D. Roosevelt have been meeting aboard two warships. The location of the conference [in a Newfoundland harbor] remains a military secret. In the pact the two leaders signed, Roosevelt also commits himself to working for post-war reconstruction in Europe. The two leaders also pledged themselves to "a permanent system of general security with disarmament."

Details of the talks are skimpy. But speculation surrounds the main point not covered in the pact: the growing Japanese threat. Officials say the two leaders probably discussed mutual use of British and American bases in the South Pacific and the possibility of Soviet leader Joseph Stalin opening a front in Siberia if Pacific war breaks out.

Preparations for the talks were a closely guarded secret. Roosevelt sailed Aug. 3 on the presidential yacht, ostensibly for some fishing.

Wage and price controls imposed to take on wartime inflation

Oct. 18, 1941

OTTAWA – The federal government today set limits on wages and prices to combat wartime inflation. The plan is imposed under authority of the War Measures Act. Prime Minister W.L. Mackenzie King said it "represents an experiment hitherto untried on this continent, and perhaps having regard to its breadth and variety, hitherto untried by the will and consent of any free people anywhere."

Increases in basic wages are banned, except for cost-of-living bonuses calculated by a government formula. Salaries of executives are not covered by the regulations. Prices and rents are fixed at the highest level they reached during the past month.

Toronto women march in a parade urging war savings. Public support for all wartime financial programs is urgently needed.

Inuit pair found guilty of manslaughter

Aug. 21, 1941

BELCHER ISLANDS, N.W.T. – A jury returned verdicts today in the strange murder trial of four Inuit here, in southeastern Hudson Bay. A white jury acquitted two accused and found two others guilty only of manslaughter in the deaths of nine Inuit last spring. The nine apparently died after a religious argument.

Found not guilty were Alec Apawkok and a woman named Akeevik who was acquitted because of temporary insanity. Apawkok's sister Sarah was one of those killed. Peter Sala and Ablaykok were both found guilty of manslaughter, while three other people who are accused of the same murders have not yet come to trial.

Evidence at the trial, before Justice C.P. Plaxton, showed that an argument arose from a contention by some natives that Christ had returned to Earth. Sala testified he believed himself God in thought but not body. Charlie Oyerack, another of the accused, testified he believed himself Jesus Christ. The claims of these two people to divine power are believed to have touched off the violence.

When Sarah Apawkok, 15 years old, said she did not believe that Sala was God, she was beaten to death. Witnesses testified that when Sarah was killed the natives believed Satan had been killed. After her death, religious books were burned as no longer necessary.

The jury consisted of a newspaperman, a mining party, and a schooner crew. It took Justice Plaxton 13 days to get here from Moose Factory.

At least 21 dead in mine explosion

Oct. 31, 1941

NORDEGG, Alta. – Twenty-one miners are known to be dead and six others are missing after an explosion today in Brazeau Collieries. The theatre in this mining town has been turned into a temporary morgue. Among the first bodies recovered was that of pit boss John Armstrong.

Company officials said the scene of the blast was the fourth left level of the mine. It is located 1.2 kilometres from the entrance. At press time, officials of the provincial mines branch and the provincial coroner were en route to the scene.

Brazeau Collieries is one of the largest mines in the province. It employs 400 workers and is open 24 hours a day.

Japanese triumph in Hong Kong attack

Canadian troops sailed for Hong Kong in October on HMCS Prince Robert.

Dec. 25, 1941

HONG KONG – Japanese forces, operating with air superiority, overwhelmed the last resistance at this garrison today. Their attack began Dec. 8. After capturing defences on the mainland, they landed on Hong Kong island proper on Dec. 19. Allied losses are estimated at more than 1,700 dead and 10,000 captured. The troops represented British, Canadian, and Indian army formations, plus Singapore and Hong Kong volunteers.

The defeat is particularly tragic to Canadians. A month before the attack, two Canadian regiments, the Royal Rifles of Canada and the Winnipeg Grenadiers, 1,975 men in all, were sent to strengthen the garrison. By mishap and mistake, none of their vehicles went with them. About 10 percent were only partially trained when dispatched. Both units were heavily engaged. Many brave acts are attributed to their members. Some 290 were killed, including their commander, Brig. J.K. Lawson. The rest are consigned to harsh captivity which may bring more deaths.

Given that Canada had no direct interests in Hong Kong and that the outpost was obviously vulnerable and received no outside aid throughout the battle, questions must be raised as to why Canadian troops were sent there in the first place. Was there a reason, or was it an inexcusable blunder?

Canada, Japan at war

Dec. 7, 1941

OTTAWA – Tonight, Canada is at war with Japan after a series of surprise Japanese attacks on Pacific installations. Prime Minister W.L. Mackenzie King, in a terse announcement after a long cabinet meeting, said that it was necessary to widen the theatre of war. Britain and the United States are also expected to declare war, probably tomorrow.

Today, the Japanese launched major attacks on Hong Kong, Hawaii, Singapore, Malaya, Thailand, the Phillipines, and a number of South Pacific islands. The first attack was on the American Pearl Harbor naval base in Hawaii, where the Japanese are believed to have dealt a crippling blow to the American fleet. It is probable that five big battleships were sunk and more than 2,000 people killed.

The Japanese have established beachheads in northern Malaya, and British troops are engaged in fierce fighting there. This is also the case at Singapore. At Hong Kong, an air raid was beaten back, but Japanese ground troops have taken some control. A contingent of Canadian troops is stationed at Hong Kong.

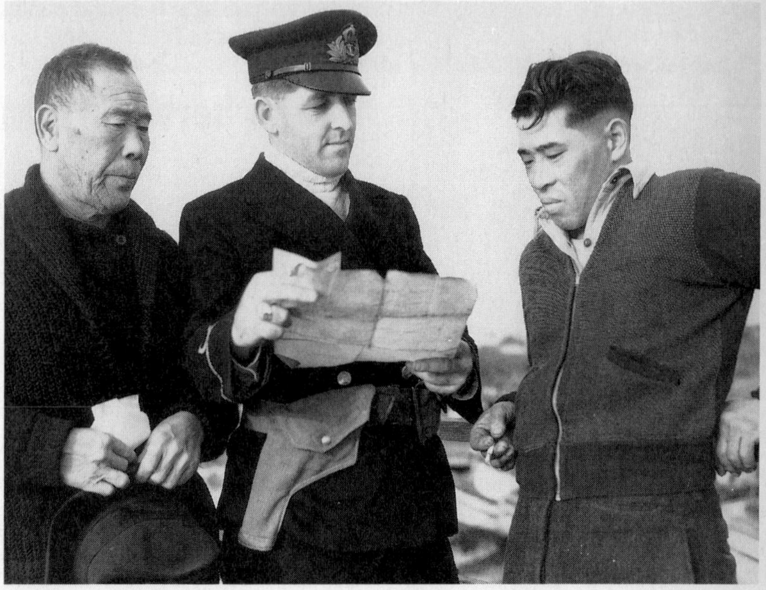

A Japanese Canadian fisherman is questioned by an RCN officer in B.C.

"Some chicken, some neck": Churchill electrifies Parliament

British PM Winston Churchill.

Dec. 30, 1941

OTTAWA – British Prime Minister Winston Churchill electrified Canada's Parliament today with a truly inspirational speech. Churchill addressed a joint session of the House of Commons and the Senate. The public galleries were filled. In the aisles were judges and representatives of foreign delegations. "We have suffered together, and we shall conquer together," Churchill declared. There can be no thought "except the total and final extirpation of the Hitler tyranny, the Japanese frenzy and the Mussolini flop."

Having just come from his meetings with Franklin D. Roosevelt, Churchill described the American president as a "great man whom destiny had marked for this climax of human fortunes." The French had given up, Churchill said, and some of their leaders "thought and said that England would in three weeks have her neck wrung like a chicken." Then, in that growl he has made famous, Churchill added: "Some chicken, some neck!"

In introducing Churchill, Prime Minister W.L. Mackenzie King said Canadians regard him as "the personification of Britain's greatness." It is impossible to exaggerate the impression the British prime minister made on his audience today. He got a tremendous ovation.

SAVE
TO BEAT
THE DEVIL!
Buy
VICTORY
BONDS

The devil's face bears an uncanny resemblance to Adolf Hitler on a Victory Bond poster. Big sales of Victory Bonds are crucial to pay for Canada's war involvement.

1942

Ottawa, Feb. 2. Defence of Canada Regulations define B.C. west of the Cascade Mountains as a "protected area." Japanese in the area will be relocated.

Ottawa, March 11. The government sets up Polymer Corp. to make synthetic rubber.

Canada, March 24. Canadian Pacific Airlines Ltd. is formed.

Toronto, April 18. Toronto Maple Leafs defeat the Detroit Red Wings four games to three to win the Stanley Cup before a crowd of 16,200 at Maple Leaf Gardens, a Canadian hockey attendance record.

St. Lawrence River, May 11. A German U-boat torpedoes two freighters, the first enemy action in inland Canadian waters. Fourteen crewmen are dead or missing.

Europe, June 29. It is believed the Germans have killed more than 1 million Jews.

Kingston, Ont., June. The CIL's Kingston Works opens, the first Canadian nylon plant and the second nylon plant in the world.

Ottawa, Oct. 6. The government announces the "conditional release" of Tim Buck, secretary of the Canadian Communist party who was arrested in September after eluding authorities for two and a half years.

Ottawa, Oct. 9. The External Affairs Department says German PoWs will be put in chains unless Germany rescinds its order for the fettering of Canadian prisoners.

Ottawa, November. The Vichy French legation leaves Ottawa, marking an end to Canadian relations with Vichy France.

Toronto, Dec. 5. Toronto RCAF Hurricanes beat the Winnipeg RCAF Bombers 8-5 for the Grey Cup.

Edmonton. The Social Credit government passes the Land Sales Prohibition Act, prohibiting sale of land to all enemy aliens and Hutterites until the end of the war, regardless of whether the Hutterites are British subjects.

British Columbia. Japanese-operated fishing boats seized at the outbreak of the war are used for coastal defence.

Ontario. Earle Birney wins a Governor General's Award for his first book of poetry, *David*, published shortly after he enlisted in the army.

Japanese to be moved off west coast

Feb. 26, 1942

OTTAWA – All Japanese will be moved from the west coast, the government announced today, to quell fears of Canadian Japanese assisting an invasion. Previously, the government ordered all Japanese men between 18 and 45 moved more than 160 kilometres inland and their fishing fleet impounded. Today, the government expanded that action to include all people of Japanese origin.

Some government members opposed the mass evacuation. It's also believed the army and the RCMP see no reason to impose it. But the government has been under tremendous pressure from the public and politicians in B.C.

An RCMP constable checks the papers of Japanese Canadian evacuees in B.C.

Queen becomes a movie star for a day

Feb. 3, 1942

LONDON, England – The queen was a movie star for a day today, playing a leading role in a film being made for the Canadian Red Cross Society. She was visiting the society's headquarters here to help stir up interest in a $20-million fund drive that opens in Canada next month. The motion picture of Red Cross activities will be shown in Canada in connection with the campaign. From the very moment Her Majesty was escorted into the building until she left after inspecting relief articles and other supplies, her every move was captured on film. The queen also posed for special shots with overseas commissioner Lt.-Col. C.A. Scott.

Queen Elizabeth.

Founder and leader of the CCF is dead

March 21, 1942

VANCOUVER – Canada lost one of its most respected activists today. James S. Woodsworth died in hospital here at age 67. Founder and leader of the CCF, Woodsworth was the MP for Winnipeg North Centre since 1921. He became known as the "conscience of Canada" for his articulately stated, principled views. Recently, he was best-known as the only MP to vote against entering the present war. While few agreed with him, everyone admired his courage in sticking to his pacifist convictions. The former Methodist minister became CCF leader in 1933.

Parliament to decide on $1-billion gift

Jan. 26, 1942

OTTAWA – The government wants Canada to give Britain $1 billion worth of munitions and food. Prime Minister W.L. Mackenzie King was cheered loudly in the Commons this afternoon when he announced the government will ask Parliament to make the gift. "The adoption of the new plan will mean that Canada, at this time of intensified crisis, is giving unmistakable evidence of the determination of our people to put forth their utmost effort in the preservation of our own liberties and in the common cause of freedom," King said.

The advantage of an outright gift rather than a loan is that "it will avoid the growth to huge and unmanageable proportions of a war debt which might breed serious misunderstandings and bitterness in the future," he said. It will also relieve Britain of any anxiety about its ability to pay to maintain a Canadian source of supply. The gift is expected to meet Britain's requirements for Canadian war supplies until early 1943.

Businessmen told sacrifices a must

March 9, 1942

TORONTO – Canadians' "entire sense of economic values must undergo complete change for the duration of the war" and "civilian standards must inevitably decrease," Richard Berkinshaw, the chairman of the Wartime Industries Control Board, told a group of businessmen tonight. The activities of businessmen have been sharply curtailed by the wartime controls that Berkinshaw runs.

Japanese Canadians removed from the west coast

Japanese Canadian families are relocated to camps in the B.C. interior.

Open trucks are used to move the families and their possessions inland.

Mass evacuation of 21,000 people ends

Oct. 31, 1942

VANCOUVER – The forced removal of Japanese from the west coast is completed. In all, 21,000 people were sent to work camps or to detention camps. A number also have been interned. The mass evacuation began early this year as a result of fears Japanese Canadians might assist an invasion and because of stong anti-Japanese feeling in B.C. Most of the 21,000 people are Canadian-born.

There was little trouble with the evacuation, many of the Japanese Canadians saying they would demonstrate their patriotism by acquiescing to the government's sometimes harsh demands. Some who protested were interned. There are more than 700 Japanese Canadians now in internment camps, including those arrested after the attack on Pearl Harbor in December.

The strongest protests resulted from the separation of families. Many men were sent to road work crews in B.C. and Alberta, while their wives and children were sent to the camps at the ghost towns in the Slocan and Kootenay valleys of interior B.C. Much of the property of those evacuated remains in the government's custody.

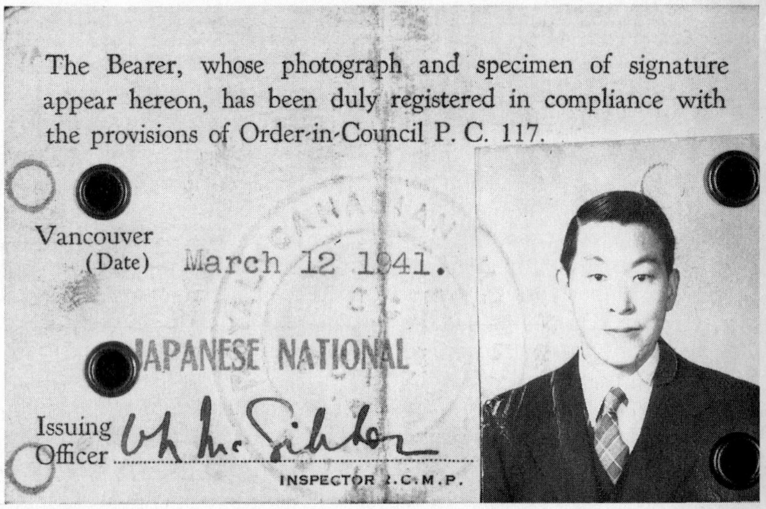

The Bearer, whose photograph and specimen of signature appear hereon, has been duly registered in compliance with the provisions of Order-in-Council P. C. 117.

Vancouver
(Date) March 12 1941.

JAPANESE NATIONAL

Issuing Officer
INSPECTOR R.C.M.P.

Special internment identification cards are issued by the federal government.

The arrival at an internment camp.

Laundry facilities must be shared.

Awaiting transportation to the interior to join their men, women and children are housed in a former cattle barn at the Pacific National Exhibition.

Canadians grouped in a new formation

April 6, 1942

LONDON, England – Canadian forces in Britain have been grouped into a new formation, the 1st Canadian Army, commanded by Lt.-Gen. A.G.L. McNaughton. In military terms, an "army" has a balance of many service arms and units which can take the field as a single fighting force. With three infantry divisions, one armored division, an armored brigade, plus supporting engineers, artillery and medical services, 1st Canadian Army fits the bill. Canadians have trained in Britain for more than two years but have seen no action. Some envy ANZAC counterparts who've fought in North Africa and Greece.

Vote gives conscription the go-ahead

W.L.M. King casts vote in plebiscite.

April 27, 1942

OTTAWA – Canadians tonight overwhelmingly gave the government the green light to impose conscription for overseas service. There was a large turnout in today's national plebiscite. With almost all the polls reporting, results show about 63 percent of voters favor allowing the government to impose conscription if necessary.

As expected, Quebec's voters strongly rejected conscription, by more than 70 percent. But in Montreal the vote was running almost even. Ontario chalked up the most impressive "yes" vote, by a margin of more than 5-to-1. That result surprised even "yes" campaigners. Toronto voted 12-to-1 in favor. Voters in rural areas were generally less strongly in favor than were city dwellers.

The specific question asked in the plebiscite was whether Canadians would release the government from Prime Minister W.L. Mackenzie King's election pledge not to impose conscription. In the plebiscite campaign, Tory leader R.B. Hanson and CCF leader M.J. Coldwell joined the prime minister in urging a "yes" vote. The turnout was heavy in most parts of the country and may set records. But voter turnout in the Maritimes was lower than that in general elections. This is only the second plebiscite in Canada's history. The first was in 1898 on the prohibition question.

King after a "yes" in conscription vote

April 7, 1942

OTTAWA – The prime minister tonight pleaded with Canadians to let him impose conscription if it becomes necessary. In urging a "yes" vote in the April 27 plebiscite, W.L. Mackenzie King said the final battles of the war might be fought in North America unless the Allies win decisively overseas. King made the speech on the CBC, and a staff member read it on the station's French service. In the coming weeks, the CBC will broadcast other pro-conscription speeches.

National selective service aids war effort

March 24, 1942

OTTAWA – The government today announced a sweeping national selective service program to more efficiently mobilize Canada's labor power for the war effort. The program increases to 30 from 26 the age limit for compulsory service in Canada and establishes a lottery system as the method of call-up. The plan also restricts civilian employment. Men are prohibited from work in a long list of non-war occupations except under certain conditions. To ease the agricultural labor shortage, farm workers are now prohibited from leaving farm work except for active military service. Farmers, farmers' sons, and agricultural workers are generally exempt from military training. Employers will be required to release technicians for essential war service and reinstate them afterward.

Reaction to the government plan is generally favorable. Canadian farmers feel their concerns have been addressed. While they are cautious, business leaders do not criticize the plan. But labor leaders complain that the war effort cannot be considered total unless wealth and resources are harnessed in the same way as labor.

Japanese sub fires at wireless station

June 21, 1942

VICTORIA, B.C. – Canada is under fire. Last night, about 10:15, a Japanese submarine off the Estevan Point lighthouse and wireless station, halfway up the west coast of Vancouver Island, lobbed about 20 shells, two of them duds, at the post. There were no casualties, but explosions broke glass and spattered the lighthouse with shell fragments. Aircraft from Victoria tried to pursue the raider, but the first bomber crashed, blocking the runway and preventing other takeoffs.

Writer Lucy Maud Montgomery dies

Feb. 24, 1942

PRINCE EDWARD ISLAND – The creator of *Anne of Green Gables*, Lucy Maud Montgomery, has died in her 68th year. She won a rapturous worldwide audience with her eight books about the spirited Prince Edward Island girl, and also gained critical acclaim for her other works, including several collections of short stories. In 1911, she married the Rev. Ewan Macdonald, and continued writing in Leaksdale and Norval, Ont. They retired to Toronto in 1936, a year after she was awarded the OBE.

This RCAF recruiting poster appeals to a mother's pride.

The aviator is a valued member of the military team which represents Canada in the war effort.

Escaped PoW's fling with freedom ends

June 15, 1942

MONTREAL – At least one American border guard knows a German officer when he sees one. At a border crossing near here today, a German Luftwaffe lieutenant tried to walk into the United States in full uniform. The man had escaped from a prisoner-of-war camp near Sherbrooke, Que., a few days ago. What is most remarkable is that the Luftwaffe man had spent part of a day wandering Montreal's streets in his uniform. No one noticed his uniform was significantly different from Canadian ones.

Developer of Ross rifle is dead at 70

June 18, 1942

ST. PETERSBURG, Fla. – Sir Charles Ross is dead. The major figure in one of Canada's biggest controversies of the First World War died here today at the age of 70. Ross developed the Ross rifle, adopted by the Canadian overseas forces in 1914 and produced at the Ross Quebec plant. The Ross jammed when overheated. Canadian troops called it the "Ross gaspipe" and dumped it on the battlefields if they could get their hands on British Lee-Enfields.

War board clarifies tea, coffee rations

Rationing supports the war effort.

Aug. 3, 1942

OTTAWA – Restaurant customers may have a cup of tea or coffee, but not both. The Wartime Prices and Trade Board today put a stop to the practice of ordering both beverages. A customer may now be served only one cup of one of the beverages at a sitting. Previously, some restaurants interpreted the regulations to permit serving one cup of each beverage. The board also ordered restaurants not to use more than one teabag per cup. Under the coupon rationing of tea and coffee, which also went into effect today, each person over 12 is entitled to one ounce of tea a week or four ounces of coffee.

Dieppe raid a disaster for Canadians

Aug. 19, 1942

LONDON, England – Allied forces today raided the port and resort town of Dieppe. The fierce eight-hour action included the largest air battle over Western Europe in nearly two years.

British commandos hit targets north and south of Dieppe, but Canadian troops made up most of the force – 4,963, of whom 3,900 actually landed on the beaches. They sustained appalling losses – 993 killed and 1,874 taken prisoner. Most of those who returned to England simply had the good fortune not to be disembarked once the state of things ashore became clear. Even so, 586 of those returning were wounded. Among these was Lt.-Col. Dollard Ménard, Fusiliers de Mont-Royal, the only regimental commander to go ashore and return to England. Landing began about 5 a.m. in the face of determined, well-entrenched defenders. By 9 a.m. our men had been fought to a standstill. The decision was made to evacuate any survivors who were not already trapped. This task was completed about 1 p.m., and the convoy sailed for England.

Although intended to test landing techniques and tactics, the Dieppe losses suggest this raid will be a model of how not to do things. The officer nominally directing the battle, Maj.-Gen. J.H. Roberts, was confined to a warship, taking reports and issuing orders without a direct view of what was happening. Troops stormed ashore after minimal bombardment of enemy positions and suffered heavy losses at the water's edge. Many tanks intended to provide fire support sank while being launched from special craft. Others had trouble negotiating the stony beaches. Reserve forces were landed in the belief that leading waves had penetrated the town. Such was not the case, and the reserves suffered as heavily as troops committed at the outset.

And in the air battle, the Allies sustained record losses. Most of Fighter Command was thrown into the operation. Nine RCAF squadrons were among those engaged. In vicious dogfights, fighters kept the German Air Force from interfering in the land battle and subsequent withdrawal by sea. Only one ship was bombed and another strafed.

Hundreds of Canadian soldiers were taken prisoner during the disastrous raid on Dieppe. Here the prisoners are led through the streets of the town.

Troops of the Cameron Highlanders board the landing craft off Dieppe.

German sub sunk in Atlantic gun battle

Aug. 6, 1942

HALIFAX – A Canadian destroyer, *HMCS Assiniboine,* today sank an enemy submarine, U-210, 645 kilometres off Newfoundland. Surface actions are quite rare with U-boats – normally they dive at the approach of warships. Today's fight began when fog lifted and *Assiniboine* found U-210 9.6 kilometres distant.

The destroyer chased for an hour, closing the distance. Even when the Germans spotted *Assiniboine,* they chose to fight a skilful surface action, running toward the destroyer until the Canadian ship could not bring her main armament to bear. The two vessels wove and dodged at close quarters for 35 minutes, trading shots with rifles, machine-guns, and medium-calibre guns. Remarked one RCN sailor: "We threw everything but the potato masher at him." The sub started fires aboard *Assiniboine,* but these were brought under control. Finally, the destroyer's guns swept the enemy bridge clear. U-210 tried to dive, but *Assiniboine* rammed twice, dropped a few depth charges, and finished her off with gunfire.

Cabinet order can impose conscription

July 23, 1942

OTTAWA – MPs today approved a measure allowing the government to impose conscription by cabinet order, rather than having to call Parliament into session. CCF members opposed the motion on the grounds that there is no provision for conscripting wealth for the war effort. Quebec Liberals also opposed, but it passed 141-45. Prime Minister W.L. Mackenzie King said he'll seek a vote of confidence if conscription is imposed. ▷

Canadian destroyer sunk; 114 are dead

Sept. 14, 1942

HALIFAX – *HMCS Ottawa,* one of the six destroyers the RCN possessed at the beginning of the war, was lost last night in a north Atlantic convoy action. She was torpedoed near midnight. At first she remained on an even keel and appeared to be seaworthy. A rescue ship closed on her but turned away to assist a sinking merchant ship. Moments later, a second torpedo struck *Ottawa.* She sank quickly. Survivors, struggling in icy waters, were hard to spot in the dark; 114 perished, including the captain, Lt.-Cmdr. C.A. Rutherford.

Lethbridge the site of new PoW centre

Nov. 15, 1942

LETHBRIDGE, Alta. – Camp No. 133, a new prisoner of war centre, is filling up as PoWs are transferred from older sites. As with other camps, guards will be members of the Veterans Guard of Canada, many of whom served in the last war. Canada has received growing numbers of PoWs since June 1940. There have been many escape attempts, including a mass breakout from Fort Henry, Kingston, but only one prisoner has made it back to Germany – Franz von Werra in 1941.

St. Roch ends Arctic trip

The Royal Canadian Mounted Police schooner St. Roch at Herschel Island.

Oct. 8, 1942

SYDNEY, N.S. – The RCMP patrol vessel *St. Roch* arrived here today after completing the first west-to-east crossing of the Northwest Passage. The 80-ton schooner, with a crew of eight, took more than two years to make the arduous trip through the icebound waters of the Canadian Arctic. It is only the second successful navigation of the passage. The Norwegian explorer Roald Amundsen did it first, east-to-west, in his vessel, the *Gjoa,* in 1903-06.

The commander of the *St. Roch* is Sgt. Henry Larsen. A native of Norway, Larsen has been with the vessel since it was launched in 1928 and has been called "the best Arctic skipper alive." It is wartime and the details of the historic voyage are shrouded in secrecy. It is known, however, that the expedition passed its first Arctic winter on the coast of Victoria Island, and the second iced-in on Boothia Peninsula. For 28 months the crew's only contact with the outside world was the ship's two-way radio.

Enemy fire downs the Eagle of Malta

Oct. 14, 1942

MALTA – Pilot Officer George F. Beurling, known as the Eagle of Malta, has been shot down and wounded. At 21, the native of Verdun, Que., is Canada's most deadly fighter pilot and the top-scoring ace in the 28-month aerial siege of Malta.

Curiously enough, Beurling is not a member of the RCAF. He was turned down when educational standards were tougher. He joined Britain's RAF, and has gone on to destroy 27 German and Italian aircraft. His success is due to his keen eyesight and instinctive aim in high-speed combat.

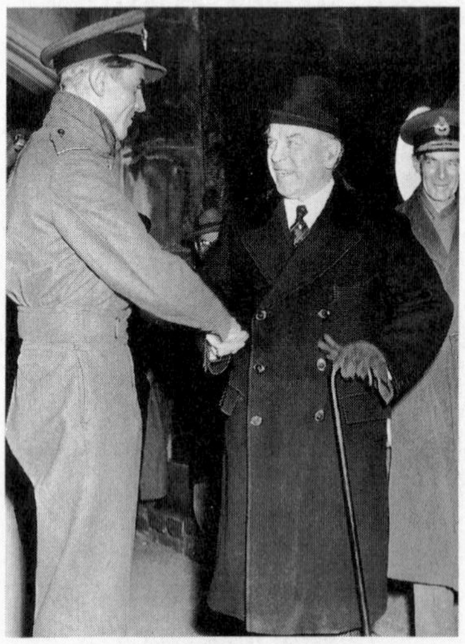

Ace pilot George F. Beurling meets Prime Minister W.L.M. King.

Compulsory call-up age lowered to 19

Sept. 30, 1942

OTTAWA – About 135,000 men were added today to the list of those liable for compulsory military service in Canada. The government lowered the age limit for compulsory call-up from 21 years to 19. As well, alien residents of non-enemy countries are now subject to call-up. Those called up under the compulsory program cannot be required to serve outside Canada. But more than 35 percent of those accepted by the army via this route volunteer for unrestricted service. Men married before July 15, 1940, are not subject to call-up.

German naval officer arrested for spying

Posters warn of the dangers of spies.

Nov. 9, 1942

NEW CARLISLE, Que. – A German naval officer was arrested here today and charged with spying. Werner Janowski, 27, was dropped off Nov. 6 by a German U-boat on the south shore of the Gaspé. He was to establish himself and inform the Germans about ship movements. Janowski checked into the hotel at this little town. Paying for his breakfast with obsolete Canadian bills was only one thing that made the hotel proprietor suspicious. As part of his cover story, Janowski said he came to this town from Chandler on a bus that stopped running weeks ago. The hotel owner alerted police.

German submarine sinks ferry off Nfld.

Oct. 15, 1942

PORT AUX BASQUES, Nfld. – Tragedy struck last night when a German U-boat torpedoed the 2,200-ton *SS Caribou* in Cabot Strait. The ship was en route here from Sydney with civilian and military passengers. A 15-year veteran of the ferry run, the *Caribou* was escorted by a single RCN vessel, which rescued 101 survivors. The *Caribou* sank quickly in the darkness. A total of 137 died, including 31 of her Newfoundland crew of 46. Among many family tragedies were the deaths of J. Tapper (Burin), his wife, and three children.

Canada-Alaska road officially opens

Nov. 20, 1942

KLUANE LAKE, Yukon – A red, white and blue ribbon marked a marvel of engineering and co-operation today. When that ribbon was cut, the Alcan Military Highway was officially open. The highway, begun only eight months ago, runs some 2,575 kilometres from Dawson Creek, B.C., through to Fairbanks, Alaska.

It was built as a military road to forestall Japanese invasion – to get troops and supplies quickly to Alaska if they are needed there. Groups of American army engineers, from various starting points, built up to 13 kilometres of road a day through the wilderness to get this project completed ahead of schedule. It is now mainly a bush road, but it will be gravel-surfaced and widened so that it can be used in all seasons.

The main addresses at the opening were delivered by Ian Mackenzie, Canadian minister of pensions and national health, and E.L. Bartlett, secretary of state for Alaska. Bartlett expects the road not only to be of military use, but to contribute significantly to the north's economic development after the war. In a message sent with Mackenzie, Prime Minister W.L. Mackenzie King said that in granting the United States permission to build a road across Canadian territory, the government demonstrated that "we are brothers-in-arms, waging a life-and-death struggle against a common enemy." American Vice-President H.A. Wallace sent a message in which he predicted the Canada-Alaska road would become part of a great highway running from southern South America to Siberia. He thinks it will soon be possible to drive from Buenos Aires to Moscow.

When the opening ceremonies finished, a convoy of trucks made its way from here to Fairbanks, the first vehicles to do so. They were led by an old weapons carrier that had been the first vehicle to travel from Dawson Creek to Whitehorse, Yukon Territory. It is expected that the ungraded, all-weather version of this highway to Alaska will be finished a year from now.

Officials from Canada and the United States sign the Alaska highway deal.

American soldier guards the bank.

This poster graphically illustrates the reasons for financially supporting the Canadian war effort.

Bracken leads Progressive Conservatives

Dec. 11, 1942

WINNIPEG – John Bracken is now the national leader of the newly named Progressive Conservative party. Bracken, for 20 years the premier of Manitoba, was elected on the second ballot. While most observers anticipated that Bracken would win the contest, many were surprised that M.A. MacPherson, a Regina lawyer, would poll 255 votes on the second ballot. In third place was Prince Albert lawyer John G. Diefenbaker.

Rare Tahltan bear-dog rapidly dying out

1942

BRITISH COLUMBIA – The Tahltan bear-dog, a fox-like canine known for its ferocity, is rapidly dying out as its Tahltan Indian masters rely less on hunting. The little carnivore, which stands 12 to 16 inches at the shoulder, was used to surround and distract the quarry as the hunter moved in for the kill. Efforts to domesticate it have failed. Almost all of the dogs removed from their northern habitat quickly succumb to heat prostration.

Butter on the list of rationed items

Dec. 21, 1942

OTTAWA – Butter is now a rationed item, and it may cause headaches for the Wartime Prices and Trade Board. As rationing went into effect today, it was expected that controlling supplies of butter will be a much more difficult task than controlling tea, coffee, sugar, and gasoline.

Butter is an easily-made domestic product. It is feared that unscrupulous entrepreneurs may take advantage of the ration system. The board realizes that with butter it will have to rely substantially on the honesty of Canadians. As well, the other items are rationed to reduce consumption. But butter is rationed to ensure equitable distribution of a short supply.

Canadians are urged to cut down on their consumption of butter.

Ration books are issued by the Wartime Prices and Trade Board.

1943

Canada, Jan. 26. Striking steel workers at Sault Ste. Marie, Ont., and Trenton, N.S., vote to return to work for 30 days, pending settlement of their dispute. Their two-week strike has cut Canada's steel output by two-thirds.

Edmonton, March. The Alberta government amends the Land Sales Prohibition Act to forbid the leasing of land to enemy aliens or Hutterites.

Boston, April 8. Detroit Red Wings beat Boston Bruins four games to none to win the Stanley Cup.

Edmonton, May 31. Ernest Manning succeeds the recently deceased William Aberhart as Social Credit premier.

Montreal, Aug. 9. Fred Rose is elected MP in a byelection, running for the Labor Progressive (Communist) Party.

Aleutian Islands, Aug. 15. Canadian and U.S. soldiers, working together for the first time in a western hemisphere operation, occupy Kiska Island, an American island held by Japan, without firing a shot.

Montreal, Aug. 16. A two-week strike against Fairchild Aircraft ends with 200,000 person days lost. Workers get full indexation of wages.

Quebec, Aug. 24. British PM Churchill, U.S. President Roosevelt, and Canadian PM King end a war strategy conference with an upbeat "forward now to victory" communiqué.

Ottawa, Sept. 20. The government orders that employees in war-related industries cannot leave their jobs or be dismissed without permission from a Selective Service officer.

France, Sept. 25. Canadian ace Flying Officer George "Buzz" Beurling shoots down his 30th German plane over France.

Ottawa, Oct. 17. PM King announces the creation of the first uniquely Canadian merit decoration, the Canada Medal.

Quebec, Oct. 20. The Roman Catholic church says its members are free to support any party upholding "basic Christian traditions," indicating it views the CCF as legitimate.

Toronto, Nov. 27. Hamilton Flying Wildcats beat the Winnipeg RCAF Bombers 23-14 to win the Grey Cup.

Canada. Bruce Hutchison wins a Governor General's Award for *The Unknown Country: Canada and her People*.

It's a girl: Dutch princess gives birth

The new princess, Margriet, is christened in Ottawa (later photo).

Jan. 19, 1943

OTTAWA – Princess Juliana of the Netherlands gave birth tonight in Ottawa Civic Hospital to her third daughter. Queen Wilhelmina in London was immediately notified by telephone, and then a statement was given to reporters. It said in part that "the little princess is a healthy baby of seven pounds, 12 ounces, which is five ounces more than the average weight. Prince Bernard, who was waiting in the suite, was the first to be informed." A few moments later, Dr. John F. Puddicombe of Ottawa, Juliana's obstetrician, announced that both mother and daughter "are doing well."

Netherlanders had been hoping for the birth of a boy who would be the first male heir in the House of Orange-Nassau since 1851.

Canadian warships sink a German sub

March 4, 1943

LONDON, England – RCN officers report the sinking today of enemy submarine U-87 west of Portugal. The vessel fell victim to two Canadian warships, *HMCS Shediac* and *HMCS Ste. Croix.* This is also the second kill accredited to *Ste. Croix,* which sank U-90 in mid-Atlantic last July 24.

Ste. Croix is one of the oldest ships in the RCN. Originally she was an American "Town" class destroyer, also known as four-stackers. In 1940, 50 such ships were transferred to Britain in exchange for bases in Newfoundland and Bermuda. Six, in turn, were handed over to the RCN. They proved to be riddled with mechanical defects. *Ste. Croix* is the only one of the six to have sunk U-boats.

U.S. firms paying "too much" for labor

An American workers' camp in the Peace River District.

March 15, 1943

EDMONTON – American companies working here will no longer be allowed to hire Canadians. Why? Because they pay them too much! At least that's what the local Chamber of Commerce says, and Ottawa agrees. So from now on, American companies will have to bring their workers with them. The trend isn't surprising, considering that a stenographer getting $56 a month from a Canadian boss can get $150 from an American one.

Social security: King moves to assure "freedom from want"

Feb. 17, 1943

OTTAWA – Today Prime Minister W.L. Mackenzie King brought Canada closer to having a "social security" program, by naming a 41-person committee to study the subject. The move follows up on this session's throne speech: "It is in the general interest that freedom from fear and from want should be the assured possession of all." The plan will include health coverage.

The move toward social security has been urged by the Co-operative Commonwealth Federation for years to prevent a repeat of the suffering that accompanied the Great Depression. At last the Liberals seem to agree, perhaps because they now see the wide-scale support the CCF has won for its programs. Should there be another depression, the poor would have something to fall back on.

Rear Admiral Murray assumes vital Atlantic post

April 30, 1943

HALIFAX – Rear Admiral Leonard W. Murray, RCN, has assumed the post of commander-in-chief, Canadian Northwest Atlantic, with headquarters at this port. He thus becomes operational commander of all anti-submarine forces – ships and aircraft – based in the Maritime provinces and in Newfoundland. Murray's authority extends to British and American units based in this area.

A native Nova Scotian, Murray has been with the RCN since its inception, graduating with the first class of the Royal Naval College of Canada in 1911. He spent much of the First World War attached to British ships. In this war Murray has commanded RCN destroyers overseas, sat on the Permanent Joint Board on Defence, and served as Commodore Commanding Newfoundland Force.

The new arrangement follows last month's Atlantic Convoy Conference in Washington, where the whole anti-submarine war was reorganized. As a result, Canada's forces are being bolstered. Additional equipment means more responsibility and makes the RCN more a partner than a mere participant in the Atlantic War.

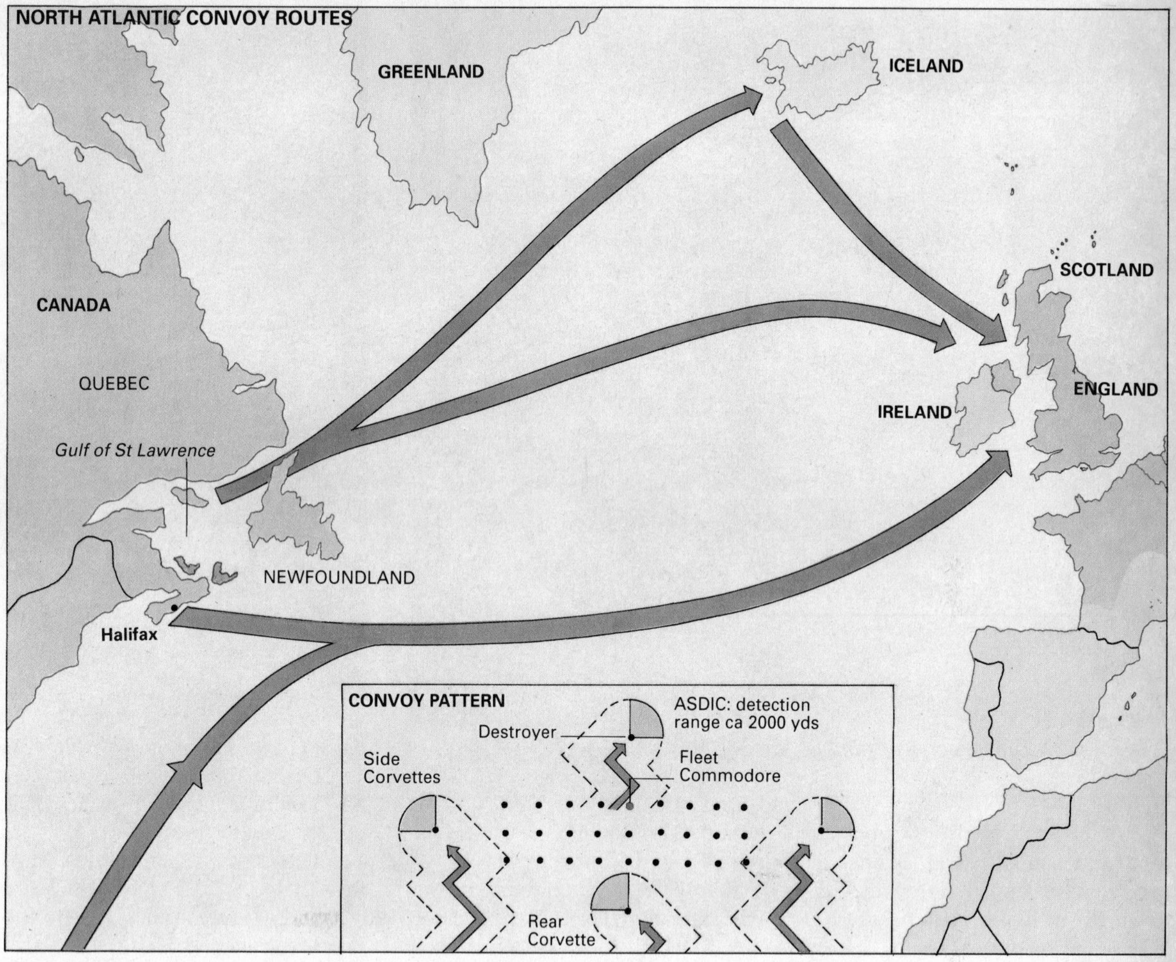

The map illustrates the convoy routes used by merchant and military shipping during the war.

Thousands strike as war fails to cool labor unrest in Canada

Strikers from the Canadian Car Munitions Ltd. block the departure of a CN Special Munitions Workers train from the Maisonneuve station in Montreal.

June 14, 1943

CANADA – This country is a hotbed of labor unrest, despite the war. At least 10,000 workers have walked off their jobs in both Ontario and Quebec. The issues are higher wages, or union recognition, or both. For example, workers at three Quebec shipyards are demanding both improved wages and a "closed shop," that is, no one but union members may work there. Responding to the demands, a spokesman for Morton Engineering and Drydock, Davie Shipbuilding and Repairing Company, and George T. Davie & Sons said the companies "consistently agreed to co-operate with their employees in seeking increased wages (rates are being regulated by the government). The only point on which there is not complete agreement" is the demand for a closed shop.

Aberhart founded Social Credit party

May 23, 1943

VANCOUVER – William "Bible Bill" Aberhart, founder of the Social Credit party and the premier of Alberta, died here today. He was 64. Aberhart was born in Perth County, Ont. While employed as a high school principal at Calgary, Aberhart became an unofficial minister for both Baptist and Pentecostal churches before forming his own church – the Prophetic Bible Institute. In 1925, Aberhart became a pioneer in radio evangelism. His *Back to the Bible Hour* was heard across the nation.

In 1932, Aberhart believed the principles of Maj. C.H. Douglas might relieve the prairies of the effects of the depression. In 1935, his Social Credit League swept the United Farmers out of office. ▷

Canadian soldiers spearhead Sicilian campaign

Three Rivers Tank Regiment rumbles through Regalbuto, Sicily on Aug. 4.

Troops from Princess Patricia's Canadian Light Infantry march through the streets of the captured Sicilian town, Valguarnera, on July 19.

July 10, 1943

PACHINO, Sicily – For the first time in the war, Canadian troops have landed on enemy-held territory with the goal of staying. The 1st Canadian Division, led by Canada's youngest general, Maj.-Gen. Guy Simonds, 39, came ashore in strength as part of a major Allied invasion of this island. Canadian casualties are light – some 60 killed or wounded – while Canadians took 650 prisoners.

Before the landings, concern was felt that an Italian position, called the Maucini battery, might give trouble. Naval gunfire suppressed the battery during the approach of Canadian landing craft; its 38-man garrison later surrendered to an RCR company when a sergeant fired a single warning shot.

Allied aircraft – including Spitfires of the RCAF's No. 417 (City of Windsor) Squadron – control the skies over the beachhead. The RCN is also present in the shape of four flotillas of the landing craft delivering troops, vehicles, and supplies to the beaches.

The 1st Division underwent intense training in Scotland before leaving for the Mediterranean in late June. Their convoy was unfortunate in running afoul of German U-boats July 4 and 5, when three transports were sunk. Fifty-eight Canadian soldiers lost their lives, and many valuable vehicles and artillery pieces went to the bottom.

TCA's transatlantic service takes flight

July 22, 1943

MONTREAL – Using a modified Lancaster bomber, Trans-Canada Airlines began the first regular Canadian transatlantic air service today with a non-stop flight to Britain. The plane, which carried three passengers and mail for the armed forces, made the 4,830-kilometre flight from Montreal in 12 hours and 25 minutes, shaving 25 minutes off the speed record. Additional fuel tanks were installed in the plane to increase its range. Canada opted for the Lancaster, a British plane, after its bid to buy three U.S. Liberators was rejected by the Americans. It is the only plane in TCA's transatlantic fleet.

The Allied leaders meet at Quebec City to discuss the progress of the war and to make future plans. Pictured here are host William Lyon Mackenzie King, Canadian prime minister, President Franklin Delano Roosevelt of the United States, and British Prime Minister Winston Churchill.

Ontario Liberals crushed at polls

Aug. 4, 1943

TORONTO – The once-mighty Ontario Liberals were chased out of power tonight, retaining only 14 of the 59 seats they held before the election. The big winners in the Ontario election are George Drew's Progressive Conservatives, who took 38 seats, and the Co-operative Commonwealth Federation, which got 34.

For Premier Harry Nixon, who only took over the post three months ago after Mitch Hepburn resigned from the party, it was a stinging defeat – softened only by the fact that he kept his seat. He'll likely hand over the reins of power very soon.

The Italian campaign: Canadian units to do battle

Soldiers on mainland virtually unopposed

Sept. 3, 1943

REGGIO CALABRIA, Italy – "We're on the mainland!" That was the word from this town, virtually at the toe of the Italian boot, as the 1st Canadian and 5th British divisions, backed by smothering airpower and massive naval firepower, crossed the Strait of Messina to begin another invasion.

The first dawn landings included the West Nova Scotia Regiment and the Carleton and York Regiment, followed almost immediately by the Royal 22nd Regiment. They landed virtually unopposed. Expected wire and mine defences were absent, and enemy troops had abandoned principal shore batteries.

Advances inland were also simple, with objectives such as the local airport falling quickly into Allied hands. Italian civilians are helping the Allies with information, including the fact that German troops have withdrawn, leaving coastal defences to demoralized, ill-trained Italian units. The most dangerous enemy met today was an escaped puma in the Reggio Zoo.

Personnel of the Seaforth Highlanders search German prisoners in Italy.

Italy signs armistice, leaves Axis alliance

Sept. 8, 1943

ROME – Plagued by fumbling leadership, disorganized industry, and military defeat, Italy has signed an armistice and is leaving the Axis alliance. Marshal Pietro Badoglio, head of government since Benito Mussolini was deposed on July 24, signed a secret agreement with the Allies five days ago. Its announcement today coincides with large Allied landings around Salerno.

Italian soldiers are being told not to attack Allied troops, though they may defend themselves. They have also been ordered to fight any Germans who come near them. King Victor Emmanuel, Badoglio, and the Italian government have fled to Brindisi, near the heel of Italy. The Italian fleet, under attack from its recent ally, the German Air Force, is steaming for Malta and Allied protection. So, for all of Mussolini's brag and bluster, Italy was never strong enough to stay in a long war.

An enthusiastic welcome for the Canadian troops in Staletti, Italy.

A Canadian tank fires on Potenza.

Troops hurl a hand grenade into a sniper's hideout in the Maltese Mountains.

Canadian soldier takes cover in a shell-blasted house in Italy.

Germans maintain tight grip on Italy

Sept. 10, 1943

ROME – The Italian government – and most of its citizens – have quit the war, but the Germans are staying in Italy, aided by a few Fascist units still loyal to the Axis. Most Italian commanders, confused at the rapid turn of events, have surrendered their arms to the Germans. Two powerful German divisions have seized Rome, disarming five Italian divisions in and around the city.

▷

Canadian Congress of Labour throws support behind CCF

Sept. 13, 1943

MONTREAL – Calling it the "political arm of the labor movement," the Canadian Congress of Labour today threw its support to the Co-operative Commonwealth Federation. The move breaks with a long-standing tradition of official political neutrality in the Canadian labor movement.

The CCL is the umbrella organization for Canadian unions aligned with the American Congress of Industrial Organizations. The CCL was formed three years ago when unions split with the Trades and Labour Congress of Canada, which adheres to the approach of political neutrality.

The CCF, formed in 1932 by western farm organizations, railway union leaders and socialist intellectuals, advocates a new anti-capitalist social order based on the supremacy of the worker.

Ships sunk in dramatic convoy battle

Sept. 24, 1943

HALIFAX – One of the most dramatic convoy battles of this war has ended. Two westbound convoys under naval and air escort were attacked by U-boat "wolf packs" over five days. Four escort ships and seven merchantmen were sunk, but the enemy also lost submarines.

Most dramatic was the loss of *HMCS Ste. Croix*, a Canadian destroyer that had previously been in at two U-boat kills. She was sunk about midnight Sept. 20. *HMS Itchen*, which had previously rescued the sole survivor of *HMS Polyanthus*, picked up 81 *Ste. Croix* survivors but was herself torpedoed on Sept. 22. From this disaster only three men survived – one from *Polyanthus*, one from *Itchen*, and one from *Ste. Croix*.

In the latter stages of the battle, four-engined Liberator bombers of the RCAF's No. 10 Squadron from Gander, Nfld., attacked U-boats far out to sea using depth charges and gunfire. The submarines often chose to stay on the surface, shooting it out with the Liberators.

Ottawa OKs funds to produce penicillin

Sept. 12, 1943

OTTAWA – Funding for plants and equipment to produce British-developed penicillin was announced today by Munitions Minister C.D. Howe. The industry, which will employ some 250 people, will be located in Montreal and Toronto. While the minister's announcement did not specify the amount of money allotted, production costs for the quantities of the new drug needed are estimated in the $1 million to $2 million range.

The bacteria-killing penicillin is ideal for combatting war wounds, the minister's announcement says. The new plants in Canada are likely to use a system developed at Banting Institute in Toronto which increases yield. With initial contracts for 26 billion units of penicillin for the armed forces, it represents the largest single order for medical supplies by his ministry, Howe says. By next February the new Canadian plants will be producing an average of 500 million units weekly.

Polymer rubber puts the bounce back in Allies' war effort

Sept. 29, 1943

SARNIA, Ont. – Synthetic rubber to replace natural supplies cut off by the enemy was produced for the first time today at the Polymer Corporation Ltd. plant here. Polymer, a Crown corporation, was established last year to produce synthetic rubber for the war effort. The need arose when the Japanese took over the Allies' access to natural rubber in the Far East. Dow Chemical, a U.S. company, built a styrene plant here last year on the invitation of C.D. Howe, Canada's minister of munitions and supply. The plant to produce styrene, essential for the synthetic rubber operation, was erected on Polymer's property.

When its plant is up to speed, Polymer is expected to produce 5,000 tons of synthetic rubber each month. The product will be used in tires as well as aircraft components, and much of it is expected to be sold to the U.S. for its war effort.

McCarthy becomes first ambassador

Nov. 11, 1943

OTTAWA – Canada took one of the last steps toward full nationhood today when it elevated the rank of its minister in Washington to that of a full-fledged ambassador. Washington returned the compliment by elevating its minister here to the same rank.

And so, the Hon. Leighton McCarthy is now Canada's first ambassador. Legations in other Allied countries are expected to be elevated to embassy rank in the near future as well.

This move is highly significant because it makes it clear that Canada, although still a member of the British Commonwealth, is now entirely in charge of her own affairs. This is a radical change from just a few decades ago when whatever international action Britain chose to take was automatically adopted by her colonies as well.

The role of the industrial workers is vital to the war effort.

More recruits for the air force are needed if Hitler is to be defeated.

Spies are a constant threat. It is essential that the routes and schedules of ships be kept secret.

Alberta delivers on hospital costs

Nov. 17, 1943

EDMONTON – The Alberta government will soon have a welcome gift for every newborn baby – it will pay the hospital costs of delivery. Dr. W.W. Cross, minister of health, made the announcement today at the hospitals' association meeting in Calgary. The new ruling takes effect next April. The subsidy is based on government's opinion that prudent health care demands that more deliveries be made in hospital maternity wards, and fewer in rural homes with only a midwife in attendance.

Report says keep status quo in Nfld. until after the war

Dec. 2, 1943

LONDON, England – Having directed that Newfoundland be governed by commission for the last nine years, the British House of Commons has finally taken up the question of the colony's future. A report was prepared recently by Lord Cochrane, secretary of state at the Dominion's Office, and presented to the Commons today by P.V. Emrys-Evans, the parliamentary undersecretary.

The report is somewhat vague, but it firmly says there will be no change in Newfoundland while the war continues, and therefore government by commission will remain in place for now. It also states an abrupt return to responsible government, terminated in 1934, is not recommended. Also, the Dominion's Office feels Confederation with Canada is not acceptable to Newfoundlanders. It seems the government wants gradual evolution to take place in the colony with an eventual return to responsible government, but Emrys-Evans emphasizes that "the (British) government will be guided by the freely expressed views of the (Newfoundland) people. It is for Newfoundland to make the choice."

This report is the end result of a parliamentary commission sent out by Clement Attlee after he visited Newfoundland last year.

Canadians seize German stronghold

After a fierce battle, Canadians now control San Leonardo di Ortona.

Soldiers rescue a buddy who has been trapped under the rubble for three days.

Dec. 28, 1943

ORTONA, Italy – Soldiers of the 1st Canadian Division have captured this Adriatic port after some of the most bitter fighting in memory. Even approaches to the town were hotly contested. An Italian farm known as Casa Barardi, located at a key crossroad, witnessed ferocious fighting before its capture by the Royal 22nd Regiment.

Canadian troops began to fight their way into the town on Dec. 21. The fighting was intense house-to-house combat – "a miniature Stalingrad," as one reporter wrote. German paratroopers – the fighting elite of a desperate army – defended the town with fanaticism, skill, and courage. Those buildings that the enemy did not defend were rigged with elaborate booby traps. The Germans dynamited houses to block some narrow streets and to force Canadian troops down others where the defences were strongest. Tanks were not designed for street fighting, but the Shermans of the Three Rivers Regiment were used at great risk to their crews in the close-quarter battle.

The battle raged even on Christmas Day. Fighting men, pulled out of the battle for an hour or two, enjoyed a full-course Christmas meal, sang a few carols, and then went back to fight. For some, Christmas dinner was the last of their lives. Both sides were ruthless as the fighting continued. Yesterday, the Germans detonated one charge under a house, killing 20 men of the Loyal Edmonton Regiment. Canadian troops identified two buildings filled with Germans, laid captured explosives under the cover of smoke, and blew them up, wiping out two enemy platoons.

Incredible as it seems, Italian civilians are still living in the town. During the battle they would crawl out of the rubble to curse Mussolini, thank the Canadians for coming, and pass around bottles of wine while machine-guns and anti-tank guns chattered and roared only metres away.

RCAF Fairey Swordfish torpedo bombers in flight formation.

A Vancouver family covers windows with blackout paper in fear of night aerial attacks.

McNaughton leaves overseas command

Dec. 26, 1943

LONDON, England – Gen. A.G.L "Andy" McNaughton has resigned as commander of First Canadian Army. Brilliant, charismatic, and outspoken, he differed with his own government about keeping Canada's overseas army as united as possible. Last June the 1st Canadian Infantry Division was sent to the Mediterranean. It is now being followed by the 5th Canadian Armoured Division. McNaughton says splitting the overseas army between two war theatres is not a good idea.

1944

Italy, Jan. 15. Canadian troops receive copies of the *Maple Leaf*, the first regular newspaper published by the Canadian army during the war.

Ottawa, March 6. The Defence Department announces Maj. Paul Triquet of Quebec has been awarded the Victoria Cross for valor in the Moro River battle in Italy. He's the fourth Canadian to win the award so far in the war.

Ottawa, March. The army finds only 14 percent of its officers and 19 percent of enlisted men speak French, manifesting low French-Canadian participation in the war effort.

Montreal, April 13. Montreal Canadiens defeat Chicago Blackhawks four games to none to win the Stanley Cup.

France, July 31. The Allies drive the Germans from Normandy.

Quebec, Aug. 8. Maurice Duplessis' Union Nationale defeats the Liberal government of Joseph-Adélard Godbout in the provincial election.

Paris, Aug. 25. Allied armies take Paris from the Germans.

Prairies, Sept. 7. More than 500 one-room rural schools in Alberta, Saskatchewan, and Manitoba can't start classes because of a teacher shortage.

Ottawa, Sept. 18. The government ends tea and coffee rationing, imposed 25 months ago because of the war.

Ottawa, Sept. 20. A government report shows 25 percent of Inuit at Eskimo Point in the N.W.T.'s Keewatin district have died of diphtheria.

Kingsville, Ont., Nov. 3. Jack Miner, famous naturalist, dies.

British Columbia, Nov. 25. Some 2,900 Home Defence soldiers protest in five towns against conscription. They are reacting to PM King's decision to send draftees overseas.

Hamilton, Nov. 25. St. Hyacinthe-Donnacona Navy beat Hamilton Wildcats 7-6 to win the Grey Cup.

Toronto. Ontario passes Canada's first Racial Discrimination Act, banning the publication or display of any expression of racial or religious discrimination.

Northwest Territories. A survey of Indian and Inuit children in the Mackenzie Delta and western Arctic shows 93 percent of the natives get no formal education.

New code smooths labor negotiations

Feb. 17, 1944

OTTAWA – Some 2.5 million workers in "war industries" now have the right to negotiate employment conditions with their bosses, thanks to a new wartime Labor Code that took effect today. The code follows investigations into last year's labor unrest, when at least 10,000 workers struck for higher wages and union recognition.

Under the code, a new eight-member board will certify bargaining units for employees. These units will have the legal right to negotiate contracts with employers. Should negotiations fail, disputes will go to a conciliation process. Strikes will be allowed, but only after all avenues of negotiation and conciliation have failed. As well, a list of unfair practices by employers, employees and unions will be drawn up. Overall, the code shows that the government knows it needs the working man to win this war, and it also wants his vote in the next election.

One "British" airman in four is Canadian

Many pilots in RAF squadrons such as this one are Canadian.

Feb. 29, 1944

OTTAWA – One-quarter of the fighting strength of the British air force is actually Canadian – though only half the RCAF is overseas. This is the measure of success of the British Commonwealth Air Training Plan, which has also turned out seven British and ANZAC airmen for every 10 Canadians trained. There are 41 RCAF squadrons overseas – 39 in Britain and one each in Ceylon and Italy.

Twelve RCAF heavy bomber squadrons constitute No. 6 Group. There is also The Lost Legion – thousands of RCAF aircrew serving in RAF squadrons and special units. Every major RAF operation involves Canadians.

Britain gives two warships to Canada

Jan. 14, 1944

OTTAWA – In what Navy Minister Angus Macdonald describes as a "token gift" for all Canada has done for Britain, the United Kingdom today gave Canada two of its new-type medium cruisers. As well, Canadian officers and seamen will be taking over two British carriers, although these ships will remain part of the Royal Navy.

This was not the only naval news in Ottawa today. Vice-Admiral Percy W. Nelles is on his way to London to act as the senior Canadian flag officer there. Although Macdonald wouldn't give details because of wartime security, it is generally understood that Nelles' transfer is related to the build-up of forces for the expected invasion of Europe. He will be joining Canada's senior army and air officers in London, says the minister. In his only hint at invasion, Macdonald added, "The fact that all three chiefs of staff are over there, I would say, is an indication that we mean business." Time will tell what that business is.

A Canadian soldier of the Perth Regiment hides and takes aim at the town of Orsogna, Italy.

Canada to pay U.S. for string of airports

Feb. 29, 1944

OTTAWA – Canada is going to foot the $46-million bill for the string of airports running from Edmonton to Alaska – at least for those that are on Canadian territory. The bases were built by U.S. army engineers and have been the chief supply line, along with the famed Alaska Highway, for the shipment of goods to Alaska and northeast Asia.

The reason for the purchase now isn't clear. These bases are already manned by Royal Canadian Air Force officers and crew, and there is no doubt that title to them was to revert to Canada as soon as the war ends. However, insiders in Ottawa say the King government may be doing this to strengthen its postwar bargaining position, and to avoid criticism that it has allowed the Americans to take over Canadian airways. For the Americans, the purchase should end complaints that they're throwing away money on what will soon be Canada's.

RCN, German navy slug it out at sea

April 29, 1944

LONDON, England – RCN destroyers have slugged it out with their German counterparts twice in the last three nights. The score stands at RCN 2, German navy 1. Early on the morning of April 26, HMC ships *Athabaskan, Huron,* and *Haida* sank the German destroyer T-29 off the coast of Brittany. They also damaged two other warships. This morning, just west of the earlier fight, *Athabaskan* and *Haida* engaged three more German destroyers. *Athabaskan* was hit by enemy torpedoes, caught fire, and blew up. *Haida* drove T-29 ashore, leaving Allied aircraft and motor torpedo boats to finish her off.

Crerar takes command

Lt. Gen. H.D.G. Crerar.

March 20, 1944

LONDON, England – Lt.-Gen. H.D.G. "Harry" Crerar has been appointed to command First Canadian Army, succeeding Gen. A.G.L. "Andy" McNaughton, who resigned in December. Crerar's most recent command has been over Canadian troops in Italy. He now leads the largest army force Canada has ever put in the field.

Like McNaughton, Crerar is a former artillery officer – he won a Distinguished Service Order in 1917. But, senior servicemen say, he lacks McNaughton's personal magnetism. His is an unenviable role – responsible both to Allied commanders and to a government on the other side of the Atlantic.

Sailors, zootsuiters in Montreal clashes

June 3, 1944

MONTREAL – Another spate of riots involving sailors and zootsuiters ripped through Montreal over the weekend, leaving dozens injured and resulting in more than 40 arrests. Clashes erupted downtown, in restaurants, dance halls, nightclubs, and in the streets. One report recounts a mob of 400 sailors sweeping through clubs hunting for zootsuiters. Witnesses say many of the sailors were armed with clubs and knives. In one restaurant zootsuiters tried to hide their trademark long coats, but the marauding sailors identified the "drugstore cowboys" by their distinctive close-cropped haircuts.

Tea, coffee lovers get more rations

May 1, 1944

OTTAWA – Coffee and tea lovers rejoice! The government is increasing the amount each Canadian is allowed to consume. The Wartime Prices and Trade Board today announced the joint coupon values for tea or coffee will be raised to eight ounces of tea or 32 ounces of coffee every month. Under the old three-week system, the limit was four ounces of tea or 16 of coffee – equal measures since tea makes four times as many cups per ounce. Neither is in short supply – rationing was implemented to free cargo ships for wartime duties.

An appeal for Canadian help.

Canadian infantry, tanks smash through Hitler Line in Italy

May 24, 1944

PONTECORVO, Italy – Canadian infantry and tanks reached this point today after fighting their way through the Hitler Line – a network of defences blocking an Allied advance on Rome. The Germans used mortars, rockets, mine fields, and tank turrets.

The main attack began yesterday. Fighting was confused. At one point German troops captured many Canadians – then marched them into territory other Canadians had just seized. Canada's 1st Division's infantry beat down the German defences, and then the 5th Division's Sherman tanks broke through. Ahead lies the Melfa River – and Rome!

Hitler Line Barrage, Italy, painted by Lawren P. Harris.

Ford workers put the brakes on strike

May 10, 1944

WINDSOR, Ont. – A strike by about 14,000 workers at the Ford Motor Co. of Canada ended tonight with a vote to return to work after the National Wartime Labor Relations Board vowed to clarify grievance procedures. The members of Local 200 of the United Auto Workers Union had been off the job since April 20, except for a two-day period which ended with a second work stoppage on May 2. The vote to return to work took place after a debate of more than two hours.

The mood swung in favor of ending the walkout after UAW of America vice-president Dick Frankensteen of Detroit argued that Ford wanted the strike in a bid to smash the union. Local 200 president Roy England told his membership that the National Wartime Labor Relations Board would not clarify the grievance procedure until the walkout ended. The strike had been ruled contrary to the labor code by the Labor Relations Board. Picket lines were withdrawn and work will resume as soon as shifts are arranged.

Humorist Leacock succumbs to cancer

March 28, 1944

TORONTO – Noted Canadian humorist Stephen Leacock has died of cancer. He was 74. Leacock, who taught economics at McGill University until 1936, published more than 25 books, including several on economics and history. He was best known for his humorous essays and novels, including *Sunshine Sketches of a Little Town. My Discovery of the West* won the 1937 Governor General's Award.

D-Day: Allied troops storm beaches at Normandy

Canadian infantrymen leave their specialized ships and wade ashore on the Normandy beaches, using ropes to guide them and carrying their bicycles.

June 6, 1944

LONDON, England – Some 175,000 American, British, Canadian, and Free French soldiers have landed in Normandy in the largest amphibious operation in military history. It involves 4,000 ships and landing craft, escorted by 600 warships. The frontal attack on the beaches was preceded by massive naval and air bombardments and by inland drops of paratroopers and glider-borne forces.

The first Canadians into France were members of the 1st Canadian Parachute Battalion who captured bridges near Cabourg. Two brigades of the 3rd Canadian Infantry Division splashed ashore between 7:45 and 8 a.m. They had to deal with booby-trapped beach obstacles and German guns in concrete bunkers. However, they captured their objectives and were reinforced by a third brigade shortly before noon. Moving inland, Canadian troops made the deepest penetrations of all Allied forces.

While the army was arriving by air and sea, other Canadian forces were involved. RCN minesweepers have been clearing the sea route, RCN landing ships launched many of the craft carrying Canadian soldiers, and RCN destroyers were involved in the preliminary shelling of enemy defences.

The RCAF was busy, too. Just before dawn, 230 heavy bombers from No. 6 (RCAF) group dropped 859 tons of explosives on shore batteries. Throughout the rest of the day, RCAF fighters flew "top cover" for Allied troops. Fighter bombers attacked enemy positions and watched for German reinforcements moving up.

The liberation of Europe has begun, but at a cost. An estimated 9,000 Allied troops have become casualties. These have included 1,074 Canadians – 359 killed, 131 captured, 584 wounded. Canadian aircrew casualties total 28 killed, including fighter pilots and crews of glider-towing aircraft shot down by intense anti-aircraft fire.

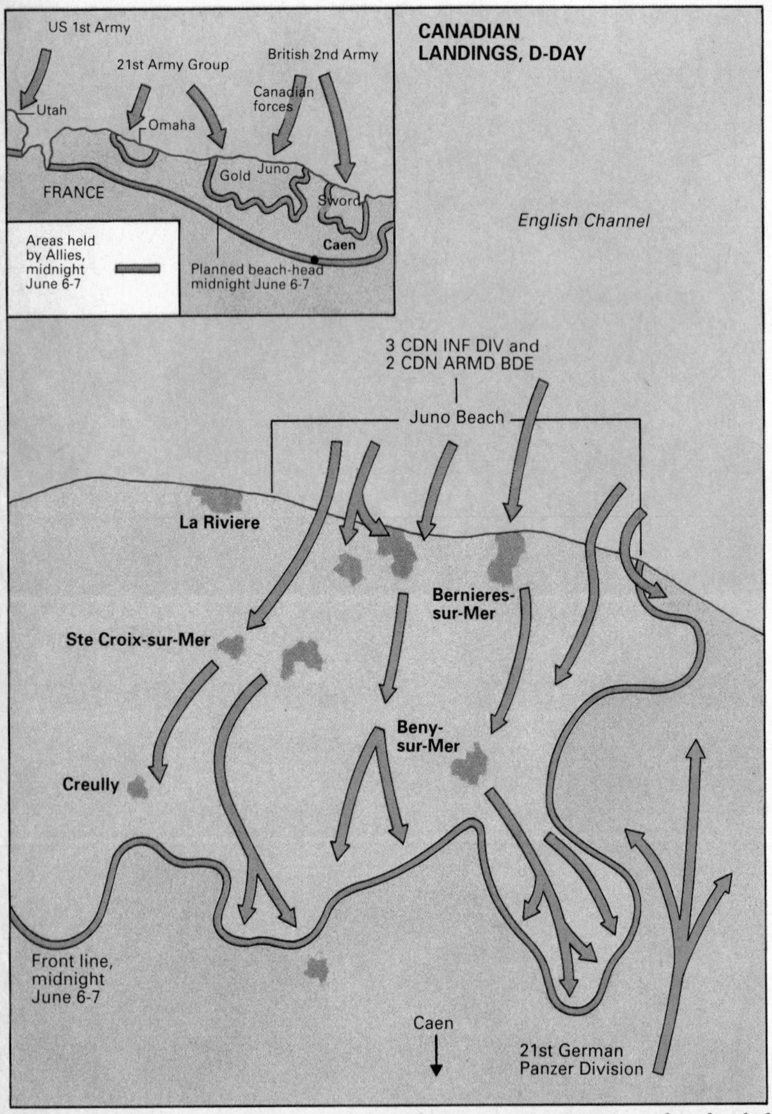

This map shows the movements of Canadian troops on D-Day as they landed on the Normandy beaches and moved inland to invade Europe.

French veteran of WWI greets Canadian tanks in Fleury-sur-Orne.

Canadian troops guard their German prisoners on Juno Beach, Normandy. The prisoners were taken during the invasion on Europe on D-Day.

Douglas guides CCF to victory in Sask.

June 15, 1944
REGINA – Calling it a "victory for the people of Saskatchewan as a whole," CCF leader Rev. T.C. Douglas led his party to a sweeping victory in the provincial election today and will become the first socialist premier in Canada. The CCF won 44 of 51 seats for which voting was held today in a house-cleaning that saw five of the nine cabinet members in the Liberal administration lose their seats.

Outgoing Liberal Premier W.J. Patterson barely kept his own seat, winning by 30 votes in Cannington. The Liberals won four seats and were leading in two others. The CCF leads in another. Voting on a 52nd seat will take place June 24.

First atomic energy plant in the works

June 15, 1944
CHALK RIVER, Ont. – The first atomic energy plant in Canada will be built at this site 210 kilometres west of Ottawa by Defence Industries Ltd. A joint project of the U.S., British, and Canadian governments, the plant will be designed by the Montreal laboratory of the National Research Council of Canada. Security and isolation were factors in selecting the site, on the Ottawa River's south bank.

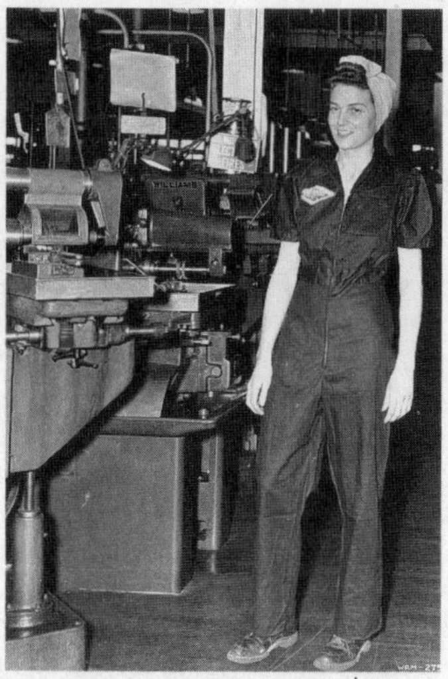

The John Inglis Company in Toronto is involved in the production of Bren guns for the military.

Attack takes its toll on Black Watch

July 25, 1944
CAEN – The Germans are falling back in Normandy, but they fight hard. Just ask members of Montreal's Canadian Black Watch – those you can find. At 3:30 a.m. today, some 300 Black Watch members moved into a village, St. Martin de Fontenay, to attack Verrières Ridge. German troops still held St. Martin. The Black Watch commander was killed as his unit cleared out the place. The action disrupted the timetable, and artillery support was not synchronized thereafter with infantry moves.

With St. Martin secured, the Black Watch advanced on their objective commencing at 9:30 a.m. They kept losing officers until one company was reportedly being led by a sergeant. Much is unclear, because radio contact was broken soon after the attack began and the intense fire ruled out communication by runner.

An earlier patrol had reported enemy defences weak. Probably the Germans were holding their fire, waiting for a better target. As the Black Watch reached the ridge summit, they fell into a trap. Camouflaged troops and dug-in tanks smothered the Canadians. They held out as long as possible; fighting on the ridge may have lasted until early afternoon. At least 123 were killed and 83 captured – scarcely 15 regained our lines. These are the heaviest single-day casualties sustained by a Canadian regiment since the Dieppe Raid.

The Maple Leaf, the Canadian forces paper, is issued for the first time at Caen.

Men of the Regina Rifles take cover in a ruined storefront in Caen.

Parents to get monthly baby bonuses

Aug. 1, 1944
OTTAWA – After years of debate, Canada now has a family allowance program. Better known as the "baby bonus," it ensures that each child in a household will receive a monthly payment from the federal government aimed at ensuring adequate nutrition and clothing. The program is universal, meaning that every family in Canada will be eligible, although those with high incomes will lose at least some of the bonus to income taxes.

The baby bonus program, which will cost a staggering $250 million this year alone, passed unanimously on second reading in the House today. However, there has been opposition. Both George Drew, premier of Ontario, and Conservative MP Dr. Herbert Bruce oppose the baby bonus on the grounds that it most benefitted those who had done the least for Canada during the war, that is, the large families of Quebec.

True or not, the feeling is indicative of the hostility between some English- and French-speaking Canadians – hostility that has only been heightened by the war. Despite this opposition, the bill finally passed without anyone voting against it.

Canada attends UN money conference

June 30, 1944
BRETTON WOODS, N.H. – World financial leaders launched a 10-day United Nations monetary conference here today in order to make money available anywhere on the globe for commerce. The conference follows up an agreement last April in which 34 countries decided to set up an $8 million international monetary fund. Its purpose is to supplement foreign exchange markets. In the past, some countries often used up their supplies of foreign exchange. ▷

Allies close Falaise gap

Canadian troops enter the ancient town of Falaise in Normandy.

Aug. 21, 1944

FALAISE – Some 50,000 Germans are prisoners tonight following linkup between American and Commonwealth armies east of this ancient Norman town. The enemy's Seventh Army and Fifth Panzer Army have ceased to exist. Those who got away are in full flight. The Battle of Normandy is over, claiming some 5,000 Canadians.

The enemy found it hard to keep open an escape route, but even as they fled they were subjected to devastating air attacks which German ack-ack could not stop. Hundreds of vehicles were abandoned on the roads. The air reeks of death – not just soldiers but horses, too, for the German army still moves as much through animal power as mechanical power.

The First Canadian Army was heavily engaged and larger than ever. Its strength has been augmented by British units, including the 51st (Highland) Division, plus Poland's crack 1st Armoured Division. Lt.-Gen. H.D.G. "Harry" Crerar thus commands a truly multinational army. Throughout the battle it has dealt with determined SS troops, deadly 88-mm guns, and the most fearsome tanks in the German army – fast Panthers and super-heavy Tigers.

Canadian Red Cross nurses care for babies of war brides going to Canada.

French citizens rejoice: Dieppe liberated

Sept. 1, 1944

DIEPPE, France – Soldiers of the 2nd Canadian Division liberated this town today – two years and two weeks after the same formation sustained terrible losses at the hands of German defenders during the notorious Dieppe Raid.

Canadians expected the enemy to defend Dieppe again, and were prepared to blast the town with naval gunfire and massive bombing. At dawn the 8th Reconnaissance Regiment learned the enemy had withdrawn. The bombing raid was cancelled with just 20 minutes to spare. All day, Canadian troops have passed through the town, welcomed by deliriously happy citizens. British engineers are now clearing debris from the port, which will help in supplying advancing forces.

The entry of the 2nd Canadian Infantry Division into Dieppe.

Conscripts called in to harvest tobacco

Aug. 17, 1944

SIMCOE, Ont. – The army will help harvest southern Ontario's tobacco harvest. Today some 500 conscripts from the Régiment de Jolliet arrived by train. Farmers welcome the help, although they look dubiously at the helpers. Officially known as NRMA men – from the 1940 National Resources Mobilization Act – the soldiers are frequently called "Zombies." They serve only in North America unless they volunteer for overseas service. NRMA men are unpopular with those who believe they should be compelled to go to combat units.

Canadians smash through Gothic Line

Sept. 2, 1944

TOMBA DE PESARO – Another German bastion, the Gothic Line, has been taken. The first Allied attacks began on Aug. 25 with 1st Canadian Corps – 1st Canadian Infantry Division, 5th Canadian Armoured Division – fighting on the eastern end of the line. The Germans fell back to their main defences, a network of mine fields, anti-tank ditches, and supporting guns. These were breached on Aug. 30 and 31, and Canadian troops advanced quickly to the Adriatic Sea. Co-operation between infantry and tanks was outstanding.

Allied leaders agree: It's on to Japan

Sept. 16, 1944

QUEBEC CITY – "On to Japan!" That seems to be the major agreement arising out of the momentous conference held here over the last few days between U.S. President Franklin D. Roosevelt, British Prime Minister Winston Churchill, and Canadian PM and host W.L. Mackenzie King.

At a short press conference held outside the governor general's residence, Roosevelt told reporters the participants had achieved "complete unanimity" concerning the mopping up of the war in Europe and the situation in Japan. In fact, since the U.S. entered the war in December 1941, Roosevelt and Churchill make all the important decisions alone. King, while physically present, appears to take no vital role in the talks, although the Canadian prime minister has complete control over where Canadian troops will be deployed. To date Canada has contributed nearly one million men and women to the struggle. Almost one out of every 10 Canadians is in uniform.

Governor General Earl of Athlone, Roosevelt, Churchill and King.

Untrained troops a hazard: Smythe

Sept. 19, 1944

TORONTO – Maj. C.F. "Conn" Smythe has dropped a bombshell on the Liberal government. In a hospital interview with George McCullagh, publisher of the *Globe and Mail*, Smythe declares that in recent fighting, inexperienced Canadian soldiers have gone into battle led by equally green non-commissioned officers. Many have never thrown a grenade or are unfamiliar with Bren guns and Piat anti-tank weapons. In action they are dangerous. They sustain high casualties in their own ranks and unnecessary losses to older soldiers who must look out for new men as well as themselves.

To provide battle-wise leaders, the army is returning wounded officers and men to action before they're fully recovered. This situation exists when Canada has well-trained troops – the NRMA conscripts – who cannot be sent overseas without their own consent.

Allies fight to consolidate Antwerp gains

Oct. 7, 1944

ANTWERP – Allied troops have made many gains in the past month, but also met some setbacks. Liberating southeastern Holland is balanced by the defeat of airborne forces at Arnhem. British troops captured Antwerp on Sept. 3 and Canadians badly need the port to supply its troops. Unfortunately, Antwerp is an inland port on the Scheldt River. Germans hold the mouth of that river and thus deny Allied forces use of the harbor.

Canadian troops have spent the last few weeks clearing the French Channel coast, capturing German "flying bomb" sites and smaller ports. They have now begun attacks to secure the Antwerp area. Geography favors the enemy. Capture of successive islands means amphibious warfare and overcoming defences at narrow causeways.

Black Watch Regiment takes bad beating

Oct. 13, 1944

ANTWERP – The Black Watch Regiment, which took a bad beating in Normandy, has been mauled again. This time, inadequate training may be as much at fault as fierce enemy resistance.

The Montreal regiment was engaged near Woensdrecht, attacking German troops well dug in behind a railway embankment. In spite of excellent artillery support, air strikes, tanks, and flame throwers, the unit repeatedly failed to reach its objectives. All four rifle company commanders became casualties. The Black Watch lost 56 killed, 62 wounded, and 27 captured in one day. Like other units, it has recently been taking former cooks, clerks, and truck drivers as replacements for earlier casualties. About half the men had less than two months training. Of these, many had only rudimentary knowledge of weapons and tactics.

Bombers stage raid on industrial centre

Oct. 7, 1944

LONDON, England – No. 6 Bomber Group, the largest RCAF formation overseas, last night launched its largest single raid. It dispatched 293 four-engined aircraft – out of a total Bomber Command force of 523 – to attack Dortmund, a German transport and industrial centre. The Canadian group chiefly flies Halifax aircraft; 248 of these were involved, as well as 45 Lancasters. They dropped more than 800 tons of high explosives to rip apart buildings, and thousands of small incendiary bombs that set the wreckage on fire. German defences were weak. Only five bombers – two of them RCAF – were lost.

Minister of defence resigns over draft

PM King is in a difficult and dangerous position trying to ride out the conscription crisis.

Nov. 13, 1944

OTTAWA – Defence Minister James Ralston, unable to persuade Prime Minister W.L. Mackenzie King that only conscription will provide desperately needed reinforcements in Europe, bowed to official pressure and resigned today. King says enough men will volunteer to fight, but with the war almost over, that is unlikely. King's stance outrages Canadians aware that front-line morale is low because so many men are wounded and exhausted.

Conscription OK'd after 2-year delay

Nov. 23, 1944

OTTAWA – After two years of hesitation, Prime Minister W.L. Mackenzie King has announced he will invoke Bill 80 to conscript troops for Europe. The National Resources Mobilization Act will send 16,000 conscripts to England.

Conscription has long been a touchy issue. In 1942, English-speaking Canadians voted for and French-Canadians voted against overseas conscription. More recently, James Ralston was forced to resign his post as defence minister when he supported conscription.

Many French-speaking Liberals feel betrayed. Quebec agreed to participate in the war on condition enlistment be voluntary, and with no conscription for overseas service. But powerful French-Canadian cabinet minister Louis St. Laurent and others feel heavy Canadian casualties and intense English-Canadian pressure for immediate conscription left King no choice.

St. Roch ends voyage in record time

Oct. 16, 1944

VANCOUVER – The RCMP patrol vessel *St. Roch* slipped almost unnoticed into this harbor today at the end of another historic voyage through the Canadian Arctic. Two years ago the 300-ton schooner made the first west-to-east transit of the Northwest Passage. Today marks the first time that any vessel has sailed through the passage in both directions.

Commanded by Sgt. Henry Larsen, the *St. Roch* has completed this latest adventure in record time. It left Halifax in July, and despite encountering thick fog, heavy ice, and a tornado, arrived here just 86 days and 11,740 kilometres later. On its first passage, the *St. Roch* followed a route through the tortuous channels close to the mainland coast of America. This time Larsen took a more northerly route through Lancaster Sound, Barrow Strait, and Prince of Wales Strait. It is the first time this route has been navigated.

Larsen has been with the *St. Roch* since it was launched in 1928 to give the RCMP a means of supplying its remote Arctic outposts. The vessel is only 32 metres long, schooner-rigged, with a hull reinforced with beams of Douglas fir and a 300-horsepower engine installed specially for this excursion. Before the war it spent eight winters locked in the ice as a "floating" RCMP detachment. The two trips through the Arctic have strengthened Canada's claim to its Arctic territories.

The Northwest Passage has always been a formidable challenge to navigators.

Opening Antwerp is costly for Canadians

Buffalo amphibious vehicles carry troops across a Belgian river.

Nov. 8, 1944

ANTWERP – Nearly 6,400 Canadians were killed or wounded in the last five weeks, but German troops have been cleared from Breskens and the islands of South Beveland, North Beveland, and Walcheren. Some ruthless methods were used, including bombers blasting the Walcheren dikes. The resultant flooding hampered the Germans but has damaged much valuable farmland. Allied ships may now clear enemy mines. After that, Allies can funnel food, fuel, men, and munitions to the front.

Houde back as the mayor of Montreal

Dec. 11, 1944

MONTREAL – Four months after his release from internment for inciting opposition to compulsory military registration and conscription for military service in Canada, Camillien Houde has been re-elected mayor of Montreal for the fifth time. Houde, imprisoned since 1940, beat incumbent Adhemar Raynault by 14,000 votes. In his victory speech, Houde offered an olive branch to his enemies, saying "the day will come when you need Quebec's stability and soundness for other purposes than war."

Company sign painter Cpl. Jack Reay works on his famous sign about trench warfare.

Dutch children welcome Canadian troops with orange flags.

PM gets vote of confidence over draft

Dec. 7, 1944

OTTAWA – Prime Minister W.L. Mackenzie King has survived a vote of confidence on his conscription policy, supported by the Co-operative Commonwealth Federation and the Social Credit party. His opponents were the Conservatives, who want the government to send more than 16,000 conscripts overseas. The vote was 143-70. The CCF's support came after King agreed to change the wording of his confidence motion. The original read "that this House will aid the government in its policy of maintaining a vigorous war effort." As CCF leader M.J. Coldwell doesn't like many of the government's policies, he moved that the words "its policy of" be taken out of the motion. King pondered this change for a moment, then agreed, leading to charges from the Tories that the Liberals and CCF were secretly working together. Despite the fireworks, and Quebec's anger over conscription, there can be no doubt that King's policy of a limited draft now stands as law.

Tenants with kids cannot be refused

Dec. 22, 1944

OTTAWA – Landlords will not be allowed to refuse accommodation to tenants with children, the Wartime Prices and Trade Board ruled today. With the housing shortage expected to worsen, the formal decree is intended to maximize the use of existing housing. Penalties for non-compliance were not announced.

Only under special permit can the law be circumvented. Area controllers will be appointed locally to decide how any dwelling can best be used, and even take possession and rent it. Also, no residence can be closed or its use as a living space restricted without the administrator's approval.

Lensman covering the war in Europe

Photographer Bell in Normandy.

1944

NORTH EUROPE – Capt. Ken Bell, one of Canada's finest photographers, is currently covering the entire campaign of First Canadian Army here. Bell enlisted in the infantry, but was assigned in March 1943 to the Directorate of Public Relations as a photographer. He photographed Canadian wartime activity, often in the new color medium. In 1944, Bell was posted to the Highland Light Infantry of Canada in Britain. On D-Day, he landed with it in Normandy.

Senio River marks limit of latest push

Dec. 25, 1944

RAVENNA, Italy – The Senio River, a small stream, marks the limit of the latest Canadian push in Italy. For the past seven months Canadian troops have been pressing up the Italian peninsula, forcing successive enemy defence lines and crossing many rivers. The latest campaign began Dec. 2 and cost 1st Canadian Corps 548 killed, 1,796 wounded, and 212 captured. These are the heaviest casualties since the Gothic Line fighting in August. On the other hand, the enemy lost ground while suffering many dead. Canadians took 1,670 prisoners.

Enemy tactics were typical. Every time Canadian troops gained ground, Germans counter-attacked. They had to be beaten off before advancing again. Bad weather limited air forces, but heavy artillery support helped; Canadian guns fired 184,000 shells. Engineers built 29 bridges, often under enemy fire.

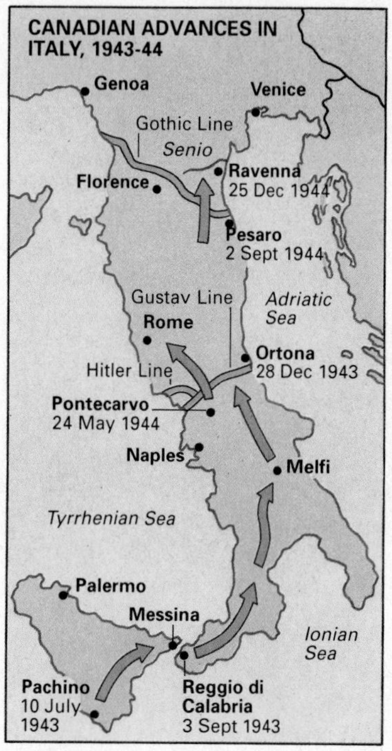

Canadian role in Italian campaign.

Comfort leads band of wartime artists

1944

LONDON, England – Since January 1943, the Canadian forces have had a select band of war artists covering their activities, from recruitment to battle – and sometimes to hospital or burial.

The scheme was set up with help from the artists themselves. Charles Comfort, a distinguished painter and teacher at the University of Toronto, chose the first batch of army painters. The army, noting that Comfort, 44, had not nominated himself, commissioned him and sent him overseas. He began painting in England, but has moved on to work in North Africa and Italy.

Comfort visited Italy before the war and now compares what he saw then with the present devastation. One general has compared the Italian campaign to "waging war in a museum." Comfort can document that observation in a unique way.

Captain Charles Comfort paints in a ruined house near Ortona, Italy.

Islanders willingly pay for health plan

Dr. Harold Trefry.

Summer 1944

ST. JOSEPH'S ISLAND, Ont. – Although this small community on St. Mary's River is sometimes isolated in spring and fall when the ferry isn't running and the ice is not solid enough for other transportation, its standard of health is as high as in any urban centre. The reason is a medical scheme set up by a doctor under which the 1,600 residents, on a voluntary basis, can each pay $2.50 a year and then not worry about physicians' fees.

The plan was started seven years ago by Dr. Harold Scott Trefry, now regarded as a local hero. The island is now almost completely free of communicable diseases.

Select group of Official War Artists sent overseas

Canadian Soldier no. 1, by Lilies Torrance Newton.

Paintings can tell story better than words

1944

LONDON, England – Canadian war artists ensure that our nation will have a unique record of the conflict when peace is restored. Although many in uniform paint and draw in their spare time, Official War Artists are a select group. As members of the armed forces they wear the same uniforms, get the same pay, and eat the same food as those in other trades. However, their job is to paint, not to fight.

It is not necessarily a safe job. RCAF artist Paul Goranson's ship was sunk in mid-Atlantic. He spent six hours in a lifeboat before rescue. Capt. George Pepper was trapped behind enemy lines for a week before our troops caught up to him. Others have come under artillery fire and air raids. A few have seen combat. Lieut. C.A. Law alternates between painting and work on a torpedo boat. Flight Lieut. R.S. Hyndman flew Spitfires before he was made a war artist.

Ordinary troops are supportive and interested. They know that the paintings will tell better than words just what our Canadian men have been going through.

Evacuation, by Charles Goldhamer.

Raid on San Giusto, Pisa, by Paul Goranson.

Normandy Dustbowl, by Robert Stewart Hyndman.

Fire On Board During Action, by Thomas Harold Beament.

The Hitler Line, by Charles Comfort.

Detail of the painting Torpedoed North Atlantic, by Paul Goranson.

Photographers capture the war up close

1944

LONDON, England – Canadians pioneered battlefield photography in the First World War and are keeping up the tradition. Many photographers are attached to Canadian units. All three services have newsphoto sections in Canada and overseas. The work can be dangerous – army photographers must often work under fire and sometimes are killed on the job. Terry Rowe died under fire in Italy, while his naval counterpart, Jack Mahoney, was lost with *HMCS Athabaskan*. Two others were decorated for bravery under fire. Capt. Ken Bell went mountain climbing to cover alpine training in Yoho Valley. The photographers' biggest problem is lack of up-todate equipment, notably a telephoto lens.

Detail of D-Day, by Tom Wood. A view of the battle on the Normandy beaches as seen from the vantage point of the offshore landing craft.

1945

Victoria, March 2. Painter and writer Emily Carr dies. Her painting was influenced by the art of northwest coast Indians.

Detroit, April 22. Toronto Maple Leafs beat Detroit Red Wings four games to three to win the Stanley Cup.

Milan, April 28. Benito Mussolini, former Fascist leader of Italy, is executed by Italian partisans and strung up by his heels in public.

Berlin, April 30. Adolf Hitler commits suicide as Russian troops occupy the city.

Poland, April 30. Russian Red Army soldiers enter concentration camps in which millions of Jews, Poles, and many others have been systematically killed by the Germans.

New York, June 26. Fifty nations, including Canada, sign the World Security Charter, creating the United Nations to keep international peace.

Japan, Sept. 2. Japan formally surrenders.

Canada, September. Almost 80,000 women in service industries have been laid off.

Toronto, Dec. 1. Toronto Argonauts beat Winnipeg Blue Bombers 35-0 for the Grey Cup.

Ottawa, Dec. 29. The government releases figures of Canadian war losses: 41,371 dead, 42,178 wounded, 10,844 taken prisoner, and 32 missing. About 20,000 more Canadians were killed in WWI than in this war.

London, December. PM Clement Attlee announces the British government will set up "an elected National Convention of Newfoundlanders" to make suggestions on forms of future government for the colony.

Canada. John Grierson resigns as government film commissioner. He has headed the National Film Board since its creation in 1939.

Canada. A returning soldier observes: "When we disembarked, smiling Red Cross and Salvation Army girls gave us a little bag with a couple of chocolate bars and a comic book. We had left as children and returned as killers and they were treating us as children."

Canada. Novels published in 1945 include Gabrielle Roy's *Bonheur d'Occasion* and Hugh MacLennan's *Two Solitudes*. In poetry, Irving Layton's *Here and Now* and Miriam Waddington's *Green World* appear.

Canadian push on Germany resumes

Feb. 8, 1945

FIRST CANADIAN ARMY HQ – The Canadians are attacking again. After three months of relative quiet – during which time their commander, Harry Crerar, was promoted to full general – this army has begun a campaign to clear out Germans west of the Rhine. The attack opened with a barrage by 1,034 guns and bombing that wiped out Goch and Cleve.

A few weeks ago the frozen ground was ideal for rapid troop and tank movement. But now, rain and thawing temperatures favor the Germans. Advancing will be difficult. But the Allies hope within months to meet the Russian Red Army, now 100 kilometres from Berlin, in central Germany.

1st Canadian Army Engineers rebuild a road in Holland during the advance.

The Rocket scores 50 goals in 50 games

Maurice "Rocket" Richard.

March 18, 1945

BOSTON – Maurice "Rocket" Richard, star of the Montreal Canadiens hockey club, has posted a new high watermark for sharpshooters: he's scored 50 goals in 50 games. Richard's 50th goal came in the last game of the season, as Montreal shaded the Boston Bruins 4-2. Boston fans gave Richard a resounding ovation befitting the new champion of the ice palace.

Toe Blake and Teeder Kennedy, Richard's closest rivals in the goal-scoring race, were 21 goals short of the Rocket's amazing 50-goal season. Richard has made it plain that he is a force to be dealt with in the NHL: his 50 goals give him 87 in just over two seasons.

Family allowance cheques in the mail

Feb. 18, 1945

OTTAWA – The first family allowance cheques are in the mail. The monthly grant, paid from the general revenues of the federal government, will help pay for medical and dental services, food, and shelter for all children under 16 attending school. A family whose taxable income is less than $1,200 per year will get 100 percent of the monthly allowance, from $5 for a child under 6 to $8 for a child 13 to 15. Families with higher incomes get a percentage of that amount. The cheque, covering the allowance for all children in the family, will be payable to the mother.

Operation Veritable cracks Siegfried Line

Feb. 21, 1945

GOCH – Operation Veritable, which began on Feb. 8, has ended with Canadian troops capturing the German defence complex, the Siegfried Line. In 1939-40 British troops sang a ditty, "We'll Hang Out Our Washing on the Siegfried Line." It took four years and much blood to make the joke a reality.

Canadians had to push through three lines of anti-tank ditches and entrenched anti-tank guns, mixed with houses turned into strongpoints. It was a simple, brutal, battering attack. Gen. Harry Crerar said there was "no room for manoeuvre and no scope for cleverness." Bad weather ruled out air support for five days in mid-battle. Mud slowed vehicles, including tanks and armored personnel carriers. Regiments lost men advancing, then had to defend the ground with minimal strength. "A" Company, the Essex Scottish, held one position for 36 hours with only 35 fit men and a few wounded.

Forestry Corps cuts trees on the Rhine

March 14, 1945

REICHWALD FOREST, Germany – Canadian Forestry Corps are cutting trees in Germany. Just weeks ago the area was a battlefield, so the trees are riddled with shell splinters. Apart from supplying wood for rail lines, bridges, and barracks, forestry troops have built log booms across rivers to prevent destruction of bridges by German mines floated from upstream.

Canada helps form the United Nations

April 1, 1945

NEW YORK – Canada is one of 50 countries which have pledged to support an international system of deliberatory bodies, functional agencies, and temporary and permanent commissions under the overall title of the United Nations. As the war in Europe appears to be ending, a major conference in San Francisco is planned. Its aim will be to promote international cooperation among sovereign states to promote peace, security, economic development, and fundamental human rights and freedoms.

Canadian overseas army is now united

April 2, 1945

NIJMEGAN – The Canadian army overseas is now united in one theatre. In February, the 1st Canadian Corps began moving from Italy to northwest Europe. They sailed from Leghorn to Marseilles, travelled overland via the Rhone Valley, and took over the Nijmegan sector in mid-March. Today they began fighting northwestward into Holland while 2nd Canadian Corps pushes north. Veterans from Italy are surprised that in Holland electric lights and running water work even in forward areas.

Allies cross the Rhine in strength

March 24, 1945

WESEL, Germany – Crushing Allied forces have crossed the Rhine. Once again, massive air power, amphibious fleets, and thousands of airborne soldiers have turned the German defences. The attack began last night on a front 30 kilometres wide, supported by some 5,500 heavy guns. It proceeded as fast as space on the east bank could be captured to accommodate new arrivals. Allied armies are now expanding their bridgeheads and advancing east. They should link up with Russian armies moving west in a few weeks.

Canadian troops and tanks make advances in Germany at Emmerich.

German artillery destroyed many Allied gliders and transport planes. However, most amphibious assault craft swam the river almost unopposed in six minutes. The first Canadian unit over, the Highland Light Infantry of Canada, crossed at 4:25 a.m. today. Next came the 1st Canadian Parachute Battalion, dropped at 11:30 a.m. as part of the British 6th Airborne Division.

Further Canadian units have been pouring across ever since. With them come an endless stream of weapons – tanks, self-propelled guns, rocket batteries, flame throwers – the whole array of modern, mechanized warfare. To handle this, army engineers assemble prefabricated bridges in a few hours, replacing those blown up by the enemy only days before. German resistance is uneven. One village falls easily, the next may be defended desperately.

Freed Canadian tells of life in a German prisoner-of-war camp

April 26, 1945

SOUTHERN GERMANY – Brig. W.W. (Bill) Southam of Toronto told today of life in a German prisoner-of-war camp, where he spent more than two-and-a-half years. Because of a leg ailment, Southam was left behind a couple of weeks ago when the Germans marched 100 other Canadian officers to a camp further south. He spoke well of his fellow-prisoners, saying "nothing ever got them down," and that they did all the camp work themselves. "If we had been forced to live on (German) rations, it would not have been comfortable, (but) Red Cross parcels came through regularly." Captured in 1942, Southam was liberated by the advancing U.S. 3rd Army.

German U-boat sinks Canadian minesweeper outside of Halifax

Survivors from the sunken HMCS Esquimalt await rescue at sea.

April 16, 1945

HALIFAX – *HMCS Esquimalt*, a minesweeper, was sunk by a German U-boat this morning just outside of Halifax. There were 65 men aboard the *Esquimalt* when the torpedo hit, of whom 39 are dead. The vessel is the eighth Canadian warship lost in home waters to enemy action in this war.

A single torpedo hit *Esquimalt* in her starboard side. The explosion killed several men outright. Then, after the blast, the ship went down so fast there was no time for crew members to send a distress signal and lifeboats could not be launched. Sailors clung to rubber Carley floats until rescued by *HMCS Sarnia* six hours later.

"Boom-bust" cycle tackled by Ottawa

April 12, 1945

OTTAWA – The federal government has released a White Paper on Employment and Income which, if it becomes law, should protect Canadians from devastating economic depressions. Based on the theories of Lord Keynes, the fundamental thrust of the paper is government intervention as a means of smoothing out the "boom-bust" cycle of capitalism. In short, when times are bad the government will invest heavily in the economy to keep things moving and to create jobs. Then, when times improve, it will pay off through taxation the deficits it has incurred.

Hitler dead, German forces give up on all fronts

Dutch civilians celebrate their liberation by the Canadian army.

German officers and troops come in to surrender and dump their arms.

A Dutch welcome for the Stormont, Dundas and Glengarry Highlanders.

May 7, 1945

EUROPE – Nazi dictator Adolf Hitler is dead – he committed suicide in his underground headquarters – and German forces have been giving up on all fronts. The end was in sight in mid-March, when the western Allies crossed the Rhine while on the eastern front Russian troops crushed opponents from the Baltic to the Balkans.

On April 16 the Soviets launched their final offensive, and on April 25 the two fronts began to merge as American and Russian troops met on the Elbe. British and Russian forces greeted one another two days later. The 1st Canadian Parachute Battalion, which penetrated further into Germany than any other Canadian unit, met Russian troops at Wismar on May 4.

The first general surrender came with the capitulation of all enemy forces in northern Italy on May 2. On the same day, German resistance in Berlin ceased after two weeks of desperate, house-to-house fighting. Russian troops control the capital. In quick succession, enemy commanders have been surrendering to their opposite numbers in Holland, Denmark, and throughout Germany itself. German submarines have been ordered to report their positions, hoist black flags, stay on the surface, and surrender to Allied ships.

While Allied fighter and fighter-bomber sorties were flown up to the last minute, major air attacks ceased more than two weeks ago. No. 6 (RCAF) Group lost four aircraft – all through collisions – when they blasted Wangerooge Island on April 25; and Bomber Command's last big raid was the night of April 25-26. Bombers have since been engaged in Operation Exodus (flying freed prisoners of war to Britain) and Operation Manna (dropping food supplies to starving Dutch civilians in Holland).

The Allies face massive problems. Sanitation systems have been shattered. Europe's railway net has been wrecked. Nearly one million German troops remain on foreign soil – in Denmark, France, Holland, Italy, and Norway – and millions of prisoners are in Allied hands. They must be returned to Germany – but Germany itself is in ruins, a country filled with its own prisoners, slave laborers, and refugees. Massive population shifts must be reversed. Civil government has collapsed. Allied armies must administer whole nations, sorting out which former enemies can be trusted to operate while ferreting out war criminals.

Some liberated countries are in bad shape, too. Germans flooded much of Holland to slow advancing Canadians. Centuries of land reclamation have been undone, the soil now tainted with salt water. The western portions of the Soviet Union have been devastated. Some cities changed hands four times, with greater destruction each time.

The fighting has stopped, but for soldiers and civilians alike there is danger everywhere. City rubble must be cleared cautiously, as there are hundreds of unexploded bombs about. Rivers and harbors have been thickly sowed with German and Allied mines, which must be swept away before normal navigation resumes. Even farm fields are often filled with "dud" shells and mines left by retreating armies.

Celebration turns into orgy of destruction

May 8, 1945

HALIFAX – Two people are dead and many shops have been looted and destroyed by fire after naval personnel rioted yesterday on the streets of Halifax. Similar uprisings occurred on a smaller scale in Sydney and Kentville. In Halifax, civil authorities, with the active assistance of the naval administration, have placed an 8 p.m. curfew in effect immediately. It is believed that this will stop the drunken and marauding bands of service personnel from continuing with more of their havoc.

Opinions are varied as to the basis of this madness, but generally it is believed that what began as a victory celebration turned into an orgy of destruction when crowds became intoxicated after storming liquor stores and breweries.

The first instances of trouble were seen two nights ago when a group of sailors burned a streetcar and two police cars. Things quieted down immediately afterward but resumed the following afternoon when crowds of looters began breaking windows on the main thoroughfares. It is expected that damage to local property may run into the millions.

Victory celebrations get out of hand in Halifax and a riot breaks out.

King: 43,500 must fight against Japan

May 18, 1945

EDMONTON – Prime Minister W.L. Mackenzie King announced today that about 43,500 Canadian soldiers will form the Pacific Force for operations against Japan, the last Axis power still in the war. The force will use U.S. equipment and organization already in place. On April 4, King had assured the Commons that any Canadians sent to the Pacific theatre would be volunteers, and last week the army issued a pamphlet advising soldiers how to apply. RCAF squadrons are also being flown home to train for the Pacific.

Western Canadians watching for bombs

May 22, 1945

OTTAWA – Western Canadians were warned today: watch out for Japanese bomb-carrying balloons. The balloons, about nine metres high and made of paper, have been crossing the Pacific and landing on the west coast and on prairie farms. But news of their arrival has been kept secret to avoid giving the Japanese information. So far no one has been hurt by the small bombs the balloons carry. Children on a prairie farm found a balloon and were about to start a bonfire with it when a farmer came up and took the bombs away.

Canadians mark VE-Day

Trafalgar Square, London, is the scene of a happy celebration on VE-Day.

King and St. Laurent broadcast the victory news to Canadians on VE-Day.

May 8, 1945

OTTAWA – Canadians are celebrating VE-Day with bells, bonfires, impromptu parades, tumultuous parties, religious services, and quiet reflective moments. King George has spoken by radio to the Empire/Commonwealth. National leaders also addressed the people. The front page of the *Maple Leaf,* a newspaper published for Canadian troops overseas, has a huge, one-word headline – "KAPUT!"

Among the most subdued celebrants are the soldiers still "in the line." Until three days ago they saw friends maimed and killed. Moreover, there is work to be done, caring for civilian refugees and keeping the forces running smoothly. Most boisterous are those with time to celebrate in rear echelons, Britain, and Canada. In London, celebrants concentrate at Buckingham Palace and Trafalgar Square.

Halifax has been hard hit by celebrations that turned into riots that are still in progress. Many blame civic authorities for poor planning that closed movie houses, leaving servicemen nothing to do but carouse. In Iceland, members of No. 162 (RCAF) Squadron were confined to base and thus kept Canada's name clean while other Allied troops rioted in Reykjavik.

Novel tells of two Canadian solitudes

1945

TORONTO – A cloistered rural Quebec community ruled by its conservative parish priest, and Montreal's wealthy anglophone community: these are the settings of Hugh MacLennan's novel *Two Solitudes*, published this year. Paul Tallard, son of French-Canadian and Irish parents, tries to bridge the gap between these vastly separate worlds when he falls in love and then marries an upper class anglo-Montreal girl. He also plans a novel about his Canadian experience. Sensitive and perceptive about French-English relations, *Two Solitudes* is a great Canadian novel.

RCN played a vital role during the war

June 7, 1945

OTTAWA – The Royal Canadian Navy played a vital role in keeping the Atlantic sea lanes to Britain open, naval headquarters announced last night. From September 1939 to last month, RCN ships escorted 25,343 merchant ships to Britain, plus many on the return run to North America. RCN vessels also protected convoys running between Britain and the Mediterranean as well as ships on the dangerous run to northern Russia. The RCN lost 1,900 men.

U.S. drops an atomic bomb on Japan

An aerial view of Hiroshima showing the complete devastation caused by the explosion of the atomic bomb.

Aug. 6, 1945

HIROSHIMA – One bomb, dropped by an American B-29 and as powerful as 20,000 tons of TNT, has destroyed two-thirds of this city of 330,000, killing nearly 80,000 persons in seconds. A towering cloud of smoke and dust rose 12 kilometres. Last March it took 334 American bombers one night and 1,667 tons of bombs to inflict similar casualties on Tokyo.

The new weapon, an atomic bomb, was a closely guarded secret. It used uranium mined at Canada's Eldorado Mine for its explosive power. The bomb was developed in the United States with help from British and European scientists. A research plant at Chalk River, Ont., was also involved. Many European participants fled their countries during Hitler's rise and assisted because they feared the Nazis might be first with such a weapon.

No one knows where atomic power will lead. Warfare as it is known may disappear. Yesterday's most modern weapon is now as obsolete as a flintlock musket.

King leads Liberals to another victory

June 11, 1945

OTTAWA – When he entered the federal election campaign that ended with tonight's victory, Prime Minister W.L. Mackenzie King told Canadians this would be his last campaign. Certainly the Progressive Conservatives under John Bracken believed this to be the case, banking on anger over King's conscription policy to win over English-speaking Canada, as well as the many French-speaking Canadians against conscription. But, aided by peace in Europe, King won 125 seats tonight, compared to the PCs' 67 and 28 for the CCF.

Canadian troops join the Berlin garrison

July 4, 1945

BERLIN – Canadian troops became part of the Berlin garrison today. A composite battalion joined British forces in the city. The Canadian unit consists of companies drawn from the Loyal Edmonton Regiment, Les Fusiliers Mont-Royal, and the Argyll and Sutherland Highlanders of Canada.

Canada's military presence in Berlin will be both symbolic and brief. More significant is the Canadian Army Occupation Force. It will police and administer a large sector of northwestern Germany.

Tories easy winners in Ontario election

June 6, 1945

TORONTO – Tonight's election proves the Conservatives' unshakable grip on Ontario. Led by Premier George Drew, the Tories took 66 of the 90 seats in the provincial legislature, up from 38. The Co-operative Commonwealth Federation, the pre-election opposition with 32 seats, is now down to six. The Liberals, with only 13 seats, are now the official opposition. Overall, it's a stunning victory for Drew. Now he can rule as he pleases.

Men reprimanded after staging riot

July 7, 1945

ALDERSHOT, England – Canada's reputation got a black eye last night when some 500 of its troops rioted here. About 25 shops were damaged, windows broken, and an amusement arcade wrecked. Maj.-Gen. Dan Spry, commanding the Canadian Repatriation Unit, has reprimanded the men, declaring that they "undermine the good reputation the Canadians had built up on the battlefields."

Morale has been undermined by slow repatriation, delayed because shipping space is needed for the continuing war in Asia.

Pacific War is over: Japan surrenders

Aug. 14, 1945

TOKYO – Stunned by military defeat and devastated by massive air raids, capped by two atomic bombs in four days plus Russia's intervention in the war, Japan has surrendered with minimal conditions. The imperial form of government will remain, and the Japanese home islands will not be partitioned, as happened with Germany after it surrendered.

The Pacific War actually began in 1931 with Japan's intervention in Manchuria. America and European powers only became involved in December 1941. It has been a terribly bloody conflict. Japan alone is estimated to have sustained 1.5 million battle deaths and some 300,000 civilian dead. China's pre-1941 losses are unknown, but they may run as high as four million dead through all causes.

Canadian troops were present at the Hong Kong disaster in December 1941, while RCAF airmen served in Ceylon (1942-45) and Burma (1944-45). Had the war continued into 1946, Canadian troops, airmen, and sailors – all volunteers – would have been present in large numbers.

Last month the government's volunteer policy led to an embarrassing incident involving *HMCS Uganda,* a cruiser serving with the British Pacific Fleet. She was recalled to Esquimalt to ensure that her crew was composed only of men who had volunteered specifically for Pacific service.

Japanese delegation signs the surrender on the U.S. ship Missouri in Tokyo.

Lieutenant last Canadian to die in war?

Aug. 9, 1945

BRITISH PACIFIC FLEET – Lieut. Robert H. Gray, Trail and Nelson, B.C., was killed in action today. Gray enlisted in the Royal Canadian Navy in July 1940, trained as a pilot, and was posted to *HMS Formidable,* a British aircraft carrier.

Last August, Gray took part in air strikes against the German battleship *Tirpitz. Formidable* and other RN ships were sent to the Far East last spring. Gray participated in air strikes in the East China Sea, on Okinawa, and against the Japanese home islands. Early this morning Gray was leading a section that attacked a small Japanese warship in Onagawa Bay (northern Honshu). His Corsair fighter was hit by enemy shells and set on fire. One bomb was shot off its mount.

Trailing flames, Gray pressed home his attack with his remaining bomb, sank the warship, then dived into the water. At no time did he try to bail out. Gray was 28 years old and may be the last Canadian to die in battle in this war.

VJ-Day festivities begin

A group of liberated Canadian and British prisoners in Kowloon, China.

Lt.-Cmdr. Fred Day greets Canadian prisoners of war in Hong Kong.

Aug. 19, 1945

OTTAWA – Allied leaders have taken to the radio again to express thanksgiving at Japan's surrender. In a special message to the forces, Prime Minister W.L. Mackenzie King thanked Canadian service personnel for everything they had endured and achieved.

In Britain, the happy crowds were even greater than those on VE-Day. Hundreds of Canadian servicemen congregated at Trafalgar Square, the west side of which is occupied by Canada House. A few fully-clothed soldiers took a dip in the fountains.

From coast to coast, Canadians cut loose with celebrations marking VJ-Day. The wildest scenes were in Sudbury, where about 3,000 people looted liquor stores, rioted, and smashed windows. Damage was estimated at $40,000, and 28 people were arrested. Halifax, scene of VE-Day riots, was more orderly this time.

Ottawa schoolchildren paraded in the streets, beating on pails and washbuckets. An impromptu conga line snaked its way down Toronto's Yonge Street. A Winnipeg celebrant drove through the streets in a 1925 automobile fitted with an ear-splitting steamboat whistle. In Quebec, VJ-Day was tame compared to the previous day, when the liner *Pasteur* arrived with 23,000 Canadian veterans. The ship was greeted by cheering crowds and a 20-gun salute. The cease-fire took effect on Aug. 15.

CANADA COMES OF AGE
1945-1989

Small ZEEP reactor said to be working

Sept. 5, 1945

CHALK RIVER, Ont. – ZEEP "went critical" today, say reliable sources. If the reports are true, it will be the first time an atomic reactor outside the United States has produced energy by nuclear fission. ZEEP, Zero Energy Experimental Pile, is a small reactor built to test design details for larger power plants. It is kept behind a veil of secrecy at the nuclear laboratories established last year here, on the Ottawa River north of Pembroke.

Reports say Soviet is trying to defect

Sept. 7, 1945

OTTAWA – A man claiming to be a Soviet embassy employee is reportedly trying to defect to Canada. Officials are tight-lipped, but the RCMP are apparently questioning a man named Igor Gouzenko. He has with him documents he claims implicate Canadian government employees in passing atomic secrets to the Soviets. Gouzenko said he left the embassy on Sept. 5 and spent two days trying to convince authorities of his sincerity.

Japanese Canadians to be deported

Dec. 15, 1945

OTTAWA – Last August, Japan surrendered to the Allies, ending the Second World War. Today, four months later, the Liberal government used the War Measures Act to pass three orders-in-council enabling Canada to deport Japanese nationals as well as native-born or naturalized Canadians of Japanese descent. The war may be over, but for Japanese Canadians, an old battle remains to be fought here – the battle for acceptance.

Embittered by their forced relocation and seizure of their property, toward the end of the war 10,000 Japanese Canadians, mostly the older generation and their dependants, requested repatriation to Japan. More than half of these have since asked to remain instead, but to no avail. Ottawa is intent on deporting as many Japanese Canadians as possible, the final solution to what it has long perceived as an "Oriental problem."

King, Truman, Attlee agree to share atomic energy secrets

Dec. 11, 1945

WASHINGTON, D.C. – The leaders of the world's three atomic powers today say they will share their knowledge, but only if there are adequate safeguards against its use in war. Canadian Prime Minister W.L. Mackenzie King, U.S. President Harry Truman, and British Prime Minister Clement Attlee say the dangers of the spread of atomic knowledge are profound.

"Faced with the terrible realities of the application of science to destruction, every nation will realize more urgently than before the overwhelming need to maintain the rule of law among nations and to banish the scourge of war from the earth." They pleaded with other countries to strongly support the United Nations organization.

Clement Attlee, Harry Truman, and W.L.M. King meet at the White House.

Capt. S.F. Banfill, prisoner since 1941, meets his son for the first time.

This model wears a lime-green spun rayon dress suggested as part of a civilian wardrobe to be purchased with the $100 clothing allowance being given to members of the CWAC.

Medicine shortage fatal for 200 PoWs

Sept. 7, 1945

MANILA – More than 200 Canadians died in Hong Kong prison camps because of a shortage of medicine, returning prisoners said here today. The Japanese captured the Canadians when Hong Kong fell on Christmas Day, 1941. The 33 men who arrived here today make a total of 300 Canadians recovered from Hong Kong. The 33 were in good spirits, and only a few were sick. They said Japanese treatment of the prisoners improved near the end of the war. The 1,985 Canadians reached Hong Kong Nov. 16, 1941. When it was attacked Dec. 7, the Canadians, inexperienced and overwhelmed by numbers and gunpower, had little chance. The PoWs crave home-cooked meals, beer, and ice cream.

Wartime brings racial intolerance to the surface

Japanese community not what it once was

1945

CANADA – All material manifestations of efforts by Canada's Japanese population to settle and assimilate in this country were wiped out by one single but far-reaching event, one over which they had no control – Japan's bombing of Pearl Harbor on Dec. 7, 1941.

From that day on, racial intolerance of Japanese Canadians has had its *raison d'être*. They lost their property and their freedom. Moved to internment camps, men, women, and children of Japanese origin now live dispersed throughout the Canadian interior. And there they must assimilate, in new and unfamiliar surroundings, if they are to remain in Canada. Have they the will to do so? Many of the second generation of immigrants, the *Nisei*, are more Canadian than Japanese. By 1941, the *Nisei* numbered 60 percent of all Japanese Canadians. Educated in Canadian schools, most of them have rejected traditional Japanese values. Assimilation depends not on their acceptance of Canada – already a *fait accompli* – but on Canada's acceptance of them.

Relocation in '42 shattered many dreams

Keiko Orida (front row, fifth from left) with her Grade 8 classmates.

TORONTO – I was born in B.C. on May 9, 1931, and was 10 when we heard on the radio that Japan had attacked Pearl Harbor. My dad was very upset by what he read in Japanese-language newspapers, wondering if we would be uprooted. I didn't understand what it meant, but I was frightened. I was the oldest of five kids and one of the two Japanese students at Aldergrove Public School in B.C.

In the fall of 1942, we received notice we would have to leave. Our house was new, big, quite nice and standing on 15 acres. My father, who worked in a pulp and paper mill, had dreamed of setting up a strawberry farm. We packed the maximum we were allowed, two suitcases each, or 150 pounds. My dad said we would be coming back, so he hid some valuables, including our Japanese festival dolls, in the attic. We never saw them again.

My dad got work as a laborer for the CPR, working outside and living in barracks except on weekends. He wasn't any good at cooking his own meals, got sick and complained a lot about stomach pains. He died of cancer when I was 13, and with the little assistance my mom got we lived in poverty. She remarried, but my stepdad was older and could only work a bit. Because we were poor, I had to turn down a McGill scholarship. My dream of becoming a teacher was shattered.

– *Keiko Orida Yamashita*

Woman recalls life in "traumatic era"

RICHMOND, B.C. – A portion of Canada's history which is considered by some as shameful is the wartime relocation of the Japanese from the B.C. coast to the interior. I would like to present a different perspective, the impressions of a frightened 14-year-old. From early memories, the Japanese had been classmates and friends. After Pearl Harbor, there was a marked change of attitude in many Japanese. Remarks such as "We'll soon be running things" were alarming. This, with news that Japanese subs had been seen off the coast, left many of us with feelings of dread. Many of us who lived through this traumatic era consider the relocation justified, and that no compensation should have been considered.

– *Geraldine Wray*

Japanese men en route to interior.

Woman wonders what became of friend

VANCOUVER – When Japan bombed Pearl Harbor, I was a 16-year-old student at Grandview High School of Commerce. The only Japanese in the class was Molly, a great favorite, full of fun and always willing to help a slower student. Near the end of term, Molly and her family were interned. She could still come to classes, but had to return to camp after school. All her vivaciousness disappeared. Two girls who had been very friendly with Molly were the first to say she deserved to be put away. What she was guilty of, I do not know. I often wonder if she stayed in Canada. If so, I hope she was compensated for the hurt she suffered.

– *Norma Price*

Japanese men await transportation to camps in B.C. interior or the prairies.

1946

Toronto, Jan. 29. Walter "Babe" Pratt of the Toronto Maple Leafs is expelled from the NHL for gambling on hockey games.

Philadelphia, Feb. 14. An "electronic brain," or computer, is operating at the University of Pennsylvania.

Ottawa, Feb. 15. PM King appoints a royal commission to investigate leakages of secret information to unauthorized persons, and the RCMP arrest people suspected of being part of a Soviet spy ring.

Montreal, April 9. Montreal Canadiens defeat Boston Bruins four games to one to win the Stanley Cup.

Northwest Territories, May 5. The Canadian government completes Exercise Musk-ox, a test of various equipment over a 4,830-kilometre roadless terrain.

Ontario, Sept. 25. The Trades and Labour Congress rejects a resolution to bar communists from union positions.

Ottawa, Oct. 29. James S. Benning is sentenced to five years in jail for communicating secrets to the U.S.S.R. while he was a government official.

Ottawa, Nov. 11. Married women are being released from jobs in the civil service and the CBC on the grounds they were employed during the war on a temporary basis.

Toronto, Nov. 30. Toronto Argonauts defeat Winnipeg Blue Bombers 28-6 for the Grey Cup.

Ottawa, Dec. 12. The wartime ministries for land, naval, and air forces are discontinued, and a unified Department of National Defence is created under Brooke Claxton.

Ottawa. The government creates the Atomic Energy Control Board to control the development of nuclear energy in Canada.

Ottawa. The government disbands the women's military services.

Regina. Saskatchewan's CCF government introduces the Swift Current Regional Health Plan to provide public health services for 53,000 people on an experimental basis.

Toronto. Dora Mavor Moore founds the New Play Society to develop Canadian theatre talent by producing plays.

Haiti. The famous Canadian schooner *Bluenose* strikes a reef off Haiti and is wrecked.

Report names Soviet spies in Canada

March 29, 1946

OTTAWA – Members of the GRU, the Russian army intelligence organization, are carrying on spy operations in this country, it was disclosed today in the third interim report of the Royal Commission on Espionage. The report was tabled in the Commons by Prime Minister W.L. Mackenzie King. It named the last five of the original 13 men and two women detained under the secret order-in-council of last October. The commission still has to hear some of these witnesses. A few have been named by other witnesses, and some others in documents obtained from defecting Soviet cipher clerk Igor Gouzenko. Names in today's report were all mentioned in the espionage hearing of Montreal MP Fred Rose.

Suspected spy, Dr. Raymond Boyer.

J. Scott Benning, another accused.

Here come the war brides – all 1,046

Leading WREN Kerr interviews British wives of Canadian sailors in London.

March 3, 1946

HALIFAX – As the band struck up *Here Comes the Bride,* the *Aquitania* steamed into harbor carrying 1,046 wives of Canadian soldiers. The women, along with 100 children, made up one of three groups to arrive the last few days. On Friday, the *Scythia* brought 800 wives and children into port. The *Letitia* will dock tomorrow with another 800. Many of the women will then meet their husbands at various points across the country.

An estimated one in five bachelor soldiers and airmen married overseas. For the past several months, their brides and young children have been arriving in Halifax. To help the women adjust to life in a new country, the federal government has set up the Canadian Wives' Bureau in London, England. The bureau provides literature and advice to women about to embark for Canada. Women's organizations in this country are also doing their part to help the brides adapt. Many of the women, used to shortages and rationing at home, were amazed to find chocolate and nylon stockings available on ship.

Ford workers told to pay their dues

Jan. 29, 1946

TORONTO – Ford workers at Windsor today come under a unique scheme that may have wide-ranging implications. The United Auto Workers is not allowed to impose union membership on all eligible employees. But the union will receive dues from all, whether or not they are members.

In his binding decision in the arbitration of the Windsor labor dispute, Justice Ivan Rand of the Supreme Court of Canada said even those who choose not to be UAW members must pay union dues and the company must collect their money. He refused a union demand that a "closed shop" be imposed on the Ford plant. But he accepted union arguments that it should get something from all those who benefit from its action. "I doubt if any circumstance provokes more resentment in a plant than this sharing of the fruits of unionist work and courage by the non-member."

Rand's arbitration came after a strike by Ford's 10,000 unionized workers late last year, provoked by the issues the Rand compromise has settled. Wage issues remain outstanding. Neither the union nor the company would comment until they studied the arbitrator's report.

Rose guilty of passing secrets to Soviets

Fred Rose, member of Parliament, enters court at his trial on charges of spying for the U.S.S.R.

June 20, 1946

MONTREAL – Fred Rose, a member of Parliament for almost three years, was sentenced today to six years in prison for having conspired to pass wartime secrets to the Soviet Union. The Polish-born Rose, 39, was the Labour Progressive party's only MP. He was found guilty last Saturday by a 12-man jury, but maintained his innocence even after being sent to jail for one year less than the maximum by Mr. Justice Wilfrid Lazure. His Lordship rebuked the MP for Montreal-Cartier: "You sacrificed the interests and security of Canada to give your loyalty to a foreign country." A key witness was Igor Gouzenko, a defector from the Soviet embassy.

Violence erupts on the Stelco picket line

Placard-bearing picketers parade in Hamilton during the Stelco strike.

July 16, 1946

HAMILTON – Violence broke out on the Stelco picket line today, 48 hours after the company's 2,700 employees walked out on their first strike. The cause? Management's decision to bring in strikebreakers in an attempt to keep the plant running. It all started when strikebreakers, their faces blackened like commandos, made a mad dash through the pickets to the front gate. Once inside, they began clearing the railway tracks of lumber placed there by the strikers to keep Stelco from shipping out steel.

Then, says striker Frank Malloy, "everything broke loose. I saw club-wielding company men leap from the flat cars and start slugging the strikers. I estimate some 300 poured off the flat cars." Some of these were armed with pick handles. Others had chains and pipes.

The ensuing melee was horrific. Scores of men on both sides were injured. But the intensity of the battle isn't surprising, given what's at stake. For Stelco, giving in to the workers would mean recognizing union power and, moreover, raising wages and cutting the work week from 48 to 40 hours. For the union, its very existence is on the line, as is the attempt by the workers to gain some degree of power and prestige in their dealings with management at the steel plant.

Tulips are a Dutch treat

Dutch tulips on Parliament Hill in Ottawa are a beautiful thank-you gift.

Spring 1946

OTTAWA – The core of the nation's capital has exploded into bloom with thousands of tulips, the Dutch royal family's way of saying thank you to all Canadians.

When the Germans invaded the Netherlands in May 1940, the royal family went into exile in London with Princess Juliana going on to Ottawa. On Jan. 19, 1943, the princess gave birth in the Ottawa Civic Hospital to her third daughter, Margriet. The 10,000 tulip bulbs donated to the city are an expression of Juliana's gratitude to this country for its hospitality to her family during the wartime years of exile. Furthermore, court officials say, the royal family and the tulip producers of Holland intend to continue to send Ottawa 25,000 bulbs a year so that the tulip festival will bloom as an annual reminder.

Canada buys part of Alaska Highway

April 3, 1946

OTTAWA – Canada paid the United States $108 million today for the 1,966-kilometre portion of the Alaska Highway between Dawson Creek, B.C., and the Alaska border. Construction began in 1942 on the road which links Dawson Creek with Fairbanks, Alaska. It was an eight-month project involving 11,000 soldiers and 16,000 civilians from both countries. Originally built for military purposes in the event of a Japanese invasion, the portion of the road in this country will now be turned over to the Canadian army.

The purchase price doesn't cover the highway construction itself, but is for airstrips, buildings, and other services such as telephones. The road, which has a gravel surface, spans five mountain ranges.

Act makes citizens "Canadians first"

May 14, 1946

OTTAWA – Citizens of Canada will soon be Canadians first, rather than British subjects first as is now the case. The passing of the Canadian Citizenship Act today means that a Canadian citizen is no longer classified as a Briton born elsewhere. Instead it identifies a Canadian as a member of an independent and sovereign state, rather than a colony.

Another change comes to the status of women who gained citizenship by marrying Canadians. Under the exisiting law, such women could lose their Canadian citizenship if their marriages broke up. Under the new law, this will no longer happen. Once you are a citizen, you are a citizen – period.

The new act comes into effect on Jan. 1 of next year.

Public health care gaining acceptance

Pregnant women get free medicals

Sept. 24, 1946

TORONTO – The women of Ontario will be receiving a letter from Health Minister Russell Kelly inviting those who are pregnant to have a free medical examination, compliments of the provincial government. It is hoped this move will reduce the number of stillbirths and infant deaths. The minister's letter urges Ontario women to put aside modesty – for the sake of their child and themselves – and consult a doctor.

Hospital expenses on the house in Sask.

Sept. 3, 1946

REGINA – Effective Jan. 1, 1947, residents of Saskatchewan will no longer pay their own hospital expenses. Premier Tommy Douglas explained the Saskatchewan Hospitalization Plan as only that, and not an insurance scheme.

A fee of $5 per person, with a limit of $30 per family, will be collected beginning Oct. 1. Payments may be made in installments. Those who pay by Dec. 31 will receive a hospital service card. After that, people will still pay doctor bills and other medical expenses, but the cost of a hospital stay will be paid from this fund, which will include government money.

The hospitalization plan is only one of the recommendations of the Saskatchewan Health Services Survey Commission set up in 1944 under Dr. Henry Sigerist of Johns Hopkins University in Baltimore. Other recommendations which have already been put in place provide for free medical and dental care and drugs for pensioners, and the provision for a college of medicine to be built in the future at the University of Saskatchewan.

Robinson destined for place in history

Jackie Robinson: struggle ahead.

Spring 1946

MONTREAL – Jackie Robinson, now playing for Montreal in the Brooklyn Dodgers' farm team in the International League, appears destined for promotion – and a place in history as the first black player in the modern-day major leagues. Robinson was approached last fall by Branch Rickey, the president and general manager of the Dodgers determined to challenge the unwritten ban on black players. Rickey warned Robinson a long, ugly struggle lay ahead, in which a wife's support could be critical. On Feb. 10, Robinson married his girlfriend Rachel.

Smallwood shocks convention delegates

Oct. 28, 1946

ST. JOHN'S, Nfld. – The National Convention meeting here since Sept. 11 "to make recommendations to His Majesty's government as to possible forms of future government to be put before the (Newfoundland) people at a national referendum" was startled today when Joseph R. Smallwood proposed that Newfoundland send representatives to Ottawa to find out what terms and conditions could be expected in the event of the colony joining Canada.

It is not expected that the motion will pass, because only 10 to 15 members support Confederation. Most delegates want the British government to fulfil its promise of 1934 and return the system of responsible government.

Ottawa launches new savings bonds

Oct. 14, 1946

OTTAWA – The success of Victory Bonds is one legacy of the recent war. And so, not wanting to give up a good thing, the federal government has launched a peacetime version, called Canada Savings Bonds. Offered in denominations of $50, $100 and $500, the CSBs offer an interest rate of 2.75 percent. Apparently sales are going well, indicating that the public is more than happy to loan the government money, as long as they can eventually get it back with interest.

A demonstration is staged by Dominion Textile strikers in Montreal.

The Canadian delegation at the Paris peace talks held at the Palais du Luxembourg. From left to right: Norman Robertson, William Lyon Mackenzie King, Brooke Claxton, and A.D.P. Heeney.

Wartime wage, salary controls end

Nov. 30, 1946

OTTAWA – One of the last vestiges of wartime will disappear at midnight tonight, when the government relinquishes its control of wages and salaries. The news came this evening from Prime Minister William Lyon Mackenzie King, in Quebec at a testimonial dinner for the minister of justice and external affairs, Louis St. Laurent. In a prepared statement, King said that "with the gradual increase in production the need for limitations on the expansion of purchasing power has decreased. ... It was only a matter of time before there would no longer be a need for wage and salary control in the battle against inflation. The government believes that time has now arrived."

However, says King, any outstanding cases still before the War Labour Boards (which regulated wages) will be heard, and heard quickly. After that, the wartime control of wages will be a thing of the past.

Those on the union side of labor will be greatly relieved to hear this news. It will allow them to go after aggressive wage hikes, in order to make up for the years of low raises. But company managers who will pay for these increases aren't likely to be rejoicing tonight.

Former PMs observe King's actions.

Toronto sells last 25 horses used for removing garbage

Dec. 4, 1946

TORONTO – The last 25 horses in the service of the city have been sold. Since 1888, when horses were first used in the collection of ashes and dust, they have been part of the street cleaning department. Housed in their own stables, they were cared for by a full-time veterinary surgeon. Six smiths kept them in shoes, with each animal receiving a new pair once a month.

The Clydesdales were purchased from Ontario farms, usually when the animals were around five to seven years. Typically, a horse spent nine years on the streets, although some were still working at 20. In 1929, the peak year, more than 400 horses were at work, with an additional 200 privately-owned animals used for winter snow removal. In the Great War, 115 of the city's horses went to France with the Royal Canadian Artillery.

In the early days, two-wheel horse-drawn dumpcarts were used to remove ashes and garbage. These were replaced by dump wagons, and then by trailers big enough to hold the waste of six yards. Drawn by horses, they were left at pick-up points and hauled to dumps and incinerators by tractor. Horse-drawn vehicles have now given way to self-loading sanitation vehicles.

Canadian war veterans back on campus

Demobilized army personnel await interviews with rehabilitation counsellors.

Nov. 25, 1946

OTTAWA – A total of 35,000 veterans are now enrolled at 29 universities in Canada, surpassing figures for the entire university enrolment in this country before the outbreak of the Second World War. In announcing the figures, the department of veterans affairs said by next year there will be 40,000 veterans on campuses as more finish their matriculation and become eligible for university entrance. The breakdown includes 16,000 veterans in their freshman year, 12,000 second-year students, 4,000 third-year, 2,000 fourth-year, and 1,000 post-graduate students.

With 9,700 veterans enrolled, the University of Toronto led the way. The University of British Columbia had the next highest veteran enrolment with 4,700, followed by McGill University at Montreal with 3,200, the University of Manitoba at Winnipeg with 2,900, and Saskatoon's University of Saskatchewan with 2,400. Veterans Minister Ian Mackenzie praised the universities for adjusting to provide the service men and women with the opportunity to resume their education. Of the Second World War veterans returning to class, about 2,000 are women. During the height of the war in 1942, there were only 24 veterans studying at Canadian universities.

Ontario to legalize liquor by the glass

Dec. 5, 1946

TORONTO – After 30 years, it will soon be legal to buy liquor by the glass in Ontario again. So says Premier George Drew, who is introducing the change Jan. 1. As strange as it seems, Drew says he's making the change to cut alcohol consumption, primarily by tourists who, having no place to buy a drink by the glass, buy a bottle instead. In addition, the government will be taking over the retailing of beer from the breweries. It will be sold from provincial stores.

The city of Halifax, Nova Scotia, as viewed from Citadel Hill.

1947

Ottawa, Jan. 30. The Commons expels communist Fred Rose, sentenced to six years in prison on spying charges.

Toronto, Feb. 19. Bell Telephone Co. gives one of the first public demonstrations of car telephones.

Ottawa, March 4. The government says it will establish nine Arctic weather stations.

Ottawa, April 1. The government passes the National Wildlife Act, establishing a week each year to promote the conservation of wildlife and natural resources.

Ottawa, April 15. A government spokesman says cabinet has made Soviet defector Igor Gouzenko a British subject.

Toronto, April 17. The Toronto Board of Education grants maternity leave and service benefits to its 50 married women teachers.

Toronto, April 19. Toronto Maple Leafs beat Montreal Canadiens four games to two to win the Stanley Cup.

Quebec, April 25. The legislature passes a motion protesting the underrepresentation of French-Canadians in the federal civil service.

Toronto, Nov. 29. Toronto Argonauts beat Winnipeg Blue Bombers 10-9 to win the Grey Cup.

Paris, Dec. 1. Gabrielle Roy wins the *Prix Fémina* for *Bonheur d'Occasion*. She's the first Canadian to win a major French literary award.

Kamloops, B.C., Dec. 8. A royal commission opens to hear Japanese Canadian claims that Ottawa gave them inadequate compensation for land it appropriated during the war.

Ottawa, Dec. 12. The government passes the Gold Mining Assistance Act, allowing for federal subsidies for gold mining companies.

Sable Island. In an effort to prevent shipwrecks, Ottawa installs a radio beacon off Sable Island, the Graveyard of the Atlantic, and ships begin carrying radar and sonar.

Alberta. Nemiskan National Park, an antelope preserve, is abolished and the land returned to the Alberta government. The antelope preservation plan has had some success.

Newfoundland. U.S. naval airplanes flying out of their base at Argentia are regularly using whales as training targets.

Japanese won't be deported after all

Jan. 24, 1947

OTTAWA – The Liberal government today revoked the 1945 orders-in-council permitting the deportation of Japanese Canadians, despite vehement opposition by MPs from British Columbia. While Japanese Canadians and white liberal-minded activists alike consider revocation of the arbitrary orders a moral victory, a larger hurdle still remains to be conquered.

The controversial exclusion order restricting Japanese Canadians from changing place of residence without a permit remains in effect, and they are still prohibited from fishing off B.C.'s coast. In 1941, 90 percent of Canada's Japanese lived there. Now, only 33 percent do.

Chinese immigrants are welcome again

Jan. 27, 1947

OTTAWA – The Chinese Immigration Act, which has restricted the entry of Chinese into Canada for 24 years, will be repealed in the next session of Parliament. Chinese Canadians welcomed the announcement by Prime Minister W.L. Mackenzie King and said that now wives and children can join husbands and fathers already in Canada. Since 1923 only students, merchants and diplomats have been allowed into Canada from China.

Child protests the rising cost of chocolate bars in Canada.

Oil's well that ends well

At Birth of New Alberta Oil Field

IMPERIAL LEDUC No. 1 WELL—Discovery for a second major Alberta oil field, blowing out its huge billow of burning oil and heavy smoke when the well was completed as a big producer last week. —Photo by H. Pollard, Calgary

Page from The Western Examiner announcing the Imperial Leduc No. 1 Well.

Feb. 13, 1947

LEDUC, Alta. – At 4 o'clock this afternoon, Mines Minister Nathan E. Tanner turned the valve which ushered in an oil strike of unusual promise. A crowd of 500 cheered as a giant smoke ring rose into the air before oil began to flow.

Officials of Imperial Oil admitted they were taking a gamble by inviting provincial officials and the media to the "spudding in" of the new well. A drill crew led by Vernon "Dry Hole" Hunter in November of last year brought in an earlier well in this district, but geologists first believed it was an anomaly. Subsequent examination of the drill logs down to the 1,520-metre level, however, assured them that this time Hunter's nickname did not apply. Observers were convinced they had witnessed the opening of a major petroleum find.

Petroleum unearthed in Alberta tar sands

Jan. 11, 1947

EDMONTON – Petroleum deposits of global significance have been found beneath the banks of the Athabasca River, 32 kilometres north of Fort McMurray. Preliminary surveys reveal that the area may have a productive capacity of up to 864,500 barrels per hectare.

The deposits are of bitumen and are located in sand which, in some of the holes, is 17 metres thick. The discovery is a result of recent diamond drilling over a five-square-kilometre area in the great tar sands deposits, and was carried out by Abasands Ltd. The announcement was made by oil authority Dr. G.S. Hume through the Department of Mines and Resources. The details of the discovery will be explained at a meeting of the Canadian Institute of Mining and Metallurgy to be held in Ottawa on Jan. 22.

Indian speaks mind for joint committee

April 21, 1947

OTTAWA – For the first time in Canadian history, a parliamentary committee has consulted Indian leaders for their views on Indian policies. Teddy Yellow Fly, a 49-year-old Blackfoot band councillor from Gleichen, Alta., spoke today to the parliamentary committee investigating Indian administration, criticizing its excessive "regimentation." A joint committee of the House of Commons and the Senate is reviewing possible amendments to the Indian Act, the legislative act that governs all aspects of Indian administration in Canada.

Blackfoot Indian Teddy Yellow Fly.

Public meeting first in council's history

April 15, 1947

NORTHWEST TERRITORIES – The Northwest Territories council met here today publicly for the first time since its creation in 1905. The appointed council, which governs the Territories for the federal government, is chaired by Dr. Hugh Keenlyside, N.W.T. commissioner and deputy mines and resources minister. Keenlyside has a new orientation. The federal government and not fur traders and Christian missionaries will be responsible for health and education in the N.W.T. It will even deal with such issues as: should beer be sold 24 hours a day?

Barbara Ann skates to a world title

Feb. 16, 1947

STOCKHOLM – Barbara Ann Scott of Ottawa soared to victory tonight in the world figure skating championships. Capping a dream of 11 years, the 18-year-old beauty won both the difficult compulsory school figures and the colorful free-skating competition, pirouetting to triumph over 21 of the top women skaters from seven countries.

The 15,000 spectators have been treated over the past three days to an exhibition of skating unparalleled since the "Norwegian Doll," Sonje Henie, flashed on the scene in 1936. Also engulfed in the cheering throng tonight was Barbara Ann's mother, Mrs. Clyde Scott, widow of a soldier, who has encouraged her daughter since the child first put on skates at age seven.

Barbara Ann Scott makes a spectacular stag jump during a performance.

Welcome mat put out for Jewish orphans

May 2, 1947

OTTAWA – The federal Liberal government announced today that in conjunction with a broadening of official immigration policy, Canada will provide sanctuary for 1,000 orphaned Jewish children from Europe. The irony of this decision cannot be missed.

The children are but a few of the sons and daughters of countless European Jews slaughtered by the Nazis in Polish and German death camps. Following Hitler's rise to power, many Jews, fearing a regime that unabashedly called for their extermination, petitioned Canada for permission to immigrate. This permission was denied them.

In fact, like most western countries, Canada through its official policy displayed absolutely no sympathy for the plight of Europe's Jews. So to some observers here today's decision begs an important question: is it not too little too late?

Leeward of the Island, by Paul-Emile Borduas.

12,188 cases of VD reported in Ontario

June 15, 1947

TORONTO – Ontario reported 12,188 cases of venereal disease last year, with even young children being infected, the Canadian Health Officers' Association learned at its meeting here today. The group was told that this total included 4,834 cases of syphilis, which can be even more deadly than polio. Even children six years old and younger were found with VD, and in one case the parents were not infected while a child was. Common bathing is one theory on the infection's source.

Heart attack claims former PM Bennett

June 26, 1947

DORKING, England – Richard B. Bennett, prime minister of Canada from 1930 to 1935, has died of a heart attack in his bath here. He was 77. Created Viscount Bennett of Mickleham in 1941, Bennett had the misfortune to become head of a Conservative government at the onset of the Great Depression. His attempts to boost the sagging economy didn't help much, and he lost power after his first term. Afterwards, Bennett moved here. ▷

NRX reactor operating

Worker dons protective footwear.

July 22, 1947

CHALK RIVER, Ont. – Canada's first large nuclear reactor, called NRX, went into operation at the research plant here today. Currently the world's most powerful reactor, NRX is just 2.4 metres in diameter and stands three metres high, but operates at a power above 10 million watts. It has the greatest density of neutrons of all known natural uranium reactors. Natural uranium rods are inside aluminum tubes, which in turn go into an aluminum tank containing heavy water. The heavy water slows down the speed of neutrons released during fission, which is critical because maintaining a chain reaction is not possible with fast neutrons.

Arsonist gangs threatening Doukhobors

Aug. 21, 1947

VANCOUVER – Night raiders are burning homes and public buildings in Doukhobor communities in the interior. One gang of arsonists is said to be led by a nude woman. The raids are believed to be the work of the radical Sons of Freedom sect, which has broken away from the main Doukhobor community. They are demanding orthodox Doukhobors join the sect. If they do not, their homes, farms, and sawmills will be burned down.

Orthodox Doukhobors await a move after being burned out by Sons of Freedom.

Miss Canada third in American pageant

Sept. 7, 1947

ATLANTIC CITY – Toronto's Margaret Marshall, crowned Miss Canada earlier this year, has truly arrived. The blue-eyed and honey-blonde beauty captured the third place today at the Miss America pageant, finishing behind Miss Memphis and Miss Minnesota. After the contest, Marshall came to her senses: "I'd so much rather be Miss Canada," she admitted.

Blind eligible to collect pensions at 21

Young Progressive Conservative Diefenbaker speaks on the pension issue.

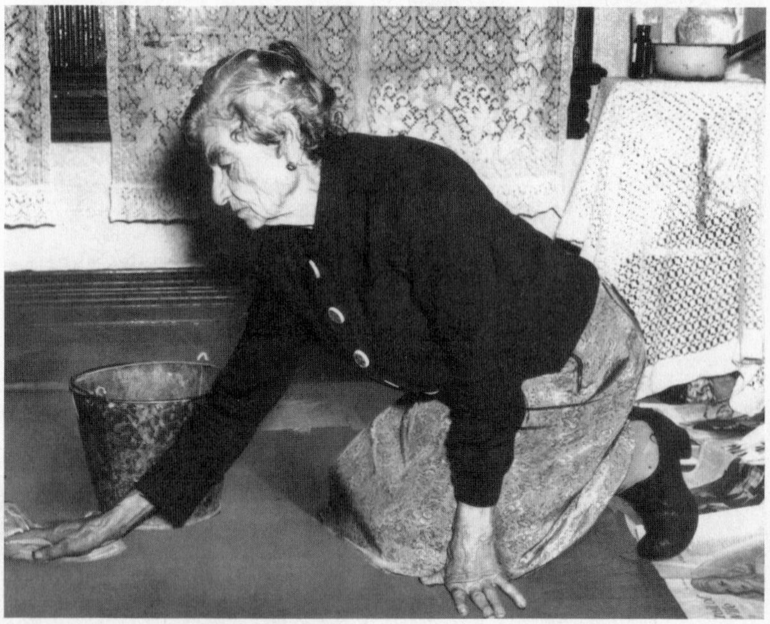

This old age pensioner scrubs floors to supplement her income.

July 1, 1947

OTTAWA – In mid-June, the Liberal government introduced a bill designed to adjust and increase pension payments for Canadians. Today, one of the new steps came into force: blind Canadians are now eligible to collect pensions from the age of 21 instead of 40. But while this move toward liberalizing social security is being widely applauded, important changes affecting the majority of Canada's elderly are still under debate.

For many of Canada's senior citizens, life is no bed of roses. Many are forced by necessity to continue working well past the accepted age of retirement. Only those 70 and over qualify for pensions, but of an estimated 500,000 in that age bracket only 207,000 actually collect. An old age pension pays a maximum $28 per month, and because other earnings render them ineligible for state aid, many must either remain in the workforce or face impoverishment. To help rectify this, the new bill proposes an increase, to $32.75 per month, and, more importantly, provides seniors with a wider margin of acceptable income.

Canada doubles DP quota to 20,000

Oct. 6, 1947

OTTAWA – Canada's doubled its quota of displaced people from Europe. In a statement today, the government said this country will accept 20,000 people, instead of the 10,000 originally planned. The increase follows recent visits of Canadian cabinet ministers to Europe. They said they found many people in Austrian and German displaced persons' camps who would be suitable Canadian settlers.

The Labor Department is working to select immigrants. So far, about 6,000 applications have been approved. The new quota is contingent on international talks that may raise further Canada's commitment. The government is not saying what numbers might be reached.

An ambassador greets Dutch immigrants to Canada at Montreal.

Terms of union cause for debate in Nfld.

Nov. 6, 1947

ST. JOHN'S, Nfld. – The National Convention was officially handed Ottawa's terms of union today, and it is expected they will create a sensation in the colony. It will be recalled that Joseph R. Smallwood's motion of October 1946 to send a delegation to Ottawa was soundly defeated. But early in the New Year he shrewdly managed to have the proposal added as an amendment to R.B. Job's motion to investigate union with the United States. Another part of that motion called for a delegation to go to London and find out what assistance Newfoundland could expect from Britain.

As Smallwood anticipated, the Commission of Government declared the U.S. option lay outside the convention's terms of reference. Then the delegation to London was bluntly told an independent Newfoundland could expect no assistance from Britain. On the other hand, the delegation – including Smallwood – to Ottawa was given every indication that Confederation with Canada would be economically advantageous to Newfoundland.

Louis St. Laurent meets F.G. Bradley of Newfoundland to discuss union.

King: marriage not out of the question

Canada's most eligible bachelor?

Oct. 22, 1947

OTTAWA – Canada's bachelor Prime Minister W.L. Mackenzie King still has hopes of getting married. He told a convention of the National Federation of Liberal women tonight: "Now my good friend (Veterans Minister Ian Mackenzie) has plunged into the matrimonial lake, I'm left all alone ... When I saw a lady prepared to take chances on him, it gave me hopes."

Canadian novelists deliver the goods

1947

CANADA – Dealing with death, poverty, and alcoholism, and ranging from the endless Saskatchewan prairie to infernal Mexico to the cramped slums of depression Montreal, Canadian novels published this year have little in common except a tendency to focus on the dark side of human existence.

Gabrielle Roy's brilliant novel *Bonheur d'occasion* (1945) has just appeared in an English translation entitled *The Tin Flute*. Roy is a quiet literary revolutionary – her novel, portraying Montreal's poor at the end of the Great Depression, sharply questions the economic system that, in the words of one character, "means the bread line ... a third of the population on relief."

Shift the camera 180 degrees, and the reader is shocked by Malcolm Lowry's masterpiece *Under the Volcano*. Cinematic in technique, metaphorical, metaphysical, and autobiographical, the novel portrays the death of an alcoholic consul in Mexico. Born in England, Lowry wrote most of the haunting novel while living in a shack at Dollarton, B.C.

Saskatchewan writer W.O. Mitchell is working yet another side of the literary street. His novel *Who Has Seen the Wind* describes the coming of age of a boy named Brian in a Saskatchewan town. While the novel criticizes the puritanism of the town, Brian experiences fleeting intimations of divine immortality on the vast windswept prairie.

Novelist Gabrielle Roy.

1948

Davos, Switzerland, Feb. 14. Canadian Barbara Ann Scott wins the world figure skating championship for the second straight year.

Toronto, March 25. The Ontario government announces the creation of a $100,000 alcoholism research foundation in conjunction with Alcoholics Anonymous.

Detroit, April 14. Toronto Maple Leafs defeat Detroit Red Wings four games to none for the Stanley Cup.

Montreal, April 30. Archbishop Joseph Charbonneau denounces graduation balls and dances.

Ottawa, May 12. Mayor Stanley Lewis says Barbara Ann Scott will accept the city's gift of a new car that she declined a year ago to protect her amateur status.

Italy, May 20. Canadian-born RAF ace George "Buzz" Beurling is killed in a crash near Rome while flying to fight in Israel's war of independence.

British Columbia, June. Floods cause millions of dollars in damage and leave more than 9,000 homeless.

Goose Bay, Nfld., July 14. Six RAF Vampires complete the first Atlantic crossing by jet-propelled aircraft.

Toronto, Nov. 27. Calgary Stampeders beat Ottawa Rough Riders 12-7 to win the Grey Cup.

New York, Dec. 10. The UN Assembly adopts the Universal Declaration of Human Rights. As a result of its provisions, women's rights to employment and equal pay are official Canadian policy.

Vancouver, Dec. 20. The first margarine goes on sale since the lifting of a ban on the product. At 53 cents a pound, it is quickly snapped up.

Quebec. Quebec censors ban Phil Rosen's *Sins of the Fathers*, an educational film on venereal disease.

Charlottetown. Prince Edward Island ends prohibition, the last province to do so.

Charlottetown. The Liberal government reacts to a meat packers' strike by prohibiting labor unions on the Island.

Canada. The RCMP revive their Musical Ride by popular demand.

Quebec. Roger Lemelin publishes his novel *Les Plouffes*.

Barbara Ann Scott as good as gold

Feb. 6, 1948

ST. MORITZ, Switzerland – Barbara Ann Scott of Ottawa, who last year became the first Canadian to win the women's world figure-skating championships, today won Canada its first Olympic crown for figure skating. To win this title, Barbara Ann, wearing the number 13, had to overcome difficult ice and 24 other competitors. Although 12 of them were still waiting to perform as the blonde Canadian beauty left the ice, the cheering crowds had already picked the superb skater as winner without waiting for results from the nine judges.

Two other Canadians, Suzanne Morrow and Marilyn Ruth Take, both of Toronto, like nearly all the skaters, had trouble with the surface, rough from a hockey game.

Barbara Ann Scott has just won a second major figure skating title.

Britain puts Nfld.'s fate to referendum

March 11, 1948

ST. JOHN'S, Nfld. – Britain announced today that a referendum will be held to decide the future of Newfoundland. Voters in the colony are offered three choices: Commission of Government for the next five years; Confederation with Canada; or responsible government. Because the National Convention decided that responsible government should be returned to Newfoundland, many accuse Britain of favoring Confederation.

Flooding leaves 2,500 homeless in west

April 26, 1948

WINNIPEG – Widespread floods are easing slightly in Alberta and Saskatchewan, but the situation remains critical in Manitoba. In the three provinces, more than 2,500 people are homeless, victims of rampaging rivers. There appears to be no end in sight for the problem of excessive moisture. Even as the danger seemed to be passing in Alberta, the province was hit by more heavy wet snows.

In the aftermath of the flooding, thousands of hectares of farmland are under water, highway bridges are washed out, and in some cases rail lines have been swept away. Some of the most pressing problems are to be found on the farms. Not only will it be necessary to reseed some flooded areas, but in many cases feed cannot be delivered to herds because so many roads are impassable. It will be several weeks before crews can begin repair work on the bridges.

In Winnipeg, rising floodwater from the Red and Assiniboine rivers is now within three blocks of Portage and Main, threatening the heart of the city.

Gélinas' Tit-Coq marks record 9th month

1948

MONTREAL – *Tit-Coq,* playwright Gratien Gélinas' tale of a woe-begone illegitimate orphan, is celebrating its record-breaking ninth month on stage, and it continues to earn raves from critics. The play is based on a character adapted from Gélinas' popular Fridolin sketches. *Tit-Coq* joins the army, falls in love with his pal's sister, then gets shipped off to war. While he's overseas, his love tires of waiting and marries another. When *Tit-Coq* returns, Marie-Ange is ready to run away with him, but a divorce is impossible.

Gratien Gélinas.

Liquor consumption plunges in Ontario

April 15, 1948

TORONTO – Relaxed liquor laws have not uncorked a flood of drunkenness, Premier George Drew told the Ontario legislature. In fact, Drew says, in the 11 months since Ontario has allowed the sale of booze by the glass, consumption has plunged by 249,700 litres. Drew says the answer to alcohol problems is not prohibition, but stepping up efforts to warn young people of the dangers of drinking. He called on parents to encourage responsible behavior in their children.

Women teachers win salary battle

June 24, 1948

TORONTO – Female public school teachers have won a battle for equal pay. The Toronto Board of Education this evening voted 9-6 to increase women's maximum salaries to $3,500, the same as their male colleagues. The increase, to be effected in 1951, will cost taxpayers an estimated $120,000.

Several trustees opposed the increase, including board chairman C.R. Conquergood, who tried to have the motion postponed. Arguing that men have extra responsibilities, he said "women belong in the home anyway."

Radios outnumber phones in Canada

Feb. 20, 1948

OTTAWA – Ninety percent of Canadian homes have radios, but only 50 percent have telephones. That is just one finding of a report issued by the Dominion Bureau of Statistics on the nation's 3,136,000 homes. However, the number of phones has increased from 40 percent since 1941.

The report also shows that 53 percent of homes are heated by coal, 28 percent by wood, 12 percent by oil, four percent by gas, and one percent by coke. The remainder use sawdust, electricity, or coal oil. Regarding the types of heating equipment used, 28 percent have hot air furnaces and 15 percent steam or hot water furnaces.

Eaton's catalogue, 1948-1949.

Veterans meeting to tackle problems

May 21, 1948

SASKATOON – The Canadian Legion's 12th annual national convention will be held at HMCS *Unicorn* in Saskatoon. About 1,000 veterans from across the country representing all branches of the armed forces are expected. The five-day convention will be kicked off on Sunday with a parade and drumhead service in one of the downtown parks. That evening the governor general, Viscount Alexander, will open the meeting.

This convention promises to be a busy one. Delegates face more than 150 resolutions submitted by members, and they will review every problem and piece of legislation affecting veterans. The agenda includes tightening restrictions on communists joining the legion and working toward more and better benefits for veterans.

The Department of Veterans' Affairs now holds in trust the profits from the wartime operation of canteens. This matter will also be discussed: it's been proposed that the Legion administer a benefit fund established with this money.

Members are pressing for the War Veterans Allowances Act to include only those veterans of the imperial army who came to Canada before the Second World War and those Canadian veterans who served in England during the First World War. At present it provides pensions to certain veterans unable to support themselves. There will also be discussion of housing and land settlement policies. This will be one of the biggest conventions ever held in this city.

Veterans parade in Montreal protesting the lack of homes for their families.

Student veterans study engineering at McGill University's Dawson College.

Newfoundlanders opt for Confederation

July 30, 1948

ST. JOHN'S, Nfld. – It has been announced that a committee will be appointed to negotiate the terms of union with Canada. The revelation comes one week after the results of the second referendum were tabulated. In the first referendum of June 3 neither of the three options received a majority of votes, so Commission of Government, with the least support, was dropped from the ballot for the second referendum, held July 22. Confederation received 78,323 votes (52.34 percent) and responsible government 71,344 (47.66 percent). Thus Newfoundland will become the 10th province of Canada.

The confederate forces, led by Joseph R. Smallwood, ran a well-financed campaign emphasizing the benefits, including old age pensions and family allowance payments, that Confederation would bring. The responsible government forces were poorly organized and could promise little except independence.

Jews and Negroes can't own property

June 11, 1948

TORONTO – A covenant that forbids Jews, Negroes and people of color from owning property in a section of the Lake Huron summer resort of Grand Bend was upheld today by Ontario's Supreme Court. Cottage-owner Annie Noble had wanted to sell her property at Beach o' Pines and argued that the restriction – which applies until Aug. 1, 1962 – was illegal. ▷

Social Credit romps to power in Alberta

Aug. 17, 1948

EDMONTON – Ernest C. Manning and the Social Credit party he now leads have virtually destroyed the opposition in the Alberta legislature. Social Credit has swept into power by winning 51 of 57 seats in the provincial election. The new opposition will be composed of two Liberals and two members of the CCF.

Premier Manning campaigned on a platform almost totally free of contention. He stood for free enterprise, small government, and what he described as a well-financed welfare state. He opposed socialism in any form. Veteran observers of the provincial scene say that a combination of the oil and post-war booms makes the Social Credit administration almost unbeatable.

St. Laurent picked to succeed King

Aug. 8, 1948

OTTAWA – The 66-year-old, fluently bilingual Louis St. Laurent, external affairs minister in W.L. Mackenzie King's last government, has been chosen to succeed King at a Liberal party convention here today. St. Laurent won on the first ballot with 838 votes, as opposed to 323 for Jimmy Gardiner, and 56 for Culby Power of Quebec.

St. Laurent is a quiet, competent corporation lawyer from Quebec City, part of the new breed of French-Canadian professionals. He also has a reputation for excellence, and a restrained kind of old world charm that has served him well since he entered politics in 1942.

Meanwhile, King retires from the post he's held on and off since 1921. He leaves office as Canada's longest-serving prime minister.

St. Laurent discusses party matters with W.L.M. King at the convention.

Bronfman insures pilots fighting for Israel

This rally in Montreal is in support of the state of Israel.

1948

MONTREAL – Samuel Bronfman, whose family-run Distillers Corp. has made him a millionaire several times over, has guaranteed to underwrite life insurance policies for Canadian pilots who sign up to help Israel fight in its war for independence. This is the latest action in a long series of charitable gestures made by Bronfman in support of Jewish causes.

In 1934, he agreed to head the Federation of Jewish Philanthropies, a post that he still holds. At the outbreak of the Second World War, he set up, with the help of Montreal lawyer Saul Hayes, the refugee committee of the Canadian Jewish Congress. The committee had its greatest success when it persuaded the Canadian government to allow 1,200 Jewish orphans to enter the country from Europe. The Canadian Jewish Congress group then astonished Ottawa officials by demanding that the parents of the "orphans" also be admitted.

DPs living under harsh conditions: report

Oct. 19, 1948

WINNIPEG – A Winnipeg newspaper claims that displaced persons are living in conditions "worse than DP camps in Germany." In a front-page story today, the *Tribune* says displaced persons in the sugar beet industry live in poor accommodations, have scanty and grimy blankets, food of poor quality, and insufficient washing and sanitation facilities.

Reaction to the story was swift. In Ottawa, Arthur MacNamara, labor department deputy, said his department will launch an immediate investigation. In Winnipeg, H.R. Richardson, director of the provincial Farm Help Service, said conditions as reported do not exist. This statement was refuted by Fred J. White, regional superintendent of the Unemployment Insurance Commission, the agency which brought the displaced persons to this province.

Lithuanian immigrant railway workers near Swift Current, Saskatchewan.

Refus Global more than just a refusal

Aug. 9, 1948

MONTREAL – "The ways of society must be abandoned once and for all; we must free ourselves from its utilitarian spirit. ... We must refuse to close our eyes to vice, to deceit perpetrated under the cloak of imparted knowledge, of services rendered, of payment due." So writes painter Paul-Emile Borduas in *Refus Global*, a passionate manifesto published today in 400 typewritten mimeographed copies. Borduas wrote the *Refus* with poet Claude Gauvreau, Bruno Cormier, painter Fernand Leduc, and dancer Françoise Sullivan, and it is signed by 15 members of Borduas' artistic group called the Automatistes.

Borduas and his collaborators are fed up – fed up with a Quebec society he calls "a colony trapped since 1760 within the slippery walls of fear"; fed up with the corrupt church that has stood guard over that fortress; fed up with western "Christian" civilization and utilitarian society; fed up with "deliberate, rational effort." The *Refus* is a clarion call for a collective, passionate rejection of all the above mentioned and more. But the *Refus* is not only a rejection. It concludes, "We foresee a time when man will be freed from his useless chains and realize in the unpredictable order of spontaneity and a resplendent anarchy the fullness of his individual gifts ... we will joyfully pursue our savage need for liberation."

Canadians not dull, MacLennan asserts

Nov. 30, 1948

TORONTO – Canadians aren't dull. They just make the world think they are, author Hugh MacLennan told the Canadian Club today. Outside Canada, people think an Eskimo dog is more interesting than former prime minister W.L. Mackenzie King, he said. "The fault is ours. People in other countries would never have considered a dog more interesting than Mr. King if it had not been for the propaganda we have been sending them." He put much blame on government publicity bureaus.

Canada and Nfld. sign terms of union

Dec. 12, 1948

OTTAWA – Yesterday in a ceremony in the Senate chamber, the terms of union were signed by Canada and Newfoundland. The two delegations have been negotiating since Oct. 6 and have produced a document containing 50 "terms" which will come into effect just before midnight on March 31, 1949. Most of the terms are obvious and expected, but a number created problems. One of the most contentious concerns the amount of financial assistance needed to support essential services in Newfoundland. Another concerns denominational education, which is guaranteed in the new province.

Joseph Smallwood signs Newfoundland's Confederation agreement.

Prime Minister Louis St. Laurent and Brooke Claxton, minister of national defence, signed on behalf of Canada. F. Gordon Bradley, Philip Gruchy, John B. McEvoy, J.R. Smallwood, Albert Walsh, and Gordon Winter signed for Newfoundland. One member of Newfoundland's delegation, Chesley A. Crosbie, refused to sign because he is convinced the financial arrangements will prove inadequate.

A reception was held after the signing and a band played *God Save the King* and *O Canada*. The *Ode to Newfoundland* could not be played because the music could not be located in time.

Many assume Smallwood will be chosen as premier to form an interim government, Bradley will join the federal cabinet, and Walsh will become lieutenant-governor.

The RCMP Musical Ride performs at New York's World's Fair.

Supreme Court kills ban on margarine

Dec. 14, 1948

OTTAWA – Margarine, banned in Canada since 1886, will be sold soon, thanks to the Supreme Court. In a ruling made today, five of the seven judges ruled the section of the Dairy Industry Act which banned margarine was *ultra vires*; that is, illegal because such a restriction was outside Parliament's powers. The dairy industry, fearing lost sales, is understandably upset.

Dairy industry promotes products.

1949

Ohsweken, Ont., Jan. 9. Famous Six Nations distance runner Tom Longboat dies.

Asbestos, Que., Feb. 14. 5,000 workers affiliated with the Canadian Catholic Confederation of Labor go on an illegal strike, paralysing major asbestos mines.

Newfoundland, March 31. Newfoundland enters Confederation under a 1948 agreement.

Newfoundland, April 4. Nutritionists report improvement in the health of Newfoundlanders due to a diet of fortified flour and fortified margarine.

Toronto, April 16. Toronto Maple Leafs beat Detroit Red Wings four games to none to win the Stanley Cup.

Toronto, April. Leslie Frost succeeds Tom Kennedy as PC premier of Ontario.

Montreal, May 1. Archbishop Joseph Charbonneau comes out in support of the strikers at Asbestos.

Asbestos, Que., May 6. Provincial police beat up and arrest strikers. Yesterday, the strikers beat police who were trying to break picket lines to put strikebreakers to work.

Ontario, June 10. Governor General's Award winners include Hugh MacLennan's *The Precipice* and A.M. Klein's *The Rocking Chair and Other Poems.*

Edmonton, June 15. The Alberta government announces the sale of a petroleum and natural gas lease in Redwater oilfield to Amerada Petroleum Corp. for a record $3,223,320.

British Columbia, Aug. 21. The biggest earthquake recorded in Canada hits the west coast, but there are no deaths and little damage reported.

Toronto, Sept. 17. More than 100 people die when the old Canadian-built cruise ship *Noronic* is destroyed by fire.

Washington, D.C., Sept. 23. President Truman reveals the Soviet Union has exploded its first atomic bomb.

Toronto, Nov. 26. Montreal Alouettes beat Calgary Stampeders 28-15 in the Grey Cup.

Victoria, Dec. 12. Nancy Hodges is named Speaker of the B.C. legislature, the first woman in the Commonwealth named Speaker to a legislature.

Ottawa. The government gives Japanese Canadians the vote, and removes all restrictions on their movement.

Plane flies across Canada – non-stop

Jan. 15, 1949

HALIFAX – Advances in aviation technology have given Canada's Arctic a pivotal strategic importance, lying as Canada does between two opposing superpowers. Manned Soviet bomber attack is a distinct possibility as the Cold War escalates. Just today the RCAF proved how far modern transport planes can fly. A North Star, based on the Douglas DC-4 airliner and fitted with a Rolls-Royce Merlin engine, has landed here after the first-ever non-stop coast-to-coast flight. Piloted by Flying Officer J. Jolicoeur, it left Vancouver yesterday and flew the 4,630-kilometre Great Circle route for eight hours, 32 minutes, 529 kilometres an hour.

Aircrew of the Canadair North Star which made the first non-stop flight.

Davies wins twice at drama festival

Feb. 19, 1949

BROCKVILLE, Ont. – Playwright, director, and editor Robertson Davies competed with himself here today and won. Davies' play *Fortune My Foe,* performed by the Ottawa Drama League, won first prize at the Eastern Ontario drama festival. But a close second was the Peterborough Little Theatre version of the classic *The Taming of the Shrew.* Davies, editor of the Peterborough *Examiner,* directed the *Shrew.* The Ottawa group won not only for a well-written play, but for its polished performances.

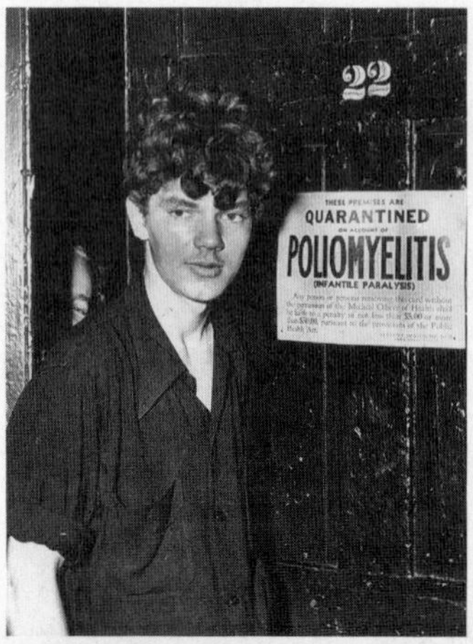

Poliomyelitis quarantine sign on the J block of Stanley Barracks in Toronto.

Communist slams Labour Congress, CCF

Feb. 4, 1949

TORONTO – The Canadian Congress of Labour and the CCF can expect no more support from Canadian Communists. In a speech at the Communist convention here tonight, leader Tim Buck denounced both the labor organization and the political party as barriers to working class progress. "CCF leaders fully support anti-Soviet, anti-democratic war alliances of capitalist states," he said.

The Communists supported the CCF in the last federal election. But that was an "opportunistic mistake," Buck said. The labor congress actively undermines militant trade unions, he said. "It encourages and facilitates treacherous anti-working class collaboration with employers against unions under progressive leadership." In his speech, Buck attacked the North Atlantic alliance as a war pact aimed at the Soviet Union.

Polio epidemic hits eastern Arctic Inuit

April 1, 1949

OTTAWA – Medical personnel have identified a polio epidemic in the Keewatin district, on the west side of Hudson Bay. Doctors have already learned of 90 cases, with 14 deaths. A number of survivors have extensive residual paralysis. Nurses and doctors in the field stations have quarantined a large area, and the authorities are discouraging the stricken coastal groups from travelling into the interior. Only four years ago, the eastern Arctic Inuit were hit by a diphtheria and then a typhoid epidemic. Now, it's polio. The federal government's current campaign to improve health services in the Northwest Territories is badly needed.

Windsor study puts auto union on top

March 11, 1949

WINDSOR, Ont. – This is a city of four warring power groups, and the auto workers' union is clearly on top. That is a conclusion a noted sociologist reached after a study of Windsor. C.W.M. Hart said today that the union, to which 18,000 of this city's 100,000 people belong, has become so powerful it's expanded its activities to include welfare services and now virtually controls life here. Everyone in Windsor is either a "violent partisan" supporting labor or opposing it, he said. Other significant groups he identified were big business (Ford and Chrysler), the Catholic church, and an old elite of those who control service organizations.

Newfoundland the 10th province to join Canada

Terrain near Rose Blanche is an example of Newfoundland's rugged beauty.

The floral emblem of Newfoundland is the Pitcher Plant.

Major natural resource? It's the fishery

March 31, 1949

NEWFOUNDLAND – The entry of this colony into Confederation is accompanied by some considerable resources. The total landmass is 111,390 square kilometres on the island and 294,330 square kilometres in Labrador. The major natural resource is the fishery, and on fishing grounds extending out more than 300 kilometres are harvested various species of groundfish but particularly cod. In addition, important pelagic fish, especially herring, mackerel, salmon and caplin, are also caught. Lobsters, scallops, squid, crab, whales and seals are available in large numbers.

Besides its ocean resources, there are deposits of fluorospar, iron ore, lead, zinc, and other minerals. Also, there are vast tracts of forests and considerable hydro power potential, as well as offshore gas and oil deposits. Although few highways are paved, there is a trans-island railway, branch rail lines, an international airport, harbor facilities, and armed forces bases. There are some 400 farms and thousands of vegetable plots.

A pastoral scene at Trinity Bay, near Queen's Cove, Newfoundland.

Economy forced to change with the times

March 31, 1949

NEWFOUNDLAND – The economy of this province was originally based on the international trade in salted dried codfish. Codfish was split, salted, and dried in the open air and sold primarily in the markets of Spain, Portugal, Italy, Greece, the West Indies, and Brazil. This was a seasonal activity, insufficient to support a large permanent population. Then in the early 1800s a spring seal fishery was developed, broadening the economic base. Later, lobster, herring and other fisheries were developed.

By the end of the 1800s it was obvious that the fisheries alone could not sustain the entire population, and a program of natural resource development was begun which resulted in the building of a trans-island railway and several branch lines and in the opening of pulp and paper mills, an iron ore mine, and a lead and zinc mine. The Second World War saw the construction of American and Canadian armed forces bases and an international airport at Gander. Newfoundland prospered – many people left the fisheries to work on the bases, and those who continued to fish received good prices for their catches.

After the war the saltfish markets became depressed, and there has been a shift toward the production of fresh frozen codfish for American markets. Meanwhile, mining and pulp and paper milling continue, as do the lesser fisheries. There has been a fledgling tourist industry ever since the construction of the railway as sports enthusiasts come to fish and hunt. It is hoped that in the future Newfoundland will build on these strengths.

Long and bitter asbestos strike ends

Members of the Federation of Mining Employees hold a meeting at Asbestos.

July 1, 1949

ASBESTOS, Que. – The bitter, violent asbestos strike is over, but it took the intervention of the Catholic archbishop of Quebec to end it. The union and the Johns-Manville company came to an agreement this morning, with the help of Msgr. Maurice Roy.

The issue slowing settlement here was rehiring strikers. Asbestos workers at Thetford Mines, Que., settled with their employers on June 24. But the Johns-Manville company was unwilling to rehire 20 strikers. The strike began illegally on Feb. 14 and quickly involved 5,000 workers at Asbestos and Thetford Mines. On May 5, the Riot Act was read in a clash between strikers and police.

NATO to counteract Soviet Union moves

Canadian ambassador H. Wrong.

April 4, 1949

WASHINGTON, D.C. – External Affairs Minister Lester Pearson signed an agreement creating the North Atlantic Treaty Organization today, making Canada part of a defensive alliance with the United States, Britain, France, and other former European allies.

NATO is designed to counteract the Soviet Union's expansionist moves in Eastern Europe since the end of the Second World War, such as the Communist coup d'etat in Czechoslovakia and the current Soviet blockade of West Berlin. Canada is a driving force for NATO, which not only protects its members but preserves peace. NATO pledges peaceful means to settle disputes, as the UN stipulates.

Smallwood guides Liberals to victory

May 31, 1949

ST. JOHN'S, Nfld. – Joseph R. Smallwood's new Liberal party has won a decisive victory over the Progressive Conservatives, taking 22 of 28 seats. Smallwood allied himself with the governing Liberals in Ottawa, while the Conservative party became dominated by the former anti-confederate forces. With old age pensions and family allowance payments beginning to flow from Ottawa, the result was a foregone conclusion.

Carving Newfoundland's arms.

St. Laurent leads Liberals to lopsided win

June 27, 1949

OTTAWA – The Liberal party under Prime Minister Louis St. Laurent has won the largest parliamentary majority ever in today's federal election: 124 seats. All told, the Liberals got 193 seats. The Progressive Conservatives under former Ontario premier George Drew took 42, the CCF 12, Social Credit 10, and independents five.

It is a resounding victory for St. Laurent, who was fighting his first election as leader since succeeding William Lyon Mackenzie King. His strategists had only been expecting 140 seats. Some are even worried that the party has too big a majority, which could hurt it at the next election.

St. Laurent meets future electors.

New commonwealth is cited by Pearson

April 28, 1949

OTTAWA – King George VI is no longer monarch of India, but he is the leader of the British Commonwealth. The agreement among Commonwealth countries means "a new commonwealth of nations is brought into being," said External Affairs Minister Lester Pearson. India is a republic and part of the Commonwealth. It recognizes the king as Commonwealth leader.

Avro's jet unique in North America

Aug. 10, 1949

TORONTO – The four-engine Avro Canada Ltd. jetliner flew for the first time at nearby Malton Airport today, establishing a first for Canada in aviation. The Canadian designed and built plane, which can carry 50 passengers at altitudes up to 9,000 metres and a speed of 692 kilometres an hour, is the only one of its type in North America. U.S. passenger jetliners have yet to fly.

Restaurants free to snub Negroes

Dec. 5, 1949

DRESDEN, Ont. – Uncle Tom could not eat lunch in some restaurants in his home town. Citizens here today voted 517-108 against a proposed bylaw that would have forced restaurants to serve customers "regardless of race, creed, or color." Dresden was the home of the man who inspired Harriet Beecher Stowe's famous Negro character Uncle Tom.

Power to amend BNA Act is limited

Dec. 16, 1949
LONDON, England – Canada's Parliament can now amend the country's Constitution without reference to Britain. King George VI today gave his assent to a statute of the British Parliament that gives Canada limited power to amend the British North America Act. The BNA Act creating Canada and establishing its constitutional framework previously could be amended only by the British Parliament. The Canadian Parliament can now amend it, but only in carefully restricted ways.

The federal government cannot infringe on provincial rights or on civil rights. It cannot use its amending power to affect French or English language use or schools. And it cannot change the rules for the longevity of a parliament or the frequency of its sessions.

Subway system construction snarls traffic

Workmen tear up Yonge Street to build the Toronto subway.

Sept. 7, 1949
TORONTO – Construction on a rapid-transit underground train system began beneath Yonge Street today, creating traffic jams among commuters who had to take detours around closed streets. The subway, a $50-million project which some day is expected to be a convenience to people coming downtown, was anything but that today. Impatient drivers blew their horns as traffic slowed to a crawl in the construction area.

Holy cow, Batman! Comic books barred

Dec. 11, 1949
TORONTO – Crime comics are no longer produced or distributed in Canada. A new Criminal Code amendment in effect as of today bans any periodical that "substantially comprises matter depicting pictorially the commission of crimes, real or fictitious."

At a weekend meeting here, a committee representing all Canadian comic publishers, distributors, and printers imposed a ban on 25 titles and established a self-censorship bureau. Committee members did not agree that comic books are dangerous to the morals of youth. But "if the government says some forms of comic books are harmful ... then we, as an industry, can only comply," the committee said.

By establishing self-censorship, the industry feels it is protecting retailers from having to make difficult decisions about what kinds of material the new law might include.

Jehovah's Witness to get a new trial

Dec. 5, 1949
OTTAWA – A new trial has been ordered in the case of a Quebec Jehovah's Witness charged with seditious libel. In a judgment issued today, three Supreme Court of Canada justices said the judge in the Aimé Boucher case incorrectly instructed the jury about the law, and therefore a new trial was warranted. But in a minority opinion, Justice I.C. Rand made a strong statement supporting the principle of religious freedom. Justice Willard Estey agreed with Rand that Boucher ought to be acquitted.

Mounties screening film board staffers

Nov. 18, 1949
OTTAWA – The RCMP are screening National Film Board employees before the government agency is allowed to work for the defence department. In the House of Commons today, cabinet ministers revealed the screenings have been taking place. During the war, private firms produced defence films and continued to do that work later. Last May, the government decided to switch to its own film agency and the screening began. The government ministers denied there was evidence that questioned the patriotism of NFB employees.

A mother and daughter wash dishes for the last time in the kitchen of their old home, slated to be razed as part of a Toronto slum clearance project.

The mother and daughter wash dishes on the first night in their new home built for them in this same Toronto slum improvement project.

1950

Quebec, Feb. 1. As an aftermath of the Asbestos strike, the Roman Catholic Church issues a Collective Pastoral Letter, removing its clergy from leadership of Quebec's Catholic trade unions.

Detroit, April 23. Detroit Red Wings defeat New York Rangers four games to three to win the Stanley Cup.

Halifax, May 29. RCMP Sgt. Frederick Farrar completes the first circumnavigation of North America in the *St. Roch*.

Ottawa, June 13. On the recommendation of royal commissioner Justice H.I. Bird, the government announces it will pay $1,222,829 in conscience money to Japanese forcibly evacuated from their west coast homes during WWII.

Korea, June 25. Communist North Korea invades South Korea [sparking the Korean War].

Toronto, June 26. The Toronto Stock Exchange registers its largest single day decline since the crash of 1929, as markets around the world plunge with the news of fighting in Korea.

New York, June 27. The UN Security Council reacts to the invasion of South Korea by recommending that UN members help South Korea defend itself.

Hawaii, July 12. Three Canadian destroyers arrive at Pearl Harbor and join the U.S. naval task force Yoke to operate against the Communists in the Far Pacific.

Ottawa, Aug. 7. PM St. Laurent announces Canada will form an expeditionary force to send to Korea to fight under the UN banner.

Ottawa, Aug. 8. Former PM Mackenzie King's two homes (Laurier House in Ottawa and the Kingsmere country estate in the Gatineau) are bequeathed to the nation as his will is made public.

Quebec, Sept. 28. At a constitutional conference, Canada's first ministers can't agree on a procedure for amending the Constitution in Canada and "domiciling" the Constitution in Canada, rather than Britain.

Toronto, Oct. 23. The *Globe and Mail* reports western Canadian oil fields lead the world in oil exploration and development.

Toronto, Nov. 25. Toronto Argonauts beat the Winnipeg Blue Bombers 13-0 for the Grey Cup.

Pension deal averts a strike at Ford

April 11, 1950

WINDSOR, Ont. – A pension plan deal, the first of its kind in Canada, has averted a strike by 12,000 Ford workers here. The union membership tonight accepted a new contract that includes the company's proposal to establish a plan that would pay retired employees as much as $55 a month.

The plan will be financed entirely by Ford. Those who retire at 65 after 30 years service will get the top pension payment. The union originally demanded the pension limit be set at $100 a month after 25 years service. After talks lasting more than a year, the union accepted the lower figure in return for a more generous eligibility for the pensions. Union officials expect the pension deal to set a precedent for other labor negotiations.

Ford president Rhys Sale is happy with the contract even though the pensions "place a heavy financial obligation on the company." The plan will cost Ford more than $1 million a year. Employees also get an expanded health program.

Avro tests a new twin-engined jet fighter

Prototype Avro CF-100 Mk. 1 flies over Rockcliffe, Ontario, on test flight.

Jan. 19, 1950

TORONTO – A new jet fighter flew at Malton today. The Avro (Canada) CF-100 is a twin-engined jet. Test pilot W.A. "Bill" Waterton afterwards described the aircraft as pleasant and safe. A native of Guelph, Ont., Waterton joined the RAF in 1939, won two Air Force Crosses in the war, and is well-known in test pilot circles.

Designed for the RCAF, the CF-100 is a long-range, radar-equipped, all-weather machine, ideal to protect Canada's vast air spaces. It weighs 10 tons empty, 15.5 tons with crew, fuel, and equipment. The CF-100 is Avro's second design. Its C-102 jetliner – the world's second jet transport – first flew on Aug. 10, 1949. CF-100 work began in October 1945, using information from wind tunnels and German sources.

"Ill health" forces archbishop to quit

Feb. 11, 1950

MONTREAL – Ill health is the official reason given for the resignation of Montreal's archbishop, Msgr. Joseph Charbonneau, 58. However, Charbonneau supported the striking workers at Asbestos last year, and some suggest this is the real reason he has quit, under intense pressure from the church hierarchy which supports Premier Maurice Duplessis.

Msgr. Joseph Charbonneau.

Nova Scotia premier Macdonald laments curse of Confederation

March 24, 1950

HALIFAX – Confederation was a deal whereby politicians sold out the people of Nova Scotia, Premier Angus Macdonald said today. And Nova Scotia continues to suffer under the curse and burden imposed on it in 1867, he told the legislature. "There never was a poorer bargain struck by any province and it has had its effects to this day," he said.

Nova Scotian delegates to the Confederation conferences were too anxious to be considered nation-builders. They forgot their loyalty to the people they represented, Macdonald said. His remarks were made in response to comments by Robert Stanfield when the opposition leader called the Confederation politicians men of great vision.

Macdonald said in the Confederation deal, the federal government reserved too much taxation power for itself. It agreed to make up the province's deficit at Confederation, but this amounted to 80 cents per capita, the price of a sheepskin. "People in the province said they had been sold for the price of a sheepskin," Macdonald said. But "we are in it now and we must make the best of it."

Pelletier, Trudeau publish Cité Libre

Pierre Elliott Trudeau.

June 15, 1950

MONTREAL – Quebec's activist intellectuals have a new weapon in their battle against Premier Maurice Duplessis and what they see as the forces of conservatism. The first issue of *Cité Libre* appeared here this month and dedicates itself to fight for modernization and democracy in Quebec. The magazine is edited by Gérard Pelletier and Pierre Trudeau.

In the first issue, Trudeau urges Quebecers "to throw out the thousand prejudices with which the past burdens the present, and to build for the new man." *Cité Libre* editors see Duplessis as imposing a traditionalist, anti-modern nationalism on Quebec that prevents the province from achieving economic and social growth.

Manitoba battles Red River flooding

May 5, 1950

WINNIPEG – Southeastern Manitoba today became a battleground as soldiers and volunteers tried to control the waters of the rampaging Red River. The Legislative Buildings have been re-named Flood Control Headquarters. Brig. R.E.A. Morton now leads a major military force which is being augmented on a daily basis. Under the brigadier's direction are 15,000 men, women and children engaged in building new dikes and topping up existing ones.

It is estimated that by the end of the week more than 100,000 Manitobans will have been forced out of their homes. The first to go were the residents of southern towns like Morris and St. Jean Baptiste. Last evening Morton first ordered the evacuation of parts of three Winnipeg suburbs, Norwood, Elmwood, and East Kildonan, and three hours later issued another order covering residents living near the University of Manitoba.

Fresh troops have been ordered to Winnipeg from commands as far apart as Calgary and B.C. The Princess Patricia's Canadian Light Infantry regiment arrives tomorrow from Calgary, as will the 23rd Field Squadron, RCE, from Chilliwack. "Frogmen" from Halifax are dealing with underwater problems.

An unusual problem has developed on the farms between Winnipeg and the U.S. border. Those farmers who first moved their herds to high ground now find the cattle must once again be relocated.

RCMP officers patrol flooded homes by canoe in East Kildonan, Manitoba.

Floodwaters cover downtown Winnipeg streets in front of the legislature.

Operation to split Siamese twins fails

May 15, 1950

EDMONTON – Brenda and Beverley Townshend, born joined face-to-face six months ago, died today shortly after an operation separated them. The operation, it quickly became apparent, was doomed from the start, as the twins' hearts were so intertwined they were unable to support the individual infants. Surgeons were stymied by the lack of space in the babies' chest cavities, where they had hoped to place their hearts.

Korean conflict: Canada offers aid to UN

June 30, 1950

ESQUIMALT, B.C. – Canada moved closer to the Korean conflict today. Three Canadian destroyers left here bound for Hawaii. This is the first visible example of Canada's determination to participate in a United Nations military effort in Korea if called upon.

In the Commons today, Prime Minister Louis St. Laurent avoided tying this country directly to American interests in Korea. But he said that if the government is informed "that a Canadian contribution to aid United Nations operations under a United Nations commander would be important to achieve the ends of peace, which is of course our only purpose, then the government wishes Parliament to know that it would immediately consider making a contribution."

Meanwhile, it is reported that the Korean army has collapsed and stopped fighting in the face of the Communist invasion. U.S. President Harry Truman today ordered ground troops into Korea. Canada is among 30 countries that have offered their military services to the United Nations in Korea.

Rats! Rodents find their way to Alberta

July 21, 1950

EDMONTON – Public health officials in Alberta, which has long boasted of being Canada's only rat-free province, are in a state of shock. The Norway or brown rat, which has followed settlements across Manitoba and Saskatchewan feeding on garbage, household food, and grain, has reached Alberta. The Alberta government vows to exterminate these unwelcome disease-carrying and grain-destroying rodents.

Talks fall through; railways shut down

Aug. 22, 1950

MONTREAL – Canada's railways shut down at 6 a.m. today, after desperate last-minute negotiations failed to avert a strike. After a cabinet meeting this morning, Prime Minister Louis St. Laurent announced that Parliament would be called into emergency session. The government is busy with plans to ensure that remote regions have adequate food supplies and essential communications are maintained during the strike. The unions have said they will provide emergency services. An airlift is being organized to bring MPs and senators to the emergency session, where they will consider legislation to end the strike.

The unions representing 125,000 workers and the railways were very close to agreement on pay issues. It was thought that compromises could have been found if the companies had not insisted on 10 revisions in working conditions. These, including replacing Sunday as a day off, the unions called "retaliatory counter proposals." The unions also objected to excluding hotel employees from the contract. The company pay offer of a four-cent-an-hour increase was only one cent below the unions' demand.

Frank Hall, chairman of the unions' negotiating committee, said the unions don't want to burden the country. "We are not fighting the country; we are fighting the railways. We hold them responsible."

Children in remote Ontario areas attend class in a railway car.

Emergency legislation ends rail strike

Aug. 30, 1950

OTTAWA – Emergency legislation ended the nine-day rail strike tonight, as union leaders applauded. The unions have directed Canada's 125,000 rail and telegraph workers to get back on the job as soon as possible. The legislation provides for compulsory arbitration to settle the outstanding issues between the railways and unions. While the unions oppose compulsory arbitration on principle, the government also directed that the settlement cannot be less than the railways' last offer. This "convinces us of the desire of the government to see that we get a fair deal," said union negotiator Frank Hall.

The legislation includes hotel and water employees in the new contract, a demand the unions had made. Normal train service should be in operation within a day.

Former Liberal prime minister King dies

July 22, 1950

OTTAWA – Former prime minister William Lyon Mackenzie King died tonight. He was 76 and a bachelor. The man who headed Canada's government for 21 years, until 1948, died of pneumonia at his summer residence, Kingsmere in the Gatineau Hills near here. His body will lie in state in the Parliament Buildings. After a state funeral, he will be buried in Toronto.

W.L. Mackenzie King's funeral cortege en route to Union Station.

King was born in Berlin (now Kitchener), Ont. He graduated from the University of Toronto in 1895 and studied economics at Chicago and Harvard. In 1909, King entered Wilfrid Laurier's cabinet as minister of labor. Defeated in 1911, he became a labor consultant and worked for the Rockefeller Foundation. In 1918 he published his book *Industry and Humanity,* in which he argued for new methods of resolving labor disputes.

King became leader of the Liberal party in 1919 and PM in 1921. He was out of power during the depression, 1930 to 1935. He will be particularly remembered as the man who led Canada in the last world war and dealt with the conscription question. He is also known as the prime minister who shaped this country's independence from Britain in international affairs, and the one who introduced social programs including pensions and unemployment insurance.

Crater the largest ever left by meteor

Aug. 7, 1950

UNGAVA, Que. – Here, in the midst of Quebec's barren Ungava Peninsula, has been discovered a scientific miracle: the largest meteor crater in the world. Ten billion tons of sheer granite were blasted out of the earth by the meteor 3,000 to 5,000 years ago, leaving a hole the size of downtown Toronto. The force has been estimated to be many times that of the atomic bomb which levelled Hiroshima.

The crater was recently discovered by Dr. V. Ben Meen, director of the Royal Ontario Museum of Geology and Mineralogy. Hard to make out on the ground, its telltale circular shape was obvious once it was seen from Meen's research aircraft. Meen has reported other interesting features: creases in the rock, resembling ripples from a stone tossed into a pool, and fields of boulders tossed from the impact.

Instructor and artist Fred Varley relaxes in his studio at the Doon Summer School of Fine Arts near Kitchener, Ontario.

Canada, U.S. to pool defence resources

Oct. 26, 1950

WASHINGTON, D.C. – Canada and the U.S. today signed an agreement formally pooling North America's defence resources. The deal, which calls for increased co-operation in sharing natural resources, information, and arms, takes effect immediately. Observers believe the pact is good for both countries – it gives Canada free access to non-nuclear U.S. technology and the Americans access to Canada's vast natural resources.

Church group wants sex report banned

Nov 16, 1950

TORONTO – After they met today in the city's Park Road United Church, members of the Canadian Council of Churches demanded that the federal government prevent copies of the controversial Kinsey report on human sexuality from entering the country. The group also asked that the showing of sexual education films be limited to qualified doctors.

Princess Patricia's fighting troops arrive in Korea

Personnel from HMCS Cayuga hand food parcel down to a Korean boat.

Members of the support company Princess Patricia's Canadian Light Infantry board the USNS Joe P. Martinez in Seattle en route to Korea.

Dec. 18, 1950

PUSAN – Canadian fighting troops are arriving here in strength. This evening the 2nd Battalion, Princess Patricia's Canadian Light Infantry – 45 officers and 873 other ranks – began disembarking at this port.

North Korean forces invaded South Korea on June 25. A Canadian Army Special Force was authorized on Aug. 7, followed by enlistment of 8,000 volunteers, sufficient for an infantry brigade with supporting artillery and other specialists. Uniforms, rifles, grenades, and other equipment are Second World War pattern. That is appropriate since nearly half of those enrolling were Second World War veterans. One man tried to enlist at age 72; another tried to join in spite of having an artificial leg. Initial training proceeded in Canada. Advanced instruction was to be conducted at Fort Lewis, Wash. The program was marred, however, by a Nov. 21 railway accident at Canoe River, B.C., which killed 17 soldiers.

The rout of North Korean forces by UN armies in early October suggested that the Canadian troops might not be needed. But the intervention of Communist Chinese armies and retreat of UN forces made them vital again. The Patricias spent only four days at Fort Lewis before leaving Seattle aboard an American troopship on Nov. 25. No liquor had been allowed aboard the ship. Men going ashore at Yokohama traded shirts for bottles before they returned aboard.

The half-trained PPCLI may be the first Canadian combat troops here, but other Canadians arrived earlier. Three RCN destroyers have been operating in Korean waters since early August. *HMCS Cayuga* first fired on a target on Aug. 15. On Nov. 7, an army advanced party of 348 reached Pusan to prepare the way for the brigade. However, this party had been inactive given uncertainties about how fast the Canadian brigade was to grow and when it would be sent into battle. Members of the advanced party were being sent back to Canada even as the Patricias arrived.

Deed can't restrict sales to gentiles

Nov. 20, 1950

OTTAWA – A clause in a deed restricting the sale of land to white gentiles is invalid, the Supreme Court of Canada ruled today. Bernard Wolf, a Jew, is trying to buy property near Grand Bend, Ont. But the deed to that property has a convenant designed to bar people "of the Jewish, Hebrew, Semitic, Negro or colored race or blood" from owning it. Wolf, and the land owner, sought a legal ruling before the sale was completed. Two Ontario courts ruled against them before they appealed to the Supreme Court. Jewish groups hail the ruling as a victory for minority rights.

One of the most popular dolls currently is the Reliable Toy Company's Barbara Ann Scott doll. The tiny blond skater won three figure skating titles in 1948.

Transportation toys such as these are always popular with boys.

1951

Nova Scotia, Jan. 17. Colchester County ends a bounty on porcupine snouts after being deluged by some 34,000 snouts at a cost of $34,000 in the past year.

Brantford, Ont., Feb. 16. The Brantford fluoride committee reports that since the city began adding fluoride to its drinking water in 1945 there has been a marked drop in tooth decay among school children.

Paris, Feb. 21. Québécois folk singer Félix Leclerc wins Le Prix du disque 1951 for his song *Moi et mes souliers*.

Ottawa, March 21. The government approves the incorporation of TransCanada PipeLines Ltd. to build a natural gas pipeline from Alberta to Quebec.

Toronto, April 21. Toronto Maple Leafs beat Montreal Canadiens four games to one to win the Stanley Cup.

Ottawa, May 4. Defence Minister Claxton announces the creation of the 27th Canadian infantry brigade to serve in Europe with NATO forces.

Ottawa, July 10. Canada formally ends her state of war with Germany.

Toronto, Nov. 12. The National Ballet of Canada, founded by Celia Franca, gives its first performance.

Toronto, Nov. 24. Ottawa Rough Riders beat Saskatchewan Roughriders 21-14 for the Grey Cup.

Victoria, December. The B.C. government allows Indians to drink alcohol in beer parlors. The move comes after a revision of the federal Indian Act ended the prohibition on Indian liquor consumption.

London, Ont. The world's first cobalt radiotherapy unit for treatment of cancer, developed in Canada by Harold Johns and others, is installed at Victoria Hospital.

Quebec. Women's rights activist Thérèse Casgrain becomes provincial leader of the CCF, the first woman to lead a political party in Canada.

Saint John, N.B. K.C. Irving, head of Irving Oil Co., founds Irving Pulp and Paper Ltd., one of four major pulp and paper firms in New Brunswick.

Canada. Books published include Morley Callaghan's *The Loved and the Lost* and Marshall McLuhan's *The Mechanical Bride*.

Trois-Rivières bridge collapse kills 4

The collapsed Duplessis Bridge at Trois-Rivières, Quebec.

Feb. 1, 1951

TROIS-RIVIERES, Que. – Premier Maurice Duplessis suspects sabotage, possibly, he claims, by Communists, in the spectacular collapse of a 600-metre bridge here that bears his name. The bridge was opened in 1948 by Duplessis, amid charges of kickbacks and the use of shoddy materials. Duplessis declared at that time that "the bridge is as solid as the Union Nationale."

At least four people died in the collapse, all of them trapped in cars as the bridge roadway gave way. Witnesses say they saw a blinding flash of light just before the bridge crumpled with a roar likened to an earthquake. The bridge was named for the premier's father, a former Trois-Rivières mayor.

Government plan gives Ontario women equal pay for equal work

March 8, 1951

TORONTO – Ontario women who do the same jobs as men are now entitled to equal pay. Under the Female Employees Fair Remuneration Act women cannot be discriminated against financially because of their sex. However, the new act allows a difference in salaries paid to women and men within the same organization if they do different jobs. Contracts signed prior to March 1 of this year are not affected, but if they are still in force on Sept. 1, 1952, the provisions of the act are binding.

The act allows for fines of up to $100 for individuals and organizations guilty of discrimination. Complaints must be submitted to the director of the Fair Employment Practices Branch. The new law reflects Canada's support of the United Nations' 1948 Universal Declaration of Human Rights, which states everyone is entitled to equal pay for equal work.

A separate act also granted women the right to sit on juries. As a result, Premier Leslie Frost commented, "This is indeed a historic day in Ontario, women are being given completely equal status and equal responsibility with men."

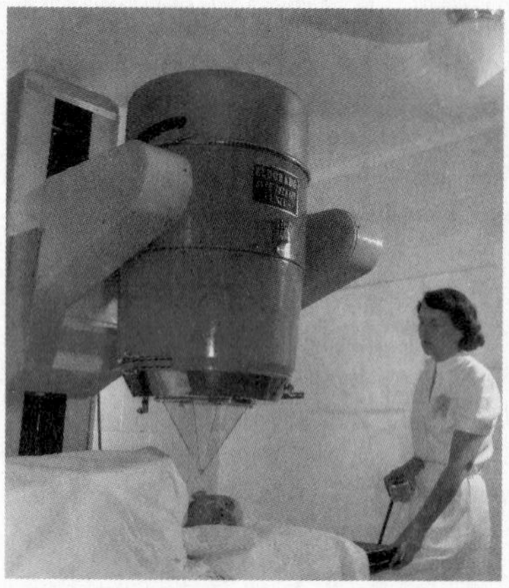

The new law does not apply to jobs which are filled by women only.

Labour Progressive a communist party

Jan. 28, 1951

TORONTO – Canada has its own communist party, even if it's known as the Labour Progressive Party, says LPP leader Tim Buck. He made the declaration before 2,400 cheering "Reds" at the party's national convention, which has just wrapped up here. Buck warned Prime Minister Louis St. Laurent not to involve Canada in a possible U.S.-China war, saying that the capitalist countries "can't succeed" against the nearly one billion people under socialism worldwide.

CBC announcer Max Ferguson characterizes Harold the Spider.

Armed forces offer women new careers

April 24, 1951

OTTAWA – Brooke Claxton, minister of national defence, announced today that the Canadian forces will resume recruiting women this summer. Qualified recruits may be commissioned. The wartime women's branches were disbanded in 1946 and not revived until Cold War expansion. Claxton says the armed forces offer women new careers. In addition to traditional female jobs – clerks, stenographers – there are openings in radar and telecommunications.

Arts need support of public: Massey

Grants would benefit such artists as the National Ballet's Celia Franca.

June 1, 1951

OTTAWA – Canadian artists should be eligible for government grants. That's one of the key recommendations in the report of the Massey Royal Commission on National Development in the Arts and Letters and Sciences.

In his report, commission head Vincent Massey proposes creating a "Canada Council," an appointed body that would decide who receives government support. More aid to universities and researchers is also recommended.

Commons moves quickly on pensions

May 7, 1951

OTTAWA – The Commons wants the Canadian Constitution amended to include old age pensions. And it is in a hurry. MPs today unanimously passed a motion asking the British government to make the amendment. The Senate will probably pass it tomorrow and it will be rushed to London. The federal government and all the provinces have agreed to a universal pension scheme for those 70 years and older by which each person would receive $40 a month. Under provincial plans now, there is a strict means test. To put the new plan in place, the BNA Act must be amended, and this must be done by the British parliament. But there is uncertainty about the stability of the Labour government. With all Canadian governments agreed, this Parliament does not want to wait until after a British election. Discussion continues about extending pensions to age 65.

Duplessis ordered to pay Jehovah's Witness $8,123 in damages

May 2, 1951

MONTREAL – Premier Maurice Duplessis has been ordered to pay $8,123.53 in damages to a restaurateur whose liquor licence he had revoked. Frank Roncarelli, a member of the Jehovah's Witnesses sect, claimed Duplessis personally intervened in the 1946 licence matter because of his religion.

Duplessis' hostility to the Jehovah's Witnesses is well known and Superior Court Justice C.G. Mackinnon accepted Roncarelli's arguments. The justice ruled Roncarelli was not guilty of a liquor law offence, and that Duplessis "committed a faulty and unauthorized act causing damages for which he should be held personally liable."

Frank Roncarelli.

Maurice Duplessis.

Evidence at the trial showed that the premier told the chairman of the Quebec liquor commission to cancel Roncarelli's licence. Roncarelli had been the chief source of bail for Jehovah's Witnesses arrested for distributing their literature in defiance of Montreal bylaws, charges that many think were spurious. Mackinnon ruled that the liquor commission was established at arm's length from the government specifically to avoid the kind of political interference that Duplessis exerted. Duplessis acted well outside the legal limits of his office, the justice said. The premier announced today he will appeal.

Doctors first to see color TV in Canada

June 21, 1951

MONTREAL – A hospital operating theatre became a television studio as some 2,000 doctors at the Canadian Medical Association convention here were the first Canadians to view color TV. The doctors had "ringside seats" at the Mount Royal Hotel as they watched a televised abdominal operation at the nearby Royal Victoria Hospital. Doctors hailed the event as a breakthrough in surgical teaching, saying color is superior to black and white. The procedure was performed by Dr. Gavin Miller, who, with a small microphone in his mask, provided running commentary.

Black pianist Peterson refused a haircut

Oscar Peterson (later photo).

May 4, 1951

HAMILTON – Brilliant black Canadian jazz pianist Oscar Peterson was returning from a practice on the driving range earlier today when he stopped in at the Commerce Barber Shop for a trim. One of the barbers turned to him and said "the shop is closed," but a few minutes later a white man walked in and the barber started cutting his hair. Mayor Lloyd Jackson has already condemned the incident as discrimination of the rankest kind, and Peterson himself said it was "an awful comedown" after his bragging about Canadian racial tolerance during a tour of the southern U.S. last year. He plans to take legal action if possible.

Canadian "doctor" exposed as a fake

Nov. 19, 1951

OTTAWA – A man serving as a doctor with the Canadian navy in Korea has been exposed as a fake and will be discharged. Naval authorities discovered that Surgeon-Lt. Joseph Cyr was an imposter when they were preparing a press release extolling his skills in performing operations under combat conditions. On checking Cyr's background for the release, they found his real name is Ferdinand Demara Jr., and the real Joseph Cyr is still practising medicine in Grand Falls, N.B. Everyone in the navy who knows Demara's work has testified he is a superlative doctor.

Indian Act gets revised

Natives such as these Chipewyans have new freedoms under the revised act.

June 1951

OTTAWA – The Indian Act, the single most important legislative enactment dealing with Canadian Indians, has been revised quite substantially. After more than a century, Canadian governmental officials have come to the realization that in attempting to train their Indian wards for independence, in effect, through the Indian Act's rigid controls, they have allowed them no independence at all.

The revised Indian Act of 1951, while it retains the old objective of assimilating Indians into the mainstream Canadian society, does permit much greater freedom. Up to 50 sections and sub-sections in the old legislation have been defeated by Parliament because they were outdated, or simply too restrictive, on Indian band members.

The revised act, for instance, eases certain restrictions on intoxicants and ends the prohibition of Indian ceremonies and dances. No longer is it necessary to obtain permits before selling one's produce or livestock. Moreover, the veto of the cabinet minister responsible for Indian Affairs over band decisions has been greatly reduced. It now appears that bands will have greater autonomy in the management of their reserves.

One group most affected by the revisions includes Indian women. For the first time, government legislation gives them the right to vote in band elections. The act does, however, end the Indian status of Indian women who "marry out" – wed someone who is not under the Indian Act. Until now women who married non-Indians could keep their dual status as an Indian and as a Canadian citizen. Although no longer Indian Act Indians after marriage, they could still collect band money if they wished, providing they did not take a money settlement for these rights.

While their children, it is true, were denied Indian status, the women themselves could remain on their band's list. Now all women marrying non-Indians automatically lose all their band rights from the date of their marriage. Government officials see this as a positive improvement, as it will speed up the entry of Indians – females at least, and their children by their non-Indian husbands – into the Canadian mainstream society.

Elizabeth calls Canada a "second home"

Princess Elizabeth arrives at the Calgary Stampede by stagecoach.

Nov. 11, 1951

ST. JOHN'S, Nfld. – Princess Elizabeth said "not goodbye, but *au revoir*" to Canada here today in a humble and heartfelt broadcast. On her five-week tour, the princess has been in every province, in cities, villages, and countryside, and seen "the future in the eyes of hundreds of thousands of your children and heard it in their voices." Canada, she said, "has become a second home in every sense. ... No words of mine can express what I would like to tell you. ... You have given me a new strength and inspiration which I know will always help me in the future."

The princess tries square dancing.

Prince Philip and Princess Elizabeth meet Louis St. Laurent.

Canadians rock-like in Un-gol, Kapyong battles

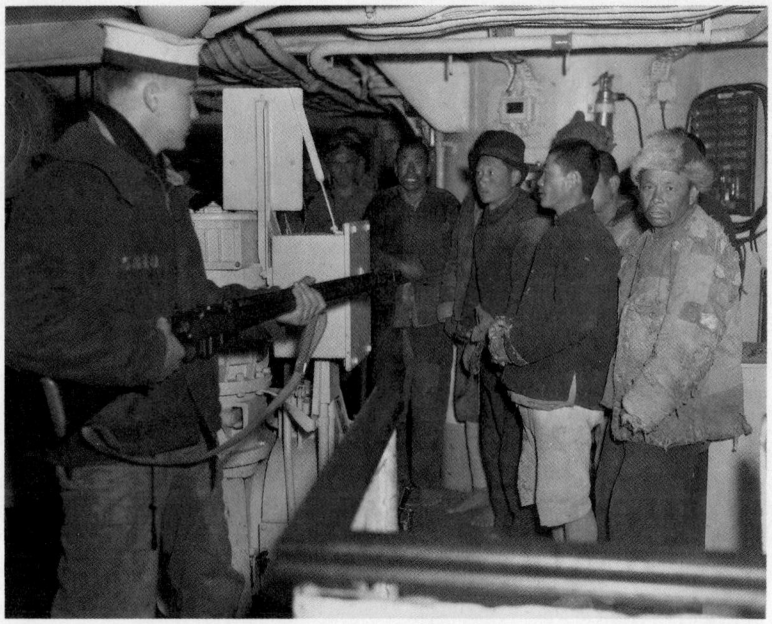

Sailor from HMCS Nootka guards fishermen captured on the Korean coast.

Contact, by Korean War artist Edward F. Zuber.

Welcome Party, The Hook, by Edward F. Zuber. The artist illustrates the inhospitable terrain which the soldiers face in the Korean War.

A Korean child, an accidental victim of napalm, shows burns to soldiers.

Nov. 25, 1951

UN-GOL, Korea – The Royal 22nd Regiment has won new honors in holding positions in face of heavy enemy attack. Chinese artillery began shelling this area on Nov. 22. Earlier, Lt.-Col. J.A. Dextraze listed what he expected of his Van Doos – "no withdrawal, no platoon overrun, and no panic."

The regiment took up a position from British troops between Hills 210 and 355 (the height of ground, in metres) and shielded the road link between them. But rain and mud forced troops to build up rather than dig down some fire positions. These so-called "hot dog stand" or "sandbag castle" posts made perfect targets. Maj. Réal Liberon, the officer on the spot, had no time to improve these posts before the enemy attacked. Chinese shellfire preceded repeated and reckless infantry attacks. Enemy soldiers often declined to take cover. The battle raged for 96 hours, on mild days and freezing nights, exhausting all ranks. Companies were sometimes surrounded before driving off enemy troops. Once, as Chinese soldiers attacked Canadian defences, a few hundred metres away Van Doos assaulted Chinese positions. During the fighting, Americans maintained delivery of 81-mm mortar shells at critical periods.

Today's victory is reminiscent of April 23-25, when Princess Patricia's Canadian Light Infantry stood rock-like at the battle of Kapyong in central Korea. As the Patricias, outnumbered by the Chinese eight-to-one, dug in to defend Hill 677, their Korean allies fled. Said one Canadian, "I am over here supposed to be helping to defend these people and they're running one way while I am going the other." By April 24, after a nearby Australian battalion had been battered into retreat, the exhausted and hungry Patricias stood alone against unrelenting waves of Chinese assaults. Facing annihilation, they held on, saved by an air drop of food and ammunition. Their final victory at Kapyong probably prevented Seoul from falling. Ten of the Patricias died, 23 were wounded.

1952

Ottawa, Feb. 11. The Dominion Bureau of Statistics reports Canada's population is 14,009,429, according to the 1951 census.

Regina, March. An epidemic of foot-and-mouth disease hits cattle in the area. Some 1,300 are killed to try to stop the spread of the disease.

Detroit, April 15. Detroit Red Wings beat Montreal Canadiens four games to none to win the Stanley Cup.

Toronto, May 13. A survey by the Toronto Women Teachers' Association shows children in homes with TV spend an average of 25-30 hours a week watching television.

Alberta, July 9. The first diesel locomotives in the Rocky Mountains go into operation, replacing steam power on the CPR between Calgary and Revelstoke, B.C.

Toronto, Sept. 8. CBLT, Canada's first English-language TV station, begins broadcasting. It is run by the CBC.

Newfoundland, Sept. 12. Many of the province's children cannot attend school because of a teacher shortage.

Ontario, Sept. 17. Simpsons-Sears Ltd. is incorporated as a Canadian catalogue order and retail company.

British Columbia, Oct. 8. The centuries-old Nechako River in northern B.C. is erased by the creation of the Keenley Dam to generate power for the Alcan aluminum smelter.

New York, Oct. 14. Canadian External Affairs Minister Lester Pearson is elected president of the UN General Assembly.

Toronto, Nov. 1. CBLT makes its first hockey TV broadcast, as the Toronto Maple Leafs defeat the Boston Bruins 3-2.

Toronto, Nov. 29. Toronto Argonauts beat Edmonton Eskimos 21-11 for the Grey Cup. It is the first Grey Cup game carried live on TV.

Marshall Islands, November. The U.S. makes one of the first hydrogen bomb tests, destroying Eniwetok Atoll.

Ottawa. The government incorporates Atomic Energy of Canada Ltd. to take over the Chalk River nuclear project from the National Research Council and investigate applications of nuclear energy.

Ontario. Ford of Canada moves its assembly plant from Windsor to Oakville.

George VI dies; Elizabeth now queen

Queen Elizabeth, Prince Philip, Princess Anne and Prince Charles.

Feb. 6, 1952

LONDON, England – King George VI, the shy monarch who led Britain bravely through the Second World War, died peacefully in his sleep this morning after a long illness. With his death, his daughter Elizabeth automatically becomes queen, including Canada in her realm. The new queen is currently winging her way home, after the news reached her as she toured East Africa with her husband Prince Philip. It is the first time in history that a British monarch has ascended to the throne while out of the country.

Elizabeth is the first British queen since the death of Queen Victoria in 1901. The 25-year-old princess is expected to take the title "Elizabeth the Second."

Massey appointed governor general

Jan. 24, 1952

OTTAWA – Vincent Massey, at one time Canada's first ambassador to the United States, has been named governor general. It's another first for Massey, whose Massey Commission report won him respect as a patron of the arts, and who is Canada's first Canadian-born governor general. His predecessors were all British-born, a fact symbolic of Canada's former colonial status. Massey's appointment is being well-received.

Right Honorable Vincent Massey.

Jaxon's identity revealed after his death

"Major" Jackson surrounded by his books and papers on a New York street.

Jan. 23, 1952

EDMONTON – Bruce Peel, chief catalogue for the Rutherford Library at the University of Alberta, has made an incredible discovery. Two weeks ago he chanced to read a Canadian Press story from New York City about the death of an eccentic individual named Honoré Jaxon who claimed to be an aide to Louis Riel in the North West Rebellion of 1885. From research he had completed on early Saskatchewan history, Peel realized Honoré Jaxon was really William Henry Jackson, Riel's English-language secretary in 1885. Just a month and a half ago the New York City dailies carried stories on Jaxon, evicted from his tenement apartment at 90. The building's owners put his books and boxes full of manuscripts, newspapers, and magazines onto the street. Now it turns out he was saving his library for the Indians of Saskatchewan. His great passion, a friend says, was to educate the Indians so "they'd get a better deal in this generation than they had in the past." Jaxon's wishes will not be realized. Most of his material has been destroyed.

CBC opens Canada's first station on TV

Sept. 6, 1952

MONTREAL – Canada's first TV station signed on the air tonight. Operated by the CBC, CBFT Montreal started broadcasting a range of Canadian programs this evening, providing an alternative for domestic viewers who have been watching U.S. signals. The programs are in both English and French, a temporary measure until a second TV station is ready to go.

Decorated Ojibwa war hero is dead

Aug. 5, 1952

PARRY ISLAND, Ont. – Francis Pegahmagabow, a decorated First World War hero who fought as a sniper and scout in the second battle of Ypres, at Passchendaele and Amiens, has died at the age of 63.

Raised at Shawanaga, an Ojibwa reserve north of Parry Island on the Georgian Bay, Pegahmagabow later attended school at Parry Sound. On his travels he came into contact with other Ojibwa bands, and this reinforced his pride in his Indian culture and heritage. Twice elected after the First World War as chief of the Parry Island Ojibwa band, he championed the old Ojibwa Indian values and fought hard to protect their treaty rights.

Canadian troops hold Little Gibraltar

Oct. 24, 1952

HILL 355, Korea – The Korean War has become a static conflict. Opponents now fight on much the same ground as a year ago. Battles are not the massive campaigns of 1914-1918 or of 1939-1945, but small, bitter actions to take or hold one hill virtually indistinguishable from the next. For the past two days the Royal Canadian Regiment has defended this feature, known as Little Gibraltar because its steep slope resembles the famous rock fortress of the same name.

Chinese artillery had pounded the area since Oct. 1. Yesterday, covered by the bombardment, they began cutting RCR barbed wire and infiltrating the area. Most of the attack fell on a single company. Survivors fell back to friendly ground and their former positions were drenched with artillery fire which forced the Chinese to withdraw. The result was a stalemate with the line unchanged.

Police recapture notorious Boyd Gang

Sept. 16, 1952

TORONTO – The notorious Boyd Gang, which broke out of Toronto's Don Jail eight days ago, has been recaptured. Edwin Alonzo Boyd and three of his henchmen were discovered in a routine police check of an old North York barn.

Despite the gang's reputation – wanted for murder and armed robbery – the capture itself was relatively calm. Boyd, Leonard Jackson, and William Russell Jackson meekly raised their hands when a pair of armed North York detectives opened the barn door and yelled, "The first one that moves gets it!" After they were escorted out at gunpoint, police returned to the barn to search for weapons. It was then that they ran into the fourth gang member, Steve Suchan, who'd been out picking apples. He also surrendered quietly.

Natural resources spark boom in Alberta

July 18, 1952

ALBERTA – The province's vast natural resources are attracting companies from all over the world. Close to $100 million in development will be spent in the Edmonton area alone. Huge petroleum reserves offer cheap power to industry, and vast, untouched forests provide sought-after raw materials for such diverse industries as pulp and paper mills and chemical refineries. Southern Alberta's "wet gas" reserves, discovered four years ago by Canadian Gulf, will soon be exploited for their natural gas, oil, and sulphur.

Conservative estimates put the value of the "wet gas" resources, whose exploitation will be stricly monitored by the provincial government, at $565 million.

Final figures put Socreds in power

July 12, 1952

VICTORIA, B.C. – The final count is in at last – the Social Credit party will form B.C.'s next government with 19 seats in the 48-seat legislature. The CCF has 18, Liberals 6, Tories 4, Independent 1. On election night a month ago, only four MLAs were declared elected, one of them the controversial W.A.C. Bennett, of Kelowna. British Columbia adopted a transferable vote system, and it has taken until now to get final figures.

The Social Credit campaign leader was Rev. George Hansell of Alberta, and the new Socred MLAs are expected to meet in three days to elect a leader from their own ranks. Bennett, once with the B.C. Conservative party, was offered the post of temporary Socred leader before the election but turned it down. Now he is favored to be the man the new MLAs will choose.

HMCS Nootka crewman works on the recovery of a minelaying junk captured in the Korean War.

Commanding officer Lt.-Col. J.A. Dextraze is interviewed by CBC announcer René Lévesque.

Inspection of equipment before a night patrol by RCR Charlie Company.

1953

Korea, Jan. 20. Canadian troops say their nylon parkas are too "swishy," betraying troops on patrol to the enemy.

North Bay, Ont., Jan. 30. Defence Minister Brooke Claxton says a chain of radar stations is operating in the north to warn Canada and the U.S. in the event of Soviet manned-bomber attack.

Hollywood, March 19. The National Film Board's *Neighbors*, made by Norman McLaren, wins an Oscar.

Ottawa, April 8. CBC chairman A.D. Dunton says it costs 20 to 30 times as much to make Canadian TV shows as it does to import American ones.

Montreal, April 16. Montreal Canadiens beat Boston Bruins four games to one to win the Stanley Cup.

Ontario, May. Joseph Hirshhorn and Franc Joubin stake a claim [near Elliot Lake] after making the biggest uranium find in Canadian history there [sparking a mining boom].

British Columbia, June 9. Premier W.A.C. Bennett's Social Credit government is re-elected with a majority. Bennett's minority government was defeated in the legislature and Lt.-Gov. Clarence Wallace refused the CCF's request to form a government.

Panmunjom, Korea, July 27. UN and North Korean delegates sign an armistice ending the Korean War.

Toronto, Nov. 28. Hamilton Tiger-Cats defeat the Winnipeg Blue Bombers 12-6 to win the Grey Cup.

London, England, Dec. 18. The Canada Company, formed in 1824 as a land and colonization company for Upper Canada, holds its final meeting following the sale of its last holdings.

Canada. There are 8,734 recorded cases of polio, the worst year ever for polio.

Toronto. Ontario creates Metropolitan Toronto, a federation of the city of Toronto and its 12 suburbs governed by a metropolitan corporation.

London. The Winnipeg Ballet is the first company in the Commonwealth granted a royal charter, becoming the Royal Winnipeg Ballet.

Canada. Hilda Neatby publishes *So Little for the Mind*, an indictment of progressive education and a call for a return to traditional education.

Millions witness queen's coronation

The RCMP take part in the coronation procession in London, England.

June 2, 1953

LONDON, England – Millions braved London's legendary rain today to witness the coronation of the new monarch, Queen Elizabeth II. Only a handful of them were actually privileged enough to see the ceremony, which was held in Westminster Abbey. Inside, world leaders sat with hereditary lords, all eyes glued to the spectacle of the young princess officially ascending to the throne of Britain, and of Canada. Fortunately, those standing outside got a close look at the new queen during her drive to the church.

The continuation of the monarchy is a symbol of tradition of staying power in a world that has seen very little of either in the last century. It also symbolizes Canada's evolving role in the Commonwealth: from colony to nation.

Government moves Inuit to High Arctic

August 1953

OTTAWA – The idea of relocating Inuit communities, popular in the 1930s, is again gaining support in Ottawa. It is felt that Inuit now living in areas where wildlife populations have greatly declined could support themselves by hunting and trapping in other uninhabited Arctic areas and thus maintain their old way of life.

Another reason advanced for relocation is the need to promote Canadian sovereignty, particularly in the High Arctic. As one spokesman of the federal government put it: "The Canadian government is anxious to have Canadians occupying as much of the north as possible and it appears in many cases the (Inuit) are the only people capable of doing this."

This month an important relocation began. Fifty-three Inuit have been transferred from Port Harrison [Inukjuak], Northern Quebec, and from Pond Inlet, Baffin Island, to Cornwallis and Ellesmere islands in the High Arctic.

Canadian officials are confident the resourceful Inuit will quickly adjust to their new homes and make a good living there.

Raid targets Royal Canadian Regiment

May 3, 1953

HILL 97, Korea – Communist forces have mounted a determined, well-planned night raid on Royal Canadian Regiment positions. In fierce fighting, the enemy killed 26, wounded 27, and took seven prisoner. The enemy also wrecked much of the RCR defence works before falling back. Canadians withdrew to their fortified bunkers and called down artillery fire on their own positions.

The enemy goal is unclear. Canadian positions were strategically unimportant. It seems both sides now launch attacks merely to keep their troops "sharp." Snatching prisoners is a means of keeping score. In these terms, despite heroic efforts, this battle must be counted as a Canadian defeat.

Dental association backs fluoridation

Jan. 27, 1953

TORONTO – The Canadian Dental Association, backed by the Canadian Medical Association, has formally approved fluoridation of community water supplies to prevent tooth decay. A joint committee of the two groups gives procedural instructions to municipalities considering the step. Health officers at the federal, provincial and municipal levels had held off implementing fluoridation recommendations until the two national official bodies had taken a stand. Today's report recommends adding one part per million of a fluoride compound to local water supplies.

The 25th Canadian Infantry Brigade uses a dog to detect mine fields in the Korean War.

St. Laurent seeking tight grip on north

Dec. 8, 1953

OTTAWA – Canada has to work harder to exert its sovereignty over its north, Prime Minister Louis St. Laurent told the House of Commons today. "We must leave no doubt about our active occupation and exercise of our sovereignty in these northern lands right up to the pole," he said.

St. Laurent was speaking to second reading of a bill that will change the name of the Resources and Development Department to the Department of Northern Affairs and Natural Resources. Jean Lesage will remain minister. St. Laurent said there have been no arguments with the United States over northern sovereignty, but he wanted to make sure American military personnel in the north recognize they are in Canadian territory.

Guinness stars in Stratford Festival

Alec Guinness plays the title role in Richard III at Stratford Festival.

July 13, 1953

STRATFORD, Ont. – Tyrone Guthrie's production of *Richard III* with Alec Guinness starring in the title role has opened the Stratford Festival. Opening night of the five-week run was hailed by *Globe and Mail* drama critic Herbert Whittaker as "the most exciting night in the history of the Canadian theatre."

Other critics were hard-pressed to find sufficient superlatives describing the cast, the direction, and the work of designer Tanya Moiseiwitsch. The theatre on the banks of the Avon, a project long sought by Stratford resident Tom Patterson, was jammed with well-wishers.

The final word of praise, Whittaker concludes, must go to the people of this festival town, and to (Patterson's) dream, "a dream come excitingly to life."

Voters hand "Uncle Louis" another term

Joey Smallwood campaigns with PM St. Laurent in Newfoundland.

Aug. 10, 1953

OTTAWA – The Liberals smashed their way to re-election tonight. The party of Prime Minister Louis St. Laurent chalked up 171 seats in the new Parliament. The best George Drew's Progressive Conservatives could manage was an uninspiring 50 House of Commons seats. The Co-operative Commonwealth Federation took 23, Social Credit got 15, and six other seats were claimed by successful independents.

If there's anything to deduce from this election, it's that Canadians are happy with the government of grandfatherly "Uncle Louis" St. Laurent. Certainly they have authorized the 18-year-old Liberal regime to retain the reins of power for at least one more term.

Church frowns on teens going "steady"

Oct. 16, 1953

OTTAWA – Canada's Roman Catholic parents have been asked by the church hierarchy to discourage the teenage custom of forming "steady" romantic attachments. In a four-page statement on Marriage and the Family, the church episcopate declares: "We call on parents to discourage the pernicious custom of boys and girls in their early teens forming permanent and exclusive steady associations which are so often an occasion of sin."

Issued after a two-day conference in Ottawa of 63 church officials, including Paul-Emile Cardinal Léger of Montreal and James Cardinal McGuigan of Toronto, the report also states that "the decline in marital morality is undoubtedly due to the unwillingness of so many to accept marriage as a sacred institution."

Report: Canadian PoWs mistreated

Oct 8, 1953

OTTAWA – The Canadian War Claims Commission today released a report which catalogues instances of gross cruelty suffered by Canadian prisoners in Nazi camps. Prisoners, who suffered from flea, rat and louse infestations, were fed skimpy meals often consisting of such items as horsehead soup and weevil-riddled beans. Medical help was frequently unavailable, and public beatings and executions caused many Canadian prisoners to suffer mental breakdowns. In contrast, Nazi prisoners in Canadian camps were very well treated.

Elaborate masks are designed by the costume department at the Stratford Shakespearean festival.

1954

Alberta, Jan. 28. Thousands of hungry elk in southwestern Alberta foothills are raiding livestock feed supplies.

Victoria, January. Mayor Claude Harrison says he will burn all books he considers communist in the public library. This statement creates a storm of protest.

Toronto, Feb. 1. University of Toronto president Sidney Smith attacks McCarthyism and upholds academic freedom in his annual report.

Stockholm, March 7. In its first appearance at the tournament, the Soviet Union defeats Canada 7-2 to win the world hockey championship.

Toronto, March 30. The Yonge Street Subway opens, Canada's first subway.

Detroit, April 16. Detroit Red Wings beat Montreal Canadiens four games to three to win the Stanley Cup.

Toronto, May 18. Peter Paul Rubens' *The Elevation of the Cross*, worth $30,000, is stolen from the Toronto Art Gallery.

Geneva, July 21. Canada is appointed to a three-member International Control Commission along with India and Poland to supervise implementation of the just-signed armistice in Indo-China.

St. Agathe, Que., Aug. 6. Emilie Dionne, one of the Dionne Quintuplets, dies during an epileptic seizure at a convent. She was 20.

Vancouver, Aug. 8. The British Empire and Commonwealth Games end. The highlight of the games was Roger Bannister running a Miracle Mile, the second fastest ever recorded.

Toronto, Oct. 15. Hurricane Hazel hits Toronto, leaving more than 60 dead and millions of dollars damage.

Manitoba, Oct. 22. The Manitoba Power Commission connects its 100,000th farm customer; 75% of Manitoba farms have been electrified.

Toronto, Nov. 27. Edmonton Eskimos beat Montreal Alouettes 26-25 for the Grey Cup.

North America. The Pinetree Line, a string of early warning radar stations in Canada and the U.S., goes into operation. The line was built by Canada and the U.S. as a joint venture.

Canada. Eighty percent of magazines sold in Canada are not Canadian. Most imported magazines are from the U.S.

U.S. agrees to join seaway project

May 13, 1954

WASHINGTON, D.C. – The United States has formally agreed to build part of the St. Lawrence Seaway. President Dwight Eisenhower today signed the bill that commits his government to the massive project and authorizes a bond issue of $103 million. The Canadian commitment is set at $300 million, but that was done when it appeared this country might have to undertake the project by itself.

In Ottawa, the cabinet is reportedly divided on whether to allow the Americans to participate in the project. Eisenhower signed the bill with a pen made of the wood of Fort Detroit, the last British fort in American territory.

Some Canadians wanted an all-Canadian St. Lawrence Seaway.

New Salk vaccine cuts polio death rate

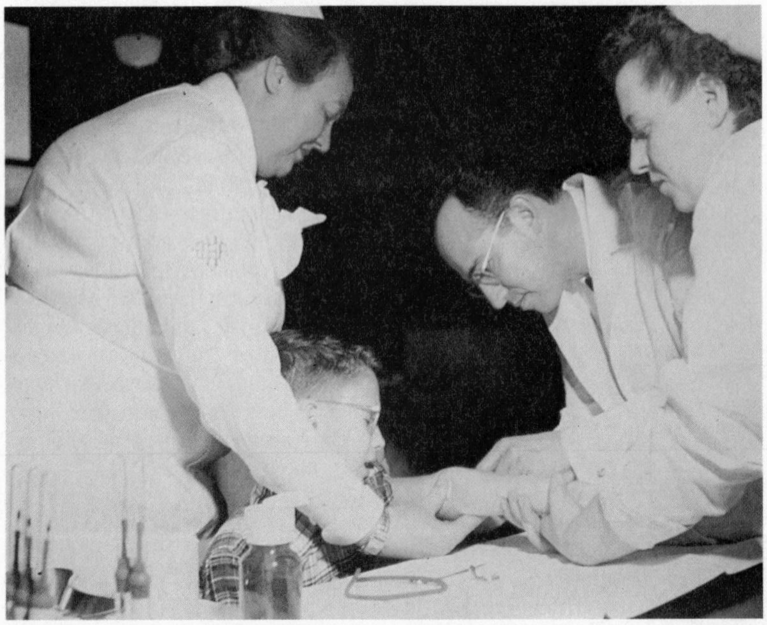

Dr. Jonas Salk, discoverer of the polio vaccine, injects a small boy.

March 26, 1954

TORONTO – Last year, cases of poliomyelitis affected more than 8,000 Canadians, crippling the majority and killing 481. But since the introduction of the Salk vaccine, the number of deaths caused by polio has plunged dramatically. Hopes of health officials are buoyed by early results from the work of American medical researcher Dr. Jonas Salk, the first person to have the courage to use large numbers of volunteers (more than 100) in his early polio virus vaccine tests.

Credit also goes to Dr. Raymond Parker at Toronto's Connaught Laboratory and to Dr. Andrew Rhodes of Toronto. Connaught was chosen in 1952 as the first laboratory to produce on a large scale the virus-containing tissue cultures. When Salk reported his results at a January 1953 meeting of the (U.S.) National Foundation's Immunization Committee, members were quick to recognize that he had scored a major triumph, "far and away the most significant work in experimental vaccination yet."

Extortion charges rock Newfoundland

April 24, 1954

ST. JOHN'S, Nfld. – Former director general of economic development Alfred Valdmanis has been charged with extorting money from firms he dealt with when he represented the government of Newfoundland. Premier Joseph R. Smallwood has been anxious to attract investment, and he hired Valdmanis in May 1950 to lead this drive. In recent months, however, Smallwood became suspicious and called in the RCMP when he was informed of the alleged extortion.

The elk or wapiti is found from Manitoba to the Rockies. It is the largest of the deer family and probably migrated to North America from Asia during the Ice Ages.

German who killed 18 PoWs released

Sept. 7, 1954

WERL, Germany – Former German Maj.-Gen. Kurt Meyer, captured 10 years ago and originally sentenced to death for shooting 18 Canadian prisoners of war, was released on parole today from the British war crimes prison here. The sentence was reduced to life imprisonment and last Jan. 15 was cut to 14 years. This is the earliest date possible that Meyer, 45, could have been freed after serving two-thirds of the sentence. Waiting for him were his wife and supporter Fred Lichtenberg of Moncton, N.B.

Bannister wins race with a Miracle Mile

Aug. 7, 1954

VANCOUVER – At today's final events of the British Empire and Commonwealth Games, England's Roger Bannister ran another Miracle Mile, winning the race with a time of 3:58.8, the second fastest ever recorded. To the cheers of 35,000 ecstatic fans at Empire Stadium, Bannister pulled ahead of his closest competitor, Australia's John Landy, with a spirited burst during the final stretch. Toronto's Rich Ferguson finished third, setting a Canadian mark of 4:04.6.

Tallest totem pole in world is erected

July 1954

VICTORIA, B.C. – The tallest totem pole in the world was erected here today. At 38 metres, it dwarfs the previous record-holder, the famous 25.8-metre totem pole at the Royal Ontario Museum in Toronto. Kwakiutl chief Mungo Martin, his son David, and Henry Hunt carved the Victoria pole. The project was sponsored by the *Victoria Times* in a campaign begun in January to sell 10,000 shares at 50 cents each.

The Victoria record effort was undertaken specifically to deny Toronto the distinction. But Toronto can still claim to have the tallest pole built for purely native use.

Marilyn Bell conquers Lake Ontario

Sept. 9, 1954

TORONTO – Marilyn Bell, a tiny 16-year-old Toronto high school student, has done what experienced lake sailors said was impossible. Tonight at dusk she touched the breakwater about a mile east of the CNE grandstand after completing the first ever swim across Lake Ontario. Some 250,000 delirious people jammed the waterfront to cheer her. Men, women, and children cried and cried, boats whistled deafeningly in unison, and one Toronto taxi driver simply said, "I'll never say women can't do anything in future." He might have said the same thing about Canadians – Bell's 52-kilometre swim was "for the honor of Canada."

She battled a rough lake for much of her 21-hour swim from Youngstown, N.Y., and often looked near the point of giving up.

Coffin found guilty of gruesome murder

Aug. 5, 1954

PERCE, Que. – A jury today found Wilbert Coffin guilty of the murder of a young American, one of three hunters slain in the Gaspé bush last summer. The jurors – six English-speaking and six French-speaking – deliberated for only 34 minutes. The burly prospector and handyman, manacled to two police constables, turned pale when he heard the verdict, but he did not appear to hear the court clerk ask him if he had anything to say. Mr. Justice Lacroix then sentenced him to be hanged.

Coffin, 43, was convicted of the murder of Richard Lindsey, 17, of Hollidaysburg, Pa. His body, and those of his father and a friend, Albert Claar, 20, were found after a search when they failed to come out of the bush. All of the bodies had been gnawed by bears. Coffin had admitted meeting them, and obtaining a part for their truck stalled in the bush, in June last year. The following month, he participated in the search when the slain men's relatives in Hollidaysburg contacted Gaspé police. Coffin's lawyer called no witnesses.

Convicted murderer Wilbert Coffin.

Ceremony kicks off $1B seaway project

Aug. 10, 1954

CORNWALL, Ont. – The $1 billion international St. Lawrence seaway and power project is under way. Americans opened the project with dynamite; Canadians with the more conventional sod-turning spades. Officiating at the dual ceremony, first on the American side then on the Canadian, were Prime Minister Louis St. Laurent, New York Gov. Thomas Dewey, and Ontario Premier Leslie Frost.

St. Laurent spoke of the importance of the project and avoided the dispute about whether the U.S. ought to share in the deep-water seaway. Frost received a standing ovation in the U.S. Then, on the other side of the river, he stressed that through history the St. Lawrence has always been considered a Canadian river, even though part of it straddles the U.S. boundary.

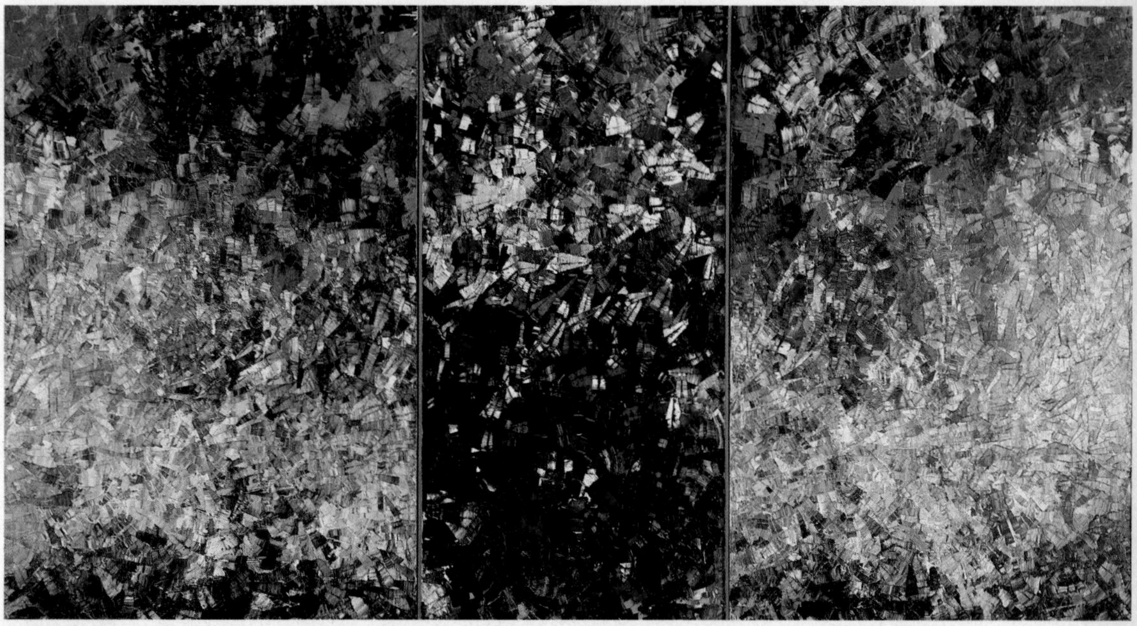

Detail of the triptych Pavane, by Montreal-born and internationally acclaimed Jean-Paul Riopelle.

1955

Ottawa, Jan. 27. The commissioner of the Northwest Territories passes a liquor control law that prohibits Inuit from having liquor, except in certain exceptional cases.

Vienna, Feb. 15. Frances Dafoe and Norris Bowden of Toronto win their second successive world pairs figure skating championship.

Ontario, March. Federal Minister of Northern Affairs Jean Lesage announces a new Inuit policy in an article in *The Beaver*. He calls for reforms in Inuit health, education, and economic conditions, and local self-government by Inuit.

Halifax, April 2. The Angus L. Macdonald Bridge linking Halifax and Dartmouth opens, the longest suspension bridge in the British Empire after Vancouver's Lion's Gate Bridge.

Ottawa, April 12. Following the successful test of the Salk polio vaccine in the U.S., the government takes steps to produce and distribute the vaccine on a large scale.

Detroit, April 14. Detroit Red Wings defeat Montreal Canadiens four games to three to win the Stanley Cup.

Nova Scotia, May 17. The first train crosses the new 1,260-metre causeway linking Cape Breton and the mainland across the Strait of Canso.

Saskatchewan, May 18. Premier T.C. Douglas opens an $8-million village for the mentally retarded near Moose Jaw, expected to house more than 1,100 people.

Toronto, June 9. Doctors at the Hospital for Sick Children perform operations on babies using a monkey's lungs to maintain blood circulation, a method never tried before.

Alberta, July 11. An avalanche kills seven Americans trying to climb Mount Temple, the worst climbing accident ever in the Canadian Rockies.

Lake Ontario, Sept. 6. Toronto's Fearnley Wheatcroft, 59, is pulled from the water after swimming 28 hours in an unsuccessful attempt to cross the lake.

Ottawa, Oct. 23. Canada marks 20 years of unbroken Liberal rule, the longest for any party since Confederation.

Vancouver, Nov. 26. Edmonton Eskimos beat Montreal Alouettes 34-19 for the Grey Cup, the first Grey Cup game ever outside of Ontario.

Six Nations hush on brief's contents

April 3, 1955

BRANTFORD, Ont. – The Six Nations of the Iroquois Confederacy are trying to develop a unified presentation to the governments of the United States and Canada. At a two-day meeting that ended here today, more than 30 representatives of the 25,000 members of the six Iroquois nations in the two countries probably worked on proposals to be included in a brief to the governments. The meeting was closed and little was said about its content.

It is known that the Iroquois leaders want to present positions on the full range of Indian treaty and other rights to the governments. A spokesman for the meeting refused to say whether the contentious issue of using Indian land for the St. Lawrence Seaway was discussed. The Confederacy has been working on a unified proposal for at least a year.

Fans riot for the Rocket

March 17, 1955

MONTREAL – A huge mob of hockey fans seeking revenge for the suspension of Rocket Richard erupted into unbelievable violence and hysteria tonight, inside and outside the Forum.

A rioting fan is led away by police.

In an unprecedented forfeiture of a National Hockey League game, the enraged fans threw tomatoes, eggs, peanuts, and coins at NHL president Clarence Campbell, who suspended hockey idol Richard last Sunday for attacking a player and a linesman in Boston. Detroit was leading Montreal 4-1 at the end of the first period tonight when a tear gas bomb went off as the game was declared over. Campbell maintained his composure – and his seat – until the bomb sent waves of gas wafting up through the spectators in the upper seats. Then he made a dash for the clinic.

Outside, the thousands who had not been able to get tickets for the game began throwing bottles and chunks of ice at the Forum, and then as police moved in, the mob moved along St. Catherine Street, wrecking streetcars, smashing windows, and looting stores. By midnight, 100 arrests were made.

Croll is first Jew named to Senate

David Arnold Croll.

July 28, 1955

OTTAWA – Lawyer and politician David Arnold Croll, 55, was today appointed Canada's first Jewish senator. The former mayor of Windsor had also been a Liberal cabinet minister in Ontario but resigned in 1937 over Premier Mitch Hepburn's opposition to industrial unionism. He served in the army during the war and was an MP from 1945 up until now.

CCF leader helped Czech anti-communists

March 29, 1955

TORONTO – M.J. Coldwell leads the Co-operative Commonwealth Federation. He is a left-leaning advocate of socialism some have labelled a communist. However, at a party meeting tonight, Coldwell revealed that he had aided Czech anti-communists in 1948 in Prague when the Communists seized power. At the time, Coldwell was having dinner with an old friend, the then-minister Frantisek Nemec. Knowing that a coup was imminent, Nemec entrusted Coldwell with the complete papers of the wartime Czech government. For four months Coldwell hid these – in his bedroom!

M.J. Coldwell, CCF leader.

U.S. to make DEW in northern Canada

May 5, 1955

OTTAWA – Some $250 million. That's the cost of a Distant Early Warning (DEW) network of radar stations the United States wants to build in the Canadian north. And that's how much it's going to pay to build the facility over the next two years, thanks to an agreement between the two countries tabled in the Commons today. The DEW Line is designed to give the Americans advance knowledge of any over-the-pole attacks by Soviet bombers. It will be primarily manned by American personnel, although Canada retains the right to take it over at any time. This will add to the 1,000 U.S. troops already here in Canada.

Ontario town hosts Scouts at jamboree

Aug. 18, 1955

NIAGARA-ON-THE-LAKE, Ont. – This little town has been turned into a giant Scout camp! Some 10,000 of the boy rangers have descended upon a campsite here for the Eighth World Scout Jamboree. They have come from 68 countries to get here – a sign of how popular scouting has become worldwide. In fact, the global nature of scouting is a key focus here, as made plain by the honorary president, U.S. President Dwight Eisenhower. He says meetings such as these build "bridges of international understanding and friendship."

Bell youngest ever to swim channel

Swimmer Marilyn Bell.

July 31, 1955

DOVER, England – Canadian Marilyn Bell, 17, stepped ashore beneath the white cliffs of Dover just before dark this evening to become the youngest person to swim the English Channel. She finished the 33.8-kilometre crossing between Cap Gris Nez, France, and Abbotscliff, near here, in 14 hours and 36 minutes. Marilyn, a Toronto schoolgirl, had a chance of beating the 12-hour, 43-minute women's record set in a race in 1951 by England's Brenda Fisher. But 4.8 kilometres from shore a tide pulled her eight kilometres to the northwest and she had to fight to avoid being pushed farther from shore. A west current also hindered her.

With thousands of people cheering her on from atop the cliffs, Marilyn made it to shore. "I'm very happy," she said before she was taken to Dover for 12 hours of rest under a doctor's supervision. The channel swim, for which Marilyn receives $15,000 from the Toronto *Telegram,* is the latest in a series of accomplishments for coach Gus Ryder's swimmer. A year ago, she won the women's division of a 42-kilometre Atlantic City marathon. Then on Sept. 9, she became the first person to swim Lake Ontario, a 52-kilometre distance.

Merger to form Canadian Labour Congress

Oct. 12, 1955

TORONTO – Most unionized workers in Canada will soon belong to a new organization. The Canadian Congress of Labour in its meeting here today approved a merger with the Trades and Labour of Canada. Out of the merger comes the Canadian Labour Congress.

The merger ends a split between industrial and craft unions in Canada. The TLC is much the older of the two organizations, with roots going back to the 19th century. The CCL was created in 1940 after the TLC expelled industrial unions, preferring to concentrate on craft unions. Industrial unions are those that organize workers by industry; craft unions organize by occupation. The CCL is now the larger of the two groups, with 360,000 workers in its affiliated unions.

There was little dissent at the CCL meeting, but some apprehension was expressed about the merger. Part of the draft merger deal is that the new organization will have no formal ties with the CCF, as the CCL has now. Some delegates said they will press the new organization to become affiliated with the political party. There was also some complaint about rules giving more power to smaller locals. The TLC approved the merger in June.

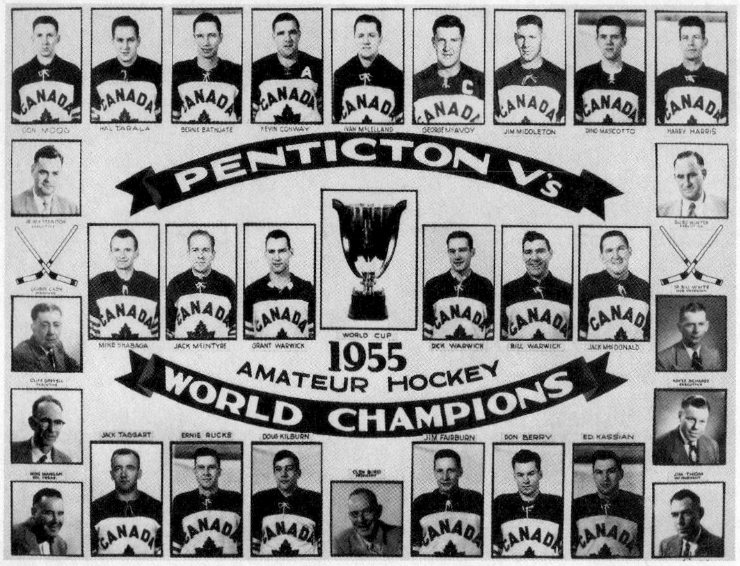

The Penticton V's have won the world championship in amateur hockey.

Molson's brewery welcomed to Toronto

A plaque is unveiled to officially open the Molson's Brewery in Toronto.

Aug. 17, 1955

TORONTO – Molson's, whose 1850 application for a brewery licence was rejected by city council, was officially welcomed to Toronto by Metro chairman Frederick Gardiner as it opened a 300,000-barrel Fleet Street facility where it will produce Crown Anchor Lager. The brewery is on 3.8 hectares of reclaimed land on Toronto's lakeshore, 2.4 bought from O'Keefe Brewing Co. Work started on the $11-million project two years ago.

Century-old B.N.A. stamp sold for $4,200

Oct. 26, 1955

TORONTO – A 104-year-old postage stamp today sold for $4,200 – the highest price ever offered for a British North America stamp. The famous Dundas 12-penny Canadian stamp of the first issue was sold by Toronto auctioneer J.N. Sissons. The stamp was named for Dundas, Ont., where it was originally found on a large legal envelope bearing the postmark of the town. Until today, the highest price paid for a mint 12-penny was $3,300.

1956

Toronto, Jan. 18. University of Toronto president Sidney Smith says government and business will have to spend more on Canadian universities to meet an unprecedented enrolment increase in the next 10 years.

Montreal, Jan. 20. Censors withdraw *The Wild Ones*, starring Marlon Brando, from cinemas on the grounds it is inspiring violence among young rowdies.

Ottawa, Jan. 31. External Affairs Minister Lester Pearson says little progress has been made toward a political solution to the struggles in Vietnam, and says Canada's peacekeeping role in Indo-China may be in jeopardy.

Montreal, April 10. Montreal Canadiens beat Detroit Red Wings four games to one for the Stanley Cup.

Toronto, April 16. Canadian piano virtuoso Glenn Gould, 23, gives a recital at Massey Hall. It's his first major appearance since recording the Bach Goldberg Variations.

Ontario, April 16. The Canadian Medical Association journal says kissing may be responsible for increases in cases of mononucleosis.

Victoria, Aug. 23. Eighteen-year-old Marilyn Bell of Toronto swims Juan de Fuca Strait in record time, 13 days after failing to finish the swim.

Toronto, Sept. 14. Thousands turn out for the funeral of WWI flying ace Billy Bishop.

Ottawa, Nov. 12. PM St. Laurent announces the formation of the Canada Council for the Arts, Humanities and Social Sciences.

Toronto, Nov. 24. Edmonton Eskimos defeat the Montreal Alouettes 50-27 to win the Grey Cup.

Ottawa, Dec. 14. John Diefenbaker is elected federal Progressive Conservative leader, succeeding George Drew.

Canada. Some 1,600 Inuit are known to have active tuberculosis, about a fifth of the Canadian Inuit population.

Quebec. Pierre Trudeau edits *The Asbestos Strike*, a book on the 1949 Asbestos strike in which he criticizes the dominant values in Quebec society.

Toronto. Robert Weaver founds the *Tamarack Review*, a magazine devoted to the work of Canadian writers.

School board ousts Little Black Sambo

Feb. 2, 1956

TORONTO – "And little Black Sambo said: Please Mr. Tiger, don't eat me up, and I'll give you my beautiful little red shoes with crimson soles." In the classic children's adventure book of the same name, Little Black Sambo outwits fierce tigers in the deep, dark jungle. But last night, *Little Black Sambo* was eaten alive when 14 Toronto Board of Education trustees voted to withdraw it from city schools on the grounds it is racist.

The vote came after black parents presented a brief arguing the book is slanderous and causes anguish to all blacks.

"OH! PLEASE MR. TIGER, DON'T EAT ME UP."

Illustration from the banned book.

Coffin hangs for murder

Feb. 10, 1956

MONTREAL – Convicted in one of Quebec's most notorious and gruesome murder cases, Wilbert Coffin was hanged early today. He maintained his innocence even in the will in which he left a few hundred dollars to the son who bears the name of the woman he lived with. But he went silently to his death on the gallows, after shaking hands with his two guards. "He said not one word," Sheriff Paul Hurteau told reporters.

Coffin was convicted in the rifle-slaying of Richard Lindsey, 17, of Hollidaysburg, Pa. Also slain in the bush were the youth's father and another American hunter.

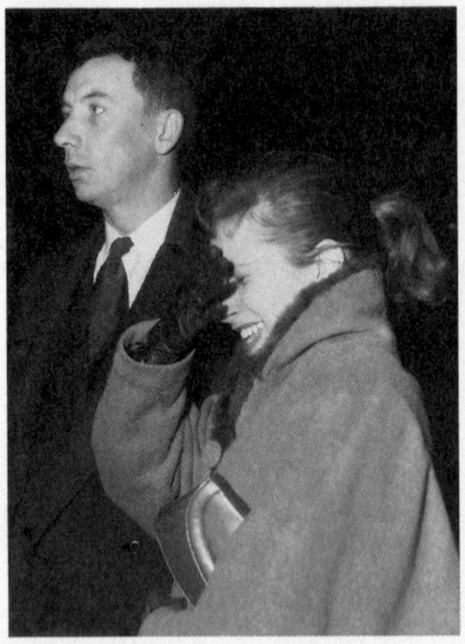

Woman cries during Coffin hanging.

Jehovah's Witness to get transfusion

April 11, 1956

ST. THOMAS, Ont. – A critically-ill seven-year-old boy will get a blood transfusion, despite his father's objections. Today the court ordered doctors to give blood to Paul Leatherdale, who was injured last Tuesday in an accidental shooting. The court order overrules father Alvin Leatherdale, a member of the Jehovah's Witnesses. This sect believes that someone who receives a transfusion will not be allowed into heaven.

Brainwashing easy if subject isolated

April 17, 1956

MONTREAL – Experiments by McGill University's department of psychology have yielded military and medical information about the techniques of brainwashing and the effects of isolation on the human mind. Reports indicate that when a subject is completely isolated he can be brainwashed no matter how strong or determined he may be. The work at McGill, said department head Dr. Donald O. Hebb, generated additional U.S. studies.

UN uses Pearson's Suez Canal peace plan

Nov. 4, 1956

NEW YORK – The United Nations has officially implemented a plan tabled by Secretary of State for External Affairs Lester B. Pearson. The resolution calls for an international emergency force to be sent to the Suez Canal to help find a peaceful solution to the conflict involving hostile British, French, Israeli and Egyptian forces currently in the area. The newly formed army, the first truly international force ever formed, will be under the command of Canadian Gen. Eedson L.M. Burns.

Howe vows to limit debate on pipeline

May 14, 1956

OTTAWA – Cries of "dictatorship" echoed in the Commons today, aimed at Trade Minister C.D. Howe. Debate began on the government's proposal to lend $80 million to TransCanada PipeLines to build a natural gas pipeline across the prairies. Howe said he'll invoke closure to limit debate on the bill. Closure is a rarely used device to stop opposition filibuster. It's never been invoked before debate began, and Howe's announcement had the Commons in an uproar. Opposition members promise a stormy debate.

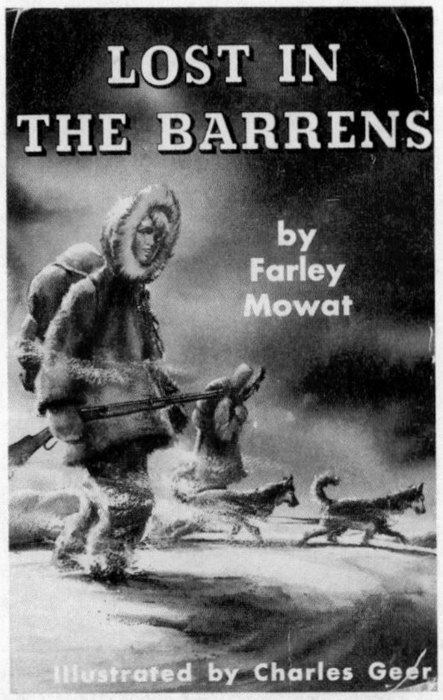
LOST IN
THE BARRENS
by
Farley
Mowat
Illustrated by Charles Geer

Farley Mowat's Lost in the Barrens has won the Governor General's Award for best juvenile novel.

Nuclear plant under construction in Ont.

Sept. 19, 1956

DES JOACHIMS, Ont. – Canada took another step into the nuclear age with the beginning of a new atomic energy plant. Federal Trade Minister C.D. Howe and Ontario Premier Leslie Frost turned the sod to start construction. The plant here, north of Pembroke on the Ottawa River, will be experimental, designed to help in building larger, commercial plants. It is a joint project of Atomic Energy of Canada, Ontario Hydro, and Canadian General Electric, with a cost of $17 million. Frost criticized Howe for saying Canada has no manpower shortage. Scientists and engineers are needed, he said.

C.D. Howe and Leslie Frost turn the first sod at Des Joachims.

Debate on the pipeline bill heats up

June 6, 1956

OTTAWA – The Senate tonight passed second reading of the pipeline bill. Third reading and royal assent tomorrow are probably mere formalities, meeting the government's June 7 deadline. But that is unlikely to end what has been the most uproarious debate in the history of Canada's Parliament.

The bill authorizes the government to loan TransCanada PipeLines $80 million to build the western section of the natural gas pipeline between Alberta and southern Ontario. The company said it could not build this year unless it got the money by June 7. But what caused the chaos and acrimony in the Commons these past three weeks was the way the Liberal government handled the debate. For the first time ever, the government has invoked closure, a time limit, on debate before the debate itself began and changed the House rules to meet the deadline. This afternoon, after passing the bill early this morning, the House abruptly adjourned as the debate claimed a victim. MP John MacDougall died of a heart attack, brought on, it is thought, by the strain of the debate.

While closure was the main battle, there were objections to the project itself. Conservatives oppose it because the company is American controlled. The CCF would prefer a state-owned pipeline.

Ottawa grants free passage to Canada for Hungarian refugees

Nov. 29, 1956

OTTAWA – Canada will provide free transportation here for refugees from the failed Hungarian Revolution. The news came tonight in Parliament, in an announcement made by Immigration Minister Jack Pickersgill.

The offer reflects the frustrating lack of help Canada and the western powers have been able to offer the brave Hungarians who tried to overthrow their oppressive Communist government. The invasion of that country by Russian tanks ensured the revolution was doomed from the start, and so the best Canada can do now is to try and help those who've escaped the terror. Many are now in Vienna, just across the border from Hungary. They're huddling in refugee camps, with few possessions, hoping for a new, free life in the west.

Refugees from the failed Hungarian Revolution gather in Vienna, Austria, and wait their turn at the Canadian embassy for visa papers to enter Canada.

Bennett's Socreds overcome scandal

Sep. 19, 1956

VICTORIA, B.C. – Premier W.A.C. Bennett's Socreds romped home for an easy 39-10 win over the CCF in today's election – despite the shadow of scandal. The opposition campaigned on accusations that bribery was involved in the granting of forest management licences. The CCF, Liberals and Tories said Robert Sommers, minister of forests, had taken gifts from the agents of forest companies. The government countered with claims about its massive bridges and highways program.

Blossoming, by Alfred Pellan. Born in Quebec City, Pellan has received considerable recognition in Europe as well as in Canada.

Vitamins to lace new biscuits sent to Inuit

July 5, 1956

TORONTO – Inuit in Canada's north will be eating a more balanced diet. F.J.G. Cunningham of the Department of Northern Affairs and Natural Resources said today the government will supply newly developed biscuits laced with vitamins to the Inuit. Cunningham expects the dietary supplement to add two inches to the average Inuit stature the next generation. It will replace the low-nutritional ship's biscuits, an Inuit staple for 100 years.

Federal equal pay legislation is enacted

Jan. 10, 1956

OTTAWA – The federal government today enacted equal pay legislation for women. The Female Employees Equal Pay Act guarantees financial equality between men and women involved in "identical or substantially identical" work. The act applies only to female employees working for the federal government, its agencies, or federal Crown corporations. Complaints of discrimination are to be directed to the minister of labor.

1957

Ottawa, March 15. The Royal Commission on Broadcasting releases a report calling for a reduction of the regulatory powers of the CBC [a prelude to the creation of private TV networks].

Ottawa, April 10. The Commons unanimously adopts the Hospital Insurance and Diagnostic Services Act, providing for a public hospitalization plan funded by the federal and provincial governments.

Montreal, April 16. Montreal Canadiens defeat Boston Bruins four games to one for the Stanley Cup.

British Columbia, May 12. Weekend climbers on Mount Slesse uncover the remains of a Trans-Canada Airlines plane missing with 62 people aboard since last December. There were no survivors in Canada's worst air disaster to date.

Edmonton, June 19. Toronto's Connaught Medical Research Laboratories announces it has developed a quadruple vaccine against polio, diphtheria, tetanus, and whooping cough.

Toronto, June 24. *Front Page Challenge,* an interview-game show featuring prominent newsmakers, is first broadcast on CBC TV.

Stratford, Ont., July 1. Canadian Christopher Plummer stars as Hamlet in the first performance at Stratford's new Shakespearean festival theatre.

Soviet Union, Oct. 4. The U.S.S.R. launches *Sputnik-I,* a manmade satellite, inaugurating the space age.

British Columbia, Oct. 7. The B.C. government and representatives of Swedish industrialist Axel Wenner-Gren sign an agreement for the construction of a huge hydroelectric project on the Peace River.

Ottawa, Oct. 21. The Northern Affairs Department says artifacts collected this summer in the Yukon establish a closer link between Asian tribes and the first North Americans.

Toronto, Nov. 30. Hamilton Tiger-Cats defeat Winnipeg Blue Bombers 32-7 to win the Grey Cup.

Montreal. Gratien Gélinas founds the Comédie-Canadienne to produce original plays in English and French.

Canada. Northrop Frye publishes *Anatomy of Criticism,* analysing the principles and techniques of literary criticism.

Royal commission: Canadians to make more for doing less

Jan. 10, 1957

OTTAWA – In 1980 Canadians will make more money for doing less work. That's one of the conclusions of the Royal Commission on Economic Prospects report released today. It estimates the work week will drop from an average of 41.3 hours now to 34.3 in 1980. But, because the Gross National Product will have tripled, wages will be much higher. As well, Canada's population will have grown to 26.5 million, up 70 percent from the current 15.6 million.

Beyond making these projections, the commission led by economist Walter Gordon has come up with some recommendations to help the government optimize developments. Among these is a call to limit foreign ownership of Canadian business, in order to keep control of the economy. Gordon also wants the government to control wheat supplies, in order to ensure a uniform price for farmers, and to radically improve Canadian universities. Whether or not the government agrees remains to be seen.

Inuit council to run N.W.T. community

Feb. 26, 1957

BAKER LAKE, N.W.T. – Under the guidance of a government officer, a group of 14 Inuit has been formed to provide the beginnings of local autonomy in this community. It is one of the first steps toward the goal of developing local, citizen-run governments in the north. The Baker Lake council, organized exactly as a council would be in southern Canada, will focus on issues such as waste disposal, clean water, fire protection, education, and the local economy.

This voice of the hitherto silent native is welcome because the Inuit now have a forum to air their opinions and make decisions. Still, some senior government bureaucrats admit the creation of the council may upset resident non-Inuit who have, to date, made all the decisions here.

Diplomat takes own life

April 4, 1957

CAIRO – Canadian ambassador E. Herbert Norman, recently re-accused of being a former communist by a muck-raking U.S. Senate committee, has committed suicide. He jumped from a seventh-floor window.

Associates say Norman was despondent over the revival of charges made in 1951 by Dr. Carl August Wittfogel. Wittfogel, once a German communist, claimed that Norman had once belonged to a student communist group. The Canadian government, for its part, responded by saying that it knew of the charges, that Norman had been cleared by the RCMP, and that it had confidence in him.

E. Herbert Norman.

Burning love: Elvis turns up the heat

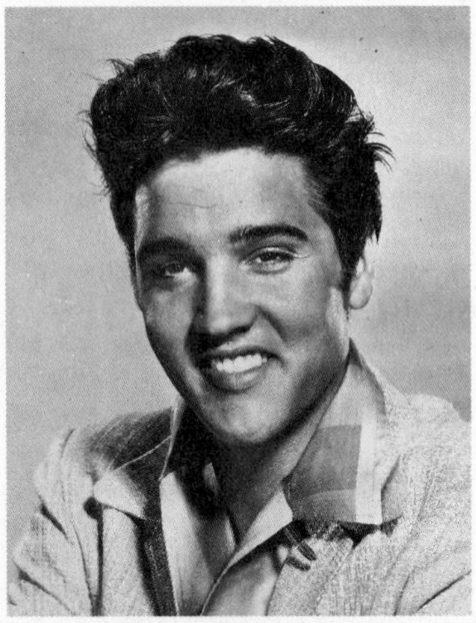

Teen idol Elvis Presley.

April 3, 1957

TORONTO – Elvis Presley, called a "whirling dervish of sex" by clergymen and "unspeakably untalented and vulgar" by critics, conquered Toronto last night. Some 24,000 screaming teenagers packed Maple Leaf Gardens for two shows, Elvis "the Pelvis" ' first in Canada. Elvis admits he knows nothing about music, but he has raw talent and physical charisma to burn. And burn he did last night. Gyrating through hits like *Hound Dog,* he ended his show in spasms, flinging himself to his knees, sweat flying in all directions, leaving a gaggle of fainting girls in his wake.

Alberta set to pay Socred "dividend"

March 1, 1957

EDMONTON – Albertans will get their long-promised Social Credit "dividend" soon. The provincial budget, tabled today in the legislature, provides for payments of $11 million to those residents who are over 21 and who have lived in this province for five years. The per capita payout will be close to $22. Provincial treasurer E.W. Hinman was careful in his budget address to spell out the basis for the dividend: it is based upon one-third of the province's oil royalties.

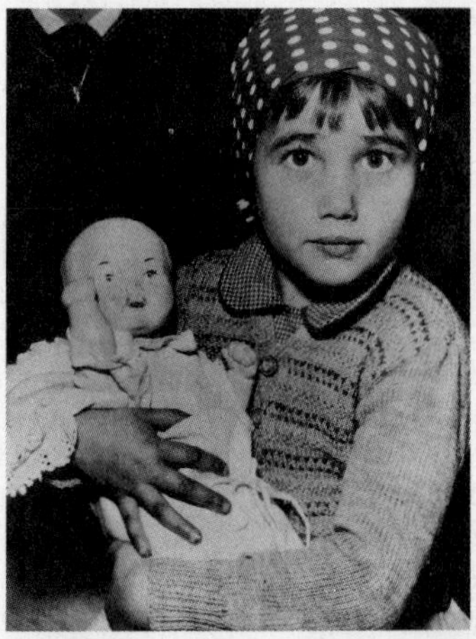

Hungarians such as this child are finding a new life in Canada after escaping their homeland.

Tory machine takes on the St. Laurent Liberals

Tough-talking Diefenbaker woos unemployed forest workers

PC leader John Diefenbaker.

May 24, 1957

KAMLOOPS, B.C. – Progressive Conservative leader John Diefenbaker put his case to this province's unemployed forest workers very neatly tonight. Asking for their votes in the upcoming federal election, he said, "I don't care about your politics. The issue is just as simple as whether or not you people want your jobs back."

Blaming the federal Liberals for the slowdown in logging wasn't the only bullet in Diefenbaker's gun. He also accused the St. Laurent government of slandering the PCs with rumors that, among other things, a Tory government would cut the pay of Canada's soldiers. And he attacked the PM's claim of "making no promises" this election by pointing to the cost of the promises already made. Said Dief, "I don't know the cost of the promises the prime minister did not make. In my opinion, they exceed at least $750 million."

Diefenbaker is swinging hard at the Liberals, and with good reason. There's a sense that the Tories have a chance this time around, something they've lacked for years. The government's rough treatment of the opposition during the pipeline debate, when it cut off debate, has not been forgotten by many Canadians. Maybe that will translate into Tory votes.

Tory leader unveils a One Canada plan

April 25, 1957

TORONTO – Tory leader John Diefenbaker wowed 'em tonight at a campaign rally held in Massey Hall. He did so not just by recycling the same old party rhetoric – though heaven knows he did that as well – but by unveiling his "One Canada" program. In it, Diefenbaker proclaims that there should be equalization of opportunities for all parts of Canada. He also stresses that the centre of the government should be returned to Parliament, rather than kept in the offices of powerful government ministers and their bureaucrats.

Tories squeak by in federal election

June 10, 1957

OTTAWA – For the first time in 22 years, the Liberals aren't in control in Ottawa. The Progressive Conservatives have taken just enough seats – 112 to the Liberals' 105 – to form a minority government. The CCF took 25 seats, Social Credit 19, and independents four. The win is a major triumph for PC leader John Diefenbaker, who has been campaigning hard to topple the regime of Louis St. Laurent. Word around the Hill is that the ousted prime minister, now 75 years old, is thinking of retiring.

While the PCs will likely form the next government, minority parties will control what gets passed in the House of Commons.

Diefenbaker appoints country's first female cabinet minister

Canada's first female cabinet minister, Ellen Fairclough of Hamilton.

June 21, 1957

OTTAWA – Prime Minister John Diefenbaker made history today. When his first cabinet was sworn in at Rideau Hall, it included Ellen Fairclough – Canada's first female cabinet minister.

Appointed as secretary of state, Fairclough is a Hamilton politician with a long history in politics. An accountant by trade, she's been an MP since 1950, and, before that, a member of Hamilton's city council. Her appointment reflects the slow but undeniable progress women are making in Canadian politics. It hasn't been that long since the notion that a woman was legally a "person" was up for debate in front of the courts. Now women are finally starting to get a share of the real power in Ottawa.

Bird cagey about giving up valuable land

June 21, 1957

VICTORIA, B.C. – Victoria real estate is going to the birds, and people are starting to squawk about it. For the past six years, Mike, a 96-year-old brandy-swigging parrot, has been the legal owner of one of the choicest pieces of property in Victoria. He inherited the land from his ex-owner, Victoria Wilson, the spinster daughter of a pioneer Victoria banker. Her will made three stipulations: that the main lot of her estate in downtown Victoria be left under lease to Mike until he dies; that the Wilson mansion and Mike's aviary on the lot be left untouched for the same period; and that Mike be fed an ounce of brandy every day to keep him in good health. So far, Mike has refused to even talk about selling.

Aerial mapping survey of Canada finished

June 30, 1957

OTTAWA – An eight-year aerial mapping survey that used wartime blind-bombing techniques was completed today by the RCAF 408 squadron. The project, which may have taken centuries using orthodox ground methods, will result in more accurate maps. One of the errors discovered involves Prince of Wales Island, site of the Magnetic North Pole used in compass navigation. The island location had been out 4.8 kilometres. Using Short Range Radio Aid to Navigation (SHORAN), a high-altitude blind-bombing instrument, survey crews in old Lancaster bombers have charted the face of Canada. SHORAN measures distance, starting with two known points to locate an uncertain third point.

NORAD defends North American skies

Sept. 12, 1957

OTTAWA – The aerial defence of North America has been entrusted to a new bi-national body, the North American Air Defence Command (NORAD). The system integrates Canadian and American radar, fighter, and missile units from coast to coast, from the Arctic to the Gulf of Mexico, into a single force, 200,000 strong, of which 17,000 are Canadians.

The continent is divided into defence zones, several of which overlap international borders. NORAD headquarters will be at Colorado Springs, Colorado. A USAF general will command NORAD with an RCAF officer as deputy commander. Air Marshal C. Roy Slemon, former chief of air staff, is the first Canadian deputy commander of NORAD.

Canada brings 14 fighter squadrons to NORAD – six auxiliary units flying single-seat Sabres and eight regular force squadrons with all-weather CF-100s. Although Canadian-U.S. cooperation in defence matters dates back to 1940, NORAD represents the greatest degree of integration to date. Some concern has been expressed as to whether Canada has surrendered too much authority over a portion of its own forces. Significantly, NORAD chiefly affects the RCAF, which is the most "continentally-minded" of the three services.

Last-ditch effort saves Dawson residents from flooding rivers

May 26, 1957

DAWSON CITY, Yukon – After several days of battling rising water levels on the Yukon and Klondike rivers, residents of this historic gold rush town are resting easily tonight, a rest no doubt welcome and certainly deserved. The flooding rivers – at one point 13 metres higher than normal – have been brought under control, at least temporarily, thanks to a determined community effort that required no less than 36 hours of continuous work by young and old alike. During that time 14,000 sandbags were filled and then piled along a 1.2-kilometre stretch of riverbank.

A state of emergency was declared in Dawson City two days ago, and military personnel in Edmonton, 1,770 kilometres southeast of here, began transporting the sandbags as well as water pumps to the stricken region. A helicopter has also been sent to an area along the McQuestion River, 145 kilometres south of Dawson, where two men are reported to be stranded without food. At Whitehorse, the territorial capital, another 40,000 sandbags plus additional pumps are ready to be sent if requested.

Famed Canadian photographer Yousuf Karsh specializes in photographing influential people.

Scientists condemn nuclear weapons at N.S. conference

British philosopher Bertrand Russell is attending the Pugwash conference.

July 11, 1957

PUGWASH, N.S. – Some of the world's greatest scientists and philosophers have concluded four days of discussion on science and world affairs with a blanket condemnation of nuclear weapons. Bringing together 22 delegates from 10 nations, the conference was the brainchild of U.S. industrialist Cyrus Eaton, originally from Pugwash.

Eaton was heeding a call from such great minds as Albert Einstein and Bertrand Russell for top scientists, including some from the Soviet Union and China, to meet and review the dangers of the nuclear age. He plans annual conferences.

Indian they called "The Lawyer" dies

Aug. 11, 1957

MICHEL INDIAN RESERVE, Alta. – John Callihoo, founding president of the Indian Association of Alberta, died today. He was 75. Callihoo was called "The Lawyer" by officials often forced into making concessions to this relentless fighter for Indian rights. Of Iroquois-Cree extraction, Callihoo first became influential organizing Alberta Métis in the early 1930s. In 1937, he became president of the League of Alberta Indians, reorganized as the IAA in 1939.

Queen Elizabeth delivers throne speech

Oct. 14, 1957

OTTAWA – History was made in Parliament today. For the first time, the throne speech was not made by the queen's representative – the governor general – but by the queen herself. Resplendent in her jewelled dress, Queen Elizabeth herself delivered the upcoming policies of the government. This visit doesn't just signify the ease of modern travel across the Atlantic. It also shows the queen views herself as queen of Canada.

Queen Elizabeth reads the speech from the throne at opening of Parliament.

Industrial training for Indians planned

1957

OTTAWA – Officials representing the federal ministry of citizenship and immigration have unveiled a program to train Indians as technicians and assembly plant workers in Canada's rapidly-growing industrial sector. The initiative is recognition of the fact that previous government arrangements for the education of Indians were not satisfactory.

"We need to help Indians move out of their primitive outposts of economic backwardness," a ministry official said. The training plan is just the first step of a number of initiatives contemplated by social scientists in the Indian Affairs branch. Other steps may include relocating whole communities from remote areas, placing Indian children who lack proper parental care in supportive foster homes in comfortable urban settings, and the increased integration of Indian youth into the mainstream of the provincial school systems.

"Our purpose is ultimately to work ourselves out of a job by helping Indians to stand on their own two feet so they will no longer have need for the government to manage their lives," the official concludes.

DEW Line detects, tracks Russian bombers

July 31, 1957

OTTAWA – The Distant Early Warning (DEW) Line became operational today. Stretching from Alaska to Greenland, roughly along the 70th Parallel, it is a series of some 50 radar posts to detect and track Russian bombers approaching across the Arctic. DEW Line bases can also direct fighters to meet the intruders. Data from the DEW Line stations is sent to USAF Air Defence Command in Colorado Springs and its RCAF counterpart in St. Hubert, Que.

A U.S.-Canadian agreement of 1954 authorized DEW Line construction. Much of the building and transport work was done by Canadian firms. All the same, nationalists are sensitive to the line, built to meet American concerns.

Nobel prize for Pearson

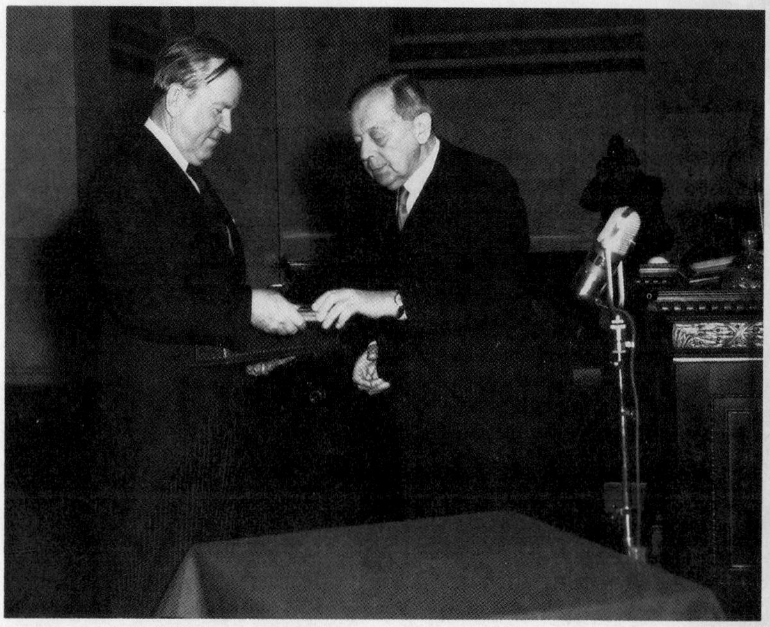

Lester B. Pearson accepts the Nobel Peace Prize in Oslo (later photo).

Oct. 14, 1957

OSLO – The former Canadian external affairs minister, Lester B. Pearson, was honored today with the Nobel Peace Prize. He's the first Canadian to win the prize, which carries with it a cash award of $40,275. The award of the 1957 Peace Prize was announced by the Nobel committee of the Norwegian Parliament after two years in which the committee was unable to find a suitable candidate.

Pearson, a 60-year-old diplomat and scholar, said today in Ottawa, where the new Parliament was in the process of being opened by the queen, that he hopes to go to Oslo to receive the award on Dec. 10. The Nobel committee does not give details as to why the Peace Prize is awarded, but signs point to Pearson's role in the setting up of the United Nations Emergency Force to defuse last year's Suez crisis.

Pearson, whose contributions to the cause of world peace began long before his call for the UN force in the Middle East, says the Peace Prize comes as a tribute to Canada as a whole and not just to him personally.

Claude Jodoin, CLC leader, addresses a rally during Murdochville strike.

1958

Ottawa, January. Lester B. Pearson is elected federal Liberal leader, following the resignation of Louis St. Laurent last year.

Ontario, April 3. The Avro Arrow crashes the sound barrier in a flight from Toronto's Malton Airport.

Boston, April 20. Montreal Canadiens defeat Boston Bruins four games to two to win the Stanley Cup.

Winnipeg, June 16. The Progressive Conservatives under Duff Roblin win the provincial election [beginning of a wave of reforms].

British Columbia, June 17. A collapse of two sections of the new Second Narrows Bridge across Burrard Inlet kills 19 workmen and injures 20.

Ottawa, July 14. PM Diefenbaker speaks to the largest radio-TV audience in Canadian history, on all the nation's radio stations and most of its TV stations, to explain his government's new conversion loan.

Ottawa, Sept. 6. The government creates the National Capital Commission to help develop and preserve the Ottawa region.

Whitehorse, Sept. 26. John Diefenbaker is the first Canadian PM to visit the Yukon. He promises to spend $100 million on northern roads.

Vancouver, Nov. 29. Winnipeg Blue Bombers beat Hamilton Tiger-Cats 35-28 to win the Grey Cup.

British Columbia, Dec. 16. Frenchman Louis Lourmais is the first to swim through the Hell's Gate Canyon of the Fraser River.

Yellowknife, N.W.T. Sir John Franklin High School opens, offering courses in an integrated setting for Inuit, Indians, Métis, and whites.

Winnipeg. Tom Hendry and John Hirsch found the Manitoba Theatre Centre, the first Canadian professional regional theatre.

Montreal. Ludmilla Chiriaeff founds *Les Grands Ballets Canadiens.*

Boston. Willie O'Ree, a Fredericton native, joins the Boston Bruins, becoming the first black to play in the National Hockey League.

Cambridge, Massachusetts. Canadian-born economist John Kenneth Galbraith publishes *The Affluent Society*.

Gladstone named first Indian senator

Gladstone shows his official appointment to his grandson (later photo).

Feb. 1, 1958

OTTAWA – Prime Minister John Diefenbaker today appointed the first Indian ever to become a Canadian senator. The honor falls on James Gladstone, 71, a Blood band member of Cree and Scottish ancestry who gained acceptance in Canada's largest Indian reserve through marriage and the study of the Blood language and culture.

The future senator is a former president of the Indian Association of Alberta, one of the most effective Indian political organizations in the country. He is widely credited with bringing about a degree of political harmony between Alberta's two main Indian groups, the Crees and the three Blackfoot nations in the southern portion of the province. Gladstone's unifying approach to leadership of the IAA allowed him to exert considerable influence on federal initiatives, such as the revision of the Indian Act in 1951.

Diefenbaker traces his vision of north

Feb. 12, 1958

WINNIPEG – Prime Minister John Diefenbaker traced his vision for development of Canada's north and did some Liberal bashing as well as he kicked off his bid for a majority government before 5,000 people here tonight. He forecast a $100-million road project in the Yukon and Northwest Territories that in turn would tie in with a joint federal-provincial proposal to commit $75 million for access roads in the north. Diefenbaker also promised a program of Arctic research to explore by land and air the continental shelf in the far north. He predicted the development of Arctic sea routes, aided by the coming of atomic icebreakers, and more self-government in the N.W.T.

Buoyed by the turnout that some observers called the prairies' largest political rally in three decades, the Conservative leader turned his guns on the Liberals. "Why didn't they do it then (while in power)?" Diefenbaker asked in response to Liberal calls for housing and small business aid, national development, and tax reductions.

Lucile Wheeler a winner in downhill race

Lucile Wheeler races to a record-setting win in Bad Gastein.

Feb. 6, 1958

BAD GASTEIN, Austria – Lucile Wheeler raced down the women's downhill course in record time today to become the first Canadian to win a race in the history of world ski championship competition. The 23-year-old skier from St. Jovite, Que., covered the 1.5-mile course in two minutes, 12.1 seconds, beating, as did the other eight top finishers, the old course record of 2:17.1. At the halfway point, Lucille was third. But she recovered in the second half, despite almost falling just before the finish. Going about 100 kilometres an hour, she suddenly faced a wall of spectators, but "my skis carried me in the right direction."

Avro Arrow's maiden flight is a success

The new delta-winged Avro CF-105 Arrow will replace the Avro CF-100.

March 25, 1958

TORONTO – Canada's Avro Arrow, the world's largest jet interceptor, made a successful 35-minute maiden flight from nearby Malton Airport today, before touching down at 296 kilometres an hour and taxiing in to be greeted by the cheers of Avro employees. Test pilot Jan Zurakowski, whom one Avro executive said was the only person that was not nervous, said the Arrow handled nicely and there was "no unexpected trouble."

The twin-engine Arrow, the size of an airliner, is capable of speeds of 2,415 kilometres an hour. About $200 million has been spent on the plane and the engine being developed for it. Each aircraft is expected to cost $4 million. In flight, Zurakowski was pursued by two photo planes, including an Avro CF-100 the Arrow is to replace.

Blast puts an end to deadly Ripple Rock

April 5, 1958

CAMPBELL RIVER, B.C. – Ripple Rock, graveyard of men and ships, was blown up today in man's biggest non-atomic explosion. The underwater rock formation, with spires reaching up to three metres below the surface, has long been a danger to ships using Seymour Narrows, part of the channel between Vancouver Island and the mainland. Since 1875 at least 114 people have died when their ships foundered on the rock.

Two years ago engineers started to dig a tunnel from the shore near here and then packed 1,375 tons of Nitramex into holes bored into the rock. Just before the explosion the people of Campbell River shut off their electricity and stacked dishes on the floor. But when the switch set off the blast they felt only a slight rumble. Then they saw a 150-metre-wide bubble swirling up through the water. Next, a tall column of water and rock shot into the sky. Clouds of smoke and gas covered the sea between Campbell River and Maud Island. When they cleared, Seymour Narrows was safe for ships.

NORAD unveils strategy

May 19, 1958

OTTAWA – One man will have authority to order Canadian and American forces into action if the continent is attacked, documents released today indicate. There will be no time for consultation and government leaders will probably not be notified until after the decision is made.

The government made public an exchange of diplomatic notes between Canada and the U.S. that establish some working principles of the North American Air Defence Command (NORAD). For security reasons, some specifics are being kept secret. But the notes indicate the NORAD commander, based in Colorado Springs, Colorado, will have full control of the air forces in a surprise attack.

The commander is American Gen. Earle Partridge. His deputy, who would act in his absence, is Canadian Air Marshal C. Roy Slemon. The commander will have the power to move Canadian or American units across the border. No mention was made of nuclear weapons, normally not flown over Canada without permission.

Diefenbaker's Tories win in a landslide

March 31, 1958

OTTAWA – Prime Minister John Diefenbaker has won a truly stunning victory tonight. With all the returns in, it's now known that the Progressive Conservatives have won 208 seats in Parliament. This means that Diefenbaker was justified in gambling last year's overthrow of the Liberals on the chance of gaining a majority government.

Now, instead of worrying about whether the opposition can get enough votes to turf him out on a moment's notice, he has a majority that will allow the PCs to rule Canada quite comfortably. As for Liberal leader Lester B. Pearson, his once-great party has been reduced to a rump of less than 50 seats! It is nothing less than humiliating.

Ontario Premier Leslie Frost was instrumental in helping Diefenbaker to massive gains in Ontario.

The Stephen Leacock Memorial Home in Orillia, Ontario.

CMA told smoking causes lung cancer

June 18, 1958

HALIFAX A frightening picture of the dangers of smoking was presented today at the annual convention of the Canadian Medical Association. An exhibit presented by Dalhousie University Medical School was a gloomy compendium of the relation of smoking to lung cancer and other fatal diseases. The exhibit claims one in 18 boys and one in 103 girls will die of lung cancer. Four out of five of the males who die of lung cancer are dead because of the smoking habit. Nine percent of heavy smokers (25 to 50 cigarettes a day) die of lung cancer.

Breeding creates Canadian horse

The Canadian.

Selective breeding, beginning with the Norman horses first brought to Quebec in 1665, has yielded an animal – the Canadian – uniquely suited to this country's demanding environment. A muscular, big-headed horse with a shiny black coat, the Canadian has been instrumental in opening up vast tracts of wilderness. It is able to travel 95 kilometers a day, and is virtually immune to the hoof and leg problems that plague other breeds. Its characteristic gentleness and intelligence make it popular with recreational riders.

U.S., Canada eye joint defence plan

Prime Minister Diefenbaker and President Dwight Eisenhower confer.

July 10, 1958

OTTAWA – Cabinet members from the United States and Canada will form a joint committee to oversee continental defence. The group was announced today at talks here between Prime Minister John Diefenbaker and U.S. President Dwight Eisenhower. The two leaders also agreed to undertake joint studies on defence against nuclear attack. The Arctic is their main concern.

Three cabinet members from each country will form the committee, designed to assert civilian authority over the military. The committee may also be a vehicle for the two governments to negotiate Canadian forces having access to the same weapons, including nuclear weapons, as the Americans. Eisenhower leaves here tomorrow.

Manmade lake to power 16 generators

Sept. 5, 1958

CORNWALL, Ont. – About 15,000 people gathered here this morning expecting a big blast. But all they saw was a small flash as 30 tons of nitrone blew gaps in the 200-metre earthen cofferdam holding back the St. Lawrence River. The bursting dam created a new lake that will power the generators of the Robert H. Saunders international power plant. The plant, with 16 generators on each side of the border, will produce more than 1.5 million kilowatts of electricity. Submerged under the lake are parts of two towns, Morrisburg and Iroquois. Morrisburg's main street has been levelled to create a waterfront park. More than 500 houses and 6,500 people had to be relocated. Some of the historic buildings in the flooded area were moved to a new historic park, Upper Canada Village. The huge power plant will begin operation in September. All 16 Canadian generators should be operating by late 1959.

Lesage new leader of Quebec Liberals

June 1, 1958

QUEBEC – Former federal cabinet minister Jean Lesage was elected leader of the Quebec Liberals today, but he probably will not seek a seat in the legislature until the next election, likely in 1960. Lesage said he will soon resign his federal seat, but will not contest a July 2 provincial byelection because he considers it to be a trap set by Premier Maurice Duplessis.

Rug hooking: the once-popular pastime is now on the decline

Traditional skills such as rug hooking and spinning are being lost today.

1958

CANADA – Post-war prosperity has led to the decline of a colorful craft, rug hooking. Developed around the beginning of the last century, the rugs were made from scraps of material, often old clothes, hooked into a foundation fabric such as burlap or canvas. Created in a time when floor coverings were a luxury, hooked rugs were a cheap and durable alternative. Women often made their own designs, although commercially-stencilled foundation cloths were available as early as 1868. The Maritimes, Newfoundland, and Quebec were noted for distinctively designed and elegantly crafted rugs.

Potlatch ceremony is practised again

1958

VANCOUVER – West coast Indians are starting to hold potlatch ceremonies openly without fear of prosecution. Potlatches, in which Haida chiefs prove their worth by showering gifts of food and valuables on a throng of guests, were banned in 1884 by the Conservative government of Sir John A. Macdonald after complaints from whites that the lavish gift-giving impoverished whole communities. Although potlatches were still held surreptitiously, there were some prosecutions, and artifacts used in the ceremonies were put in museums. The ban was lifted in 1951.

Board to regulate Canadian content

Sept. 6, 1958

OTTAWA – An act setting up a Board of Broadcast Governors to regulate public and private broadcasting stations, but at the same time establishing the CBC as a separate body with its own board, has been passed by Parliament. The 15-member BBG has authority over matters such as Canadian content, program and advertising standards, and the operation of networks. Opposition leader Lester Pearson has argued against the dual system, saying it will be confusing and that the BBG would tend to regulate only private stations.

The queen's crown tops the current model of the Royal Canadian Mounted Police badge.

Disaster strikes at Springhill mines

Nov. 5, 1958

SPRINGHILL, N.S. – The body of the last of 74 miners trapped since Oct. 23 in the bowels of the No. 2 Cumberland mine, the deepest coal mine in North America, was brought to the surface today. A rock surge is blamed for the disaster, the second to strike Springhill since 39 miners died in a rock surge in 1956. Many survivors of the shift of 167 men were brought to surface with serious injuries, some after as long as a week underground. The 74 deaths were caused by dehydration and suffocation. The miners had been trapped in gas-filled pockets at coal faces at the 3,990- and 3,960-metre depths.

A rumble like an earthquake shook the pretty town of 7,000 around 8 p.m. Disaster-wary citizens rushed to the pithead to see for themselves whether their loved ones were among those rescued or trapped. Relatives counted lamps to see who among the miners was still underground.

One teenage girl was in fitful tears as she waited for word of her father. "If I could just glimpse daddy's face even, I'd be able to go home and tell Mom that I've seen him," she sobbed. One black and grim miner reportedly said after his rescue, "They're all dead." Another distraught miner who had worked the morning shift said, "It's pretty bad down there as I understand it. I've got a brother and a brother-in-law down there. I only hope God keeps them alive."

Rescue efforts spearheaded by the fabled team of draegermen, miners trained to rescue trapped workers, have been hampered by a breakdown in communication lines and ventilation. Emergency medical supplies are being flown in from neighboring communities. Hiram Thompson, a mining expert, speculated that the cause of the rock surge may never be known. He added that the Springhill region is prone to rock shocks.

Rescue workers bring a survivor to the surface after 6 1/2 days underground.

Inuit starving to death, MP tells House

Aug. 10, 1958

OTTAWA – Inuit are starving to death and Canada does not seem to care, the House of Commons was told today. In an emotional speech, M.A. Hardie, MP for Mackenzie River, said 14 Inuit starved last winter in the far north because of the depletion of the caribou herds, and more are in danger. They ate their clothes as a last resort.

Starvation in the north "has no real or personal association to our minds," Hardie said. "But if 14 people in any part of Canada other than that part which I have the honor to represent were to die of starvation the entire country would be aroused in indignation that conditions of this kind could exist in our society." The government said a relief program has begun.

Blue Bombers capture CFL's first Grey Cup

Nov. 29, 1958

VANCOUVER – Before a crowd of more than 33,000 at Empire Stadium, the Winnipeg Blue Bombers today became the first club in the newly formed Canadian Football League to win the Grey Cup, defeating the Hamilton Tiger-Cats 35-28. Although Canadian teams have battled for the coveted trophy since 1909, the CFL only came into formal existence this year. Its nine professional teams were part of a looser amalgamation known as the Canadian Football Council, formed in 1956. Under the CFC, the teams became entirely removed from amateur jurisdiction.

Ex-minister to jail on bribery charges

Nov. 14, 1958

VANCOUVER – Robert Sommers, the former B.C. minister of forests, has been jailed for five years on bribery charges. The man who gave him some of the money, bonds, and carpets mentioned in the charges, H. Wilson Gray, was also jailed for five years.

The six-month trial did little to restore confidence in the integrity of the Social Credit government. Many feel Sommers was taking the blame for a corrupt, inept administration. Charges that "money talks" in the granting of forest management licences were made in 1955. The Socreds denied everything, but as evidence and pressure mounted there was a series of inquiries, commissions, and police investigations that ended in charges being laid.

1959

Toronto, March 26. The Ontario government incorporates York University.

Montreal, April 18. Montreal Canadiens beat Toronto Maple Leafs four games to one to win the Stanley Cup.

Toronto, May 8. The Ontario government announces the abolishment of the strap in Ontario reform institutions.

Ottawa, May 25. George Koneak is the first Inuit to speak officially to the government of Canada, addressing a meeting of the Eskimo Affairs Committee. He admits his people's problems and asks for "help in any way."

Escruminac, N.B., June 20. A fishing fleet is hit by a massive storm that drowns 35 men and sinks 22 boats.

Ottawa, July 1. Queen Elizabeth unveils a memorial to 822 Canadian and Commonwealth air force personel who died in Canada without known graves during WWII.

Kelowna, B.C., Aug. 2. $70 million worth of cancelled bonds are burned at a Social Credit gathering to symbolize the ending of the provincial debt by Social Credit Premier W.A.C. Bennett.

Ottawa, Aug. 17. Northern Affairs Minister Alvin Hamilton announces the discovery of oil and natural gas in the Yukon's Eagle Plains area.

Toronto, Sept. 9. A racial segregationist appearing on national CBC TV prompts a flood of protests.

Toronto, Sept. 14. The United Church of Canada publishes a statement of doctrine that breaks sharply with fundamentalist beliefs about the soul, hell, and prayers for the dead.

Toronto, Nov. 28. Winnipeg Blue Bombers beat Hamilton Tiger-Cats 21-7 to win the Grey Cup.

British Columbia. MacMillan Bloedel Ltd. merges with Powell River Co. Ltd., becoming one of the world's most integrated forest products firms.

Elliot Lake, Ont. The town is booming because of uranium mining, stimulated by American military demand. Twelve mining companies are operating and the town has almost 25,000 people.

Canada. Novels published include Hugh MacLennan's *The Watch that Ends the Night* and Mordecai Richler's *The Apprenticeship of Duddy Kravitz*.

Military keeping up with the times

Dief scraps plans for Avro CF-105 Arrow

Feb. 20, 1959

MALTON – Prime Minister John Diefenbaker has shocked the Canadian aircraft industry. He announced today that development of the Avro CF-105 Arrow jet fighter and the Iroquois engine is to cease. He cited as reasons the opinion that manned bombers are unlikely to be the principal threat to North America, the probability that ballistic missiles will be a greater threat, and high costs given American refusal to buy Arrows. The announcement means immediate unemployment for 13,800 Avro employees, from clerks to skilled aeronautical engineers. One labor leader describes the move as "economic treachery."

Avro began design work on the Arrow in 1951. The first was rolled out Oct. 4, 1957, and test pilot Jan Zurakowski made the first flight on March 25, 1958. Five Arrows had been built to date. Flight testing was incomplete, but examples had attained Mach 1.96 – almost twice the speed of sound.

Nuclear warheads to defend country

Feb. 20, 1959

OTTAWA – Canada's future air defences will have nuclear capability. In turning its back on manned fighters, the government has placed its trust in missiles. The prime minister has confirmed the type of missile – the Boeing Bomarc – and that it will be equipped with nuclear warheads. Short-range nuclear weapons are planned for Canadian forces in Europe.

World skiing title for Anne Heggtveit

Jan. 25, 1959

ST. MORITZ, Switzerland – Anne Heggtveit of Ottawa combined a fourth-place finish in today's downhill race and a victory in the slalom yesterday to give Canada its second overall championship in as many years in a world women's skiing competition. Her victory in the White Ribbon event here follows up the world alpine title won by Lucile Wheeler of St. Jovite, Que., in Austria a year ago. Lucile has retired. Anne, 21, has consistently placed in the top 10 at European meets this winter. This was her first combined championship.

Priceless treasures returning to Poland

Jan. 8, 1959

OTTAWA – The government announced tonight that priceless Polish art treasures stored in Canada since 1940 will be returned to Poland. Call it a victory for historical preservation over political ideology, the triumph of beauty over the ravages of a world war and a cold war, or just the anticlimactic end of a bitter diplomatic wrangle.

The move is possible because the legal custodian of the treasures, Joseph Polkowski, has agreed to their return after fighting for 13 years to keep them from Poland's Communist government. Polkowski gave in because the treasures need expert attention and he knows the Polish government has the technology to provide it. The treasures, which include the first Gutenberg Bible ever printed and the original works of Chopin, have immense national importance for the Poles. They were brought to Canada in 1940 for safekeeping after the Nazis invaded Poland. The Canadian government has consistently denied Polish demands to return the treasures.

The government said today Canada has never assumed responsibility for the treasures, and "the difficulty concerning their withdrawal was essentially one of establishing legal title and not one to which the Canadian government was a party."

Prince Albert tenor singing with opera

April 8, 1959

LONDON, England – John Vickers has arrived. The Prince Albert tenor will join the Metropolitan Opera Company in New York for a two-month stint starting in January. With his exceptional talent and the help of a good friend and fellow Prince Albertan, Prime Minister John Diefenbaker, who sponsors him, Vickers has risen quickly. He now lives in London, where his musical home is the Royal Opera House, Covent Garden. He's also sung in Vienna, and will join the San Francisco Opera Company this fall for a short time.

A long lineup forms for the anti-polio vaccination clinic in Montreal.

Grey Nuns' founder beatified by Pope

May 4, 1959

ROME – Marie-Marguerite d'Youville, who founded the Order of the Grey Nuns in 1737, was beatified today by Pope John. She is the first Canadian-born person to be elevated to holy status. Present at the ceremony was Sister Jeanne Deblois, who claimed to have regained her sight in 1927 when she prayed to Mother d'Youville. Marguerite died in 1771 while head of the General Hospital of Montreal.

Castro full of praise on visit to Montreal

Fidel Castro in Montreal.

April 26, 1959

MONTREAL – Making a pitch for Canadian dollars for both capital investment in his country and as a tourist attraction, Cuban Prime Minister Fidel Castro arrived here today full of compliments for Canada and the reception it gave him. Castro told a news conference that his welcome a few hours earlier was warm and that Canadians set an example of how working people developing their own resources could attain high living standards. Castro said he regretted missing a visit to the headquarters of the RCMP, a force he wanted to emulate. He denied Cuba has communist ties, but said it wants to establish "a real example of democracy."

Dispute in Newfoundland turns ugly

Violence in woodworkers' strike claims life of police constable

March 11, 1959

BADGER, Nfld. – Const. William Moss died today in the hospital in Grand Falls after he was hit on the head in a clash with striking loggers here last night.

The loggers' union, the International Woodworkers of America, was certified by the Newfoundland Labour Relations Board in 1958 after a supervised ballot which saw the IWA receive 85 percent support from the loggers. Two locals were started, with Local 544, representing the loggers employed by the Anglo-Newfoundland Development Company, being formed first.

When negotiations began between the IWA and the AND, the union demanded a 25 cent an hour increase in wages, a shorter work week of 54 hours, and improved camp conditions and food. The AND turned down the demands, and it also refused to accept the unanimous report of a conciliation board.

The IWA called a strike vote, received 98.8 percent support, and the strike began on Jan. 1. When it looked like the strikers might win, the government decertified the IWA, and when that did not clear the picket lines the government sent RCMP and Newfoundland officers to do so.

In a confrontation late last night, the 24-year-old Moss was injured and later died. With the full force of the government against them, the IWA and the loggers will be forced to give in.

Non-striking employees clear roadblocks left by striking members of IWA.

RCMP arrest 15 strikers from the International Woodworkers of America.

Milestone anniversary no cause for celebration in Newfoundland

March 29, 1959

ST. JOHN'S, Nfld. – Plans to hold a formal banquet to celebrate 10 years of Confederation with Canada were cancelled today. Originally 500 guests were invited to attend this banquet and to listen to speeches by Premier Joseph R. Smallwood and Lt.-Gov. Campbell L. Macpherson. However, the organizers just announced that there is nothing to celebrate, and that while the banquet will go ahead, it will be part of a celebration to honor Smallwood. Reasons for the cancellation relate to Smallwood's relationship with the Progressive Conservative prime minister, John Diefenbaker, the present depressed condition of the economy, Clause 29 of the 1949 Terms of Union, and the recent International Woodworkers of America strike.

Diefenbaker and Smallwood have not been getting along since the former's 1958 election victory. In addition, Newfoundland is suffering an economic downturn and has been counting on the extension of and an increase in the funding that has been coming from Ottawa under Clause 29. Diefenbaker said four days ago the amount would remain at $8 million and cease in 1962. Smallwood and Newfoundlanders are outraged.

The Newfoundland government is also angered by the refusal of Ottawa to send RCMP reinforcements in the recent IWA strike. There are considerable anti-Canadian feelings here at present. ▷

Judge grants Inuit couples divorce decrees

May 5, 1959

NORTHWEST TERRITORIES – A justice of the Territorial Court granted two divorce decrees to Inuit on his latest Arctic circuit. Although details of both actions are sketchy, this is probably the first time Inuit couples have sought a southern style parting of the ways.

Traditionally, Inuit children are matched early in life by parents. Under Inuit law, should they find it impossible to get along they simply separate, both being free to take on a new mate. Now there appear to be complications. The Inuit communal way of life is giving way to individuality, less sharing, and the white man's concepts of money, bank accounts, and property.

Education brings many of the white man's ideas and skills to the Inuit.

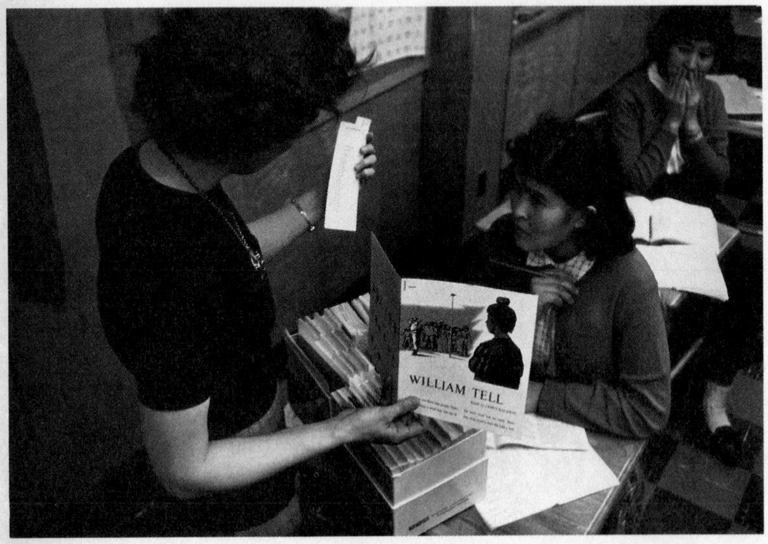

Through her study of English, this Slavey girl will pick up new concepts.

Pig project fails; Inuit to fill up on yak

May 26, 1959

NORTHWEST TERRITORIES – The Inuit apparently do not like pork. Hog raising was introduced at Great Whale River in 1957 by the government in an effort to diversify the Inuit economy and provide them with an additional source of food. But as costs have mounted and interest has dwindled, it has been decided to replace the swine with the yak, a sturdier and hardier beast, as an alternative meat supply. The yaks are still braving the elements of the government Experimental Farm in Ottawa.

Dam project under way

PM Diefenbaker starts the South Saskatchewan River dam project.

May 27, 1959

OUTLOOK, Sask. – More than 10,000 people were on hand today as Prime Minister John Diefenbaker pushed a button that triggered a blast of 1,000 pounds of dynamite. It was all part of a ceremony which kicks off construction on a $185 million power and irrigation dam on the South Saskatchewan River. It will be one of the world's largest earth dams, creating a lake 225 kilometres long which will directly irrigate 200,000 hectares of land and stabilize about four million hectares.

The ceremony featured formation flying by RCAF jets. Also, Diefenbaker was presented with an honorary chieftainship and given the name Chief Walking Buffalo by Chief William Littlecrow of the Sioux Indian band on the nearby Moose Woods Reserve. Among the dignitaries were Premier T.C. Douglas and former Liberal agriculture minister J.G. Gardiner, who unsuccessfully promoted the project years ago. The federal government will pay 75 percent of the cost of the dam and the province will pay for the power facilities.

Queen Elizabeth appears relaxed and happy with the large turnout to welcome her to Tuxford, Saskatchewan, on her current tour.

National Energy Board is created

July 18, 1959

OTTAWA – The National Energy Board, designed to regulate natural gas, oil, and electricity, has been formed by the federal government. The board, which consists of nine members, is also to play an advisory role, counselling the government on how energy resources can best be developed and used. Its powers will include jurisdiction over granting permission to construct interprovincial pipelines and other aspects relating to their safety and tolls. Exporting of natural gas, oil, and electrical power, as well as control of refined oil product exports, will come under the board.

NATO ships gather at Toronto harbor

Aug. 26, 1959

TORONTO – CNE officials, the RCN, and navies of five other NATO countries have assembled a 19-ship fleet in Toronto harbor. Their presence celebrates the new St. Lawrence Seaway. They represent several types of anti-submarine vessels. The ships and 4,000 sailors have been provided by the RCN (eight), Britain (four), France (one), Germany (two), the Netherlands (one), and the United States (three). The public will be invited to tour four of the ships.

Vanier first French governor general

Governor General Georges Vanier.

Aug. 1, 1959

OTTAWA – Maj.-Gen. Georges Vanier, the French-Canadian officer who urged Quebecers to fight in the Second World War, has been chosen to succeed retiring Gov. Gen. Vincent Massey. Like Massey, Vanier is also Canadian-born. But he is the first francophone to have been chosen for this prestigious role by the queen.

Vanier has had a distinguished military career. As well, he has been a very able diplomat, having served as Canada's first ambassador to France. He has also been a United Nations delegate, and acted as a Canadian representative during the peace talks that arose after the Second World War.

St. Lawrence Seaway officially open

An aerial view of the new St. Lawrence Seaway showing the Iroquois and Long Sault dams and the huge powerhouses between Barnhart Island and Cornwall. The international route follows the U.S. shore closely at this point.

Queen Elizabeth and Eisenhower.

June 26, 1959

ST. LAMBERT LOCK, Que. – At noon today, the royal yacht *Britannia* passed through two symbolic gates here to open the St. Lawrence Seaway. About 15,000 spectators cheered Queen Elizabeth, U.S. President Dwight Eisenhower, and Prime Minister John Diefenbaker at this lock at Montreal, the first lock of the system. Many thousands more lined the 3.2-kilometre mall built for the occasion.

As *Britannia* entered the lock, hundreds of balloons were released, rockets flared, fireworks exploded, and hundreds of little Canadian ensigns, Union Jacks, and Stars and Stripes rained down on the crowd. Ships in Montreal harbor sounded their whistles and the church bells of the city joined in the chorus. Eisenhower described the seaway as "a magnificent symbol to the entire world of the achievements possible to two democratic nations peacefully working together." Since the seaway was unofficially opened three months ago, 1,875 ships have gone through the locks.

World waits to see if Truscott to hang

Dec. 8, 1959

OTTAWA – All eyes are on the federal government to see if Prime Minister John Diefenbaker will prevent the hanging of 14-year-old Steven Truscott today. Truscott was convicted of raping and murdering a young girl.

His conviction came after a trial in which "contradiction" is the best way to sum up the testimony of the 75 witnesses. After all was said and done, many people decided that Truscott did not commit the crime, a belief which only adds to the debate over his execution.

In fact, the Truscott case has been receiving coverage around the world, with the general sentiment being that hanging a 14-year-old is hardly justice. So strong are these sentiments that Canada may one day abolish capital punishment.

Quebec's Premier Maurice Duplessis dies

Sept. 7, 1959

SCHEFFERVILLE, Que. – Le chef is dead. Premier Maurice Duplessis, 69, died after a series of strokes at one minute past midnight today. He took ill a few days ago on a tour of this mining town in northeastern Quebec. He was premier for 18 years, longer than anyone else. He was known for his one-man rule. "To be a leader is to be strong, firm and courageous," he said. Duplessis was the founder of the Union Nationale party, a coalition of Conservatives and disaffected Liberals who first won power in 1936, lost it in 1939, but regained the government in 1944 and have not been seriously challenged since. He was a workaholic who had few diversions, except that he was an avid baseball fan.

Tories end 24-year Liberal reign in P.E.I.

Sept. 1, 1959

CHARLOTTETOWN – In opposition since 1935, Prince Edward Island's Tories will finally form a government. The long Liberal reign just ending has resulted in significant changes. Rural electrification, paved roads, increased government services, and a plethora of federal programs have catapulted P.E.I. into modern times. The Liberals, however, have grown listless in power. Islanders, by the narrow margin of 50.4 percent to 49.6 percent, have decided to return Walter Shaw's Conservatives. And Liberal leader Alex Matheson seems unperturbed, saying that the province will now enjoy its first decent opposition in 24 years.

1960

Paris, Feb. 22. French-Canadian painter Paul-Emile Borduas, leader of the Automatistes and co-author of the *Refus Global,* dies. He leaves behind an outstanding body of work.

Squaw Valley, Idaho, Feb. 28. The 1960 Winter Olympics end. For Canada, Barbara Wagner and Bob Paul won the gold medal in pairs figure skating, and Anne Heggtveit won the gold in women's slalom skiing.

Montreal, April 14. Montreal Canadiens beat Toronto Maple Leafs four games to none to win the Stanley Cup.

Montreal, May 3. Roman Catholic priests Gérard Dion and Louis O'Neill publish *The Christian and the Elections*, a scathing indictment of political morality in Quebec.

Regina, June 8. Tommy Douglas' CCF government is returned to power with a majority in an election fought mainly on the government's proposed comprehensive public medical care program.

Ontario, July. The Voice of Women is formed to work for world peace.

Ottawa, Aug. 10. PM Diefenbaker's Bill of Rights, a statute specifying the rights of Canadians, becomes law.

Quebec, Aug. 30. Jean-Paul Desbiens publishes *Les Insolences du Frère Untel*, an attack on the church-dominated Quebec education system.

Vancouver, Nov. 27. Ottawa Rough Riders defeat Edmonton Eskimos 16-6 to win the Grey Cup.

Detroit, Dec. 1. Gordie Howe of the Detroit Red Wings boosts his total career points, including playoffs, to 1,093, breaking Maurice Richard's record.

Lisbon, Dec. 28. Dr. Philippe Panneton, French-Canadian novelist, physician, professor, and diplomat, dies. He wrote *Trente Arpents* (translated as *Thirty Acres*) and other novels under the pseudonym Ringuet.

Cape Dorset, N.W.T. Inuit woman artist Ashevak Kenojuak draws *The Enchanted Owl.*

Winnipeg. The provincial government passes the Metropolitan Winnipeg Act, creating the first metropolitan form of government in North America.

Sudbury, Ont. Laurentian University is founded, succeeding the University of Sudbury. It provides instruction in both French and English.

Forest resources have major impact

Paper industry workers

1960

CANADA – An estimated 15 percent of Canadian jobs are directly or indirectly connected to the nation's vast forests, which cover 4.4 million square kilometres of land. Newspapers and books in England, the United States, and Japan are printed on top-quality paper from Canada, and Canadian logs and planks grace buildings the world over. Even uncut trees are valuable, as more and more tourists visit national parks to enjoy Canada's natural scenery.

This vast resource, managed primarily by provincial governments, requires constant monitoring, as forest fires, most caused by people but sometimes by lightning, destroy millions of trees annually. In response, Canada is quickly becoming a world leader in forest fire-fighting technology and tactics, and often deploys crack firemen who are called on to parachute into otherwise inaccessible areas within minutes of receiving the alarm.

Most provincial governments endeavor to plant new seedlings to replace trees that have been cut down. But environmentalists warn that the current level of exploitation so damages the land that the new treelets may never take root in the arid, eroded soil, and may simply be washed away down mountainsides during rainstorms.

RCAF officer devises 5BX exercise plan

1960

OTTAWA – An exercise manual developed by a Royal Canadian Air Force officer for use where facilities are limited is now being offered for sale to the public. Wing Cmdr. Johnny Tett's Five Basic Exercises, thus known as 5BX, includes six charts, each consisting of five exercises that are to be done in the same sequence. Tett's program lists 12 levels of physical fitness and suggests that each person start at the bottom level and not move up until he or she can complete all the exercises in 11 minutes.

The five exercises are: touching the floor while standing with your legs straight; lying on your back and doing sit-ups to the vertical position, with both hands clasped behind your head; lying face down, hands clasped behind your back, then raising your head, shoulders and chest, as well as both legs, as high as you can; lying face down with hands under your shoulders, touching first your chin, followed by your forehead to the floor before you do a push-up; stationary run. The booklet is 35 cents and may make fitness easier to achieve.

Ottawa's Anne Heggtveit won Canada's first ever gold medal in Olympic skiing in Squaw Valley in February. She has also won the world slalom and alpine combined titles this year.

Inuit artwork helps refugees worldwide

April 14, 1960

FROBISHER BAY, N.W.T. – Today, in this remote northern community's tiny Aurora Theatre, Inuit opened their hearts to the plight of refugees worldwide and donated works of art to United Nations representative Peter Casson of Switzerland. According to one Inuit, pictures of the hardships suffered by distant refugees have had a strong impact on the community: "People are in need of food, shelter, warmth. In the past we have lived that way ourselves. We want to help." The valuable sculptures will be auctioned off in Toronto with proceeds going to a special refugee fund. One sculpture of a hunter weighs 11.25 kilograms and is believed to be worth at least $5,000.

Casson has spent the last eight months crisscrossing Canada seeking contributions in this, World Refugee Year. But, apart from the Inuit generosity, he is far from satisfied with Canadian contributions in general; the total thus far is a mere one-fifteenth of Norway's.

Casson thinks that "Canadians should now decide ... whether they care a damn or whether they don't about their fellow human beings who suffer" and hopes the Inuit example "will light a beacon which will make it possible for many Canadians to do their part in the refugee year."

Canadiens win 5th Stanley Cup in row

April 14, 1960

TORONTO – The Montreal Canadiens won the Stanley Cup for a record fifth successive year tonight at Maple Leaf Gardens, skating to a 4-0 victory over the Toronto Maple Leafs and a four-game sweep in their best-of-seven National Hockey League final series. Jean Béliveau with two goals and Henri Richard and Doug Harvey with one each did the Montreal scoring, while Jacques Plante had the shutout.

Meanwhile, Maurice "Rocket" Richard, 38, the veteran Montreal superstar, may have played his last game. He said he would decide on his hockey future this summer.

National art gallery opens in Ottawa

The new National Gallery which has just been officially opened in Ottawa.

Feb. 17, 1960

OTTAWA – The new National Gallery officially opened tonight amidst an astonishing display of high spirits and bad manners. Prime Minister John Diefenbaker momentarily stunned 2,000 guests into silence by declaring "national greatness is more than economic power, and man does not live by bread alone," but the other guest speakers were rudely drowned out by the loud chatter of a cross-section of Canada's wealthiest and most powerful art patrons. Nevertheless, the excitement bodes well for the gallery's future: its fine collection of works by Canadians the Old Masters will appease the appetites of many art lovers.

Lesage's Liberals oust the UN from power

Jean Lesage, premier of Quebec.

René Lévesque, elected to legislature.

June 22, 1960

QUEBEC CITY – Jean Lesage and the Liberals won a stunning upset victory in the provincial elections today, ending the 16-year rule of the Union Nationale. Lesage, whose Liberals won 50 of the legislature's 95 seats, campaigned primarily on the corruption of the UN government. His fears were borne out on election day. More than 100 people were arrested for election irregularities, and most of the blame was put on UN organizers. Montreal police reported an average of one election-related incident a minute today.

In the suburb of Verdun, six policemen were arrested for threatening the wife of Verdun mayor and Liberal candidate George O'Reilly. Motorcyclists raided six Montreal polling places and held voters and officials at bay while they stuffed ballot boxes with premarked ballots. Police raided the campaign offices of an independent candidate here, seized baseball bats, and arrested 10 people they described as "goons."

Police also raided the offices of the daily newspaper *Le Devoir,* which this morning ran a photograph of a ballot marked for a UN candidate. *Le Devoir* says "thousands of these ballots have been released and will be turned into ballot boxes throughout the city."

Robichaud, Liberals win election in N.B.

June 27, 1960

FREDERICTON – The first New Brunswick premier of Acadian descent won a surprise victory in elections today. Liberal Louis Robichaud, 34, ended the eight-year reign of Conservative Hugh John Flemming. The Liberals won 31 of 52 seats. Robichaud advocates abolishing premiums for hospitalization insurance. He supports bilingualism in New Brunswick.

Indians are wary of greedy whites

May 11, 1960

OTTAWA – Howard Beebe, president of the Alberta Indian Association, told federal officials today Indian women are being pursued by white fortune-seekers. Beebe said the men want to acquire shares of Indian oil and gas royalties by marrying the women. He wants legislation delaying payment of band shares for five years to Indian women who marry whites.

Georges Vanier and John Diefenbaker meet General de Gaulle in Ottawa.

Former PM Arthur Meighen dead at 86

June 5, 1960

TORONTO – A state funeral is planned for former prime minister Arthur Meighen, who died at his home here today. He was 86.

Meighen was PM twice, but he never won an election as Conservative leader. He became prime minister in 1920 when Sir Robert Borden retired, but was defeated in 1921. He was prime minister briefly again in 1926 during the celebrated Byng-King affair, but again was defeated in the election. He resigned as leader and was appointed to the Senate.

In 1941, the Tories again turned to him as leader, but he lost a by-election and retired from politics in 1942. He then became wealthy as an investment counsellor.

Arthur Meighen served two terms as prime minister during the 1920s, but never won an election as Tory leader.

Indians get right to vote

March 10, 1960

OTTAWA – Many Indians are reacting with anger and suspicion to the decision of the federal government to give them the right to vote in national elections. Albert Lightening of the Indian Association of Alberta expressed his "absolute" opposition to this initiative. "This is a trick to rob us of what we have left," said another Indian leader from Caughnawaga near Montreal. Farther up the St. Lawrence River at the Akwesasne Reserve, protesters carried banners. One urged: "Diefenbaker Drop Dead."

The laws of Canada are set up in such a way that "enfranchisement" for native people has long been equated with the loss of Indian status. Many Indian leaders see the extension of the vote to their people as a prelude to taxation and subjugation of their lands under municipal status, both running counter to treaty agreements. "What I fear," said one elder, "is that by becoming voters in Dominion elections we risk being treated as a mere interest group by Canadian politicians rather than as independent peoples with special protections for our lands that are guaranteed by ... the British Empire."

The minister of citizenship says the existing rights of Indians "will not in any way be abrogated or diminished in consequence of their having the right to vote," but many Indians remain skeptical.

Country's 2-millionth immigrant since the end of WWII arrives

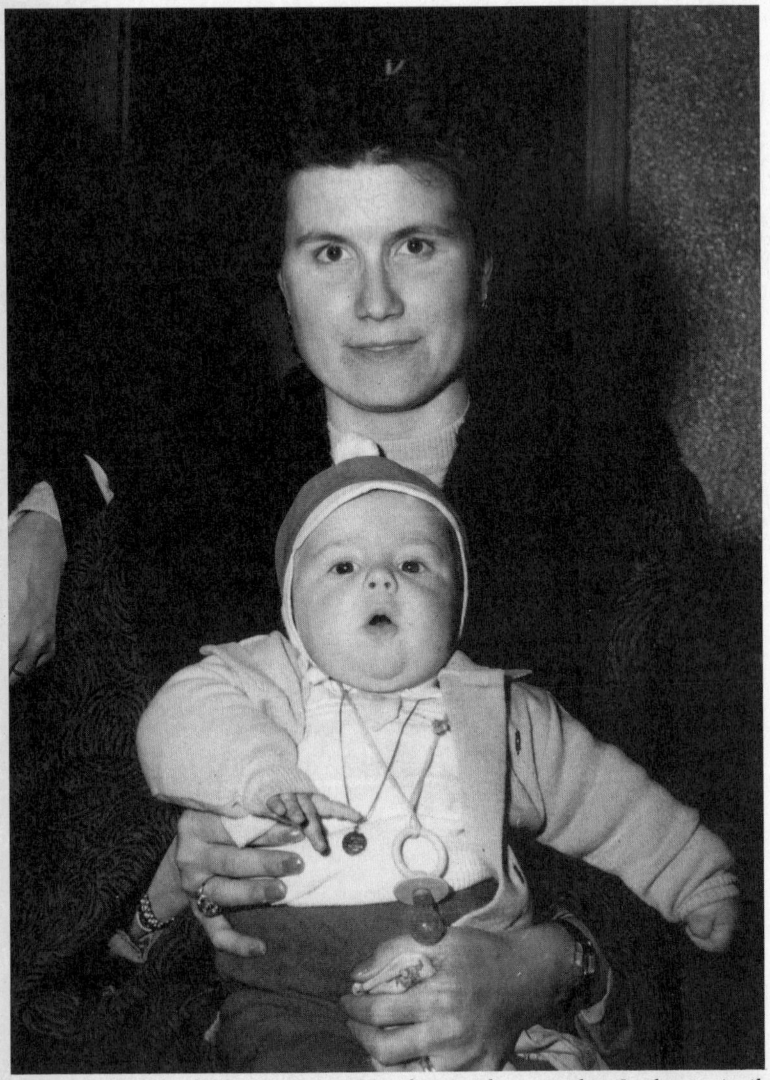

Yugoslav mother, child are among 190 refugees who arrived at Quebec in April.

Dec. 5, 1960

OTTAWA – With the arrival in Quebec of 16-year-old Anette Toft from Denmark, Canada has admitted 2 million immigrants since the end of the Second World War. But, officials say, it's unlikely a similar number will come to this country in the next 15 years. The tide of immigrants since 1945 is unsurpassed since the early days of the century.

Two factors are mainly responsible for the heavy flow. Canada was one of the first nations to offer a refuge to Europeans who lost their jobs and homes in the turmoil of war, and thousands poured in from the end of the war until 1950. After that year, Canada's unprecedented economic expansion offered new job opportunities to Europeans, still suffering the aftershocks of the war. Immigration continued at a high level until 1958, when prosperity returned to Europe and Canada's economic expansion levelled off. As unemployment in this country rose, the government had to put curbs on immigration.

Canada no longer needs large numbers of laborers and unskilled workers – the main requirement is now for professionals and immigrants with skills. But the availability of professional and skilled workers is not as great as it was up to 1957, as Britain and European nations – especially West Germany – begin to prosper.

He's back: Drapeau wins race for mayor

Montreal Mayor Jean Drapeau.

Oct. 24, 1960

MONTREAL – Jean Drapeau, 44, is back as mayor of Montreal after a landslide election victory. He first won the office in 1954 but lost a close race to Sarto Fournier in 1957. Today's was no contest. Drapeau received almost 78,000 votes to Fournier's 47,000. Drapeau's new Civic Party tonight is leading in 44 of the 66 council seats.

In a referendum question today, Montreal voters rejected the tradition of having 33 appointed seats on council. Drapeau first sought office in the Quebec election of 1944 as an anti-conscription candidate.

Study says smoking is linked to cancer

Sept. 23, 1960

OTTAWA – A survey by the federal Health Department has uncovered strong new evidence that there is a link between cigarette smoking and lung cancer, and that cigarette smokers die younger. The findings were based on questionnaires returned by 27,635 male recipients of First World War pensions. As deaths occurred, they were matched against the questionnaires and cause of death supplied by doctors. The lung cancer death rate was thus shown to be 0.35 per thousand for those who had never smoked, and 11.78 for those who reported smoking cigarettes.

Canadian exports to Cuba on the rise

Dec. 9, 1960

OTTAWA – Canada may reap big benefits from the U.S. embargo on trade with Communist Cuba. After meeting with trade officials here today, Cuban Minister of Economy Regino Boti said Canadian exports to his country should increase 10 times in the coming year, to $150 million. This would include a large volume of auto parts.

Of the Cubans, Trade Minister George Hees said "you can't do business with better businessmen anywhere." These comments have already ruffled some feathers in Washington. The Americans fear that embargoed goods will be transshipped to Cuba through Canada.

But Canadian officials said they made it clear to Boti that this country will not allow the re-export of American goods.

Yesterday, it was announced that Fidel Castro's government made a deal to buy the Cuban operation of the Royal Bank of Canada. The bank has 24 branches in Cuba and assets of $125 million. In October, Cuba nationalized all banks. But, in an effort not to alienate the Canadian government, the Royal and the Bank of Nova Scotia were exempt from the legislation. When the Royal complained it was having trouble competing with the nationalized banks, the Cubans made an offer to buy it.

PM hopes to increase trade with Cuba.

Dorval's $30M international airport opens to mixed reviews

Dec. 15, 1960

MONTREAL – It's been called "the best airport in the world." But reviews of the international air terminal at Dorval, officially opening today, are mixed. "All Canada can look with pride at this beautiful building," Transport Minister Leon Balcer said today. The attractiveness of the $30-million steel-and-glass structure is not denied. Its efficiency is. Chief among the complaints are the long walks between areas the airport design imposes on travellers. A "corridor wasteland," one critic called it, complaining that the airport is just too big.

TCA's first Vanguard sits on the tarmac at the Dorval airport.

Lady Chatterley's Lover not obscene

Nov. 15, 1960

TORONTO – A four-member panel of experts has decided that the novel *Lady Chatterley's Lover* is not obscene within the meaning of the Criminal Code. The panel was appointed by Ontario Attorney General Kelso Roberts. The panel did find objectionable six pocketbooks dealing with sexual perversion, but did not identify them in case publicity would boost sales.

Inuit artist Kenojuak draws inside her tent at Cape Dorset. A member of the Cape Dorset co-operative, Kenojuak is becoming nationally recognized.

Quebec now a part of insurance plan

Dec. 19, 1960

OTTAWA – All Canadians will soon be covered by government hospitalization insurance. Today, Quebec became the last province to sign the agreement to put the plan into effect. There are some differences among the provincial plans, but they all follow some overall principles and the federal government pays about half the cost. This year, not counting Quebec, the plan will cost Ottawa $170 million. When the signing was announced this afternoon, CCF leader Hazen Argue suggested Ottawa provide full prepaid medical care.

Bruce Kidd, young Toronto distance runner, set a Canadian record for two miles last year.

1961

Ottawa, Feb. 3. The government approves the merger of the Canadian Bank of Commerce and the Imperial Bank of Canada to form the Canadian Imperial Bank of Commerce.

Warsaw, Feb. 27. The Warsaw Museum says over 540,000 visited its four-week exhibition of Polish art treasures recently returned by Quebec.

Geneva, March 12. The Trail Smoke Eaters, Canada's entry at the world hockey championships, beat the U.S.S.R. 5-1 to win the tournament [Canada's last world championship].

Detroit, April 16. Chicago Blackhawks beat Detroit Red Wings four games to two to win the Stanley Cup.

Pretoria, May 31. South Africa is declared a republic and leaves the Commonwealth after censure from Canada and other nations.

Toronto, July 10. Mazo de la Roche, author of the Jalna novels and one of Canada's most successful writers, dies.

Ottawa, July 13. James Coyne, governor of the Bank of Canada, resigns because of a controversy over his refusal to adopt the government's expansionist monetary policy.

Detroit, Sept. 10. Bob Hayward, Canada's top powerboat racer, is killed in a race. He won the Harmsworth trophy, the world's top racing honor, the last three years.

Ottawa, Sept. 11. The Department of National Revenue says doctors were the highest paid professionals in Canada in 1959 and nurses were the lowest.

Toronto, Oct. 15. The New Democratic Party Youth's founding convention calls for an end to Protestant religious education in Ontario schools.

Toronto, Nov. 8. John P. Robarts is sworn in as Conservative premier following the resignation of Leslie Frost.

Ottawa, Nov. 30. The Five Painters from Regina Exhibition, featuring works by Regina artists [the Regina Five], opens at the National Gallery to critical acclaim.

Toronto, Dec. 2. Winnipeg Blue Bombers beat Hamilton Tiger-Cats 21-14 to win the Grey Cup.

Canada. The Canadian Television Network (CTV) begins operations with stations in major Canadian cities.

Dief and Ike sign B.C. power treaty

Jan. 17, 1961

WASHINGTON, D.C. – Prime Minister John Diefenbaker and U.S. President Dwight Eisenhower agreed here today to develop the power of the Columbia River and control its flooding. The treaty they signed provides for Canada to build three giant storage dams in southern B.C. at a cost of $345 million. The U.S. will build the power generating stations and pay Canada $64 million toward the cost of building the dams. Both countries will share the power. When the projects are finished they will have cost about $3 billion. British Columbia Premier W.A.C. Bennett says there are flaws in the agreement and he won't get the legislature to ratify the treaty. Besides, B.C. wants to wait until engineering studies are finished and a deal with Ottawa has been signed.

Formula to amend Constitution sought

Jan. 13, 1961

OTTAWA – Canada's governments are close to an agreement to bring home the Constitution. After a meeting ended here today between the federal justice minister and representatives of all the provincial cabinets, participants expressed optimism.

The stumbling block has been developing a formula to amend the British North America Act. That problem has been solved by establishing two categories of BNA Act clauses. Some would be "entrenched." To amend these, the approval of the federal government and all the provinces would be necessary. Other clauses could be amended with the approval of Ottawa plus two-thirds of the provinces having 50 percent of the population.

Priceless Poland art returned by Quebec

Jan. 2, 1961

QUEBEC CITY – The Quebec government today returned Polish art treasures worth $60 million to Polish authorities after holding them since 1948. The treasures include historic relics and jewels.

The articles were part of a batch of treasures brought to Canada for safekeeping in 1940. Ottawa returned the treasures it held in 1959, but former Quebec premier Maurice Duplessis repeatedly refused Polish demands to return the treasures his province held, on the grounds they did not belong to Poland's Communist government. Quebec governments have negotiated for the return of the treasures since Duplessis' death in September 1959.

PM pushes the principle of racial equality

John Diefenbaker and George Drew at Canada House in London, England.

Sir Winston Churchill greets Canadian Prime Minister John Diefenbaker.

March 17, 1961

OTTAWA – Prime Minister John Diefenbaker came home today a hero in the fight for equal rights. Diefenbaker is seen as the one who, at the Commonwealth conference in London the past few days, pushed hardest to force South Africa to accept the principle of racial equality. South Africa walked out of the conference on March 15 and plans to leave the Commonwealth. With South Africa gone, racial equality is now "one of the abiding principles of the Commonwealth," Diefenbaker said.

Report recommends boost for magazines

June 15, 1961

OTTAWA – American magazines shouldn't be allowed to carry Canadian ads aimed at Canadians. As well, the Canadians advertising in them shouldn't get the same tax breaks as people advertising in Canadian-produced magazines. Such are the two key recommendations of the Royal Commission on Publications. It has been looking for ways to save the domestic magazine market from stiff cross-border American competition.

Socreds elect Thompson national leader

Robert Thompson (centre) celebrates his first-ballot victory as leader of the Social Credit Party of Canada at a convention in Ottawa.

July 7, 1961

OTTAWA – Robert Thompson, a 46-year-old chiropractor from Red Deer, Alta., has been elected leader of the Social Credit party at a convention here today. After winning on the first ballot, he lashed out at the Diefenbaker government. He called for unemployment insurance to be replaced with jobs, taxes to be cut, and government to be run like business.

Canadian nationalism is exemplified in an all-Canadian designed aircraft.

Kennedy in the capital

May 16, 1961

OTTAWA – An estimated 50,000 enthusiastic Canadians today welcomed United States President John F. Kennedy to the capital. In a scene reminiscent of the 1951 visit of Queen Elizabeth and Prince Philip, huge crowds, teeming with American and Canadian flags, lined the streets of Ottawa just to get a glimpse of the popular Democratic president and his wife Jackie. The Kennedys, accompanied by Gov. Gen. Georges Vanier, rode through the city on their way to an official reception at Rideau Hall. The president and his wife are to attend a white-tie banquet organized in their honor tonight.

Jacqueline and John F. Kennedy.

President Kennedy, Gov. Gen. Vanier, and PM Diefenbaker take a stroll.

Ontario's longtime premier steps down

Aug. 3, 1961

TORONTO – Leslie Frost, premier of Ontario since 1949 and known as Old Man Ontario, has announced his retirement as head of the provincial Progressive Conservative party. Frost's tenure saw advances in health, education, and human rights legislation. And his pragmatic, small-town politics led the Tories to three election wins. Education Minister John Robarts and Attorney General Kelso Roberts are favored to replace Frost.

B.C. to take control of electric company

Aug. 2, 1961

VICTORIA, B.C. – Premier W.A.C. Bennett has introduced a bill that provides for the takeover of the B.C. Electric Company. Bill 5 is the result of months of struggle between Bennett and Dal Grauer, the ailing head of the power company, over the government's plans for Columbia and Peace River power. Now B.C. is in a much more powerful position to bargain with Ottawa over the Columbia. Bill 5 will get royal assent tomorrow.

Douglas at helm as New Democratic Party formed

Tommy Douglas speaks to the New Democratic Party convention at Ottawa.

The New Democratic founding convention is addressed by Stanley Knowles.

Aug. 3, 1961

OTTAWA – The issue in the next federal election will be socialism versus free enterprise, if Canada's newest political party has its way. In his acceptance speech as leader of the New Democratic Party, Saskatchewan Premier T.C. Douglas tonight accepted a challenge from Conservative Prime Minister John Diefenbaker. But the Conservatives must properly state what they say they want as the issue, Douglas said. The NDP supports a planned economy that provides full employment and a high standard of living, he said, and its opponents support an unplanned economy in which every person has to fend for himself.

Douglas was overwhelmingly elected leader at the NDP's founding convention here. The party was formed of an alliance of the Co-operative Commonwealth Federation, unions of the Canadian Labour Congress, and activist New Party clubs. The CCF, which has been well-established in federal politics and held the government of Saskatchewan since 1944, has seen its support decline in recent years.

Queen City corrects coat of arms snafu

Aug. 22, 1961

TORONTO – This week the city of Toronto has finally corrected an historical inaccuracy in its century-old coat of arms. Indians have become such a distant and foreign people to Torontonians that for more than 100 years they've included a representation of a plains Indian on their coat of arms instead of a Mississauga Indian, the local group with whom the British arranged for the surrender of the site of Toronto nearly 200 years ago.

Few Torontonians today even know the meaning of the Iroquois name for their city. The Mississauga had always been told by the Iroquois that "Toronto" signified "looming of trees," or trees growing out of the water. As late as one century ago, in the 1860s, looking south from Queen Street to Ashbridge's Bay on the lakefront, you could see trees that appeared to grow from the water. Now skyscrapers obscure the view.

Hockey and Sports Halls of Fame are officially declared open

Aug. 26, 1961

TORONTO – The Hockey Hall of Fame and Canada's Sports Hall of Fame were officially declared open today by Prime Minister John Diefenbaker before thousands of visitors and celebrities at the Canadian National Exhibition. On hand for the ceremonies were Livingston T. Merchant, United States ambassador to Canada, Mayor Nathan Phillips, and a host of men whose names are legendary for their prowess at hockey.

Prime Minister Diefenbaker opens the Hockey and Sports Halls of Fame.

Diefenbaker took the opportunity to announce a new $5-million initiative to encourage and develop amateur sports in Canada. The program will support coaches, athletes, and researchers, as well as Canadian competition in international sporting events. The PM stressed the importance of physical and mental fitness in the contest between freedom and communism.

The opening of the Halls of Fame took place at the height of the annual CNE, and was attended by the biggest of hockey superstars, including Cyclone Taylor, Ace Bailey, Eddie Shore, Maurice Richard, Ching Johnson, Jack Adams, Milt Schmidt, and Babe Pratt.

Funding for the Hockey Hall of Fame, which was actually founded in 1943, was provided by the National Hockey League, the city of Toronto, and the CNE Association. The hall is open to the public year-round and has a wide variety of memorabilia.

Environmentalists wind up six-day Montreal meeting

Oct. 28, 1961
MONTREAL – Since Canada's first Wildlife Conference in 1919, the country's federal government has not always considered environmental issues when making policies. But a new awareness of the finite nature of Canada's rich natural resources led Ottawa to sponsor this year's six-day Resources for Tomorrow Conference, which ended today.

Discussions revolved around the status of Canada's resources, looking into the problems and trends relating to Canadian waters, fish, forests, wildlife, and soil.

The conference was an opportunity for government representatives to weigh public concerns about certain environmental issues and to incorporate them into their deliberations. Overall, the event is being considered a success. As anticipated, some of the points raised at the Resources for Tomorrow Conference will be adopted as new conservation policies geared, it is hoped, to preserve and perpetuate Canada's resources.

Saskatchewan first to adopt medicare

Nov. 18, 1961
REGINA – The Saskatchewan legislature has passed the controversial medicare bill that will provide the province with the first prepaid medical care plan in the country. Other bills were passed to supply funding for the program. A six percent provincial surcharge was added to personal income taxes, and the corporation tax was increased from nine percent to 10 percent. On Jan. 1, the sales tax will increase from three percent to five percent. The province's health and education departments will share revenue from these increases.

The 930,000 people in Saskatchewan will be levied $12 per individual or $24 per family. The new medical insurance plan will come into effect April 1, 1962. Cost for the first year of operation is estimated at $22 million.

National Indian Council established

Dec. 31, 1961
CALGARY – William Wutunee, a Cree lawyer living in Calgary, counts the National Indian Council's first month of existence a significant success. He was one of the most forceful movers in creating the national organization. The council represents the most recent of a series of initiatives in the 20th century to create a national Indian forum along with the provincial organizations which already exist. Native people are actually a diverse lot whose ancestral roots are set in dozens of distinct native nationalities. In Wutunee's view, Indians across Canada need to become better acquainted with one another so they can present a more common political front on many matters of shared interest. Not every Indian leader shares Wutunee's confidence in the council's bright future.

Stats say 69.7% of Canadians live and work in urban areas

This Belgian immigrant has established a tobacco farm in Ontario.

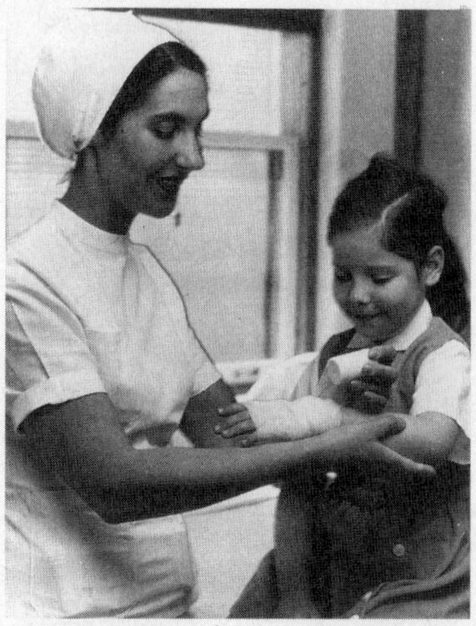

Hungarian-born Dr. Susan Gartha practises in London, Ontario.

Greek immigrant arrives in Toronto.

1961
CANADA – The demographics of Canada are changing – dramatically. Since the end of the Second World War, Canada's population has shifted, in focus and numerically, from rural to urban: 69.7 percent of Canadians now live and work in urban areas. This can be attributed to two major reasons: the migration of labor from agricultural and primary industries to the manufacturing and service-related sector, and the immigration of professional and unskilled labor.

Fewer Canadians than ever make their livings in farming, fishing, or the lumber industry. In 1901, 45 percent of all male workers were employed in agriculture – by last year, only 11 percent. The migration of young people from rural to urban areas is partly responsible. According to census reports, of those aged 15 to 19 living on farms in 1951 almost 40 percent had left by 1956, mostly for jobs in non-agricultural labor. This loss of manpower has been offset by increased mechanization and development of fertilizers and pest controls.

The majority of post-war immigrants – mostly British, Dutch, German, Italian, Polish, Jews, and some Hungarian refugees following the 1956 revolution – have added to the broad spectrum of modern urban dwellers by settling in cities and towns. Many are unskilled, but professionals, including doctors and engineers, have also arrived.

Government expands plan addressing the threat of nuclear war

Sept. 7, 1961
OTTAWA – The government is rapidly expanding its program to protect Canadians from nuclear war. Prime Minister John Diefenbaker told the House of Commons today that 100,000 men will be trained for civilian survival operations. In an atmosphere of heightened international tensions, the government also announced other measures designed to dampen the effect of nuclear war. Outside each city thought to be a nuclear target, dispersal centres will be established. These will hold supplies of food, vehicles, blankets, clothing, and medical supplies.

1962

Ottawa, Feb. 6. The government announces all federal cheques will be bilingual.

British Columbia, March 6. An explosion, believed to be the work of Sons of Freedom Doukhobors, topples a giant power transmission tower into Kootenay Lake.

Canada, March 21. The sedative drug thalidomide is withdrawn from the market after a year because of evidence it may cause birth defects.

Chicago, April 22. Toronto Maple Leafs defeat Chicago Blackhawks four games to two to win the Stanley Cup.

Toronto, May 31. Premier Robarts announces approval of plans for a university at Peterborough, Trent University.

Regina, July 1. The CCF government's Medical Care Insurance Act goes into effect, providing comprehensive public health care for the first time in Canada. Doctors across the province go on strike in opposition to the plan.

Ottawa, Aug. 7. The Health Department announces it is sending a letter to doctors and druggists warning of the possible side effects of the birth control pills Enovid and Orthonovum.

Ontario, September. The Robarts Plan, named after the minister of education who conceived it, is introduced in Ontario schools. It provides for academic and vocational education in schools to meet the needs of the baby boomers.

Toronto, Dec. 2. Winnipeg Blue Bombers beat Hamilton Tiger-Cats 28-27 to win the Grey Cup.

Niagara-on-the-Lake, Ont. Brian Doherty founds the Shaw Festival, the world's only theatre festival devoted to George Bernard Shaw plays.

Dawson, Yukon. Tom Patterson's Yukon theatre festival is held in the summer.

Esterhazy, Sask. Potash mining begins at the site of the world's largest known reserves of potash.

Canada. Marshall McLuhan publishes *The Gutenberg Galaxy: the making of typographic man*, which coins the phrase the "global village."

United States. Conservationist Rachel Carson publishes *Silent Spring*, documenting the environmental threat posed by pollution, hazardous wastes, and pesticides.

New immigration rules to open door

Jan. 19, 1962

OTTAWA – In what many regard as a long overdue step toward ridding racial discrimination from Canada's immigration regulations, the Conservative government today announced that as of next month any person from any country in the world will be considered admissible – provided he or she meets education and skills requirements and other special criteria demanded by the Immigration Department. The new rules, designed to prevent exclusion based on race or national origin, will allow a greater number of immigrants from Asia, Africa, and the Middle East. For example, agreements with India and Pakistan limiting the number of immigrants to a few hundred a year will no longer be necessary.

Among the changes, skilled persons who have difficulty supporting themselves at first will be admitted if sponsored by parents, in-laws, or a future spouse already here. Also, deportation orders can now be appealed before a special board. Still, the new steps have aroused some criticism. Liberal J.W. Pickersgill charges that by maintaining admissibility requirements, the government has merely "substituted one set of criteria for discrimination of another."

Cowichan sweaters popular with tourists and around the world

Feb. 12, 1962

DUNCAN, B.C. – The Indian women of the Cowichan Valley, north of Victoria, have always been expert weavers. But these days, instead of making blankets and clothes for themselves they are making sweaters and selling them to tourists – and to stores around the world. And they knit, instead of weave, and use the wool from sheep brought to the valley by settlers in the 1850s, instead of wool from dogs and goats. These Cowichan sweaters give superb protection against the rain and cold. Earlier sweaters were of a single color, but settlers from the Shetlands showed the Indians how to knit patterned sweaters – Fair Isle style.

Cowichan sweaters are sold at the co-operative store at Saanichton, B.C.

Canadian communications theorist Marshall McLuhan has just published The Gutenberg Galaxy: The Making of Typographic Man, in which he calls the world a "global village," because of its electronic interdependence. McLuhan has taught at the University of Toronto since 1946.

Rolphton's nuclear plant one of a kind

June 4, 1962

ROLPHTON, Ont. – For the first time, the atom has been employed to generate electricity in Canada. At 1:31 today, 3,000 kilowatts from the Rolphton experimental nuclear power plant were fed into Ontario Hydro's grid. The current is enough to power 2,000 homes. The event is the culmination of eight years research by the federal government's Atomic Energy of Canada Ltd., Ontario Hydro, and Canadian General Electric.

The plant uses heat generated by atomic chain reactions in uranium to heat water. This drives steam turbines, which generate electricity. The Rolphton plant is the first of its kind anywhere. It is also the prototype for a 200,000-kilowatt plant.

Doukhobor women burn their homes

June 8, 1962

TRAIL, B.C. – Women of the Sons of Freedom sect of the Doukhobors burned more than 50 of their own homes in the West Kootenay area today. Some stood naked as flames destroyed the tar-paper and plywood homes, while others worked in their gardens to the light of the blaze. One told reporters: "God told me to do it." Later the women threw rocks and water at police and reporters and then went to local schools and took their children home.

The women are thought to be protesting charges of intimidation laid in Vancouver recently against 71 members of the sect's Fraternal Council. Last night Freedomites held in a Nelson jail set a series of fires, but they were quickly put out. Last month nine sect members were jailed for bombing a power pylon.

Doukhobor watches home burn.

Tories are back, but with a minority

Lester Pearson during the campaign.

June 18, 1962

OTTAWA – Urban Ontario and rural Quebec voted different ways but combined to give Canada a minority government tonight. Late returns show Prime Minister John Diefenbaker's Conservatives with 116 seats, down from the 208 they won in 1958. The Liberals hold 98, the Social Credit 30, and the NDP 19.

The Liberals made their major gains in Ontario, particularly in Toronto. The biggest surprise was Works Minister David Walker, a Toronto Conservative, being defeated by Liberal Donald S. Macdonald. In Quebec, the Social Credit made its big gains, winning 26 seats. Social Credit leader Robert Thompson said tonight he will cooperate with the Conservatives to provide stable government, but only until he feels another election should be held. NDP leader T.C. Douglas lost his seat in Regina.

Some fears were expressed tonight about how a minority government might affect the country. "At a time of financial crisis no party will take hold and be able to give the kind of confidence needed in Canada," said Liberal campaign co-chairman Walter Gordon.

One Liberal success story in Toronto is the victory of popular Maple Leaf hockey player Red Kelly. He thinks he will be a bit out of place in Ottawa because, he said, he doesn't smoke, drink, or swear.

Deal ends dispute over medical care

July 23, 1962

SASKATOON – As soon as the Medical Care Insurance Act can be amended, medical care will be back to normal in Saskatchewan. At 12:45 p.m. today, mediator Lord Taylor announced a settlement of the three-week dispute between the Saskatchewan College of Physicians and Surgeons and the provincial government. Taylor is an architect of Britain's national health plan. During the dispute, the province recruited 61 British doctors on short-term contracts.

The new agreement says patients may choose their own doctors, and doctors are free to practise in or out of the act.

Detail of street scene in Montreal by artist Richard D. Wilson.

Morrisseau paintings sell out first night

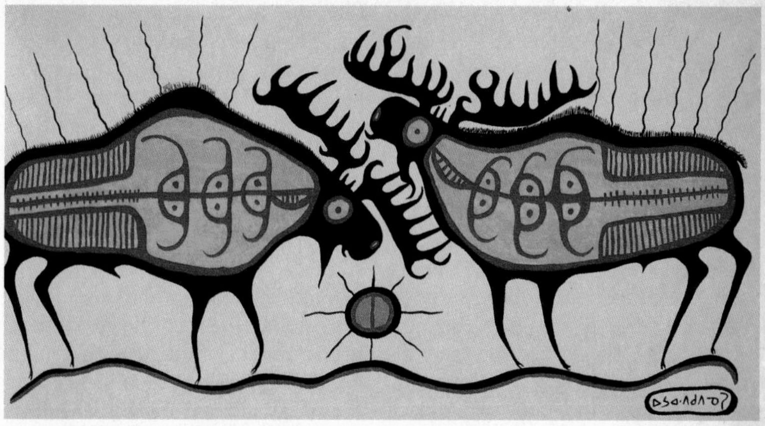

Two Bull Moose Fighting, by Norval Morrisseau.

Fall 1962

TORONTO – Seldom has a Canadian art show provoked more intense debate than Toronto's Pollock Gallery exhibition of the works of Ojibwa artist Norval Morrisseau. On opening night, all the paintings were sold, as visitors responded enthusiastically to Morrisseau's striking images of his Ojibwa people's oral tradition.

The story is all the more remarkable when one considers the 30-year-old Indian from near Beardmore in the Lake Nipigon area of northwestern Ontario is a self-taught artist.

Morrisseau lives in a cabin with his wife and four children in a Indian settlement bordering Beardmore's garbage dump. He paints "not for myself, but for my people."

Mariposa Folk Festival attracts 10,000

Aug. 12, 1962

ORILLIA, Ont. – An estimated 10,000 young people from across North America converged on this small town to attend the second annual Mariposa Folk Festival, making it one of the largest such gatherings ever. By the time they left tonight, the self-described "folkniks" had spent an estimated $40,000 in the area on food, hotels, and alcohol. The festival, which included all-night concerts, is expected to return next year.

Trans-Canada open from sea to sea

July 30, 1962

ROGERS PASS, B.C. – The Trans-Canada Highway was opened here today, and Canadians can now drive from St. John's, Nfld., to Victoria, B.C. – if they take a ferry at either end. The section between Golden and Revelstoke which passes through Rogers Pass was one of the last to be built – and one of the most expensive, for it had to be protected against snowslides that plague the area. Although there are national standards governing construction (such as shoulder width, low gradients and curvature), about 3,200 kilometres of the 7,700-kilometre highway are still unpaved.

There has been talk of a transcontinental highway since 1910, but work did not start until 1950 when the federal government paid out $150 million – half the estimated cost at that time. The provinces, which actually built the highway, were to contribute the other half. But new cost-sharing agreements increased the federal share to $825 million. Total cost when finished – $1 billion.

Alouette satellite launched by NASA

The Canadian satellite Alouette.

Sept. 29, 1962

POINT ARGUELLO, Calif. – The Canadian-built satellite *Alouette* was launched from nearby Vandenberg Air Force Base today on a mission to make a scientific study of the top side of the ionosphere. The *Alouette,* described by U.S. officials as being as sophisticated as any American spacecraft launched to date, carried the longest antennas ever sent into space. In blasting the 145-kilogram spacecraft aloft, it marked the U.S. National Aeronautics and Space Administration's initial launching on the Pacific coast. The *Alouette*, which may solve communication and space problems, went into an almost circular polar orbit after it was carried aloft by a Thor-Agena B rocket.

CNR president Gordon burns in effigy

Nov. 28, 1962

QUEBEC CITY – Hard-driving Donald Gordon, president of the Canadian National Railways and who, legend has it, drinks a bottle of scotch a day, was burned in effigy tonight by several hundred separatist supporters in Quebec City. The demonstration comes in the wake of a reported statement by Gordon that there are no French-Canadians qualified for the vice-presidency of the CNR. Gordon made the remark before the House of Commons Railway Committee. Above the straw effigy was a placard reading "Gordon, Spokesman for English-Canadians."

CNR president Donald Gordon.

The angry crowd, most of them students, gathered at Place d'Youville after being led into the downtown square by a cavalcade of cars, horns blaring. The demonstration appears to have been organized by the Rassemblement pour l'Indépendance Nationale. Two separatist leaders from the Quebec City area continued to excite the crowd after the effigy had been burned, describing the Red Ensign as a symbol of England's domination over Canada and, in turn, English Canada's domination over Quebec.

Parents of crippled babies to get help

July 31, 1962

TORONTO – Premier John Robarts has promised wide-ranging provincial aid to parents of babies crippled by the drug thalidomide in Ontario. Officials of the governments of Alberta and Saskatchewan have also announced that care will be provided for thalidomide babies. Robarts, who is on holiday at his Lake Huron cottage, issued a statement by telephone in which he said the Ontario government will do everything possible to help the parents.

Saskatchewan has no reports yet of any babies born deformed by the mother's use of thalidomide. But in Regina, the health ministry said any such children would receive care under the Medical Care Insurance Act. There have been 12 thalidomide babies born in Alberta, and they will receive the same care as other handicapped children.

Chinese refugee family arrive.

This young immigrant has just arrived in Edmonton from Hong Kong.

Britain joining ECM has Dief concerned

Sept. 11, 1962

LONDON, England – Prime Minister John Diefenbaker today expressed reservations about Britain joining the European Common Market. British Prime Minister Harold Macmillan had referred to the mere 35 kilometres between the U.K. and Europe. Diefenbaker stopped short of saying Canada opposed the move, but he wondered how it would affect Commonwealth trade and defence relations. As PM, Diefenbaker has encouraged trade with Britain, to lessen Canada's dependence on the U.S.

Conscription book fuels nationalist cause

1962

QUEBEC – Prominent Quebec journalist and politician André Laurendeau's *The Conscription Crisis, 1942*, a newly published series of nationalist essays condemning the Canadian government's behavior toward French-Canadians in the Second World War, is fast becoming a manifesto for nationalist Quebecers. In the book, Laurendeau, in 1942 the editor of the nationalist paper *L'Action Nationale*, chronicles his efforts to stop the conscription of French-Canadians at the hands of the English-Canadian majority. In his eyes, Canada is not one nation, but the result of one more populous and more powerful nation – English Canada – using its power to suppress and control the smaller nation – Quebec. Many Quebecers share this view, and some are calling for political secession in order to establish a "true democracy" in Quebec.

Chinese mark the Year of the Dog

Young Chinese Canadian wishes her pet a happy Year of the Dog.

This seeing-eye dog is special to its blind master every year.

Air defences are on alert

Oct. 24, 1962

OTTAWA – Canada's air defences have been placed on high alert as the U.S. and the U.S.S.R. face off over the issue of offensive missiles deployed in Cuba. Earlier, Canada denied the Russians access to Canadian airports. Soviet transports en route to Cuba often refuel at Gander and Halifax.

The alert was delayed one day by Prime Minister John Diefenbaker's reluctance to permit it, although Canadian units in NORAD should have been brought to the same degree of readiness as their American counterparts when the crisis broke Oct. 22.

That Canadian forces have been placed on a more vigilant standing is due to Defence Minister Douglas Harkness, whose differences with Diefenbaker led to heated arguments. Harkness simply told his service chiefs to order that precautions be taken as quietly as possible. The alert is not fully effective, however, given that Canadian CF-101 fighters have no missiles and Bomarc missiles have no warheads.

Blue Bombers edge Ti-Cats in "fog bowl"

Players were having difficulty seeing in the fog-filled stadium.

Dec. 2, 1962

TORONTO – History was made during the Grey Cup game this year – it became the only football match ever played on this continent that took a whole weekend to complete. The Winnipeg Blue Bombers were leading the Hamilton Tiger-Cats 28-27 when the contest was stopped during the fourth quarter because of fog.

The teams resumed play on Sunday, this time in bright sunshine, but the Bombers obviously enjoyed playing in Saturday's soup. They gained only four yards in nine minutes on Day II, while Hamilton racked up 105 yards. But the Ti-Cats couldn't overcome the single-point deficit. By holding on to their slim lead, the Bombers won their fourth Grey Cup in five years.

Hydro issue powers Lesage-led Liberals

Nov. 14, 1962

QUEBEC CITY – Elections today gave Premier Jean Lesage a firmer hold on power, the Liberals winning 63 seats compared to the 52 they won in 1960. The big issue in the election was the Liberal plan to nationalize 11 private power companies. That is a particular aim of Natural Resources Minister René Lévesque. Claire Kirkland-Casgrain, who won a byelection last year to become the first female member of the legislature, was re-elected. There was little violence, unlike past provincial elections.

1963

Toronto, Jan. 14. The Planned Parenthood Federation holds its first official meeting, despite uncertainty about the legality of birth control.

Toronto, March 29. At the largest political rally in Canadian history, 15,842 people jam Maple Leaf Gardens to hear NDP leader Tommy Douglas.

Toronto, April 18. Toronto Maple Leafs beat Detroit Red Wings four games to one to win the Stanley Cup.

Ottawa, April 22. Lester B. Pearson takes office as PM, heading a minority Liberal government after defeating John Diefenbaker's Conservative government at the polls.

Sao Paulo, May 4. Canada completes its most successful post-WWII athletic meet as the Pan-American Games end. Canada won 63 medals, second in total medals to the U.S.

Northwest Territories, May 4. Severe floods hit Hay River and Fort Simpson, forcing the evacuation of about 1,900.

Toronto, June 11. The Canadian Medical Association says obesity is one of Canada's major medical problems.

Lunenburg, N.S., July 26. *Bluenose II* is launched, a replica of the famous racing schooner *Bluenose*.

Orillia, Ont., Aug. 10. The annual Mariposa Folk Festival ends. Attended by 20,000, mostly young people, it is marred by liquor offences, "illicit sex," and hooliganism.

Montreal, Aug. 11. Claude *Jutras' A tout prendre* wins grand prize for feature films at the Canadian Film Festival.

Toronto, Sept. 4. Fluoridation of the water supply begins, aimed at preventing tooth decay.

Montreal, Sept. 21. Some 3,000 of Quebec's social elite attend the opening of Place des Arts concert hall, as 1,000 separatists demonstrate outside.

Montreal, Oct. 7. Eight people are sentenced to prison on charges arising from separatist-related terrorist activities last spring, including the bombing death of W.V. O'Neill.

Vancouver, Nov. 30. Hamilton Tiger-Cats defeat B.C. Lions 21-10 to win the Grey Cup.

Canada. Universities founded this year include Brock University at St. Catharines, Simon Fraser University at Burnaby, University of Victoria, and University of Moncton.

Dief's Tories in trouble

Feb. 4, 1963

OTTAWA – The House of Commons voted no-confidence in Prime Minister John Diefenbaker's Conservative government tonight. An election is likely. The vote was 142-111. Two NDP members joined Conservatives in supporting the minority government. The prime minister now must either resign or call an election. His resignation is considered highly improbable.

Yesterday, Diefenbaker delivered a hard-hitting speech in the House, one that sounded like an election address. He accused Liberal leader Lester Pearson of flip-flopping on the issue of nuclear arms. Pearson had opposed Canada having nuclear missiles, but lately he appears to be more accepting of them. Diefenbaker said he prefers storing nuclear warheads for the controversial Bomarc missile south of the border until they are needed.

Also yesterday, Defence Minister Douglas Harkness quit the cabinet in a dispute with Diefenbaker on the nuclear issue. Other cabinet ministers are reportedly unhappy and there have been rumors of a full-fledged cabinet revolt.

The Canadian debate has generated great interest in the United States. American television stations interrupted programming for bulletins on the troubles of the Diefenbaker government. U.S. President John Kennedy, no friend of Diefenbaker, has avoided comment.

Three dead, 12 wounded in loggers' strike

Feb. 13, 1963

KAPUSKASING, Ont. – The deadliest strike in Ontario's history may be near its end. Early this morning, pulp mill workers here voted to return to work. Loggers are still waging a strike that climaxed in a battle at Reesor siding near here that left three dead, 12 wounded, 19 charged with murder, and 400 charged with rioting.

On Feb. 1, 400 striking loggers descended on Reesor siding, where independent workers had been piling pulpwood. As the strikers tore apart the piles of wood, 12 police guards struggled with them. Then, says Ontario Attorney General Fred Cass, 22 independents emerged from a shack with guns blazing, shooting into the skirmishing group of strikers and police. The strikers retreated and the police arrested the independents. The mill workers had been staying off the job to support the striking loggers.

Sweet Adelines quit over ban on black

March 14, 1963

OTTAWA – About half of the members of the Ottawa branch of the Sweet Adelines have quit and will form another singing club, one of the dissidents said today. The women resigned after Mrs. Lana Clowes, a black housewife, was barred from the branch by the U.S.-based headquarters. The new group said it would affiliate with Harmony Inc., which has no ban on blacks. Branch president Jane Burns says only two resignations have been submitted, and the group would lose its international friendship by pulling out of the North American organization. "Besides," she added, "they're not going to miss 40 girls out of 13,000."

Jean Béliveau of the Montreal Canadiens is highly regarded both on and off the ice.

Defence minister Harkness resigns

Douglas Harkness.

Feb. 3, 1963

OTTAWA – Douglas Harkness has resigned as minister of national defence. He quit over policy and principle – Harkness believes that specific weapons used by Canadian forces – the CF-101 fighter, Bomarc ground-to-air missile, and the Honest John rockets, the latter deployed with NATO in Europe – should be issued with the nuclear warheads or rockets for which they were designed.

At the same time, Harkness attacked as hypocritical the stand of opposition leader Lester Pearson, who urges that Canada accept the nuclear weapons and then renegotiate defence arrangements so as to dispose of them.

Fatal blast may be work of terrorists

April 21, 1963

MONTREAL – A bomb blast tonight at the Canadian army's recruiting centre in the heart of the city killed William O'Neill, 65, a janitor who was due to retire in two weeks. Provincial deputy attorney general Charles-Edouard Cantin said: "At first sight, (the murder) is so similar to other recent acts of sabotage that the first name that comes to mind is the FLQ (the Front de libération du Québec)." The army's Provost Corps now joins three other police forces in the war against FLQ terrorists.

CMA launches drive to combat smoking

June 11, 1963

TORONTO – Smoking can lead to cancer. That's the view of the General Council of the Canadian Medical Association, to which doctors in Canada belong. The CMA has decided to launch a drive against smoking to reduce cancer, and it wants the federal government's help. In a brief being sent to the minister of national health and welfare, Judy LaMarsh, the CMA asks the government to formally recognize the link between smoking and cancer. It wants this risk made clear through public education, and warning labels stating this danger put on cigarette packages.

Liberals headed for a minority win

Victorious Lester B. Pearson.

April 8, 1963

OTTAWA – It looks like another minority government. But this time Canadians decided on a Liberal one, depending on what Prime Minister John Diefenbaker decides. In late returns tonight, Diefenbaker's Conservatives appear to have 94 seats, compared to the Liberals' 130. The Social Credit has 24 and the NDP 17.

Constitutionally, Diefenbaker can remain prime minister even though he has a clear minority. The prime minister left that option open tonight when he spoke to reporters. He referred to the situation in 1925 when W.L. Mackenzie King hung on to the government with only 101 Liberal seats to the Conservatives' 116, with the Progressives holding 24. But analysts say the politics of 1925 were fundamentally different from those of today and it appears Liberal leader Lester B. Pearson will become prime minister. All party leaders tonight were cautious in their comments. But Pearson said the Liberals are the only party capable of forming a government.

Diefenbaker appears to have lost, but he staved off disaster. Racked by dissension in his own party and calls for a new leader, his energetic campaign kept the prairies in the Tory column and partially staved off Liberal gains in the Maritimes and Ontario.

FLQ suspected as mailbox bombs triggered in Montreal suburb

Attendants work on the injured demolitions expert after a bomb blast.

May 17, 1963

MONTREAL – An army demolition expert is fighting for his life tonight after one of 17 dynamite bombs placed in mailboxes blew up in his hands. Sgt.-Maj. Walter Leja of the Royal Canadian Engineers was trying to dismantle the bomb in predominantly English-speaking Westmount. In the rash of explosions, beginning about 3 a.m., six mailboxes were shattered, five more bombs were found and disarmed, and five more were hauled away – mailboxes and all – to be set off. As Westmount Mayor Chipman Drury led explosives teams around the affluent community, he said: "It's like wartime." The terrorist Front de libération du Québec is the prime suspect.

Pearson, Kennedy issue communiqué

Kennedy meets Pearson.

May 11, 1963

HYANNIS PORT, Mass. – Prime Minister Lester Pearson and U.S. President John Kennedy issued a vague communiqué after two days of talks here. Arming Canada's missiles with nuclear warheads must have been on the agenda, but the statement says nothing specific on the issue. The leaders do plan to re-activate the joint committee on defence, which hasn't met since 1960. By all accounts, talks were friendly, but the communiqué deals with one strong disagreement. Pearson told Kennedy Canada will establish a 12-mile fishing zone. Kennedy said the U.S. intends to stick to its three-mile position.

Major Barbara a hit at Neptune Theatre

July 1, 1963

HALIFAX – Professional theatre is back in Halifax. Aided by military trumpeters, the city's glitterati turned out for the opening production of the new Neptune Theatre: George Bernard Shaw's *Major Barbara.* Under the direction of George McCowan and company leader Leon Major, the play revived live theatre in the renovated Garrick vaudeville house. It received a five-minute standing ovation.

Manning's Socreds easy Alberta winners

June 17, 1963

EDMONTON – The Social Credit party breezed to victory tonight, with little change in the political landscape in Alberta. Late returns give Ernest Manning's Socreds 60 seats. The Liberals have two and the Coalition one. At dissolution, there were 60 Socreds, one Liberal, one Conservative, one Independent Socred, one Coalition, and one vacant. A recent redistribution cut two seats from the previous legislature.

All three major political party leaders other than Manning lost their seats. Conservative lawyer Milt Harradence, a flamboyant lawyer, lost his bid in Calgary. NDP leader Neil Reimer lost in Edmonton, and Liberal leader David Hunter lost in Athabasca. The Coalition is a movement in the manner of the old Progressive movement. It does not profess to believe in party politics and therefore does not have an acknowledged party leader. In today's election, 62 of 63 legislature seats were decided.

Dief knocks makeup of B&B Commission

B&B Commission co-chairmen André Laurendeau and Davidson Dunton.

July 20, 1963

OTTAWA – The membership of the Royal Commission on Bilingualism and Biculturalism is not broad enough, opposition leader John Diefenbaker said today after Prime Minister Lester Pearson announced the commission's membership. But Diefenbaker was playing politics, and the issue is too important for politics, Social Credit leader Robert Thompson said. The commission, which is co-chaired by André Laurendeau and Davidson Dunton, includes an Acadian priest, a Ukrainian Canadian professor, a French-Canadian journalist, and Calgary's Gertrude Laing, the first woman appointed to a royal commission in Canada.

Howe passes the Rocket with 545th goal

Gordie Howe's 544th goal was scored against Gump Worsley.

Nov. 19, 1963

DETROIT – Gordie Howe became the NHL's greatest scorer when he fired his record-breaking 545th goal in a game against the Montreal Canadiens. Howe, who tied Maurice "Rocket" Richard's record five games earlier, picked up the milestone marker at 15:06 of the second stanza while the Wings were killing off a major penalty. After taking a pass from Billy McNeill, Howe slipped over the blueline and whipped a high wrist shot to the short side past Charlie Hodge in the Canadiens' net. The packed house at the Detroit Olympia saluted their hero with a standing ovation that delayed the game for almost 20 minutes.

B.C. power pact signed

July 10, 1963

OTTAWA – The federal government and B.C. have signed an agreement governing the development of the huge hydroelectric power potential of B.C.'s interior. Negotiations had been dragging on for years while Premier W.A.C. Bennett bargained with former prime minister John Diefenbaker and his justice minister, B.C.'s Davie Fulton. Then, in April, Diefenbaker and Fulton were defeated.

Lester Pearson, the new prime minister, recognized that delegating the negotiations to a minister would not work with Bennett, and so he conducted some of the bargaining himself. And he named Jack Davis, a former B.C. Electric economist who favored exporting power to the U.S., as his parliamentary assistant. The stage was set for a speedy resolution of the dispute. Pearson proposed some changes in the agreement with the U.S. and then met Bennett in Ottawa to tie up the details.

Pearson promises poorer provinces aid

Ontario Premier John Robarts.

Nov. 26, 1963

OTTAWA – The federal government will substantially increase aid to poorer provinces, Prime Minister Lester Pearson told the federal-provincial conference here today. He did not mention a specific figure, but it is expected $75 million will be added to the present $153 million in equalization payments. The federal government will do this over the strong objections of Ontario and Quebec. Ontario Premier John Robarts wants no increase in equalization payments, arguing the money will come indirectly from his province. The PM said provinces need more money to offset rising costs.

Independence movement is news to some

Nov. 2, 1963

TORONTO – An astonishing 21 percent of French-speaking Quebecers don't know an independence movement exists in their province. The results of a CBC-*Maclean's* magazine poll published today also show that both pro- and anti-separatist factions are hardening their attitudes. The poll found 13 percent favor immediate independence, 43 percent oppose it, and 23 percent are undecided. The pro-separatist percentage much increased among urban, well-educated, well-paid respondents. The trend is opposite among those unaware of the movement.

Callaghan packs a potent punch in Paris

1963

TORONTO – Once in a lifetime. That is how to describe Morley Callaghan's summer in Paris in 1929, the subject of his just-published memoir *That Summer in Paris*. With his wife Loretto, Callaghan went to Paris where he developed friendships with American writers Ernest Hemingway and F. Scott Fitzgerald. Callaghan and Hemingway became regular boxing partners, and one day Callaghan knocked Hemingway to the canvas as Fitzgerald gaped at the spectacle of the already almost-legendary Hemingway felled by an unassuming, unestablished Canadian writer.

Inuit murder cases immortalized in stone carvings

1963

IQALUIT, N.W.T. – Art imitates life, and in Canada's Northwest Territories, the old art form of soapstone or whalebone carving is imitating, preserving and publicizing a unique society and an innovative new approach to the administration of native justice there. The man most closely associated with this process – the artistic and the judicial – is Justice J.H. Sissons, the first resident judge of the Territorial Court of the N.W.T.

Since his appointment in 1955, Sissons has widely broadcast his belief that to serve the native people at this moment of immense cultural change, court practices must adapt. Lawyers say he "ruffled feathers" in Ottawa over his insistence that the court must travel on circuit, even to remote Arctic outposts. Everyone has a right, he says, to be tried by his peers. To ensure that this happens, Sissons travels more than 32,000 kilometres a year.

Justice often calls for the wisdom of Solomon in the N.W.T. as the Inuit continue to move off the land to the new government-constructed settlements. Age-old customs are called into question and the court must rule on traditional practice as well as pass judgment on crimes arising out of new societal circumstances.

Judge Sissons is so committed to his mission in the north that he often commissions Inuit artists to depict carvings of his court cases. In dramatic bas-relief these sculptures of traditional soapstone and whalebone represent the unique personalities Sissons meets in his courtroom, and record the climactic moments of brutality that led their perpetrators before this southern judge. The artworks also represent the legal history of the times and attest to the challenges the court faces as Inuit adjust to new, often confusing lifestyles.

Sissons this year passed a life sentence on Mingeriak, whose trial for murder has ended here. The convicted man killed a boy and wounded his mother. Mingeriak was charged with capital murder and pleaded guilty to non-capital murder. The court apparently considered that in all justice, the crime required a maximum sentence.

Sculpture depicts the wounded mother and her murdered son.

Regina vs. Angulalik: trader not guilty

An Inuit trader allegedly killed a man whose son had robbed his store.

FLAGSTAFF ISLAND, N.W.T. – Another celebrated case saw one of the Northwest Territories' best-known native citizens brought to trial and acquitted. In May 1957, the enterprising owner of two trading posts, Stephen Angulalik, about 60, was charged with murder after he sent to the RCMP a note accusing himself of a knife killing. Angulalik holds the Queen's Coronation Medal in recognition of his "ability to acquire the new aptitudes needed to share in the work of modern Arctic development."

The incident occurred during New Year's celebrations at Angulalik's Perry River trading post, where Inuit had gathered for dancing and drumming and there was drinking of home brew. A fight broke out between Angulalik and the victim, Otoiak, apparently because Otoiak's sons had stolen goods from his store. "I was very drunk. I got mad and we went outside, where I poked him twice with my knife," the note read. A witness saw the men struggle, but while Otoiak had blood on his clothes he thought they were playing. Otoiak died two days later.

Regina vs. Kikkik: Inuit woman innocent

RANKIN INLET, N.W.T. – Judge J.H. Sissons ordered a carving of his most challenging cases, the trial of Kikkik, an Inuit woman charged in 1958 with murder, abandonment of a child, and criminal negligence of a second child. In April, the jury returned a verdict of not guilty in the case of Regina vs. Kikkik. Sissons' court heard how the alleged crimes occurred in a period of famine for families living on the land. Kikkik's half-brother, believing wrongly that Kikkik and her husband had food they were not sharing, shot and killed her husband and then shot at Kikkik. Kikkik seized a knife and stabbed and killed her half-brother and then fled the camp with her five children. When an RCMP patrol found her on the frozen barren lands two children were missing. They eventually found the two children, but the youngest was dead.

The jury believed Kikkik had abandoned her youngest children as she struggled on so that the oldest might survive. Montreal geologist and jury foreman Henry Leavitt said, "She had a hard choice to make, and the jury felt she had made the right one. The Arctic is like that. It's full of hard choices."

This Inuit woman was charged with stabbing to death her half-brother.

Toronto, February. Leonard Braithwaite, the first black elected to a Canadian legislature, blasts the law providing for segregated schools in his first speech in the legislature.

Port Alberni, B.C., March 28. A tidal wave causes millions of dollars in damage.

Regina, April 22. Ross Thatcher's Liberals win a provincial election from Premier Woodrow Lloyd and the CCF, ending the CCF's 20-year reign.

Toronto, April 25. Toronto Maple Leafs defeat Detroit Red Wings four games to three to win the Stanley Cup.

Ottawa, April. Regulations for issuance of social insurance numbers come into effect to assist in record-keeping. Employers are required to ensure their employees have SINs.

Louisville, May 2. Canadian colt Northern Dancer wins the Kentucky Derby.

Toronto, June 8. Toronto city council votes to supply birth control pills to any woman on welfare who wants them.

Toronto, July 31. *Maclean's* editors Ken Lefolii, Peter Gzowski, Robert Fulford, Barbara Moon, Harry Bruce, and David Stein resign. They are opposed to the magazine's management eroding the traditional independence of the editorial department.

Toronto, Sept. 6. 3,000 fans greet the Beatles on arrival at Toronto International Airport.

Blaine, Washington, Sept. 16. PM Pearson and President Johnson attend celebrations for the revised Columbia River Treaty between Canada and the U.S. Under the agreement, the U.S. will pay hundreds of millions of dollars for Canada's share of downstream power.

Toronto, Oct. 4. The weekly public affairs program *This Hour Has Seven Days*, starring Patrick Watson, Laurier LaPierre, John Drainie, and Dinah Christie, debuts.

Toronto, Nov. 28. B.C. Lions defeat Hamilton Tiger-Cats 34-24 to win the Grey Cup.

Canada. Marshall McLuhan publishes *Understanding Media: the extension of man*, in which he states "the Medium is the Message."

Fort McMurray, Alta. Great Canadian Oil Sands Ltd., a subsidiary of Sun Oil Co., invests $300 million in a plant to produce oil to pipe to Edmonton.

Schlitz Brewing Co. buying into Labatt

Feb. 7, 1964

LONDON, Ont. – Risking the threat of widespread management upheaval, Labatt family and company shareholders have sold 1.5 million shares, or 34 percent, of John Labatt Ltd. to the Jos. Schlitz Brewing Co. of Milwaukee. If approved by the U.S. Department of Justice, the sale is worth $34.5 million, and it ends Power Corporation Canada Ltd.'s bid to buy the brewery. Initially, Schlitz will have two of the 16 board of director seats. Still, many see the sale as the end of 117 years of Canadian ownership.

Toronto boasts new $16-million airport

Jan. 12, 1964

TORONTO – Spectators jammed Toronto International Airport's shiny new building tonight, to watch the arrival of Trans-Canada Airlines Flight 871 from Vienna. Hundreds of them packed the $16-million circular terminal, shaped this way to minimize the walking distance for passengers.

As well, its multi-level parking garage and quiet, tranquil atmosphere are a welcome relief for travellers accustomed to the crowded, out-of-date old terminal – one that was never designed to cope with the jet age.

And the winners are...

Historian and poet take Molson Prizes

Historian Donald Creighton.

March 31, 1964

CANADA – A nationalist historian and a globe-trotting poet have been named as the first recipients of the Canada Council's Molson Prize, awarded for outstanding achievement in the arts, humanities, and social sciences. Historian Donald Creighton won the award for his dramatic, often brilliantly polemical Canadian history books such as *The Empire of the St. Lawrence* and *Dominion of the North*. The other recipient is Quebec poet Alain Grandbois, author of *Rivages de l'homme* and *L'Etoile pourpre*, collections of rich, exotic poetry.

Professor honored for book on Brown

Historian J.M.S. Careless.

March 20, 1964

OTTAWA – J.M.S. Careless, a 44-year-old professor at the University of Toronto, has just won his second Governor General's Award, for *Brown of the Globe*, his biography of George Brown. The book sheds new light on Brown, the man who founded the *Globe* newspaper in 1843 and played a crucial role in steering Canada on the road to Confederation as Reform Party leader in the 1850s and 1860s.

Garner wins a Governor General's Award

March 20, 1964

OTTAWA – Hugh Garner has been awarded the Governor General's Award for fiction published in 1963. He won for his collection of short stories called *The Best of Hugh Garner*. Garner is a breath of fresh air in the literary world – he was a hobo in the Great Depression, fought for the Republicans in the Spanish Civil War, and now fills his stories with down-and-outers, portraying them with sympathy and poignancy rather than anger at the society that has left them behind. He wrote recently that writing suits him just fine because no other career "would have interfered less with my drinking."

Novelist Hugh Garner.

Ontario to abolish segregated schools

March 12, 1964

TORONTO – Black children will soon be able to go legally to the same schools as whites in Ontario. That news came today from provincial Education Minister Bill Davis. Speaking in the legislature, he said the 114-year-old law segregating white and black schools will be abolished. In reality, the law has not been followed for some 60 years. It was originally passed in 1850 for the children of escaped American slaves who had settled in southwestern Ontario. As well, Davis says free textbooks will now be provided up to Grade 10.

Premiers mull over Constitution's fate

Sept. 1, 1964

CHARLOTTETOWN – A century after the first Charlottetown Conference, Canada's premiers are back on the Island. This time they want to bring the Constitution home. Their main obstacle? An amending formula all can agree on. Though there is hope for an agreement in principle, Premier Jean Lesage observes Quebec once regarded the BNA Act as the protector of its interests. Angered at the absence of French in today's ceremonies celebrating the centenary of the 1864 conference, he says a new constitution must make more room for French Canada's aspirations.

Plan proposes merging armed forces

Defence Minister Paul Hellyer.

March 26, 1964

OTTAWA – Paul Hellyer, minister of national defence, today tabled his White Paper on Defence in Parliament. Highlight of the proposals is the plan to merge the three Canadian military services into a single, unified force – the first of its kind in the world. Hellyer believes he will be able to reduce the forces from their present strength of 122,000 to some 110,000, chopping $100 million from the defence budget of $1.5 billion.

The forces have in the past had limited integration in such fields as dental treatment and pay accounting. But the white paper goes much further. As of Aug. 1, three posts will disappear – chief of the general staff, chief of air staff, chief of naval staff – and be replaced by a single head, the chief of defence staff, who will preside over forces which are organized purely on functional lines. In the field, the forces themselves will be integrated with common terms of rank and similar uniforms.

The new, integrated force will be particularly mobile, to move units quickly either as reinforcements for NATO or as United Nations peacekeepers available at short notice. This will mean more air transport, including increased use of Canadian civil carriers to fly troops to trouble spots.

Pearson, Johnson discuss war in Vietnam

Lester Pearson and U.S. President Lyndon Johnson at an earlier meeting.

May 28, 1964

NEW YORK – Canadian Prime Minister Lester Pearson is meeting U.S. President Lyndon Johnson here today for a briefing on the progress of the Vietnam war. It's expected Pearson will object to the possibility of the Americans using nuclear weapons in their effort to bring the North Vietnamese to heel. But Pearson, always a diplomatic realist, is not likely to take such a strong stand against conventional bombing.

Quebec's married women get legal rights

July 1, 1964

QUEBEC – Married women in Quebec now have the same legal rights as men. The passing of Bill 16 means married women no longer need their husbands' permission to conduct business transactions and can launch a lawsuit on their own. The law also liberates married women to pursue any career of their choosing. Liberal minister Claire Kirkland-Casgrain, the first and only woman elected to the Quebec Assembly, introduced the new law.

Love the Beatles? Yeah, yeah, yeah

Aug. 22, 1964

VANCOUVER – They played for only 32 minutes, but the excitement generated by the Beatles at a concert here was enough to fell at least 100 hysterical teenage girls. Following the concert, the Fab Four eluded frantic fans and made their getaway from the stage into waiting limousines. Most of the performance was drowned out by non-stop shrieking from the crowd of 16,000, which included tots and middle-aged mothers. The Beatles' next stop is the Hollywood Bowl in Los Angeles.

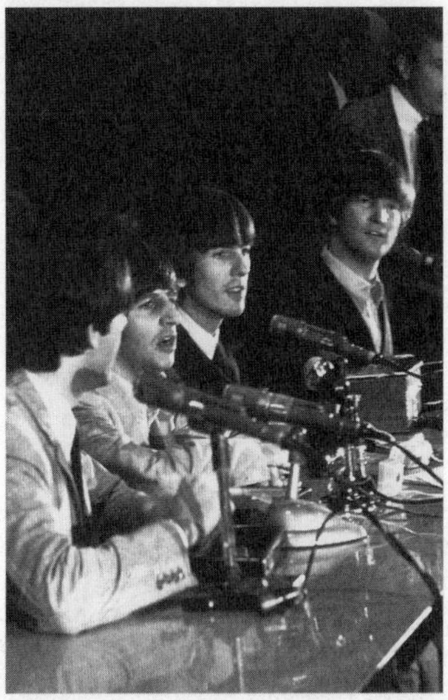

The Beatles give press conference.

Separatist students protest royal visit

The queen with Gov. Gen. Vanier.

Oct. 10, 1964

QUEBEC CITY – Thirty-two separatist-minded students have been arrested – and many more beaten – in protests against Queen Elizabeth's royal visit here. Police, clad in fluorescent red raincoats and carrying two-foot-long clubs, quickly descended on anyone who seemed hostile to the queen at her procession through the city. Separatists seized on the queen's visit as a focal point because to them she symbolizes English domination. ▷

Canadians serving in UN peace force

Canadian troops in Cyprus.

March 15, 1964

OTTAWA – The first of 1,150 Canadian troops have reached Cyprus as part of a UN peacekeeping force that will also include Swedish, Irish, and British units. A party of 29 Canadian flew to the island to prepare the way for those following. The first contingent, members of the Royal 22nd Regiment, will be flown directly to Cyprus. Vehicles and heavy equipment will be shipped aboard the RCN's only aircraft carrier, *HMCS Bonaventure*.

Greek and Turkish Cypriots have been fighting for months, but formation of a UN force moved slowly until Turkey threatened to land troops.

Formula to amend Constitution OK'd

Oct. 13, 1964

OTTAWA – Canada's attorneys general have agreed on a formula to amend this country's Constitution. This may be the mechanism that leads to agreement on bringing the British North America Act home from Britain.

The attorneys general, at meetings here, set out two main classes of amendments and a number of other provisions. Amendments designed to change the basic powers of the provinces or those that affect the use of French or English would require the unanimous consent of the provinces. Other amendments would have to be approved by seven provinces representing half Canada's population.

The federal government agreed to restrict somewhat the limited amending power it now has. The provinces agreed Ottawa could change the powers of provincial legislatures but those amendments would not take effect until the legislatures approved them.

Delegation of power from a province to the federal government was contentious. Quebec argued that each province ought to be able to do that on its own. But Ontario strongly objected and the final agreement is that a minimum of four provinces would have to agree to change of that sort. Today's amending formula differs little from one adopted in 1960.

Poll gives Northern Dancer the nod as year's top three-year-old

E.P. Taylor's championship horse Northern Dancer wins another race.

Nov. 20, 1964

NEW YORK – Canada's Northern Dancer, winner of two of the three jewels in horse racing's Triple Crown this year, has been voted the top three-year-old of the year by the *Morning Telegraph* and the *Daily Racing Form.* Northern Dancer, from E.P. Taylor's Windfields Farm, became the first Canadian-bred horse to win the Kentucky Derby this spring, finishing in a record time of two minutes flat. The horse followed up with a win in the Preakness Stakes, but hopes of a Triple Crown were dashed by a loss at the Belmont Stakes, the final race in the series. A leg injury forced Northern Dancer into retiring to stud. Kelso, a gelding that is the top money-winner with almost $2 million in purses, was voted horse of the year for the fifth time.

Smallwood slams door on reopening hydro talks with Quebec

Oct. 26, 1964

LONDON, England – The premier of Newfoundland, Joseph R. Smallwood, announced here today that negotiations between his province and neighboring Quebec over the sale of hydro power to Quebec are over. Smallwood has been trying to get development started on Hamilton Falls in Labrador since 1952, and a company called Brinco was founded for this purpose. However, Brinco has not been able to obtain the offer of a satisfactory price from Quebec.

Now Smallwood has begun to study the alternative route for power from western Labrador, across the Strait of Belle Isle to the island of Newfoundland, and then across the Cabot Strait to the mainland. Most observers think this is not feasible and an deal must be made with Quebec eventually.

Prime Minister Lester B. Pearson dons native headdress on visit to Manitoulin Island, Ontario.

Regulations to ensure the killing of seal pups is more humane

Nov. 3, 1964

OTTAWA – Following exposés of various seal hunting methods published in the spring, in-boxes at the Department of Fisheries are full of mail from outraged citizens. They insist on protective action ensuring that seal pups be killed before being skinned, rather than just knocked out as they are now.

Fisheries Minister H.J. Robichaud told the Commons yesterday about two regulations passed by his department to ensure the humane killing of pups during the March-April slaughter. The first requires a seal to be dead, rather than just knocked out, before it is skinned. The second bans lines with hooks and says fishermen must use clubs heavy enough to kill with one blow.

Elliot Lake water: is it safe or not?

Nov. 14, 1964

HALIBURTON, Ont. – Gavin Henderson, executive director of the Conservation Council of Ontario, questions Premier John Robarts' inference that there is no danger in the polluted waters of the Elliot Lake region. The Ontario Water Resources Commission confirmed radioactive contamination in the Elliot Lake and Algoma area, emanating from the radioactive waste of the surrounding uranium mills. Henderson insists radiological pollution is serious: "You never know what effect even a little radiation will have on children, even 50 years from now."

The International Union of Mine, Mill and Smelter Workers agreed that the situation is grave. It recommended the federal government take emergency action to give medical examinations and uncontaminated water to all Elliot Lake residents, and to investigate all water supplies near areas where mining or processing of radioactive materials took place.

Maple leaf to fly on nation's new flag

Canada's new flag has a single stylized red maple leaf on a white background between two red bars.

Dec. 15, 1964

OTTAWA – Canada has a new flag. After months of bitter debate, the Pearson government forced a vote on the "single red maple leaf with red bars" design at 1 this morning, winning it 152-85.

The flag that was adopted isn't Prime Minister Lester Pearson's original choice. That one was first shown in the House May 27. It has three red maple leaves, with thin blue vertical bars at the edges. However, this design raised so much fuss the flag issue was put to a special parliamentary committee. In October, it chose the present design, devised by historian George F.G. Stanley. This does not please the Tories, who oppose any flag that drops the British Union Jack.

Whitton loses bid in race for mayor

Dec. 7, 1964

OTTAWA – Canada's most combative and colorful mayor lost re-election tonight in a surprising result that saw her run third. Ottawa Mayor Charlotte Whitton, 68, lost a bid for re-election in a rancorous election campaign distinguished by personal attacks among the candidates. At one election meeting, the mayor threatened to read the Riot Act. "I do love this city, but it does not love me or want my services anymore," she said when the results were clear.

Whitton said she leaves city hall in good shape for her male successor. "It's always a woman's way to leave everything ready for the men of the household so all they have to do is eat and not wash the dishes." She became mayor first in 1951, then retired in 1956. She tried unsuccessfully for a seat in the House of Commons in 1958 and regained the mayor's post in 1960. Whitton says she will be back.

Blacks plan boycott of rat-infested school

Nov. 8, 1964

HARROW, Ont. – A school boycott is being threatened by 30 black families if the school trustees do not immediately end 34 years of segregation at the facilities known as SS 11. A delegation will ask the trustees to close the rat-ridden SS 11 by January and integrate its 94 students into the other predominantly white schools in the area. The parents say, however, that before they take the drastic step of keeping their children out of school, they'll talk to officials in the Ontario Department of Education.

Strikers block CN tracks into Inco property at Thompson, Man., in August.

Quebec and Nfld. in a war of words

Dec. 18, 1964

QUEBEC CITY – As a result of the on-again, off-again negotiations between Quebec and Newfoundland over the development of hydro power in Labrador and its being sold to Quebec, both provinces have begun to verbally attack each other. Newfoundland Premier Joseph R. Smallwood vows he will ignore Quebec and sell power to the United States via the "Anglo-Saxon route." Some Quebec nationalists respond by arguing that Labrador really belongs to Quebec. The Newfoundland iron ore mined in Labrador is shipped to and through Sept-Iles, Que., and the suggestion was made here today that Quebec should tax this ore.

The question of the location of the Labrador-Quebec boundary often arises when the provinces are at odds. In 1927, the British Privy Council ruled on the issue, setting the present boundary. Quebec has never accepted that judgment.

1965

Toronto, Feb. 13. University of Toronto professor George Langford says the Great Lakes are being killed by pollution, and warns that within 10 years the point of no return will have been reached.

St. John's, Nfld., Feb. 17. A mammoth ice field, 65 kilometres wide, is moving down the Newfoundland coast.

Montreal, May 1. Montreal Canadiens defeat Chicago Blackhawks four games to three for the Stanley Cup.

Toronto, June 2. The Ontario government announces beer and liquor will be sold in airplanes and theatre lounges, and with meals in bowling alleys and curling rinks.

Toronto, June 4. The United Church of Canada approves of legal abortions in cases of rape, incest, or when the mother's health is in question.

Ottawa, June 15. The government announces it will permit color TV in Canada, effective Jan. 1, 1967.

Saskatchewan, July 4. Cannington Manor near Carlyle, an agricultural college for the sons of wealthy Englishmen established in the 1880s, opens as a provincial historic park.

Toronto, Sept. 23. Inco, Canada's largest mining company, announces plans to extend its operations in the Sudbury area at an expected cost of $79 million.

Toronto, Nov. 27. Hamilton Tiger-Cats defeat Winnipeg Blue Bombers 22-16 to win the Grey Cup.

Canada. The Canadian Indian Youth Council is formed to help develop Indian leaders for the future.

Winnipeg. Burton Cummings, Randy Bachman and others form the rock band Chad Allen and the Expressions [The Guess Who].

Edmonton. Joseph H. Shoctor founds the Citadel Theatre in the Salvation Army Citadel.

Charlottetown. The musical version of Lucy Maud Montgomery's *Anne of Green Gables* premieres at the Charlottetown Summer Festival. It was written by Don Harron and Norman Campbell.

Saskatchewan. Religious fundamentalists, claiming racial segregation is God's will, force students at the Briercrest Bible Institute near Moose Jaw to pledge not to participate in interracial dating.

Auto pact ends tariffs

Prime Minister Pearson and President Johnson sign the auto pact.

Jan. 16, 1965

AUSTIN, Tex. – American cars and car parts can now enter Canada duty-free. Prime Minister Lester Pearson and U.S. President Lyndon Johnson signed a far-reaching agreement at the president's ranch near here today. Canada will abolish the 17.5-percent tariff on American cars and the larger duty on American parts, thereby forgoing $50 million in customs revenue each year. Johnson has committed himself to seeking the removal of the duties on Canadian cars and parts exported to the U.S.

Canadian officials say the boost to the Canadian auto industry will more than offset the loss of revenue. Last year, the Canadian auto industry had an output of $900 million. The Pearson-Johnson pact is expected to add $300 million to the total by 1968, and about 50,000 new jobs. It will have a major effect on the automotive trade deficit Canada has with the U.S.

Pearson said free trade might be extended to other industries. "The automotive industry, the organization of it on this continent, lends itself to this kind of agreement more easily than other industries. But we will certainly be anxious to have a look at the other situations to see if we can apply this."

Survey lists Canada second in affluence

Jan. 25, 1965

WASHINGTON, D.C. – Canada, according to criteria selected by the Organization for Economic Co-operation and Development, has beaten Sweden to become the second most affluent country in the world after the United States, says the latest edition of *OECD Observer*. The OECD is a policy group formed by Canada, Japan, the U.S., and 18 European nations.

In the survey, Canada was shown as producing $2,263 per capita in national output, compared to America's $3,000 and Sweden's $2,046. As well, it was found that Canadians own 347 cars and 400 radio sets per 1,000 people.

New books critical of Canadian society

Spring 1965

CANADA – Two new books, Dr. John Porter's *The Vertical Mosaic* and Pierre Berton's *The Comfortable Pew*, are creating a national uproar and becoming bestsellers in the process.

Berton's new book, like the majority of his work, invites debate by deliberately creating conflict. *The Comfortable Pew* criticizes the nation's Protestant clergy for running a church which clings tenaciously to an artificially pious past. Berton attacks the simplicity of church decisions, and insists the church often falls behind atheist philosophers. Yet critics are quick to point out that Berton's book has two major flaws: first, it overgeneralizes, and second, it ignores all those people who go to church.

Porter's book, while also provoking much debate, focuses on the apparent racial hierarchy of Canadian society. Based on decade-old statistics, *The Vertical Mosaic* criticizes the fact that of a cross section of 950 influential business people, not one was a woman, only 51 were French-Canadian, and a mere six were Jews. Furthermore, Porter, a sociology professor at Carleton University, questions the reality of a Canadian identity if virtually all that Canadians consume comes from the United States.

The Supreme Court of Canada building in Ottawa.

Mining camp buried in tragic avalanche

Feb. 18, 1965

STEWART, B.C. – A mass of snow, rock, and mud raced down a mountainside near here and buried most of a mining camp. Rescue teams went to work soon after the slide hit the camp. They managed to dig out 20 men who were injured, but found 26 bodies in the snow, rock, and wrecked buildings. Many of the men were asleep in the camp waiting their turn to go on shift at the nearby Granduc copper ore mine. The cause of the avalanche is being probed. The Granduc mine is close to the Portland Canal and borders on the Alaska Panhandle.

Johnson stays mum on Pearson speech

Pearson and Johnson: happier days.

Feb. 3, 1965

CAMP DAVID, Md. – U.S. President Lyndon Johnson did not want to talk about Prime Minister Lester Pearson's views on Vietnam after the two leaders met informally here today. Yesterday, as he received a peace award from Temple University in Philadelphia, Pearson suggested the U.S. stop bombing North Vietnam. "Continued intensification of hostilities in Vietnam could lead to uncontrollable escalation," Pearson said. "A settlement is hard to envisage in the heat of battle, but it is now imperative to seek one."

Maple Leaf flag raised

Feb. 15, 1965

OTTAWA – The old Red Ensign was hauled down from flagpoles all over Canada today, and, in its place, the new Maple Leaf flag was sent up the flagpole. Without a doubt the best-attended flag-raising was on Parliament Hill. There 10,000 people stood in cold, clear winter weather to listen to Prime Minister Lester Pearson proclaim the event as "a new stage in Canada's forward march" to national unity. They cheered as the new flag inched toward the top of the Peace Tower, although the cheering was more polite than unrestrained.

Not everybody was pleased by the event. Tory leader John Diefenbaker, a staunch supporter of the old Red Ensign with its Union Jack, was seen to dry a tear as the old flag was pulled down.

Flag is raised on the Peace Tower.

Inuit lad a stranger among own people

April 25, 1965

PORT HARRISON [Inukjuak], Que. – Toomee Elijaasiapik today returned to Port Harrison, near his parents' hunting camp. They were not there to meet him. Even if they had been, they would not have been able to talk to their four-year-old son, who has spent half his life as a tuberculosis patient in a hospital 800 kilometres to the south.

Toomee has been made a stranger among his own people through the means whereby white man's medicine saved his life. This paradox is only one of the ironies that characterize the Canadian government's growing involvement with the indigenous people of the north.

The federal government, drawn into the Arctic especially after the Second World War for strategic reasons, has sought to cultivate links with the Inuit in order to affirm Canadian sovereignty. The development of a foreign infrastructure was the result, creating new dependencies that necessitate yet further government intervention into Inuit culture.

To Prince Edward Island, by Alex Colville.

Commons approves new pension plan

March 29, 1965

OTTAWA – After 26 days of debate, the House of Commons tonight approved the Canada Pension Plan. The plan will be based on compulsory contributions beginning next January. At the end of a 10-year transition period, pension benefits will reach a maximum of $104 a month. Saying the compulsory contributions were simply a new form of taxation, 12 MPs voted against the plan. Employees will pay 1.8 percent of their earnings over $600 a year to a maximum of $5,000 annually. Employers will match the contributions.

Problems of overlapping provincial jurisdiction forced the government to revise the bill three times. The Liberal government defeated several opposition attempts to amend the bill. The closest vote came on an NDP move to make the flat-rate pension of $75 a month immediately payable at age 65 instead of 70.

Civil rights march backs U.S. Negroes

March 14, 1965

OTTAWA – In a show of solidarity with Negroes attempting to register to vote in the southern United States, 2,000 protesters today peacefully marched on the U.S. embassy. The ranks of this, Canada's biggest civil rights march, included four MPs, 25 clergymen, and countless university students. Prime Minister Lester Pearson, addressing the crowd on Parliament Hill, warmly supported "those in Alabama, or anywhere else, who are fighting within the law for their rights as free citizens."

Lafayette Surney, a Mississippi Negro and active member of the Student Non-violent Coordinating Committee, said the Canadian support lends new courage to American Negro protesters who march despite the risk of violence – and even death. A telegram supporting U.S. President Lyndon B. Johnson's plans to introduce new voting rights legislation was sent to the White House after protest leaders found the U.S. embassy empty.

Oak Island search costs trio their lives

Aug. 11, 1965

OAK ISLAND, N.S. – This tiny island, barely a mile long, today claimed the lives of three treasure-seekers. The men were exploring a mine shaft they had uncovered when gas fumes overcame them. Centuries ago, up to $30 million of loot was reportedly left here by pirates who built an elaborate series of underground tunnels to hide their treasure. Fortune-seekers have long flocked to the site, but so far they have not discovered anything of value. Despite today's tragic deaths, the search for the elusive treasure will no doubt continue.

Priest charges CNR with discrimination

Aug. 23, 1965

BARRIE, Ont. – Father Bernard Brown, a Roman Catholic missionary from the Northwest Territories, received a rude shock when he boarded a train between Toronto and North Bay with the young men on the canoe team he coaches. An employee of the Canadian National Railways allegedly told him: "Take your Indians to the rear car and kindly keep them there." The discriminatory comment angered the priest. "There is definitely segregation here if that's the way things work on our public conveyances," the coach said.

Windward Islands proposal put forth

Sept. 16, 1965

OTTAWA – Canada has been asked to provide defence and external affairs services for a proposed merger of the Windward Islands, in return for free trade with the four Caribbean states. John Compton, chief minister of St. Lucia, put out the feeler for Canadian support at a meeting with external affairs officials. He said the other islands – Dominica, St. Vincent and Grenada – support the concept and are aware of his presentation here. A political union with Canada is not part of the proposal.

Ottawa must pay Indian health costs

May 13, 1965

BATTLEFORD, Sask. – A judge has ruled that a provision in Treaty No. 6 obligates the federal government to pay the costs of the Saskatchewan government's medical insurance plan for all registered Indians in the province. This important test case was brought by Walter Johnson, a treaty Indian living in Battleford away from his home reserve. Although the federal government has been paying the medical expenses of Indians living on their reserves, officials argued that Johnson left behind his treaty rights once he moved to town.

In the 1870s, Treaty 6 Cree negotiators ceded their title to a large portion of present-day Alberta and Saskatchewan in return for a variety of commitments, including a promise that "a medicine chest will be kept at the house of each Indian agent." The Indians also demanded and received a commitment from Queen Victoria's men that Treaty 6 people would be taken care of in the event of any "pestilence or famine."

The ruling advances the idea that Indian treaties establish a framework of government-Indian relations sufficiently flexible to meet the changing requirements of successive generations. Such adaptiveness in interpretation is a necessity if treaties are truly to last as long as the sun shines and the rivers flow.

PM's collective bargaining vow puts an end to postal strike

Postal clerks and mailmen attend a meeting during the strike in Montreal.

Aug. 8, 1965

OTTAWA – Canada's postal workers have agreed to go back to work, ending a walkout that started on July 22 over wages. In accepting the government's latest offer, the 20,000 unionized postal workers have won a promise from Prime Minister Lester Pearson that collective bargaining will be brought into the public service. That means unions, and strikes, will finally be accepted as factors in the management of government employees.

The workers didn't do too badly in the wage category either. Although they fell $110-$150 short of the $660 pay raise they wanted, the final increase still works out to about 25 cents an hour more than they're getting now.

Artist named to reproduce Fathers of Confederation painting

June 30, 1965

OTTAWA – The famous Robert Harris painting of the *Fathers of Confederation,* destroyed when Parliament burned in 1916, is to be reproduced by Toronto artist Rex Woods. He'll be working from Harris' original charcoal "cartoon" of the Canadians who gathered at Charlottetown in 1864, plus a small oil rendering by Harris and three copies by other artists.

Harris' original painting incorporated those who were at Charlottetown – led by John A. Macdonald – and also delegates to a later conference in Quebec. He painted it in 1883, at the request of the government. Later, when it was destroyed, Harris touched up his charcoal sketch for public viewing.

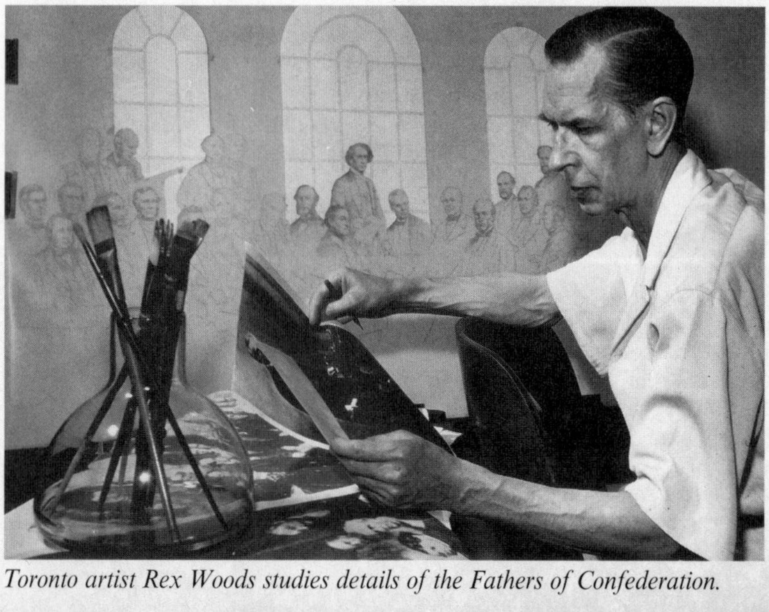

Toronto artist Rex Woods studies details of the Fathers of Confederation.

Deal signed to resettle Nfld. "outport" residents

1965

NEWFOUNDLAND – Newfoundland and Canada signed a major deal this year to facilitate the relocation of "outport" residents. The Fisheries Household Resettlement Program provides financial aid to help and encourage fishermen and their families to move from remote outports to "growth centres," areas where it is hoped that manufacturing and industry will develop. For many this means the end of a centuries-old way of life. For others, it is an escape from the trappings of isolation.

This century's ever-improving communications have brought a new awareness to the outports, causing some residents of the tiny coastal villages to grow more conscious of their isolation. Along with this, the Newfoundland and Canadian governments feel the price to maintain transportation systems, education, health, and other social services for the outports is too high. It would be cheaper to supply services – and better services at that – if people in the outports moved to growth areas.

By the time Newfoundland joined Canada in 1949, many of the small, independent inshore fisheries were facing economic ruin. Large fish processing plants are becoming increasingly necessary if Newfoundland is to compete on international markets. Since 1945, more than 150 outports have been vacated, partly because of a government urging them to do what's "best."

A new program aims to help remote outport residents move to "growth centres."

First native on N.W.T. Council appointed

Pearson chats with Abraham Okpik after naming him to the N.W.T. Council.

Oct. 18, 1965

OTTAWA – Abraham Okpik has been appointed to the Northwest Territories Council, Prime Minister Lester Pearson announced today. Okpik, whose name means "owl" in his Inuit language, is the first native named to the council, which is made up of five appointed and four elected members. The council's main purpose is to advise the Carrothers Commission on Territorial Government. Okpik, a tall, heavyset Inuit who has served as a translator, rehabilitation centre director, journalist, and town councillor, says he doesn't want special treatment because of his origin. Okpik says he'll push for increased native representation through the creation of new constituencies in the eastern Arctic. His appointment comes at a time when the Arctic governmental system is criticized as being obsolete and ineffective. Experts speculate that the N.W.T. may petition for status as a province.

Father Bauer gives up coaching position

Father David Bauer, former coach of Canada's national hockey team.

Aug. 23, 1965

WINNIPEG – Rev. David Bauer has turned over the reins of Canada's national hockey team to former New York Ranger Jackie McLeod. Bauer, who is the acknowledged father of the national team program, will stay on as an adviser to McLeod, who's now both coach and manager of the team.

The national team will relocate to Winnipeg and will be looking toward a stronger showing at next year's international competition. Training from September until spring is intended to prepare the boys for next year's world championship series in Yugoslavia. Says Father Bauer: "I don't think we can ever go back there again with anything less than an American Hockey League team." (The AHL is comprised of farm teams run by National Hockey League clubs.) The past two years have been rough for Canada's national team, with consecutive fourth-place finishes at the world championships.

▷

Nfld. tuition fees: Smallwood reveals province to foot bill

Oct. 6, 1965

ST. JOHN'S, Nfld. – Premier Joseph R. Smallwood made a major announcement today at a special assembly in Memorial University's gymnasium. He revealed that all tuition fees for undergraduates from first-year through fifth-year would be paid by the provincial government in the future.

Fees now average $350 per year, and with about 4,000 students in attendance this means the proposal will cost the government about $1.5 million annually. Smallwood also promised that beginning next year his government will phase in a plan whereby students who are attending Memorial will be paid a salary as well. It seems the sum will be set at $50 per month for students in and near St. John's and $100 per month for those who must move to the city from other parts of the province. Both plans will apply only to students whose parents reside in Newfoundland.

Smallwood has taken a keen interest in Memorial, which was granted university status only after Confederation. Under his government's direction, Memorial has expanded enrolment and added new programs. In 1961 it moved to a new campus and expansion continues. Smallwood's program will ensure continued growth, and it also makes Memorial University unique among Canadian universities.

Liberal minority is second in a row

Edmontonians welcomed Tory leader Diefenbaker during the campaign.

Whistle stop by Diefenbaker in his home province, Saskatchewan.

Pearson makes a plea for national unity at a luncheon meeting in Calgary, Alberta, during his successful election campaign.

Nov. 8, 1965

OTTAWA – The federal election today changed little and another election within a year is possible. Liberal Prime Minister Lester Pearson has another minority government. Late returns show the Liberals with 128 seats, Conservatives 99, NDP 21, Social Credit Rally 9, Social Credit 5, independent 2. One seat is still in doubt.

The Liberals won 129 seats in the 1963 election. In this campaign, Pearson said if he did not get a majority, he would call another election soon. Tonight, Pearson refused to comment on that possibility or on the statement by External Affairs Minister Paul Martin that the Liberals may seek a coalition with the NDP. Calling the election "useless," NDP leader T.C. Douglas tonight said his party would not consider a coalition except in some unforeseen crisis. The NDP will support legislation with which it agrees, but will stay in opposition.

Two Liberal cabinet ministers, one in P.E.I. and one in Alberta, lost. But it is thought Pearson might fill out his cabinet with three rising stars elected from Quebec – Pierre Trudeau, Jean Marchand, and Gérard Pelletier. These three will have a role in the growing confrontation between Ottawa and Quebec. Marchand promised an increased federal role in social policy as new provincial Family and Social Welfare Minister René Lévesque was demanding the federal government get out of the field.

N.B. set to revamp municipal structure

Nov. 19, 1965

FREDERICTON – Premier Louis Robichaud wants sweeping changes to the structure of municipal government in New Brunswick. Under legislation introduced today, the Robichaud government would take control of many municipal functions and reorganize and standardize municipal services.

The biggest changes will probably be felt in education. When Robichaud announced the program on radio and television earlier this week, one of the images he used was that of a shoddy, crowded, one-room school. He said he wanted to create equal opportunity and an acceptable minimum of services for all people in the province "regardless of the financial resources of the locality in which they live."

Under the program, the province will take over all financing and much responsibility for education from the municipalities. The 400 school districts will be consolidated into 34 large districts. Some trustees will still be appointed, but most will be elected. The legislation also wipes out county councils, with the province taking full control in the rural areas. It sets uniform assessment and maximum local tax rates.

The skeletal federal government moans that "some of the demands were a bit excessive" after a visit by the 10 provincial premiers.

Canadian fashions stay in touch with the times

Satin evening cloak, c1912.

Afternoon dresses, c1902.

Beaded jacket, c1915.

Evening dress, c1900.

Day dress and morning coat, c1927.

Afternoon dress, 1930s.

Evening dress and day dress, c1939.

Hardy Amies evening dress, 1947.

1959 evening dress by Lanvin.

This Marie-Paule obi coat, c1965, shows the Oriental influence.

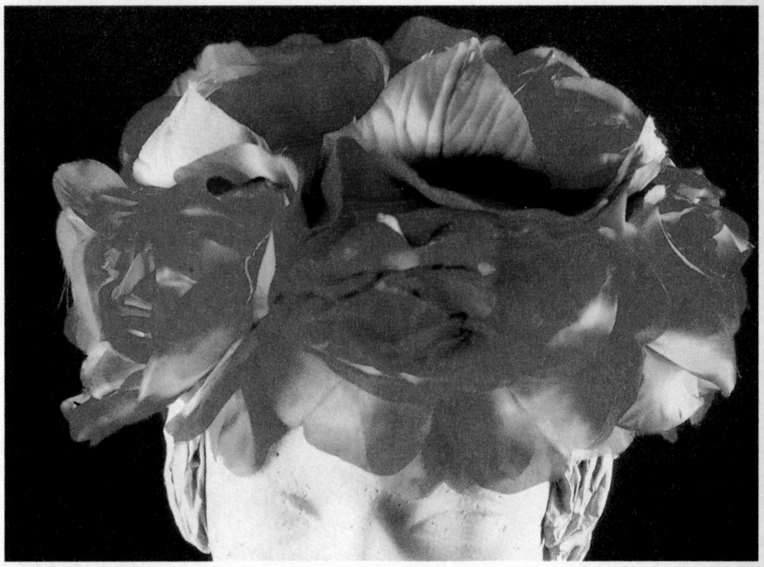

Hats are still a necessary item in the well-dressed woman's wardrobe. This 1965 hat serves no functional purpose and is simply frivolously flowery.

1966

Ontario, March 4. Studebaker of Canada announces it is closing its Hamilton car plant because of declining sales.

United States, March 12. Bobby Hull of the Chicago Blackhawks scores his 51st goal of the season, breaking Maurice Richard's record of 50 goals in a season.

Toronto, March 29. World heavyweight champion Cassius Clay [Muhammad Ali] scores a unanimous win over Canadian champion George Chuvalo.

Ottawa, April 5. The Commons votes to maintain capital punishment, though all death sentences in Canada have been commuted since 1963.

Detroit, May 5. Montreal Canadiens defeat Detroit Red Wings four games to two to win the Stanley Cup.

Fredericton, June 10. Louis Robichaud's Liberal government passes the Municipalities Act, stripping the municipalities of most powers and centralizing all municipal responsibilities for health, welfare, education, and justice in Fredericton.

Fredericton, July 17. The government passes the Schools Act, stating all schools in the province must provide identical services and making other reforms to the school system.

Regina, September. Ken and Sue Kramer found the Globe Theatre, Canada's first professional children's theatre.

Ottawa, Oct. 5. The Carrothers Report on the future government of the N.W.T. is tabled in the Commons. Its main recommendation is for the N.W.T. to remain one jurisdiction for the time being.

Ontario, Oct. 14. The National Association of Catholic Bishops announces that Roman Catholics can eat meat on Fridays, effective today.

Vancouver, Nov. 26. Saskatchewan Roughriders defeat Ottawa Rough Riders 29-14 to win the Grey Cup.

Regina, Dec. 8. The legislature ratifies an agreement with Ottawa to phase out equalization payments to Saskatchewan over the next five years. The province has ceased to qualify for equalization grants because it is no longer deemed a "have-not" province.

Victoria. The legislature incorporates the Bank of British Columbia.

Montreal. Canada's second subway system, the Métro, opens.

Taxes dip in B.C., increase in Ontario

Feb. 11, 1966

VICTORIA, B.C. – British Columbia's latest budget calls for tax cuts and help for the poor and homeowners. But in Ontario, the sales tax is going up and so are taxes on gasoline, cigarettes, and liquor. Opposition leaders called it a "soak-the-poor" budget.

B.C.'s budget, introduced by Premier W.A.C. Bennett, who is his own finance minister, showed that the provincial economy is booming – and that a provincial election is not far away. He took the five percent sales tax off restaurant meals, candies, soft drinks, newspapers, periodicals, and school supplies. The homeowner grant is going up $10 a year to $110, and British Columbia will now pay for 90 percent of medical insurance premiums for those with no taxable income. Bennett also promised that more money would be spent on highways, universities, civil service salaries and grants to municipalities. He sympathized with the people living in provinces whose government did not have the fiscal foresight of Social Credit.

In Ontario, provincial treasurer James Allan announced the tax increases, and said provincial income tax would go up, too, if Ottawa did not increase federal tax grants.

Repatriation plan dead

Former justice minister Fulton.

Privy Council president Guy Favreau, who denounces the Tories' "sentimental colonialism."

Jan. 22, 1966

MONTREAL – The latest plan to bring home Canada's Constitution appears to be dead. In a speech here today, Privy Council president Guy Favreau said it would be better to delay attempts at constitutional change. The federal government and Quebec could seek accommodation within the existing BNA Act, he said. "I would rather delay the repatriation of the Constitution – although, as everybody knows, I consider it essential – than see the reform of the Constitution entrusted to a Parliament dominated by the sentimental colonialism from which the Tories draw their conception of national unity."

Discussion of the method of amending the Constitution, key to repatriation, is based on the Fulton-Favreau formula. That method, first approved in 1964 and ratified so far by nine provinces but not Quebec, was devised by Favreau and former Conservative justice minister Davie Fulton. Quebec Premier Jean Lesage has echoed Favreau's sentiments.

Paper's publishing in three languages

Jan. 6, 1966

INUVIK, N.W.T. – A new independent newspaper has started publication here. The *Drum* reflects a coming of age for the peoples of the western Arctic who wish to not only keep abreast of the Arctic pace of economic development, but who also insist that the local population must no longer be ignored by government and industry in the decision-making process.

The paper welcomes news and opinion from residents of the Mackenzie Delta. And to reach more readers, the paper has created a precedent by publishing in English, Inuktitut (the Inuit language), and Kutchin, or Loucheux, a predominant Indian dialect of the region.

Canadair to build CL-215 water bomber

CL-215 amphibian (later photo).

Feb. 1, 1966

MONTREAL – Officials at Canadair today announced that production of the amphibious CL-215 will begin immediately. The new aircraft, which is expected to fly within the next 18 months, is designed primarily to combat forest fires in remote areas. The plane will be the world's first aircraft built specifically as a water bomber, and Canadair hopes to sell it abroad.

The twin-engined CL-215 has been designed to fly inches above a body of water, within 10 seconds scoop 5,000 litres into its cargo bay, then fly to the site of the fire to "bomb" it. This operation can be repeated as long as the plane has enough fuel to keep flying. The new aircraft will also be equipped to "bomb" with chemical agents.

Fisheries minister gets firsthand look at seal slaughter

March 7, 1966

QUEBEC – With the continued current of letters flooding federal government offices, Fisheries Minister H.J. Robichaud has decided to visit the seal slaughter and judge conditions for himself. A dispassionate Robichaud stood on the scarlet blotched ice today observing the fishermen. The minister examined the club of one of the fishermen, who offered to demonstrate killing and skinning techniques. The minister concluded, from this demonstration, that there was no doubt the pup was dead before it was skinned.

T.I. Hughes, general manager of the Ontario Humane Society, agreed with Robichaud that the fishermen did indeed kill the seal before skinning it, since it was a law passed by Robichaud in 1962. But Hughes planned a demonstration of his own. Armed with a pistol used in slaughter houses and a .22-calibre rifle equipped with specially designed plastic bullets, he proceeded to find the most humane way of killing seal pups.

Robichaud had come to observe, but even with firsthand knowledge of the goings-on at the seal hunt, he declared that it was simply impossible to answer all of the mail that overwhelmed his office, as well as the prime minister's and the governor general's.

Co-hosts LaPierre, Watson get the axe

April 15, 1966

OTTAWA – Top management of the Canadian Broadcasting Corporation has decided not to renew the contracts of co-hosts Laurier LaPierre and Patrick Watson of the controversial and hugely successful public affairs program *This Hour Has Seven Days*. The decision may be presented to the CBC board of directors which meets next week in Halifax. The Nielsen ratings, which indicate the show draws more than 3 million viewers, would seem to rule out the possibility that the program itself would be cancelled.

Major snowstorm paralyses Winnipeg

Scaling a snowbank in Winnipeg.

The rising sun casts a golden light over the snow-covered prairie.

A mail truck is buried after a severe winter storm on the prairies.

March 4, 1966

WINNIPEG – Manitoba's capital city today is virtually closed down, victim of a major blizzard. A combination of 30 centimetres of snow and winds blowing at a steady 110 kilometres per hour resulted in what the Greater Winnipeg Safety Council called the "most serious and dangerous blizzard any of us has ever experienced."

Schools are closed. Public transportation is cancelled, as is the postal service. For the first time in 60 years, the Winnipeg Grain Exchange was not able to open. All hospitals are on emergency service, and in many cases staff members cannot go home, nor can their replacements report for duty. One hazard facing hundreds of homeowners is a condition they have never seen before: the inability to get out of their homes. Residents of some entire streets are prisoners of snowbanks which cover doorways and first-floor windows.

Winnipeg's two major downtown department stores have been turned into temporary hostels. At 3 p.m. yesterday when both employees and shoppers were unable to get transportation to their homes, they remained at Eaton's and The Bay. At Eaton's there are 900 live-in guests, and at The Bay the number is around 300. A few of them slept overnight in beds that are in the display windows.

Radio stations rallied to the cause by going on emergency service with information programs providing news bulletins and helping to locate stormbound individuals. Drivers of snowmobiles and of four-wheel-drive vehicles were pressed into service by police.

Ottawa to spend $112M on improvements at Indian reserves

March 17, 1966

OTTAWA – The federal government has earmarked $112 million to develop housing and improve the basic infrastructure on reserves inhabited by some 600 Indian bands, it was revealed today. Most of the money will be spent on 12,000 prefabricated houses. The rest will be used on water, sewage, electricity and road systems.

An important impetus to the plan was a federal-provincial conference on poverty and opportunity held last year in Ottawa. A major topic was the poor living standards of many Indians. Only nine percent of Indian reserve homes have sewer connections or septic tanks, only 13 percent have running water, and seven percent have indoor baths.

One problem is that Indians fall under the jurisdiction of the federal government. Indian reserves have not been privy to the growth of services developed largely under provincial and municipal governments. ▷

Munsinger Affair crops up in the House

March 10, 1966

OTTAWA – Spies and alleged spies threw the House of Commons into chaos today. Justice Minister Lucien Cardin has made vague charges that more than one cabinet minister in the former Diefenbaker government was involved with a woman named Gerda Munsinger, who may have been a spy.

Two former Conservative defence ministers, Douglas Harkness and Gordon Churchill, proposed motions that Cardin resign unless he could immediately back up his allegations. It was so confusing that at one point Speaker Lucien Lamoureux admitted even he did not know what motion was on the floor. Opposition leader John Diefenbaker issued a statement accusing Cardin of McCarthyism.

Gerda Munsinger.

PM refuses resignation

March 10, 1966

OTTAWA – Prime Minister Lester Pearson has refused to accept Justice Minister Lucien Cardin's letter of resignation. Today, Cardin took back the letter and destroyed it. The minister is caught in a swirl of controversy. It began over his handling of the George Spencer spy case and escalated when he accused former Tory cabinet ministers of having liaisons with an East German woman who may have been a Communist spy.

Pearson has offered to hold an inquiry into espionage in Canada. But he is, for the moment at least, hanging on to the justice minister whose behavior the majority of observers believe is at most bizarre. Cardin has told reporters that the Munsinger affair was worse than Britain's infamous Profumo spy scandal. But he admits he has not seen the police Munsinger file and he refuses to supply any details.

Cardin said he was goaded into attacking the Conservatives over Munsinger because Tory leader John Diefenbaker criticized his handling of the Spencer case. The government denied Spencer, a Vancouver postal clerk, a pension because he was thought to be a Communist spy. The opposition argued Spencer didn't get a fair hearing.

Churchill Falls hydro project in the works

Oct. 6, 1966

QUEBEC CITY – Quebec plans the biggest hydroelectric project in history, Premier Daniel Johnson announced tonight. In partnership with the British Newfoundland Corp. (Brinco), Quebec will subsidize the development of Churchill Falls in Labrador. When complete in five years, Churchill Falls will produce more electricity than Egypt's Aswan Dam, under construction, and the U.S. Grand Coulee Dam combined. Construction will employ 5,000 workers.

Under terms of the agreement, Brinco will put about $650 million into developing the site. Quebec agreed to buy all surplus power from it and to spend $350 million building lines from the Labrador-Quebec border through the province to U.S. markets.

Johnson said the agreement specifies it will have no effect on the continuing Quebec-Newfoundland border disputes. Johnson said the Churchill Falls project was not Quebec's best option. But he said Hydro-Québec did not work fast enough to investigate the potential of rivers flowing into James Bay.

Johnson leads revitalized UN to power

Victorious Daniel Johnson.

June 5, 1966

QUEBEC CITY – Daniel Johnson led a revitalized Union Nationale to victory tonight, defeating Premier Jean Lesage's Liberals. The UN won 55 seats to the Liberals' 51. Two independent members were elected. Most UN gains were in rural Quebec, but the party also made surprising advances in the Liberal stronghold of Montreal. Welfare Minister René Lévesque, who was re-elected, said his party's failure resulted from not looking at Quebec from regional and local perspectives. Other commentators traced the UN's rural successes to the feeling that the Liberals had become a "big city" party.

Byelection win puts P.E.I. Grits in office

July 11, 1966

CHARLOTTETOWN – "If it doesn't move, pave it. If it does, give it a pension." Some wits have offered this as a fitting slogan for today's byelection in 1st Kings. The vote was crucial, for on it hinged majority in the House. The Liberals and the incumbent Conservatives were tied after the May 30 general election. The Liberal victory today gives them the government. In winning this squeaker, their leader, Alex Campbell, 33, also becomes the youngest man elected premier of a Canadian province.

Golden Sentinel, by Onondaga artist Arnold Jacobs.

Tree of Peace, by Arnold Jacobs.

Munsinger report is critical of Dief

Oct. 5, 1966

OTTAWA – Prime Minister Lester Pearson is praised and former prime minister John Diefenbaker criticized in the Munsinger spy scandal report released today. Justice Wishart Spence said East German Gerda Munsinger was a security risk and that former Tory associate defence minister Pierre Sevigny became a security risk by his love affair with her. Diefenbaker should have fired Sevigny when the affair came to light, Spence said. Pearson's handling of the matter was proper, he added.

Cohen's latest tells of Beautiful Losers

Author Leonard Cohen.

1966

TORONTO – What does a saintly Mohawk woman who lived in the 17th century have to do with a present-day scholar obsessed with his dead Indian wife and his dead male lover? Read Leonard Cohen's *Beautiful Losers* and maybe you'll find out. Then again maybe not. The experimental novel is just as weird and enigmatic as it is dirty and beautiful.

Cohen's concerned with the denial of the self. His "beautiful losers" are people like Catherine Tekakwitha, the Mohawk saint, and the novel's scholar-narrator who descends the treehouse of his male lover and hitchhikes to Montreal, where he is miraculously transformed before an awestruck crowd.

Dief's future as Tory leader in doubt

Nov. 16, 1966

OTTAWA – Dief may not be the chief much longer. The Conservative party conference here today instructed the party executive to hold a leadership convention before the end of next year. By a vote of 563-186, the delegates repudiated the leadership of John Diefenbaker, who led the Tories to the biggest victory in Canadian electoral history in 1958.

The vote for a leadership convention was coupled with a resolution that expressed confidence in Diefenbaker, but that sentiment was clearly hollow. Opposition to Diefenbaker's leadership has been growing, led by party president Dalton Camp. Before today's vote, Diefenbaker angrily accused the Camp forces of Hitler Youth tactics. He said Camp packed the hall on Nov. 14 to boo him during his speech. Camp denied the charge.

Pro-Diefenbaker forces are extremely angry. Nova Scotia MP Robert Muir hit an anti-Dief delegate yesterday and Alberta MP Jack Horner threatens fisticuffs.

Socreds swept back into power in B.C.

Sept. 12, 1966

VICTORIA B.C. – British Columbia's Social Credit party, running with an invigorated slate of eager new candidates, has won another impressive victory. Premier W.A.C. Bennett's party, 14 years in office, has increased its popular vote to 46 percent and held its seats at 33 in the 55-seat legislature. Many of the old Socred hands were absent from the campaign, after being defeated by urban professionals in the nomination races. The new representatives, whose ranks include five women, had a relatively uneventful campaign.

Socred policies are popular in B.C., and Bennett's party has ruled the province efficiently. The premier, who since 1953 has acted as his own finance minister, uses a "pay as you go" policy when it comes to government spending. This policy led him to declare B.C. "debt-free" in 1959.

PM lights Centennial Flame on the Hill

The Centennial Flame is surrounded by the coats of arms of the provinces.

Dec. 31, 1966

OTTAWA – Amidst cheering crowds, Prime Minister Lester Pearson kicked off Canada's 100th birthday by lighting the Centennial Flame at midnight. It's a gas-fired torch mounted in a round stone base, etched with the crests of the provinces; one that, once lit, is intended never to be extinguished.

Unlike the flame-lighting, the rest of the celebrations did not go so smoothly. Thanks to the CBC, which organized the affair, Queen Elizabeth was seen delivering a birthday message on a huge screen. But she was not heard, because nobody bothered to pipe her voice through the public address system. "Typical CBC," one spectator was heard to say. "Don't adjust your set." But, despite this, and a total lack of public seating, the mood of the crowd was festive.

The cliffs of Allan Bay at Boat Point, Devon Island, Northwest Territories.

Commons passes national medicare plan

Dec. 8, 1966

OTTAWA – On July 1, 1968, many Canadians will come under a national medical plan. But it still depends on the province in which they live. The Commons today gave final reading to the legislation that will provide a federal subsidy of about 50 percent to provincial medicare costs. But it remains up to each province to participate in and implement the scheme. The plan passed the Commons easily, despite a number of reservations. Only two of the Social Credit members voted against it. But a number of Creditistes and Conservatives refused to vote. Opposition leader John Diefenbaker supported the plan and brought most of his caucus with him in the voting. NDP members also voted in favor.

1967

Victoria, Jan. 9. The Centennial Train, a museum in train cars illustrating achievements from Canada's first 100 years, starts a trip across Canada.

Ottawa, March 5. Governor General Georges Vanier, Canada's first French-Canadian governor general, dies of heart failure.

Europe, March 26. Nancy Greene of Rossland, B.C., wins the World Cup in skiing.

Toronto, April 24. More than 350 University of Toronto faculty members march past the American consulate general to protest American involvement in Vietnam.

Toronto, May 2. Toronto Maple Leafs defeat Montreal Canadiens four games to two to win the Stanley Cup.

Montreal, May 25. The Montreal Stock Exchange is the first stock exchange in North America to admit female members.

Ottawa, July 1. On the centenary of Confederation, the government institutes the Order of Canada to recognize exemplary achievement in major fields of endeavor.

Winnipeg, Aug. 6. The Pan-American Games end. Canada won 92 medals, placing second overall to the U.S.

Yellowknife, N.W.T., Sept. 18. The territorial government of the N.W.T. is moved from Ottawa to Yellowknife, chosen as capital of the territory.

Montreal, Oct. 27. Expo 67 ends, after hosting 50 million people since opening April 28.

Ottawa, Dec. 3. Hamilton Tiger-Cats defeat Saskatchewan Roughriders 24-1 to win the Grey Cup.

London, England, Dec. 30. Vincent Massey, Canada's first native-born governor general, dies.

Canada. The six-team National Hockey League adds six new teams, the NHL's first expansion since 1942.

Canada. The Agricultural and Rural Development Administration finds 44 percent of Canadian farm families are poor.

Manitoba. The University of Winnipeg and the University of Brandon are founded.

Canada. Alberta and New Brunswick appoint ombudsmen to investigate public complaints against government action, the first Canadian governments to do so.

Michener takes his oath

April 19, 1967

OTTAWA – Amidst the red-and-wood glow of the Senate chamber, packed with Parliamentarians, senators, judges, and spectators alike, former Speaker Roland Michener was sworn in today as Canada's 20th governor general. He replaces the late Georges Vanier, whose body rested in state in this very chamber six weeks ago.

Michener is a far cry from the stuffy officials Canadians are used to. The former Conservative MP, who so impressed the Liberals with his impartiality as Speaker that they appointed him high commissioner to India in 1964, is an informal, witty man. In fact, in an interview given before today's ceremony, Michener said he doesn't want women to feel compelled to curtsy to him in his position as the queen's representative in Canada. A simple bow or handshake will do. After the swearing-in ceremony, the Micheners headed to their new home at Rideau Hall. They gave tea to about 60 dignitaries who dropped by around 4 p.m.

Governor General Roland Michener.

Top court upholds Truscott conviction

May 4, 1967

OTTAWA – Steven Truscott's appeal that he was wrongly convicted of murder eight years ago has been rejected by the Supreme Court of Canada in an 8-1 verdict. Truscott was 14 when sentenced to hang for the 1959 rape-murder of 12-year-old Lynne Harper near Clinton, Ont. It was changed to life imprisonment, and Truscott, incarcerated at Collins Bay, Ont., must serve another 30 months before he is eligible for parole. Eight justices did not believe his testimony. The ninth said grave errors in the trial warranted a new trial.

Expo 67 hosts 315,000 people on first day

April 27, 1967

MONTREAL – Canada's birthday fair, Expo 67, has received more than 315,000 visitors on its first day. That's almost three times as many as were expected. Most of the crowds went to La Ronde, the amusement section of the fair built in the St. Lawrence River. But that doesn't mean the international pavilions were not crowded. Long lines led up to the Soviet pavilion, where 5,000 people an hour passed through. The U.S. geodesic dome came close, with 3,600 an hour.

Despite the good cheer of the crowds, not all was happiness and bliss. There have been complaints of price gouging by concessionaires. One place, for example, is selling a litre of Lowenbrau beer for $3.30 – way over the usual price.

Large crowds close subway in Montreal

April 30, 1967

MONTREAL – The rush to get into Expo 67 by subway was so intense the underground system had to be closed. At the busiest stations, police helped Montreal Transportation Commission employees prevent any more people from entering the subway. Despite this, it's estimated 1.2 million fairgoers used the train and special buses today to see Expo's first day. Police had other Expo problems on their hands as well today. At one point, they went on radio to ask people not to stop on the highway to take pictures of the Expo site.

Manning's Socreds make it seven in a row

Alberta Premier E.C. Manning has returned to power for another term.

May 23, 1967

EDMONTON – Premier Ernest C. Manning's Social Credit government has been returned to power for the seventh consecutive term. With late-night results still trickling in, Social Credit has won 44 seats and seems likely to win another 10. There are 65 seats in the Alberta legislature.

With results which surprised many political observers, Calgary lawyer Peter Lougheed now heads the official opposition as leader of a recently strengthened Progressive Conservative party.

Along with the elections for legislative seats, there was a plebiscite on Daylight Saving Time which was defeated.

Armed forces debut integrated uniform

May 29, 1967

OTTAWA – Canadian forces today unveiled their new, integrated uniform – a dark green pattern almost identical for all ranks. Soldiers, sailors, and airmen will resemble each other. Rank badges on sleeves are visible from a distance, but only at close range can one discern badges that distinguish trades and regiments. The design will be worn by selected personnel, including the 100-man Honour Guard at Expo 67, for a nine-month trial period. Few changes are expected before it becomes general issue.

The world watches as Montreal hosts Expo 67

The inverted pyramid of the Canadian pavilion presides over the site.

American fine arts are displayed inside the pavilion of the United States.

The United Nations pavilion is surrounded by member countries' flags.

Expo 67 is attracting huge crowds to this site in the St. Lawrence River.

The centre of the Canadian buildings is the inverted pyramid, known by the Inuit name Katimavik, which means "meeting place."

The American geodesic dome is covered with a transparent acrylic skin.

Canada as host country welcomes the world to this international fair.

Scientists act to protect whooping crane

One of the 12 whooping crane chicks born this year in Wood Buffalo Park.

June 1967

WOOD BUFFALO NATIONAL PARK – There is nothing quite like the deep bugle-like sound of the grand snowy-white whooping crane. The mating call of these giant marsh birds, once considered extinct, echoes throughout the Canadian wilderness once more. The last live whooping crane seen in the wild was a chick that was snatched from its nest in Muddy Lake, Sask., by warden Fred Bradshaw in 1922. Ironically, the shrieking infant whooping crane was the last nestling collected in order to be immortalized in the Royal Ontario Museum in Toronto. Thirty years passed before another whooping crane was sighted.

In 1954, a nesting site was discovered at Wood Buffalo National Park, a wildlife reserve straddling the border of Alberta and the Northwest Territories, between the headwaters of the Nyarling and Klewi rivers. The birds were left to breed undisturbed for about 10 years, until the scientific community placed the whooping crane under scrutiny. This time their intention is to perpetuate the species.

Six eggs were taken from the nesting grounds at Wood Buffalo National Park and flown to a special reservation at Patuxent for artificial incubation. The whooping crane proved its vivacity when all eggs hatched, followed by the survival of four thriving chicks.

This 25-cent piece is one of the set of six coins featuring Canadian wildlife specially minted for Canada's centennial year.

Proud nation turns 100

1967

CANADA – Nine years ago, the Conservative government under Prime Minister John Diefenbaker began the task of making 1967, Canada's centennial year, one that cabinet minister Alvin Hamilton suggested should be "of significance and of national importance". Spurred on by the present Liberal government of Lester Pearson, the goal has been achieved. Countless parades, speeches and displays have marked Canada's centennial year across the country.

The queen cuts Centennial cake.

But Montreal's Expo 67, called by *Time* magazine "a symbol of the vigor and enthusiasm of the Canadians who conceived an impossible dream and made it come true", is the greatest success of all. It's theme is Man and His World and, apart from the contributions by Canadian cities and provinces, over 60 nations plus many international organizations and companies are participating. The pavillions, designed by the world's leading architects, house everything from historical and cultural displays to exhibits focusing on modern consumerism and technology.

National library's new $13M home opens

Prime Minister Pearson opens the national library and archives building.

June 20, 1967

OTTAWA – It took 14 years, but Canada's national library got its own home today when Prime Minister Lester Pearson officially opened a $13-million building just west of Parliament Hill. Both the library and national archives will be housed there. An act of Parliament created the library in 1953, but the concept was first proposed in 1883 by Sir John A. Macdonald, the first prime minister of Canada.

On display at the opening were some books presented by Britain to Canada as a Centennial gift, including a 1627 edition of a book on explorer Samuel de Champlain's voyages. The library, on Wellington Street, is Canada's equivalent of the Library of Congress in the U.S. and the British Museum in Britain.

Bluenose II thrills Expo 67 visitors

The Bluenose II is a replica of Canada's famous racing schooner of the 1920s.

July 1967

MONTREAL – Among the many attractions thrilling visitors to Expo 67 is a floating testament to a bygone era, the *Bluenose II*, a replica of the famed Lunenburg schooner that was once the pride of the Nova Scotian fishing fleet. Hundreds daily walk its deck and marvel at the intricate web of rigging, the sleek design, and the craftmanship that seldom fails to stir, in the minds and hearts of many, visions of romance and adventure associated with the lost golden age of sail.

The *Bluenose II* is Canada's official host ship at Expo. Apart from some modern additions such as radar, sonar, and engines, the *Bluenose II* resembles its namesake in almost every detail. She should, too. After all, she was built, in 1963, in the same Lunenburg shipyard as the original, Smith and Rhuland's. The most noticeable difference, however, and one in which the second may never duplicate the first, is speed.

The original *Bluenose* won her fame as the fastest saltbanker in the world. The wooden-hulled ship was a standard fishing schooner in design, from her hold to her sail plan, but was bigger than most. She sank after striking a reef off the coast of Haiti in 1946.

Orange and Green Bi-serial, by Montreal-born artist Guido Molinari.

Centennial means it's time to party

Canada's Centennial 5-cent stamp.

The celebrations on Parliament Hill.

July 1, 1967

OTTAWA – The nation's capital is throwing the biggest Canadian birthday bash yet, and as midnight approaches and thousands gather on Parliament Hill, the festive mood shows few signs of waning.

Ottawa's centennial celebrations, including a royal visit, have continued almost non-stop all day and are now about to peak in a spectacular display of fireworks above the Hill. As a prelude, car horns have become instruments of applause, a steady stream of cheers ring out from every quarter, and ad hoc renditions of *O Canada* and *God Save the Queen* occasionally burst forth from the jubilant milieu. Ottawa has never seen such a night. Because of the First World War, the 50th anniversary of Confederation was not celebrated in 1917. ▷

De Gaulle: "Vive le Québec libre!"

July 24, 1967

MONTREAL – Quebec separatists got a big boost tonight when French President Charles de Gaulle cried "Vive le Québec libre" from the balcony of city hall. More than 10,000 well-wishers, including many banner-carrying separatists, witnessed the general's declaration at the close of a brief speech.

"Vive le Québec! Vive le Québec libre! Vive le Canada français! Vive la France," de Gaulle shouted to the frenzied crowd. The remarks came on the second day of the general's four-day visit to Canada, where he is to tour the French pavilion at Expo 67. Observers got a forewarning of what was on de Gaulle's mind when he remarked that the mood of the crowds he encountered on his trip from Quebec City to Montreal reminded him of "an atmosphere resembling the liberation" of France in 1944.

At a state dinner in Quebec City yesterday, de Gaulle noted that Quebec was increasingly becoming "a particular economic reality" which wishes to govern its own destiny. The president's visit, at the invitation of the federal government, has been already the source of controversy. Protocol says a head of state should visit the national capital before continuing his travels. But the French general balked at that idea, and so his tour includes a three-day stop in Quebec before a one-day visit to Ottawa.

Charles de Gaulle visits Montreal.

Early departure for France's de Gaulle

July 26, 1967

MONTREAL – An unrepentant Charles de Gaulle cut short his Canadian visit and left for home today after stirring a diplomatic storm with his "Vive le Québec libre" declaration. At a dinner held at the French pavilion at Expo 67 last night, de Gaulle acknowledged the controversy he stirred but refused to make amends. "There may have been some difficulty ... but if the president of the French republic has helped the French of Canada, he will rejoice and so will France."

Drapeau: French "attached" to Canada

July 26, 1967

MONTREAL – In a pointed rebuke of French President Charles de Gaulle's "Vive le Québec libre" outburst, Montreal Mayor Jean Drapeau says that French-Canadians are "profoundly attached to our immense country."

Drapeau, an anti-conscription candidate in the Second World War, made the remarks at a city hall lunch for the visiting president, whose comments have buoyed separatists and angered the federal government. Drapeau told de Gaulle "our dream is to play in Canada and North America a role analogous to that which France plays in Europe and in the family of nations." He added that belonging to Canada "is the best way to serve the French language and culture."

On leaving city hall after the lunch, a subdued de Gaulle ignored pleas from separatists to deliver more words of encouragement.

Jim Day of Canada wins the gold medal in equestrian jumping at the Pan-American Games on Aug. 6, 1967.

Construction is over at the Bennett dam

Sep. 12, 1967

FORT ST. JOHN, B.C. – Premier W.A.C. Bennett climbed into a 35-ton dump truck, pulled the right levers, and out tumbled a load of rock and fill to finish the construction of the W.A.C. Bennett Dam. The dam, part of a group of hydroelectric projects in the northeast corner of the province, cost about $750 million.

Three thousand people watched the ceremony, including 200 officials from B.C. Hydro and a workman in a hard hat who joined the crowd in saluting the premier. A month ago the premier opened the Duncan Lake dam on the Columbia – the first of the three dams on this river to be completed.

Pearson's rebuttal: our nation is united

July 25, 1967

OTTAWA – "Canada will remain united and will reject any effort to destroy her unity," Prime Minister Lester Pearson says in a statement that responds to French President Charles de Gaulle's "Vive le Québec libre" pronouncement. Pearson released the statement tonight after a full day of cabinet discussions over what action the federal government should take in light of de Gaulle's provocative words. Some MPs have called for the government to cancel further events in de Gaulle's visit.

"Certain statements by the president tend to encourage a small minority of our population whose aim is to destroy Canada," says the statement. "As such they are unacceptable to the Canadian people and the Canadian government. The people of Canada are free. Every province of Canada is free. Canadians do not need to be liberated. Indeed many thousands of Canadians gave their lives in two World Wars in the liberation of France and other European countries."

The prime minister then expressed the wish that his scheduled talks with de Gaulle would foster friendly relations with France. Pearson's statement was immediately branded as "pussyfooting" by opposition leader John Diefenbaker.

Tories dump Dief; Stanfield at helm

New Tory leader, Robert Stanfield.

Sept. 9, 1967

TORONTO – Tory rebels have completed the overthrow of leader John Diefenbaker. Today they and a majority of party delegates here voted in Robert Stanfield as the new leader, on the fifth ballot.

Stanfield, the premier and provincial Tory leader in Nova Scotia, is expected to resign that post immediately and head to Ottawa. He will then run for a seat in the House. Diefenbaker is also heading back to Ottawa, to move out of Stornaway, the opposition leader's residence. His future is in doubt, following the rejection of his leadership by the party. It's a stinging blow for the former PM.

Léger plans to open African leper colony

Cardinal Léger with the Pope.

Dec. 10, 1967
MONTREAL – An emotional Paul-Emile Cardinal Léger left for Africa yesterday, saying he may never return. He told a press conference at Dorval Airport: "It may be that you will see me again ... but in my heart I leave with a resolution never to come back." He plans to meet bishops in Senegal, Cameroon and Dahomey, former French colonies in West Equatorial Africa, to discuss opening a leper colony where the need is greatest. Even before his departure, three lay diocesan organizations and a group of parish priests proposed various candidates to succeed the cardinal as archbishop of Montreal. As yet, no names have been disclosed.

CNR to swap trains for buses in Nfld.?

Nov. 17, 1967
ST. JOHN'S, Nfld. – The area manager of Canadian National Railways announced today that the CNR plans to operate a bus service across the island of Newfoundland next year on an experimental basis. He says it will give passengers an opportunity to compare the new bus with the old rail service, and he feels confident people will find the buses an improvement. Observers feel the CNR is glad the Trans-Canada Highway was completed in 1965 and that it plans to close down Newfoundland's rail service.

Where did Dollard die?

Oct. 31, 1967
OTTAWA – Adam Dollard des Ormeaux died once, but that event will be commemorated twice. The Historic Sites and Monuments Board today decided not to take sides in a dispute about whether the famous battle of Long Sault was fought in Ontario or Quebec. The board will erect two plaques, one on each side of the border.

In 1660, Dollard led a group to ambush Iroquois hunters at the Long Sault rapids on the Ottawa River, just west of Lachute, Que. Dollard's group found itself outnumbered and after a week-long siege was wiped out. A dam has flooded out the rapids themselves and there is doubt about on which side of the river Dollard and his friends met their deaths.

Researcher Terry Smyth told the monuments board it is not possible to determine conclusively the location. In the 19th century, Quebec historians raised the battle to the status of an epic event in the history of New France. Historians since downplay its significance.

Robichaud's Liberals retain hold on power

Oct. 23, 1967
FREDERICTON – The political landscape in New Brunswick changed little in elections today. Premier Louis Robichaud returned to office with a slightly reduced majority. Late returns show Robichaud's Liberals with 32 seats to the Conservatives' 26. The most interesting aspect of the election was not the winners, but the losers. The flamboyant new Conservative leader Charles Van Horne lost a close race in his own riding to his former law partner. Robichaud lost three cabinet ministers. A Liberal upset K. Arthur Moore, former Speaker and dean of the legislature.

An RCMP officer tries to protect the Confederation train in Montreal.

Lévesque, Liberals split on separation

Oct. 15, 1967
QUEBEC CITY – Vowing to take his campaign for an independent Quebec across Canada, René Lévesque, a former minister in the Lesage government, today quit the Quebec Liberal party after it rejected his plan for separation-then-association. Some 150 delegates at a party convention left with Lévesque after Liberals endorsed a resolution rejecting separation but calling for "special status" for Quebec. Party leader Jean Lesage regretted Lévesque's departure, but said "he did what he had to do."

René Lévesque explains his position.

B&B report urges linguistic equality

Dec. 5, 1967
OTTAWA – Linguistic equality between French and English is imperative if Canada is to remain unified, the Royal Commission on Bilingualism and Biculturalism declares. Prime Minister Lester Pearson tabled the first volume of the commission's report today.

The commission says the Constitution should be amended to declare clearly that French and English are the official languages of the federal government and its agencies. Ontario and New Brunswick, which have large French-speaking minorities, should declare themselves bilingual and ensure that their French-speaking citizens have the same rights as Quebec accords its English-speaking minority, the commission says.

1968

Ottawa, Feb. 15. The Watkins Report on foreign investment recommends closer scrutiny of foreign subsidiaries to ensure Canadian economic independence.

Ottawa, March 4. Canada suspends diplomatic relations with Gabon over that central African country's invitation of the Quebec government to an international conference on education.

Fredericton, April 12. The legislature passes the Official Languages Act, recognizing English and French as official languages.

Montreal, May 11. Montreal Canadiens defeat St. Louis Blues four games to none to win the Stanley Cup.

Quebec, June 2. André Laurendeau, noted intellectual, journalist and co-chair of the Royal Commission on Bilingualism and Biculturalism, dies.

Quebec, Aug. 28. Michel Tremblay's play *Les Belles-Soeurs* premieres, one of the first artistic uses of joual.

Manicouagan, Que., Sept. 26. Quebec Premier Daniel Johnson dies.

Edmonton, Sept. 27. Ernest Manning retires after seven straight terms as Social Credit premier.

Montreal, Nov. 21. Two bombs directed at the Quebec Liquor Commission explode within three hours. Police suspect it is the work of Marxist revolutionaries working on behalf of striking liquor board employees.

Toronto, Nov. 30. Ottawa Rough Riders defeat Calgary Stampeders 24-21 to win the Grey Cup.

Britain. The *Nonsuch II* is launched to celebrate the 300th anniversary of the voyage of the *Nonsuch*, which helped demonstrate the fur-trading potential of Hudson Bay.

Europe. Nancy Greene wins the World Cup in skiing for the second straight year.

Calgary. The 190-metre Husky [Calgary] Tower opens.

Toronto. The Toronto Dominion Bank, the Royal Bank of Canada, the Canadian Imperial Bank of Commerce, and the Banque canadienne nationale form Chargex Ltd. [Visa].

Winnipeg. Chad Allen and the Expressions are renamed The Guess Who.

Greene skis to Olympic gold medal

Feb. 17, 1968

GRENOBLE, France – Canadian spectators lining the icy trail cheered wildly as British Columbia native Nancy Greene roared down the slopes on her way to an Olympic gold medal in the giant slalom and a silver in the slalom earlier today. Greene, whose aggressive style and persistence have made her the world's premier female skier, has been pursuing Olympic gold ever since she watched her Team Canada roommate Anne Heggtveit win in Squaw Valley in 1960.

Nagged by frequent injuries and monetary problems, Greene managed to bounce back to win the World Cup last season, and she is favored to win it again this year. Yet despite her successes, Greene says she wants to leave the circuit at the end of the season in order to concentrate on her personal life.

Nancy Greene (centre) wins the gold medal in the giant slalom.

Canada, U.S. agree on defence system

March 7, 1968

OTTAWA – Minister of External Affairs Paul Martin today announced that Canada will participate with the U.S. in the development of an airborne radar warning system as additional protection for North America against manned bombers. This is the new method of AWACS (Airborne Warning and Aircraft Control System) – relays of aircraft, some of which will always be aloft, carrying elaborate radar equipment which can "see" further than radar sets that are located on the ground.

Canada will be important if only because its territory will be used to base the aircraft, and their patrols will be largely in Canadian airspace. Although Martin said Canada is ready to renew the 10-year-old NORAD pact, he also stressed that Canada's role in the new defence scheme is unrelated to the planned American system of Anti-Ballistic Missiles. The American radar and missile project, intended to destroy intercontinental ballistic missiles in the stratosphere, is to be developed and built exclusively by the U.S. and will function independently of the NORAD system.

Top CRTC posts filled: Juneau is chairman

March 1968

OTTAWA – The Canadian Radio-television and Telecommunications Commission, established last month by an act of Parliament, moved closer to becoming operational with the appointments of Pierre Juneau as its chairman and Harry Boyle as vice-chairman. The CRTC will be the new regulatory body for broadcasting, with control over a wide variety of areas, such as licensing and program standards. The Broadcasting Act gives the fledgling organization some teeth. It allows for fines of up to $25,000 for a first offence by a private broadcaster, up to $50,000 for each subsequent offence, and a ceiling of $100,000 for all infractions. The CRTC was preceded by the Board of Broadcast Governors, formed 10 years ago to regulate public and private broadcasting stations.

Canadian Pacific airplane after a crash at Vancouver on Feb. 7, 1968.

Trudeau sworn in as prime minister

Pierre Elliott Trudeau is victorious at the Liberal leadership convention.

April 20, 1968

OTTAWA – After an abrupt change of plans that may signal an election soon, Pierre Trudeau became Canada's prime minister this morning. Trudeau, who succeeded Lester Pearson as Liberal leader on April 6, had planned to be sworn in as prime minister next week. But if he had done that, the rules stipulate he would not have been able to call an election until fall.

Trudeau's becoming prime minister today opens the door to an election as early as June. But his aides said yesterday the change in swearing-in timing was due only to Trudeau completing his cabinet appointments earlier than expected. The cabinet is reported decidedly split on the timing of the election, with Trudeau himself favoring an early date.

Trudeau, and others in his cabinet, want to capitalize on the momentum his leadership campaign created. But cabinet veteran Paul Martin is reported to have had an emotional confrontation with the new prime minister. Martin argued that Trudeau's victory at the leadership convention was so slim he should wait to establish himself and the new administration before calling an election. Martin also wanted badly to remain as external affairs minister. Trudeau offered him a choice between justice minister or government leader in the Senate and Martin finally chose the Senate appointment.

Both the Conservatives and the NDP have been preparing for a June election. Yesterday, the NDP unveiled its election platform. At the same time, Conservative leader Robert Stanfield announced the formation of a high-profile policy advisory committee.

Trudeau surrounded by supporters.

Leadership candidate Paul Martin is interviewed by the press.

Big league baseball coming to Montreal

May 27, 1968

CHICAGO – Play ball! That familiar cry will be heard at the major league level for the first time in Canada next year with today's announcement that Montreal has been awarded one of two expansion baseball franchises in the National League. San Diego is the other new team. A group led by Blue Bonnets Raceway president J. Louis Lévesque paid $10 million for the franchise and will draft its players from existing clubs. Gerry Snyder, vice-chairman of Montreal's executive committee, made the pitch to the league's officials at a meeting here.

Recipient of heart dies after 41 hours

June 1, 1968

MONTREAL – Canada's first heart transplant patient died after 41 hours of life with a new heart. The Montreal Heart Institute's Dr. Pierre Grondin, who performed the procedure on Albert Murphy, 58, said the patient died of complications brought on by anti-coagulant drugs which allow a mechanical heart to be used while surgeons install the new heart. Doctors had to use the mechanical device because the new heart couldn't carry its full load. Murphy was the world's 18th heart transplant recipient. Grondin says he's undeterred.

Alexander becomes the first black MP

April 12, 1968

HAMILTON – Lincoln Alexander, a lawyer running for the Conservative party, has been elected, making him the first black MP in Canadian history. Despite this distinction, Alexander insists he is not just a spokesman for blacks, but a member for all the people in his riding. Nevertheless, his election signifies the gradual progress black Canadians are making in politics, although it's a slow progress indeed. For his part, Alexander is encouraging blacks of all parties to run for office.

Trudeaumania runs wild in federal vote: Liberals win majority

June 25, 1968

OTTAWA – Trudeaumania swept the nation tonight. The Liberals under their new leader Pierre Trudeau will form the first majority government since 1958. Late returns showed the Liberals with 154 seats, the Conservatives with 72, the NDP with 22, and the Creditistes with 15.

The only bright spot for the Conservatives was the Maritime provinces. Trudeau's charm had not caught on there and the Conservatives picked up a few seats. But Ontario voted solidly Liberal and Trudeau even established a foothold on the prairies.

Some prominent opposition candidates went down to defeat, including NDP leader T.C. Douglas, former Conservative justice minister Davie Fulton, former Manitoba premier Duff Roblin, and Conservative president Dalton Camp. Michael Starr, the popular former Conservative labor minister, lost his Oshawa seat to NDP newcomer Edward Broadbent. Quebec voted mainly for the federalist Liberals. ▷

Basilica fire costly; priceless relics lost

The fire at St. Boniface Basilica.

July 22, 1968

WINNIPEG – Fire today destroyed the 60-year-old St. Boniface Basilica. Damage may run in excess of $2.5 million and many priceless relics were destroyed.

A crew had just finished painting the roof and its twin towers when the blaze broke out. Fire trucks were delayed en route to the scene as pedestrians clogged the bridge over the Red River. The cathedral is the third to stand on the same location.

Rand commission: change labor laws

Sept. 5, 1968

TORONTO – Labor disputes in Ontario will be radically different if recommendations by the Rand Royal Commission are put into effect. The two-year task force under Ivan C. Rand has set out numerous ideas for smoothing out labor relations in Ontario. Among them is a ban on mass picketing, job protection for strikers, no strikes by public workers, and the creation of an industrial tribunal to handle labor disputes.

The report, says Rand, is based on the notion that labor and management have to accept limits on their impact on the public interest. That's a view unlikely to be popular with either side. Labor has already rejected the report.

Lévesque named first leader of PQ

Oct. 15, 1968

QUEBEC CITY – A year after he split with the Quebec Liberal party, René Lévesque leads his own party dedicated to splitting Quebec from Canada. The Parti Québécois was born this weekend at a convention attended by some 2,000 separatist sympathizers. The new party is made up of Lévesque's breakaway ex-Liberals and members of the Ralliement National, a rural separatist group boasting 4,600 members led by former Creditiste MP Gilles Grégoire. The new party claims more than 20,000 paid-up members.

The Parti Québécois goals were spelled out last April when Lévesque released the 13-page manifesto *Option Québec*. It calls for Quebec to become a sovereign French state with its own ministries dealing with foreign affairs, the interior, finance, economics, education, social affairs, and the prime ministership. French will be the official language at work and for all business and labor contracts.

But, unlike the Rassemblement pour l'Indépendance Nationale, led by extremist Pierre Bourgault, the PQ is not calling for a complete and unequivocal break from Canada. It's position is more moderate – sovereignty-association.

René Lévesque left the Liberal party to form the Parti Québécois.

Prime minister introduces Official Languages Bill to Parliament

Prime Minister Pierre Trudeau explains his policies to a press conference.

Oct. 17, 1968

OTTAWA – With the words, "We believe in two official languages and in a pluralist society, not merely as a political necessity but as an enrichment," Prime Minister Pierre Trudeau today introduced the Official Languages Bill to Parliament. Essentially, it would make English and French "co-equal" official languages for all of the federal courts, the civil service, and Crown agencies.

This official bilingualism would apply in the English areas where French people make up 10 percent of the population, or the reverse in French areas. A languages commissioner will investigate infractions. The bill is likely to be criticized by western Tory MPs leery of "French domination" by Quebec.

Arrests end militant students' protest

Nov. 23, 1968

BRITISH COLUMBIA – With cries of "Sieg Heil" and "Police Brutality" echoing in the corridors, 114 student militants were arrested this morning at Simon Fraser University. Their red and black battle flag – with its portrait of dead Cuban revolutionary Ernesto "Che" Guevara – has been torn down from the second-storey wall of the school's administrative centre. The arrests, on charges of obstructing public property, end an occupation that has lasted three days.

As in the United States and Europe, student activism is on the rise in Canada. Most of the militants arrested today belong to the radical Students for a Democratic University, an organization similar to Students for a Democratic Society in the U.S. Embracing liberal ideologies associated with the New Left movement – participatory democracy, equal opportunity, non-violent protest against "the Establishment" – the SDU has demanded greater student autonomy, broader admission policies, and increased funding.

Postal workers OK deal; strike ends

Aug. 8, 1968

OTTAWA – Postal workers are back on the job, having ratified an deal that gives them 39-45 cents an hour more over a 26-month period dating back to Aug. 1 of last year. Because of this retroactivity clause, workers can expect a hefty bonus cheque soon. The increase is a far cry from the 75 cents an hour raise the union wanted, a fact that led union members in Vancouver and Montreal to vote against it.

Language bill leads students to protest

Dec. 5, 1968

QUEBEC CITY – After windows in government buildings were broken in a student demonstration today, Premier Jean-Jacques Bertrand vowed to use force against extremists if it becomes necessary. Police estimate that 90 percent of the thousands of high school and college demonstrators were under 16. They were protesting against proposed legislation to safeguard the province's English-language schools. Bertrand again promised to introduce the language bill before the end of the legislature's present session.

Minority education commission's focus

Dec. 9, 1968

OTTAWA – The federal government should revoke its hands-off approach to education by spending more on minority-language schooling in French and English. That's the recommendation of the Royal Commission on Bilingualism and Biculturalism, looking at ways to bring French- and English-speaking Canada closer. It calls for Ottawa to pay an additional 10 percent of the per-student cost of education so that minority-language schools can be set up in areas where there's a more than 10 percent English- or French-speaking minority.

Hijacker sentenced to six years in jail

Dec. 10, 1968

MONTREAL – A Texan who describes himself as a black militant was sentenced today to six years imprisonment as Canada's first air hijacker. Charles Lavern Beasley, 23, pleaded guilty to kidnapping, assault, and public mischief in his Sept. 11 attempt to force an Air Canada Viscount on a flight from Saint John, N.B., to Toronto to divert to Cuba. He had held a gun to the pilot's head, forcing him to land in Montreal for refuelling. Beasley allowed the passengers off and was talked into surrendering.

Duff's Ditch tackles Red River floods

Oct. 11, 1968

WINNIPEG – The Red River Floodway was opened today, 18 years after the original announcement that it would be constructed. It was during the disastrous flood of 1950 that then-premier D.L. Campbell declared that engineering studies would be carried out on two major flood-control measures; ring dikes for the southern Manitoba towns located on the Red River, and a water diversion canal around the capital city. That news was released at a time when uncontrolled flooding had forced 100,000 Manitobans to leave their homes and material damage from that year's flooding was estimated to be about $100 million.

The Red River Floodway cost $63 million. It follows a semi-circular route, 35 kilometres in length, around the east side of Winnipeg. During periods of high water, the flows of both the Red River and the Assiniboine River are diverted into this channel. The strongest proponent of the diversion was former premier Duff Roblin, as a result of which the mammoth earth-moving project is popularly known as Duff's Ditch. Between Winnipeg and the U.S. border, five other towns at risk of flooding are now ringed by earthen embankments.

Thinkers' Conference favors a multicultural Canadian society

A Ukrainian Canadian Christmas.

Dec. 15, 1968

TORONTO – The concept of Canada as a French-English society was rejected in favor of a broader-based multicultural society at a Thinkers' Conference on Cultural Rights that drew together 20 major ethnic groups today. In urging Ottawa to form an advisory group that would look after the interests of ethnic groups, the 151 delegates were trying to ensure their participation in Canada's cultural development. English and French groups were invited, but few came.

A spokesman said the conference favored bilingualism but not biculturalism because it does not reflect the diverse cultural makeup of this country. The delegates got a different opinion from *Le Devoir* editor Claude Ryan, a guest speaker at today's wrap-up session. Ryan said Canada is mainly a bilingual and bicultural society and substituting either of the official languages at the policy level would be challenging this country's cornerstones.

Hutterites in Canada preserve their heritage in special schools.

Two Portuguese immigrant couples seem happy to be in Canada. Canada is home to immigrants from many different European nations.

1969

Windsor, Ont., Feb. 20. University of Windsor students end a nine-day occupation of the theology department, having failed to win more say in university decision-making.

Old Crow, Yukon, March 11. The RCMP's last northern dog sled patrol leaves for Fort McPherson. The dog sleds are being replaced by snowmobiles.

Quebec, March 19. Premier Bertrand announces Bill 85 introduced in 1968 to protect rights to English-language education will not be pursued due to widespread opposition.

Toronto, April 6. Some 5,000 people attend a rally against U.S. involvement in Vietnam.

Saskatoon, April. An important showing of works by Cree artist Allen Sapp draws widespread attention.

Ottawa, May 2. Indian Affairs Minister Jean Chrétien agrees to the establishment of a committee, to include natives, to investigate treaty and related rights questions.

St. Louis, May 4. Montreal Canadiens defeat St. Louis Blues four games to none to win the Stanley Cup.

Winnipeg, June 25. The NDP under Edward Schreyer wins the provincial election, Manitoba's first NDP victory.

Montreal, July 10. Sir George Williams University professor Perry Anderson is cleared of charges of racism that gave rise to violent student demonstrations.

Toronto, July 20. Up to 35,000 gather at Nathan Phillips Square to watch the first moonwalk on a giant screen.

Toronto, Sept. 14. John Lennon and Yoko Ono perform at the Toronto Rock 'n' Roll Festival. It's Lennon's first performance in four years.

Montreal, Nov. 30. Ottawa Rough Riders defeat Saskatchewan Roughriders 24-21 to win the Grey Cup.

Toronto. Pollution Probe is founded at University of Toronto to work toward environmental preservation.

Ontario. The Waffle group, led by Mel Watkins and James Laxer, is established as a caucus of the NDP. Its policies are radically socialist and nationalist.

Montreal. The Montreal Expos, Canada's first major league baseball team, begin play in the National League.

Legislation softens stance on abortion

May 14, 1969

OTTAWA – A wide-ranging Criminal Code amendment bill that includes the liberalization of laws on abortion and homosexuality passed its third and final reading in the House of Commons today with the Conservatives split in their opposition.

The sections of the bill dealing with abortion and homosexuality split the Conservatives. The new legislation will allow abortions if the mother's health is in jeopardy, but a three-person hospital panel must make the decision. The bill also legalizes homosexual acts if they are carried out in private between consenting adults.

Stock exchange bombed

The Montreal Stock Exchange after a bomb caused $1 million in damage.

Feb. 13, 1969

MONTREAL – A bomb exploded in the Montreal Stock Exchange at 2:45 this afternoon, showering the crowded floor with broken glass, plaster, and other debris, and causing an estimated $1 million damage. Miraculously, nobody was killed and most of the 27 injuries were minor, even though the blast was strong enough to cause extensive damage to floors above and below the exchange. The bomb, which was detonated by a timer, was planted in the visitors' gallery one floor above the exchange itself. Police suspect the blast was the work of the Front de libération du Québec, a nationalist terrorist organization dedicated to securing Quebec's independence and responsible for scores of similar bombings in the Montreal area. Stocks usually handled by the exchange will be traded in Toronto until officials can reopen here.

Students destroy campus computer

Smoke billows from the university.

Feb. 11, 1969

MONTREAL – Students today destroyed the main computer and set fire to the data centre of Sir George Williams University. Two weeks ago, about 150 to 200 students occupied the data centre to protest the university's investigation into racism charges against a biology professor.

This morning, angry at new developments, the students wrecked the main computer with fire axes and wrenches and threw computer records and tapes into the street below. When riot police tried to force their way in, the students set fire to the premises. Police later arrested 96. Damage to the main computer alone is estimated at $1.4 million.

"Tiny" Tymm the 21-millionth Canadian

March 7, 1969

WINNIPEG – An infant born today at Winnipeg General Hospital is already in the history books, and she hasn't even been named. Miss Tymm, known to maternity ward staff as "Tiny," made her arrival at 11:15 p.m. and became the 21-millionth Canadian. Her parents are Mr. and Mrs. Bruno Tymm. The population clock at the Dominion Bureau of Statistics in Ottawa ticked over to 21 million at 14 minutes and 44 seconds after 11 p.m. On a theoretical basis, births occur in Canada every 87 seconds.

RCMP sled dog patrols like this are a thing of the past. The last dog patrol was on March 11 this year, using Siberian huskies descended from those donated by Walt Disney after the filming of Nikki: Wild Dog of the North.

John and Yoko plan "lie-in" for peace

Yoko Ono and John Lennon.

June 1969

TORONTO – Beatle John Lennon and his wife Yoko Ono have been detained at Toronto International Airport for more than two hours. The couple are bound for Montreal, where they plan to hold a lie-in in their hotel bed to promote peace. Lennon hopes to visit Prime Minister Pierre Trudeau. "We want to give him acorns to plant for peace." The Lennons have been refused entry to the U.S. because of a previous drug charge.

Abolish Indian Affairs, report urges

June 19, 1969

OTTAWA – The federal government has approved a Department of Indian Affairs plan to abolish itself. Indian Affairs Minister Jean Chrétien told the House of Commons today his department has outlived its usefulness. In a brief but wide-ranging report, the department recommended that Indians no longer maintain a special status and that the federal government is no longer responsible for them. The report suggested the government bring natives into the mainstream of Canadian society within five years. This would involve gradually ending all federal support natives have received since treaties were signed with them. "The anomoly of treaties between groups within society and the government of that society will require that these treaties be reviewed to see how they can be equitably ended," the report said. Chrétien said the report would be a basis for discussions with natives. Tory Indian Affairs critic Ged Baldwin said he hoped the government was establishing a serious policy, not making a radical proposal "merely as a bargaining instrument."

U.S. tanker the first commercial ship to take Northwest Passage

The SS Manhattan pushes through ice near Baffin Island early in its voyage through the Northwest Passage en route to the oil fields northwest of Alaska.

Sept. 14, 1969

ARCTIC OCEAN – The *SS Manhattan*, an American oil company-owned giant tanker as long as three football fields, successfully completed a voyage through the Northwest Passage today, the first commercial vessel to do so. The trip was an experiment to discover if a ship the size of the *Manhattan* could withstand the punishment of breaking through the heavy ice floes. The voyage has raised the issue of Canada's sovereignty over the Arctic, as the American owners sought no prior permission to use the Northwest Passage. The U.S. considers the Northwest Passage to be international waters.

Feed grain to pay for student tuitions

Aug. 7, 1969

REGINA – At a meeting that included Ken Sunquist, president of Regina Campus Student Union, Saskatoon student representatives, and the education minister and his deputy minister and staff, final plans were made for 200 university students to pay tuition fees in grain.

Students will make applications to a committee of university administrators, student representatives, and the Department of Agriculture which will select the most needy. Payment may be made in wheat, oats, or barley by delivering to certain terminals in the province. Cheques will go directly to the university. The grain will be used on farms owned by the government. A total of 200 students from both the Saskatoon and Regina campuses will be eligible.

Cardinal's Unjust Society is a best-seller

December 1969

CANADA – Harold Cardinal, 42-year-old president of the Indian Association of Alberta, has written a Canadian best-seller. *The Unjust Society: The Tragedy of Canada's Indians* is a scathing attack on the attempts of Prime Minister Pierre Trudeau and Jean Chrétien, minister of Indian Affairs and Northern Development, to eliminate Indian status in Canada.

Cardinal terms the government's proposed policy, outlined in a government white paper, a blueprint for cultural genocide. As he writes: "The history of Canada's Indians is a shameful chronicle of the white man's disinterest, his deliberate trampling of Indian rights and his repeated betrayal of our trust." All of those who want to understand the viewpoint and the grievances of Canada's treaty Indians must read this book.

Alberta native leader Harold Cardinal criticizes the government.

Official Languages Act is now in force

Sept. 9, 1969

OTTAWA – Canada is officially bilingual. The Official Languages Act, passed in July over a determined protest by some MPs, goes into force today. The law makes French and English equal in all agencies under federal jurisdiction. It also establishes "bilingual districts," where a minority group of either language is 10 percent or more of the population and where all federal services will be offered in either language.

Former prime minister John Diefenbaker led a small group of Conservative MPs in opposing the bill. They defied orders from their leader, Robert Stanfield, to support the bill. Earlier, the government agreed to change the bill to remove the appearance that all courts would have to be bilingual. ▷

Military restores order in Montreal

Oct. 13, 1969

MONTREAL – Canadian soldiers began pulling out of Montreal today after quelling the wildest spree of lawlessness the city has ever seen. The troops, from CFB Valcartier, were called in by Quebec Premier Jean-Jacques Bertrand to restore order as a 16-hour strike by police and firemen unleashed a binge of rioting, looting, arson, and vandalism.

The trouble began five days ago while police gathered at Paul Sauvé Arena to vote on a return-to-work order. Gangs of hoodlums quickly formed and began to roam the streets. They attacked the U.S. consulate, McGill University, Place Ville-Marie, and several downtown stores and hotels, leaving shattered glass and destruction in their wake.

At least two deaths are blamed on the outbreak. A senior officer of the Quebec Provincial Police antisubversion unit was gunned down by a sniper. In the suburb of Westmount, a physician shot dead a burglar in his home. Dozens of other policemen and civilians were injured in the storm of anarchy that swept the city. By the time police began returning to work, the QPP and some 600 heavily armed troops had stepped in to contain the violence. Fights were reported between drunken city policemen and their provincial replacements. All forces were called on a day later to keep a close watch on a parade of some 300 separatists who tried to march on city hall.

Injuries occurred during the recent riots in Montreal.

UN education bill sparks ugly riots in Quebec capital

Oct. 31, 1969

QUEBEC CITY – Police used tear gas and fire hoses to subdue riots that erupted outside the provincial legislature and in the old capital as about 20,000 demonstrators gathered to protest Bill 63. The bill, under study by the Union Nationale government, would grant Quebecers the right to choose to be educated in French or English.

Thirty-four people were arrested in the melee in which protesters threw rocks, broke windows, and spray-painted separatist slogans on walls. At least 20 people were treated for injuries. Many of the protesters came from Montreal led by the Ligue pour l'Intégration Scolaire, which wants to force all immigrants in Quebec to attend French schools. About 80 percent of immigrants enter the English-speaking community here. This worries French-Canadian nationalists, particularly as the French-Canadian birthrate, in contrast to a generation ago, is now so low.

The unruly demonstration follows several other peaceful ones in Montreal the past two days. More than 10,000 students and teachers marched and attended fiery nationalist rallies to lend their voice to the fight against Bill 63. At one point the UN's headquarters was surrounded by crowds chanting slogans against the government.

Supreme Court rules Drybones not guilty of violating Indian Act

Nov. 20, 1969

OTTAWA – In one of the most significant rulings made to date on the Canadian Bill of Rights, the Supreme Court of Canada found Joseph Drybones not guilty of violating the liquor provisions of the Indian Act. The federal act which governs virtually every aspect of the lives of registered Indians in Canada has many sections that made it an offence for those covered by the act to purchase or consume alcohol. Those provisions go back to articles in the numbered Indian treaties negotiated in the 1870s. Now this particular variety of treaty provision has been struck down by the courts as inconsistent with the equality provisions of the Bill of Rights.

First Jewish cabinet minister appointed

Oct. 15, 1969

OTTAWA – The appointment of Herbert Gray, Canada's first Jewish cabinet minister, was announced today by Prime Minister Pierre Trudeau. Gray, the MP for Windsor West, will join Canada's largest ever cabinet as a minister without portfolio. His mandate will be to concentrate on any financial issues. He will also be responsible for advising Finance Minister E. J. Benson on issues of student loan legislation, tariff policy, and financial institution policies. Gray, 38, is a fully bilingual lawyer.

George "Punch" Imlach completes 10 years as coach of the Leafs.

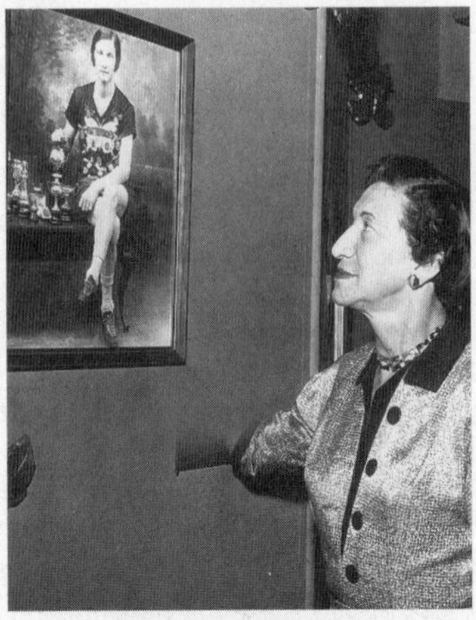

Fanny "Bobbie" Rosenfeld, Canada's female athlete of the half century, studies a photo of herself with her many trophies.

Birth control guide becomes best-seller

Nov. 1, 1969

MONTREAL – Much to the dismay of the hierarchy of the Roman Catholic church in Quebec, the *Birth-Control Handbook* has become a best-seller. Estimates put sales of the family-planning guide, published by two medical students, in excess of two million. This is the latest indication that this is the year when the women's liberation movement has taken hold in the province. The Montreal Women's Liberation Movement, with financial help from Dr. Henry Morgentaler, has opened a centre downtown.

CRTC: Air of Death is not misleading

March 18, 1969

TORONTO – The Canadian Radio-television and Telecommunications Commission hearings on the CBC broadcast *Air of Death* have opened. The radio program dealing with air pollution in Canada provoked some controversy as to its candidness. *Air of Death* producers testified that none of the facts were distorted or taken from obscure sources. The CRTC concluded that the program delivered unfeigned facts, from respectable sources, presenting a clear picture of the air pollution in Canada, and ruled that producers of *Air of Death* did not mislead their audience.

Toronto bans use of pesticide DDT

Sept. 24, 1969

ONTARIO – Reports revealing the damage being done to wildlife by pesticides have awakened an awareness in Canadian citizens about the release of chemicals in the atmosphere. Scientists find that birds of prey are mostly affected.

Bald eagles are rendered infertile by DDT intoxication. Similarly affected, the peregrine falcon is on the verge of extinction. This evidence prompted several concerned Ontario residents to lobby for the ban of the pesticide DDT. Today, they rejoiced when Toronto announced the complete ban of DDT, to become effective Jan. 1, 1971.

Environmentalists form pressure group

October 1969

BRITISH COLUMBIA – A group of Americans and Canadians has organized a blockade at the Douglas border crossing to protest the nuclear testing on Amchitka Island. Letters and phone calls from sympathetic patrons stormed the British Columbia chapter of the Sierra Club with pledges of membership and financial endowments.

The success of the Amchitka protest has inspired three participants – Jim Bohlen, Paul Côté and Irving Stowe – to harness this fervor toward the anti-nuclear campaign and organize an ecological strike force. As a result, the Don't Make a Wave Committee was instituted on Oct. 1.

When asked what their plans were, the three founders replied that they intended to pursue the anti-nuclear convictions of their group; maybe sail the waters as a vigilante committee. When Stowe held up two fingers in the V-sign for peace, Canadian member Bob Darnell said "make it a green peace." The three founders bounded with zeal, declaring that if they ever owned a boat they would call it the *Greenpeace.*

The protesters' intensity grew, and within a few days the Don't Make a Wave Committee followed its purpose and rented a boat. Their strategy to sit in the middle of the nuclear-testing area clearly signals the group's dedication to ecology.

Africville slum succumbs

A young resident of Africville, Halifax's notorious Negro slum area.

An old man at his Africville home.

Dec. 30, 1969

HALIFAX – In a move which finally marks the death of Africville, Canada's worst Negro slum, Aaron "Pa" Miller, 72, has accepted a city offer of $14,387 to sell his home and leave the area.

Nestled on the edge of the city dump, Africville has for 150 years provided the worst living conditions of any Canadian slum. Residents, who had to rely on a single contaminated well for their water supply, were crowded into filthy, rat-infested tenements. As a result, many of them suffered from skin and lung diseases. Unemployment was rampant, and wages were so low that almost the entire population of Africville lived in poverty. Such conditions often led residents to commit desperate acts. In 1962, a man arrested for trespassing at the nearby city dump told officials that he was looking for breakfast for his family.

Local politicians have long been aware of Africville's problems, but have been slow to take action. A report calling for the slum's destruction was tabled as early as 1945, but little was done until 1963, when Dr. Albert Rose, a University of Toronto professor hired to study the area, announced that previous studies were more than adequate and that swift action, and not more political stalling, was needed. In his recommendations, Rose expressed the hope that Canadians would never again be forced to live under such appalling conditions.

Factories such as these in Hamilton are becoming targets for ecology groups.

Canadians are very influenced by the lifestyle of hippies like these at Woburn Alley, England.

Hippies gather in San Francisco.

1970

Lac la Biche, Alta., Jan. 19. Some 200 native people occupy the Alberta Newstart centre to protest Ottawa's cancellation of its research program.

Ottawa, January. The government establishes a Preparatory Commission [Metric Commission Canada] to co-ordinate metric conversion throughout the Canadian economy and distribute information on metric.

Montreal, March 14. Eight West Indians are fined a total of $32,500 for conspiracy to obstruct the use of the computer centre at Sir George Williams University last year.

Toronto, March 26. University of Toronto agrees to renovate its day-care centre, ending an occupation of its administrative building by students to back demands for the renovation.

Ottawa, March 31. The government bans fishing in Lake Erie after a report shows high mercury content in pickerel from the lake.

Toronto, April 8. The CBC announces it has bought the children's show *Sesame Street* to show on its TV network.

Toronto, May 10. Some 5,000 people demonstrate outside the U.S. consulate against American involvement in Cambodia. Police arrest 91 demonstrators.

Boston, May 10. Boston Bruins defeat St. Louis Blues four games to none to win the Stanley Cup.

Ottawa, May 11. Thirty women from the Cross-Canada Abortion Caravan lobbying for abortion on demand create a disturbance in the Commons.

Ottawa, June 3. The Indian Association of Alberta presents a "red paper" to the government proposing Indians, rather than the provinces, assume some federal responsibilities.

Montreal, Oct. 5. The FLQ kidnaps British Trade Commissioner James Cross and demands $500,000 ransom and the release of 21 "political prisoners."

New Brunswick, Oct. 26. Richard Hatfield's Conservatives win the provincial election.

Toronto, Nov. 28. Montreal Alouettes defeat the Calgary Stampeders 23-10 to win the Grey Cup.

Quebec, Dec. 23. PM Trudeau announces federal troops will be withdrawn from Quebec on Jan. 4.

Farmers in Perdue help hungry Métis

Feb. 23, 1970

PERDUE, Sask. – In open defiance of the Canadian Wheat Board, farmers of this small community 80 kilometres west of Saskatoon today ground wheat they will send to hungry Métis. The Wheat Board, unconvinced by a report that 5,000 Métis in northern parts of the province are near starvation, has refused to grant permits for transfer of surplus wheat, claiming its role is that of a marketing and not a charitable organization.

Farmers consider the donations logical given that much of the stored wheat will spoil over the winter. It's "surely not a crime to feed hungry people," one farmer said.

Oil spills off Nova Scotia

The Liberian tanker with its cargo of bunker oil has been grounded for the last nine days while crews have tried to free it and prevent oil spills.

Feb. 12, 1970

ARICHAT, N.S. – Half of the oil tanker *Arrow* sank this morning. The ship, carrying 15.9 million litres of bunker oil, ran onto rocks nine days ago in Chedabucto Bay near this small Cape Breton community. On Feb. 8, the tanker split in two. As crews tried to pump air into it so it could be floated out to sea and sunk, the stern section slipped off the rocks into 30 metres of water. Both sections of the tanker have been leaking oil steadily.

A spokesman for Imperial Oil, which leased the Liberian-registered tanker, said the leakage rate has increased dramatically, but there are no estimates of the total amount leaked. A large oil slick has drifted out to sea, but oil continues to pollute water off Janvrin and Crichton islands near here. Government and company experts are trying to find ways to burn off some of the oil. Plastic booms have been constructed to protect fish plants at Arichat Harbor and the Bay of Canso. People here are critical of the clean-up operation. They say the government had no contingency plan and failed to react quickly enough.

Yellowknife hosts first Arctic games

PM Trudeau in the Arctic.

March 9, 1970

YELLOWKNIFE – In lighting torches held by three of the athletes, Prime Minister Pierre Trudeau officially opened the first Arctic Winter Games today under bright sunshine but sub-zero temperatures. Trudeau later watched Inuit games, such as hitting pop cans with a whip, before visiting hockey and basketball matches as the main competition for 800 athletes from Yukon, the Northwest Territories, and Alaska began.

Laundry detergent phosphates targeted

Feb. 19, 1970

OTTAWA – Energy and Resources Minister J.J. Greene has announced a federal ban on phosphates in laundry detergent. With all 10 provinces at the federal-provincial meetings approving the ban, phosphate pollution of water will be made a criminal offence. Ottawa plans to progressively reduce phosphates in laundry detergents until they're totally outlawed by 1973. Greene also proposed an amendment to the Canada Water Act, prohibiting phosphates and substitutes, which pollute by stimulating the growth of algae that depletes oxygen, killing other marine forms.

Farmers offered $140M to not grow wheat

Feb. 27, 1970

OTTAWA – Implementing a plan to strengthen the price of grain on international markets, the federal government today offered western farmers with surplus amounts up to $140 million not to grow wheat next year. Instead, the government wants the farmers to convert 8.8 million hectares to summer fallow. One official says "foreign buyers are not willing to pay top prices when they know we are sitting on a mountain of grains." Operation LIFT – Lower Inventory For Tomorrow – will pay farmers $2.40 per hectare. The average farm size is 288 hectares.

New constitution's a must, UN asserts

April 4, 1970

MONTREAL – The Quebec government demands Ottawa sign a new constitution within four years. If it doesn't, the Union Nationale promises to hold a referendum on independence. The ultimatum was written into the UN platform for the April 29 election at a special meeting here today. Premier Jean-Jacques Bertrand refused to take a personal stand on separation.

Bourassa, Liberals win Quebec election

April 29, 1970

QUEBEC CITY – The Parti Québécois made big gains in the popular vote, but the Liberals won most seats, decisively beating the reigning Union Nationale in elections today. The Liberals, under new leader Robert Bourassa, won 72 seats. The UN was reduced from 55 to 16. Premier Jean-Jacques Bertrand won his seat, but 12 of his cabinet ministers were defeated.

The separatist Parti Québécois came an impressive second in the popular vote, 24 percent to the Liberals' 44 percent, but won only seven seats. Quebec electoral structure favors rural constituencies and the PQ strength is urban. PQ leader René Lévesque and his deputy, Jacques Parizeau, failed to win seats. The Creditistes won 13 seats. The voter turnout of 80 percent was a record.

Bourassa celebrates election victory.

Ease marijuana laws, probe suggests

June 19, 1970

OTTAWA – People who use marijuana should not be put behind bars, the LeDain Drug Inquiry Commission says in its interim report tabled in the House of Commons today. The report does not endorse the legalization of marijuana, saying not enough is known about effects of long-term use. But it recommends that drug offences be taken out of the Narcotic Control Act and placed under the less severe Food and Drug Act.

The report is critical of drug enforcement officials, saying their methods are doing more harm than good. It calls for improved educational programs to alert young people to the hazards of drug use. The commission, led by law dean Gerald LeDain, also calls for more research into the effects of drugs.

Health Minister John Munro said in response to the report that he would soon introduce a law easing penalties for simple possession of marijuana – but not hashish, its more potent derivative. Stiff penalties for trafficking will remain.

No mention of abortion in Canadian doctors' new code of ethics

Protesters oppose Canada's abortion law in this demonstration in Montreal.

June 16, 1970

WINNIPEG – A new code of ethics adopted by the Canadian Medical Association omits all reference to abortion. Written in 1930, the former code was last revised in 1963 and described abortion as "a violation of moral law and the Criminal Code of Canada." Doctors who believe abortion is justified only if a mother's life is in danger base their objections on the Oath of Hippocrates. Written nearly 2,500 years ago in ancient Greece, the oath forbids abortion. But Toronto's Dr. R.J.M. Galloway, chairman of the CMA committee on ethics, commented, "We don't live back in the time of Greece."

Tomorrow, representatives of the Women's Liberation Movement will urge CMA directors to have abortion removed from the Criminal Code. Although Galloway said this move is possible where doctors perform abortions, he added, "We are not ready for that yet."

Bomb spree rattles suburb of Montreal

May 31, 1970

MONTREAL – The worst wave of terrorist bombings in seven years rocked Westmount early this morning. Five bombs blasted an office building and four homes between 1:58 a.m. and 4:55 a.m. No one was seriously injured. Mrs. Peter Bronfman, whose home suffered extensive damage, said, "We were particularly lucky. I just hope the police get them before they kill somebody." Premier Robert Bourassa said it was a "futile gesture of despair by fanatics" against the Liberal victory in the April 29 election.

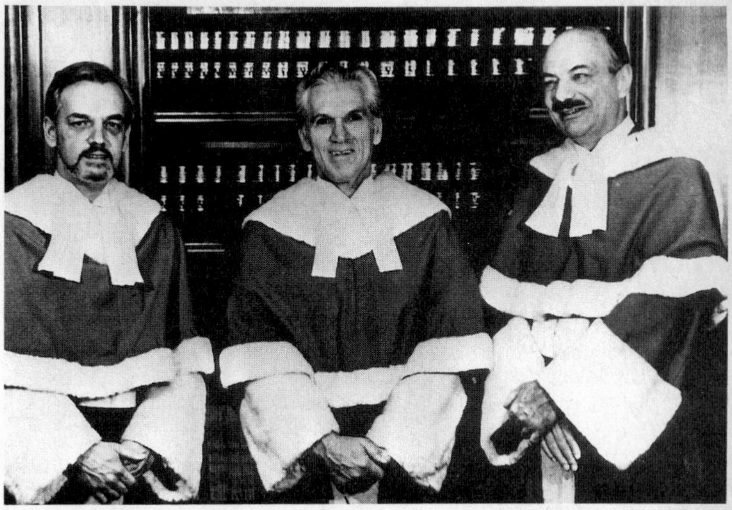

Three new Supreme Court Justices have just been appointed – Jean Beetz (left), Bora Laskin (centre), and Louis-Philippe de Grandpré.

Day-care services urged

Sept. 28, 1970

OTTAWA – The Royal Commission on the Status of Women wants the government to establish better day-care facilities across the country. According to the report, of the 608,000 children of working mothers in Canada, 15 percent are cared for outside the home, with only one percent going to day nurseries or nursery school.

While the report stresses there is no intention to force women to work outside the home, it states, "Women do not have the opportunity to choose or the choice may carry unfair penalties." Those penalties include the cost of private day care, worry over inadequate arrangements, or reduced work hours. Many mothers must work part-time or on weekends because of the lack of day care. The report recommends the government create a network of day-care centres, with parents to pay fees on a sliding scale, depending on their incomes. The report estimates day care for 450,000 children across the country could cost $500 million a year.

Mohawks leave island as sign of goodwill

July 9, 1970

CORNWALL, Ont. – A group of Mohawk Indians from St. Regis Reserve near here today agreed to leave Loon Island, a small cottagers' retreat in the St. Lawrence River. The Mohawks peacefully took over the six-hectare site two months ago. They justified their actions with documentation they say proves unequivocally their formal title not only to Loon Island, but also to 41 other islands along the busy water transportation route between Montreal and Cornwall.

A Mohawk spokesman said the Indians are leaving the island as a sign of "good faith," giving the federal government two weeks to investigate and resolve their claim.

Quebec, personified by an enraged revolutionary, bares its teeth in this cartoon on the October Crisis by Duncan MacPherson. The "teeth" are recognizable as current political leaders of the province at the federal, provincial and municipal levels of government.

Labor minister kidnapped; FLQ suspected

Trade Commissioner James Cross.

Labor Minister Pierre Laporte.

Oct. 10, 1970

ST. LAMBERT, Que. – Provincial Labor Minister Pierre Laporte was kidnapped outside his home today, 25 minutes after terrorists' terms for the return of kidnapped British Trade Commissioner James Cross had been rejected by the federal and Quebec governments. The abduction of Laporte as he played touch football with his nephew outside his suburban home is believed to be the work of another cell of the Front de libération du Québec, whose ransom demands for Cross were turned down.

The public and the politicians, shocked by the kidnapping of the British trade official last Monday, are now totally outraged by the acts of two men who pushed the cabinet minister into a car that sped off into the dusk. The burly kidnappers were not disguised.

Ottawa sends armed forces into Quebec

Soldiers patrol Montreal streets.

Oct. 15, 1970

MONTREAL – Canada's armed forces are taking up guard positions here and in Quebec City after Premier Robert Bourassa requested Ottawa to send in the troops, previously stationed in the nation's capital. The provincial cabinet has passed an order-in-council placing all policemen in Quebec under the control of Maurice St. Pierre, director of the Quebec Provincial Police.

A QPP information officer said, "We know (the soldiers) are coming ... we're clearing the parking lot for the army. They're going to do some protection work for ministers and so on. We need some rest. We've been working 20 to 22 hours a day." An army official emphasized the troops are an aid to civil authority "for the maintenance of law and order" and will work with, and for, police forces in both cities.

Ottawa invokes War Measures Act

A newsboy holds up a paper with a banner headline reporting that the War Measures Act has been invoked to deal with the crisis situation in Quebec.

Soldier guards Montreal building.

Oct. 16, 1970

OTTAWA – In a speech broadcast to the nation tonight, Prime Minister Pierre Trudeau defended his government's use of wartime powers as vital to the life and liberty of all Canadians. The government is not acting out of fear, but "to prevent fear spreading."

Earlier, in the Commons, leaders of the Conservative and New Democratic parties had agreed that emergency powers were needed, but that the government has been far too drastic in invoking the War Measures Act. Trudeau responded in his nationwide radio and TV hookup in French and English by saying the extraordinary measures are essential to combat the FLQ kidnapping crisis.

Suspects nabbed

Dec. 28, 1970

MONTREAL – Canada's biggest manhunt ended this morning when three suspects in the kidnapping and murder of Quebec Labor Minister Pierre Laporte surrendered. Brothers Jacques and Paul Rose and Francis Simard had been tracked to a farmhouse 32 kilometres south of the city. They dropped their guns and gave up. Marc Charbonneau was a fourth suspect.

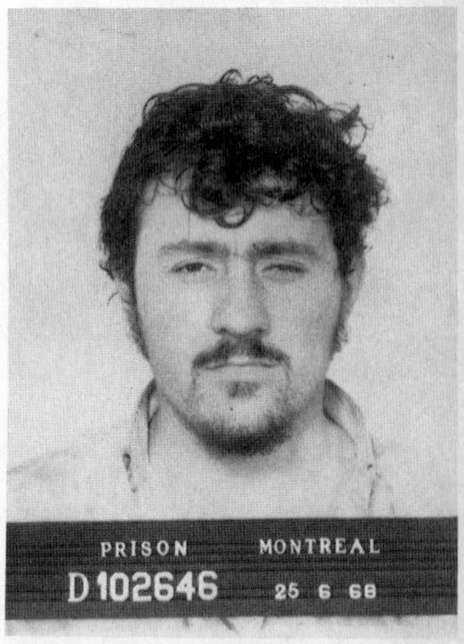

Police photo of Paul Rose.

Laporte found dead in the trunk of a car

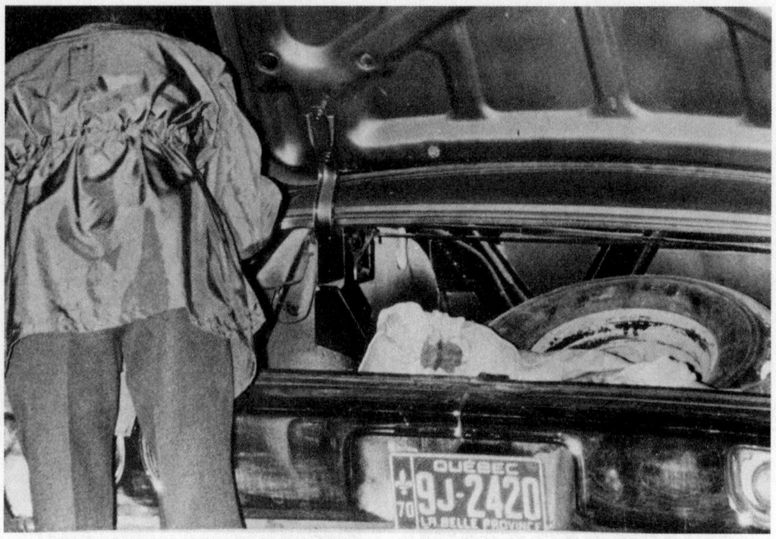

The body of Pierre Laporte is found in the trunk of a car at St. Hubert.

Oct. 18, 1970

MONTREAL – The body of kidnapped Quebec Labor Minister Pierre Laporte was found at 12:25 this morning in the trunk of a car parked beside an airplane hangar in St. Hubert. Police say he had apparently been strangled with the chain of his religious medallion. Members of the terrorist Front de libération du Québec are objects of a massive manhunt in the kidnappings of Laporte and British Trade Commissioner James Cross.

New law to replace War Measures Act

Nov. 3, 1970

OTTAWA – The government is bringing in new legislation to modify its powers for the fight against the Front de libération du Québec. The new law has substantially the same powers as those of the War Measures Act, which will be withdrawn. The bill has been given first reading, debate begins tomorrow, and despite some opposition from Tories and New Democrats it is expected to become law next week. Its expiry date is April 30, but it could be withdrawn sooner.

Kidnap suspect Marc Charbonneau.

Kidnappers free British diplomat Cross

Dec. 3, 1970

MONTREAL – Two FLQ kidnappers and five other people including an infant were flown to Cuba tonight after troops and police had forced them to surrender in their hideout and release their hostage of 60 days, British Trade Commissioner James Cross. The Cuban flight was the main condition for the safe release of Cross, kidnapped from his Montreal home on Oct. 5. The 49-year-old Cross, an official said, "is in excellent condition."

1971

Toronto, Feb. 13. William Davis succeeds John Robarts as Ontario Conservative leader and premier.

Ottawa, April 24. David Lewis is elected national NDP leader, defeating James Laxer, representing the left-wing Waffle faction of the party.

Chicago, May 18. Montreal Canadiens defeat the Chicago Blackhawks four games to three to win the Stanley Cup.

Montreal, May 20. Francis Simard is sentenced to life in jail after being found guilty of non-capital murder in the death of Pierre Laporte.

Halifax, June 8. The Canadian Medical Association agrees that abortion should be a matter for decision between a woman and her doctor.

Vancouver, July 1. PM Trudeau announces $2.5 million will be set aside for the construction of a museum on the University of British Columbia campus to house Indian art and artifacts.

Quebec, July 14. The government adopts a bill establishing Hydro-Québec to oversee the development of the $6-billion James Bay hydroelectric power project.

Canada, July. The Alberta and Ontario governments adopt 18 as the legal age of majority.

Alberta, Aug. 30. The Conservatives led by Peter Lougheed win the provincial election, ending 36 years of Social Credit rule in Alberta.

Vancouver, Nov. 28. Calgary Stampeders defeat Toronto Argonauts 14-11 to win the Grey Cup.

Quebec, Dec. 5. The Quebec Federation of Labor votes to recognize Quebec's right to self-determination and independence, reversing its stand on the issue.

Quebec. Claude Jutra makes *Mon Oncle Antoine* for the National Film Board.

Canada. Mordecai Richler's novel *St. Urbain's Horseman* appears.

Ontario. The federal and Ontario governments establish Pukaskwa National Park as a semi-wilderness region on the north shore of Lake Superior.

Ottawa. The government White Paper on metric conversion states a single, coherent system based on metric units should be used for all measurements in Canada.

Abortion is all right in some situations, United Church says

Feb. 1, 1971

NIAGARA FALLS, Ont. – The General Council of the United Church of Canada has ruled that abortion is morally justifiable "in certain medical, social and economic circumstances." The statement came after a two-hour debate. Recommending abortion be a matter between a woman and her doctor, the council urged it be removed from the Criminal Code of Canada. The council also noted abortion is "morally undesirable, medically dangerous and socially expensive" as a method of birth control, supporting instead contraception and voluntary sterilization.

The council urged that doctors, nurses, clergymen and others who perform abortions, assist in the operation or counsel pregnant women be permitted to follow their consciences. If they object to abortion, they should refer women to others who can assist. Also recommended were discussions between the clergy and laity on abortion.

Indian municipality the country's first

July 5, 1971

CAPE MUDGE, B.C. – Cape Mudge is the first Indian reserve in Canada to become a municipality. The 300 people of this community on Quadra Island, some 250 kilometres north of Victoria and near the east coast of Vancouver Island, today witnessed the legal transformation of Cape Mudge from an Indian reserve to a provincial municipality. Although a municipal government will be put in place, the agreement says Cape Mudge remains eligible for "funds, services and programs" from the Department of Indian Affairs in Ottawa.

Some see Cape Mudge's change in status as a logical fulfilment of the Indian Act, the legislation which since 1876 has governed Indian reserves in Canada. In any case, a precedent has now been set which may see other Indian bands follow suit and abandon their reserve status.

Trudeau, Margaret Sinclair tie the knot

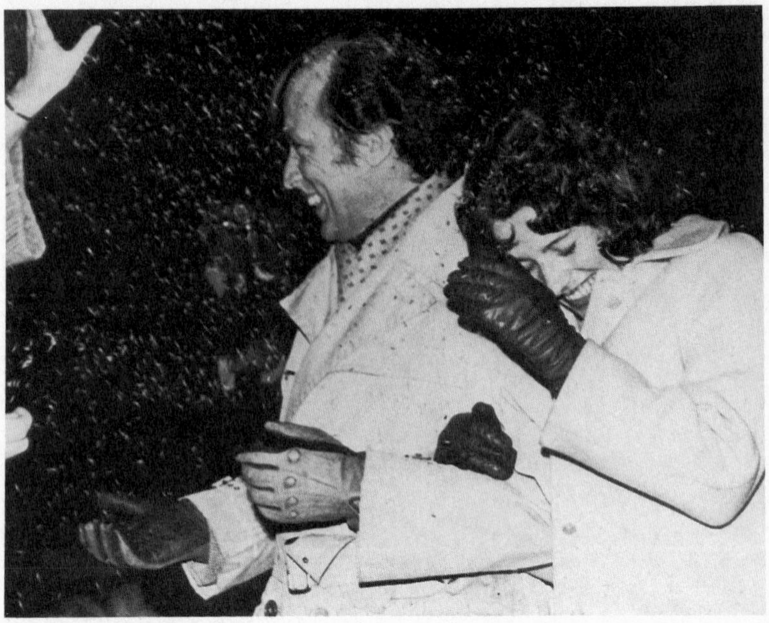

Pierre and Margaret Trudeau leave for a honeymoon in the Rockies.

March 4, 1971

NORTH VANCOUVER – The marriage here today of Prime Minister Pierre Trudeau and 22-year-old Margaret Sinclair comes as a stunning surprise to all but a few friends and relatives. At 51, the prime minister had been considered a confirmed bachelor, although he often dated such glamorous celebrities as singing star Barbra Streisand. He first met his bride, the daughter of former Liberal cabinet minister James Sinclair, on holiday in Tahiti in 1968. They saw each other often the past three years.

Rose found guilty of murdering Laporte

March 13, 1971

MONTREAL – Paul Rose, a member of the terrorist Front de libération du Québec, was found guilty today of the murder last Oct. 17 of provincial cabinet minister Pierre Laporte. His lawyer, Robert Lemieux, who has done little else for three years but defend accused or convicted Quebec separatists and terrorists, said immediately he will launch an appeal early next week. Rose, 27, was sentenced to life imprisonment and will be eligible for parole in 10 years. Laporte had been kidnapped a week before his body was found in a car trunk.

Jacques Rose, brother of Paul.

Trudeau helps settle Commonwealth split

Jan. 22, 1971

JAKARTA, Indonesia – Prime Minister Pierre Trudeau has defused a split between Britain and black African nations. At the Commonwealth conference, he's gotten antagonists in a dispute over Britain's arms sales to apartheid South Africa to accept the idea that "no country will afford to regimes which practise racial discrimination assistance which, in its own judgment, directly contributes to the pursuit or consolidation of this evil policy."

Constitutional talks under way in B.C.

June 14, 1971

VICTORIA, B.C. – Quebec's demands for a freer hand in social policy are setting the tone for debate at the three-day constitutional conference which opens here today. Quebec wants to introduce its own guaranteed income plan – with Ottawa meeting half the cost. Federal officials have already told reporters that Ottawa will reject Quebec's demand as too comprehensive. But the federal government seems ready to give in to some of Quebec's demands which are based on proposals to amend Section 94A of the BNA Act. This empowered Ottawa to pass laws governing old age pensions.

Anti-Confederation separatists march

July 1, 1971

MONTREAL – Led at one point by a separatist stripper, some 2,500 marchers celebrated Canada's birthday by denouncing Confederation. The near-nude young woman, brandishing a red, green, and white *patriote* flag, was among representatives of nationalist and left-wing groups which paraded and heard speeches demanding Quebec independence. Not all were pleased with the woman's naked display. "It took us two months to prepare this parade and she's ruining it," one organizer complained.

Talks focus on Great Lakes pollution

May 12, 1971

CANADA – Discussions are taking place between the governments of Canada and the United States centre on the quality of water in the Great Lakes. Both governments are concerned about the possibility of water from the Great Lakes contributing harm to health and property.

The continued growth of population and resource development, on both sides of the border, is increasing the use of water and contributing to the pollution of the Great Lakes Basin ecosystem. The Boundary Waters' Treaty signed on Jan. 11, 1909, recognizes the rights of both countries to use the water, and more specifically, their obligation not to pollute the boundary waters. And now, both sides agree that a new policy must be adopted to prevent the deterioration of the Great Lakes basin ecosystem.

Deliberations to find common objectives for the enhancement of water quality and for the development and implementation of co-operative programs are under way.

Critics: "Fortune" falls flat as movie

June 23, 1971

TORONTO – John Herbert's acclaimed play *Fortune and Men's Eyes*, the story of a young inmate's gradual brutalization in prison, has been adapted for the big screen – but with little success. The film, directed by Canadian Harvey Hart, made its Toronto debut this week and met with a chorus of criticism slamming its failure to bring the core issue – the need for prison reform – to the forefront.

Herbert's semi-autobiographical play raged at a penal system that not only punishes but also demoralizes and corrupts. The film version, however, loses Herbert's reformist perspective and sense of outrage. Explicit scenes of homosexual rape of young inmates sensationalize without drawing conclusions about the grim realities of Canada's penal system. Even the abandoned Quebec jail where *Fortune and Men's Eyes* was filmed, is not identified.

Quetico Park off limits to lumber industry

Ontario Premier Bill Davis.

May 13, 1971

TORONTO – Bowing to environmentalist demands, Ontario Premier William Davis announced an end to commercial logging in Quetico Provincial Park. Speaking in the legislature, Davis said the government was simply accepting the recommendations of the 12-man Quetico Advisory Committee, set up by the province to decide the future of the 2,800-square-kilometre park, west of Thunder Bay.

Davis also promised to compensate the one logging company still working in Quetico with "alternative cutting rights" elsewhere in Ontario. This came as news to Eldon Harvey, manager of the affected Jim Mathieu lumber operation. He says nobody has talked to him about such a deal.

Whale watching is growing in popularity on the British Columbia coast.

The women's rights movement is gaining in strength. Women are demanding equality everywhere! Cartoonist Bob Bierman seems to suggest here that some women are getting carried away in their demands.

PCs squeak by Liberals in Newfoundland

Oct. 30, 1971

ST. JOHN'S, Nfld. – A cliff-hanger of an election has resulted in 21 Progressive Conservatives, 20 Liberals, and one New Labrador Party member. It's a far cry from the results of the last provincial election in 1966 which resulted in Joseph R. Smallwood leading the Liberals to a 39-3 victory. While some recounts will be needed and the PCs do not have a majority, most observers think Smallwood's political career is coming to an end.

Blakeney, NDP winners

June 23, 1971

REGINA – Allan Blakeney is Saskatchewan's new premier. His New Democratic Party defeated Ross Thatcher's Liberal government by 45 seats to 14. The remaining seat of Athabasca is undecided. The Progressive Conservatives were shut out in the provincial election.

This is the third defeat in 10 elections for Thatcher. In his address to the much-subdued group at Liberal headquarters, he said, "I accept full and complete responsibility (for the loss). It must have been because of something I did, and something where my leadership went wrong. But I don't think even a socialist government can ruin the future for Saskatchewan. ... I would not wish to continue as leader of the opposition for too long."

The NDP promises to abolish medical and hospital fees, and to rescind a Liberal deal to underwrite much of a northern pulp mill. The mill was to be 70 percent owned by a New York developer, and the deal would result in few jobs and plenty of pollution.

Saskatchewan's Allan Blakeney.

Arctic status no big issue with Kosygin

President Nixon and PM Trudeau confront each other on Arctic sovereignty.

The question of the north has Trudeau in a difficult position.

Oct. 20, 1971

OTTAWA – Arctic sovereignty was not a big issue in discussions during Soviet Premier Alexis Kosygin's recent visit to Canada. Answering questions in the Commons today, Prime Minister Pierre Trudeau said there is little likelihood of a treaty between the Soviet Union and Canada on the matter in the near future. Ownership of the oil-rich and strategically-important Arctic islands remains contentious. While most Canadians believe their country extends to the North Pole, Soviets and Americans privately say Canada's lack of real occupation of the area places its sovereignty in doubt.

Toronto abolishes use of the strap

July 22, 1971

TORONTO – Teachers here will no longer be able to discipline children with "the strap." In an 11-6 vote, trustees of the Board of Education agreed to abolish this last vestige of corporal punishment in Toronto schools. It's a reform that comes despite the protests of teachers and the board's own director of education, Ronald Jones. He told the meeting, "I think to make such a thing mandatory is wrong." Jones pleaded with the trustees to leave the strap in place until disciplinary alternatives could be found. But he was overridden by the elected trustees.

The strap is a length of leather belt used to strike children's palms.

Leaders back policy on multiculturalism

Oct. 8, 1971

OTTAWA – Opposition parties in the House of Commons united in giving rare support to a government policy today. All party leaders supported in principle Prime Minister Pierre Trudeau's policy statement on multiculturalism. In announcing the intention to give greater support to cultural groups, Trudeau said "a policy of multiculturalism within a bilingual framework is basically the conscious support of individual freedom of choice. We are free to be ourselves. But this cannot be left to chance." The government must use its resources to ensure that individuals are able to participate in the activities of Canada's many ethnic groups, he said.

Indian dies after being shot by Mountie

Aug. 27, 1971

YELLOWKNIFE – Chief Ed Bird, secretary of the Northwest Territories Indian Brotherhood, died yesterday after he was shot by an RCMP officer. The victim, leader of the Fitz-Smith Indian band, was 30. Details of the shooting are sketchy. All that's certain is that the incident occurred after the officer went to check a complaint involving a domestic dispute. Justice Minister John Turner has promised an investigation and a "full public report." No charges have been laid against the officer.

Four seasons spring into life each and every year

Spring flowers bloom in Vancouver's Queen Elizabeth Park.

Fall colors are reflected in the lake at Manitoba's Whiteshell Provincial Park.

A crisp and clear late summer day in Nova Scotia's Peggy's Cove.

Ontario's maples are ablaze with color every autumn.

Nature's life cycle just can't be missed

CANADA – This country's vastness, its geographic diversity, and its climate have shaped a national psyche that sets Canadians apart in this world. When speaking of the land – its rocky shores, its temperate, fertile areas, or its barren northern tundra – one cannot avoid thinking in terms of the one variable that touches all Canada's regions – the seasons. Nature's life cycle cannot be missed in this country, largely because it's so extreme. The seasons affect the economy and labor, health and moods, rest and recreation. People change as the seasons change, whether battling the storms or relishing the warmth, always adapting, always reaffirming their place.

Winter's fresh snow makes the land a paradise for skiers.

1972

Winnipeg, Jan. 1. Winnipeg adopts a new municipal government system called the central city concept, amalgamating 12 municipalities into one and making Winnipeg the third largest Canadian city.

Canada, April 20. Saskatchewan novelist Max Braithwaite wins the Leacock Memorial Medal for Humour for *The Night We Stole the Mountie's Car*.

Ottawa, May 5. Northern Quebec natives file suit to have the James Bay hydroelectric project ruled unconstitutional.

New York, May 11. Boston Bruins defeat New York Rangers four games to two to win the Stanley Cup.

Ontario, July 21. The CRTC grants Global Communications Ltd. a broadcast licence to operate a TV network [Global Television Network] in southern Ontario.

Ottawa, July 31. The government eliminates jail sentences for those convicted of marijuana possesion and takes other steps to reduce punishments for marijuana-related offences.

Moscow, Sept. 28. Team Canada, composed of Canadian professionals, narrowly defeats the Soviet Union in an eight-game hockey series when Paul Henderson scores with 34 seconds left in the final game.

Toronto, Oct. 20. Maple Leaf Gardens president Harold Ballard is sentenced to three years in jail for fraud and theft.

Hamilton, Dec. 3. Hamilton Tiger-Cats beat Saskatchewan Roughriders 13-10 for the Grey Cup.

Victoria, Dec. 21. In an effort to preserve agricultural land, the B.C. government passes an order-in-council forbidding the use of farmland for any purpose except farming.

North America. The World Hockey Association launches its first season, a professional league competing with the NHL and including Canadian teams in Edmonton, Ottawa, Quebec City, and Winnipeg.

Victoria. Nishga Indian Frank Arthur Calder is named to the cabinet of Dave Barrett's newly elected NDP provincial government, becoming the first Indian cabinet minister.

Canada. Margaret Atwood publishes the novel *Surfacing*, and *Survival: A Thematic Guide to Canadian Literature*.

Nuclear power plant now officially open

The Pickering Nuclear Power Generating Station (later image).

Feb. 25, 1972

PICKERING, Ont. – Ontario Hydro's nuclear power generating station, which first produced electricity last April, was officially opened here today by Premier William Davis and Hydro chairman George Gathercole. The $750-million plant is expected to be the largest nuclear station in the world that uses natural uranium fuel. Under construction since 1965, the plant has two of its four reactors in operation. The remainder of the plant will be operational next year. At that time it is expected to produce 2 million kilowatts of power.

The Pickering station, about 30 kilometres east of Toronto, uses Candu (Canadian deuterium uranium) reactors. The 47-metre-high domed reactor buildings are to contain radioactivity the reactors or their cooling systems might release. A vacuum building acts as an additional safety device. If reactor cooling piping breaks, it sucks in released steam and condenses it with water sprayed from a tank with a capacity of nine million litres.

Technicians' strike slowing air traffic

Feb. 6, 1972

OTTAWA – Air travel in Canada hasn't ground to a halt, but it's going very, very slowly now that 1,700 radar technicians have walked off the job across Canada. Their strike began at 6 p.m., as their negotiators entered the 34th consecutive hour of mediation talks between the union and the government. The reason the whole system has not collapsed is that 486 members of Local 2228 of the International Brotherhood of Electrical Workers must, by law, provide basic safe air service. The strike follows the union's rejection of a conciliation board offer of a 15.5 percent wage hike over 28 months.

Conservatives win majority in Nfld.; Moores is premier

March 25, 1972

ST. JOHN'S, Nfld. – After 23 years in opposition and the last several months trying to govern under impossible conditions, the Progressive Conservatives, led by Frank Moores, swept to victory yesterday taking 33 of the 42 seats. It will be recalled that this election was preceded by five months of political confusion, as Joseph R. Smallwood took some time to resign as premier and only recently stepped down as leader of the Liberals.

Moores credits his win to the fact that the people of Newfoundland want a change and to enter a new political era. Smallwood blames the loss by the Liberals, now led by Edward Roberts, on the fact that the voters are bored with his party. Roberts seems resigned to the loss, and points out that "it was not a Liberal year."

The Progressive Conservatives have finally laid to rest the reputation which they acquired when the party was first organized in 1949; that they were all former anti-confederates and would turn back the clock if given a chance. Smallwood, never one to rest, has decided that he will compile and publish an "encyclopedia of Newfoundland and Labrador."

George and Hubert Buck, by Rick Hill. Singing is an important part of the social, cultural and spiritual life of the Iroquois. These two singers have helped to keep music alive. Their costumes illustrate another traditional skill – that of artistic beadwork.

Davies' novels full of myth and mirth

1972

TORONTO – A fateful rock buried in a snowball has given wing to one of the most fascinating novel series in Canadian history. Robertson Davies has just published *The Manticore*, the sequel to *Fifth Business* (1970), in which Boy Staunton tosses the snowball in question, setting off a series of events that carries throughout both novels. The novels are frisky confessional romps, detailing the lives of schoolmaster Dunstan Ramsay, business mogul Boy Staunton, and his lawyer-son David. Along Davies' fictional journey, we meet saints, a famous magician, and the devil in the form of a beautiful woman with lesbian tendencies.

Royal commission to probe land use

Aug. 14, 1972

CHARLOTTETOWN – Premier Alex Campbell today appointed a royal commission to look into the issues of land use and ownership on Prince Edward Island. Both arose in last year's election.

Land use and ownership are familiar issues to Islanders. In 1767, the British government gave all of P.E.I. away in a single afternoon. It took residents 150 years to buy it all back. Thus it is not strange that Islanders are sensitive about the topic. With patterns of land use changing and non-resident ownership on the rise, residents fear losing control of their own land again.

Pollution act aims to safeguard Arctic

Aug. 2, 1972

OTTAWA – The Arctic Waters Pollution Prevention Act was proclaimed law today, largely in response to recent challenges to Canada's sovereignty over the Arctic. The spectre of American tankers plying northern waters with impunity and increased chances of disastrous oil spills led Ottawa to act, asserting its right to control these waters to prevent pollution.

Barrett, NDP end Socred reign in B.C.

Aug. 30, 1972

VICTORIA, B.C. – A weary Premier W.A.C. Bennett and his lacklustre government were kicked out of office by brash Dave Barrett and his "socialist hordes" today. When the counting stopped, the Socreds, who had won seven elections in a row, were down to 10 seats and only 31 percent of the popular vote. Eleven cabinet ministers were defeated, but Bennett kept his seat in the Okanagan. The NDP won 38 seats with about 40 percent of the popular vote. The other parties continued their slides to oblivion. The Liberals are down to five seats and the Tories to two.

Bennett campaigned with little of his old zest, and just before the vote the most controversial of his cabinet ministers, Phil Gagliardi, said that his premier was too old and should step down. In contrast, Barrett campaigned vigorously and steered clear of any socialist dogma. He promised government auto insurance, day-care centres, public transit for the Lower Mainland, and better pensions.

U.S. and Canada sign Great Lakes Water Quality Agreement

April 15, 1972

OTTAWA – In a brief ceremony on Parliament Hill today, Prime Minister Pierre Trudeau, External Affairs Minister Mitchell Sharp, U.S. President Richard Nixon, and U.S. Secretary of State William Rogers signed the Great Lakes Water Quality Agreement. The agreement outlines anti-pollution objectives for Canada and the U.S. One major point is the 50-percent reduction of phosphorus dumping, expected to cost the U.S. some $2 billion and Canada $250 million. An icy downpour kept the crowd to under 1,000 people, most of whom protested Nixon's visit. The RCMP kept protesters away from Nixon as he left Parliament.

President Nixon and PM Trudeau sign pact targeting pollution.

The vibrant colors of fall make this season Canada's most spectacular.

LeDain probe says legalize marijuana

May 17, 1972

OTTAWA – If the LeDain Commission has its way, Canadians will be able to light up a marijuana cigarette in public or grow their own "grass," but traffickers would risk jail terms. These recommendations are in the final report released today by Osgoode law school dean Gerald LeDain and the four other members of the drug inquiry. "We were attempting to strike a balance between social benefit and social cost and we don't pretend that our work is a marvel of logic and consistency," LeDain said.

While advocating the legal personal use of marijuana, the probe says police should still have the power to seize drugs or plants wherever they see them. The report recommends that traffickers face five years in jail.

Liberals govern clinging to power

Former PM Pearson dies in the capital

Pearson funeral at Christ Church.

Dec. 27, 1972
OTTAWA – Lester B. Pearson, former Liberal prime minister and Nobel Peace Prize winner, died tonight of cancer. He was 75. The good-natured Pearson, nicknamed "Mike," never held a majority government as PM from 1963 to 1968, but the legacies of his administration – particularly the Canadian Pension Plan and universal medicare – will long be felt by Canadians. As an international diplomat, Pearson won the Nobel for his instrumental role in establishing the United Nations peacekeeping force during the 1956 Suez Crisis.

Election all even; Trudeau won't quit

Nov. 2, 1972
OTTAWA – Prime Minister Pierre Trudeau said tonight he will not resign. Returns from the Oct. 30 election now show his Liberals deadlocked with Robert Stanfield's Conservatives. An official count added one seat to the Liberal total, bringing the government up to 109, the same number the Tories won. Recounts may alter results in tight races. The NDP holds a strong balance of power with 30 seats. The Social Credit won 16.

Trudeau said the election results show Canadians found his government's performance "not satisfactory." But the voters did not "express any clear degree of approval for any single party." Trudeau said he would not seek NDP support to keep the government in power.

NDP leader David Lewis said today his party will not force a new election but will also not abandon its principles. "On many issues we will have to accept less than we would otherwise want, keeping in mind the good of Canada. But there will be limits to our willingness to accept less than we would otherwise want." The NDP will not support tax breaks to corporations.

Talks tackle problems of Canadian cities

Prime Minister Trudeau and his wife Margaret in Vancouver.

Nov. 21, 1972
TORONTO – Despite its shaky position, Prime Minister Pierre Trudeau's government continues to function. One important issue being dealt with is the problem facing Canadian cities. Today, federal, provincial and municipal governments decided to hold continuing talks, the first time thorny constitutional issues have been overcome to permit finding a possible solution. Yesterday, the Ontario government appeared to have scuttled the talks by declaring that Ottawa had no business involving itself in what is provincial jurisdiction. But today, Ontario was persuaded to soften its line to permit future negotiations among all three levels of government. Federal Urban Affairs Minister Ron Basford was pleased.

Early morning at Peggy's Cove. Fishermen prepare for the day's trip.

Team Canada gets a hero's welcome

Oct. 1, 1972
TORONTO – At least 30,000 fans, some who had waited in the rain for four hours, turned out at Nathan Phillips Square tonight to greet Team Canada on its return from the Soviet Union. The biggest cheers were reserved for series heroes Phil Esposito of the Boston Bruins and Paul Henderson of the Toronto Maple Leafs. Henderson scored the winning goal in each of the three final games in Moscow, as Canada won the series four games to three, with one tie. It was the first time Canadian professionals faced a Soviet team. Earlier, the club was met in Montreal by a group that included the prime minister.

Radio gets a boost from new satellite

Nov. 9, 1972
UNITED STATES – Canada's first telecommunications satellite, the Anik A-1, designed and built by the American Hughes Aircraft Corp. with the help of Canada's Northern Electric and Spar Aerospace, was launched today. More than 100 ground stations are now being installed to act as relays for radio signals to and from the satellite. By placing Anik A-1 in orbit, scientists expect to overcome radio signal distance limitations caused by the curvature of the earth's surface. Once the system is operational, a message sent from Halifax to Vancouver will take only a few seconds to reach its destination.

Canadians celebrate: it's the best of the fest

Edmonton commemorates the gold rush every year with Klondike Days.

Dragons lead the Chinese New Year's Parade in Vancouver.

Bonhomme's ice palace at the Quebec Winter Carnival.

A highlight of the Quebec Winter Carnival is a night parade.

Toronto's Caribana Festival.

A Caribana Festival dancer.

Ice boat races are held on the St. Lawrence River.

1973

Ottawa, Jan. 31 The Supreme Court of Canada rules Nishga Indians in B.C. have no rights over land in the Nass River Valley, but accepts the concept of aboriginal rights.

Montreal, Feb. 22. Jacques Rose is acquitted on charges of murdering Pierre Laporte.

Ottawa, March 28. The Heritage Canada Foundation is established with a federal government grant as a private non-profit trust for the preservation of significant Canadian heritage sites.

Chicago, May 10. Montreal Canadiens defeat Chicago Blackhawks four games to two to win the Stanley Cup.

Ottawa, May 29. Canada announces it will withdraw from the ICCS truce observance force in Vietnam because other participating countries do not favor keeping an impartial role.

New Brunswick, June 8. Delegates approve the establishment of the New Brunswick Society of Acadians.

Niagara-on-the-Lake, Ont., June 28. Queen Elizabeth II inaugurates the new Shaw Festival Theatre, designed by Ronald Thom.

Ottawa, Aug. 30. Some 200 striking railway workers occupy the Centre Block of Parliament to protest the government's plans to force 56,000 striking railway employees back to work.

Ottawa, Aug. 30. Some 200 natives occupy the Indian Affairs building to protest the government's failure to consult Indians for its Indian Affairs programs, and its failure to deal with native grievances.

Montreal, Nov. 13. A jury acquits Dr. Henry Morgentaler of performing an illegal abortion, despite the fact that he has admitted to performing more than 5,000 abortions.

Toronto, Nov. 25. Ottawa Rough Riders defeat Edmonton Eskimos 22-18 to win the Grey Cup.

Ottawa, Dec. 25. PM Trudeau's second son, Alexandre Emmanuel, is born. His first son – Justin Pierre James – was also born Christmas Day.

Winnipeg. Premier Ed Schreyer's NDP government bans the killing of beluga whales in Manitoba waters. Ottawa refuses to recognize the ban, as it claims jurisdiction over sea mammals.

Canada and U.S. agree on a cleanup plan for oil spills

April 9, 1973

CANADA – Three years ago, the International Joint Commission put out a special Report on Potential Oil Pollution. That report helped spawn the joint Canada-U.S. Working Group on Great Lakes Pollution, which has devised a Canada-U.S. Marine Pollution Contingency Plan to deal with oil spills and other noxious substances.

Central to the plan is a recognition of the need for joint contingency plans relating to bodies of water of mutual interest to Canada and the U.S. These plans would require as well co-operative measures and responses to potential pollution accidents or episodes: joint policy, joint response centre teams, and officials to organize the activities of joint response teams. The point of the plan is to anticipate what pollution crises the U.S. and Canada might confront in either continental or coastal waters and to determine how to solve them.

The main objectives of the plan are: to develop appropriate measures to discover pollution problems, and to alert authorities about them; to take measures to prevent the spread of oil; to provide continuous joint resources to assist during a pollution incident; to develop reporting and notification procedures and cleanup systems.

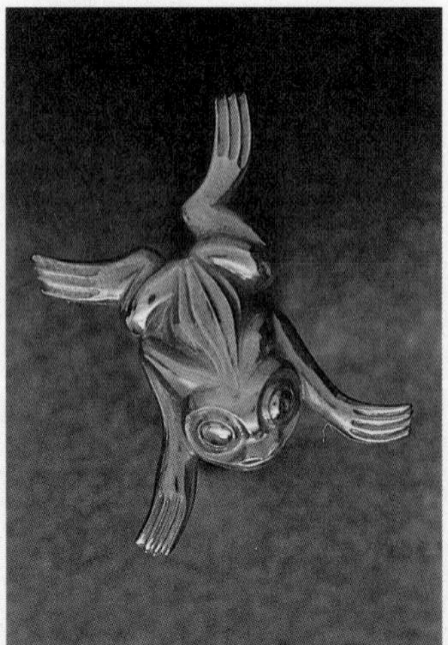

The Haida often depict animals in their carvings. This gold brooch represents a swimming frog.

Canadian truce observers reach Vietnam

Canadians serve as truce observers for the ICCS.

Jan. 29, 1973

SAIGON – The first contingent of Canadian truce observers arrived this morning. It consists of 130 soldiers and 15 civilians. Their numbers will grow to about 300. The party left Montreal two days ago. The prime minister, the minister of national defence, and the chief of defence staff all delivered good luck messages, and Gov. Gen. Roland Michener was on hand to shake every man's hand before boarding.

The Canadians join observers from Hungary, Indonesia, and Poland – fellow-members of the International Commission of Control and Supervision at sites throughout South Vietnam. Their task is to monitor observance of the Paris Agreement and Protocols encompassing withdrawal of American forces, prisoner exchanges, and a hoped-for cease-fire between the South Vietnamese government and Communist opponents.

Hardy Boys books gutted by publisher

1973

WHITBY, Ontario – Leslie McFarlane, author of 18 Hardy Boys books under the pen name Franklin W. Dixon, is not happy with the fate of his work. In 1959, the books' publisher, the Stratemeyer Syndicate, gutted the books of their funniest scenes and richest language, presumably to streamline the stories. McFarlane recently called the cuts "a literary fraud."

Get your kicks from Sourtoe Cocktail

1973

DAWSON, Yukon – Local resident Dick Stevenson deserves points for creative drinking. His Sourtoe Cocktail is a bizarre blend of one old toe dropped into a glass of champagne, and people actually seem anxious to join the illustrious ranks of those who've braved the gruesome mix. Drinkers don't swallow the dismembered appendage, but must let it touch their lips.

Highest court admits aboriginal claims

Jan. 31, 1973

OTTAWA – In an extremely important British Columbia Indian land case ruled upon today by the Supreme Court of Canada, the majority of the judges acknowledged that aboriginal title exists in law. No longer can the aboriginal claims of native peoples who have not entered into a treaty relationship with the Canadian government be ignored. This decision runs counter to the federal government's denial of the existence of aboriginal rights.

Court upholds Indian Act marriage clause

July 12, 1973

OTTAWA – A Supreme Court of Canada ruling handed down today demonstrates the limitations of the Canadian Bill of Rights. Top court judges have ruled 5-4 against Jeannette Corbière-Lavell, of the Wikwemikong reserve in Ontario. She brought her case against the government after losing her registered Indian status when she married a non-Indian in 1970. (By comparison, Indian men do not lose their status by marrying non-Indians. Their non-Indian wives and children gain Indian status.)

Corbière-Lavell argued that the Indian Act provision which resulted in her loss of status runs counter to guarantees of equality in the Bill of Rights. But the court ruled the act could be enforced reasonably without infringing on the rights of Indian women to equality before the law. The decision is expected to trigger protests from international human rights groups, which consider the clause an infringement on civil liberties. Tension arising from differing views on inter-marriage may also surface within the Indian community.

Former PM Louis St. Laurent dead at 91

The funeral of former prime minister Louis St. Laurent at Quebec City.

July 25, 1973

QUEBEC CITY – Louis St. Laurent, 91, courtly constitutional lawyer and prime minister from 1948 to 1957, died this afternoon. He entered politics reluctantly in 1942, at the request of the PM W.L. Mackenzie King, but immediately made an impression by courageously supporting King's conscription plans during World War II, the only Liberal minister from Quebec to do so. Fervently patriotic, he promoted Canadian membership in NATO after becoming Minister of External Affairs in 1946. St. Laurent was chosen King's successor in 1948 despite not running a leadership campaign. He retired soon after the 1957 election loss.

Captain says he was beaten during arrest

Aug. 19, 1973

VANCOUVER – Capt. David McTaggart, of the protest ship *Greenpeace III,* was taken to a Vancouver military hospital after his vessel was seized in the nuclear test zone at Mururoa by the French army. Sources say McTaggart was injured during his arrest. In a phone conversation with his brother, McTaggart said he was beaten by French seamen, sustaining internal injuries and an eye injury. McTaggart does not know the whereabouts of his vessel or the other members of his crew.

Kain and Augustyn star

June 19, 1973

MOSCOW – Karen Kain and Frank Augustyn swept away two top awards at the prestigious Moscow International Ballet Competition, a feat unprecedented in Canada's dance history. The pair are the shining stars of the National Ballet of Canada.

Kain took the silver medal in the women's division, while Augustyn narrowly missed the bronze in the men's test. The pair beat an elite field of dancers to take top honors in duet ensemble work for their performance of the Bluebird Pas de Deux from *Sleeping Beauty.* They received 2,000-ruble prizes. Kain and Augustyn and the rest of the winners are now embarking on a tour of Russian cities to showcase the year's best in ballet.

Karen Kain and Frank Augustyn.

Ottawa to renew treaty-making tradition

Aug. 8, 1973

OTTAWA – The treaty tradition lives again. The federal government today announced it will start accepting applications from Indian groups to initiate the negotiation of comprehensive land claims. An Office of Native Claims is being established, mainly to deal with natives in parts of the country not covered by Indian treaties and where aboriginal title to the land therefore remains unextinguished. The new policy emanates from a Supreme Court of Canada ruling involving Nishga Indians in B.C.

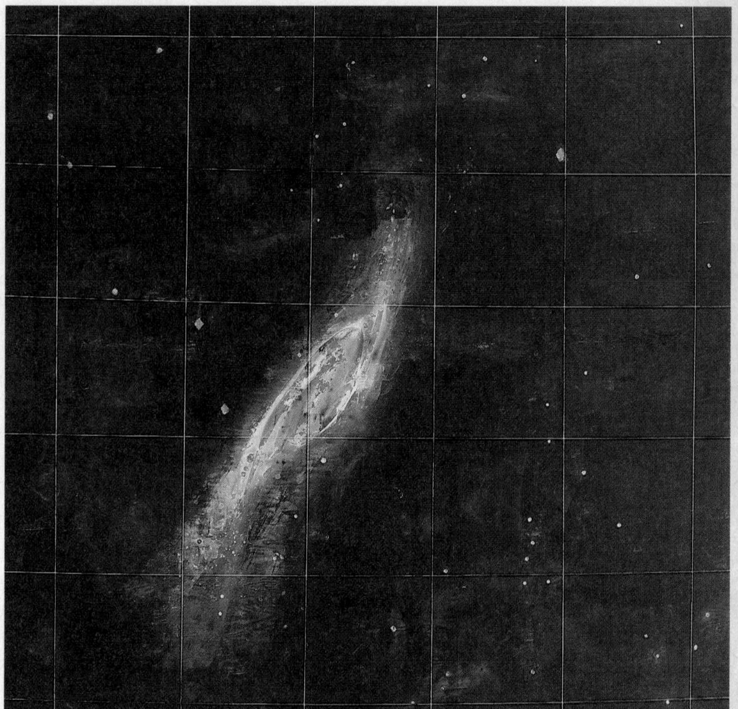

Paterson Ewen's Galaxie. Acrylic, galvanized iron and string on plywood.

Jules Léger named governor general

Governor General Jules Léger.

Oct. 5, 1973

OTTAWA – A diplomat who has held several ambassadorial posts will be Canada's next governor general. Buckingham Palace and the Prime Minister's Office announced today Jules Léger, 60, will take over in mid-January from retiring Gov. Gen. Roland Michener. Léger is ambassador to Belgium and Luxembourg and has been ambassador to Italy, France, and Mexico. He has held several posts in the Department of External Affairs here and was executive assistant to former prime minister Louis St. Laurent. Léger is the brother of Paul-Emile Cardinal Léger, retired archbishop of Montreal. He will be Canada's 21st governor general.

Arab nations raise price of oil 70%

Oct. 17, 1973

MIDDLE EAST – To protest western support for Israel in the Yom Kippur War, oil-producing Arab states today increased the price of oil 70 percent and pledged to cut production by five percent a month. The announcement came soon after U.S. President Richard Nixon called for $2.2-billion US in emergency aid for Israel. The embargo, aimed primarily at the U.S., threatens to cause widespread gasoline and oil shortages all over the west. Hardest hit will be western Europe, which imports four-fifths of its oil from Arab nations. In Britain, the price hike will weaken an economy already crippled by a balance of payments deficit.

Canadians are also likely to suffer from the embargo. Although there is plenty of oil in Canada, most of it has yet to be exploited because it is difficult to get to and expensive to extract and transport. Today's announcement, however, makes it economically viable for Canada to push toward petroleum self-sufficiency.

Indians have right to file land claim

Sept. 6, 1973

YELLOWKNIFE – Justice William Morrow of the Supreme Court of the Northwest Territories has just made a landmark decision in the area of aboriginal rights in Canada. Six months ago, 16 Dene Indian chiefs in the N.W.T. claimed an area some 1 million square kilometres in extent. They argued that Treaties 8 and 11 were friendship or peace treaties which did not involve the surrender of land rights. Morrow has spent the summer visiting all the Dene communities to listen to testimony from the Indians and others who remembered the treaty-making talks, particularly those for Treaty 11 in 1921.

Morrow ruled today that the Indians had aboriginal rights to the western section of the Northwest Territories, and that they had the right to put forward a claim to land, which in extent is roughly 10 percent of Canada.

Bourassa's Liberals swept back to power

PQ leader René Lévesque greets his supporters on election night.

Oct. 29, 1973

QUEBEC CITY – Robert Bourassa's Liberals swept to victory tonight, shutting out the Union Nationale and defeating the resurgent Parti Québécois. In winning 101 seats, up from the 68 they had in the last Assembly, the Liberals appear to have benefitted from the collapse of both the UN and the Creditistes. The UN, with 15 seats in the last Assembly and once virtually unbeatable in provincial politics, did not win a single seat and received only about five percent of the popular vote. Late returns showed the Creditistes with only two seats. They had 11 in the last Assembly. The PQ increased its popular vote to about 31 percent, but did not increase the seven seats it held. PQ leader René Lévesque lost in his riding. Bourassa campaigned mostly on his own considerable popularity, but claimed the results are a victory for federalism.

Pianist Oscar Peterson is invested as an Officer of the Order of Canada.

Frustrated Canadians pull out of Vietnam

July 31, 1973

SAIGON – Canadian participation on the International Commission of Control and Supervision ceased today, in accordance with government statements made May 28. The step is occasioned by frustration at Cold War deadlocks, as Polish and Hungarian observers worked at cross-purposes with the Canadians and Indonesians. Equally important is the fact that the Vietnamese have no intention of complying with the Paris accords aimed at ending what is officially seen as a civil war. This endangers observer lives. Capt. Charles E. Laviolette was one of eight people killed when an ICCS helicopter was shot down near Lao Bao on April 7.

More concern being paid to social welfare issues

'Well, the demonstration worked–we got better living conditions..."

Living conditions for Canadian natives often need improvement.

Canada's national identity is constantly threatened by American influence.

MPs debate interim report on food prices

April 10, 1973

OTTAWA – MPs debated at length the interim report of their food prices review committee in the House of Commons today. Consumer and Corporate Affairs Minister Herb Gray said the report "shows a real concern for those living on low incomes, for whom the recent rapid increase in the cost of food has created hardship."

But the debate demonstrated little attention to those for whom, it is widely agreed, recent inflation has made it tougher to sustain life and health. Indeed, the long debate was mostly about politics. The NDP said it always advocated controlling food prices and accused the Liberals of blocking controls. The Liberals accused the Conservatives of fostering the increase in prices.

There was little attention paid to the complaints of small grocers who testified before the committee that they were squeezed by the large corporations. Politicians' rhetoric did not highlight the plight of the low-income family, not even the statements by the NDP members who made the rising cost of living their major target in the last election campaign.

MP Grace MacInnis, an NDP member of the committee, supported the report's major recommendation that a food prices review board be established. She hopes the board has teeth. "Food prices are still spiralling, and the government will pigeonhole and water down these recommendations at its peril."

Tory MP James McGrath, also a committee member, argued for an overall prices and wages freeze, part of the PC platform. "To approach the whole problem of spiralling prices you cannot isolate food prices. It must be approached in an overall context, and that has to include the whole spectrum of prices, incomes, salaries and wages."

McGrath said the Conservative members of the committee did not support the report because it did not advocate an overall prices and wages freeze. But McGrath also said the committee heard evidence that "in this country nourishment is a problem of major proportions. There is evidence to indicate that there are children in this country today who are undernourished because of an inadequate diet; they are going to school on an inadequate breakfast."

"We have ways of making you talk French..."

Bilingualism is becoming essential in government employment.

1974

Edmonton, Jan. 14. The Alberta government plans to spend $100 million in the next five years on technology to develop the crude oil potential of the Alberta tar sands.

Washington, D.C., Feb. 13. Twelve major oil consuming nations, including Canada, reach general agreement to co-ordinate their response to the energy crisis.

Ottawa, Feb. 21. New immigration policies stipulate that immigrants will need a firm job offer, or be prepared to go to an area where their skills are in demand, before they are allowed into the country.

British Columbia, March 1. The Court of Appeals rules Indian children can be adopted by non-Indian parents without losing their Indian status.

Victoria, March 14. Dave Barrett's NDP government introduces rent controls to B.C.

Hay River, N.W.T., March 18. The first Indian reserve in the N.W.T. is created.

Philadelphia, May 19. Philadelphia Flyers defeat Boston Bruins four games to two to win the Stanley Cup.

Ottawa, May 21. Canada suspends shipments to India of nuclear equipment and technology in response to India's detonation of a nuclear device.

Toronto, June 29. Leading Soviet ballet dancer Mikhail Baryshnikov defects from the Soviet Union while on tour.

Edmonton, July 2. Ralph Steinhauer becomes lieutenant-governor of Alberta, the first Indian lieutenant-governor in Canada.

Quebec, Nov. 17. The Parti Québécois promises that if it wins power it will hold a referendum on the question of sovereignty-association.

Vancouver, Nov. 24. Montreal Alouettes beat Edmonton Eskimos 20-7 for the Grey Cup.

Regina. Saskatchewan's NDP government introduces health plans to provide free dental care for children aged 3-12, and to subsidize certain prescription drugs.

Toronto. Pauline McGibbon is appointed lieutenant-governor of Ontario, the first female lieutenant-governor in Canada.

Canada. The Waffle, founded in 1969 as a left-wing caucus of the NDP, disintegrates. The Waffle was purged from the Ontario NDP in 1972.

Beaufort Sea drilling banned till '76

March 6, 1974

OTTAWA – Jean Chrétien, minister of Indian and Northern Affairs, announced today that drilling in the Beaufort Sea will not be allowed to start before the summer of 1976.

The past two weeks, representatives of the Indian and northern affairs and environment departments and the oil companies holding permits in the Beaufort Sea region, have deliberated on the condition of the marine environment of the Beaufort Sea. The oil companies have agreed to pay more than $3 million and participate in a crash program of environmental studies. With the emphasis on protecting the marine mammals and the aquatic ecology in the region, the minister said only the latest technology and drilling systems will be accepted. Yet environmentalists like Douglas Pimlot note that "there simply is no existing technology and no equipment available which can be considered even remotely adequate for cleaning up a massive oil spill in arctic waters."

Group of Seven painter A.Y. Jackson dies

A.Y. Jackson is seen here with a class at the Banff School of Fine Arts.

April 5, 1974

KLEINBURG, Ont. – A.Y. Jackson, the last surviving member of the Group of Seven, died at a nursing home near here today. He was 91. "His integrity, his love of the land, his artistic perseverance are indelibly recorded in the history of Canadian art," commented Ian Trowell, president of the Ontario Society of Artists. Born in Montreal, Alexander Young Jackson helped organize the Group of Seven in 1920. Since 1968, Jackson has lived with Robert and Signe McMichael, who own the McMichael Canadian Collection in Kleinburg. Jackson will be buried on the Kleinburg grounds, near other Group of Seven members.

Liberals' minority defeated in House

May 8, 1974

OTTAWA – There will be a federal election in July, Prime Minister Pierre Trudeau said tonight. His announcement followed the defeat of his government in the House of Commons earlier this evening. By a vote of 137-123, the Commons voted no-confidence during debate on the budget, the first time in Canadian history a government has been defeated in a budget debate. Standings in the House were Liberals 109, Conservatives 106, NDP 31, Creditistes 15. There was one independent and two vacancies.

The Tories will mount an election campaign based on the party plan for wage and price controls. Liberals say controls wouldn't curb inflation but would disrupt the economy. NDP MPs predict the party standings will change little. The minority Liberal government survived 19 confidence votes since it came to power in 1972.

Trudeau smiles despite defeat.

First ministers approve oil and gas deal

Jan. 23, 1974

OTTAWA – The oil price freeze will come off but gasoline and heating oil prices will be equalized across the country. In a complicated deal that leaves some crucial matters unresolved, the prime minister and the 10 premiers today decided the crude oil price freeze will be removed in April. But on what increases will be imposed after April, the first ministers are, in the words of Alberta Premier Peter Lougheed, back at square one. Key to the equalization deal is where the revenues will be found to support it. Alberta and Saskatchewan say the federal government has no right to share in provincial oil revenues. Quebec and the Maritimes want a subsidy to remove the seven cents a gallon more for gasoline their consumers pay compared to those in western Canada. Alberta wants a one-price system applied to other commodities.

UN mission in Syria claims 9 Canadians

Aug. 9, 1974

SYRIA – Nine Canadians, members of the United Nations peacekeeping force trying to prevent war between Syria and Israel, died after their Buffalo transport plane was shot down. Details are sketchy, but it appears the plane may have been mistakenly shot down by a Syrian missile. Syria claims that the downing occurred as Israeli planes were bombing nearby Lebanese and Syrian anti-aircraft batteries attempting to drive off the attackers. Israel, for its part, denies any such raid was taking place when the Buffalo was shot down.

Lake Ontario swim done in record time

Aug. 16, 1974

TORONTO – Sixteen-year-old Scarborough swimmer Cindy Nicholas stepped ashore to the sound of cheers and boat horns at Ontario Place late this afternoon after setting a record of 15 hours and 18 minutes for the 52-kilometre crossing of Lake Ontario. It was three hours faster than the previous record for that distance. Nicholas, who set out from Youngstown, N.Y., at 2:20 this morning, kept up a pace of at least 70 strokes a minute in the crossing. She decided six weeks ago to make the swim, and trained with coach Al Waites.

Largest object in universe is found

Aug. 29, 1974

NETHERLANDS – Canadian astronomer Dr. A.G. Willis, working with Dutch scientists at the Leiden Observatory, has found the largest object in the universe. The object, known to scientists as 3C 286, is a cloud of energy sources which stretches 105,582,528,000,000,000,000 miles from end to end. The cloud is so far away that light from it takes 1.8 billion years to reach the Earth. Willis is in the Netherlands under a two-year appointment sponsored by Canada's National Research Council.

Liberals to govern with a majority

July 8, 1974

OTTAWA – Pierre Trudeau's Liberals swept the country today, making gains from the Conservatives in the east and from the NDP in the west. Late election returns tonight show the Liberals with 139 seats, the Conservatives with 96, the NDP with 16, the Creditistes with 12, and one independent. The most prominent loser in the election was NDP leader David Lewis, victim of a Liberal sweep of most Toronto-area ridings.

Despite the attention Robert Stanfield paid to Quebec, the Conservatives managed to win only the three seats they previously held there. Leonard Jones, the anti-French former Moncton mayor, won handily as an independent. Stanfield had refused to allow him to run as a Conservative. Many observers attribute the impressive Liberal victory to voter uneasiness about the Conservative wage and price control platform.

Salmon fishing on agenda at conference

July 4, 1974

CARACAS, Venezuela – The third Law of the Sea Conference has been held here. Discussions by Canadian fisheries representatives emphasized deep-sea salmon fishing. Fisheries Minister Jack Davis introduced a proposal at the conference concerning the baselines of the Canadian territorial sea for purposes of exploitation and preservation.

To secure control of fisheries from the point of view of marine conservation, Davis moved to extend Canada's coastal jurisdiction to 200 nautical miles from shore. The new fishing zone and the interdiction of high seas fishing are, Davis argued, conservation measures aimed at the management of salmon throughout their entire migratory range.

Fisheries Minister Jack Davis.

Canada's brilliant pianist Glenn Gould performs rarely on the concert stage. He prefers the technical perfection of the recording studio.

B.C. judge upholds Indian right to hunt

July 20, 1974

PENTICTON, B.C. – Some observers believe a British Columbia court ruling on aboriginal hunting rights could become a landmark in aboriginal law. Judge A.D.C. Washington has found Jacob Kruger and Robert Manual, both of the Penticton Indian band, not guilty of breaking provincial laws when they killed wild animals out of season.

Washington said Kruger and Manual acted in a manner consistent with the long-standing Crown tradition of allowing Indians unmolested access to unoccupied sections of their ancestral hunting grounds. Only explicit legislation, he added, can restrict these aboriginal rights to hunt and fish according to Indian custom.

French the official language of Quebec

July 30, 1974

QUEBEC CITY – The government of Premier Robert Bourassa passed its language legislation today, angering both Quebec nationalists and English Quebecers. The new law establishes only French as Quebec's official language and puts restrictions on English-language education. It passed 92-10, with two Liberals joining the six Parti Québécois members and two Creditistes to oppose the government.

One of the dissident Liberals, George Springate, voted against because "I believe in the complete and utter freedom of choice in linguistic matters." PQ members said there were too many loopholes in the education sections. They want French more firmly established. ▷

Female Mounties a first

Sept. 17, 1974

TORONTO – Four women pledged oaths of allegiance to the Royal Canadian Mounted Police today, completing an initial step toward becoming the first female constables in the history of the 101-year-old police force. Now it's on to training in Regina, where they'll learn marching, shooting and various other aspects of law enforcement. Because the Mounties are structured on the cavalry system of 32 to a troop, they'll soon be joined by 28 other women to round out the female contingent.

Women have long been attached to the force, but only in civilian capacities such as communications services, laboratory work, and as interpreters. In what many consider an overdue step toward equal opportunity for women in Canada's elite law enforcement agency, the new recruits will perform duties once restricted to males only, including undercover narcotics work, commercial fraud investigation, and highway patrol. They will receive the regular starting salary of $10,794 per annum.

RCMP now have female members.

NDP comes out of the political wilderness

September 1974

OTTAWA – Founded 13 years ago in an enthusiastic atmosphere at the largest, longest political convention in Canadian history up to that time, the New Democratic Party is now enjoying a considerable amount of success at the polls and can look back on an arduous ascent with a list of solid political achievements behind it.

Electoral success has never come as easily for the NDP as it has for the Liberals and the Conservatives. The party has never come close to forming a federal government. But the NDP is in power in British Columbia, Manitoba, and Saskatchewan, with governments headed by Dave Barrett, Edward Schreyer, and Allan Blakeney, respectively. All three NDP premiers are oriented away from dogmatic socialism and toward pragmatic social democratic reform. They have improved welfare payments and services, gotten involved in resource industries, and set up medical programs for the young and elderly.

The federal fortunes of the NDP do not appear to be on the upswing. Led by David Lewis, the party held the balance of power in Pierre Trudeau's minority government elected in 1972. This July, when Trudeau's Liberals won a majority government, NDP representation in the House was almost cut in half, dipping from 30 to 16 seats. The NDP could take credit for some reforms introduced by Trudeau's minority government, such as higher pensions and family allowances.

Ed Broadbent (later photo) ran for the federal NDP leadership in 1971.

Welfare costs $100M over budget in B.C.

Sept. 18, 1974

VICTORIA, B.C. – Everyone's in a $100-million tizzy about NDP bookkeeping. Welfare costs, shared by three levels of government, have apparently gone about $100 million over budget. There were stories about clerical errors, but only about $5 million can be blamed on accounting mistakes, says Premier Dave Barrett. The rest seems to have been spent on welfare programs. Municipal leaders refuse to pay for the overruns.

RCMP quash native protest on the Hill

Sept. 29, 1974

OTTAWA – The RCMP riot squad was turned on about 300 native people who tried to present their grievances to officials on Parliament Hill today. The protesters, some of whom came from as far away as Vancouver, are part of the Native People's Caravan. They hope to draw government attention to a range of native grievances, including the need for better housing and medical care. Today's confrontation resulted in several injuries.

The mythological Water Spirit Mishapishoo, by Ojibwa artist Norval Morrisseau.

Top court to hear Morgentaler case

Oct. 2, 1974

OTTAWA – Dr. Henry Morgentaler's final legal battle begins this afternoon before the Supreme Court. Last year, a Quebec court acquitted Morgentaler, 50, of performing an illegal abortion. Morgentaler's defence focused on a section of the Criminal Code relieving anyone who performs an operation with skill, care and concern for the patient's health from criminal responsibility. However, the Quebec Court of Appeal overturned the decision in April.

Natives end opposition to James Bay

Nov. 15, 1974

MONTREAL – In an historic development tonight, officials representing the federal and Quebec governments and leaders of the Cree and Inuit of northern Quebec signed an elaborate document suspending native opposition to the James Bay hydroelectric project.

The agreement-in-principle covers more than 647,000 square kilometres of relatively pristine territory in the Canadian Shield. In this vast expanse, many of the 10,000 Cree and Inuit have lived off the land as hunters and fishermen. Their way of life was threatened when Robert Bourassa's Liberal government targeted the land for massive waterworks to generate hydroelectricity.

Federal, provincial and native representatives ready to sign James Bay pact.

Essentially, the agreement-in-principle amounts to a modern-day Indian treaty. In return for their agreeing to suspend court challenges to the project and to recognize Quebec's sovereignty over the area, native negotiators secured exclusive hunting and fishing rights over a 129,500-square-kilometre area. Reserve-like communities will be established on federal land in the hunting grounds.

The Cree will be paid $150 million over a 10-year period. The major innovation in the deal is a provision to allow the development of a limited degree of self-government in the fields of health, social services, education, and economic development.

"...AND IF IT GETS ENOUGH RAIN, AND SUN, AND IF IT ISN'T KILLED BY HAIL, AND IF IT ISN'T DAMAGED BY FROST, AND IF WE CAN GET IT OFF BEFORE IT'S COVERED BY SNOW, AND IF WE GET IT TO THE ELEVATORS, AND IF THE TRAINS ARE RUNNING, AND IF THE GRAIN HANDLERS AREN'T ON STRIKE, AND IF..."
Rodewalt/Calgary/Albertan

The prosperity of the prairie farmer is dependent on many external forces over which he has no control.

Drapeau re-elected, but party hit hard

Nov. 11, 1974

MONTREAL – Jean Drapeau has been re-elected mayor for his fifth term, but his Civic Party suffered its worst setback in 14 years, losing 19 of the seats it won in a complete sweep of the 55-member council in the 1970 FLQ kidnapping crisis. That year, the mayor won 92 percent of the popular vote, but today that was cut to 55 percent. His party lost one seat to a neophyte candidate for the Democracy Montreal party, and 18 seats to the Montreal Citizens' Movement, which began organizing only a year ago. The MCM is a true grassroots organization, drawing support from separatists, federalists, pensioners, and intellectuals.

Montreal Mayor Jean Drapeau.

Room for 18 more seats in the House

Dec. 20, 1974

OTTAWA – The number of seats in the House of Commons will increase at the next election, from 264 to 282. The change comes after the bill enabling expansion was approved by the Senate and given royal assent.

The expansion, MPs agree, is a response to the needs of a population that is continually growing. Critics ask if Canada, already incurring huge deficits, can afford such an expansion.

1975

Ottawa, Jan. 25. Charlotte Whitton, women's rights activist, former mayor of Ottawa, and Canada's first female mayor, dies.

Ottawa, March 4. TV cameras are allowed to record the regular proceedings of Parliament for the first time.

British Columbia, March 18. Two Indian bands declare they have sole title to hundreds of square kilometres of Blackwater and Nasko River watersheds in central B.C. and forbid government and industry to enter the area without permission.

Toronto, April 2. The last section of the CN Tower, the world's tallest free-standing structure, is lifted into place.

Blood Indian Reserve, Alta., April 3. Gerald Tailfeathers, noted Blood Indian artist, dies.

Quebec, April 20. The Quebec government says convicted abortionist Henry Morgentaler won't be allowed out of jail to accept an American award as Humanist of the Year.

Cannes, France, May 23. *Les Ordres*, a Canadian feature film by Michel Brault about the October Crisis of 1970, is named co-winner of the "best direction" award at the Cannes Film Festival.

Buffalo, May 27. Philadelphia Flyers beat Buffalo Sabres four games to two to win the Stanley Cup.

Montreal, June 9. A jury acquits Dr. Henry Morgentaler of performing an illegal abortion, Morgentaler's second such acquittal.

Helsinki, Aug. 1. Canada and 34 other nations sign the Helsinki Accords, vowing to uphold the sovereignty of individual nations and human rights.

Ottawa, September. Finance Minister John Turner resigns suddenly from cabinet without explanation.

Calgary, Nov. 23. Edmonton Eskimos defeat Montreal Alouettes 9-8 to win the Grey Cup.

Toronto. Robertson Davies' novel *World of Wonders* is released, the sequel to *Fifth Business* and *The Manticore*, completing his Deptford trilogy.

Canada. F.R. "Budge" Crawley's film *The Man Who Skied Down Everest* is a big success.

Stratford, Ont. British actor-director Robin Phillips becomes artistic director of the Stratford Festival.

Hull of a game lets Bobby equal record

Feb. 14, 1975

WINNIPEG – Bobby Hull tied Rocket Richard's professional hockey record of 50 goals in 50 games tonight with a three-goal performance that led the Winnipeg Jets to a 5-3 victory over the Houston Aeros. The milestone came in the Jets' 50th game of the World Hockey Association season, 30 years after Richard of the Montreal Canadiens set the record in the National Hockey League. Hull, a star with Chicago of the NHL before the Jets lured him to the WHA, beat Aeros' goalie Ron Grahame for the historic goal. The capacity crowd littered the ice with debris in celebrating Hull's achievement.

Morgentaler goes to jail

Dr. Henry Morgentaler.

March 26, 1975

OTTAWA – Dr. Henry Morgentaler begins an 18-month jail term today. The Supreme Court dismissed the Montreal-based doctor's appeal in a 6-3 vote, despite arguments that inability to obtain abortions on request violated Canadian civil rights. Morgentaler went to trial in 1973 on charges of performing an abortion without the approval of a three-man hospital committee required by law. An acquittal from a Quebec court was overturned on appeal.

Morgentaler told reporters he has no regrets about the jail term, and that in performing abortions he has saved hundreds of women from "death and injury."

Mackenzie pipeline inquiry set to start

March 3, 1975

YELLOWKNIFE – Judge Thomas Berger of the B.C. Supreme Court opens the Mackenzie Valley Pipeline Inquiry's public hearings here today. Berger, provincial NDP leader before he became a judge, was appointed by Prime Minister Pierre Trudeau to head the inquiry a year ago. His task: to try to assess the social and economic impact on the north of the plans by two consortiums to build a 3,860-kilometre pipeline – first for gas, then oil – from the Arctic to Alberta.

Property law victory for Ontario women

May 12, 1975

TORONTO – Married women in Ontario have gained ground in their fight for equality, thanks to new legislation introduced in the legislature today. Under the new law, a married woman will be able to claim for her contribution to a house, or property, owned by her spouse. This change should prevent situations such as the Irene Murdoch case in Alberta, in which a separated woman was denied a share in a house she helped pay for.

Number of Senate seats increased to 104

May 30, 1975

OTTAWA – Two seats have been added to the 102-member Senate, one each for the Yukon and the Northwest Territories. But the move, which is aimed at improving the north's representation in Ottawa, drew fire from Liberal MP Ian Watson. He said, "The Senate is non-representative and non-elective ... it is inappropriate that we should now move toward adding members to that body before we have made fundamental reforms."

Low tide on the Bay of Fundy at St. Andrews, New Brunswick.

No doctor or nurse in tiny Yukon town

May 9, 1975

WATSON LAKE, Yukon – The 800 residents of this community 455 kilometres east of Whitehorse have been particularly careful to avoid illness or injury in recent days – there's been no doctor or nurse to help them. The only doctor is in jail for refusing to register under the territory's compulsory health plan. He is not opposed to the principle of health plans, but considers the Yukon's too expensive. His only assistant has joined a nationwide nurses' strike.

Historic park set up on Viking territory

June 27, 1975

L'ANSE AUX MEADOWS, Nfld. – Prime Minister Pierre Trudeau cut the ribbon opening the temporary visitors' centre today as an agreement was signed transferring 8,000 hectares of land surrounding North America's only authenticated Viking site to the federal government to establish a national historic park. Dignitaries at the ceremony included ambassadors from four Scandinavian countries and Dr. and Mrs. Ingstad, Norse archeologists whose work confirmed this as a Viking site.

Soviet fishing fleet banned from ports

July 23, 1975

CANADA – For years, the great Soviet commercial fishing fleet has been a factor in Canadian waters. But recently, the Canadian government announced that the Soviet Union's Atlantic fishing fleet will be barred from Canadian ports. The Soviet fleet has violated Canadian fishing laws by overfishing its quota. With a spirited campaign toward conservation and to secure further control and management of commercial fisheries, the Department of Fisheries and Oceans is cracking down on all offenders.

Compensate captain, France ordered

June 17, 1975

FRANCE – The French government has been ordered to compensate Canadian navigator and Greenpeace activist Capt. David McTaggart for damages incurred to his ship in 1973. McTaggart refused a French admiral's orders to leave the high seas in 1973, prompting two French ships, *La Bayonnaise* and *Hippopotame,* to close in on his ketch, the *Greenpeace III.* McTaggart ran up the international signal for "manoeuvring with difficulty" that any seaman would immediately respond to, but to his astonishment *La Bayonnaise* edged even closer to *Greenpeace III.* This assault resulted in the ramming and boarding of *Greenpeace III.*

This April 8, proceedings began in the French courts. The purpose of the court action was to protect freedom of navigation on the high seas. France, it appears, violated this right, established by the Geneva Convention of 1958, when it declared a nuclear test zone around Mururoa, where the 1973 incident involving *Greenpeace III* occurred.

Broadbent elected national leader of the New Democratic Party

July 7, 1975

WINNIPEG – Ed Broadbent is the new leader of the New Democratic Party. His election on the fourth ballot concluded the party's four-day convention.

To the surprise of many delegates, Broadbent had to fight off a strong bid by Rosemary Brown, a British Columbia MLA. Brown was supported by feminists, as well as by many members of the party's left wing. When she acknowledged the Broadbent victory, Brown said she viewed her defeat as a partial win on the grounds she had moved the party farther to the left. In coming in second, Brown edged out MP Lorne Nystrom and university professor John Harney.

In his acceptance speech, Broadbent said his major challenge was to convert democratic socialism into a workable political program. The convention drew 1,661 delegates.

Ed Broadbent speaks to the convention just after his election as party leader. He promises to start a campaign agaist the government immediately.

The Alberta Badlands near Drumheller feature impressive rock formations.

Hoodoo rocks rise majestically from the arid sand of the Badlands.

Petro-Canada to combat energy crisis

July 30, 1975

OTTAWA – Alarmed by the oil shortages caused by the energy crisis, the Liberal government has moved into the oil game. Today, by statute, it established Petro-Canada, a publicly owned oil company. Petro-Canada is a child of the government's mistrust of multinationals, which have tended to favor their parent countries' interests over those of Canadians. As well, now that these companies have downgraded their estimates of Canadian inground reserves – making the country ever-more reliant on undependable foreign supplies – the government wants a company to look for more reserves here.

A key target of such development will likely be the Alberta Tar Sands, which are made up of oil embedded in sand. Only a federally-funded corporation such as Petro-Canada is likely to be able to afford the risk of backing such costly explorations.

Petro-Canada is also intended to give the federal government a "window on the oil industry."

University of Sask. bans gay professor

Oct. 1, 1975

SASKATOON – Claiming it's not a violation of civil rights, the head of the University of Saskatchewan today upheld a decision banning self-declared homosexual Doug Wilson from supervising the school's practice teachers. The ban came as the result of an advertisement placed in the university's student newspaper by Wilson seeking members for an academic gay club. Wilson, 24, is a graduate student in education and a lecturer at the university.

University president Dr. R.W. Begg, in upholding the faculty of education's ban on Wilson, said the man's identification with the gay movement would create a "catastrophe" if he were allowed to oversee teachers in schools. At the same time, Begg declared "there has been no discrimination against Mr. Wilson as a student or as a teacher. ... It was a managerial decision." The publicity the issue has attracted, not the university's decision, would harm Wilson's career, he said.

C-c-cold helps Eskimos win the Grey Cup

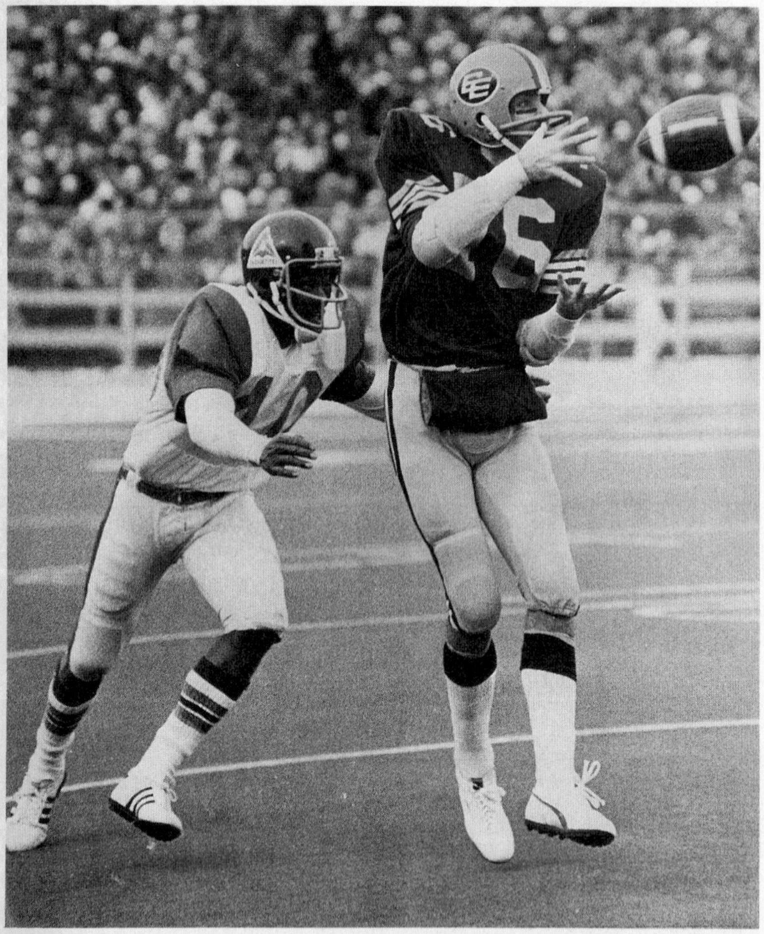

Edmonton's George McGowan makes a key interception against Montreal.

Nov. 23, 1975

CALGARY – The Edmonton Eskimos won the first Grey Cup game ever played in this city, holding on to beat the Montreal Alouettes 9-8 today when a last-minute field goal attempt by Montreal's Don Sweet went wide. Played in -10 degree weather and with a 25-kilometre-an-hour wind, it was the first Canadian Football League championship final that failed to produce a touchdown since Toronto beat Winnipeg 4-3 in 1937.

Edmonton's Dave Cutler kicked field goals of 40, 25 and 52 yards, the latter a Grey Cup record, to score all of his team's points. Sweet had field goals of 35 and 47 yards for Montreal, and two other tries went wide for singles. One of them was the crucial last-minute attempt from 19 yards, a miss that wasn't his fault. Jimmy Jones, who holds the ball on placekicks, said wind and cold led to a bad exchange from centre. Jones was late placing the ball, throwing off Sweet's timing.

American invasion of Quebec re-lived

Oct. 4, 1975

QUEBEC CITY – Two hundred years after they last tried, American invaders failed again to capture Quebec City. This time, though, there were no casualties in a costumed re-enactment of the Dec. 31, 1775, attack Gen. Benedict Arnold led on Quebec. The battle, staged on the Plains of Abraham, is a prelude to American bicentennial celebrations. It was organized by military history buffs from Maine.

Ceremony marks Mirabel airport opening

Visitors inspect the Concorde at the official opening of Mirabel airport.

Oct. 4, 1975

MIRABEL, Que. – Canada's newest airport was inaugurated in a ceremony this afternoon led by Prime Minister Pierre Trudeau. He said the half-billion-dollar facility 55 kilometres northwest of Montreal is such a great achievement "Torontonians will be down here on their knees." Last week, under great public pressure, the Ontario government pulled out of the Pickering project, forcing the federal government to abandon plans for a second major Toronto airport. Critics label Mirabel a white elephant.

Quebec natives sign the James Bay Agreement

Nov. 11, 1975
QUEBEC CITY – The James Bay and Northern Quebec Agreement, the first aboriginal treaty to be negotiated since 1923, was formalized tonight. The signing ceremony involved an array of officials from many organizations and agencies, including the government of Quebec, Hydro-Québec, the federal Department of Indian and Northern Affairs, the Grand Council of the Crees of Quebec, and the Northern Quebec Inuit Association. The deal was signed almost one year after the original acceptance of an agreement-in-principle.

The signing represents the meeting of a variety of national and territorial visions – a confluence of competing political agendas and varying philosophical orientations toward the land and its creatures. For officials under Quebec Premier Robert Bourassa, the large quantity of water running out to sea is an unexploited source of energy to fuel the economic enterprises of a nationalistically-inclined Quebec.

The James Bay Agreement includes a framework for a future regime in northern Quebec that will give native people a modest degree of capacity to cope with the invading technocracy from the south. The agreement lays a basis for Cree and Inuit schools, hospitals, social service agencies, and business enterprises. It has provisions to ensure native trapping and fishing.

Postal workers vote to end 6-week strike by close 51.8% margin

Dec. 2, 1975
CANADA – Across the country, striking postal workers are returning reluctantly to work after crippling the mail for the past six weeks. It was a close vote, with a scant 51.8-percent margin for the winning side.

The reason for the margin is simple: the government essentially succeeded in outwaiting the workers. That's why they went along with the same terms offered weeks ago by conciliator Judge Jean Moisin – a $1.70-per-hour wage increase over 30 months, without the desired reduction of the 40-hour work week. Also missed was the union's attempt to protect jobs against the new postal code, a six-number identification system that will allow the use of automated sorting machines in the post office.

Edmonton postal workers returned to work at midnight before the final vote.

Despite this defeat, Canadian Union of Postal Workers vice-president Jean-Claude Parrot warns that the union "is going back to work, but all of us, including those who accepted the offer, will be fighting every day during this contract for the things that are missing." His bitter defiance is essentially somewhat toothless, because the union itself is split, with 2,000 workers crossing the picket lines during the strike.

Wages and prices controlled by board

Dec. 3, 1975
OTTAWA – The Trudeau government has made good its threat to deal harshly with inflation, by establishing wage and price controls. Specific measures will be decided on by the new Anti-Inflation Board, headed by former Liberal cabinet minister Jean-Luc Pepin.

Pepin's first target are wage demands, such as the 39.2-percent wage hike offered by the Toronto Board of Education to striking high school teachers. Even though the teachers believe that offer isn't high enough, Pepin says it's too high, and thus it will be disallowed by the AIB. Pepin acknowledges "that the decision was seen by the teachers as cruel." And the head of the AIB adds: "It's their bad luck that they were first on the list."

"Ugly broads" not sought for Olympics

Nov. 11, 1975
MONTREAL – Gals who wear glasses won't be leading the masses. At least that appears to be the policy of the organizers now selecting hostesses for next year's Olympic Games. Spectacles don't look good with the uniform hats, the organizers say. And one applicant, Nancy Gelfand, was told that because she wears specs, there was no point in even filling in a form. The former hostess at Expo 67, a 26-year-old MA student, has all the other qualifications: Canadian, bilingual, and between 20 and 35. She says she was told by an organizer the no-glasses rule "helps screen out ugly broads ... real dogs."

Stanley Park offers the beauty of nature in the busy city of Vancouver.

Socreds oust NDP from office in B.C.

Dec. 11, 1975
VICTORIA, B.C. – Despite a shaky campaign start by the new Socred leader, Bill Bennett, his party easily beat Dave Barrett's NDP in the provincial election today. The Socreds won 35 seats in the 55-seat legislature. The NDP, plagued by controversy and dissension in its three-year reign, held on to only 18 seats. The Liberals and Conservatives got one seat each. W.A.C. Bennett, the new premier's father, had stepped in to block the formation of another "free enterprise" party, and so prevented a split in the anti-NDP vote. But the Old Man of B.C. politics was not allowed to do any campaigning.

1976

Montreal, Jan. 5. The Society for the Prevention of Cruelty to Animals opens a dog blood bank, the first in Canada.

Montreal, Jan. 20. The Quebec Court of Appeal upholds the acquittal of Dr. Henry Morgentaler on charges of performing an illegal abortion.

Toronto, Feb. 7. Darryl Sittler of the Toronto Maple Leafs scores six goals and four assists for a record 10 points as the Leafs beat the Boston Bruins.

Ottawa, Feb. 27. Inuit leaders present their land claim to 1.9 million square kilometres of land in the north and 2 million square kilometres of ocean to Prime Minister Trudeau.

Montreal, April 18. The architect who designed the Olympic Stadium admits he made an error in calculations and left 15,000 seats with a bad view of the track.

Ottawa, May 5. PM Trudeau tells the Commons that a "deep loyalty" to the Parti Québécois could disqualify someone from getting a job in the federal civil service.

Philadelphia, May 16. Montreal Canadiens defeat Philadelphia Flyers four games to none to win the Stanley Cup.

Montreal, July 11. The International Olympic Committee accepts Canada's position that Taiwan not be allowed to compete in the Olympics under the name "Republic of China."

Ottawa, July 14. MPs vote to abolish the death penalty for all civilian offences.

London, England, Aug. 4. Canadian newspaper tycoon Roy Herbert Thompson, Baron Thompson, dies.

Quebec, Sept. 15. Team Canada wins the first Canada Cup, an invitational international tournament, by beating Czechoslovakia 5-4.

Quebec, Nov. 19. Robert Bourassa resigns as leader of the Quebec Liberal party.

Toronto, Nov. 28. Ottawa Rough Riders defeat Saskatchewan Roughriders 23-20 to win the Grey Cup.

Toronto. After heavy losses, the T. Eaton Co. announces the end of its catalogue sales operation established in 1884.

Canada. The RCMP establish a Native Policing Branch to police native communities. The Mounties also hire natives to serve in the branch.

Trudeau tells Castro to butt out of Angola

Trudeau joined Castro for a sing-a-long during his Cuban visit.

Feb. 3, 1976

OTTAWA – Prime Minister Pierre Trudeau told Cuban premier Fidel Castro to get his troops out of Angola. In the Commons today, the PM answered questions about his 11-day tour of Mexico, Cuba, and Venezuela. Conservatives said Trudeau should have cancelled the Cuban portion of the trip to protest Castro's intervention in the Angolan civil war. But Trudeau said he took the opportunity to talk to Castro about the African situation.

Saskatchewan bills eye potash industry

Jan. 28, 1976

REGINA – The Blakeney government has not yet announced its intentions, but two bills which passed this session allow the provincial government to expropriate the potash industry in whole or in part. The Liberals filibustered the legislation, arguing that the bills furthered socialism in the province. Conservatives did not aggressively support one side or the other.

Kathy Kreiner won the gold medal in giant slalom at the Olympic Games in Innsbruck, Austria.

Dome free to drill in the Beaufort Sea

April 15, 1976

OTTAWA – Environmentalists and natives oppose it. But the federal cabinet today decided to allow oil and gas drilling in the Beaufort Sea this summer. The debate in cabinet was reported as "vigorous." To deal with one environmental concern, the government shortened the drilling season by one month to allow time to clear up an oil spill, if there is one, before winter. Also, Dome Petroleum will have to carry $50 million in insurance to cover environmental damage. But that did not comfort natives. "You can't put a price on the Beaufort Sea," said John Amagoalik, director of land claims for the Inuit Tapirisat. "The risks are too high."

Joe who? A fourth ballot victory gives Clark PC leadership

Feb. 22, 1976

OTTAWA – Tonight at the Progressive Conservative leadership convention, Joe Clark, a Tory MP virtually unknown in eastern Canada, won the party leadership by the slimmest of margins. Clark got only 65 votes more than the front-runner, Claude Wagner, on the fourth ballot in a victory won by so many lesser, losing candidates throwing their support behind him.

Clark's victory was a surprise both to Wagner, a law-and-order style Quebec politician, and Brian Mulroney, the third-place candidate with no parliamentary experience. Mulroney mounted a slick campaign – "too slick," according to those who opposed him.

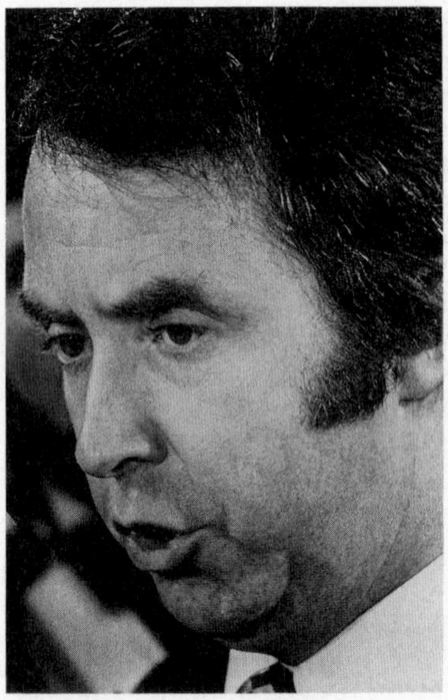

New PC leader Joe Clark.

CRTC to regulate telecommunications

April 1, 1976

OTTAWA – Telecommunications and broadcasting are now regulated by the same agency. Effective today, the Canadian Radio-television and Telecommunications Commission takes over the increasingly complex and controversial field of telecommunications in the federal sphere. This brings Bell Canada and CN-CP Telecommunications under its control.

Pilots walk out in language dispute

June 22, 1976

CANADA – Canadian pilots are refusing to fly, thanks to an ongoing dispute about the extension of bilingualism to three Quebec airports by the federal government. The air traffic controllers, claiming that such a change will threaten safety, have only stayed on the job because of a court injunction forbidding a walkout. This chaos in the control tower is why the 2,800 members of the Canadian Air Line Pilots Association walked off the job. They're worried about the increased risk of air accidents in the current environment. That's a fear shared by foreign pilots at KLM, Scandinavian Airlines, and British Airways. They, like their Canadian counterparts at Air Canada and Canadian Pacific [Canadian Airlines International], also refuse to fly in Canada.

This crisis is a debacle for the Trudeau government, which has been trying to promote bilingualism in Canada. There's little doubt that the government didn't anticipate the trouble its policy has caused.

RCMP letter leaked to destroy me: PM

June 9, 1976

OTTAWA – A top secret letter about RCMP surveillance of Quebec political parties was leaked to "destroy my reputation and credibility," Prime Minister Pierre Trudeau declared today in the House.

The letter, sent anonymously to the Toronto *Sun,* was from the head of the RCMP security service to another top Mountie official. It said the prime minister had issued guidelines to curb RCMP monitoring of the Parti Québécois. The *Sun* then published an editorial condemning Trudeau for being soft on separatists: "Trudeau, personally, has made it easier for separatists to subvert Confederation and break up Canada from within." Trudeau denied issuing hands-off orders and called the charges "scurrilous, inaccurate and venomous."

Solicitor General Warren Allmand said there was nothing to block the RCMP from investigating genuine subversion. Meanwhile, the RCMP raided the Toronto office of *Sun* editor Peter Worthington and seized the leaked letter after a four-hour search. The letter had been in a top drawer of Worthington's desk. "We'll make it tougher for them next time. We'll probably put it on the table in the vestibule," Worthington quipped.

Ending tax writeoff angers TV stations

U.S. Ambassador Thomas Enders.

June 12, 1976

OTTAWA – "Canada can't simply unilaterally cut back on its relations with the United States, and expect there won't be reaction from us." So says Thomas Enders, U.S. ambassador to Canada. His comments come in the wake of protests by U.S. border TV stations of Canada's decision to revoke a 100-percent tax writeoff for Canadians who advertise on the stations.

Air traffic walkout ends after 9 days

June 29, 1976

CANADA – Canadian pilots and air traffic controllers are back on the job, ending a nine-day walkout over increased use of French at Quebec airports. The strikers, worried the extension of French services would lead to misunderstandings, and thus more accidents, came back to work after Liberal Transport Minister Otto Lang agreed to add a third member to the commission looking into the dangers of bilingual air traffic control. He's also consented to a free vote – not along party lines – on whether to go ahead with the expansion, if the commission decides airport bilingualism is safe.

For now, the pilots are satisifed with this solution. But they have warned they might strike again, if bilingualism is brought to Montreal's airport.

This poster for the 1976 Olympics at Montreal suggests current issues of global concern.

Unemployment hits 15-year high of 7.4%

May 20, 1976

OTTAWA – Unemployment has hit the highest rate in 15 years, with 7.4 percent of Canadians out of work. High levels of unemployment are expected to continue for the next few years. To cope with the situation, the federal government is contemplating a new job creation program. Last month, the Economic Council of Canada recommended the federal government allocate $1 billion to create 100,000 to 200,000 new jobs.

Parliament Hill site of farmers' protest

Whelan is hit with milk jug.

June 3, 1976

OTTAWA – Angry at cuts both to subsidies and production quotas, 5,000 Quebec dairy farmers went on a rampage on Parliament Hill today. They hurled plastic bottles full of milk, bouncing one off Agriculture Minister Eugene Whelan as he tried to calm them down. They smashed windows and ornamental lamps, and torched both trees and park benches on Parliament Hill.

In fact, things got so tense the RCMP called in its riot squad to disperse the demonstrators, only the second time in Canadian history this has happened. The farmers want the cuts more evenly distributed between all the provinces.

National body joins provincial workers

May 14, 1976

QUEBEC CITY – Government employees in six provinces should have more clout at the bargaining table, now that they've joined into one national union. At a convention held here, the public service unions from B.C., Alberta, Saskatchewan, Manitoba, P.E.I., and Newfoundland signed up for the new National Union of Provincial Government Employees. Conspicuous by their absence are the unions of Ontario and Nova Scotia, both expelled from the Canadian Labour Congress for refusing to endorse the new national body.

All eyes on Montreal as Olympic Games begin

Queen on hand to open Summer Games

The official Olympic banner is raised at the opening ceremonies.

July 17, 1976

MONTREAL – Amidst tight security, and political rumblings by African nations, Queen Elizabeth today declared the 21st Olympic Games officially open. Since arriving in Quebec, the royal couple have been sped around in an armor-plated limousine. Few people, apart from those who could afford seats for the opening ceremonies or were invited to official functions, have caught more than a glimpse of the queen. Standing-room tickets – not easy to procure – for today's opening sold for some $30 apiece. It is reported the queen has asked to be driven around Montreal tomorrow in an open car, a white Cadillac convertible.

CANADA
158

Canadian high jumper Greg Joy.

Expensive Olympics draw to joyful end

Aug. 1 1976

MONTREAL – The Olympic Games ended today, proving that one person's financial disaster is another's joy. Who can forget Vancouver's Greg Joy flying over the bar on his way to capturing a silver medal in the high jump before thousands of ecstatic fans at the Olympic Stadium? Who can forget Mayor Jean Drapeau declaring that "the Montreal Olympics can no more have a deficit than a man can have a baby?" With the games now headed for a huge deficit, Drapeau has Pablum all over his face.

Canada has become the only host country in Olympic history not to win a gold medal, but there was still lots to cheer for Canadians. Silver medals went to Joy and fellow-Canadians John Wood in canoeing and Michel Vaillancourt in equestrian jumping. Still, these games will be best remembered for Romanian Nadia Comaneci's perfect 10s in gymnastics and American Bruce Jenner's decathlon triumph.

Comaneci's perfect 10 is an Olympic first

Romanian gymnast Nadia Comaneci practises before a perfect performance.

July 18, 1976

MONTREAL – The 14-year-old Romanian gymnast Nadia Comaneci shattered tradition tonight when she scored a perfect 10, the first ever awarded at the Games in the compulsory section of the program on the uneven bars. Nadia, who weighs only 88 pounds on a four-foot 10-inch frame, is the new darling of the gymnastics world, replacing the Soviet Union's Olga Korbut, who in 1972 won three golds and a silver medal.

Olympic Games hit by African boycott

July 18, 1976

MONTREAL – Almost all of the nations of Africa pulled out of the Olympic Games today, as well as two Arab and Caribbean countries. The organization of the 21st Games has been thrown into confusion in the most dramatic exodus on political grounds since the modern Olympics began in 1896. The past three days, 28 African nations, with 770 athletes, or 10 percent of the total, have pulled out.

They are protesting against the refusal by the International Olympic Committee to censure or expel New Zealand because a rugby team from that country is touring South Africa, which has been expelled by the IOC and has not sent any athletes to these Games. The IOC says it can't do anything more.

'ELLO, MORGENTALER?
"THE OLYMPICS CAN NO MORE HAVE A DEFICIT THAN A MAN CAN HAVE A BABY."
JEAN DRAPEAU.

Montreal Mayor Jean Drapeau is under fire for the enormous costs of the Olympic Games.

More than one million workers stay home in day of protest

Oct. 14, 1976

CANADA – More than one million members of unions stayed off the job across Canada today in a day of protest marking the first anniversary of the imposition of wage and price controls. Support for the protest was greatest in northern mining centres such as Elliot Lake, Ont., where at least 95 percent of workers stayed off the job. In the east end of Montreal, some protesters disrupted public transit by stopping buses.

On the whole, however, union organizers could claim only partial success. Just 7,500 people showed up for a rally at Queen's Park in Toronto, far below expectations, and an Ottawa rally attracted fewer than 2,000 protesters.

The Communist contingent in the Day of Protest demonstration in Toronto.

Strikes legal when the AIB rolls back wages, board rules

Sept. 17, 1976

OTTAWA – Strikes are legal when the Anti-Inflation Board rolls back wages, the Canada Labor Relations Board ruled today. In a precedent-setting decision, the CLRB rejected an application by a Yukon mining company to declare illegal a strike protesting an AIB rollback. The board said the rollback meant that a collective agreement was not in effect.

The AIB was established to oversee federal government wage and price controls. The CLRB has under its jurisdiction about 500,000 workers, but the provincial labor boards may use the federal decision as a precedent. Board rulings may be appealed to the court.

While some labor unions hailed the ruling as a victory, others were cautious. Lynn Williams, Ontario director of the United Steelworkers of America, whose union is involved in the Yukon strike, said workers can use the strike as a weapon to force Ottawa to change its anti-inflation policies. That thinking worried Dennis McDermott, Canadian director of the United Auto Workers. Striking against AIB decisions "is a political strike – it's against the government." McDermot opposes political strikes.

Premiers OK revenue-sharing compromise

Dec. 13, 1976

OTTAWA – The provinces and federal government reached a compromise on revenue sharing at dinner tonight. In talks with the 10 premiers, Prime Minister Pierre Trudeau had said he would not budge from his offer to give the provinces one percentage point of the personal income tax Ottawa collects. The premiers initially were united in their demand for four points. At dinner they accepted Trudeau's new offer of two points, one point of it as an immediate cash payment. In return, the provinces agreed to accept a formula for equalization payments for cost-shared programs that will represent a lower value than they wanted.

The premiers have not yet officially accepted the compromise but they are expected to do so tomorrow. Earlier today, the prime minister and premiers were forced to move to another meeting room when reporters demanding an open conference staged a sit-in.

Air Canada to allow French in cockpits

Sept. 29, 1976

MONTREAL – Bowing to a court order, Air Canada says it will allow French in its planes' cockpits. The order came after Liberal MP Serge Joyal, backed by 41 French Air Canada pilots, applied to Quebec's Superior Court to override the airline's ban on French. The use of any language besides English concerns pilots, who fear misunderstandings may cause accidents.

Indians described as lazy, apathetic

Sept. 17, 1976

YELLOWKNIFE, N.W.T. – Racism has forced the chief of the territorial corrections service, Clare Wilkins, to resign. The issue arose over a Yellowknife Correctional Institute training manual describing Indians as "lazy, apathetic, adolescent and credulous." To make amends, Territories Commissioner Stuart Hodgson and Social Development Minister Peter Ernerk, an Inuit, issued a public apology. Feelings were already high: last year at Fort Simpson 300 native delegates from throughout the Mackenzie River Valley passed the Dene Declaration proclaiming the Dene's "right to self-determination."

The Snowbirds fly in formation over Montreal's Olympic Stadium.

Three views of Montreal's Olympic Stadium are seen in this promotional poster for the Olympic Games. The roof is to be retracted by mechanisms in the tower.

Separatist Parti Québécois steamrollers to power

Nov. 15, 1976

MONTREAL – In an election result that stunned even René Lévesque, the separatist Parti Québécois swept to power tonight. Late returns show the PQ with 69 seats to the Liberals' 28 and the Union Nationale's 11. Liberal Premier Robert Bourassa lost his own seat. "You understand I have not yet had time to assimilate all this," Lévesque told throngs of delirious supporters here after the magnitude of his victory become clear.

René Lévesque casts election ballot.

Of the three former federal MPs who switched to provincial politics to help stem the PQ tide, only Bryce Mackasey won a seat. "It's not the end of the world," Mackasey said. "Life will go on tomorrow. We're still a long way from separation. Let a few days pass before we assess it. The important thing is not to panic. Your money is protected in the banks."

It was his party's moderation that lost the election, Bourassa said. "It is more and more difficult in modern societies to take a middle-of-the-road approach." But others attributed his defeat to the scandals and the financial crises that have plagued his government and to the PQ playing down separatism in favor of economic and social issues.

Premier-elect René Lévesque speaks to his supporters after the win.

Outside the province, reaction ranged from caution to shock. In a prepared statement, Prime Minister Pierre Trudeau said, "We must conclude that the people of Quebec did not vote on constitutional but on economic and administrative issues." New Brunswick Premier Richard Hatfield was "extremely upset" by the PQ victory. But former Newfoundland premier Joey Smallwood predicted the PQ will provide "good government ... perhaps the best Quebec has had in quite some time." Saskatchewan Premier Allan Blakeney said the PQ may force Ottawa to be more responsive to the provinces' needs.

Lionel Remillard, founding principal of Toronto's first French-language high school, asked "what other choice did the Québécois have? The way I see it now is that Quebec has been born again."

PQ members swear allegiance to queen

Nov. 24, 1976

QUEBEC – Nine newly elected members of the Parti Québécois government swore their allegiance to the queen today. But they were uncomfortable. The nine Members of the National Assembly from the Quebec area were the first of the separatist government to be sworn in. They quietly took the oath in the Assembly before the chief clerk. "This is the second time I've done this," said Adrien Ouellette. "The first time was when I got my commission in the army. I hope it's the last time."

Premier-elect René Lévesque plans to be sworn in tomorrow. A day later, the new cabinet will be introduced and sworn in. Lévesque has given no hint of whom he will choose to be ministers. Then, a party will be held at Quebec's convention centre to which everyone is invited to meet their new premier.

Picnic with Birthday Cake and Blue Sky, by Gathie Falk. A Manitoba-born artist, Falk has gained recognition across the country.

Control on coastal waters to expand

Dec. 31, 1976

OTTAWA – Tomorrow Canada's 320-kilometre jurisdiction over its coastal waters comes into effect on both the east and west coasts. It will be extended to the Arctic waters on March 1.

East coast fishermen have long complained about overfishing by foreign ships, and last year the Canadian government concluded the International Commission for the Northwest Atlantic Fisheries was not going to solve the problem. Fisheries Minister Romeo Leblanc and External Affairs Minister Don Jamieson began the negotiations that led most other nations to accept Canada's decision. Last June Canada announced it would extend its jurisdiction on Jan. 1, 1977, and other coastal nations, including the United States, are doing likewise. Negotiations will be required to resolve problems of overlap.

English Canada has mixed reactions to PQ victory

Parent founders of young Canada keep an eye on their squabbling children.

Kamienski / Winnipeg / Tribune / 17 November 1976

Cartoonist Kamienski portrays René Lévesque's disdain for BNA Act.

Nov. 15, 1976

QUEBEC – The first reaction from political leaders across Canada to the Parti Québécois victory over the Liberals in today's provincial election is one of surprise, either pleased or dismayed.

Former Newfoundland premier Joey Smallwood says PQ leader René Lévesque will provide "good government ... perhaps the best Quebec has had in quite some time." He predicts that if Premier Lévesque holds a referendum on sovereignty-association, it will be defeated. Newfoundland premier Frank Moores said he's "very worried" about the PQ victory.

New Brunswick's Premier Richard Hatfield is "extremely upset." Leonard Jones, an independent from Moncton who has often voiced anti-French views, says it's time the rest of Canada called Quebec's bluff and invited it to separate.

The Parti Québécois position includes both separatism and association. Quebec would leave Canada to gain political sovereignty, or independence in all domestic and foreign affairs. Sovereignty, however, would be accompanied by an economic association with English-speaking Canada.

Prince Andrew set to study in Ontario

Dec. 9, 1976

LAKEFIELD, Ont. – Boys living at the exclusive Lakefield College School will soon have a new classmate – Prince Andrew. The second son of Queen Elizabeth will attend the school from January to June next year. He'll be taking a Grade 12 program. College headmaster Terence Guest says the prince will not live any better than the other students boarding here. He will, however, be accompanied by an RCMP bodyguard at all times. Lakefield is a private school with a reputation for strictness. Boys caught smoking are expelled.

Canadair produces components for the Lockheed CP-140 Aurora.

Smokey sniffs out library fire hazard

Dec. 16, 1976

OTTAWA – Smokey the service dog put out a fire before it started today. Two weeks ago the National Library went to the Dorval Police Dog Service with a crisis that threatened to destroy the archive's invaluable photo collection, possibly even lives: film negatives with a nitrocellulose base were deteriorating, creating a highly explosive gas. The problem was finding the dangerous negatives among the 5 million photos packed, row upon row, in 10,000 boxes. Within six hours, Smokey narrowed it down to 20 to 25 containers.

1977

Ottawa, March 4. Noted Ojibwa artist Benjamin Chee Chee commits suicide while in jail for disturbing the peace.

Ottawa, March 24. PM Trudeau tells university students that if the are upset with the job climate in Canada they should move elsewhere.

Quebec, March 29. Premier René Lévesque and federal NDP leader Ed Broadbent agree at a meeting that they share the same views about social democracy in Canada.

Toronto, April 5. A student-run survey shows that more than 70 percent of students at Osgoode Hall Law School have smoked marijuana.

Toronto, April 7. Toronto Blue Jays, Canada's second major league baseball team, play their first home game, beating the Chicago White Sox 11-5 in a snowstorm.

Quebec, April 14. The Parti Québécois says that francophones living outside Quebec will have to fend for themselin defending their language and culture.

Boston, May 14. Montreal Canadiens defeat Boston Bruins four games to none to win the Stanley Cup.

Ottawa, Aug. 3. The government rejects native demands for their own political territory in the Northwest Territories. PM Trudeau says Ottawa will never agree to a political territory based solely on race.

Canada, Sept. 6. Highway signs across Canada, except in Quebec and Nova Scotia, are converted to metric.

England, Sept. 8. Canadian Cindy Nicholas becomes the first woman to make a return swim of the English Channel, beating the male record for the swim by 10 hours.

Winnipeg, Oct. 11. The Conservatives led by Sterling Lyon defeat the NDP government of Ed Schreyer in a provincial election.

Montreal, Nov. 27. Montreal Alouettes beat Edmonton Eskimos 41-6 for the Grey Cup.

Ottawa. The Department of Indian Affairs and Northern Development sponsors a Band Constables Program, using native constables on reserves to enforce local band bylaws.

Canada. Native representation in penitentiaries is 280 per 100,000 population, compared to a rate of 40 per 100,000 population for non-natives.

PM proposes bringing home Constitution

Jan. 21, 1977

OTTAWA – Prime Minister Pierre Trudeau has made a new proposal to provincial premiers to bring the Canadian Constitution home from Britain. In a letter to the premiers, Trudeau said today the federal government is willing to reopen negotiations regarding the contentious issues of an amending formula and language rights. With agreement on the two issues, Trudeau said broader talks could begin on changing the Constitution.

Trudeau prefers the so-called Victoria Formula for amendments. It requires for changing the Constitution the approval of Ontario, Quebec, at least two Maritime provinces, British Columbia, and at least one other western province.

Prime Minister Pierre Trudeau.

Lévesque woos financial bigwigs in N.Y.

Jan. 25, 1977

NEW YORK – Quebec independence is inevitable, Premier René Lévesque told investors here today. Lévesque's speech to about 1,600 members of the elite Economic Club of New York was carefully prepared, calculated to preserve confidence among the American financial community. But it appeared to have a more reassuring effect in Canada than it did here. "I never heard a seditious speech like that before – that guy ought to be strung up," one audience member said when the premier finished.

René Lévesque wants independence.

Lévesque said "independence for Quebec now appears as normal, I might say almost inevitable, as it was for the American states of 200 years ago." Most audience members praised Lévesque for his confidence and an eloquent speech. But they were not swayed by arguments of an independent Quebec being a good place for their money.

Politicians crowded around televisions in House of Commons lobbies to watch Lévesque. "He naturally wanted to reassure the financiers, bankers and businessmen," said Conservative finance critic Sinclair Stevens. "He gave them what they wanted to hear."

Fear of separation not used to lure industries to Ont.

Feb. 13, 1977

MONTREAL – Ontario does not want to use the separatist threat to drain Quebec of its industry. Several firms have – or are suspected of having – moved their offices from Quebec to Ontario as a result of René Lévesque's Parti Québécois election victory last year. But Ontario Minister of Industry and Tourism Claude Bennett said here today his government will not encourage such action.

Ontario has "nothing to gain economically for our province or for our country if we decide to go in and because of some discontent that could prevail or exist in the province of Quebec, to try and bring those industries out of this province and into the province of Ontario," Bennett said.

Last Thursday, Prime Minister Pierre Trudeau said he believes companies are moving their offices and individuals are shifting their savings from Quebec to Ontario because of the fear of separation. He said investors have been uncertain for years about the financial climate in Quebec because of the separatist policies of some provincial politicians. This uncertainty increased to fear with the election last November of the PQ, Trudeau said.

Bennett said Ontario only considers helping moves from Quebec if it is convinced the moves are made for genuine reasons. If a company might move to the U.S., the Ontario government will consider incentives. "We will not beg them to come to the province of Ontario." But if the company is looking to the U.S., "then I feel we're in a real competitive position. We must then move in and show what we have in Ontario that will equal or better what they're looking for."

Trudeau's vow: I'll resign if Quebec votes for independence

Jan. 28, 1977

QUEBEC CITY – Prime Minister Pierre Trudeau will resign if Quebec votes for independence. In a low-key but emotional speech here today, Trudeau also challenged Quebec Premier René Lévesque to quit if Quebec votes for federalism. He told the Quebec Chamber of Commerce the PQ referendum should be held soon. "The choice must be definitive and final. If the referendum is lost, it should not be reopened for 15 years," he said.

Trudeau's audience, mainly small businessmen who fear the consequences of separation, received the PM's speech enthusiastically. Trudeau replied to the arguments Lévesque made recently in a speech to the Economic Club of New York.

Quebec won't separate, Trudeau says

Feb. 22, 1977
WASHINGTON, D.C. – Quebec will not separate, Prime Minister Pierre Trudeau told Americans today. In the first speech ever by a Canadian prime minister to a joint session of the U.S. Congress, Trudeau said that "with all the certainty I can command that Canada's unity will not be fractured."

Constitutional accommodations must be made to protect French-speaking Canadians, Trudeau said. "We have not, however, created the conditions in which French-speaking Canadians have felt they were fully equal or could fully develop the richness of the culture they had inherited." But only "a small minority of the people of Quebec" believe the problems should be solved by separation. Trudeau's speech was poorly attended but very enthusiastically received.

President prefers a united Canada

Feb. 2, 1977
WASHINGTON, D.C. – U.S. President Jimmy Carter said today he prefers a united Canada "but that's a judgment for the Canadian people to make." In an interview with the CTV network, Carter said he did not know if the U.S. would recognize a sovereign Quebec. "We will cross that bridge when we come to it." After meeting with Prime Minister Pierre Trudeau, Carter avoided seeming to interfere in Canadian affairs. Canadian stability is "of crucial importance" to the U.S., but "I've seen nothing yet that would cause me concern."

Lévesque: Trudeau speech too vague

Feb. 23, 1977
QUEBEC CITY – Premier René Lévesque today congratulated Prime Minister Pierre Trudeau for "a good speech" to the American Congress yesterday, but then qualified his praise. Trudeau's speech seemed "like a desperate appeal to English-Canadian opinion, maybe thinking they'll listen better from Washington." Trudeau should spell out exactly what constitutional changes he favors. Lévesque criticized Trudeau for saying only a small number of Quebecers support the Parti Québécois proposal of sovereignty-association.

Passenger railway called Via on tap

Feb. 28, 1977
OTTAWA – The federal government is creating a new, publicly owned passenger railway. Called Via, the new line will take over routes from Canadian Pacific and Canadian National, both of which have been trying to get out of the money-losing business for years. Via is intended to provide cheaper passenger service than at present, and to require something less than the $160 million currently paid out by Ottawa to CN and CP to keep passenger trains on the rails. Via will rent its track from the railways.

Unions may boycott firms that leave Quebec, Laberge warns

Louis Laberge, president of the Quebec Federation of Labor.

Feb. 17, 1977
TORONTO – Quebec unions may boycott firms that leave the province because of the possibility of separatism. In a speech here tonight, Louis Laberge, president of the Quebec Federation of Labor, said he believes big business is trying to squeeze Quebec by moving or threatening to move. The Royal Bank is moving some of its headquarter operations from Montreal to Toronto. Laberge said that if the bank is trying "in a sneaky way to move to Toronto, it would be easy to boycott the bank." The Royal has said its reorganization has nothing to do with Quebec politics.

Laberge doesn't support separation and the federation has taken no position on the issue. But the federation supports the Parti Québécois because of its social and labor programs. Laberge criticized "a few hotheads" for making separatism seem attractive.

Indian writer dies after long illness

Jan. 31, 1977
PARIS, Ont. – Edith Brant Monture, author of *Famous Indians* and *West to the Setting Sun* and *Joseph Brant: Mohawk,* written with Harvey Chalmers, died last evening after a lengthy illness.

The great-great-granddaughter of the famous war chief Joseph Brant was born in 1894 on the New Credit Reserve, adjoining the Six Nations Reserve near Brantford, Ont. She wrote and lectured on the history of the North American Indian, she was first president of the women's section of the Ontario Agricultural Society, and she became an Associate of the Canadian Council of Christians and Jews.

The Ojibwa artist Benjamin Chee Chee is seen here with an exhibition of his early geometric works. Chee Chee was gaining national recognition for his art when he committed suicide in an Ottawa jail cell where he was being held for disturbing the peace in a restaurant.

Commission urges moratorium on pipeline

Mr. Justice Thomas Berger examines a copy of his pipeline report.

May 8, 1977

OTTAWA – A pipeline down the Mackenzie Valley in Canada's north could result in civil disorder among natives and greater American involvement in this country's affairs, Justice Thomas Berger reported today. Berger headed the commission established in 1974 to study the effects of the proposed natural gas pipeline.

In the report released today, Berger wrote about opposition to the pipeline from natives and environmentalists. The justice of the B.C. Supreme Court recommended that no major energy project be built in the Mackenzie River valley for 10 years to allow settlement of native land claims. He also said no pipeline should be constructed across the environmentally sensitive northern part of the Yukon. But he said the Mackenzie Valley pipeline is environmentally feasible if strict guidelines are enforced.

The Americans will decide this fall if they want to bring Alaskan natural gas through a Canadian pipeline or on tankers. Natives are elated with the report. "The judge has recognized the Dene nation," said George Erasmus, N.W.T. Indian Brotherhood president.

Language battle brews

April 4, 1977

TORONTO – Ontario is preparing to fight the proposed Quebec language law in the courts. Premier William Davis said today he has asked government lawyers for an opinion on the Parti Québécois white paper on language released last week. The document suggests legislation to make Quebec essentially unilingual French. All communications in Quebec would have to be in French and children could attend an English-language school only if one parent had attended English primary school in Quebec.

Davis said he would co-operate with the federal government in launching a constitutional challenge to the proposed law. In the Commons today, Prime Minister Pierre Trudeau agreed with opposition leader Joe Clark that the Quebec law may violate the federal Official Languages Act and might be unconstitutional. But reaction from his government would have to wait until the Quebec government actually introduced a specific law.

Schooling provisions in the white paper appear to be a victory for PQ hard-liners over those, including Premier René Lévesque, who wanted a less restrictive provision. In Toronto today, influential Montreal newspaper publisher Claude Ryan described the white paper as "a shock and a possible warning of things to come." He said the proposed law was "a dubious restriction of liberty."

Meanwhile, a spokesman for Montreal's Italian community accused the PQ of trying to make Italian immigrants "white niggers in America." Angelo Montini said the proposed law would make immigrants third- or fourth-class Canadian citizens.

Lévesque's demands are upsetting.

"Dirty" Canadians upend the Swedes

May 4, 1977

VIENNA, Austria – In a game which Swedish player Roland Eriksson termed "a wrestling match," Team Canada today pummelled the Swedes 7-0 in World Hockey Tournament play.

Sweden, which defeated Team Canada 4-2 earlier in the tournament, was appalled by the brutal tactics of the Canadian team. Team Canada defenceman Carol Vadnais, commenting on an incident in which he used the butt end of his stick to send a Swedish player to the hospital, says that coach Johnny Wilson told the players to "go out and get" whomever they wanted. Despite the uproar, captain Phil Esposito says Canada will continue to use "just a little intimidation."

Senate appointee the first Inuit to sit in Canadian Parliament

Willy Adams (right) with Bud Olson and Senate Speaker Renaude Lapointe.

May 5, 1977

OTTAWA – Willy Adams of Rankin Inlet, N.W.T., has been appointed senator for the Northwest Territories. Adams, an electrical contractor, will be the first Inuit to sit in Parliament. He will be in a unique position to speak out on issues that concern the Inuit: land claims, pipeline development, and oil, gas and mineral exploration.

Adams' appointment by Prime Minister Pierre Trudeau is being hailed as a landmark for Canada's northern natives. The Inuit Tapirisat, an organization that represents more than 22,000 Inuit across northern Canada, has welcomed the move, as they feel they now have someone in Ottawa who is sympathetic to their cause and who understands the problems confronting the Inuit.

Clean up Yonge St., protesters demand

Aug. 8, 1977

TORONTO – An estimated 15,000 protesters, most of them from this city's Portuguese community, marched on city hall today demanding the notorious Yonge Street strip be cleaned up. The action follows the murder last week of 12-year-old Emanuel Jacques. His body was found on the roof of a Yonge Street sex shop.

With countless placards calling for justice, the marchers demanded greater government controls over the strip. Perhaps the most telling sign of all was held aloft by a young boy. It read: "We love people. We love our police force. We love our government. Please love us too."

Bill 101 Quebec's new language law

Unilingual postal service.

Aug. 26, 1977

QUEBEC CITY – The Charter of the French Language is the law of Quebec tonight, despite what appears to be lukewarm support from Premier René Lévesque. The controversial Bill 101 passed third reading in the National Assembly this afternoon by a vote of 54-32 and received royal assent tonight.

Earlier today, in his first speech about Bill 101 in the Assembly, Lévesque said the law may contain "errors," but he urged it be given "an honest tryout for one or two years." The premier has softened his stand on the law over the past few months. Previously he said he was uneasy about the severe restrictions the law places on admission to English-language schools. The law forces all children to attend French school, unless one of their parents has attended an English primary school in Quebec.

Cultural Development Minister Camille Laurin, the bill's author, described it as a law "for generations to come." In an eloquent address that drew cheering and applause, Laurin said the law is "a decisive gesture for the liberation and promotion of Quebec workers."

Lévesque urged English-speaking Quebecers not to overreact, pointing to the law's safeguards for the use of English in communications and law. He also said the law will be applied "with all the flexibility that will appear necessary."

Maggie and Pierre separate after 6 years

The Trudeaus are seen here in happier days during a visit to China in 1973.

May 27, 1977

OTTAWA – After six years of marriage and months of rumors of strife, Prime Minister Pierre Trudeau made it official today: he and Margaret are officially separated. He made it clear that the separation is at his wife's instigation, and that he will have custody of their three sons, "giving Margaret generous access to them."

He is 57, she's 28, and acquaintances say that the 29-year gap has played a large part in the breakup.

Trudeau and Carter OK pipeline project

Sept. 8, 1977

WASHINGTON, D.C. – The leaders of Canada and the United States today agreed on constructing a pipeline to bring Alaskan natural gas south. Prime Minister Pierre Trudeau and U.S. President Jimmy Carter reached a deal that will see the pipeline built along the Alaska Highway through Canada's north.

The decision ignores the findings of the recent Berger Commission. Justice Thomas Berger said there should be a 10-year moratorium on pipeline construction until native land claims are settled. Berger also said the Alaska Highway route was less environmentally sensitive than the competing proposal to build along the Mackenzie Valley.

Trudeau and Carter said the $10-billion pipeline will be the largest single energy project in history. Eventually a connecting line will be built to Canadian gas fields. The agreement says American consumers would pay a large part of the cost of that connection. The project will employ directly about 8,000 at its peak of construction.

Inflation, unity are government priorities

Oct. 18, 1977

OTTAWA – Inflation and national unity still top the government agenda. In the throne speech read today by Queen Elizabeth, the government said wage and price controls will continue through early 1978. It also proposed increased constitutional protection for the use of English and French. The queen emphasized national unity by alternating between the two languages. It was the first time since 1957 she has read the speech in person.

Loon, carved in green stone by Cape Dorset artist Sheokjuk Oqutaq.

1978

Montreal, Jan. 6. Sun Life, the largest Canadian-owned life insurance company, announces it will move its head office from Montreal to Toronto because of the new Quebec language law, Bill 101.

Ottawa, Jan. 30. The government announces searchers have found the impact crater of a nuclear-powered Soviet spy satellite that crashed in northern Canada last week. The satellite left a radioactive trail across the north.

Ottawa, Feb. 9. The government orders 11 Soviet officials out of Canada for plotting to infiltrate the RCMP security service.

Quebec, April 15. Claude Ryan, editor of Montreal's *Le Devoir*, is elected leader of the Quebec Liberal party.

Boston, May 25. Montreal Canadiens defeat Boston Bruins four games to two to win the Stanley Cup.

Rome, June 12. The Vatican confers the title of venerable on Brother André, "the Miracle Man of Montreal," for his remarkable healing feats.

Ottawa, July 6. The government prohibits all new development in a 38,850-square-kilometre area of the Yukon so a national wilderness area can be set up. The area extends from the Porcupine and Bell rivers to the Beaufort Sea.

Ottawa, July 14. The government agrees to pay $45 million to 2,500 Inuit of the western Arctic from 1981 to 1994. In return, the Inuit agree to give up any aboriginal rights to 270,480 square kilometres of land they traditionally used.

Edmonton, Aug. 11. The 11th Commonwealth Games wrap up. Canada has captured 109 medals, winning the games for the first time.

Toronto, Nov. 26. Edmonton Eskimos defeat Montreal Alouettes 20-13 for the Grey Cup.

Alberta. The Métis Association of Alberta passes a motion to seek a posthumous pardon for Louis Riel from Ottawa.

Alberta. Syncrude opens a plant to produce crude oil from the Athabasca Tar Sands.

Newfoundland. L'Anse aux Meadows, the first authentic site of Viking explorations in North America, is made a United Nations World Heritage Site. It is located on the northern tip Newfoundland's Great Northern Peninsula.

Gazette celebrates its 200th birthday

June 3, 1978

MONTREAL – Employees of *The Gazette,* some of them wearing period costumes, gathered tonight in a renovated house in the Old Quarter to celebrate the daily newspaper's 200th anniversary. Editor Mark Harrison did his best to dress like American Benjamin Franklin, who brought Fleury Mesplet and his hand-operated press here to publicize the Revolution. When the Americans fled, so did Franklin, but Mesplet stayed on to put out a four-page French weekly. English articles began appearing in 1822, and *The Montreal Gazette* became a daily in 1853. In 1968, the White family, which had owned the paper for almost 100 years, sold *The Gazette* to Southam Press.

Business booms at Potash Corporation

April 1, 1978

REGINA – The Saskatchewan government is making bigger profits on potash. The new provincial Crown company Potash Corporation of Saskatchewan now owns 32 percent of the productive capacity of potash mines in the province, and has tentatively bought 60 percent ownership in mines that control another 11 percent of capacity.

In his report for the fiscal year ending yesterday, Minister of Natural Resources John Messer said provincial revenues from potash production totalled $99.8 million, up 21.6 percent from the previous year. Messer said that sales outside the continent increased by about 40 percent, due mainly to renewed interest in potash in India and Japan. Last year there was a record production of 6.7 million tons of the mineral, used mainly as fertilizer.

Gay given custody of his two children

March 21, 1978

OTTAWA – In a precedent-setting decision, an Ottawa County Court judge today awarded custody of two children to their homosexual father, a 37-year-old businessman from Montreal. Judge Elmer Smith declared him "the parent with the most meaningful emotional ties with the children," an eight-year-old girl and a 13-year-old boy. The ruling overturns an interim divorce decree that granted the mother custody. In making the decision, Smith admitted having a hard time "determining at what point sexual preference becomes significant" in custody battles and that the father's non-aggressive lifestyle as a homosexual was a factor.

Jones-Konihowski pentathlon winner

Diane Jones-Konihowski wins the second heat of the 100-metre hurdles.

Aug. 6, 1978

EDMONTON – Canada's Diane Jones-Konihowski, with a record 4,768 points, won the pentathlon today at the Commonwealth Games. She won the high jump, long jump, shot put, and hurdles, and was second to fellow-Canadian Jill Ross of London in the 800 metres, for a total surpassed only once in international competition. The Soviet Union's Nadyezhda Tkachenko had 4,839 points in 1977. Jones-Konihowski, 27, beat the second-place finisher in the pentathlon by 546 points.

Quebec gets bigger say on immigration

Feb. 20, 1978

MONTREAL – Quebec will have greater control over immigration under an agreement signed with Ottawa here today. The province will have final approval of most immigrants and a new system will favor those who speak French or who can be easily assimilated into French-speaking society. Today's deal, under negotiation for almost a year, is the third of its kind in recent years. Under the British North America Act, immigration is a joint responsibility of the federal and provincial governments. Quebec's desire for increased powers over immigration stems from the need to attract immigrants willing to stay in the province on a permanent basis. Most immigrants who came to Quebec over the last 20 years assimilated into the English-speaking community. Now, they, too, are joining the exodus of anglophones leaving the province. Immigrants willing to assimilate into Quebec's French-speaking society, however, will help counter the province's declining birthrate.

Postal workers set to return to work

Oct. 25, 1978

OTTAWA – After a week of defiance, postal workers have decided to obey back-to-work legislation passed by the federal government. The compliance came only after the RCMP raided several offices of the Canadian Union of Postal Workers and charged five of its leaders with disobeying the Public Service Staff Relations Act. Speaking in the House, Justice Minister Otto Lang said that the charges will be prosecuted, even though the strike is over.

Adding to the iron fist of the government is its threat to fire any postal workers who are not back to work by midnight tonight. CUPW president Jean-Claude Parrot said the union decided to give in because "we don't consider this to be a bluff." The standoff started two days after the postal workers went out on strike, after 18 months of fruitless negotiations with the federal government.

Basque ship from 16th century found

Sept. 1, 1978

RED BAY, Nfld. – Divers today discovered what they believe are the remains of the *San Juan,* a Basque whaling vessel that sank in 1535. If they are correct, it provides an important missing link in Canadian history.

Research shows that in the 16th century the Basques, from the southeast corner of the Bay of Biscay on the France-Spain border, fished in the waters of what is now Canada. The *San Juan,* found here on the south coast of Labrador just north of the tip of Newfoundland island, is a significant indication of the Basque activity. Robert Grenier, a Parks Canada employee, and his team found the wreck after only three days of searching. Archeological remains of Basque whaling stations have been found on the shores of Red Bay and documents recently unearthed in Spanish archives pinpointed the wreck's location. The documents concerned a legal dispute about the ownership of the whale oil the *San Juan* carried. The discovery of the 300-ton *San Juan* is said to be the earliest archeological find in Canadian waters. Until very recently, the Basque connection to Canada was only vaguely realized. Now it is thought that the seasonal Basque outpost at Red Bay maintained a population of 500 or 600 in the 16th century. Grenier wants to bring the *San Juan,* piece by piece, to the surface next year, if he can get federal government funding.

Majolica earthenware jug.

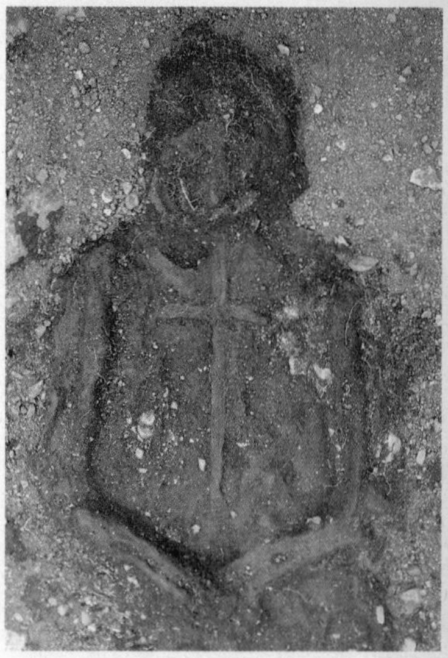

Remains of a whaler.

Greenpeace to launch new protest ship

The Greenpeace international protest ship, the Rainbow Warrior.

1978

ENGLAND – Greenpeace expects its newest protest ship, the *Rainbow Warrior,* to be on the high seas this summer, off on a mission in the north Atlantic to intercept the Icelandic whaling fleet.

Not long ago, following pained discussions with European whalers, Greenpeace activist Robert Hunter, a major voice in the movement to protect whales, was invited to appear on a Dutch television station to solicit funds for Greenpeace to purchase a 50-metre trawler, the *Sir William Hardy.* The campaign was successful. After buying the trawler, Greenpeace converted the vessel into a protest ship and rebaptized it the *Rainbow Warrior.*

Once plentiful caplin stock is on decline

1978

NEWFOUNDLAND – For decades, tiny caplin fish inundated the beaches of Conception Bay. They piled on the banks in multitudes, converting the shore into a spongy knee-thick layer of eggs. Folk came from all around, scooping caplin by the bucketful until their horses could barely haul the loads. Incredibly, this opulence has been decimated by commercial fishing to near extinction of the caplin. The depletion of the offshore stock has shifted fisheries to pilfer inshore stock. The caplin is a main food source of sea birds. The continual decline of the tiny fish has created deficiencies that are influencing the stability of bird colonies.

Queen Elizabeth, PM Trudeau and Prince Philip at Commonwealth Games.

1979

Ottawa, Jan. 25. The Pepin-Robarts Task Force on Canadian Unity makes its report, recommending an overhaul of the federal system to reflect regional diversity and special powers for Quebec.

Montreal, May 21. Montreal Canadiens defeat New York Rangers four games to one to win the Stanley Cup.

Charlottetown, April 23. The Conservatives led by J. Angus MacLean defeat the Liberal government of Bennett Campbell in a provincial election, the last Liberal provincial government left in Canada.

St. John's, Nfld., June 18. Premier Brian Peckford wins his first election as Newfoundland Conservative leader as the Conservatives retain power.

Canada, June 22. The World Hockey Association officially disbands after seven seasons. Edmonton, Hartford, Quebec, and Winnipeg are taken into the NHL.

Ontario, June 28. Atomic Energy of Canada introduces the Therascan, a Canadian-invented brain scanner that shows how the brain functions, a revolutionary advance in brain scanning.

Ontario, Sept. 6. Archeologists are studying the remains of perhaps the last complete Neutral Indian village, a 3.6-hectare camp near Thorold. The Iroquois wiped out the Neutral Confederacy in 1651.

Montreal, Sept. 25. The Montreal *Star* closes its doors after 110 years of publication.

Ottawa, Sept. 26. A Canadian Human Rights Commission study concludes that tolerance of homosexuality is more widespread in Canada than tolerance of different political opinions.

Ottawa, Oct. 15. A team of Canadian and U.S. scientists reports for the first time that acid rain is damaging vegetable crops and forests. The situation is called "almost irreversible."

Montreal, Nov. 25. Edmonton Eskimos defeat Montreal Alouettes 17-9 for the Grey Cup.

Ottawa, Dec. 13. PM Joe Clark's Conservative government is defeated in the Commons on a non-confidence motion against its first budget.

Ottawa, Dec. 18. Pierre Trudeau announces he will postpone his retirement and lead the Liberals in the next election.

Schreyer sworn in as governor general

New Governor General Ed Schreyer.

Jan. 17, 1979

OTTAWA – Edward Schreyer, former New Democrat premier of Manitoba, was sworn in today as Canada's 22nd governor general. Schreyer, who at 43 is considered a relatively young man for this job, set the stage of his five-year term at Rideau Hall by taking a shot at Quebec separatists. He said there is "a minority view that does not acknowledge that in an enlightened federal Canada there is scope for the fullest expression of cultural and linguistic heritage."

Schreyer takes over from Jules Léger, who has had trouble performing his duties since 1974, when a stroke left him with impaired speech. Schreyer is expected to be populist in his approach to the vice-regal office.

Bilingual air traffic control safe: report

Jan. 4, 1979

OTTAWA – Bilingual air traffic control is not a hazard, the federal Transport Department has concluded, three years after the subject caused a bitter language debate and disruption of air traffic.

At that time, English pilots argued that expanded bilingual air traffic control proposed by the Trudeau government would be unsafe. The transport report, conducted for a commission of inquiry, refutes that claim, and says bilingual air traffic control may even be safer than English-only. The study was based on 18 months of tests simulating air traffic over Dorval and Mirabel airports, which both serve Montreal.

The report states that bilingual services can be introduced at these airports within 11 weeks of receiving final approval. However, it could take as long as eight years before the services are in effect provincewide, partly because the Transport Department's plan also calls for the expansion of airspace controlled by Quebec. The total cost of implementing the services will be about $12 million.

Peckford triumphs at Tory leadership convention in Nfld.

March 19, 1979

ST. JOHN'S, Nfld. – Brian Peckford has become the third premier of Newfoundland since the province joined Confederation in 1949. With a good organization behind him, Peckford, a 36-year-old former school teacher, has won the leadership of Newfoundland's Progressive Conservative party. With former premier Frank Moores recently retiring from office, Peckford's victory at the PC convention not only makes him party leader, but the province's premier.

Peckford's been in politics seven years and has always been an energetic and vigorous member. He was minister of mines and energy in Moores' administration. He is committed to provincial rights in general and to the development of the offshore gas and oil resources for the benefit of this province.

After the results of the first ballot, Peckford led with 200 votes to Bill Doody's 157, Walter Carter's 87, Leo Barry's 84, Jim Morgan's 56, Ed Maynard's 26, Tom Hickey's 24, and Ralph Trask's two. Kenneth Prowse and Dorothy Wyatt were shut out. Peckford forged ahead on the second ballot, and on the third he got 331 votes, defeating his two remaining rivals. Moores did not publicly support any candidate, but came onto the stage at the end and congratulated Peckford.

The cat came back the very next year

Jan. 30, 1979

VERNON, B.C. – Nouchka the cat disappeared last August in the East Kootenay region, escaping from the Schellenberg family car. This week, a scratching was heard at the door of the Schellenberg home here, 525 highway kilometres away from the last point Nouchka was seen. Yes, they thought it was a goner, but the cat came back, almost six months later and having crossed some of the heaviest mountain country in Canada. Shocked but purrfectly pleased, the Schellenbergs greeted her with open arms.

The presence of sod houses such as these vividly illustrates Newfoundland's early European settlement, when Vikings established communities here.

Anti-Ottawa approach sparks Lougheed

March 14, 1979

CALGARY – Premier Peter Lougheed vowed to continue his fight for provincial rights after voters returned him with his largest majority yet. "I do not think all the decision-making in Canada should be done in Ottawa and Toronto," he said here tonight. Results of today's election give Lougheed's Conservatives 74 seats, the Social Credit four, and the NDP one. The lone NDP member is leader Grant Notley, whose party ran a surprising second in all 18 Edmonton ridings. Social Credit leader Bob Clark said Lougheed's anti-Ottawa attitude won him the mandate. "The people of Alberta strongly endorse the premier's fight with Ottawa," he said.

Peter Lougheed celebrates victory with son Joe and wife Jeanne.

Trudeau vows to bring back Constitution

May 9, 1979

TORONTO – Prime Minister Pierre Trudeau has vowed to bring the Constitution back to Canada even if he has to go to the people with a national referendum, despite any provincial objections. He pledged this before a capacity crowd of 16,000 people in Maple Leaf Gardens, while 3,000 others holding tickets were prevented from entering. The Liberals had printed 100,000 tickets and distributed many in schools, advertising that the prime minister's appearance would precede a concert with ethnic, rock and country-western bands.

Trudeau speaks to Toronto rally.

Trudeau says Canada is the only country in the world that is unable to amend its own constitution, and he's making this the main issue in these last days of the general election campaign.

Chanting "Trudeau, Trudeau, Trudeau," the crowd responded enthusiastically to criticism of Tory leader Joe Clark, a pledge of equality for women, and the promise a Liberal government would ensure Alberta shares its profits from oil resources. But Trudeau may have a tough time keeping tonight's promises, if elected; none of Canada's 10 provincial governments are Liberal.

Minority win for Tories

Joe Clark and wife Maureen McTeer wave to supporters.

June 4, 1979

OTTAWA – Two weeks ago, Prime Minister Joe Clark vowed to make national unity his priority. After an election that left Parliament deeply divided on regional and linguistic lines, he has his work cut out for him. At least he'll be starting fresh. Today, he unveiled the first Conservative cabinet in 16 years and it contains a lot of new young faces.

Clark, who will be 40 tomorrow, ignored the old guard in appointing the ministers sworn in today. Only two have previous cabinet experience. One of the most powerful of the new ministers is Flora MacDonald, the first woman to hold a post as senior as external affairs. The new labor minister, Lincoln Alexander, is the first black in a federal cabinet.

The May 22 election gave Clark's Conservatives 136 seats, Pierre Trudeau's Liberals 114, the NDP 26, and the Social Credit six. Clark will have only two members from Quebec to back his minority government, but he has said that in supporting the Liberals, Quebecers voted for a strong federalism and "I pledge to make it work, to make it grow and to keep this Canada together." Both Quebec Tory MPs have been named to cabinet posts.

Judgment has English-only law in doubt

April 26, 1979

WINNIPEG – In a judgment that may have far-reaching implications, a $5 parking ticket has been ruled invalid because it was printed in English only. Chief Justice Samuel Freedman of the Manitoba Court of Appeal said in a judgment released today that the English-only ticket contravened the constitutional deal that brought Manitoba into Confederation in 1870. Freedman ruled unconstitutional Manitoba's Official Language Act, as it applies to court proceedings. That law, passed in 1890, established English as the only official language in the province. But Freedman ruled the two-language provisions of the Manitoba Act of 1870 clearly take precedence.

Freedman's ruling will undoubtedly be appealed to the Supreme Court of Canada. If it is upheld, it may mean all Manitoba laws since 1890 are technically invalid. More importantly, one provision of the Manitoba law is similar to a section of Quebec's Bill 101 limiting the use of English in courts and setting French as the only language in which laws need be written.

PQ convention OKs 2-referendum plan

June 3, 1979

QUEBEC CITY – Full Quebec independence would take at least two referendums, the Parti Québécois has decided. At its convention here today, the PQ said a positive vote in a referendum on independence would lead to talks with Canada on economic association. If those negotiations failed, the PQ would hold another referendum before unilateral separation. Finance Minister Jacques Parizeau, a separatist hard-liner, said the so-called "hyphen policy" was necessary to ensure the clearest possible mandate for independence.

Acid rain labelled a serious problem

July 13, 1979

OTTAWA – Environment Minister John Fraser says acid rain is the most serious problem Canada has ever faced. Prime Minister Joe Clark says it is a priority issue. And a report by the Great Lakes Water Quality Board states that unless sulphur dioxide, the main antagonist in acid rain, is not reduced, extensive, irreversible damage will occur in 10 to 15 years.

Another report by the Great Lakes advisory board indicates that all parts of the Great Lakes receive up to 40 times more acid than found in natural precipitation.

Silent screen star Mary Pickford dies

May 29, 1979

HOLLYWOOD – Star of the silent screen and North America's sweetheart of the 1920s, Toronto-born Mary Pickford died today in a Santa Monica hospital at age 86. She'll be remembered by millions of fans around the world as the innocent little girl with golden curls. Soon after the arrival of talking pictures, Mary Pickford quit while she was ahead, retiring to the mansion she shared with her second husband, Douglas Fairbanks Sr. She reapplied for and got her Canadian citizenship in 1978.

Power flows from James Bay project

Oct. 27, 1979

LA GRANDE, Que. – Lights stayed on but television screens went blank as the first electricity surged from the James Bay project. Quebec Premier René Lévesque turned a switch here this afternoon to connect the $15.1-billion project to the province's power grid. As he did, a technician's mistake denied television viewers the planned live coverage of the ceremony.

Only one generator went into production today, but over the next year 15 more will make this power station the second largest in the world. When Phase I is complete in 1985, it will produce the equivalent of 16 nuclear reactors the size of the Pickering plant in Ontario. Further phases will double that capacity. "This is a grand day for Quebec and a tribute to our expertise," Lévesque said. "Quebec can now choose, in all serenity, its energy and political future."

Lévesque paid tribute to former premier Robert Bourassa, who attended the ceremony, for initiating the James Bay project in 1971. Bourassa said Quebec should develop all its hydroelectric resources as quickly as possible. It could then export large surpluses and invest the profits in an Alberta-style Heritage Fund. Lévesque said the province is willing to export more energy, but Quebec needs take priority. Quebec Natural Resources Minister Yves Berubé said the huge projects allows the province to postpone decisions on nuclear power for at least six years.

Quebec Premier René Lévesque flips switch to open the James Bay plant.

Diefenbaker dies preparing for session

Former PM John Diefenbaker.

Aug. 16, 1979

OTTAWA – The Chief died just as he said he would – working. John Diefenbaker, 83, rose at 5 this morning and went to his study to organize papers for a parliamentary session. At 7 a.m. he was found dead, the papers still in his hand. The Prince Albert MP was first elected in 1940 and was prime minister from 1957 to 1963, leading his party to the greatest electoral triumph in Canadian history in 1958. His leadership was often controversial, but no one denied his sincerity in sticking up for the little guy. He considered the Canadian Bill of Rights his greatest achievement.

All-weather road spans Arctic Circle

Aug. 18, 1979

ARCTIC CIRCLE – The 645-kilometre Dempster Highway, Canada's first all-weather road across the Arctic Circle, is officially open. Starting in Dawson City on the Yukon River, it ends in Inuvik on the Mackenzie River Delta. The completion of the road is seen as the final symbolic act in former prime minister John Diefenbaker's Conservative government's Northern Vision Road to Resources program, started in 1959 and ridiculed by the Liberals as building roads "from igloo to igloo."

Convention delegates hope to attain provincial status for Acadia

Oct. 8, 1979

EDMUNDSTON, N.B. – Delegates at a convention organized by the Society of New Brunswick Acadians today made it clear they want new political status for Acadia – but within a Canadian context and not as part of Quebec. Forty-eight percent of delegates favor provincial status for Acadia, while four percent support joining Quebec. New Brunswick's 223,780 Acadians are worried by calls for Maritime union and Quebec separation: the former would decrease political representation and the latter would emphasize their position as a French-speaking minority.

First gold bullion coin goes on sale

Sept. 6, 1979

WINNIPEG – Canada's first gold bullion coin, made here at the Royal Canadian Mint, went on sale today. Eventually 5 million of the $50 face value coins will be minted over the next three years – all from domestic gold. That's because the government is making these coins with an eye to stimulating gold mining in Canada.

Despite the $50 face value, the actual price of the one-ounce gold coin will sit slightly higher than the world price, currently $329 US an ounce. On one side there is a maple leaf. On the other, a portrait of Queen Elizabeth II.

Gas leak remedied; citizens head home

Nov. 16, 1979

MISSISSAUGA, Ont. – All of the 250,000 residents evacuated from this area are being allowed to return home, now that the remaining chlorine has been drained from a derailed railway tank car. The news ends six days of disruption for Mississauga residents and for their businesses. Mississauga businesses are estimated to have lost $40 million worth of revenue due to the evacuation. The massive evacuation was ordered after the CP Rail car jumped the tracks and started leaking lethal chlorine gas. An inquiry will be held later.

Woodcarver Nelphas Prévost uses symbols representing the sky and earth to decorate his work.

PQ referendum question made public

The cartoonist's interpretation of René Lévesque's political theories as a referendum is introduced.

Dec. 20, 1979

QUEBEC CITY – The Parti Québécois government today unveiled the wording of its sovereignty-association referendum. Opponents immediately decried the text as unfair.

The referendum question is a full four paragraphs, setting out what the government means by sovereignty-association. An agreement between Quebec and the rest of Canada "would enable Quebec to acquire the exclusive power to make its laws, administer its taxes and establish relations abroad – in other words, sovereignty – and at the same time, to maintain with Canada an economic association including a common currency." Voters are asked to agree or disagree on giving the Quebec government a mandate to negotiate such an agreement.

Liberal leader Claude Ryan denounced the wording as confusing and fraudulent. The referendum wording also promises a second referendum asking the electorate whether they agree with the results of the negotiations.

"Do you have a readable broad outline of the incredible cultural awakening and overt striving for nationhood which has wracked Quebec in the past decade... in English...?"

English-speaking Canadians have problems understanding Quebec nationalism. One of the major difficulties is the language barrier.

1980

Tehran, Jan. 28. Canadian ambassador Ken Taylor engineers the escape from Iran of six Americans who have been in hiding since Iranian revolutionaries seized the American embassy three months ago and took 66 hostages.

Ottawa, Feb. 29. PM Trudeau announces the appointment of Jeanne Sauvé as Speaker of the Commons, the first woman to hold this position in Canada.

Quebec, March 20. The Parti Québécois-dominated legislature approves the wording for the upcoming referendum on Quebec sovereignty.

St. John's, Nfld., April 12. One-legged runner Terry Fox begins his Marathon of Hope, a cross-Canada run to raise money and generate publicity for cancer research.

United States, April 30. Fifty-two-year-old Gordie Howe of the Hartford Whalers announces his retirement from hockey. He holds the NHL records for most games, most goals, assists and points.

New York, May 24. New York Islanders defeat Philadelphia Flyers four games to two to win the Stanley Cup.

Newfoundland, July 21. The province's fishing industry is completely shut down by strikes, lockouts, and layoffs, leaving 35,000 without work.

Canada, Aug. 27. Southam Inc. closes the Winnipeg *Tribune* and Thomson Newspapers closes the Ottawa *Journal*. The companies say both papers have been losing money.

Ottawa, Oct. 2. PM Trudeau announces his intention to entrench, unilaterally through Parliament, a constitution embracing a Charter of Rights and a domestic amending formula.

Canada, Oct. 23. The *Globe and Mail* prints its new national edition using satellite communications, a first for a Canadian newspaper.

Toronto, Nov. 23. Edmonton Eskimos defeat Hamilton Tiger-Cats 48-10 to win the Grey Cup.

Northwest Territories, Dec. 1. An Inuit-run TV station beaming Inuktitut-language programs to the eastern Arctic officially opens.

Varna, Bulgaria. Evelyn Hart of the Royal Winnipeg Ballet wins the women's solo gold medal at the Varna International Ballet Competition.

Problems dog Clark's Conservatives

Jan. 21, 1980

TORONTO – Prime Minister Joe Clark gets a "bum rap" among the electorate, but the Conservatives themselves are to blame. Communications Minister David MacDonald today gave his candid views of the problems dogging the Conservatives as they seek re-election.

When they became government last year, the Conservatives forgot why they had been elected, MacDonald said. "We became a government essentially because the people wanted to get rid of Trudeau. We have had to, in effect, prove our credentials in office and that has been no easy task."

The result has been that Clark is portrayed as a weak, ineffectual leader who broke most of the promises he made in the last campaign. Polls show the Conservatives trailing Pierre Trudeau's Liberals by about 20 percent as the Feb. 18 election approaches. "We forgot some of the basic rules of politics," MacDonald said. "We allowed ourselves to get defensive about things that we shouldn't have spent a great deal of time being defensive about." The minority Conservative government has spent most of its time dealing with matters left over from the previous Liberal administration. Only three Conservative bills have moved past first reading and only one of these has become law. As he campaigns, voters at almost every meeting remind Clark of his government's record. Clark said he would govern "as if with a majority." On the campaign trail, he attributes his problems to his government's minority position.

Revamped immigration law harder on American draft dodgers

Feb. 8, 1980

WINNIPEG – Changes in Canada's immigration laws will make it harder for U.S. draft resisters to settle in Canada, Prime Minister Joe Clark said on a campaign stop.

Clark said the new law requires all would-be immigrants to apply for entry to Canada from their country of origin. Canada would accept conscientious objectors, but not those seeking to avoid the draft proposed by President Jimmy Carter. Clark was reacting to comments by External Affairs Minister Flora MacDonald that draft evaders would not be welcome here. During the Vietnam War, draft dodgers could apply for landed immigrant status from within Canada.

U.S. army deserters such as these will find it more difficult to enter Canada.

Another Voice, by Rick Hill. Iroquois tradition names clans after animals. The artist's son is shown here as a member of his mother's Bear Clan.

New Year's blaze claims at least 42

Jan. 1, 1980

CHAPAIS, Que. – Police say a fire that broke out during a New Year's Eve party in a community hall here, taking at least 42 lives, was "definitely of criminal origin." Fifty people are being treated for severe burns, and 30 children have been orphaned by the blaze at Le Club Opemiska in this remote copper mining town. The tragedy started when flames engulfed dry fir branches in a huge ceiling arch. Witnesses among the 400 guests report seeing a reveller showing off his cigarette lighter by trying to set fire to the arch. Police are holding a young man as a material witness.

Silverheels played Tonto on TV series

Jay Silverheels as Tonto.

March 5, 1980

HOLLYWOOD – Canadian-born Jay Silverheels, who played the Lone Ranger's sidekick Tonto in the television series, has died of pneumonia at the age of 62. The Mohawk Indian from the Six Nations reserve at Brantford, Ont., co-starred with Clayton Moore in the long-running Lone Ranger series. Silverheels was the founder of the Indian Actors Workshop and the first North American Indian with a star on Hollywood's Walk of Fame.

He's back: Trudeau elected next PM

Feb. 18, 1980

OTTAWA – Joe Clark's nine-month reign as prime minister ended tonight. And Pierre Trudeau staged one of the most impressive comebacks in Canadian political history. Late returns show Trudeau's Liberals with a majority government, 148 seats to the Conservatives' 101 and the NDP's 32.

Trudeau, who only three months ago resigned as Liberal leader but stayed on when the election was called, picked up seats in the Maritimes, Quebec, and Ontario. The NDP lost ground from Ontario to the east but did much better than expected on the prairies and in B.C. Liberals won 48 percent of the popular vote. Trudeau's major problem is that his party won only two seats west of Ontario and the biggest issue is the confrontation between Ottawa and Alberta over energy pricing. Clark's proposal for higher energy prices was unpopular in consuming provinces.

Supporters pin a rose on Pierre Trudeau during the victory celebration.

Liberals say nyet to Moscow Olympics: Canada to join boycott

April 22, 1980

OTTAWA – Canada will join an international movement to boycott the Olympic Games in Moscow in retaliation for the Soviet Union's invasion of Afghanistan, the Liberal government announced today. Canadian athletes will not be forbidden to go on their own, but they will receive no financial support from the government.

External Affairs Minister Mark MacGuigan called it "wholly inappropriate" to hold the Olympics in Moscow in light of the Soviet action in Afghanistan, which began four months ago. Dick Pound, president of the Canadian Olympic Association, said the U.S.-led boycott is flagrantly using the Olympics for political purposes. Canada's Diane Jones-Konihowski, a strong pentathlon competitor, also opposed the decision and still hopes to compete.

Ottawa pays $2.7B for F-18 jet fighters

April 9, 1980

OTTAWA – The federal cabinet today gave a $2.7-billion contract to the U.S. aircraft maker McDonnell Douglas Corp. for 137 twin-engine F-18 Hornet fighters. The cabinet turned aside a last-minute bid by General Dynamics, whose F-16 was the other plane competing to be the fighter Canadian airmen will fly till the end of the century. The selection process has dragged on since 1977. Ottawa says the total payout will climb to $4 billion when all the planes have been delivered by 1989, because the new aircraft require hangars, flight simulators, and weaponry.

Peggy's Cove Lighthouse on the south shore of Nova Scotia.

Governments help to bail out Chrysler

May 10, 1980

OTTAWA – Chrysler Corp. and its sister company Chrysler of Canada have been given a new lease on life with loan guarantees and subsidies from three levels of government. After warning signals that Chrysler, an automobile-manufacturing firm with a 54-year history, would run out of money by the end of the month, the U.S. government came through with $1.5 billion in federal loan guarantees. Ottawa has agreed to $200 million in loan guarantees and Ontario has pledged a $10-million subsidy. The automaker has lost market shares on both sides of the border.

Cancer stops Fox's Marathon of Hope

Terry Fox as he left St. John's.

Sept. 2, 1980

NEW WESTMINSTER, B.C. – Runner Terry Fox has had to end his Marathon of Hope and begin his second grim battle against cancer. Three years ago, cancer forced the amputation of his right leg above the knee. His coast-to-coast marathon to raise funds for cancer research came to an end in Thunder Bay when doctors diagnosed the cancer had spread to his lungs. He told reporters in Thunder Bay after getting the test results: "It's an unbelievable shock. I really didn't think this could happen."

The 22-year-old British Columbian was then flown home in a chartered aircraft and immediately taken to hospital in this Vancouver suburb. The Marathon of Hope has raised $2 million since the runner set out in St. John's on April 12.

Terry Fox and his mother Betty.

Quebec voters say "yes" to Canada

May 22, 1980

MONTREAL – Canada won and René Lévesque lost. "This hurts me more than any election defeat. I know of what I speak," the Quebec premier told supporters tonight after Quebecers strongly rejected sovereignty-association.

About 60 percent of the referendum total voted not to give the Quebec government a mandate to negotiate sovereignty-association with the rest of Canada. These appeared to include a slight majority of francophone voters. It was a particular defeat for Lévesque, who softened the referendum question to make it more palatable. The government asked for a mandate only to negotiate, not to declare independence. If it had won this referendum another would have been held on results of the negotiations.

Prime Minister Pierre Trudeau said tonight the referendum showed the maturity of Quebec voters. But he warned against premature rejoicing. Fully 40 percent voted to renegotiate Confederation. "We have all lost a little in this referendum. If you take account of the broken friendships, the strained family relationships, the hurt pride, there is no one among us who has not suffered some wound which we must try to heal in the days and weeks to come."

Lévesque was bitter about the "scandalous, immoral" Ottawa intervention in the campaign. But he said the results must be accepted as a victory for the federalists.

Two sides of the sovereignty issue are illustrated on this "house divided."

Trudeau details views on new constitution

Prime Minister Pierre Trudeau.

May 21, 1980

OTTAWA – Prime Minister Pierre Trudeau has told Canadians his bottom-line position on a new constitution: a federal parliament with real powers applying to the whole country; provincial parliaments with powers no less real in their own territories; and a charter of rights and freedoms, including language rights. He was given sustained applause in the Commons from MPs, including the leaders of both opposition parties, when he ended a half-hour statement by declaring, "For us, everything else is negotiable." Asked if a constitutional conference could be set for July, he said he couldn't be specific.

O Canada made national anthem

June 27, 1980

OTTAWA – *O Canada.* At last it's officially our national anthem. That status was declared by Parliament today and a proclamation to the same effect by Gov. Gen. Ed Schreyer on Dominion Day will be greeted by a fanfare of trumpets. There were minor revisions in the English lyrics of the anthem but the French words remain unchanged. The National Anthem Act took less than an hour to complete after all three House leaders agreed to limit debate on the issue. To mark the occasion of the act's passing, MPs stood and sang the anthem.

Alberta and Saskatchewan raise price of crude oil $2 a barrel

Aug. 1, 1980

EDMONTON – First Alberta and then Saskatchewan announced a $2 increase in the price of a barrel of crude oil. The increases come after Prime Minister Pierre Trudeau and Alberta Premier Peter Lougheed were unable to come to an agreement last week over pricing and revenue-sharing negotiations. However, the federal government will not oppose the increase. The wellhead price of a barrel of Alberta and Saskatchewan crude is still $16.75 less than average U.S. prices and $20 less than world prices.

Of the $2 increase, the provinces will receive 90 cents, the companies 90 cents, and the federal government 20 cents. When the increase takes effect 60 days from now, consumers will be paying an extra 1.5 cents per litre for gasoline and heating oil.

No deal reached in constitutional talks

Sept. 13, 1980

OTTAWA – The premiers of all 10 provinces have apparently failed to reach an agreement on a large number of issues leading to constitutional reform, after a week of talks. They came out of a private negotiating session last night with Prime Minister Pierre Trudeau, and sources say they can agree on only three or four items on the 12-point agenda. Today, however, a testy, tired, and angry prime minister wound up the conference and admitted failure. He plans to meet with his caucus within the week to decide what action Ottawa should take by itself.

All summer, Trudeau and federal officials have warned that should the premiers fail to agree on a package of constitutional reforms, Ottawa might have to take unilateral action before the end of this year. "That's still my wish," the prime minister said when asked at the end of the conference about his deadline. "My wishes and desires have not changed since 1968."

Premiers split on Constitution's fate

Oct. 13, 1980

TORONTO – The provincial premiers seem unable to forge a common position on the package Prime Minister Pierre Trudeau wants on the Constitution. The Canadian premiers were converging in Toronto tonight for new emergency talks. But they seem to have separated into three camps in their opinions expressed since Ottawa announced its intention to patriate the British North America Act with an amending formula.

All alone is William Davis of Ontario, who wholeheartedly backs the prime minister. Then there are the premiers who, for different reasons, have pledged all-out efforts to stop unilateral federal action. This group includes the premiers of Quebec, Newfoundland, Nova Scotia, Prince Edward Island, Alberta, and Manitoba.

Somewhere in between, apparently trying to find a middle ground, are Saskatchewan's Allan Blakeney, New Brunswick's Richard Hatfield, and William Bennett of British Columbia.

Lesage the father of Quiet Revolution

Dec. 11, 1980

QUEBEC CITY – The father of the Quiet Revolution is dead. Jean Lesage, former lawyer and Liberal premier from 1960 to 1966, has died of cancer at 68. Lesage became leader of the Quebec Liberals in 1958 after 13 years as a federal MP. His impact was immediate and profound. With a series of social and political reforms, he eliminated corruption and patronage and created ministries for education and cultural affairs.

Starvation blamed as scores of ponies die

August 1980

SABLE ISLAND, N.S. – A recent survey conducted by the Canadian Wildlife Service shows that more than half of the ponies on Sable Island died last winter, apparently of starvation. The die-off supports a theory by scientists that there is only enough natural food on the sand-spit to feed roughly 200 of the ponies. The population, before last winter, had risen to 359. Wild herds have roamed Sable for more than three centuries and are thought to have originated from shipwrecks in the area.

The Burgess Shale fossil site has been placed on the UN Heritage List.

Greenpeace vessel in daring escape

Greenpeace sailor David McTaggart.

Nov. 8, 1980

VANCOUVER – Members of Greenpeace have learned that the Greenpeace ship *Rainbow Warrior* has escaped from the Spanish port of El Ferro, where she was being held by the Spanish armed forces.

Rainbow Warrior was forced into port in June by Spanish naval vessels and its crew was accused of obstructing Spanish whalers and of aiding a school of whales to escape. Fines of $142,000 were levied against the ship's captain, Jonathan Castle, and the ship was held in El Ferro. Spanish naval engineers then disabled the *Rainbow Warrior* by removing a propellor shaft bearing. But the ship's crew, working secretly, managed to fit a substitute bearing so the propulsion system could work again.

Then, at night, when the Spanish guards were relaxing, *Rainbow Warrior* slipped her mooring, started her engine, and sailed out to sea – and international waters.

Marshall McLuhan, media guru, dies

Dec. 31, 1980

TORONTO – Canadian scholar Marshall McLuhan died today. Deeply literate, undoubtedly revolutionary, often misunderstood, McLuhan's contribution to communications theory's been compared to the work of Freud and Darwin for its universal importance.

A professor at the University of Toronto, McLuhan established a worldwide reputation with *Understanding Media* (1964), which studied the changes in human perceptions caused by electronic communications such as TV. "The medium is the message," he stated, meaning the form of communication determines the way information is perceived and interpreted. McLuhan also coined the phrase the "global village" to describe the electronic interdependence of today's world.

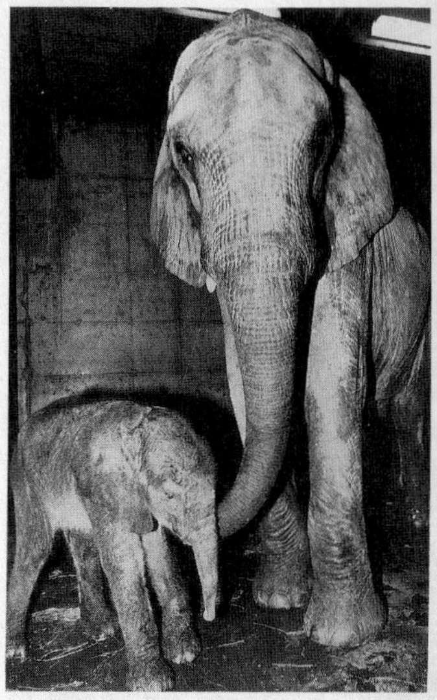

As of Oct. 18 Toronto boasts the western hemisphere's fourth African elephant born in captivity.

1981

Ottawa, March 23. The Supreme Court rules that Saskatchewan resident André Mercure has the right to be tried on a speeding charge in French, overturning a Saskatchewan court decision.

New York, May 21. New York Islanders defeat Minnesota North Stars four games to one to win the Stanley Cup.

Labrador, July 15. Evidence is found that a secret German naval mission landed on the Labrador coast in 1943 and established an automatic weather station.

Montreal, Sept. 13. The Soviet Union defeats Canada 8-1 to win the Canada Cup, the first time Canada has lost the cup.

Ottawa, Sept. 25. The post office announces increased postal rates, including raising the first class postage in Canada from $0.17 to $0.30, effective Jan. 1, 1982.

Baden Baden, West Germany, Sept. 30. The International Olympic Committee announces that Calgary will be the site of the 1988 Winter Olympics.

Ottawa, Nov. 5. PM Trudeau and the premiers of all the provinces except Quebec reach an agreement for the patriation of the Constitution.

Montreal, Nov. 22. Edmonton Eskimos defeat Ottawa Rough Riders 26-23 in the Grey Cup.

Ottawa, Dec. 8. The Senate votes in favor of the constitutional package and it is sent to Britain for final approval by Parliament.

Ottawa, Dec. 16. The government announces it is setting aside more than $4 billion and huge tracts of land in the Yukon and N.W.T. in hopes of settling native land claims there by 1985.

Edmonton, Dec. 27. Wayne Gretzky of the Edmonton Oilers scores five goals in a game against Philadelphia, giving him 50 goals in 39 games, shattering Maurice Richard's long-standing NHL record of 50 goals in 50 games.

Canada, Dec. 31. Inflation hits a 33-year high in 1981.

Toronto. Lawren Harris' *South Shore, Baffin Island* is sold for $240,000, a record price for a Canadian painting.

United States. Reports suggest the appearance of an alarming new disease, common in homosexuals, that appears to destroy the body's immune system [AIDS].

Aboriginal, treaty rights recognized

Natives protest for treaty rights.

Jan. 30, 1981

OTTAWA – Aboriginal leaders are greeting with cautious optimism a series of constitutional changes the federal government has agreed to include in its patriation package. The principal provision to be added to the new Canadian Constitution is an assertion that "the aboriginal and treaty rights" of the aboriginal people of Canada are both "recognized and affirmed." Aboriginal people are defined as Indians, Inuit, and Métis.

The adoption of this legal wording marks the fruition of high-level discussions over a two-year period about the place of aboriginal people in Canada's new constitutional order. Three national aboriginal organizations made presentations to a parliamentary committee studying how the rights and freedoms of all Canadians can be safeguarded in the new Constitution.

The Inuit Committee on National Issues was especially effective making its case that significant innovations are required to protect Canada's aboriginal people from being overwhelmed by others once the Constitution is brought home from Britain.

While the Inuit gained approval for many of the points they made, they were not able to secure federal agreement of the principle that aboriginal assent is required to any constitutional amendment affecting aboriginal and treaty rights. In this sense, aboriginal people have been left as outsiders in the process of redefining Canada through the process of constitutional renewal.

PQ rebounds from referendum loss to win election in Quebec

April 13, 1981

QUEBEC CITY – Premier René Lévesque's Parti Québécois has roared back from its referendum defeat last year to score a resounding victory at the polls. The PQ took 80 seats in the 122-seat National Assembly, leaving Liberal Claude Ryan with 42 members. The Union Nationale, led by former Tory federal minister Roch LaSalle, was shut out and LaSalle says he plans to quit.

The PQ's win was even more sweeping than the 1976 landslide, when it won 71 seats and 41 percent of the popular vote. This time the party picked up 49 percent of all votes cast, to the Liberals' 46.

The key to the win was the PQ's focus on continued good government and a strong economic performance. Lévesque and his troops carefully downplayed talk of an agenda for Quebec independence.

René Lévesque (later photo), whose Parti Québécois took 80 out of 122 seats.

Nation mourns as cancer claims courageous Canadian Terry Fox

June 28, 1981

NEW WESTMINSTER, B.C. – Terry Fox, the 22-year-old one-legged runner who inspired a nation to rally to the fight against cancer, died at dawn today in hospital with his family at his side. Tributes poured in from across Canada, and the federal government ordered all its flags to fly at half-mast until Fox's funeral. Since launching his Marathon of Hope last year at St. John's, Fox has raised $23 million for cancer research as Canadians poured their hearts out in donations. When he reached Toronto, he said his run was not "nearly as hard as the struggle being faced by hundreds of cancer patients in this country." It all came to a sad end last September at Thunder Bay when he was diagnosed with lung cancer and flown home to New Westminster.

Contractor accused of murdering 9 kids

Clifford Olson leaves courthouse.

Aug. 31, 1981

VANCOUVER – Eight additional counts of first-degree murder have been laid against Clifford Robert Olson, bringing to nine the number of children he is accused of killing. The charges, laid in Burnaby court, were confirmed by Insp. Larry Proke, who, as head of the RCMP serious crimes unit, is in charge of the investigation.

Olson, 41, a self-employed contractor from Coquitlam, is married and has a baby son. He was arrested on Aug. 14 and charged several days later with the murder of Judy Kozma. The nude body of the 14-year-old girl was found in the Weaver Lake area, 80 kilometres east of Vancouver. She had been stabbed 19 times. Olson has been remanded in custody for psychiatric evaluation until Sept. 18.

The eight new charges laid are in connection with the deaths of six B.C. children, a boy visiting here from Saskatchewan, and a girl believed to be visiting from Germany. Police have recovered nine bodies, all nude, since Christmas Day, and are searching for two more children. Crown prosecutor John Hall holds out little hope that the two additional bodies will be found. "I can't postpone this indefinitely – waiting for the other bodies," he said. At least one of the bodies had been torn apart by wild animals.

Final changes made to Constitution

April 24, 1981

OTTAWA – The Senate is in step with the House of Commons, approving today the same final touches to the proposed new Constitution the MPs passed yesterday.

But eight Liberal senators, including six who have condemned the constitutional reform plans put forward by Prime Minister Pierre Trudeau, broke party ranks when they refused to register a vote on a government-sponsored amendment. They were joined in abstaining by 21 Progressive Conservatives and one independent as the upper chamber voted 46-0 in favor of the government proposal to include a mention of God in the new constitution and to include a slight alteration of the amending formula and a strengthening of rights for women and native peoples.

They then rejected by 44-21 a Tory proposal to make the entire new Constitution conditional on approval by seven provinces representing at least half of the population. Today's votes end more than six months of debate and study.

PM, Lougheed sign historic energy deal

Sept. 1, 1981

OTTAWA – An 18-month stalemate between the federal government and Alberta has come to an end. Prime Minister Pierre Trudeau and Alberta Premier Peter Lougheed have signed an agreement that sets consumer oil and natural gas prices and resolves taxation issues. Federal Energy Minister Marc Lalonde and his Alberta counterpart Mervin Leitch spent six days bargaining. A subsequent meeting between Lougheed and Trudeau resulted in the agreement. The next five years will see consumer prices more than triple and natural gas prices more than double. Starting as early as Oct. 1, gasoline and home heating oil will go up by at least 40 cents a litre. There will be one price schedule for oil produced in existing fields and another for oil produced from new fields, oil sands plants, and frontier oil. Oil sands projects which were stalled when negotiations began will resume.

French-only signs a must in Quebec

Sept. 1, 1981

MONTREAL – The ban on non-French storefront signs is in effect. And there'll be no exceptions or extensions. Businesses have had three years to get ready, said an official of the language office. Offenders face fines of up to $500. Some businesses vow to defy the law. Stationer Allan Singer says he'll take the fight for English signs to the Supreme Court if necessary.

South Shore, Baffin Island, by Lawren Harris is auctioned for $240,000, the most ever paid for a Canadian painting.

Patriation plan legal, top court says

Sept. 28, 1981

OTTAWA – In a 7-2 judgment, the Supreme Court of Canada has ruled that Ottawa's plans to patriate the Constitution without provincial consent are legal. But the court also ruled 6-3 that there is a tradition in Canada that provincial consent is necessary for constitutional change. Both the pro and anti forces immediately claimed that the split decision gives them a victory. Both sides, however, also left open the possibility of further discussion, before starting vigorous lobbying in London.

More than three dozen lawyers stood under TV lights in the steamy courtroom, their faces bathed in sweat, as Chief Justice Bora Laskin read the complicated judgment on national television. Prime Minister Pierre Trudeau reacted to the decision of the court in a speech beamed by satellite TV from Seoul, South Korea. He said he "hasn't ruled out the possibility of listening to what the provinces have to say," and may even delay the final stage of debate on the resolution in Parliament if there is a serious offer forthcoming. Quebec's Premier René Lévesque vowed to continue fighting the PM.

Potential prize pumpkin pilfered

Oct. 4, 1981

KLEINBURG, Ont. – A 300-pound Atlantic giant pumpkin has been stolen from a patch owned by Frazier Mohawk, Anthony D'Atri, and Mark Parr, squashing the trio's hopes of a prize in the town's pumpkin competition. When one of the thieves phoned, Mohawk offered $300 for the fruit, but the kidnapper refused the offer.

The farmers suspect the criminals are either pranksters, greedy pie makers, or seed merchants. Parr pointed out that five such seeds go for $1.25 in stores.

Canadarm waves to Earth from U.S. space shuttle Columbia

Nov. 14, 1981

ABOARD THE COLUMBIA – The Remote Manipulator System, better known as the Canadarm, today waved to Earth from the cargo bay of the American space shuttle *Columbia*, surpassing all engineers' expectations. The 15-metre device, conceived and built by Spar Aerospace of Toronto, is designed to move cargo such as satellites in and out of the NASA craft's 18-metre cargo bay. As Spar technicians on the ground celebrated, pilot Richard Truly turned the arm's camera onto himself and held up a sign that read "Hi Mom."

The success of the device comes as a positive sign in a mission which has been cut short by consistent technical difficulties. NASA officials today announced that the shuttle will limp back to Earth tomorrow, less than halfway through its second mission.

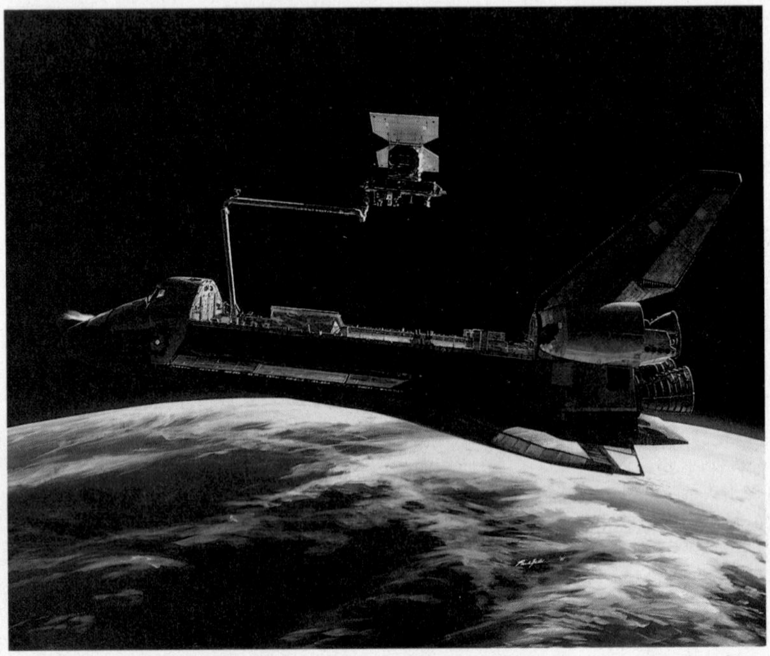

Canada's contribution to space age technology, the Remote Manipulator System, or Canadarm, is shown here in operation aboard the Columbia.

Deal OKs aboriginal and women's rights

Nov. 24, 1981

OTTAWA – The Canadian first ministers have relented somewhat in their collective assault on aboriginal rights and gender equality. They are responding to massive criticism that greeted their decision to cut provisions from the new Constitution that aboriginal and feminist activists worked hard to secure. Women are to be fully restored in their constitutional gains, while native people face a more ambivalent outcome.

Little of substance comes out of leaders' 2-day economic summit

Meeting for the final session of the economic summit conference in Ottawa.

July 21, 1981

OTTAWA – Despite the self-congratulatory speeches at the wrap-up of the two-day economic summit, the seven leaders of the top western industrialized nations agreed to little of substance. A communiqué reflects the conservative philosophies of British Prime Minister Margaret Thatcher and U.S. President Ronald Reagan. Prime Minister Pierre Trudeau won a vague commitment to talks on improved North-South relations.

Leaders agreed fighting inflation and unemployment are top priorities as their economies continue to slump, but Reagan escaped attack for his policy of high interest rates.

High interest rates spark huge protest

Nov. 21, 1981

OTTAWA – In the largest demonstration in Canadian history, 100,000 people today crowded onto Parliament Hill to protest high interest rates and other government economic policies. Dennis McDermott, president of the Canadian Labour Congress and organizer of today's rally, spoke in front of a banner which referred to Canadians as the "victims of government bungling."

Demonstrators, many of whom are facing unemployment or even bankruptcy because of the slowdown in the economy caused by interest rates now around 15 percent, came from across the country to join the protest.

Landmarks looking good from coast to coast

Beaconsfield House, Charlottetown, Prince Edward Island, was built in 1877.

Casa Loma, Toronto, was built for industrialist Henry Pellatt in 1911.

Window boxes add to this colorful street scene in Lunenburg, Nova Scotia.

A federal government building in Lower Town, old Quebec City.

McDougall Memorial United Church near Morley, Alberta. A simple spire and pointed arch windows are typical of early Canadian church architecture.

West coast Indians use totem poles as symbolic and decorative additions to their houses. This child figure is from one of these totems.

1982

Vancouver, Jan. 14. Clifford Olson is sentenced to life in prison for murdering at least 11 people. The RCMP paid Olson's family $100,000 for his revealing where his victims' bodies were buried.

Newfoundland, Feb. 15. The *Ocean Ranger*, a Mobil Oil of Canada Ltd. oil rig, sinks in a storm off St. John's; 84 lives are lost.

Ontario, Feb. 15. *The Tamarack Review*, a central influence on Canadian literature during its 25-year history, folds because of financial difficulties.

Ottawa, March 30. Justice Bertha Wilson, the first woman appointed to the Supreme Court of Canada, is sworn in.

Zolder, Belgium, May 9. Gilles Villeneuve, Canada's premier high-speed racer, dies in a crash during a qualifying race.

Vancouver, May 16. New York Islanders defeat Vancouver Canucks four games to none to win the Stanley Cup.

Nepal, Oct. 5. Laurie Skreslet, accompanied by two Sherpa guides, is the first Canadian to reach the summit of Mount Everest, part of the Canadian Mount Everest Expedition.

Ontario, Oct. 18. Former premier John Robarts commits suicide.

Ottawa, Oct. 26. Legislation is passed renaming Dominion Day, Canada Day.

Rome, Oct. 31. Mother Marguerite Bourgeoys, an early settler to Canada who devoted her life to the poor, is declared a saint by the Pope. She is Canada's first female saint.

Ottawa, Nov. 2. Brian Mulroney, president of Iron Ore Co. of Canada, announces the company's mining operations at Schefferville, Que., will close next year, affecting hundreds of miners and other workers.

Ottawa, Nov. 16. The Applebaum-Hébert Report on Canadian cultural policy is released, recommending greater arts funding and more Canadian content in film and TV.

Toronto, Nov. 28. Edmonton Eskimos beat Toronto Argonauts 32-16 to win a record fifth straight Grey Cup.

Yukon, Dec. 17. The federal government announces it will pay Yukon Indians $183 million to settle land claims. In return, the Council of Yukon Indians agrees to give up land claims to most of the Yukon.

Unemployed search for jobs in Calgary

March 1, 1982

CALGARY – Job-seekers from across the country are sleeping in Calgary's emergency shelters. Mostly from Quebec and Ontario, the unemployed migrated here in hopes of sharing in the region's increasing wealth, but they have instead found a market which has no room for their skills.

Moreover, the situation appears to be getting worse. The city's shelters, run by the Salvation Army and various church groups, are overflowing with people. Jean Schumacher, who manages Calgary's Inner City Welcome Centre, said there are "wall-to-wall bodies" on the floor every night. If it can stay open, the shelter expects to serve 95,000 free meals this year, nearly three times last year's total.

Many fear the hostels now in operation may have to close because of insufficient funding. A motion to increase annual support for the Inner City Welcome Centre by $9,000 was recently defeated by provincial legislators.

Test-tube tots born to Oakville couple

March 26, 1982

OAKVILLE, Ont. – The first test-tube twins in the world have been born to 35-year-old Canadian Katherine Rankin of Oakville. Unable to conceive normally, Rankin and her husband Ian attended the clinic of Dr. Steptoe in Cambridge, England, for an *in vitro* conception. The procedure involved removing two eggs from the ovaries of Mrs. Rankin and placing them in a special fluid, where they were fertilized with sperm from Mr. Rankin. After two days, both fertilized eggs were implanted into Mrs. Rankin's womb, where at least one egg would develop normally.

To the great delight of the Rankins and their doctors, each egg generated a healthy baby boy: Colin Patrick Hugh Rankin, weighing six pounds 15 ounces, and Gregory Robert Ian Rankin, weighing six pounds four ounces. The twins arrived two weeks early and were born 11 minutes apart.

Britain OKs patriation

March 8, 1982

LONDON, England – British MPs have given final approval to patriation of the Canadian Constitution, after 19 hours of debate stretched over four days. But the vote in the House of Commons was 177-33, showing that fewer than a third of the 635 members of Parliament bothered to turn up for third reading. The Canada Bill now goes to the House of Lords. Second reading, debate in principle, will start on March 18 and debate on details on March 23.

Many MPs expressed relief that Britain would finally be rid of an "anomaly," whereby amendments to the Canadian Constitution had to be approved by Westminster. Opposition in the Commons debate came from a group of MPs which felt the British government should await the results of court appeals against patriation from Quebec – and from another group criticizing inadequate protection in the patriation package for native rights.

George Cunningham, an independent Labour MP who summarized the majority feeling, said British MPs had no right to legislate for Canada. But Conservative backbencher Sir Bernard Braine warned Britain would stand severely judged for acquiescing "in a blind act of expediency," and that the bill offers no real protection of native rights.

Athlete of the Year Award – Aquatic Hall of Fame and Museum of Canada.

Sask. voters choose Devine government

April 26, 1982

REGINA – Grant Devine is the new premier of Saskatchewan, taking 54 percent of the popular vote in the provincial election. It took less than 30 minutes after the polls closed for the Conservatives to be declared winners. The New Democratic Party under Allan Blakeney, in power for the last 11 years, took 38 percent of the vote. Although Ralph Goodale was defeated, his Liberal party had five percent of the vote. The Western Canada Concept party had three percent.

If Devine keeps his promises, residents of Saskatchewan may look forward to: removal of the 20 percent sales tax on gasoline; subsidization of new and renewable home mortgages for three years; reduction of personal income tax by 10 percent; gradual elimination of the five percent provincial sales tax; eight percent first-time loans to farmers; free telephones for senior citizens; and a comprehensive daycare program.

Blakeney's main issue was the retention of the Crow's Nest Pass Agreement freight rate. About his loss, Blakeney said "clearly errors were made by your government for which I take full responsibility." He warned Devine he would be held to his promises.

New Canadian Constitution in force

Queen Elizabeth signs the new Canadian Constitution.

April 17, 1982

OTTAWA – A jubilant crowd of 32,000 watched on Parliament Hill today as the queen signed the royal proclamation of the Constitution, cutting this country's last colonial tie to Britain. Even a sudden outburst of rain didn't dampen the crowd's spirits, although high winds drowned out much of the queen's address and thunderclaps punctuated Prime Minister Pierre Trudeau's speech.

The prime minister praised the Constitution for strengthening protection for French-speaking Canadians outside Quebec and for that province's English-speaking residents. He said: "History will show that nothing essential to the originality of Quebec has been sacrificed." In Montreal, Premier René Lévesque led a protest rally.

Alsands megaproject falls by the wayside

April 30, 1982

OTTAWA – The Alsands oil sands project will be no more as of this July 31 and completion of the Alaska Highway natural gas pipeline will be delayed by another two years. The news comes despite generous government offers. According to an Alsands spokesman, the offers came too late.

The Alsands project was part of a plan to make Canada self-sufficient in oil by 1990. Energy-related megaprojects have been falling by the wayside, crumbling the federal government's economic development strategy. There are some projects still in place. They include the Norman Wells natural gas pipeline and some oil upgrading projects.

Podborski skis way to World Cup title

Canada's Steve Podborski.

March 5, 1982

ASPEN, Col. – Toronto skier Steve Podborski today became the first North American to win the World Cup men's downhill championship, despite his worst finish in two and a half years. He was 14th in today's race, the second to last of the season, but took the title when Austria's Harti Weirather finished second, 11/100ths of a second behind Switzerland's Peter Mueller. Weirather had to win both today and tomorrow's finale. The top five races of each skier count. Podborski had three wins and two seconds. ▷

What a romance! The public loves those Harlequin paperbacks

1982

DON MILLS, Ont. – True love can conquer all, and better yet, it's as authentically Canadian as maple syrup! But wait – hasn't romance always been mankind's oldest preoccupation? It has, and that goes far to explain the phenomenal success of Canada's Harlequin Enterprises Ltd., the biggest Canadian publisher and the world's largest publisher of romance novels.

The pioneer of quality romantic fiction, Harlequin has since the 1950s sold more than a billion books to millions of mainly female readers in 100 international markets and in more than a dozen languages. A line of Harlequins sold each year would stretch 1,000 times round the Earth – what a way to wrap the world in romantic fantasy!

Sample title from Harlequin's extremely successful publications.

Nelles off the hook for infant murders

A relieved and happy Susan Nelles.

May 21, 1982

TORONTO – Nurse Susan Nelles, accused of murdering four babies in the Hospital for Sick Children, had her case dismissed by Provincial Court Judge David Vaneck earlier today. While pointing out there is no doubt the infants were murdered, Vaneck cited the weakness of the prosecution's circumstantial evidence and Nelles' excellent professional reputation as reasons for his decision to dismiss the case. After the judgment was announced, Metro Toronto police launched an investigation of 43 suspicious deaths in the hospital's infant ward.

Trudeau criticizes U.S. foreign policy

June 10, 1982

BONN, West Germany – Canadian Prime Minister Pierre Trudeau today ended all speculation about his being critical of U.S. foreign policy by lashing out at the Americans. Trudeau, honorary president at the NATO summit, voiced objections to the American approach to the meeting, which has U.S. leaders reading pre-prepared speeches which leave no time for discussion of the issues at hand. Among the unpopular policies levied by the U.S. against the Eastern Bloc are economic sanctions.

Permits OK drilling off Nova Scotia

July 30, 1982

HALIFAX – Federal Energy Minister Marc Lalonde today announced that permits for a $500-million, three-year drilling project off Nova Scotia's north coast have been awarded to Petro-Canada, Bow Valley Industries Ltd., and Husky Oil Operations Ltd. The drilling, which is to begin almost immediately, will take place in a 1.7-million hectare area about 30 kilometres north of Sable Island. Two rigs, whose crews must be at least 90 percent Canadian according to the agreement, will drill a minimum of eight wells over the next three years. Lalonde denied allegations he used favoritism in rendering his decision.

Petro-Canada, unlikely to go ahead with plans to build an offshore drilling platform, intends to operate a Swedish-owned rig on the project. Finance Minister Allan MacEachen warned that high labor costs and inefficiency in Canada's rig-building facilities mean Canadian companies are often forced to operate cheaper foreign-built rigs.

Archambault prison riot ends with 3 guards, 2 inmates dead

Dec. 14, 1982

MONTREAL – One prison guard was hanged and two others stabbed to death in a bloody riot at the maximum security Archambault Institute. The two inmates who sparked the riot with a botched escape attempt committed suicide. One of the dead guards was working his last shift before retiring after 25 years in the correctional service.

The riot broke out around 10:30 p.m. when inmates were returning to their cells from the prison yard. Some tried to take unarmed guards hostage in an escape attempt. It took 20 minutes for the anti-riot squad to quell the outbreak with tear gas. Meanwhile, guards had been brutalized by their captives.

Montreal's Archambault Institute where the riot took place.

Quebec pair among five to be beatified

May 23, 1982

VATICAN CITY – Pope John Paul II today announced the beatifications of five religious leaders, two of whom were French-Canadians who lived in Quebec. Citing dedication and charity, the Pope granted beatification, the first major step toward achieving sainthood, to Brother André Bessette and Mother Marie Rose.

Bessette, whom the Pope referred to as "a man of miracles," is best known as the curator of Montreal's St. Joseph's Oratory from 1909 to 1936. Rose, the founder of Longueuil's the Sisters of the Holy Names of Jesus and Mary, died in 1849 at the age of 39. Following the announcement, Quebec Premier René Lévesque invited the Pope to pay an official visit to the province.

Pianist Glenn Gould dies in Toronto

Oct. 4, 1982

TORONTO – Famous Canadian pianist, broadcaster and writer Glenn Gould died today. The 50-year-old, considered by many a musical genius, had been in a coma since suffering a stroke a week ago. A Toronto native who never married, Gould was an intensely shy personality. But with 65 albums and numerous articles to his credit, the eccentric musician was one of Canada's best-known intellectuals.

Known for his radio documentaries, his fiery passion, and his unrelenting wit, Gould was far more than a pianist. He was a creative artist who used his instrument to liven classic pieces with a unique and innovative new sound.

Access to Info Act fulfils Grit promise

June 28, 1982

OTTAWA – The Liberal government today delivered on its two-year-old promise to pass a freedom of information law. The Access to Information Act, which goes into effect in about a year, allows public access to non-restricted documents produced in the last three years. Older documents will be made available within the next two years.

NDP members of Parliament did not vote for the bill, complaining that the section which excludes cabinet-generated documents is too restrictive. The law also calls for the restriction of access to any information which falls under the Official Secrets Act. Passed alongside the new act was a bill designed to protect individual privacy by limiting access to personal information in government files.

UN recognizes Canadian fishing zone

Dec. 10, 1982

CANADA – Along with 159 other countries, Canada today signed the Law of the Sea instituting a 322-kilometre offshore economic zone. For almost a decade, Canadian fisheries have tried to institute a minimum 322-kilometre zone from the baselines of the Canadian territorial sea. Their objective was to get control over fisheries for the purpose of conservation and exploitation. On Jan. 1, 1977, Canada officially declared a 322-kilometre zone. The extension of jurisdiction was accepted by Poland, Spain, Portugal, France, Norway, and the U.S.S.R. Together, these six countries accounted for 88 percent of the catch taken by foreign fishermen, other than those of the United States, within 322 kilometres of the Canadian Atlantic coast. At the time, these countries recognized Canada's 322-kilometre zone, but demanded guarantees of surplus allocations. Today, the 322-kilometre zone is incorporated in the United Nations' convention on the Law of the Sea.

Karen Baldwin wins Miss Universe title

Miss Universe, Karen Baldwin.

July 26, 1982

LIMA, Peru – Canada's Karen Baldwin was named Miss Universe 1982 tonight, winning the judges' nod over 76 other women. "Tell me this is a dream," the five-foot-nine model from London, Ont., marvelled as she left the stage. Karen, 18, who will receive $150,000 in cash and prizes, will go on tour for a year. The judging consisted of interviews, as well as evening gown and swimsuit appearances.

Ecological concerns expressed by Frye

1982

TORONTO – The new collection of Northrop Frye's essays on Canadian culture, *Divisions on a Ground,* reveals the views of Canada's foremost literary critic on his own country. The professor of English, who has taught at the University of Toronto for more than 40 years, is one of the authors most quoted by critics and scholars.

This anthology explodes with new insights, including an emphasis in his essay "Sharing the Continent" on the need for global respect for the Earth. "It seems to me," he writes, "that the capitalist-socialist controversy is out of date, and that a detente with an outraged nature is what is important now."

Carling Bassett wins the Women's National Tennis Championship.

Newfoundland seal fishery: end in sight

A white seal is killed with one blow from a Norwegian hakapik. Animal rights groups object to this method of killing, considering it cruel and inhumane.

April 15, 1982

ST. JOHN'S, Nfld. – After nearly 200 years in operation, the annual spring seal fishery in Newfoundland is coming to a close. Due to protests from animal rights groups, the markets for seal skins and seal oil have declined in recent years, and the Canadian government must face the fact that this traditional industry is bad for Canada's international image.

The seal in question, the harp seal – *phoca groenlandica* – belongs to the family of phocid seals of which seven species can be found in Canada. Of these seven only two – the harp and hooded – are migratory, while two others are Arctic and three are temperate. The Arctic and the migratory bear their young on ice, while the others use beaches and reefs.

Harp seals are found in three major stocks, but only one frequents the Canadian waters. This northwest Atlantic herd migrates from the Arctic to the waters off Newfoundland in the autumn to feed on the rich feeding grounds. In February the herd begins its journey back to the Arctic and later that month it meets the Arctic ice drifting south. The young are born on that ice, where they are nursed by the mothers as the ice continues to drift south and the adults continue to feed. In April, after the pups take to the water, the herd resumes its northward migration.

The seal fishery became the second industry of Newfoundland in the 1790s and provided spring employment for the cod fishermen. This allowed more of them to make permanent homes in colony and the population grew. However, in recent years the seal fishery has been a minor industry. Nevertheless, if it ends, about 4,000 fishermen will lose an important part of their income and there are fears that the seal stocks will increase and deplete the fish stocks.

1983

New Brunswick, January. The Point Lepreau Nuclear Generating Station near Saint John, Atlantic Canada's first nuclear generating station, begins commercial operation.

Canada, April 23. More than 80,000 people protest across the country against the arms race and U.S. plans to test the Cruise Missile in Canada.

New York, May 17. New York Islanders defeat Edmonton Oilers four games to none to win the Stanley Cup.

Toronto, June 2. The Ontario government announces the creation of five wilderness parks and promises the creation of 155 provincial parks.

Vancouver, June 19. B.C. Place, a beautiful 60,000-seat domed stadium, is officially opened.

Quebec, July 13. French-Canadian writer Gabrielle Roy, author of *Bonheur d'occasion* (*The Tin Flute*), dies.

Ottawa, July 15. The government approves plans to test the American Cruise Missile in Canada at the request of the U.S. government.

Ottawa, Sept. 5. The government suspends all flights into Montreal by the Soviet airline Aeroflot to protest the Soviets' shooting down of South Korean Airlines Flight 007 last week that killed 269 people.

Windsor, Ont., Oct. 2. Chrysler Corp. chairman Lee Iacocca presides at the official re-opening of the Windsor assembly plant, renovated to become one of the most advanced car factories in the world.

British Columbia, Nov. 13. A labor war ends when the B.C. government signs peace treaties with its striking civil servants and with Operation Solidarity, the huge anti-government coalition. The strikers were protesting government cutbacks.

Ottawa, Nov. 16. Margaret Trudeau files for divorce from her husband PM Trudeau after a six-year separation.

Vancouver, Nov. 27. Toronto Argonauts defeat B.C. Lions 18-17 to win the Grey Cup.

Ottawa. The House of Commons Special Committee on Indian Self-Government (the Penner Committee) releases its report. It recommends Indian communities be allowed to develop new forms of band government as an order of government separate from federal and provincial levels.

Clark steps down as leader of the Tories

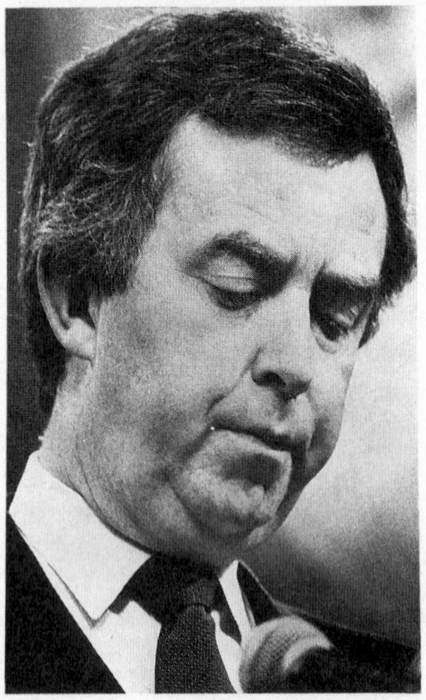

Joe Clark has resigned as PC leader.

Jan. 2, 1983

OTTAWA – None of the all-too-familiar jeers and catcalls greeted Joe Clark as he took his seat in the House of Commons this morning. Instead, he received a nonpartisan standing ovation from his fellow members of Parliament. Clark has announced his impending resignation as leader of both the Progressive Conservatives and the official opposition.

Since the last election, the Tories have been increasingly divided over Clark's leadership. Three days ago, hoping to resolve the bitter infighting, national delegates voted in favor of holding a leadership convention later this year. Clark has every intention of running for the top job again, but must resign his present positions if he is to do so.

Chrysler builds 5-millionth car in Windsor

Chrysler Corp. chairman Lee Iacocca and some of his company's line of cars.

May 9, 1983

WINDSOR, Ont. – A shiny white 1983 Chrysler New Yorker Fifth Avenue rolled off the assembly line today, the five-millionth car churned out by the Windsor plant. The factory, expanded to 225,000 square metres last year, has been putting out Chrysler products since 1929. Among its most famous products are the Chrysler Royal convertible used for the 1939 royal tour and special military trucks used in the Second World War.

Supporting the Windsor factory are numerous parts plants across North America. Chrysler takes full advantage of the Auto Pact, a conditional free-trade agreement signed with the United States in 1965, by building about half of its products in Canada.

If You Love This Planet takes home an Academy Award

April 12, 1983

LOS ANGELES – At the Academy Awards in Los Angeles, Canada triumphed in the category of best short subject documentary with the National Film Board production *If You Love This Planet.*

The documentary graphically portrays the evils of nuclear war, exposing the resultant ravages to the biosphere and cautioning the world about the long-term ecological upheaval of nuclear arms. The film's dramatic presentation inflames the emotions of its audiences, invoking the activist spirit in the most complacent. It is one Canadian film that has received a great deal of controversy. It even has been labelled as being "propagandistic" by the U.S government.

Ironically, the derision contributed to the popularity of the film and to the impact the documentary seemed to have on Canadian and American populations. In her acceptance speech, director Terri Nash directed some humorous gratitude to the U.S. Department of Justice for its criticism of the film. The strong opposition added credence to the film's message.

A symbol of achievement for Canadian film-makers, this Oscar also represents a victory for environmentalists.

About 1.4 million people out of work

Jan. 7, 1983

OTTAWA – The national unemployment rate of 12.8 percent is the highest this country has seen since the Great Depression, Statistics Canada reported today. Fully 1,454,000 people are searching for jobs. Another 156,000 are so discouraged they've stopped looking for jobs they say simply don't exist. Conservative employment critic David Crombie called for the government to reconvene Parliament immediately to deal with the issue. Experts speculate Prime Minister Pierre Trudeau's caucus may increase the federal deficit to $30 billion to stimulate the economy.

Marshall cleared after 11 years in jail

May 10, 1983

HALIFAX – After spending 11 years in jail for a murder he did not commit, Micmac Donald Marshall Jr. was acquitted yesterday. Marshall, incarcerated when he was 17, hails from the Shubenacadie Reserve near Sydney.

Marshall was convicted in 1971 for killing his friend Sandy Seale in Sydney's Wentworth Park. Subsequent investigation has shown the conviction was gained with perjured evidence. Moreover, vital information was withheld by Crown officials from the defendant's lawyer. Ten days after Marshall's conviction, James MacNeil came forward to Sydney police with the story that the real killer was Roy Ebsary. RCMP officials soon dismissed this revelation after conducting a brief inquiry.

MacNeil's story, however, became part of a growing body of evidence that was eventually forced on the attention of the judiciary through the efforts of Marshall's lawyer. The Supreme Court of Nova Scotia finally corroborated the wrongfulness of Marshall's conviction.

Donald Marshall answers questions from reporters after his acquittal.

The five judges' unanimous decision still holds Marshall largely responsible for his difficulties. "In attempting to defend himself against the charge of murder," the judges state, "Mr. Marshall admittedly committed perjury for which he could still be charged. By lying he helped secure his own conviction. ... By planning a robbery with the aid of Mr. Seale he triggered a series of events which unfortunately ended in the death of Mr. Seale."

They've got a deal: Manitoba restores right to use French

May 25, 1983

WINNIPEG – Franco-Manitobans tonight ratified a deal to restore French language rights in this province for the first time since 1890. The provincial government will make French an official language of the legislature and courts. It also agrees to provide French services at head offices of government departments and agencies. "We got everything that any court could have given us, and more," said Leo Robert, president of the Société Franco-Manitobaine.

Three years ago, the Supreme Court of Canada ruled unconstitutional an 1890 law making English the only official language of Manitoba. That law violated the deal that brought Manitoba into Confederation in 1870. The deal with the French community is a political hot potato, but the alternative for the NDP government was an expensive court-imposed settlement.

Mulroney wins Conservative leadership

New PC leader Brian Mulroney and his wife Mila.

June 11, 1983

OTTAWA – Brian Mulroney, a 44-year-old lawyer and former president of Iron Ore Canada, has been chosen new leader of the Progressive Conservative party, capturing a dramatic fourth ballot victory tonight over his nearest rival, former prime minister Joe Clark. The decision by delegates at the national convention, held here in the tense, steamy atmosphere of the Civic Centre, is thought to signal an end to the bitter infighting that has plagued Clark's leadership in recent years. Mulroney's top priority is to restore party unity, but because he is not yet a member of Parliament he must also seek election to the House of Commons.

Quebec court: charter overrules Bill 101

June 9, 1983

MONTREAL – Quebec's highest court decided in less than five hours today that Canadians who were educated in English anywhere in this country can send their children to English schools in Quebec. Three judges of the Quebec Court of Appeals ruled that Chief Justice Jules Deschênes of Quebec Superior Court was right last September when he ruled that the Canadian Charter of Rights and Freedoms overrules Quebec's Bill 101, or the French-language charter, in deciding the schooling issue. An official says Quebec will appeal to the Supreme Court of Canada.

Air show jet crash proves fatal for 6

May 22, 1983

FRANKFURT, West Germany – At a NATO air show, a CF-104, the fighter which Canadian pilots call the "Widowmaker," crashed into a crowded highway today, claiming the pilot and five civilians. The jet, flown by Capt. Allan Stephenson, was the 101st CF-104 to crash. Experts speculate a bird entered the unforgiving plane's single engine. Despite their record, officials insist CF-104s will remain in service until they are replaced by F-18s later in the decade.

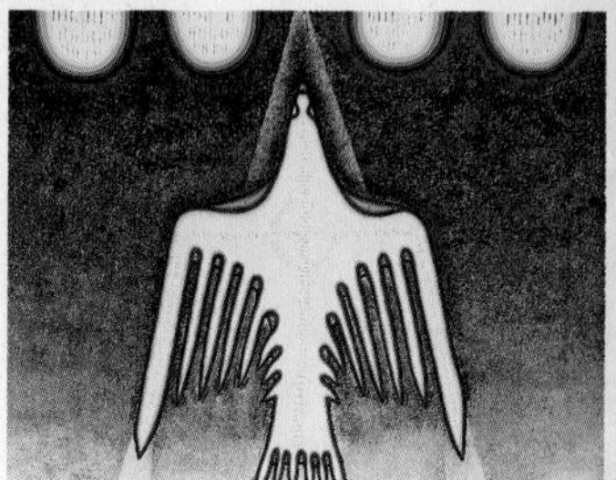

The Enlightenment, by Blake Debassige, an Ojibwa artist influenced by Norval Morrisseau.

Sauvé first female governor general

Jeanne and Maurice Sauvé.

Dec. 23, 1983
OTTAWA – To the delight of Canadian women's groups, Jeanne Sauvé, former Speaker of the House and three-time Liberal cabinet minister, has been appointed governor general. She'll be the first woman to hold the post. Sauvé, married to businessman and former Liberal cabinet minister Maurice Sauvé, admits she'll have to watch for conflicts of interest.

Experts warning of greenhouse effect

Oct. 22, 1983
CANADA – Burning fossil fuels emit carbon dioxide which forms a shield around the Earth, allowing sunlight to penetrate, but preventing escape of infrared heat rays. Recent scientific reports by the United States indicate that the resultant warming of the planet will cause dramatic weather changes, becoming noticeable within a decade and progressively worse over the next century.

Specifically, the greenhouse effect could mean: the desert Sahel area of Africa will get more rain, but agriculture zones of Canada, the U.S., Soviet Union, and China will become drier and less prolific; the dry area of the prairies will become scorched, but the Hudson Bay lowland could become a farming zone; farming belts in central and southwestern parts of the United States that already suffer from water shortage will become convulsive. Overall, researchers predict that Canada, with its steep coastlines, will fare better than other parts of the world.

Interest is high for space program jobs

Aug. 3, 1983
OTTAWA – The National Research Council today reported that publicity surrounding Canada's space program has created a "tidal wave" of applications for two positions. More than 1,500 people have applied to be payload specialists or motion sickness researchers aboard NASA space shuttle missions, and most of the applicants are serious. Once chosen, the astronauts will be trained both in Canada and in the United States before one becomes the first Canadian in space.

Charles calls acid rain a major hazard

Prince Charles and Princess Diana attend a state dinner during Ottawa visit.

June 22, 1983
OTTAWA – Acid rain was rated a major hazard to Canadian lakes and forests by Prince Charles in his address to a group of 600 Kiwanis members. Sulphur dioxide, the main component of acid rain, is killing lake ecosystems in Ontario and Quebec. Ottawa blames emissions from industries in the northeast United States.

Since Canada's urging the U.S. to clean up sulphur dioxide emissions, acid rain has become a sensitive subject which has chafed relations between Canada and the U.S. Prince Charles' comments awakened the diplomatic dispute. The Prince of Wales added further fuel to the fire by advising his audience to take an active role on the issue and join the crusade against acid rain. He expounded by saying that disparagement of the environment disrupts a human's inner being and leaves one "psychologically confused." The prince advocates a greater harmony between man and nature.

Canada heads killing of all Haiti's pigs

This black Creole pig was one of the few to escape slaughter in Haiti.

November 1983
PORT-AU-PRINCE – The Canadian-directed, U.S.-financed, 18-month slaughter of all Haiti's 1.2 million pigs is complete, ending fears that the African Swine Fever infecting many of them will spread to North America's commercial herds. ASF, an incurable, infectious, AIDS-like virus, kills its victims within 48 hours of the first symptoms, but has no effect on humans who eat contaminated meat. ASF, exceptionally resistant, can survive even six months in refrigerated, treated ham. Its presence was confirmed in Haiti in 1978, and intense Canadian and U.S. pressure forced president Jean-Claude Duvalier to permit eradication of all Haiti's pigs, though they were the backbone of the peasants' economy.

CBC ordered to increase Canadian content

Oct. 24, 1983
OTTAWA – Federal Communications Minister Francis Fox today ordered the CBC to raise Canadian content to 80 percent during peak evening hours. The changes, to take place within the next five years, will be made without a substantial increase in the corporation budget. To fund the new demands, the CBC will lay off workers and try to attract more advertisers. In an effort to stifle CBC Quebec's image as a hotbed of separatism, Fox said the CBC must be "consciously partial to the success of Canada." The minister's revelation has already raised fears that future reports on separatist issues will be one-sided.

Putting Canada's natural resources to good use

Petroleum industry meets energy needs

This northern Alberta oil rig makes a dramatic sight on the horizon.

1983

CANADA – Petroleum is the major energy source of the industrialized world, and Canadians are among the world's highest petroleum consumers per capita due to our cold climate, high standard of living, and relatively low petroleum prices. Canada produces most of the petroleum it consumes, mainly in Alberta from crude oil and natural gas fields and bitumen deposits, or oil sands. From there, much of the petroleum is shipped by pipeline to eastern Canada, where it's made into products ranging from gasoline to lubricating oils to plastics and shampoo. Multinational companies control a big part of Canada's petroleum industry.

Billions of tons of grain produced yearly

Grain elevators such as these in Alberta are built beside the railway.

1983

CANADA – Grain elevators silhouetted against the flaming red prairie sky, trains of boxcars filled with prairie grain snaking their way through the Rocky Mountains to west coast port terminals, massive ocean-going ships waiting in Vancouver harbor to receive the grain, the fruits of Canada's breadbasket – these are the operations of Canada's grain industry, one of the country's most important.

Canada produces billions of tons of grain each year, mostly on the prairies, the annual amount depending on weather conditions. Wheat accounts for 67 percent of Canadian-grown grain, and Canada is one of the world's largest wheat exporters. Oats and barley are also important Canadian grain crops. Harvested in the late summer and early fall, grain is trucked from prairie farms to primary elevators. From there, it is shipped by rail to Thunder Bay, Churchill, and west coast ports, where it is either stored or loaded onto ships. The Canadian Wheat Board markets western grains intended for human consumption or export.

Forestry industry generates 780,000 jobs

1983

CANADA – Canada's forestry industries, ranging from logging to wood industries such as sawmills to pulp and paper industries to Christmas trees and maple sugar, generate 780,000 jobs in Canada. But it is essential to look beyond the economics of Canadian forestry. Unbridled exploitation of the forests can cause soil erosion, harm waterways, and imperil fish and wildlife. Forests are home to many native people and are an important place of recreation.

B.C. truck with huge load of logs.

Governments have not been blind to these considerations. Canada has thousands of hectares of parks and wilderness preserves, and has enacted environmental laws to control forest industries. But, due to these measures and a neglect of forest renewal, Canada is on the threshold of a wood shortage. With world consumption of forest products due to rise substantially in coming decades, Canadian governments and the forestry industry have realized the importance of forest management techniques such as replanting and site preparation and have begun to practise these techniques.

The CL-289 drone, a surveillance system, was developed by Canadair Inc.

1984

Winnipeg, Feb. 27. The Manitoba government abandons its controversial bill to extend French-language rights and services because of widespread opposition.

Ottawa, Feb. 29. PM Trudeau announces his retirement after 16 years in office.

Ottawa, March 26. Chief Justice Bora Laskin of the Supreme Court of Canada dies.

Quebec, May 8. Canadian soldier Cpl. Denis Lortie kills three and wounds 13 when he storms the National Assembly with a submachine-gun. He gives himself up.

Edmonton, May 19. Edmonton Oilers defeat New York Islanders four games to one to win the Stanley Cup.

Alberta, July 8. Johnny Bob Smallboy, an Indian leader who drew attention to Indian problems when he led a group of Indian followers to live at an isolated bush camp, dies.

Los Angeles, Aug. 12. The Summer Olympics close. Canada won 44 medals, its best showing ever at the games, due in part to a boycott of the games by the U.S.S.R. and other communist countries.

Montreal, Sept. 3. A bomb blast at Central Station kills three and injures 21.

Quebec, Sept. 9. Pope John Paul II begins a 12-day Canadian visit, the first visit to Canada by a pope.

Edmonton, Sept. 18. Team Canada defeats Sweden two games to none to win the Canada Cup hockey tournament.

United States, Oct. 5. Marc Garneau becomes the first Canadian astronaut in space as part of a mission of the American space shuttle *Challenger*.

Washington, D.C., Nov. 13. PM Pierre Trudeau is awarded the Albert Einstein Peace Prize for his efforts in encouraging "North-South" dialogue, and his recent personal initiative to lower Cold War tensions.

Edmonton, Nov. 18. Winnipeg Blue Bombers defeat Hamilton Tiger-Cats 47-17 to win the Grey Cup.

Toronto, Dec. 5. Recording artist Bryan Adams wins four Juno Awards.

Ottawa, Dec. 19. Statistics Canada says Canada will need 275,000 immigrants by the year 2000 to keep the population growing because of low Canadian fertility rates.

Boucher's haul: 2 golds and a bronze

Speedskater Gaetan Boucher.

Feb. 19, 1984

SARAJEVO, Yugoslavia – The two gold medals and one bronze won by Gaetan Boucher in speed skating events at the winter Olympics here are the best performance ever by a Canadian Olympian. Boucher, of St. Hubert, Que., had won a silver at the 1980 Olympics. His two golds here tie a Canadian team record for the winter Olympics set in 1960.

Canadarm to the rescue

April 10, 1984

ABOARD THE CHALLENGER – The long arm of Canada's scientific community has passed a pivotal test thousands of kilometres above the Earth's surface. Today, the Canadarm, developed by private industry's Spar Aerospace Ltd. and the government's Canadian Aeronautical Establishment, reached out from the United States space shuttle *Challenger* and grabbed the orbiting but crippled Solar Maximum satellite, setting a precedent that will have enormous cost-saving effects on the future use of space satellites.

Now, with Solar Max tucked away in the shuttle's cargo hold, it has been proved that satellites can be serviced – or at least retrieved – while still in orbit. Capable of both loading and discharging payloads, the mechanical arm is 15 metres in length and functions much the same as a human arm, with six rotating joints operated by a remote control system.

First tested in 1981 aboard the second space shuttle mission, it has exceeded its initial design goals. Today, for example, it was used to retrieve the Solar Max only after an earlier attempt to secure the satellite, by an astronaut equipped with a rocket pack, had failed. The Canadarm's "hand" was then used to snag a handle on the satellite only eight centimetres long.

Canadian astronaut Marc Garneau.

Among its other contributions to the space shuttle program, Canada is currently training six astronauts. One of them, Marc Garneau, is expected to join a mission this fall. This will make him the first Canadian to enter space.

Lack of American action against acid rain causes deep regret

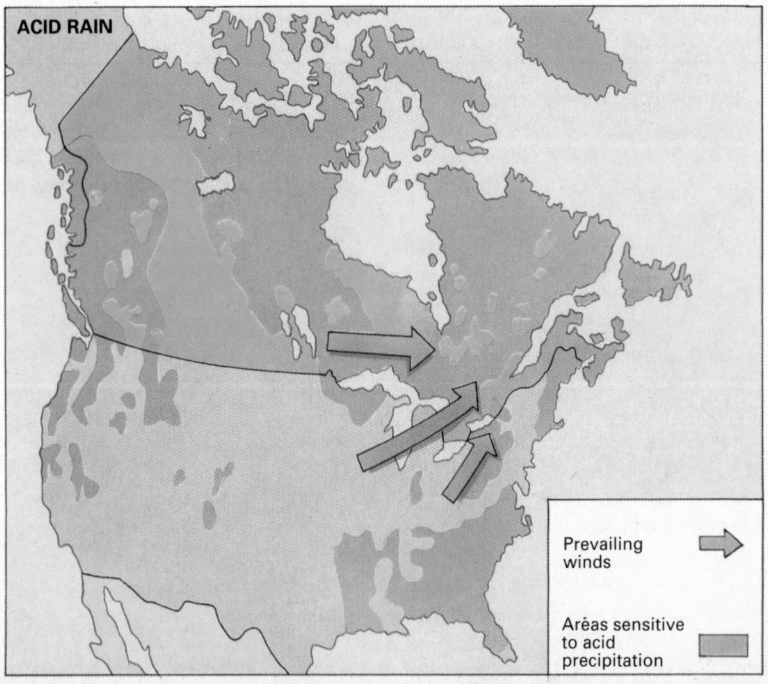

Prevailing winds determine areas most affected by acid precipitation.

Feb. 23, 1984

WASHINGTON, D.C. – In an early morning meeting at the State Department, ambassador Allan Gotlieb handed a diplomatic note to William Schneider, the undersecretary of state for security assistance, science and technology. The note, in forceful tones, stressed Canada's deep regret that the U.S. has not planned a program to curb sulphur dioxide emissions.

Canada is committed to reducing sulphur dioxide emissions. So far it has made more progress than the United States, and it aims to reduce emissions another 25 percent. A fact sheet issued by the embassy indicates up to 1,400 Canadian bodies of water are polluted by acid rain and devoid of fish. Another 48,000 lakes in Ontario are threatened. Half the acid rain damage emanates from the U.S., but no controls have yet been enforced.

Canadians shine at Olympics in L.A.

Steve Bauer of Fenwick, Ontario, won the silver medal in the men's cycling road race at the Los Angeles Summer Olympic Games.

Victor Davis won gold medals in both the 100-metre and 200-metre breaststroke as well as the silver medal with the 4 x 100 metre relay team.

Alex Baumann won gold medals in swimming in the 200- and 400-metre individual medleys.

Linda Thom proudly displays the gold medal she won in the women's sport pistol competition.

Return of the tall ships

Canada welcomes the Tall Ships 450 years after Cartier's arrival.

June 18, 1984

GASPE, Que. – Tall ships have returned to Gaspé 450 years after Jacques Cartier brought the first such vessels to the bay. When Cartier's two ships landed July 24, 1534, he was greeted by Iroquoian Indians from Stadacona [Quebec City] led by Chief Donnacona. Today, dozens of tall ships from around the world were greeted by some 15,000 visitors to the town and by a cigarette-chomping Premier René Lévesque, who declared, "the long, tenacious and often heroic road which led to modern-day Quebec began here." Lévesque also paid tribute to Canada's native peoples, "who accepted from the start to share their lands, not knowing the injustices they were to face and which we are trying to correct." In fact, back in 1534 Cartier erected a cross on the Gaspé to claim the land for France, despite protests from Chief Donnacona, and carried two of Donnacona's sons to France.

At least 70 of the tall ships are due to arrive in Quebec City in the last week of June to celebrate the 450th anniversary of Cartier's landing. Most of them will sail to Sydney, N.S., early in July to take part in a transatlantic race. Some will sail up the St. Lawrence to Montreal and Toronto, and 11 of the ships will stay in Quebec City for the summer. More than 800 events are scheduled across Quebec this summer as part of the celebrations.

Betty Hughes the first woman to head CN

June 1, 1984

OTTAWA – An Edmonton woman with lots of civic experience but no railway background was appointed the new chairman of Canadian National Railways today. Betty Hughes, 60, becomes the first woman to lead a major Crown corporation. Hughes, who has been a member of Edmonton city council for 10 years and served on its executive committee, told a press conference today that her experience qualifies her for the job. A Liberal, she assumes the post vacated by Jack Horner when he took over the job of Grain Transportation Administrator.

Tough-talking Pope condemns abortion

Pope John Paul II was greeted on his arrival by youth in ethnic dress.

Sept. 18, 1984

VANCOUVER – Popular pontiff John Paul II, the first reigning pope to set foot in Canada, addressed an enthusiastic audience at B.C. Place tonight and reaffirmed the traditional anti-abortion Catholic church stand. Anyone expecting a softening of the Vatican's position on the contentious issue has come away disappointed. Calling abortion an "unspeakable crime against human life" that "sets the stage for despising, negating and eliminating the life of adults," the Pope also spoke against artificial means of birth control, stating that marriage must include love "as well as openness to procreation."

Tonight's rally comes toward the end of a hectic 11-day tour of Canada that was to include a stopover at the remote northern community of Fort Simpson, 500 kilometres south of the Arctic Circle. There the Pope was to deliver a speech addressing Canada's native people, but when his Canadian government 707 aircraft was unable to land because of fog, the Pope flew on to Yellowknife, capital of the Northwest Territories, where his message was broadcast by CBC Radio.

In keeping with the outspoken positions the Vatican has taken lately on behalf of human rights and the oppressed, the Pope said native people here deserve "a just and equitable degree" of self-government and a "land base" that they may use to establish themselves economically.

Turner takes reins of Liberal Party

June 16, 1984

OTTAWA – John Turner sounded like he was on the election trail from the moment he won the Liberal leadership today. Delegates to the Liberal convention here decisively chose Turner to succeed Prime Minister Pierre Trudeau. On the second ballot, Turner beat Energy Minister Jean Chrétien by about 500 votes.

In his acceptance speech, Turner outlined a careful position, promising to work at "the historic task of building a new tomorrow for Canada." He dealt with a number of national issues, with an obvious eye on the national television audience rather than on the party faithful who had endured a divisive three-month leadership campaign. Turner said he'd usher in "a new era where hope, confidence and compassion will be the guiding aims."

The government has till next year to go in its mandate, but Turner will likely call an early election.

John Turner greets the press after becoming Liberal Party leader.

After his victory tonight, he embraced Chrétien on the stage and told the audience his opponent had a privileged place in the hearts of Canadians. He has offered Chrétien a senior cabinet portfolio. Turner exchanged only polite handshakes with the PM. The relationship between Turner and Trudeau has been cool since the former justice and finance minister stormed out of Trudeau's cabinet in 1975.

Mulroney's Conservatives win federal election by a landslide

Sept. 4, 1984

CANADA – Canadians responded to Tory leader Brian Mulroney's call for "unity, reconciliation and a new definition of Canada's goals" today, handing the Progressive Conservative party an election victory of unprecedented proportions. According to Mulroney, the win signals "a new day for Quebec and a new day for our wonderful Canada." Indeed, the political face of this nation has been changed – dramatically. The Tories have won 211 of 282 federal ridings, crushing the Liberal government's longtime stranglehold on Quebec in the process.

The margin of victory has shocked many – even the most optimistic of Tories – leaving in its wake great speculation over why the sudden collapse of Liberal support. Analysts are suggesting two main reasons: an emerging trend toward social and economic conservatism and the effectiveness of Mulroney's campaign in comparison to Liberal leader John Turner's. The Liberal government's inability to deal effectively with the recent recession eroded popular support, and during televised debates Turner faltered in the face of a Mulroney broadside attacking Liberal patronage appointments to the Senate.

New PM Mulroney and wife Mila.

New Brunswick's Hatfield charged with possession of marijuana

Oct. 26, 1984

FREDERICTON – Richard Hatfield became the first New Brunswick premier to be charged with a criminal offence as an RCMP officer handed him a summons on the steps of city hall today. Hatfield, 53, declined to comment on the charge of criminal possession of marijuana. If convicted, the premier could face a maximum penalty of a $1,000 fine and up to six months in jail.

Opposition parties are calling for the premier to step down until such time as the matter is resolved, but Hatfield, in his 14th year in office, refuses to let the case affect his political activities. In a letter released today, the premier, who has admitted the drug was found in his suitcase, stated he is pushing for an early trial to prove his innocence as soon as possible.

Hatfield has been critical of RCMP press leaks and procedural delays, complaining that his rights have been denied. He is expected to enter a not guilty plea within the next few days.

Ottawa and Nfld. OK offshore deal

Dec. 12, 1984

OTTAWA – Federal Energy Minister Pat Carney and Newfoundland's minister in charge of offshore negotiations, Bill Marshall, have come to an agreement over the control and revenue sharing of oil and gas reserves off the coast of Newfoundland. The agreement is based on the deal worked out between Premier Brian Peckford and Prime Minister Brian Mulroney when Mulroney led the opposition. Principal clauses give Newfoundland the right to collect royalties and taxes as if the resources were on land and recognize Newfoundland's rights as principal beneficiary of the resources.

Thatcher guilty of murdering ex-wife

Nov. 6, 1984

SASKATOON, Sask. – Colin Thatcher, a 46-year-old former MLA and cabinet minister, today was found guilty of murdering his ex-wife and was sentenced to life in prison, making him eligible for parole in 25 years. He has 30 days to appeal the verdict, although he has already announced he does not plan to do so.

The trial, one of the most sensational in Saskatchewan's history, heard from 36 witnesses. Thatcher was extremely angry with his ex-wife following a divorce settlement in which he was ordered to pay her $820,000, the jury was told. He repeatedly referred to her as a "bitch." Thatcher's ex-wife, who was living with her second husband, Anthony Wilson, was found dead after someone hacked at her head at least 20 times before shooting her. So brutal was the fight that she lost a finger trying to protect herself.

Thatcher, unemotional throughout the testimony, reportedly purchased a gun in California and smuggled it back into Canada after repeated efforts to hire killers failed. Californian Lynn Mendell, Thatcher's former girlfriend, testified the MLA told her he had killed his ex-wife, describing it as "a strange feeling to blow your wife away." The Saskatchewan cabinet is scheduled to meet later today to decide how to fill the former MLA's seat in the legislature.

Convicted murderer Colin Thatcher.

Gretzky the fastest to get 1,000 points

Dec. 19, 1984

EDMONTON – An assist early in his 424th game pushed Wayne Gretzky to the 1,000-point plateau tonight, marking the shortest time and youngest age – 23 – any National Hockey League player has reached that level. The previous fastest was Guy Lafleur, in his 720th game for Montreal Canadiens. Gretzky scored two goals and had four assists before the night was over in leading Edmonton Oilers to a 7-3 win over the Los Angeles Kings.

Wayne Gretzky scored his 1,000th career point in his 424th game.

Inuit blame Hydro-Québec for the death of 20,000 caribou

Inuit volunteers drag carcasses of drowned caribou from Caniapiscau River.

Oct. 4, 1984

QUEBEC – Every year at this time, an estimated 400,000 caribou migrate east to west across northern Quebec. This past week, the swollen Caniapiscau River at Limestone Falls has taken the lives of more than 20,000 caribou. A flotilla of Inuit canoes outfitted with hunters carrying guns, noise-makers and fences headed for the falls intent on scaring the caribou away from the falls and redirecting them to a safer crossing area upstream.

The Inuit are calling the caribou drownings a major ecological disaster and blame Hydro-Québec, saying the deadly surge was initiated when Hydro opened spillways 450 kilometres upriver. Hydro blames recent rainfall.

Premier of Ontario Davis to step down

Oct. 8, 1984

TORONTO – William Davis called it quits as leader of the Big Blue Machine today after 13 years in office as Conservative premier of Ontario, ending a successful political career that has spanned 25 years. In an emotional, at times tearful news conference, Davis cited the party's need for "new ideas and new perspectives" as the main reason behind his decision to leave.

Morgentaler acquitted in abortion case

Nov. 8, 1984

TORONTO – A Supreme Court of Ontario jury today acquitted Dr. Henry Morgentaler and two colleagues of breaking a Canadian abortion law the three have openly defied by performing abortions at their Toronto clinic.

Because Morgentaler admits to performing illegal abortions, the jury must have acquitted him on the defence of necessity that his defence lawyer, Morris Manning, mounted over the course of the trial. Manning argued that Morgentaler should be acquitted because his Toronto abortion clinic rectifies an urgent situation in which Canadian women are denied safe and fast abortions under the current legal system.

The present law states abortions can only be performed in hospitals after being approved by a therapeutic abortion committee. In effect, the jury today found the Canadian abortion law to be inadequate to meet the needs of women.

1985

Moscow, March 11. Mikhail Gorbachev succeeds Konstantin Chernenko as leader of the Soviet Union.

Edmonton, May 30. Edmonton Oilers defeat Philadelphia Flyers four games to one to win the Stanley Cup.

Ottawa, June 13. The Supreme Court rules most Manitoba laws are invalid as they are only in English, and not in French as well.

Quebec, June 20. PQ Premier René Lévesque announces his retirement.

Atlantic Ocean, June 23. An Air India jet flying from Toronto to Bombay crashes off Ireland, killing 329, including 280 Canadians. It is suspected the crash was caused by a bomb placed by Sikh extremists.

Toronto, June 26. Liberal leader David Peterson takes office as premier after the Conservative government is defeated in the legislature, ending 42 years of Conservative rule in Ontario.

Red Deer, Alta., July 22. The Alberta Court of Queen's Bench fines former schoolteacher James Keegstra $5,000 for promoting hatred against Jews. Keegstra taught his students the Holocaust didn't happen, and an evil Jewish conspiracy controls world affairs.

Arctic, Aug. 11. The U.S. icebreaker *Polar Sea* completes a voyage through the Northwest Passage, made without Canada's permission, a challenge to Canada's Arctic sovereignty.

Alberta, Sept. 25. The Tyrrell Museum of Paleontology, devoted to dinosaurs and other fossils, opens near Drumheller.

Alberta, Oct. 13. Don Getty is elected Alberta Conservative leader. He will succeed Peter Lougheed as premier.

Montreal, Nov. 24. B.C. Lions defeat Hamilton Tiger-Cats 37-24 to win the Grey Cup.

Quebec, Dec. 2. Robert Bourassa's Liberals defeat the PQ government and their new leader Premier Pierre-Marc Johnson in a provincial election.

Gander, Nfld., Dec. 12. A jet crash kills all 258 aboard, mostly U.S. soldiers.

Ottawa. The government amends the Indian Act to let Indian women who lost their Indian status through marriage to regain it, and to allow greater band control of liquor and residency on reserves.

Cruise Missile test labelled a success

Feb. 20, 1985

COLD LAKE, Alta. – The first solo flight of an American Cruise Missile took place in Canadian air space. The low-flying, unarmed missile was released from a B-52 Bomber over the Beaufort Sea. The self-propelled projectile travelled its course from its point of release to the Northern Alberta Primrose weapons range in little under an hour. At the Primrose range, the missile executed its bombing run before military cameras, then climbed to a higher altitude, released a 21-metre parachute, and drifted down on top of the frozen Primrose Lake, where a 12-member recovery crew waited.

The test went according to plan. Even a barrage of Greenpeace protest balloons was no match for the perfectly programmed missile. The Greenpeace activists say the projectile bashed through 23 weather balloons that hovered 150 metres from the ground. Canadian and U.S. military spokesmen said they took no notice of the Greenpeace demonstrators.

Top court upholds Indian band's claim

1985

OTTAWA – The Supreme Court has handed down its ruling in the Musqueam case, a landmark in the history of Indian land claims. The Musqueam case goes back to 1959, when the Department of Indian Affairs negotiated on behalf of the Musqueam band for a Vancouver golf club to lease 64 hectares of land from the band. When band officers finally saw the lease 12 years later, they concluded the government had abandoned their interests in negotiating the lease. The band took its case to court, and was awarded $10 million.

Now the Supreme Court has upheld this award, stating Ottawa has a responsibility to protect the interests of Indians under the 1875 Indian Act, which put Indians in a special category as wards of the government. The ruling may lead to other land claims where Indians can show Ottawa abandoned their interests when it negotiated land deals on their behalf.

Hatfield not guilty in marijuana case

Jan. 29, 1985

FREDERICTON – Judge Andrew Harrigan, suggesting a member of the press planted marijauna on Premier Richard Hatfield to create "the juiciest story to ever crack the media," has found the politician not guilty of possession. Hatfield was charged last September after a routine security search prior to a royal visit found 35 grams of the drug in his luggage.

Experiment with Life, by Toronto-born artist and film-maker Joyce Wieland.

Red Cross to start screening for AIDS

Aug. 1, 1985

TORONTO – The Canadian Red Cross Society today announced it will implement a national screening program within four months to prevent donors infected with a virus linked to acquired immune deficiency syndrome – or AIDS – from giving blood. At present, patients who receive Red Cross blood have no assurance it is not contaminated. Donors attest to their own good health and blood is tested only for venereal disease and hepatitis. Under the new program, donated blood will undergo a test for the HTVL III virus.

Tough times mean one in six is poor

1985

CANADA – According to a government study, more than 4.3 million Canadians – one sixth of the population – are poor because of tough economic times during the past five years and unemployment. This includes 870,000 children and young adults. According to Statistics Canada, anyone living in a city of more than 500,000 and earning less than $9,839 per year lives beneath the poverty line.

Tory dynasty days numbered in Ont.

May 28, 1985

TORONTO – Forty-two consecutive years of Tory rule in Ontario are about to end, thanks to an unprecedented deal signed today by the province's Liberal and New Democratic Party leaders, David Peterson and Bob Rae. Under the terms of the historic agreement, a Liberal administration led by Peterson will assume power backed by an NDP promise to neither instigate nor support a motion of non-confidence for the next two years. In return, the Liberals will co-operate with the NDP on a series of legislative reforms and the introduction of new bills, many of them affecting social aid programs.

Premier Frank Miller's Conservatives won only 52 of 125 seats in the election of May 2, just enough to form a minority government. But joint action by the Liberals and NDP, with a combined 73 seats, can topple the Tories. The deal made public today, despite some controversy over its legality, means the long Tory reign won't last through the end of this June.

Canada to tighten grip on Arctic land

Sept. 10, 1985

OTTAWA – External Affairs Minister Joe Clark announced today federal plans to strengthen Canada's claim of sovereignty over the Far North. The new steps include proposed construction of the world's most powerful icebreaker, increased aerial surveillance over the region, and the opening of talks with the United States aimed at settling Canada's claims to sovereignty over the Northwest Passage, long disputed by Washington.

The announcement follows vociferous condemnation by opposition MPs over the government's decision to allow the U.S. ship *Polar Sea* to sail the passage this past summer despite the fact Washington ignores Canada's claims.

Chuck wagon races at the Calgary Exhibition and Stampede.

Violent storms batter southern Ontario

The Barrie tornado destroyed many homes, leaving nearby ones unscathed.

May 31, 1985

SOUTHERN ONTARIO – A series of violent thunderstorms and severe tornadoes, moving in eight well-defined tracks, battered this part of the province this afternoon, causing 12 deaths and an estimated $200 million damage. Officials assessing the situation say it's a miracle so few people died.

The city of Barrie was the hardest hit when a tornado touched down in an industrial park at 4:35 p.m. killing eight people and razing buildings as it carved a path through the neighborhood. More deaths were miraculously avoided by a power cut caused by another tornado 100 kilometres away – it sent Barrie businessmen and students home about an hour before the storm hit there. An estimated 240 Barrie homes have been rendered uninhabitable and will have to be destroyed.

In a scene reminiscent of London during the Blitz, hundreds of residents are tonight sifting through the rubble trying to salvage what few possessions they have left. Most will stay with relatives or in hotels until they find new homes.

Fred Raymond, a blind man who painstakingly built his dream house in Orangeville, emerged from the storm relatively unscathed only to discover his home was destroyed. "It took 20 years to build it and 30 seconds to wipe it out," Raymond's wife, Devon, said. Mr. and Mrs. Raymond, like most of the storm victims, intend to rebuild.

Tornadoes are common in southern Ontario, but it is rare that they reach such intensity. Today's twisters rated an F4 – indicating wind speeds of 313-450 kilometres an hour – on T.T. Fujita's tornado intensity scale of F0 to F5. The only other F4 tornado in Canada killed 28 Regina residents in June 1912. No F5 intensity tornadoes are known to have occurred in Canada. Cleanup efforts are already under way and provincial legislators are setting up emergency relief funds.

1986

Toronto, Jan. 9. An Ontario Hospital Association Conference is told the risk to hospital workers of getting AIDS from non-sexual contact is slight.

Washington, D.C., March 19. PM Mulroney and President Reagan reach an agreement to deal with acid rain, but environmental groups say the deal is vastly inadequate.

Ottawa, March 31. Senator Jacques Hébert ends a 21-day hunger strike in protest of the government's cancellation of the Katimavik youth program.

Charlottetown, April 21. Joseph Ghiz's Liberals defeat the Conservative government in a provincial election.

Edmonton, April. Wayne Gretzky of the Edmonton Oilers ends the regular season with a record 215 points, and the Oilers' Paul Coffey finishes with 48 goals, a record for a defenceman.

Ottawa, May 8. The government orders Canadians not to drink rainwater after finding high levels of radioactive iodine, believed to be a result of the Chernobyl nuclear accident.

Vancouver, May 22. Bill Bennett announces his retirement after 10 years as Social Credit premier of B.C.

Calgary, May 24. Montreal Canadiens defeat Calgary Flames four games to one to win the Stanley Cup.

Summerside, P.E.I., June 4. The Prince County Hospital disbands its abortion committee, leaving P.E.I. as the only province where women can't get a legal abortion.

Toronto, Aug. 1. Dancer and choreographer Erik Bruhn, artistic director of the National Ballet of Canada, dies.

London, England, Aug. 4. Six Commonwealth nations, including Canada, break with Britain and impose economic sanctions on South Africa as a measure against apartheid.

Toronto, Nov. 18. An unidentified collector pays $450,000 for Lawren Harris' *Mountains in Snow*, a record sum for a Canadian painting.

Vancouver, Nov. 30. Hamilton Tiger-Cats defeat Edmonton Eskimos 39-15 to win the Grey Cup.

Canada. Films released include Denys Arcand's *Le Déclin de l'empire américain*, Yves Simoneau's *Pouvoir intime*, and Anne Wheeler's *Loyalties*.

Conservatives trim family allowances

Jan. 20, 1986

OTTAWA – The Progressive Conservatives used their Commons majority today to pass a bill that would trim family allowances by hundreds of millions of dollars over the next few years. The leader of the New Democratic Party, Ed Broadbent, told the House: "I give notice to the government that it may, because of its numbers, have won the battle, but the war for justice will continue right up to the (late February) budget." Liberal health critic Douglas Firth said the bill will hurt families living below the poverty line to the tune of $16 million this year alone. The bill still needs Senate approval and royal assent before it becomes law.

Carr elected head of CLC

New CLC president Shirley Carr.

May 1, 1986

CANADA – Shirley Carr, 56, has been elected president of the Canadian Labour Congress. She is the first woman and first public sector unionist to hold the post in the 30-year history of the CLC. A former social worker from Niagara Falls, Ont., Carr has worked for the CLC for 12 years, most recently as secretary-treasurer. She succeeds Dennis McDermott, whose 12-year term was marked by internal conflict and declining membership.

"It's time for change, it's time for peace, it's time for unity in the labor movement," Carr told delegates at the biennial convention. The CLC represents 2.1 million, or 58 percent, of the 3.6-million union members across Canada.

Former NDP leader Tommy Douglas dies

Tommy Douglas with the Parliament Buildings in the background.

Feb. 24, 1986

OTTAWA – Spokesmen for all political parties in the Commons today paid tribute to T.C. Douglas, who died yesterday at his Ottawa home after a five-year battle with cancer. Prime Minister Brian Mulroney said the former federal New Democratic Party leader and Saskatchewan premier was one of Canada's "great humanitarians and a truly great parliamentarian."

NDP leader Ed Broadbent said Douglas "was a great man, one of the rare individuals who actually changed the course of history." Said Liberal leader John Turner in praising both his oratory and gentlemanly style: "I never heard Tommy Douglas take a cheap shot at anyone." Six others paid tributes that went beyond traditional statements of party leaders, recalling Douglas' wit and sense of humor.

Ottawa to outlaw gay discrimination

March 4, 1986

OTTAWA – Justice Minister John Crosbie today announced that mandatory retirement and discrimination against homosexuals will be outlawed in the federal jurisdiction. He also said that women will be allowed a greater role in the Canadian Forces. He was specific only on the issue of ending mandatory retirement for federal civil servants and about a million other employees who come under Ottawa's jurisdiction, leaving vague the question of combat roles for women, which will be decided by the military.

Although Crosbie told the Commons the government would "take whatever measures are necessary" to ensure that sexual orientation is banned as grounds for discrimination, he didn't say what these measures would be, or whether Ottawa plans to amend the Canadian Human Rights Act to add sexual preference to the list of forbidden grounds for discrimination.

There was no indication of whether the package of reforms means that Defence Minister Erik Nielsen will repeal a Canadian Forces' order that means, in effect, that homosexuals are not recruited, or, if found, are discharged. It's also unclear whether the RCMP will end a similar, unwritten policy.

Drapeau to retire as Montreal mayor

June 27, 1986

MONTREAL – The man who put Montreal on the map with Expo 67 and the debt-laden 1976 Summer Olympics announced his retirement today. Mayor Jean Drapeau, his voice breaking in emotion, said the decision to end his 32-year political career was forced by ill health. Although polls show Drapeau's Civic Party trailing the Montreal Citizens' Movement as the November election approaches, the controversial mayor said he still retained the support of the people. Quebec Premier Robert Bourassa called the retiring mayor "a visionary."

Governor General's Award for Atwood

Novelist Margaret Atwood.

June 3, 1986

MONTREAL – Author Margaret Atwood has won the Governor General's Award for English-language fiction for her futuristic novel *The Handmaid's Tale*. This is the second Governor General's Award for Atwood. *The Circle Game* won the award for poetry in 1966. Other multiple award winners in the past have included Pierre Berton, Gabrielle Roy, and Hugh MacLennan.

Atwood was unable to attend the ceremony at Place des Arts, where Gov. Gen. Jeanne Sauvé presented awards to George F. Walker for English-language drama and Fernand Ouellette for French-language fiction.

Royal couple open Expo

Prince Charles and Princess Diana.

May 2, 1986

VANCOUVER – Outside it was windy and wet but inside B.C. Place all was joy as Prince Charles and Diana, the Princess of Wales, opened Expo 86 here. About 60,000 invited guests, singers and dancers roared their welcome and then gave a similar salute to Jimmy Pattison, the millionaire B.C. businessman who took over the direction of the fair when it was faltering. Later the royals were taken on a tour of the exposition. Its theme is transport.

One group of fair-goers was oblivious to the fuss. They were the teenagers waiting – some since dawn – to get on the roller coaster called The Scream Machine.

Church to end male-dominant references

Aug. 17, 1986

SUDBURY, Ont. – The "Father, the Son and the Holy Spirit" will stay the same, but the United Church of Canada vows to wipe out other male-dominant references in its religious literature. The General Council of the church adopted the resolution at its annual meeting here to curb male domination. The church will refrain from using the term "man" and use the inclusive term "people." King, He, Master, and Father will be stricken from church vocabulary and replaced by God, Creator, or Father-Mother.

The council stopped short of banning the incantation "in the name of the Father, the Son and the Holy Spirit." It says the phrase is an essential part of the church's sacrament ceremony.

Axel Heiberg Island fossil forest found

Aug. 28, 1986

AXEL HEIBERG ISLAND – The most stunning fossil forest in the world has been discovered by Canadian scientists on Axel Heiberg Island, about 1,100 kilometres from the North Pole. The 45-million-year-old fossil forest comprises stumps a metre wide and logs up to 10 metres. Some of the trees in the one-square-kilometre site are clearly redwoods and water firs, both of which are found in south-eastern Asia. The other species are not known to science.

Scientists are amazed at how well preserved the specimens are. Fossil wood had not petrified or turned to stone. Describing the freshness of leaves found near stumps, the University of Saskatchewan's James Basinger said "it's like you've just plucked them off the tree."

CMA says doctors should report any AIDS-related cases

Aug. 12, 1986

WINNIPEG – The public risk of AIDS justifies doctors reporting AIDS-related cases to health authorities, the Canadian Medical Association general council has ruled. "The public health concerns are such that we are going to have to know who these seropositives are and what's going to happen to them in two or three or four years," Dr. Arthur Parsons told reporters.

Parsons said he recognized disclosing who is carrying any AIDS-related viruses may trouble some doctors who consider it a breach of patients' rights, but the overriding concern must be protection of public health. He said the association would try to ensure responsible use of information to curb any abuses of patient-doctor confidentiality. Health officials say 662 AIDS cases have been reported in Canada to date, with 339 deaths.

The Canadian Medical Association also endorsed a resolution saying doctors have an ethical duty to treat people with AIDS, although no incidents of refusing treatment have been reported.

Les Ballets Jazz de Montréal in Appearances.

Arcand's Decline shines

Friends meet for a country weekend in The Decline of the American Empire.

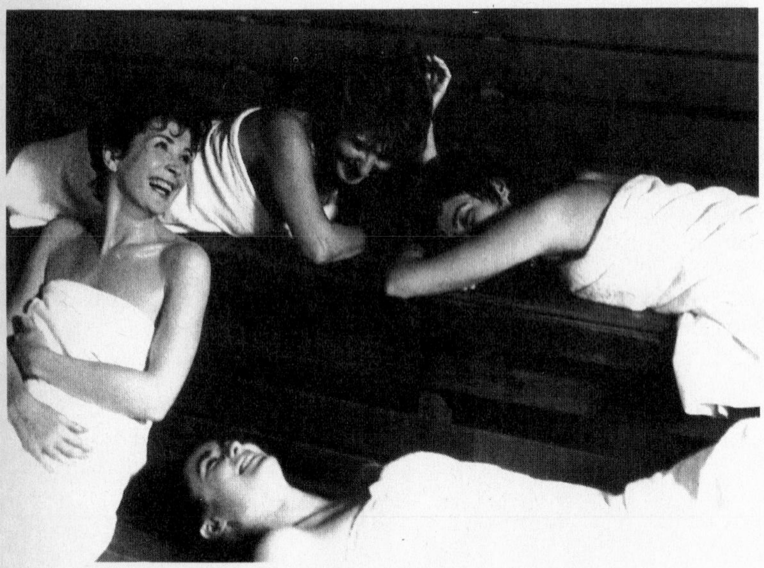

Relationships are explored in Arcand's award-winning film.

Sept. 14, 1986

TORONTO – *The Decline of the American Empire,* a movie about the sexual attitudes of Quebecers, took two top prizes at the Toronto Festival of Festivals. The film earned director Denys Arcand the most popular film award as well as laurels for best Canadian film. This is the first time in the festival's 11-year history a Canadian film has won in the most popular category. Previous winners have been *The Big Chill* and *Chariots of Fire,* both box-office hits.

The best Canadian film, determined by the seven-member international jury, carries with it a $15,000 cheque. "This big trophy and this big cheque are a bit overwhelming ...," Arcand said. "A good Canadian film does good for all Canadian films."

Arcand is to head to Hollywood soon to oversee the production of the English version of *The Decline.* The comedy features some frank dialogue about relations – sexual and social – between friends gathered for a week at a country home. A poster of the movie depicting stylized male and female genitalia has raised eyebrows.

The festival awarded other Canadian films. *Sitting in Limbo* and Martha Henry's performance in *Dancing In The Dark* got special honorary mentions.

Newfoundland has high illiteracy rate

Oct. 7, 1986

ST. JOHN'S, Nfld. – One in three Newfoundlanders is functionally illiterate, according to the royal commission report on employment and unemployment in the province. Thirty percent read at less than a Grade 9 level, compared to 19 percent for Canada as a whole.

Illiteracy has a direct bearing on unemployment. Newfoundland's youth unemployment rate is the highest in Canada at 33.2 percent. The school dropout rate is also extremely high. Only six percent of Newfoundlanders go to university.

Campeau controls giant U.S. retailer

Nov. 2, 1986

NEW YORK – Toronto businessman Robert Campeau today closed a deal to purchase the U.S. retail giant Allied Stores Corp., which operates retail franchises across America. The deal follows weeks of hostility between Campeau Corp. and Allied managers, and comes just days before the two corporations were due to meet in a Manhattan courtroom. Under the terms of the purchase agreement, Allied shareholders will receive $69 US per share, $11 more than Campeau's original offer.

Expert: Franklin's crew died naturally

The grave of a Franklin crewman.

Sept. 23, 1986

EDMONTON – University of Alberta anthropologist Owen Beattie announced today that autopsies performed this summer on the remains of two crew members of the ill-fated 1845 Franklin expedition show the men died of natural causes, probably a combination of hunger and tuberculosis.

The bodies, encased in ice for 140 years and only partially decomposed, were exhumed and examined by a team of Canadian and American scientists. The perfectly preserved remains of another crewman were examined two years ago, but so far no evidence of rumored cannibalism by the crew has been found.

Goalie mask introduced by Jacques Plante is now standard equipment.

Chemicals dumped in Welland Canal

Nov. 11, 1986

ONTARIO – The Ontario New Democratic Party today publicized a report on water pollution in the Welland Canal. The study shows that sewage treatment plants and industries dump 394,000 cubic metres of chemical waste into the canal every day. Much of the effluent contains known or suspected carcinogens. The report is highly critical of the government's half-hearted efforts to clean up the water, which, like that of the highly polluted Niagara River, eventually finds its way into Lake Ontario. Furthermore, had the study been conducted according to government guidelines, up to 90 percent of the dangerous chemicals would have gone unnoticed.

NDP environment critic Ruth Grier says that although 90 percent of the chemicals in the lake come from the U.S., Canada must set an example by cleaning up its share before asking the Americans to do the same. The government says it will pass stiffer pollution-control regulations in the coming months.

Nobel Prize honors Polanyi's research

Dec. 10, 1986

STOCKHOLM, Sweden – As trumpets blasted his praises, Canadian chemist John Polanyi received his Nobel Prize from King Carl Gustav XIV of Sweden today. Winning the Nobel Prize, in association with two fellow chemists from Harvard and Berkeley, is the latest glory in the impressive career of the unpretentious scientist from the University of Toronto. In its way, today's ceremony was just "an incident in life," said Polanyi. "But what an incident!"

Polanyi and his associates won the Nobel for research explaining that molecules interact in chemical reactions. The three prizes awarded for science – one each for physics, chemistry, medicine or physiology – are the world's greatest scientific awards. John Polanyi is the second Canadian to win the chemistry prize, the first being Gerhard Herzberg in 1971.

Expo 86 hosts 22 million

The site of Expo 86 was a narrow strip of land along False Creek in Vancouver. The new development made a magnificent setting for a world's fair.

The city of Vancouver forms the backdrop for the architectural innovation of the World Trade Centre and Canada Place at Expo 86.

Oct. 13, 1986

VANCOUVER – Expo 86 has closed its doors – and the last of the 22 million visitors has gone home. Very few of the unpleasant things feared by planners occurred – there were no terrorist attacks and no traffic jams. Although attendance was light in May and June it soon picked up as the weather got better. The final 22-million figure was nine million higher than forecast. The deficit, to be paid from lottery revenue, is forecast to be $310 million.

Expo 86, built on a narrow site on the shores of False Creek, attracted millions of foreign visitors who, it is hoped, will return for other vacations now that they have seen the beauty, the cleanliness, and relaxing charm of this city. Officials hope businessmen who came for pleasure will return to do business.

Report cites danger acid rain is posing

Dec. 2, 1986

ONTARIO – While pollution control programs levelled off toxic emissions and reduced acid in the '70s, increased sulphur and nitrogen pollution now has elevated acid rain fallout. A six-volume report by 60 federal and provincial scientists says acid rain damage has targeted rivers and small lakes stretching from central and northern Ontario to Nova Scotia.

Dry particles or weak solutions of sulphuric acid in rain or snow are devastating lakes, forests and crops. About 14,000 Canadian lakes have died and up to 40,000 are seriously threatened. The report denotes evidence that the underground water sources also are being acidified.

The national report says even humans are at risk. Metals dissolved from rocks and acids in sources of drinking water and pollution infiltrating the lungs cause considerable health risks. Children in areas of acidic air pollution in southern Ontario have decreased lung function, and they contract more colds, allergies, coughs, and stuffy noses than those living in the cleaner-air regions of western Canada.

This acidic pollution is decaying Canadian forests at an alarming rate. In some areas the veil of acidity is equivalent to vinegar. Computer analysis indicates a 40-percent reduction of acid rain could save threatened waters.

Ontario to provide services in French

Nov. 18, 1986

TORONTO – In a move aimed at showing Ontario's commitment to a bilingual Canada, MPPs from all three political parties unanimously approved a bill providing Ontario government services in French, as well as English. Bill 8, as it's known, means that some ministries will be able to provide French services within three years, says Bernard Grandmaitre, minister responsible for francophone affairs. All this means that "eventually this province will be bilingual," says Grandmaitre.

1987

Toronto, March 16. The *Globe and Mail* reports condom use is becoming standard in gay bathhouses, a reflection of concerns about AIDS.

Toronto, March 18. *Le Déclin de l'empire américain* wins eight Genie Awards.

Ottawa, March 27. Federal, provincial and aboriginal leaders fail to agree on a constitutional amendment guaranteeing native self-government.

Toronto, April 3. Industry spokesmen say Canadians buying large amounts of life or health insurance must now take a mandatory AIDS test.

London, England, April 27. The World Commission on the Environment and Development releases *Our Common Future* (the Brundtland Report), a landmark report on the global environmental crisis.

Edmonton, May 31. Edmonton Oilers defeat Philadelphia Flyers four games to three to win the Stanley Cup.

Canada, June 30. The $1 loonie coin makes its debut in circulation in major cities.

Yellowknife, N.W.T., June. The N.W.T. government announces a $400,000 AIDS education program for northerners, among the most sexually active Canadians.

Halifax, July 29. Most of the 174 illegal South Asian refugees who landed here July 13 have been cleared for release in Canada after sponsors posted performance bonds. Federal authorities detained the refugees for two weeks.

Alberta, Sept. 4. Researchers reveal they have made the first discovery of dinosaur fetuses in eggs. The find shows dinosaurs lived in colonies and mothered their young.

Ontario, Sept. 10. David Peterson's Liberals win a landslide victory in a provincial election.

Fort Simpson, N.W.T., Sept. 20. Pope John Paul II meets with native people and says Canada must grant natives self-government.

Washington, D.C., Oct. 4. Canada and the U.S. agree on the terms of a free-trade agreement.

Ottawa, Oct. 26. The Commons ratifies the Meech Lake accord with a large majority.

Vancouver, Nov. 29. Edmonton Eskimos defeat Toronto Argonauts 38-36 for the Grey Cup.

First ministers OK Meech Lake accord

June 3, 1987

OTTAWA – "Today, we welcome Quebec back to the Canadian constitutional family," Prime Minister Brian Mulroney said at a noontime signing ceremony of an agreement reached by the first ministers on April 30 at Meech Lake, Que., and fine-tuned in 19 straight hours of deliberation.

Just before dawn, the 11 weary first ministers approved legal wording for proposed constitutional amendments that recognize Quebec as a distinct society. Said that province's Premier Robert Bourassa at the signing ceremony, "Canada is one of the greatest countries in the world." He looked as if emotion and fatigue might overcome him as the prime minister rushed to his side and shook his hand as the other premiers applauded loudly.

In Montreal, former prime minister Pierre Trudeau said that although what is now known as the Meech Lake accord was signed, it is far from ratified. He called the prime minister "a weakling," and the premiers "snivellers."

Orser claims world figure skating title

March 12, 1987

CINCINNATI – Brian Orser of Penetanguishene, Ont., became the first Canadian since 1963 to win the men's world figure skating title, dethroning defending champ Brian Boitano of the United States. Orser, who last month won his seventh successive national title, put to an end a long string of disappointment for Canadian men skaters. He is the first gold medal winner since Donald McPherson of Stratford, Ont.

Brian Orser practises in Cincinnati before winning the world title.

Novelist Margaret Laurence passes away

Margaret Laurence won the Canada Council Molson Award in 1975.

Jan. 5, 1987

LAKEFIELD, Ont. – Novelist Margaret Laurence died at her home this morning after a battle with lung cancer. She was 60.

Born Margaret Wemyss in Neepawa, Man., she drew on her experiences in a small town for novels, several of which chronicled lives of women in a conservative fictional town called Manawaka. Of these, *The Stone Angel* is considered her best work. Another, *The Diviners*, caused controversy because of descriptions of sexual encounters and abortion. The Peterborough Board of Education, near her home, received many requests to have it removed from the high school reading lists.

Indian medicine men earn respect of health-care professionals

March 1987

MANITOBA – The traditional Indian medicine man is a popular figure in northern Manitoba these days. Just ask 87-year-old healer Nazer Linklater, or, for that matter, any one of the many doctors and nurses who show no qualms about sending patients his way. Not long ago western health professionals would have scoffed at the idea. Not so anymore. He is popular for one simple reason: more often than not, his brand of medicine works, particularly on Indians. According to one federal nurse, Linklater's an invaluable "mixture of a psychiatrist, a priest and a doctor." Health and welfare officials agree and now cover travel expenses for Indians who wish to consult medicine men.

National Assembly ratifies Meech pact

June 23, 1987

QUEBEC CITY – Quebec has become the first government to approve the Meech Lake accord that brings the province – as "a distinct society" – into the constitutional fold. "For the first time, we are winners in the constitutional debate," Premier Robert Bourassa told the National Assembly just before the 95-18 vote that ended a 35-hour emergency debate. Parti Québécois leader Pierre-Marc Johnson said the Bourassa administration will go down in history as "one of the most abjectly cowardly governments on powers for Quebec."

Trudeau criticizes constitutional deal

Aug. 27, 1987

OTTAWA – In his most passionate attack yet on the Meech Lake accord, Pierre Trudeau today told a Senate-Commons committee studying the agreement that not only is there no need to entrench special status for Quebec in a new constitution, but that such a move is insulting to Quebecers. Billed at the hearings as a "private citizen," the 67-year-old former prime minister warned the committee members that if they think recognizing Quebec as a distinct society means nothing then "you're in for a superb surprise."

Hansen finishes his Man in Motion tour

May 22, 1987

VANCOUVER – Tens of thousands of supporters lined Vancouver's streets as Rick Hansen triumphantly rolled into the city 26 months and 40,000 kilometres after starting his Man in Motion round-the-world tour. Hansen, who at 29 has been confined to a wheelchair since an accident 14 years ago, has raised more than $10 million for spinal chord research from patrons in 34 countries. Like his late friend Terry Fox, Hansen's hope and determination have made him an international hero.

One million women abused each year

June 10, 1987

OTTAWA – One million Canadian women are abused each year, according to a report issued today. Battered But Not Beaten, an investigation into wife battering in Canada, defines wife abuse as more than physical attacks. It also includes bullying, threats, insults, and controls that threaten the physical, sexual, economic, or psychological well-being of women, their children, friends, or relatives. The report says women are not the only victims of such abuse. Children of battered women may become withdrawn, suicidal, or violent.

The study says more than 20,000 women were admitted to transition houses in 1985, 80 percent because of abuse from partners. Most were young, between 21 and 34. Many were teenagers or pregnant. Seventy percent were high school dropouts, and most came from households with an annual income of less than $20,000. At least another 20,000 were turned away because of the chronic lack of funds at shelters for battered women.

Vicki Keith completes her two-way swim across Lake Ontario

Vicki Keith smiles and touches a concrete pier to mark the end of her swim.

Aug. 7, 1987

TORONTO – Marathon swimmer Vicki Keith of Kingston, Ont., came ashore just before 4 p.m. today, completing a 102-kilometre, two-way crossing of Lake Ontario in 56 hours and 13 minutes. The swim, to Port Dalhousie (near St. Catharines) and back, was expected to take 48 hours, but she was delayed by strong currents and waves up to three metres in height.

Keith, who had to fight off hallucinations at one point in the swim, first tried the double crossing last year, but the attempt was called off after 36 hours because of storms. Keith, 26, said she was not a quitter and that the pain of the swim was worth the effort. One of the hazards she faced was pollution. Bacteria from sewage has been so high, all beaches in Metro Toronto are closed to the public.

Johnson sets record in 100-metre dash

Aug. 30, 1987

ROME – Canada's Ben Johnson established himself as the fastest runner in the world, winning the 100-metre dash at the world track and field championships today in a record 9.83 seconds. The former mark of 9.93, held by Calvin Smith of the United States, was tied by his countryman, Carl Lewis, in this event. The gold medal Johnson won was the first for a Canadian in track and field at the Olympics or world championships since Duncan McNaughton's gold in high jump at the Olympics of 1932. Johnson, 25, was born in Jamaica. He believes he can further improve his time for the Seoul Olympics next year.

Canadian Ben Johnson crossed the finish line ahead of American Donald Witherspoon and set a world record of 6.41 seconds in the 60 metres at the World Indoor Championships in Indianapolis on March 7.

Founder of the PQ and former premier René Lévesque dies

Founder of the Parti Québécois René Lévesque is dead at age 65.

Nov. 1, 1987

MONTREAL – René Lévesque is dead. The former Quebec premier and founder of the Parti Québécois died here tonight. He was 65. Premier Robert Bourassa said his longtime political foe "will pass into history as one of our most generous and determined patriots."

Lévesque was one of Quebec's most influential television commentators before he joined Jean Lesage's Liberal government in 1960. As minister of natural resources, he was responsible for nationalizing electric utilities.

Lévesque founded the PQ in 1968 and led it to power in 1976. In 1980, he led the referendum campaign in an unsuccessful attempt to get a mandate to negotiate sovereignty-association. Lévesque retired in 1985.

All hell breaks loose on stock market

Oct. 20, 1987

OTTAWA – Hundreds of billions of dollars in stock values were wiped out in a few brief hours today, as stock exchanges around the world were devastated by panic selling. The plunge on Wall Street knocked some $507 billion from the value of U.S. shares as the Dow Jones industrial average dive-bombed 22.62 percent. By comparison, the 1929 crash sliced 12 percent off shares. The Toronto Stock Exchange took a cruel beating. Stocks plunged $37 billion and the TSE index slumped 11 percent. The Montreal market lost 9.5 percent.

"It's just incredibly hectic here," one exhausted New York trader said. "Everybody wants to sell but there are practically no buyers." Yesterday's crash stunned investors already reeling from the shock of last Friday's crash, seen as a long-overdue correction to a wild bull market. Over the weekend panic set in, and when exchanges opened this morning all hell broke loose.

"It's a classic liquidity crisis," said one analyst based in Montreal. "Everybody wants out of everything. They're all trying to get through the keyhole at once."

Lemieux's marker good for Canada Cup

Mark Messier and his teammates celebrate Canada Cup victory.

Sept. 15, 1987

HAMILTON – Mario Lemieux scored on a pass from Wayne Gretzky late in the game to give Team Canada a 6-5 victory over the Soviet Union in the third and deciding game of the Canada Cup hockey tournament tonight. The goal capped a comeback from a 3-0 deficit in one of the most exciting games since Paul Henderson was the hero for Team Canada in the final game of the inaugural series with the Soviets 15 years ago. It was Lemieux's 11th goal of the tourney. He had seven assists in the nine games. The points leader was Gretzky, with three goals and 18 assists.

Officer in Montreal shoots black youth

Nov. 11, 1987

MONTREAL – An unarmed black youth was shot dead by a Montreal Urban Community police officer outside a west-end police station early today. Anthony Griffin, 19, died in hospital from a bullet wound to the forehead. The youth had obeyed an order to halt, Police chief Roland Bourget said. He has ordered an investigation of the shooting, which he denies was racially motivated. Griffin was picked up by police after a taxi driver reported he refused to pay a fare. A computer check revealed Griffin was wanted on a burglary charge. The officer has been suspended.

Alberta farmer Doug Murfin demonstrates the results of a 1985 drought. Canada is urged to do more to protect its arable land.

Clean sweep: McKenna's Liberals win all 58 seats in N.B. vote

Oct. 13, 1987

FREDERICTON – There's not a single opposition member of the New Brunswick legislature tonight. The results of the vote are clear: Frank McKenna's Liberals won 58 seats, the other parties won none. This ends the 17-year rule of colorful and controversial Conservative Premier Richard Hatfield, until today the longest serving of Canada's current premiers. Standings in the previous legislature were Conservatives 37, Liberal 20, and NDP one.

McKenna said tonight he expects the news media and members of his own party to become an unofficial opposition. "I think we're going to have to be very disciplined," he said. "We're going to have to self-discipline ourselves and I intend to be very tough on that."

McKenna said his positions on free trade and the Meech Lake constitutional accord remain the same. He has endorsed free trade with the U.S. and wants the Meech deal changed to protect the rights of women and francophones outside Quebec. In the campaign, McKenna refused to talk about Hatfield's personal problems, the subject of much comment by others.

Hatfield said tonight he accepts responsibility for the stunning defeat but would not say whether he intends to remain Conservative leader. McKenna's victory was so complete only one riding was won by fewer than 100 votes. Only one other shutout has been recorded in Canadian political history.

Free trade text tabled

Dec. 11, 1987

OTTAWA – After months of negotiation, the 2,500-page text of the proposed free-trade agreement was tabled in the House by Prime Minister Brian Mulroney. If approved, the package would lower most of the trade barriers between Canada and the United States. It would allow many American goods to compete freely with domestically-made products in the Canadian market, and vice versa. It also has a mechanism for settling trade disputes between the two countries, the number of which have been growing over the years.

Supporters of the FTA, such as Mulroney's Tories, say it will give Canadian industry a much bigger market to sell in. But opponents, such as Liberal leader John Turner and NDP chief Ed Broadbent, are already criticizing the deal as a "sellout" to the States. Both leaders are daring the prime minister to call an election over free trade to let the people decide the issue.

Night lights create a rainbow of color in the water in this cityscape of Halifax, the capital of Nova Scotia.

Governor General's Award Munro's third

Alice Munro receives her Governor General's Award from Jeanne Sauvé.

May 27, 1987

TORONTO – Alice Munro accepted her third Governor General's Award at Roy Thomson Hall today. Gov. Gen. Jeanne Sauvé presented the award for Munro's collection of short stories, *The Progress of Love*. Munro, 56, won her first Governor General's Award in 1968 for *Dance of the Happy Shades*. The second award winner, *Lives of Girls and Women*, published in 1971, was also a runner-up for Britain's prestigious Booker Prize.

The Territorial Capital Building in Whitehorse, Yukon Territory.

Canada, U.S. to clean up the Great Lakes

Nov. 11, 1987

TORONTO – Canada and the United States have signed a tougher version of the 1978 Great Lakes Water Quality Agreement. Instead of just identifying obvious polluters, "we are taking ... an ecosystem approach," says Canadian Environment Minister Tom McMillan. Speaking here, McMillan says that all sources of pollution will now be dealt with. These include leaking dumps, fertilizer runoff from fields, and toxic chemical seepage.

The city skyline of Yellowknife in the Northwest Territories.

1988

Ottawa, Jan. 15. A survey of provincial laboratories shows that more than 10,000 Canadians have tested positive for the AIDS virus.

Ottawa, Jan. 15. Ukrainian Canadians ask Ottawa to officially acknowledge that Ukrainians were mistreated in Canada during and after WWI, and to negotiate to provide redress for the mistreatment.

Ottawa, Feb. 25. The Supreme Court rules Saskatchewan must either translate its laws into French and allow French to be used in its courts and legislature or enact a law making English the only language of the courts and legislature.

Calgary, Feb. 28. The Winter Olympics end. Canada won five medals altogether, including silver medals for Brian Orser and Elizabeth Manley in figure skating.

Calgary, March 1. Frank King, chair of the Olympic Organizing Committee, reports the games had an unprecedented $32-million profit.

Winnipeg, March 9. Former NDP premier Howard Pawley announces his retirement from politics after his government's defeat on a non-confidence vote.

Toronto, March 22. Jean-Claude Lauzon's film *Un Zoo la nuit* wins an unprecedented 13 Genie Awards.

Toronto, May 17. The Ontario government reverses a previous decision to allow logging, mining, hunting, and trapping in wilderness and nature reserve parks. The government also says the Red Squirrel logging road in Temagami, expected to hurt the environment, will be built.

Edmonton, May 26. Edmonton Oilers defeat Boston Bruins four games to none to win the Stanley Cup.

Ottawa, May 31. The Commons passes bills directed against the tobacco industry that include measures to phase out tobacco advertising.

Winnipeg, June. Arnold Spohr retires as artistic director of the internationally acclaimed Royal Winnipeg Ballet.

Winnipeg, Sept. 2. Statistics Canada says a drought that has ravaged Canadian crops will cut Canadian wheat production 41 percent in 1988.

Ottawa, Nov. 27. Winnipeg Blue Bombers defeat B.C. Lions 22-21 for the Grey Cup.

Top court strikes down abortion law

Jan. 28, 1988

OTTAWA – The Supreme Court of Canada has overturned the federal abortion law. The law required a panel at an "accredited" hospital to determine whether a pregnancy threatened a woman's life or health before granting an abortion. The 5-2 ruling states that the law and committee process was unconstitutional, threatened women's health, and forced women to undergo painful and arbitrary delays.

The ruling came as a result of an appeal on Dr. Henry Morgentaler's fourth trial on abortion-related charges. The decision allows women in Canada to obtain abortions on demand for the first time in the history of the country.

Mulroney, Reagan sign free-trade pact

Jan. 2, 1988

OTTAWA – The Canada-U.S. trade agreement was signed this afternoon, with Prime Minister Brian Mulroney asking President Ronald Reagan to send the deal to the U.S. Congress "as expeditiously as possible." The prime minister has promised to introduce legislation on the free-trade deal early this year, but it could be months before it reaches Congress. Already, opposition members have threatened that the legislation will face a rough ride in the Commons. The Liberals have already denounced it as "a monumental disaster."

Pending approval of the deal by both Parliament and Congress, almost all trade tariffs between Canada and the U.S. will be gradually phased out over a 10-year period, beginning Jan. 1, 1989. Rules governing investment restrictions, customs procedures, and trade in energy and services will also change.

Shultz defends U.S. stance on acid rain

Jan. 11, 1988

OTTAWA – When External Affairs Minister Joe Clark and U.S. Secretary of State George Shultz met here today, acid rain was a top priority for Canadian officials. Ottawa wants the United States to match Canadian abatement of acid rain emissions with a total reduction of 50 percent by 1994. Instead of responding to the agreement, Shultz claimed acid rain is not as bad as Canada pretends. He added that Washington is spending more than $500 million to research acid rain, and that it is misleading to say the U.S. is not acting on the issue of acid rain.

Winter Olympic Games open in Calgary

Olympic opening ceremonies at the McMahon Stadium playing field.

Feb. 13, 1988

CALGARY – Canada opened its doors to the world today as the 15th Winter Olympic Games got under way here with a two-hour show that featured 6,000 entertainers. A Wild West theme was established as cowboys, Indians, and chuck wagons, as well as Mounties on horseback, paraded across the McMahon Stadium playing field. About 2,500 athletes marched into the stadium, with the 149-person Canadian team led by figure skater Brian Orser, the defending world champion. Robyn Perry, 12, of Calgary, lit the Olympic cauldron after taking the torch from two former Olympians, skier Ken Read and speed skater Cathy Priestner.

Elizabeth Manley in her award-winning silver medal performance.

James Bay II plans on Quebec agenda

March 8, 1988

QUEBEC CITY – Quebec Premier Robert Bourassa announced plans to proceed with Phase II of the massive James Bay hydroelectric project. Calling the megaproject a "form of Quebec patriotism," Bourassa said the $7.5-billion undertaking would generate 40,000 jobs and 2,500 megawatts of power, much of which has been sold already to northern U.S. states. He said contracts worth $40 billion are on the order book and clients in New York, Vermont, and Maine are expecting delivery by 1995.

Bourassa described the James Bay II announcement as "one of the most glorious moments of my career." He vowed the labor problems that plagued the first phase would not happen this time around with a new stable social climate in the province. He also said the massive project would conform to provincial environmental standards.

France recalls envoy in fish dispute

April 18, 1988

ST. JOHN'S, Nfld. – France recalled its ambassador to Canada yesterday as relations between the two countries deteriorated following the arrest of the St. Pierre vessel the *Croix de Lorraine* 65 kilometres east of this port.

After Canada extended its jurisdiction 322 kilometres to sea, it let St. Pierre fishermen continue to fish in the Gulf of St. Lawrence. However, France has also laid claim to 322 kilometres of coastal waters around St. Pierre and Miquelon, and last fall, when it broke off talks with Canada over the boundary around the islands, Canada banned all French fishing in the Gulf.

The 6,000 residents of St. Pierre and Miquelon argue that their livelihood is threatened, and in order to draw attention to their plight they decided to fish openly in Canadian waters and be arrested. Seventeen trawlermen and four government officials left St. Pierre on Wednesday in the *Croix de Lorraine* and on Thursday began fishing near here.

On Friday, Canadian fisheries patrol vessels the *Cape Roger* and the *Leonard J. Cowley* placed the *Croix de Lorraine* and crew under arrest, escorting the ship to port. The men were held in custody until Sunday and released on bail. They flew back to St. Pierre this morning. Relations between Canada and France have sunk to a new low.

These French fishermen were arrested by Canada inside the 322 km. limit.

Campeau wins battle for giant retailer

Robert Campeau discusses his deal for the Federated Department Stores.

April 1, 1988

NEW YORK – After 10 weeks of a high-priced bidding war, Canadian entrepreneur Robert Campeau has won the right to buy Federated Department Stores for a whopping $6.64 billion US. It's the biggest deal ever made by a Canadian, the record having been set by Campeau in 1986 when he bought Allied Stores for $3.4 billion.

Campeau emerged victorious after agreeing to sell his chief rival, Edward Finkelstein of Macy's, two important California chains for $1.1 billion. Still, in winning, he's probably gone into more debt than any Canadian in history.

Filmon reigns with minority government

April 26, 1988

WINNIPEG – Gary Filmon's Conservatives have won a minority government in today's provincial election. The seat count is 25 for the PCs, 20 for Sharon Carstairs' Liberals, and 12 for Gary Doer's NDP. The Liberals are the big surprise, led from near-oblivion by Carstairs. The NDP has been reduced to third place after winning the last election under Howard Pawley.

Browning first to land a quadruple jump

Kurt Browning performs his quad.

March 25, 1988

BUDAPEST – Canada's Kurt Browning became the first person to land a quadruple jump in official competition today when he opened his free skating routine with a quad toe loop at the world figure skating championships. The move upstaged American Brian Boitano, who also tried a quad jump but landed on both feet, which doesn't count. Boitano, who won the Olympic gold at Calgary, did add the world gold to his trophy case, as defending champion Brian Orser of Canada took the silver.

Browning, who finished sixth, is the latest Canadian to introduce multiple-rotation jumps. In 1962, Don Jackson landed the first triple lutz, and Vern Taylor did the first triple Axel at the 1978 worlds.

Top court overturns Keegstra conviction

June 6, 1988

CALGARY – The Supreme Court of Alberta today quashed the 1985 conviction of James Keegstra on charges of promoting hatred against Jews. The court ruled the Criminal Code section under which Keegstra was charged violates freedom-of-speech guarantees in the Charter of Rights and Freedoms.

For 14 years Keegstra taught his junior high school students at Eckville, Alta., that the Holocaust didn't happen and that an evil international Jewish conspiracy influences world events. He was the mayor of Eckville and a popular teacher in 1983 when a mother of one of his students read her son's notebooks. She complained to the school board about his teachings. He was fired, lost his teaching certificate, defeated as mayor, charged with spreading hatred against an identifiable group, and convicted in 1985 after a long trial.

Prairie drought hurts farm industry

June 15, 1988

REGINA – "Every day is just a killer. The moisture from the rains of two weeks ago has evaporated. The conditions are disastrous. There is crop being torn up because it isn't worthwhile." Garfield Stevenson, president of the Saskatchewan Wheat Pool, was commenting on present drought conditions on the prairies. It is predicted that the total harvest this year will be 35 percent below the average yield. Earl Geddes, president of Keystone Agricultural Producers in Manitoba, estimates that Canada will export 20 million tons of grain this year, 10 million less than normal.

An Alberta farmer digs deep but finds little moisture in his field.

Plagued by drought and low grain prices, many farmers are being forced to seek outside employment – or even to leave farming altogether. In the last 12 months, 24,000 prairie people have left agriculture. The figure includes farmers, farm workers, and unpaid family members.

In Alberta, 3,000 people have left the farm. In Manitoba, the number is 4,000. But the province of Saskatchewan takes the lead with some 17,000 people who have quit the farming business. And these numbers were calculated in May, when employment on farms traditionally reaches its highest point.

Farmers are cutting costs by not hiring help. In fact, unemployment rose in Manitoba at a time when the national rate went down.

Mountie raid sparks Mohawk roadblock

June 1, 1988

KAHNAWAKE, Que. – A dispute involving the right to sell tax-free cigarettes has mushroomed into a serious confrontation between Kahnawake Mohawks and RCMP officers. The episode began yesterday morning when some 200 Mounties armed with submachine-guns raided several stores on the Kahnawake Reserve, just outside Montreal. They seized $450,000 in cigarettes the RCMP say were smuggled in from the United States. The Mohawks, some heavily armed, responded by blocking highways running through the reserve. A lawyer for the shop owners says no law was broken in selling the cigarettes since Jay's Treaty, signed in 1794, gives Indians the right to duty-free cross-border commerce.

Mohawk Indians block the entrance to the Kahnawake Reserve near Montreal.

Blockbuster deal sends Gretzky to L.A.

Aug. 9, 1988

EDMONTON – In what may be the biggest trade in hockey history, the Edmonton Oilers sent Wayne Gretzky to the Los Angeles Kings in a multi-player deal that L.A. sweetened with an undisclosed sum of money. Gretzky, Marty McSorley, and Mike Krushelnyski go to the Kings, in return for Jimmy Carson, Martin Gélinas, three first-round draft choices, plus the cash. Gretzky, recently married to actress Janet Jones – they are expecting their first child – said he initiated the deal for his family and hockey. He is seen as being able to sell hockey in L.A., but that is no consolation for angry Oiler fans.

Gretzky is sad to leave Edmonton.

Sexual assaults land priest 5 years in jail

Sept. 30, 1988

ST. JOHN'S, Nfld. – Father James Hickey was sentenced today to five years imprisonment for sexually assaulting boys and young men during the 1970s and 1980s while he served as priest in several parishes. Hickey was highly regarded, and so his arrest earlier this year on 32 counts of sexual assault, indecent assault, and gross indecency has shocked the province and the Roman Catholic community. Hickey pleaded guilty to 20 charges on Sept. 9.

It appears this is not an isolated case and that other priests are about to be charged with similar offences.

Johnson sets record winning gold medal

Johnson raises his arm in victory.

Sept. 24, 1988

SEOUL – Sprinter Ben Johnson set a world record of 9.79 seconds for the 100 metres today in winning Canada's first Olympic gold medal on the track since Percy Williams won that event plus the 200 metres in 1928. In beating the former record of 9.83 he set at last year's world championships, Johnson was quick out of the blocks.

American Carl Lewis set a U.S. record of 9.92 in the final, but was a badly-beaten second to Johnson. The top four runners all finished in less than 10 seconds.

Pair in catamaran end Arctic journey

Aug. 17, 1988

POND INLET, N.W.T. – Two young Canadians have just sailed through the Northwest Passage. They are the first to make the journey in a wind-powered craft. Jeffrey MacInnis, 25, and Michael Beedell, 32, started their voyage three years ago. They spent their summers in the ice-filled Arctic sailing along the coast in their yellow 5.5-metre catamaran *Perception.* When the ice closed in each winter, they left for Ontario and returned to the Arctic to take up their trip in the spring. Their sailing time: 100 days. MacInnis and Beedell wore special clothing but said they were still numb with cold.

Ben used steroids, stripped of medal

Sept. 27, 1988

SEOUL – Gold quickly tarnished for Canada's Ben Johnson today when he was stripped of his gold medal in the Olympic Games 100-metre dash after testing positive for illegal drugs. Johnson, 26, who blew away the field and his own former world record with an incredible 9.79-second final Saturday, tested positive for a banned anabolic steroid called stanozolol. The IOC rejected suggestions of sabotage in the testing. American Carl Lewis, who finished second, was given the gold.

Johnson was banned from the Olympics and left Seoul this morning for New York. Canada's Sports Minister Jean Charest said the sprinter would receive a life ban from national teams. It will hit him in the pocketbook as well with the loss of promotional contracts estimated to be as high as $15 million.

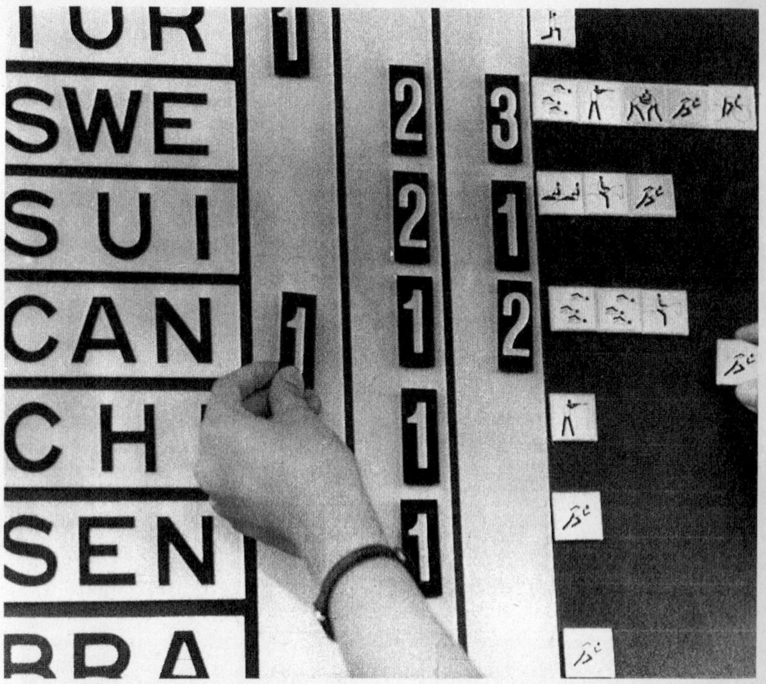

An Olympic official lowers Canada medal count after Johnson is disqualified.

Synchronized swimmer Waldo, boxer Lewis bringing home gold

Carolyn Waldo and Michelle Cameron win the gold medal in the duet synchronized swimming event. Waldo also won gold in the solo event.

Lennox Lewis shows his gold medal.

Oct. 2, 1988

SEOUL – Synchronized swimmer Carolyn Waldo is the first Canadian woman to win two gold medals in one summer Olympics, and Lennox Lewis brought Canada its first boxing gold since 1932 in weekend competition here, giving the controversy-plagued national team a much-needed boost.

Saturday, Waldo and Michelle Cameron won the gold in the duet synchronized swimming event. The night before, she won the gold in the solo competition. Waldo, of Beaconsfield, Que., and Cameron, of Calgary, won the gold on the basis of a strong earlier showing in compulsory figures. Twins Sarah and Karen Josephson of the U.S. outscored the Canadians in the final routine but couldn't overcome their lead in the compulsories.

In the ring today, Lewis, of Kitchener, won the super-heavyweight title when he stopped U.S. champion Riddick Bowe at the 43-second mark of the second round. Canada's last Olympic boxing gold was the bantamweight crown won by Horace "Lefty" Gwynne 56 years ago. Lewis, 23, had vowed he'd win the gold to make up for the one stripped from sprinter Ben Johnson after he tested positive for a banned anabolic steroid.

RCMP put an end to Lubicon blockade

Oct. 20, 1988

LITTLE BUFFALO, Alta. – The RCMP swooped down this morning on blockades maintained by Lubicon Indians and their supporters. Armed with rifles, police dogs, chain saws, and a court injunction, Mounties cleared obstacles to traffic and made 23 arrests.

The problem stems from negotiations for Treaty No. 8 in 1899 when the isolated Crees of Lubicon lake were missed by Crown officials. Their land claim is still unresolved even though millions of dollars worth of oil are removed every day from their ancestral land in northern Alberta. Alberta Premier Don Getty hopes to meet Chief Bernard Ominayak to discuss the dispute.

Canada wins a seat on Security Council

Oct. 26, 1988

NEW YORK – Canada has been elected to the United Nations Security Council by the UN General Assembly. The council, which is made up of five permanent and 10 temporary members, is designed as a sort of "cabinet" for the United Nations.

And, although superpower rivalries have often stopped it from functioning, still Canada's election to a two-year term is seen as important by External Affairs Minister Joe Clark. "It steps up our role internationally. ... Some people belittle it, but we can make an important contribution because of our history of tolerance" – and of peacekeeping troops as well.

Haida carving entitled Raven and the First Men.

PCs back in the saddle

Nov. 21, 1988

OTTAWA – The federal Tories have been returned to power in today's general election, meaning that Prime Minister Brian Mulroney has won the fight for free trade. Despite a seven-percent drop in their share of the vote – from 50 to 43 percent – the PCs have taken enough seats across Canada to form a second majority government. This comes as sweet news for Mulroney, as does his continued success in Quebec, once thought to be an impregnable Liberal stronghold.

The victory comes after an incredibly bitter campaign over the free-trade agreement with the United States, one that both pro and anti forces turned into a crusade for the future of Canada. It revitalized the career of Liberal leader John Turner, whose pinning of Mulroney in a televised debate had many wondering if he'd overthrow the Tories. But, despite doubling his share of seats in the House, neither Turner nor NDP leader Ed Broadbent will be able to stop passage of the free-trade agreement early next month.

Japanese Canadians to get compensation

Mulroney and Miki sign agreement.

Sept. 21, 1988

OTTAWA – After four long years of negotiations, the federal government today agreed to terms of compensation for 21,800 Japanese Canadians forcibly removed from the west coast during the Second World War. The settlement, signed by Prime Minister Brian Mulroney and Art Miki, president of the National Association of Japanese Canadians, could pay as much as $300 million in individual compensation. It provides those still living whose property was expropriated or who were interned with $21,000 each. The government has also agreed it would provide a $12-million community fund.

PCB fire forces residents out of homes

Aug. 21, 1988

ST. BASILE LE GRAND, Que. – Local residents have been evacuated after a fire at a PCB warehouse near this farming community sent a thick plume of toxic smoke billowing into the air. The warehouse was a storage site for the PCBs, which scientists say release cancer-causing furans and dioxins when burned. The PCBs are used mostly in power transformers. The fire has raised questions about the security of toxic waste storage sites, and angry residents wonder why it takes a potentially disastrous fire to alert environmental authorities to the hazards.

Teens warned of dangers of unsafe sex

Dec. 1, 1988

OTTAWA – A study released today warns that sexually-active teens are not taking the necessary precautions against the spread of AIDS and other sexually-transmitted diseases. The study, based on a survey of 38,000 Canadian adolescents, recommends that people with AIDS meet with students to talk about the deadly virus. Dr. Alistair Clayton, director general of the Federal Centre for AIDS, warns it could become a serious problem if teens continue to ignore the dangers of unsafe sex.

Klondike in middle of a mini-gold rush

Dec. 31, 1988

DAWSON, Yukon – About 200 family firms are hard at work taking gold from the Klondike's creeks – 92 years after the big Bonanza strike. The gradual rise in gold prices means placer miners can sift through the piles of sand and rock left on the banks of the famous creeks and find enough gold to make the day's work worthwhile. They use the techniques honed in the California gold rush. These involve washing away the lighter sand and pieces of rock to leave the heavier fragments of gold.

This fine gold is not as valuable as coarse gold nuggets, but placer miners can still make a living. They found $64 million worth last year. The original Klondike miners used this method at first but then started to dig shafts to get to veins of ore. Now placer mining is back.

Language law overruled

Bilingual and unilingual signs such as these are not allowed under Quebec's controversial language law.

Dec. 15, 1988

OTTAWA – Quebec's contentious language law has been tossed back to Premier Robert Bourassa by today's ruling of the Supreme Court of Canada that overturns the law's provisions requiring that all signs, posters, and commercial advertising be only in French. This means Quebec can order the use of French in such communications, but cannot ban the use of other languages along with French.

Bourassa must decide whether to accept the ruling of the court and change offending sections of the law, known as Bill 101, or override the court's decision by invoking the "notwithstanding" clause of the Canadian Charter of Rights and Freedoms. Bourassa told reporters today he will not announce any action until Sunday. He also warned store owners against putting up bilingual signs "prematurely."

Bourassa ensures French-only signs

Quebec Premier Robert Bourassa.

Dec. 18, 1988

QUEBEC CITY – As expected, Premier Robert Bourassa today said he'll invoke the so-called notwithstanding clauses of the Canadian and Quebec rights charters to ensure that French is the only language allowed on commercial signs outside stores. The decision was taken after a flurry of cabinet and caucus meetings following the ruling on Thursday by the Supreme Court of Canada that struck down parts of Quebec's language law, Bill 101. The premier said that some bilingual signs will be permitted inside some stores, a compromise that several political observers predict will only serve to inflame protests from both sides.

Montreal rally in support of Bill 101 attracts 18,000 people

Dec. 18, 1988

MONTREAL – Quebec's independence movement got a big boost today at a huge rally in support of the province's language law, Bill 101. Close to 12,000 people jammed into the Paul Sauvé Arena in the east end, while another 6,000 had to stand outside in the biting cold.

Former Parti Québécois cabinet minister Camille Laurin, the author 11 years ago of the language law, suggested there hasn't been such a massive demonstration in Quebec since the PQ was first elected on Nov. 15, 1976. Said Louis Laberge, president of the Quebec Federation of Labor: "Not since the death of (former PQ premier) René Lévesque have Quebecers come together in such a way." The head of the small but vocal Parti Indépendantiste, Gilles Rhéaume, said: "The Supreme Court of Canada says it is impossible to live in French in Quebec within the federal system."

The highest court in the land ruled last Thursday that Bill 101's provision requiring that all commercial signs be in French only violated both federal and provincial charters of rights and freedoms. A group of students at the rally set fire to the Canadian flag.

Quebec nationalists crowd the Paul Sauvé Arena, waving flags and placards.

Anglo trio leaving Bourassa's cabinet

Dec. 20, 1988

QUEBEC CITY – Three of the four cabinet ministers representing anglophone interests in the Bourassa government have quit, saying they can't support the decision to continue banning English on signs outside stores. Richard French, Clifford Lincoln and Herbert Marx say they can't vote for Bill 178. The fourth, John Ciaccia, says he can, "because someone has to make the first concession, the first step, toward easing confrontations."

CPR's Rogers Pass project an engineering marvel

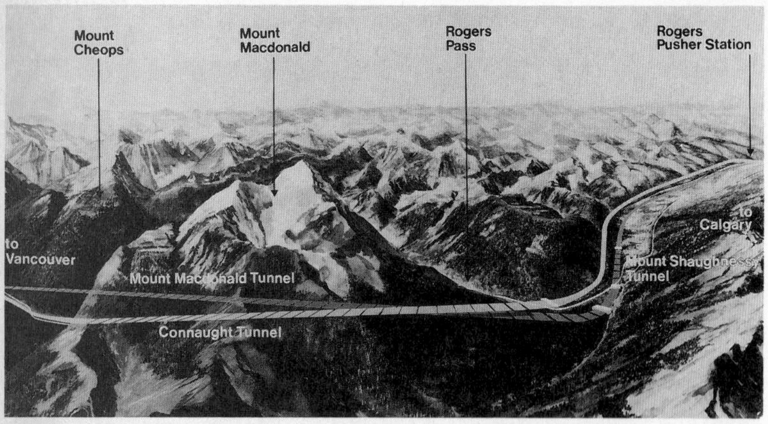

Artist's conception of the new Mount Macdonald Tunnel in the Rogers Pass.

CP Rail plants trees in a massive reclamation project.

CP Rail built three work camps such as this one to house construction workers.

Work nearly done on Macdonald Tunnel

December 1988

BRITISH COLUMBIA – The Canadian Pacific Railway has almost completed its second national dream: 33.5 kilometres of tunnel that stretches beneath Mount Macdonald and Mount Cheops and through the historic – and infamous – Rogers Pass in the Selkirk mountain range. "This is a big job," said a 40-year-old blaster, one of more than 1,000 men and women to work on the project. "If you can pull this off, you can work anywhere in the world."

He wasn't kidding. The Macdonald Tunnel, a marvel of modern engineering, runs through perhaps the most treacherous terrain in Canada. Located 131 rail kilometres away from the Alberta border, the narrow pass was discovered by an American engineer, Maj. A.B. Rogers, in 1881. At that time the area was relatively uninhabited, by man or beast. Few could survive the avalanches, insects, and harshness of the beautiful but dangerous Selkirk mountains. Giant bridges were constructed in the 1880s to carry trains through the pass, but the tracks were forced off the summit of Mount Macdonald by 1916 because of avalanches.

Now a safe and economically viable route is a *fait accompli.* The tunnel cost the CPR $500 million to build and required four years of boring through almost 15 kilometres of quartzite and philite, but it is expected to pay immediate dividends. Gone are the days when a dozen locomotives were needed to push and pull a 14,000-ton westbound freight train across the Great Divide. As few as four or five can now do the job in less time; traffic is expected to double, at least.

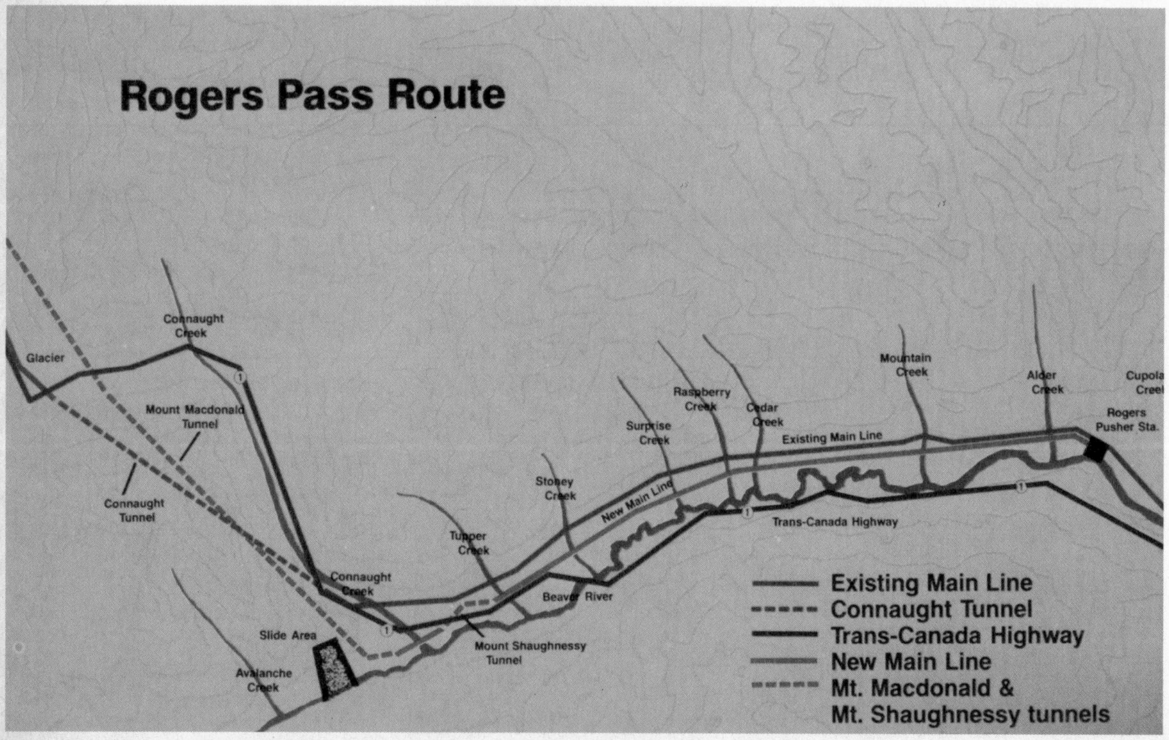

This map shows the various transportation routes through the Rogers Pass area.

Crews used this 302-ton boring machine, nicknamed the Mole, in the project.

Rails transport men and materials into tunnels under construction.

This is the nerve centre for the tunnel's sophisticated ventilation system.

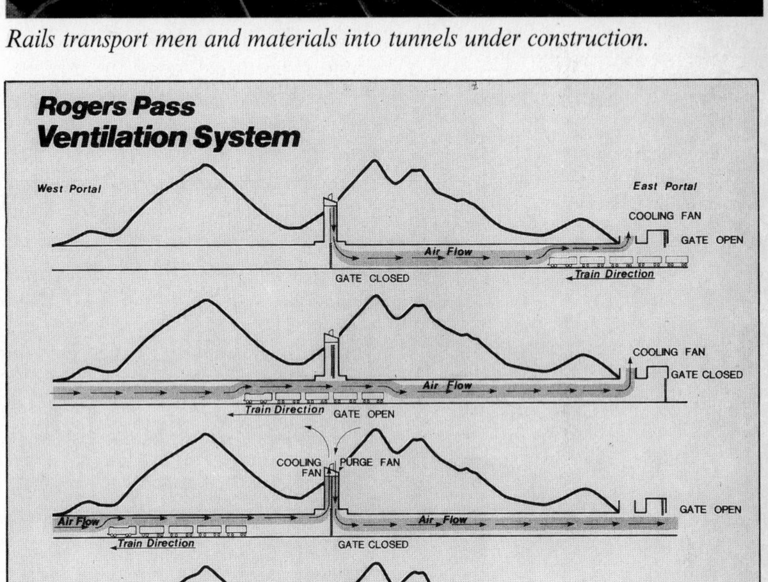

These drawings illustrate the efficiency of Rogers Pass ventilation.

The Stoney Creek Bridge is the longest of the five bridges in the project.

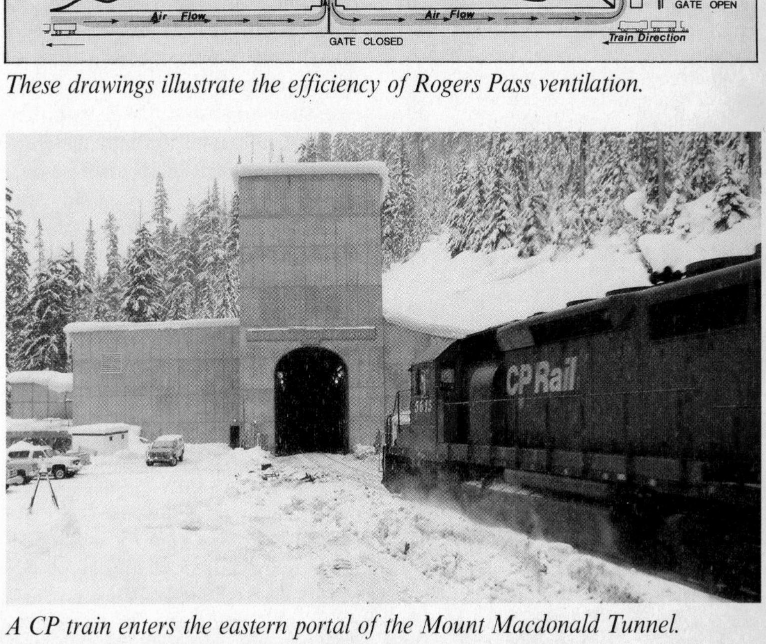

A CP train enters the eastern portal of the Mount Macdonald Tunnel.

1989

St. John's, Nfld., Jan. 21. Brian Peckford announces his resignation after 10 years as Conservative premier.

Quebec, Feb. 4. A Laval University study finds the milk of Inuit mothers in northern Quebec contains the highest level of PCBs of any mother's milk in the world.

Ontario, March 4. Ed Broadbent announces he is retiring as federal NDP leader after 14 years in the job.

Newfoundland, March 6. The Roman Catholic church announces it is establishing an inquiry into charges that priests sexually assaulted children under their care.

Montreal, May 25. Calgary Flames defeat Montreal Canadiens four games to two to win the Stanley Cup.

Toronto, June 3. Toronto's new SkyDome stadium is inaugurated with a gala spectacle.

Quebec, July 26. The Quebec Court of Appeal upholds an injunction barring Chantal Daigle from having an abortion, ruling the fetus is "a distinct human entity ... and has the right to life."

Ontario, Aug. 24. A team of scientists from Canada and the U.S. announces it has found the defective gene that causes cystic fibrosis.

Barcelona, Sept. 5. The International Amateur Athletic Federation strips Ben Johnson of the 100-metre world record he set at the 1987 world track and field championships at Rome, but will still recognize him as a champion of the meet.

Ottawa, Oct. 16. Environment Minister Lucien Bouchard announces Ottawa is giving the provinces $100 million over five years to clean up about 1,000 toxic waste sites.

Montreal, Nov. 8. Montreal's homeless will soon be eligible to receive welfare payments under an agreement between the city, the Quebec government, and community groups. It will be the first time in Canada the homeless get welfare payments.

Ontario, Nov. 26. Hundreds of protesters bring their own dishes to McDonald's restaurants across Ontario to protest the company's use of environmentally harmful packaging.

Toronto, Nov. 26. Saskatchewan Roughriders defeat Hamilton Tiger-Cats 43-40 to win the Grey Cup.

France and Canada to send boundary dispute to tribunal

April 1, 1989

ST. JOHN'S, Nfld. – International Trade Minister John Crosbie announced yesterday that France and Canada have agreed to send the boundary dispute concerning waters surrounding St. Pierre and Miquelon off Newfoundland's south coast to an international tribunal within three years. This dispute has soured relations between the two countries and has led to confrontation between the fishermen in the disputed waters.

However, as part of this agreement Canada will give 2,950 tons of fish from the stocks off Newfoundland's northeast coast to France. This is a sensitive issue in Newfoundland because these cod stocks in the zone known as 2J3KL are already depleted and fishermen on the northeast coast have been complaining of overfishing in this region for years. In addition, the provincial PCs, under their new leader Tom Rideout, are in the midst of a campaign for re-election.

Canada gets first female combat soldier

Private Heather Erxleben puts on camouflage paint during field exercise.

Jan. 19, 1989

WAINWRIGHT, Alta. – Heather Erxleben, one of 21 infantry soldiers graduating from Canadian Forces Base Wainwright, has made history. The Vancouverite is the first woman combat soldier in Canada. "I wanted to become a soldier because I like the physical aspect of the army," she said.

Erxleben, 22, was the only one of 21 women to take the infantry test who successfully completed training. The drop-out rate among females is higher than males because of the course's physical rigors. "We knew there were very few Canadian women strong enough," said Cmdr. J.E. Harper, director of combat-related employment for women.

Abortion issue left up to Conservatives

March 9, 1989

OTTAWA – The Supreme Court of Canada has tossed the abortion issue back in the federal government's lap by refusing to rule on whether a fetus has the right to life. The court declared that to decide such an abstract issue would be an intrusion into Parliament's law-making authority. It also said a ruling on fetal rights would only confuse the medical profession.

The top court ordered the federal government to pay court costs incurred by Joseph Borowski of Winnipeg, who has waged a 10-year battle against abortion in Canada. The costs were awarded as a wrist-slap to the federal government for having allowed the case to proceed while it decides how to tackle a new abortion law. An incensed Borowski said "it seems to me it was a gimmick, a charade, a trick they played on us" to hear his case but not render a decision.

Ben on steroids before world meet: coach

March 2, 1989

TORONTO – Ben Johnson had been using anabolic steroids in preparing for the 1987 world track and field championships where he set a record for the 100-metre dash, his coach Charlie Francis testified today at the federal Dubin inquiry into drug use in amateur sport. The coach pointed to a chart which detailed a steroid program leading up to the championships in Rome, at which he ran the 100 metres in 9.83 seconds. He beat his own record with a 9.79 clocking at the Olympic Games in Seoul last year, but was stripped of the gold when he tested positive for steroids.

Coach Charlie Francis explains some training techniques to the inquiry.

Despite the testimony of Francis, the International Amateur Athletics Federation said there was no grounds to wipe out the Rome record because he had passed a drug test there after the race. Francis said Furazabol was the drug being used and that he injected Johnson with it at his apartment. He said that Johnson used Winstrol, also called stanozolol, during the same period. He revealed as well that a rift developed between himself and Johnson before the Olympics. After a brief parting in the spring, Johnson returned to work with Francis.

Hijack drama on the Hill

April 7, 1989

OTTAWA – A bizarre hostage-taking which saw a Greyhound bus being surrounded by police sharpshooters on Parliament Hill ended quietly today when the single hijacker surrendered to the RCMP. The drama began shortly after Greyhound bus No. 1482 left Montreal bound for New York with 11 passengers. When the bus arrived at the tollgate at the St. Lawrence River, the gunman leapt up and took over the bus, releasing an elderly passenger at the bridge.

Because police assumed the bus was still headed for New York, they didn't tell the RCMP of the hostage-taking. So the Mounties were completely taken off-guard when the bus arrived at Parliament Hill in Ottawa at 2:20 p.m. There the hijacker released two more hostages, who told police he had dynamite and would blow the bus up if his demands weren't met. These focused on ending the war between pro-Israeli and pro-Palestinian groups in Lebanon. After a long standoff in which shots were fired, the man finally surrendered. He has been identified as Charles Yacoub.

Policeman passes radio to bus driver.

A tradition is over: last $1 bills printed

Canadian Bank Note employee inspects last sheets of $1 bills.

April 20, 1989

OTTAWA – A tradition ended here today at the Canadian Bank Note Company when the last paper $1 bills were printed. From here on in, only the new $1 brass coin – nicknamed the "loonie" because it has a loon on its front – will be produced. The new coins are cheaper to make and will last 20 years to the old bills' one. Even so, many Canadians are not happy with the thought of using the loonie. They say it's too heavy, and distorts the shape of pant pockets even worse than quarters do! At present, there are about $300 million worth of $1 bills in circulation. This last batch will be released in June.

Ruling: gay couples can be a "family"

April 13, 1989

OTTAWA – A human rights tribunal, in a landmark decision today, ruled that homosexual couples can constitute a family. This was part of the ruling in the case of a federal civil servant who had been denied bereavement leave to attend the funeral of his male partner's father. The tribunal of the Canadian Human Rights Commission ruled that the Treasury Board and a government union discriminated against Brian Mossop of Toronto. Mossop said he fought the case on a matter of principle, that "there shouldn't be any special privileges for being heterosexual." New Democrat MP Svend Robinson calls it "an enlightened decision."

Talk about your quint-essential family

Feb. 6, 1989

NEWMARKET, Ont. – It was a year ago today that Mae Collier gave birth to Canada's first test-tube quintuplets, named Wade, Lance, Remington, William, and Maxine. Since then, she and her husband Wayne have changed about 18,250 diapers, and gone through countless feedings, burpings, and so on. Despite all the work, Mae and Wayne are in high spirits. "You have a choice – either you can be miserable or you can decide to have lots of fun," Mae commented from her Newmarket home. The Colliers are getting help from family and volunteers, and the community has rallied to provide clothes, cribs, and strollers.

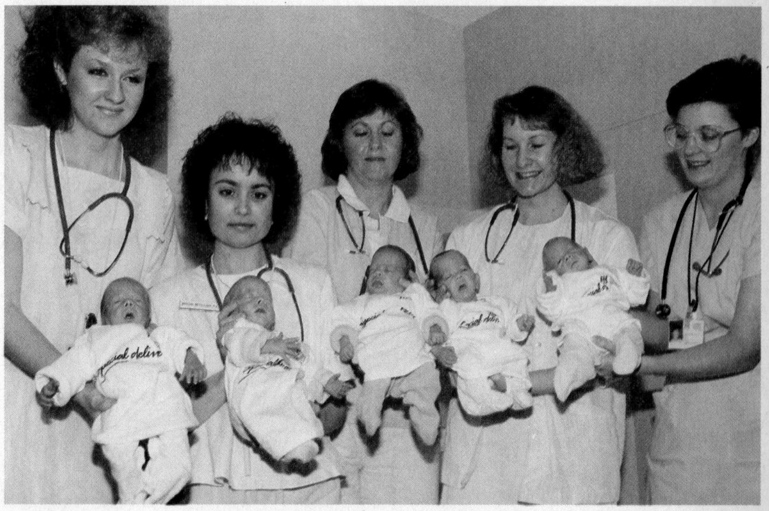

Multiple births are becoming more common. The Collier quints, pictured here, were born in Toronto a year ago – Canada's first test-tube quintuplets.

Quebec Inuit leaders to draft constitution

April 10, 1989

NORTHERN QUEBEC – In an election here today, 80 percent of 3,500 eligible Inuit voted for six leaders, including the two major leaders Charlie Watt and Harry Tulugak, to begin work on an Inuit constitution which may lead to a form of regional self-government. For the Inuit, the need for such a constitution is evident as the provincial government, in its quest for increased Hydro-Québec production, continues to implement unpopular policies. As one leader says, it's no longer a question of buying the Inuit, but of securing their cultural and economic future.

Marshmallow madness is reeling them in

Harvesting the marshmallow crop.

April 1, 1989

MONTREAL – Its first crop of hydroponically-grown marshmallows has delighted agronomists at the city's experimental station down at the Old Port. "Of 100 saleable bushels, 80 percent are category A, soft-white," a spokesman reports. Once harvested only in wintry marshes, selected mallows were cross-pollinated to produce the hardy new variety that seeded Montreal's successful attempt at controlled production in shallow, 5mm aqua-pans. The mallows will be known as April Fools.

Jesus of Montreal a winner in Cannes

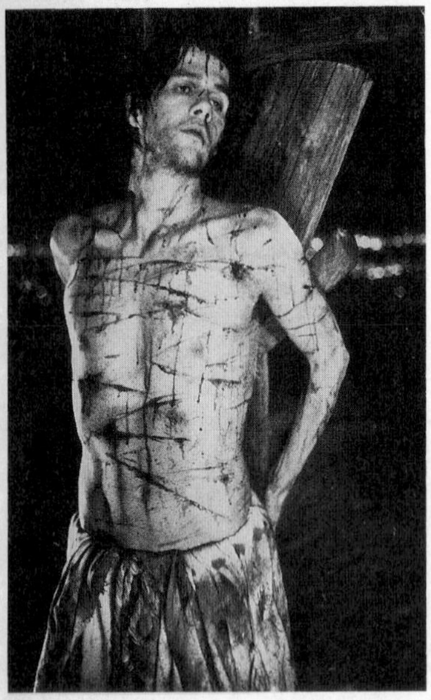

Jesus of Montreal.

May 23, 1989
CANNES – *Jesus of Montreal* is the second Cannes award for Montreal director Denys Arcand. The film took the Jury Prize at the fabled festival, but lost the Palme D'Or to *Sex, Lies and Videotape,* from the U.S.

Three years ago Arcand won the top critics' prize for *The Decline of the American Empire. Jesus of Montreal* is about a troupe of actors in Montreal who get caught up in producing a modern version of the passion play. The film is already a box-office hit in Quebec.

Ghiz guides Grits to victory in P.E.I.

May 29, 1989
CHARLOTTETOWN – Here is a quick refresher for those unfamiliar with the current trends in Prince Edward Island politics. Joe Ghiz and his provincial Liberals are popular. Quite popular. Brian Mulroney and his federal Tories are not. Emphatically not. Mel Gass and his provincial PCs are caught between the two. Politically speaking, this is an unpleasant place to be for the Tories. Today that was evident, as Gass led his party to the second worst defeat in Island electoral history.

A series of wildly unpopular federal policies seem to have made only the partisan inclined to vote for the provincial wing of the party. The extent of the Conservative defeat: 30-2, the final tally read. Not since the Liberal sweep of 1935 has a party been so badly mauled at the polls on Prince Edward Island.

Joe Ghiz celebrates his election victory with his wife and son.

Festival makes cuts in Merchant of Venice

May 18, 1989
TORONTO – After a meeting with officials of the Canadian Jewish Congress, the Stratford Festival has made two cuts in Shakespeare's *The Merchant of Venice.* But Patricia Quigley, a festival official, today denied that the theatre was bowing to pressure from any group. Quigley said a reference to the merchant Shylock's forced conversion to Christianity has been deleted because it is "outdated."

Purists say the anti-Semitic aspect of the play is part of its literary history and should not be touched. Quigley said a scene involving Lancelot and Jessica, in which he jokes that the price of pork will rise if Jews convert to Christianity, was also dropped because of its "racial overtones."

Sask. to translate its laws into French

June 1, 1989
REGINA – After sinking $4 million into GigaText Translation System Inc., the company that was to translate Saskatchewan statutes into French but which three months later is still not in operation, the provincial government has engaged a translation service affiliated with the University of New Brunswick to start the work. In the meantime, the Saskatchewan Economic Development Corporation has taken control of GigaText and loaned the company an additional $1.25 million to pay expenses until the end of the year.

Guy Montpetit, sole signing authority for GigaText and who had an earlier company of his go bankrupt, is facing a $39-million lawsuit in Montreal and is under a government-ordered RCMP investigation into how the $4 million was spent.

In February 1988, the Supreme Court of Canada ruled that Saskatchewan laws must be translated into French to be valid. To comply with the top court ruling, the provincial government then passed the Language Act, which calls for the translations.

Fireworks mark the official opening of the Canadian Museum of Civilization, designed by Douglas Cardinal. The museum is situated on the Hull shore of the Ottawa River directly opposite the Parliament Buildings.

Cars cost at least $100 a week to run

Aug. 11, 1989
OTTAWA – It costs $100 a week or more just to run the average cheap car, the Canadian Automobile Association says. In its annual report released today, the CAA says rising gas, insurance, and purchase prices have driven the cost over the $100 mark even in low-cost Alberta, where a subcompact only cost $87.58 a week last year. CAA president Michael McNeil says the costs wouldn't be so high if Ottawa didn't insist on such steep fuel taxes at the pumps. He says the taxes have an effect that is "very negative on the economy."

Johnson admits he used anabolic steroids

Ben Johnson considers his responses.

June 12, 1989

TORONTO – Ben Johnson confessed to the Dubin inquiry today that he began using anabolic steroids in 1981, although he didn't realize what they were until two years later. The testimony to the inquiry into drug use in amateur sport was a marked turnaround from his denial when stripped of the Olympic gold medal in the 100-metre dash last year in Seoul, South Korea, after a positive test.

The Toronto sprinter says he would not have taken steroids had he been aware of potential liver, kidney, and sexual dysfunction side effects. He said that coach Charlie Francis told him other athletes took them and the only way he could be the best was to follow suit.

Liberals end a 17-year drought in Nfld.

April 21, 1989

ST. JOHN'S, Nfld. – Clyde Wells and his Liberal party won at least 30 out of 52 seats yesterday and brought to an end 17 years of Progressive Conservative government. Tom Rideout, who succeeded Brian Peckford as premier only 29 days ago, was unable to sway voters concerned about the declining economy, especially the fishery sector. Wells is seen as a new vigorous leader with fresh talent around him. A swing in St. John's toward the Liberals made the difference.

Wells, who lost his bid for a seat, has several imminent problems to deal with. He will probably decide against further government support for the Sprung greenhouse – a multi-million dollar venture to hydroponically grow cucumbers – and he is expected to continue the public inquiry into allegations concerning the Mount Cashel orphanage.

Wells will have to contend with severe problems in the cod fishery due to declining fish stocks which will result in plant closures, unemployment, and emigration. There is also the Meech Lake agreement passed by the House of Assembly. Wells says he may rescind Newfoundland's support for the accord.

The Sprung Greenhouse in Newfoundland is a modern hydroponic facility. However, the owners are experiencing difficulty due to a lack of sunlight.

Via Rail cuts on the way

June 5, 1989

OTTAWA – Via Rail passenger service will be slashed in half under a cost-cutting plan announced today by the federal government. The cuts will eliminate Via's famous dome-topped *Canadian,* which has thrilled millions of tourists on its winding course through the Rockies. Also to be chopped are 13 regional services. The cutbacks will mean the loss of some 2,700 jobs as the government hopes to save $1 billion in projected losses over the next five years. The government says because of low ridership on Via's expansive network, it shells out $2 in subsidies for every $1 in revenue it receives.

Liberal opposition leader John Turner said the Conservative government has "turned the national dream into a national nightmare. The last spike has become the last straw." The government has promised a royal commission into passenger travel to try to defuse the heat of opposition to the Via cuts.

AIDS strips people of their rights, dignity

Demonstrators call for action.

An estimated 12,000 people attend meetings such as this one at the AIDS conference in Montreal.

June 5, 1989

MONTREAL – The devastating effects of AIDS are well documented – in terms of physical debilitation. What is not widely recognized, however, is the extent of emotional and mental duress AIDS sufferers face. According to Larry Gostin, a professor at the Harvard University School of Public Health speaking here today at the Fifth International Conference on AIDS, every day "human beings ... are being taken out of society, stripped of their rights, stripped of their dignity." Why? Because they either have AIDS or have tested seropositive for the HIV virus.

For the uninitiated, the revelations are startling. According to a recent global study, there are countless examples of people with AIDS being dispossessed, displaced, and disowned. In some areas of the United States, many who have tested seropositive are excluded from hospitals. They are denied housing. In one case, a child with AIDS was banned from attending school. The case went to court and judged in his favor, but on condition he attend class sitting behind a glass cubicle.

At the workplace, people with AIDS have been fired or demoted, and in some cases they have been deliberately exposed to public humiliation. Harvard's Prof. William Curan says there "is an almost total absence of legislation protecting the human rights of people with AIDS." Discrimination, caused by ignorance, is allowed to continue. ▷

Montreal homeless face hell of a life

June 24, 1989

MONTREAL – Anyone walking into Dernier Recours Montréal, an agency that shelters 100 derelicts every night, can tell you the homeless face a hell of a life. Men sleep on slabs of concrete, many of them stinking of urine, feces, and vomit. And these are the ones who have made it off the streets. A study released last week by sociologist Pierre Simard put the number of homeless people in Montreal at 15,000, with 2,000 being added to their ranks every year.

Simard's study contains startling conclusions. Two-thirds of Montreal's homeless men grew up in middle-income or affluent families. They have typically spent 15 years in the workforce. Almost all of them said they didn't choose to live on the streets. Two-thirds of them are willing and able to work. Simard says they stay down and out because there are no programs to help them fight their drug and alcohol addictions, and no job training to help them get back to work. A similar study on derelict women by Françoise-Romaine Ouellette says women are often driven to the streets by family violence, incest, and alcohol and drug dependency.

Simard says governments should give more money for public housing for derelicts, and for programs to help them fight addictions and retrain for the job market.

Man gets one year for spreading AIDS

Aug. 10, 1989

CALGARY – AIDS-carrier Gordon "Tito" Summers was sentenced to one year in jail for knowingly spreading the deadly AIDS virus to two women. Judge Robert Dinkel found Summers guilty on the reduced charge of being a common nuisance after the two women, both of whom have tested positive for AIDS, refused to testify against the man. Summers, known as Tito on the city bar circuit, has served time for breaking and entering. The Alberta Civil Liberties Association said the ruling will discourage people with AIDS from seeking help.

Daigle abortion stuns Supreme Court

Aug. 8, 1989

OTTAWA – The Supreme Court of Canada was stunned today by the announcement that a Quebec woman had obtained an abortion just as it was about to quash an injunction obtained by her jilted boyfriend preventing her from terminating the pregnancy. Daniel Bedard, lawyer for Chantal Daigle, 22, told the court his client made the decision to abort her 22-week-old fetus without his knowledge. He said he learned of the abortion on a break in the court's hearing.

Daigle's former boyfriend, Jean-Guy Tremblay, had won an injunction blocking the abortion. The Quebec Court of Appeal upheld the injunction a month ago. The case has intensified the emotional debate between pro-choice and anti-abortion forces. Both sides blame the storm of publicity surrounding Daigle's pregnancy on the federal government for failing to bring in a new abortion law.

Despite Daigle having an abortion, Tremblay said he has not given up the fight. Accusing Daigle of having "killed my child," Tremblay said he would consult his lawyers about further action. Legal experts say Daigle could be subject to contempt charges, but one abortion rights advocate said "who in their right mind would want to do that?" Tremblay's lawyer, Henry Kelada, said the court's ruling opens the door for abortion on demand.

Daigle is surrounded by the press.

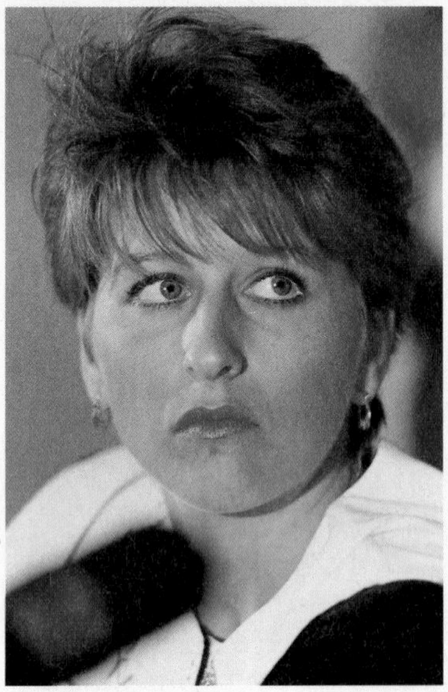

A serious Daigle during trial.

Mystery teenager "Christina" identified as psychiatric patient

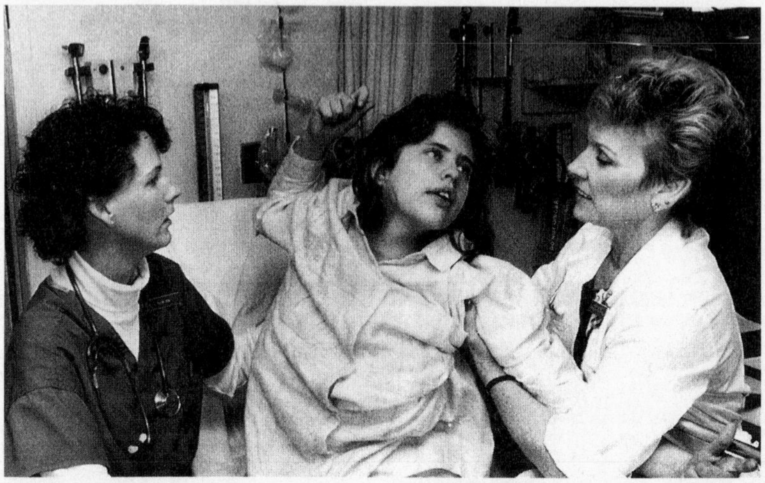

Rochelle Scholl was admitted to a Des Moines hospital in 1988.

Aug. 7, 1989

ST. JOHN'S, Nfld. – The mystery teenager found on the steps of a city cathedral has been identified. The girl, who called herself Christina Yatso, was unable to speak or walk when found July 7. At first, she appeared to be about 15 and seemed to be suffering from a neurological disorder. Investigation of the case, which received worldwide publicity, revealed her to be Rochelle Scholl, a 19-year-old psychiatric patient from Portland, Oregon. Because of a psychological ailment, Scholl believes herself to be another person. A police spokesman said Scholl has returned to Oregon.

Man making a video of legendary Okanagan Lake monster

July 17, 1989

KELOWNA, B.C. – Ken Chaplin, tired of those who doubt the existence of Ogopogo, the Okanagan Lake monster, is making a video of the creature to show scientists. Ogopogo, whose reputation goes back to the days when Indians visited the lake's shores, has been seen again this summer, swimming along, say the spotters, with his characteristic wavy motion. Cynics note that Okanagan Lake, a hot spot surrounded by hills, is often hit by squalls and freak weather. The waves that result could easily be taken for a monster.

Now Chaplin is determined to show what Ogopogo looks like and is videotaping the monster for the next few days. The National Geographic Society of Washington, D.C., wants to see the videotape and plans to get experts to analyse it. But one B.C. expert says the tape he has seen looks like a shot of a large sea otter.

Forest fires force 23,000 to flee homes

July 7, 1989

WINNIPEG – Manitoba is undergoing the most serious outbreak of forest fires in history. A combination of prolonged drought and searing heat has resulted in close to 250 fires. Some 23,000 northern residents have been forced out of their homes. By bus and by air they were evacuated first to Thompson, Wabowden, and Thicket Portage, but when facilities in those communities proved inadequate, many were flown south to Winnipeg and Brandon. They are being housed in hotels and university residences.

In most of the northern communities, only the able-bodied men were left to maintain fireguards. For them, this is a difficult assignment. The woods are tinder dry and the heat is close to unbearable.

Firefighters are trying to stop the spread of the forest fires in Manitoba.

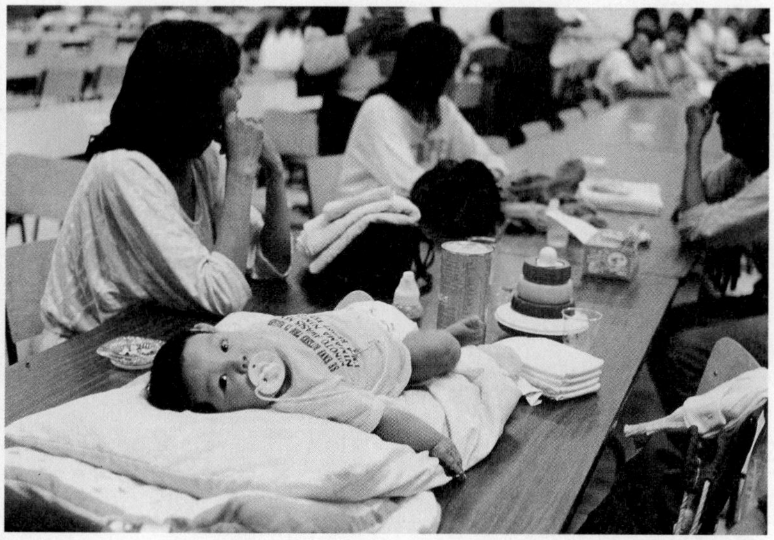

Evacuees from Nelson House are billeted in a makeshift shelter in Thompson.

PCBs return to Quebec

The Soviet Ship Nadezhda Obukhova will deliver the PCBs to Baie Comeau.

Hydro-Québec's Manic 2 site where PCBs are stored.

Aug. 17, 1989

QUEBEC – For the past two years, Canada has sent its polychlorinated biphenyl wastes to Britain for destruction by incineration. But when a Soviet freighter arrived in Liverpool yesterday, British dockworkers refused to unload the 1,500 tons of PCB wastes. The shipment was the first of about 13 shipments of PCBs taken from the storage facility destroyed by fire last year in St. Basile le Grand. Environment Minister Lise Bacon says the PCB shipment posed no danger to dockworkers and suggests the issue was inflated by the British media. The ship returning from Britain with the PCB wastes will be directed to Baie Comeau, where all the PCBs from St. Basile le Grand will be stored in Hydro-Québec's Manic 2 station, 30 kilometres west of Baie Comeau.

Oldest citizen marks her 110th birthday

Aug. 24, 1989

CORNWALL, Ont. – Lillian Ross, Canada's oldest citizen, celebrated her 110th birthday at St. Joseph's Nursing Villa today. Although quiet for most of the party, she did share a few memories. Among them, presenting flowers to Sir John A. Macdonald when she was 12 and singing in a New York opera at the turn of the century. Never married, Ross is a staunch Tory, which means she has seen many other leaders since Sir John.

The bear facts: Pooh statue gets the nod

Sept. 8, 1989

WHITE RIVER, Ont. – The Walt Disney Company has relented, and White River, a town of 1,200 residents in Northern Ontario, will soon have its Winnie. Winnie-the-Pooh, that is. For several months now, the two sides have battled publicly over whether the town can erect a big statue honoring the honey-loving bear. Author A.A. Milne based the Pooh character on a real-life Winnie, a black bear born in White River in 1914. ▷

Campeau may lose control of company

Robert Campeau.

Sept. 15, 1989

TORONTO – Robert Campeau, the swashbuckling Canadian who took over Federated Department Stores – owners of Bloomingdale's – for $6.64 billion US last year, is about to lose control of his company to his minority-shareholding creditors. They insist his share of stock go below 50 percent, allowing them to call the shots, or they'll call their loans and bankrupt him. Campeau got in trouble because he couldn't arrange new loans while his old money ran out. As it ran out, his stores began to have trouble buying new stock, thus worrying his bankers and making new financing even harder to get.

Tape re-enacts native leader's death

Aug. 21, 1989

WINNIPEG – A videotaped re-enactment of the shooting of Indian leader J.J. Harper, made by police following the incident, has been made public and was shown today at an inquest. The videotape, produced by the Winnipeg police six days after the shooting, shows Const. Robert Cross grabbing Harper by the arm after Harper refused a request to identify himself. In earlier testimony Cross said he believed that Harper was a suspect in a car theft.

The re-enactment shows that Harper, after his arm was grabbed, turned sharply and knocked Cross to the ground. Cross is depicted lying on his back, with Harper over top of him, grappling for the officer's gun. Cross has his left leg up to push Harper away when the gun goes off.

Winnipeg Police Chief Herb Stephen testifies at the J.J. Harper inquiry.

Mount Cashel orphanage for boys closing

Nov. 17, 1989

ST. JOHN'S, Nfld. – After more than 90 years in operation, the Mount Cashel orphanage for boys will close its doors as soon as alternative accommodations can be found for the 40 residents now at the institution. The orphanage, which has been run by the Christian (formerly the Irish Christian) brothers since 1898, has been the subject of a public inquiry since Sept. 11 and the focus of attention and speculation for the last nine months over allegations of the sexual abuse of young boys by brothers in the mid 1970s.

There are allegations also that the police, justice and welfare authorities failed to respond to complaints from children involved at the time. While many feel that the orphanage should remain open, under different management if necessary, others agree that this is no longer possible.

Harper case officer takes his own life

Police inspector Kenneth Dowson.

Sept. 20, 1989

WINNIPEG – Only hours before he was to testify at a provincial inquiry, police inspector Kenneth Dowson took his own life. The inquiry is trying to learn the facts surrounding the death of Indian leader J.J. Harper. As the senior officer in charge of the investigation into Harper's death, Dowson's testimony was critical. The inquiry was adjourned until further notice.

Snowbird Captain Shane Antaya's jet plunged into Lake Ontario during an air show at the Canadian National Exhibition on Sept. 4. The 24-year-old pilot was killed in the accident.

Rocks date back billions of years

Oct. 4, 1989

UNITED STATES – The U.S. National Science Foundation, a government agency that provides funding for basic science and engineering research, has reported finding rocks 3.96 billion years old. The two rocks were discovered north of the Great Slave Lake in the Northwest Territories by American and Australian scientists. According to senior scientist Samuel Bowring of Washington University, the rocks will provide valuable insight into a period of the Earth's history scientists know little about.

Gretzky the NHL's all-time top scorer

Oct. 15, 1989

EDMONTON – Wayne Gretzky broke Gordie Howe's National Hockey League career points record when he scored with 53 seconds left in the third period against the Edmonton Oilers, his former team. The goal pushed him past Howe's mark of 1,850 points, which he tied earlier in the game with an assist. It also forced overtime, and Gretzky scored the winning goal in leading the Los Angeles Kings to a 5-4 win. It was Gretzky's 780th NHL game. Howe's total came in 1,767 games.

Gretzky celebrates record goal.

Gunman kills 14 women, then himself

Murdered student on cafeteria chair.

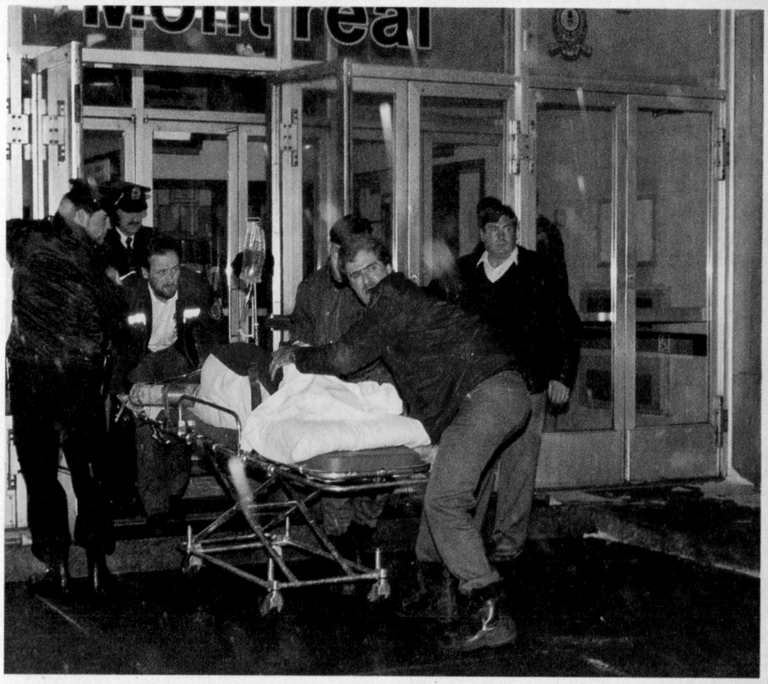

One of the injured is wheeled away by police and ambulance attendants.

Dec. 6, 1989

MONTREAL – A young gunman wearing hunting garb stalked and shot 14 women dead at the University of Montreal today before he turned his semi-automatic rifle on himself to commit suicide. Twelve other people were injured, several critically, in the worst massacre in Canadian history.

The gunman burst into a packed computer class at about 4:30 p.m., yelling "you're all a bunch of feminists." Said 24-year-old engineering student Louis Hamel: "He ordered men and women to separate sides of the classroom. We thought it was a joke, then he fired a shot and all hell broke loose."

Six women were shot dead in the second-floor classroom, a seventh was gunned down in another room, and then the gunman strode off in search of other victims.

Another student, François Bordeleau, ran up a flight of stairs and dragged other students by the collar to keep them from heading in the gunman's direction. "It was a human hunt," Bordeleau said. "We were the quarry."

As fear and panic swept through the building, the man killed three women in the ground-floor cafeteria and four more in a third-floor corridor, where he then shot himself. Police have identified the gunman as Marc Lepine, and said they've found a note naming several prominent women as potential targets.

Government OKs $150M for AIDS

Dec. 13, 1989

OTTAWA – The Conservative government announced today it will provide $150 million in "disaster relief" for Canadians who have contracted AIDS – or the virus that causes it – from tainted blood products. It is hoped the compensation will restore confidence in Canada's blood supply. According to Dept. of Health and Welfare estimates, 1,250 Canadians, including 950 hemophiliacs, were infected with the HIV virus via blood transfusions from 1979 until the Canadian Red Cross began screening donations in 1985. The money will help victims who have no insurance and can't work.

McLaughlin the first female to lead a national party in Canada

Ed Broadbent retires as NDP chief.

Dec. 2, 1989

WINNIPEG – Audrey McLaughlin has won the race to succeed outgoing New Democratic Party leader Ed Broadbent with a fourth-ballot victory over her nearest rival, former B.C. premier Dave Barrett. Her win makes her the first-ever female national party leader in Canadian history.

McLaughlin's win was overshadowed by a controversy concerning the defection of defeated candidate Simon De Jong to her camp. Based on a meeting at the convention with Barrett, it appeared De Jong had agreed to support that candidate in exchange for a powerful position in a Barrett-led NDP. Whether he agreed or not, De Jong later went to McLaughlin, giving her the win.

Audrey McLaughlin is surrounded by supporters at NDP convention.

My Canada

Canada's history is the record of its people and all they have accomplished and endured, felt and seen, known and written. What better sources, then, to compile an authentic historical record, than individual Canadians? And so we sponsored our *Chronicle of Canada* contest, and invited Canadians to submit their own stories to share with us. The following stories – "My Canada" – are those we selected from the myriad of wonderful entries we received from across Canada.

"My Canada" is organized chronologically, and the layout is typical of *Chronicle* style. Whenever necessary for reasons of length or style, the stories have been edited. However, every attempt has been made to retain as much of the original flavor as possible. Some stories are illustrated with images supplied by contest entrants. The framed pictures are meant to enhance the layout, and are unrelated to a specific narrative.

– *Elizabeth Abbott*, editor-in-chief

Heads on display after 8 hangings

Judge William D. Powell sentenced eight traitors to death by hanging.

July 20, 1814

YORK [Toronto] – Eight men died on the scaffold today, paying the penalty for high treason. They'd been convicted by a special court under Judge William D. Powell as traitors in an American-led raid on Canadian soil. The executions were at the height of bitter wartime hatred, just days before Lundy's Lane, The War of 1812's bloodiest battle.

In court, the men heard the full gruesome death sentence: they would be hanged almost to the point of strangulation, cut down, beheaded, and quartered. Then their heads would be exhibited in public, to deter others from high treason. In reality, this sentence was never fully executed, nor was it at Burlington Heights. The hangman was careful not to cut the 8 men down until they were dead. But their heads were indeed cut off and exhibited.

– *Robert W. Reid*

"Blockade runner" took contraband supplies to U.S. ports

1861-1865

HALIFAX – My grandfather, John McWhinnie, was born in 1835 and first went to sea at the age of 20. During the American Civil War (1861-65), he sailed as a "blockade runner," taking contraband supplies into ports of the southern U.S. under the guns of the North's ships. He couldn't write home for three years, and his parents thought he'd been killed. He was well-paid for the dangerous work, but believing the South's currency would be useless after the war, he spent it all. A beautiful oil painting of the first ship he captained, the *E.D. Bigelow,* hung in his home for more than 100 years.

– *Marion McWhinnie*

An oil painting of the E.D. Bigelow, the first ship John McWhinnie captained.

Tobique tribute

Early 1900s

New Brunswick pioneer Maude Carmont wrote the following poem based on the recollections of her late daughter and my aunt, Katharine Mills:

Tobique, wild Tobique,
  my childhood's happy home;
Thy shores I never shall forget,
  though far from thee I roam.
Again I roam thy wooded hills
  and fish thy sparkling streams;
The scent of thy wild flowers
  still come to me in dreams.
To all who till thy fertile soil,
  it is returned tenfold.
Oh, not in vain, shall be their
  toil; they are repaid in gold.
Let others sing of foreign lands,
  and beauty rare to see,
Tobique has all my soul
  demands,
mine own sweet country.

– *JoAnne Hall*

Patriot's medal recalls escape, bravery

Rebellion of 1837

MONTREAL – One of the leaders of the Rebellion of Lower Canada of 1837, Thomas Storrow Brown returned from exile in the United States when an amnesty was declared in 1844. In 1875, he had a gold medal struck commemorating his escape and the bravery of the man who helped him, Washington Franklin Jennings, my father-in-law James Simpson Miller's great-grandfather. The medal says in part: "In December 1837, T.S. Brown, a patriot for whose apprehension $2,000 was offered, lame and exhausted after four nights' exposure in the woods, met W.F. Jennings who regardless of the reward offered or the danger to which he exposed himself, secreted Brown in barns, supplied food and provided him a safe passage across the line to Vermont."

A gold medal commemorates T.S. Brown's escape to the U.S.

Every year, Brown sent Jennings' family, especially the Miller grandchildren, a basket of rare and exotic fruit from Florida, for the "one of nature's noblemen" who saved him would hear of no other reward. The medal is still in the Miller family.

– *Laura Neame*

Fishermen's pain eased by invention of gillnet "drum"

Little more than a large spool, the "drum" revolutionized fishing.

Early 1900s

MALCOLM ISLAND, B.C. – In the early part of this century, British Columbia fishermen worked in small, flat-bottomed rowing skiffs. Their nets – long, wet, and heavy with salmon – were pulled in by hand, gruelling work that ruined the oldtimers' fingers. Lauri Jarvis' family had immigrated to North Dakota from Finland, and in 1901 he was sent to live with an uncle and aunt in Sointula, on Malcolm Island, off Vancouver Island.

After he'd established himself as a boat-builder and worked on the gillnet fleets, in 1931 Jarvis built the first gillnet "drum" out of yellow cedar. He worked for more than a year to perfect it, and then patented it. Orders poured in as men realized they were no longer limited in their fishing by tides or weather. Jarvis, however, couldn't meet the demand for his invention, and other gillnetters, impatient or reluctant to pay the $25 fee, began to build their own drums. He hired a lawyer and won. But all he could do was force fishermen to remove "illegal" drums from their boats.

Jarvis had revolutionized the fishing industry, but as it was little more than a large thread spool, the concept was too simple to make a patent effective. He gave up.

– Paula Wild

Railroad kept its own sweet time

Post First World War

REVELSTOKE, B.C. – Our family came to live in the Kettle Valley after the war. The railroad was our lifeline to other parts of B.C., our escape and our return. Along with the general store, we bought the post office contract to meet the train with the mail, twice a day. In theory, one train arrived at 9 a.m., another at 6 p.m. In fact, the Kettle Valley Railroad (KVR) train arrived "when it did."

We'd hear the whistle sounding at the corner and dash to the track. Bemused spectators would place bets on the train or on us.

The KVR is gone now and the steel rails have been removed. Our children no longer run to stand by the track. But on a warm summer night we still hear the puffing engine grinding to our stop, and on a freezing night we hear the whistle of our friend at the corner.

– Ruth M. Des Mazes

The Kettle Valley Railroad train kept townsfolk busy guessing its arrival time.

Family hit by one tragedy after another

The Gluska family home, scene of many tales of hardship and grief.

1899-1909

MANITOBA – With many other Ukrainian immigrant families, Hrynko Gluska, 44, his wife Teklia, 37, and their family of five daughters and eldest son Michael arrived in Winnipeg in early May 1899. Two of the little daughters were among the 44 children who died of scarlet fever while families awaited designation of their homesteads. In 1903, tragedy struck again when a lightning bolt killed Teklia and three daughters. (One daughter was born in Canada.) Two years later, Hrynko was returning from a visit to son Michael near Shoal Lake when he fell into an abandoned well and died. A strong faith in God kept Michael and his sister Nastia going, both of them marrying and raising families.

– Mildred Leschasin

Hurricane on lakes kills at least 250

Nov. 9, 1913

KINCARDINE, Ont. – The Presbyterian church in this small town on the shores of Lake Huron was usually packed, but on this Sunday night, there were only six people present, including the minister, two members of his family – and young Harry Laishley Martin.

That's one of the reasons Harry recalls the night of the Great Hurricane so vividly. It had been a beautiful Indian summer day, but then the winds picked up on the Great Lakes and a blizzard developed into an incredible storm.

It wasn't until the following day when the full horror struck. Harry's father was the undertaker in Ripley and was asked by the coroner to help remove the bodies of seamen from the beaches. A dozen freighters had gone down in the storm, and the bodies had to be stacked up like cordwood behind the funeral parlor. At least 250 men had perished in the storm, and losses were estimated at close to $100 million. Timepieces found on the bodies had all stopped at 2:20.

– Margaret Gammon

Great food is just part of the deal at this boarding house

1926

TISDALE, Sask. – When the CPR train whistle blew, my grandmother Annie would take off her apron and tidy herself up. "I'll just see who is coming in on the train today," she'd tell her son John. "Build up the fire and put the kettle on. It's a long cold walk from the station."

I was 12 years old in the year when people from all over the world were rushing to the goldfields or heading north to start a new life. The CPR station was at the end of the street, and Grandma used to entice travellers into her boarding house before they'd made the chilly trek to the two hotels, some blocks away. She almost always got five or six boarders at one swoop. The food was good, the rooms clean, the cost reasonable – and then there was the entertainment in the evenings.

John was fond of a drink, making him popular with male guests who liked a snort, and he was a talented violinist. There was a gramophone and recordings of *Barnacle Bill* and *The Big Rock Candy Mountain.* Anyone who could play an instrument was invited to join in with the piano player – me. My mother wasn't all that keen on the parties, but I still cherish the memories.

– Flora Watson

A jug of ale and a house for sale

1914

PICTON, Ont. – The Turpin family – my grandparents and their five children – had been eking out a living after leaving England eight years before when the opportunity arose to buy the home they were renting for $4 a month. Grandpa was having a jug of ale in the Royal Hotel when he saw a rich reveller drop a $10 bill. That represented two weeks wages – so Grandpa put his feet on it till he could retrieve it and go home, singing. That became the down payment. My mother Agnes, then 14, had just got a job as a domestic and "donated" her pay of $12 each month to cover the rest.

– Herbert C. Franklin

A $10 bill found on a tavern floor became a down payment on the Turpin home.

Rescue worker comes back from the dead

1913-1916

THE ROCKIES – My grandfather, Daniel Fraser Kennedy, had left Nova Scotia in the 1900s for Alberta, where the Canadian Pacific Railway needed experienced hard-rock miners for the building of tunnels for their trains through the Rockies. He'd become a miner at age 14, when his father, a coal miner, had died, probably of black lung disease. Dan became one of the many hard-working men who helped build the Connaught tunnel for three years, from 1913 on.

At one point during the construction, the ventilation system failed and miners were felled by poisonous gases. Dan was one of the draegermen sent in as the rescue team when engineers got the fresh-air system working again, but while the team was in there, it failed again. A doctor was stationed at the surface, separating the living from the dead as the men were brought out.

When Dan regained consciousness, he threw off a sheet and went for the door. A watchman screamed and ran off. Dan then saw the sign on the door. It read "morgue."

– Effie I. Langer

Youngster valued his Rebellion Box

1930s

TORONTO – As a child growing up here in the '30s, I came to believe there was something different, something special, about our family, because I often heard an aged aunt referring to our "loyalist stock." I had no idea what it meant, but it sounded kind of romantic. In the house of my childhood, there was a unique object, related to our "stock" as a tiny footnote in Ontario history. It was a hand-carved wooden box, about the size of a receptacle for a ring. Inside, there was a lock of fine brown hair, and fine words written, a place, a time, and a poem.

In school, my favorite teacher told us of the Upper Canada Rebellion of 1837, and I was able to bring in the box for show-and-tell.

My great-grandfather, Eli Irwin, had been one of the number of brave York County settlers who rebelled against the Family Compact. He was jailed for his part in the rebellion, and two other victims, Samuel Lount and Peter Mathews, were hanged. The Rebellion Box was my great-grandfather's tribute to these men.

Years later, I was given a copy of our family tree, and found that we came from United Empire Loyalist "stock," those who refused to fight against England's George III.

– John L. Kennedy

Man survives his long walk to freedom

Author's impression of her father on his trek from the Ukraine to Warsaw.

1929

BATHURST, N.B. – My father came to Canada just after the depression had begun, when immigration was virtually closed. The reason he was allowed in was that there was a specific job waiting for him, one that a Canadian could not fill. The job was as a tutor for six Jewish families in Bathurst, N.B., which had been arranged by Eli Shklar, his uncle. But to get to Canada, via Liverpool, my father had to walk from Zhitomir in the Ukraine to Warsaw, a long, arduous trek. Afterwards, he was conscripted in the Canadian army, but, after three days, the survivor of the long walk was discharged: he had flat feet.

– Fruma Rothberg Sanders

Cover of The New Wind Has Wings, an anthology of poems by Canadian writers. The book has gained widespread popularity, mainly as children's literature.

Welcome to Canada just a mite bumpy for German couple

1936

EDMONTON – It must have been the wine, for it wasn't like Mother to reminisce.

"Things sure were different in 1936." (Another sip of wine.) "It wouldn't have been so bad if your Dad could have settled in Montreal or Toronto. There are a lot of German people around there. But no, he had to pick Athabasca. Imagine getting on a bus in Edmonton and driving on a highway – calling that rutty, bumpy road a highway! – for a hundred miles. And there's me and your Dad sitting in the back. The bus driver kept looking at us in the rearview mirror. What he was thinking, God only knows. There we were, the only people on the bus, and we sat in the back."

(Another sip of wine.)

"We got married on a Sunday. A Sunday! Afterwards, your Dad asked if I wanted to go to the lake. What did I know? We went in this old Model T, with a man named Cliff driving. He drove like hell. My hair was standing up all over the place and my skirt went flying. I couldn't speak any English, but I'm thinking, This guy is crazy. Anyway, we got there, and went fishing, while the mosquitoes made a meal of me." (Finishing the wine.) "But me, I caught the biggest fish!"

– Agnes Kaspersky

Elizabeth and Stefan Kaspersky on their wedding day in May, 1936.

Exploring Baffin Island

1923-31

BAFFIN ISLAND – My father logged more than 50,000 kilometres by dog sled and canoe exploring this, the world's fifth largest island, starting in 1923. My mother and I, a preschooler and the first white child to live on the island, arrived July 30, 1930, at Lake Harbour, after a 16-day voyage from Montreal with my father, J. Dewey Soper, an explorer and naturalist. There were about 300 Inuit in the general area, and we now added to the non-native population of three Mounties, four Hudson's Bay Co. men, and the Anglican missionary and his wife.

By the early 1920s, vast areas remained unexplored, and it was on these that my father focused his attention. In 1926, he'd made a remarkable journey covering 1,050 kilometres across the island. He was to write later: "I still feel extraordinary admiration for the efforts of (Inuit aides) Akatuga and Newkequak, who endured so much suffering without a murmur. It is impossible to forget the frightful cold of 70 below zero as we forged our way over Lake Nettilling, across the Great Plain, and back."

Dewey, Carrie and Roland Soper at Lake Harbour in 1930.

In the years that followed, my father's contribution to the exploration of Baffin Island was recognized by the naming after him of several geographical features.

– Roland Soper

On-to-Ottawa trek ends in Regina jail cell

July 1, 1935

REGINA – In the middle of the depression, I, Jimmie Higgins, joined the On-to-Ottawa trek, unemployed men riding the rails from Vancouver to present the federal government with demands for improvement in our conditions.

At a rally in Regina, I was making small talk with a mother who had a baby in a carriage when all hell broke loose. It seems the police had been given orders to break up the meeting, and that's what they did, in the most violent, inhumane way possible. A Mounted Policeman's horse knocked over the baby carriage, and I saw the mother trying to protect the baby with her body. As I tried to help the mother, I received a blow – and woke up in a jail cell. That was the end of the On-to-Ottawa trek.

– as told to Janette Higgins

Off we go on North America's first ski tow

1932

SHAWBRIDGE, Que. – My father, with his good friend Alec Foster, designed, built, and operated the first ski tow in North America. It was located on the big hill in the Laurentians at Shawbridge, and was commonly known as "Foster's Folly." It was installed in 1932, with Dad and Foster using a Dodge automobile engine to supply power to the rope tow around pulleys at several intervals on the slope. The skiers would take the train from Montreal in the morning, and return that same evening. The winters from 1932 to '34 were intensely cold – often going down to 35 degrees Fahrenheit – and many times they had difficulty starting the engine. Somehow, they succeeded.

–André J.M. Tellier

Grandfather known as an X-ray martyr who helped others

1862-1933

CANADA – The following testimonial to my maternal grandfather, Frank Simpson Pepperdene, was in *The Times* of London in 1910: "He was not only one of the earliest experimenters in radiography and radiotherapy, but gave his services freely to two institutions (in England.) Indeed, the greater part of his work with X-rays has been done gratuitously."

This letter, signed by six physicians and surgeons, was an appeal for funds to help the radiologist to emigrate to Canada. He, his wife Elizabeth Ann, and their six children were settled in the spring of 1911 on a fruit farm near Vineland, in the Niagara Peninsula. The previous year, he'd lost his left arm to cancer caused by the radiation. He thought his career was over, but in 1915, Pepperdene was appointed as first radiologist to the Gage Institute in Toronto and two sanatoriums. Cancer eventually claimed his other arm, and he died in 1933 at the Quebec City home of his son, Rev. Liddon Pepperdene.

In a tribute, writer Godfrey L. Gale wrote in his 1979 book of Pepperdene's work at the Weston [Toronto] "San": "He is still spoken of with affection and respect." He was one of the first X-ray martyrs.

– Marion Cameron

Frank S. Pepperdene, a pioneer in radiology, lost both arms to cancer.

Halifax explosion of 1945 felt up to 8 kilometres away

July 18, 1945

HALIFAX – When most people hear of the Halifax explosion, they think of the huge blast that devastated this city in 1917. But there was another, one much less horrific but that nevertheless sent a ripple of fear through the hearts and minds of all Haligonians. At 6:35 this evening, as I was riding my bicycle, a tremendous blast threw me off balance and onto the pavement. All around me people emerged from their homes shouting "it must be the magazine," meaning the arsenal on Bedford Basin's northeastern shore where munitions lay stockpiled.

In fact, a small barge had caught fire and the flames had quickly spread to a munitions shed. The explosion – felt by patrons at the Nova Scotian Hotel, eight kilometres away – scattered blazing debris over the harbor and the magazine. Numerous fires started, and fearing the worst, thousands climbed Citadel Hill and flocked to the Public Gardens. Halifax Commons turned into a tent city, ships were removed from the harbor, and hospitals went on alert.

Thankfully, damage to the city was not extensive and serious injuries were few. Only one person died. The fires were miraculously brought under control within 24 hours of the initial explosion.

– Anne Rockwell Fairley

Chopper plans grounded

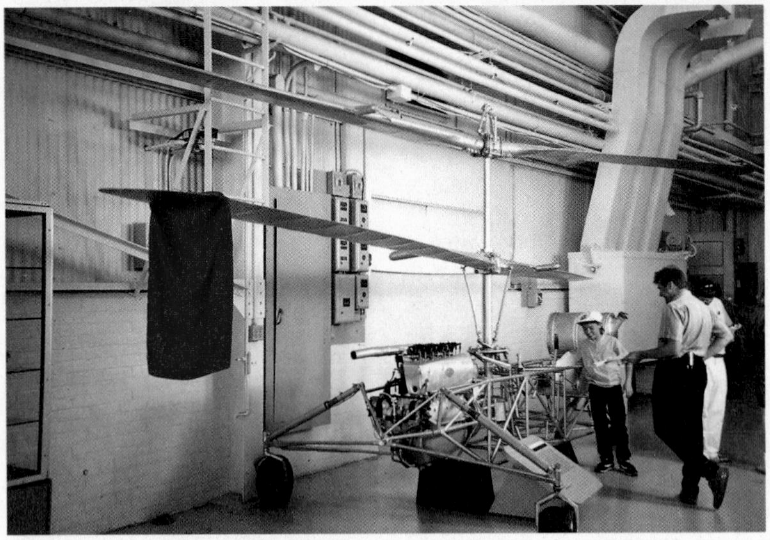

The helicopter built by the Froebe brothers was ahead of its time.

1939

CANADA – Lack of capital has unfortunately forced Douglas, Nicholas, and Theodore Froebe, three extremely inventive brothers, to quit work on their latest project – a helicopter! The prototype was built from airplane parts, some fashioned painstakingly by hand, according to their specifications. It lifts clear off the ground, but once airborne vibrates madly. By the middle of last year, the brothers were making short forward and backward flights with complete rotational control, but the severe vibrations remained a problem. Nevertheless, the machine was far in advance of contemporary designs.

– Gloria Moore

Cheated on coal? Well, not exactly

November 1934

HAMILTON – My father was an Irish immigrant with an undisguised hostility for authority. He also hadn't held a steady job in years. The depression was a factor, but we suspected he'd also been blackballed for his overzealous involvement with the union movement. It was his belligerent nature that led him to weigh the coal.

It was the first time we'd purchased hard coal. We were a family of seven and subsisted on City Relief, depending on weekly vouchers for rent, food, and fuel. We had always bought coke because it was cheaper. But it burned quickly, never lasting through the night and likely as not, next morning we'd have frozen pipes. Father ordered 225 kilograms of coal. Hang the expense. The coal barely covered the fuel-bin floor. "Sure and Bejesus, we've been gypped again!" Father shouted. He and I took it all back. It was weighed again – 238 kilograms. On the long walk home, Father never spoke a word.

– Douglas R. Greer

Most heartfelt of songs related to war and the need for peace

1942

QUEBEC – When night fell, many young men and women, part of what we called the Empire Air Training Plan, would descend upon the Rock Cliff Inn, just a few short kilometres away from their lodging at the Hotel L'Esterel in the Laurentians. Together we sang many songs, but the most heartfelt were those related to the war:

There'll be bluebirds over the white cliffs of Dover,
Tomorrow when the world is free.
There'll be love and laughter, and peace thereafter, Tomorrow...

Perhaps this song expressed best what motivated us during the war – not lust for power, but the need to restore a peaceful world.

– Bernard Jaffé

Few knew "The Silent War" was going on

May-October 1942

GASPE, Que. – A century and a quarter after American troops invaded Canada along the upper St. Lawrence waterway and lakes, another hostile encroachment around the lower part of the river and the gulf was almost successful. While no particular land action occurred, German submarines caused much concern for the government.

During a six-month period in 1942, these submarines successfully torpedoed a number of ships. Eleven were sunk in the month of September alone. Yet few people knew what was taking place virtually at our front door. War correspondents dubbed this area of conflict "The Silent War" because their coverage was so restricted by censors. Only the bare essentials were printed. The general public was purposely kept in the dark on the loss of roughly 600 men, women, children, soldiers, and sailors.

Also not mentioned in dispatches was the contribution by wives of services personnel stationed in the area. As volunteers under the direction of the Red Cross, the women took care of survivors and provided meals and lodging.

– George C. Roy

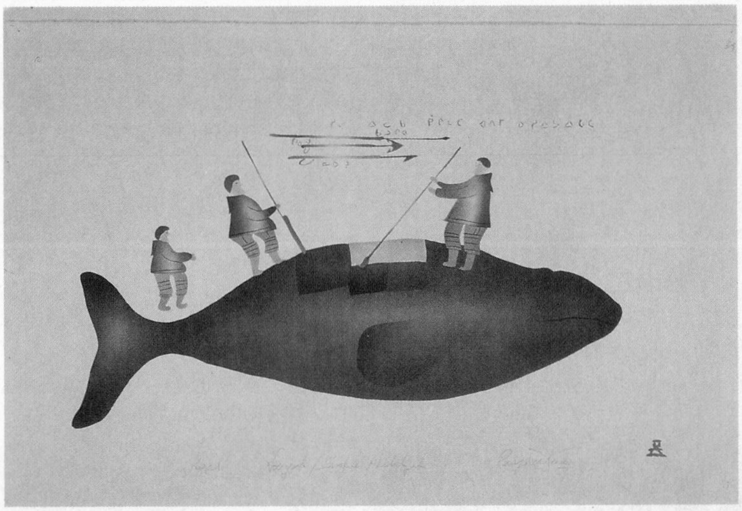

A drawing by Nicodemus Nowyook, entitled Nowyook Remembers.

Ban on thalidomide too late for some

1960s

CANADA – In March 1962, the Canadian government banned the sale of thalidomide, a drug then used in some tranquillizers and sleeping pills. Tragically, the ban came too late. Thalidomide was never properly tested for harmful side effects, the most damaging of which affected the fetus. Many children were born suffering physical deformities, the most common being phocomelia, where the hands or feet start from the shoulder or hip.

I, for example, was born without arms. This may seem a large handicap, but I learned to use my feet as if they were hands: I can eat, wash or dress using my feet, and can even drive a car. Unfortunately, many thalidomiders are worse off and suffer from lack of independence and equal opportunity. The thalidomide tragedy was a dark blotch in Canadian history. We the victims, however, are striving to survive and, ultimately, thrive.

– Gavin Bamber

Liquor's quicker if you have a permit

1950s

TORONTO – Most immigrants experience some measure of culture shock on arrival in their new country. In my case, it was not expected. I was coming to Ontario from Britain. The Union Jack flew everywhere. But an easy transition was not to be, as I discovered the day I tried to buy a bottle of whisky.

I soon learned my area of town was the Holy City, completely devoid of "liquor outlets," a term that did little but conjure up images of gentlemen's washrooms. Determined in my quest, after a roundabout journey by cab I at last entered a liquor store. To the victor go the spoils! Not quite, however. After filling out a form, with name and address as requested, I strode to the counter full of joy. The clerk then asked to see my permit. My what? Surely this was bureaucracy gone raving mad. I was beaten. It was three years before I found the courage to apply for that permit.

– Tony Jones

Application fee well worth the risk

Anand, now a Montreal engineer.

1952

MONTREAL – In June 1952, I was an unpaid engineering trainee in the Himalaya foothills, working on dam projects and living with my bride on dowry money. An ad by India's Scientific Research Council to send 10 students to Commonwealth countries made me risk the application fee. Weeks later an interview call came from Delhi.

At the council offices, I was among 60 other hopefuls from all over India. "Why should we send you?" I was asked. "India spends fabulous sums on visiting foreign experts," I replied. "Train me in Canada for a lifetime service instead." After an eternity of waiting, my name was called. Hooray!

Four days before my ship sailed from Bombay, I received my travel vouchers from Delhi but had no passport, foreign exchange, or inoculations. In a frenzy, I acquired what I needed. Then, after sailing, I received a telegraph that my wife was ill. I made plans to disembark, but three days later she wired me: "Feeling better – Proceed."

I arrived in Montreal Oct. 28. I encountered many more snafus and worked at odd jobs before managing to bring my wife and newborn son over. The next year I won a top award at McGill, and after returning to India for a brief period arrived in Canada to stay in 1956. Selection for Canadian training was an unexpected adventure. Thanks to Canada, it was worth it!

– Tilak Raj Anand

Legendary Canadian makes its last run

November 1989

CANADA – Frankly, I was apprehensive about spending three days confined to a train, but with Via's legendary *Canadian* nearing its final run, it was now or never. I packed plenty of insurance against boredom, all of which soon proved superfluous. Boarding at Toronto, I travelled to Vancouver with my nose pressed to the window, marvelling at Canada's vastness and diversity. We snaked past the lakes, narrows and rocky outcrops of the Muskokas, through dense strands of maple, oak and ash, and along the rugged shore of Lake Superior before uncoiling onto lonely, snow-dusted stretches of prairie. Then, the spectacular Rockies. I heard one passenger say "every child should be given one free ticket to this train." Indeed, no one who took this unforgettable journey could have wished to see it end.

– Mark D. Gerson

Upper Canada Village, near Morrisburg, Ontario, is a replica of a community that might have existed in the region in the 19th century.

Dief's not dead! Go ahead and ask him

1979

SASKATCHEWAN – History will record that the Rt. Hon. John George Diefenbaker died on Aug. 16, 1979. But a few months before, Diefenbaker had actually heard a premature report of his death and took great delight in the story, appealing as it did to his great sense of humor.

On May 13, the man who had been Canada's 13th prime minister was in his constituency campaigning for re-election. The Chief, 83 years old, had already served 39 years in Parliament. He was sound asleep in his room at the Sheraton-Marlboro Hotel in Prince Albert when, shortly before midnight, the hotel switchboard operator took a call from a Montreal journalist asking if it was true Dief was dead.

Within minutes, journalists from across Canada were calling with the same question. As Diefenbaker's aide, I knew the story wasn't true. But after about 25 calls I got a little nervous, so I peeked into his room. There he was sound asleep, and snoring. When asked about his health the next day at committee headquarters, he boomed "How do I look?" Then, with a mischievous grin and a tilt of his head, he asked: "Have they told you yet about my passing?"

– Michael McCafferty

Fight to save our endangered species continues

Sea mammal numbers are on the decline

Pollution and exploitation are causing the decline of many sea mammals. Among the most affected are whales, traditionally very valuable creatures. Today, the products of one right whale alone are worth as much as $50,000 in Japan.

For over 400 years, the right whale has been savagely hunted. By the mid-1800s, the whaling industry had wiped out the species in the eastern north Pacific, and only about 100 animals remain in the region today. In 1937, the International Whaling Commission protected the right whale from commercial whaling, but populations remain frail and the right whale is rare throughout its range. A relic 100 animals remain in the western north Atlantic.

The little white beluga whale is another endangered sea mammal and one of the most polluted animals in the world today. Despite their small size, these white-skinned, smiling whales carry thick blankets of blubber that sop up toxins like sponges. Autopsies on beluga whales found dead on the beaches reveal DDT, PCBs and other organochlorines in their blubber and brain cells.

Pollution virtually halves the beluga's lifespan. Populations are rapidly shrinking. Ninety years ago, 5,000 belugas leapt about the St. Lawrence River from the Saguenay to Montreal harbor. Now, only 500 Belugas roam a 130-kilometre stretch of river centred at Tadoussac. In Baffin Island, Inuit hunting and a low birthrate are also destroying the small beluga population.

The sea otter, however, has a happier story. Once so plentiful in the Maritimes it could be killed without fear of extermination, by 1830 the fur trade had exhausted sea otter populations. The last sea otter was sighted in British Columbia in 1929. Today, 500 sea otters live in Canada, the offspring of 89 animals imported from Alaska.

The future of the whales is uncertain, as populations do not seem to be increasing. But transplanted sea otters have become thriving communities, and their future in Canada looks bright.

The eastern cougar is being driven into remote wilderness areas.

Belugas are riddled with toxins.

The sea otter population, once thriving in Canada, had to be re-established by importing 89 animals from Alaska.

Eastern cougar and the leatherback turtle among Canada's 183 endangered animals

The eastern cougar that once gambolled about the forests of southern Ontario, Quebec, and New Brunswick stalking the white-tailed deer, is currently one of Canada's endangered species. In the last century, man has molested the species, exterminating populations over large parts of its range, and driving remaining animals farther into remote areas of the wilderness. Although protected in Nova Scotia, New Brunswick, and Ontario, surviving populations have failed to expand. In New Brunswick, where deer populations can sustain an estimated 200 cougars, only 33 of the cats survive.

For centuries, Canadian wildlife has been plagued by man. Many of our native animals were stalked with such rapacity that species did not merely dwindle, they vanished.

In 1535, during Jacques Cartier's second expedition, when he moored his vessels at Isle aux Coudres at Baie St. Paul, the St. Lawrence teemed with sea creatures. According to records kept by Cartier's scribe, there were schools of large white fish, known today as the beluga whales, and an inestimable number of *grande tortures,* or giant turtles we know today as leatherback turtles. Later recordings by Du Creux and Josselyn documented five species of sea turtles in the Quebec region. By the end of the 17th century, these sea turtles were so scarce that the appearance of a single leatherback anywhere in the region of Baie St. Paul was an exceptional event.

Today, a few migrating adults have been sighted off the Atlantic provinces and in British Columbia, but the current world status of this giant turtle is grim. Leatherbacks have the greatest distribution of any reptile. They nest in tropical areas from southern Mexico to Ecuador and from Florida to French Guyana. They migrate well beyond the tropics and have been sighted in southern Alaska and the U.S.S.R., in the Pacific, and mid-Labrador and Norway in the Atlantic. The leatherback turtles' southern migrations lead them to Chile and southern Australia. Considering the global range of the leatherback, the estimated population of 40,000 turtles is low. To date, Canadian summer migrant populations have not been determined.

Pollution is another factor that adversely effects wildlife. Toxins in air and water alter wild habitats, threatening the future of many species. The inability of animals to adjust naturally to their depreciated environment changes behavior patterns and breeding habits. Birds of prey are mostly affected by pesticides, which cause thinning of egg shells, egg eating by adult birds, and nest abandonment. Attempts to re-introduce a vanishing species such as the peregrine falcon into an environment constantly doused with toxic chemicals may prove futile – the peregrine is making a very slow comeback. But restrictions on pesticide use have helped the burrowing owl, a small owl that digs nest underground.

Recent efforts by wildlife associations and individuals committed to preserving wild species and their habitats will secure the future of some of the 183 endangered species now listed by the Committee on the Status of Endangered Wildlife in Canada. The hope is that management and protection measures, along with public concern, will lead to the re-emergence of threatened species, whose demise poses a terrible threat not only to Canadian wildlife, but also to human beings.

Returning the peregrine falcon to its original environment is a slow process.

"Gemini," a right whale, engages in courtship activity. Hunting has drastically reduced the right whale's numbers.

Environmental damage taking its toll on planet

The dinosaurs would not be impressed

Forest fire ravages evergreens.

Look, but don't touch: sign warns against swimming, due to excessive levels of bacteria in the water.

When the dinosaurs and some 75 percent of the animal species on Earth disappeared mysteriously 65 million years ago, the process took millions of years. Shift the camera into the future – in Kubrick-like fashion – to the year 1989. Through the destruction of tropical rain forests and other environmental damage, humans destroy some six species an hour, and it's estimated 10 to 30 percent of the Earth's species will be extinct by the year 2000. One expert says "we are facing the first human-created extinction cycle that is on the same scale as the major geological events of the past, but condensed into an incomparably small time span."

As long as the Earth's human population was relatively small, it did not fundamentally disrupt the infinitely complex network now known as the biosphere (the layer on the Earth's surface made up of the atmosphere, water, minerals, and organisms). But in the last 200 years, industrialization and rapid population growth have put unprecedented stress on the biosphere.

On a global scale, today's greatest environmental problem is the destruction of the tropical rain forests, a cause of extinctions, global warming, and other calamities. Acid rain, caused by industrial and urban sulphur dioxide emissions, is another tragic problem. Thousands of lakes and rivers in eastern North America and Scandinavia have no fish because of acid rain. Birds and vegetation are also severely threatened. Most acid rain in Canada is caused by industries in the U.S. – acid rain is a pointed illustration that the environmental crisis is global and needs global solutions.

The litany of problems goes on and on. The burning of fossil fuels and the destruction of the rain forests have caused the global warming known as the greenhouse effect, expected to lead to climatic shifts devastating to the environment. The depletion of the ozone layer caused by chlorofluorocarbons in aerosol spray cans, fridges, and plastic foam products has already led to an increase in skin cancer. Pollution has ravaged much of the world's oceans and inland waterways. Land pollution is yet another problem, reducing or destroying the soil's ability to support vegetation.

The web of life on Earth has evolved continually over 4.6 billion years according to a schedule that is infinitely slow by human perceptions. Now we are experimenting with the entire planet, speeding up the rate of change, imposing new pressures, and inflicting unforgivable wounds on the environment. The consequences are unknown. They surely cannot be good. They may be catastrophic.

Not fit for man or beast: an oily film covers water littered with garbage and a dead fish, victim of pollution.

A jumble of rusted scrap metal creates an unappealing collage at this waterside garbage dump.

Out of sight, out of mind: garbage dumps are eventually buried, but non-biodegradable trash can remain intact for decades when hidden from the elements.

Fast lane to extinction: emissions from the vehicles that crowd our highways are a major factor in the production of acid rain and the greenhouse effect.

Time to deal with environment crisis running out

Door-to-door pickup encourages people to recycle rather than throw out trash.

Orca whale watching in B.C.: will our children have the same privilege?

But the will to solve the problem is there

Canada's first environmentalists were its native peoples who lived for centuries in a complex relationship with their environment, inflicting little long-term damage. In the face of today's environmental problems such as acid rain, the greenhouse effect, and the depletion of the ozone layer, the example of their societies gives hope. We cannot return to the past to live like Canada's native peoples, but it is hoped we can work out new ways of relating to the environment that go beyond traditional western paradigms that hold the environment as either something to be feared or something to be exploited without thought of the consequences.

There is little time to deal with the environmental crisis, but lots of will and ability around the world. Considerable work has been done the last 10 years to develop global strategies to promote the health of the biosphere. The 1987 World Commission on Environment and Development, called the Brundtland Commission after its chair Dr. Gro Harlem Brundtland, prime minister of Norway, was a landmark in global environmental awareness. It stressed the harm we are causing the environment and argued for sustainable economic development that is not at odds with a healthy environment.

Progress is being made in Canada. Air pollution has been reduced by pollution control devices in factories, better tuned cars, and more efficient burning of fuel. Most provinces and the federal government have passed clean air acts specifying emission standards, and Ottawa and the eastern provinces have agreed to reduce sulphur dioxide emissions that cause acid rain by 50 percent by 1994. In the long run, however, air pollution problems will be solved by consuming less energy from less polluting sources, rather than by pollution controls.

Strides have also been made in the prevention of water and land pollution. Water treatment programs have done much to alleviate water pollution, and recycling is probably the most promising solution to problems of urban and industrial waste.

But more money is still needed for research and technology to prevent pollution at its source and to promote recycling, rather than to clean up pollution after it has been inflicted on the environment. Governments and industry are slowly realizing it is essential to consider the environmental impact of new products and production processes from the earliest stages of development. Producers and consumers will pay more for environmentally friendly products, but such products will promote the health of the environment, and the cost in the long run will be far less.

Used cardboard boxes are packed into bales to await recycling.

Rain, once a purifying force, now leaves a residue that has to be cleaned from buildings and monuments.

Douglas firs stand tall against a clear B.C. sky. Gradual improvements in the way individuals and corporations treat the environment could save these forests.

Man's best friend has a place in Canadian hearts

The yellow Labrador retriever, although related to the Newfoundland and similar in temperament, is not technically a Canadian breed.

The Tahltan bear dog, now virtually extinct, was once used for hunting.

Four strains of dogs unique to Canada

Dogs came to Canada with the first humans, experts say, and they have been an integral part of Canadian life ever since, offering loyalty, companionship, and, more practically, transportation and help with hunting. Selective breeding has yielded four uniquely Canadian strains of man's best friend.

Familiar to Canadian households is the Newfoundland, a large black dog which loves to swim, Its cousin the Labrador retriever, which can be black, golden, or yellow, is well known in Canada although it is not technically a Canadian breed. The intelligence and gentleness of both breeds make them popular pets the world over. A smaller dog, the Nova Scotia duck tolling retriever, helps the duck hunter by attracting the birds with an elaborate display. The Tahltan bear dog, a small, fox-like breed from the west coast now virtually extinct, also used to help its master hunt by distracting the quarry. Canada's best known and most spectacular breed is the Canadian Eskimo dog, or husky, which, when hitched to a sled, offers the Inuit safe and reliable transport across Canada's barren tundra.

The Newfoundland is renowned for its intelligence and gentleness.

The Canadian Eskimo dog or husky is used for dogsled transport in the North.

The Nova Scotia duck tolling retriever helps hunters by attracting ducks.

Restoration breathes new life into historical sites

Cities show renewed interest in heritage

CANADA – As we near the end of this century, we anticipate a future filled with new and innovative architectural designs. But Canadians are also looking back with growing interest on buildings of old. A sense of appreciation for heritage sites has burgeoned during the last 20 years: the bulldozer approach – out with the old, in with the new – no longer predominates.

Canada has a wealth of historic properties, from abandoned trading posts to remote towns to cities still bustling with activity, the hubs on which our nation was built. And in the cities, interest in the preservation and restoration of buildings is shared by historians and developers alike.

Halifax is one example among many of how restoration has merged with commercial interests. Old waterfront warehouses, once dilapidated and in some cases even abandoned, now house restaurants, boutiques, pubs and offices. Known as the Historic Properties, the area is capitalizing on the attractiveness of a bygone era, luring tourists – and their dollars – with its charm.

Quebec City and Montreal have also had the preservation of their historic buildings linked to commercial interests. As Canada's oldest cities, both have an abundance of buildings that date back to the 17th and 18th centuries. But, unlike Halifax, tourism – although important – is not the sole impetus behind restoration. Rather, the priority is to maintain Old Quebec and Old Montreal as communities where people still live and work. Many of the older buildings are used as residential and office space.

Vancouver's Gastown, like the restored waterfront area in Halifax, has been rejuvenated after decades of neglect. For the most part of this century it was Vancouver's "skid row" with its run-down warehouses and cheap hotels. Not so anymore. By the early 1970s it had become a main tourist attraction with shops and restaurants lining a colorful, brick-paved street.

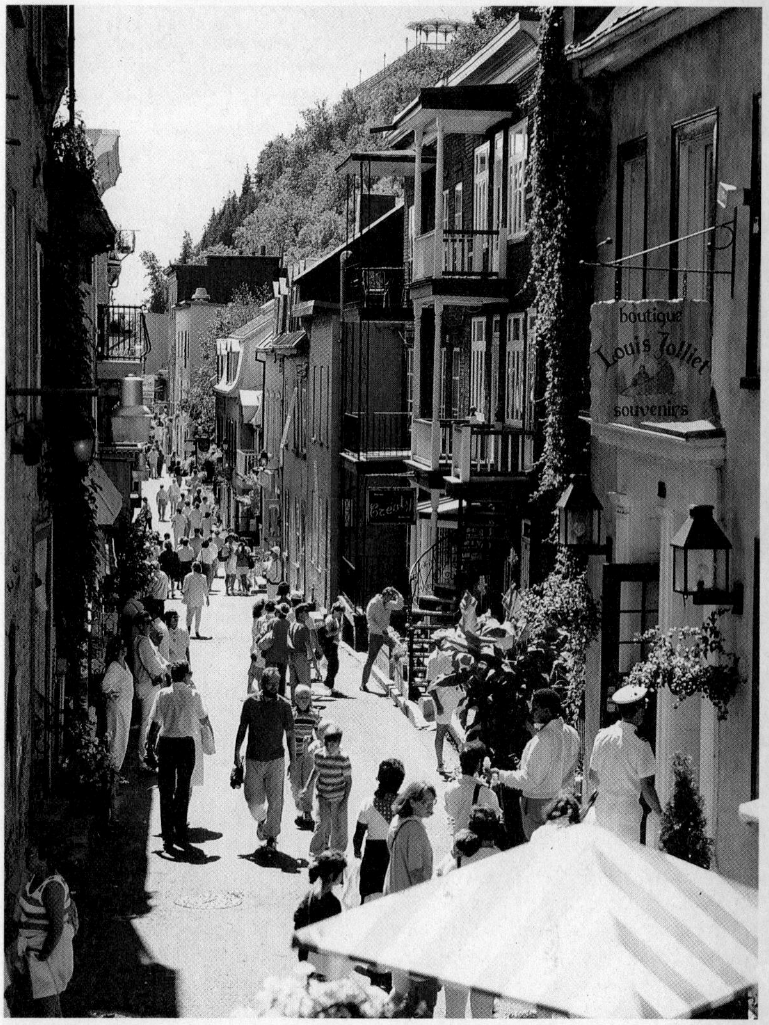

Rue Petit Champlain in Quebec City bustles with strolling tourists.

Built in 1725, the well-preserved Maison Calvet in Old Montreal now houses a delicatessen.

Gastown, once Vancouver's skid row, is now a picturesque tourist area.

A town crier evokes images of yesteryear in Halifax's Historic Properties.

Alberta

Alberta, although referred to as a prairie province, has one of the most varied landscapes in Canada. Much of the province is covered with arable soil and Alberta's Peace River valley is the northernmost permanent agricultural settlement in Canada. The rugged and spectacular Rocky Mountains lie along the western border with British Columbia and the unique Badlands in the Red Deer River valley were home to prehistoric dinosaurs.

Much of Alberta had been in the huge domain of the Hudson's Bay Company known as Rupert's Land. It was inhabited by many native tribes, including the Blackfoot and the Sarcee in the south and the Cree, Assiniboine, Slavey, and Beaver further north. In 1754, Anthony Henday, an employee of the Hudson's Bay Company, was the first white man to see what is now Alberta. The Dominion of Canada acquired Rupert's Land in 1870, renamed it the Northwest Territories, and developed plans for settlement. The North West Mounted Police built Fort Macleod in 1874 and set out to establish law and order. In the first decade of the 20th century, the development of the new fast-maturing Marquis wheat provided the necessary impetus to the homesteading program. Settlers arrived in waves from Europe, the United States, and other parts of Canada. Alberta acquired provincial status in 1905. The discovery of oil at Leduc in 1947 began a modern era of prosperity for Alberta.

The name Alberta was chosen for one of the four postal districts of the Northwest Territories in 1883 to honor the daughter of Queen Victoria, Princess Louise Caroline Alberta. The capital Edmonton is situated on the site of a Hudson's Bay Company fort by the same name.

The climate of Alberta is dry, as the prevailing winds from the Pacific lose their moisture on the windward side of the Rockies. Summers are warm and winters are very cold. However, southern Alberta can be suddenly warmed by as much as 30 degrees by a weather phenomenon known as the chinook.

Since the economy of Alberta is resource-based and dependent on external markets, it suffers from extreme fluctuations. Agriculture was once the mainstay of the economy, but it has been supplanted by the petroleum, mining, and manufacturing industries. Alberta has the largest deposits of oil and natural gas in Canada, including the oil sands of the Athabasca River. Alberta has more than 70 percent of Canada's coal supplies. The manufacturing industry is tied to the natural resources and the construction industry. Tourism is a significant source of income: besides the Rocky Mountains, the province offers the famed Calgary Stampede and Edmonton's Klondike Days.

Alberta residents pay relatively low provincial income tax and no sales tax. The province has a unique Heritage Fund established with revenue from the oil industry.

The provincial legislative assembly has 83 members. In the federal government, Alberta has 21 members of Parliament and six senators.

Edmonton, Alberta skyline with the Muttart Conservatory in the foreground.

Area: Land: 644,390 sq km; Freshwater: 16,800 sq km;
Total: 661,190 sq km (6.6% of Canada)

Elevations: Highest point: 3,747m (Mount Columbia)
Lowest point: Lake Athabasca and Slave River shores

Population (1989): 2,446,400 (9.3% of population of Canada)

Population density: 3.7 persons per sq km of land

Mother tongue: English 82.3%; French 2.4%; Other 15.3%

Date joined Confederation: Sept. 1, 1905

Motto: Fortis et Liber (Strong And Free)

Flower: Wild rose

Capital: Edmonton

Mean temperatures for typical locations:
Edmonton: January -15C; July 17.4C
Medicine Hat: January -12.6C; July 19.9C

Annual precipitation for typical locations:
Edmonton: 466.1mm; Medicine Hat: 347.9mm

Gross domestic product (1989): $63.5 billion
(10.5% of Canada's GDP)

British Columbia

British Columbia, Canada's westernmost province, is the third largest in both area and population. A region of mountains and plateaus, it has only limited agricultural land, mainly in river valleys. The many islands off the coast are part of this province. More than 70 percent of the population live in the southwest corner of the province including the cities of Victoria and Vancouver, the third largest metropolitan area in Canada.

This northwestern region of the continent was inhabited by Indians of the Athabaskan and Salish tribes in the interior and the Kwakiutl, Haida, Nootka, and Tsimshian on the coast. The coastal tribes established settled communities and lived primarily by fishing, while the interior tribes were nomadic. Capt. James Cook, the first white man on these shores, landed on Vancouver Island at Nootka Sound in 1778. The next decade was marked by conflicting claims by the British and Spanish. In 1792, Capt. George Vancouver mapped the Pacific coast and the island which bears his name. The 19th century brought a disagreement with the United States over the border. This issue was settled in 1849 by the Oregon Treaty. The British gained undisputed control of the mainland north of the 49th Parallel and the whole of Vancouver Island, which was made a colony. British Columbia gained colonial status in 1858. The two were combined under the latter name in 1866 and entered Confederation in 1871 after being promised a transcontinental railway. The Canadian Pacific Railway was completed in 1885.

Queen Victoria named this province when the colony was created in 1858. The capital Victoria was named after this popular queen. Although the furthest from Britain, this province is often described as the most British in Canada.

The southern coastal areas of British Columbia have the mildest winter temperatures in Canada. Summers are cool. Precipitation along the coast is high due to the barriers created by the mountains. The interior and northern areas have wider variations in climate.

British Columbia is rich in natural resources. About half the province is forested and most of this is commercially viable. Abundant rainfall and mild temperatures on the coastal side of the province produce the biggest coniferous trees in Canada. Although arable land is limited, the Okanagan Valley is one of Canada's major fruit-producing areas. Minerals include copper, gold, silver, lead, and zinc. British Columbia has large coal reserves as well as natural gas and oil. Hydro-electric potential is second only to that of Quebec, but means have to be found to harness the rivers without interfering with the important Pacific salmon fishing industry. Shipping, both international and coastal, is a major contributor to the economy. Tourism provides additional income.

The legislative assembly of British Columbia has 69 members. At the federal level, the province has 28 members in the House of Commons and six senators.

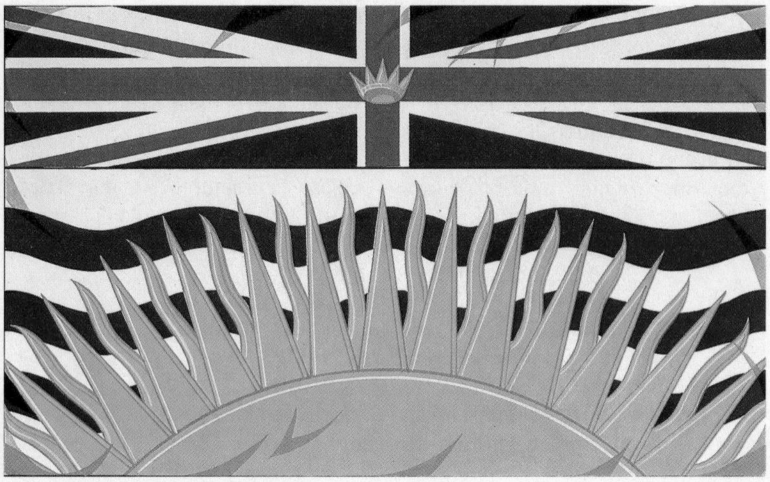

Wildflowers blanket the meadows below Mount Robson, British Columbia.

Area: Land: 929,730 sq km; Freshwater: 18,070 sq km;
Total: 947,800 sq km (9.5% of Canada)

Elevations: Highest point: 4,663m (Fairweather Mountain)
Lowest point: sea level (coastal areas)

Population (1989): 3,085,300 (11.7% of population of Canada)

Population density: 3.2 persons per sq km of land

Mother tongue: English 82.1%; French 1.6%; Other 16.3%

Date joined Confederation: July 20, 1871

Motto: Splendor Sine Occasu
(Splendor Without Diminishment)

Flower: Pacific dogwood

Capital: Victoria

Mean temperatures for typical locations:
Fort Nelson: January -23.8C; July 16.6C
Victoria: January 4.1C; July 15.4C

Annual precipitation for typical locations:
Fort Nelson: 451.8mm; Victoria: 647.2mm

Gross domestic product (1989): $68.2 billion
(11.3% of Canada's GDP)

Manitoba

Manitoba is the easternmost of Canada's three Prairie provinces. It differs from the other two in that it has an ocean coastline (on Hudson Bay) and an ocean port (Churchill). Manitoba is known as the "land of 100,000 lakes." These lakes are the creation of the last ice age. All waters of Manitoba drain toward the north and Hudson Bay. The province has an irregular shape, with a maximum width of 793 kilometres and length of 1,225 kilometres. The terrain is relatively level.

Manitoba was originally inhabited by Woods Cree, Plains Cree, Assiniboine, Ojibwa, and Chipewyan Indians. Hudson Bay provided the ocean route for the early visits by the white man to this territory. The first to visit the region was the British explorer Thomas Button, who spent the winter of 1612-13 at the mouth of the Nelson River. The rights to trade for furs in the territory drained by Hudson Bay were granted to the Hudson's Bay Company by King Charles II in 1670. The vast territory was known as Rupert's Land. While the British were developing the fur trade along the northern shores of Manitoba, the French fur traders were competing for the same business via the land and water routes of the continent. It was 1812 before the first farming settlement was established. In that year, Lord Selkirk acquired a land grant from the Hudson's Bay Company in what is now southern Manitoba and created his Red River Colony. In 1870, Canada purchased Rupert's Land. The Métis, a group of settlers of mixed French and Indian parentage under the leadership of Louis Riel, opposed plans for a new province. Nonetheless, that same year a tiny province to be known as Manitoba was created in the Red River area. Territorial extensions in 1881 and 1912 created the present limits of this province. When the railway reached Winnipeg in 1881, the modern era of the province began. Then at the hub of a growing country, Manitoba attracted large numbers of immigrants to its farmland.

The name Manitoba is an onomatopoeic Indian word for the lake by the same name. Its exact meaning is unknown. Winnipeg, the capital, gets its name from the Cree word for "murky water" – appropriate since this city is situated at the junction of the Red and Assiniboine rivers.

In Manitoba, the summers are warm and relatively damp. Winters are drier and extremely cold. Of the three Prairie provinces, Manitoba has the most precipitation during the growing season.

Modern Manitoba has a diversified economy. Furs and agriculture were the original industries and agriculture still makes a major contribution to the provincial economy. Wheat is the main crop. Minerals include copper and zinc. Hydroelectricity is plentiful and the manufacturing industry is highly developed. Winnipeg is a focal point for all national transportation systems, both land and air.

Manitoba is the province that best represents Canada's multiculturalism. In addition to the native population and descendants of British and French settlers, this province has substantial numbers from other backgrounds – Ukrainian, Polish, German, Dutch, Scandinavian, and others.

Manitoba has a 57-member provincial legislature. At the federal level, it is represented by 14 members of Parliament and six senators.

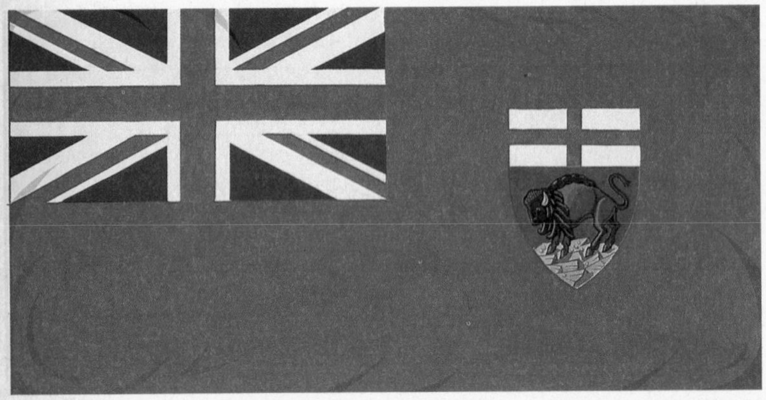

Aerial view of Cranberry Lake in Grass River Provincial Park, Manitoba.

Area: Land: 548,360 sq km; Freshwater: 101,590 sq km;
Total: 649,950 sq km (6.5% of Canada)

Elevations: Highest point: 832m (Baldy Mountain)
Lowest point: Hudson Bay shore

Population (1989): 1,085,300 (4.1% of population of Canada)

Population density: 2 persons per sq km of land

Mother tongue: English 73.4%; French 4.9%; Other 21.8%

Date joined Confederation: July 15, 1870

Motto: None

Flower: Prairie crocus

Capital: Winnipeg

Mean temperatures for typical locations:
The Pas: January -22.7C; July 17.7C
Winnipeg: January -19.3C; July 19.6C

Annual precipitation for typical locations:
The Pas 453.7mm; Winnipeg 525.5mm

Gross domestic product (1989): $21.5 billion
(3.6% of Canada's GDP)

New Brunswick

Part of New Brunswick was once called Acadia. Champlain established the original settlement on Ste. Croix Island (now in the state of Maine). The French developed the fur trade and developed a rapport with the natives. For two centuries, control of the land alternated between the French and British. Then in 1755, determined to strengthen its power, Britain demanded that the Acadians swear an oath of allegiance. Those who refused were deported. The 1763 Treaty of Paris ceded the area to Britain. Because of a common border with the state of Maine, more than 14,000 United Empire Loyalists settled in the area in 1783. As a result, the territory was made a province of Britain in 1784 and named New Brunswick, after the family name of King George III. New Brunswick was a charter member in the Confederation of Canada in 1867.

The original inhabitants of New Brunswick were the Micmac in the east and the Maliceet along the St. John River valley. Today's population is made up largely of descendants of the Acadian settlers from the French era and of the large Loyalist influx after the American Revolution. New Brunswick is an officially bilingual province. Its capital is Fredericton.

Fredericton, New Brunswick, with Christ Church Cathedral in the foreground.

New Brunswick is roughly rectangular in shape. Its maximum dimensions are 322 kilometres from north to south and 242 kilometres from east to west. Its two longest borders meet the sea on one side and the state of Maine on the other. It borders Quebec on the north and is joined to Nova Scotia on the south by a narrow land bridge, called the Isthmus of Chignecto. New Brunswick has a 1,524-kilometre seacoast. Most of the interior plateau is forest covered. The St. John River valley is rich in fertile soil. The Bay of Fundy has the world's highest tides, causing the phenomena of the Reversing Falls at Saint John and Tidal Bore at Moncton.

The climate of New Brunswick is varied. In the northern interior, the winters are quite severe while the coastal areas bear the moderating influence of the sea.

The largest natural resource of New Brunswick is its forest. More than half of this forest is softwood, making it suitable for paper production. Fishing of species such as lobster, herring, tuna, and crab is a major economic factor. Minerals include silver, lead, zinc, coal, and potash. Agricultural production centres around potatoes and dairying. The pulp and paper industry and the food processing industry make up the main elements of the manufacturing sector. With plants at Grand Falls, Beechwood, and Mactaquac, the St. John River is the main source of hydroelectricity, but a feasible means of harnessing the powerful Fundy tides is always being sought. Tourism is a significant contributor to the economy.

The New Brunswick legislative assembly has 58 members. At the federal level, the province is represented by 10 members of Parliament and 10 senators.

Area: Land: 72,090 sq km; Freshwater: 1,350 sq km;
Total: 73,440 sq km (0.7% of Canada)

Elevations: Highest point: 820m (Mount Carleton)
Lowest point: sea level (coastal areas)

Population (1989): 720,700 (2.7% of population of Canada)

Population density: 10 persons per sq km of land

Mother tongue: English 65.3%; French 33.5%; Other 1.3%

Date joined Confederation: July 1, 1867

Motto: Spem Reduxit (Hope Was Restored)

Flower: Purple violet

Capital: Fredericton

Temperatures for a typical location:
Chatham: January -9.7C; July 19.2C

Annual precipitation for a typical location:
Chatham: 1,096.7mm

Gross domestic product (1989): $11.7 billion
(1.9% of Canada's GDP)

Newfoundland

Newfoundland joined Confederation in 1949 and is Canada's newest province, even though it was the first part of North America visited by Europeans. The Vikings settled here briefly in the 10th century, and years before Columbus and Basque and Portuguese sailors fished and camped seasonally on these shores. Sailing for Henry VII, John Cabot is credited with the official discovery in 1497. Almost a century later, Humphrey Gilbert planted the flag for Elizabeth I to create Britain's first colony in America. During the next 200 years, Britain and France repeatedly fought over Newfoundland, until the Treaty of Paris in 1763 gave the British control. The tiny islands of St. Pierre and Miquelon off the south coast were ceded to France.

Newfoundland became a full British colony with responsible government in 1855, but self-rule collapsed in the depression of the 1930s. From then until 1949, it was ruled by a commission appointed by Britain. In a referendum in 1948, Newfoundlanders narrowly voted to join Canada, gaining full provincial status the following year. Historically, Newfoundland has always considered Labrador part of its territory, but there have been many disputes with Quebec on this issue.

New Founde Lande, Terra Nova, and Terre Neuve were names given the island by early fishermen and explorers. The map reveals many interesting place names, such as Come By Chance, Bumble Bee Bight, and Joe Batts Arm.

The Beothuk Indians – now extinct – were the original inhabitants. Labrador is still inhabited by various native groups – Inuit, Micmac, Naskapi, and Montagnais, but today Newfoundlanders are mainly of British descent.

Newfoundland, Canada's easternmost province, is made up of two parts – the island by the same name and the much larger area called Labrador on the mainland. Both have rocky surfaces and many parts are heavily forested.

There are great variations in climate. The northernmost area of Labrador is sub-arctic; the interior is continental; and Newfoundland's climate is moderate. Precipitation rates also vary. Much of Labrador is dry, while the maritime areas of Labrador and the island are quite wet. The Labrador current coming from the North Atlantic keeps the climate relatively cool.

Newfoundland is rich in natural resources – wood from the forest, hydroelectricity from the powerful rivers, minerals from the pre-Cambrian rock, fish from the sea, and petroleum from under the sea. Historically, the economy of this province was based on the sea. The fishing industry is in decline today but the 20th century has seen economic growth in the other sectors. This province is now Canada's largest producer of iron ore. Pulp and paper production is strong and the rich Hibernia oil fields were discovered offshore in 1979.

Newfoundland is represented in the federal government by seven members of Parliament and six senators. The provincial house of assembly in St. John's has 52 members. Newfoundland is unique in its local political structure. Because of the isolation of the settlements, county and township divisions have never been established and less than half of the communities have any form of local government.

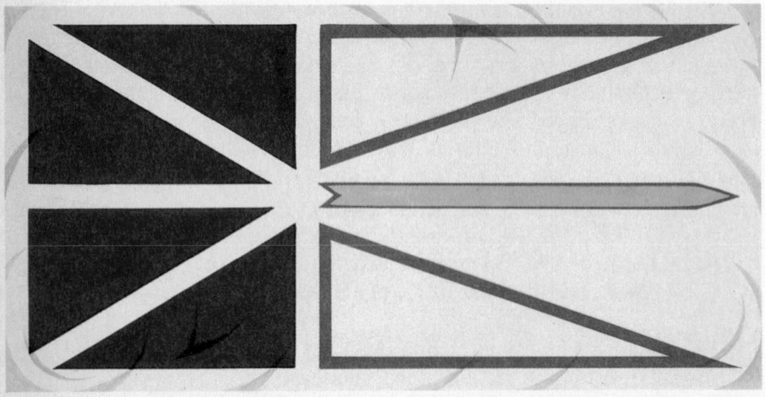

The outport of François on the southern coast of Newfoundland.

Area: Land: 371,690 sq km; Freshwater: 34,030 sq km;
Total: 405,720 sq km (4.1% of Canada)

Elevations: Highest point: 1,622m (Mount Carbrick, Labrador)
Lowest point: sea level (coastal areas)

Population (1989): 571,400 (2.2% of population of Canada)

Population density: 1.5 persons per sq km of land

Mother tongue: English 98.8%; French 0.5%; Other 0.8%

Date joined Confederation: March 31, 1949

Motto: Quaerite Prime Regnum Dei
(Seek Ye First The Kingdom Of God)

Flower: Pitcher plant

Capital: St. John's

Mean temperatures for typical locations:
Gander: January -6.2C; July 16.5C
Goose Bay: January -16.4C; July 15.8C

Annual precipitation for typical locations:
Gander: 1,130.1mm; Goose Bay: 946.1mm

Gross domestic product (1989): $7.9 billion
(1.3% of Canada's GDP)

Northwest Territories

The Northwest Territories make up one-third of Canada, with the present boundaries established in 1912. But when the Dominion of Canada acquired the region in 1870, it included present-day Alberta, Saskatchewan, Manitoba, the Yukon, and parts of northern Ontario and Quebec. However, it did not include the Arctic archipelago which was ceded to Canada by Britain in 1880. The name given to this land, Northwest Territories, came from a designation in the charter of 1670 granting the Hudson's Bay Company rights to Rupert's Land.

From the 16th century on, the Northwest Territories were visited by fur traders and explorers seeking a Northwest Passage across the continent. Samuel Hearne made the first significant land exploration for the Hudson's Bay Company in 1770-71. In 1789, Alexander Mackenzie of the North West Company discovered and travelled the river which bears his name. The disappearance of the Franklin expedition in 1845 led to stepped up exploration in this harsh land. The first man to complete a ship crossing of the Northwest Passage was the Norwegian explorer Roald Amundsen in 1903-04.

The mainland of the Northwest Territories can be divided into sub-Arctic and Arctic areas – one below and the other above the treeline. Only the southwestern part of the Northwest Territories is below the permafrost area. The largest of the Arctic islands is Baffin Island, and 17 of the other islands are also larger than Canada's smallest province, Prince Edward Island. The capital is Yellowknife, the only city in the Northwest Territories.

The population of the Northwest Territories is 58 percent native. In fact, 14 percent of the people speak neither of Canada's two official languages. Of the natives, the Inuit live in the more northerly Arctic areas while the Indian and Métis inhabit the sub-Arctic areas of the Mackenzie Valley. The white minority lives in the more settled areas.

The climate of this northern land is extremely dry and cold. The summers last from three weeks in the far north to three months in the southwest. Because of their northern latitude, the Territories are known as "the land of the midnight sun." In the middle of the summer, daylight lasts 24 hours.

The economic base of the Northwest Territories is mining. Minerals include lead, zinc, and gold. The Norman Wells in the western Arctic are the Territories' only working oil fields, but the potential for future oil extraction exists in the Beaufort Sea area. Electricity is produced by thermal-powered plants. The traditional activities of hunting, fishing, and trapping still provide some income for many of the native population. With growing interest in the north, tourism is an expanding industry. There is also a growing demand for native arts and crafts. Inuit art is appreciated worldwide.

Originally administered by an appointed council and commissioner, the Northwest Territories now have an elected 24-member territorial council. The commissioner, however, is appointed by the federal government and reports to the minister of Indian affairs and northern development. The Territories are represented in Parliament by two members in the House of Commons and one senator. Native land claims and provincial status are two ongoing major political issues.

Cumberland Sound and Baffin Island in the Northwest Territories.

Area: Land: 3,293,020 sq km; Freshwater: 133,300 sq km;
Total: 3,426,320 sq km (34.4% of Canada)

Elevations: Highest point: 2,773m (Mount Sir James MacBrien)
Lowest point: sea level (Arctic shores)

Population (1989): 53,600 (0.2% of population of Canada)

Population density: 0.02 persons per sq km of land

Mother tongue: English 55.3%; French 2.7%; Other 42%

Reconstituted to present form: Sept. 1, 1905

Motto: None

Flower: Mountain avens

Capital: Yellowknife

Mean temperatures for typical locations:
Fort Simpson: January -28.2C; July 16.6C
Resolute: January -32.1C; July 4.1C

Annual precipitation for typical locations:
Fort Simpson: 355.1mm
Resolute: 131.4mm

Gross domestic product of Yukon and Northwest territories (1989):
$2.6 billion (0.4% of Canada's GDP)

Nova Scotia

The most easterly part of mainland North America, Nova Scotia, is surrounded by water except for a 22-kilometre land boundary with New Brunswick. Cape Breton Island is joined to the rest of the province by the Canso Causeway.

The history of Nova Scotia goes back to the beginnings of European contact. Cape Breton was probably visited by the same Basque and Portuguese fishermen who visited Newfoundland and Labrador. The French began settling in what was then Acadia when Champlain and de Monts built Port-Royal in 1605. The English first attacked Port-Royal from Virginia in 1913, but a long British-French rivalry culminated in the expulsion of the Acadians in 1755, after which many New Englanders moved up. The arrival of large numbers of United Empire Loyalists after the American Revolution established Nova Scotia as predominantly British with American ties. Nova Scotia was one of the four original partners in Confederation in 1867.

The name Nova Scotia, or New Scotland, was given to the area by William Alexander, a Scot sent out to establish a colony under royal charter in 1621. The site of the capital, Halifax, was originally called Chebucto, a Micmac word meaning great, long harbor – appropriate because it is one of the finest natural deep-water harbors in the world. The majority of Nova Scotians are of British origin. The historic area of Acadia still has a considerable French-speaking population. Lunenberg was originally settled by Germans. Nova Scotia also has an established black community.

Nova Scotia is 579 kilometres long and a maximum of 130 kilometres wide. Its good harbors have been important militarily and economically. The Annapolis Valley is the agricultural centre of the province. Cape Breton, making up one-third of the province's area, is primarily rugged highlands. Its largest lakes, the Bras d'Or Lakes, are saltwater. Perhaps the most famous island off Nova Scotia is Sable Island, known as the Graveyard of the Atlantic due to the large number of ships that have run aground on its treacherous sandbars.

The climate of Nova Scotia is influenced by both continental and maritime weather patterns. South coastal areas have more moderate temperatures than those inland.

The economy is resource-based. Fish and fish products account for more than one-third of all exports; forest products account for a quarter. The coal mines of Cape Breton produce more than 3 million tons a year. Nova Scotia is the largest producer of gypsum in Canada and has the only North American primary tin mine. Although only 10 percent of the land is suitable for agriculture, dairy and fruit farming yield significant returns.

Nova Scotia has a 52-member legislative assembly and is represented federally by 11 members of Parliament and 10 senators.

Lighthouse guides ships past Enragée Point on Cape Breton Island.

Area: Land: 52,840 sq km; Freshwater: 2,650 sq km;
Total: 55,490 sq km (0.6% of Canada)

Elevations: Highest point: 532m
(Cape Breton Highlands National Park)
Lowest point: Sea level (coastal areas)

Population (1989): 888,700 (3.4% of population of Canada)

Population density: 16.5 persons per sq km of land

Mother tongue: English 93.8%; French 4.1%; Other 2.1%

Date joined Confederation: July 1, 1867

Motto: Munit Haec Et Altera Vincit
(One Defends And The Other Conquers)

Flower: Mayflower

Capital: Halifax

Mean temperatures for a typical location:
Halifax: January -3.1C; July 18.2C

Annual precipitation for a typical location:
Halifax: 1,282mm

Gross domestic product (1989): $14.8 billion
(2.5% of Canada's GDP)

Ontario

Ontario is Canada's second largest province in area. It extends from the Great Lakes in the south to the shores of Hudson Bay/James Bay in the north, and from west to east from Manitoba to Quebec. The province is made up of three physical regions – the Hudson Bay Lowlands, Canadian Shield, Great Lakes, and St. Lawrence Lowlands.

Ontario is Canada's most populous province. More than one-third of the nation's people live here – 90 percent of them within 160 kilometres of the southern border.

Originally part of the vast hinterland of New France, Ontario was home to more than 30,000 Huron Indians in the central Great Lakes area. En route to buy furs from the natives, French traders travelled the waterways of this land. The Hurons became both their military allies and trading middlemen. A rare attempt at permanent settlement ended tragically in 1649 when the Jesuit founders of Ste-Marie were killed by the Iroquois trade rivals of the Hurons. At the end of the American Revolution, about 10,000 United Empire Loyalists arrived in this territory and began to colonize it. The Constitutional Act of 1791 named this land Upper Canada. Under the Act of Union of 1840, it became known as Canada West. An original partner in Confederation in 1867, the province adopted the name Ontario, after the lake which forms much of its southern border. Ontario is Iroquoian for "beautiful water." The capital city Toronto gets its name from a Iroquoian word for either "looming of trees" or "meeting place," referring to the fact that it was the point from which the trade routes led west. The majority of the Ontario population is English-speaking, but this province is also home to the largest number of French-speaking people in Canada outside the province of Quebec. The native population is primarily of Algonquian and Iroquoian descent. The economic stability of Ontario also attracts increasing numbers of immigrants of various ethnic origins.

The climate of Ontario covers a wide range. The north is sub-Arctic with severe cold while the south is continental with milder temperatures and higher humidity.

Ontario is Canada's richest province. It has abundant natural resources and is the most highly industrialized province in Canada. The primary industries of agriculture, mining, and forestry were the origins of Ontario's prosperity and remain significant factors. Despite the fact that agricultural land is in a relatively narrow strip in the south, Ontario is Canada's leader in agricultural products. Minerals include gold, nickel, copper, zinc, silver, and uranium. Forests belong to the Crown and the right to cut is controlled by licence.

However, it is the manufacturing and service industries which have made Ontario so rich. This province accounts for more than 50 percent of the manufactured products in Canada. The automobile industry is the largest manufacturing sector in the province. Other products include machinery, chemicals, rubber, plastics, electrical and electronic equipment, and petroleum products. The service industry, including tourism, is the largest element of the economy of Ontario.

Ontario has a provincial parliament of 125 members. It has 98 members in the House of Commons and 24 senators – the largest representation of any province.

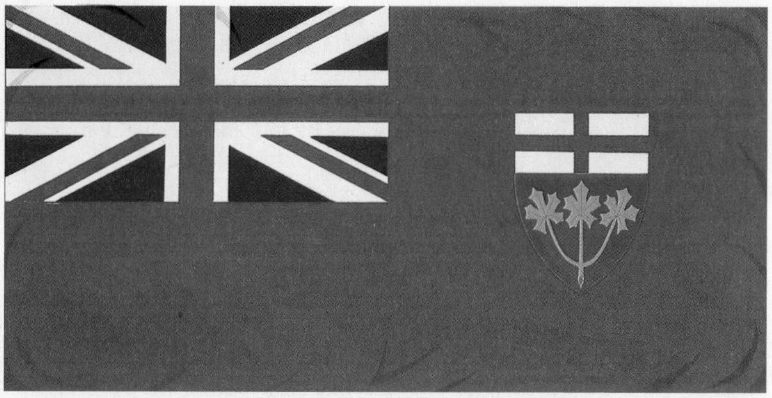

The CN Tower and SkyDome are focal points of Toronto's skyline.

Area: Land: 891,190 sq km; Freshwater: 177,390 sq km;
Total: 1,068,580 sq km (10.7% of Canada)

Elevations: Highest point: 693m (Ishpatina Ridge)
Lowest point: Hudson Bay shore

Population (1989): 9,624,500 (36.5% of population of Canada)

Population density: 10.8 persons per sq km of land

Mother tongue: English 78%; French 5.3%: Other 16.7%

Date joined Confederation: July 1, 1867

Motto: Ut Incepit Fidelis Sic Permanet
(Loyal It Began, Loyal It Remains)

Flower: White trillium

Capital: Toronto

Mean temperatures for typical locations:
Thunder Bay: January -15.4C; July 17.6C
Toronto: January -4.6C; July 22C

Annual precipitation for typical locations:
Thunder Bay: 711.8mm; Toronto: 800.5mm

Gross domestic product (1989): $248 billion
(41.2% of Canada's GDP)

Prince Edward Island

The smallest Canadian province, Prince Edward Island, extends 170 kilometres from tip to tip and ranges from six to 64 kilometres in width. Although the first of the pre-Confederation conferences was held in Charlottetown, the island did not join Canada until 1873, the seventh province to do so.

Before the arrival of the white man, this island was home to the Micmac Indians and named Abegweit (land cradled in the waves). Early French settlers called it Ile St. Jean. After the French defeat at Louisbourg in 1758, the British simply anglicized the name until 1799, when they changed it to Prince Edward Island to honor the Duke of Kent, then commander of the British troops in North America.

Most present-day inhabitants are of British origin. The French-speaking population, mainly of Acadian descent, forms the second largest ethnic group. The Micmac still live in parts of the island but now are less than one percent of the population. Due to economic conditions and its small size, this province has attracted few immigrants.

The soil of Prince Edward Island is known for its distinctive red color which is caused by large quantities of iron oxides or rust. Although much of the island consists of rolling hills, nowhere is the elevation higher than 142 metres above sea level. The coastline is deeply indented. The north shore features extensive sand dunes and beaches. The coast is dotted with small harbors suitable for shallow-draught inshore fishing vessels. Good deep-water ports exist at Charlottetown and Summerside.

The mainstay of Prince Edward Island's economy is agriculture. Because of its fertile soil, the province promotes itself as the Garden of the Gulf. Potatoes are the most important agricultural product. Tourism, though still in second place, is a rapidly increasing element of island income. Although the island is accessible only by air or water, more than 700,000 tourists a year visit, attracted by the beautiful beaches and relaxed lifestyle. Fishing, the island's oldest organized industry, still has a vital role in the economy. The leading species are lobster, herring and ocean perch. Malpeque oysters are world-famous. One secondary industry is Irish moss, sold as the thickening agent carageenan.

The resources of Prince Edward Island are primarily the soil and the sea. There is no commercial mining and no source of hydroelectricity. As a result, energy costs are the highest in Canada. Some electricity is produced by oil-fired plants, but most is imported from New Brunswick by undersea cable.

Since no part of Prince Edward Island is very far from the sea, the climate is moderate. Seasons do not exhibit the extremes of other parts of Canada, although there are occasionally severe lows in winter.

Prince Edward Island is divided into three counties: Prince, King's and Queen's. Charlottetown, the capital, is the only city. The province has a 32-member legislative assembly and is represented federally by four members of Parliament and four senators.

Red dirt roads are a distinguishing feature of P.E.I. scenes.

Area: Land: 5,660 sq km; Freshwater: 0 sq km;
Total: 5,660 sq km (0.1% of Canada)

Elevations: Highest point: 142m (Queen's County)
Lowest point: sea level (coastal areas)

Population (1989): 130,300 (0.5% of population of Canada)

Population density: 23 persons per sq km of land

Mother tongue: English 94.1%; French 4.7%; Other 1.2%

Date joined Confederation: July 1, 1873

Motto: Parva Sub Ingenti
(The Small Under The Protection Of The Great)

Flower: Lady's slipper

Capital: Charlottetown

Mean temperatures for a typical location:
Charlottetown: January -7.1C; July 18.3C

Annual precipitation for a typical location:
Charlottetown: 1,169.4mm

Gross domestic product (1989): $1.8 billion
(0.3% of Canada's GDP)

Quebec

Quebec is the largest province in Canada in landmass and second largest in population. Jacques Cartier claimed the land for France in 1534. For the next 74 years, the St. Lawrence was visited in the summer months only, for fur trading with the natives. Having failed in two earlier attempts to establish colonies in the Maritimes, Champlain built the Habitation at Quebec in 1608. This colony was successful and became the centre of the land known as New France. Most settlement took place along the St. Lawrence. With the fall of Quebec in 1759 and the Treaty of Paris in 1763, Britain gained control of the territory. The name was changed to Quebec, an Indian name which applied originally to the capital city only, because it is situated at "the place where the river narrows." With the Constitutional Act of 1791, Quebec became Lower Canada. In 1840, it was renamed Canada East. When this province joined Confederation in 1867, it again took its Indian name, Quebec.

Quebec was home to many different native groups – Iroquois, Naskapi, Montagnais, Cree, Huron, Algonquin, Malecite, Micmac, and Inuit. Today the population of Quebec is predominantly French-speaking. In fact, French is the only language authorized by the province. The English-speaking minority lives mostly in urban areas and near the Ontario and U.S. borders.

Quebec is an immense province with a maximum north-south distance of 1,967 kilometres and a maximum east-west distance of 1,553 kilometres. Settlement is concentrated in the St. Lawrence River valley. Much of the vast north is virtually uninhabited. The north is part of the Canadian Shield and the south the St. Lawrence Lowlands.

The weather of this province is as diverse as its terrain. The most northerly areas are arctic in climate while the St. Lawrence Valley has hot summers and cold winters.

Traditionally the Quebec economy was based on agriculture and forestry. Although only four percent of the province is classed as agricultural, farming is still important. In pulp and paper, Quebec ranks first in Canada and in sawmill production second. Since 80 percent of the province is in the Canadian Shield, Quebec is rich in minerals – iron, gold, copper, and zinc. The powerful rivers that drain the Shield make Quebec the largest producer of hydroelectricity in the nation. Shipping remains a significant economic factor despite the rise in air transport. The tourism industry is strong and growing. Manufacturing has long played a major role in Quebec's economy. Once dominated by textiles, this industry is now diversifying.

The provincial government of Quebec is the 122-member National Assembly. In the federal Parliament, Quebec is represented by 75 members in the House of Commons and 24 senators.

Quebec's legal system is unique in Canada. Its basis is the Napoleonic Civil Code while all other provinces base their civil laws on English Common Law.

The stately Château Frontenac overlooks Quebec City's waterfront.

Area: Land: 1,356,790 sq km; Freshwater: 183,890 sq km;
Total: 1,540,680 sq km (15.5% of Canada)

Elevations: Highest point: 1,622m (Mont d'Iberville)
Lowest point: St. Lawrence shore

Population (1989): 6,714,400 (25.5% of population of Canada)

Population density: 4.9 persons per sq km of land

Mother tongue: English 10.4%; French 82.8%; Other 6.8%

Date joined Confederation: July 1, 1867

Motto: Je Me Souviens (I Remember)

Flower: Fleur-de-lis (White garden lily)

Capital: Quebec City

Mean temperatures for typical locations:
Fort Chimo: January -23.3C; July 11.4C
Montreal: January -8.7C; July 21.8C

Annual precipitation for typical locations:
Fort Chimo: 504.2mm; Montreal: 1,020.1mm

Gross domestic product (1989): $144 billion
(23.9% of Canada's GDP)

Saskatchewan

Saskatchewan is the only Canadian province to have no natural borders. Perfectly regular in shape, it has boundaries that follow specific parallels of latitude and lines of longitude. The province is 1,224 kilometres long and an average of 539 kilometres wide. The name Saskatchewan, used for both the province and its main river, is an anglicized version of the Cree "Kisiskatchewan," which means "swiftly flowing water."

The aboriginal inhabitants of Saskatchewan were the Cree, Blackfoot, Assiniboine, and Chipewyan. A young Hudson's Bay Company employee named Henry Kelsey was the first white man to see the plains in 1690. Early settlers were the Métis, descendants of the French fur traders and their Indian wives. In 1870, when Canada took over Rupert's Land from the Hudson's Bay Company, the land including what is now Saskatchewan was named the Northwest Territories. The arrival of the Canadian Pacific Railway in 1882 provided access for immigrants of many nationalities. Saskatchewan became one of two new provinces carved from the Northwest Territories in 1905.

The capital of Saskatchewan is Regina. Originally called Wascana, the Cree word for "pile of bones," the name Regina was suggested as more suitable for a capital city by Princess Louise, wife of the governor general and daughter of Queen Victoria. The northern third of Saskatchewan is part of the Canadian Shield. The rest is a vast plain of fertile soil. Saskatchewan has more farmland than any other province – one-half of the nation's total.

Saskatchewan has a continental climate with long, cold winters and warm, dry, and comparatively short summers. Severe storms and extremes of temperature are common – blizzards and chinooks in winter, thunderstorms, hail, and even tornadoes in summer.

The population of Saskatchewan represents many cultures. Besides those of native, French or British backgrounds, there are many of Ukrainian, German, Russian, Scandinavian, and other descent. A promise of cheap or free land in the late 19th and early 20th centuries attracted homesteaders. Today, although the cities have grown, half the population is still rural.

Saskatchewan's economy has diversified this century, but agriculture remains the single most important economic contributor. The province produces 53 percent of Canada's wheat. Other crops include rapeseed, rye, flax, barley, and oats. Saskatchewan is rich in minerals. It has more than 40 percent of the recoverable potash in the world, 50 percent of Canadian uranium supplies, and is second in Canada in crude oil production. Other minerals include natural gas, coal, copper, zinc, gold, and silver. The mining industry has expanded rapidly in the last quarter century. The manufacturing sector is also expanding. Saskatchewan has large forest reserves and produces its own energy.

The provincial legislative assembly has 64 seats. At the federal level, Saskatchewan has 14 members of Parliament and six senators.

Saskatchewan's Legislative Building in the capital city of Regina.

Area: Land: 570,700 sq km; Freshwater: 81,630 sq km;
Total: 652,330 sq km (6.5% of Canada)

Elevations: Highest point: 1,468m (Cypress Hills)
Lowest point: Lake Athabasca shoreline

Population (1989): 1,003,600 (3.8% of population of Canada)

Population density: 1.8 persons per sq km of land

Mother tongue: English 81.9%; French 2.3%; Other 15.7%

Date joined Confederation: Sept. 1, 1905

Motto: Multis E Gentibus Vires
(From Many Peoples, Strength)

Flower: Western red lily

Capital: Regina

Mean temperatures for a typical location:
Regina: January -17.9%; July 18.9%

Annual precipitation for a typical location:
Regina: 384.0mm

Gross domestic product (1989): $18.6 billion
(3.1% of Canada's GDP)

Yukon Territory

The Yukon Territory is situated in Canada's extreme northwest corner. It is bounded by British Columbia on the south, the Arctic Ocean on the north, the Northwest Territories on the east, and Alaska on the west. This territory is almost triangular in shape with only a very short northern boundary.

The Yukon Territory is a rugged land covered with mountains, high plateaus, and swiftly flowing waters. The name Yukon is from the Loucheux Indian word Yu-kun-ah for "great river." The Yukon River is the fifth largest in North America and drains the whole territory.

This territory was home to Canada's northernmost Indians, the Kutchin, when the British explorer John Franklin first arrived on what's now called Herschel Island. Franklin was seeking the Northwest Passage but recognized the potential for fur trade in the area. Men of the Hudson's Bay Company explored the area before establishing a post on the Yukon River in 1847. Gold prospectors started arriving in the 1860s. The most exciting moments in Yukon history came in 1896, when gold was discovered in Bonanza Creek and the Klondike gold rush followed. Before the gold rush the Yukon was a district of the Northwest Territories, but with its new prosperity it was made a separate territory in 1898. The centre of gold country, Dawson was the capital. Whitehorse replaced Dawson in 1951.

Until the late 19th century the rivers provided the main source of transportation. The Klondike gold rush brought about the construction of the White Pass and Yukon Railway. The Americans built the Alaska Highway through the Yukon in 1942 providing the first long-distance land route in the territory. In 1979, the Dempster Highway was opened from Dawson City to Inuvik, Northwest Territories.

The climate of the Yukon is quite dry because of its high altitude and because the mountains block the moist Pacific air. Winters are very cold. The lowest temperature (-63 degrees C) on Canadian record was registered at Snag in 1947. Summers are quite warm but short. The frost-free period is only about two-and-a-half months.

The economy of the Yukon is a resource-based one. Furs, the original resource, still provide employment to many of the aboriginal people. Today the main resources are the minerals – gold, silver, lead, and zinc. Dependence to a large extent on one industry makes for a very volatile economy. With poor markets and diminishing supplies, the early 1980s were particularly poor times for the Yukon. However, the economy now seems to be on the road to recovery. The tourist industry is also developing rapidly.

The Yukon Territory is governed by a federally-appointed commissioner and an elected 16-member legislative assembly which has the power to deal with local matters. However, all legislation requires the signature of the commissioner. Full provincial status and Indian land claims are major concerns in the Yukon Territory. At the federal level, the Yukon is represented by one member in the House of Commons and one senator.

The Selwyn Mountains in the Yukon are resplendent in their fall colors.

Area: Land: 478,970 sq km; Freshwater: 4,480 sq km;
Total: 483,450 sq km (4.8% of Canada)

Elevations: Highest point: 5,951m (Mount Logan)
Lowest point: sea level (Arctic shores)

Population (1989): 25,700 (0.1% of population of Canada)

Population density: 0.05 persons per sq km of land

Mother tongue: English 89.1%; French 2.6%; Other 8.3%

Date organized: June 13, 1898

Motto: None

Flower: Fireweed

Capital: Whitehorse

Mean temperatures for typical locations:
Dawson: January -30.7C; July 15.6C
Whitehorse: January -20.7C; July 14.1C

Annual precipitation for typical locations:
Dawson: 306.1mm; Whitehorse: 261.2mm

Gross domestic product of Yukon and Northwest territories (1989):
$2.6 billion (0.4% of Canada's GDP)

General Index

This index provides rapid access to the information you seek. Each entry is followed by a page number and a letter indicating the column in which the article begins (a, b, c or d). Pages in roman refer to texts whereas pages in italic refer to the column of chronology.

A

D

I

K

L

O

Q

U

X

Y

Z

Photo Credit Index

Jacket

1. Geological Survey of Canada/J.D. Aitken, KGS-196
2. Office of the Prime Minister
3. Metro Toronto Library, # 1825
4. Moving Image and Sound Archives/National Archives of Canada
5. Hudson's Bay Company Archives/Public Archives of Manitoba
6. Miller Comstock/E. Otto
7. Canadian Museum of Nature (Museum of Natural Sciences)/Eleanor M. Kish
8. Environment Canada, Signal Hill Historic Park
9. National Archives of Canada, C11226
10. National Archives of Canada, C2771
11. Nova Scotia Department of Tourism and Culture
12. McGill Rare Books
13. Travelarctic/Dept. of Economic Development & Tourism, Northwest Territories
14. Confederation Life Gallery of Canadian History
15. The Granger Collection, # 4E800.22
16. National Gallery of Canada/Dr. Naomi Jackson Groves
17. National Archives of Canada, C3165
18. Richard Hill
19. Canapress
20. Miller Comstock/R. Hall
21. The Granger Collection, # BC42
22. National Archives of Canada, C42249
23. British Columbia Provincial Museum, # 35
24. National Archives of Canada, C3202
25. Royal Canadian Mounted Police Archives
26. Canapress
27. Canadian Space Agency, # 88-27535
28. Prince Edward Island Tourism and Parks/Kenneth Ginn
29. Miller Comstock/M. Beedell

Front end paper: The Granger Collection, New York, 4E647.05
Back end paper: Chronicle Publications

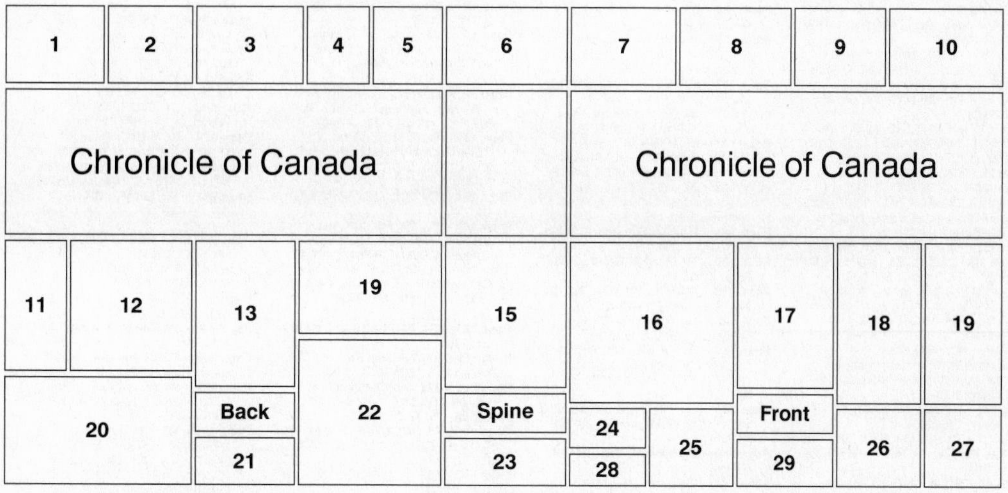

Agencies Some agency names have been abbreviated in this index. The list below provides full names of picture agencies.

AMHD-Q: Archives des Augustines du Monastère de l'Hôtel Dieu de Québec
Athlete Information Bureau: Athlete Information Bureau & Canadian Olympic Association
BC Archives: British Columbia Archives & Records Service
BCPM: British Columbia Provincial Museum
BNS: Bank of Nova Scotia Archives
BSQ: Bibliothèque du Séminaire du Québec
Bank of Montreal: Bank of Montreal Archives
Bell: Bell Telephone Historical Collection
Bettmann: Bettmann Archive, New York
CIBC: Canadian Imperial Bank of Commerce
CMC: Canadian Museum of Civilization
CP Rail: CP Rail Corporate Archives
CWM: Canadian War Museum
Canada Post: Canada Post Corporation
Canadian Jewish Congress: Canadian Jewish Congress National Archives
Canapress: Canapress Photo Service
Cater Andrews: The Literary Executors, The Cater Andrews Collection, Memorial University of Newfoundland
Centre for Nfld. Studies: Centre for Newfoundland Studies Archives, Memorial University
Chronicle: Chronicle Publications
Confederation Centre: Confederation Centre Art Gallery and Museum (Gift of the Robert Harris Trust, 1965)
Confederation Life: Confederation Life Gallery of Canadian History
Currency Museum: Currency Museum/ Bank of Canada
DND: Department of National Defence
Digby: Admiral Digby Library and Historical Society, Digby, Nova Scotia
GSC: Geological Survey of Canada
Glenbow: Glenbow Archives and Museum, Calgary, Alberta
Granger: Granger Collection, New York
Guelph: University of Guelph Collection at MacDonald Stewart Art Centre
HBCA/PAM: Hudson's Bay Company Archives, Public Archives of Manitoba
Imagewares: Imagewares International
Lande: Lawrence M. Lande Collection of Canadiana, Department of Rare Books and Special Collections of McGill University
London Free Press: London Free Press Collection of Photographic Negatives/ The D.B. Weldon Library/ University of Western Ontario
MAHD-Q: Musée des Augustines du Monastère de l'Hôtel Dieu de Québec
MTL: Metropolitan Toronto Library
Man. Archives: Public Archives of Manitoba
Maritime Museum: Maritime Museum of the Atlantic (Ballou's Pictorial)
McCord: McCord Museum of Canadian History
McGill: Department of Rare Books and Special Collections of the McGill University Libraries
McMichael: McMichael Canadian Art Collection
NAC: National Archives of Canada
NAC/Jefferys: National Archives of Canada, C.W. Jefferys Estate
NB Archives: Provincial Archives of New Brunswick
NFB: National Film Board
NGC: National Gallery of Canada
NMC: National Map Collection
National Library: National Library – Rare Books
Nature: Canadian Museum of Nature (Museum of Natural Science)
Nfld. Archives: Public Archives of Newfoundland and Labrador
Notman: Notman Photographic Archives, McCord Museum of Canadian History
Ont. Archives: Archives of Ontario, Toronto
PAA: Public Archives of Alberta
PAA – E. Brown: Public Archives of Alberta, E. Brown Collection
PAA – photo coll.: Public Archives of Alberta, photo collection
PEI Archives: Prince Edward Island Public Archives
Pangnirtung: Indian and Northern Affairs/ Pangnirtung Inuit Co-op/ Nicodemus Nowyook
Peace: Peace River Centennial Museum and Archives
RCMP: Royal Canadian Mounted Police
Sask. Archives: Saskatchewan Archives Board
Signal Hill: Environment Canada, Signal Hill National Historic Park
Steves: Howard K. Steves, Silver Spring, MD, U.S.A.
Topham: Topham Picture Source, London
Tyrrell: Tyrrell Museum of Paleontology, Drumheller, Alberta/ Neil Brown
UBC: UBC Museum of Anthropology, Vancouver, B.C.
UBC Special Coll.: UBC Museum of Anthropology Special Collections
WCPI: Western Canada Pictorial Index

Every effort has been made to trace the copyright of the illustrations used in this publication. If an error has been made in these picture credits, we apologize and ask the copyright holder to contact Chronicle Publications so that it can be investigated, and, where necessary, corrected. Regrettably, the large number of illustrations used in this book makes it impossible to acknowledge all the individual museums and art galleries who hold the various objects and paintings which appear in the photographs supplied by the agencies and libraries credited.

The position of the pictures is indicated by a combination of the following letters: B: Bottom, T: Top, M: Middle, L: Left, R: Right, X: Middle Left, Y: Middle Right, SP: Spread

Photo Credit Index

Page 4 – **MR** GSC/R.L. Christie: KGS-66 – **TR** Imagewares/Neil Brown – **TL** Miller Comstock/R. Hall: T000-59320-444 – **TY** Miller Comstock/E. Otto: 10017400 – **ML** Miller Comstock/Malak: 240F-5-7A – **BL** Miller Comstock/B. Thompson: MA032539 – **BR** Miller Comstock/M. Saunders: MSAU-1784
Page 6 & 7 – **SP** Richard Hill/Arnold Jacobs: 14
Page 8 – **MR** British Museum (Natural History): T191
Page 9 – **TM, MY** GSC/M.J. Copeland (ref: 204309, KGS-2067) – **MX** GSC: 21363
Page 10 – All pictures from Chronicle
Page 11 – **TR, BL** Nature/Eleanor M. Kish (Plate 12, Plate 15)
Pages 12 & 13 – All pictures from Tyrrell (ref: 1, 2, 4, 5, 6, 14, 15, 16, 17, 19, 20)
Page 14 – All pictures from Nature
Page 15 – **TR** Chronicle – **BM** Prof. M. Day, London
Page 16 – **TR** Chronicle/Keith Crowe – **BX, BR** CMC (ref: S754047, S754064)
Page 17 – **MM, BR** National Library (ref: C127485, NL12649)
Page 18 – **TM, BY, BL** CMC (ref: S80-8, S754499, S713830)
Page 19 – All pictures from Jean Lengellé (ref: 7, 28, 29, 32, 35, 36)
Page 20 – **MR** NAC: C5539 – **BR** Nfld. Archives: NA1757
Page 21 – **TM** CMC: S712998 – **BR** Keith Crowe
Page 22 – **TX, TY** CMC (ref: S754186, K75954)
Page 23 – **TL, TR** CMC (ref: S75569, S814371)
Page 24 – **TR, BL** CMC (ref: S75-592, S71-2176)
Page 25 – **BY** Alberta Culture and Multiculturalism – **TL** Miller Comstock/N. Lightfoot
Page 26 – **ML, MY** BCPM (ref: 31, 34)
Page 27 – **TL, MR, BR** CMC (ref: S85-3298, S82-15, S82-320)
Page 28 – **MR, ML, BX** CMC (ref: S82-260, S87-700, S80-265)
Page 29 – **BL** GSC/R.G. Blackadar: KGS-46 – **TL, TR** Miller Comstock/G. Hunter – **MR, BR** Miller Comstock/E. Otto
Page 30 – **BR** Chronicle – **TR** CMCS82-325
Page 31 – **TR, BL, BR** Granger (ref: 4EB103, 4E286.02, 4E393.23)
Page 32 – **TR** Granger: 4E829.02 – **BY** National Library: C122987 – **TL** NMC: 19268
Page 33 – **TX, BL** NAC (ref: C8907, C17525) – **BR** National Library: NL15939
Page 34 – **MR** Granger: DN6107 – **TR** NAC: C1956
Page 35 – **TL, TR, BR** NAC (ref: C5538, C12235, C10522)
Page 36 – **TL, TR, BL, BR** NAC (ref: C11210, C100717, C100719, C99259)
Page 37 – **ML, BL, BY, BR** NAC (ref: C34206, C99250, C99244, C99261) – **TL, TX, TR** National Library (ref: C92246, C92245, C92242)
Page 38 – **BR** Bettmann: E.495 – **TR, BM** NMC (ref: H310000, A-10000)
Page 39 – **TR, ML** Granger (ref: BL50E, 4EJW163) – **BR** New York Public Library
Page 40 – **TY** Confederation Life: E4 – **BR** NAC: C111502
Page 41 – **TL, TR, ML, BL, BR** NAC (ref: C99320, C25700, C1913, C1912, C21115)
Page 42 – **TY** Granger: LM1092 – **BR** NAC: C99343
Page 43 – **TR** Granger: 4E283.33 – **BR** John Carter Brown Library: 04684 – **BL** National Library: C92244
Page 44 – **TR** Maritime Museum: N16,633 – **BR, ML** NAC (ref: C2312, 6327,H3: 900)
Page 45 – **BR** NAC/Jefferys: C106968 – **MX** NAC: C23089 – **TR** National Library: NL8760
Page 46 – **ML** NAC: C-100713 – **TR, BR** NAC/Jefferys (ref: C-73611, C-13986)
Page 47 – **TR** Explorer Archives, Paris: 555072 – **MR, BR** Granger (ref: DN6108, 4E736.10) – **TL, BL** NMC (ref: H1/ 10,000, A/10,000)
Page 48 & 49 – **SP** NAC/George Reid: C-11015
Page 50 – **BY** NAC/Jefferys: C73448 – **TM** NAC: C13320
Page 51 – **TR** Granger: 4E817.06 – **BM** NAC: C6163
Page 52 – **TY** NAC: C2061 – **BR** National Library: C92243
Page 53 – **TL, BR** NAC (ref: C5749, c-8336) – **TR** NAC/Jefferys: C73635
Page 54 – **TM** WCPI: EWA043113894 – **BR** NAC: C-10622
Page 55 – **TL** Granger: 4E328.28 – **MR** National Library: NL5309 – **BX** NAC: C-16952
Page 56 – **TR** National Library: NL15087 – **MM** NAC: C-82790
Page 57 – **TY, MR** NAC (ref: C-11987, C-25597) – **BM** National Library: NL5307
Page 58 – **TL** Confederation Life: E6 – **TR, BM** NAC (ref: C-27543, C-11232)
Page 59 – **TL, BR, TM, BL,** AMHD-Q (ref: B11, B18, 11, 85-826/2) – **TR** NAC: C-34198
Page 60 – **BR** Confederation Life: P-1 – **MR** NAC: C-7704
Page 61 – **TM, MR, BM** NAC (ref: C-11237, C-12329, C-5839)
Page 62 – **TX** NAC/Jefferys: C-69795 – **TY, BM** NAC (ref: C-3165, C-354)
Page 63 – **TM** Guelph: 1 – **MM** NAC: C-1994 – **BM** NAC/Jefferys: C-70336
Page 64 – **TM** NAC/Jefferys: C-73423 – **MY** NMC: 6338
Page 65 – **TM, TR, BX** NAC (ref: C-11198, C-410, C-8986)
Page 66 – **TR** NAC: C-7695
Page 67 – **BR** MAHD-Q: 3 – **TM, BL** NAC (ref: C-13950, C-18567)
Page 68 – **TX** NAC: C-107650 – **TY, MM** NAC/Jefferys (ref: C-10689, C-10688) – **BR, BL, BX** NAC (ref: C-10368, C-14855, C-14811)
Page 69 – **TL** Granger: 4E278.18 – **BR** NAC: C-10604
Page 70 – **TR, MR** HBCA/PAM (ref: P-379, 363-C-25-6)
Page 71 – **BM** HBCA/PAM: P-448 – **MY** MAHD-Q: 2 – **TM** NAC: C-747
Page 72 – **MR** HBCA/PAM: P-382 – **TL, BX** NAC (ref: C-13325, C-7962)
Page 73 – **TR** Granger: 4E278.16 – **ML, MR** NAC (ref: C-1225, C-09627)
Page 74 – **BR** HBCA/PAM: P-424 – **TM** NAC: C-7182
Page 75 – **TL** HBCA/PAM: 1987/363-M-15 – **BX** NAC: C-5066 – **BR** National Library: NL5336
Page 76 – **TR, MR** NAC (ref: C-6007, C7063)
Page 77 – **BX** NAC/Jefferys: C-10687 – **TR, TL, MR, BR** NAC (ref: C-40383, C-6022, C-1055 (S), C-10509)
Page 78 – **TM, BX, BR** NAC (ref: C-10686, C-1854, C-15791)
Page 79 – **TX** HBCA/PAM: P-401 – **BL, BR** NMC (ref: 26825 (R) H1/2000, 26825 (R) H1/2000)
Page 80 – **TR** Confederation Life: E8 – **BR** MAHD-Q: 5 – **BX** NAC: C-10614
Page 81 – **TX, TY, MX, MY** NAC (ref: C-92417, C-92421, C-92415, C-92419)
Page 82 – **MR** HBCA/PAM: P-417 – **TM** NAC: C-10891 – **BX** National Library: C-115952
Page 83 – **BR** Granger: DN922 – **TM** NAC: C-17059 – **BL** National Library: NL-6639
Page 84 – **TR, MR, BR** NAC (ref:: C6497, C99333, C4696)
Page 85 – **TR** Granger: 4E222.29 – **ML** NAC/Simpson: C13956 – **BR** NAC: C7219
Page 86 – **BM** Archives d'Outremer, Paris: FI539 – **TR** Man. Archives: N-3923
Page 87 – **TR, ML, BR** NAC (ref: C820, C6896, C106727)
Page 88 – **TR, MR** NAC (ref: C1090, C101)
Page 89 – **TR** Confederation Life: P2 – **BR, BL** NAC (ref: C11070, 21058)
Page 90 – **TM, MR, BM** NAC (ref: C14253, C122, C4293)
Page 91 – **TL, TR** HBCA/PAM (ref: P385, P415) – **BL, BR** NAC (ref: C11295, C2705)
Page 92 – **BX, BR** NAC (ref: C7220, C24550) – **TR** NB Archives: P4-3-29
Page 93 – **TR, MR** Granger (ref: 4E486.05, 4E486.09) – **BM** NAC: C15594
Page 94 – **TR, MX, BR** NAC (ref: C27665, C8874, C297)
Page 95 – **TM** Granger: 4E328.29 – **ML** NAC/Simpson: C13955 – **BM, MR** NAC (ref: C7111, C16464)
Page 96 – **TR, BY** NAC (ref: C4298, C7223)
Page 97 – **BM** Granger: 4E78.18 – **ML, TY, MR** NAC (ref: C12327, C18720, C121919)
Page 98 – **MR** Granger: DN919 – **TL, BL** NAC (ref: C4664, C41389)
Page 99 – **TR** Granger: 4E59.19 – **TL, BL, BR** NAC (ref: C2736, C1084, C1082)
Page 100 – **TL, TR, ML, BL, BR** NAC (ref: C4501, C77769, C21457, C106743, C106740)
Page 101 – **TR, ML, BM** NAC (ref: C3699, C3759, C357)
Page 102 – **TR, MY** NAC (ref: C118259, C7700)
Page 103 – **MR** MTL: T15521 – **TM, BL, BR** NAC (ref: C11043, C361, C350)
Page 104 – **ML, BR** NAC (ref: C604, NL5368)
Page 105 – **MR, BR** Granger (ref: 4E233.12, 4E822.25) – **TR** NAC: C7224
Page 106 & 107 – **SP** NAC: C42249
Page 108 – **TX** NAC: C2834 – **MX** NAC: C2833 – **BR** NAC: C117373
Page 109 – **BR** Chronicle – **TL, TR** Granger (ref: 4E811.20, 4E988.11)
Page 110 – **TR, BL** NAC (ref: C6861, C11915) – **TL** WCPI/Tim Ball: 19
Page 111 – **TY, TR, MR** NAC (ref: C95201, C95202, C70642) – **BL** National Library: 12391
Page 112 – **TR, BR** HBCA/PAM (ref: P-387 (1923), P416 (1952)) – **TX** NAC: C20053
Page 113 – **TR, ML** Granger (ref: 4E165.05, 4E881.08) – **BR** NAC: C38989
Page 114 – **MM** Granger: 4E838.05 – **BR** NAC: C1525
Page 115 – **TR, MR, ML** NAC (ref: C5415, C46334, C8724)
Page 116 – **BM** MTL: T14880 – **ML, TM** NAC (ref: C5838, C5224)
Page 117 – **ML, MR** NAC (ref: C13203, C9672) – **TY** NB Archives: P4-3-114
Page 118 – **TM** Granger: 4E1004.07 – **BR** NB Archives: P8-30
Page 119 – **TM, MR** NAC (ref: C40577, C8711)
Page 120 – **MR** Confederation Life: E10 – **TL, ML, BY** NAC (ref: C16946, C11201, C1598)
Page 121 – **TX, TY, TR, BL** NAC (ref: C34675, C13415, C33614, C5746)
Page 122 – **BL** Miller Comstock/M. Beedell – **BR** Miller Comstock/N. Lightfoot – **TL, TR** NAC (ref: C4766, C42306)
Page 123 – **TR, BR** NAC (ref: C34677, C47916)
Page 124 – **TL, TY, TR, BL, BX, BR** NAC (ref: C2719, C113668, C6215, C6217, C6216, C2717)
Page 125 – **TY, TR, BL, BR** McCord (ref: M973.93.1, M971.105.1, M966.8.2, M966.53.1) – **TL** NAC: C113742
Page 126 – **TR** CMC: S89-1741 – **MM** MTL: T32463
Page 127 – **MM** NAC: C82981 – **TM** National Library: NL15941
Page 128 – **BR** MTL: T15799 – **TL, BL** NAC (ref: C168, –)
Page 129 – **TM, BM** NAC/Jefferys (ref: C20587, C96362) – **ML** NAC/Simpson: C13954
Page 130 – **MR, BL** NAC (ref: C16830, C23633) – **TL** Richard Hill: 1
Page 131 – **BL** Granger: BC60 – **TL, TR, MR** Richard Hill (ref: 2, 4, 5)
Page 132 – **MX** HBCA/PAM: P-420 – **TR** Oren Lyons: 17 – **TL, BL, BR** NAC (ref: C2035, C130682, C1917)
Page 133 – **BR** NAC: C2001 – **BL** National Library: NL5477 – **TY** NB Archives: P4-3-116
Page 134 – **TM** NAC/Simpson: C13936 – **BY** NAC: C5968
Page 135 – **TR** Granger: GR1045 – **BX** NAC: C32211
Page 136 – **TM** MTL: T14834 – **BL, BR** NAC (ref: C40162, C2146)
Page 137 – **TL, TR, BM** NAC (ref: C70627, C70626, C15251)
Page 138 – **TL, TR, ML, MX, MY, MR, BL, BR** UBC (ref: A50045, A4323, A6273, EPT1, A3425, A2617, A17159, NB9.50)
Page 139 – **TL, TR, ML, BL, BR** UBC (ref: A7079, EPT10, A1774, A2469, A5255)
Page 140 – **TY, MR** NAC (ref: C70664, C5536)
Page 141 – **TM** Chronicle – **MM** Granger: D745 – **BL** NAC: C12263
Page 142 – **TM** HBCA/PAM: P-435 – **MR** McCord: M12067 – **BY** NAC: C8111
Page 143 – **TR** Confederation Life: E11 – **TL, BR** NAC (ref: C12267, C3374) – **BL** NAC/Simpson: C13941
Page 144 – **MR** MTL: T1370 – **TM** NAC/Jefferys: C73712 – **BL** NAC: C100660 – **BY** NAC/Simpson: C13946
Page 145 – **ML** Granger: 4E750.10 – **BR** McCord: M965.165.1 – **TR, BL** NAC (ref: C130548, C34334)
Page 146 – **TX, MM** MTL (ref: T15089, MTL1084) – **TR** NAC: C130852
Page 147 – **BL, BR** MTL (ref: T16547, T30535) – **TR** NAC: C13875
Page 148 – **BL** MTL: T32183 – **MR** NAC/Jefferys: C121336 – **TL** NB Archives: P37-477-1
Page 149 – **TL, TM, TR, BL, MX, MY, MR** CMC (ref: S89-1726, K72-685, S72-679, S89-1725, S72-2299, S72-2320, S89-1732) – **BM** WCPI: 324-10369 – **BR** WCPI/Tim Ball: 13-52
Page 150 – **MX** MTL: 1610 – **TR** NAC: C2774
Page 151 – **TR, MY, BL** NAC (ref: C403, C3305, NMC9846)
Page 152 – **TL** Humboldt and District Museum and Gallery – **BR** Maritime Museum: N16,632 – **BL** NB Archives: P4-3-93
Page 153 – **BR** MTL: 1686 – **TM** NAC/Jefferys: C6848 – **BL** NAC: C122927
Page 154 – **TR** Canadian Jewish Congress – **BM** NAC/Jefferys: C73702
Page 155 – **BL** NAC/Jefferys: C70270 – **BR** NAC: C1626 – **MX** National Library: NL2428
Page 156 – **BY** BSQ – **TM, BL** NAC (ref: C127746, C19123)
Page 157 – All pictures from the Bank of Montreal
Page 158 – **MM** NAC: C13965 – **TM** WCPI: 272-8720
Page 159 – **BM** MTL: 1242 – **TY** NAC: C95294 – **MR** WCPI: 78-2427
Page 160 – **BR** MTL: 1574 – **TR** NAC/Jefferys: C73719 – **BL** NAC: C87907
Page 161 – **BX** HBCA/PAM: P388 – **TX, MR** NAC (ref: C16404, C273) – **BR** WCPI: 27-813
Page 162 – **TM** Granger: 4E405.32 – **MR** MTL: 18003 – **BR** NAC: C7434
Page 163 – **TM, BR, BL** NAC (ref: C40598, C974, C46498)
Page 164 – **TL, TR, MM** NAC (ref: C124, C11053, C3329)
Page 165 – **TR, BM** NAC (ref: C7762, C32708)
Page 166 – **TL, TR, ML, BM** NAC (ref: C41031, C40894, C6500, C3297)
Page 167 – **ML** Granger: 4E222-22 – **TR, BR** NAC (ref: C5586, C6147)
Page 168 – **TM, BR** NAC (ref: C795, C5743)
Page 169 – **BR** Bettmann: E.2246 – **TL** Granger: 4E758.11 – **TR** NAC: C24368
Page 170 – **TR** Granger: 4E758.12 – **TL, MR, BR** NAC (ref: C93560, C6243, C6240)
Page 171 – **BM** Currency Museum: P02C18 – **TR** NAC: C115678
Page 172 – **MR, TY** NAC (ref: C18184, C104181) – **BX** WCPI: 27-822
Page 173 – **BL** Man. Archives – **TR** WCPI: 27-821
Page 174 – **BY** Bank of Montreal – **TM** Man. Archives – **BL** MTL: 16098
Page 175 – **MR** HBCA/PAM: P-447 – **TY** Man. Archives – **BL** MTL: 30726 – **BR** NAC: C133041
Page 176 – **BM** Bank of Montreal: P764 – **TM** NAC: C114503
Page 177 – **TM, MM, BM** NAC (ref: C28781, C119416, C28782)
Page 178 – **BM** CMC: S89-1819 – **TL, TM** NAC (ref: C5149, C40364)
Page 179 – **TL, BL, BR** CMC (ref: K72-716, K72-726, K72-677) – **TR** MAHD-Q: 12
Page 180 – **TR** NAC: C38951 – **MR** WCPI: 27-825
Page 181 – **BL** Glenbow: NA1344-2 – **TL, TR, ML, MX, MR, BR** NAC (ref: 10502, C10500, C1935, C11023, C100592, C1943)
Page 182 – **TR** HBCA/PAM: 363-P-80-F – **ML** Man. Archives: N3753 – **TL, BR** NAC (ref: C40327, C5843)
Page 183 – **TL, TR** HBCA/PAM (ref: 363-M-39, P-423) – **MR, BL** NAC (ref: C-1906, C40772) – **BR** WCPI: 31-936
Page 184 – **TM** MTL: 1087 – **BM** NAC: C31205
Page 185 – **TL, TR, ML, MR, BL, BR** NAC (ref: C114504, C25705, C25699, C5528, C25704, C25702)
Page 186 – **TL, ML** NAC (ref: C1726, C8155) – **BR** NB Archives: P4-3-25
Page 187 – **TR, MX, MR** AMHD-Q (ref: C5, C4, C3)
Page 188 – **TR, BM** NAC (ref: C36597, C1938)
Page 189 – **TX, TR** Man. Archives (ref: N10444, –) – **BM** NAC: C114384
Page 190 – **TM** Confederation Life: P6 – **MY** HBCA/PAM: P-412 – **BL** Lande – **TL** NAC: C17338
Page 191 – **BL** HBCA/PAM: P402 – **TM** NAC/Jefferys: C73703 – **BR** NAC: C3256
Page 192 – **BM** HBCA/PAM: P389 – **TR** NAC: C8640
Page 193 – **BR** McCord: M472 – **TR, MR** NAC (ref: C1619, C97668)
Page 194 – **TM** HBCA/PAM: P396 – **BM** MTL: T10935
Page 195 – **TX, TR, MR** NAC (ref: C38948, C1939, C8714)
Page 196 – **TM** Confederation Life: A4 – **MM, BR** NAC (ref: C5954, C119412)
Page 197 – **TL, TR, MR, BR** NAC (ref: C28542, C28544, C87698, C38856)
Page 198 – **TM** Memorial University, Nfld. – **MM** NAC: C127959
Page 199 – **BR** MTL: T16319 – **TL, TM** NAC (ref: C5414, C9563) – **TR** Richard Hill: 8
Page 200 – **TR** County of Kent Historic Site – **TL, BL** MTL (ref: 1551, 828)
Page 201 – **TL, TR, MR, BR** NAC (ref: C11811, C23349, C103532, C103533)
Page 202 – **TM, BR** NAC (ref: C18837, C115050)
Page 203 – **TR** MTL: 832C-1 – **TL, MR** NAC (ref: C120285, C127879)
Page 204 – **TM** Confederation Life: A5 – **BY** NAC: C7964
Page 205 – **TM** MTL: T33060 – **MR** NB Archives: P4-3-100 – **BL** Victoria University Library, Toronto
Page 206 – **TL, TR** MTL (ref: 1827, 1236) – **ML** NAC: C9351
Page 207 – **BR** CMC: S89-1815 – **TM** NAC: C252 – **BL** NB Archives: P4-3-13
Page 208 – **BX** HBCA/PAM: P-405 – **TR** MTL: T14459 – **TX** NAC: C19997
Page 209 – **TL** MTL: 1749 – **BR** NAC: C93020 – **TM, MM** NB Archives (ref: P4-3-20, P4-3-21)
Page 210 – **TY** Ont. Archives: S2901 – **BM** MTL: T16264
Page 211 – **BR** Man. Archives: 617.1 – **TL** MTL: 1119
Page 212 – **TL** Man. Archives – **TR, BM** NAC (ref: C1944, C1628)
Page 213 – **BL** HBCA/PAM: P-215 – **TL** Man. Archives: P400 – **TY** MTL: 836 – **BR** NAC: RD853
Page 214 – **BR** CMC: S89-1735 – **TM** NAC: C10693
Page 215 – **TL** CMC: S89-1742 – **TX** McCord: M17935 – **TR, MR** NAC (ref: C1941, C13821)
Page 216 – **TL, MR, BR** NAC (ref: C18294, C17937, C12062)
Page 217 – **TR, ML, MX, BR** NAC (ref: C393, C85175, C4500, C41372)
Page 218 – **BR** John Deere: 4 – **BL, TL** NAC (ref: C4782, C4783) – **MM** NAC/Jefferys: C13988
Page 219 – **BR** Currency Museum: P-02-84-1 – **TM, ML, MR** NAC (ref: C396, C4788, C11095)
Page 220 – **TX, TY, BM** NAC (ref: C133484, C108292, C131921)
Page 221 – **ML, TM, BM** NAC (ref: C5456, C4785, C1242)
Page 222 – **TR, BL, ML** NAC (ref: C508, C1032, C1029)
Page 223 – **TR** HBCA/PAM: P-390 – **BR** Lande – **MM** NAC: C2739
Page 224 – **MM** MTL: T15727 – **BM** NAC: C131925
Page 225 – **TX, ML, BL** NAC (ref: C28520, C404, C416) – **BR** NB Archives: P4-3-96
Page 226 – **MY** Glenbow: NA-642-1 – **BM** MTL: T17023
Page 227 – **MR** MTL: T10850 – **MX, BR** NAC (ref: C11317, C28758)
Page 228 – **MY, BM** NAC (ref: C667, C36647)
Page 229 – **BR** MTL: 1831 – **TX** NAC/Simpson: C13945 – **TR** NAC: C727 – **BL** Steves
Page 230 – **TM** Bettmann: F2892 – **TR** Hiram Walker Historical Museum – **BY** NAC: C5655
Page 231 – **TR** Chronicle – **BY** Granger: D5207 – **TM** NB Archives: P37-463-2
Page 232 – **TL** James Mackenzie Dunkin – **TY, BR, BL** NAC (ref: C16656, C104606, C127216)
Page 233 – **TR** Lande – **BL, BR** NAC (ref: C5962, C10696)
Page 234 – **TR, BM** MTL (ref: T30794, T31826)
Page 235 – **TY, TR, ML** NAC (ref: C5453, C6070, C106725)
Page 236 – **TM** Man. Archives: N224 – **BM** MTL: T32231 – **BR** NAC: C8249
Page 237 – **TM, MR** NAC (ref: C315, C402)
Page 238 – **BY** MTL: 1248 – **TY** NAC: C6721
Page 239 – **BL** HBCA/PAM: P-63 – **MR, TR** NAC (ref: C1629, C41430)
Page 240 – **BM** Man. Archives – **MR** MTL: T13773 – **TX** NAC: C18524
Page 241 – **TL, TR, MR, BR** NAC (ref: PA103280, C114374, C10692, C40149)
Page 242 – **MR** HBCA/PAM: P-413 – **MY** NAC: C11758
Page 243 – **TM, TR, MM** Granger (ref: BC39, BC40, BC38)
Page 244 – **BR** MTL: 1680 – **TR, BY** NAC (ref: PA147987, C11218)
Page 245 – **TR** City of Quebec Archives
Page 246 – **TM** ET Archive, London – **BX** Granger: BC35
Page 247 – **ML** MTL: 845L2 – **TX** NAC/Jefferys: C73725 – **BR** NB Archives: P37-162
Page 248 – **MM** Ont. Archives: 2469S7458 – **BR** WCPI: 13 Vol. 8
Page 249 – **ML, BM, MR** NAC (ref: C33233, C30259, C40334) – **TY** Punch in Canada/Walker: 1849
Page 250 – **TL, BY** NAC (ref: C2726, C22324) – **TY** NAC/Jefferys: C73717
Page 251 – **TL, TY, MY** HBCA/PAM (ref: N7932, N85-34, N85-33) – **BR** NAC: C22325
Page 252 – **TL, TM, BL, BR, MR** Bettmann (ref: C61.24, PL3459, F8780, PG13620, PG17387)
Page 253 – **TL, TR, BR** Bettmann (ref: F3396, C29.16, F916)
Page 254 – **TM, TR, MM** Bettmann (ref: PG.992, 676.39, F.7014)
Page 255 – **BL** HBCA/PAM: P-440 – **TR** MTL: 1356 – **BR** NAC: C3101
Page 256 – **MR, BR** McCord (ref: M972.4, M982.101.5) – **TL, TY, BX** NAC (ref: C74694, C74720, C11227)
Page 257 – **BL** Bettmann: 1642 – **ML, TR, MR** NAC (ref: C4530, C100194, C16105)
Page 258 – **MX** MTL: 851J2-5 – **BR** NAC/Simpson: C13948
Page 259 – **TL, TM, MM** Bettmann (ref: 411.29, PL.7725, F.4375)
Page 260 – **BR** BC Archives: A-1232 – **TL** Canada Post – **TR, ML** NAC (ref: C1670, 10503)
Page 261 – **MX** BSQ – **MR** HBCA/PAM: P-243 – **TR, BL** NAC (ref: C3368, C22326)
Page 262 – **MR** Man. Archives – **TM, BM** MTL (ref: 2250, T17185)
Page 263 – **BX** Granger: CT827 – **TL, TR, ML, MR, BL, BR** NAC (ref: C41048, C11003, C4666, C11224, C5994, C22095)
Page 264 – **MY, BR** NAC (ref: C7043, C22762)
Page 265 – **TY** Bettmann: U695999 – **TL** NAC: PA23411 – **BR** NB Archives: P5-224
Page 266 – **TL, BR** Bettmann (ref: PG15898, 597.34)
Page 267 – **BL, TM, BR** Bettmann (ref: F2264, P1.7910, F.8102)
Page 268 – **TR, BR** NAC (ref: C40778, C122483)
Page 269 – **BL** CMC: S89-1745 – **MR** Granger: 1008.66
Page 270 – **MR** HBCA: PAM: P114 – **TM** NAC: C15494
Page 271 – **BR** MTL: 853G1 – **TM, MM** NAC (ref: C5164, C46486)
Page 272 – **TY** HBCA/PAM: 1987-363-R-2 – **BM** WCPI: 75-22624
Page 273 – **TX, TR, BL** NAC (ref: C5081, C26011, C6717)
Page 274 – **TY** Ont. Archives: ACC2801S901 – **MM** NB Archives: P37-19
Page 275 – **TR** Digby: MP221.42 – **BL** HBCA/PAM: RBFC3961.3R5 – **ML, MX** NAC (ref: C2169, C2262)
Page 276 – **BM** British Library of London – **TM** NAC: PA138681
Page 277 – **TM** AMHD-Q: C1
Page 278 – **TX, TY, BM** NAC (ref: PA149098, C1153, NMC7037)
Page 279 – **TM** MTL: 856D2 – **BR** NAC: C5317
Page 280 – **BL** BC Archives: 2143 – **TL, MR** NAC (ref: C10383, C41706)
Page 281 – **BL** MTL: 857G1 – **TY** NAC/Simpson: C13947 – **MR** NAC: C6372 – **BM** Notman: N17502-1
Page 282 – **TY** Glenbow: NA-588-1 – **BM** Man. Archives: N8722
Page 283 – **BR** NAC: C2813 – **TX, TR** Vancouver Public Library (ref: 901, 13478)
Page 284 – **TR** BC Archives: 55 – **TX** HBCA/PAM: P-397
Page 285 – **TY** Bettmann: PG.9369 – **BR** Currency Museum/Zagon – **BL** Granger: 4E1.25
Page 286 – **BL** Canada Post – **TM** HBCA/PAM: P422 – **MR** NAC: PA26435
Page 287 – **TL** Glenbow: NA-1269-16 – **BR** MTL: 1139 – **TR** NAC: C4572
Page 288 – **TR, MR** NAC (ref: C23568, C36316)
Page 289 – **TM, BR** NAC (ref: C19405, C21289) – **BL** Ont. Archives: P2014
Page 290 – **TR** Man. Archives – **BM** MTL: T16587 – **TM** NAC/CIBC: C6007
Page 291 – **TY, TR** Man. Archives (ref: N3546, –) – **ML** NAC: C18743 – **MR** WCPI: 54-1635
Page 292 – **TM** Bettmann: F7718 – **BY** NAC: C12101
Page 293 – **MR** HBCA/PAM: P-205 – **TR** NAC: C5086 – **MX** Notman: N8561-1
Page 294 – **BR** BC Archives: 2614 – **TM** NAC: C22626
Page 295 – **ML** CMC: S89-1720 – **BX** MTL: 86M1 – **TR** NAC: C33682 – **BR** Notman
Page 296 – **BR** NAC: C40180 – **TR** WCPI: 01 vol. 8
Page 297 – **TM, BR** NAC (ref: C13289, C10699) – **BL** Notman: N7086
Page 298 – **MM** MTL: T16131 – **TY, BR** NAC (ref: C6874, C10518)
Page 299 – **BL** NB Archives: P5-909 – **MR** NAC: C21006
Page 300 – **TL, TR, MR, BL, BR** BCPM (ref: 36, 35, 21, 28, 24) – **ML** UBC: 452/62
Page 301 – **TL, TX, TR, BL, BM, BR** BCPM (ref: 22, 3, 23, 2, 4, 1) – **MR** CMC: S85-3272 – **ML** UBC: A2624
Page 302 – **BX, BR** HBCA/PAM (ref: P393, P436) – **TM** NAC: C40179
Page 303 – **TM, BM** Cater Andrews (ref: M11, M12) – **BR** Currency Museum/Zagon – **ML** NAC: C4806
Page 304 – **TL, TR** BC Archives (ref: 2612, A-347) – **ML, BL** MTL (ref: T30591, 1512) – **MR** NAC: C58669
Page 305 – **TX, TR** NAC (ref: C13964, C9583) – **BR** Notman
Page 306 – **TY** Bruce Mines Museum: 3 – **BX** NB Archives: P5-217
Page 307 – **MR** McCord: M972X94 – **ML** NAC: PA149709
Page 308 – **TR** Bank of Montreal – **TL, ML, MR, BL, BR** NAC (ref: C13965, C522, C13456, C1926, C506)
Page 309 – **BY** HBCA/PAM: 363-R-13 – **TL, TR, ML, MR, BL** NAC (ref: C11914, C815, C11223, C1901, C873) – **BR** NB Archives: P4-3-15
Page 310 – **TR** Meacham's Atlas – **MY** NAC: C9958
Page 311 – **BM** NAC: PA91061 – **TR** NB Archives: P5-146
Page 312 – **ML, BR** NAC (ref: C34614, PA138680) – **TR** PEI Archives: 2755/26
Page 313 – **TR** Confederation Life – **BY** NAC: C6184
Page 314 – **BM** MTL: 1110 – **TL** NAC: C5488 – **TR** NB Archives: P4-3-52
Page 315 – **ML, MR, BR** NAC (ref: C8359, C5464, C813)
Page 316 – **BR** BC Archives – **TX** NAC: C22002
Page 317 – **BR** Granger: 4GCR320 – **TR** NAC: C13290 – **BX** Smithsonian National Portrait Gallery
Page 318 – **TM** Granger: 4E29.19 – **BL** Notman
Page 319 – **ML, TM** NAC (ref: C5371, C22893) – **MR** NB Archives: P5-66
Page 320 – **TM, BY** NAC (ref: C117841, P0S-3) – **MR** Ont. Archives: S12786
Page 321 – **MR, BL** NAC (ref: C20270, C74700, PA149709)
Page 322 – **TR** NAC: C11731
Page 323 – **TR** NAC: C18737 – **BR** NB Archives: P37-463-3
Page 324 – **TM** Confederation Life: A8 – **BM** HBCA/PAM: P-111
Page 325 – **MX, MY, BX, BR** NAC (ref: B71906, C22320, C74719, C74713)
Page 326 – **MR** HBCA/PAM: P-441 – **BX** NAC: C9480
Page 327 – **TM** Chronicle – **BR** Confederation Life: C5 – **TR** NAC: MG40EI
Page 328 & 329 – All pictures from NB Archives
Page 330 – **BX, BR** NAC (ref: C61910, C6186) – **TX, TY, TR, MX, MY, MR, BL, BY** NB Archives
Page 331 – **TR** Bank of Montreal – **BR** MTL: T13502 – **BL** NAC: PA30217
Page 332 – **TL, TR, BL** NAC (ref: C40810, –, C10662)
Page 333 – **TL, TR, BL, BR** NAC (ref: C2641, –, C2634, C2643)
Page 334 – **TL, TR, BL** NAC (ref: C11239, –, C1881)

Page 335 – TL, TR, BR NAC (ref: –, C2482, C42271)
Page 336 – BL MTL: T16871 – **TM** NAC: C11508
Page 337 – TM HBCA/PAM: P-394 – **TL, BR** NAC (ref: C11588, C106731)
Page 338 & 339 – SP BNS/Fred Finley
Page 340 – MX Canada Post – **TR** NAC: C15021
Page 341 – MR Bill Fitsell – **TL, TX** NAC (ref: C6513, C8007)
Page 342 – TM NAC: C40358 – **MM** NB Archives: P5-259
Page 343 – TL, TM, BR NAC (ref: C17572, C9945, PA138698)
Page 344 – BR AMHD-Q: C7 – **TM** HBCA/PAM: P-442 – **BL** NAC: C26481
Page 345 – TM Man. Archives – **BR** NAC: C2771
Page 346 – TM Glenbow: NA1039-1 – **TR, ML** NAC (ref: PA27387, C48503) – **BM** Notman: N28901-1
Page 347 – TM Canapress – **BL** Eleanor Fellows: PDP12 – **MR** Glenbow: NA550-18
Page 348 – TR, MM NAC (ref: C14088, C33690) – **TM** PEI Archives: 2755/27
Page 349 – TR Confederation Centre: CAGH-1892 – **TM** Glenbow: NA2929-1
Page 350 – MY McGill – **TR** HBCA/PAM: P-449 – **MX** Royal Bank of Canada Archives: 79-9
Page 351 – BM NAC: C11021 – **TM** Notman: N45121-1
Page 352 – TL, TR, MR Man. Archives (ref: N5953, N5955, –)
Page 353 – MR Man. Archives: N10307 – **TM, BM** NAC (ref: C48854, C48849)
Page 354 – TL, TR, BL NAC (ref: C31264, –, C11246)
Page 355 – TM, MM, MR NAC (ref: C48837, C48861, C48516)
Page 356 – BR HBCA/PAM: 1987/363-M-39 – **BL** Man. Archives – **TL, TR** NAC (ref: C10334, C24289)
Page 357 – ML Cater Andrews: M14 – **BR** MTL: 1161 – **TM** NAC: C11749
Page 358 – MM, BM NAC (ref: 21269, C22233)
Page 359 – TR, BY NAC (ref: C54365, C40293)
Page 360 – TM, BM NAC (ref: PA74666, C7622)
Page 361 – TL BC Archives – **TR, BR** NAC (ref: –, C1572)
Page 362 – TM Man. Archives – **MM** NAC: C56481
Page 363 – ML Currency Museum – **MR** Man. Archives – **TM, BM** NAC (ref: C56617, C56567)
Page 364 – MX, BM NAC (ref: PA120487, C66559)
Page 365 – TM Man. Archives – **BM** NAC: C108134
Page 366 – TY Man. Archives – **MR, BM** NAC (ref: C5496, PA165779)
Page 367 – ML Man. Archives – **TR** Meacham's Atlas – **BR** NAC: C58952
Page 368 – TR Glenbow: NA-1444-1 – **BM** NAC: C59209 – **TY** RCMP: 397
Page 369 – TL, TY, BR NAC (ref: C14954, C59089, C41906)
Page 370 – TL, TR, BL NAC (ref: C5796, –, C277)
Page 371 – All pictures from Bengough Grip
Page 372 – ML MTL: 1687 – **TY, BL** NAC (ref: C19026, C174)
Page 373 – MM Glenbow: NA-1255-56 – **TR** RCMP: 4190 – **BM** WCPI: EWA41213357
Page 374 – TY, BM NAC (ref: C10460, C73304)
Page 375 – TY, ML RCMP
Page 376 – ML, TM, BM NAC (ref: C17335, C61544, C41047)
Page 377 – BX, TM NAC (ref: C36080, C121077) – **BR** RCMP
Page 378 – BR NAC: C61557 – **BL** Notman: N15870-2
Page 379 – TR City of Quebec Archives: 16779 – **BL, BR** NAC (ref: C38560, C61174)
Page 380 – BM NAC: C64614 – **TM** PEI Archives: 2301/342
Page 381 – MR, BM NAC (ref: PA25443, C62795) – **TL** Notman: N82635-1
Page 382 – TL, TR Glenbow (ref: NA-1434-2, NA-13-1)
Page 383 – BM NAC: C121146 – **TR** WCPI: 173-5404
Page 384 – MR, TR Bell: – **BX** Glenbow: NA-659-44
Page 385 – BR MTL: T31780 – **TM** NAC: C40821
Page 386 – TL Bettmann: E242 – **TR** Granger: 4E424.29 – **BR, BL** NAC (ref: C64551, C64722)
Page 387 – TR Man. Archives: N10141 – **BR** NAC: PA143281
Page 388 – TR NAC: PA12332 – **BX** RCMP
Page 389 – BX MTL: 877A2 – **TR, BR** NAC (ref: C40710, C35951) – **TL** NB Archives: P7-105
Page 390 – TR Glenbow: NA-40-1 – **TL, TX, BY** NAC (ref: PA124101, PA9256, PA9479)
Page 391 – TM CP Rail: 17756 – **BR** Man. Archives: 85-1908 – **MM** NAC: C17718
Page 392 – BM Granger: 4E645.03 – **TR** NAC: C6232
Page 393 – BR NAC: C11030 – **TM** WCPI: MAA34-983
Page 394 – MR Chronicle – **TR** GSC: 91888
Page 395 – TX, TR, BY NAC (ref: C95470, C68373, C8986) – **ML** WCPI: MAA31-924
Page 396 – TR Confederation Life: A10 – **TX, BM** NAC (ref: C1652, C71839)
Page 397 – BX, BR, TX NAC (ref: PA21055, C131016, C71978) – **TY** NB Archives: P5-556
Page 398 – TR RCMP: 1109-1 – **BL** WCPI: CGA202463158
Page 399 – BR HBCA/PAM: P-61 – **TL, TR, MR, BL** NAC (ref: C41220, C13632, C131920, C114460)
Page 400 – TR Granger: 4E69.18 – **BX** NAC: C75480
Page 401 – TX, TY Bell – **BR** NAC: PA13005
Page 402 – ML CP Rail: 870 – **TL, BR** Man. Archives (ref: N7934, –)
Page 403 – MR Glenbow: NA-2627-2 – **BR** NAC: C13901 – **TL** NB Archives: P5-373
Page 404 – TR CP Rail: 7193 – **BR** NAC: PA112248
Page 405 – TL, TR, MR NAC (ref: C72985, C3862, NMC7032)
Page 406 – TM NAC: C121918 – **BM** NGC – **Royal Cdn. Academy of Arts Diploma Work: 113**
Page 407 – TL HBCA: PAM: P-197 – **TR** Man. Archives – **MR** NAC: C85854
Page 408 – TM NAC: C13884 – **BM** WCPI: MAA-2-579
Page 409 – TR, TL Glenbow (ref: NA-33-26, NA-33-16) – **MR** NAC: PA119434
Page 410 – BL BNS: Fred Finley – **TM, MM** Salvation Army
Page 411 – TL Glenbow: NA-1270-1 – **MM** PEI Archives: 2702-6 – **TR** RCMP: 3232
Page 412 – MR Bettmann: PG.6301 – **TM** WCPI: MAA-5-1513
Page 413 – TM Granger: 4E267.32 – **MR, BM** NAC (ref: PA95417, C22917)
Page 414 – All pictures from PAA – **E. Brown**
Page 415 – ML, MR, BL, BR NAC (ref: PA138856, C11774, C11784, C11783)
Page 416 – TM, MM NAC (ref: PA38576, C46676) – **BR** WCPI: 262-08392
Page 417 – TL CP Rail: A18090 – **TR** Glenbow: NA-782-13 – **BY** National Library: NL16595
Page 418 – TM BC Archives: E-4017 – **BL, BY** Glenbow (ref: NA-1365-2, NA-1365-1)
Page 419 – BM NAC: C09991 – **TM** Notman: N73328-2
Page 420 – BY ET Archive, London/MILA/I.B – **TR** NAC: C41125
Page 421 – TR, ML Glenbow (ref: NA-3988-1, NA-1353-10)
Page 422 – TR Glenbow: NA1480-20 – **TM, BR** NAC (ref: C2424, C2425)
Page 423 – TL, MR Glenbow (ref: NA1480-39, NA-1104-1) – **BL** NAC: C2769
Page 424 – TY CP Rail: 13561-2 – **ML, BR** Glenbow (ref: NA1480-31, NA1081-3)
Page 425 – TL, TY Granger (ref: 760.28, CPR22) – **BL** York Sunbury Historical Society Museum
Page 426 – BM Chronicle – **TL, TR, MR** Glenbow (ref: NA4428-10, NA1353-28, NA720-2)
Page 427 – BY Bengough Grip – **TM** CP Rail: 1960 – **MM, BL** Glenbow (ref: NA3012-4, NA3012-6)
Page 428 – TX, TR BC Archives ref: B-3592, B-3593)
Page 429 – BR Chronicle – **TL** NAC: PA31485 – **MM** Vancouver Public Library: 1094
Page 430 – TR CP Rail: 19991 – **BL** Glenbow: NA-1353-26 – **TL** NAC: C14464
Page 431 – TR CP Rail: 19724 – **MX** Glenbow: NA-13-2 – **BL** NAC: PA24339 – **BR** Notman: N83122-B2
Page 432 – TM, MR NAC (ref: PA53554, C3844) – **BM** NGC: 28063
Page 433 – MR, BR BC Archives (ref: A-6448, A-4407) – **TR** PAA – **E. Brown: B145**
Page 434 – TM Glenbow: NA-4449-1 – **MR** NAC: C18884 – **BL** NB Archives: P5-216
Page 435 – TR Glenbow: NA-1033-3 – **BL** NAC: C14426 – **BR** Ont. Archives: ACC9379-L9667
Page 436 – BR Granger: 4E645.02 – **TX, TR** NAC (ref: PA25657, C70468)
Page 437 – BL CMC: S72-2151 – **BR** Confederation Centre: CAG H-13 – **MR** NAC: PA51546 – **TM** Notman: NMP015: 89(44)
Page 438 – TL Cater Andrews: M59 – **TR** Glenbow: NA-1406-188 – **BL** Granger: 634.29
Page 439 – BR, TR, BY Granger (ref: GR1083, 4E982.14, 995.48)
Page 440 – TM Glenbow: NA-207-63 – **BM** NAC: C129778
Page 441 – MM Glenbow: NA-3049-1 – **TM, BM** NAC (ref: C41289, C6332)
Page 442 – BR NAC: PA25698 – **TM** PAA – **E. Brown: B1700** – **BL** PEI Archives: 2702-10
Page 443 – TY NAC: C11587 – **BY** Notman
Page 444 – BR Granger: DN2306 – **TR** NAC: C1229
Page 445 – TL, TR, MR Glenbow (ref: NA118-19, NA-899-4, NA-1906-14)
Page 446 – MM MTL: T13401 – **TM, ML** NAC (ref: C3206, PA50260)
Page 447 – BX CMC: S89-1856 – **TM, BR** Glenbow (ref: NA1255-20, NA-1681-6)
Page 448 – BR HBCA/PAM: 1987/363-F-121
Page 449 – TL, TY, BM NAC (ref: C6536, C97288, PA17195)
Page 450 – TR Granger: 4E892.13 – **TY, ML** NAC (ref: PA27267, C52819) – **BR** PAA – **E. Brown: B697**
Page 451 – TR, BR NAC (ref: C30291, C40712)
Page 452 – TL, TR NB Archives (ref: P5-417, P5-416A) – **BM** Notman: MP891(6)
Page 453 – TR CP Rail: 692 – **BL** NAC: C41067
Page 454 – BM Glenbow: NA-354-29 – **TY** PAA – **E. Brown: B967**
Page 455 – TR Centre for Nfld. Studies – **BR** Man. Archives – **TL** NAC: C68645
Page 456 – TL HBCA/PAM: P221 – **BL, BR** NAC (ref: C1047, PA164313) – **TR, MR** Notman (ref: N11043-2, N10983-II)
Page 457 – TL, ML, BR, MR NAC (ref: C10516, PA164320, C120628, PA164317) – **BL** NB Archives: P6-628 – **TR** Notman: N110663-BII
Page 458 – TR, BM NAC (ref: PA49464, C6794)
Page 459 – TM, BR MTL (ref: T31223, 89B1) – **TR** NAC: C7364
Page 460 – BM CMC: S89-1886 – **TR** NAC: C29977 – **TM** Ont. Archives/Amhurstburg Historical Museum: ACC2537S12008
Page 461 – ML, BR NAC (ref: PA160539, C-13876)
Page 462 – BM MTL: 89C2 – **TR** NAC: C41400
Page 463 – BR CMC: S89-1839 – **TM** NAC: PA12984 – **BL** Notman: N110.815-B2
Page 464 – BM HBCA/PAM/1987: 13/211 – **TM** GSC: 7633
Page 465 – TR NAC: PA27222 – **BM** NGC: 18023 – **TX** Ont. Archives: S1823
Page 466 – TR Cater Andrews: M69 – **BR** NAC: C11027
Page 467 – BR MTL: 2052 – **TL** NAC: C13879
Page 468 – TX, TR, MR NAC (ref: PA27436, PA122876, PA27434)
Page 469 – TY Notman: N113.576-B2 – **BR** PEI Archives: 2755: 13
Page 470 – TR, BM NAC (ref: PA43986, C11040)
Page 471 – TR Glenbow: NA-1237-1 – **ML, BR** NAC (ref: C86343, PA122914)
Page 472 – TL Daily Mail & Empire/Kahrs – **TM** Ont. Archives/Amhurstburg Historical Museum: ACC2537S12015 – **BM** WCPI: Vol.2 17
Page 473 – TR, MM, MR Glenbow (ref: NA-3684-3, NA-266-1, NA-263-1)
Page 474 – TY, BM NAC (ref: PA28880, PA41951)
Page 475 – BL MTL: 89B1 – **BR** NAC: PA16125 – **TR** PAA – **E. Brown: B5241**
Page 476 – TL NAC: C16459 – **TR, MR** PAA – **E. Brown**
Page 477 – TM Confederation Life: A11 – **BR** NAC: C8133
Page 478 – TY NAC: PA28146 – **BM** Notman: N126,528-2
Page 479 – TR CP Rail: 6679 – **BL** NAC: PA16157
Page 480 – TX NAC: C1009 – **BM** NAC/Imperial Oil: PA96275 – **ML** Sask. Archives: R88-133
Page 481 – TM NAC/Larss & Duclos: C18642 – **BR** NAC/J.G. McJury: C26413 – **TR, BM, ML, TL** NAC (ref: PA13284, PA16080, PA13482, C14477) – **MR, BL** PAA – **E. Brown**
Page 482 – TM, BM NAC (ref: C5007, PA87767)
Page 483 – TL, TR NAC (ref: C5208, C8891, –, **BR** NGC: 300
Page 484 – TM, BX NAC (ref: C5392, C81772) – **BR** Notman: N3246
Page 485 – TL Man. Archives: N123 – **TR, BR** NAC (ref: C7983, C126498)
Page 486 & 487 – All pictures from Notman
Page 488 – TL CMC: S89-1716 – **TR, MY** McCord (ref: M1-4797, M20277) – **BL, TY, BX, MR, BY, BR** Notman (ref: N76.752, N76.472, N79.402, N112.395, N82723, N80.387)
Page 489 – BR Granger: 4GCR461 – **TY, TR, ML, BY, MR, BL** McCord (ref: M971.118.6, M18825, M969.1.11, M973.1.1, M974.138, M979.33.6) – **BX, TL, TX, MX, MY** Notman (ref: N5501, N79.495, N14.647, N77.142, N111.612)
Page 490 – All pictures from Notman
Page 491 – TL, BL, TR BC Archives (ref: C-5218, A-2123, D-3846) – **ML, MR, BR** MTL (ref: 1160, 1884, 1880)
Page 492 – TM, MR NAC (ref: PA122114, C51799)
Page 493 – MM, BM NAC (ref: C6097, C14923) – **TM** PAA – **E. Brown: B5394**
Page 494 – TR CMC: S89-1722 – **BM, TL** NAC (ref: C2990, C41068) – **TM** WCPI: 34-1005
Page 495 – ML NAC: C27495 – **TM** NB Archives: P5-398 – **BR** NGC: 3343
Page 496 – TM NAC: PA28925 – **MY** Notman: N80.379-B2
Page 497 – TL, TR NAC (ref: C2083, C30944) – **BX** Ont. Archives: RG10-30-S15525
Page 498 – TL, BL NAC (ref: C13880, C9576) – **TR** Ont. Archives: ACC9789S163407
Page 499 – TM, MR, BL NAC (ref: C5945, PA60611, PA11938)
Page 500 – MR Man. Archives: N10675 – **TY, TR, BY** NAC (ref: PA61747, C46447, PA128887) – **BR, TL** Notman (ref: N109,867-B2, N115,258)
Page 501 – All pictures from CWM/William Kent
Page 502 – TR Glenbow: NA-125-27 – **BM** NAC: PA113044
Page 503 – TR Cater Andrews: M50 – **BR** Glenbow: NA1035-6 – **BL** NAC: C40183 – **TL** PAA – **E. Brown: B724**
Page 504 – TR NAC: PA16388 – **ML** NAC/Hockey Hall of Fame: PA50681 – **BL** NB Archives: P98/56
Page 505 – TR, BR NAC (ref: PA37139, C15037) – **BL** Glenbow: NC-5-61
Page 506 – TM NAC: PA130361 – **MM** NB Archives: P11-60
Page 507 – TR, BR Glenbow (ref: NA-414-2, NA-654-4) – **ML** NAC: PA67295
Page 508 – TR, ML, BY NAC (ref: C6727, PA53567, PA113304) – **BR** PAA – **E. Brown: B796**
Page 509 – BM NAC/Glenbow-Alberta Institute: C37953 – **MM** WCPI: 14
Page 510 – BM CP Rail: A4216 – **TY, TR** Glenbow (ref: NA-2740-1, NA-1528-1)
Page 511 – TR Bank of Montreal: 36 – **BM** MTL: 1411
Page 512 – TL, TR NAC (ref: C30723, PA43492) – **BX** NB Archives: P5-240
Page 513 – BR NAC: PA38445 – **ML** PAA – **E. Brown: B1180** – **TM** Philip Owen
Page 514 – BM MTL: 89B1 – **MR** NAC: PA27942
Page 515 – ML, BL NB Archives (ref: P6-184, P5-573) – **BR** Royal B.C. Museum: PN258
Page 516 – TX, TR, ML, MY NAC (ref: C20843, C20844, C30251, PA95515) – **TL, MR, BL, BR** PAA – **E. Brown**
Page 517 – TL Glenbow: NA-4433-31 – **MR** NAC: C30235 – **TR, ML, BL** PAA – **E. Brown** – **BR** Glenbow: NA-4433-29
Page 518 – BL MTL: 2284 – **TR** NAC
Page 519 – BL MTL: 2209 – **TR** NAC
Page 520 – MR Bettmann: PG7205 – **BL** NB Archives: P37-402
Page 521 – TL NAC/National Geographic: C17377 – **TY** NAC: C28214 – **BX** Lande – **BR** WCPI: 87-2691
Page 522 – TX, BM NAC (ref: C14094, C8208)
Page 523 – BM NGC: 1044 – **TR** WCPI: 87-2717
Page 524 – TM Glenbow: NA-654-5 – **BL** MTL: T10806 – **TR** Vancouver Public Library: 1786
Page 525 – BR CMC: S89-1855 – **BL** Ont. Archives: S18128 – **TM** PAA – **photo coll.: A10,499**
Page 526 – TR PAA – **photo coll.: H296**
Page 527 – TR, TX, BR NAC (ref: PA143204, C14485, C46484) – **ML** NAC/Sports Hall of Fame: PA49901
Page 528 – TX, MR, BL NAC (ref: PA20614, C29659, C35357)
Page 529 – TX, BL NAC (ref: C14118, PA28626) – **MR** Vancouver Public Library: 1773
Page 530 – BM Currency Museum – **TM** NAC: PA9639
Page 531 – MR, TL, ML NAC (ref: PA89112, PA100000, PA37797)
Page 532 – TL, TY, BY NAC (ref: C80202, C22108, PA66547)
Page 533 – TM McLennan Library, McGill – **TR, BL, BX** NAC (ref: C66950, C34337, C23933)
Page 534 – TR Bell: 14115-A – **BM** NGC: 127
Page 535 – MX Betty Tomlinson Anderson – **TR** NAC: C684 – **TL, MY** PAA – **E. Brown** – **BR** PAA: B723 – **MR** WCPI: 154451132
Page 536 – TM Man. Archives: N7935 – **BL** NAC/Sports Hall of Fame: PA50395 – **BR** Nfld. Archives: 2
Page 537 – TR BC Archives: B-9834 – **TL** Bettmann: PG9448 – **BL** NAC: PA42405
Page 538 – TM, MY Man. Archives – **BR** NAC: C56774
Page 539 – TL, TR NAC (ref: C16393, C4555) – **BR** NB Archives: P18-343
Page 540 – BR NAC: C17906 – **TR** NB Archives: P6-588 – **BL** Evelyn Grisdale, Weekes, Sask.
Page 541 – BX Glenbow: NA-273-3 – **TL, TR** NAC (ref: C9660, C30620) – **MR** Ont. Archives/Glengarry Pioneer Museum: ACC16953-S18664 – **ML** WCPI: 163-5130
Page 542 – BR BC Archives: C6062 – **TR** Man. Archives: N8997
Page 543 – TR NAC: C30953 – **MR** NAC: PA118224 – **BL, TL** Notman (ref: N180,315, N5686)
Page 544 – TM, ML Glenbow (ref: NA-4623-1, NA-1267-1) – **BR** RCMP: 544
Page 545 – MM, BR NAC (ref: PA29806, PA66852)
Page 546 – BR Biggar and District Museum – **TR, MX** NAC (ref: PA38449, C28550)
Page 547 – BR CMC: S89-1869 – **TR** Mary Evans Picture Library: 6208/01
Page 548 – BL BCPM: 32 – **TM** Chronicle – **MR** WCPI: 45814718
Page 549 – TL, TR, ML, MR, BL, BR Glenbow (ref: NA-274-3, NA-604-1A, NA-335-15, NA-2365-1, NA-370-14, NA-3620-14)
Page 550 – TR NAC: PA9808 – **ML** NB Archives: P18-164 – **TL** Ont. Archives: ACC2538-S1893 – **BR** PAA – **E. Brown: B1146** – **BL** WCPI: 163-5133
Page 551 – TX, TR, BM, BR NAC (ref: C30945, C30950, C21076, C30954)
Page 552 – BR BC Archives: D-7752 – **TX** NAC: C14141
Page 553 – BR MTL: 913B2 – **TL** NAC: PA142045
Page 554 – MY Glenbow: NA-617-1 – **TM** NAC: PA23033
Page 555 – TM, MM, BL NAC (ref: C70806, PA74041, C45389)
Page 556 – TR Miller Comstock/J.D. Markou – **BR** NAC: PA135687
Page 557 – TX, TR, MR Glenbow (ref: NA246-1, NA2736-2, NA3055-39) – **BL** NAC: C119446
Page 558 – BR Ian Bowering – **TL, ML** NAC (ref: C46574, C38613)
Page 559 – MM, BM Glenbow (ref: NA-3965-66, NA-3965-69)
Page 560 & 562 – SP CWM/William Kent: 8911
Page 562 – TL, TR, MR, BR NAC (ref: C29484, C95282, PA24970, PA5997)
Page 563 – TR, BL, BY, BR NAC (ref: PA4737, C86408, C95378, C95391)
Page 564 – MX Glenbow: NA-5032-2 – **TR** NAC: C14145
Page 565 – TR, BY, BR NAC (ref: C27331, C9038, C46284)
Page 566 – ML, BR NAC (ref: C3687, PA57607) – **BX** NB Archives: P61-405
Page 567 – BX Canada Post – **TX, TR** Man. Archives (ref: N9907, N9905)
Page 568 – TR Glenbow: NA-4174-14 – **MX** Man. Archives
Page 569 – BL Glenbow: NA-5126-1 – **TR, BM** NAC (ref: PA72524, PA41366)
Page 570 – TL, MR NAC (ref: PA1356, C80027) – **TR** PAA – **E. Brown: B5397**
Page 571 – TM, MM, BL NAC (ref: PA94, PA186, C5792)
Page 572 – TX, TR, MR, ML, BL NAC (ref: PA627, PA962, PA809, PA832, C33428)
Page 573 – TX, ML, BL, TR NAC (ref: PA647, PA868, PA988, PA590)
Page 574 – MX, TR, MR NAC (ref: C2082, PA1036, C148)
Page 575 – ML, TR NAC (ref: C6859, PA880) – **BX** WCPI
Page 576 – BR Glenbow: NA-2365-97 – **MX, TR** NAC (ref: PA121719, PA1654)
Page 577 – BR McGill – **TL, TR, ML** NAC (ref: PA1826, PA1581, PA3717)
Page 578 – BL MTL: 914F1/1 – **TR, MR** NAC (ref: PA2105, PA5544)
Page 579 – BR Chronicle – **TX, TR** NAC (ref: PA22744, C19951)
Page 580 – All pictures from CWM/William Kent (ref: 8284, 8170, 8141, 8934, 8409)
Page 581 – TL, ML, BL, BR CWM/William Kent (ref: 8021, 8095, 8592, 8882) – **MR** NAC/Mary Riter-Hamilton: C104640
Page 582 – BM Glenbow: NA-3232-25
Page 583 – MY Glenbow: NA-1258-19 – **TM, MX, BL** NAC (ref: PA128886, C100040, C26531)
Page 584 – BL Glenbow: NA-2204-5 – **MY** NAC: C88237
Page 585 – BL, TL, BR NAC (ref: C50289, PA2951, PA3490)
Page 586 – BL Chronicle – **TM** NAC: C19108
Page 587 – TR, TL, ML, MM, BR NAC (ref: C33185, PA3642, PA3442, PA3572, C87137)
Page 588 – TL, TR NAC (ref: PA25025, PA22768)
Page 589 – TL, TR, ML, MY, MR, BL, BR NAC (ref: PA2800, PA3539, 172550, PA4422, PA3211, PA2562, PA2404)
Page 590 – MM Miller Comstock/K. Sommerer – **TM** Ont. Archives: ACC9141S13340
Page 591 – MR Fondation Lionel Groulx – **BL** NGC: 1367
Page 592 – All pictures from WCPI (ref: 10, 11, 20)
Page 593 – TL, TR, BM NAC (ref: C26782, C34022, PA121929) – **MR** WCPI: 18-536
Page 594 – TL, TR, BX NAC (ref: C46315, C242, C57580)
Page 595 – BL, BR NAC (ref: PA110157, PA22376) – **TX** WCPI: 52
Page 596 – TR, BX NAC/Hockey Hall of Fame (ref: PA50719, PA50718) – **BR** WCPI: 1301-38957
Page 597 – TR, BR NAC (ref: C691, C79116) – **ML** NGC: 1519
Page 598 – MR NAC: C34840 – **TM** Ont. Archives: ACC9379S15000 – **BL** RCMP
Page 599 – TL, TR, BL, BX CP Rail (ref: 18392, A6199, 4316, 2053) – **BR** WCPI: 163-5122
Page 600 – TX, BM NAC (ref: PA66673, PA126710)
Page 601 – TL, TM Glenbow (ref: NA-789-91, NA-2204-4) – **BR, BX** NAC (ref: PA41990, C13255)
Page 602 – BL Bank of Montreal: P1388B – **TR** NAC/Kelsey Studio, Durham: C6908 – **BR** Ont. Hydro Archives: HP1043
Page 603 – ML, MY, MR, BR NAC (ref: PA10226, C9800, PA10254, PA38515) – **BL, TL** WCPI (ref: 163-5120, 30)
Page 604 – BM Cater Andrews: M57 – **TR** NAC: C1350
Page 605 – TR Glenbow: NA-3684-8 – **ML** PAA – **photo coll.: A3926** – **BY** Richard Hill: 7
Page 606 – MR BC Archives: D-6342 – **TL** NAC/Lyonde Photographers: PA53712 – **BL** PAA – **photo coll.: A5253**
Page 607 – TR Julius Cook/Richard Hill: 11 – **BM** NB Archives: P37-476-3
Page 608 – TY, BR NAC (ref: C57365, C71600)
Page 609 – MR Glenbow: NA1136-2 – **TL** NAC: C68871 – **BL, BR** NAC/Toronto Transit Commission (ref: PA55051, PA54989)
Page 610 – TR City Archives, Vancouver – **MX** NAC: C11576
Page 611 – BR Glenbow: NA-2365-33 – **TY** NAC: C3188 – **ML** PAA – **photo coll.: A11.413**
Page 612 – MM Man. Archives: N5848 – **TR** NAC
Page 613 – TR, BR NAC (ref: PA61541, PA61926) – **BL** NGC: 4301
Page 614 – MR Glenbow: NA-4447-5 – **TL, ML** NAC (ref: PA86585, PA53239)
Page 615 – TR, BL NAC (ref: C33571, PA137183) – **BR** PAA – **photo coll.: A11.415**
Page 616 – TR, BM NAC (ref: C86437, PA125248)
Page 617 – BL Chrysler Canada: 58-3109 – **TR** Glenbow: NA-1379-1 – **MX** NAC: C26070
Page 618 – BL McGill – **MR** NAC: PA43577
Page 619 – TL, TR Canadian Jewish Congress (ref: PC12/0C/1.40, PC1/L31/13) – **BR** Jewish Historical Society of Western Canada: JM2908 – **MR, BL** NAC (ref: C27596, C42732)
Page 620 – BY McGill – **TR** NAC: PA24284
Page 621 – ML NAC: PA148544 – **TR** NB Archives: P106-50 – **BM** NGC Collection: 3708
Page 622 – BY Bettmann: UP72779INP – **TR** NAC/Aitken Ltd., London: C1690 – **TL, BL** NAC (ref: C24695, C88073)
Page 623 – TL McGill – **TX, BL, TR** NAC
Page 624 – TY Chronicle – **BR** NAC/Sports Hall of Fame: PA50309
Page 625 – TY BC Archives: D-8247 – **BR** NAC: C5482
Page 626 – MX, BL NAC (ref: PA87900, PA126930) – **MR** WCPI: 13-339-12
Page 627 – BR Canada Post – **TL** NAC/Canadian Gov't Motion Picture Bureau: PA149202 – **MY, ML** NAC (ref: C30180, PA87702)
Page 628 – BR NAC/Paul Alfred: C10536 – **BX** NAC/Sports Hall of Fame: PA50382
Page 629 – MM NAC: PA62900 – **BR** McGill – **TL** Notman: N23,289
Page 630 – TR NAC/Sports Hall of Fame: PA50338 – **TX, BL** NAC (ref: PA150983, PA151007) – **BR** PAA – **photo coll.: A11-419**
Page 631 – BR CMC: S89-1727 – **ML** NAC/Finn: C53679 – **TR** RCMP: 3695
Page 632 – BR Vancouver Public Library: 22642
Page 633 – MR Glenbow: NA-1258-37 – **TM** NAC/J.D. Soper: PA101335 – **BM** NAC/L.T. Burwash: PA99678
Page 634 – BR BC Archives: D-7770 – **TR, BL** NAC (ref: PA15576, PA61938) – **ML, MR** Notman (ref: N24-506, N26.031) – **TL** PAA – **photo coll.: BA-32**
Page 635 – TR Centre for Nfld. Studies: 3 – **MR** NAC: PA55480 – **ML** Nfld. Archives
Page 636 – BR McMichael/A.J. Casson: 1966.16.128 – **TR** NGC: 1785 – **BL** NGC/F.H. Varley Estate: 1814
Page 637 – TL McMichael/Mary Mastin: 1966.16.3 – **TR** McMichael/Lawren P. Harris/Margaret Knox: 1966.16.88 – **ML** McMichael: 1968.8.26 – **MR** McMichael/Marjorie Lismer Bridges: 1966.16.112 – **BR** NGC: 1694
Page 638 – TR, MR NAC (ref: C20594, C30804) – **BR** Sask. Archives: R-A3341(1)
Page 639 – MR, BR NAC (ref: C29396, C13236) – **TL** Sask. Archives: RA3341(2)
Page 640 – TL, MX, MR, BL NAC (ref: PA126100, PA138909, 14186)
Page 641 – MR NAC: C7731 – **MM** WCPI: 203963555
Page 642 – MR NAC: C37139 – **MM** NAC/Communist Party of Canada: PA124357 – **TL** MTL: 929BI
Page 643 – BL McMichael: 1977.42 – **BY** NGC/Vincent Massey bequest: 15478 – **TR** PAA – **E. Brown: B644**

Page 644 – **TM, TR** NAC (ref: PA92386, PA117916)
Page 645 – **TM** BC Archives: D-8407 – **BL** MTL: 93D1 – **BR** NAC/W. Oliver: PA150000
Page 646 – **BL, TR** NAC (ref: PA139645, PA117649) – **MR, ML** Sask. Archives (ref: R-B9057, R-A-4822)
Page 647 – **BY** Glenbow: NA-1258-93 – **TX, TR** HBCA/PAM (ref: 363-F-75(N7339), 363-F-75(N7340))
Page 648 – **TY** Glenbow: NA-1258-119 – **MR** NAC/Kilree: C77581
Page 649 – **TR** NAC: C5114 – **ML** NAC/Richard J.C. Fabry: PA148966 – **BR** Nfld. Archives
Page 650 – **BL** Centre for Nfld. Studies: COLL-137 – **MR** Glenbow: NA-1486-1 – **TL, MX** NAC (ref: PA123609, PA150986)
Page 651 – **BL** NAC: PA55623 – **TM, TR** Sask. Archives (ref: R-A5215 (1), R-A4823)
Page 652 – All pictures from Prof. Louis Lenz, University of Manitoba (ref: 2303-79-1, 2303-79-2)
Page 653 – **TL, ML** Canadian Jewish Congress (ref: ZA1933, PC12/OC/121) – **MR** NAC/DND: PA35133
Page 654 – **TM, MR, BL** NAC (ref: PA55582, PA130443, C66621)
Page 655 – **TM** NAC/Communist Party of Canada: PA125089 – **BR** WCPI: 44314276
Page 656 – **BM** NAC/Hockey Hall of Fame: C38108 – **TR** Sask. Archives: R-A-4287
Page 657 – **TR, MM** NAC (ref: PA9642, PA139647)
Page 658 – **BL** Bettmann: UP1771484 – **BR** Moving Image and Sound Archives: 4855 – **TR** NAC: PA37030
Page 659 – **TM** Canapress – **BY** NAC: PA164759
Page 660 – **MR, BX** NAC (ref: C11569, C52024)
Page 661 – **MM** NAC: C29399 – **BL** NAC/Sask. Archives: C24840
Page 662 – **TR** NAC/Sask. Archives: C24834 – **ML** RCMP: 222 – **MR** WCPI: 128-38331
Page 663 – **TR** NAC: C13256 – **BR** Notman: N26,033 – **ML** Winnipeg Free Press/Dale
Page 664 – **TX** NAC/DND: PA34866 – **BR** WCPI: 2075-64498
Page 665 – **MR** Canapress – **TM, MM** NAC (ref: C70770, PA148874)
Page 666 – **MX, ML** Bettmann (ref: U1937, 152787) – **MR** NAC/Canadian Geographical Journal: C5144
Page 667 – **BR** CMC: S89-1843 – **TL, TR** NAC (ref: PA117423, C67451)
Page 668 – **BR** NAC/Hockey Hall of Fame: PA50720 – **TM** Sask. Archives: R-B3484
Page 669 – **BR** Donald Smith – **TM** NAC: PA57668
Page 670 – **BL** Air Canada/Programmed Communications: B2262 – **TX** NAC: C67469 – **BR** PAA – **E. Brown: B10473**
Page 671 – **TM** Glenbow: NA-1158-5 – **MR** Topham: M00827984
Page 672 – **TM** BC Archives: C-7928 – **MR** Ont. Archives: ACC9509S14971
Page 673 – **BY** Air Canada Historical Services: B3558 – **ML** Bettmann: UO24172 – **TX** Glenbow: NA-3164-349
Page 674 – **TY** Glenbow: NA-3043-1 – **TL, TR** NAC (ref: C62097, PA164746) – **BM** Nova Scotia Tourism and Culture: D90
Page 675 – **TY** NAC: NFB: PA114604 – **TR, BM** NAC (ref: C85967, C33945)
Page 676 – **TX, TR** NAC (ref: C74970, C67449)
Page 677 – All pictures from Sask. Archives (ref: R-B9049, R-B9066, R-B9050)
Page 678 – **MR, BR** Canadian Jewish Congress (ref: PC12/OC/3, PC12/OC/7.88) – **TR** Glenbow: NA-3368-19 – **BL** NAC: C42733
Page 679 – **TR** Bettmann: U878918 – **ML, BL** Popperfoto (ref: PP80990, PP80734) – **BR** Topham: 250490
Page 680 – **TL** Man. Archives: 26/1 – **TR, MR, BX, BR** NAC (ref: C35115, C23312, C7477, C85094)
Page 681 – **MY** Chronicle – **BR** Moving Image and Sound Archives: 15658
Page 682 – **BL** NAC: PA107975 – **MM** Popperfoto: PN88661
Page 683 – **TX** McGill – **BL** NAC: C87481 – **MR** Popperfoto: 73019
Page 684 – **MR** Moving Image and Sound Archives: 397 – **MX, BX** NAC (ref: C24719, C19531)
Page 685 – **TR** NAC/Montreal Gazette: PA108055 – **BR** NAC: C33446 – **BL** NAC/NFB: PA166252
Page 686 – **MR** NAC/Montreal Gazette: PA107909 – **BL, BX** NAC
Page 687 – **BL** NAC/Estate of Claude P. Dettloff: C38723 – **TR, MR** NAC (ref: PA142400, PA167952)
Page 688 – **TR, BY** NAC (ref: C9707, C97252)
Page 689 – **ML** NAC/Nicholas Morant: PA13784 – **BR** NAC: C53880 – **TX** McGill
Page 690 – **MR** NAC/Alexandra Studio: PA115551 – **ML, BL** McGill
Page 691 – **MR, BR** NAC (ref: PA112539, C5788) – **TL** NAC/DND: PA114891 – **BL** NAC/Karsh: C12600
Page 692 – **TR** NAC/Tak Toyota: C47387 – **MY** Topham: M00827985
Page 693 – **TR** NAC/Tak Toyota: C46350 – **MR, TL, BX** NAC (ref: PA103542, C46355, C67496) – **BL, BR** UBC Special Coll.
Page 694 – **BX, BY** McGill – **TX** NAC: C37127
Page 695 – **ML** McGill – **TR, MR** NAC (ref: C29588, PA113245)
Page 696 – **BX** McGill – **TM, MR** NAC (ref: C51810, C25)
Page 697 – **MR** McGill – **TM** NAC/Frank Tyrell: PA130488 – **BR, BL** NAC (ref: C29457, C90883) – **MY** Peace: 73.558.G
Page 698 – **TM** NAC: C4908 – **MR** Peace: 77.802.2
Page 699 – **TR** Jonathan Gladstone/j.b. geographics – **BL** NAC: PA137223
Page 700 – **TL, TR** NAC/DND/Smith (ref: PA170290, PA163671) – **BM** NAC: C14168
Page 701 – **TR** NAC/DND/Rowe: PA114485 – **MY** NAC/DND/Smith: PA136806 – **MR, BL** NAC/DND/Stirton (ref: PA144103, PA136198) – **BY** NAC/DND/Rowe: PA141867
Page 702 – All pictures from McGill
Page 703 – **TX, TR** NAC/DND/Rowe (ref: PA166565, PA152748) – **BL** NAC (ref: PA167610 – **BY** NAC/NFB/Long: PA112885
Page 704 – **MM, BR** NAC/DND (ref: PA37482, PA130610)
Page 705 – **MR** CWM/William Kent – **BL** McGill – **TX** NAC/DND: PA116458
Page 706 – **BL** Jonathan Gladstone/j.b. geographics – **TL** NAC: PA122765 – **MR** NAC/DND/Cooper: PA131386 – **BR** NAC/DND/Dubervill: PA133754
Page 707 – **TR** NAC/DND/Dean: PA162328 – **MR** NAC/DND/Aikman: PA115028 – **BL** NAC/NFB: PA153051
Page 708 – **TL, MR** NAC/DND/Dean (ref: PA129135, PA131233) – **BL** NAC/DND/Richer: PA136664
Page 709 – **MR** Halifax Herald/Chambers 1944 – **MX** NAC: C21525
Page 710 – **TR** Confederation Life: A14 – **ML** NAC/DND/Grant: PA136754 – **BY** NAC/DND/Dean: PA132415 – **BR** NAC/DND/Aikman: PA131256
Page 711 – **MY** Chronicle – **BR** NAC/DND/Nye: PA128286 – **ML** NAC/DND/Bell: PA131443 – **BX** St Joseph Island Museum/Elsie Mole
Pages 712 & 713 – All pictures from CWM/William Kent (ref: 11281, 11435, 11565, 10029, 12296, 11469, 10558)
Page 714 – **TR** NAC/DND/Bell: PA153099 – **MX** NAC/Hockey Hall of Fame: PA50671
Page 715 – **MM** NAC/DND/Grant: PA131818 – **BL** NAC/DND/Arless: PA157029
Page 716 – **TL** NAC/DND/Stirton: PA134376 – **TR** NAC/DND/Dean: PA134388 – **MR** NAC/DND/Grant: PA131566
Page 717 – **ML** NAC: PA79586 – **TR** NAC/DND/Cole: PA141657 – **MR** NAC/NFB: C22716
Page 718 – **TR** Popperfoto: 73056
Page 719 – **TR, MR** NAC/DND/Hawes (ref: PA145983, PA151738) – **ML** Popperfoto: 73056
Page 720 & 721 – **SP** Miller Comstock/Malak
Page 722 – **MR** NAC/Acme News Pictures, N.Y.: C23284 – **BL** NAC/Jacques: PA115236 – **BY** NAC/DND/Allan: PA128258
Page 723 – **ML** Keiko Orida Yamashita – **BR** UBC Special Coll. – **TR** Vancouver Public Library: 1380
Page 724 – **TX** NAC: PA129633 – **TR** NAC/Montreal Star: PA129637 – **MM** NAC/DND/Richer: PA128179
Page 725 – **TR** Miller Comstock/Malak: 10012232 – **TL** NAC/Weekend Magazine/Graetz: PA115249 – **ML** NAC: PA120506
Page 726 – **TR** Bettmann: 790257 – **BL** NAC/M. Parent: PA107342 – **BR** NAC/Paris-Matin: C31312
Page 727 – **BR** Courtesy Acadian and Mackenzie Bus Lines – **TY** Montreal Gazette/Collins 1946 – **ML** NAC/NFB: Jacques: C49434
Page 728 – **TR** Glenbow: NA-789-80 – **BX** NAC: PA93674
Page 729 – **ML** Glenbow: NA-1241-59 – **TR** NAC/NFB/Royal: PA112691 – **BM** NGC/Borduas: 6098
Page 730 – **TL** NAC/NFB/Lund: PA111377 – **ML** NAC: PA93948 – **TR** NAC/Weekend Magazine/Jacques: PA130735 – **MR** NAC/Canadian Tribune Publ.: PA93924
Page 731 – **TM** NAC/Hunter: PA123476 – **BR** NAC: C18347 – **BL** NAC/NFB/Hunter: PA128074 – **MY** NAC/Actualit, Brussels: C31324
Page 732 – **TR** NAC/National Photographs Reg'd.: C14176 – **BY** NAC: PA122724
Page 733 – **TR** NAC: PA93664 – **MR** NAC/NFB/Lund: C49422 – **BL** NAC
Page 734 – **TR** NAC: C23259 – **ML** NAC/Montreal Gazette: PA116478 – **BR** NAC: PA129325
Page 735 – **TR** NAC/NFB: PA128080 – **BR** NAC/Canadian Tribune Publ.: PA93682 – **BM** RCMP: 2547
Page 736 – **TR** NAC/Montreal Gazette: PA129602 – **BX** NAC/Canadian Tribune Publ.: PA93672
Page 737 – **TL** Miller Comstock/R. Hall: 10051457 – **BL** Miller Comstock/G. Hunter: CNF-018-DCQ – **TR** NAC
Page 738 – **TL** NAC/Montreal Star: PA116380 – **BL** NAC/NFB: C6255 – **MY** NAC: PA123991 – **TR** NAC/Harris Ewing: PA124427
Page 739 – **ML** NAC/Canada Pictures Ltd.: PA55029 – **BL, BR** NAC/Weekend Magazine/Milne (ref: PA128761, PA128760)
Page 740 – **MR** NAC/Jules. A. Castonguay: PA165136 – **MM** NAC/DND: PA112261
Page 741 – **TL** NAC/Walter Curtin: PA144330 – **TR, MR** WCPI (ref: 100130007, 100130018)
Page 742 – **MX** NAC/NFB/Lunney: PA108057 – **BL** NAC/H. Wright Corp.: PA142372 – **BR** NAC/Norfolk: PA121970
Page 743 – **BX, BR** CMC (ref: S89-1870, S89-1844) – **TL** NAC/DND/Gordon: PA151991 – **TR** NAC/DND/Plastow: PA128822
Page 744 – **TM** NAC/Montreal Gazette: C53625 – **MR, BY** NAC/NFB/Lund (ref: PA111355, PA111381)
Page 745 – **TL** NAC/Bell: PA153945 – **MY** NAC/Weekend Magazine: PA115281 – **MR, BX** NAC (ref: C87257, PA140565)
Page 746 – **TL** NAC/G. Hunter: PA111773 – **MR** NAC/NFB/Royal: PA154623 – **TR, BR** NAC (ref: C17824, PA123994)
Page 747 – **TR, ML** CWM/William Kent – **TL** NAC/DND/Brown: PA151996 – **MR** NAC/DND/Plastow: PA170294
Page 748 – **TM** NAC: C88552 – **BX** NAC/NFB/Lund: PA144172 – **MR** New York Daily News: PG929-185
Page 749 – **BL** NAC/DND/Stitt: PA133089 – **BX** NAC/DND/Olson: C79007 – **BR** NAC/DND/Tomelin: PA129740
Page 750 – **BR** NAC/DND/Whittaker: PA134494 – **TM** RCMP: 1615-2
Page 751 – **BR** McCord – **ML** NAC: C17219 – **TM** Stratford Festival Archives/Peter Smith
Page 752 – **BR** Miller Comstock/D. Bryan: 10699-085 – **TR** NAC/Canadian Tribune Publ.: PA93725 – **MM** Popperfoto: PLP/C/77
Page 753 – **MY** NAC: PA166908 – **BR** NGC/VIS*ART: 15038
Page 754 – **TM** Canapress – **MR, MX** NAC (ref: C1275, PA52580)
Page 755 – **TX, BL** NAC/Sports Hall of Fame (ref: PA50353, PA49618) – **MR** NAC/Metropolitan Photos/Molson Collection: PA139479
Page 756 – **MX** Granger: 4E1012.29 – **BR** McGill – **TR** NAC/Montreal Gazette: PA119854
Page 757 – **ML** NAC: C19376 – **MR** NAC/Gilliak: PA124953 – **BX** NGC: 7781
Page 758 – **MY** Bettmann: F.11659 – **TR** Canapress – **BR** NAC/Star Weekly: PA147723
Page 759 – **TL** NAC/Rapid Grip & Batten: C10434 – **MM** NAC/Cameron: PA129249
Page 760 – **BL** NAC/Lund: PA111539 – **TR** Topham: M00828516
Page 761 – **TR** NAC/Cameron: PA121704 – **ML** NAC/Malak: C7749 – **BR** NAC/Montreal Star: PA116451
Page 762 – **TM** NAC/NFB/Lunney: PA114853 – **MR** NAC/Sports Hall of Fame: PA50625
Page 763 – **TL, MR, BR** NAC (ref: C61732, PA52456, C21548)
Page 764 – **ML** Marc Cooper – **TM** NAC: Cameron/PA113742 – **BM** Nfld. Archives
Page 765 – **TR** Canapress – **BL** RCMP
Page 766 – **BR** NAC/Montreal Star/Blackman: PA137180
Page 767 – **TM, MR** Canapress – **ML** NAC/Lunney/Bier: PA152322
Page 768 – **TL, BL** NAC/NFB/Lunney (ref: PA166311, PA166310) – **TR** NAC/NFB/Hyllyard: PA111437 – **BY** NAC: PA167775
Page 769 – **TR, ML** NAC/Cameron (ref: PA121475, PA144186) – **TM** WCPI: 201362838
Page 770 – **TX** NAC: PA151642 – **BM** NAC/Sports Hall of Fame: PA50286
Page 771 – **TM** Canapress – **ML** NAC/Montreal Star: PA136678 – **MX, BR** NAC/Montreal Gazette (ref: PA117514, PA117500)
Page 772 – **MR** Canapress – **TX** NAC: C47340 – **BL** NAC/W.B. Edwards: C53922
Page 773 – **TR** Canapress – **MM** NAC: PA147993 – **BL** NAC/NFB/Gilliat: PA146503 – **BR** NAC/Sports Hall of Fame: PA49991
Page 774 – **MR** NAC/Cameron: PA112927 – **BR** NAC/Associated Press: C26229
Page 775 – **BL** Bombardier: Canadair – **TR** CP Rail: B3339-2 – **MR, ML** NAC/Cameron (ref: PA154665, PA115139)
Page 776 – **BM** Hockey Hall of Fame & Museum – **TL, TR** NAC (ref: C36222, PA149638)
Page 777 – **BX** NAC/London Free Press: PA147726 – **MM, BY** NAC(ref: PA124860, PA122562)
Page 778 – **BM** Canapress – **MR** NAC: PA139233
Page 779 – **MR** Glenbow/Morrisseau: 64.27.10 – **TX, BL** NAC (ref: C17217, C29022) – **ML** Vancouver Sun/George Diack
Page 780 – **TL, MY** Canapress – **BM** NAC/Edmonton Journal: C45079 – **BL** NAC/Hamilton Spectator: PA148760
Page 781 – **MR** Canapress – **BL** NAC/Montreal Gazette: PA157722 – **ML** NAC: PA148756
Page 782 – **TR** NAC/Cameron: PA129234 – **BY** NAC: C29510
Page 783 – **TX, MR** Canapress – **ML** NAC: PA137864
Page 784 – **TL** NAC/Montreal Star/Stall: PA128702 – **ML** NAC/Hockey Hall of Fame: PA50539 – **MY** WCPI: 100830243
Page 785 – All pictures from Richard Harrington
Page 786 – **TR, BY** Canapress – **TY** NAC: PA123984
Page 787 – **ML** Canapress – **TX** NAC/Cameron: PA129238 – **BY** NAC/Toronto Star Syndicate: PA168415 – **MR** NAC: C56999
Page 788 – **TL** Canapress – **MM** NAC/Sports Hall of Fame: PA50437 – **BR** NAC/Cameron: PA170158
Page 789 – **BM** NAC/Murray McKenzie: 120690 – **TR** Secretary of State
Page 790 – **TM** Canapress – **BR** NAC: C43954
Page 791 – **TX** NAC/Cameron: PA168019 – **ML** NAC: PA117602 – **BM** NGC: 14954
Page 792 – **BR** Canapress – **MM** NAC: PA162997
Page 793 – **TR, ML** Canapress – **MR** WCPI: 101230351
Page 794 – **MY** Canapress – **TM, MX** NAC/Cameron (ref: PA115755, C74147) – **BR** NAC/Halifax Chronicle Herald/Robert Chambers: C133855
Page 795 – **TL, TX, TY, TR, ML, MX, MY, MR, BL, BX, BR** McCord (ref: M21578, M965.162, M967.80.7, M19804, M20213, M969.41.2, M202.30, M9741.7.1, M967.29.3, M984.173.1, M22206
Page 796 – **BY** Bombardier/Canadair – **TR** NAC/Cameron: PA136780 – **TY** WCPI: 101530437
Page 797 – **TX, TR, MR** WCPI (ref: 100730214, 10, IVL245)
Page 798 – **MY** Canapress – **TX** NAC: PA152499 – **BX, BY** Richard Hill/Arnold Jacobs (ref: 13, 15)
Page 799 – **BL** GSC: KGS-98 – **TL** NAC/Allan Leishman: PA170173 – **MR** NAC/Cameron: PA113475
Page 800 – **BX** Canapress – **TY** NAC/Cameron: PA144184
Page 801 – **ML, MR** Miller Comstock/F. Frazak (ref: MA049622, MA048624) – **TL, TR, BL, BY, BR** Miller Comstock/A.H. Miller (ref: AHM-84, AHM-88, AHM-85, AHM-90, AHM-77)
Page 802 – **TL** Canapress – **TR** Canada Post – **BL** Currency Museum/Zagon: M-110870-R – **TX** NAC/Dominion-Wide: C24559 – **MR** NAC: C23715
Page 803 – **TL** N.S. Tourism and Culture: M. Crosby – **MR** NAC/Malak: C29459 – **BL** NGC/Molinari: 15452
Page 804 – **MR** Canapress – **TY** NAC/Montreal Gazette: PA117531 – **BL** WCPI: 102730809
Page 805 – **MR, BM** Canapress – **TL** NAC/Montreal Star: PA137943
Page 806 – **TR** NAC/Info Services, Health and Welf.: PA152572 – **BR** NAC: C62296
Page 807 – **TM, MX** NAC/Cameron (ref: PA111214, PA111213) – **MY** NAC/Warrander Studio: PA139803
Page 808 – **TR** Canapress – **MM** NAC/Cameron: C25000 – **TL** WCPI: 524-16712
Page 809 – **MX** NAC/Windsor Daily Star: C45118 – **MR, BR** NAC (ref: PA131846, PA137122)
Page 810 – **MX** Canapress – **TR** NAC/Montreal Gazette: PA117513 – **BR** NAC: PA29623
Page 811 – All pictures from Canapress
Page 812 – **TM** Canapress – **BX, BY** NAC/Sports Hall of Fame (ref: C29543, PA50486)
Page 813 – **BY, BR** Canapress – **BL** Miller Comstock/W. Griebeling: J140W:405:G – **TX, TR** NAC/Ted Grant (ref: PA170251, PA170247)
Page 814 – All pictures from Canapress
Page 815 – **BL, BR** Canapress – **MM** NAC: PA164027
Page 816 – **TY, TR, BY** Canapress – **BL** Toronto Star/Macpherson
Page 817 – **TL, MR, BR, BL** Canapress – **TY** NAC: PA129838
Page 818 – All pictures from Canapress
Page 819 – **MX** Canapress – **BL** Miller Comstock/C. Milne: 30738-439 – **BR** Victoria Times/Bob Bierman
Page 820 – **TR** Canapress – **TL** Hamilton Spectator/Blaine – **BL** WCPI/Peter Kuch: 108132387
Page 821 – **TL** Miller Comstock/Malak: 87-B8-294B – **ML** Miller Comstock/R. Scherer: TC00-69243-449 – **TR, MR** Miller Comstock/G. Hunter (ref: 10071458, CON-098-IAJ) – **BR** Miller Comstock/M. Beedell: MA050751
Page 822 – **TM** Canapress – **BR** Richard Hill: 9
Page 823 – **BM** Miller Comstock/W. Griebeling: 10023030 – **MR** NAC/B. Robson/G. Bird: PA152323
Page 824 – **TR** Canapress – **BL** Miller Comstock/Malak – **TL** NAC/Globe and Mail: PA137772
Page 825 – **TL, TR, BR** Miller Comstock/Malak – **MX** Miller Comstock/H. Georg – **MR** Miller Comstock/D. McColeman: 5984-446 – **ML** Miller Comstock/K. Nagai – **BL** Miller Comstock/R. Hall
Page 826 – **TR** NAC/R. Malott: PA114285 – **BX** UBC: A9349
Page 827 – **TR** Canapress – **ML** NAC/George Cree: PA137725 – **BL** NGC/Carmen Lamanna Gallery: 17953
Page 828 – **BL** Canapress – **TL** Miller Comstock/Karsh – **MR** NAC/Cameron: PA115039
Page 829 – **TL** Edmonton Sun/Windsor Star/Roschkov – **TR** Vancouver Sun/Peterson – **BR** Vancouver Sun/Norris
Page 830 – **BR** Canapress – **MM** NAC/NFB/F. Royal: PA128905
Page 831 – **MY** Canapress – **BM** NAC/Walter Curtin: PA137052
Page 832 – **BL** CMC/Morrisseau: S89-1709 – **TX** RCMP: 81-101-4 – **TR** WCPI: FPA101230365
Page 833 – **BL** Calgary Albertan/Calgary Herald/Rodewalt – **MR** Canapress – **TM** NAC: PA129351
Page 834 – **TY** Canapress – **BM** Miller Comstock/M. Madau: 77618-408
Page 835 – **MR** Canapress – **BL, BR** Imagewares/Neil Brown (ref: 6, 7)
Page 836 – All pictures from Canapress
Page 837 – **MM** Canapress – **BM** Miller Comstock/Malak: 77362-411
Page 838 – **MR** Canapress – **TM** NAC/Cameron: PA136976 – **BX** NAC/D. Paterson: PA139756
Page 839 – **TR, MX** Canapress – **BY** NAC/R. Bellemare: C99312
Page 840 – **TL, MX, TR** Canapress – **BR** Aislin
Page 841 – **BM** Bombardier/Canadair: C-38203-6 – **TM** NAC: PA126361 – **BR** NAC/R. Bellemare: C110331
Page 842 – **TL, TR** Canapress – **BM** NGC: 18772
Page 843 – **BM** Bombardier/Canadair: C17995 – **TL** Toronto Star/Macpherson – **TR** Winnipeg Tribune/Kamienski
Page 844 – **MX** Canapress – **TY** WCPI/ W. Glowacki: 101130312
Page 845 – All pictures from Canapress
Page 846 – **TL, BM** Canapress – **TR** Aislin/Toronto Star Syndicate
Page 847 – **TX** Canapress – **ML** NAC/Cameron: PA136978 – **BR** McMichael: 1989.9.4
Page 848 – **MR** Canapress
Page 849 – **ML, BR** Canapress – **TY, TR** Memorial University/James Tuck
Page 850 – **BR** Signal Hill – **TX** WCPI/W. Glowacki: 102230651
Pages 851 & 852 – All pictures from Canapress
Page 853 – **BL** CMC: S89-1723 – **TR** Toronto Star/Roschkov – **BR** Toronto Star/Barron
Page 854 – **MR** NAC: PA153762 – **BM** Richard Hill: 6
Page 855 – **TL, TR** Canapress – **BM** Miller Comstock/M. Saunders
Pages 856, 857, 858, 859 – All pictures from Canapress
Page 860 – **BL** Canapress – **MM** Canadian Space Agency
Page 861 – **TL** Alain Masson – **BL** D. Leighton – **TR** First Light/Barry Dursley – **MR** Gera Dillon – **ML** Masterfile/J. A. Kraulis – **BR** Pathfinder/Tom W. Parkin
Page 862 – **BR** Aquatic Hall of Fame + Museum of Canada Inc.
Page 863 – **MR** Canapress – **BM** Harlequin – **TM** NAC: PA140705
Page 864 – All pictures from Canapress
Page 865 – **TL** London Free Press – **MR, BL** Canapress
Page 866 – All pictures from Canapress
Page 867 – **TM, ML** Canapress – **BR** McMichael/Blake Debassige: 1984.3
Page 868 – **TL, MR** Canapress – **BL** Elizabeth Abbott
Page 869 – **BR** Bombardier/Canadair: C17136 – **TL** Miller Comstock/O. Bierwagen: 18303 – **BL** The Province/Peter Hulbert – **TR** WCPI: 2017-62961
Page 870 – **TX** Athlete Information Bureau: C84-26486 – **TR** Canadian Space Agency – **BM** Chronicle
Page 871 – **TL, ML, BL, BX** Athlete Information Bureau (ref: C84-27659, C84-27152, C84-27123, C84-27496) – **TR** Miller Comstock/Wamboldt/Waterfield: 10299
Page 872 – **MR, TL** Canapress – **TR** NAC/R. Cooper: PA152412
Page 873 – All pictures from Canapress
Page 874 – **BR** NGC/VIS*ART: 28244
Page 875 – **BL** Calgary Exhibition + Stampede/Dan Sullivan: 1163-85-35 – **MR** Canapress
Page 876 – All pictures from Canapress
Page 877 – **TX, ML** Canapress – **BR** Les Ballets Jazz de Montreal/Ian Westbury
Page 878 – All pictures from Canapress
Page 879 – **TM** Miller Comstock/W. Gordon: 10037180 – **MM** Miller Comstock/G. Hunter: CBC-482-NHJ
Pages 880, 881, 882 – All pictures from Canapress
Page 883 – **ML** Canapress – **TR** Miller Comstock/K. Wright: 10044484 – **MR** Miller Comstock/G. Hunter: 10068995 – **BR** Miller Comstock/Eric Hayes: 79345-407
Page 884 – **TR, BR** Athlete Information Bureau (ref: C88-1163, C88-1112)
Pages 885 & 886 – All pictures from Canapress
Page 887 – **TL, MM** Athlete Information Bureau (ref: C88-3516, N88-5069) – **MR, TR** Canapress
Page 888 – **MY** Canapress – **BL** UBC: NB1.481
Page 889 – All pictures from Canapress
Pages 890 & 891 – All pictures from CP Rail
Page 892 – All pictures from Canapress
Page 893 – **TX, ML, MR** Canapress – **BY** Chronicle
Page 894 – **TL, TR** Canapress – **BL** CMC
Pages 895 to 898 – All pictures from Canapress
Page 899 – **ML, TR, BX, BR** Canapress – **TX** Montreal Gazette/Allen McInnes
Page 900 – **MR** Marion McWhinnie – **BY** NAC/Laura Neame – **ML** Ont. Archives: S-17881
Page 901 – **MM** M. Leschasin – **TL** Paula Wild – **TR** R.M. Des Mazes
Page 902 – **BL** Fruma Rothberg Sanders – **TR** H.C. Franklin – **BY** McLennan Library, McGill
Page 903 – **BL** F. Kaspersky – **BR** M. Cameron – **TY** Roland Soper
Page 904 – **TM** Gloria M. Moore – **BR** Pangnirtung
Page 905 – **BM** Miller Comstock/Malak: 240G-80-22 – **TX** T.R. Anand
Page 906 – **BR** First Light/Thomas Kitchin: TK32539 – **TR** Miller Comstock/E. Deggingen: KZ-3066F – **BL** Miller Comstock/K. Scholz: 0068167-417
Page 907 – **TR** First Light/Thomas Kitchin: TK145174 – **BR** Moira Brown: 1150
Page 908 – **TL** Miller Comstock/O. Bierwagen: J320-54943 – **TR** Miller Comstock/W. Griebeling: R450/1929/83 – **ML** Miller Comstock/Heil/Runk/Shoenberger: CS2D-112G – **MR** Miller Comstock/Herbert Lamb: QP.1643R – **BL** Miller Comstock/P. St. Jacques: R450/02180/400 – **BR** Miller Comstock/M. Beedell: MA021662
Page 909 – **TL** Miller Comstock/Kroll: 32028-443 – **TR** Miller Comstock/G.D. Lepp: 16235-082 – **MY** Miller Comstock/H. Heil: R451-06486-432 – **MR** Miller Comstock/W. Wittman: R450-03310-423 – **BR** Miller Comstock/W. Fraser: 10743-401
Page 910 – **MR** Bob Strong, St. John's Nfld. – **TR** Canadian Kennel Club/Susan Pierce – **TL** Mary Browne – **BL** Miller Comstock/M. Beedell: 10008623 – **BR** Nova Scotia Duck Tolling Retriever Club of Canada
Page 911 – **TR, MX** Miller Comstock/E. Otto (ref: 78367-415, 78251-415) – **BL** Miller Comstock/H. Schade – **BR** Miller Comstock/Malak: 240E-24HS-7A
Page 912 – **BL** Miller Comstock/E. Otto: T000-0038376-41 – **ML, TR** NAC
Page 913 – **BL** Miller Comstock/E. Otto: E04389X – **ML, TR** NAC
Page 914 – **BL** Miller Comstock/G. Hunter: CMA-521-AA0 – **ML, TR** NAC
Page 915 – **BL** Miller Comstock/G. Hunter: 10068911 – **ML, TR** NAC
Page 916 – **BL** Miller Comstock/G. Hunter: CNF-022-IAJ – **ML, TR** NAC
Page 917 – **BL** Miller Comstock/M. Beedell: 10026843 – **ML, TR** NAC
Page 918 – **BL** Miller Comstock/G. Hunter: CNS-512-AAN – **ML, TR** NAC
Page 919 – **BL** Miller Comstock/B. Hoferichter: T000-91633-461 – **ML, TR** NAC
Page 920 – **BL** Miller Comstock/G. Hunter: 10068724 – **ML, TR** NAC
Page 921 – **BL** Miller Comstock/E. Otto: T000-78273-415 – **ML, TR** NAC
Page 922 – **BL** Miller Comstock/W. Griebeling: MA018368 – **ML, TR** NAC
Page 923 – **BL** Miller Comstock/G. Hunter: 10069107 – **ML, TR** NAC

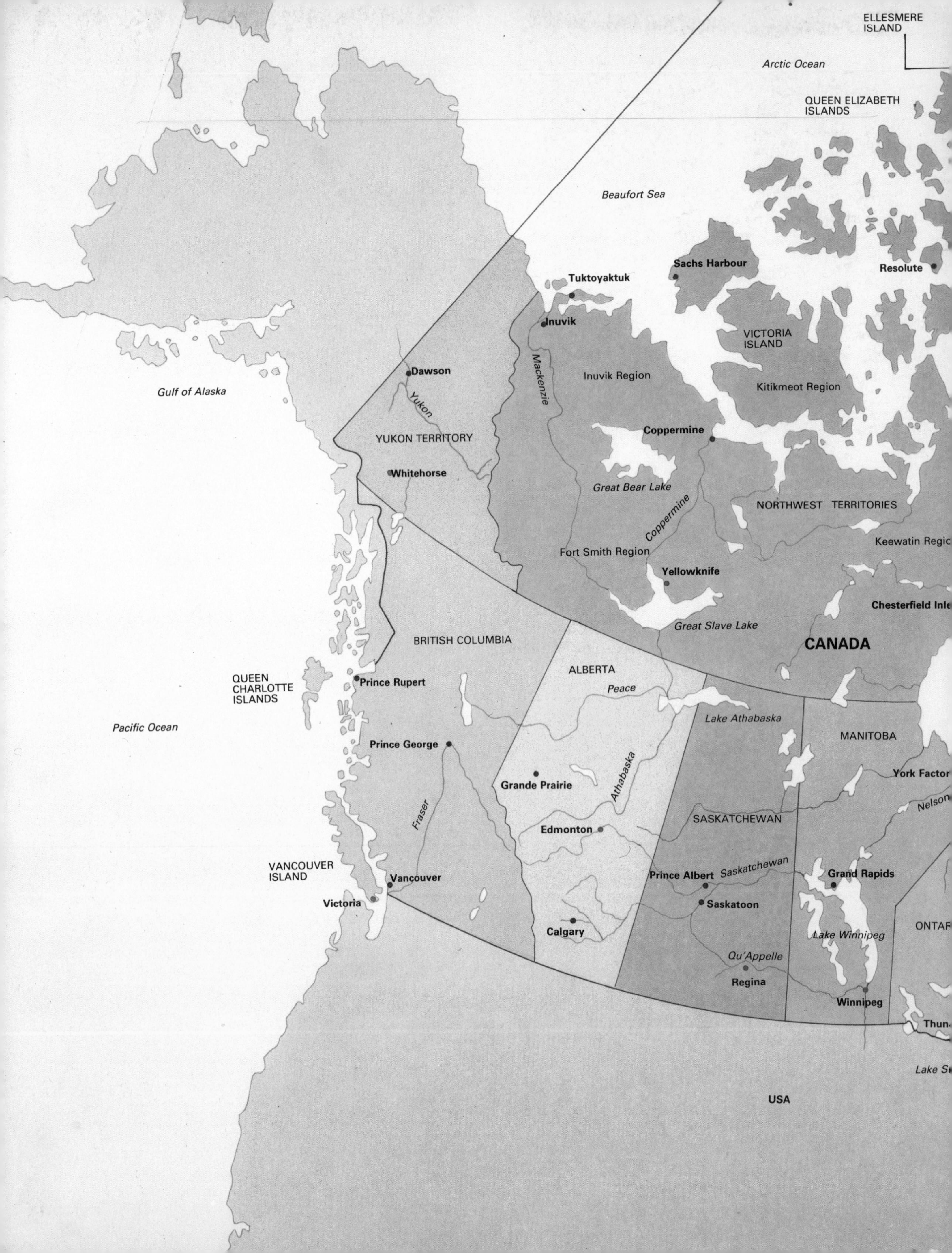
ELLESMERE ISLAND
Arctic Ocean
QUEEN ELIZABETH ISLANDS
Beaufort Sea
Sachs Harbour
Resolute
Tuktoyaktuk
Inuvik
VICTORIA ISLAND
Dawson
Mackenzie
Inuvik Region
Kitikmeot Region
Gulf of Alaska
Yukon
YUKON TERRITORY
Coppermine
Whitehorse
Great Bear Lake
Coppermine
NORTHWEST TERRITORIES
Fort Smith Region
Keewatin Regic
Yellowknife
Chesterfield Inle
Great Slave Lake
CANADA
BRITISH COLUMBIA
ALBERTA
QUEEN CHARLOTTE ISLANDS
Prince Rupert
Peace
Pacific Ocean
Lake Athabaska
MANITOBA
Prince George
Athabaska
Grande Prairie
York Factor
Fraser
Nelson
SASKATCHEWAN
Edmonton
VANCOUVER ISLAND
Prince Albert
Saskatchewan
Grand Rapids
Vancouver
Saskatoon
Victoria
Lake Winnipeg
ONTAR
Calgary
Qu'Appelle
Regina
Winnipeg
Thun
Lake S
USA